Statistical Record OF Native North Americans

ISSN 1082-7811

Statistical Record OF Native North Americans

Second Edition

Marlita A. Reddy, Editor

 **Gale Research Inc.**

An International Thomson Publishing Company

Changing the Way the World Learns

NEW YORK • LONDON • BONN • BOSTON • DETROIT • MADRID
MELBOURNE • MEXICO CITY • PARIS • SINGAPORE • TOKYO
TORONTO • WASHINGTON • ALBANY NY • BELMONT CA • CINCINNATI OH

Marlita A. Reddy, *Editor*

Editorial Code and Data, Inc. Staff

Arsen J. Darnay, *Senior Editor*
Helen S. Fisher, Robert S. Lazich, and Susan M. Turner, *Contributing Editors*
Gary Alampi, *Programmer Analyst*
Nancy Ratliff and Sherae R. Carroll, *Data Entry Associates*

Gale Research Inc. Staff

Mark Mikula, *Developmental Editor*
Neil Schlager, *Managing Editor, Multicultural Team*

Mary Beth Trimper, *Production Director*
Shanna Heilveil, *Production Assistant*
Cynthia Baldwin, *Product Design Manager*
C.J. Jonik, *Desktop Publisher*
Sherrell L. Hobbs, *Graphic Artist*
Bernadette M. Gornie, *Cover Design*

10 9 8 7 6 5 4 3 2 1

TABLE OF CONTENTS

CHAPTER 2 - DEMOGRAPHICS continued:

CHAPTER 2 - DEMOGRAPHICS continued:

CHAPTER 3 - THE FAMILY continued:

CHAPTER 4 - EDUCATION continued:

INTRODUCTION

Statistical Record of Native North Americans, 2nd edition (*SRNNA-2*) is a compilation of statistical data on the indigenous population of North America. The information compiled in this book pulls together data scattered among many federal and state agencies, tribal governments, associations, and other organizations. Much of the information is not available elsewhere in printed format. The goals in producing this book are to provide a tool which makes these diverse data accessible to the public while providing full citations of the original sources so that the researcher can do additional work using the sources, if so desired.

New features of the second edition include:

Expanded coverage of Indian areas from the 1990 Census, including Alaska Native Statistical Areas (ANVSAs), reservations and trust lands, Tribal Designated Statistical Areas (TDSAs), and Tribal Jurisdiction Statistical Areas (TJSAs).

° Updated coverage of major tribal groups from the 1990 Census.

° Updated statistics on health, education, and economic conditions.

° Data on the Aboriginal population of Canada from from the 1991 Census conducted by Statistics Canada.

Who are the Native North Americans?

There is no widely accepted name for the diversity of peoples who, together, form the indigenous nations of North America. These native inhabitants have been referred to as "Indians," "Native Americans," "First Peoples," "Aboriginal Peoples," and "Indigenous Peoples." In *SRNNA-2* we have used the term **Native North Americans**. The term includes the native populations of the United States (including Alaska) and Canada. Since *SRNNA- 2* reports on statistical data from a wide range of sources, the names used in each source have been left unchanged.

There are also many definitions of the term "American Indian." Government agencies and tribes use different criteria to determine tribal membership. Thus data from different sources are not always directly comparable. The two largest sources of statistical information are the Bureau of Indian Affairs (BIA) and the Bureau of the Census. The BIA generally regards someone as an Indian if that person is a member of one of the 510 federally recognized tribes and, in order to qualify for certain BIA services, is of at least one- quarter Indian ancestry. The Census Bureau recognizes a person as Indian if he or she claims to be such on the Census questionnaire.[1]

Scope and Coverage

Statistical Record of Native North Americans, 2nd Edition includes statistics on:

° Native North Americans as compared with other racial/ethnic groups under many specific subject headings.

° Native North Americans as compared with one another (e.g., by reservation or other Indian area, by tribe, by sex, by age, etc.). All Indian areas are represented in the *Population* chapter. In all other cases, data are shown for the largest 50 reservations or Alaska Native Areas and for selected tribal statistical areas. All areas with populations of 500 or more persons have been included in these tables.

° Individual tribal data under rare circumstances (e.g., historical data on the Yani tribe).

Historical and Current Data

The period covered in *SRNNA* extends from 20th century estimates of pre-European contact populations to population projections for 2050. Data about the original Native North American population are, by and large, estimates by specialists drawing on early accounts of explorers, traders, artists, adventurers, missionaries, and military people—some of whom had reasons for either minimizing or exaggerating their estimates of population. There is, not surprisingly, neither scholarly nor general agreement about the validity of these early estimates. In fact, the subject is embroiled in controversy. Historical data are nonetheless presented—and in all of their diversity—to make these estimates available alongside the later and more systematically collected data. The first census data came from the 1890 census.

---

1 For one discussion of the political ramifications of Indian identification the reader may refer to Jaimes, M. Annette, "Federal Indian Identification Policy: a Usurpation of Indigenous Sovereignty in North America", in Jaimes, M. Annette (ed.), *The State of Native America: Genocide, Colonization, and Resistance*, Boston: South End Press, 1992.

Indigenous Peoples of Canada

Statistical Record of Native North Americans includes in its coverage tabular data on the First Nations within Canada largely from the Census of 1991 and the First Aboriginal Peoples Survey. These data were provided through the generosity of Statistics Canada, and are supplemented by various periodical sources. The data provide information on both on-reserve and off-reserve populations.

Canadian data are presented in a separate chapter and use the chapter headings from the rest of the book as subtopics within the chapter to provide an arrangement format parallel to the book as a whole. This was done because the designations used within the Canadian statistical bureaus do not always directly correspond to those of the U.S. Census Bureau and the BIA; furthermore, governmental and monetary system differences between the two countries do not allow direct comparison of the data involved. For further background information on Canadian data, please consult the corresponding chapter overview below.

Sources

Data for *SRNNA-2* were obtained through an extensive library search and contacts with federal agencies, national organizations, and associations. Scores of agencies and organizations were consulted as well as the works of a number of recognized historians.

The source for each table is shown with the table. The source block will in many instances contain citation of a *primary* source—the source used by the author of the table.

A more detailed discussion of sources is presented in the next section, *Guide to Chapters and Contents*.

Arrangement of the Data

SRNNA-2 is organized by chapter and topic. There are twelve chapters on broad topics such as History, Demographics, The Family, etc. Within these chapters, data are organized by topics. In the chapter on Demographics, for instance, topics are Population, Tribal Enrollment, Population Trends, Geographic Mobility, and Housing and Household Characteristics. These topics are arranged in order from broad to narrow coverage of data. Tables under each topic are arranged in order of the scope of coverage. Data that compare Native Peoples to other groups come first; next are tables comparing Native Peoples to each other. These data are presented for the largest 50 ANVSAs, TDSAs, TJSAs, and reservations and trust lands; finally, data on individual tribes or reservations (where available) are presented.

Canadian data are shown in a separate chapter, as explained above. Historical data are presented within a separate chapter when the data are chronologically historical in nature; that is, if the data presented cover the years 1910 or 1930 but do not include current data, the information has been placed in the *History* chapter. If, however, the data are anthropological/historical in nature but make a comparison to available current data (e.g., *Huron Indian Population, Early 1600's to 1980*), they will be found in the appropriate chapter under the appropriate topic (in this case, *Demographics* and *Population Trends*).

Keyword Index

SRNNA-2 has a single *Keyword Index* that refers to subjects, concepts, institutions, and organizations. More than 3,500 terms will be found in the index.

Acknowledgments

The editors would like to express their thanks to Mr. George Russell of Thunderbird Enterprises, Professor Gordon Henry of the Department of Languages and Literature at Michigan State University, and Patrick LeBeau of the Department of History at Ferris State University. All three consented to serve the editorial staff in an advisory capacity on the first edition of this book and made valuable contributions in its conceptual stages. The editors would like to express thanks to the many individuals in the federal government, associations, and publishers who helped in the creation of *SRNNA* by providing reports, data, references, and permissions, especially Al Finnel of the Bureau of Indian Affairs; Bernice Campbell, Georgette Gaulin, Pauline Gibeau, Jerry G. Stinson, and John Valentine of Statistics Canada, Drew McCormick, Research Consultant; and the Senate Committee on Indian Affairs.

Many thanks go to Nancy Ratliff and Sherae Carroll who struggled valiantly with the mass and complexity of the data presented in the book in rendering many different kinds of materials into machine-readable format.

Comments and Suggestions

The editors welcome comments and suggestions for improving *SRNNA-2* in its future editions. Please write to:

Statistical Record of Native North Americans, 2nd Edition

Gale Research Inc.

835 Penobscot Building

Detroit, MI 48226-4094

GUIDE TO CHAPTERS AND CONTENTS

This section presents a discussion of *SRNNA-2*'s twelve chapters. The intent is to provide some comment on the main sources consulted, to highlight issues and controversies that surround the data presented, and to provide a brief summary of the more important contents of each chapter. After the chapter summaries, a section titled *Further Reading* provides a listing of additional sources. The listing is not—and is not intended to be—exhaustive.

Chapter 1 - History

The information presented in this chapter has been included because of reader interest in the subject. The data are from a variety of sources, including the U.S. Census Bureau, the Bureau of Indian Affairs, and various scholars in the fields of history and anthropology.

The data estimates presented range from pre-Columbian contact to the Census of 1963. However, in order to allow expanded presentation of current data, detailed population figures from the 1962-63 Census have been omitted from this edition. As explained in the *Introduction*, if estimates were juxtaposed with comparable current data, the tables were placed in chapters according to subject matter. Any information referring to years prior to 1980 are found in this chapter.

Some consider historical data questionable and objectionable, especially (but not exclusively) data collected before 1890; 1890 data are considered to be the first complete data on American Indians compiled by the federal government. The question of population counts is a prime example of this controversy, as illustrated in the table entitled, "20th Century Estimates of the Population of Aboriginal North America Before 1492." Such estimates range from as few as 900,000 persons to as many as 12,250,000. Even an estimate of 2,000,000 would indicate a population decline and a loss of some 6.1 million indigenous persons (about 81 percent of the indigenous population) by the 1890 Census. This population decline has been attributed by various scholars to genocide through the introduction of diseases, alcohol, and firearms—as well as intentional violence in the westward expansion of the European settlers.[1]

By including the historical data, the editors in no way mean to imply that they are either accurate or inaccurate. The intention is to provide a sampling of information for reader reference and provide resources for following up such data by providing full citations below each table. Further suggestions for historical background are also provided below.

The terminology and designations of tribes by different sources throughout this chapter have been reproduced with their original spellings. Names of tribes and languages may vary in appearance, depending on the time of data compilation and the source of the information.

Chapter 2 - Demographics

Data for this chapter were drawn primarily from the 1990 Census of Population and from historical data not shown in the chapter on *History*.

Population Trends

This section contains population estimates of the indigenous peoples of the United States from pre-European contact until 1990. While there is historical/anthropological content in the data, these particular tables show a trend toward the 1980 and 1990 Censuses, and were therefore included in the Demographics chapter.

Even in the most current U.S. Censuses, there has been some question about the accuracy of minority data and the validity of representation of these groups in the population.[2] Even more controversy surrounds the period before 1890. Since the turn of the century, estimates of the pre-1492 North American indigenous population have varied from 1.2 million to 18.0 million. The higher the estimate taken as the base, the more likely the contention that European arrivals engaged in intentional or involuntary genocide.[3]

SRNNA-2 presents but does not interpret these data. Rather the editors have tried to present a sampling of relevant materials (in this chapter and in the chapter titled *History*). *History* shows data that are not directly juxtaposed with current data.

---

1 For two discussions of such a viewpoint, the reader is referred to Stiffarm, Lenore A. and Phil Lane, Jr., "The Demography of North America: a Question of American Indian Survival", in Jaimes, M. Annette (ed.), *The State of Native America: Genocide, Colonization, and Resistance*, Boston: South End Press, 1992; and Thornton, Russell, *American Indian Holocaust and Survival: a Population History Since 1492*, Norman, OK: University of Oklahoma Press, 1987.

2 Stiffarm, *op. cit.*

3 Thornton, *op. cit.*

Population

This section contains current population data on the indigenous population (including American Indians, Eskimos, and Aleuts) from the 1990 Census. New to this edition is coverage by tribe, which has just recently been released by the Bureau of the Census. Please note that the designation "Indian" by the Census Bureau is entirely dependent on the individual responses of U.S. residents and does not necessarily ensure recognition by the tribe.

Population by Area. The Census Bureau estimates that in 1990 there were 1.959 million native persons living in the United States, including 57,000 Eskimos and 24,000 Aleuts, representing about 1 percent of the total U.S. population. This represents an increase of about 600,000 for the group since 1980. The majority of the population resided in the West (47 percent) and in the South (28 percent). The most populous states were Oklahoma, California, and Arizona, which were the only states to exceed a population of 200,000. Among the largest 70 major U.S. metropolitan areas, the densest Native populations were in Tulsa (6.8 percent), Tucson (3.0 percent), Phoenix (1.8 percent), Bakersfield (1.3 percent), Fresno (1.1 percent), and Sacramento (1.1 percent). The remaining 65 metro areas had less than 1 percent Native populations. The chapter also provides data for Alaska Native Village Statistical Areas, Tribal Designated Statistical Areas, and Tribal Jurisdiction Statistical Areas.

Population by Tribe. The largest tribes responding to the census were Cherokee, Navajo, Chippewa, and Sioux; as was the case with the 1980 Census, these were the only tribes whose populations exceeded 100,000. Detailed population estimates for all tribes responding to the 1990 Census, by age, by state, and by U.S. Census region are presented in this section. Again, please keep in mind that these data were compiled from the responses of individuals who identified themselves as American Indians or Native Alaskans on their census forms. Tribal enrollment status data can be found in the chapter titled *Government Relations*.

Population in Indian Areas. This section contains population data from the 1990 Census for Native areas across the U.S. There were 807,817 persons living in American Indian and Alaska Native Areas. About 54 percent of these persons were Native North Americans, constituting about 22 percent of the Native population. Data are presented by age, sex, and tribal enrollment status of persons residing in Alaska Native Village Statistical Areas (ANVSAs), Tribal Designated Statistical Areas (TDSAs), and on reservations and trust lands. A detailed description of each type of area is provided in the footnotes of the applicable tables.

Chapter 3 - The Family

About 66 percent of the 449,000 American Indian and Native Alaskan families in the U.S. were married couples; the comparable figure for the total population was 79 percent. Twenty-six percent of families were headed by a female householder with no husband present (12 percent for the general population). Detailed family characteristics are presented in this chapter, by major tribal group.

Native families in reservation states tended to be larger than those of the general population, with an average of 4.6 persons per family for American Indians and Alaska Natives versus 3.8 persons for the average family in the United States (all races).

Family income tended to be lower than that of the general population. Median income for Native families was $21,619 versus $34,213 for families of all races.

A study of nearly 14,000 Native American adolescents in 50 tribes showed that family size affected the emotional welfare of teens; teens worried about parental abuse, domestic violence, and poverty.[4] Statistics on the impact of social, economic, and health conditions on Native American children and adolescents are presented in this chapter. Additional data can be found in the chapters entitled *Education* and *Health and Health Care*.

Chapter 4 - Education

The most recent detailed data on education of the Native population of the United States come from the U.S. Department of Education. According to this information, as of April 1990, 66 percent of American Indians and Alaska Natives age 25 years and older had completed high school; in the United States as a whole, the result was 75 percent. About 9 percent of Native persons have completed four or more years of college (compared with 20 percent of all U.S. residents). Completion rates by tribe and by reservation are presented in detail for 1990 (the most current available data) in the *Educational Progress* section.

Schools

According to the 1990 Census, about 35 percent of Native children ages 3 and 4 and 93 percent of Native children between the ages of 5 and 14 were enrolled in school. A 1990 study of eighth graders by the U.S. Department of Education showed that the vast majority of Native students were enrolled in public schools (92 percent).

Higher Education

According to the National Advisory Council on Indian Education, there were an estimated 97,657 American Indian and Alaska Native students enrolled in higher education institutions in 1990. This represented less than 1 percent of the total student population. Of these Native students, about 55 percent were in 2-year colleges. There has been an overall increase in higher

---

4   Indian Health Service, Maternal and Child Health Service, Robert Wood Johnson Foundation, *The State of Native American Youth*, February, 1992.

education enrollment by Native students since 1980, when there were 84,000 enrollees, with a total enrollment of about 119,000 in the fall of 1992. Of 5,176 baccalaureate degrees awarded in the 1990-91 academic year, the greatest number (18 percent) were in Business and Management, followed by Education (13 percent) and Social Sciences and History (12 percent).

American Indians and Native Alaskans constituted only 0.4 percent of the 348,682 master's degrees conferred in the 1991-92 academic year; distribution of degrees awarded in 1990-91 showed the greatest number of degrees in Education (36 percent). One hundred eighteen Native students received doctorates in the same year, which represented 0.3 percent of all doctoral degrees. This represented a slight decline from the 1980-81 academic year, when there were 130 doctorates awarded to Native students (0.4 percent of all doctorates). As was the case with master's degrees, the largest percentage of doctoral students earned degrees in Education (1990- 91). As of 1987, American Indians and Alaska Natives made up about 1 percent of faculty in higher education institutions. This figure did not vary greatly across academic disciplines or by type of institution, except in the case of 2-year colleges; these had approximately 2 percent Native faculty.

Educational Progress

Figures from the U.S. Department of Education show that, as of 1992, American Indian and Alaska Native students had the lowest high school completion rates among all race/ethnicities. Detailed statistics on education proficiency are presented in this section.

For Native high school students taking the Scholastic Aptitude Test (SAT) in 1992, the average score was 837, the second highest among all minority groups (the highest average was 945 for Asian Americans). Native students also showed the second highest 5-year improvement (up 12 percent since 1987) among all races and ethnicities. This section presents achievement scores and trends for a variety of disciplines, as well as statistics on risks to minority students' educational progress. For additional data on these risk factors, the reader should consult the section in this chapter entitled *School Environment* and the chapters entitled *The Family* and *Health and Health Care*.

Chapter 5 - Culture

While cultural issues are not generally quantifiable, this chapter has been included to present statistical information on the areas of language and employment in traditional occupations.

Language

Of the estimated 1.7 million American Indians over age 5 surveyed in the 1990 Census, 281,990 (16 percent) persons reported speaking an American Indian or Alaska Native language at home. Detailed information is presented, by language, for major tribal groups in the United States, and for selected Indian areas.

Traditional Occupations

Data on this topic are reported from the 1980 Census, because the Census Bureau did not ask this question in 1990. Therefore, this is the most most current information available on traditional occupations. Of an estimated 4,120 employed in traditional occupations on reservations across the United States, the largest number were employed in handworking occupations (33 percent). The next most reported occupations were in jewelry-related occupations and positions in tribal government. Detailed information is presented in this chapter, for major tribal groups in the United States and for selected areas of Oklahoma.

Chapter 6 - Health and Health Care

It is the administrative responsibility of the Department of Health and Human Services to provide federal health services to American Indians and Alaskan Natives. Since 1954, pursuant to passage of a public law (P.L. 83- 568), it has provided these services through the Indian Health Service (IHS), which is part of Public Health Service.

Births

The birth rate for Native peoples has exceeded that of the general population of the United States and has exceeded the birth rate of all other minorities since at least 1955. In 1988 (the most recent year available), the birth rate for all Indians and Alaska Natives was 28.8 per 1,000 persons as compared to 15.9 per 1,000 for all races and 14.7 for all minorities.

Native births were shown to be less likely to be low-weight (5.9 percent of all Native births versus 6.9 percent of all births). Native mothers tended to give birth at an earlier age than the total U.S. population, with 45 percent of Native mothers giving birth below age 20 (for all United States, the percentage of mothers under age 20 was 24 percent).

In spite of the fact that, as with the general population, the Native maternal death rate decreased overall since 1958, as late as 1986 the maternal mortality rate exceeded that of the white population by as much as 50 percent.[5]

Deaths

Life expectancy of both sexes among the indigenous population has increased from 51.0 years in 1940 to 71.5 years in 1988, which is still lower than that of the U.S. white population. Whites had a life expectancy of 74.9 years. In 1988 the overall age-adjusted mortality rate for

---

5   U.S. Department of Health, *Health Status of Minorities and Low-Income Groups: Third Edition*, p. 87.

American Indians and Alaska Natives was 600.2 per 100,000 persons. This was greater than the United States figure of 535.5 per 100,000 persons. The rate difference was most pronounced in infancy and between the ages of 1-4 and 15-44. Overall, Native persons were much more likely than the general population to die from accidents (both motor vehicle-related and other), chronic liver disease and cirrhosis, diabetes, pneumonia or influenza, suicide or homicide, and tuberculosis. They were less likely to die from cardiovascular disease (any type), tumors, and chronic obstructive lung diseases. In 1988 the infant mortality rate for Native peoples was shown to be just slightly higher than that of the U.S. population (11.0 per 1,000 versus 10.0 per 1,000 for all U.S.). Please note, however, that some studies have shown undercounting of American Indians and Alaska Natives by as much as 26 percent in these statistics.[6]

Health Concerns

Despite the fact that among the IHS population health problems have decreased anywhere from 56 percent to 91 percent since 1955, numerous health concerns remain. The leading causes of hospitalization in 1989 were births and delivery complications, respiratory problems, and digestive system disorders. Leading causes for outpatient care were upper respiratory infections and colds, ear infections, and diabetes. Substance abuse, especially alcohol abuse, is a major health concern for Native Americans; and while alcohol related mortality declined steadily from the early 1970s to 1985, it rose from 30.8 deaths per 100,000 in 1986 to 37.3 in 1988. This most recent rate compares to a rate of only 6.3 per 100,000 for all races.

Chapter 7 - Social and Economic Conditions

Employment

Of the 851,000 American Indians and Alaska Natives participating in the U.S. civilian labor force in 1990, 14 percent were unemployed. The unemployment rate on the largest reservations varies from 13.8 percent for the Zuni Pueblo to 35.3 percent for Fort Apache.

Of an estimated 705,000 Native persons age 16 and older who were employed as of the 1990 Census, the largest percentage worked in the service industries (about 22 percent). The smallest percentage worked in the banking industry (approximately 1 percent of all employed Native persons). Detailed data are presented for all U.S. industries for Indian areas and by major tribal group.

Income and Poverty

The median annual income for American Indians and Alaska Natives dropped from $20,541 in 1980 (adjusted for inflation) to $20,025 in 1990. It was the only decrease in income among all

---

6 U.S. Department of Health and Human Services, *Health Status of Minorities and Low-Income Groups: Third Edition*, p. 89.

race/ethnicities. The percentage of Native persons living below the poverty line increased from 27.5 percent in 1980 to 30.9 percent in 1990; for children the percentage went from 32.5 percent to 37.6 percent.

Housing Characteristics

This section presents extensive data on housing from the U.S. Department of Housing and Urban Development, as well as from the 1990 Census.

Native American households represented less than 1 percent of the total 93 million households in the United States. These households were much more likely to be in non-metropolitan areas (nearly 60 percent of total, as opposed to 20 percent for all United States).

A significantly higher percentage (15 percent) of Native Americans resided in mobile homes than did the general population and the square footage of housing units was less than for all other population groups.

Chapter 8 - Business and Industry

The data in this section come from the U.S. Department of Commerce, the Department of Energy, the Department of the Interior Minerals Management Service, the U.S. Senate Sub-Committee on Indian Affairs, and the National Indian Gaming Association.

Minority-Owned and Native-Owned Firms

In 1987 there were more than 1.2 million minority-owned firms in the United States. These firms constituted 8.9 percent of all U.S. firms and 3.9 percent of all sales and receipts for U.S. firms. Native-owned firms represented 1.8 percent of minority firms and 1.2 percent of those sales and receipts. With average sales and receipts of $43,000, Native American and Alaska Native-owned firms were below average as compared to all minority firms ($64,000) and well below average for all U.S. firms ($145,000). Businesses owned by Native women had the lowest average receipts per firm in the United States. ($32,000).

In terms of growth, Native-owned businesses have shown a 57 percent increase in number of firms since 1982 (64 percent for all minority firms) and an 84 percent increase in receipts (126 percent for all minority firms).

Like all firms in the United States, the largest concentration of minority firms is in the service industries, and the largest concentration of sales and receipts is in the retail industry. Native-owned firms follow the same pattern. But while the largest *minority* share of U.S. firms was in the transportation and utilities industries, the largest *Native-owned* share was in agriculture, fishing, and forestry; the Native North American companies, however, were only 1 percent of this sector's total firms and only 0.5 percent of the sector's sales and receipts.

Overall, minority-owned firms tend to be concentrated in a few states; California, Texas, New York, and Florida are home to more than half of all minority firms in the United States and account for about 59 percent of minority firm receipts. Similarly, more than half of Native-owned firms are located in four states—Alaska, California, Oklahoma, and North Carolina—which account for about 46 percent of Native firm receipts.

Like most minority-owned businesses, Native-owned firms tend to be proprietorships rather than partnerships or corporations. Among minority firms, Native-owned firms are the least likely to incorporate—2 percent of all Native-owned firms are corporations as compared with 3 percent for all minority-owned firms and 7 percent for all U.S. firms.

Minerals Leasing

While Native-owned firms constitute less than 0.1 percent of the mining industry in number of firms and receipts, Indian land holds significant resources, including oil, gas, and coal as well other minerals such as phosphate, quartz crystal, sand and gravel, potash, and sodium.

Actual and potential oil and gas-producing Native American lands in 1993 measured more than 1.7 million acres—13 percent of all federal and Indian onshore production-capable lands. Coal-bearing land measured nearly 124,000 acres in 1990, which made up more than 31 percent of all federal and Indian coal-leased land.

SRNNA provides revenue data for these mineral leases; please note, however, that these revenues are part of an estimated $2.0 billion held in trust by the Bureau of Indian Affairs in Tribal and IIM (Individual Indian Money) accounts. The accounting of these trust funds has been under investigation over the past eight years by the Environment, Energy, and Natural Resources House Subcommittee of the Congress. For an explanation of the process of lease revenue management, please consult, "Indians Are Sold Out by the U.S.; Honor System License to Loot; U.S. Fails to Protect Oil on Indian, Federal Lands," in *The Arizona Republic*, October 4, 1987. For further discussion of the investigation, consult *Misplaced Trust: The Bureau of Indian Affairs' Mismanagement of the Indian Trust Fund*, Subcommittee on Environment, Energy and Natural Resources, March 18, 1992.

Tribal Casinos and Gaming

Since the passage of the Indian Gaming Regulatory Act by Congress in 1988, revenues from tribal gaming have reached $7.5 billion annually.[7] There has been a great deal of controversy

---

7   "The next throw," *The Economist*, March 18, 1995.

over this industry; some state governments are opposed to provisions of the federal statute in order to protect the gaming industry, because gaming is opposed in the state, and for other reasons.

The data in this section come from the Senate Subcommittee on Indian Affairs and various periodical sources. Further background information can be obtained from NIGA (The National Indian Gaming Association), an organization founded "to protect and preserve the general welfare of tribes striving for self-sufficiency through gaming enterprises in Indian country." It distributes a packet of information that provides background about issues surrounding the development of Indian gaming in the United States and is cited below under *Further Reading*.

Chapter 9 - Land and Water Management

Certain subjects do not lend themselves well to quantification and a number of issues in the forefront of the Native community are cultural in nature. An example of such an issue is religious freedom, which is the basis of a great many land claim suits brought to court by members of the indigenous population. While the editors are aware that this is an issue of great consequence, both politically and culturally, statistical data are not readily available in this context. For discussions of the issue of religious freedom, please see *References* below.

Information in this chapter includes quantitative data on land ownership, land use, BIA jurisdiction of lands, and condition of the environment on reservation lands. For additional information on minerals leasing, see the chapter entitled *Business and Industry*. Data on water rights were not available in time for publication, but suggestions for obtaining such information are provided below.

Land Ownership

This section provides data on land ownership and BIA jurisdiction and record management for these land tracts. The Department of the Interior, through the BIA, is responsible for "maintaining land ownership records and title documents, negotiating and awarding leases and permits for use of the land, and distributing to the Indian land owners the income generated by leases and permits."[8] In a study of 12 reservations, the General Accounting Office found that more than 50 percent of the 83,000 land tracts were owned in their entirety by either the tribe or an Indian individual. Twenty percent of these tracts, however, had at least one ownership interest of less than 2 percent. These small ownership interests constituted about 60 percent of the 1.1 million ownership records that the BIA is required to maintain. Detailed information is presented by reservation, by ownership type, and by land type. Additional information on ownership can be found in the section entitled *Land Use*.

---

8 U.S. General Accounting Office, *Land Ownership at Indian Reservations*, GAO/RCED- 92-96BR.

Land Use

This section provides data on use of lands under BIA jurisdiction as of 1990. The majority of lands designated for Indian use were set aside for forest grazing. The smallest amount was set aside for commercial forestlands. Detailed information is presented in this section, by BIA Area, and by type of land use.

Environmental Issues

This section presents most recent data available on the environmental conditions of selected reservations in the United States. Major environmental problems reported by tribes include water quality, solid waste management and disposal, hazardous waste and disposal, and sewage treatment. Information is provided for selected states and for selected tribes and reservations. For additional references on many of these issues, see *References*.

Chapter 10 - Government Relations

While tabular data on tribal government systems were not available at time of publication, the reader is advised to contact Americans for Indian Opportunity (address given below) which distributes a number of publications that provide background on this subject. Other suggestions for further information are also provided.

Federal Assistance Programs

This section provides budgets and expenditures for assistance programs available to Native Americans in the United States. Data are shown for fiscal years 1987 through 1989 and are arranged by federal department. Related information can also be found in the chapters entitled *Education* and *Social and Economic Conditions*.

Government Representation

This section provides statistics on Native American representation in the United States government at the federal, state, and local levels. "Local government" in this context does not refer to indigenous self-government but to employment in or appointment to U.S. city or county positions.

In 1990 there were 28,728 American Indians and Alaska Natives employed as full-time state and local government employees. This represented 0.5 percent of all employees in that year. The median income was $22,507 per year, as compared to $24,499 for all employees of the same category. This section provides detailed data, by type of occupation, for part-time, as well as full-time employees.

Chapter 11 - Law and Law Enforcement

At the time of this writing, the BIA did not have compiled statistics available on law enforcement on reservation lands. Major compilations of statistical data for the U.S., published by the Department of Justice, did not report Native Americans as a separate group except in the cases that have been included in this chapter. This does not necessarily mean that such statistics do not exist at all, only that we were unable to locate such data before publication. Other references to available information are listed below under *References*. Statistics presented in this section provide tabular data on arrest rates, crime rates, hate crimes, and law enforcement representation.

In 1992, for all ages, the proportion of arrests that were American Indians and Alaska Natives was about 1 percent of all persons arrested. These figures do not change drastically when considering the populations above and below the age of 18. Variation occurs when measuring arrests in urban versus rural areas, with Native representation being twice as high in rural areas (2.7 percent versus 1.1 percent).

The limited law enforcement data the editors were able to locate show low representation of Native Americans in this field. Because tables that only reported Native Americans as part of the category "Other" were not included in *SRNNA-2*, available information is so scant that it is impossible to draw any conclusions about the field as a whole from the data presented.

Chapter 12 - Canada

Data in this chapter are drawn largely from the 1991 Canadian Census (the most recent). Please note, however, that 78 reserves were incompletely enumerated in the 1991 census. The population figures presented here include persons citing Aboriginal origin and/or registration under the Indian Act of Canada. Statistics Canada also conducted a survey, known as the Aboriginal Peoples Survey, which showed that approximately 62 percent of those reporting Aboriginal origins identified with that background. Data from both studies are shown in this chapter, as well as supplemental information from periodical sources. Indigenous peoples of Canada are generally designated by Statistics Canada as belonging to three classifications. These are Indians, Inuits, and Métis. Within the designation **Indian**, there are three classifications: Status Indians—those registered as Indians with the federal government in the *Indian Act*, non-Status Indians—those affiliated with an Indian band ancestrally or culturally but not registered with the Canadian federal government as such; and Treaty Indians—those who can prove descent from a band having a treaty with the federal government (these persons may also be Status Indians). Persons classified as **Inuits** are those persons descended from native inhabitants of the northernmost provinces in Canada. Persons classified as **Métis** are persons of mixed Indian and European descent, through lineage from earlier Métis persons, self-proclaimed as Métis, and/or accepted as such by the Métis community.

The 1991 Census allowed respondents to provide multiple responses to ethnicity origin. Data are presented here for single, multiple, and total responses. Dollar figures in this section refer to Canadian dollars.

Population

According to Statistics Canada, there are 601 Indian bands on reserves and Crown lands. A total of 1,002,675 persons designated themselves as having Aboriginal origin, representing about 3.8 percent of the total Canadian population. Most of the Native population resides in the provinces west of Quebec. The largest Native population was in Ontario (243,550), followed by British Columbia (169,035) and Alberta (148,220), respectively. Approximately 19 percent of those reporting Aboriginal origins resided on reserves.

The Aboriginal Peoples Survey, also conducted by Statistics Canada, found that approximately 626,000 (62 percent) of persons reporting Aboriginal origins or Indian registration identified with their Aboriginal origins. Of these persons 460,680 identified themselves as North American Indian; 36,215 as Inuit; and 135,285 as Métis. Summary statistics are presented in this section.

Education

Native persons living on reserves are far more likely than the general population to have less than a 9th grade education. In 1986 36 percent of the on reserve population age 15 years and older had less than a 9th grade education; the value for all other Canadians was 14 percent. About 37 percent of the reserve population had completed at least high school (39 percent of all other Canadians). Please note that 78 reserves were not included in the Census, and this could affect results of such a survey in either direction depending on the academic achievement of the indigenous persons left uncounted.

Employment

In 1991 approximately 419,000 Aboriginal persons participated in the Canadian labor force. The Aboriginal population experienced an unemployment rate of 19.4 percent. Persons residing on reserves suffered markedly higher unemployment (30.7 percent vs. 17.7 percent off reserve).

All Aboriginal employment greatly exceeded that of the general population (10.2 percent). Of those employed, the largest percentage (15 percent) was employed in government services; the smallest percentage (1 percent) worked in the real estate and insurance industry.

Income

In 1989 the average registered Indian, whether on or off reserve, earned about $17,000. The average Aboriginal residing on reserve earned only $11,000—less than half of what Canadians on the whole reported as income ($24,000).

Culture

Of the 1.0 million persons reporting Aboriginal origin on the 1991 Census, the largest percentage reported affiliation with Catholicism (56 percent), followed by Protestantism (36 percent). Less than 1 percent reported affiliation with Aboriginal religions. (This figure was higher for off- reserve than for on-reserve populations).

Based on single responses, the majority (69 percent) of those reporting Aboriginal origin claimed English as their first language. This was followed by French (12 percent), which is also an official language. Persons reported speaking an Aboriginal language as their mother tongue numbered 171,805. Those speaking Cree constituted 43 percent of that group. The next most frequently cited languages were Inkitut (14 percent) and Ojibway (13 percent). No single other language was cited by more than 6 percent of Aboriginal persons.

Availability of Data

This chapter provides only highlights of data compiled by Statistics Canada, which made these figures available for this edition of *SRNNA*. The address for obtaining the publications cited in this book, as well as a catalogue of recent Census releases, is given below under *References*.

References

Americans for Indian Opportunity. *Survey of American Indian Environmental Needs on Reservation Lands: 1986*, Washington, D.C.: U.S. Environmental Protection Agency, Office of Federal Activities, September 1986.

Burger, Julian. *The GAIA Atlas of First Peoples: a Future for the Indigenous World*, New York: Anchor Books, 1990.

Debo, Angie. *A History of the Indians of the United States*, Norman: University of Oklahoma Press, 1970.

Department of Northern Affairs and Northern Development, Canada. *In Print: Publications Available from the Department of Indian Affairs and Northern Development*. [Available from

The Information Kiosk, Communications Branch, Dept. of Indian Affairs and Northern Development, Ottawa, ON K1A 0H4]

The Final Report of the White House Conference on Indian Education (in 2 vols.), 1849 C. Street, Washington, D.C. 20240.

Gover, Maggie. *You Don't Have to Be Poor to Be Indian*, Americans for Indian Opportunity, 1979.

Jaimes, M. Annette (ed.). *The State of Native America: Genocide, Colonization, and Resistance*, Boston: South End Press, 1992.

National Center for American Indian Enterprise Development, 953 E. Juanita Ave., Mesa, AZ 85204.

Northwest Indian Fisheries Commission, *Annual Report FY1988*.

O'Brien, Sharon. *American Indian Tribal Governments*, Norman: University of Oklahoma, 1990.

Prucha, Francis Paul. *Documents of United States Indian Policy*, Lincoln: University of Nebraska Press, 1990.

Prucha, Francis Paul. *Indian-White Relations in the United States: a Bibliography of Works Published 1975-1980*, Lincoln: University of Nebraska Press, 1982.

Ruoff, A. LaVonne. *American Indian Literature: An Introduction, Bibliographic Review & Selected Bibliography*, Modern Lang., 1990.

Ruoff, A. LaVonne, "History in *Winter in the Blood*: Background and Bibliography," *American Indian Quarterly* 4 (No. 2, 1978): 169-172.

Russell, George. *The American Indian Digest Handbook*, Phoenix: Thunderbird Enterprises, 1994.

Statistics Canada, Marketing Division, Sales and Service, Ottawa K1A OT6. Phone: (613)951-8116. Toll-Free Order Only Line (U.S. and Canada): (800) 267-6677.

Thornton, Russell. *American Holocaust and Survival: A Population History Since 1492*, Norman, OK: University of Oklahoma Press, 1987.

U.S. Department of the Interior, Bureau of Indian Affairs. *American Indians Today: Answers to Your Questions*, Third Edition, Washington, D.C., 1991.

U.S. Department of the Interior, Bureau of Indian Affairs. *Federal Register of Recognized Tribes*, Washington, D.C., 1991.

U.S. Department of the Interior, Bureau of Indian Affairs. *Indian Land Areas - 1989* (map), Washington, D.C., 1989.

U.S. Department of the Interior, Bureau of Indian Affairs, Branch of Acknowledgment and Research. *List of Tribal Petitioners by State,* Washington, D.C., 1991.

U.S. Department of the Interior, Bureau of Indian Affairs, Division of Tribal Government Services, Office of Public Information. *Tribal Leaders List*, Washington, D.C., 1991.

U.S. Department of Labor, Bureau of Labor Statistics. *Indian Labor Force. Washington, D.C., 1991.*

Vecsey, Christopher (ed.). *Handbook of American Indian Religious Freedom*, New York: The Crossroad Publishing Company, 1991.

Statistical
Record
OF Native
North
Americans

Chapter 1
HISTORY

Population

★ 1 ★

20th Century Estimates of the Population of Aboriginal North America Before 1492

Numbers are shown in thousands.

Scholar (date)	North America (000)	Conterminous United States (000)
Mooney (1910)	1,148	846
Rivet (1924)	1,148	-
Sapper (1924)	2,000-3,500	-
Mooney (1928)	1,153	849
Wilcox (1931)	1,002	-
Kroeber (1939)	900	720
Rosenblat (1945)	1,000	-
Steward (1945)	1,000	-
Ashburn (1947)	2,000-2,500	-
Steward (1949)	1,001	-
Aschmann (1959)	2,240	-
Driver (1961)	1,000-2,000	-
Dobyns (1966)	9,800-12,250	-
Driver (1969)	3,500	2,500
Ubelaker (1976)	2,171	-
Denevan (1976)	4,400	-
Thornton and Marsh-Thornton (1981)	-	1,845
Dobyns (1983)	18,000[1]	-

Source: Thornton, Russell. *American Indian Holocaust and Survival: A Population History Since 1492.* Norman, OK University of Oklahoma Press, 1987, p. 26. Published by permission. *Notes:* A dash (-) indicates no data were given. 1. North of Mesoamerica.

★ 2 ★

Population

20th Century Estimates of Western Hemisphere Total Aboriginal Population Before 1492

Numbers are shown in thousands.

Scholar (date)	Estimate (000)
Rivet (1924)	40,000-50,000
Sapper (1924)	40,000-50,000
Spinden (1928)	50,000-75,000[1]
Wilcox (1931)	13,101
Kroeber (1939)	8,400
Rosenblat (1945)	13,385
Steward (1945)	13,170
Sapper (1948)	31,000
Steward (1949)	15,491
Rivet (1952)	15,500
Borah (1964)	100,000
Dobyns (1966)	90,043-112,554
Morner (1967)	33,300
Driver (1969)	30,000
Denevan (1976)	57,300 (43,000-72,000)

Source: Thornton, Russell. *American Indian Holocaust and Survival: A Population History Since 1492.* Norman, OK: University of Oklahoma Press, 1987, p. 23. Published by permission. *Note:* 1. Circa A.D. 1200.

★ 3 ★

Population

Denevan's Population Estimates for the Western Hemisphere in 1492

Numbers are shown in thousands.

Area	Population (000)
North America	4,400
Mexico	21,400
Central America	5,650
Caribbean	5,850
Andes	11,500
Lowland South America	8,500
Western Hemisphere	57,300

Source: Thornton, Russell. *American Indian Holocaust and Survival: A Population History Since 1492.* Norman, OK: University of Oklahoma Press, 1987, p. 25. Published by permission. Primary source: Denevan, William M., "Epilogue," pp. 289-292 in William M. Denevan, ed., *The Native Population of the Americas in 1492.* Madison: University of Wisconsin Press, 1976, p. 291.

★ 4 ★

Population

Dobyns's Population Estimates for the Western Hemisphere in 1492

Numbers are shown in thousands.

Area	Population (000)
North America	9,800-12,250
Mexican Civilization	30,000-37,500
Central America	10,800-13,500
Caribbean Islands	443-554
Andean Civilization	30,000-37,500
Marginal South America	9,000-11,250
Western Hemisphere	90,043-112,554

Source: Thornton, Russell. *American Indian Holocaust and Survival: A Population History Since 1492.* Norman, OK: University of Oklahoma Press, 1987, p. 24. Published by permission. Primary source: Dobyns, Henry F., "Estimating Aboriginal American Population: An Appraisal of Techniques with a New Hemisphere Estimate," *Current Anthropology*, 1966, p. 415.

★ 5 ★

Population

Kroeber's American Indian Population Estimates for the Western Hemisphere in 1500

Numbers are shown in thousands.

Area	Population (000)
North of the Rio Grande River	900
Northwest Mexico	100
Northeast Mexico	100
Central and Southern Mexico, Guatemala, El Salvador	3,000
Honduras, Nicaragua	100
Native North America	4,200
Inca Empire	3,000
Rest of South America	1,000
West Indies	200
Native South America	4,200
Western Hemisphere	8,400

Source: Thornton, Russell. *American Indian Holocaust and Survival: A Population History Since 1492.* Norman, OK: University of Oklahoma Press, 1987, p. 24. Published by permission. Primary source: Kroeber, Alfred L., "Cultural and Natural Areas of Native North America," *University of California Publications in American Archaeology and Ethnology*, 1939, p. 166.

★ 6 ★

Population

Mooney's Population Estimates for Aboriginal North America With European Contact Dates

Area	European contact date	Population
North Atlantic States	1600	55,600
South Atlantic States	1600	52,200
Gulf States	1650	114,400
Central States	1650	75,300
Northern Plains	1780	100,800
Southern Plains	1690	41,000
Columbia Region	1780	88,800
California	1769	260,000
Central Mountain Region	1845	19,300
New Mexico and Arizona	1680	72,000
Greenland	1721	10,000
Eastern Canada	1600	54,200
Central Canada	1670	50,950
British Columbia	1780	85,800
Alaska	1740	72,600
North America		1,152,950

Source: Thornton, Russell. *American Indian Holocaust and Survival: A Population History Since 1492.* Norman, OK: University of Oklahoma Press, 1987, p. 27. Published by permission. Primary source: Mooney, James, "The Aboriginal Population of America North of Mexico," pp. 1-40 in John R. Swanton, ed., *Smithsonian Miscellaneous Collections*, vol. 80.

★ 7 ★

Population

Mooney's Population Estimates for Aboriginal North America With Ubelaker's Revised Estimates

In 1976, Douglas H. Ubelaker revised James Mooney's population estimates, which were originally published in 1929.

Area	Mooney's population	Revised estimate
North Atlantic States	55,600	157,348
South Atlantic States	52,200	92,916
Gulf States	114,400	473,616
Central States	75,300	167,919
Northern Plains	100,800	140,112
Southern Plains	41,000	264,040
Columbia Region	88,800	111,000
California	260,000	310,000
Central Mountain and Region	19,300	19,300
New Mexico and Arizona	72,000	113,760

[Continued]

★7★

Mooney's Population Estimates for Aboriginal North America With Ubelaker's Revised Estimates
[Continued]

Area	Mooney's population	Revised estimate
Conterminous United States	879,400	1,850,011
Greenland	10,000	10,000
Eastern Canada	54,200	81,842
Central Canada	50,950	36,684
British Columbia	85,800	119,262
Alaska	72,600	73,326
Other areas	273,550	321,114
North America	1,152,950	2,171,125

Source: Thornton, Russell. *American Indian Holocaust and Survival: A Population History Since 1492.* Norman, OK: University of Oklahoma Press, 1987, p. 29. Published by permission. Primary source: Ubelaker, Douglas H., "Prehistoric New World Population Size: Historical Review and Current Appraisal of North American Estimates," *American Journal of Physical Anthropology,* 1976, p. 664; Mooney, "The Aboriginal Population of America North of Mexico," pp. 1-40 in John R. Swanton, ed., *Smithsonian Miscellaneous Collections,* vol. 80.

★8★

Population

Questions Asked of American Indians in Supplemental Schedules of U.S. Census Enumerations, 1880-1970

An (X) indicates that the questions was asked; a dash (-) indicates that the question was not asked.

Question	1880	1890	1900	1910	1920	1930	1940	1950	1960	1970
Whether a chief	X	-	-	-	-	-	-	-	-	-
By what authority	X	-	-	-	-	-	-	-	-	-
Whether a war chief	X	-	-	-	-	-	-	-	-	-
Length of time on reservation	X	-	-	-	-	-	-	-	-	-
Length of time person has worn citizen's dress	X	-	-	-	-	-	-	-	-	-
Number of persons who wear citizen's dress, wholly and in part	-	X	-	-	-	-	-	-	-	-
Total population of agency, by tribe	-	X	-	-	-	-	-	-	-	-
Total population of tribe and what Indian language is spoken	-	X	-	-	-	-	-	-	-	-
Whether tribe is increasing or decreasing	-	X	-	-	-	-	-	-	-	-
Number of Negroes, mulattos, quadroons, octoroons with the tribe	-	X	-	-	-	-	-	-	-	-
Number of persons in this family	-	X	-	-	-	-	-	-	-	-
Probable wealth and wages earned	-	X	-	-	-	-	-	-	-	-
Tribe or clan (of individual)	X	X	X	X	-	-	-	X	-	-
Tribe(s) of parents	-	-	X	X	-	-	-	-	-	-
Proportions of Indian or other blood	X	X	X	X	-	-	-	X	-	-
Number of times married	-	-	-	X	-	-	-	-	-	-

[Continued]

★ 8 ★

Questions Asked of American Indians in Supplemental Schedules of U.S. Census Enumerations, 1880-1970

[Continued]

Question	1880	1890	1900	1910	1920	1930	1940	1950	1960	1970
Now living in polygamy (1890, number of wives)	-	X	X	-	-	-	-	-	-	-
If living in polygamy, whether wives are sisters	-	X	-	X	-	-	-	-	-	-
Vaccinated	X	-	-	-	-	-	-	-	-	-
Personal property:										
Number and value of horses owned	X	-	-	-	-	-	-	-	-	-
Number and value of cattle, oxen, milch cows owned	X	-	-	-	-	-	-	-	-	-
Number and value of sheep owned	X	-	-	-	-	-	-	-	-	-
Number and value of swine owned	X	-	-	-	-	-	-	-	-	-
Number and value of mules and asses owned	X	-	-	-	-	-	-	-	-	-
Number and value of domestic fowls owned	X	-	-	-	-	-	-	-	-	-
Pounds and value of wool owned	X	-	-	-	-	-	-	-	-	-
Number of dogs owned	X	-	-	-	-	-	-	-	-	-
Number and kinds of firearms owned	X	-	-	-	-	-	-	-	-	-
Land in severalty:										
Received land allotment (give year)	-	-	-	X	-	-	-	-	-	-
Number acres held by patent	X	-	-	-	-	-	-	-	-	-
Number acres held by allotment without patent	X	-	-	-	-	-	-	-	-	-
Number acres held by tribal regulation	X	-	-	-	-	-	-	-	-	-
Number of families actually living on and cultivating lands allotted in severalty	-	X	-	-	-	-	-	-	-	-
Number of other families engaged in agriculture or other civilized pursuits	-	X	-	-	-	-	-	-	-	-
How supported (wholly or fractional):										
Self-supporting, for how many years	X	-	-	-	-	-	-	-	-	-
By family	X	-	-	-	-	-	-	-	-	-
By civilized industries	X	X	-	-	-	-	-	-	-	-
By government	X	X	-	-	-	-	-	-	-	-
By hunting	X	X	-	-	-	-	-	-	-	-
By fishing	X	X	-	-	-	-	-	-	-	-
By natural products of soil, such as roots, berries, etc.	X	X	-	-	-	-	-	-	-	-
Number of Indian children of school age	-	X	-	-	-	-	-	-	-	-
Number of Indian children for whom school accommodations are provided	-	X	-	-	-	-	-	-	-	-
Number of Indian apprentices who have been learning trades during year, and trade	-	X	-	-	-	-	-	-	-	-
Number of missionaries, by sex and denomination	-	X	-	-	-	-	-	-	-	-
Number of church members, by denomination	-	X	-	-	-	-	-	-	-	-
Ability to read English	X[1]	X[1]	-	-	-	-	-	X	-	-
Ability to write English	X[1]	X[1]	-	-	-	-	-	X	-	-
Ability to speak English	X[1]	X[1]	-	X	-	-	-	X	-	-
Ability to read or write native language	X[1]	-	-	-	-	-	-	-	-	-
Ability to read any language other than English	-	-	-	-	-	-	-	X	-	-
Ability to write any language other than English	-	-	-	-	-	-	-	X	-	-
Ability to speak any other foreign language	X[1]	-	-	-	-	-	-	X	-	-

[Continued]

★8★

Questions Asked of American Indians in Supplemental Schedules of U.S. Census Enumerations, 1880-1970

[Continued]

Question	1880	1890	1900	1910	1920	1930	1940	1950	1960	1970
Graduated from educational institution (name and location)	-	-	-	X	-	-	-	-	-	-
In 1949, whether he attended or participated in any native Indian ceremonies	-	-	-	-	-	-	-	X	-	-
Military service, with time and organization	-	X	-	-	-	-	-	-	-	-
Taxed and not taxed	-	X	X	X	-	-	-	-	-	-
Number of white persons killed by Indians, according to sex	-	X	-	-	-	-	-	-	-	-
Number and kind of crimes against Indians committed by whites	-	X	-	-	-	-	-	-	-	-
Number of whites punished for above crimes	-	X	-	-	-	-	-	-	-	-
Number of whiskey sellers prosecuted, and kind and extent of punishment of each	X	-	-	-	-	-	-	-	-	-
Number of whites unlawfully on reservation	-	X	-	-	-	-	-	-	-	-
Occupation; area occupied, quality	-	X	-	-	-	-	-	-	-	-
Number of Indian criminals punished:										
By courts of Indian offenses	-	X	-	-	-	-	-	-	-	-
By other methods (civil, military, or tribal authority)	-	X	-	-	-	-	-	-	-	-
Number of Indians killed by Indians of same tribe, by hostile Indians, by U.S. soldiers, by citizens	-	X	-	-	-	-	-	-	-	-
Indian deaths during year	X	X	-	-	-	-	-	-	-	-

Housing questions

Question	1880	1890	1900	1910	1920	1930	1940	1950	1960	1970
House, pueblo, or lodge	X	-	-	X	-	-	-	-	-	-
Construction material, if a house	X	X	-	-	-	-	-	-	-	-
Type of floor construction	-	-	-	-	-	-	-	X	-	-
Number of houses owned by Indians	-	X	-	-	-	-	-	-	-	-
Number of houses built for Indians by government and cost of same	-	X	-	-	-	-	-	-	-	-
Number of houses occupied by Indians	-	X	-	-	-	-	-	-	-	-
If occupied by Indian, fixed or movable dwelling	-	-	X	-	-	-	-	-	-	-
Number of families in dwelling	-	X	-	-	-	-	-	-	-	-
Number of persons in dwelling	-	X	-	-	-	-	-	-	-	-
Owned or rented	-	X	-	-	-	-	-	-	-	-
If owned, whether mortgaged	-	X	-	-	-	-	-	-	-	-
Residing on own lands	-	-	-	X	-	-	-	-	-	-

Source: Thornton, Russell. *American Indian Holocaust and Survival: A Population History Since 1492.* Norman, OK: University of Oklahoma Press, 1987, pp. 217-219. Published by permission. Primary source: U.S. Bureau of the Census, *Population and Housing Inquiries in U.S. Decennial Censuses*, 1790-1970. U.S. Department of Commerce Working Paper 39. Washington, D.C.: U.S. Government Printing Office, 1973, pp. 27-31 and 38. *Note:* 1. Asked of adults only.

★ 9 ★

Population

Selected Population Characteristics Reported in 1872

This table shows opinions expressed by the Commissioner of Indian Affairs (or his agents) on the condition of Indians in 1872.

Characteristic	Population
Means of support	
"Supporting themselves on reservations, receiving nothing from government except interest on their own funds or annuities pursuant to treaties"	130,000
"Entirely subsisted by the government"	31,000
"In part subsisted by the government"	84,000
"Subsisting by hunting, fishing, roots, berries; begging or stealing"	55,000
Connection with the government	
"On reservations under complete control of agents"	150,000
"Visited agency at times for food or gossip, but generally roaming on or off their reservations, engaged in hunting or fishing"	95,000
"Never visited agency, and over whom government exercised practically no control, but most of whom were inoffensive"	55,000
Treaties and reservations	
"Had treaties with the government, 92 reservations"	180,000
"No treaties, but 15 reservations with agents in charge"	40,000
"No treaties, no reservations, but were more or less under the control of agents appointed for them and received more or less subsistence"	25,000
"No treaties, no reservations, practically no government control"	55,000
Degree of "Civilization" (with no degree of assurance)	
"Civilized"	97,000
"Semi-Civilized"	125,000
"Wholly barbarous"	78,000

Source: U.S. Department of the Interior. Bureau of Indian Affairs. Albuquerque Area Office. Division of Administration. *Fact Book.* U.S. Department of the Interior, February 1989, p. 3. Primary source: Commissioner of Indian Affairs, Annual Report (Washington, D.C.: Government Printing Office, 1872, pp. 15, 84).

★ 10 ★

Population

United States American Indian Population, 1870-1910

Year	Indian population		
	United States		Alaska Census returns
	Census returns	Reports of the Commissioner of Indian Affairs[1]	
1910	265,683	279,023	25,331
1900	237,196	250,000	29,536
1890	248,253	228,000	25,354
1880	-	244,000	32,996[2]
1870	-	278,000	-

Source: U.S. Bureau of the Census, *Indian Population in the United States and Alaska, 1910.* Washington, DC: U.S. Government Printing Office, 1915, p. 10. *Notes:* A dash (-) indicates data were not available. 1. Figures are exclusive of freedmen and intermarried whites, as follows: 1910, 25,927; 1900, 20,000 (estimate); 1890, 16,000 (estimate); 1880, 12,000 (estimate); and 1870, 10,000 (estimate). 2. Partly estimated.

★ 11 ★

Population

Attrition of American Indian Tribes in U.S. Regions

Region	Characteristics at European contact				Characteristics in 1907						
	Date	Population	Number of tribes	Mean size	Contact size, %	Population	Number of tribes	Mean size	Tribes extinct	Tribes nearing extinction	Tribes extinct or near extinction, %
North Atlantic	1600	55,600	24	2,317	39.4	21,900	10	2,190	14	6	83.3
South Atlantic	1600	52,200	35	1,491	4.2	2,170	15	145	20	14	97.1
Gulf States	1650	114,400	39	2,933	54.8	62,700	12	5,225	27	4	79.5
Central States	1650	75,300	12	6,275	61.3	46,126	10	4,613	2	1	25.0
Northern Plains	1780	100,800	20	5,040	50.1	50,477	19	2,804	1	1	10.0
Southern Plains	1690	41,000	12	3,417	7.0	2,861	7	409	5	0	41.7
Columbia Region	1780	88,800	95	935	17.4	15,431	83	211	12	40	54.7
Central Mountains	1845	19,300	6	3,217	59.8	11,544	6	1,924	0	0	0
New Mexico and Arizona	1680	72,000	25	2,880	74.8	53,832	19	2,833	6	1	28.0
California	1769	260,000	45	5,778	7.2	18,797	36	696	9	9	40.0
Total		849,000	313			285,838	217		96	66	
Average	1704			2,712	66.3			1,470			57.5

Source: Thornton, Russell. *We Shall Live Again: The 1870 and 1890 Ghost Dance Movements as Demographic Revitalization.* New York, NY: Cambridge University Press, 1986, p. 22. Published by permission. *Notes:* Information on which this table is based was obtained from Mooney (1928), Smith (1928), and Kroeber (1957).

★ 12 ★

Population

American Indian Population and Percent Distribution, by Age Group, 1900-1930

Age group	1900	1910	1920	1930
All ages	237,196	265,683	244,437	332,397
Under 20 years	117,779	136,804	123,102	169,091
20 to 49 years	83,819	91,906	86,151	118,090
50 years and over	30,964	36,024	34,393	44,767
Age unknown	4,634	949	791	449
Percent	100.0	100.0	100.0	100.0
Under 20 years	49.7	51.5	50.4	50.9
20 to 49 years	35.3	34.6	35.2	35.5
50 years and over	13.1	13.6	14.1	13.5
Age unknown	2.0	0.4	0.3	0.1

Source: Truesdell, Dr. Leon E. U.S. Department of Commerce. Bureau of the Census. Fifteenth Census of the United States: 1930, *The Indian Population of the United States and Alaska.* Washington, DC: U.S. Government Printing Office, 1937, p. 86.

★ 13 ★

Population

Median Ages for Selected Racial/Ethnic Groups, by Sex, 1920 and 1930

Color and nativity	Total		Male		Female	
	1920	1930	1920	1930	1920	1930
All classes	25.2	26.4	25.8	26.7	24.7	26.1
Indian	19.7	19.6	20.4	20.0	19.0	19.1
White	25.6	26.9	26.1	27.1	25.1	26.6
Native white	22.4	23.7	22.4	23.6	22.3	23.8
Foreign-born white	40.0	43.9	40.1	44.1	29.9	43.7
Black	22.3	23.4	22.8	23.7	22.0	23.2
Chinese	40.2	32.3	42.7	35.1	19.4	17.3
Japanese	30.2	24.5	34.1	29.7	24.0	15.9

Source: Truesdell, Dr. Leon E. U.S. Department of Commerce. Bureau of the Census. Fifteenth Census of the United States: 1930, *The Indian Population of the United States and Alaska.* Washington, DC: U.S. Government Printing Office, 1937, p. 88.

★ 14 ★

Population

American Indian Population Distribution and Population per 10,000 Persons, 1910 and 1930

The Indian population of the United States was 11.2 persons per 100 square miles of land in 1930, as compared with 8.9 in 1910. Only in the state of Oklahoma was the Indian population in excess of one person per single square mile. Of the states not shown in this table, Rhode Island and Massachusetts ranked highly in the number of Indians person 100 square miles.

State	1910				1930			
	Total population	Indian population	Percent distribution of Indian population	Indians per 10,000 total population	Total population	Indian population	Percent distribution of Indian population	Indians per 10,000 total population
United States	91,972,266	265,683	100.0	28.9	122,775,046	332,397	100.0	27.1
Oklahoma	1,657,155	74,825	28.2	451.5	2,396,040	92,725	27.9	387.0
Arizona	204,354	29,201	11.0	1,428.9	435,573	43,726	13.2	1,003.9
New Mexico	327,301	20,573	7.7	628.6	423,317	28,941	8.7	683.7
South Dakota	583,888	19,137	7.2	327.8	692,849	21,833	6.6	315.1
California	2,377,549	16,371	6.2	68.9	5,677,251	19,212	5.8	33.8
North Carolina	2,206,287	7,851	3.0	35.6	3,170,276	16,579	5.0	52.3
Montana	376,053	10,745	4.0	285.7	537,606	14,798	4.5	275.3
Wisconsin	2,333,860	10,142	3.8	43.5	2,939,006	11,548	3.5	39.3
Washington	1,141,990	10,997	4.1	96.3	1,563,396	11,253	3.4	72.0
Minnesota	2,075,708	9,053	3.4	43.6	2,563,953	11,077	3.3	43.2
North Dakota	577,056	6,486	2.4	112.4	680,845	8,387	2.5	123.2
Michigan	2,810,173	7,519	2.8	26.8	4,842,325	7,080	2.1	14.6
New York	9,113,614	6,046	2.3	6.6	12,588,066	6,973	2.1	5.5
Nevada	81,875	5,240	2.0	640.0	91,058	4,871	1.5	534.9
Oregon	672,765	5,090	1.9	75.7	953,786	4,776	1.4	50.1
Idaho	325,594	3,488	1.3	107.1	445,032	3,638	1.1	81.7
Nebraska	1,192,214	3,502	1.3	29.4	1,377,963	3,256	1.0	23.6
Utah	373,351	3,123	1.2	83.6	507,847	2,869	0.9	56.5
Kansas	1,690,949	2,444	0.9	14.5	1,880,999	2,454	0.7	13.0
Wyoming	145,965	1,486	0.6	101.8	225,565	1,845	0.6	81.8
All other States	61,704,565	12,364	4.7	2.0	78,782,293	14,556	4.4	1.8

Source: Truesdell, Dr. Leon E. U.S. Department of Commerce. Bureau of the Census. Fifteenth Census of the United States: 1930, *The Indian Population of the United States and Alaska*. Washington, DC: U.S. Government Printing Office, 1937, p. 5.

★ 15 ★

Population

American Indian Population Distribution, by Selected State and Full/Mixed Blood Status, 1910 and 1930

State	1910			1930		
	Full blood	Mixed blood	Not reported	Full blood	Mixed blood	Not reported
Arizona	94.2	1.4	4.3	86.4	2.2	11.3
California	70.0	28.1	1.9	39.2	36.8	24.0
Idaho	83.6	15.0	1.4	66.1	30.9	3.0
Kansas	36.5	62.9	0.6	14.2	60.6	25.1
Michigan	52.2	47.6	0.2	17.1	35.2	47.7
Minnesota	44.1	55.8	0.1	23.0	67.4	9.6
Montana	59.7	37.5	2.8	37.0	60.1	2.9
Nebraska	69.3	28.4	2.4	45.9	33.2	20.9
Nevada	86.6	10.3	3.1	72.6	26.7	0.7
New Mexico	99.0	0.9	0.1	89.7	2.1	8.2
New York	54.7	38.9	6.4	24.9	44.6	30.5
North Carolina	19.1	80.3	0.5	37.9	54.8	7.3
North Dakota	40.5	57.7	1.8	27.0	65.9	7.1
Oklahoma	36.6	62.6	0.8	28.1	66.3	5.6
Oregon	63.3	36.4	0.2	45.1	48.3	6.6
South Dakota	70.4	28.7	0.9	52.3	46.1	1.6
Utah	95.1	3.4	1.5	77.1	10.1	12.8
Washington	68.7	30.6	0.6	46.0	43.6	10.4
Wisconsin	54.7	45.1	0.2	35.1	55.2	9.6
Wyoming	80.5	19.5	-	60.5	35.3	4.2

Source: Truesdell, Dr. Leon E. U.S. Department of Commerce. Bureau of the Census. Fifteenth Census of the United States: 1930, *The Indian Population of the United States and Alaska* Washington, DC: U.S. Government Printing Office, 1937, p. 71. *Note:* A dash (-) represents zero.

★ 16 ★

Population

American Indian Population in the United States, 1800-1910

Date	Population
1800	600,000[1]
1820	471,000[2]
1847	383,000[3]
1857	313,000[4]
1870	278,000[5]
1880	244,000[5]
1890	228,000[5]

[Continued]

★ 16 ★

American Indian Population in the United States, 1800-1910
[Continued]

Date	Population
1900	250,000[5]
1910	279,000[5]

Source: Thornton, Russell. *We Shall Live Again: The 1870 and 1890 Ghost Dance Movements as Demographic Revitalization.* New York, NY: Cambridge University Press, 1986, p. 24. Published by permission. *Notes:* 1. From U.S. Bureau of Indian Affairs (1943), as cited by Hadley (1957:24). 2. From Morse (1970[1822]:375). 3. From Schoolcraft (1851-57), as cited by Mallery (1877:341). 4. From Schoolcraft (1851-57), as cited by Dobyns (1976:55). 5. From U.S. Bureau of the Census (1915:10).

★ 17 ★

Population

American Indian Population in Urban and Rural Areas, by Geographic Division, 1910-1930

Geographic division	1910			1920			1930		
	Urban	Rural	Percent urban	Urban	Rural	Percent urban	Urban	Rural	Percent urban
United States	11,925	253,758	4.5	15,219	229,218	6.2	32,816	299,581	9.9
New England	800	1,276	38.5	766	949	44.7	1,041	1,425	42.2
Middle Atlantic	825	6,892	10.7	906	5,034	15.3	2,181	5,528	28.3
East North Central	1,319	16,936	7.2	1,634	14,061	10.4	3,822	15,995	19.3
West North Central	1,629	39,777	3.9	1,815	35,448	4.9	3,497	44,748	7.2
South Atlantic	131	8,923	1.4	196	13,477	1.4	218	18,842	1.1
East South Central	137	2,475	5.2	51	1,572	3.1	99	2,007	4.7
West South Central	4,589	72,178	6.0	5,352	55,266	8.8	15,108	80,562	15.8
Mountain	1,272	74,066	1.7	1,772	75,127	2.3	2,677	99,406	2.6
Pacific	1,223	31,235	3.8	2,727	28,284	8.8	4,173	31,068	11.8

Source: Truesdell, Dr. Leon E. U.S. Department of Commerce. Bureau of the Census. Fifteenth Census of the United States: 1930, *The Indian Population of the United States and Alaska.* Washington, DC: U.S. Government Printing Office, 1937, p. 6.

★ 18 ★
Population

American Indian Population of the United States and Alaska, 1890-1930

For cautionary explanation, see notes.

Year	Continental United States	Alaska
1890	248,253	25,354
1900	237,196	29,536
1910	265,683	25,331
1920	244,437	26,558
1930	332,397	29,983

Source: Truesdell, Dr. Leon E. U.S. Department of Commerce. Bureau of the Census. Fifteenth Census of the United States: 1930, *The Indian Population of the United States and Alaska.* Washington, DC: U.S. Government Printing Office, 1937, p. 2. *Notes:* Effect of changes in the method of enumeration - In the case of the Indian population, rates of increase or decrease are of little significance, as the size of the Indian population depends entirely upon the attention paid to the enumeration of mixed bloods, and the interpretation of the term "Indian" in the instructions to enumerators. It is not without significance that at the two censuses in which specific questions were asked as to tribe and blood, the number of Indians should have been much larger than at censuses in which these questions were not asked. If the definition of the Indian population were limited to Indians maintaining tribal relations, the enumeration of the Bureau of Indian Affairs is probably more nearly accurate than that of the census. This enumeration in 1932 showed a total of 228,381. On the other hand, if all persons having even a trace of Indian blood were returned as Indians, the number would far exceed even the total returned at the census of 1930.

★ 19 ★
Population

American Indian Population per 10,000 Total Population for Selected States, 1890-1910

State	1890			1910			1900		
	Total population	Indian population		Total population	Indian population		Total population	Indian population	
		Number	Per 10,000 of the total population		Number	Per 10,000 of the total population		Number	Per 10,000 of the total population
United States	62,947,714	248,253	39.4	91,972,266	265,683	28.9	75,994,575	237,196	31.2
Arizona	88,243	29,981	3,397.5	204,354	29,201	1,428.9	122,931	26,480	2,154.1
California	1,213,398	16,624	137.0	2,377,549	16,371	68.9	1,485,053	15,377	103.5
Colorado	413,249	1,092	26.4	799,024	1,482	18.5	539,700	1,437	26.6
Idaho	88,548	4,223	476.9	325,594	3,488	107.1	161,772	4,226	261.2
Kansas	1,428,108	1,682	11.8	1,690,949	2,444	14.5	1,470,495	2,130	14.5[1]
Michigan	2,093,890	5,625	26.9	2,810,173	7,519	26.8	2,420,982	6,354	26.2
Minnesota	1,310,283	10,096	77.1	2,075,708	9,053	43.6	1,751,394	9,182	52.4
Mississippi	1,289,600	2,036	15.8	1,797,114	1,253	7.0	1,551,270	2,203	14.2
Montana	142,924	11,206	784.1	376,053	10,745	285.7	243,329	11,343	466.2
Nebraska	1,062,656	6,431	60.5	1,192,214	3,502	29.4	1,066,300	3,322	31.2
Nevada	47,355	5,156	1,088.8	81,875	5,240	640.0	42,335	5,216	1,232.1

[Continued]

★ 19 ★

American Indian Population per 10,000 Total Population for Selected States, 1890-1910
[Continued]

State	1890			1910			1900		
	Total population	Indian population		Total population	Indian population		Total population	Indian population	
		Number	Per 10,000 of the total population		Number	Per 10,000 of the total population		Number	Per 10,000 of the total population
New Mexico	160,282	160,282	938.6	327,301	20,573	628.6	195,310	13,144	673.0
New York	6,003,174	6,044	10.1	9,113,614	6,046	6.6	7,268,894	5,257	7.2
North Carolina	1,617,949	1,516	9.4	2,206,287	7,851	35.6	1,893,810	5,687	30.0
North Dakota	190,983	8,174	428.0	577,056	6,486	112.4	319,146	6,968	218.3
Oklahoma[2]	258,657	64,456	2,491.9	1,657,155	74,825	451.5	790,391	64,445	815.4
Oregon	317,704	4,971	156.5	672,765	5,090	75.7	413,536	4,951	119.7
South Dakota	348,600	19,854	569.5	583,888	19,137	327.8	401,570	20,225	503.6
Utah	210,779	3,456	164.0	373,351	3,123	83.6	276,749	2,623	94.8
Washington	357,232	11,181	313.0	1,141,990	10,997	96.3	518,103	10,039	193.8
Wisconsin	1,693,330	9,930	58.6	2,333,860	10,142	43.5	2,069,042	8,372	40.5
Wyoming	62,555	1,844	294.8	145,965	1,486	101.8	92,531	1,686	182.2
Total for 22 states	20,399,499	240,622	118.0	32,863,839	256,054	77.9	25,094,643	230,667	91.9
All other states	42,548,215	7,631	1.8	59,108,427	9,629	1.6	50,899,932	6,529	1.3

Source: U.S. Bureau of the Census. *Indian Population in the United States and Alaska, 1910.* Washington, DC: U.S. Government Printing Office, 1915, p. 13. *Notes:* 1. If 591 Indians in Haskell Institute are excluded, the number per 10,000 of the total population is 11. Similar exclusions for 1890 and 1900 cannot be made. 2. Includes population of Indian Territory for 1900 and 1890.

★ 20 ★

Population

American Indian Population per 100 Square Miles for Selected States in 1910

State	Land area in square miles	Indian population: 1910	
		Total	Per 100 square miles
United States	2,973,890	265,683	8.9
Oklahoma	69,414	74,825	107.8
Arizona	113,810	29,201	25.7
South Dakota	76,868	19,137	24.9
Wisconsin	55,256	10,142	18.4
New Mexico	122,503	20,573	16.8
Washington	66,836	10,997	16.5
North Carolina	48,740	7,851	16.1
Michigan	57,480	7,519	13.1
New York	47,654	6,046	12.7
Minnesota	80,858	9,053	11.2
California	155,652	16,371	10.5
North Dakota	70,183	6,486	9.2
Montana	146,201	10,745	7.3

[Continued]

★ 20 ★

American Indian Population per 100 Square Miles for Selected States in 1910
[Continued]

State	Land area in square miles	Indian population: 1910	
		Total	Per 100 square miles
Oregon	95,607	5,090	5.3
Nevada	109,821	5,240	4.8
Nebraska	76,808	3,502	4.6
Idaho	83,354	3,488	4.2
Utah	82,184	3,123	3.8
Mississippi	46,362	1,253	2.7
Kansas	81,774	1,853[1]	2.3
Wyoming	97,594	1,486	1.5
Colorado	103,658	1,482	1.4
Total for 22 states	1,888,617	255,463	13.5
All other states	1,085,273	10,220	0.9

Source: U.S. Bureau of the Census. *Indian Population in the United States and Alaska, 1910.* Washington, DC: U.S. Government Printing Office, 1915, p. 14. *Notes:* 1. Exclusive of 591 Indians in Haskell Institute, who are included in the total for "All other states."

★ 21 ★

Population

American Indian Population, by Geographic Division and State, 1890-1930

Geographic division and state	1890	1900	1910	1920	1930
United States	248,253	237,196	265,683	244,437	332,397
Geographic Divisions:					
New England	1,445	1,600	2,076	1,716	2,466
Middle Atlantic	7,209	6,959	7,717	5,940	7,709
East North Central	16,202	15,027	18,255	15,695	19,817
West North Central	46,822	42,339	41,406	37,263	48,245
South Atlantic	2,359	6,585	9,054	13,673	19,060
East South Central	3,396	2,590	2,612	1,623	2,106
West South Central	66,042	65,574	76,767	60,618	95,670
Mountain	72,002	66,155	75,338	76,899	102,083
Pacific	32,776	30,367	32,458	31,011	35,241
New England:					
Maine	559	798	692	839	1,012
New Hampshire	16	22	34	28	64
Vermont	34	5	26	24	36
Massachusetts	428	587	688	555	874
Rhode Island	180	35	284	110	318

[Continued]

★ 21 ★

American Indian Population, by Geographic Division and State, 1890-1930

[Continued]

Geographic division and state	1890	1900	1910	1920	1930
Connecticut	228	153	152	159	152
Middle Atlantic:					
New York	6,044	5,257	6,046	5,503	6,973
New Jersey	84	63	165	100	213
Pennsylvania	1,081	1,639	1,503	337	523
East North Central:					
Ohio	206	42	127	151	435
Indiana	343	243	279	125	285
Illinois	98	16	188	194	469
Michigan	5,625	6,354	7,519	5,614	7,080
Wisconsin	9,930	8,372	10,142	9,611	11,548
West North Central:					
Minnesota	10,096	9,162	9,053	8,761	11,077
Iowa	457	382	471	529	660
Missouri	128	130	313	171	576
North Dakota	8,174	6,968	6,486	6,254	8,387
South Dakota	19,854	20,225	19,137	16,384	21,833
Nebraska	6,431	3,322	3,502	2,888	3,256
Kansas	1,682	2,130	2,444	2,276	2,454
South Atlantic:					
Delaware	4	9	5	2	5
Maryland	44	3	55	32	50
District of Columbia	25	22	68	37	40
Virginia	349	354	539	824	779
West Virginia	9	12	36	7	18
North Carolina	1,516	5,687	7,851	11,824	16,579
South Carolina	173	121	331	304	959
Georgia	68	19	95	125	43
Florida	171	358	74	518	587
East South Central:					
Kentucky	71	102	234	57	22
Tennessee	146	108	216	56	161
Alabama	1,143	177	909	405	465
Mississippi	2,036	2,203	1,253	1,105	1,458
West South Central:					
Arkansas	250	66	460	106	408
Louisiana	628	593	780	1,066	1,536
Oklahoma	64,456	64,445	74,825	57,337	92,725
Texas	708	470	702	2,109	1,001

[Continued]

★ 21 ★

American Indian Population, by Geographic Division and State, 1890-1930

[Continued]

Geographic division and state	1890	1900	1910	1920	1930
Mountain:					
Montana	11,206	11,343	10,745	10,956	14,798
Idaho	4,223	4,226	3,488	3,098	3,638
Wyoming	1,844	1,686	1,486	1,343	1,845
Colorado	1,092	1,437	1,482	1,383	1,395
New Mexico	15,044	13,144	20,573	19,512	28,941
Arizona	29,981	26,480	29,201	32,989	43,726
Utah	3,456	2,623	3,123	2,711	2,869
Nevada	5,156	5,216	5,240	4,907	4,871
Pacific:					
Washington	11,181	10,039	10,997	9,061	11,253
Oregon	4,971	4,951	5,090	4,590	4,776
California	16,624	15,377	16,371	17,360	19,212

Source: Truesdell, Dr. Leon E. U.S. Department of Commerce. Bureau of the Census. Fifteenth Census of the United States: 1930, *The Indian Population of the United States and Alaska.* Washington, DC: U.S. Government Printing Office, 1937, p. 3.

★ 22 ★

Population

American Indian Population in Urban and Rural Areas, by Geographic Division and State, 1930

Division and state	Total Indian population	Urban		Rural-farm		Rural-nonfarm	
		Number	Percent	Number	Percent	Number	Percent
United States	332,397	32,816	9.9	188,946	56.8	110,635	33.3
Geographic divisions:							
New England	2,466	1,041	42.2	98	4.0	1,327	53.8
Middle Atlantic	7,709	2,181	28.3	1,990	25.8	3,538	45.9
East North Central	19,817	3,822	19.3	4,423	22.3	11,572	58.4
West North Central	48,245	3,497	7.2	27,026	56.0	17,722	36.7
South Atlantic	19,060	218	1.1	16,437	86.2	2,405	12.6
East South Central	2,106	99	4.7	1,803	85.6	204	9.7
West South Central	95,670	15,108	15.8	56,874	59.4	23,688	24.8
Mountain	102,083	2,677	2.6	67,138	65.8	32,268	31.6
Pacific	35,241	4,173	11.9	13,157	37.3	17,911	50.8
New England:							
Maine	1,012	390	38.5	36	3.6	586	57.9
New Hampshire	64	24	-	18	-	22	-
Vermont	36	8	-	16	-	12	-

[Continued]

★ 22 ★

American Indian Population in Urban and Rural Areas, by Geographic Division and State, 1930

[Continued]

Division and state	Total Indian population	Urban		Rural-farm		Rural-nonfarm	
		Number	Percent	Number	Percent	Number	Percent
Massachusetts	874	285	32.6	3	0.3	586	67.0
Rhode Island	318	245	77.0	6	1.9	67	21.1
Connecticut	162	89	54.9	19	11.7	54	33.3
Middle Atlantic:							
New York	6,973	1,706	24.5	1,893	27.1	3,374	48.4
New Jersey	213	151	70.9	9	4.2	53	24.9
Pennsylvania	523	324	62.0	88	16.8	111	21.2
East North Central:							
Ohio	435	268	61.6	70	16.1	97	22.3
Indian	285	160	56.1	72	25.3	53	18.6
Illinois	469	368	78.5	24	5.1	77	16.4
Michigan	7,080	1,849	26.1	1,251	17.7	3,980	56.2
Wisconsin	11,548	1,177	10.2	3,006	26.0	7,365	63.8
West North Central:							
Minnesota	11,077	918	8.3	2,189	19.8	7,970	72.0
Iowa	660	251	38.0	204	30.9	205	31.1
Missouri	578	378	65.4	101	17.5	99	17.1
North Dakota	8,387	392	4.7	5,461	65.1	2,534	30.2
South Dakota	21,833	483	2.2	16,297	74.6	5,053	23.1
Nebraska	3,256	228	7.0	1,616	49.6	1,412	43.4
Kansas	2,454	847	34.5	1,158	47.2	449	18.3
South Atlantic:							
Delaware	5	4	-	-	-	1	-
Maryland	50	25	-	11	-	14	-
District of Columbia	40	40	-	-	-	-	-
Virginia	779	35	4.5	628	80.6	116	14.9
West Virginia	18	7	-	3	-	8	-
North Carolina	16,579	51	0.3	15,000	90.5	1,528	9.2
South Carolina	959	26	2.7	765	79.8	168	17.5
Georgia	43	16	-	6	-	21	-
Florida	587	14	2.4	24	4.1	549	93.5
East South Central:							
Kentucky	22	13	-	2	-	7	-
Tennessee	161	24	14.9	84	52.2	53	32.9
Alabama	465	26	5.6	320	68.8	119	25.6
Mississippi	1,458	36	2.5	1,397	95.8	25	1.7
West South Central:							
Arkansas	408	106	26.0	91	22.3	211	51.7

[Continued]

★ 22 ★

American Indian Population in Urban and Rural Areas, by Geographic Division and State, 1930

[Continued]

Division and state	Total Indian population	Urban		Rural-farm		Rural-nonfarm	
		Number	Percent	Number	Percent	Number	Percent
Louisiana	1,536	59	3.8	605	39.4	872	56.8
Oklahoma	92,725	14,593	15.7	55,820	60.2	22,312	24.1
Texas	1,001	350	35.0	358	35.8	293	29.3
Mountain:							
Montana	14,798	389	2.6	8,069	54.5	6,340	42.8
Idaho	3,638	135	3.7	2,508	68.9	995	27.4
Wyoming	1,845	65	3.5	1,150	62.3	630	34.1
Colorado	1,395	319	22.9	727	52.1	349	25.0
New Mexico	28,941	695	2.4	18,946	65.5	9,300	32.1
Arizona	43,726	734	1.7	31,626	72.3	11,366	26.0
Utah	2,869	91	3.2	2,097	73.1	681	23.7
Nevada	4,871	249	5.1	2,015	41.4	2,607	53.5
Pacific:							
Washington	11,253	1,053	9.4	4,685	41.6	5,515	49.0
Oregon	4,776	384	8.0	2,487	52.1	1,905	39.9
California	19,212	2,736	14.2	5,985	31.1	10,491	54.6

Source: Truesdell, Dr. Leon E. U.S. Department of Commerce. Bureau of the Census. Fifteenth Census of the United States: 1930, *The Indian Population of the United States and Alaska.* Washington, DC: U.S. Government Printing Office, 1937, p.6.

★ 23 ★

Population

California Indian Population, Prehistory to 1907

Date	Population
Prehistory	310,000 +
1800	260,000
1834	210,000
1849	100,000
1852	85,000
1856	50,000
1860	35,000
1870	30,000
1880	20,500
1890	18,000

[Continued]

★ 23 ★

California Indian Population, Prehistory to 1907
[Continued]

Date	Population
1900	15,500[1]
1907	18,797

Source: Thornton, Russell. *We Shall Live Again: The 1870 and 1890 Ghost Dance Movements as Demographic Revitalization.* New York, NY: Cambridge University Press, 1986, p. 25. Published by permission. *Notes:* Information on which this table was based was obtained from Merriam (1905), Mooney (1928), Cook (1976a), and Thornton (1980). 1. Cook (1976a) disagrees with the nadir figure reported here (from Merriam, 1905), arguing that the actual nadir was between some 20,000 and 25,000 and occurred during the decade 1890-1900.

★ 24 ★

Population

Population History of Indians in Texas, 1690-1890

Tribe or group	1690 population	1890 population	Reduction (%)
Karankawan	2,800	Extinct	100
Akokisa	500	Extinct	100
Bidui	500	Extinct	100
Coahuiltecan	7,500	Extinct	100
Tonkawan	1,600	56	97
Caddo (of Texas)	8,500	536	94
Wichita (of Texas)	3,200	358	89
Kichai	500	66	87
Lipan Apache	500	60	88
Mescalero Apache	700	473	32
Kiowa-Apache	300 + (1780)	326	+9
Comanche	7,000	1,598	77
Kiowa	2,000 (1780)	1,140	43
Arapaho	3,000 (1780)	[1]	[1]
Cheyenne	3,500 + (1780)	5,630	13

Source: Thornton, Russell. *American Indian Holocaust and Survival: A Population History Since 1492.* Norman, OK: University of Oklahoma, Press, 1987, p. 131. Published by permission. Primary source: Ewers, "The Influence of Epidemics on the Indian Populations and Cultures of Texas," *Plains Anthropologist,* 1973, p. 106. *Note:* 1. Included in Cheyenne total.

★ 25 ★

Population

American Indian Population Decline on Martha's Vineyard and Nantucket Islands, 1642-1792

Date	Population	
	From	To
Martha's Vineyard		
1642-1674	3,000	1,500
1674-1698	1,500	1,000
1698-1720	1,000	800
1720-1764	800	313
Nantucket		
1659-1674	3,000	1,500
1674-1698	1,500	1,000
1698-1763	1,000	348
1763-1792	348	20

Source: Thornton, Russell. *American Indian Holocaust and Survival: A Population History Since 1492.* Norman, OK: University of Oklahoma Press, 1987, 83. Published by permission. Primary source: Cook, "The Significance of Disease in the Extinction of the New England Indians," *Human Biology*, 1973, pp. 502-503.

★ 26 ★

Population

Alaskan Indian Population, by Linguistic Stock, Tribe, Sex, and Age Group, and Mixture of Blood, 1910 - I

Tribe and mixture of blood	Both sexes	Male				Female			
		Total[1]	Under 20 yrs.	20 to 50 yrs.	51 yrs. and over	Total[1]	Under 20 yrs.	20 to 50 yrs.	51 yrs. and over
Algonquian stock									
Total	3	2	-	2	-	1	1	-	-
Full blood	1	1	-	1	-	-	-	-	-
Mixed blood (white and Indian)	2	1	-	1	-	1	1	-	-
Athapaskan stock									
Total	3,916	2,009	902	948	159	1,907	893	884	130
Full blood	3,642	1,875	797	921	157	1,767	777	861	129
Mixed blood	274	134	105	27	2	140	116	23	1
White and Indian	273	134	105	27	2	139	115	23	1
Other races and Indian (Japanese)	1	-	-	-	-	1	1	-	-
Ahtena	297	161	66	75	20	136	59	66	11
Full blood	293	158	64	74	20	135	58	66	11

[Continued]

★ 26 ★

Alaskan Indian Population, by Linguistic Stock, Tribe, Sex, and Age Group, and Mixture of Blood, 1910 - I

[Continued]

Tribe and mixture of blood	Both sexes	Male				Female			
		Total[1]	Under 20 yrs.	20 to 50 yrs.	51 yrs. and over	Total[1]	Under 20 yrs.	20 to 50 yrs.	51 yrs. and over
Mixed blood (white and Indian)	4	3	2	1	-	1	1	-	-
Hankutchin	127	79	37	31	11	48	24	23	1
Full blood	127	79	37	31	11	48	24	23	1
Kaiyuhkhotana	160	78	26	46	6	82	33	43	6
Full blood	155	75	23	46	6	80	31	43	6
Mixed blood (white and Indian)	5	3	3	-	-	2	2	-	-
Knaiakhotana	697	380	178	169	33	317	158	138	21
Full blood	672	364	165	166	33	308	151	136	21
Mixed blood (white and Indian)	25	16	13	3	-	9	7	2	-
Kutchin	359	188	83	86	19	171	80	78	13
Full blood	349	184	80	85	19	165	74	78	13
Mixed blood (white and Indian)	10	4	3	1	-	6	6	-	-
Nahane	8	5	3	2	-	3	2	1	-
Full blood	2	1	-	1	-	1	-	1	-
Mixed blood (white and Indian)	6	4	3	1	-	2	2	-	-
Natsitkutchin	177	96	39	45	12	81	35	35	11
Full blood	176	96	39	45	12	80	34	35	11
Mixed blood (Japanese and Indian)	1	-	-	-	-	1	1	-	-
Tenankutchin	415	216	97	98	21	199	89	97	13
Full blood	396	204	87	96	21	192	83	96	13
Mixed blood (white and Indian)	19	12	10	2	-	7	6	1	-
Tukkuthkutchin	6	1	1	-	-	5	2	3	-
Full blood	3	-	-	-	-	3	-	3	-
Mixed blood (white and Indian)	3	1	1	-	-	2	2	-	-
Unakhotana	193	98	37	56	5	95	50	41	4
Full blood	170	89	30	54	5	81	36	41	4
Mixed blood (white and Indian)	23	9	7	2	-	14	14	-	-
Vuntakutchin	5	2	-	2	-	3	-	3	-
Full blood	5	2	-	2	-	3	-	3	-
Tribe not reported	1,472	705	335	338	32	767	361	356	50
Full blood	1,294	623	272	321	30	671	286	336	49
Mixed blood (white and Indian)	178	82	63	17	2	96	75	20	1

[Continued]

★ 26 ★

Alaskan Indian Population, by Linguistic Stock, Tribe, Sex, and Age Group, and Mixture of Blood, 1910 - I
[Continued]

Tribe and mixture of blood	Both sexes	Male				Female			
		Total[1]	Under 20 yrs.	20 to 50 yrs.	51 yrs. and over	Total[1]	Under 20 yrs.	20 to 50 yrs.	51 yrs. and over
Eskimauan stock									
Total	14,087	7,310	3,505	3,176	557	6,777	3,135	3,019	547
Full blood	12,859	6,666	3,007	3,049	543	6,193	2,691	2,890	540
Mixed blood	1,228	644	498	127	14	584	444	129	7
White and Indian	1,209	637	491	127	14	572	433	128	7
Other races and Indian	19	7	7	-	-	12	11	1	-
Chinese	5	2	2	-	-	3	3	-	-
Japanese	14	5	5	-	-	9	8	1	-
Aleut	1,451	758	404	288	61	693	353	287	50
Full blood	999	523	249	221	52	476	207	225	44
Mixed blood	452	235	155	67	9	217	146	62	6
White and Indian	449	234	154	67	9	215	144	62	6
Other races and Indian (Japanese)	3	1	1	-	-	2	2	-	-
Chnagmiut	326	180	100	66	14	146	69	65	12
Full blood	299	165	85	66	14	134	57	65	12
Mixed blood (white and Indian)	27	15	15	-	-	12	12	-	-
Ikogmiut	782	374	172	173	29	408	186	194	28
Full blood	768	366	165	172	29	402	180	194	28
Mixed blood (white and Indian)	14	8	7	1	-	6	6	-	-
Imaklimiut	2	1	-	1	-	1	1	-	-
Full blood	2	1	-	1	-	1	1	-	-
Iprackmiut	4	3	2	1	-	1	-	1	-
Full blood	4	3	2	1	-	1	-	1	-
Kaialigmiut	192	98	49	37	12	94	37	47	10
Full blood	191	98	49	37	12	93	36	47	10
Mixed blood (white and Indian)	1	-	-	-	-	1	1	-	-
Kakuakamiut	22	10	6	3	1	12	6	4	2
Full blood	22	10	6	3	1	12	6	4	2
Kangmaligmiut	1	-	-	-	-	1	1	-	-
Full blood	1	-	-	-	-	1	1	-	-
Kaviagmiut	238	120	66	48	6	118	55	51	12
Full blood	209	109	55	48	6	100	37	51	12
Mixed blood (white and Indian)	29	11	11	-	-	18	18	-	-

[Continued]

★ 26 ★

Alaskan Indian Population, by Linguistic Stock, Tribe, Sex, and Age Group, and Mixture of Blood, 1910 - I

[Continued]

Tribe and mixture of blood	Both sexes	Male				Female			
		Total[1]	Under 20 yrs.	20 to 50 yrs.	51 yrs. and over	Total[1]	Under 20 yrs.	20 to 50 yrs.	51 yrs. and over
Kekchabukmiut	32	16	6	9	1	16	5	10	1
Full blood	32	16	6	9	1	16	5	10	1
Kinugumiut	594	330	156	148	26	264	118	120	26
Full blood	576	322	148	148	26	254	108	120	26
Mixed blood (white and Indian)	18	8	8	-	-	10	10	-	-
Kopagmiut	9	3	2	1	-	6	-	6	-
Full blood	9	3	2	1	-	6	-	6	-
Kowagmiut	561	301	141	141	19	260	114	125	21
Full blood	546	293	133	141	19	253	107	125	21
Mixed blood (white and Indian)	15	8	8	-	-	7	7	-	-

Source: U.S. Bureau of the Census. *Indian Population in the United States and Alaska, 1910.* Washington, DC: U.S. Government Printing Office, 1915, pp. 154-156. *Notes:* A dash (-) represents zero. 1. Totals include persons of unknown age.

★ 27 ★

Population

Alaskan Indian Population, by Linguistic Stock, Tribe, Sex, and Age Group, and Mixture of Blood, 1910 - II

Tribe and mixture of blood	Both sexes	Male				Female			
		Total[1]	Under 20 yrs.	20 to 50 yrs.	51 yrs. and over	Total[1]	Under 20 yrs.	20 to 50 yrs.	51 yrs. and over
Eskimauan stock (cont.)									
Kukpaurungmiut	6	4	3	1	-	2	-	1	1
Full blood	6	4	3	1	-	2	-	1	1
Kunmiut	77	43	21	20	2	34	12	19	3
Full blood	77	43	21	20	2	34	12	19	3
Kusetrinmiut	133	82	47	32	3	51	21	25	5
Full blood	125	77	42	32	3	48	18	25	5
Mixed blood (white and Indian)	8	5	5	-	-	3	3	-	-
Kuskovakmiut	370	212	135	67	10	158	82	67	9
Full blood	361	206	130	66	10	155	79	67	9
Mixed blood (white and Indian)	9	6	5	1	-	3	3	-	-
Kuskowik	37	18	11	5	2	19	7	10	2

[Continued]

★ 27 ★

Alaskan Indian Population, by Linguistic Stock, Tribe, Sex, and Age Group, and Mixture of Blood, 1910 - II
[Continued]

Tribe and mixture of blood	Both sexes	Male				Female			
		Total[1]	Under 20 yrs.	20 to 50 yrs.	51 yrs. and over	Total[1]	Under 20 yrs.	20 to 50 yrs.	51 yrs. and over
Full blood	36	17	10	5	2	19	7	10	2
Mixed blood (white and Indian)	1	1	1	-	-	-	-	-	-
Kuskwogmiut	1,480	741	344	342	55	739	337	348	54
Full blood	1,447	723	326	342	55	724	322	348	54
Mixed blood (white and Indian)	33	18	18	-	-	15	15	-	-
Magemiut	376	176	85	79	12	200	103	80	17
Full blood	376	176	85	79	12	200	103	80	17
Malemiut	563	292	149	118	21	271	136	110	19
Full blood	546	282	139	118	21	264	129	110	19
Mixed blood	17	10	10	-	-	7	7	-	-
White and Indian	14	8	8	-	-	6	6	-	-
Other races and Indian (Chinese)	3	2	2	-	-	1	1	-	-
Naparktoo	9	8	1	6	1	1	-	1	-
Full blood	9	8	1	6	1	1	-	1	-
Neechuktamiut	25	12	5	6	1	13	6	5	2
Full blood	25	12	5	6	1	13	6	5	2
Nunatogmiut	285	158	56	83	16	127	50	60	11
Full blood	277	153	52	82	16	124	47	60	11
Mixed blood (white and Indian)	8	5	4	1	-	3	3	-	-
Nunivagmiut	301	161	69	80	12	140	54	75	11
Full blood	299	160	68	80	12	139	53	75	11
Mixed blood (white and Indian)	2	1	1	-	-	1	1	-	-
Nunochogmiut	158	73	32	38	3	85	36	39	10
Full blood	158	73	32	38	3	85	36	39	10
Nushagagmiut	31	20	7	8	5	11	6	4	1
Full blood	24	16	3	8	5	8	3	4	1
Mixed blood (white and Indian)	7	4	4	-	-	3	3	-	-
Nuwukmiut	81	40	16	20	4	41	17	23	1
Full blood	71	34	12	18	4	37	16	20	1
Mixed blood (white and Indian)	10	6	4	2	-	4	1	3	-
Pitukmiut	4	3	-	1	1	1	-	-	-
Full blood	4	3	-	1	1	1	-	-	-

[Continued]

★ 27 ★

Alaskan Indian Population, by Linguistic Stock, Tribe, Sex, and Age Group, and Mixture of Blood, 1910 - II
[Continued]

Tribe and mixture of blood	Both sexes	Male				Female			
		Total[1]	Under 20 yrs.	20 to 50 yrs.	51 yrs. and over	Total[1]	Under 20 yrs.	20 to 50 yrs.	51 yrs. and over
Polazramiut	14	8	6	2	-	6	4	2	-
Full blood	14	8	6	2	-	6	4	2	-
Selawigmiut	258	140	54	79	7	118	43	65	10
Full blood	258	140	54	79	7	118	43	65	10
Sidarumiut	5	3	1	2	-	2	-	1	1
Full blood	4	2	-	2	-	2	-	1	1
Mixed blood (white and Indian)	1	1	1	-	-	-	-	-	-
Tikeramiut	320	159	60	83	15	161	67	70	23
Full blood	300	153	54	83	15	147	53	70	23
Mixed blood (white and Indian)	20	6	6	-	-	14	14	-	-
Togiagmiut	93	52	26	18	8	41	13	23	5
Full blood	89	48	22	18	8	41	13	23	5
Mixed blood (white and Indian)	4	4	4	-	-	-	-	-	-
Ukivokmiut	140	77	38	37	2	63	26	36	1
Full blood	140	77	38	37	2	63	26	36	1
Unaligmiut	441	221	131	74	16	220	101	102	17
Full blood	421	211	121	74	16	210	91	102	17
Mixed blood (white and Indian)	20	10	10	-	-	10	10	-	-
Utkiavinmiut	123	63	30	30	3	60	23	36	1
Full blood	119	62	30	29	3	57	21	35	1
Mixed blood (white and Indian)	4	1	-	1	-	3	2	1	-
Utukamiut	127	65	26	34	5	62	22	32	8
Full blood	116	57	18	34	5	59	19	32	8
Mixed blood (white and Indian)	11	8	8	-	-	3	3	-	-
Yuit	292	149	61	71	17	143	55	63	25
Full blood	290	148	60	71	17	142	54	63	25
Mixed blood (white and Indian)	2	1	1	-	-	1	1	-	-
Southern Eskimo	3,650	1,899	875	861	155	1,751	857	745	135
Full blood	3,186	1,645	678	809	150	1,541	708	686	134
Mixed blood	464	254	197	52	5	210	149	59	1
White and Indian	454	250	193	52	5	204	144	58	1
Other races and Indian (Japanese)	10	4	4	-	-	6	5	1	-
Tribe not reported	474	237	112	63	12	237	112	67	13

[Continued]

★ 27 ★

Alaskan Indian Population, by Linguistic Stock, Tribe, Sex, and Age Group, and Mixture of Blood, 1910 - II

[Continued]

Tribe and mixture of blood	Both sexes	Male				Female			
		Total[1]	Under 20 yrs.	20 to 50 yrs.	51 yrs. and over	Total[1]	Under 20 yrs.	20 to 50 yrs.	51 yrs. and over
Full blood	423	219	97	61	12	204	83	63	13
Mixed blood	51	18	15	2	-	33	29	4	-
White and Indian	48	18	2	-	30	26	4	-	-
Other races and Indian	3	-	-	-	-	3	3	-	-
Chinese	2	-	-	-	-	2	2	-	-
Japanese	1	-	-	-	-	1	1	-	-

Source: U.S. Bureau of the Census. *Indian Population in the United States and Alaska, 1910.* Washington, DC: U.S. Government Printing Office, 1915, pp. 154-156. Notes: A dash (-) represents zero. 1. Totals include persons of unknown age.

★ 28 ★

Population

Alaskan Indian Population, by Linguistic Stock, Tribe, Sex, and Age Group, and Mixture of Blood, 1910 - III

Tribe and mixture of blood	Both sexes	Male				Female			
		Total[1]	Under 20 yrs.	20 to 50 yrs.	51 yrs. and over	Total[1]	Under 20 yrs.	20 to 50 yrs.	51 yrs. and over
Hadian stock									
Total	530	281	143	106	29	249	130	95	23
Full blood	377	201	88	83	29	176	81	72	22
Mixed blood (white and Indian)	153	80	55	23	-	73	49	23	1
Tlingit stock									
Total	4,426	2,223	995	949	278	2,203	1,004	934	263
Full blood	3,890	1,945	791	879	274	1,945	792	896	255
Mixed blood	536	278	204	70	4	258	212	38	8
White and Indian	522	271	197	70	4	251	205	38	8
Other races and Indian	13	6	6	-	-	7	7	-	-
Chinese	2	1	1	-	-	1	1	-	-
Japanese	11	5	5	-	-	6	6	-	-
Mixture unknown	1	1	1	-	-	-	-	-	-
Auk	267	143	47	82	14	124	55	61	8
Full blood	242	132	37	81	14	110	43	60	7
Mixed blood (white and Indian)	25	11	10	1	-	14	12	1	1
Chilkat	690	350	140	167	43	340	144	151	45
Full blood	629	318	112	163	43	311	119	148	44
Mixed blood (white and Indian)	61	32	28	4	-	29	25	3	1

[Continued]

★ 28 ★

Alaskan Indian Population, by Linguistic Stock, Tribe, Sex, and Age Group, and Mixture of Blood, 1910 - III

[Continued]

Tribe and mixture of blood	Both sexes	Male				Female			
		Total[1]	Under 20 yrs.	20 to 50 yrs.	51 yrs. and over	Total[1]	Under 20 yrs.	20 to 50 yrs.	51 yrs. and over
Henya	214	114	50	49	15	100	52	39	9
Full blood	192	101	41	45	15	91	44	38	9
Mixed blood (white and Indian)	22	13	9	4	-	9	8	1	-
Huna	625	303	141	125	36	322	136	143	43
Full blood	590	286	127	122	36	304	120	141	43
Mixed blood (white and Indian)	35	17	14	3	-	18	16	2	-
Hutsnuwu	536	268	131	101	36	268	123	109	36
Full blood	498	247	111	100	36	251	107	108	36
Mixed blood	38	21	20	1	-	17	16	1	-
White and Indian	31	18	17	1	-	13	12	1	-
Other races and Indian	7	3	3	-	-	4	4	-	-
Chinese	1	-	-	-	-	1	1	-	-
Japanese	6	3	3	-	-	3	3	-	-
Kake	322	163	80	52	31	159	73	65	21
Full blood	276	141	63	47	31	135	54	61	20
Mixed blood	46	22	17	5	-	24	19	4	1
White and Indian	45	22	17	5	-	23	18	4	1
Other races and Indian (Japanese)	1	-	-	-	-	1	1	-	-
Kuyu	29	17	4	10	3	12	6	4	2
Full blood	29	17	4	10	3	12	6	4	2
Sitka	608	295	131	115	49	313	144	117	51
Full blood	527	248	97	104	47	279	118	109	51
Mixed blood	81	47	34	11	2	34	26	8	-
White and Indian	80	46	33	11	2	34	26	8	-
Mixture unknown	1	1	1	-	-	-	-	-	-
Stikine	189	96	35	49	12	93	44	34	15
Full blood	150	72	27	33	12	78	30	34	14
Mixed blood (white and Indian)	39	24	8	16	-	15	14	-	1
Taku	142	70	31	31	8	72	27	38	6
Full blood	128	62	23	31	8	66	22	37	6
Mixed blood	14	8	8	-	-	6	5	1	-
White and Indian	13	7	7	-	-	6	5	1	-
Other races and Indian (Chinese)	1	1	1	-	-	-	-	-	-
Tongas	184	88	42	38	8	96	52	35	9
Full blood	156	76	33	35	8	80	40	31	9
Mixed blood (white and Indian)	28	12	9	3	-	16	12	4	-

[Continued]

★ 28 ★

Alaskan Indian Population, by Linguistic Stock, Tribe, Sex, and Age Group, and Mixture of Blood, 1910 - III

[Continued]

Tribe and mixture of blood	Both sexes	Male				Female			
		Total[1]	Under 20 yrs.	20 to 50 yrs.	51 yrs. and over	Total[1]	Under 20 yrs.	20 to 50 yrs.	51 yrs. and over
Yakutat	307	143	70	65	8	164	78	77	9
Full blood	276	131	59	64	8	145	59	77	9
Mixed blood	31	12	11	1	-	19	19	-	-
White and Indian	30	12	11	1	-	18	18	-	-
Other races and Indian (Japanese)	1	-	-	-	-	1	1	-	-
Tribe not reported	313	173	93	65	15	140	70	61	9
Full blood	197	114	57	44	13	83	30	48	5
Mixed blood	116	59	36	21	2	57	40	13	4
White and Indian	113	57	34	21	2	56	39	13	4
Other races and Indian (Japanese)	3	2	2	-	-	1	1	-	-
Tsimshian stock									
Total	729	384	187	143	54	345	178	119	48
Full blood	615	333	151	131	51	282	138	96	48
Mixed blood (white and Indian)	114	51	36	12	3	63	40	23	-

Source: U.S. Bureau of the Census. *Indian Population in the United States and Alaska, 1910.* Washington, DC: U.S. Government Printing Office, 1915, pp. 154-156. *Notes:* A dash (-) represents zero. 1. Totals include persons of unknown age.

★ 29 ★

Population

American Indian Population, by Linguistic Stock, Tribe, and State, 1910 and 1930 - I

Population is shown for states which had five or more Indians of the specified tribe in either 1910 or 1930. Linguistic stocks appear in bold letters.

Linguistic stock, tribe and state	Number	
	1910	1930
Algonquian	39,926	40,670
Arapaho	1,419	1,241
Wyoming	703	863
Oklahoma	685	360
Montana	18	4
Kansas	6	3
Other states	7	11
Blackfeet	2,367	3,145
Montana	2,254	3,033
Washington	-	16

[Continued]

★ 29 ★

American Indian Population, by Linguistic Stock, Tribe, and State, 1910 and 1930 - I
[Continued]

Linguistic stock, tribe and state	Number	
	1910	1930
Ohio	-	14
Nebraska	33	12
Oklahoma	15	11
South Dakota	1	11
Idaho	3	7
California	1	6
Pennsylvania	12	6
Oregon	6	6
North Dakota	35	1
Other states	7	22
Cheyenne	3,055	2,695
Montana	1,346	1,408
Oklahoma	1,522	1,220
South Dakota	133	27
Kansas	5	9
Washington	-	8
Arizona	-	6
California	-	5
Pennsylvania	33	-
Colorado	6	-
Other states	10	12
Chippewa	20,214	21,549
Minnesota	8,234	9,495
Wisconsin	4,299	4,437
North Dakota	2,966	3,827
Michigan	3,725	1,685
Montana	486	1,549
South Dakota	73	280
Oklahoma	64	56
Oregon	48	48
Kansas	92	33
Washington	6	28
Idaho	-	18
Arizona	1	14
New Mexico	-	12
California	6	10
Illinois	-	10
Ohio	3	8
Colorado	-	7
Nebraska	64	7
Missouri	1	6
Nevada	-	6
Pennsylvania	134	2

[Continued]

★ 29 ★

American Indian Population, by Linguistic Stock, Tribe, and State, 1910 and 1930 - I
[Continued]

Linguistic stock, tribe and state	Number	
	1910	1930
Other states	12	11
Delaware	985	971
Oklahoma	895	874
Kansas	55	45
Arizona	-	12
New York	7	10
Minnesota	-	8
Arkansas	-	5
Pennsylvania	9	1
Other states	19	16
Gros Ventres (Atsina)	510	631
Montana	503	615
Wyoming	1	6
Other states	6	10
Kickapoo	348	523
Kansas	211	278
Oklahoma	135	219
Nebraska	1	8
Washington	-	8
Other states	1	10
Menominee	1,422	1,969
Wisconsin	1,350	1,950
South Dakota	3	7
Michigan	34	5
Minnesota	13	1
Oklahoma	7	1
Pennsylvania	9	-
Other states	6	5
Miami and Illinois	360	284
Oklahoma	241	222
Indiana	92	47
Kansas	11	7
Colorado	-	5
Missouri	6	-
Other states	10	3
Ottawa	2,717	1,745
Michigan	2,454	1,469
Oklahoma	170	167
Wisconsin	50	84

[Continued]

★ 29 ★

American Indian Population, by Linguistic Stock, Tribe, and State, 1910 and 1930 - I

[Continued]

Linguistic stock, tribe and state	Number	
	1910	1930
California	-	6
Illinois	-	5
Minnesota	-	5
Nebraska	23	3
Kansas	14	-
Pennsylvania	6	-
Other states	-	6
Potawatomi	2,440	1,854
Kansas	819	654
Oklahoma	866	636
Wisconsin	245	425
Michigan	461	89
Nebraska	21	14
Minnesota	1	7
Arizona	3	5
Utah	-	5
South Dakota	10	4
Iowa	6	1
Other states	8	14

Source: Truesdell, Dr. Leon E. U.S. Department of Commerce. Bureau of the Census. Fifteenth Census of the United States: 1930, *The Indian Population of the United States and Alaska.* Washington, DC: U.S. Government Printing Office, 1937, pp. 56-68. *Note:* A dash (-) indicates 5 or less Indians were counted.

★ 30 ★

Population

American Indian Population, by Linguistic Stock, Tribe, and State, 1910 and 1930 - II

Population is shown for states which had five or more Indians of the specified tribe in either 1910 or 1930. Linguistic stocks appear in bold letters.

Linguistic stock, tribe and state	Number	
	1910	1930
Algonquian (cont.)		
Sauk and Fox	724	887
Oklahoma	347	478
Iowa	257	344
Kansas	69	23
Nebraska	13	20
Michigan	1	5
Missouri	5	3

[Continued]

★ 30 ★

American Indian Population, by Linguistic Stock, Tribe, and State, 1910 and 1930 - II
[Continued]

Linguistic stock, tribe and state	Number	
	1910	1930
Washington	8	2
Pennsylvania	14	1
Tennessee	6	-
Other states	4	11
Shawnee	1,338	1,161
Oklahoma	1,300	1,107
Colorado	-	13
Texas	-	6
New Mexico	-	6
Kansas	14	4
Missouri	14	3
Other states	10	22
Eastern Algonquians	2,027	2,015
Wisconsin	693	813
Maine	634	761
New York	191	194
Rhode Island	-	130
Massachusetts	372	54
Connecticut	77	25
Minnesota	8	14
Oklahoma	9	10
Illinois	-	6
Pennsylvania	25	-
Other states	19	8
Virginia-Carolina Indians	5,195	12,975
North Carolina	5,865	12,402
South Carolina	-	352
Virginia	330	203
Oklahoma	-	8
Arizona	-	6
Other states	-	4
Athapaskan	30,402	47,418
Apache	6,119	6,537
Arizona	4,652	5,113
New Mexico	1,155	1,284
Oklahoma	282	99
California	4	14
Washington	-	7
Colorado	1	5
Kansas	13	-
Other states	12	15

[Continued]

★ 30 ★

American Indian Population, by Linguistic Stock, Tribe, and State, 1910 and 1930 - II

[Continued]

Linguistic stock, tribe and state	Number	
	1910	1930
Kiowa Apache	139	164
Oklahoma	139	183
Illinois	-	1
Navaho	22,455	39,064
Arizona	11,001	20,707
New Mexico	10,354	16,971
Utah	1,039	1,109
Colorado	8	185
California	20	42
South Dakota	4	12
Nevada	-	8
Washington	-	7
Oklahoma	4	5
Missouri	-	5
Pennsylvania	13	1
Kansas	8	1
Other states	4	11
Oregon Athapaskans	656	504
Oregon	499	489
California	129	7
Washington	23	6
Other states	5	2
California Athapaskans	1,033	1,129
California	999	1,115
Washington	15	5
Oregon	8	4
Arizona	6	2
Kansas	5	-
Other states	-	3
Caddoan	1,863	2,115
Arikara	444	420
North Dakota	425	412
New York	6	-
Other states	13	8
Caddo	452	625
Oklahoma	436	615
Kansas	5	5
Pennsylvania	8	-
Other states	3	5

[Continued]

★ 30 ★

American Indian Population, by Linguistic Stock, Tribe, and State, 1910 and 1930 - II

[Continued]

Linguistic stock, tribe and state	Number	
	1910	1930
Pawnee	633	770
Oklahoma	573	729
Arizona	19	12
Kansas	14	11
California	-	7
Pennsylvania	18	-
South Dakota	5	-
Other states	4	11
Wichita and Kichai	334	300
Oklahoma	295	292
South Dakota	20	2
Pennsylvania	15	-
Other states		
Chimakuan	306	375
Washington	306	371
Other states	-	4
Chinookan	897	561
Oregon	352	447
Washington	524	104
Oklahoma	4	8
Montana	12	1
Other states	5	1
Chitimachan	69	51
Louisiana	50	51
Pennsylvania	19	-
Chumashan	38	14
California	38	13
Arizona	-	1

Source: Truesdell, Dr. Leon E. U.S. Department of Commerce. Bureau of the Census. Fifteenth Census of the United States: 1930, *The Indian Population of the United States and Alaska.* Washington, DC: U.S. Government Printing Office, 1937, pp. 56-68. *Note:* A dash (-) indicates 5 or less Indians were counted.

★ 31 ★

Population

American Indian Population, by Linguistic Stock, Tribe, and State, 1910 and 1930 - III

Population is shown for states which had five or more Indians of the specified tribe in either 1910 or 1930. Linguistic stocks appear in bold letters.

Linguistic stock, tribe and state	Number	
	1910	1930
Costanoan (Santa Cruz)	17	-
California	17	-
Iroquoian	39,679	52,457
Iroquois	7,837[1]	6,866
New York	4,918	4,365
Wisconsin	2,122	1,732
Oklahoma	263	340
Pennsylvania	362	81
Michigan	17	78
Minnesota	8	45
California	6	30
South Dakota	10	29
Arizona	2	22
Colorado	-	17
Kansas	35	14
Illinois	1	12
Washington	-	10
North Dakota	1	9
Nebraska	5	8
Ohio	12	7
Montana	1	7
New Mexico	2	6
Arkansas	-	6
Indiana	-	6
Missouri	-	6
Nevada	-	5
Other states	11	31
Wyandot	353	353
Oklahoma	320	323
South Dakota	2	15
Kansas	21	4
California	5	1
Other states	5	10
Cherokee	31,489	45,238
Oklahoma	29,610	40,904
North Carolina	1,406	1,963
Alabama	9	287
Virginia	19	268
California	34	258
Kansas	71	191
Arkansas	-	180
Oregon	19	126

[Continued]

★ 31 ★

American Indian Population, by Linguistic Stock, Tribe, and State, 1910 and 1930 - III
[Continued]

Linguistic stock, tribe and state	Number	
	1910	1930
Texas	-	117
Arizona	4	101
Michigan	3	96
Missouri	13	88
Washington	8	82
Colorado	12	76
New Mexico	1	61
Illinois	-	51
Wisconsin	14	40
Tennessee	45	38
Idaho	8	36
Montana	12	31
Ohio	15	29
New York	5	26
Iowa	-	26
Nebraska	-	25
Pennsylvania	50	18
Georgia	-	15
South Dakota	7	13
Wyoming	-	13
Louisiana	1	12
Indiana	-	10
Nevada	-	9
Massachusetts	-	8
New Jersey	-	7
Mississippi	-	6
Minnesota	2	5
Florida	-	5
North Dakota	34	4
South Dakota	87	2
Other states	-	11
Kalapooian	106	45
Oregon	78	28
California	-	11
Washington	28	2
Other states	-	4
Karok (Orleans)	775	755
California	775	723
Oklahoma	-	18
Oregon	-	9
Other states	-	5

[Continued]

★ 31 ★

American Indian Population, by Linguistic Stock, Tribe, and State, 1910 and 1930 - III

[Continued]

Linguistic stock, tribe and state	Number	
	1910	1930
Keresan	4,027	4,134
New Mexico	3,996	4,092
Arizona	-	27
California	19	7
Oklahoma	4	6
Other states	8	2
Kiowan (Kiowa)	1,126	1,050
Oklahoma	1,107	1,046
Kansas	17	-
Other states	2	4
Kusan (Kusa)	93	107
Oregon	93	99
Other states	-	8

Source: Truesdell, Dr. Leon E. U.S. Department of Commerce, Bureau of the Census. Fifteenth Census of the United States: 1930, *The Indian Population of the United States and Alaska.* Washington, DC: U.S. Government Printing Office, 1937, pp. 56-68. *Notes:* A dash (-) indicates 5 or less Indians were counted. 1. Includes 61 of returned as "Iroquois" but with tribe not reported. Not distributed by States.

★ 32 ★

Population

American Indian Population, by Linguistic Stock, Tribe, and State, 1910 and 1930 - IV

Population is shown for states which had five or more Indians of the specified tribe in either 1910 or 1930. Linguistic stocks appear in bold letters.

Linguistic stock, tribe and state	Number	
	1910	1930
Kutenaian (Kutenai)	538	287
Montana	424	185
Idaho	107	101
Other states	7	1
Maidu	1,100	93
California	1,098	75
Wisconsin	-	11
Other states	2	7
Miwok	699	491
California	698	485

[Continued]

★ 32 ★

American Indian Population, by Linguistic Stock, Tribe, and State, 1910 and 1930 - IV

[Continued]

Linguistic stock, tribe and state	Number	
	1910	1930
Other states	1	6
Muskhogean	29,191	33,633
Chickasaw	4,204	4,745
Oklahoma	4,191	4,685
California	-	14
Missouri	-	11
Louisiana	-	8
Colorado	-	8
Texas	-	5
Other states	13	14
Choctaw	15,917	17,757
Oklahoma	14,551	16,461
Mississippi	1,162	624
Louisiana	115	190
Texas	-	66
California	-	41
Arizona	-	40
Alabama	57	27
Kansas	11	24
Colorado	-	20
New Mexico	-	18
Michigan	-	14
Missouri	-	8
Oregon	1	7
Arkansas	-	7
Wyoming	-	7
South Dakota	8	1
Virginia	8	-
Other states	4	22
Creek	7,341	9,083
Oklahoma	6,654	8,607
Texas	199	180
Louisiana	196	134
Kansas	33	43
Alabama	185	36
Oregon	1	24
Missouri	2	11
California	3	10
Arizona	-	9
New Mexico	-	7
Wisconsin	-	6
Arkansas	-	5

[Continued]

★ 32 ★

American Indian Population, by Linguistic Stock, Tribe, and State, 1910 and 1930 - IV

[Continued]

Linguistic stock, tribe and state	Number	
	1910	1930
Montana	34	3
South Dakota	9	2
North Carolina	7	1
Mississippi	6	-
Other states	12	5
Seminole	1,729	2,048
Oklahoma	1,503	1,789
Florida	16	227
California	1	7
Arizona	-	6
Oregon	-	6
Michigan	-	5
Texas	200	2
Kansas	8	-
Other states	1	6
Piman	8,034	9,587
Papago	3,798	5,205
Arizona	3,785	5,163
California	6	29
Other states	7	13
Pima	4,236	4,382
Arizona	4,167	4,322
California	60	22
South Dakota	-	13
Oklahoma	-	10
Montana	-	5
Kansas	5	2
Other states	4	8
Pomo	1,193	1,143
California	1,162	1,134
Kansas	6	-
Other states	5	9
Salinan (San Antonio)	16	-
California	16	-
Salishan	7,723	9,333
Washington Coast Salish	3,918	4,106
Oregon	57	26
Idaho	-	11
California	-	8

[Continued]

★ 32 ★

American Indian Population, by Linguistic Stock, Tribe, and State, 1910 and 1930 - IV

[Continued]

Linguistic stock, tribe and state	Number	
	1910	1930
Pennsylvania	5	1
Other states	6	5

Source: Truesdell, Dr. Leon E. U.S. Department of Commerce. Bureau of the Census. Fifteenth Census of the United States: 1930, *The Indian Population of the United States and Alaska.* Washington, DC: U.S. Government Printing Office, 1937, pp. 56-68. *Note:* A dash (-) indicates 5 or less Indians were counted.

★ 33 ★

Population

American Indian Population, by Linguistic Stock, Tribe, and State, 1910 and 1930 - V

Population is shown for states which had five or more Indians of the specified tribe in either 1910 or 1930. Linguistic stocks appear in bold letters.

Linguistic stock, tribe and state	Number	
	1910	1930
Salishan (cont.)		
Interior Salish	3,780	5,211
Washington	2,242	2,607
Montana	939	2,036
Idaho	419	480
Oregon	151	72
Nebraska	7	1
Pennsylvania	19	-
Other states	3	15
Tillamook	25	16
Oregon	18	9
Washington	6	2
Other states	1	5
Shapwailutan	5,698[1]	6,352
Klamath and Modoc	978	2,034
Oregon	858	1,057
California	36	922
Oklahoma	33	31
Washington	5	8
Nevada	-	8
Arizona	6	2
Pennsylvania	25	-
Missouri	10	-
Other states	5	6

[Continued]

★ 33 ★

American Indian Population, by Linguistic Stock, Tribe, and State, 1910 and 1930 - V

[Continued]

Linguistic stock, tribe and state	Number	
	1910	1930
Shahaptians	4,374	4,119
Washington	1,984	1,890
Idaho	1,074	1,091
Oregon	1,206	1,054
Montana	66	39
California	2	14
Nevada	-	8
Nebraska	-	6
Kansas	7	2
Pennsylvania	33	-
Other states	2	15
Cayuse and Molala	329	199
Oregon	302	193
Washington	11	1
South Dakota	5	-
Other states	11	5
Shastan	1,578	844
California	1,383	693
Oregon	177	138
Washington	2	5
Nevada	8	1
Oklahoma	7	1
Other states	1	6
Shoshonean	16,842	15,985
Bannock	413	415
Idaho	363	313
Oklahoma	-	66
Wyoming	9	11
Oregon	2	7
California	4	6
Utah	1	6
Montana	23	1
Pennsylvania	5	-
Other states	6	5
Comanche	1,171	1,423
Oklahoma	1,160	1,390
California	-	8
Kansas	7	6
Arizona	-	5
Other states	4	14

[Continued]

★ 33 ★

American Indian Population, by Linguistic Stock, Tribe, and State, 1910 and 1930 - V
[Continued]

Linguistic stock, tribe and state	Number	
	1910	1930
Hopi	2,009	2,752
Arizona	1,941	2,701
California	42	22
New Mexico	9	12
Nevada	-	7
Washington	-	7
Pennsylvania	13	-
Other states	4	3
Paiute-Mono-Paviotso	5,631	5,060
Nevada	2,782	2,660
California	1,968	1,531
Oregon	341	291
Arizona	97	249
Utah	238	193
Idaho	152	112
Montana	27	11
Oklahoma	-	5
Washington	7	4
Wyoming	8	-
Pennsylvania	5	-
Other states	6	4
Shoshoni	3,840	3,994
Nevada	1,555	1,633
Idaho	1,259	1,251
Wyoming	700	787
California	33	177
Utah	248	107
Arizona	4	9
Montana	10	8
Washington	-	6
Oregon	-	6
Pennsylvania	27	-
Other states	4	10
Ute	2,281	1,980
Utah	1,509	1,269
Colorado	725	669
Wyoming	6	18
New Mexico	-	5
Washington	-	5
Nevada	6	3
Oklahoma	14	2
Kansas	12	-

[Continued]

★ 33 ★

American Indian Population, by Linguistic Stock, Tribe, and State, 1910 and 1930 - V
[Continued]

Linguistic stock, tribe and state	Number	
	1910	1930
Other states	9	9
Southern California	1,497	361
California	1,493	350
Oklahoma	-	10
Other states	4	1

Source: Truesdell, Dr. Leon E. U.S. Department of Commerce. Bureau of the Census. Fifteenth Census of the United States: 1930, *The Indian Population of the United States and Alaska.* Washington, DC: U.S. Government Printing Office, 1937, pp. 56-68. *Notes:* A dash (-) indicates 5 or less Indians were counted. 1. Includes 17 of Shapwailutan stock, not reported by tribe or distributed by state.

★ 34 ★

Population

American Indian Population, by Linguistic Stock, Tribe, and State, 1910 and 1930 - VI

Population is shown for states which had five or more Indians of the specified tribe in either 1910 or 1930. Linguistic stocks appear in bold letters.

Linguistic stock, tribe and state	Number	
	1910	1930
Siouan	32,941	37,329
Catawba	124	166
South Carolina	99	159
Colorado	14	-
North Carolina	6	-
Other states	5	7
Crow	1,799	1,674
Montana	1,698	1,625
Oklahoma	2	13
South Dakota	53	12
Indiana	-	6
Washington	-	5
Kansas	14	1
California	11	-
North Dakota	11	-
Pennsylvania	5	-
Other states	5	12
Hidatsa	547	528
North Dakota	520	519

[Continued]

★ 34 ★

American Indian Population, by Linguistic Stock, Tribe, and State, 1910 and 1930 - VI
[Continued]

Linguistic stock, tribe and state	Number	
	1910	1930
South Dakota	1	9
Pennsylvania	10	-
Montana	9	-
Wyoming	6	-
Kansas	1	-
Iowa	244	176
Nebraska	38	83
Oklahoma	79	71
Kansas	124	19
Kansas	238	318
Oklahoma	252	313
Kansas	6	1
Other states	-	4
Mandan	209	271
North Dakota	197	258
Montana	5	12
South Dakota	5	1
District of Columbia	2	-
Oto and Missouri	345	627
Oklahoma	326	614
California	-	7
Nebraska	10	1
Kansas	6	1
Other states	3	4
Omaha	1,105	1,103
Nebraska	1,075	1,027
Oklahoma	5	48
Colorado	-	12
South Dakota	-	6
Kansas	11	2
Pennsylvania	11	-
Other states	3	8
Osage	1,373	2,344
Oklahoma	1,345	2,106
Kansas	12	112
California	-	21
Oregon	-	20
Colorado	-	19
New Mexico	1	12

[Continued]

★ 34 ★

American Indian Population, by Linguistic Stock, Tribe, and State, 1910 and 1930 - VI
[Continued]

Linguistic stock, tribe and state	Number	
	1910	1930
Arizona	2	8
Arkansas	-	7
Washington	-	7
Texas	-	6
Illinois	-	5
Pennsylvania	7	2
Other states	6	19
Ponca	875	939
Oklahoma	619	743
Nebraska	193	161
South Dakota	18	31
Kansas	42	-
Other states	3	4
Quapaw	231	222
Oklahoma	221	212
Kansas	6	10
Other states	4	-
Dakota	22,778	25,934
South Dakota	18,340	20,918
North Dakota	1,900	2,307
Montana	887	1,251
Nebraska	794	690
Minnesota	457	311
Oklahoma	56	144
California	3	49
Washington	6	28
Idaho	-	26
Arizona	3	23
Wyoming	11	22
Kansas	93	21
Michigan	1	17
Pennsylvania	97	15
Colorado	-	14
Oregon	2	14
Illinois	8	13
Nevada	2	13
New Mexico	-	13
Wisconsin	33	9
New York	1	8
Missouri	11	6
Kentucky	-	6
Tennessee	-	5

[Continued]

★ 34 ★

American Indian Population, by Linguistic Stock, Tribe, and State, 1910 and 1930 - VI
[Continued]

Linguistic stock, tribe and state	Number	
	1910	1930
Iowa	7	3
New Jersey	62	1
Other states	4	7
Assiniboin	1,253	1,581
Montana	1,229	1,467
North Dakota	8	94
Nevada	-	5
Kansas	6	1
Oregon	6	1
Other states	4	13

Source: Truesdell, Dr. Leon E. U.S. Department of Commerce. Bureau of the Census. Fifteenth Census of the United States: 1930, *The Indian Population of the United States and Alaska.* Washington, DC: U.S. Government Printing Office, 1937, pp. 56-68. *Note:* A dash (-) indicates 5 or less Indians were counted.

★ 35 ★

Population

American Indian Population, by Linguistic Stock, Tribe, and State, 1910 and 1930 - VII

Population is shown for states which had five or more Indians of the specified tribe in either 1910 or 1930. Linguistic stocks appear in bold letters.

Linguistic group, tribe and state	Number	
	1910	1930
Siouan (cont.)		
Winnebago	1,820	1,446
Wisconsin	735	937
Nebraska	1,007	423
Minnesota	8	15
Oklahoma	9	14
Kansas	5	14
South Dakota	2	12
Iowa	32	5
Illinois	-	5
Pennsylvania	17	3
Other states	5	18
Tanoan	3,140	3,412
New Mexico	3,077	3,348
California	3	32
Arizona	8	9
Texas	34	-

[Continued]

★ 35 ★

American Indian Population, by Linguistic Stock, Tribe, and State, 1910 and 1930 - VII

[Continued]

Linguistic group, tribe and state	Number	
	1910	1930
Other states	5	23
Tonkawan (Tonkawa)	42	48
Oklahoma	42	46
Other states	-	2
Tunican (Tunica)	43	1
Louisiana	43	1
Washoan (Washo)	819	668
Nevada	536	389
California	273	275
Oregon	5	-
Other states	5	4
Wintun	710	512
California	703	508
Other states	7	4
Wiyot (Humboldt Bay)	152	236
California	152	230
Oregon	-	4
Nevada	-	2
Yakonan	55	9
Oregon	47	7
Washington	7	2
South Dakota	1	-
Yuman	39	9
California	39	9
Yokuts	533	1,145
California	530	1,085
Nevada	-	29
Oregon	-	13
Oklahoma	-	9
Arizona	2	6
Other states	1	3
Yuchean	78	216
Oklahoma	74	1195
North Carolina	-	5
Other states	4	16

[Continued]

★ 35 ★

American Indian Population, by Linguistic Stock, Tribe, and State, 1910 and 1930 - VII

[Continued]

Linguistic group, tribe and state	Number	
	1910	1930
Yukian	198	177
California	194	150
Oregon	3	24
Other states	1	3
Yuman	4,267	4,537
Cocopa	245	99
Arizona	229	89
California	16	10
Diegueno	756	322
California	756	321
Nevada	-	1
Northern Yumans	988	646
Arizona	983	639
Other states	5	7
Maricopa	386	310
Arizona	382	295
California	4	5
Other states	-	10
Mohave	1,058	854
Arizona	667	574
California	389	277
Other states	2	3
Yuma	834	2,306
California	642	2,231
Arizona	191	69
Other states	1	6
Yurok	668	471
California	668	440
Nevada	-	26
Zunian (Zuni)	1,667	1,749
New Mexico	1,664	1,726
Arizona	1	10
Other states	2	13

Source: Truesdell, Dr. Leon E. U.S. Department of Commerce. Bureau of the Census. Fifteenth Census of the United States: 1930, *The Indian Population of the United States and Alaska.* Washington, DC: U.S. Government Printing Office, 1937, pp. 56-68. *Note:* A dash (-) indicates 5 or less Indians were counted.

★ 36 ★

Population

American Indian Population, by Linguistic Stock, Tribe, and State, 1910 and 1930 - VIII

Population is shown for states which had five or more Indians of the specified tribe in either 1910 or 1930. Linguistic stocks appear in bold letters.

Linguistic stock, tribe and state	Number	
	1910	1930
Other tribes of the Unites States, including stocks and tribes not reported	20,425[1]	35,150
California	1,856	5,578
Oklahoma	4,407	4,900
Michigan	790	3,291
North Carolina	565	2,197
New York	886	1,875
Arizona	498	1,345
New Mexico	313	1,267
Washington	1,343	1,173
Minnesota	314	1,090
Louisiana	375	1,089
Wisconsin	588	1,052
Kansas	500	894
Mississippi	82	824
Massachusetts	291	753
Nebraska	198	738
Texas	269	575
North Dakota	374	538
South Carolina	143	445
Montana	440	422
Missouri	246	407
Oregon	664	402
Florida	56	348
Pennsylvania	438	331
Ohio	92	323
South Dakota	372	322
Colorado	714	309
Virginia	178	301
Illinois	179	291
Iowa	169	263
Arkansas	460	194
Indiana	184	194
Rhode Island	284	184
New Jersey	106	170
Utah	85	161
Maine	87	144
Connecticut	75	121
Tennessee	155	113
Alabama	658	112
Idaho	87	104
Wyoming	29	84
Maryland	55	47
New Hampshire	31	35

[Continued]

★ 36 ★

American Indian Population, by Linguistic Stock, Tribe, and State, 1910 and 1930 - VIII
[Continued]

Linguistic stock, tribe and state	Number	
	1910	1930
District of Columbia	57	34
Nevada	336	27
Vermont	26	26
Georgia	95	25
Kentucky	234	15
West Virginia	36	14
Delaware	5	3

Source: Truesdell, Dr. Leon E. U.S. Department of Commerce. Bureau of the Census. Fifteenth Census of the United States: 1930, *The Indian Population of the United States and Alaska.* Washington, DC: U.S. Government Printing Office, 1937, pp. 56-68. *Notes:* A dash (-) indicates 5 or less Indians were counted. 1. Includes 61 of Iroquois stock, 17 of Shapwailutan stock, and 13 of Tanoan stock in totals for these stocks.

★ 37 ★

Population

American Indian Population, by Linguistic Stock, Tribe, and State, 1910 and 1930 - IX

Population is shown for states which had five or more Indians of the specified tribe in either 1910 or 1930. Linguistic stocks appear in bold letters.

Linguistic stock, tribe and state	Number	
	1910	1930
Alaskan and foreign tribes	1,781	6,253
Canadian and Mexican tribes	1,781	5,651
Arizona	534	2,097
Montana	309	1,043
Washington	596	522
New York	24	408
North Dakota	5	401
Michigan	28	289
Maine	168	106
California	38	99
Oklahoma	1	75
New Mexico	-	69
South Dakota	-	66
Minnesota	2	55
Massachusetts	24	44
Louisiana	-	44
Illinois	-	41
Idaho	2	37
Ohio	-	36
Pennsylvania	4	35

[Continued]

★ 37 ★

American Indian Population, by Linguistic Stock, Tribe, and State, 1910 and 1930 - IX
[Continued]

Linguistic stock, tribe and state	Number	
	1910	1930
Wisconsin	2	29
New Hampshire	-	29
Oregon	42	24
Texas	-	15
Colorado	-	13
Kansas	1	12
New Jersey	-	11
Wyoming	-	10
Connecticut	-	10
Vermont	-	6
Nebraska	1	5
Other states	-	20
Alaskan tribes	85	385
Washington	6	226
Oregon	79	90
Idaho	-	18
California	-	18
New York	-	8
Other states	-	25
Other foreign-born Indians	1[1]	217
New York	-	56
California	1[1]	35
New Jersey	1[1]	17
Pennsylvania	1[1]	16
Texas	1[1]	10
Missouri	1[1]	8
Louisiana	1[1]	7
Ohio	1[1]	6
Michigan	1[1]	6
Massachusetts	1[1]	5
Illinois	1[1]	5
Minnesota	1[1]	5
Washington	1[1]	5
Other states	1[1]	36

Source: Truesdell, Dr. Leon E. U.S. Department of Commerce. Bureau of the Census. Fifteenth Census of the United States: 1930, *The Indian Population of the United States and Alaska.* Washington, DC: U.S. Government Printing Office, 1937, pp. 56-68. *Notes:* A dash (-) indicates 5 or less Indians were counted. 1. Not tabulated in 1910.

★ 38 ★

Population

Cahuilla Population History from Aboriginal Times to 1980

Date	Population
Aboriginal times	2,500-10,000
1850	2,000-3,000
1890	1,100-1,200
1910	755
1970	1,000
1980	?

Source: Thornton, Russell. *American Indian Holocaust and Survival: A Population History Since 1492.* Norman, OK: University of Oklahoma Press, 1987, p. 126. Published by permission. Primary source: U.S. Bureau of the Census, *Indian Population of the United States and Alaska, 1910.* Washington, D.C.: U.S. Government Printing Office, 1915, p. 97; Harvey, "Population of the Cahuilla Indians: Decline and Its Causes," *Eugenics Quarterly,* p. 194; Bean, "Cults and Their Transformations," pp. 662-672 in Robert F. Heizer, ed., *California,* vol. 8 of *Handbook of North American Indians.* Washington, D.C.: Smithsonian Institution, 1978, p. 584.

★ 39 ★

Population

California Indian Population History, Pre-European Contact to 1980

Date	Population
Pre-European	310,000?-705,000
1800	260,000
1834	210,000
1849	100,000
1852	85,000
1856	50,000
1860	35,000
1870	30,000
1880	20,500
1890	18,000
1900	15,000-20,000

[Continued]

★ 39 ★

California Indian Population History, Pre-European Contact to 1980

[Continued]

Date	Population
1907	18,000
1980	198,275[1]

Source: Thornton, Russell. *American Indian Holocaust and Survival: A Population History Since 1492.* Norman, OK: University of Oklahoma Press, 1987, p. 109. Published by permission. Primary source: Merriam, "The Indian Population of California," *American Anthropologist,* 1905, p. 60; Mooney, "The Aboriginal Population of America North of Mexico," pp. 1-40 in John R. Swanton, ed., *Smithsonian Miscellaneous Collections,* vol. 80, 1928, p. 19; Cook, S., *The Population of the California Indians, 1669-1970.* Berkeley: University of California Press, 1976, pp. 69-71; Cook, N., *Demographic Collapse: Indian Peru, 1520- 1620.* Cambridge, England: Cambridge University Press, 1981, p. 91; Powers, *Tribes of California.* Contributions to North American Ethnology, vol. 3. Reprint. Washington, D.C.: U.S. Government Printing Office, 1976. Swagerty and Thornton, "Preliminary 1980 Census Counts for American Indians, Eskimos, and Aleuts," *American Indian Culture and Research Journal,* 1982, p. 92; U.S. Bureau of the Census, *1980 Census of Population, Supplementary Report. American Indian Areas and Alaska Native Villages: 1980.* PC80-S1-13. Washington, D.C.: U.S. Government Printing Office, 1984, p. 14. *Note:* 1. Includes recent immigrants to California.

★ 40 ★

Population

Cherokee Population History, 1650-1980

Date	Population
1650	22,000
1808-1809	13,395
1826	17,713
1835	21,542
1851-1852	15,802
1866	15,566
1875	19,717
1880	21,920
1890	28,000
1900	32,376
1910	31,489
1970	66,150
1980	232,000 +

Source: Thornton, Russell. *American Indian Holocaust and Survival: A Population History Since 1492.* Norman, OK: University of Oklahoma Press, 1987, p. 115. Published by permission. Primary source: U.S. Bureau of the Census, *Indian Population of the United States and Alaska, 1910.* Washington, D.C.: U.S. Government Printing Office, 1915, p. 83; *The Indian Population of the United States and Alaska.* Washington, D.C.: U.S. Government Printing Office, 1937, p. 188; Mooney, "The Aboriginal Population of America North of Mexico," pp. 1-40 in John R. Swanton, ed., *Smithsonian Miscellaneous Collections,* vol. 80, 1928, p. 8. Thornton, "Cherokee Population Losses During the Trail of Tears: A New Perspective and a New Estimate," *Ethnohistory,* 1984, pp. 295, 297.

★ 41 ★

Population

Cheyenne Population History, 1780-1980

Date	Population
1780	3,500+
1875	4,000
1880	3,767
1890	3,654
1900	3,446
1910	3,055
1930	2,695
1970	6,872
1980	9,918

Source: Thornton, Russell. *American Indian Holocaust and Survival: A Population History Since 1492.* Norman, OK: University of Oklahoma Press, 1987, p. 120. Published by permission. Primary source: U.S. Bureau of the Census, *Indian Population of the United States and Alaska, 1910.* Washington, D.C.; U.S. Government Printing Office, 1915, p. 73; *The Indian Population of the United States and Alaska.* Washington, D.C.: U.S. Government Printing Office, 1937, p. 37; *1970 Census of the Population Subject Report. American Indians.* Final Report PC(2)- 1F. Washington, D.C.: U.S. Government Printing Office, 1973, p. 188; Unpublished American Indian population data from 1980 census, 1981; Mooney, "The Aboriginal Population of America North of Mexico," pp. 1-40 in John R. Swanton, ed., *Smithsonian Miscellaneous Collections,* vol. 80, 1928, p. 13.

★ 42 ★

Population

Huron Population History, Early 1600s to 1980

Date	Population
Huron of Huronia	
Early 1600s	20,000-35,000
1640	10,000
Wyandot	
Mid-1660s	500
1880	251
1890	288
1900	339
1910	353
1980	1,091

[Continued]

★ 42 ★

Huron Population History, Early 1600s to 1980

[Continued]

Date	Population
Huron of Lorette 1966	979

Source: Thornton, Russell. *American Indian Holocaust and Survival: A Population History Since 1492.* Norman, OK: University of Oklahoma Press, 1987, p. 73. Published by permission. Primary source: U.S. Bureau of the Census, *Indian Population of the United States and Alaska,* 1910. Washington, D.C.: U.S. Government Printing Office, 1915, p. 85; Unpublished American Indian population data from 1980 census, 1981; Heidenreich, "Huron," pp. 368-388 in Bruce G. Trigger, ed., *Northeast,* vol. 15 of *Handbook of North American Indians.* Washington, D.C.: Smithsonian Institution, 1978 pp. 369-370; Morissonneau, "Huron of Lorette," pp. 389-393 in Bruce G. Trigger, ed., *Northeast,* vol. 15 of *Handbook of North American Indians.* Washington, D.C.: Smithsonian Institution, 1978, p. 392; Tooker, "Wyandot," pp. 398-406 in Bruce G. Trigger, ed., *Northeast,* vol. 15 of *Handbook of North American Indians.* Washington, D.C.: Smithsonian Institution, 1978, pp. 403-404.

★ 43 ★

Population

Illinois Indian Population History, 1670-1980

Date	Population
1670-80	10,500+
1700	6,000
1736	2,500
1763	1,950
1800	500
1840	200
1910	130
1956	439
1980	645

Source: Thornton, Russell. *American Indian Holocaust and Survival: A Population History Since 1492.* Norman, OK: University of Oklahoma Press, 1987, p. 88. Published by permission. Primary source: U.S. Bureau of the Census, *Indian Population of the United States and Alaska,* 1910. Washington, D.C.: U.S. Government Printing Office, 1915, p. 75; Unpublished American Indian population data from 1980 census, 1981; Blasingham, "The Depopulation of the Illinois Indians," *Ethnohistory,* 1956, p. 372; Callender, "Illinois," pp. 673-80 in Bruce G. Trigger, ed., *Northeast,* vol. 15, of *Handbook of North American Indians.* Washington, D.C.: Smithsonian Institution, 1978, p. 697.

★ 44 ★

Population

Kalapuya Population History, 1780-1980

Date	Population
1780	3,000
1910	106
1970	95
1980	65

Source: Thornton, Russell. *American Indian Holocaust and Survival: A Population History Since 1492.* Norman, OK: University of Oklahoma Press, 1987, p. 125. Published by permission. Primary source: U.S. Bureau of the Census, *Indian Population of the United States and Alaska, 1910.* Washington, D.C.: U.S. Government Printing Office, 1915, p. 85; *1970 Census of the Population Subject Report. American Indians.* Final Report PC (2)- 1F. Washington, D.C.: U.S. Government Printing Office, 1973, p. 188; Unpublished American Indian population data from 1980 census, 1981; Mooney, "The Aboriginal Population of America North of Mexico," pp. 1-40 in John R. Swanton, ed., *Smithsonian Miscellaneous Collections,* vol. 80, 1928, p. 18.

★ 45 ★

Population

Kansas Population History, From Early 1700s to 1980

Date	Size
Early 1700s	5,000
Late 1700s	3,000
Early 1800s	1,500
1861	866
1870	574
1880	397
1900	217
1910	238
1980	677

Source: Thornton, Russell. *American Indian Holocaust and Survival: A Population History Since 1492.* Norman, OK: University of Oklahoma Press, 1987, p. 127. Published by permission. Primary source: U.S. Bureau of the Census, *Indian Population of the United States and Alaska, 1910.* Washington, D.C.: U.S. Government Printing Office, 1915, p. 100; Unpublished American Indian population data from 1980 census, 1981; Mooney, "The Aboriginal Population of America North of Mexico," pp. 1-40 in John R. Swanton, ed., *Smithsonian Miscellaneous Collections,* vol. 80, 1928, p. 13; Unrau, "The Depopulation of the Dheghia-Siouan Kansa Prior to Removal," *New Mexico Historical Review,* 1973, p. 316-321.

★ 46 ★
Population
Kickapoo Population History, Late 1700s to 1980

Location	Population
Late 1700s	
United States	2,700
1832	
United States	2,000
1875	
United States	806
Kansas	380
Oklahoma	426
Mexico	350
1905	
United States	432
Kansas	185
Oklahoma	247
Mexico	400
1950s	
United States	722
Kansas	343
Oklahoma	379
Mexico	387
United States	1,249
1980	
United States	2,355

Source: Thornton, Russell. *American Indian Holocaust and Survival: A Population History Since 1492.* Norman, OK: University of Oklahoma Press 1987, p. 235. Published by permission. Primary source: U.S. Bureau of the Census, *Indian Population of the United States and Alaska,* 1910. Washington, D.C.: U.S. Government Printing Office, 1915, p. 74; 1970 *Census of the Population, Subject Report, American Indians* Final Report PC (2)- 1F. Washington, D.C.: U.S. Government Printing Office, 1973. p. 188; Unpublished American Indian population data from 1980 census, 1981. Latorre and Latorre, *The Mexican Kickapoo Indians,* Austin: University of Texas, Press; Laughlin, William S., Jorgen B. Jorgensen, and Bruno Frolich, 1976, p. 28; Callender, Pope, and Pope, "Kickapoo," pp. 656-672 in Bruce G. Trigger, ed., *Northeast,* vol. 15 of *Handbook of North American Indians.* Washington, D.C.: Smithsonian Institution, 1978, pp. 666-667.

★ 47 ★

Population

Mandan Population History, 1738-1980

Date	Population
1738	15,000
1750	9,000
1780	3,600
1837 (June)	1,600-2,000
1837 (October)	138
1855	252
1866	400
1877	420
1890	251
1904	250
1910	209
1929	329
1937	355
1980	1,013

Source: Thornton, Russell. *American Indian Holocaust and Survival: A Population History Since 1492.* Norman, OK: University of Oklahoma Press, 1987, p. 96. Published by permission. Primary source: U.S. Bureau of the Census, *Indian Population of the United States and Alaska,* 1910. Washington, D.C.: U.S. Government Printing Office, 1915, p. 100; Unpublished American Indian population data from 1980 census, 1981; Mooney, "The Aboriginal Population of American North of Mexico," pp. 1-40 in John R. Swanton, ed., *Smithsonian Miscellaneous Collections,* vol. 80; Moore, John H., 1928, p. 13; Glassner, "Population Figures for Mandan Indians," *The Indian Historian,* 1974, pp. 45-46.

★ 48 ★

Population

Omaha Indian Population History, Late 1700s to 1980

Date	Population
Late 1700s	3,000-3,500
1802	Less than 300
1876	1,076
1882	1,100
1884	1,179
1910	1,105
1930	1,103
1960	1,100 (approximately)

[Continued]

★ 48 ★

Omaha Indian Population History, Late 1700s to 1980
[Continued]

Date	Population
1975	2,600
1980	3,090

Source: Thornton, Russell. *American Indian Holocaust and Survival: A Population History Since 1492.* Norman, OK: University of Oklahoma Press, 1987, p. 93. Published by permission. Primary source: "Omaha Sociology," *Third Annual Report of the Bureau of Ethnology.* Washington, D.C.: U.S. Government Printing Office, 1884, p. 214; Fletcher and LaFlesche, *The Omaha Tribe. Twenty-Seventh Annual Report of the Bureau of American Ethnology...1905-06.* Washington, D.C.: U.S. Government Printing Office, 1911, p. 33; U.S. Bureau of the Census, *Indian Population of the United States and Alaska,* 1910. Washington, D.C.: U.S. Government Printing Office, 1915. p. 101; Unpublished American Indian population data from 1980 census, 1981; Ross, "The Omaha People," *The Indian Historian,* 1970, p. 22; Liberty, "Population Trends Among Present-Day Omaha Indians." *Plains Anthropologist,* 1975, pp. 225, 227.

★ 49 ★

Population

Tolowa Population History, Pre-European Contact to 1983

Date	Population
Pre-European	2,400+
1850s	316
1870	200
1910	121-150
1950	154
1981	396
1983	400-450

Source: Thornton, Russell. *American Indian Holocaust and Survival: A Population History Since 1492.* Norman, OK: University of Oklahoma Press, 1987, p. 207. Published by permission. Primary source: U.S. Bureau of the Census, *Indian Population of the United States and Alaska,* 1990. Washington, D.C.: U.S. Government Printing Office, 1915, p. 79; Unpublished American Indian population data from 1980 census, 1981; Kroeber, *Handbook of the Indians of California,* Washington, D.C.: U.S. Government Printing Office, 1925, p. 883; Tax, *Map of the North American Indians: 1950 Distribution of Descendants of the Aboriginal Population of Alaska, Canada and the United States.* Chicago: Department of Anthropology, University of Chicago, 1960; Baumhoff, "Ecological Determinants of Aboriginal California Populations." *University of California Publications in American Archaeology and Ethnology,* 1963, p. 231; Cook, *The Population of the California Indians,* 1769-1970. Berkeley: University of California Press, 1976b, pp. 55-56; Heth, Unpublished recording of Yurok and Tolowa Indians. Department of Music and American Indian Studies Center, University of California, Los Angeles, 1976; Thornton, "Demographic Antecedents of a Revitalization Movement: Population Change, Population Size and the 1890 Ghost Dance." *American Sociological Review,* 1981, p. 703; Bommelyn, Personal communication, 1983.

★ 50 ★

Population

Yana Population History, Pre-European Contact to 1980

Date	Population
Precontact	2,000-3,000
1848	1,900
1867	100
1864	35
1910	39
1928	12
1973	20
1980	0?

Source: Thornton, Russell. *American Indian Holocaust and Survival: A Population History Since 1492.* Norman, OK: University of Oklahoma Press, 1987, p. 111. Published by permission. Primary source: U.S. Bureau of the Census, *Indian Population of the United States and Alaska, 1910.* Washington, D.C.: U.S. Government Printing Office, 1915, p. 108; Unpublished American Indian population data from 1980 census, 1981; Johnson, "Tribal Demography: The Hopi and Navajo Population as Seen Through Manuscripts from the 1900 U.S. Census," *Social Science History,* 1978, p. 362; Thornton, "Recent Estimates of the Prehistoric California Indian Population," *Current Anthropology,* 1980, p. 703.

★ 51 ★

Population

Yuki Population History, Pre-European Contact to 1980

Date	Population
Pre-European	6,000-12,000+[1]
1858	2,300+
1864	600
1870	238
1880	168
1910	95
1973	32+
1980	96

Source: Thornton, Russell. *American Indian Holocaust and Survival: A Population History Since 1492.* Norman, OK: University of Oklahoma Press, 1987, p. 203. Published by permission. Primary source: Miller, "Whatever Happened to the Yuki." *The Indian Historian,* 1975, p. 6; "Yuki, Huchnom, and Coast Yuki," pp. 249-255 in Robert F. Heizer, ed., *California,* vol. 8 of *Handbook of North American Indians.* Washington, D.C.: Smithsonian Institution, 1978, p. 250; U.S. Bureau of the Census, unpublished American Indian population data from 1980 census, 1981. *Notes:* 1. Estimates of this population have ranged as high as 20,000 (see Miller, 1975, 1978, 1979).

Blood Status

★ 52 ★

Full-Blood and Mixed-Blood Indians in the United States and Alaska, 1910

Class	Indian population: 1910			
	United States		Alaska	
	Number	Percent of total	Number	Percent of total
Total	265,683	100.0	25,331	100.0
Full blood	150,053	56.5	21,444	84.7
Mixed blood	93,423	35.2	3,887	15.3
White and Indian[1]	88,030	33.1	3,843	15.2
Negro and Indian	2,255	0.8	-	-
White, Negro, and Indian	1,793	0.7	-	-
Other mixtures	80	[2]	43	0.2
Mixture unknown	1,265	0.5	1	[2]
Not reported	22,207	8.4	-	-

Source: U.S. Bureau of the Census. *Indian Population in the United States and Alaska, 1910.* Washington, DC: U.S. Government Printing Office, 1915, p. 31. *Notes:* A dash (-) represents zero. 1. Includes Mexican and Indian. 2. Less than one-tenth of 1 percent.

★ 53 ★

Blood Status

Full-Blood and Mixed-Blood Indians, by State, 1910

State	Indians reported on special schedule						
	Number				Percent of total		
	Total	Full-blood	Mixed-blood	Blood not reported	Full-blood	Mixed-blood	Blood not reported
United States	247,137	150,053	93,423	3,661	60.7	37.8	1.5
Arizona	28,748	27,087	414	1,247	94.2	1.4	4.3
California	14,994	10,493	4,217	284	70.0	28.1	1.9
Colorado	769	718	50	1	93.4	6.5	0.1
Idaho	3,426	2,864	514	48	83.6	15.0	1.4
Kansas	1,413[1]	516	889	8	36.5	62.9	0.6
Michigan	6,761	3,528	3,218	15	52.2	47.6	0.2
Minnesota	8,756	3,859	4,886	11	44.1	55.8	0.1
Mississippi	1,176	1,077	90	9	91.6	7.7	0.8
Montana	10,394	6,204	3,895	295	59.7	37.5	2.8
Nebraska	3,312	2,294	939	79	69.3	28.4	2.4

[Continued]

★ 53 ★

Full-Blood and Mixed-Blood Indians, by State, 1910

[Continued]

| State | Indians reported on special schedule | | | | | | |
| | Number | | | | Percent of total | | |
	Total	Full-blood	Mixed-blood	Blood not reported	Full-blood	Mixed-blood	Blood not reported
Nevada	4,949	4,287	508	154	86.6	10.3	3.1
New Mexico	20,279	20,085	175	19	99.0	0.9	0.1
New York	5,209	2,850	2,028	331	54.7	38.9	6.4
North Carolina	7,287	1,394	5,855	38	19.1	80.3	0.5
North Dakota	6,168	2,499	3,561	108	40.5	57.7	1.8
Oklahoma	70,744	25,887	44,288	599	36.6	62.6	0.8
Oregon	4,580	2,901	1,668	11	63.3	36.4	0.2
South Dakota	18,822	13,247	5,408	167	70.4	28.7	0.9
Utah	3,051	2,900	105	46	95.1	3.4	1.5
Washington	9,852	6,770	3,019	63	68.7	30.6	0.6
Wisconsin	9,597	5,249	4,330	18	54.7	45.1	0.2
Wyoming	1,458	1,174	284	-	80.5	19.5	-
Total for 22 states	241,775	147,883	90,341	3,551	61.2	37.4	1.75
All other states	5,362	2,170	3,082	110	40.5	57.5	2.1

Source: U.S. Bureau of the Census. *Indian Population in the United States and Alaska, 1910.* Washington, DC: U.S. Government Printing Office, 1915, p. 32. *Notes:* A dash (-) represents zero. 1. Exclusive of 591 Indians in Haskell Institute, who are included in the total for "All other states."

★ 54 ★

Blood Status

Full-Blood and Mixed-Blood Indians, by Linguistic Stock, Tribe, and State, 1910: A - Mi

Data are shown for tribes having 200 or more members in 1910.

| Stock, tribe, and state | Indians reported on special schedule : 1910 | | | | | | |
| | Number | | | | Percent of total | | |
	Total	Full blood	Mixed blood	Blood not reported	Full blood	Mixed blood	Blood not reported
UNITED STATES							
Algonquian stock	40,975	18,396	22,319	260	44.9	54.5	0.6
Arapaho	1,419	1,311	108	-	92.4	7.6	-
Oklahoma	685	621	64	-	90.7	9.3	-
Wyoming	703	661	42	-	94.0	6.0	-
Cheyenne	3,055	2,662	319	74	87.1	10.4	2.4
Montana	1,346	1,181	97	68	87.7	7.2	5.1
Oklahoma	1,522	1,379	139	4	90.6	9.1	0.3
South Dakota	133	74	57	2	55.6	42.9	1.5
Chippewa	20,214	6,970	13,138	106	34.5	65.0	0.5
Michigan	3,725	1,558	2,152	15	41.8	57.8	0.4
Minnesota	8,234	3,595	4,629	10	43.7	56.2	0.1

[Continued]

★ 54 ★

Full-Blood and Mixed-Blood Indians, by Linguistic Stock, Tribe, and State, 1910: A - Mi
[Continued]

Stock, tribe, and state	Indians reported on special schedule : 1910						
	Number				Percent of total		
	Total	Full blood	Mixed blood	Blood not reported	Full blood	Mixed blood	Blood not reported
Montana	486	84	402	-	17.3	82.7	-
North Dakota	2,966	58	2,829	79	2.0	95.4	2.7
Pennsylvania	134	31	103	-	23.1	76.9	-
Wisconsin	4,299	1,601	2,696	2	37.2	62.7	1
Cree	459	40	418	1	8.7	91.1	0.2
Montana	309	35	273	1	11.3	88.3	0.3
Delaware	914	279	633	2	30.5	69.3	0.2
Gros Ventres	510	390	119	1	76.5	23.3	0.2
Kickapoo	348	240	107	1	69.0	30.7	0.3
Kansas	211	112	99	-	53.1	46.9	-
Oklahoma	135	126	8	1	93.3	5.9	0.7
Mashpee	206	1	205	-	0.5	99.5	-
Menominee	1,422	704	716	2	49.5	50.4	0.1
Miami	226	59	166	1	26.1	73.5	0.4
Oklahoma	123	22	100	1	17.9	81.3	0.8
Ottawa	2,717	1,720	997	-	63.3	36.7	-
Michigan	2,454	1,664	790	-	67.8	32.2	-
Oklahoma	170	12	158	-	7.1	92.9	-
Passamaquoddy	386	295	91	-	76.4	23.6	-
Penobscot	266	85	181	-	32.0	68.0	-
Piegan	2,268	1,214	1,053	1	53.5	46.4	1
Potawatomi	2,440	960	1,478	2	39.3	60.6	0.1
Kansas	819	319	500	-	38.9	61.1	-
Michigan	461	281	180	-	61.0	39.0	-
Oklahoma	866	115	749	2	13.3	86.5	0.2
Wisconsin	245	227	18	-	92.7	7.3	-
Sauk and Fox	724	547	171	6	75.6	23.6	0.8
Iowa	257	245	12	-	95.3	4.7	-
Oklahoma	347	260	81	6	74.9	23.3	1.7
Shawnee	1,338	535	800	3	40.0	59.8	0.2
Stockbridges	533	184	340	9	34.5	63.8	1.7
Athapaskan stock	30,406	28,264	1,045	1,097	93.0	3.4	3.6
Apache	4,973	3,801	127	1,045	76.4	2.6	21.0
Arizona	4,652	3,491	116	1,045	75.0	2.5	22.5
Oklahoma	271	263	8	-	97.0	3.0	-
Hupa	639	345	294	-	54.0	46.0	-
Jicarilla Apache	694	694	-	-	100.0	-	-
Mescalero Apache	424	411	13	-	96.9	3.1	-
Navajo	22,455	22,304	99	52	99.3	0.4	0.2
Arizona	11,001	10,900	49	52	99.1	0.4	0.5
New Mexico	10,354	10,322	32	-	99.7	0.3	-
Utah	1,039	1,034	5	-	99.5	0.5	-

[Continued]

★ 54 ★

Full-Blood and Mixed-Blood Indians, by Linguistic Stock, Tribe, and State, 1910: A - Mi
[Continued]

| Stock, tribe, and state | Indians reported on special schedule : 1910 | | | | | | |
| | Number | | | | Percent of total | | |
	Total	Full blood	Mixed blood	Blood not reported	Full blood	Mixed blood	Blood not reported
Rogue River	383	223	160	-	58.2	41.8	-
Wailaki	227	82	145	-	36.1	63.9	-
Caddoan stock	1,863	1,574	277	12	84.5	14.9	0.6
Arikara	444	372	72	-	83.8	16.2	-
Caddo	452	336	116	-	74.3	25.7	-
Pawnee	633	544	77	12	85.9	12.2	1.9
Wichita	318	308	10	-	96.9	3.1	-
Chimakuan stock	306	286	20	-	93.5	6.5	-
Quileute	259	240	19	-	92.7	7.3	-
Chinookan stock	897	459	436	2	51.2	48.6	0.2
Chinook	315	53	261	1	16.8	82.9	0.3
Oregon	125	12	112	1	9.6	89.6	0.8
Washington	177	41	136	-	23.2	76.8	-
Wasco	242	159	83	-	65.7	34.3	-
Oregon	184	134	50	-	72.8	27.2	-
Wishram	274	216	57	1	78.8	20.8	0.4
Croatan group	5,865	458	5,372	35	7.8	91.6	0.6
Croatan	5,865	458	5,372	35	7.8	91.6	0.6
Iroquoian stock	39,679	11,936	27,143	600	30.1	68.4	1.5
Cherokee	31,489	6,900	24,329	260	21.9	77.3	0.8
North Carolina	1,406	934	469	3	66.4	33.4	0.2
Oklahoma	29,610	5,919	23,440	251	20.0	79.2	0.8
Mohawk	368	63	304	1	17.1	82.6	0.3
Oneida	2,436	2,098	333	5	86.1	13.7	0.2
New York	211	188	23	-	89.1	10.9	-
Wisconsin	2,107	1,854	248	5	88.0	11.8	0.2
Onondaga	365	299	64	2	81.9	17.5	0.5
St. Regis	1,219	133	1,086	-	10.9	89.1	-
Seneca	2,907	2,022	572	313	69.6	19.7	10.8
New York	2,485	1,858	314	313	74.8	12.6	12.6
Oklahoma	215	70	145	-	32.6	67.4	-
Pennsylvania	184	85	99	-	46.2	53.8	-
Tuscarora	400	305	83	12	76.3	20.8	3.0
Wyandot	353	34	318	1	9.6	90.1	0.3
Karok stock	775	364	411	-	47.0	53.0	-
Orleans	775	364	411	-	47.0	53.0	-

[Continued]

★ 54 ★

Full-Blood and Mixed-Blood Indians, by Linguistic Stock, Tribe, and State, 1910: A - Mi

[Continued]

Stock, tribe, and state	Indians reported on special schedule : 1910						
	Number				Percent of total		
	Total	Full blood	Mixed blood	Blood not reported	Full blood	Mixed blood	Blood not reported
Keresan stock	4,027	3,976	33	18	98.7	0.8	0.4
Acoma	691	686	5	-	99.3	0.7	-
Cochiti	237	237	-	-	100.0	-	-
Laguna	1,472	1,427	27	18	96.9	1.8	1.2
San Felipe	490	489	1	-	99.8	0.2	-
Santa Ana	211	211	-	-	100.0	-	-
Santo Domingo	817	817	-	-	100.0	-	-
Kiowan stock	1,126	818	296	12	72.6	26.3	1.1
Kiowa	1,126	818	296	12	72.6	26.3	1.1
Kutenaian stock	538	255	283	-	47.4	52.6	-
Kutenai	538	255	283	-	47.4	52.6	-
Idaho	107	103	4	-	96.3	3.7	
Montana	424	148	276	-	34.9	65.1	-
Lutuamian stock	978	657	320	1	67.2	32.7	0.1
Klamath	696	459	236	1	65.9	33.9	0.1
Modoc	282	198	84	-	70.2	29.8	-
Oregon	212	168	44	-	79.2	20.8	-
Maidu stock	1,100	544	541	15	49.5	49.2	1.4
Maidu	1,100	544	541	15	49.5	49.2	1.4
Miwok stock	699	343	355	1	49.1	50.8	0.1
Miwok	670	335	334	1	50.0	49.9	0.1

Source: U.S. Bureau of the Census. *Indian Population in the United States and Alaska, 1910.* Washington, DC: U.S. Government Printing Office, 1915, pp. 32-34. *Notes:* A dash (-) represents zero. 1. Less than one-tenth of 1 percent.

★ 55 ★
Blood Status

Full-Blood and Mixed-Blood Indians, by Linguistic Stock, Tribe, and State, 1910: Mu - Si

Data are shown for tribes having 200 or more members in 1910.

Stock, tribe, and state	Indians reported on special schedule : 1910						
	Number				Percent of total		
	Total	Full blood	Mixed blood	Blood not reported	Full blood	Mixed blood	Blood not reported
UNITED STATES (cont.)							
Muskhogean stock	29,191	13,625	15,321	245	46.7	52.5	0.8
Alibamu	298	288	6	4	96.6	2.0	1.3
Louisiana	111	101	6	4	91.0	5.4	3.6
Texas	187	187	-	-	100.0	-	-
Chickasaw	4,204	1,128	3,075	1	26.8	73.1	[1]
Choctaw	15,917	7,094	8,715	108	44.6	54.8	0.7
Louisiana	115	81	13	21	70.4	11.3	18.3
Mississippi	1,162	1,075	78	9	92.5	6.7	0.8
Oklahoma	14,551	5,934	8,539	78	40.8	58.7	0.5
Creek	6,945	3,730	3,131	84	53.7	45.1	1.2
Alabama	185	4	181	-	2.2	97.8	-
Oklahoma	6,654	3,702	2,872	80	55.6	43.2	1.2
Seminole	1,729	1,289	392	48	74.6	22.7	2.8
Oklahoma	1,503	1,227	228	48	81.6	15.2	3.2
Texas	200	38	162	-	19.0	81.0	-
Piman stock	8,607	8,344	167	96	96.9	1.9	1.1
Papago	3,798	3,703	55	40	97.5	1.4	1.1
Pima	4,236	4,175	19	42	98.6	0.4	1.0
Yaqui	528	426	88	14	80.7	16.7	2.7
Pomo stock	1,193	907	220	66	76.0	18.4	5.5
Pomo	777	607	117	53	78.1	15.1	6.8
Salishan stock	7,833	5,006	2,746	81	63.9	35.1	1.0
Chehalis	282	201	81	-	71.3	28.7	-
Clallam	398	252	146	-	63.3	36.7	-
Coeur d'Alene	293	236	34	23	80.5	11.6	7.8
Columbia	385	292	88	5	75.8	22.9	1.3
Colville	785	345	437	3	43.9	55.7	0.4
Flathead	486	206	280	-	42.4	57.6	-
Montana	400	180	220	-	45.0	55.0	-
Kalispel	564	361	202	1	64.0	35.8	0.2
Montana	386	226	160	-	58.5	41.5	-
Washington	157	127	30	-	80.9	19.1	-
Lummi	353	200	153	-	56.7	43.3	-
Okinagan	272	121	135	16	44.5	49.6	5.9
Puyallup	303	178	119	6	58.7	39.3	2.0
Quinaielt	288	219	69	-	76.0	24.0	-
Sanpoil	240	180	41	19	75.0	17.1	7.9
Snohomish	664	472	190	2	71.1	28.6	0.3

[Continued]

★ 55 ★

Full-Blood and Mixed-Blood Indians, by Linguistic Stock, Tribe, and State, 1910: Mu - Si

[Continued]

Stock, tribe, and state	Indians reported on special schedule : 1910						
	Number				Percent of total		
	Total	Full blood	Mixed blood	Blood not reported	Full blood	Mixed blood	Blood not reported
Spokan	643	409	233	1	63.6	36.2	0.2
Montana	134	53	81	-	39.6	60.4	-
Washington	379	281	98	-	74.1	25.9	-
Suquamish	307	177	130	-	57.7	42.3	-
Swinomish	333	279	54	-	83.8	16.2	-
Shahaptian stock	4,391	3,372	998	21	76.8	22.7	0.5
Klikitat	405	335	64	6	82.7	15.8	1.5
Nez Perces	1,259	970	276	13	77.0	21.9	1.0
Idaho	1,035	804	218	13	77.7	21.1	1.3
Umatilla	272	219	53	-	80.5	19.5	-
Oregon	152	131	21	-	86.2	13.8	-
Wallawalla	397	126	271	-	31.7	68.3	-
Warm Springs	550	538	12	-	97.8	2.2	-
Yakima	1,362	1,043	317	2	76.6	23.3	0.1
Shastan stock	1,578	1,162	413	3	73.6	26.2	0.2
Hat Creek	240	220	20	-	91.7	8.3	-
Pit River	985	841	144	-	85.4	14.6	-
Shasta	353	101	249	3	28.6	70.5	0.8
California	255	62	192	1	24.3	75.3	0.4
Shoshonean stock	16,842	14,672	1,928	242	87.1	11.4	1.4
Bannock	413	323	90	-	78.2	21.8	-
Chemehuevi	355	315	40	-	88.7	11.3	-
California	260	242	18	-	93.1	6.9	-
Comanche	1,171	736	407	28	62.9	34.8	2.4
Hopi	2,009	2,006	3	-	99.9	0.1	-
Kawia	755	702	52	1	93.0	6.9	0.7
Mono	1,448	1,215	223	10	83.9	15.4	0.7
Paiute	780	674	78	28	86.4	10.0	3.6
California	210	183	27	-	87.1	12.9	-
Nevada	247	229	18	-	92.7	7.3	-
Utah	238	198	13	27	83.2	5.5	11.3
Paviotso	3,038	2,664	227	147	87.7	7.5	4.8
California	101	80	20	1	79.2	19.8	1.0
Idaho	152	133	18	1	87.5	11.8	0.7
Nevada	2,414	2,113	156	145	87.5	6.5	6.0
Oregon	341	334	7	-	97.9	2.1	-
San Luiseno	467	351	115	1	75.2	24.6	0.2
Shoshoni	3,840	3,329	505	6	86.7	13.2	0.2
Idaho	1,259	1,153	101	5	91.6	8.0	0.4
Nevada	1,555	1,392	162	1	89.5	10.4	0.1

[Continued]

★ 55 ★

Full-Blood and Mixed-Blood Indians, by Linguistic Stock, Tribe, and State, 1910: Mu - Si
[Continued]

Stock, tribe, and state	Indians reported on special schedule : 1910						
	Number				Percent of total		
	Total	Full blood	Mixed blood	Blood not reported	Full blood	Mixed blood	Blood not reported
Utah	248	240	8	-	96.8	3.2	-
Wyoming	700	502	198	-	71.7	28.3	-
Ute	2,244	2,112	112	20	94.1	5.0	0.9
Colorado	725	707	18	-	97.5	2.5	-
Utah	1,472	1,382	71	19	93.9	4.8	1.3
Siouan stock	32,941	22,535	9,905	501	68.4	30.1	1.5
Assiniboin	1,253	793	447	13	63.3	35.7	1.0
Crow	1,799	1,242	396	161	69.0	22.0	8.9
Hidatsa	547	418	129	-	76.4	23.6	-
Iowa	244	59	185	-	24.2	75.8	-
Kansas	124	10	114	-	8.1	91.9	-
Kansa	238	71	167	-	29.8	70.2	-
Mandan	209	165	44	-	78.9	21.1	-
Omaha	1,105	885	144	76	80.1	13.0	6.9
Osage	1,373	591	779	3	43.0	56.7	0.2
Oto	332	211	121	-	63.6	36.4	-
Ponca	875	461	408	6	52.7	46.6	0.7
Nebraska	193	60	133	-	31.1	68.9	-
Oklahoma	619	374	239	6	60.4	38.6	1.0
Quapaw	231	63	118	50	27.3	51.1	21.6
Santee Sioux	1,539	799	740	-	51.9	48.1	-
Minnesota	232	100	132	-	43.1	56.9	-
Montana	107	78	29	-	72.9	27.1	-
Nebraska	708	410	298	-	57.9	42.1	-
North Dakota	100	66	34	-	66.0	34.0	-
South Dakota	378	145	233	-	38.4	61.6	-
Sioux	996	494	477	25	49.6	47.9	2.5
Minnesota	161	117	43	1	72.7	26.7	0.6
South Dakota	277	98	176	3	35.4	63.5	1.1
Sisseton Sioux	2,514	1,631	876	7	64.9	34.8	0.3
Montana	255	204	51	-	80.0	20.0	-
North Dakota	621	469	146	6	75.5	23.5	1.0
South Dakota	1,553	926	626	1	59.6	40.3	0.1
Teton Sioux	14,284	10,598	3,551	135	74.2	24.9	0.9
North Dakota	370	225	145	-	60.8	39.2	-
South Dakota	13,795	10,289	3,371	135	74.6	24.4	1.0

Source: U.S. Bureau of the Census. *Indian Population in the United States and Alaska, 1910.* Washington, DC: U.S. Government Printing Office, 1915, pp. 32-34. *Notes:* A dash (-) represents zero. 1. Less than one-tenth of 1 percent.

★ 56 ★
Blood Status

Full-Blood and Mixed-Blood Indians, by Linguistic Stock, Tribe, and State, 1910: Si - Z and Alaska

Data are shown for tribes having 200 or more members in 1910.

Stock, tribe, and state	Indians reported on special schedule: 1910						
	Number				Percent of total		
	Total	Full blood	Mixed blood	Blood not reported	Full blood	Mixed blood	Blood not reported
UNITED STATES (cont.)							
Siouan stock continued							
Teton Sioux							
Brule Sioux	806	593	212	1	73.6	26.3	0.1
Hunkpapa Sioux	1,072	954	109	9	89.0	10.2	0.8
North Dakota	142	119	23	-	83.8	16.2	-
South Dakota	930	835	86	9	89.8	9.2	1.0
Minniconjou Sioux	397	353	33	11	88.9	8.3	2.8
Oglala Sioux	6,045	4,168	1,794	83	68.9	29.7	1.4
Sans Arc Sioux	222	64	152	6	28.8	68.5	2.7
Sihasapa	485	33	143	9	68.7	29.5	1.9
North Dakota	137	50	87	-	36.5	63.5	-
South Dakota	346	282	55	9	81.5	15.9	2.6
Two Kettle Sioux	293	143	146	4	48.8	49.8	1.4
Other Teton Sioux	4,964	3,990	962	12	80.4	19.4	0.2
Winnebago	1,820	1,543	277	-	84.8	15.2	-
Nebraska	1,007	865	142	-	85.9	14.1	-
Wisconsin	735	630	105	-	85.7	14.3	-
Yankton Sioux	2,088	1,348	718	22	64.6	34.4	1.1
Montana	372	279	92	1	75.0	24.7	0.3
North Dakota	159	156	3	-	98.1	1.9	-
South Dakota	1,534	910	603	21	59.3	39.3	1.4
Yanktonai Sioux	1,357	1,144	210	3	84.3	15.5	0.2
North Dakota	551	473	78	-	85.8	14.2	-
South Dakota	803	668	132	3	83.2	16.4	0.4
Tanoan stock	3,140	3,005	101	34	95.7	3.2	1.1
Isleta	956	894	28	34	93.5	2.9	3.6
Jemez	499	499	-	-	100.0	-	-
San Juan	387	382	5	-	98.7	1.3	-
Santa Clara	277	268	9	-	96.8	3.2	-
Taos	517	509	8	-	98.5	1.5	-
Waiilatpuan stock	329	268	60	1	81.5	18.2	0.3
Cayuse	298	254	43	1	85.2	14.4	0.3
Wakashan stock	388	361	27	-	93.0	7.0	-
Makah	360	342	18	-	95.0	5.0	-

[Continued]

★ 56 ★

Full-Blood and Mixed-Blood Indians, by Linguistic Stock, Tribe, and State, 1910: Si - Z and Alaska
[Continued]

Stock, tribe, and state	Indians reported on special schedule: 1910						
	Number				Percent of total		
	Total	Full blood	Mixed blood	Blood not reported	Full blood	Mixed blood	Blood not reported
Washoan stock	819	643	170	6	78.5	20.8	0.7
Washo	819	643	170	6	78.5	20.8	0.7
California	273	228	45	-	83.5	16.5	-
Nevada	536	414	116	6	77.2	21.6	1.1
Wintun stock	710	282	373	55	39.7	52.5	7.7
Wintun	399	121	278	-	30.3	69.7	-
Yokuts stock	533	401	104	28	75.2	19.5	5.3
Yokuts	302	255	35	12	84.4	11.6	4.0
Yuman stock	4,279	4,000	221	58	93.5	5.2	1.4
Cocopa	245	243	2	-	99.2	0.8	-
Diegueno	756	585	171	-	77.4	22.6	-
Maricopa	386	367	2	17	95.1	0.5	4.4
Mohave	1,058	1,038	9	11	98.1	0.9	1.0
Arizona	667	651	5	11	97.6	0.7	1.6
California	389	385	4	-	99.0	1.0	-
Walapai	501	485	16	-	96.8	3.2	-
Yavapai	289	256	5	28	88.6	1.7	9.7
Yuma	834	816	16	2	97.8	1.9	0.2
Arizona	191	187	4	-	97.9	2.1	-
California	642	628	12	2	97.8	1.9	0.3
Yurok stock	668	528	140	-	79.0	21.0	-
Weitspec	668	528	140	-	79.0	21.0	-
Zunian stock	1,667	1,652	15	-	99.1	0.9	-
Zuni	1,667	1,652	15	-	99.1	0.9	-
ALASKA							
Athapaskan stock	3,916	3,642	274	-	93.0	7.0	-
Ahtena	297	293	4	-	98.7	1.3	-
Knaiakhotana	697	672	25	-	96.4	3.6	-
Kutchin	359	349	10	-	97.2	2.8	-
Tenankutchin	415	396	19	-	95.4	4.6	-

[Continued]

★ 56 ★

Full-Blood and Mixed-Blood Indians, by Linguistic Stock, Tribe, and State, 1910: Si - Z and Alaska
[Continued]

Stock, tribe, and state	Indians reported on special schedule: 1910						
	Number				Percent of total		
	Total	Full blood	Mixed blood	Blood not reported	Full blood	Mixed blood	Blood not reported
Eskimauan stock	14,087	12,859	1,228	-	91.3	8.7	-
Aleut	1,451	999	452	-	68.8	31.2	-
Chnagmiut	326	299	27	-	91.7	8.3	-
Ikogmiut	782	768	14	-	98.2	1.8	-
Kaviagmiut	238	209	29	-	87.8	12.2	-
Kinugumiut	594	576	18	-	97.0	3.0	-
Kowagmiut	561	546	15	-	97.3	2.7	-
Kuskovakmiut	370	361	9	-	97.6	2.4	-
Kuskwogmiut	1,480	1,447	33	-	97.8	2.2	-
Magemiut	376	376	-	-	100.0	-	-
Malemiut	563	546	17	-	97.0	3.0	-
Nunatogmiut	285	277	8	-	97.2	2.8	-
Nunivagmiut	301	299	2	-	99.3	0.7	-
Selawigmiut	258	258	-	-	100.0	-	-
Tikeramiut	320	300	20	-	93.8	6.3	-
Unaligmiut	441	421	20	-	95.5	4.5	-
Yuit	292	290	2	-	99.3	0.7	-
Southern Eskimo	3,650	3,186	464	-	87.3	12.7	-
Haidan stock	530	377	153	-	71.1	28.9	-
Haida	530	377	153	-	71.1	28.9	
Tlingit stock	4,426	3,890	536	-	87.9	12.1	-
Auk	267	242	25	-	90.6	9.4	-
Chilkat	690	629	61	-	91.2	8.8	-
Henya	214	192	22	-	89.7	10.3	-
Huna	625	590	35	-	94.4	5.6	-
Hutsnuwu	536	498	38	-	92.9	7.1	-
Kake	322	276	46	-	85.7	14.3	-
Sitka	608	527	81	-	86.7	13.3	-
Yakutat	307	276	31	-	89.9	10.1	-
Tsimshian stock	729	615	114	-	84.4	15.6	-
Tsimshian	729	615	114	-	84.4	15.6	-

Source: U.S. Bureau of the Census. *Indian Population in the United States and Alaska, 1910.* Washington, DC: U.S. Government Printing Office, 1915, pp. 32-34. *Notes:* A dash (-) represents zero. 1. Less than one-tenth of 1 percent.

★ 57 ★
Blood Status

Mixed-Tribal Status of Full-Blood Indians, by State, 1910

| State | Full-blood Indians: 1910 | | | | | | |
| | Number | | | | Percent of total | | |
	Total	Full-tribal blood	Mixed-tribal blood	Tribal blood of one parent unknown	Full-tribal blood	Mixed-tribal blood	Tribal blood of one parent unknown
United States	150,053	139,289	10,251	513	92.8	6.8	0.3
Arizona	27,087	26,519	563	5	97.9	2.1	[1]
California	10,493	9,633	791	69	91.8	7.5	0.7
Colorado	718	703	15	-	97.9	2.1	-
Idaho	2,864	2,676	176	12	93.4	6.1	0.4
Kansas[2]	516	411	101	4	79.7	19.6	0.8
Michigan	3,528	3,173	349	6	89.9	9.9	0.2
Minnesota	3,859	3,832	22	5	99.3	0.6	0.1
Mississippi	1,077	1,077	-	-	100.0	-	-
Montana	6,204	5,730	455	19	92.4	7.3	0.3
Nebraska	2,294	2,260	33	1	98.5	1.4	[1]
Nevada	4,287	4,183	102	2	97.6	2.4	[1]
New Mexico	20,085	19,726	352	7	98.2	1.8	[1]
New York	2,850	2,111	712	27	74.1	25.0	0.9
North Carolina	1,394	1,379	15	-	98.9	1.1	-
North Dakota	2,499	1,554	939	6	62.2	37.6	0.2
Oklahoma	25,8887	24,611	1,193	83	95.1	4.6	0.3
Oregon	2,901	2,219	662	20	76.5	22.8	0.7
South Dakota	13,247	11,034	2,108	105	83.3	15.9	0.8
Utah	2,900	2,800	91	9	96.6	3.1	0.3
Washington	6,770	5,444	1,227	99	80.4	18.1	1.5
Wisconsin	5,249	5,000	225	24	95.3	4.3	0.5
Wyoming	1,174	1,155	19	-	98.4	1.6	-
Total for 22 states	147,883	137,230	10,150	503	92.8	6.9	0.3
All other states	2,170	2,059	101	10	94.9	4.7	0.5

Source: U.S. Bureau of the Census. *Indian Population in the United States and Alaska, 1910.* Washington, DC: U.S. Government Printing Office, 1915, p. 38. *Notes:* A dash (-) represents zero. 1. Less than one-tenth of 1 percent. 2. Exclusive of Indians in Haskell Institute, who are included in the total for "All other states."

★ 58 ★

Blood Status

Mixed-Tribal Blood Status of Full-Blooded Indians, by Linguistic Stock, Tribe, and State, 1910: A - Ke

Data are shown for tribes having 200 or more Indians in 1910. Percentages are not shown where base is less than 50.

Tribe and state	Full-blood Indians: 1910							
	Number				Percent of total			Percent full tribal of all Indians
	Total	Full-tribal blood	Mixed-tribal blood	Tribal blood of one parent unknown	Full-tribal blood	Mixed-tribal blood	Tribal blood of one parent unknown	
Algonquian stock								
Arapaho	1,311	1,269	42	-	96.8	3.2	-	89.4
Oklahoma	621	601	20	-	96.8	3.2	-	87.7
Wyoming	661	654	7	-	98.9	1.1	-	93.0
Cheyenne	2,662	2,507	139	16	94.2	5.2	0.6	82.1
Montana	1,181	1,103	64	14	93.4	5.4	1.2	81.9
Oklahoma	1,379	1,346	33	-	97.6	2.4	-	88.4
South Dakota	74	30	42	2	40.5	56.8	2.7	22.6
Chippewa	6,970	6,784	173	13	97.3	2.5	0.2	33.6
Michigan	1,558	1,433	122	3	92.0	7.8	0.2	38.5
Minnesota	3,595	3,575	15	5	99.4	0.4	0.1	43.4
Montana	84	78	6	-	92.9	7.1	-	16.0
North Dakota	58	57	1	-	98.3	1.7	-	1.9
Pennsylvania	31	31	-	-	-	-	-	23.1
Wisconsin	1,601	1,574	22	5	98.3	1.4	0.3	36.6
Cree	40	26	13	1	-	-	-	5.7
Montana	35	24	11	-	-	-	-	7.8
Delaware	279	213	66	-	76.3	23.7	-	23.3
Gros Ventres	390	357	33	-	91.5	8.5	-	70.0
Kickapoo	240	200	36	4	83.3	15.0	1.7	57.5
Kansas	112	79	29	4	70.5	25.9	3.6	37.4
Oklahoma	126	119	7	-	94.4	5.6	-	88.1
Mashpee	1	1	-	-	-	-	-	0.5
Menominee	704	665	33	6	94.5	4.7	0.9	46.8
Miami	59	47	12	-	79.7	20.3	-	20.8
Oklahoma	22	12	10	-	-	-	-	9.8
Ottawa	1,720	1,535	180	5	89.2	10.5	0.3	56.5
Michigan	1,664	1,496	167	1	89.9	10.0	0.1	61.0
Oklahoma	12	7	5	-	-	-	-	4.1
Passamaquoddy	295	289	6	-	98.0	2.0	-	74.9
Penobscot	85	60	25	-	70.6	29.4	-	22.6
Piegan	1,214	1,206	8	-	99.3	0.7	-	53.2
Potawatomi	960	795	164	1	82.8	17.1	0.1	32.6
Kansas	319	269	50	-	84.3	15.7	-	32.8
Michigan	281	226	55	-	80.4	19.6	-	49.0
Oklahoma	115	78	36	1	67.8	31.3	0.9	9.0
Wisconsin	227	211	16	-	93.0	7.0	-	86.1
Sauk and Fox	547	490	55	2	89.6	10.1	0.4	67.7
Iowa	245	218	27	-	89.0	11.0	-	84.8
Oklahoma	260	235	24	1	90.4	9.2	0.4	67.7
Shawnee	535	467	68	-	87.3	12.7	-	34.9

[Continued]

★ 58 ★

Mixed-Tribal Blood Status of Full-Blooded Indians, by Linguistic Stock, Tribe, and State, 1910: A - Ke

[Continued]

Tribe and state	Full-blood Indians: 1910							Percent full tribal of all Indians
	Number				Percent of total			
	Total	Full-tribal blood	Mixed-tribal blood	Tribal blood of one parent unknown	Full-tribal blood	Mixed-tribal blood	Tribal blood of one parent unknown	
Stockbridges	184	143	40	1	77.7	21.7	0.5	26.8
Athapaskan stock								
Apache	3,801	3,749	50	2	98.6	1.3	0.1	75.4
Arizona	3,491	3,469	21	1	99.4	0.6	1	74.6
Oklahoma	263	245	17	1	93.2	6.5	0.4	90.4
Hupa	345	325	20	-	94.2	5.8	-	50.9
Jicarilla Apache	694	692	2	-	99.7	0.3	-	99.7
Mescalero Apache	411	392	19	-	95.4	4.6	-	92.5
Navajo	22,304	22,241	63	-	99.7	0.3	-	99.0
Arizona	10,900	10,888	12	-	99.9	0.1	-	99.0
New Mexico	10,322	10,291	31	-	99.7	0.3	-	99.4
Utah	1,034	1,023	11	-	98.9	1.1	-	98.5
Rogue River	223	167	48	8	74.9	21.5	3.6	43.6
Wailaki	82	74	8	-	90.2	9.8	-	32.6
Caddoan stock								
Arikara	372	319	50	3	85.8	13.4	0.8	71.8
Caddo	336	299	37	-	89.0	11.0	-	66.2
Pawnee	544	530	14	-	97.4	2.6	-	83.7
Wichita	308	274	34	-	89.0	11.0	-	86.2
Chimakuan stock								
Quileute	240	206	33	1	85.8	13.8	0.4	79.5
Chinookan stock								
Chinook	53	31	20	2	58.5	37.7	3.8	9.8
Oregon	12	3	7	2	-	-	-	2.4
Washington	41	28	13	-	-	-	-	15.8
Wasco	159	95	64	-	59.7	40.3	-	39.3
Oregon	134	84	50	-	62.7	37.3	-	45.7
Wishram	216	154	56	6	71.3	25.9	2.8	56.2
Croatan group								
Croatan	458	457	1	-	99.8	0.2	-	7.8

[Continued]

★ 58 ★

Mixed-Tribal Blood Status of Full-Blooded Indians, by Linguistic Stock, Tribe, and State, 1910: A - Ke
[Continued]

Tribe and state	Full-blood Indians: 1910							Percent full tribal of all Indians
	Number				Percent of total			
	Total	Full-tribal blood	Mixed-tribal blood	Tribal blood of one parent unknown	Full-tribal blood	Mixed-tribal blood	Tribal blood of one parent unknown	
Iroquoian stock								
Cherokee	6,900	6,785	95	20	98.3	1.4	0.3	21.5
North Carolina	934	920	14	-	98.5	1.5	-	65.4
Oklahoma	5,919	5,827	72	20	98.4	1.2	0.3	19.7
Mohawk	63	38	19	6	60.3	30.2	9.5	10.3
Oneida	2,098	1,904	184	10	90.8	8.8	0.5	78.2
New York	188	89	98	1	47.3	52.1	0.5	42.2
Wisconsin	1,854	1,760	85	9	94.9	4.6	0.5	83.5
Onondaga	299	135	164	-	45.2	54.8	-	37.0
St. Regis	133	94	39	-	70.7	29.3	-	7.7
Seneca	2,022	1,738	271	13	86.0	13.4	0.6	59.8
New York	1,858	1,582	263	13	85.1	14.2	0.7	63.7
Oklahoma	70	63	7	-	90.0	10.0	-	29.3
Pennsylvania	85	85	-	-	100.0	-	-	46.2
Tuscarora	305	218	86	1	71.5	28.2	0.3	54.5
Wyandot	34	12	22	-	-	-	-	3.4
Karok stock								
Orleans	364	334	30	-	91.8	8.2	-	43.1
Keresan stock								
Acoma	686	685	1	-	99.9	0.1	-	99.1
Cochiti	237	235	2	-	99.2	0.8	-	99.2
Laguna	1,427	1,396	31	-	97.8	2.2	-	94.8
San Felipe	489	487	2	-	99.6	0.4	-	99.4
Santa Ana	211	206	5	-	97.6	2.4	-	97.6
Santo Domingo	817	811	6	-	99.3	0.7	-	99.3

Source: U.S. Bureau of the Census. *Indian Population in the United States and Alaska, 1910.* Washington, DC: U.S. Government Printing Office, 1915, pp. 41-42. *Note:* 1. Less than one-tenth of 1 percent.

★ 59 ★
Blood Status

Mixed-Tribal Blood Status of Full-Blooded Indians, by Linguistic Stock, Tribe, and State, 1910: Ki - Sh

Data are shown for tribes having 200 or more Indians in 1910. Percentages are not shown where base is less than 50.

Tribe and state	Full-blood Indians: 1910							Percent full tribal of all Indians
	Number				Percent of total			
	Total	Full-tribal blood	Mixed-tribal blood	Tribal blood of one parent unknown	Full-tribal blood	Mixed-tribal blood	Tribal blood of one parent unknown	
Kiowan stock								
Kiowa	818	766	48	4	93.6	5.9	0.5	68.0
Kutenaian stock								
Kutenai	255	246	9	-	96.5	3.5	-	45.7
Idaho	103	103	-	-	100.0	-	-	96.3
Montana	148	142	6	-	95.9	4.1	-	33.5
Lutuamian stock								
Klamath	459	380	79	-	82.8	17.2	-	54.6
Modoc	198	124	74	-	62.6	37.4	-	44.0
Oregon	168	98	70	-	58.3	41.7	-	46.2
Maidu stock								
Maidu	544	513	31	-	94.3	5.7	-	46.6
Miwok stock								
Miwok	335	308	22	5	91.9	6.6	1.5	46.0
Muskhogean stock								
Alibamu	288	287	1	-	99.7	0.3	-	96.3
Louisiana	101	101	-	-	100.0	-	-	91.0
Texas	187	186	1	-	99.5	0.5	-	99.5
Chickasaw	1,128	1,040	80	8	92.2	7.1	0.7	24.7
Choctaw	7,094	6,975	106	13	98.3	1.5	0.2	43.8
Louisiana	81	80	-	1	98.8	-	1.2	69.6
Mississippi	1,075	1,075	-	-	100.0	-	-	92.5
Oklahoma	5,934	5,817	105	12	98.0	1.8	0.2	40.0
Creek	3,730	3,531	192	7	94.7	5.1	0.2	50.8
Alabama	4	4	-	-	-	-	-	2.2
Oklahoma	3,702	3,516	179	7	95.0	4.8	0.2	52.8
Seminole	1,289	1,158	131	-	89.8	10.2	-	67.0
Oklahoma	1,227	1,098	129	-	89.5	10.5	-	73.1
Texas	38	38	-	-	-	-	-	19.0

[Continued]

★ 59 ★

Mixed-Tribal Blood Status of Full-Blooded Indians, by Linguistic Stock, Tribe, and State, 1910: Ki - Sh

[Continued]

Tribe and state	Full-blood Indians: 1910							Percent full tribal of all Indians
	Number				Percent of total			
	Total	Full-tribal blood	Mixed-tribal blood	Tribal blood of one parent unknown	Full-tribal blood	Mixed-tribal blood	Tribal blood of one parent unknown	
Piman stock								
Papago	3,703	3,638	62	3	98.2	1.7	0.1	95.8
Pima	4,175	4,039	136	-	96.7	3.3	-	95.3
Yaqui	426	401	25	-	94.1	5.9	-	75.9
Pomo stock								
Pomo	607	568	34	5	93.6	5.6	0.8	73.1
Salishan stock								
Chehalis	201	109	90	2	54.2	44.8	1.0	38.7
Clallam	252	214	35	3	84.9	13.9	1.2	53.8
Coeur d'Alene	236	199	30	7	84.3	12.7	3.0	67.9
Columbia	292	215	69	8	73.6	23.6	2.7	55.8
Colville	345	321	17	7	93.0	4.9	2.0	40.9
Flathead	206	168	37	1	81.6	18.0	0.5	34.6
Montana	180	152	28	-	84.4	15.6	-	38.0
Kalispel	361	319	40	2	88.4	11.1	0.6	56.6
Montana	226	191	33	2	84.5	14.6	0.9	49.5
Washington	127	124	3	-	97.6	2.4	-	79.0
Lummi	200	101	89	10	50.5	44.5	5.0	28.6
Okinagan	121	90	28	3	74.4	23.1	2.5	33.1
Puyallup	178	143	24	11	80.3	13.5	6.2	47.2
Quinaielt	219	198	21	-	90.4	9.6	-	68.8
Sanpoil	180	169	7	4	93.9	3.9	2.2	70.4
Snohomish	472	434	38	-	91.9	8.1	-	65.4
Spokan	409	356	51	2	87.0	12.5	0.5	55.4
Montana	53	41	12	-	77.4	22.6	-	30.6
Washington	281	261	20	-	92.9	7.1	-	68.9
Suquamish	177	145	27	5	81.9	15.3	2.8	47.2
Swinomish	279	270	6	3	96.8	2.2	1.1	8.11
Shahaptian stock								
Klikitat	335	252	80	3	75.2	23.9	0.9	62.2
Nez Perces	970	865	104	1	89.2	10.7	0.1	68.7
Idaho	804	756	47	1	94.0	5.8	0.1	73.0
Umatilla	219	158	61	-	72.1	27.9	-	58.1
Oregon	131	98	33	-	74.8	25.2	-	64.5
Wallawalla	126	100	26	-	79.4	20.6	-	25.2

[Continued]

★ 59 ★

Mixed-Tribal Blood Status of Full-Blooded Indians, by Linguistic Stock, Tribe, and State, 1910: Ki - Sh

[Continued]

| Tribe and state | Full-blood Indians: 1910 | | | | | | | Percent full tribal of all Indians |
| | Number | | | | Percent of total | | | |
	Total	Full-tribal blood	Mixed-tribal blood	Tribal blood of one parent unknown	Full-tribal blood	Mixed-tribal blood	Tribal blood of one parent unknown	
Warm Springs	538	470	68	-	87.4	12.6	-	85.5
Yakima	1,043	916	125	2	87.8	12.0	0.2	67.3
Shastan stock								
Hat Creek	220	174	46	-	79.1	20.9	-	72.5
Pit River	841	697	137	7	82.9	16.3	0.8	70.8
Shasta	101	75	26	-	74.3	25.7	-	21.2
California	62	53	9	-	85.5	14.5	-	20.8
Shoshonean stock								
Bannock	323	305	18	-	94.4	5.6	-	73.8
Chemehuevi	315	297	18	-	94.3	5.7	-	83.7
California	242	235	7	-	97.1	2.9	-	90.4
Comanche	736	690	24	22	93.8	3.3	3.0	58.9
Hopi	2,006	1,995	10	1	99.5	0.5	[1]	99.3
Kawia	702	652	45	5	92.9	6.4	0.7	86.4
Mono	1,215	1,155	56	4	95.1	4.6	0.3	79.8
Paiute	674	656	15	3	97.3	2.2	0.4	84.1
California	183	175	5	3	95.6	2.7	1.6	83.3
Nevada	229	222	7	-	96.9	3.1	-	89.9
Utah	198	196	2	-	99.0	1.0	-	82.4
Paviotso	2,664	2,598	65	1	97.5	2.4	[1]	85.5
California	80	64	16	-	80.0	20.0	-	63.4
Idaho	133	132	-	1	99.2	-	0.8	86.8
Nevada	2,113	2,089	24	-	98.9	1.1	-	86.5
Oregon	334	313	21	-	93.7	6.3	-	91.8
San Luiseno	351	339	7	5	96.6	2.0	1.4	72.6
Shoshoni	3,329	3,224	103	2	96.8	3.1	0.1	84.0
Idaho	1,153	1,113	40	-	96.5	3.5	-	88.4
Nevada	1,392	1,341	49	2	96.3	3.5	0.1	86.2
Utah	240	237	3	-	98.7	1.3	-	95.6
Wyoming	502	495	7	-	98.6	1.4	-	70.7
Ute	2,112	2,088	20	4	98.9	0.9	0.2	93.0
Colorado	707	707	-	-	100.0	-	-	97.5
Utah	1,382	1,366	12	4	98.8	0.9	0.3	92.8

Source: U.S. Bureau of the Census. *Indian Population in the United States and Alaska, 1910.* Washington, DC: U.S. Government Printing Office, 1915, pp. 41-42. *Note:* 1. Less than one-tenth of 1 percent.

★ 60 ★
Blood Status

Mixed-Tribal Blood Status of Full-Blooded Indians, by Linguistic Stock, Tribe, and State, 1910: Si - Z

Data are shown for tribes having 200 or more Indians in 1910. Percentages are not shown where base is less than 50.

Tribe and state	Full-blood Indians: 1910							Percent full tribal of all Indians
	Number				Percent of total			
	Total	Full-tribal blood	Mixed-tribal blood	Tribal blood of one parent unknown	Full-tribal blood	Mixed-tribal blood	Tribal blood of one parent unknown	
Siouan stock								
Assiniboin	793	762	30	1	96.1	3.8	0.1	60.8
Crow	1,242	1,178	64	-	94.8	5.2	-	65.5
Hidatsa	418	235	182	1	56.2	43.5	0.2	43.0
Iowa	59	34	25	-	57.6	42.4	-	13.9
Kansas	10	5	5	-	-	-	-	4.0
Kansa	71	66	5	-	93.0	7.0	-	27.7
Mandan	165	79	86	-	47.9	52.1	-	37.8
Omaha	885	877	8	-	99.1	0.9	-	79.4
Osage	591	583	8	-	98.6	1.4	-	42.5
Oto	211	185	23	3	87.7	10.9	1.4	55.7
Ponca	461	455	6	-	98.7	1.3	-	52.0
Nebraska	60	58	2	-	96.7	3.3	-	30.1
Oklahoma	374	373	1	-	99.7	0.3	-	60.3
Quapaw	63	31	32	-	49.2	50.8	-	13.4
Santee Sioux	799	672	125	2	84.1	15.6	0.3	43.7
Minnesota	100	99	1	-	99.0	1.0	-	42.7
Montana	78	65	13	-	83.3	16.7	-	60.7
Nebraska	410	403	7	-	98.3	1.7	-	56.9
North Dakota	66	16	50	-	24.2	75.8	-	16.0
South Dakota	145	89	54	2	61.4	37.2	1.4	23.5
Sioux	494	441	50	3	89.3	10.1	0.6	44.3
Minnesota	117	115	2	-	98.3	1.7	-	71.4
South Dakota	98	92	5	1	93.9	5.1	1.0	33.2
Sisseton Sioux	1,631	1,394	228	9	85.5	14.0	0.6	55.4
Montana	204	162	42	-	79.4	20.6	-	63.5
North Dakota	469	424	45	-	90.4	9.6	-	68.3
South Dakota	926	786	131	9	84.9	14.1	1.0	50.6
Teton Sioux	10,598	9,747	772	79	92.0	7.3	0.7	68.2
North Dakota	225	129	96	-	57.3	42.7	-	34.9
South Dakota	10,289	9,560	650	79	92.9	6.3	0.8	69.3
Brule Sioux	593	441	145	7	74.4	24.5	1.2	54.7
Hunkpapa Sioux	954	453	469	32	47.5	49.2	3.4	42.3
North Dakota	119	25	94	-	21.0	79.0	-	17.6
South Dakota	835	428	375	32	51.3	44.9	3.8	46.0
Minniconjou Sioux	353	142	197	14	40.2	55.8	4.0	35.8
Oglala Sioux	4,168	3,744	405	19	89.8	9.7	0.5	61.9
Sans Arc Sioux	64	21	43	-	32.8	67.2	-	9.5
Sihasapa	333	122	206	5	36.6	61.9	1.5	25.2
North Dakota	50	24	26	-	48.0	52.0	-	17.5
South Dakota	282	97	180	5	34.4	63.8	1.8	28.0

[Continued]

★ 60 ★

Mixed-Tribal Blood Status of Full-Blooded Indians, by Linguistic Stock, Tribe, and State, 1910: Si - Z
[Continued]

Tribe and state	Full-blood Indians: 1910							Percent full tribal of all Indians
	Number				Percent of total			
	Total	Full-tribal blood	Mixed-tribal blood	Tribal blood of one parent unknown	Full-tribal blood	Mixed-tribal blood	Tribal blood of one parent unknown	
Two Kettle Sioux	143	55	87	1	38.5	60.8	0.7	18.8
Other Teton Sioux	3,990	3,928	61	1	98.4	1.5	[1]	79.1
Winnebago	1,543	1,530	13	-	99.2	0.8	-	84.1
Nebraska	865	860	5	-	99.4	0.6	-	85.4
Wisconsin	630	628	2	-	99.7	0.3	-	85.4
Yankton Sioux	1,348	1,026	317	5	76.1	23.5	0.4	49.1
Montana	279	220	58	1	78.9	20.8	0.4	59.1
North Dakota	156	40	116	-	25.6	74.4	-	25.2
South Dakota	910	763	143	4	83.8	15.7	0.4	49.7
Yanktonai Sioux	1,144	768	371	5	67.1	32.4	0.4	56.6
North Dakota	473	293	179	1	61.9	37.8	0.2	53.2
South Dakota	668	474	190	4	71.0	28.4	0.6	59.0
Tanoan stock								
Isleta	894	851	43	-	95.2	4.8	-	89.0
Jemez	499	418	81	-	83.8	16.2	-	83.8
San Juan	382	380	2	-	99.5	0.5	-	98.2
Santa Clara	268	251	17	-	93.7	6.3	-	90.6
Taos	509	505	4	-	99.2	0.8	-	97.7
Waiilatpuan stock								
Cayuse	254	194	59	1	76.4	23.2	0.4	65.1
Wakashan stock								
Makah	342	252	88	2	73.7	25.7	0.6	70.0
Washoan stock								
Washo	643	620	23	-	96.4	3.6	-	75.7
California	228	209	19	-	91.7	8.3	-	76.6
Nevada	414	410	4	-	99.0	1.0	-	76.5
Wintun stock								
Wintun	121	108	13	-	89.3	10.7	-	27.1
Yokuts stock								
Yokuts	255	241	12	2	94.5	4.7	0.8	79.8

[Continued]

★ 60 ★

Mixed-Tribal Blood Status of Full-Blooded Indians, by Linguistic Stock, Tribe, and State, 1910: Si - Z

[Continued]

Tribe and state	Full-blood Indians: 1910							Percent full tribal of all Indians
	Number				Percent of total			
	Total	Full-tribal blood	Mixed-tribal blood	Tribal blood of one parent unknown	Full-tribal blood	Mixed-tribal blood	Tribal blood of one parent unknown	
Yuman stock								
Cocopa	243	242	1	-	99.6	0.4	-	98.8
Diegueno	585	568	14	3	97.1	2.4	0.5	75.1
Maricopa	367	339	27	1	92.4	7.4	0.3	87.8
Mohave	1,038	966	72	-	93.1	6.9	-	91.3
Arizona	651	584	67	-	89.7	10.3	-	87.6
California	385	381	4	-	99.0	1.0	-	97.9
Walapai	485	471	14	-	97.1	2.9	-	94.0
Yavapai	256	243	13	-	94.9	5.1	-	84.1
Yuma	816	784	29	3	96.1	3.6	0.4	94.0
Arizona	187	177	10	-	94.7	5.3	-	92.7
California	628	606	19	3	96.5	3.0	0.5	94.4
Yurok stock								
Weitspec	528	514	14	-	97.3	2.7	-	76.9
Zunian stock								
Zuni	1,652	1,641	11	-	99.3	0.7	-	98.4

Source: U.S. Bureau of the Census. *Indian Population in the United States and Alaska, 1910.* Washington, DC: U.S. Government Printing Office, 1915, pp. 41-42. *Notes:* A dash (-) represents zero. 1. Less than one-tenth of 1 percent.

★ 61 ★

Blood Status

Indian and White Mixed-Bloods, by State and Degree of Mixture, 1910

State	Number					Percent of total			
	Total	Less than half white	Half white, half Indian	More than half white	Unknown proportions	Less than half white	Half white, half Indian	More than half white	Unknown proportions
United States	88,030	18,169	24,353	43,937	1,571	20.6	27.7	49.9	1.8
Arizona	393	74	115	30	174	18.8	29.3	7.6	44.3
California	4,069	1,044	2,189	651	185	25.7	53.8	16.0	4.5
Colorado	44	4	15	16	9	[1]	[1]	[1]	[1]
Idaho	503	190	193	87	33	37.8	38.4	17.3	6.6
Kansas[2]	823	340	202	280	1	41.3	24.5	34.0	0.1
Michigan	3,138	1,454	726	925	33	46.3	23.1	29.5	1.1
Minnesota	4,799	1,393	1,427	1,978	1	29.0	29.7	41.2	[3]
Mississippi	69	39	15	15	-	56.5	21.7	21.7	-

[Continued]

★ 61 ★

Indian and White Mixed-Bloods, by State and Degree of Mixture, 1910
[Continued]

State	Number					Percent of total			
	Total	Less than half white	Half white, half Indian	More than half white	Unknown proportions	Less than half white	Half white, half Indian	More than half white	Unknown proportions
Montana	3,808	676	1,646	1,424	62	17.8	43.2	37.4	1.6
Nebraska	926	367	208	351	-	39.6	22.5	37.9	-
Nevada	503	176	292	21	14	35.0	58.1	4.2	2.8
New Mexico	163	63	36	1	63	38.7	22.1	0.6	38.7
New York	1,636	242	1,200	188	6	14.8	73.3	11.5	0.4
North Carolina	5,105	2,734	1,896	475	-	53.6	37.1	9.3	-
North Dakota	3,541	273	2,481	778	9	7.7	70.1	22.0	0.3
Oklahoma	41,856	4,120	5,451	31,542	743	9.8	13.0	75.4	1.8
Oregon	1,601	362	626	590	23	22.6	39.1	36.9	1.4
South Dakota	5,263	1,810	1,888	1,470	95	34.4	35.9	27.9	1.8
Utah	102	25	48	29	-	24.5	47.1	28.4	-
Washington	2,896	758	1,233	900	5	26.2	42.6	31.1	0.2
Wisconsin	4,136	1,306	1,517	1,271	42	31.6	36.7	30.7	1.0
Wyoming	283	64	87	95	37	22.6	30.7	33.6	13.1
Total for 22 states	85,657	17,514	23,491	43,117	1,535	20.4	27.4	50.3	1.8
All other states	2,373	655	862	820	36	27.6	36.3	34.6	1.5

Source: U.S. Bureau of the Census. *Indian Population in the United States and Alaska, 1910.* Washington, DC: U.S. Government Printing Office, 1915, p. 35. *Notes:* A dash (-) represents zero. 1. Percent not shown where base is less than 50. 2. Exclusive of Indians in Haskell Institute, who are included in the total for "All other states." 3. Less than one-tenth of 1 percent.

★ 62 ★

Blood Status

Indian and White Mixed-Bloods, by Linguistic Stock, Tribe, State, and Degree of Mixture, 1910 - I

Stock, tribe, and state	Number					Percent of total			
	Total	Less than half white	Half white, half Indian	More than half white	Unknown proportions	Less than half white	Half white, half Indian	More than half white	Unknown proportions
Algonquian stock	21,318	5,565	7,780	7,804	169	26.1	36.5	36.6	0.8
Arapaho	101	53	30	10	8	52.5	29.7	9.9	7.9
Cheyenne	319	122	106	77	14	38.2	33.2	24.1	4.4
Oklahoma	139	78	38	17	6	56.1	27.3	12.2	4.3
Chippewa	13,031	3,051	5,516	4,388	76	23.4	42.3	33.7	0.6
Michigan	2,123	830	506	766	21	39.1	23.8	36.1	1.0
Minnesota	4,556	1,349	1,362	1,844	1	29.6	29.9	40.5	[1]
Montana	402	57	257	77	11	14.2	63.9	19.2	2.7
North Dakota	2,829	27	2,153	648	1	1.0	76.1	22.9	[1]
Pennsylvania	103	17	44	42	-	16.5	42.7	40.8	-
Wisconsin	2,693	714	1,121	816	42	26.5	41.6	30.3	1.6
Cree	413	10	196	204	3	2.4	47.5	49.4	0.7
Montana	273	9	177	84	3	3.3	64.8	30.8	1.1
Delaware	631	68	143	405	15	10.8	22.7	64.2	2.4
Gros Ventres	118	21	64	32	1	17.8	54.2	27.1	0.8
Kickapoo	103	61	31	10	1	59.2	30.1	9.7	1.0
Menominee	713	318	180	215	-	44.6	25.2	30.2	-

[Continued]

★ 62 ★

Indian and White Mixed-Bloods, by Linguistic Stock, Tribe, State, and Degree of Mixture, 1910 - I

[Continued]

Stock, tribe, and state	Number					Percent of total			
	Total	Less than half white	Half white, half Indian	More than half white	Unknown proportions	Less than half white	Half white, half Indian	More than half white	Unknown proportions
Miami	164	42	42	80	-	25.6	25.6	48.8	-
Oklahoma	100	18	4	78	-	18.0	4.0	78.0	-
Ottawa	966	523	213	221	9	54.1	22.0	22.9	0.9
Michigan	759	502	176	72	9	66.1	23.2	9.5	1.2
Oklahoma	158	8	17	133	-	5.1	10.8	84.2	-
Penobscot	181	115	59	7	-	63.5	32.6	3.9	-
Piegan	1,025	200	377	422	26	19.5	36.8	41.2	2.5
Potawatomi	1,461	418	212	828	3	28.6	14.5	56.7	0.2
Kansas	486	217	127	141	1	44.7	26.1	29.0	0.2
Michigan	177	118	19	38	2	66.7	10.7	21.5	1.1
Oklahoma	749	66	58	625	-	8.8	7.7	83.4	-
Sauk and Fox	154	52	45	57	-	33.8	29.2	37.0	-
Shawnee	776	139	101	527	9	17.9	13.0	67.9	1.2
Stockbridges	216	72	84	60	-	33.3	38.9	27.8	-
Athapaskan stock	1,015	235	562	142	76	23.2	55.4	14.0	7.5
Apache	122	34	52	14	22	27.9	42.6	11.5	18.0
Arizona	111	34	44	13	20	30.6	39.6	11.7	18.0
Hupa	292	22	217	53	-	7.5	74.3	18.2	-
Rogue River	159	40	72	37	10	25.2	45.3	23.3	6.3
Wailaki	143	18	106	19	-	12.6	74.1	13.3	-
Caddoan stock	261	94	84	77	6	36.0	32.2	29.5	2.3
Caddo	111	30	36	40	5	27.0	32.4	36.0	4.5
Chinookan stock	416	63	183	170	-	15.1	44.0	40.9	-
Chinook	261	18	122	121	-	6.9	46.7	46.4	-
Oregon	112	13	56	43	-	11.6	50.0	38.4	-
Washington	136	5	60	71	-	3.7	44.1	52.2	-
Croatan group	4,668	2,540	1,856	272	-	54.4	39.8	5.8	-
Croatan	4,668	2,540	1,856	272	-	54.4	39.8	5.8	-
Iroquoian stock	26,102	2,137	3,835	19,994	136	8.2	14.7	76.6	0.5
Cherokee	23,510	1,702	2,294	19,384	130	7.2	9.8	82.5	0.6
North Carolina	429	192	39	198	-	44.8	9.1	46.2	-
Oklahoma	22,722	1,429	2,172	18,997	124	6.3	9.6	83.6	0.5
Mohawk	293	14	252	27	-	4.8	86.0	9.2	-
Oneida	312	107	103	102	-	34.3	33.0	32.7	-
Wisconsin	227	78	75	74	-	34.4	33.0	32.6	-
St. Regis	1,005	44	848	107	6	4.4	84.4	10.6	0.6
Seneca	479	163	208	108	-	34.0	43.4	22.5	-
New York	221	108	59	54	-	48.9	26.7	24.4	-
Oklahoma	145	45	60	40	-	31.0	41.4	27.6	-

[Continued]

★ 62 ★

Indian and White Mixed-Bloods, by Linguistic Stock, Tribe, State, and Degree of Mixture, 1910 - I

[Continued]

Stock, tribe, and state	Number					Percent of total			
	Total	Less than half white	Half white, half Indian	More than half white	Unknown proportions	Less than half white	Half white, half Indian	More than half white	Unknown proportions
Wyandot	317	31	44	242	-	9.8	13.9	76.3	-
Karok stock	401	84	252	65	-	20.9	62.8	16.2	-
Orleans	401	84	252	65	-	20.9	62.8	16.2	-
Kiowan stock	296	103	39	1	153	34.8	13.2	0.3	51.7
Kiowa	296	103	39	1	153	34.8	13.2	0.3	51.7
Kutenaian stock	283	22	60	201	-	7.8	21.2	71.0	-
Kutenai	283	22	60	201	-	7.8	21.2	71.0	-
Montana	276	22	54	200	-	8.0	19.6	72.5	-
Lutuamian stock	294	79	148	67	-	26.9	50.3	22.8	-
Klamath	210	63	98	49	-	30.0	46.7	23.3	-
Maidu stock	525	161	290	71	3	30.7	55.2	13.5	0.6
Maidu	525	161	290	71	3	30.7	55.2	13.5	0.6
Miwok stock	354	87	169	76	22	24.6	47.7	21.5	6.2
Miwok	333	73	165	74	21	21.9	49.5	22.2	6.3
Muskhogean stock	13,723	1,648	2,336	9,586	153	12.0	17.0	69.9	1.1
Chickasaw	2,881	182	493	2,189	17	6.3	17.1	76.0	0.6
Choctaw	8,149	900	1,296	5,865	88	11.0	15.9	72.0	1.1
Oklahoma	7,995	838	1,273	5,831	53	10.5	15.9	72.9	0.7
Creek	2,527	503	490	1,497	37	19.9	19.4	59.2	1.5
Alabama	181	1	8	172	-	0.6	4.4	95.0	-
Oklahoma	2,301	498	456	1,310	37	21.6	19.8	56.9	1.6
Seminole	164	63	57	33	11	38.4	34.8	20.1	6.7
Oklahoma	157	63	53	30	11	40.1	33.8	19.1	7.0
Piman stock	166	23	19	3	121	13.9	11.4	1.8	72.9
Pomo stock	209	80	102	27	-	38.3	48.8	12.9	-
Pomo	109	43	45	21	-	39.4	41.3	19.3	-
Salishan stock	2,687	750	1,133	801	3	27.9	42.2	29.8	0.1
Clallam	132	43	54	35	-	32.6	40.9	26.5	-
Colville	428	52	215	160	1	12.1	50.2	37.4	0.2
Flathead	280	95	70	115	-	33.9	25.0	41.1	-

[Continued]

★ 62 ★

Indian and White Mixed-Bloods, by Linguistic Stock, Tribe, State, and Degree of Mixture, 1910 - I
[Continued]

Stock, tribe, and state	Number					Percent of total			
	Total	Less than half white	Half white, half Indian	More than half white	Unknown proportions	Less than half white	Half white, half Indian	More than half white	Unknown proportions
Montana	220	90	49	81	-	40.9	22.3	36.8	-
Kalispel	200	37	53	110	-	18.5	26.5	55.0	-
Montana	158	24	44	90	-	15.2	27.8	57.0	-
Lummi	141	73	46	22	-	51.8	32.6	15.6	-
Okinagan	132	18	64	50	-	13.6	48.5	37.9	-
Puyallup	119	50	45	24	-	42.0	37.8	20.2	-
Snohomish	190	57	96	37	-	30.0	50.5	19.5	-
Spokan	233	44	96	93	-	18.9	41.2	39.9	-
Suquamish	127	58	53	16	-	45.7	41.7	12.6	-

Source: U.S. Bureau of the Census. *Indian Population in the United States and Alaska, 1910.* Washington, DC: U.S. Government Printing Office, 1915, pp. 36-37. *Notes:* A dash (-) represents zero. 1. Less than one-tenth of 1 percent.

★ 63 ★

Blood Status

Indian and White Mixed-Bloods, by Linguistic Stock, Tribe, State, and Degree of Mixture, 1910 - II

Stock, tribe, and state	Number					Percent of total			
	Total	Less than half white	Half white, half Indian	More than half white	Unknown proportions	Less than half white	Half white, half Indian	More than half white	Unknown proportions
Shahaptian stock	977	272	359	338	8	27.8	36.7	34.6	0.8
Nez Perces	276	120	101	55	-	43.5	36.6	19.9	-
Idaho	218	114	71	33	-	52.3	32.6	15.1	-
Wallawalla	266	20	100	146	-	7.5	37.6	54.9	-
Yakima	312	80	135	95	2	25.6	43.3	30.4	0.6
Shastan stock	393	103	196	94	-	26.2	49.9	23.9	-
Pit River	142	43	73	26	-	30.3	51.4	18.3	-
Shasta	231	49	115	67	-	21.2	49.8	29.0	-
California	174	29	94	51	-	16.7	54.0	29.3	-
Shoshonean stock	1,884	546	771	287	280	29.9	40.9	15.2	14.9
Comanche	399	119	85	48	147	29.8	21.3	12.0	36.8
Mono	223	62	144	9	8	27.8	64.6	4.0	3.6
Paviotso	215	85	110	18	2	39.5	51.2	8.4	0.9
Nevada	155	62	88	4	1	40.0	56.8	2.6	0.6
San Luiseno	115	44	30	6	35	38.3	26.1	5.2	30.4
Shoshoni	504	132	207	117	448	26.2	41.1	23.2	9.5
Idaho	101	21	36	24	20	20.8	35.6	23.8	19.8
Nevada	161	55	99	6	1	34.2	61.5	3.7	0.6
Wyoming	198	47	52	73	26	23.7	26.3	36.9	13.1

[Continued]

★ 63 ★

Indian and White Mixed-Bloods, by Linguistic Stock, Tribe, State, and Degree of Mixture, 1910 - II

[Continued]

Stock, tribe, and state	Number					Percent of total			
	Total	Less than half white	Half white, half Indian	More than half white	Unknown proportions	Less than half white	Half white, half Indian	More than half white	Unknown proportions
Siouan stock	9,672	3,022	3,114	3,320	216	31.2	32.2	34.3	2.2
Assiniboin	441	72	203	166	-	16.3	46.0	37.6	-
Crow	372	66	195	104	7	17.7	52.4	28.0	1.9
Hidatsa	129	65	43	21	-	50.4	33.3	16.3	-
Iowa	183	46	35	99	3	25.1	19.1	54.1	1.6
Kansas	114	20	14	80	-	17.5	12.3	70.2	-
Kansa	167	15	35	115	2	9.0	21.0	68.9	1.2
Omaha	144	38	32	74	-	26.4	22.2	51.4	-
Osage	759	39	84	632	4	5.1	11.1	83.3	0.5
Oto	114	76	16	22	-	66.7	14.0	19.3	-
Ponca	369	160	64	72	73	43.4	17.3	19.5	19.8
Nebraska	133	51	22	60	-	38.3	16.5	45.1	-
Oklahoma	200	92	30	5	73	46.0	15.0	2.5	36.5
Quapaw	116	4	22	81	9	3.4	19.0	69.8	7.8
Santee Sioux	714	286	160	268	-	40.1	22.4	37.5	-
Minnesota	126	24	27	75	-	19.0	21.4	59.5	-
Nebraska	293	158	66	69	-	53.9	22.5	23.5	-
South Dakota	218	84	55	79	-	38.5	25.2	36.2	-
Sioux	474	75	187	198	14	15.8	39.5	41.8	3.0
South Dakota	173	26	77	70	-	15.0	44.5	40.5	-
Sisseton Sioux	863	354	346	157	6	41.0	40.1	18.2	0.7
North Dakota	139	33	100	2	4	23.7	71.9	1.4	2.9
South Dakota	620	292	208	118	2	47.1	33.5	19.0	0.3
Teton Sioux	3,508	1,142	1,277	995	94	32.6	36.4	28.4	2.7
North Dakota	140	35	81	24	-	25.0	57.9	17.1	-
South Dakota	3,333	1,106	1,183	952	92	33.2	35.5	28.6	2.8
Brule Sioux	200	40	63	96	1	20.0	31.5	48.0	0.5
Hunkpapa Sioux	109	48	42	19	-	44.0	38.5	17.4	-
Minniconjou Sioux	33	10	11	12	-	-	-	-	-
Oglala Sioux	1,776	512	638	534	92	28.8	35.9	30.1	5.2
Sans Arc Sioux	152	22	44	86	-	14.5	28.9	56.6	-
Sihasapa	140	45	78	17	-	32.1	55.7	12.1	-
Two Kettle Sioux	145	55	61	29	-	37.9	42.1	20.0	-
Other Teton Sioux	953	410	340	202	1	43.0	35.7	21.2	0.1
Winnebago	276	197	39	40	-	71.4	14.1	14.5	-
Nebraska	141	92	22	27	-	65.2	15.6	19.1	-
Wisconsin	105	93	9	3	-	88.6	8.6	2.9	-
Yankton Sioux	683	187	295	200	1	27.4	43.2	29.3	0.1
South Dakota	568	167	244	157	-	29.4	43.0	27.6	-
Yanktonai Sioux	198	101	58	39	-	51.0	29.3	19.7	-
South Dakota	124	74	35	15	-	59.7	28.2	12.1	-
Tanoan stock	101	36	22	3	40	35.6	21.8	3.0	39.6
Washoan stock	168	60	92	15	1	35.7	54.8	8.9	0.6
Washo	168	60	92	15	1	35.7	54.8	8.9	0.6
Nevada	115	44	65	5	1	38.3	56.5	4.3	0.9

[Continued]

★ 63 ★

Indian and White Mixed-Bloods, by Linguistic Stock, Tribe, State, and Degree of Mixture, 1910 - II

[Continued]

Stock, tribe, and state	Number					Percent of total			
	Total	Less than half white	Half white, half Indian	More than half white	Unknown proportions	Less than half white	Half white, half Indian	More than half white	Unknown proportions
Wintun stock	362	73	181	104	4	20.2	50.0	28.7	1.1
Wintun	269	39	137	93	-	14.5	50.9	34.6	-
Yokuts stock	103	30	58	3	12	29.1	56.3	2.9	11.7
Yuman stock	216	86	70	9	51	39.8	32.4	4.2	23.6
Diegueno	171	74	51	3	43	43.3	29.8	1.8	25.1
Yurok stock	134	46	82	6	-	34.3	61.2	4.5	-
Weitspec	134	46	82	6	-	34.3	61.2	4.5	-

Source: U.S. Bureau of the Census. *Indian Population in the United States and Alaska, 1910.* Washington, DC: U.S. Government Printing Office, 1915, pp. 36-37. *Notes:* A dash (-) represents zero. 1. Less than one-tenth of 1 percent.

Education

★ 64 ★

School Enrollment of Persons 5 to 20 Years Old, 1900-1930

Data include primary schools and colleges.

Year	Total			Male			Female		
	Total number	Attending school		Total number	Attending school		Total number	Attending school	
		Number	Percent		Number	Percent		Number	Percent
1900	89,632	36,243	40.4	45,440	18,688	41.1	44,192	17,555	39.7
1910	102,163	51,877	50.8	51,964	26,820	51.6	50,199	25,057	49.9
1920	90,605	50,939	53.8	47,248	25,360	53.7	47,357	25,579	54.0
1930	129,145	77,806	60.2	64,945	39,945	60.2	64,200	38,722	60.3

Source: Truesdell, Dr. Leon E. U.S. Department of Commerce, Bureau of Census, Fifteenth Census of the United States: 1930, *The Indian Population of the United States and Alaska.* Washington, DC: U.S. Government Printing Office, 1937, p. 131.

★ 65 ★
Education

Percent of Persons 5 to 20 Years Old Attending School, by Race/Ethnicity, 1900-1930

Data include primary schools and colleges.

Race and ethnicity	1900	1910	1920	1930
All classes	50.5	59.2	64.3	69.9
Indian	40.4	50.8	53.8	60.2
White	53.6	61.3	65.7	71.2
Native	54.9	62.8	66.6	71.6
Foreign born	31.1	38.7	44.2	54.1
Negro	31.0	44.7	53.5	60.0
Chinese	25.4	45.5	62.8	75.6
Japanese	4.8	24.2	52.9	84.0

Source: Truesdell, Dr. Leon E. U.S. Department of Commerce, Bureau of Census, Fifteenth Census of the United States: 1930, *The Indian Population of the United States and Alaska.* Washington, U.S. Government Printing Office, 1937, p. 131.

★ 66 ★
Education

School Attendance of American Indians 6 to 19 Years Old, by Linguistic Stock, Tribe, Principal State, and Sex, 1910: Al - Ch

Data are shown for tribes having 100 or more members in 1910.

Linguistic stock, tribe, and state	Indian males 6 to 19 years of age: 1910					Indian females 6 to 19 years of age: 1910				
	Total number	Attending school				Total number	Attending school			
		Total	6 to 9 years of age	10 to 14 years of age	15 to 19 years of age		Total	6 to 9 years of age	10 to 14 years of age	15 to 19 years of age
UNITED STATES										
Algonquian stock	7,040	4,539	1,210	2,118	1,211	6,724	4,336	1,247	1,965	1,124
Arapaho	184	139	31	63	45	187	133	46	54	33
Oklahoma	75	54	14	21	19	75	50	19	19	12
Wyoming	102	79	17	41	21	110	82	27	35	20
Brotherton	25	20	5	11	4	32	22	9	6	7
Wisconsin	25	20	5	11	4	30	21	8	6	7
Cheyenne	432	274	61	115	98	421	240	57	107	76
Montana	203	104	18	43	43	224	94	15	46	33
Oklahoma	189	141	41	65	35	164	122	37	55	30
South Dakota	22	12	1	6	5	21	13	3	3	7
Chickahominy (Virginia)	15	2	2	-	-	18	5	2	2	1
Chippewa	3,618	2,440	659	1,159	622	3,437	2,336	664	1,056	616
Kansas	20	20	1	5	14	32	30	1	4	25
Michigan	597	365	118	180	67	547	336	101	164	71
Minnesota	1,491	1,083	304	487	292	1,327	970	291	421	258

[Continued]

★ 66 ★

School Attendance of American Indians 6 to 19 Years Old, by Linguistic Stock, Tribe, Principal State, and Sex, 1910: Al - Ch

[Continued]

Linguistic stock, tribe, and state	Indian males 6 to 19 years of age: 1910					Indian females 6 to 19 years of age: 1910				
	Total number	Attending school				Total number	Attending school			
		Total	6 to 9 years of age	10 to 14 years of age	15 to 19 years of age		Total	6 to 9 years of age	10 to 14 years of age	15 to 19 years of age
Montana	86	24	5	16	3	81	24	4	14	6
Nebraska	28	28	6	11	11	30	30	3	10	17
North Dakota	568	340	66	175	99	611	356	90	190	76
Oklahoma	13	7	3	4	-	7	3	2	1	-
Pennsylvania	42	42	1	6	35	43	43	-	4	39
South Dakota	9	6	4	1	1	13	7	2	3	2
Wisconsin	752	513	149	269	95	733	527	169	241	117
Cree	83	49	9	25	15	96	68	20	31	17
Montana	54	27	5	12	10	60	46	12	23	11
Washington	21	17	4	8	5	21	14	4	6	4
Delaware	189	149	43	60	46	175	133	39	68	26
Oklahoma	185	145	43	58	44	166	126	38	63	25
Gros Ventres	66	20	-	13	7	86	35	1	20	14
Montana	65	20	-	13	7	86	35	1	20	14
Kickapoo	54	33	6	17	10	38	23	5	13	5
Kansas	38	28	3	16	9	26	18	4	11	3
Oklahoma	16	5	3	1	1	11	4	1	2	1
Malecite	27	19	8	7	4	27	18	7	7	4
Maine	26	18	8	7	3	26	17	7	6	4
Mashpee	32	25	7	9	9	31	26	8	12	6
Massachusetts	29	22	7	9	6	30	25	8	12	5
Menominee	275	190	67	99	24	255	174	61	90	23
Wisconsin	262	178	62	94	22	244	166	60	86	20
Miami	44	34	11	17	6	45	35	10	16	9
Indiana	13	8	3	5	-	17	9	3	5	1
Oklahoma	27	22	8	11	3	26	24	7	10	7
Ottawa	450	291	84	135	72	385	250	71	112	67
Michigan	376	230	72	107	51	341	214	60	101	53
Oklahoma	30	21	6	10	5	31	23	10	7	6
Wisconsin	23	20	6	9	5	5	5	1	4	-
Passamaquoddy	49	36	10	13	13	56	36	12	15	9
Maine	47	34	10	13	11	55	35	12	14	9
Penobscot	44	26	8	16	2	43	23	9	9	5
Maine	42	24	8	15	1	39	19	9	6	4
Peoria	22	20	6	8	6	29	22	7	7	8
Oklahoma	19	17	5	8	4	25	19	7	7	5
Piegan	399	84	20	41	23	390	108	25	50	33
Montana	385	71	20	39	12	379	97	25	46	26
Potawatomi	469	314	74	144	96	378	249	59	118	72
Kansas	161	117	17	57	43	120	88	12	50	26
Michigan	77	55	14	28	13	67	41	13	21	7
Oklahoma	174	124	39	50	35	149	112	31	46	35
Wisconsin	44	8	-	6	2	33	4	1	1	2
Powhatan (Virginia)	27	4	2	1	1	26	8	1	6	1
Sauk and Fox	124	83	19	34	30	115	62	17	31	14
Iowa	47	27	6	11	10	38	11	3	6	2
Kansas	20	18	2	4	12	19	15	2	8	5

[Continued]

★ 66 ★

School Attendance of American Indians 6 to 19 Years Old, by Linguistic Stock, Tribe, Principal State, and Sex, 1910: Al - Ch

[Continued]

Linguistic stock, tribe, and state	Indian males 6 to 19 years of age: 1910					Indian females 6 to 19 years of age: 1910				
	Total number	Attending school				Total number	Attending school			
		Total	6 to 9 years of age	10 to 14 years of age	15 to 19 years of age		Total	6 to 9 years of age	10 to 14 years of age	15 to 19 years of age
Oklahoma	52	34	10	17	7	49	29	10	15	4
Shawnee	208	147	41	68	38	244	170	61	66	43
Oklahoma	200	139	40	66	33	230	156	58	65	33
Shinnecock (New York)	19	15	8	3	4	29	24	12	9	3
Stockbridges	75	51	13	27	11	77	62	24	30	8
Wisconsin	74	50	13	27	10	71	56	23	27	6
Wampanoag	29	23	3	13	7	19	13	3	8	2
Massachusetts	26	20	3	13	4	18	12	3	8	1
Athapaskan stock	5,557	1,094	208	504	382	5,235	796	210	336	250
Apache	793	352	51	171	130	650	244	39	101	104
Arizona	747	314	39	162	113	611	217	29	90	98
Oklahoma	37	32	12	8	12	34	23	8	11	4
Hupa	110	26	6	10	10	102	23	1	14	8
California	106	22	5	9	8	95	18	1	13	4
Jicarilla Apache (New Mexico)	105	66	16	32	18	93	62	27	8	27
Kiowa Apache (Oklahoma)	17	11	1	7	3	19	12	2	4	6
Mescalero Apache	53	45	19	17	9	71	53	18	26	9
New Mexico	51	43	19	17	7	70	52	18	26	8
Navajo	4,302	464	76	210	178	4,138	289	81	135	73
Arizona	2,180	259	53	126	80	2,093	176	63	79	34
New Mexico	1,910	171	20	75	76	1,896	103	17	52	34
Utah	179	4	1	2	1	146	7	-	2	5
Rogue River	75	60	13	33	14	58	37	12	21	4
Oregon	75	60	13	33	14	55	36	11	21	4
Tolowa (California)	20	16	8	5	3	13	8	2	2	4
Umpqua	18	10	5	1	4	14	10	3	6	1
Oregon	15	8	3	1	4	10	7	-	6	1
Wailaki	35	26	7	10	9	37	28	12	10	6
California	31	22	7	10	5	32	24	10	10	4
Caddoan stock	324	248	63	98	87	338	271	77	107	87
Arikara	76	59	10	23	26	82	68	16	29	23
North Dakota	71	57	9	23	25	82	68	16	29	23
Caddo	93	70	23	26	21	90	73	31	29	13
Oklahoma	89	67	23	26	18	88	71	31	29	11
Pawnee	96	70	16	31	23	98	75	13	32	30
Oklahoma	82	57	16	24	17	84	61	13	26	22
Wichita	56	48	14	17	17	67	54	17	16	21
Oklahoma	45	39	14	16	9	59	48	17	15	16
Chimakuan stock	46	32	9	13	10	33	17	7	5	5
Quileute (Washington)	40	27	9	13	5	26	15	6	4	5

[Continued]

★ 66 ★

School Attendance of American Indians 6 to 19 Years Old, by Linguistic Stock, Tribe, Principal State, and Sex, 1910: Al - Ch
[Continued]

Linguistic stock, tribe, and state	Indian males 6 to 19 years of age: 1910					Indian females 6 to 19 years of age: 1910				
	Total number	Attending school				Total number	Attending school			
		Total	6 to 9 years of age	10 to 14 years of age	15 to 19 years of age		Total	6 to 9 years of age	10 to 14 years of age	15 to 19 years of age
Chimarikan stock	5	5	1	4	-	6	6	4	2	-
Chinookan stock	155	110	29	55	26	122	88	27	40	21
Chinook	55	43	11	21	11	59	46	16	23	7
Oregon	32	26	3	16	7	29	24	6	12	6
Washington	21	15	8	4	3	30	22	10	11	1
Wasco	40	34	10	16	8	29	22	7	6	9
Oregon	29	24	6	13	5	21	16	6	3	7
Washington	10	9	4	2	3	8	6	1	3	2
Wishram (Washington)	42	20	3	13	4	28	16	4	8	4

Source: U.S. Bureau of the Census. *Indian Population in the United States and Alaska, 1910.* Washington, DC: U.S. Government Printing Office, 1915, pp. 205-216. *Note:* A dash (-) represents zero.

★ 67 ★

Education

School Attendance of American Indians 6 to 19 Years Old, by Linguistic Stock, Tribe, Principal State, and Sex, 1910: Ch - Sa

Data are shown for tribes having 100 or more members in 1910.

Linguistic stock, tribe, and state	Indian males 6 to 19 years of age: 1910					Indian females 6 to 19 years of age: 1910				
	Total number	Attending school				Total number	Attending school			
		Total	6 to 9 years of age	10 to 14 years of age	15 to 19 years of age		Total	6 to 9 years of age	10 to 14 years of age	15 to 19 years of age
UNITED STATES (cont.)										
Chitimachan stock	25	22	3	10	9	10	7	1	3	3
Chumashan stock	5	4	1	2	1	7	4	1	1	2
Costanoan stock	3	2	-	2	-	4	1	-	1	-
Croatan group	1,027	602	184	251	167	1,001	602	194	269	139
Croatan (North Carolina)	1,027	602	184	251	167	1,001	602	194	269	139

[Continued]

★ 67 ★

School Attendance of American Indians 6 to 19 Years Old, by Linguistic Stock, Tribe, Principal State, and Sex, 1910: Ch - Sa

[Continued]

Linguistic stock, tribe, and state	Indian males 6 to 19 years of age: 1910					Indian females 6 to 19 years of age: 1910				
	Total number	Attending school				Total number	Attending school			
		Total	6 to 9 years of age	10 to 14 years of age	15 to 19 years of age		Total	6 to 9 years of age	10 to 14 years of age	15 to 19 years of age
Eskimauan stock	19	19	2	12	5	22	22	3	10	9
Haidan stock	17	17	1	4	12	6	6	-	-	6
Iroquoian stock	7,318	5,004	1,480	2,178	1,346	7,139	4,917	1,532	2,235	1,150
Cherokee	5,989	4,095	1,236	1,788	1,071	5,767	3,941	1,258	1,810	873
Kansas	11	7	1	5	1	15	12	3	5	4
North Carolina	225	158	41	76	41	178	129	40	52	37
Oklahoma	5,664	3,867	1,180	1,682	1,005	5,511	3,764	1,205	1,740	819
Pennsylvania	17	17	-	-	17	6	6	-	1	5
South Carolina	16	7	-	4	3	13	2	-	1	1
Mohawk	56	32	10	17	5	50	36	11	20	5
New York	46	27	10	15	2	44	30	9	16	5
Oneida	381	251	90	103	58	351	222	70	101	51
New York	39	28	11	11	6	26	13	4	7	2
Wisconsin	316	198	75	88	35	303	188	64	92	32
Onondaga	54	38	10	17	11	69	53	16	24	13
New York	44	29	10	15	4	59	44	16	22	6
St. Regis	229	153	32	73	48	252	209	62	89	58
New York	200	124	32	66	26	222	179	62	83	34
Pennsylvania	29	29	-	7	22	30	30	-	6	24
Seneca	459	312	78	134	100	473	306	86	124	96
New York	359	226	69	112	45	382	233	75	104	54
Oklahoma	35	22	5	14	3	41	24	9	11	4
Pennsylvania	61	60	4	8	48	46	45	2	9	34
Tuscarora	58	50	10	13	27	66	56	11	25	20
New York	52	44	10	13	21	61	51	11	24	16
Wyandot	76	58	10	28	20	67	58	12	27	19
Oklahoma	62	45	9	23	13	58	49	12	24	13
Kalapooian stock	13	8	1	5	2	22	14	3	9	2
Karok stock	127	60	20	29	11	110	64	13	34	17
Orleans (California)	127	60	20	29	11	110	64	13	34	17
Keresan stock	659	323	92	159	72	596	275	90	126	59
Acoma (New Mexico)	117	32	-	23	9	100	32	-	24	8
Cochiti (New Mexico)	35	27	9	16	2	29	15	6	6	3
Laguna	252	174	63	67	44	232	164	62	63	39
New Mexico	237	159	63	65	31	226	158	60	62	36
San Felipe (New Mexico)	77	38	6	23	9	73	24	9	10	5
Santa Ana (New Mexico)	25	9	2	6	1	24	12	5	7	-
Santo Domingo (New Mexico)	130	29	8	15	6	123	17	6	9	2
Sia (New Mexico)	23	14	4	9	1	15	11	2	7	2

[Continued]

★ 67 ★

School Attendance of American Indians 6 to 19 Years Old, by Linguistic Stock, Tribe, Principal State, and Sex, 1910: Ch - Sa

[Continued]

Linguistic stock, tribe, and state	Indian males 6 to 19 years of age: 1910					Indian females 6 to 19 years of age: 1910				
	Total number	Attending school				Total number	Attending school			
		Total	6 to 9 years of age	10 to 14 years of age	15 to 19 years of age		Total	6 to 9 years of age	10 to 14 years of age	15 to 19 years of age
Kiowan stock	181	129	26	62	41	194	112	29	60	23
Kiowa	181	129	26	62	41	194	112	29	60	23
Oklahoma	169	117	26	61	30	192	110	29	59	22
Kusan stock	14	8	-	8	-	13	10	5	4	1
Kutenaian stock	88	38	7	21	10	71	41	9	24	8
Kutenai	88	38	7	21	10	71	41	9	24	8
Idaho	12	1	1	-	-	7	-	-	-	-
Montana	73	34	6	20	8	64	41	9	24	8
Lutuamian stock	138	110	26	45	39	145	120	42	41	37
Klamath	96	80	17	34	29	100	85	31	27	27
Oregon	86	71	17	32	22	87	72	31	27	14
Modoc	42	30	9	11	10	45	35	11	14	10
Oregon	25	18	3	7	8	35	27	9	12	6
Maidu stock	178	111	43	50	18	197	145	52	61	32
Maidu	178	111	43	50	18	197	145	52	61	32
California	178	111	43	50	18	196	144	52	60	32
Miwok stock	104	56	20	26	10	109	48	8	27	13
Miwok (California)	99	51	19	22	10	102	45	8	26	11
Muskhogean stock	5,277	3,307	987	1,432	888	5,151	3,065	999	1,319	747
Alibamu	58	18	1	9	8	64	11	-	6	5
Louisiana	28	6	1	3	2	31	3	-	1	2
Texas	30	12	-	6	6	33	8	-	5	3
Chickasaw (Oklahoma)	821	611	171	276	164	837	602	210	252	140
Choctaw	2,953	1,921	592	811	518	2,787	1,705	552	749	404
Alabama	8	-	-	-	-	12	-	-	-	-
Louisiana	17	-	-	-	-	15	-	-	-	-
Mississippi	205	59	16	25	18	182	30	12	12	6
Oklahoma	2,721	1,860	574	786	500	2,572	1,672	538	736	398
Creek	1,120	645	189	284	172	1,155	617	200	255	162
Alabama	25	15	5	7	3	37	22	8	8	6
Oklahoma	1,074	614	180	268	166	1,105	591	191	245	155
Seminole	308	112	34	52	26	281	128	37	57	34
Oklahoma	262	105	32	47	26	254	116	35	49	32
Texas	45	7	2	5	-	24	11	2	8	1

[Continued]

★ 67 ★

School Attendance of American Indians 6 to 19 Years Old, by Linguistic Stock, Tribe, Principal State, and Sex, 1910: Ch - Sa

[Continued]

Linguistic stock, tribe, and state	Indian males 6 to 19 years of age: 1910					Indian females 6 to 19 years of age: 1910				
	Total number	Attending school				Total number	Attending school			
		Total	6 to 9 years of age	10 to 14 years of age	15 to 19 years of age		Total	6 to 9 years of age	10 to 14 years of age	15 to 19 years of age
Piman stock	1,556	800	188	326	286	1,369	710	185	306	219
Papago	693	230	58	81	91	606	190	42	86	62
Arizona	686	223	58	81	84	606	190	42	86	62
Pima	763	528	118	225	185	672	493	134	206	153
Arizona	725	492	117	220	155	648	469	134	200	135
California	34	32	1	4	27	24	24	-	6	18
Yaqui	93	40	12	20	8	82	27	9	14	4
Arizona	86	33	9	16	8	76	21	7	12	2
Pomo stock	154	94	27	39	28	167	103	29	40	34
Clear Lake (California)	26	14	4	5	5	25	13	7	4	2
Pomo (California)	103	70	20	31	19	112	75	20	33	22
Salinan stock	2	2	-	1	1	1	-	-	-	-

Source: U.S. Bureau of the Census. *Indian Population in the United States and Alaska, 1910.* Washington, DC: U.S. Government Printing Office, 1915, pp. 205-216. *Note:* A dash (-) represents zero.

★ 68 ★

Education

School Attendance of American Indians 6 to 19 Years Old, by Linguistic Stock, Tribe, Principal State, and Sex, 1910: Sa - Sh

Data are shown for tribes having 100 or more members in 1910.

Linguistic stock, tribe, and state	Indian males 6 to 19 years of age: 1910					Indian females 6 to 19 years of age: 1910				
	Total number	Attending school				Total number	Attending school			
		Total	6 to 9 years of age	10 to 14 years of age	15 to 19 years of age		Total	6 to 9 years of age	10 to 14 years of age	15 to 19 years of age
UNITED STATES (cont.)										
Salishan stock	1,292	630	142	308	180	1,161	567	136	285	146
Chehalis	48	28	4	19	5	41	31	8	14	9
Washington	46	26	3	18	5	40	30	8	13	9
Clallam	75	47	18	19	10	69	49	12	30	7
Washington	67	39	17	15	7	68	48	12	29	7
Coeur d'Alene	48	15	1	-	7	35	11	2	7	2
Idaho	45	12	1	6	5	34	10	2	6	2
Columbia	57	33	9	15	9	49	28	10	12	6

[Continued]

★ 68 ★

School Attendance of American Indians 6 to 19 Years Old, by Linguistic Stock, Tribe, Principal State, and Sex, 1910: Sa - Sh

[Continued]

Linguistic stock, tribe, and state	Indian males 6 to 19 years of age: 1910					Indian females 6 to 19 years of age: 1910				
	Total number	Attending school				Total number	Attending school			
		Total	6 to 9 years of age	10 to 14 years of age	15 to 19 years of age		Total	6 to 9 years of age	10 to 14 years of age	15 to 19 years of age
Oregon	11	3	3	-	-	9	5	1	1	3
Washington	46	30	6	15	9	40	23	9	11	3
Colville	135	43	6	21	16	122	40	5	26	9
Washington	119	29	5	17	7	108	30	4	22	4
Cowlitz (Washington)	16	9	4	4	1	10	5	-	4	1
Flathead	82	50	7	30	13	95	55	18	24	13
Montana	60	33	3	23	7	73	36	13	16	7
Kalispel	85	33	5	17	11	73	30	4	14	12
Montana	57	26	5	13	8	46	23	3	10	10
Washington	21	4	-	3	1	23	6	1	4	1
Lummi	85	34	11	15	8	67	20	5	11	4
Washington	81	30	11	12	7	67	20	5	11	4
Muckleshoot	38	24	10	6	8	33	22	5	11	6
Washington	36	22	10	6	6	33	22	5	11	6
Nisqualli	17	12	2	2	8	16	9	1	6	2
Washington	14	9	2	1	6	13	7	1	5	1
Okinagan	43	23	2	13	8	39	21	3	9	9
Washington	38	18	2	11	5	34	16	3	9	4
Puyallup	51	42	9	15	18	50	32	10	10	12
Washington	40	31	8	13	10	42	24	9	9	6
Quinaielt	37	18	4	12	2	28	18	2	10	6
Washington	36	17	4	11	2	28	18	2	10	6
Sanpoil (Washington)	27	2	1	-	1	28	3	2	1	-
Skokomish	24	16	5	10	1	41	27	5	17	5
Washington	23	15	5	10	-	40	26	5	16	5
Snohomish	116	25	7	13	5	113	21	6	12	2
Washington	115	24	7	13	4	103	21	6	13	2
Spokan	91	47	2	33	12	95	49	3	28	18
Idaho	12	4	-	4	-	12	4	1	2	1
Montana	16	9	2	4	3	18	11	-	8	3
Washington	52	25	-	21	4	57	28	1	18	9
Suquamish (Washington)	56	30	10	13	7	45	26	9	11	6
Swinomish (Washington)	62	34	5	15	14	39	22	12	5	5
Shahaptian stock	559	326	93	127	106	590	364	110	162	92
Klikitat	51	28	6	12	10	53	30	5	12	13
Washington	44	22	5	9	8	47	24	5	10	9
Nez Perces	165	92	26	40	26	163	90	24	40	26
Idaho	128	66	21	30	15	132	69	19	32	18
Montana	7	4	-	4	-	8	6	2	4	-
Oregon	11	10	4	4	2	7	7	2	3	2

[Continued]

★ 68 ★

School Attendance of American Indians 6 to 19 Years Old, by Linguistic Stock, Tribe, Principal State, and Sex, 1910: Sa - Sh

[Continued]

Linguistic stock, tribe, and state	Indian males 6 to 19 years of age: 1910					Indian females 6 to 19 years of age: 1910				
	Total number	Attending school				Total number	Attending school			
		Total	6 to 9 years of age	10 to 14 years of age	15 to 19 years of age		Total	6 to 9 years of age	10 to 14 years of age	15 to 19 years of age
Washington	10	3	1	2	-	8	-	-	-	-
Umatilla	21	14	4	4	6	32	21	8	6	7
Oregon	13	12	3	3	6	18	16	6	6	4
Washington	6	1	1	-	-	8	2	2	-	-
Wallawalla (Oregon)	72	59	19	23	17	67	59	16	29	14
Warm Springs	61	39	15	16	8	71	45	14	25	6
Oregon	55	36	13	16	7	66	43	14	23	6
Yakima	175	86	21	29	36	186	111	41	45	25
Oregon	2	2	1	-	1	7	6	-	1	5
Washington	169	81	20	29	32	177	103	41	43	19
Shastan stock	253	142	34	72	36	291	140	32	58	50
Hat Creek (California)	37	22	8	10	4	29	10	3	3	4
Pit River	152	67	16	35	16	193	84	20	35	29
California	135	50	12	29	9	169	66	16	30	20
Oregon	13	13	4	5	4	16	12	3	4	5
Shasta	64	53	10	27	16	69	46	9	20	17
California	43	32	7	15	10	48	26	8	8	10
Oregon	21	21	3	12	6	21	20	1	12	7
Shoshonean stock	2,509	1,351	321	623	407	2,334	1,180	332	541	307
Bannock	59	42	10	10	22	47	28	5	11	12
Idaho	47	34	9	9	16	37	20	5	9	6
Chemehuevi	40	15	6	5	4	41	9	4	3	2
California	32	7	2	4	1	26	1	1	-	-
Nevada	7	7	4	-	3	9	6	3	2	1
Comanche	189	131	32	56	43	172	111	24	58	29
Oklahoma	182	124	32	54	38	168	107	24	57	26
Hopi	337	278	72	133	73	278	210	97	76	37
Arizona	304	246	72	115	59	266	199	97	69	33
Kawia (California)	130	95	27	37	31	121	97	29	41	27
Kern River (California)	20	4	1	2	1	20	5	1	3	1
Mono	209	99	27	51	21	237	111	16	62	33
California	203	99	27	51	21	227	109	16	61	32
Nevada	6	-	-	-	-	10	2	-	1	1
Paiute	114	62	18	22	22	111	39	13	17	9
Arizona	10	5	2	1	2	12	1	1	-	-
California	50	42	10	16	16	40	29	9	13	7
Nevada	21	10	6	3	1	24	5	2	3	-
Utah	32	4	-	2	2	34	3	1	1	1
Paviotso	407	271	65	137	69	396	227	58	119	50

[Continued]

★ 68 ★

School Attendance of American Indians 6 to 19 Years Old, by Linguistic Stock, Tribe, Principal State, and Sex, 1910: Sa - Sh

[Continued]

Linguistic stock, tribe, and state	Indian males 6 to 19 years of age: 1910					Indian females 6 to 19 years of age: 1910				
	Total number	Attending school				Total number	Attending school			
		Total	6 to 9 years of age	10 to 14 years of age	15 to 19 years of age		Total	6 to 9 years of age	10 to 14 years of age	15 to 19 years of age
California	11	4	2	1	1	5	1	-	1	-
Idaho	21	14	1	9	4	18	7	-	4	3
Nevada	334	225	54	114	57	335	195	53	100	42
Oregon	40	27	8	12	7	34	23	5	13	5
San Luiseno (California)	83	65	9	28	28	81	60	6	27	27
Serrano (California)	83	65	9	28	28	81	60	6	27	27
Shoshoni	546	204	39	94	71	507	200	47	92	61
Idaho	171	58	12	27	19	155	63	14	26	23
Nevada	223	52	13	20	19	211	52	17	19	16
Utah	28	20	4	14	2	31	20	4	12	4
Wyoming	103	58	10	30	18	98	56	12	34	10
Ute	338	71	11	40	20	290	62	24	23	15
Colorado	118	48	11	23	14	96	42	18	16	8
Utah	208	16	-	12	4	185	12	5	5	2

Source: U.S. Bureau of the Census. *Indian Population in the United States and Alaska, 1910.* Washington, DC: U.S. Government Printing Office, 1915, pp. 205-216. *Note:* A dash (-) represents zero.

★ 69 ★

Education

School Attendance of American Indians 6 to 19 Years Old, by Linguistic Stock, Tribe, Principal State, and Sex, 1910: Si - Win

Data are shown for tribes having 100 or more members in 1910.

Linguistic stock, tribe, and state	Indian males 6 to 19 years of age: 1910					Indian females 6 to 19 years of age: 1910				
	Total number	Attending school				Total number	Attending school			
		Total	6 to 9 years of age	10 to 14 years of age	15 to 19 years of age		Total	6 to 9 years of age	10 to 14 years of age	15 to 19 years of age
UNITED STATES (cont.)										
Siouan stock	5,112	3,241	768	1,469	1,004	4,910	3,160	785	1,398	977
Assiniboin	183	110	35	44	31	156	93	28	39	26
Montana	177	105	35	44	26	154	92	27	39	26
Catawba	25	18	6	9	3	20	17	4	10	3
South Carolina	18	13	4	7	2	18	15	3	9	3
Crow	262	183	50	81	52	237	150	33	64	53
Montana	235	158	45	71	42	216	132	30	60	42
South Dakota	11	9	4	2	3	6	5	1	1	3
Hidatsa	122	86	19	32	35	99	65	20	22	23
North Dakota	119	83	19	31	33	90	56	20	19	17

[Continued]

★ 69 ★

School Attendance of American Indians 6 to 19 Years Old, by Linguistic Stock, Tribe, Principal State, and Sex, 1910: Si - Win
[Continued]

Linguistic stock, tribe, and state	Indian males 6 to 19 years of age: 1910					Indian females 6 to 19 years of age: 1910				
	Total number	Attending school				Total number	Attending school			
		Total	6 to 9 years of age	10 to 14 years of age	15 to 19 years of age		Total	6 to 9 years of age	10 to 14 years of age	15 to 19 years of age
Iowa	45	30	4	19	7	47	33	9	16	8
Kansas	26	18	3	11	4	25	19	3	9	7
Oklahoma	12	7	1	4	2	10	5	3	2	-
Kansa	41	26	6	9	11	49	35	17	14	4
Oklahoma	39	24	6	9	9	47	33	17	13	3
Mandan	35	17	3	10	4	30	21	5	5	11
North Dakota	33	17	3	10	4	30	21	5	5	11
Omaha	199	100	18	41	41	188	110	28	53	29
Nebraska	187	89	18	41	30	188	110	28	53	29
Osage	251	192	62	76	54	241	183	58	77	48
Oklahoma	245	186	62	74	50	231	173	58	76	39
Oto	73	59	19	22	18	47	36	14	14	8
Oklahoma	66	56	17	22	17	44	34	13	14	7
Ponca	148	112	35	39	38	184	154	36	65	53
Nebraska	38	23	4	13	6	37	24	7	14	3
Oklahoma	96	75	31	24	20	117	101	29	41	31
Quapaw	54	41	8	22	11	51	39	9	20	10
Oklahoma	50	37	8	22	7	48	36	9	18	9
Santee Sioux	243	150	36	82	32	236	147	32	67	48
Minnesota	39	31	12	17	2	46	30	13	12	5
Montana	16	11	4	6	1	13	8	3	-	5
Nebraska	111	55	3	32	20	117	68	9	35	24
North Dakota	11	7	4	2	1	10	5	1	3	1
South Dakota	64	44	12	25	7	45	32	4	16	12
Sioux	201	148	26	41	81	152	111	19	43	49
Minnesota	26	19	3	7	9	37	32	7	20	5
Montana	13	6	3	2	1	15	8	3	3	2
Nebraska	6	3	-	-	3	11	6	-	4	2
New Jersey	3	-	-	-	-	1	-	-	-	-
North Dakota	19	9	3	2	4	9	7	2	2	3
Oklahoma	7	4	1	2	1	6	5	1	2	2
Pennsylvania	37	37	-	2	35	17	17	-	2	15
South Dakota	68	50	14	20	16	33	16	3	2	11
Sisseton Sioux	380	226	67	97	62	359	228	71	103	54
Minnesota	10	7	3	3	1	9	5	2	3	-
Montana	37	28	9	12	7	32	22	9	7	6
North Dakota	83	51	18	20	13	102	67	20	34	13
South Dakota	243	134	36	60	38	215	133	40	58	35
Teton Sioux	2,117	1,264	252	624	388	2,020	1,248	273	551	424
Montana	11	7	2	3	2	6	6	4	-	2
North Dakota	56	44	11	14	19	59	45	8	20	17
South Dakota	2,044	1,207	239	607	361	1,940	1,183	260	527	396
Brule Sioux	107	79	24	30	25	99	74	28	22	24
South Dakota	106	78	24	30	24	97	72	28	22	22
Hunkpapa Sioux	132	87	19	40	28	154	104	28	42	34
North Dakota	14	8	1	2	5	22	12	2	7	3
South Dakota	118	79	18	38	23	132	92	26	35	31

[Continued]

★ 69 ★

School Attendance of American Indians 6 to 19 Years Old, by Linguistic Stock, Tribe, Principal State, and Sex, 1910: Si - Win
[Continued]

Linguistic stock, tribe, and state	Indian males 6 to 19 years of age: 1910					Indian females 6 to 19 years of age: 1910				
	Total number	Attending school				Total number	Attending school			
		Total	6 to 9 years of age	10 to 14 years of age	15 to 19 years of age		Total	6 to 9 years of age	10 to 14 years of age	15 to 19 years of age
Minniconjou Sioux (South Dakota)	48	16	1	10	5	47	18	4	5	9
Oglala Sioux	953	541	123	272	146	887	525	125	234	166
South Dakota	949	539	122	271	146	881	520	123	232	165
Sans Arc Sioux (South Dakota)	42	28	8	14	6	32	20	7	9	4
Sihasapa	60	43	11	15	17	60	35	7	15	13
North Dakota	21	18	8	7	3	23	19	5	7	7
South Dakota	39	25	3	8	14	37	16	2	8	6
Two Kettle Sioux (South Dakota)	43	19	3	8	8	41	18	4	10	4
Other Teton Sioux	732	451	63	235	153	700	454	70	214	170
North Dakota	20	17	2	4	11	14	14	1	6	7
South Dakota	699	423	60	228	135	673	427	66	206	155
Winnebago	296	199	47	96	56	291	176	47	78	51
Nebraska	155	98	29	43	26	123	67	20	28	19
Wisconsin	120	81	14	46	21	161	104	27	50	27
Yankton Sioux	273	163	45	68	50	315	174	52	77	45
Montana	53	38	11	11	16	54	41	12	16	13
North Dakota	15	9	2	5	2	15	10	4	3	3
South Dakota	199	110	32	49	29	238	116	35	54	27
Yanktonai Sioux	163	116	30	57	29	188	140	30	80	30
North Dakota	68	51	13	25	13	76	58	12	33	13
South Dakota	95	65	17	32	16	112	82	18	47	17
Tanoan stock	456	285	110	124	51	455	268	126	111	31
Isleta	110	72	32	25	15	105	74	38	29	7
New Mexico	102	69	31	25	13	98	71	37	27	7
Jemez (New Mexico)	77	56	12	39	5	72	45	16	24	5
Picuris (New Mexico)	15	13	8	3	2	13	8	2	5	1
San Ildefonso (New Mexico)	22	15	10	5	-	21	18	13	3	2
San Juan	71	51	17	26	8	67	45	24	16	5
New Mexico	70	50	17	26	7	65	45	24	16	5
Santa Clara (New Mexico)	34	21	11	5	5	47	23	3	12	8
Taos (New Mexico)	83	36	16	15	5	91	30	19	11	-
Tlingit stock	15	15	-	3	12	10	10	1	4	5
Tonkawan stock	5	4	1	3	-	3	2	-	1	1
Tsimshian stock	17	15	1	4	10	5	3	2	1	-
Tunican stock	11	3	2	1	-	8	1	1	-	-
Waiilatpuan stock	57	46	18	16	12	52	47	17	21	9
Cayuse	52	43	15	16	12	51	47	17	21	9
Oregon	46	37	13	15	9	47	43	14	20	9

[Continued]

★ 69 ★

School Attendance of American Indians 6 to 19 Years Old, by Linguistic Stock, Tribe, Principal State, and Sex, 1910: Si - Win

[Continued]

Linguistic stock, tribe, and state	Indian males 6 to 19 years of age: 1910					Indian females 6 to 19 years of age: 1910				
	Total number	Attending school				Total number	Attending school			
		Total	6 to 9 years of age	10 to 14 years of age	15 to 19 years of age		Total	6 to 9 years of age	10 to 14 years of age	15 to 19 years of age
Wakashan stock	54	42	17	12	13	61	44	17	20	7
Makah	52	42	17	12	13	60	44	17	20	7
Washington	50	40	17	11	12	57	41	17	18	6
Washoan stock	112	37	9	12	16	95	25	5	12	8
Washo	112	37	9	12	16	95	25	5	12	8
California	36	10	1	4	5	32	3	1	2	-
Nevada	72	23	8	7	8	60	19	4	10	5
Wintun stock	106	45	7	29	9	99	48	14	19	15
Nomelaki	22	14	3	10	1	16	10	3	3	4
California	22	14	3	10	1	14	8	3	3	2
Patwin (California)	21	-	-	-	-	27	1	1	-	-
Wintun	63	31	4	19	8	56	37	10	16	11
California	62	30	4	18	8	53	34	10	16	8

Source: U.S. Bureau of the Census. *Indian Population in the United States and Alaska, 1910.* Washington, DC: U.S. Government Printing Office, 1915, pp. 205-216. *Note:* A dash (-) represents zero.

★ 70 ★

Education

School Attendance of American Indians 6 to 19 Years Old, by Linguistic Stock, Tribe, Principal State, and Sex, 1910: Wiy - Z and Alaska

Data are shown for tribes having 100 or more members in 1910.

Linguistic stock, tribe, and state	Indian males 6 to 19 years of age: 1910					Indian females 6 to 19 years of age: 1910				
	Total number	Attending school				Total number	Attending school			
		Total	6 to 9 years of age	10 to 14 years of age	15 to 19 years of age		Total	6 to 9 years of age	10 to 14 years of age	15 to 19 years of age
UNITED STATES (cont.)										
Wiyat stock	26	21	9	9	3	13	9	3	6	-
Humboldt Bay (California)	26	21	9	9	3	13	9	3	6	-

[Continued]

★ 70 ★

School Attendance of American Indians 6 to 19 Years Old, by Linguistic Stock, Tribe, Principal State, and Sex, 1910: Wiy - Z and Alaska

[Continued]

Linguistic stock, tribe, and state	Indian males 6 to 19 years of age: 1910					Indian females 6 to 19 years of age: 1910				
	Total number	Attending school				Total number	Attending school			
		Total	6 to 9 years of age	10 to 14 years of age	15 to 19 years of age		Total	6 to 9 years of age	10 to 14 years of age	15 to 19 years of age
Yakonan stock	11	9	1	3	5	9	7	2	3	2
Yanan stock	8	4	-	2	2	6	2	1	1	-
Yokuts stock	71	32	4	15	13	78	31	7	15	9
Chukchansi	17	11	1	5	5	31	16	2	6	8
California	17	11	1	5	5	29	14	2	6	6
Yokuts (California)	47	20	3	10	7	35	14	4	9	1
Yuchean stock	21	11	1	4	6	10	2	-	1	1
Yukian stock	22	16	8	4	4	25	13	2	3	8
Yuman stock	711	469	131	192	146	593	349	99	163	87
Cocopa	40	-	-	-	-	24	1	1	-	-
Arizona	39	-	-	-	-	22	-	-	-	-
Diegueno (California)	137	94	30	32	32	141	100	25	51	24
Havasupai (Arizona)	21	18	3	8	7	15	12	3	3	6
Maricopa (Arizona)	64	52	14	23	15	64	44	10	16	18
Mohave	173	123	35	54	34	117	76	19	44	13
Arizona	111	69	20	33	16	85	52	10	32	10
California	62	54	15	21	18	32	24	9	12	3
Walapai	113	79	26	30	23	78	37	13	21	3
Arizona	111	77	26	30	21	76	35	11	21	3
Yavapai (Arizona)	58	33	11	15	7	45	23	9	9	5
Yuma	102	69	12	29	28	106	56	19	19	18
Arizona	19	9	3	3	3	23	2	1	-	1
California	82	59	9	26	24	83	54	18	19	17
Yurok stock	107	58	24	25	9	93	55	16	24	15
Weitspec (California)	107	58	24	25	9	93	55	16	24	15
Zunian stock	214	64	18	32	14	222	53	19	25	9
Zuni	214	64	18	32	14	222	53	19	25	9
New Mexico	212	63	18	32	13	222	53	19	25	9
ALASKA										
Athapaskan stock	556	225	40	108	77	526	176	35	90	51
Ahtena	50	7	-	5	2	35	3	1	1	1
Hankutchin	23	15	4	9	2	12	7	5	-	2
Kaiyuhkhotana	14	8	2	2	4	17	9	4	3	2

[Continued]

★ 70 ★

School Attendance of American Indians 6 to 19 Years Old, by Linguistic Stock, Tribe, Principal State, and Sex, 1910: Wiy - Z and Alaska

[Continued]

Linguistic stock, tribe, and state	Indian males 6 to 19 years of age: 1910					Indian females 6 to 19 years of age: 1910				
	Total number	Attending school				Total number	Attending school			
		Total	6 to 9 years of age	10 to 14 years of age	15 to 19 years of age		Total	6 to 9 years of age	10 to 14 years of age	15 to 19 years of age
Knaiakhotana	114	44	9	17	18	96	36	9	17	10
Kutchin	49	14	5	6	3	52	8	-	5	3
Natsitkutchin	34	3	-	2	1	27	1	-	-	1
Tenankutchin	56	15	4	7	4	58	12	6	4	2
Unakhotana	18	9	4	4	1	26	9	2	6	1
Eskimauan stock	2,039	707	205	315	187	1,775	513	154	240	119
Aleut	248	78	18	36	24	209	59	8	39	12
Chnagmiut	50	24	7	8	9	32	11	6	3	2
Ikogmiut	80	1	-	1	-	101	4	-	3	1
Kaialigmiut	25	2	2	-	-	22	1	1	-	-
Kaviagmiut	38	18	8	5	5	24	17	6	9	3
Kinugumiut	91	48	11	25	12	60	28	9	8	11
Kowagmiut	84	52	18	19	15	70	51	12	26	12
Kusetrinmiut	28	20	7	10	3	7	1	-	1	-
Kuskovakmiut	69	20	1	14	5	50	6	1	4	1
Kuskwogmiut	205	34	10	16	8	178	16	5	11	-
Magemiut	46	7	1	4	2	65	25	2	11	12
Malemiut	93	47	12	22	13	81	43	6	21	16
Nunatogmiut	39	7	2	4	1	30	4	1	2	1
Nunivagmiut	47	4	1	2	1	34	1	-	1	-
Nunochogmiut	8	-	-	-	-	20	-	-	-	-
Selawigmiut	21	14	5	7	2	12	5	5	-	-
Tikeramiut	37	14	3	8	3	38	7	1	3	3
Ukivokmiut	23	7	3	2	2	12	3	2	1	-
Unaligmiut	62	28	8	15	5	60	14	5	7	2
Utkiavinmiut	10	8	-	6	2	11	7	4	2	1
Utukamiut	10	8	1	5	2	10	8	3	4	1
Yuit	39	35	7	14	14	29	23	9	7	7
Southern Eskimo	560	165	61	64	40	512	131	51	56	24
Haidan stock	88	75	22	26	27	82	58	23	17	18
Haida	88	75	22	26	27	82	58	23	17	18
Tlingit stock	611	380	139	157	84	636	384	156	168	60
Auk	34	17	5	6	6	41	26	12	13	1
Chilkat	95	59	23	24	12	99	54	24	17	13
Henya	29	18	8	7	3	32	26	9	12	5
Huna	86	66	26	24	16	100	60	24	30	6
Hutsnuwu	68	37	11	23	3	76	40	21	16	3
Kake	47	37	16	11	10	46	33	14	13	6
Sitka	87	63	23	27	13	82	55	18	24	13
Stikine	21	12	3	6	3	28	18	9	9	-
Taku	19	7	1	3	3	15	9	2	7	-

[Continued]

★ 70 ★

School Attendance of American Indians 6 to 19 Years Old, by Linguistic Stock, Tribe, Principal State, and Sex, 1910: Wiy - Z and Alaska
[Continued]

Linguistic stock, tribe, and state	Indian males 6 to 19 years of age: 1910					Indian females 6 to 19 years of age: 1910				
	Total number	Attending school				Total number	Attending school			
		Total	6 to 9 years of age	10 to 14 years of age	15 to 19 years of age		Total	6 to 9 years of age	10 to 14 years of age	15 to 19 years of age
Tongas	31	13	4	5	4	32	22	9	10	3
Yakutat	42	19	9	9	1	46	17	6	6	5
Tsimshian stock	129	80	16	42	22	112	72	39	29	4
Tsimshian	129	80	16	42	22	112	72	39	29	4

Source: U.S. Bureau of the Census. *Indian Population in the United States and Alaska, 1910.* Washington, DC: U.S. Government Printing Office, 1915, pp. 205-216.
Note: A dash (-) represents zero.

★ 71 ★
Education

School Attendance of Indians 6 to 19 Years Old, by Geographic Division, State, and Age Group, 1910

Division and state	Indians 6 to 19 years of age: 1910				
	Total number	Number attending school			
		Total	6 to 9 years of age	10 to 14 years of age	15 to 19 years of age
UNITED STATES	88,786	50,115	13,984	22,446	13,685
Geographic divisions					
New England	577	398	126	196	76
Middle Atlantic	2,746	2,040	409	715	916
East North Central	5,942	3,883	1,203	1,934	746
West North Central	13,361	8,728	2,066	3,938	2,724
South Atlantic	3,091	1,797	542	788	467
East South Central	907	261	77	126	58
West South Central	27,765	18,525	5,744	8,198	4,583
Mountain	24,321	8,516	2,231	3,879	2,406
Pacific	10,076	5,967	1,586	2,672	1,709
New England					
Maine	259	163	58	70	35
New Hampshire	9	8	3	4	1
Vermont	4	3	1	2	-
Massachusetts	191	149	45	75	29
Rhode Island	81	54	12	34	8
Connecticut	33	21	7	11	3

[Continued]

★ 71 ★

School Attendance of Indians 6 to 19 Years Old, by Geographic Division, State, and Age Group, 1910

[Continued]

Division and state	Indians 6 to 19 years of age: 1910				
	Total number	Number attending school			
		Total	6 to 9 years of age	10 to 14 years of age	15 to 19 years of age
Middle Atlantic					
New York	1,855	1,239	390	574	275
New Jersey	54	25	1	9	15
Pennsylvania	837	776	18	132	626
East North Central					
Ohio	40	26	5	17	4
Indiana	111	66	20	41	5
Illinois	44	32	8	12	12
Michigan	2,303	1,448	433	719	296
Wisconsin	3,444	2,311	737	1,145	429
West North Central					
Minnesota	3,094	2,259	661	1,003	595
Iowa	111	54	17	22	15
Missouri	100	68	20	37	11
North Dakota	2,258	1,421	347	669	405
South Dakota	5,543	3,326	765	1,554	1,007
Nebraska	1,224	754	154	343	257
Kansas	1,031	846	102	310	434
South Atlantic					
Delaware	4	4	-	2	2
Maryland	29	22	3	9	10
District of Columbia	18	14	2	10	2
Virginia	192	57	23	24	10
West Virginia	17	14	5	5	4
North Carolina	2,668	1,608	490	700	418
South Carolina	115	62	15	31	16
Georgia	29	11	2	6	3
Florida	19	5	2	1	2
East South Central					
Kentucky	92	16	5	9	2
Tennessee	76	35	10	18	7
Alabama	320	112	33	55	24
Mississippi	419	98	29	44	25
West South Central					
Arkansas	167	104	33	51	20
Louisiana	321	56	13	27	16
Oklahoma	27,060	18,288	5,689	8,072	4,527
Texas	217	77	9	48	20

[Continued]

★ 71 ★

School Attendance of Indians 6 to 19 Years Old, by Geographic Division, State, and Age Group, 1910
[Continued]

Division and state	Total number	Indians 6 to 19 years of age: 1910			
		Number attending school			
		Total	6 to 9 years of age	10 to 14 years of age	15 to 19 years of age
Mountain					
Montana	3,292	1,519	363	723	433
Idaho	875	382	92	173	117
Wyoming	437	289	68	146	75
Colorado	588	403	84	167	152
New Mexico	6,794	1,799	578	817	404
Arizona	10,039	3,366	855	1,481	1,030
Utah	870	101	19	59	23
Nevada	1,426	657	172	313	172
Pacific					
Washington	3,264	1,710	496	810	404
Oregon	1,714	1,349	332	580	437
California	5,098	2,908	758	1,282	868

Source: U.S. Bureau of the Census. *Indian Population in the United States and Alaska, 1910.* Washington, DC: U.S. Government Printing Office, 1915, p. 199. *Note:* A dash (-) represents zero.

★ 72 ★

Education

School Attendance, by Tribe, Tribal Group, Age Group, and Sex, 1930 - I

Tribe or stock	Indians 5 years old and over attending school			5 and 6 years		7 to 13 years	
	Total	Male	Female	Male	Female	Male	Female
Total	79,856	40,252	39,604	2,211	2,297	24,096	23,653
Arapaho	304	163	141	16	12	89	87
Blackfeet	865	460	405	22	13	282	258
Cheyenne	609	316	293	7	4	164	165
Chippewa	5,645	2,744	2,901	141	157	1,827	1,878
Delaware	308	166	142	12	7	100	86
Gros Ventres (Atsina)	162	73	89	3	1	41	55
Kickapoo	122	61	61	2	2	35	38
Menominee	577	301	276	19	15	166	174
Ottawa	438	247	191	23	24	147	114
Potawatomie	427	206	221	4	21	146	134
Sauk and Fox	212	96	116	7	6	52	53
Shawnee	321	161	160	13	9	91	96

[Continued]

★ 72 ★

School Attendance, by Tribe, Tribal Group, Age Group, and Sex, 1930 - I
[Continued]

Tribe or stock	Indians 5 years old and over attending school			5 and 6 years		7 to 13 years	
	Total	Male	Female	Male	Female	Male	Female
Eastern Algonquians	513	243	270	21	30	157	170
Virginia-Carolina Indians	3,422	1,760	1,662	89	107	1,205	1,039
Apache	1,280	662	618	11	13	431	432
Navaho	5,249	2,882	2,367	67	66	1,461	1,299
Oregon Athapaskans	132	74	58	3	6	43	34
California Athapaskans	266	129	137	7	18	83	82
Arikara	118	51	67	1	1	30	38
Caddo	157	78	79	3	3	46	43
Pawnee	276	146	130	11	5	78	85
Chinookan Stock	143	63	80	2	7	40	43
Iroquois	1,838	901	937	70	66	574	552
Wyandot	112	56	56	4	2	27	28
Cherokee	13,241	6,702	6,539	468	488	4,064	3,972
Karok Stock (Orleans)	199	86	113	4	8	50	67
Keresan Stock	1,058	527	531	21	30	304	281
Kiowan Stock (Kiowa)	291	141	150	9	5	75	90
Miwok Stock	127	57	70	4	4	40	44
Chickasaw	1,510	737	773	39	59	448	426
Choctaw	5,365	2,716	2,649	172	183	1,606	1,576
Creek	2,610	1,320	1,290	75	85	756	729
Seminole	530	296	234	12	18	178	122
Papago	775	391	384	20	27	227	204
Pima	1,075	538	537	23	22	284	274
Pomo Stock	234	108	126	6	5	70	88
Washington Coast Salish	939	452	487	21	20	291	328
Interior Salish	1,204	603	601	24	31	390	361
Klamath and Modoc	558	286	272	27	18	179	164
Shahaptians	946	453	493	16	21	279	291
Shastan Stock	160	84	76	6	4	63	46
Comanche	387	195	192	6	6	113	105
Hopi	857	416	441	38	33	212	223
Mono-Paviotso	117	49	68	7	4	21	39
Paiute	911	448	463	18	30	278	292
Shoshoni	796	392	404	25	23	247	235
Ute	430	218	212	10	10	127	122
Crow	437	215	222	7	9	143	137
Hidatsa	133	65	68	3	5	40	38
Oto and Missouri	251	116	135	7	4	81	97

[Continued]

★ 72 ★

School Attendance, by Tribe, Tribal Group, Age Group, and Sex, 1930 - I

[Continued]

Tribe or stock	Indians 5 years old and over attending school			5 and 6 years		7 to 13 years	
	Total	Male	Female	Male	Female	Male	Female
Omaha	304	147	157	15	9	83	86
Osage	771	415	356	36	27	217	204
Ponca	272	123	149	7	4	77	114
Dakota	6,377	3,249	3,128	116	127	1,877	1,815
Assiniboin	440	215	225	9	7	123	133
Winnebago	450	208	242	7	19	120	133
Tanoan Stock	869	454	415	29	20	245	243
Washoan Stock (Washo)	111	60	51	4	1	35	34
Wintun Stock	118	54	64	1	7	29	38
Yokuts Stock	288	157	131	9	9	101	83
Northern Yumans	125	55	70	2	3	32	45
Mohave	188	91	97	6	5	54	62
Yuma	525	266	259	9	19	162	155
Yurok Stock	125	56	69	3	5	55	43
Zunian Stock (Zuni)	420	246	174	10	7	120	86

Source: Truesdell, Dr. Leon E. U.S. Department of Commerce. Bureau of the Census. Fifteenth Census of the United States: 1930, *The Indian Population of the United States and Alaska.* Washington, DC: U.S. Government Printing Office, 1937, pp. 140-141. *Notes:* A dash (-) represents zero. The statistics of school attendance obtained in the census of 1930 are based upon the answer to a question on the population schedule as to whether the person enumerated had attended school or college at any time between September 1, 1929, and the census date, April 1, 1930. The total number of persons returned as attending school is, therefore, larger than the number who were in attendance at any one time between these two dates.

★ 73 ★

Education

School Attendance, by Tribe, Tribal Group, Age Group, and Sex, 1930 - II

Tribe or stock	14 and 15 years		16 and 17 years		18 to 20 years		21 years and over	
	Male	Female	Male	Female	Male	Female	Male	Female
Total	5,921	5,998	4,184	4,307	2,672	2,467	1,168	882
Arapaho	22	19	16	15	18	6	2	2
Blackfeet	70	65	46	44	28	20	12	5
Cheyenne	65	60	37	41	28	18	15	5
Chippewa	425	428	231	278	80	125	40	35
Delaware	22	24	21	14	7	9	4	2
Gros Ventres (Atsina)	8	13	11	12	8	6	2	2
Kickapoo	11	8	8	8	5	3	-	2
Menominee	47	43	50	27	17	16	2	1
Ottawa	37	32	23	15	13	3	4	3

[Continued]

★ 73 ★

School Attendance, by Tribe, Tribal Group, Age Group, and Sex, 1930 - II
[Continued]

Tribe or stock	14 and 15 years		16 and 17 years		18 to 20 years		21 years and over	
	Male	Female	Male	Female	Male	Female	Male	Female
Potawatomie	32	31	20	21	3	8	1	6
Sauk and Fox	12	29	14	16	8	8	3	4
Shawnee	18	28	21	16	16	8	2	3
Eastern Algonquians	38	43	20	21	2	3	5	3
Virginia-Carolina Indians	227	247	161	159	56	77	22	33
Apache	87	74	68	54	49	35	16	10
Navaho	438	350	369	308	369	250	178	94
Oregon Athapaskans	13	10	5	5	7	3	3	-
California Athapaskans	21	18	9	14	5	5	4	-
Arikara	8	12	2	8	8	5	2	3
Caddo	8	14	10	7	8	11	3	1
Pawnee	29	17	9	15	11	6	8	2
Chinookan Stock	8	14	6	11	3	5	4	-
Iroquois	122	174	79	87	40	50	16	8
Wyandot	8	8	7	12	7	5	3	1
Cherokee	942	951	697	679	394	363	137	126
Karok Stock (Orleans)	16	15	7	8	5	11	4	4
Keresan Stock	93	113	56	51	41	50	12	6
Kiowan Stock (Kiowa)	26	26	16	20	13	7	2	2
Miwok Stock	9	12	3	7	1	3	-	-
Chickasaw	97	114	83	98	51	50	19	26
Choctaw	348	369	298	262	198	175	94	84
Creek	191	185	132	172	130	89	36	30
Seminole	37	42	42	33	23	17	4	2
Papago	60	66	52	57	24	22	8	8
Pima	67	73	69	71	59	75	36	22
Pomo Stock	19	19	8	11	3	3	2	-
Washington Coast Salish	76	72	41	40	18	24	5	3
Interior Salish	86	105	67	54	25	42	11	8
Klamath and Modoc	32	41	26	28	18	20	4	1
Shahaptians	60	81	53	64	35	32	10	4
Shastan Stock	11	11	3	10	-	4	1	1
Comanche	32	35	24	30	16	11	4	5
Hopi	56	66	56	59	36	43	18	17
Mono-Paviotso	9	11	9	4	-	8	3	2
Paiute	79	66	42	47	23	22	8	6
Shoshoni	56	58	37	43	16	32	11	13
Ute	29	35	22	22	23	20	7	3
Crow	31	37	18	23	15	10	1	6
Hidatsa	7	9	6	7	8	8	1	1

[Continued]

★ 73 ★

School Attendance, by Tribe, Tribal Group, Age Group, and Sex, 1930 - II
[Continued]

Tribe or stock	14 and 15 years		16 and 17 years		18 to 20 years		21 years and over	
	Male	Female	Male	Female	Male	Female	Male	Female
Oto and Missouri	16	21	6	11	6	2	-	-
Omaha	22	29	14	17	4	9	9	7
Osage	72	50	44	39	38	26	8	10
Ponca	23	14	8	10	6	5	2	2
Dakota	512	493	375	364	254	242·	115	87
Assiniboin	36	30	31	33	10	19	6	3
Winnebago	33	31	21	36	15	19	12	4
Tanoan Stock	82	75	43	54	43	20	12	3
Washoan Stock (Washo)	10	9	5	4	3	2	3	1
Wintun Stock	15	12	6	4	2	3	1	-
Yokuts Stock	28	19	8	14	5	4	6	2
Northern Yumans	10	5	1	8	8	5	2	4
Mohave	12	9	6	9	5	9	8	3
Yuma	38	37	26	30	22	10	9	8
Yurok Stock	14	10	4	10	2	1	-	-
Zunian Stock (Zuni)	52	34	33	34	19	10	12	3

Source: Truesdell, Dr. Leon E. U.S. Department of Commerce. Bureau of the Census. Fifteenth Census of the United States: 1930, *The Indian Population of the United States and Alaska.* Washington, DC: U.S. Government Printing Office, 1937, pp. 140-141. *Notes:* A dash (-) represents zero. The statistics of school attendance obtained in the census of 1930 are based upon the answer to a question on the population schedule as to whether the person enumerated had attended school or college at any time between September 1, 1929, and the census date, April 1, 1930. The total number of persons returned as attending school is, therefore, larger than the number who were in attendance at any one time between these two dates.

★ 74 ★
Education

Illiterate American Indians 10 Years Old and Older, by Linguistic Stock, Tribe, and Sex, 1910: A - K

Data are shown for linguistic stocks with 200 or more Indians and tribes with more than 100 members in 1910.

Linguistic stock and tribe	Indians 10 years of age and over; 1910			Indian males 10 years of age and over			Indian females 10 years of age and over		
	Total number	Illiterate		Total number	Illiterate		Total number	Illiterate	
		Number	Percent		Number	Percent		Number	Percent
UNITED STATES									
Algonquian stock	29,872	11,509	38.5	15,486	5,345	34.5	14,380	6,164	42.8
Arapaho	1,047	492	47.0	545	206	37.8	502	286	57.0
Brotherton	132	3	2.3	70	3	4.3	62	-	-
Cheyenne	2,427	1,404	57.8	1,176	598	50.9	1,251	806	64.4
Chickahominy	89	24	27.0	47	14	-	42	10	-
Chippewa	14,629	5,800	39.6	7,552	2,727	36.1	7,077	3,073	43.4
Cree	326	95	29.1	166	49	29.5	160	46	28.8
Delaware	636	90	14.2	312	28	9.0	324	62	19.1

[Continued]

★ 74 ★

Illiterate American Indians 10 Years Old and Older, by Linguistic Stock, Tribe, and Sex, 1910: A - K

[Continued]

Linguistic stock and tribe	Indians 10 years of age and over: 1910			Indian males 10 years of age and over			Indian females 10 years of age and over		
	Total number	Illiterate		Total number	Illiterate		Total number	Illiterate	
		Number	Percent		Number	Percent		Number	Percent
Gros Ventres	376	199	52.9	189	93	49.2	187	106	56.7
Kickapoo	251	131	52.2	139	68	48.9	112	63	56.3
Malecite	101	35	34.7	48	17	-	53	18	34.0
Mashpee	166	1	0.6	91	-	-	75	1	1.3
Menominee	1,029	381	37.0	571	198	34.7	458	183	40.0
Miami	171	17	9.9	94	8	8.5	77	9	11.7
Ottawa	2,034	664	32.6	1,083	297	27.4	951	367	38.6
Passamaquoddy	310	110	35.5	166	45	27.1	144	65	45.1
Penobscot	231	60	26.0	124	31	25.0	107	29	27.1
Peoria	83	10	12.0	40	1	-	43	9	-
Piegan	1,602	978	61.0	810	480	59.3	792	498	62.9
Potawatomi	1,697	527	31.1	968	284	29.3	729	243	33.3
Powhatan	91	19	20.9	45	14	-	46	5	-
Sauk and Fox	521	151	29.0	280	61	21.8	241	90	37.3
Shawnee	886	248	28.0	424	95	22.4	462	153	33.1
Shinnecock	121	-	-	59	-	-	62	-	-
Stockbridges	384	17	4.4	197	8	4.1	187	9	4.8
Wampanoag	133	3	2.3	79	3	3.8	54	-	-
All other tribes	399	50	12.5	211	17	8.1	188	33	17.6
Athapaskan stock	20,460	16,982	83.0	10,252	8,136	79.4	10,208	8,840	86.7
Apache	3,480	2,386	68.6	1,754	1,060	60.4	1,726	1,326	76.8
Hupa	497	204	41.0	241	95	39.4	256	109	42.6
Jicarilla Apache	486	378	77.8	252	183	72.6	234	195	83.3
Kiowa Apache	98	40	40.8	42	15	-	56	25	44.6
Mescalero Apache	312	164	52.6	129	52	40.3	183	112	61.2
Navajo	14,797	13,496	91.2	7,429	6,592	88.7	7,368	6,904	93.7
Rogue River	286	101	35.3	153	46	30.1	133	55	41.4
Tolowa	84	44	52.4	44	19	-	40	25	-
Umpqua	79	26	32.9	40	12	-	39	14	-
Wailaki	164	52	31.7	79	17	21.5	85	35	41.2
All other tribes	164	52	31.7	79	17	21.5	85	35	41.2
Caddoan stock	1,354	537	39.7	673	248	36.8	681	289	42.4
Arikara	336	190	56.5	163	92	56.4	173	98	56.6
Caddo	302	89	29.5	161	41	25.5	141	48	34.0
Pawnee	473	162	34.2	227	73	32.2	246	89	36.2
Wichita	229	92	40.2	114	39	34.2	115	53	46.1
All other tribes	14	4	-	8	3	-	6	1	-
Chimakuan stock	228	123	53.9	113	52	46.0	115	71	61.7
Quileute	193	100	51.8	95	42	44.2	98	58	59.2
All other tribes	35	23	-	18	10	-	17	13	-

[Continued]

★ 74 ★

Illiterate American Indians 10 Years Old and Older, by Linguistic Stock, Tribe, and Sex, 1910: A - K

[Continued]

Linguistic stock and tribe	Indians 10 years of age and over: 1910			Indian males 10 years of age and over			Indian females 10 years of age and over		
	Total number	Illiterate		Total number	Illiterate		Total number	Illiterate	
		Number	Percent		Number	Percent		Number	Percent
Chinookan stock	676	230	34.0	353	92	26.1	323	138	42.7
Chinook	224	40	17.9	123	20	16.3	101	20	19.8
Wasco	184	61	33.2	95	18	18.9	89	43	48.3
Wishram	222	116	52.3	112	52	46.4	110	64	58.2
All other tribes	46	13	-	23	2	-	23	11	-
Croatan group	3,943	1,932	49.0	1,954	869	44.5	1,989	1,063	53.4
Croatan	3,943	1,932	49.0	1,954	869	44.5	1,989	1,063	53.4
Iroquoian stock	26,201	5,689	21.7	13,490	2,771	20.5	12,711	2,918	23.0
Cherokee	20,154	3,999	19.8	10,319	1,883	18.2	9,835	2,116	21.5
Mohawk	291	139	47.8	136	58	42.6	155	81	52.3
Oneida	1,739	519	29.8	930	296	31.8	809	223	27.6
Onondaga	275	75	27.3	138	29	21.0	137	46	33.6
St. Regis	912	375	41.1	499	209	41.9	413	166	40.2
Seneca	2,155	501	23.2	1,109	256	23.1	1,046	245	23.4
Tuscarora	309	51	16.5	168	24	14.3	141	27	19.1
Wyandot	253	15	5.9	137	8	5.8	116	7	6.0
All other tribes	113	15	13.3	54	8	14.8	59	7	11.9
Karok stock	555	251	45.2	275	111	40.4	280	140	50.0
Orleans	555	251	45.2	275	111	40.4	280	140	50.0
Keresan stock	2,954	2,195	74.3	1,593	1,118	70.2	1,361	1,077	79.1
Acoma	518	423	81.7	257	198	77.0	261	225	86.2
Cochiti	183	109	59.6	103	54	52.4	80	55	68.8
Laguna	1,050	633	60.3	551	302	54.8	499	331	66.3
San Felipe	379	312	82.3	227	175	77.1	152	137	90.1
Santa Ana	155	135	87.1	98	87	88.8	57	48	84.2
Santo Domingo	581	518	89.2	310	268	86.5	271	250	92.3
Sia	88	65	73.9	47	34	-	41	31	-
Kiowan stock	750	330	44.0	361	140	38.8	389	190	48.8
Kiowa	750	330	44.0	361	140	38.8	389	190	48.8
Kutenaian stock	395	215	54.4	210	111	52.9	185	104	56.2
Kutenai	395	215	54.4	210	111	52.9	185	104	56.2

Source: U.S. Bureau of the Census. *Indian Population in the United States and Alaska, 1910.* Washington, DC: U.S. Government Printing Office, 1915, pp. 226-231. *Notes:* A dash (-) represents zero or a lack of 50 persons for a percentage base.

★ 75 ★
Education

Illiterate American Indians 10 Years Old and Older, by Linguistic Stock, Tribe, and Sex, 1910: L - S

Data are shown for linguistic stocks with 200 or more Indians and tribes with more than 100 members in 1910.

Linguistic stock and tribe	Indians 10 years of age and over: 1910			Indian males 10 years of age and over			Indian females 10 years of age and over		
	Total number	Illiterate		Total number	Illiterate		Total number	Illiterate	
		Number	Percent		Number	Percent		Number	Percent
UNITED STATES (cont.)									
Lutuamian stock	727	260	35.8	347	99	28.5	380	161	42.4
Klamath	521	190	36.5	249	76	30.5	272	114	41.9
Modoc	206	70	34.0	98	23	23.5	108	47	43.5
Maidu stock	810	335	41.4	421	172	40.9	389	163	41.9
Maidu	810	335	41.4	421	172	40.9	389	163	41.9
Miwok stock	530	325	61.3	254	151	59.4	276	174	63.0
Miwok	505	318	63.0	238	147	61.8	267	171	64.0
All other tribes	25	7	-	16	4	-	9	3	-
Muskhogean stock	18,957	6,357	33.5	9,608	2,785	29.0	9,349	3,572	38.2
Alibamu	225	140	62.2	114	65	57.0	111	75	67.6
Chickasaw	2,563	379	14.8	1,268	128	10.1	1,295	251	19.4
Choctaw	10,185	3,168	31.1	5,202	1,375	26.4	4,983	1,793	36.0
Creek	4,697	1,942	41.3	2,349	869	37.0	2,348	1,073	45.7
Seminole	1,216	666	54.8	639	317	49.6	577	349	60.5
All other tribes (Koasati)	71	62	87.3	36	31	-	35	31	-
Piman stock	6,149	3,901	63.4	3,234	1,936	59.9	2,915	1,965	67.4
Papago	2,655	1,953	73.6	1,365	969	71.0	1,290	984	76.3
Pima	3,083	1,614	52.4	1,631	782	47.9	1,452	832	57.3
Yaqui	378	307	81.2	222	175	78.8	156	132	84.6
All other tribes	33	27	-	16	10	-	17	17	-
Pomo stock	919	473	51.5	465	211	45.4	454	262	57.7
Clear Lake	141	57	40.4	73	27	37.0	68	30	44.1
Pomo	606	313	51.7	308	139	45.1	298	174	58.4
All other tribes	172	103	59.9	84	45	53.6	88	58	65.9
Salishan stock	5,759	2,703	46.9	2,993	1,244	41.6	2,766	1,459	52.7
Chehalis	199	73	36.7	114	36	31.6	85	37	43.5
Clallam	280	80	28.6	144	27	18.8	136	53	39.0
Coeur d'Alene	215	107	49.8	116	50	43.1	99	57	57.6
Columbia	288	200	69.4	156	102	65.4	132	98	74.2
Colville	589	341	57.9	310	180	58.1	279	161	57.7
Cowlitz	75	30	40.0	39	12	-	36	18	-
Flathead	343	140	40.8	177	61	34.5	166	79	47.6
Kalispel	430	284	66.0	216	138	63.9	214	146	68.2
Lummi	223	51	22.9	127	28	22.0	96	23	24.0
Muckleshoot	142	60	42.3	75	27	36.0	67	33	49.3

[Continued]

★ 75 ★

Illiterate American Indians 10 Years Old and Older, by Linguistic Stock, Tribe, and Sex, 1910:
L - S
[Continued]

Linguistic stock and tribe	Indians 10 years of age and over: 1910			Indian males 10 years of age and over			Indian females 10 years of age and over		
	Total number	Illiterate		Total number	Illiterate		Total number	Illiterate	
		Number	Percent		Number	Percent		Number	Percent
Nisqualli	112	53	47.3	56	21	37.5	56	32	57.1
Okinagan	206	105	51.0	103	48	46.6	103	57	55.3
Puyallup	231	54	23.4	118	21	17.8	113	33	29.2
Quinaielt	205	82	40.0	107	39	36.4	98	43	43.9
Sanpoil	184	169	91.8	87	79	90.8	97	90	92.8
Skokomish	141	51	36.2	62	21	33.9	79	30	38.0
Snohomish	478	203	42.5	251	89	35.5	227	114	50.2
Spokan	512	226	44.1	251	93	37.1	261	133	51.0
Suquamish	217	80	36.9	118	37	31.4	99	43	43.4
Swinomish	243	121	49.8	134	50	37.3	109	71	65.1
All other tribes	446	193	43.3	232	85	36.6	214	108	50.5
Shahaptian stock	3,372	1,771	52.5	1,567	728	46.5	1,805	1,043	57.8
Klikitat	325	179	55.1	148	70	47.3	177	109	61.6
Nez Perces	980	451	46.0	480	182	37.9	500	269	53.8
Umatilla	217	153	70.5	94	61	64.9	123	92	74.8
Wallawalla	290	119	41.0	143	51	35.7	147	68	46.3
Warm Springs	408	216	52.9	184	97	52.7	224	119	53.7
Yakima	1,028	563	54.8	463	228	49.2	565	335	59.3
All other tribes	124	90	72.6	55	39	70.9	69	51	73.9
Shastan stock	1,226	721	58.8	595	339	57.0	631	382	60.5
Hat Creek	190	138	72.6	100	71	71.0	90	67	74.4
Pit River	767	508	66.2	369	243	65.9	398	265	66.6
Shasta	269	75	27.9	126	25	19.8	148	50	35.0
Shoshonean stock	12,894	8,411	65.2	6,645	4,055	61.0	6,249	4,356	69.7
Bannock	338	231	68.3	176	119	67.6	162	112	69.1
Chemehuevi	262	203	77.5	136	94	69.1	126	109	86.5
Comanche	876	455	51.9	427	192	45.0	449	263	58.6
Hopi	1,420	764	53.8	795	395	49.7	625	369	59.0
Kawia	605	310	51.2	333	159	47.7	272	151	55.5
Kern River	80	50	62.5	37	23	-	43	27	-
Mono	1,090	698	64.0	501	304	60.7	589	394	66.9
Paiute	585	447	76.4	313	221	70.6	272	226	83.1
Paviotso	2,480	1,653	66.7	1,209	754	62.4	1,271	899	70.7
San Luiseno	389	124	31.9	203	48	23.6	186	76	40.9
Serrano	91	33	36.3	49	16	-	42	17	-
Shoshoni	2,955	2,078	70.3	1,515	1,010	66.7	1,440	1,068	74.2
Ute	1,641	1,293	78.8	911	689	75.6	730	604	82.7
All other tribes	82	72	87.8	40	31	-	42	41	-

[Continued]

★ 75 ★

Illiterate American Indians 10 Years Old and Older, by Linguistic Stock, Tribe, and Sex, 1910: L - S
[Continued]

Linguistic stock and tribe	Indians 10 years of age and over: 1910			Indian males 10 years of age and over			Indian females 10 years of age and over		
	Total number	Illiterate Number	Illiterate Percent	Total number	Illiterate Number	Illiterate Percent	Total number	Illiterate Number	Illiterate Percent
Siouan stock	24,598	10,784	43.8	12,350	4,670	37.8	12,248	6,114	49.9
Assiniboin	925	488	52.8	455	215	47.3	470	273	58.1
Catawba	78	30	38.5	42	16	-	36	14	-
Crow	1,402	780	55.6	702	373	53.1	700	407	58.1
Hidatsa	394	162	41.1	208	72	34.6	186	90	48.4
Iowa	179	19	10.6	94	9	9.6	85	10	11.8
Kansa	138	24	17.4	88	16	18.2	50	8	16.0
Mandan	162	87	53.7	84	42	50.0	78	45	57.7
Omaha	791	366	46.3	407	164	40.3	384	202	52.6
Osage	898	198	22.0	465	87	18.7	433	111	25.6
Oto	245	59	24.1	135	26	19.3	110	33	30.0
Ponca	643	198	30.8	307	89	29.0	336	109	32.4
Quapaw	169	46	27.2	84	19	22.6	85	27	31.8
Santee Sioux	1,112	283	25.4	564	109	19.3	548	174	31.8
Sioux	790	223	28.2	449	103	22.9	341	120	35.2
Sisseton Sioux	1,888	761	40.3	957	313	32.7	931	448	48.1
Teton Sioux	10,739	5,129	47.8	5,349	2,214	41.4	5,390	2,915	54.1
Brule Sioux	591	265	44.8	301	110	36.5	290	155	53.4
Hunkpapa Sioux	813	417	51.3	403	184	45.7	410	233	56.8
Minniconjou Sioux	318	210	66.0	150	91	60.7	168	119	70.8
Oglala Sioux	4,486	2,060	45.9	2,242	901	40.2	2,244	1,159	51.6
Sans Arc Sioux	146	52	35.6	77	23	29.9	69	29	42.0
Sihasapa	372	163	43.8	191	70	36.6	181	93	51.4
Two Kettle Sioux	216	102	47.2	125	48	38.4	91	54	59.3
Other Teton Sioux	3,797	1,860	49.0	1,860	787	42.3	1,937	1,073	55.4
Winnebago	1,406	633	45.0	714	257	36.0	692	376	54.3
Yankton Sioux	1,583	744	47.0	754	313	41.5	829	431	52.0
Yanktonai Sioux	1,045	551	52.7	486	232	47.7	559	319	57.1
All other tribes	11	3	-	6	1	-	5	2	-

Source: U.S. Bureau of the Census. *Indian Population in the United States and Alaska, 1910.* Washington, DC: U.S. Government Printing Office, 1915, pp. 226-231.
Notes: A dash (-) represents zero or a lack of 50 persons for a percentage base.

★ 76 ★
Education

Illiterate American Indians 10 Years Old and Older, by Linguistic Stock, Tribe, and Sex, 1910: T - Z and Alaska

Data are shown for linguistic stocks with 200 or more Indians and tribes with more than 100 members in 1910.

Linguistic stock and tribe	Indians 10 years of age and over: 1910			Indian males 10 years of age and over			Indian females 10 years of age and over		
	Total number	Illiterate		Total number	Illiterate		Total number	Illiterate	
		Number	Percent		Number	Percent		Number	Percent
UNITED STATES (cont.)									
Tanoan stock	2,348	1,506	64.1	1,268	762	60.1	1,080	744	68.9
Isleta	717	531	74.1	381	280	73.5	336	251	74.7
Jemez	396	300	75.8	231	169	73.2	165	131	79.4
Picuris	76	47	61.8	37	20	-	39	27	-
San Ildefonso	85	51	60.0	41	21	-	44	30	-
San Juan	297	191	64.3	165	95	57.6	132	96	72.7
Santa Clara	199	111	55.8	103	56	54.4	96	55	57.3
Taos	371	169	45.6	198	66	33.3	173	103	59.5
All other tribes	207	106	51.2	112	55	49.1	95	51	53.7
Waiilatpuan stock	247	127	51.4	118	55	46.6	129	72	55.8
Cayuse	225	123	54.7	105	54	51.4	120	69	57.5
All other tribes	22	4	-	13	1	-	9	3	-
Wakashan stock	279	116	41.6	142	52	36.6	137	64	46.7
Makah	256	104	40.6	134	52	38.8	122	52	42.6
All other tribes	23	12	-	8	-	-	15	12	-
Washoan stock	650	478	73.5	334	220	65.9	316	258	81.6
Washo	650	478	73.5	334	220	65.9	316	258	81.6
Wintun stock	545	262	48.1	297	139	46.8	248	123	49.6
Nomelaki	101	43	42.6	52	20	38.5	49	23	-
Patwin	138	100	72.5	81	56	69.1	57	44	77.2
Wintun	306	119	38.9	164	63	38.4	142	56	39.4
Yokuts stock	407	252	61.9	218	122	56.0	189	130	68.8
Chukchansi	112	57	50.9	56	21	37.5	56	36	64.3
Yokuts	231	145	62.8	133	78	58.6	98	67	68.4
All other tribes	64	50	78.1	29	23	-	35	27	-
Yuman stock	3,290	2,007	61.0	1,806	1,040	57.6	1,484	967	65.2
Cocopah	182	170	93.4	103	94	91.3	79	76	96.2
Diegueno	568	294	51.8	305	156	51.1	263	138	52.5
Havasupai	137	98	71.5	83	57	68.7	54	41	75.9
Maricopa	287	139	48.4	152	69	45.4	135	70	51.9
Mohave	822	422	51.3	460	227	49.3	362	195	53.9
Walapai	370	226	61.1	207	108	52.2	163	118	72.4
Yavapai	229	155	67.7	126	79	62.7	103	76	73.8
Yuma	667	480	72.0	355	239	67.3	312	241	77.2
All other tribes	28	23	-	15	11	-	13	12	-

[Continued]

★ 76 ★

Illiterate American Indians 10 Years Old and Older, by Linguistic Stock, Tribe, and Sex, 1910: T - Z and Alaska

[Continued]

Linguistic stock and tribe	Indians 10 years of age and over: 1910			Indian males 10 years of age and over			Indian females 10 years of age and over		
	Total number	Illiterate		Total number	Illiterate		Total number	Illiterate	
		Number	Percent		Number	Percent		Number	Percent
Yurok stock	505	330	65.3	249	152	61.0	256	178	69.5
Weitspec	505	330	65.3	249	152	61.0	256	178	69.5
Zunian stock	1,202	1,046	87.0	631	539	85.4	571	507	88.8
Zuni	1,202	1,046	87.0	631	539	85.4	571	507	88.8
ALASKA									
Athapaskan stock	2,886	2,318	80.3	1,507	1,202	79.8	1,379	1,116	80.9
Ahtena	227	214	94.3	129	120	93.0	98	94	95.9
Hankutchin	86	63	73.3	58	41	70.7	28	22	-
Kaiyuhkhotana	125	99	79.2	64	51	79.7	61	48	78.7
Knaiakhotana	516	395	76.6	283	216	76.3	233	179	76.8
Kutchin	276	233	84.4	140	117	83.6	136	116	85.3
Natsitkutchin	150	146	97.3	84	81	96.4	66	65	98.5
Tenankutchin	302	258	85.4	156	133	85.3	146	125	85.6
Unakhotana	136	118	86.8	72	63	87.5	64	55	85.9
All other tribes	1,068	792	74.2	521	380	72.9	547	412	75.3
Eskimauan stock	9,964	7,857	78.9	5,147	3,870	75.2	4,817	3,987	82.8
Aleut	1,001	650	64.9	516	305	59.1	485	345	71.1
Chnagmiut	202	167	82.7	110	87	79.1	92	80	87.0
Ikogmiut	529	499	94.3	247	233	94.3	282	266	94.3
Kaialigmiut	127	125	98.4	62	61	98.4	65	64	98.5
Kaviagmiut	163	91	55.8	81	46	56.8	82	45	54.9
Kinugumiut	424	311	73.3	236	160	67.8	188	151	80.3
Kowagmiut	410	320	78.0	214	171	79.9	196	149	76.0
Kusetrinmiut	90	63	70.0	56	35	62.5	34	28	-
Kuskovakmiut	232	199	85.8	121	97	80.2	111	102	91.9
Kuskwogmiut	1,068	996	93.3	544	502	92.3	524	494	94.3
Magemiut	262	227	86.6	118	108	91.5	144	119	82.6
Malemiut	407	225	55.3	210	114	54.3	197	111	56.3
Nunatogmiut	224	178	79.5	130	97	74.6	94	81	86.2
Nunivagmiut	236	224	94.9	127	122	96.1	109	102	93.6
Nunochogmiut	107	104	97.2	42	42	-	65	62	95.4
Selawigmiut	177	159	89.8	98	83	84.7	79	76	96.2
Tikeramiut	252	137	54.4	127	62	48.8	125	75	60.0
Ukivokmiut	94	82	87.2	50	41	82.0	44	41	-
Unaligmiut	274	188	68.6	126	73	57.9	148	115	77.7
Utkiavinmiut	86	66	76.7	43	30	-	43	36	-
Utukamiut	91	79	86.8	46	36	-	45	43	-
Yuit	226	155	68.6	119	66	55.5	107	89	83.2
Southern Eskimo	2,613	2,106	80.6	1,383	1,056	76.4	1,230	1,050	85.4

[Continued]

★ 76 ★

Illiterate American Indians 10 Years Old and Older, by Linguistic Stock, Tribe, and Sex, 1910: T - Z and Alaska

[Continued]

Linguistic stock and tribe	Indians 10 years of age and over: 1910			Indian males 10 years of age and over			Indian females 10 years of age and over		
	Total number	Illiterate		Total number	Illiterate		Total number	Illiterate	
		Number	Percent		Number	Percent		Number	Percent
All other tribes	669	506	75.6	341	243	71.3	328	263	80.2
Haidan stock	369	123	33.3	198	58	29.3	171	65	38.0
Haida	369	123	33.3	198	58	29.3	171	65	38.0
Tlingit stock	3,240	2,021	62.4	1,634	949	58.1	1,606	1,072	66.7
Auk	213	138	64.8	120	74	61.7	93	64	68.8
Chilkat	536	339	63.2	270	158	58.5	266	181	68.0
Henya	146	90	61.6	78	47	60.3	68	43	63.2
Huna	470	338	71.9	221	144	65.2	249	194	77.9
Hutsnuwu	373	249	66.8	186	120	64.5	187	129	69.0
Kake	232	134	57.8	114	66	57.9	118	68	57.6
Sitka	446	249	55.8	225	114	50.7	221	135	61.1
Stikine	139	72	51.8	69	30	43.5	70	42	60.0
Taku	111	83	74.8	54	38	70.4	57	45	78.9
Tongas	129	60	46.5	65	27	41.5	64	33	51.6
Yakutat	211	162	76.8	96	76	79.2	115	86	74.8
All other tribes	234	107	45.7	136	55	40.4	98	52	53.1
Tsimshian stock	520	117	22.5	294	45	15.3	226	72	31.9
Tsimshian	520	117	22.5	294	45	15.3	226	72	31.9

Source: U.S. Bureau of the Census. *Indian Population in the United States and Alaska, 1910*. Washington, DC: U.S. Government Printing Office, 1915, pp. 226-231.
Notes: A dash (-) represents zero or a lack of 50 persons for a percentage base.

★ 77 ★

Education

Illiterate Persons 10 Years Old and Older in the U.S. and Alaska, by Race/Ethnicity and Sex, 1900 and 1910

Race/ethnicity and year	Males 10 years of age and older			Females 10 years of age and older		
	Total number	Illiterate		Total number	Illiterate	
		Number	Percent		Number	Percent
United States						
All groups: 1910	37,027,558	2,814,950	7.6	34,552,712	2,701,213	7.8
Indian	96,582	40,104	41.5	92,176	45,341	49.2
Chinese	65,479	9,849	15.0	3,445	1,042	30.2
Japanese	60,809	5,247	8.6	6,852	966	14.1
Negro	3,637,386	1,096,000	30.1	3,680,536	1,131,731	30.7
White	33,164,229	1,662,505	5.0	30,769,641	1,522,128	4.9

[Continued]

★ 77 ★

Illiterate Persons 10 Years Old and Older in the U.S. and Alaska, by Race/Ethnicity and Sex, 1900 and 1910

[Continued]

Race/ethnicity and year	Males 10 years of age and older			Females 10 years of age and older		
	Total number	Illiterate		Total number	Illiterate	
		Number	Percent		Number	Percent
Native	25,843,033	796,055	3.1	25,146,308	738,217	2.9
Foreign born	7,321,196	866,450	11.8	5,623,333	783,911	13.9
All other	3,073	1,245	40.5	62	5	8.1
All groups: 1900	29,703,440	3,011,224	10.1	28,246,384	3,168,845	11.2
Indian	86,504	45,376	52.5	85,048	50,971	59.9
Chinese	84,141	23,052	27.4	3,541	2,344	66.2
Japanese	23,214	4,211	18.1	877	175	20.0
Negro	3,181,650	1,371,432	43.1	3,233,931	1,481,762	45.8
White	26,327,931	1,567,153	6.0	24,922,987	1,633,593	6.6
Native	20,912,940	955,517	4.6	20,323,722	958,094	4.7
Foreign born	5,414,991	611,636	11.3	4,599,265	675,499	14.7
Alaska						
All groups: 1910	41,108	7,867	19.1	13,859	6,683	48.2
Indian	9,300	6,311	67.9	8,744	6,571	75.1
Chinese	1,206	186	15.4	2	1	[1]
Japanese	884	58	6.6	25	4	[1]
Negro	141	16	11.3	62	5	8.1
White	29,285	1,234	4.2	5,025	102	2.0
Native	13,025	78	0.6	3,437	34	1.0
Foreign born	16,260	1,156	7.1	1,588	68	4.3
All other	292	62	21.2	1	-	-
All groups: 1900	41,968	13,124	31.3	14,013	10,187	72.7
Indian	11,717	9,980	85.2	11,340	10,035	88.5
Chinese	3,113	2,389	76.7	2	1	[1]
Japanese	267	124	46.4	12	11	[1]
Negro	151	6	4.0	14	-	-
White	26,720	625	2.3	2,645	140	5.3
Native	18,624	116	0.6	2,000	77	3.9
Foreign born	8,096	509	6.3	645	63	9.8

Source: U.S. Bureau of the Census. *Indian Population in the United States and Alaska, 1910.* Washington, DC: U.S. Government Printing Office, 1915, p. 212. *Notes:* A dash (-) represents zero. 1. Percentages are not shown where base is less than 50.

★ 78 ★

Education

Percent Illiterate in the Indian Population, for 20 Selected States, by Sex and Age Group, 1910 and 1930

State	1910				1930			
	10 years old and over		21 years old and over		10 years old and over		21 years old and over	
	Male	Female	Male	Female	Male	Female	Male	Female
United States	41.5	49.2	50.8	61.4	24.0	27.6	30.4	36.2
Arizona	68.4	77.8	78.0	87.8	49.9	57.2	58.7	68.6
California	45.4	52.7	57.2	67.4	18.5	23.7	23.2	32.8
Idaho	55.6	63.3	65.1	75.8	26.0	32.8	33.7	45.2
Kansas	18.7	18.7	28.9	35.6	9.3	9.4	12.7	13.6
Michigan	30.1	39.4	37.9	51.8	13.1	17.2	17.1	24.0
Minnesota	35.3	45.1	47.3	60.3	15.4	20.8	22.8	31.7
Montana	52.1	59.6	62.6	72.5	21.0	24.4	30.0	36.1
Nebraska	29.6	41.5	38.4	56.7	10.2	13.3	14.4	20.5
Nevada	67.2	76.3	76.8	86.4	37.7	46.1	48.9	61.2
New Mexico	78.5	85.0	86.4	92.9	53.9	61.4	65.4	74.1
New York	28.0	27.8	34.6	37.2	11.8	11.5	15.5	16.3
North Carolina	43.3	51.1	52.0	64.3	31.1	28.0	38.5	37.9
North Dakota	43.6	48.6	58.1	65.3	20.5	20.9	27.8	31.5
Oklahoma	22.0	28.4	28.1	38.1	10.4	12.0	14.2	17.2
Oregon	29.7	43.5	42.5	60.0	11.5	19.4	16.5	27.1
South Dakota	39.0	52.0	49.6	65.6	13.1	19.5	18.3	27.7
Utah	80.3	86.2	85.0	93.2	56.1	58.0	65.7	70.6
Washington	39.6	52.0	48.6	64.4	13.7	19.5	18.1	27.5
Wisconsin	31.2	36.4	40.6	49.7	12.6	14.5	18.1	22.5
Wyoming	45.4	57.6	57.9	74.9	23.2	25.9	30.6	37.3

Source: Truesdell, Dr. Leon E. U.S. Department of Commerce, Bureau of Census, Fifteenth Census of the United States: 1930, *The Indian Population of the United States and Alaska.* Washington, DC: U.S. Government Printing Office, 1937, p. 145. *Notes:* The Census Bureau defines as illiterate any person 10 years old or over who is not able to read and write, either in English or in some other language. The Census Bureau has never prescribed any specific test of ability to read or write. At the Census of 1930, the enumerator was instructed to write "yes" or "no" in response to the question on the schedule, "whether able to read and write." The enumerator was, however, specifically instructed not to write "yes" (which would classify the person as literate) simply because the person was able to write his or her name.

★ 79 ★

Education

Percent Illiterate in the Population, by Race/Ethnicity, 1900-1930

Data are shown for persons 10 years old and older.

Class	1900	1910	1920	1930
All classes	10.7	7.7	6.0	4.3
Indian	56.2	45.3	34.9	25.7
White	6.2	5.0	4.0	3.0
Native	4.6	3.0	2.0	1.6
Foreign born	12.9	12.7	13.1	10.8
Negro	44.5	30.4	22.9	16.3
All other races	26.6	13.1	14.5	12.3

Source: Truesdell, Dr. Leon E. U.S. Department of Commerce. Bureau of Census. Fifteenth Census of the United States: 1930, *The Indian Population of the United States and Alaska*. Washington, DC: U.S. Government Printing Office, 1937, p. 143. *Notes:* The Census Bureau defines as illiterate any person 10 years old or over who is not able to read and write, either in English or in some other language. The Census Bureau has never prescribed any specific test of ability to read or write. At the Census of 1930, the enumerator was instructed to write "yes" or "no" in response to the question on the schedule, "whether able to read and write." The enumerator was, however, specifically instructed not to write "yes" (which would classify the person as literate) simply because the person was able to write his or her name.

Health Conditions

★ 80 ★

Epidemics Among Texas Indians, 1528-1892

Tribe/area	Date	Epidemic
Karankawan	1528	Cholera(?)
Coahuiltecan	1674-75	Smallpox
La Salle's Fort	1688-89	Smallpox
Caddo	1691	?
Coahuiltecan	1706	Smallpox
Caddo	1718	?
San Antonio missions	1739	Smallpox and measles
Tonkawa and Atakapan	Before 1746	Smallpox and measles
San Xavier missions; Tonkawa and Atakapan	1750	Smallpox
San Antonio missions	1751	?
San Xavier missions; Tonkawan and Atakapan	1753	Malaria or dysentery
East Texas	1759	Smallpox
San Antonio missions	1763	?
San Lorenzo de la Santa Cruz Mission; Lipan Apache	1763-64	Smallpox
Karankawan	1766	Smallpox or measles

[Continued]

★ 80 ★

Epidemics Among Texas Indians, 1528-1892
[Continued]

Tribe/area	Date	Epidemic
Caddo, Wichita, Tonkawa, or Atakapan	1777-78	Cholera or plague
Texas	1778	Smallpox
Texas	1801-1802	Smallpox
Caddo	1803	Measles
Caddo, Wichita, Comanche, Kiowa, Kiowa-Apache	1816	Smallpox
Kiowa, Kiowa-Apache, Comanche	1839-40	Smallpox
Kiowa, Kiowa-Apache, Apache, Cheyenne, Comanche	1849	Cholera
Kiowa, Kiowa-Apache, Comanche, Cheyenne, and Arapaho	1861-62	Smallpox
Wichita, Caddo	1864	Smallpox
Wichita, Caddo	1867	Cholera
Mescalero Apache	1877	Smallpox
Kiowa, Kiowa-Apache, Cheyenne, Arapaho	1877	Measles and fever
Kiowa, Kiowa-Apache, Comanche, Arapaho	1889-90	Influenza
Comanche, Wichita, and Caddo	1892	Measles, influenza and whooping cough

Source: Thornton, Russell. *American Indian Holocaust and Survival: A Population History Since 1492.* Norman, OK: University of Oklahoma Press, 1987, p. 130. Published by permission. Primary source: Ewers, "The Influence of Epidemics on the Indian Populations and Cultures of Texas," *Plains Anthropologist,* 1973, p. 108-109.

★ 81 ★

Health Conditions

Life Expectancy of Selected American Indian and Non-Indian Populations

Population (date)	Life expectancy
American Indian	
Indian Knoll, Kentucky (3000 B.C.)	18.6-19.02?
Texas Indians (A.D. 850-1700)	30.5
Pecos Pueblo (A.D. 800-1700)	25.0-27.4-42.9?
Tidewater Potomac, I (A.D. 1500-1600)	20.9
Mississippian (A.D. 1050-1200)	33.0
Mississippian (A.D. 1200-1300)	24.3
Tidewater Potomac, II (A.D. 1500-1600)	22.9
Non-Indian	
Egypt (A.D. 1050-1600)	19.2
Ancient Greece (670 B.C.-A.D. 600)	23.0

[Continued]

★ 81 ★

Life Expectancy of Selected American Indian and Non-Indian Populations
[Continued]

Population (date)	Life expectancy
England (11th century)	35.3
European ruling families (A.D. 1480-1579)	33.7

Source: Thornton, Russell. *American Indian Holocaust and Survival: A Population History Since 1492.* Norman, OK: University of Oklahoma Press, 1987, p. 39. Published by permission. Primary source: Goldstein, "Some Vital Statistics Based on Skeletal Material," *Human Biology,* 1953, p. 4; Ubelaker, "Reconstruction of Demographic Profiles from Ossuary Skeletal Samples: A Case Study from the Tidewater Potomac," *Smithsonian Contributions to Anthropology,* no. 18. Washington, D.C.: Smithsonian Institution Press, 1974, p. 64; Lallo and Rose, "Patterns of Stress, Disease and Mortality in Two Prehistoric Populations from North America," *Journal of Human Evolution,* 1979, p. 332; Ruff, "Reasessment of Demographic Estimates for Pecos Pueblo," *American Journal of Physical Anthropology,* 1981, p. 150; Storey, "An Estimate of Mortality in a Pre-Columbian Urban Population," *American Anthropologist,* 1985, p. 530.

★ 82 ★

Health Conditions

Mortality from 19th Century Epidemics Among the Omaha Indians

Date	Epidemic	Mortality
1801-1802	Smallpox	75% (> 1,500)
1837	Smallpox	Over 300
1849	Cholera	Over 500
1874	Measles	76
1888	Measles	87
1889	Measles	50

Source: Thornton, Russell. *American Indian Holocaust and Survival: A Population History Since 1492.* Norman, OK: University of Oklahoma Press, 1987, p. 94. Published by permission. Primary source: Liberty, "Population Trends Among Present-Day Omaha Indians," *Plains Anthropologist,* 1975, p. 228. *Note:* There were, in addition, known tuberculosis epidemics.

★ 83 ★

Health Conditions

Probable Smallpox Epidemics Among North American Indians, 1520-1797

Date	Areas of outbreak
1520-1524	Total geographic area unknown; possibly from Chile across present United States
1592-1593	Central Mexico to Sinaloa; Southern New England; Eastern Great Lakes
1602	Sinola and Northward
1639	French and British Northeastern North America
1646-1648	New Spain North to Nuevo Leon, Western Sierra Madre to Florida
1649-1650	Northeastern United States, Florida
1655	Florida
1662-1663	Mid-Atlantic, Northeast, Canada
1665-1667	Florida to Virginia
1669-1670	United States and Canada
1674-1675	Texas, Northeastern New Spain
1677-1679	Northeast in New France and British Territory
1687-1691	Northeast in French and British Frontiers; Texas
1696-1699	Southeastern and Gulf Coast
1701-1703	Northeastern to Illinois
1706	Texas and Northeastern New Spain
1715-1721	Northeast to Texas
1729-1733	New England; California Tribes; Southeast
1738-1739	Southeast to Hudson Bay; Texas Peoples
1746	New York, New England; New Spain
1750-1752	Texas to Great Lakes
1755-1760	From Canada and New England and Great Lakes to Virginia, Carolinas, and Texas
1762-1766	From Central Mexico through Texas and the Southeast to Great Lakes; Northwest Coast
1779-1783	From Central Mexico across all of North America
1785-1787	Alaskan coast across northern Canada
1788	New Mexico Pueblos
1793-1797	New Spain

Source: Snipp, C. Matthew. *American Indians: The First of This Land*. New York, NY: Russell Sage Foundation, p. 22. Published by permission. Primary source: Henry F. Dobyns, *Their Number Became Thinned: Native American Population Dynamics in Eastern North America*, Knoxville, TN: University of Tennessee Press, 1983, pp. 15-16.

Land Status

★ 84 ★

Extensions of the Trust or Restricted Status of Certain Indian Lands - I

This table contains citations of Executive orders (E.O.) and acts of Congress continuing the trust or restricted period of Indian Land, which would have otherwise expired within the several Indian reservations in the states named. A numeral "1" to the right of the name of a reservation indicates that the reservation is subject to the benefits of the Indian Reorganization Act of June 18, 1934 (48 Stat. 984; 25 U.S.C. 461-479), and the trust or restricted period of the land is extended indefinitely. Where the name of a reservation is *not* preceded by a "1", such a reservation is not subject to the Reorganization Act and is not subject to the benefits of indefinite trust or a restricted period extension. Such a reservation is dependent upon acts of Congress or Executive orders for extension of the trust or restricted period of the land. For the purpose of ensuring the continuation of the trust or restricted status of Indians allotments within Indian reservations not subject to the Reorganization Act, Congress, by the act of June 15, 1935 (49 Stat. 378), reimposed such restrictions as may have been expired between the dates of June 18, 1934, and December 31, 1936.

State	Reservation	Executive order number	Date	Period of extension
Arizona	Papago[1]	2066	Oct. 27, 1914	10 years
Do.	Do.	4464	June 28, 1926	Do.
California	Agua Caliente	3446	Apr. 30, 1921	Do.
Do.	Do.	5580	Mar. 16, 1931	Do.
Do.	Cabazon and Twenty-Nine Palms	3302	July 7, 1920	5 years
Do.	Do.	4159	Feb. 19, 1925	10 years
Do.	Capitan Grande[1]	3048	Feb. 27, 1919	5 years
Do.	Do.		Act. of Feb. 8, 1927 (44 Stat. 1061)	10 years
Do.	Hoopa Valley (Klamath River)	2943	Aug. 23, 1918	1 year
Do.	Do.		Sept. 23, 1919	Do.
Do.	Do.	3304	July 10, 1920	10 years
Do.	Do.	3980	Mar. 26, 1924	15 years
Do.	Do.	5416	Aug. 4, 1930	10 years
	Mission Bands:			
Do.	Augustine	2795	Jan. 26, 1918	Do.
Do.	Campo	2795	Do.	Do.
Do.	Cuyapipe[1]	2795	Do.	Do.
Do.	Inaja	2795	Do.	Do.
Do.	Laguna[1]	2795	Do.	Do.
Do.	La Posta[1]	2795	Do.	Do.
Do.	Mazanita[1]	2795	Do.	Do.
Do.	Mesa Grande	2795	Do.	Do.
Do.	Pala	2795	Do.	Do.
Do.	Ramona	2795	Do.	Do.
Do.	Santa Ysabel	2795	Do.	Do.
Do.	Sycuan	2795	Do.	Do.
Do.	Do.	3383	Jan. 7, 1921	25 years
Do.	San Manuel	2795	Jan. 26, 1918	10 years
Do.	Temecula	2795	Do.	Do.
Do.	All of above Mission Bands	4795	Nov. 23, 1927	Do.

[Continued]

★ 84 ★

Extensions of the Trust or Restricted Status of Certain Indian Lands - I
[Continued]

State	Reservation	Executive order number	Date	Period of extension
Do.	Morongo	6341	Oct. 17, 1933	Do.
Do.	Pala	3383	Jan. 7, 1921	25 years
Do.	Do.		Act of Feb. 11, 1936 (49 Stat. 1106)	10 years
Do.	Potrero and Rincon	2684	Aug. 16, 1917	Do.
Do.	Do.	4687	July 11, 1927	Do.
Do.	Round Valley[1]	3223	Feb. 5, 1920	3 years
Do.	Do.	3805	Mar. 5, 1923	10 years
Do.	Do.	3995	Apr. 19, 1924	Do.
Do.	Do.	5953	Nov. 23, 1932	Do.
Do.	Temecula	3699	June 27, 1922	Do.
Do.	Do.	5768	Dec. 30, 1931	Do.
Do.	Torres-Martinez	7009	Apr. 10, 1935	Do.
Idaho	Nez Perce	3250	Mar. 24, 1920	Do.
Idaho	Nez Perce	4694	July 22, 1927	10 years
Do.	Do.	5305	Mar. 18, 1930	Do.
Kansas and Nebraska	Iowa[1]	2966	Sept. 23, 1918	Do.
Do.	Do.	5023	Jan. 10, 1929	Do.
Do.	Sac and Fox[1]	2607	May 4, 1917	Do.
Do.	Do.	4571	Jan. 24, 1927	Do.
Do.	Do.	5768	Dec. 30, 1931	Do.
Do.	Kickapoo	3301	July 3, 1920	1 year
Do.	Do.	3447	May 2, 1921	10 years
Do.	Do.	5415	Aug. 4, 1930	Do.
Do.	Do.	5626	May 18, 1931	Do.
Do.	Potawatomi[1]	2747	Nov. 2, 1917	Do.
Do.	Do.	2927	July 30, 1918	Do.
Do.	Do.	3312	July 21, 1920	Do.
Do.	Do.	4688	July 11, 1927	Do.
Do.	Do.	4858	Apr. 16, 1928	Do.
Do.	Do.	5299	Mar. 10, 1930	Do.
Do.	Do.	5356	May 28, 1930	Do.
Do.	Do.	5556	Feb. 11, 1931	Do.
Minnesota	Fond du Lac[1]	3445	Apr. 30, 1921	Do.
Do.	Do.	5575	Mar. 12, 1931	Do.
Do.	Grand Portage[1]	3613	Jan. 12, 1922	Do.
Do.	Do.	5768	Dec. 30, 1931	Do.
Do.	Winnibigoshish[1]	3614	Jan 12, 1922	Do.
Do.	Do.	5466	Oct. 22, 1930	Do.
Do.	Do.	5768	Dec. 30, 1931	Do.
Do.	Deer Creek[1]	4154	Feb. 10, 1925	Do.
Do.	Bois Fort[1]	4233	May 26, 1925	Do.
Do.	Leech Lake, Cass Lake[1] and White Oak Point	4298	Aug. 29, 1925	Do.
Do.	Do.	5466	Oct. 22, 1930	Do.

[Continued]

★ 84 ★

Extensions of the Trust or Restricted Status of Certain Indian Lands - I
[Continued]

State	Reservation	Executive order number	Date	Period of extension
Do.	White Earth[1]	4642	May 5, 1927	Do.
Do.	Do.	5768	Dec. 30, 1931	Do.
Do.	Do.	5953	Nov. 23, 1932	Do.
Do.	Red Lake[1]	5383	June 26, 1930	Do.
Montana	Crow	5301	Mar. 12, 1930	Do.
Do.	Do.	5768	Dec. 30, 1931	Do.
Do.	Do.	7001	Apr. 5, 1935	Do.
Do.	Do.		Act of April 1940 (54 Stat.106)	To May 23, 1940
Do.	Flathead[1]	5953	Nov. 23, 1932	Do.
Nebraska	Omaha[1]		July 3, 1909	Do.
Do.	Do.	3111	July 10, 1919	Do.
Do.	Do.	4145	Jan. 28, 1925	Do.
Do.	Do.	4548	Dec. 4, 1926	Do.
Do.	Do.	5148	July 3, 1929	Do.
Do.	Do.	5253	Dec. 31, 1929	Do.
Do.	Ponca[1]	2374	Apr. 29, 1916	Do.
Do.	Do.	4407	Mar. 30, 1926	Do.
Do.	Santee[1]		Dec. 12, 1910	Do.
Do.	Do.	3348	Nov. 5, 1920	Do.
Do.	Do.	3722	Aug. 12, 1922	Do.
Do.	Santee Sarah Jones[1] allotment	4075	Sept. 17, 1924	Do.
Do.	Santee[1]	5474	Oct. 31, 1930	Do.
Do.	Do.	5768	Dec. 30, 1931	Do.
Do.	Do.	5953	Nov. 23, 1932	Do.
Do.	Winnebago[1]	2965	Sept. 20, 1918	Do.
Do.	Do.	4548	Dec. 4, 1926	Do.
Do.	Do.	4979	Oct. 16, 1928	Do.
Do.	Do.	4994	Nov. 14, 1928	Do.
Do.	Sac and Fox, William Banks[1] allotment	3878	July 27, 1923	1 year
Nevada	Walker River[1]	5730	Oct. 8, 1931	10 years
North Dakota	Devils Lake	2804	Feb. 11, 1918	Do.
Do.	Do.	3853	May 23, 1923	Do.
Do.	Do.	4775	Nov. 30, 1927	Do.
Do.	Do.	5303	Mar. 12, 1930	Do.
Do.	Do.	5768	Dec. 30, 1931	Do.
Do.	Do.	5953	Nov. 23, 1932	Do.
Do.	Fort Berthold[1]	4293	Aug. 25, 1925	Do.
Do.	Standing Rock[1]	5768	Dec. 30, 1931	Do.
Do.	Do.	5953	Nov. 23, 1932	Do.

Source: Office of the Federal Register National Archives and Records Administration. *Code of Federal Regulations: Indians*, Title 25, Revised as of April 1, 1994, p. 757-761. *Notes:* Do. means ditto. 1. Trust or restricted period of land is extended indefinitely.

★ 85 ★

Land Status

Extensions of the Trust or Restricted Status of Certain Indian Lands - II

This table contains citations of Executive orders (E.O.) and acts of Congress continuing the trust or restricted period of Indian Land, which would have otherwise expired within the several Indian reservations in the states named. A numeral "1" to the right of the name of a reservation indicates that the reservation is subject to the benefits of the Indian Reorganization Act of June 18, 1934 (48 Stat. 984; 25 U.S.C. 461-479), and the trust or restricted period of the land is extended indefinitely. Where the name of a reservation is *not* preceded by a "1", such a reservation is not subject to the Reorganization Act and is not subject to the benefits of indefinite trust or a restricted period extension. Such a reservation is dependent upon acts of Congress or Executive orders for extension of the trust or restricted period of the land. For the purpose of ensuring the continuation of the trust or restricted status of Indians allotments within Indian reservations not subject to the Reorganization Act, Congress, by the act of June 15, 1935 (49 Stat. 378), reimposed such restrictions as may have been expired between the dates of June 18, 1934, and December 31, 1936.

State	Reservation	Executive order number	Date	Period of extension
Oklahoma	Absentee Shawnee and Citizen Potawatomi	2494	Nov. 24, 1916	Do.
Do.	Do.	2512	Jan. 15, 1917	Do.
Do.	Do.	4557	Dec. 23, 1926	Do.
Do.	Cheyenne and Arapaho	2580	Apr. 4, 1917	Do.
Do.	Do.	4587	Feb. 17, 1927	Do.
Do.	Eastern Shawnee	2317	Feb. 15, 1916	Do.
Do.	Do.	4384	Feb. 20, 1926	Do.
Do.	Do.	5768	Dec. 30, 1931	Do.
Do.	Mexican Kickapoo	3047	Feb. 27, 1919	5 years
Do.	Do.	4029	June 19, 1924	10 years
Do.	Do.		Act of Feb. 17, 1933 (47 Stat. 819)	Do.
Do.	Modoc	2453	Sept. 14, 1916	Do.
Do.	Do.	4470	July 1, 1926	Do.
Do.	Ottawa, Seneca and Wyandotte	2591	Apr. 11, 1917	Do.
Do.	Do.	4588	Feb. 17, 1927	Do.
Do.	Pawnee	2816	Mar. 2, 1918	Do.
Do.	Do.	4898	May 29, 1928	Do.
Do.	Ponca	3327	Sept. 19, 1920	1 year
Do.	Do.	3363	Dec. 1, 1920	25 years
Do.	Do.	5539	Jan. 23, 1931	10 years
Do.	Sac and Fox, and Iowa		Mar. 27, 1896	Do.
Do.	Do.		July 23, 1906	Do.
Do.	Do.		Aug. 28, 1906	Do.
Do.	Do.	2432	Aug. 1, 1916	Do.
Do.	Do.	4435	Apr. 29, 1926	Do.
Do.	Tonkawa	2866	May 25, 1918	Do.
Do.	Tonkawa (Oakland)	4816	Feb. 25, 1928	Do.
Do.	Kaw		Act of March 1923 (42 Stat. 1561)	25 years
Do.	Do.		Act of May 27, 1924 (43 Stat. 176)	20 years
Do.	Otoe and Missouri	4281	Aug. 11, 1925	10 years
Do.	Do.	5728	Sept. 29, 1931	Do.

[Continued]

★ 85 ★

Extensions of the Trust or Restricted Status of Certain Indian Lands - II
[Continued]

State	Reservation	Executive order number	Date	Period of extension
Do.	Do.	5768	Dec. 30, 1931	Do.
Do.	Kiowa, Comanche, Apache, and Wichita.	4398	Mar. 18, 1926	Do.
Do.	Do.	5953	Nov. 23, 1932	Do.
Do.	Do.	5955	Nov. 30, 1932 (Gertrude Lamb)	Do.
Do.	Seneca	5306	Mar. 18, 1930	Do.
Do.	Quapaw		Act of Mar. 3, 1921 (41 Stat. 1248) as amended Nov. 18, 1921 (42 Stat. 1570)	25 years
Do.	Do.		As supplemented or amended by the act of July 27, 1939 (53 Stat. 1127)	
Oregon	Grande Ronde[1]	2376	Apr. 29, 1916	10 years
Do.	Do.	4408	Mar. 30, 1926	Do.
Do.	Siletz	3110	July 10, 1919	Do.
Do.	Siletz (cont.)	5087	Apr. 1, 1929	Do.
Do.	Warm Springs[1]	3586	Dec. 7, 1921	Do.
Do.	Do.	5734	Oct. 17, 1931	Do.
Do.	Umatilla	4024	June 10, 1924	Do.
Do.	Do.	5516	Dec. 17, 1930	Do.
Do.	Klamath	6961	Feb. 4, 1935	Do.
Do.	Do.		Act of Dec. 24, 1942 (56 Stat. 1081)	25 years
South Dakota	Crow Creek	3362	Nov. 30, 1920	Do.
Do.	Do.	5768	Dec. 30, 1931	10 years
Do.	Do.	6968	Feb. 9, 1935	Do.
Do.	Rosebud[1]	4417	Apr. 14, 1926	Do.
Do.	Do.	5028	Jan. 16, 1929	Do.
Do.	Do.	5302	Mar. 12, 1930	Do.
Do.	Do.	5768	Dec. 30, 1931	Do.
Do.	Sisseton and Wahpeton	1916	Apr. 16, 1914	Do.
Do.	Do.	3994	Apr. 19, 1924	15 years
Do.	Yankton Sioux[1]	2363	Apr. 20, 1916	10 years
Do.	Do.	4406	Mar. 30, 1926	Do.
Do.	Crow Creek	5173	Aug. 9, 1929	10 years
Do.	Lower Brule[1]	4981	Oct. 20, 1923	Do.
Do.	Pine Ridge[1]	5557	Feb. 13, 1931	Do.
Do.	Do.	5768	Dec. 30, 1931	Do.
Do.	Do.	5953	Nov. 23, 1932	Do.
Do.	Cheyenne River[1]	5546	Jan. 31, 1931	Do.
Do.	Do.	5768	Dec. 30, 1931	Do.
Utah	Uncompahgra, Uintah and	5357	May 29, 1930	Do.

[Continued]

★ 85 ★

Extensions of the Trust or Restricted Status of Certain Indian Lands - II
[Continued]

State	Reservation	Executive order number	Date	Period of extension
Washington	White River Bands of Ute[1]s Chief Moses Band	2109	Dec. 23, 1914	Do.
Do.	Do.	4382	Feb. 10, 1926	10 years from Mar. 8, 1926
Do.	Colville	4157	Feb. 17, 1925	10 years
Do.	Do.	6962	Feb. 4, 1935	Do.
Do.	Quinaielt[1]	5768	Dec. 30, 1931	Do.
Do.	Spokane	6939	Jan. 7, 1935	10 years
Do.	Yakima	3630	Feb. 3, 1922	Do.
Do.	Do.	4168	Mar. 11, 1925	Do.
Do.	Do.	5746	Nov. 10, 1931	Do.
Do.	Do.	7036	May 8, 1935	Do.
Do.	Do.		Act of May 27, 1937 (50 Stat. 210)	To July 9, 1942
Wisconsin	Oneida[1]	2623	May 19, 1917	1 year
Do.	Do.	2856	Mar. 4, 1918	9 years
Do.	Do.	4600	Mar. 1, 1927	10 years
Wyoming	Wind River	5768	Dec. 30, 1931	Do.
Do.	Do.	5953	Nov. 23, 1932	Do.

Source: Office of the Federal Register National Archives and Records Administration. *Code of Federal Regulations: Indians,* Title 25, Revised as of April 1, 1994, p. 757-761. *Notes:* Do. means ditto. 1. Trust or restricted period of land is extended indefinitely.

Language

★ 86 ★

Ability of American Indians 10 Years Old and Older to Speak English, by Geographic Division, State, Sex, and Age Group, 1910

Geographic division and state	Indian males 10 years of age and over: 1910				Indian females 10 years of age and over: 1910			
	Total number	Unable to speak English			Total number	Unable to speak English		
		Total	10 to 19 years of age	20 years of age and over		Total	10 to 19 years of age	20 years of age and over
UNITED STATES	96,582	26,705	5,011	21,694	92,176	32,350	5,230	27,120
Geographic divisions								
New England	869	5	1	4	791	12	1	11
Middle Atlantic	3,352	191	26	165	2,816	292	28	264
East North Central	7,157	890	183	707	6,405	1,434	155	1,279

[Continued]

★ 86 ★

Ability of American Indians 10 Years Old and Older to Speak English, by Geographic Division, State, Sex, and Age Group, 1910

[Continued]

Geographic division and state	Indian males 10 years of age and over: 1910				Indian females 10 years of age and over: 1910			
	Total number	Unable to speak English			Total number	Unable to speak English		
		Total	10 to 19 years of age	20 years of age and over		Total	10 to 19 years of age	20 years of age and over
West North Central	15,625	4,508	458	4,050	15,019	5,944	485	5,459
South Atlantic	3,155	222	23	199	3,036	219	16	203
East South Central	915	119	41	78	839	146	50	96
West South Central	25,297	3,603	707	2,896	24,991	4,691	780	3,911
Mountain	27,734	15,575	3,456	12,119	26,146	17,002	3,576	13,426
Pacific	12,478	1,592	116	1,476	12,133	2,610	139	2,471
New England								
Maine	386	4	1	3	332	12	1	11
New Hampshire	14	-	-	-	13	-	-	-
Vermont	11	1	-	1	8	-	-	-
Massachusetts	290	-	-	-	258	-	-	-
Rhode Island	108	-	-	-	119	-	-	-
Connecticut	60	-	-	-	61	-	-	-
Middle Atlantic								
New York	2,359	174	26	148	2,209	285	28	257
New Jersey	107	12	-	12	47	6	-	6
Pennsylvania	886	5	-	5	560	1	-	1
East North Central								
Ohio	59	-	-	-	49	-	-	-
Indiana	120	2	-	2	102	2	-	2
Illinois	84	-	-	-	80	1	-	1
Michigan	3,028	445	118	327	2,674	675	96	579
Wisconsin	3,866	443	65	378	3,500	756	59	697
West North Central								
Minnesota	3,290	729	123	606	3,218	1,014	100	914
Iowa	259	115	4	111	114	30	10	20
Missouri	116	3	-	3	122	2	-	2
North Dakota	2,366	941	156	785	2,288	1,110	180	930
South Dakota	7,166	2,422	144	2,278	7,179	3,327	157	3,170
Nebraska	1,317	201	25	176	1,283	386	31	355
Kansas	1,111	97	6	91	815	75	7	68
South Atlantic								
Delaware	4	-	-	-	1	-	-	-
Maryland	18	-	-	-	32	-	-	-
District of Columbia	35	1	-	1	26	-	-	-
Virginia	208	-	-	-	180	-	-	-
West Virginia	14	-	-	-	12	-	-	-

[Continued]

★ 86 ★

Ability of American Indians 10 Years Old and Older to Speak English, by Geographic Division, State, Sex, and Age Group, 1910

[Continued]

Geographic division and state	Indian males 10 years of age and over: 1910				Indian females 10 years of age and over: 1910			
	Total number	Unable to speak English			Total number	Unable to speak English		
		Total	10 to 19 years of age	20 years of age and over		Total	10 to 19 years of age	20 years of age and over
North Carolina	2,698	220	23	197	2,626	219	16	203
South Carolina	112	-	-	-	105	-	-	-
Georgia	33	-	-	-	33	-	-	-
Florida	33	1	-	1	21	-	-	-
East South Central								
Kentucky	85	1	-	1	70	-	-	-
Tennessee	73	-	-	-	86	-	-	-
Alabama	287	-	-	-	292	-	-	-
Mississippi	470	118	41	77	391	146	50	96
West South Central								
Arkansas	143	1	-	1	185	-	-	-
Louisiana	271	77	36	41	262	95	34	61
Oklahoma	24,580	3,457	660	2,797	24,306	4,523	724	3,799
Texas	303	68	11	57	238	73	22	51
Mountain								
Montana	3,978	1,588	191	1,397	3,961	1,908	189	1,719
Idaho	1,355	473	34	439	1,349	607	26	581
Wyoming	575	197	5	192	523	253	8	245
Colorado	609	232	46	186	461	252	43	209
New Mexico	7,240	5,414	1,314	4,100	6,861	5,562	1,403	4,159
Arizona	10,625	6,594	1,633	4,961	9,863	7,132	1,682	5,450
Utah	1,232	747	171	576	1,058	769	152	617
Nevada	2,120	330	62	268	2,070	519	73	446
Pacific								
Washington	4,066	668	48	620	4,035	1,086	49	1,037
Oregon	1,954	213	6	207	1,950	466	8	458
California	6,458	711	62	649	6,148	1,058	85	976

Source: U.S. Bureau of the Census. *Indian Population in the United States and Alaska, 1910.* Washington, DC: U.S. Government Printing Office, 1915, p. 236. *Note:* A dash (-) represents zero.

★87★

Language

Ability of American Indians 10 Years Old and Older to Speak English, by Linguistic Stock, Tribe, and Sex, 1910: A - K

Data are shown for linguistic stocks with 200 or more Indians and tribes with more than 100 members in 1910.

Linguistic stock and tribe	Indians 10 years of age and over: 1910			Indian males 10 years of age and over			Indian females 10 years of age and over		
	Total number	Unable to speak English		Total number	Unable to speak English		Total number	Unable to speak English	
		Number	Percent		Number	Percent		Number	Percent
UNITED STATES									
Algonquian stock	29,872	7,716	25.8	15,486	3,306	21.3	14,386	4,410	30.7
Arapaho	1,047	399	38.1	545	154	28.3	502	245	48.8
Brotherton	132	-	-	70	-	-	62	-	-
Cheyenne	2,427	1,196	49.3	1,176	505	42.9	1,251	691	55.2
Chickahominy	89	-	-	47	-	-	42	-	-
Chippewa	14,629	3,875	26.5	7,552	1,692	22.4	7,077	2,183	30.8
Cree	326	25	7.7	166	6	3.6	160	19	11.9
Delaware	636	25	3.9	312	4	1.3	324	21	6.5
Gros Ventres	376	163	43.4	189	76	40.2	187	87	46.5
Kickapoo	251	81	32.3	139	37	26.6	112	44	39.3
Malecite	101	3	3.0	48	-	-	53	3	5.7
Mashpee	166	-	-	91	-	-	75	-	-
Menominee	1,029	202	19.6	571	84	14.7	458	118	25.8
Miami	171	4	2.3	94	2	2.1	77	2	2.6
Ottawa	2,034	395	19.4	139	139	12.8	951	256	26.9
Passamaquoddy	310	10	3.2	166	4	2.4	144	6	4.2
Penobscot	231	2	0.9	124	-	-	107	2	1.9
Peoria	83	2	2.4	40	1	-	43	1	-
Piegan	1,602	864	53.9	810	417	51.5	792	447	56.4
Potawatomi	1,697	241	14.2	968	111	11.5	729	130	17.8
Powhatan	91	-	-	45	-	-	46	-	-
Sauk and Fox	521	68	13.1	280	21	7.5	241	47	19.5
Shawnee	886	137	15.5	424	44	10.4	462	93	20.1
Shinnecock	121	-	-	59	-	-	62	-	-
Stockbridges	384	1	0.3	197	-	-	187	1	0.5
Wampanoag	133	-	-	79	-	-	54	-	-
All other tribes	399	23	5.8	211	9	4.3	188	14	7.4
Athapaskan stock	20,460	15,791	77.2	10,252	7,549	73.6	10,208	8,242	80.7
Apache	3,480	2,149	61.8	1,754	922	52.6	1,726	1,227	71.1
Hupa	497	-	-	241	-	-	256	-	-
Jicarilla Apache	486	361	74.3	252	174	69.0	234	187	79.9
Kiowa Apache	98	21	21.4	42	5	-	56	16	28.6
Mescalero Apache	312	158	50.6	129	50	38.8	183	108	59.0
Navajo	14,797	13,048	88.2	7,429	6,384	85.9	7,368	6,664	90.4
Rogue River	286	17	5.9	153	2	1.3	133	15	11.3
Tolowa	84	1	1.2	44	1	-	40	-	-
Umpqua	79	14	17.7	40	5	-	39	9	-
Wailaki	164	3	1.8	79	-	-	85	3	3.5
All other tribes	177	19	10.7	89	6	6.7	88	13	14.8

[Continued]

★ 87 ★

Ability of American Indians 10 Years Old and Older to Speak English, by Linguistic Stock, Tribe, and Sex, 1910: A - K

[Continued]

Linguistic stock and tribe	Indians 10 years of age and over: 1910			Indian males 10 years of age and over			Indian females 10 years of age and over		
	Total number	Unable to speak English		Total number	Unable to speak English		Total number	Unable to speak English	
		Number	Percent		Number	Percent		Number	Percent
Caddoan stock	1,354	321	23.7	673	154	22.9	681	167	24.5
Arikara	336	186	55.4	163	88	54.0	173	98	56.6
Caddo	302	58	19.2	161	28	17.4	141	30	21.3
Pawnee	473	42	8.9	227	22	9.7	246	20	8.1
Wichita	229	34	14.8	114	15	13.2	115	19	16.5
All other tribes	14	1	-	8	1	-	6	-	-
Chimakuan stock	228	104	45.6	113	41	36.3	115	63	54.8
Quileute	193	84	43.5	95	33	34.7	98	51	52.0
All other tribes	35	20	-	18	8	-	17	12	-
Chinookan stock	676	114	16.9	353	34	9.6	323	80	24.8
Chinook	224	8	3.6	123	1	0.8	101	7	6.9
Wasco	184	47	25.5	95	12	12.6	89	35	39.3
Wishram	222	54	24.3	112	21	18.8	110	33	30.0
All other tribes	46	5	-	23	-	-	23	5	-
Croatan group	3,943	-	-	1,954	-	-	1,989	-	-
Croatan	3,943	-	-	1,954	-	-	1,989	-	-
Iroquoian stock	26,201	3,121	11.9	13,490	1,441	10.7	12,711	1,680	13.2
Cherokee	20,154	2,445	12.1	10,319	1,189	11.5	9,835	1,256	12.8
Mohawk	291	95	32.6	136	25	18.4	155	70	45.2
Oneida	1,739	198	11.4	930	77	8.3	809	121	15.0
Onondaga	275	3	1.1	138	1	0.7	137	2	1.5
St. Regis	912	207	22.7	499	86	17.2	413	121	29.3
Seneca	2,155	167	7.7	1,109	62	5.6	1,046	105	10.0
Tuscarora	309	1	0.3	168	-	-	141	1	0.7
Wyandot	253	3	1.2	137	-	-	116	3	2.6
All other tribes	113	2	1.8	54	1	1.9	59	1	1.7
Karok stock	555	63	11.4	275	24	8.7	280	39	13.9
Orleans	555	63	11.4	275	24	8.7	280	39	13.9
Keresan stock	2,954	2,070	70.1	1,593	1,041	65.3	1,361	1,029	75.6
Acoma	518	421	81.3	257	197	76.7	261	224	85.8
Cochiti	183	106	57.9	103	52	50.5	80	54	67.5
Laguna	1,050	577	55.0	551	274	49.7	499	303	60.7
San Felipe	379	284	74.9	227	158	69.6	152	126	82.9
Santa Ana	155	125	80.6	98	80	81.6	57	45	78.9
Santo Domingo	581	493	84.9	310	246	79.4	271	247	91.1
Sia	88	64	72.7	47	34	-	41	30	-

[Continued]

★ 87 ★

Ability of American Indians 10 Years Old and Older to Speak English, by Linguistic Stock, Tribe, and Sex, 1910: A - K

[Continued]

Linguistic stock and tribe	Indians 10 years of age and over: 1910			Indian males 10 years of age and over			Indian females 10 years of age and over		
	Total number	Unable to speak English		Total number	Unable to speak English		Total number	Unable to speak English	
		Number	Percent		Number	Percent		Number	Percent
Kiowan stock	750	280	37.3	361	106	29.4	389	174	44.7
Kiowa	750	280	37.3	361	106	29.4	389	174	44.7
Kutenaian stock	395	74	18.7	210	37	17.6	185	37	20.0
Kutenai	395	74	18.7	210	37	17.6	185	37	20.0

Source: U.S. Bureau of the Census. *Indian Population in the United States and Alaska, 1910.* Washington, DC: U.S. Government Printing Office, Washington, 1915, pp. 244-246. *Notes:* A dash (-) represents zero or a lack of 50 persons for a percentage base.

★ 88 ★

Language

Ability of American Indians 10 Years Old and Older to Speak English, by Linguistic Stock, Tribe, and Sex, 1910: L - S

Data are shown for linguistic stocks with 200 or more Indians and tribes with more than 100 members in 1910.

Linguistic stock and tribe	Indians 10 years of age and over: 1910			Indian males 10 years of age and over			Indian females 10 years of age and over		
	Total number	Unable to speak English		Total number	Unable to speak English		Total number	Unable to speak English	
		Number	Percent		Number	Percent		Number	Percent
UNITED STATES (cont.)									
Lutuamian stock	727	140	19.3	347	44	12.7	380	96	25.3
Klamath	521	107	20.5	249	36	14.5	272	71	26.1
Modoc	206	33	16.0	98	8	8.2	108	25	23.1
Maidu stock	810	16	2.0	421	2	0.5	389	14	3.6
Maidu	810	16	2.0	421	2	0.5	389	14	3.6
Miwok stock	530	25	4.7	254	9	3.5	276	16	5.8
Miwok	505	24	4.8	238	8	3.4	267	16	6.0
All other tribes	25	1	-	16	1	-	9	-	-
Muskhogean stock	18,957	4,367	23.0	9,608	1,867	19.4	9,349	2,500	26.7
Alibamu	225	115	51.1	114	54	47.4	111	61	55.0
Chickasaw	2,563	160	6.2	1,268	38	3.0	1,295	122	9.4
Choctaw	10,185	2,184	21.4	5,202	929	17.9	4,983	1,255	25.2
Creek	4,697	1,304	27.8	2,349	560	23.8	2,348	744	31.7
Seminole	1,216	550	45.2	639	259	40.5	577	291	50.4
All other tribes (Koasati)	71	54	76.1	36	27	-	35	27	-

[Continued]

★ 88 ★

Ability of American Indians 10 Years Old and Older to Speak English, by Linguistic Stock, Tribe, and Sex, 1910: L - S
[Continued]

Linguistic stock and tribe	Indians 10 years of age and over: 1910			Indian males 10 years of age and over			Indian females 10 years of age and over		
	Total number	Unable to speak English		Total number	Unable to speak English		Total number	Unable to speak English	
		Number	Percent		Number	Percent		Number	Percent
Piman stock	6,149	3,750	61.0	3,234	1,848	57.1	2,915	1,902	65.2
Papago	2,655	1,920	72.3	1,365	944	69.2	1,290	976	75.7
Pima	3,083	1,504	48.8	1,631	726	44.5	1,452	778	53.6
Yaqui	378	300	79.4	222	169	76.1	156	131	84.0
All other tribes	33	26	-	16	9	-	17	17	-
Pomo stock	919	27	2.9	465	5	1.1	454	22	4.8
Clear Lake	141	1	0.7	73	-	-	68	1	1.5
Pomo	606	18	3.0	308	2	0.6	298	16	5.4
All other tribes	172	8	4.7	84	3	3.6	88	5	5.7
Salishan stock	5,759	974	16.9	2,993	386	12.9	2,766	588	21.3
Chehalis	199	28	14.1	114	12	10.5	85	16	18.8
Clallam	280	16	5.7	144	4	2.8	136	12	8.8
Coeur d'Alene	215	2	0.9	116	2	1.7	99	-	-
Columbia	288	122	42.4	156	59	37.8	132	63	47.7
Colville	589	54	9.2	310	20	6.5	279	34	12.2
Cowlitz	75	11	14.7	39	2	-	36	9	-
Flathead	343	64	18.7	177	27	15.3	166	37	22.3
Kalispel	430	139	32.3	216	65	30.1	214	74	34.6
Lummi	223	20	9.0	127	8	6.3	96	12	12.5
Muckleshoot	142	36	25.4	75	15	20.0	67	21	31.3
Nisqualli	112	18	16.1	56	6	10.7	56	12	21.4
Okinagan	206	46	22.3	103	19	18.4	103	27	26.2
Puyallup	231	27	11.7	118	10	8.5	113	17	15.0
Quinaielt	205	49	23.9	107	22	20.6	98	27	27.6
Sanpoil	184	61	33.2	87	22	25.3	97	39	40.2
Skokomish	141	17	12.1	62	5	8.1	79	12	15.2
Snohomish	478	46	9.6	251	16	6.4	227	30	13.2
Spokan	512	38	7.4	251	13	5.2	261	25	9.6
Suquamish	217	36	16.6	118	15	12.7	99	21	21.2
Swinomish	243	55	22.6	134	18	13.4	109	37	33.9
All other tribes	446	89	20.0	232	26	11.2	214	63	29.4
Shahaptian stock	3,372	1,098	32.6	1,567	378	24.1	1,805	720	39.9
Klikitat	325	95	29.2	148	30	20.3	177	65	36.7
Nez Perces	980	250	25.5	480	75	15.6	500	175	35.0
Umatilla	217	110	50.7	94	38	40.4	123	72	58.5
Wallawalla	290	70	24.1	143	27	18.9	147	43	29.3
Warm Springs	408	118	28.9	184	44	23.9	224	74	33.0
Yakima	1,028	377	36.7	463	136	29.4	565	241	42.7
All other tribes	124	78	62.9	55	28	50.9	69	50	72.5

[Continued]

★ 88 ★

Ability of American Indians 10 Years Old and Older to Speak English, by Linguistic Stock, Tribe, and Sex, 1910: L - S

[Continued]

Linguistic stock and tribe	Indians 10 years of age and over: 1910			Indian males 10 years of age and over			Indian females 10 years of age and over		
	Total number	Unable to speak English		Total number	Unable to speak English		Total number	Unable to speak English	
		Number	Percent		Number	Percent		Number	Percent
Shastan stock	1,226	114	9.3	595	46	7.7	631	68	10.8
Hat Creek	190	1	0.5	100	-	-	90	1	1.1
Pit River	767	98	12.8	369	41	11.1	398	57	14.3
Shasta	269	15	5.6	126	5	4.0	143	10	7.0
Shoshonean stock	12,894	4,970	38.5	6,645	2,237	33.7	6,249	2,733	43.7
Bannock	338	214	63.3	176	106	60.2	162	108	66.7
Chemehuevi	262	134	51.1	136	44	32.4	126	90	71.4
Comanche	876	328	37.4	427	132	30.9	449	196	43.7
Hopi	1,420	714	50.3	795	370	46.5	625	344	55.0
Kawia	605	166	27.4	333	82	24.6	272	84	30.9
Kern River	80	5	6.3	37	1	-	43	4	-
Mono	1,090	235	21.6	501	67	13.4	589	168	28.5
Paiute	585	240	41.0	313	101	32.3	272	139	51.1
Paviotso	2,480	537	21.7	1,209	183	15.1	1,271	354	27.9
San Luiseno	389	89	22.9	203	33	16.3	186	56	30.1
Serrano	91	27	29.7	49	12	-	42	15	-
Shoshoni	2,955	1,246	42.2	1,515	586	38.7	1,440	660	45.8
Ute	1,641	988	60.2	911	499	54.8	730	489	67.0
All other tribes	82	47	57.3	40	21	-	42	26	-
Siouan stock	24,598	8,963	36.4	12,350	3,733	30.2	12,248	5,230	42.7
Assiniboin	925	422	45.6	455	189	41.5	470	233	49.6
Catawba	78	-	-	42	-	-	36	-	-
Crow	1,402	723	51.6	7.2	345	49.1	700	378	54.0
Hidatsa	394	135	34.3	208	52	25.0	186	83	44.6
Iowa	179	7	3.9	94	4	4.3	85	3	3.5
Kansa	138	1	0.7	88	-	-	50	1	2.0
Mandan	162	77	47.5	84	33	39.3	78	44	56.4
Omaha	791	212	26.8	407	74	18.2	384	138	35.9
Osage	898	111	12.4	465	54	11.6	433	57	13.2
Oto	245	31	12.7	135	16	11.9	110	15	13.6
Ponca	643	136	21.2	307	56	18.2	336	80	23.8
Quapaw	169	5	3.0	84	-	-	85	5	5.9
Santee Sioux	1,112	193	17.4	564	61	10.8	548	132	24.1
Sioux	790	121	15.3	449	47	10.5	341	74	21.7
Sisseton Sioux	1,888	560	29.7	957	207	21.6	931	353	37.9
Teton Sioux	10,739	4,656	43.4	5,349	1,987	37.1	5,390	2,669	49.5
Brule Sioux	591	218	36.9	301	86	28.6	290	132	45.5
Hunkpapa Sioux	813	405	49.8	403	174	43.2	410	231	56.3
Minniconjou Sioux	318	195	61.3	150	77	51.3	168	118	70.2
Oglala Sioux	4,486	1,795	40.0	2,242	771	34.4	2,244	1,024	45.6

[Continued]

★ 88 ★

Ability of American Indians 10 Years Old and Older to Speak English, by Linguistic Stock, Tribe, and Sex, 1910: L - S
[Continued]

Linguistic stock and tribe	Indians 10 years of age and over: 1910			Indian males 10 years of age and over			Indian females 10 years of age and over		
	Total number	Unable to speak English		Total number	Unable to speak English		Total number	Unable to speak English	
		Number	Percent		Number	Percent		Number	Percent
Sans Arc Sioux	146	39	26.7	77	13	16.9	69	26	37.7
Sihasapa	372	143	38.4	191	63	33.0	181	80	44.2
Two Kettle Sioux	216	77	35.6	125	37	29.6	91	40	44.0
Other Teton Sioux	3,797	1,784	47.0	1,860	766	41.2	1,937	1,018	52.6
Winnebago	1,406	406	28.9	714	126	17.6	692	280	40.5
Yankton Sioux	1,583	660	41.7	754	270	35.8	829	390	47.0
Yanktonai Sioux	1,045	505	48.3	486	211	43.4	559	294	52.6
All other tribes	11	2	-	6	1	-	5	1	-

Source: U.S. Bureau of the Census. *Indian Population in the United States and Alaska, 1910.* Washington, DC: U.S. Government Printing Office, 1915, pp. 244-246.
Notes: A dash (-) represents zero or a lack of 50 persons for a percentage base.

★ 89 ★
Language

Ability of American Indians 10 Years Old and Older to Speak English, by Linguistic Stock, Tribe, and Sex, 1910: T - Z and Alaska

Data are shown for linguistic stocks with 200 or more Indians and tribes with more than 100 members in 1910.

Linguistic stock and tribe	Indians 10 years of age and over: 1910			Indian males 10 years of age and over			Indian females 10 years of age and over		
	Total number	Unable to speak English		Total number	Unable to speak English		Total number	Unable to speak English	
		Number	Percent		Number	Percent		Number	Percent
UNITED STATES (cont.)									
Tanoan stock	2,348	1,299	55.3	1,268	671	52.9	1,080	628	58.4
Isleta	717	492	68.6	381	249	65.4	336	243	72.3
Jemez	396	294	74.2	231	164	71.0	165	130	78.8
Picuris	76	44	57.9	37	20	-	39	24	-
San Ildefonso	85	41	48.2	41	16	-	44	25	-
San Juan	297	162	54.5	165	83	50.3	132	79	59.8
Santa Clara	199	92	46.2	103	46	44.7	96	46	47.9
Taos	371	92	24.8	198	50	25.3	173	42	24.3
All other tribes	207	82	39.6	112	43	38.4	95	39	41.1
Waiilatpuan stock	247	77	31.2	118	26	22.0	129	51	39.5
Cayuse	225	77	34.2	105	26	24.8	120	51	42.5
All other tribes	22	--	-	13	-	-	9	-	-

[Continued]

★ 89 ★

Ability of American Indians 10 Years Old and Older to Speak English, by Linguistic Stock, Tribe, and Sex, 1910: T - Z and Alaska
[Continued]

Linguistic stock and tribe	Indians 10 years of age and over: 1910			Indian males 10 years of age and over			Indian females 10 years of age and over		
	Total number	Unable to speak English		Total number	Unable to speak English		Total number	Unable to speak English	
		Number	Percent		Number	Percent		Number	Percent
Wakashan stock	279	102	36.6	142	44	31.0	137	58	42.3
Makah	256	92	35.9	134	44	32.8	122	48	39.3
All other tribes	23	10	-	8	-	-	15	10	-
Washoan stock	650	39	6.0	334	19	5.7	316	20	6.3
Washo	650	39	6.0	334	19	5.7	316	20	6.3
Wintun stock	545	28	5.1	297	14	4.7	248	14	5.6
Nomelaki	101	8	7.9	52	5	9.6	49	3	-
Patwin	138	2	1.4	81	-	-	57	2	3.5
Wintun	306	18	5.9	164	9	5.5	142	9	6.3
Yokuts stock	407	40	9.8	218	9	4.1	189	31	16.4
Chukchansi	112	6	5.4	56	-	-	56	6	10.7
Yokuts	231	21	9.1	133	9	6.8	98	12	12.2
All other tribes	64	13	20.3	29	-	-	35	13	-
Yuman stock	3,290	1,229	37.4	1,806	573	31.7	1,484	656	44.2
Cocopah	182	125	68.7	103	59	57.3	79	66	83.5
Diegueno	568	187	32.9	305	83	27.2	263	104	39.5
Havasupai	137	7	5.1	83	3	3.6	54	4	7.4
Maricopa	287	130	45.3	152	64	42.1	135	66	48.9
Mohave	822	245	29.8	460	121	26.3	362	124	34.3
Walapai	370	113	30.5	207	47	22.7	163	66	40.5
Yavapai	229	112	48.9	126	53	42.1	103	59	57.3
Yuma	667	289	43.3	355	133	37.5	312	156	50.0
All other tribes	28	21	-	15	10	-	13	11	-
Yurok stock	505	81	16.0	249	25	10.0	256	56	21.9
Weitspec	505	81	16.0	249	25	10.0	256	56	21.9
Zunian stock	1,202	979	81.4	631	505	80.0	571	474	83.0
Zuni	1,202	979	81.4	631	505	80.0	571	474	83.0
ALASKA									
Athapaskan stock	2,886	1,308	45.3	1,507	565	37.5	1,379	743	53.9
Ahtena	227	117	51.5	129	54	41.9	98	63	64.3
Hankutchin	86	19	22.1	58	11	19.0	28	8	-
Kaiyuhkhotana	125	68	54.4	64	29	45.3	61	39	63.9
Knaiakhotana	516	291	56.4	283	132	46.6	233	159	68.2
Kutchin	276	211	76.4	140	104	74.3	136	107	78.7

[Continued]

★ 89 ★

Ability of American Indians 10 Years Old and Older to Speak English, by Linguistic Stock, Tribe, and Sex, 1910: T - Z and Alaska

[Continued]

Linguistic stock and tribe	Indians 10 years of age and over: 1910			Indian males 10 years of age and over			Indian females 10 years of age and over		
	Total number	Unable to speak English		Total number	Unable to speak English		Total number	Unable to speak English	
		Number	Percent		Number	Percent		Number	Percent
Natsitkutchin	150	119	79.3	84	58	69.0	66	61	92.4
Tenankutchin	302	143	47.4	156	58	37.2	146	85	58.2
Unakhotana	136	80	58.8	72	37	51.4	64	43	67.2
All other tribes	1,068	260	24.3	521	82	15.7	547	178	32.5
Eskimauan stock	9,964	7,134	71.6	5,147	3,392	65.9	4,817	3,742	77.7
Aleut	1,001	616	61.5	516	305	59.1	485	311	64.1
Chnagmiut	202	132	65.3	110	58	52.7	92	74	80.4
Ikogmiut	529	486	91.9	247	223	90.3	282	263	93.3
Kaialigmiut	127	125	98.4	62	61	98.4	65	64	98.5
Kaviagmiut	163	66	40.5	81	30	37.0	82	36	43.9
Kinugumiut	424	298	70.3	236	149	63.1	188	149	79.3
Kowagmiut	410	231	56.3	214	101	47.2	196	130	66.3
Kusetrinmiut	90	28	31.1	56	22	39.3	34	6	-
Kuskovakmiut	232	190	81.5	121	91	75.2	111	99	89.2
Kuskwogmiut	1,068	994	93.1	544	502	92.3	524	492	93.9
Magemiut	262	219	83.6	118	102	86.4	144	117	81.3
Malemiut	407	168	41.3	210	79	37.6	197	89	45.2
Nunatogmiut	224	172	76.8	130	94	72.3	94	78	83.0
Nunivagmiut	236	224	94.9	127	122	96.1	109	102	93.6
Nunochogmiut	107	102	95.3	42	41	-	65	61	93.8
Selawigmiut	177	137	77.4	98	65	66.3	79	72	91.1
Tikeramiut	252	135	53.6	127	61	48.0	125	74	59.2
Ukivokmiut	94	80	85.1	50	39	78.0	44	41	-
Unaligmiut	274	152	55.5	126	54	42.9	148	98	66.2
Utkiavinmiut	86	64	74.4	43	29	-	43	35	-
Utukamiut	91	74	81.3	46	35	-	45	39	-
Yuit	226	134	59.3	119	48	40.3	107	86	80.4
Southern Eskimo	2,613	1,856	71.0	1,383	868	62.8	1,230	988	80.3
All other tribes	669	451	67.4	341	213	62.5	328	238	72.6
Hadian stock	369	58	15.7	198	23	11.6	171	35	20.5
Haida	369	58	15.7	198	23	11.6	171	35	20.5
Tlingit stock	3,240	1,343	41.5	1,634	509	31.2	1,606	834	51.9
Auk	213	58	27.2	120	22	18.3	93	36	38.7
Chilkat	536	238	44.4	270	97	35.9	266	141	53.0
Henya	146	72	49.3	78	38	48.7	68	34	50.0
Huna	470	252	53.6	221	84	38.0	249	168	67.5
Hutsnuwu	373	167	44.8	186	57	30.6	187	110	58.8
Kake	232	95	40.9	114	41	36.0	118	54	45.8
Sitka	446	191	42.8	225	77	34.2	221	114	51.6

[Continued]

★ 89 ★

Ability of American Indians 10 Years Old and Older to Speak English, by Linguistic Stock, Tribe, and Sex, 1910: T - Z and Alaska
[Continued]

Linguistic stock and tribe	Indians 10 years of age and over: 1910			Indian males 10 years of age and over			Indian females 10 years of age and over		
	Total number	Unable to speak English		Total number	Unable to speak English		Total number	Unable to speak English	
		Number	Percent		Number	Percent		Number	Percent
Stikine	139	48	34.5	69	18	26.1	70	30	42.9
Taku	111	38	34.2	54	9	16.7	57	29	50.9
Tongas	129	43	33.3	65	13	20.0	64	30	46.9
Yakutat	211	88	41.7	96	28	29.2	115	60	52.2
All other tribes	234	53	22.6	136	25	18.4	98	28	28.6
Tsimshian stock	520	94	18.1	294	30	10.2	226	64	28.3
Tsimshian	520	94	18.1	294	30	10.2	226	64	28.3

Source: U.S. Bureau of the Census. *Indian Population in the United States and Alaska, 1910.* Washington, DC: U.S. Government Printing Office, 1915, pp. 244-246.
Notes: A dash (-) represents zero or a lack of 50 persons for a percentage base.

★ 90 ★
Language

American Indian Linguistic Stocks: Classifications by the U.S. Census Bureau in 1910 and 1930 - I

See the end of the table for original notes accompanying these data.

Classification in 1910	Classification in 1930
ALGONQUIAN STOCK	ALGONQUIAN STOCK
Arapaho	Arapaho
Blackfeet, Piegan	Blackfeet
Cheyenne	Cheyenne
Chippewa	Chippewa
Delaware, Munsee	Delaware
Gros Ventres (Atsina)	Gros Ventres (Atsina)
Kickapoo	Kickapoo
Menominee	Menominee
Miami, Peoria, Piankashaw, Wea	Miami and Illinois
Ottawa	Ottawa
Potawatomi	Potawatomi
Sauk and Fox	Sauk and Fox
Shawnee	Shawnee
Brotherton, Mashpee,	Eastern Algonquians

[Continued]

American Indian Linguistic Stocks: Classifications by the U.S. Census Bureau in 1910 and 1930 - I
[Continued]

Classification in 1910	Classification in 1930
Mohegan, Montauk, Narragansett, Niantic, Passamaquoddy Penobscot, Pequot, Poospatuck, Shinnecock, Stockbridges, Wampanoag Croatan group, and Virginia Algonquians, Croatan, Chickahominy, Mattapony, Pamunkey, Powhatan	Virginia-Carolina Indians
ATHAPASKAN STOCK - Chiricahua Apache, Coyotero Apache, Jicarilla Apache, Lipan Apache, Mescalero Apache, San Carlos Apache, Tonto Apache, White Mountain Apache	ATHAPASKAN STOCK Apache
Kiowa Apache Navaho	Kiowa Apache Navaho
Chastacosta, Chetco, Cow Creek, Rogue River, Tlatskanai, Tolowa, Umpqua, Upper Coquille	Oregon Athapaskans
Hupa, Kai-Pomo, Mattole, Redwood (Whilkut), Saiaz, Wailakki	California Athapaskans
CADDOAN STOCK Arikara Caddo Pawnee	CADDOAN STOCK Arikara Caddo Pawnee
Kichai, Tawakoni, Waco, Wichita	Wichita and Kichai
CHIMAKUAN STOCK Chimakum, Hoh, Quileute	CHIMAKUAN STOCK
CHINOOKAN STOCK Chinook, Clackamas, Clatsop, Wasco, Wishram	CHINOOKAN STOCK
CHITIMACHAN STOCK Chitimacha	CHITIMACHAN STOCK Chitimacha
CHUMASHAN STOCK	CHUMASHAN STOCK

[Continued]

★ 90 ★

American Indian Linguistic Stocks: Classifications by the U.S. Census Bureau in 1910 and 1930 - I
[Continued]

Classification in 1910	Classification in 1930
San Luis Obispo, Santa Barbareno, Santa Ynez	
COSTANOAN STOCK Santa Cruz	COSTANOAN STOCK Santa Cruz
IROQUOIAN STOCK Cayuga, Mohawk, Oneida, Onondaga, St. Regis, Seneca, Tuscarora Wyandot Cherokee	IROQUOIAN STOCK Iroquois Wyandot Cherokee
KALAPOOIAN STOCK Kalapooia, Lakmiut, Mary's River, Santiam, Wapato, Yamel, Yonkalla	KALAPOOIAN STOCK
KAROK STOCK Orleans	KAROK STOCK Orleans
KERESAN STOCK Acoma, Cochiti, Laguna, San Felipe, Santa Ana, Santa Domingo, Sia	KERESAN STOCK
KIOWAN STOCK Kiowa	KIOWAN STOCK Kiowa
KUSAN STOCK Kusa	KUSAN STOCK
KUTENAIAN STOCK Kutenai	KUTENAIAN STOCK Kutenai
MAIDU STOCK Maidu	MAIDU STOCK Maidu
MIWOK STOCK Marin, Middletown, Miwok	MIWOK STOCK
MUSKHOGEAN STOCK Chickasaw Choctaw Alibamu, Creek, Koasati	MUSKHOGEAN STOCK Chickasaw Choctaw Creek

[Continued]

★ 90 ★

American Indian Linguistic Stocks: Classifications by the U.S. Census Bureau in 1910 and 1930 - I

[Continued]

Classification in 1910	Classification in 1930
Seminole	Seminole
PIMAN STOCK Papago Pima	PIMAN STOCK Papago Pima
POMO STOCK Clear Lake, Gynomehro, Little Lake, Lower Lake, Pomo	POMO STOCK
SALINAN STOCK San Antonio	SALINAN STOCK San Antonio
SALISHAN STOCK Chehalis, Clallam, Cowlitz, Dwamish, Lummi, Muckleshoot, Nisqualli, Nooksak, Puyallup, Quinaielt, Skagit, Skokomish, Snohomish, Snoqualmu, Squaxon, Suquamish, Swinomish, Twana	SALISHAN STOCK Washington Coast Salish

Source: Truesdell, Dr. Leon E. U.S. Department of Commerce. Bureau of the Census. Fifteenth Census of the United States: 1930, *The Indian Population of the United States and Alaska.* Washington, DC: U.S. Government Printing Office, 1937, pp. 33-36. *Notes: Linguistic stocks.* - On the basis of resemblances between languages, the Indian tribes are grouped into linguistic stocks or families. These linguistic stocks are analogous to the Semitic and Indo-European stocks within the white race, while the languages of the tribes within a stock differ, just as German differs from Russian, or English from Greek. Tribes with related languages were probably at a remote "period" related by blood, although the prevalence of adoption and intermarriage with other tribes has weakened the tie of blood and also the bond of common ceremonial observances until there is often little resemblance between tribes of the same stock other than that of language. *Enumeration by stock and tribe, 1930 and 1910.* - Classification by stock and tribe, on the basis of a census enumeration, is very difficult, and the results are subject to a considerable margin of error. The popular local designations of Indian tribes do not always correspond with the scientific name, and the enumerator, who is rarely an ethnologist, could do no better than to give the name by which the tribe was locally known. If this name was not readily identified with one of the recognized tribes, the Indian was necessarily assigned to the miscellaneous group and lost to the tribal classification. No instructions were given as to the tribal allocation of Indians of mixed tribal blood. Such Indians are probably included in the tribes which they prefer to claim, or in which they have the reputation of membership. The tabulation by stock and tribe from the Census of 1910 differentiated 52 linguistic stocks, divided into 280 tribes. In 1930, for convenience of tabulation, many of the smaller tribes were thrown together into groups of tribes, reducing the number of tribes and groups to 100, and the number of linguistic stocks to 40.

★ 91 ★
Language

American Indian Linguistic Stocks: Classifications by the U.S. Census Bureau in 1910 and 1930 - II

See the end of the table for original notes accompanying these data.

Classification in 1910	Classification in 1930
SALISHAN STOCK (cont.) Coeur d'Alene, Columbia, Colville, Flathead, Kalispel, Methow, Nespelim, Okinagan, Pend d'Oreilles, Pisquow, Sanpoil, Spokan	Interior Salish
Tillamook	Tillamook
LUTUAMIAN STOCK Klamath, Modoc	SHAPWAILUTAN STOCK Klamath and Modoc
SHAHAPTIAN STOCK Klickitat, Nez Perces, Paloos, Topinish, Umatilla, Walla Walla, Warm Springs, Yakima	Shahaptians
WAIILATUPUAN STOCK Cayuse, Molala	Cayuse, Molala
SHASTAN STOCK Hat Creek Pit River Shasta	SHASTAN STOCK
SHOSHONEAN STOCK Bannock Comanche Hopi Mono, Panamint, Paviotso Chemehuevi, Paiute Shoshoni Pahvant, Ute Gabrieleno, Juaneno, Kawaiisu, Kawai, Kern River, Luiseno (San Luiseno), Serrano, Tehachapi	SHOSHONEAN STOCK Bannock Comanche Hopi Mono-Paviotso Paiute Shoshoni Ute Southern California
SIOUAN STOCK Catawba Crow Hidatsa Iowa Kansa Mandan	SIOUAN STOCK Catawba Crow Hidatsa Iowa Kansa Mandan

[Continued]

★ 91 ★

American Indian Linguistic Stocks: Classifications by the U.S. Census Bureau in 1910 and 1930 - II
[Continued]

Classification in 1910	Classification in 1930
Oto, Missouri	Oto and Missouri
Omaha	Omaha
Osage	Osage
Ponca	Ponca
Quapaw	Quapaw
Santee Sioux, Sioux, Sisseton Sioux, Teton Sioux, Yanktonai Sioux, Yankton Sioux,	Dakota
Assiniboin	Assiniboin
Winnebago	Winnebago
TANOAN STOCK	TANOAN STOCK
Isleta, Jemez, Nambe, Pecos, Picuris, Pojoaque, San Ildefonso, San Juan, Sandia, Santa Clara, Taos, Tesuque	
TONKAWAN STOCK	TONKAWAN STOCK
Tonkawa	Tonkawa
TUNICAN STOCK	TUNICAN STOCK
Tunica	Tunica
WASHOAN STOCK	WASHOAN STOCK
Washo	Washo
WINTUN STOCK	WINTUN STOCK
Nomelaki, Patwin, Wintun	
WIYOT STOCK	WIYOT STOCK
Humboldt Bay	Humboldt Bay
YANAN STOCK	YANAN STOCK
Yana	Yana
YOKUTS STOCK	YOKUTS STOCK
Choinimni, Chookiminah, Chukchansi, Kashowoo, Tachi, Wechikhit, Wikchamni, Yokuts, Yowdanchi	
YUCHEAN STOCK	YUCHEAN STOCK
Yuchi	Yuchi

[Continued]

★ 91 ★

American Indian Linguistic Stocks: Classifications by the U.S. Census Bureau in 1910 and 1930 - II

[Continued]

Classification in 1910	Classification in 1930
YUKIAN STOCK Coast Yuki, Redwood (Huchnom), Wappo, Yuki	YUKIAN STOCK
YUMAN STOCK Cocopa Diegueno Havasupai, Walapai, Yavapai, Yuma Apache Maricopa Mohave Yuma	YUMAN STOCK Cocopa Diegueno Northern Yumans Maricopa Mohave Yuma
YUROK STOCK Weitspek	YUROK STOCK Weitspek
ZUNIAN STOCK Zuni	ZUNIAN STOCK Zuni
CHIMARIKAN STOCK Chimariko	Other tribes of the United States, including tribe
TAKELMAN STOCK Takelma Other tribes Tribes not reported	
ALGONQUIAN STOCK Abnaki, Cree, Malecite,	Canadian and Mexican tribes

[Continued]

★ 91 ★

American Indian Linguistic Stocks: Classifications by the U.S. Census Bureau in 1910 and 1930 - II
[Continued]

Classification in 1910	Classification in 1930
Micmac	
PIMAN STOCK Mayo, Opata, Yaqui	
SALISHAN STOCK Bellacoola, Comox, Cowichan, Shuswap, Songish	
TSIMSHIAN STOCK Tsimshian	
WAKASHAN STOCK Kitamat, Kwakiutl, Makah, Nootka	
ATHAPASKAN STOCK Ahtena, Tenankutchin Eskimauan stock Aleut, Malemiut	Alaskan tribes
HAIDAN STOCK Haida	
TLINGIT STOCK Auk, Chilkat, Kake No corresponding classification	Indians born in other foreign countries

Source: Truesdell, Dr. Leon E. U.S. Department of Commerce. Bureau of the Census. Fifteenth Census of the United States: 1930. *The Indian Population of the United States and Alaska.* Washington, DC: U.S. Government Printing Office, 1937, pp. 33-36. *Notes: Linguistic stocks.* - On the basis of resemblances between languages, the Indian tribes are grouped into linguistic stocks or families. These linguistic stocks are analogous to the Semitic and Indo-European stocks within the white race, while the languages of the tribes within a stock differ just as German differs from Russian, or English from Greek. Tribes with related languages were probably at a remote "period" related by blood, although the prevalence of adoption and intermarriage with other tribes has weakened the tie of blood and also the bond of common ceremonial observances until there is often little resemblances between tribes of the same stock other than that of language. *Enumeration by stock and tribe, 1930 and 1910.* - Classification by stock and tribe, on the basis of a census enumeration, is very difficult, and the results are subject to a considerable margin of error. The popular local designations of Indian tribes do not always correspond with the scientific name, and the enumerator, who is rarely an ethnologist, could do no better than to give the name by which the tribe was locally known. If this name was not readily identified with one of the recognized tribes the Indian was necessarily assigned to the miscellaneous group and lost to the tribal classification. No instructions were given as to the tribal allocation of Indians of mixed tribal blood. Such Indians are probably included in the tribes which they prefer to claim, or in which they have the reputation of membership. The tabulation by stock and tribe from the Census of 1910 differentiated 52 linguistic stocks, divided into 280 tribes. In 1930, for convenience of tabulation, many of the smaller tribes were thrown together into groups of tribes, reducing the number of tribes and groups to 100, and the number of linguistic stocks to 40.

Marriage

★ 92 ★

Marital Status of American Indians 15 Years Old and Older, by Sex, 1900-1930

Sex and marital status	1900		1910		1920		1930	
	Number	Percent	Number	Percent	Number	Percent	Number	Percent
Male								
Total	72,076	100.0	80,383	100.0	76,321	100.0	103,441	100.0
Single	24,323	33.7	27,391	34.1	26,450	34.7	38,021	36.8
Married	41,067	57.0	46,154	57.4	43,095	56.5	56,382	54.5
Widowed	4,974	6.9	5,319	6.6	5,711	7.5	7,173	6.9
Divorced	418	0.6	679	0.8	680	0.8	1,646	1.6
Unknown	1,294	1.8	840	1.0	385	0.5	219	0.2
Female								
Total	71,497	100.0	76,982	100.0	70,431	100.0	96,084	100.0
Single	14,350	20.1	16,324	21.2	16,238	23.1	23,335	24.3
Married	43,906	61.4	49,095	63.8	43,923	62.4	59,168	61.6
Widowed	11,458	16.0	10,071	13.1	9,217	13.1	11,541	12.0
Divorced	870	1.2	959	1.2	826	1.1	1,876	2.0
Unknown	913	1.3	533	0.7	227	0.3	164	0.2

Source: Truesdell. Dr. Leon E. U.S. Department of Commerce. Bureau of the Census. Fifteenth Census of the United States: 1930, *The Indian Population of the United States and Alaska.* Washington, DC: U.S. Government Printing Office, 1937, p. 121.

★ 93 ★

Marriage

Marital Status of American Indians Age 15 Years Old and Older, by State and Sex, 1910 and 1930

Figures are shown in percent.

State	1910						1930					
	Male			Female			Male			Female		
	Single	Married	Widowed	Single	Married	Widowed	Single	Married	Widowed	Single	Married	Widowed
United States	34.1	57.4	6.6	21.2	63.8	13.1	36.8	54.5	6.9	24.3	61.6	12.0
Arizona	28.5	61.6	6.7	17.1	67.6	12.1	34.1	57.3	7.6	22.0	64.1	12.8
California	37.1	50.3	10.4	22.6	59.2	16.0	42.7	45.7	8.9	23.9	58.8	14.1
Idaho	24.3	64.3	6.6	12.2	68.6	16.0	28.9	57.5	9.3	16.0	63.8	16.7
Kansas	56.2	34.4	7.6	45.6	46.9	6.6	41.7	50.6	5.3	22.1	66.2	9.4
Michigan	40.0	49.8	9.2	23.8	61.0	14.0	42.3	45.8	9.8	22.3	61.9	14.0
Minnesota	34.6	56.1	6.7	19.6	62.1	14.5	39.6	50.6	7.7	25.0	60.5	11.9
Montana	29.7	64.6	4.5	15.7	69.7	13.3	33.6	56.1	7.3	19.3	67.8	10.5
Nebraska	33.2	60.3	6.0	22.0	65.5	11.9	33.3	56.3	8.3	27.6	58.9	11.2
Nevada	26.8	61.9	7.4	14.4	67.1	14.8	36.7	52.9	7.8	21.7	58.0	17.5

[Continued]

★ 93 ★

Marital Status of American Indians Age 15 Years Old and Older, by State and Sex, 1910 and 1930
[Continued]

State	1910						1930					
	Male			Female			Male			Female		
	Single	Married	Widowed	Single	Married	Widowed	Single	Married	Widowed	Single	Married	Widowed
New Mexico	13.0	60.5	7.6	17.7	66.1	13.7	34.5	56.2	8.4	24.4	61.0	13.1
New York	34.5	54.1	9.0	24.7	59.4	15.6	36.9	52.9	8.7	25.4	60.6	12.3
North Carolina	33.3	62.8	3.4	27.7	63.1	8.9	36.8	58.4	4.3	30.1	60.7	8.1
North Dakota	33.1	61.1	4.6	22.6	66.1	10.3	36.3	54.7	7.7	25.8	63.5	8.7
Oklahoma	34.9	58.4	5.3	23.0	63.7	11.9	37.9	55.7	4.6	26.8	59.4	11.3
Oregon	42.0	48.4	7.7	21.1	56.6	20.5	39.1	49.4	7.4	21.4	58.8	15.8
South Dakota	29.3	63.3	5.4	20.1	65.9	12.3	33.1	58.0	7.3	22.5	65.0	11.0
Utah	23.3	63.4	10.4	9.3	74.5	13.6	28.3	61.5	8.6	13.7	73.6	11.8
Washington	32.5	57.2	7.7	15.7	65.2	17.4	36.8	53.4	7.2	18.7	64.9	13.6
Wisconsin	35.4	55.2	7.5	23.2	63.1	12.0	41.0	49.2	7.8	26.6	60.0	11.2
Wyoming	22.9	60.3	9.4	9.1	66.6	17.5	29.4	59.3	9.2	16.5	71.7	10.8

Source: Truesdell, Dr. Leon E. U.S. Department of Commerce. Bureau of the Census. Fifteenth Census of the United States: 1930, *The Indian Population of the United States and Alaska.* Washington, DC: U.S. Government Printing Office, 1937, p. 121.

★ 94 ★

Marriage

Marital Status of American Indians Age 15 Years Old and Older, by Selected Tribe and Sex, 1910 and 1930

Figures are shown in percent.

Tribe	1910						1930					
	Male			Female			Male			Female		
	Single	Married	Widowed	Single	Married	Widowed	Single	Married	Widowed	Single	Married	Widowed
All tribes	34.1	57.4	6.6	21.2	63.8	13.1	36.8	54.5	6.9	24.3	61.6	12.0
Arapaho	20.0	67.9	5.3	7.6	72.1	14.9	26.0	69.4	4.3	18.6	74.2	6.4
Blackfeet	32.3	63.8	2.0	17.4	71.0	10.0	36.2	55.4	5.4	20.1	68.9	9.3
Cheyenne	25.7	68.0	5.5	16.9	68.5	12.2	26.8	62.0	8.9	19.1	69.0	8.8
Chippewa	37.2	54.2	6.9	23.2	62.1	12.7	40.4	50.4	7.7	25.3	61.8	10.8
Menominee	32.6	57.0	9.7	22.8	63.8	12.6	41.2	49.3	7.5	24.7	63.9	9.3
Ottawa	36.2	52.7	10.2	23.8	61.4	14.0	41.9	46.8	10.4	23.2	58.6	15.1
Potawatomi	40.0	48.3	10.4	24.2	64.2	10.8	38.9	52.1	8.4	24.8	66.1	7.6
Apache	24.2	63.4	8.2	13.9	62.3	20.2	30.7	59.1	8.7	16.7	67.8	14.2
Navaho	29.8	64.4	3.9	15.1	69.8	11.4	34.5	60.1	4.5	21.1	63.6	13.7
Iroquois	37.6	52.3	7.9	25.8	59.8	11.9	38.7	51.1	8.0	26.3	60.2	11.0
Cherokee	38.2	55.8	4.7	26.3	62.0	10.5	40.5	53.6	4.4	27.6	59.9	10.1
Keresans	35.9	53.6	10.4	22.8	63.5	13.5	39.3	47.4	12.8	30.5	59.5	9.6
Chickasaw	36.3	57.1	5.0	25.9	60.0	12.6	39.0	54.1	5.1	30.9	53.4	13.1
Choctaw	33.2	59.1	6.3	22.8	62.9	12.6	38.8	54.6	4.9	27.9	57.6	12.5
Creek	32.6	60.4	6.2	22.7	61.4	14.9	35.7	55.9	6.0	27.7	56.7	13.0
Seminole	32.7	58.5	6.9	22.1	62.8	13.8	35.6	58.9	5.1	27.3	57.0	14.2
Papago	30.7	60.7	5.4	23.5	66.2	7.6	36.7	52.4	10.3	30.7	56.3	12.3
Pima	30.2	59.3	10.1	19.6	66.2	13.9	32.7	56.4	10.3	25.2	62.7	11.3
Klamath and Modoc	38.6	51.3	9.1	19.9	52.4	26.5	43.6	44.7	9.1	20.8	57.9	17.5
Shahaptians	26.1	61.9	8.0	15.6	61.4	19.9	30.7	58.1	7.2	18.8	58.8	18.4
Comanche	23.4	68.5	7.8	14.3	65.1	19.3	28.5	65.4	4.3	25.9	61.0	11.6
Hopi	26.4	56.5	10.3	16.2	66.9	10.0	29.8	57.8	11.2	26.5	65.4	7.2

[Continued]

★ 94 ★

Marital Status of American Indians Age 15 Years Old and Older, by Selected Tribe and Sex, 1910 and 1930

[Continued]

Tribe	1910						1930					
	Male			Female			Male			Female		
	Single	Married	Widowed	Single	Married	Widowed	Single	Married	Widowed	Single	Married	Widowed
Shoshoni	24.9	63.4	8.4	12.6	68.8	15.9	31.8	54.4	11.4	18.8	62.5	16.3
Ute	25.3	59.0	12.5	9.3	73.0	14.8	27.1	60.0	11.1	15.0	72.0	12.2
Crow	21.7	67.9	9.2	13.6	69.0	16.8	25.2	63.4	6.9	18.1	68.8	10.2
Omaha	30.8	63.1	6.1	15.5	70.7	13.9	30.4	59.1	10.1	22.3	64.9	12.5
Osage	29.9	64.0	3.9	23.1	67.0	8.8	28.0	65.3	2.9	19.7	66.8	9.6
Dakota	29.8	63.4	5.1	19.9	66.0	12.5	32.6	58.3	7.4	22.1	65.1	11.1
Assiniboine	26.4	69.8	3.5	13.0	74.2	12.1	31.6	57.9	8.6	20.6	66.8	10.3
Winnebago	30.9	60.5	6.0	21.6	63.4	12.9	38.1	54.3	6.5	30.2	54.5	12.1
Tanoans	31.0	57.2	10.5	18.5	68.6	12.1	36.7	50.2	11.7	26.7	60.6	11.3
Yuma	30.6	57.4	9.0	26.4	58.5	11.3	40.4	48.1	10.5	23.0	60.9	13.6

Source: Truesdell, Dr. Leon E. U.S. Department of Commerce. Bureau of the Census. Fifteenth Census of the United States: 1930, *The Indian Population of the United States and Alaska.* Washington, DC: U.S. Government Printing Office, 1937, p. 121.

★ 95 ★

Marriage

Marital Status of American Indian Females 15 Years Old and Older, by Linguistic Stock and Tribe, 1910: A - Sa

Data are shown for tribes having 200 or more members.

Linguistic stock and tribe	Indian females 15 years of age and over: 1910								
	Total	Single		Married		Widowed		Divorced	Marital condition not reported
		Number	Percent	Number	Percent	Number	Percent		
Algonquian stock	11,974	2,653	22.2	7,570	63.2	1,530	12.8	140	81
Arapaho	437	33	7.6	315	72.1	65	14.9	1	23
Cheyenne	1,107	187	16.9	758	68.5	135	12.2	24	3
Chippewa	5,830	1,353	23.2	3,620	62.1	738	12.7	79	40
Cree	126	33	26.2	79	62.7	11	8.7	1	2
Delaware	252	64	25.4	142	56.3	42	16.7	4	-
Gros Ventres	154	26	16.9	108	70.1	18	11.7	2	-
Kickapoo	97	16	16.5	66	68.0	13	13.4	-	2
Mashpee	63	17	27.0	35	55.6	10	15.9	1	-
Menominee	356	81	22.8	227	63.8	45	12.6	3	-
Miami	60	23	38.3	27	45.0	10	16.7	-	-
Ottawa	821	195	23.8	504	61.4	115	14.0	6	1
Passamaquoddy	126	29	23.0	78	61.9	19	15.1	-	-
Penobscot	97	28	28.9	58	59.8	9	9.3	2	-
Piegan	649	113	17.4	461	71.0	65	10.0	3	7
Potawatomi	590	143	24.2	379	64.2	64	10.8	4	-
Sauk and Fox	199	42	21.1	128	64.3	28	14.1	-	1
Shawnee	386	98	25.4	227	58.8	56	14.5	5	-
Stockbridges	156	33	21.2	96	61.5	24	15.4	2	1

[Continued]

★ 95 ★

Marital Status of American Indian Females 15 Years Old and Older, by Linguistic Stock and Tribe, 1910: A - Sa
[Continued]

Linguistic stock and tribe	Indian females 15 years of age and over: 1910								
	Total	Single		Married		Widowed		Divorced	Marital condition not reported
		Number	Percent	Number	Percent	Number	Percent		
Athapaskan stock	8,446	1,297	15.4	5,692	67.4	1,165	13.8	237	55
Apache	1,529	189	12.4	987	64.6	300	19.6	43	10
Hupa	218	63	28.9	119	54.6	35	16.1	-	1
Jicarilla Apache	221	49	22.2	127	57.5	34	15.4	10	1
Mescalero Apache	157	27	17.2	75	47.8	52	33.1	3	-
Navajo	5,940	897	15.1	4,148	69.8	680	11.4	174	41
Rogue River	110	17	15.5	67	60.9	21	19.1	4	1
Wailaki	74	17	23.0	46	62.2	11	14.9	-	-
Caddoan stock	566	132	23.3	353	62.4	76	13.4	4	1
Arikara	140	38	27.1	90	64.3	10	7.1	1	1
Caddo	110	21	19.1	72	65.5	16	14.5	1	-
Pawnee	212	49	23.1	129	60.8	32	15.1	2	-
Wichita	99	24	24.2	57	57.6	18	18.2	-	-
Chimakuan stock	109	9	8.3	81	74.3	17	15.6	2	-
Quileute	93	8	8.6	71	76.3	14	15.1	-	-
Chinookan stock	275	48	17.5	176	64.0	50	18.2	-	1
Chinook	75	15	20.0	50	66.7	10	13.3	-	-
Wasco	82	16	19.5	46	56.1	20	24.4	-	-
Wishram	98	15	15.3	66	67.3	16	16.3	-	1
Croatan group	1,624	467	28.8	1,010	62.2	141	8.7	1	5
Croatan	1,624	467	28.8	1,010	62.2	141	8.7	1	5
Iroquoian stock	10,132	2,658	26.2	6,225	61.4	1,096	10.8	96	57
Cherokee	7,741	2,036	26.3	4,797	62.0	814	10.5	52	42
Mohawk	131	25	19.1	91	69.5	12	9.2	1	2
Oneida	682	155	22.7	444	65.1	67	9.8	15	1
Onondaga	113	34	30.1	58	51.3	21	18.6	-	-
St. Regis	319	105	32.0	181	56.7	28	8.8	-	5
Seneca	903	219	24.3	527	58.4	126	14.0	27	4
Tuscarora	114	36	31.6	62	54.4	15	13.2	1	-
Wyandot	87	28	32.2	51	58.6	8	9.2	-	-
Karok stock	233	51	21.9	141	60.5	38	16.3	2	1
Orleans	233	51	21.9	141	60.5	38	16.3	2	1
Keresan stock	1,154	263	22.8	733	63.5	156	13.5	2	-
Acoma	214	45	21.0	132	61.7	35	16.4	2	-
Cochiti	74	9	12.2	53	71.6	12	16.2	-	-

[Continued]

★ 95 ★

Marital Status of American Indian Females 15 Years Old and Older, by Linguistic Stock and Tribe, 1910: A - Sa
[Continued]

Linguistic stock and tribe	Indian females 15 years of age and over: 1910								
	Total	Single		Married		Widowed		Divorced	Marital condition not reported
		Number	Percent	Number	Percent	Number	Percent		
Laguna	418	109	26.1	254	60.8	55	13.2	-	-
San Felipe	135	29	21.5	85	63.0	21	15.6	-	-
Santa Ana	47	8	[1]	34	[1]	5	[1]	-	-
Santo Domingo	232	56	24.1	154	66.4	22	9.5		-
Kiowan stock	314	31	9.9	251	79.9	27	8.6	1	4
Kiowa	314	31	9.9	251	79.9	27	8.6	1	4
Kutenaian stock	154	18	11.7	116	75.3	20	13.0	-	-
Kutenai	154	18	11.7	116	75.3	20	13.0	-	-
Lutuamian stock	332	66	19.9	174	52.4	88	26.5	4	-
Klamath	240	50	20.8	130	54.2	60	25.0	-	-
Modoc	92	16	17.4	44	47.8	28	30.4	4	-
Maidu stock	316	62	19.6	195	61.7	56	17.7	1	2
Maidu	316	62	19.6	195	61.7	56	17.7	1	2
Miwok stock	236	51	21.6	130	55.1	50	21.2	2	3
Miwok	229	47	20.5	127	55.5	50	21.8	2	3
Muskhogean stock	7,606	1,761	23.2	4,721	62.1	1,013	13.3	70	41
Alibamu	85	26	30.6	46	54.1	13	15.3	-	-
Chickasaw	1,012	262	25.9	607	60.0	128	12.6	7	8
Choctaw	3,995	912	22.8	2,511	62.9	504	12.6	40	28
Creek	1,994	445	22.3	1,229	61.6	299	15.0	17	4
Seminole	494	109	22.1	310	62.8	68	13.8	6	1
Piman stock	2,440	515	21.1	1,633	66.9	259	10.6	6	27
Papago	1,087	255	23.5	720	66.2	83	7.6	2	27
Pima	1,212	238	19.6	802	66.2	168	13.9	4	-
Yaqui	129	19	14.7	103	79.8	7	5.4	-	-
Pomo stock	395	71	18.0	237	60.0	72	18.2	11	4
Pomo	260	46	17.7	154	59.2	48	18.5	10	2
Salishan stock	2,351	387	16.5	1,545	65.7	388	16.5	16	15
Chehalis	69	13	18.8	45	65.2	8	11.6	3	-
Clallam	102	15	14.7	76	74.5	8	7.8	2	1
Coeur d'Alene	85	11	12.9	64	75..3	10	11.8	-	-
Columbia	118	15	12.7	73	61.9	25	21.2	1	4
Colville	237	48	20.3	149	62.9	37	15.6	2	1

[Continued]

★ 95 ★

Marital Status of American Indian Females 15 Years Old and Older, by Linguistic Stock and Tribe, 1910: A - Sa
[Continued]

Linguistic stock and tribe	Indian females 15 years of age and over: 1910								
	Total	Single		Married		Widowed		Divorced	Marital condition not reported
		Number	Percent	Number	Percent	Number	Percent		
Flathead	134	24	17.9	90	67.2	19	14.2	1	-
Kalispel	189	24	12.7	127	67.2	37	19.6	1	-
Lummi	70	15	21.4	50	71.4	4	5.7	-	1
Okinagan	92	16	17.4	57	62.0	19	20.7	-	-
Puyallup	97	30	30.9	48	49.5	18	18.6	1	-
Quinaielt	86	9	10.5	65	75.6	12	14.0	-	-
Sanpoil	87	16	18.4	51	58.6	20	23.0	-	-
Snohomish	190	29	15.3	131	68.9	24	12.6	-	6
Spokan	228	45	19.7	146	64.0	35	15.4	1	1
Suquamish	83	15	18.1	54	65.1	12	14.5	2	-
Swinomish	102	12	11.8	69	67.6	21	20.6	-	-

Source: U.S. Bureau of the Census. *Indian Population in the United States and Alaska, 1910.* Washington, DC: United States Government Printing Office, 1915, pp. 165-167. *Notes:* A dash (-) represents zero. 1. Percentages are not shown where base is less than 50.

★ 96 ★

Marriage

Marital Status of American Indian Females 15 Years Old and Older, by Linguistic Stock and Tribe, 1910: Sh - Z

Data are shown for tribes having 200 or more members.

Linguistic stock and tribe	Indian females 15 years of age and over: 1910								
	Total	Single		Married		Widowed		Divorced	Marital condition not reported
		Number	Percent	Number	Percent	Number	Percent		
Shahaptian stock	1,594	248	15.6	978	61.4	318	19.9	30	20
Klikitat	162	31	19.1	96	59.3	29	17.9	2	4
Nez Perces	447	62	13.9	279	62.4	88	19.7	10	8
Umatilla	114	13	11.4	55	48.2	38	33.3	6	2
Wallawalla	116	24	20.7	75	64.7	13	11.2	4	-
Warm Springs	193	22	11.4	131	67.9	40	20.7	-	-
Yakima	501	87	17.4	308	61.5	93	18.6	8	5
Shastan stock	537	123	22.9	311	57.9	92	17.1	6	5
Hat Creek	85	9	10.2	62	72.9	13	15.3	1	-
Pit River	337	75	22.3	206	61.1	47	13.9	4	5
Shasta	115	39	33.9	43	37.4	32	27.8	1	-

[Continued]

★ 96 ★

Marital Status of American Indian Females 15 Years Old and Older, by Linguistic Stock and Tribe, 1910: Sh - Z

[Continued]

Linguistic stock and tribe	Indian females 15 years of age and over: 1910							Divorced	Marital condition not reported
	Total	Single		Married		Widowed			
		Number	Percent	Number	Percent	Number	Percent		
Shoshonean stock	5,440	806	14.8	3,598	66.1	852	15.7	94	90
Bannock	148	22	14.9	99	66.9	25	16.9	2	-
Chemehuevi	112	8	7.1	76	67.9	26	23.2	1	1
Comanche	384	55	14.3	250	65.1	74	19.3	4	1
Hopi	538	87	16.2	360	66.9	54	10.0	37	-
Kawia	226	49	21.7	142	62.8	29	12.8	1	5
Mono	505	90	17.8	299	59.2	94	18.6	14	8
Paiute	238	39	16.4	157	66.0	40	16.8	2	-
Paviotso	1,118	143	12.8	750	67.1	173	15.5	5	47
San Luiseno	155	66	42.6	65	41.9	22	14.2	2	-
Shoshoni	1,274	161	12.6	876	68.8	202	15.9	16	19
Ute	634	59	9.3	463	73.0	94	14.8	9	9
Siouan stock	10,509	2,062	19.6	6,976	66.4	1,315	12.5	99	57
Assiniboine	414	54	13.0	307	74.2	50	12.1	2	1
Crow	626	85	13.6	432	69.0	105	16.8	2	2
Hidatsa	153	42	27.5	91	59.5	18	11.8	-	2
Iowa	68	19	27.9	46	67.6	3	4.4	-	-
Kansa	33	8	[1]	23	[1]	2	[1]	-	-
Mandan	73	21	28.8	35	47.9	13	17.8	-	4
Omaha	317	49	15.5	224	70.7	44	13.9	-	-
Osage	351	81	23.1	235	67.0	31	8.8	4	-
Oto	96	12	12.5	74	77.1	9	9.4	1	-
Ponca	268	70	26.1	176	65.7	20	7.5	1	1
Quapaw	64	15	23.4	38	59.4	9	14.1	1	1
Santee Sioux	471	101	21.4	303	64.3	60	12.7	5	2
Sioux	295	92	31.2	169	57.3	27	9.2	2	5
Sisseton Sioux	800	140	17.5	535	66.9	114	14.3	8	3
Teton Sioux	4,673	935	20.0	3,073	65.8	591	12.6	52	22
Brule Sioux	260	39	15.0	178	68.5	31	11.9	10	2
Hunkpapa Sioux	364	65	17.9	245	67.3	49	13.5	3	2
Minniconjou Sioux	154	31	20.1	93	60.4	29	18.8	1	-
Oglala Sioux	1,930	394	20.4	1,294	67.0	227	11.8	12	3
Sans Arc Sioux	58	11	19.0	37	63.8	10	17.2	-	-
Sihasapa	161	26	16.1	116	72.0	16	9.9	3	-
Two Kettle Sioux	75	14	18.7	53	70.7	8	10.7	-	-
Other Teton Sioux	1,671	355	21.2	1,057	63.3	221	13.2	23	15
Winnebago	588	127	21.6	373	63.4	76	12.9	9	3
Yankton Sioux	719	133	18.5	510	70.9	66	9.2	5	5
Yanktonai Sioux	470	75	16.0	312	66.4	72	15.3	6	5

[Continued]

★ 96 ★

Marital Status of American Indian Females 15 Years Old and Older, by Linguistic Stock and Tribe, 1910: Sh - Z
[Continued]

Linguistic stock and tribe	Indian females 15 years of age and over: 1910								
	Total	Single		Married		Widowed		Divorced	Marital condition not reported
		Number	Percent	Number	Percent	Number	Percent		
Tanoan stock	932	172	18.5	639	68.6	113	12.1	5	3
Isleta	305	31	10.2	211	69.2	58	19.0	5	-
Jemez	139	26	18.7	100	71.9	11	7.9	-	2
San Juan	113	22	19.5	79	69.9	11	9.7	-	1
Santa Clara	79	29	36.7	43	54.4	7	8.9	-	-
Taos	139	30	21.6	101	72.7	8	5.8	-	-
Waiilatpuan stock	107	12	11.2	52	48.6	36	33.6	7	-
Cayuse	99	11	11.1	46	46.5	36	36.4	6	-
Wakashan stock	117	15	12.8	83	70.9	19	16.2	-	-
Makah	102	14	13.7	71	69.6	17	16.7	-	-
Washoan stock	292	43	14.7	208	71.2	30	10.3	8	3
Washo	292	43	14.7	208	71.2	30	10.3	8	3
Wintun stock	217	34	15.7	157	72.4	24	11.1	2	-
Wintun	120	25	20.8	82	68.3	12	10.1	1	-
Yokuts stock	164	31	18.9	108	65.9	24	14.6	1	-
Yokuts	85	14	16.5	61	71.8	10	11.8	-	-
Yuman stock	1,272	205	16.1	850	66.8	185	14.5	17	15
Cocopa	78	18	23.1	45	57.7	14	17.9	-	1
Diegueno	209	42	20.1	127	60.8	30	14.4	1	9
Maricopa	118	21	17.8	82	69.5	15	12.7	-	-
Mohave	310	29	9.4	212	68.4	64	20.6	1	4
Walapai	123	6	4.9	103	83.7	14	11.4	-	-
Yavapai	88	10	11.4	63	71.6	10	11.4	5	-
Yuma	284	75	26.4	166	58.5	32	11.3	10	1
Yurok stock	224	35	15.6	137	61.2	51	22.8	1	-
Weitspec	224	35	15.6	137	61.2	51	22.8	1	-
Zunian stock	504	61	12.1	349	69.2	63	12.5	31	-
Zuni	504	61	12.1	349	69.2	63	12.5	31	-

Source: U.S. Bureau of the Census. *Indian Population in the United States and Alaska, 1910.* Washington, DC: U.S. Government Printing Office, 1915, pp. 165-167.
Notes: A dash (-) represents zero. 1. Percentages are not shown where base is less than 50.

★ 97 ★
Marriage

Marital Status of American Indian Males 15 Years Old and Older, by Linguistic Stock and Tribe, 1910: A - Sa

Data are shown for tribes having 200 or more members.

Linguistic stock and tribe	Indian males 15 years of age and over: 1910									
	Total	Single		Married		Widowed		Divorced	Marital condition not reported
		Number	Percent	Number	Percent	Number	Percent		
Algonquian stock	12,849	4,598	35.8	7,160	55.7	898	7.0	93	100
Arapaho	474	95	20.0	322	67.9	25	5.3	3	29
Cheyenne	1,020	262	25.7	694	68.0	56	5.5	5	3
Chippewa	6,180	2,297	37.2	3,352	54.2	426	6.9	56	49
Cree	132	63	47.7	64	48.5	5	3.8	-	-
Delaware	249	116	46.6	118	47.4	14	5.6	1	-
Gros Ventres	168	51	30.4	108	64.3	8	4.8	-	1
Kickapoo	117	27	23.1	73	62.4	16	13.7	-	1
Mashpee	81	38	46.9	34	42.0	6	7.4	3	-
Menominee	454	148	32.6	259	57.0	44	9.7	3	-
Miami	76	38	50.0	34	44.7	4	5.3	-	-
Ottawa	928	336	489	52.7	95	10.2	4	4	
Passamaquoddy	151	54	35.8	81	53.6	15	9.9	1	-
Penobscot	104	28	26.9	65	62.5	9	8.7	2	-
Piegan	639	212	33.2	408	63.8	13	2.0	2	4
Potawatomi	795	318	40.0	384	48.3	83	10.4	7	3
Sauk and Fox	245	85	34.7	139	56.7	18	7.3	-	3
Shawnee	347	133	38.3	193	55.6	20	5.8	-	1
Stockbridges	169	71	42.0	78	46.2	18	10.7	2	-
Athapaskan stock	8,258	2,393	28.9	5,270	63.6	423	5.1	79	120
Apache	1,472	349	23.7	940	63.9	118	8.0	17	48
Hupa	194	76	39.2	101	52.1	17	8.8	-	-
Jicarilla Apache	215	59	27.4	130	60.5	17	7.9	9	-
Mescalero Apache	112	28	25.0	70	62.5	13	11.6	1	-
Navajo	5,918	1,762	29.8	3,814	64.4	228	3.9	43	71
Rogue River	119	38	31.9	59	49.6	18	15.1	4	-
Wailaki	68	21	30.9	43	63.2	2	2.9	2	-
Caddoan stock	564	193	34.2	333	59.0	32	5.7	1	5
Arikara	136	40	29.4	81	59.6	10	7.4	1	4
Caddo	131	50	38.2	70	53.4	10	7.6	-	1
Pawnee	195	69	35.4	121	62.1	5	2.6	-	-
Wichita	95	32	33.7	57	60.0	6	6.3	-	-
Chimakuan stock	99	29	29.3	67	67.7	-	-	3	-
Quileute	81	23	28.4	55	67.9	-	-	3	-
Chinookan stock	289	103	35.6	161	55.7	24	8.3	-	1
Chinook	100	48	48.0	39	39.0	13	13.0	-	-
Wasco	78	21	26.9	55	70.5	1	1.3	-	1
Wishram	94	27	28.7	58	61.7	9	9.6	-	-

[Continued]

★ 97 ★

Marital Status of American Indian Males 15 Years Old and Older, by Linguistic Stock and Tribe, 1910: A - Sa

[Continued]

Linguistic stock and tribe	Indian males 15 years of age and over: 1910								
	Total	Single		Married		Widowed		Divorced	Marital condition not reported
		Number	Percent	Number	Percent	Number	Percent		
Croatan group	1,588	526	33.1	1,006	63.4	48	3.0	4	4
Croatan	1,588	526	33.1	1,006	63.4	48	3.0	4	4
Iroquoian stock	10,946	4,171	38.1	6,007	54.9	603	5.5	69	96
Cherokee	8,208	3,134	38.2	4,581	55.8	389	4.7	39	65
Mohawk	115	43	37.4	56	48.7	7	6.1	-	9
Oneida	805	299	37.1	443	55.0	47	5.8	16	-
Onondaga	121	51	42.1	60	49.6	10	8.3	-	-
St. Regis	420	173	41.2	207	49.4	28	6.7	-	12
Seneca	964	334	34.6	511	53.0	97	10.1	13	9
Tuscarora	155	72	46.5	72	46.5	11	7.1	-	-
Wyandot	109	49	45.0	52	47.7	6	5.5	1	1
Karok stock	229	100	43.7	108	47.2	20	8.7	1	-
Orleans	229	100	43.7	108	47.2	20	8.7	1	-
Keresan stock	1,340	481	35.9	718	53.6	140	10.4	1	-
Acoma	210	72	34.3	125	59.5	12	5.7	1	-
Cochiti	86	20	23.3	60	69.8	6	7.0	-	-
Laguna	462	165	35.7	254	55.0	43	9.3	-	-
San Felipe	198	86	43.4	80	40.4	32	16.2	-	-
Santa Ana	85	35	41.2	35	41.2	15	17.6	-	-
Santo Domingo	262	84	32.1	150	57.3	28	10.7	-	-
Kiowan stock	181	45	24.9	121	66.9	11	6.1	4	-
Kiowa	293	61	20.8	225	76.8	6	2.0	-	1
Kutenaian stock	181	45	24.9	121	66.9	11	6.1	4	-
Kutenai	181	45	24.9	121	66.9	11	6.1	4	-
Lutuamian stock	298	115	38.6	153	51.3	27	9.1	3	-
Klamath	213	86	40.4	108	50.7	17	8.0	2	-
Modoc	85	29	34.1	45	52.9	10	11.8	1	-
Maidu stock	364	130	35.7	179	49.2	45	12.4	7	3
Maidu	364	130	35.7	179	49.2	45	12.4	7	3
Miwok stock	220	72	32.7	117	53.2	24	10.9	2	5
Miwok	208	67	32.2	112	53.8	22	10.6	2	5
Muskhogean stock	7,745	2,587	33.4	4,582	59.2	478	6.2	41	57
Alibamu	93	39	41.9	46	49.5	8	8.6	-	-

[Continued]

★ 97 ★

Marital Status of American Indian Males 15 Years Old and Older, by Linguistic Stock and Tribe, 1910: A - Sa
[Continued]

Linguistic stock and tribe	Indian males 15 years of age and over: 1910								
	Total	Single		Married		Widowed		Divorced	Marital condition not reported
		Number	Percent	Number	Percent	Number	Percent		
Chickasaw	955	347	36.3	545	57.1	48	5.0	6	9
Choctaw	4,174	1,386	33.2	2,468	59.1	265	6.3	19	36
Creek	1,958	629	32.1	1,192	60.9	119	6.1	10	8
Seminole	535	175	32.7	313	58.5	37	6.9	6	4
Piman stock	2,715	843	31.0	1,622	59.7	208	7.7	8	34
Papago	1,143	351	30.7	694	60.7	62	5.4	2	34
Pima	1,369	413	30.2	812	59.3	138	10.1	6	-
Yaqui	189	71	37.6	111	58.7	7	3.7	-	-
Pomo stock	412	114	27.7	242	58.7	45	10.9	8	3
Pomo	269	73	27.1	162	60.2	23	8.6	8	3
Salishan stock	2,521	800	31.7	1,480	58.7	186	7.4	21	34
Chehalis	93	30	32.3	57	61.3	6	6.5	-	-
Clallam	121	42	34.7	74	61.2	3	2.5	2	-
Coeur d'Alene	102	29	28.4	70	68.6	2	2.0	1	-
Columbia	137	34	24.8	81	59.1	11	8.0	-	11
Colville	262	105	40.1	124	47.3	23	8.8	8	2
Flathead	144	54	37.5	81	56.3	8	5.6	1	-
Kalispel	191	58	30.4	119	62.3	12	6.3	2	-
Lummi	87	26	29.9	47	54.0	9	10.3	-	5
Okinagan	84	26	31.0	50	59.5	4	4.8	2	2
Puyallup	101	43	42.6	49	48.5	8	7.9	1	-
Quinaielt	92	22	23.9	62	67.4	7	7.6	1	-
Sanpoil	78	30	38.5	39	50.0	7	9.0	-	2
Snohomish	212	66	31.1	122	57.5	17	8.0	1	6
Spokan	207	52	25.1	133	64.3	21	10.1	-	1
Suquamish	95	32	33.7	58	61.1	4	4.2	1	-
Swinomish	110	29	26.4	74	67.3	5	4.5	-	2

Source: U.S. Bureau of the Census. *Indian Population in the United States and Alaska, 1910.* Washington, DC: U.S. Government Printing Office, 1915, pp. 165-167. *Notes:* A dash (-) represents zero. 1. Percentages are not shown where base is less than 50.

★ 98 ★

Marriage

Marital Status of American Indian Males 15 Years Old and Older, by Linguistic Stock and Tribe, 1910: Sh - Z

Data are shown for tribes having 200 or more members.

Linguistic stock and tribe	Indian males 15 years of age and over: 1910								
	Total	Single		Married		Widowed		Divorced	Marital condition not reported
		Number	Percent	Number	Percent	Number	Percent		
Shahaptian stock	1,392	363	26.1	861	61.9	112	8.0	33	23
Klikitat	131	35	26.7	84	64.1	5	3.8	6	1
Nez Perces	425	107	25.2	261	61.4	33	7.8	15	9
Umatilla	89	18	20.2	57	64.0	11	12.4	2	1
Wallawalla	119	45	37.8	65	54.6	8	6.7	1	-
Warm Springs	165	27	16.4	123	74.5	14	8.5	-	1
Yakima	411	120	29.2	236	57.4	39	9.5	8	8
Shastan stock	489	151	30.9	284	58.1	51	10.4	3	-
Hat Creek	86	18	20.9	58	67.4	10	11.6	-	-
Pit River	305	78	25.6	187	61.3	38	12.5	2	-
Shasta	98	55	56.1	39	39.8	3	3.1	1	-
Shoshonean stock	5,696	1,542	27.1	3,406	59.8	541	9.5	87	120
Bannock	160	54	33.8	91	56.9	13	8.1	2	-
Chemehuevi	122	28	23.0	79	64.8	15	12.3	-	-
Comanche	359	84	23.4	246	68.5	28	7.8	1	-
Hopi	651	172	26.4	368	56.5	67	10.3	43	1
Kawia	291	95	32.6	147	50.5	40	13.7	-	9
Mono	422	123	29.1	245	58.1	42	10.0	9	3
Paiute	274	82	29.9	161	58.8	26	9.5	2	3
Paviotso	1,032	243	23.5	655	63.5	70	6.8	4	60
San Luiseno	173	88	50.9	63	36.4	20	11.6	2	-
Shoshoni	1,320	329	24.9	837	63.4	111	8.4	15	28
Ute	783	198	25.3	462	59.0	98	12.5	9	16
Siouan stock	10,517	3,107	29.5	6,692	63.6	546	5.2	91	81
Assiniboine	397	105	26.4	277	69.8	14	3.5	-	1
Crow	608	132	21.7	413	67.9	56	9.2	6	1
Hidatsa	169	69	40.8	93	55.0	3	1.8	-	4
Iowa	72	22	30.6	46	63.9	2	2.8	1	1
Kansa	77	23	29.9	50	64.9	2	2.6	-	33
Mandan	67	18	26.9	39	58.2	5	7.5	-	5
Omaha	344	106	30.8	217	63.1	21	6.1	-	-
Osage	381	114	29.9	244	64.0	15	3.9	3	5
Oto	111	32	28.8	76	68.5	2	1.8	1	-
Ponca	264	84	31.8	170	64.4	9	3.4	1	-
Quapaw	58	21	36.2	33	56.9	3	5.2	-	1
Santee Sioux	470	144	30.6	298	63.4	22	4.7	5	1
Sioux	396	191	48.2	186	47.0	12	3.0	2	5
Sisseton Sioux	832	246	29.6	529	63.6	38	4.6	8	11
Teton Sioux	4,551	1,341	29.5	2,884	63.4	249	5.5	45	32

[Continued]

★ 98 ★

Marital Status of American Indian Males 15 Years Old and Older, by Linguistic Stock and Tribe, 1910: Sh - Z
[Continued]

Linguistic stock and tribe	Indian males 15 years of age and over: 1910								
	Total	Single		Married		Widowed		Divorced	Marital condition not reported
		Number	Percent	Number	Percent	Number	Percent		
Brule Sioux	268	66	24.6	183	68.3	13	4.9	3	3
Hunkpapa Sioux	354	102	28.8	236	66.7	16	4.5	-	-
Minniconjou Sioux	130	38	29.2	76	58.5	15	11.5	1	-
Oglala Sioux	1,866	575	30.8	1,187	63.6	89	4.8	5	10
Sans Arc Sioux	61	22	36.1	37	60.7	1	1.6	1	-
Sihasapa	173	53	30.6	109	63.0	9	5.2	2	-
Two Kettle Sioux	112	33	29.5	71	63.4	6	5.4	2	-
Other Teton Sioux	1,587	452	28.5	985	62.1	100	6.3	31	19
Winnebago	602	186	30.9	364	60.5	36	6.0	9	7
Yankton Sioux	660	162	24.5	458	69.4	35	5.3	2	3
Yanktonai Sioux	421	100	23.8	292	69.4	19	4.5	6	4
Tanoan stock	1,120	347	31.0	641	57.2	118	10.5	7	7
Isleta	352	104	29.5	213	60.5	29	8.2	6	-
Jemez	189	55	29.1	105	55.6	23	12.2	-	6
San Juan	138	44	31.9	76	55.1	17	12.3	-	1
Santa Clara	97	39	40.2	47	48.5	10	10.3	1	-
Taos	169	44	26.0	106	62.7	19	11.2	-	-
Waiilatpuan stock	99	23	23.2	61	61.6	12	12.1	3	-
Cayuse	87	20	23.0	56	64.4	8	9.2	3	-
Wakashan stock	130	28	21.5	94	72.3	8	6.2	-	-
Makah	122	27	22.1	87	71.3	8	6.6	-	-
Washoan stock	295	77	26.1	187	63.4	22	7.5	3	6
Washo	295	77	26.1	187	63.4	22	7.5	3	6
Wintun stock	261	86	33.0	130	49.8	43	16.5	2	-
Wintun	142	54	38.0	61	43.0	25	17.6	2	-
Yokuts stock	192	65	33.9	107	55.7	20	10.4	-	-
Yokuts	117	38	32.5	65	55.6	14	12.0	-	-
Yuman stock	1,561	455	29.1	875	56.1	160	10.2	16	55
Cocopa	94	35	37.2	40	42.6	13	13.8	-	6
Diegueno	267	98	36.7	131	49.1	26	9.7	2	10
Maricopa	127	33	26.0	75	59.1	18	14.2	-	1
Mohave	397	97	24.4	223	56.2	40	10.1	2	35
Walapai	165	49	29.7	101	61.2	13	7.9	1	1
Yavapai	99	22	22.2	67	67.7	9	9.1	1	-
Yuma	324	99	30.6	186	57.4	29	9.0	10	-

[Continued]

★ 98 ★

Marital Status of American Indian Males 15 Years Old and Older, by Linguistic Stock and Tribe, 1910: Sh - Z

[Continued]

Linguistic stock and tribe	Indian males 15 years of age and over: 1910								Divorced	Marital condition not reported
	Total	Single		Married		Widowed				
		Number	Percent	Number	Percent	Number	Percent		
Yurok stock	213	68	31.9	115	54.0	30	14.1	-	-
Weitspec	213	68	31.9	115	54.0	30	14.1	-	-
Zunian stock	563	144	25.6	345	61.3	57	10.1	17	-
Zuni	563	144	25.6	345	61.3	57	10.1	17	-

Source: U.S. Bureau of the Census. *Indian Population in the United States and Alaska, 1910.* Washington, DC: U.S. Government Printing Office, 1915, pp. 165-167. *Notes:* A dash (-) represents zero. 1. Percentages are not shown where base is less than 50.

U.S. Government

★ 99 ★

BIA Employees, 1852-1934

The total number of Bureau of Indian Affairs employees is shown for selected years.

Date	Number of employees
1852	108
1888	1,725
1911	6,000
1933	5,000
1934	12,000

Source: U.S. Department of the Interior. Bureau of Indian Affairs. Albuquerque Area Office Division of Administration. *Fact Book.* February 1989, p. 2. Primary source: Theodore W. Taylor, "The Regional Organization of the Bureau of Indian Affairs." (Ph.D. dissertation, Harvard University), December 1959, p. 98.

★ 100 ★

U.S. Government

Federal Restoration of Terminated American Indian Tribes

Tribe or band	State	Population	Acres	Termination statute	Date of act	Effective date	Current status
Menominee	Wisconsin	3,270	233,881	68 stat. 250	1954	1961	Restored
Klamath	Oregon	2,133	862,662	68 stat. 718	1954	1961	Restored
Western Oregon[1] (61 tribes and bands)	Oregon	2,081	3,158	68 stat. 724	1954	1956	Restored[2]
Alabama-Coushatta	Texas	450	3,200	68 stat. 768	1954	1955	Restored
Mixed blood Utes	Utah	490	211,430	68 stat. 868	1954	1961	Terminated
Southern Paiute	Utah	232	42,839	68 stat. 1099	1954	1957	Restored
Lower Lake Rancheria	California	unknown	unknown	70 stat. 58	1956	1956	Restored
Wyandotte	Oklahoma	1,157	94	70 stat. 893	1956	1959	Restored
Peoria	Oklahoma	640	unknown	70 stat. 937	1956	1959	Restored
Ottawa	Oklahoma	630	0	70 stat. 963	1957	1959	Restored
Coyote Valley Ranch	California	unknown	unknown	71 stat. 283	1957	1957	Restored
California Rancherias[1] (37-38 rancherias)	California	1,107	4,315	72 stat. 619	1958	1961-70	Restored[2]
Catawba	S. Carolina	631	3,388	73 stat. 502	1959	1962	Pending
Ponca	Nebraska	442	834	76 stat. 429	1962	1966	Restored
Total		13,263	1,365,801				

Source: Grobsmith, Elizabeth S. and Beth R. Ritter, "The Ponca Tribe of Nebraska: the process of restoration of a federally terminated tribe," *Human Organization* Vol. 51, No. 1, 1992, p. 4. Primary source: Prucha (1984:1048), Wilkinson & Biggs (1977:151), Mills (1989:4), Goodman (1990), Schmidt (1990): personal communication. *Notes:* 1. Figures are aggregates. 2. Those tribes seeking restoration have been restored.

★ 101 ★

U.S. Government

House and Senate Committees: 1838-1920

Committees having jurisdiction over Indian affairs are shown by year.

Years	Senate	House
1838		Select Committee on Indian Fighters
1878	Joint Committee on Transfer of the Indian Bureau	
1879-1880	Select Committee to Examine into Removal of Northern Cheyennes	
1881	Select Committee to Examine into Circumstances Connected With Removal of Northern Cheyennes from the Sioux Reservation to the Indian Territory	

[Continued]

★ 101 ★

House and Senate Committees: 1838-1920
[Continued]

Years	Senate	House
1836-1892	Select Committee on Indian Traders	Select Committee on Expenditures for the Indians and Yellowstone Park
1888-1892	Select Committee on Indian Traders	Select Committee on Indian Depredation Claims (1888-1891)
	Select Committee on the Five Civilized Tribes	
1893-1908	Select Committee to Investigate Trespassers on Indian (Cherokee) Lands	
	Select Committee on the Five Civilized Tribes	
	Standing Committee on Indian Depredations	
1909-1920	Standing Committee on Indian Depredations	
	Standing Committee on the Five Civilized Tribes	
	Standing Committee to Investigate Trespassers on Indian Lands	

Source: Jones, Richard. Congressional Research Service. *American Indian Policy: Background, Nature, History, Current Issues, Future Trends, Congressional Research Service Report No. 87227.* Washington, DC: CRS, 1980, p. 80.

★ 102 ★
U.S. Government

Land Units for Which Federal Trusteeship Had Been Terminated by Acts of Congress, 1963 - I

Land unit, jurisdiction	Principal Tribe		Public Law	Statute Ref.	Effective
	Name	Population			
California Sacramento Area Office					
Lower Lake	Pomo	8	84-443	(70 Stat. 58)	Mar 2, 1956
Coyote Valley	Pomo	30	85-91	(71 Stat. 283)	Jul 10, 1957
Laguna	Diegueno	0	80-335	(61 Stat. 731)	Feb 4, 1985
Buena Vista	Me-Wuk	5	85-671	(72 Stat. 619)	Apr 11, 1961
Cache Creek	Pomo	4	85-671	(72 Stat. 619)	do

[Continued]

★ 102 ★

Land Units for Which Federal Trusteeship Had Been Terminated by Acts of Congress, 1963 - I

[Continued]

Land unit, jurisdiction	Principal Tribe		Public Law	Statute Ref.	Effective
	Name	Population			
Mark West	Pomo	0	85-671	(72 Stat. 619)	do
Paskenta	Wintun	6	85-671	(72 Stat. 619)	do
Ruffeys	Ruffy	0	85-671	(72 Stat. 619)	do
Strawberry Valley	Maidu	2	85-671	(72 Stat. 619)	do
Alexander Valley	Wappo	12	85-671	(72 Stat. 619)	Aug 1, 1961
Chicken Ranch	Me-Wuk	16	86-671	(72 Stat. 619)	do
Lytton	Pomo	33	85-671	(72 Stat. 619)	do
Mooretown	Maidu	4	85-671	(72 Stat. 619)	do
Potter Valley	Pomo	11	85-671	(72 Stat. 619)	do
Redwood Valley	Pomo	27	85-671	(72 Stat. 619)	do
Table Bluff	Miami	48	85-671	(72 Stat. 619)	do
Redding	Clear Creek (mixed)	44	85-671	(72 Stat. 619)	Prior to Jun 30, 1962[1]
North Fork	Momo	1	85-671	(72 Stat. 619)	do
Scotts Valley	Pomo	45	85-671	(72 Stat. 619)	do
Table Mountain	Chukchansi	51	85-671	(72 Stat. 619)	do
Wilton	Me-Wuk	32	85-671	(72 Stat. 619)	do
Auburn	Maidu	83	85-671	(72 Stat. 619)	do
Guidiville	Pomo	21	85-671	(72 Stat. 619)	do
Nevada City	Maidu	2	85-671	(72 Stat. 619)	do
Picayunne	Chukchansi	11	85-671	(72 Stat. 619)	do
Upper Lake	Pomo	64	85-671	(72 Stat. 619)	do
Elk Valley	Cresent City	30	85-671	(72 Stat. 619)	do
Oklahoma Muskogee Area Office					
Wyandotte (also Kans)	Wyandotte[2]	423	84-887	(70 Stat. 893)	Aug 1, 1959
Peoria	Peoria[3]	230	84-921	(70 Stat. 937)	Aug 2, 1959
Ottawa	Ottawa	244	84-943	(70 Stat. 963)	Aug 13, 1961
Modoc (also Mo)	Modoc[4]	29	83-587	(68 Stat. 718)	Aug 13, 1961
Oregon Portland Area Office					
Grand Ronde & Siletz	Clackamas, Umpqua, Rogue River, and Klamath	2,100	83-588	(68 Stat. 724)	Aug 13, 1956

[Continued]

★ 102 ★

Land Units for Which Federal Trusteeship Had Been Terminated by Acts of Congress, 1963 - I

[Continued]

Land unit, jurisdiction	Principal Tribe		Public Law	Statute Ref.	Effective
	Name	Population			
Western Oregon Public Domain Allotments (Includes Coos Bay)	Kusa, Rogue River, Klamath, and Umpqua	803	83-588	(68 Stat. 724)	Aug 13, 1956
Klamath	Klamath, Modoc, and Snake[4]	1,185	83-587 85-132 85-731 86-247	(68 Stat. 718) (71 Stat. 347) (72 Stat. 816) (73 Stat. 477)	Aug 13, 1961
South Carolina Central Office Catawba	Catawba Roll	353 631	86-322	(73 Stat. 592)	Jul 2, 1962
Texas Anadarko Area Office Alabama-Coushatta	Alabama-Coushatta[5]	385	83-627	(68 Stat. 768)	Jul 1, 1955
Utah Phoenix Area Office Cedar City	Paiute	28	83-762	(68 Stat. 1099)	Mar 1, 1957
Indian Peaks	Paiute	26	83-762	(68 Stat. 1099)	do
Kanosh	Paiute	42	83-762	(68 Stat. 1099)	do
Koosharem	Paiute	34	83-762	(68 Stat. 1099)	do
Shivwitz	Paiute	130	83-762	(68 Stat. 1099)	do
Uintah and Ouray	Ute (mixed blood only) (Affiliated Ute Citizens of Ouray)[6]	269	83-671	(68 Stat. 868)	Aug 27, 1961

[Continued]

★ 102 ★

Land Units for Which Federal Trusteeship Had Been Terminated by Acts of Congress, 1963 - I

[Continued]

Land unit, jurisdiction	Principal Tribe		Public Law	Statute Ref.	Effective
	Name	Population			
Wisconsin Minneapolis Area Office Menominee	Menominee	2,221	83-399 84-715 84-718 85-488 86-733	(68 Stat. 250) (70 Stat. 544) (70 Stat. 549) (72 Stat. 290) (74 Stat. 867)	Apr 30, 1961

Source: United States Department of Interior. Bureau of Indian Affairs. *U.S. Indian Population (1962) and Land (1963).* Washington, DC: U.S. Government Printing Office, November 1963, pp. 31-33. *Notes:* 1. Land trusteeship terminated prior to June 30, 1962. Group termination effective on date of proclamation. Proclamation delayed to secure additions to sanitary facilities. 2. Termination of relations with tribal organization delayed by search for trustee to dispose of Wyandotte (Huron) Cemetery in Kansas City. 3. Termination of relations with tribal organization effective when claims pending before the Indian Claims Commission and the United States Court of Claims are settled. 4. Supervision over claims attorney contracts. 5. Tribal members are still eligible for Federal educational and medical aid. 6. Subject to distribution of unadjudicated and unliquidated claims and gas mineral rights.

★ 103 ★

U.S. Government

Land Units for Which Federal Trusteeship Had Been Terminated by Acts of Congress, 1963 - II

Land unit	Public law	Statute ref.	Effective
California			
Big Sandy (Auberry)	85-671	(72 Stat. 619)	
Big Valley (Mission)	85-671	(72 Stat. 619)	
Blue Lake	85-671	(72 Stat. 619)	
Chico (Meechupta)	85-671	(72 Stat. 619)	
Cloverdale	85-671	(72 Stat. 619)	
Cold Springs	85-671	(72 Stat. 619)	
Graton	85-671	(72 Stat. 619)	
Greenville	85-671	(72 Stat. 619)	Not later than three years after approval of each plan
Hopland	85-671	(72 Stat. 619)	
Indian Ranch	85-671	(72 Stat. 619)	
Middletown	85-671	(72 Stat. 619)	
Pinoleville	85-671	(72 Stat. 619)	
Quartz Valley	85-671	(72 Stat. 619)	
Robinson	85-671	(72 Stat. 619)	
Rohnerville	85-671	(72 Stat. 619)	
Smith River	85-671	(72 Stat. 619)	

[Continued]

★ 103 ★

Land Units for Which Federal Trusteeship Had Been Terminated by Acts of Congress, 1963 - II

[Continued]

Land unit	Public law	Statute ref.	Effective
Nebraska			
Ponca	87-629[1]	(76 Stat. 429)	Sept 5, 1965
Oklahoma			
Choctaw	86-192	(72 Stat. 420)	Aug 25, 1962
(tribal land only)	87-609[2]	(76 Stat. 405)	Aug 25, 1962

Source: United States Department of Interior. Bureau of Indian Affairs. *U.S. Indian Population (1962) and Land (1963).* Washington, DC: U.S. Government Printing Office, November 1963, pp. 36. *Notes:* 1. Act of Sept. 5, 1962. 2. Act of Aug. 24, 1962.

★ 104 ★

U.S. Government

Land Units for Which Federal Trusteeship Had Been Terminated by Other Means Than an Act of Congress, 1963

Other means include transfers, expired of restrictions, or disposal by fee patent.

State, jurisdiction, land unit	Principal tribe		Page Reference House Report 2503, 82nd Congress	Other references
	Name	Population		
Arizona				
Phoenix Area Office				
City of Tucson (lots)	Papago	0	-	Reported F.Y. 1960
New York				
Central Office				
Allegany	Seneca	1,110	p. 688	[1]
Cattaraugus	Seneca & Cayuga	2,464	p. 690	Public Law 80-881
Oil Springs	Seneca	0	p. 703	(62 Stat. 1224)
Oneida	Oneida	369	p. 703	Jul 2, 1948 (Legal Jurisdiction)
Onondaga	Onondaga	744	p. 703	
St. Regis	Mohawk	1,865	p. 708	Public Law 81-690
Tonawanda	Seneca	688	p. 712	(64 Stat. 442)
Tuscarora	Tuscarora	452	p. 713	Aug 14, 1950 (Lease income)
				Public Law 81-

[Continued]

★ 104 ★

Land Units for Which Federal Trusteeship Had Been Terminated by Other Means Than an Act of Congress, 1963

[Continued]

State, jurisdiction, land unit	Principal tribe		Page Reference House Report 2503, 82nd Congress	Other references
	Name	Population		
				785 (64 Stat. 845) Sept 13, 1950
Pennsylvania Central Office Cornplanter	Seneca[1]	30	p. 692	
Louisiana Muskogee Area Office Coushatta	Coushatta	200	p. 1,248	None
Michigan Minneapolis Area Office Scattered Ottawa and Chippewa (Beaver, Hog and Fox Islands, etc.)	Ottawa & Chippewa	3,895	p. 771 p. 1,175 p. 688 p. 695	None
Minnesota Minneapolis Area Office Pipestone Wabasha Community	Sioux Sioux	103 0	p. 705 p. 714 p. 983	None None
Nevada Phoenix Area Office Austin	Shoshone	139	p. 734 p. 1,135	None
Beowawe	Shoshone	61	p. 1,135	None
Carlin	Shoshone	13	p. 743 p. 1,135	None
Eureka	Shoshone	23	p. 804 p. 1,135	None
Wells	Shoshone	52	p. 968 p. 1,017 p. 1,135	None

Source: U.S. Department of Interior. Bureau of Indian Affairs. *U.S. Indian Population (1962) and Land (1963).* Washington, DC: U.S. Government Printing Office, November 1963, pp. 34-35. *Notes:* A dash (-) means not applicable 1. Still subject to Acts of November 11, 1794 (Annual payment of $2,700 in cloth), and of February 19, 1831 (Annual cash payment of $6,000), and the provision of legal services.

Chapter 2

DEMOGRAPHICS

Population

★ 105 ★

U.S. Population Distribution, by Race/Ethnicity, 1990

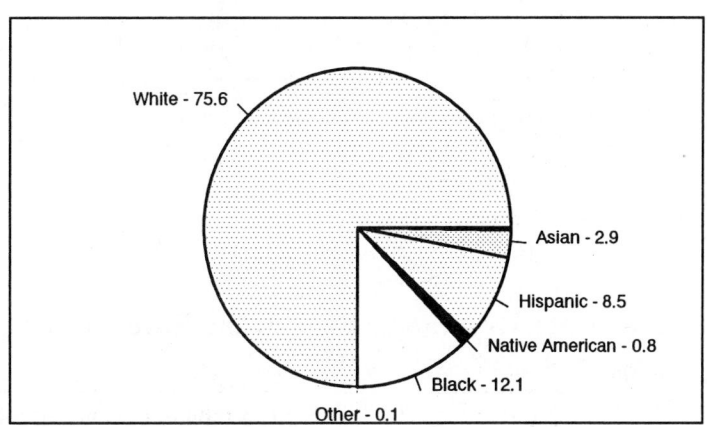

Race and ethnicity	Percent
White	75.6
Black	12.1
Hispanic[1]	8.5
Asian	2.9
Native American	0.8
Other	0.1

Source: Usdansky, Margaret L. "USA's decade of change: 'diverse' fits nation better than 'normal'." *USA TODAY* (29 May 1992), p. 1A. Primary source: U.S. Census Bureau. *Note:* 1. Persons of Hispanic origin may be of any race.

★ 106 ★
Population

Census Undercounts of Minorities, 1990

Blacks - 31,505	
Hispanics - 23,591	
Asians - 7,504	
Native Americans - 1,977	

Chart shows data from column 2.

Figures show estimates of population undercounts by the U.S. Census Bureau in 1990. Population counts directly affect the number of legislative seats in a district and impact the amount of federal funding available to geographic locations.

[Numbers shown in thousands]

Group	Official count (000)	Census estimate (000)	Undercount (percent)
Blacks	29,986	31,505	4.8
Hispanics[1]	22,354	23,591	5.2
Asians	7,273	7,504	3.1
Native Americans	1,878	1,977	5.0

Source: Welch, William M. "Census ruling may remap politics." *USA TODAY* (10 August 1994), p. 3A. Primary source: U.S. Bureau of the Census. *Note:* 1. Hispanics may be of any race.

★ 107 ★
Population

Population, by State, Geographic Region, and Race/Ethnicity, 1990

Data are shown in thousands, as of April 1.

Region, division, and state	Total[1]	White	Black	American Indian, Eskimo, Aleut				Asian/ Pacific Islander	Hispanic[2]
				Total	American Indian	Eskimo	Aleut		
United States	248,710	199,686	29,986	1,959	1,878	57	24	7,274	22,354
Northeast	50,809	42,069	5,613	125	122	2	2	1,335	3,754
New England	13,207	12,033	628	33	32	(Z)	(Z)	232	568
Maine	1,228	1,208	5	6	6	(Z)	(Z)	7	7
New Hampshire	1,109	1,087	7	2	2	(Z)	(Z)	9	11
Vermont	563	555	2	2	2	(Z)	(Z)	3	4
Massachusetts	6,016	5,405	300	12	12	(Z)	(Z)	143	288
Rhode Island	1,003	917	39	4	4	(Z)	(Z)	18	46
Connecticut	3,287	2,859	274	7	6	(Z)	(Z)	51	213
Middle Atlantic	37,602	30,036	4,986	92	90	1	2	1,104	3,186
New York	17,990	13,385	2,859	63	61	1	1	694	2,214
New Jersey	7,730	6,130	1,037	15	15	(Z)	(Z)	273	740
Pennsylvania	11,882	10,520	1,090	15	14	(Z)	(Z)	137	232
Midwest	59,669	52,018	5,716	338	334	2	2	768	1,727
East North Central	42,009	35,764	4,817	150	147	1	1	573	1,438

[Continued]

★ 107 ★

Population, by State, Geographic Region, and Race/Ethnicity, 1990
[Continued]

| Region, division, and state | Total[1] | White | Black | American Indian, Eskimo, Aleut | | | | Asian/ Pacific Islander | Hispanic[2] |
				Total	American Indian	Eskimo	Aleut		
Ohio	10,847	9,522	1,155	20	20	(Z)	(Z)	91	140
Indiana	5,544	5,021	432	13	12	(Z)	(Z)	38	99
Illinois	11,431	8,953	1,694	22	21	(Z)	(Z)	285	904
Michigan	9,295	7,756	1,292	56	55	(Z)	(Z)	105	202
Wisconsin	4,892	4,513	245	39	39	(Z)	(Z)	54	93
West North Central	17,660	16,254	899	188	187	1	1	195	289
Minnesota	4,375	4,130	95	50	49	(Z)	(Z)	78	54
Iowa	2,777	2,683	48	7	7	(Z)	(Z)	25	33
Missouri	5,117	4,486	548	20	20	(Z)	(Z)	41	62
North Dakota	639	604	4	26	26	(Z)	(Z)	3	5
South Dakota	696	638	3	51	51	(Z)	(Z)	3	5
Nebraska	1,578	1,481	57	12	12	(Z)	(Z)	12	37
Kansas	2,478	2,232	143	22	22	(Z)	(Z)	32	94
South	85,446	65,582	15,829	563	557	3	3	1,122	6,767
South Atlantic	43,567	33,391	8,924	172	170	1	1	631	2,133
Delaware	666	535	112	2	2	(Z)	(Z)	9	16
Maryland	4,781	3,394	1,190	13	13	(Z)	(Z)	140	125
District of Columbia	607	180	400	1	1	(Z)	(Z)	11	33
Virginia	6,187	4,792	1,163	15	15	(Z)	(Z)	159	160
West Virginia	1,793	1,726	56	2	2	(Z)	(Z)	7	8
North Carolina	6,629	5,008	1,456	80	80	(Z)	(Z)	52	77
South Carolina	3,487	2,407	1,040	8	8	(Z)	(Z)	22	31
Georgia	6,478	4,600	1,747	13	13	(Z)	(Z)	76	109
Florida	12,938	10,749	1,760	36	35	(Z)	(Z)	154	1,574
East South Central	15,176	12,049	2,977	41	40	(Z)	(Z)	84	95
Kentucky	3,685	3,392	263	6	6	(Z)	(Z)	18	22
Tennessee	4,877	4,048	778	10	10	(Z)	(Z)	32	33
Alabama	4,041	2,976	1,021	17	16	(Z)	(Z)	22	25
Mississippi	2,573	1,633	915	9	8	(Z)	(Z)	13	16
West South Central	26,703	20,142	3,929	350	347	1	1	407	4,539
Arkansas	2,351	1,945	374	13	13	(Z)	(Z)	13	20
Louisiana	4,220	2,839	1,299	19	18	(Z)	(Z)	41	93
Oklahoma	3,146	2,584	234	252	252	(Z)	(Z)	34	86
Texas	16,987	12,775	2,022	66	64	1	1	319	4,340
West	52,786	40,017	2,828	933	866	51	17	4,048	10,106
Mountain	13,659	11,762	374	481	478	1	1	217	1,992
Montana	799	741	2	48	48	(Z)	(Z)	4	12
Idaho	1,007	950	3	14	14	(Z)	(Z)	9	53
Wyoming	454	427	4	9	9	(Z)	(Z)	3	26
Colorado	3,294	2,905	133	28	27	(Z)	(Z)	60	424
New Mexico	1,515	1,146	30	134	134	(Z)	(Z)	14	579
Arizona	3,665	2,963	111	204	203	(Z)	(Z)	55	688
Utah	1,723	1,616	12	24	24	(Z)	(Z)	33	85
Nevada	1,202	1,013	79	20	19	(Z)	(Z)	38	124
Pacific	39,127	28,255	2,454	453	387	49	16	3,831	8,114

[Continued]

★ 107 ★

Population, by State, Geographic Region, and Race/Ethnicity, 1990

[Continued]

Region, division, and state	Total[1]	White	Black	American Indian, Eskimo, Aleut				Asian/ Pacific Islander	Hispanic[2]
				Total	American Indian	Eskimo	Aleut		
Washington	4,867	4,309	150	81	78	2	2	211	215
Oregon	2,842	2,637	46	38	37	1	1	69	113
California	29,760	20,524	2,209	242	236	3	4	2,846	7,688
Alaska	550	415	22	86	31	44	10	20	18
Hawaii	1,108	370	27	5	5	(Z)	(Z)	685	81

Source: U.S. Bureau of the Census. *Statistical Abstract of the United States, 1993.* 113th ed. Washington, DC: U.S. Government Printing Office, 1993. Primary source: U.S. Bureau of the Census, 1990 Census of Population, General Population Characteristics, United States (CP-1-1). *Notes:* Z stands for less than 500. 1. Includes other races, not shown separately. 2. Persons of Hispanic origin may be of any race.

★ 108 ★

Population

Minority Populations, by State, 1990

State	African American	American Indian[1]	Asian or Pacific Islander	Hispanic	Total combined Non-white Population[2]
Alabama	1,017,713	16,221	21,217	24,629	1,079,780
Alaska	21,799	84,594	18,730	17,803	142,926
Arizona	104,809	190,091	51,530	688,338	1,034,768
Arkansas	372,762	12,393	12,144	19,876	417,175
California	2,092,446	184,065	2,710,353	7,687,938	12,674,802
Colorado	128,057	22,068	56,773	424,302	631,200
Connecticut	260,840	5,950	49,114	213,116	529,020
Delaware	111,011	1,938	8,854	15,820	137,623
Dist. of Columbia	395,213	1,252	10,734	32,710	439,909
Florida	1,701,103	32,910	146,159	1,574,143	3,454,315
Georgia	1,737,165	12,621	73,725	108,922	1,932,433
Hawaii	25,916	4,001	646,404	81,390	757,711
Idaho	3,211	12,418	9,053	52,927	77,609
Illinois	1,673,703	18,213	275,568	904,446	2,871,930
Indiana	428,612	11,999	36,618	98,788	576,017
Iowa	47,493	6,765	24,926	32,647	111,831
Kansas	140,761	20,363	30,814	93,670	285,608
Kentucky	261,360	5,518	17,201	21,984	306,063
Louisiana	1,291,470	17,539	39,302	93,044	1,441,355
Maine	4,937	5,898	6,505	6,829	24,169
Maryland	1,177,823	12,143	136,619	125,102	1,451,687
Massachusetts	274,464	10,545	140,338	287,549	712,896
Michigan	1,282,744	52,571	102,506	201,596	1,639,417
Minnesota	93,040	48,251	76,229	53,884	271,404
Mississippi	911,891	8,316	12,543	15,931	948,681
Missouri	545,527	18,873	40,087	61,702	666,189
Montana	2,242	46,475	4,123	12,174	65,014

[Continued]

★ 108 ★

Minority Populations, by State, 1990
[Continued]

State	African American	American Indian[1]	Asian or Pacific Islander	Hispanic	Total combined Non-white Population[2]
Nebraska	56,711	11,719	12,026	36,969	117,425
Nevada	76,503	17,480	35,897	124,419	254,299
New Hampshire	6,749	2,042	9,197	11,333	29,321
New Jersey	984,845	12,490	264,341	739,861	2,001,537
New Mexico	27,642	128,068	12,587	579,224	747,521
New York	2,569,126	50,540	666,843	2,214,026	5,500,535
North Carolina	1,449,142	78,930	50,593	76,726	1,655,391
North Dakota	3,451	25,590	3,345	4,665	37,051
Ohio	1,147,440	19,137	89,195	139,696	1,395,468
Oklahoma	231,462	246,631	32,366	86,160	596,619
Oregon	44,982	35,749	67,422	112,707	260,860
Pennsylvania	1,072,459	13,505	134,056	232,262	1,452,282
Rhode Island	34,283	3,629	17,584	45,752	101,248
South Carolina	1,035,947	8,004	21,304	30,551	1,095,806
South Dakota	3,176	49,648	3,013	5,252	61,089
Tennessee	774,925	9,685	30,938	32,741	848,289
Texas	1,976,360	52,803	303,825	4,339,905	6,672,893
Utah	7,060	12,654	21,132	49,489	90,335
Vermont	1,868	1,651	3,159	3,661	10,339
Virginia	1,153,133	14,347	154,183	160,288	1,481,951
Washington	146,000	76,397	203,668	214,570	640,635
West Virginia	55,986	2,363	7,252	8,489	74,090
Wisconsin	241,697	37,769	52,284	93,194	424,944
Wyoming	3,426	8,857	2,622	25,751	40,656

Source: "Ranking of total combined non-white population of states, 1990," *Black Issues in Higher Education* vol. 8 (29 August 1991), p. 47. Primary source: *1990 Census of Population and Housing*, P.L. 94-171 Redistricting Data. *Notes:* 1. Includes Eskimo and Aleut populations. 2. Excludes other (non-white) race populations. This "Other Race" category was excluded to enable comparisons to 1980 census compilations. Nationally, nearly 10 million persons listed their race as "Other."

★ 109 ★

Population

Population in Major Metropolitan Areas

Data are shown as of April 1, for areas as defined by U.S. Office of Management and Budget, June 30, 1993.

Metropolitan area[1]	Total population	Black	American Indian, Eskimo, Aleut	Asian and Pacific Islander	Hispanic origin[2]	Percent of total metropolitan population			
						Black	American Indian, Eskimo Aleut	Asian and Pacific Islander	Hispanic origin[2]
New York-Northern New Jersey-Long Island, NY-NJ-CT-PA CMSA	19,549,649	3,453,951	48,758	899,964	2,859,162	17.7	0.2	4.6	14.6
Los Angeles-Riverside-Orange County, CA CMSA	14,531,529	1,229,809	87,487	1,339,048	4,779,118	8.5	0.6	9.2	32.9
Chicago-Gary-Kenosha, IL-IN-WI CMSA	8,239,820	1,564,193	16,031	258,445	897,697	19.0	0.2	3.1	10.9
Washington-Baltimore, DC-MD-VA-WV CMSA	6,727,050	1,695,732	18,388	247,903	259,264	25.2	0.3	3.7	3.9
San Francisco-Oakland-San Jose, CA CMSA	6,253,311	537,753	40,847	926,961	970,403	8.6	0.7	14.8	15.5

[Continued]

Population in Major Metropolitan Areas

[Continued]

Metropolitan area[1]	Total popu- lation	Black	American Indian, Eskimo, Aleut	Asian and Pacific Islander	Hispanic origin[2]	Percent of total metropolitan population			
						Black	American Indian, Eskimo, Aleut	Asian and Pacific Islander	Hispanic origin[2]
Philadelphia-Wilmington-Atlantic City, PA-NJ-DE-MD CMSA	5,892,937	1,083,264	11,552	118,855	224,175	18.4	0.2	2.0	3.8
Boston-Worcester-Lawrence, MA-NH-ME-CT CMSA	5,455,403	261,329	10,226	136,700	238,771	4.8	0.2	2.5	4.4
Detroit-Ann Arbor-Flint, MI CMSA	5,187,171	1,060,887	21,396	72,842	105,339	20.5	0.4	1.4	2.0
Dallas-Fort Worth, TX CMSA	4,037,282	566,225	19,573	98,247	525,514	14.0	0.5	2.4	13.0
Houston-Galveston-Brazoria, TX CMSA	3,731,131	667,928	11,082	132,247	773,490	17.9	0.3	3.5	20.7
Miami-Fort Lauderdale, FL CMSA	3,192,582	591,440	5,700	43,437	1,061,846	18.5	0.2	1.4	33.3
Seattle-Tacoma-Bremerton, WA CMSA	2,970,328	132,691	38,260	181,222	88,603	4.5	1.3	6.1	3.0
Atlanta, GA MSA	2,959,950	747,219	5,804	51,829	58,215	25.2	0.2	1.8	2.0
Cleveland-Akron, OH CMSA	2,859,644	445,078	5,329	28,537	54,535	15.6	0.2	1.0	1.9
Minneapolis-St. Paul, MN-WI MSA	2,538,834	90,055	24,251	65,580	37,903	3.5	1.0	2.6	1.5
San Diego, CA MSA	2,498,016	159,306	20,066	198,311	510,781	6.4	0.8	7.9	20.4
St. Louis, MO-IL MSA	2,492,525	424,285	5,095	23,773	26,385	17.0	0.2	1.0	1.1
Pittsburgh, PA MSA	2,394,811	179,667	2,366	16,719	13,415	7.5	0.1	0.7	0.6
Phoenix-Mesa, AZ MSA	2,238,480	77,905	48,802	36,796	379,560	3.5	2.2	1.6	17.0
Tampa-St. Petersburg-Clearwater, FL MSA	2,067,959	185,503	5,467	23,055	139,248	9.0	0.3	1.1	6.7
Denver-Boulder-Greeley, CO CMSA	1,980,140	98,322	14,669	43,775	253,702	5.0	0.7	2.2	12.8
Cincinnati-Hamilton, OH-KY-IN CMSA	1,817,571	204,217	2,534	14,332	9,505	11.2	0.1	0.8	0.5
Portland-Salem, OR-WA CMSA	1,793,476	44,045	18,155	57,060	71,632	2.5	1.0	3.2	4.0
Milwaukee-Racine, WI CMSA	1,607,183	214,182	8,522	19,786	60,340	13.3	0.5	1.2	3.8
Kansas City, MO-KS MSA	1,582,875	200,844	7,704	17,466	45,366	12.7	0.5	1.1	2.9
Sacramento-Yolo, CA CMSA	1,481,102	101,940	17,021	114,520	172,374	6.9	1.1	7.7	11.6
Norfolk-Virginia Beach-Newport News, VA-NC MSA	1,443,244	408,738	4,807	35,340	32,660	28.3	0.3	2.4	2.3
Indianapolis, IN MSA	1,380,491	182,196	2,809	10,496	11,969	13.2	0.2	0.8	0.9
Columbus, OH MSA	1,345,450	163,434	2,823	20,927	11,204	12.1	0.2	1.6	0.8
San Antonio, TX MSA	1,324,749	89,020	4,693	16,080	628,344	6.7	0.4	1.2	47.4
New Orleans, LA MSA	1,285,270	446,771	4,095	21,917	53,923	34.8	0.3	1.7	4.2
Orlando, FL MSA	1,224,852	147,499	3,583	21,040	100,723	12.0	0.3	1.7	8.2
Buffalo-Niagara Falls, NY MSA	1,189,288	121,956	7,611	11,026	24,347	10.3	0.6	0.9	2.0
Charlotte-Gastonia-Rock Hill, NC-SC MSA	1,162,093	231,654	4,107	11,304	10,671	19.9	0.4	1.0	0.9
Hartford, CT MSA	1,157,585	96,358	2,006	17,456	79,825	8.3	0.2	1.5	6.9
Providence-Fall River-Warwick, RI-MA MSA	1,134,350	37,079	3,876	19,990	47,375	3.3	0.3	1.8	4.2
Salt Lake City-Ogden, UT MSA	1,072,227	10,464	8,337	25,598	61,964	1.0	0.8	2.4	5.8
Rochester, NY MSA	1,062,470	94,884	3,553	14,189	31,689	8.9	0.3	1.3	3.0
Greensboro – Winston-Salem – High Point, NC MSA	1,050,304	203,106	3,499	6,868	7,832	19.3	0.3	0.7	0.7
Memphis, TN-AR-MS MSA	1,007,306	410,306	1,824	8,193	8,116	40.7	0.2	0.8	0.8
Nashville, TN MSA	985,026	152,349	2,121	10,012	7,665	15.5	0.2	1.0	0.8
Oklahoma City, OK MSA	958,839	101,082	45,720	17,742	34,152	10.5	4.8	1.9	3.6
Dayton-Springfield, OH MSA	951,270	126,238	1,915	9,278	7,254	13.3	0.2	1.0	0.8
Louisville, KY-IN MSA	948,829	122,323	1,575	5,600	5,823	12.9	0.2	0.6	0.6
Grand Rapids-Muskegon-Holland, MI MSA	937,891	64,376	5,275	8,797	29,149	6.9	0.6	0.9	3.1
Jacksonville, FL MSA	906,727	181,265	2,587	15,362	22,479	20.0	0.3	1.7	2.5
Richmond-Petersburg, VA MSA	865,640	252,340	2,705	11,864	9,327	29.2	0.3	1.4	1.1
West Palm Beach-Boca Raton, FL MSA	863,518	107,705	1,211	9,020	66,613	12.5	0.1	1.0	7.7
Albany-Schenectady-Troy, NY MSA	861,424	39,370	1,496	10,710	14,856	4.6	0.2	1.2	1.7
Raleigh-Durham-Chapel Hill, NC MSA	855,545	206,681	2,236	14,062	10,845	24.2	0.3	1.6	1.3
Las Vegas, NV-AZ MSA	852,737	71,332	9,060	26,767	89,060	8.4	1.1	3.1	10.4
Austin-San Marcos, TX MSA	846,227	79,591	3,073	18,985	176,863	9.4	0.4	2.2	20.9
Birmingham, AL MSA	840,140	241,321	1,422	3,907	3,765	28.7	0.2	0.5	0.4
Honolulu, HI MSA	836,231	25,875	3,532	526,459	56,884	3.1	0.4	63.0	6.8
Greenville-Spartanburg-Anderson, SC MSA	830,563	144,656	1,197	5,150	5,938	17.4	0.1	0.6	0.7
Fresno, CA MSA	755,580	35,917	8,537	58,503	267,034	4.8	1.1	7.7	35.3
Syracuse, NY MSA	742,177	42,090	4,223	8,071	10,128	5.7	0.6	1.1	1.4
Tulsa, OK MSA	708,954	58,186	48,196	6,563	14,534	8.2	6.8	0.9	2.1
Tucson, AZ MSA	666,880	20,795	20,330	11,964	163,262	3.1	3.0	1.8	24.5
Omaha, NE-IA MSA	639,580	51,468	3,268	6,445	16,566	8.0	0.5	1.0	2.6
Scranton – Wilkes-Barre – Hazleton, PA MSA	638,466	5,933	450	3,161	3,588	0.9	0.1	0.5	0.6
Toledo, OH MSA	614,128	69,717	1,423	6,146	20,382	11.4	0.2	1.0	3.3
Youngstown-Warren, OH MSA	600,895	56,311	959	2,177	7,805	9.4	0.2	0.4	1.3

[Continued]

★ 109 ★

Population in Major Metropolitan Areas
[Continued]

Metropolitan area[1]	Total population	Black	American Indian, Eskimo, Aleut	Asian and Pacific Islander	Hispanic origin[2]	Percent of total metropolitan population			
						Black	American Indian, Eskimo Aleut	Asian and Pacific Islander	Hispanic origin[2]
Allentown-Bethlehem-Easton, PA MSA	595,081	12,164	574	6,546	27,101	2.0	0.1	1.1	4.6
El Paso, TX MSA	591,610	22,110	2,590	6,485	411,619	3.7	0.4	1.1	69.6
Albuquerque, NM MSA	589,131	14,638	30,116	8,089	218,415	2.5	5.1	1.4	37.1
Harrisburg-Lebanon-Carlisle, PA MSA	587,986	39,472	737	6,251	10,239	6.7	0.1	1.1	1.7
Springfield, MA MSA	587,884	36,844	1,014	8,416	49,694	6.3	0.2	1.4	8.5
Knoxville, TN MSA	585,960	35,768	1,440	4,541	3,174	6.1	0.2	0.8	0.5
Bakersfield, CA MSA	543,477	30,131	7,026	16,541	151,995	5.5	1.3	3.0	28.0
Baton Rouge, LA MSA	528,264	156,509	902	5,657	7,532	29.6	0.2	1.1	1.4
Little Rock-North Little Rock, AR MSA	513,117	101,862	1,870	3,347	4,164	19.9	0.4	0.7	0.8
Charleston-North Charleston, SC MSA	506,875	153,227	1,613	6,113	7,512	30.2	0.3	1.2	1.5
Sarasota-Bradenton, FL MSA	489,483	28,473	984	2,657	15,306	5.8	0.2	0.5	3.1
Wichita, KS MSA	485,270	36,979	5,160	9,109	19,793	7.6	1.1	1.9	4.1

Source: 1994 Statistical Abstract of the United States on CD-ROM [machine-readable datafiles]. CD-8A-94. Washington, DC: U.S. Department of Commerce, Economics and Statistics Administration, Bureau of the Census, Data User Services Division, January 1995. Primary source: U.S. Bureau of the Census, 1990 Census of Population and Housing, Supplementary Reports, Metropolitan Areas as Defined by the Office of Management and Budget, June 30, 1993, (1990 CPH-S-1-1).
Notes: 1. Metropolitan areas are shown in rank order of total population of consolidated metropolitan statistical areas (CMSAs) and metropolitan statistical areas (MSAs). 2. Persons of Hispanic origin may be of any race.

★ 110 ★

Population

Native American Populations in North and South America, by Country, 1991

Estimated populations are shown, by country, for 1991.

	Estimated population	% of Total population
Mexico	10,537,000	12.4
Peru	8,097,000	38.6
Guatemala	5,423,000	60.3
Bolivia	4,985,000	71.2
Ecuador	3,753,000	37.5
United States	1,959,000	0.8
Canada	892,000	3.4
Chile	767,000	5.9
Colombia	708,000	2.2
El Salvador	500,000	10.0
Argentina	477,000	1.5
Brazil	325,000	0.2
Venezuela	290,000	1.5
Panama	194,000	8.0
Honduras	168,000	3.4
Paraguay	101,000	2.5
Nicaragua	66,000	1.7
Guyana	29,000	3.9
Costa Rica	19,000	0.6
Belize	15,000	9.1
Surinam	11,000	2.9

[Continued]

★ 110 ★

Native American Populations in North and South America, by Country, 1991

[Continued]

	Estimated population	% of Total population
French Guyana	1,000	1.2
Uruguay	0	0.0
Total	39,317,000	5.8

Source: Report on the Americas Volume XXV, No. 3, (December 1991), p. 16. Computed from: Enrique Mayer & Elio Masferrer, "La Poblacion Indigena de America," America Indigena, Vol. 39, No. 2 (1979); World Bank, Informe sobre el desarrollo mundial 1991; U.S. and Canada census.

★ 111 ★

Population

Population of the Top 50 American Indian Tribes, 1990

Population is shown in thousands.

Tribe	Population
Cherokee	308,132
Navajo	219,198
Chippewa	103,826
Sioux	103,255
Choctaw	82,299
Pueblo	52,939
Apache	50,051
Iroquois	49,038
Lumbee	48,444
Creek	43,550
Blackfoot	32,234
Canadian/Latin American	22,379
Chickasaw	20,631
Potawatomi	16,763
Tohono O'Odham	16,041
Pima	14,431
Tlingit	13,925
Seminole	13,797
Athabaskans	13,738
Cheyenne	11,456
Comanche	11,322
Paiute	11,142
Salish	10,246
Yaqui	9,931
Osage	9,527
Kiowa	9,421
Delaware	9,321
Shoshone	9,215
Crow	8,588

[Continued]

★ 111 ★

Population of the Top 50 American Indian Tribes, 1990
[Continued]

Tribe	Population
Cree	8,290
Yakima	7,850
Houma	7,810
Menominee	7,543
Ottawa	7,522
Ute	7,273
Colville	7,140
Yuman	7,128
Winnebago	6,920
Arapaho	6,350
Shawnee	6,179
Assiniboine	5,274
Pomo	4,766
Sac and Fox	4,517
Miami	4,477
Salish	4,455
Yurok	4,296
Omaha	4,143
Nez Perce	4,113
Eastern tribes	3,928

Source: Anderson, Mary. "Census figures misleading: Navajo claim to be largest tribe." *Indian Country Today* (3 December 1992), p. A1. Primary source: U.S. Census.

★ 112 ★

Population

States With The Most Native Americans, 1990

| Oklahoma - 252,089 |
| California - 236,078 |
| Arizona - 203,009 |
| New Mexico - 134,097 |
| North Carolina - 79,825 |

State	Population
Oklahoma	252,089
California	236,078
Arizona	203,009
New Mexico	134,097
North Carolina	79,825

Source: Staimer, Marcia. "USA snapshots: states with the most Native Americans." *USA TODAY* (27 November 1992), p. 1A. Primary source: U.S. Census Bureau.

★ 113 ★

Population

American Indian, Eskimo, and Aleut Population, by Geographic Region and State, 1990

Region, division, and state	American Indians, Eskimo, and Aleut			
	Total	American Indian	Eskimo	Aleut
U.S.	1,959	1,878	57	24
Northeast	125	122	2	2
New England	33	32	(Z)	(Z)
Maine	6	6	(Z)	(Z)
New Hampshire	2	2	(Z)	(Z)
Vermont	2	2	(Z)	(Z)
Maine	12	12	(Z)	(Z)
Rhode Island	4	4	(Z)	(Z)
Connecticut	7	6	(Z)	(Z)
Midwest Atlantic	92	90	1	2
New York	63	61	1	1
New Jersey	15	15	(Z)	(Z)
Pennsylvania	15	14	(Z)	(Z)
Midwest	338	334	2	2
East North Central	150	147	1	1
Ohio	20	20	(Z)	(Z)
Indiana	13	12	(Z)	(Z)
Illinois	22	21	(Z)	(Z)
Michigan	56	56	(Z)	(Z)
Wisconsin	39	39	(Z)	(Z)
West North Central	188	187	1	1
Minnesota	50	49	(Z)	(Z)
Iowa	7	7	(Z)	(Z)
Missouri	20	20	(Z)	(Z)
North Dakota	26	26	(Z)	(Z)
South Dakota	51	51	(Z)	(Z)
Nebraska	12	12	(Z)	(Z)
Kansas	22	22	(Z)	(Z)
South	563	557	3	3
South Atlantic	172	170	1	1
Delaware	2	2	(Z)	(Z)
Maryland	13	13	(Z)	(Z)
District of Columbia	1	1	(Z)	(Z)
Virginia	15	15	(Z)	(Z)
West Virginia	2	2	(Z)	(Z)
North Carolina	80	80	(Z)	(Z)
South Carolina	8	8	(Z)	(Z)
Georgia	13	13	(Z)	(Z)
Florida	36	35	(Z)	(Z)
East South Central	41	40	(Z)	(Z)
Kentucky	6	6	(Z)	(Z)

[Continued]

★ 113 ★

American Indian, Eskimo, and Aleut Population, by Geographic Region and State, 1990
[Continued]

Region, division, and state	American Indians, Eskimo, and Aleut			
	Total	American Indian	Eskimo	Aleut
Tennessee	10	10	(Z)	(Z)
Alabama	17	16	(Z)	(Z)
Mississippi	9	8	(Z)	(Z)
West South Central	350	347	1	1
Arizona	13	13	(Z)	(Z)
Louisiana	19	18	(Z)	(Z)
Oklahoma	252	252	(Z)	(Z)
Texas	66	64	1	1
West	933	866	51	17
Mountain	481	478	1	1
Montana	48	48	(Z)	(Z)
Idaho	14	14	(Z)	(Z)
Wyoming	9	9	(Z)	(Z)
Colorado	28	27	(Z)	(Z)
New Mexico	134	134	(Z)	(Z)
Arizona	204	203	(Z)	(Z)
Utah	24	24	(Z)	(Z)
Nevada	20	19	(Z)	(Z)
Pacific	453	387	49	16
Washington	81	78	2	2
Oregon	38	37	1	1
California	242	236	3	4
Alaska	86	31	44	10
Hawaii	5	5	(Z)	(Z)

Source: U.S. Bureau of the Census. *Statistical Abstract of the United States: 1992* (112th edition). Washington, DC: U.S. Government Printing Office, 1992, pp. 24-25. Primary source: U.S. Bureau of the Census, press release CB91-215. *Note:* A (Z) stands for less than 500.

★ 114 ★

Population

Population of Native North Americans by MSA in 1990 - I: A-K

Metropolitan Statistical Areas	Total area population	American Indians, Eskimos, and Aleuts				
		Total	% of area's population	American Indians	Eskimos	Aleuts
Abilene, TX MSA	119,655	450	0.4	432	6	12
Albany, GA MSA	112,561	281	0.2	279	1	1
Albany–Schenectady–Troy, NY MSA	874,304	1,560	0.2	1,520	19	21
Albuquerque, NM MSA	480,577	16,296	3.4	16,201	64	31
Alexandria, LA MSA	131,556	564	0.4	558	3	3

[Continued]

★ 114 ★

Population of Native North Americans by MSA in 1990 - I: A-K
[Continued]

Metropolitan Statistical Areas	Total area population	American Indians, Eskimos, and Aleuts				
		Total	% of area's population	American Indians	Eskimos	Aleuts
Allentown–Bethlehem–Easton, PA–NJ MSA	686,688	688	0.1	643	21	24
Altoona, PA MSA	130,542	118	0.1	115	1	2
Amarillo, TX MSA	187,547	1,355	0.7	1,350	2	3
Anchorage, AK MSA	226,338	14,569	6.4	5,985	6,034	2,550
Anderson, IN MSA	130,669	299	0.2	284	11	4
Anderson, SC MSA	145,196	173	0.1	170	2	1
Anniston, AL MSA	116,034	296	0.3	293	3	
Appleton–Oshkosh–Neenah, WI MSA	315,121	2,796	0.9	2,752	18	26
Asheville, NC MSA	174,821	486	0.3	480	1	5
Athens, GA MSA	156,267	257	0.2	241	7	9
Atlanta, GA MSA	2,833,511	5,532	0.2	5,334	64	134
Atlantic City, NJ MSA	319,416	778	0.2	750	16	12
Augusta, GA–SC MSA	396,809	941	0.2	910	23	8
Austin, TX MSA	781,572	2,827	0.4	2,662	57	108
Bakersfield, CA MSA	543,477	7,026	1.3	6,947	44	35
Baltimore, MD MSA	2,382,172	6,444	0.3	6,264	89	91
Bangor, ME MSA	88,745	1,008	1.1	997	10	1
Baton Rouge, LA MSA	528,264	902	0.2	875	9	18
Battle Creek, MI MSA	135,982	696	0.5	687	1	8
Beaumont–Port Arthur, TX MSA	361,226	890	0.2	872	3	15
Bellingham, WA MSA	127,780	4,014	3.1	3,848	54	112
Benton Harbor, MI MSA	161,378	685	0.4	676	5	4
Billings, MT MSA	113,419	3,235	2.9	3,225	5	5
Biloxi–Gulfport, MS MSA	197,125	595	0.3	571	16	8
Binghamton, NY MSA	264,497	450	0.2	436	8	6
Birmingham, AL MSA	907,810	1,506	0.2	1,458	22	26
Bismarck, ND MSA	83,831	2,016	2.4	2,016		
Bloomington, IN MSA	108,978	216	0.2	212	4	
Bloomington–Normal, IL MSA	129,180	203	0.2	192	6	5
Boise City, ID MSA	205,775	1,382	0.7	1,354	17	11
Boston–Lawrence–Salem, MA–NH CMSA	4,171,643	7,542	0.2	7,261	145	136
Bradenton, FL MSA	211,707	501	0.2	470	6	25
Bremerton, WA MSA	189,731	3,211	1.7	3,068	59	84
Brownsville–Harlingen, TX MSA	260,120	413	0.2	406	7	
Bryan–College Station, TX MSA	121,862	274	0.2	264	7	3
Buffalo–Niagara Falls, NY CMSA	1,189,288	7,611	0.6	7,567	26	18
Burlington, NC MSA	108,213	303	0.3	299	4	
Burlington, VT MSA	131,439	299	0.2	291	6	2
Canton, OH MSA	394,106	1,015	0.3	994	9	12
Casper, WY MSA	61,226	404	0.7	396	7	1
Cedar Rapids, IA MSA	168,767	363	0.2	359	4	
Champaign–Urbana–Rantoul, IL MSA	173,025	331	0.2	319	5	7
Charleston, SC MSA	506,875	1,613	0.3	1,564	29	20
Charleston, WV MSA	250,454	292	0.1	276	7	9

[Continued]

★ 114 ★

Population of Native North Americans by MSA in 1990 - I: A-K
[Continued]

Metropolitan Statistical Areas	Total area popu-lation	American Indians, Eskimos, and Aleuts				
		Total	% of area's population	American Indians	Eskimos	Aleuts
Charlotte – Gastonia – Rock Hill, NC – SC MSA	1,162,093	4,107	0.4	4,032	17	58
Charlottesville, VA MSA	131,107	148	0.1	138	4	6
Chattanooga, TN – GA MSA	433,210	891	0.2	879	5	7
Cheyenne, WY MSA	73,142	528	0.7	518	7	3
Chicago – Gary – Lake County, IL – IN – WI CMSA	8,065,633	15,758	0.2	15,098	306	354
Chico, CA MSA	182,120	3,241	1.8	3,212	20	9
Cincinnati – Hamilton, OH – KY – IN CMSA	1,744,124	2,457	0.1	2,365	34	58
Clarksville – Hopkinsville, TN – KY MSA	169,439	688	0.4	674	13	1
Cleveland – Akron – Lorain, OH CMSA	2,759,823	5,133	0.2	4,994	78	61
Colorado Springs, CO MSA	397,014	3,242	0.8	3,158	59	25
Columbia, MO MSA	112,379	394	0.4	379	3	12
Columbia, SC MSA	453,331	1,013	0.2	968	24	21
Columbus, GA – AL MSA	243,072	765	0.3	689	69	7
Columbus, OH MSA	1,377,419	2,880	0.2	2,813	29	38
Corpus Christi, TX MSA	349,894	1,394	0.4	1,373	13	8
Cumberland, MD – WV MSA	101,643	71	0.1	67	4	
Dallas – Fort Worth, TX CMSA	3,885,415	18,972	0.5	18,608	174	190
Danville, VA MSA	108,711	117	0.1	117		
Davenport – Rock Island – Moline, IA – IL MSA	350,861	902	0.3	888	8	6
Dayton – Springfield, OH MSA	951,270	1,915	0.2	1,872	17	26
Daytona Beach, FL MSA	370,712	915	0.2	898	13	4
Decatur, AL MSA	131,556	2,434	1.9	2,431	2	1
Decatur, IL MSA	117,206	157	0.1	149	8	
Denver – Boulder, CO CMSA	1,848,319	13,884	0.8	13,600	159	125
Des Moines, IA MSA	392,928	1,015	0.3	977	7	31
Detroit – Ann Arbor, MI CMSA	4,665,236	17,961	0.4	17,731	78	152
Dothan, AL MSA	130,964	526	0.4	521	5	
Dubuque, IA MSA	86,403	77	0.1	73	3	1
Duluth, MN – WI MSA	239,971	4,487	1.9	4,452	14	21
Eau Claire, WI MSA	137,543	617	0.4	599	5	13
El Paso, TX MSA	591,610	2,590	0.4	2,542	22	26
Elkhart – Goshen, IN MSA	156,198	453	0.3	440	10	3
Elmira, NY MSA	95,195	211	0.2	203	2	6
Enid, OK MSA	56,735	1,234	2.2	1,227	1	6
Erie, PA MSA	275,572	438	0.2	428	6	4
Eugene – Springfield, OR MSA	282,912	3,207	1.1	3,123	45	39
Evansville, IN – KY MSA	278,990	477	0.2	471	5	1
Fargo – Moorhead, ND – MN MSA	153,296	1,497	1.0	1,489	8	
Fayetteville, NC MSA	274,566	4,425	1.6	4,397	13	15
Fayetteville – Springdale, AR MSA	113,409	1,486	1.3	1,478	2	6
Fitchburg – Leominster, MA MSA	102,797	196	0.2	185	7	4
Flint, MI MSA	430,459	3,132	0.7	3,109	11	12
Florence, AL MSA	131,327	302	0.2	300	1	1
Florence, SC MSA	114,344	145	0.1	140	1	4

[Continued]

★ 114 ★

Population of Native North Americans by MSA in 1990 - I: A-K

[Continued]

Metropolitan Statistical Areas	Total area popu-lation	American Indians, Eskimos, and Aleuts				
		Total	% of area's population	American Indians	Eskimos	Aleuts
Fort Collins – Loveland, CO MSA	186,136	1,063	0.6	1,040	9	14
Fort Myers – Cape CoraL, Fl MSA	335,113	672	0.2	665	4	3
Fort Pierce, FL MSA	251,071	526	0.2	509	13	4
Fort Smith, AR – OK MSA	175,911	9,054	5.1	9,044	4	6
Fort Walton Beach, FL MSA	143,776	776	0.5	751	17	8
Fort Wayne, IN MSA	363,811	1,056	0.3	1,043	6	7
Fresno, CA MSA	667,490	7,119	1.1	6,954	40	125
Gadsden, AL MSA	99,840	250	0.3	243	7	
Gainesville, FL MSA	204,111	443	0.2	429	10	4
Glens Falls, NY MSA	118,539	214	0.2	211	3	
Grand Forks, ND MSA	70,683	1,244	1.8	1,236	8	
Grand Rapids, MI MSA	688,399	3,394	0.5	3,373	12	9
Great Falls, MT MSA	77,691	3,072	4.0	3,053	14	5
Greeley, CO MSA	131,821	785	0.6	759	10	16
Green Bay, WI MSA	194,594	3,869	2.0	3,843	7	19
Greensboro – Winston-Salem – High Point, NC MSA	942,091	3,196	0.3	3,167	21	8
Greenville – Spartanburg, SC MSA	640,861	959	0.1	934	9	16
Hagerstown, MD MSA	121,393	241	0.2	238	3	
Harrisburg – Lebanon – Carlisle, PA MSA	587,986	737	0.1	713	11	13
Hartford – New Britain – Middletown, CT CMSA	1,085,837	1,826	0.2	1,769	26	31
Hickory – Morganton, NC MSA	221,700	417	0.2	399	18	
Honolulu, HI MSA	836,231	3,532	0.4	3,293	83	156
Houma – Thibodaux, LA MSA	182,842	6,814	3.7	6,809	5	
Houston – Galveston – Brazoria, TX CMSA	3,711,043	11,029	0.3	10,677	170	182
Huntington – Ashland, WV – KY – OH MSA	312,529	372	0.1	368	4	
Huntsville, AL MSA	238,912	1,601	0.7	1,583	12	6
Indianapolis, IN MSA	1,249,822	2,510	0.2	2,435	49	26
Iowa City, IA MSA	96,119	176	0.2	162	9	5
Jackson, MI MSA	149,756	655	0.4	646	5	4
Jackson, MS MSA	395,396	346	0.1	338	2	6
Jackson, TN MSA	77,982	66	0.1	64	1	1
Jacksonville, FL MSA	906,727	2,587	0.3	2,529	27	31
Jacksonville, NC MSA	149,838	939	0.6	919	16	4
Jamestown – Dunkirk, NY	141,895	558	0.4	556	1	1
Janesville – Beloit, WI MSA	139,510	369	0.3	368	1	
Johnson City – Kingsport – Bristol, TN – VA MSA	436,047	766	0.2	751	7	8
Johnstown, PA MSA	241,247	152	0.1	148	4	
Joplin, MO MSA	134,910	2,452	1.8	2,440	11	1
Kalamazoo, MI MSA	223,411	1,017	0.5	1,007	1	9
Kankakee, IL MSA	96,255	150	0.2	143	6	1
Kansas City, MO – KS MSA	1,566,280	7,631	0.5	7,503	68	60
Killeen – Temple, TX MSA	255,301	1,405	0.6	1,376	13	16

[Continued]

★ 114 ★

Population of Native North Americans by MSA in 1990 - I: A-K
[Continued]

Metropolitan Statistical Areas	Total area popu-lation	American Indians, Eskimos, and Aleuts				
		Total	% of area's population	American Indians	Eskimos	Aleuts
Knoxville, TN MSA	604,816	1,505	0.2	1,485	8	12
Kokomo, IN MSA	96,946	246	0.3	243	2	1

Source: Census of Population and Housing, 1990: Summary Tape File 1 on CD-ROM, U.S. Bureau of the Census, Washington, D.C. 1991.

★ 115 ★

Population

Population of Native North Americans by MSA in 1990 - II: L-Y

Metropolitan Statistical Areas	Total area popu-lation	American Indians, Eskimos, and Aleuts				
		Total	% of area's population	American Indians	Eskimos	Aleuts
La Crosse, WI MSA	97,904	340	0.3	325	5	10
Lafayette, LA MSA	208,740	440	0.2	436	2	2
Lafayette – West Lafayette, IN MSA	130,598	320	0.2	311	8	1
Lake Charles, LA MSA	168,134	387	0.2	383	3	1
Lakeland – Winter Haven, FL MSA	405,382	1,158	0.3	1,119	27	12
Lancaster, PA MSA	422,822	484	0.1	469	5	10
Lansing – East Lansing, MI MSA	432,674	2,655	0.6	2,622	20	13
Laredo, TX MSA	133,239	201	0.2	185	3	13
Las Cruces, NM MSA	135,510	1,009	0.7	980	16	13
Las Vegas, NV MSA	741,459	6,416	0.9	6,292	67	57
Lawrence, KS MSA	81,798	2,161	2.6	2,134	21	6
Lawton, OK MSA	111,486	5,153	4.6	5,129	16	8
Lewiston – Auburn, ME MSA	88,141	197	0.2	195	2	
Lexington-Fayette, KY MSA	348,428	561	0.2	537	14	10
Lima, OH MSA	154,340	252	0.2	247	2	3
Lincoln, NE MSA	213,641	1,207	0.6	1,196	4	7
Little Rock – North Little Rock, AR MSA	513,117	1,870	0.4	1,828	27	15
Longview – Marshall, TX MSA	162,431	670	0.4	658	9	3
Los Angeles – Anaheim – Riverside, CA CMSA	14,531,529	87,487	0.6	85,004	1,036	1,447
Louisville, KY – IN MSA	952,662	1,576	0.2	1,546	13	17
Lubbock, TX MSA	222,636	686	0.3	675	5	6
Lynchburg, VA MSA	142,199	277	0.2	271	4	2
Macon – Warner Robins, GA MSA	281,103	571	0.2	558	7	6
Madison, WI MSA	367,085	1,201	0.3	1,151	23	27
Manchester, NH MSA	147,809	278	0.2	267	9	2
Mansfield, OH MSA	126,137	223	0.2	220	2	1
Mcallen – Edinburg – Mission, TX MSA	383,545	668	0.2	625	22	21
Medford, OR MSA	146,389	1,863	1.3	1,830	25	8
Melbourne – Titusville – Palm Bay, FL MSA	398,978	1,369	0.3	1,341	18	10

[Continued]

★ 115 ★

Population of Native North Americans by MSA in 1990 - II: L-Y
[Continued]

Metropolitan Statistical Areas	Total area population	American Indians, Eskimos, and Aleuts				
		Total	% of area's population	American Indians	Eskimos	Aleuts
Memphis, TN – AR – MS MSA	981,747	1,791	0.2	1,740	15	36
Merced, CA MSA	178,403	1,516	0.8	1,461	6	49
Miami – Fort Lauderdale, FL CMSA	3,192,582	5,700	0.2	5,486	79	135
Midland, TX MSA	106,611	414	0.4	412	1	1
Milwaukee – Racine, WI CMSA	1,607,183	8,522	0.5	8,430	35	57
Minneapolis – St. Paul, MN – WI MSA	2,464,124	23,956	1.0	23,621	110	225
Mobile, AL MSA	476,923	2,570	0.5	2,547	14	9
Modesto, CA MSA	370,522	4,039	1.1	3,965	27	47
Monroe, LA MSA	142,191	239	0.2	227	11	1
Montgomery, AL MSA	292,517	622	0.2	589	10	23
Muncie, IN MSA	119,659	274	0.2	268	6	
Muskegon, MI MSA	158,983	1,338	0.8	1,331	7	
Naples, FL MSA	152,099	428	0.3	424	2	2
Nashville, TN MSA	985,026	2,121	0.2	2,093	19	9
New Bedford, MA MSA	175,641	504	0.3	502	2	
New Haven – Meriden, CT MSA	530,180	947	0.2	925	10	12
New London – Norwich, CT – RI MSA	266,819	1,433	0.5	1,405	17	11
New Orleans, LA MSA	1,238,816	3,615	0.3	3,557	26	32
New York – Northern New Jersey – Long Island, NY – NJ – CT CMSA	18,087,251	46,191	0.3	44,337	726	1,128
Norfolk – Virginia Beach – Newport News, VA MSA	1,396,107	4,679	0.3	4,556	67	56
Ocala, FL MSA	194,833	638	0.3	634	4	
Odessa, TX MSA	118,934	647	0.5	641	4	2
Oklahoma City, OK MSA	958,839	45,720	4.8	45,623	58	39
Olympia, WA MSA	161,238	2,498	1.5	2,364	51	83
Omaha, NE – IA MSA	618,262	3,159	0.5	3,126	17	16
Orlando, FL MSA	1,072,748	3,199	0.3	3,109	37	53
Owensboro, KY MSA	87,189	101	0.1	100	1	
Panama City, FL MSA	126,994	949	0.7	933	1	15
Parkersburg – Marietta, WV – OH MSA	149,169	242	0.2	237	4	1
Pascagoula, MS MSA	115,243	254	0.2	248	3	3
Pensacola, FL MSA	344,406	3,347	1.0	3,326	15	6
Peoria, IL MSA	339,172	587	0.2	574	5	8
Philadelphia – Wilmington – Trenton, PA – NJ – DE – MD CMSA	5,899,345	11,307	0.2	10,962	159	186
Phoenix, AZ MSA	2,122,101	38,017	1.8	37,708	163	146
Pine Bluff, AR MSA	85,487	227	0.3	225	1	1
Pittsburgh – Beaver Valley, PA CMSA	2,242,798	2,257	0.1	2,187	42	28
Pittsfield, MA MSA	79,250	142	0.2	135	6	1
Portland, ME MSA	215,281	562	0.3	555	3	4
Portland – Vancouver, OR – WA CMSA	1,477,895	13,603	0.9	13,034	257	312
Portsmouth – Dover – Rochester, NH – ME MSA	223,578	414	0.2	400	11	3
Poughkeepsie, NY MSA	259,462	374	0.1	360	6	8
Providence – Pawtucket – Fall River, RI – MA CMSA	1,141,510	3,782	0.3	3,694	44	44

[Continued]

Population of Native North Americans by MSA in 1990 - II: L-Y
[Continued]

Metropolitan Statistical Areas	Total area population	American Indians, Eskimos, and Aleuts				
		Total	% of area's population	American Indians	Eskimos	Aleuts
Provo–Orem, UT MSA	263,590	1,913	0.7	1,883	11	19
Pueblo, CO MSA	123,051	991	0.8	979	8	4
Raleigh–Durham, NC MSA	735,480	1,933	0.3	1,896	16	21
Rapid City, SD MSA	81,343	5,835	7.2	5,804	27	4
Reading, PA MSA	336,523	333	0.1	318	10	5
Redding, CA MSA	147,036	3,954	2.7	3,885	26	43
Reno, NV MSA	254,667	4,921	1.9	4,832	53	36
Richland–Kennewick–Pasco, WA MSA	150,033	1,124	0.7	1,086	21	17
Richmond–Petersburg, VA MSA	865,640	2,705	0.3	2,681	15	9
Roanoke, VA MSA	224,477	281	0.1	277	4	
Rochester, MN MSA	106,470	295	0.3	286	8	1
Rochester, NY MSA	1,002,410	2,870	0.3	2,824	28	18
Rockford, IL MSA	283,719	697	0.2	665	19	13
Sacramento, CA MSA	1,481,102	17,021	1.1	16,650	165	206
Saginaw–Bay City–Midland, MI MSA	399,320	1,975	0.5	1,948	15	12
St. Cloud, MN MSA	190,921	637	0.3	625	9	3
St. Joseph, MO MSA	83,083	273	0.3	273		
St. Louis, MO–IL MSA	2,444,099	4,947	0.2	4,805	57	85
Salem, OR MSA	278,024	4,041	1.5	3,904	83	54
Salinas–Seaside–Monterey, CA MSA	355,660	3,017	0.8	2,944	46	27
Salt Lake City–Ogden, UT MSA	1,072,227	8,337	0.8	8,210	82	45
San Angelo, TX MSA	98,458	373	0.4	360	8	5
San Antonio, TX MSA	1,302,099	4,648	0.4	4,529	58	61
San Diego, CA MSA	2,498,016	20,066	0.8	19,564	193	309
San Francisco–Oakland–San Jose, CA CMSA	6,253,311	40,847	0.7	39,255	662	930
Santa Barbara–Santa Maria–Lompoc, CA MSA	369,608	3,351	0.9	3,279	42	30
Santa Fe, NM MSA	117,043	2,948	2.5	2,930	9	9
Sarasota, FL MSA	277,776	483	0.2	462	14	7
Savannah, GA MSA	242,622	515	0.2	489	21	5
Scranton–Wilkes-Barre, PA MSA	734,175	580	0.1	553	20	7
Seattle–Tacoma, WA CMSA	2,559,164	32,071	1.3	29,643	1,126	1,302
Sharon, PA MSA	121,003	115	0.1	111	3	1
Sheboygan, WI MSA	103,877	357	0.3	344	1	12
Sherman–Denison, TX MSA	95,021	1,046	1.1	1,028	1	17
Shreveport, LA MSA	334,341	865	0.3	849	9	7
Sioux City, IA–NE MSA	115,018	1,999	1.7	1,993	3	3
Sioux Falls, SD MSA	123,809	1,680	1.4	1,675	3	2
South Bend–Mishawaka, IN MSA	247,052	846	0.3	840	4	2
Spokane, WA MSA	361,364	5,539	1.5	5,390	95	54
Springfield, IL MSA	189,550	319	0.2	313	4	2
Springfield, MO MSA	240,593	1,471	0.6	1,450	11	10
Springfield, MA MSA	529,519	864	0.2	835	13	16
State College, PA MSA	123,786	179	0.1	168	7	4
Steubenville–Weirton, OH–WV MSA	142,523	237	0.2	224	4	9

[Continued]

★ 115 ★

Population of Native North Americans by MSA in 1990 - II: L-Y
[Continued]

Metropolitan Statistical Areas	Total area population	American Indians, Eskimos, and Aleuts				
		Total	% of area's population	American Indians	Eskimos	Aleuts
Stockton, CA MSA	480,628	5,085	1.1	4,999	38	48
Syracuse, NY MSA	659,864	3,948	0.6	3,915	18	15
Tallahassee, FL MSA	233,598	568	0.2	554	8	6
Tampa–St. Petersburg–Clearwater, FL MSA	2,067,959	5,467	0.3	5,331	76	60
Terre Haute, IN MSA	130,812	338	0.3	325	8	5
Texarkana, TX–Texarkana, AR MSA	120,132	560	0.5	554	2	4
Toledo, OH MSA	614,128	1,423	0.2	1,398	9	16
Topeka, KS MSA	160,976	1,836	1.1	1,827	4	5
Tucson, AZ MSA	666,880	20,330	3.0	20,231	56	43
Tulsa, OK MSA	708,954	48,196	6.8	48,116	45	35
Tuscaloosa, AL MSA	150,522	253	0.2	246	7	
Tyler, TX MSA	151,309	520	0.3	513	6	1
Utica–Rome, NY MSA	316,633	613	0.2	598	9	6
Victoria, TX MSA	74,361	208	0.3	194	4	10
Visalia–Tulare–Porterville, CA MSA	311,921	3,992	1.3	3,938	26	28
Waco, TX MSA	189,123	563	0.3	551	4	8
Washington, DC–MD–VA MSA	3,923,574	11,036	0.3	10,685	145	206
Waterbury, CT MSA	221,629	538	0.2	518	2	18
Waterloo–Cedar Falls, IA MSA	146,611	237	0.2	237		
Wausau, WI MSA	115,400	490	0.4	464	7	19
West Palm Beach–Boca Raton–Delray Beach, FL MSA	863,518	1,211	0.1	1,169	26	16
Wheeling, WV–OH MSA	159,301	145	0.1	143	2	
Wichita, KS MSA	485,270	5,160	1.1	5,132	13	15
Wichita Falls, TX MSA	122,378	903	0.7	876	6	21
Williamsport, PA MSA	118,710	219	0.2	216	1	2
Wilmington, NC MSA	120,284	435	0.4	433	2	
Worcester, MA MSA	436,905	891	0.2	876	11	4
Yakima, WA MSA	188,823	8,405	4.5	8,355	25	25
York, PA MSA	417,848	501	0.1	485	5	11
Youngstown–Warren, OH MSA	492,619	785	0.2	767	13	5
Yuba City, CA MSA	122,643	2,616	2.1	2,585	12	19
Yuma, AZ MSA	106,895	1,429	1.3	1,420	5	4

Source: Census of Population and Housing, 1990: Summary Tape File 1 on CD-ROM, U.S. Bureau of the Census, Washington, D.C. 1991.

★ 116 ★

Population

American Indian Population On and Off Reservations, by Selected Tribal Affiliation, 1991

The number of tribal members is shown, by residence status and tribal affiliation, for 1991.

Reservation	Tribal Affiliation	Residing on reservation	Residing off reservation	Total tribal membership
Blackfeet	Blackfeet	7,217	6,623	13,840
Cheyenne River	Cheyenne Sioux	3,690	5,970	9,660
Colville	Colville	4,170	3,475	7,645
Crow	Crow	6,210	2,382	8,592
Fort Berthold	Arikara, Mandan, Hidatsa	4,600	4,500	9,100
Fort Peck	Assiniboine-Sioux	5,146	4,485	9,631
Pine Ridge	Oglala Sioux	12,107	7,000	19,107
Rosebud	Rosebud Sioux	10,973	1,810	12,783
Standing Rock	Standing Rock-Sioux	4,799	8,611	13,410
Turtle Mountain	Chippewa	4,420	22,080	26,500
Wind River	Arapahoe, Shoshone	5,003	2,278	7,281
Yakima	Yakima	5,585	2,514	8,099
Total		73,920	71,728	145,648

Source: U.S. General Accounting Office. *Indian Programs: Profile of Land Ownership at 12 Reservations.* Washington, DC: U.S. GAO, GAO/RCED-92-96BR, February 1992, p. 8.

★ 117 ★

Population

Population by Tribe and U.S. Region, 1990: Abenaki-Chinook

Data are based on a sample and are subject to sampling variability.

Tribe	U.S.	Northeast Region		Midwest Region		South Region			West Region	
		New England	Middle Atlantic	East North Central	West North Central	South Atlantic	East South Central	West South Central	Mountain	Pacific
American Indian	1,937,391	34,013	87,173	157,555	189,904	184,637	46,015	354,711	482,400	400,983
Abenaki	1,549	1,225	86	20	5	46	26	21	26	94
Alaska Native	1,313	18	120	19	17	41	-	30	38	1,030
Alaska Indian	205	-	-	-	17	15	-	-	15	158
Alaska Native	779	18	-	-	-	15	-	3	23	720
Chaneliak	61	-	59	-	-	-	-	-	-	2
Chugach	107	-	-	-	-	-	-	27	-	80
Sealaska	131	-	61	19	-	11	-	-	-	40
Other Alaska Native	30	-	-	-	-	-	-	-	-	30
Alaskan Athabaskans	14,198	71	120	166	188	189	17	159	260	13,028
Ahtna	205	16	-	-	8	-	-	-	8	173
Alaskan Athabaskan	13,192	48	95	148	166	187	17	123	175	12,233
Doyon	265	5	19	7	14	2	-	12	-	206
Tanaina	536	2	6	11	-	-	-	24	77	416

[Continued]

Population by Tribe and U.S. Region, 1990: Abenaki-Chinook

[Continued]

Tribe	U.S.	Northeast Region		Midwest Region		South Region			West Region	
		New England	Middle Atlantic	East North Central	West North Central	South Atlantic	East South Central	West South Central	Mountain	Pacific
Algonquian	1,700	395	436	173	20	178	5	48	67	378
Apache	53,330	458	1,156	2,368	1,394	2,228	662	5,211	28,445	11,408
Apache	32,912	396	1,010	2,162	1,141	1,989	587	4,389	11,697	9,541
Chiricahua	739	14	57	42	60	66	-	86	61	353
Fort Sill Apache	103	-	-	-	19	-	8	64	12	-
Jicarilla Apache	2,750	7	-	2	2	-	-	50	2,516	173
Lipan Apache	30	-	2	10	-	-	-	7	-	11
Mescalero Apache	4,144	29	53	92	28	87	32	191	2,846	786
Oklahoma Apache	563	-	-	10	56	36	9	301	49	102
Payson Apache	89	-	-	3	-	-	-	86	-	
San Carlos Apache	2,300	4	26	42	40	38	24	47	1,889	190
White Mountain Apache	9,700	8	8	5	48	12	2	76	9,289	252
Arapaho	6,918	68	60	167	180	121	29	1,155	4,481	657
Arapaho	5,585	68	60	158	143	121	29	1,122	3,273	611
Northern Arapaho	1,319	-	-	9	37	-	-	33	1,194	46
Southern Arapaho	14	-	-	-	-	-	-	-	14	-
Arikara	1,671	3	13	31	1,104	53	-	50	207	210
Assiniboine	5,521	14	48	32	166	107	6	113	4,015	1,020
Bannock	187	-	-	6	-	-	-	9	152	20
Blackfoot	37,992	1,551	2,707	4,591	1,681	3,322	642	1,723	10,774	11,001
Brotherton	466	-	3	348	72	14	-	-	6	23
Caddo	2,984	28	16	49	68	139	9	2,149	157	369
Caddo	2,935	28	16	49	68	124	9	2,125	153	363
Oklahoma Caddo	49	-	-	-	-	15	-	24	4	6
Cahuilla	1,294	-	-	-	-	-	-	4	42	1,248
Agua Caliente Cahuilla	50	-	-	-	-	-	-	-	6	44
Cahuilla	888	-	-	-	-	-	-	4	23	861
Soboba	201	-	-	-	-	-	-	-	13	188
Torres-Martinez	129	-	-	-	-	-	-	-	-	129
Other Cahuilla	26	-	-	-	-	-	-	-	-	26
California tribes	1,331	33	-	51	10	26	7	10	46	1,148
Cahto	126	-	-	5	10	8	-	-	-	103
Chimariko	63	-	-	-	-	-	-	-	-	63
Coast Miwok	41	-	-	-	-	-	-	-	-	41
Digger	35	-	-	-	-	-	-	-	11	24
Mattole	38	-	-	-	-	-	-	-	6	32
Morongo	573	-	-	13	-	18	7	10	16	509
Santa Rosa	53	33	-	-	-	-	-	-	-	20
Wappo	54	-	-	10	-	-	-	-	7	37
Yuki	294	-	-	11	-	-	-	-	6	277
Other California	54	-	-	12	-	-	-	-	-	42
Canadian and Latin American	27,179	998	3,306	2,744	1,147	2,317	384	2,433	2,548	11,302
Canadian Indian	3,431	234	219	660	222	196	48	45	228	1,579
Central American Indian	1,744	125	218	51	62	605	31	250	49	353
French American Indian	1,018	67	141	144	64	52	10	209	73	258
Mexican American Indian	13,678	206	774	1,413	494	746	196	1,340	1,365	7,144
South American Indian	2,882	295	1,115	151	108	443	19	84	163	504
Spanish American Indian	4,426	71	839	325	197	275	80	505	670	1,464
Catawba	964	9	16	25	4	792	7	24	47	40
Cayuse	161	-	-	-	7	6	-	2	-	146
Chehalis	314	-	-	-	-	-	-	2	9	303
Chemakuan	738	-	-	-	14	-	-	7	7	710
Chemakuan	14	-	-	-	-	-	-	-	-	14
Hoh	103	-	-	-	-	-	-	-	-	103
Quileute	621	-	-	-	14	-	-	7	7	593
Chemehuevi	640	-	5	29	32	-	-	17	212	345
Cherokee	369,035	4,306	13,412	34,639	22,463	52,843	20,905	129,103	19,608	71,756
Cherokee	352,680	4,269	13,337	34,297	21,975	47,338	17,226	124,031	19,170	71,037
Cherokees of Northeast Alabama	87	-	-	-	-	-	83	4	-	-
Cherokees of Southeast Alabama	196	-	6	39	6	54	64	16	11	-
Eastern Cherokee	5,968	19	17	181	104	5,145	42	142	122	196
Echota Cherokee	3,773	-	2	27	4	117	3,462	62	6	93

[Continued]

★ 117 ★

Population by Tribe and U.S. Region, 1990: Abenaki-Chinook

[Continued]

Tribe	U.S.	Northeast Region		Midwest Region		South Region			West Region	
		New England	Middle Atlantic	East North Central	West North Central	South Atlantic	East South Central	West South Central	Mountain	Pacific
Etowah Cherokee	85	5	-	26	2	19	-	25	-	8
Northern Cherokee	285	-	2	-	88	9	-	99	25	62
United Keetoowah Band	145	-	-	-	-	-	-	126	-	19
Western Cherokee	5,811	13	48	69	284	156	28	4,598	274	341
Other Cherokee	5	-	-	-	-	5	-	-	-	-
Cherokee Shawnee	944	-	16	87	59	34	12	588	5	143
Cheyenne	11,809	70	190	501	690	264	69	3,122	5,180	1,723
Cheyenne	7,104	62	188	468	525	259	52	2,859	1,329	1,362
Northern Cheyenne	4,398	8	2	26	161	5	10	73	3,776	337
Southern Cheyenne	307	-	-	7	4	-	7	190	75	24
Cheyenne-Arapaho	2,629	9	-	16	94	47	-	1,950	205	308
Chickahominy	901	-	55	12	-	682	14	14	64	60
Chickahominy	893	-	55	12	-	674	14	14	64	60
Other Chickahominy	8	-	-	-	-	8	-	-	-	-
Chickasaw	21,522	55	99	373	434	422	218	15,525	929	3,467
Chinook	878	8	22	8	9	31	-	6	25	769
Chinook	813	8	17	8	9	31	-	6	25	709
Clatsop	32	-	-	-	-	-	-	-	-	32
Other Chinook	33	-	5	-	-	-	-	-	-	28

Source: U.S. Bureau of the Census. *1990 Census of Population: Characteristics of American Indians by Tribe and Language.* CP3-7. Washington, DC: The Bureau, 1994, p. 1. *Note:* A dash (-) represents zero or a percent that rounds to zero.

★ 118 ★

Population

Population by Tribe and U.S. Region, 1990: Chippewa-Diegueno

Data are based on a sample and are subject to sampling variability.

Tribe	U.S.	Northeast Region		Midwest Region		South Region			West Region	
		New England	Middle Atlantic	East North Central	West North Central	South Atlantic	East South Central	West South Central	Mountain	Pacific
Chippewa	105,988	623	845	35,605	46,545	2,588	641	1,749	6,233	11,159
Bad River	1,442	16	20	1,098	236	-	9	6	-	57
Bay Mills Chippewa	442	-	6	415	9	-	-	-	-	12
Bois Forte	482	-	-	21	451	-	-	-	-	10
Chippewa	69,719	522	713	23,737	26,335	2,079	538	1,516	4,783	9,496
Fond du Lac	823	-	-	133	675	-	-	-	6	9
Grand Portage	102	-	-	7	84	-	-	-	-	11
Keweenaw	699	-	6	545	39	37	15	-	20	37
Lac Courte Oreilles	2,763	-	-	2,133	460	76	8	17	21	48
Lac du Flambeau	770	-	-	710	24	-	9	-	11	16
Lac Vieux Desert Chippewa	31	-	-	28	-	-	-	-	-	3
Lake Superior	190	-	-	60	102	-	-	15	-	13
Leech Lake	1,667	-	-	28	1,608	8	-	-	11	12
Leelanau	682	-	-	569	-	48	-	4	16	45
Little Shell Chippewa	574	-	-	-	17	-	-	49	463	45
Mille Lac	660	-	-	28	632	-	-	-	-	-
Minnesota Chippewa	2,884	17	23	140	2,327	80	19	51	35	192
Red Cliff Chippewa	836	-	6	526	223	6	-	-	48	27
Red Lake Chippewa	3,796	11	-	63	3,639	21	-	-	12	50
Saginaw Chippewa	847	-	16	764	6	14	13	-	6	28
St. Croix Chippewa	485	-	-	418	67	-	-	-	-	-
Sault Ste. Marie Chippewa	3,963	7	15	3,526	17	154	14	24	48	158

[Continued]

★ 118 ★

Population by Tribe and U.S. Region, 1990: Chippewa-Diegueno
[Continued]

Tribe	U.S.	Northeast Region		Midwest Region		South Region			West Region	
		New England	Middle Atlantic	East North Central	West North Central	South Atlantic	East South Central	West South Central	Mountain	Pacific
Sokaogon Chippewa	318	-	-	309	-	-	-	-	-	9
Turtle Mountain	9,208	45	23	144	7,677	42	8	37	622	610
White Earth	2,592	5	17	190	1,917	23	8	30	131	271
Other Chippewa	13	-	-	13	-	-	-	-	-	-
Chitimacha	625	-	25	12	5	13	5	555	-	10
Choctaw	86,231	272	519	1,807	2,213	2,294	8,186	55,107	3,684	12,149
Choctaw	65,321	249	448	1,656	1,993	2,016	6,158	38,366	3,250	11,185
Mississippi Choctaw	2,624	-	17	72	9	35	1,029	1,299	49	114
Mowa Band of Choctaw	947	-	-	-	-	24	908	15	-	-
Oklahoma Choctaw	17,323	23	54	79	211	219	91	15,411	385	850
Other Choctaw	16	-	-	-	-	-	-	16	-	-
Chumash	3,208	-	6	12	7	21	-	9	34	3,119
Chumash	3,114	-	6	12	7	21	-	9	34	3,025
Santa Ynez	94	-	-	-	-	-	-	-	-	94
Coeur d'Alene	1,057	-	17	-	2	35	-	8	606	389
Coharie	1,199	-	42	16	32	1,090	2	-	11	6
Colorado River	1,645	-	-	-	49	-	-	-	1,567	29
Colville	7,057	9	37	18	62	66	15	85	352	6,413
Comanche	11,437	89	179	382	557	693	155	6,717	714	1,951
Comanche	11,267	89	179	382	544	693	155	6,566	714	1,945
Oklahoma Comanche	170	-	-	-	13	-	-	151	-	6
Coos	201	9	-	-	-	-	11	-	-	181
Coquilles	520	-	-	2	-	-	-	-	8	510
Costanoan	858	-	12	6	-	28	15	1	48	748
Coushatta	1,213	-	-	-	5	12	14	1,090	10	82
Alabama Coushatta	736	-	-	-	5	12	7	635	5	72
Coushatta	477	-	-	-	-	-	7	455	5	10
Cowlitz	804	9	11	6	-	9	6	-	47	716
Cree	8,467	150	226	519	400	334	72	252	4,773	1,741
Creek	45,872	67	580	691	1,644	5,805	3,409	27,754	1,399	4,523
Alabama Quassarte	180	-	-	-	3	-	-	160	17	-
Creek	44,168	58	535	687	1,638	5,068	2,918	27,408	1,360	4,496
Eastern Creek	589	9	45	2	-	449	13	60	2	9
Lower Muskogee	180	-	-	-	-	150	15	15	-	-
MaChis Lower Creek Indian	64	-	-	-	-	12	34	-	-	18
Poarch Band	498	-	-	2	-	95	383	11	7	-
Principal Creek Indian Nation	56	-	-	-	-	9	39	8	-	-
Thlopthlocco	102	-	-	-	-	9	-	80	13	-
Other Creek	35	-	-	-	3	13	7	12	-	-
Croatan	177	-	-	-	-	104	32	12	-	29
Crow	9,394	43	204	242	296	306	77	250	6,820	1,156
Cupeno	373	7	-	-	-	26	-	-	-	340
Agua Caliente	117	7	-	-	-	-	-	-	-	110
Cupeno	256	-	-	-	-	26	-	-	-	230
Delaware	9,800	174	2,364	755	738	433	131	3,553	540	1,112
Delaware	6,844	77	585	662	567	241	92	3,147	493	980
Eastern Delaware	558	2	27	42	50	35	13	302	22	65
Lenni-Lenape	1,351	13	1,108	29	12	146	19	-	5	19
Munsee	103	-	13	22	32	11	-	15	6	4
Oklahoma Delaware	203	-	22	-	77	-	5	89	5	5
Rampough Mountain	732	82	609	-	-	-	-	-	9	32
Sand Hill	9	-	-	-	-	-	2	-	-	7
Diegueno	2,249	-	18	30	7	26	-	46	26	2,096
Campo	103	-	-	-	-	6	-	-	-	97

[Continued]

★ 118 ★

Population by Tribe and U.S. Region, 1990: Chippewa-Diegueno

[Continued]

Tribe	U.S.	Northeast Region		Midwest Region		South Region			West Region	
		New England	Middle Atlantic	East North Central	West North Central	South Atlantic	East South Central	West South Central	Mountain	Pacific
Capitan Grande	241	-	-	-	-	-	-	-	-	241
Diegueno	1,431	-	18	27	7	20	-	31	20	1,308
Manzanita	42	-	-	-	-	-	-	-	6	36
Mesa Grande	53	-	-	-	-	-	-	-	-	53
San Pascual	262	-	-	3	-	-	-	5	-	254
Santa Ysabel	85	-	-	-	-	-	-	2	-	83
Sycuan	32	-	-	-	-	-	-	8	-	24
Other Diegueno	-	-	-	-	-	-	-	-	-	-

Source: U.S. Bureau of the Census. *1990 Census of Population: Characteristics of American Indians by Tribe and Language.* CP3-7. Washington, DC: The Bureau, 1994, p. 7.
Note: A dash (-) represents zero or a percent that rounds to zero.

★ 119 ★

Population

Population by Tribe and U.S. Region, 1990: Eastern Tribes-Miwok

Data are based on a sample and are subject to sampling variability.

Tribe	U.S.	Northeast Region		Midwest Region		South Region			West Region	
		New England	Middle Atlantic	East North Central	West North Central	South Atlantic	East South Central	West South Central	Mountain	Pacific
Eastern tribes	3,853	399	357	176	32	2,302	33	297	16	241
Moor	126	-	-	11	14	86	-	15	-	-
Nansemond	142	-	30	-	-	112	-	-	-	-
Natchez	70	-	-	6	-	12	6	40	-	6
Nipmuc	434	336	23	15	-	5	-	-	-	55
Southeastern Indians	1,642	53	228	121	18	992	27	61	13	129
Susquehanock	124	-	66	13	-	39	-	-	-	6
Tunica	44	-	-	-	-	-	-	44	-	-
Tunica Biloxi	138	-	-	10	-	-	-	128	-	-
Waccamaw-Siouan	1,006	-	3	-	-	994	-	9	-	-
Wesort	34	-	-	-	-	-	-	-	-	34
Wicomico	38	-	-	-	-	38	-	-	-	-
Other Eastern	55	10	7	-	-	24	-	-	3	11
Fort Berthold	1,643	-	-	14	1,333	49	-	-	109	138
Fort Hall	3,450	17	-	-	4	7	-	19	3,166	237
Gabrieleno	581	6	-	1	-	-	-	2	22	550
Gila River	1,484	-	-	9	8	6	-	-	1,410	51
Grand Ronde	1,253	-	-	-	-	-	-	35	23	1,195
Gras Ventres	2,875	17	66	38	96	8	-	25	2,251	374
Atsina	-	-	-	-	-	-	-	-	-	-
Gros Ventres	2,875	17	66	38	96	8	-	25	2,251	374
Haida	1,936	36	16	5	17	17	-	10	6	1,829
Haliwa	2,946	12	165	-	-	2,633	-	69	-	67
Hidatsa	1,539	-	-	4	1,111	31	-	63	195	135
Hoopa	2,390	-	-	-	-	11	8	-	78	2,293
Hoopa	2,386	-	-	-	-	11	8	-	78	2,289
Other Hoopa	4	-	-	-	-	-	-	-	-	4
Houma	7,809	-	11	34	39	129	203	7,298	4	91

[Continued]

★ 119 ★

Population by Tribe and U.S. Region, 1990: Eastern Tribes-Miwok
[Continued]

Tribe	U.S.	Northeast Region		Midwest Region		South Region			West Region	
		New England	Middle Atlantic	East North Central	West North Central	South Atlantic	East South Central	West South Central	Mountain	Pacific
Iowa	1,555	28	18	33	698	54	-	355	73	296
Iroquois	52,557	1,853	21,700	11,937	1,393	4,780	479	3,284	1,819	5,312
Cayuga	1,111	16	883	41	5	49	16	10	14	77
Iroquois	5,158	548	1,069	806	102	593	93	250	413	1,284
Mohawk	17,106	1,013	10,214	1,811	235	1,454	146	442	630	1,161
Oneida	11,307	77	1,100	8,137	418	301	40	228	280	726
Onondaga	1,729	26	1,169	104	14	111	30	99	51	125
Seneca	9,133	103	6,067	649	72	458	77	492	231	984
Seneca	8,263	103	5,455	514	72	436	63	492	209	919
Seneca Nation	461	-	243	123	-	17	14	-	22	42
Tonawanda Seneca	409	-	369	12	-	5	-	-	-	23
Seneca-Cayuga	1,225	-	23	7	145	29	9	807	20	185
Tuscarora	3,245	56	1,116	57	6	1,762	53	16	52	127
Wyandotte	2,543	14	59	325	396	23	15	940	128	643
Juaneno	1,605	-	2	-	2	26	-	7	30	1,538
Kalispel	175	-	-	-	-	-	-	2	40	133
Karok	3,077	10	9	17	-	20	-	22	216	2,783
Kaw	1,166	-	-	55	241	19	20	687	57	87
Kickapoo	3,576	10	30	105	728	35	31	2,180	222	235
Kickapoo	3,450	10	30	105	720	35	31	2,062	222	235
Oklahoma Kickapoo	126	-	-	-	8	-	-	118	-	-
Kiowa	9,460	23	99	118	509	225	19	6,945	797	725
Kiowa	8,936	23	99	118	509	225	19	6,432	786	725
Oklahoma Kiowa	524	-	-	-	-	-	-	513	11	-
Klallam	1,522	-	5	36	-	25	-	23	2	1,431
Jamestown	112	-	-	-	-	-	-	-	-	112
Klallam	725	-	5	36	-	25	-	3	-	656
Lower Elwha	230	-	-	-	-	-	-	-	2	228
Port Gamble Klallam	455	-	-	-	-	-	-	20	-	435
Klamath	3,113	-	9	14	-	7	-	70	143	2,870
Konkow	380	-	11	25	-	-	-	-	3	341
Kootenai	745	-	19	-	-	6	-	-	485	235
Long Island	488	15	435	-	-	14	-	16	-	8
Matinecock	70	6	54	-	-	-	-	10	-	-
Montauk	80	9	63	-	-	-	-	-	-	8
Poospatuck	338	-	318	-	-	14	-	6	-	-
Setauket	-	-	-	-	-	-	-	-	-	-
Luiseno	2,798	8	27	53	16	24	9	5	70	2,586
La Jolla	162	-	-	-	-	11	-	-	-	151
Luiseno	1,757	-	-	10	5	-	-	-	25	1,717
Pala	549	8	27	43	11	11	-	-	45	404
Pauma	120	-	-	-	-	-	-	-	-	120
Pechanga	210	-	-	-	-	2	9	5	-	194
Lumbee	50,888	67	431	1,172	183	47,672	232	295	159	677
Lummi	3,125	-	-	52	37	38	13	20	47	2,918
Maidu	2,334	-	-	31	-	10	-	21	115	2,157
Maidu	2,334	-	-	31	-	10	-	21	115	2,157
Nishinam	-	-	-	-	-	-	-	-	-	-

[Continued]

★ 119 ★

Population by Tribe and U.S. Region, 1990: Eastern Tribes-Miwok
[Continued]

| Tribe | U.S. | Northeast Region | | Midwest Region | | South Region | | | West Region | |
		New England	Middle Atlantic	East North Central	West North Central	South Atlantic	East South Central	West South Central	Mountain	Pacific
Makah	1,661	11	-	2	15	47	9	40	11	1,526
Maliseet	891	701	30	33	21	23	28	16	3	36
Aroostook	6	6	-	-	-	-	-	-	-	-
Maliseet	885	695	30	33	21	23	28	16	3	36
Mandan	1,273	-	2	42	774	68	-	15	170	202
Mattaponi	440	-	68	-	-	331	7	-	-	34
Menominee	8,064	39	74	7,041	209	178	7	91	146	279
Miami	4,580	5	55	2,506	550	265	49	463	250	437
Illinois Miami	72	5	-	11	10	27	-	-	-	19
Indiana Miami	307	-	19	158	37	45	-	40	-	8
Miami	3,480	-	36	2,247	273	136	49	285	225	229
Oklahoma Miami	721	-	-	90	230	57	-	138	25	181
Miccosukee	261	-	-	9	-	233	4	5	-	10
Micmac	2,726	1,819	228	107	62	165	36	25	100	184
Mission Indians	2,056	9	-	38	9	3	5	23	120	1,849
Miwok	3,438	26	7	7	34	15	11	8	154	3,176

Source: U.S. Bureau of the Census. *1990 Census of Population: Characteristics of American Indians by Tribe and Language.* CP3-7. Washington, DC: The Bureau, 1994, p. 13.
Note: A dash (-) represents zero or a percent that rounds to zero.

★ 120 ★
Population

Population by Tribe and U.S. Region, 1990: Modoc-Pueblo

Data are based on a sample and are subject to sampling variability.

| Tribe | U.S. | Northeast Region | | Midwest Region | | South Region | | | West Region | |
		New England	Middle Atlantic	East North Central	West North Central	South Atlantic	East South Central	West South Central	Mountain	Pacific
Modoc	521	-	25	13	54	-	-	20	14	395
Modoc	521	-	25	13	54	-	-	20	14	395
Oklahoma Modoc	-	-	-	-	-	-	-	-	-	-
Mohegan	996	507	195	36	-	98	12	20	73	55
Mono	1,697	-	-	23	2	3	-	20	38	1,611
Nanticoke	1,529	8	586	23	-	789	-	31	23	69
Narragansett	2,564	2,087	81	20	11	141	9	30	31	154
Navajo	225,298	366	815	1,342	1,251	1,665	297	2,991	205,388	11,183
Nez Perce	4,003	38	20	63	72	145	12	96	2,018	1,539
Nomalaki	314	-	-	-	-	21	-	-	-	293
Northwest tribes	699	43	204	22	2	43	13	128	12	232
Columbia	511	43	204	12	2	43	-	128	12	67
Kalapuya	52	-	-	1	-	-	-	-	-	51
Tillamook	93	-	-	8	-	-	-	-	-	85
Other Northwest	43	-	-	1	-	-	13	-	-	29
Omaha	4,363	8	13	165	3,483	144	7	88	206	249
Oregon Athabaskan	341	-	-	6	2	12	-	92	4	225
Osage	10,430	63	40	319	785	341	126	6,056	705	1,995
Otoe-Missouria	1,762	18	26	8	137	107	-	1,239	90	137
Ottawa	7,885	10	88	5,681	254	448	63	526	148	667
Burt Lake Ottawa	13	-	-	13	-	-	-	-	-	-

[Continued]

★ 120 ★

Population by Tribe and U.S. Region, 1990: Modoc-Pueblo
[Continued]

Tribe	U.S.	Northeast Region		Midwest Region		South Region			West Region	
		New England	Middle Atlantic	East North Central	West North Central	South Atlantic	East South Central	West South Central	Mountain	Pacific
Michigan Ottawa	73	-	-	39	-	-	-	-	-	34
Oklahoma Ottawa	80	-	-	12	18	-	-	-	-	50
Ottawa	7,719	10	88	5,617	236	448	63	526	148	583
Paiute	11,369	26	34	57	157	138	16	115	5,429	5,397
Burns Paiute	138	-	-	-	-	-	-	-	-	138
Kaibab	101	-	-	-	8	-	-	-	84	9
Moapa	51	-	-	-	-	-	-	-	51	-
Northern Paiute	234	-	-	-	5	-	-	-	78	151
Owens Valley	314	-	-	-	-	-	-	-	-	314
Paiute	9,201	-	34	57	115	120	16	113	4,061	4,685
Pyramid Lake	628	-	-	-	-	13	-	-	602	13
Southern Paiute	93	-	-	-	12	5	-	2	52	22
Walker River	373	22	-	-	-	-	-	-	317	34
Yerington Paiute	169	-	-	-	-	-	-	-	156	13
Other Paiute	67	4	-	-	17	-	-	-	28	18
Pamunkey	400	10	152	34	-	177	-	13	6	8
Passamaquoddy	2,466	2,101	30	11	14	164	-	6	50	90
Passamaquoddy	2,466	2,101	30	11	14	164	-	6	-	-
Other Passamaquoddy	-	-	-	-	-	-	-	-	-	-
Pawnee	3,387	25	89	135	197	180	6	1,842	389	524
Oklahoma Pawnee	156	-	-	-	2	-	-	154	-	-
Pawnee	3,231	25	89	135	195	180	6	1,688	389	524
Penobscot	2,407	1,642	142	81	-	250	12	75	42	163
Peoria	1,274	-	-	15	175	69	11	584	112	308
Oklahoma Peoria	56	-	-	-	-	-	-	19	19	18
Peoria	1,218	-	-	15	175	69	11	565	93	290
Pequot	679	482	44	17	11	73	-	-	12	40
Pima	15,074	18	33	76	75	114	26	160	13,314	1,258
Piscataway	824	26	22	-	-	729	3	-	-	44
Pit River	1,753	-	14	16	-	18	-	39	61	1,605
Pomo	4,898	9	-	9	47	35	-	29	144	4,625
Central Pomo	103	9	-	-	-	-	-	-	17	77
Kashaya	62	-	-	-	-	-	-	-	-	62
Northern Pomo	262	-	-	-	-	-	-	-	-	262
Pomo	4,412	-	-	9	47	35	-	29	127	4,165
Other Pomo	59	-	-	-	-	-	-	-	-	59
Ponca	2,788	20	31	2	626	9	-	1,837	138	125
Oklahoma Ponca	104	-	-	-	2	-	-	86	7	9
Ponca	2,684	20	31	2	624	9	-	1,751	131	116
Potawatomi	16,719	65	184	3,949	2,693	431	131	5,720	907	2,639
Citizen Band Potawatomi	1,954	5	36	21	314	68	38	1,154	127	191
Forest County	333	-	-	327	6	-	-	-	-	-
Hannahville	63	-	-	58	-	-	-	5	-	-
Huron Potawatomi	88	-	-	70	10	-	-	8	-	-
Popagon Potawatomi	48	-	-	48	-	-	-	-	-	-
Potawatomi	13,640	48	146	3,384	1,971	359	93	4,479	741	2,419
Prairie Band	593	12	2	41	392	4	-	74	39	29
Wisconsin Potawatomi	-	-	-	-	-	-	-	-	-	-
Powhatan	795	27	360	10	46	191	13	32	41	75
Pueblo	55,330	187	422	571	397	747	113	1,694	46,602	4,597
Acoma	3,938	-	7	30	24	13	8	22	3,562	272
Arizona Tewa	423	-	-	-	-	25	-	-	392	6
Cochiti	1,184	-	-	20	-	14	-	-	1,122	28
Hopi	11,791	23	172	125	173	171	2	150	9,841	1,134

[Continued]

★ 120 ★

Population by Tribe and U.S. Region, 1990: Modoc-Pueblo

[Continued]

Tribe	U.S.	Northeast Region		Midwest Region		South Region			West Region	
		New England	Middle Atlantic	East North Central	West North Central	South Atlantic	East South Central	West South Central	Mountain	Pacific
Isleta	3,306	25	-	-	22	67	-	57	2,944	191
Jemez	2,238	-	-	21	21	-	-	53	2,047	96
Keres	36	-	-	-	-	-	-	-	36	-
Laguna	6,424	8	45	67	21	138	20	155	5,353	617
Nambe	300	-	-	-	-	8	-	4	288	-
Picuris	245	-	21	-	2	-	-	-	191	31
Piro	15	-	-	-	-	-	-	-	-	15
Pojoaque	39	-	-	-	-	-	-	6	33	-
Pueblo	2,664	26	26	137	68	91	44	217	1,087	968
Sandia	291	-	-	-	-	-	-	-	285	6
San Felipe	2,218	-	-	16	4	21	-	8	2,137	32
San Ildefonso	411	-	-	5	-	3	-	-	396	7
San Juan	1,081	-	-	18	2	-	-	-	1,035	26
Santa Ana	596	-	6	-	-	-	11	9	552	18
Santa Clara	1,180	-	-	2	1	-	-	39	1,102	36
Santa Domingo	2,865	83	104	16	-	13	-	34	2,572	43
Taos	1,875	-	-	15	18	23	-	21	1,689	109
Tesuque	225	-	-	-	8	-	-	-	217	-
Tewa	1,640	-	12	54	10	55	9	52	1,055	393
Tigua	1,271	22	17	-	-	39	-	786	103	304
Zia	793	-	-	24	-	-	-	-	760	9
Zuni	8,281	-	12	21	23	66	19	81	7,803	256

Source: U.S. Bureau of the Census. *1990 Census of Population: Characteristics of American Indians by Tribe and Language.* CP3-7. Washington, DC: The Bureau, 1994, p. 19. *Note:* A dash (-) represents zero or a percent that rounds to zero.

★ 121 ★

Population

Population by Tribe and U.S. Region, 1990: Puget Sound Salish-Sioux

Data are based on a sample and are subject to sampling variability.

Tribe	U.S.	Northeast Region		Midwest Region		South Region			West Region	
		New England	Middle Atlantic	East North Central	West North Central	South Atlantic	East South Central	West South Central	Mountain	Pacific
Puget Sound Salish	10,384	22	53	53	124	229	12	53	204	9,634
Duwamish	215	-	7	20	-	-	-	-	2	186
Muckleshoot	1,031	-	8	-	38	-	-	-	-	985
Nisqually	436	-	-	-	7	10	-	-	3	416
Nooksack	890	-	-	-	-	-	-	17	43	830
Puyallup	1,013	22	7	17	-	27	12	3	17	908
Samish	225	-	9	5	12	20	-	-	6	173
Sauk-Suiattle	147	-	-	-	6	-	-	-	2	139
Skokomish	737	-	-	-	4	8	-	13	6	706
Snohomish	499	-	-	-	16	7	-	2	32	442
Snoqualmie	444	-	-	-	-	-	-	2	14	428
Squaxin Island	489	-	-	-	-	18	-	-	-	471
Steilacoom	150	-	-	-	-	6	-	-	-	144
Stillaguamish	140	-	-	-	-	-	-	-	-	140
Suquamish	635	-	5	11	-	29	-	2	-	588
Swinomish	716	-	-	-	-	11	-	-	50	655

[Continued]

Population by Tribe and U.S. Region, 1990: Puget Sound Salish-Sioux

[Continued]

Tribe	U.S.	Northeast Region		Midwest Region		South Region			West Region	
		New England	Middle Atlantic	East North Central	West North Central	South Atlantic	East South Central	West South Central	Mountain	Pacific
Tulalip	2,170	-	-	-	29	76	-	4	18	2,043
Upper Skagit	423	-	17	-	12	6	-	10	11	367
Other Puget Sound Salish	24	-	-	-	-	11	-	-	-	13
Quapaw	1,438	-	16	57	371	43	19	660	63	209
Quinault	2,513	-	-	52	11	53	-	7	86	2,304
Rappahannock	343	-	19	-	-	301	-	13	-	10
Sac and Fox	4,774	-	42	212	1,583	106	-	1,972	299	560
Missouri Sac and Fox	88	-	-	-	29	-	-	-	59	-
Oklahoma Sac and Fox	239	-	-	-	33	-	-	151	1	54
Sac and Fox	3,168	-	24	136	627	36	-	1,780	184	381
Sac and Fox-Mesquakie	1,279	-	18	76	894	70	-	41	55	125
Salinan	279	-	-	4	-	5	-	-	-	270
Salish	4,830	5	41	23	38	90	-	144	2,989	1,500
Salish and Kootenai	2,293	6	7	-	19	22	-	16	1,832	391
Schaghticoke	182	137	16	5	2	20	-	-	-	2
Seminole	15,564	219	764	532	563	3,367	200	7,199	601	2,119
Florida Seminole	518	-	-	11	-	405	26	11	10	55
Oklahoma Seminole	450	-	12	-	-	26	-	397	15	-
Seminole	14,596	219	752	521	563	2,936	174	6,791	576	2,064
Other Seminole	-	-	-	-	-	-	-	-	-	-
Serrano	295	-	3	-	-	-	-	22	-	270
San Manual	12	-	-	-	-	-	-	-	-	12
Serrano	283	-	3	-	-	-	-	22	-	258
Shasta	703	-	13	-	16	17	-	28	49	580
Shawnee	6,640	24	230	834	372	497	186	2,974	273	1,250
Absentee Shawnee	1,129	-	-	-	24	29	6	1,006	52	12
Eastern Shawnee	762	-	16	18	111	5	8	415	29	160
Shawnee	4,749	24	214	816	237	463	172	1,553	192	1,078
Shinnecock	1,670	115	1,300	6	-	180	2	13	4	50
Shoshone	9,506	59	135	207	168	221	32	348	5,977	2,359
Battle Mountain	82	-	-	-	-	-	-	-	82	-
Ely	153	-	-	-	15	-	-	-	138	-
Goshute	209	3	-	11	-	-	-	-	192	3
Shoshone	7,925	56	130	196	153	219	32	335	4,630	2,174
Te-Moak Western Shoshone	932	-	5	-	-	2	-	5	779	141
Timbi-Sha Shoshone	47	-	-	-	-	-	-	8	12	27
Washakie	66	-	-	-	-	-	-	-	58	8
Yomba	44	-	-	-	-	-	-	-	38	6
Other Shoshone	48	-	-	-	-	-	-	-	48	-
Shoshone-Paiute	2,320	-	9	24	19	4	-	22	1,755	487
Duck Valley	419	-	-	16	-	4	-	-	380	19
Fallon	121	-	-	-	-	-	-	-	112	9
Shoshone-Paiute	1,780	-	9	8	19	-	-	22	1,263	459
Siletz	1,726	12	24	-	4	12	-	34	70	1,570
Sioux	107,321	690	1,776	4,260	65,196	3,665	722	3,500	13,372	14,140
Blackfoot Sioux	581	-	60	139	31	26	4	26	51	244
Brule Sioux	53	4	-	9	33	-	-	-	-	7
Cheyene River Sioux	7,602	12	24	71	6,654	78	-	154	339	270
Crow Creek Sioux	2,273	-	28	21	1,863	2	16	40	147	156
Dakota Sioux	538	36	24	19	274	40	7	-	74	64
Devils Lake Sioux	2,227	-	-	-	2,150	21	-	-	35	21
Flandreau Santee	191	-	7	7	143	-	-	-	25	9
Fort Peck	847	-	-	-	261	-	-	6	472	108
Lake Traverse Sioux	52	-	-	52	-	-	-	-	-	-

[Continued]

★ 121 ★

Population by Tribe and U.S. Region, 1990: Puget Sound Salish-Sioux

[Continued]

Tribe	U.S.	Northeast Region		Midwest Region		South Region			West Region	
		New England	Middle Atlantic	East North Central	West North Central	South Atlantic	East South Central	West South Central	Mountain	Pacific
Lower Brule Sioux	1,374	-	-	10	1,228	15	-	38	21	62
Lower Sioux	81	-	-	-	81	-	-	-	-	-
Mdewakanton Sioux	294	-	-	21	258	-	-	-	-	15
Oglala Sioux	17,092	46	117	250	13,695	337	39	206	1,404	998
Pine Ridge Sioux	751	-	-	9	662	9	-	-	34	37
Prior Lake	59	8	-	5	46	-	-	-	-	-
Rosebud Sioux	11,146	21	85	65	9,809	46	42	107	480	491
Santee Sioux	2,284	2	-	98	1,729	40	9	100	136	170
Sioux	44,354	553	1,317	3,174	13,705	2,740	519	2,573	9,357	10,416
Sisseton Sioux	884	-	10	3	688	9	-	17	35	122
Sisseton-Wahpeton Sioux	3,491	1	1	43	3,105	73	42	34	66	126
Standing Rock Sioux	6,071	-	12	36	5,423	65	9	13	292	221
Teton Sioux	1,251	5	55	127	321	154	35	61	154	339
Wahpeton Sioux	51	2	6	7	19	-	-	-	-	17
Yankton Sioux	3,709	-	26	92	2,969	10	-	125	250	237
Other Sioux	65	-	4	2	49	-	-	-	-	10

Source: U.S. Bureau of the Census. *1990 Census of Population: Characteristics of American Indians by Tribe and Language.* CP3-7. Washington, DC: The Bureau, 1994, p. 25. *Note:* A dash (-) represents zero or a percent that rounds to zero.

★ 122 ★

Population

Population by Tribe and U.S. Region, 1990: Siuslaw-Yurok and Other Specified Tribes

Data are based on a sample and are subject to sampling variability.

Tribe	U.S.	Northeast Region		Midwest Region		South Region			West Region	
		New England	Middle Atlantic	East North Central	West North Central	South Atlantic	East South Central	West South Central	Mountain	Pacific
Siuslaw	48	-	-	-	-	-	-	-	14	34
Spokane	2,042	-	5	-	13	29	-	14	95	1,886
Stockbridge	2,219	105	68	1,452	103	147	29	66	78	171
Tlingit	14,417	56	87	108	161	122	19	141	181	13,542
Tohono O'Odham	16,876	32	30	149	43	37	3	143	15,099	1,340
Ak-Chin	334	-	-	-	-	-	-	-	334	-
Tohono O'Odham	16,542	32	30	149	43	37	3	143	14,765	1,340
Other Tohono O'Odham	-	-	-	-	-	-	-	-	-	-
Tolowa	451	-	-	5	-	-	-	-	-	446
Tonkawa	321	-	-	-	18	-	-	247	1	55
Tsimshian	2,157	-	-	17	5	15	-	8	32	2,080
Umatilla	1,285	-	15	4	37	-	-	47	94	1,088
Umpqua	671	7	-	-	-	-	-	5	32	627
Cow Creek Umpqua	346	-	-	-	-	-	-	-	7	339
Umpqua	325	7	-	-	-	-	-	5	25	288
Ute	7,658	25	46	116	75	123	72	218	6,053	930
Allen Canyon	-	-	-	-	-	-	-	-	-	-
Uintah Ute	572	-	8	6	2	-	-	49	479	28
Ute	5,626	25	36	110	73	117	72	169	4,163	861
Ute Mountain Ute	1,460	-	2	-	-	6	-	-	1,411	41
Wailaki	1,254	-	-	2	18	-	5	-	72	1,157
Walla-Walla	227	-	-	-	-	6	-	-	9	212

[Continued]

Population by Tribe and U.S. Region, 1990: Siuslaw-Yurok and Other Specified Tribes
[Continued]

Tribe	U.S.	Northeast Region		Midwest Region		South Region			West Region	
		New England	Middle Atlantic	East North Central	West North Central	South Atlantic	East South Central	West South Central	Mountain	Pacific
Wampanoag	2,334	1,754	158	21	43	81	20	28	49	180
Gay Head Wampanoag	128	84	13	-	-	15	-	-	2	14
Mashpee Wampanoag	61	31	22	8	-	-	-	-	-	-
Wampanoag	2,145	1,639	123	13	43	66	20	28	47	166
Warm Springs	2,685	-	-	-	3	-	-	36	11	2,635
Washo	1,489	-	-	-	9	23	-	1	806	650
Washo	1,475	-	-	-	7	23	-	1	804	640
Other Washo	14	-	-	-	2	-	-	-	2	10
Wichita	1,241	17	5	8	38	14	11	1,013	14	121
Winnebago	6,591	6	42	2,954	2,408	108	19	119	323	612
Nebraska Winnebago	167	-	-	72	67	-	-	-	28	-
Winnebago	5,153	6	39	1,956	2,114	91	19	106	230	592
Wisconsin Winnebago	1,271	-	3	926	227	17	-	13	65	20
Wintu	2,319	-	-	4	25	13	-	10	99	2,168
Wiyot	479	-	-	1	11	7	-	30	5	425
Yakima	7,577	16	7	2	52	19	6	47		
Yaqui	9,838	3	21	83	46	115	37	83	7,136	2,314
Barrio Libre	-	-	-	-	-	-	-	-	-	-
Pascua Yaqui	681	-	-	-	-	5	19	40	496	121
Yaqui	9,157	3	21	83	46	110	18	43	6,640	2,193
Yavapai Apache	644	-	-	7	-	-	-	-	617	20
Yokuts	2,967	11	22	8	15	9	-	16	82	2,804
Chukchansi	822	11	-	-	-	-	-	-	18	793
Tachi	418	-	-	8	-	9	-	-	-	401
Tule River	908	-	15	-	11	-	-	-	-	882
Yokuts	819	-	7	-	4	-	-	16	64	728
Yuchi	380	-	6	-	36	20	-	178	13	127
Yuman	7,319	-	10	7	73	28	8	176	4,846	2,171
Cocopah	612	-	-	-	20	-	-	5	521	66
Havasupai	557	-	-	-	-	-	-	30	502	25
Hualapai	1,205	-	1	-	-	-	8	109	1,020	67
Maricopa	744	-	-	-	10	-	-	-	712	22
Mohave	1,321	-	-	-	31	28	-	17	780	465
Quechan	2,194	-	9	1	12	-	-	15	678	1,479
Yavapai	686	-	-	6	-	-	-	-	633	47
Yurok	4,444	7	22	10	46	22	19	61	139	4,118
Other specified tribes	1,201	-	14	52	52	14	-	23	503	543
Burt Lake Band	45	-	-	45	-	-	-	-	-	-
Fort Belknap	158	-	-	5	19	-	-	-	123	11
Fort McDermitt	171	-	-	-	-	-	-	-	163	8
Fort McDowell	256	-	-	-	-	-	-	-	139	17
Los Coyotes	60	-	-	-	-	-	-	-	-	60
Mexican Indian Cherokee	86	-	12	-	8	14	-	23	-	29
Reno-Sparks	48	-	-	-	-	-	-	-	47	1
Round Valley	99	-	-	-	-	-	-	-	-	99
Shoalwater	85	-	-	2	-	-	-	-	-	83
Wascopum	233	-	-	-	-	-	-	-	-	233
Wind River	46	-	-	-	25	-	-	-	21	-
All other specified	14	-	2	-	-	-	-	-	10	2
Tribe not specified	23,208	619	3,301	2,241	2,127	3,079	697	2,737	1,901	6,506
Tribe not reported	195,447	6,398	24,371	21,059	14,929	27,231	6,041	25,677	23,330	46,411

Source: U.S. Bureau of the Census. *1990 Census of Population: Characteristics of American Indians by Tribe and Language.* CP3-7. Washington, DC: The Bureau, 1994, p. 31. *Note:* A dash (-) represents zero or a percent that rounds to zero.

★ 123 ★
Population

Population by Tribe, Region, and State, 1990: Abenaki-Chinook - Part I

Data are based on a sample and are subject to sampling variability.

Tribe	New England						Middle Atlantic		
	Maine	New Hampshire	Vermont	Massachusetts	Rhode Island	Connecticut	New York	New Jersey	Pennsylvania
American Indian	6,345	2,390	2,144	12,343	4,112	6,679	57,425	14,191	15,557
Abenaki	38	105	850	171	9	52	52	26	8
Alaska Native	-	18	-	-	-	-	120	-	-
Alaska Indian	-	-	-	-	-	-	-	-	-
Alaska Native	-	18	-	-	-	-	-	-	-
Chaneliak	-	-	-	-	-	-	59	-	-
Chugach	-	-	-	-	-	-	-	-	-
Sealaska	-	-	-	-	-	-	61	-	-
Other Alaska Native	-	-	-	-	-	-	-	-	-
Alaskan Athabaskans	5	-	8	26	10	22	73	16	31
Ahtna	-	-	-	16	-	-	-	-	-
Alaskan Athabaskan	3	-	8	10	10	17	67	16	12
Doyon	-	-	-	-	-	5	-	-	19
Tanaina	2	-	-	-	-	-	6	-	-
Algonquian	28	47	38	124	43	115	243	100	93
Apache	53	97	38	190	4	76	591	224	341
Apache	53	80	38	155	-	70	489	189	332
Chiricahua	-	14	-	-	-	-	40	17	-
Fort Sill Apache	-	-	-	-	-	-	-	-	-
Jicarilla Apache	-	-	-	7	-	-	-	-	-
Lipan Apache	-	-	-	-	-	-	-	-	2
Mescalero Apache	-	3	-	26	-	-	30	18	5
Oklahoma Apache	-	-	-	-	-	-	-	-	-
Payson Apache	-	-	-	-	-	-	-	-	-
San Carlos Apache	-	-	-	-	4	-	26	-	-
White Mountain Apache	-	-	-	2	-	6	6	-	2
Arapaho	9	-	3	48	-	8	30	7	23
Arapaho	9	-	3	48	-	8	30	7	23
Northern Arapaho	-	-	-	-	-	-	-	-	-
Southern Arapaho	-	-	-	-	-	-	-	-	-
Arikara	-	-	-	3	-	-	8	-	5
Assiniboine	-	-	12	2	-	-	33	9	6
Bannock	-	-	-	-	-	-	-	-	-
Blackfoot	153	235	90	617	99	357	1,545	489	673
Brotherton	-	-	-	-	-	-	3	-	-
Caddo	-	-	-	8	-	20	13	-	3
Caddo	-	-	-	8	-	20	13	-	3
Oklahoma Caddo	-	-	-	-	-	-	-	-	-
Cahuilla	-	-	-	-	-	-	-	-	-
Agua Caliente Cahuilla	-	-	-	-	-	-	-	-	-
Cahuilla	-	-	-	-	-	-	-	-	-
Soboba	-	-	-	-	-	-	-	-	-
Torres-Martinez	-	-	-	-	-	-	-	-	-
Other Cahuilla	-	-	-	-	-	-	-	-	-
California tribes	-	-	-	33	-	-	-	-	-
Cahto	-	-	-	-	-	-	-	-	-
Chimariko	-	-	-	-	-	-	-	-	-
Coast Miwok	-	-	-	-	-	-	-	-	-
Digger	-	-	-	-	-	-	-	-	-
Mattole	-	-	-	-	-	-	-	-	-
Morongo	-	-	-	-	-	-	-	-	-
Santa Rosa	-	-	-	33	-	-	-	-	-
Wappo	-	-	-	-	-	-	-	-	-
Yuki	-	-	-	-	-	-	-	-	-
Other California	-	-	-	-	-	-	-	-	-
Canadian and Latin American	126	65	11	456	80	260	2,189	595	522
Canadian Indian	56	16	-	97	25	40	136	54	29
Central American Indian	17	6	-	67	7	28	153	45	20
French American Indian	14	6	7	34	-	6	128	-	13
Mexican American Indian	18	31	4	67	38	48	475	48	251
South American Indian	19	6	-	122	10	138	780	235	100
Spanish American Indian	2	-	-	69	-	-	517	213	109

[Continued]

★ 123 ★

Population by Tribe, Region, and State, 1990: Abenaki-Chinook - Part I

[Continued]

Tribe	New England						Middle Atlantic		
	Maine	New Hampshire	Vermont	Massachusetts	Rhode Island	Connecticut	New York	New Jersey	Pennsylvania
Catawba	-	-	-	-	-	9	13	-	3
Cayuse	-	-	-	-	-	-	-	-	-
Chehalis	-	-	-	-	-	-	-	-	-
Chemakuan	-	-	-	-	-	-	-	-	-
Chemakuan	-	-	-	-	-	-	-	-	-
Hoh	-	-	-	-	-	-	-	-	-
Quileute	-	-	-	-	-	-	-	-	-
Chemehuevi	-	-	-	-	-	-	5	-	-
Cherokee	430	351	114	1,868	574	969	6,327	2,779	4,306
Cherokee	428	351	109	1,844	568	969	6,313	2,751	4,273
Cherokees of Northeast Alabama	-	-	-	-	-	-	-	-	-
Cherokees of Southeast Alabama	-	-	-	-	-	-	-	6	-
Eastern Cherokee	2	-	-	17	-	-	8	3	6
Echota Cherokee	-	-	-	-	-	-	-	-	2
Etowah Cherokee	-	-	5	-	-	-	-	-	-
Northern Cherokee	-	-	-	-	-	-	-	-	2
United Keetoowah Band	-	-	-	-	-	-	-	-	-
Western Cherokee	-	-	-	7	6	-	6	19	23
Other Cherokee	-	-	-	-	-	-	-	-	-
Cherokee Shawnee	-	-	-	-	-	-	10	6	-
Cheyenne	-	6	2	20	11	31	131	16	43
Cheyenne	-	6	2	12	11	31	131	16	41
Northern Cheyenne	-	-	-	8	-	-	-	-	2
Southern Cheyenne	-	-	-	-	-	-	-	-	-
Cheyenne-Arapaho	-	-	-	9	-	-	-	-	-
Chickahominy	-	-	-	-	-	-	44	-	11
Chickahominy	-	-	-	-	-	-	44	-	11
Other Chickahominy	-	-	-	-	-	-	-	-	-
Chickasaw	19	-	-	9	-	27	26	23	50
Chinook	-	-	-	8	-	-	19	-	3
Chinook	-	-	-	8	-	-	14	-	3
Clatsop	-	-	-	-	-	-	-	-	-
Other Chinook	-	-	-	-	-	-	5	-	-

Source: U.S. Bureau of the Census. *1990 Census of Population: Characteristics of American Indians by Tribe and Language.* CP3-7. Washington, DC: The Bureau, 1994, p. 2. *Note:* A dash (-) represents zero or a percent that rounds to zero.

★ 124 ★

Population

Population by Tribe, Region, and State, 1990: Abenaki-Chinook - Part II

Data are based on a sample and are subject to sampling variability.

Tribe	East North Central Region					West North Central Region						
	Ohio	Indiana	Illinois	Michigan	Wisconsin	Minnesota	Iowa	Missouri	North Dakota	South Dakota	Nebraska	Kansas
American Indian	21,931	14,233	23,357	58,667	39,367	49,106	7,785	21,961	25,256	50,294	12,453	23,049
Abenaki	-	7	7	6	-	-	-	5	-	-	-	-
Alaska Native	-	-	19	-	-	17	-	-	-	-	-	-
Alaska Indian	-	-	-	-	-	17	-	-	-	-	-	-
Alaska Native	-	-	-	-	-	-	-	-	-	-	-	-
Chaneliak	-	-	-	-	-	-	-	-	-	-	-	-
Chugach	-	-	-	-	-	-	-	-	-	-	-	-
Sealaska	-	-	19	-	-	-	-	-	-	-	-	-
Other Alaska Native	-	-	-	-	-	-	-	-	-	-	-	-
Alaskan Athabaskans	44	20	29	46	27	77	1	40	-	13	6	51
Ahtna	-	-	-	-	-	-	-	-	-	8	-	-
Alaskan Athabaskan	34	13	29	46	26	77	1	40	-	5	6	37
Doyon	-	7	-	-	-	-	-	-	-	-	-	14
Tanaina	10	-	-	-	1	-	-	-	-	-	-	-
Algonquian	31	10	28	48	56	4	-	-	-	-	-	16

[Continued]

★ 124 ★

Population by Tribe, Region, and State, 1990: Abenaki-Chinook - Part II
[Continued]

Tribe	East North Central Region					West North Central Region						
	Ohio	Indiana	Illinois	Michigan	Wisconsin	Minnesota	Iowa	Missouri	North Dakota	South Dakota	Nebraska	Kansas
Apache	463	285	656	820	144	161	125	550	20	9	107	422
Apache	390	271	595	767	139	128	93	527	10	9	102	272
Chiricahua	7	-	17	18	-	17	27	4	-	-	-	12
Fort Sill Apache	-	-	-	-	-	-	3	-	-	-	-	16
Jicarilla Apache	2	-	-	-	-	-	-	-	2	-	-	-
Lipan Apache	-	-	10	-	-	-	-	-	-	-	-	-
Mescalero Apache	64	14	12	-	2	-	2	19	-	-	-	7
Oklahoma Apache	-	-	-	7	3	-	-	-	-	-	-	56
Payson Apache	-	-	-	3	-	-	-	-	-	-	-	-
San Carlos Apache	-	-	22	20	-	10	-	-	-	-	-	30
White Mountain Apache	-	-	-	5	-	6	-	-	8	-	5	29
Arapaho	38	6	31	75	17	35	8	29	12	11	17	68
Arapaho	38	6	22	75	17	27	8	29	9	3	16	51
Northern Arapaho	-	-	9	-	-	8	-	-	3	8	1	17
Southern Arapaho	-	-	-	-	-	-	-	-	-	-	-	-
Arikara	-	-	19	6	6	73	5	4	963	24	9	26
Assiniboine	-	14	7	8	3	34	8	24	74	17	-	9
Bannock	6	-	-	-	-	-	-	-	-	-	-	-
Blackfoot	1,204	560	880	1,590	357	262	175	558	55	97	77	457
Brotherton	-	-	-	-	348	62	4	6	-	-	-	-
Caddo	11	-	15	5	18	-	-	9	-	7	-	52
Caddo	11	-	15	5	18	-	-	9	-	7	-	52
Oklahoma Caddo	-	-	-	-	-	-	-	-	-	-	-	-
Cahuilla	-	-	-	-	-	-	-	-	-	-	-	-
Agua Caliente Cahuilla	-	-	-	-	-	-	-	-	-	-	-	-
Cahuilla	-	-	-	-	-	-	-	-	-	-	-	-
Soboba	-	-	-	-	-	-	-	-	-	-	-	-
Torres-Martinez	-	-	-	-	-	-	-	-	-	-	-	-
Other Cahuilla	-	-	-	-	-	-	-	-	-	-	-	-
California tribes	8	11	12	20	-	-	-	-	-	-	-	10
Cahto	-	-	-	5	-	-	-	-	-	-	-	10
Chimariko	-	-	-	-	-	-	-	-	-	-	-	-
Coast Miwok	-	-	-	-	-	-	-	-	-	-	-	-
Digger	-	-	-	-	-	-	-	-	-	-	-	-
Mattole	-	-	-	-	-	-	-	-	-	-	-	-
Morongo	2	-	-	11	-	-	-	-	-	-	-	-
Santa Rosa	-	-	-	-	-	-	-	-	-	-	-	-
Wappo	6	-	-	4	-	-	-	-	-	-	-	-
Yuki	-	11	-	-	-	-	-	-	-	-	-	-
Other California	-	-	12	-	-	-	-	-	-	-	-	-
Canadian and Latin American	253	270	788	1,273	160	385	188	246	26	51	63	188
Canadian Indian	29	13	50	537	31	123	47	20	18	4	3	7
Central American Indian	18	-	-	19	14	35	10	17	-	-	-	-
French American Indian	2	32	24	79	7	45	2	8	-	9	-	-
Mexican American Indian	148	170	555	468	72	98	82	128	8	19	50	109
South American Indian	5	27	78	16	25	51	-	42	-	10	-	5
Spanish American Indian	51	28	81	154	11	33	47	31	-	9	10	67
Catawba	6	-	19	-	-	-	-	-	-	-	4	-
Cayuse	-	-	-	-	-	-	-	2	-	-	-	5
Chehalis	-	-	-	-	-	-	-	-	-	-	-	-
Chemakuan	-	-	-	-	-	-	-	14	-	-	-	-
Chemakuan	-	-	-	-	-	-	-	-	-	-	-	-
Hoh	-	-	-	-	-	-	-	-	-	-	-	-
Quileute	-	-	-	-	-	-	-	14	-	-	-	-
Chemehuevi	-	-	-	29	-	-	-	-	32	-	-	-
Cherokee	9,433	4,955	7,281	11,465	1,505	1,319	1,557	10,747	188	359	1,042	7,251
Cherokee	9,333	4,918	7,166	11,392	1,488	1,302	1,557	10,543	167	359	1,024	7,023
Cherokees of Northeast Alabama	-	-	-	-	-	-	-	-	-	-	-	-
Cherokees of Southeast Alabama	-	-	39	-	-	6	-	-	-	-	-	-
Eastern Cherokee	41	23	68	38	11	5	-	22	-	-	-	77
Echota Cherokee	22	-	-	5	-	-	-	4	-	-	-	-
Etowah Cherokee	18	-	-	8	-	-	-	2	-	-	-	-
Northern Cherokee	-	-	-	-	-	-	-	77	-	-	11	-

[Continued]

★ 124 ★

Population by Tribe, Region, and State, 1990: Abenaki-Chinook - Part II
[Continued]

Tribe	East North Central Region					West North Central Region						
	Ohio	Indiana	Illinois	Michigan	Wisconsin	Minnesota	Iowa	Missouri	North Dakota	South Dakota	Nebraska	Kansas
United Keetoowah Band	-	-	-	-	-	-	-	-	-	-	-	-
Western Cherokee	19	14	8	22	6	6	-	99	21	-	7	151
Other Cherokee	-	-	-	-	-	-	-	-	-	-	-	-
Cherokee Shawnee	71	-	-	13	3	8	4	39	-	-	-	8
Cheyenne	129	74	149	82	67	56	39	130	75	147	47	196
Cheyenne	121	63	143	82	59	19	22	119	7	129	35	194
Northern Cheyenne	8	4	6	-	8	37	17	11	68	16	12	-
Southern Cheyenne	-	7	-	-	-	-	-	-	-	2	-	2
Cheyenne-Arapaho	8	-	-	-	8	-	-	9	-	20	18	47
Chickahominy	2	7	-	3	-	-	-	-	-	-	-	-
Chickahominy	2	7	-	3	-	-	-	-	-	-	-	-
Other Chickahominy	-	-	-	-	-	-	-	-	-	-	-	-
Chickasaw	64	93	100	79	37	7	8	168	2	-	36	213
Chinook	-	-	-	-	8	-	-	9	-	-	-	-
Chinook	-	-	-	-	8	-	-	9	-	-	-	-
Clatsop	-	-	-	-	-	-	-	-	-	-	-	-
Other Chinook	-	-	-	-	-	-	-	-	-	-	-	-

Source: U.S. Bureau of the Census. *1990 Census of Population: Characteristics of American Indians by Tribe and Language.* CP3-7. Washington, DC: The Bureau, 1994, p. 3. *Note:* A dash (-) represents zero or a percent that rounds to zero.

★ 125 ★

Population

Population by Tribe, Region, and State, 1990: Abenaki-Chinook - Part III

Data are based on a sample and are subject to sampling variability.

Tribe	South Atlantic Region								
	Delaware	Maryland	District of Columbia	Virginia	West Virginia	North Carolina	South Carolina	Georgia	Florida
American Indian	2,157	13,838	1,523	16,041	3,013	82,428	8,771	15,056	41,810
Abenaki	-	-	-	24	-	-	-	12	10
Alaska Native	-	-	-	-	-	3	-	-	38
Alaska Indian	-	-	-	-	-	-	-	-	15
Alaska Native	-	-	-	-	-	3	-	-	12
Chaneliak	-	-	-	-	-	-	-	-	-
Chugach	-	-	-	-	-	-	-	-	-
Sealaska	-	-	-	-	-	-	-	-	11
Other Alaska Native	-	-	-	-	-	-	-	-	-
Alaskan Athabaskans	-	18	7	24	-	30	-	39	71
Ahtna	-	-	-	-	-	-	-	-	-
Alaskan Athabaskan	-	18	7	24	-	30	-	37	71
Doyon	-	-	-	-	-	-	-	2	-
Tanaina	-	-	-	-	-	-	-	-	-
Algonquian	9	17	-	66	-	13	7	18	48
Apache	41	191	43	283	56	270	72	303	969
Apache	41	175	43	269	56	226	64	249	866
Chiricahua	-	16	-	-	-	-	8	7	35
Fort Sill Apache	-	-	-	-	-	-	-	-	-
Jicarilla Apache	-	-	-	-	-	-	-	-	-
Lipan Apache	-	-	-	-	-	-	-	-	-
Mescalero Apache	-	-	-	14	-	15	-	14	44
Oklahoma Apache	-	-	-	-	-	-	-	33	3
Payson Apache	-	-	-	-	-	-	-	-	-
San Carlos Apache	-	-	-	-	-	29	-	-	9

[Continued]

Population by Tribe, Region, and State, 1990: Abenaki-Chinook - Part III
[Continued]

Tribe	South Atlantic Region								
	Delaware	Maryland	District of Columbia	Virginia	West Virginia	North Carolina	South Carolina	Georgia	Florida
White Mountain Apache	-	-	-	-	-	-	-	-	12
Arapaho	-	6	-	18	-	7	30	17	43
Arapaho	-	6	-	18	-	7	30	17	43
Northern Arapaho	-	-	-	-	-	-	-	-	-
Southern Arapaho	-	-	-	-	-	-	-	-	-
Arikara	11	10	-	-	12	-	-	7	13
Assiniboine	-	6	-	18	-	47	6	11	19
Bannock	-	-	-	-	-	-	-	-	-
Blackfoot	67	626	64	449	82	459	169	233	1,173
Brotherton	-	-	-	-	-	-	-	8	6
Caddo	-	-	-	38	-	-	17	53	31
Caddo	-	-	-	38	-	-	17	53	16
Oklahoma Caddo	-	-	-	-	-	-	-	-	15
Cahuilla	-	-	-	-	-	-	-	-	-
Agua Caliente Cahuilla	-	-	-	-	-	-	-	-	-
Cahuilla	-	-	-	-	-	-	-	-	-
Soboba	-	-	-	-	-	-	-	-	-
Torres-Martinez	-	-	-	-	-	-	-	-	-
Other Cahuilla	-	-	-	-	-	-	-	-	-
California tribes	-	9	-	-	-	-	9	-	8
Cahto	-	-	-	-	-	-	-	-	8
Chimariko	-	-	-	-	-	-	-	-	-
Coast Miwok	-	-	-	-	-	-	-	-	-
Digger	-	-	-	-	-	-	-	-	-
Mattole	-	-	-	-	-	-	-	-	-
Morongo	-	9	-	-	-	-	9	-	-
Santa Rosa	-	-	-	-	-	-	-	-	-
Wappo	-	-	-	-	-	-	-	-	-
Yuki	-	-	-	-	-	-	-	-	-
Other California	-	-	-	-	-	-	-	-	-
Canadian and Latin American	6	252	55	368	9	256	116	161	1,094
Canadian Indian	-	23	-	57	9	12	30	22	43
Central American Indian	-	69	8	146	-	30	-	36	316
French American Indian	-	-	-	17	-	9	-	6	20
Mexican American Indian	-	72	9	81	-	60	29	58	437
South American Indian	6	45	38	59	-	44	24	39	188
Spanish American Indian	-	43	-	8	-	101	33	-	90
Catawba	-	-	-	11	-	48	633	27	73
Cayuse	-	-	-	-	-	-	-	6	-
Chehalis	-	-	-	-	-	-	-	-	-
Chemakuan	-	-	-	-	-	-	-	-	-
Chemakuan	-	-	-	-	-	-	-	-	-
Hoh	-	-	-	-	-	-	-	-	-
Quileute	-	-	-	-	-	-	-	-	-
Chemehuevi	-	-	-	-	-	-	-	-	-
Cherokee	553	4,316	387	4,822	1,523	15,791	3,279	7,508	14,664
Cherokee	527	4,236	387	4,737	1,494	10,813	3,243	7,454	14,447
Cherokees of Northeast Alabama	-	-	-	-	-	-	-	-	-
Cherokees of Southeast Alabama	-	-	-	-	-	-	-	16	38
Eastern Cherokee	-	72	-	41	-	4,924	28	31	49
Echota Cherokee	-	-	-	9	21	-	-	7	80
Etowah Cherokee	-	-	-	-	8	-	-	-	11
Northern Cherokee	-	-	-	-	-	9	-	-	-
United Keetoowah Band	-	-	-	-	-	-	-	-	-
Western Cherokee	26	8	-	35	-	40	8	-	39

[Continued]

★ 125 ★

Population by Tribe, Region, and State, 1990: Abenaki-Chinook - Part III
[Continued]

Tribe	South Atlantic Region								
	Delaware	Maryland	District of Columbia	Virginia	West Virginia	North Carolina	South Carolina	Georgia	Florida
Other Cherokee	-	-	-	-	-	5	-	-	-
Cherokee Shawnee	-	-	-	10	-	-	-	12	12
Cheyenne	-	31	-	30	14	54	7	22	106
Cheyenne	-	31	-	30	14	54	7	22	101
Northern Cheyenne	-	-	-	-	-	-	-	-	5
Southern Cheyenne	-	-	-	-	-	-	-	-	-
Cheyenne-Arapaho	-	13	-	-	-	20	-	7	7
Chickahominy	-	38	-	633	-	-	-	-	11
Chickahominy	-	38	-	625	-	-	-	-	11
Other Chickahominy	-	-	-	8	-	-	-	-	-
Chickasaw	-	43	-	50	15	75	72	47	120
Chinook	-	-	-	5	-	-	-	-	26
Chinook	-	-	-	5	-	-	-	-	26
Clatsop	-	-	-	-	-	-	-	-	-
Other Chinook	-	-	-	-	-	-	-	-	-

Source: U.S. Bureau of the Census. *1990 Census of Population: Characteristics of American Indians by Tribe and Language.* CP3-7. Washington, DC: The Bureau, 1994, p. 4.
Note: A dash (-) represents zero or a percent that rounds to zero.

★ 126 ★
Population

Population by Tribe, Region, and State, 1990: Abenaki-Chinook - Part IV

Data are based on a sample and are subject to sampling variability.

Tribe	East South Central Region				West South Central Region				Mountain Region			
	Kentucky	Tennessee	Alabama	Mississippi	Arkansas	Louisiana	Oklahoma	Texas	Montana	Idaho	Wyoming	Colorado
American Indian	6,780	12,304	18,155	8,776	14,141	19,873	252,132	68,565	47,574	14,436	9,904	28,116
Abenaki	-	26	-	-	-	-	11	10	-	-	-	-
Alaska Native	-	-	-	-	27	-	-	3	-	14	-	8
Alaska Indian	-	-	-	-	-	-	-	-	-	-	-	8
Alaska Native	-	-	-	-	-	-	-	3	-	14	-	-
Chaneliak	-	-	-	-	-	-	-	-	-	-	-	-
Chugach	-	-	-	-	27	-	-	-	-	-	-	-
Sealaska	-	-	-	-	-	-	-	-	-	-	-	-
Other Alaska Native	-	-	-	-	-	-	-	-	-	-	-	-
Alaskan Athabaskans	-	8	-	9	13	-	57	89	27	11	30	33
Ahtna	-	-	-	-	-	-	-	-	-	8	-	-
Alaskan Athabaskan	-	8	-	9	8	-	57	58	8	3	30	33
Doyon	-	-	-	-	5	-	-	7	-	-	-	-
Tanaina	-	-	-	-	-	-	-	24	19	-	-	-
Algonquian	-	-	-	5	5	-	-	43	17	2	-	11
Apache	150	318	149	45	301	547	1,722	2,641	125	229	99	1,621
Apache	150	295	110	32	295	525	1,316	2,253	83	206	93	1,433
Chiricahua	-	-	-	-	-	-	86	-	-	-	-	-
Fort Sill Apache	-	-	-	8	6	-	53	5	-	-	6	-
Jicarilla Apache	-	-	-	-	-	-	32	18	-	9	-	44
Lipan Apache	-	-	-	-	-	-	-	7	-	-	-	-
Mescalero Apache	-	12	15	5	-	-	21	170	12	3	-	115
Oklahoma Apache	-	9	-	-	-	22	267	12	5	-	-	-
Payson Apache	-	-	-	-	-	-	-	-	-	-	-	-
San Carlos Apache	-	-	24	-	-	-	33	14	-	-	-	14
White Mountain Apache	-	2	-	-	-	-	-	76	25	11	-	15
Arapaho	6	-	23	-	6	6	1,024	119	113	114	3,607	204
Arapaho	6	-	23	-	6	6	991	119	90	107	2,581	179
Northern Arapaho	-	-	-	-	-	-	33	-	23	7	1,012	25
Southern Arapaho	-	-	-	-	-	-	-	-	-	-	14	-
Arikara	-	-	-	-	-	12	26	12	27	-	2	51
Assiniboine	6	-	-	-	7	-	45	61	3,689	97	23	44
Bannock	-	-	-	-	-	-	-	9	8	130	11	-
Blackfoot	217	173	147	105	170	92	434	1,027	8,636	256	131	482

[Continued]

Population by Tribe, Region, and State, 1990: Abenaki-Chinook - Part IV
[Continued]

Tribe	East South Central Region				West South Central Region				Mountain Region			
	Kentucky	Tennessee	Alabama	Mississippi	Arkansas	Louisiana	Oklahoma	Texas	Montana	Idaho	Wyoming	Colorado
Brotherton	-	-	-	-	-	-	-	-	6	-	-	-
Caddo	-	9	-	-	102	10	1,748	289	4	-	-	83
Caddo	-	9	-	-	102	10	1,724	289	4	-	-	83
Oklahoma Caddo	-	-	-	-	-	-	24	-	-	-	-	-
Cahuilla	-	-	-	-	-	-	-	4	-	-	-	-
Agua Caliente Cahuilla	-	-	-	-	-	-	-	-	-	-	-	-
Cahuilla	-	-	-	-	-	-	-	4	-	-	-	-
Soboba	-	-	-	-	-	-	-	-	-	-	-	-
Torres-Martinez	-	-	-	-	-	-	-	-	-	-	-	-
Other Cahuilla	-	-	-	-	-	-	-	-	-	-	-	-
California tribes	-	7	-	-	-	10	-	-	-	6	-	-
Cahto	-	-	-	-	-	-	-	-	-	-	-	-
Chimariko	-	-	-	-	-	-	-	-	-	-	-	-
Coast Miwok	-	-	-	-	-	-	-	-	-	-	-	-
Digger	-	-	-	-	-	-	-	-	-	-	-	-
Mattole	-	-	-	-	-	-	-	-	-	6	-	-
Morongo	-	7	-	-	-	10	-	-	-	-	-	-
Santa Rosa	-	-	-	-	-	-	-	-	-	-	-	-
Wappo	-	-	-	-	-	-	-	-	-	-	-	-
Yuki	-	-	-	-	-	-	-	-	-	-	-	-
Other California	-	-	-	-	-	-	-	-	-	-	-	-
Canadian and Latin American	80	210	86	8	76	276	199	1,882	117	205	29	808
Canadian Indian	22	26	-	-	9	19	-	17	84	35	8	5
Central American Indian	8	7	16	-	-	11	41	198	2	-	12	7
French American Indian	6	-	4	-	-	151	7	51	-	32	-	29
Mexican American Indian	21	115	60	-	60	63	110	1,107	28	122	9	351
South American Indian	1	18	-	-	-	5	-	79	3	2	-	90
Spanish American Indian	22	44	6	8	7	27	41	430	-	14	-	326
Catawba	-	-	7	-	-	-	4	20	-	12	-	11
Cayuse	-	-	-	-	-	-	2	-	-	-	-	-
Chehalis	-	-	-	-	-	-	-	2	-	-	-	3
Chemakuan	-	-	-	-	-	7	-	-	-	-	-	-
Chemakuan	-	-	-	-	-	-	-	-	-	-	-	-
Hoh	-	-	-	-	-	-	-	-	-	-	-	-
Quileute	-	-	-	-	-	7	-	-	-	-	-	-
Chemehuevi	-	-	-	-	-	-	17	-	-	-	36	-
Cherokee	3,303	7,217	9,407	978	7,737	2,989	99,227	19,150	900	1,835	722	5,884
Cherokee	3,295	7,139	5,840	952	7,679	2,934	94,467	18,951	878	1,827	715	5,780
Cherokees of Northeast Alabama	-	6	77	-	-	-	4	-	-	-	-	-
Cherokees of Southeast Alabama	-	6	58	-	-	-	14	2	-	-	-	-
Eastern Cherokee	8	32	2	-	-	12	52	78	10	2	-	-
Echota Cherokee	-	9	3,427	26	-	31	18	13	-	-	-	6
Etowah Cherokee	-	-	-	-	-	-	-	25	-	-	-	-
Northern Cherokee	-	-	-	-	-	6	93	-	8	-	-	4
United Keetoowah Band	-	-	-	-	-	-	126	-	-	-	-	-
Western Cherokee	-	25	3	-	58	6	4,453	81	4	6	7	94
Other Cherokee	-	-	-	-	-	-	-	-	-	-	-	-
Cherokee Shawnee	-	12	-	-	12	1	534	41	-	-	-	5
Cheyenne	36	15	18	-	21	2	2,802	297	4,158	63	224	366
Cheyenne	19	15	18	-	21	2	2,555	281	590	43	73	325
Northern Cheyenne	10	-	-	-	-	-	57	16	3,549	20	151	15
Southern Cheyenne	7	-	-	-	-	-	190	-	19	-	-	26
Cheyenne-Arapaho	-	-	-	-	-	-	1,881	69	14	10	-	81
Chickahominy	14	-	-	-	-	-	14	-	11	-	-	-
Chickahominy	14	-	-	-	-	-	14	-	11	-	-	-
Other Chickahominy	-	-	-	-	-	-	-	-	-	-	-	-
Chickasaw	49	82	53	34	198	48	12,832	2,447	41	49	10	291
Chinook	-	-	-	-	-	-	-	6	-	-	5	-
Chinook	-	-	-	-	-	-	-	6	-	-	5	-
Clatsop	-	-	-	-	-	-	-	-	-	-	-	-
Other Chinook	-	-	-	-	-	-	-	-	-	-	-	-

Source: U.S. Bureau of the Census. *1990 Census of Population: Characteristics of American Indians by Tribe and Language.* CP3-7. Washington, DC: The Bureau, 1994, p. 5. *Note:* A dash (-) represents zero or a percent that rounds to zero.

Population by Tribe, Region, and State, 1990: Abenaki-Chinook - Part V

Data are based on a sample and are subject to sampling variability.

Tribe	Mountain Region (cont.)				Pacific Region				
	New Mexico	Arizona	Utah	Nevada	Washington	Oregon	California	Alaska	Hawaii
American Indian	133,816	204,150	24,173	20,231	79,353	40,547	243,736	32,173	5,174
Abenaki	13	-	-	13	13	20	57	-	4
Alaska Native	-	9	7	-	373	53	94	510	-
Alaska Indian	-	-	7	-	56	10	45	47	-
Alaska Native	-	9	-	-	281	20	49	370	-
Chaneliak	-	-	-	-	-	-	-	2	-
Chugach	-	-	-	-	7	7	-	66	-
Sealaska	-	-	-	-	12	9	-	19	-
Other Alaska Native	-	-	-	-	17	7	-	6	-
Alaskan Athabaskans	6	84	41	28	520	234	285	11,982	7
Ahtna	-	-	-	-	-	-	-	173	-
Alaskan Athabaskan	6	32	41	22	443	220	210	11,353	7
Doyon	-	-	-	-	24	-	45	137	-
Tanaina	-	52	-	6	53	14	30	319	-
Algonquian	4	21	-	12	28	119	206	7	18
Apache	6,051	19,589	160	571	888	902	9,208	162	248
Apache	888	8,370	129	495	607	701	7,894	126	213
Chiricahua	17	26	-	18	61	8	279	5	-
Fort Sill Apache	-	6	-	-	-	-	-	-	-
Jicarilla Apache	2,441	22	-	-	7	22	135	9	-
Lipan Apache	-	-	-	-	-	-	11	-	-
Mescalero Apache	2,643	46	-	27	58	45	664	16	3
Oklahoma Apache	9	35	-	-	13	36	53	-	-
Payson Apache	-	86	-	-	-	-	-	-	-
San Carlos Apache	42	1,820	-	13	61	33	88	-	8
White Mountain Apache	11	9,178	31	18	81	57	84	6	24
Arapaho	113	111	189	30	186	55	388	17	11
Arapaho	55	83	148	30	178	47	358	17	11
Northern Arapaho	58	28	41	-	8	8	30	-	-
Southern Arapaho	-	-	-	-	-	-	-	-	-
Arikara	4	117	6	-	46	12	152	-	-
Assiniboine	38	72	33	19	392	223	334	65	6
Bannock	-	-	-	3	10	6	4	-	-
Blackfoot	117	492	209	451	3,456	1,121	6,009	251	164
Brotherton	-	-	-	-	4	-	19	-	-
Caddo	10	39	13	8	64	-	300	5	-
Caddo	6	39	13	8	64	-	294	5	-
Oklahoma Caddo	4	-	-	-	-	-	6	-	-
Cahuilla	-	42	-	-	7	20	1,221	-	-
Agua Caliente Cahuilla	-	6	-	-	-	-	44	-	-
Cahuilla	-	23	-	-	-	15	846	-	-
Soboba	-	13	-	-	7	-	181	-	-
Torres-Martinez	-	-	-	-	-	5	124	-	-
Other Cahuilla	-	-	-	-	-	-	26	-	-
California tribes	1	12	-	27	75	46	1,025	2	-
Cahto	-	-	-	-	-	-	103	-	-
Chimariko	-	-	-	-	-	-	63	-	-
Coast Miwok	-	-	-	-	7	-	34	-	-

[Continued]

Population by Tribe, Region, and State, 1990: Abenaki-Chinook - Part V
[Continued]

Tribe	Mountain Region (cont.)				Pacific Region				
	New Mexico	Arizona	Utah	Nevada	Washington	Oregon	California	Alaska	Hawaii
Digger	-	-	-	11	6	-	16	2	-
Mattole	-	-	-	-	-	-	32	-	-
Morongo	-	-	-	16	53	38	418	-	-
Santa Rosa	-	-	-	-	-	-	20	-	-
Wappo	-	7	-	-	-	-	37	-	-
Yuki	1	5	-	-	9	8	260	-	-
Other California	-	-	-	-	-	-	42	-	-
Canadian and Latin American	210	755	208	216	1,608	443	8,965	109	177
Canadian Indian	5	32	28	31	956	76	496	39	12
Central American Indian	8	14	6	-	8	21	317	-	7
French American Indian	-	12	-	-	29	-	223	-	6
Mexican American Indian	101	547	69	138	445	257	6,313	56	73
South American Indian	-	34	30	4	80	24	359	5	36
Spanish American Indian	96	116	75	43	90	65	1,257	9	43
Catawba	-	-	10	14	6	-	6	6	22
Cayuse	-	-	-	-	13	99	34	-	-
Chehalis	-	6	-	-	274	8	21	-	-
Chemakuan	-	-	-	7	611	59	40	-	-
Chemakuan	-	-	-	-	14	-	-	-	-
Hoh	-	-	-	-	103	-	-	-	-
Quileute	-	-	-	7	494	59	40	-	-
Chemehuevi	8	104	6	58	-	23	322	-	-
Cherokee	1,713	4,821	1,016	2,717	8,430	7,116	52,915	1,571	1,724
Cherokee	1,641	4,695	972	2,662	8,305	7,070	52,391	1,571	1,700
Cherokees of Northeast Alabama	-	-	-	-	-	-	-	-	-
Cherokees of Southeast Alabama	-	-	-	11	-	-	-	-	-
Eastern Cherokee	25	65	12	8	36	-	160	-	-
Echota Cherokee	-	-	-	-	9	-	68	-	16
Etowah Cherokee	-	-	-	-	-	-	-	-	8
Northern Cherokee	10	3	-	-	40	15	7	-	-
United Keetoowah Band	-	-	-	-	-	-	19	-	-
Western Cherokee	37	58	32	36	40	31	270	-	-
Other Cherokee	-	-	-	-	-	-	-	-	-
Cherokee Shawnee	-	-	-	-	14	8	107	14	-
Cheyenne	145	115	25	84	462	201	987	49	24
Cheyenne	110	101	21	66	368	125	801	44	24
Northern Cheyenne	12	7	4	18	94	68	170	5	-
Southern Cheyenne	23	7	-	-	-	8	16	-	-
Cheyenne-Arapaho	72	7	21	-	71	-	237	-	-
Chickahominy	5	48	-	-	-	-	60	-	-
Chickahominy	5	48	-	-	-	-	60	-	-
Other Chickahominy	-	-	-	-	-	-	-	-	-
Chickasaw	154	237	55	92	393	156	2,823	57	38
Chinook	-	-	13	7	341	308	120	-	-
Chinook	-	-	13	7	300	294	115	-	-
Clatsop	-	-	-	-	13	14	5	-	-
Other Chinook	-	-	-	-	28	-	-	-	-

Source: U.S. Bureau of the Census. *1990 Census of Population: Characteristics of American Indians by Tribe and Language.* CP3-7. Washington, DC: The Bureau, 1994, p. 6. *Note:* A dash (-) represents zero or a percent that rounds to zero.

★ 128 ★
Population

Population by Tribe, Region, and State, 1990: Chippewa-Diegueno - Part I

Data are based on a sample and are subject to sampling variability.

Tribe	New England						Middle Atlantic		
	Maine	New Hampshire	Vermont	Massachusetts	Rhode Island	Connecticut	New York	New Jersey	Pennsylvania
Chippewa	58	17	40	352	20	136	373	158	314
Bad River	-	-	-	16	-	-	-	20	-
Bay Mills Chippewa	-	-	-	-	-	-	-	6	-
Bois Forte	-	-	-	-	-	-	-	-	-
Chippewa	50	17	40	292	20	103	329	103	281
Fond du Lac	-	-	-	-	-	-	-	-	-
Grand Portage	-	-	-	-	-	-	-	-	-
Keweenaw	-	-	-	-	-	-	6	-	-
Lac Courte Oreilles	-	-	-	-	-	-	-	-	-
Lac du Flambeau	-	-	-	-	-	-	-	-	-
Lac Vieux Desert Chippewa	-	-	-	-	-	-	-	-	-
Lake Superior	-	-	-	-	-	-	-	-	-
Leech Lake	-	-	-	-	-	-	-	-	-
Leelanau	-	-	-	-	-	-	-	-	-
Little Shell Chippewa	-	-	-	-	-	-	-	-	-
Mille Lac	-	-	-	-	-	-	-	-	-
Minnesota Chippewa	-	-	-	-	-	17	5	13	5
Red Cliff Chippewa	-	-	-	-	-	-	6	-	-
Red Lake Chippewa	-	-	-	-	-	11	-	-	-
Saginaw Chippewa	-	-	-	-	-	-	-	16	-
St. Croix Chippewa	-	-	-	-	-	-	-	-	-
Sault Ste. Marie Chippewa	-	-	-	7	-	-	-	-	15
Sokoagon Chippewa	-	-	-	-	-	-	-	-	-
Turtle Mountain	8	-	-	37	-	-	17	-	6
White Earth	-	-	-	-	-	5	10	-	7
Other Chippewa	-	-	-	-	-	-	-	-	-
Chitimacha	-	-	-	-	-	-	-	-	25
Choctaw	27	14	3	133	28	67	249	120	150
Choctaw	27	14	3	122	28	55	229	107	112
Mississippi Choctaw	-	-	-	-	-	-	5	7	5
Mowa Band of Choctaw	-	-	-	-	-	-	-	-	-
Oklahoma Choctaw	-	-	-	11	-	12	15	6	33
Other Choctaw	-	-	-	-	-	-	-	-	-
Chumash	-	-	-	-	-	-	-	6	-
Chumash	-	-	-	-	-	-	-	6	-
Santa Ynez	-	-	-	-	-	-	-	-	-
Coeur d'Alene	-	-	-	-	-	-	17	-	-
Coharie	-	-	-	-	-	-	36	6	-
Colorado River	-	-	-	-	-	-	-	-	-
Colville	-	2	-	7	-	-	8	-	29
Comanche	2	18	-	41	-	28	61	35	83
Comanche	2	18	-	41	-	28	61	35	83
Oklahoma Comanche	-	-	-	-	-	-	-	-	-
Coos	9	-	-	-	-	-	-	-	-
Coquilles	-	-	-	-	-	-	-	-	-
Costanoan	-	-	-	-	-	-	5	7	-
Coushatta	-	-	-	-	-	-	-	-	-
Alabama Coushatta	-	-	-	-	-	-	-	-	-
Coushatta	-	-	-	-	-	-	-	-	-
Cowlitz	-	-	-	-	-	9	11	-	-
Cree	20	11	16	64	8	31	111	39	76
Creek	7	-	-	42	-	18	225	170	185
Alabama Quassarte	-	-	-	-	-	-	-	-	-
Creek	7	-	-	42	-	9	197	162	176
Eastern Creek	-	-	-	-	-	9	28	8	9
Lower Muskogee	-	-	-	-	-	-	-	-	-
MaChis Lower Creek Indian	-	-	-	-	-	-	-	-	-
Poarch Band	-	-	-	-	-	-	-	-	-
Principal Creek Indian Nation	-	-	-	-	-	-	-	-	-
Thlopthlocco	-	-	-	-	-	-	-	-	-
Other Creek	-	-	-	-	-	-	-	-	-

[Continued]

★ 128 ★

Population by Tribe, Region, and State, 1990: Chippewa-Diegueno - Part I

[Continued]

Tribe	New England						Middle Atlantic		
	Maine	New Hampshire	Vermont	Massachusetts	Rhode Island	Connecticut	New York	New Jersey	Pennsylvania
Croatan	-	-	-	-	-	-	-	-	-
Crow	2	11	8	22	-	-	53	45	106
Cupeno	7	-	-	-	-	-	-	-	-
Agua Caliente	7	-	-	-	-	-	-	-	-
Cupeno	-	-	-	-	-	-	-	-	-
Delaware	2	6	2	43	18	103	543	1,339	482
Delaware	-	6	2	39	-	30	137	209	239
Eastern Delaware	2	-	-	-	-	-	-	-	27
Lenni-Lenape	-	-	-	4	-	9	89	803	216
Munsee	-	-	-	-	-	-	13	-	-
Oklahoma Delaware	-	-	-	-	-	-	22	-	-
Rampough Mountain	-	-	-	-	18	64	282	327	-
Sand Hill	-	-	-	-	-	-	-	-	-
Diegueno	-	-	-	-	-	-	18	-	-
Campo	-	-	-	-	-	-	-	-	-
Capitan Grande	-	-	-	-	-	-	-	-	-
Diegueno	-	-	-	-	-	-	18	-	-
Manzanita	-	-	-	-	-	-	-	-	-
Mesa Grande	-	-	-	-	-	-	-	-	-
San Pascual	-	-	-	-	-	-	-	-	-
Santa Ysabel	-	-	-	-	-	-	-	-	-
Sycuan	-	-	-	-	-	-	-	-	-
Other Diegueno	-	-	-	-	-	-	-	-	-

Source: U.S. Bureau of the Census. *1990 Census of Population: Characteristics of American Indians by Tribe and Language.* CP3-7. Washington, DC: The Bureau, 1994, p. 8. *Note:* A dash (-) represents zero or a percent that rounds to zero.

★ 129 ★

Population

Population by Tribe, Region, and State, 1990: Chippewa-Diegueno - Part II

Data are based on a sample and are subject to sampling variability.

Tribe	East North Central Region					West North Central Region						
	Ohio	Indiana	Illinois	Michigan	Wisconsin	Minnesota	Iowa	Missouri	North Dakota	South Dakota	Nebraska	Kansas
Chippewa	620	419	1,707	19,912	12,947	32,050	481	298	12,337	582	285	512
Bad River	-	-	125	52	921	165	8	7	-	54	-	2
Bay Mills Chippewa	-	-	-	415	-	9	-	-	-	-	-	-
Bois Forte	-	-	-	13	8	441	-	-	-	5	5	-
Chippewa	532	383	1,380	14,076	7,366	19,465	412	264	5,197	258	278	461
Fond du Lac	-	-	-	-	133	667	-	-	8	-	-	-
Grand Portage	-	-	-	7	-	84	-	-	-	-	-	-
Keweenaw	-	-	9	501	35	39	-	-	-	-	-	-
Lac Courte Oreilles	-	-	26	17	2,090	433	-	2	7	11	2	5
Lac du Flambeau	-	-	-	5	705	24	-	-	-	-	-	-
Lac Vieux Desert Chippewa	-	-	-	25	3	-	-	-	-	-	-	-
Lake Superior	12	-	2	-	46	102	-	-	-	-	-	-
Leech Lake	-	-	10	4	14	1,598	-	-	6	-	-	4
Leelanau	-	-	8	541	20	-	-	-	-	-	-	-
Little Shell Chippewa	-	-	-	-	-	13	-	-	2	2	-	-
Mille Lac	-	-	7	-	21	632	-	-	-	-	-	-
Minnesota Chippewa	-	-	-	71	69	2,230	17	-	53	19	-	8
Red Cliff Chippewa	-	-	28	56	442	219	4	-	-	-	-	-
Red Lake Chippewa	-	-	9	4	50	3,571	12	17	22	12	-	5
Saginaw Chippewa	-	6	2	753	3	-	-	5	-	-	-	1
St. Croix Chippewa	-	-	-	-	418	67	-	-	-	-	-	-
Sault Ste. Marie Chippewa	55	18	50	3,300	103	9	-	3	2	-	-	3
Sokaogon Chippewa	-	-	-	-	309	-	-	-	-	-	-	-

[Continued]

Population by Tribe, Region, and State, 1990: Chippewa-Diegueno - Part II
[Continued]

Tribe	East North Central Region					West North Central Region						
	Ohio	Indiana	Illinois	Michigan	Wisconsin	Minnesota	Iowa	Missouri	North Dakota	South Dakota	Nebraska	Kansas
Turtle Mountain	15	12	26	45	46	460	28	-	6,983	190	-	16
White Earth	6	-	25	14	145	1,822	-	-	57	31	-	7
Other Chippewa	-	-	-	13	-	-	-	-	-	-	-	-
Chitimacha	-	-	12	-	-	5	-	-	-	-	-	-
Choctaw	481	211	576	411	128	149	101	775	47	38	112	991
Choctaw	437	173	533	388	125	145	89	707	47	35	103	867
Mississippi Choctaw	10	38	16	8	-	-	-	9	-	-	-	-
Mowa Band of Choctaw	-	-	-	-	-	-	-	-	-	-	-	-
Oklahoma Choctaw	34	-	27	15	3	4	12	59	-	3	9	124
Other Choctaw	-	-	-	-	-	-	-	-	-	-	-	-
Chumash	-	-	-	2	10	5	2	-	-	-	-	-
Chumash	-	-	-	2	10	5	2	-	-	-	-	-
Santa Ynez	-	-	-	-	-	-	-	-	-	-	-	-
Coeur d'Alene	-	-	-	-	-	2	-	-	-	-	-	-
Coharie	-	-	-	13	3	-	-	-	-	32	-	-
Colorado River	-	-	-	-	-	8	-	-	-	5	-	36
Colville	6	-	2	4	6	-	8	4	11	-	28	11
Comanche	70	70	68	113	61	25	18	188	-	39	66	221
Comanche	70	70	68	113	61	25	18	188	-	39	66	208
Oklahoma Comanche	-	-	-	-	-	-	-	-	-	-	-	13
Coos	-	-	-	-	-	-	-	-	-	-	-	-
Coquilles	-	-	-	-	2	-	-	-	-	-	-	-
Costanoan	6	-	-	-	-	-	-	-	-	-	-	-
Coushatta	-	-	-	-	-	-	5	-	-	-	-	-
Alabama Coushatta	-	-	-	-	-	-	5	-	-	-	-	-
Coushatta	-	-	-	-	-	-	-	-	-	-	-	-
Cowlitz	-	-	-	6	-	-	-	-	-	-	-	-
Cree	91	81	91	229	27	205	17	39	67	38	19	15
Creek	184	76	239	131	61	68	58	443	22	48	115	890
Alabama Quassarte	-	-	-	-	-	-	-	-	-	-	3	-
Creek	184	76	239	129	59	65	58	443	22	48	112	890
Eastern Creek	-	-	-	2	-	-	-	-	-	-	-	-
Lower Muskogee	-	-	-	-	-	-	-	-	-	-	-	-
MaChis Lower Creek Indian	-	-	-	-	-	-	-	-	-	-	-	-
Poarch Band	-	-	-	-	2	-	-	-	-	-	-	-
Principal Creek Indian Nation	-	-	-	-	-	-	-	-	-	-	-	-
Thlopthlocco	-	-	-	-	-	-	-	-	-	-	-	-
Other Creek	-	-	-	-	-	3	-	-	-	-	-	-
Croatan	-	-	-	-	-	-	-	-	-	-	-	-
Crow	25	31	42	89	55	38	12	104	59	42	11	30
Cupeno	-	-	-	-	-	-	-	-	-	-	-	-
Agua Caliente	-	-	-	-	-	-	-	-	-	-	-	-
Cupeno	-	-	-	-	-	-	-	-	-	-	3	-
Delaware	195	95	136	291	38	34	12	124	-	13	3	552
Delaware	177	77	112	279	17	22	12	74	-	13	3	443
Eastern Delaware	-	-	24	-	18	-	-	36	-	-	-	14
Lenni-Lenape	11	18	-	-	-	12	-	-	-	-	-	-
Munsee	7	-	-	12	3	-	-	-	-	-	-	32
Oklahoma Delaware	-	-	-	-	-	-	-	14	-	-	-	63
Rampough Mountain	-	-	-	-	-	-	-	-	-	-	-	-
Sand Hill	-	-	-	-	-	-	-	-	-	-	-	-
Diegueno	18	-	-	2	10	7	-	-	-	-	-	-
Campo	-	-	-	-	-	-	-	-	-	-	-	-
Capitan Grande	-	-	-	-	-	-	-	-	-	-	-	-
Diegueno	15	-	-	2	10	7	-	-	-	-	-	-
Manzanita	-	-	-	-	-	-	-	-	-	-	-	-
Mesa Grande	-	-	-	-	-	-	-	-	-	-	-	-
San Pascual	3	-	-	-	-	-	-	-	-	-	-	-
Santa Ysabel	-	-	-	-	-	-	-	-	-	-	-	-

[Continued]

★ 129 ★

Population by Tribe, Region, and State, 1990: Chippewa-Diegueno - Part II

[Continued]

| Tribe | East North Central Region | | | | | West North Central Region | | | | | | |
	Ohio	Indiana	Illinois	Michigan	Wisconsin	Minnesota	Iowa	Missouri	North Dakota	South Dakota	Nebraska	Kansas
Sycuan	-	-	-	-	-	-	-	-	-	-	-	-
Other Diegueno	-	-	-	-	-	-	-	-	-	-	-	-

Source: U.S. Bureau of the Census. *1990 Census of Population: Characteristics of American Indians by Tribe and Language.* CP3-7. Washington, DC: The Bureau, 1994, p. 9. *Note:* A dash (-) represents zero or a percent that rounds to zero.

★ 130 ★

Population

Population by Tribe, Region, and State, 1990: Chippewa-Diegueno - Part III

Data are based on a sample and are subject to sampling variability.

| Tribe | South Atlantic Region | | | | | | | | |
	Delaware	Maryland	District of Columbia	Virginia	West Virginia	North Carolina	South Carolina	Georgia	Florida
Chippewa	-	217	13	293	24	505	127	289	1,120
Bad River	-	-	-	-	-	-	-	-	-
Bay Mills Chippewa	-	-	-	-	-	-	-	-	-
Bois Forte	-	-	-	-	-	-	-	-	-
Chippewa	-	138	5	247	13	392	72	216	996
Fond du Lac	-	-	-	-	-	-	-	-	-
Grand Portage	-	-	-	-	-	-	-	-	-
Keweenaw	-	37	-	-	-	-	-	-	-
Lac Courte Oreilles	-	-	-	8	-	15	48	-	5
Lac du Flambeau	-	-	-	-	-	-	-	-	-
Lac Vieux Desert Chippewa	-	-	-	-	-	-	-	-	-
Lake Superior	-	-	-	-	-	-	-	-	-
Leech Lake	-	-	-	-	-	-	-	-	8
Leelanau	-	-	-	22	-	-	-	-	26
Little Shell Chippewa	-	-	-	-	-	-	-	-	-
Mille Lac	-	-	-	-	-	-	-	-	-
Minnesota Chippewa	-	6	-	-	11	33	7	23	-
Red Cliff Chippewa	-	-	-	-	-	-	-	6	-
Red Lake Chippewa	-	11	8	-	-	-	-	2	-
Saginaw Chippewa	-	5	-	5	-	-	-	-	4
St. Croix Chippewa	-	-	-	-	-	-	-	-	-
Sault Ste. Marie Chippewa	-	20	-	-	-	17	-	42	75
Sokaogon Chippewa	-	-	-	-	-	-	-	-	-
Turtle Mountain	-	-	-	-	-	42	-	-	-
White Earth	-	-	-	11	-	6	-	-	6
Other Chippewa	-	-	-	-	-	-	-	-	-
Chitimacha	-	-	-	7	-	-	-	-	6
Choctaw	-	205	5	481	30	243	104	247	979
Choctaw	-	191	5	405	11	204	83	223	894
Mississippi Choctaw	-	-	-	-	-	22	-	8	5
Mowa Band of Choctaw	-	-	-	-	-	-	-	-	24
Oklahoma Choctaw	-	14	-	76	19	17	21	16	56
Other Choctaw	-	-	-	-	-	-	-	-	-
Chumash	-	-	-	-	-	-	-	-	21
Chumash	-	-	-	-	-	-	-	-	21
Santa Ynez	-	-	-	-	-	-	-	-	-
Coeur d'Alene	-	-	-	26	-	9	-	-	-

[Continued]

★ 130 ★

Population by Tribe, Region, and State, 1990: Chippewa-Diegueno - Part III
[Continued]

Tribe	South Atlantic Region								
	Delaware	Maryland	District of Columbia	Virginia	West Virginia	North Carolina	South Carolina	Georgia	Florida
Coharie	-	-	-	5	-	1,039	-	37	9
Colorado River	-	-	-	-	-	-	-	-	-
Colville	-	2	-	8	9	47	-	-	-
Comanche	6	46	-	162	18	96	51	15	299
Comanche	6	46	-	162	18	96	51	15	299
Oklahoma Comanche	-	-	-	-	-	-	-	-	-
Coos	-	-	-	-	-	-	-	-	-
Coquilles	-	-	-	-	-	-	-	-	-
Costanoan	-	5	-	-	-	-	-	7	16
Coushatta	-	-	-	-	-	-	12	-	-
Alabama Coushatta	-	-	-	-	-	-	12	-	-
Coushatta	-	-	-	-	-	-	-	-	-
Cowlitz	-	-	-	-	-	-	-	-	9
Cree	32	36	5	14	-	32	50	21	144
Creek	-	143	16	164	8	175	61	1,179	4,059
Alabama Quassarte	-	-	-	-	-	-	-	-	-
Creek	-	118	16	157	8	160	61	1,098	3,450
Eastern Creek	-	6	-	-	-	6	-	2	435
Lower Muskogee	-	19	-	7	-	9	-	61	54
MaChis Lower Creek Indian	-	-	-	-	-	-	-	3	9
Poarch Band	-	-	-	-	-	-	-	12	83
Principal Creek Indian Nation	-	-	-	-	-	-	-	-	9
Thlopthlocco	-	-	-	-	-	-	-	-	9
Other Creek	-	-	-	-	-	-	-	3	10
Croatan	-	-	-	48	-	47	9	-	-
Crow	-	29	-	13	-	49	29	43	143
Cupeno	-	-	-	-	-	-	26	-	-
Agua Caliente	-	-	-	-	-	-	-	-	-
Cupeno	-	-	-	-	-	-	26	-	-
Delaware	100	62	-	62	10	2	18	27	152
Delaware	12	40	-	62	2	2	5	27	91
Eastern Delaware	-	-	-	-	2	-	-	-	33
Lenni-Lenape	88	11	-	-	6	-	13	-	28
Munsee	-	11	-	-	-	-	-	-	-
Oklahoma Delaware	-	-	-	-	-	-	-	-	-
Rampough Mountain	-	-	-	-	-	-	-	-	-
Sand Hill	-	-	-	-	-	-	-	-	-
Diegueno	-	9	-	7	-	4	-	-	6
Campo	-	-	-	-	-	-	-	-	6
Capitan Grande	-	-	-	-	-	-	-	-	-
Diegueno	-	9	-	7	-	4	-	-	-
Manzanita	-	-	-	-	-	-	-	-	-
Mesa Grande	-	-	-	-	-	-	-	-	-
San Pascual	-	-	-	-	-	-	-	-	-
Santa Ysabel	-	-	-	-	-	-	-	-	-
Sycuan	-	-	-	-	-	-	-	-	-
Other Diegueno	-	-	-	-	-	-	-	-	-

Source: U.S. Bureau of the Census. *1990 Census of Population: Characteristics of American Indians by Tribe and Language.* CP3-7. Washington, DC: The Bureau, 1994, p. 10.
Note: A dash (-) represents zero or a percent that rounds to zero.

Population by Tribe, Region, and State, 1990: Chippewa-Diegueno - Part IV

Data are based on a sample and are subject to sampling variability.

Tribe	East South Central Region				West South Central Region				Mountain Region			
	Kentucky	Tennessee	Alabama	Mississippi	Arkansas	Louisiana	Oklahoma	Texas	Montana	Idaho	Wyoming	Colorado
Chippewa	207	278	121	35	155	186	546	862	3,233	437	272	572
Bad River	-	9	-	-	-	-	-	6	-	-	-	-
Bay Mills Chippewa	-	-	-	-	-	-	-	-	-	-	-	-
Bois Forte	-	-	-	-	-	-	-	-	-	-	-	-
Chippewa	150	243	110	35	97	163	463	793	2,266	368	191	502
Fond du Lac	-	-	-	-	-	-	-	-	-	6	-	-
Grand Portage	-	-	-	-	-	-	-	-	-	-	-	-
Keweenaw	15	-	-	-	-	-	-	-	7	-	-	-
Lac Courte Oreilles	8	-	-	-	-	-	17	-	-	-	-	15
Lac du Flambeau	-	-	9	-	-	-	-	-	-	-	-	-
Lac Vieux Desert Chippewa	-	-	-	-	-	-	-	-	-	-	-	-
Lake Superior	-	-	-	-	-	-	15	-	-	-	-	-
Leech Lake	-	-	-	-	-	-	-	-	-	-	-	6
Leelanau	-	-	-	-	-	-	4	-	-	-	-	16
Little Shell Chippewa	-	-	-	-	-	-	25	24	454	5	4	-
Mille Lac	-	-	-	-	-	-	-	-	-	-	-	-
Minnesota Chippewa	12	7	-	-	36	-	9	6	3	2	-	8
Red Cliff Chippewa	-	-	-	-	-	-	-	-	8	-	-	-
Red Lake Chippewa	-	-	-	-	-	-	-	-	-	-	2	-
Saginaw Chippewa	8	5	-	-	-	-	-	-	-	-	-	-
St. Croix Chippewa	-	-	-	-	-	-	-	-	-	-	-	-
Sault Ste. Marie Chippewa	-	14	-	-	15	-	-	9	-	2	24	2
Sokaogon Chippewa	-	-	-	-	-	-	-	-	-	-	-	-
Turtle Mountain	6	-	2	-	-	17	13	7	396	48	51	23
White Earth	8	-	-	-	7	6	-	17	99	6	-	-
Other Chippewa	-	-	-	-	-	-	-	-	-	-	-	-
Chitimacha	-	5	-	-	-	477	-	78	-	-	-	-
Choctaw	148	474	2,212	5,352	1,473	1,868	42,716	9,050	88	209	103	705
Choctaw	142	452	1,252	4,312	1,321	1,695	27,711	7,639	74	173	103	630
Mississippi Choctaw	-	-	-	1,029	-	12	1,127	160	11	-	-	23
Mowa Band of Choctaw	-	-	908	-	-	9	6	-	-	-	-	-
Oklahoma Choctaw	6	22	52	11	152	136	13,872	1,251	3	36	-	52
Other Choctaw	-	-	-	-	-	16	-	-	-	-	-	-
Chumash	-	-	-	-	-	-	9	-	-	-	3	18
Chumash	-	-	-	-	-	-	9	-	-	-	3	18
Santa Ynez	-	-	-	-	-	-	-	-	-	-	-	-
Coeur d'Alene	-	-	-	-	-	8	-	-	-	577	-	-
Coharie	-	2	-	-	-	-	-	-	-	-	-	11
Colorado River	-	-	-	-	-	-	-	-	-	4	7	12
Colville	-	15	-	-	-	-	62	23	85	157	-	23
Comanche	50	41	42	22	80	100	5,059	1,478	30	24	28	146
Comanche	50	41	42	22	80	100	4,908	1,478	30	24	28	146
Oklahoma Comanche	-	-	-	-	-	-	151	-	-	-	-	-
Coos	-	-	-	11	-	-	-	-	-	-	-	-
Coquilles	-	-	-	-	-	-	-	-	-	-	-	8
Costanoan	-	15	-	-	-	-	-	1	15	-	-	13
Coushatta	-	-	-	14	-	389	34	667	-	-	-	-
Alabama Coushatta	-	-	-	7	-	42	22	571	-	-	-	-
Coushatta	-	-	-	7	-	347	12	96	-	-	-	-
Cowlitz	-	-	6	-	-	-	-	-	6	-	41	-
Cree	16	39	9	8	46	28	56	122	4,312	128	59	64
Creek	40	165	3,021	183	315	287	24,657	2,495	11	79	68	209
Alabama Quassarte	-	-	-	-	-	9	9	142	-	-	8	-
Creek	38	165	2,542	173	300	272	24,547	2,289	11	79	60	207
Eastern Creek	-	-	13	-	10	-	13	37	-	-	-	2
Lower Muskogee	-	-	15	-	-	-	-	15	-	-	-	-
MaChis Lower Creek Indian	-	-	34	-	-	-	-	-	-	-	-	-
Poarch Band	-	-	373	10	5	6	-	-	-	-	-	-
Principal Creek Indian Nation	-	-	39	-	-	-	-	8	-	-	-	-
Thlopthlocco	-	-	-	-	-	-	80	-	-	-	-	-
Other Creek	2	-	5	-	-	-	8	4	-	-	-	-

[Continued]

★ 131 ★

Population by Tribe, Region, and State, 1990: Chippewa-Diegueno - Part IV

[Continued]

Tribe	East South Central Region				West South Central Region				Mountain Region			
	Kentucky	Tennessee	Alabama	Mississippi	Arkansas	Louisiana	Oklahoma	Texas	Montana	Idaho	Wyoming	Colorado
Croatan	32	-	-	-	8	-	-	4	-	-	-	-
Crow	-	12	28	37	-	21	129	100	6,281	33	205	23
Cupeno	-	-	-	-	-	-	-	-	-	-	-	-
Agua Caliente	-	-	-	-	-	-	-	-	-	-	-	-
Cupeno	-	-	-	-	-	-	-	-	-	-	-	-
Delaware	12	95	24	-	127	9	3,066	351	9	38	26	200
Delaware	12	56	24	-	125	-	2,703	319	9	20	26	182
Eastern Delaware	-	13	-	-	2	9	271	20	-	13	-	9
Lenni-Lenape	-	19	-	-	-	-	-	-	-	5	-	-
Munsee	-	-	-	-	-	-	15	-	-	-	-	-
Oklahoma Delaware	-	5	-	-	-	-	77	12	-	-	-	-
Rampough Mountain	-	-	-	-	-	-	-	-	-	-	-	9
Sand Hill	-	2	-	-	-	-	-	-	-	-	-	-
Diegueno	-	-	-	-	-	5	33	8	-	-	6	-
Campo	-	-	-	-	-	-	-	-	-	-	-	-
Capitan Grande	-	-	-	-	-	-	-	-	-	-	-	-
Diegueno	-	-	-	-	-	-	31	-	-	-	-	-
Manzanita	-	-	-	-	-	-	-	-	-	-	6	-
Mesa Grande	-	-	-	-	-	-	-	-	-	-	-	-
San Pascual	-	-	-	-	-	5	-	-	-	-	-	-
Santa Ysabel	-	-	-	-	-	-	2	-	-	-	-	-
Sycuan	-	-	-	-	-	-	-	8	-	-	-	-
Other Diegueno	-	-	-	-	-	-	-	-	-	-	-	-

Source: U.S. Bureau of the Census. *1990 Census of Population: Characteristics of American Indians by Tribe and Language.* CP3-7. Washington, DC: The Bureau, 1994, p. 11.
Note: A dash (-) represents zero or a percent that rounds to zero.

★ 132 ★

Population

Population by Tribe, Region, and State, 1990: Chippewa-Diegueno - Part V

Data are based on a sample and are subject to sampling variability.

Tribe	Mountain Region (cont.)				Pacific Region				
	New Mexico	Arizona	Utah	Nevada	Washington	Oregon	California	Alaska	Hawaii
Chippewa	506	626	278	309	4,021	1,606	5,010	322	200
Bad River	-	-	-	-	17	-	40	-	-
Bay Mills Chippewa	-	-	-	-	-	-	6	-	6
Bois Forte	-	-	-	-	10	-	-	-	-
Chippewa	461	575	135	285	3,363	1,357	4,408	208	160
Fond du Lac	-	-	-	-	4	-	5	-	-
Grand Portage	-	-	-	-	-	11	-	-	-
Keweenaw	-	13	-	-	7	-	30	-	-
Lac Courte Oreilles	-	6	-	-	-	6	42	-	-
Lac du Flambeau	-	11	-	-	6	-	10	-	-
Lac Vieux Desert Chippewa	-	-	-	-	-	-	3	-	-
Lake Superior	-	-	-	-	5	-	8	-	-
Leech Lake	-	-	-	5	2	-	10	-	-
Leelanau	-	-	-	-	-	-	45	-	-
Little Shell Chippewa	-	-	-	-	3	29	13	-	-
Mille Lac	-	-	-	-	-	-	-	-	-
Minnesota Chippewa	3	6	-	13	151	18	23	-	-
Red Cliff Chippewa	-	-	40	-	-	-	27	-	-
Red Lake Chippewa	-	-	10	-	15	17	18	-	-

[Continued]

★ 132 ★

Population by Tribe, Region, and State, 1990: Chippewa-Diegueno - Part V
[Continued]

Tribe	Mountain Region (cont.)				Pacific Region				
	New Mexico	Arizona	Utah	Nevada	Washington	Oregon	California	Alaska	Hawaii
Saginaw Chippewa	-	6	-	-	7	-	21	-	-
St. Croix Chippewa	-	-	-	-	-	-	-	-	-
Sault Ste. Marie Chippewa	20	-	-	-	26	-	57	41	34
Sokaogon Chippewa	-	-	-	-	9	-	-	-	-
Turtle Mountain	22	9	71	2	286	110	146	68	-
White Earth	-	-	22	4	110	58	98	5	-
Other Chippewa	-	-	-	-	-	-	-	-	-
Chitimacha	-	-	-	-	-	-	10	-	-
Choctaw	841	1,135	146	457	919	1,101	9,714	236	179
Choctaw	684	1,024	113	449	848	958	8,995	223	161
Mississippi Choctaw	-	15	-	-	24	5	83	2	-
Mowa Band of Choctaw	-	-	-	-	-	-	-	-	-
Oklahoma Choctaw	157	96	33	8	47	138	636	11	18
Other Choctaw	-	-	-	-	-	-	-	-	-
Chumash	4	-	-	9	18	59	3,013	-	29
Chumash	4	-	-	9	18	59	2,919	-	29
Santa Ynez	-	-	-	-	-	-	94	-	-
Coeur d'Alene	-	29	-	-	289	58	42	-	-
Coharie	-	-	-	-	6	-	-	-	-
Colorado River	5	1,510	13	16	-	17	12	-	-
Colville	15	58	3	11	5,970	125	283	35	-
Comanche	150	274	18	44	202	148	1,519	45	37
Comanche	150	274	18	44	202	148	1,513	45	37
Oklahoma Comanche	-	-	-	-	-	-	6	-	-
Coos	-	-	-	-	7	149	18	7	-
Coquilles	-	-	-	-	25	444	32	9	-
Costanoan	2	18	-	-	-	-	739	9	-
Coushatta	5	5	-	-	16	9	22	-	35
Alabama Coushatta	-	5	-	-	16	5	16	-	35
Coushatta	5	-	-	-	-	4	6	-	-
Cowlitz	-	-	-	-	582	65	49	20	-
Cree	62	52	42	54	704	254	674	91	18
Creek	291	466	96	179	447	395	3,591	47	43
Alabama Quassarte	-	-	-	9	-	-	-	-	-
Creek	278	466	96	163	447	395	3,564	47	43
Eastern Creek	-	-	-	-	-	-	9	-	-
Lower Muskogee	-	-	-	-	-	-	-	-	-
MaChis Lower Creek Indian	-	-	-	-	-	-	18	-	-
Poarch Band	-	-	-	7	-	-	-	-	-
Principal Creek Indian Nation	-	-	-	-	-	-	-	-	-
Thlopthlocco	13	-	-	-	-	-	-	-	-
Other Creek	-	-	-	-	-	-	-	-	-
Croatan	-	-	-	-	-	-	29	-	-
Crow	22	68	91	97	289	133	666	43	25
Cupeno	-	-	-	-	-	40	300	-	-
Agua Caliente	-	-	-	-	-	-	110	-	-
Cupeno	-	-	-	-	-	40	190	-	-
Delaware	64	108	47	48	127	84	853	27	21

[Continued]

★ 132 ★

Population by Tribe, Region, and State, 1990: Chippewa-Diegueno - Part V
[Continued]

Tribe	Mountain Region (cont.)				Pacific Region				
	New Mexico	Arizona	Utah	Nevada	Washington	Oregon	California	Alaska	Hawaii
Delaware	64	102	47	43	122	84	733	27	14
Eastern Delaware	-	-	-	-	-	-	65	-	-
Lenni-Lenape	-	-	-	-	-	-	19	-	-
Munsee	-	6	-	-	-	-	4	-	-
Oklahoma Delaware	-	-	-	5	5	-	-	-	-
Rampough Mountain	-	-	-	-	-	-	25	-	7
Sand Hill	-	-	-	-	-	-	7	-	-
Diegueno	-	20	-	-	7	32	2,048	-	9
Campo	-	-	-	-	-	-	97	-	-
Capitan Grande	-	-	-	-	-	-	241	-	-
Diegueno	-	20	-	-	6	14	1,288	-	-
Manzanita	-	-	-	-	-	-	36	-	-
Mesa Grande	-	-	-	-	-	-	44	-	9
San Pascual	-	-	-	-	1	18	235	-	-
Santa Ysabel	-	-	-	-	-	-	83	-	-
Sycuan	-	-	-	-	-	-	24	-	-
Other Diegueno	-	-	-	-	-	-	-	-	-

Source: U.S. Bureau of the Census. *1990 Census of Population: Characteristics of American Indians by Tribe and Language.* CP3-7. Washington, DC: The Bureau, 1994, p. 12. *Note:* A dash (-) represents zero or a percent that rounds to zero.

★ 133 ★
Population

Population by Tribe, Region, and State, 1990: Eastern Tribes-Miwok - Part I

Data are based on a sample and are subject to sampling variability.

Tribe	New England						Middle Atlantic		
	Maine	New Hampshire	Vermont	Massachusetts	Rhode Island	Connecticut	New York	New Jersey	Pennsylvania
Eastern tribes	5	7	6	276	31	74	194	38	125
Moor	-	-	-	-	-	-	-	-	-
Nansemond	-	-	-	-	-	-	-	12	18
Natchez	-	-	-	-	-	-	-	-	-
Nipmuc	5	7	-	261	22	41	23	-	-
Southeastern Indians	-	-	-	11	9	33	155	26	47
Susquehanock	-	-	-	-	-	-	9	-	57
Tunica	-	-	-	-	-	-	-	-	-
Tunica Biloxi	-	-	-	-	-	-	-	-	-
Waccamaw-Siouan	-	-	-	-	-	-	-	-	3
Wesort	-	-	-	-	-	-	-	-	-
Wicomico	-	-	-	-	-	-	-	-	-
Other Eastern	-	-	6	4	-	-	7	-	-
Fort Berthold	-	-	-	-	-	-	-	-	-
Fort Hall	-	-	-	-	-	17	-	-	-
Gabrieleno	-	-	-	-	-	6	-	-	-
Gila River	-	-	-	-	-	-	-	-	-
Grand Ronde	-	-	-	-	-	-	-	-	-
Gros Ventres	2	-	-	15	-	-	-	-	66
Atsina	-	-	-	-	-	-	-	-	-
Gros Ventres	2	-	-	15	-	-	-	-	66
Haida	-	-	-	12	-	24	16	-	-

[Continued]

★ 133 ★

Population by Tribe, Region, and State, 1990: Eastern Tribes-Miwok - Part I
[Continued]

Tribe	New England						Middle Atlantic		
	Maine	New Hampshire	Vermont	Massachusetts	Rhode Island	Connecticut	New York	New Jersey	Pennsylvania
Haliwa	-	-	-	12	-	-	13	28	124
Hidatsa	-	-	-	-	-	-	-	-	-
Hoopa	-	-	-	-	-	-	-	-	-
Hoopa	-	-	-	-	-	-	-	-	-
Other Hoopa	-	-	-	-	-	-	-	-	-
Houma	-	-	-	-	-	-	11	-	-
Iowa	-	-	-	28	-	-	6	6	6
Iroquois	62	212	216	750	68	545	19,638	907	1,155
Cayuga	-	-	7	9	-	-	856	13	14
Iroquois	40	103	57	160	27	161	721	208	140
Mohawk	5	91	116	433	21	347	9,420	412	382
Oneida	-	2	24	42	-	9	1,026	37	37
Onondaga	2	-	3	16	5	-	1,095	45	29
Seneca	2	16	2	59	15	9	5,432	135	500
Seneca	2	16	2	59	15	9	4,849	135	471
Seneca Nation	-	-	-	-	-	-	222	-	21
Tonawanda Seneca	-	-	-	-	-	-	361	-	8
Seneca-Cayuga	-	-	-	-	-	-	23	-	-
Tuscarora	6	-	-	31	-	19	1,043	29	44
Wyandotte	7	-	7	-	-	-	22	28	9
Juaneno	-	-	-	-	-	-	-	2	-
Kalispel	-	-	-	-	-	-	-	-	-
Karok	-	10	-	-	-	-	-	-	9
Kaw	-	-	-	-	-	-	-	-	-
Kickapoo	-	-	10	-	-	-	9	11	10
Kickapoo	-	-	10	-	-	-	9	11	10
Oklahoma Kickapoo	-	-	-	-	-	-	-	-	-
Kiowa	-	18	-	5	-	-	89	-	10
Kiowa	-	18	-	5	-	-	89	-	10
Oklahoma Kiowa	-	-	-	-	-	-	-	-	-
Klallam	-	-	-	-	-	-	5	-	-
Jamestown	-	-	-	-	-	-	-	-	-
Klallam	-	-	-	-	-	-	5	-	-
Lower Elwha	-	-	-	-	-	-	-	-	-
Port Gamble Klallam	-	-	-	-	-	-	-	-	-
Klamath	-	-	-	-	-	-	-	-	9
Konkow	-	-	-	-	-	-	-	-	11
Kootenai	-	-	-	-	-	-	19	-	-
Long Island	-	-	-	6	-	9	408	27	-
Matinecock	-	-	-	6	-	-	45	9	-
Montauk	-	-	-	-	-	9	63	-	-
Poospatuck	-	-	-	-	-	-	300	18	-
Setauket	-	-	-	-	-	-	-	-	-
Luiseno	8	-	-	-	-	-	-	-	27
La Jolla	-	-	-	-	-	-	-	-	-
Luiseno	-	-	-	-	-	-	-	-	-
Pala	8	-	-	-	-	-	-	-	27
Pauma	-	-	-	-	-	-	-	-	-
Pechanga	-	-	-	-	-	-	-	-	-
Lumbee	12	10	-	10	7	28	70	105	256
Lummi	-	-	-	-	-	-	-	-	-
Maidu	-	-	-	-	-	-	-	-	-
Maidu	-	-	-	-	-	-	-	-	-
Nishinam	-	-	-	-	-	-	-	-	-
Makah	-	-	-	-	-	11	-	-	-

[Continued]

★ 133 ★

Population by Tribe, Region, and State, 1990: Eastern Tribes-Miwok - Part I
[Continued]

Tribe	New England						Middle Atlantic		
	Maine	New Hampshire	Vermont	Massachusetts	Rhode Island	Connecticut	New York	New Jersey	Pennsylvania
Maliseet	609	-	4	36	6	46	25	-	5
Aroostook	-	-	-	6	-	-	-	-	-
Maliseet	609	-	4	30	6	46	25	-	5
Mandan	-	-	-	-	-	-	-	-	2
Mattaponi	-	-	-	-	-	-	-	8	60
Menominee	2	16	-	9	-	12	19	17	38
Miami	-	-	-	5	-	-	16	4	35
Illinois Miami	-	-	-	5	-	-	-	-	-
Indiana Miami	-	-	-	-	-	-	2	-	17
Miami	-	-	-	-	-	-	14	4	18
Oklahoma Miami	-	-	-	-	-	-	-	-	-
Miccosukee	-	-	-	-	-	-	-	-	-
Micmac	828	179	20	677	49	66	164	14	50
Mission Indians	-	-	-	9	-	-	-	-	-
Miwok	-	-	-	-	-	26	7	-	-

Source: U.S. Bureau of the Census. *1990 Census of Population: Characteristics of American Indians by Tribe and Language.* CP3-7. Washington, DC: The Bureau, 1994, p. 14.
Note: A dash (-) represents zero or a percent that rounds to zero.

★ 134 ★
Population

Population by Tribe, Region, and State, 1990: Eastern Tribes-Miwok - Part II

Data are based on a sample and are subject to sampling variability.

Tribe	East North Central Region					West North Central Region						
	Ohio	Indiana	Illinois	Michigan	Wisconsin	Minnesota	Iowa	Missouri	North Dakota	South Dakota	Nebraska	Kansas
Eastern tribes	61	11	41	57	6	-	9	14	-	-	2	7
Moor	-	-	-	11	-	-	-	14	-	-	-	-
Nansemond	-	-	-	-	-	-	-	-	-	-	-	-
Natchez	-	-	-	6	-	-	-	-	-	-	-	-
Nipmuc	9	6	-	-	-	-	-	-	-	-	-	-
Southeastern Indians	46	5	24	40	6	-	9	-	-	-	2	7
Susquehanock	6	-	7	-	-	-	-	-	-	-	-	-
Tunica	-	-	-	-	-	-	-	-	-	-	-	-
Tunica Biloxi	-	-	10	-	-	-	-	-	-	-	-	-
Waccamaw-Siouan	-	-	-	-	-	-	-	-	-	-	-	-
Wesort	-	-	-	-	-	-	-	-	-	-	-	-
Wicomico	-	-	-	-	-	-	-	-	-	-	-	-
Other Eastern	-	-	-	-	-	-	-	-	-	-	-	-
Fort Berthold	-	-	-	-	14	46	4	-	1,189	81	8	5
Fort Hall	-	-	-	-	-	-	-	2	2	-	-	-
Gabrieleno	-	-	-	1	-	-	-	-	-	-	-	-
Gila River	-	-	9	-	-	-	-	-	-	-	-	8
Grand Ronde	-	-	-	-	-	-	-	-	-	-	-	-
Gros Ventres	-	-	5	-	33	10	-	8	59	7	4	8
Atsina	-	-	-	-	-	-	-	-	-	-	-	-
Gros Ventres	-	-	5	-	33	10	-	8	59	7	4	8
Haida	-	-	-	-	5	-	2	-	-	-	-	15
Haliwa	-	-	-	-	-	-	-	-	-	-	-	-
Hidatsa	-	2	-	-	2	8	-	47	1,012	44	-	-
Hoopa	-	-	-	-	-	-	-	-	-	-	-	-

[Continued]

★ 134 ★

Population by Tribe, Region, and State, 1990: Eastern Tribes-Miwok - Part II
[Continued]

Tribe	East North Central Region					West North Central Region						
	Ohio	Indiana	Illinois	Michigan	Wisconsin	Minnesota	Iowa	Missouri	North Dakota	South Dakota	Nebraska	Kansas
Hoopa	-	-	-	-	-	-	-	-	-	-	-	-
Other Hoopa	-	-	-	-	-	-	-	-	-	-	-	-
Houma	14	7	13	-	-	-	-	34	5	-	-	-
Iowa	25	-	-	7	1	26	11	104	-	-	161	396
Iroquois	984	373	956	2,393	7,231	281	103	566	54	64	34	291
Cayuga	-	-	25	13	3	-	-	-	-	-	5	-
Iroquois	102	64	96	501	43	25	12	38	4	-	14	9
Mohawk	286	148	86	1,209	82	31	56	27	9	33	10	69
Oneida	76	48	577	397	7,039	197	31	126	10	19	5	30
Onondaga	50	-	-	35	19	-	-	-	-	9	-	5
Seneca	318	51	103	138	39	26	-	20	-	3	-	23
Seneca	211	51	86	127	39	26	-	20	-	3	-	23
Seneca Nation	107	-	5	11	-	-	-	-	-	-	-	-
Tonawanda Seneca	-	-	12	-	-	-	-	-	-	-	-	-
Seneca-Cayuga	-	5	-	-	2	-	-	131	-	-	-	14
Tuscarora	25	-	-	32	-	2	4	-	-	-	-	-
Wyandotte	127	57	69	68	4	-	-	224	31	-	-	141
Juaneno	-	-	-	-	-	-	-	2	-	-	-	-
Kalispel	-	-	-	-	-	-	-	-	-	-	-	-
Karok	8	-	-	9	-	-	-	-	-	-	-	-
Kaw	23	23	9	-	-	-	-	81	-	-	41	119
Kickapoo	9	5	30	33	28	11	18	43	4	15	7	630
Kickapoo	9	5	30	33	28	11	18	43	4	15	7	622
Oklahoma Kickapoo	-	-	-	-	-	-	-	-	-	-	-	8
Kiowa	23	9	37	32	17	40	32	64	3	11	14	345
Kiowa	23	9	37	32	17	40	32	64	3	11	14	345
Oklahoma Kiowa	-	-	-	-	-	-	-	-	-	-	-	-
Klallam	8	-	-	17	11	-	-	-	-	-	-	-
Jamestown	-	-	-	-	-	-	-	-	-	-	-	-
Klallam	8	-	-	17	11	-	-	-	-	-	-	-
Lower Elwha	-	-	-	-	-	-	-	-	-	-	-	-
Port Gamble Klallam	-	-	-	-	-	-	-	-	-	-	-	-
Klamath	-	7	7	-	-	-	-	-	-	-	-	-
Konkow	-	-	25	-	-	-	-	-	-	-	-	-
Kootenai	-	-	-	-	-	-	-	-	-	-	-	-
Long Island	-	-	-	-	-	-	-	-	-	-	-	-
Matinecock	-	-	-	-	-	-	-	-	-	-	-	-
Montauk	-	-	-	-	-	-	-	-	-	-	-	-
Poospatuck	-	-	-	-	-	-	-	-	-	-	-	-
Setauket	-	-	-	-	-	-	-	-	-	-	-	-
Luiseno	10	-	43	-	-	-	-	5	-	-	5	6
La Jolla	-	-	-	-	-	-	-	-	-	-	-	-
Luiseno	10	-	-	-	-	-	-	5	-	-	-	-
Pala	-	-	43	-	-	-	-	-	-	-	5	6
Pauma	-	-	-	-	-	-	-	-	-	-	-	-
Pechanga	-	-	-	-	-	-	-	-	-	-	-	-
Lumbee	177	79	121	783	12	14	-	93	32	-	-	44
Lummi	-	45	-	7	-	13	-	-	24	-	-	-
Maidu	7	-	24	-	-	-	-	-	-	-	-	-
Maidu	7	-	24	-	-	-	-	-	-	-	-	-
Nishinam	-	-	-	-	-	-	-	-	-	-	-	-
Makah	-	-	-	-	2	-	-	-	15	-	-	-
Maliseet	-	26	-	7	-	2	-	19	-	-	-	-
Aroostook	-	-	-	-	-	-	-	-	-	-	-	-

[Continued]

★ 134 ★

Population by Tribe, Region, and State, 1990: Eastern Tribes-Miwok - Part II

[Continued]

| Tribe | East North Central Region | | | | | West North Central Region | | | | | | |
	Ohio	Indiana	Illinois	Michigan	Wisconsin	Minnesota	Iowa	Missouri	North Dakota	South Dakota	Nebraska	Kansas
Maliseet	-	26	-	7	-	2	-	19	-	-	-	-
Mandan	-	-	14	5	23	136	4	16	564	12	42	-
Mattaponi	-	-	-	-	-	-	-	-	-	-	-	-
Menominee	43	32	487	124	6,355	99	30	24	8	15	-	33
Miami	109	2,122	122	147	6	16	37	180	-	-	9	308
Illinois Miami	-	-	11	-	-	-	-	-	-	-	2	8
Indiana Miami	-	143	6	9	-	-	-	16	-	-	-	21
Miami	96	1,945	99	101	6	16	27	86	-	-	5	139
Oklahoma Miami	13	34	6	37	-	-	10	78	-	-	2	140
Miccosukee	-	-	9	-	-	-	-	-	-	-	-	-
Micmac	42	8	23	28	6	8	-	15	11	-	-	28
Mission Indians	9	29	-	-	-	2	-	7	-	-	-	-
Miwok	-	-	-	-	7	12	-	22	-	-	-	-

Source: U.S. Bureau of the Census. *1990 Census of Population: Characteristics of American Indians by Tribe and Language.* CP3-7. Washington, DC: The Bureau, 1994, p. 15. *Note:* A dash (-) represents zero or a percent that rounds to zero.

★ 135 ★

Population

Population by Tribe, Region, and State, 1990: Eastern Tribes-Miwok - Part III

Data are based on a sample and are subject to sampling variability.

| Tribe | South Atlantic Region | | | | | | | | |
	Delaware	Maryland	District of Columbia	Virginia	West Virginia	North Carolina	South Carolina	Georgia	Florida
Eastern tribes	12	178	19	266	3	1,370	345	17	92
Moor	12	37	19	18	-	-	-	-	-
Nansemond	-	-	-	91	-	4	-	-	17
Natchez	-	-	-	-	-	-	12	-	-
Nipmuc	-	-	-	-	-	-	-	-	5
Southeastern Indians	-	59	-	140	3	387	333	9	61
Susquehanock	-	29	-	-	-	8	-	-	2
Tunica	-	-	-	-	-	-	-	-	-
Tunica Biloxi	-	-	-	-	-	-	-	-	-
Waccamaw-Siouan	-	-	-	8	-	971	-	8	7
Wesort	-	-	-	-	-	-	-	-	-
Wicomico	-	38	-	-	-	-	-	-	-
Other Eastern	-	15	-	9	-	-	-	-	-
Fort Berthold	-	-	-	-	-	49	-	-	-
Fort Hall	-	7	-	-	-	-	-	-	-
Gabrieleno	-	-	-	-	-	-	-	-	-
Gila River	-	-	6	-	-	-	-	-	-
Grand Ronde	-	-	-	-	-	-	-	-	-
Gros Ventres	-	8	-	-	-	-	-	-	-
Atsina	-	-	-	-	-	-	-	-	-
Gros Ventres	-	8	-	-	-	-	-	-	-
Haida	-	-	-	-	-	-	-	-	17
Haliwa	6	192	4	131	-	2,287	-	-	13
Hidatsa	-	-	23	-	-	8	-	-	-
Hoopa	-	-	-	5	-	-	-	-	6
Hoopa	-	-	-	5	-	-	-	-	6

[Continued]

Population by Tribe, Region, and State, 1990: Eastern Tribes-Miwok - Part III

[Continued]

Tribe	South Atlantic Region								
	Delaware	Maryland	District of Columbia	Virginia	West Virginia	North Carolina	South Carolina	Georgia	Florida
Other Hoopa	-	-	-	-	-	-	-	-	-
Houma	-	-	-	12	-	-	-	94	23
Iowa	-	15	-	9	-	23	-	7	-
Iroquois	16	479	31	507	33	1,930	116	195	1,473
Cayuga	-	37	-	8	-	4	-	-	-
Iroquois	-	63	16	74	4	59	21	30	326
Mohawk	8	149	15	257	10	142	77	63	722
Oneida	-	68	-	72	-	49	9	30	73
Onondaga	-	29	-	-	-	22	-	21	39
Seneca	-	98	-	23	19	87	-	42	189
Seneca	-	98	-	23	19	81	-	37	178
Seneca Nation	-	-	-	-	-	6	-	-	11
Tonawanda Seneca	-	-	-	-	-	-	-	5	-
Seneca-Cayuga	-	15	-	-	-	-	-	-	14
Tuscarora	8	20	-	73	-	1,567	9	9	76
Wyandotte	-	-	-	-	-	-	-	-	23
Juaneno	-	-	-	-	-	-	-	26	-
Kalispel	-	-	-	-	-	-	-	-	-
Karok	-	-	-	20	-	-	-	-	-
Kaw	-	-	-	-	-	9	-	-	10
Kickapoo	-	-	-	18	-	-	6	11	-
Kickapoo	-	-	-	18	-	-	6	11	-
Oklahoma Kickapoo	-	-	-	-	-	-	-	-	-
Kiowa	-	24	-	21	-	27	-	75	78
Kiowa	-	24	-	21	-	27	-	75	78
Oklahoma Kiowa	-	-	-	-	-	-	-	-	-
Klallam	-	-	-	15	-	10	-	-	-
Jamestown	-	-	-	-	-	-	-	-	-
Klallam	-	-	-	15	-	10	-	-	-
Lower Elwha	-	-	-	-	-	-	-	-	-
Port Gamble Klallam	-	-	-	-	-	-	-	-	-
Klamath	-	-	-	7	-	-	-	-	-
Konkow	-	-	-	-	-	-	-	-	-
Kootenai	-	-	-	-	-	-	-	-	6
Long Island	-	-	-	-	-	-	-	-	14
Matinecock	-	-	-	-	-	-	-	-	-
Montauk	-	-	-	-	-	-	-	-	-
Poospatuck	-	-	-	-	-	-	-	-	14
Setauket	-	-	-	-	-	-	-	-	-
Luiseno	-	13	-	-	-	2	-	9	-
La Jolla	-	11	-	-	-	-	-	-	-
Luiseno	-	-	-	-	-	-	-	-	-
Pala	-	2	-	-	-	-	-	9	-
Pauma	-	-	-	-	-	-	-	-	-
Pechanga	-	-	-	-	-	2	-	-	-
Lumbee	7	1,167	11	450	30	44,535	486	327	659
Lummi	-	-	-	-	-	1	-	-	37
Maidu	-	-	-	-	-	6	4	-	-
Maidu	-	-	-	-	-	6	4	-	-
Nishinam	-	-	-	-	-	-	-	-	-
Makah	-	12	-	8	27	-	-	-	-
Maliseet	6	-	-	-	-	-	-	6	11
Aroostook	-	-	-	-	-	-	-	-	-
Maliseet	6	-	-	-	-	-	-	6	11

[Continued]

★ 135 ★

Population by Tribe, Region, and State, 1990: Eastern Tribes-Miwok - Part III

[Continued]

Tribe	South Atlantic Region								
	Delaware	Maryland	District of Columbia	Virginia	West Virginia	North Carolina	South Carolina	Georgia	Florida
Mandan	-	15	-	13	-	-	-	40	-
Mattaponi	-	11	6	303	8	3	-	-	-
Menominee	-	2	7	50	6	-	12	15	86
Miami	-	-	15	36	-	-	12	40	162
Illinois Miami	-	-	-	-	-	-	-	11	16
Indiana Miami	-	-	-	11	-	-	-	-	34
Miami	-	-	-	25	-	-	12	22	77
Oklahoma Miami	-	-	15	-	-	-	-	7	35
Miccosukee	-	-	-	-	-	-	11	-	222
Micmac	-	16	-	17	-	33	13	-	86
Mission Indians	-	-	-	3	-	-	-	-	-
Miwok	-	-	-	-	-	-	8	7	-

Source: U.S. Bureau of the Census. *1990 Census of Population: Characteristics of American Indians by Tribe and Language.* CP3-7. Washington, DC: The Bureau, 1994, p. 16. *Note:* A dash (-) represents zero or a percent that rounds to zero.

★ 136 ★
Population

Population by Tribe, Region, and State, 1990: Eastern Tribes-Miwok - Part IV

Data are based on a sample and are subject to sampling variability.

Tribe	East South Central Region				West South Central Region				Mountain Region			
	Kentucky	Tennessee	Alabama	Mississippi	Arkansas	Louisiana	Oklahoma	Texas	Montana	Idaho	Wyoming	Colorado
Eastern tribes	12	-	21	-	-	147	21	129	1	-	-	7
Moor	-	-	-	-	-	-	15	-	-	-	-	-
Nansemond	-	-	-	-	-	-	-	-	-	-	-	-
Natchez	-	-	6	-	-	6	-	34	-	-	-	-
Nipmuc	-	-	-	-	-	-	-	-	-	-	-	-
Southeastern Indians	12	-	15	-	-	-	6	55	-	-	-	7
Susquehanock	-	-	-	-	-	-	-	-	-	-	-	-
Tunica	-	-	-	-	-	27	-	17	-	-	-	-
Tunica Biloxi	-	-	-	-	-	114	-	14	-	-	-	-
Waccamaw-Siouan	-	-	-	-	-	-	-	9	-	-	-	-
Wesort	-	-	-	-	-	-	-	-	-	-	-	-
Wicomico	-	-	-	-	-	-	-	-	-	-	-	-
Other Eastern	-	-	-	-	-	-	-	-	1	-	-	-
Fort Berthold	-	-	-	-	-	-	-	-	44	-	9	4
Fort Hall	-	-	-	-	-	12	7	-	32	2,911	65	6
Gabrieleno	-	-	-	-	-	2	-	-	-	-	-	17
Gila River	-	-	-	-	-	-	-	-	-	-	-	3
Grand Ronde	-	-	-	-	-	-	13	22	-	8	-	-
Gros Ventres	-	-	-	-	-	-	23	2	2,082	16	50	5
Atsina	-	-	-	-	-	-	-	-	-	-	-	-
Gros Ventres	-	-	-	-	-	-	23	2	2,082	16	50	5
Haida	-	-	-	-	-	-	-	10	2	4	-	-
Haliwa	-	-	-	-	-	24	45	-	-	-	-	-
Hidatsa	-	-	-	-	-	-	42	21	91	3	-	24
Hoopa	8	-	-	-	-	-	-	-	-	41	-	11
Hoopa	8	-	-	-	-	-	-	-	-	41	-	11
Other Hoopa	-	-	-	-	-	-	-	-	-	-	-	-
Houma	-	6	46	151	25	7,204	-	69	-	-	-	4
Iowa	-	-	-	-	-	4	314	37	2	-	-	27
Iroquois	176	149	143	11	99	273	2,143	769	73	143	34	496
Cayuga	-	-	16	-	-	-	10	-	-	-	-	-
Iroquois	43	16	34	-	20	42	61	127	26	74	-	99

[Continued]

★ 136 ★

Population by Tribe, Region, and State, 1990: Eastern Tribes-Miwok - Part IV
[Continued]

Tribe	East South Central Region				West South Central Region				Mountain Region			
	Kentucky	Tennessee	Alabama	Mississippi	Arkansas	Louisiana	Oklahoma	Texas	Montana	Idaho	Wyoming	Colorado
Mohawk	75	43	17	11	10	130	154	148	10	33	27	156
Oneida	9	11	20	-	12	12	59	145	17	16	-	78
Onondaga	1	29	-	-	-	7	18	74	-	-	-	13
Seneca	48	14	15		-	21	284	187	20	18	7	67
Seneca	34	14	15	-	-	21	284	187	-	18	7	67
Seneca Nation	14	-	-	-	-	-	-	-	20	-	-	-
Tonawanda Seneca	-	-	-	-	-	-	-	-	-	-	-	-
Seneca-Cayuga	-	-	9	-	9	27	761	10	-	2	-	10
Tuscarora	-	21	32	-	-	-	16	-	-	-	-	41
Wyandotte	-	15	-	-	48	34	780	78	-	-	-	32
Juaneno	-	-	-	-	-	-	7	-	-	8	-	-
Kalispel	-	-	-	-	2	-	-	-	34	6	-	-
Karok	-	-	-	-	-	-	5	17	36	31	14	35
Kaw	20	-	-	-	-	-	624	63	3	-	-	-
Kickapoo	-	14	8	9	18	18	1,354	790	12	2	-	21
Kickapoo	-	14	8	9	18	18	1,236	790	12	2	-	21
Oklahoma Kickapoo	-	-	-	-	-	-	118	-	-	-	-	-
Kiowa	-	6	4	9	32	7	6,438	468	4	61	-	143
Kiowa	-	6	4	9	32	7	5,925	468	4	61	-	143
Oklahoma Kiowa	-	-	-	-	-	-	513	-	-	-	-	-
Klallam	-	-	-	-	3	-	20	-	2	-	-	-
Jamestown	-	-	-	-	-	-	-	-	-	-	-	-
Klallam	-	-	-	-	3	-	-	-	-	-	-	-
Lower Elwha	-	-	-	-	-	-	-	-	2	-	-	-
Port Gamble Klallam	-	-	-	-	-	-	20	-	-	-	-	-
Klamath	-	-	-	-	-	-	60	10	18	8	13	26
Konkow	-	-	-	-	-	-	-	-	-	-	-	-
Kootenai	-	-	-	-	-	-	-	-	349	116	-	-
Long Island	-	-	-	-	-	-	6	10	-	-	-	-
Matinecock	-	-	-	-	-	-	-	10	-	-	-	-
Montauk	-	-	-	-	-	-	-	-	-	-	-	-
Poospatuck	-	-	-	-	-	-	6	-	-	-	-	-
Setauket	-	-	-	-	-	-	-	-	-	-	-	-
Luiseno	-	-	9	-	-	-	-	5	-	33	-	11
La Jolla	-	-	-	-	-	-	-	-	-	-	-	-
Luiseno	-	-	-	-	-	-	-	-	-	-	-	9
Pala	-	-	-	-	-	-	-	-	-	33	-	2
Pauma	-	-	-	-	-	-	-	-	-	-	-	-
Pechanga	-	-	9	-	-	-	-	5	-	-	-	-
Lumbee	58	115	57	2	29	62	88	116	8	4	-	86
Lummi	7	-	6	-	2	-	-	18	8	18	-	-
Maidu	-	-	-	-	-	5	6	10	7	29	25	5
Maidu	-	-	-	-	-	5	6	10	7	29	25	5
Nishinam	-	-	-	-	-	-	-	-	-	-	-	-
Makah	-	-	-	9	-	-	40	-	-	7	-	4
Maliseet	2	22	-	4	-	-	-	16	-	-	3	-
Aroostook	-	-	-	-	-	-	-	-	-	-	-	-
Maliseet	2	22	-	4	-	-	-	16	-	-	3	-
Mandan	-	-	-	-	-	-	9	6	45	16	20	43
Mattaponi	-	-	-	7	-	-	-	-	-	-	-	-
Menominee	-	7	-	-	17	-	34	40	10	-	-	35
Miami	8	31	-	10	-	6	398	59	45	16	-	69
Illinois Miami	-	-	-	-	-	-	-	-	-	-	-	-
Indiana Miami	-	-	-	-	-	-	32	8	-	-	-	-
Miami	8	31	-	10	-	6	247	32	45	14	-	46
Oklahoma Miami	-	-	-	-	-	-	119	19	-	2	-	23
Miccosukee	-	-	4	-	-	-	-	5	-	-	-	-
Micmac	16	-	17	3	-	-	13	12	2	-	-	8
Mission Indians	-	5	-	-	9	-	-	14	-	15	-	13
Miwok	-	-	11	-	-	-	-	8	-	23	-	22

Source: U.S. Bureau of the Census. *1990 Census of Population: Characteristics of American Indians by Tribe and Language.* CP3-7. Washington, DC: The Bureau, 1994, p. 17. *Note:* A dash (-) represents zero or a percent that rounds to zero.

Population by Tribe, Region, and State, 1990: Eastern Tribes-Miwok - Part V

Data are based on a sample and are subject to sampling variability.

Tribe	Mountain Region (cont.)				Pacific Region				
	New Mexico	Arizona	Utah	Nevada	Washington	Oregon	California	Alaska	Hawaii
Eastern tribes	5	3	-	-	45	11	153	17	15
Moor	-	-	-	-	-	-	-	-	-
Nansemond	-	-	-	-	-	-	-	-	-
Natchez	-	-	-	-	-	-	6	-	-
Nipmuc	-	-	-	-	-	-	43	12	-
Southeastern Indians	3	3	-	-	34	-	75	5	15
Susquehanock	-	-	-	-	6	-	-	-	-
Tunica	-	-	-	-	-	-	-	-	-
Tunica Biloxi	-	-	-	-	-	-	-	-	-
Waccamaw-Siouan	-	-	-	-	-	-	-	-	-
Wesort	-	-	-	-	5	-	29	-	-
Wicomico	-	-	-	-	-	-	-	-	-
Other Eastern	2	-	-	-	-	11	-	-	-
Fort Berthold	19	-	23	10	64	63	11	-	-
Fort Hall	-	8	83	61	42	75	102	12	6
Gabrieleno	-	5	-	-	-	-	550	-	-
Gila River	-	1,407	-	-	10	41	-	-	-
Grand Ronde	-	15	-	-	154	973	68	-	-
Gros Ventres	32	41	6	19	297	22	41	14	-
Atsina	-	-	-	-	-	-	-	-	-
Gros Ventres	32	41	6	19	297	22	41	14	-
Haida	-	-	-	-	464	135	120	1,110	-
Haliwa	-	-	-	-	10	26	16	-	15
Hidatsa	12	27	8	30	60	-	70	5	-
Hoopa	3	9	6	8	89	158	2,025	13	8
Hoopa	3	9	6	8	89	154	2,025	13	8
Other Hoopa	-	-	-	-	-	4	-	-	-
Houma	-	-	-	-	-	-	76	7	8
Iowa	24	5	15	-	59	20	206	11	-
Iroquois	198	434	181	260	767	545	3,681	166	153
Cayuga	-	10	4	-	10	6	61	-	-
Iroquois	22	60	66	66	135	78	975	29	67
Mohawk	59	162	81	102	128	57	945	21	10
Oneida	50	88	13	18	35	87	529	28	47
Onondaga	12	22	-	4	56	14	44	-	11
Seneca	55	50	-	14	162	117	618	69	18
Seneca	53	50	-	14	128	117	593	69	18
Seneca Nation	2	-	-	-	34	-	8	-	-
Tonawanda Seneca	-	-	-	-	-	-	17	6	-
Seneca-Cayuga	-	6	2	-	2	92	91	-	-
Tuscarora	-	-	-	11	25	2	83	17	-
Wyandotte	-	36	15	45	214	92	335	2	-
Juaneno	-	-	-	22	2	8	1,528	-	-

[Continued]

★ 137 ★

Population by Tribe, Region, and State, 1990: Eastern Tribes-Miwok - Part V
[Continued]

Tribe	Mountain Region (cont.)				Pacific Region				
	New Mexico	Arizona	Utah	Nevada	Washington	Oregon	California	Alaska	Hawaii
Kalispel	-	-	-	-	114	1	-	18	-
Karok	-	32	22	46	77	359	2,300	26	21
Kaw	39	7	-	8	11	15	61	-	-
Kickapoo	9	76	51	51	36	13	163	23	-
Kickapoo	9	76	51	51	36	13	163	23	-
Oklahoma Kickapoo	-	-	-	-	-	-	-	-	-
Kiowa	240	301	11	37	60	72	557	4	32
Kiowa	231	301	11	35	60	72	557	4	32
Oklahoma Kiowa	9	-	-	2	-	-	-	-	-
Klallam	-	-	-	-	1,253	16	158	4	-
Jamestown	-	-	-	-	91	-	17	4	-
Klallam	-	-	-	-	555	11	90	-	-
Lower Elwha	-	-	-	-	213	5	10	-	-
Port Gamble Klallam	-	-	-	-	394	-	41	-	-
Klamath	16	4	-	58	157	2,312	346	29	26
Konkow	-	-	3	-	9	4	328	-	-
Kootenai	-	6	14	-	144	68	3	20	-
Long Island	-	-	-	-	-	-	8	-	-
Matinecock	-	-	-	-	-	-	-	-	-
Montauk	-	-	-	-	-	-	8	-	-
Poospatuck	-	-	-	-	-	-	-	-	-
Setauket	-	-	-	-	-	-	-	-	-
Luiseno	-	7	-	19	81	4	2,501	-	-
La Jolla	-	-	-	-	15	-	136	-	-
Luiseno	-	7	-	9	46	-	1,671	-	-
Pala	-	-	-	10	20	-	384	-	-
Pauma	-	-	-	-	-	-	120	-	-
Pechanga	-	-	-	-	-	4	190	-	-
Lumbee	4	23	11	23	80	25	479	41	52
Lummi	8	6	5	2	2,713	63	118	21	3
Maidu	-	14	2	33	42	88	2,005	22	-
Maidu	-	14	2	33	42	88	2,005	22	-
Nishinam	-	-	-	-	-	-	-	-	-
Makah	-	-	-	-	1,418	15	84	9	-
Maliseet	-	-	-	-	11	-	21	4	-
Aroostook	-	-	-	-	-	-	-	-	-
Maliseet	-	-	-	-	11	-	21	4	-
Mandan	-	24	22	-	17	43	142	-	-
Mattaponi	-	-	-	-	-	-	34	-	-
Menominee	13	53	28	7	28	89	136	12	14
Miami	47	22	14	37	140	46	221	30	-
Illinois Miami	-	-	-	-	6	-	7	6	-
Indiana Miami	-	-	-	-	-	8	-	-	-
Miami	47	22	14	37	49	25	155	-	-

[Continued]

★ 137 ★

Population by Tribe, Region, and State, 1990: Eastern Tribes-Miwok - Part V
[Continued]

Tribe	Mountain Region (cont.)				Pacific Region				
	New Mexico	Arizona	Utah	Nevada	Washington	Oregon	California	Alaska	Hawaii
Oklahoma Miami	-	-	-	-	85	13	59	24	-
Miccosukee	-	-	-	-	-	-	10	-	-
Micmac	-	90	-	-	51	11	122	-	-
Mission Indians	26	49	-	17	98	51	1,685	7	8
Miwok	-	20	14	75	46	54	3,047	4	25

Source: U.S. Bureau of the Census. *1990 Census of Population: Characteristics of American Indians by Tribe and Language.* CP3-7. Washington, DC: The Bureau, 1994, p. 18. *Note:* A dash (-) represents zero or a percent that rounds to zero.

★ 138 ★

Population

Population by Tribe, Region, and State, 1990: Modoc-Pueblo - Part I

Data are based on a sample and are subject to sampling variability.

Tribe	New England						Middle Atlantic		
	Maine	New Hampshire	Vermont	Massachusetts	Rhode Island	Connecticut	New York	New Jersey	Pennsylvania
Modoc	-	-	-	-	-	-	-	-	25
Modoc	-	-	-	-	-	-	-	-	25
Oklahoma Modoc	-	-	-	-	-	-	-	-	-
Mohegan	9	9	7	7	42	433	130	12	53
Mono	-	-	-	-	-	-	-	-	-
Nanticoke	-	-	-	-	-	8	15	515	56
Narragansett	10	8	-	213	1,698	158	69	-	12
Navajo	30	13	64	140	59	60	364	272	179
Nez Perce	-	18	-	9	6	5	5	10	5
Nomalaki	-	-	-	-	-	-	-	-	-
Northwest tribes	-	-	9	10	14	10	103	101	-
Columbia	-	-	9	10	14	10	103	101	-
Kalapuya	-	-	-	-	-	-	-	-	-
Tillamook	-	-	-	-	-	-	-	-	-
Other Northwest	-	-	-	-	-	-	-	-	-
Omaha	-	8	-	-	-	-	8	-	5
Oregon Athabaskan	-	-	-	-	-	-	-	-	-
Osage	-	-	3	37	-	23	28	-	12
Otoe-Missouria	-	18	-	-	-	-	-	26	-
Ottawa	-	10	-	-	-	-	22	13	53
Burt Lake Ottawa	-	-	-	-	-	-	-	-	-
Michigan Ottawa	-	-	-	-	-	-	-	-	-
Oklahoma Ottawa	-	-	-	-	-	-	-	-	-
Ottawa	-	10	-	-	-	-	22	13	53
Paiute	-	-	-	26	-	-	27	5	2
Burns Paiute	-	-	-	-	-	-	-	-	-
Kaibab	-	-	-	-	-	-	-	-	-
Moapa	-	-	-	-	-	-	-	-	-
Northern Paiute	-	-	-	-	-	-	-	-	-
Owens Valley	-	-	-	-	-	-	-	-	-
Paiute	-	-	-	-	-	-	27	5	2
Pyramid Lake	-	-	-	-	-	-	-	-	-
Southern Paiute	-	-	-	-	-	-	-	-	-

[Continued]

★ 138 ★

Population by Tribe, Region, and State, 1990: Modoc-Pueblo - Part I

[Continued]

Tribe	New England						Middle Atlantic		
	Maine	New Hampshire	Vermont	Massachusetts	Rhode Island	Connecticut	New York	New Jersey	Pennsylvania
Walker River	-	-	-	-	-	-	-	-	-
Yerington Paiute	-	-	-	-	-	-	-	-	-
Other Paiute	-	-	-	4	-	-	-	-	-
Pamunkey	-	-	-	10	-	-	84	17	51
Passamaquoddy	1,750	108	2	169	-	72	15	-	15
Passamaquoddy	1,750	108	2	169	-	72	15	-	15
Other Passamaquoddy	-	-	-	-	-	-	-	-	-
Pawnee	7	2	-	16	-	-	29	15	45
Oklahoma Pawnee	-	-	-	-	-	-	-	-	-
Pawnee	7	2	-	16	-	-	29	15	45
Penobscot	1,090	104	31	182	28	207	75	38	29
Peoria	-	-	-	-	-	-	-	-	-
Oklahoma Peoria	-	-	-	-	-	-	-	-	-
Peoria	-	-	-	-	-	-	-	-	-
Pequot	-	-	6	65	88	323	12	-	32
Pima	7	-	-	11	-	-	4	20	9
Piscataway	-	-	-	26	-	-	5	-	17
Pit River	-	-	-	-	-	-	7	-	7
Pomo	-	-	9	-	-	-	-	-	-
Central Pomo	-	-	9	-	-	-	-	-	-
Kashaya	-	-	-	-	-	-	-	-	-
Northern Pomo	-	-	-	-	-	-	-	-	-
Pomo	-	-	-	-	-	-	-	-	-
Other Pomo	-	-	-	-	-	-	-	-	-
Ponca	11	-	-	9	-	-	31	-	-
Oklahoma Ponca	-	-	-	-	-	-	-	-	-
Ponca	11	-	-	9	-	-	31	-	-
Potawatomi	6	-	5	37	-	17	113	4	67
Citizen Band Potawatomi	5	-	-	-	-	-	34	-	2
Forest County	-	-	-	-	-	-	-	-	-
Hannahville	-	-	-	-	-	-	-	-	-
Huron Potawatomi	-	-	-	-	-	-	-	-	-
Popagon Potawatomi	-	-	-	-	-	-	-	-	-
Potawatomi	1	-	5	25	-	17	79	4	63
Prairie Band	-	-	-	12	-	-	-	-	2
Wisconsin Potawatomi	-	-	-	-	-	-	-	-	-
Powhatan	2	-	-	12	-	13	39	244	77
Pueblo	3	-	16	126	17	25	284	90	48
Acoma	-	-	-	-	-	-	-	-	7
Arizona Tewa	-	-	-	-	-	-	-	-	-
Cochiti	-	-	-	-	-	-	-	-	-
Hopi	3	-	-	13	-	7	90	78	4
Isleta	-	-	-	8	17	-	-	-	-
Jemez	-	-	-	-	-	-	-	-	-
Keres	-	-	-	-	-	-	-	-	-
Laguna	-	-	8	-	-	-	24	6	15
Nambe	-	-	-	-	-	-	-	-	-
Picuris	-	-	-	-	-	-	21	-	-
Piro	-	-	-	-	-	-	-	-	-
Pojoaque	-	-	-	-	-	-	-	-	-
Pueblo	-	-	8	-	-	18	21	-	5
Sandia	-	-	-	-	-	-	-	-	-
San Felipe	-	-	-	-	-	-	-	-	-
San Ildefonso	-	-	-	-	-	-	-	-	-
San Juan	-	-	-	-	-	-	-	-	-

[Continued]

★ 138 ★

Population by Tribe, Region, and State, 1990: Modoc-Pueblo - Part I
[Continued]

Tribe	New England						Middle Atlantic		
	Maine	New Hampshire	Vermont	Massachusetts	Rhode Island	Connecticut	New York	New Jersey	Pennsylvania
Santa Ana	-	-	-	-	-	-	6	-	-
Santa Clara	-	-	-	-	-	-	-	-	-
Santa Domingo	-	-	-	83	-	-	98	6	-
Taos	-	-	-	-	-	-	-	-	-
Tesuque	-	-	-	-	-	-	-	-	-
Tewa	-	-	-	-	-	-	5	-	7
Tigua	-	-	-	22	-	-	17	-	-
Zia	-	-	-	-	-	-	-	-	-
Zuni	-	-	-	-	-	-	8	-	10

Source: U.S. Bureau of the Census. *1990 Census of Population: Characteristics of American Indians by Tribe and Language.* CP3-7. Washington, DC: The Bureau, 1994, p. 20.
Note: A dash (-) represents zero or a percent that rounds to zero.

★ 139 ★
Population

Population by Tribe, Region, and State, 1990: Modoc-Pueblo - Part II

Data are based on a sample and are subject to sampling variability.

Tribe	East North Central Region					West North Central Region						
	Ohio	Indiana	Illinois	Michigan	Wisconsin	Minnesota	Iowa	Missouri	North Dakota	South Dakota	Nebraska	Kansas
Modoc	-	6	7	-	-	-	-	21	-	-	2	31
Modoc	-	6	7	-	-	-	-	21	-	-	2	31
Oklahoma Modoc	-	-	-	-	-	-	-	-	-	-	-	-
Mohegan	4	-	22	5	5	-	-	-	-	-	-	-
Mono	-	-	15	-	8	-	-	2	-	-	-	-
Nanticoke	11	-	-	12	-	-	-	-	-	-	-	-
Narragansett	-	-	-	13	7	5	-	-	6	-	-	-
Navajo	303	205	450	257	127	153	21	268	89	220	39	461
Nez Perce	20	-	-	20	23	18	7	13	-	17	6	11
Nomalaki	-	-	-	-	-	-	-	-	-	-	-	-
Northwest tribes	8	-	-	13	1	-	-	-	2	-	-	-
Columbia	-	-	-	12	-	-	-	-	2	-	-	-
Kalapuya	-	-	-	-	1	-	-	-	-	-	-	-
Tillamook	8	-	-	-	-	-	-	-	-	-	-	-
Other Northwest	-	-	-	1	-	-	-	-	-	-	-	-
Omaha	29	2	21	55	58	37	282	56	30	88	2,862	128
Oregon Athabaskan	-	-	6	-	-	2	-	-	-	-	-	-
Osage	70	15	67	142	25	19	23	257	-	2	31	453
Otoe-Missouria	8	-	-	-	-	7	7	9	3	7	10	94
Ottawa	123	19	74	5,141	324	47	11	113	-	-	-	83
Burt Lake Ottawa	-	-	-	13	-	-	-	-	-	-	-	-
Michigan Ottawa	-	-	-	39	-	-	-	-	-	-	-	-
Oklahoma Ottawa	-	-	-	12	-	-	-	-	-	-	-	18
Ottawa	123	19	74	5,077	324	47	11	113	-	-	-	65
Paiute	-	-	21	8	28	44	6	21	2	45	-	39
Burns Paiute	-	-	-	-	-	-	-	-	-	-	-	-
Kaibab	-	-	-	-	-	-	-	-	-	-	-	8
Moapa	-	-	-	-	-	-	-	-	-	-	-	-
Northern Paiute	-	-	-	-	-	-	-	-	-	5	-	-
Owens Valley	-	-	-	-	-	-	-	-	-	-	-	-

[Continued]

★ 139 ★

Population by Tribe, Region, and State, 1990: Modoc-Pueblo - Part II
[Continued]

Tribe	East North Central Region					West North Central Region						
	Ohio	Indiana	Illinois	Michigan	Wisconsin	Minnesota	Iowa	Missouri	North Dakota	South Dakota	Nebraska	Kansas
Paiute	-	-	21	8	28	27	6	21	2	40	-	19
Pyramid Lake	-	-	-	-	-	-	-	-	-	-	-	-
Southern Paiute	-	-	-	-	-	-	-	-	-	-	-	12
Walker River	-	-	-	-	-	-	-	-	-	-	-	-
Yerington Paiute	-	-	-	-	-	-	-	-	-	-	-	-
Other Paiute	-	-	-	-	-	17	-	-	-	-	-	-
Pamunkey	32	-	-	2	-	-	-	-	-	-	-	-
Passamaquoddy	-	-	-	11	-	-	-	-	-	7	-	7
Passamaquoddy	-	-	-	11	-	-	-	-	-	7	-	7
Other Passamaquoddy	-	-	-	-	-	-	-	-	-	-	-	-
Pawnee	47	8	37	35	8	6	22	27	3	3	9	127
Oklahoma Pawnee	-	-	-	-	-	-	-	-	-	2	-	-
Pawnee	47	8	37	35	8	6	22	27	3	1	9	127
Penobscot	31	24	8	16	2	-	-	-	-	-	-	-
Peoria	-	-	15	-	-	7	15	101	-	-	-	52
Oklahoma Peoria	-	-	-	-	-	-	-	-	-	-	-	-
Peoria	-	-	15	-	-	7	15	101	-	-	-	52
Pequot	-	15	-	2	-	-	11	-	-	-	-	-
Pima	18	13	-	34	11	35	12	5	-	13	-	10
Piscataway	-	-	-	-	-	-	-	-	-	-	-	-
Pit River	-	-	-	16	-	-	-	-	-	-	-	-
Pomo	7	-	2	-	-	21	7	8	-	-	11	-
Central Pomo	-	-	-	-	-	-	-	-	-	-	-	-
Kashaya	-	-	-	-	-	-	-	-	-	-	-	-
Northern Pomo	-	-	-	-	-	-	-	-	-	-	-	-
Pomo	7	-	2	-	-	21	7	8	-	-	11	-
Other Pomo	-	-	-	-	-	-	-	-	-	-	-	-
Ponca	-	-	-	-	2	15	-	9	-	41	266	295
Oklahoma Ponca	-	-	-	-	-	-	-	-	-	-	2	-
Ponca	-	-	-	-	2	15	-	9	-	41	264	295
Potawatomi	86	272	290	2,261	1,040	81	39	300	4	36	51	2,182
Citizen Band Potawatomi	-	17	-	-	4	4	-	25	-	-	-	285
Forest County	-	-	-	4	323	-	-	-	-	-	-	6
Hannahville	-	-	-	42	16	-	-	-	-	-	-	-
Huron Potawatomi	-	-	-	52	18	-	-	2	-	-	8	-
Popagon Potawatomi	-	5	-	43	-	-	-	-	-	-	-	-
Potawatomi	86	247	277	2,120	654	74	29	273	4	18	43	1,530
Prairie Band	-	3	13	-	25	3	10	-	-	18	-	361
Wisconsin Potawatomi	-	-	-	-	-	-	-	-	-	-	-	-
Powhatan	5	-	-	3	2	9	-	6	-	-	-	31
Pueblo	190	62	123	144	52	85	33	78	8	29	10	154
Acoma	30	-	-	-	-	-	-	7	-	-	-	17
Arizona Tewa	-	-	-	-	-	-	-	-	-	-	-	-
Cochiti	-	-	-	7	13	-	-	-	-	-	-	-
Hopi	25	-	12	56	32	41	4	37	-	22	-	69
Isleta	-	-	-	-	-	10	-	-	-	7	-	5
Jemez	21	-	-	-	-	-	21	-	-	-	-	-
Keres	-	-	-	-	-	-	-	-	-	-	-	-
Laguna	10	20	33	4	-	-	-	8	-	-	-	13
Nambe	-	-	-	-	-	-	-	-	-	-	-	-
Picuris	-	-	-	-	-	-	2	-	-	-	-	-
Piro	-	-	-	-	-	-	-	-	-	-	-	-
Pojoaque	-	-	-	-	-	-	-	-	-	-	-	-
Pueblo	61	18	28	30	-	25	-	17	-	-	9	17

[Continued]

★ 139 ★

Population by Tribe, Region, and State, 1990: Modoc-Pueblo - Part II

[Continued]

Tribe	East North Central Region					West North Central Region						
	Ohio	Indiana	Illinois	Michigan	Wisconsin	Minnesota	Iowa	Missouri	North Dakota	South Dakota	Nebraska	Kansas
Sandia	-	-	-	-	-	-	-	-	-	-	-	-
San Felipe	-	-	16	-	-	-	-	-	-	-	-	4
San Ildefonso	-	5	-	-	-		-	-	-	-	-	-
San Juan	18	-	-	-	-	2	-	-	-	-	-	-
Santa Ana	-	-	-	-	-	-	-	-	-	-	1	-
Santa Clara	-	-	2	-	-	-	-	-	-	-		-
Santa Domingo	-	-	6	10	-	-	-	-	-	-	-	
Taos	6	-	-	9	-	-	6	-	-	-	-	12
Tesuque	-	-	-	-	-	-	-	-	-	-	-	18
Tewa	14	19	13	8	-	2	-	-	8	-	-	-
Tigua	-	-	-	-	-	-	-	-	-	-	-	-
Zia	-	-	13	11	-	-	-	-	-	-	-	9
Zuni	5	-	-	9	7	5	-	9	-	-	-	

Source: U.S. Bureau of the Census. *1990 Census of Population: Characteristics of American Indians by Tribe and Language.* CP3-7. Washington, DC: The Bureau, 1994, p. 21.
Note: A dash (-) represents zero or a percent that rounds to zero.

★ 140 ★
Population

Population by Tribe, Region, and State, 1990: Modoc-Pueblo - Part III

Data are based on a sample and are subject to sampling variability.

Tribe	South Atlantic Region								
	Delaware	Maryland	District of Columbia	Virginia	West Virginia	North Carolina	South Carolina	Georgia	Florida
Modoc	-	-	-	-	-	-	-	-	-
Modoc	-	-	-	-	-	-	-	-	-
Oklahoma Modoc	-	-	-	-	-	-	-	-	25
Mohegan	-	19	-	46	-	8	-	-	-
Mono	-	-	-	-	-	3	-	-	8
Nanticoke	639	53	-	31	2	56	-	-	35
Narragansett	8	40	-	26	-	18	-	14	349
Navajo	9	323	5	337	96	243	120	183	11
Nez Perce	-	23	-	84	-	7	13	7	-
Nomalaki	-	-	-	-	-	-	-	21	
Northwest tribes	-	-	-	8	-	6	-	-	29
Columbia	-	-	-	8	-	6	-	-	29
Kalapuya	-	-	-	-	-	-	-	-	-
Tillamook	-	-	-	-	-	-	-	-	-
Other Northwest	-	-	-	-	-	-	-	-	117
Omaha	-	9	-	12	-	6	-	-	-
Oregon Athabaskan	-	1	-	-	-	-	11	-	-
Osage	-	56	-	109	-	43	24	26	83
Otoe-Missouria	-	26	-	42	-	6	-	-	33
Ottawa	34	72	-	71	-	61	28	105	77
Burt Lake Ottawa	-	-	-	-	-	-	-	-	-
Michigan Ottawa	-	-	-	-	-	-	-	-	-
Oklahoma Ottawa	-	-	-	-	-	-	-	-	-
Ottawa	34	72	-	71	-	61	28	105	77
Paiute	-	15	8	6	-	4	6	-	99

[Continued]

★ 140 ★

Population by Tribe, Region, and State, 1990: Modoc-Pueblo - Part III
[Continued]

Tribe	South Atlantic Region								
	Delaware	Maryland	District of Columbia	Virginia	West Virginia	North Carolina	South Carolina	Georgia	Florida
Burns Paiute	-	-	-	-	-	-	-	-	-
Kaibab	-	-	-	-	-	-	-	-	-
Moapa	-	-	-	-	-	-	-	-	-
Northern Paiute	-	-	-	-	-	-	-	-	-
Owens Valley	-	-	-	-	-	-	-	-	-
Paiute	-	15	8	6	-	4	6	-	81
Pyramid Lake	-	-	-	-	-	-	-	-	13
Southern Paiute	-	-	-	-	-	-	-	-	5
Walker River	-	-	-	-	-	-	-	-	-
Yerington Paiute	-	-	-	-	-	-	-	-	-
Other Paiute	-	-	-	-	-	-	-	-	-
Pamunkey	-	4	-	119	25	5	17	7	-
Passamaquoddy	-	16	-	55	-	4	7	11	71
Passamaquoddy	-	16	-	55	-	4	7	11	71
Other Passamaquoddy	-	-	-	-	-	-	-	-	-
Pawnee	3	14	-	9	-	105	-	10	39
Oklahoma Pawnee	-	-	-	-	-	-	-	-	-
Pawnee	3	14	-	9	-	105	-	10	39
Penobscot	3	-	-	20	-	6	80	8	133
Peoria	-	-	-	-	-	-	-	34	35
Oklahoma Peoria	-	-	-	-	-	-	-	-	-
Peoria	-	-	-	-	-	-	-	34	35
Pequot	-	10	-	-	-	-	-	6	57
Pima	6	-	4	42	1	13	19	13	16
Piscataway	-	665	22	26	-	-	-	-	16
Pit River	-	-	-	15	-	-	-	3	-
Pomo	-	-	-	7	-	23	-	5	-
Central Pomo	-	-	-	-	-	-	-	-	-
Kashaya	-	-	-	-	-	-	-	-	-
Northern Pomo	-	-	-	-	-	-	-	-	-
Pomo	-	-	-	7	-	23	-	5	-
Other Pomo	-	-	-	-	-	-	-	-	-
Ponca	-	-	-	-	-	-	-	-	9
Oklahoma Ponca	-	-	-	-	-	-	-	-	-
Ponca	-	-	-	-	-	-	-	-	9
Potawatomi	-	33	8	39	2	29	12	11	297
Citizen Band Potawatomi	-	-	-	14	-	6	-	-	48
Forest County	-	-	-	-	-	-	-	-	-
Hannahville	-	-	-	-	-	-	-	-	-
Huron Potawatomi	-	-	-	-	-	-	-	-	-
Popagon Potawatomi	-	-	-	-	-	-	-	-	-
Potawatomi	-	33	8	25	2	23	12	7	249
Prairie Band	-	-	-	-	-	-	-	4	-
Wisconsin Potawatomi	-	-	-	-	-	-	-	-	-
Powhatan	3	82	4	54	-	17	-	-	31
Pueblo	-	112	-	264	1	74	29	122	145
Acoma	-	8	-	-	-	-	-	-	5
Arizona Tewa	-	25	-	-	-	-	-	-	-
Cochiti	-	-	-	-	-	-	-	14	-
Hopi	-	21	-	63	1	15	23	10	38
Isleta	-	-	-	25	-	32	-	10	-
Jemez	-	-	-	-	-	-	-	-	-
Keres	-	-	-	-	-	-	-	-	-
Laguna	-	12	-	54	-	5	6	17	44
Nambe	-	-	-	-	-	-	-	8	-

[Continued]

★ 140 ★

Population by Tribe, Region, and State, 1990: Modoc-Pueblo - Part III
[Continued]

Tribe	South Atlantic Region								
	Delaware	Maryland	District of Columbia	Virginia	West Virginia	North Carolina	South Carolina	Georgia	Florida
Picuris	-	-	-	-		-	-	-	-
Piro	-	-	-	-	-	-	-	-	-
Pojoaque	-	-	-	-	-	-	-	-	-
Pueblo	-	8	-	14	-	15	-	37	17
Sandia	-	-	-	-	-	-	-	-	-
San Felipe	-	21	-	-	-	-	-	-	-
San Ildefonso	-	3	-	-	-	-	-	-	-
San Juan	-	-	-	-	-	-	-	-	-
Santa Ana	-	-	-	-	-	-	-	-	-
Santa Clara	-	-	-	-	-	-	-	-	-
Santa Domingo	-	-	-	-	-	-	-	13	-
Taos	-	-	-	17	-	-	-	-	6
Tesuque	-	-	-	-	-	-	-	-	-
Tewa	-	-	-	48	-	-	-	-	7
Tigua	-	7	-	9	-	4	-	-	19
Zia	-	-	-	-	-	-	-	-	-
Zuni	-	7	-	34	-	3	-	13	9

Source: U.S. Bureau of the Census. *1990 Census of Population: Characteristics of American Indians by Tribe and Language.* CP3-7. Washington, DC: The Bureau, 1994, p. 22. *Note:* A dash (-) represents zero or a percent that rounds to zero.

★ 141 ★
Population

Population by Tribe, Region, and State, 1990: Modoc-Pueblo - Part IV

Data are based on a sample and are subject to sampling variability.

Tribe	East South Central Region				West South Central Region				Mountain Region			
	Kentucky	Tennessee	Alabama	Mississippi	Arkansas	Louisiana	Oklahoma	Texas	Montana	Idaho	Wyoming	Colorado
Modoc	-	-	-	-	4	-	16	-	-	2	-	-
Modoc	-	-	-	-	4	-	16	-	-	2	-	-
Oklahoma Modoc	-	-	-	-	-	-	-	-	-	-	-	-
Mohegan	9	-	3	-	-	-	7	13	6	-	-	45
Mono	-	-	-	-	-	-	2	18	-	9	-	-
Nanticoke	-	-	-	-	24	-	7	-	-	-	-	21
Narragansett	-	9	-	-	-	-	-	30	-	-	-	10
Navajo	135	106	45	11	84	126	872	1,909	393	574	194	3,794
Nez Perce	-	-	12	-	21	10	13	52	114	1,804	4	11
Nomalaki	-	-	-	-	-	-	-	-	-	-	-	-
Northwest tribes	-	13	-	-	-	-	-	128	-	-	-	-
Columbia	-	-	-	-	-	-	-	128	-	-	-	-
Kalapuya	-	-	-	-	-	-	-	-	-	-	-	-
Tillamook	-	-	-	-	-	-	-	-	-	-	-	-
Other Northwest	-	13	-	-	-	-	-	-	-	-	-	-
Omaha	-	-	-	7	-	-	66	22	28	21	8	77
Oregon Athabaskan	-	-	-	-	-	-	40	52	-	-	-	-
Osage	31	38	27	30	180	69	5,050	757	25	38	9	262
Otoe-Missouria	-	-	-	-	10	-	1,199	30	-	15	-	8
Ottawa	38	-	25	-	23	15	303	185	5	14	18	33
Burt Lake Ottawa	-	-	-	-	-	-	-	-	-	-	-	-
Michigan Ottawa	-	-	-	-	-	-	-	-	-	-	-	-
Oklahoma Ottawa	-	-	-	-	-	-	-	-	-	-	-	-
Ottawa	38	-	25	-	23	15	303	185	5	14	18	33
Paiute	-	16	-	-	11	2	13	89	55	170	36	18

[Continued]

Population by Tribe, Region, and State, 1990: Modoc-Pueblo - Part IV

[Continued]

Tribe	East South Central Region				West South Central Region				Mountain Region			
	Kentucky	Tennessee	Alabama	Mississippi	Arkansas	Louisiana	Oklahoma	Texas	Montana	Idaho	Wyoming	Colorado
Burns Paiute	-	-	-	-	-	-	-	-	-	-	-	-
Kaibab	-	-	-	-	-	-	-	-	-	-	-	-
Moapa	-	-	-	-	-	-	-	-	-	-	-	3
Northern Paiute	-	-	-	-	-	-	-	-	3	2	-	-
Owens Valley	-	-	-	-	-	-	-	-	-	-	-	-
Paiute	-	16	-	-	11	-	13	89	50	155	36	7
Pyramid Lake	-	-	-	-	-	-	-	-	2	13	-	2
Southern Paiute	-	-	-	-	-	2	-	-	-	-	-	-
Walker River	-	-	-	-	-	-	-	-	-	-	-	6
Yerington Paiute	-	-	-	-	-	-	-	-	-	-	-	-
Other Paiute	-	-	-	-	-	-	-	-	-	-	-	-
Pamunkey	-	-	-	-	-	-	6	7	-	-	-	6
Passamaquoddy	-	-	-	-	-	3	-	3	-	-	-	7
Passamaquoddy	-	-	-	-	-	3	-	3	-	-	-	7
Other Passamaquoddy	-	-	-	-	-	-	-	-	-	-	-	-
Pawnee	3	-	-	3	14	44	1,614	170	13	7	-	126
Oklahoma Pawnee	-	-	-	-	-	3	151	-	-	-	-	-
Pawnee	3	-	-	3	14	41	1,463	170	13	7	-	126
Penobscot	-	-	12	-	-	11	5	59	4	-	3	17
Peoria	-	11	-	-	23	-	506	55	7	22	7	44
Oklahoma Peoria	-	-	-	-	-	-	10	9	-	-	-	-
Peoria	-	11	-	-	23	-	496	46	7	22	7	44
Pequot	-	-	-	-	-	-	-	-	-	-	-	-
Pima	8	8	10	-	21	7	64	68	29	24	25	75
Piscataway	-	3	-	-	-	-	-	-	-	-	-	-
Pit River	-	-	-	-	-	-	24	15	-	2	-	8
Pomo	-	-	-	-	-	-	15	14	-	29	-	23
Central Pomo	-	-	-	-	-	-	-	-	-	-	-	-
Kashaya	-	-	-	-	-	-	-	-	-	-	-	-
Northern Pomo	-	-	-	-	-	-	-	-	-	-	-	-
Pomo	-	-	-	-	-	-	15	14	-	29	-	23
Other Pomo	-	-	-	-	-	-	-	-	-	-	-	-
Ponca	-	-	-	-	16	8	1,705	108	7	-	-	57
Oklahoma Ponca	-	-	-	-	-	-	86	-	-	-	-	7
Ponca	-	-	-	-	16	8	1,619	108	7	-	-	50
Potawatomi	23	81	27	-	167	66	4,314	1,173	154	121	6	270
Citizen Band Potawatomi	10	28	-	-	2	-	875	277	43	18	-	30
Forest County	-	-	-	-	-	-	-	-	-	-	-	-
Hannahville	-	-	-	-	-	-	-	5	-	-	-	-
Huron Potawatomi	-	-	-	-	-	-	8	-	-	-	-	-
Popagon Potawatomi	-	-	-	-	-	-	-	-	-	-	-	-
Potawatomi	13	53	27	-	165	66	3,372	876	99	97	6	229
Prairie Band	-	-	-	-	-	-	59	15	12	6	-	11
Wisconsin Potawatomi	-	-	-	-	-	-	-	-	-	-	-	-
Powhatan	5	8	-	-	-	-	18	14	-	-	-	15
Pueblo	66	32	9	6	22	20	372	1,280	65	57	109	752
Acoma	2	-	-	6	-	-	22	-	-	-	-	80
Arizona Tewa	-	-	-	-	-	-	-	-	-	-	-	-
Cochiti	-	-	-	-	-	-	-	-	-	-	-	28
Hopi	-	2	-	-	12	-	76	62	37	30	31	132
Isleta	-	-	-	-	-	15	-	42	-	-	-	15
Jemez	-	-	-	-	-	-	5	48	7	-	-	29
Keres	-	-	-	-	-	-	-	-	-	-	-	-
Laguna	20	-	-	-	-	-	86	69	4	7	-	70
Nambe	-	-	-	-	-	-	-	4	-	-	-	-
Picuris	-	-	-	-	-	-	-	-	-	-	-	13
Piro	-	-	-	-	-	-	-	-	-	-	-	-
Pojoaque	-	-	-	-	-	-	6	-	-	-	-	-
Pueblo	44	-	-	-	10	5	104	98	-	18	40	110
Sandia	-	-	-	-	-	-	-	-	-	-	-	-
San Felipe	-	-	-	-	-	-	8	-	-	-	-	-
San Ildefonso	-	-	-	-	-	-	-	-	-	-	-	-
San Juan	-	-	-	-	-	-	-	-	-	-	7	-

[Continued]

★ 141 ★

Population by Tribe, Region, and State, 1990: Modoc-Pueblo - Part IV
[Continued]

Tribe	East South Central Region				West South Central Region				Mountain Region			
	Kentucky	Tennessee	Alabama	Mississippi	Arkansas	Louisiana	Oklahoma	Texas	Montana	Idaho	Wyoming	Colorado
Santa Ana	-	11	-	-	-	-	9	-	10	-	-	-
Santa Clara	-	-	-	-	-	-	3	36	-	-	-	-
Santa Domingo	-	-	-	-	-	-	16	18	-	-	-	30
Taos	-	-	-	-	-	-	5	16	7	-	8	112
Tesuque	-	-	-	-	-	-	-	-	-	-	-	-
Tewa	-	-	9	-	-	-	-	52	-	-	-	61
Tigua	-	-	-	-	-	-	25	761	-	-	23	-
Zia	-	-	-	-	-	-	-	-	-	-	-	37
Zuni	-	19	-	-	-	-	7	74	-	2	-	35

Source: U.S. Bureau of the Census. *1990 Census of Population: Characteristics of American Indians by Tribe and Language.* CP3-7. Washington, DC: The Bureau, 1994, p. 23. *Note:* A dash (-) represents zero or a percent that rounds to zero.

★ 142 ★

Population

Population by Tribe, Region, and State, 1990: Modoc-Pueblo - Part V

Data are based on a sample and are subject to sampling variability.

Tribe	Mountain Region (cont.)				Pacific Region				
	New Mexico	Arizona	Utah	Nevada	Washington	Oregon	California	Alaska	Hawaii
Modoc	4	8	-	-	17	178	200	-	-
Modoc	4	8	-	-	17	178	200	-	-
Oklahoma Modoc	-	-	-	-	-	-	-	-	-
Mohegan	-	22	-	-	-	-	55	-	-
Mono	-	24	-	5	25	6	1,559	9	12
Nanticoke	2	-	-	-	29	4	36	-	-
Narragansett	-	12	-	9	17	8	129	-	-
Navajo	79,079	107,543	13,153	658	744	745	9,420	123	151
Nez Perce	6	38	33	8	801	386	323	29	-
Nomalaki	-	-	-	-	7	6	280	-	-
Northwest tribes	-	12	-	-	67	32	133	-	-
Columbia	-	12	-	-	-	-	67	-	-
Kalapuya	-	-	-	-	30	9	12	-	-
Tillamook	-	-	-	-	31	21	33	-	-
Other Northwest	-	-	-	-	6	2	21	-	-
Omaha	41	27	4	-	86	56	103	-	4
Oregon Athabaskan	-	-	-	4	55	101	60	9	-
Osage	115	126	40	90	117	328	1,465	60	25
Otoe-Missouria	30	37	-	-	13	15	92	-	17
Ottawa	21	7	31	19	80	34	553	-	-
Burt Lake Ottawa	-	-	-	-	-	-	-	-	-
Michigan Ottawa	-	-	-	-	19	-	15	-	-
Oklahoma Ottawa	-	-	-	-	-	-	50	-	-
Ottawa	21	7	31	19	61	34	488	-	-
Paiute	89	421	753	3,887	245	478	4,605	22	47

[Continued]

★ 142 ★

Population by Tribe, Region, and State, 1990: Modoc-Pueblo - Part V
[Continued]

Tribe	Mountain Region (cont.)				Pacific Region				
	New Mexico	Arizona	Utah	Nevada	Washington	Oregon	California	Alaska	Hawaii
Burns Paiute	-	-	-	-	3	135	-	-	-
Kaibab	-	61	23	-	-	-	9	-	-
Moapa	-	-	-	48	-	-	-	-	-
Northern Paiute	4	10	2	57	34	13	104	-	-
Owens Valley	-	-	-	-	-	-	314	-	-
Paiute	79	345	688	2,701	187	325	4,104	22	47
Pyramid Lake	-	-	38	547	-	2	11	-	-
Southern Paiute	-	-	2	50	-	-	22	-	-
Walker River	-	5	-	306	21	-	13	-	-
Yerington Paiute	6	-	-	150	-	-	13	-	-
Other Paiute	-	-	-	28	-	3	15	-	-
Pamunkey	-	-	-	-	-	-	8	-	-
Passamaquoddy	31	12	-	-	-	4	70	16	-
Passamaquoddy	31	12	-	-	-	4	70	16	-
Other Passamaquoddy	-	-	-	-	-	-	-	-	-
Pawnee	53	86	15	89	108	24	360	12	20
Oklahoma Pawnee	-	-	-	-	-	-	-	-	-
Pawnee	53	86	15	89	108	24	360	12	20
Penobscot	7	11	-	-	19	8	127	-	9
Peoria	-	13	-	19	60	33	197	18	-
Oklahoma Peoria	-	-	-	19	18	-	-	-	-
Peoria	-	13	-	-	42	33	197	18	-
Pequot	-	-	6	6	-	7	33	-	-
Pima	86	13,034	21	20	84	67	1,093	7	7
Piscataway	-	-	-	-	36	-	8	-	-
Pit River	-	1	-	50	52	207	1,322	19	5
Pomo	-	60	13	19	80	43	4,480	4	18
Central Pomo	-	-	-	17	-	-	77	-	-
Kashaya	-	-	-	-	-	-	62	-	-
Northern Pomo	-	-	-	-	-	-	262	-	-
Pomo	-	60	13	2	80	43	4,020	4	18
Other Pomo	-	-	-	-	-	-	59	-	-
Ponca	-	65	7	2	-	24	100	1	-
Oklahoma Ponca	-	-	-	-	-	-	9	-	-
Ponca	-	65	7	2	-	24	91	1	-
Potawatomi	28	165	62	101	365	153	2,098	16	7
Citizen Band Potawatomi	-	3	-	33	14	27	150	-	-
Forest County	-	-	-	-	-	-	-	-	-
Hannahville	-	-	-	-	-	-	-	-	-
Huron Potawatomi	-	-	-	-	-	-	-	-	-
Popagon Potawatomi	-	-	-	-	-	-	-	-	-
Potawatomi	28	152	62	68	351	124	1,921	16	7
Prairie Band	-	10	-	-	-	2	27	-	-
Wisconsin Potawatomi	-	-	-	-	-	-	-	-	-

[Continued]

★ 142 ★

Population by Tribe, Region, and State, 1990: Modoc-Pueblo - Part V

[Continued]

Tribe	Mountain Region (cont.)				Pacific Region				
	New Mexico	Arizona	Utah	Nevada	Washington	Oregon	California	Alaska	Hawaii
Powhatan	-	24	2	-	12	-	63	-	-
Pueblo	34,458	10,446	394	321	248	144	3,950	184	71
Acoma	3,386	84	-	12	16	-	243	13	-
Arizona Tewa	3	385	4	-	-	-	6	-	-
Cochiti	1,067	27	-	-	9	10	9	-	-
Hopi	505	8,837	176	93	71	31	1,007	25	-
Isleta	2,873	22	-	34	14	2	175	-	-
Jemez	1,985	26	-	-	8	6	78	4	-
Keres	17	19	-	-	-	-	-	-	-
Laguna	4,741	414	42	75	27	12	521	11	46
Nambe	288	-	-	-	-	-	-	-	-
Picuris	166	12	-	-	-	-	31	-	-
Piro	-	-	-	-	-	-	15	-	-
Pojoaque	33	-	-	-	-	-	-	-	-
Pueblo	776	85	19	39	51	32	802	83	-
Sandia	266	-	19	-	-	-	6	-	-
San Felipe	2,126	11	-	-	-	-	24	8	-
San Ildefonso	396	-	-	-	-	-	7	-	-
San Juan	1,006	9	7	6	-	-	26	-	-
Santa Ana	536	6	-	-	-	-	18	-	-
Santa Clara	1,081	16	5	-	-	-	11	25	-
Santa Domingo	2,516	26	-	-	6	-	37	-	-
Taos	1,485	37	14	26	2	-	107	-	-
Tesuque	213	4	-	-	-	-	-	-	-
Tewa	764	169	42	19	7	44	316	15	11
Tigua	42	38	-	-	31	-	268	-	5
Zia	723	-	-	-	-	-	9	-	-
Zuni	7,464	219	66	17	6	7	234	-	9

Source: U.S. Bureau of the Census. *1990 Census of Population: Characteristics of American Indians by Tribe and Language.* CP3-7. Washington, DC: The Bureau, 1994, p. 24.
Note: A dash (-) represents zero or a percent that rounds to zero.

★ 143 ★

Population

Population by Tribe, Region, and State, 1990: Puget Sound Salish-Sioux - Part I

Data are based on a sample and are subject to sampling variability.

Tribe	New England						Middle Atlantic		
	Maine	New Hampshire	Vermont	Massachusetts	Rhode Island	Connecticut	New York	New Jersey	Pennsylvania
Puget Sound Salish	-	-	-	22	-	-	8	7	38
Duwamish	-	-	-	-	-	-	-	7	-
Muckleshoot	-	-	-	-	-	-	8	-	-
Nisqually	-	-	-	-	-	-	-	-	-
Nooksack	-	-	-	-	-	-	-	-	-
Puyallup	-	-	-	22	-	-	-	-	7

[Continued]

★ 143 ★

Population by Tribe, Region, and State, 1990: Puget Sound Salish-Sioux - Part I
[Continued]

Tribe	New England						Middle Atlantic		
	Maine	New Hampshire	Vermont	Massachusetts	Rhode Island	Connecticut	New York	New Jersey	Pennsylvania
Samish	-	-	-	-	-	-	-	-	9
Sauk-Suiattle	-	-	-	-	-	-	-	-	-
Skokomish	-	-	-	-	-	-	-	-	-
Snohomish	-	-	-	-	-	-	-	-	-
Snoqualmie	-	-	-	-	-	-	-	-	-
Squaxin Island	-	-	-	-	-	-	-	-	-
Steilacoom	-	-	-	-	-	-	-	-	-
Stillaguamish	-	-	-	-	-	-	-	-	-
Suquamish	-	-	-	-	-	-	-	-	5
Swinomish	-	-	-	-	-	-	-	-	-
Tulalip	-	-	-	-	-	-	-	-	-
Upper Skagit	-	-	-	-	-	-	-	-	17
Other Puget Sound Salish	-	-	-	-	-	-	-	-	-
Quapaw	-	-	-	-	-	-	9	7	-
Quinault	-	-	-	-	-	-	-	-	-
Rappahannock	-	-	-	-	-	-	8	5	6
Sac and Fox	-	-	-	-	-	-	13	16	13
Missouri Sac and Fox	-	-	-	-	-	-	-	-	-
Oklahoma Sac and Fox	-	-	-	-	-	-	-	-	-
Sac and Fox	-	-	-	-	-	-	8	16	-
Sac and Fox-Mesquakie	-	-	-	-	-	-	5	-	13
Salinan	-	-	-	-	-	-	-	-	-
Salish	-	-	-	5	-	-	32	9	-
Salish and Kootenai	-	-	-	6	-	-	7	-	-
Schaghticoke	-	7	-	14	-	116	16	-	-
Seminole	2	31	4	71	-	111	305	190	269
Florida Seminole	-	-	-	-	-	-	-	-	-
Oklahoma Seminole	-	-	-	-	-	-	12	-	-
Seminole	2	31	4	71	-	111	293	190	269
Other Seminole	-	-	-	-	-	-	-	-	-
Serrano	-	-	-	-	-	-	-	-	3
San Manual	-	-	-	-	-	-	-	-	-
Serrano	-	-	-	-	-	-	-	-	3
Shasta	-	-	-	-	-	-	7	-	6
Shawnee	-	8	-	16	-	-	54	-	176
Absentee Shawnee	-	-	-	-	-	-	-	-	-
Eastern Shawnee	-	-	-	-	-	-	-	-	16
Shawnee	-	8	-	16	-	-	54	-	160
Shinnecock	-	-	-	-	30	85	1,284	9	7
Shoshone	-	8	12	13	13	13	62	20	53
Battle Mountain	-	-	-	-	-	-	-	-	-
Ely	-	-	-	-	-	-	-	-	-
Goshute	-	-	3	-	-	-	-	-	-
Shoshone	-	8	9	13	13	13	62	15	53
Te-Moak Western Shoshone	-	-	-	-	-	-	-	5	-
Timbi-Sha Shoshone	-	-	-	-	-	-	-	-	-
Washakie	-	-	-	-	-	-	-	-	-
Yomba	-	-	-	-	-	-	-	-	-
Other Shoshone	-	-	-	-	-	-	-	-	-
Shoshone-Paiute	-	-	-	-	-	-	-	9	-
Duck Valley	-	-	-	-	-	-	-	-	-
Fallon	-	-	-	-	-	-	-	-	-
Shoshone-Paiute	-	-	-	-	-	-	-	9	-
Siletz	-	-	-	12	-	-	24	-	-
Sioux	77	62	31	320	80	120	868	261	647
Blackfoot Sioux	-	-	-	-	-	-	27	-	33
Brule Sioux	-	4	-	-	-	-	-	-	-
Cheyenne River Sioux	2	-	-	-	-	10	15	4	5
Crow Creek Sioux	-	-	-	-	-	-	21	-	7
Dakota Sioux	-	5	-	-	26	5	-	-	24
Devils Lake Sioux	-	-	-	-	-	-	-	-	-
Flandreau Santee	-	-	-	-	-	-	-	-	7

[Continued]

★ 143 ★

Population by Tribe, Region, and State, 1990: Puget Sound Salish-Sioux - Part I

[Continued]

Tribe	New England						Middle Atlantic		
	Maine	New Hampshire	Vermont	Massachusetts	Rhode Island	Connecticut	New York	New Jersey	Pennsylvania
Fort Peck	-	-	-	-	-	-	-	-	-
Lake Traverse Sioux	-	-	-	-	-	-	-	-	-
Lower Brule Sioux	-	-	-	-	-	-	-	-	-
Lower Sioux	-	-	-	-	-	-	-	-	-
Mdewakanton Sioux	-	-	-	-	-	-	-	-	-
Oglala Sioux	-	-	8	38	-	-	61	15	41
Pine Ridge Sioux	-	-	-	-	-	-	-	-	-
Prior Lake	-	-	-	8	-	-	-	-	-
Rosebud Sioux	-	9	6	-	6	-	72	-	13
Santee Sioux	-	2	-	-	-	-	-	-	-
Sioux	74	42	15	274	48	100	594	227	496
Sisseton Sioux	-	-	-	-	-	-	10	-	-
Sisseton-Wahpeton Sioux	1	-	-	-	-	-	1	-	-
Standing Rock Sioux	-	-	-	-	-	-	12	-	-
Teton Sioux	-	-	-	-	-	5	19	15	21
Wahpeton Sioux	-	-	2	-	-	-	6	-	-
Yankton Sioux	-	-	-	-	-	-	26	-	-
Other Sioux	-	-	-	-	-	-	4	-	-

Source: U.S. Bureau of the Census. *1990 Census of Population: Characteristics of American Indians by Tribe and Language.* CP3-7. Washington, DC: The Bureau, 1994, p. 26. *Note:* A dash (-) represents zero or a percent that rounds to zero.

★ 144 ★

Population

Population by Tribe, Region, and State, 1990: Puget Sound Salish-Sioux - Part II

Data are based on a sample and are subject to sampling variability.

Tribe	East North Central Region					West North Central Region						
	Ohio	Indiana	Illinois	Michigan	Wisconsin	Minnesota	Iowa	Missouri	North Dakota	South Dakota	Nebraska	Kansas
Puget Sound Salish	-	16	-	29	8	15	6	37	-	32	18	16
Duwamish	-	-	-	20	-	-	-	-	-	-	-	-
Muckleshoot	-	-	-	-	-	-	-	6	-	32	-	-
Nisqually	-	-	-	-	-	7	-	-	-	-	-	-
Nooksack	-	-	-	-	-	-	-	-	-	-	-	-
Puyallup	-	-	-	9	8	-	-	-	-	-	-	-
Samish	-	5	-	-	-	-	-	12	-	-	-	-
Sauk-Suiattle	-	-	-	-	-	-	-	-	-	-	6	-
Skokomish	-	-	-	-	-	-	-	4	-	-	-	-
Snohomish	-	-	-	-	-	-	-	-	-	-	-	16
Snoqualmie	-	-	-	-	-	-	-	-	-	-	-	-
Squaxin Island	-	-	-	-	-	-	-	-	-	-	-	-
Steilacoom	-	-	-	-	-	-	-	-	-	-	-	-
Stillaguamish	-	-	-	-	-	-	-	-	-	-	-	-
Suquamish	-	11	-	-	-	-	-	-	-	-	-	-
Swinomish	-	-	-	-	-	-	-	-	-	-	-	-
Tulalip	-	-	-	-	-	8	6	15	-	-	-	-
Upper Skagit	-	-	-	-	-	-	-	-	-	-	12	-
Other Puget Sound Salish	-	-	-	-	-	-	-	-	-	-	-	-
Quapaw	-	6	37	7	7	-	-	141	-	-	-	230
Quinault	-	-	-	15	37	2	3	6	-	-	-	-
Rappahannock	-	-	-	-	-	-	-	-	-	-	-	-
Sac and Fox	7	41	62	45	57	14	1,120	138	7	3	51	250

[Continued]

★ 144 ★

Population by Tribe, Region, and State, 1990: Puget Sound Salish-Sioux - Part II

[Continued]

Tribe	East North Central Region					West North Central Region						
	Ohio	Indiana	Illinois	Michigan	Wisconsin	Minnesota	Iowa	Missouri	North Dakota	South Dakota	Nebraska	Kansas
Missouri Sac and Fox	-	-	-	-	-	-	-	-	-	-	5	24
Oklahoma Sac and Fox	-	-	-	-	-	6	-	10	-	-	-	17
Sac and Fox	7	7	29	45	48	2	329	67	2	3	44	180
Sac and Fox-Mesquakie	-	34	33	-	9	6	791	61	5	-	2	29
Salinan	-	-	-	-	4	-	-	-	-	-	-	-
Salish	-	9	-	3	11	-	20	6	10	-	-	2
Salish and Kootenai	-	-	-	-	-	-	-	-	-	19	-	-
Schaghticoke	-	5	-	-	-	-	-	2	-	-	-	-
Seminole	195	57	143	127	10	66	24	149	18	36	24	246
Florida Seminole	7	4	-	-	-	-	-	-	-	-	-	-
Oklahoma Seminole	-	-	-	-	-	-	-	-	-	-	-	-
Seminole	188	53	143	127	10	66	24	149	18	36	24	246
Other Seminole	-	-	-	-	-	-	-	-	-	-	-	-
Serrano	-	-	-	-	-	-	-	-	-	-	-	-
San Manual	-	-	-	-	-	-	-	-	-	-	-	-
Serrano	-	-	-	-	-	-	-	-	-	-	-	-
Shasta	-	-	-	-	-	-	-	13	-	3	-	-
Shawnee	410	300	33	74	17	-	8	126	2	13	15	208
Absentee Shawnee	-	-	-	-	-	-	-	-	-	-	-	24
Eastern Shawnee	-	9	-	9	-	-	-	63	-	-	7	41
Shawnee	410	291	33	65	17	-	8	63	2	13	8	143
Shinnecock	-	-	-	6	-	-	-	-	-	-	-	-
Shoshone	61	16	35	74	21	17	2	53	20	25	10	41
Battle Mountain	-	-	-	-	-	-	-	-	-	-	-	-
Ely	-	-	-	-	-	-	-	15	-	-	-	-
Goshute	11	-	-	-	-	-	-	-	-	-	-	-
Shoshone	50	16	35	74	21	17	2	38	20	25	10	41
Te-Moak Western Shoshone	-	-	-	-	-	-	-	-	-	-	-	-
Timbi-Sha Shoshone	-	-	-	-	-	-	-	-	-	-	-	-
Washakie	-	-	-	-	-	-	-	-	-	-	-	-
Yomba	-	-	-	-	-	-	-	-	-	-	-	-
Other Shoshone	-	-	-	-	-	-	-	-	-	-	-	-
Shoshone-Paiute	-	-	8	16	-	-	6	-	6	5	2	-
Duck Valley	-	-	-	16	-	-	-	-	-	-	-	-
Fallon	-	-	-	-	-	-	-	-	-	-	-	-
Shoshone-Paiute	-	-	8	-	-	-	6	-	6	5	2	-
Siletz	-	-	-	-	-	-	-	-	-	-	-	4
Sioux	710	663	1,059	1,096	732	6,122	1,432	859	6,856	45,127	3,952	848
Blackfoot Sioux	21	81	6	-	31	22	6	3	-	-	-	-
Brule Sioux	-	-	9	-	-	-	-	8	-	25	-	-
Cheyenne River Sioux	22	-	22	8	19	89	3	6	249	6,198	73	36
Crow Creek Sioux	7	-	-	6	8	57	-	15	12	1,736	43	-
Dakota Sioux	-	-	16	-	3	205	6	5	7	46	5	-
Devils Lake Sioux	-	-	-	-	-	139	-	-	1,987	13	11	-
Flandreau Santee	-	-	-	-	7	28	-	-	8	100	-	7
Fort Peck	-	-	-	-	-	88	-	-	107	54	-	12
Lake Traverse Sioux	-	-	-	41	11	-	-	-	-	-	-	-
Lower Brule Sioux	-	-	-	10	-	2	-	2	7	1,215	2	-
Lower Sioux	-	-	-	-	-	81	-	-	-	-	-	-
Mdewakanton Sioux	-	-	-	12	9	248	2	-	-	8	-	-
Oglala Sioux	52	45	81	35	37	238	55	66	105	12,218	957	56
Pine Ridge Sioux	-	3	6	-	-	27	-	-	14	577	39	5
Prior Lake	5	-	-	-	-	46	-	-	-	-	-	-
Rosebud Sioux	8	6	16	26	9	76	73	27	70	9,085	428	50

[Continued]

★ 144 ★

Population by Tribe, Region, and State, 1990: Puget Sound Salish-Sioux - Part II
[Continued]

Tribe	East North Central Region					West North Central Region						
	Ohio	Indiana	Illinois	Michigan	Wisconsin	Minnesota	Iowa	Missouri	North Dakota	South Dakota	Nebraska	Kansas
Santee Sioux	3	38	27	30	-	198	527	37	7	404	533	23
Sioux	553	451	786	900	484	3,394	577	646	1,772	5,047	1,685	584
Sisseton Sioux	-	-	-	-	3	181	-	-	27	455	11	14
Sisseton-Wahpeton Sioux	-	12	23	-	8	405	8	2	94	2,588	8	-
Standing Rock Sioux	-	-	-	13	23	321	-	2	2,369	2,704	16	11
Teton Sioux	32	6	35	5	49	143	5	35	4	102	22	10
Wahpeton Sioux	-	-	5	2	-	13	-	-	-	6	-	-
Yankton Sioux	7	19	27	8	31	81	170	3	17	2,539	119	40
Other Sioux	-	2	-	-	-	40	-	2	-	7	-	-

Source: U.S. Bureau of the Census. *1990 Census of Population: Characteristics of American Indians by Tribe and Language.* CP3-7. Washington, DC: The Bureau, 1994, p. 27.
Note: A dash (-) represents zero or a percent that rounds to zero.

★ 145 ★
Population

Population by Tribe, Region, and State, 1990: Puget Sound Salish-Sioux - Part III

Data are based on a sample and are subject to sampling variability.

Tribe	South Atlantic Region								
	Delaware	Maryland	District of Columbia	Virginia	West Virginia	North Carolina	South Carolina	Georgia	Florida
Puget Sound Salish	-	17	-	142	6	18	-	13	33
Duwamish	-	-	-	-	-	-	-	-	-
Muckleshoot	-	-	-	-	-	-	-	-	-
Nisqually	-	-	-	-	-	-	-	-	10
Nooksack	-	-	-	-	-	-	-	-	-
Puyallup	-	-	-	20	-	-	-	-	7
Samish	-	-	-	20	-	-	-	-	-
Sauk-Suiattle	-	-	-	-	-	-	-	-	-
Skokomish	-	-	-	8	-	-	-	-	-
Snohomish	-	-	-	-	-	-	-	7	-
Snoqualmie	-	-	-	-	-	-	-	-	-
Squaxin Island	-	-	-	-	-	18	-	-	-
Steilacoom	-	-	-	-	-	-	-	6	-
Stillaguamish	-	-	-	-	-	-	-	-	-
Suquamish	-	11	-	18	-	-	-	-	-
Swinomish	-	6	-	-	-	-	-	-	5
Tulalip	-	-	-	76	-	-	-	-	-
Upper Skagit	-	-	-	-	6	-	-	-	-
Other Puget Sound Salish	-	-	-	-	-	-	-	-	11
Quapaw	-	-	9	8	-	-	7	-	19
Quinault	-	-	-	4	-	40	-	-	9
Rappahannock	-	11	-	290	-	-	-	-	-
Sac and Fox	-	7	-	5	-	-	-	23	71
Missouri Sac and Fox	-	-	-	-	-	-	-	-	-
Oklahoma Sac and Fox	-	-	-	-	-	-	-	-	-
Sac and Fox	-	-	-	5	-	-	-	6	25
Sac and Fox-Mesquakie	-	7	-	-	-	-	-	17	46
Salinan	-	-	-	5	-	-	-	-	-
Salish	-	9	-	39	8	-	-	7	27

[Continued]

★145★

Population by Tribe, Region, and State, 1990: Puget Sound Salish-Sioux - Part III
[Continued]

Tribe	South Atlantic Region								
	Delaware	Maryland	District of Columbia	Virginia	West Virginia	North Carolina	South Carolina	Georgia	Florida
Salish and Kootenai	-	-	-	18	-	-	-	-	4
Schaghticoke	-	-	-	10	-	-	-	-	10
Seminole	9	75	25	172	6	117	70	213	2,680
Florida Seminole	-	-	-	-	-	-	-	-	405
Oklahoma Seminole	-	9	-	-	-	-	-	-	17
Seminole	9	66	25	172	6	117	70	213	2,258
Other Seminole	-	-	-	-	-	-	-	-	-
Serrano	-	-	-	-	-	-	-	-	-
San Manual	-	-	-	-	-	-	-	-	-
Serrano	-	-	-	-	-	-	-	-	-
Shasta	-	6	-	-	-	-	11	-	-
Shawnee	19	20	-	33	23	146	25	-	231
Absentee Shawnee	-	-	-	-	4	16	-	-	9
Eastern Shawnee	-	-	-	-	-	-	-	-	5
Shawnee	19	20	-	33	19	130	25	-	217
Shinnecock	-	43	7	44	-	18	-	-	68
Shoshone	-	38	-	20	4	3	7	7	142
Battle Mountain	-	-	-	-	-	-	-	-	-
Ely	-	-	-	-	-	-	-	-	-
Goshute	-	-	-	-	-	-	-	-	-
Shoshone	-	38	-	20	4	3	7	7	140
Te-Moak Western Shoshone	-	-	-	-	-	-	-	-	2
Timbi-Sha Shoshone	-	-	-	-	-	-	-	-	-
Washakie	-	-	-	-	-	-	-	-	-
Yomba	-	-	-	-	-	-	-	-	-
Other Shoshone	-	-	-	-	-	-	-	-	-
Shoshone-Paiute	-	-	-	-	-	-	-	-	4
Duck Valley	-	-	-	-	-	-	-	-	4
Fallon	-	-	-	-	-	-	-	-	-
Shoshone-Paiute	-	-	-	-	-	-	-	-	-
Siletz	-	-	-	-	-	-	-	12	-
Sioux	33	243	7	628	98	1,088	147	265	1,156
Blackfoot Sioux	-	6	-	7	-	-	13	-	-
Brule Sioux	-	-	-	-	-	-	-	-	-
Cheyenne River Sioux	-	-	-	13	43	-	6	-	16
Crow Creek Sioux	-	-	-	2	-	-	-	-	-
Dakota Sioux	-	14	-	-	-	-	2	-	24
Devils Lake Sioux	-	-	-	8	-	-	-	13	-
Flandreau Santee	-	-	-	-	-	-	-	-	-
Fort Peck	-	-	-	-	-	-	-	-	-
Lake Traverse Sioux	-	-	-	-	-	-	-	-	-
Lower Brule Sioux	-	-	-	8	-	-	-	7	-
Lower Sioux	-	-	-	-	-	-	-	-	-
Mdewakanton Sioux	-	-	-	-	-	-	-	-	-
Oglala Sioux	-	17	-	133	13	39	7	30	98
Pine Ridge Sioux	-	-	-	9	-	-	-	-	-
Prior Lake	-	-	-	-	-	-	-	-	-
Rosebud Sioux	-	-	-	8	-	12	-	19	7
Santee Sioux	-	-	-	-	-	3	12	9	16
Sioux	33	168	7	391	31	948	105	180	877
Sisseton Sioux	-	-	-	9	-	-	-	-	-
Sisseton-Wahpeton Sioux	-	22	-	-	-	11	2	-	38
Standing Rock Sioux	-	7	-	32	-	26	-	-	-

[Continued]

★ 145 ★

Population by Tribe, Region, and State, 1990: Puget Sound Salish-Sioux - Part III
[Continued]

Tribe	South Atlantic Region								
	Delaware	Maryland	District of Columbia	Virginia	West Virginia	North Carolina	South Carolina	Georgia	Florida
Teton Sioux	-	9	-	-	9	49	-	7	80
Wahpeton Sioux	-	-	-	-	-	-	-	-	-
Yankton Sioux	-	-	-	8	2	-	-	-	-
Other Sioux	-	-	-	-	-	-	-	-	-

Source: U.S. Bureau of the Census. *1990 Census of Population: Characteristics of American Indians by Tribe and Language.* CP3-7. Washington, DC: The Bureau, 1994, p. 28. *Note:* A dash (-) represents zero or a percent that rounds to zero.

★ 146 ★

Population

Population by Tribe, Region, and State, 1990: Puget Sound Salish-Sioux - Part IV

Data are based on a sample and are subject to sampling variability.

Tribe	East South Central Region				West South Central Region				Mountain Region			
	Kentucky	Tennessee	Alabama	Mississippi	Arkansas	Louisiana	Oklahoma	Texas	Montana	Idaho	Wyoming	Colorado
Puget Sound Salish	-	-	12	-	-	5	13	35	25	11	-	20
Duwamish	-	-	-	-	-	-	-	-	2	-	-	-
Muckleshoot	-	-	-	-	-	-	-	-	-	-	-	-
Nisqually	-	-	-	-	-	-	-	-	-	3	-	-
Nooksack	-	-	-	-	-	-	-	17	-	-	-	18
Puyallup	-	-	12	-	-	3	-	-	-	6	-	-
Samish	-	-	-	-	-	-	-	-	6	-	-	-
Sauk-Suiattle	-	-	-	-	-	-	-	-	2	-	-	-
Skokomish	-	-	-	-	-	-	13	-	-	-	-	-
Snohomish	-	-	-	-	-	-	-	2	-	-	-	-
Snoqualmie	-	-	-	-	-	2	-	-	6	-	-	-
Squaxin Island	-	-	-	-	-	-	-	-	-	-	-	-
Steilacoom	-	-	-	-	-	-	-	-	-	-	-	-
Stillaguamish	-	-	-	-	-	-	-	-	-	-	-	-
Suquamish	-	-	-	-	-	-	-	2	-	-	-	-
Swinomish	-	-	-	-	-	-	-	-	-	2	-	2
Tulalip	-	-	-	-	-	-	-	4	9	-	-	-
Upper Skagit	-	-	-	-	-	-	-	10	-	-	-	-
Other Puget Sound Salish	-	-	-	-	-	-	-	-	-	-	-	-
Quapaw	-	-	19	-	49	12	523	76	7	-	-	18
Quinault	-	-	-	-	-	-	2	5	29	13	2	25
Rappahannock	-	-	-	-	-	-	13	-	-	-	-	-
Sac and Fox	-	-	-	-	33	18	1,784	137	20	-	14	70
Missouri Sac and Fox	-	-	-	-	-	-	-	-	-	-	-	-
Oklahoma Sac and Fox	-	-	-	-	10	-	139	2	-	-	-	1
Sac and Fox	-	-	-	-	23	7	1,615	135	20	-	14	37
Sac and Fox-Mesquakie	-	-	-	-	-	11	30	-	-	-	-	32
Salinan	-	-	-	-	-	-	-	-	-	-	-	-
Salish	-	-	-	-	18	19	49	58	2,658	97	-	50
Salish and Kootenai	-	-	-	-	-	-	16	-	1,693	32	13	12
Schaghticoke	-	-	-	-	-	-	-	-	-	-	-	-
Seminole	53	72	73	2	71	91	6,432	605	46	102	22	105
Florida Seminole	-	26	-	-	-	-	11	-	-	-	-	-
Oklahoma Seminole	-	-	-	-	-	-	397	-	-	-	-	-
Seminole	53	46	73	2	71	91	6,024	605	46	102	22	105
Other Seminole	-	-	-	-	-	-	-	-	-	-	-	-
Serrano	-	-	-	-	-	-	-	22	-	-	-	-
San Manual	-	-	-	-	-	-	-	-	-	-	-	-
Serrano	-	-	-	-	-	-	-	22	-	-	-	-
Shasta	-	-	-	-	22	-	-	6	-	3	-	9
Shawnee	40	99	3	44	125	48	2,442	359	7	2	16	42

[Continued]

★ 146 ★

Population by Tribe, Region, and State, 1990: Puget Sound Salish-Sioux - Part IV

[Continued]

Tribe	East South Central Region				West South Central Region				Mountain Region			
	Kentucky	Tennessee	Alabama	Mississippi	Arkansas	Louisiana	Oklahoma	Texas	Montana	Idaho	Wyoming	Colorado
Absentee Shawnee	-	6	-	-	7	-	950	49	-	-	-	-
Eastern Shawnee	-	8	-	-	45	-	333	37	-	-	8	6
Shawnee	40	85	3	44	73	48	1,159	273	7	2	8	36
Shinnecock	-	2	-	-	-	-	-	13	-	-	-	4
Shoshone	16	8	2	6	21	25	86	216	47	676	1,752	116
Battle Mountain	-	-	-	-	-	-	-	-	-	2	-	-
Ely	-	-	-	-	-	-	-	-	-	-	-	-
Goshute	-	-	-	-	-	-	-	-	-	45	-	-
Shoshone	16	8	2	6	21	25	86	203	47	563	1,729	112
Te-Moak Western Shoshone	-	-	-	-	-	-	-	5	-	49	23	-
Timbi-Sha Shoshone	-	-	-	-	-	-	-	8	-	-	-	-
Washakie	-	-	-	-	-	-	-	-	-	17	-	-
Yomba	-	-	-	-	-	-	-	-	-	-	-	-
Other Shoshone	-	-	-	-	-	-	-	-	-	-	-	4
Shoshone-Paiute	-	-	-	-	-	-	22	-	6	277	3	32
Duck Valley	-	-	-	-	-	-	-	-	-	105	-	-
Fallon	-	-	-	-	-	-	-	-	-	-	-	-
Shoshone-Paiute	-	-	-	-	-	-	22	-	6	172	3	32
Siletz	-	-	-	-	-	-	34	-	15	44	-	-
Sioux	193	314	155	60	229	275	1,255	1,741	4,721	657	1,032	2,840
Blackfoot Sioux	4	-	-	-	2	-	5	19	33	-	-	-
Brule Sioux	-	-	-	-	-	-	-	-	-	-	-	-
Cheyenne River Sioux	-	-	-	-	-	15	67	72	53	1	42	122
Crow Creek Sioux	-	8	8	-	-	-	40	-	48	5	-	21
Dakota Sioux	6	-	1	-	-	-	-	-	-	-	-	34
Devils Lake Sioux	-	-	-	-	-	-	-	-	17	-	-	-
Flandreau Santee	-	-	-	-	-	-	-	-	-	-	-	-
Fort Peck	-	-	-	-	-	6	-	-	424	-	-	8
Lake Traverse Sioux	-	-	-	-	-	-	-	-	-	-	-	-
Lower Brule Sioux	-	-	-	-	-	7	-	31	-	-	-	5
Lower Sioux	-	-	-	-	-	-	-	-	-	-	-	-
Mdewakanton Sioux	-	-	-	-	-	-	-	-	-	-	-	-
Oglala Sioux	12	23	4	-	14	5	76	111	108	86	311	550
Pine Ridge Sioux	-	-	-	-	-	-	-	-	3	-	-	15
Prior Lake	-	-	-	-	-	-	-	-	-	-	-	-
Rosebud Sioux	-	32	-	10	-	54	37	16	21	49	28	196
Santee Sioux	-	9	-	-	2	-	55	43	25	9	21	38
Sioux	147	217	112	43	206	144	932	1,291	3,826	446	571	1,717
Sisseton Sioux	-	-	-	-	-	17	-	-	17	-	10	-
Sisseton-Wahpeton Sioux	-	6	30	6	-	-	25	9	22	-	11	27
Standing Rock Sioux	7	2	-	-	5	-	3	5	68	37	20	19
Teton Sioux	17	17	-	1	-	8	-	53	15	6	6	34
Wahpeton Sioux	-	-	-	-	-	-	-	-	-	-	-	-
Yankton Sioux	-	-	-	-	-	19	15	91	41	18	12	54
Other Sioux	-	-	-	-	-	-	-	-	-	-	-	-

Source: U.S. Bureau of the Census. *1990 Census of Population: Characteristics of American Indians by Tribe and Language.* CP3-7. Washington, DC: The Bureau, 1994, p. 29.
Note: A dash (-) represents zero or a percent that rounds to zero.

★ 147 ★
Population

Population by Tribe, Region, and State, 1990: Puget Sound Salish-Sioux - Part V

Data are based on a sample and are subject to sampling variability.

Tribe	Mountain Region (cont.)				Pacific Region				
	New Mexico	Arizona	Utah	Nevada	Washington	Oregon	California	Alaska	Hawaii
Puget Sound Salish	55	22	15	56	8,865	254	403	100	12
Duwamish	-	-	-	-	141	17	28	-	-
Muckleshoot	-	-	-	-	969	3	9	4	-
Nisqually	-	-	-	-	379	15	11	11	-
Nooksack	-	10	15	-	766	26	12	26	-
Puyallup	-	-	-	11	865	35	-	8	-
Samish	-	-	-	-	134	12	27	-	-
Sauk-Suiattle	-	-	-	-	135	-	4	-	-
Skokomish	-	6	-	-	671	16	17	2	-
Snohomish	-	6	-	26	338	31	34	27	12
Snoqualmie	-	-	-	8	407	10	3	8	-
Squaxin Island	-	-	-	-	409	22	40	-	-
Steilacoom	-	-	-	-	133	4	7	-	-
Stillaguamish	-	-	-	-	127	-	13	-	-
Suquamish	-	-	-	-	548	16	19	5	-
Swinomish	46	-	-	-	622	2	31	-	-
Tulalip	9	-	-	-	1,899	10	131	3	-
Upper Skagit	-	-	-	11	309	35	17	6	-
Other Puget Sound Salish	-	-	-	-	13	-	-	-	-
Quapaw	5	16	-	17	46	5	114	27	17
Quinault	-	17	-	-	2,138	112	33	21	-
Rappahannock	-	-	-	-	-	-	10	-	-
Sac and Fox	133	14	4	44	130	69	361	-	-
Missouri Sac and Fox	59	-	-	-	-	-	-	-	-
Oklahoma Sac and Fox	-	-	-	-	-	54	-	-	-
Sac and Fox	74	14	-	25	111	15	255	-	-
Sac and Fox-Mesquakie	-	-	4	19	19	-	106	-	-
Salinan	-	-	-	-	7	22	241	-	-
Salish	5	45	80	54	785	328	334	48	5
Salish and Kootenai	32	9	28	13	209	65	110	7	-
Schaghticoke	-	-	-	-	-	-	-	2	-
Seminole	76	141	16	93	376	111	1,475	104	53
Florida Seminole	-	10	-	-	-	-	55	-	-
Oklahoma Seminole	-	15	-	-	-	-	-	-	-
Seminole	76	116	16	93	376	111	1,420	104	53
Other Seminole	-	-	-	-	-	-	-	-	-
Serrano	-	-	-	-	-	28	242	-	-
San Manual	-	-	-	-	-	-	12	-	-
Serrano	-	-	-	-	-	28	230	-	-
Shasta	-	-	-	37	60	172	339	-	9
Shawnee	84	80	13	29	244	175	804	4	23
Absentee Shawnee	22	30	-	-	-	-	12	-	-
Eastern Shawnee	15	-	-	-	35	117	8	-	-
Shawnee	47	50	13	29	209	58	784	4	23
Shinnecock	-	-	-	-	-	-	50	-	-
Shoshone	157	165	427	2,637	359	292	1,595	64	49
Battle Mountain	-	-	-	80	-	-	-	-	-

[Continued]

246

★ 147 ★

Population by Tribe, Region, and State, 1990: Puget Sound Salish-Sioux - Part V
[Continued]

Tribe	Mountain Region (cont.)				Pacific Region				
	New Mexico	Arizona	Utah	Nevada	Washington	Oregon	California	Alaska	Hawaii
Ely	-	19	-	119	-	-	-	-	-
Goshute	-	-	100	47	-	3	-	-	-
Shoshone	131	141	305	1,602	351	251	1,459	64	49
Te-Moak Western Shoshone	-	5	-	702	-	38	103	-	-
Timbi-Sha Shoshone	-	-	-	12	-	-	27	-	-
Washakie	23	-	18	-	8	-	-	-	-
Yomba	-	-	-	38	-	-	6	-	-
Other Shoshone	3	-	4	37	-	-	-	-	-
Shoshone-Paiute	8	23	25	1,381	32	45	380	10	20
Duck Valley	8	8	-	259	-	19	-	-	-
Fallon	-	-	-	112	-	-	9	-	-
Shoshone-Paiute	-	15	25	1,010	32	26	371	10	20
Siletz	-	-	11	-	150	1,333	80	7	-
Sioux	886	1,754	820	662	3,206	2,038	8,217	442	237
Blackfoot Sioux	8	10	-	-	56	-	162	-	26
Brule Sioux	-	-	-	-	-	-	7	-	-
Cheyenne River Sioux	22	47	46	6	70	74	110	16	-
Crow Creek Sioux	-	52	21	-	61	21	68	2	4
Dakota Sioux	-	6	16	18	6	3	55	-	-
Devils Lake Sioux	8	10	-	-	6	15	-	-	-
Flandreau Santee	25	-	-	-	-	-	9	-	-
Fort Peck	-	-	40	-	70	8	30	-	-
Lake Traverse Sioux	-	-	-	-	-	-	-	-	-
Lower Brule Sioux	-	8	-	8	37	20	5	-	-
Lower Sioux	-	-	-	-	-	-	-	-	-
Mdewakanton Sioux	-	-	-	-	7	8	-	-	-
Oglala Sioux	73	233	20	23	256	128	566	42	6
Pine Ridge Sioux	7	9	-	-	20	3	14	-	-
Prior Lake	-	-	-	-	-	-	-	-	-
Rosebud Sioux	29	95	50	12	107	85	281	12	6
Santee Sioux	-	9	-	34	47	29	74	20	-
Sioux	620	1,087	582	508	2,113	1,496	6,330	314	163
Sisseton Sioux	2	6	-	-	68	-	45	9	-
Sisseton-Wahpeton Sioux	-	-	6	-	55	40	31	-	-
Standing Rock Sioux	24	117	-	7	93	14	79	9	26
Teton Sioux	54	19	6	14	48	48	243	-	-
Wahpeton Sioux	-	-	-	-	-	-	17	-	-
Yankton Sioux	14	46	33	32	86	46	81	18	6
Other Sioux	-	-	-	-	-	-	10	-	-

Source: U.S. Bureau of the Census. *1990 Census of Population: Characteristics of American Indians by Tribe and Language.* CP3-7. Washington, DC: The Bureau, 1994, p. 30. *Note:* A dash (-) represents zero or a percent that rounds to zero.

★ 148 ★
Population

Population by Tribe, Region, and State, 1990: Siuslaw-Yurok and Other Specified Tribes - Part I

Data are based on a sample and are subject to sampling variability.

Tribe	New England						Middle Atlantic		
	Maine	New Hampshire	Vermont	Massachusetts	Rhode Island	Connecticut	New York	New Jersey	Pennsylvania
Siuslaw	-	-	-	-	-	-	-	-	-
Spokane	-	-	-	-	-	-	5	-	-
Stockbridge	6	-	11	17	-	71	36	32	-
Tlingit	-	11	2	33	-	10	56	18	13
Tohono O'Odham	6	7	-	-	-	19	27	-	3
Ak-Chin	-	-	-	-	-	-	-	-	-
Tohono O'Odham	6	7	-	-	-	19	27	-	3
Other Tohono O'Odham	-	-	-	-	-	-	-	-	-
Tolowa	-	-	-	-	-	-	-	-	-
Tonkawa	-	-	-	-	-	-	-	-	-
Tsimshian	-	-	-	-	-	-	-	-	-
Umatilla	-	-	-	-	-	-	15	-	-
Umpqua	-	-	-	7	-	-	-	-	-
Cow Creek Umpqua	-	-	-	-	-	-	-	-	-
Umpqua	-	-	-	7	-	-	-	-	-
Ute	4	12	-	9	-	-	16	24	6
Allen Canyon	-	-	-	-	-	-	-	-	-
Uintah Ute	-	-	-	-	-	-	-	8	-
Ute	4	12	-	9	-	-	16	16	4
Ute Mountain Ute	-	-	-	-	-	-	-	-	2
Wailaki	-	-	-	-	-	-	-	-	-
Walla-Walla	-	-	-	-	-	-	-	-	-
Wampanoag	8	62	18	1,555	92	19	97	24	37
Gay Head Wampanoag	-	-	-	84	-	-	13	-	-
Mashpee Wampanoag	2	-	-	18	11	-	5	-	17
Wampanoag	6	62	18	1,453	81	19	79	24	20
Warm Springs	-	-	-	-	-	-	-	-	-
Washo	-	-	-	-	-	-	-	-	-
Washo	-	-	-	-	-	-	-	-	-
Other Washo	-	-	-	-	-	-	-	-	-
Wichita	-	-	-	-	-	17	5	-	-
Winnebago	-	6	-	-	-	-	21	5	16
Nebraska Winnebago	-	-	-	-	-	-	-	-	-
Winnebago	-	6	-	-	-	-	21	5	13
Wisconsin Winnebago	-	-	-	-	-	-	-	-	3
Wintu	-	-	-	-	-	-	-	-	-
Wiyot	-	-	-	-	-	-	-	-	-
Yakima	16	-	-	-	-	-	2	-	5
Yaqui	-	-	-	3	-	-	19	-	2
Barrio Libre	-	-	-	-	-	-	-	-	-
Pascua Yaqui	-	-	-	-	-	-	-	-	-
Yaqui	-	-	-	3	-	-	19	-	2
Yavapai Apache	-	-	-	-	-	-	-	-	-
Yokuts	-	-	-	-	-	11	15	7	-
Chukchansi	-	-	-	-	-	11	-	-	-
Tachi	-	-	-	-	-	-	-	-	-
Tule River	-	-	-	-	-	-	15	-	-
Yokuts	-	-	-	-	-	-	-	7	-
Yuchi	-	-	-	-	-	-	-	6	-
Yuman	-	-	-	-	-	-	9	-	1
Cocopah	-	-	-	-	-	-	-	-	-
Havasupai	-	-	-	-	-	-	-	-	-
Hualapai	-	-	-	-	-	-	-	-	1
Maricopa	-	-	-	-	-	-	-	-	-
Mohave	-	-	-	-	-	-	-	-	-
Quechan	-	-	-	-	-	-	9	-	-
Yavapai	-	-	-	-	-	-	-	-	-
Yurok	-	-	-	-	-	7	-	-	22
Other specified tribes	-	-	-	-	-	-	12	-	2
Burt Lake Band	-	-	-	-	-	-	-	-	-
Fort Belknap	-	-	-	-	-	-	-	-	-

[Continued]

Population by Tribe, Region, and State, 1990: Siuslaw-Yurok and Other Specified Tribes - Part I

[Continued]

Tribe	New England						Middle Atlantic		
	Maine	New Hampshire	Vermont	Massachusetts	Rhode Island	Connecticut	New York	New Jersey	Pennsylvania
Fort McDermitt	-	-	-	-	-	-	-	-	-
Fort McDowell	-	-	-	-	-	-	-	-	-
Los Coyotes	-	-	-	-	-	-	-	-	-
Mexican Indian Cherokee	-	-	-	-	-	-	12	-	-
Reno-Sparks	-	-	-	-	-	-	-	-	-
Round Valley	-	-	-	-	-	-	-	-	-
Shoalwater	-	-	-	-	-	-	-	-	-
Wascopum	-	-	-	-	-	-	-	-	-
Wind River	-	-	-	-	-	-	-	-	2
All other specified	-	-	-	-	-	-	-	-	-
Tribe not specified	55	24	47	234	72	167	2,169	833	299
Tribe not reported	723	399	376	2,755	788	1,357	16,861	3,945	3,565

Source: U.S. Bureau of the Census. *1990 Census of Population: Characteristics of American Indians by Tribe and Language.* CP3-7. Washington, DC: The Bureau, 1994, p. 32. *Note:* A dash (-) represents zero or a percent that rounds to zero.

Population by Tribe, Region, and State, 1990: Siuslaw-Yurok and Other Specified Tribes - Part II

Data are based on a sample and are subject to sampling variability.

Tribe	East North Central Region					West North Central Region						
	Ohio	Indiana	Illinois	Michigan	Wisconsin	Minnesota	Iowa	Missouri	North Dakota	South Dakota	Nebraska	Kansas
Siuslaw	-	-	-	-	-	-	-	-	-	-	-	-
Spokane	-	-	-	-	13	-	-	-	-	-	-	-
Stockbridge	67	34	53	12	1,286	53	-	16	-	-	34	-
Tlingit	16	17	20	40	15	7	-	79	2	16	25	32
Tohono O'Odham	26	18	59	44	2	18	-	8	-	-	-	17
Ak-Chin	-	-	-	-	-	-	-	-	-	-	-	-
Tohono O'Odham	26	18	59	44	2	18	-	8	-	-	-	17
Other Tohono O'Odham	-	-	-	-	-	-	-	-	-	-	-	-
Tolowa	-	5	-	-	-	-	-	-	-	-	-	-
Tonkawa	-	-	-	-	-	-	-	-	-	-	-	18
Tsimshian	-	-	8	-	9	-	-	-	-	-	5	-
Umatilla	-	-	-	-	4	-	-	9	-	-	18	10
Umpqua	-	-	-	-	-	-	-	-	-	-	-	-
Cow Creek Umpqua	-	-	-	-	-	-	-	-	-	-	-	-
Umpqua	-	-	-	-	-	-	-	-	-	-	-	-
Ute	23	31	37	20	5	3	2	16	4	-	20	30
Allen Canyon	-	-	-	-	-	-	-	-	-	-	-	-
Uintah Ute	6	-	-	-	-	-	-	-	2	-	-	-
Ute	17	31	37	20	5	3	2	16	2	-	20	30
Ute Mountain Ute	-	-	-	-	-	-	-	-	-	-	-	-
Wailaki	-	-	-	-	2	-	-	8	-	-	10	-
Walla-Walla	-	-	-	-	-	-	-	-	-	-	-	-
Wampanoag	7	-	-	10	4	16	-	-	-	-	7	20
Gay Head Wampanoag	-	-	-	-	-	-	-	-	-	-	-	-
Mashpee Wampanoag	-	-	-	8	-	-	-	-	-	-	-	-
Wampanoag	7	-	-	2	4	16	-	-	-	-	7	20
Warm Springs	-	-	-	-	-	-	3	-	-	-	-	-
Washo	-	-	-	-	-	-	-	4	-	-	-	5
Washo	-	-	-	-	-	-	-	2	-	-	-	5
Other Washo	-	-	-	-	-	-	-	2	-	-	-	-

[Continued]

Population by Tribe, Region, and State, 1990: Siuslaw-Yurok and Other Specified Tribes - Part II
[Continued]

Tribe	East North Central Region					West North Central Region						
	Ohio	Indiana	Illinois	Michigan	Wisconsin	Minnesota	Iowa	Missouri	North Dakota	South Dakota	Nebraska	Kansas
Wichita	-	-	8	-	-	-	-	-	-	-	-	38
Winnebago	26	18	291	52	2,567	592	426	37	20	75	1,197	61
Nebraska Winnebago	-	-	25	-	47	22	16	-	-	-	29	-
Winnebago	26	18	261	52	1,599	389	401	36	8	70	1,157	53
Wisconsin Winnebago	-	-	5	-	921	181	9	1	12	5	11	8
Wintu	-	4	-	-	-	-	-	12	13	-	-	-
Wiyot	-	-	-	1	-	-	-	-	-	4	-	7
Yakima	-	-	-	2	-	20	-	23	-	-	-	9
Yaqui	-	-	62	7	14	28	-	7	-	11	-	-
Barrio Libre	-	-	-	-	-	-	-	-	-	-	-	-
Pascua Yaqui	-	-	-	-	-	-	-	-	-	-	-	-
Yaqui	-	-	62	7	14	28	-	7	-	11	-	-
Yavapai Apache	-	7	-	-	-	-	-	-	-	-	-	-
Yokuts	-	-	-	-	8	-	-	-	-	11	4	-
Chukchansi	-	-	-	-	-	-	-	-	-	-	-	-
Tachi	-	-	-	-	8	-	-	-	-	-	-	-
Tule River	-	-	-	-	-	-	-	-	-	11	-	-
Yokuts	-	-	-	-	-	-	-	-	-	-	4	-
Yuchi	-	-	-	-	-	-	-	-	-	-	-	36
Yuman	-	-	-	6	1	12	12	15	-	-	5	29
Cocopah	-	-	-	-	-	5	-	15	-	-	-	-
Havasupai	-	-	-	-	-	-	-	-	-	-	-	-
Hualapai	-	-	-	-	-	-	-	-	-	-	-	-
Maricopa	-	-	-	-	-	-	10	-	-	-	-	-
Mohave	-	-	-	-	-	-	2	-	-	-	-	29
Quechan	-	-	-	-	1	7	-	-	-	-	5	-
Yavapai	-	-	-	6	-	-	-	-	-	-	-	-
Yurok	10	-	-	-	-	-	-	3	-	-	6	37
Other specified tribes	-	-	5	47	-	-	-	-	12	32	-	8
Burt Lake Band	-	-	-	45	-	-	-	-	-	-	-	-
Fort Belknap	-	-	5	-	-	-	-	-	12	7	-	-
Fort McDermitt	-	-	-	-	-	-	-	-	-	-	-	-
Fort McDowell	-	-	-	-	-	-	-	-	-	-	-	-
Los Coyotes	-	-	-	-	-	-	-	-	-	-	-	-
Mexican Indian Cherokee	-	-	-	-	-	-	-	-	-	-	-	8
Reno-Sparks	-	-	-	-	-	-	-	-	-	-	-	-
Round Valley	-	-	-	-	-	-	-	-	-	-	-	-
Shoalwater	-	-	-	2	-	-	-	-	-	-	-	-
Wascopum	-	-	-	-	-	-	-	-	-	-	-	-
Wind River	-	-	-	-	-	-	-	-	-	25	-	-
All other specified	-	-	-	-	-	-	-	-	-	-	-	-
Tribe not specified	448	207	592	683	311	744	131	250	243	295	165	299
Tribe not reported	3,914	2,065	4,799	7,640	2,641	4,953	1,008	2,740	924	2,238	1,196	1,870

Source: U.S. Bureau of the Census. *1990 Census of Population: Characteristics of American Indians by Tribe and Language.* CP3-7. Washington, DC: The Bureau, 1994, p. 33.
Note: A dash (-) represents zero or a percent that rounds to zero.

★ 150 ★
Population

Population by Tribe, Region, and State, 1990: Siuslaw-Yurok and Other Specified Tribes - Part III

Data are based on a sample and are subject to sampling variability.

Tribe	South Atlantic Region								
	Delaware	Maryland	District of Columbia	Virginia	West Virginia	North Carolina	South Carolina	Georgia	Florida
Siuslaw	-	-	-	-	-	-	-	-	-
Spokane	-	-	-	17	-	-	12	-	-
Stockbridge	-	27	-	24	7	8	-	15	66
Tlingit	-	47	-	12	-	-	9	7	47
Tohono O'Odham	-	6	-	24	-	2	-	-	5
Ak-Chin	-	-	-	-	-	-	-	-	-
Tohono O'Odham	-	6	-	24	-	2	-	-	5
Other Tohono O'Odham	-	-	-	-	-	-	-	-	-
Tolowa	-	-	-	-	-	-	-	-	-
Tonkawa	-	-	-	-	-	-	-	-	-
Tsimshian	-	9	-	-	-	-	-	-	6
Umatilla	-	-	-	-	-	-	-	-	-
Umpqua	-	-	-	-	-	-	-	-	-
Cow Creek Umpqua	-	-	-	-	-	-	-	-	-
Umpqua	-	-	-	-	-	-	-	-	-
Ute	-	9	4	26	4	43	10	18	9
Allen Canyon	-	-	-	-	-	-	-	-	-
Uintah Ute	-	-	-	-	-	-	-	-	-
Ute	-	9	4	26	4	37	10	18	9
Ute Mountain Ute	-	-	-	-	-	6	-	-	-
Wailaki	-	-	-	-	-	-	-	-	-
Walla-Walla	-	6	-	-	-	-	-	-	-
Wampanoag	-	9	5	16	15	-	7	-	29
Gay Head Wampanoag	-	-	-	-	-	-	-	-	15
Mashpee Wampanoag	-	-	-	-	-	-	-	-	-
Wampanoag	-	9	5	16	15	-	7	-	14
Warm Springs	-	-	-	-	-	-	-	-	-
Washo	-	-	-	3	-	20	-	-	-
Washo	-	-	-	3	-	20	-	-	-
Other Washo	-	-	-	-	-	-	-	-	-
Wichita	-	7	-	-	-	-	-	-	7
Winnebago	-	20	-	6	-	25	-	8	49
Nebraska Winnebago	-	-	-	-	-	-	-	-	-
Winnebago	-	20	-	6	-	15	-	8	42
Wisconsin Winnebago	-	-	-	-	-	10	-	-	7
Wintu	-	-	-	-	-	5	-	-	8
Wiyot	-	-	-	7	-	-	-	-	-
Yakima	2	6	-	-	-	-	-	5	6
Yaqui	-	-	-	65	-	7	-	13	30
Barrio Libre	-	-	-	-	-	-	-	-	-
Pascua Yaqui	-	-	-	-	-	-	-	5	-
Yaqui	-	-	-	65	-	7	-	8	30
Yavapai Apache	-	-	-	-	-	-	-	-	-
Yokuts	-	-	-	-	-	9	-	-	-
Chukchansi	-	-	-	-	-	-	-	-	-
Tachi	-	-	-	-	-	9	-	-	-
Tule River	-	-	-	-	-	-	-	-	-
Yokuts	-	-	-	-	-	-	-	-	-
Yuchi	-	14	-	-	-	-	-	-	6
Yuman	-	-	-	6	-	13	-	9	-
Cocopah	-	-	-	-	-	-	-	-	-
Havasupai	-	-	-	-	-	-	-	-	-

[Continued]

★ 150 ★

Population by Tribe, Region, and State, 1990: Siuslaw-Yurok and Other Specified Tribes - Part III

[Continued]

Tribe	South Atlantic Region								
	Delaware	Maryland	District of Columbia	Virginia	West Virginia	North Carolina	South Carolina	Georgia	Florida
Hualapai	-	-	-	-	-	-	-	-	-
Maricopa	-	-	-	-	-	-	-	-	-
Mohave	-	-	-	6	-	13	-	9	-
Quechan	-	-	-	-	-	-	-	-	-
Yavapai	-	-	-	-	-	-	-	-	-
Yurok	-	-	-	8	-	2	-	-	12
Other specified tribes	-	14	-	-	-	-	-	-	-
Burt Lake Band	-	-	-	-	-	-	-	-	-
Fort Belknap	-	-	-	-	-	-	-	-	-
Fort McDermitt	-	-	-	-	-	-	-	-	-
Fort McDowell	-	-	-	-	-	-	-	-	-
Los Coyotes	-	-	-	-	-	-	-	-	-
Mexican Indian Cherokee	-	14	-	-	-	-	-	-	-
Reno-Sparks	-	-	-	-	-	-	-	-	-
Round Valley	-	-	-	-	-	-	-	-	-
Shoalwater	-	-	-	-	-	-	-	-	-
Wascopum	-	-	-	-	-	-	-	-	-
Wind River	-	-	-	-	-	-	-	-	-
All other specified	-	-	-	-	-	-	-	-	-
Tribe not specified	139	325	54	446	65	1,004	124	280	642
Tribe not reported	378	2,828	644	2,511	733	9,509	2,059	2,350	6,219

Source: U.S. Bureau of the Census. *1990 Census of Population: Characteristics of American Indians by Tribe and Language.* CP3-7. Washington, DC: The Bureau, 1994, p. 34. *Note:* A dash (-) represents zero or a percent that rounds to zero.

★ 151 ★

Population

Population by Tribe, Region, and State, 1990: Siuslaw-Yurok and Other Specified Tribes - Part IV

Data are based on a sample and are subject to sampling variability.

Tribe	East South Central Region				West South Central Region				Mountain Region			
	Kentucky	Tennessee	Alabama	Mississippi	Arkansas	Louisiana	Oklahoma	Texas	Montana	Idaho	Wyoming	Colorado
Siuslaw	-	-	-	-	-	-	-	-	-	-	-	-
Spokane	-	-	-	-	-	-	-	14	21	48	-	26
Stockbridge	2	4	23	-	2	4	4	56	-	12	-	38
Tlingit	13	6	-	-	-	6	-	135	5	56	-	37
Tohono O'Odham	-	-	3	-	8	-	37	98	28	20	-	25
Ak-Chin	-	-	-	-	-	-	-	-	8	-	-	-
Tohono O'Odham	-	-	3	-	8	-	37	98	20	20	-	25
Other Tohono O'Odham	-	-	-	-	-	-	-	-	-	-	-	-
Tolowa	-	-	-	-	-	-	-	-	-	-	-	-
Tonkawa	-	-	-	-	-	-	227	20	-	1	-	-
Tsimshian	-	-	-	-	-	-	8	-	6	3	-	7
Umatilla	-	-	-	-	9	-	38	-	11	39	9	8
Umpqua	-	-	-	-	-	-	5	-	-	15	5	10
Cow Creek Umpqua	-	-	-	-	-	-	-	-	-	5	-	-
Umpqua	-	-	-	-	-	-	5	-	-	10	5	10
Ute	18	34	20	-	10	4	92	112	36	114	88	2,421
Allen Canyon	-	-	-	-	-	-	-	-	-	-	-	-
Uintah Ute	-	-	-	-	-	-	49	-	14	59	5	34
Ute	18	34	20	-	10	4	43	112	2	55	67	1,303
Ute Mountain Ute	-	-	-	-	-	-	-	-	20	-	16	1,084
Wailaki	5	-	-	-	-	-	-	-	-	13	-	35

[Continued]

Population by Tribe, Region, and State, 1990: Siuslaw-Yurok and Other Specified Tribes - Part IV
[Continued]

Tribe	East South Central Region				West South Central Region				Mountain Region			
	Kentucky	Tennessee	Alabama	Mississippi	Arkansas	Louisiana	Oklahoma	Texas	Montana	Idaho	Wyoming	Colorado
Walla-Walla	-	-	-	-	-	-	-	-	-	-	-	-
Wampanoag	8	12	-	-	-	-	9	19	11	-	-	29
Gay Head Wampanoag	-	-	-	-	-	-	-	-	-	-	-	-
Mashpee Wampanoag	-	-	-	-	-	-	-	-	-	-	-	-
Wampanoag	8	12	-	-	-	-	9	19	11	-	-	29
Warm Springs	-	-	-	-	-	-	31	5	-	9	-	-
Washo	-	-	-	-	-	-	1	-	27	-	-	8
Washo	-	-	-	-	-	-	1	-	27	-	-	8
Other Washo	-	-	-	-	-	-	-	-	-	-	-	-
Wichita	-	6	5	-	-	-	926	87	-	6	-	8
Winnebago	4	15	-	-	17	15	10	77	16	3	8	60
Nebraska Winnebago	-	-	-	-	-	-	-	-	-	-	8	-
Winnebago	4	15	-	-	17	15	10	64	16	3	-	38
Wisconsin Winnebago	-	-	-	-	-	-	-	13	-	-	-	22
Wintu	-	-	-	-	-	-	2	8	-	13	-	6
Wiyot	-	-	-	-	-	-	24	6	-	-	5	-
Yakima	6	-	-	-	6	-	11	30	35	71	-	34
Yaqui	-	18	-	19	6	-	2	75	-	7	-	70
Barrio Libre	-	-	-	-	-	-	-	-	-	-	-	-
Pascua Yaqui	-	-	-	19	6	-	-	34	-	-	-	-
Yaqui	-	18	-	-	-	-	2	41	-	7	-	70
Yavapai Apache	-	-	-	-	-	-	-	-	-	-	-	-
Yokuts	-	-	-	-	2	-	7	7	-	4	10	-
Chukchansi	-	-	-	-	-	-	-	-	-	2	10	-
Tachi	-	-	-	-	-	-	-	-	-	-	-	-
Tule River	-	-	-	-	-	-	-	-	-	-	-	-
Yokuts	-	-	-	-	2	-	7	7	-	2	-	-
Yuchi	-	-	-	-	-	-	173	5	-	-	-	-
Yuman	-	8	-	-	15	14	70	77	20	28	25	35
Cocopah	-	-	-	-	5	-	-	-	-	-	-	-
Havasupai	-	-	-	-	10	8	12	-	-	-	-	-
Hualapai	-	8	-	-	-	6	42	61	-	28	19	-
Maricopa	-	-	-	-	-	-	-	-	-	-	-	-
Mohave	-	-	-	-	-	-	12	5	-	-	-	-
Quechan	-	-	-	-	-	-	4	11	20	-	6	32
Yavapai	-	-	-	-	-	-	-	-	-	-	-	3
Yurok	15	4	-	-	20	7	-	34	-	18	-	33
Other specified tribes	-	-	-	-	-	-	-	23	127	18	2	7
Burt Lake Band	-	-	-	-	-	-	-	-	-	-	-	-
Fort Belknap	-	-	-	-	-	-	-	-	114	-	2	7
Fort McDermitt	-	-	-	-	-	-	-	-	-	10	-	-
Fort McDowell	-	-	-	-	-	-	-	-	-	-	-	-
Los Coyotes	-	-	-	-	-	-	-	-	-	-	-	-
Mexican Indian Cherokee	-	-	-	-	-	-	-	23	-	-	-	-
Reno-Sparks	-	-	-	-	-	-	-	-	-	-	-	-
Round Valley	-	-	-	-	-	-	-	-	-	-	-	-
Shoalwater	-	-	-	-	-	-	-	-	-	-	-	-
Wascopum	-	-	-	-	-	-	-	-	-	-	-	-
Wind River	-	-	-	-	-	-	-	-	13	8	-	-
All other specified	-	-	-	-	-	-	-	-	-	-	-	-
Tribe not specified	199	185	112	201	218	488	830	1,201	196	30	67	401
Tribe not reported	1,217	1,619	1,879	1,326	1,525	3,319	10,067	10,766	1,983	847	432	2,681

Source: U.S. Bureau of the Census. *1990 Census of Population: Characteristics of American Indians by Tribe and Language.* CP3-7. Washington, DC: The Bureau, 1994, p. 35.
Note: A dash (-) represents zero or a percent that rounds to zero.

★ 152 ★
Population

Population by Tribe, Region, and State, 1990: Siuslaw-Yurok and Other Specified Tribes - Part V

Data are based on a sample and are subject to sampling variability.

Tribe	Mountain Region (cont.)				Pacific Region				
	New Mexico	Arizona	Utah	Nevada	Washington	Oregon	California	Alaska	Hawaii
Siuslaw	-	-	-	14	5	25	4	-	-
Spokane	-	-	-	-	1,731	76	72	7	-
Stockbridge	5	7	-	16	39	2	109	-	21
Tlingit	12	25	9	37	2,131	441	723	10,235	12
Tohono O'Odham	114	14,876	10	26	18	31	1,240	7	44
Ak-Chin	-	326	-	-	-	-	-	-	-
Tohono O'Odham	114	14,550	10	26	18	31	1,240	7	44
Other Tohono O'Odham	-	-	-	-	-	-	-	-	-
Tolowa	-	-	-	-	45	62	328	11	-
Tonkawa	-	-	-	-	-	-	55	-	-
Tsimshian	4	12	-	-	468	40	39	1,524	9
Umatilla	6	19	-	2	88	896	100	4	-
Umpqua	-	-	-	2	33	452	142	-	-
Cow Creek Umpqua	-	-	-	2	-	289	50	-	-
Umpqua	-	-	-	-	33	163	92	-	-
Ute	162	138	3,027	67	126	39	725	27	13
Allen Canyon	-	-	-	-	-	-	-	-	-
Uintah Ute	-	5	357	5	26	-	2	-	-
Ute	152	122	2,400	62	98	39	684	27	13
Ute Mountain Ute	10	11	270	-	2	-	39	-	-
Wailaki	-	19	-	5	7	61	1,088	1	-
Walla-Walla	-	-	-	9	55	144	13	-	-
Wampanoag	-	5	4	-	24	-	146	-	10
Gay Head Wampanoag	-	-	2	-	-	-	14	-	-
Mashpee Wampanoag	-	-	-	-	-	-	-	-	-
Wampanoag	-	5	2	-	24	-	132	-	10
Warm Springs	-	-	-	2	144	2,450	41	-	-
Washo	-	24	-	747	18	27	605	-	-
Washo	-	24	-	745	18	27	595	-	-
Other Washo	-	-	-	2	-	-	10	-	-
Wichita	-	-	-	-	-	44	38	22	17
Winnebago	91	56	54	35	84	149	376	-	3
Nebraska Winnebago	-	-	20	-	-	-	-	-	-
Winnebago	59	45	34	35	79	149	361	-	3
Wisconsin Winnebago	32	11	-	-	5	-	15	-	-
Wintu	7	23	6	44	37	198	1,904	17	12
Wiyot	-	-	-	-	17	20	388	-	-
Yakima	32	66	18	-	6,154	643	317	48	10
Yaqui	41	6,986	15	17	47	85	2,162	5	15
Barrio Libre	-	-	-	-	-	-	-	-	-
Pascua Yaqui	-	496	-	-	-	-	121	-	-
Yaqui	41	6,490	15	17	47	85	2,041	5	15
Yavapai Apache	11	606	-	-	-	-	20	-	-

[Continued]

★ 152 ★

Population by Tribe, Region, and State, 1990: Siuslaw-Yurok and Other Specified Tribes - Part V
[Continued]

Tribe	Mountain Region (cont.)				Pacific Region				
	New Mexico	Arizona	Utah	Nevada	Washington	Oregon	California	Alaska	Hawaii
Yokuts	-	37	-	31	44	19	2,701	40	-
Chukchansi	-	6	-	-	21	6	726	40	-
Tachi	-	-	-	-	-	-	401	-	-
Tule River	-	-	-	-	5	-	877	-	-
Yokuts	-	31	-	31	18	13	697	-	-
Yuchi	6	7	-	-	10	-	117	-	-
Yuman	90	4,551	46	51	27	53	2,087	4	-
Cocopah	-	511	10	-	-	-	66	-	-
Havasupai	-	492	2	8	-	-	25	-	-
Hualapai	21	919	7	26	-	-	67	-	-
Maricopa	-	701	11	-	7	3	12	-	-
Mohave	3	768	7	2	5	9	451	-	-
Quechan	7	594	4	15	15	41	1,419	4	-
Yavapai	59	566	5	-	-	-	47	-	-
Yurok	14	60	-	14	205	386	3,496	21	10
Other specified tribes	12	137	-	200	91	236	216	-	-
Burt Lake Band	-	-	-	-	-	-	-	-	-
Fort Belknap	-	-	-	-	9	2	-	-	-
Fort McDermitt	-	-	-	153	-	8	-	-	-
Fort McDowell	2	137	-	-	-	17	-	-	-
Los Coyotes	-	-	-	-	-	-	60	-	-
Mexican Indian Cherokee	-	-	-	-	-	-	29	-	-
Reno-Sparks	-	-	-	47	-	-	1	-	-
Round Valley	-	-	-	-	-	-	99	-	-
Shoalwater	-	-	-	-	67	-	16	-	-
Wascopum	-	-	-	-	13	209	11	-	-
Wind River	-	-	-	-	-	-	-	-	-
All other specified	10	-	-	-	2	-	-	-	-
Tribe not specified	352	570	101	184	890	482	4,793	170	171
Tribe not reported	6,040	7,708	1,645	1,994	6,278	3,969	34,242	1,338	584

Source: U.S. Bureau of the Census. *1990 Census of Population: Characteristics of American Indians by Tribe and Language.* CP3-7. Washington, DC: The Bureau, 1994, p. 36.
Note: A dash (-) represents zero or a percent that rounds to zero.

★ 153 ★
Population

Population of Alaska Native Villages, by Age, 1990 - Akhiok-Kasaan, Part I

Alaska Native Village Statistical Area[1]	Number of persons										
	< 1 year	1-2 years	3-4 years	5 years	6 years	7-9 years	10-11 years	12-13 years	14 years	15 years	16 years
Akhiok	0	9	4	3	2	0	6	2	0	2	3
Akiachak	18	30	13	6	8	6	5	15	22	25	3
Akiak	4	31	15	9	9	23	18	9	2	4	4
Akutan	0	2	9	2	6	5	2	5	5	0	0
Alakanuk	19	20	35	10	17	37	26	30	12	20	10
Alatna	0	2	0	0	0	5	0	2	0	0	3
Aleknagik	2	11	6	9	4	15	7	7	6	0	2
Alexander	0	0	0	0	0	0	0	3	0	0	0
Allakaket	4	8	11	0	5	13	2	5	4	3	1
Ambler	8	30	20	12	10	24	13	19	7	8	6
Anaktuvuk Pass	2	22	19	14	3	23	18	6	6	5	7
Andreafsky	14	21	31	10	15	27	17	8	2	12	5
Angoon	12	43	35	22	21	45	26	29	12	8	13
Aniak	14	18	31	11	23	49	33	22	8	3	11
Anvik	2	3	4	2	0	8	2	6	3	0	0
Arctic Village	2	10	7	1	0	10	2	0	1	0	1
Atka	0	1	2	4	0	10	0	5	2	5	10
Atkasook	9	8	9	4	1	8	15	11	2	4	8
Atmautluak	5	11	12	8	5	25	12	24	8	0	5
Barrow	74	192	141	74	73	174	94	85	36	46	37
Beaver	0	7	6	7	0	5	0	0	2	3	2
Belkofski	0	0	0	0	0	0	0	0	0	0	0
Bethel	101	290	201	94	116	270	160	169	56	44	79
Bill Moore's	0	0	0	0	0	0	0	0	0	0	0
Birch Creek	0	2	3	3	0	0	2	4	0	2	0
Brevig Mission	4	14	9	2	12	16	12	14	6	2	0
Buckland	9	21	22	11	11	34	23	14	4	8	3
Cantwell	3	4	0	0	2	7	4	0	0	0	3
Canyon Village	0	0	0	0	0	0	0	0	0	0	0
Chalkyitsik	0	2	2	4	2	11	6	8	0	2	3
Chefornak	2	24	30	0	7	25	12	11	11	4	7
Chenega	0	4	3	1	3	1	8	5	3	4	0
Chevak	19	53	56	15	17	33	16	26	15	16	12
Chignik	2	0	5	5	7	14	8	15	4	1	0
Chignik Lagoon	0	2	5	2	0	4	6	7	0	2	4
Chignik Lake	0	14	13	0	0	5	0	5	0	0	0
Chilkat	4	6	7	0	4	16	2	4	0	9	3
Chilkoot	4	2	7	2	4	14	9	7	3	0	2
Chistochina	0	1	5	0	1	2	4	1	3	2	0
Chitina	0	1	2	0	1	1	0	4	2	1	0
Chuathbaluk	0	6	2	2	0	16	8	4	0	0	2
Chulloonawick	0	0	0	0	0	0	0	0	0	0	0
Circle	2	0	4	0	0	7	1	2	0	6	0
Clark's Point	0	7	0	2	0	9	3	0	0	3	0
Copper Center	11	17	29	7	10	19	7	19	2	2	2
Council	0	0	0	0	0	0	0	0	0	0	0

[Continued]

★ 153 ★

Population of Alaska Native Villages, by Age, 1990 - Akhiok-Kasaan, Part I
[Continued]

Alaska Native Village Statistical Area[1]	Number of persons										
	< 1 year	1-2 years	3-4 years	5 years	6 years	7-9 years	10-11 years	12-13 years	14 years	15 years	16 years
Craig	26	60	58	43	32	73	41	32	31	10	6
Crooked Creek	4	14	5	0	0	14	0	0	3	0	3
Deering	6	3	9	3	7	8	3	11	8	3	1
Dillingham	53	102	85	49	57	145	62	47	35	31	11
Dot Lake	0	0	2	0	0	2	4	9	1	0	0
Eagle	0	0	0	2	0	0	0	1	0	0	0
Eek	11	12	15	8	7	18	8	6	4	3	2
Egegik	0	5	0	2	0	13	5	2	0	1	0
Eklutna	6	11	14	0	6	23	14	13	14	5	11
Ekuk	0	0	0	0	0	0	0	0	0	0	0
Ekwok	3	2	6	2	0	4	2	2	0	0	0
Elim	13	21	14	8	7	21	2	14	6	6	4
Emmonak	30	52	47	12	22	28	15	21	7	8	8
English Bay	6	8	8	6	7	8	6	9	4	9	2
Evansville	2	3	1	0	0	5	0	2	0	0	0
Eyak	3	14	9	0	13	10	2	2	0	2	4
False Pass	4	2	3	3	0	4	2	0	0	0	3
Fort Yukon	12	29	23	15	12	33	26	26	9	13	10
Gakona	0	0	4	0	0	0	0	0	0	0	0
Galena	6	32	29	7	9	34	15	24	3	7	16
Gambell	13	41	24	10	14	27	26	37	7	7	8
Georgetown	0	0	0	0	0	0	0	0	0	0	0
Golovin	0	12	3	0	5	3	4	3	3	0	0
Goodnews Bay	0	23	18	10	6	13	2	4	4	0	4
Grayling	12	9	13	5	2	11	6	13	7	5	4
Grouse Creek Group	13	25	22	17	15	41	27	22	5	13	10
Gulkana	2	4	3	4	0	12	5	2	2	0	0
Hamilton	0	0	0	0	0	0	0	0	0	0	0
Healy Lake	2	0	0	4	0	8	2	0	2	2	0
Holy Cross	0	0	0	0	0	0	0	0	0	0	0
Hoonah	13	45	20	22	14	61	10	7	7	33	5
Hooper Bay	42	74	59	47	23	60	27	20	16	9	13
Hughes	0	0	3	0	3	3	2	2	0	0	3
Huslia	6	12	11	3	2	11	12	6	6	0	3
Hydaburg	10	7	17	11	5	26	16	16	8	9	5
Igiugig	4	4	3	2	3	0	0	0	0	0	1
Iliamna	2	2	2	5	0	9	4	2	0	2	0
Inalik	0	15	18	5	5	12	11	5	5	5	0
Ivanof Bay	0	4	0	0	0	5	5	0	0	0	0
Kake	16	38	32	9	8	30	25	26	21	6	12
Kaktovik	6	10	15	8	8	15	7	0	2	6	1
Kalskag	5	7	16	14	1	5	0	2	0	2	8
Kaltag	11	12	5	6	11	14	19	8	11	6	4

[Continued]

★ 153 ★

Population of Alaska Native Villages, by Age, 1990 - Akhiok-Kasaan, Part I
[Continued]

Alaska Native Village Statistical Area[1]	Number of persons										
	< 1 year	1-2 years	3-4 years	5 years	6 years	7-9 years	10-11 years	12-13 years	14 years	15 years	16 years
Karluk	1	6	2	4	2	6	2	9	0	0	5
Kasaan	2	4	2	0	0	4	0	0	0	0	0

Source: Census of Population and Housing, 1990: Summary Tape File 3C on CD-ROM [machine-readable datafiles]. Prepared by the Bureau of the Census. Washington, DC: The Bureau, 1992. *Notes:* 1. Alaska Native villages (ANVs) constitute tribes, bands, clans, groups, villages, communities, or associations in Alaska that are recognized pursuant to the Alaska Native Claims Settlement Act of 1972, Public Law 92-203. Because ANVs do not have legally designated boundaries, the Census Bureau has established Alaska Native village statistical areas (ANVSAs) for statistical purposes. For the 1990 census, the Census Bureau cooperated with officials of the nonprofit corporation within each participating Alaska Native Regional Corporation (ANRC), as well as other knowledgeable officials, to delineate boundaries that encompass the settled area associated with each ANV.

★ 154 ★

Population

Population of Alaska Native Villages, by Age, 1990 - Akhiok-Kasaan, Part II

Alaska Native Village Statistical Area[1]	Number of persons									
	17 years	18 years	19 years	20 years	21 years	22-24 years	25-29 years	30-34 years	35-39 years	40-44 years
Akhiok	2	0	0	0	4	5	13	5	8	2
Akiachak	0	10	23	0	14	24	53	35	44	8
Akiak	7	2	2	7	3	9	22	29	17	10
Akutan	0	16	15	28	37	67	96	141	87	34
Alakanuk	11	11	11	8	10	22	28	35	38	28
Alatna	0	0	0	0	0	0	2	2	3	0
Aleknagik	2	3	3	2	0	5	12	15	30	16
Alexander	0	0	0	0	0	0	4	0	0	0
Allakaket	0	3	0	0	1	4	12	12	10	2
Ambler	9	0	9	0	4	19	13	21	24	19
Anaktuvuk Pass	5	0	8	0	0	8	27	25	15	17
Andreafsky	9	2	10	3	10	15	48	39	20	28
Angoon	11	14	0	3	6	25	48	43	61	28
Aniak	5	0	7	1	7	20	46	51	45	35
Anvik	0	0	0	0	0	0	14	6	0	3
Arctic Village	0	3	0	4	0	7	3	10	5	8
Atka	0	3	3	0	0	1	0	5	19	11
Atkasook	3	5	3	4	2	17	14	14	16	8
Atmautluak	12	2	2	3	3	7	18	25	23	17
Barrow	34	46	23	25	34	106	273	259	271	180
Beaver	3	0	5	2	0	3	8	7	11	10
Belkofski	0	0	0	0	0	0	0	0	0	0
Bethel	60	76	47	60	63	241	542	473	476	313
Bill Moore's	0	0	0	0	0	0	0	0	0	0
Birch Creek	0	0	0	0	0	2	3	8	5	0
Brevig Mission	0	4	0	0	4	2	14	22	18	7
Buckland	9	6	6	4	7	16	23	17	20	8
Cantwell	0	0	0	0	0	1	11	17	17	22

[Continued]

★ 154 ★

Population of Alaska Native Villages, by Age, 1990 - Akhiok-Kasaan, Part II
[Continued]

Alaska Native Village Statistical Area[1]	Number of persons									
	17 years	18 years	19 years	20 years	21 years	22-24 years	25-29 years	30-34 years	35-39 years	40-44 years
Canyon Village	0	0	0	0	0	0	0	0	0	0
Chalkyitsik	0	0	0	0	0	2	9	6	9	3
Chefornak	2	8	12	3	2	14	17	17	23	18
Chenega	2	2	0	4	0	13	6	8	9	9
Chevak	5	8	8	14	7	31	61	48	25	27
Chignik	2	0	13	0	0	0	7	35	17	23
Chignik Lagoon	0	0	0	2	2	0	2	5	12	7
Chignik Lake	0	0	0	6	5	13	24	10	4	0
Chilkat	7	0	2	2	2	7	10	12	10	6
Chilkoot	2	1	0	0	0	4	7	31	14	33
Chistochina	0	2	2	2	0	2	3	6	3	8
Chitina	2	2	0	0	0	2	4	2	6	5
Chuathbaluk	4	2	3	0	0	5	9	6	7	4
Chulloonawick	0	0	0	0	0	0	0	0	0	0
Circle	0	0	0	0	0	0	1	8	11	7
Clark's Point	0	0	0	1	0	6	5	11	7	2
Copper Center	7	10	3	0	6	3	35	39	51	48
Council	0	0	0	2	0	0	0	0	0	0
Craig	18	15	14	13	22	39	169	108	167	86
Crooked Creek	0	0	4	2	3	8	14	0	3	8
Deering	4	0	1	0	0	18	9	10	2	13
Dillingham	40	22	15	20	17	63	193	196	192	176
Dot Lake	1	0	0	0	2	1	0	1	0	4
Eagle	0	0	0	2	0	2	7	6	3	1
Eek	6	0	4	6	6	14	28	35	12	13
Egegik	2	0	0	0	0	7	11	23	7	10
Eklutna	10	4	9	4	6	0	9	34	66	62
Ekuk	0	0	0	0	0	0	0	0	0	0
Ekwok	0	3	2	1	0	1	4	11	11	1
Elim	0	3	1	4	4	11	22	22	34	20
Emmonak	6	9	9	13	13	47	57	38	44	23
English Bay	8	3	0	2	2	7	10	20	17	7
Evansville	0	0	2	0	0	0	2	4	10	8
Eyak	0	0	1	3	3	6	12	19	22	15
False Pass	3	0	0	0	0	0	3	15	7	0
Fort Yukon	4	7	5	11	6	19	63	50	66	42
Gakona	0	0	0	0	0	0	0	0	4	0
Galena	12	4	2	3	34	65	137	125	50	65
Gambell	11	8	3	4	8	39	47	45	63	30
Georgetown	0	0	0	0	0	0	0	0	0	0
Golovin	2	3	0	6	3	6	19	3	14	3
Goodnews Bay	4	7	0	4	5	14	19	24	12	9
Grayling	9	0	3	3	5	14	17	8	17	9
Grouse Creek Group	3	11	1	3	3	10	47	68	78	67
Gulkana	2	0	1	2	0	0	5	19	13	2

[Continued]

★ 154 ★

Population of Alaska Native Villages, by Age, 1990 - Akhiok-Kasaan, Part II
[Continued]

Alaska Native Village Statistical Area[1]	Number of persons									
	17 years	18 years	19 years	20 years	21 years	22-24 years	25-29 years	30-34 years	35-39 years	40-44 years
Hamilton	0	0	0	0	0	0	0	0	0	0
Healy Lake	0	0	0	0	0	0	7	4	5	4
Holy Cross	0	0	0	0	0	0	0	0	0	0
Hoonah	0	5	11	9	5	28	77	48	74	49
Hooper Bay	9	15	4	15	8	33	96	65	44	44
Hughes	0	0	0	4	0	6	2	3	8	7
Huslia	0	0	2	0	5	11	16	6	15	13
Hydaburg	6	7	2	0	5	24	26	30	29	25
Igiugig	0	0	0	0	0	0	0	5	3	0
Iliamna	0	0	0	2	0	2	7	2	5	6
Inalik	0	7	2	2	2	9	17	12	17	11
Ivanof Bay	4	3	0	0	0	0	0	8	4	5
Kake	10	11	11	10	11	31	54	47	76	52
Kaktovik	0	4	0	4	5	11	32	19	16	13
Kalskag	2	0	1	0	5	6	26	21	6	11
Kaltag	4	0	4	2	0	11	19	30	17	17
Karluk	2	0	2	2	4	4	0	8	12	2
Kasaan	2	0	4	0	0	0	6	3	10	10

Source: Census of Population and Housing, 1990: Summary Tape File 3C on CD-ROM [machine-readable datafiles]. Prepared by the Bureau of the Census. Washington, DC: The Bureau, 1992. *Notes:* 1. Alaska Native villages (ANVs) constitute tribes, bands, clans, groups, villages, communities, or associations in Alaska that are recognized pursuant to the Alaska Native Claims Settlement Act of 1972, Public Law 92-203. Because ANVs do not have legally designated boundaries, the Census Bureau has established Alaska Native village statistical areas (ANVSAs) for statistical purposes. For the 1990 census, the Census Bureau cooperated with officials of the nonprofit corporation within each participating Alaska Native Regional Corporation (ANRC), as well as other knowledgeable officials, to delineate boundaries that encompass the settled area associated with each ANV.

★ 155 ★

Population

Population of Alaska Native Villages, by Age, 1990 - Akhiok-Kasaan, Part III

Alaska Native Village Statistical Area[1]	Number of persons									
	45-49 years	50-54 years	55-59 years	60-61 years	62-64 years	65-69 years	70-74 years	75-79 years	80-84 years	85 + years
Akhiok	4	4	2	0	1	0	0	0	0	0
Akiachak	23	14	34	5	0	11	0	13	0	0
Akiak	9	9	10	2	4	6	9	0	0	0
Akutan	19	11	10	5	0	2	1	0	0	0
Alakanuk	12	24	35	9	2	12	6	2	0	0
Alatna	2	0	0	0	0	2	0	0	0	0
Aleknagik	6	3	9	0	7	3	2	5	0	2
Alexander	0	0	7	7	0	0	16	0	0	0
Allakaket	18	5	10	1	0	2	5	2	0	0
Ambler	7	13	6	3	0	9	2	2	0	0
Anaktuvuk Pass	17	11	10	2	0	0	2	0	0	0
Andreafsky	19	8	15	4	2	7	1	3	0	1

[Continued]

★ 155 ★

Population of Alaska Native Villages, by Age, 1990 - Akhiok-Kasaan, Part III
[Continued]

Alaska Native Village Statistical Area[1]	Number of persons									
	45-49 years	50-54 years	55-59 years	60-61 years	62-64 years	65-69 years	70-74 years	75-79 years	80-84 years	85 + years
Angoon	47	36	20	3	2	10	4	10	4	2
Aniak	25	24	14	3	8	6	2	6	0	1
Anvik	11	0	2	2	4	2	2	0	2	0
Arctic Village	0	0	11	0	0	1	0	2	4	0
Atka	5	4	1	0	2	4	2	0	2	0
Atkasook	11	15	8	5	5	3	1	0	0	0
Atmautluak	17	3	2	2	1	5	5	0	0	0
Barrow	161	97	67	21	46	24	26	23	3	5
Beaver	0	3	2	0	0	3	2	3	2	0
Belkofski	0	0	0	0	0	0	0	0	0	0
Bethel	276	146	115	41	44	65	33	21	11	4
Bill Moore's	0	0	0	0	0	0	0	0	0	0
Birch Creek	3	4	0	0	0	0	0	0	0	0
Brevig Mission	11	0	3	0	4	8	0	0	0	0
Buckland	6	10	1	3	4	4	4	7	2	0
Cantwell	8	6	15	8	0	3	4	6	4	0
Canyon Village	0	0	0	0	0	0	0	0	0	0
Chalkyitsik	0	8	4	3	0	6	0	5	0	0
Chefornak	17	6	3	1	5	5	8	6	10	0
Chenega	1	2	3	0	0	3	0	0	0	0
Chevak	15	13	17	8	9	14	2	2	5	0
Chignik	9	0	2	0	0	0	2	0	0	0
Chignik Lagoon	2	0	5	0	5	2	2	0	0	0
Chignik Lake	5	0	0	4	0	17	0	0	0	0
Chilkat	7	2	5	3	0	2	5	0	0	3
Chilkoot	12	20	21	3	3	7	4	3	0	0
Chistochina	0	1	3	4	0	0	4	0	3	0
Chitina	1	5	2	0	0	1	0	2	0	0
Chuathbaluk	2	4	6	2	0	2	2	1	0	0
Chulloonawick	0	0	0	0	0	0	0	0	0	0
Circle	8	2	6	0	0	2	3	1	2	0
Clark's Point	0	0	0	0	0	6	0	0	0	0
Copper Center	23	14	28	3	3	21	0	2	5	0
Council	2	0	0	0	0	0	2	0	0	0
Craig	63	45	37	7	21	14	6	2	2	0
Crooked Creek	0	6	0	0	6	5	0	2	0	4
Deering	11	6	10	0	0	8	1	0	2	0
Dillingham	141	72	64	16	24	34	14	18	17	6
Dot Lake	12	4	2	0	0	0	0	2	0	2
Eagle	2	1	0	0	2	3	0	0	3	0
Eek	11	6	8	6	1	8	0	6	0	0
Egegik	13	3	3	2	5	4	0	2	0	0
Eklutna	15	11	21	0	8	4	1	0	0	0
Ekuk	0	0	0	0	0	0	0	0	0	0
Ekwok	5	2	2	0	2	0	0	5	0	2

[Continued]

★ 155 ★

Population of Alaska Native Villages, by Age, 1990 - Akhiok-Kasaan, Part III

[Continued]

Alaska Native Village Statistical Area[1]	Number of persons									
	45-49 years	50-54 years	55-59 years	60-61 years	62-64 years	65-69 years	70-74 years	75-79 years	80-84 years	85 + years
Elim	2	9	7	2	3	5	0	2	2	0
Emmonak	29	20	14	8	6	19	0	3	2	0
English Bay	4	2	0	0	0	2	4	0	0	0
Evansville	0	10	8	2	2	3	0	0	0	0
Eyak	13	7	4	0	2	0	0	2	0	0
False Pass	6	4	0	0	0	8	0	0	0	0
Fort Yukon	26	19	15	6	12	0	8	6	6	0
Gakona	0	4	0	0	0	0	4	4	0	0
Galena	25	34	18	8	25	9	4	0	0	4
Gambell	9	21	14	2	9	6	11	0	4	0
Georgetown	0	0	0	0	0	0	0	0	0	0
Golovin	0	10	2	0	4	10	2	0	3	0
Goodnews Bay	13	8	10	0	3	6	4	6	0	0
Grayling	3	12	4	8	6	6	2	0	4	0
Grouse Creek Group	23	28	28	11	15	16	8	0	0	0
Gulkana	5	9	6	2	4	4	3	2	0	0
Hamilton	0	0	0	0	0	0	0	0	0	0
Healy Lake	8	0	0	0	0	0	0	0	0	0
Holy Cross	0	0	0	0	0	0	0	0	0	0
Hoonah	35	50	37	19	3	13	16	5	3	5
Hooper Bay	29	19	13	9	2	27	6	8	2	8
Hughes	2	0	2	2	0	2	0	3	3	0
Huslia	18	9	4	0	8	2	7	2	0	2
Hydaburg	27	19	24	4	4	7	0	4	15	0
Igiugig	2	0	2	0	0	0	0	0	0	0
Iliamna	9	2	0	0	0	0	2	1	0	0
Inalik	9	8	5	2	2	6	0	0	0	0
Ivanof Bay	0	0	0	0	0	0	0	0	0	0
Kake	30	47	15	11	11	15	12	6	4	0
Kaktovik	19	15	8	0	4	2	3	2	0	0
Kalskag	2	2	9	0	5	3	1	3	0	0
Kaltag	12	6	2	3	0	5	1	0	1	0
Karluk	4	0	0	0	1	0	0	0	4	0
Kasaan	0	2	5	0	0	0	0	0	0	0

Source: Census of Population and Housing, 1990: Summary Tape File 3C on CD-ROM [machine-readable datafiles]. Prepared by the Bureau of the Census. Washington, DC: The Bureau, 1992. *Notes:* 1. Alaska Native villages (ANVs) constitute tribes, bands, clans, groups, villages, communities, or associations in Alaska that are recognized pursuant to the Alaska Native Claims Settlement Act of 1972, Public Law 92-203. Because ANVs do not have legally designated boundaries, the Census Bureau has established Alaska Native village statistical areas (ANVSAs) for statistical purposes. For the 1990 census, the Census Bureau cooperated with officials of the nonprofit corporation within each participating Alaska Native Regional Corporation (ANRC), as well as other knowledgeable officials, to delineate boundaries that encompass the settled area associated with each ANV.

★ 156 ★

Population

Population of Alaska Native Villages, by Age, 1990 - Kasigluk-Takotna, Part I

Alaska Native Village Statistical Area[1]	Number of persons										
	< 1 year	1-2 years	3-4 years	5 years	6 years	7-9 years	10-11 years	12-13 years	14 years	15 years	16 years
Kasigluk	10	25	35	14	15	22	24	14	11	9	9
Kiana	7	40	18	13	5	27	20	14	9	8	5
King Cove	6	11	10	4	8	22	6	17	7	3	5
King Salmon	6	12	15	7	3	15	17	12	9	7	8
Kipnuk	17	29	16	15	7	30	24	18	8	12	13
Kivalina	6	23	13	18	4	25	9	17	13	8	10
Klawock	12	29	20	10	16	27	24	20	18	12	2
Knik	6	7	10	12	12	20	8	5	2	2	3
Kobuk	6	6	4	2	1	3	4	5	0	2	1
Kokhanok	5	4	8	2	9	14	5	4	3	3	2
Koliganek	11	17	9	13	0	8	3	4	7	3	4
Kongiganak	9	25	23	10	6	21	21	12	4	7	5
Kotlik	20	27	25	11	16	45	15	23	7	3	4
Kotzebue	90	172	150	71	77	170	108	79	49	29	41
Koyuk	8	16	4	6	7	20	8	12	8	4	5
Koyukuk	2	6	7	2	7	9	6	2	0	0	0
Kwethluk	12	34	31	23	12	46	34	26	11	11	5
Kwigillingok	6	15	16	3	12	9	7	2	0	2	3
Lake Minchumina	0	0	0	0	0	0	0	0	0	0	0
Larsen Bay	8	8	6	2	8	8	6	5	2	0	4
Levelock	4	5	7	0	2	0	5	9	0	0	3
Lime Village	0	1	2	1	4	1	6	2	0	0	2
Lower Kalskag	8	16	17	6	14	19	12	10	19	8	6
McGrath	5	21	25	10	7	43	20	22	11	16	25
Manley Hot Springs	0	5	5	2	3	3	3	6	3	0	0
Manokotak	10	33	29	5	11	39	16	16	0	3	3
Marshall	0	13	8	6	6	18	17	19	8	6	13
Mary's Igloo	0	0	0	0	0	0	0	0	0	0	0
Medfra	0	0	0	0	0	0	0	0	0	0	0
Mekoryuk	0	6	6	8	4	14	6	6	6	2	3
Mentasta Lake	1	8	1	2	0	8	8	0	2	0	0
Minto	6	8	8	5	2	18	11	9	2	3	2
Mountain Village	27	42	28	14	9	51	39	34	18	7	27
Naknek	11	37	27	18	7	37	29	21	7	7	5
Napaimute	0	0	0	0	0	0	0	0	0	0	0
Napakiak	3	16	19	9	8	21	24	17	0	5	4
Napaskiak	12	21	21	4	10	26	15	9	8	9	12
Nelson Lagoon	0	7	0	0	0	0	0	0	0	0	0
Nenana	0	20	13	0	5	25	9	18	12	6	16
Newhalen	11	16	15	12	6	19	5	8	2	0	2
New Stuyahok	11	41	23	7	7	15	17	9	7	2	12
Newtok	7	11	9	4	8	18	8	14	6	0	5
Nightmute	3	2	4	2	2	17	4	8	4	7	3
Nikolai	0	5	2	2	4	7	9	6	2	2	0
Nikolski	0	0	3	0	0	2	0	3	0	0	0
Ninilchik	230	383	429	205	277	670	378	344	162	130	148

[Continued]

★ 156 ★

Population of Alaska Native Villages, by Age, 1990 - Kasigluk-Takotna, Part I
[Continued]

Alaska Native Village Statistical Area[1]	Number of persons										
	< 1 year	1-2 years	3-4 years	5 years	6 years	7-9 years	10-11 years	12-13 years	14 years	15 years	16 years
Noatak	7	22	20	12	7	26	7	11	6	9	2
Nondalton	2	12	9	4	3	6	3	3	0	0	4
Noorvik	16	52	16	11	13	54	15	27	10	11	7
Northway	0	12	2	0	5	11	6	7	7	3	2
Nuiqsut	16	21	22	17	19	10	7	8	4	12	8
Nulato	12	32	20	5	10	28	15	26	10	7	7
Nunapitchuk	11	35	18	6	12	19	12	11	4	2	6
Ohogamiut	0	0	0	0	0	0	0	0	0	0	0
Old Harbor	3	10	15	8	7	22	15	11	7	4	4
Oscarville	2	3	2	2	0	3	4	0	0	3	0
Ouzinkie	8	7	15	6	2	6	2	2	6	0	5
Paimiut	0	0	0	0	0	0	0	0	0	0	0
Pedro Bay	0	0	0	8	0	5	2	0	0	3	2
Pelican	2	3	5	1	3	19	4	4	0	2	2
Perryville	2	1	6	3	2	9	11	4	2	0	3
Pilot Point	0	4	4	3	0	3	0	0	2	0	0
Pilot Station	21	41	40	22	17	25	15	18	3	6	7
Pitkas Point	4	3	11	2	0	4	0	11	8	2	2
Platinum	0	4	3	0	3	4	0	3	0	0	0
Point Hope	27	47	34	24	15	41	50	16	12	21	19
Point Lay	3	5	4	7	3	8	3	2	2	1	0
Portage Creek	0	0	0	0	0	0	0	0	0	0	0
Port Graham	2	8	2	0	4	12	4	4	0	0	2
Port Heiden	8	7	11	3	2	7	2	4	6	2	1
Port Lions	0	9	13	7	4	13	9	4	1	0	0
Quinhagak	24	29	27	14	11	18	29	12	12	8	11
Rampart	4	2	3	4	0	0	0	3	0	0	4
Red Devil	2	3	2	0	0	6	3	3	0	2	0
Ruby	1	7	11	6	6	25	17	8	7	0	2
Russian Mission	12	21	19	14	8	12	16	5	6	1	7
St. George	2	4	14	6	4	17	7	3	0	1	0
St. Mary's	0	3	4	2	1	2	0	0	0	0	0
St. Michael	8	13	12	9	3	33	27	16	4	2	12
St. Paul	8	24	27	19	19	25	30	12	7	5	9
Salamatof	4	28	15	16	5	68	37	29	9	15	13
Sand Point	25	19	25	8	15	57	15	22	16	12	9
Savoonga	9	29	25	11	12	33	15	23	11	8	18
Saxman	2	7	18	4	7	28	23	18	7	12	6
Scammon Bay	20	30	24	14	13	18	18	16	4	6	13
Selawik	11	70	31	17	13	57	38	7	15	18	10
Seldovia	6	14	15	13	7	27	5	23	3	7	7
Shageluk	4	13	10	2	0	7	4	5	2	5	0
Shaktoolik	4	19	15	9	0	13	4	4	0	4	0
Sheldon Point	4	12	9	10	2	3	0	2	1	1	2
Shishmaref	11	30	22	8	13	35	17	21	7	8	12

[Continued]

★ 156 ★

Population of Alaska Native Villages, by Age, 1990 - Kasigluk-Takotna, Part I

[Continued]

Alaska Native Village Statistical Area[1]	Number of persons										
	< 1 year	1-2 years	3-4 years	5 years	6 years	7-9 years	10-11 years	12-13 years	14 years	15 years	16 years
Shungnak	8	10	12	2	3	9	15	8	4	3	11
Slana	0	4	2	0	3	5	2	4	0	3	0
Sleetmute	5	6	4	5	2	0	5	5	0	0	0
Solomon	0	0	0	0	0	0	0	0	0	0	0
South Naknek	5	4	6	3	3	13	3	4	4	0	0
Stebbins	24	45	19	9	7	19	25	15	9	9	10
Stevens Village	0	7	6	1	5	9	8	0	1	2	2
Stony River	6	4	0	3	3	0	2	0	0	0	0
Takotna	0	0	0	2	0	5	0	0	2	2	3

Source: Census of Population and Housing, 1990: Summary Tape File 3C on CD-ROM [machine-readable datafiles]. Prepared by the Bureau of the Census. Washington, DC: The Bureau, 1992. *Notes:* 1. Alaska Native villages (ANVs) constitute tribes, bands, clans, groups, villages, communities, or associations in Alaska that are recognized pursuant to the Alaska Native Claims Settlement Act of 1972, Public Law 92-203. Because ANVs do not have legally designated boundaries, the Census Bureau has established Alaska Native village statistical areas (ANVSAs) for statistical purposes. For the 1990 census, the Census Bureau cooperated with officials of the nonprofit corporation within each participating Alaska Native Regional Corporation (ANRC), as well as other knowledgeable officials, to delineate boundaries that encompass the settled area associated with each ANV.

★ 157 ★

Population

Population of Alaska Native Villages, by Age, 1990 - Kasigluk-Takotna, Part II

Alaska Native Village Statistical Area[1]	Number of persons									
	17 years	18 years	19 years	20 years	21 years	22-24 years	25-29 years	30-34 years	35-39 years	40-44 years
Kasigluk	4	0	7	4	3	30	38	40	41	19
Kiana	7	7	9	2	5	6	23	31	6	26
King Cove	0	9	13	11	2	22	72	62	37	28
King Salmon	9	4	10	4	14	72	116	127	59	41
Kipnuk	9	11	6	7	6	25	41	28	36	34
Kivalina	6	2	4	4	5	13	38	11	15	13
Klawock	24	12	14	11	8	45	62	65	79	74
Knik	0	0	0	0	0	8	17	32	34	20
Kobuk	2	0	2	0	3	0	6	4	4	4
Kokhanok	2	3	0	0	0	4	27	16	13	6
Koliganek	2	0	2	2	6	8	24	12	12	9
Kongiganak	0	0	9	2	4	22	27	24	24	9
Kotlik	7	6	7	8	10	18	44	27	23	39
Kotzebue	41	46	46	40	35	138	278	271	221	164
Koyuk	0	5	10	4	0	16	10	17	20	11
Koyukuk	0	3	2	2	0	1	13	14	14	4
Kwethluk	9	9	4	12	9	16	44	42	52	18
Kwigillingok	2	4	4	5	8	21	23	35	22	7
Lake Minchumina	0	0	0	0	0	0	0	0	0	0
Larsen Bay	1	10	8	4	3	8	14	7	11	9
Levelock	4	0	2	2	0	3	14	8	11	10

[Continued]

★ 157 ★

Population of Alaska Native Villages, by Age, 1990 - Kasigluk-Takotna, Part II
[Continued]

Alaska Native Village Statistical Area[1]	Number of persons									
	17 years	18 years	19 years	20 years	21 years	22-24 years	25-29 years	30-34 years	35-39 years	40-44 years
Lime Village	0	0	0	0	0	0	3	2	4	10
Lower Kalskag	4	0	5	3	4	17	24	17	17	20
McGrath	8	1	8	0	5	8	26	47	60	56
Manley Hot Springs	0	0	0	0	0	5	15	14	19	11
Manokotak	0	9	3	6	4	29	57	30	28	5
Marshall	6	4	2	0	2	11	25	14	42	16
Mary's Igloo	0	0	0	0	0	0	0	0	0	0
Medfra	0	0	0	0	0	0	0	0	0	0
Mekoryuk	4	2	0	0	2	4	12	22	15	8
Mentasta Lake	3	2	1	0	2	2	13	6	5	5
Minto	3	4	2	0	2	6	23	13	17	9
Mountain Village	21	24	8	25	10	40	47	40	34	48
Naknek	8	4	2	4	5	12	48	81	75	36
Napaimute	0	0	0	0	0	0	0	0	0	0
Napakiak	0	10	7	2	4	10	34	9	37	13
Napaskiak	12	8	6	4	0	14	23	16	21	17
Nelson Lagoon	0	0	0	0	0	26	17	0	0	13
Nenana	10	6	3	2	0	1	16	30	50	45
Newhalen	0	4	4	1	2	11	12	22	15	5
New Stuyahok	5	11	7	16	11	21	23	41	14	24
Newtok	10	4	6	4	2	10	20	12	14	13
Nightmute	4	6	1	6	10	8	19	7	4	13
Nikolai	0	0	2	2	0	4	11	10	11	6
Nikolski	0	0	0	3	0	0	3	1	0	4
Ninilchik	189	114	81	120	39	268	652	1,152	1,283	844
Noatak	10	5	2	10	8	17	44	28	22	14
Nondalton	0	2	2	0	7	7	31	9	8	3
Noorvik	9	20	0	2	5	35	36	53	24	22
Northway	1	2	0	2	0	0	2	14	10	2
Nuiqsut	2	4	3	0	2	20	46	18	9	14
Nulato	3	2	5	5	4	17	42	30	38	18
Nunapitchuk	7	3	7	5	4	21	42	45	22	17
Ohogamiut	0	0	0	0	0	0	0	0	0	0
Old Harbor	5	8	6	0	4	14	11	30	44	16
Oscarville	2	3	0	0	0	0	6	4	0	2
Ouzinkie	1	2	1	3	0	10	20	19	25	24
Paimiut	0	0	0	0	0	0	0	0	0	0
Pedro Bay	0	2	0	0	0	0	2	2	7	0
Pelican	0	13	4	4	2	5	19	34	31	24
Perryville	4	0	4	0	0	3	7	9	6	6
Pilot Point	1	1	0	0	0	5	3	4	4	6
Pilot Station	9	5	6	7	19	22	37	46	22	16
Pitkas Point	4	2	0	0	0	10	6	17	17	12
Platinum	4	0	0	0	4	5	9	7	2	3
Point Hope	3	4	4	6	7	27	48	57	44	33

[Continued]

★ 157 ★

Population of Alaska Native Villages, by Age, 1990 - Kasigluk-Takotna, Part II
[Continued]

Alaska Native Village Statistical Area[1]	Number of persons								
	17 years	18 years	19 years	20 years	21 years	22-24 years	25-29 years	30-34 years	35-39 years	40-44 years
Point Lay	0	0	3	9	3	15	17	2	11	9
Portage Creek	0	0	0	0	0	0	0	0	0	0
Port Graham	0	6	0	0	2	3	10	22	8	11
Port Heiden	2	0	0	0	2	6	10	17	5	4
Port Lions	2	2	1	2	12	9	19	27	21	11
Quinhagak	4	8	8	9	0	26	49	42	37	25
Rampart	0	0	0	0	5	8	2	0	0	9
Red Devil	0	3	0	0	0	3	2	9	2	6
Ruby	3	0	0	0	0	4	5	17	18	9
Russian Mission	1	2	3	2	5	11	18	27	9	7
St. George	0	3	0	0	0	3	20	9	9	10
St. Mary's	2	0	0	0	0	0	4	7	2	0
St. Michael	11	9	8	0	3	5	8	37	26	22
St. Paul	3	2	15	19	17	78	114	72	58	53
Salamatof	20	10	24	10	10	69	120	105	121	108
Sand Point	11	2	11	10	10	88	104	87	62	74
Savoonga	8	10	2	4	8	30	60	44	31	15
Saxman	7	5	2	8	4	17	31	34	28	28
Scammon Bay	3	3	6	4	10	17	34	22	22	11
Selawik	8	3	2	5	2	23	44	64	37	25
Seldovia	7	2	2	0	0	3	9	39	36	28
Shageluk	0	1	0	0	2	16	12	11	6	6
Shaktoolik	2	0	3	3	4	10	19	8	13	9
Sheldon Point	3	0	3	2	0	8	5	8	4	3
Shishmaref	2	3	17	5	8	24	39	31	23	14
Shungnak	0	2	2	3	0	22	20	16	15	9
Slana	2	0	0	0	0	0	0	15	7	6
Sleetmute	0	0	3	2	0	4	4	11	2	14
Solomon	0	0	0	0	0	0	0	0	2	0
South Naknek	2	3	0	2	0	4	8	21	3	12
Stebbins	10	4	14	5	19	21	42	19	35	28
Stevens Village	2	2	0	0	0	2	6	7	11	11
Stony River	0	2	0	2	0	2	8	7	0	10
Takotna	0	0	0	0	0	0	5	0	5	1

Source: Census of Population and Housing, 1990: Summary Tape File 3C on CD-ROM [machine-readable datafiles]. Prepared by the Bureau of the Census. Washington, DC: The Bureau, 1992. *Notes:* 1. Alaska Native villages (ANVs) constitute tribes, bands, clans, groups, villages, communities, or associations in Alaska that are recognized pursuant to the Alaska Native Claims Settlement Act of 1972, Public Law 92-203. Because ANVs do not have legally designated boundaries, the Census Bureau has established Alaska Native village statistical areas (ANVSAs) for statistical purposes. For the 1990 census, the Census Bureau cooperated with officials of the nonprofit corporation within each participating Alaska Native Regional Corporation (ANRC), as well as other knowledgeable officials, to delineate boundaries that encompass the settled area associated with each ANV.

★ 158 ★

Population

Population of Alaska Native Villages, by Age, 1990 - Kasigluk-Takotna, Part III

Alaska Native Village Statistical Area[1]	Number of persons									
	45-49 years	50-54 years	55-59 years	60-61 years	62-64 years	65-69 years	70-74 years	75-79 years	80-84 years	85 + years
Kasigluk	14	8	8	2	0	12	15	4	3	0
Kiana	16	12	17	2	12	9	7	2	0	2
King Cove	49	13	21	0	7	11	1	0	0	0
King Salmon	57	30	5	14	6	3	2	0	0	0
Kipnuk	21	12	14	3	2	4	1	10	3	0
Kivalina	4	23	9	4	1	0	0	6	0	0
Klawock	31	31	16	11	6	21	5	0	0	0
Knik	15	8	13	6	6	11	15	4	0	0
Kobuk	3	1	3	0	0	0	0	6	0	0
Kokhanok	5	10	5	6	2	2	1	0	0	0
Koliganek	4	3	10	2	0	8	4	0	4	0
Kongiganak	19	5	4	2	3	2	7	0	5	2
Kotlik	21	9	9	3	4	14	8	7	2	0
Kotzebue	123	83	77	13	33	33	18	24	15	16
Koyuk	11	12	2	2	2	3	0	16	1	0
Koyukuk	0	4	5	0	0	3	2	4	0	0
Kwethluk	20	14	23	5	6	11	10	12	0	7
Kwigillingok	8	4	6	4	0	9	10	4	5	2
Lake Minchumina	7	8	7	0	7	0	0	0	0	0
Larsen Bay	8	3	9	0	4	4	4	0	0	0
Levelock	2	2	0	9	2	6	0	2	0	0
Lime Village	2	0	0	0	0	2	0	3	0	2
Lower Kalskag	8	13	6	1	0	4	6	0	4	1
McGrath	51	12	10	9	2	4	4	3	5	0
Manley Hot Springs	9	6	5	0	0	3	3	3	0	0
Manokotak	10	18	10	4	4	4	9	0	3	0
Marshall	13	12	3	0	2	4	6	5	2	0
Mary's Igloo	0	0	0	0	0	0	0	0	0	0
Medfra	0	0	0	0	0	0	0	0	0	0
Mekoryuk	8	2	2	6	0	5	8	5	0	2
Mentasta Lake	2	6	2	2	4	9	6	2	0	0
Minto	7	6	6	2	1	4	12	3	0	3
Mountain Village	28	17	22	9	11	4	12	7	3	0
Naknek	30	27	23	2	3	5	9	5	5	0
Napaimute	0	0	0	0	0	0	0	0	0	0
Napakiak	17	20	9	7	0	12	6	7	2	2
Napaskiak	14	6	13	6	8	5	4	0	1	1
Nelson Lagoon	4	8	0	0	0	5	0	0	0	0
Nenana	23	8	7	12	14	5	12	2	5	2
Newhalen	11	0	3	0	2	2	1	1	0	0
New Stuyahok	28	11	6	4	3	3	4	7	2	6
Newtok	8	10	8	0	0	1	2	3	0	0
Nightmute	9	4	9	3	2	2	4	1	0	6
Nikolai	4	5	11	0	0	2	2	2	2	0
Nikolski	3	6	0	0	0	0	4	4	2	0
Ninilchik	695	439	318	123	196	296	90	127	82	27

[Continued]

★ 158 ★

Population of Alaska Native Villages, by Age, 1990 - Kasigluk-Takotna, Part III
[Continued]

Alaska Native Village Statistical Area[1]	Number of persons								
	45-49 years	50-54 years	55-59 years	60-61 years	62-64 years	65-69 years	70-74 years	75-79 years	80-84 years	85 + years
Noatak	11	16	15	6	0	5	7	0	1	2
Nondalton	17	3	10	4	10	6	2	5	0	0
Noorvik	22	10	27	12	11	15	7	4	0	2
Northway	13	2	6	1	0	7	0	0	0	4
Nuiqsut	22	14	18	1	1	9	4	2	2	0
Nulato	17	10	11	4	6	3	5	7	0	0
Nunapitchuk	20	6	4	5	6	10	9	7	9	0
Ohogamiut	0	0	0	0	0	0	0	0	0	0
Old Harbor	6	9	5	0	3	4	5	0	0	0
Oscarville	2	0	2	3	0	0	0	1	0	0
Ouzinkie	17	6	7	5	1	0	4	2	5	3
Paimiut	0	0	0	0	0	0	0	0	0	0
Pedro Bay	2	0	2	0	2	0	2	0	0	0
Pelican	4	2	8	1	0	12	2	2	0	0
Perryville	13	2	2	1	2	1	5	0	0	2
Pilot Point	0	7	0	0	0	3	3	1	0	0
Pilot Station	15	6	9	11	8	5	5	0	4	0
Pitkas Point	3	7	2	0	0	2	0	0	2	0
Platinum	4	4	2	0	0	2	4	0	0	0
Point Hope	23	19	25	5	2	6	0	5	5	0
Point Lay	24	2	4	0	6	3	2	0	0	0
Portage Creek	0	0	0	0	0	0	0	4	0	0
Port Graham	10	15	5	9	0	1	0	5	0	0
Port Heiden	6	4	0	0	2	0	0	0	0	0
Port Lions	3	9	6	2	2	3	13	2	0	0
Quinhagak	24	15	14	5	16	11	13	6	2	0
Rampart	15	3	3	0	4	0	0	3	0	0
Red Devil	0	0	2	0	0	6	0	0	0	0
Ruby	3	11	1	0	4	0	3	2	3	2
Russian Mission	2	5	5	0	4	15	3	0	0	0
St. George	1	8	7	0	5	0	0	6	2	2
St. Mary's	0	1	4	2	0	0	0	0	0	0
St. Michael	16	12	6	2	1	2	4	2	2	0
St. Paul	41	28	28	8	6	7	8	10	0	0
Salamatof	36	22	38	10	10	14	23	9	9	0
Sand Point	58	43	37	14	9	5	9	2	0	0
Savoonga	22	23	31	9	0	10	3	10	0	0
Saxman	23	21	9	1	6	15	9	0	0	0
Scammon Bay	11	9	3	0	3	4	4	0	0	4
Selawik	10	13	5	6	13	7	5	7	6	7
Seldovia	21	6	6	4	6	5	2	6	2	4
Shageluk	0	2	5	5	5	8	3	1	0	0
Shaktoolik	3	6	6	2	2	6	3	4	0	0
Sheldon Point	10	3	7	0	4	6	0	0	0	0
Shishmaref	17	12	22	6	12	2	8	4	0	0

[Continued]

★ 158 ★

Population of Alaska Native Villages, by Age, 1990 - Kasigluk-Takotna, Part III
[Continued]

Alaska Native Village Statistical Area[1]	Number of persons									
	45-49 years	50-54 years	55-59 years	60-61 years	62-64 years	65-69 years	70-74 years	75-79 years	80-84 years	85 + years
Shungnak	3	9	8	9	6	10	3	3	0	0
Slana	4	0	0	0	2	0	0	0	2	2
Sleetmute	8	11	10	4	3	2	0	2	3	0
Solomon	0	0	0	2	0	2	0	0	0	0
South Naknek	9	9	9	0	0	6	0	0	0	0
Stebbins	9	2	7	10	4	8	4	11	2	3
Stevens Village	3	3	2	0	2	5	2	2	0	0
Stony River	0	0	0	0	0	0	0	0	0	0
Takotna	7	2	0	2	0	0	0	0	0	0

Source: Census of Population and Housing, 1990: Summary Tape File 3C on CD-ROM [machine-readable datafiles]. Prepared by the Bureau of the Census. Washington, DC: The Bureau, 1992. *Notes:* 1. Alaska Native villages (ANVs) constitute tribes, bands, clans, groups, villages, communities, or associations in Alaska that are recognized pursuant to the Alaska Native Claims Settlement Act of 1972, Public Law 92-203. Because ANVs do not have legally designated boundaries, the Census Bureau has established Alaska Native village statistical areas (ANVSAs) for statistical purposes. For the 1990 census, the Census Bureau cooperated with officials of the nonprofit corporation within each participating Alaska Native Regional Corporation (ANRC), as well as other knowledgeable officials, to delineate boundaries that encompass the settled area associated with each ANV.

★ 159 ★

Population

Population of Alaska Native Villages, by Age, 1990 - Tanacross-Yakutat, Part I

Alaska Native Village Statistical Area[1]	Number of persons										
	< 1 year	1-2 years	3-4 years	5 years	6 years	7-9 years	10-11 years	12-13 years	14 years	15 years	16 years
Tanacross	0	1	2	3	0	8	0	8	4	2	5
Tanana	3	12	15	13	9	32	15	7	0	2	8
Tatitlek	4	3	10	1	3	9	7	7	1	4	0
Tazlina	3	9	13	4	15	20	15	11	0	3	2
Telida	0	0	0	0	0	0	0	0	0	0	0
Teller	0	14	11	2	6	5	11	6	4	0	5
Tenakee Springs	3	2	2	0	0	4	2	2	0	0	0
Tetlin	4	0	9	0	0	5	3	4	1	0	0
Togiak	16	36	38	12	29	42	28	14	9	5	8
Tok	17	24	33	20	13	69	20	34	18	13	16
Toksook Bay	5	31	25	5	7	22	18	13	12	8	4
Tuluksak	5	22	19	7	26	25	16	10	4	10	8
Tuntutuliak	10	14	13	3	6	24	16	15	6	8	2
Tununak	15	17	23	10	8	17	6	8	2	2	10
Twin Hills	6	1	2	0	0	0	2	0	0	0	0
Tyonek	0	2	1	2	4	5	3	7	4	0	5
Ugashik	0	0	0	0	0	0	0	0	0	0	0
Ukivok	0	0	0	0	0	0	0	0	0	0	0
Unalakleet	4	27	51	13	28	34	45	14	22	17	10
Unalaska	23	59	67	34	26	74	26	18	12	20	9
Venetie	3	4	12	2	0	11	15	5	6	8	5

[Continued]

★ 159 ★

Population of Alaska Native Villages, by Age, 1990 - Tanacross-Yakutat, Part I
[Continued]

Alaska Native Village Statistical Area[1]	Number of persons										
	< 1 year	1-2 years	3-4 years	5 years	6 years	7-9 years	10-11 years	12-13 years	14 years	15 years	16 years
Wainwright	3	32	32	15	18	51	27	14	10	3	7
Wales	2	12	17	2	0	13	9	3	2	0	2
White Mountain	6	12	8	5	7	14	4	6	4	1	2
Wiseman	0	0	0	8	0	10	0	0	0	0	0
Yakutat	7	16	20	12	15	31	27	19	8	6	5

Source: Census of Population and Housing, 1990: Summary Tape File 3C on CD-ROM [machine-readable datafiles]. Prepared by the Bureau of the Census. Washington, DC: The Bureau, 1992. *Notes:* 1. Alaska Native villages (ANVs) constitute tribes, bands, clans, groups, villages, communities, or associations in Alaska that are recognized pursuant to the Alaska Native Claims Settlement Act of 1972, Public Law 92-203. Because ANVs do not have legally designated boundaries, the Census Bureau has established Alaska Native village statistical areas (ANVSAs) for statistical purposes. For the 1990 census, the Census Bureau cooperated with officials of the nonprofit corporation within each participating Alaska Native Regional Corporation (ANRC), as well as other knowledgeable officials, to delineate boundaries that encompass the settled area associated with each ANV.

★ 160 ★
Population

Population of Alaska Native Villages, by Age, 1990 - Tanacross-Yakutat, Part II

Alaska Native Village Statistical Area[1]	Number of persons									
	17 years	18 years	19 years	20 years	21 years	22-24 years	25-29 years	30-34 years	35-39 years	40-44 years
Tanacross	2	3	0	0	0	5	3	4	10	7
Tanana	0	7	11	2	0	14	13	55	27	30
Tatitlek	5	4	2	3	1	3	7	8	18	1
Tazlina	2	6	0	0	0	3	11	35	22	28
Telida	0	0	0	0	0	0	0	0	0	0
Teller	2	0	0	0	3	2	16	20	8	6
Tenakee Springs	0	0	0	0	0	0	4	5	13	10
Tetlin	2	0	0	0	3	5	10	5	6	9
Togiak	10	11	9	10	5	23	48	62	85	13
Tok	12	9	10	3	14	31	52	95	112	84
Toksook Bay	18	20	10	8	10	21	41	20	23	11
Tuluksak	3	4	2	4	13	19	26	32	29	22
Tuntutuliak	8	1	3	5	7	21	19	25	24	14
Tununak	4	8	7	3	3	25	31	30	7	7
Twin Hills	0	0	0	0	0	0	5	14	0	2
Tyonek	4	2	3	0	0	12	6	6	10	9
Ugashik	0	1	0	0	0	1	0	2	1	0
Ukivok	0	0	0	0	0	0	0	0	0	0
Unalakleet	15	0	9	0	4	15	67	43	40	76
Unalaska	18	12	48	116	38	286	780	369	349	245
Venetie	2	6	7	0	3	6	15	18	12	8
Wainwright	7	6	0	2	3	21	37	64	39	16
Wales	2	3	3	0	2	8	8	22	7	12
White Mountain	4	0	0	2	2	3	15	19	19	11

[Continued]

★ 160 ★

Population of Alaska Native Villages, by Age, 1990 - Tanacross-Yakutat, Part II
[Continued]

Alaska Native Village Statistical Area[1]	Number of persons									
	17 years	18 years	19 years	20 years	21 years	22-24 years	25-29 years	30-34 years	35-39 years	40-44 years
Wiseman	0	0	0	0	0	0	0	16	0	0
Yakutat	8	3	10	9	9	33	41	54	58	57

Source: Census of Population and Housing, 1990: Summary Tape File 3C on CD-ROM [machine-readable datafiles]. Prepared by the Bureau of the Census. Washington, DC: The Bureau, 1992. *Notes:* 1. Alaska Native villages (ANVs) constitute tribes, bands, clans, groups, villages, communities, or associations in Alaska that are recognized pursuant to the Alaska Native Claims Settlement Act of 1972, Public Law 92-203. Because ANVs do not have legally designated boundaries, the Census Bureau has established Alaska Native village statistical areas (ANVSAs) for statistical purposes. For the 1990 census, the Census Bureau cooperated with officials of the nonprofit corporation within each participating Alaska Native Regional Corporation (ANRC), as well as other knowledgeable officials, to delineate boundaries that encompass the settled area associated with each ANV.

★ 161 ★

Population

Population of Alaska Native Villages, by Age, 1990 - Tanacross-Yakutat, Part III

Alaska Native Village Statistical Area[1]	Number of persons									
	45-49 years	50-54 years	55-59 years	60-61 years	62-64 years	65-69 years	70-74 years	75-79 years	80-84 years	85 + years
Tanacross	7	13	6	2	0	4	0	3	0	3
Tanana	7	19	12	4	5	6	8	6	7	0
Tatitlek	4	5	0	1	0	0	0	0	0	0
Tazlina	33	3	10	4	1	2	0	0	0	3
Telida	10	0	0	0	0	0	0	0	0	0
Teller	14	4	5	4	0	4	0	2	0	0
Tenakee Springs	3	3	7	0	3	7	13	6	3	0
Tetlin	2	2	7	2	1	3	3	5	0	0
Togiak	18	14	18	6	7	10	7	9	4	0
Tok	91	43	26	5	21	13	28	6	3	0
Toksook Bay	26	15	9	10	5	5	0	1	2	0
Tuluksak	9	7	8	12	0	4	2	3	0	2
Tuntutuliak	10	11	8	5	6	11	2	3	0	0
Tununak	17	8	10	3	7	0	10	2	0	0
Twin Hills	0	4	5	0	0	0	1	2	0	0
Tyonek	13	3	4	0	1	3	8	0	4	0
Ugashik	0	0	0	0	1	0	0	0	0	0
Ukivok	0	0	0	0	0	0	0	0	0	0
Unalakleet	24	21	15	0	14	14	14	2	8	0
Unalaska	190	166	72	9	7	6	5	1	2	2
Venetie	6	2	15	1	1	3	0	6	0	0
Wainwright	6	33	17	12	6	2	6	8	0	5
Wales	3	3	4	0	5	7	5	0	0	3
White Mountain	1	6	5	0	2	6	3	2	5	0

[Continued]

★ 161 ★

Population of Alaska Native Villages, by Age, 1990 - Tanacross-Yakutat, Part III
[Continued]

Alaska Native Village Statistical Area[1]	Number of persons									
	45-49 years	50-54 years	55-59 years	60-61 years	62-64 years	65-69 years	70-74 years	75-79 years	80-84 years	85 + years
Wiseman	0	0	0	0	0	0	0	0	0	0
Yakutat	27	14	10	6	11	12	5	3	8	0

Source: Census of Population and Housing, 1990: Summary Tape File 3C on CD-ROM [machine-readable datafiles]. Prepared by the Bureau of the Census. Washington, DC: The Bureau, 1992. *Notes:* 1. Alaska Native villages (ANVs) constitute tribes, bands, clans, groups, villages, communities, or associations in Alaska that are recognized pursuant to the Alaska Native Claims Settlement Act of 1972, Public Law 92-203. Because ANVs do not have legally designated boundaries, the Census Bureau has established Alaska Native village statistical areas (ANVSAs) for statistical purposes. For the 1990 census, the Census Bureau cooperated with officials of the nonprofit corporation within each participating Alaska Native Regional Corporation (ANRC), as well as other knowledgeable officials, to delineate boundaries that encompass the settled area associated with each ANV.

★ 162 ★

Population

Population of Alaska Native Villages, by Sex and Race, 1990 - Akhiok-Kasaan

Alaska Native Village Statistical Area[1]	Number of persons							
	Total	Sex		Race				
		Male	Female	White	Black	American Indian, Eskimo, or Aleut	Asian or Pacific Islander	Other race
Akhiok	81	50	31	0	0	81	0	0
Akiachak	462	232	230	42	0	416	4	0
Akiak	285	134	151	13	0	272	0	0
Akutan	605	497	108	250	7	81	237	30
Alakanuk	540	269	271	22	0	518	0	0
Alatna	23	14	9	0	0	23	0	0
Aleknagik	194	95	99	19	0	175	0	0
Alexander	37	23	14	37	0	0	0	0
Allakaket	143	78	65	12	0	131	0	0
Ambler	317	185	132	25	0	290	2	0
Anaktuvuk Pass	272	145	127	34	0	238	0	0
Andreafsky	406	221	185	61	0	345	0	0
Angoon	643	353	290	122	0	507	5	9
Aniak	529	270	259	154	16	352	5	2
Anvik	78	33	45	7	0	71	0	0
Arctic Village	92	35	57	6	0	86	0	0
Atka	101	51	50	8	0	93	0	0
Atkasook	213	114	99	8	4	201	0	0
Atmautluak	262	144	118	9	0	253	0	0
Barrow	2,750	1,428	1,322	754	14	1,756	198	28
Beaver	96	56	40	3	0	93	0	0
Belkofski	0	0	0	0	0	0	0	0
Bethel	4,687	2,448	2,239	1,574	37	2,994	65	17
Bill Moore's	0	0	0	0	0	0	0	0
Birch Creek	41	23	18	5	0	36	0	0

[Continued]

★ 162 ★

Population of Alaska Native Villages, by Sex and Race, 1990 - Akhiok-Kasaan
[Continued]

Alaska Native Village Statistical Area[1]	Number of persons							
	Total	Sex		Race				
						American Indian, Eskimo, or Aleut	Asian or Pacific Islander	Other race
		Male	Female	White	Black			
Brevig Mission	188	92	96	20	0	168	0	0
Buckland	317	174	143	2	0	315	0	0
Cantwell	145	82	63	104	2	39	0	0
Canyon Village	0	0	0	0	0	0	0	0
Chalkyitsik	95	46	49	4	0	91	0	0
Chefornak	310	168	142	8	0	302	0	0
Chenega	94	55	39	32	0	62	0	0
Chevak	597	336	261	34	0	559	4	0
Chignik	171	118	53	90	0	78	3	0
Chignik Lagoon	78	46	32	32	0	46	0	0
Chignik Lake	125	68	57	19	0	106	0	0
Chilkat	140	71	69	16	0	122	0	2
Chilkoot	219	130	89	201	0	16	2	0
Chistochina	62	32	30	19	0	43	0	0
Chitina	46	26	20	28	1	17	0	0
Chuathbaluk	99	58	41	10	0	89	0	0
Chulloonawick	0	0	0	0	0	0	0	0
Circle	73	41	32	12	0	58	0	3
Clark's Point	62	33	29	16	0	46	0	0
Copper Center	426	221	205	282	0	144	0	0
Council	6	4	2	2	0	4	0	0
Craig	1,260	674	586	964	0	288	2	6
Crooked Creek	108	58	50	10	0	98	0	0
Deering	157	88	69	5	0	152	0	0
Dillingham	2,017	1,014	1,003	831	0	1,122	53	11
Dot Lake	49	28	21	31	0	18	0	0
Eagle	35	22	13	5	0	30	0	0
Eek	264	141	123	10	0	254	0	0
Egegik	120	67	53	36	0	84	0	0
Eklutna	381	204	177	326	6	31	16	2
Ekuk	0	0	0	0	0	0	0	0
Ekwok	73	34	39	8	0	65	0	0
Elim	269	155	114	21	0	248	0	0
Emmonak	610	314	296	54	3	538	12	3
English Bay	161	86	75	14	0	147	0	0
Evansville	64	36	28	35	0	27	2	0
Eyak	168	92	76	150	0	13	2	3
False Pass	67	41	26	8	0	59	0	0
Fort Yukon	579	330	249	77	0	502	0	0
Gakona	20	8	12	20	0	0	0	0
Galena	806	549	257	398	30	368	10	0
Gambell	548	315	233	6	0	542	0	0

[Continued]

★ 162 ★

Population of Alaska Native Villages, by Sex and Race, 1990 - Akhiok-Kasaan
[Continued]

Alaska Native Village Statistical Area[1]	Number of persons							
	Total	Sex		Race				
				White	Black	American Indian, Eskimo, or Aleut	Asian or Pacific Islander	Other race
		Male	Female					
Georgetown	0	0	0	0	0	0	0	0
Golovin	123	66	57	10	0	113	0	0
Goodnews Bay	232	121	111	14	0	218	0	0
Grayling	217	118	99	9	0	208	0	0
Grouse Creek Group	630	335	295	526	0	104	0	0
Gulkana	113	68	45	38	0	75	0	0
Hamilton	0	0	0	0	0	0	0	0
Healy Lake	48	27	21	6	0	42	0	0
Holy Cross	0	0	0	0	0	0	0	0
Hoonah	729	363	366	202	0	527	0	0
Hooper Bay	846	428	418	29	0	817	0	0
Hughes	60	38	22	9	0	51	0	0
Huslia	192	91	101	16	0	176	0	0
Hydaburg	388	227	161	32	1	353	2	0
Igiugig	29	12	17	9	0	20	0	0
Iliamna	66	31	35	16	0	48	0	2
Inalik	192	101	91	9	0	183	0	0
Ivanof Bay	38	22	16	8	0	30	0	0
Kake	687	380	307	171	0	516	0	0
Kaktovik	235	127	108	39	0	194	2	0
Kalskag	163	90	73	26	1	136	0	0
Kaltag	241	132	109	20	0	221	0	0
Karluk	82	46	36	8	0	74	0	0
Kasaan	54	26	28	12	0	42	0	0

Source: Census of Population and Housing, 1990: Summary Tape File 3C on CD-ROM [machine-readable datafiles]. Prepared by the Bureau of the Census. Washington, DC: The Bureau, 1992. *Notes:* 1. Alaska Native villages (ANVs) constitute tribes, bands, clans, groups, villages, communities, or associations in Alaska that are recognized pursuant to the Alaska Native Claims Settlement Act of 1972, Public Law 92-203. Because ANVs do not have legally designated boundaries, the Census Bureau has established Alaska Native village statistical areas (ANVSAs) for statistical purposes. For the 1990 census, the Census Bureau cooperated with officials of the nonprofit corporation within each participating Alaska Native Regional Corporation (ANRC), as well as other knowledgeable officials, to delineate boundaries that encompass the settled area associated with each ANV.

★ 163 ★
Population

Population of Alaska Native Villages, by Sex and Race, 1990 - Kasigluk-Takotna

Alaska Native Village Statistical Area[1]	Number of persons							
	Total	Sex		Race				
		Male	Female	White	Black	American Indian, Eskimo, or Aleut	Asian or Pacific Islander	Other race
Kasigluk	440	211	229	24	0	416	0	0
Kiana	367	174	193	28	0	339	0	0
King Cove	457	256	201	119	0	184	138	16
King Salmon	684	463	221	528	31	105	13	7
Kipnuk	462	260	202	8	0	452	2	0
Kivalina	304	165	139	5	0	299	0	0
Klawock	705	395	310	324	0	377	4	0
Knik	276	160	116	237	0	37	2	0
Kobuk	72	36	36	11	0	61	0	0
Kokhanok	161	86	75	10	0	151	0	0
Koliganek	191	87	104	9	0	182	0	0
Kongiganak	313	182	131	6	0	307	0	0
Kotlik	462	235	227	11	3	448	0	0
Kotzebue	2,751	1,399	1,352	637	7	2,065	42	0
Koyuk	240	133	107	8	0	232	0	0
Koyukuk	112	68	44	2	0	110	0	0
Kwethluk	568	308	260	10	13	543	0	2
Kwigillingok	258	144	114	8	0	250	0	0
Lake Minchumina	29	15	14	22	0	7	0	0
Larsen Bay	164	82	82	21	0	143	0	0
Levelock	112	61	51	14	0	98	0	0
Lime Village	47	27	20	3	0	44	0	0
Lower Kalskag	289	152	137	2	2	285	0	0
McGrath	524	256	268	266	0	258	0	0
Manley Hot Springs	123	69	54	84	0	39	0	0
Manokotak	398	229	169	17	0	381	0	0
Marshall	283	152	131	20	5	252	6	0
Mary's Igloo	0	0	0	0	0	0	0	0
Medfra	0	0	0	0	0	0	0	0
Mekoryuk	168	96	72	0	0	168	0	0
Mentasta Lake	102	50	52	22	0	80	0	0
Minto	197	102	95	5	0	192	0	0
Mountain Village	706	361	345	57	4	640	5	0
Naknek	590	300	290	338	0	252	0	0
Napaimute	0	0	0	0	0	0	0	0
Napakiak	334	176	158	9	2	323	0	0
Napaskiak	326	162	164	16	0	310	0	0
Nelson Lagoon	80	44	36	9	0	71	0	0
Nenana	377	204	173	206	12	156	3	0
Newhalen	192	93	99	15	0	177	0	0
New Stuyahok	398	208	190	17	0	381	0	0
Newtok	217	103	114	18	0	199	0	0
Nightmute	174	80	94	3	0	168	0	3

[Continued]

★ 163 ★

Population of Alaska Native Villages, by Sex and Race, 1990 - Kasigluk-Takotna
[Continued]

Alaska Native Village Statistical Area[1]	Number of persons							
	Total	Sex		Race				
		Male	Female	White	Black	American Indian, Eskimo, or Aleut	Asian or Pacific Islander	Other race
Nikolai	113	69	44	9	0	104	0	0
Nikolski	38	25	13	13	0	25	0	0
Ninilchik	10,491	5,517	4,974	9,926	61	411	85	8
Noatak	352	208	144	8	0	344	0	0
Nondalton	172	97	75	18	0	154	0	0
Noorvik	548	284	264	29	0	519	0	0
Northway	121	76	45	6	0	113	0	2
Nuiqsut	335	181	154	16	0	319	0	0
Nulato	399	203	196	7	0	392	0	0
Nunapitchuk	385	203	182	10	0	375	0	0
Ohogamiut	0	0	0	0	0	0	0	0
Old Harbor	276	156	120	16	0	253	0	7
Oscarville	44	26	18	0	0	44	0	0
Ouzinkie	214	119	95	31	0	183	0	0
Paimiut	0	0	0	0	0	0	0	0
Pedro Bay	41	14	27	0	0	41	0	0
Pelican	212	131	81	130	0	74	1	7
Perryville	110	71	39	5	0	105	0	0
Pilot Point	54	29	25	7	0	47	0	0
Pilot Station	467	239	228	15	0	452	0	0
Pitkas Point	131	63	68	8	0	123	0	0
Platinum	67	39	28	3	0	64	0	0
Point Hope	629	365	264	39	2	585	3	0
Point Lay	148	92	56	27	0	121	0	0
Portage Creek	4	4	0	4	0	0	0	0
Port Graham	145	78	67	19	0	124	2	0
Port Heiden	111	63	48	27	0	84	0	0
Port Lions	206	116	90	73	0	133	0	0
Quinhagak	509	266	243	39	0	468	2	0
Rampart	72	44	28	0	0	72	0	0
Red Devil	54	29	25	14	0	40	0	0
Ruby	175	105	70	44	0	129	2	0
Russian Mission	240	137	103	11	0	229	0	0
St. George	143	59	84	5	0	138	0	0
St. Mary's	34	17	17	7	0	27	0	0
St. Michael	315	157	158	25	0	290	0	0
St. Paul	752	489	263	160	24	531	25	12
Salamatof	1,007	613	394	872	24	110	1	0
Sand Point	859	531	328	287	0	422	87	63
Savoonga	514	259	255	19	0	495	0	0
Saxman	380	209	171	55	0	321	2	2
Scammon Bay	346	164	182	7	0	337	2	0

[Continued]

★ 163 ★

Population of Alaska Native Villages, by Sex and Race, 1990 - Kasigluk-Takotna
[Continued]

Alaska Native Village Statistical Area[1]	Number of persons							
	Total	Sex		Race				
		Male	Female	White	Black	American Indian, Eskimo, or Aleut	Asian or Pacific Islander	Other race
Selawik	579	331	248	21	3	555	0	0
Seldovia	315	155	160	262	0	39	7	7
Shageluk	135	74	61	4	0	131	0	0
Shaktoolik	175	93	82	8	0	167	0	0
Sheldon Point	112	61	51	7	0	99	6	0
Shishmaref	433	224	209	15	0	418	0	0
Shungnak	225	112	113	8	0	217	0	0
Slana	63	29	34	61	0	2	0	0
Sleetmute	115	56	59	22	0	93	0	0
Solomon	6	6	0	0	0	6	0	0
South Naknek	133	77	56	28	0	105	0	0
Stebbins	448	224	224	21	0	427	0	0
Stevens Village	101	56	45	0	0	101	0	0
Stony River	49	20	29	0	0	49	0	0
Takotna	36	18	18	25	0	9	2	0

Source: Census of Population and Housing, 1990: Summary Tape File 3C on CD-ROM [machine-readable datafiles]. Prepared by the Bureau of the Census. Washington, DC: The Bureau, 1992. *Notes:* 1. Alaska Native villages (ANVs) constitute tribes, bands, clans, groups, villages, communities, or associations in Alaska that are recognized pursuant to the Alaska Native Claims Settlement Act of 1972, Public Law 92-203. Because ANVs do not have legally designated boundaries, the Census Bureau has established Alaska Native village statistical areas (ANVSAs) for statistical purposes. For the 1990 census, the Census Bureau cooperated with officials of the nonprofit corporation within each participating Alaska Native Regional Corporation (ANRC), as well as other knowledgeable officials, to delineate boundaries that encompass the settled area associated with each ANV.

★ 164 ★

Population

Population of Alaska Native Villages, by Sex and Race, 1990 - Tanacross-Yakutat

Alaska Native Village Statistical Area[1]	Number of persons							
	Total	Sex		Race				
		Male	Female	White	Black	American Indian, Eskimo, or Aleut	Asian or Pacific Islander	Other race
Tanacross	105	57	48	0	0	105	0	0
Tanana	349	202	147	75	0	274	0	0
Tatitlek	111	36	75	13	0	98	0	0
Tazlina	258	147	111	177	0	80	1	0
Telida	10	0	10	10	0	0	0	0
Teller	154	94	60	21	0	133	0	0
Tenakee Springs	92	47	45	76	0	13	3	0
Tetlin	91	55	36	7	0	84	0	0
Togiak	606	322	284	85	2	519	0	0

[Continued]

★ 164 ★

Population of Alaska Native Villages, by Sex and Race, 1990 - Tanacross-Yakutat
[Continued]

Alaska Native Village Statistical Area[1]	Number of persons							
	Total	Sex		Race				
		Male	Female	White	Black	American Indian, Eskimo, or Aleut	Asian or Pacific Islander	Other race
Tok	935	509	426	840	0	87	8	0
Toksook Bay	405	204	201	13	0	389	3	0
Tuluksak	353	183	170	21	0	329	3	0
Tuntutuliak	300	161	139	15	0	283	0	2
Tununak	300	158	142	11	0	286	3	0
Twin Hills	44	28	16	7	0	37	0	0
Tyonek	121	69	52	12	0	109	0	0
Ugashik	6	5	1	2	0	4	0	0
Ukivok	0	0	0	0	0	0	0	0
Unalakleet	646	364	282	129	0	510	7	0
Unalaska	3,089	2,180	909	1,917	49	273	597	253
Venetie	182	97	85	11	0	171	0	0
Wainwright	502	242	260	30	0	472	0	0
Wales	159	88	71	16	0	140	0	3
White Mountain	174	87	87	25	2	145	2	0
Wiseman	34	18	16	34	0	0	0	0
Yakutat	544	287	257	241	0	290	13	0

Source: Census of Population and Housing, 1990: Summary Tape File 3C on CD-ROM [machine-readable datafiles]. Prepared by the Bureau of the Census. Washington, DC: The Bureau, 1992. Notes: 1. Alaska Native villages (ANVs) constitute tribes, bands, clans, groups, villages, communities, or associations in Alaska that are recognized pursuant to the Alaska Native Claims Settlement Act of 1972, Public Law 92-203. Because ANVs do not have legally designated boundaries, the Census Bureau has established Alaska Native village statistical areas (ANVSAs) for statistical purposes. For the 1990 census, the Census Bureau cooperated with officials of the nonprofit corporation within each participating Alaska Native Regional Corporation (ANRC), as well as other knowledgeable officials, to delineate boundaries that encompass the settled area associated with each ANV.

★ 165 ★

Population

Population of American Indian Reservations and Trust Lands, by Age, 1990 - Acoma-Colville, Part I

American Indian Reservation and Trust Lands[1,2]	Number of persons										
	< 1 year	1-2 years	3-4 years	5 years	6 years	7-9 years	10-11 years	12-13 years	14 years	15 years	16 years
Acoma Pueblo and Trust Lands, NM	74	95	106	72	41	168	117	131	51	63	40
Agua Caliente Reservation	66	278	284	98	86	350	321	159	107	148	74
Alabama and Coushatta Reservation	5	17	21	13	6	21	21	49	7	10	9
Alamo Navajo Reservation	23	49	64	22	41	76	67	63	39	33	35
Allegany Reservation	124	229	227	101	99	334	185	209	102	94	86
Alturas Rancheria	0	0	0	0	0	0	0	0	0	0	0
Annette Islands Reserve	10	78	64	34	52	98	70	54	9	35	27
Augustine Reservation	0	0	0	0	0	0	0	0	0	0	0
Bad River Reservation	31	43	47	36	26	64	47	30	17	17	25
Barona Rancheria	16	8	14	8	10	24	22	23	13	5	25

[Continued]

★ 165 ★

Population of American Indian Reservations and Trust Lands, by Age, 1990 - Acoma-Colville, Part I
[Continued]

American Indian Reservation and Trust Lands[1,2]	Number of persons										
	< 1 year	1-2 years	3-4 years	5 years	6 years	7-9 years	10-11 years	12-13 years	14 years	15 years	16 years
Bay Mills Reservation	5	18	22	11	14	19	29	15	11	5	6
Benton Paiute Reservation	0	4	6	1	1	8	4	0	3	0	0
Berry Creek Rancheria	0	0	0	0	0	0	0	0	0	0	0
Big Bend Rancheria	0	0	0	0	3	0	0	0	0	0	0
Big Cypress Reservation	3	22	8	0	3	19	29	25	7	6	11
Big Lagoon Rancheria	0	0	0	0	0	3	0	2	0	0	0
Big Pine Rancheria	5	21	16	6	18	20	23	23	8	12	8
Big Sandy Rancheria	3	6	2	0	0	2	4	2	0	0	0
Big Valley Rancheria	0	0	0	0	0	0	0	10	7	0	0
Bishop Rancheria	26	61	45	30	42	106	53	57	30	25	15
Blackfeet Reservation	143	456	455	251	203	645	367	380	139	180	134
Blue Lake Rancheria	0	0	0	0	2	4	3	2	0	0	0
Bois Forte (Nett Lake) Reservation	5	25	13	6	7	13	19	22	8	5	3
Bridgeport Colony	0	3	4	0	0	2	0	2	0	0	1
Brighton Reservation	6	16	0	6	0	47	17	53	0	17	7
Burns Paiute Reservation and Trust Lands, OR	4	8	9	2	0	13	6	12	3	8	13
Cabazon Reservation	20	24	43	17	22	74	38	34	29	20	15
Cahuilla Reservation	2	6	1	5	1	2	10	6	3	2	2
Campo Reservation	6	10	25	4	8	13	6	3	6	0	0
Camp Verde Reservation	10	60	38	19	23	57	13	31	12	9	7
Canoncito Reservation	49	56	68	24	18	94	35	44	35	24	31
Capitan Grande Reservation	0	0	0	0	0	0	0	0	0	0	0
Carson Colony	9	9	10	3	2	13	11	16	6	1	11
Catawba Reservation (state)	0	15	2	9	8	4	6	12	0	4	0
Cattaraugus Reservation	20	140	63	44	76	157	69	59	55	22	57
Cedarville Rancheria	0	0	0	0	0	3	0	3	2	0	0
Chehalis Reservation	12	24	19	6	13	33	26	25	13	3	10
Chemehuevi Reservation	2	21	7	0	6	8	4	0	0	9	2
Cheyenne River Reservation	178	368	398	182	192	546	387	308	155	142	141
Chicken Ranch Rancheria	0	5	0	0	0	0	0	0	0	0	0
Chitimacha Reservation	8	18	5	2	3	28	17	12	10	3	3
Cochiti Pueblo	23	35	33	19	29	73	35	33	34	21	36
Cocopah Reservation	12	24	30	11	22	53	15	25	7	21	16
Coeur d'Alene Reservation and Trust Lands, ID	65	172	180	85	101	304	196	153	94	108	105
Cold Springs Rancheria	3	18	28	7	2	6	3	2	3	3	1
Colorado River Reservation	94	291	292	135	138	413	267	255	181	109	151

[Continued]

★ 165 ★

Population of American Indian Reservations and Trust Lands, by Age, 1990 - Acoma-Colville, Part I
[Continued]

American Indian Reservation and Trust Lands[1,2]	Number of persons										
	< 1 year	1-2 years	3-4 years	5 years	6 years	7-9 years	10-11 years	12-13 years	14 years	15 years	16 years
Colusa (Cachil Dehe) Rancheria	0	0	0	0	0	1	4	2	0	0	0
Colville Reservation	107	244	311	101	138	494	303	258	111	119	124

Source: Census of Population and Housing, 1990: Summary Tape File 3C on CD-ROM [machine-readable datafiles]. Prepared by the Bureau of the Census. Washington, DC: The Bureau, 1992. *Notes:* 1. Federal American Indian reservations are areas with boundaries established by treaty, statute, and/or executive or court order, and recognized by the federal government as territory in which American Indian tribes have jurisdiction. State reservations are lands held in trust by state governments for the use and benefit of a given tribe. The reservations and their boundaries were identified for the 1990 census by the Bureau of Indian Affairs (BIA), Department of Interior (for federal reservations), and state governments (for state reservations). The names of American Indian reservations recognized by state governments, but not by the federal government, are followed by "state." Areas composed of reservation lands that are administered jointly and/or are claimed by two reservations, as identified by the BIA, are called "joint areas," and are treated as separate American Indian reservations for census purposes. Federal reservations may cross state boundaries, and federal and state reservations may cross county, county subdivision, and place boundaries. For reservations that cross state boundaries, only the portion of the reservations in a given state is shown in the data products for that state; the entire reservations are shown in data products for the United States. 2. Trust lands are property associated with a particular American Indian reservation or tribe, held in trust by the federal government. Trust lands may be held in trust either for a tribe (tribal trust lands) or for an individual member of a tribe (individual trust land). Trust lands recognized for the 1990 census comprised all tribal trust lands and inhabited individual trust lands located outside of a reservation boundary. As with other American Indian areas, trust lands may be located in more than one state. Only the trust lands in a given state are shown in the data products for that state; all trust lands associated with a reservation or tribe are shown in data products for the United States. The Census Bureau first reported data for tribal trust lands for the 1980 census.

★ 166 ★

Population

Population of American Indian Reservations and Trust Lands, by Age, 1990 - Acoma-Colville, Part II

American Indian Reservation and Trust Lands[1,2]	Number of persons									
	17 years	18 years	19 years	20 years	21 years	22-24 years	25-29 years	30-34 years	35-39 years	40-44 years
Acoma Pueblo and Trust Lands, NM	50	32	55	35	44	125	188	248	164	115
Agua Caliente Reservation	124	144	115	98	152	414	968	993	1,040	1,001
Alabama and Coushatta Reservation	18	5	8	16	10	22	45	29	39	22
Alamo Navajo Reservation	32	30	22	14	29	69	107	102	91	64
Allegany Reservation	118	121	106	89	98	322	563	520	469	412
Alturas Rancheria	0	0	0	0	0	0	0	0	0	0
Annette Islands Reserve	18	17	22	15	25	50	112	134	125	114
Augustine Reservation	0	0	0	0	0	0	0	0	0	0
Bad River Reservation	15	7	9	6	19	37	108	79	51	66
Barona Rancheria	10	16	13	2	21	33	49	52	57	41
Bay Mills Reservation	11	16	5	4	7	23	46	36	36	27
Benton Paiute Reservation	2	2	0	0	0	0	0	2	6	6
Berry Creek Rancheria	0	0	0	0	0	0	0	0	0	0
Big Bend Rancheria	0	0	0	0	0	0	0	0	0	0
Big Cypress Reservation	0	11	41	15	7	32	39	7	25	17
Big Lagoon Rancheria	0	0	0	0	0	0	0	7	0	0
Big Pine Rancheria	11	18	3	3	0	11	31	26	51	35
Big Sandy Rancheria	0	3	0	0	0	2	7	11	0	0
Big Valley Rancheria	0	0	0	0	0	0	0	0	5	5
Bishop Rancheria	34	30	24	10	26	48	115	160	118	101

[Continued]

Population of American Indian Reservations and Trust Lands, by Age, 1990 - Acoma-Colville, Part II

[Continued]

American Indian Reservation and Trust Lands[1,2]	Number of persons									
	17 years	18 years	19 years	20 years	21 years	22-24 years	25-29 years	30-34 years	35-39 years	40-44 years
Blackfeet Reservation	154	118	107	65	79	336	658	814	540	460
Blue Lake Rancheria	4	0	0	0	0	0	3	0	12	10
Bois Forte (Nett Lake) Reservation	9	8	5	4	11	17	25	15	18	19
Bridgeport Colony	0	0	0	0	0	0	4	0	0	2
Brighton Reservation	15	7	2	11	12	21	38	22	44	30
Burns Paiute Reservation and Trust Lands, OR	4	7	0	2	8	11	9	14	15	20
Cabazon Reservation	17	25	23	7	10	30	94	68	30	41
Cahuilla Reservation	0	0	0	2	3	0	17	1	11	4
Campo Reservation	2	0	2	0	0	4	16	34	21	14
Camp Verde Reservation	13	12	8	6	17	22	44	45	29	40
Canoncito Reservation	24	23	18	18	51	54	119	104	59	60
Capitan Grande Reservation	0	0	0	0	0	0	0	0	0	0
Carson Colony	4	2	2	6	5	13	20	24	23	18
Catawba Reservation (state)	2	4	3	0	2	7	18	25	4	14
Cattaraugus Reservation	39	45	26	33	34	74	175	190	126	116
Cedarville Rancheria	0	0	0	0	0	0	0	0	0	2
Chehalis Reservation	3	8	14	10	3	24	27	29	38	28
Chemehuevi Reservation	9	1	2	2	0	2	10	19	25	29
Cheyenne River Reservation	179	86	113	75	47	290	632	644	430	381
Chicken Ranch Rancheria	0	0	0	0	0	0	5	6	0	0
Chitimacha Reservation	3	2	0	0	0	11	43	47	15	4
Cochiti Pueblo	23	24	19	30	7	64	91	79	83	65
Cocopah Reservation	5	12	6	6	4	13	12	61	31	46
Coeur d'Alene Reservation and Trust Lands, ID	106	73	71	34	58	166	346	419	488	432
Cold Springs Rancheria	0	6	1	0	2	6	15	12	10	4
Colorado River Reservation	109	121	134	124	100	314	493	581	540	517
Colusa (Cachil Dehe) Rancheria	0	0	0	0	0	0	0	3	5	3
Colville Reservation	109	112	83	74	78	219	462	545	558	466

Source: Census of Population and Housing, 1990: Summary Tape File 3C on CD-ROM [machine-readable datafiles]. Prepared by the Bureau of the Census. Washington, DC: The Bureau, 1992. *Notes:* 1. Federal American Indian reservations are areas with boundaries established by treaty, statute, and/or executive or court order, and recognized by the federal government as territory in which American Indian tribes have jurisdiction. State reservations are lands held in trust by state governments for the use and benefit of a given tribe. The reservations and their boundaries were identified for the 1990 census by the Bureau of Indian Affairs (BIA), Department of Interior (for federal reservations), and state governments (for state reservations). The names of American Indian reservations recognized by state governments, but not by the federal government, are followed by "state." Areas composed of reservation lands that are administered jointly and/or are claimed by two reservations, as identified by the BIA, are called "joint areas," and are treated as separate American Indian reservations for census purposes. Federal reservations may cross state boundaries, and federal and state reservations may cross county, county subdivision, and place boundaries. For reservations that cross state boundaries, only the portion of the reservations in a given state is shown in the data products for that state; the entire reservations are shown in data products for the United States. 2. Trust lands are property associated with a particular American Indian reservation or tribe, held in trust by the federal government. Trust lands may be held in trust either for a tribe (tribal trust lands) or for an individual member of a tribe (individual trust land). Trust lands recognized for the 1990 census comprised all tribal trust lands and inhabited individual trust lands located outside of a reservation boundary. As with other American Indian areas, trust lands may be located in more than one state. Only the trust lands in a given state are shown in the data products for that state; all trust lands associated with a reservation or tribe are shown in data products for the United States. The Census Bureau first reported data for tribal trust lands for the 1980 census.

Population of American Indian Reservations and Trust Lands, by Age, 1990 - Acoma-Colville, Part III

American Indian Reservation and Trust Lands[1,2]	Number of persons									
	45-49 years	50-54 years	55-59 years	60-61 years	62-64 years	65-69 years	70-74 years	75-79 years	80-84 years	85 + years
Acoma Pueblo and Trust Lands, NM	106	116	81	20	58	46	55	40	28	26
Agua Caliente Reservation	961	1,122	1,230	559	1,135	2,060	2,073	1,915	983	781
Alabama and Coushatta Reservation	35	32	17	6	21	13	14	4	12	1
Alamo Navajo Reservation	34	38	34	8	12	17	24	8	3	9
Allegany Reservation	330	333	321	150	232	347	380	221	211	179
Alturas Rancheria	0	0	0	0	0	3	0	0	0	0
Annette Islands Reserve	89	48	49	24	22	27	16	12	7	7
Augustine Reservation	0	0	0	0	0	0	0	0	0	0
Bad River Reservation	53	51	40	6	24	20	27	16	8	6
Barona Rancheria	38	25	21	0	6	5	7	3	0	6
Bay Mills Reservation	14	7	23	1	12	9	5	2	2	0
Benton Paiute Reservation	6	4	5	0	3	3	2	7	0	0
Berry Creek Rancheria	0	0	0	0	0	0	0	0	0	0
Big Bend Rancheria	0	0	0	0	0	0	2	0	0	0
Big Cypress Reservation	54	31	11	0	7	0	0	19	0	0
Big Lagoon Rancheria	0	0	0	0	0	0	0	0	0	0
Big Pine Rancheria	14	35	9	4	12	6	4	17	5	0
Big Sandy Rancheria	7	0	0	0	3	5	0	2	0	0
Big Valley Rancheria	10	0	7	0	13	0	6	13	5	0
Bishop Rancheria	42	35	71	18	27	31	34	17	0	6
Blackfeet Reservation	402	387	291	66	156	194	109	105	57	37
Blue Lake Rancheria	4	0	3	0	0	6	0	0	0	0
Bois Forte (Nett Lake) Reservation	11	17	14	7	5	12	8	4	0	0
Bridgeport Colony	0	4	3	0	0	3	0	0	0	0
Brighton Reservation	33	29	16	4	4	26	36	9	0	0
Burns Paiute Reservation and Trust Lands, OR	7	11	5	0	2	2	3	0	0	0
Cabazon Reservation	41	30	29	5	3	27	13	8	15	6
Cahuilla Reservation	5	5	8	3	1	3	0	2	0	2
Campo Reservation	39	10	7	3	3	8	9	15	2	0
Camp Verde Reservation	19	33	12	0	2	11	12	9	3	8
Canoncito Reservation	67	48	23	7	11	3	11	6	6	3
Capitan Grande Reservation	0	0	0	0	0	0	0	0	0	0
Carson Colony	15	20	14	0	5	0	2	0	0	1
Catawba Reservation (state)	16	0	6	7	4	5	0	0	0	0
Cattaraugus Reservation	95	95	105	32	37	61	67	26	27	18
Cedarville Rancheria	0	0	0	0	0	0	0	0	0	0
Chehalis Reservation	42	15	13	19	8	18	9	2	3	7
Chemehuevi Reservation	23	11	16	2	23	44	19	17	9	3
Cheyenne River Reservation	357	323	299	105	153	222	150	125	87	48
Chicken Ranch Rancheria	7	0	5	0	0	22	11	5	0	0
Chitimacha Reservation	2	2	13	5	7	18	21	7	2	0
Cochiti Pueblo	67	81	108	12	48	82	56	45	35	20
Cocopah Reservation	9	38	23	6	17	5	24	30	0	0
Coeur d'Alene Reservation and Trust Lands, ID	350	304	282	105	182	261	215	146	133	44

[Continued]

★ 167 ★

Population of American Indian Reservations and Trust Lands, by Age, 1990 - Acoma-Colville, Part III

[Continued]

American Indian Reservation and Trust Lands[1,2]	Number of persons									
	45-49 years	50-54 years	55-59 years	60-61 years	62-64 years	65-69 years	70-74 years	75-79 years	80-84 years	85 + years
Cold Springs Rancheria	16	0	9	0	0	0	0	6	0	0
Colorado River Reservation	433	355	338	156	275	396	267	182	119	64
Colusa (Cachil Dehe) Rancheria	0	0	0	0	0	0	0	0	0	2
Colville Reservation	396	324	304	90	171	216	193	148	104	72

Source: Census of Population and Housing, 1990: Summary Tape File 3C on CD-ROM [machine-readable datafiles]. Prepared by the Bureau of the Census. Washington, DC: The Bureau, 1992. *Notes:* 1. Federal American Indian reservations are areas with boundaries established by treaty, statute, and/or executive or court order, and recognized by the federal government as territory in which American Indian tribes have jurisdiction. State reservations are lands held in trust by state governments for the use and benefit of a given tribe. The reservations and their boundaries were identified for the 1990 census by the Bureau of Indian Affairs (BIA), Department of Interior (for federal reservations), and state governments (for state reservations). The names of American Indian reservations recognized by state governments, but not by the federal government, are followed by "state." Areas composed of reservation lands that are administered jointly and/or are claimed by two reservations, as identified by the BIA, are called "joint areas," and are treated as separate American Indian reservations for census purposes. Federal reservations may cross state boundaries, and federal and state reservations may cross county, county subdivision, and place boundaries. For reservations that cross state boundaries, only the portion of the reservations in a given state in shown in the data products for that state; the entire reservations are shown in data products for the United States. 2. Trust lands are property associated with a particular American Indian reservation or tribe, held in trust by the federal government. Trust lands may be held in trust either for a tribe (tribal trust lands) or for an individual member of a tribe (individual trust land). Trust lands recognized for the 1990 census comprised all tribal trust lands and inhabited individual trust lands located outside of a reservation boundary. As with other American Indian areas, trust lands may be located in more than one state. Only the trust lands in a given state are shown in the data products for that state; all trust lands associated with a reservation or tribe are shown in data products for the United States. The Census Bureau first reported data for tribal trust lands for the 1980 census.

★ 168 ★

Population

Population of American Indian Reservations and Trust Lands, by Age, 1990 - Coos-Grindstone Creek, Part I

American Indian Reservation and Trust Lands[1,2]	Number of persons										
	< 1 year	1-2 years	3-4 years	5 years	6 years	7-9 years	10-11 years	12-13 years	14 years	15 years	16 years
Coos, Lower Umpqua, and Siuslaw Reservation	0	0	0	0	0	0	0	0	0	0	0
Cortina Rancheria	0	0	2	0	0	0	0	4	3	0	0
Coushatta Reservation	0	1	0	2	2	1	2	0	2	0	4
Cow Creek Reservation	5	8	2	0	4	5	6	0	0	3	4
Coyote Valley Reservation	0	16	8	4	3	9	8	7	4	0	3
Crow Reservation and Trust Lands, MT	124	324	233	165	161	437	209	263	147	120	115
Crow Creek Reservation	56	83	98	49	47	144	119	84	30	40	39
Cuyapaipe Reservation	0	0	0	0	0	0	0	0	0	0	0
Deer Creek Reservation	3	3	6	2	4	2	7	6	7	5	9
Devils Lake Sioux Reservation	90	183	179	71	96	268	228	162	71	61	65
Dresslerville Colony	5	14	10	0	4	7	4	6	0	0	0
Dry Creek Rancheria	0	5	3	0	7	7	6	0	3	0	0
Duck Valley Reservation	20	47	47	24	25	81	56	50	22	16	19
Duckwater Reservation	2	4	10	0	2	10	6	8	6	4	0
Eastern Cherokee Reservation	103	292	186	116	118	357	300	235	90	84	137
Elk Valley Rancheria	0	0	18	13	0	4	6	4	4	0	0
Ely Colony	0	0	0	0	0	6	6	12	6	6	4
Enterprise Rancheria	0	0	0	0	0	0	0	0	0	0	0
Fallon Colony	2	17	14	3	0	4	15	8	2	0	3
Fallon Reservation	1	5	15	18	6	20	8	23	5	3	5

[Continued]

★ 168 ★

Population of American Indian Reservations and Trust Lands, by Age, 1990 - Coos-Grindstone Creek, Part I
[Continued]

American Indian Reservation and Trust Lands[1,2]	Number of persons										
	< 1 year	1-2 years	3-4 years	5 years	6 years	7-9 years	10-11 years	12-13 years	14 years	15 years	16 years
Flandreau Reservation	1	13	20	2	5	26	13	6	14	8	8
Flathead Reservation	282	677	714	335	335	1,247	793	698	296	372	353
Fond du Lac Reservation	34	137	136	53	78	170	122	105	56	67	41
Fort Apache Reservation	309	678	619	366	286	781	515	378	223	201	227
Fort Belknap Reservation and Trust Lands, MT	63	156	125	73	59	190	108	122	38	51	60
Fort Berthold Reservation	83	220	282	126	137	354	238	173	84	52	111
Fort Bidwell Reservation	1	4	1	4	2	12	11	6	5	5	2
Fort Hall Reservation and Trust Lands, ID	134	198	175	121	125	361	195	211	96	96	58
Fort Independence Reservation	2	2	0	3	0	7	3	0	0	5	0
Fort McDermitt Reservation	5	31	8	7	4	31	13	19	3	13	7
Fort McDowell Reservation	15	47	48	25	13	33	19	20	15	7	0
Fort Mojave Reservation and Trust Lands, AZ–CA–NV	14	49	29	10	20	42	34	18	9	5	2
Fort Peck Reservation	255	500	507	224	223	673	490	391	186	204	191
Fort Yuma (Quechan) Reservation	45	71	85	35	35	117	75	38	46	36	28
Gila Bend Reservation and Trust Lands, AZ	0	0	0	0	0	0	0	0	0	0	0
Gila River Reservation	212	481	529	272	255	699	380	346	223	102	214
Golden Hill Reservation (state)	0	0	0	0	0	0	0	0	0	0	0
Goshute Reservation	0	3	3	6	6	3	2	0	0	0	0
Grand Portage Reservation	0	3	20	8	0	19	6	16	3	7	0
Grand Ronde Reservation	0	0	0	0	0	0	0	0	0	3	0
Grand Traverse Reservation and Trust Lands, MI	8	17	12	3	10	31	7	8	4	10	11
Greenville Rancheria	0	0	0	0	0	0	0	0	0	0	0
Grindstone Creek Rancheria	4	4	7	2	4	7	8	15	0	3	3

Source: Census of Population and Housing, 1990: Summary Tape File 3C on CD-ROM [machine-readable datafiles]. Prepared by the Bureau of the Census. Washington, DC: The Bureau, 1992. *Notes:* 1. Federal American Indian reservations are areas with boundaries established by treaty, statute, and/or executive or court order, and recognized by the federal government as territory in which American Indian tribes have jurisdiction. State reservations are lands held in trust by state governments for the use and benefit of a given tribe. The reservations and their boundaries were identified for the 1990 census by the Bureau of Indian Affairs (BIA), Department of Interior (for federal reservations), and state governments (for state reservations). The names of American Indian reservations recognized by state governments, but not by the federal government, are followed by "state." Areas composed of reservation lands that are administered jointly and/or are claimed by two reservations, as identified by the BIA, are called "joint areas," and are treated as separate American Indian reservations for census purposes. Federal reservations may cross state boundaries, and federal and state reservations may cross county, county subdivision, and place boundaries. For reservations that cross state boundaries, only the portion of the reservations in a given state is shown in the data products for that state; the entire reservations are shown in data products for the United States. 2. Trust lands are property associated with a particular American Indian reservation or tribe, held in trust by the federal government. Trust lands may be held in trust either for a tribe (tribal trust lands) or for an individual member of a tribe (individual trust land). Trust lands recognized for the 1990 census comprised all tribal trust lands and inhabited individual trust lands located outside of a reservation boundary. As with other American Indian areas, trust lands may be located in more than one state. Only the trust lands in a given state are shown in the data products for that state; all trust lands associated with a reservation or tribe are shown in data products for the United States. The Census Bureau first reported data for tribal trust lands for the 1980 census.

★ 169 ★
Population

Population of American Indian Reservations and Trust Lands, by Age, 1990 - Coos-Grindstone Creek, Part II

American Indian Reservation and Trust Lands[1,2]	Number of persons									
	17 years	18 years	19 years	20 years	21 years	22-24 years	25-29 years	30-34 years	35-39 years	40-44 years
Coos, Lower Umpqua, and Siuslaw Reservation	0	0	0	0	0	0	0	0	0	0
Cortina Rancheria	0	0	0	0	0	0	0	2	1	8
Coushatta Reservation	2	1	0	0	0	0	4	0	8	7
Cow Creek Reservation	0	2	0	0	0	4	15	7	8	5
Coyote Valley Reservation	0	0	2	5	2	10	15	7	7	9
Crow Reservation and Trust Lands, MT	130	95	98	37	121	222	501	494	576	434
Crow Creek Reservation	34	24	24	23	15	94	116	135	104	64
Cuyapaipe Reservation	0	0	0	0	0	0	0	0	0	0
Deer Creek Reservation	7	0	3	0	0	4	0	4	24	21
Devils Lake Sioux Reservation	66	64	87	36	53	164	252	220	261	162
Dresslerville Colony	0	2	9	0	6	3	23	12	3	7
Dry Creek Rancheria	0	4	0	3	0	10	12	0	5	0
Duck Valley Reservation	19	22	7	12	15	50	98	55	88	57
Duckwater Reservation	2	0	0	3	0	2	13	14	13	4
Eastern Cherokee Reservation	100	102	136	143	106	235	568	457	438	466
Elk Valley Rancheria	0	0	0	9	0	16	10	0	7	0
Ely Colony	8	4	0	0	0	0	0	0	9	16
Enterprise Rancheria	0	0	0	0	0	0	0	0	0	0
Fallon Colony	8	2	0	0	0	19	21	10	3	9
Fallon Reservation	3	3	3	0	3	10	22	36	37	13
Flandreau Reservation	0	6	4	1	2	5	34	26	16	24
Flathead Reservation	333	328	246	202	195	530	1,018	1,743	1,661	1,443
Fond du Lac Reservation	43	39	53	37	31	96	300	273	231	196
Fort Apache Reservation	103	124	124	136	222	541	1,034	789	679	626
Fort Belknap Reservation and Trust Lands, MT	54	30	26	27	17	112	199	191	167	117
Fort Berthold Reservation	101	87	55	70	51	182	356	452	385	304
Fort Bidwell Reservation	2	0	0	0	3	0	8	11	12	10
Fort Hall Reservation and Trust Lands, ID	114	48	115	68	52	248	448	391	413	260
Fort Independence Reservation	0	0	0	0	0	0	3	16	2	0
Fort McDermitt Reservation	7	11	7	15	3	21	38	17	23	23
Fort McDowell Reservation	7	13	8	2	10	35	77	79	32	19
Fort Mojave Reservation and Trust Lands, AZ–CA–NV	16	5	12	2	13	45	82	71	27	37
Fort Peck Reservation	173	168	98	84	111	392	746	999	798	654
Fort Yuma (Quechan) Reservation	46	38	15	18	20	64	98	119	133	133
Gila Bend Reservation and Trust Lands, AZ	0	0	0	0	0	0	0	0	0	0
Gila River Reservation	135	201	178	166	148	522	849	708	558	458
Golden Hill Reservation (state)	0	0	0	0	0	3	3	0	0	0
Goshute Reservation	0	2	0	0	0	3	9	11	9	4
Grand Portage Reservation	0	0	0	0	9	4	16	29	44	38
Grand Ronde Reservation	0	0	0	0	0	3	3	3	0	11
Grand Traverse Reservation and Trust Lands, MI	7	0	6	4	0	7	18	21	25	14

[Continued]

★ 169 ★

Population of American Indian Reservations and Trust Lands, by Age, 1990 - Coos-Grindstone Creek, Part II

[Continued]

American Indian Reservation and Trust Lands[1,2]	Number of persons									
	17 years	18 years	19 years	20 years	21 years	22-24 years	25-29 years	30-34 years	35-39 years	40-44 years
Greenville Rancheria	0	0	0	0	0	0	0	0	0	0
Grindstone Creek Rancheria	0	0	4	6	0	0	0	14	0	7

Source: Census of Population and Housing, 1990: Summary Tape File 3C on CD-ROM [machine-readable datafiles]. Prepared by the Bureau of the Census. Washington, DC: The Bureau, 1992. Notes: 1. Federal American Indian reservations are areas with boundaries established by treaty, statute, and/or executive or court order, and recognized by the federal government as territory in which American Indian tribes have jurisdiction. State reservations are lands held in trust by state governments for the use and benefit of a given tribe. The reservations and their boundaries were identified for the 1990 census by the Bureau of Indian Affairs (BIA), Department of Interior (for federal reservations), and state governments (for state reservations). The names of American Indian reservations recognized by state governments, but not by the federal government, are followed by "state." Areas composed of reservation lands that are administered jointly and/or are claimed by two reservations, as identified by the BIA, are called "joint areas," and are treated as separate American Indian reservations for census purposes. Federal reservations may cross state boundaries, and federal and state reservations may cross county, county subdivision, and place boundaries. For reservations that cross state boundaries, only the portion of the reservations in a given state is shown in the data products for that state; the entire reservations are shown in data products for the United States. 2. Trust lands are property associated with a particular American Indian reservation or tribe, held in trust by the federal government. Trust lands may be held in trust either for a tribe (tribal trust lands) or for an individual member of a tribe (individual trust land). Trust lands recognized for the 1990 census comprised all tribal trust lands and inhabited individual trust lands located outside of a reservation boundary. As with other American Indian areas, trust lands may be located in more than one state. Only the trust lands in a given state are shown in the data products for that state; all trust lands associated with a reservation or tribe are shown in data products for the United States. The Census Bureau first reported data for tribal trust lands for the 1980 census.

★ 170 ★

Population

Population of American Indian Reservations and Trust Lands, by Age, 1990 - Coos-Grindstone Creek, Part III

American Indian Reservation and Trust Lands[1,2]	Number of persons									
	45-49 years	50-54 years	55-59 years	60-61 years	62-64 years	65-69 years	70-74 years	75-79 years	80-84 years	85 + years
Coos, Lower Umpqua, and Siuslaw Reservation	0	0	0	0	0	0	0	0	0	0
Cortina Rancheria	3	2	0	0	0	0	2	0	0	2
Coushatta Reservation	0	0	0	3	3	0	0	0	0	0
Cow Creek Reservation	6	0	0	2	3	0	0	0	0	0
Coyote Valley Reservation	3	3	0	5	0	0	5	0	0	4
Crow Reservation and Trust Lands, MT	310	330	199	57	109	119	100	62	44	5
Crow Creek Reservation	84	80	33	16	38	45	25	10	10	0
Cuyapaipe Reservation	0	0	0	0	0	0	0	0	0	0
Deer Creek Reservation	3	12	3	6	3	8	19	6	2	3
Devils Lake Sioux Reservation	174	124	110	40	45	80	54	46	30	32
Dresslerville Colony	8	15	13	0	2	0	0	0	0	0
Dry Creek Rancheria	0	10	0	0	0	0	0	0	0	0
Duck Valley Reservation	79	42	40	15	10	28	7	27	5	13
Duckwater Reservation	2	12	11	3	0	6	4	6	4	0
Eastern Cherokee Reservation	334	274	244	93	110	186	132	83	52	34
Elk Valley Rancheria	10	9	18	0	0	0	0	0	0	0
Ely Colony	0	6	2	0	0	0	0	0	0	0
Enterprise Rancheria	0	0	0	0	0	0	0	0	0	0
Fallon Colony	5	0	4	0	6	3	2	0	0	2
Fallon Reservation	20	22	31	10	10	16	5	7	6	3
Flandreau Reservation	8	11	8	0	5	6	6	2	0	0
Flathead Reservation	1,101	931	802	316	629	1,004	924	731	389	433
Fond du Lac Reservation	169	149	116	62	72	128	106	72	10	29

[Continued]

★ 170 ★

Population of American Indian Reservations and Trust Lands, by Age, 1990 - Coos-Grindstone Creek, Part III

[Continued]

American Indian Reservation and Trust Lands[1,2]	Number of persons									
	45-49 years	50-54 years	55-59 years	60-61 years	62-64 years	65-69 years	70-74 years	75-79 years	80-84 years	85 + years
Fort Apache Reservation	351	277	297	95	114	167	99	62	74	9
Fort Belknap Reservation and Trust Lands, MT	106	81	79	14	51	72	32	37	14	14
Fort Berthold Reservation	275	122	234	84	108	207	188	96	77	93
Fort Bidwell Reservation	2	4	3	3	8	3	8	3	0	3
Fort Hall Reservation and Trust Lands, ID	311	167	186	53	84	118	115	83	26	44
Fort Independence Reservation	5	0	0	0	4	4	0	0	0	2
Fort McDermitt Reservation	25	20	10	7	0	11	6	6	6	2
Fort McDowell Reservation	8	16	31	16	17	2	0	4	7	3
Fort Mojave Reservation and Trust Lands, AZ–CA–NV	22	20	42	3	12	38	5	0	6	2
Fort Peck Reservation	455	519	389	137	208	320	255	183	111	78
Fort Yuma (Quechan) Reservation	131	86	92	41	83	131	113	75	34	21
Gila Bend Reservation and Trust Lands, AZ	0	0	0	0	0	0	0	0	0	0
Gila River Reservation	454	368	288	97	148	203	170	76	50	88
Golden Hill Reservation (state)	3	0	0	0	0	0	0	0	0	0
Goshute Reservation	0	2	7	0	0	0	0	0	9	0
Grand Portage Reservation	10	15	19	12	6	14	3	4	0	3
Grand Ronde Reservation	2	3	2	0	9	3	3	2	2	0
Grand Traverse Reservation and Trust Lands, MI	6	0	15	4	0	15	0	0	0	0
Greenville Rancheria	0	0	0	0	0	25	0	0	0	0
Grindstone Creek Rancheria	0	13	0	0	0	0	0	0	0	0

Source: Census of Population and Housing, 1990: Summary Tape File 3C on CD-ROM [machine-readable datafiles]. Prepared by the Bureau of the Census. Washington, DC: The Bureau, 1992. *Notes:* 1. Federal American Indian reservations are areas with boundaries established by treaty, statute, and/or executive or court order, and recognized by the federal government as territory in which American Indian tribes have jurisdiction. State reservations are lands held in trust by state governments for the use and benefit of a given tribe. The reservations and their boundaries were identified for the 1990 census by the Bureau of Indian Affairs (BIA), Department of Interior (for federal reservations), and state governments (for state reservations). The names of American Indian reservations recognized by state governments, but not by the federal government, are followed by "state." Areas composed of reservation lands that are administered jointly and/or are claimed by two reservations, as identified by the BIA, are called "joint areas," and are treated as separate American Indian reservations for census purposes. Federal reservations may cross state boundaries, and federal and state reservations may cross county, county subdivision, and place boundaries. For reservations that cross state boundaries, only the portion of the reservations in a given state is shown in the data products for that state; the entire reservations are shown in data products for the United States. 2. Trust lands are property associated with a particular American Indian reservation or tribe, held in trust by the federal government. Trust lands may be held in trust either for a tribe (tribal trust lands) or for an individual member of a tribe (individual trust land). Trust lands recognized for the 1990 census comprised all tribal trust lands and inhabited individual trust lands located outside of a reservation boundary. As with other American Indian areas, trust lands may be located in more than one state. Only the trust lands in a given state are shown in the data products for that state; all trust lands associated with a reservation or tribe are shown in data products for the United States. The Census Bureau first reported data for tribal trust lands for the 1980 census.

★ 171 ★

Population

Population of American Indian Reservations and Trust Lands, by Age, 1990 - Hannahville-Lummi, Part I

American Indian Reservation and Trust Lands[1,2]	Number of persons										
	< 1 year	1-2 years	3-4 years	5 years	6 years	7-9 years	10-11 years	12-13 years	14 years	15 years	16 years
Hannahville Community and Trust Lands, MI	3	7	14	4	0	11	8	23	3	2	4
Hassanamisco Reservation (state)	0	0	0	0	0	0	0	0	0	0	0
Havasupai Reservation	9	22	27	3	7	39	20	23	6	10	4
Hoh Reservation	6	2	7	2	7	11	5	0	3	3	2
Hollywood Reservation	10	19	46	17	25	38	33	27	12	18	6

[Continued]

★ 171 ★

Population of American Indian Reservations and Trust Lands, by Age, 1990 - Hannahville-Lummi, Part I

[Continued]

American Indian Reservation and Trust Lands[1,2]	Number of persons										
	< 1 year	1-2 years	3-4 years	5 years	6 years	7-9 years	10-11 years	12-13 years	14 years	15 years	16 years
Hoopa Valley Reservation	53	108	93	51	59	171	108	72	23	38	55
Hopi Reservation and Trust Lands, AZ	146	279	345	113	146	475	321	384	155	138	127
Hopland Rancheria	0	16	8	15	8	28	21	10	3	0	0
Hualapai Reservation and Trust Lands, AZ	13	54	47	24	34	58	26	39	15	24	13
Inaja-Cosmit Reservation	0	0	0	0	0	0	0	0	0	0	0
Indian Township Reservation	15	28	35	20	25	46	26	14	8	10	10
Iowa Reservation	2	17	14	15	16	15	9	3	3	2	0
Isabella Reservation and Trust Lands, MI	369	708	663	345	362	1,098	728	635	336	314	291
Isleta Pueblo	42	129	119	75	66	215	101	85	45	60	37
Jackson Rancheria	0	0	3	0	0	2	0	0	0	0	3
Jamestown Klallam Reservation and Trust Lands, WA	0	0	0	4	0	5	1	0	0	0	0
Jamul Village	0	0	0	0	0	0	0	0	0	0	0
Jemez Pueblo	36	78	78	43	45	124	66	63	44	39	25
Jicarilla Apache Reservation	68	144	142	83	75	207	92	109	38	57	40
Kaibab Reservation	0	5	12	5	2	5	5	0	0	8	4
Kalispel Reservation	4	4	2	4	0	0	0	0	0	2	0
Karok Reservation and Trust Lands, CA	0	13	11	7	19	37	35	7	0	6	0
Kickapoo Reservation	21	26	28	16	0	23	21	11	6	13	7
Kootenai Reservation	9	3	5	6	0	7	14	3	0	0	3
Lac Courte Oreilles Reservation and Trust Lands, WI	49	120	98	58	53	141	113	88	55	34	47
Lac du Flambeau Reservation	23	107	89	43	44	109	51	88	37	36	22
Lac Vieux Desert Reservation	6	5	9	0	3	6	3	13	3	0	11
Laguna Pueblo and Trust Lands, NM	55	111	114	73	67	254	162	182	63	59	96
La Jolla Reservation	1	33	4	10	4	21	15	6	2	2	2
Lake Traverse (Sisseton) Reservation	196	322	325	211	230	532	370	354	209	209	167
L'Anse Reservation and Trust Lands, MI	52	95	111	46	56	143	124	121	53	42	54
La Posta Reservation	0	0	0	0	0	0	0	0	0	0	0
Las Vegas Colony	6	0	6	0	3	6	10	0	3	2	0
Laytonville Rancheria	9	6	10	2	4	7	4	5	0	0	5
Leech Lake Reservation	157	342	332	177	171	540	371	296	133	167	150
Likely Rancheria	0	0	0	0	0	0	0	0	0	0	0
Lone Pine Rancheria	0	13	4	9	8	9	13	3	6	2	2
Lookout Rancheria	0	6	0	0	0	7	7	0	0	0	0
Los Coyotes Reservation	38	7	7	0	12	0	8	0	0	0	0
Lovelock Colony	0	0	0	3	0	4	6	10	0	5	9
Lower Brule Reservation	20	74	51	17	26	104	65	51	29	25	24
Lower Elwha Reservation and Trust Lands, WA	0	5	3	0	4	5	6	4	2	1	0

[Continued]

★ 171 ★

Population of American Indian Reservations and Trust Lands, by Age, 1990 - Hannahville-Lummi, Part I
[Continued]

American Indian Reservation and Trust Lands[1,2]	Number of persons										
	< 1 year	1-2 years	3-4 years	5 years	6 years	7-9 years	10-11 years	12-13 years	14 years	15 years	16 years
Lower Sioux Community	4	15	16	9	6	26	8	10	2	4	5
Lummi Reservation	67	138	109	73	44	164	101	95	47	49	36

Source: Census of Population and Housing, 1990: Summary Tape File 3C on CD-ROM [machine-readable datafiles]. Prepared by the Bureau of the Census. Washington, DC: The Bureau, 1992. *Notes:* 1. Federal American Indian reservations are areas with boundaries established by treaty, statute, and/or executive or court order, and recognized by the federal government as territory in which American Indian tribes have jurisdiction. State reservations are lands held in trust by state governments for the use and benefit of a given tribe. The reservations and their boundaries were identified for the 1990 census by the Bureau of Indian Affairs (BIA), Department of Interior (for federal reservations), and state governments (for state reservations). The names of American Indian reservations recognized by state governments, but not by the federal government, are followed by "state." Areas composed of reservation lands that are administered jointly and/or are claimed by two reservations, as identified by the BIA, are called "joint areas," and are treated as separate American Indian reservations for census purposes. Federal reservations may cross state boundaries, and federal and state reservations may cross county, county subdivision, and place boundaries. For reservations that cross state boundaries, only the portion of the reservations in a given state is shown in the data products for that state; the entire reservations are shown in data products for the United States. 2. Trust lands are property associated with a particular American Indian reservation or tribe, held in trust by the federal government. Trust lands may be held in trust either for a tribe (tribal trust lands) or for an individual member of a tribe (individual trust land). Trust lands recognized for the 1990 census comprised all tribal trust lands and inhabited individual trust lands located outside of a reservation boundary. As with other American Indian areas, trust lands may be located in more than one state. Only the trust lands in a given state are shown in the data products for that state; all trust lands associated with a reservation or tribe are shown in data products for the United States. The Census Bureau first reported data for tribal trust lands for the 1980 census.

★ 172 ★

Population

Population of American Indian Reservations and Trust Lands, by Age, 1990 - Hannahville-Lummi, Part II

American Indian Reservation and Trust Lands[1,2]	Number of persons									
	17 years	18 years	19 years	20 years	21 years	22-24 years	25-29 years	30-34 years	35-39 years	40-44 years
Hannahville Community and Trust Lands, MI	0	8	11	11	3	8	15	27	8	7
Hassanamisco Reservation (state)	0	0	0	0	0	0	0	0	0	0
Havasupai Reservation	8	1	1	6	6	16	38	48	47	20
Hoh Reservation	0	9	0	0	0	4	4	8	13	0
Hollywood Reservation	6	35	10	9	5	28	77	62	120	46
Hoopa Valley Reservation	32	23	17	19	34	69	198	182	175	61
Hopi Reservation and Trust Lands, AZ	151	135	112	117	68	225	484	741	504	424
Hopland Rancheria	0	4	0	0	3	9	15	21	12	10
Hualapai Reservation and Trust Lands, AZ	13	6	6	8	8	36	84	78	83	32
Inaja-Cosmit Reservation	0	0	0	0	0	0	0	0	0	0
Indian Township Reservation	18	18	7	10	14	35	75	29	42	33
Iowa Reservation	0	0	0	3	4	6	33	20	18	6
Isabella Reservation and Trust Lands, MI	339	278	351	430	640	1,521	1,997	2,063	1,973	1,433
Isleta Pueblo	62	38	39	43	31	107	250	289	222	233
Jackson Rancheria	0	0	0	0	0	3	0	3	5	5
Jamestown Klallam Reservation and Trust Lands, WA	0	0	2	0	2	0	0	0	3	8
Jamul Village	0	0	0	0	0	0	0	0	0	0
Jemez Pueblo	33	26	23	16	25	103	174	140	100	95
Jicarilla Apache Reservation	53	46	61	64	37	116	293	182	161	143
Kaibab Reservation	0	3	7	0	4	0	8	8	14	6
Kalispel Reservation	0	6	3	5	2	0	16	8	5	4
Karok Reservation and Trust Lands, CA	0	0	0	0	0	9	36	84	69	15
Kickapoo Reservation	13	7	7	7	6	11	35	29	40	27

[Continued]

★ 172 ★

Population of American Indian Reservations and Trust Lands, by Age, 1990 - Hannahville-Lummi, Part II

[Continued]

American Indian Reservation and Trust Lands[1,2]	Number of persons									
	17 years	18 years	19 years	20 years	21 years	22-24 years	25-29 years	30-34 years	35-39 years	40-44 years
Kootenai Reservation	2	1	2	0	0	3	13	10	13	4
Lac Courte Oreilles Reservation and Trust Lands, WI	38	36	40	39	32	79	183	183	145	143
Lac du Flambeau Reservation	33	38	29	26	24	88	184	143	132	114
Lac Vieux Desert Reservation	3	3	0	3	5	6	9	6	7	12
Laguna Pueblo and Trust Lands, NM	31	67	47	45	35	137	286	317	263	206
La Jolla Reservation	0	0	0	0	0	3	6	16	10	2
Lake Traverse (Sisseton) Reservation	176	139	85	90	99	317	651	647	650	606
L'Anse Reservation and Trust Lands, MI	49	71	36	47	47	120	233	202	237	224
La Posta Reservation	0	0	0	0	0	0	0	0	0	0
Las Vegas Colony	0	0	0	9	0	0	8	7	7	2
Laytonville Rancheria	2	7	3	1	0	7	23	12	6	3
Leech Lake Reservation	146	96	80	68	69	249	551	591	577	555
Likely Rancheria	0	0	0	0	0	0	0	0	0	0
Lone Pine Rancheria	2	4	9	2	2	16	14	16	19	17
Lookout Rancheria	7	0	0	0	0	0	14	0	14	0
Los Coyotes Reservation	0	0	0	8	0	0	48	13	0	10
Lovelock Colony	4	0	0	0	3	3	3	17	2	0
Lower Brule Reservation	15	33	20	7	9	62	93	59	67	60
Lower Elwha Reservation and Trust Lands, WA	3	2	2	7	6	8	6	12	12	1
Lower Sioux Community	0	3	9	5	0	11	16	21	9	11
Lummi Reservation	70	42	29	44	37	113	275	266	234	177

Source: Census of Population and Housing, 1990: Summary Tape File 3C on CD-ROM [machine-readable datafiles]. Prepared by the Bureau of the Census. Washington, DC: The Bureau, 1992. *Notes:* 1. Federal American Indian reservations are areas with boundaries established by treaty, statute, and/or executive or court order, and recognized by the federal government as territory in which American Indian tribes have jurisdiction. State reservations are lands held in trust by state governments for the use and benefit of a given tribe. The reservations and their boundaries were identified for the 1990 census by the Bureau of Indian Affairs (BIA), Department of Interior (for federal reservations), and state governments (for state reservations). The names of American Indian reservations recognized by state governments, but not by the federal government, are followed by "state." Areas composed of reservation lands that are administered jointly and/or are claimed by two reservations, as identified by the BIA, are called "joint areas," and are treated as separate American Indian reservations for census purposes. Federal reservations may cross state boundaries, and federal and state reservations may cross county, county subdivision, and place boundaries. For reservations that cross state boundaries, only the portion of the reservations in a given state is shown in the data products for that state; the entire reservations are shown in data products for the United States. 2. Trust lands are property associated with a particular American Indian reservation or tribe, held in trust by the federal government. Trust lands may be held in trust either for a tribe (tribal trust lands) or for an individual member of a tribe (individual trust land). Trust lands recognized for the 1990 census comprised all tribal trust lands and inhabited individual trust lands located outside of a reservation boundary. As with other American Indian areas, trust lands may be located in more than one state. Only the trust lands in a given state are shown in the data products for that state; all trust lands associated with a reservation or tribe are shown in data products for the United States. The Census Bureau first reported data for tribal trust lands for the 1980 census.

★ 173 ★

Population

Population of American Indian Reservations and Trust Lands, by Age, 1990 - Hannahville-Lummi, Part III

American Indian Reservation and Trust Lands[1,2]	Number of persons									
	45-49 years	50-54 years	55-59 years	60-61 years	62-64 years	65-69 years	70-74 years	75-79 years	80-84 years	85 + years
Hannahville Community and Trust Lands, MI	4	4	0	0	2	7	1	1	0	0
Hassanamisco Reservation (state)	0	0	0	0	0	0	0	0	0	0
Havasupai Reservation	21	13	14	4	2	0	8	6	0	4
Hoh Reservation	9	5	0	12	0	2	0	2	0	0

[Continued]

★ 173 ★

Population of American Indian Reservations and Trust Lands, by Age, 1990 - Hannahville-Lummi, Part III

[Continued]

American Indian Reservation and Trust Lands[1,2]	Number of persons									
	45-49 years	50-54 years	55-59 years	60-61 years	62-64 years	65-69 years	70-74 years	75-79 years	80-84 years	85 + years
Hollywood Reservation	42	44	98	53	64	151	138	133	31	9
Hoopa Valley Reservation	112	111	68	27	36	48	68	52	22	14
Hopi Reservation and Trust Lands, AZ	251	326	230	82	120	194	136	96	90	100
Hopland Rancheria	5	2	6	4	1	4	2	0	0	1
Hualapai Reservation and Trust Lands, AZ	22	31	10	7	14	19	12	5	12	0
Inaja-Cosmit Reservation	0	0	0	0	0	0	0	0	0	0
Indian Township Reservation	22	34	10	4	1	15	11	1	6	2
Iowa Reservation	11	8	8	4	3	3	2	0	0	2
Isabella Reservation and Trust Lands, MI	1,104	946	944	342	481	717	586	448	214	275
Isleta Pueblo	90	145	84	48	53	57	64	70	32	22
Jackson Rancheria	0	0	0	0	0	0	3	0	0	0
Jamestown Klallam Reservation and Trust Lands, WA	0	0	0	4	0	3	0	2	0	0
Jamul Village	0	0	0	0	0	0	0	0	0	0
Jemez Pueblo	85	77	44	21	18	27	47	28	7	4
Jicarilla Apache Reservation	101	97	79	33	24	36	21	17	10	7
Kaibab Reservation	7	3	6	0	2	2	2	2	0	0
Kalispel Reservation	10	0	4	0	5	2	2	0	2	0
Karok Reservation and Trust Lands, CA	12	0	8	6	0	20	0	6	0	0
Kickapoo Reservation	6	21	23	12	17	15	21	3	4	2
Kootenai Reservation	0	0	0	0	2	1	0	0	0	0
Lac Courte Oreilles Reservation and Trust Lands, WI	116	84	123	26	58	108	58	47	34	9
Lac du Flambeau Reservation	124	122	167	54	77	162	78	99	42	23
Lac Vieux Desert Reservation	2	11	11	0	0	3	2	2	0	3
Laguna Pueblo and Trust Lands, NM	212	149	173	66	60	119	91	59	61	64
La Jolla Reservation	8	0	1	5	8	0	0	0	3	0
Lake Traverse (Sisseton) Reservation	666	532	493	211	382	547	471	378	247	328
L'Anse Reservation and Trust Lands, MI	184	164	142	56	68	138	152	92	82	76
La Posta Reservation	0	0	0	0	0	0	0	0	0	0
Las Vegas Colony	8	6	3	0	0	0	0	0	0	0
Laytonville Rancheria	4	1	4	0	2	8	0	2	0	0
Leech Lake Reservation	444	499	452	165	262	315	293	254	188	93
Likely Rancheria	0	0	0	0	0	0	0	0	0	0
Lone Pine Rancheria	17	7	10	8	1	14	0	2	0	6
Lookout Rancheria	0	0	0	0	0	0	0	0	0	7
Los Coyotes Reservation	15	0	0	0	0	0	0	0	15	0
Lovelock Colony	3	2	3	2	5	3	5	0	0	0
Lower Brule Reservation	51	46	24	7	13	19	17	4	3	0
Lower Elwha Reservation and Trust Lands, WA	4	4	3	0	0	0	4	3	2	3

[Continued]

★ 173 ★

Population of American Indian Reservations and Trust Lands, by Age, 1990 - Hannahville-Lummi, Part III

[Continued]

American Indian Reservation and Trust Lands[1,2]	Number of persons									
	45-49 years	50-54 years	55-59 years	60-61 years	62-64 years	65-69 years	70-74 years	75-79 years	80-84 years	85 + years
Lower Sioux Community	15	4	6	2	5	3	6	5	0	5
Lummi Reservation	196	136	128	64	106	139	100	54	19	12

Source: Census of Population and Housing, 1990: Summary Tape File 3C on CD-ROM [machine-readable datafiles]. Prepared by the Bureau of the Census. Washington, DC: The Bureau, 1992. Notes: 1. Federal American Indian reservations are areas with boundaries established by treaty, statute, and/or executive or court order, and recognized by the federal government as territory in which American Indian tribes have jurisdiction. State reservations are lands held in trust by state governments for the use and benefit of a given tribe. The reservations and their boundaries were identified for the 1990 census by the Bureau of Indian Affairs (BIA), Department of Interior (for federal reservations), and state governments (for state reservations). The names of American Indian reservations recognized by state governments, but not by the federal government, are followed by "state." Areas composed of reservation lands that are administered jointly and/or are claimed by two reservations, as identified by the BIA, are called "joint areas," and are treated as separate American Indian reservations for census purposes. Federal reservations may cross state boundaries, and federal and state reservations may cross county, county subdivision, and place boundaries. For reservations that cross state boundaries, only the portion of the reservations in a given state is shown in the data products for that state; the entire reservations are shown in data products for the United States. 2. Trust lands are property associated with a particular American Indian reservation or tribe, held in trust by the federal government. Trust lands may be held in trust either for a tribe (tribal trust lands) or for an individual member of a tribe (individual trust land). Trust lands recognized for the 1990 census comprised all tribal trust lands and inhabited individual trust lands located outside of a reservation boundary. As with other American Indian areas, trust lands may be located in more than one state. Only the trust lands in a given state are shown in the data products for that state; all trust lands associated with a reservation or tribe are shown in data products for the United States. The Census Bureau first reported data for tribal trust lands for the 1980 census.

★ 174 ★

Population

Population of American Indian Reservations and Trust Lands, by Age, 1990 - Makah-Papago, Part I

American Indian Reservation and Trust Lands[1,2]	Number of persons										
	< 1 year	1-2 years	3-4 years	5 years	6 years	7-9 years	10-11 years	12-13 years	14 years	15 years	16 years
Makah Reservation	26	79	60	34	27	75	63	38	30	11	11
Manchester (Point Arena) Rancheria	0	17	2	8	4	26	15	5	0	2	4
Manzanita Reservation	0	0	0	2	0	0	6	4	2	6	6
Maricopa (Ak-Chin) Reservation	15	16	31	8	6	33	16	12	13	14	8
Mashantucket Pequot Reservation	2	5	4	3	3	8	0	3	0	0	0
Mattaponi Reservation (state)	0	3	0	0	0	0	0	7	0	0	0
Menominee Reservation	59	227	168	121	110	236	168	125	56	61	44
Mesa Grande Reservation	0	5	2	2	1	5	2	0	2	2	0
Mescalero Apache Reservation	70	115	185	70	103	216	127	139	46	49	53
Miccosukee Reservation	4	6	6	2	0	5	2	5	2	2	5
Middletown Rancheria	0	2	2	0	0	0	2	4	3	6	2
Mille Lacs Reservation	6	18	24	12	4	29	23	14	5	0	2
Mississippi Choctaw Reservation and Trust Lands, MS	146	191	229	132	154	363	198	197	98	65	123
Moapa River Reservation	10	9	17	18	18	41	25	12	3	10	12
Montgomery Creek Rancheria	0	0	3	0	1	0	0	0	0	0	0
Morongo Reservation	16	55	41	26	23	77	42	37	23	12	4
Muckleshoot Reservation and Trust Lands, WA	92	152	147	90	53	227	148	116	70	61	65
Nambe Pueblo and Trust Lands, NM	11	43	36	32	16	69	44	43	20	27	18
Narragansett Reservation	3	0	1	0	0	3	0	0	0	0	0
Navajo Reservation and Trust Lands, AZ–NM–UT	3,623	8,041	8,062	3,479	3,556	10,674	7,148	6,590	3,220	3,243	3,030
Nez Perce Reservation	181	357	429	226	225	720	576	551	258	247	303
Nisqually Reservation	18	35	23	26	12	53	42	22	10	10	31
Nooksack Reservation and Trust Lands, WA	14	53	30	20	11	56	49	33	9	11	25
Northern Cheyenne Reservation and Trust Lands, MT–SD	61	259	231	81	133	273	145	191	119	75	106
North Fork Rancheria	0	0	0	0	0	0	0	0	0	0	0
Northwestern Shoshoni Reservation	0	0	0	0	0	0	0	0	0	0	0

[Continued]

★ 174 ★

Population of American Indian Reservations and Trust Lands, by Age, 1990 - Makah-Papago, Part I

[Continued]

American Indian Reservation and Trust Lands[1,2]	Number of persons										
	< 1 year	1-2 years	3-4 years	5 years	6 years	7-9 years	10-11 years	12-13 years	14 years	15 years	16 years
Oil Springs Reservation	0	0	0	0	0	0	0	0	0	0	0
Omaha Reservation	95	230	233	124	76	307	216	191	83	88	60
Oneida (East) Reservation	19	0	0	0	0	0	0	0	0	0	0
Oneida (West) Reservation	235	661	702	353	347	1,035	669	660	353	312	359
Onondaga Reservation	13	15	42	0	0	81	52	0	46	0	0
Ontonagon Reservation	0	0	0	0	0	0	0	0	0	0	0
Osage Reservation	442	1,173	1,234	689	623	2,084	1,415	1,276	699	644	681
Ozette Reservation	0	0	0	0	0	0	0	0	0	0	0
Paiute of Utah Reservation	14	5	38	21	7	63	18	31	12	8	6
Pala Reservation	36	78	58	32	25	106	51	37	5	18	17
Pamunkey Reservation (state)	0	0	0	0	0	0	0	0	0	0	0
Papago Reservation	92	400	416	272	296	622	365	399	162	105	198

Source: *Census of Population and Housing, 1990: Summary Tape File 3C on CD-ROM* [machine-readable datafiles]. Prepared by the Bureau of the Census. Washington, DC: The Bureau, 1992. *Notes:* 1. Federal American Indian reservations are areas with boundaries established by treaty, statute, and/or executive or court order, and recognized by the federal government as territory in which American Indian tribes have jurisdiction. State reservations are lands held in trust by state governments for the use and benefit of a given tribe. The reservations and their boundaries were identified for the 1990 census by the Bureau of Indian Affairs (BIA), Department of Interior (for federal reservations), and state governments (for state reservations). The names of American Indian reservations recognized by state governments, but not by the federal government, are followed by "state." Areas composed of reservation lands that are administered jointly and/or are claimed by two reservations, as identified by the BIA, are called "joint areas," and are treated as separate American Indian reservations for census purposes. Federal reservations may cross state boundaries, and federal and state reservations may cross county, county subdivision, and place boundaries. For reservations that cross state boundaries, only the portion of the reservations in a given state is shown in the data products for that state; the entire reservations are shown in data products for the United States. 2. Trust lands are property associated with a particular American Indian reservation or tribe, held in trust by the federal government. Trust lands may be held in trust either for a tribe (tribal trust lands) or for an individual member of a tribe (individual trust land). Trust lands recognized for the 1990 census comprised all tribal trust lands and inhabited individual trust lands located outside of a reservation boundary. As with other American Indian areas, trust lands may be located in more than one state. Only the trust lands in a given state are shown in the data products for that state; all trust lands associated with a reservation or tribe are shown in data products for the United States. The Census Bureau first reported data for tribal trust lands for the 1980 census.

★ 175 ★

Population

Population of American Indian Reservations and Trust Lands, by Age, 1990 - Makah-Papago, Part II

American Indian Reservation and Trust Lands[1,2]	Number of persons									
	17 years	18 years	19 years	20 years	21 years	22-24 years	25-29 years	30-34 years	35-39 years	40-44 years
Makah Reservation	19	29	13	11	23	70	116	106	84	80
Manchester (Point Arena) Rancheria	0	2	0	0	0	7	35	12	10	4
Manzanita Reservation	9	0	0	0	1	0	6	4	6	3
Maricopa (Ak-Chin) Reservation	4	6	2	17	15	23	54	25	29	28
Mashantucket Pequot Reservation	3	0	0	0	0	3	10	8	2	4
Mattaponi Reservation (state)	3	2	6	0	5	8	0	0	0	12
Menominee Reservation	89	46	52	42	41	147	253	301	188	159
Mesa Grande Reservation	1	0	0	1	0	0	4	11	5	4
Mescalero Apache Reservation	36	46	50	43	28	144	262	265	171	103
Miccosukee Reservation	1	2	0	3	0	0	5	7	11	0
Middletown Rancheria	2	7	0	2	0	0	0	5	10	6
Mille Lacs Reservation	8	10	9	6	6	9	27	29	19	18
Mississippi Choctaw Reservation and Trust Lands, MS	85	69	66	38	43	217	377	285	294	268
Moapa River Reservation	4	6	2	11	10	6	55	30	13	30
Montgomery Creek Rancheria	0	0	0	0	0	0	0	4	0	0

[Continued]

★ 175 ★

Population of American Indian Reservations and Trust Lands, by Age, 1990 - Makah-Papago, Part II

[Continued]

American Indian Reservation and Trust Lands[1,2]	Number of persons									
	17 years	18 years	19 years	20 years	21 years	22-24 years	25-29 years	30-34 years	35-39 years	40-44 years
Morongo Reservation	23	17	17	12	21	29	100	105	57	60
Muckleshoot Reservation and Trust Lands, WA	51	49	57	47	24	153	329	285	271	246
Nambe Pueblo and Trust Lands, NM	24	24	13	18	8	31	103	111	139	104
Narragansett Reservation	0	0	0	0	3	0	2	1	0	2
Navajo Reservation and Trust Lands, AZ–NM–UT	2,919	2,828	2,471	2,242	2,113	6,610	12,243	11,209	9,088	7,592
Nez Perce Reservation	255	219	115	126	128	430	974	1,239	1,225	1,141
Nisqually Reservation	4	3	5	7	4	24	52	46	59	57
Nooksack Reservation and Trust Lands, WA	12	18	0	3	0	29	55	42	58	30
Northern Cheyenne Reservation and Trust Lands, MT–SD	92	54	69	67	36	221	250	322	232	308
North Fork Rancheria	0	0	0	0	0	0	0	0	0	0
Northwestern Shoshoni Reservation	0	0	0	0	0	0	0	0	0	0
Oil Springs Reservation	0	0	0	0	0	0	0	0	0	1
Omaha Reservation	76	91	64	39	50	187	358	333	311	299
Oneida (East) Reservation	0	0	0	0	0	0	22	0	0	0
Oneida (West) Reservation	309	281	206	208	171	567	1,469	1,733	1,742	1,546
Onondaga Reservation	0	0	11	34	14	0	39	109	127	104
Ontonagon Reservation	0	0	0	0	0	0	0	0	0	0
Osage Reservation	648	423	471	371	374	1,129	2,941	3,493	3,074	3,085
Ozette Reservation	0	0	0	0	0	0	0	0	0	0
Paiute of Utah Reservation	5	7	5	12	2	19	36	63	41	39
Pala Reservation	7	7	17	12	21	60	113	110	85	41
Pamunkey Reservation (state)	0	0	0	3	0	3	0	0	2	0
Papago Reservation	142	134	133	67	144	400	543	665	553	444

Source: Census of Population and Housing, 1990: Summary Tape File 3C on CD-ROM [machine-readable datafiles]. Prepared by the Bureau of the Census. Washington, DC: The Bureau, 1992. *Notes:* 1. Federal American Indian reservations are areas with boundaries established by treaty, statute, and/or executive or court order, and recognized by the federal government as territory in which American Indian tribes have jurisdiction. State reservations are lands held in trust by state governments for the use and benefit of a given tribe. The reservations and their boundaries were identified for the 1990 census by the Bureau of Indian Affairs (BIA), Department of Interior (for federal reservations), and state governments (for state reservations). The names of American Indian reservations recognized by state governments, but not by the federal government, are followed by "state." Areas composed of reservation lands that are administered jointly and/or are claimed by two reservations, as identified by the BIA, are called "joint areas," and are treated as separate American Indian reservations for census purposes. Federal reservations may cross state boundaries, and federal and state reservations may cross county, county subdivision, and place boundaries. For reservations that cross state boundaries, only the portion of the reservations in a given state is shown in the data products for that state; the entire reservations are shown in data products for the United States. 2. Trust lands are property associated with a particular American Indian reservation or tribe, held in trust by the federal government. Trust lands may be held in trust either for a tribe (tribal trust lands) or for an individual member of a tribe (individual trust land). Trust lands recognized for the 1990 census comprised all tribal trust lands and inhabited individual trust lands located outside of a reservation boundary. As with other American Indian areas, trust lands may be located in more than one state. Only the trust lands in a given state are shown in the data products for that state; all trust lands associated with a reservation or tribe are shown in data products for the United States. The Census Bureau first reported data for tribal trust lands for the 1980 census.

★ 176 ★

Population

Population of American Indian Reservations and Trust Lands, by Age, 1990 - Makah-Papago, Part III

American Indian Reservation and Trust Lands[1,2]	Number of persons									
	45-49 years	50-54 years	55-59 years	60-61 years	62-64 years	65-69 years	70-74 years	75-79 years	80-84 years	85 + years
Makah Reservation	56	60	28	12	4	23	34	5	7	4
Manchester (Point Arena) Rancheria	8	22	6	5	0	4	11	3	0	0
Manzanita Reservation	4	3	2	0	0	0	0	0	2	0
Maricopa (Ak-Chin) Reservation	10	18	4	8	6	5	20	4	0	0
Mashantucket Pequot Reservation	3	4	0	3	3	0	0	0	0	0
Mattaponi Reservation (state)	6	0	3	0	0	4	8	3	0	4
Menominee Reservation	138	108	126	42	55	93	61	53	17	25
Mesa Grande Reservation	0	0	2	0	3	3	8	0	0	0
Mescalero Apache Reservation	103	73	34	23	29	41	20	12	8	0
Miccosukee Reservation	0	0	4	0	0	0	0	0	0	0
Middletown Rancheria	5	6	2	1	2	0	2	5	0	0
Mille Lacs Reservation	8	15	27	5	11	8	10	8	0	10
Mississippi Choctaw Reservation and Trust Lands, MS	96	196	61	82	70	64	10	29	11	0
Moapa River Reservation	10	4	5	3	1	12	0	0	0	0
Montgomery Creek Rancheria	0	0	0	0	0	0	0	0	0	0
Morongo Reservation	48	45	32	15	29	61	41	11	22	8
Muckleshoot Reservation and Trust Lands, WA	209	163	196	44	64	128	159	58	43	39
Nambe Pueblo and Trust Lands, NM	86	92	39	26	57	44	31	22	14	13
Narragansett Reservation	4	6	0	0	0	0	0	2	0	0
Navajo Reservation and Trust Lands, AZ–NM–UT	5,777	5,573	4,530	2,009	2,001	3,060	2,199	1,539	988	1,001
Nez Perce Reservation	972	892	892	328	511	826	728	508	367	210
Nisqually Reservation	31	18	21	17	7	11	1	0	0	0
Nooksack Reservation and Trust Lands, WA	22	31	4	25	24	28	0	0	5	0
Northern Cheyenne Reservation and Trust Lands, MT–SD	157	125	82	32	62	85	33	5	0	0
North Fork Rancheria	0	0	0	0	0	0	0	0	0	0
Northwestern Shoshoni Reservation	0	0	0	0	0	0	0	0	0	0
Oil Springs Reservation	0	2	0	0	0	0	0	0	0	1
Omaha Reservation	266	219	244	114	134	213	212	132	93	100
Oneida (East) Reservation	0	0	0	0	0	0	0	0	0	0
Oneida (West) Reservation	1,021	959	572	244	303	373	220	186	112	32
Onondaga Reservation	0	0	37	0	0	0	22	25	0	0
Ontonagon Reservation	0	0	0	0	0	0	0	0	0	0
Osage Reservation	2,663	2,197	2,007	775	1,178	1,724	1,606	1,080	690	504
Ozette Reservation	0	0	0	0	0	0	0	0	0	0
Paiute of Utah Reservation	32	24	49	5	27	21	4	5	1	4
Pala Reservation	30	32	32	5	24	20	19	16	2	9
Pamunkey Reservation (state)	0	6	12	0	3	3	15	0	0	0
Papago Reservation	483	357	302	108	207	213	124	123	45	73

Source: Census of Population and Housing, 1990: Summary Tape File 3C on CD-ROM [machine-readable datafiles]. Prepared by the Bureau of the Census. Washington, DC: The Bureau, 1992. Notes: 1. Federal American Indian reservations are areas with boundaries established by treaty, statute, and/or executive or court order, and recognized by the federal government as territory in which American Indian tribes have jurisdiction. State reservations are lands held in trust by state governments for the use and benefit of a given tribe. The reservations and their boundaries were identified for the 1990 census by the Bureau of Indian Affairs (BIA), Department of Interior (for federal reservations), and state governments (for state reservations). The names of American Indian reservations recognized by state governments, but not by the federal government, are followed by "state." Areas composed of reservation lands that are administered jointly and/or are claimed by two reservations, as identified by the BIA, are called "joint areas," and are treated as separate American Indian reservations for census purposes. Federal reservations may cross state boundaries, and federal and state reservations may cross county, county subdivision, and place boundaries. For reservations that cross state boundaries, only the portion of the reservations in a given state is shown in the data products for that state; the entire reservations are shown in data products for the United States. 2. Trust lands are property associated with a particular American Indian reservation or tribe, held in trust by the federal government. Trust lands may be held in trust either for a tribe (tribal trust lands) or for an individual member of a tribe (individual trust land). Trust lands recognized for the 1990 census comprised all tribal trust lands and inhabited individual trust lands located outside of a reservation boundary. As with other American Indian areas, trust lands may be located in more than one state. Only the trust lands in a given state are shown in the data products for that state; all trust lands associated with a reservation or tribe are shown in data products for the United States. The Census Bureau first reported data for tribal trust lands for the 1980 census.

★ 177 ★
Population

Population of American Indian Reservations and Trust Lands, by Age, 1990 - Pascua-Rocky Boy's, Part I

American Indian Reservation and Trust Lands[1,2]	Number of persons										
	< 1 year	1-2 years	3-4 years	5 years	6 years	7-9 years	10-11 years	12-13 years	14 years	15 years	16 years
Pascua Yaqui Reservation	74	179	145	68	85	191	138	115	84	36	36
Paucatuck Eastern Pequot Reservation (state)	0	0	0	0	0	0	0	0	0	0	0
Pauma Reservation	6	17	12	2	9	15	11	1	1	0	2
Payson (Yavapai-Apache) Community	0	0	0	0	13	0	0	13	0	0	0
Pechanga Reservation	4	15	10	7	6	24	22	6	10	9	12
Penobscot Reservation and Trust Lands, ME	12	9	13	10	22	34	12	8	8	4	7
Picayune Rancheria	0	0	0	0	0	0	0	0	0	0	0
Picuris Pueblo	21	51	100	25	35	93	41	89	24	46	34
Pine Creek Reservation (state)	0	0	0	2	0	0	0	0	0	0	0
Pine Ridge Reservation and Trust Lands, NE–SD	289	845	846	298	415	890	558	481	310	210	210
Pinoleville Rancheria	4	2	3	0	0	5	0	0	0	0	0
Pleasant Point Reservation	19	13	23	7	10	59	21	30	4	5	13
Poarch Creek Reservation and Trust Lands, AL	9	20	5	15	4	20	2	5	4	12	6
Pojoaque Pueblo	33	64	80	50	48	117	130	81	28	31	40
Poospatuck Reservation (state)	0	16	0	0	4	31	8	0	0	3	0
Port Gamble Reservation	9	33	22	19	8	42	21	24	14	10	13
Port Madison Reservation	69	105	231	106	93	248	163	150	87	49	50
Potawatomi (Kansas) Reservation	25	54	57	26	24	71	42	35	13	14	11
Potawatomi (Wisconsin) Reservation and Trust Lands, WI	2	13	12	9	9	23	15	19	7	4	2
Prairie Island Community	0	1	2	0	0	1	1	2	0	0	0
Puyallup Reservation and Trust Lands, WA	539	1,208	1,231	563	635	1,804	1,108	937	437	384	443
Pyramid Lake Reservation	15	57	75	34	36	98	50	39	21	22	16
Quartz Valley Rancheria	0	2	3	0	0	4	0	8	0	0	0
Quileute Reservation	20	13	19	12	2	22	21	7	2	7	10
Quinault Reservation	39	79	50	33	22	72	61	25	16	37	10
Ramah Navajo Community	2	13	6	4	0	9	7	6	2	5	7
Ramona Reservation	0	0	0	0	0	0	0	0	0	0	0
Rankokus Reservation (state)	0	0	0	0	0	0	0	0	0	0	0
Red Cliff Reservation and Trust Lands, WI	17	44	43	25	33	46	30	37	8	14	30
Redding Rancheria	0	0	3	0	0	0	0	3	0	0	4
Red Lake Reservation	72	201	228	136	50	301	155	190	73	48	82
Redwood Valley Rancheria	0	0	0	0	8	17	0	0	0	0	0
Reno-Sparks Colony	0	4	17	6	8	24	10	0	2	14	2
Resighini Rancheria	0	0	5	6	0	7	5	0	0	0	0
Rincon Reservation	33	56	60	22	26	82	45	62	16	30	19
Roaring Creek Rancheria	5	5	4	0	0	0	3	0	0	0	0
Robinson Rancheria	6	9	9	3	10	9	22	9	4	1	9
Rocky Boy's Reservation and Trust Lands, MT	54	102	117	50	41	158	107	76	51	36	42

Source: Census of Population and Housing, 1990: Summary Tape File 3C on CD-ROM [machine-readable datafiles]. Prepared by the Bureau of the Census. Washington, DC: The Bureau, 1992. *Notes:* 1. Federal American Indian reservations are areas with boundaries established by treaty, statute, and/or executive or court order, and recognized by the federal government as territory in which American Indian tribes have jurisdiction. State reservations are lands held in trust by state governments for the use and benefit of a given tribe. The reservations and their boundaries were identified for the 1990 census by the Bureau of Indian Affairs (BIA), Department of Interior (for federal reservations), and state governments (for state reservations). The names of American Indian reservations recognized by state governments, but not by the federal government, are followed by "state." Areas composed of reservation lands that are administered jointly and/or are claimed by two reservations, as identified by the BIA, are called "joint areas," and are treated as separate American Indian reservations for census purposes. Federal reservations may cross state boundaries, and federal and state reservations may cross county, county subdivision, and place boundaries. For reservations that cross state boundaries, only the portion of the reservations in a given state is shown in the data products for that state; the entire reservations are shown in data products for the United States. 2. Trust lands are property associated with a particular American Indian reservation or tribe, held in trust by the federal government. Trust lands may be held in trust either for a tribe (tribal trust lands) or for an individual member of a tribe (individual trust land). Trust lands recognized for the 1990 census comprised all tribal trust lands and inhabited individual trust lands located outside of a reservation boundary. As with other American Indian areas, trust lands may be located in more than one state. Only the trust lands in a given state are shown in the data products for that state; all trust lands associated with a reservation or tribe are shown in data products for the United States. The Census Bureau first reported data for tribal trust lands for the 1980 census.

★ 178 ★

Population

Population of American Indian Reservations and Trust Lands, by Age, 1990 - Pascua-Rocky Boy's, Part II

American Indian Reservation and Trust Lands[1,2]	Number of persons									
	17 years	18 years	19 years	20 years	21 years	22-24 years	25-29 years	30-34 years	35-39 years	40-44 years
Pascua Yaqui Reservation	29	53	54	47	40	104	215	158	137	123
Paucatuck Eastern Pequot Reservation (state)	0	4	0	0	0	0	0	4	4	0
Pauma Reservation	0	3	3	0	0	2	19	19	8	11
Payson (Yavapai-Apache) Community	0	0	0	0	0	0	26	0	13	12
Pechanga Reservation	4	4	2	3	10	18	29	24	35	32
Penobscot Reservation and Trust Lands, ME	7	5	0	4	13	12	40	61	53	30
Picayune Rancheria	0	0	0	0	0	0	0	0	0	0
Picuris Pueblo	37	41	27	19	12	74	171	135	137	110
Pine Creek Reservation (state)	2	0	0	0	2	0	0	0	2	4
Pine Ridge Reservation and Trust Lands, NE–SD	207	199	216	153	168	534	959	749	736	621
Pinoleville Rancheria	0	0	0	0	0	15	10	0	5	6
Pleasant Point Reservation	3	5	15	17	10	39	45	28	10	30
Poarch Creek Reservation and Trust Lands, AL	2	6	11	7	2	4	22	15	21	3
Pojoaque Pueblo	43	33	19	24	28	92	214	274	235	179
Poospatuck Reservation (state)	0	14	16	8	0	8	7	23	0	3
Port Gamble Reservation	9	10	8	17	13	18	60	51	49	26
Port Madison Reservation	62	52	38	44	38	104	359	467	483	403
Potawatomi (Kansas) Reservation	27	11	13	11	17	39	74	62	90	77
Potawatomi (Wisconsin) Reservation and Trust Lands, WI	5	2	8	0	2	5	35	14	15	13
Prairie Island Community	0	3	0	0	2	0	1	1	10	1
Puyallup Reservation and Trust Lands, WA	413	395	438	465	429	1,375	2,782	3,170	2,740	2,201
Pyramid Lake Reservation	11	23	12	12	10	52	128	110	92	66
Quartz Valley Rancheria	0	0	0	0	0	0	3	3	7	0
Quileute Reservation	1	0	10	3	13	11	55	43	24	7
Quinault Reservation	35	10	10	22	14	45	142	104	63	121
Ramah Navajo Community	5	2	7	5	4	5	7	21	6	11
Ramona Reservation	0	0	0	0	0	0	0	0	0	0
Rankokus Reservation (state)	0	0	0	0	0	0	0	0	0	0
Red Cliff Reservation and Trust Lands, WI	14	14	7	12	15	54	75	63	78	41
Redding Rancheria	4	4	4	0	0	0	0	11	8	7
Red Lake Reservation	76	89	66	40	64	185	296	256	232	189
Redwood Valley Rancheria	0	0	0	0	0	0	19	12	18	0
Reno-Sparks Colony	5	5	5	10	10	12	18	10	16	13
Resighini Rancheria	0	0	0	0	0	0	3	10	15	0
Rincon Reservation	32	41	53	10	24	63	142	107	163	112
Roaring Creek Rancheria	0	0	0	0	0	0	0	3	0	0
Robinson Rancheria	0	4	0	1	0	3	27	6	20	11
Rocky Boy's Reservation and Trust Lands, MT	29	37	29	36	30	88	166	155	131	124

Source: Census of Population and Housing, 1990: Summary Tape File 3C on CD-ROM [machine-readable datafiles]. Prepared by the Bureau of the Census. Washington, DC: The Bureau, 1992. *Notes:* 1. Federal American Indian reservations are areas with boundaries established by treaty, statute, and/or executive or court order, and recognized by the federal government as territory in which American Indian tribes have jurisdiction. State reservations are lands held in trust by state governments for the use and benefit of a given tribe. The reservations and their boundaries were identified for the 1990 census by the Bureau of Indian Affairs (BIA), Department of Interior (for federal reservations), and state governments (for state reservations). The names of American Indian reservations recognized by state governments, but not by the federal government, are followed by "state." Areas composed of reservation lands that are administered jointly and/or are claimed by two reservations, as identified by the BIA, are called "joint areas," and are treated as separate American Indian reservations for census purposes. Federal reservations may cross state boundaries, and federal and state reservations may cross county, county subdivision, and place boundaries. For reservations that cross state boundaries, only the portion of the reservations in a given state is shown in the data products for that state; the entire reservations are shown in data products for the United States. 2. Trust lands are property associated with a particular American Indian reservation or tribe, held in trust by the federal government. Trust lands may be held in trust either for a tribe (tribal trust lands) or for an individual member of a tribe (individual trust land). Trust lands recognized for the 1990 census comprised all tribal trust lands and inhabited individual trust lands located outside of a reservation boundary. As with other American Indian areas, trust lands may be located in more than one state. Only the trust lands in a given state are shown in the data products for that state; all trust lands associated with a reservation or tribe are shown in data products for the United States. The Census Bureau first reported data for tribal trust lands for the 1980 census.

★ 179 ★

Population

Population of American Indian Reservations and Trust Lands, by Age, 1990 - Pascua-Rocky Boy's, Part III

American Indian Reservation and Trust Lands[1,2]	Number of persons									
	45-49 years	50-54 years	55-59 years	60-61 years	62-64 years	65-69 years	70-74 years	75-79 years	80-84 years	85 + years
Pascua Yaqui Reservation	63	94	39	17	34	21	15	12	0	0
Paucatuck Eastern Pequot Reservation (state)	4	0	0	0	0	0	0	0	0	0
Pauma Reservation	7	0	0	0	0	2	1	0	0	0
Payson (Yavapai-Apache) Community	0	26	0	0	0	0	0	0	0	0
Pechanga Reservation	28	11	11	5	18	12	4	7	7	2
Penobscot Reservation and Trust Lands, ME	24	17	17	4	7	16	7	4	6	3
Picayune Rancheria	0	0	0	0	0	0	0	0	0	0
Picuris Pueblo	114	93	74	31	40	61	52	44	38	30
Pine Creek Reservation (state)	2	0	0	0	2	3	3	0	0	0
Pine Ridge Reservation and Trust Lands, NE–SD	435	408	263	113	309	318	113	161	68	37
Pinoleville Rancheria	5	5	0	0	5	5	0	0	0	0
Pleasant Point Reservation	56	11	23	4	13	10	4	7	4	4
Poarch Creek Reservation and Trust Lands, AL	18	5	3	0	14	10	4	6	0	0
Pojoaque Pueblo	136	121	120	19	52	55	56	44	24	11
Poospatuck Reservation (state)	24	16	0	8	0	0	7	0	0	0
Port Gamble Reservation	22	13	24	0	8	8	2	0	2	0
Port Madison Reservation	325	185	163	84	113	184	181	126	41	31
Potawatomi (Kansas) Reservation	60	48	49	20	15	27	19	23	21	4
Potawatomi (Wisconsin) Reservation and Trust Lands, WI	11	3	10	8	5	7	0	4	2	2
Prairie Island Community	0	0	0	0	0	4	1	0	0	0
Puyallup Reservation and Trust Lands, WA	1,964	1,515	1,174	438	717	1,022	820	553	341	194
Pyramid Lake Reservation	56	54	74	16	15	56	49	36	12	11
Quartz Valley Rancheria	0	3	3	6	11	0	0	2	0	2
Quileute Reservation	12	24	7	0	2	2	3	0	0	0
Quinault Reservation	73	69	19	13	11	25	36	2	7	6
Ramah Navajo Community	7	11	4	0	1	8	2	6	0	2
Ramona Reservation	0	0	0	0	0	0	0	0	0	0
Rankokus Reservation (state)	0	0	0	0	0	0	0	0	0	0
Red Cliff Reservation and Trust Lands, WI	38	39	25	9	12	23	13	7	6	4
Redding Rancheria	5	5	0	0	0	0	14	0	0	0
Red Lake Reservation	138	88	124	50	72	61	53	37	24	14
Redwood Valley Rancheria	0	0	9	9	9	0	10	0	0	0
Reno-Sparks Colony	13	18	4	4	3	0	4	3	2	0
Resighini Rancheria	0	0	0	0	0	0	0	0	0	0
Rincon Reservation	45	40	58	14	31	18	54	0	12	8
Roaring Creek Rancheria	0	0	0	0	0	0	0	0	0	0
Robinson Rancheria	0	0	3	1	0	0	0	0	0	0
Rocky Boy's Reservation and Trust Lands, MT	63	53	35	21	18	46	18	7	8	3

Source: Census of Population and Housing, 1990: Summary Tape File 3C on CD-ROM [machine-readable datafiles]. Prepared by the Bureau of the Census. Washington, DC: The Bureau, 1992. *Notes:* 1. Federal American Indian reservations are areas with boundaries established by treaty, statute, and/or executive or court order, and recognized by the federal government as territory in which American Indian tribes have jurisdiction. State reservations are lands held in trust by state governments for the use and benefit of a given tribe. The reservations and their boundaries were identified for the 1990 census by the Bureau of Indian Affairs (BIA), Department of Interior (for federal reservations), and state governments (for state reservations). The names of American Indian reservations recognized by state governments, but not by the federal government, are followed by "state." Areas composed of reservation lands that are administered jointly and/or are claimed by two reservations, as identified by the BIA, are called "joint areas," and are treated as separate American Indian reservations for census purposes. Federal reservations may cross state boundaries, and federal and state reservations may cross county, county subdivision, and place boundaries. For reservations that cross state boundaries, only the portion of the reservations in a given state is shown in the data products for that state; the entire reservations are shown in data products for the United States. 2. Trust lands are property associated with a particular American Indian reservation or tribe, held in trust by the federal government. Trust lands may be held in trust either for a tribe (tribal trust lands) or for an individual member of a tribe (individual trust land). Trust lands recognized for the 1990 census comprised all tribal trust lands and inhabited individual trust lands located outside of a reservation boundary. As with other American Indian areas, trust lands may be located in more than one state. Only the trust lands in a given state are shown in the data products for that state; all trust lands associated with a reservation or tribe are shown in data products for the United States. The Census Bureau first reported data for tribal trust lands for the 1980 census.

★ 180 ★

Population

Population of American Indian Reservations and Trust Lands, by Age, 1990 - Rohnerville-Soboba, Part I

American Indian Reservation and Trust Lands[1,2]	Number of persons										
	< 1 year	1-2 years	3-4 years	5 years	6 years	7-9 years	10-11 years	12-13 years	14 years	15 years	16 years
Rohnerville Rancheria	0	0	0	0	0	0	0	0	0	0	0
Rosebud Reservation and Trust Lands, SD	299	537	441	276	299	753	401	469	252	215	241
Round Valley Reservation and Trust Lands, CA	24	48	50	29	25	77	37	40	8	22	13
Rumsey Rancheria	0	0	0	0	0	0	0	0	0	0	0
Sac and Fox (Iowa) Reservation	12	26	23	5	16	50	42	32	12	12	6
Sac and Fox (KS-NE) Reservation and Trust Lands, KS–NE	0	6	15	0	4	11	3	4	6	0	3
St. Croix Reservation	20	16	23	23	11	31	11	17	10	12	5
St. Regis Mohawk Reservation	23	75	123	27	35	73	88	80	24	15	45
Salt River Reservation	89	227	197	120	66	291	181	197	57	34	75
San Carlos Reservation	218	362	391	234	221	579	315	379	95	109	191
Sandia Pueblo	74	140	147	106	73	173	171	169	76	40	82
Sandy Lake Reservation	0	3	2	1	0	2	1	1	0	0	0
San Felipe Pueblo	71	123	124	74	74	127	109	103	49	47	48
San Ildefonso Pueblo	18	50	78	56	30	95	52	49	24	28	26
San Juan Pueblo	96	211	189	85	84	257	177	189	84	122	91
San Manuel Reservation	0	12	0	0	0	8	0	3	0	0	0
San Pasqual Reservation	8	2	19	24	13	27	18	25	23	20	8
Santa Ana Pueblo	8	26	39	23	17	42	28	22	4	12	3
Santa Clara Pueblo	159	338	344	191	179	608	353	354	138	157	176
Santa Rosa Rancheria	17	13	16	9	10	24	9	11	10	11	19
Santa Rosa Reservation	8	0	5	2	2	3	3	0	0	0	3
Santa Ynez Reservation	0	11	20	11	5	19	27	11	2	0	3
Santa Ysabel Reservation	3	1	1	0	1	11	14	5	3	8	11
Santee Reservation	14	24	27	10	8	46	43	31	14	18	9
Santo Domingo Pueblo	56	158	116	86	112	183	46	71	77	55	64
San Xavier Reservation	37	30	53	17	33	100	70	24	9	19	18
Sauk-Suiattle Reservation	3	6	6	3	3	0	9	5	4	0	2
Sault Ste. Marie Reservation and Trust Lands, MI	22	23	44	15	27	65	47	45	23	11	7
Schaghticoke Reservation (state)	0	0	0	0	0	0	0	2	0	0	0
Shakopee Community	7	12	13	13	4	10	5	3	2	3	3
Sheep Ranch Rancheria	0	0	0	0	0	0	0	0	0	0	0
Sherwood Valley Rancheria	0	0	0	0	0	0	0	0	0	0	0
Shingle Springs Rancheria	0	0	0	0	0	0	0	0	0	0	0
Shinnecock Reservation (state)	5	13	7	6	8	26	5	7	9	7	4
Shoalwater Reservation	10	11	0	3	0	3	3	15	5	6	3
Siletz Reservation	0	0	0	0	0	0	0	0	0	0	0
Skokomish Reservation	6	23	26	19	19	30	21	16	7	9	7
Skull Valley Reservation	0	0	0	0	0	0	0	0	0	0	0
Smith River Rancheria	0	7	5	0	0	9	26	16	0	7	0
Soboba Reservation	0	28	14	10	11	44	24	23	5	2	8

Source: Census of Population and Housing, 1990: Summary Tape File 3C on CD-ROM [machine-readable datafiles]. Prepared by the Bureau of the Census. Washington, DC: The Bureau, 1992. *Notes:* 1. Federal American Indian reservations are areas with boundaries established by treaty, statute, and/or executive or court order, and recognized by the federal government as territory in which American Indian tribes have jurisdiction. State reservations are lands held in trust by state governments for the use and benefit of a given tribe. The reservations and their boundaries were identified for the 1990 census by the Bureau of Indian Affairs (BIA), Department of Interior (for federal reservations), and state governments (for state reservations). The names of American Indian reservations recognized by state governments, but not by the federal government, are followed by "state." Areas composed of reservation lands that are administered jointly and/or are claimed by two reservations, as identified by the BIA, are called "joint areas," and are treated as separate American Indian reservations for census purposes. Federal reservations may cross state boundaries, and federal and state reservations may cross county, county subdivision, and place boundaries. For reservations that cross state boundaries, only the portion of the reservations in a given state is shown in the data products for that state; the entire reservations are shown in data products for the United States. 2. Trust lands are property associated with a particular American Indian reservation or tribe, held in trust by the federal government. Trust lands may be held in trust either for a tribe (tribal trust lands) or for an individual member of a tribe (individual trust land). Trust lands recognized for the 1990 census comprised all tribal trust lands and inhabited individual trust lands located outside of a reservation boundary. As with other American Indian areas, trust lands may be located in more than one state. Only the trust lands in a given state are shown in the data products for that state; all trust lands associated with a reservation or tribe are shown in data products for the United States. The Census Bureau first reported data for tribal trust lands for the 1980 census.

★ 181 ★

Population

Population of American Indian Reservations and Trust Lands, by Age, 1990 - Rohnerville-Soboba, Part II

American Indian Reservation and Trust Lands[1,2]	Number of persons									
	17 years	18 years	19 years	20 years	21 years	22-24 years	25-29 years	30-34 years	35-39 years	40-44 years
Rohnerville Rancheria	0	0	0	0	0	0	0	0	0	0
Rosebud Reservation and Trust Lands, SD	222	138	195	118	182	358	654	623	712	471
Round Valley Reservation and Trust Lands, CA	7	26	12	17	5	33	106	83	57	98
Rumsey Rancheria	0	0	0	0	0	0	0	0	0	19
Sac and Fox (Iowa) Reservation	6	12	24	8	6	23	59	27	35	25
Sac and Fox (KS-NE) Reservation and Trust Lands, KS–NE	2	5	0	0	0	2	10	20	11	10
St. Croix Reservation	11	11	15	6	10	16	44	30	25	39
St. Regis Mohawk Reservation	55	14	36	16	41	100	136	202	142	118
Salt River Reservation	76	57	63	70	83	168	326	400	353	164
San Carlos Reservation	118	131	108	109	116	444	507	600	481	373
Sandia Pueblo	57	33	60	38	51	129	324	434	351	301
Sandy Lake Reservation	0	0	0	0	0	3	2	7	1	0
San Felipe Pueblo	47	52	54	34	39	125	239	200	161	168
San Ildefonso Pueblo	12	12	6	15	30	49	149	173	143	124
San Juan Pueblo	83	63	132	67	69	221	469	424	380	433
San Manuel Reservation	4	0	4	3	0	7	5	3	3	0
San Pasqual Reservation	14	8	10	12	6	16	30	32	59	55
Santa Ana Pueblo	7	8	7	11	7	20	71	65	63	37
Santa Clara Pueblo	172	148	137	131	165	358	705	882	871	700
Santa Rosa Rancheria	10	3	12	9	3	18	33	8	12	8
Santa Rosa Reservation	0	4	0	1	4	2	10	0	0	8
Santa Ynez Reservation	21	0	2	11	4	16	21	20	31	21
Santa Ysabel Reservation	0	5	6	3	2	0	12	4	17	25
Santee Reservation	15	13	12	10	12	27	45	39	58	67
Santo Domingo Pueblo	44	35	78	58	50	166	290	172	205	182
San Xavier Reservation	50	21	10	28	30	27	101	96	87	75
Sauk-Suiattle Reservation	2	4	0	0	2	2	9	10	13	8
Sault Ste. Marie Reservation and Trust Lands, MI	27	9	9	15	21	24	43	87	46	26
Schaghticoke Reservation (state)	0	0	0	0	0	2	0	0	3	3
Shakopee Community	3	0	7	7	3	16	20	19	12	6
Sheep Ranch Rancheria	0	0	0	0	0	0	0	0	0	0
Sherwood Valley Rancheria	0	0	0	0	0	0	0	0	0	2
Shingle Springs Rancheria	0	0	3	0	0	0	0	0	0	4
Shinnecock Reservation (state)	2	9	2	5	4	11	28	39	29	18
Shoalwater Reservation	2	8	0	2	0	0	16	7	9	9
Siletz Reservation	0	0	0	0	0	0	0	0	0	0
Skokomish Reservation	14	6	12	7	8	20	62	57	31	41
Skull Valley Reservation	0	0	0	5	5	0	0	0	2	0

[Continued]

★ 181 ★

Population of American Indian Reservations and Trust Lands, by Age, 1990 - Rohnerville-Soboba, Part II

[Continued]

American Indian Reservation and Trust Lands[1,2]	Number of persons									
	17 years	18 years	19 years	20 years	21 years	22-24 years	25-29 years	30-34 years	35-39 years	40-44 years
Smith River Rancheria	0	10	0	0	0	12	16	19	15	0
Soboba Reservation	3	9	9	11	4	14	44	54	25	28

Source: Census of Population and Housing, 1990: Summary Tape File 3C on CD-ROM [machine-readable datafiles]. Prepared by the Bureau of the Census. Washington, DC: The Bureau, 1992. *Notes:* 1. Federal American Indian reservations are areas with boundaries established by treaty, statute, and/or executive or court order, and recognized by the federal government as territory in which American Indian tribes have jurisdiction. State reservations are lands held in trust by state governments for the use and benefit of a given tribe. The reservations and their boundaries were identified for the 1990 census by the Bureau of Indian Affairs (BIA), Department of Interior (for federal reservations), and state governments (for state reservations). The names of American Indian reservations recognized by state governments, but not by the federal government, are followed by "state." Areas composed of reservation lands that are administered jointly and/or are claimed by two reservations, as identified by the BIA, are called "joint areas," and are treated as separate American Indian reservations for census purposes. Federal reservations may cross state boundaries, and federal and state reservations may cross county, county subdivision, and place boundaries. For reservations that cross state boundaries, only the portion of the reservations in a given state is shown in the data products for that state; the entire reservations are shown in data products for the United States. 2. Trust lands are property associated with a particular American Indian reservation or tribe, held in trust by the federal government. Trust lands may be held in trust either for a tribe (tribal trust lands) or for an individual member of a tribe (individual trust land). Trust lands recognized for the 1990 census comprised all tribal trust lands and inhabited individual trust lands located outside of a reservation boundary. As with other American Indian areas, trust lands may be located in more than one state. Only the trust lands in a given state are shown in the data products for that state; all trust lands associated with a reservation or tribe are shown in data products for the United States. The Census Bureau first reported data for tribal trust lands for the 1980 census.

★ 182 ★

Population

Population of American Indian Reservations and Trust Lands, by Age, 1990 - Rohnerville-Soboba, Part III

American Indian Reservation and Trust Lands[1,2]	Number of persons									
	45-49 years	50-54 years	55-59 years	60-61 years	62-64 years	65-69 years	70-74 years	75-79 years	80-84 years	85 + years
Rohnerville Rancheria	0	0	0	0	0	0	0	0	0	0
Rosebud Reservation and Trust Lands, SD	387	274	259	90	138	253	176	102	59	38
Round Valley Reservation and Trust Lands, CA	52	95	38	29	27	52	41	7	11	12
Rumsey Rancheria	0	0	0	0	0	0	0	0	0	0
Sac and Fox (Iowa) Reservation	27	18	27	8	12	9	13	9	0	2
Sac and Fox (KS-NE) Reservation and Trust Lands, KS–NE	11	10	9	2	2	11	0	3	0	2
St. Croix Reservation	25	18	31	0	12	8	0	0	2	3
St. Regis Mohawk Reservation	47	154	81	18	25	43	75	35	28	0
Salt River Reservation	276	136	179	48	110	216	201	219	122	55
San Carlos Reservation	242	240	272	57	86	101	60	38	42	20
Sandia Pueblo	186	150	146	48	69	127	67	66	41	15
Sandy Lake Reservation	0	3	2	0	0	0	0	0	0	0
San Felipe Pueblo	143	64	60	34	22	50	45	16	10	13
San Ildefonso Pueblo	57	68	63	22	11	57	20	36	25	8
San Juan Pueblo	299	239	203	73	103	122	101	82	61	28
San Manuel Reservation	5	0	0	0	0	0	2	0	0	0
San Pasqual Reservation	23	16	9	0	13	11	5	9	2	0
Santa Ana Pueblo	28	7	9	4	18	17	13	2	2	4
Santa Clara Pueblo	521	500	407	140	215	405	245	189	174	168
Santa Rosa Rancheria	5	18	3	6	3	6	8	3	2	0
Santa Rosa Reservation	2	1	0	0	0	0	0	0	0	0
Santa Ynez Reservation	15	4	9	8	0	5	6	9	5	0
Santa Ysabel Reservation	6	10	9	4	3	5	0	0	4	0

[Continued]

★ 182 ★

Population of American Indian Reservations and Trust Lands, by Age, 1990 - Rohnerville-Soboba, Part III

[Continued]

American Indian Reservation and Trust Lands[1,2]	Number of persons									
	45-49 years	50-54 years	55-59 years	60-61 years	62-64 years	65-69 years	70-74 years	75-79 years	80-84 years	85 + years
Santee Reservation	39	27	20	16	25	24	16	16	9	6
Santo Domingo Pueblo	89	105	40	44	39	47	55	15	35	0
San Xavier Reservation	36	37	76	6	0	14	19	0	6	0
Sauk-Suiattle Reservation	13	8	0	0	0	0	0	0	0	0
Sault Ste. Marie Reservation and Trust Lands, MI	27	21	2	1	2	16	0	18	0	0
Schaghticoke Reservation (state)	0	0	0	0	0	0	0	0	0	0
Shakopee Community	14	13	7	0	12	0	6	8	1	0
Sheep Ranch Rancheria	0	0	0	0	0	0	0	0	0	0
Sherwood Valley Rancheria	0	0	0	0	0	4	0	0	0	0
Shingle Springs Rancheria	3	0	0	2	0	0	0	0	0	0
Shinnecock Reservation (state)	20	32	18	6	11	28	21	3	11	3
Shoalwater Reservation	7	0	10	0	0	0	0	0	0	0
Siletz Reservation	0	0	0	0	0	0	0	0	0	0
Skokomish Reservation	29	38	27	8	11	20	10	10	21	3
Skull Valley Reservation	0	5	0	0	0	0	0	0	0	0
Smith River Rancheria	0	17	0	7	23	0	0	0	0	0
Soboba Reservation	8	12	19	2	7	10	3	3	5	3

Source: Census of Population and Housing, 1990: Summary Tape File 3C on CD-ROM [machine-readable datafiles]. Prepared by the Bureau of the Census. Washington, DC: The Bureau, 1992. *Notes:* 1. Federal American Indian reservations are areas with boundaries established by treaty, statute, and/or executive or court order, and recognized by the federal government as territory in which American Indian tribes have jurisdiction. State reservations are lands held in trust by state governments for the use and benefit of a given tribe. The reservations and their boundaries were identified for the 1990 census by the Bureau of Indian Affairs (BIA), Department of Interior (for federal reservations), and state governments (for state reservations). The names of American Indian reservations recognized by state governments, but not by the federal government, are followed by "state." Areas composed of reservation lands that are administered jointly and/or are claimed by two reservations, as identified by the BIA, are called "joint areas," and are treated as separate American Indian reservations for census purposes. Federal reservations may cross state boundaries, and federal and state reservations may cross county, county subdivision, and place boundaries. For reservations that cross state boundaries, only the portion of the reservations in a given state is shown in the data products for that state; the entire reservations are shown in data products for the United States. 2. Trust lands are property associated with a particular American Indian reservation or tribe, held in trust by the federal government. Trust lands may be held in trust either for a tribe (tribal trust lands) or for an individual member of a tribe (individual trust land). Trust lands recognized for the 1990 census comprised all tribal trust lands and inhabited individual trust lands located outside of a reservation boundary. As with other American Indian areas, trust lands may be located in more than one state. Only the trust lands in a given state are shown in the data products for that state; all trust lands associated with a reservation or tribe are shown in data products for the United States. The Census Bureau first reported data for tribal trust lands for the 1980 census.

★ 183 ★

Population

Population of American Indian Reservations and Trust Lands, by Age, 1990 - Sokaogan-Ute, Part I

American Indian Reservation and Trust Lands[1,2]	Number of persons										
	< 1 year	1-2 years	3-4 years	5 years	6 years	7-9 years	10-11 years	12-13 years	14 years	15 years	16 years
Sokaogon Chippewa Community and Trust Lands, WI	13	32	23	5	7	27	8	27	6	4	7
Southern Ute Reservation	119	271	284	169	168	487	292	271	138	126	120
Spokane Reservation	36	80	73	23	30	103	69	45	21	28	27
Squaxin Island Reservation and Trust Lands, WA	11	7	10	5	2	11	7	8	2	1	2
Standing Rock Reservation	162	368	382	152	177	555	364	379	214	158	180
Stewarts Point Rancheria	6	4	5	5	0	0	4	0	5	0	0
Stillaguamish Reservation	2	5	2	0	1	7	13	11	4	0	2
Stockbridge Reservation	4	23	12	9	18	19	33	24	6	11	5
Sulphur Bank (El-Em) Rancheria	0	5	3	0	0	0	8	6	4	4	5

[Continued]

★ 183 ★

Population of American Indian Reservations and Trust Lands, by Age, 1990 - Sokaogan-Ute, Part I

[Continued]

American Indian Reservation and Trust Lands[1,2]	Number of persons										
	< 1 year	1-2 years	3-4 years	5 years	6 years	7-9 years	10-11 years	12-13 years	14 years	15 years	16 years
Summit Lake Reservation	0	0	0	0	0	0	2	0	0	0	0
Susanville Reservation	6	34	30	16	11	32	17	12	13	18	3
Swinomish Reservation	17	52	55	20	37	79	44	51	23	18	35
Sycuan Reservation	0	0	0	0	0	0	0	0	0	0	0
Table Bluff Rancheria	0	0	3	0	0	1	0	4	0	2	0
Table Mountain Rancheria	3	3	0	3	0	2	0	0	0	0	1
Tama Reservation (state)	0	0	0	0	0	1	4	2	0	0	4
Taos Pueblo and Trust Lands, NM	76	130	135	79	98	230	156	96	65	55	48
Te-Moak Reservation and Trust Lands, NV	19	50	45	17	30	59	34	32	8	16	25
Tesuque Pueblo and Trust Lands, NM	16	35	34	13	14	24	19	16	2	2	7
Tonawanda Reservation	0	34	25	3	0	32	18	10	3	3	9
Torres-Martinez Reservation	35	83	68	34	37	115	80	55	39	26	26
Trinidad Rancheria	0	4	0	0	0	0	2	0	3	2	3
Tulalip Reservation	95	222	246	151	128	408	234	222	90	89	87
Tule River Reservation	7	58	30	20	14	69	44	42	19	16	11
Tunica-Biloxi Reservation	0	3	0	0	0	4	2	0	0	0	0
Tuolumne Rancheria	3	0	6	0	0	2	6	0	0	3	0
Turtle Mountain Reservation and Trust Lands, ND – SD	140	375	413	208	223	465	306	369	136	141	105
Tuscarora Reservation	9	40	10	5	0	48	37	16	16	44	20
Twenty-Nine Palms Reservation	0	0	0	0	0	0	0	0	0	0	0
Uintah and Ouray Reservation	279	767	815	417	379	1,350	964	935	397	436	375
Umatilla Reservation	36	80	71	53	43	138	93	91	46	43	31
Upper Lake Rancheria	0	4	1	0	0	8	12	3	0	0	0
Upper Sioux Community	0	0	2	0	2	0	0	0	0	0	0
Upper Skagit Reservation	4	14	4	2	2	10	11	11	6	0	0
Ute Mountain Reservation and Trust Lands, CO – NM – UT	22	76	71	38	25	63	37	70	31	39	21

Source: Census of Population and Housing, 1990: Summary Tape File 3C on CD-ROM [machine-readable datafiles]. Prepared by the Bureau of the Census. Washington, DC: The Bureau, 1992. *Notes:* 1. Federal American Indian reservations are areas with boundaries established by treaty, statute, and/or executive or court order, and recognized by the federal government as territory in which American Indian tribes have jurisdiction. State reservations are lands held in trust by state governments for the use and benefit of a given tribe. The reservations and their boundaries were identified for the 1990 census by the Bureau of Indian Affairs (BIA), Department of Interior (for federal reservations), and state governments (for state reservations). The names of American Indian reservations recognized by state governments, but not by the federal government, are followed by "state." Areas composed of reservation lands that are administered jointly and/or are claimed by two reservations, as identified by the BIA, are called "joint areas," and are treated as separate American Indian reservations for census purposes. Federal reservations may cross state boundaries, and federal and state reservations may cross county, county subdivision, and place boundaries. For reservations that cross state boundaries, only the portion of the reservations in a given state is shown in the data products for that state; the entire reservations are shown in data products for the United States. 2. Trust lands are property associated with a particular American Indian reservation or tribe, held in trust by the federal government. Trust lands may be held in trust either for a tribe (tribal trust lands) or for an individual member of a tribe (individual trust land). Trust lands recognized for the 1990 census comprised all tribal trust lands and inhabited individual trust lands located outside of a reservation boundary. As with other American Indian areas, trust lands may be located in more than one state. Only the trust lands in a given state are shown in the data products for that state; all trust lands associated with a reservation or tribe are shown in data products for the United States. The Census Bureau first reported data for tribal trust lands for the 1980 census.

★ 184 ★

Population

Population of American Indian Reservations and Trust Lands, by Age, 1990 - Sokaogan-Ute, Part II

American Indian Reservation and Trust Lands[1,2]	Number of persons									
	17 years	18 years	19 years	20 years	21 years	22-24 years	25-29 years	30-34 years	35-39 years	40-44 years
Sokaogon Chippewa Community and Trust Lands, WI	5	7	7	0	2	25	28	33	21	10
Southern Ute Reservation	120	105	88	93	79	216	470	723	760	582
Spokane Reservation	33	26	19	22	25	55	97	138	90	80
Squaxin Island Reservation and Trust Lands, WA	6	5	0	4	5	0	11	7	15	22
Standing Rock Reservation	157	106	87	110	61	235	597	584	523	401
Stewarts Point Rancheria	0	0	0	0	0	18	6	5	0	0
Stillaguamish Reservation	0	6	0	3	0	0	12	11	9	7
Stockbridge Reservation	13	13	4	6	9	33	53	36	24	13
Sulphur Bank (El-Em) Rancheria	3	3	4	6	0	0	7	1	5	6
Summit Lake Reservation	0	0	0	0	0	0	0	6	0	0
Susanville Reservation	4	3	4	7	0	19	71	58	58	16
Swinomish Reservation	38	22	20	16	23	41	68	145	164	166
Sycuan Reservation	0	0	0	0	0	0	0	0	0	0
Table Bluff Rancheria	0	0	0	0	0	2	3	8	6	5
Table Mountain Rancheria	0	0	2	0	0	0	5	5	10	0
Tama Reservation (state)	0	0	0	0	0	0	0	4	3	0
Taos Pueblo and Trust Lands, NM	90	58	69	50	58	154	349	336	398	425
Te-Moak Reservation and Trust Lands, NV	21	22	19	10	13	31	92	71	68	51
Tesuque Pueblo and Trust Lands, NM	4	12	7	8	11	19	99	91	54	38
Tonawanda Reservation	4	6	2	2	4	18	56	21	19	30
Torres-Martinez Reservation	24	47	26	30	41	120	150	105	131	73
Trinidad Rancheria	0	0	4	0	0	0	9	3	9	7
Tulalip Reservation	78	107	67	62	62	167	510	674	688	511
Tule River Reservation	16	17	10	27	7	23	78	73	65	54
Tunica-Biloxi Reservation	0	0	0	0	0	9	4	0	0	0
Tuolumne Rancheria	0	0	2	3	0	1	4	10	4	0
Turtle Mountain Reservation and Trust Lands, ND – SD	141	135	135	84	118	308	606	539	378	381
Tuscarora Reservation	0	5	0	16	0	8	9	45	84	35
Twenty-Nine Palms Reservation	0	0	0	0	0	0	0	0	0	0
Uintah and Ouray Reservation	295	266	211	145	179	497	1,051	1,314	1,211	958
Umatilla Reservation	50	32	27	31	17	65	181	178	200	157
Upper Lake Rancheria	0	0	0	0	0	0	11	15	9	0
Upper Sioux Community	0	0	2	2	0	0	2	2	1	0
Upper Skagit Reservation	5	2	4	0	3	7	19	17	17	12
Ute Mountain Reservation and Trust Lands, CO – NM – UT	15	16	28	19	33	79	146	127	101	71

Source: Census of Population and Housing, 1990: Summary Tape File 3C on CD-ROM [machine-readable datafiles]. Prepared by the Bureau of the Census. Washington, DC: The Bureau, 1992. *Notes:* 1. Federal American Indian reservations are areas with boundaries established by treaty, statute, and/or executive or court order, and recognized by the federal government as territory in which American Indian tribes have jurisdiction. State reservations are lands held in trust by state governments for the use and benefit of a given tribe. The reservations and their boundaries were identified for the 1990 census by the Bureau of Indian Affairs (BIA), Department of Interior (for federal reservations), and state governments (for state reservations). The names of American Indian reservations recognized by state governments, but not by the federal government, are followed by "state." Areas composed of reservation lands that are administered jointly and/or are claimed by two reservations, as identified by the BIA, are called "joint areas," and are treated as separate American Indian reservations for census purposes. Federal reservations may cross state boundaries, and federal and state reservations may cross county, county subdivision, and place boundaries. For reservations that cross state boundaries, only the portion of the reservations in a given state is shown in the data products for that state; the entire reservations are shown in data products for the United States. 2. Trust lands are property associated with a particular American Indian reservation or tribe, held in trust by the federal government. Trust lands may be held in trust either for a tribe (tribal trust lands) or for an individual member of a tribe (individual trust land). Trust lands recognized for the 1990 census comprised all tribal trust lands and inhabited individual trust lands located outside of a reservation boundary. As with other American Indian areas, trust lands may be located in more than one state. Only the trust lands in a given state are shown in the data products for that state; all trust lands associated with a reservation or tribe are shown in data products for the United States. The Census Bureau first reported data for tribal trust lands for the 1980 census.

★ 185 ★
Population

Population of American Indian Reservations and Trust Lands, by Age, 1990 - Sokaogon-Ute, Part III

American Indian Reservation and Trust Lands[1,2]	Number of persons									
	45-49 years	50-54 years	55-59 years	60-61 years	62-64 years	65-69 years	70-74 years	75-79 years	80-84 years	85 + years
Sokaogon Chippewa Community and Trust Lands, WI	13	0	13	0	1	6	5	2	0	0
Southern Ute Reservation	479	363	327	130	195	248	186	115	89	73
Spokane Reservation	99	40	49	16	36	26	16	22	11	16
Squaxin Island Reservation and Trust Lands, WA	0	17	0	2	2	26	4	0	2	0
Standing Rock Reservation	394	319	304	132	171	232	167	140	116	29
Stewarts Point Rancheria	6	6	16	0	0	3	0	0	0	0
Stillaguamish Reservation	10	7	0	0	0	0	0	0	0	0
Stockbridge Reservation	29	33	20	12	16	32	16	18	15	6
Sulphur Bank (El-Em) Rancheria	2	8	7	0	3	3	0	3	0	0
Summit Lake Reservation	0	0	0	0	0	0	0	0	0	0
Susanville Reservation	20	15	7	4	0	5	6	2	0	0
Swinomish Reservation	110	134	137	75	140	258	147	92	36	22
Sycuan Reservation	0	0	0	0	0	0	0	0	0	0
Table Bluff Rancheria	6	0	2	3	0	0	0	0	0	0
Table Mountain Rancheria	0	0	4	0	0	4	0	0	2	0
Tama Reservation (state)	2	0	0	0	0	0	0	0	0	0
Taos Pueblo and Trust Lands, NM	320	239	172	78	117	162	163	152	83	60
Te-Moak Reservation and Trust Lands, NV	56	42	35	18	15	12	11	17	5	6
Tesuque Pueblo and Trust Lands, NM	34	40	35	16	11	15	12	3	4	7
Tonawanda Reservation	34	18	42	3	22	29	13	7	16	0
Torres-Martinez Reservation	53	42	60	17	44	38	20	3	2	4
Trinidad Rancheria	0	0	5	8	4	0	8	0	0	0
Tulalip Reservation	475	328	316	135	195	239	201	196	94	26
Tule River Reservation	17	24	4	9	30	6	1	5	7	0
Tunica-Biloxi Reservation	3	0	0	0	4	2	2	3	0	0
Tuolumne Rancheria	8	2	5	5	7	7	5	2	0	0
Turtle Mountain Reservation and Trust Lands, ND–SD	389	239	144	106	115	178	69	86	52	17
Tuscarora Reservation	43	26	28	7	45	66	16	31	0	0
Twenty-Nine Palms Reservation	0	0	0	0	0	0	0	0	0	0
Uintah and Ouray Reservation	823	724	536	203	322	473	356	268	192	97
Umatilla Reservation	130	165	138	38	90	115	93	49	41	27
Upper Lake Rancheria	0	2	0	0	0	1	3	0	1	0
Upper Sioux Community	2	0	0	0	5	2	0	2	2	0
Upper Skagit Reservation	5	5	3	0	2	3	0	1	4	0
Ute Mountain Reservation and Trust Lands, CO–NM–UT	50	44	37	24	22	10	28	3	12	8

Source: Census of Population and Housing, 1990: Summary Tape File 3C on CD-ROM [machine-readable datafiles]. Prepared by the Bureau of the Census. Washington, DC: The Bureau, 1992. *Notes:* 1. Federal American Indian reservations are areas with boundaries established by treaty, statute, and/or executive or court order, and recognized by the federal government as territory in which American Indian tribes have jurisdiction. State reservations are lands held in trust by state governments for the use and benefit of a given tribe. The reservations and their boundaries were identified for the 1990 census by the Bureau of Indian Affairs (BIA), Department of Interior (for federal reservations), and state governments (for state reservations). The names of American Indian reservations recognized by state governments, but not by the federal government, are followed by "state." Areas composed of reservation lands that are administered jointly and/or are claimed by two reservations, as identified by the BIA, are called "joint areas," and are treated as separate American Indian reservations for census purposes. Federal reservations may cross state boundaries, and federal and state reservations may cross county, county subdivision, and place boundaries. For reservations that cross state boundaries, only the portion of the reservations in a given state is shown in the data products for that state; the entire reservations are shown in data products for the United States. 2. Trust lands are property associated with a particular American Indian reservation or tribe, held in trust by the federal government. Trust lands may be held in trust either for a tribe (tribal trust lands) or for an individual member of a tribe (individual trust land). Trust lands recognized for the 1990 census comprised all tribal trust lands and inhabited individual trust lands located outside of a reservation boundary. As with other American Indian areas, trust lands may be located in more than one state. Only the trust lands in a given state are shown in the data products for that state; all trust lands associated with a reservation or tribe are shown in data products for the United States. The Census Bureau first reported data for tribal trust lands for the 1980 census.

★ 186 ★

Population

Population of American Indian Reservations and Trust Lands, by Age, 1990 - Vermillion-Zuni, Part I

American Indian Reservation and Trust Lands[1,2]	Number of persons										
	< 1 year	1-2 years	3-4 years	5 years	6 years	7-9 years	10-11 years	12-13 years	14 years	15 years	16 years
Vermillion Lake Reservation	0	0	0	0	0	6	0	0	0	0	0
Viejas Rancheria	8	29	24	8	10	29	23	20	6	7	2
Walker River Reservation	23	38	38	15	13	38	22	29	3	23	45
Warm Springs Reservation and Trust Lands, OR	79	174	195	65	98	252	141	145	71	81	61
Washoe Reservation	0	5	0	2	0	3	4	0	0	0	27
White Earth Reservation	149	291	283	150	157	544	334	357	172	155	152
Wind River Reservation	277	790	777	541	372	1,326	1,029	785	318	372	361
Winnebago Reservation	50	89	104	62	34	178	113	93	50	33	26
Winnemucca Colony	0	6	0	0	0	0	0	0	0	0	0
Wisconsin Winnebago Reservation and Trust Lands, WI	10	21	27	10	6	24	46	28	15	19	17
Woodfords Community	0	0	0	0	0	0	2	1	0	0	0
XL Ranch Reservation	0	0	0	0	0	0	0	0	0	2	0
Yakima Reservation and Trust Lands, WA	349	1,337	1,152	573	574	1,447	1,173	1,049	564	477	489
Yankton Reservation	113	197	264	118	126	347	204	197	139	99	137
Yavapai Reservation	7	17	12	5	10	9	1	8	0	0	0
Yerington Reservation and Trust Lands, NV	8	16	21	11	4	28	15	13	7	14	35
Yomba Reservation	0	4	6	0	4	6	8	4	4	0	2
Ysleta Del Sur Pueblo	8	12	16	3	15	18	20	7	8	4	3
Yurok Reservation	26	56	45	16	23	45	64	70	16	4	15
Zia Pueblo and Trust Lands, NM	12	19	34	25	19	37	21	30	7	10	14
Zuni Pueblo	140	360	343	180	182	480	226	323	155	166	158

Source: Census of Population and Housing, 1990: Summary Tape File 3C on CD-ROM [machine-readable datafiles]. Prepared by the Bureau of the Census. Washington, DC: The Bureau, 1992. *Notes:* 1. Federal American Indian reservations are areas with boundaries established by treaty, statute, and/or executive or court order, and recognized by the federal government as territory in which American Indian tribes have jurisdiction. State reservations are lands held in trust by state governments for the use and benefit of a given tribe. The reservations and their boundaries were identified for the 1990 census by the Bureau of Indian Affairs (BIA), Department of Interior (for federal reservations), and state governments (for state reservations). The names of American Indian reservations recognized by state governments, but not by the federal government, are followed by "state." Areas composed of reservation lands that are administered jointly and/or are claimed by two reservations, as identified by the BIA, are called "joint areas," and are treated as separate American Indian reservations for census purposes. Federal reservations may cross state boundaries, and federal and state reservations may cross county, county subdivision, and place boundaries. For reservations that cross state boundaries, only the portion of the reservations in a given state is shown in the data products for that state; the entire reservations are shown in data products for the United States. 2. Trust lands are property associated with a particular American Indian reservation or tribe, held in trust by the federal government. Trust lands may be held in trust either for a tribe (tribal trust lands) or for an individual member of a tribe (individual trust land). Trust lands recognized for the 1990 census comprised all tribal trust lands and inhabited individual trust lands located outside of a reservation boundary. As with other American Indian areas, trust lands may be located in more than one state. Only the trust lands in a given state are shown in the data products for that state; all trust lands associated with a reservation or tribe are shown in data products for the United States. The Census Bureau first reported data for tribal trust lands for the 1980 census.

★ 187 ★
Population

Population of American Indian Reservations and Trust Lands, by Age, 1990 - Vermillion-Zuni, Part II

American Indian Reservation and Trust Lands[1,2]	Number of persons									
	17 years	18 years	19 years	20 years	21 years	22-24 years	25-29 years	30-34 years	35-39 years	40-44 years
Vermillion Lake Reservation	0	0	0	0	0	0	5	5	0	0
Viejas Rancheria	4	5	7	0	5	6	56	49	39	11
Walker River Reservation	63	13	10	7	3	28	67	65	39	47
Warm Springs Reservation and Trust Lands, OR	52	54	47	64	38	126	314	264	198	185
Washoe Reservation	2	17	0	12	2	0	7	7	15	8
White Earth Reservation	171	151	68	76	81	205	530	618	521	572
Wind River Reservation	372	295	253	231	179	666	1,434	1,887	1,714	1,500
Winnebago Reservation	34	28	25	39	14	83	141	206	196	116
Winnemucca Colony	0	0	0	0	12	6	6	0	0	6
Wisconsin Winnebago Reservation and Trust Lands, WI	11	20	12	13	5	32	34	14	52	43
Woodfords Community	3	2	0	0	0	0	0	0	0	4
XL Ranch Reservation	0	0	0	0	2	0	0	4	0	5
Yakima Reservation and Trust Lands, WA	552	531	457	465	419	1,129	2,145	2,075	1,906	1,520
Yankton Reservation	111	110	48	52	56	156	438	387	381	328
Yavapai Reservation	5	6	11	4	1	11	38	22	2	3
Yerington Reservation and Trust Lands, NV	34	8	7	10	10	25	50	27	27	19
Yomba Reservation	0	0	4	3	0	6	12	10	14	2
Ysleta Del Sur Pueblo	19	4	6	8	0	29	29	34	22	12
Yurok Reservation	11	5	52	18	40	72	72	99	108	73
Zia Pueblo and Trust Lands, NM	18	8	16	6	9	36	81	39	46	28
Zuni Pueblo	85	154	146	108	120	407	756	679	533	456

Source: Census of Population and Housing, 1990: Summary Tape File 3C on CD-ROM [machine-readable datafiles]. Prepared by the Bureau of the Census. Washington, DC: The Bureau, 1992. *Notes:* 1. Federal American Indian reservations are areas with boundaries established by treaty, statute, and/or executive or court order, and recognized by the federal government as territory in which American Indian tribes have jurisdiction. State reservations are lands held in trust by state governments for the use and benefit of a given tribe. The reservations and their boundaries were identified for the 1990 census by the Bureau of Indian Affairs (BIA), Department of Interior (for federal reservations), and state governments (for state reservations). The names of American Indian reservations recognized by state governments, but not by the federal government, are followed by "state." Areas composed of reservation lands that are administered jointly and/or are claimed by two reservations, as identified by the BIA, are called "joint areas," and are treated as separate American Indian reservations for census purposes. Federal reservations may cross state boundaries, and federal and state reservations may cross county, county subdivision, and place boundaries. For reservations that cross state boundaries, only the portion of the reservations in a given state is shown in the data products for that state; the entire reservations are shown in data products for the United States. 2. Trust lands are property associated with a particular American Indian reservation or tribe, held in trust by the federal government. Trust lands may be held in trust either for a tribe (tribal trust lands) or for an individual member of a tribe (individual trust land). Trust lands recognized for the 1990 census comprised all tribal trust lands and inhabited individual trust lands located outside of a reservation boundary. As with other American Indian areas, trust lands may be located in more than one state. Only the trust lands in a given state are shown in the data products for that state; all trust lands associated with a reservation or tribe are shown in data products for the United States. The Census Bureau first reported data for tribal trust lands for the 1980 census.

★ 188 ★

Population

Population of American Indian Reservations and Trust Lands, by Age, 1990 - Vermillion-Zuni, Part III

American Indian Reservation and Trust Lands[1,2]	Number of persons									
	45-49 years	50-54 years	55-59 years	60-61 years	62-64 years	65-69 years	70-74 years	75-79 years	80-84 years	85 + years
Vermillion Lake Reservation	0	8	0	4	4	3	0	0	0	0
Viejas Rancheria	15	25	20	5	6	8	2	0	2	0
Walker River Reservation	36	22	27	22	12	33	23	7	0	0
Warm Springs Reservation and Trust Lands, OR	114	97	88	18	32	39	29	17	4	1
Washoe Reservation	11	6	7	0	0	5	4	0	2	0
White Earth Reservation	418	437	405	163	261	450	323	292	173	126
Wind River Reservation	1,289	1,037	921	353	571	788	575	390	332	180
Winnebago Reservation	82	88	96	49	69	104	56	48	26	14
Winnemucca Colony	9	0	0	4	0	5	0	0	0	0
Wisconsin Winnebago Reservation and Trust Lands, WI	38	16	32	10	15	16	12	7	0	3
Woodfords Community	2	2	4	0	0	0	0	0	0	0
XL Ranch Reservation	0	0	0	0	0	4	3	0	3	0
Yakima Reservation and Trust Lands, WA	1,119	1,273	901	330	623	879	821	561	328	230
Yankton Reservation	324	324	301	97	198	257	262	195	161	154
Yavapai Reservation	3	4	4	2	3	5	0	0	0	0
Yerington Reservation and Trust Lands, NV	24	2	3	4	12	18	6	6	3	3
Yomba Reservation	2	0	2	2	5	0	4	2	0	0
Ysleta Del Sur Pueblo	14	22	16	11	7	8	8	7	0	0
Yurok Reservation	56	41	50	36	53	72	45	32	21	7
Zia Pueblo and Trust Lands, NM	34	26	11	6	5	11	15	10	3	2
Zuni Pueblo	314	224	176	59	129	100	96	116	53	21

Source: Census of Population and Housing, 1990: Summary Tape File 3C on CD-ROM [machine-readable datafiles]. Prepared by the Bureau of the Census. Washington, DC: The Bureau, 1992. *Notes:* 1. Federal American Indian reservations are areas with boundaries established by treaty, statute, and/or executive or court order, and recognized by the federal government as territory in which American Indian tribes have jurisdiction. State reservations are lands held in trust by state governments for the use and benefit of a given tribe. The reservations and their boundaries were identified for the 1990 census by the Bureau of Indian Affairs (BIA), Department of Interior (for federal reservations), and state governments (for state reservations). The names of American Indian reservations recognized by state governments, but not by the federal government, are followed by "state." Areas composed of reservation lands that are administered jointly and/or are claimed by two reservations, as identified by the BIA, are called "joint areas," and are treated as separate American Indian reservations for census purposes. Federal reservations may cross state boundaries, and federal and state reservations may cross county, county subdivision, and place boundaries. For reservations that cross state boundaries, only the portion of the reservations in a given state is shown in the data products for that state; the entire reservations are shown in data products for the United States. 2. Trust lands are property associated with a particular American Indian reservation or tribe, held in trust by the federal government. Trust lands may be held in trust either for a tribe (tribal trust lands) or for an individual member of a tribe (individual trust land). Trust lands recognized for the 1990 census comprised all tribal trust lands and inhabited individual trust lands located outside of a reservation boundary. As with other American Indian areas, trust lands may be located in more than one state. Only the trust lands in a given state are shown in the data products for that state; all trust lands associated with a reservation or tribe are shown in data products for the United States. The Census Bureau first reported data for tribal trust lands for the 1980 census.

Population of American Indian Reservations and Trust Lands, by Sex and Race, 1990 - Acoma-Colville

American Indian Reservation and Trust Lands[1,2]	Number of persons							
	Total	Sex		Race				
						American Indian, Eskimo, or Aleut	Asian or Pacific Islander	Other race
		Male	Female	White	Black			
Acoma Pueblo and Trust Lands, NM	2,590	1,237	1,353	20	0	2,566	0	4
Agua Caliente Reservation	19,839	9,273	10,566	18,107	409	135	380	808
Alabama and Coushatta Reservation	548	290	258	0	0	548	0	0
Alamo Navajo Reservation	1,259	579	680	29	0	1,226	4	0
Allegany Reservation	7,312	3,398	3,914	6,179	16	1,068	20	29
Alturas Rancheria	3	0	3	0	0	3	0	0
Annette Islands Reserve	1,464	788	676	248	3	1,206	3	4
Augustine Reservation	0	0	0	0	0	0	0	0
Bad River Reservation	1,031	508	523	192	0	837	0	2
Barona Rancheria	573	279	294	151	0	351	10	61
Bay Mills Reservation	441	213	228	59	2	380	0	0
Benton Paiute Reservation	75	35	40	14	0	61	0	0
Berry Creek Rancheria	0	0	0	0	0	0	0	0
Big Bend Rancheria	5	5	0	0	0	5	0	0
Big Cypress Reservation	449	163	286	5	0	444	0	0
Big Lagoon Rancheria	12	7	5	3	0	9	0	0
Big Pine Rancheria	455	222	233	99	0	344	10	2
Big Sandy Rancheria	59	25	34	20	0	36	0	3
Big Valley Rancheria	81	40	41	23	0	31	13	14
Bishop Rancheria	1,437	745	692	422	0	979	5	31
Blackfeet Reservation	8,488	4,241	4,247	1,440	6	7,031	0	11
Blue Lake Rancheria	53	28	25	26	0	27	0	0
Bois Forte (Nett Lake) Reservation	335	180	155	9	0	326	0	0
Bridgeport Colony	28	4	24	0	0	28	0	0
Brighton Reservation	528	220	308	102	11	415	0	0
Burns Paiute Reservation and Trust Lands, OR	198	97	101	48	0	150	0	0
Cabazon Reservation	858	436	422	495	29	37	0	297
Cahuilla Reservation	107	50	57	15	0	77	0	15
Campo Reservation	270	140	130	148	5	106	6	5
Camp Verde Reservation	624	321	303	26	10	574	1	13
Canoncito Reservation	1,193	577	616	10	0	1,183	0	0
Capitan Grande Reservation	0	0	0	0	0	0	0	0
Carson Colony	265	110	155	8	0	251	0	6
Catawba Reservation (state)	177	96	81	63	0	111	0	3
Cattaraugus Reservation	2,183	1,041	1,142	187	0	1,979	4	13
Cedarville Rancheria	10	8	2	3	0	7	0	0
Chehalis Reservation	504	254	250	209	0	286	4	5
Chemehuevi Reservation	325	144	181	224	3	88	0	10
Cheyenne River Reservation	7,743	3,820	3,923	2,625	16	5,092	4	6
Chicken Ranch Rancheria	66	29	37	66	0	0	0	0
Chitimacha Reservation	311	155	156	80	0	231	0	0

[Continued]

★ 189 ★

Population of American Indian Reservations and Trust Lands, by Sex and Race, 1990 - Acoma-Colville

[Continued]

American Indian Reservation and Trust Lands[1,2]	Number of persons							
	Total	Sex		Race				
		Male	Female	White	Black	American Indian, Eskimo, or Aleut	Asian or Pacific Islander	Other race
Cochiti Pueblo	1,410	696	714	521	5	792	2	90
Cocopah Reservation	584	283	301	28	6	549	0	1
Coeur d'Alene Reservation and Trust Lands, ID	5,778	2,974	2,804	4,995	3	756	3	21
Cold Springs Rancheria	163	74	89	27	0	136	0	0
Colorado River Reservation	7,944	3,838	4,106	4,759	16	2,374	54	741
Colusa (Cachil Dehe) Rancheria	20	8	12	0	0	18	2	0
Colville Reservation	7,034	3,564	3,470	3,056	7	3,779	27	165

Source: Census of Population and Housing, 1990: Summary Tape File 3C on CD-ROM [machine-readable datafiles]. Prepared by the Bureau of the Census. Washington, DC: The Bureau, 1992. *Notes:* 1. Federal American Indian reservations are areas with boundaries established by treaty, statute, and/or executive or court order, and recognized by the federal government as territory in which American Indian tribes have jurisdiction. State reservations are lands held in trust by state governments for the use and benefit of a given tribe. The reservations and their boundaries were identified for the 1990 census by the Bureau of Indian Affairs (BIA), Department of Interior (for federal reservations), and state governments (for state reservations). The names of American Indian reservations recognized by state governments, but not by the federal government, are followed by "state." Areas composed of reservation lands that are administered jointly and/or are claimed by two reservations, as identified by the BIA, are called "joint areas," and are treated as separate American Indian reservations for census purposes. Federal reservations may cross state boundaries, and federal and state reservations may cross county, county subdivision, and place boundaries. For reservations that cross state boundaries, only the portion of the reservations in a given state is shown in the data products for that state; the entire reservations are shown in data products for the United States. 2. Trust lands are property associated with a particular American Indian reservation or tribe, held in trust by the federal government. Trust lands may be held in trust either for a tribe (tribal trust lands) or for an individual member of a tribe (individual trust land). Trust lands recognized for the 1990 census comprised all tribal trust lands and inhabited individual trust lands located outside of a reservation boundary. As with other American Indian areas, trust lands may be located in more than one state. Only the trust lands in a given state are shown in the data products for that state; all trust lands associated with a reservation or tribe are shown in data products for the United States. The Census Bureau first reported data for tribal trust lands for the 1980 census.

★ 190 ★

Population

Population of American Indian Reservations and Trust Lands, by Sex and Race, 1990 - Coos-Grindstone Creek

American Indian Reservation and Trust Lands[1,2]	Number of persons							
	Total	Sex		Race				
		Male	Female	White	Black	American Indian, Eskimo, or Aleut	Asian or Pacific Islander	Other race
Coos, Lower Umpqua, and Siuslaw Reservation	0	0	0	0	0	0	0	0
Cortina Rancheria	29	18	11	10	0	19	0	0
Coushatta Reservation	42	22	20	0	0	42	0	0
Cow Creek Reservation	89	45	44	64	0	25	0	0
Coyote Valley Reservation	139	70	69	13	0	124	0	2
Crow Reservation and Trust Lands, MT	6,341	3,217	3,124	1,622	0	4,706	13	0
Crow Creek Reservation	1,763	947	816	239	3	1,521	0	0
Cuyapaipe Reservation	0	0	0	0	0	0	0	0
Deer Creek Reservation	182	81	101	182	0	0	0	0
Devils Lake Sioux Reservation	3,574	1,805	1,769	898	0	2,665	2	9

[Continued]

★ 190 ★

Population of American Indian Reservations and Trust Lands, by Sex and Race, 1990 - Coos-Grindstone Creek

[Continued]

American Indian Reservation and Trust Lands[1,2]	Number of persons							
	Total	Sex		Race				
		Male	Female	White	Black	American Indian, Eskimo, or Aleut	Asian or Pacific Islander	Other race
Dresslerville Colony	153	60	93	12	0	141	0	0
Dry Creek Rancheria	75	31	44	6	0	69	0	0
Duck Valley Reservation	1,096	554	542	82	0	1,003	2	9
Duckwater Reservation	151	76	75	15	0	136	0	0
Eastern Cherokee Reservation	6,311	3,129	3,182	967	11	5,287	14	32
Elk Valley Rancheria	128	61	67	78	0	50	0	0
Ely Colony	85	31	54	6	0	79	0	0
Enterprise Rancheria	0	0	0	0	0	0	0	0
Fallon Colony	162	60	102	15	0	143	4	0
Fallon Reservation	369	191	178	22	0	338	0	9
Flandreau Reservation	280	151	129	28	0	252	0	0
Flathead Reservation	21,061	10,377	10,684	15,855	8	5,128	21	49
Fond du Lac Reservation	3,211	1,629	1,582	2,122	0	1,083	4	2
Fort Apache Reservation	10,506	5,124	5,382	551	29	9,902	0	24
Fort Belknap Reservation and Trust Lands, MT	2,485	1,241	1,244	162	2	2,308	3	10
Fort Berthold Reservation	5,387	2,553	2,834	2,313	3	3,054	10	7
Fort Bidwell Reservation	136	70	66	5	0	131	0	0
Fort Hall Reservation and Trust Lands, ID	5,114	2,554	2,560	1,774	0	3,085	26	229
Fort Independence Reservation	58	27	31	16	0	42	0	0
Fort McDermitt Reservation	399	222	177	13	0	382	0	4
Fort McDowell Reservation	628	299	329	60	0	568	0	0
Fort Mojave Reservation and Trust Lands, AZ–CA–NV	692	311	381	117	3	535	0	37
Fort Peck Reservation	10,722	5,212	5,510	4,852	8	5,822	26	14
Fort Yuma (Quechan) Reservation	2,102	1,019	1,083	703	37	1,123	4	235
Gila Bend Reservation and Trust Lands, AZ	0	0	0	0	0	0	0	0
Gila River Reservation	9,578	4,645	4,933	203	13	9,101	13	248
Golden Hill Reservation (state)	9	6	3	9	0	0	0	0
Goshute Reservation	79	45	34	0	0	76	0	3
Grand Portage Reservation	308	160	148	99	4	205	0	0
Grand Ronde Reservation	49	29	20	47	0	2	0	0
Grand Traverse Reservation and Trust Lands, MI	263	124	139	18	0	233	4	8
Greenville Rancheria	25	17	8	25	0	0	0	0
Grindstone Creek Rancheria	101	43	58	0	0	101	0	0

Source: Census of Population and Housing, 1990: Summary Tape File 3C on CD-ROM [machine-readable datafiles]. Prepared by the Bureau of the Census. Washington, DC: The Bureau, 1992. *Notes:* 1. Federal American Indian reservations are areas with boundaries established by treaty, statute, and/or executive or court order, and recognized by the federal government as territory in which American Indian tribes have jurisdiction. State reservations are lands held in trust by state governments for the use and benefit of a given tribe. The reservations and their boundaries were identified for the 1990 census by the Bureau of Indian Affairs (BIA), Department of Interior (for federal reservations), and state governments (for state reservations). The names of American Indian reservations recognized by state governments, but not by the federal government, are followed by "state." Areas composed of reservation lands that are administered jointly and/or are claimed by two reservations, as identified by the BIA, are called "joint areas," and are treated as separate American Indian reservations for census purposes. Federal reservations may cross state boundaries, and federal and state reservations may cross county, county subdivision, and place boundaries. For reservations that cross state boundaries, only the portion of the reservations in a given state is shown in the data products for that state; the entire reservations are shown in data products for the United States. 2. Trust lands are property associated with a particular American Indian reservation or tribe, held in trust by the federal government. Trust lands may be held in trust either for a tribe (tribal trust lands) or for an individual member of a tribe (individual trust land). Trust lands recognized for the 1990 census comprised all tribal trust lands and inhabited individual trust lands located outside of a reservation boundary. As with other American Indian areas, trust lands may be located in more than one state. Only the trust lands in a given state are shown in the data products for that state; all trust lands associated with a reservation or tribe are shown in data products for the United States. The Census Bureau first reported data for tribal trust lands for the 1980 census.

★ 191 ★
Population

Population of American Indian Reservations and Trust Lands, by Sex and Race, 1990 - Hannahville-Lummi

American Indian Reservation and Trust Lands[1,2]	Number of persons							
	Total	Sex		Race				
		Male	Female	White	Black	American Indian, Eskimo, or Aleut	Asian or Pacific Islander	Other race
Hannahville Community and Trust Lands, MI	196	109	87	4	0	190	0	2
Hassanamisco Reservation (state)	0	0	0	0	0	0	0	0
Havasupai Reservation	433	209	224	17	0	416	0	0
Hoh Reservation	116	64	52	9	0	107	0	0
Hollywood Reservation	1,412	653	759	924	6	480	2	0
Hoopa Valley Reservation	2,199	1,058	1,141	400	4	1,780	3	12
Hopi Reservation and Trust Lands, AZ	7,215	3,498	3,717	171	4	7,002	30	8
Hopland Rancheria	208	80	128	29	0	160	0	19
Hualapai Reservation and Trust Lands, AZ	833	403	430	17	0	812	0	4
Inaja-Cosmit Reservation	0	0	0	0	0	0	0	0
Indian Township Reservation	624	326	298	82	0	542	0	0
Iowa Reservation	227	126	101	131	0	96	0	0
Isabella Reservation and Trust Lands, MI	22,931	11,267	11,664	21,597	158	872	153	151
Isleta Pueblo	2,953	1,400	1,553	182	0	2,723	6	42
Jackson Rancheria	27	11	16	11	0	16	0	0
Jamestown Klallam Reservation and Trust Lands, WA	34	18	16	24	0	10	0	0
Jamul Village	0	0	0	0	0	0	0	0
Jemez Pueblo	1,734	838	896	0	0	1,734	0	0
Jicarilla Apache Reservation	2,636	1,273	1,363	167	8	2,404	6	51
Kaibab Reservation	120	67	53	55	0	65	0	0
Kalispel Reservation	90	46	44	6	0	84	0	0
Karok Reservation and Trust Lands, CA	400	139	261	377	0	12	0	11
Kickapoo Reservation	478	243	235	107	0	368	0	3
Kootenai Reservation	101	43	58	5	0	96	0	0
Lac Courte Oreilles Reservation and Trust Lands, WI	2,437	1,211	1,226	654	2	1,767	2	12
Lac du Flambeau Reservation	2,408	1,187	1,221	973	0	1,431	2	2
Lac Vieux Desert Reservation	147	71	76	0	0	147	0	0
Laguna Pueblo and Trust Lands, NM	3,724	1,744	1,980	54	2	3,649	0	19
La Jolla Reservation	162	57	105	9	0	151	2	0
Lake Traverse (Sisseton) Reservation	10,840	5,496	5,344	7,989	0	2,810	3	38
L'Anse Reservation and Trust Lands, MI	3,317	1,647	1,670	2,615	5	697	0	0
La Posta Reservation	0	0	0	0	0	0	0	0
Las Vegas Colony	86	54	32	5	0	71	0	10
Laytonville Rancheria	137	57	80	6	0	123	2	6
Leech Lake Reservation	8,783	4,401	4,382	5,339	12	3,421	9	2
Likely Rancheria	0	0	0	0	0	0	0	0
Lone Pine Rancheria	235	112	123	66	0	164	0	5
Lookout Rancheria	62	34	28	0	0	62	0	0
Los Coyotes Reservation	181	98	83	73	0	93	0	15
Lovelock Colony	92	48	44	14	0	78	0	0
Lower Brule Reservation	1,095	541	554	107	2	984	0	2
Lower Elwha Reservation and Trust Lands, WA	112	67	45	7	0	103	2	0

[Continued]

★ 191 ★

Population of American Indian Reservations and Trust Lands, by Sex and Race, 1990 - Hannahville-Lummi

[Continued]

American Indian Reservation and Trust Lands[1,2]	Number of persons							
	Total	Sex		Race				
		Male	Female	White	Black	American Indian, Eskimo, or Aleut	Asian or Pacific Islander	Other race
Lower Sioux Community	241	136	105	29	0	212	0	0
Lummi Reservation	3,164	1,603	1,561	1,515	13	1,608	10	18

Source: Census of Population and Housing, 1990: Summary Tape File 3C on CD-ROM [machine-readable datafiles]. Prepared by the Bureau of the Census. Washington, DC: The Bureau, 1992. *Notes:* 1. Federal American Indian reservations are areas with boundaries established by treaty, statute, and/or executive or court order, and recognized by the federal government as territory in which American Indian tribes have jurisdiction. State reservations are lands held in trust by state governments for the use and benefit of a given tribe. The reservations and their boundaries were identified for the 1990 census by the Bureau of Indian Affairs (BIA), Department of Interior (for federal reservations), and state governments (for state reservations). The names of American Indian reservations recognized by state governments, but not by the federal government, are followed by "state." Areas composed of reservation lands that are administered jointly and/or are claimed by two reservations, as identified by the BIA, are called "joint areas," and are treated as separate American Indian reservations for census purposes. Federal reservations may cross state boundaries, and federal and state reservations may cross county, county subdivision, and place boundaries. For reservations that cross state boundaries, only the portion of the reservations in a given state is shown in the data products for that state; the entire reservations are shown in data products for the United States. 2. Trust lands are property associated with a particular American Indian reservation or tribe, held in trust by the federal government. Trust lands may be held in trust either for a tribe (tribal trust lands) or for an individual member of a tribe (individual trust land). Trust lands recognized for the 1990 census comprised all tribal trust lands and inhabited individual trust lands located outside of a reservation boundary. As with other American Indian areas, trust lands may be located in more than one state. Only the trust lands in a given state are shown in the data products for that state; all trust lands associated with a reservation or tribe are shown in data products for the United States. The Census Bureau first reported data for tribal trust lands for the 1980 census.

★ 192 ★

Population

Population of American Indian Reservations and Trust Lands, by Sex and Race, 1990 - Makah-Papago

American Indian Reservation and Trust Lands[1,2]	Number of persons							
	Total	Sex		Race				
		Male	Female	White	Black	American Indian, Eskimo, or Aleut	Asian or Pacific Islander	Other race
Makah Reservation	1,238	640	598	263	10	956	3	6
Manchester (Point Arena) Rancheria	212	121	91	28	0	173	11	0
Manzanita Reservation	66	44	22	16	13	37	0	0
Maricopa (Ak-Chin) Reservation	450	204	246	6	0	411	0	33
Mashantucket Pequot Reservation	71	44	27	20	0	50	1	0
Mattaponi Reservation (state)	74	43	31	2	0	72	0	0
Menominee Reservation	3,411	1,679	1,732	192	0	3,216	0	3
Mesa Grande Reservation	63	30	33	3	0	54	0	6
Mescalero Apache Reservation	2,664	1,335	1,329	93	2	2,519	0	50
Miccosukee Reservation	72	36	36	0	0	72	0	0
Middletown Rancheria	76	37	39	53	0	18	5	0
Mille Lacs Reservation	380	184	196	23	0	354	3	0
Mississippi Choctaw Reservation and Trust Lands, MS	4,257	2,027	2,230	190	11	4,056	0	0
Moapa River Reservation	377	171	206	115	0	177	6	79
Montgomery Creek Rancheria	8	2	6	0	0	8	0	0
Morongo Reservation	1,109	525	584	519	18	526	41	5
Muckleshoot Reservation and Trust Lands, WA	3,836	1,892	1,944	2,858	17	875	33	53

[Continued]

★ 192 ★

Population of American Indian Reservations and Trust Lands, by Sex and Race, 1990 - Makah-Papago
[Continued]

American Indian Reservation and Trust Lands[1,2]	Number of persons							
	Total	Sex		Race				
		Male	Female	White	Black	American Indian, Eskimo, or Aleut	Asian or Pacific Islander	Other race
Nambe Pueblo and Trust Lands, NM	1,358	696	662	874	0	313	3	168
Narragansett Reservation	30	8	22	11	0	19	0	0
Navajo Reservation and Trust Lands, AZ–NM–UT	148,658	73,157	75,501	4,455	169	143,507	99	428
Nez Perce Reservation	16,159	8,293	7,866	14,168	15	1,885	54	37
Nisqually Reservation	649	292	357	175	3	460	6	5
Nooksack Reservation and Trust Lands, WA	697	365	332	204	12	456	25	0
Northern Cheyenne Reservation and Trust Lands, MT–SD	3,906	1,894	2,012	333	0	3,564	0	9
North Fork Rancheria	0	0	0	0	0	0	0	0
Northwestern Shoshoni Reservation	0	0	0	0	0	0	0	0
Oil Springs Reservation	4	2	2	4	0	0	0	0
Omaha Reservation	5,238	2,555	2,683	3,306	2	1,925	5	0
Oneida (East) Reservation	41	22	19	0	0	41	0	0
Oneida (West) Reservation	17,940	9,073	8,867	15,322	69	2,450	65	34
Onondaga Reservation	771	345	426	771	0	0	0	0
Ontonagon Reservation	0	0	0	0	0	0	0	0
Osage Reservation	41,393	20,382	21,011	30,902	4,225	6,100	17	149
Ozette Reservation	0	0	0	0	0	0	0	0
Paiute of Utah Reservation	624	297	327	321	0	285	1	17
Pala Reservation	1,125	627	498	454	7	581	0	83
Pamunkey Reservation (state)	47	21	26	10	0	37	0	0
Papago Reservation	8,587	4,157	4,430	79	0	8,490	0	18

Source: Census of Population and Housing, 1990: Summary Tape File 3C on CD-ROM [machine-readable datafiles]. Prepared by the Bureau of the Census. Washington, DC: The Bureau, 1992. *Notes:* 1. Federal American Indian reservations are areas with boundaries established by treaty, statute, and/or executive or court order, and recognized by the federal government as territory in which American Indian tribes have jurisdiction. State reservations are lands held in trust by state governments for the use and benefit of a given tribe. The reservations and their boundaries were identified for the 1990 census by the Bureau of Indian Affairs (BIA), Department of Interior (for federal reservations), and state governments (for state reservations). The names of American Indian reservations recognized by state governments, but not by the federal government, are followed by "state." Areas composed of reservation lands that are administered jointly and/or are claimed by two reservations, as identified by the BIA, are called "joint areas," and are treated as separate American Indian reservations for census purposes. Federal reservations may cross state boundaries, and federal and state reservations may cross county, county subdivision, and place boundaries. For reservations that cross state boundaries, only the portion of the reservations in a given state is shown in the data products for that state; the entire reservations are shown in data products for the United States. 2. Trust lands are property associated with a particular American Indian reservation or tribe, held in trust by the federal government. Trust lands may be held in trust either for a tribe (tribal trust lands) or for an individual member of a tribe (individual trust land). Trust lands recognized for the 1990 census comprised all tribal trust lands and inhabited individual trust lands located outside of a reservation boundary. As with other American Indian areas, trust lands may be located in more than one state. Only the trust lands in a given state are shown in the data products for that state; all trust lands associated with a reservation or tribe are shown in data products for the United States. The Census Bureau first reported data for tribal trust lands for the 1980 census.

★ 193 ★

Population

Population of American Indian Reservations and Trust Lands, by Sex and Race, 1990 - Pascua-Rocky Boy's

American Indian Reservation and Trust Lands[1,2]	Total	Sex		Race				
		Male	Female	White	Black	American Indian, Eskimo, or Aleut	Asian or Pacific Islander	Other race
Pascua Yaqui Reservation	2,406	1,177	1,229	21	28	2,270	0	87
Paucatuck Eastern Pequot Reservation (state)	16	4	12	0	0	16	0	0
Pauma Reservation	151	66	85	6	3	132	0	10
Payson (Yavapai-Apache) Community	103	77	26	0	0	103	0	0
Pechanga Reservation	391	182	209	147	2	242	0	0
Penobscot Reservation and Trust Lands, ME	469	226	243	76	0	393	0	0
Picayune Rancheria	0	0	0	0	0	0	0	0
Picuris Pueblo	1,899	931	968	1,092	0	164	0	643
Pine Creek Reservation (state)	22	9	13	0	0	22	0	0
Pine Ridge Reservation and Trust Lands, NE–SD	12,119	6,187	5,932	1,021	19	11,006	11	62
Pinoleville Rancheria	70	29	41	10	0	51	0	9
Pleasant Point Reservation	542	257	285	28	0	514	0	0
Poarch Creek Reservation and Trust Lands, AL	255	136	119	65	0	190	0	0
Pojoaque Pueblo	2,481	1,211	1,270	2,081	0	159	2	239
Poospatuck Reservation (state)	196	68	128	24	8	164	0	0
Port Gamble Reservation	555	281	274	158	0	386	5	6
Port Madison Reservation	4,834	2,449	2,385	4,263	14	374	169	14
Potawatomi (Kansas) Reservation	1,079	568	511	574	2	503	0	0
Potawatomi (Wisconsin) Reservation and Trust Lands, WI	266	144	122	11	0	247	0	8
Prairie Island Community	30	19	11	4	0	26	0	0
Puyallup Reservation and Trust Lands, WA	32,435	16,092	16,343	25,621	2,248	977	3,073	516
Pyramid Lake Reservation	1,358	657	701	375	4	967	0	12
Quartz Valley Rancheria	57	34	23	57	0	0	0	0
Quileute Reservation	352	192	160	53	0	290	9	0
Quinault Reservation	1,271	692	579	288	3	967	7	6
Ramah Navajo Community	175	83	92	0	0	175	0	0
Ramona Reservation	0	0	0	0	0	0	0	0
Rankokus Reservation (state)	0	0	0	0	0	0	0	0
Red Cliff Reservation and Trust Lands, WI	876	435	441	140	5	729	0	2
Redding Rancheria	72	43	29	28	0	44	0	0
Red Lake Reservation	3,690	1,859	1,831	118	0	3,560	12	0
Redwood Valley Rancheria	111	58	53	111	0	0	0	0
Reno-Sparks Colony	242	112	130	0	0	242	0	0
Resighini Rancheria	51	28	23	2	0	49	0	0
Rincon Reservation	1,478	786	692	937	2	432	2	105
Roaring Creek Rancheria	20	5	15	0	0	20	0	0

[Continued]

★ 193 ★

Population of American Indian Reservations and Trust Lands, by Sex and Race, 1990 - Pascua-Rocky Boy's

[Continued]

American Indian Reservation and Trust Lands[1,2]	Number of persons							
	Total	Sex		Race				
		Male	Female	White	Black	American Indian, Eskimo, or Aleut	Asian or Pacific Islander	Other race
Robinson Rancheria	167	86	81	42	0	125	0	0
Rocky Boy's Reservation and Trust Lands, MT	1,931	1,007	924	64	0	1,860	0	7

Source: Census of Population and Housing, 1990: Summary Tape File 3C on CD-ROM [machine-readable datafiles]. Prepared by the Bureau of the Census. Washington, DC: The Bureau, 1992. Notes: 1. Federal American Indian reservations are areas with boundaries established by treaty, statute, and/or executive or court order, and recognized by the federal government as territory in which American Indian tribes have jurisdiction. State reservations are lands held in trust by state governments for the use and benefit of a given tribe. The reservations and their boundaries were identified for the 1990 census by the Bureau of Indian Affairs (BIA), Department of Interior (for federal reservations), and state governments (for state reservations). The names of American Indian reservations recognized by state governments, but not by the federal government, are followed by "state." Areas composed of reservation lands that are administered jointly and/or are claimed by two reservations, as identified by the BIA, are called "joint areas," and are treated as separate American Indian reservations for census purposes. Federal reservations may cross state boundaries, and federal and state reservations may cross county, county subdivision, and place boundaries. For reservations that cross state boundaries, only the portion of the reservations in a given state is shown in the data products for that state; the entire reservations are shown in data products for the United States. 2. Trust lands are property associated with a particular American Indian reservation or tribe, held in trust by the federal government. Trust lands may be held in trust either for a tribe (tribal trust lands) or for an individual member of a tribe (individual trust land). Trust lands recognized for the 1990 census comprised all tribal trust lands and inhabited individual trust lands located outside of a reservation boundary. As with other American Indian areas, trust lands may be located in more than one state. Only the trust lands in a given state are shown in the data products for that state; all trust lands associated with a reservation or tribe are shown in data products for the United States. The Census Bureau first reported data for tribal trust lands for the 1980 census.

★ 194 ★

Population

Population of American Indian Reservations and Trust Lands, by Sex and Race, 1990 - Rohnerville-Soboba

American Indian Reservation and Trust Lands[1,2]	Number of persons							
	Total	Sex		Race				
		Male	Female	White	Black	American Indian, Eskimo, or Aleut	Asian or Pacific Islander	Other race
Rohnerville Rancheria	0	0	0	0	0	0	0	0
Rosebud Reservation and Trust Lands, SD	9,632	4,742	4,890	1,585	15	7,998	0	34
Round Valley Reservation and Trust Lands, CA	1,181	562	619	598	5	549	0	29
Rumsey Rancheria	19	10	9	9	0	10	0	0
Sac and Fox (Iowa) Reservation	586	299	287	12	2	572	0	0
Sac and Fox (KS-NE) Reservation and Trust Lands, KS–NE	162	78	84	127	0	35	0	0
St. Croix Reservation	485	224	261	49	0	436	0	0
St. Regis Mohawk Reservation	1,974	936	1,038	48	3	1,923	0	0
Salt River Reservation	4,856	2,319	2,537	1,274	0	3,547	0	35
San Carlos Reservation	7,239	3,419	3,820	77	32	7,060	0	70
Sandia Pueblo	3,944	1,896	2,048	2,794	5	405	6	734
Sandy Lake Reservation	28	8	20	2	0	26	0	0
San Felipe Pueblo	2,525	1,234	1,291	334	0	1,884	8	299
San Ildefonso Pueblo	1,586	772	814	933	9	334	12	298
San Juan Pueblo	5,237	2,642	2,595	3,438	13	1,275	1	510
San Manuel Reservation	59	36	23	18	0	38	0	3
San Pasqual Reservation	517	268	249	296	0	221	0	0

[Continued]

★ 194 ★

Population of American Indian Reservations and Trust Lands, by Sex and Race, 1990 - Rohnerville-Soboba
[Continued]

American Indian Reservation and Trust Lands[1,2]	Number of persons							
	Total	Sex		Race				
						American Indian, Eskimo, or Aleut	Asian or Pacific Islander	Other race
		Male	Female	White	Black			
Santa Ana Pueblo	624	300	324	67	0	491	0	66
Santa Clara Pueblo	10,230	4,885	5,345	8,091	46	1,295	25	773
Santa Rosa Rancheria	319	173	146	14	0	281	0	24
Santa Rosa Reservation	58	33	25	13	0	39	0	6
Santa Ynez Reservation	317	138	179	35	0	254	24	4
Santa Ysabel Reservation	173	105	68	22	3	144	0	4
Santee Reservation	740	363	377	302	0	438	0	0
Santo Domingo Pueblo	2,773	1,401	1,372	45	7	2,721	0	0
San Xavier Reservation	1,129	522	607	18	0	1,087	15	9
Sauk-Suiattle Reservation	112	61	51	59	3	50	0	0
Sault Ste. Marie Reservation and Trust Lands, MI	723	369	354	220	0	501	0	2
Schaghticoke Reservation (state)	10	5	5	5	0	5	0	0
Shakopee Community	229	110	119	40	0	182	0	7
Sheep Ranch Rancheria	0	0	0	0	0	0	0	0
Sherwood Valley Rancheria	6	2	4	0	0	6	0	0
Shingle Springs Rancheria	12	3	9	10	0	2	0	0
Shinnecock Reservation (state)	397	184	213	8	31	355	3	0
Shoalwater Reservation	129	64	65	46	0	83	0	0
Siletz Reservation	0	0	0	0	0	0	0	0
Skokomish Reservation	618	330	288	201	0	415	2	0
Skull Valley Reservation	17	15	2	0	0	17	0	0
Smith River Rancheria	189	101	88	93	0	96	0	0
Soboba Reservation	442	211	231	53	1	372	1	15

Source: Census of Population and Housing, 1990: Summary Tape File 3C on CD-ROM [machine-readable datafiles]. Prepared by the Bureau of the Census. Washington, DC: The Bureau, 1992. *Notes:* 1. Federal American Indian reservations are areas with boundaries established by treaty, statute, and/or executive or court order, and recognized by the federal government as territory in which American Indian tribes have jurisdiction. State reservations are lands held in trust by state governments for the use and benefit of a given tribe. The reservations and their boundaries were identified for the 1990 census by the Bureau of Indian Affairs (BIA), Department of Interior (for federal reservations), and state governments (for state reservations). The names of American Indian reservations recognized by state governments, but not by the federal government, are followed by "state." Areas composed of reservation lands that are administered jointly and/or are claimed by two reservations, as identified by the BIA, are called "joint areas," and are treated as separate American Indian reservations for census purposes. Federal reservations may cross state boundaries, and federal and state reservations may cross county, county subdivision, and place boundaries. For reservations that cross state boundaries, only the portion of the reservations in a given state is shown in the data products for that state; the entire reservations are shown in data products for the United States. 2. Trust lands are property associated with a particular American Indian reservation or tribe, held in trust by the federal government. Trust lands may be held in trust either for a tribe (tribal trust lands) or for an individual member of a tribe (individual trust land). Trust lands recognized for the 1990 census comprised all tribal trust lands and inhabited individual trust lands located outside of a reservation boundary. As with other American Indian areas, trust lands may be located in more than one state. Only the trust lands in a given state are shown in the data products for that state; all trust lands associated with a reservation or tribe are shown in data products for the United States. The Census Bureau first reported data for tribal trust lands for the 1980 census.

★ 195 ★

Population

Population of American Indian Reservations and Trust Lands, by Sex and Race, 1990 - Sokaogon-Ute

American Indian Reservation and Trust Lands[1,2]	Number of persons							
	Total	Sex		Race				
						American Indian, Eskimo, or Aleut	Asian or Pacific Islander	Other race
		Male	Female	White	Black			
Sokaogon Chippewa Community and Trust Lands, WI	337	163	174	30	4	303	0	0
Southern Ute Reservation	7,886	3,949	3,937	6,405	15	1,037	22	407
Spokane Reservation	1,451	710	741	219	2	1,213	3	14
Squaxin Island Reservation and Trust Lands, WA	194	90	104	46	0	146	0	2
Standing Rock Reservation	7,956	4,058	3,898	3,057	14	4,872	10	3
Stewarts Point Rancheria	89	42	47	0	0	89	0	0
Stillaguamish Reservation	112	58	54	17	0	95	0	0
Stockbridge Reservation	565	291	274	117	0	448	0	0
Sulphur Bank (El-Em) Rancheria	96	40	56	5	0	91	0	0
Summit Lake Reservation	8	5	3	0	0	8	0	0
Susanville Reservation	491	239	252	323	0	148	12	8
Swinomish Reservation	2,285	1,176	1,109	1,690	3	581	7	4
Sycuan Reservation	0	0	0	0	0	0	0	0
Table Bluff Rancheria	45	26	19	6	0	39	0	0
Table Mountain Rancheria	44	23	21	9	0	35	0	0
Tama Reservation (state)	20	6	14	11	0	9	0	0
Taos Pueblo and Trust Lands, NM	4,701	2,219	2,482	2,561	19	1,252	43	826
Te-Moak Reservation and Trust Lands, NV	950	481	469	89	4	853	0	4
Tesuque Pueblo and Trust Lands, NM	702	349	353	476	3	223	0	0
Tonawanda Reservation	483	234	249	35	0	448	0	0
Torres-Martinez Reservation	1,628	930	698	1,344	6	158	87	33
Trinidad Rancheria	71	38	33	10	0	61	0	0
Tulalip Reservation	7,103	3,545	3,558	5,775	26	1,204	61	37
Tule River Reservation	803	412	391	48	0	750	0	5
Tunica-Biloxi Reservation	36	19	17	18	0	18	0	0
Tuolumne Rancheria	85	44	41	13	0	68	2	2
Turtle Mountain Reservation and Trust Lands, ND – SD	7,101	3,495	3,606	371	0	6,730	0	0
Tuscarora Reservation	709	362	347	356	0	353	0	0
Twenty-Nine Palms Reservation	0	0	0	0	0	0	0	0
Uintah and Ouray Reservation	17,235	8,658	8,577	14,327	15	2,667	56	170
Umatilla Reservation	2,549	1,235	1,314	1,492	8	1,030	4	15
Upper Lake Rancheria	70	32	38	59	0	11	0	0
Upper Sioux Community	26	7	19	3	0	23	0	0
Upper Skagit Reservation	173	83	90	6	0	161	3	3
Ute Mountain Reservation and Trust Lands, CO – NM – UT	1,366	713	653	62	0	1,299	0	5

Source: Census of Population and Housing, 1990: Summary Tape File 3C on CD-ROM [machine-readable datafiles]. Prepared by the Bureau of the Census. Washington, DC: The Bureau, 1992. *Notes:* 1. Federal American Indian reservations are areas with boundaries established by treaty, statute, and/or executive or court order, and recognized by the federal government as territory in which American Indian tribes have jurisdiction. State reservations are lands held in trust by state governments for the use and benefit of a given tribe. The reservations and their boundaries were identified for the 1990 census by the Bureau of Indian Affairs (BIA), Department of Interior (for federal reservations), and state governments (for state reservations). The names of American Indian reservations recognized by state governments, but not by the federal government, are followed by "state." Areas composed of reservation lands that are administered jointly and/or are claimed by two reservations, as identified by the BIA, are called "joint areas," and are treated as separate American Indian reservations for census purposes. Federal reservations may cross state boundaries, and federal and state reservations may cross county, county subdivision, and place boundaries. For reservations that cross state boundaries, only the portion of the reservations in a given state is shown in the data products for that state; the entire reservations are shown in data products for the United States. 2. Trust lands are property associated with a particular American Indian reservation or tribe, held in trust by the federal government. Trust lands may be held in trust either for a tribe (tribal trust lands) or for an individual member of a tribe (individual trust land). Trust lands recognized for the 1990 census comprised all tribal trust lands and inhabited individual trust lands located outside of a reservation boundary. As with other American Indian areas, trust lands may be located in more than one state. Only the trust lands in a given state are shown in the data products for that state; all trust lands associated with a reservation or tribe are shown in data products for the United States. The Census Bureau first reported data for tribal trust lands for the 1980 census.

★ 196 ★

Population

Population of American Indian Reservations and Trust Lands, by Sex and Race, 1990 - Vermillion-Zuni

American Indian Reservation and Trust Lands[1,2]	Number of persons							
	Total	Sex		Race				
						American Indian, Eskimo, or Aleut	Asian or Pacific Islander	Other race
		Male	Female	White	Black			
Vermillion Lake Reservation	35	23	12	0	0	35	0	0
Viejas Rancheria	431	244	187	196	2	229	0	4
Walker River Reservation	811	452	359	140	18	612	13	28
Warm Springs Reservation and Trust Lands, OR	3,143	1,614	1,529	234	4	2,871	6	28
Washoe Reservation	146	89	57	54	34	58	0	0
White Earth Reservation	8,785	4,471	4,314	5,979	2	2,798	6	0
Wind River Reservation	21,915	11,015	10,900	15,732	15	5,717	85	366
Winnebago Reservation	2,346	1,177	1,169	1,174	5	1,154	2	11
Winnemucca Colony	54	17	37	0	0	54	0	0
Wisconsin Winnebago Reservation and Trust Lands, WI	608	317	291	80	2	526	0	0
Woodfords Community	20	12	8	20	0	0	0	0
XL Ranch Reservation	23	13	10	0	0	23	0	0
Yakima Reservation and Trust Lands, WA	27,448	14,060	13,388	10,688	108	6,198	517	9,937
Yankton Reservation	6,281	3,109	3,172	4,273	2	2,002	3	1
Yavapai Reservation	193	102	91	24	0	151	0	18
Yerington Reservation and Trust Lands, NV	470	277	193	68	9	349	0	44
Yomba Reservation	106	65	41	4	0	100	0	2
Ysleta Del Sur Pueblo	370	196	174	118	0	248	0	4
Yurok Reservation	1,343	721	622	845	0	494	2	2
Zia Pueblo and Trust Lands, NM	638	306	332	0	0	638	0	0
Zuni Pueblo	7,445	3,630	3,815	311	20	7,094	7	13

Source: Census of Population and Housing, 1990: Summary Tape File 3C on CD-ROM [machine-readable datafiles]. Prepared by the Bureau of the Census. Washington, DC: The Bureau, 1992. *Notes:* 1. Federal American Indian reservations are areas with boundaries established by treaty, statute, and/or executive or court order, and recognized by the federal government as territory in which American Indian tribes have jurisdiction. State reservations are lands held in trust by state governments for the use and benefit of a given tribe. The reservations and their boundaries were identified for the 1990 census by the Bureau of Indian Affairs (BIA), Department of Interior (for federal reservations), and state governments (for state reservations). The names of American Indian reservations recognized by state governments, but not by the federal government, are followed by "state." Areas composed of reservation lands that are administered jointly and/or are claimed by two reservations, as identified by the BIA, are called "joint areas," and are treated as separate American Indian reservations for census purposes. Federal reservations may cross state boundaries, and federal and state reservations may cross county, county subdivision, and place boundaries. For reservations that cross state boundaries, only the portion of the reservations in a given state is shown in the data products for that state; the entire reservations are shown in data products for the United States. 2. Trust lands are property associated with a particular American Indian reservation or tribe, held in trust by the federal government. Trust lands may be held in trust either for a tribe (tribal trust lands) or for an individual member of a tribe (individual trust land). Trust lands recognized for the 1990 census comprised all tribal trust lands and inhabited individual trust lands located outside of a reservation boundary. As with other American Indian areas, trust lands may be located in more than one state. Only the trust lands in a given state are shown in the data products for that state; all trust lands associated with a reservation or tribe are shown in data products for the United States. The Census Bureau first reported data for tribal trust lands for the 1980 census.

★ 197 ★

Population

Population of Tribal Designated Statistical Areas, by Age, 1990 - Part I

Tribal Designated Statistical Area[1]	Number of persons										
	< 1 year	1-2 years	3-4 years	5 years	6 years	7-9 years	10-11 years	12-13 years	14 years	15 years	16 years
Apache Choctaw TDSA (state)	325	590	777	422	399	1,202	750	661	345	364	301
Chickahominy TDSA (state)	15	70	24	26	36	141	128	85	33	34	43
Clifton Choctaw TDSA (state)	22	28	28	0	0	36	10	24	14	0	0
Coharie TDSA (state)	1,615	3,453	3,472	1,431	1,470	4,790	3,268	3,474	1,748	1,755	1,618
Coquille Indian TDSA	4,566	11,377	11,126	5,527	5,882	16,503	10,921	11,115	5,124	5,029	5,059
Delaware-Muncie TDSA (state)	0	31	20	0	12	12	0	12	6	7	0
Eastern Chickahominy TDSA (state)	0	13	0	6	0	5	0	0	0	0	0
Florida Tribe of Eastern Creek TDSA (state)	0	0	21	0	0	9	0	0	0	0	0
Haliwa-Saponi TDSA (state)	122	250	165	109	78	284	252	252	107	169	101
Jena Band of Choctaw TDSA (state)	828	1,949	1,632	995	877	2,882	2,092	1,748	967	859	945
Klamath TDSA	482	1,298	1,148	718	620	1,642	1,234	1,276	504	579	615
Lumbee TDSA (state)	848	1,797	1,721	1,060	755	2,588	1,771	2,027	927	1,048	1,012
Meherrin TDSA (state)	671	1,670	1,566	887	775	2,617	1,670	1,782	786	928	847
Mohegan TDSA (state)	305	866	661	390	278	1,061	715	506	178	306	271
Ponca TDSA (state)	0	0	0	0	0	0	0	0	2	0	0
Ramapough TDSA (state)	3	23	41	0	0	15	11	8	0	7	0
United Houma Nation TDSA (state)	11,432	26,279	26,104	13,506	13,374	40,875	27,016	25,284	12,708	12,570	11,568
Waccamaw Siouan TDSA (state)	5	78	97	25	85	194	136	67	33	65	79
Wampanoag-Gay Head TDSA	98	379	272	227	184	492	318	306	124	82	101

Source: Census of Population and Housing, 1990: Summary Tape File 3C on CD-ROM [machine-readable datafiles]. Prepared by the Bureau of the Census. Washington, DC: The Bureau, 1992. *Notes:* 1. Tribal designated statistical areas (TDSAs) are areas, delineated outside Oklahoma by federally- and state-recognized tribes without a land base or associated trust lands, to provide statistical areas for which the Census Bureau tabulates data. TDSAs represent areas generally containing the American Indian population over which federally-recognized tribes have jurisdiction and areas in which state tribes provide benefits and services to their members. The names of TDSAs delineated by state-recognized tribes are followed by "(state)." The Census Bureau did not recognize TDSAs before the 1990 census.

★ 198 ★

Population

Population of Tribal Designated Statistical Areas, by Age, 1990 - Part II

Tribal Designated Statistical Area[1]	Number of persons									
	17 years	18 years	19 years	20 years	21 years	22-24 years	25-29 years	30-34 years	35-39 years	40-44 years
Apache Choctaw TDSA (state)	288	358	275	296	245	751	1,561	1,559	1,423	1,293
Chickahominy TDSA (state)	59	34	51	20	56	74	285	217	204	238
Clifton Choctaw TDSA (state)	14	15	18	7	5	28	19	77	50	13
Coharie TDSA (state)	1,719	1,791	1,687	1,723	1,900	4,976	9,111	9,193	8,593	7,741
Coquille Indian TDSA	5,017	5,856	7,022	7,089	6,562	17,121	29,178	32,041	34,068	30,689
Delaware-Muncie TDSA (state)	6	0	0	5	0	0	29	47	23	12
Eastern Chickahominy TDSA (state)	0	0	0	4	6	14	13	14	0	13
Florida Tribe of Eastern Creek TDSA (state)	0	0	17	0	0	0	9	0	0	26
Haliwa-Saponi TDSA (state)	126	109	110	135	94	212	424	507	466	389
Jena Band of Choctaw TDSA (state)	828	995	1,001	931	818	2,522	5,048	4,912	4,659	4,221
Klamath TDSA	722	613	594	601	658	1,694	2,852	3,118	3,124	2,853
Lumbee TDSA (state)	1,123	1,132	1,110	980	782	2,108	3,689	4,143	3,838	3,110
Meherrin TDSA (state)	807	894	923	761	642	1,794	3,985	4,500	3,855	3,330

[Continued]

★ 198 ★

Population of Tribal Designated Statistical Areas, by Age, 1990 - Part II

[Continued]

Tribal Designated Statistical Area[1]	Number of persons									
	17 years	18 years	19 years	20 years	21 years	22-24 years	25-29 years	30-34 years	35-39 years	40-44 years
Mohegan TDSA (state)	318	291	304	378	363	1,417	2,839	2,121	1,854	1,430
Ponca TDSA (state)	0	0	3	0	0	0	0	0	2	4
Ramapough TDSA (state)	0	9	4	3	6	44	64	39	56	73
United Houma Nation TDSA (state)	12,441	11,772	11,968	11,644	11,097	36,962	71,920	74,029	65,104	57,754
Waccamaw Siouan TDSA (state)	37	38	56	43	47	54	229	220	212	309
Wampanoag-Gay Head TDSA	138	74	119	75	64	341	722	992	1,179	1,187

Source: Census of Population and Housing, 1990: Summary Tape File 3C on CD-ROM [machine-readable datafiles]. Prepared by the Bureau of the Census. Washington, DC: The Bureau, 1992. *Notes:* 1. Tribal designated statistical areas (TDSAs) are areas, delineated outside Oklahoma by federally- and state-recognized tribes without a land base or associated trust lands, to provide statistical areas for which the Census Bureau tabulates data. TDSAs represent areas generally containing the American Indian population over which federally-recognized tribes have jurisdiction and areas in which state tribes provide benefits and services to their members. The names of TDSAs delineated by state-recognized tribes are followed by "(state)." The Census Bureau did not recognize TDSAs before the 1990 census.

★ 199 ★

Population

Population of Tribal Designated Statistical Areas, by Age, 1990 - Part III

Tribal Designated Statistical Area[1]	Number of persons									
	45-49 years	50-54 years	55-59 years	60-61 years	62-64 years	65-69 years	70-74 years	75-79 years	80-84 years	85 + years
Apache Choctaw TDSA (state)	1,254	1,159	1,149	482	684	1,127	1,053	735	490	328
Chickahominy TDSA (state)	223	159	200	32	79	73	70	27	13	0
Clifton Choctaw TDSA (state)	14	11	21	0	37	30	18	8	5	0
Coharie TDSA (state)	6,223	6,032	5,525	2,129	3,676	5,526	4,220	3,079	1,983	1,303
Coquille Indian TDSA	22,732	17,729	16,509	7,088	11,059	18,947	16,237	12,490	8,145	5,713
Delaware-Muncie TDSA (state)	24	0	0	0	6	13	11	16	0	7
Eastern Chickahominy TDSA (state)	0	0	2	0	0	0	0	0	0	8
Florida Tribe of Eastern Creek TDSA (state)	0	7	35	10	17	18	26	10	0	10
Haliwa-Saponi TDSA (state)	349	388	335	95	166	208	200	113	60	56
Jena Band of Choctaw TDSA (state)	3,438	2,990	2,734	911	1,441	2,386	1,981	1,449	772	583
Klamath TDSA	2,318	1,773	1,857	752	1,089	1,888	1,681	1,281	741	558
Lumbee TDSA (state)	2,667	2,213	1,657	728	1,063	1,517	1,053	938	464	359
Meherrin TDSA (state)	2,975	2,748	2,557	1,178	1,774	2,897	2,075	1,760	973	647
Mohegan TDSA (state)	1,119	1,115	1,057	529	647	1,192	848	589	393	295
Ponca TDSA (state)	0	0	0	0	0	0	0	0	0	0
Ramapough TDSA (state)	29	60	50	14	11	13	40	22	0	7
United Houma Nation TDSA (state)	47,364	38,129	32,991	14,325	20,230	29,767	20,331	14,630	8,866	5,334
Waccamaw Siouan TDSA (state)	135	139	129	33	67	46	44	46	16	7
Wampanoag-Gay Head TDSA	602	502	598	210	363	633	490	355	251	161

Source: Census of Population and Housing, 1990: Summary Tape File 3C on CD-ROM [machine-readable datafiles]. Prepared by the Bureau of the Census. Washington, DC: The Bureau, 1992. *Notes:* 1. Tribal designated statistical areas (TDSAs) are areas, delineated outside Oklahoma by federally- and state-recognized tribes without a land base or associated trust lands, to provide statistical areas for which the Census Bureau tabulates data. TDSAs represent areas generally containing the American Indian population over which federally-recognized tribes have jurisdiction and areas in which state tribes provide benefits and services to their members. The names of TDSAs delineated by state-recognized tribes are followed by "(state)." The Census Bureau did not recognize TDSAs before the 1990 census.

★ 200 ★

Population

Population of Tribal Designated Statistical Areas, by Sex and Race, 1990

Tribal Designated Statistical Area[1]	Number of persons							
	Total	Sex		Race				
		Male	Female	White	Black	American Indian, Eskimo, or Aleut	Asian or Pacific Islander	Other race
Apache Choctaw TDSA (state)	22,646	10,981	11,665	17,918	3,955	684	26	63
Chickahominy TDSA (state)	2,749	1,304	1,445	714	1,553	482	0	0
Clifton Choctaw TDSA (state)	552	291	261	371	0	181	0	0
Coharie TDSA (state)	116,224	54,711	61,513	68,982	44,772	1,422	505	543
Coquille Indian TDSA	403,521	195,851	207,670	383,961	1,994	6,236	6,956	4,374
Delaware-Muncie TDSA (state)	299	142	157	276	0	23	0	0
Eastern Chickahominy TDSA (state)	98	49	49	67	23	8	0	0
Florida Tribe of Eastern Creek TDSA (state)	215	112	103	215	0	0	0	0
Haliwa-Saponi TDSA (state)	6,431	3,203	3,228	521	3,646	2,244	0	20
Jena Band of Choctaw TDSA (state)	60,394	29,373	31,021	52,616	6,895	336	497	50
Klamath TDSA	40,883	20,414	20,469	37,742	338	1,858	271	674
Lumbee TDSA (state)	50,228	23,771	26,457	8,689	12,632	28,775	32	100
Meherrin TDSA (state)	55,274	25,769	29,505	24,135	30,744	201	119	75
Mohegan TDSA (state)	24,636	12,087	12,549	21,902	1,718	240	341	435
Ponca TDSA (state)	11	6	5	11	0	0	0	0
Ramapough TDSA (state)	652	304	348	343	156	139	0	14
United Houma Nation TDSA (state)	817,374	394,903	422,471	646,952	139,381	10,018	13,109	7,914
Waccamaw Siouan TDSA (state)	2,771	1,306	1,465	792	629	1,297	8	45
Wampanoag-Gay Head TDSA	11,639	5,665	5,974	10,748	500	283	41	67

Source: Census of Population and Housing, 1990: Summary Tape File 3C on CD-ROM [machine-readable datafiles]. Prepared by the Bureau of the Census. Washington, DC: The Bureau, 1992. Notes: 1. Tribal designated statistical areas (TDSAs) are areas, delineated outside Oklahoma by federally- and state-recognized tribes without a land base or associated trust lands, to provide statistical areas for which the Census Bureau tabulates data. TDSAs represent areas generally containing the American Indian population over which federally-recognized tribes have jurisdiction and areas in which state tribes provide benefits and services to their members. The names of TDSAs delineated by state-recognized tribes are followed by "(state)." The Census Bureau did not recognize TDSAs before the 1990 census.

★ 201 ★

Population

Population of Tribal Jurisdiction Statistical Areas, by Age, 1990 - Part I

Tribal Jurisdiction Statistical Area[1]	Number of persons										
	< 1 year	1-2 years	3-4 years	5 years	6 years	7-9 years	10-11 years	12-13 years	14 years	15 years	16 years
Absentee Shawnee-Citizens Band of Potawatomi TJSA	970	2,426	2,514	1,375	1,263	4,500	3,462	3,338	1,519	1,529	1,623
Caddo-Wichita-Delaware TJSA	109	200	273	82	127	433	265	227	141	115	171
Cherokee TJSA	4,712	11,930	11,659	6,504	6,446	19,104	13,417	12,152	6,035	6,046	6,174
Cheyenne-Arapaho TJSA	1,816	4,267	4,688	2,378	2,488	7,781	5,040	4,907	2,623	2,190	2,118
Chickasaw TJSA	3,102	6,483	7,013	3,789	3,604	12,228	7,969	7,650	3,741	4,067	3,692
Choctaw TJSA	2,733	5,422	5,678	2,975	2,789	9,372	6,240	6,899	3,755	3,512	3,173
Creek TJSA	7,921	19,248	19,178	9,398	9,854	29,147	18,912	17,451	8,955	9,068	8,609
Iowa TJSA	40	128	116	50	65	217	170	176	74	69	74

[Continued]

★ 201 ★

Population of Tribal Jurisdiction Statistical Areas, by Age, 1990 - Part I
[Continued]

Tribal Jurisdiction Statistical Area[1]	Number of persons										
	< 1 year	1-2 years	3-4 years	5 years	6 years	7-9 years	10-11 years	12-13 years	14 years	15 years	16 years
Kaw TJSA	115	347	446	235	265	533	339	477	198	192	180
Kiowa-Comanche-Apache-Fort Sill Apache TJSA	2,832	6,893	6,402	3,478	2,990	10,172	6,260	6,491	3,004	3,034	2,878
Otoe-Missouria TJSA	32	88	98	48	61	172	100	117	36	39	33
Pawnee TJSA	198	430	414	265	197	695	496	523	226	250	218
Sac and Fox TJSA	590	1,466	1,420	707	804	2,476	1,648	1,289	743	835	738
Seminole TJSA	274	535	687	338	349	1,165	739	695	241	356	358
Tonkawa TJSA	127	360	329	171	150	643	376	368	140	176	171
Creek-Seminole Joint Area TJSA	29	57	53	36	19	136	76	76	50	31	36
Iowa-Sac and Fox Joint Area TJSA	9	23	31	17	3	58	42	25	8	17	15

Source: Census of Population and Housing, 1990: Summary Tape File 3C on CD-ROM [machine-readable datafiles]. Prepared by the Bureau of the Census. Washington, DC: The Bureau, 1992. *Notes:* 1. Tribal jurisdiction statistical areas (TJSAs) are areas, delineated by federally recognized tribes in Oklahoma without a reservation, for which the Census Bureau tabulates data. TJSAs represent areas generally containing the American Indian population over which one or more tribal governments have jurisdiction. If tribal officials delineated adjacent TJSAs so that they include some duplicate territory, the overlap area is called a "joint use area," which is treated as a separate TJSA for census purposes.

★ 202 ★
Population

Population of Tribal Jurisdiction Statistical Areas, by Age, 1990 - Part II

Tribal Jurisdiction Statistical Area[1]	Number of persons									
	17 years	18 years	19 years	20 years	21 years	22-24 years	25-29 years	30-34 years	35-39 years	40-44 years
Absentee Shawnee-Citizens Band of Potawatomi TJSA	1,601	1,334	1,187	995	935	2,808	6,557	8,166	8,242	7,309
Caddo-Wichita-Delaware TJSA	119	124	77	61	81	213	606	538	575	485
Cherokee TJSA	6,131	5,843	5,450	5,071	4,639	13,092	27,891	30,688	29,125	26,774
Cheyenne-Arapaho TJSA	2,463	2,193	2,304	1,827	1,791	5,100	11,559	12,648	11,932	10,187
Chickasaw TJSA	4,138	3,792	3,596	3,192	2,846	8,113	17,454	19,524	18,328	16,896
Choctaw TJSA	3,215	3,330	3,038	2,766	2,306	7,415	14,305	14,641	14,385	13,290
Creek TJSA	8,626	8,561	8,802	8,867	8,201	25,337	53,186	56,673	50,605	46,946
Iowa TJSA	91	36	48	32	38	133	294	394	295	264
Kaw TJSA	207	159	134	131	106	278	738	906	1,001	1,131
Kiowa-Comanche-Apache-Fort Sill Apache TJSA	3,158	3,379	3,944	4,311	4,024	9,976	17,881	17,389	14,939	11,573
Otoe-Missouria TJSA	30	45	39	32	22	104	187	240	210	182
Pawnee TJSA	238	239	178	163	154	432	935	1,190	1,159	1,121
Sac and Fox TJSA	797	694	584	601	561	1,676	3,851	3,619	3,373	3,223
Seminole TJSA	430	306	324	258	261	709	1,533	1,578	1,526	1,399
Tonkawa TJSA	137	170	331	193	146	353	816	789	854	701
Creek-Seminole Joint Area TJSA	29	47	31	34	20	69	144	154	150	192
Iowa-Sac and Fox Joint Area TJSA	25	4	16	8	7	9	51	102	98	36

Source: Census of Population and Housing, 1990: Summary Tape File 3C on CD-ROM [machine-readable datafiles]. Prepared by the Bureau of the Census. Washington, DC: The Bureau, 1992. *Notes:* 1. Tribal jurisdiction statistical areas (TJSAs) are areas, delineated by federally recognized tribes in Oklahoma without a reservation, for which the Census Bureau tabulates data. TJSAs represent areas generally containing the American Indian population over which one or more tribal governments have jurisdiction. If tribal officials delineated adjacent TJSAs so that they include some duplicate territory, the overlap area is called a "joint use area," which is treated as a separate TJSA for census purposes.

★ 203 ★

Population

Population of Tribal Jurisdiction Statistical Areas, by Age, 1990 - Part III

Tribal Jurisdiction Statistical Area[1]	Number of persons									
	45-49 years	50-54 years	55-59 years	60-61 years	62-64 years	65-69 years	70-74 years	75-79 years	80-84 years	85 + years
Absentee Shawnee-Citizens Band of Potawatomi TJSA	5,663	4,891	4,144	1,696	2,385	3,330	2,002	1,490	1,106	652
Caddo-Wichita-Delaware TJSA	509	430	381	200	250	388	351	289	220	168
Cherokee TJSA	23,609	20,724	20,243	7,577	11,441	18,302	14,713	11,125	7,393	5,124
Cheyenne-Arapaho TJSA	8,424	6,828	6,460	2,300	3,542	5,522	5,009	4,331	3,434	2,515
Chickasaw TJSA	14,478	12,868	12,996	4,915	7,452	12,640	10,403	9,179	6,605	4,760
Choctaw TJSA	12,282	10,301	10,004	3,983	6,576	10,488	8,476	7,311	5,016	3,677
Creek TJSA	38,074	29,626	27,391	10,526	16,339	26,331	18,975	15,885	10,436	8,326
Iowa TJSA	237	214	152	90	85	180	140	111	94	30
Kaw TJSA	846	771	721	261	429	706	451	404	224	296
Kiowa-Comanche-Apache-Fort Sill Apache TJSA	9,816	8,662	8,256	3,478	4,687	7,541	6,385	5,195	3,821	2,891
Otoe-Missouria TJSA	140	145	102	49	91	104	64	72	45	23
Pawnee TJSA	919	793	762	311	415	705	684	458	394	251
Sac and Fox TJSA	2,878	2,551	2,331	1,029	1,521	2,487	2,218	2,030	1,410	942
Seminole TJSA	1,317	1,030	1,185	373	703	1,281	1,029	946	592	476
Tonkawa TJSA	600	598	553	214	358	704	517	524	371	328
Creek-Seminole Joint Area TJSA	186	104	129	54	61	98	128	74	82	34
Iowa-Sac and Fox Joint Area TJSA	70	40	24	18	11	30	18	9	4	7

Source: Census of Population and Housing, 1990: Summary Tape File 3C on CD-ROM [machine-readable datafiles]. Prepared by the Bureau of the Census. Washington, DC: The Bureau, 1992. *Notes:* 1. Tribal jurisdiction statistical areas (TJSAs) are areas, delineated by federally recognized tribes in Oklahoma without a reservation, for which the Census Bureau tabulates data. TJSAs represent areas generally containing the American Indian population over which one or more tribal governments have jurisdiction. If tribal officials delineated adjacent TJSAs so that they include some duplicate territory, the overlap area is called a "joint use area," which is treated as a separate TJSA for census purposes.

★ 204 ★

Population

Population of Tribal Jurisdiction Statistical Areas, by Sex and Race, 1990

Tribal Jurisdiction Statistical Area[1]	Number of persons							
	Total	Sex		Race				
		Male	Female	White	Black	American Indian, Eskimo, or Aleut	Asian or Pacific Islander	Other race
Absentee Shawnee-Citizens Band of Potawatomi TJSA	91,012	46,577	44,435	78,281	5,791	6,129	287	524
Caddo-Wichita-Delaware TJSA	8,208	4,046	4,162	7,262	76	599	11	260
Cherokee TJSA	399,134	193,940	205,194	295,141	34,398	66,435	1,115	2,045
Cheyenne-Arapaho TJSA	150,665	73,654	77,011	135,810	3,731	6,824	1,279	3,021
Chickasaw TJSA	257,513	123,922	133,591	224,799	8,666	21,013	739	2,296
Choctaw TJSA	209,353	101,890	107,463	170,189	9,499	28,245	419	1,001
Creek TJSA	635,454	306,413	329,041	540,721	38,800	45,190	6,512	4,231
Iowa TJSA	4,137	2,035	2,102	3,679	142	307	5	4
Kaw TJSA	13,227	6,482	6,745	12,366	47	687	91	36
Kiowa-Comanche-Apache-Fort Sill Apache TJSA	205,740	103,925	101,815	154,534	25,788	12,979	3,604	8,835
Otoe-Missouria TJSA	2,750	1,370	1,380	2,202	41	475	9	23
Pawnee TJSA	15,413	7,614	7,799	13,650	105	1,628	14	16

[Continued]

★ 204 ★

Population of Tribal Jurisdiction Statistical Areas, by Sex and Race, 1990

[Continued]

Tribal Jurisdiction Statistical Area[1]	Number of persons							
	Total	Sex		Race				
		Male	Female	White	Black	American Indian, Eskimo, or Aleut	Asian or Pacific Islander	Other race
Sac and Fox TJSA	51,092	24,294	26,798	44,495	1,544	4,575	212	266
Seminole TJSA	22,993	10,947	12,046	17,406	1,748	3,772	12	55
Tonkawa TJSA	12,268	5,941	6,327	11,197	18	881	43	129
Creek-Seminole Joint Area TJSA	2,419	1,187	1,232	1,686	173	531	19	10
Iowa-Sac and Fox Joint Area TJSA	835	435	400	784	28	20	0	3

Source: Census of Population and Housing, 1990: Summary Tape File 3C on CD-ROM [machine-readable datafiles]. Prepared by the Bureau of the Census. Washington, DC: The Bureau, 1992. *Notes:* 1. Tribal jurisdiction statistical areas (TJSAs) are areas, delineated by federally recognized tribes in Oklahoma without a reservation, for which the Census Bureau tabulates data. TJSAs represent areas generally containing the American Indian population over which one or more tribal governments have jurisdiction. If tribal officials delineated adjacent TJSAs so that they include some duplicate territory, the overlap area is called a "joint use area," which is treated as a separate TJSA for census purposes.

★ 205 ★

Population

Population of Urban and Rural Areas in Selected Alaska Native Villages

Data are shown for the 50 areas with the largest populations, in number of persons.

Alaska Native Village Statistical Area[1]	Number of persons			
	Urban		Rural	
	Inside urbanized area	Outside urbanized area	Farm	Nonfarm
Akiachak	0	0	0	462
Akutan	0	0	0	605
Alakanuk	0	0	0	540
Andreafsky	0	0	0	406
Angoon	0	0	2	641
Aniak	0	0	0	529
Barrow	0	2,340	0	410
Bethel	0	4,239	0	448
Chevak	0	0	0	597
Copper Center	0	0	0	426
Craig	0	0	0	1,260
Dillingham	0	0	0	2,017
Emmonak	0	0	0	610
Fort Yukon	0	0	20	559
Galena	0	0	0	806
Gambell	0	0	0	548
Grouse Creek Group	0	0	6	624
Hoonah	0	0	0	729
Hooper Bay	0	0	0	846

[Continued]

★ 205 ★

Population of Urban and Rural Areas in Selected Alaska Native Villages
[Continued]

Alaska Native Village Statistical Area[1]	Number of persons			
	Urban		Rural	
	Inside urbanized area	Outside urbanized area	Farm	Nonfarm
Kake	0	0	0	687
Kasigluk	0	0	0	440
King Cove	0	0	0	457
King Salmon	0	0	0	684
Kipnuk	0	0	0	462
Klawock	0	0	0	705
Kotlik	0	0	0	462
Kotzebue	0	2,743	0	8
Kwethluk	0	0	0	568
McGrath	0	0	0	524
Mountain Village	0	0	0	706
Naknek	0	0	0	590
Ninilchik	0	3,660	81	6,750
Noorvik	0	0	0	548
Pilot Station	0	0	0	467
Point Hope	0	0	0	629
Quinhagak	0	0	0	509
St. Paul	0	0	0	752
Salamatof	0	0	11	996
Sand Point	0	0	0	859
Savoonga	0	0	0	514
Selawik	0	0	0	579
Shishmaref	0	0	0	433
Stebbins	0	0	0	448
Togiak	0	0	0	606
Tok	0	0	5	930
Toksook Bay	0	0	0	405
Unalakleet	0	0	0	646
Unalaska	0	3,089	0	0
Wainwright	0	0	0	502
Yakutat	0	0	0	544

Source: Census of Population and Housing, 1990: Summary Tape File 3C on CD-ROM [machine-readable datafiles]. Prepared by the Bureau of the Census. Washington, DC: The Bureau, 1992. *Notes:* 1. Alaska Native villages (ANVs) constitute tribes, bands, clans, groups, villages, communities, or associations in Alaska that are recognized pursuant to the Alaska Native Claims Settlement Act of 1972, Public Law 92-203. Because ANVs do not have legally designated boundaries, the Census Bureau has established Alaska Native village statistical areas (ANVSAs) for statistical purposes. For the 1990 census, the Census Bureau cooperated with officials of the nonprofit corporation within each participating Alaska Native Regional Corporation (ANRC), as well as other knowledgeable officials, to delineate boundaries that encompass the settled area associated with each ANV.

★ 206 ★

Population

Population of Urban and Rural Areas in Selected Tribal Designated Statistical Areas

Tribal Designated Statistical Area[1]	Number of persons			
	Urban		Rural	
	Inside urbanized area	Outside urbanized area	Farm	Nonfarm
Apache Choctaw TDSA (state)	0	3,126	655	18,865
Chickahominy TDSA (state)	0	0	61	2,688
Clifton Choctaw TDSA (state)	0	0	39	513
Coharie TDSA (state)	34,653	28,062	2,246	51,263
Coquille Indian TDSA	209,676	103,742	3,645	86,458
Delaware-Muncie TDSA (state)	0	0	45	254
Florida Tribe of Eastern Creek TDSA (state)	0	0	0	215
Haliwa-Saponi TDSA (state)	0	0	179	6,252
Jena Band of Choctaw TDSA (state)	26,509	2,262	380	31,243
Klamath TDSA	0	35,903	289	4,691
Lumbee TDSA (state)	0	6,489	1,668	42,071
Meherrin TDSA (state)	0	7,041	2,538	45,695
Mohegan TDSA (state)	24,636	0	0	0
Ramapough TDSA (state)	571	0	0	81
United Houma Nation TDSA (state)	609,551	110,591	1,387	95,845
Waccamaw Siouan TDSA (state)	0	0	89	2,682
Wampanoag-Gay Head TDSA	0	0	71	11,568

Source: Census of Population and Housing, 1990: Summary Tape File 3C on CD-ROM [machine-readable datafiles]. Prepared by the Bureau of the Census. Washington, DC: The Bureau, 1992. *Notes:* 1. Tribal designated statistical areas (TDSAs) are areas, delineated outside Oklahoma by federally- and state-recognized tribes without a land base or associated trust lands, to provide statistical areas for which the Census Bureau tabulates data. TDSAs represent areas generally containing the American Indian population over which federally-recognized tribes have jurisdiction and areas in which state tribes provide benefits and services to their members. The names of TDSAs delineated by state-recognized tribes are followed by "(state)." The Census Bureau did not recognize TDSAs before the 1990 census.

★ 207 ★

Population

Population of Urban and Rural Areas in Selected Tribal Jurisdiction Statistical Areas

Tribal Jurisdiction Statistical Area[1]	Number of persons			
	Urban		Rural	
	Inside urbanized area	Outside urbanized area	Farm	Nonfarm
Absentee Shawnee-Citizens Band of Potawatomi TJSA	43,054	7,768	1,389	38,801
Caddo-Wichita-Delaware TJSA	0	0	1,152	7,056
Cherokee TJSA	73,646	120,414	14,945	190,129
Cheyenne-Arapaho TJSA	33,594	59,139	8,041	49,891
Chickasaw TJSA	0	118,809	10,672	128,032
Choctaw TJSA	2,393	69,521	11,896	125,543
Creek TJSA	395,603	114,351	6,639	118,861
Iowa TJSA	0	0	467	3,670
Kaw TJSA	0	7,711	472	5,044
Kiowa-Comanche-Apache-Fort Sill Apache TJSA	92,582	46,345	5,858	60,955
Otoe-Missouria TJSA	0	745	330	1,675
Pawnee TJSA	0	3,156	715	11,542
Sac and Fox TJSA	0	30,015	2,082	18,995
Seminole TJSA	0	10,071	688	12,234
Tonkawa TJSA	0	10,665	404	1,199
Creek-Seminole Joint Area TJSA	0	1,035	139	1,245
Iowa-Sac and Fox Joint Area TJSA	0	0	65	770

Source: Census of Population and Housing, 1990: Summary Tape File 3C on CD-ROM [machine-readable datafiles]. Prepared by the Bureau of the Census. Washington, DC: The Bureau, 1992. *Notes:* 1. Tribal jurisdiction statistical areas (TJSAs) are areas, delineated by federally recognized tribes in Oklahoma without a reservation, for which the Census Bureau tabulates data. TJSAs represent areas generally containing the American Indian population over which one or more tribal governments have jurisdiction. If tribal officials delineated adjacent TJSAs so that they include some duplicate territory, the overlap area is called a "joint use area," which is treated as a separate TJSA for census purposes.

★ 208 ★

Population

Population of Urban and Rural Areas on Selected Reservations and Trust Lands

Data are shown for the 50 areas with the largest populations, in number of persons.

American Indian Reservation and Trust Lands[1,2]	Number of persons			
	Urban		Rural	
	Inside urbanized area	Outside urbanized area	Farm	Nonfarm
Agua Caliente Reservation	19,651	0	0	188
Allegany Reservation	0	6,175	22	1,115
Blackfeet Reservation	0	0	488	8,000
Cheyenne River Reservation	0	0	1,119	6,624

[Continued]

★ 208 ★

Population of Urban and Rural Areas on Selected Reservations and Trust Lands
[Continued]

American Indian Reservation and Trust Lands[1,2]	Number of persons			
	Urban		Rural	
	Inside urbanized area	Outside urbanized area	Farm	Nonfarm
Coeur d'Alene Reservation and Trust Lands, ID	0	0	490	5,288
Colorado River Reservation	0	2,924	51	4,969
Colville Reservation	0	851	306	5,877
Crow Reservation and Trust Lands, MT	0	0	638	5,703
Eastern Cherokee Reservation	0	0	109	6,202
Flathead Reservation	0	3,254	2,509	15,298
Fort Apache Reservation	0	3,738	7	6,761
Fort Berthold Reservation	0	0	421	4,966
Fort Hall Reservation and Trust Lands, ID	31	2,735	162	2,186
Fort Peck Reservation	0	2,880	1,190	6,652
Gila River Reservation	0	0	122	9,456
Hopi Reservation and Trust Lands, AZ	0	0	0	7,215
Isabella Reservation and Trust Lands, MI	0	8,717	639	13,575
Laguna Pueblo and Trust Lands, NM	0	0	23	3,701
Lake Traverse (Sisseton) Reservation	0	0	2,355	8,485
Leech Lake Reservation	0	0	320	8,463
Mississippi Choctaw Reservation and Trust Lands, MS	0	25	39	4,193
Muckleshoot Reservation and Trust Lands, WA	3,095	0	17	724
Navajo Reservation and Trust Lands, AZ–NM–UT	0	32,004	1,422	115,232
Nez Perce Reservation	0	2,868	1,082	12,209
Northern Cheyenne Reservation and Trust Lands, MT–SD	0	0	173	3,733
Omaha Reservation	0	0	889	4,349
Oneida (West) Reservation	10,377	0	512	7,051
Osage Reservation	6,054	7,105	1,092	27,142
Papago Reservation	0	2,622	80	5,885
Pine Ridge Reservation and Trust Lands, NE–SD	0	2,598	734	8,787
Port Madison Reservation	0	3,105	26	1,703
Puyallup Reservation and Trust Lands, WA	31,525	0	76	834
Red Lake Reservation	0	0	45	3,645
Rosebud Reservation and Trust Lands, SD	0	0	744	8,888
Salt River Reservation	1,167	0	54	3,635
San Carlos Reservation	0	2,954	0	4,285
Sandia Pueblo	282	2,831	8	823
San Juan Pueblo	0	839	52	4,346
Santa Clara Pueblo	0	5,937	33	4,260
Southern Ute Reservation	0	0	940	6,946
Standing Rock Reservation	0	0	1,457	6,499
Taos Pueblo and Trust Lands, NM	0	2,010	11	2,680
Tulalip Reservation	1,559	0	95	5,449
Turtle Mountain Reservation and Trust Lands, ND–SD	0	0	194	6,907
Uintah and Ouray Reservation	0	3,915	1,677	11,643
White Earth Reservation	0	0	1,540	7,245
Wind River Reservation	0	9,202	1,530	11,183

[Continued]

★ 208 ★

Population of Urban and Rural Areas on Selected Reservations and Trust Lands
[Continued]

American Indian Reservation and Trust Lands[1,2]	Number of persons			
	Urban		Rural	
	Inside urbanized area	Outside urbanized area	Farm	Nonfarm
Yakima Reservation and Trust Lands, WA	95	13,969	1,682	11,702
Yankton Reservation	0	0	1,343	4,938
Zuni Pueblo	0	5,883	0	1,562

Source: Census of Population and Housing, 1990: Summary Tape File 3C on CD-ROM [machine-readable datafiles]. Prepared by the Bureau of the Census. Washington, DC: The Bureau, 1992. *Notes:* 1. Federal American Indian reservations are areas with boundaries established by treaty, statute, and/or executive or court order, and recognized by the federal government as territory in which American Indian tribes have jurisdiction. State reservations are lands held in trust by state governments for the use and benefit of a given tribe. The reservations and their boundaries were identified for the 1990 census by the Bureau of Indian Affairs (BIA), Department of Interior (for federal reservations), and state governments (for state reservations). The names of American Indian reservations recognized by state governments, but not by the federal government, are followed by "state." Areas composed of reservation lands that are administered jointly and/or are claimed by two reservations, as identified by the BIA, are called "joint areas," and are treated as separate American Indian reservations for census purposes. Federal reservations may cross state boundaries, and federal and state reservations may cross county, county subdivision, and place boundaries. For reservations that cross state boundaries, only the portion of the reservations in a given state is shown in the data products for that state; the entire reservations are shown in data products for the United States. 2. Trust lands are property associated with a particular American Indian reservation or tribe, held in trust by the federal government. Trust lands may be held in trust either for a tribe (tribal trust lands) or for an individual member of a tribe (individual trust land). Trust lands recognized for the 1990 census comprised all tribal trust lands and inhabited individual trust lands located outside of a reservation boundary. As with other American Indian areas, trust lands may be located in more than one state. Only the trust lands in a given state are shown in the data products for that state; all trust lands associated with a reservation or tribe are shown in data products for the United States. The Census Bureau first reported data for tribal trust lands for the 1980 census.

★ 209 ★

Population

Population, by Race and Hispanic Origin in Selected Alaska Native Villages

Data are shown for the 50 areas with the largest populations, in number of persons.

Alaska Native Village Statistical Area[1]	Not of Hispanic origin					Hispanic origin				
	White	Black	Am. Indian, Eskimo, or Aleut	Asian or Pacific Islander	Other race	White	Black	Am. Indian, Eskimo, or Aleut	Asian or Pacific Islander	Other race
Akiachak	42	0	416	4	0	0	0	0	0	0
Akutan	247	7	81	219	0	3	0	0	18	30
Alakanuk	22	0	518	0	0	0	0	0	0	0
Andreafsky	61	0	343	0	0	0	0	2	0	0
Angoon	122	0	505	5	0	0	0	2	0	9
Aniak	154	16	352	5	2	0	0	0	0	0
Barrow	742	8	1,745	182	5	12	6	11	16	23
Bethel	1,531	37	2,970	63	5	43	0	24	2	12
Chevak	34	0	557	4	0	0	0	2	0	0
Copper Center	280	0	144	0	0	2	0	0	0	0
Craig	939	0	279	2	0	25	0	9	0	6
Dillingham	830	0	1,109	53	1	1	0	13	0	10
Emmonak	54	3	534	12	2	0	0	4	0	1
Fort Yukon	77	0	502	0	0	0	0	0	0	0
Galena	396	30	368	10	0	2	0	0	0	0
Gambell	6	0	542	0	0	0	0	0	0	0
Grouse Creek Group	518	0	104	0	0	8	0	0	0	0
Hoonah	202	0	527	0	0	0	0	0	0	0

[Continued]

★ 209 ★

Population, by Race and Hispanic Origin in Selected Alaska Native Villages
[Continued]

Alaska Native Village Statistical Area[1]	Not of Hispanic origin					Hispanic origin				
	White	Black	Am. Indian, Eskimo, or Aleut	Asian or Pacific Islander	Other race	White	Black	Am. Indian, Eskimo, or Aleut	Asian or Pacific Islander	Other race
Hooper Bay	29	0	817	0	0	0	0	0	0	0
Kake	171	0	514	0	0	0	0	2	0	0
Kasigluk	24	0	416	0	0	0	0	0	0	0
King Cove	111	0	184	86	0	8	0	0	52	16
King Salmon	506	31	105	13	0	22	0	0	0	7
Kipnuk	8	0	452	2	0	0	0	0	0	0
Klawock	322	0	371	2	0	2	0	6	2	0
Kotlik	11	3	448	0	0	0	0	0	0	0
Kotzebue	614	7	2,057	42	0	23	0	8	0	0
Kwethluk	10	13	543	0	0	0	0	0	0	2
McGrath	266	0	256	0	0	0	0	2	0	0
Mountain Village	57	4	640	3	0	0	0	0	2	0
Naknek	338	0	252	0	0	0	0	0	0	0
Ninilchik	9,726	55	404	85	0	200	6	7	0	8
Noorvik	29	0	519	0	0	0	0	0	0	0
Pilot Station	15	0	450	0	0	0	0	2	0	0
Point Hope	39	2	585	3	0	0	0	0	0	0
Quinhagak	37	0	468	2	0	2	0	0	0	0
St. Paul	159	24	529	25	0	1	0	2	0	12
Salamatof	829	24	110	1	0	43	0	0	0	0
Sand Point	268	0	422	87	0	19	0	0	0	63
Savoonga	19	0	494	0	0	0	0	1	0	0
Selawik	21	3	555	0	0	0	0	0	0	0
Shishmaref	15	0	418	0	0	0	0	0	0	0
Stebbins	21	0	427	0	0	0	0	0	0	0
Togiak	85	2	519	0	0	0	0	0	0	0
Tok	833	0	87	8	0	7	0	0	0	0
Toksook Bay	13	0	389	3	0	0	0	0	0	0
Unalakleet	125	0	510	7	0	4	0	0	0	0
Unalaska	1,826	49	271	566	26	91	0	2	31	227
Wainwright	30	0	469	0	0	0	0	3	0	0
Yakutat	241	0	285	13	0	0	0	5	0	0

Source: Census of Population and Housing, 1990: Summary Tape File 3C on CD-ROM [machine-readable datafiles]. Prepared by the Bureau of the Census. Washington, DC: The Bureau, 1992. *Notes:* 1. Alaska Native villages (ANVs) constitute tribes, bands, clans, groups, villages, communities, or associations in Alaska that are recognized pursuant to the Alaska Native Claims Settlement Act of 1972, Public Law 92-203. Because ANVs do not have legally designated boundaries, the Census Bureau has established Alaska Native village statistical areas (ANVSAs) for statistical purposes. For the 1990 census, the Census Bureau cooperated with officials of the nonprofit corporation within each participating Alaska Native Regional Corporation (ANRC), as well as other knowledgeable officials, to delineate boundaries that encompass the settled area associated with each ANV.

★ 210 ★

Population

Population, by Race and Hispanic Origin in Selected Tribal Designated Statistical Areas

Tribal Designated Statistical Area[1]	Not of Hispanic origin					Hispanic origin				
	White	Black	Am. Indian, Eskimo, or Aleut	Asian or Pacific Islander	Other race	White	Black	Am. Indian, Eskimo, or Aleut	Asian or Pacific Islander	Other race
Apache Choctaw TDSA (state)	16,988	3,938	478	26	0	930	17	206	0	63
Chickahominy TDSA (state)	714	1,533	482	0	0	0	20	0	0	0
Clifton Choctaw TDSA (state)	326	0	171	0	0	45	0	10	0	0
Coharie TDSA (state)	68,229	44,565	1,422	503	14	753	207	0	2	529
Coquille Indian TDSA	376,623	1,917	5,932	6,805	125	7,338	77	304	151	4,249
Delaware-Muncie TDSA (state)	276	0	23	0	0	0	0	0	0	0
Florida Tribe of Eastern Creek TDSA (state)	215	0	0	0	0	0	0	0	0	0
Haliwa-Saponi TDSA (state)	521	3,646	2,244	0	20	0	0	0	0	0
Jena Band of Choctaw TDSA (state)	52,210	6,872	315	428	0	406	23	21	69	50
Klamath TDSA	36,562	338	1,715	252	10	1,180	0	143	19	664
Lumbee TDSA (state)	8,643	12,577	28,558	32	0	46	55	217	0	100
Meherrin TDSA (state)	24,103	30,712	197	119	32	32	32	4	0	43
Mohegan TDSA (state)	21,482	1,648	240	314	87	420	70	0	27	348
Ramapough TDSA (state)	343	153	139	0	0	0	3	0	0	14
United Houma Nation TDSA (state)	619,806	138,591	9,808	12,723	362	27,146	790	210	386	7,552
Waccamaw Siouan TDSA (state)	792	629	1,276	8	25	0	0	21	0	20
Wampanoag-Gay Head TDSA	10,696	491	273	41	54	52	9	10	0	13

Source: Census of Population and Housing, 1990: Summary Tape File 3C on CD-ROM [machine-readable datafiles]. Prepared by the Bureau of the Census. Washington, DC: The Bureau, 1992. *Notes:* 1. Tribal designated statistical areas (TDSAs) are areas, delineated outside Oklahoma by federally- and state-recognized tribes without a land base or associated trust lands, to provide statistical areas for which the Census Bureau tabulates data. TDSAs represent areas generally containing the American Indian population over which federally-recognized tribes have jurisdiction and areas in which state tribes provide benefits and services to their members. The names of TDSAs delineated by state-recognized tribes are followed by "(state)." The Census Bureau did not recognize TDSAs before the 1990 census.

★ 211 ★

Population

Population, by Race and Hispanic Origin in Selected Tribal Jurisdiction Statistical Areas

Tribal Jurisdiction Statistical Area[1]	Not of Hispanic origin					Hispanic origin				
	White	Black	Am. Indian, Eskimo, or Aleut	Asian or Pacific Islander	Other race	White	Black	Am. Indian, Eskimo, or Aleut	Asian or Pacific Islander	Other race
Absentee Shawnee-Citizens Band of Potawatomi TJSA	77,421	5,778	5,885	273	54	860	13	244	14	470
Caddo-Wichita-Delaware TJSA	7,161	76	574	11	2	101	0	25	0	258
Cherokee TJSA	292,354	34,207	65,601	1,059	119	2,787	191	834	56	1,926
Cheyenne-Arapaho TJSA	134,177	3,688	6,583	1,204	55	1,633	43	241	75	2,966
Chickasaw TJSA	222,864	8,507	20,684	737	47	1,935	159	329	2	2,249
Choctaw TJSA	168,876	9,458	27,917	388	49	1,313	41	328	31	952
Creek TJSA	533,357	38,576	44,673	6,362	278	7,364	224	517	150	3,953
Iowa TJSA	3,660	142	307	5	0	19	0	0	0	4
Kaw TJSA	12,273	47	684	91	0	93	0	3	0	36
Kiowa-Comanche-Apache-Fort Sill Apache TJSA	150,300	25,371	12,227	3,403	289	4,234	417	752	201	8,546
Otoe-Missouria TJSA	2,187	41	460	9	0	15	0	15	0	23
Pawnee TJSA	13,572	105	1,622	14	3	78	0	6	0	13
Sac and Fox TJSA	44,135	1,544	4,511	206	19	360	0	64	6	247
Seminole TJSA	17,220	1,748	3,743	12	0	186	0	29	0	55
Tonkawa TJSA	11,109	18	854	41	13	88	0	27	2	116

[Continued]

★ 211 ★

Population, by Race and Hispanic Origin in Selected Tribal Jurisdiction Statistical Areas

[Continued]

Tribal Jurisdiction Statistical Area[1]	Not of Hispanic origin					Hispanic origin				
	White	Black	Am. Indian, Eskimo, or Aleut	Asian or Pacific Islander	Other race	White	Black	Am. Indian, Eskimo, or Aleut	Asian or Pacific Islander	Other race
Creek-Seminole Joint Area TJSA	1,683	173	531	19	0	3	0	0	0	10
Iowa-Sac and Fox Joint Area TJSA	784	28	20	0	0	0	0	0	0	3

Source: Census of Population and Housing, 1990: Summary Tape File 3C on CD-ROM [machine-readable datafiles]. Prepared by the Bureau of the Census. Washington, DC: The Bureau, 1992. *Notes:* 1. Tribal jurisdiction statistical areas (TJSAs) are areas, delineated by federally recognized tribes in Oklahoma without a reservation, for which the Census Bureau tabulates data. TJSAs represent areas generally containing the American Indian population over which one or more tribal governments have jurisdiction. If tribal officials delineated adjacent TJSAs so that they include some duplicate territory, the overlap area is called a "joint use area," which is treated as a separate TJSA for census purposes.

★ 212 ★

Population

Population, by Race and Hispanic Origin on Selected Reservations and Trust Lands

Data are shown for the 50 areas with the largest populations, in number of persons.

American Indian Reservation and Trust Lands[1,2]	Not of Hispanic origin					Hispanic origin				
	White	Black	Am. Indian, Eskimo, or Aleut	Asian or Pacific Islander	Other race	White	Black	Am. Indian, Eskimo, or Aleut	Asian or Pacific Islander	Other race
Agua Caliente Reservation	17,135	379	120	380	27	972	30	15	0	781
Allegany Reservation	6,161	16	1,068	20	0	18	0	0	0	29
Blackfeet Reservation	1,420	6	6,965	0	0	20	0	66	0	11
Cheyenne River Reservation	2,620	16	5,043	4	0	5	0	49	0	6
Coeur d'Alene Reservation and Trust Lands, ID	4,923	2	709	3	0	72	1	47	0	21
Colorado River Reservation	3,507	16	1,913	54	18	1,252	0	461	0	723
Colville Reservation	2,987	7	3,664	27	28	69	0	115	0	137
Crow Reservation and Trust Lands, MT	1,617	0	4,693	13	0	5	0	13	0	0
Eastern Cherokee Reservation	962	11	5,277	14	0	5	0	10	0	32
Flathead Reservation	15,748	8	4,952	21	0	107	0	176	0	49
Fort Apache Reservation	541	29	9,769	0	0	10	0	133	0	24
Fort Berthold Reservation	2,311	3	3,042	10	0	2	0	12	0	7
Fort Hall Reservation and Trust Lands, ID	1,739	0	2,966	26	6	35	0	119	0	223
Fort Peck Reservation	4,774	8	5,773	26	0	78	0	49	0	14
Gila River Reservation	167	13	8,325	13	9	36	0	776	0	239
Hopi Reservation and Trust Lands, AZ	159	4	6,866	30	0	12	0	136	0	8
Isabella Reservation and Trust Lands, MI	21,420	158	822	153	12	177	0	50	0	139
Laguna Pueblo and Trust Lands, NM	48	2	3,614	0	0	6	0	35	0	19
Lake Traverse (Sisseton) Reservation	7,979	0	2,791	3	10	10	0	19	0	28
Leech Lake Reservation	5,326	12	3,404	9	0	13	0	17	0	2
Mississippi Choctaw Reservation and Trust Lands, MS	190	11	4,043	0	0	0	0	13	0	0
Muckleshoot Reservation and Trust Lands, WA	2,836	17	842	30	0	22	0	33	3	53
Navajo Reservation and Trust Lands, AZ–NM–UT	4,405	169	142,694	99	32	50	0	813	0	396
Nez Perce Reservation	14,024	15	1,816	45	0	144	0	69	9	37
Northern Cheyenne Reservation and Trust Lands, MT–SD	333	0	3,486	0	0	0	0	78	0	9
Omaha Reservation	3,306	2	1,891	5	0	0	0	34	0	0
Oneida (West) Reservation	15,269	69	2,372	59	0	53	0	78	6	34
Osage Reservation	30,686	4,091	5,959	17	0	216	134	141	0	149
Papago Reservation	79	0	8,181	0	0	0	0	309	0	18
Pine Ridge Reservation and Trust Lands, NE–SD	1,021	19	10,870	11	0	0	0	136	0	62
Port Madison Reservation	4,199	14	343	169	3	64	0	31	0	11
Puyallup Reservation and Trust Lands, WA	25,122	2,196	909	3,057	19	499	52	68	16	497
Red Lake Reservation	118	0	3,537	12	0	0	0	23	0	0
Rosebud Reservation and Trust Lands, SD	1,583	15	7,921	0	0	2	0	77	0	34
Salt River Reservation	1,103	0	3,089	0	0	171	0	458	0	35
San Carlos Reservation	77	32	6,988	0	0	0	0	72	0	70
Sandia Pueblo	806	5	375	6	0	1,988	0	30	0	734
San Juan Pueblo	286	5	1,215	0	8	3,152	8	60	1	502
Santa Clara Pueblo	1,469	44	1,231	21	29	6,622	2	64	4	744
Southern Ute Reservation	5,647	12	831	20	2	758	3	206	2	405
Standing Rock Reservation	3,054	14	4,826	10	0	3	0	46	0	3

[Continued]

★ 212 ★

Population, by Race and Hispanic Origin on Selected Reservations and Trust Lands
[Continued]

American Indian Reservation and Trust Lands[1,2]	Not of Hispanic origin					Hispanic origin				
	White	Black	Am. Indian, Eskimo, or Aleut	Asian or Pacific Islander	Other race	White	Black	Am. Indian, Eskimo, or Aleut	Asian or Pacific Islander	Other race
Taos Pueblo and Trust Lands, NM	1,243	8	1,232	38	18	1,318	11	20	5	808
Tulalip Reservation	5,715	26	1,169	54	0	60	0	35	7	37
Turtle Mountain Reservation and Trust Lands, ND – SD	371	0	6,707	0	0	0	0	23	0	0
Uintah and Ouray Reservation	14,143	15	2,558	40	15	184	0	109	16	155
White Earth Reservation	5,972	2	2,779	6	0	7	0	19	0	0
Wind River Reservation	15,415	15	5,443	85	6	317	0	274	0	360
Yakima Reservation and Trust Lands, WA	9,665	85	5,708	444	75	1,023	23	490	73	9,862
Yankton Reservation	4,268	2	1,993	3	0	5	0	9	0	1
Zuni Pueblo	273	20	6,992	7	0	38	0	102	0	13

Source: Census of Population and Housing, 1990: Summary Tape File 3C on CD-ROM [machine-readable datafiles]. Prepared by the Bureau of the Census. Washington, DC: The Bureau, 1992. *Notes:* 1. Federal American Indian reservations are areas with boundaries established by treaty, statute, and/or executive or court order, and recognized by the federal government as territory in which American Indian tribes have jurisdiction. State reservations are lands held in trust by state governments for the use and benefit of a given tribe. The reservations and their boundaries were identified for the 1990 census by the Bureau of Indian Affairs (BIA), Department of Interior (for federal reservations), and state governments (for state reservations). The names of American Indian reservations recognized by state governments, but not by the federal government, are followed by "state." Areas composed of reservation lands that are administered jointly and/or are claimed by two reservations, as identified by the BIA, are called "joint areas," and are treated as separate American Indian reservations for census purposes. Federal reservations may cross state boundaries, and federal and state reservations may cross county, county subdivision, and place boundaries. For reservations that cross state boundaries, only the portion of the reservations in a given state is shown in the data products for that state; the entire reservations are shown in data products for the United States. 2. Trust lands are property associated with a particular American Indian reservation or tribe, held in trust by the federal government. Trust lands may be held in trust either for a tribe (tribal trust lands) or for an individual member of a tribe (individual trust land). Trust lands recognized for the 1990 census comprised all tribal trust lands and inhabited individual trust lands located outside of a reservation boundary. As with other American Indian areas, trust lands may be located in more than one state. Only the trust lands in a given state are shown in the data products for that state; all trust lands associated with a reservation or tribe are shown in data products for the United States. The Census Bureau first reported data for tribal trust lands for the 1980 census.

Geographic Mobility

★ 213 ★

Geographic Mobility of Persons in Selected Alaska Native Villages

Data are shown for the 50 areas with the largest populations, in number of persons.

Alaska Native Village Statistical Area[1]	Persons age 5 years and older									
	Same house in 1985	Different house in the United States in 1985								
		Same county	Different county					Abroad in 1985		
			Same State	Different State				Puerto Rico	Outlying U.S. area	Foreign country
				Northeast	Midwest	South	West			
Akiachak	241	136	0	0	0	0	24	0	0	0
Akutan	132	6	25	0	0	60	217	0	0	154
Alakanuk	406	43	7	0	2	2	6	0	0	0
Andreafsky	209	67	43	0	9	0	8	0	0	4
Angoon	376	47	55	3	31	13	22	0	0	6
Aniak	177	187	80	8	0	0	14	0	0	0
Barrow	1,076	710	292	12	19	36	167	0	0	31
Bethel	1,674	1,327	556	42	77	127	249	0	6	37
Chevak	349	73	40	0	0	0	7	0	0	0
Copper Center	178	106	55	2	2	17	9	0	0	0
Craig	273	304	187	11	42	19	276	0	0	4
Dillingham	880	399	277	7	69	39	98	0	0	8
Emmonak	297	148	14	4	2	0	16	0	0	0

[Continued]

★ 213 ★

Geographic Mobility of Persons in Selected Alaska Native Villages
[Continued]

Alaska Native Village Statistical Area[1]	Persons age 5 years and older									
	Same house in 1985	Different house in the United States in 1985								
		Same county	Different county					Abroad in 1985		
			Same State	Different State				Puerto Rico	Outlying U.S. area	Foreign country
				Northeast	Midwest	South	West			
Fort Yukon	224	230	26	2	2	11	16	0	0	4
Galena	216	146	67	27	62	80	90	0	0	51
Gambell	419	24	19	0	2	0	6	0	0	0
Grouse Creek Group	220	188	85	19	11	3	42	0	0	2
Hoonah	453	104	20	0	0	10	64	0	0	0
Hooper Bay	510	123	28	0	2	0	8	0	0	0
Kake	376	150	28	0	4	0	43	0	0	0
Kasigluk	300	58	2	0	2	0	8	0	0	0
King Cove	204	32	30	0	0	9	86	0	0	69
King Salmon	112	102	103	13	65	136	94	0	0	26
Kipnuk	369	26	2	0	0	0	3	0	0	0
Klawock	166	221	43	0	13	0	196	0	0	5
Kotlik	322	51	15	0	0	0	2	0	0	0
Kotzebue	1,017	826	255	8	31	40	162	0	0	0
Kwethluk	409	79	0	0	0	1	2	0	0	0
McGrath	273	115	41	0	10	4	30	0	0	0
Mountain Village	459	96	28	0	7	0	19	0	0	0
Naknek	240	110	62	0	28	6	67	0	0	2
Ninilchik	4,451	2,498	902	154	160	256	964	0	0	64
Noorvik	352	85	15	0	5	0	7	0	0	0
Pilot Station	288	68	6	0	3	0	0	0	0	0
Point Hope	406	55	43	6	0	0	11	0	0	0
Quinhagak	297	116	6	0	0	0	10	0	0	0
St. Paul	350	104	78	28	1	24	84	0	0	24
Salamatof	344	275	226	0	8	21	83	0	0	3
Sand Point	276	198	78	0	15	8	185	0	0	30
Savoonga	320	118	0	0	13	0	0	0	0	0
Selawik	387	76	2	0	0	0	2	0	0	0
Shishmaref	289	71	5	0	2	0	3	0	0	0
Stebbins	277	46	27	0	0	0	10	0	0	0
Togiak	380	79	29	0	0	6	22	0	0	0
Tok	414	209	128	4	25	9	67	0	0	5
Toksook Bay	40	299	5	0	0	0	0	0	0	0
Unalakleet	380	103	50	0	16	3	12	0	0	0
Unalaska	545	303	383	54	65	55	1,263	3	8	261
Wainwright	349	60	1	2	4	6	13	0	0	0
Yakutat	150	197	59	2	11	3	79	0	0	0

Source: Census of Population and Housing, 1990: Summary Tape File 3C on CD-ROM [machine-readable datafiles]. Prepared by the Bureau of the Census. Washington, DC: The Bureau, 1992. *Notes:* 1. Alaska Native villages (ANVs) constitute tribes, bands, clans, groups, villages, communities, or associations in Alaska that are recognized pursuant to the Alaska Native Claims Settlement Act of 1972, Public Law 92-203. Because ANVs do not have legally designated boundaries, the Census Bureau has established Alaska Native village statistical areas (ANVSAs) for statistical purposes. For the 1990 census, the Census Bureau cooperated with officials of the nonprofit corporation within each participating Alaska Native Regional Corporation (ANRC), as well as other knowledgeable officials, to delineate boundaries that encompass the settled area associated with each ANV.

★ 214 ★

Geographic Mobility

Geographic Mobility of Persons in Selected Tribal Designated Statistical Areas

Tribal Designated Statistical Area[1]	Same house in 1985	Different house in the United States in 1985							Abroad in 1985		
		Same county	Different county						Puerto Rico	Outlying U.S. area	Foreign country
			Same State	Different State							
				Northeast	Midwest	South	West			
Apache Choctaw TDSA (state)	13,531	4,831	1,483	30	114	783	152	0	2	28
Chickahominy TDSA (state)	1,928	284	301	61	0	55	0	0	7	4
Clifton Choctaw TDSA (state)	379	68	0	15	0	5	7	0	0	0
Coharie TDSA (state)	63,536	25,304	8,897	2,151	1,442	4,546	777	0	42	989
Coquille Indian TDSA	158,033	114,793	35,810	2,432	5,262	6,078	48,876	19	195	4,954
Delaware-Muncie TDSA (state)	155	65	28	0	0	0	0	0	0	0
Florida Tribe of Eastern Creek TDSA (state)	65	57	0	0	25	28	0	0	0	19
Haliwa-Saponi TDSA (state)	4,602	874	176	69	0	162	11	0	0	0
Jena Band of Choctaw TDSA (state)	32,139	13,438	6,768	160	309	2,380	510	0	0	281
Klamath TDSA	18,218	10,806	2,955	195	381	614	4,472	0	0	314
Lumbee TDSA (state)	30,482	11,362	2,425	432	191	761	110	0	0	99
Meherrin TDSA (state)	34,956	8,889	3,158	1,161	165	2,702	105	0	0	231
Mohegan TDSA (state)	12,137	7,061	1,148	979	219	918	185	35	34	88
Ramapough TDSA (state)	436	106	23	0	0	0	20	0	0	0
United Houma Nation TDSA (state)	462,801	184,727	68,613	2,547	4,415	20,073	4,932	113	162	5,176
Waccamaw Siouan TDSA (state)	2,021	387	114	29	0	40	0	0	0	0
Wampanoag-Gay Head TDSA	5,606	2,853	1,034	947	34	235	152	0	0	29

Source: Census of Population and Housing, 1990: Summary Tape File 3C on CD-ROM [machine-readable datafiles]. Prepared by the Bureau of the Census. Washington, DC: The Bureau, 1992. *Notes:* 1. Tribal designated statistical areas (TDSAs) are areas, delineated outside Oklahoma by federally- and state-recognized tribes without a land base or associated trust lands, to provide statistical areas for which the Census Bureau tabulates data. TDSAs represent areas generally containing the American Indian population over which federally-recognized tribes have jurisdiction and areas in which state tribes provide benefits and services to their members. The names of TDSAs delineated by state-recognized tribes are followed by "(state)." The Census Bureau did not recognize TDSAs before the 1990 census.

★ 215 ★

Geographic Mobility

Geographic Mobility of Persons in Selected Tribal Jurisdiction Statistical Areas

Tribal Jurisdiction Statistical Area[1]	Same house in 1985	Different house in the United States in 1985							Abroad in 1985		
		Same county	Different county						Puerto Rico	Outlying U.S. area	Foreign country
			Same State	Different State							
				Northeast	Midwest	South	West			
Absentee Shawnee-Citizens Band of Potawatomi TJSA	49,391	18,701	11,383	141	961	2,057	1,744	0	0	724
Caddo-Wichita-Delaware TJSA	5,044	1,461	838	4	15	129	66	0	0	69
Cherokee TJSA	208,860	90,172	39,216	1,087	8,929	13,490	7,738	16	0	1,325
Cheyenne-Arapaho TJSA	73,825	32,612	21,870	402	2,316	5,408	2,699	26	0	736
Chickasaw TJSA	138,639	55,223	28,999	228	2,411	10,555	3,960	9	22	869
Choctaw TJSA	112,890	44,553	19,306	286	1,761	11,823	4,552	0	8	341
Creek TJSA	294,479	162,177	64,028	4,235	18,207	26,363	15,047	69	27	4,475
Iowa TJSA	2,169	717	771	6	65	56	64	0	0	5
Kaw TJSA	6,960	2,927	1,129	38	463	438	257	0	8	99
Kiowa-Comanche-Apache-Fort Sill Apache TJSA	88,312	44,875	12,871	2,866	5,836	17,027	7,775	180	128	9,743
Otoe-Missouria TJSA	1,620	477	305	0	13	58	53	0	0	6
Pawnee TJSA	8,535	2,761	2,397	3	195	280	174	0	0	26
Sac and Fox TJSA	27,403	10,759	6,349	75	591	1,285	987	0	0	167
Seminole TJSA	13,066	5,430	2,231	34	155	290	247	0	0	44
Tonkawa TJSA	6,497	3,221	974	23	288	249	153	0	0	47

[Continued]

★ 215 ★

Geographic Mobility of Persons in Selected Tribal Jurisdiction Statistical Areas
[Continued]

Tribal Jurisdiction Statistical Area[1]	Persons age 5 years and older									
	Same house in 1985	Different house in the United States in 1985							Abroad in 1985		
		Same county	Different county						Puerto Rico	Outlying U.S. area	Foreign country
			Same State	Different State							
				Northeast	Midwest	South	West			
Creek-Seminole Joint Area TJSA	1,362	602	239	0	24	42	11	0	0	0
Iowa-Sac and Fox Joint Area TJSA	383	198	143	0	2	16	25	0	0	5

Source: Census of Population and Housing, 1990: Summary Tape File 3C on CD-ROM [machine-readable datafiles]. Prepared by the Bureau of the Census. Washington, DC: The Bureau, 1992. *Notes:* 1. Tribal jurisdiction statistical areas (TJSAs) are areas, delineated by federally recognized tribes in Oklahoma without a reservation, for which the Census Bureau tabulates data. TJSAs represent areas generally containing the American Indian population over which one or more tribal governments have jurisdiction. If tribal officials delineated adjacent TJSAs so that they include some duplicate territory, the overlap area is called a "joint use area," which is treated as a separate TJSA for census purposes.

★ 216 ★

Geographic Mobility

Geographic Mobility of Persons on Selected Reservations and Trust Lands

Data are shown for the 50 areas with the largest populations, in number of persons.

American Indian Reservation and Trust Lands[1,2]	Persons age 5 years and older									
	Same house in 1985	Different house in the United States in 1985							Abroad in 1985		
		Same county	Different county						Puerto Rico	Outlying U.S. area	Foreign country
			Same State	Different State							
				Northeast	Midwest	South	West			
Agua Caliente Reservation	8,208	4,108	4,044	348	631	432	861	0	12	567
Allegany Reservation	4,233	1,867	266	92	38	119	52	23	0	42
Blackfeet Reservation	4,691	1,998	373	2	66	95	185	0	3	21
Cheyenne River Reservation	3,734	1,813	761	6	254	27	186	0	0	18
Coeur d'Alene Reservation and Trust Lands, ID	2,854	1,335	469	37	47	36	561	0	0	22
Colorado River Reservation	3,355	2,165	572	25	102	128	716	0	0	204
Colville Reservation	3,490	1,644	813	22	50	17	262	0	0	74
Crow Reservation and Trust Lands, MT	3,377	1,791	269	10	52	35	109	0	0	17
Eastern Cherokee Reservation	4,042	755	577	13	43	245	50	0	0	5
Flathead Reservation	10,613	4,963	1,737	73	172	216	1,582	0	0	32
Fort Apache Reservation	5,226	2,894	559	0	28	64	129	0	0	0
Fort Berthold Reservation	2,732	1,088	638	7	40	54	237	0	0	6
Fort Hall Reservation and Trust Lands, ID	2,687	960	707	0	18	4	187	0	0	44
Fort Peck Reservation	4,995	3,284	703	0	198	14	239	0	0	27
Gila River Reservation	5,100	2,202	786	29	21	5	146	0	0	67
Hopi Reservation and Trust Lands, AZ	4,112	1,767	419	5	26	47	69	0	0	0
Isabella Reservation and Trust Lands, MI	11,216	5,145	3,632	85	279	392	341	0	0	101
Laguna Pueblo and Trust Lands, NM	2,739	442	194	0	15	5	44	0	0	5
Lake Traverse (Sisseton) Reservation	6,476	2,177	613	44	530	45	102	0	0	10
Leech Lake Reservation	4,837	1,752	960	27	161	42	164	0	0	9
Mississippi Choctaw Reservation and Trust Lands, MS	2,207	1,240	187	0	3	54	0	0	0	0
Muckleshoot Reservation and Trust Lands, WA	1,860	854	349	17	55	67	218	0	0	25
Navajo Reservation and Trust Lands, AZ–NM–UT	94,196	22,784	5,461	159	395	463	5,336	0	11	127
Nez Perce Reservation	9,045	2,529	1,612	54	176	128	1,573	0	0	75

[Continued]

★ 216 ★

Geographic Mobility of Persons on Selected Reservations and Trust Lands
[Continued]

American Indian Reservation and Trust Lands[1,2]	Same house in 1985	Persons age 5 years and older								
		Different house in the United States in 1985								
		Same county	Different county					Abroad in 1985		
			Same State	Different State				Puerto Rico	Outlying U.S. area	Foreign country
				Northeast	Midwest	South	West			
Northern Cheyenne Reservation and Trust Lands, MT–SD	1,978	920	314	6	57	9	64	0	0	7
Omaha Reservation	3,118	928	413	0	161	13	38	0	0	9
Oneida (West) Reservation	8,849	4,312	1,911	106	668	248	208	0	0	40
Osage Reservation	22,659	6,303	7,395	18	560	933	530	0	0	146
Papago Reservation	6,301	1,100	234	0	7	0	30	0	0	7
Pine Ridge Reservation and Trust Lands, NE–SD	6,350	2,849	506	27	161	50	142	43	0	11
Port Madison Reservation	2,161	1,191	494	27	66	111	335	6	0	38
Puyallup Reservation and Trust Lands, WA	13,834	6,855	4,691	207	594	678	1,774	2	9	813
Red Lake Reservation	2,137	850	100	0	0	0	102	0	0	0
Rosebud Reservation and Trust Lands, SD	4,337	2,740	553	52	371	51	251	0	0	0
Salt River Reservation	2,246	1,766	42	25	57	12	120	0	10	65
San Carlos Reservation	3,847	958	1,268	20	10	6	159	0	0	0
Sandia Pueblo	2,227	646	468	6	4	91	133	0	0	8
San Juan Pueblo	3,602	791	193	0	11	2	102	0	0	40
Santa Clara Pueblo	6,279	1,513	1,065	39	44	138	272	0	0	39
Southern Ute Reservation	3,906	1,722	514	52	88	232	662	8	0	28
Standing Rock Reservation	4,146	1,836	343	13	484	23	188	0	0	11
Taos Pueblo and Trust Lands, NM	2,489	1,115	277	58	34	94	241	10	8	34
Tulalip Reservation	3,531	1,975	589	1	60	35	292	0	0	57
Turtle Mountain Reservation and Trust Lands, ND–SD	3,331	2,339	263	0	43	44	153	0	0	0
Uintah and Ouray Reservation	9,594	3,428	1,292	2	130	170	693	0	0	65
White Earth Reservation	5,848	1,280	689	3	153	16	71	0	0	2
Wind River Reservation	10,780	5,891	1,159	139	578	299	1,180	0	0	45
Yakima Reservation and Trust Lands, WA	13,287	7,138	1,232	11	110	503	1,368	0	18	943
Yankton Reservation	3,661	1,363	426	3	153	18	71	0	8	4
Zuni Pueblo	5,236	893	210	0	31	65	159	0	0	8

Source: Census of Population and Housing, 1990: Summary Tape File 3C on CD-ROM [machine-readable datafiles]. Prepared by the Bureau of the Census. Washington, DC: The Bureau, 1992. *Notes:* 1. Federal American Indian reservations are areas with boundaries established by treaty, statute, and/or executive or court order, and recognized by the federal government as territory in which American Indian tribes have jurisdiction. State reservations are lands held in trust by state governments for the use and benefit of a given tribe. The reservations and their boundaries were identified for the 1990 census by the Bureau of Indian Affairs (BIA), Department of Interior (for federal reservations), and state governments (for state reservations). The names of American Indian reservations recognized by state governments, but not by the federal government, are followed by "state." Areas composed of reservation lands that are administered jointly and/or are claimed by two reservations, as identified by the BIA, are called "joint areas," and are treated as separate American Indian reservations for census purposes. Federal reservations may cross state boundaries, and federal and state reservations may cross county, county subdivision, and place boundaries. For reservations that cross state boundaries, only the portion of the reservations in a given state is shown in the data products for that state; the entire reservations are shown in data products for the United States. 2. Trust lands are property associated with a particular American Indian reservation or tribe, held in trust by the federal government. Trust lands may be held in trust either for a tribe (tribal trust lands) or for an individual member of a tribe (individual trust land). Trust lands recognized for the 1990 census comprised all tribal trust lands and inhabited individual trust lands located outside of a reservation boundary. As with other American Indian areas, trust lands may be located in more than one state. Only the trust lands in a given state are shown in the data products for that state; all trust lands associated with a reservation or tribe are shown in data products for the United States. The Census Bureau first reported data for tribal trust lands for the 1980 census.

★ 217 ★
Geographic Mobility

Place of Birth of Persons in Selected Alaska Native Villages

Data are shown for the 50 areas with the largest populations, in number of persons.

Alaska Native Village Statistical Area[1]	State of residence	Born in other State in the United States				Born outside the United States			Foreign born
		Northeast	Midwest	South	West	Puerto Rico	U.S. outlying area	Born abroad of American parents	
Akiachak	441	5	5	3	4	0	0	4	0
Akutan	79	13	25	53	139	0	5	37	254
Alakanuk	517	2	4	0	17	0	0	0	0
Andreafsky	357	2	18	4	12	0	0	2	11
Angoon	522	9	44	8	58	0	0	0	2
Aniak	379	14	58	22	52	0	0	0	4
Barrow	1,852	86	176	95	375	0	0	26	140
Bethel	3,214	167	388	230	566	2	3	10	107
Chevak	563	2	4	1	23	0	0	3	1
Copper Center	204	2	79	39	100	0	0	2	0
Craig	413	30	99	60	641	0	0	7	10
Dillingham	1,258	79	255	72	323	2	0	5	23
Emmonak	548	16	5	6	22	0	3	2	8
Fort Yukon	491	11	15	25	23	0	0	2	12
Galena	355	111	132	93	78	0	0	11	26
Gambell	539	0	7	0	0	0	0	0	2
Grouse Creek Group	255	35	113	49	161	0	0	2	15
Hoonah	541	11	22	32	112	0	0	5	6
Hooper Bay	818	2	9	0	17	0	0	0	0
Kake	508	2	20	17	138	0	0	2	0
Kasigluk	416	0	14	0	10	0	0	0	0
King Cove	193	8	10	22	64	0	0	0	160
King Salmon	126	26	201	148	155	0	0	13	15
Kipnuk	442	2	0	0	16	0	0	0	2
Klawock	322	6	40	14	321	0	0	0	2
Kotlik	448	5	2	0	7	0	0	0	0
Kotzebue	2,141	62	158	92	259	0	0	13	26
Kwethluk	553	0	5	1	7	0	0	0	2
McGrath	313	37	36	21	105	0	0	2	10
Mountain Village	647	6	21	7	18	0	3	2	2
Naknek	313	16	60	34	161	0	0	0	6
Ninilchik	3,333	946	1,530	904	3,204	0	0	131	443
Noorvik	520	3	14	4	4	0	0	3	0
Pilot Station	447	0	8	9	3	0	0	0	0
Point Hope	569	10	14	16	20	0	0	0	0
Quinhagak	484	0	6	7	12	0	0	0	37
St. Paul	500	34	27	41	113	0	0	7	22
Salamatof	382	36	111	124	325	0	0	3	147
Sand Point	460	6	39	8	196	0	0	0	0
Savoonga	495	2	17	0	0	0	0	0	0
Selawik	549	0	4	15	11	0	0	0	0
Shishmaref	416	0	7	1	9	0	0	0	0
Stebbins	427	0	6	0	15	0	0	2	0
Togiak	543	7	12	12	30	0	0	3	12
Tok	313	91	217	57	240	0	2	0	0
Toksook Bay	399	0	2	0	4	0	0	7	6
Unalakleet	539	5	36	35	18	0	0	27	843
Unalaska	334	207	209	152	1,313	4	0		

[Continued]

★ 217 ★

Place of Birth of Persons in Selected Alaska Native Villages
[Continued]

Alaska Native Village Statistical Area[1]	State of residence	Born in other State in the United States				Born outside the United States			Foreign born
		Northeast	Midwest	South	West	Puerto Rico	U.S. outlying area	Born abroad of American parents	
Wainwright	472	0	14	6	10	0	0	0	0
Yakutat	308	19	39	30	135	0	4	2	7

Source: Census of Population and Housing, 1990: Summary Tape File 3C on CD-ROM [machine-readable datafiles]. Prepared by the Bureau of the Census. Washington, DC: The Bureau, 1992. *Notes:* 1. Alaska Native villages (ANVs) constitute tribes, bands, clans, groups, villages, communities, or associations in Alaska that are recognized pursuant to the Alaska Native Claims Settlement Act of 1972, Public Law 92-203. Because ANVs do not have legally designated boundaries, the Census Bureau has established Alaska Native village statistical areas (ANVSAs) for statistical purposes. For the 1990 census, the Census Bureau cooperated with officials of the nonprofit corporation within each participating Alaska Native Regional Corporation (ANRC), as well as other knowledgeable officials, to delineate boundaries that encompass the settled area associated with each ANV.

★ 218 ★

Geographic Mobility

Place of Birth of Persons in Selected Tribal Designated Statistical Areas

Tribal Designated Statistical Area[1]	State of residence	Born in other State in the United States				Born outside the United States			Foreign born
		Northeast	Midwest	South	West	Puerto Rico	U.S. outlying area	Born abroad of American parents	
Apache Choctaw TDSA (state)	18,330	169	621	2,919	400	0	0	108	99
Chickahominy TDSA (state)	2,386	103	65	163	32	0	0	0	0
Clifton Choctaw TDSA (state)	478	21	0	28	0	0	0	7	18
Coharie TDSA (state)	94,308	4,974	3,396	9,911	1,442	85	38	741	1,329
Coquille Indian TDSA	169,314	16,863	58,553	29,415	111,539	110	206	3,306	14,215
Delaware-Muncie TDSA (state)	256	0	25	11	7	0	0	0	0
Florida Tribe of Eastern Creek TDSA (state)	72	25	63	46	0	0	0	0	9
Haliwa-Saponi TDSA (state)	6,132	38	40	185	27	0	0	0	9
Jena Band of Choctaw TDSA (state)	47,305	867	2,109	7,819	1,206	21	0	423	644
Klamath TDSA	18,428	1,113	5,053	3,343	11,326	12	5	343	1,260
Lumbee TDSA (state)	45,138	1,125	427	2,969	219	14	11	131	194
Meherrin TDSA (state)	44,386	2,041	608	7,444	366	9	11	104	305
Mohegan TDSA (state)	15,173	5,081	912	1,435	413	238	53	181	1,150
Ramapough TDSA (state)	464	83	5	62	11	4	0	4	19
United Houma Nation TDSA (state)	658,262	15,086	23,270	73,717	10,845	941	278	3,377	31,598
Waccamaw Siouan TDSA (state)	2,562	86	0	109	0	6	0	0	8
Wampanoag-Gay Head TDSA	7,016	2,813	628	495	262	0	0	89	336

Source: Census of Population and Housing, 1990: Summary Tape File 3C on CD-ROM [machine-readable datafiles]. Prepared by the Bureau of the Census. Washington, DC: The Bureau, 1992. *Notes:* 1. Tribal designated statistical areas (TDSAs) are areas, delineated outside Oklahoma by federally- and state-recognized tribes without a land base or associated trust lands, to provide statistical areas for which the Census Bureau tabulates data. TDSAs represent areas generally containing the American Indian population over which federally-recognized tribes have jurisdiction and areas in which state tribes provide benefits and services to their members. The names of TDSAs delineated by state-recognized tribes are followed by "(state)." The Census Bureau did not recognize TDSAs before the 1990 census.

★ 219 ★

Geographic Mobility

Place of Birth of Persons in Selected Tribal Jurisdiction Statistical Areas

Tribal Jurisdiction Statistical Area[1]	State of residence	Born in other State in the United States				Born outside the United States			Foreign born
		Northeast	Midwest	South	West	Puerto Rico	U.S. outlying area	Born abroad of American parents	
Absentee Shawnee-Citizens Band of Potawatomi TJSA	63,707	1,600	7,735	10,893	5,380	7	25	829	836
Caddo-Wichita-Delaware TJSA	6,549	33	337	712	378	0	0	31	168
Cherokee TJSA	259,643	6,148	51,100	54,963	22,273	80	61	1,545	3,321
Cheyenne-Arapaho TJSA	104,307	1,882	13,824	19,436	7,876	51	22	620	2,647
Chickasaw TJSA	185,048	2,636	13,971	38,547	13,829	32	42	1,080	2,328
Choctaw TJSA	132,770	1,726	9,827	48,370	14,767	21	26	534	1,312
Creek TJSA	384,774	19,104	90,425	85,701	38,023	356	154	3,663	13,254
Iowa TJSA	2,990	77	343	426	274	0	0	10	17
Kaw TJSA	7,925	219	2,742	1,390	721	4	0	66	160
Kiowa-Comanche-Apache-Fort Sill Apache TJSA	105,187	8,218	19,392	45,529	13,204	773	268	5,801	7,368
Otoe-Missouria TJSA	2,075	34	225	212	163	0	2	23	16
Pawnee TJSA	11,271	235	1,568	1,397	832	0	0	50	60
Sac and Fox TJSA	37,862	505	3,917	5,079	3,086	7	0	160	476
Seminole TJSA	17,884	195	1,071	2,411	1,259	0	0	66	107
Tonkawa TJSA	8,749	74	1,972	809	530	0	3	33	98
Creek-Seminole Joint Area TJSA	2,008	10	95	194	85	0	0	13	14
Iowa-Sac and Fox Joint Area TJSA	645	2	92	42	41	0	0	2	11

Source: Census of Population and Housing, 1990: Summary Tape File 3C on CD-ROM [machine-readable datafiles]. Prepared by the Bureau of the Census. Washington, DC: The Bureau, 1992. *Notes:* 1. Tribal jurisdiction statistical areas (TJSAs) are areas, delineated by federally recognized tribes in Oklahoma without a reservation, for which the Census Bureau tabulates data. TJSAs represent areas generally containing the American Indian population over which one or more tribal governments have jurisdiction. If tribal officials delineated adjacent TJSAs so that they include some duplicate territory, the overlap area is called a "joint use area," which is treated as a separate TJSA for census purposes.

★ 220 ★

Geographic Mobility

Place of Birth of Persons on Selected Reservations and Trust Lands

Data are shown for the 50 areas with the largest populations, in number of persons.

American Indian Reservation and Trust Lands[1,2]	State of residence	Born in other State in the United States				Born outside the United States			Foreign born
		Northeast	Midwest	South	West	Puerto Rico	U.S. outlying area	Born abroad of American parents	
Agua Caliente Reservation	4,807	3,106	5,075	1,637	1,757	0	0	233	3,224
Allegany Reservation	6,166	638	140	169	58	27	0	34	80
Blackfeet Reservation	7,515	32	276	70	400	2	0	83	110
Cheyenne River Reservation	6,667	36	692	75	237	0	0	9	27
Coeur d'Alene Reservation and Trust Lands, ID	2,151	146	631	245	2,521	0	2	24	58
Colorado River Reservation	2,899	244	906	798	1,938	0	0	75	1,084
Colville Reservation	5,239	77	435	173	844	0	2	55	209
Crow Reservation and Trust Lands, MT	5,116	46	348	117	687	0	0	27	0
Eastern Cherokee Reservation	5,421	148	181	414	104	0	0	11	32
Flathead Reservation	12,959	463	2,975	639	3,662	0	0	133	230
Fort Apache Reservation	9,902	55	150	115	256	0	0	24	4
Fort Berthold Reservation	4,556	19	275	87	400	0	0	10	40
Fort Hall Reservation and Trust Lands, ID	3,997	8	131	144	689	0	0	4	141
Fort Peck Reservation	8,282	44	1,669	92	519	0	0	13	103
Gila River Reservation	8,955	13	68	95	263	0	0	6	178
Hopi Reservation and Trust Lands, AZ	6,750	7	96	87	246	0	0	5	24
Isabella Reservation and Trust Lands, MI	19,316	441	1,424	832	432	8	2	120	356

[Continued]

★ 220 ★

Place of Birth of Persons on Selected Reservations and Trust Lands

[Continued]

American Indian Reservation and Trust Lands[1,2]	State of residence	Born in other State in the United States				Born outside the United States			
		Northeast	Midwest	South	West	Puerto Rico	U.S. outlying area	Born abroad of American parents	Foreign born
Laguna Pueblo and Trust Lands, NM	3,229	5	31	43	395	0	0	10	11
Lake Traverse (Sisseton) Reservation	7,775	51	2,581	111	267	0	0	16	39
Leech Lake Reservation	7,054	69	1,176	162	241	0	0	23	58
Mississippi Choctaw Reservation and Trust Lands, MS	3,964	0	57	220	16	0	0	0	0
Muckleshoot Reservation and Trust Lands, WA	2,299	147	479	159	644	0	2	15	91
Navajo Reservation and Trust Lands, AZ–NM–UT	123,869	415	1,410	1,912	20,682	8	5	93	264
Nez Perce Reservation	9,086	290	1,514	725	4,305	0	2	80	157
Northern Cheyenne Reservation and Trust Lands, MT–SD	3,320	11	274	56	239	0	0	6	0
Omaha Reservation	3,890	19	1,134	58	102	0	0	3	32
Oneida (West) Reservation	14,675	247	2,139	378	302	4	2	62	131
Osage Reservation	29,843	572	4,562	4,061	2,015	0	9	113	218
Papago Reservation	8,221	18	35	108	125	0	0	40	40
Pine Ridge Reservation and Trust Lands, NE–SD	10,518	73	1,002	144	290	57	0	0	35
Port Madison Reservation	2,452	236	650	298	917	4	10	43	224
Puyallup Reservation and Trust Lands, WA	16,819	1,076	3,837	2,283	4,842	60	45	455	3,018
Red Lake Reservation	3,489	7	120	16	34	0	0	6	18
Rosebud Reservation and Trust Lands, SD	7,799	120	1,212	88	372	0	0	25	16
Salt River Reservation	3,477	153	625	141	266	0	0	30	164
San Carlos Reservation	6,711	14	83	81	305	0	0	0	45
Sandia Pueblo	3,110	58	111	221	318	2	0	13	111
San Juan Pueblo	4,673	40	49	80	330	0	0	8	57
Santa Clara Pueblo	8,059	161	349	430	971	11	0	47	202
Southern Ute Reservation	4,268	274	862	733	1,646	3	0	25	75
Standing Rock Reservation	5,197	24	2,304	43	361	0	0	4	23
Taos Pueblo and Trust Lands, NM	3,248	221	312	305	467	2	0	30	116
Tulalip Reservation	4,624	184	853	249	944	6	2	45	196
Turtle Mountain Reservation and Trust Lands, ND–SD	6,523	25	193	60	268	0	0	22	10
Uintah and Ouray Reservation	13,650	57	641	458	2,193	0	0	54	182
White Earth Reservation	7,415	49	1,014	68	173	0	0	20	46
Wind River Reservation	12,599	510	3,857	1,089	3,596	8	0	57	199
Yakima Reservation and Trust Lands, WA	15,514	164	1,616	1,693	3,276	6	0	173	5,006
Yankton Reservation	5,446	18	567	76	147	0	2	4	21
Zuni Pueblo	6,969	32	84	61	272	0	0	9	18

Source: Census of Population and Housing, 1990: Summary Tape File 3C on CD-ROM [machine-readable datafiles]. Prepared by the Bureau of the Census. Washington, DC: The Bureau, 1992. *Notes:* 1. Federal American Indian reservations are areas with boundaries established by treaty, statute, and/or executive or court order, and recognized by the federal government as territory in which American Indian tribes have jurisdiction. State reservations are lands held in trust by state governments for the use and benefit of a given tribe. The reservations and their boundaries were identified for the 1990 census by the Bureau of Indian Affairs (BIA), Department of Interior (for federal reservations), and state governments (for state reservations). The names of American Indian reservations recognized by state governments, but not by the federal government, are followed by "state." Areas composed of reservation lands that are administered jointly and/or are claimed by two reservations, as identified by the BIA, are called "joint areas," and are treated as separate American Indian reservations for census purposes. Federal reservations may cross state boundaries, and federal and state reservations may cross county, county subdivision, and place boundaries. For reservations that cross state boundaries, only the portion of the reservations in a given state is shown in the data products for that state; the entire reservations are shown in data products for the United States. 2. Trust lands are property associated with a particular American Indian reservation or tribe, held in trust by the federal government. Trust lands may be held in trust either for a tribe (tribal trust lands) or for an individual member of a tribe (individual trust land). Trust lands recognized for the 1990 census comprised all tribal trust lands and inhabited individual trust lands located outside of a reservation boundary. As with other American Indian areas, trust lands may be located in more than one state. Only the trust lands in a given state are shown in the data products for that state; all trust lands associated with a reservation or tribe are shown in data products for the United States. The Census Bureau first reported data for tribal trust lands for the 1980 census.

Population Trends

★ 221 ★

Population of American Indians and the Total United States Population, 1890-1980

Date	American Indian		Total United States	
	Size	Change from previous decade (%)	Size	Change from previous decade (%)
1890	248,253		62,947,714	
1900	237,196	-4.5	75,994,575	20.7
1910	276,927	16.8	91,972,266	21.0
1920	244,437	-11.7	105,710,620	14.9
1930	343,352	40.5	122,775,046	16.1
1940	345,252	0.6	131,669,275	7.2
1950	357,499	3.5	151,325,798	14.5
1960	523,591	46.5	179,323,175	18.5
1970	792,730	51.4	203,302,031	13.4
1980	1,366,676	72.4	226,545,805	11.4

Source: Thornton, Russell. *American Indian Holocaust and Survival: A Population History Since 1492.* Norman, OK: University of Oklahoma Press, 1987, p. 160. Published by permission. Primary source: U.S. Bureau of the Census, *Indian Population of the United States and Alaska,* 1910. Washington, D.C.: U.S. Government Printing Office, 1915. p. 10; *1970 Census of the Population. Subject Report. American Indians.* Final Report PC (2)- 1F. Washington, D.C.: U.S. Government Printing Office, 1973, p. 11; *Statistical Abstract of the United States, 1982-1983.* Washington, D.C.: U.S. Government Printing Office, 1982-1983, p. 6; *1980 Census of the Population, Supplementary Report, American Indians Areas and Alaska Native Villages: 1980.* PC80-S1-13. Washington, D.C.: U.S. Government Printing Office, 1984, p. 14; Swagerty and Thornton, "Preliminary 1980 Census Counts for American Indians, Eskimos and Aleuts," *American Indian Culture and Research Journal,* 1982, p. 92.

★ 222 ★

Population Trends

American Indian Population, by State, 1900-1980

State	1900	1910	1920	1930	1940	1950	1960	1970	1980
Alabama	177	909	405	465	464	928	1,276	2,443	7,502
Alaska	13,152?	11,244	9,918?	10,955	11,283	14,089	14,444	16,276	21,869
Arizona	26,480	29,201	32,989	43,726	55,076	65,761	83,387	95,812	152,498
Arkansas	66	460	106	408	278	533	580	2,014	9,364
California	15,377	16,371	17,360	19,212	18,675	19,947	39,014	91,018	198,275
Colorado	1,437	1,482	1,383	1,395	1,360	1,567	4,238	8,336	17,734
Connecticut	153	152	159	162	201	333	923	2,222	4,431
Delaware	9	5	2	5	14	?	597	656	1,307
District of Columbia	22	68	37	40	190	330	587	956	996

[Continued]

★ 222 ★

American Indian Population, by State, 1900-1980

[Continued]

State	1900	1910	1920	1930	1940	1950	1960	1970	1980
Florida	358	74	518	587	690	1,011	2,504	6,677	19,134
Georgia	19	95	125	43	106	333	749	2,347	7,442
Hawaii	?	?	?	?	?	?	472	1,126	2,655
Idaho	4,226	3,488	3,098	3,638	3,537	3,800	5,231	6,687	10,418
Illinois	16	188	194	469	624	1,443	4,704	11,413	15,846
Indiana	243	279	125	285	223	438	948	3,887	7,682
Iowa	382	471	529	660	733	1,084	1,708	2,992	5,369
Kansas	2,130	2,444	2,276	2,454	1,165?	2,381	5,069	8,672	15,256
Kentucky	102	234	57	22	44	234	391	1,531	3,518
Louisiana	593	780	1,066	1,536	1,801	409?	3,587	5,294	11,969
Maine	798	892	839	1,012	1,251	1,522	1,879	2,195	4,057
Maryland	3	55	32	50	73	314	1,538	4,239	7,823
Massachusetts	587	688	555	874	769	1,201	2,118	4,475	7,483
Michigan	6,354	7,519	5,614	7,080	6,282	7,000	9,701	16,854	39,734
Minnesota	9,182	9,053	8,761	11,077	12,528	12,533	15,496	23,128	34,831
Mississippi	2,203	1,253	1,105	1,458	2,134	2,502	3,442	4,113	6,131
Missouri	130	313	171	578	330	547	1,723	5,405	12,129
Montana	11,343	10,745	10,956	14,798	16,841	16,606	21,181	27,130	37,598
Nebraska	3,322	3,502	2,888	3,256	3,401	3,954	5,545	6,624	9,145
Nevada	5,216	5,240	4,907	4,871	4,747	5,025	6,681	7,933	13,306
New Hampshire	22	34	23	64	50	74	135	361	1,297
New Jersey	63	168	100	213	211	621	1,699	4,706	8,176
New Mexico	13,144	20,573	19,512	28,941	34,510	41,901	56,255	72,788	107,338
New York	5,257	6,046	5,503	6,973	8,651	10,640	16,491	28,355	38,967
North Carolina	5,687	7,851	11,824	16,579	22,546	3,742?	38,129	44,406	64,536
North Dakota	6,968	6,486	6,254	8,387	10,114	10,766	11,736	14,369	20,120
Ohio	42	127	151	435	338	1,146	1,910	6,654	11,985
Oklahoma	64,445	74,825	57,337	92,725	63,125	53,769	64,689	98,468	169,292
Oregon	4,951	5,090	4,590	4,776	4,594	5,820	8,026	13,510	26,591
Pennsylvania	1,629	1,503	337	523	441	1,141	2,122	5,533	9,179
Rhode Island	35	234	110	318	196	385	932	1,390	2,872
South Carolina	121	331	304	959	1,234	554	1,098	2,241	5,665
South Dakota	20,225	19,137	16,384?	21,833	23,347	23,344	25,794	32,365	44,948
Tennessee	108	216	56	161	114	339	638	2,276	5,013
Texas	470	702	2,109	1,001	1,103	2,736	5,750	17,957	39,740
Utah	2,623	3,123	2,711	2,869	3,611	4,201	6,961	11,273	19,158
Vermont	5	26	24	36	16	30	57	229	968
Virginia	354	539	824	779	198	1,056	2,155	4,853	9,211
Washington	10,039	10,997	9,061	11,253	11,394	13,816	21,076	33,386	58,186
West Virginia	12	36	7	18	25	160	181	751	1,555

[Continued]

★ 222 ★

American Indian Population, by State, 1900-1980
[Continued]

State	1900	1910	1920	1930	1940	1950	1960	1970	1980
Wisconsin	8,372	10,142	9,611	11,548	12,265	12,196	14,297	18,924	29,320
Wyoming	1,686	1,486	1,343	1,845	2,349	3,237	4,020	4,980	7,057

Source: Thornton, Russell. *American Indian Holocaust and Survival: A Population History Since 1492.* Norman, OK: University of Oklahoma Press, 1987, p. 162-163. Published by permission. Primary source: U.S. Bureau of the Census, *Indian Population of the United States and Alaska,* 1910. Washington, D.C.: U.S. Government Printing Office, 1915. p. 10, and 112; *The Indian Population of the United States and Alaska,* Washington, D.C.: U.S. Government Printing Office, 1937, p. 231; *General Population Characteristics: United States Summary.* PC80-1-B1, Pt. 1 Washington, D.C.: U.S. Government Printing Office, 1983, p. 3; *1980 Census of Population, Supplementary Report. American Indian Areas and Alaska Native Villages: 1980.* PC80-S1-13. Washington, D.C.: U.S. Government Printing Office, 1984, p. 14; Stanley and Thomas, "Current Demographics and Social Trends Among North American Indians," *Annals of the American Academy of Political and Social Science,* 1978, p. 114; Swagerty and Thornton, "Preliminary 1980 Census Counts for American Indians, Eskimos and Aleuts," *American Indian Culture and Research Journal,* 1982, pp. 92-93.

★ 223 ★

Population Trends

Native American Population Growth Compared With Other Groups, 1980 to 1990

Asian - 107.8

Hispanic - 53.0

Native American - 37.9

Black - 13.2

White - 6.0

There are now nearly 2 million Native Americans living in the United States.

Race and ethnicity	Population increase (%)
Asian	107.8
Hispanic[1]	53.0
Native American	37.9
Black	13.2
White	6.0

Source: Carter, James and Dominique de Menil. "USA can't point finger at others on human rights." *USA TODAY* (10 December 1992), p. 11A. Primary source: U.S. Census Bureau. *Note:* 1. Hispanics may be of any race.

★ 224 ★

Population Trends

Percentage of the United States Indian Population Who Are Urban, 1890-1980

Year	Percent
1890	0.0
1900	0.4
1910	4.5
1920	6.1
1930	9.9
1940	7.2
1950	13.4
1960	27.9
1970	44.5
1980	49.0

Source: Thornton, Russell *American Indian Holocaust and Survival: A Population History Since 1492.* Norman, OK: University of Oklahoma Press, 1987, p. 227. Published by permission. Primary source: Thornton, Sandefur, and Grasmick, *The Urbanization of American Indians: A Critical Bibliography.* Bloomington: Indiana University Press, 1982, p. 14. U.S. Bureau of the Census, *General Social and Economic Characteristics: United States Summary.* PC80-1-C1. Washington, D.C.: U.S. Government Printing Office, 1983, p. 92.

★ 225 ★

Population Trends

Population Projections for 2040

By the middle of the next century, minority groups will make up 47% of the total U.S. population.

Race/ethnicity	1992 (in millions)	Projected population for 2040 (in millions)
Total	254.9	382.7
Whites	190.6	201.8
Blacks	30.4	57.3
Hispanics[1]	24.1	80.7
Asians	7.9	38.8
Native Americans	1.9	4.1

Source: Usdansky, Margaret L. "California's mix offers a look at the future." *USA TODAY* (4 December 1992), p. 8A. Primary source: U.S. Census Bureau. *Note:* 1. Hispanics can be of any race.

★ 226 ★

Population Trends

Projections of Hispanic and Non-Hispanic Populations, by Age and Sex: 1995 to 2025

Data, from middle series projections, are shown as of July 1 of each year based on the resident population.

Age and sex	Population (000)					Percent distribution		
	1995	2000	2005	2010	2025	2000	2010	2025
Hispanic origin, total[1]	26,798	31,166	35,702	40,525	56,927	100.0	100.0	100.0
Under 5 years old	3,090	3,293	3,579	3,983	5,337	10.6	9.8	9.4
5 to 13 years old	4,560	5,542	6,196	6,651	9,020	17.8	16.4	15.8
14 to 17 years old	1,817	2,102	2,582	2,909	3,750	6.7	7.2	6.6
18 to 24 years old	3,204	3,547	4,070	4,863	6,300	11.4	12.0	11.1
25 to 34 years old	5,021	5,145	5,301	5,834	8,464	16.5	14.4	14.9
35 to 44 years old	3,894	4,830	5,396	5,519	7,043	15.5	13.6	12.4
45 to 54 years old	2,274	3,046	3,930	4,828	5,668	9.8	11.9	10.0
55 to 64 years old	1,407	1,734	2,281	3,020	5,266	5.6	7.5	9.3
65 to 74 years old	955	1,137	1,333	1,637	3,609	3.6	4.0	6.3
75 to 84 years old	436	586	767	914	1,744	1.9	2.3	3.1
85 years old and over	141	203	267	367	725	0.7	0.9	1.3
Male	13,610	15,777	18,022	20,410	28,531	50.6	50.4	50.1
Female	13,188	15,388	17,679	20,115	28,396	49.4	49.6	49.9
Non-Hispanic White, total	193,900	197,872	200,842	203,441	209,863	100.0	100.0	100.0
Under 5 years old	13,020	11,936	11,326	11,273	11,267	6.0	5.5	5.4
5 to 13 years old	23,032	23,506	22,605	21,141	21,096	11.9	10.4	10.1
14 to 17 years old	9,892	10,507	10,751	10,564	9,494	5.3	5.2	4.5
18 to 24 years old	17,413	17,245	18,458	19,001	16,691	8.7	9.3	8.0
25 to 34 years old	29,455	25,852	24,077	24,421	25,531	13.1	12.0	12.2
35 to 44 years old	31,542	32,741	29,965	26,370	26,262	16.5	13.0	12.5
45 to 54 years old	23,777	27,760	30,735	31,928	24,094	14.0	15.7	11.5
55 to 64 years old	17,064	18,751	22,605	26,459	28,104	9.5	13.0	13.4
65 to 74 years old	15,938	15,174	14,837	16,503	26,348	7.7	8.1	12.6
75 to 84 years old	9,629	10,674	11,153	10,768	15,129	5.4	5.3	7.2
85 years old and over	3,138	3,726	4,331	5,013	5,846	1.9	2.5	2.8
Male	94,716	96,846	98,472	99,903	103,362	48.9	49.1	49.3
Female	99,184	101,025	102,370	103,538	106,501	51.1	50.9	50.7
Non-Hispanic Black, total	31,648	33,741	35,793	37,930	44,705	100.0	100.0	100.0
Under 5 years old	3,076	3,033	3,109	3,289	3,790	9.0	8.7	8.5
5 to 13 years old	5,027	5,519	5,678	5,735	6,704	16.4	15.1	15.0
14 to 17 years old	2,187	2,312	2,587	2,676	2,955	6.9	7.1	6.6
18 to 24 years old	3,593	3,705	3,990	4,400	4,769	11.0	11.6	10.7
25 to 34 years old	5,196	4,953	4,886	5,084	6,214	14.7	13.4	13.9
35 to 44 years old	4,863	5,338	5,207	4,967	5,526	15.8	13.1	12.4
45 to 54 years old	2,996	3,781	4,584	5,023	4,647	11.2	13.2	10.4
55 to 64 years old	2,049	2,274	2,752	3,480	4,561	6.7	9.2	10.2
65 to 74 years old	1,583	1,626	1,698	1,903	3,593	4.8	5.0	8.0
75 to 84 years old	814	880	945	978	1,447	2.6	2.6	3.2
85 years old and over	263	319	356	397	500	0.9	1.0	1.1
Male	14,958	15,939	16,891	17,890	21,089	47.2	47.2	47.2

[Continued]

★ 226 ★

Projections of Hispanic and Non-Hispanic Populations, by Age and Sex: 1995 to 2025

[Continued]

Age and sex	Population (000)					Percent distribution		
	1995	2000	2005	2010	2025	2000	2010	2025
Female	16,689	17,802	18,901	20,040	23,616	52.8	52.8	52.8
Non-Hispanic American Indian, Eskimo, Aleut, total	1,927	2,055	2,190	2,336	2,796	100.0	100.0	100.0
Under 5 years old	188	185	198	214	246	9.0	9.2	8.8
5 to 13 years old	347	361	359	372	453	17.6	15.9	16.2
14 to 17 years old	144	164	176	170	205	8.0	7.3	7.3
18 to 24 years old	222	232	265	286	310	11.3	12.2	11.1
25 to 34 years old	310	304	313	341	403	14.8	14.6	14.4
35 to 44 years old	284	302	293	290	363	14.7	12.4	13.0
45 to 54 years old	189	225	255	272	269	10.9	11.6	9.6
55 to 64 years old	117	134	161	191	226	6.5	8.2	8.1
65 to 74 years old	76	82	91	106	174	4.0	4.5	6.2
75 to 84 years old	38	46	53	58	92	2.2	2.5	3.3
85 years old and over	13	20	27	34	55	1.0	1.5	2.0
Male	948	1,010	1,075	1,146	1,370	49.1	49.1	49.0
Female	979	1,045	1,115	1,190	1,426	50.9	50.9	51.0
Non-Hispanic Asian, Pacific Islander, total	9,161	11,407	13,759	16,199	24,046	100.0	100.0	100.0
Under 5 years old	807	984	1,122	1,258	1,732	8.6	7.8	7.2
5 to 13 years old	1,295	1,617	2,006	2,314	3,184	14.2	14.3	13.2
14 to 17 years old	552	727	850	1,070	1,492	6.4	6.6	6.2
18 to 24 years old	1,034	1,181	1,454	1,670	2,515	10.4	10.3	10.5
25 to 34 years old	1,688	1,983	2,215	2,499	3,687	17.4	15.4	15.3
35 to 44 years old	1,567	1,914	2,214	2,513	3,394	16.8	15.5	14.1
45 to 54 years old	988	1,357	1,715	2,048	2,857	11.9	12.6	11.9
55 to 64 years old	604	795	1,071	1,403	2,298	7.0	8.7	9.6
65 to 74 years old	412	532	663	829	1,637	4.7	5.1	6.8
75 to 84 years old	170	251	346	441	861	2.2	2.7	3.6
85 years old and over	42	66	102	157	389	0.6	1.0	1.6
Male	4,453	5,529	6,660	7,838	11,660	48.5	48.4	48.5
Female	4,708	5,879	7,099	8,361	12,386	51.5	51.6	51.5

Source: 1994 Statistical Abstract of the United States on CD-ROM [machine-readable datafiles]. CD-8A-94. Washington, DC: U.S. Department of Commerce, Economics and Statistics Administration, Bureau of the Census, Data User Services Division, January 1995. Primary source: U.S. Bureau of the Census, Current Population Reports, P25-1104. *Note:* 1. Persons of Hispanic origin may be of any race.

Chapter 3
THE FAMILY

Characteristics

★ 227 ★

Families, by Type, and Presence and Age of Children in Selected Alaska Native Villages

Data are shown for the 50 areas with the largest populations, in number of persons.

| Alaska Native Village Statistical Area[1] | Married-couple family | | Other family | | | |
| | | | Male householder, no wife present | | Female householder, No husband present | |
	With children 18 years and older	No children 18 years and older	With children 18 years and older	No children 18 years and older	With children 18 years and older	No children 18 years and older
Akiachak	27	44	2	7	9	6
Akutan	0	6	2	5	0	2
Alakanuk	27	39	0	6	6	18
Andreafsky	15	40	3	7	5	12
Angoon	30	75	7	3	5	8
Aniak	7	86	0	9	3	10
Barrow	89	309	15	49	41	82
Bethel	111	594	14	69	62	154
Chevak	13	48	5	9	17	8
Copper Center	1	87	2	5	9	20
Craig	27	215	2	21	10	38
Dillingham	64	327	6	16	15	68
Emmonak	18	47	8	21	14	11
Fort Yukon	15	60	13	22	16	21
Galena	2	81	4	22	0	10
Gambell	28	32	4	22	9	4
Grouse Creek Group	2	129	0	6	9	12
Hoonah	28	88	4	13	16	28
Hooper Bay	35	62	10	9	15	23
Kake	26	119	4	8	5	15
Kasigluk	12	59	0	0	6	8
King Cove	10	44	0	1	3	5
King Salmon	15	94	0	6	2	7
Kipnuk	27	40	2	2	5	4

[Continued]

★ 227 ★

Families, by Type, and Presence and Age of Children in Selected Alaska Native Villages
[Continued]

| Alaska Native Village Statistical Area[1] | Married-couple family | | Other family | | | |
| | | | Male householder, no wife present | | Female householder, No husband present | |
	With children 18 years and older	No children 18 years and older	With children 18 years and older	No children 18 years and older	With children 18 years and older	No children 18 years and older
Klawock	29	108	0	3	10	27
Kotlik	23	48	0	4	8	6
Kotzebue	91	262	8	89	45	78
Kwethluk	19	56	11	7	11	4
McGrath	7	93	0	11	4	19
Mountain Village	36	55	4	10	15	14
Naknek	19	94	2	7	4	5
Ninilchik	255	2,047	16	39	46	228
Noorvik	41	22	0	14	11	9
Pilot Station	14	52	0	6	6	13
Point Hope	14	59	4	20	2	25
Quinhagak	25	52	10	11	10	7
St. Paul	14	73	14	16	11	4
Salamatof	15	130	0	9	1	19
Sand Point	15	104	5	13	7	21
Savoonga	27	39	10	8	21	0
Selawik	10	50	2	14	12	24
Shishmaref	23	21	0	18	8	17
Stebbins	20	32	0	14	6	13
Togiak	30	47	0	15	8	27
Tok	12	203	0	13	6	21
Toksook Bay	27	38	0	2	1	2
Unalakleet	8	98	0	23	15	5
Unalaska	20	236	1	15	5	20
Wainwright	11	68	3	7	15	8
Yakutat	21	54	3	15	11	10

Source: *Census of Population and Housing, 1990: Summary Tape File 3C on CD-ROM* [machine-readable datafiles]. Prepared by the Bureau of the Census. Washington, DC: The Bureau, 1992. *Notes:* 1. Alaska Native villages (ANVs) constitute tribes, bands, clans, groups, villages, communities, or associations in Alaska that are recognized pursuant to the Alaska Native Claims Settlement Act of 1972, Public Law 92-203. Because ANVs do not have legally designated boundaries, the Census Bureau has established Alaska Native village statistical areas (ANVSAs) for statistical purposes. For the 1990 census, the Census Bureau cooperated with officials of the nonprofit corporation within each participating Alaska Native Regional Corporation (ANRC), as well as other knowledgeable officials, to delineate boundaries that encompass the settled area associated with each ANV.

★ 228 ★
Characteristics
Families, by Type, and Presence and Age of Children in Selected Tribal Designated Statistical Areas

Tribal Designated Statistical Area[1]	Married-couple family		Other family			
			Male householder, no wife present		Female householder, No husband present	
	With children 18 years and older	No children 18 years and older	With children 18 years and older	No children 18 years and older	With children 18 years and older	No children 18 years and older
Apache Choctaw TDSA (state)	779	4,314	70	163	374	590
Chickahominy TDSA (state)	154	422	4	26	106	72
Clifton Choctaw TDSA (state)	22	69	0	31	21	19
Coharie TDSA (state)	4,199	18,908	460	1,041	2,666	4,586
Coquille Indian TDSA	10,214	76,978	1,175	3,890	4,279	10,534
Delaware-Muncie TDSA (state)	6	84	0	0	7	0
Florida Tribe of Eastern Creek TDSA (state)	0	55	0	0	0	19
Haliwa-Saponi TDSA (state)	347	847	18	96	169	242
Jena Band of Choctaw TDSA (state)	2,106	11,085	144	406	878	1,372
Klamath TDSA	989	7,979	99	399	446	1,083
Lumbee TDSA (state)	2,187	6,062	219	499	1,377	2,156
Meherrin TDSA (state)	2,163	8,737	302	536	1,422	1,987
Mohegan TDSA (state)	909	4,155	83	208	436	830
Ramapough TDSA (state)	74	47	3	0	6	13
United Houma Nation TDSA (state)	36,250	133,524	3,589	6,642	15,790	21,968
Waccamaw Siouan TDSA (state)	137	419	9	34	72	67
Wampanoag-Gay Head TDSA	254	2,210	9	74	99	331

Source: Census of Population and Housing, 1990: Summary Tape File 3C on CD-ROM [machine-readable datafiles]. Prepared by the Bureau of the Census. Washington, DC: The Bureau, 1992. *Notes:* 1. Tribal designated statistical areas (TDSAs) are areas, delineated outside Oklahoma by federally- and state-recognized tribes without a land base or associated trust lands, to provide statistical areas for which the Census Bureau tabulates data. TDSAs represent areas generally containing the American Indian population over which federally-recognized tribes have jurisdiction and areas in which state tribes provide benefits and services to their members. The names of TDSAs delineated by state-recognized tribes are followed by "(state)." The Census Bureau did not recognize TDSAs before the 1990 census.

★ 229 ★

Characteristics

Families, by Type, and Presence and Age of Children in Selected Tribal Jurisdiction Statistical Areas

| Tribal Jurisdiction Statistical Area[1] | Married-couple family | | Other family | | | |
| | | | Male householder, no wife present | | Female householder, No husband present | |
	With children 18 years and older	No children 18 years and older	With children 18 years and older	No children 18 years and older	With children 18 years and older	No children 18 years and older
Absentee Shawnee-Citizens Band of Potawatomi TJSA	3,570	18,622	334	652	986	1,548
Caddo-Wichita-Delaware TJSA	246	1,784	29	50	111	135
Cherokee TJSA	14,337	78,696	1,295	2,796	5,846	9,946
Cheyenne-Arapaho TJSA	4,386	30,917	390	1,056	1,501	3,003
Chickasaw TJSA	8,490	53,802	683	1,531	3,132	5,707
Choctaw TJSA	7,157	40,877	634	1,439	3,049	5,542
Creek TJSA	19,015	125,197	1,530	4,306	8,136	16,343
Iowa TJSA	139	855	13	13	42	82
Kaw TJSA	429	3,071	58	90	60	128
Kiowa-Comanche-Apache-Fort Sill Apache TJSA	5,712	39,489	552	1,303	2,811	5,438
Otoe-Missouria TJSA	104	485	12	24	65	46
Pawnee TJSA	551	3,350	32	86	176	279
Sac and Fox TJSA	1,734	10,422	110	343	684	1,222
Seminole TJSA	795	4,304	86	237	455	541
Tonkawa TJSA	341	2,600	35	87	133	232
Creek-Seminole Joint Area TJSA	101	407	7	25	39	59
Iowa-Sac and Fox Joint Area TJSA	28	187	0	0	9	10

Source: Census of Population and Housing, 1990: Summary Tape File 3C on CD-ROM [machine-readable datafiles]. Prepared by the Bureau of the Census. Washington, DC: The Bureau, 1992. *Notes:* 1. Tribal jurisdiction statistical areas (TJSAs) are areas, delineated by federally recognized tribes in Oklahoma without a reservation, for which the Census Bureau tabulates data. TJSAs represent areas generally containing the American Indian population over which one or more tribal governments have jurisdiction. If tribal officials delineated adjacent TJSAs so that they include some duplicate territory, the overlap area is called a "joint use area," which is treated as a separate TJSA for census purposes.

★ 230 ★

Characteristics

Families, by Type, and Presence and Age of Children on Selected Reservations and Trust Lands

Data are shown for the 50 areas with the largest populations, in number of persons.

| American Indian Reservation and Trust Lands[1,2] | Married-couple family | | Other family | | | |
| | | | Male householder, no wife present | | Female householder, No husband present | |
	With children 18 years and older	No children 18 years and older	With children 18 years and older	No children 18 years and older	With children 18 years and older	No children 18 years and older
Agua Caliente Reservation	362	4,301	59	161	292	426
Allegany Reservation	258	1,081	33	67	144	273
Blackfeet Reservation	258	982	34	170	168	303
Cheyenne River Reservation	215	994	54	122	172	276

[Continued]

★ 230 ★

Families, by Type, and Presence and Age of Children on Selected Reservations and Trust Lands
[Continued]

American Indian Reservation and Trust Lands[1,2]	Married-couple family		Other family			
			Male householder, no wife present		Female householder, No husband present	
	With children 18 years and older	No children 18 years and older	With children 18 years and older	No children 18 years and older	With children 18 years and older	No children 18 years and older
Coeur d'Alene Reservation and Trust Lands, ID	122	1,347	20	62	31	91
Colorado River Reservation	226	1,310	63	109	134	254
Colville Reservation	151	1,047	27	147	137	298
Crow Reservation and Trust Lands, MT	290	874	22	56	97	113
Eastern Cherokee Reservation	200	874	38	54	234	277
Flathead Reservation	478	3,944	103	243	285	599
Fort Apache Reservation	326	1,153	40	121	245	327
Fort Berthold Reservation	136	718	7	120	95	204
Fort Hall Reservation and Trust Lands, ID	173	710	39	88	74	127
Fort Peck Reservation	288	1,550	43	168	244	376
Gila River Reservation	324	659	106	188	313	485
Hopi Reservation and Trust Lands, AZ	300	586	18	64	214	321
Isabella Reservation and Trust Lands, MI	855	3,900	41	206	238	553
Laguna Pueblo and Trust Lands, NM	177	416	23	29	122	78
Lake Traverse (Sisseton) Reservation	278	1,936	72	176	188	258
Leech Lake Reservation	249	1,453	47	185	128	274
Mississippi Choctaw Reservation and Trust Lands, MS	99	359	24	77	179	138
Muckleshoot Reservation and Trust Lands, WA	141	593	19	43	43	117
Navajo Reservation and Trust Lands, AZ–NM–UT	6,033	13,549	677	2,228	3,576	4,599
Nez Perce Reservation	402	3,494	48	183	144	301
Northern Cheyenne Reservation and Trust Lands, MT–SD	96	446	7	54	106	168
Omaha Reservation	157	824	26	40	100	131
Oneida (West) Reservation	784	3,325	51	117	162	343
Osage Reservation	1,350	8,432	96	273	549	860
Papago Reservation	304	301	99	250	311	559
Pine Ridge Reservation and Trust Lands, NE–SD	332	922	122	148	329	482
Port Madison Reservation	111	1,018	8	59	43	108
Puyallup Reservation and Trust Lands, WA	1,032	5,511	137	310	409	1,074
Red Lake Reservation	162	238	16	83	98	224
Rosebud Reservation and Trust Lands, SD	226	836	30	157	283	527
Salt River Reservation	93	598	30	106	185	164
San Carlos Reservation	301	673	7	78	200	246
Sandia Pueblo	163	548	8	87	86	163
San Juan Pueblo	275	653	34	104	154	143
Santa Clara Pueblo	437	1,517	56	141	216	408
Southern Ute Reservation	237	1,522	20	91	107	168
Standing Rock Reservation	236	1,013	34	116	137	306
Taos Pueblo and Trust Lands, NM	170	636	37	55	130	191
Tulalip Reservation	214	1,422	24	60	76	157
Turtle Mountain Reservation and Trust Lands, ND–SD	211	571	100	141	198	487
Uintah and Ouray Reservation	486	3,011	44	139	155	341
White Earth Reservation	302	1,471	39	135	115	228
Wind River Reservation	631	4,026	106	166	240	670
Yakima Reservation and Trust Lands, WA	897	3,683	96	408	420	826

[Continued]

★ 230 ★

Families, by Type, and Presence and Age of Children on Selected Reservations and Trust Lands
[Continued]

American Indian Reservation and Trust Lands[1,2]	Married-couple family		Other family			
			Male householder, no wife present		Female householder, No husband present	
	With children 18 years and older	No children 18 years and older	With children 18 years and older	No children 18 years and older	With children 18 years and older	No children 18 years and older
Yankton Reservation	195	999	30	84	86	150
Zuni Pueblo	400	531	55	55	248	191

Source: Census of Population and Housing, 1990: Summary Tape File 3C on CD-ROM [machine-readable datafiles]. Prepared by the Bureau of the Census. Washington, DC: The Bureau, 1992. *Notes:* 1. Federal American Indian reservations are areas with boundaries established by treaty, statute, and/or executive or court order, and recognized by the federal government as territory in which American Indian tribes have jurisdiction. State reservations are lands held in trust by state governments for the use and benefit of a given tribe. The reservations and their boundaries were identified for the 1990 census by the Bureau of Indian Affairs (BIA), Department of Interior (for federal reservations), and state governments (for state reservations). The names of American Indian reservations recognized by state governments, but not by the federal government, are followed by "state." Areas composed of reservation lands that are administered jointly and/or are claimed by two reservations, as identified by the BIA, are called "joint areas," and are treated as separate American Indian reservations for census purposes. Federal reservations may cross state boundaries, and federal and state reservations may cross county, county subdivision, and place boundaries. For reservations that cross state boundaries, only the portion of the reservations in a given state is shown in the data products for that state; the entire reservations are shown in data products for the United States. 2. Trust lands are property associated with a particular American Indian reservation or tribe, held in trust by the federal government. Trust lands may be held in trust either for a tribe (tribal trust lands) or for an individual member of a tribe (individual trust land). Trust lands recognized for the 1990 census comprised all tribal trust lands and inhabited individual trust lands located outside of a reservation boundary. As with other American Indian areas, trust lands may be located in more than one state. Only the trust lands in a given state are shown in the data products for that state; all trust lands associated with a reservation or tribe are shown in data products for the United States. The Census Bureau first reported data for tribal trust lands for the 1980 census.

★ 231 ★

Characteristics

Non-Immediate Relatives in Households - 1991

Numbers are shown in thousands of occupied units. Households of Hispanic origin may be of any race.

Characteristics	All households	White	Black	American Indian, Eskimo, or Aleut	Asian or Pacific Islander	Hispanic origin	Not of Hispanic origin	
							Total	White
Persons other than spouse or children								
Households with other relatives	20,847	16,351	3,398	141	747	1,988	18,859	14,603
Single adult offspring 18 to 29	11,785	9,443	1,831	75	344	1,006	10,778	8,544
Single adult offspring 30 years of age or over	3,204	2,520	588	15	60	242	2,962	2,313
Households with three generations	2,234	1,460	594	16	115	353	1,881	1,165
Households with related subfamilies	2,227	1,416	606	23	142	371	1,857	1,099
Households with other types of relatives	7,055	5,083	1,426	64	369	855	6,200	4,352
Households with nonrelatives	6,519	5,414	761	72	184	652	5,867	4,860

Source: Woodward, Jeanne M. *America's Racial and Ethnic Groups: Their Housing in the Early Nineties.* Bureau of the Census. Current Housing Reports, Series H121/94-3. Washington, DC: U.S. Government Printing Office, p. 45. Primary source: American Housing Survey (AHS), 1991 National Internal User File.

Households

★ 232 ★

American Indian and Alaska Native Households by Type and Presence and Age of Children in Selected Alaska Native Villages

Data are shown for the 50 areas with the largest populations, in number of persons.

Alaska Native Village Statistical Area[1]	Family households						Nonfamily households
	Married-couple family		Other family				
			Male householder, no wife present		Female householder, no husband present		
	With own children under 18 years	No own children under 18 years	With own children under 18 years	No own children under 18 years	With own children under 18 years	No own children under 18 years	
Akiachak	43	21	4	5	15	0	19
Akutan	6	0	0	4	0	2	6
Alakanuk	51	13	4	2	9	15	21
Andreafsky	27	15	5	1	11	2	16
Angoon	35	24	4	6	8	5	18
Aniak	26	15	4	3	8	3	23
Barrow	139	57	14	19	63	27	85
Bethel	208	79	28	22	113	74	177
Chevak	40	7	11	3	16	9	43
Copper Center	7	5	4	3	9	7	17
Craig	36	14	3	0	13	4	26
Dillingham	119	50	7	9	43	18	77
Emmonak	37	17	17	8	17	8	23
Fort Yukon	36	14	11	18	25	12	42
Galena	14	21	19	3	10	0	41
Gambell	48	12	3	23	7	6	19
Grouse Creek Group	6	2	2	0	9	0	13
Hoonah	47	31	8	4	11	24	36
Hooper Bay	77	14	10	9	28	10	28
Kake	56	42	8	4	11	9	27
Kasigluk	46	15	0	0	8	6	9
King Cove	18	9	1	0	5	3	8
King Salmon	9	5	0	0	2	3	9
Kipnuk	54	9	2	2	4	5	13
Klawock	43	16	3	0	23	7	21
Kotlik	51	16	4	0	4	10	15
Kotzebue	145	48	48	20	74	40	87
Kwethluk	49	18	6	12	11	4	17
McGrath	25	3	7	2	9	2	23
Mountain Village	55	11	14	0	17	12	12
Naknek	26	6	5	2	3	2	36
Ninilchik	25	49	0	7	7	0	26
Noorvik	32	23	11	3	9	10	9
Pilot Station	52	11	6	0	13	6	10

[Continued]

★ 232 ★

American Indian and Alaska Native Households by Type and Presence and Age of Children in Selected Alaska Native Villages

[Continued]

Alaska Native Village Statistical Area[1]	Family households						Nonfamily households
	Married-couple family		Other family				
			Male householder, no wife present		Female householder, no husband present		
	With own children under 18 years	No own children under 18 years	With own children under 18 years	No own children under 18 years	With own children under 18 years	No own children under 18 years	
Point Hope	54	7	11	11	24	3	15
Quinhagak	53	13	6	15	9	8	15
St. Paul	41	27	2	28	8	7	20
Salamatof	4	4	0	0	3	1	11
Sand Point	44	22	8	7	18	5	38
Savoonga	40	17	3	15	15	6	18
Selawik	39	9	8	8	26	10	12
Shishmaref	27	10	13	5	15	10	22
Stebbins	35	15	12	2	10	6	7
Togiak	56	11	5	8	13	16	16
Tok	4	6	0	0	2	3	6
Toksook Bay	53	8	2	0	2	1	9
Unalakleet	56	19	14	9	10	10	31
Unalaska	6	12	4	1	5	5	15
Wainwright	52	13	5	5	10	13	27
Yakutat	16	12	9	4	13	6	31

Source: Census of Population and Housing, 1990: Summary Tape File 3C on CD-ROM [machine-readable datafiles]. Prepared by the Bureau of the Census. Washington, DC: The Bureau, 1992. *Notes:* 1. Alaska Native villages (ANVs) constitute tribes, bands, clans, groups, villages, communities, or associations in Alaska that are recognized pursuant to the Alaska Native Claims Settlement Act of 1972, Public Law 92-203. Because ANVs do not have legally designated boundaries, the Census Bureau has established Alaska Native village statistical areas (ANVSAs) for statistical purposes. For the 1990 census, the Census Bureau cooperated with officials of the nonprofit corporation within each participating Alaska Native Regional Corporation (ANRC), as well as other knowledgeable officials, to delineate boundaries that encompass the settled area associated with each ANV.

★ 233 ★

Households

American Indian and Alaska Native Households by Type and Presence and Age of Children in Selected Tribal Jurisdiction Statistical Areas

Tribal Jurisdiction Statistical Area[1]	Family households						Nonfamily households
	Married-couple family		Other family				
			Male householder, no wife present		Female householder, no husband present		
	With own children under 18 years	No own children under 18 years	With own children under 18 years	No own children under 18 years	With own children under 18 years	No own children under 18 years	
Absentee Shawnee-Citizens Band of Potawatomi TJSA	619	566	51	15	155	88	349
Caddo-Wichita-Delaware TJSA	48	37	11	4	21	16	27
Cherokee TJSA	6,738	5,642	358	446	1,728	1,056	4,581
Cheyenne-Arapaho TJSA	646	320	71	49	235	169	363

[Continued]

★ 233 ★

American Indian and Alaska Native Households by Type and Presence and Age of Children in Selected Tribal Jurisdiction Statistical Areas

[Continued]

Tribal Jurisdiction Statistical Area[1]	Family households						Nonfamily households
	Married-couple family		Other family				
			Male householder, no wife present		Female householder, no husband present		
	With own children under 18 years	No own children under 18 years	With own children under 18 years	No own children under 18 years	With own children under 18 years	No own children under 18 years	
Chickasaw TJSA	2,070	1,645	167	150	575	387	1,566
Choctaw TJSA	2,741	2,399	181	152	820	538	2,153
Creek TJSA	4,129	3,926	269	280	1,295	823	3,897
Iowa TJSA	28	20	4	2	5	3	12
Kaw TJSA	96	37	0	6	5	3	55
Kiowa-Comanche-Apache-Fort Sill Apache TJSA	1,089	728	80	102	543	367	573
Otoe-Missouria TJSA	25	9	6	9	21	27	32
Pawnee TJSA	189	132	6	0	37	47	98
Sac and Fox TJSA	474	325	32	14	176	97	206
Seminole TJSA	341	231	9	40	59	141	203
Tonkawa TJSA	87	61	9	3	22	13	53
Creek-Seminole Joint Area TJSA	45	41	12	2	11	16	24
Iowa-Sac and Fox Joint Area TJSA	2	0	0	0	0	0	3

Source: Census of Population and Housing, 1990: Summary Tape File 3C on CD-ROM [machine-readable datafiles]. Prepared by the Bureau of the Census. Washington, DC: The Bureau, 1992. *Notes:* 1. Tribal jurisdiction statistical areas (TJSAs) are areas, delineated by federally recognized tribes in Oklahoma without a reservation, for which the Census Bureau tabulates data. TJSAs represent areas generally containing the American Indian population over which one or more tribal governments have jurisdiction. If tribal officials delineated adjacent TJSAs so that they include some duplicate territory, the overlap area is called a "joint use area," which is treated as a separate TJSA for census purposes.

★ 234 ★

Households

American Indian and Alaska Native Households by Type and Presence and Age of Children in Selected Tribal Designated Statistical Areas

Tribal Designated Statistical Area[1]	Family households						Nonfamily households
	Married-couple family		Other family				
			Male householder, no wife present		Female householder, no husband present		
	With own children under 18 years	No own children under 18 years	With own children under 18 years	No own children under 18 years	With own children under 18 years	No own children under 18 years	
Apache Choctaw TDSA (state)	112	37	10	11	5	14	13
Chickahominy TDSA (state)	23	60	0	9	18	23	24
Clifton Choctaw TDSA (state)	14	7	0	12	19	9	0
Coharie TDSA (state)	135	146	36	0	22	43	123
Coquille Indian TDSA	512	497	50	82	284	101	626
Delaware-Muncie TDSA (state)	6	0	0	0	0	0	0
Florida Tribe of Eastern Creek TDSA (state)	0	0	0	0	0	0	0
Haliwa-Saponi TDSA (state)	215	174	35	33	115	42	116
Jena Band of Choctaw TDSA (state)	71	35	0	0	14	6	0
Klamath TDSA	122	79	17	7	56	47	216
Lumbee TDSA (state)	2,982	1,870	283	174	1,032	710	1,567

[Continued]

★ 234 ★

American Indian and Alaska Native Households by Type and Presence and Age of Children in Selected Tribal Designated Statistical Areas

[Continued]

Tribal Designated Statistical Area[1]	Family households						Nonfamily households
	Married-couple family		Other family				
			Male householder, no wife present		Female householder, no husband present		
	With own children under 18 years	No own children under 18 years	With own children under 18 years	No own children under 18 years	With own children under 18 years	No own children under 18 years	
Meherrin TDSA (state)	9	9	0	0	14	10	32
Mohegan TDSA (state)	0	17	0	0	22	0	25
Ramapough TDSA (state)	0	12	0	3	0	6	33
United Houma Nation TDSA (state)	1,246	602	71	89	296	97	373
Waccamaw Siouan TDSA (state)	148	109	11	23	8	44	29
Wampanoag-Gay Head TDSA	23	12	0	0	12	2	46

Source: Census of Population and Housing, 1990: Summary Tape File 3C on CD-ROM [machine-readable datafiles]. Prepared by the Bureau of the Census. Washington, DC: The Bureau, 1992. *Notes:* 1. Tribal designated statistical areas (TDSAs) are areas, delineated outside Oklahoma by federally- and state-recognized tribes without a land base or associated trust lands, to provide statistical areas for which the Census Bureau tabulates data. TDSAs represent areas generally containing the American Indian population over which federally-recognized tribes have jurisdiction and areas in which state tribes provide benefits and services to their members. The names of TDSAs delineated by state-recognized tribes are followed by "(state)." The Census Bureau did not recognize TDSAs before the 1990 census.

★ 235 ★

Households

American Indian and Alaska Native Households by Type and Presence and Age of Children on Selected Reservations and Trust Lands

Data are shown for the 50 areas with the largest populations, in number of persons.

American Indian Reservation and Trust Lands[1,2]	Family households						Nonfamily households
	Married-couple family		Other family				
			Male householder, no wife present		Female householder, no husband present		
	With own children under 18 years	No own children under 18 years	With own children under 18 years	No own children under 18 years	With own children under 18 years	No own children under 18 years	
Agua Caliente Reservation	18	19	0	0	0	0	17
Allegany Reservation	86	58	21	14	65	33	119
Blackfeet Reservation	715	281	127	61	268	178	258
Cheyenne River Reservation	417	129	94	43	244	150	234
Coeur d'Alene Reservation and Trust Lands, ID	76	37	11	12	40	9	60
Colorado River Reservation	183	105	51	13	106	91	112
Colville Reservation	251	210	86	53	228	90	278
Crow Reservation and Trust Lands, MT	582	137	18	31	108	92	107
Eastern Cherokee Reservation	548	317	48	44	289	165	322
Flathead Reservation	507	213	110	65	278	176	410
Fort Apache Reservation	1,041	291	71	90	277	295	242
Fort Berthold Reservation	183	131	69	30	184	68	136
Fort Hall Reservation and Trust Lands, ID	248	170	37	59	88	71	123
Fort Peck Reservation	503	191	117	28	300	216	255
Gila River Reservation	552	306	132	123	454	336	320
Hopi Reservation and Trust Lands, AZ	497	343	51	31	273	262	210
Isabella Reservation and Trust Lands, MI	92	29	11	0	51	13	53
Laguna Pueblo and Trust Lands, NM	307	268	23	25	72	128	179

[Continued]

American Indian and Alaska Native Households by Type and Presence and Age of Children on Selected Reservations and Trust Lands
[Continued]

American Indian Reservation and Trust Lands[1,2]	Family households						Nonfamily households
	Married-couple family		Other family				
			Male householder, no wife present		Female householder, no husband present		
	With own children under 18 years	No own children under 18 years	With own children under 18 years	No own children under 18 years	With own children under 18 years	No own children under 18 years	
Lake Traverse (Sisseton) Reservation	129	48	92	39	213	75	186
Leech Lake Reservation	198	102	106	59	203	98	209
Mississippi Choctaw Reservation and Trust Lands, MS	315	107	71	24	167	150	90
Muckleshoot Reservation and Trust Lands, WA	38	26	17	6	52	17	9
Navajo Reservation and Trust Lands, AZ–NM–UT	12,613	5,836	2,008	847	4,837	3,142	5,842
Nez Perce Reservation	156	103	38	31	83	60	122
Northern Cheyenne Reservation and Trust Lands, MT–SD	342	105	35	12	177	92	99
Omaha Reservation	88	55	24	17	132	45	50
Oneida (West) Reservation	178	160	29	27	129	37	132
Osage Reservation	556	462	22	22	156	105	532
Papago Reservation	282	289	189	160	511	359	380
Pine Ridge Reservation and Trust Lands, NE–SD	648	353	130	131	535	263	363
Port Madison Reservation	43	20	6	3	13	10	28
Puyallup Reservation and Trust Lands, WA	48	45	16	7	66	26	103
Red Lake Reservation	218	155	56	43	214	102	135
Rosebud Reservation and Trust Lands, SD	512	135	138	46	475	304	358
Salt River Reservation	256	66	57	79	162	157	92
San Carlos Reservation	701	236	50	35	261	185	213
Sandia Pueblo	39	26	5	5	10	8	16
San Juan Pueblo	92	45	32	11	34	83	63
Santa Clara Pueblo	138	56	8	17	64	43	91
Southern Ute Reservation	82	34	22	14	58	36	58
Standing Rock Reservation	324	98	80	33	274	123	251
Taos Pueblo and Trust Lands, NM	84	106	23	19	56	34	97
Tulalip Reservation	118	55	5	12	54	27	47
Turtle Mountain Reservation and Trust Lands, ND–SD	506	240	136	87	505	164	323
Uintah and Ouray Reservation	223	79	56	22	124	76	80
White Earth Reservation	189	141	59	23	170	77	182
Wind River Reservation	560	249	52	70	234	94	216
Yakima Reservation and Trust Lands, WA	391	209	90	98	371	172	208
Yankton Reservation	101	61	36	21	121	49	111
Zuni Pueblo	531	333	29	72	223	209	80

Source: Census of Population and Housing, 1990: Summary Tape File 3C on CD-ROM [machine-readable datafiles]. Prepared by the Bureau of the Census. Washington, DC: The Bureau, 1992. *Notes:* 1. Federal American Indian reservations are areas with boundaries established by treaty, statute, and/or executive or court order, and recognized by the federal government as territory in which American Indian tribes have jurisdiction. State reservations are lands held in trust by state governments for the use and benefit of a given tribe. The reservations and their boundaries were identified for the 1990 census by the Bureau of Indian Affairs (BIA), Department of Interior (for federal reservations), and state governments (for state reservations). The names of American Indian reservations recognized by state governments, but not by the federal government, are followed by "state." Areas composed of reservation lands that are administered jointly and/or are claimed by two reservations, as identified by the BIA, are called "joint areas," and are treated as separate American Indian reservations for census purposes. Federal reservations may cross state boundaries, and federal and state reservations may cross county, county subdivision, and place boundaries. For reservations that cross state boundaries, only the portion of the reservations in a given state is shown in the data products for that state; the entire reservations are shown in data products for the United States. 2. Trust lands are property associated with a particular American Indian reservation or tribe, held in trust by the federal government. Trust lands may be held in trust either for a tribe (tribal trust lands) or for an individual member of a tribe (individual trust land). Trust lands recognized for the 1990 census comprised all tribal trust lands and inhabited individual trust lands located outside of a reservation boundary. As with other American Indian areas, trust lands may be located in more than one state. Only the trust lands in a given state are shown in the data products for that state; all trust lands associated with a reservation or tribe are shown in data products for the United States. The Census Bureau first reported data for tribal trust lands for the 1980 census.

★ 236 ★

Households

Households by Type and Presence and Age of Children in Selected Alaska Native Villages

Data are shown for the 50 areas with the largest populations, in number of persons.

Alaska Native Village Statistical Area[1]	Family households						Nonfamily households
	Married-couple family		Other family				
			Male householder, no wife present		Female householder, no husband present		
	With own children under 18 years	No own children under 18 years	With own children under 18 years	No own children under 18 years	With own children under 18 years	No own children under 18 years	
Akiachak	50	21	4	5	15	0	23
Akutan	6	0	3	4	0	2	12
Alakanuk	53	13	4	2	9	15	25
Andreafsky	36	19	9	1	15	2	19
Angoon	62	43	4	6	8	5	24
Aniak	66	27	6	3	10	3	40
Barrow	278	120	35	29	92	31	255
Bethel	477	228	56	27	135	81	433
Chevak	52	9	11	3	16	9	48
Copper Center	44	44	4	3	20	9	40
Craig	147	95	19	4	36	12	138
Dillingham	235	156	13	9	63	20	187
Emmonak	48	17	20	9	17	8	37
Fort Yukon	46	29	17	18	25	12	58
Galena	47	36	23	3	10	0	73
Gambell	48	12	3	23	7	6	25
Grouse Creek Group	83	48	4	2	14	7	71
Hoonah	58	58	13	4	20	24	56
Hooper Bay	81	16	10	9	28	10	38
Kake	77	68	8	4	11	9	38
Kasigluk	52	19	0	0	8	6	13
King Cove	37	17	1	0	5	3	14
King Salmon	54	55	6	0	6	3	47
Kipnuk	56	11	2	2	4	5	14
Klawock	74	63	3	0	30	7	64
Kotlik	51	20	4	0	4	10	18
Kotzebue	243	110	73	24	78	45	194
Kwethluk	57	18	6	12	11	4	22
McGrath	74	26	9	2	18	5	48
Mountain Village	69	22	14	0	17	12	19
Naknek	82	31	7	2	5	4	75
Ninilchik	1,338	964	24	31	213	61	1,136
Noorvik	36	27	11	3	9	11	12
Pilot Station	53	13	6	0	13	6	13
Point Hope	64	9	13	11	24	3	19
Quinhagak	59	18	6	15	9	8	17
St. Paul	55	32	2	28	8	7	29
Salamatof	88	57	6	3	18	2	69
Sand Point	78	41	8	10	23	5	80
Savoonga	45	21	3	15	15	6	20

[Continued]

★ 236 ★

Households by Type and Presence and Age of Children in Selected Alaska Native Villages
[Continued]

Alaska Native Village Statistical Area[1]	Family households						Nonfamily households
	Married-couple family		Other family				
			Male householder, no wife present		Female householder, no husband present		
	With own children under 18 years	No own children under 18 years	With own children under 18 years	No own children under 18 years	With own children under 18 years	No own children under 18 years	
Selawik	51	9	8	8	26	10	14
Shishmaref	27	17	13	5	15	10	24
Stebbins	37	15	12	2	10	9	11
Togiak	64	13	7	8	19	16	27
Tok	127	88	7	6	21	6	115
Toksook Bay	57	8	2	0	2	1	11
Unalakleet	87	19	14	9	10	10	48
Unalaska	150	106	11	5	17	8	277
Wainwright	54	25	5	5	10	13	30
Yakutat	43	32	14	4	13	8	63

Source: Census of Population and Housing, 1990: Summary Tape File 3C on CD-ROM [machine-readable datafiles]. Prepared by the Bureau of the Census. Washington, DC: The Bureau, 1992. Notes: 1. Alaska Native villages (ANVs) constitute tribes, bands, clans, groups, villages, communities, or associations in Alaska that are recognized pursuant to the Alaska Native Claims Settlement Act of 1972, Public Law 92-203. Because ANVs do not have legally designated boundaries, the Census Bureau has established Alaska Native village statistical areas (ANVSAs) for statistical purposes. For the 1990 census, the Census Bureau cooperated with officials of the nonprofit corporation within each participating Alaska Native Regional Corporation (ANRC), as well as other knowledgeable officials, to delineate boundaries that encompass the settled area associated with each ANV.

★ 237 ★

Households

Households by Type and Presence and Age of Children in Selected Tribal Designated Statistical Areas

Tribal Designated Statistical Area[1]	Family households						Nonfamily households
	Married-couple family		Other family				
			Male householder, no wife present		Female householder, no husband present		
	With own children under 18 years	No own children under 18 years	With own children under 18 years	No own children under 18 years	With own children under 18 years	No own children under 18 years	
Apache Choctaw TDSA (state)	2,359	2,734	86	147	534	430	2,085
Chickahominy TDSA (state)	260	316	0	30	66	112	174
Clifton Choctaw TDSA (state)	58	33	10	21	26	14	16
Coharie TDSA (state)	9,847	13,260	668	833	4,280	2,972	12,573
Coquille Indian TDSA	36,390	50,802	2,920	2,145	10,151	4,662	54,197
Delaware-Muncie TDSA (state)	70	20	0	0	0	7	0
Florida Tribe of Eastern Creek TDSA (state)	0	55	0	0	19	0	33
Haliwa-Saponi TDSA (state)	598	596	50	64	253	158	385
Jena Band of Choctaw TDSA (state)	6,697	6,494	300	250	1,347	903	5,007
Klamath TDSA	3,835	5,133	290	208	1,076	453	5,126

[Continued]

★ 237 ★

Households by Type and Presence and Age of Children in Selected Tribal Designated Statistical Areas
[Continued]

Tribal Designated Statistical Area[1]	Family households						Nonfamily households
	Married-couple family		Other family				
			Male householder, no wife present		Female householder, no husband present		
	With own children under 18 years	No own children under 18 years	With own children under 18 years	No own children under 18 years	With own children under 18 years	No own children under 18 years	
Lumbee TDSA (state)	4,609	3,640	433	285	2,139	1,394	3,369
Meherrin TDSA (state)	4,790	6,110	272	566	1,810	1,599	5,197
Mohegan TDSA (state)	2,178	2,886	134	157	829	437	3,178
Ramapough TDSA (state)	28	93	0	3	0	19	61
United Houma Nation TDSA (state)	87,423	82,351	4,515	5,716	21,417	16,341	72,740
Waccamaw Siouan TDSA (state)	314	242	20	23	72	67	126
Wampanoag-Gay Head TDSA	1,160	1,304	55	28	282	148	2,099

Source: Census of Population and Housing, 1990: Summary Tape File 3C on CD-ROM [machine-readable datafiles]. Prepared by the Bureau of the Census. Washington, DC: The Bureau, 1992. *Notes:* 1. Tribal designated statistical areas (TDSAs) are areas, delineated outside Oklahoma by federally- and state-recognized tribes without a land base or associated trust lands, to provide statistical areas for which the Census Bureau tabulates data. TDSAs represent areas generally containing the American Indian population over which federally-recognized tribes have jurisdiction and areas in which state tribes provide benefits and services to their members. The names of TDSAs delineated by state-recognized tribes are followed by "(state)." The Census Bureau did not recognize TDSAs before the 1990 census.

★ 238 ★
Households

Households by Type and Presence and Age of Children in Selected Tribal Jurisdiction Statistical Areas

Tribal Jurisdiction Statistical Area[1]	Family households						Nonfamily households
	Married-couple family		Other family				
			Male householder, no wife present		Female householder, no husband present		
	With own children under 18 years	No own children under 18 years	With own children under 18 years	No own children under 18 years	With own children under 18 years	No own children under 18 years	
Absentee Shawnee-Citizens Band of Potawatomi TJSA	11,000	11,192	514	472	1,483	1,051	5,388
Caddo-Wichita-Delaware TJSA	911	1,119	37	42	108	138	783
Cherokee TJSA	42,339	50,694	2,123	1,968	9,435	6,357	36,950
Cheyenne-Arapaho TJSA	17,867	17,436	817	629	2,725	1,779	14,290
Chickasaw TJSA	28,014	34,278	1,125	1,089	5,393	3,446	25,897
Choctaw TJSA	21,683	26,351	982	1,091	5,061	3,530	20,780
Creek TJSA	67,793	76,419	2,954	2,882	15,194	9,285	76,737
Iowa TJSA	519	475	12	14	69	55	311
Kaw TJSA	1,513	1,987	55	93	120	68	1,224
Kiowa-Comanche-Apache-Fort Sill Apache TJSA	22,380	22,821	925	930	5,396	2,853	17,790
Otoe-Missouria TJSA	285	304	15	21	44	67	227
Pawnee TJSA	1,749	2,152	60	58	261	194	1,439
Sac and Fox TJSA	5,359	6,797	260	193	1,116	790	5,818
Seminole TJSA	2,313	2,786	127	196	414	582	2,373
Tonkawa TJSA	1,291	1,650	70	52	207	158	1,449

[Continued]

★ 238 ★

Households by Type and Presence and Age of Children in Selected Tribal Jurisdiction Statistical Areas

[Continued]

Tribal Jurisdiction Statistical Area[1]	Family households						Nonfamily households
	Married-couple family		Other family				
			Male householder, no wife present		Female householder, no husband present		
	With own children under 18 years	No own children under 18 years	With own children under 18 years	No own children under 18 years	With own children under 18 years	No own children under 18 years	
Creek-Seminole Joint Area TJSA	215	293	14	18	56	42	224
Iowa-Sac and Fox Joint Area TJSA	118	97	0	0	10	9	67

Source: Census of Population and Housing, 1990: Summary Tape File 3C on CD-ROM [machine-readable datafiles]. Prepared by the Bureau of the Census. Washington, DC: The Bureau, 1992. *Notes:* 1. Tribal jurisdiction statistical areas (TJSAs) are areas, delineated by federally recognized tribes in Oklahoma without a reservation, for which the Census Bureau tabulates data. TJSAs represent areas generally containing the American Indian population over which one or more tribal governments have jurisdiction. If tribal officials delineated adjacent TJSAs so that they include some duplicate territory, the overlap area is called a "joint use area," which is treated as a separate TJSA for census purposes.

★ 239 ★

Households

Households by Type and Presence and Age of Children on Selected Reservations and Trust Lands

Data are shown for the 50 areas with the largest populations, in number of persons.

American Indian Reservation and Trust Lands[1,2]	Family households						Nonfamily households
	Married-couple family		Other family				
			Male householder, no wife present		Female householder, no husband present		
	With own children under 18 years	No own children under 18 years	With own children under 18 years	No own children under 18 years	With own children under 18 years	No own children under 18 years	
Agua Caliente Reservation	697	3,966	69	151	307	411	4,834
Allegany Reservation	616	723	57	43	275	142	1,047
Blackfeet Reservation	816	424	141	63	285	186	446
Cheyenne River Reservation	718	491	112	64	271	177	539
Coeur d'Alene Reservation and Trust Lands, ID	659	810	43	39	93	29	529
Colorado River Reservation	696	840	111	61	227	161	653
Colville Reservation	589	609	105	69	314	121	614
Crow Reservation and Trust Lands, MT	733	431	25	53	118	92	240
Eastern Cherokee Reservation	632	442	48	44	309	202	389
Flathead Reservation	2,085	2,337	209	137	572	312	2,262
Fort Apache Reservation	1,135	344	71	90	277	295	378
Fort Berthold Reservation	433	421	81	46	218	81	440
Fort Hall Reservation and Trust Lands, ID	467	416	41	86	117	84	273
Fort Peck Reservation	1,069	769	152	59	357	263	720
Gila River Reservation	639	344	154	140	462	336	346
Hopi Reservation and Trust Lands, AZ	527	359	51	31	273	262	294
Isabella Reservation and Trust Lands, MI	2,394	2,361	163	84	551	240	2,569
Laguna Pueblo and Trust Lands, NM	323	270	23	29	72	128	196
Lake Traverse (Sisseton) Reservation	1,006	1,208	114	134	294	152	1,103
Leech Lake Reservation	775	927	131	101	259	143	758
Mississippi Choctaw Reservation and Trust Lands, MS	330	128	77	24	167	150	99
Muckleshoot Reservation and Trust Lands, WA	335	399	40	22	116	44	368
Navajo Reservation and Trust Lands, AZ–NM–UT	13,282	6,300	2,058	847	4,996	3,179	6,719
Nez Perce Reservation	1,617	2,279	132	99	271	174	1,615
Northern Cheyenne Reservation and Trust Lands, MT–SD	415	127	49	12	182	92	150

[Continued]

★ 239 ★

Households by Type and Presence and Age of Children on Selected Reservations and Trust Lands
[Continued]

American Indian Reservation and Trust Lands[1,2]	Family households						Nonfamily households
	Married-couple family		Other family				
			Male householder, no wife present		Female householder, no husband present		
	With own children under 18 years	No own children under 18 years	With own children under 18 years	No own children under 18 years	With own children under 18 years	No own children under 18 years	
Omaha Reservation	463	518	34	32	161	70	448
Oneida (West) Reservation	2,400	1,709	94	74	358	147	931
Osage Reservation	4,598	5,184	245	124	850	559	3,751
Papago Reservation	316	289	189	160	511	359	411
Pine Ridge Reservation and Trust Lands, NE–SD	781	473	135	135	535	276	499
Port Madison Reservation	536	593	43	24	105	46	516
Puyallup Reservation and Trust Lands, WA	3,128	3,415	227	220	1,055	428	3,315
Red Lake Reservation	229	171	56	43	214	108	135
Rosebud Reservation and Trust Lands, SD	729	333	138	49	500	310	503
Salt River Reservation	282	409	57	79	162	187	450
San Carlos Reservation	738	236	50	35	261	185	242
Sandia Pueblo	380	331	75	20	168	81	255
San Juan Pueblo	582	346	114	24	123	174	305
Santa Clara Pueblo	1,029	925	115	82	408	216	865
Southern Ute Reservation	917	842	77	34	180	95	569
Standing Rock Reservation	738	511	102	48	300	143	503
Taos Pueblo and Trust Lands, NM	363	443	55	37	194	127	693
Tulalip Reservation	743	893	29	55	123	110	611
Turtle Mountain Reservation and Trust Lands, ND–SD	512	270	139	102	514	171	398
Uintah and Ouray Reservation	2,194	1,303	131	52	345	151	789
White Earth Reservation	852	921	88	86	228	115	718
Wind River Reservation	2,418	2,239	102	170	632	278	1,692
Yakima Reservation and Trust Lands, WA	2,467	2,113	233	271	784	462	1,501
Yankton Reservation	578	616	48	66	155	81	611
Zuni Pueblo	571	360	38	72	230	209	189

Source: Census of Population and Housing, 1990: Summary Tape File 3C on CD-ROM [machine-readable datafiles]. Prepared by the Bureau of the Census. Washington, DC: The Bureau, 1992. *Notes:* 1. Federal American Indian reservations are areas with boundaries established by treaty, statute, and/or executive or court order, and recognized by the federal government as territory in which American Indian tribes have jurisdiction. State reservations are lands held in trust by state governments for the use and benefit of a given tribe. The reservations and their boundaries were identified for the 1990 census by the Bureau of Indian Affairs (BIA), Department of Interior (for federal reservations), and state governments (for state reservations). The names of American Indian reservations recognized by state governments, but not by the federal government, are followed by "state." Areas composed of reservation lands that are administered jointly and/or are claimed by two reservations, as identified by the BIA, are called "joint areas," and are treated as separate American Indian reservations for census purposes. Federal reservations may cross state boundaries, and federal and state reservations may cross county, county subdivision, and place boundaries. For reservations that cross state boundaries, only the portion of the reservations in a given state is shown in the data products for that state; the entire reservations are shown in data products for the United States. 2. Trust lands are property associated with a particular American Indian reservation or tribe, held in trust by the federal government. Trust lands may be held in trust either for a tribe (tribal trust lands) or for an individual member of a tribe (individual trust land). Trust lands recognized for the 1990 census comprised all tribal trust lands and inhabited individual trust lands located outside of a reservation boundary. As with other American Indian areas, trust lands may be located in more than one state. Only the trust lands in a given state are shown in the data products for that state; all trust lands associated with a reservation or tribe are shown in data products for the United States. The Census Bureau first reported data for tribal trust lands for the 1980 census.

★ 240 ★
Households

Households by Type and Relationship in Selected Alaska Native Villages - Part I

Data are shown for the 50 areas with the largest populations, in number of persons.

Alaska Native Village Statistical Area[1]	Persons in family households						
	Householder	Spouse	Child		Grand-child	Other relatives	Non-relatives
			Natural-born or adopted	Step-child			
Akiachak	95	75	178	4	32	34	21
Akutan	15	6	35	0	2	4	7
Alakanuk	96	69	253	1	32	54	4
Andreafsky	82	61	202	6	8	10	11
Angoon	128	106	267	14	62	28	11
Aniak	115	95	213	9	2	16	29
Barrow	585	396	1,135	24	80	93	77
Bethel	1,004	693	1,637	45	136	156	180
Chevak	100	64	276	9	48	37	10
Copper Center	124	89	127	10	16	6	6
Craig	313	241	427	12	19	20	33
Dillingham	496	390	749	28	36	45	33
Emmonak	119	63	291	3	46	24	22
Fort Yukon	147	65	235	2	20	23	27
Galena	119	84	181	14	0	4	23
Gambell	99	54	254	2	61	43	10
Grouse Creek Group	158	128	210	9	5	11	17
Hoonah	177	134	271	0	34	25	28
Hooper Bay	154	99	464	7	48	17	13
Kake	177	142	249	4	23	13	20
Kasigluk	85	71	208	2	20	38	3
King Cove	63	57	121	0	0	2	7
King Salmon	124	98	136	3	0	5	12
Kipnuk	80	74	251	0	20	19	0
Klawock	177	139	240	7	2	22	31
Kotlik	89	71	229	2	20	23	6
Kotzebue	573	357	1,062	59	139	154	103
Kwethluk	108	76	290	8	29	29	3
McGrath	134	96	213	6	5	6	14
Mountain Village	134	84	386	0	36	29	12
Naknek	131	104	200	20	5	13	24
Ninilchik	2,631	2,240	3,572	202	80	128	110
Noorvik	97	59	220	3	124	13	14
Pilot Station	91	64	261	2	9	12	15
Point Hope	124	76	283	2	34	47	41
Quinhagak	115	79	246	0	25	13	11
St. Paul	132	87	193	8	45	54	9
Salamatof	174	147	249	26	10	23	9
Sand Point	165	121	242	7	4	17	17
Savoonga	105	57	259	0	52	21	0
Selawik	112	59	304	5	36	34	15
Shishmaref	87	45	200	2	23	27	20
Stebbins	85	47	191	2	61	36	12

[Continued]

★ 240 ★

Households by Type and Relationship in Selected Alaska Native Villages - Part I
[Continued]

Alaska Native Village Statistical Area[1]	Persons in family households						
	Householder	Spouse	Child		Grand-child	Other relatives	Non-relatives
			Natural-born or adopted	Step-child			
Togiak	127	77	274	0	17	67	10
Tok	255	210	287	15	6	11	15
Toksook Bay	70	59	234	0	17	7	4
Unalakleet	149	111	263	0	29	33	7
Unalaska	297	237	374	21	21	53	31
Wainwright	112	84	217	2	33	7	10
Yakutat	114	77	181	13	9	21	30

Source: Census of Population and Housing, 1990: Summary Tape File 3C on CD-ROM [machine-readable datafiles]. Prepared by the Bureau of the Census. Washington, DC: The Bureau, 1992. Notes: 1. Alaska Native villages (ANVs) constitute tribes, bands, clans, groups, villages, communities, or associations in Alaska that are recognized pursuant to the Alaska Native Claims Settlement Act of 1972, Public Law 92-203. Because ANVs do not have legally designated boundaries, the Census Bureau has established Alaska Native village statistical areas (ANVSAs) for statistical purposes. For the 1990 census, the Census Bureau cooperated with officials of the nonprofit corporation within each participating Alaska Native Regional Corporation (ANRC), as well as other knowledgeable officials, to delineate boundaries that encompass the settled area associated with each ANV.

★ 241 ★

Households

Households by Type and Relationship in Selected Alaska Native Villages - Part II

Data are shown for the 50 areas with the largest populations, in number of persons.

Alaska Native Village Statistical Area[1]	Living in nonfamily households					Living in group quarters	
	Male householders		Female householders		Non-relatives	Institu-tionalized persons	Other persons in group quarters
	Living alone	Not living alone	Living alone	Not living alone			
Akiachak	15	0	8	0	0	0	0
Akutan	6	4	0	2	9	0	515
Alakanuk	15	4	4	2	6	0	0
Andreafsky	8	6	5	0	7	0	0
Angoon	22	2	0	0	3	0	0
Aniak	19	9	12	0	10	0	0
Barrow	103	48	87	17	84	10	11
Bethel	183	87	123	40	175	140	88
Chevak	39	4	3	2	5	0	0
Copper Center	16	8	16	0	8	0	0
Craig	71	29	19	19	57	0	0
Dillingham	87	27	53	20	49	1	3
Emmonak	22	4	9	2	5	0	0
Fort Yukon	40	3	15	0	2	0	0
Galena	42	16	15	0	23	0	285
Gambell	19	0	6	0	0	0	0
Grouse Creek Group	38	11	15	7	21	0	0
Hoonah	44	0	8	4	4	0	0

[Continued]

★ 241 ★

Households by Type and Relationship in Selected Alaska Native Villages - Part II
[Continued]

Alaska Native Village Statistical Area[1]	Living in nonfamily households					Living in group quarters	
	Male householders		Female householders		Non-relatives	Institu-tionalized persons	Other persons in group quarters
	Living alone	Not living alone	Living alone	Not living alone			
Hooper Bay	30	2	2	4	6	0	0
Kake	23	4	9	2	13	0	8
Kasigluk	11	0	2	0	0	0	0
King Cove	8	2	3	1	4	0	189
King Salmon	28	3	12	4	8	0	251
Kipnuk	12	0	0	2	2	0	2
Klawock	30	14	15	5	23	0	0
Kotlik	12	4	2	0	4	0	0
Kotzebue	85	38	54	17	63	41	6
Kwethluk	15	2	5	0	3	0	0
McGrath	29	1	18	0	2	0	0
Mountain Village	10	3	4	2	6	0	0
Naknek	39	8	25	3	18	0	0
Ninilchik	576	144	311	105	304	19	69
Noorvik	7	5	0	0	6	0	0
Pilot Station	10	0	3	0	0	0	0
Point Hope	11	3	4	1	3	0	0
Quinhagak	10	3	4	0	3	0	0
St. Paul	21	3	5	0	4	0	191
Salamatof	20	10	37	2	13	287	0
Sand Point	52	15	8	5	26	0	180
Savoonga	18	0	2	0	0	0	0
Selawik	14	0	0	0	0	0	0
Shishmaref	13	5	6	0	5	0	0
Stebbins	8	3	0	0	3	0	0
Togiak	13	5	6	3	7	0	0
Tok	72	14	27	2	21	0	0
Toksook Bay	8	3	0	0	3	0	0
Unalakleet	40	6	2	0	6	0	0
Unalaska	141	97	28	11	171	0	1,607
Wainwright	20	3	4	3	7	0	0
Yakutat	26	12	21	4	19	0	17

Source: Census of Population and Housing, 1990: Summary Tape File 3C on CD-ROM [machine-readable datafiles]. Prepared by the Bureau of the Census. Washington, DC: The Bureau, 1992. *Notes:* 1. Alaska Native villages (ANVs) constitute tribes, bands, clans, groups, villages, communities, or associations in Alaska that are recognized pursuant to the Alaska Native Claims Settlement Act of 1972, Public Law 92-203. Because ANVs do not have legally designated boundaries, the Census Bureau has established Alaska Native village statistical areas (ANVSAs) for statistical purposes. For the 1990 census, the Census Bureau cooperated with officials of the nonprofit corporation within each participating Alaska Native Regional Corporation (ANRC), as well as other knowledgeable officials, to delineate boundaries that encompass the settled area associated with each ANV.

★ 242 ★

Households

Households by Type and Relationship in Selected Tribal Designated Statistical Areas - Part I

Tribal Designated Statistical Area[1]	Persons in family households						
	Householder	Spouse	Child		Grand-child	Other relatives	Non-relatives
			Natural-born or adopted	Step-child			
Apache Choctaw TDSA (state)	6,290	4,938	6,904	389	675	537	189
Chickahominy TDSA (state)	784	585	901	51	106	116	25
Clifton Choctaw TDSA (state)	162	82	205	10	20	49	8
Coharie TDSA (state)	31,860	22,941	33,553	1,781	2,994	3,652	1,411
Coquille Indian TDSA	107,070	86,834	100,567	7,813	3,949	6,895	8,411
Delaware-Muncie TDSA (state)	97	85	117	0	0	0	0
Florida Tribe of Eastern Creek TDSA (state)	74	52	30	0	0	10	9
Haliwa-Saponi TDSA (state)	1,719	1,159	2,514	54	265	244	58
Jena Band of Choctaw TDSA (state)	15,991	13,259	17,847	1,244	1,103	1,104	549
Klamath TDSA	10,995	8,965	10,634	1,091	498	749	712
Lumbee TDSA (state)	12,500	8,321	18,756	923	2,213	1,624	836
Meherrin TDSA (state)	15,147	11,023	16,415	1,025	2,407	1,745	738
Mohegan TDSA (state)	6,621	4,964	6,877	482	271	505	499
Ramapough TDSA (state)	143	122	144	17	39	102	13
United Houma Nation TDSA (state)	217,763	169,666	271,559	13,866	19,213	23,667	9,890
Waccamaw Siouan TDSA (state)	738	610	982	84	117	56	43
Wampanoag-Gay Head TDSA	2,977	2,444	2,857	109	98	207	223

Source: Census of Population and Housing, 1990: Summary Tape File 3C on CD-ROM [machine-readable datafiles]. Prepared by the Bureau of the Census. Washington, DC: The Bureau, 1992. *Notes:* 1. Tribal designated statistical areas (TDSAs) are areas, delineated outside Oklahoma by federally- and state-recognized tribes without a land base or associated trust lands, to provide statistical areas for which the Census Bureau tabulates data. TDSAs represent areas generally containing the American Indian population over which federally-recognized tribes have jurisdiction and areas in which state tribes provide benefits and services to their members. The names of TDSAs delineated by state-recognized tribes are followed by "(state)." The Census Bureau did not recognize TDSAs before the 1990 census.

★ 243 ★

Households

Households by Type and Relationship in Selected Tribal Designated Statistical Areas - Part II

Tribal Designated Statistical Area[1]	Living in nonfamily households					Living in group quarters	
	Male householders		Female householders		Non-relatives	Institu-tionalized persons	Other persons in group quarters
	Living alone	Not living alone	Living alone	Not living alone			
Apache Choctaw TDSA (state)	697	73	1,294	21	102	284	253
Chickahominy TDSA (state)	89	0	78	7	7	0	0
Clifton Choctaw TDSA (state)	0	0	16	0	0	0	0
Coharie TDSA (state)	3,986	659	7,596	332	1,390	3,629	440
Coquille Indian TDSA	16,582	6,830	25,871	4,914	15,593	4,879	7,313
Delaware-Muncie TDSA (state)	0	0	0	0	0	0	0
Florida Tribe of Eastern Creek TDSA (state)	26	0	0	7	7	0	0
Haliwa-Saponi TDSA (state)	170	18	181	16	33	0	0

[Continued]

★ 243 ★

Households by Type and Relationship in Selected Tribal Designated Statistical Areas - Part II
[Continued]

Tribal Designated Statistical Area[1]	Living in nonfamily households					Living in group quarters	
	Male householders		Female householders		Non-relatives	Institu-tionalized persons	Other persons in group quarters
	Living alone	Not living alone	Living alone	Not living alone			
Jena Band of Choctaw TDSA (state)	1,510	262	3,081	154	553	3,273	464
Klamath TDSA	1,908	594	2,371	253	1,085	316	712
Lumbee TDSA (state)	1,205	204	1,854	106	454	496	736
Meherrin TDSA (state)	1,853	231	3,049	64	446	526	605
Mohegan TDSA (state)	1,057	364	1,512	245	776	412	51
Ramapough TDSA (state)	0	0	52	9	11	0	0
United Houma Nation TDSA (state)	26,345	5,986	36,927	3,482	11,526	5,924	1,560
Waccamaw Siouan TDSA (state)	39	6	75	6	15	0	0
Wampanoag-Gay Head TDSA	622	284	1,064	129	541	74	10

Source: Census of Population and Housing, 1990: Summary Tape File 3C on CD-ROM [machine-readable datafiles]. Prepared by the Bureau of the Census. Washington, DC: The Bureau, 1992. *Notes:* 1. Tribal designated statistical areas (TDSAs) are areas, delineated outside Oklahoma by federally- and state-recognized tribes without a land base or associated trust lands, to provide statistical areas for which the Census Bureau tabulates data. TDSAs represent areas generally containing the American Indian population over which federally-recognized tribes have jurisdiction and areas in which state tribes provide benefits and services to their members. The names of TDSAs delineated by state-recognized tribes are followed by "(state)." The Census Bureau did not recognize TDSAs before the 1990 census.

★ 244 ★

Households

Households by Type and Relationship in Selected Tribal Jurisdiction Statistical Areas - Part I

Tribal Jurisdiction Statistical Area[1]	Persons in family households						
			Child				
	Householder	Spouse	Natural-born or adopted	Step-child	Grand-child	Other relatives	Non-relatives
Absentee Shawnee-Citizens Band of Potawatomi TJSA	25,712	22,264	27,243	2,911	1,507	1,533	1,037
Caddo-Wichita-Delaware TJSA	2,355	2,075	2,314	155	181	115	64
Cherokee TJSA	112,916	92,026	116,867	9,834	8,028	7,444	4,374
Cheyenne-Arapaho TJSA	41,253	35,389	44,088	3,437	1,921	2,320	1,336
Chickasaw TJSA	73,345	62,533	70,730	6,496	3,909	4,075	1,944
Choctaw TJSA	58,698	47,702	57,552	5,691	4,445	4,291	2,108
Creek TJSA	174,527	143,475	176,479	13,802	7,697	10,786	5,822
Iowa TJSA	1,144	1,043	1,296	134	54	56	56
Kaw TJSA	3,836	3,540	3,660	270	109	163	37
Kiowa-Comanche-Apache-Fort Sill Apache TJSA	55,305	44,772	58,804	4,773	3,719	3,892	2,339
Otoe-Missouria TJSA	736	581	857	99	90	59	52
Pawnee TJSA	4,474	3,915	4,397	407	213	254	99
Sac and Fox TJSA	14,515	11,995	14,363	1,055	714	839	617
Seminole TJSA	6,418	5,168	6,494	465	734	667	219
Tonkawa TJSA	3,428	2,839	3,322	285	102	146	92

[Continued]

★ 244 ★

Households by Type and Relationship in Selected Tribal Jurisdiction Statistical Areas - Part I
[Continued]

Tribal Jurisdiction Statistical Area[1]	Persons in family households						
	Householder	Spouse	Child		Grand-child	Other relatives	Non-relatives
			Natural-born or adopted	Step-child			
Creek-Seminole Joint Area TJSA	638	498	674	51	56	33	15
Iowa-Sac and Fox Joint Area TJSA	234	218	282	6	7	6	10

Source: Census of Population and Housing, 1990: Summary Tape File 3C on CD-ROM [machine-readable datafiles]. Prepared by the Bureau of the Census. Washington, DC: The Bureau, 1992. *Notes:* 1. Tribal jurisdiction statistical areas (TJSAs) are areas, delineated by federally recognized tribes in Oklahoma without a reservation, for which the Census Bureau tabulates data. TJSAs represent areas generally containing the American Indian population over which one or more tribal governments have jurisdiction. If tribal officials delineated adjacent TJSAs so that they include some duplicate territory, the overlap area is called a "joint use area," which is treated as a separate TJSA for census purposes.

★ 245 ★
Households

Households by Type and Relationship in Selected Tribal Jurisdiction Statistical Areas - Part II

Tribal Jurisdiction Statistical Area[1]	Living in nonfamily households					Living in group quarters	
	Male householders		Female householders		Non-relatives	Institu-tionalized persons	Other persons in group quarters
	Living alone	Not living alone	Living alone	Not living alone			
Absentee Shawnee-Citizens Band of Potawatomi TJSA	2,097	263	2,826	202	587	2,647	183
Caddo-Wichita-Delaware TJSA	295	34	443	11	76	90	0
Cherokee TJSA	12,185	1,961	21,734	1,070	3,942	4,069	2,684
Cheyenne-Arapaho TJSA	4,756	774	8,220	540	1,608	3,808	1,215
Chickasaw TJSA	8,121	970	16,139	667	2,158	4,829	1,597
Choctaw TJSA	6,744	735	12,860	441	1,646	5,203	1,237
Creek TJSA	26,070	5,444	41,940	3,283	10,606	9,581	5,942
Iowa TJSA	111	26	169	5	34	9	0
Kaw TJSA	368	61	768	27	128	254	6
Kiowa-Comanche-Apache-Fort Sill Apache TJSA	6,241	881	10,155	513	1,818	3,612	8,916
Otoe-Missouria TJSA	97	13	111	6	49	0	0
Pawnee TJSA	521	57	833	28	108	101	6
Sac and Fox TJSA	1,652	307	3,736	123	583	578	15
Seminole TJSA	811	43	1,470	49	89	350	16
Tonkawa TJSA	435	67	908	39	136	219	250
Creek-Seminole Joint Area TJSA	48	11	158	7	24	180	26
Iowa-Sac and Fox Joint Area TJSA	46	3	18	0	5	0	0

Source: Census of Population and Housing, 1990: Summary Tape File 3C on CD-ROM [machine-readable datafiles]. Prepared by the Bureau of the Census. Washington, DC: The Bureau, 1992. *Notes:* 1. Tribal jurisdiction statistical areas (TJSAs) are areas, delineated by federally recognized tribes in Oklahoma without a reservation, for which the Census Bureau tabulates data. TJSAs represent areas generally containing the American Indian population over which one or more tribal governments have jurisdiction. If tribal officials delineated adjacent TJSAs so that they include some duplicate territory, the overlap area is called a "joint use area," which is treated as a separate TJSA for census purposes.

★ 246 ★
Households

Households by Type and Relationship on Selected Reservations and Trust Lands - Part I

Data are shown for the 50 areas with the largest populations, in number of persons.

American Indian Reservation and Trust Lands[1,2]	Persons in family households						
			Child				
	Householder	Spouse	Natural-born or adopted	Step-child	Grand-child	Other relatives	Non-relatives
Agua Caliente Reservation	5,601	4,681	2,521	133	146	431	265
Allegany Reservation	1,856	1,346	2,216	117	112	139	172
Blackfeet Reservation	1,915	1,266	3,282	119	516	218	244
Cheyenne River Reservation	1,833	1,208	3,088	111	418	304	193
Coeur d'Alene Reservation and Trust Lands, ID	1,673	1,455	1,589	154	94	99	96
Colorado River Reservation	2,096	1,546	2,524	119	230	257	322
Colville Reservation	1,807	1,191	2,320	166	204	238	260
Crow Reservation and Trust Lands, MT	1,452	1,178	2,547	95	406	307	47
Eastern Cherokee Reservation	1,677	1,083	2,237	135	293	170	144
Flathead Reservation	5,652	4,413	6,247	463	314	396	436
Fort Apache Reservation	2,212	1,472	4,556	201	736	485	377
Fort Berthold Reservation	1,280	870	1,949	76	257	174	169
Fort Hall Reservation and Trust Lands, ID	1,211	905	1,876	89	254	328	103
Fort Peck Reservation	2,669	1,848	4,106	208	338	310	338
Gila River Reservation	2,075	973	3,939	349	746	551	419
Hopi Reservation and Trust Lands, AZ	1,503	887	2,968	61	703	498	236
Isabella Reservation and Trust Lands, MI	5,793	4,689	7,026	309	157	259	367
Laguna Pueblo and Trust Lands, NM	845	667	1,333	40	358	191	55
Lake Traverse (Sisseton) Reservation	2,908	2,164	3,513	125	191	266	291
Leech Lake Reservation	2,336	1,716	3,062	133	191	237	230
Mississippi Choctaw Reservation and Trust Lands, MS	876	455	1,823	44	341	277	189
Muckleshoot Reservation and Trust Lands, WA	956	732	1,306	62	143	69	112
Navajo Reservation and Trust Lands, AZ–NM–UT	30,662	19,529	68,033	3,187	9,944	5,594	3,180
Nez Perce Reservation	4,572	3,868	4,301	407	214	247	202
Northern Cheyenne Reservation and Trust Lands, MT–SD	877	530	1,620	100	314	112	153
Omaha Reservation	1,278	1,003	1,832	65	240	134	90
Oneida (West) Reservation	4,782	4,086	6,831	287	113	197	230
Osage Reservation	11,560	9,743	12,097	996	707	651	432
Papago Reservation	1,824	608	3,339	81	703	718	725
Pine Ridge Reservation and Trust Lands, NE–SD	2,335	1,201	4,776	238	1,351	935	567
Port Madison Reservation	1,347	1,133	1,440	80	33	84	85
Puyallup Reservation and Trust Lands, WA	8,473	6,610	10,296	710	421	767	644
Red Lake Reservation	821	394	1,594	80	273	148	177
Rosebud Reservation and Trust Lands, SD	2,059	1,078	3,986	215	791	496	381
Salt River Reservation	1,176	718	1,489	46	260	343	233
San Carlos Reservation	1,505	968	3,264	69	511	429	214
Sandia Pueblo	1,055	739	1,444	82	65	98	146
San Juan Pueblo	1,363	909	2,120	67	189	106	113
Santa Clara Pueblo	2,775	1,935	3,563	151	312	191	191
Southern Ute Reservation	2,145	1,741	2,667	188	154	159	136
Standing Rock Reservation	1,842	1,206	3,060	213	404	378	276
Taos Pueblo and Trust Lands, NM	1,219	793	1,507	30	160	107	77
Tulalip Reservation	1,953	1,603	2,083	174	106	222	159
Turtle Mountain Reservation and Trust Lands, ND–SD	1,708	783	3,329	65	273	143	290
Uintah and Ouray Reservation	4,176	3,499	7,466	342	282	278	252
White Earth Reservation	2,290	1,805	3,202	107	165	150	193
Wind River Reservation	5,839	4,521	7,386	442	587	533	302
Yakima Reservation and Trust Lands, WA	6,330	4,595	9,631	220	971	1,584	1,047

[Continued]

★ 246 ★

Households by Type and Relationship on Selected Reservations and Trust Lands - Part I

[Continued]

American Indian Reservation and Trust Lands[1,2]	Persons in family households						
	Householder	Spouse	Child		Grand-child	Other relatives	Non-relatives
			Natural-born or adopted	Step-child			
Yankton Reservation	1,544	1,205	2,168	51	160	186	116
Zuni Pueblo	1,480	989	2,817	76	991	791	82

Source: Census of Population and Housing, 1990: Summary Tape File 3C on CD-ROM [machine-readable datafiles]. Prepared by the Bureau of the Census. Washington, DC: The Bureau, 1992. *Notes:* 1. Federal American Indian reservations are areas with boundaries established by treaty, statute, and/or executive or court order, and recognized by the federal government as territory in which American Indian tribes have jurisdiction. State reservations are lands held in trust by state governments for the use and benefit of a given tribe. The reservations and their boundaries were identified for the 1990 census by the Bureau of Indian Affairs (BIA), Department of Interior (for federal reservations), and state governments (for state reservations). The names of American Indian reservations recognized by state governments, but not by the federal government, are followed by "state." Areas composed of reservation lands that are administered jointly and/or are claimed by two reservations, as identified by the BIA, are called "joint areas," and are treated as separate American Indian reservations for census purposes. Federal reservations may cross state boundaries, and federal and state reservations may cross county, county subdivision, and place boundaries. For reservations that cross state boundaries, only the portion of the reservations in a given state is shown in the data products for that state; the entire reservations are shown in data products for the United States. 2. Trust lands are property associated with a particular American Indian reservation or tribe, held in trust by the federal government. Trust lands may be held in trust either for a tribe (tribal trust lands) or for an individual member of a tribe (individual trust land). Trust lands recognized for the 1990 census comprised all tribal trust lands and inhabited individual trust lands located outside of a reservation boundary. As with other American Indian areas, trust lands may be located in more than one state. Only the trust lands in a given state are shown in the data products for that state; all trust lands associated with a reservation or tribe are shown in data products for the United States. The Census Bureau first reported data for tribal trust lands for the 1980 census.

★ 247 ★

Households

Households by Type and Relationship on Selected Reservations and Trust Lands - Part II

Data are shown for the 50 areas with the largest populations, in number of persons.

American Indian Reservation and Trust Lands[1,2]	Living in nonfamily households					Living in group quarters	
	Male householders		Female householders		Non-relatives	Institu-tionalized persons	Other persons in group quarters
	Living alone	Not living alone	Living alone	Not living alone			
Agua Caliente Reservation	1,436	572	2,572	254	947	216	64
Allegany Reservation	310	58	621	58	148	144	15
Blackfeet Reservation	245	40	142	19	64	54	364
Cheyenne River Reservation	235	18	264	22	45	0	4
Coeur d'Alene Reservation and Trust Lands, ID	247	54	212	16	89	0	0
Colorado River Reservation	226	87	320	20	155	25	17
Colville Reservation	249	84	255	26	152	54	28
Crow Reservation and Trust Lands, MT	101	17	108	14	29	14	26
Eastern Cherokee Reservation	126	49	191	23	95	88	0
Flathead Reservation	799	162	1,219	82	310	313	255
Fort Apache Reservation	139	24	170	45	69	20	0
Fort Berthold Reservation	254	22	151	13	57	115	0
Fort Hall Reservation and Trust Lands, ID	142	26	100	5	32	43	0
Fort Peck Reservation	296	24	377	23	76	109	0
Gila River Reservation	127	53	132	34	95	85	0
Hopi Reservation and Trust Lands, AZ	143	24	122	5	38	27	0
Isabella Reservation and Trust Lands, MI	724	435	1,108	302	1,202	416	144
Laguna Pueblo and Trust Lands, NM	76	5	102	13	17	22	0
Lake Traverse (Sisseton) Reservation	437	55	598	13	92	153	34
Leech Lake Reservation	343	61	313	41	120	0	0
Mississippi Choctaw Reservation and Trust Lands, MS	7	50	10	32	141	12	0
Muckleshoot Reservation and Trust Lands, WA	102	35	193	38	74	0	14
Navajo Reservation and Trust Lands, AZ–NM–UT	3,357	389	2,826	147	677	635	498
Nez Perce Reservation	700	142	721	52	256	470	7

[Continued]

★ 247 ★

Households by Type and Relationship on Selected Reservations and Trust Lands - Part II
[Continued]

American Indian Reservation and Trust Lands[1,2]	Living in nonfamily households					Living in group quarters	
	Male householders		Female householders			Institutionalized persons	Other persons in group quarters
	Living alone	Not living alone	Living alone	Not living alone	Nonrelatives		
Northern Cheyenne Reservation and Trust Lands, MT–SD	87	10	40	13	30	20	0
Omaha Reservation	180	31	228	9	59	89	0
Oneida (West) Reservation	335	162	360	74	282	153	48
Osage Reservation	1,257	146	2,287	61	262	1,164	30
Papago Reservation	120	61	158	72	178	0	0
Pine Ridge Reservation and Trust Lands, NE–SD	251	27	161	60	117	45	55
Port Madison Reservation	196	72	229	19	113	0	3
Puyallup Reservation and Trust Lands, WA	1,223	492	1,314	286	918	0	281
Red Lake Reservation	87	3	26	19	20	48	0
Rosebud Reservation and Trust Lands, SD	266	32	185	20	53	34	36
Salt River Reservation	135	10	277	28	43	98	0
San Carlos Reservation	152	0	80	10	11	26	0
Sandia Pueblo	94	31	108	22	60	0	0
San Juan Pueblo	121	29	140	15	47	0	18
Santa Clara Pueblo	343	65	431	26	130	117	0
Southern Ute Reservation	242	65	218	44	109	18	0
Standing Rock Reservation	230	39	216	18	74	0	0
Taos Pueblo and Trust Lands, NM	239	61	369	24	105	0	10
Tulalip Reservation	229	114	231	37	192	0	0
Turtle Mountain Reservation and Trust Lands, ND–SD	188	17	166	27	71	27	14
Uintah and Ouray Reservation	321	36	399	33	79	72	0
White Earth Reservation	322	31	349	16	68	71	16
Wind River Reservation	613	121	855	103	321	236	56
Yakima Reservation and Trust Lands, WA	603	117	750	31	289	208	1,072
Yankton Reservation	242	22	337	10	45	132	63
Zuni Pueblo	88	4	89	8	13	17	0

Source: Census of Population and Housing, 1990: Summary Tape File 3C on CD-ROM [machine-readable datafiles]. Prepared by the Bureau of the Census. Washington, DC: The Bureau, 1992. *Notes:* 1. Federal American Indian reservations are areas with boundaries established by treaty, statute, and/or executive or court order, and recognized by the federal government as territory in which American Indian tribes have jurisdiction. State reservations are lands held in trust by state governments for the use and benefit of a given tribe. The reservations and their boundaries were identified for the 1990 census by the Bureau of Indian Affairs (BIA), Department of Interior (for federal reservations), and state governments (for state reservations). The names of American Indian reservations recognized by state governments, but not by the federal government, are followed by "state." Areas composed of reservation lands that are administered jointly and/or are claimed by two reservations, as identified by the BIA, are called "joint areas," and are treated as separate American Indian reservations for census purposes. Federal reservations may cross state boundaries, and federal and state reservations may cross county, county subdivision, and place boundaries. For reservations that cross state boundaries, only the portion of the reservations in a given state is shown in the data products for that state; the entire reservations are shown in data products for the United States. 2. Trust lands are property associated with a particular American Indian reservation or tribe, held in trust by the federal government. Trust lands may be held in trust either for a tribe (tribal trust lands) or for an individual member of a tribe (individual trust land). Trust lands recognized for the 1990 census comprised all tribal trust lands and inhabited individual trust lands located outside of a reservation boundary. As with other American Indian areas, trust lands may be located in more than one state. Only the trust lands in a given state are shown in the data products for that state; all trust lands associated with a reservation or tribe are shown in data products for the United States. The Census Bureau first reported data for tribal trust lands for the 1980 census.

★ 248 ★

Households

Persons in Households in Selected Alaska Native Villages

Data are shown for the 50 areas with the largest populations, in number of persons.

Alaska Native Village Statistical Area[1]	One person	Two persons	Three persons	Four persons	Five persons	Six persons	7 or more persons
Akiachak	23	15	17	27	14	5	17
Akutan	6	9	2	0	4	6	0
Alakanuk	19	16	11	12	18	4	41
Andreafsky	13	17	23	13	14	11	10
Angoon	22	29	18	26	25	22	10
Aniak	31	38	25	14	13	18	16
Barrow	190	167	144	129	104	57	49
Bethel	306	344	256	238	148	76	69
Chevak	42	10	16	22	17	9	32
Copper Center	32	56	27	25	20	4	0
Craig	90	137	87	66	41	17	13
Dillingham	140	195	123	110	78	25	12
Emmonak	31	14	27	16	24	31	13
Fort Yukon	55	44	38	35	16	12	5
Galena	57	59	28	18	13	11	6
Gambell	25	16	6	19	22	12	24
Grouse Creek Group	53	69	29	52	19	2	5
Hoonah	52	65	46	41	23	3	3
Hooper Bay	32	20	20	19	29	45	27
Kake	32	66	34	41	28	10	4
Kasigluk	13	10	13	17	4	13	28
King Cove	11	17	14	10	18	5	2
King Salmon	40	52	38	18	14	0	9
Kipnuk	12	7	11	10	15	19	20
Klawock	45	74	36	32	29	18	7
Kotlik	14	19	9	18	16	10	21
Kotzebue	139	163	127	105	104	71	58
Kwethluk	20	14	14	19	23	16	24
McGrath	47	37	41	16	30	7	4
Mountain Village	14	28	9	26	30	17	29
Naknek	64	35	26	39	24	15	3
Ninilchik	887	1,173	606	607	289	86	119
Noorvik	7	17	12	20	4	8	41
Pilot Station	13	15	14	11	21	11	19
Point Hope	15	11	23	16	35	19	24
Quinhagak	14	20	25	17	31	14	11
St. Paul	26	38	31	16	20	18	12
Salamatof	57	62	58	22	25	6	13
Sand Point	60	61	50	42	16	13	3
Savoonga	20	16	11	22	4	18	34
Selawik	14	10	20	19	24	19	20
Shishmaref	19	17	22	14	12	14	13
Stebbins	8	14	12	10	22	7	23
Togiak	19	26	24	30	21	19	15
Tok	99	110	70	51	22	15	3
Toksook Bay	8	7	9	11	8	10	28

[Continued]

★ 248 ★

Persons in Households in Selected Alaska Native Villages
[Continued]

Alaska Native Village Statistical Area[1]	One person	Two persons	Three persons	Four persons	Five persons	Six persons	7 or more persons
Unalakleet	42	30	29	48	33	10	5
Unalaska	169	163	104	91	40	1	6
Wainwright	24	33	11	24	24	14	12
Yakutat	47	44	24	23	23	10	6

Source: Census of Population and Housing, 1990: Summary Tape File 3C on CD-ROM [machine-readable datafiles]. Prepared by the Bureau of the Census. Washington, DC: The Bureau, 1992. *Notes:* 1. Alaska Native villages (ANVs) constitute tribes, bands, clans, groups, villages, communities, or associations in Alaska that are recognized pursuant to the Alaska Native Claims Settlement Act of 1972, Public Law 92-203. Because ANVs do not have legally designated boundaries, the Census Bureau has established Alaska Native village statistical areas (ANVSAs) for statistical purposes. For the 1990 census, the Census Bureau cooperated with officials of the nonprofit corporation within each participating Alaska Native Regional Corporation (ANRC), as well as other knowledgeable officials, to delineate boundaries that encompass the settled area associated with each ANV.

★ 249 ★

Households

Persons in Households in Selected Tribal Designated Statistical Areas

Tribal Designated Statistical Area[1]	One person	Two persons	Three persons	Four persons	Five persons	Six persons	7 or more persons
Apache Choctaw TDSA (state)	1,991	2,712	1,409	1,251	624	274	114
Chickahominy TDSA (state)	167	282	231	178	57	23	20
Clifton Choctaw TDSA (state)	16	47	51	31	18	15	0
Coharie TDSA (state)	11,582	14,085	8,529	6,184	2,622	798	633
Coquille Indian TDSA	42,453	59,522	24,853	21,363	8,635	3,087	1,354
Delaware-Muncie TDSA (state)	0	27	35	7	28	0	0
Florida Tribe of Eastern Creek TDSA (state)	26	52	29	0	0	0	0
Haliwa-Saponi TDSA (state)	351	625	396	354	204	82	92
Jena Band of Choctaw TDSA (state)	4,591	6,568	4,071	3,562	1,507	407	292
Klamath TDSA	4,279	5,721	2,568	2,040	1,072	298	143
Lumbee TDSA (state)	3,059	3,823	3,185	2,863	1,858	613	468
Meherrin TDSA (state)	4,902	6,156	3,741	3,132	1,331	673	409
Mohegan TDSA (state)	2,569	3,230	1,826	1,412	533	122	107
Ramapough TDSA (state)	52	51	31	18	29	6	17
United Houma Nation TDSA (state)	63,272	82,135	56,616	50,218	24,464	8,799	4,999
Waccamaw Siouan TDSA (state)	114	231	174	200	96	41	8
Wampanoag-Gay Head TDSA	1,686	1,658	740	660	249	42	41

Source: Census of Population and Housing, 1990: Summary Tape File 3C on CD-ROM [machine-readable datafiles]. Prepared by the Bureau of the Census. Washington, DC: The Bureau, 1992. *Notes:* 1. Tribal designated statistical areas (TDSAs) are areas, delineated outside Oklahoma by federally- and state-recognized tribes without a land base or associated trust lands, to provide statistical areas for which the Census Bureau tabulates data. TDSAs represent areas generally containing the American Indian population over which federally-recognized tribes have jurisdiction and areas in which state tribes provide benefits and services to their members. The names of TDSAs delineated by state-recognized tribes are followed by "(state)." The Census Bureau did not recognize TDSAs before the 1990 census.

★ 250 ★

Households

Persons in Households in Selected Tribal Jurisdiction Statistical Areas

Tribal Jurisdiction Statistical Area[1]	One person	Two persons	Three persons	Four persons	Five persons	Six persons	7 or more persons
Absentee Shawnee-Citizens Band of Potawatomi TJSA	4,923	10,183	6,101	6,057	2,686	812	338
Caddo-Wichita-Delaware TJSA	738	1,099	483	479	255	56	28
Cherokee TJSA	33,919	50,793	26,085	23,064	10,574	3,558	1,873
Cheyenne-Arapaho TJSA	12,976	18,226	9,179	9,358	4,363	1,115	326
Chickasaw TJSA	24,260	34,196	16,603	15,412	6,198	1,873	700
Choctaw TJSA	19,604	26,437	13,488	12,225	5,132	1,816	776
Creek TJSA	68,010	83,563	42,044	36,366	15,166	4,418	1,697
Iowa TJSA	280	479	237	291	115	40	13
Kaw TJSA	1,136	1,913	767	792	329	68	55
Kiowa-Comanche-Apache-Fort Sill Apache TJSA	16,396	23,525	13,445	12,044	5,116	1,800	769
Otoe-Missouria TJSA	208	287	150	170	85	40	23
Pawnee TJSA	1,354	2,083	964	910	423	124	55
Sac and Fox TJSA	5,388	6,944	3,305	2,822	1,305	415	154
Seminole TJSA	2,281	2,878	1,406	1,278	642	202	104
Tonkawa TJSA	1,343	1,747	684	625	332	116	30
Creek-Seminole Joint Area TJSA	206	297	135	102	92	13	17
Iowa-Sac and Fox Joint Area TJSA	64	94	48	54	41	0	0

Source: Census of Population and Housing, 1990: Summary Tape File 3C on CD-ROM [machine-readable datafiles]. Prepared by the Bureau of the Census. Washington, DC: The Bureau, 1992. *Notes:* 1. Tribal jurisdiction statistical areas (TJSAs) are areas, delineated by federally recognized tribes in Oklahoma without a reservation, for which the Census Bureau tabulates data. TJSAs represent areas generally containing the American Indian population over which one or more tribal governments have jurisdiction. If tribal officials delineated adjacent TJSAs so that they include some duplicate territory, the overlap area is called a "joint use area," which is treated as a separate TJSA for census purposes.

★ 251 ★

Households

Persons in Households on Selected Reservations and Trust Lands

Data are shown for the 50 areas with the largest populations, in number of persons.

American Indian Reservation and Trust Lands[1,2]	One person	Two persons	Three persons	Four persons	Five persons	Six persons	7 or more persons
Agua Caliente Reservation	4,008	4,822	930	420	156	63	36
Allegany Reservation	931	824	447	401	198	70	32
Blackfeet Reservation	387	490	422	363	338	229	132
Cheyenne River Reservation	499	522	353	371	247	163	217
Coeur d'Alene Reservation and Trust Lands, ID	459	820	335	355	153	52	28
Colorado River Reservation	546	951	377	451	212	89	123
Colville Reservation	504	733	390	403	200	130	61
Crow Reservation and Trust Lands, MT	209	373	277	302	197	160	174
Eastern Cherokee Reservation	317	576	468	344	242	65	54
Flathead Reservation	2,018	2,710	1,151	1,009	610	255	161
Fort Apache Reservation	309	366	364	442	491	259	359
Fort Berthold Reservation	405	426	242	271	234	54	88
Fort Hall Reservation and Trust Lands, ID	242	411	229	220	131	125	126

[Continued]

★ 251 ★

Persons in Households on Selected Reservations and Trust Lands
[Continued]

American Indian Reservation and Trust Lands[1,2]	One person	Two persons	Three persons	Four persons	Five persons	Six persons	7 or more persons
Fort Peck Reservation	673	810	571	568	418	207	142
Gila River Reservation	259	418	428	437	360	336	183
Hopi Reservation and Trust Lands, AZ	265	251	331	272	293	173	212
Isabella Reservation and Trust Lands, MI	1,832	2,662	1,461	1,446	682	171	108
Laguna Pueblo and Trust Lands, NM	178	199	195	165	134	88	82
Lake Traverse (Sisseton) Reservation	1,035	1,288	519	533	381	138	117
Leech Lake Reservation	656	1,052	486	380	316	130	74
Mississippi Choctaw Reservation and Trust Lands, MS	17	160	159	257	205	90	87
Muckleshoot Reservation and Trust Lands, WA	295	430	186	217	91	44	61
Navajo Reservation and Trust Lands, AZ–NM–UT	6,183	5,517	5,375	5,932	5,660	3,931	4,783
Nez Perce Reservation	1,421	2,387	904	819	427	165	64
Northern Cheyenne Reservation and Trust Lands, MT–SD	127	181	148	189	167	83	132
Omaha Reservation	408	502	222	264	154	100	76
Oneida (West) Reservation	695	1,635	1,136	1,301	624	239	83
Osage Reservation	3,544	5,081	2,566	2,554	978	412	176
Papago Reservation	278	495	332	374	296	211	249
Pine Ridge Reservation and Trust Lands, NE–SD	412	441	381	371	377	295	557
Port Madison Reservation	425	678	299	294	95	47	25
Puyallup Reservation and Trust Lands, WA	2,537	3,931	2,033	1,851	899	320	217
Red Lake Reservation	113	169	158	190	128	119	79
Rosebud Reservation and Trust Lands, SD	451	421	485	391	296	191	327
Salt River Reservation	412	509	182	181	199	69	74
San Carlos Reservation	232	179	233	348	267	249	239
Sandia Pueblo	202	375	291	243	131	51	17
San Juan Pueblo	261	367	371	361	182	84	42
Santa Clara Pueblo	774	1,039	706	627	318	129	47
Southern Ute Reservation	460	855	486	510	267	95	41
Standing Rock Reservation	446	532	365	360	291	143	208
Taos Pueblo and Trust Lands, NM	608	538	323	259	108	45	31
Tulalip Reservation	460	954	387	402	200	84	77
Turtle Mountain Reservation and Trust Lands, ND–SD	354	410	418	408	254	137	125
Uintah and Ouray Reservation	720	1,327	694	773	626	458	367
White Earth Reservation	671	899	485	401	298	157	97
Wind River Reservation	1,468	2,368	1,223	1,263	715	284	210
Yakima Reservation and Trust Lands, WA	1,353	2,057	1,262	1,226	862	378	693
Yankton Reservation	579	627	279	283	201	105	81
Zuni Pueblo	177	181	240	292	306	199	274

Source: Census of Population and Housing, 1990: Summary Tape File 3C on CD-ROM [machine-readable datafiles]. Prepared by the Bureau of the Census. Washington, DC: The Bureau, 1992. *Notes:* 1. Federal American Indian reservations are areas with boundaries established by treaty, statute, and/or executive or court order, and recognized by the federal government as territory in which American Indian tribes have jurisdiction. State reservations are lands held in trust by state governments for the use and benefit of a given tribe. The reservations and their boundaries were identified for the 1990 census by the Bureau of Indian Affairs (BIA), Department of Interior (for federal reservations), and state governments (for state reservations). The names of American Indian reservations recognized by state governments, but not by the federal government, are followed by "state." Areas composed of reservation lands that are administered jointly and/or are claimed by two reservations, as identified by the BIA, are called "joint areas," and are treated as separate American Indian reservations for census purposes. Federal reservations may cross state boundaries, and federal and state reservations may cross county, county subdivision, and place boundaries. For reservations that cross state boundaries, only the portion of the reservations in a given state is shown in the data products for that state; the entire reservations are shown in data products for the United States. 2. Trust lands are property associated with a particular American Indian reservation or tribe, held in trust by the federal government. Trust lands may be held in trust either for a tribe (tribal trust lands) or for an individual member of a tribe (individual trust land). Trust lands recognized for the 1990 census comprised all tribal trust lands and inhabited individual trust lands located outside of a reservation boundary. As with other American Indian areas, trust lands may be located in more than one state. Only the trust lands in a given state are shown in the data products for that state; all trust lands associated with a reservation or tribe are shown in data products for the United States. The Census Bureau first reported data for tribal trust lands for the 1980 census.

Employment

★ 252 ★

Number of Workers in Families (1989) in Selected Alaska Native Villages

Data are shown for the 50 areas with the largest populations, in number of persons.

Alaska Native Village Statistical Area[1]	No workers	One worker	Two workers	Three or more workers
Akiachak	12	19	41	23
Akutan	2	3	8	2
Alakanuk	8	29	35	24
Andreafsky	1	21	36	24
Angoon	13	16	66	33
Aniak	2	39	63	11
Barrow	25	137	327	96
Bethel	40	282	538	144
Chevak	6	20	55	19
Copper Center	8	46	65	5
Craig	6	77	195	35
Dillingham	16	139	272	69
Emmonak	11	37	35	36
Fort Yukon	22	59	55	11
Galena	4	48	58	9
Gambell	5	24	42	28
Grouse Creek Group	1	44	100	13
Hoonah	17	35	78	47
Hooper Bay	16	39	62	37
Kake	10	54	91	22
Kasigluk	5	15	45	20
King Cove	5	18	30	10
King Salmon	0	34	61	29
Kipnuk	21	26	26	7
Klawock	12	56	85	24
Kotlik	8	26	34	21
Kotzebue	32	171	256	114
Kwethluk	11	50	28	19
McGrath	5	32	76	21
Mountain Village	8	52	40	34
Naknek	3	18	90	20
Ninilchik	238	799	1,320	274
Noorvik	2	36	28	31
Pilot Station	9	31	41	10
Point Hope	2	39	69	14
Quinhagak	9	17	68	21
St. Paul	10	36	54	32
Salamatof	13	43	92	26
Sand Point	9	68	73	15

[Continued]

★ 252 ★

Number of Workers in Families (1989) in Selected Alaska Native Villages

[Continued]

Alaska Native Village Statistical Area[1]	No workers	One worker	Two workers	Three or more workers
Savoonga	24	31	35	15
Selawik	11	38	49	14
Shishmaref	4	36	36	11
Stebbins	2	41	27	15
Togiak	11	34	53	29
Tok	20	56	151	28
Toksook Bay	3	6	37	24
Unalakleet	5	39	77	28
Unalaska	4	52	209	32
Wainwright	12	42	48	10
Yakutat	11	23	50	30

Source: Census of Population and Housing, 1990: Summary Tape File 3C on CD-ROM [machine-readable datafiles]. Prepared by the Bureau of the Census. Washington, DC: The Bureau, 1992. Notes: 1. Alaska Native villages (ANVs) constitute tribes, bands, clans, groups, villages, communities, or associations in Alaska that are recognized pursuant to the Alaska Native Claims Settlement Act of 1972, Public Law 92-203. Because ANVs do not have legally designated boundaries, the Census Bureau has established Alaska Native village statistical areas (ANVSAs) for statistical purposes. For the 1990 census, the Census Bureau cooperated with officials of the nonprofit corporation within each participating Alaska Native Regional Corporation (ANRC), as well as other knowledgeable officials, to delineate boundaries that encompass the settled area associated with each ANV.

★ 253 ★

Employment

Number of Workers in Families (1989) in Selected Tribal Designated Statistical Areas

Tribal Designated Statistical Area[1]	No workers	One worker	Two workers	Three or more workers
Apache Choctaw TDSA (state)	1,444	2,160	2,325	361
Chickahominy TDSA (state)	57	204	388	135
Clifton Choctaw TDSA (state)	21	86	55	0
Coharie TDSA (state)	4,313	9,469	14,131	3,947
Coquille Indian TDSA	18,551	31,329	47,202	9,988
Delaware-Muncie TDSA (state)	5	45	41	6
Florida Tribe of Eastern Creek TDSA (state)	47	27	0	0
Haliwa-Saponi TDSA (state)	325	547	661	186
Jena Band of Choctaw TDSA (state)	2,408	5,404	6,910	1,269
Klamath TDSA	1,880	3,151	4,884	1,080
Lumbee TDSA (state)	1,717	3,417	5,361	2,005
Meherrin TDSA (state)	2,315	4,521	6,667	1,644
Mohegan TDSA (state)	946	1,621	3,188	866
Ramapough TDSA (state)	9	43	45	46

[Continued]

★ 253 ★

Number of Workers in Families (1989) in Selected Tribal Designated Statistical Areas

[Continued]

Tribal Designated Statistical Area[1]	No workers	One worker	Two workers	Three or more workers
United Houma Nation TDSA (state)	29,148	71,689	92,262	24,664
Waccamaw Siouan TDSA (state)	100	200	318	120
Wampanoag-Gay Head TDSA	343	785	1,543	306

Source: Census of Population and Housing, 1990: Summary Tape File 3C on CD-ROM [machine-readable datafiles]. Prepared by the Bureau of the Census. Washington, DC: The Bureau, 1992. *Notes:* 1. Tribal designated statistical areas (TDSAs) are areas, delineated outside Oklahoma by federally- and state-recognized tribes without a land base or associated trust lands, to provide statistical areas for which the Census Bureau tabulates data. TDSAs represent areas generally containing the American Indian population over which federally- recognized tribes have jurisdiction and areas in which state tribes provide benefits and services to their members. The names of TDSAs delineated by state-recognized tribes are followed by "(state)." The Census Bureau did not recognize TDSAs before the 1990 census.

★ 254 ★

Employment

Number of Workers in Families (1989) in Selected Tribal Jurisdiction Statistical Areas

Tribal Jurisdiction Statistical Area[1]	No workers	One worker	Two workers	Three or more workers
Absentee Shawnee-Citizens Band of Potawatomi TJSA	3,168	6,960	12,404	3,180
Caddo-Wichita-Delaware TJSA	350	776	1,023	206
Cherokee TJSA	17,817	36,119	47,829	11,151
Cheyenne-Arapaho TJSA	4,287	11,971	20,566	4,429
Chickasaw TJSA	12,352	23,363	30,745	6,885
Choctaw TJSA	11,605	19,238	23,078	4,777
Creek TJSA	21,745	52,450	82,667	17,665
Iowa TJSA	147	371	530	96
Kaw TJSA	561	1,080	1,705	490
Kiowa-Comanche-Apache-Fort Sill Apache TJSA	6,836	18,487	25,500	4,482
Otoe-Missouria TJSA	64	251	334	87
Pawnee TJSA	647	1,464	1,898	465
Sac and Fox TJSA	2,403	4,410	6,421	1,281
Seminole TJSA	1,340	1,888	2,619	571
Tonkawa TJSA	523	1,022	1,524	359
Creek-Seminole Joint Area TJSA	131	242	213	52
Iowa-Sac and Fox Joint Area TJSA	22	53	143	16

Source: Census of Population and Housing, 1990: Summary Tape File 3C on CD-ROM [machine-readable datafiles]. Prepared by the Bureau of the Census. Washington, DC: The Bureau, 1992. *Notes:* 1. Tribal jurisdiction statistical areas (TJSAs) are areas, delineated by federally recognized tribes in Oklahoma without a reservation, for which the Census Bureau tabulates data. TJSAs represent areas generally containing the American Indian population over which one or more tribal governments have jurisdiction. If tribal officials delineated adjacent TJSAs so that they include some duplicate territory, the overlap area is called a "joint use area," which is treated as a separate TJSA for census purposes.

★ 255 ★

Employment

Number of Workers in Families (1989) on Selected Reservations and Trust Lands

Data are shown for the 50 areas with the largest populations, in number of persons.

American Indian Reservation and Trust Lands[1,2]	No workers	One worker	Two workers	Three or more workers
Agua Caliente Reservation	1,850	1,900	1,574	277
Allegany Reservation	300	564	748	244
Blackfeet Reservation	239	754	749	173
Cheyenne River Reservation	303	564	765	201
Coeur d'Alene Reservation and Trust Lands, ID	248	534	735	156
Colorado River Reservation	422	714	731	229
Colville Reservation	317	597	730	163
Crow Reservation and Trust Lands, MT	194	410	686	162
Eastern Cherokee Reservation	178	541	777	181
Flathead Reservation	874	1,893	2,382	503
Fort Apache Reservation	349	900	739	224
Fort Berthold Reservation	182	426	517	155
Fort Hall Reservation and Trust Lands, ID	146	313	585	167
Fort Peck Reservation	303	809	1,273	284
Gila River Reservation	644	754	505	172
Hopi Reservation and Trust Lands, AZ	265	603	471	164
Isabella Reservation and Trust Lands, MI	726	1,585	2,790	692
Laguna Pueblo and Trust Lands, NM	132	250	371	92
Lake Traverse (Sisseton) Reservation	284	970	1,320	334
Leech Lake Reservation	555	698	893	190
Mississippi Choctaw Reservation and Trust Lands, MS	123	274	366	113
Muckleshoot Reservation and Trust Lands, WA	142	278	406	130
Navajo Reservation and Trust Lands, AZ–NM–UT	8,461	11,182	8,308	2,711
Nez Perce Reservation	752	1,451	1,959	410
Northern Cheyenne Reservation and Trust Lands, MT–SD	101	326	362	88
Omaha Reservation	180	380	569	149
Oneida (West) Reservation	268	1,176	2,508	830
Osage Reservation	1,633	3,611	5,136	1,180
Papago Reservation	656	968	148	52
Pine Ridge Reservation and Trust Lands, NE–SD	589	862	717	167
Port Madison Reservation	226	374	633	114
Puyallup Reservation and Trust Lands, WA	1,343	2,362	3,876	892
Red Lake Reservation	250	300	226	45
Rosebud Reservation and Trust Lands, SD	483	753	632	191
Salt River Reservation	314	382	399	81
San Carlos Reservation	358	593	451	103
Sandia Pueblo	123	443	380	109
San Juan Pueblo	192	482	465	224
Santa Clara Pueblo	454	944	1,099	278
Southern Ute Reservation	208	624	1,075	238
Standing Rock Reservation	307	661	695	179
Taos Pueblo and Trust Lands, NM	175	427	495	122
Tulalip Reservation	306	482	952	213
Turtle Mountain Reservation and Trust Lands, ND–SD	497	607	433	171

[Continued]

★ 255 ★

Number of Workers in Families (1989) on Selected Reservations and Trust Lands
[Continued]

American Indian Reservation and Trust Lands[1,2]	No workers	One worker	Two workers	Three or more workers
Uintah and Ouray Reservation	462	1,415	1,844	455
White Earth Reservation	430	680	913	267
Wind River Reservation	828	1,769	2,564	678
Yakima Reservation and Trust Lands, WA	1,017	1,920	2,366	1,027
Yankton Reservation	259	452	678	155
Zuni Pueblo	90	356	537	497

Source: Census of Population and Housing, 1990: Summary Tape File 3C on CD-ROM [machine-readable datafiles]. Prepared by the Bureau of the Census. Washington, DC: The Bureau, 1992. *Notes:* 1. Federal American Indian reservations are areas with boundaries established by treaty, statute, and/or executive or court order, and recognized by the federal government as territory in which American Indian tribes have jurisdiction. State reservations are lands held in trust by state governments for the use and benefit of a given tribe. The reservations and their boundaries were identified for the 1990 census by the Bureau of Indian Affairs (BIA), Department of Interior (for federal reservations), and state governments (for state reservations). The names of American Indian reservations recognized by state governments, but not by the federal government, are followed by "state." Areas composed of reservation lands that are administered jointly and/or are claimed by two reservations, as identified by the BIA, are called "joint areas," and are treated as separate American Indian reservations for census purposes. Federal reservations may cross state boundaries, and federal and state reservations may cross county, county subdivision, and place boundaries. For reservations that cross state boundaries, only the portion of the reservations in a given state is shown in the data products for that state; the entire reservations are shown in data products for the United States. 2. Trust lands are property associated with a particular American Indian reservation or tribe, held in trust by the federal government. Trust lands may be held in trust either for a tribe (tribal trust lands) or for an individual member of a tribe (individual trust land). Trust lands recognized for the 1990 census comprised all tribal trust lands and inhabited individual trust lands located outside of a reservation boundary. As with other American Indian areas, trust lands may be located in more than one state. Only the trust lands in a given state are shown in the data products for that state; all trust lands associated with a reservation or tribe are shown in data products for the United States. The Census Bureau first reported data for tribal trust lands for the 1980 census.

Income and Earnings

★ 256 ★

Median Family Income (1989) in Selected Alaska Native Villages

Data are shown for the 50 areas with the largest populations, in number of persons.

Alaska Native Village Statistical Area[1]	Median income (dollars)
Akiachak	29,250
Akutan	31,875
Alakanuk	23,250
Andreafsky	30,833
Angoon	35,625
Aniak	34,792
Barrow	68,960
Bethel	45,203

[Continued]

★ 256 ★

Median Family Income (1989) in Selected Alaska Native Villages
[Continued]

Alaska Native Village Statistical Area[1]	Median income (dollars)
Chevak	22,083
Copper Center	42,500
Craig	50,562
Dillingham	47,857
Emmonak	26,406
Fort Yukon	20,417
Galena	34,375
Gambell	17,188
Grouse Creek Group	50,775
Hoonah	40,781
Hooper Bay	19,688
Kake	37,375
Kasigluk	26,719
King Cove	63,419
King Salmon	62,152
Kipnuk	4,999
Klawock	43,304
Kotlik	22,083
Kotzebue	44,632
Kwethluk	16,786
McGrath	39,167
Mountain Village	25,500
Naknek	56,195
Ninilchik	42,546
Noorvik	32,708
Pilot Station	16,563
Point Hope	41,667
Quinhagak	17,969
St. Paul	48,000
Salamatof	42,955
Sand Point	43,125
Savoonga	12,411
Selawik	21,833
Shishmaref	14,875
Stebbins	23,250
Togiak	15,781
Tok	32,039
Toksook Bay	23,125
Unalakleet	40,347
Unalaska	61,927

[Continued]

★ 256 ★

Median Family Income (1989) in Selected Alaska Native Villages
[Continued]

Alaska Native Village Statistical Area[1]	Median income (dollars)
Wainwright	38,929
Yakutat	40,714

Source: Census of Population and Housing, 1990: Summary Tape File 3C on CD-ROM [machine-readable datafiles]. Prepared by the Bureau of the Census. Washington, DC: The Bureau, 1992.
Notes: 1. Alaska Native villages (ANVs) constitute tribes, bands, clans, groups, villages, communities, or associations in Alaska that are recognized pursuant to the Alaska Native Claims Settlement Act of 1972, Public Law 92-203. Because ANVs do not have legally designated boundaries, the Census Bureau has established Alaska Native village statistical areas (ANVSAs) for statistical purposes. For the 1990 census, the Census Bureau cooperated with officials of the nonprofit corporation within each participating Alaska Native Regional Corporation (ANRC), as well as other knowledgeable officials, to delineate boundaries that encompass the settled area associated with each ANV.

★ 257 ★

Income and Earnings

Median Family Income (1989) in Selected Tribal Designated Statistical Areas

Tribal Designated Statistical Area[1]	Median income (dollars)
Apache Choctaw TDSA (state)	20,705
Chickahominy TDSA (state)	33,640
Clifton Choctaw TDSA (state)	16,389
Coharie TDSA (state)	24,502
Coquille Indian TDSA	29,179
Delaware-Muncie TDSA (state)	32,344
Florida Tribe of Eastern Creek TDSA (state)	30,139
Haliwa-Saponi TDSA (state)	17,018
Jena Band of Choctaw TDSA (state)	25,348
Klamath TDSA	27,734
Lumbee TDSA (state)	22,601
Meherrin TDSA (state)	22,499
Mohegan TDSA (state)	38,519
Ramapough TDSA (state)	29,821
United Houma Nation TDSA (state)	30,050
Waccamaw Siouan TDSA (state)	26,702
Wampanoag-Gay Head TDSA	41,369

Source: Census of Population and Housing, 1990: Summary Tape File 3C on CD-ROM [machine-readable datafiles]. Prepared by the Bureau of the Census. Washington, DC: The Bureau, 1992.
Notes: 1. Tribal designated statistical areas (TDSAs) are areas, delineated outside Oklahoma by federally- and state-recognized tribes without a land base or associated trust lands, to provide statistical areas for which the Census Bureau tabulates data. TDSAs represent areas generally containing the American Indian population over which federally-recognized tribes have jurisdiction and areas in which state tribes provide benefits and services to their members. The names of TDSAs delineated by state-recognized tribes are followed by "(state)." The Census Bureau did not recognize TDSAs before the 1990 census.

★ 258 ★

Income and Earnings

Median Family Income (1989) in Selected Tribal Jurisdiction Statistical Areas

Tribal Jurisdiction Statistical Area[1]	Median income (dollars)
Absentee Shawnee-Citizens Band of Potawatomi TJSA	30,914
Caddo-Wichita-Delaware TJSA	23,639
Cherokee TJSA	25,561
Cheyenne-Arapaho TJSA	29,426
Chickasaw TJSA	25,316
Choctaw TJSA	20,453
Creek TJSA	32,329
Iowa TJSA	22,541
Kaw TJSA	42,652
Kiowa-Comanche-Apache-Fort Sill Apache TJSA	24,757
Otoe-Missouria TJSA	25,455
Pawnee TJSA	25,424
Sac and Fox TJSA	25,580
Seminole TJSA	21,787
Tonkawa TJSA	24,392
Creek-Seminole Joint Area TJSA	18,654
Iowa-Sac and Fox Joint Area TJSA	29,900

Source: Census of Population and Housing, 1990: Summary Tape File 3C on CD-ROM [machine-readable datafiles]. Prepared by the Bureau of the Census. Washington, DC: The Bureau, 1992. *Notes:* 1. Tribal jurisdiction statistical areas (TJSAs) are areas, delineated by federally recognized tribes in Oklahoma without a reservation, for which the Census Bureau tabulates data. TJSAs represent areas generally containing the American Indian population over which one or more tribal governments have jurisdiction. If tribal officials delineated adjacent TJSAs so that they include some duplicate territory, the overlap area is called a "joint use area," which is treated as a separate TJSA for census purposes.

★ 259 ★

Income and Earnings

Median Family Income (1989) on Selected Reservations and Trust Lands

Data are shown for the 50 areas with the largest populations, in number of persons.

American Indian Reservation and Trust Lands[1,2]	Median income (dollars)
Agua Caliente Reservation	35,335
Allegany Reservation	23,259
Blackfeet Reservation	15,371
Cheyenne River Reservation	15,797
Coeur d'Alene Reservation and Trust Lands, ID	25,123
Colorado River Reservation	21,816
Colville Reservation	22,154
Crow Reservation and Trust Lands, MT	18,726

[Continued]

★ 259 ★

Median Family Income (1989) on Selected Reservations and Trust Lands
[Continued]

American Indian Reservation and Trust Lands[1,2]	Median income (dollars)
Eastern Cherokee Reservation	17,121
Flathead Reservation	22,548
Fort Apache Reservation	13,371
Fort Berthold Reservation	20,000
Fort Hall Reservation and Trust Lands, ID	22,997
Fort Peck Reservation	21,019
Gila River Reservation	10,220
Hopi Reservation and Trust Lands, AZ	14,464
Isabella Reservation and Trust Lands, MI	30,246
Laguna Pueblo and Trust Lands, NM	18,641
Lake Traverse (Sisseton) Reservation	21,148
Leech Lake Reservation	20,276
Mississippi Choctaw Reservation and Trust Lands, MS	16,479
Muckleshoot Reservation and Trust Lands, WA	33,646
Navajo Reservation and Trust Lands, AZ–NM–UT	11,672
Nez Perce Reservation	24,903
Northern Cheyenne Reservation and Trust Lands, MT–SD	14,815
Omaha Reservation	21,677
Oneida (West) Reservation	44,418
Osage Reservation	28,812
Papago Reservation	7,940
Pine Ridge Reservation and Trust Lands, NE–SD	11,760
Port Madison Reservation	34,399
Puyallup Reservation and Trust Lands, WA	36,119
Red Lake Reservation	12,734
Rosebud Reservation and Trust Lands, SD	13,266
Salt River Reservation	16,000
San Carlos Reservation	9,891
Sandia Pueblo	19,556
San Juan Pueblo	18,739
Santa Clara Pueblo	25,255
Southern Ute Reservation	27,735
Standing Rock Reservation	16,545
Taos Pueblo and Trust Lands, NM	17,104
Tulalip Reservation	36,349
Turtle Mountain Reservation and Trust Lands, ND–SD	10,671
Uintah and Ouray Reservation	24,770
White Earth Reservation	19,300
Wind River Reservation	25,072
Yakima Reservation and Trust Lands, WA	20,926

[Continued]

★ 259 ★

Median Family Income (1989) on Selected Reservations and Trust Lands
[Continued]

American Indian Reservation and Trust Lands[1,2]	Median income (dollars)
Yankton Reservation	19,073
Zuni Pueblo	15,918

Source: Census of Population and Housing, 1990: Summary Tape File 3C on CD-ROM [machine-readable datafiles]. Prepared by the Bureau of the Census. Washington, DC: The Bureau, 1992. *Notes:* 1. Federal American Indian reservations are areas with boundaries established by treaty, statute, and/or executive or court order, and recognized by the federal government as territory in which American Indian tribes have jurisdiction. State reservations are lands held in trust by state governments for the use and benefit of a given tribe. The reservations and their boundaries were identified for the 1990 census by the Bureau of Indian Affairs (BIA), Department of Interior (for federal reservations), and state governments (for state reservations). The names of American Indian reservations recognized by state governments, but not by the federal government, are followed by "state." Areas composed of reservation lands that are administered jointly and/or are claimed by two reservations, as identified by the BIA, are called "joint areas," and are treated as separate American Indian reservations for census purposes. Federal reservations may cross state boundaries, and federal and state reservations may cross county, county subdivision, and place boundaries. For reservations that cross state boundaries, only the portion of the reservations in a given state is shown in the data products for that state; the entire reservations are shown in data products for the United States. 2. Trust lands are property associated with a particular American Indian reservation or tribe, held in trust by the federal government. Trust lands may be held in trust either for a tribe (tribal trust lands) or for an individual member of a tribe (individual trust land). Trust lands recognized for the 1990 census comprised all tribal trust lands and inhabited individual trust lands located outside of a reservation boundary. As with other American Indian areas, trust lands may be located in more than one state. Only the trust lands in a given state are shown in the data products for that state; all trust lands associated with a reservation or tribe are shown in data products for the United States. The Census Bureau first reported data for tribal trust lands for the 1980 census.

Marriage

★ 260 ★

Marital Status of Females in Selected Alaska Native Villages

Data are shown for the 50 areas with the largest populations, in number of persons.

Alaska Native Village Statistical Area[1]	Never married	Now married			Widowed	Divorced
		Married, spouse present	Married, spouse absent			
			Separated	Other		
Akiachak	70	80	0	3	9	4
Akutan	38	6	10	10	11	16
Alakanuk	72	74	0	0	15	0
Andreafsky	43	62	4	6	5	0
Angoon	35	113	2	6	8	6
Aniak	31	96	8	2	11	7
Barrow	253	401	24	24	39	106
Bethel	484	696	56	55	101	145
Chevak	71	64	0	3	17	2
Copper Center	18	89	9	2	12	19
Craig	70	243	17	2	7	45

[Continued]

★ 260 ★

Marital Status of Females in Selected Alaska Native Villages
[Continued]

Alaska Native Village Statistical Area[1]	Never married	Now married			Widowed	Divorced
		Married, spouse present	Married, spouse absent			
			Separated	Other		
Dillingham	149	408	13	6	49	73
Emmonak	91	63	1	2	17	8
Fort Yukon	67	70	8	2	10	11
Galena	53	83	0	3	11	27
Gambell	58	58	0	7	11	3
Grouse Creek Group	36	125	12	2	8	26
Hoonah	61	136	0	3	18	24
Hooper Bay	76	99	4	3	19	7
Kake	36	144	2	2	18	12
Kasigluk	49	74	0	2	15	3
King Cove	19	57	0	41	17	13
King Salmon	54	94	5	10	5	12
Kipnuk	43	80	1	2	9	0
Klawock	39	136	5	0	15	32
Kotlik	46	71	0	0	11	7
Kotzebue	306	366	20	38	67	73
Kwethluk	34	83	2	6	18	0
McGrath	57	96	0	8	8	17
Mountain Village	91	87	3	0	23	7
Naknek	39	103	5	7	15	20
Ninilchik	598	2,266	72	27	154	392
Noorvik	65	59	4	5	9	9
Pilot Station	52	66	1	6	6	2
Point Hope	68	73	2	12	5	7
Quinhagak	46	82	10	2	7	2
St. Paul	55	91	2	12	16	15
Salamatof	60	150	8	0	23	34
Sand Point	71	121	0	10	23	21
Savoonga	68	62	0	2	24	5
Selawik	47	59	2	2	13	8
Shishmaref	76	45	2	0	12	2
Stebbins	74	49	0	4	7	3
Togiak	57	83	4	3	21	10
Tok	47	210	9	10	17	22
Toksook Bay	66	59	0	0	3	0
Unalakleet	31	117	0	0	12	5
Unalaska	214	235	13	93	12	184
Wainwright	36	84	0	5	19	5
Yakutat	46	81	7	5	18	19

Source: Census of Population and Housing, 1990: Summary Tape File 3C on CD-ROM [machine-readable datafiles]. Prepared by the Bureau of the Census. Washington, DC: The Bureau, 1992. *Notes:* 1. Alaska Native villages (ANVs) constitute tribes, bands, clans, groups, villages, communities, or associations in Alaska that are recognized pursuant to the Alaska Native Claims Settlement Act of 1972, Public Law 92-203. Because ANVs do not have legally designated boundaries, the Census Bureau has established Alaska Native village statistical areas (ANVSAs) for statistical purposes. For the 1990 census, the Census Bureau cooperated with officials of the nonprofit corporation within each participating Alaska Native Regional Corporation (ANRC), as well as other knowledgeable officials, to delineate boundaries that encompass the settles area associated with each ANV.

★ 261 ★

Marriage

Marital Status of Females in Selected Tribal Designated Statistical Areas

| Tribal Designated Statistical Area[1] | Never married | Now married | | | Widowed | Divorced |
| | | Married, spouse present | Married, spouse absent | | | |
			Separated	Other		
Apache Choctaw TDSA (state)	1,490	4,999	315	204	1,479	490
Chickahominy TDSA (state)	281	586	17	6	115	95
Clifton Choctaw TDSA (state)	40	87	0	25	49	0
Coharie TDSA (state)	11,151	23,080	2,294	767	8,305	3,900
Coquille Indian TDSA	33,528	87,305	3,473	2,441	19,831	20,847
Delaware-Muncie TDSA (state)	11	85	0	0	7	0
Florida Tribe of Eastern Creek TDSA (state)	0	52	0	14	0	19
Haliwa-Saponi TDSA (state)	783	1,145	126	38	310	84
Jena Band of Choctaw TDSA (state)	4,512	13,374	637	393	3,382	1,820
Klamath TDSA	2,622	9,009	350	316	2,016	1,873
Lumbee TDSA (state)	6,130	8,329	990	407	2,467	1,403
Meherrin TDSA (state)	5,386	11,113	1,012	367	3,821	1,591
Mohegan TDSA (state)	2,373	4,972	201	93	1,325	1,177
Ramapough TDSA (state)	102	130	0	3	43	12
United Houma Nation TDSA (state)	71,499	171,697	11,750	4,896	36,334	29,770
Waccamaw Siouan TDSA (state)	249	625	37	8	85	116
Wampanoag-Gay Head TDSA	1,102	2,417	115	45	539	716

Source: Census of Population and Housing, 1990: Summary Tape File 3C on CD-ROM [machine-readable datafiles]. Prepared by the Bureau of the Census. Washington, DC: The Bureau, 1992. *Notes:* 1. Tribal designated statistical areas (TDSAs) are areas, delineated outside Oklahoma by federally- and state-recognized tribes without a land base or associated trust lands, to provide statistical areas for which the Census Bureau tabulates data. TDSAs represent areas generally containing the American Indian population over which federally-recognized tribes have jurisdiction and areas in which state tribes provide benefits and services to their members. The names of TDSAs delineated by state-recognized tribes are followed by "(state)." The Census Bureau did not recognize TDSAs before the 1990 census.

★ 262 ★

Marriage

Marital Status of Females in Selected Tribal Jurisdiction Statistical Areas

| Tribal Jurisdiction Statistical Area[1] | Never married | Now married | | | Widowed | Divorced |
| | | Married, spouse present | Married, spouse absent | | | |
			Separated	Other		
Absentee Shawnee-Citizens Band of Potawatomi TJSA	4,704	22,381	444	413	3,188	3,017
Caddo-Wichita-Delaware TJSA	354	2,091	40	41	500	215
Cherokee TJSA	24,492	92,469	3,054	2,398	21,590	16,699
Cheyenne-Arapaho TJSA	9,010	35,497	903	915	8,150	4,744
Chickasaw TJSA	14,409	62,836	1,760	1,398	16,925	9,300
Choctaw TJSA	11,899	47,906	1,693	1,167	14,409	8,298
Creek TJSA	45,840	144,273	4,411	3,720	31,018	31,579
Iowa TJSA	189	1,057	16	26	202	111
Kaw TJSA	632	3,545	27	86	712	324
Kiowa-Comanche-Apache-Fort Sill Apache TJSA	11,718	45,089	1,678	1,481	10,291	7,961
Otoe-Missouria TJSA	145	595	20	11	127	112
Pawnee TJSA	785	3,931	92	55	830	497

[Continued]

★ 262 ★

Marital Status of Females in Selected Tribal Jurisdiction Statistical Areas
[Continued]

| Tribal Jurisdiction Statistical Area[1] | Never married | Now married | | | Widowed | Divorced |
| | | Married, spouse present | Married, spouse absent | | | |
			Separated	Other		
Sac and Fox TJSA	2,978	12,020	348	220	3,694	2,152
Seminole TJSA	1,457	5,240	118	156	1,914	683
Tonkawa TJSA	721	2,845	41	76	951	421
Creek-Seminole Joint Area TJSA	180	504	27	12	152	85
Iowa-Sac and Fox Joint Area TJSA	49	218	3	0	22	16

Source: Census of Population and Housing, 1990: Summary Tape File 3C on CD-ROM [machine-readable datafiles]. Prepared by the Bureau of the Census. Washington, DC: The Bureau, 1992. *Notes:* 1. Tribal jurisdiction statistical areas (TJSAs) are areas, delineated by federally recognized tribes in Oklahoma without a reservation, for which the Census Bureau tabulates data. TJSAs represent areas generally containing the American Indian population over which one or more tribal governments have jurisdiction. If tribal officials delineated adjacent TJSAs so that they include some duplicate territory, the overlap area is called a "joint use area," which is treated as a separate TJSA for census purposes.

★ 263 ★

Marriage

Marital Status of Females on Selected Reservations and Trust Lands

Data are shown for the 50 areas with the largest populations, in number of persons.

| American Indian Reservation and Trust Lands[1,2] | Never married | Now married | | | Widowed | Divorced |
| | | Married, spouse present | Married, spouse absent | | | |
			Separated	Other		
Agua Caliente Reservation	1,084	4,726	179	126	2,192	1,443
Allegany Reservation	716	1,346	131	37	616	257
Blackfeet Reservation	826	1,280	65	118	282	176
Cheyenne River Reservation	667	1,206	37	87	315	269
Coeur d'Alene Reservation and Trust Lands, ID	288	1,461	22	51	202	126
Colorado River Reservation	677	1,566	78	122	311	334
Colville Reservation	565	1,173	104	26	293	318
Crow Reservation and Trust Lands, MT	503	1,251	41	60	109	191
Eastern Cherokee Reservation	556	1,090	65	60	284	276
Flathead Reservation	1,366	4,404	156	81	1,177	856
Fort Apache Reservation	982	1,504	58	194	238	327
Fort Berthold Reservation	512	875	62	39	249	207
Fort Hall Reservation and Trust Lands, ID	348	935	34	53	159	213
Fort Peck Reservation	960	1,836	90	58	431	368
Gila River Reservation	1,522	976	93	56	430	173
Hopi Reservation and Trust Lands, AZ	865	917	72	91	280	238
Isabella Reservation and Trust Lands, MI	2,456	4,705	98	78	929	800
Laguna Pueblo and Trust Lands, NM	330	705	47	59	212	70
Lake Traverse (Sisseton) Reservation	756	2,180	67	69	713	249
Leech Lake Reservation	732	1,726	39	37	411	234
Mississippi Choctaw Reservation and Trust Lands, MS	515	498	57	30	131	187
Muckleshoot Reservation and Trust Lands, WA	305	732	53	13	155	147
Navajo Reservation and Trust Lands, AZ–NM–UT	17,686	19,928	2,007	2,219	4,314	2,807
Nez Perce Reservation	817	3,879	117	100	697	552
Northern Cheyenne Reservation and Trust Lands, MT–SD	429	524	28	45	68	181
Omaha Reservation	413	1,006	60	32	283	95
Oneida (West) Reservation	1,484	4,093	92	57	294	451
Osage Reservation	2,157	9,813	257	206	2,220	1,572

[Continued]

★ 263 ★

Marital Status of Females on Selected Reservations and Trust Lands
[Continued]

| American Indian Reservation and Trust Lands[1,2] | Never married | Now married | | | | Widowed | Divorced |
| | | Married, spouse present | Married, spouse absent | | | |
			Separated	Other		
Papago Reservation	1,599	601	74	89	363	234
Pine Ridge Reservation and Trust Lands, NE–SD	1,401	1,278	96	126	352	344
Port Madison Reservation	268	1,145	21	22	156	192
Puyallup Reservation and Trust Lands, WA	2,440	6,658	383	199	1,006	1,498
Red Lake Reservation	554	398	36	10	115	55
Rosebud Reservation and Trust Lands, SD	1,136	1,096	59	81	322	429
Salt River Reservation	483	723	63	88	326	169
San Carlos Reservation	748	966	40	104	227	213
Sandia Pueblo	344	746	37	19	106	208
San Juan Pueblo	507	910	36	17	232	192
Santa Clara Pueblo	1,049	1,940	96	22	465	422
Southern Ute Reservation	509	1,760	33	57	221	267
Standing Rock Reservation	705	1,220	33	39	220	355
Taos Pueblo and Trust Lands, NM	525	794	49	23	245	308
Tulalip Reservation	416	1,610	58	41	203	308
Turtle Mountain Reservation and Trust Lands, ND–SD	961	779	99	18	234	271
Uintah and Ouray Reservation	1,061	3,521	100	83	464	307
White Earth Reservation	624	1,799	28	42	420	207
Wind River Reservation	1,417	4,529	145	156	870	869
Yakima Reservation and Trust Lands, WA	2,454	4,696	355	264	988	663
Yankton Reservation	533	1,203	28	62	378	133
Zuni Pueblo	801	1,163	130	157	265	150

Source: Census of Population and Housing, 1990: Summary Tape File 3C on CD-ROM [machine-readable datafiles]. Prepared by the Bureau of the Census. Washington, DC: The Bureau, 1992. *Notes:* 1. Federal American Indian reservations are areas with boundaries established by treaty, statute, and/or executive or court order, and recognized by the federal government as territory in which American Indian tribes have jurisdiction. State reservations are lands held in trust by state governments for the use and benefit of a given tribe. The reservations and their boundaries were identified for the 1990 census by the Bureau of Indian Affairs (BIA), Department of Interior (for federal reservations), and state governments (for state reservations). The names of American Indian reservations recognized by state governments, but not by the federal government, are followed by "state." Areas composed of reservation lands that are administered jointly and/or are claimed by two reservations, as identified by the BIA, are called "joint areas," and are treated as separate American Indian reservations for census purposes. Federal reservations may cross state boundaries, and federal and state reservations may cross county, county subdivision, and place boundaries. For reservations that cross state boundaries, only the portion of the reservations in a given state is shown in the data products for that state; the entire reservations are shown in data products for the United States. 2. Trust lands are property associated with a particular American Indian reservation or tribe, held in trust by the federal government. Trust lands may be held in trust either for a tribe (tribal trust lands) or for an individual member of a tribe (individual trust land). Trust lands recognized for the 1990 census comprised all tribal trust lands and inhabited individual trust lands located outside of a reservation boundary. As with other American Indian areas, trust lands may be located in more than one state. Only the trust lands in a given state are shown in the data products for that state; all trust lands associated with a reservation or tribe are shown in data products for the United States. The Census Bureau first reported data for tribal trust lands for the 1980 census.

★ 264 ★

Marriage

Marital Status of Females, by Age in Selected Alaska Native Villages

Data are shown for the 50 areas with the largest populations, in number of persons.

| Alaska Native Village Statistical Area[1] | Never married | | | | Ever married | | | |
	15 to 24 years	25 to 34 years	35 to 44 years	45 years and older	15 to 24 years	25 to 34 years	35 to 44 years	45 years and older
Akiachak	54	16	0	0	3	20	25	48
Akutan	26	12	0	0	0	36	14	3
Alakanuk	56	11	5	0	2	13	28	46
Andreafsky	32	9	0	2	4	29	12	32

[Continued]

★ 264 ★

Marital Status of Females, by Age in Selected Alaska Native Villages
[Continued]

Alaska Native Village Statistical Area[1]	Never married				Ever married			
	15 to 24 years	25 to 34 years	35 to 44 years	45 years and older	15 to 24 years	25 to 34 years	35 to 44 years	45 years and older
Angoon	21	14	0	0	16	25	40	54
Aniak	23	6	2	0	7	45	27	45
Barrow	134	84	23	12	41	177	170	206
Bethel	255	163	51	15	78	329	293	353
Chevak	46	21	2	2	4	26	20	36
Copper Center	13	3	2	0	4	34	50	43
Craig	30	34	4	2	33	99	106	76
Dillingham	79	50	13	7	33	149	163	204
Emmonak	62	18	9	2	2	22	25	42
Fort Yukon	36	19	8	4	3	32	28	38
Galena	39	14	0	0	7	26	38	53
Gambell	27	16	11	4	2	22	24	31
Grouse Creek Group	22	11	3	0	5	51	65	52
Hoonah	33	17	8	3	8	33	45	95
Hooper Bay	41	25	6	4	6	41	30	55
Kake	32	4	0	0	13	37	49	79
Kasigluk	21	21	7	0	15	20	22	37
King Cove	8	11	0	0	6	37	31	54
King Salmon	35	19	0	0	9	40	39	38
Kipnuk	31	5	7	0	6	20	30	36
Klawock	33	6	0	0	21	40	84	43
Kotlik	33	9	4	0	6	20	28	35
Kotzebue	187	90	20	9	25	173	168	198
Kwethluk	21	8	2	3	10	36	23	40
McGrath	39	11	0	7	2	28	64	35
Mountain Village	59	28	4	0	7	20	39	54
Naknek	18	14	5	2	6	52	43	49
Ninilchik	327	175	82	14	166	747	947	1,051
Noorvik	37	22	6	0	0	24	17	45
Pilot Station	36	13	1	2	2	31	19	29
Point Hope	42	17	4	5	6	31	30	32
Quinhagak	24	11	9	2	11	35	20	37
St. Paul	39	13	0	3	15	42	31	48
Salamatof	47	13	0	0	24	43	49	99
Sand Point	37	34	0	0	8	55	51	61
Savoonga	42	22	2	2	2	22	24	45
Selawik	22	14	2	9	4	35	12	33
Shishmaref	41	20	8	7	4	9	12	36
Stebbins	41	19	14	0	8	9	16	30
Togiak	34	18	5	0	2	33	41	45
Tok	22	5	16	4	28	71	69	100
Toksook Bay	51	11	3	1	5	12	10	35
Unalakleet	8	11	5	7	15	44	36	39
Unalaska	75	119	20	0	61	163	183	130

[Continued]

★ 264 ★

Marital Status of Females, by Age in Selected Alaska Native Villages
[Continued]

Alaska Native Village Statistical Area[1]	Never married				Ever married			
	15 to 24 years	25 to 34 years	35 to 44 years	45 years and older	15 to 24 years	25 to 34 years	35 to 44 years	45 years and older
Wainwright	23	11	2	0	2	42	20	49
Yakutat	36	8	2	0	0	30	56	44

Source: Census of Population and Housing, 1990: Summary Tape File 3C on CD-ROM [machine-readable datafiles]. Prepared by the Bureau of the Census. Washington, DC: The Bureau, 1992. *Notes:* 1. Alaska Native villages (ANVs) constitute tribes, bands, clans, groups, villages, communities, or associations in Alaska that are recognized pursuant to the Alaska Native Claims Settlement Act of 1972, Public Law 92-203. Because ANVs do not have legally designated boundaries, the Census Bureau has established Alaska Native village statistical areas (ANVSAs) for statistical purposes. For the 1990 census, the Census Bureau cooperated with officials of the nonprofit corporation within each participating Alaska Native Regional Corporation (ANRC), as well as other knowledgeable officials, to delineate boundaries that encompass the settled area associated with each ANV.

★ 265 ★

Marriage

Marital Status of Females, by Age in Selected Tribal Designated Statistical Areas

Tribal Designated Statistical Area[1]	Never married				Ever married			
	15 to 24 years	25 to 34 years	35 to 44 years	45 years and older	15 to 24 years	25 to 34 years	35 to 44 years	45 years and older
Apache Choctaw TDSA (state)	946	278	94	172	499	1,320	1,267	4,401
Chickahominy TDSA (state)	126	106	10	39	19	151	206	443
Clifton Choctaw TDSA (state)	5	18	10	7	19	32	27	83
Coharie TDSA (state)	6,457	2,477	940	1,277	2,250	6,905	7,488	21,703
Coquille Indian TDSA	23,125	6,159	2,480	1,764	6,652	24,603	30,270	72,372
Delaware-Muncie TDSA (state)	11	0	0	0	0	36	20	36
Florida Tribe of Eastern Creek TDSA (state)	0	0	0	0	0	9	17	59
Haliwa-Saponi TDSA (state)	475	181	53	74	67	288	432	916
Jena Band of Choctaw TDSA (state)	3,034	685	296	497	1,388	4,229	4,142	9,847
Klamath TDSA	2,080	309	126	107	698	2,707	2,803	7,356
Lumbee TDSA (state)	4,077	1,190	380	483	696	2,979	3,224	6,697
Meherrin TDSA (state)	3,308	1,113	393	572	617	3,319	3,408	10,560
Mohegan TDSA (state)	1,279	625	137	332	485	1,766	1,381	4,136
Ramapough TDSA (state)	30	48	17	7	0	18	37	133
United Houma Nation TDSA (state)	45,598	15,506	4,732	5,663	14,827	60,088	58,016	121,516
Waccamaw Siouan TDSA (state)	198	34	0	17	35	227	272	337
Wampanoag-Gay Head TDSA	508	278	142	174	49	571	1,079	2,133

Source: Census of Population and Housing, 1990: Summary Tape File 3C on CD-ROM [machine-readable datafiles]. Prepared by the Bureau of the Census. Washington, DC: The Bureau, 1992. *Notes:* 1. Tribal designated statistical areas (TDSAs) are areas, delineated outside Oklahoma by federally- and state-recognized tribes without a land base or associated trust lands, to provide statistical areas for which the Census Bureau tabulates data. TDSAs represent areas generally containing the American Indian population over which federally-recognized tribes have jurisdiction and areas in which state tribes provide benefits and services to their members. The names of TDSAs delineated by state-recognized tribes are followed by "(state)." The Census Bureau did not recognize TDSAs before the 1990 census.

★ 266 ★
Marriage

Marital Status of Females, by Age in Selected Tribal Jurisdiction Statistical Areas

Tribal Jurisdiction Statistical Area[1]	Never married				Ever married			
	15 to 24 years	25 to 34 years	35 to 44 years	45 years and older	15 to 24 years	25 to 34 years	35 to 44 years	45 years and older
Absentee Shawnee-Citizens Band of Potawatomi TJSA	3,788	528	184	204	1,662	6,680	7,410	13,691
Caddo-Wichita-Delaware TJSA	248	38	17	51	179	535	499	1,674
Cherokee TJSA	17,488	3,713	1,486	1,805	8,363	26,075	27,055	74,717
Cheyenne-Arapaho TJSA	6,970	994	291	755	3,042	11,026	10,563	25,578
Chickasaw TJSA	11,059	1,738	638	974	5,355	17,205	17,418	52,241
Choctaw TJSA	8,951	1,351	671	926	4,960	13,031	13,344	42,138
Creek TJSA	30,418	9,202	2,982	3,238	12,550	46,216	47,220	109,015
Iowa TJSA	158	13	2	16	80	348	292	692
Kaw TJSA	505	58	31	38	155	789	977	2,773
Kiowa-Comanche-Apache-Fort Sill Apache TJSA	8,552	1,766	543	857	5,835	15,078	12,555	33,032
Otoe-Missouria TJSA	113	19	3	10	55	204	176	430
Pawnee TJSA	587	99	33	66	292	998	1,100	3,015
Sac and Fox TJSA	2,151	425	167	235	1,054	3,367	3,242	10,771
Seminole TJSA	1,009	228	91	129	447	1,363	1,377	4,924
Tonkawa TJSA	581	59	34	47	250	729	717	2,638
Creek-Seminole Joint Area TJSA	89	26	28	37	60	112	145	463
Iowa-Sac and Fox Joint Area TJSA	46	0	3	0	4	88	56	111

Source: Census of Population and Housing, 1990: Summary Tape File 3C on CD-ROM [machine-readable datafiles]. Prepared by the Bureau of the Census. Washington, DC: The Bureau, 1992. *Notes:* 1. Tribal jurisdiction statistical areas (TJSAs) are areas, delineated by federally recognized tribes in Oklahoma without a reservation, for which the Census Bureau tabulates data. TJSAs represent areas generally containing the American Indian population over which one or more tribal governments have jurisdiction. If tribal officials delineated adjacent TJSAs so that they include some duplicate territory, the overlap area is called a "joint use area," which is treated as a separate TJSA for census purposes.

★ 267 ★
Marriage

Marital Status of Females, by Age on Selected Reservations and Trust Lands

Data are shown for the 50 areas with the largest populations, in number of persons.

American Indian Reservation and Trust Lands[1,2]	Never married				Ever married			
	15 to 24 years	25 to 34 years	35 to 44 years	45 years and older	15 to 24 years	25 to 34 years	35 to 44 years	45 years and older
Agua Caliente Reservation	486	257	126	215	122	617	920	7,007
Allegany Reservation	395	161	39	121	127	393	387	1,480
Blackfeet Reservation	447	225	96	58	118	560	376	867
Cheyenne River Reservation	449	139	63	16	114	489	361	950
Coeur d'Alene Reservation and Trust Lands, ID	223	35	19	11	103	355	408	996
Colorado River Reservation	459	123	47	48	159	415	543	1,294
Colville Reservation	363	151	40	11	61	360	462	1,031
Crow Reservation and Trust Lands, MT	328	120	29	26	123	406	480	643
Eastern Cherokee Reservation	342	139	38	37	143	399	429	804
Flathead Reservation	912	255	83	116	286	1,178	1,524	3,686
Fort Apache Reservation	564	243	103	72	233	703	571	814
Fort Berthold Reservation	305	136	28	43	74	287	317	754
Fort Hall Reservation and Trust Lands, ID	288	48	12	0	90	346	339	619
Fort Peck Reservation	573	291	63	33	114	642	646	1,381
Gila River Reservation	807	480	135	100	66	352	351	959
Hopi Reservation and Trust Lands, AZ	511	239	28	87	37	333	413	815
Isabella Reservation and Trust Lands, MI	1,698	444	171	143	377	1,555	1,494	3,184
Laguna Pueblo and Trust Lands, NM	203	94	19	14	57	212	228	596

[Continued]

★ 267 ★

Marital Status of Females, by Age on Selected Reservations and Trust Lands
[Continued]

American Indian Reservation and Trust Lands[1,2]	Never married				Ever married			
	15 to 24 years	25 to 34 years	35 to 44 years	45 years and older	15 to 24 years	25 to 34 years	35 to 44 years	45 years and older
Lake Traverse (Sisseton) Reservation	435	141	52	128	150	466	570	2,092
Leech Lake Reservation	448	185	85	14	90	404	495	1,458
Mississippi Choctaw Reservation and Trust Lands, MS	304	121	58	32	95	190	277	341
Muckleshoot Reservation and Trust Lands, WA	212	63	21	9	49	264	205	582
Navajo Reservation and Trust Lands, AZ–NM–UT	10,485	4,435	1,492	1,274	1,990	7,904	7,215	14,166
Nez Perce Reservation	625	101	48	43	202	979	1,090	3,074
Northern Cheyenne Reservation and Trust Lands, MT–SD	305	84	8	32	105	190	258	293
Omaha Reservation	253	101	19	40	56	244	305	871
Oneida (West) Reservation	1,032	288	92	72	120	1,357	1,538	1,972
Osage Reservation	1,566	281	144	166	652	2,840	2,907	7,669
Papago Reservation	671	450	243	235	22	187	312	840
Pine Ridge Reservation and Trust Lands, NE–SD	809	339	141	112	169	543	512	972
Port Madison Reservation	176	29	39	24	38	383	398	717
Puyallup Reservation and Trust Lands, WA	1,637	538	167	98	483	2,489	2,292	4,480
Red Lake Reservation	328	169	47	10	16	110	179	309
Rosebud Reservation and Trust Lands, SD	756	258	73	49	140	403	553	891
Salt River Reservation	258	135	53	37	45	223	214	887
San Carlos Reservation	507	141	31	69	153	419	373	605
Sandia Pueblo	179	124	28	13	44	326	301	445
San Juan Pueblo	305	112	57	33	83	300	355	649
Santa Clara Pueblo	595	261	97	96	131	568	736	1,510
Southern Ute Reservation	342	118	39	10	110	523	643	1,062
Standing Rock Reservation	449	148	80	28	73	424	384	986
Taos Pueblo and Trust Lands, NM	246	136	58	85	37	212	378	792
Tulalip Reservation	275	96	32	13	82	517	517	1,104
Turtle Mountain Reservation and Trust Lands, ND–SD	556	270	98	37	70	362	344	625
Uintah and Ouray Reservation	821	126	62	52	341	1,123	1,041	1,970
White Earth Reservation	422	138	35	29	84	425	492	1,495
Wind River Reservation	976	276	83	82	308	1,513	1,522	3,226
Yakima Reservation and Trust Lands, WA	1,559	606	130	159	480	1,425	1,540	3,521
Yankton Reservation	329	91	46	67	58	323	301	1,122
Zuni Pueblo	506	208	64	23	170	513	481	701

Source: Census of Population and Housing, 1990: Summary Tape File 3C on CD-ROM [machine-readable datafiles]. Prepared by the Bureau of the Census. Washington, DC: The Bureau, 1992. *Notes:* 1. Federal American Indian reservations are areas with boundaries established by treaty, statute, and/or executive or court order, and recognized by the federal government as territory in which American Indian tribes have jurisdiction. State reservations are lands held in trust by state governments for the use and benefit of a given tribe. The reservations and their boundaries were identified for the 1990 census by the Bureau of Indian Affairs (BIA), Department of Interior (for federal reservations), and state governments (for state reservations). The names of American Indian reservations recognized by state governments, but not by the federal government, are followed by "state." Areas composed of reservation lands that are administered jointly and/or are claimed by two reservations, as identified by the BIA, are called "joint areas," and are treated as separate American Indian reservations for census purposes. Federal reservations may cross state boundaries, and federal and state reservations may cross county, county subdivision, and place boundaries. For reservations that cross state boundaries, only the portion of the reservations in a given state is shown in the data products for that state; the entire reservations are shown in data products for the United States. 2. Trust lands are property associated with a particular American Indian reservation or tribe, held in trust by the federal government. Trust lands may be held in trust either for a tribe (tribal trust lands) or for an individual member of a tribe (individual trust land). Trust lands recognized for the 1990 census comprised all tribal trust lands and inhabited individual trust lands located outside of a reservation boundary. As with other American Indian areas, trust lands may be located in more than one state. Only the trust lands in a given state are shown in the data products for that state; all trust lands associated with a reservation or tribe are shown in data products for the United States. The Census Bureau first reported data for tribal trust lands for the 1980 census.

★ 268 ★

Marriage

Marital Status of Males in Selected Alaska Native Villages

Data are shown for the 50 areas with the largest populations, in number of persons.

| Alaska Native Village Statistical Area[1] | Never married | Now married | | | Widowed | Divorced |
| | | Married, spouse present | Married, spouse absent | | | |
			Separated	Other		
Akiachak	81	74	12	6	0	0
Akutan	219	6	12	169	4	68
Alakanuk	88	72	4	2	5	2
Andreafsky	63	54	0	15	0	9
Angoon	84	109	1	6	4	24
Aniak	54	96	0	0	4	11
Barrow	380	419	10	46	22	83
Bethel	711	708	37	73	29	135
Chevak	111	61	0	0	12	6
Copper Center	43	88	0	0	4	21
Craig	132	250	18	16	6	58
Dillingham	198	395	17	8	7	59
Emmonak	103	65	5	6	9	6
Fort Yukon	109	78	0	9	12	18
Galena	142	84	6	205	7	26
Gambell	135	56	4	2	5	10
Grouse Creek Group	53	134	7	6	3	31
Hoonah	114	114	0	14	4	42
Hooper Bay	152	97	10	0	7	4
Kake	84	147	3	4	0	30
Kasigluk	41	77	4	4	0	1
King Cove	86	54	0	61	2	16
King Salmon	94	113	16	143	0	42
Kipnuk	83	71	3	2	1	3
Klawock	109	140	8	12	3	30
Kotlik	53	74	2	0	2	7
Kotzebue	395	354	16	41	20	89
Kwethluk	81	82	16	2	15	0
McGrath	44	100	6	4	1	19
Mountain Village	122	95	5	0	6	5
Naknek	52	114	0	14	2	25
Ninilchik	1,040	2,325	92	44	50	353
Noorvik	103	63	4	5	1	7
Pilot Station	55	64	2	3	6	2
Point Hope	89	76	3	10	7	11
Quinhagak	72	78	5	2	21	6
St. Paul	180	90	7	48	15	50
Salamatof	219	147	0	15	0	140
Sand Point	152	119	19	65	6	50
Savoonga	105	72	0	2	3	3
Selawik	111	60	0	0	13	5
Shishmaref	79	44	0	0	0	9
Stebbins	69	50	4	10	0	6
Togiak	98	77	5	9	3	12
Tok	96	215	3	15	2	41

[Continued]

★ 268 ★

Marital Status of Males in Selected Alaska Native Villages
[Continued]

| Alaska Native Village Statistical Area[1] | Never married | Now married | | | Widowed | Divorced |
| | | Married, spouse present | Married, spouse absent | | | |
			Separated	Other		
Toksook Bay	70	65	3	0	0	1
Unalakleet	100	107	8	0	3	25
Unalaska	894	273	66	409	2	355
Wainwright	58	79	3	2	3	6
Yakutat	84	75	7	6	5	36

Source: Census of Population and Housing, 1990: Summary Tape File 3C on CD-ROM [machine-readable datafiles]. Prepared by the Bureau of the Census. Washington, DC: The Bureau, 1992. *Notes:* 1. Alaska Native villages (ANVs) constitute tribes, bands, clans, groups, villages, communities, or associations in Alaska that are recognized pursuant to the Alaska Native Claims Settlement Act of 1972, Public Law 92-203. Because ANVs do not have legally designated boundaries, the Census Bureau has established Alaska Native village statistical areas (ANVSAs) for statistical purposes. For the 1990 census, the Census Bureau cooperated with officials of the nonprofit corporation within each participating Alaska Native Regional Corporation (ANRC), as well as other knowledgeable officials, to delineate boundaries that encompass the settled area associated with each ANV.

★ 269 ★

Marriage

Marital Status of Males in Selected Tribal Designated Statistical Areas

| Tribal Designated Statistical Area[1] | Never married | Now married | | | Widowed | Divorced |
| | | Married, spouse present | Married, spouse absent | | | |
			Separated	Other		
Apache Choctaw TDSA (state)	1,780	5,189	112	290	354	473
Chickahominy TDSA (state)	414	585	28	7	25	32
Clifton Choctaw TDSA (state)	83	99	0	7	0	0
Coharie TDSA (state)	11,821	23,416	1,593	1,147	1,137	2,892
Coquille Indian TDSA	41,600	88,115	2,666	2,616	3,804	15,154
Delaware-Muncie TDSA (state)	13	90	0	0	0	0
Florida Tribe of Eastern Creek TDSA (state)	17	55	0	0	10	18
Haliwa-Saponi TDSA (state)	759	1,232	107	54	77	97
Jena Band of Choctaw TDSA (state)	6,079	13,257	508	569	493	1,400
Klamath TDSA	4,178	9,036	348	278	382	1,553
Lumbee TDSA (state)	6,303	8,314	680	363	453	895
Meherrin TDSA (state)	5,544	10,982	944	337	748	1,005
Mohegan TDSA (state)	3,055	5,119	150	85	182	944
Ramapough TDSA (state)	103	137	4	4	13	0
United Houma Nation TDSA (state)	82,851	172,286	7,473	5,122	6,719	20,399
Waccamaw Siouan TDSA (state)	259	581	36	7	17	31
Wampanoag-Gay Head TDSA	1,175	2,501	114	78	129	308

Source: Census of Population and Housing, 1990: Summary Tape File 3C on CD-ROM [machine-readable datafiles]. Prepared by the Bureau of the Census. Washington, DC: The Bureau, 1992. *Notes:* 1. Tribal designated statistical areas (TDSAs) are areas, delineated outside Oklahoma by federally- and state-recognized tribes without a land base or associated trust lands, to provide statistical areas for which the Census Bureau tabulates data. TDSAs represent areas generally containing the American Indian population over which federally-recognized tribes have jurisdiction and areas in which state tribes provide benefits and services to their members. The names of TDSAs delineated by state-recognized tribes are followed by "(state)." The Census Bureau did not recognize TDSAs before the 1990 census.

★ 270 ★

Marriage

Marital Status of Males in Selected Tribal Jurisdiction Statistical Areas

| Tribal Jurisdiction Statistical Area[1] | Never married | Now married | | | Widowed | Divorced |
| | | Married, spouse present | Married, spouse absent | | | |
			Separated	Other		
Absentee Shawnee-Citizens Band of Potawatomi TJSA	7,788	22,430	606	940	744	2,990
Caddo-Wichita-Delaware TJSA	619	2,043	21	48	106	273
Cherokee TJSA	31,689	93,843	2,228	2,537	4,041	12,135
Cheyenne-Arapaho TJSA	12,491	35,426	611	1,328	1,473	4,129
Chickasaw TJSA	19,644	62,719	1,128	1,733	2,889	7,193
Choctaw TJSA	17,384	48,499	1,313	1,773	2,478	6,671
Creek TJSA	55,805	145,290	2,853	4,651	4,899	21,051
Iowa TJSA	335	1,000	16	27	28	94
Kaw TJSA	977	3,518	6	68	116	261
Kiowa-Comanche-Apache-Fort Sill Apache TJSA	21,663	45,575	1,200	3,063	1,879	5,620
Otoe-Missouria TJSA	230	610	20	19	29	80
Pawnee TJSA	1,102	3,949	71	57	155	445
Sac and Fox TJSA	3,927	12,243	235	259	477	1,396
Seminole TJSA	1,912	5,170	131	109	298	782
Tonkawa TJSA	948	2,964	31	98	185	323
Creek-Seminole Joint Area TJSA	259	511	17	23	53	64
Iowa-Sac and Fox Joint Area TJSA	62	215	3	9	4	18

Source: Census of Population and Housing, 1990: Summary Tape File 3C on CD-ROM [machine-readable datafiles]. Prepared by the Bureau of the Census. Washington, DC: The Bureau, 1992. *Notes:* 1. Tribal jurisdiction statistical areas (TJSAs) are areas, delineated by federally recognized tribes in Oklahoma without a reservation, for which the Census Bureau tabulates data. TJSAs represent areas generally containing the American Indian population over which one or more tribal governments have jurisdiction. If tribal officials delineated adjacent TJSAs so that they include some duplicate territory, the overlap area is called a "joint use area," which is treated as a separate TJSA for census purposes.

★ 271 ★

Marriage

Marital Status of Males on Selected Reservations and Trust Lands

Data are shown for the 50 areas with the largest populations, in number of persons.

| American Indian Reservation and Trust Lands[1,2] | Never married | Now married | | | Widowed | Divorced |
| | | Married, spouse present | Married, spouse absent | | | |
			Separated	Other		
Agua Caliente Reservation	1,796	4,705	156	186	419	1,078
Allegany Reservation	759	1,346	107	39	131	217
Blackfeet Reservation	938	1,260	53	154	86	211
Cheyenne River Reservation	871	1,229	31	69	49	199
Coeur d'Alene Reservation and Trust Lands, ID	451	1,476	30	32	72	217
Colorado River Reservation	755	1,546	52	104	90	243
Colville Reservation	826	1,221	68	53	79	241
Crow Reservation and Trust Lands, MT	632	1,222	25	79	40	125
Eastern Cherokee Reservation	692	1,119	102	31	38	201
Flathead Reservation	1,879	4,446	93	137	325	764
Fort Apache Reservation	1,163	1,508	20	124	75	158
Fort Berthold Reservation	666	852	17	17	66	128
Fort Hall Reservation and Trust Lands, ID	481	894	51	63	20	247
Fort Peck Reservation	1,170	1,885	23	85	47	320

[Continued]

Marital Status of Males on Selected Reservations and Trust Lands
[Continued]

American Indian Reservation and Trust Lands[1,2]	Never married	Now married				Widowed	Divorced
		Married, spouse present	Married, spouse absent				
			Separated	Other			
Gila River Reservation	1,363	1,026	130	28	140	244
Hopi Reservation and Trust Lands, AZ	1,010	924	78	93	51	232
Isabella Reservation and Trust Lands, MI	2,980	4,782	64	67	156	572
Laguna Pueblo and Trust Lands, NM	404	623	57	59	30	47
Lake Traverse (Sisseton) Reservation	1,229	2,240	98	79	164	247
Leech Lake Reservation	923	1,711	25	48	130	248
Mississippi Choctaw Reservation and Trust Lands, MS	405	505	56	57	74	34
Muckleshoot Reservation and Trust Lands, WA	381	739	34	23	30	129
Navajo Reservation and Trust Lands, AZ–NM–UT	19,700	20,009	821	2,067	957	1,750
Nez Perce Reservation	1,437	3,924	102	136	205	670
Northern Cheyenne Reservation and Trust Lands, MT–SD	396	548	13	13	15	153
Omaha Reservation	558	985	33	32	71	115
Oneida (West) Reservation	1,724	4,119	100	64	66	381
Osage Reservation	3,281	9,882	239	373	267	1,491
Papago Reservation	1,493	626	47	90	111	236
Pine Ridge Reservation and Trust Lands, NE–SD	1,463	1,331	147	86	197	366
Port Madison Reservation	392	1,136	37	10	34	169
Puyallup Reservation and Trust Lands, WA	3,311	6,622	198	234	268	1,156
Red Lake Reservation	558	401	33	18	41	65
Rosebud Reservation and Trust Lands, SD	1,205	1,075	61	67	51	323
Salt River Reservation	563	736	5	66	80	129
San Carlos Reservation	872	1,003	45	81	16	130
Sandia Pueblo	433	726	0	13	14	169
San Juan Pueblo	705	940	32	21	26	247
Santa Clara Pueblo	1,039	1,958	60	43	111	361
Southern Ute Reservation	681	1,768	29	43	75	244
Standing Rock Reservation	997	1,261	10	37	71	255
Taos Pueblo and Trust Lands, NM	585	805	27	12	50	213
Tulalip Reservation	608	1,660	35	33	74	261
Turtle Mountain Reservation and Trust Lands, ND–SD	838	786	43	49	100	288
Uintah and Ouray Reservation	1,327	3,513	58	73	96	329
White Earth Reservation	1,060	1,779	19	39	111	220
Wind River Reservation	1,845	4,692	104	157	201	715
Yakima Reservation and Trust Lands, WA	3,496	4,672	132	639	239	632
Yankton Reservation	719	1,200	32	55	111	122
Zuni Pueblo	804	1,084	119	200	53	130

Source: Census of Population and Housing, 1990: Summary Tape File 3C on CD-ROM [machine-readable datafiles]. Prepared by the Bureau of the Census. Washington, DC: The Bureau, 1992. *Notes:* 1. Federal American Indian reservations are areas with boundaries established by treaty, statute, and/or executive or court order, and recognized by the federal government as territory in which American Indian tribes have jurisdiction. State reservations are lands held in trust by state governments for the use and benefit of a given tribe. The reservations and their boundaries were identified for the 1990 census by the Bureau of Indian Affairs (BIA), Department of Interior (for federal reservations), and state governments (for state reservations). The names of American Indian reservations recognized by state governments, but not by the federal government, are followed by "state." Areas composed of reservation lands that are administered jointly and/or are claimed by two reservations, as identified by the BIA, are called "joint areas," and are treated as separate American Indian reservations for census purposes. Federal reservations may cross state boundaries, and federal and state reservations may cross county, county subdivision, and place boundaries. For reservations that cross state boundaries, only the portion of the reservations in a given state are shown in the data products for that state; the entire reservations are shown in data products for the United States. 2. Trust lands are property associated with a particular American Indian reservation or tribe, held in trust by the federal government. Trust lands may be held in trust either for a tribe (tribal trust lands) or for an individual member of a tribe (individual trust land). Trust lands recognized for the 1990 census comprised all tribal trust lands and inhabited individual trust lands located outside of a reservation boundary. As with other American Indian areas, trust lands may be located in more than one state. Only the trust lands in a given state are shown in the data products for that state; all trust lands associated with a reservation or tribe are shown in data products for the United States. The Census Bureau first reported data for tribal trust lands for the 1980 census.

Child Care

★ 272 ★

Latchkey Children

```
White - 18.6
Black - 17.6
American Indian and Alaska Native - 13.8
Asian and Pacific Islander - 14.4
Hispanic - 12.4
```

Data reflect results of a 1988 survey of eighth graders. Affirmative responses are shown as percentages for each race/ethnicity.

Race and ethnicity	Usually no one home when returns home from school
Hispanic	12.4
American Indian and Alaska Native	13.8
Asian and Pacific Islander	14.4
Black	17.6
White	18.6

Source: U.S. Department of Education. *A Profile of the American Eighth Grader.* Washington, DC: U.S. Department of Education, 1990, p. 52. Primary source: U.S. Department of Education, National Center for Education Statistics, "National Education Longitudinal Study of 1988: Base Year Student Survey".

★ 273 ★

Child Care

Time Spent by Eighth Graders at Home Alone

Figures represent results of a 1988 survey. Students' affirmative responses are shown in percent for each race/ethnicity.

Race/ethnicity	Number of hours				
	None/never happens	Less than 1 hour	1-2 hours	2-3 hours	More than 3 hours
Total	13.3	32.4	27.8	12.9	13.6
Black	16.2	28.1	23.2	12.8	19.5
American Indian/Native Alaskan	16.0	30.8	21.1	13.3	18.8
Hispanic	20.7	29.0	22.8	11.2	16.3

[Continued]

★ 273 ★

Time Spent by Eighth Graders at Home Alone
[Continued]

Race/ethnicity	Number of hours				
	None/never happens	Less than 1 hour	1-2 hours	2-3 hours	More than 3 hours
Asian and Pacific Islander	16.7	29.0	25.8	12.6	15.9
White	11.6	33.8	29.5	13.1	12.0

Source: U.S. Department of Education. *A Profile of the American Eighth Grader.* Washington, DC: U.S. Department of Education, 1990, p. 53. Primary source: U.S. Department of Education, National Center for Education Statistics, "National Education Longitudinal Study 1988: Base Year Student Survey".

Children

★ 274 ★

Number of Single Children Under Age 18 per Household - 1991

Numbers are shown in thousands of occupied units. Households of Hispanic origin may be of any race.

Characteristics	All households	White	Black	American Indian, Eskimo, or Aleut	Asian or Pacific Islander	Hispanic origin	Not of Hispanic origin	
							Total	White
Number of single children under 18 years old								
None	58,559	51,276	5,708	219	1,065	2,802	55,757	48,826
One	14,517	11,769	2,181	96	359	1,164	13,352	10,734
Two	12,701	10,436	1,628	78	426	1,183	11,519	9,411
Three	5,177	4,088	839	58	139	678	4,499	3,465
Four	1,505	1,138	273	22	48	283	1,222	876
Five	457	296	122	11	22	84	373	219
Six or more	230	137	81	2	8	45	185	94

Source: Woodward, Jeanne M. *America's Racial and Ethnic Groups: Their Housing in the Early Nineties.* Bureau of the Census. Current Housing Reports, Series H121/94-3. Washington, DC: U.S. Government Printing Office, p. 45. Primary source: American Housing Survey (AHS), 1991 National Internal User File.

★ 275 ★

Children

Ages of Single Children in Households - 1991

Numbers are shown in thousands of occupied units. Households of Hispanic origin may be of any race.

Characteristics	All households	White	Black	American Indian, Eskimo, or Aleut	Asian or Pacific Islander	Hispanic origin	Not of Hispanic origin	
							Total	White
Ages of single children								
Households with children	34,588	27,864	5,124	267	1,001	3,437	31,150	24,799
One child under 6 only	5,741	4,727	804	27	142	471	5,270	4,306
One child under 6, one or more 6 to 17	5,808	4,528	896	65	218	786	5,023	3,845
Two or more under 6 only	3,161	2,572	421	18	109	341	2,820	2,273
Two or more under 6, one or more 6 to 17	1,916	1,460	376	34	32	314	1,602	1,160
One or more 6 to 17 only	17,961	14,577	2,628	123	502	1,526	16,435	13,216

Source: Woodward, Jeanne M. *America's Racial and Ethnic Groups: Their Housing in the Early Nineties.* Bureau of the Census. Current Housing Reports, Series H121/94-3. Washington, DC: U.S. Government Printing Office, p. 45. Primary source: American Housing Survey (AHS), 1991 National Internal User File.

★ 276 ★

Children

Child Abuse Investigations by the BIA

Data show number of investigations by each Area office from 1 January 1992 through 30 May 1993.

	Sexual	Other
Aberdeen Area	158	82
Albuquerque Area	103	153
Anadarko Area	11	8
Billings Area	183	52
Eastern Area	24	29
Minneapolis Area	70	8
Muskogee Area	13	0
Navajo Area	84	11
Phoenix Area	273	461
Portland Area	51	25

Source: U.S. Senate Committee on Indian Affairs. *Indian Child Protection and Family Violence Prevention Act: Hearing Before the Committee on Indian Affairs.* 103rd Cong., 1st sess., (28 October 1993), p. 45.

★ 277 ★
Children

Child Abuse and Neglect Cases Substantiated and Indicated, by Race/ Ethnicity of Victim

Data shown are based on reports alleging child abuse and neglect that were referred for investigation by the respective child protective services agency in each State. The reporting period may be either calendar or fiscal year. The majority of States were unable to provide unduplicated counts. Also, a varying number of States reported the various characteristics presented below. Excludes the Armed Forces. A substantiated case represents a type of investigation disposition that determines that there is sufficient evidence under State law to conclude that maltreatment occurred or that the child is at risk of maltreatment.

Race/ethnic group of victim[1]	1990		1991		1992	
	Number	Percent	Number	Percent	Number	Percent
Victims, total	775,409	100.0	818,527	99.9	952,620	100.0
White	424,470	54.7	454,059	55.5	525,399	55.2
Black	197,400	25.5	218,044	26.6	245,777	25.8
Asian and Pacific Islander	6,408	0.8	6,585	0.8	8,007	0.8
American Indian, Eskimo, and Aleut	10,283	1.3	10,873	1.3	13,087	1.4
Other races	11,749	1.5	12,982	1.6	15,969	1.7
Hispanic origin	73,132	9.4	77,985	9.5	90,840	9.5
Unknown	51,967	6.7	37,999	4.6	53,541	5.6

Source: 1994 Statistical Abstract of the United States on CD-ROM [machine-readable datafiles]. CD-8A-94. Washington, DC: U.S. Department of Commerce, Economics and Statistics Administration, Bureau of the Census, Data User Services Division, January 1995. Primary source: U.S. Department of Health and Human Services, National Center on Child Abuse and Neglect, National Child Abuse and Neglect Data System, *Working Paper 2, 1991 Summary Data Component*, May 1993; *Child Maltreatment - 1992*, May 1994. *Notes:* 1. Some States were unable to report on the number of Hispanic victims, thus it is probable that nationwide the percentage of Hispanic victims is higher.

★ 278 ★
Children

Child Abuse of American Indians in South Dakota - FY 1992

Data show number of substantiated cases of child abuse of American Indian children in South Dakota, by age group and sex, in fiscal year 1992.

Age group	Male	Female	All
0-2 years	105	97	202
2-5 years	197	201	398
6-11 years	257	303	560
12-15 years	93	126	219
16+ years	36	65	101
Unknown	0	0	0
All	688	792	1,480

Source: U.S. Senate Committee on Indian Affairs. *Indian Child Protection and Family Violence Prevention Act: Hearing Before the Committee on Indian Affairs.* 103rd Cong., 1st sess., (28 October 1993), p. 104. Primary source: Rosebud Sioux Tribe Child & Family Services, testimony before the Oversight Hearing on Child Abuse, 28 October 1993.

Adolescents

★ 279 ★

Adolescent Suicide Attempts, by History of Family Attempts or Completions

22% of the sample reported knowledge of a suicide attempt or completion by a family member. Data are shown in percent and are based on a survey of 13,923 rural American Indian/Alaska Native adolescents living on or near reservations[1].

Youth suicide attempts	Family history	
	No attempts	Attempts/ completions
No attempts	86.8	69.7
Ever attempted suicide	13.2	30.3
Total	100.0	100.0

Source: Indian Health Service, Maternal and Child Health Bureau, and the Robert Wood Johnson Foundation. *The State of Native American Youth Health, February, 1992,* p. 32. *Notes:* 1. Caution: Sample was not random and does not fully represent all Native American/Alaska Native groups.

★ 280 ★

Adolescents

Adolescents Participating in Motor Vehicle Risk Behaviors

Data are shown in percent and are based on a survey of 13,923 rural American Indian/Alaska Native adolescents living on or near reservations[1].

Motor vehicle risk behaviors	Males		Females	
	Grades 7-9	Grades 10-12	Grades 7-9	Grades 10-12
Among those who drive, percent who have driven while under the influence of drugs/alcohol	30.9	44.8	22.2	34.1
Often or sometimes ride with a drinking/drug using driver	20.2	27.8	18.1	23.9
Believe it is OK to drive after three or more drinks	4.9	11.7	2.7	4.1
Ride a motorcycle more often than once a month	44.2	38.9	30.1	24.9
Among motorcyclists, percent who rarely or never wear a helmet when on a motorcycle	37.8	44.0	44.2	57.8
Rarely or never wear seatbelts in a car	45.6	46.7	42.8	42.6

[Continued]

★ 280 ★

Adolescents Participating in Motor Vehicle Risk Behaviors
[Continued]

Motor vehicle risk behaviors	Males		Females	
	Grades 7-9	Grades 10-12	Grades 7-9	Grades 10-12
Frequently ride in the back of a pickup truck	48.2	40.8	35.6	21.5
High risk for motor vehicle injuries[2]	11.8	15.9	8.7	7.9

Source: Indian Health Service, Maternal and Child Health Bureau, and the Robert Wood Johnson Foundation. *The State of Native American Youth Health, February, 1992,* p. 18. *Notes:* 1. Caution: Sample was not random and does not fully represent all Native American/Alaska Native groups. 2. High risk is based on respondents affirming four or more vehicle related risk factors.

★ 281 ★

Adolescents

Adolescents' School Performance, by Associated Behavior

Data show percentage of Native American youths who report above or below average school performance and selected risk behaviors. Data are based on a survey of 13,923 rural American Indian/Alaska Native adolescents living on or near reservations[1].

Risk behavior	Below average school performance	Above average school performance
Daily/weekly cigarette use	30.9	13.4
Daily/weekly alcohol use	19.6	8.5
Drink five times/drinks per sittings	54.7	41.9
Daily/weekly marijuana use	17.9	7.8
Ever had sexual intercourse	32.5	26.6
Ever caused/gotten pregnant	3.7	4.2
Feel school people don't care	41.6	22.0
Feel family doesn't understand	35.6	19.8
Feel extremely hopeless	13.7	10.0
Would like to commit suicide	16.6	7.5
Have attempted suicide	22.2	14.9
Ever been sexually abused	11.3	10.1
Ever been physically abused	16.9	12.5

Source: Indian Health Service, Maternal and Child Health Bureau, and the Robert Wood Johnson Foundation. *The State of Native American Youth Health, February, 1992,* p. 10. *Notes:* 1. Caution: Sample was not random and does not fully represent all Native American/Alaska Native groups.

★ 282 ★

Adolescents

Characteristics of Adolescents Who Had Reported Emotional Stress in the Previous Month

Data are based on a survey of 13,923 rural American Indian/Alaska Native adolescents living on or near reservations[1].

Characteristic	High stress (N = 750)	All adolescents (N = 13,226)
Family relations		
Live in single parent or alternative family structures	60.3	54.1
Biological parents divorced or separated	36.4	31.3
Worries a great deal that parents will divorce	30.4	26.2
Feels family does not understand them	44.0	24.4
Physical/sexual abuse		
Reports have been sexually abused	21.9	10.1
Reports have been physically abused	31.7	13.3
School problems		
Reports doing below average in school	17.3	11.9
Frequently absent from school due to illness	12.8	7.6
Suicidal tendencies		
Has ever attempted suicide	44.6	16.9
Reports they would like to commit suicide or would if they had the chance	26.0	9.2
Sexual risk taking		
Has had sexual intercourse	42.8	30.9
Has been pregnant or caused a pregnancy	10.8	6.1

Source: Indian Health Service, Maternal and Child Health Bureau, and the Robert Wood Johnson Foundation. *The State of Native American Youth Health, February, 1992,* p. 27. *Notes:* An (N) refers to the number of students answering in the affirmative. 1. Caution: Sample was not random and does not fully represent all Native American/Alaska Native groups.

★ 283 ★

Adolescents

Comparisons of Adolescents for High and Low Risk of Suicide

Data are shown in percent and are based on a survey of 13,923 rural American Indian/Alaska Native adolescents living on or near reservations[1].

Characteristic	High (N = 2,171)	Low (N = 11,283)	Percent difference
Associated behaviors			
Heavy drinking	30.6	17.4	13.2
Marijuana weekly or daily	20.1	10.2	9.9
Had sexual intercourse	44.0	28.4	15.6
Caused/had pregnancy	10.2	5.3	4.9
Sexual/physical abuse	12.5	4.0	8.5
Induced vomiting weekly	7.6	3.2	4.3
Support system factors			
Family doesn't understand	39.3	21.3	18.0
Friend attempted suicide	26.6	16.4	10.2
Adults don't care	26.6	15.0	11.6
Friend completed suicide	18.9	7.6	11.3
Family member tried suicide	36.4	18.8	17.6

Source: Indian Health Service, Maternal and Child Health Bureau, and the Robert Wood Johnson Foundation. *The State of Native American Youth Health, February, 1992,* p. 33. *Notes:* An (N) indicates the number of adolescents in each group. For the purpose of better understanding who is at high risk for suicide, further analysis was undertaken for youths who: 1) attempted suicide within the past year; 2) think seriously about killing themselves; and 3) have made repeated attempts, even though the attempts may have been more than a year ago. Eighty-four percent of youths surveyed do not have any of these elements of suicide history or ideation. Nine percent have one out of the three characteristics, five percent have two of the three, and two percent (N = 293) have all three characteristics. 1. Caution: Sample was not random and does not fully represent all Native American/Alaska Native groups.

★ 284 ★

Adolescents

Delinquent Behaviors of Rural Adolescents

Data are shown in percent, by sex and grade, and are based on a survey of 13,923 rural American Indian/Alaska Native adolescents living on or near reservations[1].

Anti-social activity in past 12 months	Males		Females	
	Grades 7-9	Grades 10-12	Grades 7-9	Grades 10-12
Damaged, destroyed or vandalized property				
Once or twice	23.1	22.5	16.5	12.6
3 or more times	8.9	7.3	4.3	3.0
Stolen from a store/shoplifted				
Once or twice	18.5	22.6	16.3	16.1
3 or more times	10.8	9.8	7.4	6.9

[Continued]

★ 284 ★

Delinquent Behaviors of Rural Adolescents

[Continued]

Anti-social activity in past 12 months	Males		Females	
	Grades 7-9	Grades 10-12	Grades 7-9	Grades 10-12
Stolen from parents or other family members				
Once or twice	15.4	12.0	17.0	12.4
3 or more times	5.2	3.9	4.4	2.5
Ran away from home				
Once or twice	9.5	6.7	10.8	9.8
3 or more times	4.8	2.7	5.4	3.9

Source: Indian Health Service, Maternal and Child Health Bureau, and the Robert Wood Johnson Foundation. *The State of Native American Youth Health, February, 1992*, p. 23. *Notes:* 1. Caution: Sample was not random and does not fully represent all Native American/Alaska Native groups.

★ 285 ★

Adolescents

Reasons Given for Sexual Abstinence by Adolescents

Data are shown in percent and are based on a survey of 13,923 rural American Indian/Alaska Native adolescents living on or near reservations[1].

Reasons for sexual abstinence	Males	Females
Want to wait until older	42.7	45.5
Don't want risk of pregnancy	20.4	48.0
Want to wait until marriage	29.0	41.3
Not ready emotionally	16.2	37.1
Fear of disease	21.7	28.3
Parents' values are against it	8.0	23.8
No one has asked me to do it	14.1	7.9
Haven't met anyone yet	11.8	12.6
Haven't had the opportunity	7.1	5.3
Religious values are against it	4.0	7.0

Source: Indian Health Service, Maternal and Child Health Bureau, and the Robert Wood Johnson Foundation. *The State of Native American Youth Health, February, 1992*, p. 36. *Notes:* 1. Caution: Sample was not random and does not fully represent all Native American/Alaska Native groups.

★ 286 ★

Adolescents

Risk Behaviors and Perceived Health Status of Adolescents

Data are based on a survey of 13,923 rural American Indian/Alaska Native adolescents living on or near reservations[1].

Risk behavior	Perceived health status	
	Poor (N = 264)	Good or excellent (N = 10,386)
Ever attempted suicide	33.9	14.8
Below average school performance	34.8	9.2
Use three or more drugs at least monthly	10.6	4.7
Feel overweight	64.1	26.1
Sexually active	36.7	29.9
Experienced abuse	29.2	15.1

Source: Indian Health Service, Maternal and Child Health Bureau, and the Robert Wood Johnson Foundation. *The State of Native American Youth Health, February, 1992,* p. 12. *Notes:* An (N) refers to the number of students who reported a certain health status. 1. Caution: Sample was not random and does not fully represent all Native American/Alaska Native groups.

★ 287 ★

Adolescents

Risk Factors for Alcohol or Drug Dependency

Data show responses to a survey of program managers of OSAP (Office for Substance Abuse Prevention) American Indian Alaska Native grants. Managers were asked to indicate the most significant risks for substance abuse. Percentages reflect affirmative responses.

Risk Factor	Significance			
	None	Some	Moderate	Great
Parental alcoholism	-	-	13	88
Poor self-esteem	-	-	13	88
Substance abuse by friends and peers	-	-	17	81
Abuse/neglect	-	6	25	69
Family disruption or conflict	-	13	17	69
Emotional/psychological difficulties	-	6	44	56
Sexual abuse as a child	6	17	17	56
Person's early substance use	-	6	38	50
Poor and inconsistent family management	6	13	31	50
Alienation from social values of Native American culture	6	25	17	50
Previous suicide threat or attempt	17	13	17	50
Poor or undefined racial identity	-	6	50	44
Poor relations with family members	-	13	44	44
High absenteeism	-	25	31	44
School dropout	6	25	25	44

[Continued]

★ 287 ★

Risk Factors for Alcohol or Drug Dependency
[Continued]

Risk Factor	Significance			
	None	Some	Moderate	Great
Personal physical assault	17	13	25	44
High unemployment in community	-	17	44	38
Multiple home placements	6	17	38	38
Sensation seeking	13	13	38	38
Community disorganization	6	31	25	38
Inadequate healthy recreational activity	-	17	50	31
Risk taking	6	13	50	31
Criminal behavior in parents or siblings	6	25	38	31
Delinquency/crime	-	38	31	31
Recent death of relative or friend	6	31	31	31
Poor academic performance	6	38	25	31
Inability to metabolize alcohol efficiently	17	31	17	31
Alienation from social values of white culture	13	38	25	25
Frequent moves	17	31	25	25
Parental divorce	13	44	17	25
Low socioeconomic background	17	38	17	25
Low commitment to education	13	50	13	25
Attention deficit disorder and hyperactivity	25	25	31	17
Negative boarding school experience	17	38	25	17
Cognitive deficits	25	44	13	17
Lack of attachment to neighborhood	38	17	31	13
Depressed autonomic and central nervous system arousal	17	56	13	13
Physical handicap/illness	31	50	17	-
Other				
Rapid cultural change	-	-	-	6
Community-wide unresolved grief	-	-	-	6
Lack of family education	-	-	6	-
Perception of alcohol as normal	-	-	6	-

Source: U.S. Department of Health and Human Services. Public Health Service. Alcohol, Drug Abuse, and Mental Health Administration. Office for Substance Abuse Prevention. *Breaking New Ground For American Indian and Alaska Native Youth: Program Summaries* (OSAP Technical Report-3). Rockville, MD: U.S. DHHS, p. 34.

★ 288 ★

Adolescents

School-Based Intervention Approaches to Substance Abuse Prevention

The Office for Substance Abuse Prevention (OSAP) funds 18 prevention programs in Native communities in 12 states. Figures show the percentage of projects that provided each type of intervention.

School-based interventions	Percent of projects
Education/training not using established curriculum	69.0
Referral for counseling/psychotherapy	50.0
Group counseling/psychotherapy	44.0
Self-help groups	44.0
Education/training using established curriculum	44.0
Individual counseling/psychotherapy	38.0
Cultural activities	31.0
Case/program consultation	31.0
Recreational activities	25.0
Special facility	25.0
No school-based intervention	17.0
Social action groups	13.0
Special register	6.0
Legal intervention	-
Other assessment	13.0

Source: U.S. Department of Health and Human Services. Public Health Service. Alcohol, Drug Abuse, and Mental Health Administration. Office for Substance Abuse Prevention. *Breaking New Ground For American Indian and Alaska Native Youth: Program Summaries* (OSAP Technical Report-3). Rockville, MD: U.S. DHHS, p. 39.

★ 289 ★

Adolescents

Sexual Activity Among Adolescents

Data are shown in percent and are based on a survey of 13,923 rural American Indian/Alaska Native adolescents living on or near reservations[1].

Frequency of sexual intercourse	Males	Females
Not sure	24.6	21.1
Once or twice	14.7	16.9
Rarely (a few times a year or less)	30.6	32.2
Sometimes (1-4 times per month)	22.6	20.4
Frequently (several times a week)	7.6	9.4

Source: Indian Health Service, Maternal and Child Health Bureau, and the Robert Wood Johnson Foundation. *The State of Native American Youth Health, February, 1992,* p. 35. *Notes:* 1. Caution: Sample was not random and does not fully represent all Native American/Alaska Native groups.

★ 290 ★

Adolescents

Student Reports of Risk Behaviors

Data show the percentage of Native American youths who reported that the following activities occur on or off school grounds. Data are based on a survey of 13,923 rural American Indian/Alaska Native adolescents living on or near reservations[1].

Activity	Grades 7-9	Grades 10-12
Using drugs	23.4	48.4
Drinking	32.3	54.7
Inhaling paint, gas	12.2	8.3
Destroying things	22.2	26.2
Getting into fights	36.1	20.0
Stealing things	26.2	25.8

Source: Indian Health Service, Maternal and Child Health Bureau, and the Robert Wood Johnson Foundation. *The State of Native American Youth Health, February, 1992*, p. 10. *Notes:* 1. Caution: Sample was not random and does not fully represent all Native American/Alaska Native groups.

★ 291 ★

Adolescents

Substance Abuse Among Adolescents

Data show the percentage of youths who reported having tried each substance. Results are based on a survey of 13,923 rural American Indian/Alaska Native adolescents living on or near reservations[1].

Substance	Grades 7-9		Grades 10-12	
	Males	Females	Males	Females
Cigarettes	41.6	46.3	50.1	54.2
Beer/wine	45.3	45.3	74.0	69.1
Hard liquor	28.8	24.2	56.2	46.2
Chewing tobacco/snuff	44.8	29.4	49.3	25.1
Marijuana	32.9	29.5	51.7	48.4
Peyote	23.4	20.4	25.0	21.5
Inhalants	12.7	15.0	6.6	7.4
Amphetamines	7.8	7.7	13.8	12.7
Cocaine	4.6	4.1	8.9	6.7
Sedatives	3.6	3.2	3.9	3.8
Codeine/morphine/other opiates	2.9	2.1	5.7	5.0
Psychedelics	4.3	2.9	9.3	6.3
Diet pills to lose weight	4.2	8.4	3.7	14.6
Look-a-like drugs	4.5	4.5	2.7	3.0
PCP/angel dust	2.5	2.5	3.7	2.4
Crack/rock cocaine	2.7	2.5	4.1	2.8
Heroin	1.6	1.2	1.1	1.0

Source: Indian Health Service, Maternal and Child Health Bureau, and the Robert Wood Johnson Foundation. *The State of Native American Youth Health, February, 1992*, p. 41. *Notes:* 1. Caution: Sample was not random and does not fully represent all Native American/Alaska Native groups.

★ 292 ★

Adolescents

Suicide Attempts Reported by Rural Native American Adolescents, by Sex and Grade: Females

| 12th - 16.2 |
| 11th - 13.2 |
| 10th - 13.0 |
| 7th - 10.9 |
| 9th - 9.8 |
| 8th - 10.4 |

Data are based on a survey of 13,923 rural American Indian/Alaska Native adolescents living on or near reservations.[1].

Grade	Percent
7th	10.9
8th	10.4
9th	9.8
10th	13.0
11th	13.2
12th	16.2

Source: Indian Health Service, Maternal and Child Health Bureau, and the Robert Wood Johnson Foundation. *The State of Native American Youth Health, February, 1992,* p. 31. *Notes:* 1. Caution: Sample was not truly random and does not fully represent all Native American/Alaska Native groups.

★ 293 ★

Adolescents

Suicide Attempts Reported by Rural Native American Adolescents, by Sex and Grade: Males

```
11th - 26.6
9th - 24.6
12th - 24.1
10th - 24.4
8th - 19.9
7th - 15.0
```

Data are based on a survey of 13,923 rural American Indian/Alaska Native adolescents living on or near reservations.[1].

Grade	Percent
7th	15.0
8th	19.9
9th	24.6
10th	24.4
11th	26.6
12th	24.1

Source: Indian Health Service, Maternal and Child Health Bureau, and the Robert Wood Johnson Foundation, *The State of Native American Youth Health, February, 1992*, p. 31. *Notes:* 1. Caution: Sample was not truly random and does not fully represent all Native American/Alaska Native groups.

★ 294 ★

Adolescents

Top Concerns of Rural Adolescents: Females

Data are based on a survey of 13,923 rural American Indian/Alaska Native adolescents living on or near reservations[1].

Concerns, by age group	%
Grades 7-9	
School performance	64.5
Parent dying	63.2
Losing best friend	61.6
Getting AIDS	49.7
Appearance/looks	48.6
Grades 10-12	
School performance	72.9
Parent dying	63.8
Losing best friend	57.1

[Continued]

★ 294 ★

Top Concerns of Rural Adolescents: Females
[Continued]

Concerns, by age group	%
Future employment	48.8
Getting AIDS	48.4

Source: Indian Health Service, Maternal and Child Health Bureau, and the Robert Wood Johnson Foundation, *The State of Native American Youth Health, February, 1992,* p. 26. *Notes:* 1. Caution: Sample was not random and does not fully represent all Native American/Alaska Native groups.

★ 295 ★

Adolescents

Top Concerns of Rural Adolescents: Males

Data are based on a survey of 13,923 rural American Indian/Alaska Native adolescents living on or near reservations[1].

Concerns	%
Grades 7-9	
Parent dying	55.3
School performance	51.1
Getting AIDS	49.3
Losing best friend	38.6
Body development	35.6
Grades 10-12	
Parent dying	55.4
School performance	54.6
Getting AIDS	48.6
Losing best friend	39.9
Future employment	37.7

Source: Indian Health Service, Maternal and Child Health Bureau, and the Robert Wood Johnson Foundation. *The State of Native American Youth Health, February, 1992,* p. 26. *Notes:* 1. Caution: Sample was not random and does not fully represent all Native American/Alaska Native groups.

★ 296 ★

Adolescents

Whom Adolescents Confide in When Physically or Sexually Abused

Data are shown in percent for those who did confide in someone. Results are based on a survey of 13,923 rural American Indian/Alaska Native adolescents living on or near reservations[1].

Abuse confidant	Physical abuse		Sexual abuse	
	Males (N=198)	Females (N=711)	Males (N=74)	Females (N=558)
Family member	67.6	59.6	49.3	67.9
Close friend	57.6	83.3	55.6	77.4
School counselor or teacher	25.7	27.5	22.6	16.5
Social worker	23.0	25.8	27.0	25.9
School nurse/public health nurse	13.1	9.6	17.6	8.3
Physician	11.9	6.8	19.1	7.7
Mental health counselor	11.4	11.8	18.6	13.8
Dorm aide or counselor	13.2	9.4	16.4	7.8
CHR Village Health aide	6.9	1.4	14.3	2.5
Minister or priest	9.1	4.8	14.7	4.8

Source: Indian Health Service, Maternal and Child Health Bureau, and the Robert Wood Johnson Foundation. *The State of Native American Youth Health, February, 1992,* p. 30. *Notes:* An (N) indicates the number of respondents. 1. Caution: Sample was not random and does not fully represent all Native American/Alaska Native groups.

The Elderly

★ 297 ★

Elderly Households by Type and Relationship in Selected Alaska Native Villages

Data are shown for the 50 areas with the largest populations, in number of persons.

ANVSA[1]	Persons in family households				Persons in nonfamily households					Persons in group quarters	
					Male householder		Female householder				
	Householder	Spouse	Other relatives	Non-relatives	Living alone	Not living alone	Living alone	Not living alone	Non-relatives	Institu-tionalized persons	Other persons in group quarters
Akiachak	20	4	0	0	0	0	0	0	0	0	0
Akutan	2	0	1	0	0	0	0	0	0	0	0
Alakanuk	8	7	5	0	0	0	0	0	0	0	0
Andreafsky	8	2	2	0	0	0	0	0	0	0	0
Angoon	16	9	1	0	4	0	0	0	0	0	0
Aniak	0	2	3	0	4	0	6	0	0	0	0
Barrow	38	22	7	0	7	0	7	0	0	0	0
Bethel	79	17	7	0	13	2	16	0	0	0	0
Chevak	16	2	2	0	3	0	0	0	0	0	0
Copper Center	17	3	0	0	8	0	0	0	0	0	0
Craig	12	6	0	0	3	0	3	0	0	0	0
Dillingham	33	13	9	0	5	0	20	6	3	0	0
Emmonak	15	3	2	0	0	0	4	0	0	0	0

[Continued]

★ 297 ★

Elderly Households by Type and Relationship in Selected Alaska Native Villages
[Continued]

ANVSA[1]	Persons in family households				Persons in nonfamily households					Persons in group quarters	
					Male householder		Female householder		Non-relatives	Institu-tionalized persons	Other persons in group quarters
	Householder	Spouse	Other relatives	Non-relatives	Living alone	Not living alone	Living alone	Not living alone			
Fort Yukon	9	3	2	2	2	0	2	0	0	0	0
Galena	8	4	1	0	4	0	0	0	0	0	0
Gambell	11	4	6	0	0	0	0	0	0	0	0
Grouse Creek Group	12	6	3	0	3	0	0	0	0	0	0
Hoonah	12	9	4	0	9	0	8	0	0	0	0
Hooper Bay	34	13	2	0	0	0	2	0	0	0	0
Kake	18	9	2	0	1	0	7	0	0	0	0
Kasigluk	14	11	8	0	1	0	0	0	0	0	0
King Cove	7	0	2	2	1	0	0	0	0	0	0
King Salmon	2	0	0	0	0	0	3	0	0	0	0
Kipnuk	10	5	0	0	1	0	0	2	0	0	0
Klawock	10	8	0	0	3	0	5	0	0	0	0
Kotlik	15	8	2	0	4	0	2	0	0	0	0
Kotzebue	41	16	6	0	4	0	10	0	0	29	0
Kwethluk	23	8	2	0	5	0	2	0	0	0	0
McGrath	7	2	2	2	1	0	2	0	0	0	0
Mountain Village	17	5	2	0	0	0	2	0	0	0	0
Naknek	5	2	0	0	4	0	13	0	0	0	0
Ninilchik	227	204	24	11	88	0	49	0	0	19	0
Noorvik	22	6	0	0	0	0	0	0	0	0	0
Pilot Station	7	0	5	0	2	0	0	0	0	0	0
Point Hope	5	4	6	0	1	0	0	0	0	0	0
Quinhagak	21	4	2	2	3	0	0	0	0	0	0
St. Paul	15	7	2	0	0	1	0	0	0	0	0
Salamatof	9	9	8	0	4	1	22	0	2	0	0
Sand Point	8	0	0	0	4	0	0	2	2	0	0
Savoonga	15	5	3	0	0	0	0	0	0	0	0
Selawik	23	2	5	0	2	0	0	0	0	0	0
Shishmaref	8	4	0	0	0	0	2	0	0	0	0
Stebbins	19	8	1	0	0	0	0	0	0	0	0
Togiak	18	0	6	0	0	0	3	0	3	0	0
Tok	20	12	0	0	9	3	4	0	2	0	0
Toksook Bay	5	2	1	0	0	0	0	0	0	0	0
Unalakleet	25	8	0	0	3	0	2	0	0	0	0
Unalaska	8	0	1	0	4	0	0	2	1	0	0
Wainwright	12	5	2	0	0	0	2	0	0	0	0
Yakutat	14	2	0	0	3	0	9	0	0	0	0

Source: Census of Population and Housing, 1990: Summary Tape File 3C on CD-ROM [machine-readable datafiles]. Prepared by the Bureau of the Census. Washington, DC: The Bureau, 1992. *Notes:* 1. Alaska Native villages (ANVs) constitute tribes, bands, clans, groups, villages, communities, or associations in Alaska that are recognized pursuant to the Alaska Native Claims Settlement Act of 1972, Public Law 92-203. Because ANVs do not have legally designated boundaries, the Census Bureau has established Alaska Native village statistical areas (ANVSAs) for statistical purposes. For the 1990 census, the Census Bureau cooperated with officials of the nonprofit corporation within each participating Alaska Native Regional Corporation (ANRC), as well as other knowledgeable officials, to delineate boundaries that encompass the settled area associated with each ANV.

★ 298 ★

The Elderly

Elderly Households by Type and Relationship in Selected Tribal Designated Statistical Areas

TDSA[1]	Persons in family households				Persons in nonfamily households					Persons in group quarters	
					Male householder		Female householder		Non-relatives	Institu-tionalized persons	Other persons in group quarters
	Householder	Spouse	Other relatives	Non-relatives	Living alone	Not living alone	Living alone	Not living alone			
Apache Choctaw TDSA (state)	1,383	808	181	5	233	4	882	3	5	229	0
Chickahominy TDSA (state)	79	32	12	0	21	0	39	0	0	0	0
Clifton Choctaw TDSA (state)	36	9	0	0	0	0	16	0	0	0	0
Coharie TDSA (state)	5,411	3,011	1,042	50	968	23	4,342	52	77	1,130	5
Coquille Indian TDSA	21,199	15,337	1,940	438	3,659	408	13,827	438	852	2,848	586

[Continued]

★ 298 ★

Elderly Households by Type and Relationship in Selected Tribal Designated Statistical Areas

[Continued]

| TDSA[1] | Persons in family households | | | | Persons in nonfamily households | | | | | Persons in group quarters | |
| | | | | | Male householder | | Female householder | | | | |
	Householder	Spouse	Other relatives	Non-relatives	Living alone	Not living alone	Living alone	Not living alone	Non-relatives	Institu-tionalized persons	Other persons in group quarters
Delaware-Muncie TDSA (state)	27	20	0	0	0	0	0	0	0	0	0
Florida Tribe of Eastern Creek TDSA (state)	27	18	10	0	9	0	0	0	0	0	0
Haliwa-Saponi TDSA (state)	218	133	89	0	73	10	114	0	0	0	0
Jena Band of Choctaw TDSA (state)	2,445	1,353	296	20	313	19	1,856	38	40	766	25
Klamath TDSA	2,135	1,480	235	74	412	23	1,404	53	89	237	7
Lumbee TDSA (state)	1,722	888	259	23	238	17	949	21	6	189	19
Meherrin TDSA (state)	3,093	1,821	515	27	574	20	1,908	13	33	348	0
Mohegan TDSA (state)	1,040	761	168	17	234	0	910	36	46	105	0
Ramapough TDSA (state)	39	17	7	0	0	0	19	0	0	0	0
United Houma Nation TDSA (state)	29,285	16,543	7,037	272	4,451	263	16,976	318	462	3,253	68
Waccamaw Siouan TDSA (state)	77	36	9	0	15	0	22	0	0	0	0
Wampanoag-Gay Head TDSA	606	481	78	14	181	6	454	16	12	42	0

Source: Census of Population and Housing, 1990: Summary Tape File 3C on CD-ROM [machine-readable datafiles]. Prepared by the Bureau of the Census. Washington, DC: The Bureau, 1992. *Notes:* 1. Tribal designated statistical areas (TDSAs) are areas, delineated outside Oklahoma by federally- and state-recognized tribes without a land base or associated trust lands, to provide statistical areas for which the Census Bureau tabulates data. TDSAs represent areas generally containing the American Indian population over which federally-recognized tribes have jurisdiction and areas in which state tribes provide benefits and services to their members. The names of TDSAs delineated by state-recognized tribes are followed by "(state)." The Census Bureau did not recognize TDSAs before the 1990 census.

★ 299 ★

The Elderly

Elderly Households by Type and Relationship in Selected Tribal Jurisdiction Statistical Areas

| Tribal Jurisdiction Statistical Area[1] | Persons in family households | | | | Persons in nonfamily households | | | | | Persons in group quarters | |
| | | | | | Male householder | | Female householder | | | | |
	Householder	Spouse	Other relatives	Non-relatives	Living alone	Not living alone	Living alone	Not living alone	Non-relatives	Institu-tionalized persons	Other persons in group quarters
Absentee Shawnee-Citizens Band of Potawatomi TJSA	3,363	2,057	456	14	554	29	1,631	25	37	383	31
Caddo-Wichita-Delaware TJSA	518	338	47	0	125	0	309	0	0	79	0
Cherokee TJSA	20,537	13,331	2,024	152	3,555	185	13,296	163	316	2,949	149
Cheyenne-Arapaho TJSA	6,896	4,696	600	7	1,164	36	5,378	56	64	1,914	0
Chickasaw TJSA	14,669	10,126	1,356	35	2,906	81	11,038	78	152	3,091	55
Choctaw TJSA	11,950	7,361	1,472	96	2,551	103	8,832	108	144	2,316	35
Creek TJSA	27,096	18,077	3,446	158	4,517	227	20,725	309	393	4,897	108
Iowa TJSA	210	141	30	0	36	5	128	0	5	0	0
Kaw TJSA	762	533	50	0	104	0	529	0	0	103	0
Kiowa-Comanche-Apache-Fort Sill Apache TJSA	8,925	5,725	919	39	1,673	38	6,668	61	79	1,682	24
Otoe-Missouria TJSA	127	61	6	2	43	0	69	0	0	0	0
Pawnee TJSA	926	621	83	5	181	9	578	0	6	83	0
Sac and Fox TJSA	3,122	2,196	283	7	491	6	2,469	22	22	469	0
Seminole TJSA	1,553	909	218	11	337	3	1,046	16	22	197	12
Tonkawa TJSA	761	560	51	0	161	11	652	7	22	219	0
Creek-Seminole Joint Area TJSA	153	99	13	0	18	0	116	0	2	15	0
Iowa-Sac and Fox Joint Area TJSA	23	16	0	0	15	0	14	0	0	0	0

Source: Census of Population and Housing, 1990: Summary Tape File 3C on CD-ROM [machine-readable datafiles]. Prepared by the Bureau of the Census. Washington, DC: The Bureau, 1992. *Notes:* 1. Tribal jurisdiction statistical areas (TJSAs) are areas, delineated by federally recognized tribes in Oklahoma without a reservation, for which the Census Bureau tabulates data. TJSAs represent areas generally containing the American Indian population over which one or more tribal governments have jurisdiction. If tribal officials delineated adjacent TJSAs so that they include some duplicate territory, the overlap area is called a "joint use area," which is treated as a separate TJSA for census purposes.

★ 300 ★
The Elderly

Elderly Households by Type and Relationship on Selected Reservations and Trust Lands

Data are shown for the 50 areas with the largest populations, in number of persons.

American Indian Reservation and Trust Lands[1,2]	Persons in family households				Persons in nonfamily households					Persons in group quarters	
					Male householder		Female householder			Institutionalized persons	Other persons in group quarters
	Householder	Spouse	Other relatives	Non-relatives	Living alone	Not living alone	Living alone	Not living alone	Non-relatives		
Agua Caliente Reservation	2,743	2,060	229	27	457	136	1,708	67	158	216	11
Allegany Reservation	352	227	47	10	126	12	412	7	10	129	6
Blackfeet Reservation	198	85	31	8	69	2	51	0	2	28	28
Cheyenne River Reservation	250	127	45	0	47	3	160	0	0	0	0
Coeur d'Alene Reservation and Trust Lands, ID	333	218	32	0	73	3	127	3	10	0	0
Colorado River Reservation	388	266	30	31	60	17	214	5	17	0	0
Colville Reservation	285	156	30	2	81	2	138	0	3	36	0
Crow Reservation and Trust Lands, MT	163	91	10	0	25	0	36	0	0	0	5
Eastern Cherokee Reservation	227	124	13	0	24	0	90	3	6	0	0
Flathead Reservation	1,203	842	107	13	305	19	754	14	39	185	0
Fort Apache Reservation	232	67	83	7	17	0	5	0	0	0	0
Fort Berthold Reservation	199	132	24	0	98	1	103	0	0	104	0
Fort Hall Reservation and Trust Lands, ID	151	100	37	0	20	0	78	0	0	0	0
Fort Peck Reservation	377	230	66	0	65	0	159	0	0	50	0
Gila River Reservation	241	89	77	0	31	0	40	13	25	71	0
Hopi Reservation and Trust Lands, AZ	300	140	93	8	17	0	58	0	0	0	0
Isabella Reservation and Trust Lands, MI	773	528	91	15	125	9	467	9	7	178	38
Laguna Pueblo and Trust Lands, NM	163	83	27	0	21	0	66	8	4	22	0
Lake Traverse (Sisseton) Reservation	673	418	139	1	171	9	415	0	8	137	0
Leech Lake Reservation	429	269	53	1	128	8	225	11	19	0	0
Mississippi Choctaw Reservation and Trust Lands, MS	70	34	0	0	0	0	6	0	4	0	0
Muckleshoot Reservation and Trust Lands, WA	155	107	18	1	19	3	105	8	11	0	0
Navajo Reservation and Trust Lands, AZ–NM–UT	4,258	1,734	604	54	772	44	1,123	23	84	31	60
Nez Perce Reservation	1,035	699	69	14	224	13	467	18	28	72	0
Northern Cheyenne Reservation and Trust Lands, MT–SD	67	37	0	0	8	0	11	0	0	0	0
Omaha Reservation	268	156	16	2	54	0	168	4	4	78	0
Oneida (West) Reservation	350	244	45	3	58	3	122	6	19	39	34
Osage Reservation	2,010	1,279	172	12	282	16	1,564	17	21	225	6
Papago Reservation	269	99	87	18	0	13	59	11	22	0	0
Pine Ridge Reservation and Trust Lands, NE–SD	340	121	81	0	51	0	50	6	14	34	0
Port Madison Reservation	223	157	19	4	24	7	121	5	3	0	0
Puyallup Reservation and Trust Lands, WA	1,071	771	180	9	208	21	568	22	28	0	52
Red Lake Reservation	106	42	7	0	4	0	0	0	0	30	0
Rosebud Reservation and Trust Lands, SD	306	86	38	3	80	7	103	0	5	0	0
Salt River Reservation	317	191	26	0	62	0	207	5	5	0	0
San Carlos Reservation	95	38	46	0	29	0	40	0	0	13	0
Sandia Pueblo	120	93	27	4	16	4	45	6	1	0	0
San Juan Pueblo	195	75	38	0	14	0	72	0	0	0	0
Santa Clara Pueblo	450	262	58	0	67	0	230	2	0	112	0
Southern Ute Reservation	299	171	39	2	67	3	102	3	7	18	0
Standing Rock Reservation	315	167	58	15	42	0	87	0	0	0	0
Taos Pueblo and Trust Lands, NM	224	117	32	0	45	0	201	0	1	0	0
Tulalip Reservation	298	229	45	2	67	0	108	3	4	0	0
Turtle Mountain Reservation and Trust Lands, ND–SD	213	40	28	25	21	0	75	0	0	0	0
Uintah and Ouray Reservation	577	352	56	2	88	2	265	2	1	41	0
White Earth Reservation	505	304	67	5	140	4	268	2	7	56	6
Wind River Reservation	913	545	97	0	134	11	436	4	6	119	0
Yakima Reservation and Trust Lands, WA	1,059	622	206	17	262	22	493	17	23	98	0

[Continued]

★ 300 ★

Elderly Households by Type and Relationship on Selected Reservations and Trust Lands
[Continued]

American Indian Reservation and Trust Lands[1,2]	Persons in family households				Persons in nonfamily households					Persons in group quarters	
					Male householder		Female householder				
	Householder	Spouse	Other relatives	Non-relatives	Living alone	Not living alone	Living alone	Not living alone	Non-relatives	Institu-tionalized persons	Other persons in group quarters
Yankton Reservation	317	200	50	5	90	4	235	0	3	125	0
Zuni Pueblo	213	96	49	0	5	0	23	0	0	0	0

Source: Census of Population and Housing, 1990: Summary Tape File 3C on CD-ROM [machine-readable datafiles]. Prepared by the Bureau of the Census. Washington, DC: The Bureau, 1992. *Notes:* 1. Federal American Indian reservations are areas with boundaries established by treaty, statute, and/or executive or court order, and recognized by the federal government as territory in which American Indian tribes have jurisdiction. State reservations are lands held in trust by state governments for the use and benefit of a given tribe. The reservations and their boundaries were identified for the 1990 census by the Bureau of Indian Affairs (BIA), Department of Interior (for federal reservations), and state governments (for state reservations). The names of American Indian reservations recognized by state governments, but not by the federal government, are followed by "state." Areas composed of reservation lands that are administered jointly and/or are claimed by two reservations, as identified by the BIA, are called "joint areas," and are treated as separate American Indian reservations for census purposes. Federal reservations may cross state boundaries, and federal and state reservations may cross county, county subdivision, and place boundaries. For reservations that cross state boundaries, only the portion of the reservations in a given state is shown in the data products for that state; the entire reservations are shown in data products for the United States. 2. Trust lands are property associated with a particular American Indian reservation or tribe, held in trust by the federal government. Trust lands may be held in trust either for a tribe (tribal trust lands) or for an individual member of a tribe (individual trust land). Trust lands recognized for the 1990 census comprised all tribal trust lands and inhabited individual trust lands located outside of a reservation boundary. As with other American Indian areas, trust lands may be located in more than one state. Only the trust lands in a given state are shown in the data products for that state; all trust lands associated with a reservation or tribe are shown in data products for the United States. The Census Bureau first reported data for tribal trust lands for the 1980 census.

Chapter 4
EDUCATION

░░░

Educational Attainment

░░░

★ 301 ★

Educational Attainment of American Indians and Alaska Natives Age 25 and Older in Selected Alaska Native Villages

Data are shown for the 50 areas with the largest populations, in number of persons.

Alaska Native Village Statistical Area[1]	Less than 9th grade	9th to 12th grade no diploma	High school graduate or equiv.	Some college, no degree	Assoc. degree	Bachelor's degree	Graduate or profess. degree
Akiachak	107	13	73	6	16	0	0
Akutan	3	22	17	0	2	0	0
Alakanuk	80	39	74	12	2	4	3
Andreafsky	44	14	52	37	4	6	0
Angoon	30	55	92	46	6	3	0
Aniak	35	18	72	18	2	3	2
Barrow	205	114	257	133	43	35	9
Bethel	307	143	527	270	86	56	27
Chevak	62	18	70	57	3	7	0
Copper Center	19	15	33	13	0	3	0
Craig	11	33	60	20	11	6	2
Dillingham	108	60	210	120	26	32	10
Emmonak	86	11	93	18	5	2	3
Fort Yukon	74	57	104	16	2	6	0
Galena	40	20	79	31	0	4	0
Gambell	80	64	73	28	6	0	4
Grouse Creek Group	7	3	20	10	10	0	4
Hoonah	31	39	129	45	8	20	9
Hooper Bay	103	35	156	43	5	5	0
Kake	17	55	104	61	4	9	5
Kasigluk	68	21	70	15	6	2	0
King Cove	23	16	28	16	1	0	0
King Salmon	11	9	18	12	7	0	0
Kipnuk	84	21	80	10	2	2	0
Klawock	9	36	85	35	5	3	8
Kotlik	77	17	75	19	5	6	0

[Continued]

★ 301 ★

Educational Attainment of American Indians and Alaska Natives Age 25 and Older in Selected Alaska Native Villages

[Continued]

Alaska Native Village Statistical Area[1]	Less than 9th grade	9th to 12th grade no diploma	High school graduate or equiv.	Some college, no degree	Assoc. degree	Bachelor's degree	Graduate or profess. degree
Kotzebue	220	115	379	134	42	22	4
Kwethluk	108	32	72	27	4	6	0
McGrath	23	15	33	25	9	7	3
Mountain Village	99	15	75	33	6	3	2
Naknek	21	16	39	34	12	3	3
Ninilchik	44	24	96	33	19	5	0
Noorvik	94	30	61	29	0	8	0
Pilot Station	60	30	63	15	6	0	0
Point Hope	60	41	96	35	3	3	0
Quinhagak	86	53	52	31	6	9	0
St. Paul	82	56	117	37	7	0	0
Salamatof	7	28	8	41	6	2	2
Sand Point	52	46	83	22	4	3	0
Savoonga	94	53	85	8	1	0	0
Selawik	78	50	75	22	6	0	0
Shishmaref	65	14	52	43	1	3	0
Stebbins	68	45	38	17	0	0	0
Togiak	87	28	93	40	0	5	0
Tok	9	8	10	6	3	2	0
Toksook Bay	72	11	46	21	4	2	1
Unalakleet	58	23	96	40	13	16	0
Unalaska	21	48	53	14	5	9	12
Wainwright	77	40	95	9	0	0	0
Yakutat	25	36	49	25	6	6	3

Source: Census of Population and Housing, 1990: Summary Tape File 3C on CD-ROM [machine-readable datafiles]. Prepared by the Bureau of the Census. Washington, DC: The Bureau, 1992. *Notes:* 1. Alaska Native villages (ANVs) constitute tribes, bands, clans, groups, villages, communities, or associations in Alaska that are recognized pursuant to the Alaska Native Claims Settlement Act of 1972, Public Law 92-203. Because ANVs do not have legally designated boundaries, the Census Bureau has established Alaska Native village statistical areas (ANVSAs) for statistical purposes. For the 1990 census, the Census Bureau cooperated with officials of the nonprofit corporation within each participating Alaska Native Regional Corporation (ANRC), as well as other knowledgeable officials, to delineate boundaries that encompass the settled area associated with each ANV.

★ 302 ★

Educational Attainment

Educational Attainment of American Indians and Alaska Natives Age 25 and Older in Selected Tribal Designated Statistical Areas

Tribal Designated Statistical Area[1]	Less than 9th grade	9th to 12th grade no diploma	High school graduate or equiv.	Some college, no degree	Assoc. degree	Bachelor's degree	Graduate or profess. degree
Apache Choctaw TDSA (state)	81	91	183	17	0	0	9
Chickahominy TDSA (state)	49	93	127	46	6	21	0
Clifton Choctaw TDSA (state)	41	26	39	0	0	0	0
Coharie TDSA (state)	222	240	290	50	39	16	21
Coquille Indian TDSA	337	807	1,042	872	282	208	92
Delaware-Muncie TDSA (state)	0	0	6	0	0	0	0
Florida Tribe of Eastern Creek TDSA (state)	0	0	0	0	0	0	0
Haliwa-Saponi TDSA (state)	506	357	264	74	62	0	0
Jena Band of Choctaw TDSA (state)	33	32	37	74	0	0	2
Klamath TDSA	89	229	305	180	40	17	9
Lumbee TDSA (state)	3,524	4,243	3,740	1,540	575	1,138	360
Meherrin TDSA (state)	14	19	23	13	17	8	12
Mohegan TDSA (state)	6	32	55	30	7	8	18
Ramapough TDSA (state)	56	33	7	7	0	16	0
United Houma Nation TDSA (state)	2,218	1,015	1,020	301	87	85	52
Waccamaw Siouan TDSA (state)	202	170	263	100	15	0	0
Wampanoag-Gay Head TDSA	14	11	50	26	34	14	8

Source: Census of Population and Housing, 1990: Summary Tape File 3C on CD-ROM [machine-readable datafiles]. Prepared by the Bureau of the Census. Washington, DC: The Bureau, 1992. *Notes:* 1. Tribal designated statistical areas (TDSAs) are areas, delineated outside Oklahoma by federally- and state-recognized tribes without a land base or associated trust lands, to provide statistical areas for which the Census Bureau tabulates data. TDSAs represent areas generally containing the American Indian population over which federally-recognized tribes have jurisdiction and areas in which state tribes provide benefits and services to their members. The names of TDSAs delineated by state-recognized tribes are followed by "(state)." The Census Bureau did not recognize TDSAs before the 1990 census.

★ 303 ★

Educational Attainment

Educational Attainment of American Indians and Alaska Natives Age 25 and Older in Selected Tribal Jurisdiction Statistical Areas

Tribal Jurisdiction Statistical Area[1]	Less than 9th grade	9th to 12th grade no diploma	High school graduate or equiv.	Some college, no degree	Assoc. degree	Bachelor's degree	Graduate or profess. degree
Absentee Shawnee-Citizens Band of Potawatomi TJSA	324	841	1,103	720	88	163	36
Caddo-Wichita-Delaware TJSA	24	86	139	33	0	17	9
Cherokee TJSA	5,117	6,943	10,718	6,331	1,781	2,270	1,183
Cheyenne-Arapaho TJSA	238	808	889	879	177	180	97
Chickasaw TJSA	1,439	2,373	3,556	1,972	420	746	322
Choctaw TJSA	2,410	3,143	4,516	2,472	748	806	492
Creek TJSA	2,076	4,625	7,911	5,306	1,671	1,881	821
Iowa TJSA	14	48	65	14	4	7	2
Kaw TJSA	13	38	106	104	19	50	18
Kiowa-Comanche-Apache-Fort Sill Apache TJSA	563	1,403	2,210	1,297	236	468	241
Otoe-Missouria TJSA	13	60	82	43	22	11	0

[Continued]

★ 303 ★

Educational Attainment of American Indians and Alaska Natives Age 25 and Older in Selected Tribal Jurisdiction Statistical Areas
[Continued]

Tribal Jurisdiction Statistical Area[1]	Less than 9th grade	9th to 12th grade no diploma	High school graduate or equiv.	Some college, no degree	Assoc. degree	Bachelor's degree	Graduate or profess. degree
Pawnee TJSA	74	154	366	156	51	32	27
Sac and Fox TJSA	262	526	744	430	128	143	50
Seminole TJSA	374	466	480	316	116	79	73
Tonkawa TJSA	26	123	106	68	32	24	8
Creek-Seminole Joint Area TJSA	38	82	62	48	15	14	6
Iowa-Sac and Fox Joint Area TJSA	0	2	2	1	6	0	0

Source: Census of Population and Housing, 1990: Summary Tape File 3C on CD-ROM [machine-readable datafiles]. Prepared by the Bureau of the Census. Washington, DC: The Bureau, 1992. *Notes:* 1. Tribal jurisdiction statistical areas (TJSAs) are areas, delineated by federally recognized tribes in Oklahoma without a reservation, for which the Census Bureau tabulates data. TJSAs represent areas generally containing the American Indian population over which one or more tribal governments have jurisdiction. If tribal officials delineated adjacent TJSAs so that they include some duplicate territory, the overlap area is called a "joint use area," which is treated as a separate TJSA for census purposes.

★ 304 ★

Educational Attainment

Educational Attainment of American Indians and Alaska Natives Age 25 and Older on Selected Reservations and Trust Lands

Data are shown for the 50 areas with the largest populations, in number of persons.

American Indian Reservation and Trust Lands[1,2]	Less than 9th grade	9th to 12th grade no diploma	High school graduate or equiv.	Some college, no degree	Assoc. degree	Bachelor's degree	Graduate or profess. degree
Agua Caliente Reservation	0	7	24	30	0	11	0
Allegany Reservation	53	117	217	107	36	8	9
Blackfeet Reservation	303	806	969	756	242	132	86
Cheyenne River Reservation	295	555	687	425	106	72	30
Coeur d'Alene Reservation and Trust Lands, ID	58	62	90	85	32	17	1
Colorado River Reservation	172	246	369	191	69	43	4
Colville Reservation	217	389	654	418	111	85	27
Crow Reservation and Trust Lands, MT	215	443	455	825	98	115	30
Eastern Cherokee Reservation	333	677	914	460	252	90	14
Flathead Reservation	317	355	823	638	243	109	29
Fort Apache Reservation	774	1,429	1,287	497	221	50	7
Fort Berthold Reservation	161	237	286	418	115	83	27
Fort Hall Reservation and Trust Lands, ID	217	389	460	253	117	28	7
Fort Peck Reservation	290	724	836	446	178	113	42
Gila River Reservation	905	1,710	1,021	369	109	47	8
Hopi Reservation and Trust Lands, AZ	605	738	1,175	610	339	66	54
Isabella Reservation and Trust Lands, MI	78	122	114	69	23	7	8
Laguna Pueblo and Trust Lands, NM	247	318	933	298	178	65	19
Lake Traverse (Sisseton) Reservation	143	303	440	225	72	28	16
Leech Lake Reservation	254	365	489	290	93	53	10
Mississippi Choctaw Reservation and Trust Lands, MS	545	275	530	231	82	31	9
Muckleshoot Reservation and Trust Lands, WA	80	112	69	60	3	8	3
Navajo Reservation and Trust Lands, AZ–NM–UT	23,900	14,584	15,573	6,829	2,492	1,340	637
Nez Perce Reservation	80	200	253	282	71	38	30
Northern Cheyenne Reservation and Trust Lands, MT–SD	145	412	384	361	67	40	41
Omaha Reservation	108	199	245	136	72	9	4
Oneida (West) Reservation	166	230	444	215	86	50	25
Osage Reservation	235	523	1,193	843	202	250	69

[Continued]

★ 304 ★

Educational Attainment of American Indians and Alaska Natives Age 25 and Older on Selected Reservations and Trust Lands

[Continued]

American Indian Reservation and Trust Lands[1,2]	Less than 9th grade	9th to 12th grade no diploma	High school graduate or equiv.	Some college, no degree	Assoc. degree	Bachelor's degree	Graduate or profess. degree
Papago Reservation	1,318	865	1,730	182	31	17	0
Pine Ridge Reservation and Trust Lands, NE–SD	823	1,206	1,056	762	386	220	72
Port Madison Reservation	13	37	47	43	17	17	3
Puyallup Reservation and Trust Lands, WA	47	107	145	124	35	15	17
Red Lake Reservation	249	426	530	254	78	22	5
Rosebud Reservation and Trust Lands, SD	528	761	899	567	248	89	73
Salt River Reservation	137	596	533	239	29	14	8
San Carlos Reservation	428	1,100	1,005	297	132	13	46
Sandia Pueblo	27	17	48	86	6	20	8
San Juan Pueblo	57	88	283	156	92	12	25
Santa Clara Pueblo	65	63	221	190	103	53	18
Southern Ute Reservation	34	89	222	91	20	29	10
Standing Rock Reservation	233	538	625	321	205	72	25
Taos Pueblo and Trust Lands, NM	55	159	305	134	41	30	11
Tulalip Reservation	61	180	152	114	38	20	6
Turtle Mountain Reservation and Trust Lands, ND–SD	615	737	576	517	320	217	29
Uintah and Ouray Reservation	97	442	312	188	45	32	14
White Earth Reservation	229	308	497	190	113	31	23
Wind River Reservation	241	701	729	541	163	102	55
Yakima Reservation and Trust Lands, WA	361	693	919	533	155	159	25
Yankton Reservation	135	241	252	157	24	31	4
Zuni Pueblo	436	1,092	1,200	460	118	95	28

Source: Census of Population and Housing, 1990: Summary Tape File 3C on CD-ROM [machine-readable datafiles]. Prepared by the Bureau of the Census. Washington, DC: The Bureau, 1992. *Notes:* 1. Federal American Indian reservations are areas with boundaries established by treaty, statute, and/or executive or court order, and recognized by the federal government as territory in which American Indian tribes have jurisdiction. State reservations are lands held in trust by state governments for the use and benefit of a given tribe. The reservations and their boundaries were identified for the 1990 census by the Bureau of Indian Affairs (BIA), Department of Interior (for federal reservations), and state governments (for state reservations). The names of American Indian reservations recognized by state governments, but not by the federal government, are followed by "state." Areas composed of reservation lands that are administered jointly and/or are claimed by two reservations, as identified by the BIA, are called "joint areas," and are treated as separate American Indian reservations for census purposes. Federal reservations may cross state boundaries, and federal and state reservations may cross county, county subdivision, and place boundaries. For reservations that cross state boundaries, only the portion of the reservations in a given state is shown in the data products for that state; the entire reservations are shown in data products for the United States. 2. Trust lands are property associated with a particular American Indian reservation or tribe, held in trust by the federal government. Trust lands may be held in trust either for a tribe (tribal trust lands) or for an individual member of a tribe (individual trust land). Trust lands recognized for the 1990 census comprised all tribal trust lands and inhabited individual trust lands located outside of a reservation boundary. As with other American Indian areas, trust lands may be located in more than one state. Only the trust lands in a given state are shown in the data products for that state; all trust lands associated with a reservation or tribe are shown in data products for the United States. The Census Bureau first reported data for tribal trust lands for the 1980 census.

★ 305 ★

Educational Attainment

Educational Attainment of Persons Age 25 and Older in Selected Alaska Native Villages

Data are shown for the 50 areas with the largest populations, in number of persons.

Alaska Native Village Statistical Area[1]	Less than 9th grade	9th to 12th grade no diploma	High school graduate or equiv.	Some college, no degree	Assoc. degree	Bachelor's degree	Graduate or profess. degree
Akiachak	107	13	78	6	16	15	5
Akutan	33	79	102	66	38	53	35
Alakanuk	80	39	81	12	6	6	7
Andreafsky	44	14	56	48	6	23	4
Angoon	33	60	98	67	8	25	27
Aniak	37	18	108	52	6	23	22
Barrow	219	145	380	302	116	190	104
Bethel	324	183	770	545	178	340	220
Chevak	64	18	72	61	3	13	15
Copper Center	22	39	82	64	21	40	4
Craig	26	101	262	192	26	87	33
Dillingham	124	80	337	281	93	171	77
Emmonak	86	11	100	24	7	16	19
Fort Yukon	76	57	126	21	7	25	7
Galena	42	24	151	168	43	52	24
Gambell	80	64	73	28	6	6	4
Grouse Creek Group	21	39	131	96	23	62	17
Hoonah	31	55	184	85	30	35	14
Hooper Bay	103	35	157	47	5	18	7
Kake	22	69	157	84	6	26	16
Kasigluk	68	21	70	15	6	17	7
King Cove	59	33	98	56	21	31	3
King Salmon	13	12	98	209	46	38	44
Kipnuk	84	21	84	13	2	5	0
Klawock	11	79	185	55	8	28	35
Kotlik	77	17	75	21	5	10	5
Kotzebue	228	134	463	243	78	136	87
Kwethluk	108	32	75	29	4	13	3
McGrath	35	29	63	72	22	38	30
Mountain Village	99	17	83	42	6	12	23
Naknek	30	21	100	98	23	52	25
Ninilchik	328	563	1,993	1,633	439	1,075	293
Noorvik	94	30	61	32	0	21	7
Pilot Station	60	30	63	15	6	7	3
Point Hope	60	45	102	43	3	14	5
Quinhagak	86	55	54	33	8	14	9
St. Paul	82	84	140	97	16	9	5
Salamatof	15	112	173	205	59	41	20
Sand Point	114	80	162	93	9	35	11
Savoonga	94	55	85	8	1	9	6
Selawik	78	50	78	25	6	10	2
Shishmaref	65	14	53	43	2	11	2
Stebbins	68	45	40	17	0	12	2
Togiak	87	33	99	48	2	14	18

[Continued]

★ 305 ★

Educational Attainment of Persons Age 25 and Older in Selected Alaska Native Villages

[Continued]

Alaska Native Village Statistical Area[1]	Less than 9th grade	9th to 12th grade no diploma	High school graduate or equiv.	Some college, no degree	Assoc. degree	Bachelor's degree	Graduate or profess. degree
Tok	37	58	180	128	52	78	46
Toksook Bay	72	11	49	21	4	10	1
Unalakleet	58	23	113	62	30	35	17
Unalaska	121	356	595	657	170	248	56
Wainwright	77	40	99	12	0	15	8
Yakutat	27	53	96	75	10	20	25

Source: Census of Population and Housing, 1990: Summary Tape File 3C on CD-ROM [machine-readable datafiles]. Prepared by the Bureau of the Census. Washington, DC: The Bureau, 1992. *Notes:* 1. Alaska Native villages (ANVs) constitute tribes, bands, clans, groups, villages, communities, or associations in Alaska that are recognized pursuant to the Alaska Native Claims Settlement Act of 1972, Public Law 92-203. Because ANVs do not have legally designated boundaries, the Census Bureau has established Alaska Native village statistical areas (ANVSAs) for statistical purposes. For the 1990 census, the Census Bureau cooperated with officials of the nonprofit corporation within each participating Alaska Native Regional Corporation (ANRC), as well as other knowledgeable officials, to delineate boundaries that encompass the settled area associated with each ANV.

★ 306 ★

Educational Attainment

Educational Attainment of Persons Age 25 and Older in Selected Tribal Designated Statistical Areas

Tribal Designated Statistical Area[1]	Less than 9th grade	9th to 12th grade no diploma	High school graduate or equiv.	Some college, no degree	Assoc. degree	Bachelor's degree	Graduate or profess. degree
Apache Choctaw TDSA (state)	2,666	2,777	5,697	1,677	287	710	483
Chickahominy TDSA (state)	333	498	575	226	51	109	28
Clifton Choctaw TDSA (state)	96	79	112	11	5	0	0
Coharie TDSA (state)	11,737	14,895	23,110	11,483	4,728	5,685	2,696
Coquille Indian TDSA	16,024	34,501	76,621	64,949	17,355	33,226	19,949
Delaware-Muncie TDSA (state)	9	7	89	40	7	36	0
Florida Tribe of Eastern Creek TDSA (state)	19	50	43	56	0	0	0
Haliwa-Saponi TDSA (state)	1,314	851	1,031	293	146	92	29
Jena Band of Choctaw TDSA (state)	5,538	6,430	13,159	6,461	1,098	3,164	1,675
Klamath TDSA	1,993	3,907	9,022	5,833	1,903	2,247	980
Lumbee TDSA (state)	5,602	7,220	7,423	3,327	1,208	1,943	716
Meherrin TDSA (state)	6,648	8,353	11,086	4,065	1,823	2,273	1,006
Mohegan TDSA (state)	1,693	2,330	5,626	2,657	1,078	1,689	955
Ramapough TDSA (state)	128	107	85	94	7	49	8
United Houma Nation TDSA (state)	74,183	76,963	167,168	89,256	19,307	50,463	23,434
Waccamaw Siouan TDSA (state)	306	411	553	214	71	35	42
Wampanoag-Gay Head TDSA	253	542	2,431	1,541	829	1,784	865

Source: Census of Population and Housing, 1990: Summary Tape File 3C on CD-ROM [machine-readable datafiles]. Prepared by the Bureau of the Census. Washington, DC: The Bureau, 1992. *Notes:* 1. Tribal designated statistical areas (TDSAs) are areas, delineated outside Oklahoma by federally- and state-recognized tribes without a land base or associated trust lands, to provide statistical areas for which the Census Bureau tabulates data. TDSAs represent areas generally containing the American Indian population over which federally-recognized tribes have jurisdiction and areas in which state tribes provide benefits and services to their members. The names of TDSAs delineated by state-recognized tribes are followed by "(state)." The Census Bureau did not recognize TDSAs before the 1990 census.

★ 307 ★

Educational Attainment

Educational Attainment of Persons Age 25 and Older in Selected Tribal Jurisdiction Statistical Areas

Tribal Jurisdiction Statistical Area[1]	Less than 9th grade	9th to 12th grade no diploma	High school graduate or equiv.	Some college, no degree	Assoc. degree	Bachelor's degree	Graduate or profess. degree
Absentee Shawnee-Citizens Band of Potawatomi TJSA	5,341	10,868	19,081	12,788	2,923	4,478	2,154
Caddo-Wichita-Delaware TJSA	812	986	2,073	817	91	387	224
Cherokee TJSA	30,929	47,109	82,494	47,956	13,139	22,158	10,944
Cheyenne-Arapaho TJSA	9,487	14,039	32,388	19,974	4,640	9,009	5,154
Chickasaw TJSA	22,667	31,334	56,461	30,457	5,521	14,400	7,658
Choctaw TJSA	25,247	26,604	41,181	21,040	6,400	8,532	5,731
Creek TJSA	29,998	55,945	118,665	91,522	25,250	60,997	26,942
Iowa TJSA	328	512	1,094	363	81	142	60
Kaw TJSA	372	841	2,327	2,009	551	1,893	892
Kiowa-Comanche-Apache-Fort Sill Apache TJSA	13,047	18,468	39,508	26,805	5,664	12,603	6,419
Otoe-Missouria TJSA	131	284	691	263	119	118	48
Pawnee TJSA	997	1,729	4,151	1,749	422	740	309
Sac and Fox TJSA	4,244	5,987	11,954	6,011	1,166	2,749	1,352
Seminole TJSA	2,332	3,233	4,595	2,698	695	875	540
Tonkawa TJSA	765	1,527	2,590	1,481	556	641	367
Creek-Seminole Joint Area TJSA	378	332	436	210	62	84	88
Iowa-Sac and Fox Joint Area TJSA	34	43	218	106	21	70	26

Source: Census of Population and Housing, 1990: Summary Tape File 3C on CD-ROM [machine-readable datafiles]. Prepared by the Bureau of the Census. Washington, DC: The Bureau, 1992. *Notes:* 1. Tribal jurisdiction statistical areas (TJSAs) are areas, delineated by federally recognized tribes in Oklahoma without a reservation, for which the Census Bureau tabulates data. TJSAs represent areas generally containing the American Indian population over which one or more tribal governments have jurisdiction. If tribal officials delineated adjacent TJSAs so that they include some duplicate territory, the overlap area is called a "joint use area," which is treated as a separate TJSA for census purposes.

★ 308 ★

Educational Attainment

Educational Attainment of Persons Age 25 and Older on Selected Reservations and Trust Lands

Data are shown for the 50 areas with the largest populations, in number of persons.

American Indian Reservation and Trust Lands[1,2]	Less than 9th grade	9th to 12th grade no diploma	High school graduate or equiv.	Some college, no degree	Assoc. degree	Bachelor's degree	Graduate or profess. degree
Agua Caliente Reservation	875	2,109	4,652	4,792	936	2,074	1,383
Allegany Reservation	563	920	1,874	628	296	230	157
Blackfeet Reservation	505	913	1,137	899	277	350	195
Cheyenne River Reservation	593	759	1,274	715	224	282	109
Coeur d'Alene Reservation and Trust Lands, ID	272	523	1,325	845	305	340	97
Colorado River Reservation	828	989	1,470	760	271	243	155
Colville Reservation	418	704	1,434	882	215	296	100
Crow Reservation and Trust Lands, MT	353	574	804	1,095	161	279	74
Eastern Cherokee Reservation	487	789	1,117	574	335	127	42
Flathead Reservation	1,579	1,713	4,574	2,731	764	1,247	517
Fort Apache Reservation	791	1,473	1,358	528	221	216	86
Fort Berthold Reservation	431	412	749	708	310	289	82
Fort Hall Reservation and Trust Lands, ID	396	656	867	479	191	97	13
Fort Peck Reservation	603	1,158	1,879	1,072	525	445	170
Gila River Reservation	1,100	1,738	1,059	414	109	87	8

[Continued]

★ 308 ★

Educational Attainment of Persons Age 25 and Older on Selected Reservations and Trust Lands
[Continued]

American Indian Reservation and Trust Lands[1,2]	Less than 9th grade	9th to 12th grade no diploma	High school graduate or equiv.	Some college, no degree	Assoc. degree	Bachelor's degree	Graduate or profess. degree
Hopi Reservation and Trust Lands, AZ	610	753	1,187	652	364	98	114
Isabella Reservation and Trust Lands, MI	1,315	1,629	4,516	2,393	718	1,617	1,335
Laguna Pueblo and Trust Lands, NM	251	320	959	310	181	73	32
Lake Traverse (Sisseton) Reservation	1,659	903	2,164	888	492	512	191
Leech Lake Reservation	730	821	1,816	985	347	398	142
Mississippi Choctaw Reservation and Trust Lands, MS	554	308	600	236	82	48	15
Muckleshoot Reservation and Trust Lands, WA	151	343	782	536	151	207	64
Navajo Reservation and Trust Lands, AZ–NM–UT	24,035	14,771	16,155	7,382	2,657	2,290	1,519
Nez Perce Reservation	1,201	1,616	3,856	2,265	682	871	322
Northern Cheyenne Reservation and Trust Lands, MT–SD	164	431	448	399	77	98	76
Omaha Reservation	469	450	1,103	535	200	187	84
Oneida (West) Reservation	622	777	3,872	1,887	1,078	1,616	660
Osage Reservation	2,371	4,934	9,663	5,135	1,379	2,520	1,015
Papago Reservation	1,370	865	1,730	182	31	29	33
Pine Ridge Reservation and Trust Lands, NE–SD	914	1,289	1,247	851	465	364	160
Port Madison Reservation	98	343	805	890	215	571	223
Puyallup Reservation and Trust Lands, WA	1,372	2,415	6,097	4,722	1,441	2,615	969
Red Lake Reservation	261	434	552	266	85	23	13
Rosebud Reservation and Trust Lands, SD	625	853	1,260	735	304	267	192
Salt River Reservation	265	906	879	524	56	121	54
San Carlos Reservation	438	1,113	1,033	297	139	38	61
Sandia Pueblo	377	498	756	404	64	136	90
San Juan Pueblo	457	532	963	564	320	94	87
Santa Clara Pueblo	956	723	1,938	1,250	432	545	278
Southern Ute Reservation	331	549	1,668	1,020	240	615	317
Standing Rock Reservation	729	689	1,352	610	310	315	104
Taos Pueblo and Trust Lands, NM	310	424	982	589	135	368	246
Tulalip Reservation	245	671	1,386	1,185	407	547	147
Turtle Mountain Reservation and Trust Lands, ND–SD	676	749	629	561	334	280	70
Uintah and Ouray Reservation	481	1,907	3,070	1,726	450	662	232
White Earth Reservation	1,102	737	1,873	646	470	345	116
Wind River Reservation	953	2,246	4,279	2,874	847	1,247	525
Yakima Reservation and Trust Lands, WA	4,055	2,810	3,811	2,263	635	871	266
Yankton Reservation	876	478	1,275	601	242	263	72
Zuni Pueblo	441	1,092	1,247	466	131	204	131

Source: Census of Population and Housing, 1990: Summary Tape File 3C on CD-ROM [machine-readable datafiles]. Prepared by the Bureau of the Census. Washington, DC: The Bureau, 1992. *Notes:* 1. Federal American Indian reservations are areas with boundaries established by treaty, statute, and/or executive or court order, and recognized by the federal government as territory in which American Indian tribes have jurisdiction. State reservations are lands held in trust by state governments for the use and benefit of a given tribe. The reservations and their boundaries were identified for the 1990 census by the Bureau of Indian Affairs (BIA), Department of Interior (for federal reservations), and state governments (for state reservations). The names of American Indian reservations recognized by state governments, but not by the federal government, are followed by "state." Areas composed of reservation lands that are administered jointly and/or are claimed by two reservations, as identified by the BIA, are called "joint areas," and are treated as separate American Indian reservations for census purposes. Federal reservations may cross state boundaries, and federal and state reservations may cross county, county subdivision, and place boundaries. For reservations that cross state boundaries, only the portion of the reservations in a given state is shown in the data products for that state; the entire reservations are shown in data products for the United States. 2. Trust lands are property associated with a particular American Indian reservation or tribe, held in trust by the federal government. Trust lands may be held in trust either for a tribe (tribal trust lands) or for an individual member of a tribe (individual trust land). Trust lands recognized for the 1990 census comprised all tribal trust lands and inhabited individual trust lands located outside of a reservation boundary. As with other American Indian areas, trust lands may be located in more than one state. Only the trust lands in a given state are shown in the data products for that state; all trust lands associated with a reservation or tribe are shown in data products for the United States. The Census Bureau first reported data for tribal trust lands for the 1980 census.

★ 309 ★

Educational Attainment

Educational Attainment, by Age Group, for Major Tribal Groups, 1990: Abenaki-Menominee

Data, shown for selected tribes with at least 100 persons, are based on a sample and are subject to sampling variability.

Group	Total persons 25 years and older	Less than 9th grade	High school graduate or higher	Male	Female	Some college or higher	Bachelor's degree or higher	Male	Female
American Indian	1,040,955	13.7	65.6	65.8	65.4	36.7	9.4	10.1	8.7
Abenaki	938	14.7	68.6	69.8	67.0	34.9	9.4	13.8	3.7
Alaska Native	695	10.8	68.3	63.3	73.9	40.1	15.4	12.6	18.5
Alaskan Athabaskans	7,048	19.3	65.1	65.2	65.0	27.5	5.1	5.8	4.4
Algonquian	1,201	5.7	76.1	84.4	68.9	55.2	20.0	24.4	16.2
Apache	27,717	11.5	63.8	64.4	63.1	35.3	6.9	8.4	5.4
Arapaho	3,340	7.2	68.9	67.4	70.2	36.8	7.1	7.3	6.9
Arikara	724	6.9	68.0	69.2	66.8	47.9	12.7	10.6	14.6
Assiniboine	2,915	8.3	74.8	72.5	76.6	46.3	10.4	13.2	8.1
Bannock	81	-	76.5	61.5	90.5	69.1	28.4	20.5	35.7
Blackfoot	22,345	7.9	71.4	70.9	71.8	44.0	9.5	10.1	8.9
Brotherton	314	8.9	76.8	76.4	77.1	34.7	10.2	13.0	7.2
Caddo	1,494	3.8	76.7	73.4	79.8	46.0	11.9	12.4	11.5
Cahuilla	577	4.7	70.7	74.6	67.0	35.4	2.9	3.2	2.7
California tribes	806	4.7	70.6	67.5	73.9	39.3	8.1	8.0	8.2
Canadian Indian	1,927	10.9	68.7	69.2	68.3	47.2	11.4	12.4	10.5
Central American Indian	945	33.0	43.2	44.1	42.0	27.1	10.2	11.0	9.1
French American Indian	769	17.9	73.2	79.7	69.6	44.2	13.1	6.5	16.8
Mexican American Indian	6,636	26.0	55.0	53.4	57.2	32.1	8.2	9.2	7.0
South American Indian	1,740	15.2	61.7	62.2	61.2	44.0	21.0	21.8	20.4
Spanish American Indian	2,140	19.4	62.4	62.1	62.6	33.8	7.1	8.6	6.0
Catawba	511	18.0	68.7	72.1	65.8	30.5	8.2	18.0	-
Cayuse	110	3.6	61.8	89.4	41.3	44.5	15.5	21.3	11.1
Chehalis	135	17.0	65.2	64.3	66.2	35.6	31.9	40.0	23.1
Chemakuan	342	5.3	57.3	56.7	58.1	31.9	.6	-	1.3
Chemehuevi	292	1.0	57.5	46.8	65.5	30.5	.7	-	1.2
Cherokee	229,231	11.7	68.2	68.6	67.8	40.1	11.1	12.4	9.9
Cherokee Shawnee	531	14.9	65.7	67.4	64.4	38.2	12.6	21.3	5.5
Cheyenne	5,480	9.4	69.5	74.1	64.4	41.7	6.9	7.9	5.9
Cheyenne-Arapaho	936	2.4	75.4	74.1	76.5	42.8	6.3	2.1	9.9
Chickahominy	663	10.7	61.5	60.6	62.2	31.8	11.5	13.2	10.1
Chickasaw	12,631	7.8	74.2	74.0	74.5	46.8	14.6	16.5	13.1
Chinook	561	7.3	77.2	75.2	79.3	37.1	8.9	13.4	4.1
Chippewa	54,804	9.8	69.7	68.6	70.6	37.8	8.2	8.5	8.0
Chitimacha	299	21.4	66.2	75.0	55.6	17.7	6.0	7.9	3.7
Choctaw	49,128	11.6	70.3	71.5	69.3	41.7	13.3	15.2	11.8
Chumash	1,861	9.8	64.3	64.0	64.5	37.1	5.2	2.4	7.6
Coeur d'Alene	465	11.4	63.9	63.9	63.9	41.9	7.7	7.4	8.0
Coharie	745	11.4	61.5	61.3	61.6	26.7	9.3	2.0	14.2
Colorado River	694	12.8	68.6	64.0	71.4	35.3	2.0	3.0	1.4
Colville	3,548	10.1	73.5	75.7	71.8	39.8	9.1	9.2	9.0
Comanche	6,560	6.6	74.2	75.8	72.3	45.4	14.2	14.9	13.3
Coos	125	-	94.4	100.0	92.6	44.8	4.8	-	6.4
Coquilles	224	4.5	69.6	66.7	72.3	49.6	28.6	34.3	23.5

[Continued]

★ 309 ★

Educational Attainment, by Age Group, for Major Tribal Groups, 1990: Abenaki-Menominee
[Continued]

Group	Total persons 25 years and older	Less than 9th grade	High school graduate or higher	Male	Female	Some college or higher	Bachelor's degree or higher	Male	Female
Costanoan	545	14.3	61.3	66.3	57.4	41.5	14.3	15.4	13.4
Coushatta	633	14.8	64.3	60.4	68.7	32.5	8.8	12.3	5.0
Cowlitz	548	10.6	81.2	77.9	84.2	38.7	10.9	17.5	4.9
Cree	4,334	10.8	70.9	71.0	70.9	45.5	11.6	10.9	12.2
Creek	25,182	8.4	73.2	72.6	73.8	42.7	12.7	13.9	11.6
Croatan	131	19.8	66.4	61.4	72.1	42.0	14.5	27.1	-
Crow	4,535	9.0	70.1	70.1	70.2	46.5	10.8	9.0	12.8
Cupeno	167	3.0	59.3	45.8	72.6	30.5	-	-	-
Delaware	5,931	6.5	76.3	74.5	77.7	44.6	17.2	17.3	17.1
Diegueno	1,256	10.4	58.5	62.5	54.9	33.3	2.5	3.2	1.8
Eastern tribes	2,396	17.4	62.4	64.2	60.9	33.8	9.0	9.4	8.7
Fort Berthold	687	10.5	76.4	78.2	75.1	49.1	12.5	8.4	15.4
Fort Hall	1,591	10.9	64.9	57.8	71.7	30.7	1.9	2.1	1.8
Gabrieleno	372	3.2	69.6	69.8	69.5	47.3	10.5	8.5	11.5
Gila River	662	14.0	58.8	70.7	46.1	26.9	5.0	7.6	2.2
Grand Ronde	670	6.7	64.9	61.6	68.7	33.6	6.4	3.6	9.6
Gros Ventres	1,383	11.4	71.6	66.2	75.8	40.3	9.7	12.0	7.9
Haida	945	5.5	76.1	77.7	73.9	46.6	8.1	8.4	7.8
Haliwa	1,597	28.9	42.6	43.0	42.3	19.7	2.4	2.9	2.1
Hidatsa	708	3.4	87.1	88.5	86.1	64.7	17.5	19.1	16.3
Hoopa	1,180	4.2	67.6	64.7	70.8	33.6	7.2	7.3	7.1
Houma	3,634	51.7	30.1	27.3	32.7	10.6	1.5	2.1	.9
Iowa	842	7.5	77.4	79.9	75.0	41.7	12.0	10.4	13.6
Iroquois	30,882	10.4	71.9	71.2	72.5	41.1	11.3	11.2	11.5
Juaneno	928	5.0	68.6	76.0	61.5	42.8	8.6	14.2	3.2
Kalispel	82	14.6	73.2	73.0	73.3	40.2	12.2	27.0	-
Karok	1,704	7.8	73.3	78.9	67.8	39.9	8.9	12.0	5.8
Kaw	728	3.4	80.4	86.5	74.8	53.8	20.3	23.1	17.8
Kickapoo	1,727	15.2	69.0	75.8	64.1	37.8	9.7	12.2	7.9
Kiowa	4,692	3.7	79.1	82.2	76.0	48.4	14.1	14.9	13.3
Klallam	797	8.4	63.0	65.9	61.1	29.9	6.0	8.3	4.6
Klamath	1,461	6.5	69.8	72.7	67.8	34.8	8.3	9.0	7.7
Konkow	212	26.4	40.6	35.4	44.8	15.1	1.4	3.1	-
Kootenai	378	6.3	80.2	79.3	80.9	37.3	7.9	3.4	12.1
Long Island	261	-	73.6	72.2	75.0	53.6	23.4	10.5	36.7
Luiseno	1,479	5.8	73.2	77.2	69.7	43.9	10.5	10.6	10.5
Lumbee	27,343	22.4	51.6	48.5	54.3	25.2	9.4	8.2	10.6
Lummi	1,435	12.3	65.0	69.4	60.0	34.4	7.1	10.8	2.8
Maidu	1,210	8.7	66.4	64.0	68.6	40.7	5.2	6.9	3.6
Makah	754	11.8	66.6	71.0	63.1	36.2	11.4	13.6	9.7
Maliseet	463	14.9	71.1	75.6	68.6	27.6	16.0	10.6	18.8
Mandan	607	6.6	77.4	75.3	78.8	51.6	13.3	8.9	16.1

[Continued]

★ 309 ★

Educational Attainment, by Age Group, for Major Tribal Groups, 1990: Abenaki-Menominee

[Continued]

Group	Total persons 25 years and older	Less than 9th grade	High school graduate or higher	Male	Female	Some college or higher	Bachelor's degree or higher	Male	Female
Mattaponi	311	16.7	67.2	71.2	58.3	45.3	16.7	20.9	7.3
Menominee	4,026	9.4	66.4	64.1	68.4	30.3	5.2	5.7	4.8

Source: U.S. Bureau of the Census. *1990 Census of Population: Characteristics of American Indians by Tribe and Language.* CP3-7. Washington, DC: The Bureau, 1994, pp. 95-121.

★ 310 ★

Educational Attainment

Educational Attainment, by Age Group, for Major Tribal Groups, 1990: Miami-Yurok and Other Specified Tribes

Data, shown for selected tribes with at least 100 persons, are based on a sample and are subject to sampling variability.

Group	Total persons 25 years and older	Less than 9th grade	High school graduate or higher	Male	Female	Some college or higher	Bachelor's degree or higher	Male	Female
Miami	2,505	3.5	81.9	78.9	84.2	45.5	15.3	17.5	13.7
Miccosukee	150	48.7	28.7	17.8	39.0	18.0	4.0	8.2	-
Micmac	1,487	13.9	68.9	68.1	69.7	40.9	12.7	15.0	10.6
Mission Indians	1,399	10.9	68.2	63.8	71.6	34.2	7.6	6.4	8.6
Miwok	1,818	8.6	59.3	63.1	55.7	31.2	6.2	6.8	5.7
Modoc	297	4.0	80.1	74.0	89.7	50.2	13.1	12.7	13.8
Mohegan	696	4.7	75.1	77.4	72.8	38.5	11.8	4.2	19.8
Mono	894	7.9	62.3	63.4	61.2	36.2	4.4	8.9	-
Nanticoke	1,054	19.6	64.6	62.4	67.1	34.1	15.5	17.8	12.7
Narragansett	1,474	11.7	68.1	63.7	71.7	36.1	8.1	6.9	9.0
Navajo	100,594	28.2	51.0	51.8	50.3	24.9	4.5	4.2	4.7
Nez Perce	2,179	8.9	77.1	75.6	78.3	52.3	11.9	12.6	11.3
Nomalaki	171	8.8	52.6	68.2	37.2	29.8	6.4	-	12.8
Northwest tribes	529	4.7	56.1	63.8	48.7	29.9	5.1	5.0	5.2
Omaha	1,920	11.0	66.2	70.1	62.9	37.2	5.3	8.1	2.9
Oregon Athabaskan	165	3.0	84.8	81.6	88.5	33.9	12.7	24.1	-
Osage	6,212	3.1	86.7	88.5	84.8	59.6	22.1	23.8	20.4
Otoe-Missouria	918	4.4	73.9	74.5	73.3	44.4	14.6	19.9	9.9
Ottawa	4,245	8.1	70.1	71.7	68.5	37.6	8.3	8.2	8.3
Paiute	5,773	9.0	66.2	65.3	67.0	32.7	5.4	4.5	6.2
Pamunkey	264	8.3	81.1	66.2	86.8	56.1	26.5	17.6	30.0
Passamaquoddy	1,167	12.3	73.6	71.0	75.8	34.5	5.0	5.1	4.8
Pawnee	1,996	3.0	81.3	79.2	82.9	56.8	17.3	18.2	16.7
Penobscot	1,581	6.8	80.0	80.2	79.9	44.9	16.8	17.3	16.4
Peoria	765	4.2	82.0	85.8	78.1	43.9	14.2	17.6	10.8
Pequot	431	7.0	69.1	67.4	70.4	33.2	8.4	8.8	8.0

[Continued]

★ 310 ★

Educational Attainment, by Age Group, for Major Tribal Groups, 1990: Miami-Yurok and Other Specified Tribes
[Continued]

Group	Total persons 25 years and older	Less than 9th grade	High school graduate or higher	Male	Female	Some college or higher	Bachelor's degree or higher	Male	Female
Pima	6,621	16.5	47.5	45.5	49.0	18.8	2.8	1.9	3.5
Piscataway	443	8.4	70.4	63.5	76.6	37.7	10.8	6.3	14.9
Pit River	838	8.7	64.3	67.8	61.8	36.3	1.7	3.2	.6
Pomo	2,393	10.7	59.0	62.9	56.0	31.7	2.4	2.6	2.2
Ponca	1,385	8.3	64.0	65.4	62.9	31.9	6.0	11.2	2.0
Potawatomi	9,428	7.2	76.5	73.1	79.4	43.6	14.1	15.3	13.1
Powhatan	469	6.8	79.5	85.2	73.3	53.9	21.5	29.1	13.3
Pueblo	28,597	9.8	71.5	72.4	70.6	35.3	7.3	7.7	6.9
Puget Sound Salish	5,266	10.8	69.1	64.0	73.6	37.9	7.7	7.9	7.5
Quapaw	783	3.3	81.4	83.5	79.0	48.0	19.3	26.8	11.2
Quinault	1,246	10.9	65.8	68.7	63.5	36.9	6.3	5.5	7.0
Rappahannock	245	35.1	46.5	45.8	47.1	24.1	7.8	15.0	2.2
Sac and Fox	2,686	7.7	74.6	76.5	73.0	39.1	9.3	13.1	6.3
Salinan	179	11.2	38.5	36.8	40.5	22.9	-	-	-
Salish	2,743	10.6	72.7	71.7	73.5	43.8	9.7	11.0	8.7
Salish and Kootenai	1,321	9.5	76.8	76.6	76.9	42.1	9.3	9.9	8.8
Schaghticoke	114	14.9	60.5	44.0	73.4	30.7	9.6	4.0	14.1
Seminole	8,319	11.4	70.5	70.2	70.7	41.9	11.1	13.0	9.4
Serrano	111	7.2	50.5	43.6	57.1	28.8	-	-	-
Shasta	435	4.1	83.7	83.9	83.5	56.8	8.5	12.2	5.2
Shawnee	3,787	7.7	73.0	73.5	72.7	47.5	12.6	12.5	12.7
Shinnecock	1,087	3.3	74.2	67.4	78.5	39.3	15.9	16.7	15.5
Shoshone	5,180	9.8	67.8	67.8	67.9	39.2	8.8	8.6	8.9
Shoshone Paiute	1,062	7.4	76.6	71.5	79.9	41.0	4.1	1.4	5.9
Siletz	804	4.4	77.4	80.8	74.3	37.9	1.2	1.1	1.4
Sioux	51,014	9.6	69.7	70.0	69.4	40.0	8.9	8.9	8.9
Spokane	1,050	9.3	73.1	77.4	69.4	41.0	11.4	11.3	11.5
Stockbridge	1,385	11.1	70.5	65.1	75.1	40.2	7.3	6.6	7.9
Tlingit	7,382	9.0	73.3	74.1	72.6	36.8	6.7	6.3	6.9
Tohono O'Odham	8,043	23.8	53.4	54.6	52.5	15.0	1.2	.9	1.5
Tolowa	200	4.0	82.5	84.3	81.2	48.5	23.5	10.8	32.5
Tonkawa	138	21.7	54.3	48.7	61.3	21.7	10.1	17.1	1.6
Tsimshian	1,180	6.3	78.6	77.0	79.8	35.3	7.3	9.6	5.5
Umatilla	695	4.3	77.8	75.5	79.8	45.0	6.2	10.7	2.4
Umpqua	306	3.6	68.0	67.4	68.4	35.0	4.2	-	7.3
Ute	3,616	10.2	62.7	61.7	63.7	33.0	5.5	5.4	5.5
Wailaki	732	9.6	67.3	57.7	74.5	42.6	10.1	5.8	13.3
Walla-Walla	146	4.8	84.9	91.9	77.8	32.9	10.3	8.1	12.5
Wampanoag	1,480	10.7	75.1	77.1	73.3	38.4	15.1	13.1	16.9
Warm Springs	972	9.8	61.4	63.9	59.5	29.3	2.9	4.6	1.6
Washo	850	9.2	64.2	61.8	66.2	33.9	7.6	7.9	7.5
Wichita	495	5.7	76.6	83.2	72.4	48.3	12.9	14.7	11.8
Winnebago	3,146	8.0	76.2	74.0	78.0	45.5	9.6	9.4	9.8

[Continued]

★ 310 ★

Educational Attainment, by Age Group, for Major Tribal Groups, 1990: Miami-Yurok and Other Specified Tribes

[Continued]

Group	Total persons 25 years and older	Less than 9th grade	High school graduate or higher	Male	Female	Some college or higher	Bachelor's degree or higher	Male	Female
Wintu	1,373	6.0	72.0	76.7	68.4	35.8	3.6	3.0	4.1
Wiyot	302	2.0	69.5	73.8	67.2	39.4	1.0	2.8	-
Yakima	3,780	10.0	66.4	66.1	66.7	34.1	8.0	8.6	7.5
Yaqui	4,746	28.0	48.5	52.0	44.7	26.4	4.3	5.4	3.2
Yavapai Apache	232	8.6	59.1	47.6	63.3	38.8	2.2	1.6	2.4
Yokuts	1,379	13.1	57.1	52.6	61.5	30.7	4.8	4.0	5.6
Yuchi	241	7.1	85.1	84.4	85.7	61.0	14.9	22.1	7.6
Yuman	3,683	12.1	61.0	62.5	59.8	29.7	4.5	5.6	3.5
Yurok	2,280	6.8	68.3	64.9	70.9	38.0	9.3	9.1	9.4
Tribe not specified	12,483	18.3	60.7	61.1	60.2	34.7	10.7	12.4	8.9
Tribe not reported	105,183	17.7	58.9	60.2	57.4	31.7	8.7	9.8	7.4

Source: U.S. Bureau of the Census. *1990 Census of Population: Characteristics of American Indians by Tribe and Language.* CP3-7. Washington, DC: The Bureau, 1994, pp. 95-121.

★ 311 ★

Educational Attainment

Employment Status and Educational Attainment of American Indians and Alaska Natives Age 16-19 in Selected Alaska Native Villages - Part I

Data are shown for the 50 areas with the largest populations, in number of persons.

Alaska Native Village Statistical Area[1]	In Armed Forces				Civilian		
	Enrolled in school		Not enrolled in school		Enrolled in school		
	High school graduate	Not h.s. graduate	High school graduate	Not h.s. graduate	Employed	Unemployed	Not in labor force
Akiachak	0	0	0	0	0	0	8
Akutan	0	0	0	0	0	0	0
Alakanuk	0	0	0	0	0	0	26
Andreafsky	0	0	0	0	2	2	8
Angoon	0	0	0	0	2	0	28
Aniak	0	0	0	0	7	0	0
Barrow	0	0	0	0	8	4	38
Bethel	0	0	0	0	30	8	80
Chevak	0	0	0	0	8	0	12
Copper Center	0	0	0	0	0	0	3
Craig	0	0	0	0	2	3	2
Dillingham	0	0	0	0	10	1	41
Emmonak	0	0	0	0	0	2	16
Fort Yukon	0	0	0	0	2	1	13
Galena	0	0	0	0	0	2	25
Gambell	0	0	0	0	0	0	12
Grouse Creek Group	0	0	0	0	0	0	0
Hoonah	0	0	0	0	0	0	10

[Continued]

★ 311 ★

Employment Status and Educational Attainment of American Indians and Alaska Natives Age 16-19 in Selected Alaska Native Villages - Part I

[Continued]

Alaska Native Village Statistical Area[1]	In Armed Forces				Civilian		
	Enrolled in school		Not enrolled in school		Enrolled in school		
	High school graduate	Not h.s. graduate	High school graduate	Not h.s. graduate	Employed	Unemployed	Not in labor force
Hooper Bay	0	0	0	0	0	3	26
Kake	0	0	0	0	2	0	27
Kasigluk	0	0	0	0	0	4	9
King Cove	0	0	0	0	0	0	11
King Salmon	0	0	0	0	0	0	8
Kipnuk	0	0	0	0	0	0	27
Klawock	0	0	0	0	3	2	17
Kotlik	0	0	0	0	0	2	11
Kotzebue	0	0	0	0	6	4	74
Kwethluk	0	0	0	0	0	0	22
McGrath	0	0	0	0	10	0	19
Mountain Village	0	0	0	0	0	4	51
Naknek	0	0	0	0	0	0	11
Ninilchik	0	0	0	0	7	0	18
Noorvik	0	0	0	0	2	0	24
Pilot Station	0	0	0	0	0	0	15
Point Hope	0	0	0	0	1	2	15
Quinhagak	0	0	0	0	6	0	14
St. Paul	0	0	0	0	2	0	11
Salamatof	0	0	0	0	0	0	0
Sand Point	0	0	0	0	7	0	13
Savoonga	0	0	0	0	0	0	31
Selawik	0	0	0	0	0	0	16
Shishmaref	0	0	0	0	0	3	20
Stebbins	0	0	0	0	0	2	18
Togiak	0	0	0	0	3	0	19
Tok	0	0	0	0	0	0	6
Toksook Bay	0	0	0	0	15	7	28
Unalakleet	0	0	0	0	0	0	18
Unalaska	0	0	0	0	6	3	12
Wainwright	0	0	0	0	5	0	13
Yakutat	0	0	0	0	4	0	4

Source: Census of Population and Housing, 1990: Summary Tape File 3C on CD-ROM [machine-readable datafiles]. Prepared by the Bureau of the Census. Washington, DC: The Bureau, 1992. *Notes:* 1. Alaska Native villages (ANVs) constitute tribes, bands, clans, groups, villages, communities, or associations in Alaska that are recognized pursuant to the Alaska Native Claims Settlement Act of 1972, Public Law 92-203. Because ANVs do not have legally designated boundaries, the Census Bureau has established Alaska Native village statistical areas (ANVSAs) for statistical purposes. For the 1990 census, the Census Bureau cooperated with officials of the nonprofit corporation within each participating Alaska Native Regional Corporation (ANRC), as well as other knowledgeable officials, to delineate boundaries that encompass the settled area associated with each ANV.

★ 312 ★

Educational Attainment

Employment Status and Educational Attainment of American Indians and Alaska Natives Age 16-19 in Selected Alaska Native Villages - Part II

Data are shown for the 50 areas with the largest populations, in number of persons.

Alaska Native Village Statistical Area[1]	Civilian (cont.) Not enrolled in school					
	High school graduate			Not high school graduate		
	Employed	Unemployed	Not in labor force	Employed	Unemployed	Not in labor force
Akiachak	12	5	11	0	0	0
Akutan	0	0	0	0	0	0
Alakanuk	5	6	2	0	2	2
Andreafsky	4	0	6	4	0	0
Angoon	2	0	0	0	0	2
Aniak	2	0	3	0	0	0
Barrow	22	4	0	2	9	6
Bethel	27	2	9	6	9	31
Chevak	4	2	6	0	0	1
Copper Center	0	0	0	0	5	2
Craig	0	0	0	4	0	0
Dillingham	0	0	6	0	0	2
Emmonak	2	1	1	0	2	8
Fort Yukon	2	0	2	2	0	2
Galena	5	0	0	0	0	0
Gambell	0	0	3	0	0	15
Grouse Creek Group	0	0	0	0	0	0
Hoonah	0	0	0	7	4	0
Hooper Bay	4	2	2	0	2	2
Kake	3	2	6	0	0	0
Kasigluk	0	2	3	0	0	0
King Cove	0	0	0	0	0	0
King Salmon	3	0	2	0	2	0
Kipnuk	3	0	2	0	0	7
Klawock	2	0	2	0	2	3
Kotlik	2	5	4	0	0	0
Kotzebue	9	6	4	11	4	19
Kwethluk	0	0	3	0	0	2
McGrath	0	3	0	0	0	4
Mountain Village	5	2	5	0	0	8
Naknek	0	0	0	0	0	0
Ninilchik	3	0	0	0	0	7
Noorvik	0	0	3	0	0	7
Pilot Station	3	0	2	0	0	7
Point Hope	3	0	0	0	2	2
Quinhagak	3	0	6	0	0	2
St. Paul	1	0	0	1	0	2
Salamatof	1	0	0	0	0	0
Sand Point	0	0	5	0	0	0
Savoonga	0	0	1	0	0	6
Selawik	2	0	0	0	1	2
Shishmaref	4	0	5	0	2	0

[Continued]

★ 312 ★

Employment Status and Educational Attainment of American Indians and Alaska Natives Age 16-19 in Selected Alaska Native Villages - Part II
[Continued]

Alaska Native Village Statistical Area[1]	Civilian (cont.) Not enrolled in school					
	High school graduate			Not high school graduate		
	Employed	Unemployed	Not in labor force	Employed	Unemployed	Not in labor force
Stebbins	5	2	2	0	1	8
Togiak	0	0	9	0	0	0
Tok	0	0	0	0	0	0
Toksook Bay	0	2	0	0	0	0
Unalakleet	3	0	6	0	0	0
Unalaska	0	0	0	0	0	0
Wainwright	2	0	0	0	0	0
Yakutat	3	0	0	2	0	2

Source: Census of Population and Housing, 1990: Summary Tape File 3C on CD-ROM [machine-readable datafiles]. Prepared by the Bureau of the Census. Washington, DC: The Bureau, 1992. *Notes:* 1. Alaska Native villages (ANVs) constitute tribes, bands, clans, groups, villages, communities, or associations in Alaska that are recognized pursuant to the Alaska Native Claims Settlement Act of 1972, Public Law 92-203. Because ANVs do not have legally designated boundaries, the Census Bureau has established Alaska Native village statistical areas (ANVSAs) for statistical purposes. For the 1990 census, the Census Bureau cooperated with officials of the nonprofit corporation within each participating Alaska Native Regional Corporation (ANRC), as well as other knowledgeable officials, to delineate boundaries that encompass the settled area associated with each ANV.

★ 313 ★

Educational Attainment

Employment Status and Educational Attainment of American Indians and Alaska Natives Age 16-19 in Selected TDSAs - Part I

Tribal Designated Statistical Area[1]	In Armed Forces				Civilian		
	Enrolled in school		Not enrolled in school		Enrolled in school		
	High school graduate	Not h.s. graduate	High school graduate	Not h.s. graduate	Employed	Unemployed	Not in labor force
Apache Choctaw TDSA (state)	0	0	0	0	8	0	24
Chickahominy TDSA (state)	0	0	0	0	5	0	20
Clifton Choctaw TDSA (state)	0	0	0	0	0	0	22
Coharie TDSA (state)	0	0	0	0	26	8	47
Coquille Indian TDSA	0	0	0	0	68	24	144
Delaware-Muncie TDSA (state)	0	0	0	0	0	0	6
Florida Tribe of Eastern Creek TDSA (state)	0	0	0	0	0	0	0
Haliwa-Saponi TDSA (state)	0	0	0	0	5	0	80
Jena Band of Choctaw TDSA (state)	0	0	5	0	0	0	49
Klamath TDSA	0	0	0	0	20	6	83
Lumbee TDSA (state)	0	0	0	0	377	122	1,213
Meherrin TDSA (state)	0	0	0	0	2	0	8
Mohegan TDSA (state)	0	0	0	0	0	0	0
Ramapough TDSA (state)	0	0	0	0	0	0	0
United Houma Nation TDSA (state)	0	0	0	0	55	24	346

[Continued]

★ 313 ★

Employment Status and Educational Attainment of American Indians and Alaska Natives Age 16-19 in Selected TDSAs - Part I

[Continued]

Tribal Designated Statistical Area[1]	In Armed Forces				Civilian		
	Enrolled in school		Not enrolled in school		Enrolled in school		
	High school graduate	Not h.s. graduate	High school graduate	Not h.s. graduate	Employed	Unemployed	Not in labor force
Waccamaw Siouan TDSA (state)	0	0	0	0	7	0	58
Wampanoag-Gay Head TDSA	0	0	0	0	11	0	6

Source: Census of Population and Housing, 1990: Summary Tape File 3C on CD-ROM [machine-readable datafiles]. Prepared by the Bureau of the Census. Washington, DC: The Bureau, 1992. *Notes:* 1. Tribal designated statistical areas (TDSAs) are areas, delineated outside Oklahoma by federally- and state-recognized tribes without a land base or associated trust lands, to provide statistical areas for which the Census Bureau tabulates data. TDSAs represent areas generally containing the American Indian population over which federally-recognized tribes have jurisdiction and areas in which state tribes provide benefits and services to their members. The names of TDSAs delineated by state-recognized tribes are followed by "(state)." The Census Bureau did not recognize TDSAs before the 1990 census.

★ 314 ★

Educational Attainment

Employment Status and Educational Attainment of American Indians and Alaska Natives Age 16-19 in Selected TDSAs - Part II

Tribal Designated Statistical Area[1]	Civilian (cont.)					
	Not enrolled in school					
	High school graduate			Not high school graduate		
	Employed	Unemployed	Not in labor force	Employed	Unemployed	Not in labor force
Apache Choctaw TDSA (state)	12	0	0	3	0	0
Chickahominy TDSA (state)	6	0	0	0	0	0
Clifton Choctaw TDSA (state)	0	0	0	0	0	0
Coharie TDSA (state)	0	0	9	0	0	0
Coquille Indian TDSA	28	38	0	15	42	53
Delaware-Muncie TDSA (state)	0	0	0	0	0	0
Florida Tribe of Eastern Creek TDSA (state)	0	0	0	0	0	0
Haliwa-Saponi TDSA (state)	12	0	4	30	6	16
Jena Band of Choctaw TDSA (state)	0	0	0	0	0	0
Klamath TDSA	29	0	0	11	7	12
Lumbee TDSA (state)	199	35	75	211	78	222
Meherrin TDSA (state)	0	0	0	0	0	0
Mohegan TDSA (state)	0	0	0	0	0	0
Ramapough TDSA (state)	0	0	0	0	4	0
United Houma Nation TDSA (state)	80	13	33	72	35	110
Waccamaw Siouan TDSA (state)	27	0	0	0	0	0
Wampanoag-Gay Head TDSA	5	0	0	0	0	0

Source: Census of Population and Housing, 1990: Summary Tape File 3C on CD-ROM [machine-readable datafiles]. Prepared by the Bureau of the Census. Washington, DC: The Bureau, 1992. *Notes:* 1. Tribal designated statistical areas (TDSAs) are areas, delineated outside Oklahoma by federally- and state-recognized tribes without a land base or associated trust lands, to provide statistical areas for which the Census Bureau tabulates data. TDSAs represent areas generally containing the American Indian population over which federally-recognized tribes have jurisdiction and areas in which state tribes provide benefits and services to their members. The names of TDSAs delineated by state-recognized tribes are followed by "(state)." The Census Bureau did not recognize TDSAs before the 1990 census.

★ 315 ★

Educational Attainment

Employment Status and Educational Attainment of American Indians and Alaska Natives Age 16-19 in Selected TJSAs - Part I

Tribal Jurisdiction Statistical Area[1]	In Armed Forces				Civilian Enrolled in school		
	Enrolled in school		Not enrolled in school				
	High school graduate	Not h.s. graduate	High school graduate	Not h.s. graduate	Employed	Unemployed	Not in labor force
Absentee Shawnee-Citizens Band of Potawatomi TJSA	0	0	0	0	171	21	158
Caddo-Wichita-Delaware TJSA	0	0	0	0	3	2	23
Cherokee TJSA	0	0	6	0	1,069	345	2,588
Cheyenne-Arapaho TJSA	0	0	0	0	54	13	240
Chickasaw TJSA	6	0	5	0	378	104	931
Choctaw TJSA	0	0	0	0	321	168	1,173
Creek TJSA	0	0	4	0	675	180	1,307
Iowa TJSA	0	0	0	0	0	2	5
Kaw TJSA	0	0	0	0	16	0	7
Kiowa-Comanche-Apache-Fort Sill Apache TJSA	0	0	13	7	100	62	499
Otoe-Missouria TJSA	0	0	0	0	2	5	17
Pawnee TJSA	0	0	0	0	19	1	75
Sac and Fox TJSA	0	0	0	0	94	48	176
Seminole TJSA	0	0	0	0	23	10	188
Tonkawa TJSA	0	0	0	0	16	10	39
Creek-Seminole Joint Area TJSA	0	0	0	0	2	0	32
Iowa-Sac and Fox Joint Area TJSA	0	0	0	0	2	0	0

Source: Census of Population and Housing, 1990: Summary Tape File 3C on CD-ROM [machine-readable datafiles]. Prepared by the Bureau of the Census. Washington, DC: The Bureau, 1992. *Notes:* 1. Tribal jurisdiction statistical areas (TJSAs) are areas, delineated by federally recognized tribes in Oklahoma without a reservation, for which the Census Bureau tabulates data. TJSAs represent areas generally containing the American Indian population over which one or more tribal governments have jurisdiction. If tribal officials delineated adjacent TJSAs so that they include some duplicate territory, the overlap area is called a "joint use area," which is treated as a separate TJSA for census purposes.

★ 316 ★

Educational Attainment

Employment Status and Educational Attainment of American Indians and Alaska Natives Age 16-19 in Selected TJSAs - Part II

Tribal Jurisdiction Statistical Area[1]	Civilian (cont.) Not enrolled in school					
	High school graduate			Not high school graduate		
	Employed	Unemployed	Not in labor force	Employed	Unemployed	Not in labor force
Absentee Shawnee-Citizens Band of Potawatomi TJSA	82	7	8	39	18	30
Caddo-Wichita-Delaware TJSA	4	6	0	0	0	3
Cherokee TJSA	391	87	148	200	192	304
Cheyenne-Arapaho TJSA	2	10	3	28	27	33
Chickasaw TJSA	113	36	32	46	39	140
Choctaw TJSA	171	41	78	82	51	131
Creek TJSA	305	71	112	146	50	213
Iowa TJSA	9	0	0	0	3	13
Kaw TJSA	0	0	0	0	0	0
Kiowa-Comanche-Apache-Fort Sill Apache TJSA	67	41	55	28	18	47
Otoe-Missouria TJSA	3	2	3	0	0	7

[Continued]

★ 316 ★

Employment Status and Educational Attainment of American Indians and Alaska Natives Age 16-19 in Selected TJSAs - Part II

[Continued]

| Tribal Jurisdiction Statistical Area[1] | Civilian (cont.) Not enrolled in school | | | | | |
| | High school graduate | | | Not high school graduate | | |
	Employed	Unemployed	Not in labor force	Employed	Unemployed	Not in labor force
Pawnee TJSA	4	1	8	6	2	8
Sac and Fox TJSA	12	11	10	6	23	35
Seminole TJSA	10	21	8	10	0	34
Tonkawa TJSA	0	5	0	5	7	5
Creek-Seminole Joint Area TJSA	5	0	2	4	3	0
Iowa-Sac and Fox Joint Area TJSA	0	0	0	0	0	0

Source: Census of Population and Housing, 1990: Summary Tape File 3C on CD-ROM [machine-readable datafiles]. Prepared by the Bureau of the Census. Washington, DC: The Bureau, 1992. *Notes:* 1. Tribal jurisdiction statistical areas (TJSAs) are areas, delineated by federally recognized tribes in Oklahoma without a reservation, for which the Census Bureau tabulates data. TJSAs represent areas generally containing the American Indian population over which one or more tribal governments have jurisdiction. If tribal officials delineated adjacent TJSAs so that they include some duplicate territory, the overlap area is called a "joint use area," which is treated as a separate TJSA for census purposes.

★ 317 ★

Educational Attainment

Employment Status and Educational Attainment of American Indians and Alaska Natives Age 16-19 on Selected Reservations and Trust Lands - Part I

Data are shown for the 50 areas with the largest populations, in number of persons.

| American Indian Reservation and Trust Lands[1,2] | In Armed Forces | | | | Civilian | | |
| | Enrolled in school | | Not enrolled in school | | Enrolled in school | | |
	High school graduate	Not h.s. graduate	High school graduate	Not h.s. graduate	Employed	Unemployed	Not in labor force
Agua Caliente Reservation	0	0	0	0	7	0	0
Allegany Reservation	0	0	0	0	4	2	35
Blackfeet Reservation	0	0	0	0	15	31	285
Cheyenne River Reservation	0	0	0	0	28	20	253
Coeur d'Alene Reservation and Trust Lands, ID	0	0	0	0	3	0	51
Colorado River Reservation	0	0	0	0	6	9	107
Colville Reservation	0	0	0	0	54	24	150
Crow Reservation and Trust Lands, MT	0	0	0	0	31	59	182
Eastern Cherokee Reservation	0	0	0	0	31	28	214
Flathead Reservation	2	0	0	0	75	10	199
Fort Apache Reservation	0	0	0	0	13	54	289
Fort Berthold Reservation	0	0	0	0	12	7	174
Fort Hall Reservation and Trust Lands, ID	0	0	0	0	0	18	126
Fort Peck Reservation	0	0	0	0	19	4	264
Gila River Reservation	0	0	0	0	69	27	410
Hopi Reservation and Trust Lands, AZ	0	0	0	0	22	51	341
Isabella Reservation and Trust Lands, MI	0	0	0	0	1	0	38

[Continued]

★ 317 ★

Employment Status and Educational Attainment of American Indians and Alaska Natives Age 16-19 on Selected Reservations and Trust Lands - Part I

[Continued]

American Indian Reservation and Trust Lands[1,2]	In Armed Forces				Civilian		
	Enrolled in school		Not enrolled in school		Enrolled in school		
	High school graduate	Not h.s. graduate	High school graduate	Not h.s. graduate	Employed	Unemployed	Not in labor force
Laguna Pueblo and Trust Lands, NM	0	0	0	0	0	9	162
Lake Traverse (Sisseton) Reservation	0	0	0	0	19	16	92
Leech Lake Reservation	0	0	0	0	22	11	136
Mississippi Choctaw Reservation and Trust Lands, MS	0	0	0	0	0	0	221
Muckleshoot Reservation and Trust Lands, WA	0	0	0	0	4	0	35
Navajo Reservation and Trust Lands, AZ–NM–UT	0	0	0	0	668	556	7,238
Nez Perce Reservation	0	0	0	0	17	7	89
Northern Cheyenne Reservation and Trust Lands, MT–SD	0	0	0	0	32	22	160
Omaha Reservation	0	0	0	0	21	3	69
Oneida (West) Reservation	0	0	0	0	31	9	99
Osage Reservation	0	0	0	0	28	29	232
Papago Reservation	0	0	0	0	25	20	372
Pine Ridge Reservation and Trust Lands, NE–SD	0	0	0	0	17	60	473
Port Madison Reservation	0	0	0	0	8	0	8
Puyallup Reservation and Trust Lands, WA	0	0	0	0	7	3	36
Red Lake Reservation	0	0	0	0	20	0	184
Rosebud Reservation and Trust Lands, SD	0	0	0	0	37	67	374
Salt River Reservation	0	0	0	0	31	0	155
San Carlos Reservation	0	0	0	0	53	45	298
Sandia Pueblo	0	0	0	0	9	3	7
San Juan Pueblo	0	0	0	0	0	9	54
Santa Clara Pueblo	0	0	0	0	5	5	45
Southern Ute Reservation	0	0	0	0	11	0	64
Standing Rock Reservation	0	0	0	0	31	13	254
Taos Pueblo and Trust Lands, NM	0	0	0	0	7	5	46
Tulalip Reservation	0	0	0	0	15	2	30
Turtle Mountain Reservation and Trust Lands, ND–SD	0	0	0	0	33	22	259
Uintah and Ouray Reservation	0	0	0	0	11	6	92
White Earth Reservation	0	0	0	0	10	11	119
Wind River Reservation	0	0	0	0	47	31	194
Yakima Reservation and Trust Lands, WA	0	0	0	0	42	10	292

[Continued]

★ 317 ★

Employment Status and Educational Attainment of American Indians and Alaska Natives Age 16-19 on Selected Reservations and Trust Lands - Part I

[Continued]

American Indian Reservation and Trust Lands[1,2]	In Armed Forces				Civilian		
	Enrolled in school		Not enrolled in school		Enrolled in school		
	High school graduate	Not h.s. graduate	High school graduate	Not h.s. graduate	Employed	Unemployed	Not in labor force
Yankton Reservation	0	0	0	0	12	6	133
Zuni Pueblo	0	0	0	0	40	49	332

Source: Census of Population and Housing, 1990: Summary Tape File 3C on CD-ROM [machine-readable datafiles]. Prepared by the Bureau of the Census. Washington, DC: The Bureau, 1992. *Notes:* 1. Federal American Indian reservations are areas with boundaries established by treaty, statute, and/or executive or court order, and recognized by the federal government as territory in which American Indian tribes have jurisdiction. State reservations are lands held in trust by state governments for the use and benefit of a given tribe. The reservations and their boundaries were identified for the 1990 census by the Bureau of Indian Affairs (BIA), Department of Interior (for federal reservations), and state governments (for state reservations). The names of American Indian reservations recognized by state governments, but not by the federal government, are followed by "state." Areas composed of reservation lands that are administered jointly and/or are claimed by two reservations, as identified by the BIA, are called "joint areas," and are treated as separate American Indian reservations for census purposes. Federal reservations may cross state boundaries, and federal and state reservations may cross county, county subdivision, and place boundaries. For reservations that cross state boundaries, only the portion of the reservations in a given state is shown in the data products for that state; the entire reservations are shown in data products for the United States. 2. Trust lands are property associated with a particular American Indian reservation or tribe, held in trust by the federal government. Trust lands may be held in trust either for a tribe (tribal trust lands) or for an individual member of a tribe (individual trust land). Trust lands recognized for the 1990 census comprised all tribal trust lands and inhabited individual trust lands located outside of a reservation boundary. As with other American Indian areas, trust lands may be located in more than one state. Only the trust lands in a given state are shown in the data products for that state; all trust lands associated with a reservation or tribe are shown in data products for the United States. The Census Bureau first reported data for tribal trust lands for the 1980 census.

★ 318 ★

Educational Attainment

Employment Status and Educational Attainment of American Indians and Alaska Natives Age 16-19 on Selected Reservations and Trust Lands - Part II

Data are shown for the 50 areas with the largest populations, in number of persons.

American Indian Reservation and Trust Lands[1,2]	Civilian (cont.)					
	Not enrolled in school					
	High school graduate			Not high school graduate		
	Employed	Unemployed	Not in labor force	Employed	Unemployed	Not in labor force
Agua Caliente Reservation	0	0	0	17	0	0
Allegany Reservation	9	4	6	6	4	4
Blackfeet Reservation	11	5	4	1	19	60
Cheyenne River Reservation	10	23	3	11	14	58
Coeur d'Alene Reservation and Trust Lands, ID	2	0	13	0	0	13
Colorado River Reservation	12	0	3	0	3	17
Colville Reservation	0	23	11	6	19	12
Crow Reservation and Trust Lands, MT	10	4	8	9	16	38
Eastern Cherokee Reservation	40	14	15	34	28	35
Flathead Reservation	22	2	15	37	8	64
Fort Apache Reservation	0	0	17	8	51	130
Fort Berthold Reservation	10	9	6	11	0	9
Fort Hall Reservation and Trust Lands, ID	14	7	9	10	0	44

[Continued]

★ 318 ★

Employment Status and Educational Attainment of American Indians and Alaska Natives Age 16-19 on Selected Reservations and Trust Lands - Part II

[Continued]

American Indian Reservation and Trust Lands[1,2]	Civilian (cont.) Not enrolled in school					
	High school graduate			Not high school graduate		
	Employed	Unemployed	Not in labor force	Employed	Unemployed	Not in labor force
Fort Peck Reservation	15	9	18	12	29	30
Gila River Reservation	8	17	31	33	45	79
Hopi Reservation and Trust Lands, AZ	34	5	13	11	25	23
Isabella Reservation and Trust Lands, MI	9	5	0	31	0	6
Laguna Pueblo and Trust Lands, NM	8	6	32	0	5	19
Lake Traverse (Sisseton) Reservation	11	0	0	4	8	38
Leech Lake Reservation	9	5	0	3	3	14
Mississippi Choctaw Reservation and Trust Lands, MS	16	6	0	30	11	43
Muckleshoot Reservation and Trust Lands, WA	0	0	0	17	2	10
Navajo Reservation and Trust Lands, AZ–NM–UT	182	161	465	259	370	1,141
Nez Perce Reservation	2	2	10	0	14	26
Northern Cheyenne Reservation and Trust Lands, MT–SD	8	16	19	0	11	43
Omaha Reservation	2	2	12	2	10	9
Oneida (West) Reservation	17	0	3	6	4	4
Osage Reservation	12	8	9	4	5	15
Papago Reservation	5	0	21	48	8	108
Pine Ridge Reservation and Trust Lands, NE–SD	18	16	25	19	29	157
Port Madison Reservation	10	0	0	0	0	0
Puyallup Reservation and Trust Lands, WA	4	0	0	3	6	5
Red Lake Reservation	8	30	15	2	20	34
Rosebud Reservation and Trust Lands, SD	17	8	39	8	29	130
Salt River Reservation	11	0	0	15	11	48
San Carlos Reservation	5	16	9	0	19	103
Sandia Pueblo	6	3	0	0	0	0
San Juan Pueblo	5	7	7	0	0	13
Santa Clara Pueblo	6	0	1	0	3	0
Southern Ute Reservation	8	4	0	4	4	9
Standing Rock Reservation	12	27	2	1	11	35
Taos Pueblo and Trust Lands, NM	7	7	0	5	2	3
Tulalip Reservation	1	2	0	4	0	7

[Continued]

★ 318 ★

Employment Status and Educational Attainment of American Indians and Alaska Natives Age 16-19 on Selected Reservations and Trust Lands - Part II

[Continued]

| American Indian Reservation and Trust Lands[1,2] | Civilian (cont.) Not enrolled in school | | | | | |
| | High school graduate | | | Not high school graduate | | |
	Employed	Unemployed	Not in labor force	Employed	Unemployed	Not in labor force
Turtle Mountain Reservation and Trust Lands, ND–SD	17	31	20	0	31	97
Uintah and Ouray Reservation	4	5	14	2	10	29
White Earth Reservation	6	2	11	3	0	18
Wind River Reservation	11	8	20	6	16	47
Yakima Reservation and Trust Lands, WA	14	0	9	22	8	44
Yankton Reservation	2	2	9	0	7	32
Zuni Pueblo	47	5	16	11	7	29

Source: Census of Population and Housing, 1990: Summary Tape File 3C on CD-ROM [machine-readable datafiles]. Prepared by the Bureau of the Census. Washington, DC: The Bureau, 1992. Notes: 1. Federal American Indian reservations are areas with boundaries established by treaty, statute, and/or executive or court order, and recognized by the federal government as territory in which American Indian tribes have jurisdiction. State reservations are lands held in trust by state governments for the use and benefit of a given tribe. The reservations and their boundaries were identified for the 1990 census by the Bureau of Indian Affairs (BIA), Department of Interior (for federal reservations), and state governments (for state reservations). The names of American Indian reservations recognized by state governments, but not by the federal government, are followed by "state." Areas composed of reservation lands that are administered jointly and/or are claimed by two reservations, as identified by the BIA, are called "joint areas," and are treated as separate American Indian reservations for census purposes. Federal reservations may cross state boundaries, and federal and state reservations may cross county, county subdivision, and place boundaries. For reservations that cross state boundaries, only the portion of the reservations in a given state is shown in the data products for that state; the entire reservations are shown in data products for the United States. 2. Trust lands are property associated with a particular American Indian reservation or tribe, held in trust by the federal government. Trust lands may be held in trust either for a tribe (tribal trust lands) or for an individual member of a tribe (individual trust land). Trust lands recognized for the 1990 census comprised all tribal trust lands and inhabited individual trust lands located outside of a reservation boundary. As with other American Indian areas, trust lands may be located in more than one state. Only the trust lands in a given state are shown in the data products for that state; all trust lands associated with a reservation or tribe are shown in data products for the United States. The Census Bureau first reported data for tribal trust lands for the 1980 census.

Enrollment

★ 319 ★

School Enrollment, by Sector

Percent of eighth graders enrolled in each school sector in 1988 is shown for each race/ethnicity.

Race/ethnicity	Public school	Catholic school	Independent school	Other private school
Total	87.9	7.5	1.0	3.6
American Indian and Native Alaskan	92.0	3.4	0.3	4.3
Asian and Pacific Islander	83.8	8.8	3.2	4.2
Black	92.9	5.7	0.5	0.9

[Continued]

★ 319 ★

School Enrollment, by Sector

[Continued]

Race/ethnicity	Public school	Catholic school	Independent school	Other private school
Hispanic	90.5	7.9	0.4	1.2
White	86.7	7.8	1.1	4.4

Source: U.S. Department of Education. *A Profile of the American Eighth Grader.* Washington, DC: U.S. Department of Education, 1990, p. 19. Primary source: U.S. Department of Education, National Center for Education Statistics, "National Education Longitudinal Study of 1988: Base Year Student Survey".

★ 320 ★

Enrollment

Public School Enrollment, 1986 and 1992

Percent distribution of enrolled students is shown, by race/ethnicity, for 1986 and for 1992, as reported by States to the Department of Education.

Race/ethnicity	Percent distribution	
	1986	1992[2]
Total U.S.	100.0	100.0
White, non-Hispanic[1]	70.4	66.7
Black, non-Hispanic[1]	16.1	16.5
Hispanic	9.9	12.3
Asian/Pacific Islander	2.8	3.5
American Indian/Alaskan Native	0.9	1.0

Source: U.S. Department of Education. National Center for Education Statistics. Office of Educational Research and Improvement. *Digest of Education Statistics, 1994.* Lanham, MD: Bernan, November 1994, p. 60. Primary source: U.S. Department of Education, Office for Civil Rights, 1986 State Summaries of Elementary and Secondary School Civil Rights Survey; and National Center for Education Statistics, Common Core of Data Survey. (This table was prepared May 1994.) *Notes:* A dash (-) stands for data not available. 1. Excludes persons of Hispanic origin. 2. Data include estimates for non-responding states.

★ 321 ★

Enrollment

Percent Enrolled in School, by Age Group, for Major Tribal Groups, 1990: Abenaki-Menominee

Data, shown for selected tribes with at least 100 persons, are based on a sample and are subject to sampling variability.

Group	Percent enrolled in school						
	3 and 4 years	5 to 14 years	15 to 17 years	18 and 19 years	20 to 24 years	25 to 34 years	35 years and older
American Indian	24.6	92.6	89.2	54.4	23.1	12.0	5.7
Abenaki	-	88.6	82.8	61.6	37.6	5.6	2.4
Alaska Native	36.5	91.4	92.3	18.2	17.9	4.2	7.6
Alaskan Athabaskans	30.8	91.0	91.5	52.0	13.0	7.3	6.5
Algonquian	50.0	93.4	89.9	69.2	18.7	9.1	8.2
Apache	18.3	94.0	87.2	49.2	19.7	11.6	6.3
Arapaho	28.8	93.1	87.8	46.2	21.4	13.8	7.4
Arikara	34.1	94.8	97.1	56.6	29.1	16.5	4.6
Assiniboine	26.8	92.6	85.4	42.2	19.8	13.7	6.6
Bannock	-	100.0	100.0	-	23.3	28.6	23.3
Blackfoot	28.1	92.9	86.0	53.9	19.8	11.3	8.5
Brotherton	13.3	100.0	100.0	30.0	59.3	9.7	3.3
Caddo	3.3	89.9	85.2	63.8	26.5	14.5	7.0
Cahuilla	30.6	93.0	100.0	45.8	-	4.6	2.6
California tribes	10.6	97.3	59.2	13.8	1.0	8.3	2.9
Canadian Indian	24.7	88.4	84.9	54.3	19.5	16.6	4.8
Central American Indian	25.9	88.2	69.5	39.3	36.7	7.0	10.1
French American Indian	77.8	100.0	85.4	100.0	-	21.7	8.2
Mexican American Indian	22.6	92.9	79.8	52.1	27.2	12.7	9.2
South American Indian	47.4	99.1	88.3	45.9	44.0	22.6	12.1
Spanish American Indian	22.2	92.4	96.1	76.7	32.9	17.1	8.1
Catawba	3.9	97.3	100.0	50.0	35.9	13.2	1.4
Cayuse	-	78.3	100.0	100.0	60.0	-	-
Chehalis	36.0	71.0	100.0	20.0	23.5	16.9	14.3
Chemakuan	15.3	96.3	93.8	10.7	13.0	6.7	1.4
Chemehuevi	36.4	98.1	75.0	73.3	24.1	7.6	5.5
Cherokee	21.8	92.8	88.6	50.7	22.2	11.0	5.2
Cherokee Shawnee	-	99.1	100.0	65.0	14.7	13.8	.5
Cheyenne	27.9	93.1	88.4	54.0	20.5	10.8	6.6
Cheyenne-Arapaho	19.1	90.7	92.0	59.5	10.2	14.8	9.2
Chickahominy	-	80.6	100.0	71.9	40.0	-	-
Chickasaw	31.8	93.0	93.7	62.3	25.6	13.9	3.8
Chinook	-	96.2	82.1	70.0	20.0	7.3	5.7
Chippewa	28.6	93.4	89.9	53.3	19.6	11.8	5.6
Chitimacha	-	100.0	84.8	40.6	-	3.7	4.1
Choctaw	23.8	93.5	91.4	59.6	26.2	12.7	4.8
Chumash	18.7	93.3	96.4	60.3	22.6	15.0	8.5
Coeur d'Alene	57.9	94.1	96.8	59.0	16.5	21.3	4.9
Coharie	-	80.9	100.0	58.3	26.4	17.2	2.2
Colorado River	37.5	91.6	94.3	58.3	23.1	8.1	3.3
Colville	28.1	94.0	91.2	60.6	18.6	11.0	5.3
Comanche	26.9	88.0	95.4	38.8	25.3	14.1	4.8
Coos	-	100.0	100.0	100.0	-	-	-

[Continued]

★ 321 ★

Percent Enrolled in School, by Age Group, for Major Tribal Groups, 1990: Abenaki-Menominee
[Continued]

| Group | Percent enrolled in school | | | | | | |
	3 and 4 years	5 to 14 years	15 to 17 years	18 and 19 years	20 to 24 years	25 to 34 years	35 years and older
Coquilles	63.9	90.3	100.0	60.0	60.0	33.3	-
Costanoan	33.3	100.0	87.7	65.4	29.2	27.5	2.9
Coushatta	31.4	87.5	92.3	66.7	26.3	16.5	7.3
Cowlitz	57.1	100.0	100.0	95.5	33.3	1.7	6.0
Cree	24.0	93.6	83.9	53.5	22.6	16.1	10.7
Creek	20.7	91.6	91.3	59.4	27.3	12.4	5.6
Croatan	-	50.0	100.0	-	100.0	23.7	-
Crow	35.2	92.7	83.3	54.4	25.6	15.5	11.4
Cupeno	40.0	83.3	100.0	-	23.1	3.7	4.7
Delaware	17.0	94.2	88.0	50.8	27.6	9.8	5.0
Diegueno	21.2	92.9	93.8	32.9	20.9	5.8	6.4
Eastern tribes	29.8	96.6	90.8	56.9	28.1	13.0	4.1
Fort Berthold	19.8	97.2	100.0	59.7	17.2	12.4	13.6
Fort Hall	18.1	91.8	94.3	36.0	8.5	8.6	5.2
Gabrieleno	-	100.0	76.5	73.3	30.2	8.1	1.9
Gila River	55.9	95.2	81.0	58.7	32.8	11.4	5.5
Grand Ronde	14.3	97.4	82.4	88.6	7.1	18.8	3.7
Gros Ventres	35.3	97.1	99.0	57.9	21.9	10.7	6.8
Haida	27.9	90.6	84.7	54.8	19.6	14.9	5.6
Haliwa	-	89.3	87.0	46.8	10.2	8.7	3.3
Hidatsa	33.7	94.3	95.6	68.2	38.9	23.1	5.6
Hoopa	24.7	95.3	91.4	54.7	21.4	11.0	5.7
Houma	19.0	89.2	87.4	28.4	12.3	5.0	2.6
Iowa	13.8	92.5	76.3	50.6	24.5	4.9	3.5
Iroquois	29.9	94.5	89.9	59.0	28.1	14.9	6.1
Juaneno	19.4	97.5	96.7	15.7	9.1	19.4	6.5
Kalispel	-	82.6	100.0	37.5	-	-	-
Karok	19.7	97.4	94.4	48.8	23.1	5.5	3.1
Kaw	37.0	95.7	85.3	60.0	39.6	9.7	4.9
Kickapoo	20.7	90.4	91.4	43.7	27.2	7.5	5.2
Kiowa	21.1	89.2	90.3	59.0	19.1	12.6	5.7
Klallam	19.5	91.2	90.2	68.8	7.8	28.8	3.3
Klamath	16.1	92.4	93.5	60.5	12.5	10.5	3.8
Konkow	23.8	94.9	100.0	-	-	18.0	2.5
Kootenai	50.0	94.7	100.0	69.7	21.8	11.3	3.7
Long Island	-	100.0	100.0	53.7	-	9.9	-
Luiseno	35.0	97.0	89.8	62.6	32.2	6.1	5.8
Lumbee	18.9	92.3	88.8	55.4	23.7	8.0	3.6
Lummi	32.7	92.0	87.6	72.3	15.8	17.8	9.6
Maidu	24.4	97.2	100.0	39.1	7.6	14.0	6.4
Makah	23.3	86.8	68.4	32.9	16.5	4.8	2.7
Maliseet	19.4	87.4	90.9	64.8	33.3	21.1	5.0
Mandan	23.6	95.7	84.6	61.8	41.6	4.2	4.6

[Continued]

★ 321 ★

Percent Enrolled in School, by Age Group, for Major Tribal Groups, 1990: Abenaki-Menominee

[Continued]

Group	Percent enrolled in school						
	3 and 4 years	5 to 14 years	15 to 17 years	18 and 19 years	20 to 24 years	25 to 34 years	35 years and older
Mattaponi	-	100.0	100.0	62.2	19.4	25.6	2.1
Menominee	32.7	95.0	91.0	38.9	17.9	10.5	4.9

Source: U.S. Bureau of the Census. *1990 Census of Population: Characteristics of American Indians by Tribe and Language.* CP3-7. Washington, DC: The Bureau, 1994, pp. 95-121.

★ 322 ★

Enrollment

Percent Enrolled in School, by Age Group, for Major Tribal Groups, 1990: Miami-Yurok and Other Specified Tribes

Data, shown for selected tribes with at least 100 persons, are based on a sample and are subject to sampling variability.

Group	Percent enrolled in school						
	3 and 4 years	5 to 14 years	15 to 17 years	18 and 19 years	20 to 24 years	25 to 34 years	35 years and older
Miami	20.9	91.6	88.8	47.7	30.5	13.5	4.1
Miccosukee	50.0	80.4	62.5	50.0	40.9	21.1	-
Micmac	-	94.7	78.9	38.6	28.8	10.4	8.9
Mission Indians	-	92.1	90.6	55.9	13.2	26.1	3.3
Miwok	31.2	94.7	95.2	59.8	16.2	13.8	4.4
Modoc	-	91.0	88.0	64.5	32.9	17.8	.4
Mohegan	-	94.0	67.5	25.0	38.2	11.9	5.1
Mono	1.8	93.3	100.0	59.5	18.7	7.9	6.9
Nanticoke	13.1	100.0	87.0	71.6	14.5	-	3.1
Narragansett	17.6	96.3	100.0	79.2	34.5	9.5	4.2
Navajo	24.7	91.6	90.0	62.9	24.7	12.8	5.5
Nez Perce	38.0	92.9	83.2	63.2	26.5	20.9	5.5
Nomalaki	-	100.0	-	100.0	-	-	-
Northwest tribes	-	100.0	100.0	80.8	38.1	17.1	-
Omaha	25.9	88.3	85.4	51.4	11.3	10.8	4.5
Oregon Athabaskan	-	97.0	100.0	76.0	22.5	9.5	-
Osage	27.2	93.2	95.5	59.0	30.3	11.0	5.5
Otoe-Missouria	38.1	96.8	92.6	65.4	35.7	5.7	9.6
Ottawa	14.3	93.1	94.5	47.9	22.8	12.7	5.8
Paiute	22.9	92.9	84.6	41.2	16.3	8.0	5.7
Pamunkey	-	100.0	100.0	100.0	26.5	12.5	9.2
Passamaquoddy	33.8	93.6	92.2	68.2	41.8	9.9	10.1
Pawnee	41.3	93.5	87.0	65.9	17.0	12.6	5.7
Penobscot	26.8	96.2	77.8	85.1	29.3	15.9	8.0
Peoria	32.1	89.8	90.1	87.5	13.8	11.3	5.7
Pequot	63.6	100.0	100.0	22.2	8.6	9.8	5.1

[Continued]

★ 322 ★

Percent Enrolled in School, by Age Group, for Major Tribal Groups, 1990: Miami-Yurok and Other Specified Tribes
[Continued]

Group	Percent enrolled in school						
	3 and 4 years	5 to 14 years	15 to 17 years	18 and 19 years	20 to 24 years	25 to 34 years	35 years and older
Pima	23.1	93.5	84.4	55.6	26.3	9.4	8.8
Piscataway	-	96.0	100.0	29.4	25.8	14.5	4.2
Pit River	21.7	96.8	87.4	15.4	31.6	30.0	3.8
Pomo	31.5	96.5	100.0	88.1	27.7	8.9	6.3
Ponca	16.0	94.0	93.8	31.9	33.8	5.4	7.6
Potawatomi	24.6	93.1	92.7	56.7	35.9	11.2	5.0
Powhatan	-	83.2	100.0	76.2	28.0	10.9	6.3
Pueblo	32.1	94.0	93.0	55.9	23.1	10.4	5.8
Puget Sound Salish	30.7	89.7	88.2	46.6	18.4	12.5	6.7
Quapaw	22.0	98.1	100.0	56.7	30.1	21.5	4.9
Quinault	28.6	92.8	85.4	25.0	10.0	5.4	8.2
Rappahannock	-	82.6	100.0	50.0	-	14.3	-
Sac and Fox	14.3	94.4	93.9	34.3	25.3	12.1	6.1
Salinan	66.7	100.0	-	-	33.3	53.8	9.6
Salish	19.9	97.4	91.8	58.8	29.9	13.2	7.4
Salish and Kootenai	10.1	95.0	96.0	41.1	15.4	17.4	8.8
Schaghticoke	-	100.0	-	100.0	-	-	9.5
Seminole	24.9	91.3	90.2	53.7	24.8	12.8	6.7
Serrano	50.0	96.4	100.0	-	31.8	-	-
Shasta	10.7	100.0	100.0	17.6	21.4	16.8	2.3
Shawnee	15.2	94.5	94.6	54.9	32.2	13.6	5.6
Shinnecock	7.7	95.8	80.9	96.1	37.5	13.7	5.8
Shoshone	22.8	93.3	94.0	50.7	27.7	14.1	4.7
Shoshone Paiute	14.4	97.6	88.4	58.1	13.1	10.0	2.1
Siletz	4.9	97.9	82.3	60.8	32.2	8.2	4.0
Sioux	21.5	92.7	86.9	51.9	21.7	11.8	6.8
Spokane	21.9	95.5	84.2	50.0	22.1	18.3	7.7
Stockbridge	41.3	94.0	91.4	84.6	21.0	10.0	3.5
Tlingit	34.3	92.1	89.3	41.6	22.9	10.0	5.8
Tohono O'Odham	20.4	93.7	84.5	47.4	17.7	8.5	2.8
Tolowa	16.1	86.9	100.0	33.3	-	10.7	7.6
Tonkawa	31.3	96.9	100.0	100.0	40.0	3.0	7.0
Tsimshian	55.3	97.8	96.3	51.7	6.7	17.4	7.2
Umatilla	3.4	89.5	93.8	30.8	20.8	10.4	3.2
Umpqua	-	77.4	100.0	100.0	21.8	6.6	-
Ute	42.3	93.7	91.1	56.1	20.1	11.5	5.8
Wailaki	61.7	88.0	90.8	64.3	29.3	20.7	12.7
Walla-Walla	-	97.4	87.5	-	-	18.8	2.0
Wampanoag	66.7	94.1	93.8	70.0	44.5	13.4	7.1
Warm Springs	46.7	92.8	86.7	63.8	7.9	6.8	4.2
Washo	31.3	97.5	94.9	34.5	9.8	14.8	2.3
Wichita	7.5	91.4	100.0	40.0	23.4	7.8	4.7
Winnebago	28.5	93.5	95.6	63.3	18.8	13.0	7.3
Wintu	20.2	88.8	100.0	54.7	15.9	4.5	-

[Continued]

★ 322 ★

Percent Enrolled in School, by Age Group, for Major Tribal Groups, 1990: Miami-Yurok and Other Specified Tribes
[Continued]

Group	Percent enrolled in school						
	3 and 4 years	5 to 14 years	15 to 17 years	18 and 19 years	20 to 24 years	25 to 34 years	35 years and older
Wiyot	-	75.4	63.6	75.8	76.7	-	-
Yakima	26.1	91.0	95.7	65.3	24.6	11.5	12.0
Yaqui	19.7	91.1	79.7	52.1	25.7	21.4	16.8
Yavapai Apache	45.5	98.5	100.0	45.5	-	2.7	8.8
Yokuts	24.3	92.0	97.8	37.7	31.5	10.3	4.9
Yuchi	11.1	89.0	100.0	100.0	-	12.3	-
Yuman	36.0	90.1	86.0	64.1	19.2	12.1	4.6
Yurok	24.6	94.3	89.5	49.0	16.5	15.9	3.1
Tribe not specified	20.8	91.0	89.1	56.8	22.5	17.9	6.7
Tribe not reported	23.9	91.1	86.9	50.7	23.9	13.1	6.1

Source: U.S. Bureau of the Census. *1990 Census of Population: Characteristics of American Indians by Tribe and Language.* CP3-7. Washington, DC: The Bureau, 1994, pp. 123-151.

★ 323 ★

Enrollment

School Enrollment of Persons Age 3 and Older, by Race/Ethnicity in Selected Alaska Native Villages - Part I

Data are shown for the 50 areas with the largest populations, in number of persons.

ANVSA[1]	White				Black				American Indian, Eskimo, or Aleut			
	Enrolled in pre-primary school	Enrolled in elementary or high school	Enrolled in college	Not enrolled in school	Enrolled in pre-primary school	Enrolled in elementary or high school	Enrolled in college	Not enrolled in school	Enrolled in preprimary primary school	Enrolled in elementary or high school	Enrolled in college	Not enrolled in school
Akiachak	0	12	0	21	0	0	0	0	6	71	7	293
Akutan	0	1	16	233	0	0	0	7	7	22	2	48
Alakanuk	0	0	2	16	0	0	0	0	36	162	2	283
Andreafsky	6	11	4	36	0	0	0	0	30	78	12	194
Angoon	5	15	5	89	0	0	0	0	35	136	0	289
Aniak	1	38	11	100	0	11	2	3	17	102	9	196
Barrow	23	110	69	520	0	6	2	4	134	397	63	947
Bethel	27	242	123	1,103	6	2	1	21	99	656	129	1,816
Chevak	2	2	7	21	0	0	0	0	40	137	12	300
Copper Center	5	44	23	195	0	0	0	0	14	19	9	89
Craig	16	155	13	708	0	0	0	0	15	69	2	188
Dillingham	15	132	52	593	0	0	0	0	31	265	24	690
Emmonak	4	13	0	35	0	0	0	3	44	104	2	311
Fort Yukon	0	6	9	58	0	0	0	0	17	93	13	342
Galena	0	26	35	333	0	0	0	30	2	99	1	232
Gambell	0	0	4	2	0	0	0	0	18	135	11	324
Grouse Creek Group	20	110	21	342	0	0	0	0	6	28	0	65
Hoonah	0	13	5	170	0	0	0	0	11	129	17	326
Hooper Bay	0	0	0	27	0	0	0	0	64	192	2	445
Kake	0	29	7	130	0	0	0	0	16	118	4	329
Kasigluk	0	2	10	12	0	0	0	0	35	97	2	247
King Cove	2	14	0	99	0	0	0	0	16	54	3	98
King Salmon	12	59	77	366	0	0	0	31	0	19	8	74
Kipnuk	0	0	0	8	0	0	0	0	13	142	28	223
Klawock	0	58	18	237	0	0	0	0	9	73	5	260
Kotlik	0	0	2	9	0	3	0	0	26	118	6	251
Kotzebue	6	99	38	463	0	0	0	7	73	506	62	1,193

[Continued]

★ 323 ★

School Enrollment of Persons Age 3 and Older, by Race/Ethnicity in Selected Alaska Native Villages - Part I

[Continued]

ANVSA[1]	White				Black				American Indian, Eskimo, or Aleut			
	Enrolled in pre-primary school	Enrolled in elementary or high school	Enrolled in college	Not enrolled in school	Enrolled in pre-primary school	Enrolled in elementary or high school	Enrolled in college	Not enrolled in school	Enrolled in preprimary primary school	Enrolled in elementary or high school	Enrolled in college	Not enrolled in school
Kwethluk	0	1	3	6	0	4	0	9	12	155	12	318
McGrath	15	52	23	162	0	0	0	0	8	102	7	129
Mountain Village	0	9	3	45	0	0	0	4	38	191	22	320
Naknek	8	63	10	238	0	0	0	0	10	66	2	145
Ninilchik	294	1,958	481	6,601	6	10	6	36	12	115	21	251
Noorvik	0	4	0	23	0	0	0	0	12	145	2	294
Pilot Station	0	2	0	10	0	0	0	0	35	102	44	212
Point Hope	4	5	5	25	0	0	0	2	34	179	16	282
Quinhagak	5	4	2	22	0	0	0	0	25	109	2	285
St. Paul	0	1	6	151	0	0	0	24	37	96	5	363
Salamatof	7	196	56	583	0	0	18	5	2	22	1	84
Sand Point	2	35	34	204	0	0	0	0	25	108	8	251
Savoonga	0	2	10	7	0	0	0	0	18	133	0	306
Selawik	2	4	2	13	0	0	0	3	33	158	4	279
Shishmaref	0	0	0	15	0	0	0	0	19	122	19	217
Stebbins	0	5	4	12	0	0	0	0	15	101	3	239
Togiak	2	27	17	34	0	0	0	2	27	141	12	292
Tok	27	167	87	525	0	0	0	0	12	22	2	44
Toksook Bay	3	1	2	7	0	0	0	0	20	124	31	178
Unalakleet	3	22	13	87	0	0	0	0	53	143	5	282
Unalaska	26	95	82	1,665	0	0	0	49	8	61	3	178
Wainwright	0	0	0	30	0	0	0	0	44	131	3	259
Yakutat	9	46	13	167	0	0	0	0	12	57	7	197

Source: *Census of Population and Housing, 1990: Summary Tape File 3C on CD-ROM* [machine-readable datafiles]. Prepared by the Bureau of the Census. Washington, DC: The Bureau, 1992. *Notes:* 1. Alaska Native villages (ANVs) constitute tribes, bands, clans, groups, villages, communities, or associations in Alaska that are recognized pursuant to the Alaska Native Claims Settlement Act of 1972, Public Law 92-203. Because ANVs do not have legally designated boundaries, the Census Bureau has established Alaska Native village statistical areas (ANVSAs) for statistical purposes. For the 1990 census, the Census Bureau cooperated with officials of the nonprofit corporation within each participating Alaska Native Regional Corporation (ANRC), as well as other knowledgeable officials, to delineate boundaries that encompass the settled area associated with each ANV.

★ 324 ★

Enrollment

School Enrollment of Persons Age 3 and Older, by Race/Ethnicity in Selected Alaska Native Villages - Part II

Data are shown for the 50 areas with the largest populations, in number of persons.

ANVSA[1]	Asian or Pacific Islander				Other race				Hispanic origin			
	Enrolled in in pre-primary school	Enrolled in elementary or high school	Enrolled in college	Not enrolled in school	Enrolled in in pre-primary school	Enrolled in elementary or high school	Enrolled in college	Not enrolled in school	Enrolled in in pre-primary school	Enrolled in elementary or high school	Enrolled in college	Not enrolled in school
Akiachak	0	0	4	0	0	0	0	0	0	0	0	0
Akutan	0	0	0	237	0	0	0	30	0	0	0	51
Alakanuk	0	0	0	0	0	0	0	0	0	0	0	0
Andreafsky	0	0	0	0	0	0	0	0	0	0	0	2
Angoon	0	3	0	2	0	6	0	3	0	6	0	5
Aniak	0	3	0	2	0	0	0	2	0	0	0	0
Barrow	9	41	15	118	0	4	0	22	2	12	3	43
Bethel	0	9	1	48	1	2	0	10	2	3	2	59
Chevak	0	3	0	1	0	0	0	0	0	0	0	2
Copper Center	0	0	0	0	0	0	0	0	0	0	0	2
Craig	0	0	0	2	0	2	0	4	0	14	0	22
Dillingham	6	23	0	20	0	0	2	9	0	8	2	14
Emmonak	3	0	0	6	0	0	0	3	0	2	0	3
Fort Yukon	0	0	0	0	0	0	0	0	0	0	0	0

[Continued]

★ 324 ★

School Enrollment of Persons Age 3 and Older, by Race/Ethnicity in Selected Alaska Native Villages - Part II

[Continued]

ANVSA[1]	Asian or Pacific Islander				Other race				Hispanic origin			
	Enrolled in in pre-primary school	Enrolled in elementary or high school	Enrolled in college	Not enrolled in school	Enrolled in in pre-primary school	Enrolled in elementary or high school	Enrolled in college	Not enrolled in school	Enrolled in in pre-primary school	Enrolled in elementary or high school	Enrolled in college	Not enrolled in school
Galena	0	0	7	3	0	0	0	0	0	0	0	2
Gambell	0	0	0	0	0	0	0	0	0	0	0	0
Grouse Creek Group	0	0	0	0	0	0	0	0	0	6	0	2
Hoonah	0	0	0	0	0	0	0	0	0	0	0	0
Hooper Bay	0	0	0	0	0	0	0	0	0	0	0	0
Kake	0	0	0	0	0	0	0	0	0	2	0	0
Kasigluk	0	0	0	0	0	0	0	0	0	0	0	0
King Cove	0	0	4	134	0	0	0	16	0	0	0	76
King Salmon	0	3	0	10	0	0	0	7	0	2	7	20
Kipnuk	0	0	0	2	0	0	0	0	0	0	0	0
Klawock	0	0	0	4	0	0	0	0	2	0	0	8
Kotlik	0	0	0	0	0	0	0	0	0	0	0	0
Kotzebue	0	16	0	26	0	0	0	0	2	7	0	22
Kwethluk	0	0	0	0	0	0	0	2	0	0	0	2
McGrath	0	0	0	0	0	0	0	0	0	0	0	2
Mountain Village	0	3	0	2	0	0	0	0	0	0	0	2
Naknek	0	0	0	0	0	0	0	0	0	0	0	0
Ninilchik	4	26	0	49	0	0	0	8	0	66	12	121
Noorvik	0	0	0	0	0	0	0	0	0	0	0	0
Pilot Station	0	0	0	0	0	0	0	0	0	0	0	0
Point Hope	0	0	0	3	0	0	0	0	0	0	0	0
Quinhagak	0	2	0	0	0	0	0	0	0	0	0	2
St. Paul	0	0	0	25	0	0	0	12	0	1	0	13
Salamatof	0	0	0	1	0	0	0	0	0	10	0	33
Sand Point	0	0	3	84	0	4	0	57	0	6	0	74
Savoonga	0	0	0	0	0	0	0	0	0	1	0	0
Selawik	0	0	0	0	0	0	0	0	0	0	0	0
Shishmaref	0	0	0	0	0	0	0	0	0	0	0	0
Stebbins	0	0	0	0	0	0	0	0	0	0	0	0
Togiak	0	0	0	0	0	0	0	0	0	0	0	0
Tok	0	0	0	8	0	0	0	0	0	3	2	2
Toksook Bay	0	0	0	3	0	0	0	0	0	0	0	0
Unalakleet	4	3	0	0	0	0	0	0	0	0	4	0
Unalaska	0	26	0	561	0	10	55	188	4	17	29	297
Wainwright	0	0	0	0	0	0	0	0	0	3	0	0
Yakutat	0	4	0	9	0	0	0	0	0	0	0	5

Source: Census of Population and Housing, 1990: Summary Tape File 3C on CD-ROM [machine-readable datafiles]. Prepared by the Bureau of the Census. Washington, DC: The Bureau, 1992. *Notes:* 1. Alaska Native villages (ANVs) constitute tribes, bands, clans, groups, villages, communities, or associations in Alaska that are recognized pursuant to the Alaska Native Claims Settlement Act of 1972, Public Law 92-203. Because ANVs do not have legally designated boundaries, the Census Bureau has established Alaska Native village statistical areas (ANVSAs) for statistical purposes. For the 1990 census, the Census Bureau cooperated with officials of the nonprofit corporation within each participating Alaska Native Regional Corporation (ANRC), as well as other knowledgeable officials, to delineate boundaries that encompass the settled area associated with each ANV.

★ 325 ★

Enrollment

School Enrollment of Persons Age 3 and Older, by Race/Ethnicity in Selected Tribal Designated Statistical Areas - Part I

TDSA[1]	White				Black				American Indian, Eskimo, or Aleut			
	Enrolled in in pre-primary school	Enrolled in elementary or high school	Enrolled in college	Not enrolled in school	Enrolled in in pre-primary school	Enrolled in elementary or high school	Enrolled in college	Not enrolled in school	Enrolled in in pre-primary school	Enrolled in elementary or high school	Enrolled in college	Not enrolled in school
Apache Choctaw TDSA (state)	183	3,087	516	13,499	48	1,166	91	2,396	14	185	9	448
Chickahominy TDSA (state)	9	126	28	509	4	340	57	1,109	0	86	17	379
Clifton Choctaw TDSA (state)	0	67	9	255	0	0	0	0	0	46	0	125
Coharie TDSA (state)	805	9,870	3,829	52,063	777	10,218	2,061	29,215	7	319	73	964

[Continued]

★ 325 ★

School Enrollment of Persons Age 3 and Older, by Race/Ethnicity in Selected Tribal Designated Statistical Areas - Part I
[Continued]

TDSA[1]	White				Black				American Indian, Eskimo, or Aleut			
	Enrolled in pre-primary school	Enrolled in elementary or high school	Enrolled in college	Not enrolled in school	Enrolled in pre-primary school	Enrolled in elementary or high school	Enrolled in college	Not enrolled in school	Enrolled in pre-primary school	Enrolled in elementary or high school	Enrolled in college	Not enrolled in school
Coquille Indian TDSA	6,633	59,483	32,479	270,605	49	408	453	911	86	1,146	384	4,277
Delaware-Muncie TDSA (state)	5	38	0	202	0	0	0	0	0	12	0	11
Florida Tribe of Eastern Creek TDSA (state)	0	9	17	189	0	0	0	0	0	0	0	0
Haliwa-Saponi TDSA (state)	0	62	19	405	32	856	73	2,472	5	483	51	1,581
Jena Band of Choctaw TDSA (state)	772	9,288	2,775	37,498	110	1,588	237	4,505	5	114	14	188
Klamath TDSA	725	6,302	2,507	26,700	36	91	33	164	49	437	77	1,132
Lumbee TDSA (state)	108	1,309	938	6,073	190	3,303	767	7,583	374	7,284	1,311	18,211
Meherrin TDSA (state)	277	3,500	1,234	18,420	363	7,070	1,152	20,556	0	76	8	112
Mohegan TDSA (state)	462	3,075	1,388	15,995	32	388	102	1,042	0	24	30	173
Ramapough TDSA (state)	0	17	20	283	9	12	17	118	0	13	4	122
United Houma Nation TDSA (state)	12,216	113,923	37,264	456,096	2,559	37,442	6,597	84,245	156	2,689	192	6,325
Waccamaw Siouan TDSA (state)	0	211	6	567	8	156	13	417	31	269	72	885
Wampanoag-Gay Head TDSA	304	1,529	370	8,127	10	86	70	293	11	47	26	181

Source: Census of Population and Housing, 1990: Summary Tape File 3C on CD-ROM [machine-readable datafiles]. Prepared by the Bureau of the Census. Washington, DC: The Bureau, 1992. *Notes:* 1. Tribal designated statistical areas (TDSAs) are areas, delineated outside Oklahoma by federally- and state-recognized tribes without a land base or associated trust lands, to provide statistical areas for which the Census Bureau tabulates data. TDSAs represent areas generally containing the American Indian population over which federally-recognized tribes have jurisdiction and areas in which state tribes provide benefits and services to their members. The names of TDSAs delineated by state-recognized tribes are followed by "(state)." The Census Bureau did not recognize TDSAs before the 1990 census.

★ 326 ★

Enrollment

School Enrollment of Persons Age 3 and Older, by Race/Ethnicity in Selected Tribal Designated Statistical Areas - Part II

TDSA[1]	Asian or Pacific Islander				Other race				Hispanic origin			
	Enrolled in pre-primary school	Enrolled in elementary or high school	Enrolled in college	Not enrolled in school	Enrolled in pre-primary school	Enrolled in elementary or high school	Enrolled in college	Not enrolled in school	Enrolled in pre-primary school	Enrolled in elementary or high school	Enrolled in college	Not enrolled in school
Apache Choctaw TDSA (state)	0	0	0	26	3	4	0	56	14	257	26	869
Chickahominy TDSA (state)	0	0	0	0	0	0	0	0	0	0	0	20
Clifton Choctaw TDSA (state)	0	0	0	0	0	0	0	0	0	9	0	28
Coharie TDSA (state)	12	99	38	333	14	89	42	328	19	228	92	1,006
Coquille Indian TDSA	141	1,211	2,259	2,978	118	956	429	2,572	343	2,763	1,135	6,973
Delaware-Muncie TDSA (state)	0	0	0	0	0	0	0	0	0	0	0	0
Florida Tribe of Eastern Creek TDSA (state)	0	0	0	0	0	0	0	0	0	0	0	0
Haliwa-Saponi TDSA (state)	0	0	0	0	0	0	0	20	0	0	0	0
Jena Band of Choctaw TDSA (state)	7	218	49	199	0	6	5	39	7	126	35	369
Klamath TDSA	12	31	87	136	5	147	13	419	37	517	52	1,173
Lumbee TDSA (state)	0	0	8	24	0	12	40	48	0	114	56	230
Meherrin TDSA (state)	0	28	45	38	0	0	6	48	0	12	8	73
Mohegan TDSA (state)	0	92	31	208	22	192	36	173	33	253	47	468
Ramapough TDSA (state)	0	0	0	0	0	4	0	7	0	7	0	7
United Houma Nation TDSA (state)	284	3,556	1,064	7,483	107	1,613	801	5,051	551	7,098	2,914	23,679
Waccamaw Siouan TDSA (state)	0	0	0	8	0	31	0	14	0	27	0	14
Wampanoag-Gay Head TDSA	0	0	9	32	0	26	0	41	2	13	0	63

Source: Census of Population and Housing, 1990: Summary Tape File 3C on CD-ROM [machine-readable datafiles]. Prepared by the Bureau of the Census. Washington, DC: The Bureau, 1992. *Notes:* 1. Tribal designated statistical areas (TDSAs) are areas, delineated outside Oklahoma by federally- and state-recognized tribes without a land base or associated trust lands, to provide statistical areas for which the Census Bureau tabulates data. TDSAs represent areas generally containing the American Indian population over which federally-recognized tribes have jurisdiction and areas in which state tribes provide benefits and services to their members. The names of TDSAs delineated by state-recognized tribes are followed by "(state)." The Census Bureau did not recognize TDSAs before the 1990 census.

★ 327 ★

Enrollment

School Enrollment of Persons Age 3 and Older, by Race/Ethnicity in Selected Tribal Jurisdiction Statistical Areas - Part I

TJSA[1]	White				Black				American Indian, Eskimo, or Aleut			
	Enrolled in preprimary school	Enrolled in elementary or high school	Enrolled in college	Not enrolled in school	Enrolled in preprimary school	Enrolled in elementary or high school	Enrolled in college	Not enrolled in school	Enrolled in preprimary school	Enrolled in elementary or high school	Enrolled in college	Not enrolled in school
Absentee Shawnee-Citizens Band of Potawatomi TJSA	946	15,899	4,377	54,221	176	1,436	317	3,633	131	1,588	332	3,787
Caddo-Wichita-Delaware TJSA	88	1,285	273	5,392	2	21	0	49	27	121	30	358
Cherokee TJSA	4,322	49,721	14,725	215,574	557	8,201	2,060	21,812	1,266	16,850	3,399	40,981
Cheyenne-Arapaho TJSA	2,350	25,824	8,488	93,953	64	803	341	2,333	188	1,861	383	3,890
Chickasaw TJSA	3,448	38,712	10,438	164,546	127	2,124	493	5,483	555	5,557	1,201	12,415
Choctaw TJSA	1,934	28,977	7,929	125,370	186	2,312	542	6,044	482	7,583	1,220	17,322
Creek TJSA	10,480	88,239	36,148	383,880	700	8,858	3,265	23,801	975	11,055	2,614	28,119
Iowa TJSA	34	787	175	2,535	0	22	23	87	5	94	2	196
Kaw TJSA	354	2,083	481	9,030	0	0	0	47	39	162	27	415
Kiowa-Comanche-Apache- Fort Sill Apache TJSA	2,121	26,459	8,779	110,535	456	5,909	2,012	15,752	260	3,299	675	7,973
Otoe-Missouria TJSA	46	470	70	1,532	0	7	0	34	12	128	8	291
Pawnee TJSA	168	2,450	487	10,031	11	9	0	72	30	433	60	1,004
Sac and Fox TJSA	561	7,707	1,811	32,716	27	304	107	1,036	69	1,281	152	2,812
Seminole TJSA	282	2,954	883	12,771	5	419	70	1,178	57	1,007	127	2,366
Tonkawa TJSA	118	1,872	636	8,155	0	6	6	6	9	262	75	472
Creek-Seminole Joint Area TJSA	17	235	83	1,315	0	62	11	90	11	154	20	306
Iowa-Sac and Fox Joint Area TJSA	14	180	27	531	0	13	4	11	3	1	7	9

Source: Census of Population and Housing, 1990: Summary Tape File 3C on CD-ROM [machine-readable datafiles]. Prepared by the Bureau of the Census. Washington, DC: The Bureau, 1992. *Notes:* 1. Tribal jurisdiction statistical areas (TJSAs) are areas, delineated by federally recognized tribes in Oklahoma without a reservation, for which the Census Bureau tabulates data. TJSAs represent areas generally containing the American Indian population over which one or more tribal governments have jurisdiction. If tribal officials delineated adjacent TJSAs so that they include some duplicate territory, the overlap area is called a "joint use area," which is treated as a separate TJSA for census purposes.

★ 328 ★

Enrollment

School Enrollment of Persons Age 3 and Older, by Race/Ethnicity in Selected Tribal Jurisdiction Statistical Areas - Part II

TJSA[1]	Asian or Pacific Islander				Other race				Hispanic origin			
	Enrolled in preprimary school	Enrolled in elementary or high school	Enrolled in college	Not enrolled in school	Enrolled in preprimary school	Enrolled in elementary or high school	Enrolled in college	Not enrolled in school	Enrolled in preprimary school	Enrolled in elementary or high school	Enrolled in college	Not enrolled in school
Absentee Shawnee-Citizens Band of Potawatomi TJSA	6	57	12	212	12	150	37	287	38	421	84	948
Caddo-Wichita-Delaware TJSA	0	5	0	6	8	48	12	174	17	94	14	222
Cherokee TJSA	34	298	215	552	72	499	183	1,171	178	1,618	459	3,260
Cheyenne-Arapaho TJSA	18	406	159	641	74	797	109	1,900	119	1,425	320	2,823
Chickasaw TJSA	8	204	106	409	63	669	61	1,309	158	1,437	214	2,501
Choctaw TJSA	9	135	64	182	43	323	50	491	78	831	155	1,408
Creek TJSA	190	1,407	1,119	3,518	66	824	540	2,487	354	2,787	1,290	6,950
Iowa TJSA	0	0	0	5	0	0	2	2	0	8	5	8
Kaw TJSA	21	50	0	20	0	26	0	10	13	39	5	67
Kiowa-Comanche-Apache- Fort Sill Apache TJSA	37	685	339	2,414	117	2,371	566	5,256	210	3,907	933	8,116
Otoe-Missouria TJSA	0	2	0	7	0	1	0	22	0	8	2	38
Pawnee TJSA	0	2	0	12	0	0	0	16	0	21	10	53
Sac and Fox TJSA	8	18	21	140	6	83	16	161	19	225	52	362
Seminole TJSA	0	2	2	8	0	6	3	44	0	103	3	147
Tonkawa TJSA	0	20	0	21	2	34	5	82	4	65	6	140
Creek-Seminole Joint Area TJSA	0	9	0	10	0	4	0	6	0	7	0	6

[Continued]

★ 328 ★

School Enrollment of Persons Age 3 and Older, by Race/Ethnicity in Selected Tribal Jurisdiction Statistical Areas - Part II
[Continued]

TJSA[1]	Asian or Pacific Islander				Other race				Hispanic origin			
	Enrolled in preprimary school	Enrolled in elementary or high school	Enrolled in college	Not enrolled in school	Enrolled in preprimary school	Enrolled in elementary or high school	Enrolled in college	Not enrolled in school	Enrolled in preprimary school	Enrolled in elementary or high school	Enrolled in college	Not enrolled in school
Iowa-Sac and Fox Joint Area TJSA	0	0	0	0	0	0	0	3	0	0	0	3

Source: Census of Population and Housing, 1990: Summary Tape File 3C on CD-ROM [machine-readable datafiles]. Prepared by the Bureau of the Census. Washington, DC: The Bureau, 1992. *Notes:* 1. Tribal jurisdiction statistical areas (TJSAs) are areas, delineated by federally recognized tribes in Oklahoma without a reservation, for which the Census Bureau tabulates data. TJSAs represent areas generally containing the American Indian population over which one or more tribal governments have jurisdiction. If tribal officials delineated adjacent TJSAs so that they include some duplicate territory, the overlap area is called a "joint use area," which is treated as a separate TJSA for census purposes.

★ 329 ★
Enrollment

School Enrollment of Persons Age 3 and Older, by Race/Ethnicity on Selected Reservations and Trust Lands - Part I

Data are shown for the 50 areas with the largest populations, in number of persons.

American Indian Reservation and Trust Lands[1,2]	White				Black				American Indian, Eskimo, or Aleut			
	Enrolled in pre-primary school	Enrolled in elementary or high school	Enrolled in college	Not enrolled in school	Enrolled in pre-primary school	Enrolled in elementary or high school	Enrolled in college	Not enrolled in school	Enrolled in pre-primary school	Enrolled in elementary or high school	Enrolled in college	Not enrolled in school
Agua Caliente Reservation	108	1,041	626	16,140	0	71	17	270	0	18	0	108
Allegany Reservation	84	996	258	4,571	0	0	0	5	39	250	71	640
Blackfeet Reservation	36	181	93	1,037	0	0	0	6	324	2,031	418	3,752
Cheyenne River Reservation	24	448	74	1,962	0	0	0	16	207	1,622	166	2,668
Coeur d'Alene Reservation and Trust Lands, ID	78	928	157	3,648	0	0	0	3	37	236	19	411
Colorado River Reservation	65	836	158	3,536	1	6	0	9	81	654	55	1,413
Colville Reservation	48	593	120	2,193	0	5	0	2	138	1,082	140	2,185
Crow Reservation and Trust Lands, MT	14	220	96	1,215	0	0	0	0	165	1,414	323	2,433
Eastern Cherokee Reservation	5	141	23	778	0	0	0	11	131	1,300	226	3,255
Flathead Reservation	260	3,075	390	11,520	0	0	0	8	128	1,343	408	2,900
Fort Apache Reservation	0	134	53	353	0	6	0	23	348	2,556	318	5,704
Fort Berthold Reservation	24	452	55	1,720	0	0	0	3	154	836	140	1,683
Fort Hall Reservation and Trust Lands, ID	24	455	107	1,117	0	0	0	0	71	781	72	1,900
Fort Peck Reservation	99	1,045	71	3,453	0	2	0	4	181	1,503	241	3,330
Gila River Reservation	5	33	14	139	0	0	0	13	237	2,714	308	5,171
Hopi Reservation and Trust Lands, AZ	0	18	36	117	0	0	0	0	162	1,930	227	4,262
Isabella Reservation and Trust Lands, MI	471	3,719	2,414	13,999	0	17	25	104	37	243	71	460
Laguna Pueblo and Trust Lands, NM	0	2	11	41	0	0	0	2	91	930	90	2,372
Lake Traverse (Sisseton) Reservation	98	1,434	133	6,066	0	0	0	0	90	824	110	1,526
Leech Lake Reservation	71	987	154	3,937	3	0	0	9	156	986	162	1,812
Mississippi Choctaw Reservation and Trust Lands, MS	3	15	5	153	0	6	0	5	183	1,343	256	1,951
Muckleshoot Reservation and Trust Lands, WA	54	495	108	2,067	1	2	0	12	58	276	5	438
Navajo Reservation and Trust Lands, AZ–NM–UT	52	716	308	3,098	5	19	32	100	3,138	42,086	5,634	81,285
Nez Perce Reservation	173	2,673	357	10,541	1	2	0	11	60	503	93	1,121
Northern Cheyenne Reservation and Trust Lands, MT–SD	11	56	37	217	0	0	0	0	86	1,071	144	1,955
Omaha Reservation	60	595	102	2,424	0	0	0	2	51	527	65	1,082
Oneida (West) Reservation	469	3,332	879	9,947	2	10	2	48	152	639	149	1,319
Osage Reservation	485	5,487	1,088	22,792	41	1,033	377	2,583	155	1,579	279	3,725
Papago Reservation	0	0	11	68	0	0	0	0	161	2,423	180	5,234
Pine Ridge Reservation and Trust Lands, NE–SD	33	71	45	827	0	11	0	8	292	3,297	505	5,830
Port Madison Reservation	133	694	210	3,069	0	3	3	8	7	120	2	230
Puyallup Reservation and Trust Lands, WA	553	4,171	1,317	18,390	55	666	88	1,211	29	278	35	572

[Continued]

★ 329 ★

School Enrollment of Persons Age 3 and Older, by Race/Ethnicity on Selected Reservations and Trust Lands - Part I

[Continued]

American Indian Reservation and Trust Lands[1,2]	White				Black				American Indian, Eskimo, or Aleut			
	Enrolled in pre-primary school	Enrolled in elementary or high school	Enrolled in college	Not enrolled in school	Enrolled in pre-primary school	Enrolled in elementary or high school	Enrolled in college	Not enrolled in school	Enrolled in pre-primary school	Enrolled in elementary or high school	Enrolled in college	Not enrolled in school
Red Lake Reservation	3	23	4	76	0	0	0	0	170	981	144	2,004
Rosebud Reservation and Trust Lands, SD	28	314	131	1,055	0	10	2	0	211	2,507	345	4,161
Salt River Reservation	0	13	31	1,219	0	0	0	0	121	1,033	130	1,962
San Carlos Reservation	0	14	17	46	0	0	0	32	134	2,038	241	4,067
Sandia Pueblo	50	573	100	1,908	0	0	2	3	18	99	9	256
San Juan Pueblo	50	667	225	2,282	0	5	1	5	26	267	62	854
Santa Clara Pueblo	100	1,636	436	5,542	0	5	13	26	34	340	115	739
Southern Ute Reservation	182	1,377	264	4,296	0	5	0	7	53	271	20	616
Standing Rock Reservation	37	601	58	2,245	0	14	0	0	204	1,560	187	2,507
Taos Pueblo and Trust Lands, NM	20	445	91	1,928	0	2	0	12	23	255	49	856
Tulalip Reservation	112	995	215	4,249	3	13	2	5	55	288	35	723
Turtle Mountain Reservation and Trust Lands, ND–SD	5	54	21	289	0	0	0	0	186	1,946	294	3,791
Uintah and Ouray Reservation	450	4,268	494	8,340	0	0	0	11	132	804	98	1,384
White Earth Reservation	69	1,282	160	4,206	0	2	0	0	130	808	84	1,598
Wind River Reservation	295	3,293	790	10,805	0	0	9	6	198	1,648	228	3,175
Yakima Reservation and Trust Lands, WA	124	1,781	499	7,877	0	19	0	89	141	1,878	436	3,272
Yankton Reservation	36	738	73	3,264	0	2	0	0	51	621	65	1,117
Zuni Pueblo	0	56	36	219	0	0	6	8	217	1,932	356	4,095

Source: Census of Population and Housing, 1990: Summary Tape File 3C on CD-ROM [machine-readable datafiles]. Prepared by the Bureau of the Census. Washington, DC: The Bureau, 1992. *Notes:* 1. Federal American Indian reservations are areas with boundaries established by treaty, statute, and/or executive or court order, and recognized by the federal government as territory in which American Indian tribes have jurisdiction. State reservations are lands held in trust by state governments for the use and benefit of a given tribe. The reservations and their boundaries were identified for the 1990 census by the Bureau of Indian Affairs (BIA), Department of Interior (for federal reservations), and state governments (for state reservations). The names of American Indian reservations recognized by state governments, but not by the federal government, are followed by "state." Areas composed of reservation lands that are administered jointly and/or are claimed by two reservations, as identified by the BIA, are called "joint areas," and are treated as separate American Indian reservations for census purposes. Federal reservations may cross state boundaries, and federal and state reservations may cross county, county subdivision, and place boundaries. For reservations that cross state boundaries, only the portion of the reservations in a given state is shown in the data products for that state; the entire reservations are shown in data products for the United States. 2. Trust lands are property associated with a particular American Indian reservation or tribe, held in trust by the federal government. Trust lands may be held in trust either for a tribe (tribal trust lands) or for an individual member of a tribe (individual trust land). Trust lands recognized for the 1990 census comprised all tribal trust lands and inhabited individual trust lands located outside of a reservation boundary. As with other American Indian areas, trust lands may be located in more than one state. Only the trust lands in a given state are shown in the data products for that state; all trust lands associated with a reservation or tribe are shown in data products for the United States. The Census Bureau first reported data for tribal trust lands for the 1980 census.

★ 330 ★

Enrollment

School Enrollment of Persons Age 3 and Older, by Race/Ethnicity on Selected Reservations and Trust Lands - Part II

Data are shown for the 50 areas with the largest populations, in number of persons.

American Indian Reservation and Trust Lands[1,2]	Asian or Pacific Islander				Other race				Hispanic origin			
	Enrolled in pre-primary school	Enrolled in elementary or high school	Enrolled in college	Not enrolled in school	Enrolled in pre-primary school	Enrolled in elementary or high school	Enrolled in college	Not enrolled in school	Enrolled in pre-primary school	Enrolled in elementary or high school	Enrolled in college	Not enrolled in school
Agua Caliente Reservation	7	67	21	275	8	160	17	541	16	333	50	1,258
Allegany Reservation	0	8	0	10	2	10	0	15	2	12	0	28
Blackfeet Reservation	0	0	0	0	0	4	0	7	0	38	4	49
Cheyenne River Reservation	0	4	0	0	0	0	0	6	1	40	0	14
Coeur d'Alene Reservation and Trust Lands, ID	0	0	0	3	0	6	7	8	4	56	17	53
Colorado River Reservation	0	7	10	37	15	198	39	439	60	696	73	1,438
Colville Reservation	4	2	0	21	0	30	3	117	12	80	11	170
Crow Reservation and Trust Lands, MT	0	0	0	13	0	0	0	0	0	7	0	3
Eastern Cherokee Reservation	0	0	14	0	0	0	0	32	0	15	0	32
Flathead Reservation	0	4	0	17	0	4	11	34	4	91	29	153

[Continued]

★ 330 ★

School Enrollment of Persons Age 3 and Older, by Race/Ethnicity on Selected Reservations and Trust Lands - Part II

[Continued]

American Indian Reservation and Trust Lands[1,2]	Asian or Pacific Islander				Other race				Hispanic origin			
	Enrolled in pre-primary school	Enrolled in elementary or high school	Enrolled in college	Not enrolled in school	Enrolled in pre-primary school	Enrolled in elementary or high school	Enrolled in college	Not enrolled in school	Enrolled in pre-primary school	Enrolled in elementary or high school	Enrolled in college	Not enrolled in school
Fort Apache Reservation	0	0	0	0	0	0	0	24	0	31	12	114
Fort Berthold Reservation	0	0	0	10	0	0	0	7	0	10	0	9
Fort Hall Reservation and Trust Lands, ID	0	0	0	26	7	67	6	149	7	137	0	205
Fort Peck Reservation	3	8	0	15	0	2	0	10	0	31	3	81
Gila River Reservation	0	0	0	13	0	20	33	185	23	391	54	495
Hopi Reservation and Trust Lands, AZ	0	0	0	30	0	0	0	8	17	41	23	72
Isabella Reservation and Trust Lands, MI	1	32	53	62	7	28	34	77	21	114	40	166
Laguna Pueblo and Trust Lands, NM	0	0	0	0	0	0	2	17	3	19	5	33
Lake Traverse (Sisseton) Reservation	0	0	0	3	0	22	5	11	0	18	5	33
Leech Lake Reservation	2	0	0	4	0	0	0	1	0	8	0	17
Mississippi Choctaw Reservation and Trust Lands, MS	0	0	0	0	0	0	0	0	0	13	0	0
Muckleshoot Reservation and Trust Lands, WA	1	11	6	11	0	5	0	42	13	18	3	50
Navajo Reservation and Trust Lands, AZ–NM–UT	0	0	17	76	13	101	35	279	72	352	52	694
Nez Perce Reservation	0	11	0	38	0	4	4	29	7	77	14	140
Northern Cheyenne Reservation and Trust Lands, MT–SD	0	0	0	0	0	4	0	5	0	4	0	75
Omaha Reservation	0	0	0	5	0	0	0	0	0	24	0	7
Oneida (West) Reservation	2	28	10	22	0	14	0	20	2	74	10	71
Osage Reservation	0	0	0	17	0	35	17	85	12	263	32	318
Papago Reservation	0	0	0	0	0	0	0	18	7	57	0	242
Pine Ridge Reservation and Trust Lands, NE–SD	0	0	0	11	14	0	0	41	14	27	0	150
Port Madison Reservation	6	59	13	89	0	6	0	8	7	24	0	64
Puyallup Reservation and Trust Lands, WA	74	1,020	162	1,589	10	130	28	310	21	318	62	652
Red Lake Reservation	0	6	0	6	0	0	0	0	0	0	0	16
Rosebud Reservation and Trust Lands, SD	0	0	0	0	0	13	5	14	0	64	7	37
Salt River Reservation	0	0	0	0	0	0	0	31	27	195	29	321
San Carlos Reservation	0	0	0	0	5	35	6	24	5	82	10	41
Sandia Pueblo	0	0	0	6	11	200	14	481	50	659	54	1,836
San Juan Pueblo	0	0	0	1	6	127	26	326	56	755	233	2,442
Santa Clara Pueblo	0	7	0	17	7	130	62	524	87	1,585	401	4,978
Southern Ute Reservation	0	7	0	10	11	110	19	248	69	351	41	830
Standing Rock Reservation	0	5	0	5	0	0	0	3	10	5	5	26
Taos Pueblo and Trust Lands, NM	3	15	0	25	11	158	29	573	20	463	78	1,489
Tulalip Reservation	3	0	0	53	0	14	6	15	2	48	14	63
Turtle Mountain Reservation and Trust Lands, ND–SD	0	0	0	0	0	0	0	0	0	12	0	11
Uintah and Ouray Reservation	0	22	6	24	9	66	6	75	17	149	13	237
White Earth Reservation	0	4	2	0	0	0	0	0	0	17	0	7
Wind River Reservation	0	12	44	29	11	69	16	220	28	248	20	512
Yakima Reservation and Trust Lands, WA	6	79	45	381	246	2,720	347	5,822	288	3,275	443	6,501
Yankton Reservation	0	0	0	3	0	0	0	1	0	6	4	5
Zuni Pueblo	0	0	0	7	0	0	0	13	6	53	0	82

Source: Census of Population and Housing, 1990: Summary Tape File 3C on CD-ROM [machine-readable datafiles]. Prepared by the Bureau of the Census. Washington, DC: The Bureau, 1992. *Notes:* 1. Federal American Indian reservations are areas with boundaries established by treaty, statute, and/or executive or court order, and recognized by the federal government as territory in which American Indian tribes have jurisdiction. State reservations are lands held in trust by state governments for the use and benefit of a given tribe. The reservations and their boundaries were identified for the 1990 census by the Bureau of Indian Affairs (BIA), Department of Interior (for federal reservations), and state governments (for state reservations). The names of American Indian reservations recognized by state governments, but not by the federal government, are followed by "state." Areas composed of reservation lands that are administered jointly and/or are claimed by two reservations, as identified by the BIA, are called "joint areas," and are treated as separate American Indian reservations for census purposes. Federal reservations may cross state boundaries, and federal and state reservations may cross county, county subdivision, and place boundaries. For reservations that cross state boundaries, only the portion of the reservations in a given state is shown in the data products for that state; the entire reservations are shown in data products for the United States. 2. Trust lands are property associated with a particular American Indian reservation or tribe, held in trust by the federal government. Trust lands may be held in trust either for a tribe (tribal trust lands) or for an individual member of a tribe (individual trust land). Trust lands recognized for the 1990 census comprised all tribal trust lands and inhabited individual trust lands located outside of a reservation boundary. As with other American Indian areas, trust lands may be located in more than one state. Only the trust lands in a given state are shown in the data products for that state; all trust lands associated with a reservation or tribe are shown in data products for the United States. The Census Bureau first reported data for tribal trust lands for the 1980 census.

★ 331 ★
Enrollment

School Enrollment of Persons Age 3 and Older, by Type of School in Selected Alaska Native Villages

Data are shown for the 50 areas with the largest populations, in number of persons.

Alaska Native Village Statistical Area[1]	Enrolled in preprimary school		Enrolled in elementary or high school		Enrolled in college		Not enrolled in school
	Public school	Private school	Public school	Private school	Public school	Private school	
Akiachak	6	0	83	0	7	4	314
Akutan	7	0	23	0	18	0	555
Alakanuk	36	0	162	0	4	0	299
Andreafsky	36	0	89	0	10	6	230
Angoon	40	0	160	0	5	0	383
Aniak	18	0	146	8	18	4	303
Barrow	164	2	552	6	136	13	1,611
Bethel	123	10	909	2	237	17	2,998
Chevak	42	0	142	0	19	0	322
Copper Center	19	0	63	0	29	3	284
Craig	31	0	226	0	15	0	902
Dillingham	52	0	415	5	69	9	1,312
Emmonak	51	0	117	0	2	0	358
Fort Yukon	17	0	99	0	20	2	400
Galena	2	0	125	0	40	3	598
Gambell	18	0	135	0	13	2	326
Grouse Creek Group	26	0	129	9	21	0	407
Hoonah	11	0	142	0	17	5	496
Hooper Bay	64	0	192	0	2	0	472
Kake	16	0	147	0	7	4	459
Kasigluk	35	0	99	0	12	0	259
King Cove	18	0	64	4	7	0	347
King Salmon	12	0	81	0	81	4	488
Kipnuk	13	0	142	0	28	0	233
Klawock	8	1	131	0	17	6	501
Kotlik	26	0	121	0	8	0	260
Kotzebue	74	5	606	15	96	4	1,689
Kwethluk	12	0	160	0	15	0	335
McGrath	23	0	154	0	22	8	291
Mountain Village	38	0	203	0	8	17	371
Naknek	18	0	118	11	11	1	383
Ninilchik	217	99	1,900	209	430	78	6,945
Noorvik	12	0	149	0	2	0	317
Pilot Station	35	0	102	2	44	0	222
Point Hope	38	0	184	0	20	1	312
Quinhagak	30	0	113	2	4	0	307
St. Paul	37	0	97	0	7	4	575
Salamatof	6	3	208	10	57	18	673
Sand Point	27	0	147	0	45	0	596
Savoonga	18	0	135	0	10	0	313
Selawik	35	0	162	0	6	0	295
Shishmaref	19	0	122	0	19	0	232
Stebbins	15	0	104	2	7	0	251

[Continued]

★ 331 ★

School Enrollment of Persons Age 3 and Older, by Type of School in Selected Alaska Native Villages
[Continued]

Alaska Native Village Statistical Area[1]	Enrolled in preprimary school		Enrolled in elementary or high school		Enrolled in college		Not enrolled in school
	Public school	Private school	Public school	Private school	Public school	Private school	
Togiak	29	0	165	3	29	0	328
Tok	34	5	189	0	86	3	577
Toksook Bay	23	0	125	0	33	0	188
Unalakleet	60	0	168	0	18	0	369
Unalaska	34	0	183	9	110	30	2,641
Wainwright	44	0	131	0	3	0	289
Yakutat	21	0	104	3	15	5	373

Source: Census of Population and Housing, 1990: Summary Tape File 3C on CD-ROM [machine-readable datafiles]. Prepared by the Bureau of the Census. Washington, DC: The Bureau, 1992. Notes: 1. Alaska Native villages (ANVs) constitute tribes, bands, clans, groups, villages, communities, or associations in Alaska that are recognized pursuant to the Alaska Native Claims Settlement Act of 1972, Public Law 92-203. Because ANVs do not have legally designated boundaries, the Census Bureau has established Alaska Native village statistical areas (ANVSAs) for statistical purposes. For the 1990 census, the Census Bureau cooperated with officials of the nonprofit corporation within each participating Alaska Native Regional Corporation (ANRC), as well as other knowledgeable officials, to delineate boundaries that encompass the settled area associated with each ANV.

★ 332 ★
Enrollment

School Enrollment of Persons Age 3 and Older, by Type of School in Selected Tribal Designated Statistical Areas

Tribal Designated Statistical Area[1]	Enrolled in preprimary school		Enrolled in elementary or high school		Enrolled in college		Not enrolled in school
	Public school	Private school	Public school	Private school	Public school	Private school	
Apache Choctaw TDSA (state)	220	28	4,355	87	523	93	16,425
Chickahominy TDSA (state)	4	9	518	34	90	12	1,997
Clifton Choctaw TDSA (state)	0	0	105	8	9	0	380
Coharie TDSA (state)	1,182	433	20,004	591	4,747	1,296	82,903
Coquille Indian TDSA	4,258	2,769	59,635	3,569	33,734	2,270	281,343
Delaware-Muncie TDSA (state)	5	0	50	0	0	0	213
Florida Tribe of Eastern Creek TDSA (state)	0	0	9	0	17	0	189
Haliwa-Saponi TDSA (state)	37	0	1,363	38	143	0	4,478
Jena Band of Choctaw TDSA (state)	569	325	10,539	675	1,999	1,081	42,429
Klamath TDSA	540	287	6,751	257	2,570	147	28,551
Lumbee TDSA (state)	563	109	11,721	187	2,776	288	31,939
Meherrin TDSA (state)	529	111	10,140	534	1,787	658	39,174
Mohegan TDSA (state)	355	161	3,401	370	1,291	296	17,591
Ramapough TDSA (state)	9	0	46	0	24	17	530
United Houma Nation TDSA (state)	6,391	8,931	120,207	39,016	34,601	11,317	559,200

[Continued]

★ 332 ★

School Enrollment of Persons Age 3 and Older, by Type of School in Selected Tribal Designated Statistical Areas

[Continued]

Tribal Designated Statistical Area[1]	Enrolled in preprimary school		Enrolled in elementary or high school		Enrolled in college		Not enrolled in school
	Public school	Private school	Public school	Private school	Public school	Private school	
Waccamaw Siouan TDSA (state)	39	0	658	9	68	23	1,891
Wampanoag-Gay Head TDSA	207	118	1,589	99	314	161	8,674

Source: Census of Population and Housing, 1990: Summary Tape File 3C on CD-ROM [machine-readable datafiles]. Prepared by the Bureau of the Census. Washington, DC: The Bureau, 1992. *Notes:* 1. Tribal designated statistical areas (TDSAs) are areas, delineated outside Oklahoma by federally- and state-recognized tribes without a land base or associated trust lands, to provide statistical areas for which the Census Bureau tabulates data. TDSAs represent areas generally containing the American Indian population over which federally-recognized tribes have jurisdiction and areas in which state tribes provide benefits and services to their members. The names of TDSAs delineated by state-recognized tribes are followed by "(state)." The Census Bureau did not recognize TDSAs before the 1990 census.

★ 333 ★

Enrollment

School Enrollment of Persons Age 3 and Older, by Type of School in Selected Tribal Jurisdiction Statistical Areas

Tribal Jurisdiction Statistical Area[1]	Enrolled in preprimary school		Enrolled in elementary or high school		Enrolled in college		Not enrolled in school
	Public school	Private school	Public school	Private school	Public school	Private school	
Absentee Shawnee-Citizens Band of Potawatomi TJSA	902	369	18,111	1,019	4,400	675	62,140
Caddo-Wichita-Delaware TJSA	121	4	1,467	13	297	18	5,979
Cherokee TJSA	4,700	1,551	72,491	3,078	17,838	2,744	280,090
Cheyenne-Arapaho TJSA	1,844	850	28,958	733	8,672	808	102,717
Chickasaw TJSA	3,305	896	46,194	1,072	11,446	853	184,162
Choctaw TJSA	2,280	374	38,748	582	9,186	619	149,409
Creek TJSA	6,822	5,589	100,777	9,606	29,475	14,211	441,805
Iowa TJSA	33	6	892	11	187	15	2,825
Kaw TJSA	197	217	2,225	96	476	32	9,522
Kiowa-Comanche-Apache-Fort Sill Apache TJSA	2,375	616	37,938	785	10,965	1,406	141,930
Otoe-Missouria TJSA	55	3	601	7	67	11	1,886
Pawnee TJSA	141	68	2,822	72	456	91	11,135
Sac and Fox TJSA	467	204	9,109	284	1,693	414	36,865
Seminole TJSA	256	88	4,367	21	979	106	16,367
Tonkawa TJSA	87	42	2,137	57	684	38	8,736
Creek-Seminole Joint Area TJSA	21	7	446	18	104	10	1,727
Iowa-Sac and Fox Joint Area TJSA	17	0	194	0	38	0	554

Source: Census of Population and Housing, 1990: Summary Tape File 3C on CD-ROM [machine-readable datafiles]. Prepared by the Bureau of the Census. Washington, DC: The Bureau, 1992. *Notes:* 1. Tribal jurisdiction statistical areas (TJSAs) are areas, delineated by federally recognized tribes in Oklahoma without a reservation, for which the Census Bureau tabulates data. TJSAs represent areas generally containing the American Indian population over which one or more tribal governments have jurisdiction. If tribal officials delineated adjacent TJSAs so that they include some duplicate territory, the overlap area is called a "joint use area," which is treated as a separate TJSA for census purposes.

★ 334 ★

Enrollment

School Enrollment of Persons Age 3 and Older, by Type of School on Selected Reservations and Trust Lands

Data are shown for the 50 areas with the largest populations, in number of persons.

American Indian Reservation and Trust Lands[1,2]	Enrolled in preprimary school		Enrolled in elementary or high school		Enrolled in college		Not enrolled in school
	Public school	Private school	Public school	Private school	Public school	Private school	
Agua Caliente Reservation	66	57	1,239	118	550	131	17,334
Allegany Reservation	106	19	1,229	35	292	37	5,241
Blackfeet Reservation	355	5	2,173	43	480	31	4,802
Cheyenne River Reservation	231	0	2,065	9	205	35	4,652
Coeur d'Alene Reservation and Trust Lands, ID	108	7	1,107	63	147	36	4,073
Colorado River Reservation	150	12	1,690	11	228	34	5,434
Colville Reservation	175	15	1,639	73	250	13	4,518
Crow Reservation and Trust Lands, MT	162	17	1,420	214	383	36	3,661
Eastern Cherokee Reservation	124	12	1,346	95	196	67	4,076
Flathead Reservation	326	62	4,313	113	725	84	14,479
Fort Apache Reservation	324	24	2,540	156	329	42	6,104
Fort Berthold Reservation	163	15	1,276	12	169	26	3,423
Fort Hall Reservation and Trust Lands, ID	96	6	1,283	20	164	21	3,192
Fort Peck Reservation	253	30	2,516	44	285	27	6,812
Gila River Reservation	224	18	2,660	107	323	32	5,521
Hopi Reservation and Trust Lands, AZ	150	12	1,810	138	207	56	4,417
Isabella Reservation and Trust Lands, MI	389	127	3,614	425	2,464	133	14,702
Laguna Pueblo and Trust Lands, NM	77	14	925	7	86	17	2,432
Lake Traverse (Sisseton) Reservation	167	21	2,096	184	214	34	7,606
Leech Lake Reservation	222	10	1,872	101	292	24	5,763
Mississippi Choctaw Reservation and Trust Lands, MS	107	79	1,029	335	117	144	2,109
Muckleshoot Reservation and Trust Lands, WA	99	15	719	70	107	12	2,570
Navajo Reservation and Trust Lands, AZ–NM–UT	2,974	234	40,893	2,029	5,365	661	84,838
Nez Perce Reservation	214	20	3,101	92	424	30	11,740
Northern Cheyenne Reservation and Trust Lands, MT–SD	90	7	860	271	144	37	2,177
Omaha Reservation	89	22	1,116	6	150	17	3,513
Oneida (West) Reservation	411	214	3,274	749	873	167	11,356
Osage Reservation	515	166	7,822	312	1,414	347	29,202
Papago Reservation	153	8	2,254	169	170	21	5,320
Pine Ridge Reservation and Trust Lands, NE–SD	314	25	3,040	339	464	86	6,717
Port Madison Reservation	85	61	847	35	175	53	3,404
Puyallup Reservation and Trust Lands, WA	506	215	5,871	394	1,310	320	22,072
Red Lake Reservation	173	0	999	11	148	0	2,086
Rosebud Reservation and Trust Lands, SD	237	2	2,745	99	414	69	5,230
Salt River Reservation	113	8	1,001	45	155	6	3,212
San Carlos Reservation	126	13	1,873	214	237	27	4,169
Sandia Pueblo	76	3	830	42	99	26	2,654
San Juan Pueblo	75	7	996	70	293	21	3,468
Santa Clara Pueblo	120	21	1,846	272	518	108	6,848
Southern Ute Reservation	211	35	1,724	46	276	27	5,177
Standing Rock Reservation	229	12	2,126	54	207	38	4,760
Taos Pueblo and Trust Lands, NM	42	15	800	75	134	35	3,394
Tulalip Reservation	115	58	1,264	46	200	58	5,045
Turtle Mountain Reservation and Trust Lands, ND–SD	191	0	1,949	51	286	29	4,080
Uintah and Ouray Reservation	524	67	5,101	59	574	30	9,834
White Earth Reservation	188	11	2,012	84	231	15	5,804
Wind River Reservation	373	131	4,815	207	1,011	76	14,235
Yakima Reservation and Trust Lands, WA	461	56	6,201	276	1,086	241	17,441

[Continued]

★ 334 ★

School Enrollment of Persons Age 3 and Older, by Type of School on Selected Reservations and Trust Lands
[Continued]

American Indian Reservation and Trust Lands[1,2]	Enrolled in preprimary school		Enrolled in elementary or high school		Enrolled in college		Not enrolled in school
	Public school	Private school	Public school	Private school	Public school	Private school	
Yankton Reservation	80	7	1,143	218	97	41	4,385
Zuni Pueblo	217	0	1,830	158	368	30	4,342

Source: Census of Population and Housing, 1990: Summary Tape File 3C on CD-ROM [machine-readable datafiles]. Prepared by the Bureau of the Census. Washington, DC: The Bureau, 1992. *Notes:* 1. Federal American Indian reservations are areas with boundaries established by treaty, statute, and/or executive or court order, and recognized by the federal government as territory in which American Indian tribes have jurisdiction. State reservations are lands held in trust by state governments for the use and benefit of a given tribe. The reservations and their boundaries were identified for the 1990 census by the Bureau of Indian Affairs (BIA), Department of Interior (for federal reservations), and state governments (for state reservations). The names of American Indian reservations recognized by state governments, but not by the federal government, are followed by "state." Areas composed of reservation lands that are administered jointly and/or are claimed by two reservations, as identified by the BIA, are called "joint areas," and are treated as separate American Indian reservations for census purposes. Federal reservations may cross state boundaries, and federal and state reservations may cross county, county subdivision, and place boundaries. For reservations that cross state boundaries, only the portion of the reservations in a given state is shown in the data products for that state; the entire reservations are shown in data products for the United States. 2. Trust lands are property associated with a particular American Indian reservation or tribe, held in trust by the federal government. Trust lands may be held in trust either for a tribe (tribal trust lands) or for an individual member of a tribe (individual trust land). Trust lands recognized for the 1990 census comprised all tribal trust lands and inhabited individual trust lands located outside of a reservation boundary. As with other American Indian areas, trust lands may be located in more than one state. Only the trust lands in a given state are shown in the data products for that state; all trust lands associated with a reservation or tribe are shown in data products for the United States. The Census Bureau first reported data for tribal trust lands for the 1980 census.

Academic Progress

★ 335 ★

ACT Average Scores, by Race/Ethnicity, 1994

Data show average ACT (American College Testing Assessment) scores for 1994 and percent change from 1993. The ACT is scored on a scale of 1 to 36.

Race/ethnicity	Score	1-yr. chg.
American Indian	18.5	+0.1
Asian	21.7	0.0
Black	17.0	-0.1
Mexican American	18.4	-0.1
Other Hispanic	19.3	0.0
White	21.4	0.0
All students	20.8	+0.1

Source: Chronicle of Higher Education Almanac (7 September 1994), p. A54. Primary source: American College Testing.

★ 336 ★

Academic Progress

Adult Document Literacy Skills, 1992

Data show percent of persons age 16 and older at each proficiency level. Document literacy reflects the knowledge and skills used to process information from documents. A level 1 score of 0 to 225 requires the reader to locate pieces of information based on a literal match. A level 2 score of 225 to 275 requires the reader to match a single piece of information among several distractors. A level 3 score of 276 to 325 requires the reader to integrate multiple pieces of information from one or more documents. A level 4 score of 326 to 375 requires the performance of multiple-feature matches, cycling through documents, and integrating information. A level 5 score of 376 to 500 requires the reader to search through complex displays that contain multiple distractors, to make high-level text-based inferences.

Race/ethnicity	Average score	Percent of adults with proficiency level -				
		1	2	3	4	5
Total	267	23	28	31	15	3
White	280	16	27	34	19	3
Black	230	43	36	18	3	0
Asian or Pacific Islander	245	34	25	28	12	2
American Indian	254	27	37	29	7	0
Hispanic						
Mexican	205	54	25	16	4	0
Cuban	212	48	30	16	4	2
Puerto Rican	215	49	29	18	3	0
Central/South American	206	53	25	16	4	0
Other	254	28	26	32	12	2

Source: U.S. Department of Education. National Center for Education Statistics. Office of Educational Research and Improvement. *Digest of Education Statistics, 1994.* Lanham, MD: Bernan, November 1994, p. 408. U.S. Department of Education, National Center for Education Statistics, National Adult Literacy Survey, *Adult Literacy in America, 1992,* prepared by Educational Testing Service. (This table was prepared February 1994.).

★ 337 ★

Academic Progress

Adult Prose Literacy Skills, 1992

Data show percent of persons age 16 and older at each proficiency level. Prose literacy is the ability to understand and use information contained in various kinds of textual material. A level 1 score of 0 to 225 requires the reader to locate a single piece of information in a short text. A level 2 score of 226 to 275 requires the reader to locate a single piece of information in the text with several distractors or to make low-level inferences. A level 3 score of 276 to 325 requires the reader to make literal or synonymous matches between the text and information given in the task, or to make low-level inferences. A level 4 score of 326 to 375 requires the reader to perform multiple-feature matches and to integrate or synthesize information from complex passages. A level 5 score of 376 to 500 requires the reader to search for information in dense text which contains a number of distractors.

Race/ethnicity	Average score	Percent of adults with proficiency level -				
		1	2	3	4	5
Total	272	21	27	32	17	3
White	286	14	25	36	21	4
Black	237	38	37	21	4	0
Asian or Pacific Islander	242	36	25	25	12	2
American Indian	254	25	39	28	7	1
Hispanic						
Mexican	206	54	25	16	5	0
Cuban	211	53	24	17	6	1
Puerto Rican	218	47	32	17	3	0
Central/South American	207	56	22	17	4	0
Other	260	25	27	33	13	2

Source: U.S. Department of Education. National Center for Education Statistics. Office of Educational Research and Improvement. *Digest of Education Statistics, 1994.* Lanham, MD: Bernan, November 1994, p. 408. U.S. Department of Education, National Center for Education Statistics, National Adult Literacy Survey, *Adult Literacy in America, 1992,* prepared by Educational Testing Service. (This table was prepared February 1994.).

★ 338 ★

Academic Progress

Adult Quantitative Literacy Skills, 1992

Data show percent of persons age 16 and older at each proficiency level. Quantitative literacy is the ability to perform numerical operations in everyday life. A level 1 score of 0 to 225 requires the reader to perform a single, relatively simple, arithmetic operation. A level 2 score of 226 to 275 requires the reader to perform a single operation using numbers that are either stated in the task or easily located in the material. A level 3 score of 276 to 325 requires the reader to use two or more numbers to solve the problem. A level 4 score of 326 to 375 requires the reader to perform two or more sequential operations or a single operation in which the quantities are found in different types of displays. A level 5 score of 376 to 500 requires the reader to perform multiple operations sequentially. They must extract the features of the problem from text or rely on background knowledge to determine the quantities or operations needed.

Race/ethnicity	Average score	Percent of adults with proficiency level -				
		1	2	3	4	5
Total	271	22	25	31	17	4
White	287	14	24	35	21	5
Black	224	46	34	17	3	0
Asian or Pacific Islander	256	30	23	27	16	4
American Indian	250	33	32	28	7	1
Hispanic						
Mexican	205	54	25	17	4	0
Cuban	223	46	20	25	6	3
Puerto Rican	212	51	28	17	3	1
Central/South American	203	53	25	18	4	0
Other	246	31	25	31	11	1

Source: U.S. Department of Education. National Center for Education Statistics. Office of Educational Research and Improvement. *Digest of Education Statistics, 1994.* Lanham, MD: Bernan, November 1994, p. 408. U.S. Department of Education, National Center for Education Statistics, National Adult Literacy Survey, *Adult Literacy in America, 1992,* prepared by Educational Testing Service. (This table was prepared February 1994.).

★ 339 ★

Academic Progress

Average Carnegie Units Completed by High School Graduates, by Subject Field and Race/Ethnicity: 1982 and 1992

The Carnegie unit is a standard of measurement that represents one credit for the completion of a one-year course. Data refer to public high school students.

Subject field	Academic year and race/ethnicity of student											
	1982 graduates						1992 graduates					
	Total	White	Black	Hispanic	Asian	Am. Indian	Total	White	Black	Hispanic	Asian	Am. Indian
Total	21.44	21.51	21.13	21.19	22.18	21.32	23.76	23.83	23.21	23.62	23.45	23.38
English	3.87	3.84	4.06	3.88	3.82	3.92	4.18	4.17	4.20	4.26	4.14	4.09
History/social studies	3.16	3.19	3.09	3.02	3.19	3.22	3.58	3.61	3.59	3.38	3.51	3.63
Mathematics												
Total	2.55	2.59	2.53	2.26	3.14	2.09	3.39	3.38	3.37	3.36	3.65	3.16

[Continued]

★ 339 ★

Average Carnegie Units Completed by High School Graduates, by Subject Field and Race/Ethnicity: 1982 and 1992

[Continued]

Subject field	Academic year and race/ethnicity of student											
	1982 graduates						1992 graduates					
	Total	White	Black	Hispanic	Asian	Am. Indian	Total	White	Black	Hispanic	Asian	Am. Indian
Less than algebra	0.92	0.80	1.39	1.24	0.74	1.14	0.98	0.87	1.35	1.24	0.74	1.55
Algebra or higher	1.62	1.79	1.14	1.03	2.41	0.95	2.41	2.51	2.02	2.12	2.91	1.61
Science												
Total	2.16	2.24	2.04	1.79	2.59	1.96	2.87	2.93	2.74	2.60	3.22	2.55
General science	0.74	0.73	0.81	0.77	0.51	0.72	0.84	0.83	0.94	0.81	0.73	1.03
Biology	0.93	0.96	0.89	0.79	1.09	0.78	1.19	1.21	1.15	1.16	1.20	0.99
Chemistry	0.34	0.37	0.25	0.16	0.60	0.35	0.58	0.61	0.47	0.47	0.79	0.35
Physics	0.16	0.19	0.09	0.07	0.39	0.11	0.26	0.28	0.18	0.16	0.50	0.18
Foreign languages	0.96	1.02	0.70	0.76	1.89	0.45	1.67	1.70	1.28	1.76	2.43	0.92
Arts	1.45	1.51	1.25	1.30	1.32	1.67	1.62	1.68	1.45	1.44	1.38	1.53
Vocational education[1]	4.64	4.53	4.82	5.26	3.12	5.09	3.76	3.73	3.92	3.79	3.18	4.53
Personal use[2]	2.64	2.59	2.64	2.92	3.10	2.93	2.69	2.63	2.66	3.03	2.93	2.97
Computer science[3]	0.08	0.09	0.08	0.04	0.14	0.04	0.35	0.34	0.38	0.41	0.43	0.25

Source: U.S. Department of Education. National Center for Education Statistics. Office of Educational Research and Improvement. *Digest of Education Statistics, 1994.* Lanham, MD: Bernan, November 1994, p. 133. Primary source: U.S. Department of Education, National Center for Education Statistics. "High School and Beyond," First Followup survey; "1990 High School Transcript Study" and the "National Education Longitudinal Study of 1988," Second Followup survey. (This table was prepared August 1994.) *Notes:* 1. Includes nonoccupational vocational education, vocational general introduction, agriculture, business, marketing, health, occupational home economics, trade and industry, and technical courses. 2. Includes personal and social courses, religion and theology, and courses not included in other subject fields. 3. Computer courses are included in mathematics and vocational categories.

★ 340 ★

Academic Progress

Classroom Preparedness of High School Sophomores

Motivation to learn is an important factor in the academic achievement of a student. This table shows the percentage of students of each race/ethnicity who arrived at school without schoolbooks, pens and paper, or completed homework assignments.

Characteristics	Come to school without books		Come to school without paper, pen, or pencil		Come to school without homework completed	
	1980	1990	1980	1990	1980	1990
All sophomores	8.5	6.3	15.1	10.5	22.1	18.1
Sex						
Male	10.4	7.6	19.6	15.2	27.0	22.4
Female	6.0	5.0	10.2	5.8	16.8	13.8
Race/ethnicity						
White	6.7	5.1	13.9	10.2	21.2	18.1
Black	13.7	8.1	17.6	9.6	22.9	16.0
Hispanic	13.8	10.9	20.1	13.5	27.7	20.6
Asian	13.0	9.5	14.6	11.0	17.1	17.6

[Continued]

★ 340 ★

Classroom Preparedness of High School Sophomores
[Continued]

Characteristics	Come to school without books		Come to school without paper, pen, or pencil		Come to school without homework completed	
	1980	1990	1980	1990	1980	1990
American Indian	17.5	11.1	25.9	11.8	30.9	21.9
Control of school						
Public	8.9	6.6	15.2	10.2	22.6	18.5
Catholic	4.5	3.4	14.7	10.5	17.2	12.6
Other private	5.4	4.6	13.6	18.9	17.7	19.8
SES quartile[1]						
Lowest	11.3	8.4	16.8	10.7	25.1	19.6
Middle	7.7	6.4	14.2	9.9	21.5	18.4
Highest	5.5	3.5	13.6	10.8	18.4	15.3
Test quartile[2]						
Lowest	17.1	12.8	21.9	15.1	28.5	23.8
Second	8.1	6.4	14.3	10.0	22.8	19.3
Third	4.8	3.8	12.1	7.8	19.8	16.2
Highest	3.0	2.5	10.8	8.2	16.2	14.3

Source: U.S. Department of Education. National Center for Education Statistics. *The Condition of Education 1994.* Washington, DC: U.S. Government Printing Office, p. 126. Primary source: U.S. Department of Education, National Center for Education Statistics, *America's High School Sophomores: A Ten Year Comparison; High School and Beyond,* Base Year Survey (1980); and National Longitudinal Study of 1988, First Follow-up Student Survey (1990). *Notes:* 1. SES quartiles provide a relative measure of the socioeconomic status of families. The middle two quartiles were collapsed, creating a three-level SES scale with the values "lowest (lowest quartile)", "middle" (the two middle quartiles), and "highest" (the highest quartile). 2. Test quartiles provide a general ability measure of students. The composite test quartile was computed from the average weighted nonmissing responses to standardized test scores for reading, vocabulary, and mathematics.

★ 341 ★
Academic Progress

College Completion Rates, by Race/Ethnicity

This table shows results of a study of 534,981 students who enrolled as first-time freshmen on a full-time basis in the fall of 1984. Percentages reflect how many of the students had graduated from those institutions by fall of 1990.

Race/ethnicity	Percent of students graduated
Total	53.0
American Indian	29.0
Asian	62.0
Black	31.0

[Continued]

★ 341 ★

College Completion Rates, by Race/Ethnicity
[Continued]

Race/ethnicity	Percent of students graduated
Hispanic	40.0
White	56.0

Source: Cage, Mary Crystal. "Fewer Students Get Bachelor's Degrees in 4 Years, Study Finds". *Chronicle of Higher Education* (15 July 1992), p. A29. Primary source: National Collegiate Athletic Association.

★ 342 ★

Academic Progress

Foreign Language Credits Earned

Foreign language courses are generally recommended in preparation for higher education. Language training contributes to understanding of different cultures, a heightened awareness of one's native language, and preparation for careers in the global market. This table shows the percentage of students of each race/ethnicity who earned foreign language credits in 1982 and in 1992. A course unit is also known as a "Carnegie unit," which is a standard of measurement assigning one credit for completion of each hour-per-day course over one academic year.

Race/ethnicity	1982					1992				
	Average number of course units	Percentage of graduates earning various number of course units				Average number of course units	Percentage of graduates earning various number of course units			
		1	2	3	4		1	2	3	4
All graduates	1.1	49.8	33.7	14.4	5.2	1.8	73.9	58.2	26.6	10.6
White	1.2	52.2	36.6	15.9	6.0	1.8	74.4	58.9	27.9	11.5
Black	0.8	40.6	21.7	6.8	1.4	1.3	62.8	45.6	15.0	3.9
Hispanic	0.8	41.4	23.9	10.1	3.4	1.8	80.1	62.6	23.1	7.1
Asian	1.9	76.2	61.8	34.3	11.2	2.4	85.7	76.6	44.4	19.7
American Indian	0.4	22.4	14.0	4.4	1.4	0.9	49.7	34.0	6.2	1.0

Source: U.S. Department of Education. National Center for Education Statistics. *The Condition of Education 1994.* Washington, DC: U.S. Government Printing Office, 1994, p. 248. Primary source: U.S. Department of Education, National Center for Education Statistics, 1982 High School and Beyond Transcript Study and the National Education Longitudinal Study Transcripts, 1992.

★ 343 ★

Academic Progress

Mathematics Course Enrollment

As industry becomes more technically oriented, exposure to mathematics and science is essential in preparing a student for future employment and the rate of student enrollment in such courses can be used to predict the availability of candidates in technical fields. This table shows the precentage of high school graduates who have taken each course.

Mathematics courses (credits)	White	Black	Hispanic	Asian	American Indian
1990					
Any mathematics (1.00)	99.7	98.7	99.8	99.9	100.0
Remedial/below grade level math (1.00)	20.0	35.4	38.3	19.9	37.7
Algebra I (1.00)	77.2	77.6	81.4	71.6	72.2
Algebra II (.50)	52.4	39.0	38.6	59.5	47.3
Geometry (1.00)	67.2	56.3	54.4	72.1	54.5
Trigonometry (0.50)	19.6	14.1	11.0	35.2	15.6
Analysis/pre-calculus (.50)	15.0	6.2	7.3	25.5	8.5
Calculus (1.00)	7.0	2.8	3.9	18.6	6.1
AP calculus (1.00)	4.3	1.2	3.0	15.6	4.2
Algebra II and geometry (1.50)	47.2	32.9	34.5	53.2	37.8
Algebra II, geometry, and trigonometry (2.0)	13.6	8.1	8.6	21.5	10.3
Algebra II, geometry, trigonometry, and calculus (3.00)	2.3	1.1	1.5	6.5	3.2
1992					
Any mathematics (1.00)	99.7	99.1	99.8	100.0	100.0
Remedial/below grade level math (1.00)	14.6	30.9	24.2	14.5	35.2
Algebra I (1.00)	79.6	78.0	84.4	71.9	80.8
Algebra II (.50)	59.2	40.9	46.9	60.8	42.1
Geometry (1.00)	72.6	60.4	62.9	77.1	53.6
Trigonometry (0.50)	22.5	13.0	15.2	31.3	10.0
Analysis/pre-calculus (.50)	17.9	12.6	10.6	33.9	3.0
Calculus (1.00)	10.7	6.9	4.7	20.1	1.4
AP calculus (1.00)	5.8	2.5	2.2	16.1	1.3
Algebra II and geometry (1.50)	53.1	35.0	41.9	55.5	35.7
Algebra II, geometry, and trigonometry (2.0)	15.9	6.8	10.9	18.2	5.9
Algebra II, geometry, trigonometry, and calculus (3.00)	3.0	0.9	1.2	5.4	0.6

Source: U.S. Department of Education. National Center for Education Statistics. *The Condition of Education 1994.* Washington, DC: U.S. Government Printing Office, 1994, p. 243. Primary source: U.S. Department of Education, National Center for Education Statistics, *The 1990 High School Transcript Study Tabulations, 1993* (based on the 1987 and 1990 NAEP High School Transcript Studies), High School and Beyond Transcript Study, and the National Education Logitudinal Study Transcripts, 1992. *Note:* AP stands for advanced placement.

★ 344 ★

Academic Progress

Mathematics Proficiency

This table shows mathematics standardized scores percent distribution of students among score quartiles, by race/ethnicity. Twenty-five percent of all students fall into each quartile grouping. Data are shown for 1990.

Score and quartile	Total	Race/ethnicity				
		White	Black	Hispanic	Asian	American Indian
Standardized score[1]	53.5	54.5	49.3	52.2	57.3	44.9

Percent distribution, by score quartile

Score quartile distribution	100.0	100.0	100.0	100.0	100.0	100.0
Lower quartile	23.6	18.0	44.0	36.7	14.4	54.6
Lower middle quartile	25.3	23.6	31.1	31.6	20.2	24.7
Upper middle quartile	25.3	27.6	17.2	19.9	26.8	14.9
Upper quartile	25.8	30.7	7.8	11.9	38.6	5.9

Source: U.S. Department of Education. National Center for Education Statistics. Office of Educational Research and Improvement. *Digest of Education Statistics, 1994.* Lanham, MD: Bernan, November 1994, p. 127. U.S. Department of Education, National Center for Education Statistics, "National Longitudinal Study of 1988, First Followup" survey. (This table was prepared May 1992.) *Notes:* Because of rounding, details may not add to totals. 1. Standardized scores with a mean of 50 and a standard deviation of 10.

★ 345 ★

Academic Progress

Occupational Goals of of High School Seniors in 1992

Data show percent distribution of intended occupations at age 30 for each race/ethnicity.

Expected occupation at age 30	Total	Race/ethnicity				
		White	Black	Hispanic	Asian	American Indian
Total	100.0	100.0	100.0	100.0	100.0	100.0
Craftsperson or operator	3.5	3.7	3.4	2.7	2.4	2.7
Farmer or farm manager	0.9	1.0	0.6	0.7	0.1	[1]
Housewife/homemaker	1.0	1.2	0.4	0.7	0.8	[1]
Laborer or farmworker	0.7	0.7	0.3	0.6	1.2	1.9
Military, police, or security officer	6.6	6.4	7.7	7.4	5.1	10.0
Professional, business, or managerial	50.8	50.0	55.1	47.1	61.3	43.3
Teacher	7.5	8.4	3.7	6.7	3.4	4.8
Business owner	6.0	5.6	6.8	7.7	7.0	6.4
Technical	5.4	5.0	5.5	7.5	6.0	8.2
Salesperson, clerical, or office worker	4.8	4.6	5.3	6.4	4.1	5.2
Service worker	2.4	2.3	3.1	2.5	0.6	5.8

[Continued]

★ 345 ★

Occupational Goals of of High School Seniors in 1992
[Continued]

Expected occupation at age 30	Total	Race/ethnicity				
		White	Black	Hispanic	Asian	American Indian
Other employment	10.2	10.8	8.0	9.6	8.0	10.6
Don't know or no plans	0.2	0.2	0.2	0.5	0.2	1.0

Source: U.S. Department of Education. National Center for Education Statistics. Office of Educational Research and Improvement. *Digest of Education Statistics, 1994.* Lanham, MD: Bernan, November 1994, p. 136. *Note:* 1. Less than 0.05 percent.

★ 346 ★

Academic Progress

SAT Average Scores, by Race/Ethnicity, 1994

Data show average SAT (Scholastic Aptitude Test) scores for 1994 and percent change from 1993.

Race/ethnicity	Verbal		Mathematics	
	Score	1-yr. chg.	Score	1-yr. chg.
American Indian	396	-3	441	-6
Asian	416	+1	535	0
Black	352	-1	388	0
Mexican American	372	-2	427	-1
Puerto Rican	367	0	411	+2
Other Hispanic	383	-1	435	+2
White	443	-1	495	+1
Other	425	+3	480	+3
All students	423	-1	479	+1

Source: Chronicle of Higher Education Almanac (1 September 1994), p. 13. Primary source: The College Board.

★ 347 ★

Academic Progress

SAT Scores, by Race/Ethnicity, 1987 and 1994

| White - 452 |
| National averages - 435 |
| Other - 415 |
| Asian American - 408 |
| American Indian - 396 |
| Other Hispanic - 393 |
| Mexican American - 387 |
| Puerto Rican - 366 |
| Black - 354 |

Chart shows data from column 1.

Race/ethnicity	1987				1994			
	Verbal		Mathematics		Verbal		Mathematics	
	Men	Women	Men	Women	Men	Women	Men	Women
American Indian	396	391	452	413	397	395	459	425
Asian American	408	403	543	498	417	414	557	514
Black	354	349	391	367	348	354	399	381
Mexican American	387	373	449	402	375	368	448	410
Puerto Rican	366	355	423	380	371	365	432	395
Other Hispanic	393	382	459	408	389	379	462	414
White	452	442	514	466	445	441	519	475
Other	415	396	485	428	426	424	505	459
National averages	435	425	500	453	425	421	501	460

Source: "Gender gap continues to close on S.A.T.'s." *New York Times (National Edition)* (25 August 1994), p. 12A. Primary source: The College Board.

★ 348 ★

Academic Progress

Science Course Enrollment

As industry becomes more technically oriented, exposure to mathematics and science is essential in preparing a student for future employment and the rate of student enrollment in such courses can be used to predict the availability of candidates in technical fields. This table shows the percentage of high school graduates who have taken each course.

Science courses (credits)	White	Black	Hispanic	Asian	American Indian
1990					
Any science (1.00)	99.5	99.0	99.3	99.8	99.5
Biology (1.00)	92.0	91.0	90.3	90.5	91.1
AP/honors biology (1.00)	5.1	3.8	2.4	6.4	3.2
Chemistry (1.00)	52.3	40.3	38.8	64.1	38.6

[Continued]

★ 348 ★

Science Course Enrollment
[Continued]

Science courses (credits)	White	Black	Hispanic	Asian	American Indian
AP/honors chemistry (1.00)	3.8	2.5	1.2	7.7	4.8
Physics (1.00)	23.1	14.5	13.0	38.4	18.9
AP/honors physics (1.00)	2.1	0.7	1.0	5.9	2.7
Engineering (1.00)	0.1	0.1	0.0	0.0	0.0
Astronomy (1.00)	1.4	0.4	1.1	0.7	2.2
Geology (1.00)	28.3	15.8	14.2	15.6	30.6
Biology and chemistry (2.00)	50.9	39.6	36.8	60.5	37.6
Biology, chemistry, and physics (3.00)	20.7	12.1	10.2	33.8	16.0
1992					
Any science (1.00)	99.5	100.0	99.7	100.0	100.0
Biology (1.00)	93.5	92.2	91.2	93.4	84.5
AP/honors biology (1.00)	6.5	3.2	2.4	6.8	5.0
Chemistry (1.00)	58.0	45.9	42.6	67.4	32.9
AP/honors chemistry (1.00)	4.2	2.3	2.5	9.1	1.8
Physics (1.00)	25.9	17.6	15.7	41.6	13.3
AP/honors physics (1.00)	2.9	1.4	2.4	9.2	0.6
Engineering (1.00)	0.3	0.2	0.1	0.5	0.0
Astronomy (1.00)	1.0	0.1	0.1	0.1	0.0
Geology (1.00)	19.3	17.6	11.5	16.6	29.7
Biology and chemistry (2.00)	56.5	44.2	40.5	65.4	31.2
Biology, chemistry, and physics (3.00)	22.6	15.5	12.8	38.2	10.8

Source: U.S. Department of Education. National Center for Education Statistics. *The Condition of Education 1994.* Washington, DC: U.S. Government Printing Office, 1994, p. 243. Primary source: U.S. Department of Education, National Center for Education Statistics, *The 1990 High School Transcript Study Tabulations, 1993* (based on the 1987 and 1990 NAEP High School Transcript Studies), High School and Beyond Transcript Study, and the National Education Longitudinal Study Transcripts, 1992.

★ 349 ★

Academic Progress

Science Experiments and Projects

Data show the percentage of students providing affirmative responses to the question "Have you ever done experiments or projects at home or in school with...?" Standard error for each result is shown in parentheses.

Group	Plants or animals	Electricity	Chemicals	Rocks or minerals	Telescope	Thermometer or barometer
Grade 4						
White	58 (1.0)	53 (1.5)	42 (1.0)	51 (1.4)	42 (0.9)	45 (1.3)
Black	53 (1.5)	53 (1.6)	38 (1.8)	47 (1.5)	40 (2.0)	49 (2.0)
Hispanic	57 (1.6)	55 (1.9)	40 (1.5)	47 (1.8)	46 (2.0)	48 (1.8)
Asian/Pacific Islander	64 (3.8)	52 (6.1)	38 (4.7)	48 (5.9)	46 (3.4)	37 (6.0)
American Indian	70 (3.4)	58 (3.6)	39 (4.7)	53 (3.0)	45 (3.9)	57 (3.5)
Male	58 (1.0)	60 (1.4)	41 (1.1)	50 (1.2)	43 (1.1)	46 (1.4)
Female	57 (1.3)	46 (1.5)	41 (1.0)	51 (1.7)	41 (1.0)	46 (1.4)
Total	58 (0.8)	53 (1.2)	41 (0.7)	50 (1.2)	42 (0.8)	46 (1.1)

[Continued]

★ 349 ★

Science Experiments and Projects
[Continued]

Group	Plants or animals	Electricity	Chemicals	Rocks or minerals	Telescope	Thermometer or barometer
Grade 8						
White	74 (1.2)	67 (1.4)	65 (1.6)	60 (1.5)	49 (1.1)	56 (1.5)
Black	64 (2.0)	58 (2.5)	57 (2.3)	51 (2.1)	36 (2.3)	47 (2.6)
Hispanic	68 (1.8)	60 (2.3)	55 (1.9)	54 (2.5)	44 (1.7)	49 (2.5)
Asian/Pacific Islander	73 (4.2)	70 (3.0)	64 (3.3)	54 (4.8)	36 (3.3)	46 (5.1)
American Indian	59 (14.4)[1]	60 (7.8)[1]	60 (12.5)[1]	58 (9.2)[1]	49 (5.0)[1]	56 (6.4)[1]
Male	71 (1.2)	75 (1.2)	64 (1.5)	57 (1.4)	49 (1.2)	52 (1.3)
Female	73 (1.5)	54 (1.4)	61 (1.6)	59 (1.6)	45 (1.1)	56 (1.6)
Total	72 (1.1)	65 (1.2)	63 (1.4)	58 (1.3)	47 (0.9)	54 (1.2)
Grade 12						
White	86 (0.7)	74 (1.1)	83 (0.8)	70 (1.0)	55 (1.0)	71 (1.2)
Black	79 (1.8)	65 (2.0)	77 (1.8)	62 (2.3)	51 (2.3)	63 (1.6)
Hispanic	83 (1.9)	64 (2.2)	76 (1.8)	64 (2.5)	53 (2.4)	63 (2.1)
Asian/Pacific Islander	84 (1.9)	74 (2.3)	81 (5.6)	63 (5.2)	49 (3.6)	74 (2.4)
American Indian	78 (7.0)[1]	72 (9.9)[1]	74 (7.2)[1]	61 (5.2)[1]	42 (8.5)[1]	62 (6.6)[1]
Male	84 (0.9)	82 (0.9)	83 (0.7)	68 (1.2)	56 (1.1)	70 (1.1)
Female	85 (0.8)	63 (1.4)	80 (1.0)	68 (1.3)	52 (1.1)	69 (1.3)
Total	85 (0.7)	72 (1.0)	81 (0.7)	68 (1.0)	54 (0.8)	69 (1.0)

Source: Jones, Lee R., and others, *The 1990 Science Report Card: NAEP's Assessment of Fourth, Eighth, and Twelfth Graders,* Prepared by Educational Testing Service under contract with the National Center for Education Statistics, Office of Educational Research and Improvement, U.S. Department of Education, March, 1992, p. 83. *Notes:* 1. Interpret with caution - the nature of the sample does not allow accurate determination of the variability of these estimated statistics.

★ 350 ★

Academic Progress

Science Experiments and Projects Performed by Students and Average Proficiencies

Percent of students reporting the number of projects or experiments done and their average proficiencies based on IRT (item response theory) scaling procedures. Progress is estimated on a scale of 0 to 500. Scores are assigned to five proficiency levels: Level 150—Knows everyday science facts; Level 200—Understands simple scientific principles; Level 250—Applies general scientific information; Level 300—Analyzes scientific procedures and data; and Level 350—Integrates specialized scientific information. Data presented are proficiency scores, not levels.

Group	Five or six		Three or four		One or two		None	
	% of students	Avg. profic.	% of students	Avg. profic.	% of students	Avg. profic.	% of students	Avg. profic.
Grade 4								
White	16 (0.7)	246 (1.3)	44 (0.8)	240 (1.3)	32 (0.9)	243 (1.2)	8 (0.6)	243 (2.0)
Black	11 (0.9)	212 (3.4)	49 (1.6)	203 (2.0)	33 (1.4)	206 (1.6)	8 (0.9)	213 (3.0)
Hispanic	12 (1.2)	216 (3.2)	51 (1.8)	210 (1.6)	31 (1.3)	215 (1.9)	6 (0.6)	215 (4.2)
Asian/Pacific Islander	15 (5.5)	234 (7.9)	41 (3.4)	231 (4.0)	39 (5.5)	236 (6.1)	4 (1.6)	228 (10.9)
American Indian	17 (2.9)	231 (4.4)	56 (4.2)	225 (3.4)	22 (3.7)	224 (6.0)	5 (1.5)	233 (10.7)
Male	16 (0.9)	243 (1.7)	47 (1.1)	230 (1.3)	31 (1.1)	235 (1.5)	6 (0.5)	237 (2.9)
Female	13 (0.8)	235 (2.0)	45 (1.1)	230 (1.4)	34 (1.0)	232 (1.3)	8 (0.8)	234 (2.4)
Total	15 (0.6)	239 (1.2)	46 (0.6)	230 (1.2)	32 (1.1)	234 (1.1)	7 (0.5)	235 (1.7)
Grade 8								
White	38 (1.6)	283 (1.5)	37 (1.0)	272 (1.5)	20 (0.9)	262 (2.1)	5 (0.5)	246 (2.8)
Black	22 (1.9)	246 (3.6)	40 (2.0)	232 (2.4)	32 (1.5)	223 (3.2)	6 (1.1)	216 (6.5)
Hispanic	28 (2.0)	253 (2.8)	40 (1.6)	242 (2.7)	26 (1.7)	234 (2.9)	7 (1.1)	222 (5.0)
Asian/Pacific Islander	29 (3.1)	284 (4.5)	41 (3.2)	270 (4.1)	26 (3.2)	260 (6.1)	5 (1.6)	253 (18.2)

[Continued]

★ 350 ★

Science Experiments and Projects Performed by Students and Average Proficiencies
[Continued]

Group	Five or six		Three or four		One or two		None	
	% of students	Avg. profic.	% of students	Avg. profic.	% of students	Avg. profic.	% of students	Avg. profic.
American Indian	34 (10.6)[1]	266 (5.6)[1]	35 (6.0)[1]	251 (10.7)[1]	20 (9.9)[1]	245 (6.0)[1]	11 (3.7)[1]	223 (9.1)[1]
Male	36 (1.5)	278 (1.6)	38 (0.9)	264 (1.8)	20 (0.9)	252 (1.9)	6 (0.5)	239 (4.0)
Female	33 (1.6)	276 (1.8)	37 (1.2)	261 (1.2)	24 (1.0)	248 (2.1)	6 (0.6)	238 (3.1)
Total	35 (1.3)	277 (1.4)	38 (0.9)	262 (1.3)	22 (0.8)	250 (1.6)	6 (0.4)	238 (2.4)
Grade 12								
White	58 (1.3)	311 (1.1)	28 (0.9)	298 (1.9)	10 (0.6)	282 (2.8)	4 (0.4)	270 (3.6)
Black	46 (2.2)	266 (2.8)	34 (1.7)	253 (3.6)	15 (1.3)	243 (3.9)	6 (0.8)	233 (6.7)
Hispanic	46 (2.1)	283 (2.5)	34 (1.7)	270 (5.2)	16 (1.6)	258 (3.8)	4 (0.9)	238 (9.0)
Asian/Pacific Islander	55 (4.1)	316 (8.6)	27 (2.7)	306 (7.3)	15 (2.1)	289 (7.5)	3 (1.2)	274 (32.2)
American Indian	47 (6.9)[1]	288 (6.6)[1]	31 (6.7)[1]	294 (7.0)[1]	12 (7.4)[1]	270 (5.6)[1]	10 (5.3)[1]	268 (7.5)[1]
Male	59 (1.3)	308 (1.6)	27 (1.0)	293 (2.1)	10 (0.7)	277 (2.9)	4 (0.4)	266 (4.4)
Female	51 (1.5)	299 (1.3)	31 (1.0)	284 (1.8)	13 (0.9)	270 (2.4)	5 (0.4)	256 (3.8)
Total	55 (1.2)	304 (1.2)	29 (0.8)	288 (1.6)	12 (0.6)	273 (2.2)	4 (0.3)	260 (2.9)

Source: Jones, Lee R., and others, *The 1990 Science Report Card: NAEP's Assessment of Fourth, Eighth, and Twelfth Graders,* Prepared by Educational Testing Service under contract with the National Center for Education Statistics, Office of Educational Research and Improvement, U.S. Department of Education, March, 1992, p. 84. *Notes:* Achievement results were analyzed using item response theory (IRT) scaling procedures, which allowed the National Assessment of Educational Progress to estimate students' average proficiency on a scale ranging from 0 to 500. The standard errors of the estimated percentages and proficiencies appear in parentheses. It can be said with 95 percent certainty that for each population of interest, the value for the whole population is within plus or minus two standard errors of the estimate for the sample. 1. Interpret with caution - the nature of the sample does not allow accurate determination of the variability of these estimated statistics.

★ 351 ★
Academic Progress

Science Instruction: Frequency Reported by 4th Graders

Frequency of instruction is shown in percent. Proficiency is based on IRT (item response theory) scaling procedures. Progress is estimated on a scale of 0 to 500. Scores are assigned to five proficiency levels: Level 150—Knows everyday science facts; Level 200—Understands simple scientific principles; Level 250—Applies general scientific information; Level 300—Analyzes scientific procedures and data; and Level 350—Integrates specialized scientific information. Data presented are proficiency scores, not levels.

Group	Almost every day		Several times a week		About once a week		Less than once a week		Never	
	% of students	Avg. profic.	% of students	Avg. profic.	% of students	Avg. profic.	% of students	Avg. profic.	% of students	Avg. profic.
White	54 (2.1)	243 (1.1)	22 (1.1)	246 (1.6)	12 (1.1)	242 (1.7)	8 (0.8)	238 (2.2)	5 (0.8)	230 (3.3)
Black	46 (2.9)	209 (1.8)	20 (1.9)	207 (3.0)	17 (1.7)	203 (1.9)	10 (1.1)	201 (4.0)	7 (1.1)	192 (4.0)
Hispanic	44 (3.4)	216 (2.1)	20 (1.5)	213 (2.2)	18 (1.9)	211 (3.0)	9 (1.0)	205 (2.9)	10 (1.4)	203 (4.0)
Asian/Pacific Islander	39 (5.3)	240 (6.5)	24 (2.6)	230 (4.5)	21 (3.2)	230 (4.1)	8 (2.1)	232 (8.8)	9 (4.1)	223 (10.9)
American Indian	51 (5.0)	228 (3.6)	19 (3.0)	229 (6.4)	13 (3.8)	233 (6.9)	10 (3.2)	216 (8.6)	6 (2.8)	201 (7.6)
Male	51 (1.9)	237 (1.3)	22 (1.1)	237 (2.2)	13 (1.1)	232 (1.9)	8 (0.7)	226 (2.7)	6 (0.8)	218 (3.2)
Female	51 (2.2)	234 (1.3)	20 (1.2)	235 (1.6)	15 (1.3)	228 (2.1)	8 (0.8)	227 (2.6)	5 (0.8)	216 (4.4)
Total	51 (1.9)	235 (1.1)	21 (0.9)	236 (1.5)	14 (1.0)	230 (1.5)	8 (0.7)	227 (2.0)	6 (0.7)	217 (2.8)

Source: Jones, Lee R., and others, *The 1990 Science Report Card: NAEP's Assessment of Fourth, Eighth, and Twelfth Graders,* Prepared by Educational Testing Service under contract with the National Center for Education Statistics, Office of Educational Research and Improvement, U.S. Department of Education, March, 1992, p. 79. *Notes:* Achievement results were analyzed using item response theory (IRT) scaling procedures, which allowed the National Assessment of Educational Progress to estimate students' average proficiency on a scale ranging from 0 to 500. The standard errors of the estimated percentages and proficiencies appear in parentheses. It can be said with 95 percent certainty that for each population of interest, the value for the whole population is within plus or minus two standard errors of the estimate for the sample.

★ 352 ★

Academic Progress

Student Attitudes Toward Science

Responses to the question "Do you like science?" Average proficiencies are based on IRT (item response theory) scaling procedures. Progress is estimated on a scale of 0 to 500. Scores are assigned to five proficiency levels: Level 150—Knows everyday science facts; Level 200—Understands simple scientific principles; Level 250—Applies general scientific information; Level 300—Analyzes scientific procedures and data; and Level 350—Integrates specialized scientific information. Data presented are proficiency scores, not levels.

Race/ethnicity	Yes		No	
	Percent of students	Average proficiency	Percent of students	Average proficiency
Grade 4				
White	81 (0.9)	245 (1.1)	19 (0.9)	231 (1.5)
Black	75 (1.9)	208 (1.7)	25 (1.9)	199 (2.3)
Hispanic	76 (1.4)	217 (1.5)	24 (1.4)	199 (2.5)
Asian/Pacific Islander	78 (5.7)	238 (2.9)	22 (5.7)	217 (4.3)
American Indian	80 (4.1)	230 (3.1)	21 (4.1)	212 (5.1)
Male	81 (1.0)	238 (1.2)	19 (1.0)	218 (2.0)
Female	78 (1.0)	235 (1.2)	22 (1.0)	222 (1.6)
Total	80 (0.8)	237 (1.0)	20 (0.8)	220 (1.4)
Grade 8				
White	67 (1.1)	280 (1.2)	33 (1.1)	258 (1.6)
Black	70 (2.1)	235 (2.3)	30 (2.1)	223 (2.9)
Hispanic	71 (2.1)	245 (2.7)	29 (2.1)	233 (2.9)
Asian/Pacific Islander	70 (4.6)	277 (4.5)	31 (4.6)	256 (5.0)
American Indian	71 (5.9)[1]	254 (12.5)[1]	29 (5.9)[1]	246 (6.8)[1]
Male	72 (1.1)	272 (1.5)	28 (1.1)	248 (2.0)
Female	64 (1.2)	266 (1.5)	36 (1.2)	253 (1.6)
Total	68 (1.0)	269 (1.2)	32 (1.0)	251 (1.4)
Grade 12				
White	66 (0.9)	312 (1.4)	34 (0.9)	284 (1.3)
Black	60 (1.8)	263 (2.9)	40 (1.8)	247 (3.0)
Hispanic	68 (2.3)	279 (3.0)	32 (2.3)	261 (3.9)
Asian/Pacific Islander	69 (3.5)	320 (7.8)	31 (3.5)	284 (5.0)
American Indian	71 (6.5)[1]	298 (5.3)[1]	29 (6.5)[1]	257 (6.0)[1]
Male	74 (0.9)	307 (1.6)	26 (0.9)	275 (1.9)
Female	57 (1.1)	298 (1.3)	43 (1.1)	277 (1.4)
Total	65 (0.7)	303 (1.3)	35 (0.7)	276 (1.2)

Source: Jones, Lee R., and others, *The 1990 Science Report Card: NAEP's Assessment of Fourth, Eighth, and Twelfth Graders,* Prepared by Educational Testing Service under contract with the National Center for Education Statistics, Office of Educational Research and Improvement, U.S. Department of Education, March, 1992, p. 81. *Notes:* Achievement results were analyzed using item response theory (IRT) scaling procedures, which allowed the National Assessment of Educational Progress to estimate students' average proficiency on a scale ranging from 0 to 500. The standard errors of the estimated percentages and proficiencies appear in parentheses. It can be said with 95 percent certainty, that for each population of interest, the value for the whole population is within plus or minus two standard errors of the estimate for the sample. 1. Interpret with caution - the nature of the sample does not allow accurate determination of the variability of these estimated statistics.

★ 353 ★

Academic Progress

Students in the Top and Bottom Thirds of Their Classes in Science

Percentages are shown for 1990, by race/ethnicity. Standard error for each result is shown in parentheses.

Level	White	Black	Hispanic	Asian/ Pacific Islander	American Indian
Grade 4					
Top one-third	38 (3.2)	8 (1.8)	15 (2.3)	25 (9.7)	27 (6.0)
Bottom one-third	18 (2.2)	73 (3.9)	53 (3.4)	39 (9.0)	33 (4.7)
Grade 8					
Top one-third	31 (3.5)	11 (2.3)	13 (7.7)	36 (7.7)	15 (11.8)[1]
Bottom one-third	25 (3.4)	69 (4.7)	59 (5.9)	33 (8.5)	59 (26.9)[1]
Grade 12					
Top one-third	41 (3.8)	13 (3.3)	22 (4.4)	37 (15.4)	29 (8.4)[1]
Bottom one-third	16 (3.6)	64 (4.6)	47 (6.8)	17 (5.9)	28 (11.2)[1]

Source: Jones, Lee R., and others, *The 1990 Science Report Card: NAEP's Assessment of Fourth, Eighth, and Twelfth Graders,* Prepared by Educational Testing Service under contract with the National Center for Education Statistics, Office of Educational Research and Improvement, U.S. Department of Education, March, 1992, p. 20. *Notes:* Achievement results were analyzed using item response theory (IRT) scaling procedures, which allowed the National Assessment of Educational Progress to estimate students' average proficiency on a scale ranging from 0 to 500. The standard errors of the estimated percentages and proficiencies appear in parentheses. It can be said with 95 percent certainty, that for each population of interest, the value for the whole population is within plus or minus two standard errors of the estimate for the sample. 1. Interpret with caution - the nature of the sample does not allow accurate determination of the variability of these estimated statistics.

★ 354 ★

Academic Progress

Students' Average Science Proficiency, by Content Area

Proficiency is based on IRT (item response theory) scaling procedures. Progress is estimated on a scale of 0 to 500. Scores are assigned to five proficiency levels: Level 150—Knows everyday science facts; Level 200—Understands simple scientific principles; Level 250—Applies general scientific information; Level 300—Analyzes scientific procedures and data; and Level 350—Integrates specialized scientific information. Data presented are proficiency scores, not levels.

Race/ethnicity	Distribution of students (percent)	Life sciences	Physical sciences	Earth and space sciences	Nature of science
Grade 4					
White	70 (0.5)	238 (1.0)	245 (1.2)	243 (1.1)	242 (1.1)
Black	15 (0.4)	204 (1.6)	207 (2.0)	204 (1.5)	212 (1.7)
Hispanic	11 (0.3)	209 (1.8)	213 (1.6)	215 (1.6)	212 (1.7)
Asian/Pacific Islander	2 (0.3)	227 (4.1)	238 (3.9)	233 (3.6)	238 (3.5)
American Indian	2 (0.3)	222 (3.8)	229 (4.0)	228 (3.6)	226 (3.8)
Grade 8					
White	71 (0.4)	273 (1.4)	271 (1.4)	276 (1.5)	270 (1.5)

[Continued]

★ 354 ★

Students' Average Science Proficiency, by Content Area
[Continued]

Race/ethnicity	Distribution of students (percent)	Life sciences	Physical sciences	Earth and space sciences	Nature of science
Black	15 (0.4)	233 (2.3)	232 (2.3)	228 (2.6)	230 (2.7)
Hispanic	10 (0.3)	242 (2.4)	241 (2.2)	242 (2.3)	236 (2.4)
Asian/Pacific Islander	3 (0.4)	272 (4.0)	271 (3.9)	270 (4.3)	267 (5.2)
American Indian	1 (0.5)[1]	252 (9.7)[1]	250 (7.8)[1]	257 (7.3)[1]	244 (15.6)[1]
Grade 12					
White	73 (0.4)	305 (1.1)	300 (1.7)	301 (1.3)	307 (1.4)
Black	14 (0.5)	262 (2.0)	253 (3.1)	247 (2.8)	267 (3.0)
Asian/Pacific Islander	4 (0.2)	309 (7.1)	310 (8.3)	304 (6.6)	312 (6.9)
Hispanic	8 (0.3)	275 (2.7)	271 (3.2)	270 (2.9)	277 (3.9)
American Indian	1 (0.2)[1]	287 (4.5)[1]	283 (5.6)[1]	289 (6.1)[1]	283 (9.6)[1]

Source: Jones, Lee R., and others, *The 1990 Science Report Card: NAEP's Assessment of Fourth, Eighth, and Twelfth Graders,* Prepared by Educational Testing Service under contract with the National Center for Education Statistics, Office of Educational Research and Improvement, U.S. Department of Education, March, 1992, p. 64. *Notes:* Achievement results were analyzed using item response theory (IRT) scaling procedures, which allowed the National Assessment of Educational Progress to estimate students' average proficiency on a scale ranging from 0 to 500. The standard errors of the estimated percentages and proficiencies appear in parentheses. It can be said with 95 percent certainty that for each population of interest, the value for the whole population is within plus or minus two standard errors of the estimate for the sample. 1. Interpret with caution - the nature of the sample does not allow accurate determination of the variability of these estimated statistics.

★ 355 ★

Academic Progress

Students' Science Proficiency

Students' average proficiency is shown, based on IRT (item response theory) scaling procedures. Progress is estimated on a scale of 0 to 500. Scores are assigned to five proficiency levels: Level 150—Knows everyday science facts; Level 200—Understands simple scientific principles; Level 250—Applies general scientific information; Level 300—Analyzes scientific procedures and data; and Level 350—Integrates specialized scientific information. Data presented are proficiency scores, not levels.

Race/ethnicity	Students		Proficiency	
	Percent distribution	Standard error	Average score	Standard error
Grade 4				
White	70	0.5	242	1.0
Black	15	0.4	205	1.5
Hispanic	11	0.3	212	1.5
Asian/Pacific Islander	2	0.3	233	3.0
American Indian	2	0.3	226	2.7
Grade 8				
White	71	0.4	273	1.4
Black	15	0.4	231	2.2
Hispanic	10	0.3	241	2.1
Asian/Pacific Islander	3	0.4	271	4.0
American Indian	1	0.5[1]	252	8.5[1]

[Continued]

★ 355 ★

Students' Science Proficiency
[Continued]

Race/ethnicity	Students		Proficiency	
	Percent distribution	Standard error	Average score	Standard error
Grade 12				
White	73	0.4	303	1.3
Black	14	0.5	256	2.4
Hispanic	8	0.3	273	2.8
Asian/Pacific Islander	4	0.2	308	7.1
American Indian	1	0.2[1]	286	4.6[1]

Source: Jones, Lee R., and others, *The 1990 Science Report Card: NAEP's Assessment of Fourth, Eighth, and Twelfth Graders,* Prepared by Educational Testing Service under contract with the National Center for Education Statistics, Office of Educational Research and Improvement, U.S. Department of Education, March, 1992, p. *Notes:* Achievement results were analyzed using item response theory (IRT) scaling procedures, which allowed the National Assessment of Educational Progress to estimate students' average proficiency on a scale ranging from 0 to 500. It can be said with 95 percent certainty that for each population of interest, the value for the whole population is within plus or minus two standard errors of the estimate for the sample. 1. Interpret with caution-the nature of the sample does not allow accurate determination of the variability of these estimated statistics.

★ 356 ★

Academic Progress

Students' Science Proficiency Levels

Percent of students at or above four proficiency levels based on IRT (item response theory) scaling procedures. Progress is estimated on a scale of 0 to 500. Scores are assigned to five proficiency levels: Level 150—Knows everyday science facts; Level 200—Understands simple scientific principles; Level 250—Applies general scientific information; Level 300—Analyzes scientific procedures and data; and Level 350—Integrates specialized scientific information. Standard error is shown in parentheses.

Race/ethnicity	Level 200	Level 250	Level 300	Level 350
Grade 4				
White	93 (0.8)	40 (1.6)	1 (0.3)	0 (0.0)
Black	58 (2.7)	5 (1.1)	0 (0.2)	0 (0.2)
Hispanic	66 (2.4)	10 (1.2)	0 (0.0)	0 (0.0)
Asian/Pacific Islander	88 (3.1)	29 (5.2)	2 (1.5)	0 (0.0)
American Indian	81 (5.3)	20 (4.8)	0 (0.0)	0 (0.0)
Grade 8				
White	97 (0.5)	74 (1.3)	23 (1.3)	1 (0.3)
Black	80 (2.5)	31 (2.5)	3 (0.8)	0 (0.1)
Hispanic	87 (1.7)	42 (2.8)	5 (0.9)	0 (0.1)
Asian/Pacific Islander	96 (1.9)	71 (4.8)	23 (4.1)	1 (0.6)
American Indian	92 (2.8)[1]	54 (11.6)[1]	8 (2.8)[1]	0 (0.0)[1]
Grade 12				
White	100 (0.1)	91 (0.8)	53 (1.4)	12 (0.9)
Black	94 (1.4)	57 (3.0)	12 (2.0)	1 (0.6)
Asian/Pacific Islander	99 (1.4)	90 (3.2)	60 (7.4)	17 (5.0)

[Continued]

★ 356 ★

Students' Science Proficiency Levels
[Continued]

Race/ethnicity	Level 200	Level 250	Level 300	Level 350
American Indian	100 (0.7)[1]	89 (5.6)[1]	33 (9.3)[1]	2 (0.0)[1]
Hispanic	98 (0.8)	70 (3.4)	23 (2.9)	3 (1.0)

Source: Jones, Lee R., and others, *The 1990 Science Report Card: NAEP's Assessment of Fourth, Eighth, and Twelfth Graders*, Prepared by Educational Testing Service under contract with the National Center for Education Statistics, Office of Educational Research and Improvement, U.S. Department of Education, March, 1992, p. 52. *Notes:* Achievement results were analyzed using item response theory (IRT) scaling procedures, which allowed the National Assessment of Educational Progress to estimate students' average proficiency on a scale ranging from 0 to 500. The standard errors of the estimated percentages and proficiencies appear in parentheses. It can be said with 95 percent certainty that for each population of interest, the value for the whole population is within plus or minus two standard errors of the estimate for the sample. When the percentage of students is either 0 or 100, the standard error is inestimatable. However, percentages 99.5 percent and greater were rounded to 100 percent and percentages less than 0.5 were rounded to 0 percent. 1. Interpret with caution - the nature of the sample does not allow accurate determination of the variability of these estimated statistics.

Extracurriculars

★ 357 ★

Extracurricular Activities at School

Data show percentage of high school seniors participating in each type of activity in 1992.

Activity	White	Black	Hispanic	Asian	American Indian
Athletics					
Interscholastic team sport	30.8	32.3	25.8	28.3	30.4
Interscholastic individual sport	20.9	21.2	14.9	21.6	20.7
Intramural team sport	22.3	25.8	20.8	24.9	27.9
Intramural individual sport	12.5	16.7	14.0	14.7	18.2
Performing arts					
Cheerleading	7.4	10.6	6.7	5.1	11.9
School band or orchestra	19.6	24.4	16.9	17.7	16.8
School play or musical	16.1	15.9	10.6	13.7	14.0
Student govt./clubs					
Student government	15.4	16.7	14.7	14.6	14.3
Academic honor society	19.6	14.0	12.5	27.2	13.6
School yearbook/newspaper	19.7	14.3	16.8	18.9	21.2
School service clubs	13.6	13.6	14.4	19.3	11.6
School academic clubs	25.8	20.7	22.6	32.3	17.7

[Continued]

★ 357 ★

Extracurricular Activities at School
[Continued]

Activity	White	Black	Hispanic	Asian	American Indian
School hobby clubs	7.4	6.6	9.1	11.3	10.8
School FTA, FHA, and FFA[1]	17.6	22.5	16.4	8.8	22.1

Source: U.S. Department of Education. National Center for Education Statistics. Office of Educational Research and Improvement. *Digest of Education Statistics, 1994.* Lanham, MD: Bernan, November 1994, p. 138. Primary source: U.S. Department of Education, National Center for Education Statistics, "National Education Longitudinal Study of 1988," First and Second Followup surveys. (This table was prepared March 1994.) *Notes:* 1. FTA stands for Future Teachers of America; FHA stands for Future Homemakers of America; FFA stands for Future Farmers of America.

★ 358 ★

Extracurriculars

Leisure Activity, by Type

Data show the percentage of high school seniors who said they engaged in each activity in 1982 and 1992.

Activity	Total	White	Black	Hispanic	Asian	American Indian
Percent of 12th graders, 1982						
At least once a week						
Talking with friends	92.7	94.2	89.1	88.9	86.7	91.3
Reading for pleasure	50.4	51.0	53.9	43.1	56.4	50.3
Going on dates	61.3	63.9	51.9	58.1	40.3	54.5
Driving or riding around	62.4	65.2	48.9	60.7	42.4	62.3
Thinking or daydreaming	68.5	71.1	64.6	58.0	62.4	53.9
Talking with parents	83.9	85.6	80.1	78.0	79.8	76.0
Reading front page of newspaper	69.1	69.7	71.9	63.3	73.5	61.8
Five or more weekday hours						
Watches television	11.5	9.4	22.2	13.8	8.1	20.9
Percent of 12th graders, 1992						
At least once a week						
Use a personal computer	23.7	23.9	23.6	20.9	27.0	23.8
Work on hobbies	40.9	42.0	34.8	39.9	37.8	49.8
Attend religious activities	31.0	31.4	33.7	26.9	30.4	14.6
Attend youth groups	22.4	22.5	23.3	18.5	26.4	22.1
Perform community service	11.3	11.1	12.1	10.9	14.0	9.2
Driving or riding around	73.3	75.7	67.8	66.2	66.7	71.0
Do things with friends	88.1	90.7	79.8	82.4	85.9	77.2
Do things with parent	66.7	68.2	62.0	63.8	63.4	61.2
Talk with other adult	47.7	48.8	44.3	46.2	43.0	44.0
Take music, art, or dance class	10.1	9.9	9.7	9.8	14.0	10.6
Take sports lessons	7.3	7.0	7.4	8.2	9.4	11.6
Play ball or other sport	26.3	27.1	22.9	23.6	28.7	29.4

[Continued]

★ 358 ★

Leisure Activity, by Type
[Continued]

Activity	Total	White	Black	Hispanic	Asian	American Indian
More than an hour a day						
Reading for pleasure	55.4	56.3	51.0	53.5	54.4	59.3
Plays video games	13.0	11.7	19.9	13.0	13.5	21.1
Five or more weekday hours						
Watches television	8.4	6.4	21.3	9.3	6.4	12.7

Source: U.S. Department of Education. National Center for Education Statistics. Office of Educational Research and Improvement. *Digest of Education Statistics, 1994.* Lanham, MD: Bernan, November 1994, p. 139. Primary source: U.S. Department of Education, National Center for Education Statistics, "National Education Longitudinal Study of 1988," Second Followup survey, and "High School and Beyond," First Followup survey. (This table was prepared April 1994.).

★ 359 ★

Extracurriculars

School-Sponsored Extracurriculars

Data show the percentage of high school seniors who participated in each activity in 1982 and 1992.

Race/ethnicity	Academic clubs, 1992	Athletics		Cheerleading/drill team		Hobby clubs		Music		Vocational clubs	
		1982	1992	1982	1992	1982	1992	1982	1992	1982	1992
All seniors	25.1	50.0	40.0	13.5	7.6	19.5	7.7	27.6	19.8	23.5	17.7
White	25.8	49.8	41.1	13.1	7.4	18.7	7.4	26.7	19.6	21.9	17.6
Black	20.7	51.8	38.9	16.9	10.6	18.5	6.6	34.7	24.4	31.0	22.5
Hispanic	22.6	49.9	32.9	14.1	6.7	23.6	9.1	26.8	16.9	27.5	16.4
Asian	32.3	43.7	42.3	6.3	5.1	26.1	11.3	20.6	17.7	7.0	8.8
American Indian	17.7	52.8	42.5	11.5	11.9	30.3	10.8	26.5	16.8	30.0	22.1

Source: U.S. Department of Education. National Center for Education Statistics. Office of Educational Research and Improvement. *Digest of Education Statistics, 1994.* Lanham, MD: Bernan, November 1994, p. 139. Primary source: U.S. Department of Education, National Center for Education Statistics, "High School and Beyond," First Followup survey, 1980 Sophomore Cohort; and "National Education Longitudinal Study of 1988," Second Followup survey. (This table was prepared April 1994.).

School Environment

★ 360 ★

Drug Exposure in School

Aside from the fact that drug use by youth is a contributing risk factor in their education, the sale of drugs in school is an indication of the overall learning environment. This table shows the percentage of students who were offered drugs in school during the first semester, for 1988, 1990, and 1992. Data are shown by race/ethnicity of the student.

Race/ethnicity	8th graders in 1988		10th graders in 1990		12th graders in 1992	
	Once or twice	More than twice	Once or twice	More than twice	Once or twice	More than twice
All students	6.9	3.1	10.1	6.9	9.5	6.5
White	6.9	3.1	10.6	7.3	9.7	6.9
Black	5.8	1.8	7.1	3.8	6.5	2.8
Hispanic	8.9	5.3	9.4	7.9	12.2	8.9
Asian	3.5	1.3	8.5	4.9	6.7	4.8
American Indian	11.3	5.1	16.5	8.1	10.8	10.3

Source: U.S. Department of Education. National Center for Education Statistics. *The Condition of Education 1994.* Washington, DC: U.S. Government Printing Office, 1994, p. 310. U.S. Department of Education, National Center for Education Statistics, National Education Longitudinal Study of 1988, Base Year (1988), First Follow-up (1990), and Second Follow-up (1992) Student Surveys.

★ 361 ★

School Environment

Federal Compliance of BIA School Libraries

Data show results of a survey of 182 libraries at BIA (Bureau of Indian Affairs) or BIA-tribally controlled schools and are based on a total of 122 valid responses. Figures reflect how many respondents were in compliance with Public Law 95-561, which set certain minimum standards for BIA schools.

Characteristic	In compliance:	
	Number	Percent
Has a school library in the school	102	83.6
Has a full-time or 2/3-time librarian	58	45.0
Has book collection equal to or larger than 15 books per K-8 student and 10 books per 9-12 student	114	93.0
Has audio-visual materials equal to required 750 total or 5 per student	50	40.9
Has at least one magazine per ten students for small school or one magazine per 20 students for large school[1]	86	70.0
Has a reference collection	104	85.0

[Continued]

★ 361 ★

Federal Compliance of BIA School Libraries
[Continued]

Characteristic	In compliance:	
	Number	Percent
Has a professional collection for staff use	90	73.0
Has a collection of Native American materials	109	87.7

Source: McCauley, Elfrieda. "Native American school libraries: a survey." *School Library Journal* (April 1991), p. 34. Primary source: American Association of School Libraries, Native American Librarians Roundtable.

★ 362 ★

School Environment

Parental Involvement in Students' Academic Training

Parental involvement is thought to be an integral component in the academic progress of a student. This table shows the percentage of eighth grade students who reported each type of parental involvement, by race/ethnicity of student.

Type of parent involvement	Total	Sex		Race/ethnicity					Urbanicity		
		Male	Female	White	Black	Hispanic	Asian	American Indian	Urban	Suburban	Rural
Talked about:											
Selecting courses	85.0	82.0	89.0	87.0	80.0	82.0	85.0	78.0	82.0	87.0	85.0
School activities	91.0	89.0	93.0	92.0	91.0	86.0	90.0	87.0	90.0	91.0	91.0
Class studies	88.0	86.0	91.0	89.0	88.0	84.0	87.0	87.0	88.0	89.0	88.0
Checked homework	90.0	91.0	89.0	90.0	93.0	90.0	90.0	90.0	92.0	90.0	89.0
Limited T.V. viewing	65.0	64.0	63.0	63.0	60.0	67.0	77.0	59.0	65.0	64.0	60.0
Limited going out with friends	89.0	88.0	90.0	89.0	86.0	89.0	88.0	82.0	90.0	89.0	88.0
Spoke with teacher/counselor	60.0	64.0	56.0	59.0	68.0	57.0	48.0	59.0	64.0	61.0	54.0
Visited classes	29.0	29.0	28.0	26.0	36.0	34.0	28.0	32.0	34.0	28.0	25.0

Source: U.S. Department of Education. National Center for Education Statistics. *The Condition of Education 1994.* Washington, DC: U.S. Government Printing Office, 1994, p. 124. Primary source: U.S. Department of Education, National Center for Education Statistics, National Education Longitudinal Study of 1988.

★ 363 ★

School Environment

Reasons for Attending School

Figures represent percentage of tenth grade students who agree or strongly agree with each statement. Data are shown by race/ethnicity, for 1990.

Reason given	Total	White	Black	Hispanic	Asian	American Indian
Think subjects are interesting	71.0	68.8	79.1	74.5	77.3	81.2
Get a feeling of satisfaction	76.9	74.8	85.8	81.3	79.6	81.6
Nothing else to do	30.3	30.1	29.0	31.1	32.4	31.3
Need education to get a job	96.6	96.5	96.7	96.8	97.1	93.4

[Continued]

★ 363 ★

Reasons for Attending School
[Continued]

Reason given	Total	White	Black	Hispanic	Asian	American Indian
To meet friends	82.7	85.5	66.1	80.1	84.9	80.8
Play on a team or belong to a club	53.6	55.3	49.3	45.3	56.3	46.2
Teachers care and expect student to succeed	74.0	72.4	81.6	76.0	74.6	79.4

Source: U.S. Department of Education. National Center for Education Statistics. Office of Educational Research and Improvement. *Digest of Education Statistics, 1994.* Lanham, MD: Bernan, November 1994, p. 144. Primary source: U.S. Department of Education, National Center for Education Statistics, "National Education Longitudinal Survey of 1988," First Followup survey. (This table was prepared February 1993.).

★ 364 ★

School Environment

School Attendance Patterns, 1990 and 1992

This table shows attendance patterns of students who were in tenth grade in 1990 and in 12th grade in 1992, by race/ethnicity.

	Total	Race/ethnicity				
		White	Black	Hispanic	Asian Pacific Is.	American Indian
Percent of 10th graders in 1990						
Number of days missed first half of current school year						
None	14.3	13.0	21.2	12.5	23.1	12.0
1 or 2 days	23.2	22.8	27.2	20.6	28.6	12.5
3 or 4 days	27.7	28.8	24.5	25.0	23.9	33.7
5 or more days	34.8	35.4	27.1	41.9	24.4	41.9
Number of times late first half of current school year						
None	25.2	27.8	17.8	17.8	22.0	18.6
1 or 2 days	38.2	38.0	41.1	36.7	39.7	31.3
3 or more days	36.7	34.2	41.1	45.5	38.3	50.1
Cut classes						
Never or almost never	84.8	85.8	86.5	75.8	87.1	81.4
At least sometimes	15.2	14.2	13.5	24.2	12.9	18.6
Percent of 12th graders in 1992						
Number of days missed first half of current school year						
None	8.7	7.4	15.8	6.9	15.6	11.3
1 or 2 days	30.3	29.9	29.9	31.0	31.6	34.3
3 to 6 days	35.0	36.2	31.2	34.4	27.4	37.8

[Continued]

★ 364 ★

School Attendance Patterns, 1990 and 1992

[Continued]

	Total	Race/ethnicity				
		White	Black	Hispanic	Asian Pacific Is.	American Indian
7 or more days	25.9	26.5	22.1	27.1	22.7	28.6
Number of times late first half of current school year						
None	19.0	20.6	14.0	14.7	16.2	19.1
1 or 2 days	33.5	34.4	32.1	28.7	33.8	25.3
3 or more days	47.6	45.0	53.9	56.6	50.0	55.6
Cut classes						
Never or almost never	75.6	76.5	77.7	67.9	72.7	73.7
At least sometimes	24.4	23.5	22.3	32.1	27.3	26.3

Source: U.S. Department of Education. National Center for Education Statistics. Office of Educational Research and Improvement. *Digest of Education Statistics, 1994.* Lanham, MD: Bernan, November 1994, p. 144. Primary source: U.S. Department of Education, National Center for Education Statistics, "National Education Longitudinal Study of 1988," First and Second Followup surveys. (This table was prepared March 1994.).

School Personnel

★ 365 ★

Math Teacher Qualifications

Data show the percentage of eighth graders whose math teachers majored or minored in math in college. Data are shown for 1988.

Students' race/ethnicity	Teacher			
	Major in math/math educ.	Minor in math/math educ.	Major in education	Other major
All students	43.3	27.1	18.2	11.4
White	45.7	27.2	17.7	9.4
Asian	44.1	23.5	15.0	17.5
Black	40.0	26.6	21.5	12.9
Hispanic	33.3	28.5	17.5	20.8
Native American	30.5	23.5	23.4	22.6

Source: National Science Board. *Science & Engineering Indicators—1993* (NSB 93-1). Washington, DC: U.S. Government Printing Office, 1993, p. 20. Primary source: Research, Evaluation, and Dissemination Division, *Indicators of Science and Mathematics Education 1992*, NSF-95 (Washington, DC: National Science Foundation, 1993).

★ 366 ★

School Personnel

School Board Members, by Race/Ethnicity

Data show the racial and ethnic distribution of school board members in the United States and in U.S. regions in 1992 and 1993. The percentage of American Indian board members was highest in the Western U.S.

Race/ethnicity	Northeast		Central		Southern		Western		Pacific		National	
	1992	1993	1992	1993	1992	1993	1992	1993	1992	1993	1992	1993
Black	1.6	0.9	2.5	1.8	10.8	10.5	2.3	-	-	1.1	3.2	2.4
White	96.4	98.1	96.3	95.5	84.8	84.8	91.7	94.0	94.4	90.3	93.9	93.8
Hispanic	1.2	-	0.7	0.4	2.5	2.3	3.8	3.0	0.8	3.4	1.5	1.3
Native American Indian	-	0.3	0.5	0.4	1.3	-	2.3	2.2	1.6	2.3	0.8	0.7
Asian	0.4	0.6	-	0.8	0.6	1.2	-	-	-	2.3	0.2	0.9
Other	0.4	-	-	0.6	-	1.2	-	-	3.2	0.6	0.5	0.4

Source: "The demographics of school board service." *American School Board Journal* (January 1993), p. 39. *Note:* A dash (-) stands for data not given in original source.

★ 367 ★

School Personnel

School Teachers and Administrators, by Race/Ethnicity

Data show percent distribution of public school teachers in secondary school, by race/ethnicity, for the 1990-91 school year. Distribution is shown for both vocational and non-vocational programs.

Race/ethnicity	Total	Teacher type	
		Non-voca-tional	Voca-tional
Total	100.0	100.0	100.0
White	89.1	89.4	87.8
Black	6.6	6.1	8.7
Hispanic	2.8	3.0	2.0
Asian	0.8	0.8	0.7
American Indian/Alaskan Native	0.7	0.7	0.9

Source: U.S. Department of Education. National Center for Education Statistics. Office of Educational Research and Improvement. *Digest of Education Statistics, 1994.* Lanham, MD: Bernan, November 1994, p. 80. Primary source: U.S. Department of Education, National Center for Education Statistics, "Schools and Staffing Survey, 1990-91." (This table was prepared July 1994.).

Federal Government Support

★ 368 ★

Budget for the Office of Indian Education

Budget allocations are shown for fiscal year 1988-90.

Program	Number of dollars		
	FY 1988 appropriation	FY 1989 appropriation	FY 1990 appropriation
Subpart 1			
Local Educational Agencies	45,670,000	49,248,000	50,825,000
Indian-Controlled Schools	3,500,000	3,500,000	3,451,000
Subpart 1 subtotal	49,170,000	52,748,000	54,276,000
Subpart 2			
Education Services for Indian Children	3,710,000	3,710,000	4,138,000
Planning, Pilot & Demonstration	1,935,000	1,935,000	1,841,000
Fellowships	1,600,000	1,600,000	1,587,000
Education Personnel Development	2,262,000	2,262,000	2,230,000
Resource & Evaluation Centers	2,200,000	2,300,000	2,268,000
Gifted & Talented Program	0	500,000	493,000[1]
Subpart 2 subtotal	11,707,000	12,307,000	12,307,000
Subpart 3			
Education Services for Adults	3,000,000	4,000,000	4,078,000
Planning, Pilot & Demonstration	0	0	0
Subpart 3 subtotal	3,000,000	4,000,000	4,078,000
Subpart 4			
Office of Indian Education	2,163,000	2,206,000	2,403,000
National Advisory Council on Indian Education	286,000	292,000	306,000
Subpart 4 subtotal	2,449,000	2,449,000	2,709,000
Indian Education Program totals	66,326,000	71,553,000	73,620,000

Source: National Advisory Council on Indian Education. *Toward the Year 2000: Listening to the Voice of Native America*, 17th Annual Report to the United States Congress, Fiscal Year 1990, p. 53. Primary source: Office of Indian Education budget reports. *Notes:* 1. The Gifted and Talented budget was reduced to $493,000 from $500,000 by the Gramm-Rudman Hollings sequester. The Gifted and Talented appropriation for fiscal year 1990 was carried over from fiscal year 1989.

★ 369 ★

Federal Government Support

Budgets for Federal Education Programs Which Serve the Indian Population

Figures are shown for fiscal year 1990.

Program	($)
U.S. Department of Education	
Elementary and Secondary Education	
Indian Education Act	73,620,000
Impact Aid - Maintenance & Operations	243,690,065
Impact Aid - Construction	11,798,215
Adult and Vocational Education	
Vocational Education Set-Aside	11,009,952
Special Education and Rehabilitation Services	
Vocational Rehabilitation Set-Aside	3,821,000
Postsecondary Education	
Minority Science Improvement Program	803,106
Institutional Aid	6,585,342
Bilingual Education	14,194,000
Educational Research & Improvement	
Library Services for Tribes	2,419,120
Total	367,940,800
Operated by BIA but funded through Education Department	
Chapter 1 (Set-Aside)	27,344,592
Education of the Handicapped	19,034,529
Math and Science Handicapped Set-Aside	686,660
Drug-Free Schools and Communities (Set-Aside)	5,332,000
Total	52,397,781
Other Department of Education Programs Serving Indians	
Chapter 1, ECIA[2]	79,334,000[1]
Subtotal	499,672,581
U.S. Department of the Interior Bureau of Indian Affairs	
School Operations	
ISEP[3] (Formula & Adjustments)	176,052,000
Institutionalized Handicapped	3,382,000
School Boards (Expense & Training)	1,183,200
Student Transportation	12,489,000
Solo Parent Program	131,000
Technical Support (Agency & MIS)[4]	6,990,000
Indian School Program Adjustments	1,885,000
Tribal Departments of Education	99,000
Substance Abuse/Alcohol-Educ. Prog.	
School Counselors	2,330,000
Johnson O'Malley	23,252,000

[Continued]

★ 369 ★

Budgets for Federal Education Programs Which Serve the Indian Population
[Continued]

Program	($)
Continuing Education	
Postsecondary Schools	12,110,000
Special Higher Education Scholarships	2,131,000
Tribally Controlled Comm. Colleges (Operations & Endowment)	15,825,000
Mansfield University	395,000
Tribe/Agency Operations	
Scholarships	27,635,000
Adult Education	3,167,000
Tribal Colleges Snyder Act Supplement	904,000
BIA total	289,960,200
Other programs	
Office of Construction (Interior)	33,710,000
Indian Health Service Scholarships	8,799,000
Head Start (Health and Human Services)	48,256,821
Job Training Partnership Act (Dept. of Labor, American Indian/Alaska Native JPTA program)	57,910,602
Grand total	938,309,204

Source: National Advisory Council on Indian Education. *Toward the Year 2000: Listening to the Voice of Native America,* 17th Annual Report to the United States Congress, Fiscal Year 1990, p. 54. *Notes:* 1. Figures from the Office of Planning, Budget & Evaluation. 2. Education Consolidation and Improvement Act. 3. Indian Schools Education Program. 4. Management Information System.

★ 370 ★

Federal Government Support

Department of Education Programs Specifically Targeted to Indians

Figures are shown in thousands of dollars.

	FY 1993 Actual	FY1994 Appropriation	FY1995 Request
Goals 2000	-	455[1]	3,470[1]
School-to-Work	-	250[2]	750[2]
Chapter 1 LEA Grants	34,696	35,919	35,722
Chapter 1 Even Start	1,339	1,371	1,770
Impact Aid Basic Support Payments	252,140	260,000	203,000
Impact Aid Supplemental Payments for Children with Disabilities	0	0	21,300
Impact Aid Construction	3,770	3,700	5,000
Eisenhower Professional Development	1,309[3]	1,335[3]	1,880
Safe and Drug-Free Schools and Communities	5,620	5,437	4,800
Homeless Children and Youth	50	50	50

[Continued]

★ 370 ★

Department of Education Programs Specifically Targeted to Indians
[Continued]

	FY 1993 Actual	FY1994 Appropriation	FY1995 Request
Indian Education	80,583	83,500	86,000
Special Education:			
Grants to states	25,342	26,539	29,050
Infants and families	2,607	3,094	3,974
Vocational rehabilitation	6,203	6,515	8,422
Vocational education	12,554	12,635	12,484
Tribally Controlled Postsecondary Vocational institutions	2,946	2,946	3,000
Library services for Indian tribes	1,793	1,811	1,545
Total	430,952	445,557	422,217

Source: U.S. Senate Committee on Indian Affairs. *Fiscal Year 1995 Budget.* 103rd Cong., 2nd sess., March 3, 9, 1994 and April 13, 1994. Washington, DC: U.S. Government Printing Office, 1994, p. 105. Primary source: U.S. Department of Housing, Assistant Secretary for Public and Indian Housing. *Notes:* 1. Estimates only. The Administration's proposed Goals 2000: Educate America Act would reserve 1 percent of the funds appropriated for Title III of the Act for the Territories and for the Secretary of the Interior to benefit children attending BIA-funded schools. 2. Data reflect total program, which includes funds appropriated to and requested by the Department of Labor. 3. Funds provided under Eisenhower Mathematics and Science Education State Grants are shown for comparability.

★ 371 ★

Federal Government Support

Educational Fellowships Given by the Office of Indian Education, by Field

The number of fellows, total awards by field, and the average amount given per pupil are shown for fiscal year 1990. 59 of the fellows were new, and 69 were continuing from the previous year.

Field	Number of fellows	Total award by field ($)	Avg. per pupil award ($)
Business administration	14	174,063	12,433
Clinical psychology	9	118,149	13,128
Education	19	241,831	12,728
Engineering	20	173,729	8,686
Law	19	307,964	16,209
Medicine	23	357,953	15,563
Natural resources	15	131,302	8,753
Psychology	9	95,663	10,629
Total	128	1,600,654	12,505

Source: National Advisory Council on Indian Education. *Toward the Year 2000: Listening to the Voice of Native America,* 17th Annual Report to the United States Congress, Fiscal Year 1990, p. 12. Primary source: Office of Indian Education, Fellowship Program.

★ 372 ★

Federal Government Support

Educational Personnel Recruitment

The dollars granted for the Educational Personnel Development (EPD) Program are shown, by state, fiscal year 1990. The EPD Program provides training for American Indian/Alaska Native students for careers in education. The ultimate objective of the program is to train educational personnel to serve the Indian community. Under the authorizing legislation, awards are made primarily to universities for graduate programs in education. A majority of the projects offer graduate degrees in social work, educational administration, counseling, and doctoral degrees in educational development.

State	Amount ($)
California	
Humboldt State University, Arcata	190,654
Montana (3)	
Blackfeet Community College, Browning	67,628
Montana State University, Bozeman	283,540
Stone Child College, Box Elder	142,663
Montana total	493,831
New Mexico	
Ramah Navajo School Board, Inc., Pine Hill	49,902
Oklahoma (3)	
American Indian Research & Development, Norman	229,551
American Indian Resource Center, Talequah	156,879
Cross Cultural Education Center, Park Hill	247,627
Oklahoma total	634,057
Pennsylvania	
Pennsylvania State University, University Park	197,945
South Dakota (2)	
Oglala Lakota College, Kyle	213,188
Sinte Gleska College, Rosebud	101,487
South Dakota total	314,675
Wisconsin	
Menominee Indian Tribe of Wisconsin, Keshena	180,853
Wyoming	
Univ. of Wyoming, Student Educational Opp., Laramie	167,499
Educational Personnel Development total	2,229,416
Applications awarded (number)	14

Source: National Advisory Council on Indian Education. *Toward the Year 2000: Listening to the Voice of Native America*, 17th Annual Report to the United States Congress, Fiscal Year 1990, pp. 43-44. Primary source: Office of Indian Education.

★ 373 ★

Federal Government Support

Educational Services for Indian Adults

Dollars granted under the Indian Education Act for special programs relating to adult education are shown for fiscal year 1990.

State/ organization city	Grant amount ($)
Arizona (2)	
Cocopah Indian Tribe, Somerton	137,603
Native Americans for Community Action, Flagstaff	105,458
Arizona total	243,061
Colorado	
Denver Indian Center, Denver	134,134
Massachusetts	
Boston Indian Council, Boston	205,461
Michigan (3)	
Genesee Valley Indian Assn., Flint	50,824
Grand Traverse Band of Ottawa/Chippewa, Suttons Bay	169,886
Sault Ste. Marie Chippewa Indian, Sault Ste. Marie	77,688
Michigan total	298,398
Minnesota (4)	
American Indian OIC., Inc., Minneapolis	115,048
Heart of the Earth Survival School, Minneapolis	250,226
Migizi Communications, Inc., Minneapolis	218,725
Red School House, Inc., St. Paul	208,489
Minnesota total	832,488
Nebraska	
Lincoln Indian Center, Lincoln	45,367
Montana (4)	
Dull Knife Memorial College	119,008
Fort Belknap Community Council, Harlem	128,389
Little Bighorn College, Crow Agency	138,255
Stonechild College, Box Elder	129,408
Montana total	515,060
New York (1)	
Seneca Nation of Indians, Irving	79,920
North Carolina (1)	
Cumberland Co. Assn. for Indian People, Fayetteville	143,021
Oklahoma (4)	
American Indian Resource Center, Tahlequah	128,337
Cherokee Nation of Oklahoma, Tahlequah	208,670
Miami Inter-Tribal Council, Miami	118,749

[Continued]

★ 373 ★

Educational Services for Indian Adults
[Continued]

State/ organization city	Grant amount ($)
Sac and Fox Nation Education Dept., Stroud	156,870
Oklahoma total	611,870
South Dakota (2)	
Oglala Lakota College, Kyle	91,024
Sisseton-Wahpeton Sioux Tribe, Sisseton	89,377
South Dakota total	180,401
Utah	
Ute Indian Tribe, Ft. Duchesne	182,538
Washington (4)	
Nisqually Indian Tribe, Olympia	141,084
Seattle Indian Center, Seattle	143,686
Snoqualmie Tribal Learning Center, Seattle	134,991
United Indians of all Tribes, Seattle	186,520
Washington total	606,281
Educational Services for Indian Adults total	4,078,000
Total applications awarded in FY 1990	30

Source: National Advisory Council on Indian Education. *Toward the Year 2000: Listening to the Voice of Native America*, 17th Annual Report to the United States Congress, Fiscal Year 1990, pp. 46-47. Primary source: Office of Indian Education.

★ 374 ★
Federal Government Support

Federal Education Support, 1994

Data show estimated federal support for education, by agency and type of recipient. Outlays by type of recipient are estimated based on obligation data. Data do not include federal tax expenditures.

(In millions of dollars)

Agency	Total	Local education agencies	State education agencies	College students	Institutions of higher education	Federal	Multiple types of recipients	Other
Total[1]	87,569.4	20,017.4	4,975.4	15,214.4	27,093.5	3,049.1	10,131.3	7,088.4
Total program funds - on-budget	68,364.2	20,017.4	4,528.0	7,623.4	20,351.9	3,049.1	10,131.3	2,663.0
Department of Education	28,879.7	11,635.6	3,683.5	4,789.4	4,890.9	530.1	1,368.2	1,982.1
Department of Agriculture	8,728.5	7,728.6	72.4	-	474.9	18.2	-	434.6
Department of Commerce	91.4	-	-	-	91.4	-	-	-
Department of Defense	3,747.9	108.8	-	183.9	1,996.1	1,241.0	218.1	-
Department of Energy	2,647.2	5.1	-	3.0	2,638.0	-	1.2	-
Department of Health and Human Services	11,706.8	332.6	-	913.0	6,398.0	110.1	3,953.1	-
Department of Housing and Development	0.4	-	-	-	0.4	-	-	-

[Continued]

★ 374 ★

Federal Education Support, 1994
[Continued]

Agency	Total	Local education agencies	State education agencies	College students	Institutions of higher education	Federal	Multiple types of recipients	Other
Department of the Interior	765.8	64.6	124.0	33.7	101.1	399.2	43.2	-
Department of Justice	155.9	-	-	-	3.4	152.4	-	-
Department of Labor	4,536.5	-	636.1	-	0.6	-	3,899.8	-
Department of State	48.0	-	-	-	7.5	38.5	-	2.0
Department of Transportation	109.9	-	-	0.3	48.6	43.0	6.4	11.7
Department of Treasury	58.4	-	-	-	0.2	58.3	-	-
Department of Veterans Affairs	1,393.2	-	12.0	1,378.6	2.6	-	-	-
Other agencies and programs								
Agency for International Development	257.0	-	-	-	25.9	-	-	231.2
Appalachian Regional Commission	7.8	-	-	-	1.5	-	6.3	-
Barry Goldwater Scholarship and Excellence in Education Foundation	3.1	-	-	-	-	-	3.1	-
Corporation for National and Community Service	180.0	-	-	-	-	-	180.0	-
Environmental Protection Agency	169.5	-	-	-	169.5	-	-	-
Estimated education share of federal aid to the District of Columbia	146.3	127.3	-	-	14.3	-	4.8	-
Federal Emergency Management Agency	65.7	15.0	-	-	50.0	-	0.2	0.5
General Services Administration	-	-	-	-	-	-	-	-
Harry S. Truman scholarship fund	3.2	-	-	-	-	-	3.2	-
Institute of American Indian and Alaska Native Culture and Arts Development	12.9	-	-	-	-	-	12.9	-
James Madison Memorial Fellowship Foundation	2.3	-	-	-	-	-	2.3	-
Japanese-United States Friendship Commission	1.8	-	-	-	-	-	1.8	-
Library of Congress	320.3	-	-	-	-	320.3	-	-
National Aeronautics and Space Administration	1,457.5	-	-	-	1,451.2	-	6.3	-
National Archives and Records Administration	108.2	-	-	-	-	108.2	-	-
National Commission on Libraries and Information Science	1.0	-	-	-	-	-	-	1.0
National Endowment for the Arts	7.3	-	-	-	-	-	7.3	-
National Endowment for the Humanities	157.5	-	-	-	-	-	157.5	-
National Science Foundation	2,241.3	-	-	283.0	1,958.3	-	-	-
Nuclear Regulatory Commission	26.3	-	-	-	26.3	-	-	-
Office of Economic Opportunity	-	-	-	-	-	-	-	-
Smithsonian Institution	7.7	-	-	-	-	0.8	6.9	-
U.S. Arms Control and Disarmament Agency	2	-	-	-	-	2	-	-
U.S. Information Agency	304.7	-	-	38.3	-	29.0	237.3	-
U.S. Institute of Peace	11.5	-	-	-	-	-	11.5	-
Other agencies	1.6	-	-	-	1.6	-	-	-
Nonfederal funds generated by federal legislation and off-budget support	19,205.3	-	447.4	7,590.9	6,741.6	-	-	4,425.4

Source: U.S. Department of Education. National Center for Education Statistics. Office of Educational Research and Improvement. *Digest of Education Statistics, 1994.* Lanham, MD: Bernan, November 1994, p. 377. U.S. Department of Education, Office of Management and Budget, unpublished tabulations; U.S. Office of Management and Budget, *Budget of the U.S. Government, Fiscal Year 1995,* and *Catalog of Federal Domestic Assistance*; National Science Foundation, *Federal Funds for Research and Development, Fiscal Years 1992, 1993, and 1994*; and unpublished data obtained from various federal agencies. (This table was prepared May 1994.) *Notes:* A dash stands for data not available or not applicable. Because of rounding, details may not add to totals. Includes on-budget support, and nonfederal funds generated by federal legislation, and off-budget support. 2. Less than $50,000.

Higher Education Enrollment

★ 375 ★

Enrollment Trends in Higher Education

Total fall enrollment and percent distribution of students, by race and ethnicity, are shown biennially from 1980 through 1990.

Control of institution and race/ethnicity	Number in thousands						Percent distribution					
	1980	1982	1984	1986	1988	1990	1980	1982	1984	1986	1988	1990
All institutions												
Total	12,087	12,388	12,235	12,504	13,043	13,710	100.0	100.0	100.0	100.0	100.0	100.0
White, non-Hispanic	9,833	9,997	9,815	9,921	10,283	10,675	81.4	80.7	80.2	79.3	78.8	77.9
Black, non-Hispanic	1,107	1,101	1,076	1,082	1,130	1,223	9.2	8.9	8.8	8.7	8.7	8.9
Hispanic	472	519	535	618	680	758	3.9	4.2	4.4	4.9	5.2	5.5
Asian or Pacific Islander	286	351	390	448	497	555	2.4	2.8	3.2	3.6	3.8	4.0
American Indian or Alaskan Native	84	88	84	90	93	103	0.7	0.7	0.7	0.7	0.7	0.7
Nonresident alien	305	331	335	345	361	397	2.5	2.7	2.7	2.8	2.8	2.9
Public												
Total	9,456	9,695	9,458	9,714	10,156	10,741	78.2	78.3	77.3	77.7	77.9	78.3
White, non-Hispanic	7,656	7,785	7,543	7,654	7,964	8,340	63.3	62.8	61.6	61.2	61.1	60.8
Black, non-Hispanic	876	873	844	854	881	952	7.2	7.0	6.9	6.8	6.8	6.9
Hispanic	406	446	456	532	587	648	3.4	3.6	3.7	4.3	4.5	4.7
Asian or Pacific Islander	240	296	323	371	406	445	2.0	2.4	2.6	3.0	3.1	3.2
American Indian or Alaskan Native	74	77	72	79	81	90	0.6	0.6	0.6	0.6	0.6	0.7
Nonresident alien	204	219	219	224	238	265	1.7	1.8	1.8	1.8	1.8	1.9
Private												
Total	2,630	2,693	2,777	2,790	2,887	2,970	21.8	21.7	22.7	22.3	22.1	21.7
White, non-Hispanic	2,177	2,212	2,272	2,267	2,319	2,335	18.0	17.9	18.6	18.1	17.8	17.0
Black, non-Hispanic	231	228	232	228	248	271	1.9	1.8	1.9	1.8	1.9	2.0
Hispanic	66	74	79	86	93	110	0.5	0.6	0.6	0.7	0.7	0.8
Asian or Pacific Islander	47	55	67	77	91	109	0.4	0.4	0.5	0.6	0.7	0.8
American Indian or Alaskan Native	10	10	11	11	11	12	0.1	0.1	0.1	0.1	0.1	0.1
Nonresident	101	113	116	120	123	132	0.8	0.9	0.9	1.0	0.9	1.0

Source: U.S. Department of Education. Office of Educational Research and Improvement. Postsecondary Education Statistics Division. *Trends in Racial/Ethnic Enrollment in Higher Education: Fall 1980 Through Fall 1990.* Washington, DC: U.S. Government Printing Office, p. 1. Primary source: U.S. Department of Education, National Center for Education Statistics, Higher Education General Information Survey "Fall Enrollment in Colleges and Universities" (1978-1984) and Integrated Postsecondary Education Data System "Fall Enrollment" surveys 1986, 1988, and 1990, p. 1. *Notes:* Because of underreporting/nonreporting of racial/ethnic data, data prior to 1986 were estimated when possible. Also, due to rounding, detail may not add to totals.

★ 376 ★

Higher Education Enrollment

Enrollment Trends, by Level of Institution

Total fall enrollment and percent distributions are shown, by race/ethnicity, for 1984-92.

Level of institution and race/ethnicity	Numbers in thousands					Percent distribution by type and control[1]				
	1984	1988	1990	1991	1992[2]	1984	1988	1990	1991	1992[2]
All institutions	12,233.0	13,043.1	13,818.6	14,359.0	14,491.2	100.0	100.0	100.0	100.0	100.0
White, non-Hispanic	9,814.7	10,283.2	10,722.5	10,989.8	10,870.0	82.5	81.1	79.9	78.8	77.5
Total minority	2,083.8	2,398.8	2,704.7	2,952.8	3,163.6	17.5	18.9	20.1	21.2	22.5
Black, non-Hispanic	1,075.8	1,129.6	1,247.0	1,335.4	1,393.5	9.0	8.9	9.3	9.6	9.9
Hispanic	534.9	680.0	782.4	8966.6	954.4	4.5	5.4	5.8	6.2	6.8
Asian or Pacific Islander	389.5	496.7	572.4	637.2	696.8	63.3	3.9	4.3	4.6	5.0
American Indian or Alaskan Native	83.6	92.5	102.8	113.7	118.8	0.7	0.7	0.8	0.8	0.8
Nonresident alien	334.6	361.2	391.5	416.4	457.6	-	-	-	-	-
4-year institutions	7,706.1	8,175.0	8,578.6	8,707.1	8,768.0	100.0	100.0	100.0	100.0	100.0
White, non-Hispanic	6,300.4	6,581.6	6,768.1	6,791.0	6,746.9	84.9	83.6	82.0	81.2	80.2
Total minority	1,123.6	1,291.8	1,486.1	1,573.3	1,663.8	15.1	16.4	18.0	18.8	19.8
Black, non-Hispanic	617.0	656.3	722.8	757.8	791.5	8.3	8.3	8.8	9.1	9.4
Hispanic	246.1	296.0	358.2	382.9	409.9	3.3	3.8	4.3	4.6	4.9
Asian or Pacific Islander	222.4	297.4	357.2	381.5	407.6	3.0	3.8	4.3	4.6	4.8
American Indian or Alaskan Native	38.1	42.1	47.9	51.1	54.9	0.5	0.5	0.6	0.6	0.7
Nonresident alien	282.1	301.5	324.3	342.8	357.2	-	-	-	-	-
2-year institutions[1]	4,526.9	4,868.1	5,240.1	5,651.9	5,723.2	100.0	100.0	100.0	100.0	100.0
White, non-Hispanic	3,514.3	3,701.5	3,954.3	4,198.8	4,123.1	78.5	77.0	76.4	75.3	73.3
Total minority	960.1	1,106.9	1,218.6	1,379.6	1,499.7	21.5	23.0	23.6	24.7	26.7
Black, non-Hispanic	458.7	473.3	524.3	577.6	602.0	10.3	9.8	10.1	10.4	10.7
Hispanic	288.8	383.9	424.2	483.7	544.5	6.5	8.0	8.2	8.7	9.7
Asian or Pacific Islander	167.1	199.3	215.2	255.7	289.2	3.7	4.1	4.2	4.6	5.1
American Indian or Alaskan Native	45.5	50.4	54.9	62.6	64.0	1.0	1.0	1.1	1.1	1.1
Nonresident alien	52.5	59.6	67.1	73.5	100.4	-	-	-	-	-

Source: U.S. Department of Education. National Center for Education Statistics. Office of Educational Research and Improvement. *Digest of Education Statistics, 1994.* Lanham, MD: Bernan, November 1994, p. 207. Primary source: U.S. Department of Education, National Center for Education Statistics, "Fall Enrollment in Colleges and Universities," and Integrated Postsecondary Education Data System "Fall Enrollment" surveys. (This table was prepared March 1994.) *Notes:* A dash (-) stands for not applicable. Because of underreporting/nonreporting of racial/ethnic data, some figures are slightly lower than corresponding data in other tables. Because of rounding, detail may not add to totals. 1. Distribution for U.S. citizens only. 2. Preliminary data.

★ 377 ★

Higher Education Enrollment

Enrollment Trends, by Level of Study

Fall enrollment and percent distribution are shown biennially from 1980 through 1990.

Level of institution and race/ethnicity	Numbers in thousands						Percent distribution by level of study					
	1980	1982	1984	1986	1988	1990	1980	1982	1984	1986	1988	1990
Undergraduate enrollment												
Total	10,560	10,875	10,610	10,798	11,304	11,863	100.0	100.0	100.0	100.0	100.0	100.0
White, non-Hispanic	8,556	8,749	8,484	8,558	8,907	9,231	81.0	80.5	80.0	79.3	76.8	77.8
Total minority	1,797	1,907	1,911	2,036	2,192	2,406	17.0	17.5	18.0	18.9	19.4	20.3
Black, non-Hispanic	1,028	1,028	995	996	1,039	1,124	9.7	9.4	9.4	9.2	9.2	9.5
Hispanic	438	485	495	563	631	702	4.1	4.5	4.7	5.2	5.6	5.9
Asian or Pacific Islander	253	313	343	393	437	485	2.4	2.9	3.2	3.6	3.9	4.1
American Indian or Alaskan Native	79	82	78	83	86	95	0.7	0.8	0.7	0.8	0.8	0.8
Nonresident alien	208	220	216	205	205	226	2.0	2.0	2.0	1.9	1.8	1.9

[Continued]

★ 377 ★

Enrollment Trends, by Level of Study
[Continued]

Level of institution and race/ethnicity	Numbers in thousands						Percent distribution by level of study					
	1980	1982	1984	1986	1988	1990	1980	1982	1984	1986	1988	1990
Graduate enrollment												
Total	1,250	1,235	1,344	1,435	1,472	1,574	100.0	100.0	100.0	100.0	100.0	100.0
White, non-Hispanic	1,030	1,002	1,087	1,133	1,153	1,221	82.4	81.1	80.9	78.9	78.4	77.6
Total minority	125	123	141	167	167	187	10.0	10.0	10.5	11.6	11.4	11.9
Black, non-Hispanic	66	61	67	72	76	84	5.3	4.9	5.0	5.0	5.2	5.3
Hispanic	27	27	32	46	39	46	2.2	2.2	2.4	3.2	2.7	2.9
Asian or Pacific Islander	28	30	37	43	46	52	2.2	2.5	2.8	3.0	3.1	3.3
American Indian or Alaskan Native	4	5	5	5	6	6	0.4	0.4	0.4	0.4	0.4	0.4
Nonresident alien	94	108	115	136	151	165	7.5	8.8	8.6	9.5	10.3	10.5
First-professional enrollment												
Total	277	278	278	270	267	274	100.0	100.0	100.0	100.0	100.0	100.0
White, non-Hispanic	248	246	243	231	223	222	89.5	88.5	87.4	85.3	83.6	81.3
Total minority	26	29	32	36	39	46	9.5	10.4	11.4	13.2	14.6	16.7
Black, non-Hispanic	13	13	13	14	14	16	4.6	4.7	4.8	5.2	5.4	5.8
Hispanic	7	7	8	9	9	10	2.4	2.5	2.9	3.4	3.5	3.8
Asian or Pacific Islander	6	6	9	11	14	18	2.2	2.9	3.4	4.2	5.4	6.7
American Indian or Alaskan Native	1	1	1	1	1	1	0.3	0.4	0.4	0.4	0.4	0.4
Nonresident alien	3	3	3	4	5	5	1.0	1.1	1.2	1.5	1.8	2.0

Source: U.S. Department of Education. Office of Educational Research and Improvement. Postsecondary Education Statistics Division. *Trends in Racial/Ethnic Enrollment in Higher Education: Fall 1980 Through Fall 1990.* Washington, DC: U.S. Government Printing Office, p. 4. Primary source: U.S. Department of Education, National Center for Education Statistics, Higher Education General Information Survey "Fall Enrollment in Colleges and Universities" (1978-1984) and Integrated Postsecondary Education Data System "Fall Enrollment" surveys (1986, 1988, and 1990). *Notes:* Because of underreporting/nonreporting of racial/ethnic data, data prior to 1986 were estimated when possible. Also, due to rounding, detail may not add to totals.

★ 378 ★

Higher Education Enrollment

Enrollment Trends, by Sex

Total fall enrollment and percent distribution of students are shown biennially from 1980 through 1990.

Race/ethnicity and sex	Number, in thousands						Percent distribution					
	1980	1982	1984	1986	1988	1990	1980	1982	1984	1986	1988	1990
All students												
Total	12,087	12,388	12,235	12,504	13,043	13,710	100.0	100.0	100.0	100.0	100.0	100.0
White, non-Hispanic	9,833	9,997	9,815	9,921	10,283	10,675	81.4	80.7	80.2	79.3	78.8	77.9
Black, non-Hispanic	1,107	1,101	1,076	1,082	1,130	1,223	9.2	8.9	8.8	8.7	8.7	8.9
Hispanic	472	519	535	618	680	758	3.9	4.2	4.4	4.9	5.2	5.5
Asian or Pacific Islander	286	351	390	448	497	555	2.4	2.8	3.2	3.6	3.8	4.0
American Indian or Alaskan Native	84	88	84	90	93	103	0.7	0.7	0.7	0.7	0.7	0.7
Nonresident alien	305	331	335	345	361	397	2.5	2.7	2.7	2.8	2.8	2.9
Men												
Total	5,868	5,999	5,859	5,885	5,998	6,239	48.5	48.4	47.9	47.1	46.0	45.5
White, non-Hispanic	4,773	4,830	4,690	4,647	4,712	4,841	39.5	39.0	38.3	37.2	36.1	35.3
Black, non-Hispanic	464	458	437	436	443	476	3.8	3.7	3.6	3.5	3.4	3.5
Hispanic	232	252	254	290	310	344	1.9	2.0	2.1	2.3	2.4	2.5
Asian or Pacific Islander	151	189	210	239	259	287	1.3	1.5	1.7	1.9	2.0	2.1
American Indian or Alaskan Native	38	40	38	39	39	43	0.3	0.3	0.3	0.3	0.3	0.3

[Continued]

★ 378 ★

Enrollment Trends, by Sex
[Continued]

Race/ethnicity and sex	Number, in thousands						Percent distribution					
	1980	1982	1984	1986	1988	1990	1980	1982	1984	1986	1988	1990
Nonresident alien	211	230	231	233	235	248	1.7	1.9	1.9	1.9	1.8	1.8
Women												
Total	6,219	6,389	6,376	6,619	7,045	7,472	51.5	51.6	52.1	52.9	54.0	54.5
White, non-Hispanic	5,060	5,167	5,125	5,273	5,572	5,834	41.9	41.7	41.9	42.2	42.7	42.6
Black, non-Hispanic	643	644	639	646	687	747	5.3	5.2	5.2	5.2	5.3	5.4
Hispanic	240	267	281	328	370	414	2.0	2.2	2.3	2.6	2.8	3.0
Asian or Pacific Islander	135	162	180	209	237	268	1.1	1.3	1.5	1.7	1.8	2.0
Nonresident alien	94	101	104	112	126	149	0.8	0.8	0.9	0.9	1.0	1.1

Source: U.S. Department of Education. Office of Educational Research and Improvement. Postsecondary Education Statistics Division. *Trends in Racial/Ethnic Enrollment in Higher Education: Fall 1980 Through Fall 1990.* Washington, DC: U.S. Government Printing Office, p. 6. Primary source: U.S. Department of Education, National Center for Education Statistics, Higher Education Data System "Fall Enrollment" surveys (1986, 1988, and 1990). *Notes:* Because of underreporting/nonreporting of racial/ethnic data, data prior to 1986 were estimated when possible. Also, due to rounding, detail may not add to totals.

★ 379 ★

Higher Education Enrollment

Fall Enrollment Distribution in Higher Education Institutions, by Year

Distribution of students is shown, for U.S. citizens, by race/ethnicity for selected years.

Race/ethnicity	Percent distribution						
	1976	1980	1984	1988	1990	1991	1992[1]
Total	100.0	100.0	100.0	100.0	100.0	100.0	100.0
White, non-Hispanic	84.3	83.5	82.5	81.1	79.9	78.8	77.5
Total minority	15.7	16.5	17.5	18.9	20.1	21.2	22.5
Black, non-Hispanic	9.6	9.4	9.0	8.9	9.3	9.6	9.9
Hispanic	3.6	4.0	4.5	5.4	5.8	6.2	6.8
Asian or Pacific Islander	1.8	2.4	3.3	3.9	4.3	4.6	5.0
American Indian/Alaskan Native	0.7	0.7	0.7	0.7	0.8	0.8	0.8
Men	52.4	48.0	47.3	45.4	45.0	44.8	44.5
White, non-Hispanic	44.7	40.5	39.4	37.2	36.2	35.6	34.8
Total minority	7.7	7.5	7.9	8.3	8.8	9.2	9.7
Black, non-Hispanic	4.4	3.9	3.7	3.5	3.6	3.7	3.8
Hispanic	1.9	2.0	2.1	2.4	2.6	2.8	3.0
Asian or Pacific Islander	1.0	1.3	1.8	2.0	2.2	2.3	2.5
American Indian/Alaskan Native	0.4	0.3	0.3	0.3	0.3	0.3	0.4
Women	47.6	52.0	52.7	54.6	550	55.2	55.5
White, non-Hispanic	39.6	42.9	43.1	43.9	43.7	43.2	42.7
Total minority	8.0	9.0	9.6	10.6	11.4	12.0	12.8
Black, non-Hispanic	5.2	5.5	5.4	5.4	5.7	5.9	6.1
Hispanic	1.6	2.0	2.4	2.9	3.2	3.4	3.8

[Continued]

★ 379 ★

Fall Enrollment Distribution in Higher Education Institutions, by Year
[Continued]

Race/ethnicity	Percent distribution						
	1976	1980	1984	1988	1990	1991	1992[1]
Asian or Pacific Islander	0.8	1.1	1.5	1.9	2.1	2.2	2.5
American Indian/Alaskan Native	0.3	0.4	0.4	0.4	0.4	0.5	0.5

Source: U.S. Department of Education. National Center for Education Statistics. Office of Educational Research and Improvement. *Digest of Education Statistics, 1994.* Lanham, MD: Bernan, November 1994, p. 208. Primary source: U.S. Department of Education, National Center for Education Statistics, "Fall Enrollment in Colleges and Universities"; and Integrated Postsecondary Education Data System (IPEDS), "Fall Enrollment" survey. (This Table was prepared March 1994.) *Notes:* Because of underreporting and nonreporting of racial/ethnic data, some figures are slightly lower than corresponding data in other tables. Because of rounding, details may not add to totals. 1. Preliminary data.

★ 380 ★

Higher Education Enrollment

College Enrollment, by Selected Characteristics

Data are shown in thousands, as of fall of each year. Totals may differ from other tables because of adjustments to underreported and nonreported racial/ethnic data. Nonresident alien students are not distributed among racial/ethnic groups.

Characteristic	1978	1980	1984	1988	1990	1991, est.	1992, prel.
Total	11,231.2	12,086.8	12,233.0	13,043.1	13,819.5	14,359.0	14,491.2
Male	5,621.5	5,868.1	5,858.3	5,998.2	6,284.4	6,501.8	6,526.1
Female	5,609.6	6,218.7	6,374.7	7,044.9	7,535.1	7,857.1	7,965.1
Public	8,769.8	9,456.4	9,456.4	10,156.4	10,844.7	11,309.6	11,387.8
Private	2,461.4	2,630.4	2,776.6	2,886.7	2,974.8	3,049.4	3,103.5
Two-year	4,028.8	4,521.4	4,526.9	4,868.1	5,240.1	5,651.9	5,723.2
Four-year	7,202.4	7,565.4	7,706.1	8,175.0	8,579.4	8,707.1	8,768.0
Undergraduate	9,665.8	10,469.1	10,610.8	11,304.2	11,959.2	12,439.3	12,539.8
Graduate	1,310.4	1,340.9	1,343.7	1,471.9	1,586.2	1,639.1	1,670.0
First professional	255.0	276.8	278.5	267.1	274.1	280.5	281.4
White[1]	9,194.0	9,833.0	9,814.7	10,283.2	10,723.0	10,989.8	10,870.0
Male	4,613.1	4,772.9	4,689.9	4,711.6	4,861.3	4,962.2	4,882.5
Female	4,580.9	5,060.1	5,124.7	5,571.6	5,861.7	6,027.6	5,987.6
Public	7,136.1	7,656.1	7,542.4	7,963.8	8,385.4	8,622.2	8,486.9
Private	2,057.9	2,176.9	2,272.3	2,319.4	2,337.6	2,367.5	2,383.1
Two-year	3,166.9	3,558.5	3,514.3	3,701.5	3,954.3	4,198.8	4,123.1
Four-year	6,027.1	6,274.5	6,300.4	6,581.6	6,768.7	6,791.0	6,746.9
Undergraduate	7,870.6	8,480.7	8,484.0	8,906.7	9,272.6	9,507.7	9,380.6

[Continued]

★ 380 ★

College Enrollment, by Selected Characteristics

[Continued]

Characteristic	1978	1980	1984	1988	1990	1991, est.	1992, prel.
Graduate	1,094.1	1,104.7	1,087.3	1,153.2	1,228.4	1,258.0	1,268.4
First professional	229.3	247.7	243.4	223.2	222.0	224.0	220.9
Black[1]	1,054.4	1,106.8	1,075.8	1,129.6	1,247.1	1,335.4	1,393.5
Male	453.3	463.7	436.8	442.7	484.7	517.0	537.1
Female	601.1	643.0	639.0	686.9	762.4	818.4	856.4
Public	839.5	876.1	844.0	881.1	976.5	1,053.4	1,101.1
Private	214.9	230.7	231.8	248.5	270.6	281.9	292.4
Two-year	442.6	472.5	458.7	473.3	524.3	577.6	602.0
Four-year	611.8	634.3	617.0	656.3	722.8	757.8	791.5
Undergraduate	966.5	1,018.8	994.9	1,038.8	1,147.2	1,229.3	1,281.2
Graduate	76.4	75.1	67.4	76.5	83.9	88.9	94.1
First professional	11.4	12.8	13.4	14.3	16.0	17.2	18.2
Hispanic	417.3	471.7	534.9	680.0	782.6	866.6	954.4
Male	212.5	231.6	253.8	310.3	354.0	390.5	427.4
Female	204.7	240.1	281.2	369.6	428.6	476.0	527.1
Public	362.5	406.2	456.1	586.9	671.4	742.1	821.7
Private	54.7	65.5	78.9	93.1	111.1	124.5	132.7
Two-year	226.9	255.1	288.8	383.9	424.2	483.7	544.5
Four-year	190.4	216.6	246.1	296.0	358.3	382.9	409.9
Undergraduate	384.0	433.1	495.2	631.2	724.6	804.2	887.2
Graduate	28.0	32.1	31.7	39.5	47.2	50.9	55.2
First professional	5.4	6.5	8.0	9.3	10.9	11.4	12.0
American Indian[1]	77.9	83.9	83.6	92.5	102.8	113.7	118.8
Male	36.8	37.8	37.4	39.1	43.1	47.6	50.1
Female	41.0	46.1	46.1	53.4	59.7	66.1	68.8
Public	68.5	74.2	72.1	81.1	90.4	100.2	103.0
Private	9.5	9.7	11.4	11.5	12.4	13.6	15.9
Two-year	43.1	47.0	45.5	50.4	54.9	62.6	64.0
Four-year	34.8	36.9	38.1	42.1	47.9	51.1	54.9
Undergraduate	71.9	77.9	77.8	85.9	95.5	105.8	110.4
Graduate	4.9	5.2	4.8	5.6	6.2	6.6	7.0
First professional	1.1	0.8	1.0	1.1	1.1	1.3	1.5
Asian[1]	235.1	286.4	389.5	496.7	572.5	637.2	696.8

[Continued]

★ 380 ★

College Enrollment, by Selected Characteristics
[Continued]

Characteristic	1978	1980	1984	1988	1990	1991, est.	1992, prel.
Male	126.3	151.3	210.0	259.2	294.9	325.1	351.3
Female	108.7	135.2	179.5	237.5	277.6	312.0	345.5
Public	195.4	239.7	322.7	405.7	461.0	516.3	565.6
Private	39.6	46.7	66.8	91.0	111.6	120.9	131.1
Two-year	97.2	124.3	167.1	199.3	215.2	255.7	289.2
Four-year	137.8	162.1	222.4	297.4	357.3	381.5	407.6
Undergraduate	202.8	248.7	343.0	436.6	500.5	558.7	612.7
Graduate	27.5	31.6	37.1	45.7	53.2	57.6	61.6
First professional	4.8	6.1	9.3	14.4	18.8	20.8	22.5
Nonresident alien	252.6	305.0	334.6	361.2	391.5	416.4	457.6
Male	179.5	210.8	230.4	235.3	246.3	259.4	277.8
Female	73.1	94.2	104.1	125.9	145.2	157.0	179.8
Public	167.7	204.1	219.0	237.8	260.0	275.3	309.4
Private	84.8	100.8	115.5	123.3	131.5	141.0	148.2
Two-year	52.0	64.1	52.5	59.6	67.1	73.5	100.4
Four-year	200.5	240.9	282.1	301.5	324.4	342.8	357.2
Undergraduate	170.1	209.9	215.8	205.0	218.7	233.6	267.7
Graduate	79.5	92.2	115.3	151.4	167.3	177.0	183.7
First professional	3.0	2.9	3.4	4.7	5.4	5.8	6.3

Source: 1994 Statistical Abstract of the United States on CD-ROM [machine-readable datafiles]. CD-8A-94. Washington, DC: U.S. Department of Commerce, Economics and Statistics Administration, Bureau of the Census, Data User Services Division, January 1995. Primary source: U.S. National Center for Education Statistics, Digest of Education Statistics, annual. *Note:* 1. Non-Hispanic.

★ 381 ★

Higher Education Enrollment

Enrollment Distribution in Public and Private Higher Education Institutions

Universities have been seeking to increase cultural diversity on campuses by attracting greater numbers of minority students. This table shows percent distribution of total enrollment, by race/ethnicity of students. American Indians and Alaska Natives made up approximately one percent of enrollment in public institutions but only half a percent of private school enrollment in 1992.

Control and type of institution and race/ethnicity of student	Number, in thousands			
	1986	1988	1990	1992
All institutions	100.0	100.0	100.0	100.0
White	79.3	78.8	77.9	75.0
Minority	17.9	18.4	19.2	21.8
Black	8.7	8.7	8.9	9.6
Hispanic	4.9	5.2	5.5	6.6
Asian or Pacific Islander	3.6	3.8	4.0	4.8
American Indian/Alaskan Native	0.7	0.7	0.8	0.8
Nonresident alien	2.8	2.8	2.9	3.2
Public institutions	100.0	100.0	100.0	100.0
White	78.8	78.4	77.6	74.5
Minority	18.9	19.2	19.9	22.8
Black	8.8	8.7	8.9	9.7
Hispanic	5.5	5.8	6.0	7.2
Asian or Pacific Islander	3.8	4.0	4.1	5.0
American Indian/Alaskan Native	0.8	0.8	0.8	0.9
Nonresident alien	2.3	2.3	2.5	2.7
Private institutions	100.0	100.0	100.0	100.0
White	81.3	80.3	78.6	76.8
Minority	14.4	15.4	16.9	18.4
Black	8.2	8.6	9.1	9.4
Hispanic	3.1	3.2	3.7	4.3
Asian or Pacific Islander	2.8	3.2	3.7	4.3
American Indian/Alaskan Native	0.4	0.4	0.4	0.5
Nonresident alien	4.3	4.3	4.4	4.8

Source: U.S. Department of Education. National Center for Education Statistics. *The Condition of Education 1994.* Washington, DC: U.S. Government Printing Office, 1994, p. 319. Primary source: U.S. Department of Education, National Center for Education Statistics, *Digest of Education 1993*, table 201 and unpublished tabulations (based on the IPEDS/HEGIS survey of fall enrollment in postsecondary and higher education, various years).

★ 382 ★

Higher Education Enrollment

Science and Engineering Graduate Students, by Field and Race/Ethnicity, 1983-91

Data show number of graduate students enrolled in science and engineering programs.

Field	1983	1984	1985	1986	1987	1988	1989	1990	1991
Total enrollment									
Total science and engineering	348,315	350,755	359,554	369,047	373,762	376,821	384,691	395,298	415,240
Natural sciences	103,213	103,784	104,347	105,803	105,485	406,085	107,851	108,486	113,242
Math and computer sciences	40,996	43,269	47,424	49,364	50,661	51,657	51,936	54,155	54,720
Social and behavioral sciences	112,995	110,922	111,623	111,740	113,727	115,920	120,585	125,328	132,871
Engineering	91,111	92,780	96,160	102,140	103,889	103,159	104,319	107,329	114,407
White enrollment									
Total science and engineering	225,313	223,420	224,177	227,998	229,011	229,950	231,001	237,686	245,172
Natural sciences	74,538	74,244	72,170	71,885	69,496	69,169	68,545	68,341	69,989
Math and computer sciences	23,762	23,942	25,367	26,015	26,799	27,653	26,634	27,864	27,119
Social and behavioral sciences	78,318	75,809	76,249	77,017	79,000	80,621	84,244	88,357	93,044
Engineering	48,695	49,425	50,391	53,081	53,716	52,507	51,578	53,124	55,020
Asian enrollment									
Total science and engineering	9,368	10,185	12,024	12,788	14,590	15,182	15,682	17,039	18,217
Natural sciences	2,389	2,535	2,727	2,771	3,061	3,450	3,581	3,874	4,305
Math and computer sciences	1,663	1,816	2,475	2,767	3,232	3,446	3,449	3,679	3,704
Social and behavioral sciences	1,911	2,019	2,010	2,127	2,441	2,370	2,659	2,789	3,005
Engineering	3,405	3,815	4,812	5,123	5,856	5,916	5,993	6,697	7,203
Black enrollment									
Total science and engineering	10,980	10,724	10,534	10,471	10,443	11,216	11,800	12,635	13,696
Natural sciences	1,983	2,004	1,993	1,839	1,821	1,980	2,097	2,137	2,311
Math and computer sciences	967	954	1,017	1,135	1,191	1,247	1,299	1,472	1,605
Social and behavioral sciences	6,637	6,306	6,115	6,024	6,009	6,469	6,765	7,228	7,746
Engineering	1,393	1,460	1,409	1,473	1,422	1,520	1,639	1,798	2,034
Hispanic enrollment									
Total science and engineering	8,901	8,692	8,623	8,659	8,812	9,093	9,464	10,132	11,168
Natural sciences	1,922	1,895	2,097	2,123	2,075	2,230	2,394	2,360	2,576
Math and computer sciences	612	584	743	715	810	845	851	920	978
Social and behavioral sciences	4,926	4,713	4,303	4,218	4,199	4,301	4,508	4,960	5,435
Engineering	1,441	1,500	1,480	1,603	1,728	1,717	1,711	1,892	2,179
Native American enrollment									
Total science and engineering	915	831	740	746	786	926	864	1,048	1,201
Natural sciences	224	207	169	198	183	220	180	251	329
Math and computer sciences	53	70	78	51	75	72	75	63	62
Social and behavioral sciences	457	362	371	366	404	490	485	583	621
Engineering	181	192	122	131	124	144	124	151	189
Foreign citizen enrollment									
Total science and engineering	70,381	72,297	76,853	84,035	88,806	93,849	98,272	101,835	108,408
Natural sciences	18,286	18,853	20,360	22,729	24,487	26,220	28,166	29,478	31,342
Math and computer sciences	10,502	11,552	12,803	13,816	14,857	15,422	16,337	17,356	18,021

[Continued]

★ 382 ★

Science and Engineering Graduate Students, by Field and Race/Ethnicity, 1983-91

[Continued]

Field	1983	1984	1985	1986	1987	1988	1989	1990	1991
Social and behavioral sciences	14,105	14,006	14,836	15,479	16,082	16,878	16,959	17,034	17,726
Engineering	27,488	27,886	28,854	32,011	33,380	35,329	36,810	37,967	41,319

Source: National Science Board. *Science & Engineering Indicators—1993* (NSB 93-1). Washington, DC: U.S. Government Printing Office, 1993, p. 279. Primary source: Science resources Studies Division, National Science Foundation, *Academic Science and Engineering, Graduate Enrollment and Support, Fall 1991*, Detailed Statistical Tables, NSF 93-309 (washington, DC: NSF, 1993). *Notes:* The natural sciences include all physical, environmental, biological, and agricultural sciences. The social and behavioral sciences include psychology, sociology, and other social sciences.

★ 383 ★

Higher Education Enrollment

Tribally Controlled Community Colleges, Enrollment 1980-1990

Numbers show full-time equivalent enrollment from 1980-1990.

	Fiscal years										
	1980	1981	1982	1983	1984	1985	1986	1987	1988	1989	1990
Blackfeet	83	184	211	176	179	174	207	213	263	315	268
Cheyenne	-	-	66	73	52	45	42	49	61	75	66
D-Q University	76	91	99	100	107	112	108	112	121	127	91
Dull Knife	93	73	104	146	190	178	95	100	116	155	106
Fond du Lac	-	-	-	-	-	-	-	-	-	115	162
Fort Belknap	-	-	-	-	-	76	85	89	114	123	120
Fort Berthold	-	46	49	41	63	61	106	113	115	120	145
Fort Peck	-	52	60	50	57	59	100	126	180	176	221
Lac Courte Oreilles	-	-	-	-	57	66	85	79	136	150	180
Little Big Horn	-	-	32	81	95	80	84	92	100	100	211
Little Hoop	35	21	41	39	57	66	83	85	86	100	238
Lummi (NWIC)	-	40	33	26	77	104	150	175	243	421	471
Nebraska	109	128	183	162	149	146	157	144	132	88	166
Oglala	282	282	331	371	421	480	467	473	710	701	629
Salish Kootenai	90	118	162	190	182	179	268	272	342	353	369
Sinte Gleska	173	197	181	194	252	269	291	278	316	373	339
Sisseton-Wapeton	-	72	84	71	116	126	110	87	81	105	123
Standing Rock	111	142	147	172	214	225	227	215	242	217	230
Stone Child	-	-	-	-	-	-	-	123	135	135	156
Turtle Mountain	107	159	198	172	191	225	259	240	300	338	376
Bay Mills[1]	-	-	-	-	-	-	-	-	-	65	169
Ganado[1]	131	84	49	130	157	182	135	-	-	-	-

Source: Walke, Roger. *Federal Programs of Assistance to Native Americans: A Report Prepared for the Senate Select Committee on Indian Affairs of the United States Senate.* Washington, DC: U.S. Government Printing Office, December 1991, p. 164. *Note:* 1. Ganado closed Fall 1986; Bay Mills Community College joined in 1989.

Higher Education Degrees

★ 384 ★

Bachelor's Degrees Conferred, by Sex and Race/Ethnicity, 1976-92

Distribution of bachelor's degrees awarded in each academic year is shown in percent, by sex and race/ethnicity.

Year and sex of student	Percentage distribution of degrees conferred						
	Total	White, non-Hispanic	Black, non-Hispanic	Hispanic	Asian or Pacific Islander	American Indian/ Alaskan Native	Non-resident alien
1976-77							
Total[1]	100.0	88.0	6.4	2.0	1.5	0.4	1.7
Men	100.0	88.6	5.1	2.1	1.5	0.4	2.3
Women	100.0	87.3	7.9	2.0	1.5	0.4	1.0
1978-79							
Total[2]	100.0	87.3	6.6	2.2	1.7	0.4	1.9
Men	100.0	87.8	5.2	2.2	1.7	0.4	2.7
Women	100.0	86.7	8.0	2.2	1.6	0.4	1.1
1980-81							
Total[3]	100.0	86.4	6.5	2.3	2.0	0.4	2.4
Men	100.0	86.5	5.2	2.3	2.2	0.4	3.5
Women	100.0	86.2	7.8	2.4	1.9	0.4	1.3
1984-85							
Total[4]	100.0	85.3	5.9	2.7	2.6	0.4	3.0
Men	100.0	85.1	4.8	2.6	2.8	0.4	4.2
Women	100.0	85.5	7.0	2.7	2.4	0.5	1.9
1986-87							
Total[5]	100.0	84.9	5.7	2.7	3.3	0.4	3.0
Men	100.0	84.6	4.7	2.7	3.6	0.4	4.1
Women	100.0	85.2	6.7	2.8	3.0	0.4	1.9
1988-89							
Total[6]	100.0	84.6	5.7	2.9	3.7	0.4	2.7
Men	100.0	84.5	4.6	2.9	4.0	0.4	3.6
Women	100.0	84.7	6.7	3.0	3.4	0.4	1.8
1989-90							
Total[7]	100.0	84.3	5.8	3.1	3.7	0.4	2.5
Men	100.0	84.3	4.7	3.0	4.0	0.4	3.5
Women	100.0	84.3	6.8	3.2	3.5	0.5	1.7
1990-91							
Total[8]	100.0	83.6	6.0	3.4	3.8	0.4	2.7
Men	100.0	83.7	4.9	3.3	4.2	0.4	3.6
Women	100.0	83.5	7.0	3.5	3.6	0.4	1.9
1991-92							
Total[9]	100.0	82.9	6.4	3.6	4.1	0.5	2.5

[Continued]

★ 384 ★

Bachelor's Degrees Conferred, by Sex and Race/Ethnicity, 1976-92
[Continued]

Year and sex of student	Percentage distribution of degrees conferred						
	Total	White, non-Hispanic	Black, non-Hispanic	Hispanic	Asian or Pacific Islander	American Indian/ Alaskan Native	Non-resident alien
Men	100.0	83.1	5.2	3.5	4.5	0.4	3.2
Women	100.0	82.7	7.4	3.7	3.8	0.5	1.8

Source: U.S. Department of Education. National Center for Education Statistics. Office of Educational Research and Improvement. *Digest of Education Statistics, 1994.* Lanham, MD: Bernan, November 1994, p. 278. Primary source: U.S. Department of Education, National Center for Education Statistics, "Degrees and Other Formal Awards Conferred" surveys, and Integrated Postsecondary Education Data System (IPEDS), "Completions" surveys. (This table was prepared March 1994.) *Notes:* Some data have been revised from previously published data. 1. Excludes 1,121 men and 528 women whose racial/ethnic group was not available. 2. Excludes 1,279 men and 571 women whose racial/ethnic group was not available. 3. Excludes 258 men and 82 women whose racial/ethnic group was not available. 4. Exclude 6,380 men and 4,786 women whose racial/ethnic group was not available. 5. Reported racial/ethnic distributions of students by level of degree, field of degree, and sex were used to estimate race/ethnicity for students whose race/ethnicity was not reported. 6. Reported racial/ethnic distributions of students by level of degree, field of degree, and sex were used to estimate race/ethnicity for students whose race/ethnicity was not reported. Excludes 1,400 men and 1,005 women whose racial/ethnic group and field of study were not available. 7. Reported racial/ethnic distributions of students by level of degree, field of degree, and sex were used to estimate race/ethnicity for students whose race/ethnicity was not reported. Excludes 1,379 men and 1,334 women whose racial/ethnic group and field of study were not available. 8. Reported racial/ethnic distributions of students by level of degree, field of degree, and sex were used to estimate race/ethnicity for students whose race/ethnicity was not reported. Excludes 7,621 men and 5,637 women whose racial/ethnic group and field of study were not available. 9. Reported racial/ethnic distributions of students by level of degree, field of degree, and sex were used to estimate race/ethnicity for students whose race/ethnicity was not reported. Excludes 3,835 men and 2,885 women whose racial/ethnic group and field of study were not available.

★ 385 ★

Higher Education Degrees

Master's Degrees Conferred, 1978-89

Figures show the total number of degrees conferred, the number of American Indian/Alaska Natives receiving degrees, and the percent received by American Indian/Alaska Natives are shown for selected years, from 1978 to 1989.

Year	Total degrees conferred	American Indian/Alaska Natives receiving degrees	% received by American Indian/ Alaska Natives
1988-89	308,872	1,133	.37
1986-87	289,341	1,104	.39
1984-85	280,421	1,256	.45
1980-81	294,183	1,034	.35
1978-79	301,707	999	.33

Source: National Advisory Council on Indian Education. *Toward the Year 2000: Listening to the Voice of Native America,* 17th Annual Report to the United States Congress, Fiscal Year 1990, p. 81.

★ 386 ★

Higher Education Degrees

Master's Degree Distribution, by Race/Ethnicity, 1976-92

Distribution of degrees awarded in each academic year is shown in percent, by sex and race/ethnicity.

Year and sex of student	Percentage of degrees conferred						
	Total	White, non-Hispanic	Black, non-Hispanic	Hispanic	Asian or Pacific Islander	American Indian/ Alaskan Native	Non-resident alien
1976-77							
Total[1]	100.0	84.0	6.6	1.9	1.6	0.3	5.5
Men	100.0	83.25	4.6	2.0	1.9	0.3	8.1
Women	100.0	85.0	8.9	1.9	1.3	0.3	2.6
1978-79							
Total[2]	100.0	83.0	6.5	1.9	1.8	0.3	6.5
Men	100.0	81.3	4.6	1.8	2.2	0.3	9.8
Women	100.0	84.9	8.4	1.9	1.5	0.3	3.1
1980-81							
Total[3]	100.0	82.0	5.8	2.2	2.1	0.4	7.5
Men	100.0	79.3	4.2	2.1	2.6	0.3	11.4
Women	100.0	84.6	7.4	2.3	1.7	0.4	3.7
1984-85							
Total[4]	100.0	79.7	5.0	2.4	2.8	0.4	9.6
Men	100.0	76.1	3.7	2.2	3.5	0.4	14.1
Women	100.0	83.4	6.2	2.7	2.1	0.5	5.2
1986-87							
Total[5]	100.0	79.1	4.8	2.4	3.0	0.4	10.3
Men	100.0	74.7	3.6	2.4	3.7	0.4	15.2
Women	100.0	83.3	5.9	2.5	2.2	0.4	5.7
1988-89							
Total[6]	100.0	78.4	4.6	2.3	3.3	0.4	11.0
Men	100.0	73.7	3.5	2.2	4.1	0.3	16.2
Women	100.0	82.7	5.5	2.5	2.7	0.4	6.3
1989-90							
Total[7]	100.0	78.1	4.8	2.5	3.3	0.3	11.1
Men	100.0	73.8	3.6	2.3	3.9	0.3	16.0
Women	100.0	81.9	5.8	2.6	2.7	0.4	6.6
1990-91							
Total[8]	100.0	77.7	4.9	2.6	3.4	0.3	11.1
Men	100.0	73.3	3.8	2.4	4.2	0.3	16.1
Women	100.0	81.5	5.9	2.7	2.7	0.4	6.8
1991-92							
Total[9]	100.0	77.0	5.2	2.7	3.6	0.4	11.2

[Continued]

★ 386 ★

Master's Degree Distribution, by Race/Ethnicity, 1976-92
[Continued]

Year and sex of student	Percentage of degrees conferred						
	Total	White, non-Hispanic	Black, non-Hispanic	Hispanic	Asian or Pacific Islander	American Indian/ Alaskan Native	Non-resident alien
Men	100.0	72.8	3.8	2.6	4.4	0.3	16.1
Women	100.0	80.5	6.4	2.8	3.0	0.4	7.0

Source: U.S. Department of Education. National Center for Education Statistics. Office of Educational Research and Improvement. *Digest of Education Statistics, 1994.* Lanham, MD: Bernan, November 1994, p. 281. Primary source: U.S. Department of Education, National Center for Education Statistics, "Degrees and Other Formal Awards Conferred" surveys, and Integrated Postsecondary Education Data System (IPEDS), "Completions" survey. (This table was prepared March 1994.) *Notes:* Some data have been revised from previously published figures. 1. Excludes 387 men and 175 women whose racial/ethnic group was not available. 2. Excludes 733 men and 91 women whose racial/ ethnic group was not available. 3. Excludes 1,377 men and 179 women whose racial/ethnic group was not available. 4. Excludes 3,973 men and 1,857 women whose racial/ethnic group was not available. 5. Reported racial/ethnic distributions of students by level of degree, field of degree, and sex were used to estimate race/ethnicity for students whose race/ethnicity was not reported. 6. Reported racial/ethnic distributions of students by level of degree, field of degree, and sex were used to estimate race/ethnicity for students whose race/ethnicity was not reported. Excludes 482 men and 369 women whose racial/ethnic group and field of study were not available. 7. Reported racial/ ethnic distributions of students by level of degree, field of degree, and sex were used to estimate race/ethnicity for students whose race/ ethnicity was not reported. Excludes 727 men and 1,109 women whose racial/ethnic group and field of study were not available. 8. Reported racial/ethnic distributions of students by level of degree, field of degree, and sex were used to estimate race/ethnicity for students whose race/ethnicity was not reported. Excludes 4,686 men and 3,837 women whose racial/ethnic group and field of study were not available. 9. Reported racial/ethnic distributions of students by level of degree, field of degree, and sex were used to estimate race/ethnicity for students whose race/ethnicity was not reported. Excludes 2,299 men and 1,857 women whose racial/ethnic group and field of study were not available.

★ 387 ★

Higher Education Degrees

Master's Degrees Conferred, by Major Field of Study, 1991-92

The number of degrees conferred is shown by major field of study and race/ethnicity for the 1991-92 academic year.

Major field of study	Total	White, non-Hispanic	Black, non-Hispanic	Hispanic	Asian/ Pacific Islander	American Indian/ Alaskan Native	Nonresident alien
All fields, total[1]	348,682	268,371	18,116	9,358	12,658	1,273	38,906
Agricultural and natural resources	3,735	2,546	82	61	74	7	965
Architecture and related programs	3,640	2,530	135	121	191	10	653
Area, ethnic, and cultural studies	1,385	957	91	86	69	16	166
Biological/life sciences	4,785	3,404	156	141	276	13	795
Business management and administrative svcs.	84,642	65,320	3,966	1,944	3,635	220	9,557
Communications	4,180	3,109	258	78	110	15	610
Communications technologies	284	170	18	5	9	0	82
Computer and information sciences	9,530	4,678	334	158	1,171	16	3,173
Education	92,668	78,874	6,444	2,838	1,192	457	2,863
Engineering	24,983	13,640	498	521	2,377	45	7,902
Engineering-related technologies	994	728	52	20	55	6	133
English language and literature/letters	7,450	6,462	220	152	146	37	433
Foreign languages and literature	2,926	1,896	37	280	101	6	606
Health professions and related sciences	23,065	19,220	1,136	559	739	94	1,317
Home economics and vocational home economics	2,412	1,920	121	61	45	6	259
Law and legal studies	2,369	1,253	46	76	77	2	915

[Continued]

★ 387 ★

Master's Degrees Conferred, by Major Field of Study, 1991-92

[Continued]

Major field of study	Total	White, non-Hispanic	Black, non-Hispanic	Hispanic	Asian/ Pacific Islander	American Indian/ Alaskan Native	Nonresident alien
Liberal arts and sciences, general studies, and humanities	2,394	2,057	107	48	36	8	138
Library science	4,893	4,230	159	106	148	8	242
Mathematics	4,011	2,523	84	64	216	4	1,120
Multi/interdisciplinary studies	2,126	1,721	87	60	63	8	187
Parks, recreation, leisure and fitness studies	1,358	1,191	49	32	11	2	73
Philosophy and religion	1,146	931	50	26	39	7	93
Physical sciences and science technologies	5,374	3,296	105	91	318	19	1,545
Precision production trades	0	0	0	0	0	0	0
Protective services	1,249	973	182	35	15	6	38
Psychology	10,215	8,737	562	379	194	41	302
Public administration & services	19,243	15,231	2,001	771	422	124	694
Social sciences and history	12,702	9,034	602	301	396	50	2,319
Theological studies/religious vocations	5,185	4,085	240	116	189	12	543
Transportation and material moving	385	340	22	9	8	3	3
Visual and performing arts	9,353	7,315	272	219	336	31	1,180

Source: U.S. Department of Education. National Center for Education Statistics. Office of Educational Research and Improvement. *Digest of Education Statistics, 1994.* Lanham, MD: Bernan, November 1994, p. 279. Primary source: U.S. Department of Education, National Center for Education Statistics, Integrated Postsecondary Education Data System (IPEDS), "Completions" survey. (This table was prepared April 1994.) *Notes:* To facilitate trend comparisons, certain aggregations have been made of the degree fields as reported in the IPEDS "Completions" survey: "Agriculture and natural resources" includes Agribusiness and agriculture production, Agricultural sciences, and Conservation and renewable natural resources; "Business and management and administrative services" includes Business and management, Business and office, Marketing and distribution, and Consumer and personal services. 1. Reported racial/ethnic distributions of students by level of degree, field of degree, and sex were used to estimate race/ethnicity for students whose race/ethnicity was not reported. Excludes 2,299 men and 1,857 women whose racial/ethnic group and field of study were not available.

★ 388 ★

Higher Education Degrees

Doctoral Degrees Conferred, 1978-89

Figures show the total number of degrees conferred, the number of American Indian/Alaska Natives receiving degrees, and the percentage received by American Indian/Alaska Natives is shown for selected years, from 1978 to 1989.

Year	Total degrees conferred	American Indian/ Alaska Natives receiving degrees	% received by American Indian/ Alaska Natives
1988-89	35,692	84	.23
1986-87	34,033	104	.30
1984-85	32,307	119	.37
1980-81	32,839	130	.40
1978-79	32,664	104	.32

Source: National Advisory Council on Indian Education. *Toward the Year 2000: Listening to the Voice of Native America,* 17th Annual Report to the United States Congress, Fiscal Year 1990, p. 81.

★ 389 ★

Higher Education Degrees

Doctoral Degrees Awarded, 1982 and 1992

| Total - 24,391 |
| White - 21,680 |
| African American - 1,057 |
| Hispanic - 535 |
| Asian American - 452 |
| Native American - 77 |

Chart shows data from column 1.

The number of American Indians earning Ph.D.s nearly doubled between 1982 and 1992. Data show number of doctorates awarded to U.S. citizens, by race/ethnicity of recipient.

Race/ethnicity	1982	1992
Total	24,391	25,759
White	21,680	22,718
African American	1,057	951
Hispanic	535	755
Asian American	452	828
Native American	77	148

Source: "Students of color earn more Ph.D.s". *Higher Education & National Affairs, ACE* (10 January 1994), p. 3. Primary source: Cecelia Ottinger, Robin Sikula, and Charles Washington, *Production of Minority Doctorates*, ACE Research Brief Series, Vol. 4, no. 8, 1993.

★ 390 ★

Higher Education Degrees

Doctoral Degrees Conferred, by Major Field of Study, 1991-92

The number of degrees conferred is shown by major field of study and race/ethnicity for the 1991-92 academic year.

Major field of study	Total	White, non-Hispanic	Black, non-Hispanic	Hispanic	Asian/ Pacific Islander	American Indian/ Alaskan Native	Nonresident alien
All fields, total[1]	1,129,833	936,771	72,326	40,761	46,720	5,176	28,079
Agricultural and natural resources	15,124	13,743	413	296	300	83	289
Architecture and related programs	8,753	7,050	294	407	551	33	418
Area, ethnic, and cultural studies	5,342	3,875	517	355	382	48	165
Biological/life sciences	42,941	33,179	2,428	1,673	4,488	185	988
Business management and administrative svcs.	256,603	209,768	18,304	8,466	10,592	949	8,524
Communications	54,257	46,554	3,970	1,650	1,088	177	818
Communication technologies	720	588	99	14	6	2	11
Computer and information sciences	24,557	17,311	2,147	901	2,140	81	1,977
Construction trades	67	52	11	1	1	1	1
Education	108,006	97,460	5,226	3,116	977	654	573
Engineering	61,206	45,923	2,406	2,087	6,387	186	4,217
Engineering-related technologies	16,190	13,071	1,174	558	794	88	505

[Continued]

★ 390 ★

Doctoral Degrees Conferred, by Major Field of Study, 1991-92
[Continued]

Major field of study	Total	White, non-Hispanic	Black, non-Hispanic	Hispanic	Asian/ Pacific Islander	American Indian/ Alaskan Native	Nonresident alien
English language and literature/letters	54,951	48,543	2,658	1,623	1,447	222	458
Foreign languages and literature	13,903	11,157	427	1,426	480	46	367
Health professions and related sciences	61,720	52,281	4,222	1,765	2,261	332	859
Home economics and vocational home economics	14,898	12,980	868	340	425	67	218
Law and legal studies	2,144	1,835	149	69	67	16	8
Liberal arts and sciences, general studies, and humanities	32,174	26,457	2,670	1,581	817	205	444
Library science	97	85	5	1	2	0	4
Mathematics	14,783	11,906	916	455	868	46	592
Mechanics and repairers	78	70	4	1	1	0	2
Multi/interdisciplinary studies	20,647	16,853	1,290	957	1,056	126	365
Parks, recreation, leisure and fitness studies	8,446	7,679	393	181	85	38	70
Philosophy and religion	7,526	6,559	311	229	276	27	124
Physical sciences and science technologies	16,960	14,044	836	382	1,025	66	607
Precision production trades	378	303	42	2	11	6	14
Protective services	18,855	14,574	2,699	1,075	262	135	110
Psychology	63,513	53,242	4,271	2,827	319	660	
Public administration & services	15,987	12,169	2,369	798	302	174	175
Military sciences	184	149	20	14	0	1	0
Social sciences and history	133,974	110,086	9,188	5,808	5,470	606	2,816
Theological studies/religious vocations	4,729	4,143	159	102	136	21	168
Transportation and material moving	3,598	3,156	174	123	55	28	62
Visual and performing arts	46,522	39,926	1,666	1,478	1,774	208	1,470

Source: U.S. Department of Education. National Center for Education Statistics. Office of Educational Research and Improvement. *Digest of Education Statistics, 1994.* Lanham, MD: Bernan, November 1994, p. 285. Primary source: U.S. Department of Education, National Center for Education Statistics, Integrated Postsecondary Education Data System (IPEDS), "Completions" survey. (This table was prepared April 1994.) *Notes:* To facilitate trend comparisons, certain aggregations have been made of the degree fields as reported in the IPEDS "Completions" survey: "Agriculture and natural resources" includes Agribusiness and agriculture production, Agricultural sciences, and Conservation and renewable natural resources; "Business and management and administrative services" includes Business and management, Business and office, Marketing and distribution, and Consumer and personal services. 1. Reported racial/ethnic distributions of students by level of degree, field of degree, and sex were used to estimate race/ethnicity for students whose race/ethnicity was not reported. Excludes 389 men and 180 women whose racial/ethnic group and field of study were not available.

★ 391 ★

Higher Education Degrees

First-Professional Degrees Conferred, 1978-89

Figures show the total number of degrees conferred, the number of American Indian/Alaska Natives receiving degrees, and the percentage received by American Indian/Alaska Natives is shown for selected years, from 1978 to 1989.

Year	Total degrees conferred	AI/AN's receiving degrees	Percent received by AI/AN's
1988-89	70,758	268	.38
1986-87	71,617	304	.42
1984-85	75,057	248	.33
1980-81	71,340	192	.27
1978-79	68,503	216	.32

Source: National Advisory Council on Indian Education. *Toward the Year 2000: Listening to the Voice of Native America,* 17th Annual Report to the United States Congress, Fiscal Year 1990, p. 82.

★ 392 ★

Higher Education Degrees

First-Professional Degrees Conferred, by Race/Ethnicity

The percentage of American Indians and Alaska Natives receiving first-professional degrees in the U.S. has remained well below one percent over the past fifteen years. Figures show the number of degrees conferred and percent distribution by race and ethnicity for both men and women from 1976 through 1992.

Year and sex of student	Total (number)	Percent distribution					
		White, non-Hispanic	Black, non-Hispanic	Hispanic	Asian or Pacific Islander	American Indian/Alaskan Native	Nonresident alien
1976-77, total[1]	63,953	91.4	4.0	1.7	1.6	0.3	1.1
Men	51,980	91.9	3.4	1.7	1.5	0.3	1.2
Women	11,973	88.9	6.5	1.5	2.0	0.3	0.7
1978-79, total[2]	68,611	91.0	4.1	1.9	1.8	0.3	0.9
Men	52,425	91.8	3.4	1.9	1.6	0.3	1.0
Women	16,186	88.4	6.5	1.8	2.1	0.4	0.7
1980-81, total[3]	71,340	90.5	4.1	2.2	2.0	0.3	0.9
Men	52,194	91.3	3.4	2.2	1.9	0.3	1.0
Women	19,146	88.4	6.1	2.1	2.4	0.3	0.7
1984-84, total[4]	71,057	89.0	4.3	2.7	2.6	0.3	1.2
Men	47,501	89.7	3.4	2.6	2.4	0.4	1.4
Women	23,556	87.4	6.0	2.7	2.8	0.3	0.8
1986-87, total	71,617	87.5	4.8	2.9	3.2	0.4	1.2
Men	46,523	88.4	3.9	2.8	3.1	0.4	1.4
Women	25,094	85.8	6.3	3.0	3.4	0.5	1.0
1988-89, total	70,856	86.4	4.4	3.2	4.2	0.4	1.4
Men	45,046	87.5	3.6	3.1	4.0	0.3	1.5
Women	25,810	84.5	5.9	3.5	4.5	0.4	1.2

[Continued]

★ 392 ★

First-Professional Degrees Conferred, by Race/Ethnicity

[Continued]

Year and sex of student	Total (number)	Percent distribution					
		White, non-Hispanic	Black, non-Hispanic	Hispanic	Asian or Pacific Islander	American Indian/Alaskan Native	Nonresident alien
1989-90, total[5]	70,744	85.2	4.8	3.4	4.8	0.4	1.5
Men	43,778	86.5	3.8	3.3	4.5	0.3	1.6
Women	26,966	83.0	6.4	3.6	5.2	0.5	1.3
1990-91, total[6]	71,515	84.4	5.0	3.5	5.3	0.4	1.5
Men	43,601	85.7	3.8	3.5	5.0	0.3	1.7
Women	27,914	82.3	6.8	3.7	5.6	0.4	1.1
1991-92, total[7]	72,129	82.9	4.9	3.8	6.2	0.4	1.7
Men	43,812	84.3	3.7	3.7	5.9	0.4	2.0
Women	28,317	80.7	6.9	4.0	6.6	0.5	1.3

Source: U.S. Department of Education. National Center for Education Statistics. Office of Educational Research and Improvement. *Digest of Education Statistics, 1994.* Lanham, MD: Bernan, November 1994, p. 287. U.S. Department of Education, National Center for Education Statistics, "Degrees and Other Formal Awards Conferred" survey, and Integrated Postsecondary Education Data System (IPEDS), "Completions" survey. (this table was prepared April 1994.) *Notes:* For years 1984-85, reported distributions of students by level of degree, field of degree, and sex were used to estimate race/ethnicity for students whose race/ethnicity was not reported. 1. Excludes 394 men and 12 women whose racial/ethnic group was not available. 2. Excludes 227 men and 10 women whose racial/ethnic group was not available. 3. Excludes 598 men and 18 women whose racial/ethnic group was not available. 4. Excludes 2,954 men and 1,052 women whose racial/ethnic group was not available. 5. Excludes 183 men and 61 women whose racial/ethnic group was not available. 6. Excludes 245 men and 188 women whose racial/ethnic group was not available. 7. Excludes 1,259 men and 758 women whose racial/ethnic group was not available.

★ 393 ★

Higher Education Degrees

Science and Engineering Bachelor's Degrees, 1977-91

Data show number of degrees earned in each field, by race/ethnicity of recipient, for each year.

Race/ethnicity and field	1977	1979	1981	1985	1987	1989	1990	1991
Total								
All degrees	928,228	931,340	946,877	990,877	1,003,532	1,030,171	1,062,151	1,107,997
Science and engineering	374,579	373,431	374,693	355,253	355,873	351,150	360,242	371,658
Natural sciences[1]	98,342	96,186	90,254	75,670	68,929	63,073	62,865	65,401
Math and computer sciences	20,729	20,670	26,406	54,388	56,442	46,277	42,369	40,194
Social and behavioral sciences[2]	205,831	193,775	182,638	147,624	156,079	174,853	190,305	203,877
Engineering	49,677	62,800	75,395	77,571	74,423	66,947	64,703	62,186
Engineering technology	NA	NA	NA	20,533	20,577	20,098	19,150	18,294

U.S. citizens and permanent residents

Race/ethnicity and field	1977	1979	1981	1985	1987	1989	1990	1991
White								
All degrees	807,857	802,665	807,509	826,356	819,477	840,326	856,686	892,363
Science and engineering	323,845	318,819	313,486	290,388	281,588	277,106	280,889	289,253
Natural sciences[1]	88,308	85,403	78,778	63,592	55,898	50,580	49,527	51,113
Math and computer sciences	18,110	17,633	22,013	43,484	42,446	33,998	30,683	28,998
Social and behavioral sciences[2]	175,355	163,132	151,839	122,320	126,753	142,447	153,185	163,980
Engineering	42,072	52,651	60,856	60,992	56,491	50,081	47,494	45,162
Engineering technology	NA	NA	NA	16,673	16,541	16,156	15,251	14,279

[Continued]

★ 393 ★

Science and Engineering Bachelor's Degrees, 1977-91
[Continued]

Race/ethnicity and field	1977	1979	1981	1985	1987	1989	1990	1991
Asian								
All degrees	13,907	15,542	18,908	25,562	31,921	37,573	38,027	41,725
Science and engineering	6,558	7,591	9,572	13,454	17,114	19,383	19,698	20,860
Natural sciences[1]	1,935	2,227	2,406	2,880	3,641	3,973	4,308	4,670
Math and computer sciences	479	587	1,061	2,929	3,489	3,287	3,018	2,925
Social and behavioral sciences[2]	2,933	2,919	3,039	3,163	4,394	6,048	6,360	7,045
Engineering	1,211	1,858	3,066	4,482	5,590	6,075	6,012	6,220
Engineering technology	NA	NA	NA	542	807	839	755	768
Black								
All degrees	58,700	60,301	60,729	57,563	55,103	56,837	59,301	65,009
Science and engineering	23,134	23,324	23,767	18,946	18,955	19,273	20,074	21,943
Natural sciences[1]	3,416	3,541	3,561	3,096	2,870	2,756	2,815	3,026
Math and computer sciences	1,073	1,159	1,371	2,913	3,654	3,249	2,967	2,808
Social and behavioral sciences[2]	17,260	16,849	16,386	10,898	10,116	11,201	12,220	13,880
Engineering	1,385	1,775	2,449	2,039	2,315	2,067	2,072	2,229
Engineering technology	NA	NA	NA	1,277	1,269	1,208	1,200	1,227
Hispanic								
All degrees	27,043	29,719	33,167	36,391	38,196	41,361	43,864	49,027
Science and engineering	11,002	12,163	13,107	12,848	13,182	14,177	14,896	16,290
Natural sciences[1]	2,271	2,634	2,958	2,979	2,964	2,849	2,859	3,010
Math and computer sciences	435	495	688	1,380	1,696	1,568	1,498	1,695
Social and behavioral sciences[2]	7,006	7,479	7,641	6,302	5,968	7,199	8,028	9,019
Engineering	1,290	1,555	1,820	2,187	2,554	2,561	2,511	2,566
Engineering technology	NA	NA	NA	525	664	634	784	731
Native American								
All degrees	3,328	3,410	3,593	4,246	3,866	3,967	4,212	4,486
Science and engineering	1,368	1,411	1,430	1,500	1,409	1,361	1,416	1,519
Natural sciences[1]	338	296	298	313	259	265	262	298
Math and computer sciences	41	52	39	198	164	143	129	123
Social and behavioral sciences[2]	854	899	898	780	776	776	879	940
Engineering	135	164	195	209	210	177	146	158
Engineering technology	NA	NA	NA	103	78	105	69	75
Foreign citizens								
All degrees	15,744	17,853	22,631	29,258	28,592	26,457	26,553	29,657
Science and engineering	8,486	10,039	13,282	14,249	13,838	12,479	12,489	12,879
Natural sciences[1]	2,042	2,061	2,251	2,132	1,786	1,744	1,736	1,941
Math and computer sciences	583	741	1,233	2,879	3,233	2,678	2,590	3,741
Social and behavioral sciences[2]	2,287	2,473	2,835	3,048	2,930	2,985	3,246	3,741

[Continued]

★ 393 ★

Science and Engineering Bachelor's Degrees, 1977-91

[Continued]

Race/ethnicity and field	1977	1979	1981	1985	1987	1989	1990	1991
Engineering	3,574	4,764	6,963	6,190	5,889	5,072	4,917	4,582
Engineering technology	NA	NA	NA	1,277	986	659	727	712

Source: National Science Board. *Science & Engineering Indicators—1993* (NSB 93-1). Washington, DC: U.S. Government Printing Office, 1993, pp. 274-275. Primary source: Science Resources Studies Division, National Science foundation, *Science and Engineering Degrees, by Race/Ethnicity of Recipients: 1977-91*, Detailed Statistical Tables (Washington, DC: NSF, forthcoming). *Notes:* NA stands for data not available. Data by racial/ethnic group were collected on a biennial schedule until 1990. Data are not available by racial/ethnic group for foreign citizens on temporary visas. Data by racial/ethnic group are collected by broad fields of study only; therefore, these data cannot be adjusted to the exact field taxonomies used by the National Science Foundation. 1. The natural sciences include all physical, environmental, biological, and agricultural sciences. 2. The social and behavioral sciences include psychology, sociology, and other social sciences.

★ 394 ★

Higher Education Degrees

Science and Engineering Master's Degrees Conferred, 1977-91

Data show number of degrees earned in each field for each year.

Race/ethnicity and field	1977	1979	1981	1985	1987	1989	1990	1991
Total								
All degrees	318,241	302,075	296,798	287,213	290,532	311,050	324,947	338,498
Science and engineering	83,475	79,785	79,869	80,630	83,515	87,783	89,826	91,126
Natural sciences[1]	16,234	16,350	15,332	14,045	13,461	13,260	12,966	12,713
Math and computer sciences	6,496	6,101	6,787	9,989	11,808	12,829	13,327	12,956
Social and behavioral sciences[2]	44,494	41,824	41,034	35,661	36,189	37,959	39,548	41,450
Engineering	16,251	15,510	1,716	20,935	22,057	23,735	23,985	24,007
Engineering technology	NA	NA	NA	816	883	1,135	1,194	1,188

U.S. citizens and permanent residents

Race/ethnicity and field	1977	1979	1981	1985	1987	1989	1990	1991
White								
All degrees	266,109	249,401	241,255	223,649	216,807	230,322	236,874	247,524
Science and engineering	66,661	62,158	60,407	56,101	55,790	56,864	57,606	58,435
Natural sciences[1]	13,405	13,282	12,411	10,559	9,623	9,262	8,722	8,300
Math and computer sciences	5,256	4,625	4,708	6,176	6,729	6,818	7,020	6,705
Social and behavioral sciences[2]	36,556	34,169	33,141	27,180	26,601	27,952	29,005	30,795
Engineering	11,444	10,082	10,147	12,186	12,837	12,832	12,859	12,635
Engineering technology	NA	NA	NA	526	581	802	823	830
Asian								
All degrees	5,145	5,519	6,304	7,805	8,129	10,174	9,994	11,070
Science and engineering	2,021	2,232	2,481	3,543	3,745	4,482	4,393	4,676
Natural sciences[1]	388	469	365	450	464	545	504	532
Math and computer sciences	198	253	376	779	962	1,072	1,125	1,203
Social and behavioral sciences[2]	698	660	661	763	669	873	901	933
Engineering	737	850	1,079	1,551	1,650	1,992	1,863	2,008
Engineering technology	NA	NA	NA	25	46	40	79	60
Black								
All degrees	21,041	19,422	17,152	13,960	13,173	13,455	14,473	15,857
Science and engineering	4,197	4,042	3,695	3,152	3,223	3,151	3,559	3,825

[Continued]

★ 394 ★

Science and Engineering Master's Degrees Conferred, 1977-91
[Continued]

Race/ethnicity and field	1977	1979	1981	1985	1987	1989	1990	1991
Natural sciences[1]	351	382	351	290	301	238	225	261
Math and computer sciences	200	136	137	233	280	257	302	383
Social and behavioral sciences[2]	3,406	3,278	2,947	2,299	2,239	2,301	2,645	2,783
Engineering	240	246	260	330	403	355	387	398
Engineering technology	NA	NA	NA	37	42	55	44	47
Hispanic								
All degrees	7,071	6,470	7,439	7,730	7,781	8,133	8,495	9,684
Science and engineering	2,078	1,702	2,052	2,231	2,291	2,339	2,321	2,575
Natural sciences[1]	245	227	251	332	310	266	262	281
Math and computer sciences	91	61	102	149	183	178	169	213
Social and behavioral sciences[2]	1,491	1,199	1,414	1,404	1,286	1,427	1,444	1,613
Engineering	251	215	285	346	512	468	446	468
Engineering technology	NA	NA	NA	6	17	10	9	19
Native American								
All degrees	968	999	1,034	1,257	1,049	1,082	1,050	1,125
Science and engineering	225	246	257	313	270	302	258	294
Natural sciences[1]	48	50	33	45	23	41	31	34
Math and computer sciences	15	24	19	48	25	45	13	23
Social and behavioral sciences[2]	139	148	174	173	184	183	179	197
Engineering	23	24	31	47	38	33	35	40
Engineering technology	NA	NA	NA	2	26	2	5	3
Foreign citizens								
All degrees	17,345	19,427	22,058	26,952	28,264	32,123	34,602	37,611
Science and engineering	8,282	9,111	10,468	13,132	13,764	15,949	17,077	17,841
Natural sciences[1]	1,797	1,895	1,864	2,178	2,132	2,504	2,732	2,856
Math and computer sciences	736	937	1,368	2,394	2,903	3,418	3,598	3,878
Social and behavioral sciences[2]	2,204	2,319	2,673	2,866	2,948	3,280	3,508	3,587
Engineering	3,545	3,960	4,563	5,694	5,781	6,747	7,239	7,520
Engineering technology	NA	NA	NA	124	127	131	162	172

Source: National Science Board. *Science & Engineering Indicators—1993* (NSB 93-1). Washington, DC: U.S. Government Printing Office, 1993, pp. 282-83. Primary source: Science resources Studies Division, National Science Foundation, *Science and Engineering Degrees, by Race/Ethnicity of Recipients: 1977-91*, Detailed Statistical Tables (Washington, DC: NSF, forthcoming). *Notes:* Data by racial/ethnic group were collected on a biennial schedule until 1990. Data are not available by racial/ethnic group for foreign citizens on temporary visas. Data by racial/ethnic group are collected by broad fields of study only; therefore, these data cannot be adjusted to the exact field taxonomies used by the National Science Foundation. NA stands for not available. 1. The natural sciences include all physical, environmental, biological, and agricultural sciences. 2. The social and behavioral sciences include psychology, sociology, and other social sciences.

★ 395 ★
Higher Education Degrees

Science and Engineering Doctoral Degrees Conferred, 1977-91

Data show number of degrees awarded in each field for each year.

Race/ethnicity and field	1977	1979	1981	1985	1987	1989	1990	1991
				Total[1]				
Total								
All degrees	31,716	31,239	31,357	31,297	32,363	34,318	36,057	37,451
Science and engineering	8,016	17,872	18,258	18,935	19,890	21,727	22,857	23,979
Natural sciences[2]	6,622	7,817	7,996	8,437	8,655	9,185	9,766	10,152
Math and computer sciences	1,618	979	960	998	1,190	1,471	1,597	1,837
Social and behavioral sciences[3]	7,135	6,463	6,659	6,223	6,227	6,425	6,507	6,653
Engineering	2,633	2,494	2,528	3,166	3,712	4,544	4,893	5,212
			Total U.S. citizens and permanent residents					
Total								
All degrees	27,487	26,784	26,342	24,694	24,561	25,026	26,581	26,535
Science and engineering	14,889	14,711	14,655	14,065	14,055	14,592	15,346	15,360
Natural sciences[2]	6,427	6,604	6,641	6,634	6,450	6,628	6,942	6,898
Math and computer sciences	769	778	713	631	671	824	825	935
Social and behavioral sciences[3]	5,886	5,712	5,830	5,206	5,021	4,911	5,239	5,169
Engineering	1,799	1,617	1,471	1,594	1,913	2,229	2,340	2,358
White								
All degrees	23,654	22,396	22,470	21,297	21,116	21,569	22,862	22,604
Science and engineering	12,875	12,314	12,573	12,166	12,051	12,501	13,156	12,983
Natural sciences[2]	5,598	5,620	5,771	5,902	5,662	5,800	6,078	5,993
Math and computer sciences	671	658	610	527	548	688	711	758
Social and behavioral sciences[3]	5,177	4,879	5,099	4,549	4,383	4,287	4,531	4,444
Engineering	1,429	1,157	1,093	1,188	1,458	1,726	1,836	1,788
Asian								
All degrees	910	1,102	1,073	1,069	1,167	1,261	1,302	1,491
Science and engineering	745	884	827	809	924	981	1,006	1,157
Natural sciences[2]	342	377	344	346	369	400	411	462
Math and computer sciences	42	55	56	50	67	76	75	122
Social and behavioral sciences[3]	112	146	142	132	161	145	163	172
Engineering	249	306	285	281	327	360	357	401
Black								
All degrees	1,194	1,114	1,110	1,043	907	962	1,046	1,082
Science and engineering	344	347	346	374	319	366	371	431
Natural sciences[2]	85	84	89	100	95	105	98	108
Math and computer sciences	10	12	11	10	13	9	5	19
Social and behavioral sciences[3]	234	231	227	230	186	219	228	249
Engineering	15	20	19	34	25	33	40	55
Hispanic								
All degrees	474	539	526	634	709	694	835	843
Science and engineering	194	231	239	296	357	384	465	478
Natural sciences[2]	74	83	92	107	138	158	196	187

[Continued]

★ 395 ★

Science and Engineering Doctoral Degrees Conferred, 1977-91
[Continued]

Race/ethnicity and field	1977	1979	1981	1985	1987	1989	1990	1991
Math and computer sciences	10	12	5	18	15	15	15	20
Social and behavioral sciences[3]	88	112	126	149	170	163	200	212
Engineering	22	24	16	22	34	48	54	59
Native American								
All degrees	66	81	85	96	115	94	96	130
Science and engineering	31	29	28	41	53	53	42	56
Natural sciences[2]	14	6	8	21	20	25	12	27
Math and computer sciences	1	1	1	0	3	2	1	1
Social and behavioral sciences[3]	15	19	15	19	23	19	25	22
Engineering	1	3	4	1	7	7	4	6
Foreign citizens								
Total								
All degrees	3,448	3,587	3,940	5,228	5,610	6,647	8,074	8,852
Science and engineering	2,675	2,689	2,983	4,048	4,468	5,392	6,555	7,281
Natural sciences[2]	1,079	1,046	1,140	1,518	1,704	1,975	2,531	2,843
Math and computer sciences	170	181	226	327	445	524	695	818
Social and behavioral sciences[3]	651	645	675	784	787	952	1,056	1,147
Engineering	775	817	942	1,419	1,532	1,941	2,273	2,473
Unknown citizenship								
Total								
All degrees	781	868	1,075	1,375	2,192	2,645	1,402	2,064
Science and engineering	452	472	620	822	1,367	1,743	956	1,338
Natural sciences[2]	170	167	215	285	501	582	293	411
Math and computer sciences	25	20	21	40	74	123	77	84
Social and behavioral sciences[3]	183	225	269	344	525	664	306	462
Engineering	74	60	115	153	267	374	280	381

Source: National Science Board. *Science & Engineering Indicators—1993* (NSB 93-1). Washington, DC: U.S. Government Printing Office, 1993, p. 286-87. Primary source: Science resources Studies Division, National Science Foundation, *Science and Engineering Doctorates: 1960-91,* Detailed Statistical Tables NSF 93-301 (Washington, DC: NSF 1993). *Notes:* Data by racial/ethnic group were collected on a biennial schedule until 1990. Data are not available by racial/ethnic group for foreign citizens on temporary visas. Data by racial/ethnic group are collected by broad fields of study only; therefore, these data cannot be adjusted to the exact field taxonomies used by the National Science Foundation. 1. Includes all doctorates awarded to U.S. citizens and permanent residents, temporary residents, and persons whose citizenship is unknown. 2. The natural sciences include all physical, environmental, biological, and agricultural sciences. 3. The Social and behavioral sciences include psychology, sociology, and other social sciences.

★ 396 ★

Higher Education Degrees

Engineering Bachelor's Degree Conferrals

Conferrals of engineering degrees serve as indicators of future workforce availability. This table shows number of bachelor's degrees earned in selected years and percent change in number of degrees awarded between 1983 and 1993.

	1983	1988	1993	% chg. 1983-93
Total	72,471	71.386	65,001	-10.5
Women	9,566	10,940	10,453	801
as percent of total	13.2	15.3	16.1	
Black	1,862	2,211	2,637	35.1
as percent of total	2.6	3.1	4.1	
Hispanic[1]	1,883	2,441	2,845	39.4
as percent of total	2.6	3.4	4.4	
Asian	3,098	5,591	6,764	65.6
as percent of total	4.3	7.8	10.4	
Indian	97	187	175	41.7
as percent of total	0.1	0.3	0.3	
Foreign	6,151	5,763	4,604	-26.8
as percent of total	8.5	8.1	7.1	

Source: Manpower Comments (December 1993), p. 24. Engineering Workforce Commission. *Note:* 1. Includes 338, 516, and 546 BS from U. of Puerto Rico.

★ 397 ★

Higher Education Degrees

Engineering Master's Degree Conferrals

Conferrals of engineering degrees serve as indicators of future workforce availability. This table shows number of master's degrees earned in selected years and percent change in number of degrees awarded between 1983 and 1993.

	1983	1988	1993	% chg. 1983-93
Total	19,909	25,616	31,104	43.7
Women	1,796	3,377	4,876	91.2
as percent of total	9.0	13.2	15.7	
Black	261	365	638	13.3
as percent of total	1.3	1.4	2.1	
Hispanic	310	479	629	66.6
as percent of total	1.6	1.9	2.0	
Asian	1,294	1,785	2,512	68.2
as percent of total	6.5	7.0	8.1	
Indian	16	32	57	128.1

[Continued]

★ 397 ★

Engineering Master's Degree Conferrals
[Continued]

	1983	1988	1993	% chg. 1983-93
as percent of total	0.1	0.1	0.2	
Foreign	5,145	7,329	10,122	67.9
as percent of total	25.8	28.6	32.5	

Source: *Manpower Comments* (December 1993), p. 24. Engineering Workforce Commission.

★ 398 ★

Higher Education Degrees

Engineering Doctoral Degree Conferrals

Conferrals of engineering degrees serve as indicators of future workforce availability. This table shows number of doctoral degrees earned in selected years and percent change in number of degrees awarded between 1983 and 1993.

	1983	1988	1993	% chg. 1983-93
Total	3,023	4,571	6,198	69.5
Women	142	313	600	146.3
as percent of total	4.7	6.8	9.7	
Black	19	29	46	93.1
as percent of total	0.6	0.6	0.7	
Hispanic	41	36	55	38.9
as percent of total	1.4	0.8	0.9	
Asian	173	275	383	76.4
as percent of total	5.7	6.0	6.2	
Indian	0	3	2	66.7
as percent of total	0.0	0.1	0.0	
Foreign	1,192	2,033	3,306	104.0
as percent of total	39.4	44.5	53.3	

Source: *Manpower Comments* (December 1993), p. 24. Engineering Workforce Commission. *Note:* 1. Includes 338, 516, and 546 BS from U. of Puerto Rico.

Higher Education Faculty

★ 399 ★

Full-Time Faculty at Institutions of Higher Education, 1987 - I

Figures are shown, by the type of position and race/ethnicity, for 1987.

Selected characteristics	Number in thousands	Percent total	Public research	Private research	Public doctoral	Private doctoral	Public comprehensive
Total (in thousands)	489	-	96	39	396	15	93
Percent	-	100.0	19.7	8.0	7.3	3.0	19.0
Percent distribution							
Total	-	100.0	100.0	100.0	100.0	100.0	100.0
Race							
White, non-Hispanic	438	89.5	90.4	85.4	92.0	91.3	88.0
Black, non-Hispanic	16	3.2	1.6	6.1	1.8	0.1	3.5
Hispanic	11	2.3	2.4	5.0	1.1	2.2	2.1
Asian	21	4.2	4.8	3.5	4.5	5.9	5.8
American Indian	3	0.7	0.7	[1]	0.6	0.5	0.6

Source: U.S. Department of Education. National Center for Education Statistics. Office of Educational Research and Improvement. *Digest of Education Statistics, 1994.* Lanham, MD: Bernan, November 1994, p. 231. Primary source: U.S. Department of Education, National Center for Education Statistics, National Survey of Postsecondary Faculty (NSOPF), 1988. (This table was prepared June 1990.) *Notes:* Data may not add to totals because of rounding or missing data. A dash (-) stands for not applicable. 1. Less than 0.5 percent.

★ 400 ★

Higher Education Faculty

Full-Time Faculty at Institutions of Higher Education, 1987 - II

Figures are shown, by the type of position and race/ethnicity, for 1987.

Selected characteristics	Private comprehensive	Liberal arts	Public 2-year	Private 2-year	Medical	Other
Total (in thousands)	35	39	91	4	25	15
Percent	7.2	8.0	18.7	0.8	5.2	3.0
Percent distribution						
Total	100.0	100.0	100.0	100.0	100.0	100.0
Race						
White, non-Hispanic	91.2	86.9	91.0	94.1	85.3	95.1
Black, non-Hispanic	1.7	8.0	3.0	3.1	3.0	2.3
Hispanic	1.6	1.2	3.5	2.3	[1]	1.6
Asian	4.4	2.7	1.6	0.5	10.3	1.0
American Indian	1.1	1.2	0.9	[1]	1.4	[1]

Source: U.S. Department of Education. National Center for Education Statistics. Office of Educational Research and Improvement. *Digest of Education Statistics, 1994.* Lanham, MD: Bernan, November 1994, p. 231. Primary source: U.S. Department of Education, National Center for Education Statistics, National Survey of Postsecondary Faculty (NSOPF), 1988. (This table was prepared June 1990.) *Notes:* Data may not add to totals because of rounding or missing data. A dash (-) stands for not applicable. 1. Less than 0.5 percent.

★ 401 ★

Higher Education Faculty

Full-Time Faculty at Institutions of Higher Education, by Field, 1987-88

Figures are shown, by field and race/ethnicity, for 1987-88.

Faculty characteristics	Number in thousands	All fields	Agricultural and home economics	Business	Education	Engineering	Fine arts	Health	Humanities	Natural sciences	Social sciences	Other
Total, in thousands	489	-	13	37	35	25	32	85	62	84	53	64
Percentage	-	100.0	3.0	7.0	7.0	5.0	7.0	17.0	13.0	17.0	11.0	13.0
Percent distribution												
Total	489	100.0	100.0	100.0	100.0	100.0	100.0	100.0	100.0	100.0	100.0	100.0
Race/ethnicity												
White, non-Hispanic	438	90.0	94.0	88.0	88.0	87.0	92.0	88.0	90.0	91.0	90.0	89.0
Black, non-Hispanic	16	3.0	0.0	4.0	6.0	[1]	3.0	2.0	3.0	2.0	5.0	5.0
Hispanic	11	2.0	3.0	1.0	4.0	2.0	3.0	1.0	5.0	1.0	3.0	2.0
Asian	21	4.0	2.0	6.0	1.0	11.0	1.0	7.0	2.0	6.0	2.0	3.0
American Indian	4	1.0	1.0	1.0	1.0	[1]	[1]	1.0	1.0	[1]	1.0	1.0

Source: U.S. Department of Education. National Center for Education Statistics. Office of Educational Research and Improvement. *Digest of Education Statistics, 1994.* Lanham, MD: Bernan, November 1994, p. 232. Primary source: U.S. Department of Education, National Survey of Postsecondary Faculty (NSOPF), 1987-88. (This table was prepared April 1991.) *Notes:* Because of rounding and survey item nonresponse, details may not add to totals. A dash (-) stands for not applicable. 1. Less than 0.5 percent.

Higher Education Costs

★ 402 ★

Financial Aid Received by Undergraduates, 1989-90 - I

Figures are shown, by type of aid given and race/ethnicity of student.

Selected student characteristics	Enrollment of under-graduates[1] (000)	Any aid			Grants		
		Total[2]	Federal	Non Federal	Total	Federal	Non Federal
Percent of all undergraduates receiving aid							
All undergraduates	12,600	44.0	30.0	32.3	37.2	21.4	28.4
Race/ethnicity							
White, non-Hispanic	9,410	41.2	26.3	31.2	34.2	17.5	27.2
Black, non-Hispanic	1,142	61.2	50.0	40.5	55.3	42.2	37.0
Hispanic	840	44.2	34.4	31.6	38.7	27.6	28.1
Asian American	575	35.5	25.5	28.2	31.2	20.2	25.9
American Indian	83	51.6	31.8	44.1	46.8	27.5	38.4
Average 1989-90 award for full-time, full-year undergraduates enrolled in fall 1989							
All full-time, full-year undergraduates	3,947	4,732	3,511	2,836	3,095	1,770	2,544
Race/ethnicity							
White, non-Hispanic	3,208	4,597	3,488	2,785	2,976	1,702	2,494
Black, non-Hispanic	301	5,116	3,586	2,902	3,433	1,997	2,668
Hispanic	189	5,139	3,502	3,002	3,388	1,867	2,698
Asian American	174	5,614	3,650	3,304	3,836	1,886	2,874
American Indian	19	6,299	4,004	3,510	3,921	2,099	2,908

[Continued]

★ 402 ★

Financial Aid Received by Undergraduates, 1989-90 - I
[Continued]

Selected student characteristics	Enrollment of under- graduates[1] (000)	Any aid			Grants		
		Total[2]	Federal	Non Federal	Total	Federal	Non Federal
Average 1989-90 award for other undergraduates enrolled in fall 1989							
All other undergraduates[3]	7,285	2,798	2,728	1,577	1,715	1,370	1,324
Race/ethnicity							
White, non-Hispanic	5,465	2,699	2,758	1,544	1,619	1,341	1,282
Black, non-Hispanic	665	3,021	2,580	1,599	1,948	1,396	1,434
Hispanic	556	2,946	2,680	1,490	1,798	1,345	1,287
Asian American	339	3,624	2,904	2,274	2,388	1,654	1,758
American Indian	52	2,945	3,265	1,762	2,131	1,787	1,601

Source: U.S. Department of Education. National Center for Education Statistics. Office of Educational Research and Improvement. *Digest of Education Statistics, 1994.* Lanham, MD: Bernan, November 1994, p. 315-316. Primary source: U.S. Department of Education, National Center for Education Statistics, *National Postsecondary Student Aid Study, 1989-90.* (This table was prepared June 1992.) *Notes:* Because of rounding and/or the fact that some students receive aid from multiple sources, details may not add to totals. Because of rounding and survey nonresponse, row details may not add to totals. Data include undergraduates in noncollegiate and collegiate institutions. 1. Numbers of undergraduates may not equal figures reported in other tables, since these data are based on a sample survey. 2. Includes students who reported they were awarded aid, but did not specify the source or type of aid. 3. Enrollment data include persons whose attendance was not reported.

★ 403 ★

Higher Education Costs

Financial Aid Received by Undergraduates, 1989-90 - II

Figures are shown, by type of aid given and race/ethnicity of student.

Selected student characteristics	Loans			Work study total[3]	Other		
	Total	Federal	Non Federal		Total	Federal	Non Federal
Percent of all undergraduates receiving aid							
All undergraduates	20.4	19.3	2.3	5.4	8.2	1.8	6.5
Race/ethnicity							
White, non-Hispanic	19.1	18.0	2.4	5.2	8.3	1.8	6.7
Black, non-Hispanic	28.2	27.2	2.4	8.4	7.8	2.3	5.7
Hispanic	19.9	19.2	2.4	5.3	7.9	1.6	6.4
Asian American	14.7	13.7	2.0	5.7	6.5	1.2	5.2
American Indian	16.2	15.5	1.5	6.9	11.9	3.4	9.6
Average 1989-90 award for full-time,							
full-year undergraduates enrolled in fall 1989							
All full-time, full-year undergraduates	2,764	2,660	2,252	1,071	2,091	3,133	1,694
Race/ethnicity							
White, non-Hispanic	2,783	2,671	2,305	1,033	2,028	3,222	1,602
Black, non-Hispanic	2,543	2,501	1,565	1,143	2,442	2,443	2,348
Hispanic	2,755	2,632	2,047	1,252	1,919	3,058	1,606
Asian American	2,915	2,840	2,541	1,296	2,758	3,500	2,584
American Indian	3,361	3,387	1,610	1,182	3,362	4,404	2,893
Average 1989-90 award for other undergraduates enrolled in fall 1989							
All other undergraduates[4]	2,668	2,527	2,004	1,063	1,523	2,783	1,248
Race/ethnicity							
White, non-Hispanic	2,665	2,511	2,066	989	1,537	2,840	1,261
Black, non-Hispanic	2,558	2,521	1,510	1,048	1,609	2,381	1,334
Hispanic	2,789	2,630	1,962	1,280	1,114	3,088	710

[Continued]

★ 403 ★

Financial Aid Received by Undergraduates, 1989-90 - II
[Continued]

Selected student characteristics	Loans			Work study total[3]	Other		
	Total	Federal	Non Federal		Total	Federal	Non Federal
Asian American	2,795	2,568	2,065	1,549	1,902	2,434	1,917
American Indian	3,472	3,094	3,240	1,187	1,188	2,019	1,029

Source: U.S. Department of Education. National Center for Education Statistics. Office of Educational Research and Improvement. *Digest of Education Statistics, 1994.* Lanham, MD: Bernan, November 1994, p. 315-316. Primary source: U.S. Department of Education, National Center for Education Statistics, *National Postsecondary Student Aid Study, 1989-90.* (This table was prepared June 1992.) *Notes:* Because of rounding and/or the fact that some students receive aid from multiple sources, details may not add to totals. Because of rounding and survey nonresponse, row details may not add to totals. Data include undergraduates in noncollegiate and collegiate institutions. 1. Numbers of undergraduates may not equal figures reported in other tables, since these data are based on a sample survey. 2. Includes students who reported they were awarded aid, but did not specify the source or type of aid. 3. Details on Federal and nonfederal Work Study programs were not available. 4. Enrollment data include persons whose attendance was not reported.

Chapter 5
CULTURE AND TRADITION

~~~~~~

Language

~~~~~~

★ 404 ★

American Indian Languages Spoken at Home, by Age and Sex, 1990 - Part I

Data show number of persons speaking each language in households in the United States, for both sexes and females. Data are based on a sample and are subject to variability.

Language	Both sexes					Females				
	5 yrs. and older	5 to 17 years	18 to 54 years	55 to 64 years	65 yrs. & older	5 yrs. and older	5 to 17 years	18 to 54 years	55 to 64 years	65 yrs. & older
All American Indian languages	281,900	64,952	167,811	23,419	25,808	146,901	31,664	87,701	12,751	14,785
Algonquian languages	12,887	2,358	7,061	1,547	1,921	6,571	1,106	3,495	822	1,148
Algonquian	625	162	404	51	8	330	83	221	26	-
Arapaho	882	184	385	158	155	415	71	173	94	77
Atsina	42	5	14	8	15	19	-	5	3	8
Blackfoot	740	65	481	93	101	380	34	241	53	52
Cheyenne	1,570	144	1,087	158	181	795	64	524	96	111
Cree	775	128	416	86	145	389	50	195	52	92
Delaware	53	8	40	2	3	26	3	21	-	2
Fox	614	139	340	79	56	328	66	188	26	48
French Cree	326	50	146	44	86	163	13	67	36	47
Kickapoo	509	185	227	23	74	316	86	155	12	63
Menominee	512	251	159	32	70	276	149	80	12	35
Miami	6	-	6	-	-	6	-	6	-	-
Micmac	173	9	134	30	-	80	9	59	12	-
Ojibwa	4,518	722	2,399	638	759	2,200	327	1,131	327	415
Ottawa	308	42	168	29	69	160	4	89	19	48
Passamaquoddy	762	173	457	59	73	436	96	262	28	50
Penobscot	47	19	28	-	-	31	15	16	-	-
Potawatomi	175	52	59	19	45	84	28	19	12	25
Shawnee	107	2	44	21	40	78	-	30	9	39
Yurok	143	18	67	17	41	59	5	13	5	36
Other Algonquian languages	-	-	-	-	-	-	-	-		
Athapascan-Eyak languages	157,694	42,848	94,510	10,279	10,057	82,223	20,854	50,182	5,720	5,467

[Continued]

★ 404 ★

American Indian Languages Spoken at Home, by Age and Sex, 1990 - Part I
[Continued]

Language	Both sexes					Females				
	5 yrs. and older	5 to 17 years	18 to 54 years	55 to 64 years	65 yrs. & older	5 yrs. and older	5 to 17 years	18 to 54 years	55 to 64 years	65 yrs. & older
Ahtena	16	6	10	-	-	13	3	10	-	-
Apache languages	12,897	2,814	8,339	1,032	712	6,636	1,360	4,249	573	454
Apache	11,563	2,648	7,387	904	624	5,943	1,281	3,755	506	401
Chiricahua	259	43	194	13	9	123	20	95	4	4
Jicarilla	786	76	556	102	52	430	29	301	63	37
Kiowa-Apache	18	-	3	9	6	3	-	3	-	-
San Carlos	271	47	199	4	21	137	30	95	-	12
Athapascan	1,414	193	675	251	295	738	83	335	164	156
Chasta Costa	20	2	18	-	-	7	-	7	-	-
Han	7	-	-	-	7	7	-	-	-	7
Hupa	93	29	38	7	19	52	13	21	7	11
Koyukon	20	-	5	2	13	9	-	3	-	6
Kuchin	313	51	206	27	29	138	28	86	14	10
Navaho	142,886	39,751	85,203	8,960	8,972	74,612	19,367	45,464	4,962	4,819
Tanaina	18	-	11	-	7	6	-	2	-	4
Other Athapascan-Eyak languages	10	2	5	-	3	5	-	5	-	-
Caddoan languages	354	42	163	52	97	211	33	93	27	58
Arikara	80	9	41	6	24	48	-	30	2	16
Caddo	125	10	50	23	42	86	10	22	18	36
Pawnee	111	11	58	11	31	48	11	28	3	6
Wichita	38	12	14	12	-	29	12	13	4	-
Central and South American languages	431	144	242	33	12	158	64	79	13	2
Arawakian	19	-	19	-	-	9	-	9	-	-
Aymara	-	-	-	-	-	-	-	-	-	-
Chibchan	3	-	3	-	-	2	-	2	-	-
Mapuche	-	-	-	-	-	-	-	-	-	-
Mayan languages	190	89	89	-	12	73	39	32	-	2
Misumalpan	146	45	92	9	-	50	20	21	9	-
Oto-Manguen	24	-	-	24	-	4	-	-	4	-
Quechua	49	10	39	-	-	20	5	15	-	-
Tupi-Guarani	-	-	-	-	-	-	-	-	-	-
Haida	110	44	36	3	27	66	27	26	3	10
Hokan languages	2,430	367	1,352	281	430	1,335	221	710	140	264
Achumawi	81	30	33	-	18	40	17	23	-	-
Atsugewi	-	-	-	-	-	-	-	-	-	-
Karok	68	17	36	-	15	32	8	11	-	13
Pomo	112	4	39	30	39	41	-	30	10	11
Shastan	12	-	12	-	-	-	-	-	-	-
Washo	111	4	74	21	12	58	2	43	9	4
Yuman languages	2,046	312	1,158	230	346	1,164	194	613	121	236
Cocomaricopa	149	-	79	27	43	113	-	61	9	43
Delta River Yuman	310	51	178	36	45	163	51	76	6	30

[Continued]

★ 404 ★

American Indian Languages Spoken at Home, by Age and Sex, 1990 - Part I
[Continued]

Language	Both sexes					Females				
	5 yrs. and older	5 to 17 years	18 to 54 years	55 to 64 years	65 yrs. & older	5 yrs. and older	5 to 17 years	18 to 54 years	55 to 64 years	65 yrs. & older
Diegueno	87	16	44	5	22	59	13	25	5	16
Havasupai	396	124	224	17	31	205	66	114	7	18
Mohave	176	22	58	33	63	100	7	26	25	42
Walapai	437	69	290	38	40	222	35	147	13	27
Yavapai	163	13	86	32	32	87	13	44	16	14
Yuma	328	17	199	42	70	215	9	120	40	46
Other Yuman languages	-	-	-	-	-	-	-	-	-	-
Iroquoian languages	12,046	1,484	7,243	1,462	1,857	6,028	644	3,582	710	1,092
Cayuga	40	-	28	-	12	17	-	12	-	5
Cherokee	9,285	1,002	5,825	1,097	1,361	4,592	436	2,827	537	792
Iroquois	50	-	43	2	5	20	-	15	-	5
Mohawk	1,504	188	809	244	263	797	83	443	111	160
Oneida	314	60	114	40	100	182	33	62	14	73
Onondaga	29	15	7	-	7	9	9	-	-	-
Seneca	686	182	316	79	109	344	65	174	48	57
Tuscarora	138	37	101	-	-	67	18	49	-	-
Wyandot	-	-	-	-	-	-	-	-	-	-
Keres	8,346	1,776	5,128	639	803	4,189	832	2,549	359	449
Muskogean languages	13,772	3,027	7,419	1,529	1,797	7,202	1,433	3,918	804	1,047
Alabama	165	32	80	32	21	67	14	29	18	6
Choctaw	8,147	2,107	4,437	789	814	4,233	890	2,360	418	475
Hichita	-	-	-	-	-	-	-	-	-	-
Koasati	281	47	170	29	35	156	25	99	12	20
Mikasuki	473	143	260	35	35	290	85	157	24	24
Muskogee	4,706	698	2,472	644	892	2,456	329	1,273	332	522

Source: U.S. Bureau of the Census. *1990 Census of Population and Housing, Characteristics of American Indians by Tribe and Language,* pp. 874-875. *Note:* A dash (-) stands for zero or rounds to zero.

★ 405 ★

Language

American Indian Languages Spoken at Home, by Age and Sex, 1990 - Part II

Data show number of persons speaking each language in households in the United States, for both sexes and females. Data are based on a sample and are subject to variability.

Language	Both sexes					Females				
	5 yrs. and older	5 to 17 years	18 to 54 years	55 to 64 years	65 yrs. & older	5 yrs. and older	5 to 17 years	18 to 54 years	55 to 64 years	65 yrs. & older
Penutian languages	8,190	2,092	4,794	589	715	4,384	1,023	2,616	337	408
Chinook Jargon	17	-	12	-	5	17	-	12	-	5
Foothill North Yokuts	78	6	63	4	5	29	-	20	4	5
Klamath	80	31	24	3	22	49	14	13	-	22
Mountain Maidu	59	-	30	15	14	30	-	16	-	14
Nez Perce	644	119	349	81	95	333	56	182	36	59
Sahaptian	712	109	407	87	109	419	46	237	78	58
Sierra Miwok	65	-	45	7	13	59	-	45	7	7
Siuslaw	3	-	3	-	-	-	-	-	-	-
Tachi	25	-	9	3	13	14	-	-	3	11
Tarascan	-	-	-	-	-	-	-	-	-	-
Tsimshian	113	6	52	22	33	73	6	35	14	18
Upper Chinook	41	3	20	3	15	17	2	7	3	5
Wintun	10	-	4	-	6	4	-	-	-	4
Zuni	6,343	1,818	3,776	364	385	3,340	899	2,049	192	200
Other Penutian languages	-	-	-	-	-	-	-	-	-	-
Siouan languages	19,683	3,373	11,962	2,038	2,310	10,278	1,672	6,210	1,069	1,327
Chiwere	136	57	54	3	22	69	30	28	2	9
Crow	4,143	1,310	2,559	141	133	2,183	635	1,403	77	68
Dakota	13,387	1,679	8,302	1,577	1,829	6,985	835	4,271	802	1,077
Hidatsa	437	44	281	66	46	230	23	133	47	27
Kansa	3	-	-	-	3	-	-	-	-	-
Mandan	7	-	7	-	-	1	-	1	-	-
Omaha	450	105	229	42	74	212	46	102	26	38
Osage	101	38	45	8	10	65	21	34	-	10
Ponca	212	21	102	41	48	92	7	46	17	22
Quapaw	14	-	2	12	-	14	-	2	12	-
Winnebago	793	119	381	148	145	427	75	190	86	76
Tanoan languages	8,255	1,533	4,980	732	1,010	4,179	726	2,409	446	598
Kiowa	936	91	486	111	248	468	28	211	68	161
Picuris	101	18	47	27	9	57	4	26	23	4
Sandia	43	-	39	2	2	27	-	27	-	-
Tewa	3,447	587	2,222	292	349	1,790	302	1,099	184	205
Tiwa	2,338	451	1,367	208	312	1,173	224	667	107	175
Towa	1,390	389	819	92	90	664	168	379	64	53
Tlingit	1,088	81	455	246	306	512	27	190	105	190
Tonkawa	3	-	3	-	-	-	-	-	-	-
Uto-Aztecan languages	23,493	3,797	14,444	2,514	2,738	12,396	1,972	7,426	1,363	1,635
Aztecan	15	7	2	6	-	6	-	-	6	-
Cahuilla	35	7	14	2	12	19	4	4	2	9

[Continued]

★ 405 ★

American Indian Languages Spoken at Home, by Age and Sex, 1990 - Part II

[Continued]

Language	Both sexes					Females				
	5 yrs. and older	5 to 17 years	18 to 54 years	55 to 64 years	65 yrs. & older	5 yrs. and older	5 to 17 years	18 to 54 years	55 to 64 years	65 yrs. & older
Cupeno	9	7	2	-	-	2	-	2	-	-
Hopi	5,264	989	3,309	388	578	2,642	502	1,570	224	346
Luiseno	41	9	16	8	8	16	3	9	-	4
Numic languages	6,345	871	3,756	783	935	3,378	458	1,935	418	567
Chemehuevi	3	-	3	-	-	2	-	2	-	-
Comanche	693	111	302	111	169	409	57	166	64	122
Mono	159	24	54	9	72	68	24	5	3	36
Paiute	1,534	208	825	233	268	838	91	440	135	172
Shoshoni	2,142	251	1,350	282	259	1,101	145	654	158	144
Ute	1,184	277	1,222	148	167	960	141	668	58	93
Other Numic languages	-	-	-	-	-	-	-	-	-	-
Pima	11,449	1,845	7,181	1,262	1,161	6,168	971	3,818	680	699
Serrano	2	-	2	-	-	-	-	-	-	-
Sonoran, n.e.c.	-	-	-	-	-	-	-	-	-	-
Tubatulabal	-	-	-	-	-	-	-	-	-	-
Yaqui	333	62	162	65	44	165	34	88	33	10
Wakashan and Salish languages	1,105	305	539	68	193	663	156	315	44	148
Clallam	5	-	3	-	2	2	-	-	-	2
Coeur d'Alene	30	-	7	4	19	13	-	4	-	9
Columbia	-	-	-	-	-	-	-	-	-	-
Kalispel	4	-	2	-	2	-	-	-	-	-
Kutenai	102	29	60	3	10	69	19	39	1	10
Kwakiutl	21	7	12	-	2	14	5	7	-	2
Makah	109	36	52	6	15	53	12	31	2	8
Nootsack	12	-	12	-	-	-	-	-	-	-
Okanogan	104	18	44	10	32	72	6	36	8	22
Puget Sound Salish	81	19	25	10	27	53	8	13	8	24
Quinault	21	12	6	-	3	5	3	2	-	-
Salish	540	181	270	25	64	331	103	153	21	54
Spokane	57	3	29	10	15	35	-	16	4	15
Tillamook	3	-	3	-	-	-	-	-	-	-
Twana	14	-	14	-	-	14	-	14	-	-
Upper Chehalis	2	-	-	-	2	2	-	-	-	2
Other Wakashan and Salish languages	-	-	-	-	-	-	-	-	-	-
Yuchi	65	5	37	-	23	42	3	18	-	21
Yuki	-	-	-	-	-	-	-	-	-	-
Unspecified American Indian languages	12,038	1,676	7,443	1,407	1,512	6,464	871	3,883	789	921

Source: U.S. Bureau of the Census. *1990 Census of Population and Housing, Characteristics of American Indians by Tribe and Language.* pp. 874-875. *Note:* A dash (-) stands for zero or rounds to zero.

American Indian Languages Spoken at Home, by Region and State, 1990

Data show number of persons speaking an American Indian language at home for the United States, U.S. regions, and states. Data are based on a sample and are subject to variability.

United States, region and division, and state	Persons speaking American Indian languages at home
United States total	281,990
Region and division	
Northeast	5,195
New England	1,524
Middle Atlantic	3,671
Midwest	23,618
East North Central	4,809
West North Central	18,809
South	29,466
South Atlantic	4,181
East South Central	4,718
West South Central	20,567
West	223,711
Mountain	209,756
Pacific	13,955
State	
New England	1,524
Maine	879
New Hampshire	65
Vermont	38
Massachusetts	412
Rhode Island	66
Connecticut	64
Middle Atlantic	3,671
New York	3,213
New Jersey	273
Pennsylvania	185
East North Central	4,809
Ohio	303
Indiana	276
Illinois	676
Michigan	1,265
Wisconsin	2,289
West North Central	18,809
Minnesota	3,870
Iowa	985
Missouri	528
North Dakota	2,400

[Continued]

★ 406 ★

American Indian Languages Spoken at Home, by Region and State, 1990
[Continued]

United States, region and division, and state	Persons speaking American Indian languages at home
South Dakota	9,229
Nebraska	1,140
Kansas	657
South Atlantic	4,181
Delaware	8
Maryland	255
District of Columbia	-
Virginia	392
West Virginia	30
North Carolina	1,338
South Carolina	85
Georgia	287
Florida	1,786
East South Central	4,718
Kentucky	118
Tennessee	244
Alabama	141
Mississippi	4,215
West South Central	20,567
Arkansas	279
Louisiana	320
Oklahoma	17,235
Texas	2,733
Mountain	209,756
Montana	7,527
Idaho	1,987
Wyoming	1,513
Colorado	2,738
New Mexico	76,738
Arizona	107,373
Utah	9,645
Nevada	2,235
Pacific	13,955
Washington	2,960
Oregon	1,304
California	6,629
Alaska	3,013
Hawaii	49

Source: U.S. Bureau of the Census. *1990 Census of Population and Housing, Characteristics of American Indians by Tribe and Language.* pp. 874-875. *Note:* A dash (-) stands for zero or rounds to zero.

★ 407 ★

Language

Indigenous Languages by State

Data show the number of indigenous languages still spoken in the United States.

State	Number of languages
Oklahoma	23
California	22
Alaska	20
Washington	15
Arizona	12
New Mexico	11
Montana	9
Oregon	7
New York	6
North Dakota	6
Idaho	5
Wisconsin	5
Kansas	4
Nebraska	4

Source: Schwartz, John. "Preserving endangered speeches: researchers begin an aggressive effort to keep Native American languages alive." *The Washington Post National Weekly Edition* (21-27 March 1995), p. 38. Primary source: Michael Krauss, linguist, University of Alaska at Fairbanks.

★ 408 ★

Language

Household Language and Linguistic Isolation in Selected Alaska Native Villages

Data are shown for the 50 areas with the largest populations, in number of persons.

Alaska Native Village Statistical Area[1]	English	Spanish		Asian or Pacific Island language		Other language	
		Linguistically isolated	Not linguistically isolated	Linguistically isolated	Not linguistically isolated	Linguistically isolated	Not linguistically isolated
Akiachak	11	0	0	0	0	25	82
Akutan	19	0	0	0	0	0	8
Alakanuk	8	0	0	0	0	11	102
Andreafsky	32	0	0	0	0	5	64
Angoon	106	0	0	1	0	2	43
Aniak	94	0	4	0	4	0	53
Barrow	330	8	20	5	43	46	388
Bethel	682	0	34	3	20	84	614
Chevak	13	0	0	0	0	15	120
Copper Center	135	0	0	0	0	6	23
Craig	439	0	4	0	3	0	5
Dillingham	481	0	13	2	5	25	157

[Continued]

★ 408 ★

Household Language and Linguistic Isolation in Selected Alaska Native Villages
[Continued]

Alaska Native Village Statistical Area[1]	English	Spanish		Asian or Pacific Island language		Other language	
		Linguistically isolated	Not linguistically isolated	Linguistically isolated	Not linguistically isolated	Linguistically isolated	Not linguistically isolated
Emmonak	29	0	0	0	5	10	112
Fort Yukon	117	0	0	0	0	17	71
Galena	139	0	4	3	3	2	41
Gambell	6	0	0	0	0	5	113
Grouse Creek Group	210	0	4	0	0	2	13
Hoonah	125	0	0	0	4	5	99
Hooper Bay	14	0	0	0	0	38	140
Kake	177	0	0	0	0	2	36
Kasigluk	11	0	0	0	0	29	58
King Cove	65	0	3	0	5	0	4
King Salmon	164	0	4	0	0	3	0
Kipnuk	1	0	0	0	0	79	14
Klawock	206	0	5	0	5	0	25
Kotlik	26	0	0	0	0	27	54
Kotzebue	414	0	20	0	12	19	302
Kwethluk	5	0	0	0	0	66	59
McGrath	156	0	3	0	0	0	23
Mountain Village	36	0	0	0	0	9	108
Naknek	186	0	0	0	0	2	18
Ninilchik	3,364	13	73	0	14	90	213
Noorvik	17	0	0	0	0	18	74
Pilot Station	10	0	0	0	0	24	70
Point Hope	47	0	0	0	0	6	90
Quinhagak	7	0	1	0	0	54	70
St. Paul	108	0	0	0	0	8	45
Salamatof	238	0	4	0	0	1	0
Sand Point	232	0	5	0	0	0	8
Savoonga	9	0	0	0	0	24	92
Selawik	40	0	0	0	0	11	75
Shishmaref	17	0	0	0	0	6	88
Stebbins	13	0	0	0	0	4	79
Togiak	17	0	0	0	0	27	110
Tok	311	0	14	0	0	2	43
Toksook Bay	4	0	0	0	0	4	73
Unalakleet	121	0	0	0	0	8	68
Unalaska	426	3	26	41	41	5	32
Wainwright	15	0	0	0	0	28	99
Yakutat	145	2	0	0	2	0	28

Source: Census of Population and Housing, 1990: Summary Tape File 3C on CD-ROM [machine-readable datafiles]. Prepared by the Bureau of the Census. Washington, DC: The Bureau, 1992. *Notes:* 1. Alaska Native villages (ANVs) constitute tribes, bands, clans, groups, villages, communities, or associations in Alaska that are recognized pursuant to the Alaska Native Claims Settlement Act of 1972, Public Law 92-203. Because ANVs do not have legally designated boundaries, the Census Bureau has established Alaska Native village statistical areas (ANVSAs) for statistical purposes. For the 1990 census, the Census Bureau cooperated with officials of the nonprofit corporation within each participating Alaska Native Regional Corporation (ANRC), as well as other knowledgeable officials, to delineate boundaries that encompass the settled area associated with each ANV.

★ 409 ★

Language

Household Language and Linguistic Isolation in Selected Tribal Designated Statistical Areas

Tribal Designated Statistical Area[1]	English	Spanish		Asian or Pacific Island language		Other language	
		Linguistically isolated	Not linguistically isolated	Linguistically isolated	Not linguistically isolated	Linguistically isolated	Not linguistically isolated
Apache Choctaw TDSA (state)	8,026	19	118	0	0	17	195
Chickahominy TDSA (state)	886	6	23	0	0	6	37
Clifton Choctaw TDSA (state)	145	0	20	0	0	0	13
Coharie TDSA (state)	41,483	91	1,582	28	229	83	937
Coquille Indian TDSA	148,817	588	4,379	584	1,491	397	5,011
Delaware-Muncie TDSA (state)	97	0	0	0	0	0	0
Florida Tribe of Eastern Creek TDSA (state)	100	0	0	0	0	0	7
Haliwa-Saponi TDSA (state)	1,991	0	40	0	0	7	66
Jena Band of Choctaw TDSA (state)	19,251	0	228	19	152	49	1,299
Klamath TDSA	14,815	159	487	19	57	38	546
Lumbee TDSA (state)	14,906	23	590	8	50	4	288
Meherrin TDSA (state)	19,370	20	354	13	18	13	556
Mohegan TDSA (state)	8,160	72	269	22	93	155	1,028
Ramapough TDSA (state)	160	0	20	0	0	9	15
United Houma Nation TDSA (state)	234,482	1,892	10,814	1,103	2,271	4,668	35,273
Waccamaw Siouan TDSA (state)	791	0	52	0	0	0	21
Wampanoag-Gay Head TDSA	4,760	7	35	0	12	24	238

Source: Census of Population and Housing, 1990: Summary Tape File 3C on CD-ROM [machine-readable datafiles]. Prepared by the Bureau of the Census. Washington, DC: The Bureau, 1992. *Notes:* 1. Tribal designated statistical areas (TDSAs) are areas, delineated outside Oklahoma by federally- and state-recognized tribes without a land base or associated trust lands, to provide statistical areas for which the Census Bureau tabulates data. TDSAs represent areas generally containing the American Indian population over which federally-recognized tribes have jurisdiction and areas in which state tribes provide benefits and services to their members. The names of TDSAs delineated by state-recognized tribes are followed by "(state)." The Census Bureau did not recognize TDSAs before the 1990 census.

★ 410 ★

Language

Household Language and Linguistic Isolation in Selected Tribal Jurisdiction Statistical Areas

Tribal Jurisdiction Statistical Area[1]	English	Spanish		Asian or Pacific Island language		Other language	
		Linguistically isolated	Not linguistically isolated	Linguistically isolated	Not linguistically isolated	Linguistically isolated	Not linguistically isolated
Absentee Shawnee-Citizens Band of Potawatomi TJSA	29,400	18	829	2	183	40	628
Caddo-Wichita-Delaware TJSA	2,898	37	148	0	2	11	42
Cherokee TJSA	140,167	294	2,722	71	467	713	5,432
Cheyenne-Arapaho TJSA	51,674	232	1,723	62	176	134	1,542
Chickasaw TJSA	94,741	302	2,124	35	316	120	1,604
Choctaw TJSA	75,255	137	1,413	45	211	225	2,192
Creek TJSA	234,307	769	5,697	446	1,371	881	7,793
Iowa TJSA	1,382	0	34	0	2	8	29
Kaw TJSA	4,792	0	113	0	0	0	155

[Continued]

★ 410 ★

Household Language and Linguistic Isolation in Selected Tribal Jurisdiction Statistical Areas

[Continued]

Tribal Jurisdiction Statistical Area[1]	English	Number of households					
		Spanish		Asian or Pacific Island language		Other language	
		Linguistically isolated	Not linguistically isolated	Linguistically isolated	Not linguistically isolated	Linguistically isolated	Not linguistically isolated
Kiowa-Comanche-Apache-Fort Sill Apache TJSA	63,679	518	3,744	135	1,283	220	3,516
Otoe-Missouria TJSA	901	0	20	0	8	8	26
Pawnee TJSA	5,687	7	72	2	12	10	123
Sac and Fox TJSA	19,257	6	417	21	50	47	535
Seminole TJSA	8,125	0	191	2	15	25	433
Tonkawa TJSA	4,712	7	85	4	14	10	45
Creek-Seminole Joint Area TJSA	791	0	16	0	6	6	43
Iowa-Sac and Fox Joint Area TJSA	290	0	3	0	0	0	8

Source: Census of Population and Housing, 1990: Summary Tape File 3C on CD-ROM [machine-readable datafiles]. Prepared by the Bureau of the Census. Washington, DC: The Bureau, 1992. *Notes:* 1. Tribal jurisdiction statistical areas (TJSAs) are areas, delineated by federally recognized tribes in Oklahoma without a reservation, for which the Census Bureau tabulates data. TJSAs represent areas generally containing the American Indian population over which one or more tribal governments have jurisdiction. If tribal officials delineated adjacent TJSAs so that they include some duplicate territory, the overlap area is called a "joint use area," which is treated as a separate TJSA for census purposes.

★ 411 ★

Language

Household Language and Linguistic Isolation on Selected Reservations and Trust Lands

Data are shown for the 50 areas with the largest populations, in number of persons.

American Indian Reservations and Trust Lands[1,2]	English	Number of households					
		Spanish		Asian or Pacific Island language		Other language	
		Linguistically isolated	Not linguistically isolated	Linguistically isolated	Not linguistically isolated	Linguistically isolated	Not linguistically isolated
Agua Caliente Reservation	8,696	134	556	26	106	113	804
Allegany Reservation	2,617	3	41	0	2	31	209
Blackfeet Reservation	1,906	0	31	0	2	6	416
Cheyenne River Reservation	1,581	0	11	0	0	87	693
Coeur d'Alene Reservation and Trust Lands, ID	2,065	5	38	0	0	13	81
Colorado River Reservation	1,784	112	594	4	9	6	240
Colville Reservation	2,181	3	62	6	8	2	159
Crow Reservation and Trust Lands, MT	694	0	5	0	0	160	833
Eastern Cherokee Reservation	1,559	0	16	0	6	50	435
Flathead Reservation	7,302	4	90	0	4	11	503
Fort Apache Reservation	377	0	37	0	0	662	1,514
Fort Berthold Reservation	1,345	0	10	0	0	21	344
Fort Hall Reservation and Trust Lands, ID	916	39	55	0	7	40	427
Fort Peck Reservation	2,852	4	19	0	8	30	476
Gila River Reservation	654	51	119	0	0	236	1,361

[Continued]

★ 411 ★

Household Language and Linguistic Isolation on Selected Reservations and Trust Lands
[Continued]

American Indian Reservations and Trust Lands[1,2]	Number of households						
	English	Spanish		Asian or Pacific Island language		Other language	
		Linguistically isolated	Not linguistically isolated	Linguistically isolated	Not linguistically isolated	Linguistically isolated	Not linguistically isolated
Hopi Reservation and Trust Lands, AZ	210	11	13	0	5	368	1,190
Isabella Reservation and Trust Lands, MI	7,725	20	206	9	38	26	338
Laguna Pueblo and Trust Lands, NM	231	9	22	0	5	52	722
Lake Traverse (Sisseton) Reservation	3,376	2	17	0	0	31	585
Leech Lake Reservation	2,584	2	30	0	2	41	435
Mississippi Choctaw Reservation and Trust Lands, MS	92	0	0	0	0	401	482
Muckleshoot Reservation and Trust Lands, WA	1,208	2	38	0	13	5	58
Navajo Reservation and Trust Lands, AZ – NM – UT	2,803	40	232	9	26	11,066	23,205
Nez Perce Reservation	5,679	6	100	6	28	37	331
Northern Cheyenne Reservation and Trust Lands, MT – SD	425	0	10	0	0	63	529
Omaha Reservation	1,520	2	19	0	3	26	156
Oneida (West) Reservation	5,296	0	92	0	22	12	291
Osage Reservation	14,528	9	357	0	33	17	367
Papago Reservation	191	20	7	0	0	685	1,332
Pine Ridge Reservation and Trust Lands, NE – SD	1,291	11	7	0	13	172	1,340
Port Madison Reservation	1,745	1	20	8	31	4	54
Puyallup Reservation and Trust Lands, WA	10,120	72	315	394	419	41	427
Red Lake Reservation	603	0	3	0	5	10	335
Rosebud Reservation and Trust Lands, SD	1,395	0	25	0	0	118	1,024
Salt River Reservation	1,049	9	104	0	5	36	423
San Carlos Reservation	241	0	32	0	0	439	1,035
Sandia Pueblo	431	57	738	0	0	2	82
San Juan Pueblo	112	206	1,076	1	0	12	261
Santa Clara Pueblo	654	354	2,254	0	10	70	298
Southern Ute Reservation	2,025	45	416	0	12	6	210
Standing Rock Reservation	1,610	0	28	0	5	101	601
Taos Pueblo and Trust Lands, NM	650	136	683	3	5	61	374
Tulalip Reservation	2,352	0	49	2	31	4	126
Turtle Mountain Reservation and Trust Lands, ND – SD	1,586	0	7	0	0	16	497
Uintah and Ouray Reservation	4,243	22	192	0	33	36	439
White Earth Reservation	2,701	0	44	2	1	45	215
Wind River Reservation	6,464	18	270	7	3	67	702
Yakima Reservation and Trust Lands, WA	4,899	617	1,709	34	91	52	429
Yankton Reservation	1,700	0	24	0	2	70	359
Zuni Pueblo	188	0	16	0	7	360	1,098

Source: Census of Population and Housing, 1990: Summary Tape File 3C on CD-ROM [machine-readable datafiles]. Prepared by the Bureau of the Census. Washington, DC: The Bureau, 1992. *Notes:* 1. Federal American Indian reservations are areas with boundaries established by treaty, statute, and/or executive or court order, and recognized by the federal government as territory in which American Indian tribes have jurisdiction. State reservations are lands held in trust by state governments for the use and benefit of a given tribe. The reservations and their boundaries were identified for the 1990 census by the Bureau of Indian Affairs (BIA), Department of Interior (for federal reservations), and state governments (for state reservations). The names of American Indian reservations recognized by state governments, but not by the federal government, are followed by "state." Areas composed of reservation lands that are administered jointly and/or are claimed by two reservations, as identified by the BIA, are called "joint areas," and are treated as separate American Indian reservations for census purposes. Federal reservations may cross state boundaries, and federal and state reservations may cross county, county subdivision, and place boundaries. For reservations that cross state boundaries, only the portion of the reservations in a given state is shown in the data products for that state; the entire reservations are shown in data products for the United States. 2. Trust lands are property associated with a particular American Indian reservation or tribe, held in trust by the federal government. Trust lands may be held in trust either for a tribe (tribal trust lands) or for an individual member of a tribe (individual trust land). Trust lands recognized for the 1990 census comprised all tribal trust lands and inhabited individual trust lands located outside of a reservation boundary. As with other American Indian areas, trust lands may be located in more than one state. Only the trust lands in a given state are shown in the data products for that state; all trust lands associated with a reservation or tribe are shown in data products for the United States. The Census Bureau first reported data for tribal trust lands for the 1980 census.

★ 412 ★

Language

Language Spoken at Home and English Ability, by Age in Selected Alaska Native Villages - Part I

Data are shown for the 50 areas with the largest populations, in number of persons.

ANVSA[1]	Speak only English	Speak Spanish			Speak Asian/Pacific Island language			Speak other language		
		Speak English very well	Speak English well	Speak English not well/at all	Speak English very well	Speak English well	Speak English not well/at all	Speak English very well	Speak English well	Speak English not well/at all
Akiachak	4	0	0	0	0	0	0	41	37	8
Akutan	25	0	0	0	0	0	0	0	0	0
Alakanuk	78	0	0	0	0	0	0	95	0	0
Andreafsky	60	0	0	0	0	0	0	39	6	0
Angoon	183	0	0	0	0	0	0	2	2	0
Aniak	152	0	0	0	5	0	0	8	0	0
Barrow	339	0	0	0	11	0	0	273	30	0
Bethel	741	2	0	0	11	0	0	198	85	11
Chevak	5	0	0	0	0	0	0	99	38	13
Copper Center	73	0	0	0	0	0	0	2	0	0
Craig	286	0	0	0	0	0	0	0	0	0
Dillingham	428	2	0	0	5	0	0	15	23	4
Emmonak	92	0	0	0	0	0	0	31	4	0
Fort Yukon	140	0	0	0	0	0	0	4	4	0
Galena	124	0	0	0	0	0	0	3	0	0
Gambell	0	0	0	0	0	0	0	129	15	3
Grouse Creek Group	143	3	0	0	0	0	0	7	0	0
Hoonah	152	0	0	0	0	0	0	7	0	0
Hooper Bay	40	0	0	0	0	0	0	65	108	11
Kake	145	0	0	0	0	0	0	2	0	0
Kasigluk	4	0	0	0	0	0	0	53	40	25
King Cove	72	0	0	0	0	0	0	0	0	0
King Salmon	87	0	0	0	0	0	0	0	0	0
Kipnuk	0	0	0	0	0	0	0	0	134	2
Klawock	151	2	0	0	0	0	0	0	0	0
Kotlik	84	0	0	0	0	0	0	27	17	3
Kotzebue	577	0	0	0	0	0	0	58	19	11
Kwethluk	6	0	0	0	0	0	0	56	84	31
McGrath	143	0	0	0	0	0	0	19	0	0
Mountain Village	198	0	0	0	0	0	0	14	8	0
Naknek	133	0	0	0	0	0	0	6	0	0
Ninilchik	2,085	20	0	0	7	0	0	71	235	85
Noorvik	110	0	0	0	0	0	0	27	19	1
Pilot Station	89	0	0	0	0	0	0	29	4	0
Point Hope	156	0	0	0	0	0	0	39	2	4
Quinhagak	8	0	0	0	0	0	0	14	70	27
St. Paul	127	0	0	0	0	0	0	0	2	0
Salamatof	211	0	1	0	0	0	0	0	0	0
Sand Point	161	4	0	0	0	0	0	0	0	0
Savoonga	11	0	0	0	0	0	0	81	45	2
Selawik	138	0	0	0	0	0	0	40	5	0
Shishmaref	97	0	0	0	0	0	0	26	0	0
Stebbins	82	0	0	0	0	0	0	19	10	2
Togiak	28	0	0	0	0	0	0	73	44	12
Tok	210	3	0	0	0	0	0	0	2	0
Toksook Bay	0	0	0	0	0	0	0	68	34	5
Unalakleet	164	0	0	0	0	0	0	34	0	0
Unalaska	226	0	0	0	11	0	0	0	0	0

[Continued]

★ 412 ★

Language Spoken at Home and English Ability, by Age in Selected Alaska Native Villages - Part I
[Continued]

ANVSA[1]	Speak only English	Persons age 5 to 17 years								
		Speak Spanish			Speak Asian/Pacific Island language			Speak other language		
		Speak English very well	Speak English well	Speak English not well/at all	Speak English very well	Speak English well	Speak English not well/at all	Speak English very well	Speak English well	Speak English not well/at all
Wainwright	62	0	0	0	0	0	0	78	12	0
Yakutat	128	0	0	0	0	0	0	0	3	0

Source: Census of Population and Housing, 1990: Summary Tape File 3C on CD-ROM [machine-readable datafiles]. Prepared by the Bureau of the Census. Washington, DC: The Bureau, 1992. Notes: 1. Alaska Native villages (ANVs) constitute tribes, bands, clans, groups, villages, communities, or associations in Alaska that are recognized pursuant to the Alaska Native Claims Settlement Act of 1972, Public Law 92-203. Because ANVs do not have legally designated boundaries, the Census Bureau has established Alaska Native village statistical areas (ANVSAs) for statistical purposes. For the 1990 census, the Census Bureau cooperated with officials of the nonprofit corporation within each participating Alaska Native Regional Corporation (ANRC), as well as other knowledgeable officials, to delineate boundaries that encompass the settled area associated with each ANV.

★ 413 ★

Language

Language Spoken at Home and English Ability, by Age in Selected Alaska Native Villages - Part II

Data are shown for the 50 areas with the largest populations, in number of persons.

ANVSA[1]	Speak only English	Persons age 18 to 64 years								
		Speak Spanish			Speak Asian/Pacific Island language			Speak other language		
		Speak English very well	Speak English well	Speak English not well/at all	Speak English very well	Speak English well	Speak English not well/at all	Speak English very well	Speak English well	Speak English not well/at all
Akiachak	25	0	0	0	0	0	0	141	82	39
Akutan	225	0	39	12	72	97	66	20	0	35
Alakanuk	47	0	0	0	0	0	0	192	18	16
Andreafsky	104	0	0	0	0	0	0	90	26	3
Angoon	304	0	0	0	0	3	0	27	2	0
Aniak	214	4	0	0	4	0	0	61	3	0
Barrow	726	23	10	3	63	23	13	618	108	22
Bethel	1,664	38	2	0	18	20	5	790	322	54
Chevak	30	0	0	0	1	0	0	231	19	10
Copper Center	246	0	0	0	0	0	0	15	5	0
Craig	791	2	3	0	3	0	0	7	0	0
Dillingham	975	16	2	0	7	4	0	139	53	15
Emmonak	125	0	0	0	2	4	0	160	26	13
Fort Yukon	250	0	0	0	0	0	0	65	32	0
Galena	528	3	2	0	10	3	0	36	4	9
Gambell	8	0	0	0	0	0	0	260	34	0
Grouse Creek Group	373	5	0	0	0	0	0	7	4	4
Hoonah	350	0	0	0	4	0	0	61	35	0
Hooper Bay	30	0	0	0	0	0	0	235	107	24
Kake	394	0	0	0	0	0	0	23	0	0
Kasigluk	23	0	0	0	0	0	0	68	96	27
King Cove	173	13	8	16	59	42	24	3	0	8
King Salmon	520	25	0	0	0	0	0	14	0	0
Kipnuk	9	0	0	0	2	0	0	7	215	13
Klawock	434	0	3	0	4	0	0	24	0	0
Kotlik	79	0	0	0	0	0	0	58	69	22
Kotzebue	1,109	24	0	4	10	2	6	352	43	18
Kwethluk	15	0	0	0	0	0	0	85	155	19
McGrath	266	6	0	0	0	0	0	21	2	0
Mountain Village	164	0	0	0	0	0	0	92	102	5
Naknek	336	0	0	0	0	0	0	8	6	2
Ninilchik	5,706	74	29	14	27	0	0	218	161	95

[Continued]

★ 413 ★

Language Spoken at Home and English Ability, by Age in Selected Alaska Native Villages - Part II
[Continued]

ANVSA[1]	Speak only English	Speak Spanish			Speak Asian/Pacific Island language			Speak other language		
		Speak English very well	Speak English well	Speak English not well/at all	Speak English very well	Speak English well	Speak English not well/at all	Speak English very well	Speak English well	Speak English not well/at all
Noorvik	87	0	0	0	0	0	0	121	38	33
Pilot Station	43	0	0	0	0	0	0	112	61	13
Point Hope	146	0	0	0	0	0	0	125	14	19
Quinhagak	25	1	0	0	0	0	0	101	101	50
St. Paul	449	0	0	0	0	12	13	44	21	0
Salamatof	637	8	3	0	0	0	0	27	0	18
Sand Point	491	7	20	7	39	28	6	11	0	0
Savoonga	17	0	0	0	0	0	0	168	104	0
Selawik	114	0	0	0	0	0	0	79	57	2
Shishmaref	75	0	0	0	0	0	0	141	17	0
Stebbins	62	0	0	0	0	0	0	133	24	0
Togiak	46	0	0	0	0	0	0	179	67	37
Tok	531	19	0	0	0	0	0	46	0	0
Toksook Bay	11	0	0	0	3	0	0	155	22	38
Unalakleet	239	0	0	0	0	0	0	67	18	4
Unalaska	1,817	83	97	102	145	171	190	46	17	19
Wainwright	38	0	0	0	0	0	0	168	43	13
Yakutat	323	2	2	0	3	0	0	11	1	0

Source: Census of Population and Housing, 1990: Summary Tape File 3C on CD-ROM [machine-readable datafiles]. Prepared by the Bureau of the Census. Washington, DC: The Bureau, 1992. Notes: 1. Alaska Native villages (ANVs) constitute tribes, bands, clans, groups, villages, communities, or associations in Alaska that are recognized pursuant to the Alaska Native Claims Settlement Act of 1972, Public Law 92-203. Because ANVs do not have legally designated boundaries, the Census Bureau has established Alaska Native village statistical areas (ANVSAs) for statistical purposes. For the 1990 census, the Census Bureau cooperated with officials of the nonprofit corporation within each participating Alaska Native Regional Corporation (ANRC), as well as other knowledgeable officials, to delineate boundaries that encompass the settled area associated with each ANV.

★ 414 ★
Language

Language Spoken at Home and English Ability, by Age in Selected Alaska Native Villages - Part III

Data are shown for the 50 areas with the largest populations, in number of persons.

ANVSA[1]	Speak only English	Speak Spanish			Speak Asian/Pacific Island language			Speak other language		
		Speak English very well	Speak English well	Speak English not well/at all	Speak English very well	Speak English well	Speak English not well/at all	Speak English very well	Speak English well	Speak English not well/at all
Akiachak	0	0	0	0	0	0	0	5	3	16
Akutan	0	0	0	0	0	0	0	0	2	1
Alakanuk	0	0	0	0	0	0	0	8	0	12
Andreafsky	1	0	0	0	0	0	0	0	5	6
Angoon	2	0	0	0	0	0	0	20	8	0
Aniak	6	0	0	0	0	0	0	6	0	3
Barrow	0	0	0	0	3	0	0	29	19	30
Bethel	24	2	0	0	0	0	0	39	16	53
Chevak	0	0	0	0	0	0	0	0	2	21
Copper Center	13	0	0	0	0	0	0	5	8	2
Craig	24	0	0	0	0	0	0	0	0	0
Dillingham	25	0	0	0	0	0	0	30	15	19
Emmonak	0	0	0	0	0	0	0	4	12	8
Fort Yukon	7	0	0	0	0	0	0	5	0	8
Galena	10	0	0	0	0	0	0	7	0	0
Gambell	0	0	0	0	0	0	0	11	2	8

[Continued]

★ 414 ★

Language Spoken at Home and English Ability, by Age in Selected Alaska Native Villages - Part III
[Continued]

ANVSA[1]	Speak only English	Speak Spanish			Speak Asian/Pacific Island language			Speak other language		
		Speak English very well	Speak English well	Speak English not well/at all	Speak English very well	Speak English well	Speak English not well/at all	Speak English very well	Speak English well	Speak English not well/at all
Grouse Creek Group	21	0	0	0	0	0	0	0	3	0
Hoonah	14	0	0	0	0	0	0	21	6	1
Hooper Bay	0	0	0	0	0	0	0	0	14	37
Kake	13	0	0	0	0	0	0	20	4	0
Kasigluk	0	0	0	0	0	0	0	2	5	27
King Cove	10	0	0	0	0	0	0	2	0	0
King Salmon	2	0	0	0	0	0	0	0	3	0
Kipnuk	0	0	0	0	0	0	0	1	6	11
Klawock	16	0	0	0	2	0	0	8	0	0
Kotlik	4	0	0	0	0	0	0	4	6	17
Kotzebue	21	0	0	0	0	0	0	36	28	21
Kwethluk	0	0	0	0	0	0	0	5	5	30
McGrath	14	0	0	0	0	0	0	0	0	2
Mountain Village	0	0	0	0	0	0	0	2	15	9
Naknek	21	0	0	0	0	0	0	3	0	0
Ninilchik	591	0	0	0	0	0	0	18	2	11
Noorvik	0	0	0	0	0	0	0	4	10	14
Pilot Station	0	0	0	0	0	0	0	0	1	13
Point Hope	4	0	0	0	0	0	0	8	3	1
Quinhagak	0	0	0	0	0	0	0	0	2	30
St. Paul	4	0	0	0	0	0	0	11	10	0
Salamatof	54	0	0	0	0	0	0	0	1	0
Sand Point	14	0	0	0	0	0	0	2	0	0
Savoonga	0	0	0	0	0	0	0	0	20	3
Selawik	2	0	0	0	0	0	0	4	9	17
Shishmaref	0	0	0	0	0	0	0	6	8	0
Stebbins	2	0	0	0	0	0	0	3	11	12
Togiak	3	0	0	0	0	0	0	3	0	24
Tok	41	0	0	0	0	0	0	4	4	1
Toksook Bay	0	0	0	0	0	0	0	0	0	8
Unalakleet	7	0	0	0	0	0	0	12	15	4
Unalaska	11	0	0	0	0	0	0	1	4	0
Wainwright	0	0	0	0	0	0	0	5	6	10
Yakutat	10	0	0	0	0	0	0	15	3	0

Source: Census of Population and Housing, 1990: Summary Tape File 3C on CD-ROM [machine-readable datafiles]. Prepared by the Bureau of the Census. Washington, DC: The Bureau, 1992. *Notes:* 1. Alaska Native villages (ANVs) constitute tribes, bands, clans, groups, villages, communities, or associations in Alaska that are recognized pursuant to the Alaska Native Claims Settlement Act of 1972, Public Law 92-203. Because ANVs do not have legally designated boundaries, the Census Bureau has established Alaska Native village statistical areas (ANVSAs) for statistical purposes. For the 1990 census, the Census Bureau cooperated with officials of the nonprofit corporation within each participating Alaska Native Regional Corporation (ANRC), as well as other knowledgeable officials, to delineate boundaries that encompass the settled area associated with each ANV.

★ 415 ★

Language

Language Spoken at Home and English Ability, by Age in Selected Tribal Designated Statistical Areas - Part I

TDSA[1]	Speak only English	Persons age 5 to 17 years								
		Speak Spanish			Speak Asian/Pacific Island language			Speak other language		
		Speak English very well	Speak English well	Speak English not well/at all	Speak English very well	Speak English well	Speak English not well/at all	Speak English very well	Speak English well	Speak English not well/at all
Apache Choctaw TDSA (state)	4,670	10	12	9	0	0	0	12	0	19
Chickahominy TDSA (state)	551	0	27	0	0	0	0	0	0	7
Clifton Choctaw TDSA (state)	98	0	0	0	0	0	0	0	0	0
Coharie TDSA (state)	20,179	409	257	174	38	8	12	107	63	26
Coquille Indian TDSA	66,739	1,302	365	362	299	93	22	846	60	89
Delaware-Muncie TDSA (state)	55	0	0	0	0	0	0	0	0	0
Florida Tribe of Eastern Creek TDSA (state)	9	0	0	0	0	0	0	0	0	0
Haliwa-Saponi TDSA (state)	1,441	7	0	0	0	0	0	30	0	0
Jena Band of Choctaw TDSA (state)	11,789	39	15	16	51	77	25	137	41	3
Klamath TDSA	7,418	186	104	57	22	16	0	90	17	0
Lumbee TDSA (state)	11,777	166	184	46	7	0	0	99	15	17
Meherrin TDSA (state)	10,702	115	25	25	16	0	0	118	43	55
Mohegan TDSA (state)	3,714	139	40	29	24	3	0	60	14	0
Ramapough TDSA (state)	41	0	0	0	0	0	0	0	0	0
United Houma Nation TDSA (state)	155,968	3,786	993	739	1,641	648	448	3,651	894	574
Waccamaw Siouan TDSA (state)	707	14	0	0	0	0	0	0	0	0
Wampanoag-Gay Head TDSA	1,937	14	6	0	0	0	0	12	2	1

Source: Census of Population and Housing, 1990: Summary Tape File 3C on CD-ROM [machine-readable datafiles]. Prepared by the Bureau of the Census. Washington, DC: The Bureau, 1992. *Notes:* 1. Tribal designated statistical areas (TDSAs) are areas, delineated outside Oklahoma by federally- and state-recognized tribes without a land base or associated trust lands, to provide statistical areas for which the Census Bureau tabulates data. TDSAs represent areas generally containing the American Indian population over which federally-recognized tribes have jurisdiction and areas in which state tribes provide benefits and services to their members. The names of TDSAs delineated by state-recognized tribes are followed by "(state)." The Census Bureau did not recognize TDSAs before the 1990 census.

★ 416 ★

Language

Language Spoken at Home and English Ability, by Age in Selected Tribal Designated Statistical Areas - Part II

TDSA[1]	Speak only English	Persons age 18 to 64 years								
		Speak Spanish			Speak Asian/Pacific Island language			Speak other language		
		Speak English very well	Speak English well	Speak English not well/at all	Speak English very well	Speak English well	Speak English not well/at all	Speak English very well	Speak English well	Speak English not well/at all
Apache Choctaw TDSA (state)	12,170	47	27	14	0	0	0	209	20	2
Chickahominy TDSA (state)	1,819	0	11	10	0	0	0	19	13	0
Clifton Choctaw TDSA (state)	283	10	0	8	0	0	0	7	7	0
Coharie TDSA (state)	67,565	871	334	315	155	106	25	717	119	93
Coquille Indian TDSA	230,237	3,856	1,273	1,248	1,513	1,070	546	4,017	629	354
Delaware-Muncie TDSA (state)	146	0	0	0	0	0	0	0	0	0
Florida Tribe of Eastern Creek TDSA (state)	121	0	0	0	0	0	0	0	0	0
Haliwa-Saponi TDSA (state)	3,669	23	13	10	0	0	0	24	15	25
Jena Band of Choctaw TDSA (state)	34,996	232	33	4	115	68	41	988	110	34
Klamath TDSA	22,472	455	215	254	34	17	25	361	40	23
Lumbee TDSA (state)	28,472	205	126	70	20	14	21	211	67	14
Meherrin TDSA (state)	31,102	218	64	49	24	28	23	279	49	80
Mohegan TDSA (state)	14,087	246	147	70	74	42	42	536	151	69
Ramapough TDSA (state)	424	18	0	0	0	0	0	6	6	8

[Continued]

★ 416 ★

Language Spoken at Home and English Ability, by Age in Selected Tribal Designated Statistical Areas - Part II

[Continued]

TDSA[1]	Speak only English	Speak Spanish			Speak Asian/Pacific Island language			Speak other language		
		Speak English very well	Speak English well	Speak English not well/at all	Speak English very well	Speak English well	Speak English not well/at all	Speak English very well	Speak English well	Speak English not well/at all
United Houma Nation										
TDSA (state)	439,929	11,149	4,497	3,241	2,741	1,926	1,694	29,657	8,086	2,369
Waccamaw Siouan TDSA (state)	1,631	9	24	26	0	0	0	0	0	21
Wampanoag-Gay Head TDSA	6,772	36	7	3	10	0	0	175	14	11

Source: Census of Population and Housing, 1990: Summary Tape File 3C on CD-ROM [machine-readable datafiles]. Prepared by the Bureau of the Census. Washington, DC: The Bureau, 1992. *Notes:* 1. Tribal designated statistical areas (TDSAs) are areas, delineated outside Oklahoma by federally- and state-recognized tribes without a land base or associated trust lands, to provide statistical areas for which the Census Bureau tabulates data. TDSAs represent areas generally containing the American Indian population over which federally-recognized tribes have jurisdiction and areas in which state tribes provide benefits and services to their members. The names of TDSAs delineated by state-recognized tribes are followed by "(state)." The Census Bureau did not recognize TDSAs before the 1990 census.

★ 417 ★

Language

Language Spoken at Home and English Ability, by Age in Selected Tribal Designated Statistical Areas - Part III

TDSA[1]	Speak only English	Speak Spanish			Speak Asian/Pacific Island language			Speak other language		
		Speak English very well	Speak English well	Speak English not well/at all	Speak English very well	Speak English well	Speak English not well/at all	Speak English very well	Speak English well	Speak English not well/at all
Apache Choctaw TDSA (state)	3,631	13	36	5	0	0	0	23	25	0
Chickahominy TDSA (state)	172	0	0	0	0	0	0	0	11	0
Clifton Choctaw TDSA (state)	61	0	0	0	0	0	0	0	0	0
Coharie TDSA (state)	15,839	28	32	16	17	8	0	46	71	54
Coquille Indian TDSA	58,988	419	107	70	105	38	49	1,258	355	143
Delaware-Muncie TDSA (state)	47	0	0	0	0	0	0	0	0	0
Florida Tribe of Eastern										
Creek TDSA (state)	55	0	0	0	0	0	0	9	0	0
Haliwa-Saponi TDSA (state)	631	0	0	0	0	0	0	6	0	0
Jena Band of Choctaw										
TDSA (state)	6,821	16	0	4	0	11	0	223	71	25
Klamath TDSA	5,815	35	17	31	11	0	0	182	40	18
Lumbee TDSA (state)	4,228	28	0	12	0	21	0	16	6	20
Meherrin TDSA (state)	8,218	16	0	0	0	0	14	82	18	4
Mohegan TDSA (state)	2,620	10	0	0	8	0	10	465	134	70
Ramapough TDSA (state)	58	0	0	0	0	0	0	6	9	9
United Houma Nation										
TDSA (state)	61,029	721	448	543	63	65	162	10,076	4,420	1,401
Waccamaw Siouan TDSA (state)	153	0	0	0	0	0	0	6	0	0
Wampanoag-Gay Head TDSA	1,775	4	3	0	0	0	0	76	15	17

Source: Census of Population and Housing, 1990: Summary Tape File 3C on CD-ROM [machine-readable datafiles]. Prepared by the Bureau of the Census. Washington, DC: The Bureau, 1992. *Notes:* 1. Tribal designated statistical areas (TDSAs) are areas, delineated outside Oklahoma by federally- and state-recognized tribes without a land base or associated trust lands, to provide statistical areas for which the Census Bureau tabulates data. TDSAs represent areas generally containing the American Indian population over which federally-recognized tribes have jurisdiction and areas in which state tribes provide benefits and services to their members. The names of TDSAs delineated by state-recognized tribes are followed by "(state)." The Census Bureau did not recognize TDSAs before the 1990 census.

★ 418 ★

Language

Language Spoken at Home and English Ability, by Age in Selected Tribal Jurisdiction Statistical Areas - Part I

TJSA[1]	Speak only English	Speak Spanish			Speak Asian/Pacific Island language			Speak other language		
		Persons age 5 to 17 years								
		Speak English very well	Speak English well	Speak English not well/at all	Speak English very well	Speak English well	Speak English not well/at all	Speak English very well	Speak English well	Speak English not well/at all
Absentee Shawnee-Citizens Band of Potawatomi TJSA	19,720	201	29	32	25	0	6	116	43	38
Caddo-Wichita-Delaware TJSA	1,571	85	10	11	0	0	0	3	0	0
Cherokee TJSA	79,298	896	172	232	44	10	34	800	333	190
Cheyenne-Arapaho TJSA	30,369	797	255	106	137	50	8	204	27	35
Chickasaw TJSA	49,280	659	157	91	81	33	41	451	48	37
Choctaw TJSA	40,723	378	85	141	64	5	6	349	138	41
Creek TJSA	115,103	1,546	352	433	446	173	163	1,421	195	188
Iowa TJSA	971	13	1	0	0	0	0	1	0	0
Kaw TJSA	2,509	43	23	0	0	0	0	23	16	12
Kiowa-Comanche-Apache- Fort Sill Apache TJSA	38,131	1,663	385	267	212	59	38	484	124	102
Otoe-Missouria TJSA	625	2	2	0	0	0	0	0	0	7
Pawnee TJSA	3,036	18	9	11	2	0	0	30	0	2
Sac and Fox TJSA	9,788	33	45	21	0	0	0	124	20	6
Seminole TJSA	4,473	23	10	14	0	0	0	96	10	45
Tonkawa TJSA	2,278	21	11	2	0	5	4	4	3	4
Creek-Seminole Joint Area TJSA	469	0	0	0	0	0	0	11	0	9
Iowa-Sac and Fox Joint Area TJSA	207	0	0	0	0	0	0	0	3	0

Source: Census of Population and Housing, 1990: Summary Tape File 3C on CD-ROM [machine-readable datafiles]. Prepared by the Bureau of the Census. Washington, DC: The Bureau, 1992. *Notes:* 1. Tribal jurisdiction statistical areas (TJSAs) are areas, delineated by federally recognized tribes in Oklahoma without a reservation, for which the Census Bureau tabulates data. TJSAs represent areas generally containing the American Indian population over which one or more tribal governments have jurisdiction. If tribal officials delineated adjacent TJSAs so that they include some duplicate territory, the overlap area is called a "joint use area," which is treated as a separate TJSA for census purposes.

★ 419 ★

Language

Language Spoken at Home and English Ability, by Age in Selected Tribal Jurisdiction Statistical Areas - Part II

TJSA[1]	Speak only English	Speak Spanish			Speak Asian/Pacific Island language			Speak other language		
		Persons age 18 to 64 years								
		Speak English very well	Speak English well	Speak English not well/at all	Speak English very well	Speak English well	Speak English not well/at all	Speak English very well	Speak English well	Speak English not well/at all
Absentee Shawnee-Citizens Band of Potawatomi TJSA	54,513	676	74	107	130	62	34	510	98	108
Caddo-Wichita-Delaware TJSA	4,251	132	18	73	3	0	0	25	11	17
Cherokee TJSA	221,843	2,047	566	551	383	202	39	4,556	1,420	560
Cheyenne-Arapaho TJSA	82,433	1,384	784	455	262	205	106	1,105	248	113
Chickasaw TJSA	141,846	1,702	545	366	173	181	39	1,147	394	57
Choctaw TJSA	114,579	827	314	325	158	63	38	1,654	482	182
Creek TJSA	370,536	4,374	1,392	1,257	1,526	902	563	6,595	1,330	659
Iowa TJSA	2,237	17	5	0	2	0	0	28	23	0
Kaw TJSA	7,396	62	27	6	0	0	0	95	6	20
Kiowa-Comanche-Apache- Fort Sill Apache TJSA	109,153	4,333	1,470	796	1,143	753	261	3,349	739	318
Otoe-Missouria TJSA	1,530	18	2	0	10	3	0	11	3	11
Pawnee TJSA	8,599	36	11	8	6	11	0	80	17	3
Sac and Fox TJSA	27,444	353	42	45	37	31	16	370	121	33

[Continued]

★ 419 ★

Language Spoken at Home and English Ability, by Age in Selected Tribal Jurisdiction Statistical Areas - Part II
[Continued]

TJSA[1]	Speak only English	Speak Spanish			Speak Asian/Pacific Island language			Speak other language		
		Speak English very well	Speak English well	Speak English not well/at all	Speak English very well	Speak English well	Speak English not well/at all	Speak English very well	Speak English well	Speak English not well/at all
					Persons age 18 to 64 years					
Seminole TJSA	11,811	132	32	18	3	2	6	356	110	32
Tonkawa TJSA	6,520	52	33	6	8	4	4	41	2	6
Creek-Seminole Joint Area TJSA	1,275	9	10	0	8	2	0	62	7	2
Iowa-Sac and Fox Joint Area TJSA	484	4	0	0	0	0	0	6	0	0

Source: Census of Population and Housing, 1990: Summary Tape File 3C on CD-ROM [machine-readable datafiles]. Prepared by the Bureau of the Census. Washington, DC: The Bureau, 1992. *Notes:* 1. Tribal jurisdiction statistical areas (TJSAs) are areas, delineated by federally recognized tribes in Oklahoma without a reservation, for which the Census Bureau tabulates data. TJSAs represent areas generally containing the American Indian population over which one or more tribal governments have jurisdiction. If tribal officials delineated adjacent TJSAs so that they include some duplicate territory, the overlap area is called a "joint use area," which is treated as a separate TJSA for census purposes.

★ 420 ★
Language

Language Spoken at Home and English Ability, by Age in Selected Tribal Jurisdiction Statistical Areas - Part III

TJSA[1]	Speak only English	Speak Spanish			Speak Asian/Pacific Island language			Speak other language		
		Speak English very well	Speak English well	Speak English not well/at all	Speak English very well	Speak English well	Speak English not well/at all	Speak English very well	Speak English well	Speak English not well/at all
					Persons age 65 years and older					
Absentee Shawnee-Citizens Band of Potawatomi TJSA	8,358	51	13	9	0	0	6	117	17	9
Caddo-Wichita-Delaware TJSA	1,399	6	0	0	0	0	0	8	0	3
Cherokee TJSA	54,618	151	77	55	26	0	11	842	464	413
Cheyenne-Arapaho TJSA	19,932	121	12	26	7	0	6	474	146	87
Chickasaw TJSA	42,672	307	31	47	32	0	31	337	101	29
Choctaw TJSA	33,879	87	35	44	0	3	8	618	179	115
Creek TJSA	77,224	397	151	109	87	40	62	1,103	580	200
Iowa TJSA	540	5	0	0	0	0	0	4	6	0
Kaw TJSA	2,075	0	0	0	0	0	0	3	3	0
Kiowa-Comanche-Apache-Fort Sill Apache TJSA	24,539	298	95	75	48	11	16	627	102	22
Otoe-Missouria TJSA	295	0	0	0	0	0	0	5	4	4
Pawnee TJSA	2,437	4	2	0	3	2	0	24	13	7
Sac and Fox TJSA	8,890	13	12	0	7	0	0	120	23	22
Seminole TJSA	4,038	13	0	0	6	0	0	186	65	16
Tonkawa TJSA	2,415	8	0	3	0	0	0	10	8	0
Creek-Seminole Joint Area TJSA	393	3	0	0	0	0	0	8	8	4
Iowa-Sac and Fox Joint Area TJSA	65	0	0	0	0	0	0	3	0	0

Source: Census of Population and Housing, 1990: Summary Tape File 3C on CD-ROM [machine-readable datafiles]. Prepared by the Bureau of the Census. Washington, DC: The Bureau, 1992. *Notes:* 1. Tribal jurisdiction statistical areas (TJSAs) are areas, delineated by federally recognized tribes in Oklahoma without a reservation, for which the Census Bureau tabulates data. TJSAs represent areas generally containing the American Indian population over which one or more tribal governments have jurisdiction. If tribal officials delineated adjacent TJSAs so that they include some duplicate territory, the overlap area is called a "joint use area," which is treated as a separate TJSA for census purposes.

★ 421 ★

Language

Language Spoken at Home and English Ability, by Age on Selected Reservations and Trust Lands - Part I

Data are shown for the 50 areas with the largest populations, in number of persons.

American Indian Reservation and Trust Lands[1,2]	Speak only English	Persons age 5 to 17 years								
		Speak Spanish			Speak Asian/Pacific Island language			Speak other language		
		Speak English very well	Speak English well	Speak English not well/ at all	Speak English very well	Speak English well	Speak English not well/ at all	Speak English very well	Speak English well	English not well/ at all
Agua Caliente Reservation	1,088	188	41	50	21	0	3	71	5	0
Allegany Reservation	1,245	17	0	0	0	0	0	64	2	0
Blackfeet Reservation	2,295	2	0	0	0	0	0	52	70	34
Cheyenne River Reservation	2,118	2	0	0	0	0	0	56	28	28
Coeur d'Alene Reservation and Trust Lands, ID	1,208	7	1	2	0	0	0	10	8	16
Colorado River Reservation	1,217	380	93	39	0	0	0	26	3	0
Colville Reservation	1,702	15	4	1	0	0	0	20	3	12
Crow Reservation and Trust Lands, MT	693	0	0	0	0	0	0	496	455	103
Eastern Cherokee Reservation	1,408	11	7	0	0	0	0	92	5	14
Flathead Reservation	4,505	28	0	3	0	0	0	182	34	10
Fort Apache Reservation	1,136	0	0	0	0	0	0	774	996	174
Fort Berthold Reservation	1,331	2	0	0	0	0	0	25	18	0
Fort Hall Reservation and Trust Lands, ID	1,229	37	13	9	0	0	0	64	22	3
Fort Peck Reservation	2,680	6	1	0	0	0	0	47	21	0
Gila River Reservation	2,351	29	2	42	0	0	0	160	22	20
Hopi Reservation and Trust Lands, AZ	1,117	3	0	0	0	0	0	307	322	261
Isabella Reservation and Trust Lands, MI	4,277	9	12	26	18	5	3	54	9	35
Laguna Pueblo and Trust Lands, NM	837	3	0	0	0	0	0	125	22	0
Lake Traverse (Sisseton) Reservation	2,357	7	5	0	0	0	0	85	0	4
Leech Lake Reservation	2,041	3	3	2	0	0	0	68	20	14
Mississippi Choctaw Reservation and Trust Lands, MS	158	0	0	0	0	0	0	390	590	277
Muckleshoot Reservation and Trust Lands, WA	858	5	0	0	1	5	4	2	0	6
Navajo Reservation and Trust Lands, AZ–NM–UT	12,976	78	6	0	0	0	0	14,923	12,370	3,506
Nez Perce Reservation	3,233	13	0	2	2	0	0	60	35	16
Northern Cheyenne Reservation and Trust Lands, MT–SD	1,119	0	0	0	0	0	0	80	0	16
Omaha Reservation	1,186	7	2	0	0	0	0	10	0	16
Oneida (West) Reservation	4,242	37	5	5	0	0	5	72	19	12
Osage Reservation	8,422	135	27	36	0	0	0	107	28	4
Papago Reservation	1,287	0	0	0	0	0	0	529	635	110
Pine Ridge Reservation and Trust Lands, NE–SD	3,157	0	0	15	0	0	0	350	31	26
Port Madison Reservation	965	0	0	0	15	13	0	10	3	2
Puyallup Reservation and Trust Lands, WA	5,633	91	28	22	184	324	356	72	12	2
Red Lake Reservation	1,001	0	0	0	0	0	0	62	26	22
Rosebud Reservation and Trust Lands, SD	2,812	14	0	0	0	0	0	175	118	9
Salt River Reservation	1,039	20	0	7	0	0	0	31	0	0
San Carlos Reservation	1,681	28	0	0	0	0	0	241	240	51
Sandia Pueblo	565	358	10	0	0	0	0	14	0	0
San Juan Pueblo	546	279	142	72	0	0	0	66	67	0

[Continued]

★ 421 ★

Language Spoken at Home and English Ability, by Age on Selected Reservations and Trust Lands - Part I

[Continued]

American Indian Reservation and Trust Lands[1,2]	Persons age 5 to 17 years									
	Speak only English	Speak Spanish			Speak Asian/Pacific Island language			Speak other language		
		Speak English very well	Speak English well	Speak English not well/ at all	Speak English very well	Speak English well	Speak English not well/ at all	Speak English very well	Speak English well	English not well/ at all
Santa Clara Pueblo	1,169	729	184	95	0	2	0	92	28	29
Southern Ute Reservation	1,716	102	0	9	3	0	0	48	8	5
Standing Rock Reservation	2,241	6	0	0	0	0	0	55	19	15
Taos Pueblo and Trust Lands, NM	479	168	31	29	8	0	1	142	55	4
Tulalip Reservation	1,461	11	2	0	0	0	0	10	3	0
Turtle Mountain Reservation and Trust Lands, ND – SD	1,976	0	0	0	0	0	0	110	8	0
Uintah and Ouray Reservation	5,286	100	2	15	10	4	0	77	38	16
White Earth Reservation	2,136	20	3	5	0	0	0	21	3	4
Wind River Reservation	5,051	42	15	11	12	0	0	284	34	27
Yakima Reservation and Trust Lands, WA	4,036	1,558	730	392	0	20	0	123	39	0
Yankton Reservation	1,384	11	0	7	0	0	0	41	25	10
Zuni Pueblo	208	0	0	0	0	0	0	539	1,013	195

Source: Census of Population and Housing, 1990: Summary Tape File 3C on CD-ROM [machine-readable datafiles]. Prepared by the Bureau of the Census. Washington, DC: The Bureau, 1992. *Notes:* 1. Federal American Indian reservations are areas with boundaries established by treaty, statute, and/or executive or court order, and recognized by the federal government as territory in which American Indian tribes have jurisdiction. State reservations are lands held in trust by state governments for the use and benefit of a given tribe. The reservations and their boundaries were identified for the 1990 census by the Bureau of Indian Affairs (BIA), Department of Interior (for federal reservations), and state governments (for state reservations). The names of American Indian reservations recognized by state governments, but not by the federal government, are followed by "state." Areas composed of reservation lands that are administered jointly and/or are claimed by two reservations, as identified by the BIA, are called "joint areas," and are treated as separate American Indian reservations for census purposes. Federal reservations may cross state boundaries, and federal and state reservations may cross county, county subdivision, and place boundaries. For reservations that cross state boundaries, only the portion of the reservations in a given state is shown in the data products for that state; the entire reservations are shown in data products for the United States. 2. Trust lands are property associated with a particular American Indian reservation or tribe, held in trust by the federal government. Trust lands may be held in trust either for a tribe (tribal trust lands) or for an individual member of a tribe (individual trust land). Trust lands recognized for the 1990 census comprised all tribal trust lands and inhabited individual trust lands located outside of a reservation boundary. As with other American Indian areas, trust lands may be located in more than one state. Only the trust lands in a given state are shown in the data products for that state; all trust lands associated with a reservation or tribe are shown in data products for the United States. The Census Bureau first reported data for tribal trust lands for the 1980 census.

★ 422 ★

Language

Language Spoken at Home and English Ability, by Age on Selected Reservations and Trust Lands - Part II

Data are shown for the 50 areas with the largest populations, in number of persons.

American Indian Reservation and Trust Lands[1,2]	Persons age 18 to 64 years									
	Speak only English	Speak Spanish			Speak Asian/Pacific Island language			Speak other language		
		Speak English very well	Speak English well	Speak English not well/ at all	Speak English very well	Speak English well	Speak English not well/ at all	Speak English very well	Speak English well	English not well/ at all
Agua Caliente Reservation	8,062	515	188	246	102	40	60	561	125	33
Allegany Reservation	3,862	33	4	2	2	0	0	145	9	9
Blackfeet Reservation	3,789	40	0	0	2	0	0	433	209	6
Cheyenne River Reservation	3,012	12	0	0	0	0	0	640	238	33
Coeur d'Alene Reservation and Trust Lands, ID	3,204	23	13	10	0	0	0	38	2	20
Colorado River Reservation	2,972	705	271	315	10	4	4	173	27	0
Colville Reservation	3,649	63	6	38	2	9	2	81	14	18

[Continued]

★ 422 ★

Language Spoken at Home and English Ability, by Age on Selected Reservations and Trust Lands - Part II

[Continued]

American Indian Reservation and Trust Lands[1,2]	Speak only English	Persons age 18 to 64 years								
		Speak Spanish			Speak Asian/Pacific Island language			Speak other language		
		Speak English very well	Speak English well	Speak English not well/ at all	Speak English very well	Speak English well	Speak English not well/ at all	Speak English very well	Speak English well	English not well/ at all
Crow Reservation and Trust Lands, MT	1,367	5	0	0	0	0	0	1,446	738	27
Eastern Cherokee Reservation	3,129	18	0	8	6	0	0	376	101	68
Flathead Reservation	10,513	89	7	13	4	0	0	424	92	3
Fort Apache Reservation	932	56	0	0	0	0	0	2,332	1,654	435
Fort Berthold Reservation	2,414	16	0	0	0	0	0	258	77	0
Fort Hall Reservation and Trust Lands, ID	1,957	36	22	80	0	0	0	528	189	32
Fort Peck Reservation	5,256	10	9	6	10	0	0	395	64	8
Gila River Reservation	2,340	93	97	102	0	0	0	1,598	777	136
Hopi Reservation and Trust Lands, AZ	877	6	0	15	5	0	0	1,600	1,040	276
Isabella Reservation and Trust Lands, MI	13,842	126	31	46	63	42	6	183	86	78
Laguna Pueblo and Trust Lands, NM	828	37	12	0	15	0	0	980	179	12
Lake Traverse (Sisseton) Reservation	5,014	8	8	0	0	0	0	499	20	19
Leech Lake Reservation	4,292	16	7	2	2	0	0	242	57	40
Mississippi Choctaw Reservation and Trust Lands, MS	222	0	0	0	0	0	0	858	842	240
Muckleshoot Reservation and Trust Lands, WA	2,026	32	7	8	15	0	0	40	7	2
Navajo Reservation and Trust Lands, AZ–NM–UT	8,792	328	24	44	44	35	0	36,116	20,862	10,041
Nez Perce Reservation	8,610	80	9	7	29	15	2	295	102	43
Northern Cheyenne Reservation and Trust Lands, MT–SD	1,182	11	0	0	0	0	0	483	337	4
Omaha Reservation	2,524	11	4	5	1	0	0	91	40	33
Oneida (West) Reservation	10,659	47	7	7	22	7	0	223	44	6
Osage Reservation	23,442	252	23	55	13	17	0	257	84	38
Papago Reservation	877	0	28	23	0	0	0	1,844	1,270	498
Pine Ridge Reservation and Trust Lands, NE–SD	3,422	14	18	0	13	0	0	1,876	348	172
Port Madison Reservation	2,713	5	0	17	35	28	12	45	3	0
Puyallup Reservation and Trust Lands, WA	17,487	304	122	128	353	300	636	382	68	23
Red Lake Reservation	1,371	3	0	0	6	0	0	470	30	9
Rosebud Reservation and Trust Lands, SD	3,209	22	2	2	0	0	0	1,055	263	46
Salt River Reservation	1,659	91	40	31	13	0	0	409	181	9
San Carlos Reservation	1,040	19	0	21	0	0	0	1,114	1,180	392
Sandia Pueblo	901	1,200	41	64	0	0	0	104	10	0
San Juan Pueblo	459	1,784	371	91	0	0	1	438	31	0
Santa Clara Pueblo	1,470	3,306	445	115	11	2	0	377	149	5
Southern Ute Reservation	3,745	559	37	13	11	5	0	216	22	2
Standing Rock Reservation	3,181	19	18	0	7	0	0	584	149	66
Taos Pueblo and Trust Lands, NM	1,094	862	125	60	2	5	0	554	117	4
Tulalip Reservation	4,088	40	9	4	21	19	0	100	16	0
Turtle Mountain Reservation and Trust Lands, ND–SD	3,203	7	0	0	0	0	0	420	34	13
Uintah and Ouray Reservation	7,533	155	44	20	21	2	0	525	109	31
White Earth Reservation	4,347	17	2	0	2	0	0	108	20	10

[Continued]

★ 422 ★

Language Spoken at Home and English Ability, by Age on Selected Reservations and Trust Lands - Part II

[Continued]

American Indian Reservation and Trust Lands[1,2]	Speak only English	Speak Spanish			Speak Asian/Pacific Island language			Speak other language		
		Speak English very well	Speak English well	Speak English not well/ at all	Speak English very well	Speak English well	Speak English not well/ at all	Speak English very well	Speak English well	English not well/ at all
Wind River Reservation	11,119	169	66	33	20	0	14	643	199	67
Yakima Reservation and Trust Lands, WA	8,600	2,402	971	2,254	78	73	9	428	78	0
Yankton Reservation	2,805	10	7	2	2	0	0	246	96	32
Zuni Pueblo	422	28	5	0	7	0	0	1,943	1,643	213

Source: Census of Population and Housing, 1990: Summary Tape File 3C on CD-ROM [machine-readable datafiles]. Prepared by the Bureau of the Census. Washington, DC: The Bureau, 1992. *Notes:* 1. Federal American Indian reservations are areas with boundaries established by treaty, statute, and/or executive or court order, and recognized by the federal government as territory in which American Indian tribes have jurisdiction. State reservations are lands held in trust by state governments for the use and benefit of a given tribe. The reservations and their boundaries were identified for the 1990 census by the Bureau of Indian Affairs (BIA), Department of Interior (for federal reservations), and state governments (for state reservations). The names of American Indian reservations recognized by state governments, but not by the federal government, are followed by "state." Areas composed of reservation lands that are administered jointly and/or are claimed by two reservations, as identified by the BIA, are called "joint areas," and are treated as separate American Indian reservations for census purposes. Federal reservations may cross state boundaries, and federal and state reservations may cross county, county subdivision, and place boundaries. For reservations that cross state boundaries, only the portion of the reservations in a given state is shown in the data products for that state; the entire reservations are shown in data products for the United States. 2. Trust lands are property associated with a particular American Indian reservation or tribe, held in trust by the federal government. Trust lands may be held in trust either for a tribe (tribal trust lands) or for an individual member of a tribe (individual trust land). Trust lands recognized for the 1990 census comprised all tribal trust lands and inhabited individual trust lands located outside of a reservation boundary. As with other American Indian areas, trust lands may be located in more than one state. Only the trust lands in a given state are shown in the data products for that state; all trust lands associated with a reservation or tribe are shown in data products for the United States. The Census Bureau first reported data for tribal trust lands for the 1980 census.

★ 423 ★

Language

Language Spoken at Home and English Ability, by Age on Selected Reservations and Trust Lands - Part III

Data are shown for the 50 areas with the largest populations, in number of persons.

American Indian Reservation and Trust Lands[1,2]	Speak only English	Speak Spanish			Speak Asian/Pacific Island language			Speak other language		
		Speak English very well	Speak English well	Speak English not well/ at all	Speak English very well	Speak English well	Speak English not well/ at all	Speak English very well	Speak English well	English not well/ at all
Agua Caliente Reservation	7,072	175	17	17	12	0	5	410	74	30
Allegany Reservation	1,207	9	0	0	0	0	0	65	35	22
Blackfeet Reservation	373	0	0	0	0	0	0	90	35	4
Cheyenne River Reservation	421	0	0	0	0	0	0	160	39	12
Coeur d'Alene Reservation and Trust Lands, ID	769	1	0	2	0	0	0	22	3	2
Colorado River Reservation	814	41	29	0	6	0	5	110	15	8
Colville Reservation	619	0	0	0	10	2	0	100	2	0
Crow Reservation and Trust Lands, MT	210	0	0	0	0	0	0	106	12	2
Eastern Cherokee Reservation	346	0	0	0	0	0	0	98	43	0
Flathead Reservation	3,331	0	0	0	0	0	0	111	28	11
Fort Apache Reservation	58	0	0	0	0	0	0	88	146	119
Fort Berthold Reservation	483	0	0	0	0	0	0	155	20	3
Fort Hall Reservation and Trust Lands, ID	283	14	0	0	0	0	7	31	26	25
Fort Peck Reservation	729	0	0	0	0	0	0	159	37	22

[Continued]

★ 423 ★

Language Spoken at Home and English Ability, by Age on Selected Reservations and Trust Lands - Part III

[Continued]

American Indian Reservation and Trust Lands[1,2]	Speak only English	Persons age 65 years and older								
		Speak Spanish			Speak Asian/Pacific Island language			Speak other language		
		Speak English very well	Speak English well	Speak English not well/ at all	Speak English very well	Speak English well	Speak English not well/ at all	Speak English very well	Speak English well	English not well/ at all
Gila River Reservation	90	0	13	7	0	0	0	209	212	56
Hopi Reservation and Trust Lands, AZ	25	0	0	0	0	0	0	237	168	186
Isabella Reservation and Trust Lands, MI	2,076	19	14	10	0	0	0	85	17	19
Laguna Pueblo and Trust Lands, NM	44	3	0	0	0	0	0	217	104	26
Lake Traverse (Sisseton) Reservation	1,639	4	0	2	0	0	0	246	61	19
Leech Lake Reservation	919	0	2	0	0	0	0	168	35	19
Mississippi Choctaw Reservation and Trust Lands, MS	24	0	0	0	0	0	0	0	16	74
Muckleshoot Reservation and Trust Lands, WA	406	0	0	0	0	0	0	18	3	0
Navajo Reservation and Trust Lands, AZ–NM–UT	787	0	0	0	0	0	0	1,820	1,374	4,806
Nez Perce Reservation	2,500	14	2	0	2	0	0	110	9	2
Northern Cheyenne Reservation and Trust Lands, MT–SD	34	0	0	0	0	0	0	31	32	26
Omaha Reservation	651	2	0	0	0	0	0	67	24	6
Oneida (West) Reservation	808	14	4	0	0	0	0	82	12	3
Osage Reservation	5,489	43	5	0	4	0	0	47	16	0
Papago Reservation	21	0	8	0	0	0	0	91	125	333
Pine Ridge Reservation and Trust Lands, NE–SD	237	0	0	0	0	0	0	325	110	25
Port Madison Reservation	552	0	0	0	0	0	2	5	4	0
Puyallup Reservation and Trust Lands, WA	2,680	8	7	10	34	23	45	80	28	15
Red Lake Reservation	114	0	0	0	0	0	0	70	0	5
Rosebud Reservation and Trust Lands, SD	264	0	0	0	0	0	0	228	107	29
Salt River Reservation	685	5	0	0	0	0	0	111	12	0
San Carlos Reservation	30	7	0	0	0	0	0	117	31	76
Sandia Pueblo	91	116	29	74	0	0	0	6	0	0
San Juan Pueblo	32	141	73	73	0	0	0	61	14	0
Santa Clara Pueblo	242	424	203	216	0	0	0	49	34	13
Southern Ute Reservation	541	60	27	31	0	0	0	41	7	4
Standing Rock Reservation	423	0	0	0	0	0	0	185	60	16
Taos Pueblo and Trust Lands, NM	180	167	85	49	0	0	0	51	72	16
Tulalip Reservation	718	4	0	0	0	1	0	31	2	0
Turtle Mountain Reservation and Trust Lands, ND–SD	158	0	0	0	0	0	0	206	38	0
Uintah and Ouray Reservation	1,273	14	8	0	0	0	2	63	15	11
White Earth Reservation	1,169	2	0	0	0	0	2	109	67	15
Wind River Reservation	1,938	36	19	13	0	0	0	173	64	22
Yakima Reservation and Trust Lands, WA	2,256	104	69	136	67	15	10	104	48	10

[Continued]

★ 423 ★

Language Spoken at Home and English Ability, by Age on Selected Reservations and Trust Lands - Part III

[Continued]

American Indian Reservation and Trust Lands[1,2]	Persons age 65 years and older									
	Speak only English	Speak Spanish			Speak Asian/Pacific Island language			Speak other language		
		Speak English very well	Speak English well	Speak English not well/ at all	Speak English very well	Speak English well	Speak English not well/ at all	Speak English very well	Speak English well	English not well/ at all
Yankton Reservation	765	0	1	0	0	0	0	170	80	13
Zuni Pueblo	8	0	0	0	0	0	0	110	98	170

Source: Census of Population and Housing, 1990: Summary Tape File 3C on CD-ROM [machine-readable datafiles]. Prepared by the Bureau of the Census. Washington, DC: The Bureau, 1992. *Notes:* 1. Federal American Indian reservations are areas with boundaries established by treaty, statute, and/or executive or court order, and recognized by the federal government as territory in which American Indian tribes have jurisdiction. State reservations are lands held in trust by state governments for the use and benefit of a given tribe. The reservations and their boundaries were identified for the 1990 census by the Bureau of Indian Affairs (BIA), Department of Interior (for federal reservations), and state governments (for state reservations). The names of American Indian reservations recognized by state governments, but not by the federal government, are followed by "state." Areas composed of reservation lands that are administered jointly and/or are claimed by two reservations, as identified by the BIA, are called "joint areas," and are treated as separate American Indian reservations for census purposes. Federal reservations may cross state boundaries, and federal and state reservations may cross county, county subdivision, and place boundaries. For reservations that cross state boundaries, only the portion of the reservations in a given state is shown in the data products for that state; the entire reservations are shown in data products for the United States. 2. Trust lands are property associated with a particular American Indian reservation or tribe, held in trust by the federal government. Trust lands may be held in trust either for a tribe (tribal trust lands) or for an individual member of a tribe (individual trust land). Trust lands recognized for the 1990 census comprised all tribal trust lands and inhabited individual trust lands located outside of a reservation boundary. As with other American Indian areas, trust lands may be located in more than one state. Only the trust lands in a given state are shown in the data products for that state; all trust lands associated with a reservation or tribe are shown in data products for the United States. The Census Bureau first reported data for tribal trust lands for the 1980 census.

Employment

★ 424 ★

Traditional Occupations Held by Residents of Reservations, 1980: Acoma Pueblo - Isabella - I

Data are the latest available.

Identified reservation	Persons 16 years and over working in 1980 reference period	Traditional occupations										
		Tribal government occupations				Native healers	Sheep workers	Artists and performers				
		Total	Officials and administrators	Legislators	Judicial administrators			Total	Dancers	Drummers and singers	Painters	Potters
Total American Indian, Eskimo, and Aleut	89,697	834	563	200	71	31	276	290	6	3	70	211
Acoma Pueblo, NM	632	2	2	-	-	-	3	4	-	-	-	4
Agua Caliente, CA	-	-	-	-	-	-	-	-	-	-	-	-
Alabama-Coushatta, TX	234	-	-	-	-	-	-	10	1	1	1	6
Alamo, NM	204	-	-	-	-	-	-	-	-	-	-	-
Allegany, NY	381	2	2	-	-	-	-	-	-	-	-	-
Alturas Rancheria, CA	...	...	...	...	...	...	...	...	...	...	...	...
Annette Islands Reserve, AK	398	-	-	-	-	-	-	-	-	-	-	-
Augustine, CA	-	-	-	-	-	-	-	-	-	-	-	-
Bad River, WI	197	4	4	-	-	-	-	-	-	-	-	-
Barona Rancheria, CA	79	-	-	-	-	-	-	-	-	-	-	-
Bay Mills, MI	99	1	1	-	-	-	-	-	-	-	-	-
Benton Paiute, CA	...	...	...	...	...	...	...	...	...	...	...	...
Berry Creek Rancheria, CA	-	-	-	-	-	-	-	-	-	-	-	-
Big Bend Rancheria, CA	...	...	...	...	...	...	...	...	...	...	...	...
Big Cypress, FL	108	2	2	-	-	2	-	-	-	-	-	-
Big Lagoon Rancheria, CA	...	...	...	...	...	...	...	...	...	...	...	...
Big Pine Rancheria, CA	79	-	-	-	-	-	-	-	-	-	-	-

[Continued]

★ 424 ★

Traditional Occupations Held by Residents of Reservations, 1980: Acoma Pueblo - Isabella - I

[Continued]

Identified reservation	Persons 16 years and over working in 1980 reference period	Traditional occupations										
		Tribal government occupations				Native healers	Sheep workers	Artists and performers				
		Total	Officials and administrators	Legislators	Judicial administrators			Total	Dancers	Drummers and singers	Painters	Potters
Bishop Rancheria, CA	276	1	1	-	-	-	-	-	-	-	-	-
Blackfeet, MT	1,665	16	7	7	2	-	2	-	-	-	-	-
Bois Forte (Nett Lake), MN	123	2	2	-	-	-	-	-	-	-	-	-
Bridgeport Colony, CA	23	-	-	-	-	-	-	-	-	-	-	-
Brighton, FL	132	-	-	-	-	-	-	-	-	-	-	-
Burns, Oregon	55	2	2	-	-	-	-	-	-	-	-	-
Cabazon, CA	...	...	...	...	...	...	...	...	...	...	...	...
Cachil Dehe Rancheria, CA	...	...	...	...	...	...	...	...	...	...	...	...
Cahuilla, CA	...	...	...	...	...	...	...	...	...	...	...	...
Campo, CA	17	-	-	-	-	-	-	-	-	-	-	-
Camp Verde, AZ	42	-	-	-	-	-	-	1	-	-	-	1
Canoncito, NM	156	1	1	-	-	-	-	-	-	-	-	-
Capitan Grande, CA	-	-	-	-	-	-	-	-	-	-	-	-
Carson Colony, NV	73	1	1	-	-	-	-	-	-	-	-	-
Catawba, SC	395	-	-	-	-	-	-	6	-	-	4	2
Cattaraugus, NY	559	3	2	-	1	-	-	-	-	-	-	-
Cedarville Rancheria, CA	...	...	...	...	...	...	...	...	...	...	...	...
Chehalis, WA	52	2	2	-	-	-	-	-	-	-	-	-
Chemehuevi, CA	...	...	...	...	...	...	...	...	...	...	...	...
Cheyenne River, SD	399	1	-	-	1	-	-	-	-	-	-	-
Chitimacha, LA	65	-	-	-	-	-	-	-	-	-	-	-
Cochiti Pueblo, NM	167	-	-	-	-	-	-	2	-	-	-	2
Cocopah, AZ	83	2	2	-	-	-	-	-	-	-	-	-
Coeur D'Alene, Idaho	146	-	-	-	-	-	-	-	-	-	-	-
Cold Springs Rancheria, CA	11	1	1	-	-	-	-	1	-	-	-	1
Colorado River, AZ-CA	650	8	5	-	3	-	-	1	-	-	-	1
Colville, WA	1,304	18	7	9	2	-	-	1	-	-	1	-
Cortina Rancheria, CA	...	...	...	...	...	...	...	...	...	...	...	...
Coushatta, LA	...	...	...	...	...	...	...	...	...	...	...	...
Coyote Valley Rancheria, CA	-	-	-	-	-	-	-	-	-	-	-	-
Crow, MT	1,039	16	12	-	3	-	-	-	-	-	-	-
Crow Creek, SD	322	2	-	2	-	-	-	1	-	-	1	-
Cuyapaipe, CA	...	...	...	...	...	...	...	...	...	...	...	...
Deer Creek, MN	...	...	...	...	...	...	...	...	...	...	...	...
Dresslerville Colony, NV	50	-	-	-	-	-	-	-	-	-	-	-
Dry Creek Rancheria, CA	4	-	-	-	-	-	-	-	-	-	-	-
Duck Valley, ID-NV	278	2	1	-	1	-	-	-	-	-	-	-
Duckwater, NV	40	-	-	-	-	-	-	-	-	-	-	-
Eastern Cherokee, NC	1,800	7	6	1	-	-	-	7	4	1	-	1
Eastern Pequot, CT	...	...	...	...	...	...	...	...	...	...	...	...
Ely Colony, NV	21	-	-	-	-	-	-	-	-	-	-	-
Enterprise Rancheria, CA	...	...	...	...	...	...	...	...	...	...	...	...
Fallon Colony, NV	16	1	1	-	-	-	-	-	-	-	-	-
Fallon, NV	100	1	1	-	-	-	-	-	-	-	-	-
Flandreau, SD	60	-	-	-	-	-	-	-	-	-	-	-
Flathead, MT	1,216	10	9	1	-	-	-	-	-	-	-	-
Fond du Lac, MN	142	4	2	2	-	-	-	-	-	-	-	-
Fort Apache, AZ	1,837	2	1	1	-	-	-	1	-	-	1	-
Fort Belknap, MT	493	5	5	-	-	-	-	-	-	-	-	-
Fort Berthold, ND	740	14	9	5	-	-	-	-	-	-	-	-
Fort Bidwell, CA	19	-	-	-	-	-	-	-	-	-	-	-
Fort Hall, Idaho	675	5	3	2	-	-	-	-	-	-	-	-
Fort Independence, CA	16	-	-	-	-	-	-	-	-	-	-	-
Fort McDermitt, NV-OR	101	1	1	-	-	-	-	-	-	-	-	-
Fort McDowell, AZ	129	1	1	-	-	-	-	-	-	-	-	-
Fort Mojave, AZ-CA-NV	39	-	-	-	-	-	-	-	-	-	-	-
Fort Peck, MT	1,262	18	16	-	2	-	-	-	-	-	-	-
Fort Totten, ND	462	4	4	-	-	-	-	-	-	-	-	-
Fort Yuma, AZ-CA	339	3	3	-	-	-	-	-	-	-	-	-
Gila Bend, AZ	-	-	-	-	-	-	-	-	-	-	-	-
Gila River, AZ	1,762	19	12	4	4	1	-	-	-	-	-	-
Golden Hill, CT	...	...	...	...	...	...	...	...	...	...	...	...
Goshute, NV-UT	17	-	-	-	-	-	-	-	-	-	-	-
Grand Portage, MN	88	-	-	-	-	-	-	-	-	-	-	-
Grindstone Creek Rancheria, CA	20	-	-	-	-	-	-	-	-	-	-	-
Hannahville Community, MI	76	2	2	-	-	-	-	-	-	-	-	-
Hassanamisco, MA	...	...	...	...	...	...	...	...	...	...	...	...
Havasupai, AZ	86	1	1	-	-	-	-	-	-	-	-	-
Hoh, WA	14	-	-	-	-	-	-	-	-	-	-	-
Hollywood, FL	197	7	7	-	-	-	-	-	-	-	-	-
Hoopa Valley, CA	441	1	1	-	-	-	2	-	-	-	-	-
Hoopa Valley Extension, CA	100	1	-	-	1	-	-	-	-	-	-	-

[Continued]

★ 424 ★

Traditional Occupations Held by Residents of Reservations, 1980: Acoma Pueblo - Isabella - I

[Continued]

Identified reservation	Persons 16 years and over working in 1980 reference period	Traditional occupations										
		Tribal government occupations				Native healers	Sheep workers	Artists and performers				
		Total	Officials and administrators	Legislators	Judicial administrators			Total	Dancers	Drummers and singers	Painters	Potters
Hopi, AZ	1,435	7	7	-	-	-	-	49	-	-	3	46
Hopland Rancheria, CA	-											
Hualapai, AZ	236	3	1	-	2	-	-	-	-	-	-	-
Inaja-Cosmit, CA	-	-	-	-	-	-	-	-	-	-	-	-
Indian Township, ME	104	1	1	-	-	-	-	-	-	-	-	-
Iowa, KS-NE	15	-	-	-	-	-	-	-	-	-	-	-
Isabella, MI	146	-	-	-	-	-	-	-	-	-	-	-

Source: U.S. Bureau of the Census, Subject Reports, PC80-2-1D, Part II, *American Indians, Eskimos, and Aleuts on Identified Reservations and in the Historic Areas of Oklahoma (Excluding Urbanized Areas)*, U.S. Government Printing Office, Washington, D.C., 1986, pp. 482-520. *Notes:* A dash (-) represents zero or a percent which rounds to less than 0.1. Also, a dash (-) is used because the number of supplementary questionnaires for the areas was insufficient to produce reliable estimates. Three dots (...) means not applicable, or that the data are being withheld to avoid disclosure of information for individuals.

★ 425 ★

Employment

Traditional Occupations Held by Residents of Reservations, 1980: Acoma Pueblo - Isabella - II

Data are the latest available.

Identified reservation	Jewelers	Traditional occupations										
		Handworking occupations										
		Total	Basket makers	Beaders	Bustle makers	Carvers	Fan makers	Moccasin makers	Quilters	Rattle makers	Weavers	Other handworking occupations
American Indian, Eskimo, and Aleut	1,323	1,365	156	193	2	54	2	20	47	-	806	85
Acoma Pueblo, NM	-	-	-	-	-	-	-	-	-	-	-	-
Agua Caliente, CA	-	-	-	-	-	-	-	-	-	-	-	-
Alabama-Coushatta, TX	-	1	-	1	-	-	-	-	-	-	-	-
Alamo, NM	9	9	-	-	-	-	-	-	1	-	6	2
Allegany, NY	-	3	-	3	-	-	-	-	-	-	-	-
Alturas Rancheria, CA	...	...	...	...	...	...	...	...	...	...	...	...
Annette Islands Reserve, AK	-	-	-	-	-	-	-	-	-	-	-	-
Augustine, CA	-	-	-	-	-	-	-	-	-	-	-	-
Bad River, WI	-	-	-	-	-	-	-	-	-	-	-	-
Barona Rancheria, CA	-	-	-	-	-	-	-	-	-	-	-	-
Bay Mills, MI	-	-	-	-	-	-	-	-	-	-	-	-
Benton Paiute, CA	...	...	...	...	...	...	...	...	...	...	...	...
Berry Creek Rancheria, CA	-	-	-	-	-	-	-	-	-	-	-	-
Big Bend Rancheria, CA	...	...	...	...	...	...	...	...	...	...	...	...
Big Cypress, FL	-	1	-	-	-	-	-	-	-	-	-	1
Big Lagoon Rancheria, CA	...	...	...	...	...	...	...	...	...	...	...	...
Big Pine Rancheria, CA	-	-	-	-	-	-	-	-	-	-	-	-
Bishop Rancheria, CA	2	-	-	-	-	-	-	-	-	-	-	-
Blackfeet, MT	-	8	2	3	-	2	-	-	2	-	-	-
Bois Forte (Nett Lake), MN	-	-	-	-	-	-	-	-	-	-	-	-
Bridgeport Colony, CA	-	-	-	-	-	-	-	-	-	-	-	-
Brighton, FL	1	-	-	-	-	-	-	-	-	-	-	-
Burns, Oregon	-	-	-	-	-	-	-	-	-	-	-	-
Cabazon, CA	...	...	...	...	...	...	...	...	...	...	...	...
Cachil Dehe Rancheria, CA	...	...	...	...	...	...	...	...	...	...	...	...
Cahuilla, CA	...	...	...	...	...	...	...	...	...	...	...	...
Campo, CA	-	-	-	-	-	-	-	-	-	-	-	-
Camp Verde, AZ	-	2	-	-	-	-	-	-	-	-	-	-
Canoncito, NM	9	2	-	-	-	-	-	-	-	-	-	2

[Continued]

Traditional Occupations Held by Residents of Reservations, 1980: Acoma Pueblo - Isabella - II

[Continued]

Identified reservation	Jewelers	Traditional occupations										
		Handworking occupations										
		Total	Basket makers	Beaders	Bustle makers	Carvers	Fan makers	Moccasin makers	Quilters	Rattle makers	Weavers	Other handworking occupations
Capitan Grande, CA	-	-	-	-	-	-	-	-	-	-	-	-
Carson Colony, NV	-	-	-	-	-	-	-	-	-	-	-	-
Catawba, SC	-	-	-	-	-	-	-	-	-	-	-	-
Cattaraugus, NY	-	-	-	-	-	-	-	-	-	-	-	-
Cedarville Rancheria, CA	...	...	...	...	...	...	...	...	...	...	...	...
Chehalis, WA	-	1	-	1	-	-	-	-	-	-	-	-
Chemehuevi, CA	...	...	...	...	...	...	...	...	...	...	...	...
Cheyenne River, SD	-	2	-	2	-	-	-	-	-	-	-	-
Chitimacha, LA	-	-	-	-	-	-	-	-	-	-	-	-
Cochiti Pueblo, NM	6	-	-	-	-	-	-	-	-	-	-	-
Cocopah, AZ	-	-	-	-	-	-	-	-	-	-	-	-
Coeur D'Alene, Idaho	-	-	-	-	-	-	-	-	-	-	-	-
Cold Springs Rancheria, CA	-	-	-	-	-	-	-	-	-	-	-	-
Colorado River, AZ-CA	2	2	-	-	-	-	-	-	-	-	2	-
Colville, WA	2	6	-	4	-	-	-	-	-	-	2	-
Cortina Rancheria, CA	...	...	...	...	...	...	...	...	...	...	...	...
Coushatta, LA	...	...	...	...	...	...	...	...	...	...	...	...
Coyote Valley Rancheria, CA	-	-	-	-	-	-	-	-	-	-	-	-
Crow, MT	-	5	-	5	-	-	-	-	-	-	-	-
Crow Creek, SD	-	4	-	1	-	-	-	-	3	-	-	-
Cuyapaipe, CA	...	...	...	...	...	...	...	...	...	...	...	...
Deer Creek, MN	...	...	...	...	...	...	...	...	...	...	...	...
Dresslerville Colony, NV	-	-	-	-	-	-	-	-	-	-	-	-
Dry Creek Rancheria, CA	-	-	-	-	-	-	-	-	-	-	-	-
Duck Valley, ID-NV	-	-	-	-	-	-	-	-	-	-	-	-
Duckwater, NV	-	-	-	-	-	-	-	-	-	-	-	-
Eastern Cherokee, NC	2	61	20	6	-	8	2	4	6	-	-	15
Eastern Pequot, CT	...	...	...	...	...	...	...	...	...	...	...	-
Ely Colony, NV	-	-	-	-	-	-	-	-	-	-	-	-
Enterprise Rancheria, CA	...	...	...	...	...	...	...	...	...	...	...	-
Fallon Colony, NV	-	1	-	1	-	-	-	-	-	-	-	-
Fallon, NV	-	-	-	-	-	-	-	-	-	-	-	-
Flandreau, SD	-	-	-	-	-	-	-	-	-	-	-	-
Flathead, MT	-	9	-	5	-	4	-	-	-	-	-	-
Fond du Lac, MN	-	3	-	-	-	-	-	-	2	-	1	2
Fort Apache, AZ	1	12	1	-	-	1	-	-	2	-	8	-
Fort Belknap, MT	-	1	-	-	-	-	-	-	1	-	-	-
Fort Berthold, ND	-	20	3	14	-	-	-	2	2	-	-	-
Fort Bidwell, CA	-	-	-	-	-	-	-	-	-	-	-	-
Fort Hall, Idaho	4	13	1	7	-	-	-	-	2	-	-	3
Fort Independence, CA	-	-	-	-	-	-	-	-	-	-	-	-
Fort McDermitt, NV-OR	-	-	-	-	-	-	-	-	-	-	-	-
Fort McDowell, AZ	1	3	-	-	-	1	-	-	-	-	-	2
Fort Mojave, AZ-CA-NV	-	-	-	-	-	-	-	-	-	-	-	-
Fort Peck, MT	-	6	1	3	-	-	-	-	1	-	-	-
Fort Totten, ND	-	5	-	5	-	-	-	-	-	-	-	-
Fort Yuma, AZ-CA	-	1	-	1	-	-	-	-	-	-	-	-
Gila Bend, AZ	-	-	-	-	-	-	-	-	-	-	-	-
Gila River, AZ	3	4	3	-	-	-	-	-	-	-	2	-
Golden Hill, CT	...	...	...	...	...	...	...	...	...	...	...	...
Goshute, NV-UT	-	-	-	-	-	-	-	-	-	-	-	-
Grand Portage, MN	-	2	-	2	-	-	-	-	-	-	-	-
Grindstone Creek Rancheria, CA	-	-	-	-	-	-	-	-	-	-	-	-
Hannahville Community, MI	-	-	-	-	-	-	-	-	-	-	-	-
Hassanamisco, MA	...	...	...	...	...	...	...	...	...	...	...	...
Havasupai, AZ	-	-	-	-	-	-	-	-	-	-	-	-
Hoh, WA	-	-	-	1	-	-	-	-	-	-	-	-
Hollywood, FL	-	6	-	3	-	-	-	-	-	-	1	3
Hoopa Valley, CA	2	-	-	-	-	-	-	-	-	-	-	-
Hoopa Valley Extension, CA	-	-	-	-	-	-	-	-	-	-	-	-
Hopi, AZ	26	69	3	-	-	11	-	-	-	-	34	20
Hopland Rancheria, CA	-	-	-	-	-	-	-	-	-	-	-	-
Hualapai, AZ	-	1	-	-	-	1	-	-	-	-	-	-

[Continued]

★ 425 ★

Traditional Occupations Held by Residents of Reservations, 1980: Acoma Pueblo - Isabella - II

[Continued]

| Identified reservation | Jewelers | Traditional occupations | | | | | | | | | | |
| | | Handworking occupations | | | | | | | | | | |
		Total	Basket makers	Beaders	Bustle makers	Carvers	Fan makers	Moccasin makers	Quilters	Rattle makers	Weavers	Other handworking occupations
Inaja-Cosmit, CA	-	-	-	-	-	-	-	-	-	-	-	-
Indian Township, ME	-	-	-	-	-	-	-	-	-	-	-	-
Iowa, KS-NE	-	-	-	-	-	-	-	-	-	-	-	-
Isabella, MI	-	7	2	5	-	-	-	-	-	-	-	-

Source: U.S. Bureau of the Census, Subject Reports, PC80-2-1D, Part II, *American Indians, Eskimos, and Aleuts on Identified Reservations and in the Historic Areas of Oklahoma (Excluding Urbanized Areas),* U.S. Government Printing Office, Washington, D.C., 1986, pp. 482-520. *Notes:* A dash (-) represents zero or a percent which rounds to less than 0.1. Also, a dash (-) is used because the number of supplementary questionnaires for the areas was insufficient to produce reliable estimates. Three dots (...) means not applicable, or that the data are being withheld to avoid disclosure of information for individuals.

★ 426 ★

Employment

Traditional Occupations Held by Residents of Reservations, 1980: Isleta - Santa Clara Pueblo - I

Data are the latest available.

| Identified reservation | Persons 16 years and over working in 1980 reference period | Traditional occupations | | | | | | | | | | |
| | | Tribal governmental occupations | | | | Native healers | Sheep workers | Artists and performers | | | | |
		Total	Officials and administrators	Legislators	Judicial administrators			Total	Dancers	Drummers and singers	Painters	Potters
Isleta Pueblo, NM	874	10	10	-	-	-	-	7	-	-	3	3
Jackson Rancheria, CA	...	...	...	...	...	...	...	...	...	...	...	...
Jemez Pueblo, NM	383	5	5	-	-	-	-	3	-	-	-	3
Jicarilla Apache, NM	656	1	-	-	1	-	4	-	-	-	-	-
Kaibab, AZ	42	3	3	-	-	-	-	-	-	-	-	-
Kalispel, WA	36	1	1	-	-	-	-	-	-	-	-	-
Kickapoo, KS	108	-	-	-	-	-	-	1	-	-	1	-
Kootenai, ID	-	-	-	-	-	-	-	-	-	-	-	-
Lac Courte Oreilles, WI	331	13	7	5	1	-	-	-	-	-	-	-
Lac du Flambeau, WI	322	4	4	-	-	-	-	-	-	-	-	-
Laguna Pueblo, NM	1,300	2	1	-	1	-	1	5	-	-	-	5
La Jolla, CA	43	-	-	-	-	-	-	-	-	-	-	-
L'Anse, MI	177	2	2	-	-	-	-	-	-	-	-	-
La Posta, CA	...	...	...	...	...	...	...	...	...	...	...	...
Las Vegas Colony, NV	35	-	-	-	-	-	-	-	-	-	-	-
Laytonville Rancheria, CA	24	-	-	-	-	-	-	-	-	-	-	-
Leech Lake, MN	728	11	11	-	-	-	-	-	-	-	-	-
Likely Rancheria, CA	-	-	-	-	-	-	-	-	-	-	-	-
Lone Pine Rancheria, CA	49	-	-	-	-	-	-	-	-	-	-	-
Lookout Rancheria, CA	...	...	...	...	...	...	...	...	...	...	...	...
Los Coyotes, CA	11	-	-	-	-	-	-	-	-	-	-	-
Lovelock Colony, NV	34	-	-	-	-	-	-	-	-	-	-	-
Lower Brule, SD	243	4	2	2	-	-	-	-	-	-	-	-
Lower Elwah, WA	17	-	-	-	-	-	-	-	-	-	-	-
Lower Sioux Community, MN	25	-	-	-	-	-	-	-	-	-	-	-
Lummi, WA	347	6	6	-	-	-	-	-	-	-	-	-
Makah, WA	318	10	8	2	-	-	-	-	-	-	-	-
Manchester Rancheria, CA	15	-	-	-	-	-	-	-	-	-	-	-
Manzanita, CA	...	...	...	...	...	...	...	...	...	...	...	...
Maricopa, AZ	95	1	1	-	-	-	-	-	-	-	-	-
Mattaponi, VA	23	-	-	-	-	-	-	-	-	-	-	-
Menominee, WI	699	16	13	1	2	-	-	-	-	-	-	-
Mesa Grande, CA	-	-	-	-	-	-	-	-	-	-	-	-
Mescalero Apache, NM	548	8	-	-	8	-	-	2	-	-	2	-
Miccosukee, Florida	134	-	-	-	-	-	-	-	-	-	-	-
Middletown Rancheria, CA	9	-	-	-	-	-	-	-	-	-	-	-
Mille Lacs, MN	-	-	-	-	-	-	-	-	-	-	-	-
Mississippi Choctaw Reservation, MS	909	11	8	1	1	-	-	-	-	-	-	-
Moapa River, NV	47	4	4	-	-	-	-	-	-	-	-	-

[Continued]

★ 426 ★

Traditional Occupations Held by Residents of Reservations, 1980: Isleta - Santa Clara Pueblo - I
[Continued]

Identified reservation	Persons 16 years and over working in 1980 reference period	Traditional occupations										
		Tribal governmental occupations				Native healers	Sheep workers	Artists and performers				
		Total	Officials and administrators	Legislators	Judicial administrators			Total	Dancers	Drummers and singers	Painters	Potters
Montgomery Creek Rancheria, CA	...	...	...	...	...	...	...	...	...	...	...	...
Morongo, CA	96	-	-	-	-	-	-	-	-	-	-	-
Muckleshoot, WA	98	3	1	2	-	-	-	-	-	-	-	-
Nambe Pueblo, NM	82	4	4	-	-	-	-	1	-	-	-	1
Navajo, AZ-NM-UT	22,636	116	55	57	4	28	209	25	-	-	22	2
Nez Perce, ID	469	13	11	1	1	-	-	1	-	-	1	-
Nisqually, WA	13	-	-	-	-	-	-	-	-	-	-	-
Nooksack, WA	-	-	-	-	-	-	-	-	-	-	-	-
Northern Cheyenne, MT	839	16	5	10	1	-	-	-	-	-	-	-
Oil Springs, NY	-	-	-	-	-	-	-	-	-	-	-	-
Omaha, IO-NE	339	1	-	1	-	-	-	-	-	-	-	-
Oneida, WI	608	11	8	3	-	-	-	2	-	-	1	1
Onondaga, NY	-	-	-	-	-	-	-	-	-	-	-	-
Ontonagon, MI	-	-	-	-	-	-	-	-	-	-	-	-
Osage, OK	1,755	7	7	-	-	-	-	2	-	-	2	-
Ozette, WA	...	...	...	...	...	...	...	...	...	...	...	...
Pala, CA	142	-	-	-	-	-	-	-	-	-	-	-
Pamunkey, VA	19	1	1	-	-	-	-	3	-	-	-	3
Papago, AZ	1,607	6	6	-	-	-	1	2	-	-	1	1
Pascua Yaqui, AZ	110	3	3	-	-	-	-	-	-	-	-	-
Pauma, CA	26	-	-	-	-	-	-	-	-	-	-	-
Payson Comm. of Yavapai-Apache, AZ	-	-	-	-	-	-	-	-	-	-	-	-
Pechanga, CA	36	-	-	-	-	-	-	-	-	-	-	-
Penobscot, MA	127	7	6	-	1	-	-	-	-	-	-	-
Picuris Pueblo, NM	52	-	-	-	-	-	-	-	-	-	-	-
Pine Creek, MI	...	...	...	...	...	...	...	...	...	...	...	...
Pine Ridge, SD	2,482	56	22	28	6	...	-	3	-	-	1	1
Pleasant Point, MA	101	3	3	-	-	-	-	2	-	-	-	2
Pojoaque Pueblo, NM	41	-	-	-	-	-	-	-	-	-	-	-
Poospatuck, NY	13	-	-	-	-	-	-	-	-	-	-	-
Port Gamble, WA	97	-	-	-	-	-	-	-	-	-	-	-
Port Madison, WA	56	-	-	-	-	-	-	2	-	-	-	2
Potawatomi, WI	61	4	4	-	-	-	-	-	-	-	-	-
Pottawatomi, KS	128	-	-	-	-	-	-	-	-	-	-	-
Prairie Island Community, MN	28	1	1	-	-	-	-	-	-	-	-	-
Puyallup, WA	237	2	2	-	-	-	-	-	-	-	-	-
Pyramid Lake, NV	226	2	2	-	-	-	-	-	-	-	-	-
Quileute, WA	69	-	-	-	-	-	-	-	-	-	-	-
Quinault, WA	324	4	3	-	1	-	-	-	-	-	-	-
Ramah Community, NM	335	2	1	1	-	-	11	1	-	-	1	-
Ramona, CA	-	-	-	-	-	-	-	-	-	-	-	-
Red Cliff, WI	149	4	4	-	-	-	-	-	-	-	-	-
Red Lake, MN	707	4	2	-	2	-	-	1	-	-	1	-
Reno-Sparks Colony, NV	186	1	1	-	-	-	-	2	-	-	2	-
Resighini Rancheria, CA	...	...	...	...	...	...	...	...	...	...	...	...
Rincon, CA	91	-	-	-	-	...	...	...	...	...	...	...
Roaring Creek Rancheria, CA	...	...	...	...	...	...	* ...	...	...	...	...	...
Rocky Boy's, MT	391	11	6	3	1	-	-	...	...	...	...	...
Rosebud, SD	1,279	11	9	2	-	-	-	3	-	-	-	3
Round Valley, CA	142	-	-	-	-	-	-	-	-	-	-	-
Rumsey Rancheria, CA	...	...	...	...	...	...	...	...	...	...	...	...
Sac and Fox, Iowa	141	-	-	-	-	-	-	-	-	-	-	-
Sac and Fox, KS-NE	...	...	...	...	...	...	...	...	...	...	...	...
St. Croix, WI	116	13	10	2	-	-	-	-	-	-	-	-
St. Regis Mohawk, NY	491	9	9	-	-	-	-	-	-	-	-	-
Salt River, AZ	880	1	-	1	-	-	-	4	-	-	4	-
San Carlos, AZ	1,442	14	7	5	2	-	-	1	-	-	1	-
Sandia Pueblo, NM	86	2	1	1	-	-	-	-	-	-	-	-
Sandy Lake, MN	-	-	-	-	-	-	-	-	-	-	-	-
San Felipe Pueblo, NM	469	4	4	-	-	-	-	1	-	-	1	-
San Ildefonso Pueblo, NM	197	-	-	-	-	-	-	23	-	-	-	23
San Juan Pueblo, NM	287	-	-	-	-	-	-	3	-	-	-	3
San Manuel, CA	-	-	-	-	-	-	-	-	-	-	-	-
San Pasqual, CA	34	-	-	-	-	-	-	-	-	-	-	-
Santa Ana Pueblo, NM	184	4	4	-	-	-	-	-	-	-	-	-
Santa Clara Pueblo, NM	706	8	8	-	-	-	-	64	-	-	3	61

Source: U.S. Bureau of the Census, Subject Reports, PC80-2-1D, Part II, *American Indians, Eskimos, and Aleuts on Identified Reservations and in the Historic Areas of Oklahoma (Excluding Urbanized Areas)*, U.S. Government Printing Office, Washington, D.C., 1986, pp. 482-520. *Notes:* A dash (-) represents zero or a percent which rounds to less than 0.1. Also, a dash (-) is used because the number of supplementary questionnaires for the areas was insufficient to produce reliable estimates. Three dots (...) means not applicable, or that the data are being withheld to avoid disclosure of information for individuals.

★ 427 ★

Employment

Traditional Occupations Held by Residents of Reservations, 1980: Isleta - Santa Clara Pueblo - II

Data are the latest available.

| Identified reservation | Jewelers | Traditional occupations | | | | | | | | | | |
| | | Handworking occupations | | | | | | | | | | |
		Total	Basket makers	beaders	Bustle makers	Carvers	Fan makers	Moccasin makers	Quilters	Rattle makers	Weavers	Other handworking occupations
Isleta Pueblo, NM	6	1	-	-	-	-	-	-	-	-	1	-
Jackson Rancheria, CA	...	...	...	...	...	...	...	...	...	...	...	...
Jemez Pueblo, NM	3	-	-	-	-	-	-	-	-	-	-	-
Jicarilla Apache, NM	-	17	6	5	-	-	-	-	-	-	5	1
Kaibab, AZ	-	-	-	-	-	-	-	-	-	-	-	-
Kalispel, WA	-	-	-	-	-	-	-	-	-	-	-	-
Kickapoo, KS	4	-	-	-	-	-	-	-	-	-	4	-
Kootenai, ID	-	-	-	-	-	-	-	-	-	-	-	-
Lac Courte Oreilles, WI	-	-	-	-	-	-	-	-	-	-	-	-
Lac du Flambeau, WI	-	-	-	-	-	-	-	-	-	-	-	-
Laguna Pueblo, NM	2	1	-	-	-	-	-	-	-	-	1	-
La Jolla, CA	-	-	-	-	-	-	-	-	-	-	-	-
L'Anse, MI	-	3	-	1	-	-	-	-	-	-	1	-
La Posta, CA	...	...	...	...	...	...	...	...	...	...	...	...
Las Vegas Colony, NV	-	-	-	-	-	-	-	-	-	-	-	-
Laytonville Rancheria, CA	-	-	-	-	-	-	-	-	-	-	-	-
Leech Lake, MN	-	1	-	-	-	-	-	-	-	-	1	-
Likely Rancheria, CA	-	-	-	-	-	-	-	-	-	-	-	-
Lone Pine Rancheria, CA	-	-	-	-	-	-	-	-	-	-	-	-
Lookout Rancheria, CA	...	...	...	...	...	...	...	...	...	...	...	...
Los Coyotes, CA	-	-	-	-	-	-	-	-	-	-	-	-
Lovelock Colony, NV	-	-	-	-	-	-	-	-	-	-	-	-
Lower Brule, SD	-	-	-	-	-	-	-	-	-	-	-	-
Lower Elwah, WA	-	-	-	-	-	-	-	-	-	-	-	-
Lower Sioux Community, MN	-	-	-	-	-	-	-	-	-	-	-	1
Lummi, WA	-	1	-	-	-	-	-	-	-	-	-	1
Makah, WA	1	6	2	-	-	3	-	-	-	-	-	-
Manchester Rancheria, CA	-	-	-	-	-	-	-	-	-	-	-	-
Manzanita, CA	...	...	...	...	...	...	...	...	...	...	...	...
Maricopa, AZ	-	-	-	-	-	-	-	-	-	-	-	-
Mattaponi, VA	-	-	-	-	-	-	-	-	-	-	-	-
Menominee, WI	-	3	-	1	-	-	-	-	-	-	-	1
Mesa Grande, CA	-	-	-	-	-	-	-	-	-	-	-	-
Mescalero Apache, NM	1	4	-	-	-	-	-	-	3	-	1	-
Miccosukee, Florida	1	3	-	-	1	1	-	-	-	-	-	1
Middletown Rancheria, CA	-	-	-	-	-	-	-	-	-	-	-	-
Mille Lacs, MN	-	-	-	-	-	-	-	-	-	-	-	-
Mississippi Choctaw Reservation, MS	-	2	-	1	-	-	-	-	1	-	-	-
Moapa River, NV	-	-	-	-	-	-	-	-	-	-	-	-
Montgomery Creek Rancheria, CA	...	...	...	...	...	...	...	...	...	...	...	...
Morongo, CA	-	-	-	-	-	-	-	-	-	-	-	-
Muckleshoot, WA	-	-	-	-	-	-	-	-	-	-	-	-
Nambe Pueblo, NM	-	-	-	-	-	-	-	-	-	-	-	-
Navajo, AZ-NM-UT	121	775	28	16	1	3	-	-	2	-	719	6
Nez Perce, ID	-	3	-	3	-	-	-	-	-	-	-	-
Nisqually, WA	-	1	-	1	-	-	-	-	-	-	-	-
Nooksack, WA	-	-	-	-	-	-	-	-	-	-	-	-
Northern Cheyenne, MT	-	5	-	5	-	-	-	-	-	-	-	-
Oil Springs, NY	-	-	-	-	-	-	-	-	-	-	-	-
Omaha, IO-NE	-	-	-	-	-	-	-	-	-	-	-	-
Oneida, WI	1	1	-	-	-	-	-	-	-	-	-	1
Onondaga, NY	-	-	-	-	-	-	-	-	-	-	-	-
Ontonagon, MI	-	-	-	-	-	-	-	-	-	-	-	-
Osage, OK	-	4	-	1	-	1	-	-	-	-	-	1
Ozette, WA	...	...	...	...	...	...	...	...	...	...	...	...
Pala, CA	-	-	-	-	-	-	-	-	-	-	-	-
Pamunkey, VA	-	-	-	-	-	-	-	-	-	-	-	-
Papago, AZ	-	55	54	-	-	-	-	-	-	-	1	-
Pascua Yaqui, AZ	-	-	-	-	-	-	-	-	-	-	-	-
Pauma, CA	-	1	-	1	-	-	-	-	-	-	-	-
Payson Comm. of Yavapai-Apache, AZ	-	-	-	-	-	-	-	-	-	-	-	-
Pechanga, CA	-	-	-	-	-	-	-	-	-	-	-	-

[Continued]

★ 427 ★

Traditional Occupations Held by Residents of Reservations, 1980: Isleta - Santa Clara Pueblo - II
[Continued]

| Identified reservation | Jewelers | Traditional occupations | | | | | | | | | | |
| | | Handworking occupations | | | | | | | | | | |
		Total	Basket makers	beaders	Bustle makers	Carvers	Fan makers	Moccasin makers	Quilters	Rattle makers	Weavers	Other handworking occupations
Penobscot, MA	-	2	1	-	-	1	-	-	-	-	-	-
Picuris Pueblo, NM	-	-	-	-	-	-	-	-	-	-	-	-
Pine Creek, MI	...	...	...	...	...	...	...	...	...	...	...	...
Pine Ridge, SD	3	30	-	11	-	-	-	9	5	-	.	5
Pleasant Point, MA	-	-	-	-	-	-	-	-	-	-	.	-
Pojoaque Pueblo, NM	-	-	-	-	-	-	-	-	-	-	-	-
Poospatuck, NY	-	-	-	-	-	-	-	-	-	-	-	-
Port Gamble, WA	-	1	1	-	-	-	-	-	-	-	-	-
Port Madison, WA	-	-	-	-	-	-	-	-	-	-	-	-
Potawatomi, WI	-	6	-	6	-	-	-	-	-	-	-	-
Pottawatomi, KS	-	-	-	-	-	-	-	-	-	-	-	-
Prairie Island Community, MN	-	1	-	1	-	-	-	-	-	-	-	-
Puyallup, WA	-	-	-	-	-	-	-	-	-	-	-	-
Pyramid Lake, NV	3	-	-	-	-	-	-	-	-	-	-	-
Quileute, WA	-	-	-	-	-	-	-	-	-	-	-	-
Quinault, WA	-	1	1	-	-	-	-	-	-	-	-	-
Ramah Community, NM	4	9	4	-	-	2	-	-	-	-	4	-
Ramona, CA	-	-	-	-	-	-	-	-	-	-	-	-
Red Cliff, WI	-	-	-	-	-	-	-	-	-	-	-	-
Red Lake, MN	-	-	-	-	-	-	-	-	-	-	-	-
Reno-Sparks Colony, NV	2	1	-	1	-	-	-	-	-	-	-	-
Resighini Rancheria, CA	...	...	...	...	...	...	...	...	...	...	...	-
Rincon, CA	-	-	-	-	-	-	-	-	-	-	-	-
Roaring Creek Rancheria, CA	...	...	...	...	...	...	...	...	...	...	...	-
Rocky Boy's, MT	-	10	9	1	-	-	-	-	-	-	-	-
Rosebud, SD	-	5	-	1	-	-	-	-	4	-	-	-
Round Valley, CA	-	-	-	-	-	-	-	-	-	-	-	-
Rumsey Rancheria, CA	...	...	...	...	...	...	...	...	...	...	...	-
Sac and Fox, Iowa	-	1	-	1	-	-	-	-	-	-	-	-
Sac and Fox, KS-NE	...	...	...	...	...	...	...	...	...	...	...	-
St. Croix, WI	-	-	-	-	-	-	-	-	-	-	-	-
St. Regis Mohawk, NY	-	-	-	-	-	-	-	-	-	-	-	-
Salt River, AZ	2	1	-	-	-	-	-	-	-	-	-	1
San Carlos, AZ	7	7	6	-	-	-	-	-	-	-	1	-
Sandia Pueblo, NM	4	2	-	-	-	-	-	1	-	-	1	-
Sandy Lake, MN	-	-	-	-	-	-	-	-	-	-	-	-
San Felipe Pueblo, NM	9	-	-	-	-	-	-	-	-	-	-	-
San Ildefonso Pueblo, NM	7	-	-	-	-	-	-	-	-	-	-	-
San Juan Pueblo, NM	2	-	-	-	-	-	-	-	-	-	-	-
San Manuel, CA	-	-	-	-	-	-	-	-	-	-	-	-
San Pasqual, CA	-	-	-	-	-	-	-	-	-	-	-	-
Santa Ana Pueblo, NM	-	-	-	-	-	-	-	-	-	-	-	-
Santa Clara Pueblo, NM	10	-	-	-	-	-	-	-	-	-	-	-

Source: U.S. Bureau of the Census, Subject Reports, PC80-2-1D, Part II, *American Indians, Eskimos, and Aleuts on Identified Reservations and in the Historic Areas of Oklahoma (Excluding Urbanized Areas)*, U.S. Government Printing Office, Washington, D.C., 1986, pp. 482-520. *Notes:* A dash (-) represents zero or a percent which rounds to less than 0.1. Also, a dash (-) is used because the number of supplementary questionnaires for the areas was insufficient to produce reliable estimates. Three dots (...) means not applicable, or that the data are being withheld to avoid disclosure of information for individuals.

★ 428 ★

Employment

Traditional Occupations Held by Residents of Reservations, 1980: Santa Rosa Rancheria - Zuni Pueblo - I

Data are the latest available.

Identified reservation	Persons 16 years and over working in 1980 reference period	Traditional occupations										
		Tribal governmental occupations				Native healers	Sheep workers	Artists and performers				
		Total	Officials and administrators	Legislators	Judicial administrators			Total	Dancers	Drummers and singers	Painters	Potters
Santa Rosa Rancheria, CA	31	-	-	-	-	-	1	-	-	-	-	-
Santa Rosa, CA	...	...	...	...	...	...	...	...	...	...	...	...
Santa Ynez, CA	56	1	1	-	-	-	-	-	-	-	-	-
Santa Ysabel, CA	63	-	-	-	-	-	-	-	-	-	-	-
Santee, Nebraska	124	-	-	-	-	-	-	-	-	-	-	-
Santo Domingo Pueblo, NM	712	3	3	-	-	-	-	11	-	-	-	11
San Xavier, AZ	247	3	3	-	-	-	-	2	-	-	2	-
Sauk-Suiattle, WA	-	-	-	-	-	-	-	-	-	-	-	-
Sault Ste. Marie, MI	-	-	-	-	-	-	-	-	-	-	-	-
Schaghticoke, CT	...	...	...	...	...	...	...	...	...	...	...	...
Shakopee Community, MN	30	-	-	-	-	-	-	-	-	-	-	-
Sheep Ranch Rancheria, CA	...	...	...	...	...	...	...	...	...	...	...	...
Sherwood Valley Rancheria, CA	...	...	...	...	...	...	...	...	...	...	...	...
Shingle Springs Rancheria, CA	-	-	-	-	-	-	-	-	-	-	-	-
Shinnecock, NY	72	-	-	-	-	-	-	-	-	-	-	-
Shoalwater, WA	...	...	...	...	...	...	...	...	...	...	...	...
Sisseton, ND-SD	591	3	-	3	-	-	-	-	-	-	-	-
Skokomish, WA	61	1	1	-	-	-	-	-	-	-	-	-
Skull Valley, UT	-	-	-	-	-	-	-	-	-	-	-	-
Soboba, CA	57	-	-	-	-	-	-	-	-	-	-	-
Sokaogon Chippewa Community, WI	44	1	1	-	-	-	-	2	-	-	-	2
Southern Paiute, UT	50	-	-	-	-	-	-	-	-	-	-	-
Southern Ute, CO	291	6	3	3	-	-	1	2	-	1	1	-
Spokane, WA	451	10	6	2	2	-	-	-	-	-	-	-
Squaxin Island, WA	9	-	-	-	-	-	-	-	-	-	-	-
Standing Rock, ND-SD	1,077	14	3	8	3	-	-	-	-	-	-	-
Stewart's Point Rancheria, CA	20	-	-	-	-	-	-	-	-	-	-	-
Stockbridge, WI	207	2	2	-	-	-	-	-	-	-	-	-
Sulphur Bank Rancheria, CA	18	-	-	-	-	-	-	-	-	-	-	-
Summit Lake, NV	...	...	...	...	...	...	...	...	...	...	...	...
Susanville, CA	30	-	-	-	-	-	-	-	-	-	-	-
Swinomish, WA	139	2	2	-	-	-	-	-	-	-	-	-
Sycuan, CA	8	-	-	-	-	-	-	-	-	-	-	-
Tama, GA	17	1	1	-	-	-	-	-	-	-	-	-
Taos Pueblo, NM	307	-	-	-	-	-	-	2	-	-	-	2
Te-Moak, NV	38	-	-	-	-	-	-	-	-	-	-	-
Tesuque Pueblo, NM	83	1	1	-	-	-	-	-	-	-	-	-
Tigua, TX	105	-	-	-	-	-	-	3	-	-	-	3
Tonawanda, NY	168	-	-	-	-	-	-	-	-	-	-	-
Torres-Martinez, CA	-	-	-	-	-	-	-	-	-	-	-	-
Trinidad Rancheria, CA	20	-	-	-	-	-	-	-	-	-	-	-
Tulalip, WA	241	1	1	-	-	-	-	-	-	-	-	-
Tule River, CA	134	3	3	-	-	-	-	-	-	-	-	-
Tunicabiloxi, LA	...	...	...	...	...	...	...	...	...	...	...	...
Tuolumne Rancheria, CA	26	-	-	-	-	-	-	-	-	-	-	-
Turtle Mountain, ND	961	11	9	-	2	-	-	-	-	-	-	-
Tuscarora, NY	-	-	-	-	-	-	-	-	-	-	-	-
Twenty-Nine Palms, CA	-	-	-	-	-	-	-	-	-	-	-	-
Uintah and Ouray, UT	588	3	3	-	-	-	-	1	-	-	-	1
Umatilla, OR	297	8	8	-	-	-	-	-	-	-	-	-
Upper Sioux Community, MN	21	-	-	-	-	-	-	-	-	-	-	-
Upper Skagit, WA	-	-	-	-	-	-	-	-	-	-	-	-
Ute Mountain, CO-NM	308	1	-	1	-	-	-	8	-	-	4	4
Vermillion Lake, MN	27	-	-	-	-	-	-	-	-	-	-	-
Viejas Rancheria, CA	51	-	-	-	-	-	-	-	-	-	-	-
Walker River, NV	162	1	1	-	-	-	-	-	-	-	-	-
Wampanoag, MA	-	-	-	-	-	-	-	-	-	-	-	-
Warm Springs, OR	602	7	4	1	2	-	-	-	-	-	-	-
Washoe, NV	-	-	-	-	-	-	-	-	-	-	-	-
Western Pequot, CT	...	...	...	...	...	...	...	...	...	...	...	...
White Earth, MN	734	9	8	-	1	-	-	-	-	-	-	-
Wind River, WY	1,119	14	11	1	1	-	-	-	-	-	-	-
Winnebago, Nebraska	317	4	2	2	-	-	-	-	-	-	-	-
Winnemucca Colony, NV	9	-	-	-	-	-	-	-	-	-	-	-
Wisconsin Winnebago Reservation	105	-	-	-	-	-	-	-	-	-	-	-
Woodfords Community, CA	-	-	-	-	-	-	-	-	-	-	-	-
XL Ranch, CA	...	...	...	...	...	...	...	...	...	...	...	...
Yakima, WA	1,532	33	19	13	1	-	-	9	-	-	1	8
Yankton, SD	359	-	-	-	-	-	-	-	-	-	-	-
Yavapai, AZ	28	1	1	-	-	-	-	-	-	-	-	-
Yerington, NV	40	1	1	-	-	-	-	-	-	-	-	-

[Continued]

★ 428 ★

Traditional Occupations Held by Residents of Reservations, 1980: Santa Rosa Rancheria - Zuni Pueblo - I

[Continued]

Identified reservation	Persons 16 years and over working in 1980 reference period	Traditional occupations										
		Tribal governmental occupations				Native healers	Sheep workers	Artists and performers				
		Total	Officials and administrators	Legislators	Judicial administrators			Total	Dancers	Drummers and singers	Painters	Potters
Yomba, NV	20	-	-	-	-	-	-	-	-	-	-	-
Zia Pueblo, NM	179	6	6	-	-	-	-	-	-	-	-	-
Zuni Pueblo, NM	2,000	12	8	2	1	-	41	4	-	-	2	1
San Felipe/Santa Ana Joint Area, NM	-	-	-	-	-	-	-	-	-	-	-	-
San Felipe/Santo Domingo Joint Area, NM	26	-	-	-	-	-	-	-	-	-	-	-
Other Reservation Lands in MT	-	-	-	-	-	-	-	-	-	-	-	-

Source: U.S. Bureau of the Census, Subject Reports, PC80-2-1D, Part II, *American Indians, Eskimos, and Aleuts on Identified Reservations and in the Historic Areas of Oklahoma (Excluding Urbanized Areas)*, U.S. Government Printing Office, Washington, D.C., 1986, pp. 482-520. *Notes:* A dash (-) represents zero or a percent which rounds to less than 0.1. Also, a dash (-) is used because the number of supplementary questionnaires for the areas was insufficient to produce reliable estimates. Three dots (...) means not applicable, or that the data are being withheld to avoid disclosure of information for individuals.

★ 429 ★

Employment

Traditional Occupations Held by Residents of Reservations, 1980: Santa Rosa Rancheria - Zuni Pueblo - II

Data are the latest available.

Identified reservation	Traditional occupations											
	Jewelers	Handworking occupations										
		Total	Basket makers	Beaders	Bustle makers	Carvers	Fan makers	Moccasin makers	Quilters	Rattle makers	Weavers	Other handworking occupations
Santa Rosa Rancheria, CA	-	-	-	-	-	-	-	-	-	-	-	-
Santa Rosa, CA	...	...	...	...	...	...	...	...	...	...	...	-
Santa Ynez, CA	-	-	-	-	-	-	-	-	-	-	-	-
Santa Ysabel, CA	-	1	-	1	-	-	-	-	-	-	-	-
Santee, Nebraska	-	-	-	-	-	-	-	-	-	-	-	-
Santo Domingo Pueblo, NM	325	1	-	-	-	-	-	1	-	-	-	-
San Xavier, AZ	-	4	4	-	-	-	-	-	-	-	-	-
Sauk-Suiattle, WA	-	-	-	-	-	-	-	-	-	-	-	-
Sault Ste. Marie, MI	-	-	-	-	-	-	-	-	-	-	-	-
Schaghticoke, CT	...	...	...	...	...	...	...	...	...	...	...	-
Shakopee Community, MN	-	-	-	-	-	-	-	-	-	-	-	-
Sheep Ranch Rancheria, CA	...	...	...	...	...	...	...	...	...	...	-	-
Sherwood Valley Rancheria, CA	...	...	...	...	...	...	...	...	...	...	...	-
Shingle Springs Rancheria, CA	-	-	-	-	-	-	-	-	-	-	-	-
Shinnecock, NY	-	-	-	-	-	-	-	-	-	-	-	-
Shoalwater, WA	...	...	...	...	...	...	...	...	...	...	...	-
Sisseton, ND-SD	-	9	-	-	-	-	-	1	6	-	-	2
Skokomish, WA	-	-	-	-	-	-	-	-	-	-	-	-
Skull Valley, UT	-	-	-	-	-	-	-	-	-	-	-	-
Soboba, CA	-	-	-	-	-	-	-	-	-	-	-	-
Sokaogon Chippewa Community, WI	-	-	-	-	-	-	-	-	-	-	-	2
Southern Paiute, UT	-	2	-	-	-	-	-	-	-	-	-	-
Southern Ute, CO	1	-	-	-	-	-	-	-	-	-	-	-
Spokane, WA	-	4	-	4	-	-	-	-	-	-	-	-
Squaxin Island, WA	-	-	-	-	-	-	-	-	-	-	-	-
Standing Rock, ND-SD	-	9	-	2	-	-	-	-	5	-	2	-
Stewart's Point Rancheria, CA	-	-	-	-	-	-	-	-	-	-	-	-
Stockbridge, WI	-	-	-	-	-	-	-	-	-	-	-	-
Sulphur Bank Rancheria, CA	-	-	-	-	-	-	-	-	-	-	-	-
Summit Lake, NV	...	...	...	...	...	...	...	...	...	...	...	-
Susanville, CA	-	-	-	-	-	-	-	-	-	-	-	-
Swinomish, WA	-	-	-	-	-	-	-	-	-	-	-	-
Sycuan, CA	-	-	-	-	-	-	-	-	-	-	-	-

[Continued]

★ 429 ★

Traditional Occupations Held by Residents of Reservations, 1980: Santa Rosa Rancheria - Zuni Pueblo - II

[Continued]

Identified reservation	Jewelers	Traditional occupations										
		Handworking occupations										
		Total	Basket makers	Beaders	Bustle makers	Carvers	Fan makers	Moccasin makers	Quilters	Rattle makers	Weavers	Other handworking occupations
Tama, GA	-	-	-	-	-	-	-	-	-	-	-	-
Taos Pueblo, NM	2	6	-	-	-	-	-	2	-	-	-	4
Te-Moak, NV	-	-	-	-	-	-	-	-	-	-	-	-
Tesuque Pueblo, NM	-	1	-	1	-	-	-	-	-	-	-	-
Tigua, TX	3	1	-	-	-	-	-	-	-	-	1	-
Tonawanda, NY	-	-	-	-	-	-	-	-	-	-	-	-
Torres-Martinez, CA	-	-	-	-	-	-	-	-	-	-	-	-
Trinidad Rancheria, CA	-	-	-	-	-	-	-	-	-	-	-	-
Tulalip, WA	-	4	-	-	-	3	-	-	-	-	-	1
Tule River, CA	-	-	-	-	-	-	-	-	-	-	-	-
Tunicabiloxi, LA	...	...	...	...	...	...	...	...	...	...	...	...
Tuolumne Rancheria, CA	1	-	-	-	-	-	-	-	-	-	-	-
Turtle Mountain, ND	-	1	-	1	-	-	-	-	-	-	-	-
Tuscarora, NY	-	-	-	-	-	-	-	-	-	-	-	-
Twenty-Nine Palms, CA	-	-	-	-	-	-	-	-	-	-	-	-
Uintah and Ouray, UT	-	1	1	-	-	-	-	-	-	-	-	-
Umatilla, OR	-	1	-	1	-	-	-	-	-	-	-	-
Upper Sioux Community, MN	-	-	-	-	-	-	-	-	-	-	-	-
Upper Skagit, WA	-	-	-	-	-	-	-	-	-	-	-	-
Ute Mountain, CO-NM	-	-	-	-	-	-	-	-	-	-	-	-
Vermillion Lake, MN	-	-	-	-	-	-	-	-	-	-	-	-
Viejas Rancheria, CA	-	-	-	-	-	-	-	-	-	-	-	-
Walker River, NV	-	-	-	-	-	-	-	-	-	-	-	-
Wampanoag, MA	-	-	-	-	-	-	-	-	-	-	-	-
Warm Springs, OR	1	10	-	10	-	-	-	-	-	-	-	-
Washoe, NV	-	-	-	-	-	-	-	-	-	-	-	-
Western Pequot, CT	...	...	...	...	...	...	...	...	...	...	...	...
White Earth, MN	-	6	3	-	-	-	-	-	1	-	2	-
Wind River, WY	3	16	-	15	-	-	-	-	-	-	1	-
Winnebago, Nebraska	-	-	-	-	-	-	-	-	-	-	-	-
Winnemucca Colony, NV	-	-	-	-	-	-	-	-	-	-	-	-
Wisconsin Winnebago Reservation	-	2	-	2	-	-	-	-	-	-	-	-
Woodfords Community, CA	-	-	-	-	-	-	-	-	-	-	-	-
XL Ranch, CA	...	...	...	...	...	...	...	...	...	...	...	...
Yakima, WA	2	9	-	6	-	2	-	-	-	-	-	-
Yankton, SD	-	1	-	-	-	-	-	-	-	-	-	1
Yavapai, AZ	-	-	-	-	-	-	-	-	-	-	-	-
Yerington, NV	-	-	-	-	-	-	-	-	-	-	-	-
Yomba, NV	-	-	-	-	-	-	-	-	-	-	-	-
Zia Pueblo, NM	-	-	-	-	-	-	-	-	-	-	-	-
Zuni Pueblo, NM	718	32	-	16	-	9	-	-	-	-	-	7
San Felipe/Santa Ana Joint Area, NM	-	-	-	-	-	-	-	-	-	-	-	-
San Felipe/Santo Domingo Joint Area, NM	5	-	-	-	-	-	-	-	-	-	-	-
Other Reservation Lands in MT	-	-	-	-	-	-	-	-	-	-	-	-

Source: U.S. Bureau of the Census, Subject Reports, PC80-2-1D, Part II, *American Indians, Eskimos, and Aleuts on Identified Reservations and in the Historic Areas of Oklahoma (Excluding Urbanized Areas)*, U.S. Government Printing Office, Washington, D.C., 1986, pp. 482-520. *Notes:* A dash (-) represents zero or a percent which rounds to less than 0.1. Also, a dash (-) is used because the number of supplementary questionnaires for the areas was insufficient to produce reliable estimates. Three dots (...) means not applicable, or that the data are being withheld to avoid disclosure of information for individuals.

Nature

★ 430 ★

Cultural Significance of Indian Plants for Selected Tribes

Plants are ranked from highest to lowest significance according to their CICS (cumulative index of cultural significance) scores. The CICS score is the total of all EICS (ethnic index of cultural significance) scores[1].

Scientific and common name	Gosiute	Southern Paiute	Ute	CICS
Juniperus osteosperma (juniper/cedar)	12	18	42	72
Chrysothamnus nauseosus (rabbitbrush)	36	18	12	66
Gutierrezia sarothrae (matchweed)	36	18	-	54
Opuntia erinacea (Mojave prickly pear)	18	18	12	48
Artemisia nova (sagebrush)	12	12	12	36
Ephedra nevadensis (Indian tea)	12	6	6	24
Coryphantha vivipara (fishhook cactus)	18	6	-	24
Sarcobatus vermiculatus (greasewood)	18	6	-	24
Echinocereus engelmannii (hedgehog cactus)	18	6	-	24
Rorippa nasturtium-aquaticum (watercress)	6	12	-	18
Atriplex confertifolia (shadscale)	18	-	-	18
Elymus sp. (ryegrass)	18	-	-	18
Sclerocactus pubispinus (fishhook cactus)	18	-	-	18
Stipa hymenoides (Indian ricegrass)	6	6	-	12
Carex sp. (sedge)	9	3	-	12
Artemisia spinescens (budsage)	-	-	12	12
Yucca harrimaniae (yucca)	6	3	-	9
Lipidium sp. (wild carrot)	6	3	-	9
Cowania mexicana (cliffrose)	3	3	-	6

Source: Halmo, David B., Richard W. Stoffle, and Michael J. Evans. "Paitu Nanasuagaindu Pahonupi (Three Sacred Valleys): cultural significance of Gosiute, Paiute, and Ute plants." *Human Organization* Vol. 52, No. 2, 1993, p. 142. *Notes:* 1. EICS is equal to the sum of the total uses and/or parts used for a specific purpose, multiplied by the intensity of use, the exclusivity of use, and the contemporary use values.

Perceptions of Native Americans

★ 431 ★

Perceived Social Standing of Selected Racial/Ethnic Groups, 1964-89

In polls taken in 1964 and 1989, adults nationwide were asked to rate the "social standing" of the following groups in the United States, using a scale in which 1 was the lowest standing and 9 was the highest. The figures shown are averages. The Wisians, a fictitious group, were included in 1989.

Ethnic Group	1964	1989	Change
Native white Americans	7.25	7.03	0.22
People of my own ethnic background	6.16	6.57	0.41
British	6.37	6.46	0.09
Protestants	6.59	6.39	0.20
Catholics	6.36	6.33	0.03
French	5.73	6.07	0.34
Irish	5.94	6.05	0.11
Swiss	5.50	6.03	0.53
Swedes	5.41	5.99	0.58
Austrians	5.06	5.94	0.88
Dutch	5.60	5.90	0.30
Norwegians	5.48	5.87	0.39
Scotch	5.73	5.85	0.12
Germans	5.63	5.78	0.15
Southerners	5.25	5.77	0.52
Italians	5.03	5.69	0.66
Danes	5.20	5.63	0.43
French Canadians	5.08	5.62	0.54
Japanese	3.95	5.56	1.61
Jews	4.71	5.55	0.84
People of foreign ancestry	4.84	5.38	0.54
Finns	5.08	5.34	0.26
Greeks	4.31	5.09	0.78
Lithuanians	4.42	4.96	0.54
Spanish-Americans	4.81	4.79	0.02
Chinese	3.44	4.76	1.32
Hungarians	4.57	4.70	0.13
Czechs	4.40	4.64	0.24
Poles	4.54	4.63	0.09
Russians	3.88	4.58	0.70
Latin Americans	4.27	4.42	0.15
American Indians	4.04	4.27	0.23
Negroes[1]	2.75	4.17	1.42
"Wisians"[2]		4.12	
Mexicans	3.00	3.52	0.52

[Continued]

★ 431 ★

Perceived Social Standing of Selected Racial/Ethnic Groups, 1964-89
[Continued]

Ethnic Group	1964	1989	Change
Puerto Ricans	2.91	3.32	0.41
Gypsies	2.29	2.65	0.36

Source: Lewin, Tamar. "Study points to increase in tolerance of ethnicity." *The New York Times* (8 January 1992), p. A10. Primary source: National Opinion Research Center. The 1989 survey included 1,537 adults. *Notes:* 1. Blacks were referred to as Negroes by the National Opinion Research Center in the 1989 survey to conform with the wording in the 1964 survey. 2. The Wisians, a fictitious group, were included in 1989.

Chapter 6
HEALTH AND HEALTH CARE

Births and Deaths

★ 432 ★

Live Births, by Year

Births and birth rates (per 1,000 population) are shown for American Indians and Alaska Natives and U.S. all races, 1955-1989.

Calendar year	Indian and Alaska Native		U.S. all races		U.S. White
	Number	Rate	Number	Rate	Rate
(1989)	34,143				
1987-1989 (1988)	32,544	28.8	3,909,510	15.9	14.7
1986-1988 (1987)	31,133	28.5	3,809,394	15.7	14.5
1985-1987 (1986)	29,966	28.7	3,756,547	15.6	14.5
1984-1986 (1985)	30,194	28.8	3,760,561	15.6	14.8
1983-1985 (1984)	28,416	29.8	3,669,141	15.5	14.5
1982-1984 (1983)	29,352	30.6	3,638,933	15.5	14.6
1981-1983 (1982)	28,701	30.9	3,680,537	15.9	14.9
1980-1982 (1981)	25,595	30.7	3,629,238	15.8	14.8
1979-1981 (1980)	25,346	29.9	3,612,258	15.9	14.9
1978-1980 (1979)	23,252	30.1	3,494,398	15.6	14.5
1977-1979 (1978)	20,250	29.3	3,333,279	15.0	14.0
1976-1978 (1977)	19,458	29.7	3,326,632	15.1	14.1
1975-1977 (1976)	18,797	30.6	3,167,788	14.6	13.6
1974-1976 (1975)	17,852	30.6	3,144,198	14.6	13.6
1973-1975 (1974)	17,099	30.8	3,159,958	14.8	13.9
1972-1974 (1973)	16,662	31.7	3,136,965	14.8	13.8
(1972)	16,801		3,258,411		
1954-1956 (1955)	17,028	37.5	4,097,000	25.0	23.8

Source: U.S. Department of Health and Human Services. Public Health Service. Indian Health Service. Office of Planning, Evaluation, and Legislation. Division of Program Statistics. *Trends in Indian Health - 1993,* Rockville, MD: U.S. Department of Health and Human Services, Public Health Service, p. 31.

★ 433 ★

Births and Deaths

Live Births, by Race, Type of Hispanic Origin, and Selected Characteristics

Figures represent registered births. Data exclude births to nonresidents of the U.S. and are based on race and Hispanic-origin of mother. Prior to 1990, data are for race of child and are not comparable. Hispanic-origin data are available from only 48 States and DC in 1990. However, approximately 99.6 percent of all births to Hispanic mothers in 1990 occurred in these states.

Race/ethnicity	Number of births (000)		Births to teenage mothers, percent of total		Births to unmarried mothers, percent of total		Percent of mothers beginning prenatal care during				Percent of births with low birth weight[1]	
							First trimester		Third trimester or no care			
	1990	1991	1990	1991	1990	1991	1990	1991	1990	1991	1990	1991
Total	4,158	4,111	12.8	12.9	26.6	28.0	74.2	76.2	6.0	5.8	7.0	7.1
White	3,290	3,241	10.9	11.0	16.9	18.0	77.7	79.5	4.9	4.7	5.7	5.8
Black	684	683	23.1	23.1	66.7	68.2	60.7	61.9	10.9	10.7	13.3	13.6
American Indian, Eskimo, Aleut	39	39	19.5	20.3	53.6	55.3	57.9	59.9	12.9	12.2	6.1	6.2
Asian and Pacific Islander[2]	142	145	5.7	5.8	NA	NA	NA	NA	NA	NA	NA	NA
Filipino	26	26	6.1	6.1	15.9	16.8	77.1	77.1	4.5	5.0	7.3	7.3
Chinese	23	22	1.2	1.1	5.0	5.5	81.3	82.3	3.4	3.4	4.7	5.1
Japanese	9	9	2.9	2.7	9.6	9.8	87.0	87.7	2.9	2.5	6.2	5.9
Hawaiian	6	6	18.4	18.1	45.0	45.0	65.8	68.1	8.7	7.5	7.2	6.7
Hispanic origin[3]	595	623	16.8	17.2	36.7	38.5	60.2	61.0	12.0	11.0	6.1	6.1
Mexican	386	411	17.7	18.1	33.3	35.3	57.8	58.7	13.2	12.2	5.5	5.6
Puerto Rican	59	60	21.7	21.7	55.9	57.5	63.5	65.0	10.6	9.1	9.0	9.4
Cuban	11	11	7.7	7.1	18.2	19.5	84.8	85.4	2.8	2.4	5.7	5.6
Central and South American	83	87	9.0	9.4	41.2	43.1	61.5	63.4	10.9	9.5	5.8	5.9

Source: 1994 Statistical Abstract of the United States on CD-ROM [machine-readable datafiles]. CD-8A-94. Washington, DC: U.S. Department of Commerce, Economics and Statistics Administration, Bureau of the Census, Data User Services Division, January 1995. Primary source: U.S. National Center for Health Statistics; Vital Statistics of the United States, annual; Monthly Vital Statistics Report; and unpublished data. *Notes:* NA stands for not available. 1. Births less than 2,500 grams (5 lbs.- 8 oz.). 2. Includes other races not shown separately. 3. Hispanic persons may be of any race. Includes other types not shown separately.

★ 434 ★

Births and Deaths

Live Births per Year, by Race and Hispanic Origin of Mother

Live births in selected years are shown by race and Hispanic origin of the mother. Data are based on the National Vital Statistics System of the Centers for Disease Control and Prevention.

Race and Hispanic origin of mother	Total number of live births								
	1970	1975	1980	1985	1987	1988	1989	1990	1991
All races	3,731,386	3,144,198	3,612,258	3,760,561	3,809,394	3,909,510	4,040,958	4,158,212	4,110,907
White	3,109,956	2,576,818	2,936,351	3,037,913	3,043,828	3,102,083	3,192,355	3,290,273	3,241,273
Black	561,992	496,829	568,080	581,824	611,173	638,562	673,124	684,336	682,602
American Indian or Alaskan Native	22,264	22,690	29,389	34,037	35,322	37,088	39,478	39,051	38,841
Asian or Pacific Islander	-	-	74,355	104,606	116,560	129,035	133,075	141,635	145,372
Chinese	7,044	7,778	11,671	16,405	17,818	21,322	20,982	22,737	22,498
Japanese	7,744	6,725	7,482	8,035	8,054	8,658	6,689	8,674	8,500
Filipino	8,066	10,359	13,968	20,058	22,134	23,207	24,585	25,770	26,227
Other Asian or Pacific Islander[1]	-	-	41,234	60,108	68,554	75,848	78,819	84,454	88,147
Hispanic origin (selected States)[2,3]	-	-	307,163	372,814	406,153	449,604	532,249	595,073	632,085
Mexican American	-	-	215,439	242,976	251,189	271,170	327,233	385,640	411,233
Puerto Rican	-	-	33,671	35,147	38,139	46,232	56,229	58,807	59,833
Cuban	-	-	7,163	10,024	9,987	10,189	10,842	11,311	11,058
Central and South American	-	-	21,268	40,985	50,350	57,610	72,443	83,008	86,908
Other and unknown Hispanic	-	-	29,622	43,682	56,488	64,403	65,502	56,307	54,053

[Continued]

★ 434 ★

Live Births per Year, by Race and Hispanic Origin of Mother
[Continued]

Race and Hispanic origin of mother	Total number of live births								
	1970	1975	1980	1985	1987	1988	1989	1990	1991
Non-Hispanic white (selected States)[2]	-	-	1,245,221	1,394,729	1,399,129	1,664,239	2,526,367	2,626,500	2,589,878
Non-Hispanic black (selected States)[2]	-	-	299,646	336,029	355,644	434,843	611,269	661,701	666,758

Source: U.S. Department of Health and Human Services. National Center for Health Statistics. *Health, United States, 1993.* Hyattsville, MD: Public Health Service, May 1994, p. 68. Primary source: Centers for Disease Control and Prevention, National Center for Health Statistics. Data computed by the Division of Analysis from data compiled by the Division of Vital Statistics. *Notes:* The race groups, white and black, include persons of Hispanic and non-Hispanic origin. Conversely, persons of Hispanic origin may be of any race. 1. Includes Hawaiians and part Hawaiians. 2. Trend data for Hispanics and non-Hispanics are affected by expansion of the reporting area for an Hispanic-origin item on the birth certificate and by immigration. These two factors affect the numbers of events, composition of the Hispanic population, and maternal and infant health characteristics. The number of States in the reporting area increased from 22 in 1980, to 23 plus the District of Columbia (DC) in 1983, 30 plus DC in 1988, 47 plus DC in 1989, 48 plus DC in 1990, and 49 plus DC in 1991. 3. Includes mothers of all races.

★ 435 ★

Births and Deaths

Live Birth Rates, by Birth Order and Age of Mother

Forty-five percent of mothers among the Indian population were age 20 or younger when giving birth for the first time. Nineteen percent of mothers were at least 25 years old. Data show number and percent of live births, by age of mother for each birth order.

Age of mother	Total live births	Live birth order					
		1st child	2nd child	3rd child	4th child	5th child	6th + child
American Indians and Alaska Natives, 1987-1989							
All ages (number)	97,568[1]	30,157	26,838	18,999	10,752	5,624	5,198
All ages	100.0	100.0	100.0	100.0	100.0	100.0	100.0
Under 20 years	19.3	45.3	15.6	4.6	1.1	0.3	0.1
20-24 years	34.0	35.6	44.6	36.3	23.8	13.2	4.6
25-29 years	26.2	13.3	26.6	36.1	39.1	37.5	24.3
30-34 years	14.3	4.5	10.2	17.2	25.9	32.1	37.8
35-39 years	5.2	1.2	2.7	5.0	8.9	13.9	25.6
40 years and over	1.0	0.2	0.3	0.8	1.2	2.9	7.6
U.S. all races, 1988							
All ages (number)	3,887,484[2]	1,595,587	1,272,610	631,040	236,149	85,429	66,669
All ages	100.0	100.0	100.0	100.0	100.0	100.0	100.0
Under 20 years	12.6	23.5	7.2	2.8	1.2	0.4	0.1
20-24 years	27.5	31.7	28.4	22.2	17.2	12.1	5.2
25-29 years	31.9	28.0	34.9	35.3	33.4	30.0	20.6
30-34 years	20.7	13.0	22.56	28.4	31.6	34.2	34.7
35-39 years	6.9	3.4	6.4	10.0	14.2	19.0	28.6
40 years and over	1.0	0.4	0.7	1.3	2.4	4.3	10.9
White, 1988							
All ages (number)	3,030,335[3]	1,259,158	1,014,991	486,177	170,738	57,242	42,029
All ages	100.0	100.0	100.0	100.0	100.0	100.0	100.0
Under 20 years	10.5	20.2	5.4	1.7	0.6	0.2	0.1
20-24 years	26.6	31.9	27.1	19.5	13.6	8.4	3.3

[Continued]

★ 435 ★

Live Birth Rates, by Birth Order and Age of Mother

[Continued]

Age of mother	Total live births	Live birth order					
		1st child	2nd child	3rd child	4th child	5th child	6th + child
25-29 years	33.4	30.0	36.5	36.4	33.4	28.3	17.2
30-34 years	21.8	13.8	23.7	30.5	34.2	36.8	35.0
35-39 years	7.2	3.6	6.6	10.6	15.6	21.2	32.0
40 years and over	1.1	0.4	0.7	1.4	2.6	5.0	12.4

Source: U.S. Department of Health and Human Services. Public Health Service. Indian Health Service. Office of Planning, Evaluation, and Legislation. Division of Program Statistics. *Trends in Indian Health - 1993*, Rockville, MD: U.S. Department of Health and Human Services, Public Health Service, p. 34. *Notes:* 1. Excludes 252 American Indian and Alaska Native births (0.3 percent) with live birth order not reported. 2. Excludes 22,026 U.S. all races births (0.6 percent) with birth order not reported. 3. Excludes 15,827 U.S. white births (0.5 percent) with birth order not reported.

★ 436 ★

Births and Deaths

Maternal Age and Marital Status for Live Births, by Race and Hispanic Origin of Mother

Data show percent distribution of live births in selected years according to age, marital status, and race/ethnicity of the mother.

Age, marital status, race, and Hispanic origin of mother	Percent of live births								
	1970	1975	1980	1985	1987	1988	1989	1990	1991
Age of mother less than 18 years									
All mothers	6.3	7.6	5.8	4.7	4.8	4.8	4.8	4.7	4.9
White	4.8	6.0	4.5	3.7	3.7	3.7	3.6	3.6	3.8
Black	14.8	16.3	12.5	10.6	10.7	10.6	10.5	10.1	10.3
American Indian or Alaskan Native	7.5	11.2	9.4	7.6	7.9	7.8	7.5	7.2	7.9
Asian or Pacific Islander	-	-	1.5	1.6	1.8	1.8	2.0	2.1	2.1
Chinese	1.1	0.4	0.3	0.3	0.2	0.3	0.3	0.4	0.3
Japanese	2.0	1.7	1.0	0.9	0.9	0.8	0.9	0.8	1.0
Filipino	3.7	2.4	1.6	1.6	1.8	1.7	1.9	2.0	2.0
Other Asian or Pacific Islander[1]	-	-	1.8	2.1	2.3	2.4	2.6	2.7	2.7
Hispanic origin (selected States)[2,3]	-	-	7.4	6.4	6.6	6.6	6.7	6.6	6.9
Mexican American	-	-	7.7	6.9	7.0	7.0	6.9	6.9	7.2
Puerto Rican	-	-	10.0	8.5	8.7	9.2	9.4	9.4	9.5
Cuban	-	-	3.8	2.2	2.1	2.2	2.7	2.7	2.6
Central and South American	-	-	2.4	2.4	2.7	2.7	3.0	3.2	3.5
Other and unknown Hispanic	-	-	6.5	7.0	7.7	7.6	8.0	8.0	8.3
Non-Hispanic white (selected States)[2]	-	-	4.0	3.2	3.2	3.2	3.0	3.0	3.1
Non-Hispanic black (selected States)[2]	-	-	12.7	10.7	10.7	10.8	10.5	10.2	10.3
Age of mother 18-19 years									
All mothers	11.3	11.3	9.8	8.0	7.6	7.7	8.1	8.1	8.1
White	10.4	10.3	9.0	7.1	6.8	6.9	7.2	7.3	7.2

[Continued]

★ 436 ★

Maternal Age and Marital Status for Live Births, by Race and Hispanic Origin of Mother
[Continued]

Age, marital status, race, and Hispanic origin of mother	Percent of live births								
	1970	1975	1980	1985	1987	1988	1989	1990	1991
Black	16.6	16.9	14.5	12.9	12.2	12.3	12.9	13.0	12.8
American Indian or Alaskan Native	12.8	15.2	14.6	12.4	11.8	11.4	12.1	12.3	12.4
Asian or Pacific Islander	-	-	3.9	3.4	3.3	3.4	3.7	3.7	3.7
Chinese	3.9	1.7	1.0	0.6	0.6	0.5	0.7	0.8	0.8
Japanese	4.1	3.3	2.3	1.9	1.6	1.8	1.8	2.0	1.7
Filipino	7.1	5.0	4.0	3.7	3.4	3.8	4.0	4.1	4.0
Other Asian or Pacific Islander[1]	-	-	4.9	4.2	4.1	4.3	4.6	4.5	4.6
Hispanic origin (selected States)[2,3]	-	-	11.6	10.1	9.7	9.8	10.0	10.2	10.3
Mexican American	-	-	12.0	10.6	10.3	10.3	10.5	10.7	10.9
Puerto Rican	-	-	13.3	12.4	11.8	12.2	12.6	12.6	12.2
Cuban	-	-	9.2	4.9	4.1	3.9	4.3	5.0	4.5
Central and South American	-	-	6.0	5.8	5.3	5.4	5.6	5.9	6.0
Other and unknown Hispanic	-	-	10.8	10.5	10.5	10.8	11.2	11.1	11.4
Non-Hispanic white (selected States)[2]	-	-	8.5	6.6	6.2	6.6	6.5	6.6	6.5
Non-Hispanic black (selected States)[2]	-	-	14.7	12.9	12.2	12.4	13.0	13.0	12.9
Unmarried mothers									
All mothers	10.7	14.3	18.4	22.0	24.5	25.7	27.1	28.0	29.5
White	5.5	7.1	11.2	14.7	16.9	18.0	19.2	20.4	21.8
Black	37.5	49.5	56.1	61.2	63.4	64.7	65.7	66.5	67.9
American Indian or Alaskan Native	22.4	632.7	39.2	46.8	51.1	51.7	52.7	53.6	55.3
Asian or Pacific Islander	-	-	7.3	9.5	11.0	11.5	12.4	13.2	13.9
Chinese	3.0	1.6	2.7	3.0	4.5	3.9	4.2	5.0	5.5
Japanese	4.6	4.6	5.2	7.9	7.9	8.8	9.4	9.6	9.8
Filipino	9.1	6.9	8.6	11.4	12.7	13.6	14.8	15.9	16.8
Other Asian or Pacific Islander[1]	-	-	8.5	10.9	12.4	13.2	14.2	14.9	15.6
Hispanic origin (selected States)[2,3]	-	-	23.6	29.5	32.6	34.0	35.5	36.7	38.5
Mexican American	-	-	20.3	25.7	28.9	30.6	31.7	33.3	35.3
Puerto Rican	-	-	46.3	51.1	53.0	53.3	55.2	55.9	57.5
Cuban	-	-	10.0	16.1	16.1	16.3	17.5	18.2	19.5
Central and South American	-	-	27.1	34.9	37.1	36.4	38.9	41.2	43.1
Other and unknown Hispanic	-	-	22.4	31.1	34.2	35.5	37.0	37.2	37.9
Non-Hispanic white (selected States)[2]	-	-	9.6	12.4	14.3	15.2	16.1	16.9	18.0
Non-Hispanic black (selected States)[2]	-	-	57.3	62.1	64.2	64.8	66.0	66.7	68.2

Source: National Center for Health Statistics. *Health, United States, 1993.* Hyattsville, MD: Public Health Service, May 1994, p. 72. Primary source: Centers for Disease Control and Prevention, National Center for Health Statistics. Data computed by the Division of Analysis from data compiled by the Division of Vital Statistics. *Notes:* A dash (-) stands for data not available. Data for 1970 and 1975 exclude births that occurred in States not reporting marital status. The race groups, white and black, include persons of Hispanic and non-Hispanic origin. Conversely, persons of Hispanic origin may be of any race. 1. Includes Hawaiians and part Hawaiians. 2. Trend data for Hispanics and non-Hispanics are affected by expansion of the reporting area for an Hispanic-origin item on the birth certificate and by immigration. These two factors affect numbers of events, composition of the Hispanic population, and maternal and infant health characteristics. The number of States in the reporting area increased from 22 in 1980, to 30 plus the District of Columbia (DC) in 1988, 47 plus DC in 1989, 48 plus DC in 1990, and 49 plus DC in 1991. 3. Includes mothers of all races.

★ 437 ★

Births and Deaths

Maternal Education for Live Births, by Race and Hispanic Origin

Data show distribution of live births, by educational status of mother, for selected years.

Education and race and Hispanic origin of mother	Percent of live births[1]								
	1970	1975	1980	1985	1987	1988	1989	1990	1991
Education of mother less than 12 years									
All mothers	30.8	28.6	23.7	20.6	20.2	20.4	23.2	23.8	23.9
White	27.1	25.1	20.8	17.8	17.4	17.6	21.6	22.4	22.5
Black	51.2	45.3	36.4	32.6	31.6	31.4	30.4	30.2	30.4
American Indian or Alaskan Native	60.5	52.7	44.2	39.0	38.5	37.9	37.2	36.4	36.3
Asian or Pacific Islander	-	-	21.0	19.4	17.9	17.9	19.5	20.0	19.7
Chinese	23.0	16.5	15.2	15.5	13.5	14.2	14.9	15.8	15.7
Japanese	11.8	9.1	5.0	4.8	3.1	3.5	3.3	3.5	3.0
Filipino	26.4	22.3	16.4	13.9	12.3	11.8	10.2	10.3	10.1
Other Asian or Pacific Islander[2]	-	-	26.4	23.5	21.7	21.7	26.1	26.2	25.5
Hispanic origin (selected states)[3,4]	-	-	51.1	44.5	42.8	42.5	52.8	53.9	54.3
Mexican American	-	-	62.8	59.0	58.4	56.9	61.3	61.4	61.7
Puerto Rican	-	-	55.3	46.6	44.3	45.2	43.7	42.7	41.9
Cuban	-	-	24.1	21.1	18.7	18.1	17.9	17.8	16.7
Central and South American	-	-	41.2	37.0	34.1	31.8	43.6	44.2	44.5
Other and unknown Hispanic	-	-	40.1	36.5	34.3	34.1	34.5	33.3	34.4
Non-Hispanic white (selected states)[3]	-	-	18.3	15.8	15.3	16.7	15.3	15.2	15.0
Non-Hispanic black (selected states)[3]	-	-	37.4	33.5	32.2	31.8	29.9	30.0	30.3
Education of mother 16 years or more									
All mothers	8.6	11.4	14.0	16.7	17.6	17.7	17.4	17.5	18.1
White	9.6	12.7	15.5	18.6	19.8	20.1	19.2	19.3	19.9
Black	2.8	4.3	6.2	7.0	7.1	7.1	7.2	7.2	7.3
American Indian or Alaskan Native	2.7	2.2	3.5	3.7	3.7	3.7	4.3	4.4	4.0
Asian or Pacific Islander	-	-	30.8	30.3	32.0	31.7	31.2	31.0	31.8
Chinese	34.0	37.8	41.5	35.2	36.8	36.4	40.5	40.3	41.7
Japanese	20.7	30.6	36.8	38.1	41.8	42.3	43.6	44.1	45.0
Filipino	28.1	36.6	37.1	35.2	36.9	35.5	36.0	34.5	34.1
Other Asian or Pacific Islander[2]	-	-	25.5	27.1	28.8	28.6	25.3	25.7	27.1
Hispanic origin (selected states)[3,4]	-	-	4.2	6.0	6.6	7.0	5.1	5.1	5.2
Mexican American	-	-	2.2	3.0	3.2	3.7	3.2	3.3	3.3
Puerto Rican	-	-	3.0	4.6	5.4	5.3	6.3	6.5	6.8
Cuban	-	-	11.6	15.0	17.3	18.2	19.2	20.4	21.9
Central and South American	-	-	6.1	8.1	8.8	10.1	8.2	8.6	9.1
Other and unknown Hispanic	-	-	5.5	7.2	7.6	8.0	7.7	8.5	8.2

[Continued]

★ 437 ★

Maternal Education for Live Births, by Race and Hispanic Origin
[Continued]

Education and race and Hispanic origin of mother	Percent of live births[1]								
	1970	1975	1980	1985	1987	1988	1989	1990	1991
Non-Hispanic white (selected states)[3]	-	-	16.4	19.3	20.4	20.4	22.0	22.6	23.3
Non-Hispanic black (selected states)[3]	-	-	5.7	6.7	6.8	6.9	7.2	7.3	7.3

Source: National Center for Health Statistics. *Health, United States, 1993.* Hyattsville, MD: Public Health Service, May 1994, p. 71. Centers for Disease Control and Prevention, National Center for Health Statistics: Data computed by the Division of Analysis from data compiled by the Division of Vital Statistics. *Notes:* A dash (-) stands for data not available. Excludes births that occurred in States not reporting education. The race groups, white and black, include persons of Hispanic and non-Hispanic origin. Conversely, persons of Hispanic origin may be of any race. 1. Excludes live births for whom education of mother is not known. 2. Includes Hawaiians and part Hawaiians. 3. Trend data for Hispanics and non-Hispanics are affected by expansion of the reporting area for an Hispanic-origin item on the birth certificate and by immigration. These two factors affect numbers of events, composition of the Hispanic population, and maternal and infant health characteristics. The number of States in the reporting area increased from 22 in 1980, to 30 plus the District of Columbia (DC) in 1988, 47 plus DC in 1989, 48 plus DC in 1990, and 49 plus DC in 1991.

★ 438 ★

Births and Deaths

Births of Low Birth Weight

Data show births under 2,500 grams in weight, by age and race of mother. Data for Americans Indians and Alaska Natives are for 1987-1989; data for all races and for white populations are for 1988.

Age of mother	Indian and Alaska Native			U.S. all races			U.S. white		
	Total live births	Number low weight	Percent low weight	Total live births	Number low weight	Percent low weight	Total live births	Number low weight	Percent low weight
All ages	97,648[1]	5,727	5.9	3,905,276[1]	207,681	6.9	3,043,092[1]	171,775	5.5
Under 20 years	18,835	1,157	6.1	488,292	45,664	9.4	319,180	24,140	7.6
Under 15 years	351	30	8.5	10,560	1,433	13.6	4,073	445	10.9
15-19 years	18,533	1,127	6.1	477,732	44,231	9.3	315,471	23,695	7.5
20-24 years	33,202	1,725	5.2	1,066,369	76,442	7.2	804,622	46,776	5.8
25-29 years	25,585	1,420	5.6	1,238,031	75,953	6.1	1,010,748	50,814	5.0
30-34 years	13,914	982	7.1	802,668	50,243	6.3	661,414	34,559	5.2
35-39 years	5,092	359	7.1	269,213	19,025	7.1	217,754	13,175	6.1
40 years and older	971	84	8.7	40,703	3,354	8.2	32,080	2,311	7.2

Source: U.S. Department of Health and Human Services. Public Health Service. Indian Health Service. Office of Planning, Evaluation, and Legislation. Division of Program Statistics. *Trends in Indian Health - 1993*, Rockville, MD: U.S. Department of Health and Human Services, Public Health Service, p. 32. *Notes:* 1. Excludes 172 American Indian and Alaska Native live births, 4,234 U.S. all races live births, and 3,070 U.S. white births with weight not stated.

★ 439 ★

Births and Deaths

Low-Birthweight Live Births per Year, by Race and Hispanic Origin of Mother

Percent of live births that are of low or very low birthweight are shown for selected years from 1970 to 1991.

Birthweight and race and Hispanic origin of mother	Percent of live births[1]								
	1970	1975	1980	1985	1987	1988	1989	1990	1991
Low birthweight (less than 2,500 grams)									
All mothers	7.93	7.38	6.84	6.75	6.90	6.93	7.05	6.97	7.12
White	6.85	6.27	5.72	5.65	5.70	5.67	5.72	5.70	5.80
Black	13.90	13.19	12.69	12.65	12.98	13.26	13.51	13.25	13.55
American Indian or Alaskan Native	7.97	6.41	6.44	5.86	6.15	6.00	6.26	6.11	6.15
Asian or Pacific Islander	-	-	6.68	6.16	6.41	6.31	6.51	6.45	6.54
Chinese	6.67	5.29	5.21	4.98	5.02	4.63	4.89	4.69	5.10
Japanese	9.03	7.47	6.60	6.21	6.49	6.69	6.67	6.16	5.90
Filipino	10.02	8.08	7.40	6.95	7.30	7.15	7.35	7.30	7.31
Other Asian or Pacific Islander[2]	-	-	12.71	12.61	13.10	13.28	13.61	13.32	13.62
Hispanic origin (selected States)[3,4]	-	-	6.12	6.16	6.24	6.17	6.18	6.06	6.15
Mexican American	-	-	5.62	5.77	5.74	5.60	5.60	5.55	5.60
Puerto Rican	-	-	8.95	8.69	9.30	9.42	9.50	8.99	9.42
Cuban	-	-	5.62	6.02	5.89	5.94	5.77	5.67	5.57
Central and South American	-	-	5.76	5.68	5.74	5.58	5.81	5.84	5.87
Other and unknown Hispanic	-	-	6.96	6.83	6.91	6.85	6.74	6.87	7.25
Non-Hispanic white (selected States)[3]	-	-	5.67	5.60	5.63	5.62	5.62	5.61	5.72
Non-Hispanic black (selected States)[3]	-	-	12.71	12.61	13.10	13.28	13.61	13.32	13.62
Very low birthweight (less than 1,500 grams)									
All mothers	1.17	1.16	1.15	1.21	1.24	1.24	1.28	1.27	1.29
White	0.95	0.92	0.90	0.94	0.94	0.93	0.95	0.95	0.96
Black	2.40	2.40	2.48	2.71	2.79	2.86	2.95	2.92	2.96
American Indian or Alaskan Native	0.98	0.95	0.92	1.01	1.13	1.00	1.00	1.01	1.07
Asian or Pacific Islander	-	-	0.92	0.85	0.83	0.84	0.90	0.87	0.85
Chinese	0.80	0.52	0.66	0.57	0.65	0.57	0.61	0.51	0.65
Japanese	1.48	0.89	0.94	0.84	0.80	0.92	0.86	0.73	0.62
Filipino	1.08	0.93	0.99	0.86	0.94	0.91	1.12	1.05	0.97
Other Asian or Pacific Islander[2]	-	-	0.97	0.92	0.84	0.89	0.91	0.92	0.88
Hispanic origin (selected States)[3,4]	-	-	0.98	1.01	1.06	1.01	1.05	1.03	1.02
Mexican American	-	-	0.92	0.97	0.96	0.89	0.94	0.92	0.92
Puerto Rican	-	-	1.29	1.30	1.63	1.61	1.71	1.62	1.66
Cuban	-	-	1.02	1.18	0.97	1.17	1.13	1.20	1.15
Central and South American	-	-	0.99	1.01	1.02	0.97	1.05	1.05	1.02
Other and unknown Hispanic	-	-	1.01	0.96	1.15	1.11	1.04	1.09	1.09

[Continued]

★ 439 ★

Low-Birthweight Live Births per Year, by Race and Hispanic Origin of Mother

[Continued]

Birthweight and race and Hispanic origin of mother	Percent of live births[1]								
	1970	1975	1980	1985	1987	1988	1989	1990	1991
Non-Hispanic white (selected States)[3]	-	-	0.86	0.90	0.91	0.89	0.93	0.93	0.94
Non-Hispanic black (selected States)[3]	-	-	2.46	2.66	2.73	2.82	2.97	2.93	2.97

Source: National Center for Health Statistics. *Health, United States, 1993.* Hyattsville, MD: Public Health Service, May 1994, p. 69. Primary source: Centers for Disease Control and Prevention, National Center for Health Statistics. Data computed by the Division of Analysis from data compiled by the Division of Vital Statistics. *Notes:* A dash (-) stands for data not available. The race groups, white and black, include persons of Hispanic and non-Hispanic origin. Conversely, persons of Hispanic origin can be of any race. 1. Excludes live births with unknown birth weight. Percent based on births with known birth weight. 2. Includes Hawaiians and part Hawaiians. 3. Trend data for Hispanics and non-Hispanics are affected by expansion of the reporting area for an Hispanic-origin item on the birth certificate and by immigration. These two factors affect numbers of events, composition of the Hispanic population, and maternal and infant health characteristics. The number of States in the reporting area increased from 22 in 1980, to 30 plus the District of Columbia (DC) in 1988, 47 plus DC in 1989, 48 plus DC in 1990, and 49 plus DC in 1991. 4. Includes mothers of all races.

★ 440 ★

Births and Deaths

Birth Rates for Teenage Mothers, 1991-92

Black - 81.3
American Indian - 53.8
White - 51.8
Asian - 15.2

Chart shows data from column 2.

Data show live birth rate per 1,000 mothers 15 to 17 years of age.

Race/ethnicity	Live births per 1,000 girls age 15-17 years	
	1991	1992
Black	84.1	81.3
American Indian	52.7	53.8
White	52.8	51.8
Asian	16.1	15.2

Source: Vobejda, Barbara. "Birth rate among teenage girls declines slightly." *The Washington Post* (26 October 1994), p. A3. Primary source: National Center for Health Statistics, *Statistical Abstract of the United States.*

★ 441 ★

Births and Deaths

Age-Adjusted Mortality Rates and Life Expectancy, 1972-89

The age-adjusted mortality rate of American Indians and Alaska Natives has decreased 40 percent from 1972-1974 to 1987-89. This is more than twice the decrease in death rates for whites and for all races.

Characteristic and year	Life expectancy at birth (years)	Years of productive life lost (rate per 1,000 population)	Age-adjusted mortality rate per 1,000 population)
IHS Service Area			
1987-1989	71.5	93.1	600.2
1980-1982	68.5	119.1	710.1
1972-1974	61.0	188.3	1,007.4
U.S. all races			
1988	74.9	58.8	535.5
1981	74.2	63.3	568.6
1973	71.4	78.9	692.9
U.S. white			
1988	75.6	49.2	512.8
1981	74.8	57.4	544.8
1973	72.2	70.8	659.3
Ratio: IHS to U.S. all races			
1987-1989/1988	0.95	1.58	1.12
1980-1982/1981	0.92	1.88	1.25
1972-1974/1973	0.85	2.39	1.45
Ratio: IHS to U.S. white			
1987-1989/1988	0.95	1.89	1.17
1980-1982/1981	0.92	2.07	1.30
1972-1974/1973	0.84	2.66	1.53

Source: U.S. Department of Health and Human Services. Public Health Service. Indian Health Service. Office of Planning, Evaluation, and Legislation. Division of Program Statistics. *Trends in Indian Health - 1993*, Rockville, MD: U.S. Department of Health and Human Services, Public Health Service, p. 72.

★ 442 ★

Births and Deaths

Death Rate Reductions: 1972-1989

```
┌─────────────────────────────────────────────────────────────┐
│  ┌─────────────────────────────────────────────────────────┐ │
│  │ Accidents - 216.0                                       │ │
│  └─────────────────────────────────────────────────────────┘ │
│  ┌──────────────────────┐                                    │
│  │        Alcoholism - 57.8                                  │
│  └──────────────────────┘                                    │
│  ┌──────────────────┐                                        │
│  │      Pneumonia and influenza - 45.2                       │
│  └──────────────────┘                                        │
│  ┌──────────┐                                                │
│  │   Homicide - 28.6                                         │
│  └──────────┘                                                │
│  ┌──────────┐                                                │
│  │   Maternal - 27.7                                         │
│  └──────────┘                                                │
│  ┌─────────┐                                                 │
│  │  Suicide - 25.5                                           │
│  └─────────┘                                                 │
│  ┌────────┐                                                  │
│  │ Infant - 22.2                                             │
│  └────────┘                                                  │
│  ┌─────┐                                                     │
│  │ Tuberculosis, all forms - 11.7                            │
│  └─────┘                                                     │
│  ┌──┐                                                        │
│  │ Gastrointestinal diseases - 6.94                          │
│  └──┘                                                        │
│              Chart shows data from column 1.                 │
└─────────────────────────────────────────────────────────────┘
```

Chart shows percentage decreases, as shown in column three of table.

Health improvements	Calendar year 1972/74 rate	Calendar year 1987/89 rate	Percentage decrease
Infant[1]	22.2	11.0	50.0
Maternal[2]	27.7	102	63.0
Pneumonia and influenza[3]	45.2	20.6	54.0
Tuberculosis, all forms[3]	11.7	3.1	74.0
Gastrointestinal diseases[3]	6.94	1.4	80.0
Accidents[3]	216.0	93.1	57.0
Suicide[3]	25.5	17.5	31.0
Homicide[3]	28.6	15.4	46.0
Alcoholism[3]	57.8[4]	37.3	35.0

Source: U.S. Department of Health and Human Services. Public Health Service. Indian Health Service. Office of Planning, Evaluation, and Legislation. Division of Program Statistics. *Trends in Indian Health - 1993*, Rockville, MD: U.S. Department of Health and Human Services, Public Health Service, p. 73. *Notes:* 1. Rates per 1,000 live births. 2. Rates per 100,000 live births. 3. Age-adjusted rate per 100,000 population. 4. 1979-81 age-adjusted alcoholism mortality rate, since specific mortality codes currently used to identify alcoholism deaths were not in use prior to 1979.

★ 443 ★

Births and Deaths

Death Rates for Selected Years, by Race/Ethnicity, Age, and Sex

Race and age	Both sexes			Male			Female		
	1980-82	1985-87	1989-91	1980-82	1985-87	1989-91	1980-82	1985-87	1989-91
	Deaths per 100,000 resident population								
All ages, age adjusted[1]	568.6	544.2	519.9	753.7	715.3	678.7	420.9	407.5	390.9
All ages, crude	863.3	876.7	864.3	955.3	944.1	918.0	776.4	812.7	813.2
1-14 years	38.1	33.9	31.4	44.5	39.8	36.2	31.4	27.7	26.3
15-24 years	107.7	97.8	99.1	159.9	143.4	146.1	54.5	50.9	50.0
25-44 years	166.4	166.4	178.3	228.5	232.1	252.9	105.7	101.7	104.6

[Continued]

★ 443 ★

Death Rates for Selected Years, by Race/Ethnicity, Age, and Sex

[Continued]

Race and age	Both sexes			Male			Female		
	1980-82	1985-87	1989-91	1980-82	1985-87	1989-91	1980-82	1985-87	1989-91
45-64 years	940.2	884.9	805.2	1,243.5	1,149.5	1,035.2	664.8	642.4	592.3
65-74 years	2,929.6	2,828.1	2,650.8	4,005.3	3,785.9	3,492.0	2,106.0	2,087.2	1,994.1
75-84 years	6,482.6	6,308.9	5,979.2	8,567.3	8,364.9	7,821.3	5,254.7	5,097.5	4,873.7
85 years and over	15,404.8	15,618.5	15,231.2	18,262.5	18,386.5	17,898.3	14,189.5	14,520.4	14,198.6
White									
All ages, age adjusted[1]	544.6	519.5	492.5	724.5	684.1	642.7	401.4	388.0	370.3
All ages, crude	881.4	900.2	888.5	966.0	958.3	930.5	800.9	844.7	848.2
1-14 years	35.6	31.2	28.4	41.7	36.8	32.8	29.2	25.3	23.8
15-24 years	104.9	93.9	89.3	155.7	137.2	129.5	52.7	49.0	47.0
25-44 years	146.0	145.5	153.8	199.6	202.6	218.7	92.5	88.1	88.4
45-64 years	886.8	833.7	752.9	1,174.9	1,083.7	966.5	621.6	601.2	551.6
65-74 years	2,864.1	2,755.6	2,574.6	3,939.3	3,698.7	3,397.5	2,038.5	2,020.3	1,925.7
75-84 years	6,464.5	6,267.4	5,931.1	8,594.6	8,341.9	7,775.7	5,222.1	5,051.3	4,824.3
85 years and over	15,658.7	15,814.9	15,367.5	18,609.3	18,696.9	18,113.3	14,423.8	14,692.4	14,321.7
Black									
All ages, age adjusted[1]	808.5	795.6	790.4	1,070.2	1,059.8	1,062.0	604.9	593.8	582.4
All ages, crude	845.3	863.2	873.2	995.5	999.5	1,009.4	710.8	740.5	750.8
1-14 years	53.0	49.2	48.3	61.7	57.3	56.1	44.2	40.9	40.3
15-24 years	127.6	125.7	161.9	191.7	188.9	254.9	66.1	64.1	69.8
25-44 years	334.1	337.4	373.8	485.3	491.5	547.1	204.5	203.4	221.5
45-64 years	1,523.1	1,446.6	1,374.9	2,045.6	1,931.0	1,847.7	1,099.7	1,055.4	994.2
65-74 years	3,811.2	3,854.5	3,734.7	5,034.8	5,149.8	4,962.4	2,928.2	2,947.2	2,880.2
75-84 years	7,080.8	7,193.0	6,962.0	8,862.7	9,275.5	9,087.6	5,968.2	5,968.5	5,767.6
85 years and over	12,917.1	13,956.3	14,336.4	15,240.0	16,200.3	16,740.5	11,771.5	12,934.2	13,312.5
Asian or Pacific Islander[2]									
All ages, age adjusted[1]	298.0	300.2	289.7	391.6	389.3	369.0	214.8	223.1	222.2
All ages, crude	276.9	279.4	279.0	345.6	339.2	329.7	211.6	222.2	230.5
1-14 years	25.5	24.6	22.7	28.3	28.0	25.3	22.6	21.1	20.0
15-24 years	52.0	51.3	50.1	71.4	71.4	70.8	31.6	29.5	28.1
25-44 years	75.7	73.8	76.1	92.9	95.8	100.2	60.2	53.7	53.9
45-64 years	410.5	404.2	380.4	537.3	511.6	468.1	302.5	310.9	303.6
65-74 years	1,516.0	1,504.9	1,458.7	2,087.4	2,036.5	1,952.2	969.9	1,063.5	1,064.7
75-84 years	3,832.7	4,051.2	3,895.6	5,176.0	5,439.1	5,007.3	2,617.7	2,784.3	2,923.4
85 years and over	9,617.6	10,902.5	11,058.3	12,305.2	12,277.8	12,496.9	7,975.6	9,944.1	10,039.5
American Indian or Alaskan Native[3]									
All ages, age adjusted[1]	521.5	459.1	452.6	676.4	590.8	582.6	383.8	344.5	340.6
All ages, crude	453.8	412.1	412.5	553.4	490.1	484.9	356.5	335.7	341.3
1-14 years	48.0	45.2	37.3	57.0	56.3	45.1	38.6	33.7	29.2
15-24 years	186.7	149.9	142.0	276.8	222.2	208.3	94.2	73.3	71.1
25-44 years	289.6	226.5	214.3	400.1	317.6	304.1	84.1	139.6	127.4
45-64 years	846.7	733.5	712.8	1,091.7	911.3	891.5	621.1	569.2	547.8
65-74 years	2,148.9	2,033.4	2,083.4	2,761.2	2,579.8	2,593.2	1,653.7	1,597.7	1,676.5
75-84 years	4,114.0	4,020.8	4,121.2	5,128.3	5,224.7	5,326.9	3,370.9	3,225.9	3,338.2
85 years and over	9,225.3	8,714.0	9,122.4	11,048.4	9,945.4	11,237.3	8,079.3	7,964.7	7,964.5
Hispanic[4]									
All ages, age adjusted[1]	-	-	395.8	-	-	521.3	-	-	284.5
All ages, crude	-	-	344.2	-	-	401.4	-	-	284.1

[Continued]

★ 443 ★

Death Rates for Selected Years, by Race/Ethnicity, Age, and Sex
[Continued]

Race and age	Both sexes			Male			Female		
	1980-82	1985-87	1989-91	1980-82	1985-87	1989-91	1980-82	1985-87	1989-91
1-14 years	-	-	30.2	-	-	34.7	-	-	25.5
15-24 years	-	-	103.3	-	-	156.5	-	-	40.9
25-44 years	-	-	162.2	-	-	242.7	-	-	74.2
45-64 years	-	-	566.8	-	-	746.1	-	-	400.4
65-74 years	-	-	1,874.8	-	-	2,413.5	-	-	1,447.0
75-84 years	-	-	4,282.5	-	-	5,541.8	-	-	3,471.2
85 years and over	-	-	11,021.7	-	-	12,514.5	-	-	10,182.5

Source: National Center for Health Statistics. *Health, United States, 1993.* Hyattsville, MD: Public Health Service, May 1994, p. 101. Primary source: Centers for Disease Control and Prevention, National Center for Health Statistics. Data computed by the Division of Analysis from data compiled by the Division of Vital Statistics and from national population estimates for race groups from the Census Bureau and State or U.S. aggregate population estimates for Hispanics provided by the Census Bureau. *Notes:* The race groups, white, black, Asian or Pacific Islander, and American Indian or Alaskan Native, include persons of Hispanic and non-Hispanic origin. Conversely, persons of Hispanic origin may be of any race. Consistency of race and Hispanic origin identification between the death certificate (source of data for numerator of death rates) and data from the Census Bureau (denominator) is high for individual white, black, and Hispanic persons; however, persons identified as American Indian or Asian in data from the Census Bureau are sometimes misreported as white on the death certificate, causing death rates to be underestimated by 20-30 percent for American Indians and by about 12 percent for Asians. (Sorlie, P.D., Rogot, E., and Johnson, N.J.: Validity of demographic characteristics on the death certificate, *Epidemiology*, 3(2):181-184, 1992.) A dash (-) stands for data not available. 1. Age adjusted by the direct method based on 11 age groups. 2. Interpretation of trends should take into account that the Asian population in the United States more than doubled between 1980 and 1990, primarily due to immigration. 3. Interpretation of trends should take into account that population estimates for American Indians increased by 45 percent between 1980 and 1990, partly due to better enumeration techniques in the 1990 Decennial Census and to the increased tendency for people to identify themselves as American Indian in 1990. 4. Excludes data from States lacking an Hispanic-origin item on their death certificates and from New York. It is estimated that death rates for persons 25-44 years of age are underestimated by about 12-13 percent; other death rates are generally over- or understated by about 5 percent or less due to excluding New York data.

★ 444 ★

Births and Deaths

Death Rates, by Race/Ethnicity and Age Group

Data show death rates for all causes, by detailed race, Hispanic origin, age, and sex for the United States in 1980-82, 1985-87, and 1989-91.

Race/ethnicity and age	Deaths per 100,000 resident population								
	Both sexes			Male			Female		
	1980-82	1985-87	1989-91	1980-82	1985-87	1989-91	1980-82	1985-87	1989-91
All races									
All ages, age adjusted[1]	568.6	544.2	519.9	753.7	715.3	678.7	420.9	407.5	390.9
All ages, crude	863.3	876.7	864.3	955.3	944.1	918.0	776.4	812.7	813.2
1-14 years	38.1	33.9	31.4	44.5	39.8	36.2	31.4	27.7	26.3
15-24 years	107.7	97.8	99.1	159.9	143.4	146.1	54.5	50.9	50.0
25-44 years	166.4	166.4	178.3	228.5	232.1	252.9	105.7	101.7	104.6
45-64 years	940.2	884.9	805.2	1,243.5	1,149.5	1,035.2	664.8	642.4	592.3
65-74 years	2,929.6	2,828.1	2,650.8	4,005.3	3,785.9	3,492.0	2,106.0	2,087.2	1,994.1
75-84 years	6,482.6	6,308.9	5,979.2	8,567.3	8,364.9	7,821.3	5,254.7	5,097.5	4,873.7
85 years and over	15,404.8	15,618.5	15,231.2	18,262.5	18,386.5	17,898.3	14,189.5	14,520.4	14,198.6
White									
All ages, age adjusted[1]	544.6	519.5	492.5	724.5	684.1	642.7	401.4	388.0	370.3
All ages, crude	881.4	900.2	888.5	966.0	958.3	930.5	800.9	844.7	848.2
1-14 years	35.6	31.2	28.4	41.7	36.8	32.8	29.2	25.3	23.8

[Continued]

★ 444 ★

Death Rates, by Race/Ethnicity and Age Group
[Continued]

Race/ethnicity and age	Deaths per 100,000 resident population								
	Both sexes			Male			Female		
	1980-82	1985-87	1989-91	1980-82	1985-87	1989-91	1980-82	1985-87	1989-91
15-24 years	104.9	93.9	89.3	155.7	137.2	129.5	52.7	49.0	47.0
25-44 years	146.0	145.5	153.8	199.6	202.6	218.7	92.5	88.1	88.4
45-64 years	886.8	833.7	752.9	1,174.9	1,083.7	966.5	621.6	601.2	551.6
65-74 years	2,864.1	2,755.6	2,574.6	3,939.3	3,698.7	3,397.5	2,038.5	2,020.3	1,925.7
75-84 years	6,464.5	6,267.2	5,931.1	8,594.6	8,341.9	7,775.7	5,222.1	5,051.3	4,824.3
85 years and over	15,658.7	15,814.9	15,367.5	18,609.3	18,696.9	18,113.3	14,423.8	14,692.4	14,321.7
Black									
All ages, age adjusted[1]	808.5	795.6	790.4	1,070.2	1,059.8	1,062.0	604.9	593.8	582.4
All ages, crude	845.3	863.0	873.2	995.5	999.5	1,009.4	710.8	740.5	750.8
1-14 years	53.0	49.2	48.3	61.7	57.3	56.1	44.2	40.9	40.3
15-24 years	127.6	125.7	161.9	191.7	188.9	254.9	66.1	64.1	69.8
25-44 years	334.1	337.4	373.8	485.3	491.5	547.1	204.5	203.4	221.5
45-64 years	1,523.1	1,446.6	1,374.9	2,045.6	1,931.0	1,847.7	1,099.7	1,055.4	994.2
65-74 years	3,811.2	3,854.5	3,734.7	5,034.8	5,149.8	4,962.4	2,928.2	2,947.2	2,880.2
75-84 years	7,080.8	7,193.0	6,962.0	8,862.7	9,275.5	9,087.6	5,968.2	5,968.6	5,767.6
85 years and over	12,917.1	13,956.3	14,336.4	15,240.0	16,200.3	16,740.5	11,771.5	12,934.2	13,312.5
Asian or Pacific Islander[2]									
All ages, age adjusted[1]	298.0	300.2	289.7	391.6	389.3	369.0	214.8	223.1	222.2
All ages, crude	276.9	279.4	279.0	345.6	339.2	329.7	211.6	222.2	230.5
1-14 years	25.5	24.6	22.7	28.3	28.0	25.3	22.6	21.1	20.0
15-24 years	52.0	51.3	50.1	71.4	71.4	70.8	31.6	29.5	28.1
25-44 years	75.7	73.8	76.1	92.9	95.8	100.2	60.2	53.7	53.9
45-64 years	410.5	404.2	380.4	537.3	511.6	468.1	302.5	310.9	303.6
65-74 years	1,516.0	1,504.9	1,458.7	2,087.4	2,036.5	1,952.2	969.9	1,063.5	1,064.7
75-84 years	3,832.7	4,051.2	3,895.6	5,176.0	5,439.1	5,007.3	2,617.7	2,784.3	2,923.4
85 years and over	9,617.6	10,902.5	11,058.3	12,305.2	12,277.8	12,496.9	7,975.6	9,944.1	10,039.5
American Indian or Alaskan Native[3]									
All ages, age adjusted[1]	521.5	459.1	452.6	676.4	590.8	582.6	383.8	344.5	340.6
All ages, crude	453.8	412.1	412.5	553.4	490.1	484.9	356.5	335.7	341.3
1-14 years	48.0	45.2	37.3	57.0	56.3	45.1	38.6	33.7	29.2
15-24 years	186.7	149.9	142.0	276.8	222.2	208.3	94.2	73.3	71.1
25-44 years	289.6	226.5	214.3	400.1	317.6	304.1	184.1	139.6	127.4
45-64 years	846.7	733.5	712.8	1,091.7	911.3	891.5	621.1	569.2	547.8
65-74 years	2,148.9	2,033.4	2,083.4	2,761.2	2,579.8	2,593.2	1,653.7	1,597.7	1,676.5
75-84 years	4,114.0	4,020.8	4,121.2	5,128.3	5,224.7	5,326.9	3,370.9	3,225.9	3,338.2
85 years and over	9,225.3	8,714.0	9,122.4	11,048.4	9,945.4	11,237.3	8,079.3	7,964.7	7,964.5
Hispanic[4]									
All ages, age adjusted[1]	---	---	395.8	---	---	521.3	---	---	284.5
All ages, crude	---	---	344.2	---	---	401.4	---	---	284.1

[Continued]

★ 444 ★

Death Rates, by Race/Ethnicity and Age Group

[Continued]

Race/ethnicity and age	Deaths per 100,000 resident population								
	Both sexes			Male			Female		
	1980-82	1985-87	1989-91	1980-82	1985-87	1989-91	1980-82	1985-87	1989-91
1-14 years	---	---	30.2	---	---	34.7	---	---	25.5
15-24 years	---	---	103.3	---	---	156.5	---	---	40.9
25-44 years	---	---	162.2	---	---	242.7	---	---	74.2
45-64 years	---	---	566.8	---	---	746.1	---	---	400.4
65-74 years	---	---	1,874.8	---	---	2,413.5	---	---	1,447.0
75-84 years	---	---	4,282.5	---	---	5,541.8	---	---	3,471.2
85 years and over	---	---	11,021.7	---	---	12,514.5	---	---	10,182.5

Source: National Center for Health Statistics. *Health United States, 1993.* Hyattsville, MD: Public Health Service, May 1994, p. 101. Primary source: Centers for Disease Control and Prevention, National Center for Health Statistics. Data computed by the Division of Vital Statistics and from national population estimates for race groups from the Census Bureau and State or U.S. aggregate population estimates for Hispanics provided by the Census Bureau. *Notes:* The race groups, white, black, Asian or Pacific Islander, and American Indian or Alaskan Native, include persons of Hispanic and non-Hispanic origin. Conversely, persons of Hispanic origin may be of any race. Consistency of race and Hispanic origin identification between the death certificate (source of data for numerator of death rates) and data from the Census Bureau (denominator) is high for individual white, black, and Hispanic persons; however, persons identified as American Indian or Asian in data from the Census Bureau are sometimes misreported as white on the death certificate, causing death rates to be underestimated by 22-30 percent for American Indians and by about 12 percent for Asians. (Sortie, P.D., Rogot, E., and Johnson, N.J.: Validity of demographic characteristics on the death certificate. Epidemiology 3(2):181-184, 1992.) 1. Age adjusted by the direct method based on 11 age groups. 2. Interpretation of trends should take into account that the Asian population in the United States more than doubled between 1980 and 1990, primarily due to immigration. 3. Interpretation of trends should take into account that population estimates for American Indians increased by 45 percent between 1980 and 1990, partly due to better enumeration techniques in the 1990 decennial census and to the increased tendency for people to identify themselves as American Indian in 1990. 4. Excludes data from States lacking an Hispanic-origin item on their death certificates and from New York. It is estimated that death rates for persons 25-44 years of age are understated by about 12-13 percent; other death rates are generally over or understated by about 5 percent or less due to excluding New York data.

★ 445 ★

Births and Deaths

Deaths Among AIDS Cases

Deaths among AIDS (acquired immunodeficiency syndrome) cases in the United States, but not those of including residents of U.S. territories, are shown for selected years, by age at death, sex, race, and Hispanic origin. Data are based on reporting by State health departments.

Age at death, sex, race, and Hispanic origin	Percent distribution All years[1]	Number, by year of death								
		All years[1]	1985	1987	1988	1989	1990	1991	1992	January-September 1993
All races	NA	197,727	6,704	15,504	19,773	26,005	29,022	32,573	34,228	16,885
Male										
All males, 13 years and over at diagnosis	100.0	174,556	6,138	13,812	17,482	23,097	25,579	28,540	29,778	14,662
White, not Hispanic	58.1	101,443	3,814	8,232	10,106	13,424	14,964	16,424	16,596	8,345
Black, not Hispanic	27.5	48,058	1,497	3,629	4,823	6,314	6,943	7,906	8,839	4,315
Hispanic	13.4	23,309	790	1,841	2,391	3,128	3,428	3,870	4,017	1,810
American Indian[2]	0.2	314	4	22	23	31	39	71	55	53
Asian or Pacific Islander[3]	0.7	1,152	29	76	110	156	169	214	208	117
Age at death										
13-19 years	0.2	389	21	40	37	55	49	58	48	26
20 to 29 years	15.0	26,123	1,129	2,502	3,005	3,635	3,696	3,763	3,726	1,821
30 to 39 years	45.2	78,907	2,810	6,313	7,871	10,498	11,605	12,839	13,262	6,572
40 to 49 years	26.9	47,016	1,386	3,190	4,252	5,970	7,049	8,253	8,958	4,369

[Continued]

★ 445 ★

Deaths Among AIDS Cases
[Continued]

Age at death, sex, race, and Hispanic origin	Percent distribution All years[1]	Number, by year of death								
		All years[1]	1985	1987	1988	1989	1990	1991	1992	January-September 1993
50 to 59 years	9.1	15,825	584	1,201	1,615	2,124	2,296	2,550	2,730	1,371
60 years and over	3.6	6,296	208	566	702	815	884	1,077	1,054	503
Female										
All females, 13 years and over at diagnosis	100.0	20,670	460	1,420	1,998	2,571	3,083	3,684	4,097	2,044
White, not Hispanic	26.2	5,406	146	445	555	666	804	920	988	529
Black, not Hispanic	56.6	11,708	227	782	1,097	1,454	1,766	2,096	2,396	1,180
Hispanic	16.3	3,367	84	185	328	420	488	632	679	315
American Indian[2]	0.2	38	3	2	1	6	5	11	5	3
Asian or Pacific Islander[3]	0.6	115	-	6	16	19	12	21	19	13
Age at death										
13-19 years	0.7	137	5	10	12	13	24	24	20	14
20-29 years	21.4	4,424	128	356	453	551	650	766	750	382
30-39 yeas	46.5	9,602	210	637	954	1,276	1,470	1,642	1,902	920
40-49 years	19.0	3,929	54	194	300	431	571	791	972	471
50-59 years	6.6	1,357	22	92	118	153	193	284	275	157
60 years and over	5.9	1,221	41	131	161	147	175	177	178	100
Children										
All children under 13 years at diagnosis	100.0	2,501	106	272	293	337	360	349	353	179
White, not Hispanic	22.7	568	28	69	68	91	63	77	72	41
Black, not Hispanic	55.6	1,390	60	132	161	168	221	198	210	101
Hispanic	20.6	514	16	68	61	74	72	69	69	33
American Indian[2]	0.4	10	-	2	-	2	1	4	-	1
Asian or Pacific Islander[3]	0.6	16	2	1	3	1	2	1	1	3
Age at death										
Under 1 year	29.6	741	34	84	93	113	109	84	90	25
1 year and over	70.4	1,760	72	188	200	224	251	265	263	154

Source: National Center for Health Statistics. *Health, United States, 1993.* Hyattsville, MD: Public Health Service, May 1994, p. 144. Primary source: Centers for Disease Control and Prevention, National Center for Infectious Diseases, Division of HIV/AIDS. *Notes:* NA stands for not applicable. A dash (-) stands for data not available. The AIDS case reporting definitions were expanded in 1985, 1987, and 1993. Data are updated periodically because of reporting delays and have been updated through September, 1993 for all years. 1. Includes cases prior to 1985. 2. Includes Aleut and Eskimo. 3. Includes Chinese, Japanese, Filipino, Hawaiian and part Hawaiian, and other Asian or Pacific Islander.

★ 446 ★

Births and Deaths

Mortality Rates, by Age

Figures represent death rate per 100,000 population for American Indians and Alaska Natives in 1987-1989, and for selected U.S. populations in 1988.

Age group	Indian and Alaska Native		U.S. rate			Ratio American Indian and Alaska Native to:	
	Number	Rate	All races	White	All other	U.S. all races	U.S. white
Under 1	1,077	1201.5	1,008.3	832.0	1,745.3	1.2	1.4
1-4	296	92.1	50.9	45.7	72.3	1.8	2.0
5-14	259	35.3	25.8	23.9	33.4	1.4	1.5
15-24	1,329	221.0	102.1	95.1	133.2	2.2	2.3
25-34	1,559	272.2	135.4	116.2	235.2	2.0	2.3
35-44	1,494	348.1	219.6	188.0	408.4	1.6	1.9
45-54	1,861	694.7	486.2	438.8	783.7	1.4	1.6
55-64	2,522	1,363.7	1,235.6	1,173.0	1,684.2	1.1	1.2
65-74	3,192	2,652.4	2,729.8	2,667.6	3,249.8	1.0	1.0
75-84	2,937	5,046.7	6,321.3	6,282.9	6,692.0	0.8	0.8
85+	1,796	11,021.8	15,594.0	15,875.6	12,789.6	0.7	0.7

Source: U.S. Department of Health and Human Services. Public Health Service. Indian Health Service. Office of Planning, Evaluation, and Legislation. Division of Program Statistics. *Trends in Indian Health - 1993*, Rockville, MD: U.S. Department of Health and Human Services, Public Health Service, p. 53. Primary source: U.S. Data by Race: National Center for Health Statistics, HHS, Monthly Vital Statistics Report, Vol. 38, No. 5, Supplement Advance Report—Final Mortality Statistics, 1988, and Final Mortality Statistics, 1988, NCHS Volume II, Part A, Table 1-10.

★ 447 ★

Births and Deaths

Mortality Rates, by Selected Cause

Age-adjusted rate per 100,000 population for American Indians and Alaska Natives in 1987-1989 and selected U.S. populations in 1988.

Cause of death	Indian and Alaska Native	United States			Ratio American Indian and Alaska Native to:	
		All races	White	All other	U.S. all races	U.S. white
All causes	600.2	535.5	509.8	692.5	1.1	1.2
Major cardiovascular disease	172.6	206.6	199.2	256.4	0.8	0.9
Diseases of heart	138.7	166.3	161.5	197.8	0.8	0.9
Cerebrovascular diseases	27.0	29.7	27.5	45.6	0.9	1.0
Atherosclerosis	2.5	3.4	3.4	3.3	0.7	0.7

[Continued]

★ 447 ★

Mortality Rates, by Selected Cause
[Continued]

Cause of death	Indian and Alaska Native	United States			Ratio American Indian and Alaska Native to:	
		All races	White	All other	U.S. all races	U.S. white
Hypertension	1.4	1.8	1.5	4.7	1.0	0.9
Accidents	93.1	35.0	34.1	40.7	2.7	2.7
Motor vehicle	52.2	19.7	20.0	18.5	2.6	2.6
All other	41.0	15.3	14.1	22.2	2.7	2.9
Malignant neoplasms	90.9	132.7	130.0	151.9	0.7	0.7
Chronic liver disease and cirrhosis	30.0	9.0	8.4	12.9	3.3	3.6
Diabetes mellitus	29.1	10.1	9.0	18.7	2.9	3.2
Pneumonia and influenza	20.6	14.2	13.6	17.5	1.5	1.5
Suicide	17.5	11.4	12.2	6.9	1.5	1.4
Homicide	15.4	9.0	5.3	28.2	1.7	2.9
Chronic obstructive pulmonary diseases and allied conditions	13.1	19.4	19.8	14.8	0.7	0.7
Tuberculosis, all forms	3.1	0.5	0.3	1.9	6.2	10.3

Source: U.S. Department of Health and Human Services. Public Health Service. Indian Health Service. Office of Planning, Evaluation, and Legislation. Division of Program Statistics. *Trends in Indian Health - 1993*, Rockville, MD: U.S. Department of Health and Human Services, Public Health Service, p. 51. Primary source: U.S. Mortality Rates: Monthly Vital Statistics Report, NCHS, DHHS Pub. No. (PHS) 91-1120, Vol. 39, No. 7, Supplement, Nov. 28, 1990, Table 12.

★ 448 ★

Births and Deaths

Number and Percent Distribution of Deaths, by Age and Sex

Data are shown for American Indians and Alaska Natives in 1987-1989 and for selected U.S. populations in 1988. Thirty-eight percent of deaths in Indian males occurred in persons age 45 and younger; 26 percent of deaths occurred in the same race and age group for females.

Age group	American Indians and Alaska Natives						United States		
	Both sexes		Male		Female		All races	White	Black
	Number	Percent	Number	Percent	Number	Percent			
All ages	18,336	100.0	10,776	100.0	7,560	100.0	2,167,999	1,876,906	264,019
Under 1	1,077	5.9	581	5.4	496	6.6	100.0	100.0	100.0
1 to 4	296	1.6	165	1.5	131	1.7	1.8	1.4	4.5
5 to 14	259	1.4	163	1.5	96	1.3	0.3	0.3	0.7
15 to 24	1,329	7.2	1,014	9.4	315	4.2	0.4	0.4	0.7
25 to 34	1,559	8.5	1,130	10.5	429	5.7	1.8	1.5	3.0
35 to 44	1,494	8.1	1,008	9.4	486	6.4	2.7	2.3	5.7
45 to 54	1,861	10.1	1,157	10.7	704	9.3	3.6	3.0	7.2
55 to 64	2,522	13.8	1,480	13.7	1,042	13.8	5.4	4.9	9.0
65 to 74	3,192	17.4	1,794	16.6	1,398	18.5	12.4	12.0	15.6
75 to 84	2,937	16.0	1,479	13.7	1,458	19.3	22.5	22.7	21.4

[Continued]

★ 448 ★

Number and Percent Distribution of Deaths, by Age and Sex
[Continued]

| Age group | American Indians and Alaska Natives | | | | | | United States | | |
| | Both sexes | | Male | | Female | | | | |
	Number	Percent	Number	Percent	Number	Percent	All races	White	Black
85 and older	1,796	9.8	793	7.4	1,003	13.3	27.8	28.9	20.5
Age not stated	14	0.1	12	0.1	2	0.0	0.0	0.0	0.1

Source: U.S. Department of Health and Human Services. Public Health Service. Indian Health Service. Office of Planning, Evaluation, and Legislation. Division of Program Statistics. *Trends in Indian Health - 1993*, Rockville, MD: U.S. Department of Health and Human Services, Public Health Service, p. 55. *Note:* 0.0 rounds to zero.

★ 449 ★

Births and Deaths

Leading Causes of Death

Figures represent death rate per 100,000 population for American Indians and Alaska Natives of all ages in 1987-1989. Data refer to persons in IHS (Indian Health Service) Area. The leading cause of death overall in the United States was heart disease. While the second leading cause for all races and white populations was tumors, the second leading cause of death for American Indians and Alaska Natives was accidents.

Cause of death	Number	Rate
All causes	18,336	539.9
Diseases of the heart	4,079	120.1
Accidents	2,981	87.8
Motor vehicles	1,675	49.3
Other accidents	1,306	38.5
Malignant neoplasms	2,512	74.0
Cerebrovascular diseases	827	24.4
Chronic liver disease and cirrhosis	790	23.3
Diabetes mellitus	788	23.2
Pneumonia and influenza	689	20.3
Suicide	564	16.6
Homicide and legal intervention	500	14.7
Chronic obstructive pulmonary diseases	376	11.1
All other causes	4,230	

Source: U.S. Department of Health and Human Services. Public Health Service. Indian Health Service. Office of Planning, Evaluation, and Legislation. Division of Program Statistics. *Trends in Indian Health - 1993*, Rockville, MD: U.S. Department of Health and Human Services, Public Health Service, p. 48.

★ 450 ★

Births and Deaths

Leading Causes of Death, by Sex

Figures represent death rate per 100,000 population for American Indians and Alaska Natives, 1987-1989.

Cause of death	Number	Rate
Male		
All causes	10,776	644.5
Diseases of the heart	2,393	143.1
Accidents	2,224	133.0
Motor vehicles	1,214	72.6
Other accidents	1,010	60.4
Malignant neoplasms	1,252	74.9
Suicide	477	28.5
Chronic liver disease and cirrhosis	427	25.5
Cerebrovascular diseases	413	24.7
Pneumonia and influenza	380	22.7
Homicide and legal intervention	377	22.5
Diabetes mellitus	327	19.6
Chronic obstructive pulmonary diseases and allied conditions	232	13.9
All other causes	2,274	
Female		
All causes	7,560	438.5
Disease of the heart	1,686	97.8
Malignant neoplasms	1,260	73.1
Accidents	757	43.9
Motor vehicles	461	26.7
Other accidents	296	17.2
Diabetes mellitus	461	26.7
Cerebrovascular diseases	414	24.0
Chronic liver disease and cirrhosis	363	21.1
Pneumonia and influenza	309	17.9
Certain conditions originating in the perinatal period	145	8.4
Chronic obstructive pulmonary diseases and allied conditions	144	8.4
Nephritis, nephrotic syndrome, and nephrosis	143	8.3
All other causes	1,878	

Source: U.S. Department of Health and Human Services. Public Health Service. Indian Health Service. Office of Planning, Evaluation, and Legislation. Division of Program Statistics. *Trends in Indian Health - 1993*, Rockville, MD: U.S. Department of Health and Human Services, Public Health Service, p. 50.

★ 451 ★

Births and Deaths

Ten Leading Causes of Death, 1 to 14 Years of Age

Figures represent death rate per 100,000 population in 1987-1989 for American Indians and Alaska Natives and in 1988 for all others. The leading causes of death in this age group for American Indians and Alaska Natives were accidents and congenital anomalies; the leading causes for all races and white populations were accidents and neoplasms.

Cause of death	Indian and Alaska Native		U.S. all races Rate	U.S. white Rate	Ratio American Indian and Alaska Native to -	
	Number	Rate			U.S. all races	U.S. white
All causes	555	52.6	33.6	23.1	1.6	2.3
Accidents	292	27.7	14.5	13.4	1.9	2.1
Motor vehicles	126	11.9	7.0	6.9	1.7	1.7
Other accidents	166	15.7	7.5	6.5	2.1	2.4
Congenital anomalies	34	3.2	29	2.9	1.1	1.1
Malignant neoplasms	33	3.1	3.4	3.4	0.9	0.9
Homicide	19	1.8	1.7	1.2	1.1	1.5
Diseases of the heart	17	1.6	1.4	1.2	1.1	1.3
Pneumonia and influenza	13	1.2	0.6	0.6	2.0	2.0
Suicide	10	0.9	0.5	0.5	1.8	1.8
Benign neoplasms	8	0.8	0.4	0.4	2.0	2.0
Septicemia	7	0.7	0.3	0.3	2.3	2.3
Meningitis	5	0.5	0.4	0.3	1.3	1.7
All other causes	117					

Source: U.S. Department of Health and Human Services. Public Health Service. Indian Health Service. Office of Planning, Evaluation, and Legislation. Division of Program Statistics. *Trends in Indian Health - 1993*, Rockville, MD: U.S. Department of Health and Human Services, Public Health Service, p. 43.

★ 452 ★

Births and Deaths

Ten Leading Causes of Death, 15 to 24 Years of Age

Figures represent death rate per 100,000 population in 1987-1989 for American Indians and Alaska Natives and in 1988 for all others. The leading causes of death in this age group for American Indians and Alaska Natives were accidents and suicide; the leading causes for all races and white populations were accidents and homicide.

Cause of death	Indian and Alaska Native		U.S. all races Rate	U.S. white Rate	Ratio American Indian and Alaska Native to -	
	Number	Rate			U.S. all races	U.S. white
All causes	1,329	221.0	102.1	95.1	2.2	2.3
Accidents	754	125.4	49.5	52.0	2.5	2.4
Motor vehicles	541	90.0	38.5	41.3	2.3	2.2

[Continued]

★ 452 ★

Ten Leading Causes of Death, 15 to 24 Years of Age
[Continued]

Cause of death	Indian and Alaska Native		U.S. all races Rate	U.S. white Rate	Ratio American Indian and Alaska Native to -	
	Number	Rate			U.S. all races	U.S. white
Other accidents	213	35.4	11.0	10.7	3.2	3.3
Suicide	230	38.3	13.2	14.1	2.9	2.7
Homicide	140	23.3	15.4	7.8	1.5	3.0
Malignant neoplasms	29	4.8	5.1	5.1	0.9	0.9
Diseases of the heart	15	2.5	2.9	2.4	0.9	1.0
Chronic liver disease and cirrhosis	7	1.2	0.1	0.1	12.0	12.0
Viral hepatitis	5	0.8	0.1	0.1	8.0	8.0
Nephritis, nephrotic syndrome, and nephrosis	5	0.8	0.2	0.1	4.0	8.0
Congenital anomalies	4	0.7	1.3	1.3	0.5	0.5
Cerebrovascular diseases	3	0.5	0.7	0.7	0.7	0.7
All other causes	137					

Source: U.S. Department of Health and Human Services. Public Health Service. Indian Health Service. Office of Planning, Evaluation, and Legislation. Division of Program Statistics. *Trends in Indian Health - 1993*, Rockville, MD: U.S. Department of Health and Human Services, Public Health Service, p. 44.

★ 453 ★

Births and Deaths

Ten Leading Causes of Death, 25 to 44 Years of Age

Figures represent death rate per 100,000 population in 1987-1989 for American Indians and Alaska Natives and in 1988 for all others. The leading causes of death in this age group for American Indians and Alaska Natives were accidents and chronic liver disease and cirrhosis; the leading causes of death for all races and white populations were accidents and malignant neoplasms.

Cause of death	Indian and Alaska Native		U.S. all races Rate	U.S. white Rate	Ratio American Indian and Alaska Native to -	
	Number	Rate			U.S. all races	U.S. white
All causes	3,053	304.7	174.4	150.6	1.7	2.0
Accidents	1,124	112.2	36.1	34.7	3.1	3.2
Motor vehicles	693	69.2	21.2	21.0	3.3	3.3
Other accidents	431	43.0	14.9	13.7	2.9	3.1
Chronic liver disease and cirrhosis	279	27.8	5.9	4.9	4.7	5.7
Suicide	263	26.2	15.2	16.1	1.7	1.6
Homicide	259	25.8	13.8	8.0	1.9	3.2
Diseases of the heart	219	21.9	20.0	17.1	1.1	1.3
Malignant neoplasms	193	19.3	26.6	25.4	0.7	0.8
Cerebrovascular diseases	62	6.2	4.3	3.2	1.4	1.9
Pneumonia and influenza	43	4.3	2.8	2.1	1.5	2.0
Diabetes mellitus	36	3.6	2.6	2.3	1.4	1.6

[Continued]

★ 453 ★

Ten Leading Causes of Death, 25 to 44 Years of Age

[Continued]

Cause of death	Indian and Alaska Native		U.S. all races Rate	U.S. white Rate	Ratio American Indian and Alaska Native to -	
	Number	Rate			U.S. all races	U.S. white
Nephritis, nephrotic syndrome, and nephrosis	22	2.2	1.0	0.6	2.2	3.7
All other causes	553					

Source: U.S. Department of Health and Human Services. Public Health Service. Indian Health Service. Office of Planning, Evaluation, and Legislation. Division of Program Statistics. *Trends in Indian Health - 1993*, Rockville, MD: U.S. Department of Health and Human Services, Public Health Service, p. 45.

★ 454 ★

Births and Deaths

Ten Leading Causes of Death, 45 to 64 Years of Age

Figures represent death rate per 100,000 population in 1987-1989 for American Indians and Alaska Natives and in 1988 for all others. The leading causes of death in this age group for American Indians and Alaska Natives were heart disease and tumors; the leading causes of death for all races and white populations were tumors and heart disease.

Cause of death	Indian and Alaska Native		U.S. all races Rate	U.S. white Rate	Ratio American Indian and Alaska Native to -	
	Number	Rate			U.S. all races	U.S. white
All causes	4,383	968.0	851.7	797.8	1.1	1.2
Diseases of the heart	1,124	248.2	262.4	246.5	0.9	1.0
Malignant neoplasms	817	180.4	300.1	291.4	0.6	0.6
Accidents	441	97.4	33.4	31.2	2.9	3.1
Motor vehicles	205	45.3	15.9	15.5	2.8	2.9
Other accidents	236	52.1	17.4	15.7	3.0	3.3
Chronic liver disease and cirrhosis	381	84.1	25.9	24.2	3.2	3.5
Diabetes mellitus	294	64.9	18.9	16.0	3.4	4.1
Cerebrovascular diseases	171	37.8	34.8	28.8	1.1	1.3
Pneumonia and influenza	133	29.4	13.0	11.1	2.3	2.6
Chronic obstructive pulmonary diseases and allied conditions	85	18.8	28.4	29.1	0.7	0.6
Nephritis, nephrotic syndrome and nephrosis	66	14.6	6.3	4.7	2.3	3.1
Septicemia	51	11.3	6.0	4.8	1.9	2.4
All other causes	820					

Source: U.S. Department of Health and Human Services. Public Health Service. Indian Health Service. Office of Planning, Evaluation, and Legislation. Division of Program Statistics. *Trends in Indian Health - 1993*, Rockville, MD: U.S. Department of Health and Human Services, Public Health Service, p. 46.

★ 455 ★

Births and Deaths

Ten Leading Causes of Death, 65 Years Old and Older

Figures represent death rate per 100,000 population in 1987-1989 for American Indians and Alaska Natives and in 1988 for all others. The leading causes of death in this age group for all races shown were heart disease and tumors.

Cause of death	Indian and Alaska Native		U.S. all races Rate	U.S. white Rate	Ratio American Indian and Alaska Native to -	
	Number	Rate			U.S. all races	U.S. white
All causes	7,925	4,067.5	5,146.1	5,127.6	0.8	0.8
Diseases of the heart	2,667	1,368.8	2,083.1	2,088.1	0.7	0.7
Malignant neoplasms	1,439	738.6	1,076.2	1,066.5	0.7	0.7
Cerebrovascular diseases	584	299.7	434.0	427.1	0.7	0.7
Diabetes mellitus	456	234.0	98.1	90.9	2.4	2.6
Pneumonia and influenza	453	232.5	226.9	231.7	1.0	1.0
Accidents	316	162.2	89.6	88.1	1.8	1.8
Motor vehicles	93	47.7	23.8	23.6	2.0	2.0
Other accidents	223	114.5	65.9	64.5	1.7	1.8
Chronic obstructive pulmonary diseases and allied conditions	269	138.1	227.8	237.3	0.6	0.6
Nephritis, nephrotic syndrome and nephrosis	163	83.7	61.3	56.6	1.4	1.5
Chronic liver disease and cirrhosis	120	61.6	33.0	33.3	1.9	1.8
Septicemia	92	47.2	56.0	52.2	0.8	0.9
All other causes	1,366					

Source: U.S. Department of Health and Human Services. Public Health Service. Indian Health Service. Office of Planning, Evaluation, and Legislation. Division of Program Statistics. *Trends in Indian Health - 1993,* Rockville, MD: U.S. Department of Health and Human Services, Public Health Service, p. 47.

★ 456 ★

Births and Deaths

Death Rates by Cause for Urban Indians, 1979-87

From the source: "Heart disease was the leading cause of mortality in urban Indians between 1979-1987. Accidents, cancer, and cirrhosis were among the remainder of the top four causes of urban Indian mortality, while homicide ranked consistently as the fifth leading cause of death." Data show crude rates per 100,000 population. A dash indicates that an ailment did not rank in the top ten as a leading cause of death in year shown.

	Crude rates per 1,000		
	1979-1981	1982-1984	1985-1987
Heart disease	72.8	70.6	82.0
Accidents	58.5	41.0	53.2
Cancer	32.2	44.6	49.8
Cirrhosis	46.5	34.0	36.9
Homicide	18.7	18.5	17.4

[Continued]

★ 456 ★

Death Rates by Cause for Urban Indians, 1979-87
[Continued]

	Crude rates per 1,000		
	1979-1981	1982-1984	1985-1987
Stroke	13.8	11.3	14.7
Suicide	11.5	8.9	13.4
Pneumonia	11.8	9.2	11.5
Other infection	-	-	9.7
Diabetes	8.9	-	9.5
Other respiratory	-	6.3	-
Total mortality	386.8	340.9	386.7

Source: U.S. Senate Committee on Indian Affairs. *Health Care Reform in Indian Country, and the American Health Care Security Act: Hearing Before the Committee on Indian Affairs.* 103rd Cong., 2nd sess. on S. 1757, 31 January 1994. Washington, DC: U.S. Government Printing Office, 1994, p. 139.

★ 457 ★

Births and Deaths

Years of Productive Life Lost, by IHS Area, 1989-91

YPLL (Years of Productive Life Lost) is a mortality indicator which measures the burden of premature deaths. It is calculated by subtracting the age at death from age 65 and summing the result over all deaths. YPLL and death rates are shown for each IHS area for all causes of death.

	Number of YPLL	Rate[1]
U.S. all races (1990)	12,237,379	56.2
All IHS Areas	296,436	86.7
9 Areas[2]	222,548	109.2
Aberdeen Area	32,099	147.0
Alaska Area	34,336	139.1
Albuquerque Area	16,555	87.0
Bemidji Area	15,305	88.0
Billings Area	17,875	132.6
California Area[2]	12,390	41.9
Nashville Area	10,608	75.0
Navajo Area	54,797	106.0
Oklahoma Area[2]	31,992	44.4
Phoenix Area	33,144	96.0
Portland Area[2]	29,506	80.9
Tucson Area	7,829	112.6

Source: U.S. Department of Health and Human Services. Public Health Service. Indian Health Service. Office of Planning, Evaluation, and Legislation. Division of Program Statistics. *Regional Differences in Indian Health - 1994*, Rockville, MD: U.S. Department of Health and Human Services, Public Health Service, p. 46. *Notes:* 1. Rate per 1,000 population under 65 years of age. 2. The 3 IHS Areas marked (California, Oklahoma, and Portland) appear to have a problem with underreporting of Indian race on death certificates. Therefore, a separate IHS rate was calculated excluding these three Areas.

AIDS

★ 458 ★

AIDS Cases

AIDS cases, by age at diagnosis, sex, and race/ethnicity are shown for selected years from 1985 to 1993. Data based on reporting by State health departments are shown for the United States but do not include the U.S. territories.

Age at diagnosis, sex, race, and Hispanic origin	Percent distribution All years[1]	Number, by year of report									Cases per 100,000 population[2]
		All years[1]	1985	1987	1988	1989	1990	1991	1992	January-September 1993	12 months ending September 30, 1993
All races	-	328,392	8,189	21,048	30,648	33,511	41,558	43,574	45,603	83,814	37.0
Male											
All males, 13 years and over	100.0	285,063	7,538	19,047	27,049	29,549	36,300	37,530	38,917	70,369	80.2
White, not Hispanic	56.4	160,861	4,787	12,304	16,008	17,470	20,903	20,613	20,763	36,336	54.3
Black, not Hispanic	28.8	82,110	1,704	4,315	7,153	8,031	10,268	11,082	12,107	23,047	244.3
Hispanic	13.7	38,914	987	2,245	3,647	3,714	4,731	5,403	5,540	10,125	125.3
American Indian[3]	0.2	614	7	24	34	60	72	75	97	223	36.9
Asian or Pacific Islander[4]	0.7	1,992	48	131	163	214	255	259	283	540	20.0
13-19 years	0.3	934	31	67	84	90	102	99	94	299	-
20-29 years	18.2	51,845	1,468	3,784	5,449	5,692	6,814	6,459	6,350	12,052	-
30-39 years	46.3	131,858	3,610	8,855	12,581	13,868	16,802	17,332	17,819	32,116	-
40-49 years	24.8	70,729	1,657	4,283	6,105	6,809	8,908	9,628	10,337	18,935	-
50-59 years	7.6	21,657	605	1,474	1,990	2,240	2,651	2,896	3,079	5,289	-
60 years and over	2.8	7,940	167	584	840	850	1,023	1,116	1,238	1,705	-
Female											
All females, 13 years and over	100.0	38,684	522	1,682	3,034	3,370	4,540	5,375	5,942	12,789	13.4
White, not Hispanic	26.6	10,288	141	544	854	948	1,225	1,358	1,454	3,379	4.6
Black, not Hispanic	56.1	21,707	285	894	1,650	1,893	2,539	3,109	3,398	7,171	64.3
Hispanic	16.2	6,285	92	230	497	493	736	859	1,024	2,091	27.0
American Indian[3]	0.3	103	3	3	6	9	10	11	15	43	6.5
Asian or Pacific Islander[4]	0.6	228	1	11	22	17	19	25	37	86	3.1
13-19 years	1.1	418	4	11	23	29	63	55	57	157	-
20-29 years	24.3	9,418	173	480	768	889	1,104	1,223	1,370	2,962	-
30-39 years	47.1	18,224	236	750	1,503	1,615	2,091	2,538	2,715	6,131	-
40-49 years	17.9	6,919	44	229	411	507	788	995	1,245	2,523	-
50-59 years	5.6	2,148	26	92	151	172	275	342	344	681	-
60 years and over	4.0	1,557	39	120	178	158	219	222	211	335	-
Children											
All children, under 13 years	100.0	4,645	129	319	565	592	718	669	744	629	1.7
White, not Hispanic	21.1	979	27	85	149	111	159	146	128	110	0.4
Black, not Hispanic	57.7	2,680	83	160	300	339	384	403	470	380	6.9
Hispanic	20.2	937	19	71	112	135	168	113	137	128	2.6
American Indian[3]	0.3	14	-	2	-	2	3	2	3	2	0.4
Asian or Pacific Islander[4]	0.5	22	-	1	4	3	4	4	1	4	0.2

[Continued]

★ 458 ★

AIDS Cases
[Continued]

Age at diagnosis, sex, race, and Hispanic origin	Percent distribution All years[1]	Number, by year of report									Cases per 100,000 population[2] 12 months ending September 30, 1993
		All years[1]	1985	1987	1988	1989	1990	1991	1992	January-September 1993	
Under 1 year	39.2	1,820	54	141	190	241	284	247	302	224	-
1-12 years	60.8	2,825	75	178	375	351	434	422	405	-	

Source: National Center for Health Statistics. *Health, United States, 1993.* Hyattsville, MD: Public Health Service, May 1994, p. 143. Primary source: Centers for Disease Control and Prevention, National Center for Infectious Diseases, Division of HIV/AIDS. *Notes:* A dash (-) stands for zero. NA stands for not applicable. The AIDS case reporting definitions were expanded in 1985, 1987, and 1993. Data are updated periodically because of reporting delays and have been updated through September 30, 1993 for all years and are shown as of December 31, 1993. 1. Includes cases prior to 1985. 2. Resident population estimates for 1992 are based on extrapolation from 1990 census counts from the U.S. Bureau of the Census. 3. Includes Aleut and Eskimo. 4. Includes Chinese, Japanese, Filipino, Hawaiian and part Hawaiian, and other Asian or Pacific Islander.

★ 459 ★

AIDS

AIDS Education of 8th and 10th Graders

Based on 1988 national study of 3,617 eighth and tenth graders. Percentages reflect responses to the question "Since the beginning of the 7th grade, have you received instruction in school on AIDS?"

Response	American Indian/ Alaskan	White	Black	Hispanic	Asian/ Pacific Islander	Other
Yes	50.1	33.3	40.2	39.4	30.2	38.4
No	24.8	48.7	41.9	32.1	39.5	38.8
Don't remember	25.1	18.0	18.0	28.6	30.3	22.8

Source: Anderson, D. Michael and Gregory M. Christenson, "Ethnic breakdown of AIDS related knowledge and attitudes from the National Adolescent Student Health Survey," *Journal of Health Education*, Vol. 22, No. 1, January/February 1991, p. 31. Primary source: *The National Adolescent Student Health Survey: A Report on the Health of America's Youth.* 1989. Third Party Publishing Co., Oakland, CA; American School Health Association, Association for the Advancement of Health Education, Society for Public Health Education, Inc. (Subset of original data).

★ 460 ★

AIDS

AIDS Prevention Awareness of 8th and 10th Graders

Percentages reflect responses to a 1988 national survey of 3,617 eighth and tenth graders.

Question/response	American Indian/ Alaskan	White	Black	Hispanic	Asian/ Pacific Islander	Other
Does this behavior make infection LESS likely?						
Using condoms (rubbers) during sex:						
Yes[1]	75.4	88.3	84.3	75.0	76.4	74.8
No	6.4	5.6	11.6	14.8	14.7	12.0
Don't know	18.2	6.1	4.0	10.2	8.9	13.3
Not having sex:						
Yes[1]	65.2	79.7	665	62.4	66.8	75.4
No	17.6	15.0	26.1	28.2	24.3	19.0
Don't know	17.3	5.4	7.4	9.4	8.9	5.6
Going to the bathroom after having sex:						
Yes	18.9	6.4	16.7	9.7	11.7	18.4
No[1]	42.9	61.8	55.1	57.3	52.3	54.5
Don't know	38.4	31.8	28.3	33.1	36.1	27.0
Washing after having sex:						
Yes	40.0	20.0	41.0	33.5	23.1	20.5
No[1]	33.1	52.5	41.0	36.4	49.5	46.1
Don't know	26.9	27.5	18.1	30.1	27.4	33.4

Source: Anderson, D. Michael and Gregory M. Christenson, "Ethnic breakdown of AIDS related knowledge and attitudes from the National Adolescent Student Health Survey," *Journal of Health Education*, Vol. 22, No. 1, January/February 1991, p. 33. Primary source: *The National Adolescent Student Health Survey: A Report on the Health of America's Youth.* 1989. Third Party Publishing Co., Oakland, CA; American School Health Association, Association for the Advancement of Health Education, Society for Public Health Education, Inc. (Subset of original data). *Note:* 1. Indicates a correct response.

★ 461 ★

AIDS

AIDS Risk Awareness of 8th and 10th Graders

Percentages reflect responses to a 1988 national survey of 3,617 eighth and tenth graders.

Question/response	American Indian/ Alaskan	White	Black	Hispanic	Asian/ Pacific Islander	Other
Does this behavior make infection MORE likely?						
Having sexual intercourse with someone who has AIDS:						
Yes[1]	92.2	96.8	90.3	87.8	86.9	89.4

[Continued]

★ 461 ★

AIDS Risk Awareness of 8th and 10th Graders
[Continued]

Question/response	American Indian/ Alaskan	White	Black	Hispanic	Asian/ Pacific Islander	Other
No	3.5	2.9	7.2	10.4	11.3	8.6
Don't know	4.3	0.3	2.5	1.8	1.8	2.0
Being in the same classroom with someone who has AIDS:						
Yes	0.0	4.3	5.9	5.0	3.8	5.1
No[1]	84.2	88.2	79.6	75.9	84.1	77.9
Don't know	15.8	7.6	14.5	19.1	21.1	17.0
Having more than one sex partner:						
Yes[1]	85.3	85.0	74.1	75.8	75.0	82.9
No	10.4	7.2	15.4	11.4	17.3	8.1
Don't know	4.3	7.7	10.6	12.9	7.7	9.1
Having sex with someone who has had several sex partners:						
Yes[1]	82.0	86.7	74.4	75.8	73.7	81.7
No	10.8	5.0	12.8	10.4	14.9	7.2
Don't know	7.2	8.3	12.9	13.8	11.5	11.1
A male having sex with another male:						
Yes[1]	85.9	82.4	79.7	73.7	74.6	75.1
No	8.0	7.6	11.4	12.2	15.5	10.3
Don't know	6.1	10.0	8.8	14.1	9.9	14.6
Sharing drug needles:						
Yes[1]	79.3	93.8	86.8	85.9	83.3	80.2
No	6.4	3.3	8.4	10.7	14.0	11.5
Don't know	14.2	2.9	4.8	3.4	2.7	8.3
Donating blood:						
Yes	49.7	43.0	55.0	54.7	45.1	63.9
No[1]	19.0	43.3	27.4	31.3	44.8	28.4
Don't know	31.3	13.7	17.6	14.0	10.1	7.8

Source: Anderson, D. Michael and Gregory M. Christenson, "Ethnic breakdown of AIDS related knowledge and attitudes from the National Adolescent Student Health Survey," *Journal of Health Education*, Vol. 22, No. 1, January/February 1991, p. 32. Primary source: *The National Adolescent Student Health Survey: A Report on the Health of America's Youth.* 1989. Third Party Publishing Co., Oakland, CA; American School Health Association, Association for the Advancement of Health Education, Society for Public Health Education, Inc. (Subset of original data). *Note:* 1. Indicates a correct response.

★ 462 ★

AIDS

AIDS, Basic Knowledge of 8th and 10th Graders

Percentages reflect responses to a 1988 national survey of 3,617 eighth and tenth graders.

Question/response	American Indian/ Alaskan	White	Black	Hispanic	Asian/ Pacific Islander	Other
There is no known cure for AIDS:						
True[1]	73.7	88.9	84.0	82.5	82.3	75.8
False	19.8	4.1	6.7	9.0	8.4	7.8
Don't know	6.6	7.0	9.3	8.6	9.3	16.5
A test to determine whether a person has the AIDS virus is now available:						
True[1]	82.5	85.0	73.3	76.2	84.4	78.3
False	9.6	5.1	10.7	7.0	2.2	5.6
Don't know	8.0	9.9	16.1	16.8	13.4	16.1
A vaccine that protects people from getting the AIDS virus is available:						
True	8.8	8.5	17.6	14.2	8.8	13.0
False[1]	56.2	66.9	47.0	51.3	58.1	56.2
Don't know	35.0	24.7	35.5	34.5	33.4	30.8
A pregnant woman who has the AIDS virus can give AIDS to her baby:						
True[1]	62.1	80.8	84.3	85.0	79.9	71.7
False	0.0	1.4	2.4	2.5	4.4	1.4
Don't know	37.9	17.8	13.3	12.5	15.8	26.9

Source: Anderson, D. Michael and Gregory M. Christenson, "Ethnic breakdown of AIDS related knowledge and attitudes from the National Adolescent Student Health Survey," *Journal of Health Education*, Vol. 22, No. 1, January/February 1991, p. 33. Primary source: *The National Adolescent Student Health Survey: A Report on the Health of America's Youth*. 1989. Third Party Publishing Co., Oakland, CA; American School Health Association, Association for the Advancement of Health Education, Society for Public Health Education, Inc. (Subset of original data). *Note:* 1. Indicates a correct response.

★ 463 ★

AIDS

Heterosexual HIV Transmission, by Race/Ethnicity, 1993

Data show rate of HIV (human immunodeficiency virus) transmissions among heterosexuals in the United States in 1993, by race/ethnicity. Figures are based on a total of 9,288 cases reported, of which 6,056 were among women and 3,232 were among men. A disproportionate number of these cases occurred among the black and Hispanic populations.

Race/ethnicity	Rate per 100,000 population
Black, not Hispanic	20.0
Hispanic	10.0
American Indian/Alaskan Native	2.0
Asian/Pacific Islander	1.0
White, not Hispanic	1.0

Source: "Heterosexually acquired AIDS - United States, 1993." *JAMA*, vol. 271, no. 13 (6 April 1994), p. 975. Primary source: Centers for Disease Control and Prevention. *Morbidity and Mortality Weekly Report* 1994;43:155-160.

Accidents and Injuries

★ 464 ★

Fatal Accidents, by Age and Sex

Figures represent rate per 100,000 population for American Indians and Alaska Natives in 1987-1989 and for U.S. all races in 1988. The age-specific accidental death rate for Indian males was more than three times the rate for U.S. all race in the age groups 15 to 34 years and 55 to 74 years. The rate for Indian females was more than twice that for U.S. all races for all age groups.

Age group	Male				Female			
	Indian and Alaska Native		U.S. all races	Ratio Indian to U.S. all	Indian and Alaska Native		U.S. all races	Ratio Indian to U.S. all
	Number	Rate	Rate	races	Number	Rate	Rate	races
Motor vehicle accidents								
Under 1 year	10	22.1	6.0	3.7	5	11.3	5.2	2.2
1 to 4 years	33	20.2	7.3	2.8	33	20.9	6.5	3.2
5 to 14 years	38	10.2	8.7	1.2	22	6.1	5.2	1.2
15 to 24 years	411	134.2	56.6	2.4	130	44.1	20.1	2.2
25 to 34 years	330	117.9	36.2	3.3	118	40.3	11.6	3.5
35 to 44 years	178	85.8	25.8	3.3	67	30.2	9.3	3.2
45 to 54 years	83	64.8	22.5	2.9	39	27.9	9.5	2.9
55 to 64 years	64	74.5	21.5	3.5	19	19.2	10.5	1.8
65 to 74 years	37	69.5	25.5	2.7	15	22.4	14.1	1.6
78 to 84 years	26	110.9	43.5	2.5	10	28.8	22.1	1.3
85 years and over	2	33.4	60.0	0.6	3	29.1	17.1	1.7

[Continued]

★ 464 ★

Fatal Accidents, by Age and Sex
[Continued]

Age group	Male				Female			
	Indian and Alaska Native		U.S. all races Rate	Ratio Indian to U.S. all races	Indian and Alaska Native		U.S. all races Rate	Ratio Indian to U.S. all races
	Number	Rate			Number	Rate		
Other accidents								
Under 1 year	21	46.4	20.9	2.2	13	29.3	16.4	1.8
1 to 4 years	56	34.3	15.9	2.2	29	18.3	9.4	1.9
5 to 14 years	60	16.1	7.1	2.3	21	5.8	3.2	1.8
15 to 24 years	180	58.8	18.6	3.2	33	11.2	3.2	3.5
25 to 34 years	209	74.7	23.8	3.2	35	12.0	5.0	2.4
35 to 44 years	149	71.8	25.2	2.8	38	17.1	5.7	3.0
45 to 54 years	89	69.5	24.5	2.8	2.2	15.7	6.6	2.4
55 to 64 years	100	116.5	29.7	3.9	25	25.2	10.2	2.5
65 to 74 years	79	148.4	43.1	3.4	27	40.2	21.3	1.9
75 to 84 years	41	174.9	100.2	1.7	24	69.0	62.0	1.1
85 years and over	23	384.4	314.5	1.2	29	281.2	208.4	1.3

Source: U.S. Department of Health and Human Services. Public Health Service. Indian Health Service. Office of Planning, Evaluation, and Legislation. Division of Program Statistics. *Trends in Indian Health - 1993*, Rockville, MD: U.S. Department of Health and Human Services, Public Health Service, p. 59.

★ 465 ★

Accidents and Injuries

Fatal Accidents, by Year

Figures represent age-adjusted death rate per 100,000 population for American Indians and Alaska Natives and U.S. all races and white populations from 1955-1988. Although the age-adjusted accident death rate decreased by 57 percent from 1972-1974 to 1987-1989, it was still almost 2.7 times the rate among all U.S. races in 1988.

Calendar year[1]	Indian and Alaska Native				U.S. all races			U.S. other than white		
	Total deaths	All accidents	Motor vehicle	Other	All accidents	Motor vehicle	Other	All accidents	Motor vehicle	Other
(1989)	968									
1987-1989 (1988)	1,010	93.1	52.2	41.0	35.0	19.7	15.3	34.1	20.0	14.1
1986-1988 (1987)	998	96.1	54.7	41.4	34.6	19.5	15.2	33.9	19.8	14.0
1985-1987 (1986)	981	95.8	54.7	41.1	35.2	19.4	15.7	34.5	19.8	14.7
1984-1986 (1985)	912	96.3	53.2	43.0	34.7	18.8	16.0	34.1	19.1	15.0
1983-1985 (1984)	920	98.6	53.1	45.5	35.0	19.1	15.9	34.6	19.6	15.0
1982-1984 (1983)	905	107.2	56.3	50.8	35.3	18.5	16.8	34.7	19.0	15.7
1981-1983 (1982)	999	113.4	61.6	51.8	36.6	19.3	17.3	36.1	19.8	16.3
1980-1982 (1981)	972	124.1	69.0	55.1	39.8	21.8	18.0	39.3	22.5	16.8
1979-1981 (1980)	1,058	131.7	74.6	57.1	42.3	22.9	19.5	41.5	23.4	18.0
1978-1980 (1979)	1,095	147.7	82.9	64.8	43.7	23.7	20.0	42.9	24.3	18.6
1977-1979 (1978)	1,070	153.8	86.2	67.5	44.3	23.4	20.9	43.3	23.8	19.5
1976-1978 (1977)	1,004	163.2	92.1	71.1	43.8	22.4	21.4	42.5	22.5	20.0
1975-1977 (1976)	994	171.1	96.0	75.1	43.2	21.5	21.7	41.8	21.5	20.3
1974-1976 (1975)	999	178.7	98.4	80.3	44.8	21.3	23.5	43.1	21.2	21.9
1973-1972 (1974)	921	199.0	111.1	87.9	46.0	21.8	24.2	44.3	21.7	22.6
1972-1974 (1973)	1,089	216.0	122.0	94.0	51.7	26.4	25.3	49.5	26.0	23.5

[Continued]

★ 465 ★

Fatal Accidents, by Year
[Continued]

Calendar year[1]	Indian and Alaska Native				U.S. all races			U.S. other than white		
	Total deaths	All accidents	Motor vehicle	Other	All accidents	Motor vehicle	Other	All accidents	Motor vehicle	Other
(1972)	987									
1954-1956 (1955)	714	184.0	97.6	90.3	54.3	24.6	29.7	52.2	24.3	27.9

Source: U.S. Department of Health and Human Services. Public Health Service. Indian Health Service. Office of Planning, Evaluation, and Legislation. Division of Program Statistics. *Trends in Indian Health - 1993*, Rockville, MD: U.S. Department of Health and Human Services, Public Health Service, p. 56.
Notes: 1. Data are presented for the year in which IHS was established (1955). For this year Reservation State data are shown. Starting in 1972 data are first available, and are shown, for the specific counties in the IHS service area. Data for these two geographic boundary systems are not directly comparable. American Indian and Alaska Native rates are for 3-year periods specified. Numbers of deaths and U.S. rates are for the single year specified.

Chronic Diseases

★ 466 ★

Death Rates for Diabetes-Related Causes, 1986-91

Age-adjusted rate per 100,000 population for American Indians and Alaska Natives, blacks, and U.S. all races.

Group	1986	1988	1989	1990	1991	2000 target
All persons	38.0	38.0	38.0	38.0	38.0	34.0
Black	67.0	69.0	71.0	71.0	71.0	58.0
American Indian/Alaska Native	46.0	52.0	56.0	53.0	51.0	48.0

Source: U.S. Department of Health and Human Services. Public Health Service. *Healthy People 2000*. Washington, DC: U.S. Government Printing Office, 1993, p. 108. Centers for Disease Control and Prevention, National Center for Health Statistics, National Vital Statistics System.

★ 467 ★

Chronic Diseases

Diabetes Mellitus Deaths and Mortality Rates, by Year

Age-adjusted rate per 100,000 population for American Indians, Alaska Natives, and U.S. all races, 1955-1989.

Calendar year(s)	Indian and Alaska Native		U.S. all races		U.S. white Rate	Ratio Indian to:	
	Number	Rate	Number	Rate		U.S. all races	U.S. other than White
(1989)	301						
1987-1989 (1988)	260	29.1	40,368	10.1	9.0	2.9	3.2
1986-1988 (1987)	227	26.2	38,532	9.8	8.7	2.7	3.0
1985-1987 (1986)	195	25.2	37,184	9.6	8.5	2.6	3.0
1984-1986 (1985)	208	24.9	36,969	9.6	8.6	2.6	2.9
1983-1985 (1984)	189	25.7	35,787	9.5	8.5	2.7	3.0
1982-1984 (1983)	179	25.3	36,246	9.9	8.9	2.6	2.8
1981-1983 (1982)	164	24.9	34,583	9.6	8.7	2.6	2.9
1980-1982 (1981)	156	25.8	34,642	9.8	8.8	2.6	2.9
1979-1981 (1980)	173	26.2	34,851	10.1	9.1	2.6	2.9
1978-1980 (1979)	153	27.7	33,192	10.0	9.0	2.8	3.1
1977-1979 (1978)	147	27.0	33,841	10.4	9.4	2.6	2.9
1976-1978 (1977)	133	27.6	32,989	10.4	9.4	2.7	2.9
1975-1977 (1976)	125	28.0	34,508	11.1	10.0	2.5	2.8
1974-1976 (1975)	123	27.5	35,230	11.6	10.4	2.4	2.6
1973-1975 (1974)	110	28.6	37,329	12.5	11.4	2.3	2.5
1972-1974 (1973)	117	31.0	38,208	13.2	11.8	2.3	2.6
1971-1973 (1972)	129						
(1955)	64	17.0	25,488	13.0	12.6	1.3	1.3

Source: U.S. Department of Health and Human Services. Public Health Service. Indian Health Service. Office of Planning, Evaluation, and Legislation. Division of Program Statistics. *Trends in Indian Health - 1993*, Rockville, MD: U.S. Department of Health and Human Services, Public Health Service, p. 69. *Notes:* Data are presented above for the year in which IHS was established (1955). For this year Reservation State data are shown. Starting in 1972 data are first available, and are shown above, for specific counties in the IHS service area. Data for these two geographic boundary systems are not directly comparable. American Indian and Alaska Native rates are for 3-year periods centered in the single years specified.

★ 468 ★

Chronic Diseases

Diabetes Prevalence Among Selected Groups

U.S. population group[1]	Percent rate	Rate relative to whites
American Indian[2]	9.1	1.5
Pima Indian[3]	43.4	7.0
White	6.2	1.0
Cuban	9.3	1.5
Black	10.2	1.6

[Continued]

★ 468 ★

Diabetes Prevalence Among Selected Groups
[Continued]

U.S. population group[1]	Percent rate	Rate relative to whites
Mexican American	13.0	2.1
Puerto Rican	13.4	2.2

Source: U.S. General Accounting Office. *Diabetes: Status of the Disease Among American Indians, Blacks, and Hispanics.* Washington, DC: U.S. GAO, 1992, p. 4. Primary source: Hispanic Health and Nutrition Examination Survey 1982-84 (HHANES); National Health and Nutrition Examination Survey 1976-80 (NHANES); Indian Health Service, 1991; W.C. Knowler, et al., "Diabetes Mellitus in the Pima Indians: Incidence, Risk Factors and Pathogenesis," Diabetes/Metabolism Reviews, 6:1 (1990), 1-27. *Notes:* 1. Rates for Whites, Cubans, Blacks, Mexican Americans, and Puerto Ricans are based on previously diagnosed and undiagnosed cases of diabetes. Undiagnosed cases were detected by administering an oral glucose test to a subsample of the study population. Rates for American Indians and Pima Indians are based on previously diagnosed cases of diabetes. It is likely that there are fewer undiagnosed cases of diabetes in American Indians than other racial groups because of the numerous community education programs and free health care services that are available to American Indians. Thus, it is reasonable to compare the rates, although it is likely that the total prevalence of diabetes in American Indians and Pima Indians is higher than indicated in the table. 2. The rate for American Indians is based on persons 15 years of age and older, 1990 (age-adjusted to the 1980 U.S. population). It is likely that the prevalence rate for American Indians 20 to 74 years of age would be higher than the rate for persons 15 years of age and older because increasing age is a risk factor for diabetes. 3. The rate for Pima Indians is based on persons 25-64 years of age, 1981-88. The rates are not age-adjusted. The Pima Indians, who have the highest recorded prevalence rate of diabetes in the world, have been studied for over 25 years.

★ 469 ★

Chronic Diseases

Diabetes-Related Amputation Rates, 1982-90

Data show average annual rate of all lower extremity amputations for fiscal years 1982-90 in selected IHS (Indian Health Service) service areas.

Area	FY 82-87		FY 88-90	
	Patients	Rate[1]	Patients	Rate[1]
Navajo Area	179	6.4	141	7.3
Oklahoma Area	409	8.2	169	5.3
Phoenix/Tucson Area	714	17.9	337	14.1
Total	1032	11.03	647	8.6

Source: Rith-Najarian, Stephen J. MD and others. "Reducing amputations caused by diabetes in American Indians: a simple strategy." *The (IHS) Provider* (February 1993), p. 33. Primary source: IHS Inpatient Database, IHS and Contract Care Hospital Discharges. *Notes:* Excludes Eagle Pass, and Yaqui Service Units. Also excludes VA hospitalization and those paid entirely by Medicaid and private insurance. Rate per 1,000 diabetic patients.

★ 470 ★

Chronic Diseases

Malignant Neoplasm Deaths and Mortality Rates, by Year

Age-adjusted rate per 100,000 population for American Indians, Alaska Natives, and U.S. all races, 1955-1989.

Calendar year(s)	Indian and Alaska Native		U.S. all races		U.S. white Rate	Ratio Indian to:	
	Number	Rate	Number	Rate		U.S. all races	U.S. other than White
(1989)	913						
1987-1989 (1988)	831	90.8	485,048	132.7	130.0	0.7	0.7
1986-1988 (1987)	768	88.2	476,927	132.9	130.1	0.7	0.7
1985-1987 (1986)	756	86.6	469,376	133.2	130.4	0.7	0.7
1984-1986 (1985)	714	89.7	461,563	133.6	130.4	0.7	0.7
1983-1985 (1984)	712	91.1	453,492	133.5	130.2	0.7	0.7
1982-1984 (1983)	662	92.8	442,986	133.6	129.4	0.7	0.7
1981-1983 (1982)	617	90.7	433,795	132.5	129.4	0.7	0.7
1980-1982 (1981)	578	89.7	422,094	131.6	128.5	0.7	0.7
1979-1981 (1980)	567	86.0	416,509	132.8	129.6	0.6	0.7
1978-1980 (1979)	480	88.4	403,395	130.8	130.2	0.7	0.7
1977-1979 (1978)	508	87.6	396,992	133.8	130.8	0.7	0.7
1976-1978 (1977)	456	93.2	386,686	133.0	130.0	0.7	0.7
1975-1977 (1976)	441	92.5	377,312	132.3	129.5	0.7	0.7
1974-1976 (1975)	395	92.5	365,693	129.4	128.1	0.7	0.7
1973-1975 (1974)	403	92.2	360,472	131.8	129.0	0.7	0.7
1972-1974 (1973)	385	94.4	351,055	130.7	127.7	0.7	0.7
1971-1973 (1972)	354		345,618				
(1955)	296	95.0	240,681	125.8	0.8	0.8	

Source: U.S. Department of Health and Human Services. Public Health Service. Indian Health Service. Office of Planning, Evaluation, and Legislation. Division of Program Statistics. *Trends in Indian Health - 1993*, Rockville, MD: U.S. Department of Health and Human Services, Public Health Service, p. 66. *Notes:* Data are presented above for the year in which IHS was established (1955). For this year Reservation State data are shown. Starting in 1972 data are first available, and are shown above, for specific counties in the IHS service area. Data for these two geographic boundary systems are not directly comparable. American Indian and Alaska Native rates are for 3-year periods centered in the single years specified.

★ 471 ★

Chronic Diseases

Malignant Neoplasm Mortality Rates, by Age and Sex

Rate per 100,000 population for American Indians, Alaska Natives, and U.S. all races, 1955-1989.

Age group	Indian and Alaska Native			U.S. all races			U.S. white		
	Both sexes	Male	Female	Both sexes	Male	Female	Both sexes	Male	Female
Under 1	1.1	2.2	-	2.3	2.3	2.3	2.2	2.3	2.2
1-4 years	5.3	3.7	7.0	3.7	3.8	3.7	3.8	3.9	3.7
5-14 years	2.2	3.2	1.1	3.2	3.6	2.7	3.2	3.7	2.6
15-24 years	4.8	4.2	5.4	5.1	5.9	4.2	5.1	5.9	4.2
25-34 years	11.7	9.3	14.0	11.9	11.7	12.2	11.5	11.5	11.5
35-44 years	29.4	27.5	31.1	44.2	39.7	48.5	41.6	36.9	46.2

[Continued]

★ 471 ★

Malignant Neoplasm Mortality Rates, by Age and Sex
[Continued]

Age group	Indian and Alaska Native			U.S. all races			U.S. white		
	Both sexes	Male	Female	Both sexes	Male	Female	Both sexes	Male	Female
45-54 years	114.2	106.2	121.6	160.4	166.3	154.9	152.3	153.5	151.3
55-64 years	276.3	308.6	248.3	447.3	526.7	376.6	437.1	508.6	372.5
65-74 years	595.8	706.1	508.2	842.7	1,072.7	659.2	833.8	1,050.4	660.0
75-84 years	884.9	1,113.6	730.7	1,313.3	1,861.0	982.6	1,305.6	1,839.7	984.4
85 years +	1,270.3	1,654.7	1,047.3	1,638.9	2,527.9	1,292.8	1,640.2	2,533.0	1,300.1

Source: U.S. Department of Health and Human Services. Public Health Service. Indian Health Service. Office of Planning, Evaluation, and Legislation. Division of Program Statistics. *Trends in Indian Health - 1993*, Rockville, MD: U.S. Department of Health and Human Services, Public Health Service, p. 18. *Notes:* A dash (-) represents zero. 1. Includes deaths with ICD-9 codes 140-208.

★ 472 ★

Chronic Diseases

Projects and Funding for Diabetes Research by the U.S. Government, 1991

Type of research and population group	Projects		Funding	
	Number	%	($000)	%
Human (total)[1]				
Hispanic	4	2.0	1,671	5.0
American Indian	46	28.0	7,458	21.0
Black	15	9.0	4,145	11.0
Multiracial[2]	19	12.0	5,965	17.0
White	77	47.0	16,728	46.0
Total	163	100.0	36,089	100.0
Prevention/behavioral				
Hispanic	0	0.0	70[3]	2.0
American Indian	5	36.0	358	8.0
Black	5	36.0	2,048	47.0
Multiracial[2]	1	7.0	258	7.0
White	3	21.0	1,600	37.0
Total	14	100.0	4,361	100.0
Clinical[1]				
Hispanic	1	<1.0	293	1.0
American Indian	35	28.0	6,042	25.0
Black	6	5.0	1,095	4.0
Multiracial[2]	12	10.0	2,559	11.0
White	69	55.0	14,246	58.0
Total	125	100.0	24,357	100.0
Epidemiologic				
Hispanic	3	13.0	1,308	18.0
American Indian	6	26.0	1,058	15.0
Black	4	17.0	1,002	14.0

[Continued]

★ 472 ★

Projects and Funding for Diabetes Research by the U.S. Government, 1991

[Continued]

Type of research and population group	Projects		Funding	
	Number	%	($000)	%
Multiracial	6	26.0	3,121	44.0
White	4	17.0	666	9.0
Total	23	100.0	7,155	100.0

Source: U.S. General Accounting Office. *Diabetes: Status of the Disease Among American Indians, Blacks and Hispanics.* Washington, DC: U.S. GAO, 1992, p. 13. National Institute of Diabetes and Digestive and Kidney Diseases, 1991. *Notes:* 1. Totals for human and clinical research categories include two projects ($122,000) that were targeted to another population group; the human research for whites includes another type of project ($216,000). 2. Involved only non-white populations. 3. The amount from two multiracial projects that targeted Hispanics.

★ 473 ★

Chronic Diseases

Tuberculosis Deaths and Mortality Rates, by Year

Age-adjusted rate per 100,000 population for American Indians, Alaska Natives, and U.S. all races, 1955-1989.

Calendar year(s)	Indian and Alaska Native		U.S. all races		U.S. white Rate	Ratio Indian to:	
	Number	Rate	Number	Rate		U.S. all races	U.S. other than White
(1989)	33						
1987-1989 (1988)	25	3.1	1,921	0.5	0.3	6.2	10.3
1986-1988 (1987)	28	2.9	1,755	0.5	0.3	5.8	9.7
1985-1987 (1986)	24	2.6	1,782	0.5	0.3	5.2	8.7
1984-1986 (1985)	18	2.3	1,752	0.5	0.3	4.6	7.7
1983-1985 (1984)	17	2.7	1,729	0.5	0.3	5.4	9.0
1982-1984 (1983)	30	3.0	1,779	0.5	0.3	6.0	10.0
1981-1983 (1982)	22	3.8	1,807	0.6	0.4	6.3	9.5
1980-1982 (1981)	30	4.0	1,937	0.6	0.4	6.7	10.0
1979-1981 (1980)	31	4.8	1,978	0.6	0.4	8.0	12.0
1978-1980 (1979)	33	5.8	2,007	0.7	0.4	8.3	14.5
1977-1979 (1978)	40	6.4	2,914	1.0	0.7	6.4	9.1
1976-1978 (1977)	33	8.1	2,968	1.0	0.7	8.1	11.6
1975-1977 (1976)	48	9.5	3,130	1.1	0.8	8.6	11.9
1974-1976 (1975)	53	10.9	3,333	1.2	0.9	9.1	12.1
1973-1975 (1974)	48	11.2	3,513	1.3	0.9	8.6	12.4
1972-1974 (1973)	45	11.7	3,875	1.5	1.1	7.8	10.6
1971-1973 (1972)	50		4,376				
(1955)	253	57.9	14,940	8.4	6.2	6.9	9.3

Source: U.S. Department of Health and Human Services. Public Health Service. Indian Health Service. Office of Planning, Evaluation, and Legislation. Division of Program Statistics. *Trends in Indian Health - 1993,* Rockville, MD: U.S. Department of Health and Human Services, Public Health Service, p. 68. *Notes:* Data are presented above for the year in which IHS was established (1955). For this year Reservation State data are shown. Starting in 1972 data are first available, and are shown above, for specific counties in the IHS service area. Data for these two geographic boundary systems are not directly comparable. American Indian and Alaska Native rates are for 3-year periods centered in the single years specified.

Dental Health

★ 474 ★

Dental Services Provided by IHS and Tribal Hospitals, by Year

Numbers of dental services provided by IHS (Indian Health Service), contact, tribal, and urban programs, are shown for FY 1955-1992.

Fiscal year	Number of services provided				% contract of total	% tribal and urban of total	% increase of total since 1955
	Total	IHS		Tribal and urban			
		Direct	Contract[1]				
1992	2,458,811	1,618,679	92,447	747,685	3.8	30.4	1,266.0
1991	2,369,484	1,516,233	133,253	719,998	5.6	30.4	1,216.4
1990	2,362,228	1,563,934	139,425	658,869	5.9	27.9	1,212.3
1989	2,207,082	1,466,812	132,918	607,352	6.0	27.5	1,126.2
1988	2,106,741	1,415,815	194,784	496,142	9.2	23.6	1,070.4
1987	2,130,690	1,397,262	191,639	541,789	9.0	25.4	1,083.7
1986	1,984,522	1,322,794	155,939	505,789	7.9	25.5	1,002.5
1985	1,914,820	1,276,623	210,508	427,689	11.0	22.3	963.8
1984	2,011,326	1,348,599	224,918	437,809	11.2	21.8	1,017.4
1983	1,907,336	1,325,187	149,741	432,408	7.9	22.7	959.6
1982	1,666,263	1,202,422	153,030	311,341	9.2	18.6	825.7
1981	1,801,982	1,319,913	182,880	299,189	10.1	16.6	901.1
1980	1,833,206	1,357,809	216,574	258,823	11.8	14.1	918.4
1979[2]	1,618,383	1,239,108	215,997	163,278	13.3	10.1	799.1
1978	1,099,019	885,019	214,000		19.5		510.6
1977	1,037,640	823,328	214,312		20.7		476.5
1976	975,647	798,709	176,938		18.1		442.0
1975	946,722	745,831	200,891		21.2		426.0
1974	927,701	775,747	151,954		16.4		415.4
1973	863,057	728,909	134,148		15.5		379.5
1972	844,724	718,176	126,548		15.0		369.3
1971	776,168	684,612	91,556		11.8		331.2
1970	737,206	646,580	90,626		12.3		309.6
1969	703,232	634,479	68,753		9.8		290.7
1968	681,745	613,084	68,661		10.1		278.7
1967	626,458	545,509	80,949		12.9		248.0
1966[2]	570,779	502,710	60,069		11.9		217.1
1965	572,079	495,006	77,073		13.5		217.8
1964	525,010	462,981	62,029		11.8		191.7
1963	453,906	398,452	55,454		12.2		152.2
1962	421,597	364,988	56,609		13.4		134.2
1961	403,528	348,776	54,752		13.6		124.2
1960[2]	364,423	307,248	57,175		15.7		102.5
1959	328,613	283,206	45,407		13.8		82.6
1958	282,372	282,372	-		-		56.9
1957	249,048	249,048	-		-		38.4

[Continued]

★ 474 ★

Dental Services Provided by IHS and Tribal Hospitals, by Year

[Continued]

Fiscal year	Number of services provided			Tribal and urban	% contract of total	% tribal and urban of total	% increase of total since 1955
	Total	IHS					
		Direct	Contract[1]				
1956	219,353	219,353	-		-		21.9
1955	180,000	180,000	-	-	-		-

Source: U.S. Department of Health and Human Services. Public Health Service. Indian Health Service. Office of Planning, Evaluation, and Legislation. Division of Program Statistics. *Trends in Indian Health - 1993*, Rockville, MD: U.S. Department of Health and Human Services, Public Health Service, p. 92. *Notes:* 1. Beginning with FY 1979 this category excludes contract services purchased from the private sector by Tribes. 2. Data systems were modified in 1960, 1966 and 1978. In 1978 the IHS began to use the dental services coding list adopted by the American Dental Association (ADA). The ADA list identifies individual clinical services. Previously the IHS had reported specified clinical services combined into major dental service groupings. Excluded from the 1978 count are diagnostic and adjunctive services. Excluded from the clinical counts since 1979 are diagnostic services other than examinations, revisits, and non-clinical adjunctive services.

★ 475 ★

Dental Health

Dental Services Provided by IHS and Tribal Hospitals, FY 1993

Number of services provided by each type of facility is shown, by IHS (Indian Health Service) Area, for fiscal year (FY) 1993.

	Total		IHS direct		IHS contract		Tribal direct		Tribal contract	
	Patients	Svcs.	Patients	Svcs.	Patients	Svcs.	Patients	Svcs.	Patients	Svcs.
All IHS Areas	382303	2593799	250231	1730753	17924	97897	108552	734411	5596	30738
Aberdeen Area	37810	234168	29796	185149	1942	11361	5269	33423	803	4235
Alaska Area	39647	245285	9665	70211	90	2159	29892	172915	-	-
Albuquerque Area	24667	174378	22749	153854	9	21	1909	20503	-	-
Bemidji Area	21408	148553	6687	43202	1015	9018	12614	89555	1092	6778
Billings Area	24776	166046	24346	163953	430	2093				
California Area	21849	176049	-	-	-	-	21596	174937	253	1112
Nashville Area	14232	94274	3285	23179	25	168	9896	64781	1026	6146
Navajo Area	63215	409747	57261	388182	5954	21565				
Oklahoma Area	66695	489697	47577	355493	904	21974	17254	105219	960	7011
Phoenix Area	33298	236978	28182	207961	1299	3756	3801	25156	16	106
Portland Area	27075	181238	15672	110082	3636	17884	6321	47922	1446	5350
Tucson Area	7631	37385	5011	29487	2620	7898	-	-	-	-

Source: U.S. Department of Health and Human Services. Public Health Service. Indian Health Service. Office of Planning, Evaluation, and Legislation. Division of Program Statistics. *Regional Differences in Indian Health - 1994*, Rockville, MD: U.S. Department of Health and Human Services, Public Health Service, p. 89. Primary source: IHS Dental Data Reporting System.

Infant Mortality

★ 476 ★

Infant, Neonatal, and Postneonatal Mortality Rates

Infant, neonatal, and postneonatal deaths and mortality rates are shown for selected birth cohorts, by race and Hispanic origin of mother.

Race and Hispanic origin of mother	Birth cohort						
	1960[1]	1983	1984	1985	1986	1987	1985-87
	Infant deaths per 1,000 live births						
All mothers	25.1	10.9	10.4	10.4	10.1	9.8	10.1
White	22.2	9.3	8.9	8.9	8.5	8.2	8.5
Black	42.1	19.2	18.2	18.6	18.2	17.8	18.2
American Indian or Alaskan Native	-	15.2	13.4	13.1	13.9	18.0	13.3
Asian or Pacific Islander	-	8.3	8.9	7.8	7.8	7.3	7.6
Chinese	-	9.5	7.2	5.8	5.9	6.2	6.0
Japanese	-	5	5	6.0[6]	7.2[6]	6.6[6]	6.6
Filipino	-	8.4	8.5	7.7	7.2	6.6	7.2
Other Asian or Pacific Islander[2]	-	8.3	937	8.6	8.6	7.9	8.3
Hispanic origin[3,4]	-	9.5	9.3	8.8	8.4	8.2	8.5
Mexican American	-	9.1	8.9	8.5	7.9	8.0	8.1
Puerto Rican	-	12.9	12.9	11.1	11.7	9.9	10.9
Cuban	-	7.5[6]	8.1[6]	8.5	7.5[6]	7.1	7.7
Central and South American	-	8.5	8.3	8.0	7.8	7.8	7.8
Other and unknown Hispanic	-	10.6	9.6	9.5	9.2	8.7	9.1
Non-Hispanic white[4]	-	9.2	8.7	8.7	8.4	8.1	8.4
Non-Hispanic black[4]	-	19.1	18.1	18.3	18.0	17.4	17.9
	Neonatal deaths per 1,000 live births						
All mothers	18.4	7.1	6.8	6.8	6.5	6.2	6.6
White	16.9	6.1	5.8	5.8	5.5	5.2	5.5
Black	27.3	12.5	11.9	12.3	11.9	11.8	12.0
American Indian or Alaskan Native	-	7.5	6.4	6.1	6.1	6.2	6.1
Asian or Pacific Islander	-	5.2	5.7	4.8	4.8	4.5	4.7
Chinese	-	5.5	4.4	3.3	3.1	3.7	3.4
Japanese	-	5	5	3.1[6]	4.7[6]	4.0[6]	3.9
Filipino	-	5.6	5.3	5.1	4.9	4.1	4.7
Other Asian or Pacific Islander[2]	-	5.2	6.5	5.4	5.3	4.9	5.2
Hispanic origin[3,4]	-	6.2	6.2	5.7	5.5	5.3	5.5
Mexican American	-	5.9	5.8	5.4	5.1	5.1	5.2
Puerto Rican	-	8.7	8.6	7.6	7.6	6.7	7.3
Cuban	-	5.0[6]	6.4[6]	6.2	5.1[6]	5.3	5.5
Central and South American	-	5.8	5.9	5.6	5.2	5.0	5.2
Other and unknown Hispanic	-	6.4	6.5	5.6	6.0	5.6	5.7

[Continued]

★ 476 ★

Infant, Neonatal, and Postneonatal Mortality Rates
[Continued]

Race and Hispanic origin of mother	Birth cohort						
	1960[1]	1983	1984	1985	1986	1987	1985-87
Non-Hispanic white[4]	-	6.0	5.7	5.7	5.4	5.0	5.4
Non-Hispanic black[4]	-	12.1	11.5	11.9	11.5	11.3	11.6
	Postneonatal deaths per 1,000 live births						
All mothers	6.7	3.8	3.6	3.6	3.6	3.5	3.6
White	5.3	3.2	3.1	3.1	3.0	3.0	3.0
Black	14.8	6.7	6.3	6.3	6.3	6.1	6.2
American Indian or Alaskan Native	-	7.7	7.0	7.0	7.8	6.8	7.2
Asian or Pacific Islander	-	3.1	3.1	2.9	3.0	2.8	2.9
Chinese	-	5	5	2.5[6]	2.8[6]	2.5[6]	2.6
Japanese	-	5	5	5	2.5[6]	5	2.7
Filipino	-	2.8[6]	3.2[6]	2.7[6]	2.3	2.5	2.5
Other Asian or Pacific Islander[2]	-	3.1	3.2	3.1	3.3	3.0	3.2
Hispanic origin[3,4]	-	3.3	3.1	3.2	2.9	2.9	3.0
Mexican American	-	3.2	3.2	3.2	2.8	2.9	2.9
Puerto Rican	-	4.2	4.3	3.5	4.2	3.2	3.6
Cuban	-	5	1.7[6]	5	2.4[6]	5	2.2
Central and South American	-	2.6	2.4	2.4	2.6	2.8	2.6
Other and unknown Hispanic	-	4.2	3.1	3.9	3.2	3.2	3.4
Non-Hispanic white[4]	-	3.2	3.0	3.0	3.0	3.0	3.0
Non-Hispanic black[4]	-	7.0	6.6	6.4	6.5	6.2	6.3

Source: National Center for Health Statistics. *Health, United States, 1993.* Hyattsville, MD: Public Health Service, May 1994, p. 80. Primary source: Centers for Disease Control and Prevention, National Center for Health Statistics. Data computed by the Division of Analysis from data compiled by the Division of Vital Statistics for the National Linked Files of Live Births and Infant Deaths. *Notes:* A dash (-) stands for data not available. 1. Data are shown by race of child in 1960. 2. Includes Hawaiians and part Hawaiians. 3. Includes mothers of all races. 4. Data shown only for States with an Hispanic-origin item on their birth certificates. In 1983-87, 23 States and the District of Columbia included this item. 5. Infant and neonatal mortality rates for groups with fewer than 7,500 births are considered highly unreliable and are not shown. Postneonatal mortality rates for groups with fewer than 15,000 births are considered highly unreliable and are not shown. 6. Infant and neonatal mortality rates for groups with fewer than 10,000 births are considered unreliable. Postneonatal mortality rates for groups with fewer than 20,000 births are considered unreliable.

★ 477 ★

Infant Mortality

Infant Deaths, by Leading Cause

Figures represent mortality rate per 1,000 live births for American Indians and Alaska Natives from 1987-1989 and for U.S. all races and U.S. white populations in 1988.

Cause of death	Indian and Alaska Native		U.S. all races Rate	U.S. white Rate	Ratio American Indian and Alaska Native to:	
	Number	Rate			U.S. all races	U.S. white
All causes	1,077	11.0	10.0	8.5	1.1	1.3
Sudden infant death syndrome	277	2.8	1.4	1.2	2.0	2.3
Congenital anomalies	196	2.0	2.1	2.1	1.0	1.0
Disorders relating to short gestation and low birth weight	50	0.5	0.8	0.6	0.6	0.8
Accidents	49	0.5	0.2	0.2	2.5	2.5
Respiratory distress syndrome	49	0.5	0.8	0.7	0.6	0.7
Pneumonia and influenza	45	0.5	0.2	0.1	2.5	5.0
Infections specific to the perinatal period	28	0.3	0.2	0.2	1.5	1.5
Newborn affected by complications of placenta, cord, and membranes	20	0.2	0.2	0.2	1.0	1.0
Intrauterine hypoxia and birth asphyxia	17	0.2	0.2	0.2	1.0	1.0
Newborn affected by maternal complications of pregnancy	17	0.2	0.4	0.3	0.5	0.7
All other causes	329					

Source: U.S. Department of Health and Human Services. Public Health Service. Indian Health Service. Office of Planning, Evaluation, and Legislation. Division of Program Statistics. *Trends in Indian Health - 1993*, Rockville, MD: U.S. Department of Health and Human Services, Public Health Service, p. 41. Primary source: National Center for Health Statistics (NCHS), U.S. infant mortality rates (all ages) - Monthly Vital Statistics Report, Advance Report of Final Mortality Statistics, 1988, Vol. 39 No. 7, Supplement, November 28, 1990, Table 15; and infant mortality rates by age and race published in Vital Statistics of the United States, 1988, Volume II, Part A, Mortality, Tables 2-6 and 2-16. *Note:* 0.0 stands for rounds to zero. A dash (-) stands for not applicable.

★ 478 ★

Infant Mortality

Infant Mortalities in Oklahoma, by Estimated Actual Indian Deaths Based on Matched Records, 1975-88

Death rates are shown per 1,000 live births. Matching (linking) of infant deaths to birth certificates from 1975 to 1988 indicates that infants born Indian had a 28 percent chance of being misclassified as another race (usually white) on the death certificate. Infants born white or black had less than a 1 percent chance of being misclassified.

Years	Reported born Indian	Estimated infant deaths	Reported live births	Estimated mortality rate	Reported mortality rate
1975-76	108	117.3	7,015	16.72	12.97
1977-78	108	118.6	7,660	15.48	13.71
1979-80	98	109.8	9,073	12.10	10.76
1981-82	110	126.2	10,568	11.93	8.80
1983-84	115	126.9	10,513	12.07	7.61
1985-86	101	110.5	10,310	10.72	5.40
1987-88	97	111.2	10,650	10.44	5.79
Totals	737	820.5	65,789	12.47	8.87

Source: Kennedy, Richard D. M.S. and Roger E. Deapen, Ph.D., "Differences between Oklahoma Indian infant mortality and other races," *Public Health Reports* Vol. 106, No. 1 (January-February 1991), p. 99.

★ 479 ★

Infant Mortality

Infant Mortalities in Oklahoma, by Matches for Race Classifications of Indians on Birth and Death Certificates, 1975-88

Misclassification of Indian deaths strongly alters the overall infant mortality rate for the Oklahoma Indian population form the currently reported 5.8 per 1,000 (1987-88) to an estimated actual rate of 10.4 per 1,000 for the same period.

Years	Identified Indian		Percent other race on death certificate
	On birth certificate	On death certificate	
1975-76	108	87	19.44
1977-78	108	98	9.26
1979-80	98	85	13.27
1981-82	110	81	26.36
1983-84	115	68	40.87
1985-86	101	52	48.51

[Continued]

★ 479 ★

Infant Mortalities in Oklahoma, by Matches for Race Classifications of Indians on Birth and Death Certificates, 1975-88
[Continued]

Years	Identified Indian		Percent other race on death certificate
	On birth certificate	On death certificate	
1987-88	97	57	41.24
Totals	737	528	28.35

Source: Kennedy, Richard D. M.S. and Roger E. Deapen, Ph.D., "Differences between Oklahoma Indian infant mortality and other races," *Public Health Reports* Vol. 106, No. 1 (January-February 1991), p. 99.

★ 480 ★

Infant Mortality

Infant Mortalities in Oklahoma, by Race Classifications at Birth and at Death, 1975-88

Matching (linking) of infant deaths to birth certificates from 1975 to 1988 indicates that infants born Indian had a 28 percent chance of being misclassified as another race (usually white) on the death certificate. Infants born white or black had less than a 1 percent chance of being misclassified.

Race at death	Race at birth					
	Indian	White	Black	Other	Unknown	Total
Indian	484	37	2	4	1	528
White	246	5,549	26	35	18	5,874
Black	4	42	1,103	1	2	1,152
Other	0	7	2	49	0	58
Unknown	3	11	3	1	1	19
Total	737	5,646	1,136	90	22	7,631

Source: Kennedy, Richard D. M.S. and Roger E. Deapen, Ph.D., "Differences between Oklahoma Indian infant mortality and other races," *Public Health Reports* Vol. 106, No.1 (January-February) 1991, p.98.

★ 481 ★

Infant Mortality

Infant Mortalities in Oklahoma, by Race Classified at Birth and at Death, 1975-88

The registered race, at birth and death, is shown. Matching (linking) of infant deaths to birth certificates from 1975 to 1988 indicates that infants born Indian had a 28 percent chance of being misclassified as another race (usually white) on the death certificate. Infants born white or black had less than a 1 percent chance of being misclassified.

Years	Indian at birth white at death	Percent of Indians	White at birth Indian at death	Percent of whites	Indian at birth black at death	Black at birth Indian at death
1975-76	25	23.1	6	0.6	1	0
1977-78	13	12.0	4	0.5	1	1
1979-80	18	18.4	6	0.7	1	0
1981-82	37	33.6	5	0.6	0	0
1983-84	53	46.1	7	0.9	1	1
1985-86	54	53.5	5	0.7	0	0
1987-88	46	47.4	4	0.7	0	0
Totals	246	33.4	37	0.7	4	2

Source: Kennedy, Richard D. M.S. and Roger E. Deapen, Ph.D., "Differences between Oklahoma Indian infant mortality and other races," *Public Health Reports* Vol. 106, No. 1 (January-February 1991), p. 99.

★ 482 ★

Infant Mortality

Infant Mortality Rates in Oklahoma, 1975-88

Mortality rates per 1,000 live births are shown.

Years	All races	Indian	White	Black
1975-76	16.38	12.97	15.71	26.02
1977-78	13.98	13.71	13.01	21.43
1979-80	12.58	10.76	11.87	20.23
1981-82	12.05	8.80	11.87	17.40
1983-84	10.65	7.61	10.62	14.45
1985-86	10.55	5.40	10.35	18.19
1987-88	9.33	5.79	9.32	13.47
14 year average[1]	12.10	8.87	11.75	18.43

Source: Kennedy, Richard D. M.S. and Roger E. Deapen, Ph.D., "Differences between Oklahoma Indian infant mortality and other races," *Public Health Reports* Vol. 106, No. 1 (January-February 1991), p. 98. *Notes:* 1. Computed by dividing all infant deaths from 1975 to 1988 by total number of live births for the same period.

★ 483 ★

Infant Mortality

Infant Mortality Rates, by Age

Figures represent rate per 1,000 live births from 1973 to 1988.

Calendar year[1]	Infant mortality rate	Neonatal (under 28 days)	Postnatal (28 days- 11 mos.)
American Indians and Alaska Natives			
1987-1989	11.0	5.1	5.9
1986-1988	11.1	5.2	5.9
1985-1987	11.1	5.3	5.9
1984-1986	11.1	5.0	6.0
1983-1985	11.1	5.1	6.0
1982-1984	11.5	5.1	6.4
1981-1983	12.3	5.3	7.0
1980-1982	13.2	5.9	7.3
1979-1981	15.4	7.2	8.1
1978-1980	16.5	8.2	8.4
1977-1979	17.9	8.9	9.0
1976-1978	19.2	9.3	9.9
1975-1977	20.5	10.0	10.5
1974-1976	21.6	10.4	11.2
1973-1975	21.4	10.4	11.1
1972-1974	22.2	10.2	12.0
U.S. all races			
1988	10.0	6.3	3.7
1987	10.1	6.5	3.6
1986	10.4	6.7	3.6
1985	10.6	7.0	3.7
1984	10.8	7.0	3.8
1983	11.2	7.3	3.9
1982	11.5	7.7	3.8
1981	11.9	8.0	3.9
1980	12.6	8.5	4.1
1979	13.1	8.9	4.2
1978	13.8	9.5	4.3
1977	14.1	9.9	4.2
1976	15.2	10.9	4.3
1975	16.1	11.6	4.5
1974	16.7	12.3	4.4
1973	17.7	13.0	4.7
U.S. white			
1988	8.5	5.4	3.1
1987	8.6	5.5	3.1
1986	8.9	5.8	3.1
1985	9.3	6.1	3.2
1984	9.4	6.2	3.3
1983	9.7	6.4	3.3
1982	10.1	6.8	3.3
1981	10.5	7.1	3.4

[Continued]

★ 483 ★

Infant Mortality Rates, by Age

[Continued]

Calendar year[1]	Infant mortality rate	Neonatal (under 28 days)	Postnatal (28 days- 11 mos.)
1980	11.0	7.5	3.5
1979	11.4	7.9	3.5
1978	12.0	8.4	3.6
1977	12.3	8.7	3.6
1976	13.3	9.7	3.6
1975	14.2	10.4	3.8
1974	14.8	11.1	3.7
1973	15.8	11.8	4.0

Source: U.S. Department of Health and Human Services. Public Health Service. Indian Health Service. Office of Planning, Evaluation, and Legislation. Division of Program Statistics. *Trends in Indian Health - 1993*, Rockville, MD: U.S. Department of Health and Human Services, Public Health Service, p. 38. *Notes:* 1. Starting in 1972 data on infant mortality by age are first available, and are show, for the specific counties in the IHS service area.

★ 484 ★

Infant Mortality

Infant Mortality Rates, by Year

Figures represent the mortality rate per 1,000 live births from 1955 to 1988. The infant mortality rate among American Indians and Alaska Natives decreased 50 percent between the periods 1972-1974 and 1987-1989.

Calendar year[1]	Indian and Alaska Native	U.S. all races	U.S. white	Ratio Indian and Alaska Native to:	
				U.S. all races	U.S. white
1987-1989 (1988)	11.0	10.0	8.5	1.1	1.3
1986-1988 (1987)	11.1	10.1	8.6	1.1	1.3
1985-1987 (1986)	11.1	10.4	8.9	1.1	1.2
1984-1986 (1985)	11.1	10.6	9.3	1.0	1.2
1983-1985 (1984)	11.1	10.8	9.4	1.0	1.2
1982-1984 (1983)	11.5	11.2	9.7	1.0	1.2
1981-1983 (1982)	12.3	11.5	10.1	1.1	1.2
1980-1982 (1981)	13.2	11.9	10.5	1.1	1.3
1979-1981 (1980)	15.4	12.6	11.0	1.2	1.4
1978-1980 (1979)	16.5	13.1	11.4	1.3	1.4
1977-1979 (1978)	17.9	13.8	12.0	1.3	1.5
1976-1978 (1977)	19.2	14.1	12.3	1.4	1.6
1975-1977 (1976)	20.5	15.2	13.3	1.3	1.5
1974-1976 (1975)	21.6	16.1	14.2	1.3	1.5
1973-1975 (1974)	21.4	16.7	14.8	1.3	1.4

[Continued]

★ 484 ★

Infant Mortality Rates, by Year
[Continued]

Calendar year[1]	Indian and Alaska Native	U.S. all races	U.S. white	Ratio Indian and Alaska Native to:	
				U.S. all races	U.S. white
1972-1974 (1973)	22.2	17.7	15.8	1.3	1.4
1954-1956 (1955)	62.7	26.4	23.6	2.4	2.7

Source: U.S. Department of Health and Human Services. Public Health Service. Indian Health Service. Office of Planning, Evaluation, and Legislation. Division of Program Statistics. *Trends in Indian Health - 1993*, Rockville, MD: U.S. Department of Health and Human Services, Public Health Service, p. 36. *Notes:* 1. Data are presented for the year in which IHS was established (1955). For this year Reservation State data are shown. Starting in 1972 data are first available, and are shown, for the specific counties in the IHS service area. Data for these two geographic boundary systems are not directly comparable. American Indian and Alaska Native mortality rates are for 3-year periods specified. U.S. rates are for the single years specified.

★ 485 ★

Infant Mortality

Maternal Deaths and Death Rates

Figures represent rate of maternal deaths per 100,000 live births from 1958 to 1989. The maternal death rate for American Indians and Alaska Natives decreased 63 percent between the periods 1972-1974 and 1987-1989.

Calendar year[1]	Indian and Alaska Native		U.S. all races		U.S. white Rate	Ratio Indian to:	
	Number	Rate	Number	Rate		U.S. all races	U.S. white
(1989)	3						
1987-1989 (1988)	5	10.2	330	8.4	5.9	1.2	1.7
1986-1988 (1987)	2	8.5	251	6.6	5.1	1.3	1.7
1985-1987 (1986)	1	5.5	272	7.2	4.9	0.8	1.1
1984-1986 (1985)	2	4.5	295	7.8	5.2	0.6	0.9
1983-1985 (1984)	1	8.0	285	7.8	5.4	1.0	1.5
1982-1984 (1983)	4	6.9	290	8.0	5.9	0.9	1.2
1981-1983 (1982)	1	7.2	292	7.9	5.8	0.9	1.2
1980-1982 (1981)	1	5.0	309	8.5	6.3	0.6	0.8
1979-1981 (1980)	2	9.4	334	9.2	6.7	1.0	1.4
1978-1980 (1979)	4	13.1	336	9.6	6.4	1.4	2.0
1977-1979 (1978)	3	12.7	321	9.6	6.4	1.3	2.0
1976-1978 (1977)	1	8.5	373	11.2	7.7	0.8	1.1
1975-1977 (1976)	1	8.9	390	12.3	9.0	0.7	1.0
1974-1976 (1975)	3	13.0	340	12.8	9.1	1.0	1.4
1973-1975 (1974)	3	15.5	462	14.6	10.0	1.1	1.6
1972-1974 (1973)	2	27.7	477	15.2	10.7	1.8	2.6

[Continued]

★ 485 ★

Maternal Deaths and Death Rates
[Continued]

Calendar year[1]	Indian and Alaska Native		U.S. all races		U.S. white Rate	Ratio Indian to:	
	Number	Rate	Number	Rate		U.S. all races	U.S. white
(1972)	9						
1957-1959 (1958)	16	82.6	1,581	37.6	26.3	2.2	3.1

Source: U.S. Department of Health and Human Services. Public Health Service. Indian Health Service. Office of Planning, Evaluation, and Legislation. Division of Program Statistics. *Trends in Indian Health - 1993*, Rockville, MD: U.S. Department of Health and Human Services, Public Health Service, p. 35. *Notes:* 1. Data are presented for the year in which maternal mortality data were first collected (1958) and as close to the year in which IHS was established (1955) as is possible. For this year Reservation State data are shown. Starting in 1972 data are first available, and are shown above, for the specific counties in the IHS service area. Data for these two geographic boundary systems are not directly comparable. American Indian and Alaska Native maternal mortality rates are for 3-year periods specified. Maternal deaths include deaths with ICD-9 codes 630-676.

★ 486 ★

Infant Mortality

Neonatal Deaths, by Leading Cause

Figures represent mortality rate per 1,000 live births for American Indians and Alaska Natives from 1987-1989 and for U.S. all races and U.S. white populations in 1988.

Cause of death	Indian and Alaska Native		U.S. all races Rate	U.S. white Rate	Ratio American Indian and Alaska Native to:	
	Number	Rate			U.S. all races	U.S. white
All causes	495	5.1	6.3	5.4	0.8	0.9
Congenital anomalies	132	1.3	1.5	1.6	0.9	0.8
Disorders relating to short gestation and low birth weight	48	0.5	0.8	0.6	0.6	0.8
Respiratory distress syndrome	46	0.5	0.8	0.7	0.6	0.7
Sudden infant death syndrome	32	0.3	0.1	0.1	3.0	3.0
Infections specific to the perinatal period	26	0.3	0.2	0.2	1.5	1.5
Newborn affected by complications of placenta, cord, and membranes	20	0.2	0.2	0.2	1.0	1.0
Newborn affected by maternal complications of pregnancy	17	0.2	0.4	0.3	2.0	0.7
Intrauterine hypoxia and birth asphyxia	17	0.2	0.2	0.2	1.0	1.0
Neonatal hemorrhage	8	0.1	0.1	0.1	1.0	1.0
Birth trauma	7	0.1	0.1	0.0	1.0	-
All other causes	142					

Source: U.S. Department of Health and Human Services. Public Health Service. Indian Health Service. Office of Planning, Evaluation, and Legislation. Division of Program Statistics. *Trends in Indian Health - 1993*, Rockville, MD: U.S. Department of Health and Human Services, Public Health Service, p. 41. Primary source: National Center for Health Statistics (NCHS), U.S. infant mortality rates (all ages) - Monthly Vital Statistics Report, Advance Report of Final Mortality Statistics, 1988, Vol. 39 No. 7, Supplement, November 28, 1990, Table 15; and infant mortality rates by age and race published in Vital Statistics of the United States, 1988, Volume II, Part A, Mortality, Tables 2-6 and 2-16. *Note:* 0.0 stands for rounds to zero. A dash (-) stands for not applicable.

★ 487 ★

Infant Mortality

Postneonatal Deaths, by Leading Cause

Figures represent mortality rate per 1,000 live births for American Indians and Alaska Natives from 1987-1989 and for U.S. all races and U.S. white populations in 1988.

Cause of death	Indian and Alaska Native		U.S. all races Rate	U.S. white Rate	Ratio American Indian and Alaska Native to:	
	Number	Rate			U.S. all races	U.S. white
All causes	582	5.9	3.7	3.1	1.6	1.9
Sudden infant death syndrome	245	2.5	1.3	1.2	1.9	2.1
Congenital anomalies	64	0.7	0.6	0.6	1.2	1.2
Pneumonia and influenza	42	0.4	0.1	0.1	4.0	4.0
Accidents	31	0.3	0.2	0.2	1.5	1.5
Meningitis	11	0.1	0.0	0.0	-	-
Homicide	11	0.1	0.1	0.0	1.0	-
Viral diseases	8	0.1	0.0	0.0	-	-
Bronchitis and bronchiolitis	5	0.1	0.0	0.0	-	-
Septicemia	4	0.0	0.1	0.1	-	-
Acute upper respiratory infections	4	0.0	0.0	0.0	-	-
All other causes	157					

Source: U.S. Department of Health and Human Services. Public Health Service. Indian Health Service. Office of Planning, Evaluation, and Legislation. Division of Program Statistics. *Trends in Indian Health - 1993*, Rockville, MD: U.S. Department of Health and Human Services, Public Health Service, p. 41. Primary source: National Center for Health Statistics (NCHS), U.S. infant mortality rates (all ages) - Monthly Vital Statistics Report, Advance Report of Final Mortality Statistics, 1988, Vol. 39 No. 7, Supplement, November 28, 1990, Table 15; and infant mortality rates by age and race published in Vital Statistics of the United States, 1988, Volume II, Part A, Mortality, Tables 2-6 and 2-16. *Note:* 0.0 stands for rounds to zero. A dash (-) stands for not applicable.

Mental Health

★ 488 ★

Psychiatric Patients in Private Care, by Race/Ethnicity, 1990

Data show percent distribution of patients in private psychiatric hospitals. Figures are based on the following total numbers of patients: 30,182 patients in inpatient care; 2,615 persons in residential treatment care programs; 1,439 persons in residential supportive programs; 9,930 patients in partial care programs; and 84,918 patients in outpatient care.

Race/ethnicity	Type of private care				
	Inpatient care	Residential treatment care	Residential supportive care	Partial care	Outpatient care
White	87.3	81.5	91.9	86.7	91.0
Black	11.2	16.4	7.6	12.4	8.1
Native American	0.8	0.5	0.1	0.7	0.4
Asian/Pacific Islander	0.7	1.6	0.3	0.2	0.5
Hispanic	11.3	4.2	2.4	10.6	4.8
Non-Hispanic	88.7	95.8	97.6	89.4	95.2

Source: Mental Health, United States, 1994. Manderscheid, R.W. and Sonnenschein, M.A., eds. DHHS Pub. No. (SMA)94-3000. Washington, DC: U.S. Government Printing Office, 1994, p. 137. Primary source: 1990 Inventory of Mental Health Organizations (IMHO), survey and Analysis Branch, Division of State and Community Systems Development, Center for Mental Health Services (CMHS).

★ 489 ★

Mental Health

Suicide Deaths and Mortality Rates, by Year

Figures represent age-adjusted death rate per 100,000 population for American Indians and Alaska Natives and for U.S. all races, 1955-1989.

Calendar year[1]	Indian and Alaska Native		U.S. all races		U.S. white Rate	Ratio Indian to:	
	Number	Rate	Number	Rate		U.S. all races	U.S. white
(1989)							
1987-1989 (1988)	192						
1986-1988 (1987)	185	17.5	30,407	11.4	12.2	105	104
1985-1987 (1986)	158	17.1	30,904	11.9	12.7	1.4	1.3
1984-1986 (1985)	172	16.1	29,453	11.5	12.3	1.4	1.3
1983-1985 (1984)	148	16.5	29,286	11.6	12.4	1.4	1.3
1982-1984 (1983)	161	16.4	28,295	11.4	12.2	1.4	1.3
1981-1983 (1982)	154	17.6	28,242	11.6	12.4	1.5	1.4
1980-1982 (1981)	157	17.5	27,596	11.5	12.2	1.5	1.4
1979-1981 (1980)	146	18.6	26,869	11.4	12.1	1.6	1.5

[Continued]

★ 489 ★

Suicide Deaths and Mortality Rates, by Year
[Continued]

Calendar year[1]	Indian and Alaska Native		U.S. all races		U.S. white Rate	Ratio Indian to:	
	Number	Rate	Number	Rate		U.S. all races	U.S. white
1978-1980 (1979)	162	18.1	27,204	11.7	12.4	1.5	1.5
1977-1979 (1978)	117	20.3	27,294	12.0	12.7	1.7	1.6
1976-1978 (1977)	161	21.4	28,681	12.9	13.6	1.7	1.6
1975-1977 (1976)	143	24.5	26,832	12.3	12.9	2.0	1.9
1974-1976 (1975)	139	24.0	27,063	12.6	13.3	1.9	1.8
1973-1972 (1974)	122	24.7	25,683	12.2	12.8	2.0	1.9
1972-1974 (1973)	116	25.5	25,118	12.0	12.6	2.1	2.0
(1972)	113		25,004				
1954-1956 (1955)	39	11.9	16,760	9.9	10.4	1.2	1.1

Source: U.S. Department of Health and Human Services. Public Health Service. Indian Health Service. Office of Planning, Evaluation, and Legislation. Division of Program Statistics. *Trends in Indian Health - 1993*, Rockville, MD: U.S. Department of Health and Human Services, Public Health Service, p. 60. *Notes:* 1. Data are presented for the year in which IHS was established (1955). For this year Reservation State data are shown. Starting in 1972 data are first available, and are shown, for the specific counties in the IHS service area. Data for these two geographic boundary systems are not directly comparable. American Indian and Alaska Native rates are for the 3-year periods specified. Numbers of deaths and U.S. rates are for the single year specified.

★ 490 ★

Mental Health

Suicide Mortality Rates, by Age and Sex

Figures represent death rate per 100,000 population for American Indians and Alaska Natives in 1987-1989 and for U.S. all races and white populations in 1988. The rate was higher for Indian males than Indian females in all age groups through age 74, and was highest from the ages of 15 through 34.

Age group	Indian and Alaska Native			U.S. all races			U.S. white		
	Both sexes	Male	Female	Both sexes	Male	Female	Both sexes	Male	Female
Under 5 years	-	-	-	-	-	-	-	-	-
5-14 years	1.4	2.1	0.6	0.7	1.0	0.4	0.7	1.1	0.4
15-24 years	38.3	64.0	11.5	13.2	21.9	4.2	14.1	23.4	4.6
25-34 years	33.3	61.1	6.8	15.4	25.0	5.7	16.0	25.7	6.1
35-44 years	16.8	26.5	7.7	14.8	22.9	6.9	15.7	24.1	7.4
45-54 years	12.3	22.6	2.9	14.6	21.7	7.9	15.8	23.2	8.6
55-64 years	9.2	12.8	6.1	15.6	25.0	7.2	16.9	27.0	7.9
65-74 years	6.6	11.3	3.0	18.4	33.0	6.8	19.8	35.4	7.3
75-84 years	5.2	4.3	5.8	25.9	57.2	6.9	27.7	61.5	7.4
85 years +	-	-	-	20.5	60.4	5.0	21.9	65.8	5.3

Source: U.S. Department of Health and Human Services. Public Health Service. Indian Health Service. Office of Planning, Evaluation, and Legislation. Division of Program Statistics. *Trends in Indian Health - 1993*, Rockville, MD: U.S. Department of Health and Human Services, Public Health Service, p. 61. *Note:* - Represents zero.

Native American Adolescents

★ 491 ★

Nutritional Inadequacies of Adolescents

Data show the percent of adolescents who reported not consuming items from each food group on a daily basis. Data are based on a survey of 13,923 rural American Indian/Alaska Native adolescents living on or near reservations[1].

Food groups	Males	Females
Meat & meat substitutes	23.7	30.7
Dairy food	14.6	19.9
Bread & rice	30.4	29.2
Fruit & vegetables	14.4	12.8
Eats from all four groups daily	49.2	44.5
Misses 1-2 groups daily	42.7	46.3
Misses 3-4 groups daily	8.1	9.2

Source: Indian Health Service, Maternal and Child Health Bureau, and the Robert Wood Johnson Foundation. *The State of Native American Youth Health, February, 1992,* p. 14. *Notes:* 1. Caution: Sample was not random and does not fully represent all Native American/Alaska Native groups.

★ 492 ★

Native American Adolescents

Physical Illnesses Reported by Rural Adolescents

Data are based on a survey of 13,923 rural American Indian/Alaska Native adolescents living on or near reservations[1].

Condition	Percent of total reporting having the condition	Percent of total reporting limitations from the condition
Nerve-sensory		
Hearing impairments	5.0	0.8
Speech problems	12.7	1.4
Vision problems	30.0	4.0
Learning disabilities	12.6	1.7
Emotional/somatic		
Seizures/convulsions	1.5	0.5
Nervous/emotional problems	16.4	2.4
Abdominal problems	27.1	2.0
Chronic		
Headaches	73.5	4.9
Respiratory problems	11.8	1.5

[Continued]

★ 492 ★

Physical Illnesses Reported by Rural Adolescents
[Continued]

Condition	Percent of total reporting having the condition	Percent of total reporting limitations from the condition
Diabetes	1.7	0.4
Allergies/hay fever	19.1	1.6
Other		
Mononucleosis	1.8	0.3
Concentration problems	27.0	2.7
Sexually transmitted diseases	1.8	0.4
Condition limiting school	8.4	8.4

Source: Indian Health Service, Maternal and Child Health Bureau, and the Robert Wood Johnson Foundation. *The State of Native American Youth Health, February, 1992,* p. 15. *Notes:* 1. Caution: Sample was not random and does not fully represent all Native American/Alaska Native groups.

★ 493 ★

Native American Adolescents

Unhealthy Characteristics of Adolescents

Data are shown in percent and are based on a survey of 13,923 rural American Indian/Alaska Native adolescents living on or near reservations[1].

Characteristic	Males	Females	Total
Are obese	24.7	25.0	24.9
Eat red meat daily	41.4	37.1	39.2
Eat eggs daily	40.6	33.8	37.2
Eat fruit and vegetables less than daily	14.4	12.8	13.6
Eat junk food three or more times daily	39.6	42.3	41.0
Smoke cigarettes daily	10.8	12.5	11.7
Use chewing tobacco daily	14.5	7.7	11.1
Never exercise	18.3	19.4	18.9
Have at least four of these problems	15.8	13.1	14.4

Source: Indian Health Service, Maternal and Child Health Bureau, and the Robert Wood Johnson Foundation. *The State of Native American Youth Health, February, 1992,* p. 13. *Notes:* 1. Caution: Sample was not random and does not fully represent all Native American/Alaska Native groups.

Substance Abuse

★ 494 ★

Alcoholism Deaths and Mortality Rates, 1979-89

Age adjusted rates are shown, per 100,000 population, for American Indians and Alaska Natives, U.S. all races, and U.S. whites.

Calendar year(s)	Indian and Alaska Native		U.S. all races		U.S. white Rate	Ratio Indian to:	
	Number	Rate	Number	Rate		U.S. all races	U.S. other than white
(1989)	374						
1987-1989 (1988)	372	37.3	18,715	7.0	5.9	5.3	6.3
1986-1988 (1987)	260	32.5	17,656	6.7	5.7	4.9	5.7
1985-1987 (1986)	260	30.8	17,283	6.7	5.6	4.6	5.5
1984-1986 (1985)	272	34.1	17,609	6.9	5.8	4.9	5.9
1983-1985 (1984)	300	37.8	17,452	6.9	5.9	5.5	6.4
1982-1984 (1983)	291	41.0	17,237	6.9	5.9	5.9	6.9
1981-1983 (1982)	286	45.0	17,334	7.1	6.1	6.3	7.4
1980-1982 (1981)	344	50.9	18,469	7.7	6.5	6.6	7.8
1979-1981 (1980)	368	57.8	19,560	8.3	6.9	7.0	8.4
(1979)	377						

Source: U.S. Department of Health and Human Services. Public Health Service. Indian Health Service. Office of Planning, Evaluation, and Legislation. Division of Program Statistics. *Trends in Indian Health - 1993*, Rockville, MD: U.S. Department of Health and Human Services, Public Health Service, p. 64. *Notes:* Includes deaths previously classified as alcoholism deaths (alcoholic psychosis—291, alcohol dependence syndrome—303, and chronic liver disease and cirrhosis, specified as alcoholic, 571.0-571.3), *plus* deaths caused by alcohol abuse—305.0, alcohol cardiomyopathy—425.5, alcoholic gastritis—535.3, excessive blood level of alcohol—790.3, and accidental poisoning by alcohol—E860.0 and E860.1. American Indian and Alaska Native rates are for the 3-year periods specified. Numbers of deaths and U.S. rates are for the single year specified.

★ 495 ★

Substance Abuse

Community-Based Intervention Approaches to Substance Abuse Prevention

The Office for Substance Abuse Prevention (OSAP) funds 18 prevention programs in Native communities in 12 states. Figures show the percentage of programs which make use of each intervention strategy.

Community-based interventions	Percent of projects
Education/training not using established curriculum	81.0
Referral for counseling/psychotherapy	63.0
Individual counseling/psychotherapy	63.0
Recreational activities	63.0
Case/program consultation	63.0
Group counseling/psychotherapy	56.0

[Continued]

★ 495 ★

Community-Based Intervention Approaches to Substance Abuse Prevention

[Continued]

Community-based interventions	Percent of projects
Education/training using established curriculum	56.0
Cultural activities	56.0
Self-help groups	38.0
Special facility	31.0
Legal intervention	17.0
Social action groups	13.0
Special register	13.0
No community-based intervention	-
Other:	
Community service for elders	6.0
Education/training for service provider	6.0

Source: U.S. Department of Health and Human Services. Public Health Service. Alcohol, Drug Abuse, and Mental Health Administration. Office for Substance Abuse Prevention. *Breaking New Ground For American Indian and Alaska Native Youth: Program Summaries* (OSAP Technical Report-3). Rockville, MD: U.S. DHHS, p. 39.

★ 496 ★

Substance Abuse

OSAP Prevention Program Settings

Figures show availability of prevention programs sponsored by OSAP (Office for Substance Abuse Prevention) by location.

Setting	Percent of projects
Community	63
Home	31
School	
Preschool	31
Elementary	44
Junior High	44
Senior High	38
Community College	13
Four-Year College	13
Human Service Agency	
Child Welfare Agency	25
Court/Legal Agency	25
Other	13
Outpatient Clinic	
Medical Health Clinic/Program	31
Substance Abuse Clinic/Program	44

[Continued]

★ 496 ★

OSAP Prevention Program Settings
[Continued]

Setting	Percent of projects
Mental Health Clinic/Program	25
Hospital	17

Source: U.S. Department of Health and Human Services. Public Health Service. Alcohol, Drug Abuse, and Mental Health Administration. Office for Substance Abuse Prevention. *Breaking New Ground For American Indian and Alaska Native Youth: Program Summaries* (OSAP Technical Report-3). Rockville, MD: U.S. DHHS, p. 36.

★ 497 ★

Substance Abuse

OSAP Target Population by Tribe

The Office for Substance Abuse Prevention (OSAP) funds 18 prevention programs in Native communities in 12 states. These programs serve a client population of 25 tribes. Figures show the percentage of programs which address the needs of each tribe.

Tribe	Percent of programs
Aleut	13
Apache	6
Athabaskan	13
Blackfeet	6
Chippewa/Cree	6
Chippewa	17
Clallam	6
Cocopaw	6
Eastern Band of Cherokee	6
Eskimo	6
Haida	6
Hopi	6
Inupiat	6
Makah	6
Navajo	13
Pima	6
Pomo	6
Salish-Kootenai	6
Shoshone-Bannock	6
Sioux	13
Tlingit	6
Tohono O'Odham	6

[Continued]

★ 497 ★

OSAP Target Population by Tribe
[Continued]

Tribe	Percent of programs
Tsimshian	6
Yupic	13

Source: U.S. Department of Health and Human Services. Public Health Service. Alcohol, Drug Abuse, and Mental Health Administration. Office for Substance Abuse Prevention. *Breaking New Ground For American Indian and Alaska Native Youth: Program Summaries* (OSAP Technical Report-3). Rockville, MD: U.S. DHHS, pp. 36-37.

★ 498 ★
Substance Abuse

Substance Abuse Treatment Availability for Adolescents

From the source: "Recent studies show high rates of alcohol, inhalant, and drug use among Indian youth—rates that exceed those of non-Indian youth. Recognizing the severity of the problems, in recent years, IHS [Indian Health Service] has developed additional treatment services for youth and dramatically increased the prevention services. Despite these efforts, our survey indicated that alcohol and substance abuse treatment services were often not available....As the table shows, only about one-fourth of the user population in the five areas was served by units that could provide services to more than 90 percent of those seeking care"[1].

Type of care	Pct. of pop. served by service units able to provide care to	
	More than 90 percent seeking care	Less than 50 percent seeking care
Residential treatment	24.0	38.0
Outpatient counseling	29.0	40.0
Aftercare	29.0	36.0

Source: U.S. General Accounting Office. *Indian Health Service: Basic Service Mostly Available - Substance Abuse Problems Need Attention* (GAO/HRD-93-48). Washington, DC: U.S. GAO, 1993, p. 37. *Notes:* 1. Because service units vary significantly in the sizes of their user population, in measuring service availability, [GAO] first counted the number of service units reporting each service to be available to over 90 percent of their user population, and then summed the user population of these units and computed the percentages of the user population in the five areas represented by these service units.

★ 499 ★

Substance Abuse

Substance Abuse Treatment Availability for Adults

From the source: "For the five types of adult services [that were] surveyed, about one-fourth to one-third of the user population was served by units that could provide services to 90 percent or more of those seeking care. By comparison, about one-third to one-half of the user population was served by units that could provide the services to less than 50 percent of those seeking help."

Type of care	Pct. of pop. served by service units able to provide care to	
	More than 90 percent seeking care	Less than 50 percent seeking care
Residential treatment	22.0	47.0
Outpatient counseling	29.0	41.0
Aftercare	29.0	41.0
Medical detoxification	36.0	38.0
Social-setting detoxification	25.0	51.0

Source: U.S. General Accounting Office. *Indian Health Service: Basic Service Mostly Available - Substance Abuse Problems Need Attention* (GAO/HRD-93-48). Washington, DC: U.S. GAO, 1993, p. 39.

★ 500 ★

Substance Abuse

Target Client Population for Substance Abuse Prevention

The Office for Substance Abuse Prevention (OSAP) funds 18 prevention programs in Native communities in 12 states. Figures show the percentage of programs which address the needs of each age group.

Age	Percent
Infants (0-3)	17.0
Preschool (4-5)	50.0
School (6-12)	69.0
Adolescents (13-19)	94.0
Young adults (20-35)	31.0
Middle age (36-45)	31.0
Elders (56 and older)	31.0

Source: U.S. Department of Health and Human Services. Public Health Service. Alcohol, Drug Abuse, and Mental Health Administration. Office for Substance Abuse Prevention. *Breaking New Ground For American Indian and Alaska Native Youth: Program Summaries* (OSAP Technical Report-3). Rockville, MD: U.S. DHHS, p. 37.

Venereal Disease

★ 501 ★

Gonorrhea Cases - IHS vs. Non-IHS Areas

Figures contrast reported gonorrhea cases in Indian Health Service (IHS) service areas and non-service areas of selected states, 1988.

State	IHS service areas		Non-service areas	
	Number cases	Cases per 100,000	Number cases	Cases per 100,000
California	115	138.1	58	37.1
Colorado	7	215.5	15	77.4
Montana	181	445.1	6	78.4
North Carolina	18	277.3	158	232.9
North Dakota	81	370.3	9	220.9
South Dakota	224	437.6	29	585.0
Utah	15	131.3	16	126.7

Source: Toomey, Kathleen, E., Alisa G. Oberschelp, and Joel R. Greenspan, "Sexually transmitted diseases and Native Americans: trends in reported gonorrhea and syphilis morbidity, 1984-88," *Public Health Reports* Vol. 104, No. 6, (November/December 1989), p. 570.

★ 502 ★

Venereal Disease

Gonorrhea Cases in Selected States

Figures are given for the number of cases, and cases per 100,000, from 1984-1988.

State	Native Americans		Non-Native Americans	
	Number cases	Cases per 100,000	Number cases	Cases per 100,000
Alaska[1]	5,526	1,469.66	5,984	283.66
Arizona[1]	5,074	569.22	31,835	209.08
Colorado	139	131.25	30,905	194.32
Minnesota[1]	1,171	564.59	25,230	120.94
Montana[1]	1,350	595.78	2,114	54.98
New Mexico[1]	2,647	441.31	9,908	149.41
North Carolina[2]	867	241.41	163,231	531.56
North Dakota[1]	527	428.37	996	30.89
Oklahoma	2,401	247.38	50,898	331.86
Oregon	272	178.02	25,504	190.92
South Dakota[1]	1,680	637.53	1,985	61.18
Utah[3]	268	238.27	4,757	58.59
Washington[1]	1,751	508.78	43,390	199.78

[Continued]

★ 502 ★

Gonorrhea Cases in Selected States
[Continued]

State	Native Americans		Non-Native Americans	
	Number cases	Cases per 100,000	Number cases	Cases per 100,000
13 States combined	23,673	500.83	396,737	247.52
United States	25,533	316.42	4,146,346	349.18

Source: Toomey, Kathleen E., Alisa G. Oberschelp, and Joel R. Greenspan, "Sexually transmitted diseases and Native Americans: trends in reported gonorrhea and syphilis morbidity, 1984-88," *Public Health Reports* Vol. 104, No. 6, (November/December 1989), p. 568. *Notes:* 1. Rates for Native Americans exceeded 349 per 100,000 and were higher than rates for non-Native Americans. 2. Rates for non-Native Americans exceeded 349 per 100,000. 3. Rates for Native Americans exceeded rates for non-Native Americans.

★ 503 ★

Venereal Disease

Gonorrhea Cases, by Race/Ethnicity

Blacks - 2,045	
	Native Americans - 501
	Hispanics - 279
	Whites - 97

Figures are for 13 selected states from 1984-1988.

Race and ethnicity	Cases per 100,000
Blacks	2,045
Native Americans	501
Hispanics	279
Whites	97

Source: Toomey, Kathleen E., Alisa G. Oberschelp, and Joel R. Greenspan, "Sexually transmitted diseases and Native Americans: trends in reported gonorrhea and syphilis morbidity, 1984-88," *Public Health Reports* Vol. 104, No. 6, (November/December 1989), p. 569.

★ 504 ★

Venereal Disease

Syphilis Cases in Selected States

Figures are given for 1984-1988.

State	Native Americans		Non-Native Americans	
	Number cases	Cases per 100,000	Number cases	Cases per 100,000
Alaska	7	1.83	23	1.10
Arizona	351	39.52	900	5.87
Colorado	981	8.73	694	4.36
Minnesota	24	12.05	175	0.84
Montana	6	2.64	25	0.65
New Mexico	102	17.06	304	4.58
North Carolina	14	3.91	3,657	11.89
North Dakota	3	2.73	15	0.46
Oklahoma	34	3.56	859	5.61
Oregon	15	9.60	973	7.23
South Dakota	3	1.14	16	0.49
Utah	6	5.24	92	1.13
Washington	35	10.09	873	3.99

Source: Toomey, Kathleen E., Alisa G. Oberschelp, and Joel R. Greenspan, "Sexually transmitted diseases and Native Americans: trends in reported gonorrhea and syphilis morbidity, 1984-88," *Public Health Reports* Vol. 104, No. 6, (November/December 1989), p. 569. *Notes:* Primary and secondary syphilis rates for Native Americans exceeded the rates for non-Native Americans in all States except Oklahoma and North Carolina.

Health Care

★ 505 ★

Health Care Facilities

Data show number of facilities operated by Indian Health Service (IHS) and tribes as of October 1, 1992.

Type of facility	IHS	Tribal
Hospitals	42	8
Outpatient facilities	123	332
Health centers	66	98
School health centers	4	3
Health stations	53	59
Alaska village clinics	-	172

Source: U.S. Department of Health and Human Services. Public Health Service. Indian Health Service. Office of Planning, Evaluation, and Legislation. Division of Program Statistics. *Trends in Indian Health - 1993*, Rockville, MD: U.S. Department of Health and Human Services, Public Health Service, p. 17. *Note:* A dash (-) represents zero.

Institutionalized Populations on Reservations, Tribal Jurisdiction Statistical Areas, and Tribal Designated Statistical Areas

Area	State	In Nursing Homes	In Mental Hospitals	In College Dormitories	In Military Quarters	In Emergency Shelters	Visible in Streets
Agua Caliente Reservation	CA	208	4				
Allegany Reservation	NY	119					
Blackfeet Reservation	MT	36	24				
Cabazon Reservation	CA	16					
Coeur d'Alene Reservation and Trust Lands	ID	1					
Colorado River Reservation	CO	2	6	28			
Colville Reservation	WA	49					
Crow Creek Reservation	SD	12					
Devils Lake Sioux Reservation	ND	7					
Flathead Reservation	MT	229					
Fort Berthold Reservation	ND	118					
Fort Hall Reservation and Trust Lands	ID	13					
Fort McDowell Reservation	AZ	9					
Fort Peck Reservation	MT	71	3				
Gila River Reservation	AZ	72					
Hoopa Valley Reservation	CA	12					
Isabella Reservation and Trust Lands	MI	168	11				
Lac Courte Oreilles Reservation and Trust Lands	WI	14					
Lac du Flambeau Reservation	WI	14					
Laguna Pueblo and Trust Lands	NM	22					
Lake Traverse (Sisseton) Reservation		150	4	29			
L'Anse Reservation and Trust Lands	MI	59					
Leech Lake Reservation	MN	4					
Makah Reservation	WA	20					
Muckleshoot Reservation and Trust Lands	WA	10					
Navajo Reservation and Trust Lands, AZ–NM–UT		124	172	15			
Nez Perce Reservation	ID	61	20				
Omaha Reservation	NE	79					
Oneida (West) Reservation	WI	42	5				
Osage Reservation	OK	229	5				
Ozette Reservation	WA	12					
Pine Ridge Reservation and Trust Lands, NE–SD		48	51				
Pinoleville Rancheria	CA	5					
Puyallup Reservation and Trust Lands	WA	5					
Red Lake Reservation	MN	32					
Rocky Boy's Reservation and Trust Lands	MT	1					
Salt River Reservation	AZ	4	36				
San Carlos Reservation	AZ	26					
Santa Clara Pueblo	NM	108					
Southern Ute Reservation	CO	15					
Turtle Mountain Reservation and Trust Lands, ND–SD		11					
Uintah and Ouray Reservation	UT	38	3				
Umatilla Reservation	OR	53					
White Earth Reservation	MN	61					
Wind River Reservation	WY	118	32	19			
Yakima Reservation and Trust Lands	WA	164					
Yankton Reservation	SD	123	63				
Zuni Pueblo	AZ-NM	5					
Absentee Shawnee-Citizens Band of Potawatomi TJSA	OK	495	57				
Caddo-Wichita-Delaware TJSA	OK	90					
Cherokee TJSA	OK	3379	644	1088	21	154	3
Cheyenne-Arapaho TJSA	OK	1849	937	137			
Chickasaw TJSA	OK	3318	1029	103			
Choctaw TJSA	OK	2620	924	28			
Creek TJSA	OK	5339	279	4108	449	91	
Kaw TJSA	OK	121					
Kiowa-Comanche-Apache-Fort Sill Apache TJSA	OK	1944	483	7666	87	2	
Pawnee TJSA	OK	90	4				

[Continued]

★ 506 ★

Institutionalized Populations on Reservations, Tribal Jurisdiction Statistical Areas, and Tribal Designated Statistical Areas

[Continued]

Area	State	In Nursing Homes	In Mental Hospitals	In College Dormitories	In Military Quarters	In Emergency Shelters	Visible in Streets
Sac and Fox TJSA	OK	528	7	5			
Seminole TJSA	OK	327	5				
Tonkawa TJSA	OK	197	227				
Creek-Seminole Joint Area TJSA	OK	171					
Barrow	AK	9					
Bethel	AK	26					
Galena	AK	303					
King Salmon	AK	267					
Kotzebue	AK	33					
Ninilchik	AK	16	12	50	6		
St. Paul	AK	17					
Tanana	AK	13					
Apache Choctaw TDSA (state)	LA	256					
Coharie TDSA (state)	NC	1221	627	272	49		
Coquille Indian TDSA	OR	3673	55	5115	771	166	
Jena Band of Choctaw TDSA (state)	LA	761	388	378	10	23	
Klamath TDSA	OR	249	4	359	84	2	
Lumbee TDSA (state)	NC	166	639	1			
Meherrin TDSA (state)	NC	372	583	3			
Mohegan TDSA (state)	CT	144	6	10			
United Houma Nation TDSA (state)	LA	3659	38	734	157	260	44

Source: Census of Population and Housing, 1990: Summary Tape File 1 on CD-ROM, U.S. Bureau of the Census, Washington, D.C. 1991.

★ 507 ★

Health Care

Ten Leading Causes of Hospitalization - Females

Data are shown for Indian Health Service and Tribal Direct and Contract General Hospitals, for Fiscal Year 1991.

Diagnostic category	Female	
	Number of discharges	Percent of total
All categories	56,006	100.0
Obstetric deliveries and complications of pregnancy and puerperium	19,511	35.5
Respiratory system diseases	5,362	9.7
Digestive system diseases	5,073	9.0
Genitourinary system diseases	3,638	6.6
Injuries and poisonings	3,501	6.4
Circulatory system diseases	2,835	5.2
Symptoms and ill-defined conditions	2,753	5.0
Endocrine, nutritional and metabolic disorders	2,038	3.7
Supplementary conditions	1,850	3.4

[Continued]

★ 507 ★

Ten Leading Causes of Hospitalization - Females
[Continued]

Diagnostic category	Female	
	Number of discharges	Percent of total
Mental disorders	1,370	2.5
All other	7,075	12.8

Source: U.S. Department of Health and Human Services. Public Health Service. Indian Health Service. Office of Planning, Evaluation, and Legislation. Division of Program Statistics. *Trends in Indian Health - 1993*, Rockville, MD: U.S. Department of Health and Human Services, Public Health Service, p. 81. Primary source: IHS and Tribal Direct: On-Request Report 21. IHS Contract: On-Request Report 19.

★ 508 ★

Health Care

Ten Leading Causes of Hospitalization - Males

Data are shown for Indian Health Service and Tribal Direct and Contract General Hospitals, for Fiscal Year 1991.

Diagnostic category	Male	
	Number of discharges	Percent of total
All categories	34,092	100.0
Respiratory system diseases	5,676	16.6
Injuries and poisonings	5,450	16.0
Digestive system diseases	4,280	12.6
Circulatory system diseases	3,126	9.2
Symptoms and ill-defined conditions	2,553	7.5
Mental disorders	2,442	7.2
Endocrine, nutritional and metabolic disorders	1,647	4.8
Skin and subcutaneous tissue diseases	1,611	4.7
Genitourinary system	1,169	3.4
Supplementary conditions	1,166	3.4
All other	4,972	14.6

Source: U.S. Department of Health and Human Services. Public Health Service. Indian Health Service. Office of Planning, Evaluation, and Legislation. Division of Program Statistics. *Trends in Indian Health - 1993*, Rockville, MD: U.S. Department of Health and Human Services, Public Health Service, p. 81. Primary source: IHS and Tribal Direct: On-Request Report 21. IHS Contract: On-Request Report 19.

Indian Health Service

★ 509 ★

Accreditation of IHS Health Centers

Indian Health Services (IHS) Health Center accreditation status is shown as of January 1, 1993. All health centers operated by the IHS and eligible for accreditation were accredited as of that date.

Area	IHS Health Centers			
	Total[1]	Accredited[2]	Not accredited	Accredited as percent of total
All areas	57	57	0	100.0
Aberdeen	4	4	0	100.0
Alaska	1	1	0	100.0
Albuquerque	8	8	0	100.0
Bemidji	1	1	0	100.0
Billings	7	7	0	100.0
California	-	-	-	-
Nashville	-	-	-	-
Navajo	6	6	0	100.0
Oklahoma	11	11	0	100.0
Phoenix	6	6	0	100.0
Portland	11	11	0	100.0
Tucson	2	2	0	100.0

Source: U.S. Department of Health and Human Services. Public Health Service. Indian Health Service. Office of Planning, Evaluation, and Legislation. Division of Program Statistics. *Trends in Indian Health - 1993*, Rockville, MD: U.S. Department of Health and Human Services, Public Health Service, p. 18. *Notes:* A dash (-) stands for zero. 1. Excludes health centers not eligible for accreditation survey and under tribal management pursuant to Public Law 93-638. 2. Health centers are accredited by the Joint Commission on the Accreditation of Healthcare Organizations.

★ 510 ★

Indian Health Service

Accreditation of IHS Labs

Data show Indian Health Service (IHS) laboratory accreditation status are shown as of January 1, 1993. Eighty-seven percent of health center laboratories and all of the hospital laboratories were accredited as of that date.

Area	IHS health laboratories					IHS health center laboratories				
	Total	Accredited[1]	Not accredited	Percent accredited	Percent in proficiency testing program[2]	Total	Accredited[1]	Not accredited	Percent accredited	Percent in proficiency testing program[2]
All areas	42	42	0	100.0	100.0	47	41	6	87	100.0
Aberdeen	9	9	0	100.0	100.0	4	4	0	100	100.0
Alaska	2	2	0	100.0	100.0	-	-	-	-	-
Albuquerque	5	5	0	100.0	100.0	4	4	0	100	100.0
Bemidji	2	2	0	100.0	100.0	2	1	1	50	100.0
Billings	3	3	0	100.0	100.0	6	6	0	100	100.0
California	-	-	-	-	-	-	-	-	-	-
Nashville	1	1	0	100.0	100.0	-	-	-	-	-
Navajo	6	6	0	100.0	100.0	5	5	0	100	100.0
Oklahoma	5	5	0	100.0	100.0	11	7	4	64	100.0
Phoenix	8	8	0	100.0	100.0	3	3	0	100	100.0
Portland	-	-	-	-	-	11	11	0	100	100.0
Tucson	1	1	0	100.0	100.0	1	0	1	0	100.0

Source: U.S. Department of Health and Human Services. Public Health Service. Indian Health Service. Office of Planning, Evaluation, and Legislation. Division of Program Statistics. *Trends in Indian Health - 1993*, Rockville, MD: U.S. Department of Health and Human Services, Public Health Service, p. 18. *Notes:* A dash (-) stands for zero. 1. Laboratories accredited by the College of American Pathologists, the Joint Commission on the Accreditation of Healthcare Organizations and the Health Care Financing Administration, DHHS. Excludes laboratories under tribal management pursuant to Public Law 93-638. 2. Laboratories participating in the College of American Pathologist (CAP) national proficiency testing program.

★ 511 ★

Indian Health Service

Bed size - IHS vs. U.S. Hospitals

Indian Health Service hospitals, FY 1990, and U.S. Short-Stay hospitals, calendar year 1991.

Bed size	Number of hospitals		Percent of total	
	IHS[1]	U.S.	IHS	U.S.
All	50	5,342	100.0	100.0
6-24	17	222	34.0	4.2
25-49	21	922	42.0	17.3
50-99	9	1,244	18.0	23.3
100-199	3	1,311	6.0	24.5
200+	-	1,643	-	30.8

Source: U.S. Department of Health and Human Services. Public Health Service. Indian Health Service. Office of Planning, Evaluation, and Legislation. Division of Program Statistics. *Trends in Indian Health - 1993*, Rockville, MD: U.S. Department of Health and Human Services, Public Health Service, p. 83. Primary source: IHS - Monthly Report of Inpatient Services. U.S. - Hospital Statistics, 1992-1993 Edition, American Hospital Association, Table 5A. *Note:* 1. Operated by IHS or the Tribes on September 30, 1992.

★ 512 ★

Indian Health Service

Discharge Rates - IHS vs. U.S. Hospitals

Data are shown for Indian Health Service (IHS) and all U.S. hospitals, for calendar year 1991.

Age at admission	Discharges per 1,000 population		% difference IHS rate to U.S. rate
	IHS	U.S.	
All ages	78.6	124.1	-36.7
Under 1 year	288.5	200.8	43.7
1-4 years	35.7	48.3	-26.1
5-14 years	18.1	26.7	-32.2
15-19 years	63.3	80.2	-20.7
20-24 years	101.9	113.3	-10.1
25-44 years	87.9	99.5	-11.7
45-64 years	121.3	132.2	-8.2
65 years and over	184.8	340.3	-45.7

Source: U.S. Department of Health and Human Services. Public Health Service. Indian Health Service. Office of Planning, Evaluation, and Legislation. Division of Program Statistics. *Trends in Indian Health - 1993*, Rockville, MD: U.S. Department of Health and Human Services, Public Health Service, p. 82. Primary source: IHS - Annual Reports 2C and 31. U.S. - Utilization of Short-Stay Hospitals, Annual Summary of the U.S., NCHS. *Notes:* IHS discharge rates were calculated using the IHS FY 1991 user population.

★ 513 ★

Indian Health Service

IHS Hospital Inpatient Workload, by Area and Facility - Part I

Workload statistics for IHS (Indian Health Service) hospitals are shown for October through March of fiscal year 1994.

	Beds available 06/30/94	Admissions	Discharges	Average daily census	Average length of stay	Newborns		Hospital days	
						Births	ADPL[1]	Adults & Pediatrics	Newborn
All tribal totals	278	3,801	3,816	96.7	4.6	493	5.9	17,607	1,605
Alaska total	169	2,476	2,472	63.3	4.7	378	4.4	11,517	802
Kanakanak, AK	16	282	279	4.2	2.7	32	0.3	763	52
Maniilaq, AK	25	402	398	5.8	2.6	62	0.5	1,050	84
Mount Edgecumbe, AK	78	875	876	35.5	7.4	59	0.8	6,468	154
Norton Sound, AK	NR	NR	NR	NR	NR	NR	NR	NR	NR
Y-K-D, Bethel, AK	50	917	919	17.8	3.5	225	2.8	3,236	512
Nashville total	37	415	419	12.4	5.4	0	0.0	2,256	0
Choctaw, MS	37	415	419	12.4	5.4	0	0.0	2,256	0
Oklahoma Nation	72	910	925	21.1	4.2	115	1.4	3,834	263

[Continued]

★ 513 ★

IHS Hospital Inpatient Workload, by Area and Facility - Part I
[Continued]

| | Beds available 06/30/94 | Admissions | Discharges | Average daily census | Average length of stay | Newborns | | Hospital days | |
						Births	ADPL[1]	Adults & Pediatrics	Newborn
Creek Nation, OK	20	256	263	6.7	4.8	1	0.0	1,228	3
Choctaw Nation, OK	52	654	662	14.3	4.0	114	1.4	2,606	260

Source: U.S. Department of Health. Public Health Service. Indian Health Service. *Inpatient Summary Data for Tribally Operated Hospitals by Area and Facility October Through March, Fiscal Year 1994.* Rockville, MD: IHS, 6 June 1994. *Notes:* NR stands for not reported through the Monthly Inpatient Services Reporting System. 1. Average daily patient load.

★ 514 ★

Indian Health Service

IHS Hospital Inpatient Workload, by Area and Facility - Part II

Workload statistics for IHS (Indian Health Service) hospitals are shown for October through March of fiscal year 1994.

| | Beds available 03/31/94 | Admissions | Discharges | Average daily census | Average length of stay | Newborns | | Hospital days | |
						Births	ADPL[1]	Adults & Pediatrics	Newborn
All IHS areas	1,611	30,989	31,053	729.8	4.3	4,8986	55.6	132,832	10,114
Aberdeen Area	242	3,513	3,518	77.3	4.0	272	3.5	14,076	635
Belcourt, ND	29	147	150	2.7	3.4	-	-	494	-
Eagle Butte, SD	27	473	476	7.3	2.8	40	0.4	1,326	66
Fort Yates, ND	16	343	345	4.5	2.4	3	-	822	4
Pine Ridge, SD	46	851	84602	16.0	3.4	155	2.2	2,914	405
Rapid City, SD	41	392	390	12.5	5.8	-	-	2,275	-
Rosebud, SD	35	782	783	11.2	2.6	74	0.9	2,034	160
Sisseton, SD	18	207	206	4.4	3.9	-	-	808	-
Winnebago, NE	30	318	322	18.7	10.7	-	-	3,403	-
Alaska Area	160	2,838	2,842	102.6	6.6	495	6.6	18,677	1,207
Anchorage, AK	146	2,589	2,593	99.1	7.0	466	6.4	18,032	1,167
Barrow, AK	14	249	249	3.5	2.6	29	0.2	645	40
Albuquerque Area	142	2,391	2,384	57.0	4.3	207	2.2	10,383	409
Acoma-Laguna, NM	25	309	304	10.6	6.3	-	-	1,934	-
Albuquerque, NM	28	329	336	10.1	5.6	-	-	1,834	-
Mescalero, NM	13	199	197	4.2	3.8	-	-	759	-
Santa Fe, NM	39	1,002	998	21.4	3.9	132	1.5	3,893	278
Zuni, NM	37	552	549	10.8	3.6	75	0.7	1,963	131
Bemidji Area	36	535	536	11.9	4.0	-	-	2,161	-
Cass Lake, MN	13	173	172	4.6	4.9	-	-	846	-
Red Lake, MN	23	362	364	7.2	3.6	-	-	1,315	-
Billings Area	77	1,505	1,507	25.0	3.0	164	2.2	4,552	404
Browning, MT	27	712	712	12.8	3.3	80	1.0	2,326	178
Crow Agency, MT	34	547	549	9.3	3.1	84	1.2	1,684	226
Harlem, MT	16	246	246	3.0	2.2	-	-	542	-
Nashville Area	29	430	432	13.9	5.9	1	-	2,528	1

[Continued]

★ 514 ★

IHS Hospital Inpatient Workload, by Area and Facility - Part II

[Continued]

	Beds available 03/31/94	Admissions	Discharges	Average daily census	Average length of stay	Newborns		Hospital days	
						Births	ADPL[1]	Adults & Pediatrics	Newborn
Cherokee, NC	29	430	432	13.9	5.9	1	-	2,528	1
Navajo Area	390	9,604	9,626	200.4	3.8	1,971	21.1	36,473	3,834
Chinle, AZ	60	1,563	1,564	35.8	4.2	384	4.1	6,521	750
Crownpoint, NM	39	528	532	12.0	4.1	97	0.8	2,190	146
Fort Defiance, AZ	49	1,038	1,030	22.1	3.9	230	2.7	4,020	499
Gallup, NM	107	2,626	2,638	59.6	4.1	563	5.9	10,847	1,075
Shiprock, NM	50	1,437	1,439	30.2	3.8	381	4.0	5,489	730
Tuba City, AZ	85	2,412	2,423	40.7	3.1	316	3.5	7,406	634
Oklahoma Area	216	4,814	4,816	100.9	3.8	1,412	16.0	18,369	2,291
Carl Albert (ADA), OK	53	1,249	1,253	25.2	3.7	329	3.3	4,583	594
Claremore, OK	50	1,224	1,236	29.0	4.3	429	4.4	5,269	809
Clinton, OK	11	139	139	3.0	3.9	-	-	549	-
Lawton, OK	42	629	623	12.3	3.5	141	2.0	2,230	356
Wm. W. Hastings (Tahlequah)	60	1,573	1,565	31.5	3.6	513	6.4	5,738	1,162
Phoenix Area	285	4,973	5,002	128.8	4.7	366	3.7	23,447	679
Fort Yuma (Winterhaven), CA	17	78	78	2.0	4.7	-	-	365	-
Hu-Hu-Kam (Sacaton), AZ	20	287	289	7.6	4.9	-	-	1,392	-
Keams Canyon, AZ	18	340	343	5.0	2.7	47	0.4	916	77
Owyhee, NV	15	66	68	2.3	6.2	-	-	410	-
Parker, AZ	20	154	157	5.2	6.1	-	-	941	-
Phoenix, AZ	142	2,918	2,933	81.5	5.1	243	2.7	14,841	500
San Carlos, AZ	8	165	164	3.6	4.0	-	-	659	-
Whiteriver, AZ	45	965	970	21.6	4.1	76	0.6	3,923	102
Tucson Area	34	386	390	11.9	5.6	10	0.1	2,166	24
Sells, AZ	34	386	390	11.9	5.6	10	0.1	2,166	24

Source: U.S. Department of Health. Public Health Service. Indian Health Service. Inpatient Summary Data for Indian Health Service Hospitals by Area and Facility October Through March, Fiscal Year 1994. Rockville, MD: IHS, April 1994, p. 24. Note: 1. Average daily patient load.

★ 515 ★

Indian Health Service

IHS Service Population Trends, by Area

IHS (Indian Health Service) service population is shown, by service area, for fiscal years 1990 through 1988 and projected for 1999 and 2000. Growth factor between years is shown in percent. The service population is increasing at a rate of approximately 2.35% per year and is predicted to be about 1.36 million persons in fiscal year 1995.

Area	1990 Census	1991	1992	1993	1994	1995	1996	1997	1998	1999	2000
All areas (Growth factor)	1,206,724 -	1,243,717 (3.07)	1,272,905 (2.35)	1,302,723 (2.34)	1,333,291 (2.35)	1,364,526 (2.34)	1,396,472 (2.34)	1,429,112 (2.34)	1,462,446 (2.33)	1,496,500 (2.33)	1,531,238 (2.32)
Aberdeen	74,789	81,197	83,501	85,800	88,147	90,512	92,912	95,330	97,785	100,262	102,770
Alaska	86,251	88,815	91,454	94,170	96,967	99,842	102,798	105,829	108,937	112,126	115,391
Albuquerque	67,175	68,758	70,389	72,067	73,795	75,566	77,383	79,245	81,156	83,118	85,125
Bemidji	61,349	62,788	64,276	65,799	67,364	68,966	70,604	72,290	74,012	75,775	77,573

[Continued]

★ 515 ★

IHS Service Population Trends, by Area
[Continued]

Area	1990 Census	1991	1992	1993	1994	1995	1996	1997	1998	1999	2000
Billings	47,008	48,320	49,657	51,019	52,406	53,820	55,256	56,722	58,211	59,729	61,269
California	105,690	108,218	110,894	113,684	116,588	119,604	122,733	125,975	129,331	132,804	136,387
Nashville	48,943	54,262	55,147	56,045	56,973	57,927	58,901	59,898	60,920	61,963	63,030
Navajo	183,862	189,058	194,402	199,836	205,387	211,033	216,801	222,671	228,651	234,737	240,932
Oklahoma	262,517	267,106	271,740	276,411	281,125	285,880	290,673	295,509	300,381	305,294	310,252
Phoenix	115,830	118,750	121,779	124,445	127,660	130,980	134,398	137,921	141,543	145,269	149,094
Portland	127,774	130,422	133,146	136,422	139,338	142,331	145,414	148,580	151,825	155,166	158,587
Tucson	25,536	26,023	26,520	27,025	27,541	28,065	28,599	29,142	29,694	30,257	30,828

Source: U.S. Department of Health and Human Services. Public Health Service. Indian Health Service. Office of Planning, Evaluation, and Legislation. Division of Program Statistics. *Trends in Indian Health - 1993*, Rockville, MD: U.S. Department of Health and Human Services, Public Health Service, p. 26. Primary source: Estimated American Indian and Alaska Native service population by Area based on 1980-1989 vital events and the 1990 Census modified age, race and sex file.

★ 516 ★

Indian Health Service

Indian Health Service Employees, New Hires, 1989

The total number of health professionals and support staff hired in the IHS during FY 89, is shown.

Category	Indians Hired	Non-Indians Hired	Total
Physicians	23	581	604
Medical Records Librarians	6	3	9
Sanitarians/Engineers	10	39	49
Pharmacists	6	78	84
Physician Assistants	11	61	72
Graduate Nurses	165	503	668
Practical Nurses	66	24	90
Nutritionists/Dietitians	1	14	15
Dentists	11	131	142
Health Educators	2	2	4
Social Workers	11	15	26
Medical Clerks	120	6	126
Medical Record Technicians	98	8	106
Dental Auxiliaries	72	6	78
Medical Auxiliaries (Medical Aid, Physical Therapist, Occupational Therapist, Rehabilitation Therapist, Medical Technologist, Medical Technician, Medical Radiology Technician, Medical Machine Technician, Pharmacy Technician, Health Aid/Technician	156	169	325
Speech Pathologists/Audiologist	0	0	0

[Continued]

★ 516 ★

Indian Health Service Employees, New Hires, 1989
[Continued]

Category	Indians Hired	Non-Indians Hired	Total
All Others[1]	280	105	385
Total[2]	1,038	1,745	2,783

Source: Annual Report to Congress: Indian Civil Service Retirement Act, P.L. 96-135, FY 89, p. 19. Notes: During FY 89, the IHS continued its efforts to recruit, hire, and train Indian health professionals and support staff. During FY 89, approximately 3,537 health professionals and support staff were hired in the IHS. Of that number, 1,597 or 45.1 percent were Indian health professionals and support staff working in hospitals and Service Units in the IHS. 1. Includes staff in the direct patient care and direct patient care support activities category. 2. Data are based on official personnel records. Data may vary in various professional support categories from the IHS program information since some positions are coded to other administrative and management occupational categories and do not reflect the professional category under which the incumbent was initially appointed.

★ 517 ★

Indian Health Service

Indian Health Service Employees, Support Staff, 1989

Indian and non-Indian IHS administrative support staff as of September 30, 1989, is shown.

Organizational Identity	Indians	Non-Indians	Total
Headquarters and Area Offices	2,310	614	2,744

Source: Annual Report to Congress: Indian Civil Service Retirement Act, P.L. 96-135, FY 89, p. 19.

★ 518 ★

Indian Health Service

Indian Health Service Employees, by Race/Ethnicity, 1989

The number of full-time permanent Indian and non-Indian professional (direct patient care and direct patient care support activities) and administrative support staff employed by the Indian Health Service (IHS) during FY 89 is shown below. The data show that Indian people constituted 56.6 percent of the IHS professional and support staff as of September 30, 1989[1].

Category	Indians	Non-Indians	Total
Physicians	47	757	804
Dentists	18	295	313
Graduate Nurses	755	1,358	2,113
Physician Assistants	76	17	93
Practical Nurses	388	34	422
Nursing Assistants	289	5	294
Sanitarians/Engineering	39	127	166
Pharmacists	44	291	335
Social Worker	84	35	119

[Continued]

★ 518 ★

Indian Health Service Employees, by Race/Ethnicity, 1989
[Continued]

Category	Indians	Non-Indians	Total
Health Educator	19	8	27
Nutritionists/Dietitians	16	77	93
Medical Clerks	276	5	281
Medical Records Librarians	46	21	67
Medical Records Technicians	271	7	278
Dental Auxiliaries	376	17	393
Medical Auxiliaries (Medical Aide, Physical Therapist, Occupational Therapist, Rehabilitation Therapist, Medical Technologist, Medical Technician, Medical Radiology Technician, Medical Machine Technician, Pharmacy Technician, Health Aid/Technician)	459	421	880
Speech Pathologist/Audiologist	3	4	7
All Others[2]	1,679	271	1,950
Total[3]	4,885	3,750	8,635

Source: *Annual Report to Congress: Indian Civil Service Retirement Act, P.L. 96-135, FY 89*, p. 18. Notes: 1. Health professions are considered to be the MODVOPP—medicine, osteopathy, dentistry, engineers/sanitarians, optometry, podiatry, pharmacy, nursing, and various allied health professions. 2. Includes staff in the direct patient care and direct patient care support activities category. 3. Data are based on official personnel records. Data may vary in various professional and professional support categories from the Indian Health Service (IHS) program information since some positions are coded to other administrative and management occupational categories and do not reflect the professional category under which the incumbent was initially appointed.

Outpatient Services

★ 519 ★

Community Health Representative Contacts

Distribution of community health representative[1] client contacts for leading health problems, is shown for FY 1990-1992.

Detailed activity	1992	1991	1990
Total client contacts[2]	3,773,693	3,796,978	3,340,533
Percent distribution			
Total client contacts	100.0	100.0	100.0
Health education	18.5	14.9	11.6
Case management	16.2	9.7	7.8
Case finding and screening	14.1	12.4	11.3
Transport patient	12.0	16.2[3]	18.0[3]
Provide patient care	10.8	10.3	11.3
Monitor patient	9.6	9.9	10.2
Provide environmental services	5.6	8.5	7.3
Provide homemaker services	2.2	1.2	1.2

[Continued]

★ 519 ★

Community Health Representative Contacts
[Continued]

Detailed activity	1992	1991	1990
Interpret/translate for patient	1.1	2.6	1.2
Provide emergency care	0.6	0.5	0.4
Provide other patient services	8.0	13.8[4]	19.8[4]

Source: U.S. Department of Health and Human Services. Public Health Service. Indian Health Service. Office of Planning, Evaluation, and Legislation. Division of Program Statistics. *Trends in Indian Health - 1993*, Rockville, MD: U.S. Department of Health and Human Services, Public Health Service, p. 111. *Notes:* 1. Estimated data based on CHR client contact reports completed during 12 sample reporting weeks between October 1, 1991 and September 30, 1992 and inflated to represent all weeks during each fiscal year. 2. Total includes activity unspecified, not shown separately. 3. Includes the delivery of medical supplies to patients in 1990 and 1991. 4. Includes the provision of patient clerical services.

★ 520 ★

Outpatient Services

IHS Public Health Nursing Visits

Number and percent distribution of hours devoted to patient service in the home are shown, by type of activity, for fiscal year 1992.

Type of activity	Number of hours	Percent distribution
Total hours	255,450	100.0
Patient service-home	99,269	38.9
Patient service-other	39,054	15.3
Administration	22,514	8.8
Register/record maintenance	15,050	5.9
Coordinating	10,202	4.0
Education received	9,820	3.8
Not home	6,522	2.6
Program management	5,266	2.1
Client classes	5,112	2.0
Community development	4,276	1.7
School	3,819	1.5
Education provided	2,303	0.9
Supervision provided	2,088	0.8
Supervision received	1,671	0.7
Discharge planning/hospital rounds	1,364	0.5
Interpreting	976	0.4
Clinic	759	0.3
Technical assistance received	384	0.2
Other	24,217	9.5

Source: U.S. Department of Health and Human Services. Public Health Service. Indian Health Service. Office of Planning, Evaluation, and Legislation. Division of Program Statistics. *Trends in Indian Health - 1993*, Rockville, MD: U.S. Department of Health and Human Services, Public Health Service, p. 107. Primary source: Indian Health Service, Public Health Nursing Report No. 2, Fiscal Year 1992. *Note:* Percentages do not sum to 100.0 due to rounding.

★ 521 ★

Outpatient Services

Outpatient Clinical Impressions for Leading Specific Conditions: Females

Prenatal care - 214,966

Upper respiratory infection, common cold - 177,603

Diabetes mellitus - 174,435

Otitis media - 153,237

Hypertensive disease - 121,799

Tests only

Prescription refills - 117,204

Immunization - 109,319

Family planning - 88,852

Urinary tract infection - 78,677

Data are shown for Indian Health Service direct and contract facilities, for fiscal year 1991.

Condition	Number of clinical impressions
Prenatal care	214,966
Upper respiratory infection, common cold	177,603
Diabetes mellitus	174,435
Otitis media	153,237
Hypertensive disease	121,799
Tests only (lab, x-ray)	121,487
Prescription refills	117,204
Immunization	109,319
Family planning	88,852
Urinary tract infection	78,677

Source: U.S. Department of Health and Human Services. Public Health Service. Indian Health Service. Office of Planning, Evaluation, and Legislation. Division of Program Statistics. *Trends in Indian Health - 1993*, Rockville, MD: U.S. Department of Health and Human Services, Public Health Service, p. 87. Primary source: Direct: Annual Report 1C. Contract: Annual Report 3A.

★ 522 ★

Outpatient Services

Outpatient Clinical Impressions for Leading Specific Conditions: Males

Otitis media - 149,259	
Upper respiratory infection, common cold - 125,034	
Diabetes mellitus - 104,059	
Immunization - 96,639	
Hypertensive disease - 95,358	
Prescription refills - 74,689	
Well child care - 70,240	
Tests only	
	Hospital medical/surgical follow-up - 50,338
	Respiratory allergy, asthma, hay fever - 49,273

Data are shown for Indian Health Service direct and contract facilities, for fiscal year 1991.

Condition	Number of clinical impressions
Otitis media	149,259
Upper respiratory infection, common cold	125,034
Diabetes mellitus	104,059
Immunization	96,639
Hypertensive disease	95,358
Prescription refills	74,689
Well child care	70,240
Tests only (lab, x-ray)	55,579
Hospital medical/surgical follow-up	50,338
Respiratory allergy, asthma, hay fever	49,273

Source: U.S. Department of Health and Human Services. Public Health Service. Indian Health Service. Office of Planning, Evaluation, and Legislation. Division of Program Statistics. *Trends in Indian Health - 1993*, Rockville, MD: U.S. Department of Health and Human Services, Public Health Service, p. 87. Primary source: Direct: Annual Report 1C. Contract: Annual Report 3A.

★ 523 ★

Outpatient Services

Outpatient Visits, by Type of Provider

Data are shown for Indian Health Service and Tribal Direct Facilities, for fiscal year 1992.

Type of provider	Number of visits	total
Total, all providers	5,192,906	100.0
Primary care providers	3,385,601	65.2
Physician	2,604,697	50.2
Physician assistant	319,331	6.1
Nurse practitioner	245,378	4.7
Contract physician	86,785	1.7
Nurse midwife	45,189	0.9
Pediatric nurse practitioner	36,405	0.7
All other	47,816	0.9
Other providers	1,807,305	34.8
Pharmacist	819,983	15.8
Clinic R.N.	212,172	4.1
Optometrist	141,268	2.7
Licensed practical nurse	80,890	1.5
Public health nurse	77,727	1.6
Physical therapist	56,942	1.1
All other	418,323	8.1

Source: U.S. Department of Health and Human Services. Public Health Service. Indian Health Service. Office of Planning, Evaluation, and Legislation. Division of Program Statistics. *Trends in Indian Health - 1993*, Rockville, MD: U.S. Department of Health and Human Services, Public Health Service, p. 89. Primary source: Annual Report 1A.

Preventative Health Care

★ 524 ★

Nutritional Counseling

Data show number and percent distribution of patient/client contacts for the IHS nutrition and dietetics program in fiscal year 1992. Approximately 60 percent of these contacts were made for general nutrition and diabetes nutrition counseling.

Purpose	Number	% distribution
Total contacts[1]	140,414	100.0
General nutrition	41,928	29.9
Diabetes	40,719	29.0
Weight control	25,801	18.4
Prenatal	11,935	8.5
Fat controlled	6,315	4.5
Alcohol related	4,212	3.0
Gestational diabetes	3,418	2.2
Renal	1,814	1.3
Sodium controlled	1,016	0.7
Undernutrition	973	0.7
Anemia	578	0.4
All other	1,975	1.4

Source: U.S. Department of Health and Human Services. Public Health Service. Indian Health Service. Office of Planning, Evaluation, and Legislation. Division of Program Statistics. *Trends in Indian Health - 1993*, Rockville, MD: U.S. Department of Health and Human Services, Public Health Service, p. 105. *Notes:* 1. Excludes activities that are not direct patient/client services, and activities associated with program planning, administration, evaluation, and continuing education.

★ 525 ★

Preventative Health Care

Prenatal Care for Live Births, by Race and Hispanic Origin of Mother

Data show the percentage of babies born to women obtaining prenatal care in the first trimester and the percentage born to women receiving prenatal care in the third trimester or not all. Data are shown for selected years.

Prenatal care, education, race of mother, and Hispanic origin of mother	Percent of live births[1]								
	1970	1975	1980	1985	1987	1988	1989	1990	1991
Prenatal care began during 1st trimester									
All mothers	68.0	72.4	76.3	76.2	76.0	75.9	75.5	75.8	76.2
White	72.3	75.8	79.2	79.3	79.3	79.3	78.9	79.2	79.5
Black	44.2	55.5	62.4	61.5	60.8	60.7	60.0	60.6	61.9

[Continued]

★ 525 ★

Prenatal Care for Live Births, by Race and Hispanic Origin of Mother
[Continued]

Prenatal care, education, race of mother, and Hispanic origin of mother	Percent of live births[1]								
	1970	1975	1980	1985	1987	1988	1989	1990	1991
American Indian or Alaskan Native	38.2	45.4	55.8	57.5	57.6	58.1	57.9	57.9	59.9
Asian or Pacific Islander	-	-	73.7	74.1	75.0	75.5	74.8	75.1	75.3
Chinese	71.8	76.7	82.6	82.0	81.5	82.3	81.5	81.3	82.3
Japanese	78.1	82.7	86.1	84.7	86.6	86.3	86.2	87.0	87.7
Filipino	60.6	70.6	77.3	76.5	77.9	78.4	77.6	77.1	77.1
Other Asian or Pacific Islander[2]	-	-	67.6	69.7	71.0	71.5	70.8	71.4	71.7
Hispanic origin (selected states)[3,4]	-	-	60.2	61.2	61.0	61.3	59.5	60.2	61.0
Mexican American	-	-	59.6	60.0	60.0	58.3	56.7	57.8	58.7
Puerto Rican	-	-	55.1	58.3	57.4	63.2	62.7	63.5	65.0
Cuban	-	-	82.7	82.5	83.1	83.4	83.2	84.8	85.4
Central and South American	-	-	58.8	60.6	59.1	62.8	60.8	61.5	63.4
Other and unknown Hispanic	-	-	66.4	65.8	65.5	67.3	66.0	66.4	65.6
Non-Hispanic white (selected states)[3]	-	-	81.2	81.4	81.7	81.8	82.7	83.3	83.7
Non-Hispanic black (selected states)[3]	-	-	60.7	60.1	60.0	60.4	59.9	60.7	61.9
Prenatal care began during 3rd trimester or no prenatal care									
All mothers	7.9	6.0	5.1	5.7	6.1	6.1	6.4	6.1	5.8
White	6.3	5.0	4.3	4.8	5.0	5.0	5.2	4.9	4.7
Black	16.6	10.5	8.9	10.2	11.2	11.0	11.9	11.3	10.7
American Indian or Alaskan Native	28.9	22.4	15.2	12.9	13.1	13.2	13.4	12.9	12.2
Asian or Pacific Islander	-	-	6.5	6.5	6.3	5.9	6.1	5.8	5.7
Chinese	6.5	4.4	3.7	4.4	4.2	3.4	3.6	3.4	3.4
Japanese	4.1	2.7	2.1	3.1	2.8	3.3	2.7	2.9	2.5
Filipino	7.2	4.1	4.0	4.8	4.9	4.8	4.7	4.5	5.0
Other Asian or Pacific Islander[2]	-	-	9.0	8.1	7.8	7.3	7.6	7.2	6.8
Hispanic origin (selected states)[3,4]	-	-	12.0	12.4	12.7	12.1	13.0	12.0	11.0
Mexican American	-	-	11.8	12.9	13.0	13.9	14.6	13.2	12.2
Puerto Rican	-	-	16.2	15.5	17.1	10.2	11.3	10.6	9.1
Cuban	-	-	3.9	3.7	3.9	3.6	4.0	2.8	2.4
Central and South American	-	-	13.1	12.5	13.5	9.9	11.9	10.9	9.5
Other and unknown Hispanic	-	-	9.2	9.4	9.3	8.8	9.3	8.5	8.2
Non-Hispanic white (selected states)[3]	-	-	3.5	4.0	4.1	4.1	3.7	3.4	3.2
Non-Hispanic black (selected states)[3]	-	-	9.7	10.9	11.8	11.0	12.0	11.2	10.7

Source: National Center for Health Statistics. *Health, United States, 1993.* Hyattsville, MD: Public Health Service, May 1994, p. 70. Centers for Disease Control and Prevention, National Center for Health Statistics: Data computed by the Division of Analysis from data compiled by the Division of Vital Statistics. *Notes:* A dash (-) stands for data not available. Excludes births that occurred in States not reporting prenatal care. The race groups, white and black, include persons of Hispanic and non-Hispanic origin. Conversely, persons of Hispanic origin may be of any race. 1. Excludes live births for whom trimester prenatal care began is unknown. 2. Includes Hawaiians and part Hawaiians. 3. Trend data for Hispanics and non-Hispanics are affected by expansion of the reporting area for an Hispanic-origin item on the birth certificate and by immigration. These two factors affect numbers of events, composition of the Hispanic population, and maternal and infant health characteristics. The number of States in the reporting area increased from 22 in 1980, to 30 plus the District of Columbia (DC) in 1988, 47 plus DC in 1989, 48 plus DC in 1990, and 49 plus DC in 1991. 4. Includes mothers of all races.

★ 526 ★

Preventative Health Care

Substance Risk Factors Among Chippewa Indians in Wisconsin

Data show alcohol and tobacco risk factors among Chippewa men and women, as compared to the Wisconsin general population. Results are based on a study of 175 Chippewa adults (465 were originally randomly chosen to participate) and data from the 1989 Wisconsin Behavioral Risk Factor Surveillance System.

	Men		Women	
	Chippewa	Wisconsin	Chippewa	Wisconsin
Tobacco:				
Ever smoked (percent)	88.0	58.0	78.0	48.0
Current smoker (percent)	69.0	29.0	63.0	25.0
Cigarettes per day (mean)	16	23	15	18
Alcohol:				
Drank during preceding month (percent)[1]	67.0	79.0	55.0	63.0
Days per week drank (mean)[2]	2	2	2	2
Drinks per day (mean)[3,4]	11	4	7	2
Heavy drinking (percent)[3,5]	59.0	43.0	40.0	15.0
Drink and drive (percent)[3,6]	19.0	12.0	10.0	3.0

Source: Peterson, Dan E., MD, MPH and others. "Behavioral risk factors of Chippewa Indians living on Wisconsin reservations." *Public Health Reports* vol. 109, no. 6 (November/December 1994), p. 822. *Notes:* 1. Reported drinking alcohol during the month preceding the survey. 2. Usual number of days a week drinks alcohol (among drinkers). 3. Asked only of the original survey respondents. 4. Average number drinks consumed on a day one drinks (among drinkers). 5. Drank 5 or more drinks on 1 or more days during the month preceding the survey month (among all respondents). 6. Reported driving after having had "perhaps too much to drink" at least once in the last month (among all respondents).

Substance Abuse Treatment

★ 527 ★

Alcohol Treatment Program Admissions

State-funded client treatment admissions, by race/ethnicity and state and U.S. territory are shown for fiscal year 1992.

State	White, not of Hispanic origin	Black, not of Hispanic origin	Hispanic	Asian or Pacific Islander	Native American	Other	Not reported	Total
Alabama	5,917	2,335	NA	NA	NA	27	NA	8,279
Alaska	5,135	221	141	40	6,009	37	81	11,664
Arizona	7,160	681	2,647	54	2,472	0	3,973	16,987[1]
Arkansas	6,115	2,281	48	4	49	0	0	8,497[2]
California	37,316	12,404	10,222	690	1,116	0	547	62,295
Colorado	33,461	3,445	14,271	164	3,226	109	0	54,676
Connecticut	8,657	3,148	1,537	NA	NA	81	4,932	18,355
Delaware	2,426	1,075	22	0	4	22	1	3,550
District of Columbia	236	1,980	158	0	13	6	5	2,398

[Continued]

★ 527 ★

Alcohol Treatment Program Admissions
[Continued]

State	White, not of Hispanic origin	Black, not of Hispanic origin	Hispanic	Asian or Pacific Islander	Native American	Other	Not reported	Total
Florida	21,932	4,022	3,232	68	104	125	38,035	67,518
Georgia	20,526	10,410	102	26	33	64	0	31,161
Guam	38	0	1	55	0	1	0	95
Hawaii	1,180	94	158	904	107	65	19	2,527
Idaho	4,501	38	366	15	287	48	0	5,255
Illinois	27,202	10,742	3,319	161	480	289	0	42,193
Indiana	12,896	2,293	116	13	58	137	2,645	18,158
Iowa	17,524	729	448	46	247	46	0	19,040
Kansas	10,684	1,195	966	53	420	388	0	13,706
Kentucky	22,550	1,784	1	0	0	0	289	24,624
Louisiana	6,220	3,594	NA	25	26	NA	NA	9,865
Maine	6,800	36	0	8	104	25	0	6,973
Maryland	12,290	5,386	205	37	73	33	1	18,025
Massachusetts	41,244	4,867	3,034	193	228	2,087	0	51,653
Michigan	38,059	7,562	1,585	29	1,163	99	63	48,560
Minnesota	38,621	4,035	1,941	90	8,800	285	388	54,160
Mississippi	3,746	2,997	0	0	28	0	0	6,771
Missouri	18,807	4,373	125	21	195	48	0	23,569
Montana	4,459	27	101	8	1,317	0	13	5,925
Nebraska	17,972	1,541	0	49	3,343	1,231	2	24,138
Nevada	2,899	319	279	37	209	30	1,237	5,010
New Hampshire	3,931	88	13	4	21	0	0	4,057
New Jersey	15,800	6,464	2,097	98	64	214	13	24,750
New Mexico	4,507	163	3,266	34	2,192	0	152	10,314
New York	54,553	29,424	7,864	133	2,013	760	0	94,747
North Carolina	19,152	9,055	192	10	430	57	74	28,970
North Dakota	3,361	18	0	6	931	26	2	4,344
Ohio	32,830	7,145	737	102	162	98	181	41,255
Oklahoma	8,722	1,279	263	13	1,564	0	0	11,841
Oregon	NA	NA	NA	NA	NA	NA	NA	NA
Pennsylvania	27,294	5,901	973	39	80	4	0	34,291
Puerto Rico	0	0	8,710	0	0	0	0	8,710
Rhode Island	6,132	938	330	25	90	152	0	7,667
South Carolina	13,732	7,034	220	27	40	24	106	21,183
South Dakota	7,043	103	0	0	3,090	155	0	10,391
Tennessee	5,181	1,379	72	6	15	0	17	6,670
Texas	10,968	3,347	5,877	33	175	7	0	20,407
Utah	8,691	378	1,272	74	1,890	150	18	12,473
Vermont	4,953	46	11	12	50	111	0	5,183
Virginia	11,807	3,616	603	62	99	0	923	17,110
Washington	NA	NA	NA	NA	NA	NA	NA	NA
West Virginia	9,812	490	45	9	11	0	0	10,367
Wisconsin	90,338	3,313	1,431	216	2,868	0	0	98,166
Wyoming	NA	NA	NA	NA	NA	NA	NA	NA

[Continued]

★ 527 ★

Alcohol Treatment Program Admissions
[Continued]

State	White, not of Hispanic origin	Black, not of Hispanic origin	Hispanic	Asian or Pacific Islander	Native American	Other	Not reported	Total
Total	775,380	173,795	79,001	3,693	45,896	7,041	53,717	1,138,523
Percent of total	68.1	15.3	6.9	.3	4.0	.6	4.7	100.0

Source: U.S. Department of Health and Human Services. Public Health Service. Substance Abuse and Mental Health Services Administration. Office of Applied Studies. *State Resources and Services Related to Alcohol and Other Drug Problems, Fiscal Year 1992: An Analysis of State Alcohol and Drug Abuse Profile Data.* Prepared by the National Association of State Alcohol and Drug Abuse Directors, Incorporated. DHHS Publication No. (SMA) 94-2092. Rockville, MD: Department of Health and Human Services, 1994, p. 29. Primary source: State Alcohol and Drug Abuse Profile (SADAP), FY 1992; data are included for only those programs that received at least some funds administered by the State Alcohol/Drug Agency during the states' fiscal year (FY) 1992. *Notes:* NA stands for information not available. 1. Figures represent clients "served." 2. Native American category includes American Indian and Alaskan Native (Aleut, Eskimo Indian).

★ 528 ★

Substance Abuse Treatment

Alcohol and Drug Abuse Treatment Programs

Data show number and percent distribution of clients in treatment, by treatment setting and by race/ethnicity of client. Data are current as of September 30, 1991.

Client diagnosis and race/ethnicity	Treatment setting					
	Hospital/ residential setting		Ambulatory setting		All clients	
	Number	Percent	Number	Percent	Number	Percent
Drug abuse clients						
White, not Hispanic	10,215	37.2	96,849	50.5	107,064	48.9
Black, not Hispanic	12,536	45.6	55,800	29.1	68,336	31.2
Hispanic	4,244	15.4	35,391	18.5	39,635	18.1
Asian	151	0.5	1,232	0.6	1,383	0.6
Indian	178	0.6	1,434	0.7	1,612	0.7
Other	147	0.5	941	0.5	1,088	0.5
Subtotal	27,471	100.0	191,647	100.0	219,118	100.0
Unknown[1]	1,229		16,661		17,890	
All clients	28,700		208,308		237,008	
Units reporting	1,937		4,196		5,548	
Alcoholism clients						
White, not Hispanic	18,976	67.3	209,644	67.8	228,620	67.8
Black, not Hispanic	5,949	21.1	40,040	12.9	45,989	13.6
Hispanic	2,043	7.2	46,858	15.2	48,901	14.5
Asian	154	0.5	3,768	1.2	3,922	1.2
Indian	994	3.5	7,122	2.3	8,116	2.4
Other	72	0.3	1,771	0.6	1,843	0.5
Subtotal	28,188	100.0	309,203	100.0	337,391	100.0
Unknown[1]	1,642		26,114		27,756	
All clients	29,830		335,317		365,147	

[Continued]

★ 528 ★

Alcohol and Drug Abuse Treatment Programs
[Continued]

Client diagnosis and race/ethnicity	Treatment setting					
	Hospital/ residential setting		Ambulatory setting		All clients	
	Number	Percent	Number	Percent	Number	Percent
Units reporting	2,681		4,832		6,682	
Clients with both problems						
White, not Hispanic	20,497	54.3	95,990	67.8	116,487	65.0
Black, not Hispanic	10,659	28.3	31,030	21.9	41,689	23.3
Hispanic	5,419	14.4	10,029	7.1	15,448	8.6
Asian	193	0.5	953	0.7	1,146	0.6
Indian	796	2.1	2,941	2.1	3,737	2.1
Other	157	0.4	576	0.4	733	0.4
Subtotal	37,721	100.0	141,519	100.0	179,240	100.0
Unknown[1]	2,899		27,525		30,424	
All clients	40,620		169,044		209,664	
Units reporting	2,546		4,008		5,707	
All clients						
White, not Hispanic	49,688	53.2	402,483	62.7	452,171	61.5
Black, not Hispanic	29,144	31.2	126,870	19.8	156,014	21.2
Hispanic	11,706	12.5	92,278	14.4	103,984	14.1
Asian	498	0.5	5,953	0.9	6,451	0.9
Indian	1,968	2.1	11,497	1.8	13,465	1.8
Other	376	0.4	3,288	0.5	3,664	0.5
Subtotal	93,380	100.0	642,369	100.0	735,749	100.0
Unknown[1]	5,770		70,300		76,070	
All clients	99,150		712,669		811,819	
Units reporting	3,682		6,428		8,928	

Source: U.S. Department of Health and Human Services. Public Health Service. Substance Abuse and Mental Health Services Administration. Office of Applied Studies. *National Drug and Alcoholism Treatment Unit Survey (NDATUS)*, 1991 Main Findings Report. DHHS Publication No. (SMA) 92-2007, 1993, p. 32. Primary source: NIDA and NIAA, 1991 National Drug and Alcoholism Treatment Unit Survey. *Notes:* Sum of units reporting in a hospital/residential setting and units reporting clients in an ambulatory setting does not equal total units, because units may treat clients in both types of setting. Column percentages are based on subtotals, excluding unknowns for race/ethnicity. Percentages may not sum to 100 because of rounding. Excludes 127 units that reported no clients. 1. Where units did not report clients by race/ethnicity, race/ethnicity is classified as "unknown."

★ 529 ★

Substance Abuse Treatment

Drug Treatment Program Admissions

State-funded client treatment admissions, by race/ethnicity and state and U.S. territory are shown for fiscal year 1992.

State	White, not of Hispanic origin	Black, not of Hispanic origin	Hispanic	Asian or Pacific Islander	Native American	Other	Not reported	Total
Alabama	3,773	3,830	NA	NA	NA	25	NA	7,628
Alaska	1,498	303	65	16	694	7	19	2,602
Arizona	4,512	864	1,605	21	276	0	1,427	8,705[1]
Arkansas	2,626	2,305	21	6	13	0	0	4,971[2]
California	34,940	15,650	18,522	1,338	782	0	906	72,138
Colorado	5,396	1,796	2,200	48	135	28	0	9,603
Connecticut	4,447	3,856	2,311	NA	NA	55	3,159	13,828
Delaware	773	1,505	34	1	3	31	2	2,349
District of Columbia	325	8,114	114	11	22	27	602	9,215
Florida	12,943	13,339	3,358	47	83	119	20	29,909
Georgia	10,142	17,396	73	15	14	36	1	27,677
Guam	6	0	0	22	0	1	5	34
Hawaii	599	46	56	1,069	66	68	0	1,904
Idaho	2,006	19	112	3	73	29	0	2,242
Illinois	11,617	25,235	2,081	126	339	284	0	39,682
Indiana	3,695	412	35	2	9	46	1,554	5,753
Iowa	2,861	429	62	11	51	14	0	3,428
Kansas	2,446	1,554	98	9	82	93	0	4,282
Kentucky	7,402	1,528	0	0	0	0	74	9,004
Louisiana	5,781	10,261	NA	23	26	NA	NA	16,091
Maine	1,163	18	0	0	21	12	0	1,214
Maryland	5,637	11,615	124	57	41	29	1	17,504
Massachusetts	16,535	9,297	5,066	59	106	1,608	0	32,671
Michigan	13,018	13,496	552	37	220	62	51	27,436
Minnesota	3,587	1,741	164	25	355	69	37	5,978
Mississippi	1,657	2,730	0	0	1	0	0	4,388
Missouri	5,260	5,065	44	11	23	41	0	10,444
Montana	1,475	21	38	3	287	0	0	1,824
Nebraska	1,767	480	0	11	53	85	0	2,396
Nevada	1,872	491	147	28	47	15	263	2,863
New Hampshire	1,658	66	11	3	13	0	0	1,751
New Jersey	9,783	13,283	4,959	75	52	10	0	28,162
New Mexico	1,120	96	831	5	139	0	174	2,365
New York	21,633	21,390	9,751	90	303	531	0	53,698
North Carolina	5,412	8,549	20	4	147	16	24	14,172
North Dakota	182	4	0	0	34	4	9	233
Ohio	14,249	12,075	462	45	87	75	236	27,229
Oklahoma	3,392	1,524	137	8	332	0	0	5,393
Oregon	NA	NA	NA	NA	NA	NA	NA	NA
Pennsylvania	11,534	17,520	2,032	40	21	0	0	31,147
Puerto Rico	0	0	14,886	0	0	0	0	14,886
Rhode Island	3,473	580	331	6	40	76	0	4,506
South Carolina	2,767	4,019	87	6	14	8	60	6,961
South Dakota	568	18	0	0	189	7	1,237	2,019
Tennessee	4,405	1,927	58	5	15	0	17	6,427

[Continued]

★ 529 ★

Drug Treatment Program Admissions
[Continued]

State	White, not of Hispanic origin	Black, not of Hispanic origin	Hispanic	Asian or Pacific Islander	Native American	Other	Not reported	Total
Texas	11,011	12,022	6,439	53	84	118	0	29,727
Utah	2,481	130	252	15	60	71	30	3,039
Vermont	822	51	9	1	13	42	0	938
Virginia	9,493	8,027	294	56	64	0	1,596	19,530
Washington	NA	NA	NA	NA	NA	NA	NA	NA
West Virginia	1,147	160	12	15	2	0	0	1,336
Wisconsin	13,090	8,353	1,293	74	307	0	0	23,117
Wyoming	NA	NA	NA	NA	NA	NA	NA	NA
Total	287,979	263,190	78,746	3,500	5,738	3,742	11,504	654,399
Percent of total	44.0	40.2	12.0	.5	.9	.6	1.8	100.0

Source: U.S. Department of Health and Human Services. Public Health Service. Substance Abuse and Mental Health Services Administration. Office of Applied Studies. *State Resources and Services Related to Alcohol and Other Drug Problems, Fiscal Year 1992: An Analysis of State Alcohol and Drug Abuse Profile Data.* Prepared by the National Association of State Alcohol and Drug Abuse Directors, Incorporated. DHHS Publication No. (SMA) 94-2092. Rockville, MD: Department of Health and Human Services, 1994, p. 35. Primary source: State Alcohol and Drug Abuse Profile (SADAP), FY 1992; data are included for only those programs that received at least some funds administered by the State Alcohol/Drug Agency during the states' fiscal year (FY) 1992. *Notes:* NA stands for information not available. 1. Figures represent clients "served." 2. Native American category includes American Indian and Alaskan Native (Aleut, Eskimo Indian).

Chapter 7
SOCIAL AND ECONOMIC CONDITIONS

Employment

★ 530 ★

Racial/Ethnic Distribution of the U.S. Workforce

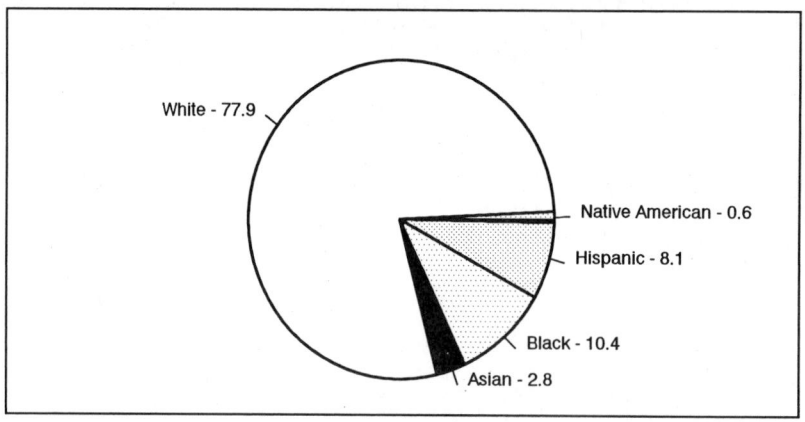

Characteristic	Percent
White	77.9
Black	10.4
Hispanic	8.1
Asian	2.8
Native American	0.6

Source: Usdansky, Margaret L. "A new U.S. workforce evolves: job shifts reflect progress of Hispanics and women." *USA TODAY* (29 January 1993), p. 7A. Primary source: U.S. Census Bureau; Bureau of Labor Statistics; *USA TODAY* analysis of Census data.

★ 531 ★

Employment

Percentage Change in the Workforce, by Race/Ethnicity, 1980-1990

Characteristic	Percent	
	Men	Women
Whites	5.7	21.5
Blacks	16.2	29.8
Hispanics[1]	63.9	72.3
Asians	105.2	107.2
Native Americans	36.7	56.0
Total workforce	11.8	26.9

Source: Usdansky, Margaret L. "A new U.S. workforce evolves: job shifts reflect progress of Hispanics and women." *USA TODAY* (29 January 1993), p. 7A. U.S. Census Bureau; Bureau of Labor Statistics; USA TODAY analysis of Census data. *Note:* 1. Hispanics may be of any race.

★ 532 ★

Employment

Continuing Education of Employed Workers, 1990-91

Continued training of workers in the face of new technology is an indication of the willingness of industry to invest in the future of its employees. This table shows the percentage of currently employed persons who took at least one course during the past year in order to improve their skills on their current job. Data are shown by race/ethnicity of the worker.

Worker characteristics	All workers	Full-time workers	Part-time workers
Total	29.5	33.1	16.4
White, non-Hispanic	31.6	35.3	18.0
Black, non-Hispanic	20.1	22.6	7.5
Hispanic	22.7	26.8	10.7
Asian	20.6	22.4	15.1
American Indian	33.5	35.0	24.6

Source: U.S. Department of Education. National Center for Education Statistics. *The Condition of Education 1994.* Washington, DC: U.S. Government Printing Office, 1994, p. 191. U.S. Department of Education, National Center for Education Statistics, National Household Education Survey, 1991 (Adult Education Component).

★ 533 ★

Employment

Minority Representation Among Engineers

Data show results of a survey of a random sample of members of 22 engineering societies. Distribution by race/ethnicity is shown in percent.

Race/ethnicity	Percent
Asian American	5.7
Hispanic	2.1
African American	1.3
Native American	0.5

Source: Lewin, David I. "Washington window: across the gender divide." *Mechanical Engineering* (October 1993), p. 34. Primary source: Society of Women Engineers survey.

★ 534 ★

Employment

Minority Representation in Newspapers, 1993

Minorities made up just over 10 percent of the 53,700 persons who worked at newspapers in 1993. Distribution of minority employees is shown by race/ethnicity.

Race/ethnicity	Percent
African-American	5.0
Hispanic	3.0
Asian American	2.0
Native American	0.3
Total	10.49

Source: Atkins, Elizabeth. "Racial bias still widespread in the media, study finds." *Detroit News* (24 July 1994), p. 2A. Primary source: American Society of Newspaper Editors.

★ 535 ★

Employment

Minority Representation in Radio Newsrooms, 1993

Minorities made up 13 percent of the 15,000 persons who worked in radio news in 1993. Distribution of minority employees is shown by race/ethnicity.

Race/ethnicity	Percent
African-American	6.0
Hispanic	4.0
Asian American	3.0
Native American	0.2
Total	13.0

Source: Atkins, Elizabeth. "Racial bias still widespread in the media, study finds." *Detroit News* (24 July 1994), p. 2A. Primary source: Radio and Television News Directors of America.

★ 536 ★

Employment

Minority Representation in Television Newsrooms, 1993

Minorities accounted for approximately 19 percent of the 25,000 persons who worked in television newsrooms in 1993. Distribution of minority employees is shown by race/ethnicity.

Race/ethnicity	Percent
African-American	11.0
Hispanic	5.0
Asian American	2.0
Native American	0.5
Total	19.0

Source: Atkins, Elizabeth. "Racial bias still widespread in the media, study finds." *Detroit News* (24 July 1994), p. 2A. Primary source: Radio and Television News Directors of America.

★ 537 ★

Employment

Science and Engineering Doctoral Workforce, by Race/Ethnicity and Degree Field, 1991

Data show proportion of the workforce that is made up of each minority, in percent.

	Portion of science & engineering workforce				
	Female	Black	Asian	Native American	Hispanic
Total science and engineering	18.8	2.1	9.8	0.2	1.8
Sciences	21.7	2.2	7.3	0.2	1.8
Physical sciences	8.9	1.1	11.3	0.1	1.7
Mathematics	10.2	1.1	10.7	0.1	2.2
Computer sciences	11.8	0.5	20.3	0.1	1.7
Environmental sciences	9.6	0.2	5.3	0.2	1.0
Life sciences	24.0	1.9	7.8	0.2	1.6
Psychology	38.1	3.1	1.6	0.2	2.0
Social sciences	23.9	4.2	5.6	0.2	2.1
Engineering	3.4	1.2	23.1	0.2	1.9
Aeronautical/astronautical	2.0	1.4	19.3	[1]	1.5
Chemical	3.7	0.8	24.4	[1]	1.2
Civil	3.6	2.4	23.0	0.2	2.0
Electrical/electronic	2.5	1.3	23.3	0.1	1.9
Materials	6.0	0.9	25.2	0.2	3.0
Mechanical	2.1	1.4	26.7	0.1	2.0
Nuclear	2.8	0.3	18.8	[1]	2.8
Systems design	13.4	5.8	15.8	[1]	4.3
Other engineering	3.2	0.3	20.9	0.4	1.5

Source: National Science Board. *Science & Engineering Indicators—1993* (NSB 93-1). Washington, DC: U.S. Government Printing Office, 1993, p. 81. Primary source: Science Resources Studies division, National Science Foundation, *Characteristics of Doctoral Scientists and Engineers: 1991* (Washington, DC: NSF, forthcoming). *Note:* 1. No cases reported.

★ 538 ★

Employment

Class of Workers Age 16 and Older in Selected Alaska Native Villages

Data are shown for the 50 areas with the largest populations, in number of persons.

Alaska Native Village Statistical Area[1]	Employed persons age 16 years and older						
	Private for profit wage and salary workers	Private not-for-profit wage and salary workers	Local government workers	State government workers	Federal government workers	Self-employed workers	Unpaid family workers
Akiachak	4	6	55	57	13	0	0
Akutan	406	2	22	0	97	0	0
Alakanuk	36	9	44	13	5	5	0
Andreafsky	34	5	59	9	15	8	2

[Continued]

★ 538 ★

Class of Workers Age 16 and Older in Selected Alaska Native Villages
[Continued]

Alaska Native Village Statistical Area[1]	Employed persons age 16 years and older						
	Private for profit wage and salary workers	Private not-for-profit wage and salary workers	Local government workers	State government workers	Federal government workers	Self-employed workers	Unpaid family workers
Angoon	43	16	22	74	19	5	0
Aniak	79	37	16	62	15	6	0
Barrow	281	52	790	39	68	17	0
Bethel	550	239	254	485	350	113	0
Chevak	47	9	71	22	3	0	0
Copper Center	47	24	24	18	13	20	0
Craig	420	23	62	23	32	69	2
Dillingham	320	175	127	98	65	56	0
Emmonak	55	8	12	49	8	4	0
Fort Yukon	42	26	29	61	8	4	0
Galena	69	15	58	30	21	4	0
Gambell	22	13	51	9	4	0	0
Grouse Creek Group	137	15	43	59	8	23	0
Hoonah	176	28	16	55	20	26	0
Hooper Bay	33	8	41	71	5	0	0
Kake	142	19	50	12	10	20	0
Kasigluk	8	17	14	47	2	0	0
King Cove	243	3	12	6	1	11	0
King Salmon	92	0	30	26	81	0	0
Kipnuk	21	2	23	13	2	0	0
Klawock	175	11	45	10	13	13	0
Kotlik	12	7	39	26	6	0	0
Kotzebue	398	159	219	134	85	24	0
Kwethluk	3	2	20	36	29	0	0
McGrath	59	34	19	68	34	5	0
Mountain Village	22	2	84	27	4	1	0
Naknek	95	6	107	10	7	19	0
Ninilchik	2,250	344	473	179	130	802	61
Noorvik	42	20	18	40	2	5	0
Pilot Station	11	0	35	46	0	4	0
Point Hope	37	1	104	6	15	0	1
Quinhagak	19	2	37	52	17	0	0
St. Paul	166	37	71	18	36	2	0
Salamatof	196	11	21	19	3	20	4
Sand Point	299	11	63	11	5	47	2
Savoonga	12	2	24	49	0	0	0
Selawik	15	14	33	29	3	5	0
Shishmaref	28	7	22	29	5	0	0
Stebbins	15	0	43	33	5	0	0
Togiak	22	3	30	39	4	2	0
Tok	151	19	7	134	31	24	4
Toksook Bay	38	33	23	1	6	1	0
Unalakleet	81	8	20	89	6	7	0
Unalaska	1,726	33	111	18	476	92	26
Wainwright	44	0	121	0	7	2	3
Yakutat	138	12	46	18	12	24	4

Source: Census of Population and Housing, 1990: Summary Tape File 3C on CD-ROM [machine-readable datafiles]. Prepared by the Bureau of the Census. Washington, DC: The Bureau, 1992. *Notes:* 1. Alaska Native villages (ANVs) constitute tribes, bands, clans, groups, villages, communities, or associations in Alaska that are recognized pursuant to the Alaska Native Claims Settlement Act of 1972, Public Law 92-203. Because ANVs do not have legally designated boundaries, the Census Bureau has established Alaska Native village statistical areas (ANVSAs) for statistical purposes. For the 1990 census, the Census Bureau cooperated with officials of the nonprofit corporation within each participating Alaska Native Regional Corporation (ANRC), as well as other knowledgeable officials, to delineate boundaries that encompass the settled area associated with each ANV.

Employment

Class of Workers Age 16 and Older in Selected Tribal Designated Statistical Areas

TDSA[1]	Employed persons age 16 years and older						
	Private for profit wage and salary workers	Private not-for-profit wage and salary workers	Local government workers	State government workers	Federal government workers	Self-employed workers	Unpaid family workers
Apache Choctaw TDSA (state)	5,115	297	497	608	152	750	98
Chickahominy TDSA (state)	964	33	144	138	44	135	13
Clifton Choctaw TDSA (state)	99	0	9	0	8	24	0
Coharie TDSA (state)	34,503	1,966	3,121	4,829	1,555	3,395	272
Coquille Indian TDSA	115,853	13,414	14,370	9,416	4,659	17,078	825
Delaware-Muncie TDSA (state)	74	0	18	0	15	27	0
Florida Tribe of Eastern Creek TDSA (state)	52	0	0	0	0	0	0
Haliwa-Saponi TDSA (state)	1,773	136	104	149	16	125	0
Jena Band of Choctaw TDSA (state)	14,574	1,276	1,759	2,452	1,488	1,580	42
Klamath TDSA	11,241	1,140	1,481	875	540	1,439	129
Lumbee TDSA (state)	15,163	607	1,132	1,879	324	1,205	105
Meherrin TDSA (state)	16,036	860	1,514	1,834	802	1,734	111
Mohegan TDSA (state)	8,025	841	751	902	546	594	34
Ramapough TDSA (state)	193	26	24	18	7	23	7
United Houma Nation TDSA (state)	264,058	16,275	23,158	13,738	9,885	20,135	1,529
Waccamaw Siouan TDSA (state)	972	3	67	60	30	49	5
Wampanoag-Gay Head TDSA	3,239	424	518	150	84	1,417	36

Source: Census of Population and Housing, 1990: Summary Tape File 3C on CD-ROM [machine-readable datafiles]. Prepared by the Bureau of the Census. Washington, DC: The Bureau, 1992. *Notes:* 1. Tribal designated statistical areas (TDSAs) are areas, delineated outside Oklahoma by federally- and state-recognized tribes without a land base or associated trust lands, to provide statistical areas for which the Census Bureau tabulates data. TDSAs represent areas generally containing the American Indian population over which federally-recognized tribes have jurisdiction and areas in which state tribes provide benefits and services to their members. The names of TDSAs delineated by state-recognized tribes are followed by "(state)." The Census Bureau did not recognize TDSAs before the 1990 census.

Employment

Class of Workers Age 16 and Older in Selected Tribal Jurisdiction Statistical Areas

TJSA[1]	Employed persons age 16 years and older						
	Private for profit wage and salary workers	Private not-for-profit wage and salary workers	Local government workers	State government workers	Federal government workers	Self-employed workers	Unpaid family workers
Absentee Shawnee-Citizens Band of Potawatomi TJSA	22,994	1,662	2,326	3,760	5,156	3,061	176
Caddo-Wichita-Delaware TJSA	1,973	117	148	286	62	586	26
Cherokee TJSA	112,641	9,555	9,734	11,888	4,795	14,519	1,382
Cheyenne-Arapaho TJSA	43,478	3,419	3,950	5,392	2,388	8,427	576
Chickasaw TJSA	66,910	5,737	6,231	9,636	3,073	11,633	989
Choctaw TJSA	45,615	3,956	5,073	9,043	3,165	7,971	911
Creek TJSA	218,423	21,204	14,780	12,167	6,428	23,396	1,665
Iowa TJSA	956	66	123	199	89	210	11
Kaw TJSA	4,485	353	333	247	101	590	24

[Continued]

★ 540 ★

Class of Workers Age 16 and Older in Selected Tribal Jurisdiction Statistical Areas
[Continued]

TJSA[1]	Employed persons age 16 years and older						
	Private for profit wage and salary workers	Private not-for-profit wage and salary workers	Local government workers	State government workers	Federal government workers	Self-employed workers	Unpaid family workers
Kiowa-Comanche-Apache- Fort Sill Apache TJSA	40,153	3,753	5,755	5,911	7,785	6,992	621
Otoe-Missouria TJSA	742	42	48	159	24	146	12
Pawnee TJSA	4,188	402	424	504	226	750	68
Sac and Fox TJSA	13,259	1,049	1,338	1,571	1,093	2,084	252
Seminole TJSA	5,413	297	546	721	368	889	55
Tonkawa TJSA	3,378	272	326	417	74	556	47
Creek-Seminole Joint Area TJSA	488	32	89	97	29	53	5
Iowa-Sac and Fox Joint Area TJSA	198	9	37	42	17	59	11

Source: Census of Population and Housing, 1990: Summary Tape File 3C on CD-ROM [machine-readable datafiles]. Prepared by the Bureau of the Census. Washington, DC: The Bureau, 1992. *Notes:* 1. Tribal jurisdiction statistical areas (TJSAs) are areas, delineated by federally recognized tribes in Oklahoma without a reservation, for which the Census Bureau tabulates data. TJSAs represent areas generally containing the American Indian population over which one or more tribal governments have jurisdiction. If tribal officials delineated adjacent TJSAs so that they include some duplicate territory, the overlap area is called a "joint use area," which is treated as a separate TJSA for census purposes.

★ 541 ★

Employment

Class of Workers Age 16 and Older on Selected Reservations and Trust Lands

Data are shown for the 50 areas with the largest populations, in number of persons.

American Indian Reservation and Trust Lands[1,2]	Employed persons age 16 years and older						
	Private for profit wage and salary workers	Private not-for-profit wage and salary workers	Local government workers	State government workers	Federal government workers	Self-employed workers	Unpaid family workers
Agua Caliente Reservation	5,405	418	383	102	76	1,140	67
Allegany Reservation	1,810	264	455	215	66	130	2
Blackfeet Reservation	654	96	668	292	344	179	105
Cheyenne River Reservation	684	153	494	92	441	554	47
Coeur d'Alene Reservation and Trust Lands, ID	1,221	118	239	118	125	391	23
Colorado River Reservation	1,854	111	357	121	269	212	16
Colville Reservation	1,012	145	349	189	455	174	8
Crow Reservation and Trust Lands, MT	626	156	275	61	248	263	29
Eastern Cherokee Reservation	1,214	219	452	54	297	131	8
Flathead Reservation	4,164	478	1,062	299	600	1,409	129
Fort Apache Reservation	642	144	706	269	549	5	0
Fort Berthold Reservation	682	182	225	106	268	302	30
Fort Hall Reservation and Trust Lands, ID	1,102	97	286	63	99	56	5
Fort Peck Reservation	1,576	254	587	118	483	615	50
Gila River Reservation	1,062	150	372	43	286	49	0

[Continued]

★ 541 ★

Class of Workers Age 16 and Older on Selected Reservations and Trust Lands
[Continued]

American Indian Reservation and Trust Lands[1,2]	Employed persons age 16 years and older						
	Private for profit wage and salary workers	Private not-for-profit wage and salary workers	Local government workers	State government workers	Federal government workers	Self-employed workers	Unpaid family workers
Hopi Reservation and Trust Lands, AZ	555	52	425	67	503	122	0
Isabella Reservation and Trust Lands, MI	6,833	669	712	1,555	184	791	62
Laguna Pueblo and Trust Lands, NM	394	73	284	76	272	60	0
Lake Traverse (Sisseton) Reservation	1,763	377	421	179	305	1,103	74
Leech Lake Reservation	1,092	197	401	202	338	391	23
Mississippi Choctaw Reservation and Trust Lands, MS	748	62	244	54	155	24	0
Muckleshoot Reservation and Trust Lands, WA	1,210	100	69	64	87	74	2
Navajo Reservation and Trust Lands, AZ–NM–UT	14,133	1,547	4,657	2,830	5,370	687	26
Nez Perce Reservation	3,023	224	557	580	554	977	33
Northern Cheyenne Reservation and Trust Lands, MT–SD	333	226	131	71	218	37	7
Omaha Reservation	838	98	202	71	209	337	8
Oneida (West) Reservation	6,793	689	636	218	212	586	54
Osage Reservation	11,600	1,056	1,264	870	473	1,771	203
Papago Reservation	622	167	349	82	342	0	0
Pine Ridge Reservation and Trust Lands, NE–SD	418	366	713	100	541	305	0
Port Madison Reservation	1,225	124	157	140	293	239	4
Puyallup Reservation and Trust Lands, WA	10,859	738	831	634	515	968	33
Red Lake Reservation	199	108	300	80	140	44	0
Rosebud Reservation and Trust Lands, SD	741	393	313	110	523	276	30
Salt River Reservation	976	50	272	12	101	29	6
San Carlos Reservation	562	37	410	140	160	16	0
Sandia Pueblo	1,064	68	166	140	71	100	0
San Juan Pueblo	980	74	189	215	405	119	8
Santa Clara Pueblo	1,852	280	279	460	804	340	16
Southern Ute Reservation	1,873	183	474	182	169	433	49
Standing Rock Reservation	534	109	354	144	493	570	65
Taos Pueblo and Trust Lands, NM	1,165	77	142	124	98	281	2
Tulalip Reservation	2,266	143	347	145	75	278	6
Turtle Mountain Reservation and Trust Lands, ND–SD	547	95	444	44	364	68	0
Uintah and Ouray Reservation	3,065	201	855	351	344	852	105
White Earth Reservation	1,268	233	431	82	134	547	35
Wind River Reservation	5,066	511	774	690	369	1,052	80
Yakima Reservation and Trust Lands, WA	6,217	594	679	525	585	786	72

[Continued]

★ 541 ★

Class of Workers Age 16 and Older on Selected Reservations and Trust Lands
[Continued]

American Indian Reservation and Trust Lands[1,2]	Employed persons age 16 years and older						
	Private for profit wage and salary workers	Private not-for-profit wage and salary workers	Local government workers	State government workers	Federal government workers	Self-employed workers	Unpaid family workers
Yankton Reservation	903	277	197	66	214	590	104
Zuni Pueblo	416	50	477	264	313	1,282	0

Source: Census of Population and Housing, 1990: Summary Tape File 3C on CD-ROM [machine-readable datafiles]. Prepared by the Bureau of the Census. Washington, DC: The Bureau, 1992. *Notes:* 1. Federal American Indian reservations are areas with boundaries established by treaty, statute, and/or executive or court order, and recognized by the federal government as territory in which American Indian tribes have jurisdiction. State reservations are lands held in trust by state governments for the use and benefit of a given tribe. The reservations and their boundaries were identified for the 1990 census by the Bureau of Indian Affairs (BIA), Department of Interior (for federal reservations), and state governments (for state reservations). The names of American Indian reservations recognized by state governments, but not by the federal government, are followed by "state." Areas composed of reservation lands that are administered jointly and/or are claimed by two reservations, as identified by the BIA, are called "joint areas," and are treated as separate American Indian reservations for census purposes. Federal reservations may cross state boundaries, and federal and state reservations may cross county, county subdivision, and place boundaries. For reservations that cross state boundaries, only the portion of the reservations in a given state is shown in the data products for that state; the entire reservations are shown in data products for the United States. 2. Trust lands are property associated with a particular American Indian reservation or tribe, held in trust by the federal government. Trust lands may be held in trust either for a tribe (tribal trust lands) or for an individual member of a tribe (individual trust land). Trust lands recognized for the 1990 census comprised all tribal trust lands and inhabited individual trust lands located outside of a reservation boundary. As with other American Indian areas, trust lands may be located in more than one state. Only the trust lands in a given state are shown in the data products for that state; all trust lands associated with a reservation or tribe are shown in data products for the United States. The Census Bureau first reported data for tribal trust lands for the 1980 census.

★ 542 ★

Employment

Employment Status of American Indians and Alaska Natives Age 16 and Older in Selected Alaska Native Villages

Data are shown for the 50 areas with the largest populations, in number of persons.

Alaska Native Village Statistical Area[1]	Male				Female			
	In labor force			Not in labor force	In labor force			Not in labor force
	In armed forces	Civilian			In armed forces	Civilian		
		Employed	Unemployed			Employed	Unemployed	
Akiachak	10	54	7	85	0	56	12	65
Akutan	0	20	0	5	0	16	0	5
Alakanuk	7	46	34	65	0	53	7	85
Andreafsky	8	51	20	35	0	47	12	38
Angoon	0	49	64	46	0	67	20	48
Aniak	0	53	10	22	0	65	4	36
Barrow	0	260	85	136	0	303	43	172
Bethel	13	382	90	401	5	559	67	381
Chevak	2	47	32	79	0	80	1	61
Copper Center	0	4	28	24	0	6	10	27
Craig	2	43	14	27	0	49	2	34
Dillingham	0	135	25	156	0	162	23	193
Emmonak	4	47	39	77	0	49	30	77
Fort Yukon	0	51	42	84	0	65	12	60
Galena	13	35	14	64	0	51	3	55
Gambell	0	54	12	141	0	39	8	82
Grouse Creek Group	0	24	0	3	0	27	1	8
Hoonah	0	126	20	41	0	74	6	68
Hooper Bay	0	76	74	95	0	61	37	101
Kake	0	89	21	72	0	72	6	75

[Continued]

★ 542 ★

Employment Status of American Indians and Alaska Natives Age 16 and Older in Selected Alaska Native Villages

[Continued]

Alaska Native Village Statistical Area[1]	Male				Female			
	In labor force			Not in labor force	In labor force			Not in labor force
	In armed forces	Civilian			In armed forces	Civilian		
		Employed	Unemployed			Employed	Unemployed	
Kasigluk	0	38	36	38	0	31	11	83
King Cove	0	30	2	32	0	14	3	28
King Salmon	6	22	6	18	0	15	0	16
Kipnuk	0	31	6	108	0	25	3	103
Klawock	0	56	28	47	0	27	9	89
Kotlik	4	36	29	60	0	45	21	64
Kotzebue	10	248	91	225	0	319	53	276
Kwethluk	2	41	10	125	0	37	2	96
McGrath	0	33	12	26	0	48	2	41
Mountain Village	0	46	45	103	0	57	27	100
Naknek	0	31	7	28	0	26	0	55
Ninilchik	0	68	7	65	0	39	13	96
Noorvik	0	57	21	83	0	51	6	82
Pilot Station	0	50	21	57	0	36	31	54
Point Hope	0	88	20	51	0	45	30	68
Quinhagak	1	50	4	113	0	57	2	74
St. Paul	3	107	30	66	0	67	9	76
Salamatof	0	13	10	56	0	4	0	17
Sand Point	0	85	3	76	0	43	2	57
Savoonga	7	36	8	122	0	34	7	107
Selawik	0	40	40	85	0	39	5	73
Shishmaref	0	39	13	65	0	37	7	85
Stebbins	0	50	41	40	0	30	21	69
Togiak	2	27	23	108	0	37	5	120
Tok	0	5	7	6	0	10	8	16
Toksook Bay	4	67	16	43	0	27	19	72
Unalakleet	0	80	30	57	0	59	15	51
Unalaska	0	90	13	29	0	31	0	35
Wainwright	0	91	16	27	0	58	4	71
Yakutat	0	51	16	29	0	55	12	30

Source: Census of Population and Housing, 1990: Summary Tape File 3C on CD-ROM [machine-readable datafiles]. Prepared by the Bureau of the Census. Washington, DC: The Bureau, 1992. *Notes:* 1. Alaska Native villages (ANVs) constitute tribes, bands, clans, groups, villages, communities, or associations in Alaska that are recognized pursuant to the Alaska Native Claims Settlement Act of 1972, Public Law 92-203. Because ANVs do not have legally designated boundaries, the Census Bureau has established Alaska Native village statistical areas (ANVSAs) for statistical purposes. For the 1990 census, the Census Bureau cooperated with officials of the nonprofit corporation within each participating Alaska Native Regional Corporation (ANRC), as well as other knowledgeable officials, to delineate boundaries that encompass the settled area associated with each ANV.

★ 543 ★

Employment

Employment Status of American Indians and Alaska Natives Age 16 and Older in Selected Tribal Designated Statistical Areas

Tribal Designated Statistical Area[1]	Male				Female			
	In labor force			Not in labor force	In labor force			Not in labor force
	In armed forces	Civilian			In armed forces	Civilian		
		Employed	Unemployed			Employed	Unemployed	
Apache Choctaw TDSA (state)	0	124	33	100	0	102	2	118
Chickahominy TDSA (state)	0	140	6	35	0	140	12	58
Clifton Choctaw TDSA (state)	0	19	0	36	0	23	11	44
Coharie TDSA (state)	0	279	11	179	0	205	36	346
Coquille Indian TDSA	0	1,261	260	698	0	1,094	200	1,040
Delaware-Muncie TDSA (state)	0	6	0	0	0	5	0	6
Florida Tribe of Eastern Creek TDSA (state)	0	0	0	0	0	0	0	0
Haliwa-Saponi TDSA (state)	0	416	66	294	0	379	42	381
Jena Band of Choctaw TDSA (state)	5	94	10	31	0	32	7	74
Klamath TDSA	0	304	70	188	0	301	60	293
Lumbee TDSA (state)	32	6,323	597	2,431	0	5,514	505	4,449
Meherrin TDSA (state)	2	26	0	9	0	37	14	39
Mohegan TDSA (state)	4	55	9	10	0	48	0	59
Ramapough TDSA (state)	0	14	4	36	0	46	0	23
United Houma Nation TDSA (state)	0	1,780	310	1,109	10	928	196	2,008
Waccamaw Siouan TDSA (state)	0	283	11	169	0	220	16	216
Wampanoag-Gay Head TDSA	0	60	16	20	0	70	2	40

Source: Census of Population and Housing, 1990: Summary Tape File 3C on CD-ROM [machine-readable datafiles]. Prepared by the Bureau of the Census. Washington, DC: The Bureau, 1992. *Notes:* 1. Tribal designated statistical areas (TDSAs) are areas, delineated outside Oklahoma by federally- and state-recognized tribes without a land base or associated trust lands, to provide statistical areas for which the Census Bureau tabulates data. TDSAs represent areas generally containing the American Indian population over which federally-recognized tribes have jurisdiction and areas in which state tribes provide benefits and services to their members. The names of TDSAs delineated by state-recognized tribes are followed by "(state)." The Census Bureau did not recognize TDSAs before the 1990 census.

★ 544 ★

Employment

Employment Status of American Indians and Alaska Natives Age 16 and Older in Selected Tribal Jurisdiction Statistical Areas

Tribal Jurisdiction Statistical Area[1]	Male				Female			
	In labor force			Not in labor force	In labor force			Not in labor force
	In armed forces	Civilian			In armed forces	Civilian		
		Employed	Unemployed			Employed	Unemployed	
Absentee Shawnee-Citizens Band of Potawatomi TJSA	0	1,282	128	742	0	1,090	104	820
Caddo-Wichita-Delaware TJSA	0	101	17	56	0	66	13	117
Cherokee TJSA	47	13,044	1,696	6,505	35	10,679	1,362	10,868
Cheyenne-Arapaho TJSA	3	1,059	218	741	0	1,003	222	942
Chickasaw TJSA	20	3,753	599	2,133	6	3,178	398	3,910
Choctaw TJSA	8	4,654	738	3,257	0	4,085	608	5,267
Creek TJSA	28	9,498	1,013	3,897	0	8,098	787	7,255
Iowa TJSA	0	53	23	25	0	43	5	53
Kaw TJSA	0	150	8	22	0	119	2	113
Kiowa-Comanche-Apache-Fort Sill Apache TJSA	192	1,738	605	1,511	24	1,859	393	2,223

[Continued]

★ 544 ★

Employment Status of American Indians and Alaska Natives Age 16 and Older in Selected Tribal Jurisdiction Statistical Areas

[Continued]

Tribal Jurisdiction Statistical Area[1]	Male				Female			
	In labor force			Not in labor force	In labor force			Not in labor force
	In armed forces	Civilian			In armed forces	Civilian		
		Employed	Unemployed			Employed	Unemployed	
Otoe-Missouria TJSA	0	59	14	55	0	64	7	95
Pawnee TJSA	0	287	47	168	0	282	31	266
Sac and Fox TJSA	0	733	230	450	0	662	175	752
Seminole TJSA	1	497	174	496	0	567	68	664
Tonkawa TJSA	0	155	46	73	0	91	23	151
Creek-Seminole Joint Area TJSA	0	85	23	87	0	59	6	67
Iowa-Sac and Fox Joint Area TJSA	0	4	0	6	0	6	0	0

Source: Census of Population and Housing, 1990: Summary Tape File 3C on CD-ROM [machine-readable datafiles]. Prepared by the Bureau of the Census. Washington, DC: The Bureau, 1992. *Notes:* 1. Tribal jurisdiction statistical areas (TJSAs) are areas, delineated by federally recognized tribes in Oklahoma without a reservation, for which the Census Bureau tabulates data. TJSAs represent areas generally containing the American Indian population over which one or more tribal governments have jurisdiction. If tribal officials delineated adjacent TJSAs so that they include some duplicate territory, the overlap area is called a "joint use area," which is treated as a separate TJSA for census purposes.

★ 545 ★

Employment

Employment Status of American Indians and Alaska Natives Age 16 and Older on Selected Reservations and Trust Lands

Data are shown for the 50 areas with the largest populations, in number of persons.

American Indian Reservation and Trust Lands[1,2]	Male				Female			
	In labor force			Not in labor force	In labor force			Not in labor force
	In armed forces	Civilian			In armed forces	Civilian		
		Employed	Unemployed			Employed	Unemployed	
Agua Caliente Reservation	0	47	4	4	0	29	0	15
Allegany Reservation	0	183	67	94	0	186	34	146
Blackfeet Reservation	0	759	456	834	0	853	272	988
Cheyenne River Reservation	0	560	269	511	0	572	168	809
Coeur d'Alene Reservation and Trust Lands, ID	0	100	34	123	0	100	9	120
Colorado River Reservation	0	305	61	253	0	391	37	410
Colville Reservation	0	538	251	384	0	548	133	573
Crow Reservation and Trust Lands, MT	0	489	408	463	0	376	273	827
Eastern Cherokee Reservation	5	989	269	480	0	958	150	728
Flathead Reservation	2	900	231	581	0	743	105	769
Fort Apache Reservation	0	1,182	609	982	0	847	500	1,601
Fort Berthold Reservation	0	370	168	265	0	408	113	484
Fort Hall Reservation and Trust Lands, ID	0	417	182	388	0	378	105	474
Fort Peck Reservation	3	694	399	588	0	714	196	890
Gila River Reservation	0	967	502	1,186	0	804	279	1,968
Hopi Reservation and Trust Lands, AZ	0	802	334	1,077	0	787	247	1,275
Isabella Reservation and Trust Lands, MI	3	151	17	94	0	148	12	133
Laguna Pueblo and Trust Lands, NM	0	537	178	425	0	553	85	733
Lake Traverse (Sisseton) Reservation	0	322	148	277	0	372	67	420
Leech Lake Reservation	0	329	228	381	0	409	102	526
Mississippi Choctaw Reservation and Trust Lands, MS	0	562	109	345	0	640	94	578
Muckleshoot Reservation and Trust Lands, WA	0	80	12	131	0	101	32	101
Navajo Reservation and Trust Lands, AZ–NM–UT	84	14,109	6,611	20,917	8	12,664	4,570	28,155
Nez Perce Reservation	0	268	121	225	0	281	73	291
Northern Cheyenne Reservation and Trust Lands, MT–SD	0	379	240	344	0	456	143	523

[Continued]

★ 545 ★

Employment Status of American Indians and Alaska Natives Age 16 and Older on Selected Reservations and Trust Lands

[Continued]

American Indian Reservation and Trust Lands[1,2]	Male				Female			
	In labor force			Not in labor force	In labor force			Not in labor force
	In armed forces	Civilian			In armed forces	Civilian		
		Employed	Unemployed			Employed	Unemployed	
Omaha Reservation	0	159	90	252	0	171	73	320
Oneida (West) Reservation	0	428	69	245	0	425	17	347
Osage Reservation	0	1,128	97	588	0	882	132	1,105
Papago Reservation	0	724	268	1,480	0	759	185	1,945
Pine Ridge Reservation and Trust Lands, NE – SD	7	1,102	597	1,403	0	871	360	1,768
Port Madison Reservation	4	61	17	44	0	65	12	23
Puyallup Reservation and Trust Lands, WA	0	179	20	93	0	161	16	171
Red Lake Reservation	0	443	188	437	0	374	91	619
Rosebud Reservation and Trust Lands, SD	2	796	430	836	0	801	239	1,377
Salt River Reservation	0	526	117	341	0	503	98	545
San Carlos Reservation	0	763	405	844	0	493	158	1,565
Sandia Pueblo	0	106	12	21	0	77	3	40
San Juan Pueblo	0	243	58	147	0	262	21	181
Santa Clara Pueblo	0	211	40	128	0	208	35	246
Southern Ute Reservation	0	179	41	94	0	181	28	159
Standing Rock Reservation	0	488	274	607	0	430	181	754
Taos Pueblo and Trust Lands, NM	0	206	72	172	0	191	59	213
Tulalip Reservation	0	181	27	110	0	168	22	198
Turtle Mountain Reservation and Trust Lands, ND – SD	0	624	448	831	0	735	255	1,128
Uintah and Ouray Reservation	0	310	124	272	0	260	104	428
White Earth Reservation	0	290	136	416	0	285	54	537
Wind River Reservation	0	660	343	628	0	490	209	1,043
Yakima Reservation and Trust Lands, WA	0	711	329	742	0	696	128	1,137
Yankton Reservation	0	169	82	303	0	180	68	365
Zuni Pueblo	0	1,184	205	800	0	1,368	205	838

Source: Census of Population and Housing, 1990: Summary Tape File 3C on CD-ROM [machine-readable datafiles]. Prepared by the Bureau of the Census. Washington, DC: The Bureau, 1992. *Notes:* 1. Federal American Indian reservations are areas with boundaries established by treaty, statute, and/or executive or court order, and recognized by the federal government as territory in which American Indian tribes have jurisdiction. State reservations are lands held in trust by state governments for the use and benefit of a given tribe. The reservations and their boundaries were identified for the 1990 census by the Bureau of Indian Affairs (BIA), Department of Interior (for federal reservations), and state governments (for state reservations). The names of American Indian reservations recognized by state governments, but not by the federal government, are followed by "state." Areas composed of reservation lands that are administered jointly and/or are claimed by two reservations, as identified by the BIA, are called "joint areas," and are treated as separate American Indian reservations for census purposes. Federal reservations may cross state boundaries, and federal and state reservations may cross county, county subdivision, and place boundaries. For reservations that cross state boundaries, only the portion of the reservations in a given state is shown in the data products for that state; the entire reservations are shown in data products for the United States. 2. Trust lands are property associated with a particular American Indian reservation or tribe, held in trust by the federal government. Trust lands may be held in trust either for a tribe (tribal trust lands) or for an individual member of a tribe (individual trust land). Trust lands recognized for the 1990 census comprised all tribal trust lands and inhabited individual trust lands located outside of a reservation boundary. As with other American Indian areas, trust lands may be located in more than one state. Only the trust lands in a given state are shown in the data products for that state; all trust lands associated with a reservation or tribe are shown in data products for the United States. The Census Bureau first reported data for tribal trust lands for the 1980 census.

★ 546 ★

Employment

Labor Force Status of Families, for Major Tribal Groups, 1990: Abenaki-Menominee - Part I

Data, shown for selected tribes with at least 100 persons, are based on sample and are subject to sampling variability.

		Married-couple families							
		Husband employed or in Armed Forces				Husband unemployed			
	Total	Total	Wife employed or in Armed Forces	Wife unemployed	Wife not in labor force	Total	Wife employed or in Armed Forces	Wife unemployed	Wife not in labor force
American Indian	295,600	212,558	132,208	10,337	70,013	20,365	9,815	2,816	7,734
Abenaki	335	226	129	19	78	48	31	-	17
Alaska Native	170	82	11	21	50	38	8	2	28
Alaskan Athabaskans	1,251	684	458	16	210	187	85	31	71
Algonquian	326	263	197	11	55	18	12	6	-
Apache	8,234	6,002	3,413	389	2,200	775	325	139	311
Arapaho	991	660	385	33	242	145	23	27	95
Arikara	188	108	75	19	14	54	13	3	38
Assinibone	770	529	323	39	167	91	42	9	40
Bannock	23	13	13	-	-	-	-	-	-
Blackfoot	6,354	4,708	3,502	175	1,481	617	302	91	224
Brotherton	110	86	33	14	39	2	2	-	-
Caddo	425	291	198	5	88	18	-	-	18
Cahuilla	166	112	51	5	56	11	-	8	3
California tribes	259	186	103	16	67	19	19	-	-
Canadian Indian	508	364	271	16	77	42	25	-	17
Central American Indian	221	180	95	19	66	11	-	-	11
French American Indian	164	140	94	15	31	5	5	-	-
Mexican American Indian	1,589	1,284	720	67	497	107	36	23	48
South American Indian	323	271	191	29	51	-	-	-	-
Spanish American Indian	473	347	172	34	141	33	13	2	18
Catawba	223	190	114	3	73	16	10	-	6
Cayuse	15	15	5	-	10	-	-	-	-
Chehalis	57	38	17	2	19	11	11	-	-
Chemakuan	93	59	25	-	34	9	6	-	3
Chemehuevi	72	49	27	-	22	2	2	-	-
Cherokee	72,108	54,085	34,583	2,280	17,222	3,529	1,923	325	1,281
Cherokee Shawnee	142	123	94	-	29	-	-	-	-
Cheyenne	1,706	1,191	747	81	363	166	80	33	53
Cheyenne-Arapaho	219	161	122	11	28	31	8	8	15
Chickahominy	159	132	76	10	46	-	-	-	-
Chickasaw	4,447	3,205	2,128	82	995	211	100	15	96
Chinook	118	103	93	5	5	6	6	-	-
Chippewa	14,633	10,187	6,768	473	2,946	1,479	764	165	550
Chitimacha	147	111	50	-	61	-	-	-	-
Choctaw	16,440	12,182	7,355	471	4,356	867	460	104	303
Chumash	494	424	275	4	145	15	-	3	12
Coeur d'Alene	116	70	33	12	25	3	2	-	1
Coharie	258	184	136	-	48	-	-	-	-
Colorado River	188	126	104	9	13	13	10	3	-
Colville	887	619	357	24	238	104	47	24	33
Comanche	2,107	1,527	959	57	511	203	128	25	50
Coos	16	16	14	-	2	-	-	-	-
Coquilles	61	50	44	6	-	3	-	3	-
Costanoan	148	100	74	11	15	25	25	-	-
Coushatta	253	186	106	20	60	6	-	-	6
Cowlitz	168	120	97	-	23	-	-	-	-
Cree	1,137	786	523	45	218	112	36	30	46
Creek	8,458	6,577	4,140	167	2,270	268	109	34	125
Croatan	63	59	49	-	10	-	-	-	-
Crow	1,497	942	431	99	412	253	83	92	78
Cupeno	71	46	26	2	18	12	3	-	9
Delaware	1,994	1,533	1,069	92	372	34	22	5	7
Diegueno	305	206	125	2	79	38	13	3	22
Eastern tribes	719	532	328	63	141	41	25	-	16

[Continued]

★ 546 ★

Labor Force Status of Families, for Major Tribal Groups, 1990: Abenaki-Menominee - Part I
[Continued]

		Married-couple families							
		Husband employed or in Armed Forces				Husband unemployed			
	Total	Total	Wife employed or in Armed Forces	Wife unemployed	Wife not in labor force	Total	Wife employed or in Armed Forces	Wife unemployed	Wife not in labor force
Fort Berthold	156	116	52	16	48	14	-	2	12
Fort Hall	441	231	122	21	88	97	36	22	39
Gabrieleno	72	64	31	5	28	2	2	-	-
Gila River	203	121	73	-	48	53	22	6	25
Grand Ronde	181	130	92	5	33	18	14	-	4
Gros Ventres	323	218	147	-	71	36	21	7	8
Haida	237	189	104	17	68	13	5	4	4
Haliwa	540	378	251	8	119	14	10	-	4
Hidatsa	130	84	52	7	25	19	12	-	7
Hoopa	312	215	148	8	59	38	24	7	7
Houma	1,365	1,002	332	63	607	45	12	-	33
Iowa	292	222	176	5	41	2	2	-	-
Iroquois	8,767	6,394	4,282	256	1,856	584	286	74	224
Juaneno	350	272	211	10	51	28	24	-	4
Kalispel	7	3	3	-	-	2	-	-	2
Karok	564	427	13	171	11	20	11	-	9
Kaw	231	150	96	-	54	10	-	7	3
Kickapoo	360	271	179	14	78	20	13	-	7
Kiowa	1,308	962	601	54	307	86	55	16	15
Klallam	193	135	80	4	51	-	-	-	-
Klamath	327	256	135	25	96	29	21	2	6
Konkaw	40	36	4	-	32	4	-	-	4
Kootenai	82	70	58	-	12	5	3	-	2
Long Island	43	24	16	-	8	4	-	-	4
Luiseno	414	287	151	6	130	40	13	-	27
Lumbee	8,671	7,104	5,027	232	1,845	224	121	22	81
Lummi	360	201	115	11	75	41	31	-	10
Maidu	339	254	118	22	114	22	11	4	7
Makah	192	142	71	4	67	24	19	5	-
Maliseet	92	66	58	2	6	17	9	-	8
Mandan	123	114	56	-	58	2	-	2	-
Mattaponi	120	104	65	-	39	3	-	-	3
Menominee	911	645	405	31	209	113	50	16	47

Source: U.S. Bureau of the Census. *1990 Census of Population: Characteristics of American Indians by Tribe and Language.* CP3-7. Washington, DC: The Bureau, 1994, pp. 96-122.

★ 547 ★

Employment

Labor Force Status of Families, for Major Tribal Groups, 1990: Abenaki-Menominee - Part II

Data, shown for selected tribes with at least 100 persons, are based on sample and are subject to sampling variability.

	Married-couple families (cont.) Husband not in labor force				Female householder, no husband present			
	Total	Wife employed or in Armed Forces	Wife unemployed	Wife not in labor force	Total	Employed or in Armed Forces	Unemployed	Not in labor force
American Indian	62,677	18,150	2,158	42,369	117,790	57,265	10,172	50,353
Abenaki	61	15	-	46	131	40	13	78
Alaska Native	50	16	11	23	76	61	3	12
Alaskan Athabaskans	380	135	36	209	998	417	125	456
Algonquian	45	24	-	21	108	95	-	13
Apache	1,457	510	53	894	3,043	1,452	255	1,336
Arapaho	186	31	9	146	480	151	79	250
Arikara	26	6	-	20	135	68	25	42
Assinibone	150	54	9	87	392	225	10	157
Bannock	10	6	-	4	8	8	-	-
Blackfoot	1,029	405	54	570	2,564	1,249	272	1,043
Brotherton	22	8	-	14	5	-	-	5
Caddo	116	34	-	82	210	91	17	102
Cahuilla	43	9	-	34	86	34	8	44
California tribes	54	-	1	53	98	60	10	28
Canadian Indian	102	46	3	53	185	69	35	81
Central American Indian	30	6	-	24	68	51	-	17
French American Indian	19	-	-	19	100	53	5	42
Mexican American Indian	198	52	4	142	567	336	24	207
South American Indian	52	8	-	44	165	77	20	68
Spanish American Indian	93	36	-	57	239	115	15	109
Catawba	17	-	-	17	14	1	2	11
Cayuse	-	-	-	-	11	5	3	3
Chehalis	8	1	-	7	37	23	3	11
Chemakuan	25	3	2	20	48	30	3	15
Chemehuevi	21	3	-	18	45	25	4	16
Cherokee	14,494	4,363	398	9,733	20,492	11,021	1,586	7,885
Cherokee Shawnee	19	-	-	19	43	21	-	22
Cheyenne	349	137	33	179	685	271	66	348
Cheyenne-Arapaho	27	14	-	13	182	97	17	68
Chickahominy	27	18	-	9	80	43	3	34
Chickasaw	1,031	321	36	674	1,082	584	50	448
Chinook	9	5	-	4	37	27	4	6
Chippewa	2,967	1,072	132	1,763	8,305	3,603	778	3,924
Chitimacha	36	8	-	28	44	25	-	19
Choctaw	3,391	846	116	2,429	4,363	2,424	316	1,623
Chumash	55	22	-	33	259	142	24	93
Coeur d'Alene	43	22	-	21	65	43	-	22
Coharie	74	49	4	21	60	34	-	26
Colorado River	49	22	-	27	154	73	-	81
Colville	164	36	8	120	540	286	29	66
Comanche	377	129	22	226	631	332	66	233
Coos	-	-	-	-	-	-	-	-
Coquilles	8	-	-	8	21	15	-	6
Costanoan	23	6	-	17	54	48	-	6
Coushatta	61	27	9	25	59	28	6	25
Cowlitz	48	19	-	29	31	14	2	15
Cree	239	75	3	161	510	226	66	218

[Continued]

★ 547 ★

Labor Force Status of Families, for Major Tribal Groups, 1990: Abenaki-Menominee - Part II
[Continued]

	Married-couple families (cont.) Husband not in labor force			Female householder, no husband present			
	Total	Wife employed or in Armed Forces	Wife unemployed	Wife not in labor force	Total	Employed or in Armed Forces	Unemployed	Not in labor force
Creek	1,613	493	30	1,090	2,252	1,326	164	762
Croatan	4	4	-	-	21	12	-	9
Crow	302	65	17	220	451	120	107	224
Cupeno	13	11	-	2	36	19	4	13
Delaware	427	118	8	301	563	337	45	181
Diegueno	61	7	-	54	165	64	17	84
Eastern tribes	146	57	-	89	215	125	7	83
Fort Berthold	26	6	-	20	111	43	2	66
Fort Hall	113	29	-	84	202	109	27	66
Gabrieleno	6	-	-	6	56	28	11	17
Gila River	29	22	-	7	95	-	4	91
Grand Ronde	33	5	7	21	68	31	-	37
Gros Ventres	69	15	2	52	216	75	25	116
Haida	35	11	3	21	103	56	10	37
Haliwa	148	60	-	88	175	76	15	84
Hidatsa	27	10	-	17	141	51	15	75
Hoopa	59	21	-	38	145	58	15	72
Houma	318	79	9	230	284	85	54	145
Iowa	68	35	-	33	67	45	-	22
Iroquois	1,789	633	104	1,052	3,309	1,749	221	1,339
Juaneno	50	8	-	42	36	18	2	16
Kalispel	2	-	-	2	8	6	-	2
Karok	117	47	-	70	130	31	-	99
Kaw	71	12	-	59	33	27	-	6
Kickapoo	69	16	6	47	324	113	51	160
Kiowa	260	88	11	161	574	319	93	162
Klallam	58	12	2	44	97	66	7	24
Klamath	42	23	-	19	293	146	31	116
Konkaw	-	-	-	-	17	5	2	10
Kootenai	7	7	-	-	103	55	27	21
Long Island	15	-	-	15	50	21	7	22
Luiseno	87	24	-	63	179	107	12	60
Lumbee	1,343	417	9	917	3,020	1,568	193	1,259
Lummi	118	38	2	78	214	83	9	122
Maidu	63	23	-	40	168	63	17	88
Makah	26	10	2	14	136	71	20	45
Maliseet	9	7	-	2	59	37	2	20
Mandan	7	2	-	5	95	58	1	36
Mattaponi	13	-	-	13	16	8	8	-
Menominee	153	57	-	96	680	304	74	302

Source: U.S. Bureau of the Census. *1990 Census of Population: Characteristics of American Indians by Tribe and Language.* CP3-7. Washington, DC: The Bureau, 1994, pp. 96-122.

★ 548 ★
Employment

Labor Force Status of Families, for Major Tribal Groups, 1990: Miami-Yurok and Other Specified Tribes - Part I

Data, shown for selected tribes with at least 100 persons, are based on sample and are subject to sampling variability.

	Total	Married-couple families							
		Husband employed or in Armed Forces				Husband unemployed			
		Total	Wife employed or in Armed Forces	Wife unemployed	Wife not in labor force	Total	Wife employed or in Armed Forces	Wife unemployed	Wife not in labor force
Miami	872	739	543	40	156	4	4	-	-
Miccosukee	40	31	15	-	16	6	4	-	2
Micmac	436	378	274	3	101	28	22	-	6
Mission Indians	411	239	205	7	27	33	18	12	3
Miwok	457	341	251	11	79	37	22	-	15
Modoc	115	86	59	-	27	7	7	-	-
Mohegan	113	93	68	12	13	2	-	-	2
Mono	215	157	98	14	45	23	19	2	2
Nanticoke	296	202	128	6	68	-	-	-	-
Narragansett	312	188	160	14	14	31	20	-	11
Navajo	27,406	15,891	8,170	1,269	6,452	2,999	1,182	625	1,192
Nez Perce	547	390	225	28	137	58	39	2	17
Nomalaki	39	28	19	-	9	2	-	-	2
Northwest tribes	68	57	15	-	42	-	-	-	-
Omaha	314	183	73	14	96	34	14	12	8
Orgeon Athabaskan	66	44	26	8	10	7	7	-	-
Osage	2,233	1,805	1,199	35	571	88	55	-	33
Otoe-Missouria	215	149	88	6	55	8	4	2	2
Ottawa	1,299	992	661	40	291	97	35	29	33
Paiute	1,401	962	588	43	331	122	54	3	65
Pamunkey	46	36	11	-	25	-	-	-	-
Passamaquoddy	256	182	129	12	41	26	16	6	4
Pawnee	482	358	240	12	106	32	22	4	6
Penobscot	412	322	203	17	102	21	9	-	12
Peoria	344	290	192	6	92	2	-	-	2
Pequot	88	51	26	5	20	-	-	-	-
Pima	1,370	824	439	40	345	118	43	20	55
Piscataway	130	107	84	-	23	-	-	-	-
Pit River	222	186	139	11	36	20	3	-	17
Pomo	531	385	259	34	92	47	17	6	24
Ponca	338	200	117	5	78	61	24	5	32
Potawatomi	3,217	2,428	1,590	91	747	143	59	29	55
Powhatan	143	112	68	-	44	14	14	-	-
Pueblo	7,236	5,015	3,122	271	1,622	520	312	64	144
Puget Sound Salish	1,511	1,013	598	41	374	125	40	8	77
Quapaw	319	245	161	13	71	7	5	2	-
Quinault	327	207	127	5	75	26	4	11	11
Rappahannock	70	43	43	-	-	5	-	-	5
Sac and Fox	732	520	362	8	150	58	23	4	31
Salinan	81	69	56	6	7	12	-	-	12
Salish	667	517	345	16	156	26	15	9	3
Salish and Kootenai	414	289	191	4	94	23	9	2	12
Schaghticoke	28	28	26	2	-	-	-	-	-
Seminole	2,430	1,843	1,229	112	502	135	87	12	36
Serrano	46	38	11	-	27	2	2	-	-
Shasta	143	107	47	-	60	13	9	-	4
Shawnee	1,203	927	555	47	325	75	73	-	2
Shinnecock	188	128	110	-	18	7	7	-	-
Shoshone	1,467	1,020	645	17	358	119	49	23	47
Shoshone Paiute	208	134	99	4	31	28	11	2	15
Siletz	240	170	120	-	50	13	3	-	10
Sioux	12,291	8,473	5,559	395	2,519	1,145	519	196	430
Spokane	311	197	139	12	46	40	19	6	15

[Continued]

★ 548 ★

Labor Force Status of Families, for Major Tribal Groups, 1990: Miami-Yurok and Other Specified Tribes - Part I
[Continued]

		Married-couple families							
		Husband employed or in Armed Forces				Husband unemployed			
	Total	Total	Wife employed or in Armed Forces	Wife unemployed	Wife not in labor force	Total	Wife employed or in Armed Forces	Wife unemployed	Wife not in labor force
Stockbridge	406	314	196	18	100	5	-	1	4
Tlingit	1,622	1,089	689	54	346	198	99	35	64
Tohono O'Odham	1,328	758	346	25	387	123	28	27	68
Tolowa	61	51	32	8	11	10	10	-	-
Tonkawa	48	18	10	2	6	12	-	8	4
Tsimshian	305	212	119	17	76	15	10	-	5
Umatilla	134	102	50	20	32	19	5	5	9
Umpqua	93	85	38	5	42	-	-	-	-
Ute	1,090	811	565	23	223	90	44	5	41
Wailaki	139	77	50	6	21	16	16	-	-
Walla-Walla	30	14	5	-	9	-	-	-	-
Wampanoag	294	216	157	16	43	24	24	-	-
Warm Springs	238	166	103	2	61	27	3	6	18
Washo	138	84	64	5	15	32	17	-	15
Wichita	174	149	56	41	52	15	13	-	2
Winnebago	684	515	355	48	112	50	27	4	19
Wintu	404	288	179	20	89	40	13	1	26
Wiyot	58	33	8	2	23	-	-	-	-
Yakima	823	554	366	8	180	64	25	-	39
Yaqui	1,330	994	484	37	473	133	58	32	43
Yavapai Apache	55	32	23	-	9	10	8	-	2
Yokuts	343	208	130	12	66	20	6	3	11
Yuchi	91	54	41	-	13	5	-	-	5
Yuman	834	544	303	8	233	80	58	-	22
Yurok	583	407	260	45	102	83	58	3	22
Tribe not specified	3,034	2,256	1,287	127	842	124	54	7	63
Tribe not reported	26,638	19,664	11,397	1,227	6,740	1,395	679	174	542

Source: U.S. Bureau of the Census. *1990 Census of Population: Characteristics of American Indians by Tribe and Language*. CP3-7. Washington, DC: The Bureau, 1994, pp. 124-152.

★ 549 ★

Employment

Labor Force Status of Families, for Major Tribal Groups, 1990: Miami-Yurok and Other Specified Tribes - Part II

Data, shown for selected tribes with at least 100 persons, are based on a sample and are subject to sampling variability.

	Married-couple families (cont.) Husband not in labor force				Female householder, no husband present			
Group	Total	Wife employed or in Armed Forces	Wife unemployed	Wife not in labor force	Total	Employed or in Armed Forces	Unemployed	Not in labor force
Miami	129	48	-	81	190	120	11	59
Miccosukee	3	3	-	-	14	11	3	-
Micmac	30	13	2	15	187	77	38	72
Mission Indians	139	52	1	86	136	41	4	91
Miwok	79	28	-	51	231	108	11	112
Modoc	22	10	-	12	24	9	3	12

[Continued]

★ 549 ★

Labor Force Status of Families, for Major Tribal Groups, 1990: Miami-Yurok and Other Specified Tribes - Part II
[Continued]

Group	Married-couple families (cont.) Husband not in labor force				Female householder, no husband present			
	Total	Wife employed or in Armed Forces	Wife unemployed	Wife not in labor force	Total	Employed or in Armed Forces	Unemployed	Not in labor force
Mohegan	18	8	-	10	71	50	-	21
Mono	35	12	-	23	145	57	1	87
Nanticoke	94	24	2	68	94	69	11	14
Narragansett	93	16	8	69	256	147	15	94
Navajo	8,516	1,545	412	6,559	12,828	5,569	1,125	6,134
Nez Perce	99	28	4	67	313	185	34	94
Nomalaki	9	-	-	9	41	9	-	32
Northwest tribes	11	-	-	11	23	-	15	8
Omaha	97	20	13	64	461	180	52	229
Oregon Athabaskan	15	1	-	14	15	8	-	7
Osage	340	130	5	205	481	175	66	140
Otoe-Missouria	58	18	-	40	150	84	9	57
Ottawa	210	83	2	125	476	241	54	181
Paiute	317	74	6	237	913	480	61	372
Pamunkey	10	3	-	7	24	14	-	10
Passamaquoddy	48	16	-	32	151	86	6	59
Pawnee	92	25	7	60	233	156	22	55
Penobscot	69	10	-	59	101	65	7	29
Peoria	52	15	-	37	72	24	10	38
Pequot	37	28	-	9	46	38	-	8
Pima	428	110	28	290	1,304	422	138	744
Piscataway	23	13	-	10	22	12	-	10
Pit River	16	4	-	12	141	50	30	61
Pomo	99	6	11	82	390	124	59	207
Ponca	77	31	5	41	136	72	9	55
Potawatomi	646	177	11	458	814	467	64	283
Powhatan	17	-	-	17	65	59	-	6
Pueblo	1,701	523	54	1,124	3,449	1,975	203	1,271
Puget Sound Salish	373	99	7	267	698	332	68	298
Quapaw	67	21	-	46	46	30	9	7
Quinault	94	26	6	62	163	97	7	59
Rappahannock	22	2	-	20	35	22	-	13
Sac and Fox	154	46	-	108	456	216	50	190
Salinan	-	-	-	-	-	-	-	-
Salish	124	20	2	102	370	226	11	133
Salish and Kootenai	102	16	2	84	148	53	11	84
Schaghticoke	-	-	-	-	9	-	3	6
Seminole	452	165	20	267	1,045	590	63	392
Serrano	6	3	-	3	18	9	3	6
Shasta	23	6	-	17	42	22	7	13
Shawnee	201	65	17	119	321	170	24	127
Shinnecock	53	18	5	30	173	115	11	47
Shoshone	328	107	9	212	645	384	44	217
Shoshone Paiute	46	16	-	30	210	99	44	67
Siletz	57	25	-	32	55	37	5	13
Sioux	2,673	912	131	1,630	8,152	3,543	833	3,776
Spokane	74	36	10	28	126	51	19	56

[Continued]

★ 549 ★

Labor Force Status of Families, for Major Tribal Groups, 1990: Miami-Yurok and Other Specified Tribes - Part II

[Continued]

Group	Married-couple families (cont.) Husband not in labor force				Female householder, no husband present			
	Total	Wife employed or in Armed Forces	Wife unemployed	Wife not in labor force	Total	Employed or in Armed Forces	Unemployed	Not in labor force
Stockbridge	87	17	-	70	151	85	16	50
Tlingit	335	91	12	232	868	440	76	352
Tohono O'Odham	447	91	13	343	1,558	625	103	830
Tolowa	-	-	-	-	36	19	-	17
Tonkawa	18	5	-	13	22	3	14	5
Tsimshian	78	15	4	59	152	55	32	65
Umatilla	13	4	-	9	96	58	14	24
Umpqua	8	3	-	5	43	20	9	14
Ute	189	75	13	101	531	244	50	237
Wailaki	46	13	4	29	102	47	8	47
Walla-Walla	16	11	-	5	14	6	2	6
Wampanoag	54	18	-	36	205	126	-	79
Warm Springs	45	21	2	22	169	67	6	96
Washo	22	8	-	14	179	115	3	61
Wichita	10	10	-	-	74	28	8	38
Winnebago	119	39	6	74	582	301	45	236
Wintu	76	19	-	57	144	73	22	49
Wiyot	25	18	-	7	37	30	-	7
Yakima	205	73	-	132	610	240	65	305
Yaqui	203	26	-	177	572	246	24	302
Yavapai Apache	13	4	-	9	53	26	-	27
Yokuts	115	29	-	86	215	90	19	106
Yuchi	32	2	-	30	8	8	-	-
Yuman	210	68	2	140	548	228	66	254
Yurok	93	14	-	79	268	102	15	151
Tribe not specified	654	175	-	479	1,337	608	83	646
Tribe not reported	5,579	1,569	167	3,843	9,974	4,457	966	4,551

Source: U.S. Bureau of the Census. *1990 Census of Population: Characteristics of American Indians by Tribe and Language.* CP3-7. Washington, DC: The Bureau, 1994, pp. 124-152.

★ 550 ★

Employment

Employment by Industry, for Major Tribal Groups, 1990: Abenaki-Menominee - Part I

Data, shown for tribes with at least 100 persons, are based on a sample and are subject to sampling variability.

Group	Agriculture, forestry, fishing	Mining	Construction	Manufacturing	Transportation	Communications, public utilities	Wholesale trade	Retail trade
American Indian	24,771	8,045	60,164	115,051	30,059	18,683	22,703	115,083
Abenaki	42	-	90	137	36	17	62	114
Alaska Native	6	5	23	88	64	22	6	110
Alaskan Athabaskans	69	68	242	208	231	110	70	494
Algonquian	3	-	82	218	43	33	31	237
Apache	755	186	1,440	2,621	751	422	595	2,972
Arapaho	62	42	159	167	57	92	49	322

[Continued]

★ 550 ★

Employment by Industry, for Major Tribal Groups, 1990: Abenaki-Menominee - Part I
[Continued]

Group	Agriculture, forestry, fishing	Mining	Construction	Manufacturing	Transportation	Communications, public utilities	Wholesale trade	Retail trade
Arikara	6	2	17	58	8	8	14	44
Assiniboine	67	19	189	215	31	39	24	240
Bannock	-	-	18	6	-	-	-	-
Blackfoot	462	74	1,427	2,192	701	372	555	2,563
Brotherton	6	-	6	53	11	-	14	57
Caddo	25	2	108	105	61	40	43	163
Cahuilla	15	5	44	42	-	19	7	50
California tribes	19	2	58	103	23	4	12	72
Canadian Indian	39	2	120	245	45	31	56	240
Central American Indian	60	-	145	101	37	-	27	115
French American Indian	13	-	27	23	5	7	4	111
Mexican American Indian	395	-	556	879	310	93	290	943
South American Indian	13	-	20	181	31	28	28	293
Spanish American Indian	43	3	72	215	71	31	86	334
Catawba	14	-	26	91	22	21	24	55
Cayuse	6	-	5	23	-	-	-	-
Chehalis	2	-	7	10	-	-	-	13
Chemakuan	18	-	10	23	7	2	-	66
Chemehuevi	-	9	8	31	-	6	25	40
Cherokee	5,090	1,602	14,738	28,463	8,113	3,953	5,597	29,048
Cherokee Shawnee	18	11	39	57	19	-	21	50
Cheyenne	189	57	314	435	214	104	109	484
Cheyenne-Arapaho	20	7	28	102	18	7	20	89
Chickahominy	22	-	21	119	53	5	35	72
Chickasaw	300	229	656	1,252	384	278	332	1,212
Chinook	17	-	19	68	13	12	11	79
Chippewa	1,078	295	2,501	6,306	1,585	917	1,025	6,395
Chitimacha	-	37	12	52	14	6	-	30
Choctaw	1,290	573	2,688	5,954	1,329	961	1,265	5,050
Chumash	86	8	153	158	49	50	78	233
Coeur d'Alene	17	-	25	19	6	-	2	30
Coharie	14	-	57	100	33	-	17	88
Colorado River	40	10	18	39	14	19	17	61
Colville	237	15	151	357	53	21	79	286
Comanche	87	36	512	524	282	167	146	708
Coos	-	-	-	28	-	5	-	3
Coquilles	24	-	4	26	-	2	5	28
Costanoan	21	-	32	48	30	2	32	84
Coushatta	12	21	25	59	23	9	-	67
Cowlitz	30	3	13	65	37	28	11	76
Cree	127	11	210	292	133	39	51	480
Creek	600	230	1,544	3,270	815	481	723	2,741
Croatan	-	-	28	7	-	12	1	40
Crow	181	38	274	216	47	39	67	394
Cupeno	13	3	8	11	3	9	-	10
Delaware	112	53	318	754	219	132	172	725
Diegueno	20	5	90	52	41	37	9	142
Eastern tribes	27	-	178	367	85	60	31	184
Fort Berthold	12	24	14	37	24	17	7	39
Fort Hall	55	48	103	85	43	17	31	160
Gabrieleno	-	-	10	60	12	16	11	40
Gila River	31	-	17	50	-	7	14	57
Grand Ronde	14	-	42	82	21	32	7	61
Gros Ventres	34	13	37	37	32	4	20	90
Haida	33	-	28	88	31	15	26	145
Haliwa	15	-	105	568	18	18	22	138
Hidatsa	9	6	28	16	5	15	17	28
Hoopa	59	2	28	61	24	34	27	120

[Continued]

★ 550 ★

Employment by Industry, for Major Tribal Groups, 1990: Abenaki-Menominee - Part I
[Continued]

Group	Agriculture, forestry, fishing	Mining	Construction	Manufacturing	Transportation	Communications, public utilities	Wholesale trade	Retail trade
Houma	259	120	149	266	246	45	111	376
Iowa	23	-	49	96	36	2	43	94
Iroquois	453	89	1,863	4,059	1,202	551	717	3,696
Juaneno	-	-	54	77	57	36	25	102
Kalispel	8	-	-	27	-	-	-	-
Karok	100	3	97	327	20	4	10	233
Kaw	19	8	33	85	19	6	13	75
Kickapoo	38	11	88	272	54	72	6	168
Kiowa	146	16	105	419	126	84	70	648
Klallam	36	-	25	95	7	27	25	76
Klamath	51	-	58	164	23	13	35	157
Konkow	-	-	9	30	4	8	5	7
Kootenai	8	-	16	28	-	25	2	36
Long Island	9	-	6	32	8	-	18	7
Luiseno	28	5	149	142	36	43	-	163
Lumbee	978	32	3,135	7,967	616	380	386	2,409
Lummi	82	-	55	135	33	17	26	151
Maidu	41	3	90	113	28	13	32	132
Makah	102	-	22	64	7	2	19	94
Maliseet	13	-	33	45	6	-	-	50
Mandan	11	-	22	57	30	9	-	34
Mattaponi	8	-	14	50	21	10	7	32
Menominee	38	-	202	651	96	20	47	428

Source: U.S. Bureau of the Census. *1990 Census of Population: Characteristics of American Indians by Tribe and Language.* CP3-7. Washington, DC: The Bureau, 1994, pp. 153-181.

★ 551 ★

Employment

Employment by Industry, for Major Tribal Groups, 1990: Abenaki-Menominee - Part II

Data, shown for tribes with at least 100 persons, are based on a sample and are subject to sampling variability.

Group	Banking & credit agencies	Insurance, real estate & other finance	Business & repair svcs.	Private households	Other personal svcs.	Entertainment & recreation services	Professional & related services	Public administration
American Indian	7,099	20,790	32,638	4,925	21,959	12,163	155,516	55,869
Abenaki	-	6	42	-	30	-	104	40
Alaska Native	-	2	12	13	19	10	79	33
Alaskan Athabaskans	29	139	202	9	113	14	1,243	461
Algonquian	6	38	28	12	20	9	145	78
Apache	122	609	771	179	635	319	3,858	1,645
Arapaho	9	60	89	6	71	38	479	151
Arikara	4	2	45	-	28	4	172	68
Assiniboine	12	53	52	-	90	34	518	273
Bannock	-	-	-	-	-	-	42	13
Blackfoot	234	556	953	183	483	339	3,341	1,125
Brotherton	14	-	8	-	-	-	48	23
Caddo	17	9	56	2	59	39	249	88
Cahuilla	-	-	32	7	29	27	64	21
California tribes	18	-	23	-	16	17	130	59
Canadian Indian	23	48	40	32	43	23	263	52
Central American Indian	-	14	33	48	13	-	157	8
French American Indian	16	40	35	-	4	5	147	49

[Continued]

★ 551 ★

Employment by Industry, for Major Tribal Groups, 1990: Abenaki-Menominee - Part II

[Continued]

Group	Banking & credit agencies	Insurance, real estate & other finance	Business & repair svcs.	Private households	Other personal svcs.	Entertainment & recreation services	Professional & related services	Public administration
Mexican American Indian	44	99	250	102	172	127	956	151
South American Indian	38	28	135	50	79	8	318	48
Spanish American Indian	14	52	94	32	77	-	310	71
Catawba	-	2	15	-	-	5	120	18
Cayuse	-	3	-	-	-	-	13	12
Chehalis	-	-	4	-	-	7	30	25
Chemakuan	-	5	7	-	11	-	41	29
Chemehuevi	-	2	4	3	52	5	32	13
Cherokee	1,818	5,581	8,151	1,028	4,461	2,477	32,213	9,571
Cherokee Shawnee	13	11	24	-	-	-	100	24
Cheyenne	-	60	106	32	103	98	836	369
Cheyenne-Arapaho	6	12	13	-	22	29	176	87
Chickahominy	21	11	10	8	25	-	83	34
Chickasaw	115	405	328	48	298	172	2,106	758
Chinook	8	9	44	-	5	-	89	29
Chippewa	353	1,046	1,632	169	1,073	1,026	8,780	3,292
Chitimacha	4	7	6	-	-	26	49	9
Choctaw	305	1,135	1,278	265	898	463	8,009	2,552
Chumash	25	35	78	17	44	23	278	83
Coeur d'Alene	2	7	2	2	-	17	72	48
Coharie	-	13	26	-	12	-	154	73
Colorado River	5	24	16	-	9	3	107	96
Colville	4	81	77	12	67	51	430	354
Comanche	39	174	222	-	112	49	968	358
Coos	-	7	-	-	-	8	6	-
Coquilles	-	-	-	-	11	-	45	14
Costanoan	-	-	30	12	29	-	55	38
Coushatta	-	-	26	6	22	12	79	67
Cowlitz	10	14	2	-	2	18	80	7
Cree	23	94	129	9	123	63	862	318
Creek	194	735	772	61	567	339	4,317	1,568
Croatan	-	-	-	-	-	12	22	-
Crow	-	35	133	6	97	34	684	221
Cupeno	-	-	2	-	11	-	33	6
Delaware	118	129	186	23	94	134	915	172
Diegueno	18	31	44	6	32	43	107	41
Eastern tribes	6	60	92	11	90	26	328	125
Fort Berthold	-	8	8	-	9	3	194	31
Fort Hall	-	10	14	3	11	-	164	124
Gabrieleno	13	16	5	-	5	-	88	16
Gila River	-	7	8	17	-	-	60	60
Grand Ronde	3	13	-	-	19	2	59	45
Gros Ventres	-	12	20	8	18	33	216	152
Haida	5	10	34	11	29	6	123	82
Haliwa	18	18	68	8	6	15	130	52
Hidatsa	7	25	20	9	-	-	143	104
Hoopa	-	18	36	40	19	9	230	93
Houma	24	6	97	30	32	20	281	111
Iowa	7	57	37	4	18	41	135	21
Iroquois	279	848	1,141	151	555	502	5,039	1,581
Juaneno	11	37	47	10	27	34	137	38
Kalispel	-	-	3	-	-	-	19	6
Karok	-	34	34	5	16	5	221	109
Kaw	-	16	13	-	25	17	180	18
Kickapoo	4	16	31	29	37	14	314	97
Kiowa	37	96	155	13	45	39	887	303
Klallam	2	29	15	-	11	12	123	46
Klamath	11	4	40	7	53	15	291	62

[Continued]

★ 551 ★

Employment by Industry, for Major Tribal Groups, 1990: Abenaki-Menominee - Part II
[Continued]

Group	Banking & credit agencies	Insurance, real estate & other finance	Business & repair svcs.	Private households	Other personal svcs.	Entertainment & recreation services	Professional & related services	Public administration
Konkow	-	-	-	-	-	-	22	7
Kootenai	-	6	8	-	-	-	33	61
Long Island	8	-	14	9	-	-	83	15
Luiseno	2	26	44	2	22	37	319	99
Lumbee	228	343	698	83	274	81	3,370	764
Lummi	-	2	48	-	27	5	235	69
Maidu	-	14	35	11	19	18	166	67
Makah	-	9	27	4	12	2	153	48
Maliseet	10	18	7	2	-	-	104	12
Mandan	-	7	16	-	6	2	144	91
Mattaponi	-	42	3	-	9	-	28	13
Menominee	18	53	114	8	73	85	542	330

Source: U.S. Bureau of the Census. *1990 Census of Population: Characteristics of American Indians by Tribe and Language.* CP3-7. Washington, DC: The Bureau, 1994, pp. 153-181.

★ 552 ★

Employment

Employment by Industry, for Major Tribal Groups, 1990: Miami-Yurok and Other Specified Tribes - Part I

Data, shown for tribes with at least 100 persons, are based on a sample and are subject to sampling variability.

Group	Agriculture, forestry, fishing	Mining	Construction	Manufacturing	Transportation	Communications, public utilities	Wholesale trade	Retail trade
Miami	49	30	119	462	76	35	114	355
Miccosukee	5	-	12	-	-	-	-	19
Micmac	13	-	107	216	32	49	58	174
Mission Indians	7	-	51	125	46	31	81	118
Miwok	85	9	93	139	26	24	35	207
Modoc	10	-	17	42	13	12	24	60
Mohegan	24	-	40	51	45	15	5	77
Mono	51	6	55	102	23	-	16	83
Nanticoke	19	-	68	134	34	18	49	148
Narragansett	-	6	54	194	42	15	20	160
Navajo	1,383	1,995	4,914	5,762	1,660	2,461	1,300	9,366
Nez Perce	100	-	85	259	36	34	33	183
Nomalaki	-	-	13	14	-	-	-	7
Northwest tribes	11	7	31	58	18	-	-	107
Omaha	17	6	43	90	40	4	42	229
Oregon Athabaskan	9	4	2	33	12	-	-	26
Osage	195	171	290	635	172	167	186	734
Otoe-Missouria	6	6	52	76	20	16	14	66
Ottawa	77	19	272	743	136	79	69	553
Paiute	225	74	336	599	87	160	95	604
Pamunkey	2	-	-	38	6	2	4	27
Passamaquoddy	14	-	66	88	30	24	35	128
Pawnee	11	3	44	189	17	30	11	247
Penobscot	32	-	82	211	45	17	35	158

[Continued]

★ 552 ★

Employment by Industry, for Major Tribal Groups, 1990: Miami-Yurok and Other Specified Tribes - Part I

[Continued]

Group	Agriculture, forestry, fishing	Mining	Construction	Manufacturing	Transportation	Communications, public utilities	Wholesale trade	Retail trade
Peoria	25	4	49	99	29	21	47	67
Pequot	-	-	20	88	4	5	8	38
Pima	264	54	225	332	82	140	89	597
Piscataway	16	2	41	9	37	19	9	70
Pit River	32	-	39	117	25	11	26	68
Pomo	35	5	133	215	74	16	58	232
Ponca	10	12	52	111	26	2	13	92
Potawatomi	167	102	534	1,076	243	262	237	1,085
Powhatan	10	-	33	34	24	13	16	30
Pueblo	391	129	1,617	2,490	432	380	919	2,796
Puget Sound Salish	275	14	237	499	94	39	161	504
Quapaw	9	-	52	88	31	22	42	102
Quinault	73	-	47	125	39	23	55	98
Rappahannock	4	-	27	18	7	16	5	32
Sac and Fox	46	14	112	279	65	74	85	212
Salinan	-	12	22	7	-	7	-	25
Salish	94	11	138	347	31	93	60	252
Salish and Kootenai	63	2	55	84	17	30	46	98
Schaghticoke	-	-	14	15	9	-	-	9
Seminole	177	126	477	930	259	195	157	1,094
Serrano	-	1	3	13	10	2	-	23
Shasta	8	8	27	42	40	11	-	36
Shawnee	63	33	160	531	102	66	67	563
Shinnecock	20	-	37	77	26	24	41	89
Shoshone	148	159	394	416	93	64	81	451
Shoshone Paiute	50	29	45	66	51	23	8	95
Siletz	18	5	19	89	53	7	30	101
Sioux	1,259	152	2,633	3,954	1,256	837	866	5,007
Spokane	46	24	29	70	8	8	12	82
Stockbridge	21	10	63	206	44	15	45	167
Tlingit	384	17	283	671	284	120	106	933
Tohono O'Odham	440	99	349	327	66	94	29	679
Tolowa	6	6	5	14	8	15	5	32
Tonkawa	-	3	-	14	-	-	-	7
Tsimshian	41	-	36	132	70	34	9	104
Umatilla	46	-	39	56	12	3	10	60
Umpqua	-	-	42	97	-	-	-	38
Ute	130	37	176	199	72	45	47	313
Wailaki	17	-	33	30	24	9	19	98
Walla-Walla	3	-	7	10	5	9	-	16
Wampanoag	15	-	87	120	54	21	37	144
Warm Springs	56	3	9	143	2	19	12	46
Washo	17	3	64	80	6	33	11	87
Wichita	-	6	23	48	11	2	9	65
Winnebago	41	-	148	339	82	66	48	272
Wintu	16	-	88	163	58	38	19	164
Wiyot	-	-	20	26	30	7	9	60
Yakima	250	-	134	328	61	30	56	290
Yaqui	158	20	284	490	131	92	89	350

[Continued]

★ 552 ★

Employment by Industry, for Major Tribal Groups, 1990: Miami-Yurok and Other Specified Tribes - Part I

[Continued]

Group	Agriculture, forestry, fishing	Mining	Construction	Manufacturing	Transportation	Communications, public utilities	Wholesale trade	Retail trade
Yavapai Apache	14	2	15	6	-	9	4	37
Yokuts	80	8	97	90	14	3	17	112
Yuchi	-	-	18	5	16	8	-	11
Yuman	70	18	129	225	86	53	49	293
Yurok	58	3	115	256	50	9	46	289
Tribe not specified	244	34	760	1,424	457	242	379	1,343
Tribe not reported	2,485	495	6,656	13,491	3,572	1,804	2,610	12,670

Source: U.S. Bureau of the Census. *1990 Census of Population: Characteristics of American Indians by Tribe and Language.* CP3-7. Washington, DC: The Bureau, 1994, pp. 153-181.

★ 553 ★

Employment

Employment by Industry, for Major Tribal Groups, 1990: Miami-Yurok and Other Specified Tribes - Part II

Data, shown for tribes with at least 100 persons, are based on a sample and are subject to sampling variability.

Group	Banking & credit agencies	Insurance, real estate & other finance	Business & repair svcs.	Private households	Other personal svcs.	Entertainment & recreation services	Professional & related services	Public administration
Miami	62	57	90	14	101	38	504	113
Miccosukee	-	-	11	-	-	11	14	41
Micmac	22	20	84	12	53	-	223	110
Mission Indians	6	25	28	6	54	33	147	24
Miwok	18	55	35	25	64	23	282	94
Modoc	-	-	-	4	-	7	37	14
Mohegan	16	30	15	-	34	-	56	43
Mono	-	12	22	-	11	70	110	45
Nanticoke	-	26	26	7	16	5	201	31
Narragansett	11	45	21	9	29	31	317	104
Navajo	331	935	2,161	260	2,837	477	15,314	4,943
Nez Perce	19	64	60	12	61	2	323	233
Nomalaki	3	-	3	-	3	-	28	-
Northwest tribes	-	6	42	9	7	24	50	-
Omaha	-	30	53	4	23	17	314	125
Orgeon Athabaskan	-	-	-	2	2	-	39	6
Osage	53	166	137	32	178	71	1,072	402
Otoe-Missouria	7	7	46	17	51	46	158	47
Ottawa	47	74	185	32	116	45	576	190
Paiute	33	79	254	15	243	74	807	366
Pamunkey	3	7	-	-	-	-	92	14
Passamaquoddy	2	21	25	-	21	10	189	147
Pawnee	13	34	107	6	54	28	405	186
Penobscot	23	56	43	-	22	24	249	90
Peoria	14	15	17	8	11	8	140	55
Pequot	16	11	22	-	9	11	88	4

[Continued]

★ 553 ★

Employment by Industry, for Major Tribal Groups, 1990: Miami-Yurok and Other Specified Tribes - Part II
[Continued]

Group	Banking & credit agencies	Insurance, real estate & other finance	Business & repair svcs.	Private households	Other personal svcs.	Entertainment & recreation services	Professional & related services	Public administration
Pima	15	135	165	38	91	93	1,067	337
Piscataway	-	-	27	5	16	-	83	89
Pit River	4	12	51	5	31	-	116	38
Pomo	36	38	64	16	85	45	289	121
Ponca	7	27	59	-	64	20	228	105
Potawatomi	110	290	301	19	253	128	1,498	615
Powhatan	5	23	15	-	-	-	93	17
Pueblo	152	423	743	191	524	339	5,616	2,599
Puget Sound Salish	14	65	120	6	84	189	771	529
Quapaw	8	18	22	21	27	4	152	50
Quinault	3	12	22	3	20	6	168	98
Rappahannock	-	6	6	-	-	-	5	23
Sac and Fox	7	35	115	2	47	79	365	202
Salinan	-	-	11	-	-	-	54	5
Salish	-	52	48	-	50	11	504	220
Salish and Kootenai	-	24	51	-	-	6	200	107
Schaghticoke	-	5	2	-	-	-	17	7
Seminole	55	213	220	27	204	146	1,350	544
Serrano	-	-	-	-	3	40	6	2
Shasta	-	-	31	-	29	7	52	13
Shawnee	31	92	90	18	99	60	728	233
Shinnecock	4	22	64	-	18	33	314	46
Shoshone	41	86	229	28	151	123	739	446
Shoshone Paiute	-	14	24	12	27	20	169	126
Siletz	-	4	42	3	18	-	62	91
Sioux	242	1,010	1,423	219	787	716	8,324	3,682
Spokane	9	11	66	3	13	1	165	106
Stockbridge	22	31	60	-	27	56	194	72
Tlingit	34	100	140	11	132	73	1,104	644
Tohono O'Odham	19	123	205	94	116	84	1,096	358
Tolowa	-	-	10	-	-	-	21	17
Tonkawa	-	-	-	-	-	-	28	9
Tsimshian	3·	9	17	-	32	2	174	82
Umatilla	-	8	5	11	7	14	161	73
Umpqua	-	-	3	-	13	-	28	7
Ute	34	83	99	32	73	46	521	483
Wailaki	-	9	21	-	7	-	112	25
Walla-Walla	-	7	3	-	3	-	31	6
Wampanoag	3	30	53	-	26	13	275	91
Warm Springs	-	7	11	-	50	19	76	169
Washo	2	14	26	6	44	17	127	102
Wichita	5	-	7	-	7	11	79	54
Winnebago	28	82	106	10	50	127	560	209
Wintu	11	15	63	-	42	29	153	55
Wiyot	-	-	7	10	-	-	22	11
Yakima	-	41	69	20	24	20	519	279
Yaqui	-	55	191	27	128	77	572	241
Yavapai Apache	6	19	-	4	18	-	23	15
Yokuts	19	21	29	14	29	28	232	112

[Continued]

★ 553 ★

Employment by Industry, for Major Tribal Groups, 1990: Miami-Yurok and Other Specified Tribes - Part II
[Continued]

Group	Banking & credit agencies	Insurance, real estate & other finance	Business & repair svcs.	Private households	Other personal svcs.	Entertainment & recreation services	Professional & related services	Public administration
Yuchi	-	6	16	-	9	-	27	7
Yuman	21	63	72	13	66	75	481	391
Yurok	15	34	58	16	83	24	312	112
Tribe not specified	102	254	419	59	331	142	1,496	517
Tribe not reported	953	2,092	4,232	651	2,348	1,028	13,093	4,178

Source: U.S. Bureau of the Census. *1990 Census of Population: Characteristics of American Indians by Tribe and Language.* CP3-7. Washington, DC: The Bureau, 1994, pp. 153-181.

★ 554 ★

Employment

Employment by Occupation, for Major Tribal Groups, 1990: Abenaki-Menominee - Part I

Data, shown for tribes with at least 100 persons, are based on a sample and are subject to sampling variability.

Group	Executive, admin. & managerial occupations	Professional specialty occupations	Technicians & related support occupations	Sales occupations	Admin. support & clerical occupations	Private household occupations
American Indian	60,681	68,109	22,293	61,424	104,457	3,724
Abenaki	26	36	57	88	90	-
Alaska Native	14	16	29	35	81	13
Alaskan Athabaskans	367	392	60	290	829	9
Algonquian	130	74	49	134	140	12
Apache	1,497	1,455	557	1,578	2,737	130
Arapaho	178	159	99	127	214	6
Arikara	59	48	6	17	52	-
Assiniboine	208	261	48	136	298	-
Bannock	14	9	-	-	19	-
Blackfoot	1,400	1,548	560	1,336	2,129	124
Brotherton	27	24	2	25	64	-
Caddo	116	66	19	72	225	-
Cahuilla	17	36	-	28	53	7
California tribes	98	41	16	28	76	-
Canadian Indian	112	148	33	112	160	32
Central American Indian	44	39	19	20	64	48
French American Indian	78	67	3	49	78	-
Mexican American Indian	292	410	122	410	581	88
South American Indian	99	178	50	156	184	50
Spanish American Indian	88	66	27	117	271	32
Catawba	25	65	6	23	95	-
Cayuse	6	10	3	-	13	-
Chehalis	25	28	2	3	25	-
Chemakuan	2	7	24	6	31	-

[Continued]

★ 554 ★

Employment by Occupation, for Major Tribal Groups, 1990: Abenaki-Menominee - Part I

[Continued]

Group	Executive, admin. & managerial occupations	Professional specialty occupations	Technicians & related support occupations	Sales occupations	Admin. support & clerical occupations	Private household occupations
Chemehuevi	33	2	-	15	28	3
Cherokee	15,174	16,099	5,346	16,361	22,128	780
Cherokee Shawnee	96	25	7	25	51	-
Cheyenne	346	280	146	214	608	32
Cheyenne-Arapaho	44	55	21	6	97	-
Chickahominy	37	36	16	38	100	8
Chickasaw	932	959	356	733	1,405	18
Chinook	11	51	36	36	40	-
Chippewa	3,564	3,612	1,009	2,942	5,763	110
Chitimacha	18	26	20	23	31	-
Choctaw	3,112	4,028	1,294	3,381	4,848	135
Chumash	83	142	68	169	193	17
Coeur d'Alene	30	33	-	21	67	2
Coharie	52	91	-	53	97	-
Colorado River	37	30	13	25	126	-
Colville	221	233	63	181	327	10
Comanche	460	447	193	477	623	-
Coos	13	-	12	11	-	-
Coquilles	16	25	-	13	14	-
Costanoan	40	18	22	38	86	12
Coushatta	30	52	5	36	83	6
Cowlitz	24	45	5	40	84	-
Cree	266	341	142	213	486	5
Creek	1,861	2,102	763	1,669	2,949	40
Croatan	13	12	-	9	22	-
Crow	182	280	119	202	392	-
Cupeno	14	11	-	2	23	-
Delaware	547	522	132	543	558	23
Diegueno	62	56	7	50	146	2
Eastern tribes	200	119	33	136	244	11
Fort Berthold	24	88	10	6	68	-
Fort Hall	81	26	36	87	116	3
Gabrieleno	7	63	-	22	94	-
Gila River	22	26	7	25	52	17
Grand Ronde	29	24	-	52	63	-
Gros Ventres	72	108	24	62	128	-
Haida	48	94	26	72	62	11
Haliwa	34	75	14	68	160	2
Hidatsa	60	49	47	13	89	9
Hoopa	73	103	18	71	153	5
Houma	102	107	38	193	173	30
Iowa	77	70	16	68	104	-
Iroquois	2,031	2,437	824	1,963	3,829	107
Juaneno	57	37	48	87	174	-

[Continued]

★ 554 ★

Employment by Occupation, for Major Tribal Groups, 1990: Abenaki-Menominee - Part I
[Continued]

Group	Executive, admin. & managerial occupations	Professional specialty occupations	Technicians & related support occupations	Sales occupations	Admin. support & clerical occupations	Private household occupations
Kalispel	-	13	3	-	9	-
Karok	79	99	47	139	159	5
Kaw	37	113	13	47	107	-
Kickapoo	106	107	34	69	198	9
Kiowa	363	339	148	206	591	7
Klallam	40	30	18	46	90	-
Klamath	99	84	27	81	129	-
Konkow	5	7	-	-	21	-
Kootenai	21	33	25	25	21	-
Long Island	17	56	8	7	57	-
Luiseno	86	140	28	93	233	2
Lumbee	1,164	1,704	446	1,303	1,831	71
Lummi	50	74	27	55	185	-
Maidu	65	53	7	52	105	11
Makah	50	67	23	61	64	4
Maliseet	3	62	3	38	52	2
Mandan	28	73	31	15	113	-
Mattaponi	16	40	6	21	55	-
Menominee	227	209	50	199	440	8

Source: U.S. Bureau of the Census. *1990 Census of Population: Characteristics of American Indians by Tribe and Language.* CP3-7. Washington, DC: The Bureau, 1994, pp. 153-181.

★ 555 ★

Employment

Employment by Occupation, for Major Tribal Groups, 1990: Abenaki-Menominee - Part II

Data, shown for tribes with at least 100 persons, are based on a sample and are subject to sampling variability.

Group	Protective service occupations	Service occupations[1]	Agriculture, forestry & fishing occupations	Prec. prod., craft & repair occupations	Machine operators assemblers & inspectors	Transportation & material moving occupations	Handlers, equipment cleaners, helpers & laborers
American Indian	16,718	109,392	23,707	97,200	59,225	38,349	40,239
Abenaki	6	59	27	121	102	66	42
Alaska Native	-	120	15	30	62	31	46
Alaskan Athabaskans	63	756	79	380	126	126	225
Algonquian	9	78	5	203	74	35	40
Apache	600	3,153	649	2,112	1,066	1,214	1,132
Arapaho	20	437	61	271	136	47	98
Arikara	19	150	-	66	30	25	8
Assiniboine	63	326	58	202	120	90	46
Bannock	5	8	-	4	6	-	14
Blackfoot	515	2,460	434	2,222	1,115	1,003	714

[Continued]

★ 555 ★

Employment by Occupation, for Major Tribal Groups, 1990: Abenaki-Menominee - Part II
[Continued]

Group	Protective service occupations	Service occupations[1]	Agriculture, forestry & fishing occupations	Prec. prod., craft & repair occupations	Machine operators assemblers & inspectors	Transportation & material moving occupations	Handlers, equipment cleaners, helpers & laborers
Brotherton	-	24	4	33	8	23	6
Caddo	31	197	32	150	68	44	46
Cahuilla	13	85	12	21	32	27	31
California tribes	12	67	21	72	43	42	40
Canadian Indian	13	190	36	210	119	48	89
Central American Indian	9	159	98	112	46	21	79
French American Indian	12	89	13	60	3	5	29
Mexican American Indian	112	977	362	732	541	311	429
South American Indian	37	277	15	99	102	34	17
Spanish American Indian	19	322	62	122	172	90	117
Catawba	2	35	-	81	47	12	22
Cayuse	3	3	6	9	2	7	-
Chehalis	6	9	-	-	-	-	-
Chemakuan	-	65	13	22	16	21	12
Chemehuevi	7	80	-	33	9	10	10
Cherokee	3,660	22,667	4,574	23,779	13,366	9,699	8,271
Cherokee Shawnee	-	57	16	61	21	13	15
Cheyenne	110	567	135	411	235	246	180
Cheyenne-Arapaho	38	166	18	49	69	12	61
Chickahominy	5	68	22	34	59	47	49
Chickasaw	172	1,404	258	1,271	575	419	371
Chinook	5	84	17	53	39	16	15
Chippewa	961	6,816	1,101	4,426	3,325	1,774	2,070
Chitimacha	18	37	-	24	40	13	2
Choctaw	777	4,197	1,274	4,375	3,013	1,862	1,719
Chumash	67	169	26	167	100	92	105
Coeur d'Alene	7	28	11	16	15	2	17
Coharie	20	59	14	69	52	73	7
Colorado River	35	90	27	51	16	21	7
Colville	51	338	228	192	134	128	169
Comanche	165	741	88	512	304	204	170
Coos	-	-	9	5	2	5	-
Coquilles	14	30	15	25	7	-	-
Costanoan	7	69	24	47	26	9	15
Coushatta	19	49	11	93	11	18	15
Cowlitz	-	22	34	55	26	47	14
Cree	67	571	87	302	122	185	177
Creek	457	2,607	507	2,459	1,595	1,044	904
Croatan	-	18	-	24	-	12	12
Crow	43	426	162	269	126	141	124
Cupeno	-	2	13	19	5	7	13
Delaware	104	484	87	413	366	266	211
Diegueno	29	105	21	89	47	73	31
Eastern tribes	49	199	31	250	221	84	93
Fort Berthold	2	94	12	51	8	50	14
Fort Hall	20	114	52	79	101	72	81
Gabrieleno	7	21	7	32	28	-	11
Gila River	8	29	25	17	22	51	27
Grand Ronde	6	65	30	42	39	28	22

[Continued]

★ 555 ★

Employment by Occupation, for Major Tribal Groups, 1990: Abenaki-Menominee - Part II
[Continued]

Group	Protective service occupations	Service occupations[1]	Agriculture, forestry & fishing occupations	Prec. prod., craft & repair occupations	Machine operators assemblers & inspectors	Transportation & material moving occupations	Handlers, equipment cleaners, helpers & laborers
Gros Ventres	26	148	29	50	23	33	23
Haida	8	113	37	71	28	52	44
Haliwa	22	101	38	191	285	77	132
Hidatsa	8	41	16	45	9	23	23
Hoopa	13	134	65	68	17	48	32
Houma	77	236	254	362	146	274	181
Iowa	5	111	31	67	40	38	36
Iroquois	455	3,365	414	2,849	1,936	1,206	1,310
Juaneno	7	71	7	57	46	32	69
Kalispel	-	7	3	21	7	-	-
Karok	57	111	122	98	95	115	92
Kaw	14	71	23	56	38	8	-
Kickapoo	5	265	61	132	124	73	68
Kiowa	88	565	99	334	211	117	221
Klallam	27	83	49	19	62	19	46
Klamath	35	181	58	108	68	48	66
Konkow	-	12	15	11	12	4	5
Kootenai	-	32	12	33	8	-	13
Long Island	-	33	-	7	-	17	7
Luiseno	16	133	60	153	55	81	37
Lumbee	327	1,899	1,060	4,592	4,726	1,242	1,379
Lummi	9	186	66	111	64	22	36
Maidu	18	148	50	138	36	80	19
Makah	18	73	92	35	35	29	14
Maliseet	-	39	13	36	33	12	7
Mandan	6	40	11	53	29	23	7
Mattaponi	7	15	14	23	30	6	4
Menominee	83	488	70	306	338	145	142

Source: U.S. Bureau of the Census. *1990 Census of Population: Characteristics of American Indians by Tribe and Language.* CP3-7. Washington, DC: The Bureau, 1994, pp. 153-181. *Note:* 1. Except protective and household.

★ 556 ★

Employment

Employment by Occupation, for Major Tribal Groups, 1990: Miami-Yurok and Other Specified Tribes - Part I

Data, shown for tribes with at least 100 persons, are based on a sample and are subject to sampling variability.

Group	Executive, admin. & managerial occupations	Professional specialty occupations	Technicians & related support occupations	Sales occupations	Admin. support & clerical occupations	Private household occupations
Miami	228	270	96	213	307	4
Miccosukee	23	5	-	5	25	-
Micmac	116	125	21	134	152	12
Mission Indians	112	62	31	61	155	6
Miwok	85	80	18	116	173	14
Modoc	7	15	5	20	56	-
Mohegan	40	24	12	36	96	-
Mono	21	32	12	92	116	-
Nanticoke	91	72	34	66	108	2
Narragansett	147	64	10	119	221	7
Navajo	3,481	5,561	1,693	4,572	8,305	245
Nez Perce	191	161	47	102	263	-
Nomalaki	3	9	-	-	7	-
Northwest tribes	41	24	6	22	31	9
Omaha	89	86	38	83	155	4
Oregon Athabaskan	14	2	-	6	14	2
Osage	661	717	176	563	583	32
Otoe-Missouria	49	44	43	90	81	17
Ottawa	191	240	118	293	424	25
Paiute	379	279	154	303	684	6
Pamunkey	26	52	2	27	14	-
Passamaquoddy	80	53	67	94	140	-
Pawnee	182	163	68	111	311	6
Penobscot	134	195	13	95	178	-
Peoria	53	50	45	74	82	8
Pequot	33	45	25	32	56	-
Pima	136	264	92	206	685	24
Piscataway	64	13	5	8	128	5
Pit River	2	36	39	45	92	5
Pomo	107	46	47	127	251	8
Ponca	76	84	40	52	127	-
Potawatomi	734	737	218	719	1,117	10
Powhatan	16	46	11	27	48	-
Pueblo	1,512	2,359	747	1,289	3,662	175
Puget Sound Salish	423	271	119	330	620	-
Quapaw	94	90	15	53	60	21
Quinault	72	57	29	47	199	3
Rappahannock	27	-	-	8	28	-
Sac and Fox	138	160	77	137	301	2
Salinan	16	-	9	29	7	-
Salish	178	265	50	133	287	-
Salish and Kootenai	117	60	25	47	119	-
Schaghticoke	-	4	7	9	19	-

[Continued]

★ 556 ★

Employment by Occupation, for Major Tribal Groups, 1990: Miami-Yurok and Other Specified Tribes - Part I
[Continued]

Group	Executive, admin. & managerial occupations	Professional specialty occupations	Technicians & related support occupations	Sales occupations	Admin. support & clerical occupations	Private household occupations
Seminole	564	608	294	644	934	17
Serrano	10	2	-	17	25	-
Shasta	32	14	5	34	56	-
Shawnee	298	363	126	316	421	16
Shinnecock	102	138	13	69	188	-
Shoshone	293	342	122	280	666	26
Shoshone Paiute	40	46	13	37	159	10
Siletz	27	53	8	40	106	-
Sioux	2,981	3,381	999	2,225	5,025	172
Spokane	121	74	30	60	77	3
Stockbridge	127	65	27	87	141	-
Tlingit	442	374	133	404	1,072	11
Tohono O'Odham	205	246	77	291	764	74
Tolowa	22	23	-	5	44	-
Tonkawa	5	10	1	15	2	-
Tsimshian	64	91	18	42	164	-
Umatilla	20	81	21	35	62	-
Umpqua	13	11	3	20	12	-
Ute	295	199	69	170	434	28
Wailaki	21	45	9	69	50	-
Walla-Walla	6	-	9	14	23	-
Wampanoag	101	128	50	90	117	-
Warm Springs	62	55	14	36	105	-
Washo	35	40	22	42	145	6
Wichita	46	21	14	63	68	-
Winnebago	170	251	29	139	381	1
Wintu	77	46	13	90	151	-
Wiyot	10	12	-	29	31	10
Yakima	158	252	85	146	442	10
Yaqui	154	240	90	114	359	18
Yavapai Apache	13	14	12	20	36	4
Yokuts	55	94	6	63	98	12
Yuchi	41	27	-	17	8	-
Yuman	160	145	48	184	471	13
Yurok	132	103	17	126	236	-
Tribe not specified	589	766	209	734	1,253	51
Tribe not reported	5,330	5,275	1,772	6,354	9,721	522

Source: U.S. Bureau of the Census. *1990 Census of Population: Characteristics of American Indians by Tribe and Language.* CP3-7. Washington, DC: The Bureau, 1994, pp. 153-181.

★ 557 ★
Employment

Employment by Occupation, for Major Tribal Groups, 1990: Miami-Yurok and Other Specified Tribes - Part II

Data, shown for tribes with at least 100 persons, are based on a sample and are subject to sampling variability.

Group	Protective service occupations	Service occupations[1]	Agriculture, forestry & fishing occupations	Prec. prod., craft & repair occupations	Machine operators assemblers & inspectors	Transportation & material moving occupations	Handlers, equipment cleaners, helpers & laborers
Miami	51	318	53	274	232	90	83
Miccosukee	2	19	6	21	-	2	5
Micmac	57	139	27	177	58	78	77
Mission Indians	3	57	7	121	70	68	29
Miwok	13	198	74	202	66	74	101
Modoc	13	40	18	13	13	19	21
Mohegan	12	106	24	32	36	2	31
Mono	33	74	37	82	36	42	29
Nanticoke	19	104	19	94	62	59	52
Narragansett	49	154	3	88	77	51	68
Navajo	1,030	9,963	1,227	9,187	4,142	2,653	4,040
Nez Perce	19	237	92	131	117	44	100
Nomalaki	7	15	-	3	14	13	-
Northwest tribes	4	90	18	64	45	14	2
Omaha	47	263	17	80	62	59	54
Oregon Athabaskan	1	49	12	9	16	8	2
Osage	107	460	188	547	300	149	178
Otoe-Missouria	26	75	4	52	87	41	26
Ottawa	59	515	91	492	397	168	200
Paiute	101	679	217	365	424	224	236
Pamunkey	14	14	2	-	38	6	-
Passamaquoddy	29	107	18	105	45	25	37
Pawnee	15	164	21	133	100	63	48
Penobscot	46	98	34	163	63	41	27
Peoria	10	77	12	78	53	36	31
Pequot	9	36	-	41	23	10	14
Pima	75	751	311	351	229	278	322
Piscataway	19	22	18	47	2	50	42
Pit River	7	118	32	53	83	30	33
Pomo	25	284	61	168	85	95	158
Ponca	42	138	5	114	78	26	46
Potawatomi	155	1,023	129	875	526	321	356
Powhatan	3	63	4	42	20	28	5
Pueblo	534	2,902	355	3,596	993	701	916
Puget Sound Salish	86	588	244	397	187	138	198
Quapaw	12	110	9	75	60	29	20
Quinault	12	105	51	66	67	31	53
Rappahannock	-	11	4	36	11	13	11
Sac and Fox	53	292	43	217	161	67	91
Salinan	5	15	-	55	7	-	-
Salish	26	299	107	238	140	63	125
Salish and Kootenai	22	107	62	107	41	36	40

[Continued]

★ 557 ★

Employment by Occupation, for Major Tribal Groups, 1990: Miami-Yurok and Other Specified Tribes - Part II

[Continued]

Group	Protective service occupations	Service occupations[1]	Agriculture, forestry & fishing occupations	Prec. prod., craft & repair occupations	Machine operators assemblers & inspectors	Transportation & material moving occupations	Handlers, equipment cleaners, helpers & laborers
Schaghticoke	-	8	-	11	2	9	9
Seminole	158	851	171	796	593	235	309
Serrano	-	14	10	11	4	10	-
Shasta	-	80	28	20	8	13	14
Shawnee	32	433	76	298	326	113	118
Shinnecock	33	132	19	49	30	19	23
Shoshone	95	593	140	433	226	230	203
Shoshone Paiute	7	156	54	91	38	41	67
Siletz	4	101	7	43	34	81	38
Sioux	898	5,868	1,234	4,006	2,201	1,470	1,907
Spokane	31	93	41	50	28	19	26
Stockbridge	40	181	22	143	100	47	53
Tlingit	80	864	358	505	241	236	316
Tohono O'Odham	86	780	474	351	200	239	391
Tolowa	-	3	6	-	11	8	17
Tonkawa	-	15	-	5	-	5	3
Tsimshian	7	96	28	112	37	37	49
Umatilla	11	111	31	47	26	37	23
Umpqua	-	43	22	28	48	9	19
Ute	106	355	96	314	99	120	105
Wailaki	16	73	19	52	10	25	15
Walla-Walla	-	19	4	4	9	5	7
Wampanoag	22	178	17	144	38	67	17
Warm Springs	39	101	42	27	55	32	54
Washo	19	136	22	82	38	13	39
Wichita	5	55	-	18	19	2	16
Winnebago	66	365	33	247	233	87	166
Wintu	6	206	31	122	79	64	29
Wiyot	-	36	10	10	7	32	15
Yakima	48	293	192	223	139	47	86
Yaqui	92	495	237	498	243	153	212
Yavapai Apache	3	27	6	18	8	-	11
Yokuts	30	215	49	172	46	44	21
Yuchi	-	9	-	-	5	16	-
Yuman	79	412	116	239	69	73	96
Yurok	44	274	109	182	102	54	101
Tribe not specified	193	1,303	236	1,118	681	538	532
Tribe not reported	1,771	12,279	2,398	10,567	7,211	4,287	4,871

Source: U.S. Bureau of the Census. *1990 Census of Population: Characteristics of American Indians by Tribe and Language.* CP3-7. Washington, DC: The Bureau, 1994, pp. 153-181. *Note:* 1. Except protective and household.

★ 558 ★
Employment

Employment, by Industry, for Persons Age 16 and Older in Selected Alaska Native Villages - Part I

Data are shown for the 50 areas with the largest populations, in number of persons.

Alaska Native Village Statistical Area[1]	Employed persons age 16 years and older								
	Agriculture, forestry & fisheries	Mining	Construction	Manufact., nondurable goods	Manufact., durable goods	Transportation	Communic. & public utilities	Wholesale trade	Retail trade
Akiachak	0	0	8	0	0	5	8	0	0
Akutan	15	0	5	378	0	46	9	2	14
Alakanuk	2	0	4	0	0	4	5	0	21
Andreafsky	0	0	5	0	0	17	5	0	11
Angoon	18	0	5	0	6	5	7	0	15
Aniak	3	0	2	0	0	31	14	0	30
Barrow	8	23	157	8	4	74	75	6	65
Bethel	15	2	62	8	5	227	77	18	219
Chevak	0	0	2	2	0	2	8	3	30
Copper Center	2	0	8	0	6	13	8	0	27
Craig	80	2	57	2	141	42	13	13	121
Dillingham	25	0	25	24	5	94	35	14	104
Emmonak	2	0	2	0	1	17	2	9	33
Fort Yukon	12	6	5	0	0	13	4	4	10
Galena	0	0	24	0	2	21	10	0	27
Gambell	0	0	0	3	2	7	10	0	11
Grouse Creek Group	4	4	17	14	22	18	4	6	51
Hoonah	58	0	7	18	30	33	3	4	32
Hooper Bay	4	0	0	5	0	5	5	0	33
Kake	30	0	20	5	55	12	4	2	27
Kasigluk	8	0	0	0	0	6	2	0	13
King Cove	35	0	16	119	0	4	0	33	32
King Salmon	6	3	14	0	6	46	10	0	17
Kipnuk	0	0	4	2	0	4	5	0	8
Klawock	11	2	20	3	92	25	0	2	32
Kotlik	0	0	0	0	0	4	10	0	12
Kotzebue	7	26	42	2	4	101	49	3	149
Kwethluk	0	0	4	2	0	4	1	0	2
McGrath	6	2	7	2	5	23	20	2	24
Mountain Village	0	0	1	0	0	6	0	2	14
Naknek	11	0	13	7	6	17	13	0	44
Ninilchik	532	155	419	174	250	291	132	126	635
Noorvik	0	12	0	0	0	3	1	0	18
Pilot Station	0	0	7	0	0	0	5	0	10
Point Hope	0	0	21	0	10	7	14	2	29
Quinhagak	0	0	4	0	0	4	13	3	16
St. Paul	44	0	32	71	0	12	15	6	12
Salamatof	27	36	18	9	15	7	4	13	50
Sand Point	76	0	15	180	4	18	8	13	27
Savoonga	0	0	2	0	0	7	2	0	7
Selawik	0	2	4	0	3	0	12	0	17
Shishmaref	9	0	0	0	1	5	4	0	11
Stebbins	1	0	7	0	0	4	5	0	15
Togiak	0	0	2	0	2	2	10	0	14
Tok	31	2	38	0	7	14	6	0	75
Toksook Bay	3	0	1	5	0	4	7	0	16
Unalakleet	0	0	0	7	0	26	8	0	24
Unalaska	147	0	228	668	67	379	84	121	401

[Continued]

★ 558 ★

Employment, by Industry, for Persons Age 16 and Older in Selected Alaska Native Villages - Part I

[Continued]

Alaska Native Village Statistical Area[1]	Employed persons age 16 years and older								
	Agriculture, forestry & fisheries	Mining	Construc-tion	Manufact., nondurable goods	Manufact., durable goods	Transpor-tation	Communic. & public utilities	Wholesale trade	Retail trade
Wainwright	0	0	38	0	0	12	11	3	18
Yakutat	18	0	18	50	13	18	5	8	24

Source: Census of Population and Housing, 1990: Summary Tape File 3C on CD-ROM [machine-readable datafiles]. Prepared by the Bureau of the Census. Washington, DC: The Bureau, 1992. *Notes:* 1. Alaska Native villages (ANVs) constitute tribes, bands, clans, groups, villages, communities, or associations in Alaska that are recognized pursuant to the Alaska Native Claims Settlement Act of 1972, Public Law 92-203. Because ANVs do not have legally designated boundaries, the Census Bureau has established Alaska Native village statistical areas (ANVSAs) for statistical purposes. For the 1990 census, the Census Bureau cooperated with officials of the nonprofit corporation within each participating Alaska Native Regional Corporation (ANRC), as well as other knowledgeable officials, to delineate boundaries that encompass the settled area associated with each ANV.

★ 559 ★

Employment

Employment, by Industry, for Persons Age 16 and Older in Selected Alaska Native Villages - Part II

Data are shown for the 50 areas with the largest populations, in number of persons.

Alaska Native Village Statistical Area[1]	Employed persons age 16 years and older							
	Finance, insurance & real estate	Business & repair services	Personal services	Enter-tainment & recreation services	Professional & related services			Public admini-stration
					Health services	Educ. services	Other prof. & related services	
Akiachak	0	0	4	7	6	69	10	18
Akutan	0	2	0	2	0	19	10	25
Alakanuk	2	0	1	0	10	39	0	24
Andreafsky	0	3	0	0	8	52	10	21
Angoon	2	0	5	0	4	83	14	15
Aniak	12	8	0	0	9	70	23	13
Barrow	20	30	29	4	72	233	62	377
Bethel	34	51	36	15	320	361	186	355
Chevak	0	2	4	0	11	66	10	12
Copper Center	6	7	2	3	12	23	12	17
Craig	10	9	26	3	14	35	32	31
Dillingham	18	36	27	5	145	127	61	96
Emmonak	2	0	0	3	2	49	8	6
Fort Yukon	0	0	4	0	12	51	18	31
Galena	3	0	2	0	13	47	8	40
Gambell	0	2	0	0	1	41	3	19
Grouse Creek Group	3	14	8	9	25	48	7	31
Hoonah	10	3	7	13	9	46	23	25
Hooper Bay	0	0	4	0	8	63	6	25
Kake	0	2	3	4	9	42	15	23
Kasigluk	0	0	2	0	7	45	3	2
King Cove	3	11	2	1	0	7	2	11
King Salmon	2	3	0	0	0	28	3	91
Kipnuk	0	0	0	0	5	29	2	2
Klawock	5	0	5	0	4	40	15	11
Kotlik	0	3	1	0	5	37	2	16
Kotzebue	11	16	36	11	90	163	125	184

[Continued]

★ 559 ★

Employment, by Industry, for Persons Age 16 and Older in Selected Alaska Native Villages - Part II

[Continued]

Alaska Native Village Statistical Area[1]	Employed persons age 16 years and older							
	Finance, insurance & real estate	Business & repair services	Personal services	Entertainment & recreation services	Professional & related services			Public administration
					Health services	Educ. services	Other prof. & related services	
Kwethluk	2	0	0	0	9	48	2	16
McGrath	0	2	0	0	10	65	13	38
Mountain Village	2	2	3	0	2	83	10	15
Naknek	3	2	4	1	5	78	19	21
Ninilchik	138	89	162	51	232	340	254	259
Noorvik	2	7	5	2	9	42	7	19
Pilot Station	0	0	3	0	10	41	7	13
Point Hope	3	2	2	0	2	46	10	16
Quinhagak	0	5	2	0	3	48	0	29
St. Paul	0	2	12	2	19	34	28	41
Salamatof	4	13	13	7	13	8	9	28
Sand Point	5	9	7	0	4	52	6	14
Savoonga	3	2	1	3	4	46	2	8
Selawik	3	0	0	0	3	27	8	20
Shishmaref	2	0	2	6	4	30	3	14
Stebbins	3	0	2	0	2	31	0	26
Togiak	0	2	0	0	6	42	3	17
Tok	0	4	36	2	6	78	19	52
Toksook Bay	0	7	0	0	4	28	0	27
Unalakleet	5	10	9	6	8	76	9	23
Unalaska	18	60	57	0	31	70	14	137
Wainwright	4	5	0	4	2	42	2	36
Yakutat	3	8	8	2	4	38	20	17

Source: Census of Population and Housing, 1990: Summary Tape File 3C on CD-ROM [machine-readable datafiles]. Prepared by the Bureau of the Census. Washington, DC: The Bureau, 1992. *Notes:* 1. Alaska Native villages (ANVs) constitute tribes, bands, clans, groups, villages, communities, or associations in Alaska that are recognized pursuant to the Alaska Native Claims Settlement Act of 1972, Public Law 92-203. Because ANVs do not have legally designated boundaries, the Census Bureau has established Alaska Native village statistical areas (ANVSAs) for statistical purposes. For the 1990 census, the Census Bureau cooperated with officials of the nonprofit corporation within each participating Alaska Native Regional Corporation (ANRC), as well as other knowledgeable officials, to delineate boundaries that encompass the settled area associated with each ANV.

★ 560 ★

Employment

Employment, by Industry, for Persons Age 16 and Older in Selected Tribal Designated Statistical Areas - Part I

TDSA[1]	Employed persons age 16 years and older								
	Agriculture, forestry & fisheries	Mining	Construction	Manufact., nondurable goods	Manufact., durable goods	Transportation	Communic. & public utilities	Wholesale trade	Retail trade
Apache Choctaw TDSA (state)	296	493	473	278	1,401	320	178	183	1,218
Chickahominy TDSA (state)	45	12	124	204	144	116	17	98	160
Clifton Choctaw TDSA (state)	0	12	27	12	5	10	0	10	23
Coharie TDSA (state)	2,374	55	3,335	8,206	4,487	1,106	926	2,197	8,396
Coquille Indian TDSA	6,997	247	9,091	6,401	22,670	6,702	3,422	6,419	37,263
Delaware-Muncie TDSA (state)	15	0	9	7	33	8	0	6	0
Florida Tribe of Eastern Creek TDSA (state)	0	0	9	0	9	10	0	0	24

[Continued]

★ 560 ★

Employment, by Industry, for Persons Age 16 and Older in Selected Tribal Designated Statistical Areas - Part I

[Continued]

TDSA[1]	Employed persons age 16 years and older								
	Agriculture, forestry & fisheries	Mining	Construction	Manufact., nondurable goods	Manufact., durable goods	Transportation	Communic. & public utilities	Wholesale trade	Retail trade
Haliwa-Saponi TDSA (state)	83	10	155	657	529	50	18	36	231
Jena Band of Choctaw TDSA (state)	489	803	1,547	754	1,555	905	993	756	4,170
Klamath TDSA	775	12	808	345	3,100	804	333	613	3,588
Lumbee TDSA (state)	807	22	2,456	5,904	2,457	315	309	275	2,362
Meherrin TDSA (state)	1,834	21	1,341	3,764	3,675	661	378	734	3,331
Mohegan TDSA (state)	172	0	939	833	1,862	315	327	287	2,010
Ramapough TDSA (state)	7	0	20	20	56	0	12	58	11
United Houma Nation TDSA (state)	6,046	14,242	23,247	17,269	21,405	22,553	11,284	19,935	65,032
Waccamaw Siouan TDSA (state)	42	0	230	287	128	52	48	0	145
Wampanoag-Gay Head TDSA	328	2	971	68	122	207	157	102	1,337

Source: Census of Population and Housing, 1990: Summary Tape File 3C on CD-ROM [machine-readable datafiles]. Prepared by the Bureau of the Census. Washington, DC: The Bureau, 1992. *Notes:* 1. Tribal designated statistical areas (TDSAs) are areas, delineated outside Oklahoma by federally- and state-recognized tribes without a land base or associated trust lands, to provide statistical areas for which the Census Bureau tabulates data. TDSAs represent areas generally containing the American Indian population over which federally-recognized tribes have jurisdiction and areas in which state tribes provide benefits and services to their members. The names of TDSAs delineated by state-recognized tribes are followed by "(state)." The Census Bureau did not recognize TDSAs before the 1990 census.

★ 561 ★

Employment

Employment, by Industry, for Persons Age 16 and Older in Selected Tribal Designated Statistical Areas - Part II

Tribal Designated Statistical Area[1]	Employed persons age 16 years and older				Professional & related services			Public administration
	Finance, insurance & real estate	Business & repair services	Personal services	Entertainment & recreation services	Health services	Educ. services	Other prof. & related services	
Apache Choctaw TDSA (state)	266	264	239	51	517	822	226	292
Chickahominy TDSA (state)	101	34	47	0	80	86	96	107
Clifton Choctaw TDSA (state)	5	0	10	0	9	0	0	17
Coharie TDSA (state)	1,849	1,590	1,400	351	4,519	4,141	2,179	2,530
Coquille Indian TDSA	8,530	7,660	6,278	2,853	14,661	18,189	11,735	6,497
Delaware-Muncie TDSA (state)	20	10	0	0	0	0	0	26
Florida Tribe of Eastern Creek TDSA (state)	0	0	0	0	0	0	0	0
Haliwa-Saponi TDSA (state)	45	71	46	11	92	140	46	83
Jena Band of Choctaw TDSA (state)	1,108	904	625	171	3,201	2,853	1,103	1,234
Klamath TDSA	757	629	566	227	1,162	1,574	829	723
Lumbee TDSA (state)	388	462	403	109	830	1,935	655	726
Meherrin TDSA (state)	561	536	647	64	1,205	2,287	853	999
Mohegan TDSA (state)	707	418	283	71	1,193	765	868	643
Ramapough TDSA (state)	16	23	0	0	14	44	13	4
United Houma Nation TDSA (state)	23,082	18,623	11,271	3,970	28,868	27,033	19,808	15,110
Waccamaw Siouan TDSA (state)	5	26	5	0	74	67	37	40
Wampanoag-Gay Head TDSA	434	220	292	68	446	313	540	261

Source: Census of Population and Housing, 1990: Summary Tape File 3C on CD-ROM [machine-readable datafiles]. Prepared by the Bureau of the Census. Washington, DC: The Bureau, 1992. *Notes:* 1. Tribal designated statistical areas (TDSAs) are areas, delineated outside Oklahoma by federally- and state-recognized tribes without a land base or associated trust lands, to provide statistical areas for which the Census Bureau tabulates data. TDSAs represent areas generally containing the American Indian population over which federally-recognized tribes have jurisdiction and areas in which state tribes provide benefits and services to their members. The names of TDSAs delineated by state-recognized tribes are followed by "(state)." The Census Bureau did not recognize TDSAs before the 1990 census.

★ 562 ★

Employment

Employment, by Industry, for Persons Age 16 and Older in Selected Tribal Jurisdiction Statistical Areas - Part I

TJSA[1]	Employed persons age 16 years and older								
	Agriculture, forestry & fisheries	Mining	Construc-tion	Manufact., nondurable goods	Manufact., durable goods	Transpor-tation	Communic. & public utilities	Wholesale trade	Retail trade
Absentee Shawnee-Citizens									
Band of Potawatomi TJSA	899	674	2,593	1,298	4,370	1,957	1,008	1,626	5,856
Caddo-Wichita-Delaware TJSA	635	109	202	102	238	88	102	132	469
Cherokee TJSA	7,276	4,558	10,832	11,162	20,794	9,785	4,341	5,978	26,865
Cheyenne-Arapaho TJSA	5,611	3,582	3,959	2,968	4,643	2,908	2,068	2,879	11,578
Chickasaw TJSA	5,538	7,306	6,485	7,754	8,203	3,825	2,514	3,423	17,172
Choctaw TJSA	4,719	1,576	5,319	5,456	7,635	2,990	2,135	2,569	12,560
Creek TJSA	4,868	8,797	16,053	13,692	33,411	17,066	8,691	15,787	51,805
Iowa TJSA	164	84	119	119	100	79	62	53	180
Kaw TJSA	182	447	218	1,065	506	164	94	262	1,008
Kiowa-Comanche-Apache-									
Fort Sill Apache TJSA	4,603	925	3,434	4,709	2,384	2,866	1,887	1,846	13,579
Otoe-Missouria TJSA	106	45	128	35	172	46	28	43	141
Pawnee TJSA	255	342	454	326	741	331	252	242	1,109
Sac and Fox TJSA	879	620	1,201	1,182	2,016	805	472	555	3,889
Seminole TJSA	290	615	381	915	559	260	195	231	1,347
Tonkawa TJSA	278	227	256	558	633	159	124	148	808
Creek-Seminole									
Joint Area TJSA	43	46	65	88	40	30	13	5	111
Iowa-Sac and Fox									
Joint Area TJSA	21	0	26	37	39	5	0	0	49

Source: Census of Population and Housing, 1990: Summary Tape File 3C on CD-ROM [machine-readable datafiles]. Prepared by the Bureau of the Census. Washington, DC: The Bureau, 1992. *Notes:* 1. Tribal jurisdiction statistical areas (TJSAs) are areas, delineated by federally recognized tribes in Oklahoma without a reservation, for which the Census Bureau tabulates data. TJSAs represent areas generally containing the American Indian population over which one or more tribal governments have jurisdiction. If tribal officials delineated adjacent TJSAs so that they include some duplicate territory, the overlap area is called a "joint use area," which is treated as a separate TJSA for census purposes.

★ 563 ★

Employment

Employment, by Industry, for Persons Age 16 and Older in Selected Tribal Jurisdiction Statistical Areas - Part II

TJSA[1]	Employed persons age 16 years and older							
	Finance, insurance & real estate	Business & repair services	Personal services	Enter-tainment & recreation services	Professional & related services			Public admini-stration
					Health services	Educ. services	Other prof. & related services	
Absentee Shawnee-Citizens								
Band of Potawatomi TJSA	1,881	1,667	848	405	2,838	3,309	1,930	5,976
Caddo-Wichita-Delaware TJSA	124	96	101	23	195	325	145	112
Cherokee TJSA	7,129	6,813	5,244	1,808	13,167	14,301	8,118	6,343
Cheyenne-Arapaho TJSA	3,519	2,758	2,023	589	5,464	5,825	3,489	3,767
Chickasaw TJSA	4,552	3,330	3,139	1,059	8,979	10,022	5,396	5,512
Choctaw TJSA	2,500	2,634	2,280	691	6,238	7,846	3,436	5,150
Creek TJSA	19,949	15,262	9,062	3,737	25,325	22,532	22,436	9,590

[Continued]

★ 563 ★

Employment, by Industry, for Persons Age 16 and Older in Selected Tribal Jurisdiction Statistical Areas - Part II
[Continued]

TJSA[1]	Employed persons age 16 years and older							
	Finance, insurance & real estate	Business & repair services	Personal services	Entertainment & recreation services	Professional & related services			Public administration
					Health services	Educ. services	Other prof. & related services	
Iowa TJSA	70	74	38	40	69	237	76	90
Kaw TJSA	300	128	117	162	408	432	398	242
Kiowa-Comanche-Apache-Fort Sill Apache TJSA	3,379	2,636	2,501	620	6,738	7,409	4,351	7,103
Otoe-Missouria TJSA	43	27	40	28	76	125	35	55
Pawnee TJSA	306	239	187	83	556	443	316	380
Sac and Fox TJSA	1,101	683	592	233	1,768	1,894	1,132	1,624
Seminole TJSA	306	365	212	109	714	794	325	671
Tonkawa TJSA	238	132	149	44	409	514	214	179
Creek-Seminole Joint Area TJSA	30	12	9	8	91	104	33	65
Iowa-Sac and Fox Joint Area TJSA	51	18	7	2	24	49	6	39

Source: Census of Population and Housing, 1990: Summary Tape File 3C on CD-ROM [machine-readable datafiles]. Prepared by the Bureau of the Census. Washington, DC: The Bureau, 1992. *Notes:* 1. Tribal jurisdiction statistical areas (TJSAs) are areas, delineated by federally recognized tribes in Oklahoma without a reservation, for which the Census Bureau tabulates data. TJSAs represent areas generally containing the American Indian population over which one or more tribal governments have jurisdiction. If tribal officials delineated adjacent TJSAs so that they include some duplicate territory, the overlap area is called a "joint use area," which is treated as a separate TJSA for census purposes.

★ 564 ★

Employment

Employment, by Industry, for Persons Age 16 and Older on Selected Reservations and Trust Lands - Part I

Data are shown for the 50 areas with the largest populations, in number of persons.

American Indian Reservation and Trust Lands[1,2]	Employed persons age 16 years and older								
	Agriculture, forestry & fisheries	Mining	Construction	Manufact., nondurable goods	Manufact., durable goods	Transportation	Communic. & public utilities	Wholesale trade	Retail trade
Agua Caliente Reservation	101	19	562	143	282	265	199	156	1,780
Allegany Reservation	21	1	192	144	523	104	61	51	525
Blackfeet Reservation	337	2	181	42	85	46	23	8	211
Cheyenne River Reservation	605	2	213	13	7	65	56	34	282
Coeur d'Alene Reservation and Trust Lands, ID	275	34	161	39	384	83	29	76	349
Colorado River Reservation	452	44	180	38	133	75	65	90	643
Colville Reservation	363	6	162	23	246	61	52	71	305
Crow Reservation and Trust Lands, MT	336	41	84	16	40	36	29	31	239
Eastern Cherokee Reservation	91	0	317	388	138	40	55	11	261
Flathead Reservation	1,140	4	645	169	736	199	250	194	1,350
Fort Apache Reservation	187	8	190	6	404	0	40	14	226
Fort Berthold Reservation	233	75	118	27	92	33	78	23	216
Fort Hall Reservation and Trust Lands, ID	204	59	138	230	51	137	22	31	297
Fort Peck Reservation	585	29	163	224	145	151	81	101	601

[Continued]

★ 564 ★

Employment, by Industry, for Persons Age 16 and Older on Selected Reservations and Trust Lands - Part I

[Continued]

American Indian Reservation and Trust Lands[1,2]	Employed persons age 16 years and older								
	Agriculture, forestry & fisheries	Mining	Construc-tion	Manufact., nondurable goods	Manufact., durable goods	Transpor-tation	Communic. & public utilities	Wholesale trade	Retail trade
Gila River Reservation	289	16	108	43	119	31	74	51	270
Hopi Reservation and Trust Lands, AZ	44	35	122	11	96	18	17	10	222
Isabella Reservation and Trust Lands, MI	322	298	624	457	791	282	111	346	2,189
Laguna Pueblo and Trust Lands, NM	22	17	106	9	266	40	16	15	72
Lake Traverse (Sisseton) Reservation	1,038	1	250	240	57	133	41	103	628
Leech Lake Reservation	174	3	189	73	248	70	37	32	399
Mississippi Choctaw Reservation and Trust Lands, MS	55	0	59	160	367	50	0	26	116
Muckleshoot Reservation and Trust Lands, WA	34	2	136	50	371	76	28	78	261
Navajo Reservation and Trust Lands, AZ–NM–UT	769	1,453	2,595	352	1,093	852	1,323	562	4,024
Nez Perce Reservation	1,036	19	394	143	992	186	70	171	783
Northern Cheyenne Reservation and Trust Lands, MT–SD	57	12	103	8	37	38	57	13	61
Omaha Reservation	314	3	75	90	104	60	13	66	279
Oneida (West) Reservation	288	4	507	1,243	706	502	275	480	1,631
Osage Reservation	680	1,179	1,202	1,127	1,920	876	573	842	2,567
Papago Reservation	119	51	152	20	0	23	91	0	201
Pine Ridge Reservation and Trust Lands, NE–SD	229	10	167	23	27	70	43	30	217
Port Madison Reservation	79	3	264	56	175	89	47	45	364
Puyallup Reservation and Trust Lands, WA	375	13	955	697	2,273	1,123	289	918	2,398
Red Lake Reservation	52	0	30	27	76	25	4	8	52
Rosebud Reservation and Trust Lands, SD	343	11	210	36	13	77	62	19	189
Salt River Reservation	71	45	98	12	66	12	34	48	214
San Carlos Reservation	138	54	95	7	42	21	54	7	137
Sandia Pueblo	39	9	218	47	205	45	54	50	270
San Juan Pueblo	77	8	223	11	121	80	43	36	313
Santa Clara Pueblo	59	3	407	39	139	126	109	63	619
Southern Ute Reservation	387	58	325	75	103	156	134	118	568
Standing Rock Reservation	657	0	86	25	8	91	25	29	204
Taos Pueblo and Trust Lands, NM	41	23	218	85	71	40	44	53	474
Tulalip Reservation	83	9	327	117	682	116	92	116	478
Turtle Mountain Reservation and Trust Lands, ND–SD	44	0	115	56	208	66	11	10	180
Uintah and Ouray Reservation	727	436	407	180	177	304	202	136	898
White Earth Reservation	458	5	219	113	108	145	51	66	406
Wind River Reservation	722	419	754	323	375	369	191	222	1,528
Yakima Reservation and Trust Lands, WA	2,722	7	330	595	498	413	207	417	1,224

[Continued]

★ 564 ★

Employment, by Industry, for Persons Age 16 and Older on Selected Reservations and Trust Lands - Part I

[Continued]

American Indian Reservation and Trust Lands[1,2]	Employed persons age 16 years and older								
	Agriculture, forestry & fisheries	Mining	Construc-tion	Manufact., nondurable goods	Manufact., durable goods	Transpor-tation	Communic. & public utilities	Wholesale trade	Retail trade
Yankton Reservation	757	4	155	49	37	66	28	56	294
Zuni Pueblo	24	10	150	7	510	21	22	540	436

Source: Census of Population and Housing, 1990: Summary Tape File 3C on CD-ROM [machine-readable datafiles]. Prepared by the Bureau of the Census. Washington, DC: The Bureau, 1992. *Notes:* 1. Federal American Indian reservations are areas with boundaries established by treaty, statute, and/or executive or court order, and recognized by the federal government as territory in which American Indian tribes have jurisdiction. State reservations are lands held in trust by state governments for the use and benefit of a given tribe. The reservations and their boundaries were identified for the 1990 census by the Bureau of Indian Affairs (BIA), Department of Interior (for federal reservations), and state governments (for state reservations). The names of American Indian reservations recognized by state governments, but not by the federal government, are followed by "state." Areas composed of reservation lands that are administered jointly and/or are claimed by two reservations, as identified by the BIA, are called "joint areas," and are treated as separate American Indian reservations for census purposes. Federal reservations may cross state boundaries, and federal and state reservations may cross county, county subdivision, and place boundaries. For reservations that cross state boundaries, only the portion of the reservations in a given state is shown in the data products for that state; the entire reservations are shown in data products for the United States. 2. Trust lands are property associated with a particular American Indian reservation or tribe, held in trust by the federal government. Trust lands may be held in trust either for a tribe (tribal trust lands) or for an individual member of a tribe (individual trust land). Trust lands recognized for the 1990 census comprised all tribal trust lands and inhabited individual trust lands located outside of a reservation boundary. As with other American Indian areas, trust lands may be located in more than one state. Only the trust lands in a given state are shown in the data products for that state; all trust lands associated with a reservation or tribe are shown in data products for the United States. The Census Bureau first reported data for tribal trust lands for the 1980 census.

★ 565 ★

Employment

Employment, by Industry, for Persons Age 16 and Older on Selected Reservations and Trust Lands - Part II

Data are shown for the 50 areas with the largest populations, in number of persons.

American Indian Reservation and Trust Lands[1,2]	Employed persons age 16 years and older							
	Finance, insurance & real estate	Business & repair services	Personal services	Enter-tainment & recreation services	Professional & related services			Public admini-stration
					Health services	Educ. services	Other prof. & related services	
Agua Caliente Reservation	975	401	853	198	628	346	538	145
Allegany Reservation	113	63	92	108	276	278	173	217
Blackfeet Reservation	29	31	68	49	281	564	105	276
Cheyenne River Reservation	104	39	30	20	102	357	173	363
Coeur d'Alene Reservation and Trust Lands, ID	85	66	43	11	141	250	107	102
Colorado River Reservation	122	116	132	38	177	223	144	268
Colville Reservation	51	60	48	47	135	220	130	352
Crow Reservation and Trust Lands, MT	41	50	18	45	157	237	113	145
Eastern Cherokee Reservation	48	64	139	66	141	144	221	251
Flathead Reservation	274	264	235	61	696	842	536	546
Fort Apache Reservation	39	13	52	32	259	303	127	415
Fort Berthold Reservation	63	29	37	2	195	308	108	158
Fort Hall Reservation and Trust Lands, ID	40	48	9	14	98	127	42	161
Fort Peck Reservation	103	69	41	41	335	451	201	362
Gila River Reservation	110	71	30	29	232	167	183	139
Hopi Reservation and Trust Lands, AZ	33	71	33	41	158	323	136	354

[Continued]

★ 565 ★

Employment, by Industry, for Persons Age 16 and Older on Selected Reservations and Trust Lands - Part II

[Continued]

American Indian Reservation and Trust Lands[1,2]	Employed persons age 16 years and older							
	Finance, insurance & real estate	Business & repair services	Personal services	Enter-tainment & recreation services	Professional & related services			Public admini-stration
					Health services	Educ. services	Other prof. & related services	
Isabella Reservation and Trust Lands, MI	500	372	409	214	941	1,790	726	434
Laguna Pueblo and Trust Lands, NM	10	33	36	2	93	152	81	189
Lake Traverse (Sisseton) Reservation	153	99	81	73	325	403	352	245
Leech Lake Reservation	84	93	168	87	234	260	198	295
Mississippi Choctaw Reservation and Trust Lands, MS	13	11	11	0	126	144	47	102
Muckleshoot Reservation and Trust Lands, WA	81	45	35	49	80	123	71	86
Navajo Reservation and Trust Lands, AZ–NM–UT	410	756	1,169	148	2,142	5,526	3,081	2,995
Nez Perce Reservation	166	158	158	58	371	521	235	487
Northern Cheyenne Reservation and Trust Lands, MT–SD	6	15	17	21	81	216	140	141
Omaha Reservation	65	54	29	16	205	184	96	110
Oneida (West) Reservation	544	347	225	172	714	665	513	372
Osage Reservation	806	574	379	185	1,182	1,217	1,087	841
Papago Reservation	54	63	51	22	97	212	192	214
Pine Ridge Reservation and Trust Lands, NE–SD	53	30	14	5	160	732	155	478
Port Madison Reservation	118	100	86	36	98	181	213	228
Puyallup Reservation and Trust Lands, WA	834	674	344	178	1,004	890	883	730
Red Lake Reservation	37	14	4	19	179	134	118	92
Rosebud Reservation and Trust Lands, SD	55	57	40	18	193	578	143	342
Salt River Reservation	79	68	134	72	128	64	112	189
San Carlos Reservation	36	44	11	11	153	236	94	185
Sandia Pueblo	78	76	50	48	54	120	90	156
San Juan Pueblo	45	100	74	27	151	180	207	294
Santa Clara Pueblo	187	229	173	24	306	414	623	511
Southern Ute Reservation	121	119	121	43	245	363	189	238
Standing Rock Reservation	49	33	25	16	127	384	111	399
Taos Pueblo and Trust Lands, NM	69	76	155	22	117	114	174	113
Tulalip Reservation	136	91	69	79	258	247	169	191
Turtle Mountain Reservation and Trust Lands, ND–SD	45	15	15	16	116	440	56	169
Uintah and Ouray Reservation	124	198	104	82	373	716	251	458
White Earth Reservation	89	95	86	25	220	355	122	167
Wind River Reservation	298	353	189	134	463	1,165	492	545
Yakima Reservation and Trust Lands, WA	190	207	207	84	516	892	464	485

[Continued]

★ 565 ★

Employment, by Industry, for Persons Age 16 and Older on Selected Reservations and Trust Lands - Part II

[Continued]

American Indian Reservation and Trust Lands[1,2]	Employed persons age 16 years and older							
	Finance, insurance & real estate	Business & repair services	Personal services	Enter-tainment & recreation services	Professional & related services			Public admini-stration
					Health services	Educ. services	Other prof. & related services	
Yankton Reservation	60	54	50	15	231	250	110	135
Zuni Pueblo	22	32	7	10	217	465	123	206

Source: Census of Population and Housing, 1990: Summary Tape File 3C on CD-ROM [machine-readable datafiles]. Prepared by the Bureau of the Census. Washington, DC: The Bureau, 1992. *Notes:* 1. Federal American Indian reservations are areas with boundaries established by treaty, statute, and/or executive or court order, and recognized by the federal government as territory in which American Indian tribes have jurisdiction. State reservations are lands held in trust by state governments for the use and benefit of a given tribe. The reservations and their boundaries were identified for the 1990 census by the Bureau of Indian Affairs (BIA), Department of Interior (for federal reservations), and state governments (for state reservations). The names of American Indian reservations recognized by state governments, but not by the federal government, are followed by "state." Areas composed of reservation lands that are administered jointly and/or are claimed by two reservations, as identified by the BIA, are called "joint areas," and are treated as separate American Indian reservations for census purposes. Federal reservations may cross state boundaries, and federal and state reservations may cross county, county subdivision, and place boundaries. For reservations that cross state boundaries, only the portion of the reservations in a given state is shown in the data products for that state; the entire reservations are shown in data products for the United States. 2. Trust lands are property associated with a particular American Indian reservation or tribe, held in trust by the federal government. Trust lands may be held in trust either for a tribe (tribal trust lands) or for an individual member of a tribe (individual trust land). Trust lands recognized for the 1990 census comprised all tribal trust lands and inhabited individual trust lands located outside of a reservation boundary. As with other American Indian areas, trust lands may be located in more than one state. Only the trust lands in a given state are shown in the data products for that state; all trust lands associated with a reservation or tribe are shown in data products for the United States. The Census Bureau first reported data for tribal trust lands for the 1980 census.

★ 566 ★

Employment

Occupations of Persons Age 16 and Older in Selected Alaska Native Villages - Part I

Data are shown for the 50 areas with the largest populations, in number of persons.

Alaska Native Village Statistical Area[1]	Managerial and professional specialty					Service occupations		
	Exec. admin. & manager. occup.	Profess. spec. occup.	Tech., sales & admin. support occup.	Technicians & related support occup.	Admin. occup. including clerical	Private household occup.	Protect. service occup.	Service occup. except protect. & household
Akiachak	12	26	0	4	52	4	0	21
Akutan	33	2	1	2	23	0	2	47
Alakanuk	8	27	5	18	15	0	8	10
Andreafsky	11	34	5	4	20	0	4	37
Angoon	21	52	0	15	24	0	2	28
Aniak	30	50	13	23	40	0	3	25
Barrow	172	209	35	41	277	2	41	188
Bethel	274	456	95	111	410	9	58	271
Chevak	4	50	1	18	23	2	0	32
Copper Center	34	29	3	8	31	0	3	9
Craig	59	58	5	67	80	0	7	70
Dillingham	160	166	43	41	139	5	21	96
Emmonak	18	33	7	9	26	0	3	24
Fort Yukon	21	41	6	13	33	0	8	21
Galena	33	53	3	21	31	0	8	14
Gambell	10	36	3	2	21	0	2	10
Grouse Creek Group	41	55	1	21	31	0	12	48
Hoonah	11	30	0	27	57	0	11	53

[Continued]

★ 566 ★

Occupations of Persons Age 16 and Older in Selected Alaska Native Villages - Part I

[Continued]

Alaska Native Village Statistical Area[1]	Managerial and professional specialty					Service occupations		
	Exec. admin. & manager. occup.	Profess. spec. occup.	Tech., sales & admin. support occup.	Technicians & related support occup.	Admin. occup. including clerical	Private household occup.	Protect. service occup.	Service occup. except protect. & household
Hooper Bay	22	49	2	7	21	0	6	20
Kake	11	44	5	21	19	0	4	27
Kasigluk	5	37	0	4	21	0	5	6
King Cove	22	9	0	17	27	0	0	7
King Salmon	38	26	29	15	40	0	5	13
Kipnuk	2	13	0	4	8	0	1	16
Klawock	19	36	0	18	31	0	3	19
Kotlik	7	18	0	9	27	1	2	18
Kotzebue	177	149	49	82	202	2	26	144
Kwethluk	6	23	0	2	15	0	2	33
McGrath	34	63	8	6	43	0	3	18
Mountain Village	12	48	0	7	34	0	0	24
Naknek	28	66	8	27	39	0	0	26
Ninilchik	463	573	135	321	488	26	66	453
Noorvik	10	33	4	15	6	0	4	24
Pilot Station	8	24	0	6	7	3	0	30
Point Hope	13	20	2	2	32	0	8	21
Quinhagak	5	23	0	11	30	0	6	23
St. Paul	30	35	13	3	38	0	20	33
Salamatof	25	27	2	27	26	8	10	30
Sand Point	14	38	7	9	15	0	13	35
Savoonga	7	22	2	5	18	0	3	22
Selawik	13	17	0	10	7	0	10	21
Shishmaref	6	21	2	9	12	2	3	16
Stebbins	16	14	0	6	13	0	6	18
Togiak	10	35	3	3	11	0	7	11
Tok	38	81	2	31	65	0	6	65
Toksook Bay	7	15	2	8	20	0	6	21
Unalakleet	24	57	2	12	19	0	10	23
Unalaska	183	66	107	98	189	2	16	316
Wainwright	18	19	0	9	31	0	3	17
Yakutat	40	36	2	9	18	0	4	26

Source: Census of Population and Housing, 1990: Summary Tape File 3C on CD-ROM [machine-readable datafiles]. Prepared by the Bureau of the Census. Washington, DC: The Bureau, 1992. *Notes:* 1. Alaska Native villages (ANVs) constitute tribes, bands, clans, groups, villages, communities, or associations in Alaska that are recognized pursuant to the Alaska Native Claims Settlement Act of 1972, Public Law 92-203. Because ANVs do not have legally designated boundaries, the Census Bureau has established Alaska Native village statistical areas (ANVSAs) for statistical purposes. For the 1990 census, the Census Bureau cooperated with officials of the nonprofit corporation within each participating Alaska Native Regional Corporation (ANRC), as well as other knowledgeable officials, to delineate boundaries that encompass the settled area associated with each ANV.

★ 567 ★

Employment

Occupations of Persons Age 16 and Older in Selected Alaska Native Villages - Part II

Data are shown for the 50 areas with the largest populations, in number of persons.

Alaska Native Village Statistical Area[1]	Farming, forestry & fishing occup.	Prec. prod., craft, & repair occup.	Operators, fabricators & laborers		
			Machine operators assemblers, inspectors	Transp. & material moving occup.	Handlers, equipment cleaners, helpers & laborers
Akiachak	0	12	0	0	4
Akutan	19	80	194	36	88
Alakanuk	0	11	3	0	7
Andreafsky	0	8	0	2	7
Angoon	15	17	0	2	3
Aniak	0	21	3	2	5
Barrow	0	162	11	66	43
Bethel	7	147	25	75	53
Chevak	0	7	6	0	9
Copper Center	0	11	0	14	4
Craig	107	75	27	47	29
Dillingham	20	73	16	30	31
Emmonak	0	7	0	4	5
Fort Yukon	12	6	4	3	2
Galena	0	21	1	4	8
Gambell	0	6	2	3	4
Grouse Creek Group	9	29	11	14	13
Hoonah	62	9	29	29	3
Hooper Bay	3	8	0	0	20
Kake	62	26	5	17	12
Kasigluk	0	5	2	1	2
King Cove	25	53	72	9	35
King Salmon	0	43	0	17	3
Kipnuk	3	3	2	0	9
Klawock	25	21	24	50	21
Kotlik	0	4	0	0	4
Kotzebue	4	97	11	40	36
Kwethluk	0	5	2	0	2
McGrath	3	24	7	0	10
Mountain Village	0	7	0	0	8
Naknek	7	34	5	2	2
Ninilchik	390	700	166	287	171
Noorvik	0	13	7	1	10
Pilot Station	0	14	0	2	2
Point Hope	0	36	7	13	10
Quinhagak	0	11	0	14	4
St. Paul	32	55	20	15	36
Salamatof	11	47	14	19	28
Sand Point	77	66	117	22	25
Savoonga	0	5	1	0	2
Selawik	0	9	0	2	10

[Continued]

★ 567 ★

Occupations of Persons Age 16 and Older in Selected Alaska Native Villages - Part II

[Continued]

Alaska Native Village Statistical Area[1]	Farming, forestry & fishing occup.	Prec. prod., craft, & repair occup.	Operators, fabricators & laborers		
			Machine operators assemblers, inspectors	Transp. & material moving occup.	Handlers, equipment cleaners, helpers & laborers
Shishmaref	9	8	0	2	1
Stebbins	1	9	0	4	9
Togiak	0	11	0	5	4
Tok	8	34	4	15	21
Toksook Bay	0	11	1	0	11
Unalakleet	0	31	11	4	18
Unalaska	93	368	475	310	259
Wainwright	0	51	0	23	6
Yakutat	29	12	37	22	19

Source: Census of Population and Housing, 1990: Summary Tape File 3C on CD-ROM [machine-readable datafiles]. Prepared by the Bureau of the Census. Washington, DC: The Bureau, 1992. *Notes:* 1. Alaska Native villages (ANVs) constitute tribes, bands, clans, groups, villages, communities, or associations in Alaska that are recognized pursuant to the Alaska Native Claims Settlement Act of 1972, Public Law 92-203. Because ANVs do not have legally designated boundaries, the Census Bureau has established Alaska Native village statistical areas (ANVSAs) for statistical purposes. For the 1990 census, the Census Bureau cooperated with officials of the nonprofit corporation within each participating Alaska Native Regional Corporation (ANRC), as well as other knowledgeable officials, to delineate boundaries that encompass the settled area associated with each ANV.

★ 568 ★

Employment

Occupations of Persons Age 16 and Older in Selected Tribal Designated Statistical Areas - Part I

Tribal Designated Statistical Area[1]	Managerial and professional specialty					Service occupations		
	Exec. admin. & manager. occup.	Profess. spec. occup.	Tech., sales & admin. support occup.	Technicians & related support occup.	Admin. occup. including clerical	Private household occup.	Protect. service occup.	Service occup. except protect. & household
Apache Choctaw TDSA (state)	552	869	135	731	795	41	104	820
Chickahominy TDSA (state)	70	94	45	69	286	15	9	131
Clifton Choctaw TDSA (state)	0	0	9	13	23	0	9	0
Coharie TDSA (state)	3,865	5,676	1,383	5,798	5,970	228	842	5,345
Coquille Indian TDSA	18,541	24,822	4,753	22,533	24,422	900	2,722	23,145
Delaware-Muncie TDSA (state)	15	0	0	6	7	0	18	10
Florida Tribe of Eastern Creek TDSA (state)	0	0	0	0	0	0	0	24
Haliwa-Saponi TDSA (state)	61	140	31	156	180	5	39	213
Jena Band of Choctaw TDSA (state)	2,269	3,303	944	3,216	3,559	132	473	2,874
Klamath TDSA	1,440	1,929	403	1,860	2,159	77	289	2,541
Lumbee TDSA (state)	872	1,844	387	1,297	1,720	86	314	1,890
Meherrin TDSA (state)	1,383	2,189	354	2,035	2,422	202	390	2,196
Mohegan TDSA (state)	1,132	1,562	533	1,310	1,807	7	282	1,520
Ramapough TDSA (state)	22	25	7	0	59	0	0	54
United Houma Nation TDSA (state)	38,851	43,489	13,152	47,800	61,832	1,253	7,048	33,343

[Continued]

★ 568 ★

Occupations of Persons Age 16 and Older in Selected Tribal Designated Statistical Areas - Part I
[Continued]

Tribal Designated Statistical Area[1]	Managerial and professional specialty					Service occupations		
	Exec. admin. & manager. occup.	Profess. spec. occup.	Tech., sales & admin. support occup.	Technicians & related support occup.	Admin. occup. including clerical	Private household occup.	Protect. service occup.	Service occup. except protect. & household
Waccamaw Siouan TDSA (state)	25	60	33	52	135	0	11	108
Wampanoag-Gay Head TDSA	759	901	111	952	708	21	69	582

Source: Census of Population and Housing, 1990: Summary Tape File 3C on CD-ROM [machine-readable datafiles]. Prepared by the Bureau of the Census. Washington, DC: The Bureau, 1992. *Notes:* 1. Tribal designated statistical areas (TDSAs) are areas, delineated outside Oklahoma by federally- and state-recognized tribes without a land base or associated trust lands, to provide statistical areas for which the Census Bureau tabulates data. TDSAs represent areas generally containing the American Indian population over which federally-recognized tribes have jurisdiction and areas in which state tribes provide benefits and services to their members. The names of TDSAs delineated by state-recognized tribes are followed by "(state)." The Census Bureau did not recognize TDSAs before the 1990 census.

★ 569 ★

Employment

Occupations of Persons Age 16 and Older in Selected Tribal Designated Statistical Areas - Part II

Tribal Designated Statistical Area[1]	Farming, forestry & fishing occup.	Prec. prod., craft, & repair occup.	Operators, fabricators & laborers		
			Machine operators assemblers, inspectors	Transp. & material moving occup.	Handlers, equipment cleaners, helpers & laborers
Apache Choctaw TDSA (state)	472	1,126	744	710	418
Chickahominy TDSA (state)	53	258	190	173	78
Clifton Choctaw TDSA (state)	0	11	22	36	17
Coharie TDSA (state)	1,985	6,638	6,687	2,338	2,886
Coquille Indian TDSA	7,141	17,601	11,525	8,941	8,569
Delaware-Muncie TDSA (state)	21	17	40	0	0
Florida Tribe of Eastern Creek TDSA (state)	0	10	9	9	0
Haliwa-Saponi TDSA (state)	100	316	627	179	256
Jena Band of Choctaw TDSA (state)	431	2,725	1,028	1,289	928
Klamath TDSA	675	1,963	1,552	1,062	895
Lumbee TDSA (state)	825	3,939	4,925	822	1,494
Meherrin TDSA (state)	1,718	3,432	3,554	1,688	1,328
Mohegan TDSA (state)	125	1,622	952	439	402
Ramapough TDSA (state)	13	46	23	41	8
United Houma Nation TDSA (state)	5,918	46,475	15,661	20,430	13,526
Waccamaw Siouan TDSA (state)	50	248	274	124	66
Wampanoag-Gay Head TDSA	261	1,065	85	181	173

Source: Census of Population and Housing, 1990: Summary Tape File 3C on CD-ROM [machine-readable datafiles]. Prepared by the Bureau of the Census. Washington, DC: The Bureau, 1992. *Notes:* 1. Tribal designated statistical areas (TDSAs) are areas, delineated outside Oklahoma by federally- and state-recognized tribes without a land base or associated trust lands, to provide statistical areas for which the Census Bureau tabulates data. TDSAs represent areas generally containing the American Indian population over which federally-recognized tribes have jurisdiction and areas in which state tribes provide benefits and services to their members. The names of TDSAs delineated by state-recognized tribes are followed by "(state)." The Census Bureau did not recognize TDSAs before the 1990 census.

Employment

Occupations of Persons Age 16 and Older in Selected Tribal Jurisdiction Statistical Areas - Part I

Tribal Jurisdiction Statistical Area[1]	Managerial and professional specialty					Service occupations		
	Exec. admin. & manager. occup.	Profess. spec. occup.	Tech., sales & admin. support occup.	Technicians & related support occup.	Admin. occup. including clerical	Private household occup.	Protect. service occup.	Service occup. except protect. & household
Absentee Shawnee-Citizens Band of Potawatomi TJSA	3,997	3,769	1,382	3,838	6,482	95	814	4,526
Caddo-Wichita-Delaware TJSA	166	337	72	246	385	33	27	399
Cherokee TJSA	14,195	18,339	5,429	16,438	24,286	1,014	2,410	21,039
Cheyenne-Arapaho TJSA	6,661	7,694	2,101	7,972	9,914	305	929	8,132
Chickasaw TJSA	9,095	12,129	3,142	10,477	14,529	547	1,415	13,651
Choctaw TJSA	5,656	8,895	2,021	7,211	9,162	428	1,753	9,835
Creek TJSA	40,004	42,904	11,349	39,636	49,691	1,119	4,303	32,239
Iowa TJSA	123	129	29	117	190	6	15	246
Kaw TJSA	808	1,152	376	725	880	35	79	503
Kiowa-Comanche-Apache-Fort Sill Apache TJSA	7,529	9,666	2,332	8,038	10,374	367	1,140	10,235
Otoe-Missouria TJSA	74	71	29	92	158	8	26	194
Pawnee TJSA	677	625	188	649	949	45	106	835
Sac and Fox TJSA	2,218	2,303	625	2,406	2,843	79	322	2,772
Seminole TJSA	760	966	200	827	1,087	44	133	1,021
Tonkawa TJSA	472	521	148	426	655	35	67	684
Creek-Seminole Joint Area TJSA	50	133	25	66	76	0	4	101
Iowa-Sac and Fox Joint Area TJSA	37	39	14	46	82	0	0	28

Source: Census of Population and Housing, 1990: Summary Tape File 3C on CD-ROM [machine-readable datafiles]. Prepared by the Bureau of the Census. Washington, DC: The Bureau, 1992. *Notes:* 1. Tribal jurisdiction statistical areas (TJSAs) are areas, delineated by federally recognized tribes in Oklahoma without a reservation, for which the Census Bureau tabulates data. TJSAs represent areas generally containing the American Indian population over which one or more tribal governments have jurisdiction. If tribal officials delineated adjacent TJSAs so that they include some duplicate territory, the overlap area is called a "joint use area," which is treated as a separate TJSA for census purposes.

Employment

Occupations of Persons Age 16 and Older in Selected Tribal Jurisdiction Statistical Areas - Part II

Tribal Jurisdiction Statistical Area[1]	Farming, forestry & fishing occup.	Prec. prod., craft, & repair occup.	Operators, fabricators & laborers		
			Machine operators assemblers, inspectors	Transp. & material moving occup.	Handlers, equipment cleaners, helpers & laborers
Absentee Shawnee-Citizens Band of Potawatomi TJSA	847	6,086	3,145	2,496	1,658
Caddo-Wichita-Delaware TJSA	568	408	232	157	168
Cherokee TJSA	6,789	24,529	13,904	8,535	7,607
Cheyenne-Arapaho TJSA	5,137	8,510	3,563	4,109	2,603
Chickasaw TJSA	5,100	14,338	8,321	6,959	4,506
Choctaw TJSA	4,760	9,934	6,826	5,328	3,925
Creek TJSA	4,630	33,968	17,825	10,918	9,477
Iowa TJSA	148	303	109	171	68

[Continued]

★ 571 ★

Occupations of Persons Age 16 and Older in Selected Tribal Jurisdiction Statistical Areas - Part II

[Continued]

Tribal Jurisdiction Statistical Area[1]	Farming, forestry & fishing occup.	Prec. prod., craft, & repair occup.	Operators, fabricators & laborers		
			Machine operators assemblers, inspectors	Transp. & material moving occup.	Handlers, equipment cleaners, helpers & laborers
Kaw TJSA	172	761	273	190	179
Kiowa-Comanche-Apache-Fort Sill Apache TJSA	4,157	6,758	4,083	3,450	2,841
Otoe-Missouria TJSA	108	165	103	83	62
Pawnee TJSA	242	949	597	403	297
Sac and Fox TJSA	772	2,698	1,737	1,196	675
Seminole TJSA	259	1,206	919	549	318
Tonkawa TJSA	274	665	569	266	288
Creek-Seminole Joint Area TJSA	40	99	88	66	45
Iowa-Sac and Fox Joint Area TJSA	11	78	21	12	5

Source: Census of Population and Housing, 1990: Summary Tape File 3C on CD-ROM [machine-readable datafiles]. Prepared by the Bureau of the Census. Washington, DC: The Bureau, 1992. *Notes:* 1. Tribal jurisdiction statistical areas (TJSAs) are areas, delineated by federally recognized tribes in Oklahoma without a reservation, for which the Census Bureau tabulates data. TJSAs represent areas generally containing the American Indian population over which one or more tribal governments have jurisdiction. If tribal officials delineated adjacent TJSAs so that they include some duplicate territory, the overlap area is called a "joint use area," which is treated as a separate TJSA for census purposes.

★ 572 ★

Employment

Occupations of Persons Age 16 and Older on Selected Reservations and Trust Lands - Part I

Data are shown for the 50 areas with the largest populations, in number of persons.

American Indian Reservation and Trust Lands[1,2]	Managerial and professional specialty					Service occupations		
	Exec. admin. & manager. occup.	Profess. spec. occup.	Tech., sales & admin. support occup.	Technicians & related support occup.	Admin. occup. including clerical	Private household occup.	Protect. service occup.	Service occup. except protect. & household
Agua Caliente Reservation	1,287	1,012	185	1,538	1,057	53	133	1,107
Allegany Reservation	247	295	79	280	378	6	78	490
Blackfeet Reservation	172	596	36	120	303	35	41	452
Cheyenne River Reservation	234	378	45	133	284	16	29	298
Coeur d'Alene Reservation and Trust Lands, ID	133	252	45	201	230	12	23	276
Colorado River Reservation	290	212	52	294	456	13	89	467
Colville Reservation	260	256	49	160	280	10	42	326
Crow Reservation and Trust Lands, MT	124	230	51	130	244	0	23	255
Eastern Cherokee Reservation	180	202	59	154	361	0	49	326
Flathead Reservation	639	1,074	162	687	1,071	30	77	1,224
Fort Apache Reservation	103	300	57	151	342	12	136	454
Fort Berthold Reservation	137	256	59	125	233	14	31	305
Fort Hall Reservation and Trust Lands, ID	126	123	27	121	151	3	33	227
Fort Peck Reservation	273	438	92	232	577	9	64	554
Gila River Reservation	63	117	50	123	358	25	35	289
Hopi Reservation and Trust Lands, AZ	188	233	26	108	356	11	35	280
Isabella Reservation and Trust Lands, MI	1,243	1,665	294	1,304	1,601	82	105	1,672
Laguna Pueblo and Trust Lands, NM	74	161	25	26	186	21	68	174
Lake Traverse (Sisseton) Reservation	255	504	34	352	554	16	23	573
Leech Lake Reservation	268	301	74	226	350	8	34	508

[Continued]

★ 572 ★

Occupations of Persons Age 16 and Older on Selected Reservations and Trust Lands - Part I

[Continued]

American Indian Reservation and Trust Lands[1,2]	Managerial and professional specialty					Service occupations		
	Exec. admin. & manager. occup.	Profess. spec. occup.	Tech., sales & admin. support occup.	Technicians & related support occup.	Admin. occup. including clerical	Private household occup.	Protect. service occup.	Service occup. except protect. & household
Mississippi Choctaw Reservation and Trust Lands, MS	13	90	45	62	137	0	10	168
Muckleshoot Reservation and Trust Lands, WA	126	188	73	161	264	2	27	217
Navajo Reservation and Trust Lands, AZ–NM–UT	1,873	4,662	720	2,015	3,918	152	671	4,992
Nez Perce Reservation	481	710	115	425	744	25	129	709
Northern Cheyenne Reservation and Trust Lands, MT–SD	131	169	12	21	183	17	49	147
Omaha Reservation	120	205	64	111	256	4	35	262
Oneida (West) Reservation	1,290	1,355	299	1,189	1,438	14	123	865
Osage Reservation	1,683	1,827	617	1,602	2,788	78	226	1,738
Papago Reservation	75	164	31	66	267	10	30	279
Pine Ridge Reservation and Trust Lands, NE–SD	211	480	55	59	448	6	108	336
Port Madison Reservation	241	341	82	215	318	14	58	256
Puyallup Reservation and Trust Lands, WA	1,943	1,801	507	1,685	2,283	41	246	1,549
Red Lake Reservation	60	148	29	35	147	0	49	146
Rosebud Reservation and Trust Lands, SD	172	439	74	110	361	5	45	377
Salt River Reservation	67	108	16	81	231	13	29	375
San Carlos Reservation	54	167	66	13	247	0	73	297
Sandia Pueblo	120	121	22	171	242	8	39	270
San Juan Pueblo	169	175	126	192	300	6	67	338
Santa Clara Pueblo	423	499	257	317	799	24	155	535
Southern Ute Reservation	307	435	87	378	461	10	52	395
Standing Rock Reservation	171	306	52	98	337	11	33	355
Taos Pueblo and Trust Lands, NM	228	246	47	250	210	11	26	334
Tulalip Reservation	347	436	99	365	437	0	78	289
Turtle Mountain Reservation and Trust Lands, ND–SD	156	293	24	85	192	2	39	278
Uintah and Ouray Reservation	423	760	117	513	750	14	70	704
White Earth Reservation	220	355	37	180	311	12	37	377
Wind River Reservation	787	1,085	290	833	1,186	21	74	1,166
Yakima Reservation and Trust Lands, WA	533	873	162	680	1,110	42	103	1,043
Yankton Reservation	149	254	33	143	223	11	21	363
Zuni Pueblo	123	412	85	248	193	7	51	257

Source: Census of Population and Housing, 1990: Summary Tape File 3C on CD-ROM [machine-readable datafiles]. Prepared by the Bureau of the Census. Washington, DC: The Bureau, 1992. *Notes:* 1. Federal American Indian reservations are areas with boundaries established by treaty, statute, and/or executive or court order, and recognized by the federal government as territory in which American Indian tribes have jurisdiction. State reservations are lands held in trust by state governments for the use and benefit of a given tribe. The reservations and their boundaries were identified for the 1990 census by the Bureau of Indian Affairs (BIA), Department of Interior (for federal reservations), and state governments (for state reservations). The names of American Indian reservations recognized by state governments, but not by the federal government, are followed by "state." Areas composed of reservation lands that are administered jointly and/or are claimed by two reservations, as identified by the BIA, are called "joint areas," and are treated as separate American Indian reservations for census purposes. Federal reservations may cross state boundaries, and federal and state reservations may cross county, county subdivision, and place boundaries. For reservations that cross state boundaries, only the portion of the reservations in a given state is shown in the data products for that state; the entire reservations are shown in data products for the United States. 2. Trust lands are property associated with a particular American Indian reservation or tribe, held in trust by the federal government. Trust lands may be held in trust either for a tribe (tribal trust lands) or for an individual member of a tribe (individual trust land). Trust lands recognized for the 1990 census comprised all tribal trust lands and inhabited individual trust lands located outside of a reservation boundary. As with other American Indian areas, trust lands may be located in more than one state. Only the trust lands in a given state are shown in the data products for that state; all trust lands associated with a reservation or tribe are shown in data products for the United States. The Census Bureau first reported data for tribal trust lands for the 1980 census.

★ 573 ★
Employment

Occupations of Persons Age 16 and Older on Selected Reservations and Trust Lands - Part II

Data are shown for the 50 areas with the largest populations, in number of persons.

American Indian Reservation and Trust Lands[1,2]	Farming, forestry & fishing occup.	Prec. prod., craft, & repair occup.	Operators, fabricators & laborers		
			Machine operators assemblers, inspectors	Transp. & material moving occup.	Handlers, equipment cleaners, helpers & laborers
Agua Caliente Reservation	131	665	131	167	125
Allegany Reservation	64	333	331	175	186
Blackfeet Reservation	217	151	73	82	60
Cheyenne River Reservation	565	164	50	144	125
Coeur d'Alene Reservation and Trust Lands, ID	282	278	189	191	123
Colorado River Reservation	402	287	91	156	131
Colville Reservation	355	189	128	144	133
Crow Reservation and Trust Lands, MT	294	101	59	59	88
Eastern Cherokee Reservation	81	362	329	116	156
Flathead Reservation	1,066	1,046	373	375	317
Fort Apache Reservation	132	176	82	174	196
Fort Berthold Reservation	180	236	38	114	67
Fort Hall Reservation and Trust Lands, ID	204	206	185	153	149
Fort Peck Reservation	514	431	204	162	133
Gila River Reservation	291	140	130	149	192
Hopi Reservation and Trust Lands, AZ	31	264	47	71	74
Isabella Reservation and Trust Lands, MI	339	1,005	612	453	431
Laguna Pueblo and Trust Lands, NM	22	165	112	67	58
Lake Traverse (Sisseton) Reservation	923	423	201	198	166
Leech Lake Reservation	148	274	130	174	149
Mississippi Choctaw Reservation and Trust Lands, MS	43	175	387	75	82
Muckleshoot Reservation and Trust Lands, WA	28	250	117	86	67
Navajo Reservation and Trust Lands, AZ–NM–UT	591	4,448	1,277	1,562	2,369
Nez Perce Reservation	769	652	452	401	336
Northern Cheyenne Reservation and Trust Lands, MT–SD	61	79	36	69	49
Omaha Reservation	281	156	93	87	89
Oneida (West) Reservation	275	969	613	363	395
Osage Reservation	633	2,941	1,414	1,039	651
Papago Reservation	139	103	53	137	208
Pine Ridge Reservation and Trust Lands, NE–SD	243	230	22	121	124
Port Madison Reservation	76	329	64	95	93
Puyallup Reservation and Trust Lands, WA	294	1,923	845	807	654
Red Lake Reservation	68	36	42	81	30
Rosebud Reservation and Trust Lands, SD	328	211	27	108	129
Salt River Reservation	116	201	66	67	76
San Carlos Reservation	87	132	38	63	88
Sandia Pueblo	27	247	125	128	89
San Juan Pueblo	59	270	53	68	167
Santa Clara Pueblo	53	541	132	138	158
Southern Ute Reservation	353	423	115	210	137
Standing Rock Reservation	625	101	21	126	33
Taos Pueblo and Trust Lands, NM	23	263	109	47	95

[Continued]

★ 573 ★

Occupations of Persons Age 16 and Older on Selected Reservations and Trust Lands - Part II
[Continued]

American Indian Reservation and Trust Lands[1,2]	Farming, forestry & fishing occup.	Prec. prod., craft, & repair occup.	Operators, fabricators & laborers		
			Machine operators assemblers, inspectors	Transp. & material moving occup.	Handlers, equipment cleaners, helpers & laborers
Tulalip Reservation	86	625	217	147	134
Turtle Mountain Reservation and Trust Lands, ND–SD	37	202	134	53	67
Uintah and Ouray Reservation	673	827	169	529	224
White Earth Reservation	420	324	125	188	144
Wind River Reservation	675	1,156	368	525	376
Yakima Reservation and Trust Lands, WA	2,448	704	865	404	491
Yankton Reservation	704	224	66	69	91
Zuni Pueblo	14	1,230	57	43	82

Source: Census of Population and Housing, 1990: Summary Tape File 3C on CD-ROM [machine-readable datafiles]. Prepared by the Bureau of the Census. Washington, DC: The Bureau, 1992. Notes: 1. Federal American Indian reservations are areas with boundaries established by treaty, statute, and/or executive or court order, and recognized by the federal government as territory in which American Indian tribes have jurisdiction. State reservations are lands held in trust by state governments for the use and benefit of a given tribe. The reservations and their boundaries were identified for the 1990 census by the Bureau of Indian Affairs (BIA), Department of Interior (for federal reservations), and state governments (for state reservations). The names of American Indian reservations recognized by state governments, but not by the federal government, are followed by "state." Areas composed of reservation lands that are administered jointly and/or are claimed by two reservations, as identified by the BIA, are called "joint areas," and are treated as separate American Indian reservations for census purposes. Federal reservations may cross state boundaries, and federal and state reservations may cross county, county subdivision, and place boundaries. For reservations that cross state boundaries, only the portion of the reservations in a given state is shown in the data products for that state; the entire reservations are shown in data products for the United States. 2. Trust lands are property associated with a particular American Indian reservation or tribe, held in trust by the federal government. Trust lands may be held in trust either for a tribe (tribal trust lands) or for an individual member of a tribe (individual trust land). Trust lands recognized for the 1990 census comprised all tribal trust lands and inhabited individual trust lands located outside of a reservation boundary. As with other American Indian areas, trust lands may be located in more than one state. Only the trust lands in a given state are shown in the data products for that state; all trust lands associated with a reservation or tribe are shown in data products for the United States. The Census Bureau first reported data for tribal trust lands for the 1980 census.

★ 574 ★

Employment

Unemployment Rates on the 10 Largest Indian Reservations, 1990

Reservation	Persons 16 & over	Total civilian labor force	Civilian unemployment rate (%)
Fort Apache (White Mountain Apache)	5,721	3,138	35.3
Pine Ridge & trust lands	6,108	2,930	32.7
Blackfeet	4,162	2,340	31.1
San Carlos Apache	4,228	1,819	31.0
Gila River	5,706	2,552	30.6
Navajo & trust lands	87,118	37,954	29.5
Rosebud & trust lands	4,481	2,266	29.5
Hopi & trust lands	4,522	2,170	26.8
Papago (Tohono O'odham)	5,361	1,936	23.4
Zuni Pueblo	4,600	2,962	13.8

Source: Anquoe, Bunty. "1990 Census shows Indians still high in unemployment." Lakota Times (12 August 1992), p. A2. Primary source: 1990 Census of Population and Housing, U.S. Bureau of Census. Note: All data shown are for persons counted as Indian, Eskimo or Aleut.

★ 575 ★

Employment

Unemployment Trends in South Dakota and Its Reservations

Data show percent of persons unemployed in reservation counties from 1987-1992.

	All South Dakota	Yankton	Rosebud	Pine Ridge	Lower Brule	Crow Creek	Standing Rock
1987	4.2	4.5	7.4	8.2	5.0	10.8	7.3
1988	3.9	4.3	6.0	8.1	3.4	7.4	5.5
1989	4.2	4.7	6.5	7.7	5.0	11.1	13.9
1990	3.7	3.7	7.6	7.6	4.7	8.9	13.3
1991	3.4	3.4	6.4	7.4	5.5	0.8	13.4
1992	3.1	2.7	5.6	6.3	3.7	7.7	12.0

Source: U.S. Senate Committee on Small Business. *Small Business Development in Indian Country.* 103rd Cong., 1st sess. on Small Business Development in Indian Country. Washington, DC: U.S. Government Printing Office (3 September 1993), pp. 118-119. Primary source: State Data Center, USD. *Notes:* Data are for the major county within the reservation, except the Pine Ridge Reservation information which includes both Shannon and Jackson Counties.

Housing

★ 576 ★

Households and Distribution of Households by Size of Geographic Location - 1991

Numbers are shown in thousands of occupied units, excluding percentages. Households of Hispanic origin may be of any race.

Characteristics	All households	White	Black	American Indian, Eskimo, or Aleut	Asian or Pacific Islander	Hispanic origin	Not of Hispanic origin	
							Total	White
Place size								
Total	65,441	53,723	9,117	248	1,794	5,409	60,033	48,984
Less than 2,500 persons	4,292	4,094	178	9	9	111	4,182	3,994
2,500 to 9,999 persons	9,102	8,350	599	39	91	460	8,642	7,916
10,000 to 19,999 persons	8,036	7,129	731	35	114	474	7,563	6,688
20,000 to 49,999 persons	12,303	10,655	1,219	43	325	836	11,467	9,913
50,000 to 99,999 persons	8,112	6,875	836	31	296	753	7,359	6,215
100,000 to 249,000 persons	7,464	5,885	1,307	32	192	682	6,782	5,269
250,000 to 499,999 persons	5,119	3,720	1,128	18	200	526	4,593	3,256
500,000 to 999,999 persons	4,455	3,042	1,174	13	190	416	4,038	2,657
1,000,000 persons or more	6,558	3,972	1,945	27	377	1,150	5,408	3,076
Percent	100.0	100.0	100.0	100.0	100.0	100.0	100.0	100.0
Less than 2,500 persons	7.0	8.0	2.0	4.0	1.0	2.0	7.0	8.0

[Continued]

★ 576 ★

Households and Distribution of Households by Size of Geographic Location - 1991
[Continued]

Characteristics	All households	White	Black	American Indian, Eskimo, or Aleut	Asian or Pacific Islander	Hispanic origin	Not of Hispanic origin	
							Total	White
2,500 to 9,999 persons	14.0	16.0	7.0	16.0	5.0	9.0	14.0	16.0
10,000 to 19,999 persons	12.0	13.0	8.0	14.0	6.0	9.0	13.0	14.0
20,000 to 49,999 persons	19.0	20.0	13.0	18.0	18.0	15.0	19.0	20.0
50,000 to 99,999 persons	12.0	13.0	9.0	13.0	17.0	14.0	12.0	13.0
100,000 to 249,000 persons	11.0	11.0	14.0	13.0	11.0	13.0	11.0	11.0
250,000 to 499,999 persons	8.0	7.0	12.0	7.0	11.0	10.0	8.0	7.0
500,000 to 999,999 persons	7.0	6.0	13.0	5.0	11.0	8.0	7.0	5.0
1,000,000 persons or more	10.0	7.0	21.0	11.0	21.0	21.0	9.0	6.0

Source: Woodward, Jeanne M. *America's Racial and Ethnic Groups: Their Housing in the Early Nineties.* Bureau of the Census. Current Housing Reports, Series H121/94-3. Washington, DC: U.S. Government Printing Office, p. 42. Primary source: American Housing Survey (AHS), 1991 National Internal User File.

★ 577 ★

Housing

Housing Distribution in Metropolitan and Non-Metropolitan Areas - 1991

Numbers are shown in thousands of occupied units, excluding percentages. Households of Hispanic origin may be of any race.

Characteristics	All households	White	Black	American Indian, Eskimo, or Aleut	Asian or Pacific Islander	Hispanic origin	Not of Hispanic origin	
							Total	White
Metropolitan-Nonmetropolitan residence								
Inside MSAs	72,723	60,635	9,295	218	1,982	5,589	67,134	55,714
Inside central cities	29,687	21,759	6,396	116	1,006	3,216	26,471	19,023
Suburbs	43,036	38,876	2,899	102	976	2,374	40,663	36,691
Outside MSAs	20,423	18,504	1,537	268	84	650	19,773	17,911
Percent	100.0	100.0	100.0	100.0	100.0	100.0	100.0	100.0
Inside MSAs	78.0	77.0	86.0	45.0	96.0	90.0	77.0	76.0
Inside central cities	32.0	27.0	59.0	24.0	49.0	52.0	30.0	26.0
Suburbs	46.0	49.0	27.0	21.0	47.0	38.0	47.0	50.0
Outside MSAs	22.0	23.0	14.0	55.0	4.0	10.0	23.0	24.0

Source: Woodward, Jeanne M. *America's Racial and Ethnic Groups: Their Housing in the Early Nineties.* Bureau of the Census. Current Housing Reports, Series H121/94-3. Washington, DC: U.S. Government Printing Office, p. 42. Primary source: American Housing Survey (AHS), 1991 National Internal User File.

★ 578 ★

Housing

Household Characteristics for American Indians, Eskimos, and Aleuts - 1991

Numbers are shown in thousands of households.

Characteristics	1991 median			1987 median		
	Number	Value (dollars)	Standard error (dollars)	Number	(in 1991 dollars)	Standard error (dollars)
American Indian, Eskimo, or **Aleut Households**						
Income of families and primarily individuals						
Owner-occupied units	257	21,770	1,480	215	24,600	2,630
Renter-occupied units	229	13,800	3,200	191	16,050	2,150
Value of unit	257	62,900	6,380	215	65,100	6,180
Monthly housing costs						
Mortgaged owners	87	625	86	122	505	34
Renters	187	389	26	212	417	23

Source: Woodward, Jeanne M. *America's Racial and Ethnic Groups: Their Housing in the Early Nineties.* Bureau of the Census. Current Housing Reports, Series H121/94-3. Washington, DC: U.S. Government Printing Office, p. 63. Primary source: American Housing Survey (AHS), 1991 National Internal User File.

★ 579 ★

Housing

Household Composition - 1991

Numbers are shown in thousands of occupied units. Households of Hispanic origin may be of any race.

Characteristics	All households	White	Black	American Indian, Eskimo, or Aleut	Asian or Pacific Islander	Hispanic origin	Not of Hispanic origin	
							Total	White
Household composition								
Two-or-more person households	70,754	60,130	7,956	403	1,743	5,207	65,547	55,500
Married-couple families, no nonrelatives	49,745	44,665	3,412	207	1,221	3,083	46,662	41,802
Other male householders	7,298	5,983	868	72	271	740	6,558	5,359
Other female householders	13,711	9,482	3,676	123	251	1,384	12,327	8,339
One-person households	22,393	19,011	2,876	83	323	1,032	21,361	18,124
Male householder	8,866	7,279	1,326	40	166	530	8,337	6,841
Female householder	13,526	11,732	1,550	43	157	502	13,024	11,283

Source: Woodward, Jeanne M. *America's Racial and Ethnic Groups: Their Housing in the Early Nineties.* Bureau of the Census. Current Housing Reports, Series H121/94-3. Washington, DC: U.S. Government Printing Office, p. 45. Primary source: American Housing Survey (AHS), 1991 National Internal User File.

★ 580 ★

Housing

Housing Tenure in the U.S. by Race/Ethnicity, 1987 and 1991

Numbers are shown in thousands of occupied units, excluding percentages. Households of Hispanic origin may be of any race.

| Characteristics | 1991 | | | 1987 | | | 1987 to 1991 change | | | | | |
| | | | | | | | Number | | | Percent | | |
	Total	Owners	Renters	Total	Owners	Renters	Total	Owners	Renters	Total	Owners	Renters
United States	93,147	59,796	33,351	88,534	56,649	31,885	4,613	3,147	1,466	5.2	5.6	4.6
White	79,140	53,748	25,391	76,157	51,290	24,864	2,983	2,458	527	3.9	4.8	2.1
Black	10,832	4,635	6,197	9,987	4,339	5,647	845	296	550	8.5	6.8	9.7
AIEA[1]	486	257	229	407	215	191	79	42	38	19.4	19.5	19.9
API[2]	2,066	1,035	1,032	1,594	736	864	472	299	168	29.6	40.6	19.4
Other	623	121	502	390	68	319	233	53	183	59.7	77.9	57.4
Hispanic origin	6,239	2,423	3,816	5,445	2,198	3,243	794	225	573	14.6	10.2	17.7
Not of Hispanic origin	86,907	57,373	29,534	83,089	54,451	28,642	3,818	2,922	892	4.6	5.4	3.1
White	73,625	51,465	22,160	71,252	49,211	22,042	2,373	2,254	118	3.3	4.6	1.0

Source: Woodward, Jeanne M. *America's Racial and Ethnic Groups: Their Housing in the Early Nineties.* Bureau of the Census. Current Housing Reports, Series H121/94-3. Washington, DC: U.S. Government Printing Office, p. 41. Primary source: American Housing Survey (AHS), 1991 and 1987 National Internal User File. *Notes:* 1. AIEA = American Indian, Eskimo, or Aleut. 2. API = Asian or Pacific Islander.

★ 581 ★

Housing

Housing Tenure in the Midwest Region, 1987 and 1991

Numbers are shown in thousands of occupied units, excluding percentages. Households of Hispanic origin may be of any race.

| Characteristics | 1991 | | | 1987 | | | 1987 to 1991 change | | | | | |
| | | | | | | | Number | | | Percent | | |
	Total	Owners	Renters	Total	Owners	Renters	Total	Owners	Renters	Total	Owners	Renters
Midwest	22,593	15,238	7,355	21,829	14,696	7,133	764	542	222	3.5	3.7	3.1
White	20,021	14,248	5,773	19,570	13,800	5,769	451	448	4	2.3	3.2	-
Black	2,150	832	1,317	1,984	802	1,183	166	30	134	8.4	3.7	11.3
AIEA[1]	84	30	54	55	13	41	29	17	13	52.7	130.8	31.7
API[2]	277	112	165	170	65	105	107	47	60	62.9	72.3	57.1
Other	61	16	46	50	16	35	11	-	11	22.0	-	31.4
Hispanic origin	415	167	248	365	151	213	50	16	35	13.7	10.6	16.4
Not of Hispanic origin	22,179	15,071	7,107	21,464	14,545	6,920	715	526	187	3.3	3.6	2.7
White	19,669	14,096	5,573	19,253	13,660	5,592	416	436	(19)	2.2	3.2	-

Source: Woodward, Jeanne M. *America's Racial and Ethnic Groups: Their Housing in the Early Nineties.* Bureau of the Census. Current Housing Reports, Series H121/94-3. Washington, DC: U.S. Government Printing Office, p. 41. Primary source: American Housing Survey (AHS), 1991 and 1987 National Internal User File. *Notes:* A dash (-) represents zero or a percent that rounds to less than 1. 1. AIEA = American Indian, Eskimo, or Aleut. 2. API = Asian or Pacific Islander.

★ 582 ★
Housing

Housing Tenure in the Northeast Region, 1987 and 1991

Numbers are shown in thousands of occupied units, excluding percentages. Households of Hispanic origin may be of any race.

| Characteristics | 1991 | | | 1987 | | | 1987 to 1991 change | | | | | |
| | | | | | | | Number | | | Percent | | |
	Total	Owners	Renters	Total	Owners	Renters	Total	Owners	Renters	Total	Owners	Renters
Northeast	18,962	11,869	7,093	18,507	11,418	7,089	455	451	4	2.5	3.9	-
White	16,349	10,981	5,368	16,232	10,651	5,581	117	330	(213)	1.0	3.1	-3.8
Black	1,927	648	1,279	1,749	598	1,151	178	50	128	10.2	8.4	11.1
AIEA[1]	51	39	12	43	18	23	8	21	(11)	18.6	116.7	-47.8
API[2]	370	169	201	289	128	160	81	41	41	28.0	32.0	25.6
Other	265	32	233	194	23	173	71	9	60	36.6	39.1	34.7
Hispanic origin	1,140	221	919	1,064	199	865	76	22	54	7.1	11.1	6.2
Not of Hispanic origin	17,822	11,648	6,174	17,443	11,219	6,224	379	429	(50)	2.2	3.8	-1.0
White	15,505	10,786	4,719	15,439	10,482	4,955	66	304	(236)	-	2.9	-4.8

Source: Woodward, Jeanne M. *America's Racial and Ethnic Groups: Their Housing in the Early Nineties.* Bureau of the Census. Current Housing Reports, Series H121/94-3. Washington, DC: U.S. Government Printing Office, p. 41. Primary source: American Housing Survey (AHS), 1991 and 1987 National Internal User File. *Notes:* A dash (-) represents zero or a percent that rounds to less than 1. 1. AIEA = American Indian, Eskimo, or Aleut. 2. API = Asian or Pacific Islander.

★ 583 ★
Housing

Housing Tenure in the South, 1987 and 1991

Numbers are shown in thousands of occupied units, excluding percentages. Households of Hispanic origin may be of any race.

| Characteristics | 1991 | | | 1987 | | | 1987 to 1991 change | | | | | |
| | | | | | | | Number | | | Percent | | |
	Total	Owners	Renters	Total	Owners	Renters	Total	Owners	Renters	Total	Owners	Renters
South	32,190	21,272	10,918	30,175	19,985	10,190	2,015	1,287	728	6.7	6.4	7.1
White	25,898	18,193	7,705	24,556	17,255	7,302	1,342	938	403	5.5	5.4	5.5
Black	5,790	2,840	2,950	5,290	2,584	2,705	500	256	245	9.5	9.9	9.1
AIEA[1]	102	58	44	81	48	33	21	10	11	25.9	20.8	33.3
API[2]	293	153	141	196	82	115	97	71	26	49.5	86.6	22.6
Other	107	28	78	51	16	35	56	12	43	109.8	75.0	122.9
Hispanic origin	1,977	951	1,026	1,753	879	873	224	72	153	12.8	8.2	17.5
Not of Hispanic origin	30,213	20,321	9,892	28,422	19,106	9,317	1,791	1,215	575	6.3	6.4	6.2
White	24,060	17,279	6,782	22,885	16,412	6,472	1,175	867	310	5.1	5.3	4.8

Source: Woodward, Jeanne M. *America's Racial and Ethnic Groups: Their Housing in the Early Nineties.* Bureau of the Census. Current Housing Reports, Series H121/94-3. Washington, DC: U.S. Government Printing Office, p. 41. Primary source: American Housing Survey (AHS), 1991 and 1987 National Internal User File. *Notes:* A dash (-) represents zero or a percent that rounds to less than 1. 1. AIEA = American Indian, Eskimo, or Aleut. 2. API = Asian or Pacific Islander.

★ 584 ★

Housing

Housing Tenure in the West, 1987 and 1991

Numbers are shown in thousands of occupied units, excluding percentages. Households of Hispanic origin may be of any race.

| Characteristics | 1991 | | | 1987 | | | 1987 to 1991 change | | | | | |
| | | | | | | | Number | | | Percent | | |
	Total	Owners	Renters	Total	Owners	Renters	Total	Owners	Renters	Total	Owners	Renters
West	19,401	11,416	7,985	18,022	10,550	7,472	1,379	866	513	7.7	8.2	6.9
White	16,872	10,327	6,545	15,814	9,596	6,220	1,058	731	325	6.7	7.6	5.2
Black	965	315	650	932	340	593	33	(25)	57	3.5	-7.4	9.6
AIEA[1]	249	130	119	233	135	97	16	(5)	22	6.9	-3.7	22.7
API[2]	1,126	601	525	948	462	486	178	139	39	18.8	30.1	8.0
Other	189	43	146	94	17	75	95	26	71	101.1	152.9	94.7
Hispanic origin	2,708	1,083	1,624	2,264	971	1,293	444	112	331	19.6	11.5	25.6
Not of Hispanic origin	16,694	10,333	6,361	15,758	9,579	6,179	936	754	182	5.9	7.9	2.9
White	14,390	9,304	5,086	13,699	8,668	5,031	691	636	55	5.0	7.3	1.1

Source: Woodward, Jeanne M. *America's Racial and Ethnic Groups: Their Housing in the Early Nineties*. Bureau of the Census. Current Housing Reports, Series H121/94-3. Washington, DC: U.S. Government Printing Office, p. 41. Primary source: American Housing Survey (AHS), 1991 and 1987 National Internal User File. *Notes:* A dash (-) represents zero or a percent that rounds to less than 1. 1. AIEA = American Indian, Eskimo, or Aleut. 2. API = Asian or Pacific Islander.

★ 585 ★

Housing

Occupancy Status of Housing in Selected Alaska Native Villages

Data are shown for the 50 areas with the largest populations, in number of housing units.

| Alaska Native Village Statistical Area[1] | Housing units | |
	Occupied	Vacant
Akiachak	111	17
Akutan	27	0
Alakanuk	120	19
Andreafsky	110	28
Angoon	151	10
Aniak	154	21
Barrow	821	101
Bethel	1,437	193
Chevak	141	17
Copper Center	160	77
Craig	444	60
Dillingham	691	160
Emmonak	166	11
Fort Yukon	208	67
Galena	173	96
Gambell	121	12
Grouse Creek Group	207	35

[Continued]

★ 585 ★

Occupancy Status of Housing in Selected Alaska Native Villages
[Continued]

Alaska Native Village Statistical Area[1]	Housing units	
	Occupied	Vacant
Hoonah	225	26
Hooper Bay	196	13
Kake	218	46
Kasigluk	88	14
King Cove	90	39
King Salmon	161	72
Kipnuk	103	29
Klawock	233	42
Kotlik	101	9
Kotzebue	764	147
Kwethluk	127	11
McGrath	175	35
Mountain Village	143	43
Naknek	202	66
Ninilchik	3,753	1,446
Noorvik	109	18
Pilot Station	101	23
Point Hope	143	31
Quinhagak	123	9
St. Paul	153	22
Salamatof	266	158
Sand Point	243	31
Savoonga	116	13
Selawik	127	25
Shishmaref	118	17
Stebbins	90	1
Togiak	154	49
Tok	367	194
Toksook Bay	89	17
Unalakleet	200	34
Unalaska	575	98
Wainwright	133	27
Yakutat	182	12

Source: Census of Population and Housing, 1990: Summary Tape File 3C on CD-ROM [machine-readable datafiles]. Prepared by the Bureau of the Census. Washington, DC: The Bureau, 1992. *Notes:* 1. Alaska Native villages (ANVs) constitute tribes, bands, clans, groups, villages, communities, or associations in Alaska that are recognized pursuant to the Alaska Native Claims Settlement Act of 1972, Public Law 92-203. Because ANVs do not have legally designated boundaries, the Census Bureau has established Alaska Native village statistical areas (ANVSAs) for statistical purposes. For the 1990 census, the Census Bureau cooperated with officials of the nonprofit corporation within each participating Alaska Native Regional Corporation (ANRC), as well as other knowledgeable officials, to delineate boundaries that encompass the settled area associated with each ANV.

★ 586 ★

Housing

Occupancy Status of Housing in Selected Tribal Designated Statistical Areas

Tribal Designated Statistical Area[1]	Housing units	
	Occupied	Vacant
Apache Choctaw TDSA (state)	8,361	4,428
Chickahominy TDSA (state)	929	60
Clifton Choctaw TDSA (state)	176	12
Coharie TDSA (state)	44,289	4,081
Coquille Indian TDSA	160,872	9,654
Delaware-Muncie TDSA (state)	91	0
Florida Tribe of Eastern Creek TDSA (state)	88	40
Haliwa-Saponi TDSA (state)	2,098	204
Jena Band of Choctaw TDSA (state)	21,057	2,591
Klamath TDSA	16,182	1,440
Lumbee TDSA (state)	16,099	1,101
Meherrin TDSA (state)	20,117	2,290
Mohegan TDSA (state)	9,823	859
Ramapough TDSA (state)	202	3
United Houma Nation TDSA (state)	290,246	31,539
Waccamaw Siouan TDSA (state)	882	86
Wampanoag-Gay Head TDSA	5,003	6,601

Source: Census of Population and Housing, 1990: Summary Tape File 3C on CD-ROM [machine-readable datafiles]. Prepared by the Bureau of the Census. Washington, DC: The Bureau, 1992. *Notes:* 1. Tribal designated statistical areas (TDSAs) are areas, delineated outside Oklahoma by federally- and state-recognized tribes without a land base or associated trust lands, to provide statistical areas for which the Census Bureau tabulates data. TDSAs represent areas generally containing the American Indian population over which federally-recognized tribes have jurisdiction and areas in which state tribes provide benefits and services to their members. The names of TDSAs delineated by state-recognized tribes are followed by "(state)." The Census Bureau did not recognize TDSAs before the 1990 census.

★ 587 ★

Housing

Occupancy Status of Housing in Selected Tribal Jurisdiction Statistical Areas

Tribal Jurisdiction Statistical Area[1]	Housing units	
	Occupied	Vacant
Absentee Shawnee-Citizens Band of Potawatomi TJSA	30,972	3,414
Caddo-Wichita-Delaware TJSA	3,144	964
Cherokee TJSA	149,891	29,677
Cheyenne-Arapaho TJSA	55,342	10,508
Chickasaw TJSA	99,458	18,406
Choctaw TJSA	79,368	12,956
Creek TJSA	251,320	31,403

[Continued]

★ 587 ★

Occupancy Status of Housing in Selected Tribal Jurisdiction Statistical Areas

[Continued]

Tribal Jurisdiction Statistical Area[1]	Housing units	
	Occupied	Vacant
Iowa TJSA	1,561	312
Kaw TJSA	5,152	575
Kiowa-Comanche-Apache-Fort Sill Apache TJSA	72,798	12,723
Otoe-Missouria TJSA	977	212
Pawnee TJSA	5,953	1,380
Sac and Fox TJSA	20,232	2,928
Seminole TJSA	8,795	1,541
Tonkawa TJSA	4,838	1,115
Creek-Seminole Joint Area TJSA	870	198
Iowa-Sac and Fox Joint Area TJSA	303	92

Source: Census of Population and Housing, 1990: Summary Tape File 3C on CD-ROM [machine-readable datafiles]. Prepared by the Bureau of the Census. Washington, DC: The Bureau, 1992. Notes: 1. Tribal jurisdiction statistical areas (TJSAs) are areas, delineated by federally recognized tribes in Oklahoma without a reservation, for which the Census Bureau tabulates data. TJSAs represent areas generally containing the American Indian population over which one or more tribal governments have jurisdiction. If tribal officials delineated adjacent TJSAs so that they include some duplicate territory, the overlap area is called a "joint use area," which is treated as a separate TJSA for census purposes.

★ 588 ★

Housing

Occupancy Status of Housing on Selected Reservations and Trust Lands

Data are shown for the 50 areas with the largest populations, in number of persons.

American Indian Reservation and Trust Lands[1,2]	Housing units	
	Occupied	Vacant
Agua Caliente Reservation	10,201	11,064
Allegany Reservation	2,901	237
Blackfeet Reservation	2,309	664
Cheyenne River Reservation	2,351	572
Coeur d'Alene Reservation and Trust Lands, ID	2,226	1,516
Colorado River Reservation	2,669	2,108
Colville Reservation	2,416	600
Crow Reservation and Trust Lands, MT	1,705	376
Eastern Cherokee Reservation	2,045	267
Flathead Reservation	7,863	2,519
Fort Apache Reservation	2,549	759
Fort Berthold Reservation	1,735	976
Fort Hall Reservation and Trust Lands, ID	1,510	253
Fort Peck Reservation	3,450	541
Gila River Reservation	2,471	216
Hopi Reservation and Trust Lands, AZ	1,810	601
Isabella Reservation and Trust Lands, MI	8,260	763
Laguna Pueblo and Trust Lands, NM	1,055	287

[Continued]

★ 588 ★

Occupancy Status of Housing on Selected Reservations and Trust Lands

[Continued]

American Indian Reservation and Trust Lands[1,2]	Housing units	
	Occupied	Vacant
Lake Traverse (Sisseton) Reservation	3,903	1,569
Leech Lake Reservation	3,109	3,163
Mississippi Choctaw Reservation and Trust Lands, MS	974	77
Muckleshoot Reservation and Trust Lands, WA	1,333	58
Navajo Reservation and Trust Lands, AZ–NM–UT	36,395	19,246
Nez Perce Reservation	6,141	806
Northern Cheyenne Reservation and Trust Lands, MT–SD	1,037	250
Omaha Reservation	1,745	201
Oneida (West) Reservation	5,734	153
Osage Reservation	15,283	2,813
Papago Reservation	2,159	346
Pine Ridge Reservation and Trust Lands, NE–SD	2,748	628
Port Madison Reservation	1,874	259
Puyallup Reservation and Trust Lands, WA	12,000	988
Red Lake Reservation	948	110
Rosebud Reservation and Trust Lands, SD	2,528	464
Salt River Reservation	1,581	556
San Carlos Reservation	1,705	394
Sandia Pueblo	1,267	158
San Juan Pueblo	1,659	217
Santa Clara Pueblo	3,656	520
Southern Ute Reservation	2,724	633
Standing Rock Reservation	2,325	407
Taos Pueblo and Trust Lands, NM	1,961	735
Tulalip Reservation	2,524	1,502
Turtle Mountain Reservation and Trust Lands, ND–SD	2,105	247
Uintah and Ouray Reservation	4,942	2,607
White Earth Reservation	3,005	1,582
Wind River Reservation	7,499	1,259
Yakima Reservation and Trust Lands, WA	7,886	527

[Continued]

★ 588 ★

Occupancy Status of Housing on Selected Reservations and Trust Lands
[Continued]

American Indian Reservation and Trust Lands[1,2]	Housing units	
	Occupied	Vacant
Yankton Reservation	2,156	332
Zuni Pueblo	1,646	254

Source: Census of Population and Housing, 1990: Summary Tape File 3C on CD-ROM [machine-readable datafiles]. Prepared by the Bureau of the Census. Washington, DC: The Bureau, 1992. *Notes:* 1. Federal American Indian reservations are areas with boundaries established by treaty, statute, and/or executive or court order, and recognized by the federal government as territory in which American Indian tribes have jurisdiction. State reservations are lands held in trust by state governments for the use and benefit of a given tribe. The reservations and their boundaries were identified for the 1990 census by the Bureau of Indian Affairs (BIA), Department of Interior (for federal reservations), and state governments (for state reservations). The names of American Indian reservations recognized by state governments, but not by the federal government, are followed by "state." Areas composed of reservation lands that are administered jointly and/or are claimed by two reservations, as identified by the BIA, are called "joint areas," and are treated as separate American Indian reservations for census purposes. Federal reservations may cross state boundaries, and federal and state reservations may cross county, county subdivision, and place boundaries. For reservations that cross state boundaries, only the portion of the reservations in a given state is shown in the data products for that state; the entire reservations are shown in data products for the United States. 2. Trust lands are property associated with a particular American Indian reservation or tribe, held in trust by the federal government. Trust lands may be held in trust either for a tribe (tribal trust lands) or for an individual member of a tribe (individual trust land). Trust lands recognized for the 1990 census comprised all tribal trust lands and inhabited individual trust lands located outside of a reservation boundary. As with other American Indian areas, trust lands may be located in more than one state. Only the trust lands in a given state are shown in the data products for that state; all trust lands associated with a reservation or tribe are shown in data products for the United States. The Census Bureau first reported data for tribal trust lands for the 1980 census.

★ 589 ★

Housing

Housing Tenure by Race in Selected Alaska Native Villages

Data are shown for the 50 areas with the largest populations, in number of persons.

Alaska Native Village Statistical Area[1]	Owner occupied units					Renter occupied units				
	White	Black	American Indian, Eskimo, or Aleut	Asian or Pacific Islander	Other race	White	Black	American Indian, Eskimo, or Aleut	Asian or Pacific Islander	Other race
Akiachak	0	0	74	0	0	8	0	26	3	0
Akutan	7	0	17	0	0	1	0	2	0	0
Alakanuk	0	0	104	0	0	6	0	10	0	0
Andreafsky	9	0	59	0	0	19	0	23	0	0
Angoon	10	0	45	0	0	30	0	64	0	2
Aniak	19	1	35	0	1	46	2	50	0	0
Barrow	43	0	186	2	2	295	2	221	50	20
Bethel	261	0	314	7	2	434	18	389	5	7
Chevak	5	0	87	0	0	12	0	37	0	0
Copper Center	78	0	30	0	0	41	0	11	0	0
Craig	219	0	59	0	2	133	0	24	3	4
Dillingham	158	0	194	5	0	185	0	139	6	4
Emmonak	5	0	96	0	3	20	2	38	2	0
Fort Yukon	17	0	145	0	0	26	0	20	0	0
Galena	33	0	65	0	0	39	0	33	3	0
Gambell	0	0	101	0	0	6	0	14	0	0
Grouse Creek Group	135	0	27	0	0	42	0	3	0	0

[Continued]

★ 589 ★

Housing Tenure by Race in Selected Alaska Native Villages
[Continued]

Alaska Native Village Statistical Area[1]	Owner occupied units					Renter occupied units				
	White	Black	American Indian, Eskimo, or Aleut	Asian or Pacific Islander	Other race	White	Black	American Indian, Eskimo, or Aleut	Asian or Pacific Islander	Other race
Hoonah	42	0	123	0	0	16	0	44	0	0
Hooper Bay	0	0	141	0	0	14	0	41	0	0
Kake	30	0	137	0	0	27	0	24	0	0
Kasigluk	1	0	47	0	0	10	0	30	0	0
King Cove	5	0	40	0	0	27	0	10	8	0
King Salmon	35	0	18	0	0	103	0	5	0	0
Kipnuk	2	0	94	2	0	2	0	3	0	0
Klawock	61	0	68	0	0	64	0	40	0	0
Kotlik	0	0	79	0	0	4	0	18	0	0
Kotzebue	89	2	230	0	0	185	2	249	7	0
Kwethluk	2	2	96	0	0	6	3	16	0	2
McGrath	42	0	19	0	0	64	0	50	0	0
Mountain Village	2	0	76	3	0	21	5	36	0	0
Naknek	51	0	54	0	0	71	0	26	0	0
Ninilchik	2,458	0	114	19	0	1,105	22	33	2	0
Noorvik	8	0	79	0	0	6	0	16	0	0
Pilot Station	0	0	64	0	0	7	0	30	0	0
Point Hope	3	0	54	0	0	14	0	72	0	0
Quinhagak	4	0	82	0	0	7	0	30	0	0
St. Paul	1	0	104	0	0	26	0	22	0	0
Salamatof	139	0	6	0	0	94	7	18	2	0
Sand Point	26	0	109	3	5	68	0	32	0	0
Savoonga	0	0	83	0	0	9	0	24	0	0
Selawik	9	2	83	0	0	3	0	30	0	0
Shishmaref	0	0	83	0	0	10	0	25	0	0
Stebbins	0	0	66	0	0	9	0	15	0	0
Togiak	7	0	121	0	0	20	0	6	0	0
Tok	251	0	20	0	0	90	0	6	0	0
Toksook Bay	2	0	69	0	0	5	0	13	0	0
Unalakleet	5	0	120	0	0	42	0	33	0	0
Unalaska	92	0	53	3	0	342	7	16	53	9
Wainwright	4	0	91	0	0	15	0	23	0	0
Yakutat	52	0	53	0	0	40	0	34	3	0

Source: Census of Population and Housing, 1990: Summary Tape File 3C on CD-ROM [machine-readable datafiles]. Prepared by the Bureau of the Census. Washington, DC: The Bureau, 1992. *Notes:* 1. Alaska Native villages (ANVs) constitute tribes, bands, clans, groups, villages, communities, or associations in Alaska that are recognized pursuant to the Alaska Native Claims Settlement Act of 1972, Public Law 92-203. Because ANVs do not have legally designated boundaries, the Census Bureau has established Alaska Native village statistical areas (ANVSAs) for statistical purposes. For the 1990 census, the Census Bureau cooperated with officials of the nonprofit corporation within each participating Alaska Native Regional Corporation (ANRC), as well as other knowledgeable officials, to delineate boundaries that encompass the settled area associated with each ANV.

★ 590 ★

Housing

Housing Tenure by Race in Selected Tribal Designated Statistical Areas

TDSA[1]	Owner occupied units					Renter occupied units				
	White	Black	American Indian, Eskimo, or Aleut	Asian or Pacific Islander	Other race	White	Black	American Indian, Eskimo, or Aleut	Asian or Pacific Islander	Other race
Apache Choctaw TDSA (state)	5,731	759	178	9	18	1,118	493	36	6	13
Chickahominy TDSA (state)	229	462	159	0	0	20	59	0	0	0
Clifton Choctaw TDSA (state)	83	0	51	0	0	31	0	11	0	0
Coharie TDSA (state)	19,654	7,013	300	76	26	8,571	8,297	188	39	125
Coquille Indian TDSA	93,916	173	1,057	641	394	60,944	411	1,194	1,408	734
Delaware-Muncie TDSA (state)	79	0	5	0	0	7	0	0	0	0
Florida Tribe of Eastern Creek TDSA (state)	70	0	0	0	0	18	0	0	0	0
Haliwa-Saponi TDSA (state)	184	839	489	0	3	38	324	221	0	0
Jena Band of Choctaw TDSA (state)	14,125	774	73	39	11	4,892	1,063	60	15	5
Klamath TDSA	9,566	20	255	34	105	5,639	68	320	65	110
Lumbee TDSA (state)	2,545	2,489	6,605	12	14	811	1,531	2,076	0	16
Meherrin TDSA (state)	7,876	6,774	65	8	10	1,934	3,418	21	11	0
Mohegan TDSA (state)	5,058	120	11	61	17	3,972	352	52	72	108
Ramapough TDSA (state)	100	34	41	0	0	20	0	7	0	0
United Houma Nation TDSA (state)	169,861	21,950	1,822	1,914	1,061	70,503	19,561	938	1,358	1,278
Waccamaw Siouan TDSA (state)	179	163	360	0	9	84	47	40	0	0
Wampanoag-Gay Head TDSA	3,395	101	63	4	20	1,273	95	34	0	18

Source: Census of Population and Housing, 1990: Summary Tape File 3C on CD-ROM [machine-readable datafiles]. Prepared by the Bureau of the Census. Washington, DC: The Bureau, 1992. *Notes:* 1. Tribal designated statistical areas (TDSAs) are areas, delineated outside Oklahoma by federally- and state-recognized tribes without a land base or associated trust lands, to provide statistical areas for which the Census Bureau tabulates data. TDSAs represent areas generally containing the American Indian population over which federally-recognized tribes have jurisdiction and areas in which state tribes provide benefits and services to their members. The names of TDSAs delineated by state-recognized tribes are followed by "(state)." The Census Bureau did not recognize TDSAs before the 1990 census.

★ 591 ★

Housing

Housing Tenure by Race in Selected Tribal Jurisdiction Statistical Areas

TJSA[1]	Owner occupied units					Renter occupied units				
	White	Black	American Indian, Eskimo, or Aleut	Asian or Pacific Islander	Other race	White	Black	American Indian, Eskimo, or Aleut	Asian or Pacific Islander	Other race
Absentee Shawnee-Citizens Band of Potawatomi TJSA	23,020	1,434	1,411	35	89	4,279	381	291	10	22
Caddo-Wichita-Delaware TJSA	2,224	21	125	0	26	610	9	65	0	64
Cherokee TJSA	89,037	7,447	14,095	131	266	27,751	4,599	6,188	116	261
Cheyenne-Arapaho TJSA	38,393	551	985	206	385	12,890	507	923	74	428
Chickasaw TJSA	67,390	1,731	4,428	77	285	21,648	1,229	2,266	73	331
Choctaw TJSA	50,043	1,919	6,399	51	118	16,642	1,161	2,863	36	136
Creek TJSA	146,043	5,188	8,920	863	501	73,480	8,742	5,811	976	796
Iowa TJSA	1,161	27	67	0	3	268	20	14	0	1
Kaw TJSA	4,027	27	150	10	5	853	13	67	0	0

[Continued]

★ 591 ★

Housing Tenure by Race in Selected Tribal Jurisdiction Statistical Areas
[Continued]

TJSA[1]	Owner occupied units					Renter occupied units				
	White	Black	American Indian, Eskimo, or Aleut	Asian or Pacific Islander	Other race	White	Black	American Indian, Eskimo, or Aleut	Asian or Pacific Islander	Other race
Kiowa-Comanche-Apache-Fort Sill Apache TJSA	40,846	2,933	2,089	483	1,102	17,646	4,772	1,390	260	1,277
Otoe-Missouria TJSA	646	8	57	0	7	160	15	81	0	3
Pawnee TJSA	4,307	30	357	5	6	1,070	20	158	0	0
Sac and Fox TJSA	13,430	349	926	16	37	4,670	254	448	30	72
Seminole TJSA	5,437	332	664	3	3	1,641	302	399	0	14
Tonkawa TJSA	3,404	0	139	4	9	1,159	2	99	8	14
Creek-Seminole Joint Area TJSA	488	24	103	4	0	158	24	64	0	5
Iowa-Sac and Fox Joint Area TJSA	233	8	5	0	3	54	0	0	0	0

Source: *Census of Population and Housing, 1990: Summary Tape File 3C on CD-ROM* [machine-readable datafiles]. Prepared by the Bureau of the Census. Washington, DC: The Bureau, 1992. *Notes:* 1. Tribal jurisdiction statistical areas (TJSAs) are areas, delineated by federally recognized tribes in Oklahoma without a reservation, for which the Census Bureau tabulates data. TJSAs represent areas generally containing the American Indian population over which one or more tribal governments have jurisdiction. If tribal officials delineated adjacent TJSAs so that they include some duplicate territory, the overlap area is called a "joint use area," which is treated as a separate TJSA for census purposes.

★ 592 ★

Housing

Housing Tenure by Race on Selected Reservations and Trust Lands

Data are shown for the 50 areas with the largest populations, in number of persons.

American Indian Reservation and Trust Lands[1,2]	Owner occupied units					Renter occupied units				
	White	Black	American Indian, Eskimo, or Aleut	Asian or Pacific Islander	Other race	White	Black	American Indian, Eskimo, or Aleut	Asian or Pacific Islander	Other race
Agua Caliente Reservation	6,942	22	31	48	61	2,758	123	23	36	157
Allegany Reservation	1,597	0	223	4	0	902	0	163	0	12
Blackfeet Reservation	260	2	976	0	0	182	2	887	0	0
Cheyenne River Reservation	778	4	431	0	0	287	0	851	0	0
Coeur d'Alene Reservation and Trust Lands, ID	1,565	3	145	0	1	428	0	82	0	2
Colorado River Reservation	1,318	5	422	9	148	474	5	213	6	69
Colville Reservation	827	0	695	6	9	336	0	508	3	32
Crow Reservation and Trust Lands, MT	427	0	672	8	0	195	0	403	0	0
Eastern Cherokee Reservation	165	6	1,420	0	0	109	5	340	0	0
Flathead Reservation	4,418	0	1,059	2	10	1,692	0	682	0	0
Fort Apache Reservation	45	13	1,609	0	11	158	0	713	0	0
Fort Berthold Reservation	681	0	372	0	7	212	0	457	6	0
Fort Hall Reservation and Trust Lands, ID	498	0	639	6	40	101	0	191	0	35
Fort Peck Reservation	1,363	0	768	0	0	480	0	834	5	0
Gila River Reservation	37	0	1,588	0	55	10	0	747	5	29

[Continued]

★ 592 ★

Housing Tenure by Race on Selected Reservations and Trust Lands
[Continued]

American Indian Reservation and Trust Lands[1,2]	Owner occupied units					Renter occupied units				
	White	Black	American Indian, Eskimo, or Aleut	Asian or Pacific Islander	Other race	White	Black	American Indian, Eskimo, or Aleut	Asian or Pacific Islander	Other race
Hopi Reservation and Trust Lands, AZ	7	0	1,360	0	7	60	0	360	16	0
Isabella Reservation and Trust Lands, MI	5,649	17	129	23	32	2,222	43	106	10	29
Laguna Pueblo and Trust Lands, NM	25	3	771	0	0	12	0	244	0	0
Lake Traverse (Sisseton) Reservation	2,323	0	211	0	5	825	0	539	0	0
Leech Lake Reservation	1,839	2	628	0	0	251	0	387	0	2
Mississippi Choctaw Reservation and Trust Lands, MS	52	0	626	0	0	0	0	296	0	0
Muckleshoot Reservation and Trust Lands, WA	796	0	102	6	0	334	2	74	0	19
Navajo Reservation and Trust Lands, AZ–NM–UT	526	0	26,462	14	78	1,396	74	7,707	58	80
Nez Perce Reservation	4,204	6	395	4	0	1,329	0	197	4	2
Northern Cheyenne Reservation and Trust Lands, MT–SD	75	0	544	0	0	91	0	327	0	0
Omaha Reservation	935	0	146	0	0	377	0	287	0	0
Oneida (West) Reservation	3,912	11	452	7	6	1,066	13	259	4	4
Osage Reservation	9,560	948	1,470	8	9	2,397	405	474	0	12
Papago Reservation	37	0	1,570	0	0	22	0	530	0	0
Pine Ridge Reservation and Trust Lands, NE–SD	264	0	1,015	3	0	140	10	1,287	10	19
Port Madison Reservation	1,366	3	85	30	6	335	0	44	5	0
Puyallup Reservation and Trust Lands, WA	6,682	248	160	208	48	3,452	397	174	504	127
Red Lake Reservation	16	0	581	0	0	15	0	336	0	0
Rosebud Reservation and Trust Lands, SD	354	0	816	0	1	247	0	1,108	0	2
Salt River Reservation	657	0	593	0	5	62	0	264	0	0
San Carlos Reservation	24	0	1,076	0	0	27	7	560	0	11
Sandia Pueblo	695	6	97	0	176	242	0	15	2	34
San Juan Pueblo	976	3	312	2	156	153	6	33	0	18
Santa Clara Pueblo	2,129	5	335	0	220	792	12	85	2	76
Southern Ute Reservation	1,805	0	174	0	104	491	0	135	0	15
Standing Rock Reservation	901	0	317	0	0	287	0	818	2	0
Taos Pueblo and Trust Lands, NM	654	3	359	2	231	566	2	65	4	75
Tulalip Reservation	1,848	2	195	0	5	349	2	112	5	6
Turtle Mountain Reservation and Trust Lands, ND–SD	57	0	1,159	0	0	66	0	823	0	0
Uintah and Ouray Reservation	3,541	4	421	1	20	702	2	235	5	11
White Earth Reservation	1,849	0	499	0	0	323	0	334	0	0
Wind River Reservation	4,268	0	885	17	32	1,555	0	651	0	91
Yakima Reservation and Trust Lands, WA	2,860	35	831	130	950	1,222	24	713	21	1,100

[Continued]

★ 592 ★

Housing Tenure by Race on Selected Reservations and Trust Lands

[Continued]

American Indian Reservation and Trust Lands[1,2]	Owner occupied units					Renter occupied units				
	White	Black	American Indian, Eskimo, or Aleut	Asian or Pacific Islander	Other race	White	Black	American Indian, Eskimo, or Aleut	Asian or Pacific Islander	Other race
Yankton Reservation	1,234	0	166	0	0	434	0	322	0	0
Zuni Pueblo	25	0	1,142	0	0	139	15	320	5	0

Source: Census of Population and Housing, 1990: Summary Tape File 3C on CD-ROM [machine-readable datafiles]. Prepared by the Bureau of the Census. Washington, DC: The Bureau, 1992. *Notes:* 1. Federal American Indian reservations are areas with boundaries established by treaty, statute, and/or executive or court order, and recognized by the federal government as territory in which American Indian tribes have jurisdiction. State reservations are lands held in trust by state governments for the use and benefit of a given tribe. The reservations and their boundaries were identified for the 1990 census by the Bureau of Indian Affairs (BIA), Department of Interior (for federal reservations), and state governments (for state reservations). The names of American Indian reservations recognized by state governments, but not by the federal government, are followed by "state." Areas composed of reservation lands that are administered jointly and/or are claimed by two reservations, as identified by the BIA, are called "joint areas," and are treated as separate American Indian reservations for census purposes. Federal reservations may cross state boundaries, and federal and state reservations may cross county, county subdivision, and place boundaries. For reservations that cross state boundaries, only the portion of the reservations in a given state is shown in the data products for that state; the entire reservations are shown in data products for the United States. 2. Trust lands are property associated with a particular American Indian reservation or tribe, held in trust by the federal government. Trust lands may be held in trust either for a tribe (tribal trust lands) or for an individual member of a tribe (individual trust land). Trust lands recognized for the 1990 census comprised all tribal trust lands and inhabited individual trust lands located outside of a reservation boundary. As with other American Indian areas, trust lands may be located in more than one state. Only the trust lands in a given state are shown in the data products for that state; all trust lands associated with a reservation or tribe are shown in data products for the United States. The Census Bureau first reported data for tribal trust lands for the 1980 census.

★ 593 ★

Housing

Tenure Status of Housing in Selected Alaska Native Villages

Data are shown for the 50 areas with the largest populations, in number of housing units.

Alaska Native Village Statistical Area[1]	Occupied housing units	
	Owner occupied	Renter occupied
Akiachak	74	37
Akutan	24	3
Alakanuk	104	16
Andreafsky	68	42
Angoon	55	96
Aniak	56	98
Barrow	233	588
Bethel	584	853
Chevak	92	49
Copper Center	108	52
Craig	280	164
Dillingham	357	334
Emmonak	104	62
Fort Yukon	162	46
Galena	98	75
Gambell	101	20
Grouse Creek Group	162	45
Hoonah	165	60
Hooper Bay	141	55
Kake	167	51

[Continued]

★ 593 ★

Tenure Status of Housing in Selected Alaska Native Villages
[Continued]

Alaska Native Village Statistical Area[1]	Occupied housing units	
	Owner occupied	Renter occupied
Kasigluk	48	40
King Cove	45	45
King Salmon	53	108
Kipnuk	98	5
Klawock	129	104
Kotlik	79	22
Kotzebue	321	443
Kwethluk	100	27
McGrath	61	114
Mountain Village	81	62
Naknek	105	97
Ninilchik	2,591	1,162
Noorvik	87	22
Pilot Station	64	37
Point Hope	57	86
Quinhagak	86	37
St. Paul	105	48
Salamatof	145	121
Sand Point	143	100
Savoonga	83	33
Selawik	94	33
Shishmaref	83	35
Stebbins	66	24
Togiak	128	26
Tok	271	96
Toksook Bay	71	18
Unalakleet	125	75
Unalaska	148	427
Wainwright	95	38
Yakutat	105	77

Source: Census of Population and Housing, 1990: Summary Tape File 3C on CD-ROM [machine-readable datafiles]. Prepared by the Bureau of the Census. Washington, DC: The Bureau, 1992. *Notes:* 1. Alaska Native villages (ANVs) constitute tribes, bands, clans, groups, villages, communities, or associations in Alaska that are recognized pursuant to the Alaska Native Claims Settlement Act of 1972, Public Law 92-203. Because ANVs do not have legally designated boundaries, the Census Bureau has established Alaska Native village statistical areas (ANVSAs) for statistical purposes. For the 1990 census, the Census Bureau cooperated with officials of the nonprofit corporation within each participating Alaska Native Regional Corporation (ANRC), as well as other knowledgeable officials, to delineate boundaries that encompass the settled area associated with each ANV.

★ 594 ★

Housing

Tenure Status of Housing in Selected Tribal Designated Statistical Areas

Tribal Designated Statistical Area[1]	Occupied housing units	
	Owner occupied	Renter occupied
Apache Choctaw TDSA (state)	6,695	1,666
Chickahominy TDSA (state)	850	79
Clifton Choctaw TDSA (state)	134	42
Coharie TDSA (state)	27,069	17,220
Coquille Indian TDSA	96,181	64,691
Delaware-Muncie TDSA (state)	84	7
Florida Tribe of Eastern Creek TDSA (state)	70	18
Haliwa-Saponi TDSA (state)	1,515	583
Jena Band of Choctaw TDSA (state)	15,022	6,035
Klamath TDSA	9,980	6,202
Lumbee TDSA (state)	11,665	4,434
Meherrin TDSA (state)	14,733	5,384
Mohegan TDSA (state)	5,267	4,556
Ramapough TDSA (state)	175	27
United Houma Nation TDSA (state)	196,608	93,638
Waccamaw Siouan TDSA (state)	711	171
Wampanoag-Gay Head TDSA	3,583	1,420

Source: Census of Population and Housing, 1990: Summary Tape File 3C on CD-ROM [machine-readable datafiles]. Prepared by the Bureau of the Census. Washington, DC: The Bureau, 1992. *Notes:* 1. Tribal designated statistical areas (TDSAs) are areas, delineated outside Oklahoma by federally- and state-recognized tribes without a land base or associated trust lands, to provide statistical areas for which the Census Bureau tabulates data. TDSAs represent areas generally containing the American Indian population over which federally-recognized tribes have jurisdiction and areas in which state tribes provide benefits and services to their members. The names of TDSAs delineated by state-recognized tribes are followed by "(state)." The Census Bureau did not recognize TDSAs before the 1990 census.

★ 595 ★

Housing

Tenure Status of Housing in Selected Tribal Jurisdiction Statistical Areas

Tribal Jurisdiction Statistical Area[1]	Occupied housing units	
	Owner occupied	Renter occupied
Absentee Shawnee-Citizens Band of Potawatomi TJSA	25,989	4,983
Caddo-Wichita-Delaware TJSA	2,396	748
Cherokee TJSA	110,976	38,915
Cheyenne-Arapaho TJSA	40,520	14,822
Chickasaw TJSA	73,911	25,547
Choctaw TJSA	58,530	20,838
Creek TJSA	161,515	89,805
Iowa TJSA	1,258	303
Kaw TJSA	4,219	933

[Continued]

★ 595 ★

Tenure Status of Housing in Selected Tribal Jurisdiction Statistical Areas
[Continued]

Tribal Jurisdiction Statistical Area[1]	Occupied housing units	
	Owner occupied	Renter occupied
Kiowa-Comanche-Apache-Fort Sill Apache TJSA	47,453	25,345
Otoe-Missouria TJSA	718	259
Pawnee TJSA	4,705	1,248
Sac and Fox TJSA	14,758	5,474
Seminole TJSA	6,439	2,356
Tonkawa TJSA	3,556	1,282
Creek-Seminole Joint Area TJSA	619	251
Iowa-Sac and Fox Joint Area TJSA	249	54

Source: Census of Population and Housing, 1990: Summary Tape File 3C on CD-ROM [machine-readable datafiles]. Prepared by the Bureau of the Census. Washington, DC: The Bureau, 1992. Notes: 1. Tribal jurisdiction statistical areas (TJSAs) are areas, delineated by federally recognized tribes in Oklahoma without a reservation, for which the Census Bureau tabulates data. TJSAs represent areas generally containing the American Indian population over which one or more tribal governments have jurisdiction. If tribal officials delineated adjacent TJSAs so that they include some duplicate territory, the overlap area is called a "joint use area," which is treated as a separate TJSA for census purposes.

★ 596 ★

Housing

Tenure Status of Housing on Selected Reservations and Trust Lands

Data are shown for the 50 areas with the largest populations, in number of housing units.

American Indian Reservation and Trust Lands[1,2]	Occupied housing units	
	Owner occupied	Renter occupied
Agua Caliente Reservation	7,104	3,097
Allegany Reservation	1,824	1,077
Blackfeet Reservation	1,238	1,071
Cheyenne River Reservation	1,213	1,138
Coeur d'Alene Reservation and Trust Lands, ID	1,714	512
Colorado River Reservation	1,902	767
Colville Reservation	1,537	879
Crow Reservation and Trust Lands, MT	1,107	598
Eastern Cherokee Reservation	1,591	454
Flathead Reservation	5,489	2,374
Fort Apache Reservation	1,678	871
Fort Berthold Reservation	1,060	675
Fort Hall Reservation and Trust Lands, ID	1,183	327
Fort Peck Reservation	2,131	1,319
Gila River Reservation	1,680	791
Hopi Reservation and Trust Lands, AZ	1,374	436
Isabella Reservation and Trust Lands, MI	5,850	2,410
Laguna Pueblo and Trust Lands, NM	799	256
Lake Traverse (Sisseton) Reservation	2,539	1,364
Leech Lake Reservation	2,469	640
Mississippi Choctaw Reservation and Trust Lands, MS	678	296
Muckleshoot Reservation and Trust Lands, WA	904	429
Navajo Reservation and Trust Lands, AZ–NM–UT	27,080	9,315

[Continued]

★ 596 ★

Tenure Status of Housing on Selected Reservations and Trust Lands
[Continued]

American Indian Reservation and Trust Lands[1,2]	Occupied housing units	
	Owner occupied	Renter occupied
Nez Perce Reservation	4,609	1,532
Northern Cheyenne Reservation and Trust Lands, MT–SD	619	418
Omaha Reservation	1,081	664
Oneida (West) Reservation	4,388	1,346
Osage Reservation	11,995	3,288
Papago Reservation	1,607	552
Pine Ridge Reservation and Trust Lands, NE–SD	1,282	1,466
Port Madison Reservation	1,490	384
Puyallup Reservation and Trust Lands, WA	7,346	4,654
Red Lake Reservation	597	351
Rosebud Reservation and Trust Lands, SD	1,171	1,357
Salt River Reservation	1,255	326
San Carlos Reservation	1,100	605
Sandia Pueblo	974	293
San Juan Pueblo	1,449	210
Santa Clara Pueblo	2,689	967
Southern Ute Reservation	2,083	641
Standing Rock Reservation	1,218	1,107
Taos Pueblo and Trust Lands, NM	1,249	712
Tulalip Reservation	2,050	474
Turtle Mountain Reservation and Trust Lands, ND–SD	1,216	889
Uintah and Ouray Reservation	3,987	955
White Earth Reservation	2,348	657
Wind River Reservation	5,202	2,297
Yakima Reservation and Trust Lands, WA	4,806	3,080
Yankton Reservation	1,400	756
Zuni Pueblo	1,167	479

Source: Census of Population and Housing, 1990: Summary Tape File 3C on CD-ROM [machine-readable datafiles]. Prepared by the Bureau of the Census. Washington, DC: The Bureau, 1992. *Notes:* 1. Federal American Indian reservations are areas with boundaries established by treaty, statute, and/or executive or court order, and recognized by the federal government as territory in which American Indian tribes have jurisdiction. State reservations are lands held in trust by state governments for the use and benefit of a given tribe. The reservations and their boundaries were identified for the 1990 census by the Bureau of Indian Affairs (BIA), Department of Interior (for federal reservations), and state governments (for state reservations). The names of American Indian reservations recognized by state governments, but not by the federal government, are followed by "state." Areas composed of reservation lands that are administered jointly and/or are claimed by two reservations, as identified by the BIA, are called "joint areas," and are treated as separate American Indian reservations for census purposes. Federal reservations may cross state boundaries, and federal and state reservations may cross county, county subdivision, and place boundaries. For reservations that cross state boundaries, only the portion of the reservations in a given state is shown in the data products for that state; the entire reservations are shown in data products for the United States. 2. Trust lands are property associated with a particular American Indian reservation or tribe, held in trust by the federal government. Trust lands may be held in trust either for a tribe (tribal trust lands) or for an individual member of a tribe (individual trust land). Trust lands recognized for the 1990 census comprised all tribal trust lands and inhabited individual trust lands located outside of a reservation boundary. As with other American Indian areas, trust lands may be located in more than one state. Only the trust lands in a given state are shown in the data products for that state; all trust lands associated with a reservation or tribe are shown in data products for the United States. The Census Bureau first reported data for tribal trust lands for the 1980 census.

★ 597 ★

Housing

Housing Units by Year Built in Selected Alaska Native Villages

Data are shown for the 50 areas with the largest populations, in number of housing units.

Alaska Native Village Statistical Area[1]	Year structure built							
	1989 to March 1990	1985 to 1988	1980 to 1984	1970 to 1979	1960 to 1969	1950 to 1959	1940 to 1949	1939 or earlier
Akiachak	6	26	18	23	36	8	11	0
Akutan	0	0	16	0	0	2	5	4
Alakanuk	0	3	36	86	5	9	0	0
Andreafsky	5	16	26	61	19	11	0	0
Angoon	2	17	29	71	4	12	0	26
Aniak	4	33	50	53	17	14	2	2
Barrow	35	117	248	318	99	34	59	12
Bethel	23	138	462	580	211	116	34	66
Chevak	0	19	62	57	15	5	0	0
Copper Center	5	27	73	74	22	15	3	18
Craig	12	38	139	186	74	17	8	30
Dillingham	31	153	257	244	57	46	20	43
Emmonak	1	12	23	88	39	3	5	6
Fort Yukon	6	36	38	100	31	22	18	24
Galena	0	38	77	114	32	3	2	3
Gambell	0	1	7	78	8	7	14	18
Grouse Creek Group	43	70	36	32	26	13	11	11
Hoonah	0	0	31	112	29	4	56	19
Hooper Bay	0	50	30	66	31	16	2	14
Kake	0	50	33	110	21	16	13	21
Kasigluk	4	2	35	50	7	2	2	0
King Cove	1	4	23	62	26	2	4	7
King Salmon	0	40	75	37	25	15	33	8
Kipnuk	0	17	11	100	4	0	0	0
Klawock	12	79	40	116	4	3	9	12
Kotlik	0	7	40	40	14	9	0	0
Kotzebue	3	143	177	316	127	88	30	27
Kwethluk	2	19	9	38	46	20	2	2
McGrath	8	35	31	87	9	7	22	11
Mountain Village	0	4	44	119	7	3	8	1
Naknek	14	44	47	81	30	24	6	22
Ninilchik	142	1,028	1,588	1,409	467	413	102	50
Noorvik	0	4	16	69	22	16	0	0
Pilot Station	3	7	52	42	11	7	2	0
Point Hope	0	2	81	61	23	5	0	2
Quinhagak	7	8	18	71	15	0	6	7
St. Paul	0	46	14	26	21	10	24	34
Salamatof	0	21	70	89	72	166	4	2
Sand Point	17	63	38	75	62	9	8	2
Savoonga	6	6	19	58	33	2	5	0
Selawik	2	5	31	80	13	7	13	1
Shishmaref	0	4	38	52	28	4	4	5
Stebbins	5	4	8	37	23	10	4	0
Togiak	15	35	26	72	38	14	3	0
Tok	39	109	155	155	64	21	18	0

[Continued]

★ 597 ★

Housing Units by Year Built in Selected Alaska Native Villages
[Continued]

Alaska Native Village Statistical Area[1]	Year structure built							
	1989 to March 1990	1985 to 1988	1980 to 1984	1970 to 1979	1960 to 1969	1950 to 1959	1940 to 1949	1939 or earlier
Toksook Bay	0	0	42	45	18	0	0	1
Unalakleet	3	6	56	95	19	31	16	8
Unalaska	104	102	115	95	5	3	211	38
Wainwright	0	0	53	63	24	9	4	7
Yakutat	6	19	28	88	19	14	10	10

Source: Census of Population and Housing, 1990: Summary Tape File 3C on CD-ROM [machine-readable datafiles]. Prepared by the Bureau of the Census. Washington, DC: The Bureau, 1992. Notes: 1. Alaska Native villages (ANVs) constitute tribes, bands, clans, groups, villages, communities, or associations in Alaska that are recognized pursuant to the Alaska Native Claims Settlement Act of 1972, Public Law 92-203. Because ANVs do not have legally designated boundaries, the Census Bureau has established Alaska Native village statistical areas (ANVSAs) for statistical purposes. For the 1990 census, the Census Bureau cooperated with officials of the nonprofit corporation within each participating Alaska Native Regional Corporation (ANRC), as well as other knowledgeable officials, to delineate boundaries that encompass the settled area associated with each ANV.

★ 598 ★
Housing

Housing Units by Year Built in Selected Tribal Designated Statistical Areas

Tribal Designated Statistical Area[1]	Year structure built							
	1989 to March 1990	1985 to 1988	1980 to 1984	1970 to 1979	1960 to 1969	1950 to 1959	1940 to 1949	1939 or earlier
Apache Choctaw TDSA (state)	228	1,469	2,351	3,786	2,073	1,160	827	895
Chickahominy TDSA (state)	63	83	157	283	179	109	51	64
Clifton Choctaw TDSA (state)	13	11	38	17	30	38	28	13
Coharie TDSA (state)	916	4,224	4,961	11,847	8,864	6,991	4,375	6,192
Coquille Indian TDSA	3,717	7,746	12,964	49,980	30,771	26,130	18,237	20,981
Delaware-Muncie TDSA (state)	0	0	22	49	7	0	0	13
Florida Tribe of Eastern Creek TDSA (state)	8	64	41	0	0	15	0	0
Haliwa-Saponi TDSA (state)	59	235	327	624	476	177	213	191
Jena Band of Choctaw TDSA (state)	406	1,804	3,314	6,853	4,166	2,896	2,375	1,834
Klamath TDSA	126	452	1,039	4,655	2,565	2,432	2,587	3,766
Lumbee TDSA (state)	499	1,948	2,479	5,700	2,819	1,643	923	1,189
Meherrin TDSA (state)	470	1,997	2,237	5,645	3,797	3,108	1,932	3,221
Mohegan TDSA (state)	96	288	223	1,172	1,690	1,542	597	5,074
Ramapough TDSA (state)	0	14	0	25	17	41	25	83
United Houma Nation TDSA (state)	2,559	19,129	42,393	95,691	75,074	49,096	20,842	17,001
Waccamaw Siouan TDSA (state)	38	162	162	293	111	76	41	85
Wampanoag-Gay Head TDSA	469	1,902	1,818	1,921	762	788	642	3,302

Source: Census of Population and Housing, 1990: Summary Tape File 3C on CD-ROM [machine-readable datafiles]. Prepared by the Bureau of the Census. Washington, DC: The Bureau, 1992. Notes: 1. Tribal designated statistical areas (TDSAs) are areas, delineated outside Oklahoma by federally- and state-recognized tribes without a land base or associated trust lands, to provide statistical areas for which the Census Bureau tabulates data. TDSAs represent areas generally containing the American Indian population over which federally-recognized tribes have jurisdiction and areas in which state tribes provide benefits and services to their members. The names of TDSAs delineated by state-recognized tribes are followed by "(state)." The Census Bureau did not recognize TDSAs before the 1990 census.

★ 599 ★
Housing

Housing Units by Year Built in Selected Tribal Jurisdiction Statistical Areas

TJSA[1]	Year structure built							
	1989 to March 1990	1985 to 1988	1980 to 1984	1970 to 1979	1960 to 1969	1950 to 1959	1940 to 1949	1939 or earlier
Absentee Shawnee-Citizens Band of Potawatomi TJSA	297	3,294	8,160	10,361	4,739	3,583	1,804	2,148
Caddo-Wichita-Delaware TJSA	34	135	805	1,034	693	296	236	875
Cherokee TJSA	2,290	11,651	25,386	46,610	29,163	29,912	16,439	18,117
Cheyenne-Arapaho TJSA	344	2,680	13,206	16,308	10,364	6,459	5,278	11,211
Chickasaw TJSA	1,008	6,688	18,803	30,234	16,737	18,031	11,244	15,119
Choctaw TJSA	1,311	7,274	13,067	26,794	15,070	10,184	7,603	11,021
Creek TJSA	2,584	18,591	44,196	78,801	47,411	36,950	21,588	32,602
Iowa TJSA	2	98	391	469	257	134	83	439
Kaw TJSA	72	374	974	1,527	1,121	762	291	606
Kiowa-Comanche-Apache-Fort Sill Apache TJSA	712	4,723	9,405	19,656	15,435	14,806	8,220	12,564
Otoe-Missouria TJSA	7	48	219	307	87	101	134	286
Pawnee TJSA	77	389	1,174	2,177	1,083	521	385	1,527
Sac and Fox TJSA	156	1,123	3,120	4,923	3,141	3,392	2,173	5,132
Seminole TJSA	20	457	1,301	2,673	1,121	1,173	1,428	2,163
Tonkawa TJSA	32	115	355	832	522	959	786	2,352
Creek-Seminole Joint Area TJSA	0	24	142	182	181	197	118	224
Iowa-Sac and Fox Joint Area TJSA	7	65	59	108	36	28	29	63

Source: Census of Population and Housing, 1990: Summary Tape File 3C on CD-ROM [machine-readable datafiles]. Prepared by the Bureau of the Census. Washington, DC: The Bureau, 1992. *Notes:* 1. Tribal jurisdiction statistical areas (TJSAs) are areas, delineated by federally recognized tribes in Oklahoma without a reservation, for which the Census Bureau tabulates data. TJSAs represent areas generally containing the American Indian population over which one or more tribal governments have jurisdiction. If tribal officials delineated adjacent TJSAs so that they include some duplicate territory, the overlap area is called a "joint use area," which is treated as a separate TJSA for census purposes.

★ 600 ★
Housing

Housing Units by Year Built on Selected Reservations and Trust Lands

Data are shown for the 50 areas with the largest populations, in number of housing units.

American Indian Reservation and Trust Lands[1,2]	Year structure built							
	1989 to March 1990	1985 to 1988	1980 to 1984	1970 to 1979	1960 to 1969	1950 to 1959	1940 to 1949	1939 or earlier
Agua Caliente Reservation	393	3,236	4,322	7,909	3,667	1,249	303	186
Allegany Reservation	61	49	173	314	275	235	187	1,844
Blackfeet Reservation	51	349	498	1,034	415	142	92	392
Cheyenne River Reservation	25	274	268	1,031	456	325	138	406
Coeur d'Alene Reservation and Trust Lands, ID	92	283	586	1,107	568	408	237	461

[Continued]

★ 600 ★

Housing Units by Year Built on Selected Reservations and Trust Lands

[Continued]

American Indian Reservation and Trust Lands[1,2]	Year structure built							
	1989 to March 1990	1985 to 1988	1980 to 1984	1970 to 1979	1960 to 1969	1950 to 1959	1940 to 1949	1939 or earlier
Colorado River Reservation	155	392	679	2,176	935	288	60	92
Colville Reservation	35	142	394	1,119	393	159	318	456
Crow Reservation and Trust Lands, MT	35	236	243	782	276	124	129	256
Eastern Cherokee Reservation	55	259	576	871	243	133	95	80
Flathead Reservation	331	767	1,242	3,313	1,274	1,036	806	1,613
Fort Apache Reservation	104	650	326	1,243	600	151	47	187
Fort Berthold Reservation	38	175	238	1,059	357	329	108	407
Fort Hall Reservation and Trust Lands, ID	5	114	215	864	191	155	98	121
Fort Peck Reservation	126	202	537	944	460	520	369	833
Gila River Reservation	85	551	318	1,053	421	159	77	23
Hopi Reservation and Trust Lands, AZ	37	194	362	516	452	207	174	469
Isabella Reservation and Trust Lands, MI	199	575	697	2,458	1,334	990	745	2,025
Laguna Pueblo and Trust Lands, NM	20	59	59	525	192	74	134	279
Lake Traverse (Sisseton) Reservation	84	203	255	1,238	761	485	321	2,125
Leech Lake Reservation	145	589	834	1,933	1,060	497	374	840
Mississippi Choctaw Reservation and Trust Lands, MS	41	249	238	308	79	54	30	52
Muckleshoot Reservation and Trust Lands, WA	16	72	77	505	664	28	8	21
Navajo Reservation and Trust Lands, AZ–NM–UT	2,305	8,130	9,553	15,533	11,517	5,030	1,654	1,919
Nez Perce Reservation	92	244	565	2,159	1,035	888	487	1,477
Northern Cheyenne Reservation and Trust Lands, MT–SD	93	119	239	510	223	16	6	81
Omaha Reservation	4	91	136	415	191	131	94	884
Oneida (West) Reservation	204	1,070	922	2,144	730	269	155	393
Osage Reservation	284	985	2,795	5,180	2,261	2,110	1,388	3,093
Papago Reservation	36	493	534	650	307	141	121	223
Pine Ridge Reservation and Trust Lands, NE–SD	45	284	364	1,373	524	237	180	369
Port Madison Reservation	63	217	438	692	175	157	118	273
Puyallup Reservation and Trust Lands, WA	663	1,461	1,592	2,811	1,751	1,380	1,677	1,653
Red Lake Reservation	108	207	183	293	173	34	12	48
Rosebud Reservation and Trust Lands, SD	191	308	308	894	798	104	92	297
Salt River Reservation	98	374	446	921	147	105	39	7
San Carlos Reservation	73	544	289	523	356	117	72	125
Sandia Pueblo	17	206	118	428	304	86	101	165

[Continued]

★ 600 ★

Housing Units by Year Built on Selected Reservations and Trust Lands

[Continued]

American Indian Reservation and Trust Lands[1,2]	Year structure built							
	1989 to March 1990	1985 to 1988	1980 to 1984	1970 to 1979	1960 to 1969	1950 to 1959	1940 to 1949	1939 or earlier
San Juan Pueblo	95	203	240	544	253	155	124	262
Santa Clara Pueblo	90	541	539	1,246	693	429	270	368
Southern Ute Reservation	69	376	572	1,158	321	260	165	436
Standing Rock Reservation	66	138	186	905	579	259	63	536
Taos Pueblo and Trust Lands, NM	42	264	245	456	304	198	293	894
Tulalip Reservation	97	797	627	1,418	540	214	145	188
Turtle Mountain Reservation and Trust Lands, ND – SD	100	479	363	674	507	101	59	69
Uintah and Ouray Reservation	43	449	1,354	2,918	712	722	483	868
White Earth Reservation	71	353	483	1,124	700	506	286	1,064
Wind River Reservation	28	444	1,349	3,000	1,396	1,093	664	784
Yakima Reservation and Trust Lands, WA	70	552	696	1,981	1,319	1,441	1,192	1,162
Yankton Reservation	23	56	273	486	228	211	90	1,121
Zuni Pueblo	31	170	227	691	318	135	84	244

Source: Census of Population and Housing, 1990: Summary Tape File 3C on CD-ROM [machine-readable datafiles]. Prepared by the Bureau of the Census. Washington, DC: The Bureau, 1992. *Notes:* 1. Federal American Indian reservations are areas with boundaries established by treaty, statute, and/or executive or court order, and recognized by the federal government as territory in which American Indian tribes have jurisdiction. State reservations are lands held in trust by state governments for the use and benefit of a given tribe. The reservations and their boundaries were identified for the 1990 census by the Bureau of Indian Affairs (BIA), Department of Interior (for federal reservations), and state governments (for state reservations). The names of American Indian reservations recognized by state governments, but not by the federal government, are followed by "state." Areas composed of reservation lands that are administered jointly and/or are claimed by two reservations, as identified by the BIA, are called "joint areas," and are treated as separate American Indian reservations for census purposes. Federal reservations may cross state boundaries, and federal and state reservations may cross county, county subdivision, and place boundaries. For reservations that cross state boundaries, only the portion of the reservations in a given state is shown in the data products for that state; the entire reservations are shown in data products for the United States. 2. Trust lands are property associated with a particular American Indian reservation or tribe, held in trust by the federal government. Trust lands may be held in trust either for a tribe (tribal trust lands) or for an individual member of a tribe (individual trust land). Trust lands recognized for the 1990 census comprised all tribal trust lands and inhabited individual trust lands located outside of a reservation boundary. As with other American Indian areas, trust lands may be located in more than one state. Only the trust lands in a given state are shown in the data products for that state; all trust lands associated with a reservation or tribe are shown in data products for the United States. The Census Bureau first reported data for tribal trust lands for the 1980 census.

★ 601 ★

Housing

Number of Rooms in Housing Units in Selected Alaska Native Villages

Data are shown for the 50 areas with the largest populations, in number of housing units.

Alaska Native Village Statistical Area[1]	Housing units with -								
	1 room	2 rooms	3 rooms	4 rooms	5 rooms	6 rooms	7 rooms	8 rooms	9 or more
Akiachak	22	32	24	19	26	0	5	0	0
Akutan	0	0	2	1	5	4	12	3	0
Alakanuk	21	34	23	35	16	7	3	0	0
Andreafsky	17	19	36	39	17	5	0	0	5
Angoon	4	11	22	63	26	18	13	3	1
Aniak	32	27	41	30	24	10	4	1	6
Barrow	68	143	210	205	171	81	26	12	6
Bethel	154	206	309	424	317	119	58	16	27
Chevak	24	26	42	34	22	10	0	0	0
Copper Center	19	27	17	50	39	54	10	16	5

[Continued]

★ 601 ★

Number of Rooms in Housing Units in Selected Alaska Native Villages

[Continued]

Alaska Native Village Statistical Area[1]	Housing units with -								
	1 room	2 rooms	3 rooms	4 rooms	5 rooms	6 rooms	7 rooms	8 rooms	9 or more
Craig	32	68	69	94	127	69	26	17	2
Dillingham	58	127	160	115	171	72	82	38	28
Emmonak	44	18	16	51	31	14	0	3	0
Fort Yukon	72	81	60	44	11	3	2	0	2
Galena	31	44	74	59	38	18	0	2	3
Gambell	3	24	22	36	41	7	0	0	0
Grouse Creek Group	24	8	20	63	69	22	19	6	11
Hoonah	12	31	23	36	53	67	12	13	4
Hooper Bay	49	29	41	39	47	3	0	1	0
Kake	4	33	39	42	68	39	25	7	7
Kasigluk	17	25	19	26	8	7	0	0	0
King Cove	0	15	18	29	31	18	5	5	8
King Salmon	6	14	36	75	63	24	2	5	8
Kipnuk	2	31	32	44	19	4	0	0	0
Klawock	33	65	49	35	50	21	12	6	4
Kotlik	10	33	17	37	11	0	2	0	0
Kotzebue	129	148	167	199	153	74	19	11	11
Kwethluk	30	34	27	34	8	5	0	0	0
McGrath	10	21	43	39	43	37	13	2	2
Mountain Village	15	32	25	40	41	23	10	0	0
Naknek	4	17	46	65	44	36	27	11	18
Ninilchik	594	721	730	1,037	848	519	300	200	250
Noorvik	13	17	19	49	16	8	0	0	5
Pilot Station	15	22	31	37	15	4	0	0	0
Point Hope	4	11	31	28	72	12	11	3	2
Quinhagak	19	27	11	36	32	7	0	0	0
St. Paul	4	8	16	14	59	33	17	18	6
Salamatof	7	12	74	87	91	89	32	16	16
Sand Point	1	16	33	77	49	64	20	5	9
Savoonga	11	7	36	53	15	7	0	0	0
Selawik	23	29	47	39	10	4	0	0	0
Shishmaref	11	21	31	52	13	3	2	2	0
Stebbins	23	11	23	14	19	1	0	0	0
Togiak	18	54	42	42	29	13	3	2	0
Tok	110	96	108	73	76	48	29	12	9
Toksook Bay	11	21	32	7	30	3	2	0	0
Unalakleet	27	36	68	45	35	14	7	2	0
Unalaska	103	83	112	181	89	44	38	14	9
Wainwright	13	14	35	58	35	4	0	1	0
Yakutat	12	30	8	35	58	32	6	0	13

Source: Census of Population and Housing, 1990: Summary Tape File 3C on CD-ROM [machine-readable datafiles]. Prepared by the Bureau of the Census. Washington, DC: The Bureau, 1992. *Notes:* 1. Alaska Native villages (ANVs) constitute tribes, bands, clans, groups, villages, communities, or associations in Alaska that are recognized pursuant to the Alaska Native Claims Settlement Act of 1972, Public Law 92-203. Because ANVs do not have legally designated boundaries, the Census Bureau has established Alaska Native village statistical areas (ANVSAs) for statistical purposes. For the 1990 census, the Census Bureau cooperated with officials of the nonprofit corporation within each participating Alaska Native Regional Corporation (ANRC), as well as other knowledgeable officials, to delineate boundaries that encompass the settled area associated with each ANV.

★ 602 ★

Housing

Number of Rooms in Housing Units in Selected Tribal Designated Statistical Areas

TDSA[1]	Housing units with -								
	1 room	2 rooms	3 rooms	4 rooms	5 rooms	6 rooms	7 rooms	8 rooms	9 or more
Apache Choctaw TDSA (state)	101	289	1,393	3,665	3,646	2,108	923	332	332
Chickahominy TDSA (state)	5	9	31	145	335	229	137	75	23
Clifton Choctaw TDSA (state)	0	0	8	51	86	43	0	0	0
Coharie TDSA (state)	236	786	3,412	12,225	13,317	9,500	4,807	2,273	1,814
Coquille Indian TDSA	4,609	8,996	17,289	36,874	39,271	30,985	16,807	8,131	7,564
Delaware-Muncie TDSA (state)	0	0	8	0	31	26	18	0	8
Florida Tribe of Eastern Creek TDSA (state)	0	9	7	18	27	22	25	20	0
Haliwa-Saponi TDSA (state)	13	27	146	575	640	467	259	91	84
Jena Band of Choctaw TDSA (state)	108	500	1,896	4,840	6,927	5,112	2,445	1,097	723
Klamath TDSA	294	785	1,803	3,910	4,068	3,334	1,743	939	746
Lumbee TDSA (state)	74	201	1,219	3,989	5,894	3,250	1,578	591	404
Meherrin TDSA (state)	116	255	1,142	4,562	6,520	4,787	2,599	1,311	1,115
Mohegan TDSA (state)	130	337	1,194	2,233	2,598	1,939	1,055	679	517
Ramapough TDSA (state)	0	0	3	50	51	46	40	12	3
United Houma Nation TDSA (state)	3,619	11,472	33,173	64,869	76,256	64,637	36,089	17,795	13,875
Waccamaw Siouan TDSA (state)	0	7	45	212	370	181	113	17	23
Wampanoag-Gay Head TDSA	152	427	728	1,658	2,444	2,482	1,563	1,035	1,115

Source: Census of Population and Housing, 1990: Summary Tape File 3C on CD-ROM [machine-readable datafiles]. Prepared by the Bureau of the Census. Washington, DC: The Bureau, 1992. *Notes:* 1. Tribal designated statistical areas (TDSAs) are areas, delineated outside Oklahoma by federally- and state-recognized tribes without a land base or associated trust lands, to provide statistical areas for which the Census Bureau tabulates data. TDSAs represent areas generally containing the American Indian population over which federally-recognized tribes have jurisdiction and areas in which state tribes provide benefits and services to their members. The names of TDSAs delineated by state-recognized tribes are followed by "(state)." The Census Bureau did not recognize TDSAs before the 1990 census.

★ 603 ★

Housing

Number of Rooms in Housing Units in Selected Tribal Jurisdiction Statistical Areas

TJSA[1]	Housing units with -								
	1 room	2 rooms	3 rooms	4 rooms	5 rooms	6 rooms	7 rooms	8 rooms	9 or more
Absentee Shawnee-Citizens Band of Potawatomi TJSA	76	451	1,560	6,361	11,363	8,485	3,682	1,530	878
Caddo-Wichita-Delaware TJSA	35	83	305	1,000	1,228	837	404	111	105
Cherokee TJSA	1,352	4,022	13,875	39,506	55,500	37,026	16,250	7,222	4,815
Cheyenne-Arapaho TJSA	281	1,206	4,177	12,952	20,939	15,146	6,450	2,835	1,864
Chickasaw TJSA	678	2,489	8,135	26,099	37,885	25,883	10,213	3,867	2,615
Choctaw TJSA	731	2,141	7,143	22,002	29,450	18,738	7,444	2,816	1,859
Creek TJSA	3,342	9,232	30,248	50,605	71,152	62,603	29,505	13,861	12,175
Iowa TJSA	7	34	83	355	611	498	206	63	16
Kaw TJSA	34	87	298	761	1,505	1,504	932	376	230
Kiowa-Comanche-Apache-Fort Sill Apache TJSA	645	2,199	7,604	17,683	26,373	18,636	7,753	2,771	1,857
Otoe-Missouria TJSA	3	12	39	226	487	270	103	36	13

[Continued]

★ 603 ★

Number of Rooms in Housing Units in Selected Tribal Jurisdiction Statistical Areas

[Continued]

TJSA[1]	Housing units with -								
	1 room	2 rooms	3 rooms	4 rooms	5 rooms	6 rooms	7 rooms	8 rooms	9 or more
Pawnee TJSA	50	152	427	1,775	2,286	1,565	643	247	188
Sac and Fox TJSA	103	429	1,755	4,664	7,103	5,028	2,411	995	672
Seminole TJSA	67	250	685	2,210	3,614	2,230	797	262	221
Tonkawa TJSA	57	130	477	1,215	1,907	1,280	483	255	149
Creek-Seminole Joint Area TJSA	0	17	48	220	453	206	71	21	32
Iowa-Sac and Fox Joint Area TJSA	3	12	7	68	106	100	55	24	20

Source: Census of Population and Housing, 1990: Summary Tape File 3C on CD-ROM [machine-readable datafiles]. Prepared by the Bureau of the Census. Washington, DC: The Bureau, 1992. Notes: 1. Tribal jurisdiction statistical areas (TJSAs) are areas, delineated by federally recognized tribes in Oklahoma without a reservation, for which the Census Bureau tabulates data. TJSAs represent areas generally containing the American Indian population over which one or more tribal governments have jurisdiction. If tribal officials delineated adjacent TJSAs so that they include some duplicate territory, the overlap area is called a "joint use area," which is treated as a separate TJSA for census purposes.

★ 604 ★

Housing

Number of Rooms in Housing Units on Selected Reservations and Trust Lands

Data are shown for the 50 areas with the largest populations, in number of housing units.

American Indian Reservation and Trust Lands[1,2]	Housing units with -								
	1 room	2 rooms	3 rooms	4 rooms	5 rooms	6 rooms	7 rooms	8 rooms	9 or more
Agua Caliente Reservation	197	886	2,560	5,411	7,300	3,391	944	352	224
Allegany Reservation	35	71	214	351	610	745	579	304	229
Blackfeet Reservation	29	179	364	838	682	468	227	111	75
Cheyenne River Reservation	39	277	429	626	741	411	212	103	85
Coeur d'Alene Reservation and Trust Lands, ID	90	133	337	753	937	544	395	268	285
Colorado River Reservation	111	270	734	1,243	1,468	667	220	33	31
Colville Reservation	45	80	330	698	815	503	244	156	145
Crow Reservation and Trust Lands, MT	17	76	136	477	696	426	146	48	59
Eastern Cherokee Reservation	15	56	172	476	814	468	234	45	32
Flathead Reservation	200	478	1,114	2,281	2,279	1,661	1,011	626	732
Fort Apache Reservation	189	388	522	648	941	455	137	8	20
Fort Berthold Reservation	23	106	309	721	740	361	188	147	116
Fort Hall Reservation and Trust Lands, ID	26	100	193	448	393	286	134	125	58
Fort Peck Reservation	34	107	291	634	1,178	887	343	243	274
Gila River Reservation	208	361	520	654	608	234	81	12	9
Hopi Reservation and Trust Lands, AZ	481	385	372	474	413	190	69	20	7
Isabella Reservation and Trust Lands, MI	53	236	561	1,803	2,037	1,822	1,213	663	635
Laguna Pueblo and Trust Lands, NM	62	126	150	329	391	194	77	13	0
Lake Traverse (Sisseton) Reservation	60	234	699	960	1,122	895	708	419	375

[Continued]

★ 604 ★

Number of Rooms in Housing Units on Selected Reservations and Trust Lands
[Continued]

American Indian Reservation and Trust Lands[1,2]	Housing units with -								
	1 room	2 rooms	3 rooms	4 rooms	5 rooms	6 rooms	7 rooms	8 rooms	9 or more
Leech Lake Reservation	111	230	755	1,697	1,536	883	566	255	239
Mississippi Choctaw Reservation and Trust Lands, MS	0	22	197	136	451	182	56	7	0
Muckleshoot Reservation and Trust Lands, WA	5	31	165	291	346	209	168	98	78
Navajo Reservation and Trust Lands, AZ–NM–UT	17,217	8,673	8,601	8,781	8,082	3,122	720	273	172
Nez Perce Reservation	55	142	554	1,459	1,662	1,215	789	480	591
Northern Cheyenne Reservation and Trust Lands, MT–SD	16	46	137	307	435	258	50	26	12
Omaha Reservation	14	26	147	339	412	401	298	190	119
Oneida (West) Reservation	11	62	199	855	1,381	1,271	861	632	615
Osage Reservation	81	279	1,163	3,701	5,655	3,957	1,798	899	563
Papago Reservation	139	329	632	608	525	216	52	4	0
Pine Ridge Reservation and Trust Lands, NE–SD	245	337	611	791	648	499	151	58	36
Port Madison Reservation	28	102	180	435	473	422	277	117	99
Puyallup Reservation and Trust Lands, WA	124	478	1,333	2,686	2,596	1,929	1,695	1,023	1,124
Red Lake Reservation	10	74	85	299	332	204	21	18	15
Rosebud Reservation and Trust Lands, SD	70	162	343	842	647	464	270	82	112
Salt River Reservation	108	305	554	604	372	155	32	0	7
San Carlos Reservation	179	257	326	412	634	229	58	0	4
Sandia Pueblo	7	45	126	345	515	201	122	47	17
San Juan Pueblo	13	80	159	476	556	283	190	60	59
Santa Clara Pueblo	36	198	373	866	1,220	734	405	213	131
Southern Ute Reservation	63	137	227	706	966	610	284	174	190
Standing Rock Reservation	18	130	275	596	728	475	176	159	175
Taos Pueblo and Trust Lands, NM	200	372	438	571	484	357	141	72	61
Tulalip Reservation	446	552	529	589	667	465	416	197	165
Turtle Mountain Reservation and Trust Lands, ND–SD	27	119	225	538	831	348	150	80	34
Uintah and Ouray Reservation	95	272	723	1,507	1,819	1,242	726	566	599
White Earth Reservation	65	193	555	926	1,121	764	448	277	238
Wind River Reservation	59	206	846	1,660	2,497	1,391	865	592	642
Yakima Reservation and Trust Lands, WA	201	595	877	1,682	1,863	1,523	791	463	418
Yankton Reservation	6	89	199	408	678	486	282	190	150
Zuni Pueblo	106	79	123	334	620	289	206	66	77

Source: Census of Population and Housing, 1990: Summary Tape File 3C on CD-ROM [machine-readable datafiles]. Prepared by the Bureau of the Census. Washington, DC: The Bureau, 1992. *Notes:* 1. Federal American Indian reservations are areas with boundaries established by treaty, statute, and/or executive or court order, and recognized by the federal government as territory in which American Indian tribes have jurisdiction. State reservations are lands held in trust by state governments for the use and benefit of a given tribe. The reservations and their boundaries were identified for the 1990 census by the Bureau of Indian Affairs (BIA), Department of Interior (for federal reservations), and state governments (for state reservations). The names of American Indian reservations recognized by state governments, but not by the federal government, are followed by "state." Areas composed of reservation lands that are administered jointly and/or are claimed by two reservations, as identified by the BIA, are called "joint areas," and are treated as separate American Indian reservations for census purposes. Federal reservations may cross state boundaries, and federal and state reservations may cross county, county subdivision, and place boundaries. For reservations that cross state boundaries, only the portion of the reservations in a given state is shown in the data products for that state; the entire reservations are shown in data products for the United States. 2. Trust lands are property associated with a particular American Indian reservation or tribe, held in trust by the federal government. Trust lands may be held in trust either for a tribe (tribal trust lands) or for an individual member of a tribe (individual trust land). Trust lands recognized for the 1990 census comprised all tribal trust lands and inhabited individual trust lands located outside of a reservation boundary. As with other American Indian areas, trust lands may be located in more than one state. Only the trust lands in a given state are shown in the data products for that state; all trust lands associated with a reservation or tribe are shown in data products for the United States. The Census Bureau first reported data for tribal trust lands for the 1980 census.

★ 605 ★

Housing

Number of Persons in Occupied Units - 1991

Numbers are shown in thousands of occupied units, excluding medians. Households of Hispanic origin may be of any race.

Characteristics	All households	White	Black	American Indian, Eskimo, or Aleut	Asian or Pacific Islander	Hispanic origin	Not of Hispanic origin	
							Total	White
Persons								
One	22,393	19,011	2,876	83	323	1,032	21,361	18,124
Two	30,589	27,170	2,698	129	461	1,381	29,209	25,952
Three	16,290	13,498	2,175	88	386	1,192	15,098	12,459
Four	14,140	11,879	1,578	86	472	1,173	12,966	10,845
Five	6,244	5,057	867	58	198	770	5,474	4,359
Six	2,107	1,649	302	15	109	377	1,730	1,299
Seven or more	1,384	875	337	28	116	314	1,069	586
Median	2.3	2.3	2.4	2.9	3.1	3.1	2.3	2.2

Source: Woodward, Jeanne M. *America's Racial and Ethnic Groups: Their Housing in the Early Nineties.* Bureau of the Census. Current Housing Reports, Series H121/94-3. Washington, DC: U.S. Government Printing Office, p. 45. Primary source: American Housing Survey (AHS), 1991 National Internal User File.

★ 606 ★

Housing

Number of Persons in Occupied Housing Units by Race of Householder in Selected Alaska Native Villages

Data are shown for the 50 areas with the largest populations, in number of persons.

Alaska Native Village Statistical Area[1]	Owner occupied units					Renter occupied units				
	White	Black	American Indian, Eskimo, or Aleut	Asian or Pacific Islander	Other race	White	Balck	American Indian, Eskimo, or Aleut	Asian or Pacific Islander	Other race
Akiachak	0	0	268	0	0	24	0	166	4	0
Akutan	19	0	63	0	0	4	0	4	0	0
Alakanuk	0	0	484	0	0	13	0	43	0	0
Andreafsky	34	0	232	0	0	45	0	95	0	0
Angoon	34	0	155	0	0	129	0	314	0	11
Aniak	95	5	141	0	10	121	13	144	0	0
Barrow	154	0	758	28	10	800	2	762	178	37
Bethel	800	0	1,226	16	5	1,074	62	1,245	16	15
Chevak	40	0	414	0	0	29	0	114	0	0
Copper Center	192	0	87	0	0	97	0	50	0	0
Craig	607	0	207	0	2	358	0	71	4	11
Dillingham	471	0	717	5	0	422	0	345	44	9
Emmonak	25	0	415	0	8	38	11	111	2	0
Fort Yukon	57	0	418	0	0	58	0	46	0	0
Galena	142	0	166	0	0	84	0	126	3	0
Gambell	0	0	477	0	0	6	0	65	0	0
Grouse Creek Group	420	0	82	0	0	126	0	2	0	0

[Continued]

★ 606 ★

Number of Persons in Occupied Housing Units by Race of Householder in Selected Alaska Native Villages
[Continued]

Alaska Native Village Statistical Area[1]	Owner occupied units					Renter occupied units				
	White	Black	American Indian, Eskimo, or Aleut	Asian or Pacific Islander	Other race	White	Balck	American Indian, Eskimo, or Aleut	Asian or Pacific Islander	Other race
Hoonah	121	0	401	0	0	54	0	153	0	0
Hooper Bay	0	0	637	0	0	36	0	173	0	0
Kake	95	0	474	0	0	63	0	47	0	0
Kasigluk	10	0	262	0	0	19	0	149	0	0
King Cove	13	0	151	0	0	62	0	18	24	0
King Salmon	100	0	47	0	0	255	0	31	0	0
Kipnuk	11	0	438	6	0	1	0	4	0	0
Klawock	114	0	241	0	0	204	0	146	0	0
Kotlik	0	0	405	0	0	10	0	47	0	0
Kotzebue	297	6	1,067	0	0	534	2	779	19	0
Kwethluk	16	13	454	0	0	13	5	65	0	2
McGrath	142	0	42	0	0	183	0	157	0	0
Mountain Village	13	0	351	23	0	62	13	244	0	0
Naknek	167	0	162	0	0	203	0	58	0	0
Ninilchik	7,196	0	252	27	0	2,798	80	48	2	0
Noorvik	15	0	462	0	0	14	0	57	0	0
Pilot Station	0	0	323	0	0	13	0	131	0	0
Point Hope	15	0	246	0	0	43	0	325	0	0
Quinhagak	26	0	337	0	0	22	0	124	0	0
St. Paul	14	0	415	0	0	75	0	57	0	0
Salamatof	424	0	28	0	0	216	22	29	1	0
Sand Point	52	0	367	8	17	156	0	79	0	0
Savoonga	0	0	354	0	0	25	0	135	0	0
Selawik	35	12	432	0	0	2	0	98	0	0
Shishmaref	0	0	347	0	0	18	0	68	0	0
Stebbins	0	0	368	0	0	19	0	61	0	0
Togiak	28	0	504	0	0	57	0	17	0	0
Tok	601	0	43	0	0	279	0	12	0	0
Toksook Bay	8	0	349	0	0	9	0	39	0	0
Unalakleet	21	0	416	0	0	125	0	84	0	0
Unalaska	239	0	181	17	0	802	7	36	170	30
Wainwright	4	0	410	0	0	35	0	53	0	0
Yakutat	148	0	168	0	0	95	0	114	2	0

Source: Census of Population and Housing, 1990: Summary Tape File 3C on CD-ROM [machine-readable datafiles]. Prepared by the Bureau of the Census. Washington, DC: The Bureau, 1992. *Notes:* 1. Alaska Native villages (ANVs) constitute tribes, bands, clans, groups, villages, communities, or associations in Alaska that are recognized pursuant to the Alaska Native Claims Settlement Act of 1972, Public Law 92-203. Because ANVs do not have legally designated boundaries, the Census Bureau has established Alaska Native village statistical areas (ANVSAs) for statistical purposes. For the 1990 census, the Census Bureau cooperated with officials of the nonprofit corporation within each participating Alaska Native Regional Corporation (ANRC), as well as other knowledgeable officials, to delineate boundaries that encompass the settled area associated with each ANV.

★ 607 ★

Housing

Number of Persons in Occupied Housing Units by Race of Householder in Selected Tribal Designated Statistical Areas

TDSA[1]	Owner occupied units					Renter occupied units				
	White	Black	American Indian, Eskimo, or Aleut	Asian or Pacific Islander	Other race	White	Balck	American Indian, Eskimo, or Aleut	Asian or Pacific Islander	Other race
Apache Choctaw TDSA (state)	14,597	2,345	580	30	35	2,879	1,548	72	6	17
Chickahominy TDSA (state)	647	1,318	461	0	0	61	262	0	0	0
Clifton Choctaw TDSA (state)	238	0	147	0	0	128	0	39	0	0
Coharie TDSA (state)	49,027	20,731	721	263	69	17,672	22,382	608	142	540
Coquille Indian TDSA	240,021	586	2,994	2,167	1,347	134,869	941	2,979	2,900	2,525
Delaware-Muncie TDSA (state)	239	0	28	0	0	32	0	0	0	0
Florida Tribe of Eastern Creek TDSA (state)	170	0	0	0	0	45	0	0	0	0
Haliwa-Saponi TDSA (state)	415	2,812	1,338	0	20	75	838	933	0	0
Jena Band of Choctaw TDSA (state)	38,916	2,242	272	168	30	11,360	3,362	176	125	6
Klamath TDSA	24,429	50	695	78	255	12,706	241	819	162	420
Lumbee TDSA (state)	6,282	8,320	22,707	41	77	1,981	3,997	5,548	0	43
Meherrin TDSA (state)	19,121	20,248	134	58	20	4,425	10,070	56	11	0
Mohegan TDSA (state)	13,153	394	27	166	40	8,547	1,133	102	209	402
Ramapough TDSA (state)	275	153	131	0	0	64	0	29	0	0
United Houma Nation TDSA (state)	487,014	76,067	6,915	8,226	4,253	155,327	61,004	2,944	4,239	3,901
Waccamaw Siouan TDSA (state)	540	497	1,285	0	41	228	105	75	0	0
Wampanoag-Gay Head TDSA	8,073	176	149	7	24	2,655	359	62	0	50

Source: Census of Population and Housing, 1990: Summary Tape File 3C on CD-ROM [machine-readable datafiles]. Prepared by the Bureau of the Census. Washington, DC: The Bureau, 1992. *Notes:* 1. Tribal designated statistical areas (TDSAs) are areas, delineated outside Oklahoma by federally- and state-recognized tribes without a land base or associated trust lands, to provide statistical areas for which the Census Bureau tabulates data. TDSAs represent areas generally containing the American Indian population over which federally-recognized tribes have jurisdiction and areas in which state tribes provide benefits and services to their members. The names of TDSAs delineated by state-recognized tribes are followed by "(state)." The Census Bureau did not recognize TDSAs before the 1990 census.

★ 608 ★

Housing

Number of Persons in Occupied Housing Units by Race of Householder in Selected Tribal Jurisdiction Statistical Areas

TJSA[1]	Owner occupied units					Renter occupied units				
	White	Black	American Indian, Eskimo, or Aleut	Asian or Pacific Islander	Other race	White	Balck	American Indian, Eskimo, or Aleut	Asian or Pacific Islander	Other race
Absentee Shawnee-Citizens Band of Potawatomi TJSA	65,368	3,610	4,211	74	247	12,048	1,408	1,048	39	129
Caddo-Wichita-Delaware TJSA	5,651	50	332	0	84	1,596	39	169	0	197
Cherokee TJSA	231,132	20,525	42,340	405	1,155	65,692	12,962	17,059	273	838
Cheyenne-Arapaho TJSA	100,166	1,564	3,134	985	1,633	31,898	1,649	2,994	163	1,456
Chickasaw TJSA	170,346	4,482	12,741	297	1,274	50,150	3,783	6,766	150	1,098
Choctaw TJSA	125,708	5,153	18,183	168	450	41,775	3,368	7,607	60	441

[Continued]

★ 608 ★

Number of Persons in Occupied Housing Units by Race of Householder in Selected Tribal Jurisdiction Statistical Areas

[Continued]

TJSA[1]	Owner occupied units					Renter occupied units				
	White	Black	American Indian, Eskimo, or Aleut	Asian or Pacific Islander	Other race	White	Balck	American Indian, Eskimo, or Aleut	Asian or Pacific Islander	Other race
Creek TJSA	380,663	13,884	25,836	3,315	1,814	152,688	22,185	14,868	2,414	2,264
Iowa TJSA	2,936	93	174	0	2	824	35	58	0	6
Kaw TJSA	10,298	34	433	91	23	1,898	13	177	0	0
Kiowa-Comanche-Apache- Fort Sill Apache TJSA	103,504	9,601	7,285	1,420	4,275	44,353	13,345	4,444	753	4,232
Otoe-Missouria TJSA	1,756	21	197	0	29	463	20	251	0	13
Pawnee TJSA	10,992	71	1,074	21	5	2,574	40	529	0	0
Sac and Fox TJSA	33,679	780	3,078	49	150	10,499	735	1,247	88	194
Seminole TJSA	14,096	845	2,278	16	5	3,282	865	1,226	0	14
Tonkawa TJSA	8,240	0	446	17	35	2,670	17	300	20	54
Creek-Seminole Joint Area TJSA	1,158	80	268	17	0	338	93	235	0	24
Iowa-Sac and Fox Joint Area TJSA	673	28	8	0	4	122	0	0	0	0

Source: Census of Population and Housing, 1990: Summary Tape File 3C on CD-ROM [machine-readable datafiles]. Prepared by the Bureau of the Census. Washington, DC: The Bureau, 1992. *Notes:* 1. Tribal jurisdiction statistical areas (TJSAs) are areas, delineated by federally recognized tribes in Oklahoma without a reservation, for which the Census Bureau tabulates data. TJSAs represent areas generally containing the American Indian population over which one or more tribal governments have jurisdiction. If tribal officials delineated adjacent TJSAs so that they include some duplicate territory, the overlap area is called a "joint use area," which is treated as a separate TJSA for census purposes.

★ 609 ★

Housing

Number of Persons in Occupied Housing Units by Race of Householder on Selected Reservations and Trust Lands

Data are shown for the 50 areas with the largest populations, in number of persons.

American Indian Reservation and Trust Lands[1,2]	Owner occupied units					Renter occupied units				
	White	Black	American Indian, Eskimo, or Aleut	Asian or Pacific Islander	Other race	White	Balck	American Indian, Eskimo, or Aleut	Asian or Pacific Islander	Other race
Agua Caliente Reservation	12,752	47	43	192	281	5,098	328	105	160	553
Allegany Reservation	4,006	0	662	15	0	1,954	0	477	0	39
Blackfeet Reservation	719	6	3,850	0	0	362	8	3,125	0	0
Cheyenne River Reservation	2,002	9	1,544	0	0	691	0	3,493	0	0
Coeur d'Alene Reservation and Trust Lands, ID	3,968	7	515	0	8	1,004	0	270	0	6
Colorado River Reservation	3,282	3	1,455	32	673	1,416	13	756	4	268
Colville Reservation	2,138	0	2,345	17	40	904	0	1,388	6	114
Crow Reservation and Trust Lands, MT	1,157	0	2,616	13	0	407	0	2,108	0	0
Eastern Cherokee Reservation	549	7	4,423	0	0	287	4	953	0	0
Flathead Reservation	11,209	0	3,558	4	27	3,844	0	1,851	0	0
Fort Apache Reservation	139	23	7,209	0	72	411	0	2,632	0	0

[Continued]

★ 609 ★

Number of Persons in Occupied Housing Units by Race of Householder on Selected Reservations and Trust Lands

[Continued]

American Indian Reservation and Trust Lands[1,2]	Owner occupied units					Renter occupied units				
	White	Black	American Indian, Eskimo, or Aleut	Asian or Pacific Islander	Other race	White	Balck	American Indian, Eskimo, or Aleut	Asian or Pacific Islander	Other race
Fort Berthold Reservation	1,718	0	1,174	0	40	519	0	1,811	10	0
Fort Hall Reservation and Trust Lands, ID	1,379	0	2,328	21	119	357	0	740	0	127
Fort Peck Reservation	3,641	0	2,441	0	0	1,169	0	3,358	4	0
Gila River Reservation	204	0	5,207	0	224	69	0	3,502	34	253
Hopi Reservation and Trust Lands, AZ	11	0	5,719	0	8	165	0	1,255	30	0
Isabella Reservation and Trust Lands, MI	15,492	27	415	97	178	5,479	140	429	50	64
Laguna Pueblo and Trust Lands, NM	64	11	2,740	0	0	24	0	863	0	0
Lake Traverse (Sisseton) Reservation	5,858	0	830	0	11	2,114	0	1,840	0	0
Leech Lake Reservation	4,822	3	2,114	0	0	560	0	1,282	0	2
Mississippi Choctaw Reservation and Trust Lands, MS	150	0	2,918	0	0	0	0	1,177	0	0
Muckleshoot Reservation and Trust Lands, WA	2,156	0	468	22	0	703	4	432	0	37
Navajo Reservation and Trust Lands, AZ–NM–UT	1,521	0	106,466	42	267	3,145	251	35,549	55	229
Nez Perce Reservation	10,535	15	1,377	8	0	3,217	0	513	14	3
Northern Cheyenne Reservation and Trust Lands, MT–SD	209	0	2,181	0	0	278	0	1,218	0	0
Omaha Reservation	2,321	0	595	0	0	944	0	1,289	0	0
Oneida (West) Reservation	12,975	27	1,364	25	27	2,369	38	875	18	21
Osage Reservation	25,182	2,658	4,252	37	69	5,703	1,222	1,046	0	30
Papago Reservation	152	0	6,708	0	0	31	0	1,696	0	0
Pine Ridge Reservation and Trust Lands, NE–SD	732	0	4,136	4	0	232	8	6,799	35	73
Port Madison Reservation	3,526	5	253	111	14	774	0	132	16	0
Puyallup Reservation and Trust Lands, WA	17,684	769	413	631	188	7,938	1,441	472	2,186	432
Red Lake Reservation	48	0	2,272	0	0	66	0	1,256	0	0
Rosebud Reservation and Trust Lands, SD	1,018	0	3,017	0	6	706	0	4,801	0	14
Salt River Reservation	1,068	0	2,544	0	15	152	0	979	0	0
San Carlos Reservation	76	0	4,767	0	0	29	22	2,256	0	63
Sandia Pueblo	1,827	17	330	0	575	961	0	59	6	169
San Juan Pueblo	2,951	10	1,152	1	450	484	5	106	0	60
Santa Clara Pueblo	5,806	11	1,031	0	605	2,118	40	280	9	213
Southern Ute Reservation	5,139	0	623	0	390	1,276	0	401	0	39
Standing Rock Reservation	2,499	0	1,092	0	0	640	0	3,718	7	0
Taos Pueblo and Trust Lands, NM	1,503	2	1,084	4	577	1,079	3	156	30	253
Tulalip Reservation	5,103	8	719	0	13	757	11	474	9	9
Turtle Mountain Reservation and Trust Lands, ND–SD	157	0	4,302	0	0	125	0	2,476	0	0
Uintah and Ouray Reservation	12,277	13	1,595	9	77	2,137	4	967	27	57

[Continued]

★ 609 ★

Number of Persons in Occupied Housing Units by Race of Householder on Selected Reservations and Trust Lands

[Continued]

American Indian Reservation and Trust Lands[1,2]	Owner occupied units					Renter occupied units				
	White	Black	American Indian, Eskimo, or Aleut	Asian or Pacific Islander	Other race	White	Balck	American Indian, Eskimo, or Aleut	Asian or Pacific Islander	Other race
White Earth Reservation	5,133	0	1,587	0	0	779	0	1,199	0	0
Wind River Reservation	11,909	0	3,410	26	121	3,583	0	2,346	0	228
Yakima Reservation and Trust Lands, WA	6,693	66	3,472	452	4,872	3,593	47	2,569	94	4,310
Yankton Reservation	3,093	0	663	0	0	1,103	0	1,227	0	0
Zuni Pueblo	65	0	5,645	0	0	264	71	1,376	7	0

Source: Census of Population and Housing, 1990: Summary Tape File 3C on CD-ROM [machine-readable datafiles]. Prepared by the Bureau of the Census. Washington, DC: The Bureau, 1992. Notes: 1. Federal American Indian reservations are areas with boundaries established by treaty, statute, and/or executive or court order, and recognized by the federal government as territory in which American Indian tribes have jurisdiction. State reservations are lands held in trust by state governments for the use and benefit of a given tribe. The reservations and their boundaries were identified for the 1990 census by the Bureau of Indian Affairs (BIA), Department of Interior (for federal reservations), and state governments (for state reservations). The names of American Indian reservations recognized by state governments, but not by the federal government, are followed by "state." Areas composed of reservation lands that are administered jointly and/or are claimed by two reservations, as identified by the BIA, are called "joint areas," and are treated as separate American Indian reservations for census purposes. Federal reservations may cross state boundaries, and federal and state reservations may cross county, county subdivision, and place boundaries. For reservations that cross state boundaries, only the portion of the reservations in a given state is shown in the data products for that state; the entire reservations are shown in data products for the United States. 2. Trust lands are property associated with a particular American Indian reservation or tribe, held in trust by the federal government. Trust lands may be held in trust either for a tribe (tribal trust lands) or for an individual member of a tribe (individual trust land). Trust lands recognized for the 1990 census comprised all tribal trust lands and inhabited individual trust lands located outside of a reservation boundary. As with other American Indian areas, trust lands may be located in more than one state. Only the trust lands in a given state are shown in the data products for that state; all trust lands associated with a reservation or tribe are shown in data products for the United States. The Census Bureau first reported data for tribal trust lands for the 1980 census.

Housing Costs and Conditions

★ 610 ★

Housing Value by Region - 1991

Numbers are shown in thousands of owner-occupied units, excluding medians and standard errors. Households of Hispanic origin may be of any race.

Characteristics	All households	White	Black	American Indian, Eskimo, or Aleut	Asian or Pacific Islander	Hispanic origin	Not of Hispanic origin	
							Total	White
Value of owner-occupied units by region								
Total	59,796	53,748	4,635	257	1,035	2,423	57,373	51,465
Median ($)	80,281	81,974	55,412	62,895	195,893	80,912	80,259	82,072
Standard error ($)	422	383	1,124	6,381	8,785	2,556	428	442
Northeast	11,869	10,981	648	39	169	221	11,648	10,786
Median ($)	116,776	118,199	74,634	...	173,780	134,625	116,427	117,882
Standard error ($)	1,232	1,245	5,097	...	11,207	8,570	1,233	1,244
Midwest	15,238	14,248	832	30	112	167	15,071	14,097
Median ($)	65,632	66,794	46,549	...	117,000	67,106	65,614	66,801

[Continued]

★ 610 ★

Housing Value by Region - 1991
[Continued]

Characteristics	All households	White	Black	American Indian, Eskimo, or Aleut	Asian or Pacific Islander	Hispanic origin	Not of Hispanic origin	
							Total	White
Standard error ($)	604	626	2,099	...	11,597	6,172	608	631
South	21,272	18,193	2,840	58	153	951	20,321	17,279
Median ($)	65,651	68,203	51,860	...	108,409	53,736	66,182	68,980
Standard error ($)	548	613	1,274	...	13,454	2,766	559	628
West	11,416	10,327	315	130	601	1,083	10,333	9,304
Median ($)	129,426	124,440	133,056	71,818	241,223	126,731	129,616	124,740
Standard error ($)	2,082	2,465	8,108	7,106	11,076	9,745	2,375	2,523

Source: Woodward, Jeanne M. *America's Racial and Ethnic Groups: Their Housing in the Early Nineties.* Bureau of the Census. Current Housing Reports, Series H121/94-3. Washington, DC: U.S. Government Printing Office, p. 60. Primary source: American Housing Survey (AHS), 1991 National Internal User File. *Note:* ... means that the base is too small to provide reliable statistics.

★ 611 ★

Housing Costs and Conditions

Monthly Housing Costs of Owner-Occupied Units - 1991

Numbers are shown in thousands of units, excluding percentages, medians, and standard errors. Households of Hispanic origin may be of any race.

Characteristics	All households	White	Black	American Indian, Eskimo, or Aleut	Asian or Pacific Islander	Hispanic origin	Not of Hispanic origin	
							Total	White
Monthly housing costs								
Mortgaged owners	30,149	26,897	2,344	87	749	1,376	28,773	25,599
Median ($)	761	767	618	625	1,326	790	760	766
Standard error($)	4	5	14	86	57	24	5	5
Non-mortgaged owners	24,454	22,307	1,812	142	165	852	23,602	21,499
Median ($)	225	229	187	157	237	181	227	230
Standard error($)	2	3	5	17	22	6	2	2
Monthly housing costs as percent of income								
Mortgaged owners	30,003	26,783	2,316	87	747	1,366	28,637	25,493
Percent	100.0	100.0	100.0	100.0	100.0	100.0	100.0	100.0
Less than 30 percent	72	73	63	66	55	60	72	74
30 to 49 percent	19	19	23	11	32	26	19	18
50 percent or more	9	8	14	22	13	14	8	8
Median	22	22	24	26	28	26	22	22
Standard error	0.13	0.14	0.48	2.92	1.07	0.82	0.13	0.14
Non-mortgaged owners	24,160	22,056	1,773	142	163	838	23,322	21,262
Percent	100.0	100.0	100.0	100.0	100.0	100.0	100.0	100.0
Less than 30 percent	85	85	79	85	88	84	85	85
30 to 49 percent	9	9	11	11	9	10	9	9
50 percent or more	6	6	10	4	2	6	6	6

[Continued]

★ 611 ★

Monthly Housing Costs of Owner-Occupied Units - 1991
[Continued]

Characteristics	All households	White	Black	American Indian, Eskimo, or Aleut	Asian or Pacific Islander	Hispanic origin	Not of Hispanic origin	
							Total	White
Median	14	14	15	12	(-10)	12	14	14
Standard error	0.14	0.14	0.68	3.02	1.25	0.94	0.14	0.14
Low income owners[1]	4,1796	3,313	769	46	34	273	3,903	3,055
Percent	100.0	100.0	100.0	100.0	100.0	100.0	100.0	100.0
Less than 30 percent	31	31	31	52	6	44	30	29
30 to 49 percent	27	26	31	20	32	24	27	26
50 to 69 percent	13	12	14	15	18	10	13	12
70 percent or more	30	31	24	13	44	22	30	32
Median	44	44	43	25	66	36	44	45

Source: Woodward, Jeanne M. *America's Racial and Ethnic Groups: Their Housing in the Early Nineties.* Bureau of the Census. Current Housing Reports, Series H121/94-3. Washington, DC: U.S. Government Printing Office, p. 60. Primary source: American Housing Survey (AHS), 1991 National Internal User File. *Note:* 1. Incomes below household poverty level.

★ 612 ★

Housing Costs and Conditions

Monthly Housing Costs of Renters - 1991

Numbers are shown in thousands, excluding percents, medians, and standard errors. Households of Hispanic origin may be of any race.

Characteristics	All households	White	Black	American Indian, Eskimo, or Aleut	Asian or Pacific Islander	Hispanic origin	Not of Hispanic origin	
							Total	White
Monthly housing costs								
Renters	30,825	23,426	5,747	187	988	3,585	27,239	20,402
Median ($)	463	475	397	389	557	476	461	474
Standard error ($)	2	3	6	26	14	7	2	3
Monthly housing costs as percent of income								
Renters	30,278	23,057	5,634	182	938	3,520	26,757	20,090
Percent	100.0	100.0	100.0	100.0	100.0	100.0	100.0	100.0
Less than 30 percent	54	56	49	54	53	43	56	58
30 to 49 percent	25	24	27	20	23	30	24	23
50 percent or more	21	20	24	25	24	27	20	19
Median	28	28	31	28	29	34	28	27
Standard error	0.17	0.19	0.62	3.22	0.93	0.73	0.17	0.20
Low income renters[1]	6,384	4,039	1,949	63	212	1,027	5,356	3,171
Percent	100.0	100.0	100.0	100.0	100.0	100.0	100.0	100.0
Less than 30 percent	21	19	25	22	13	16	22	20
30 to 49 percent	24	24	24	25	19	24	24	24
50 to 69 percent	18	19	17	7	18	20	17	18

[Continued]

★ 612 ★

Monthly Housing Costs of Renters - 1991

[Continued]

Characteristics	All households	White	Black	American Indian, Eskimo, or Aleut	Asian or Pacific Islander	Hispanic origin	Not of Hispanic origin	
							Total	White
70 percent or more	37	38	34	46	50	40	37	38
Median	56	57	50	58	70	60	55	57

Source: Woodward, Jeanne M. *America's Racial and Ethnic Groups: Their Housing in the Early Nineties.* Bureau of the Census. Current Housing Reports, Series H121/94-3. Washington, DC: U.S. Government Printing Office, p. 61. Primary source: American Housing Survey (AHS), 1991 National Internal User File. *Note:* 1. Incomes below household poverty level.

★ 613 ★

Housing Costs and Conditions

Neighborhood Conditions - 1991

Numbers are shown in thousands of occupied units. Households of Hispanic origin may be of any race.

Characteristics	All households	White	Black	American Indian, Eskimo, or Aleut	Asian or Pacific Islander	Hispanic origin	Not of Hispanic origin	
							Total	White
Neighborhood conditions								
With neighborhood	91,296	77,609	10,588	455	2,034	6,119	85,177	72,183
No problems	56,412	48,431	6,038	236	1,347	3,787	52,625	45,056
With problems	34,548	28,878	4,524	215	681	2,308	32,240	26,851
Crime	6,701	4,615	1,754	41	186	737	5,964	3,999
Noise	7,017	5,557	1,074	46	250	616	6,401	5,045
Traffic	6,651	5,896	587	30	100	424	6,228	5,508
Litter or housing deterioration	4,147	3,352	666	23	71	270	3,878	3,122
Poor city or county services	1,484	1,173	279	4	15	107	1,377	1,077
Undesirable commercial, institutional, industrial	1,583	1,409	148	-	14	114	1,469	1,302
People	11,369	9,333	1,603	112	234	884	10,485	8,548
Other	8,376	7,321	821	58	143	380	7,996	6,979
Type of problem not reported	607	521	77	1	2	18	589	505
Presence of problems not reported	335	299	27	4	6	24	312	276

Source: Woodward, Jeanne M. *America's Racial and Ethnic Groups: Their Housing in the Early Nineties.* Bureau of the Census. Current Housing Reports, Series H121/94-3. Washington, DC: U.S. Government Printing Office, p. 55. Primary source: American Housing Survey (AHS), 1991 National Internal User File. *Note:* A dash (-) represents zero or a percent that rounds to less than .1.

★ 614 ★

Housing Costs and Conditions

Opinion of Neighborhood Conditions - 1991

Numbers are in thousands of occupied units. Households of Hispanic origin may be of any race.

Characteristics	All households	White	Black	American Indian, Eskimo, or Aleut	Asian or Pacific Islander	Hispanic origin	Not of Hispanic origin	
							Total	White
Overall opinion of neighborhood								
Poor (3 or less)	3,645	2,470	992	46	90	441	3,204	2,084
Fair (4-7)	23,799	19,218	3,478	162	720	1,864	21,935	17,611
Good (8-10)	63,851	55,921	6,119	246	1,224	3,813	60,038	52,488
No neighborhood	796	715	50	24	5	29	767	692
Not reported	1,055	816	193	7	28	92	963	750

Source: Woodward, Jeanne M. *America's Racial and Ethnic Groups: Their Housing in the Early Nineties.* Bureau of the Census. Current Housing Reports, Series H121/94-3. Washington, DC: U.S. Government Printing Office, p. 55. Primary source: American Housing Survey (AHS), 1991 National Internal User File. *Note:* A dash (-) represents zero or a percent that rounds to less than .1.

★ 615 ★

Housing Costs and Conditions

Equipment in Housing - 1991

Numbers are shown in percent of occupied units. Households of Hispanic origin may be of any race.

Characteristics	All households	White	Black	American Indian, Eskimo, or Aleut	Asian or Pacific Islander	Hispanic origin	Not of Hispanic origin	
							Total	White
All occupied units, total	93,147	79,140	10,832	486	2,066	6,239	86,907	73,625
Equipment								
Percent with complete kitchen (sink, refrigerator, and burners)	99.0	99.0	98.0	99.0	98.0	98.0	99.0	99.0
Percent with all plumbing facilities (piped water, bathtub or shower, flush toilet)	98.0	98.0	97.0	96.0	98.0	97.0	98.0	98.0
Percent with washing machine	76.0	79.0	58.0	70.0	61.0	57.0	77.0	81.0
Percent with clothes dryer	69.0	74.0	42.0	58.0	54.0	41.0	71.0	76.0
Percent with heating equipment:								
Percent with central, built-in units	88.0	89.0	83.0	81.0	86.0	80.0	89.0	90.0
Percent with other types	11.0	10.0	16.0	18.0	7.0	16.0	11.0	10.0
Percent with air-conditioning:								
Percent with central	42.0	44.0	33.0	21.0	38.0	32.0	43.0	45.0
Percent with room units	29.0	28.0	33.0	30.0	23.0	28.0	29.0	28.0

Source: Woodward, Jeanne M. *America's Racial and Ethnic Groups: Their Housing in the Early Nineties.* Bureau of the Census. Current Housing Reports, Series H121/94-3. Washington, DC: U.S. Government Printing Office, p. 52. Primary source: American Housing Survey (AHS), 1991 National Internal User File.

★ 616 ★

Housing Costs and Conditions

Opinion of Housing Structure - 1991

Numbers are shown in thousands of occupied units. Households of Hispanic origin may be of any race.

Characteristics	All households	White	Black	American Indian, Eskimo, or Aleut	Asian or Pacific Islander	Hispanic origin	Not of Hispanic origin	
							Total	White
Overall opinion of structure								
Poor (3 or less)	1,659	1,153	398	19	61	206	1,453	978
Fair (4-7)	22,712	18,285	3,262	169	731	1,975	20,737	16,594
Good (8-10)	68,025	59,104	7,050	294	1,253	3,987	64,039	55,513
Not reported	750	597	123	3	21	71	679	540

Source: Woodward, Jeanne M. *America's Racial and Ethnic Groups: Their Housing in the Early Nineties.* Bureau of the Census. Current Housing Reports, Series H121/94-3. Washington, DC: U.S. Government Printing Office, p. 53. Primary source: American Housing Survey (AHS), 1991 National Internal User File.

★ 617 ★

Housing Costs and Conditions

Physical Problems in Housing - 1991

Numbers in thousands of occupied units. Households of Hispanic origin may be of any race.

Characteristics	All households	White	Black	American Indian, Eskimo, or Aleut	Asian or Pacific Islander	Hispanic origin	Not of Hispanic origin	
							Total	White
Selected physical problems								
Severe physical problems	2,874	2,221	526	29	52	267	2,607	2,008
Plumbing	2,278	1,862	334	19	37	182	2,096	1,722
Heating	341	212	97	7	6	48	293	176
Electric	67	46	19	2	-	7	60	40
Upkeep	249	139	93	2	11	43	206	100
Hallways	3	3	-	-	-	-	3	3
Moderate physical problems	4,531	3,032	1,358	18	78	564	3,966	2,519
Plumbing	295	213	74	3	-	44	251	177
Heating	1,977	1,248	700	2	16	271	1,707	995
Kitchen	560	403	119	1	26	58	502	352
Upkeep	1,914	1,284	557	14	38	224	1,690	1,080
Hallways	47	30	14	-	-	12	35	23

Source: Woodward, Jeanne M. *America's Racial and Ethnic Groups: Their Housing in the Early Nineties.* Bureau of the Census. Current Housing Reports, Series H121/94-3. Washington, DC: U.S. Government Printing Office, p. 53. Primary source: American Housing Survey (AHS), 1991 National Internal User File. *Note:* A dash (-) represents zero or a percent that rounds to less than .1.

★ 618 ★

Housing Costs and Conditions

Selected Housing Deficiencies - 1991

Numbers are shown in thousands of occupied units. Households of Hispanic origin may be of any race.

Characteristics	All households	White	Black	American Indian, Eskimo, or Aleut	Asian or Pacific Islander	Hispanic origin	Not of Hispanic origin	
							Total	White
Selected deficiencies								
Signs of rats in last 3 months	3,341	1,946	1,190	23	116	597	2,745	1,439
Holes in floor	1,139	778	309	14	24	132	1,007	660
Open cracks or holes (interior)	4,705	3,372	1,097	50	127	503	4,202	2,946
Broken plaster or peeling paint (interior)	3,847	2,794	910	27	68	432	3,416	2,407
No electrical wiring	31	29	-	2	-	-	31	29
Exposed wiring	1,491	1,091	312	15	47	206	1,285	910
Rooms without electrical outlets	1,637	1,262	326	8	28	154	1,482	1,120

Source: Woodward, Jeanne M. *America's Racial and Ethnic Groups: Their Housing in the Early Nineties*, p. 53. Primary source: American Housing Survey (AHS), 1991 National Internal User File. *Note:* A dash (-) represents zero or a percent that rounds to less than .1.

★ 619 ★

Housing Costs and Conditions

Home Heating Fuel Used in Selected Alaska Native Villages

Data are shown for the 50 areas with the largest populations, in number of housing units.

Alaska Native Village Statistical Area[1]	Occupied units using -								
	Utility gas	Bottled, tank, or LP gas	Electricity	Fuel oil, kerosene, etc.	Coal or coke	Wood	Solar energy	Other fuel	No fuel used
Akiachak	0	0	7	65	0	39	0	0	0
Akutan	0	0	0	27	0	0	0	0	0
Alakanuk	0	0	0	82	0	38	0	0	0
Andreafsky	0	0	0	79	0	31	0	0	0
Angoon	0	0	1	110	0	40	0	0	0
Aniak	0	0	8	121	2	23	0	0	0
Barrow	807	0	10	4	0	0	0	0	0
Bethel	2	2	39	1,276	0	19	0	75	24
Chevak	0	0	0	141	0	0	0	0	0
Copper Center	0	9	8	124	0	19	0	0	0
Craig	0	51	16	238	0	136	0	3	0
Dillingham	0	0	17	664	0	6	4	0	0
Emmonak	0	0	1	129	0	36	0	0	0
Fort Yukon	0	0	0	89	0	119	0	0	0
Galena	0	7	0	125	0	41	0	0	0
Gambell	0	1	0	118	0	2	0	0	0
Grouse Creek Group	0	27	13	119	4	44	0	0	0
Hoonah	0	5	17	153	0	45	0	0	5
Hooper Bay	0	0	2	191	0	3	0	0	0
Kake	0	3	9	175	0	31	0	0	0
Kasigluk	0	2	0	86	0	0	0	0	0
King Cove	0	5	2	81	0	0	0	2	0
King Salmon	0	4	3	147	0	2	0	5	0
Kipnuk	0	0	0	103	0	0	0	0	0
Klawock	0	35	0	161	0	33	0	0	4
Kotlik	0	0	0	66	0	35	0	0	0

[Continued]

★ 619 ★

Home Heating Fuel Used in Selected Alaska Native Villages
[Continued]

Alaska Native Village Statistical Area[1]	Occupied units using -								
	Utility gas	Bottled, tank, or LP gas	Electricity	Fuel oil, kerosene, etc.	Coal or coke	Wood	Solar energy	Other fuel	No fuel used
Kotzebue	11	0	47	686	0	12	0	6	2
Kwethluk	0	0	0	97	0	30	0	0	0
McGrath	0	0	4	100	0	66	0	3	2
Mountain Village	0	0	0	112	0	31	0	0	0
Naknek	0	0	0	198	0	4	0	0	0
Ninilchik	0	175	1,057	1,291	353	868	0	0	9
Noorvik	0	2	2	88	0	17	0	0	0
Pilot Station	0	0	6	73	0	22	0	0	0
Point Hope	0	0	0	141	0	2	0	0	0
Quinhagak	0	2	5	107	0	9	0	0	0
St. Paul	0	0	9	144	0	0	0	0	0
Salamatof	189	9	9	15	3	24	0	0	17
Sand Point	0	0	2	239	2	0	0	0	0
Savoonga	0	0	0	113	0	3	0	0	0
Selawik	0	0	0	113	0	14	0	0	0
Shishmaref	0	0	0	118	0	0	0	0	0
Stebbins	0	0	6	39	0	45	0	0	0
Togiak	0	0	8	146	0	0	0	0	0
Tok	0	14	0	209	2	140	0	2	0
Toksook Bay	0	0	0	89	0	0	0	0	0
Unalakleet	0	0	0	176	0	24	0	0	0
Unalaska	2	7	49	504	0	8	0	5	0
Wainwright	0	0	0	126	7	0	0	0	0
Yakutat	0	0	10	159	0	11	0	0	2

Source: Census of Population and Housing, 1990: Summary Tape File 3C on CD-ROM [machine-readable datafiles]. Prepared by the Bureau of the Census. Washington, DC: The Bureau, 1992. *Notes:* 1. Alaska Native villages (ANVs) constitute tribes, bands, clans, groups, villages, communities, or associations in Alaska that are recognized pursuant to the Alaska Native Claims Settlement Act of 1972, Public Law 92-203. Because ANVs do not have legally designated boundaries, the Census Bureau has established Alaska Native village statistical areas (ANVSAs) for statistical purposes. For the 1990 census, the Census Bureau cooperated with officials of the nonprofit corporation within each participating Alaska Native Regional Corporation (ANRC), as well as other knowledgeable officials, to delineate boundaries that encompass the settled area associated with each ANV.

★ 620 ★

Housing Costs and Conditions

Home Heating Fuel Used in Selected Tribal Designated Statistical Areas

TDSA[1]	Occupied units using -								
	Utility gas	Bottled, tank, or LP gas	Electricity	Fuel oil, kerosene, etc.	Coal or coke	Wood	Solar energy	Other fuel	No fuel used
Apache Choctaw TDSA (state)	2,587	2,524	2,051	89	0	1,056	0	33	21
Chickahominy TDSA (state)	0	44	401	310	0	174	0	0	0
Clifton Choctaw TDSA (state)	36	78	54	0	0	8	0	0	0
Coharie TDSA (state)	7,798	8,232	17,236	9,142	6	1,759	0	59	57
Coquille Indian TDSA	21,674	2,899	97,845	8,543	22	28,819	78	736	256
Delaware-Muncie TDSA (state)	7	22	27	0	0	29	0	6	0
Florida Tribe of Eastern Creek TDSA (state)	0	24	64	0	0	0	0	0	0
Haliwa-Saponi TDSA (state)	10	338	437	535	12	766	0	0	0
Jena Band of Choctaw TDSA (state)	10,249	1,508	7,992	93	0	1,181	0	7	27
Klamath TDSA	5,501	336	4,483	1,156	2	3,571	43	802	288
Lumbee TDSA (state)	1,450	3,937	5,875	2,781	13	1,957	0	32	54
Meherrin TDSA (state)	644	3,599	5,497	6,941	14	3,314	11	29	68

[Continued]

★ 620 ★

Home Heating Fuel Used in Selected Tribal Designated Statistical Areas

[Continued]

TDSA[1]	Occupied units using -								
	Utility gas	Bottled, tank, or LP gas	Electricity	Fuel oil, kerosene, etc.	Coal or coke	Wood	Solar energy	Other fuel	No fuel used
Mohegan TDSA (state)	2,502	178	1,381	5,654	22	64	0	22	0
Ramapough TDSA (state)	102	11	0	89	0	0	0	0	0
United Houma Nation TDSA (state)	171,558	4,770	112,612	248	0	353	31	107	567
Waccamaw Siouan TDSA (state)	23	160	291	258	0	145	0	0	5
Wampanoag-Gay Head TDSA	4	157	1,629	2,633	38	496	32	4	10

Source: Census of Population and Housing, 1990: Summary Tape File 3C on CD-ROM [machine-readable datafiles]. Prepared by the Bureau of the Census. Washington, DC: The Bureau, 1992. Notes: 1. Tribal designated statistical areas (TDSAs) are areas, delineated outside Oklahoma by federally- and state-recognized tribes without a land base or associated trust lands, to provide statistical areas for which the Census Bureau tabulates data. TDSAs represent areas generally containing the American Indian population over which federally-recognized tribes have jurisdiction and areas in which state tribes provide benefits and services to their members. The names of TDSAs delineated by state-recognized tribes are followed by "(state)." The Census Bureau did not recognize TDSAs before the 1990 census.

★ 621 ★

Housing Costs and Conditions

Home Heating Fuel Used in Selected Tribal Jurisdiction Statistical Areas

TJSA[1]	Occupied units using -								
	Utility gas	Bottled, tank, or LP gas	Electricity	Fuel oil, kerosene, etc.	Coal or coke	Wood	Solar energy	Other fuel	No fuel used
Absentee Shawnee-Citizens Band of Potawatomi TJSA	10,413	7,948	9,872	80	0	2,582	17	40	20
Caddo-Wichita-Delaware TJSA	1,404	824	729	2	0	184	1	0	0
Cherokee TJSA	86,070	22,327	22,926	145	2	17,959	81	300	81
Cheyenne-Arapaho TJSA	34,919	7,605	11,398	73	3	1,288	0	43	13
Chickasaw TJSA	52,482	17,122	23,128	213	10	6,149	23	268	63
Choctaw TJSA	35,166	17,048	13,770	61	23	13,021	13	234	32
Creek TJSA	177,161	12,519	54,624	99	4	5,967	83	654	209
Iowa TJSA	365	652	291	6	0	232	0	11	4
Kaw TJSA	4,026	509	515	10	0	75	0	17	0
Kiowa-Comanche-Apache-Fort Sill Apache TJSA	49,479	7,099	14,707	88	0	1,197	33	162	33
Otoe-Missouria TJSA	289	430	221	0	0	32	2	3	0
Pawnee TJSA	2,848	1,465	1,045	4	0	559	2	22	8
Sac and Fox TJSA	13,661	1,942	3,380	19	0	1,113	0	79	38
Seminole TJSA	5,037	1,629	1,410	10	0	675	5	29	0
Tonkawa TJSA	4,336	192	274	0	0	26	2	8	0
Creek-Seminole Joint Area TJSA	514	206	97	0	0	49	0	4	0
Iowa-Sac and Fox Joint Area TJSA	66	66	126	0	0	45	0	0	0

Source: Census of Population and Housing, 1990: Summary Tape File 3C on CD-ROM [machine-readable datafiles]. Prepared by the Bureau of the Census. Washington, DC: The Bureau, 1992. Notes: 1. Tribal jurisdiction statistical areas (TJSAs) are areas, delineated by federally recognized tribes in Oklahoma without a reservation, for which the Census Bureau tabulates data. TJSAs represent areas generally containing the American Indian population over which one or more tribal governments have jurisdiction. If tribal officials delineated adjacent TJSAs so that they include some duplicate territory, the overlap area is called a "joint use area," which is treated as a separate TJSA for census purposes.

★ 622 ★

Housing Costs and Conditions

Home Heating Fuel Used on Selected Reservations and Trust Lands

Data are shown for the 50 areas with the largest populations, in number of housing units.

American Indian Reservation and Trust Lands[1,2]	Occupied units using -								
	Utility gas	Bottled, tank, or LP gas	Electricity	Fuel oil, kerosene, etc.	Coal or coke	Wood	Solar energy	Other fuel	No fuel used
Agua Caliente Reservation	7,080	134	2,963	12	0	3	0	0	9
Allegany Reservation	2,098	35	528	74	0	160	0	4	2
Blackfeet Reservation	959	165	702	16	0	464	0	0	3
Cheyenne River Reservation	2	1,303	463	389	12	164	0	18	0
Coeur d'Alene Reservation and Trust Lands, ID	0	44	633	265	5	1,264	0	13	2
Colorado River Reservation	657	654	1,267	2	0	52	0	0	37
Colville Reservation	0	21	1,208	30	3	1,133	0	11	10
Crow Reservation and Trust Lands, MT	369	585	366	55	147	130	0	43	10
Eastern Cherokee Reservation	11	74	320	444	0	1,196	0	0	0
Flathead Reservation	2	772	2,652	1,805	11	2,580	3	38	0
Fort Apache Reservation	289	1,107	162	0	0	960	0	8	23
Fort Berthold Reservation	67	906	472	239	25	0	0	26	0
Fort Hall Reservation and Trust Lands, ID	199	167	752	70	49	267	0	0	6
Fort Peck Reservation	2,107	647	453	133	18	66	0	19	7
Gila River Reservation	540	674	804	0	0	408	0	0	45
Hopi Reservation and Trust Lands, AZ	77	412	100	11	634	576	0	0	0
Isabella Reservation and Trust Lands, MI	5,200	1,428	410	591	3	588	2	25	13
Laguna Pueblo and Trust Lands, NM	438	301	49	37	0	230	0	0	0
Lake Traverse (Sisseton) Reservation	0	1,319	1,084	1,290	0	206	0	4	0
Leech Lake Reservation	14	792	387	823	0	1,090	0	3	0
Mississippi Choctaw Reservation and Trust Lands, MS	25	322	308	4	0	297	0	9	9
Muckleshoot Reservation and Trust Lands, WA	507	8	684	17	0	117	0	0	0
Navajo Reservation and Trust Lands, AZ–NM–UT	4,992	5,071	3,289	594	2,424	19,666	22	167	170
Nez Perce Reservation	0	122	2,096	750	16	3,064	4	86	3
Northern Cheyenne Reservation and Trust Lands, MT–SD	5	296	636	0	52	45	0	3	0
Omaha Reservation	866	612	116	100	0	45	2	2	2
Oneida (West) Reservation	3,532	714	321	842	7	265	8	36	9
Osage Reservation	9,638	2,563	2,040	13	0	928	11	74	16
Papago Reservation	237	355	704	17	12	794	0	0	40
Pine Ridge Reservation and Trust Lands, NE–SD	110	1,702	225	119	0	551	0	41	0
Port Madison Reservation	0	61	1,074	142	0	594	0	3	0
Puyallup Reservation and Trust Lands, WA	1,644	172	7,978	1,425	10	680	8	69	14
Red Lake Reservation	0	31	406	186	0	320	0	5	0
Rosebud Reservation and Trust Lands, SD	28	1,284	678	179	0	345	0	14	0
Salt River Reservation	241	275	978	7	0	26	0	0	54
San Carlos Reservation	619	347	381	0	0	327	0	0	31

[Continued]

★ 622 ★

Home Heating Fuel Used on Selected Reservations and Trust Lands
[Continued]

American Indian Reservation and Trust Lands[1,2]	Occupied units using -								
	Utility gas	Bottled, tank, or LP gas	Electricity	Fuel oil, kerosene, etc.	Coal or coke	Wood	Solar energy	Other fuel	No fuel used
Sandia Pueblo	1,024	109	28	6	0	88	7	3	2
San Juan Pueblo	1,012	248	76	0	0	297	7	11	8
Santa Clara Pueblo	2,975	204	168	2	4	280	23	0	0
Southern Ute Reservation	455	930	242	33	139	761	46	116	2
Standing Rock Reservation	7	1,525	292	329	31	139	0	2	0
Taos Pueblo and Trust Lands, NM	1,047	281	115	8	0	497	11	0	2
Tulalip Reservation	14	180	1,677	54	0	586	0	13	0
Turtle Mountain Reservation and Trust Lands, ND–SD	80	828	685	309	0	143	0	45	15
Uintah and Ouray Reservation	1,530	1,088	790	62	242	1,206	13	11	0
White Earth Reservation	4	626	455	1,017	2	896	0	5	0
Wind River Reservation	3,438	1,485	1,341	82	114	985	26	28	0
Yakima Reservation and Trust Lands, WA	1,134	107	4,445	756	44	1,335	5	23	37
Yankton Reservation	3	961	389	716	0	79	0	8	0
Zuni Pueblo	55	458	42	0	12	1,079	0	0	0

Source: Census of Population and Housing, 1990: Summary Tape File 3C on CD-ROM [machine-readable datafiles]. Prepared by the Bureau of the Census. Washington, DC: The Bureau, 1992. *Notes:* 1. Federal American Indian reservations are areas with boundaries established by treaty, statute, and/or executive or court order, and recognized by the federal government as territory in which American Indian tribes have jurisdiction. State reservations are lands held in trust by state governments for the use and benefit of a given tribe. The reservations and their boundaries were identified for the 1990 census by the Bureau of Indian Affairs (BIA), Department of Interior (for federal reservations), and state governments (for state reservations). The names of American Indian reservations recognized by state governments, but not by the federal government, are followed by "state." Areas composed of reservation lands that are administered jointly and/or are claimed by two reservations, as identified by the BIA, are called "joint areas," and are treated as separate American Indian reservations for census purposes. Federal reservations may cross state boundaries, and federal and state reservations may cross county, county subdivision, and place boundaries. For reservations that cross state boundaries, only the portion of the reservations in a given state is shown in the data products for that state; the entire reservations are shown in data products for the United States. 2. Trust lands are property associated with a particular American Indian reservation or tribe, held in trust by the federal government. Trust lands may be held in trust either for a tribe (tribal trust lands) or for an individual member of a tribe (individual trust land). Trust lands recognized for the 1990 census comprised all tribal trust lands and inhabited individual trust lands located outside of a reservation boundary. As with other American Indian areas, trust lands may be located in more than one state. Only the trust lands in a given state are shown in the data products for that state; all trust lands associated with a reservation or tribe are shown in data products for the United States. The Census Bureau first reported data for tribal trust lands for the 1980 census.

★ 623 ★

Housing Costs and Conditions

Sewage Disposal for Housing in Selected Alaska Native Villages

Data are shown for the 50 areas with the largest populations, in number of housing units.

Alaska Native Village Statistical Area[1]	Public sewer	Septic tank or cesspool	Other means
Akiachak	14	0	114
Akutan	27	0	0
Alakanuk	0	8	131
Andreafsky	99	3	36
Angoon	140	13	8
Aniak	76	60	39
Barrow	527	28	367
Bethel	654	532	444

[Continued]

★ 623 ★

Sewage Disposal for Housing in Selected Alaska Native Villages
[Continued]

Alaska Native Village Statistical Area[1]	Public sewer	Septic tank or cesspool	Other means
Chevak	10	0	148
Copper Center	21	165	51
Craig	468	0	36
Dillingham	375	396	80
Emmonak	99	0	78
Fort Yukon	12	143	120
Galena	50	118	101
Gambell	0	4	129
Grouse Creek Group	33	188	21
Hoonah	237	0	14
Hooper Bay	5	26	178
Kake	221	39	4
Kasigluk	1	0	101
King Cove	124	5	0
King Salmon	28	195	10
Kipnuk	0	2	130
Klawock	259	2	14
Kotlik	3	3	104
Kotzebue	786	6	119
Kwethluk	9	0	129
McGrath	13	164	33
Mountain Village	122	0	64
Naknek	141	110	17
Ninilchik	1,408	2,620	1,171
Noorvik	76	0	51
Pilot Station	77	2	45
Point Hope	0	2	172
Quinhagak	3	3	126
St. Paul	171	4	0
Salamatof	181	235	8
Sand Point	263	9	2
Savoonga	7	4	118
Selawik	3	0	149
Shishmaref	0	0	135
Stebbins	0	5	86
Togiak	119	2	82
Tok	3	335	223
Toksook Bay	96	0	10
Unalakleet	214	0	20
Unalaska	556	53	64

[Continued]

★ 623 ★

Sewage Disposal for Housing in Selected Alaska Native Villages
[Continued]

Alaska Native Village Statistical Area[1]	Public sewer	Septic tank or cesspool	Other means
Wainwright	3	0	157
Yakutat	159	16	19

Source: Census of Population and Housing, 1990: Summary Tape File 3C on CD-ROM [machine-readable datafiles]. Prepared by the Bureau of the Census. Washington, DC: The Bureau, 1992. *Notes:* 1. Alaska Native villages (ANVs) constitute tribes, bands, clans, groups, villages, communities, or associations in Alaska that are recognized pursuant to the Alaska Native Claims Settlement Act of 1972, Public Law 92-203. Because ANVs do not have legally designated boundaries, the Census Bureau has established Alaska Native village statistical areas (ANVSAs) for statistical purposes. For the 1990 census, the Census Bureau cooperated with officials of the nonprofit corporation within each participating Alaska Native Regional Corporation (ANRC), as well as other knowledgeable officials, to delineate boundaries that encompass the settled area associated with each ANV.

★ 624 ★

Housing Costs and Conditions

Sewage Disposal for Housing in Selected Tribal Designated Statistical Areas

Tribal Designated Statistical Area[1]	Public sewer	Septic tank or cesspool	Other means
Apache Choctaw TDSA (state)	2,981	9,240	568
Chickahominy TDSA (state)	18	893	78
Clifton Choctaw TDSA (state)	9	179	0
Coharie TDSA (state)	28,953	18,808	609
Coquille Indian TDSA	136,699	32,936	891
Delaware-Muncie TDSA (state)	0	91	0
Florida Tribe of Eastern Creek TDSA (state)	48	74	6
Haliwa-Saponi TDSA (state)	28	1,829	445
Jena Band of Choctaw TDSA (state)	12,490	10,617	541
Klamath TDSA	15,348	2,242	32
Lumbee TDSA (state)	4,516	12,006	678
Meherrin TDSA (state)	6,542	14,565	1,300
Mohegan TDSA (state)	8,570	2,104	8
Ramapough TDSA (state)	96	109	0
United Houma Nation TDSA (state)	274,976	43,803	3,006
Waccamaw Siouan TDSA (state)	43	905	20
Wampanoag-Gay Head TDSA	963	10,557	84

Source: Census of Population and Housing, 1990: Summary Tape File 3C on CD-ROM [machine-readable datafiles]. Prepared by the Bureau of the Census. Washington, DC: The Bureau, 1992. *Notes:* 1. Tribal designated statistical areas (TDSAs) are areas, delineated outside Oklahoma by federally- and state-recognized tribes without a land base or associated trust lands, to provide statistical areas for which the Census Bureau tabulates data. TDSAs represent areas generally containing the American Indian population over which federally-recognized tribes have jurisdiction and areas in which state tribes provide benefits and services to their members. The names of TDSAs delineated by state-recognized tribes are followed by "(state)." The Census Bureau did not recognize TDSAs before the 1990 census.

★ 625 ★

Housing Costs and Conditions

Sewage Disposal for Housing in Selected Tribal Jurisdiction Statistical Areas

Tribal Jurisdiction Statistical Area[1]	Public sewer	Septic tank or cesspool	Other means
Absentee Shawnee-Citizens Band of Potawatomi TJSA	7,959	26,029	398
Caddo-Wichita-Delaware TJSA	1,504	2,474	130
Cherokee TJSA	101,827	75,778	1,963
Cheyenne-Arapaho TJSA	48,321	17,075	454
Chickasaw TJSA	67,801	48,837	1,226
Choctaw TJSA	44,971	45,201	2,152
Creek TJSA	228,859	52,734	1,130
Iowa TJSA	539	1,250	84
Kaw TJSA	4,557	1,135	35
Kiowa-Comanche-Apache-Fort Sill Apache TJSA	70,260	14,775	486
Otoe-Missouria TJSA	751	427	11
Pawnee TJSA	3,136	4,116	81
Sac and Fox TJSA	16,661	6,279	220
Seminole TJSA	6,011	4,174	151
Tonkawa TJSA	5,246	615	92
Creek-Seminole Joint Area TJSA	558	495	15
Iowa-Sac and Fox Joint Area TJSA	49	327	19

Source: Census of Population and Housing, 1990: Summary Tape File 3C on CD-ROM [machine-readable datafiles]. Prepared by the Bureau of the Census. Washington, DC: The Bureau, 1992. *Notes:* 1. Tribal jurisdiction statistical areas (TJSAs) are areas, delineated by federally recognized tribes in Oklahoma without a reservation, for which the Census Bureau tabulates data. TJSAs represent areas generally containing the American Indian population over which one or more tribal governments have jurisdiction. If tribal officials delineated adjacent TJSAs so that they include some duplicate territory, the overlap area is called a "joint use area," which is treated as a separate TJSA for census purposes.

★ 626 ★

Housing Costs and Conditions

Sewage Disposal for Housing on Selected Reservations and Trust Lands

Data are shown for the 50 areas with the largest populations, in number of housing units.

American Indian Reservation and Trust Lands[1,2]	Public sewer	Septic tank or cesspool	Other means
Agua Caliente Reservation	19,577	1,629	59
Allegany Reservation	2,641	483	14
Blackfeet Reservation	1,820	957	196
Cheyenne River Reservation	1,753	875	295
Coeur d'Alene Reservation and Trust Lands, ID	1,101	2,420	221
Colorado River Reservation	2,331	2,403	43
Colville Reservation	1,375	1,592	49
Crow Reservation and Trust Lands, MT	739	1,129	213
Eastern Cherokee Reservation	794	1,364	154
Flathead Reservation	3,769	6,270	343

[Continued]

★ 626 ★

Sewage Disposal for Housing on Selected Reservations and Trust Lands
[Continued]

American Indian Reservation and Trust Lands[1,2]	Public sewer	Septic tank or cesspool	Other means
Fort Apache Reservation	2,290	611	407
Fort Berthold Reservation	1,535	960	216
Fort Hall Reservation and Trust Lands, ID	314	1,321	128
Fort Peck Reservation	2,727	1,138	126
Gila River Reservation	1,200	1,218	269
Hopi Reservation and Trust Lands, AZ	1,097	221	1,093
Isabella Reservation and Trust Lands, MI	4,468	4,497	58
Laguna Pueblo and Trust Lands, NM	1,048	261	33
Lake Traverse (Sisseton) Reservation	2,058	3,085	329
Leech Lake Reservation	647	5,087	538
Mississippi Choctaw Reservation and Trust Lands, MS	565	462	24
Muckleshoot Reservation and Trust Lands, WA	1,015	374	2
Navajo Reservation and Trust Lands, AZ–NM–UT	18,479	10,053	27,109
Nez Perce Reservation	3,971	2,840	136
Northern Cheyenne Reservation and Trust Lands, MT–SD	771	498	18
Omaha Reservation	1,162	751	33
Oneida (West) Reservation	3,720	2,062	105
Osage Reservation	9,716	8,176	204
Papago Reservation	926	818	761
Pine Ridge Reservation and Trust Lands, NE–SD	1,547	1,113	716
Port Madison Reservation	708	1,404	21
Puyallup Reservation and Trust Lands, WA	8,729	4,171	88
Red Lake Reservation	297	706	55
Rosebud Reservation and Trust Lands, SD	1,853	976	163
Salt River Reservation	1,369	636	132
San Carlos Reservation	1,380	326	393
Sandia Pueblo	850	550	25
San Juan Pueblo	498	1,313	65
Santa Clara Pueblo	2,695	1,429	52
Southern Ute Reservation	584	2,557	216
Standing Rock Reservation	1,594	1,016	122
Taos Pueblo and Trust Lands, NM	1,500	705	491
Tulalip Reservation	1,010	2,964	52
Turtle Mountain Reservation and Trust Lands, ND–SD	1,082	1,108	162
Uintah and Ouray Reservation	2,729	4,449	371
White Earth Reservation	1,119	3,218	250
Wind River Reservation	4,545	3,994	219
Yakima Reservation and Trust Lands, WA	4,214	4,066	133

[Continued]

★ 626 ★

Sewage Disposal for Housing on Selected Reservations and Trust Lands
[Continued]

American Indian Reservation and Trust Lands[1,2]	Public sewer	Septic tank or cesspool	Other means
Yankton Reservation	1,374	1,015	99
Zuni Pueblo	1,658	111	131

Source: Census of Population and Housing, 1990: Summary Tape File 3C on CD-ROM [machine-readable datafiles]. Prepared by the Bureau of the Census. Washington, DC: The Bureau, 1992. *Notes:* 1. Federal American Indian reservations are areas with boundaries established by treaty, statute, and/or executive or court order, and recognized by the federal government as territory in which American Indian tribes have jurisdiction. State reservations are lands held in trust by state governments for the use and benefit of a given tribe. The reservations and their boundaries were identified for the 1990 census by the Bureau of Indian Affairs (BIA), Department of Interior (for federal reservations), and state governments (for state reservations). The names of American Indian reservations recognized by state governments, but not by the federal government, are followed by "state." Areas composed of reservation lands that are administered jointly and/or are claimed by two reservations, as identified by the BIA, are called "joint areas," and are treated as separate American Indian reservations for census purposes. Federal reservations may cross state boundaries, and federal and state reservations may cross county, county subdivision, and place boundaries. For reservations that cross state boundaries, only the portion of the reservations in a given state is shown in the data products for that state; the entire reservations are shown in data products for the United States. 2. Trust lands are property associated with a particular American Indian reservation or tribe, held in trust by the federal government. Trust lands may be held in trust either for a tribe (tribal trust lands) or for an individual member of a tribe (individual trust land). Trust lands recognized for the 1990 census comprised all tribal trust lands and inhabited individual trust lands located outside of a reservation boundary. As with other American Indian areas, trust lands may be located in more than one state. Only the trust lands in a given state are shown in the data products for that state; all trust lands associated with a reservation or tribe are shown in data products for the United States. The Census Bureau first reported data for tribal trust lands for the 1980 census.

★ 627 ★

Housing Costs and Conditions

Source of Water for Housing in Selected Alaska Native Villages

Data are shown for the 50 areas with the largest populations, in number of housing units.

Alaska Native Village Statistical Area[1]	Public system or private company	Individual well		Some other source
		Drilled	Dug	
Akiachak	11	3	0	114
Akutan	27	0	0	0
Alakanuk	68	0	0	71
Andreafsky	117	3	0	18
Angoon	155	0	0	6
Aniak	8	125	11	31
Barrow	893	0	0	29
Bethel	1,356	84	10	180
Chevak	147	2	0	9
Copper Center	30	150	17	40
Craig	484	0	0	20
Dillingham	359	428	12	52
Emmonak	141	0	0	36
Fort Yukon	238	2	0	35
Galena	170	12	5	82
Gambell	95	2	0	36
Grouse Creek Group	38	182	6	16
Hoonah	248	0	0	3
Hooper Bay	40	8	0	161

[Continued]

★ 627 ★

Source of Water for Housing in Selected Alaska Native Villages
[Continued]

Alaska Native Village Statistical Area[1]	Public system or private company	Individual well		Some other source
		Drilled	Dug	
Kake	257	0	0	7
Kasigluk	0	1	0	101
King Cove	129	0	0	0
King Salmon	32	182	4	15
Kipnuk	0	0	0	132
Klawock	259	2	0	14
Kotlik	5	0	0	105
Kotzebue	814	0	0	97
Kwethluk	38	2	0	98
McGrath	186	4	4	16
Mountain Village	121	0	0	65
Naknek	40	213	2	13
Ninilchik	1,668	1,698	362	1,471
Noorvik	75	0	0	52
Pilot Station	122	2	0	0
Point Hope	152	0	0	22
Quinhagak	82	0	0	50
St. Paul	175	0	0	0
Salamatof	189	208	16	11
Sand Point	274	0	0	0
Savoonga	129	0	0	0
Selawik	101	0	0	51
Shishmaref	27	0	0	108
Stebbins	90	1	0	0
Togiak	168	0	0	35
Tok	3	432	0	126
Toksook Bay	91	0	0	15
Unalakleet	220	0	0	14
Unalaska	619	0	0	54
Wainwright	120	0	0	40
Yakutat	170	11	2	11

Source: Census of Population and Housing, 1990: Summary Tape File 3C on CD-ROM [machine-readable datafiles]. Prepared by the Bureau of the Census. Washington, DC: The Bureau, 1992. *Notes:* 1. Alaska Native villages (ANVs) constitute tribes, bands, clans, groups, villages, communities, or associations in Alaska that are recognized pursuant to the Alaska Native Claims Settlement Act of 1972, Public Law 92-203. Because ANVs do not have legally designated boundaries, the Census Bureau has established Alaska Native village statistical areas (ANVSAs) for statistical purposes. For the 1990 census, the Census Bureau cooperated with officials of the nonprofit corporation within each participating Alaska Native Regional Corporation (ANRC), as well as other knowledgeable officials, to delineate boundaries that encompass the settled area associated with each ANV.

★ 628 ★

Housing Costs and Conditions

Source of Water for Housing in Selected Tribal Designated Statistical Areas

Data are shown in number of housing units.

Tribal Designated Statistical Area[1]	Public system or private company	Individual well		Some other source
		Drilled	Dug	
Apache Choctaw TDSA (state)	6,120	5,032	1,044	593
Chickahominy TDSA (state)	10	504	471	4
Clifton Choctaw TDSA (state)	114	66	8	0
Coharie TDSA (state)	34,963	10,456	2,821	130
Coquille Indian TDSA	145,092	19,558	2,171	3,705
Delaware-Muncie TDSA (state)	46	28	17	0
Florida Tribe of Eastern Creek TDSA (state)	103	25	0	0
Haliwa-Saponi TDSA (state)	148	1,020	1,113	21
Jena Band of Choctaw TDSA (state)	22,339	1,120	153	36
Klamath TDSA	15,880	1,672	40	30
Lumbee TDSA (state)	10,393	4,782	1,896	129
Meherrin TDSA (state)	12,130	7,702	2,282	293
Mohegan TDSA (state)	9,172	1,163	320	27
Ramapough TDSA (state)	138	67	0	0
United Houma Nation TDSA (state)	320,870	134	46	735
Waccamaw Siouan TDSA (state)	42	867	59	0
Wampanoag-Gay Head TDSA	7,507	3,809	257	31

Source: Census of Population and Housing, 1990: Summary Tape File 3C on CD-ROM [machine-readable datafiles]. Prepared by the Bureau of the Census. Washington, DC: The Bureau, 1992. *Notes:* 1. Tribal designated statistical areas (TDSAs) are areas, delineated outside Oklahoma by federally- and state-recognized tribes without a land base or associated trust lands, to provide statistical areas for which the Census Bureau tabulates data. TDSAs represent areas generally containing the American Indian population over which federally-recognized tribes have jurisdiction and areas in which state tribes provide benefits and services to their members. The names of TDSAs delineated by state-recognized tribes are followed by "(state)." The Census Bureau did not recognize TDSAs before the 1990 census.

★ 629 ★

Housing Costs and Conditions

Source of Water for Housing in Selected Tribal Jurisdiction Statistical Areas

Data are shown in number of housing units.

Tribal Jurisdiction Statistical Area[1]	Public system or private company	Individual well		Some other source
		Drilled	Dug	
Absentee Shawnee-Citizens Band of Potawatomi TJSA	9,831	23,006	1,510	39
Caddo-Wichita-Delaware TJSA	1,802	2,195	102	9
Cherokee TJSA	152,912	22,579	1,746	2,331
Cheyenne-Arapaho TJSA	54,916	10,291	513	130
Chickasaw TJSA	93,430	22,108	1,939	387
Choctaw TJSA	73,192	15,380	2,501	1,251

[Continued]

★ 629 ★

Source of Water for Housing in Selected Tribal Jurisdiction Statistical Areas
[Continued]

Tribal Jurisdiction Statistical Area[1]	Public system or private company	Individual well		Some other source
		Drilled	Dug	
Creek TJSA	270,848	10,068	1,053	754
Iowa TJSA	695	1,102	72	4
Kaw TJSA	5,569	123	28	7
Kiowa-Comanche-Apache-Fort Sill Apache TJSA	78,788	5,554	838	341
Otoe-Missouria TJSA	920	210	43	16
Pawnee TJSA	5,690	1,504	83	56
Sac and Fox TJSA	18,251	4,613	237	59
Seminole TJSA	7,514	2,662	134	26
Tonkawa TJSA	5,507	363	63	20
Creek-Seminole Joint Area TJSA	941	116	9	2
Iowa-Sac and Fox Joint Area TJSA	63	314	8	10

Source: Census of Population and Housing, 1990: Summary Tape File 3C on CD-ROM [machine-readable datafiles]. Prepared by the Bureau of the Census. Washington, DC: The Bureau, 1992. *Notes:* 1. Tribal jurisdiction statistical areas (TJSAs) are areas, delineated by federally recognized tribes in Oklahoma without a reservation, for which the Census Bureau tabulates data. TJSAs represent areas generally containing the American Indian population over which one or more tribal governments have jurisdiction. If tribal officials delineated adjacent TJSAs so that they include some duplicate territory, the overlap area is called a "joint use area," which is treated as a separate TJSA for census purposes.

★ 630 ★

Housing Costs and Conditions

Source of Water for Housing on Selected Reservations and Trust Lands

Data are shown for the 50 areas with the largest populations, in number of housing units.

American Indian Reservation and Trust Lands[1,2]	Public system or private company	Individual well		Some other source
		Drilled	Dug	
Agua Caliente Reservation	21,231	20	0	14
Allegany Reservation	2,938	165	19	16
Blackfeet Reservation	1,889	775	153	156
Cheyenne River Reservation	2,257	461	64	141
Coeur d'Alene Reservation and Trust Lands, ID	1,503	1,521	183	535
Colorado River Reservation	3,470	1,031	140	136
Colville Reservation	1,756	979	130	151
Crow Reservation and Trust Lands, MT	749	1,071	69	192
Eastern Cherokee Reservation	1,025	672	36	579
Flathead Reservation	4,614	3,954	409	1,405
Fort Apache Reservation	2,962	115	0	231
Fort Berthold Reservation	1,578	750	157	226
Fort Hall Reservation and Trust Lands, ID	403	1,259	55	46
Fort Peck Reservation	2,722	1,061	168	40
Gila River Reservation	2,603	79	0	5
Hopi Reservation and Trust Lands, AZ	1,823	155	13	420
Isabella Reservation and Trust Lands, MI	4,270	4,591	136	26
Laguna Pueblo and Trust Lands, NM	1,275	34	0	33

[Continued]

★ 630 ★

Source of Water for Housing on Selected Reservations and Trust Lands
[Continued]

American Indian Reservation and Trust Lands[1,2]	Public system or private company	Individual well		Some other source
		Drilled	Dug	
Lake Traverse (Sisseton) Reservation	2,509	2,072	615	276
Leech Lake Reservation	756	4,958	408	150
Mississippi Choctaw Reservation and Trust Lands, MS	1,038	13	0	0
Muckleshoot Reservation and Trust Lands, WA	1,282	97	10	2
Navajo Reservation and Trust Lands, AZ–NM–UT	33,935	11,122	2,063	8,521
Nez Perce Reservation	4,226	1,878	168	675
Northern Cheyenne Reservation and Trust Lands, MT–SD	772	496	19	0
Omaha Reservation	1,457	386	100	3
Oneida (West) Reservation	3,513	2,306	65	3
Osage Reservation	15,659	2,042	140	255
Papago Reservation	1,978	464	31	32
Pine Ridge Reservation and Trust Lands, NE–SD	1,655	1,413	165	143
Port Madison Reservation	1,784	301	26	22
Puyallup Reservation and Trust Lands, WA	11,072	1,719	121	76
Red Lake Reservation	491	513	11	43
Rosebud Reservation and Trust Lands, SD	1,980	860	105	47
Salt River Reservation	2,069	37	0	31
San Carlos Reservation	1,810	60	9	220
Sandia Pueblo	1,012	384	27	2
San Juan Pueblo	694	974	179	29
Santa Clara Pueblo	2,610	1,444	99	23
Southern Ute Reservation	624	2,242	215	276
Standing Rock Reservation	1,699	905	55	73
Taos Pueblo and Trust Lands, NM	1,604	555	92	445
Tulalip Reservation	2,788	864	277	97
Turtle Mountain Reservation and Trust Lands, ND–SD	2,072	147	20	113
Uintah and Ouray Reservation	4,727	1,976	192	654
White Earth Reservation	1,207	3,079	82	219
Wind River Reservation	5,201	3,250	160	147
Yakima Reservation and Trust Lands, WA	4,322	3,738	339	14
Yankton Reservation	2,076	277	17	118
Zuni Pueblo	1,714	30	0	156

Source: Census of Population and Housing, 1990: Summary Tape File 3C on CD-ROM [machine-readable datafiles]. Prepared by the Bureau of the Census. Washington, DC: The Bureau, 1992. *Notes:* 1. Federal American Indian reservations are areas with boundaries established by treaty, statute, and/or executive or court order, and recognized by the federal government as territory in which American Indian tribes have jurisdiction. State reservations are lands held in trust by state governments for the use and benefit of a given tribe. The reservations and their boundaries were identified for the 1990 census by the Bureau of Indian Affairs (BIA), Department of Interior (for federal reservations), and state governments (for state reservations). The names of American Indian reservations recognized by state governments, but not by the federal government, are followed by "state." Areas composed of reservation lands that are administered jointly and/or are claimed by two reservations, as identified by the BIA, are called "joint areas," and are treated as separate American Indian reservations for census purposes. Federal reservations may cross state boundaries, and federal and state reservations may cross county, county subdivision, and place boundaries. For reservations that cross state boundaries, only the portion of the reservations in a given state is shown in the data products for that state; the entire reservations are shown in data products for the United States. 2. Trust lands are property associated with a particular American Indian reservation or tribe, held in trust by the federal government. Trust lands may be held in trust either for a tribe (tribal trust lands) or for an individual member of a tribe (individual trust land). Trust lands recognized for the 1990 census comprised all tribal trust lands and inhabited individual trust lands located outside of a reservation boundary. As with other American Indian areas, trust lands may be located in more than one state. Only the trust lands in a given state are shown in the data products for that state; all trust lands associated with a reservation or tribe are shown in data products for the United States. The Census Bureau first reported data for tribal trust lands for the 1980 census.

Telephone Availability

★ 631 ★

Householder Age by Telephone Availability in Selected Alaska Native Villages

Data are shown for the 50 areas with the largest populations, in number of housing units.

Alaska Native Village Statistical Area[1]	Occupied housing units with householder age -							
	15 to 59 years		60 to 64 years		65 to 74 years		75+ years	
	With telephone	Without telephone	With telephone	Without telephone	With telephone	Without telephone	With telephone	Without telephone
Akiachak	38	53	0	0	3	7	4	6
Akutan	14	11	0	0	2	0	0	0
Alakanuk	38	63	3	8	2	4	0	2
Andreafsky	55	42	1	0	9	0	3	0
Angoon	89	36	1	0	7	3	12	3
Aniak	116	16	9	0	0	4	9	0
Barrow	649	79	35	0	36	3	19	0
Bethel	1,119	157	49	3	69	6	30	4
Chevak	38	72	9	4	4	11	2	1
Copper Center	113	24	0	2	14	3	2	2
Craig	359	59	8	4	11	0	3	0
Dillingham	563	39	22	0	36	0	28	3
Emmonak	91	47	6	5	12	2	3	0
Fort Yukon	83	94	9	7	1	4	5	5
Galena	109	40	10	6	6	0	0	2
Gambell	74	32	4	0	11	0	0	0
Grouse Creek Group	151	23	19	0	10	4	0	0
Hoonah	130	35	12	3	28	0	17	0
Hooper Bay	61	85	0	8	14	11	2	15
Kake	147	28	12	0	23	3	5	0
Kasigluk	49	27	0	3	8	1	0	0
King Cove	78	3	2	0	7	0	0	0
King Salmon	130	13	13	0	5	0	0	0
Kipnuk	56	25	3	0	5	3	9	2
Klawock	163	46	9	0	12	3	0	0
Kotlik	37	41	0	2	12	1	4	4
Kotzebue	541	125	36	5	33	0	20	4
Kwethluk	45	50	2	5	4	7	10	4
McGrath	138	23	3	0	5	0	6	0
Mountain Village	84	30	9	3	12	0	5	0
Naknek	160	16	1	0	14	0	11	0
Ninilchik	2,860	338	178	31	191	35	113	7
Noorvik	45	29	8	5	10	7	5	0
Pilot Station	49	30	10	4	4	2	0	2
Point Hope	69	61	1	4	2	0	4	2
Quinhagak	56	32	2	8	7	11	2	5
St. Paul	103	17	8	3	13	2	7	0
Salamatof	177	28	18	0	28	0	15	0
Sand Point	188	29	13	2	9	0	2	0
Savoonga	61	34	2	4	7	4	0	4
Selawik	31	61	8	5	6	4	4	8
Shishmaref	64	30	13	0	6	0	5	0
Stebbins	22	43	0	5	0	7	0	13
Togiak	90	41	6	0	6	3	8	0

[Continued]

★ 631 ★

Householder Age by Telephone Availability in Selected Alaska Native Villages
[Continued]

Alaska Native Village Statistical Area[1]	Occupied housing units with householder age -							
	15 to 59 years		60 to 64 years		65 to 74 years		75+ years	
	With telephone	Without telephone	With telephone	Without telephone	With telephone	Without telephone	With telephone	Without telephone
Tok	249	64	5	5	25	10	3	6
Toksook Bay	40	33	11	0	0	3	2	0
Unalakleet	103	50	3	4	10	12	14	4
Unalaska	432	116	8	3	7	4	5	0
Wainwright	81	27	10	2	6	0	5	2
Yakutat	117	33	5	6	11	2	8	0

Source: Census of Population and Housing, 1990: Summary Tape File 3C on CD-ROM [machine-readable datafiles]. Prepared by the Bureau of the Census. Washington, DC: The Bureau, 1992. *Notes:* 1. Alaska Native villages (ANVs) constitute tribes, bands, clans, groups, villages, communities, or associations in Alaska that are recognized pursuant to the Alaska Native Claims Settlement Act of 1972, Public Law 92-203. Because ANVs do not have legally designated boundaries, the Census Bureau has established Alaska Native village statistical areas (ANVSAs) for statistical purposes. For the 1990 census, the Census Bureau cooperated with officials of the nonprofit corporation within each participating Alaska Native Regional Corporation (ANRC), as well as other knowledgeable officials, to delineate boundaries that encompass the settled area associated with each ANV.

★ 632 ★

Telephone Availability

Householder Age by Telephone Availability in Selected Tribal Designated Statistical Areas

Tribal Designated Statistical Area[1]	Occupied housing units with householder age -							
	15 to 59 years		60 to 64 years		65 to 74 years		75+ years	
	With telephone	Without telephone	With telephone	Without telephone	With telephone	Without telephone	With telephone	Without telephone
Apache Choctaw TDSA (state)	4,306	860	641	41	1,398	83	959	73
Chickahominy TDSA (state)	680	41	83	0	74	18	33	0
Clifton Choctaw TDSA (state)	66	29	13	7	47	0	5	9
Coharie TDSA (state)	26,211	3,741	3,238	229	6,333	311	4,086	140
Coquille Indian TDSA	103,344	6,745	10,222	371	21,816	520	17,597	257
Delaware-Muncie TDSA (state)	63	0	0	0	13	0	15	0
Florida Tribe of Eastern Creek TDSA (state)	34	6	18	0	21	0	9	0
Haliwa-Saponi TDSA (state)	1,163	357	142	35	208	29	148	16
Jena Band of Choctaw TDSA (state)	13,373	1,663	1,212	111	2,696	130	1,784	88
Klamath TDSA	10,125	910	962	67	2,144	113	1,812	49
Lumbee TDSA (state)	9,293	2,419	1,197	73	1,682	175	1,149	111
Meherrin TDSA (state)	10,384	2,271	1,735	142	2,999	233	2,220	133
Mohegan TDSA (state)	6,462	310	769	7	1,317	35	908	15
Ramapough TDSA (state)	143	0	14	0	26	0	19	0
United Houma Nation TDSA (state)	201,964	14,100	20,684	829	32,673	1,055	18,449	492
Waccamaw Siouan TDSA (state)	575	96	95	8	41	14	44	9
Wampanoag-Gay Head TDSA	3,287	50	353	3	745	31	532	2

Source: Census of Population and Housing, 1990: Summary Tape File 3C on CD-ROM [machine-readable datafiles]. Prepared by the Bureau of the Census. Washington, DC: The Bureau, 1992. *Notes:* 1. Tribal designated statistical areas (TDSAs) are areas, delineated outside Oklahoma by federally- and state-recognized tribes without a land base or associated trust lands, to provide statistical areas for which the Census Bureau tabulates data. TDSAs represent areas generally containing the American Indian population over which federally-recognized tribes have jurisdiction and areas in which state tribes provide benefits and services to their members. The names of TDSAs delineated by state-recognized tribes are followed by "(state)." The Census Bureau did not recognize TDSAs before the 1990 census.

★ 633 ★

Telephone Availability

Householder Age by Telephone Availability in Selected Tribal Jurisdiction Statistical Areas

Tribal Jurisdiction Statistical Area[1]	Occupied housing units with householder age -							
	15 to 59 years		60 to 64 years		65 to 74 years		75+ years	
	With telephone	Without telephone	With telephone	Without telephone	With telephone	Without telephone	With telephone	Without telephone
Absentee Shawnee-Citizens Band of Potawatomi TJSA	21,118	1,829	2,271	78	3,225	148	2,226	77
Caddo-Wichita-Delaware TJSA	1,697	228	255	16	490	19	422	17
Cherokee TJSA	85,507	13,411	11,148	805	20,675	1,187	16,339	819
Cheyenne-Arapaho TJSA	34,888	3,546	3,414	198	6,404	251	6,469	172
Chickasaw TJSA	53,422	9,243	6,959	500	14,641	891	13,265	537
Choctaw TJSA	39,262	9,782	5,969	570	11,787	967	10,287	744
Creek TJSA	164,128	16,421	15,419	700	29,283	1,207	23,680	482
Iowa TJSA	910	147	90	13	210	16	161	14
Kaw TJSA	3,184	218	436	8	759	0	521	26
Kiowa-Comanche-Apache-Fort Sill Apache TJSA	44,147	6,522	4,433	322	8,506	462	8,118	288
Otoe-Missouria TJSA	518	120	94	0	108	10	110	17
Pawnee TJSA	3,166	568	386	16	947	39	819	12
Sac and Fox TJSA	10,553	1,934	1,461	92	2,865	113	3,100	114
Seminole TJSA	4,236	978	564	47	1,390	127	1,356	97
Tonkawa TJSA	2,410	492	315	28	701	31	838	23
Creek-Seminole Joint Area TJSA	328	175	67	12	116	9	152	11
Iowa-Sac and Fox Joint Area TJSA	194	35	22	0	28	2	21	1

Source: Census of Population and Housing, 1990: Summary Tape File 3C on CD-ROM [machine-readable datafiles]. Prepared by the Bureau of the Census. Washington, DC: The Bureau, 1992. *Notes:* 1. Tribal jurisdiction statistical areas (TJSAs) are areas, delineated by federally recognized tribes in Oklahoma without a reservation, for which the Census Bureau tabulates data. TJSAs represent areas generally containing the American Indian population over which one or more tribal governments have jurisdiction. If tribal officials delineated adjacent TJSAs so that they include some duplicate territory, the overlap area is called a "joint use area," which is treated as a separate TJSA for census purposes.

★ 634 ★

Telephone Availability

Householder Age by Telephone Availability on Selected Reservations and Trust Lands

Data are shown for the 50 areas with the largest populations, in number of housing units.

American Indian Reservation and Trust Lands[1,2]	Occupied housing units with householder age -							
	15 to 59 years		60 to 64 years		65 to 74 years		75+ years	
	With telephone	Without telephone	With telephone	Without telephone	With telephone	Without telephone	With telephone	Without telephone
Agua Caliente Reservation	4,152	116	916	19	2,466	0	2,510	22
Allegany Reservation	1,488	261	246	8	472	15	398	13
Blackfeet Reservation	1,343	524	141	11	126	43	84	37
Cheyenne River Reservation	1,142	561	143	23	197	62	203	20
Coeur d'Alene Reservation and Trust Lands, ID	1,301	207	156	25	294	16	210	17
Colorado River Reservation	1,280	459	223	41	372	26	250	18
Colville Reservation	1,324	423	135	19	238	30	225	22
Crow Reservation and Trust Lands, MT	777	561	91	44	122	45	36	29
Eastern Cherokee Reservation	983	583	101	40	164	65	98	11
Flathead Reservation	4,364	713	486	57	1,125	84	988	46
Fort Apache Reservation	874	1,266	36	85	81	112	17	78
Fort Berthold Reservation	805	362	129	15	224	19	174	7

[Continued]

★ 634 ★

Householder Age by Telephone Availability on Selected Reservations and Trust Lands
[Continued]

American Indian Reservation and Trust Lands[1,2]	Occupied housing units with householder age -							
	15 to 59 years		60 to 64 years		65 to 74 years		75+ years	
	With telephone	Without telephone	With telephone	Without telephone	With telephone	Without telephone	With telephone	Without telephone
Fort Hall Reservation and Trust Lands, ID	930	233	61	33	116	31	100	6
Fort Peck Reservation	1,989	617	180	44	300	28	284	8
Gila River Reservation	444	1,470	55	136	59	174	23	110
Hopi Reservation and Trust Lands, AZ	670	601	72	29	145	105	70	118
Isabella Reservation and Trust Lands, MI	5,902	500	461	19	751	21	576	30
Laguna Pueblo and Trust Lands, NM	525	209	36	33	97	20	117	18
Lake Traverse (Sisseton) Reservation	1,881	414	338	31	576	42	574	47
Leech Lake Reservation	1,686	353	226	17	362	32	387	46
Mississippi Choctaw Reservation and Trust Lands, MS	295	506	24	69	19	26	23	12
Muckleshoot Reservation and Trust Lands, WA	925	70	59	4	162	5	108	0
Navajo Reservation and Trust Lands, AZ-NM-UT	7,234	20,550	324	2,242	413	3,070	159	2,403
Nez Perce Reservation	3,470	451	455	19	908	39	745	54
Northern Cheyenne Reservation and Trust Lands, MT-SD	406	477	16	43	56	32	7	0
Omaha Reservation	809	283	140	11	231	32	222	17
Oneida (West) Reservation	4,735	115	332	0	358	28	163	3
Osage Reservation	8,940	1,348	1,104	49	2,175	73	1,545	49
Papago Reservation	850	786	38	122	41	152	57	113
Pine Ridge Reservation and Trust Lands, NE-SD	951	1,079	193	89	124	133	99	80
Port Madison Reservation	1,342	56	111	0	231	2	132	0
Puyallup Reservation and Trust Lands, WA	8,885	420	690	4	1,144	19	826	12
Red Lake Reservation	441	335	70	23	42	13	19	5
Rosebud Reservation and Trust Lands, SD	1,021	921	115	38	154	130	85	64
Salt River Reservation	474	447	59	11	255	12	298	25
San Carlos Reservation	268	1,191	39	69	9	84	5	40
Sandia Pueblo	873	117	68	11	110	11	75	2
San Juan Pueblo	829	430	93	8	116	22	131	30
Santa Clara Pueblo	1,990	678	188	23	392	31	317	37
Southern Ute Reservation	1,776	282	194	22	248	28	156	18
Standing Rock Reservation	1,071	574	165	44	229	50	166	26
Taos Pueblo and Trust Lands, NM	1,024	329	96	10	209	35	221	37
Tulalip Reservation	1,762	127	151	22	204	57	189	12
Turtle Mountain Reservation and Trust Lands, ND-SD	1,138	584	120	14	141	23	75	10
Uintah and Ouray Reservation	3,110	590	275	12	484	48	397	26
White Earth Reservation	1,535	331	228	21	457	39	363	31
Wind River Reservation	4,649	877	520	24	791	99	513	26
Yakima Reservation and Trust Lands, WA	4,280	1,034	496	60	1,002	75	842	97

[Continued]

★ 634 ★

Householder Age by Telephone Availability on Selected Reservations and Trust Lands
[Continued]

American Indian Reservation and Trust Lands[1,2]	Occupied housing units with householder age -							
	15 to 59 years		60 to 64 years		65 to 74 years		75+ years	
	With telephone	Without telephone	With telephone	Without telephone	With telephone	Without telephone	With telephone	Without telephone
Yankton Reservation	1,030	275	157	15	352	35	274	18
Zuni Pueblo	923	362	81	22	79	48	71	60

Source: Census of Population and Housing, 1990: Summary Tape File 3C on CD-ROM [machine-readable datafiles]. Prepared by the Bureau of the Census. Washington, DC: The Bureau, 1992. *Notes:* 1. Federal American Indian reservations are areas with boundaries established by treaty, statute, and/or executive or court order, and recognized by the federal government as territory in which American Indian tribes have jurisdiction. State reservations are lands held in trust by state governments for the use and benefit of a given tribe. The reservations and their boundaries were identified for the 1990 census by the Bureau of Indian Affairs (BIA), Department of Interior (for federal reservations), and state governments (for state reservations). The names of American Indian reservations recognized by state governments, but not by the federal government, are followed by "state." Areas composed of reservation lands that are administered jointly and/or are claimed by two reservations, as identified by the BIA, are called "joint areas," and are treated as separate American Indian reservations for census purposes. Federal reservations may cross state boundaries, and federal and state reservations may cross county, county subdivision, and place boundaries. For reservations that cross state boundaries, only the portion of the reservations in a given state is shown in the data products for that state; the entire reservations are shown in data products for the United States. 2. Trust lands are property associated with a particular American Indian reservation or tribe, held in trust by the federal government. Trust lands may be held in trust either for a tribe (tribal trust lands) or for an individual member of a tribe (individual trust land). Trust lands recognized for the 1990 census comprised all tribal trust lands and inhabited individual trust lands located outside of a reservation boundary. As with other American Indian areas, trust lands may be located in more than one state. Only the trust lands in a given state are shown in the data products for that state; all trust lands associated with a reservation or tribe are shown in data products for the United States. The Census Bureau first reported data for tribal trust lands for the 1980 census.

Income and Earnings

★ 635 ★

Household Income - 1991

Numbers are shown in thousands of occupied housing units, excluding medians. Households of Hispanic origin may be of any race.

Characteristics	All households	White	Black	American Indian, Eskimo, or Aleut	Asian or Pacific Islander	Hispanic origin	Not of Hispanic origin	
							Total	White
Household income								
Percent	100.0	100.0	100.0	100.0	100.0	100.0	100.0	100.0
Under $10,000	16.0	14.0	31.0	25.0	14.0	20.0	16.0	14.0
$10,000-$14,999	9.0	9.0	12.0	13.0	6.0	12.0	9.0	9.0
$15,000-$19,999	9.0	9.0	10.0	10.0	6.0	12.0	8.0	8.0
$20,000-$24,999	9.0	9.0	10.0	13.0	7.0	11.0	9.0	8.0
$25,000-$29,999	9.0	10.0	8.0	7.0	8.0	11.0	9.0	9.0
$30,000-$34,999	7.0	7.0	6.0	8.0	6.0	7.0	7.0	7.0
$35,000-$39,999	6.0	6.0	5.0	3.0	5.0	5.0	6.0	6.0
$40,000-$49,999	10.0	10.0	7.0	10.0	10.0	8.0	10.0	10.0
$50,000-$59,999	7.0	8.0	4.0	3.0	9.0	5.0	8.0	8.0
$60,000-$79,999	9.0	9.0	4.0	4.0	12.0	5.0	9.0	9.0
$80,000-$99,999	4.0	4.0	1.0	1.0	7.0	2.0	4.0	4.0

[Continued]

★ 635 ★

Household Income - 1991
[Continued]

Characteristics	All households	White	Black	American Indian, Eskimo, or Aleut	Asian or Pacific Islander	Hispanic origin	Not of Hispanic origin	
							Total	White
$100,000 or more	5.0	6.0	1.0	2.0	10.0	3.0	5.0	6.0
Median (dollars)	28,890	30,840	18,960	20,700	39,390	22,910	29,630	31,300

Source: Woodward, Jeanne M. *America's Racial and Ethnic Groups: Their Housing in the Early Nineties.* Bureau of the Census. Current Housing Reports, Series H121/94-3. Washington, DC: U.S. Government Printing Office, p. 57. Primary source: American Housing Survey (AHS), 1991 National Internal User File.

★ 636 ★

Income and Earnings

Income of Families and Primary Individuals in Households - 1991

Numbers are shown in thousands of occupied units, excluding medians. Households of Hispanic origin may be of any race.

Characteristics	All households	White	Black	American Indian, Eskimo, or Aleut	Asian or Pacific Islander	Hispanic origin	Not of Hispanic origin	
							Total	White
Income of families and primary individuals								
Percent	100.0	100.0	100.0	100.0	100.0	100.0	100.0	100.0
Under $5,000	6.0	5.0	14.0	14.0	9.0	9.0	6.0	5.0
$5,000-$9,999	11.0	10.0	17.0	13.0	6.0	14.0	10.0	10.0
$10,000-$14,999	10.0	9.0	12.0	13.0	7.0	13.0	10.0	9.0
$15,000-$19,999	9.0	9.0	10.0	10.0	6.0	12.0	9.0	9.0
$20,000-$24,999	9.0	9.0	10.0	13.0	8.0	11.0	9.0	9.0
$25,000-$29,999	10.0	10.0	9.0	8.0	8.0	10.0	9.0	10.0
$30,000-$34,999	7.0	7.0	5.0	8.0	6.0	6.0	7.0	7.0
$35,000-$39,999	6.0	6.0	5.0	3.0	5.0	4.0	6.0	6.0
$40,000-$49,999	9.0	10.0	7.0	10.0	10.0	7.0	10.0	10.0
$50,000-$59,999	7.0	7.0	4.0	2.0	9.0	4.0	7.0	8.0
$60,000-$79,999	8.0	9.0	4.0	3.0	11.0	5.0	8.0	9.0
$80,000-$99,999	4.0	4.0	1.0	-	7.0	2.0	4.0	4.0
$100,000 or more	5.0	5.0	1.0	1.0	9.0	2.0	5.0	6.0
Median (dollars)	27,750	30,360	17,830	20,040	36,050	20,890	36,340	29,710

Source: Woodward, Jeanne M. *America's Racial and Ethnic Groups: Their Housing in the Early Nineties.* Bureau of the Census. Current Housing Reports, Series H121/94-3. Washington, DC: U.S. Government Printing Office, p. 57. Primary source: American Housing Survey (AHS), 1991 National Internal User File. *Note:* A dash (-) represents zero or a percent that rounds to less than .1.

★ 637 ★

Income and Earnings

Personal Income Trends in South Dakota and Its Reservations

Data show per capita personal income in reservation counties from 1986-1991.

	All South Dakota	Yankton	Rosebud	Pine Ridge	Lower Brule	Crow Creek	Standing Rock
1986	11,887	9,865	6,225	5,287	11,305	7,390	7,658
1987	12,561	10,791	6,475	5,520	11,873	9,117	8,545
1988	12,775	10,151	6,497	5,836	10,749	8,639	8,771
1989	14,080	10,973	7,259	7,066	14,245	9,760	10,558
1990	15,566	13,011	7,950	8,057	15,054	10,818	11,925
1991	16,095	13,516	8,574	8,405	14,555	11,986	13,618

Source: U.S. Senate Committee on Small Business. *Small Business Development in Indian Country.* 103rd Cong., 1st sess. on Small Business Development in Indian Country. Washington, DC: U.S. Government Printing Office (3 September 1993), pp. 118 and 122. Primary source: State Data Center, USD. *Notes:* Data are for the major county within the reservation, except the Pine Ridge Reservation information which includes both Shannon and Jackson Counties.

★ 638 ★

Income and Earnings

Aggregate and Per Capita Income (1989), by Race, in Selected Alaska Native Villages

Data are shown for the 50 areas with the largest populations.

ANVSA[1]	Aggregate income (dollars)					Per capita income (dollars)				
	White	Black	American Indian, Eskimo, or Aleut	Asian or Pacific Islander	Other race	White	Black	American Indian, Eskimo, Aleut	Asian or Pacific Islander	Other race
Akiachak	753,800	0	2,579,629	76,000	0	17,948	0	6,201	19,000	0
Akutan	4,061,267	77,000	633,415	3,184,980	362,000	16,245	11,000	7,820	13,439	12,067
Alakanuk	500,289	0	2,449,060	0	0	22,740	0	4,728	0	0
Andreafsky	1,110,252	0	2,335,293	0	0	18,201	0	6,769	0	0
Angoon	3,632,520	0	3,496,018	13,726	32,092	29,775	0	6,895	2,745	3,566
Aniak	3,271,141	144,428	2,496,804	3,342	46,558	21,241	9,027	7,093	668	23,279
Barrow	27,496,940	477,746	24,485,693	3,712,000	682,308	36,468	34,125	13,944	18,747	24,368
Bethel	38,576,784	469,056	27,376,949	830,879	298,546	24,509	12,677	9,144	12,783	17,562
Chevak	1,009,485	0	2,405,215	13,500	0	29,691	0	4,303	3,375	0
Copper Center	5,410,727	0	1,201,420	0	0	19,187	0	8,343	0	0
Craig	17,317,377	0	5,188,493	0	59,746	17,964	0	18,016	0	9,958
Dillingham	21,645,307	0	16,303,358	409,083	347,346	26,047	0	14,531	7,719	31,577
Emmonak	1,465,122	21,000	3,346,608	83,240	98,459	27,132	7,000	6,220	6,937	32,820
Fort Yukon	2,426,319	0	3,395,759	0	0	31,511	0	6,764	0	0
Galena	8,125,374	361,000	3,106,107	210,019	0	20,416	12,033	8,441	21,002	0
Gambell	194,200	0	2,041,563	0	0	32,367	0	3,767	0	0
Grouse Creek Group	11,343,861	0	1,263,136	0	0	21,566	0	12,146	0	0
Hoonah	3,346,574	0	7,172,436	0	0	16,567	0	13,610	0	0
Hooper Bay	749,662	0	3,554,666	0	0	25,850	0	4,351	0	0

[Continued]

★ 638 ★

Aggregate and Per Capita Income (1989), by Race, in Selected Alaska Native Villages
[Continued]

ANVSA[1]	Aggregate income (dollars)					Per capita income (dollars)				
	White	Black	American Indian, Eskimo, or Aleut	Asian or Pacific Islander	Other race	White	Black	American Indian, Eskimo, Aleut	Asian or Pacific Islander	Other race
Kake	3,072,216	0	5,991,625	0	0	17,966	0	11,612	0	0
Kasigluk	892,357	0	2,013,276	0	0	37,182	0	4,840	0	0
King Cove	2,953,898	0	2,715,864	2,461,795	198,664	24,823	0	14,760	17,839	12,417
King Salmon	11,312,362	788,976	1,765,301	281,592	84,420	21,425	25,451	16,812	21,661	12,060
Kipnuk	186,238	0	968,237	4,146	0	23,280	0	2,142	2,073	0
Klawock	5,850,403	0	4,980,862	41,300	0	18,057	0	13,212	10,325	0
Kotlik	595,238	0	2,398,870	0	0	54,113	0	5,355	0	0
Kotzebue	16,875,002	154,647	19,384,254	1,841,163	0	26,491	22,092	9,387	43,837	0
Kwethluk	255,638	103,706	2,417,589	0	67,746	25,564	7,977	4,452	0	33,873
McGrath	4,901,805	0	2,012,856	0	0	18,428	0	7,802	0	0
Mountain Village	1,706,398	116,960	3,582,986	74,185	0	29,937	29,240	5,598	14,837	0
Naknek	7,874,370	0	3,536,570	0	0	23,297	0	14,034	0	0
Ninilchik	180,243,340	616,678	5,609,646	1,157,663	86,984	18,159	10,109	13,649	13,620	10,873
Noorvik	667,503	0	3,346,189	0	0	23,017	0	6,447	0	0
Pilot Station	462,059	0	1,850,120	0	0	30,804	0	4,093	0	0
Point Hope	1,370,355	41,746	5,654,721	159,750	0	35,137	20,873	9,666	53,250	0
Quinhagak	740,978	0	2,232,569	0	0	18,999	0	4,770	0	0
St. Paul	4,163,270	213,230	6,471,260	518,349	0	26,020	8,885	12,187	20,734	0
Salamatof	11,617,684	401,965	961,522	5,541	0	13,323	16,749	8,741	5,541	0
Sand Point	5,126,634	0	10,411,037	1,291,989	537,341	17,863	0	24,671	14,850	8,529
Savoonga	690,692	0	1,655,202	0	0	36,352	0	3,344	0	0
Selawik	567,758	53,619	2,892,464	0	0	27,036	17,873	5,212	0	0
Shishmaref	388,236	0	2,000,038	0	0	25,882	0	4,785	0	0
Stebbins	672,550	0	1,806,036	0	0	32,026	0	4,230	0	0
Togiak	1,415,498	17,746	2,131,585	0	0	15,040	8,873	4,107	0	0
Tok	12,633,753	0	928,954	49,984	0	17,088	0	10,678	6,248	0
Toksook Bay	222,144	0	1,783,804	0	0	22,990	0	4,586	0	0
Unalakleet	2,965,741	0	4,803,850	0	0	22,990	0	9,419	0	0
Unalaska	44,812,241	339,570	3,673,786	10,686,642	2,438,105	23,376	6,930	13,457	17,901	9,637
Wainwright	1,278,945	0	4,292,675	0	0	42,632	0	9,095	0	0
Yakutat	4,086,148	0	3,467,139	278,126	0	16,955	0	11,956	21,394	0

Source: Census of Population and Housing, 1990: Summary Tape File 3C on CD-ROM [machine-readable datafiles]. Prepared by the Bureau of the Census. Washington, DC: The Bureau, 1992. *Notes:* 1. Alaska Native villages (ANVs) constitute tribes, bands, clans, groups, villages, communities, or associations in Alaska that are recognized pursuant to the Alaska Native Claims Settlement Act of 1972, Public Law 92-203. Because ANVs do not have legally designated boundaries, the Census Bureau has established Alaska Native village statistical areas (ANVSAs) for statistical purposes. For the 1990 census, the Census Bureau cooperated with officials of the nonprofit corporation within each participating Alaska Native Regional Corporation (ANRC), as well as other knowledgeable officials, to delineate boundaries that encompass the settled area associated with each ANV.

★ 639 ★

Income and Earnings

Aggregate and Per Capita Income (1989), by Race, in Selected Tribal Designated Statistical Areas

TDSA[1]	Aggregate income (dollars)					Per capita income (dollars)				
	White	Black	American Indian, Eskimo, or Aleut	Asian or Pacific Islander	Other race	White	Black	American Indian, Eskimo, Aleut	Asian or Pacific Islander	Other race
Apache Choctaw TDSA (state)	171,192,287	16,550,382	4,584,738	294,876	752,461	9,554	4,185	6,703	11,341	11,944
Chickahominy TDSA (state)	9,338,039	17,615,031	5,640,048	0	0	13,078	11,343	11,701	0	0
Clifton Choctaw TDSA (state)	2,056,480	0	507,639	0	0	5,543	0	2,805	0	0
Coharie TDSA (state)	866,978,747	297,401,394	8,670,701	4,581,330	3,287,923	12,568	6,643	6,098	9,072	6,055
Coquille Indian TDSA	4,753,108,323	14,777,078	51,766,382	63,857,901	28,755,134	12,379	7,411	8,301	9,180	6,574
Delaware-Muncie TDSA (state)	2,659,945	0	211,216	0	0	9,637	0	9,183	0	0
Florida Tribe of Eastern Creek TDSA (state)	3,029,058	0	0	0	0	14,089	0	0	0	0
Haliwa-Saponi TDSA (state)	6,468,228	20,999,143	11,921,281	0	372,722	12,415	5,760	5,313	0	18,636
Jena Band of Choctaw TDSA (state)	532,754,701	32,194,032	2,704,075	3,964,127	397,200	10,125	4,669	8,048	7,976	7,944
Klamath TDSA	426,954,943	1,784,779	10,538,872	2,524,087	4,092,824	11,312	5,280	5,672	9,314	6,072
Lumbee TDSA (state)	106,952,771	76,453,616	226,278,384	593,900	486,126	12,309	6,052	7,864	18,559	4,861
Meherrin TDSA (state)	309,732,990	200,495,230	1,211,916	193,360	727,992	12,833	6,521	6,029	1,625	9,707
Mohegan TDSA (state)	336,162,255	16,220,684	2,951,203	6,974,706	3,425,949	15,348	9,442	12,297	20,454	7,876
Ramapough TDSA (state)	5,465,913	1,439,226	1,315,333	0	80,000	15,936	9,226	9,463	0	5,714
United Houma Nation TDSA (state)	8,309,205,191	836,594,626	54,732,275	120,379,820	68,682,480	12,844	6,002	5,463	9,183	8,679
Waccamaw Siouan TDSA (state)	6,984,814	6,006,158	11,394,087	40,000	36,000	8,819	9,549	8,785	5,000	800
Wampanoag-Gay Head TDSA	203,268,293	5,510,237	2,659,320	471,600	850,226	18,912	11,020	9,397	11,502	12,690

Source: Census of Population and Housing, 1990: Summary Tape File 3C on CD-ROM [machine-readable datafiles]. Prepared by the Bureau of the Census. Washington, DC: The Bureau, 1992. Notes: 1. Tribal designated statistical areas (TDSAs) are areas, delineated outside Oklahoma by federally- and state-recognized tribes without a land base or associated trust lands, to provide statistical areas for which the Census Bureau tabulates data. TDSAs represent areas generally containing the American Indian population over which federally-recognized tribes have jurisdiction and areas in which state tribes provide benefits and services to their members. The names of TDSAs delineated by state-recognized tribes are followed by "(state)." The Census Bureau did not recognize TDSAs before the 1990 census.

★ 640 ★

Income and Earnings

Aggregate and Per Capita Income (1989), by Race, in Selected Tribal Jurisdiction Statistical Areas

TJSA[1]	Aggregate income (dollars)					Per capita income (dollars)				
	White	Black	American Indian, Eskimo, or Aleut	Asian or Pacific Islander	Other race	White	Black	American Indian, Eskimo, Aleut	Asian or Pacific Islander	Other race
Absentee Shawnee-Citizens Band of Potawatomi TJSA	932,337,180	41,233,209	46,552,052	2,577,336	3,703,600	11,910	7,120	7,595	8,980	7,068
Caddo-Wichita-Delaware TJSA	71,638,113	412,152	2,926,488	36,000	1,273,922	9,865	5,423	4,886	3,273	4,900
Cherokee TJSA	3,454,443,968	229,553,406	452,686,042	9,020,284	13,320,101	11,704	6,673	6,814	8,090	6,513
Cheyenne-Arapaho TJSA	1,586,777,687	25,255,214	41,026,066	13,981,426	19,138,044	11,684	6,769	6,012	10,932	6,335
Chickasaw TJSA	2,437,546,620	55,895,271	143,153,497	5,221,688	12,100,386	10,843	6,450	6,813	7,066	5,270
Choctaw TJSA	1,585,170,682	57,777,596	175,194,707	2,025,874	5,704,052	9,314	6,082	6,203	4,835	5,698
Creek TJSA	8,074,473,428	261,488,010	378,340,514	89,257,036	32,930,695	14,933	6,739	8,372	13,707	7,783
Iowa TJSA	33,410,156	1,190,368	1,876,531	0	234,000	9,081	8,383	6,112	0	58,500
Kaw TJSA	213,047,821	217,735	5,659,417	1,420,000	488,395	17,229	4,633	8,238	15,604	13,567
Kiowa-Comanche-Apache-Fort Sill Apache TJSA	1,715,717,828	191,489,028	70,308,097	29,464,142	49,430,192	11,103	7,426	5,417	8,175	5,595
Otoe-Missouria TJSA	22,338,802	223,202	1,648,925	90,957	232,700	10,145	5,444	3,471	10,106	10,117
Pawnee TJSA	149,399,994	612,898	10,312,967	198,000	140,168	10,945	5,837	6,335	14,143	8,761
Sac and Fox TJSA	501,978,936	10,575,307	28,381,803	5,863,004	1,907,305	11,282	6,849	6,204	27,656	7,170

[Continued]

★ 640 ★

Aggregate and Per Capita Income (1989), by Race, in Selected Tribal Jurisdiction Statistical Areas

[Continued]

TJSA[1]	Aggregate income (dollars)					Per capita income (dollars)				
	White	Black	American Indian, Eskimo, or Aleut	Asian or Pacific Islander	Other race	White	Black	American Indian, Eskimo, Aleut	Asian or Pacific Islander	Other race
Seminole TJSA	180,329,791	9,549,295	20,797,838	144,998	338,636	10,360	5,463	5,514	12,083	6,157
Tonkawa TJSA	116,808,511	56,732	4,894,587	839,578	735,372	10,432	3,152	5,556	19,525	5,701
Creek-Seminole Joint Area TJSA	14,709,412	742,370	2,580,596	578,400	49,000	8,724	4,291	4,860	30,442	4,900
Iowa-Sac and Fox Joint Area TJSA	8,188,845	144,189	156,596	0	108,000	10,445	5,150	7,830	0	36,000

Source: Census of Population and Housing, 1990: Summary Tape File 3C on CD-ROM [machine-readable datafiles]. Prepared by the Bureau of the Census. Washington, DC: The Bureau, 1992. *Notes:* 1. Tribal jurisdiction statistical areas (TJSAs) are areas, delineated by federally recognized tribes in Oklahoma without a reservation, for which the Census Bureau tabulates data. TJSAs represent areas generally containing the American Indian population over which one or more tribal governments have jurisdiction. If tribal officials delineated adjacent TJSAs so that they include some duplicate territory, the overlap area is called a "joint use area," which is treated as a separate TJSA for census purposes.

★ 641 ★

Income and Earnings

Aggregate and Per Capita Income (1989), by Race, on Selected Reservations and Trust Lands

Data are shown for the 50 areas with the largest populations.

American Indian Reservation and Trust Lands[1,2]	Aggregate income (dollars)					Per capita income (dollars)				
	White	Black	American Indian, Eskimo, or Aleut	Asian or Pacific Islander	Other race	White	Black	American Indian, Eskimo, Aleut	Asian or Pacific Islander	Other race
Agua Caliente Reservation	440,093,991	4,281,884	1,456,170	4,738,467	5,874,609	24,305	10,469	10,786	12,470	7,271
Allegany Reservation	59,755,013	0	8,192,333	61,600	41,230	9,671	0	7,671	3,080	1,422
Blackfeet Reservation	13,986,082	150,000	33,172,271	0	552	9,713	25,000	4,718	0	50
Cheyenne River Reservation	28,770,362	48,412	20,759,456	200	18,000	10,960	3,026	4,077	50	3,000
Coeur d'Alene Reservation and Trust Lands, ID	56,336,112	70,000	4,359,391	5,082	185,588	11,279	23,333	5,766	1,694	8,838
Colorado River Reservation	55,819,404	172,594	14,147,741	637,872	3,710,075	11,729	10,787	5,959	11,812	5,007
Colville Reservation	32,834,691	29,100	28,572,829	268,979	876,320	10,744	4,157	7,561	9,962	5,311
Crow Reservation and Trust Lands, MT	16,107,739	0	19,968,501	254,000	0	9,931	0	4,243	19,538	0
Eastern Cherokee Reservation	7,664,668	117,600	33,742,534	21,000	176,000	7,926	10,691	6,382	1,500	5,500
Flathead Reservation	157,049,289	2,052	32,964,316	318,188	460,714	9,905	257	6,428	15,152	9,402
Fort Apache Reservation	6,384,213	238,426	37,680,467	0	257,000	11,587	8,222	3,805	0	10,708
Fort Berthold Reservation	25,231,087	0	14,809,504	180,000	13,000	10,908	0	4,849	18,000	1,857
Fort Hall Reservation and Trust Lands, ID	18,197,792	0	14,222,619	186,760	1,297,180	10,258	0	4,610	7,183	5,665
Fort Peck Reservation	49,048,392	0	27,819,666	123,200	81,550	10,109	0	4,778	4,738	5,825
Gila River Reservation	1,871,117	0	28,901,509	117,000	1,230,967	9,217	0	3,176	9,000	4,964
Hopi Reservation and Trust Lands, AZ	3,303,900	0	31,969,783	423,050	40,000	19,321	0	4,566	14,102	5,000
Isabella Reservation and Trust Lands, MI	255,317,174	1,818,556	4,755,465	1,660,362	1,235,278	11,822	11,510	5,454	10,852	8,181
Laguna Pueblo and Trust Lands, NM	896,723	42,440	22,204,309	0	189,750	16,606	21,220	6,085	0	9,987
Lake Traverse (Sisseton) Reservation	70,986,934	0	11,403,400	0	185,995	8,886	0	4,058	0	4,895
Leech Lake Reservation	51,136,213	13,308	16,095,680	19,200	0	9,578	1,109	4,705	2,133	0
Mississippi Choctaw Reservation and Trust Lands, MS	1,853,868	73,960	18,008,256	0	0	9,757	6,724	4,440	0	0

[Continued]

★ 641 ★

Aggregate and Per Capita Income (1989), by Race, on Selected Reservations and Trust Lands
[Continued]

American Indian Reservation and Trust Lands[1,2]	Aggregate income (dollars)					Per capita income (dollars)				
	White	Black	American Indian, Eskimo, or Aleut	Asian or Pacific Islander	Other race	White	Black	American Indian, Eskimo, Aleut	Asian or Pacific Islander	Other race
Muckleshoot Reservation and Trust Lands, WA	39,614,298	174,600	3,247,111	210,000	373,280	13,861	10,271	3,711	6,364	7,043
Navajo Reservation and Trust Lands, AZ–NM–UT	68,870,442	2,981,687	535,973,710	1,411,400	3,792,609	15,459	17,643	3,735	14,257	8,861
Nez Perce Reservation	153,829,524	125,004	11,502,604	239,926	227,389	10,858	8,334	6,102	4,443	6,146
Northern Cheyenne Reservation and Trust Lands, MT–SD	3,443,884	0	15,961,787	0	5,360	10,342	0	4,479	0	596
Omaha Reservation	34,218,463	1,700	6,575,445	18,000	0	10,350	850	3,416	3,600	0
Oneida (West) Reservation	256,375,381	2,210,134	17,417,835	785,406	357,550	16,733	32,031	7,109	12,083	10,516
Osage Reservation	369,166,516	45,025,307	44,139,760	283,500	1,387,508	11,946	10,657	7,236	16,676	9,312
Papago Reservation	1,466,796	0	26,426,455	0	108,000	18,567	0	3,113	0	6,000
Pine Ridge Reservation and Trust Lands, NE–SD	8,198,737	128,000	34,288,250	47,008	854,920	8,030	6,737	3,115	4,273	13,789
Port Madison Reservation	62,756,708	286,000	2,550,716	1,602,325	94,312	14,721	20,429	6,820	9,481	6,737
Puyallup Reservation and Trust Lands, WA	399,528,604	17,210,352	8,884,324	16,607,860	4,058,731	15,594	7,656	9,093	5,404	7,866
Red Lake Reservation	1,284,208	0	15,262,882	54,000	0	10,883	0	4,287	4,500	0
Rosebud Reservation and Trust Lands, SD	16,264,434	45,440	29,901,993	0	50,785	10,261	3,029	3,739	0	1,494
Salt River Reservation	16,348,086	0	14,950,150	0	367,200	12,832	0	4,215	0	10,491
San Carlos Reservation	1,026,783	423,312	22,404,800	0	514,892	13,335	13,229	3,173	0	7,356
Sandia Pueblo	20,720,380	101,693	2,866,083	4,800	5,126,227	7,416	20,339	7,077	800	6,984
San Juan Pueblo	25,807,693	13,912	7,156,177	2,000	3,879,125	7,507	1,070	5,613	2,000	7,606
Santa Clara Pueblo	80,611,781	451,796	8,564,548	87,216	5,892,509	9,963	9,822	6,614	3,489	7,623
Southern Ute Reservation	72,548,264	149,348	6,350,492	329,200	2,799,049	11,327	9,957	6,124	14,964	6,877
Standing Rock Reservation	29,086,197	0	16,668,678	160,300	9,000	9,515	0	3,421	16,030	3,000
Taos Pueblo and Trust Lands, NM	29,792,136	103,750	5,880,843	279,700	4,895,067	11,633	5,461	4,697	6,505	5,926
Tulalip Reservation	90,844,337	102,000	8,281,475	615,826	451,620	15,731	3,923	6,878	10,096	12,206
Turtle Mountain Reservation and Trust Lands, ND–SD	4,876,547	0	31,502,914	0	0	13,144	0	4,681	0	0
Uintah and Ouray Reservation	117,252,498	104,510	12,055,308	224,818	706,275	8,184	6,967	4,520	4,015	4,155
White Earth Reservation	53,604,319	0	13,758,380	42,050	0	8,965	0	4,917	7,008	0
Wind River Reservation	174,440,426	69,000	24,810,445	506,111	1,620,375	11,088	4,600	4,340	5,954	4,427
Yakima Reservation and Trust Lands, WA	120,908,639	435,558	30,538,550	6,628,844	42,591,844	11,313	4,033	4,927	12,822	4,286
Yankton Reservation	37,676,600	0	5,672,855	0	0	8,817	0	2,834	0	0
Zuni Pueblo	5,230,263	198,160	27,694,507	172,200	106,824	16,818	9,908	3,904	24,600	8,217

Source: Census of Population and Housing, 1990: Summary Tape File 3C on CD-ROM [machine-readable datafiles]. Prepared by the Bureau of the Census. Washington, DC: The Bureau, 1992. *Notes:* 1. Federal American Indian reservations are areas with boundaries established by treaty, statute, and/or executive or court order, and recognized by the federal government as territory in which American Indian tribes have jurisdiction. State reservations are lands held in trust by state governments for the use and benefit of a given tribe. The reservations and their boundaries were identified for the 1990 census by the Bureau of Indian Affairs (BIA), Department of Interior (for federal reservations), and state governments (for state reservations). The names of American Indian reservations recognized by state governments, but not by the federal government, are followed by "state." Areas composed of reservation lands that are administered jointly and/or are claimed by two reservations, as identified by the BIA, are called "joint areas," and are treated as separate American Indian reservations for census purposes. Federal reservations may cross state boundaries, and federal and state reservations may cross county, county subdivision, and place boundaries. For reservations that cross state boundaries, only the portion of the reservations in a given state is shown in the data products for that state; the entire reservations are shown in data products for the United States. 2. Trust lands are property associated with a particular American Indian reservation or tribe, held in trust by the federal government. Trust lands may be held in trust either for a tribe (tribal trust lands) or for an individual member of a tribe (individual trust land). Trust lands recognized for the 1990 census comprised all tribal trust lands and inhabited individual trust lands located outside of a reservation boundary. As with other American Indian areas, trust lands may be located in more than one state. Only the trust lands in a given state are shown in the data products for that state; all trust lands associated with a reservation or tribe are shown in data products for the United States. The Census Bureau first reported data for tribal trust lands for the 1980 census.

★ 642 ★

Income and Earnings

Household Earnings and Income (1989) in Selected Alaska Native Villages - Part I

Data are shown for the 50 areas with the largest populations, in number of persons.

ANVSA[1]	With earnings	Without earnings	Wage or salary income		Nonfarm self-employment income		Farm self-employment income		Interest, dividend, or net rental income	
			With wage or salary income	No wage or salary income	With nonfarm self-empl. income	No nonfarm self-empl. income	With farm self-empl. income	No farm self-empl. income	With interest, dividend, or net rental income	No interest, dividend, or net rental income
Akiachak	102	16	102	16	24	94	0	118	111	7
Akutan	27	0	25	2	16	11	0	27	25	2
Alakanuk	111	10	100	21	52	69	0	121	119	2
Andreafsky	100	1	100	1	49	52	0	101	95	6
Angoon	137	15	133	19	25	127	1	151	123	29
Aniak	143	12	141	14	19	136	0	155	148	7
Barrow	789	51	785	55	73	767	7	833	718	122
Bethel	1,363	74	1,330	107	315	1,122	53	1,384	1,274	163
Chevak	140	8	140	8	2	146	3	145	136	12
Copper Center	142	22	130	34	34	130	0	164	142	22
Craig	441	10	409	42	136	315	3	448	385	66
Dillingham	648	35	613	70	249	434	3	680	612	71
Emmonak	141	15	139	17	47	109	0	156	147	9
Fort Yukon	176	29	172	33	13	192	0	205	183	22
Galena	175	17	174	18	29	163	0	192	153	39
Gambell	114	10	114	10	17	107	0	124	122	2
Grouse Creek Group	219	10	211	18	65	164	0	229	207	22
Hoonah	210	23	202	31	30	203	0	233	218	15
Hooper Bay	169	23	166	26	33	159	4	188	187	5
Kake	201	14	199	16	43	172	9	206	196	19
Kasigluk	90	8	90	8	37	61	0	98	94	4
King Cove	69	8	62	15	31	46	3	74	60	17
King Salmon	171	0	171	0	14	157	2	169	141	30
Kipnuk	63	31	63	31	8	86	0	94	90	4
Klawock	224	17	216	25	28	213	4	237	193	48
Kotlik	91	16	86	21	51	56	0	107	105	2
Kotzebue	708	59	702	65	100	667	0	767	689	78
Kwethluk	112	18	112	18	11	119	11	119	127	3
McGrath	175	7	172	10	31	151	0	182	155	27
Mountain Village	141	12	135	18	57	96	0	153	135	18
Naknek	193	13	177	29	83	123	0	206	173	33
Ninilchik	3,319	448	2,933	834	1,183	2,584	68	3,699	3,413	354
Noorvik	105	4	103	6	8	101	0	109	105	4
Pilot Station	91	13	85	19	34	70	0	104	101	3
Point Hope	137	6	137	6	4	139	0	143	143	0
Quinhagak	120	12	120	12	59	73	4	128	110	22
St. Paul	151	10	151	10	9	152	0	161	148	13
Salamatof	204	39	196	47	55	188	2	241	228	15
Sand Point	230	15	198	47	80	165	4	241	198	47
Savoonga	84	41	82	43	4	121	7	118	117	8
Selawik	116	10	114	12	7	119	0	126	124	2
Shishmaref	97	14	97	14	12	99	0	111	110	1
Stebbins	93	3	90	6	11	85	0	96	95	1
Togiak	142	12	123	31	88	66	0	154	147	7
Tok	323	47	315	55	89	281	4	366	345	25

[Continued]

★ 642 ★

Household Earnings and Income (1989) in Selected Alaska Native Villages - Part I
[Continued]

ANVSA[1]	With earnings	Without earnings	Wage or salary income		Nonfarm self-employment income		Farm self-employment income		Interest, dividend, or net rental income	
			With wage or salary income	No wage or salary income	With nonfarm self-empl. income	No nonfarm self-empl. income	With farm self-empl. income	No farm self-empl. income	With interest, dividend, or net rental income	No interest, dividend, or net rental income
Toksook Bay	77	4	77	4	7	74	2	79	79	2
Unalakleet	188	9	185	12	93	104	0	197	174	23
Unalaska	566	8	542	32	124	450	2	572	372	202
Wainwright	125	17	125	17	4	138	0	142	137	5
Yakutat	156	21	144	33	84	93	2	175	162	15

Source: Census of Population and Housing, 1990: Summary Tape File 3C on CD-ROM [machine-readable datafiles]. Prepared by the Bureau of the Census. Washington, DC: The Bureau, 1992. *Notes:* 1. Alaska Native villages (ANVs) constitute tribes, bands, clans, groups, villages, communities, or associations in Alaska that are recognized pursuant to the Alaska Native Claims Settlement Act of 1972, Public Law 92-203. Because ANVs do not have legally designated boundaries, the Census Bureau has established Alaska Native village statistical areas (ANVSAs) for statistical purposes. For the 1990 census, the Census Bureau cooperated with officials of the nonprofit corporation within each participating Alaska Native Regional Corporation (ANRC), as well as other knowledgeable officials, to delineate boundaries that encompass the settled area associated with each ANV.

★ 643 ★

Income and Earnings

Household Earnings and Income (1989) in Selected Alaska Native Villages - Part II

Data are shown for the 50 areas with the largest populations, in number of persons.

ANVSA[1]	Social Security income		Public assistance income		Retirement income		Other type of income	
	With Social Security income	No Social Security income	With public assistance income	No public assistance income	With retirement income	No retirement income	With other income	No other income
Akiachak	15	103	20	98	8	110	8	110
Akutan	4	23	4	23	0	27	2	25
Alakanuk	14	107	24	97	19	102	18	103
Andreafsky	7	94	21	80	6	95	27	74
Angoon	33	119	16	136	25	127	21	131
Aniak	21	134	21	134	23	132	2	153
Barrow	76	764	68	772	88	752	52	788
Bethel	117	1,320	148	1,289	104	1,333	113	1,324
Chevak	32	116	40	108	21	127	20	128
Copper Center	30	134	28	136	38	126	25	139
Craig	26	425	8	443	28	423	99	352
Dillingham	71	612	74	609	63	620	59	624
Emmonak	38	118	28	128	17	139	18	138
Fort Yukon	24	181	27	178	20	185	28	177
Galena	12	180	4	188	23	169	17	175
Gambell	31	93	19	105	12	112	15	109
Grouse Creek Group	23	206	14	215	35	194	49	180
Hoonah	26	207	35	198	22	211	54	179

[Continued]

★ 643 ★

Household Earnings and Income (1989) in Selected Alaska Native Villages - Part II

[Continued]

ANVSA[1]	Social Security income		Public assistance income		Retirement income		Other type of income	
	With Social Security income	No Social Security income	With public assistance income	No public assistance income	With retirement income	No retirement income	With other income	No other income
Hooper Bay	25	167	71	121	34	158	44	148
Kake	31	184	18	197	23	192	31	184
Kasigluk	19	79	40	58	25	73	7	91
King Cove	9	68	2	75	7	70	2	75
King Salmon	8	163	6	165	17	154	26	145
Kipnuk	0	94	0	94	0	94	1	93
Klawock	28	213	13	228	14	227	25	216
Kotlik	30	77	49	58	16	91	17	90
Kotzebue	91	676	67	700	88	679	62	705
Kwethluk	19	111	38	92	17	113	10	120
McGrath	14	168	11	171	13	169	31	151
Mountain Village	33	120	31	122	16	137	22	131
Naknek	19	187	8	198	22	184	16	190
Ninilchik	561	3,206	363	3,404	441	3,326	706	3,061
Noorvik	18	91	24	85	26	83	20	89
Pilot Station	16	88	40	64	21	83	13	91
Point Hope	10	133	9	134	20	123	15	128
Quinhagak	7	125	63	69	33	99	17	115
St. Paul	22	139	20	141	42	119	23	138
Salamatof	44	199	58	185	28	215	47	196
Sand Point	8	237	14	231	12	233	21	224
Savoonga	22	103	23	102	23	102	6	119
Selawik	36	90	49	77	33	93	13	113
Shishmaref	26	85	30	81	27	84	18	93
Stebbins	23	73	24	72	2	94	9	87
Togiak	29	125	33	121	16	138	15	139
Tok	46	324	35	335	68	302	92	278
Toksook Bay	2	79	26	55	5	76	4	77
Unalakleet	42	155	36	161	28	169	48	149
Unalaska	24	550	18	556	20	554	34	540
Wainwright	17	125	23	119	14	128	8	134
Yakutat	32	145	20	157	37	140	31	146

Source: Census of Population and Housing, 1990: Summary Tape File 3C on CD-ROM [machine-readable datafiles]. Prepared by the Bureau of the Census. Washington, DC: The Bureau, 1992. *Notes:* 1. Alaska Native villages (ANVs) constitute tribes, bands, clans, groups, villages, communities, or associations in Alaska that are recognized pursuant to the Alaska Native Claims Settlement Act of 1972, Public Law 92-203. Because ANVs do not have legally designated boundaries, the Census Bureau has established Alaska Native village statistical areas (ANVSAs) for statistical purposes. For the 1990 census, the Census Bureau cooperated with officials of the nonprofit corporation within each participating Alaska Native Regional Corporation (ANRC), as well as other knowledgeable officials, to delineate boundaries that encompass the settled area associated with each ANV.

★ 644 ★

Income and Earnings

Household Earnings and Income (1989) in Selected Tribal Designated Statistical Areas - Part I

Data are shown in number of persons.

TDSA[1]	With earnings	Without earnings	Wage or salary income		Nonfarm self-employment income		Farm self-employment income		Interest, dividend, or net rental income	
			With wage or salary income	No wage or salary income	With nonfarm self-empl. income	No nonfarm self-empl. income	With farm self-empl. income	No farm self-empl. income	With interest, dividend, or net rental income	No interest, dividend, or net rental income
Apache Choctaw TDSA (state)	5,641	2,734	5,276	3,099	927	7,448	202	8,173	1,973	6,402
Chickahominy TDSA (state)	832	126	815	143	114	844	14	944	180	778
Clifton Choctaw TDSA (state)	141	37	134	44	24	154	0	178	21	157
Coharie TDSA (state)	34,391	10,042	33,105	11,328	4,033	40,400	1,228	43,205	9,838	34,595
Coquille Indian TDSA	122,630	38,637	116,530	44,737	22,893	138,374	2,693	158,574	68,021	93,246
Delaware-Muncie TDSA (state)	92	5	85	12	31	66	22	75	57	40
Florida Tribe of Eastern Creek TDSA (state)	61	46	61	46	0	107	0	107	47	60
Haliwa-Saponi TDSA (state)	1,568	536	1,499	605	130	1,974	80	2,024	257	1,847
Jena Band of Choctaw TDSA (state)	16,184	4,814	15,627	5,371	2,078	18,920	288	20,710	5,922	15,076
Klamath TDSA	12,185	3,936	11,626	4,495	1,915	14,206	267	15,854	6,325	9,796
Lumbee TDSA (state)	12,886	2,983	12,490	3,379	1,368	14,501	515	15,354	2,034	13,835
Meherrin TDSA (state)	15,417	4,927	14,701	5,643	1,787	18,557	986	19,358	4,560	15,784
Mohegan TDSA (state)	7,674	2,125	7,554	2,245	915	8,884	50	9,749	4,300	5,499
Ramapough TDSA (state)	176	28	150	54	32	172	0	204	95	109
United Houma Nation TDSA (state)	235,526	54,977	227,666	62,837	30,476	260,027	1,825	288,678	98,920	191,583
Waccamaw Siouan TDSA (state)	707	157	692	172	90	774	30	834	96	768
Wampanoag-Gay Head TDSA	4,086	990	3,525	1,551	1,483	3,593	91	4,985	2,141	2,935

Source: Census of Population and Housing, 1990: Summary Tape File 3C on CD-ROM [machine-readable datafiles]. Prepared by the Bureau of the Census. Washington, DC: The Bureau, 1992. *Notes:* 1. Tribal designated statistical areas (TDSAs) are areas, delineated outside Oklahoma by federally- and state-recognized tribes without a land base or associated trust lands, to provide statistical areas for which the Census Bureau tabulates data. TDSAs represent areas generally containing the American Indian population over which federally-recognized tribes have jurisdiction and areas in which state tribes provide benefits and services to their members. The names of TDSAs delineated by state-recognized tribes are followed by "(state)." The Census Bureau did not recognize TDSAs before the 1990 census.

★ 645 ★

Income and Earnings

Household Earnings and Income (1989) in Selected Tribal Designated Statistical Areas - Part II

Data are shown in number of persons.

TDSA[1]	Social Security income		Public assistance income		Retirement income		Other type of income	
	With Social Security income	No Social Security income	With public assistance income	No public assistance income	With retirement income	No retirement income	With other income	No other income
Apache Choctaw TDSA (state)	2,746	5,629	1,126	7,249	1,407	6,968	1,009	7,366
Chickahominy TDSA (state)	200	758	51	907	128	830	104	854
Clifton Choctaw TDSA (state)	84	94	12	166	31	147	17	161
Coharie TDSA (state)	13,486	30,947	5,114	39,319	6,256	38,177	5,222	39,211
Coquille Indian TDSA	47,867	113,400	11,372	149,895	28,193	133,074	23,485	137,782
Delaware-Muncie TDSA (state)	21	76	9	88	5	92	0	97

[Continued]

★ 645 ★

Household Earnings and Income (1989) in Selected Tribal Designated Statistical Areas - Part II

[Continued]

TDSA[1]	Social Security income		Public assistance income		Retirement income		Other type of income	
	With Social Security income	No Social Security income	With public assistance income	No public assistance income	With retirement income	No retirement income	With other income	No other income
Florida Tribe of Eastern Creek TDSA (state)	46	61	10	97	36	71	15	92
Haliwa-Saponi TDSA (state)	599	1,505	576	1,528	175	1,929	198	1,906
Jena Band of Choctaw TDSA (state)	5,626	15,372	1,933	19,065	3,670	17,328	2,385	18,613
Klamath TDSA	4,793	11,328	1,124	14,997	2,480	13,641	2,154	13,967
Lumbee TDSA (state)	3,897	11,972	2,841	13,028	1,808	14,061	1,675	14,194
Meherrin TDSA (state)	6,726	13,618	2,697	17,647	2,949	17,395	2,102	18,242
Mohegan TDSA (state)	2,738	7,061	905	8,894	1,734	8,065	1,070	8,729
Ramapough TDSA (state)	70	134	29	175	44	160	21	183
United Houma Nation TDSA (state)	68,955	221,548	22,238	268,265	37,824	252,679	26,115	264,388
Waccamaw Siouan TDSA (state)	180	684	116	748	31	833	95	769
Wampanoag-Gay Head TDSA	1,399	3,677	250	4,826	856	4,220	445	4,631

Source: Census of Population and Housing, 1990: Summary Tape File 3C on CD-ROM [machine-readable datafiles]. Prepared by the Bureau of the Census. Washington, DC: The Bureau, 1992. Notes: 1. Tribal designated statistical areas (TDSAs) are areas, delineated outside Oklahoma by federally- and state-recognized tribes without a land base or associated trust lands, to provide statistical areas for which the Census Bureau tabulates data. TDSAs represent areas generally containing the American Indian population over which federally-recognized tribes have jurisdiction and areas in which state tribes provide benefits and services to their members. The names of TDSAs delineated by state-recognized tribes are followed by "(state)." The Census Bureau did not recognize TDSAs before the 1990 census.

★ 646 ★

Income and Earnings

Household Earnings and Income (1989) in Selected Tribal Jurisdiction Statistical Areas - Part I

Data are shown in number of persons.

TJSA[1]	With earnings	Without earnings	Wage or salary income		Nonfarm self-employment income		Farm self-employment income		Interest, dividend, or net rental income	
			With wage or salary income	No wage or salary income	With nonfarm self-empl. income	No nonfarm self-empl. income	With farm self-empl. income	No farm self-empl. income	With interest, dividend, or net rental income	No interest, dividend, or net rental income
Absentee Shawnee-Citizens Band of Potawatomi TJSA	25,433	5,667	24,378	6,722	4,053	27,047	1,181	29,919	10,205	20,895
Caddo-Wichita-Delaware TJSA	2,416	722	2,126	1,012	366	2,772	495	2,643	1,086	2,052
Cherokee TJSA	113,379	36,487	107,838	42,028	17,158	132,708	6,636	143,230	46,288	103,578
Cheyenne-Arapaho TJSA	45,275	10,268	41,695	13,848	7,700	47,843	5,837	49,706	21,865	33,678
Chickasaw TJSA	72,240	27,002	67,136	32,106	13,039	86,203	5,663	93,579	31,277	67,965
Choctaw TJSA	55,109	24,369	51,334	28,144	8,634	70,844	4,900	74,578	19,334	60,144
Creek TJSA	202,259	49,005	193,566	57,698	33,518	217,746	5,225	246,039	95,958	155,306
Iowa TJSA	1,156	299	1,080	375	184	1,271	163	1,292	388	1,067
Kaw TJSA	3,918	1,142	3,677	1,383	659	4,401	290	4,770	2,793	2,267
Kiowa-Comanche-Apache-Fort Sill Apache TJSA	58,012	15,083	54,664	18,431	7,759	65,336	4,346	68,749	22,228	50,867
Otoe-Missouria TJSA	807	156	750	213	116	847	127	836	267	696
Pawnee TJSA	4,512	1,401	4,184	1,729	869	5,044	413	5,500	2,021	3,892
Sac and Fox TJSA	14,699	5,634	13,832	6,501	2,515	17,818	1,111	19,222	6,542	13,791
Seminole TJSA	5,998	2,793	5,692	3,099	1,035	7,756	352	8,439	2,421	6,370

[Continued]

★ 646 ★

Household Earnings and Income (1989) in Selected Tribal Jurisdiction Statistical Areas - Part I

[Continued]

TJSA[1]	With earnings	Without earnings	Wage or salary income		Nonfarm self-employment income		Farm self-employment income		Interest, dividend, or net rental income	
			With wage or salary income	No wage or salary income	With nonfarm self-empl. income	No nonfarm self-empl. income	With farm self-empl. income	No farm self-empl. income	With interest, dividend, or net rental income	No interest, dividend, or net rental income
Tonkawa TJSA	3,585	1,292	3,334	1,543	604	4,273	341	4,536	1,708	3,169
Creek-Seminole Joint Area TJSA	599	263	567	295	65	797	51	811	197	665
Iowa-Sac and Fox Joint Area TJSA	242	59	221	80	55	246	23	278	90	211

Source: Census of Population and Housing, 1990: Summary Tape File 3C on CD-ROM [machine-readable datafiles]. Prepared by the Bureau of the Census. Washington, DC: The Bureau, 1992. *Notes:* 1. Tribal jurisdiction statistical areas (TJSAs) are areas, delineated by federally recognized tribes in Oklahoma without a reservation, for which the Census Bureau tabulates data. TJSAs represent areas generally containing the American Indian population over which one or more tribal governments have jurisdiction. If tribal officials delineated adjacent TJSAs so that they include some duplicate territory, the overlap area is called a "joint use area," which is treated as a separate TJSA for census purposes.

★ 647 ★

Income and Earnings

Household Earnings and Income (1989) in Selected Tribal Jurisdiction Statistical Areas - Part II

Data are shown in number of persons.

TJSA[1]	Social Security income		Public assistance income		Retirement income		Other type of income	
	With Social Security income	No Social Security income	With public assistance income	No public assistance income	With retirement income	No retirement income	With other income	No other income
Absentee Shawnee-Citizens Band of Potawatomi TJSA	7,284	23,816	1,919	29,181	5,664	25,436	3,946	27,154
Caddo-Wichita-Delaware TJSA	1,070	2,068	201	2,937	356	2,782	248	2,890
Cherokee TJSA	46,071	103,795	13,354	136,512	23,121	126,745	16,852	133,014
Cheyenne-Arapaho TJSA	15,519	40,024	3,275	52,268	6,475	49,068	5,088	50,455
Chickasaw TJSA	33,081	66,161	8,598	90,644	15,457	83,785	10,509	88,733
Choctaw TJSA	27,934	51,544	11,377	68,101	12,354	67,124	10,822	68,656
Creek TJSA	63,009	188,255	15,243	236,021	34,206	217,058	25,851	225,413
Iowa TJSA	424	1,031	82	1,373	221	1,234	161	1,294
Kaw TJSA	1,587	3,473	183	4,877	787	4,273	326	4,734
Kiowa-Comanche-Apache- Fort Sill Apache TJSA	19,908	53,187	6,180	66,915	13,149	59,946	9,169	63,926
Otoe-Missouria TJSA	282	681	83	880	82	881	115	848
Pawnee TJSA	1,940	3,973	430	5,483	878	5,035	678	5,235
Sac and Fox TJSA	6,964	13,369	1,883	18,450	3,316	17,017	1,961	18,372
Seminole TJSA	3,340	5,451	1,199	7,592	1,455	7,336	1,046	7,745
Tonkawa TJSA	1,781	3,096	321	4,556	692	4,185	436	4,441
Creek-Seminole Joint Area TJSA	308	554	132	730	133	729	83	779

[Continued]

★ 647 ★

Household Earnings and Income (1989) in Selected Tribal Jurisdiction Statistical Areas - Part II

[Continued]

TJSA[1]	Social Security income		Public assistance income		Retirement income		Other type of income	
	With Social Security income	No Social Security income	With public assistance income	No public assistance income	With retirement income	No retirement income	With other income	No other income
Iowa-Sac and Fox Joint Area TJSA	53	248	17	284	40	261	23	278

Source: Census of Population and Housing, 1990: Summary Tape File 3C on CD-ROM [machine-readable datafiles]. Prepared by the Bureau of the Census. Washington, DC: The Bureau, 1992. *Notes:* 1. Tribal jurisdiction statistical areas (TJSAs) are areas, delineated by federally recognized tribes in Oklahoma without a reservation, for which the Census Bureau tabulates data. TJSAs represent areas generally containing the American Indian population over which one or more tribal governments have jurisdiction. If tribal officials delineated adjacent TJSAs so that they include some duplicate territory, the overlap area is called a "joint use area," which is treated as a separate TJSA for census purposes.

★ 648 ★

Income and Earnings

Household Earnings and Income (1989) on Selected Reservations and Trust Lands - Part I

Data are shown for the 50 areas with the largest populations, in number of persons.

American Indian Reservation and Trust Lands[1,2]	With earnings	Without earnings	Wage or salary income		Nonfarm self-employment income		Farm self-employment income		Interest, dividend, or net rental income	
			With wage or salary income	No wage or salary income	With nonfarm self-empl. income	No nonfarm self-empl. income	With farm self-empl. income	No farm self-empl. income	With interest, dividend, or net rental income	No interest, dividend, or net rental income
Agua Caliente Reservation	6,303	4,132	5,597	4,838	1,484	8,951	75	10,360	5,011	5,424
Allegany Reservation	2,042	861	1,992	911	230	2,673	14	2,889	1,065	1,838
Blackfeet Reservation	2,010	351	1,892	469	240	2,121	136	2,225	364	1,997
Cheyenne River Reservation	1,881	491	1,663	709	238	2,134	519	1,853	665	1,707
Coeur d'Alene Reservation and Trust Lands, ID	1,722	480	1,536	666	400	1,802	194	2,008	690	1,512
Colorado River Reservation	2,000	749	1,929	820	191	2,558	79	2,670	543	2,206
Colville Reservation	1,847	574	1,785	636	173	2,248	114	2,307	662	1,759
Crow Reservation and Trust Lands, MT	1,431	261	1,322	370	161	1,531	227	1,465	566	1,126
Eastern Cherokee Reservation	1,720	346	1,645	421	203	1,863	26	2,040	255	1,811
Flathead Reservation	5,910	2,004	5,283	2,631	1,292	6,622	877	7,037	2,756	5,158
Fort Apache Reservation	2,135	455	2,135	455	78	2,512	3	2,587	125	2,465
Fort Berthold Reservation	1,379	341	1,183	537	222	1,498	325	1,395	512	1,208
Fort Hall Reservation and Trust Lands, ID	1,224	260	1,209	275	85	1,399	122	1,362	379	1,105
Fort Peck Reservation	2,878	511	2,603	786	450	2,939	555	2,834	983	2,406
Gila River Reservation	1,663	758	1,630	791	70	2,351	48	2,373	139	2,282
Hopi Reservation and Trust Lands, AZ	1,429	368	1,357	440	212	1,585	36	1,761	185	1,612
Isabella Reservation and Trust Lands, MI	6,942	1,420	6,699	1,663	1,097	7,265	362	8,000	2,808	5,554
Laguna Pueblo and Trust Lands, NM	814	227	796	245	85	956	8	1,033	69	972
Lake Traverse (Sisseton) Reservation	3,259	752	2,751	1,260	690	3,321	1,018	2,993	1,565	2,446
Leech Lake Reservation	2,146	948	1,977	1,117	505	2,589	110	2,984	750	2,344

[Continued]

★ 648 ★

Household Earnings and Income (1989) on Selected Reservations and Trust Lands - Part I
[Continued]

American Indian Reservation and Trust Lands[1,2]	With earnings	Without earnings	Wage or salary income		Nonfarm self-employment income		Farm self-employment income		Interest, dividend, or net rental income	
			With wage or salary income	No wage or salary income	With nonfarm self-empl. income	No nonfarm self-empl. income	With farm self-empl. income	No farm self-empl. income	With interest, dividend, or net rental income	No interest, dividend, or net rental income
Mississippi Choctaw Reservation and Trust Lands, MS	825	150	825	150	12	963	9	966	12	963
Muckleshoot Reservation and Trust Lands, WA	1,060	264	1,050	274	125	1,199	11	1,313	504	820
Navajo Reservation and Trust Lands, AZ–NM–UT	24,924	12,457	24,578	12,803	1,143	36,238	346	37,035	1,140	36,241
Nez Perce Reservation	4,694	1,493	4,244	1,943	869	5,318	604	5,583	2,203	3,984
Northern Cheyenne Reservation and Trust Lands, MT–SD	895	132	867	160	108	919	48	979	183	844
Omaha Reservation	1,370	356	1,195	531	210	1,516	360	1,366	591	1,135
Oneida (West) Reservation	5,249	464	5,135	578	716	4,997	173	5,540	3,107	2,606
Osage Reservation	11,652	3,659	10,925	4,386	2,075	13,236	650	14,661	5,437	9,874
Papago Reservation	1,479	756	1,463	772	30	2,205	8	2,227	118	2,117
Pine Ridge Reservation and Trust Lands, NE–SD	2,082	752	1,921	913	230	2,604	236	2,598	434	2,400
Port Madison Reservation	1,492	371	1,425	438	302	1,561	14	1,849	877	986
Puyallup Reservation and Trust Lands, WA	9,564	2,224	9,241	2,547	1,396	10,392	110	11,678	4,579	7,209
Red Lake Reservation	657	299	639	317	71	885	25	931	68	888
Rosebud Reservation and Trust Lands, SD	1,913	649	1,825	737	186	2,376	257	2,305	452	2,110
Salt River Reservation	1,085	541	1,055	571	53	1,573	24	1,602	463	1,163
San Carlos Reservation	1,286	461	1,281	466	32	1,715	16	1,731	98	1,649
Sandia Pueblo	1,098	212	1,039	271	137	1,173	16	1,294	167	1,143
San Juan Pueblo	1,353	315	1,317	351	163	1,505	15	1,653	105	1,563
Santa Clara Pueblo	2,807	833	2,686	954	396	3,244	36	3,604	523	3,117
Southern Ute Reservation	2,288	426	2,127	587	459	2,255	381	2,333	911	1,803
Standing Rock Reservation	1,802	543	1,550	795	234	2,111	495	1,850	733	1,612
Taos Pueblo and Trust Lands, NM	1,461	451	1,318	594	348	1,564	37	1,875	418	1,494
Tulalip Reservation	2,081	483	2,007	557	391	2,173	37	2,527	1,030	1,534
Turtle Mountain Reservation and Trust Lands, ND–SD	1,418	688	1,385	721	109	1,997	43	2,063	210	1,896
Uintah and Ouray Reservation	4,118	847	3,790	1,175	747	4,218	660	4,305	1,804	3,161
White Earth Reservation	2,220	788	1,964	1,044	482	2,526	499	2,509	869	2,139
Wind River Reservation	6,082	1,449	5,737	1,794	994	6,537	612	6,919	2,753	4,778
Yakima Reservation and Trust Lands, WA	6,028	1,803	5,721	2,110	697	7,134	590	7,241	2,109	5,722
Yankton Reservation	1,586	569	1,343	812	218	1,937	517	1,638	698	1,457
Zuni Pueblo	1,564	105	1,254	415	789	880	47	1,622	92	1,577

Source: Census of Population and Housing, 1990: Summary Tape File 3C on CD-ROM [machine-readable datafiles]. Prepared by the Bureau of the Census. Washington, DC: The Bureau, 1992. *Notes:* 1. Federal American Indian reservations are areas with boundaries established by treaty, statute, and/or executive or court order, and recognized by the federal government as territory in which American Indian tribes have jurisdiction. State reservations are lands held in trust by state governments for the use and benefit of a given tribe. The reservations and their boundaries were identified for the 1990 census by the Bureau of Indian Affairs (BIA), Department of Interior (for federal reservations), and state governments (for state reservations). The names of American Indian reservations recognized by state governments, but not by the federal government, are followed by "state." Areas composed of reservation lands that are administered jointly and/or are claimed by two reservations, as identified by the BIA, are called "joint areas," and are treated as separate American Indian reservations for census purposes. Federal reservations may cross state boundaries, and federal and state reservations may cross county, county subdivision, and place boundaries. For reservations that cross state boundaries, only the portion of the reservations in a given state is shown in the data products for that state; the entire reservations are shown in data products for the United States. 2. Trust lands are property associated with a particular American Indian reservation or tribe, held in trust by the federal government. Trust lands may be held in trust either for a tribe (tribal trust lands) or for an individual member of a tribe (individual trust land). Trust lands recognized for the 1990 census comprised all tribal trust lands and inhabited individual trust lands located outside of a reservation boundary. As with other American Indian areas, trust lands may be located in more than one state. Only the trust lands in a given state are shown in the data products for that state; all trust lands associated with a reservation or tribe are shown in data products for the United States. The Census Bureau first reported data for tribal trust lands for the 1980 census.

★ 649 ★

Income and Earnings

Household Earnings and Income (1989) on Selected Reservations and Trust Lands - Part II

Data are shown for the 50 areas with the largest populations, in number of persons.

American Indian Reservation and Trust Lands[1,2]	Social Security income		Public assistance income		Retirement income		Other type of income	
	With Social Security income	No Social Security income	With public assistance income	No public assistance income	With retirement income	No retirement income	With other income	No other income
Agua Caliente Reservation	5,320	5,115	595	9,840	2,278	8,157	792	9,643
Allegany Reservation	1,118	1,785	299	2,604	541	2,362	476	2,427
Blackfeet Reservation	386	1,975	598	1,763	258	2,103	266	2,095
Cheyenne River Reservation	514	1,858	574	1,798	206	2,166	285	2,087
Coeur d'Alene Reservation and Trust Lands, ID	718	1,484	130	2,072	390	1,812	367	1,835
Colorado River Reservation	874	1,875	267	2,482	530	2,219	205	2,544
Colville Reservation	631	1,790	408	2,013	435	1,986	438	1,983
Crow Reservation and Trust Lands, MT	338	1,354	387	1,305	108	1,584	263	1,429
Eastern Cherokee Reservation	430	1,636	348	1,718	185	1,881	346	1,720
Flathead Reservation	2,884	5,030	822	7,092	1,276	6,638	1,118	6,796
Fort Apache Reservation	359	2,231	692	1,898	134	2,456	367	2,223
Fort Berthold Reservation	515	1,205	373	1,347	148	1,572	209	1,511
Fort Hall Reservation and Trust Lands, ID	335	1,149	119	1,365	172	1,312	194	1,290
Fort Peck Reservation	739	2,650	635	2,754	225	3,164	391	2,998
Gila River Reservation	443	1,978	798	1,623	155	2,266	321	2,100
Hopi Reservation and Trust Lands, AZ	382	1,415	413	1,384	149	1,648	194	1,603
Isabella Reservation and Trust Lands, MI	1,850	6,512	776	7,586	1,166	7,196	955	7,407
Laguna Pueblo and Trust Lands, NM	318	723	140	901	134	907	65	976
Lake Traverse (Sisseton) Reservation	1,526	2,485	442	3,569	313	3,698	294	3,717
Leech Lake Reservation	1,007	2,087	599	2,495	523	2,571	467	2,627
Mississippi Choctaw Reservation and Trust Lands, MS	162	813	223	752	92	883	134	841
Muckleshoot Reservation and Trust Lands, WA	343	981	113	1,211	250	1,074	181	1,143
Navajo Reservation and Trust Lands, AZ–NM–UT	7,205	30,176	11,917	25,464	2,617	34,764	3,127	34,254
Nez Perce Reservation	2,134	4,053	469	5,718	1,106	5,081	1,014	5,173
Northern Cheyenne Reservation and Trust Lands, MT–SD	99	928	384	643	61	966	149	878
Omaha Reservation	558	1,168	236	1,490	137	1,589	136	1,590
Oneida (West) Reservation	848	4,865	339	5,374	432	5,281	662	5,051
Osage Reservation	4,548	10,763	1,334	13,977	2,263	13,048	1,638	13,673
Papago Reservation	352	1,883	1,092	1,143	155	2,080	245	1,990
Pine Ridge Reservation and Trust Lands, NE–SD	666	2,168	1,136	1,698	308	2,526	372	2,462
Port Madison Reservation	463	1,400	90	1,773	397	1,466	198	1,665
Puyallup Reservation and Trust Lands, WA	2,334	9,454	1,364	10,424	1,714	10,074	1,364	10,424
Red Lake Reservation	158	798	440	516	53	903	169	787
Rosebud Reservation and Trust Lands, SD	654	1,908	984	1,578	168	2,394	251	2,311

[Continued]

★ 649 ★

Household Earnings and Income (1989) on Selected Reservations and Trust Lands - Part II
[Continued]

American Indian Reservation and Trust Lands[1,2]	Social Security income		Public assistance income		Retirement income		Other type of income	
	With Social Security income	No Social Security income	With public assistance income	No public assistance income	With retirement income	No retirement income	With other income	No other income
Salt River Reservation	636	990	307	1,319	402	1,224	111	1,515
San Carlos Reservation	187	1,560	621	1,126	101	1,646	193	1,554
Sandia Pueblo	237	1,073	170	1,140	188	1,122	129	1,181
San Juan Pueblo	341	1,327	228	1,440	174	1,494	137	1,531
Santa Clara Pueblo	919	2,721	486	3,154	515	3,125	404	3,236
Southern Ute Reservation	619	2,095	246	2,468	367	2,347	404	2,310
Standing Rock Reservation	526	1,819	635	1,710	158	2,187	329	2,016
Taos Pueblo and Trust Lands, NM	492	1,420	287	1,625	228	1,684	235	1,677
Tulalip Reservation	665	1,899	168	2,396	467	2,097	301	2,263
Turtle Mountain Reservation and Trust Lands, ND–SD	472	1,634	1,007	1,099	135	1,971	280	1,826
Uintah and Ouray Reservation	1,219	3,746	502	4,463	579	4,386	712	4,253
White Earth Reservation	1,067	1,941	522	2,486	378	2,630	410	2,598
Wind River Reservation	1,911	5,620	888	6,643	939	6,592	963	6,568
Yakima Reservation and Trust Lands, WA	2,120	5,711	1,402	6,429	976	6,855	1,139	6,692
Yankton Reservation	746	1,409	372	1,783	227	1,928	153	2,002
Zuni Pueblo	262	1,407	343	1,326	169	1,500	307	1,362

Source: Census of Population and Housing, 1990: Summary Tape File 3C on CD-ROM [machine-readable datafiles]. Prepared by the Bureau of the Census. Washington, DC: The Bureau, 1992. *Notes:* 1. Federal American Indian reservations are areas with boundaries established by treaty, statute, and/or executive or court order, and recognized by the federal government as territory in which American Indian tribes have jurisdiction. State reservations are lands held in trust by state governments for the use and benefit of a given tribe. The reservations and their boundaries were identified for the 1990 census by the Bureau of Indian Affairs (BIA), Department of Interior (for federal reservations), and state governments (for state reservations). The names of American Indian reservations recognized by state governments, but not by the federal government, are followed by "state." Areas composed of reservation lands that are administered jointly and/or are claimed by two reservations, as identified by the BIA, are called "joint areas," and are treated as separate American Indian reservations for census purposes. Federal reservations may cross state boundaries, and federal and state reservations may cross county, county subdivision, and place boundaries. For reservations that cross state boundaries, only the portion of the reservations in a given state is shown in the data products for that state; the entire reservations are shown in data products for the United States. 2. Trust lands are property associated with a particular American Indian reservation or tribe, held in trust by the federal government. Trust lands may be held in trust either for a tribe (tribal trust lands) or for an individual member of a tribe (individual trust land). Trust lands recognized for the 1990 census comprised all tribal trust lands and inhabited individual trust lands located outside of a reservation boundary. As with other American Indian areas, trust lands may be located in more than one state. Only the trust lands in a given state are shown in the data products for that state; all trust lands associated with a reservation or tribe are shown in data products for the United States. The Census Bureau first reported data for tribal trust lands for the 1980 census.

★ 650 ★

Income and Earnings

Household Income (1989) of American Indians and Alaska Natives in Selected Alaska Native Villages

Data are shown for the 50 areas with the largest populations, in number of persons.

Alaska Native Village Statistical Area[1]	Less than $5,000	$5,000 to $9,999	$10,000 to $14,999	$15,000 to $24,999	$25,000 to $34,999	$35,000 to $49,999	$50,000 to $74,999	$75,000 to $99,999	$100,000 or more
Akiachak	12	18	13	15	15	19	12	3	0
Akutan	0	0	3	2	8	3	2	0	0
Alakanuk	4	25	22	25	11	18	10	0	0
Andreafsky	8	16	5	12	8	17	9	2	0
Angoon	16	12	4	10	16	20	14	8	0
Aniak	9	11	6	12	22	8	10	2	2
Barrow	15	32	26	37	35	63	73	79	44

[Continued]

★ 650 ★

Household Income (1989) of American Indians and Alaska Natives in Selected Alaska Native Villages

[Continued]

Alaska Native Village Statistical Area[1]	Less than $5,000	$5,000 to $9,999	$10,000 to $14,999	$15,000 to $24,999	$25,000 to $34,999	$35,000 to $49,999	$50,000 to $74,999	$75,000 to $99,999	$100,000 or more
Bethel	45	50	89	111	113	104	135	42	12
Chevak	9	37	20	30	26	7	0	0	0
Copper Center	3	5	18	10	5	7	4	0	0
Craig	4	3	2	16	12	20	24	4	11
Dillingham	20	26	33	38	38	63	29	35	41
Emmonak	10	10	19	32	26	16	12	0	2
Fort Yukon	26	28	35	17	15	24	11	2	0
Galena	19	14	14	14	17	16	14	0	0
Gambell	21	27	8	24	28	6	4	0	0
Grouse Creek Group	1	0	5	14	5	5	0	0	2
Hoonah	0	3	26	26	26	35	18	23	4
Hooper Bay	25	21	36	38	32	12	10	2	0
Kake	3	7	7	29	34	34	34	6	3
Kasigluk	6	17	2	19	20	13	7	0	0
King Cove	3	3	6	1	2	5	7	4	13
King Salmon	0	2	2	4	0	0	8	6	6
Kipnuk	55	11	7	3	6	4	3	0	0
Klawock	4	7	11	10	24	19	23	3	12
Kotlik	4	13	9	39	12	17	4	2	0
Kotzebue	30	34	37	67	63	73	75	67	16
Kwethluk	22	16	16	32	18	7	2	4	0
McGrath	3	5	17	7	15	15	6	3	0
Mountain Village	9	11	15	29	13	24	15	5	0
Naknek	5	5	9	14	5	12	16	6	8
Ninilchik	8	13	9	4	19	22	26	4	9
Noorvik	2	4	6	23	26	22	7	5	2
Pilot Station	8	21	21	23	13	10	2	0	0
Point Hope	3	8	10	4	18	34	38	7	3
Quinhagak	17	25	14	28	20	13	2	0	0
St. Paul	9	0	8	22	12	36	27	9	10
Salamatof	3	1	2	1	4	8	3	0	1
Sand Point	8	6	8	15	11	37	24	11	22
Savoonga	46	9	16	12	14	13	4	0	0
Selawik	12	2	26	29	20	12	5	6	0
Shishmaref	8	16	27	21	18	10	2	0	0
Stebbins	8	12	15	23	15	9	2	3	0
Togiak	17	32	26	26	9	9	3	3	0
Tok	0	1	4	3	3	6	2	0	2
Toksook Bay	6	10	13	18	18	1	7	2	0
Unalakleet	22	5	13	37	17	37	10	0	8
Unalaska	3	3	8	6	0	7	6	9	6
Wainwright	5	5	15	27	21	27	18	7	0
Yakutat	2	11	5	7	22	22	12	8	2

Source: Census of Population and Housing, 1990: Summary Tape File 3C on CD-ROM [machine-readable datafiles]. Prepared by the Bureau of the Census. Washington, DC: The Bureau, 1992. *Notes:* 1. Alaska Native villages (ANVs) constitute tribes, bands, clans, groups, villages, communities, or associations in Alaska that are recognized pursuant to the Alaska Native Claims Settlement Act of 1972, Public Law 92-203. Because ANVs do not have legally designated boundaries, the Census Bureau has established Alaska Native village statistical areas (ANVSAs) for statistical purposes. For the 1990 census, the Census Bureau cooperated with officials of the nonprofit corporation within each participating Alaska Native Regional Corporation (ANRC), as well as other knowledgeable officials, to delineate boundaries that encompass the settled area associated with each ANV.

★ 651 ★

Income and Earnings

Household Income (1989) of American Indians and Alaska Natives in Selected Tribal Designated Statistical Areas

Data are shown in number of persons.

TDSA[1]	Less than $5,000	$5,000 to $9,999	$10,000 to $14,999	$15,000 to $24,999	$25,000 to $34,999	$35,000 to $49,999	$50,000 to $74,999	$75,000 to $99,999	$100,000 or more
Apache Choctaw TDSA (state)	8	34	63	41	35	10	6	4	1
Chickahominy TDSA (state)	4	0	0	45	60	14	34	0	0
Clifton Choctaw TDSA (state)	25	9	0	27	0	0	0	0	0
Coharie TDSA (state)	78	125	73	107	81	39	2	0	0
Coquille Indian TDSA	227	329	226	475	419	247	184	35	10
Delaware-Muncie TDSA (state)	0	0	0	0	0	6	0	0	0
Florida Tribe of Eastern Creek TDSA (state)	0	0	0	0	0	0	0	0	0
Haliwa-Saponi TDSA (state)	156	133	164	99	71	88	19	0	0
Jena Band of Choctaw TDSA (state)	2	12	30	31	12	13	26	0	0
Klamath TDSA	138	97	76	87	58	54	31	3	0
Lumbee TDSA (state)	1,140	1,243	1,014	1,875	1,355	1,226	505	144	116
Meherrin TDSA (state)	22	8	6	21	7	8	0	2	0
Mohegan TDSA (state)	0	18	10	9	10	7	0	10	0
Ramapough TDSA (state)	17	0	7	0	21	0	0	9	0
United Houma Nation TDSA (state)	418	555	412	627	233	357	137	5	30
Waccamaw Siouan TDSA (state)	38	70	36	39	52	73	42	14	8
Wampanoag-Gay Head TDSA	7	25	9	21	9	11	13	0	0

Source: Census of Population and Housing, 1990: Summary Tape File 3C on CD-ROM [machine-readable datafiles]. Prepared by the Bureau of the Census. Washington, DC: The Bureau, 1992. *Notes:* 1. Tribal designated statistical areas (TDSAs) are areas, delineated outside Oklahoma by federally- and state-recognized tribes without a land base or associated trust lands, to provide statistical areas for which the Census Bureau tabulates data. TDSAs represent areas generally containing the American Indian population over which federally-recognized tribes have jurisdiction and areas in which state tribes provide benefits and services to their members. The names of TDSAs delineated by state-recognized tribes are followed by "(state)." The Census Bureau did not recognize TDSAs before the 1990 census.

★ 652 ★

Income and Earnings

Household Income (1989) of American Indians and Alaska Natives in Selected Tribal Jurisdiction Statistical Areas

Data are shown in number of persons.

TJSA[1]	Less than $5,000	$5,000 to $9,999	$10,000 to $14,999	$15,000 to $24,999	$25,000 to $34,999	$35,000 to $49,999	$50,000 to $74,999	$75,000 to $99,999	$100,000 or more
Absentee Shawnee-Citizens Band of Potawatomi TJSA	124	325	214	398	294	310	141	35	2
Caddo-Wichita-Delaware TJSA	30	17	10	70	23	8	6	0	0
Cherokee TJSA	2,252	3,776	3,005	4,707	2,971	2,414	1,125	187	112
Cheyenne-Arapaho TJSA	406	244	213	363	244	221	114	24	24
Chickasaw TJSA	755	1,237	1,010	1,372	920	694	417	95	60
Choctaw TJSA	1,199	1,775	1,528	2,042	1,116	805	381	75	63
Creek TJSA	1,431	1,875	2,156	3,092	2,301	2,001	1,348	258	157
Iowa TJSA	7	9	20	14	5	10	9	0	0
Kaw TJSA	17	18	14	40	27	38	41	7	0
Kiowa-Comanche-Apache-Fort Sill Apache TJSA	556	639	486	793	403	378	163	43	21
Otoe-Missouria TJSA	28	42	18	26	10	5	0	0	0
Pawnee TJSA	43	94	88	117	99	35	22	8	3
Sac and Fox TJSA	157	268	184	248	210	160	84	11	2

[Continued]

★ 652 ★

Household Income (1989) of American Indians and Alaska Natives in Selected Tribal Jurisdiction Statistical Areas

[Continued]

TJSA[1]	Less than $5,000	$5,000 to $9,999	$10,000 to $14,999	$15,000 to $24,999	$25,000 to $34,999	$35,000 to $49,999	$50,000 to $74,999	$75,000 to $99,999	$100,000 or more
Seminole TJSA	89	217	204	216	136	112	41	4	5
Tonkawa TJSA	32	40	44	50	49	26	5	0	2
Creek-Seminole Joint Area TJSA	20	37	30	34	19	4	7	0	0
Iowa-Sac and Fox Joint Area TJSA	3	0	0	0	2	0	0	0	0

Source: Census of Population and Housing, 1990: Summary Tape File 3C on CD-ROM [machine-readable datafiles]. Prepared by the Bureau of the Census. Washington, DC: The Bureau, 1992. *Notes:* 1. Tribal jurisdiction statistical areas (TJSAs) are areas, delineated by federally recognized tribes in Oklahoma without a reservation, for which the Census Bureau tabulates data. TJSAs represent areas generally containing the American Indian population over which one or more tribal governments have jurisdiction. If tribal officials delineated adjacent TJSAs so that they include some duplicate territory, the overlap area is called a "joint use area," which is treated as a separate TJSA for census purposes.

★ 653 ★

Income and Earnings

Household Income (1989) of American Indians and Alaska Natives on Selected Reservations and Trust Lands

Data are shown for the 50 areas with the largest populations, in number of persons.

American Indian Reservation and Trust Lands[1,2]	Less than $5,000	$5,000 to $9,999	$10,000 to $14,999	$15,000 to $24,999	$25,000 to $34,999	$35,000 to $49,999	$50,000 to $74,999	$75,000 to $99,999	$100,000 or more
Agua Caliente Reservation	0	10	4	8	16	10	3	3	0
Allegany Reservation	33	65	61	105	57	53	22	0	0
Blackfeet Reservation	280	465	292	390	239	135	70	17	0
Cheyenne River Reservation	329	331	167	243	124	59	45	5	8
Coeur d'Alene Reservation and Trust Lands, ID	36	31	37	77	36	14	6	1	7
Colorado River Reservation	151	86	74	107	122	64	52	5	0
Colville Reservation	164	206	167	197	203	153	73	19	14
Crow Reservation and Trust Lands, MT	130	245	216	240	80	98	66	0	0
Eastern Cherokee Reservation	266	285	232	461	299	142	31	3	14
Flathead Reservation	236	407	242	353	216	201	89	14	1
Fort Apache Reservation	542	377	396	447	286	187	65	7	0
Fort Berthold Reservation	144	209	128	100	89	74	51	6	0
Fort Hall Reservation and Trust Lands, ID	133	141	144	134	150	70	24	0	0
Fort Peck Reservation	270	291	301	339	188	158	49	12	2
Gila River Reservation	652	498	422	333	180	104	34	0	0
Hopi Reservation and Trust Lands, AZ	390	303	212	362	196	164	23	8	9
Isabella Reservation and Trust Lands, MI	38	49	28	60	32	31	11	0	0
Laguna Pueblo and Trust Lands, NM	160	131	151	254	136	100	56	6	8
Lake Traverse (Sisseton) Reservation	195	169	192	115	81	6	15	0	9
Leech Lake Reservation	145	293	140	221	91	59	15	11	0
Mississippi Choctaw Reservation and Trust Lands, MS	143	107	155	309	91	105	7	0	7
Muckleshoot Reservation and Trust Lands, WA	25	28	28	34	16	20	14	0	0

[Continued]

★ 653 ★

Household Income (1989) of American Indians and Alaska Natives on Selected Reservations and Trust Lands

[Continued]

American Indian Reservation and Trust Lands[1,2]	Less than $5,000	$5,000 to $9,999	$10,000 to $14,999	$15,000 to $24,999	$25,000 to $34,999	$35,000 to $49,999	$50,000 to $74,999	$75,000 to $99,999	$100,000 or more
Navajo Reservation and Trust Lands, AZ–NM–UT	11,295	6,734	4,348	5,596	3,083	2,549	1,184	291	45
Nez Perce Reservation	83	85	72	166	74	71	40	2	0
Northern Cheyenne Reservation and Trust Lands, MT–SD	143	162	168	153	138	73	25	0	0
Omaha Reservation	49	115	86	79	54	21	2	2	3
Oneida (West) Reservation	42	141	99	149	110	79	59	5	8
Osage Reservation	233	309	232	351	264	284	173	1	8
Papago Reservation	684	496	259	460	182	76	13	0	0
Pine Ridge Reservation and Trust Lands, NE–SD	576	586	402	482	221	125	19	6	6
Port Madison Reservation	13	21	10	32	11	21	7	8	0
Puyallup Reservation and Trust Lands, WA	27	46	41	56	54	34	35	13	5
Red Lake Reservation	152	258	121	162	148	60	18	4	0
Rosebud Reservation and Trust Lands, SD	511	459	332	322	169	103	60	1	11
Salt River Reservation	208	123	192	140	92	69	39	6	0
San Carlos Reservation	520	410	195	279	140	63	74	0	0
Sandia Pueblo	7	14	9	26	17	32	2	2	0
San Juan Pueblo	55	54	42	117	37	23	28	4	0
Santa Clara Pueblo	38	67	80	97	71	42	19	2	1
Southern Ute Reservation	32	57	45	77	42	28	20	2	1
Standing Rock Reservation	345	263	132	220	138	54	26	5	0
Taos Pueblo and Trust Lands, NM	97	84	74	101	37	18	5	0	3
Tulalip Reservation	15	46	36	72	65	42	34	2	6
Turtle Mountain Reservation and Trust Lands, ND–SD	424	530	241	295	226	166	57	19	3
Uintah and Ouray Reservation	167	87	94	140	69	88	9	3	3
White Earth Reservation	113	250	137	169	69	63	36	2	2
Wind River Reservation	269	292	230	330	200	71	71	12	0
Yakima Reservation and Trust Lands, WA	260	282	232	297	248	114	73	19	14
Yankton Reservation	183	113	64	105	22	6	4	3	0
Zuni Pueblo	184	286	237	369	211	127	60	3	0

Source: Census of Population and Housing, 1990: Summary Tape File 3C on CD-ROM [machine-readable datafiles]. Prepared by the Bureau of the Census. Washington, DC: The Bureau, 1992. *Notes:* 1. Federal American Indian reservations are areas with boundaries established by treaty, statute, and/or executive or court order, and recognized by the federal government as territory in which American Indian tribes have jurisdiction. State reservations are lands held in trust by state governments for the use and benefit of a given tribe. The reservations and their boundaries were identified for the 1990 census by the Bureau of Indian Affairs (BIA), Department of Interior (for federal reservations), and state governments (for state reservations). The names of American Indian reservations recognized by state governments, but not by the federal government, are followed by "state." Areas composed of reservation lands that are administered jointly and/or are claimed by two reservations, as identified by the BIA, are called "joint areas," and are treated as separate American Indian reservations for census purposes. Federal reservations may cross state boundaries, and federal and state reservations may cross county, county subdivision, and place boundaries. For reservations that cross state boundaries, only the portion of the reservations in a given state is shown in the data products for that state; the entire reservations are shown in data products for the United States. 2. Trust lands are property associated with a particular American Indian reservation or tribe, held in trust by the federal government. Trust lands may be held in trust either for a tribe (tribal trust lands) or for an individual member of a tribe (individual trust land). Trust lands recognized for the 1990 census comprised all tribal trust lands and inhabited individual trust lands located outside of a reservation boundary. As with other American Indian areas, trust lands may be located in more than one state. Only the trust lands in a given state are shown in the data products for that state; all trust lands associated with a reservation or tribe are shown in data products for the United States. The Census Bureau first reported data for tribal trust lands for the 1980 census.

Poverty

★ 654 ★

Characteristics of Low-Income Households - 1991

Numbers are shown in thousands of occupied units, excluding percentages. Households of Hispanic origin may be of any race.

Characteristics	All households	White	Black	American Indian, Eskimo, or Aleut	Asian or Pacific Islander	Hispanic origin	Not of Hispanic origin	
							Total	White
Low-income status								
Total	93,147	79,140	10,832	486	2,066	6,239	86,907	73,625
Households with low income[1]	12,836	8,978	3,236	148	317	1,501	11,335	7,674
Percent of total	14.0	11.0	30.0	30.0	15.0	24.0	13.0	10.0
Income sources								
Total	93,147	79,140	10,832	486	2,066	6,239	86,907	73,625
Percent with								
Welfare or SSI	7.0	5.0	19.0	24.0	7.0	14.0	6.0	4.0
Alimony or child support	4.0	4.0	6.0	7.0	2.0	4.0	4.0	4.0
Selected characteristics								
Income of $25,000 or less	43,712	35,052	7,204	313	769	3,785	39,927	31,736
Percent with								
No savings or investments	49.0	43.0	73.0	69.0	47.0	71.0	47.0	41.0
Received food stamps	15.0	12.0	33.0	35.0	12.0	27.0	14.0	10.0
Households with low income[1]	12,836	8,978	3,236	148	317	1,501	11,335	7,674
Percent with								
Welfare or SSI	31.0	25.0	46.0	58.0	22.0	39.0	30.0	23.0
Alimony or child support	6.0	6.0	8.0	7.0	1.0	5.0	6.0	6.0
No savings or investments	67.0	60.0	85.0	84.0	59.0	84.0	65.0	56.0
Received food stamps	39.0	32.0	57.0	66.0	22.0	50.0	37.0	29.0

Source: Woodward, Jeanne M. *America's Racial and Ethnic Groups: Their Housing in the Early Nineties.* Bureau of the Census. Current Housing Reports, Series H121/94-3. Washington, DC: U.S. Government Printing Office, p. 57. Primary source: American Housing Survey (AHS), 1991 National Internal User File. *Note:* 1. Incomes below household poverty levels.

★ 655 ★

Poverty

American Indian, Eskimo, and Aleut Child Poverty Rates by State, 1990

Shown are the number of American Indian, Eskimo, and Aleut persons below age 18, and the number and percentage of those persons below poverty level.

State	Persons under 18	Below poverty level	Rank	Percent	
				Poor	Rank
Alabama	6,164	1,519	25	24.6	6
Alaska	33,562	8,621	43	25.7	11
Arizona	84,053	44,607	51	53.1	46
Arkansas	4,041	1,053	17	26.1	12
California	67,811	17,982	48	26.5	16
Colorado	8,497	3,008	33	35.4	31
Connecticut	1,466	313	5	21.4	3
Delaware	372	80	2	21.5	4
District of Columbia	154	55	1	35.7	32
Florida	9,750	2,541	31	26.1	12
Georgia	3,758	938	16	25.0	7
Hawaii	1,619	408	7	25.2	8
Idaho	5,081	2,056	30	40.5	36
Illinois	5,950	1,422	22	23.9	5
Indiana	3,751	1,132	19	30.2	23
Iowa	2,672	1,160	20	43.4	38
Kansas	7,207	1,932	28	26.8	17
Kentucky	1,631	681	13	41.8	37
Louisiana	6,753	3,166	34	46.9	42
Maine	2,063	583	9	28.3	19
Maryland	3,578	661	11	18.5	1
Massachusetts	3,707	1,309	21	35.3	30
Michigan	18,929	6,147	39	32.5	28
Minnesota	19,088	10,459	46	54.8	48
Mississippi	3,131	1,429	23	45.6	40
Missouri	5,656	1,483	24	26.2	14
Montana	19,166	10,238	45	53.4	47
Nebraska	4,900	2,795	32	57.0	49
Nevada	5,864	1,745	27	29.8	21
New Hampshire	464	119	3	25.6	9
New Jersey	3,387	886	14	26.2	14
New Mexico	53,163	26,643	49	50.1	45
New York	16,243	4,800	37	29.6	20
North Carolina	26,128	7,820	42	29.9	22
North Dakota	10,607	6,179	40	58.3	50
Ohio	5,222	1,588	26	30.4	24
Oklahoma	91,961	31,977	50	34.8	29
Oregon	13,277	4,288	35	32.3	27
Pennsylvania	3,625	1,128	18	31.1	26
Rhode Island	1,115	440	8	39.5	35
South Carolina	2,189	599	10	27.4	18
South Dakota	22,365	14,160	47	63.3	51
Tennessee	2,940	906	15	30.8	25
Texas	17,594	4,501	36	25.6	9

[Continued]

★ 655 ★

American Indian, Eskimo, and Aleut Child Poverty Rates by State, 1990

[Continued]

State	Persons under 18	Below poverty level	Rank	Percent Poor	Rank
Utah	18,355	4,893	38	47.3	43
Vermont	691	251	4	36.3	33
Virginia	3,513	666	12	19.0	2
Washington	27,151	10,228	44	37.7	34
West Virginia	755	337	6	44.6	39
Wisconsin	14,102	6,505	41	46.1	41
Wyoming	4,010	1,966	29	49.0	44
United States	671,231	260,403	n/a	38.6	n/a

Source: U.S. Senate Committee on Indian Affairs and Committee on Agriculture. *Barriers to Participation in Food Stamp and Other Nutrition Programs of the Department of Agriculture by People Residing on Indian Lands.* 103rd Cong., 1st sess., 25 May 1993, p. 271. Primary source: 1990 Census sample data.

★ 656 ★

Poverty

Poverty Status (1989), by Age, in Selected Alaska Native Villages - Part I

Data are shown for the 50 areas with the largest populations, in number of persons.

Alaska Native Village Statistical Area[1]	Persons whose income was above poverty level						
	Under 5 years	5 years	6 to 11 years	12 to 17 years	18 to 64 years	65 to 74 years	75 years and older
Akiachak	39	6	15	49	227	3	13
Akutan	11	2	13	4	35	3	0
Alakanuk	46	7	48	70	175	11	2
Andreafsky	41	7	42	25	148	8	4
Angoon	60	16	55	46	184	10	7
Aniak	43	8	56	20	122	8	2
Barrow	265	53	216	155	792	42	25
Bethel	355	61	317	252	1,266	76	30
Chevak	85	11	46	48	194	9	5
Copper Center	10	1	7	11	53	14	5
Craig	40	14	52	16	145	16	0
Dillingham	145	15	137	86	527	27	22
Emmonak	76	8	42	44	219	19	5
Fort Yukon	29	9	52	46	175	3	8
Galena	43	7	36	39	131	3	0
Gambell	46	7	28	32	162	8	2
Grouse Creek Group	7	6	22	5	60	0	0
Hoonah	51	22	72	52	287	17	13
Hooper Bay	63	12	61	52	227	24	12
Kake	64	8	43	56	275	17	7
Kasigluk	56	8	40	38	157	22	5
King Cove	19	3	32	26	87	12	0
King Salmon	11	0	4	11	57	3	0

[Continued]

★ 656 ★

Poverty Status (1989), by Age, in Selected Alaska Native Villages - Part I
[Continued]

Alaska Native Village Statistical Area[1]	Persons whose income was above poverty level						
	Under 5 years	5 years	6 to 11 years	12 to 17 years	18 to 64 years	65 to 74 years	75 years and older
Kipnuk	10	6	24	25	37	1	0
Klawock	38	10	34	43	193	14	0
Kotlik	59	8	59	35	174	22	9
Kotzebue	297	46	256	163	879	29	29
Kwethluk	34	13	44	39	173	15	17
McGrath	15	5	31	46	106	4	2
Mountain Village	60	11	56	78	236	16	10
Naknek	42	10	36	21	116	10	5
Ninilchik	17	9	60	42	215	15	8
Noorvik	67	11	65	50	214	15	6
Pilot Station	35	4	31	20	111	7	4
Point Hope	84	18	95	64	245	6	10
Quinhagak	24	9	28	29	170	18	8
St. Paul	52	19	64	32	305	15	10
Salamatof	1	0	6	0	28	3	1
Sand Point	32	4	65	43	199	10	2
Savoonga	29	5	39	20	127	10	3
Selawik	69	11	72	51	187	11	20
Shishmaref	43	6	39	39	158	10	4
Stebbins	55	8	29	33	134	12	11
Togiak	30	2	29	16	164	6	9
Tok	11	4	7	6	34	5	2
Toksook Bay	34	2	35	29	126	4	3
Unalakleet	56	10	84	58	196	21	10
Unalaska	29	2	17	26	152	3	3
Wainwright	64	15	93	39	220	8	11
Yakutat	23	7	32	25	139	12	6

Source: Census of Population and Housing, 1990: Summary Tape File 3C on CD-ROM [machine-readable datafiles]. Prepared by the Bureau of the Census. Washington, DC: The Bureau, 1992. *Notes:* 1. Alaska Native villages (ANVs) constitute tribes, bands, clans, groups, villages, communities, or associations in Alaska that are recognized pursuant to the Alaska Native Claims Settlement Act of 1972, Public Law 92-203. Because ANVs do not have legally designated boundaries, the Census Bureau has established Alaska Native village statistical areas (ANVSAs) for statistical purposes. For the 1990 census, the Census Bureau cooperated with officials of the nonprofit corporation within each participating Alaska Native Regional Corporation (ANRC), as well as other knowledgeable officials, to delineate boundaries that encompass the settled area associated with each ANV.

★ 657 ★

Poverty

Poverty Status (1989), by Age, in Selected Alaska Native Villages - Part II

Data are shown for the 50 areas with the largest populations, in number of persons.

Alaska Native Village Statistical Area[1]	Persons whose income was below poverty level						
	Under 5 years	5 years	6 to 11 years	12 to 17 years	18 to 64 years	65 to 74 years	75 years and older
Akiachak	0	0	8	35	8	0	0
Akutan	0	0	0	8	0	0	0
Alakanuk	3	32	13	81	7	0	0
Andreafsky	3	2	11	37	0	0	0
Angoon	3	18	19	60	2	9	0
Aniak	0	14	3	46	0	5	0
Barrow	7	19	7	85	5	6	5
Bethel	9	57	31	269	5	4	2
Chevak	4	16	23	68	7	2	0
Copper Center	0	8	0	20	2	0	0
Craig	0	0	0	5	0	0	0
Dillingham	9	19	15	73	7	6	0
Emmonak	4	12	4	66	0	0	0
Fort Yukon	4	17	14	105	5	4	0
Galena	0	5	14	52	6	4	0
Gambell	0	37	38	134	9	2	0
Grouse Creek Group	0	1	0	3	0	0	0
Hoonah	0	0	0	10	3	0	0
Hooper Bay	35	49	15	144	9	6	0
Kake	0	4	4	14	1	3	0
Kasigluk	6	21	7	35	5	2	0
King Cove	0	0	0	5	0	0	0
King Salmon	0	0	4	9	0	0	0
Kipnuk	9	37	35	199	4	13	0
Klawock	0	6	4	28	3	0	0
Kotlik	3	14	9	43	0	0	0
Kotzebue	12	36	29	165	5	7	0
Kwethluk	10	43	20	86	6	2	0
McGrath	0	10	16	18	2	0	0
Mountain Village	3	36	24	73	0	0	0
Naknek	0	0	0	4	0	3	0
Ninilchik	0	8	2	27	0	0	0
Noorvik	0	15	12	42	7	0	0
Pilot Station	18	26	21	108	3	0	0
Point Hope	4	7	2	24	0	0	0
Quinhagak	2	24	14	84	6	0	0
St. Paul	0	6	2	18	0	0	0
Salamatof	1	0	0	5	0	0	0
Sand Point	2	9	2	33	2	0	0
Savoonga	6	21	46	145	3	7	0
Selawik	6	35	4	47	1	0	0
Shishmaref	2	24	11	60	0	0	0
Stebbins	0	18	20	69	0	5	0
Togiak	7	52	25	115	8	4	0
Tok	0	5	4	7	0	0	0

[Continued]

★ 657 ★

Poverty Status (1989), by Age, in Selected Alaska Native Villages - Part II
[Continued]

Alaska Native Village Statistical Area[1]	Persons whose income was below poverty level						
	Under 5 years	5 years	6 to 11 years	12 to 17 years	18 to 64 years	65 to 74 years	75 years and older
Toksook Bay	3	12	25	92	1	0	0
Unalakleet	0	8	6	44	3	0	0
Unalaska	0	9	5	21	2	2	0
Wainwright	0	3	2	12	0	2	0
Yakutat	0	5	2	24	0	3	0

Source: Census of Population and Housing, 1990: Summary Tape File 3C on CD-ROM [machine-readable datafiles]. Prepared by the Bureau of the Census. Washington, DC: The Bureau, 1992. Notes: 1. Alaska Native villages (ANVs) constitute tribes, bands, clans, groups, villages, communities, or associations in Alaska that are recognized pursuant to the Alaska Native Claims Settlement Act of 1972, Public Law 92-203. Because ANVs do not have legally designated boundaries, the Census Bureau has established Alaska Native village statistical areas (ANVSAs) for statistical purposes. For the 1990 census, the Census Bureau cooperated with officials of the nonprofit corporation within each participating Alaska Native Regional Corporation (ANRC), as well as other knowledgeable officials, to delineate boundaries that encompass the settled area associated with each ANV.

★ 658 ★
Poverty

Poverty Status (1989), by Age, in Selected Tribal Designated Statistical Areas - Part I

Tribal Designated Statistical Area[1]	Persons whose income was above poverty level						
	Under 5 years	5 years	6 to 11 years	12 to 17 years	18 to 64 years	65 to 74 years	75 years and older
Apache Choctaw TDSA (state)	39	7	42	55	309	42	0
Chickahominy TDSA (state)	0	9	57	39	359	14	0
Clifton Choctaw TDSA (state)	10	0	10	0	48	0	8
Coharie TDSA (state)	39	19	70	116	542	124	29
Coquille Indian TDSA	320	59	360	356	2,832	208	124
Delaware-Muncie TDSA (state)	0	0	0	12	11	0	0
Florida Tribe of Eastern Creek TDSA (state)	0	0	0	0	0	0	0
Haliwa-Saponi TDSA (state)	61	26	153	191	917	70	34
Jena Band of Choctaw TDSA (state)	7	0	5	46	126	9	6
Klamath TDSA	61	27	109	118	637	43	36
Lumbee TDSA (state)	1,763	392	2,274	2,773	13,279	717	471
Meherrin TDSA (state)	8	2	14	8	70	13	4
Mohegan TDSA (state)	10	3	6	0	142	6	0
Ramapough TDSA (state)	3	0	13	0	89	14	3
United Houma Nation TDSA (state)	519	131	637	541	3,291	113	29
Waccamaw Siouan TDSA (state)	74	23	152	89	686	13	17
Wampanoag-Gay Head TDSA	22	8	20	25	129	11	15

Source: Census of Population and Housing, 1990: Summary Tape File 3C on CD-ROM [machine-readable datafiles]. Prepared by the Bureau of the Census. Washington, DC: The Bureau, 1992. Notes: 1. Tribal designated statistical areas (TDSAs) are areas, delineated outside Oklahoma by federally- and state-recognized tribes without a land base or associated trust lands, to provide statistical areas for which the Census Bureau tabulates data. TDSAs represent areas generally containing the American Indian population over which federally-recognized tribes have jurisdiction and areas in which state tribes provide benefits and services to their members. The names of TDSAs delineated by state-recognized tribes are followed by "(state)." The Census Bureau did not recognize TDSAs before the 1990 census.

★ 659 ★

Poverty

Poverty Status (1989), by Age, in Selected Tribal Designated Statistical Areas - Part II

Tribal Designated Statistical Area[1]	Persons whose income was below poverty level						
	Under 5 years	5 years	6 to 11 years	12 to 17 years	18 to 64 years	65 to 74 years	75 years and older
Apache Choctaw TDSA (state)	14	14	20	74	0	15	0
Chickahominy TDSA (state)	0	0	0	0	4	0	0
Clifton Choctaw TDSA (state)	0	0	28	54	9	0	0
Coharie TDSA (state)	11	27	50	220	21	30	0
Coquille Indian TDSA	48	258	165	1,012	44	28	175
Delaware-Muncie TDSA (state)	0	0	0	0	0	0	0
Florida Tribe of Eastern Creek TDSA (state)	0	0	0	0	0	0	0
Haliwa-Saponi TDSA (state)	17	89	75	400	59	19	0
Jena Band of Choctaw TDSA (state)	5	26	26	72	0	0	0
Klamath TDSA	34	104	71	349	31	13	0
Lumbee TDSA (state)	209	842	939	3,157	524	213	0
Meherrin TDSA (state)	0	0	34	32	0	0	8
Mohegan TDSA (state)	0	13	5	37	0	0	0
Ramapough TDSA (state)	0	0	0	17	0	0	0
United Houma Nation TDSA (state)	165	768	671	2,210	152	94	347
Waccamaw Siouan TDSA (state)	0	38	13	95	52	22	0
Wampanoag-Gay Head TDSA	0	6	0	38	3	0	0

Source: Census of Population and Housing, 1990: Summary Tape File 3C on CD-ROM [machine-readable datafiles]. Prepared by the Bureau of the Census. Washington, DC: The Bureau, 1992. *Notes:* 1. Tribal designated statistical areas (TDSAs) are areas, delineated outside Oklahoma by federally- and state-recognized tribes without a land base or associated trust lands, to provide statistical areas for which the Census Bureau tabulates data. TDSAs represent areas generally containing the American Indian population over which federally-recognized tribes have jurisdiction and areas in which state tribes provide benefits and services to their members. The names of TDSAs delineated by state-recognized tribes are followed by "(state)." The Census Bureau did not recognize TDSAs before the 1990 census.

★ 660 ★

Poverty

Poverty Status (1989), by Age, in Selected Tribal Jurisdiction Statistical Areas - Part I

Tribal Jurisdiction Statistical Area[1]	Persons whose income was above poverty level						
	Under 5 years	5 years	6 to 11 years	12 to 17 years	18 to 64 years	65 to 74 years	75 years and older
Absentee Shawnee-Citizens Band of Potawatomi TJSA	336	118	565	594	2,795	175	90
Caddo-Wichita-Delaware TJSA	60	7	36	44	208	9	2
Cherokee TJSA	3,939	1,015	5,632	5,870	26,604	2,449	1,504
Cheyenne-Arapaho TJSA	387	81	583	410	2,285	84	56
Chickasaw TJSA	1,013	281	1,575	1,852	8,045	791	542
Choctaw TJSA	1,535	476	2,199	2,374	10,445	1,182	622
Creek TJSA	2,737	590	4,124	3,438	19,998	1,775	937
Iowa TJSA	20	2	29	43	136	9	0
Kaw TJSA	77	22	73	67	290	14	11

[Continued]

★ 660 ★

Poverty Status (1989), by Age, in Selected Tribal Jurisdiction Statistical Areas - Part I

[Continued]

Tribal Jurisdiction Statistical Area[1]	Persons whose income was above poverty level						
	Under 5 years	5 years	6 to 11 years	12 to 17 years	18 to 64 years	65 to 74 years	75 years and older
Kiowa-Comanche-Apache-Fort Sill Apache TJSA	515	112	874	812	4,259	367	181
Otoe-Missouria TJSA	13	0	28	30	113	9	8
Pawnee TJSA	92	21	133	156	623	65	27
Sac and Fox TJSA	262	62	371	424	1,707	147	72
Seminole TJSA	179	51	323	259	1,327	208	56
Tonkawa TJSA	51	7	92	78	316	15	9
Creek-Seminole Joint Area TJSA	27	9	37	26	165	10	10
Iowa-Sac and Fox Joint Area TJSA	0	3	1	0	13	0	0

Source: Census of Population and Housing, 1990: Summary Tape File 3C on CD-ROM [machine-readable datafiles]. Prepared by the Bureau of the Census. Washington, DC: The Bureau, 1992. *Notes:* 1. Tribal jurisdiction statistical areas (TJSAs) are areas, delineated by federally recognized tribes in Oklahoma without a reservation, for which the Census Bureau tabulates data. TJSAs represent areas generally containing the American Indian population over which one or more tribal governments have jurisdiction. If tribal officials delineated adjacent TJSAs so that they include some duplicate territory, the overlap area is called a "joint use area," which is treated as a separate TJSA for census purposes.

★ 661 ★

Poverty

Poverty Status (1989), by Age, in Selected Tribal Jurisdiction Statistical Areas - Part II

Tribal Jurisdiction Statistical Area[1]	Persons whose income was below poverty level						
	Under 5 years	5 years	6 to 11 years	12 to 17 years	18 to 64 years	65 to 74 years	75 years and older
Absentee Shawnee-Citizens Band of Potawatomi TJSA	20	158	179	601	33	54	0
Caddo-Wichita-Delaware TJSA	2	36	32	103	7	3	0
Cherokee TJSA	442	2,839	2,325	8,780	814	825	15
Cheyenne-Arapaho TJSA	94	469	331	1,271	93	56	6
Chickasaw TJSA	154	1,061	902	2,871	243	274	0
Choctaw TJSA	174	1,452	1,228	3,875	519	422	9
Creek TJSA	318	1,771	1,414	4,933	422	388	65
Iowa TJSA	5	8	14	31	9	1	0
Kaw TJSA	4	8	13	35	17	7	0
Kiowa-Comanche-Apache-Fort Sill Apache TJSA	193	835	718	2,606	184	150	69
Otoe-Missouria TJSA	8	47	23	128	6	17	0
Pawnee TJSA	12	85	56	237	15	23	0
Sac and Fox TJSA	27	284	179	664	75	41	0
Seminole TJSA	53	186	220	572	78	25	0
Tonkawa TJSA	4	58	44	111	6	12	2
Creek-Seminole Joint Area TJSA	12	46	44	90	8	5	0
Iowa-Sac and Fox Joint Area TJSA	0	0	0	3	0	0	0

Source: Census of Population and Housing, 1990: Summary Tape File 3C on CD-ROM [machine-readable datafiles]. Prepared by the Bureau of the Census. Washington, DC: The Bureau, 1992. *Notes:* 1. Tribal jurisdiction statistical areas (TJSAs) are areas, delineated by federally recognized tribes in Oklahoma without a reservation, for which the Census Bureau tabulates data. TJSAs represent areas generally containing the American Indian population over which one or more tribal governments have jurisdiction. If tribal officials delineated adjacent TJSAs so that they include some duplicate territory, the overlap area is called a "joint use area," which is treated as a separate TJSA for census purposes.

★ 662 ★

Poverty

Poverty Status (1989), by Age, on Selected Reservations and Trust Lands - Part I

Data are shown for the 50 areas with the largest populations, in number of persons.

American Indian Reservation and Trust Lands[1,2]	Persons whose income was above poverty level						
	Under 5 years	5 years	6 to 11 years	12 to 17 years	18 to 64 years	65 to 74 years	75 years and older
Agua Caliente Reservation	17	8	3	15	76	12	4
Allegany Reservation	54	15	74	74	478	42	25
Blackfeet Reservation	350	90	497	466	1,876	131	60
Cheyenne River Reservation	175	27	337	307	1,085	85	19
Coeur d'Alene Reservation and Trust Lands, ID	33	2	53	72	250	23	20
Colorado River Reservation	162	37	199	188	809	56	23
Colville Reservation	221	47	347	299	1,385	120	63
Crow Reservation and Trust Lands, MT	229	86	301	310	1,339	50	19
Eastern Cherokee Reservation	262	58	428	392	2,035	162	98
Flathead Reservation	253	59	424	360	1,778	142	69
Fort Apache Reservation	614	171	688	459	2,490	119	88
Fort Berthold Reservation	148	31	196	135	889	65	18
Fort Hall Reservation and Trust Lands, ID	163	49	160	168	964	22	24
Fort Peck Reservation	407	43	338	311	1,765	98	55
Gila River Reservation	279	112	318	361	1,977	96	66
Hopi Reservation and Trust Lands, AZ	321	35	420	483	1,945	137	179
Isabella Reservation and Trust Lands, MI	64	10	80	63	311	16	17
Laguna Pueblo and Trust Lands, NM	178	34	267	293	1,484	118	115
Lake Traverse (Sisseton) Reservation	95	23	110	97	619	22	23
Leech Lake Reservation	152	22	177	200	905	64	45
Mississippi Choctaw Reservation and Trust Lands, MS	261	77	338	280	1,201	18	32
Muckleshoot Reservation and Trust Lands, WA	66	9	59	47	197	17	3
Navajo Reservation and Trust Lands, AZ–NM–UT	7,166	1,222	8,484	7,968	32,469	1,793	976
Nez Perce Reservation	88	28	159	199	728	63	27
Northern Cheyenne Reservation and Trust Lands, MT–SD	230	24	208	250	928	67	0
Omaha Reservation	81	19	94	76	385	34	20
Oneida (West) Reservation	138	23	163	214	943	99	54
Osage Reservation	369	103	649	506	2,404	248	140
Papago Reservation	273	44	437	373	1,612	50	85
Pine Ridge Reservation and Trust Lands, NE–SD	462	74	503	345	2,026	109	83
Port Madison Reservation	10	6	47	32	147	7	5
Puyallup Reservation and Trust Lands, WA	40	6	96	93	391	28	25
Red Lake Reservation	182	42	230	233	931	60	28
Rosebud Reservation and Trust Lands, SD	321	79	490	475	1,591	118	66
Salt River Reservation	190	23	243	155	958	19	28
San Carlos Reservation	266	93	391	388	1,378	67	38
Sandia Pueblo	43	8	45	33	182	15	0
San Juan Pueblo	66	0	99	103	502	32	24
Santa Clara Pueblo	79	24	115	116	535	35	25
Southern Ute Reservation	77	26	76	96	392	33	16
Standing Rock Reservation	247	44	310	343	931	63	28
Taos Pueblo and Trust Lands, NM	58	11	59	49	453	41	46
Tulalip Reservation	96	41	117	89	469	23	16
Turtle Mountain Reservation and Trust Lands, ND–SD	228	54	343	388	1,744	149	52
Uintah and Ouray Reservation	140	35	237	201	724	45	18
White Earth Reservation	71	13	149	147	762	94	39
Wind River Reservation	258	116	454	286	1,589	99	20
Yakima Reservation and Trust Lands, WA	300	40	377	467	1,873	146	31

[Continued]

★ 662 ★

Poverty Status (1989), by Age, on Selected Reservations and Trust Lands - Part I

[Continued]

American Indian Reservation and Trust Lands[1,2]	Persons whose income was above poverty level						
	Under 5 years	5 years	6 to 11 years	12 to 17 years	18 to 64 years	65 to 74 years	75 years and older
Yankton Reservation	44	18	96	94	344	29	12
Zuni Pueblo	334	78	374	325	2,064	107	76

Source: Census of Population and Housing, 1990: Summary Tape File 3C on CD-ROM [machine-readable datafiles]. Prepared by the Bureau of the Census. Washington, DC: The Bureau, 1992. *Notes:* 1. Federal American Indian reservations are areas with boundaries established by treaty, statute, and/or executive or court order, and recognized by the federal government as territory in which American Indian tribes have jurisdiction. State reservations are lands held in trust by state governments for the use and benefit of a given tribe. The reservations and their boundaries were identified for the 1990 census by the Bureau of Indian Affairs (BIA), Department of Interior (for federal reservations), and state governments (for state reservations). The names of American Indian reservations recognized by state governments, but not by the federal government, are followed by "state." Areas composed of reservation lands that are administered jointly and/or are claimed by two reservations, as identified by the BIA, are called "joint areas," and are treated as separate American Indian reservations for census purposes. Federal reservations may cross state boundaries, and federal and state reservations may cross county, county subdivision, and place boundaries. For reservations that cross state boundaries, only the portion of the reservations in a given state is shown in the data products for that state; the entire reservations are shown in data products for the United States. 2. Trust lands are property associated with a particular American Indian reservation or tribe, held in trust by the federal government. Trust lands may be held in trust either for a tribe (tribal trust lands) or for an individual member of a tribe (individual trust land). Trust lands recognized for the 1990 census comprised all tribal trust lands and inhabited individual trust lands located outside of a reservation boundary. As with other American Indian areas, trust lands may be located in more than one state. Only the trust lands in a given state are shown in the data products for that state; all trust lands associated with a reservation or tribe are shown in data products for the United States. The Census Bureau first reported data for tribal trust lands for the 1980 census.

★ 663 ★

Poverty

Poverty Status (1989), by Age, on Selected Reservations and Trust Lands - Part II

Data are shown for the 50 areas with the largest populations, in number of persons.

American Indian Reservation and Trust Lands[1,2]	Persons whose income was below poverty level						
	Under 5 years	5 years	6 to 11 years	12 to 17 years	18 to 64 years	65 to 74 years	75 years and older
Agua Caliente Reservation	0	0	0	0	0	0	0
Allegany Reservation	11	43	37	116	11	10	0
Blackfeet Reservation	111	634	394	1,621	98	69	0
Cheyenne River Reservation	98	520	425	1,320	61	60	0
Coeur d'Alene Reservation and Trust Lands, ID	6	52	48	134	4	7	0
Colorado River Reservation	20	142	90	426	29	27	0
Colville Reservation	18	216	132	582	34	40	0
Crow Reservation and Trust Lands, MT	58	414	329	1,138	54	15	0
Eastern Cherokee Reservation	31	290	165	955	78	35	0
Flathead Reservation	43	267	242	1,011	68	19	0
Fort Apache Reservation	171	801	572	2,548	129	33	0
Fort Berthold Reservation	63	253	187	653	24	17	0
Fort Hall Reservation and Trust Lands, ID	51	286	133	699	47	30	0
Fort Peck Reservation	97	475	280	1,261	28	32	3
Gila River Reservation	149	963	637	2,823	209	101	0
Hopi Reservation and Trust Lands, AZ	78	497	455	1,674	180	102	0
Isabella Reservation and Trust Lands, MI	8	50	37	144	6	3	0
Laguna Pueblo and Trust Lands, NM	39	213	133	509	89	47	0
Lake Traverse (Sisseton) Reservation	67	266	281	699	62	48	0
Leech Lake Reservation	87	337	248	718	56	65	5
Mississippi Choctaw Reservation and Trust Lands, MS	40	315	243	823	32	8	0
Muckleshoot Reservation and Trust Lands, WA	24	71	78	190	5	7	0
Navajo Reservation and Trust Lands, AZ–NM–UT	2,192	12,418	10,487	39,547	3,316	2,446	0
Nez Perce Reservation	14	70	57	285	7	14	4

[Continued]

★ 663 ★

Poverty Status (1989), by Age, on Selected Reservations and Trust Lands - Part II

[Continued]

American Indian Reservation and Trust Lands[1,2]	Persons whose income was below poverty level						
	Under 5 years	5 years	6 to 11 years	12 to 17 years	18 to 64 years	65 to 74 years	75 years and older
Northern Cheyenne Reservation and Trust Lands, MT–SD	48	305	301	842	40	0	0
Omaha Reservation	57	200	134	495	33	5	0
Oneida (West) Reservation	43	150	80	269	17	14	0
Osage Reservation	53	217	213	667	73	63	0
Papago Reservation	206	783	623	2,831	287	156	0
Pine Ridge Reservation and Trust Lands, NE–SD	177	1,196	1,041	3,113	202	120	0
Port Madison Reservation	7	25	10	47	3	3	0
Puyallup Reservation and Trust Lands, WA	12	52	27	132	11	5	316
Red Lake Reservation	87	258	227	868	38	21	0
Rosebud Reservation and Trust Lands, SD	164	766	753	2,036	180	75	0
Salt River Reservation	83	279	238	840	45	31	0
San Carlos Reservation	141	679	482	2,287	87	49	0
Sandia Pueblo	3	4	16	49	0	0	0
San Juan Pueblo	9	34	52	249	17	26	0
Santa Clara Pueblo	6	63	26	194	12	22	0
Southern Ute Reservation	14	32	36	180	2	4	3
Standing Rock Reservation	62	434	466	1,358	49	55	0
Taos Pueblo and Trust Lands, NM	15	89	41	274	29	32	0
Tulalip Reservation	14	61	41	157	0	3	0
Turtle Mountain Reservation and Trust Lands, ND–SD	148	578	478	1,651	71	81	0
Uintah and Ouray Reservation	39	193	118	553	31	25	0
White Earth Reservation	53	273	189	619	44	38	0
Wind River Reservation	123	536	250	1,358	65	36	0
Yakima Reservation and Trust Lands, WA	40	533	285	1,320	71	45	0
Yankton Reservation	40	212	182	560	35	27	0
Zuni Pueblo	102	483	531	1,897	89	114	0

Source: Census of Population and Housing, 1990: Summary Tape File 3C on CD-ROM [machine-readable datafiles]. Prepared by the Bureau of the Census. Washington, DC: The Bureau, 1992. *Notes:* 1. Federal American Indian reservations are areas with boundaries established by treaty, statute, and/or executive or court order, and recognized by the federal government as territory in which American Indian tribes have jurisdiction. State reservations are lands held in trust by state governments for the use and benefit of a given tribe. The reservations and their boundaries were identified for the 1990 census by the Bureau of Indian Affairs (BIA), Department of Interior (for federal reservations), and state governments (for state reservations). The names of American Indian reservations recognized by state governments, but not by the federal government, are followed by "state." Areas composed of reservation lands that are administered jointly and/or are claimed by two reservations, as identified by the BIA, are called "joint areas," and are treated as separate American Indian reservations for census purposes. Federal reservations may cross state boundaries, and federal and state reservations may cross county, county subdivision, and place boundaries. For reservations that cross state boundaries, only the portion of the reservations in a given state is shown in the data products for that state; the entire reservations are shown in data products for the United States. 2. Trust lands are property associated with a particular American Indian reservation or tribe, held in trust by the federal government. Trust lands may be held in trust either for a tribe (tribal trust lands) or for an individual member of a tribe (individual trust land). Trust lands recognized for the 1990 census comprised all tribal trust lands and inhabited individual trust lands located outside of a reservation boundary. As with other American Indian areas, trust lands may be located in more than one state. Only the trust lands in a given state are shown in the data products for that state; all trust lands associated with a reservation or tribe are shown in data products for the United States. The Census Bureau first reported data for tribal trust lands for the 1980 census.

Mortgages

★ 664 ★

Mortgages on Property - 1991

Numbers are shown in thousands of households. Households of Hispanic origin may be of any race.

Characteristics	All households	White	Black	American Indian, Eskimo, or Aleut	Asian or Pacific Islander	Hispanic origin	Not of Hispanic origin	
							Total	White
Mortgages currently on property								
None, owned free and clear	24,454	22,307	1,812	142	165	852	23,602	21,499
With mortgage or land contract	35,342	31,441	2,823	115	870	1,571	33,771	29,965
One mortgage	29,753	26,500	2,365	102	709	1,355	28,398	23,224
Two or more mortgages	4,838	4,341	354	11	124	175	4,663	4,174
Number of mortgages not reported	750	601	105	2	37	41	710	568

Source: Woodward, Jeanne M. *America's Racial and Ethnic Groups: Their Housing in the Early Nineties.* Bureau of the Census. Current Housing Reports, Series H121/94-3. Washington, DC: U.S. Government Printing Office, p. 61. Primary source: American Housing Survey (AHS), 1991 National Internal User File.

★ 665 ★

Mortgages

Farmers Home Loans to Native Americans, FY 1992

Data show the different types of assistance provided to Native Americans by the Farmers Home Administration, including number of grants and dollar amounts loaned.

Type of loan	Number	Amount
Indian land acquisition loans	3	1,000,000
Rural housing loans (single family)	242	8,064,000
Housing reservation grants (units)	52	384,750
Farm operating loans	193	5,704,000
Farm ownership loans	37	3,386,000
Farm emergency loans	7	344,000
Technical assistance grant	1	320,000

Source: U.S. Senate Committee on Indian Affairs. *Indian Housing and Related Facilities.* 103rd Cong., 1st. sess., 12 January 1993, p. 94.

★ 666 ★

Mortgages

Mortgage Status and Monthly Owner Costs as Percent of Household Income (1989) in Selected Alaska Native Villages

Data are shown for the 50 areas with the largest populations, in number of housing units.

Alaska Native Village Statistical Area[1]	Specified owner-occupied housing units -											
	With a mortgage						Not mortgaged					
	< 20 %	20 to 24 %	25 to 29 %	25 to 34 %	35 % or more	Not computed	< 20 %	20 to 24 %	25 to 29 %	25 to 34 %	35 % or more	Not computed
Akiachak	0	0	0	0	0	0	53	7	0	7	7	0
Akutan	10	2	0	0	0	0	10	0	2	0	0	0
Alakanuk	20	2	0	0	3	0	52	9	8	6	1	0
Andreafsky	10	0	2	0	6	0	37	2	2	0	3	0
Angoon	6	0	0	0	0	0	37	0	0	5	6	0
Aniak	6	2	5	3	2	0	27	0	0	0	0	0
Barrow	70	4	9	2	13	0	98	4	0	0	16	2
Bethel	115	26	29	33	24	0	174	10	7	6	20	6
Chevak	19	1	8	5	13	0	27	3	0	4	9	0
Copper Center	24	2	0	3	11	0	11	7	0	2	2	0
Craig	27	11	19	0	4	0	20	0	0	0	0	0
Dillingham	107	16	13	13	20	0	74	1	4	2	12	2
Emmonak	11	0	0	0	1	0	75	2	0	3	4	2
Fort Yukon	1	0	0	0	3	0	83	9	4	6	36	0
Galena	6	1	3	0	2	0	50	3	6	3	5	11
Gambell	15	0	2	3	12	0	36	12	2	2	16	0
Grouse Creek Group	60	10	10	2	7	0	10	0	2	0	0	0
Hoonah	54	6	0	0	0	0	42	13	3	0	4	0
Hooper Bay	21	2	3	0	17	0	69	1	6	2	19	0
Kake	49	4	4	3	4	0	42	5	2	0	8	0
Kasigluk	9	0	0	0	0	0	26	0	5	0	8	0
King Cove	4	0	0	0	0	0	32	0	0	0	0	0
King Salmon	12	2	0	0	3	0	17	2	0	0	0	4
Kipnuk	3	0	4	0	12	0	18	0	4	6	48	3
Klawock	24	0	2	0	4	0	14	3	0	0	0	0
Kotlik	14	3	2	0	9	0	40	4	2	2	3	0
Kotzebue	47	9	9	3	13	0	123	10	6	7	29	3
Kwethluk	5	2	0	0	3	0	57	12	4	0	15	0
McGrath	7	2	3	0	1	0	37	1	0	0	0	4
Mountain Village	29	5	0	0	8	0	23	0	3	2	4	0
Naknek	7	5	0	0	6	0	60	1	0	2	0	2
Ninilchik	536	152	93	89	179	0	564	27	7	3	24	20
Noorvik	19	4	0	0	4	0	34	14	0	0	2	0
Pilot Station	24	4	3	4	3	0	22	1	0	1	2	0
Point Hope	21	4	1	0	4	0	24	0	1	0	2	0
Quinhagak	25	0	0	4	4	0	33	2	0	1	8	0
St. Paul	18	5	4	0	5	0	55	5	0	0	4	0
Salamatof	44	2	0	6	6	0	17	4	0	0	0	0
Sand Point	33	0	0	0	4	0	48	3	0	0	10	2
Savoonga	9	2	0	0	15	0	17	3	0	8	22	0
Selawik	22	9	4	3	14	0	30	3	0	4	3	0
Shishmaref	22	1	2	12	9	0	15	4	0	0	4	0
Stebbins	2	0	0	0	0	0	52	4	3	3	2	0
Togiak	6	0	0	0	3	0	64	4	7	6	35	0
Tok	26	6	6	2	15	0	91	7	3	2	8	0
Toksook Bay	11	6	10	0	1	0	31	4	0	2	2	0
Unalakleet	27	0	2	0	8	4	64	3	0	0	12	0
Unalaska	28	12	10	0	6	0	34	2	0	0	17	1

[Continued]

★ 666 ★

Mortgage Status and Monthly Owner Costs as Percent of Household Income (1989) in Selected Alaska Native Villages
[Continued]

Alaska Native Village Statistical Area[1]	Specified owner-occupied housing units -											
	With a mortgage						Not mortgaged					
	< 20 %	20 to 24 %	25 to 29 %	25 to 34 %	35 % or more	Not computed	< 20 %	20 to 24 %	25 to 29 %	25 to 34 %	35 % or more	Not computed
Wainwright	28	15	0	1	10	0	30	4	3	0	4	0
Yakutat	31	9	6	2	5	0	27	3	0	0	0	0

Source: Census of Population and Housing, 1990: Summary Tape File 3C on CD-ROM [machine-readable datafiles]. Prepared by the Bureau of the Census. Washington, DC: The Bureau, 1992. *Notes:* 1. Alaska Native villages (ANVs) constitute tribes, bands, clans, groups, villages, communities, or associations in Alaska that are recognized pursuant to the Alaska Native Claims Settlement Act of 1972, Public Law 92-203. Because ANVs do not have legally designated boundaries, the Census Bureau has established Alaska Native village statistical areas (ANVSAs) for statistical purposes. For the 1990 census, the Census Bureau cooperated with officials of the nonprofit corporation within each participating Alaska Native Regional Corporation (ANRC), as well as other knowledgeable officials, to delineate boundaries that encompass the settled area associated with each ANV.

★ 667 ★
Mortgages

Mortgage Status and Monthly Owner Costs as Percent of Household Income (1989) in Selected Tribal Designated Statistical Areas

Tribal Designated Statistical Area[1]	Specified owner-occupied housing units -											
	With a mortgage						Not mortgaged					
	< 20%	20 to 24 %	25 to 29 %	25 to 34 %	35 % or more	Not computed	< 20 %	20 to 24 %	25 to 29 %	25 to 34 %	35 % or more	Not computed
Apache Choctaw TDSA (state)	455	156	127	72	266	15	1,423	183	121	58	145	65
Chickahominy TDSA (state)	156	60	18	17	78	0	156	6	0	0	0	4
Clifton Choctaw TDSA (state)	0	7	0	0	0	0	37	0	0	0	9	0
Coharie TDSA (state)	5,126	1,761	1,362	692	2,052	57	6,332	755	575	356	1,099	102
Coquille Indian TDSA	21,269	8,874	5,426	3,025	6,929	193	18,116	1,935	1,191	826	1,984	243
Delaware-Muncie TDSA (state)	15	0	0	0	0	0	0	0	0	0	0	0
Florida Tribe of Eastern Creek TDSA (state)	5	0	7	0	0	0	25	0	0	0	0	0
Haliwa-Saponi TDSA (state)	170	17	29	21	86	0	309	32	18	12	83	0
Jena Band of Choctaw TDSA (state)	2,714	951	687	326	820	53	3,519	264	267	128	495	56
Klamath TDSA	2,645	917	487	268	699	45	2,073	222	113	56	189	122
Lumbee TDSA (state)	1,466	558	243	214	736	8	2,304	205	202	155	298	61
Meherrin TDSA (state)	2,090	552	470	342	921	39	3,670	391	239	262	543	52
Mohegan TDSA (state)	982	471	377	284	472	0	1,102	113	74	53	208	6
Ramapough TDSA (state)	24	0	0	21	56	0	46	0	9	6	0	0
United Houma Nation TDSA (state)	49,025	17,265	10,774	7,378	17,478	707	46,977	3,613	2,048	1,630	4,711	1,208
Waccamaw Siouan TDSA (state)	108	18	26	4	10	8	106	6	15	6	19	7
Wampanoag-Gay Head TDSA	518	282	244	170	518	12	895	109	65	76	200	22

Source: Census of Population and Housing, 1990: Summary Tape File 3C on CD-ROM [machine-readable datafiles]. Prepared by the Bureau of the Census. Washington, DC: The Bureau, 1992. *Notes:* 1. Tribal designated statistical areas (TDSAs) are areas, delineated outside Oklahoma by federally- and state-recognized tribes without a land base or associated trust lands, to provide statistical areas for which the Census Bureau tabulates data. TDSAs represent areas generally containing the American Indian population over which federally-recognized tribes have jurisdiction and areas in which state tribes provide benefits and services to their members. The names of TDSAs delineated by state-recognized tribes are followed by "(state)." The Census Bureau did not recognize TDSAs before the 1990 census.

★ 668 ★

Mortgages

Mortgage Status and Monthly Owner Costs as Percent of Household Income (1989) in Selected Tribal Jurisdiction Statistical Areas

Tribal Jurisdiction Statistical Area[1]	Specified owner-occupied housing units -											
	With a mortgage						Not mortgaged					
	< 20 %	20 to 24 %	25 to 29 %	25 to 34 %	35 % or more	Not computed	< 20 %	20 to 24 %	25 to 29 %	25 to 34 %	35 % or more	Not computed
Absentee Shawnee-Citizens Band of Potawatomi TJSA	5,047	1,853	1,348	550	1,531	28	4,496	358	279	112	374	112
Caddo-Wichita-Delaware TJSA	209	76	34	43	116	16	576	84	44	45	97	16
Cherokee TJSA	20,235	6,909	4,497	2,603	6,528	235	25,468	2,599	1,383	983	2,642	367
Cheyenne-Arapaho TJSA	8,684	3,163	1,894	977	2,442	77	10,024	897	559	406	1,104	159
Chickasaw TJSA	12,349	4,017	2,780	1,333	4,083	234	18,650	2,067	1,171	803	1,840	433
Choctaw TJSA	7,971	2,542	1,517	990	3,319	139	13,620	1,544	949	500	1,621	357
Creek TJSA	43,778	15,811	9,784	5,589	12,076	460	35,258	2,627	1,853	1,206	3,395	694
Iowa TJSA	78	29	34	19	35	3	169	28	10	7	26	5
Kaw TJSA	1,312	433	168	123	230	0	966	45	59	7	68	8
Kiowa-Comanche-Apache- Fort Sill Apache TJSA	10,179	3,835	2,512	1,559	3,970	212	11,858	1,152	699	448	1,261	288
Otoe-Missouria TJSA	125	47	16	15	40	0	152	9	9	9	6	0
Pawnee TJSA	594	180	137	111	239	13	1,057	106	74	58	148	25
Sac and Fox TJSA	2,509	989	602	336	765	36	4,312	463	226	167	414	89
Seminole TJSA	727	309	159	68	312	9	1,680	197	125	114	271	19
Tonkawa TJSA	719	217	140	65	207	9	1,290	106	69	61	128	23
Creek-Seminole Joint Area TJSA	77	28	5	5	37	0	157	14	14	6	16	0
Iowa-Sac and Fox Joint Area TJSA	26	22	28	8	11	0	15	0	4	9	2	0

Source: Census of Population and Housing, 1990: Summary Tape File 3C on CD-ROM [machine-readable datafiles]. Prepared by the Bureau of the Census. Washington, DC: The Bureau, 1992. *Notes:* 1. Tribal jurisdiction statistical areas (TJSAs) are areas, delineated by federally recognized tribes in Oklahoma without a reservation, for which the Census Bureau tabulates data. TJSAs represent areas generally containing the American Indian population over which one or more tribal governments have jurisdiction. If tribal officials delineated adjacent TJSAs so that they include some duplicate territory, the overlap area is called a "joint use area," which is treated as a separate TJSA for census purposes.

★ 669 ★

Mortgages

Mortgage Status and Monthly Owner Costs as Percent of Household Income (1989) on Selected Reservations and Trust Lands

Data are shown for the 50 areas with the largest populations, in number of housing units.

American Indian Reservation and Trust Lands[1,2]	Specified owner-occupied housing units -											
	With a mortgage						Not mortgaged					
	< 20 %	20 to 24 %	25 to 29 %	25 to 34 %	35 % or more	Not computed	< 20 %	20 to 24 %	25 to 29 %	25 to 34 %	35 % or more	Not computed
Agua Caliente Reservation	801	286	211	178	918	29	945	125	75	64	192	57
Allegany Reservation	294	55	37	16	38	0	819	63	38	33	63	8
Blackfeet Reservation	160	22	30	7	45	0	210	29	18	15	46	6
Cheyenne River Reservation	103	3	5	13	11	0	237	27	11	14	56	0
Coeur d'Alene Reservation and Trust Lands, ID	235	68	25	12	41	2	339	25	12	11	29	4
Colorado River Reservation	293	95	43	46	119	7	236	18	4	23	51	9
Colville Reservation	296	35	16	11	45	0	336	30	7	8	21	0
Crow Reservation and Trust Lands, MT	99	9	22	34	47	0	176	23	11	7	19	19
Eastern Cherokee Reservation	503	23	22	15	33	0	399	17	6	21	35	15

[Continued]

★ 669 ★

Mortgage Status and Monthly Owner Costs as Percent of Household Income (1989) on Selected Reservations and Trust Lands

[Continued]

American Indian Reservation and Trust Lands[1,2]	Specified owner-occupied housing units -											
	With a mortgage						Not mortgaged					
	< 20 %	20 to 24 %	25 to 29 %	25 to 34 %	35 % or more	Not computed	< 20 %	20 to 24 %	25 to 29 %	25 to 34 %	35 % or more	Not computed
Flathead Reservation	762	291	108	88	226	0	1,027	126	82	30	121	2
Fort Apache Reservation	231	56	13	6	23	7	824	56	16	33	50	127
Fort Berthold Reservation	140	24	10	11	51	3	248	27	20	6	27	2
Fort Hall Reservation and Trust Lands, ID	148	47	7	0	35	0	163	13	0	0	24	10
Fort Peck Reservation	332	107	84	18	80	2	435	61	38	24	68	8
Gila River Reservation	214	25	7	17	53	0	659	61	4	39	118	64
Hopi Reservation and Trust Lands, AZ	76	35	5	3	17	4	658	28	23	4	90	57
Isabella Reservation and Trust Lands, MI	1,278	428	258	185	335	5	1,153	114	80	30	99	12
Laguna Pueblo and Trust Lands, NM	240	5	10	0	28	7	282	2	5	15	45	12
Lake Traverse (Sisseton) Reservation	231	67	21	46	70	0	602	66	46	48	72	6
Leech Lake Reservation	276	74	35	24	98	5	449	52	37	16	87	10
Mississippi Choctaw Reservation and Trust Lands, MS	185	25	19	16	23	8	213	6	13	5	27	17
Muckleshoot Reservation and Trust Lands, WA	205	81	30	22	52	7	90	5	0	3	10	0
Navajo Reservation and Trust Lands, AZ–NM–UT	806	85	103	42	252	83	9,463	664	387	339	1,204	2,992
Nez Perce Reservation	747	153	94	53	138	8	1,196	46	32	20	62	17
Northern Cheyenne Reservation and Trust Lands, MT–SD	126	24	19	0	14	0	143	21	8	29	20	24
Omaha Reservation	162	20	26	14	39	5	410	30	15	4	26	4
Oneida (West) Reservation	1,485	590	351	188	229	3	558	45	38	21	49	5
Osage Reservation	2,271	724	377	363	695	14	2,735	222	165	129	289	71
Papago Reservation	183	0	8	16	13	0	765	63	9	9	180	147
Pine Ridge Reservation and Trust Lands, NE–SD	68	8	0	1	7	0	176	36	23	9	36	39
Port Madison Reservation	340	150	121	76	136	0	221	8	0	0	3	4
Puyallup Reservation and Trust Lands, WA	1,949	901	574	320	542	17	1,278	126	53	51	109	22
Red Lake Reservation	188	30	27	13	78	8	123	15	10	8	19	0
Rosebud Reservation and Trust Lands, SD	105	29	3	15	37	0	273	37	10	19	41	8
Salt River Reservation	209	6	0	12	47	0	143	16	0	0	43	29
San Carlos Reservation	26	7	0	0	18	0	574	49	19	5	122	109
Sandia Pueblo	83	44	51	27	75	0	245	11	18	16	17	8
San Juan Pueblo	89	18	11	13	49	8	489	47	38	17	94	20
Santa Clara Pueblo	317	113	65	41	74	7	814	78	35	24	72	9
Southern Ute Reservation	186	85	59	36	90	0	160	7	18	8	19	7
Standing Rock Reservation	50	10	0	7	23	0	253	25	42	7	29	2
Taos Pueblo and Trust Lands, NM	137	26	24	21	59	0	403	74	63	19	77	12
Tulalip Reservation	432	165	77	47	115	7	300	9	3	5	8	0
Turtle Mountain Reservation and Trust Lands, ND–SD	238	33	33	17	47	2	221	34	16	28	54	5
Uintah and Ouray Reservation	514	221	142	100	158	7	661	57	42	19	117	11
White Earth Reservation	261	69	53	32	113	4	411	84	43	14	73	6
Wind River Reservation	1,030	269	187	98	180	6	901	71	81	27	79	24
Yakima Reservation and Trust Lands, WA	767	215	169	86	246	32	1,241	59	85	16	136	34

[Continued]

★ 669 ★

Mortgage Status and Monthly Owner Costs as Percent of Household Income (1989) on Selected Reservations and Trust Lands

[Continued]

American Indian Reservation and Trust Lands[1,2]	Specified owner-occupied housing units -											
	With a mortgage						Not mortgaged					
	< 20 %	20 to 24 %	25 to 29 %	25 to 34 %	35 % or more	Not computed	< 20 %	20 to 24 %	25 to 29 %	25 to 34 %	35 % or more	Not computed
Yankton Reservation	170	39	19	16	45	4	371	36	38	18	46	2
Zuni Pueblo	61	0	8	0	34	9	642	43	47	9	43	7

Source: Census of Population and Housing, 1990: Summary Tape File 3C on CD-ROM [machine-readable datafiles]. Prepared by the Bureau of the Census. Washington, DC: The Bureau, 1992. *Notes:* 1. Federal American Indian reservations are areas with boundaries established by treaty, statute, and/or executive or court order, and recognized by the federal government as territory in which American Indian tribes have jurisdiction. State reservations are lands held in trust by state governments for the use and benefit of a given tribe. The reservations and their boundaries were identified for the 1990 census by the Bureau of Indian Affairs (BIA), Department of Interior (for federal reservations), and state governments (for state reservations). The names of American Indian reservations recognized by state governments, but not by the federal government, are followed by "state." Areas composed of reservation lands that are administered jointly and/or are claimed by two reservations, as identified by the BIA, are called "joint areas," and are treated as separate American Indian reservations for census purposes. Federal reservations may cross state boundaries, and federal and state reservations may cross county, county subdivision, and place boundaries. For reservations that cross state boundaries, only the portion of the reservations in a given state is shown in the data products for that state; the entire reservations are shown in data products for the United States. 2. Trust lands are property associated with a particular American Indian reservation or tribe, held in trust by the federal government. Trust lands may be held in trust either for a tribe (tribal trust lands) or for an individual member of a tribe (individual trust land). Trust lands recognized for the 1990 census comprised all tribal trust lands and inhabited individual trust lands located outside of a reservation boundary. As with other American Indian areas, trust lands may be located in more than one state. Only the trust lands in a given state are shown in the data products for that state; all trust lands associated with a reservation or tribe are shown in data products for the United States. The Census Bureau first reported data for tribal trust lands for the 1980 census.

★ 670 ★

Mortgages

Mortgage Status and Monthly Owner Costs of American Indians/Alaska Natives in Selected Alaska Native Villages

Data are shown for the 50 areas with the largest populations, in number of housing units.

Alaska Native Village Statistical Area[1]	Specified owner-occupied housing units -										
	With a mortgage						Not mortgaged				
	Less than $300	$400 $499	$500 $699	$700 $999	$1,000 $1,499	$1,500 or more	Less than $100	$100 $199	$200 $299	$300 $399	$400 or more
Akiachak	0	0	0	0	0	0	15	44	7	8	0
Akutan	7	0	0	0	0	0	0	6	4	0	0
Alakanuk	20	5	0	0	0	0	32	28	13	0	3
Andreafsky	2	7	4	0	0	0	3	16	11	9	1
Angoon	0	2	0	2	2	0	5	16	13	0	5
Aniak	2	2	0	0	4	2	6	14	0	0	0
Barrow	2	11	23	15	24	4	9	23	27	25	19
Bethel	4	3	8	41	27	10	16	56	69	22	13
Chevak	11	35	0	0	0	0	6	15	13	4	3
Copper Center	0	6	6	2	0	0	2	3	5	2	3
Craig	0	3	2	3	3	0	0	2	0	7	0
Dillingham	8	21	14	8	12	11	7	17	16	8	18
Emmonak	7	4	1	0	0	0	7	40	31	2	1
Fort Yukon	0	0	0	0	0	0	28	50	33	13	8
Galena	0	0	0	4	0	0	23	18	6	7	4
Gambell	13	19	0	0	0	0	5	25	24	8	6
Grouse Creek Group	15	8	0	0	0	0	0	2	0	1	0
Hoonah	9	30	3	2	4	0	0	22	19	16	0
Hooper Bay	32	11	0	0	0	0	0	60	35	0	2
Kake	6	39	13	3	2	0	0	18	27	0	0
Kasigluk	7	0	0	1	0	0	2	17	19	1	0

[Continued]

★ 670 ★

Mortgage Status and Monthly Owner Costs of American Indians/Alaska Natives in Selected Alaska Native Villages
[Continued]

Alaska Native Village Statistical Area[1]	Specified owner-occupied housing units -										
	With a mortgage						Not mortgaged				
	Less than $300	$400 $499	$500 $699	$700 $999	$1,000 $1,499	$1,500 or more	Less than $100	$100 $199	$200 $299	$300 $399	$400 or more
King Cove	2	0	0	0	2	0	1	7	12	6	1
King Salmon	0	0	0	0	1	0	0	2	7	1	0
Kipnuk	4	15	0	0	0	0	3	18	9	45	0
Klawock	7	15	5	0	0	0	0	7	7	3	0
Kotlik	19	3	6	0	0	0	10	16	8	12	5
Kotzebue	1	19	4	13	6	9	10	34	50	43	23
Kwethluk	4	2	0	0	2	0	14	46	24	0	2
McGrath	0	0	0	3	0	0	3	7	4	2	0
Mountain Village	7	30	0	0	2	0	2	12	9	4	3
Naknek	0	5	0	0	2	0	0	17	12	2	7
Ninilchik	0	10	0	3	5	0	6	26	16	3	6
Noorvik	8	12	7	0	0	0	0	8	15	15	8
Pilot Station	13	18	7	0	0	0	2	16	3	4	1
Point Hope	0	18	5	5	0	0	0	8	2	11	5
Quinhagak	14	17	0	0	0	0	9	18	4	1	10
St. Paul	0	27	2	2	0	0	0	3	11	20	30
Salamatof	0	0	0	1	0	0	0	2	0	0	0
Sand Point	22	7	2	1	0	0	4	19	13	6	6
Savoonga	13	8	5	0	0	0	2	5	23	16	4
Selawik	5	35	7	0	0	0	3	6	22	0	5
Shishmaref	5	35	6	0	0	0	0	3	12	5	3
Stebbins	0	2	0	0	0	0	7	42	6	4	5
Togiak	9	0	0	0	0	0	2	47	43	15	5
Tok	0	0	1	0	0	0	0	6	2	0	2
Toksook Bay	13	15	0	0	0	0	3	7	18	11	0
Unalakleet	4	31	4	2	0	0	0	10	56	13	0
Unalaska	0	15	5	0	0	0	1	11	4	1	7
Wainwright	10	21	17	6	0	0	0	8	9	9	11
Yakutat	3	10	11	2	0	0	2	5	6	0	4

Source: Census of Population and Housing, 1990: Summary Tape File 3C on CD-ROM [machine-readable datafiles]. Prepared by the Bureau of the Census. Washington, DC: The Bureau, 1992. *Notes:* 1. Alaska Native villages (ANVs) constitute tribes, bands, clans, groups, villages, communities, or associations in Alaska that are recognized pursuant to the Alaska Native Claims Settlement Act of 1972, Public Law 92-203. Because ANVs do not have legally designated boundaries, the Census Bureau has established Alaska Native village statistical areas (ANVSAs) for statistical purposes. For the 1990 census, the Census Bureau cooperated with officials of the nonprofit corporation within each participating Alaska Native Regional Corporation (ANRC), as well as other knowledgeable officials, to delineate boundaries that encompass the settled area associated with each ANV.

★ 671 ★

Mortgages

Mortgage Status and Monthly Owner Costs of American Indians/Alaska Natives in Selected Tribal Designated Statistical Areas

| Tribal Designated Statistical Area[1] | Specified owner-occupied housing units - | | | | | | | | | | |
| | With a mortgage | | | | | | Not mortgaged | | | | |
	Less than $300	$400 $499	$500 $699	$700 $999	$1,000 $1,499	$1,500 or more	Less than $100	$100 $199	$200 $299	$300 $399	$400 or more
Apache Choctaw TDSA (state)	0	15	0	0	0	0	28	53	4	0	0
Chickahominy TDSA (state)	0	14	46	0	0	0	10	19	8	11	0
Clifton Choctaw TDSA (state)	0	7	0	0	0	0	9	0	0	0	0
Coharie TDSA (state)	17	56	7	12	0	0	4	96	28	6	0
Coquille Indian TDSA	35	202	145	67	16	6	0	112	84	26	5
Delaware-Muncie TDSA (state)	0	0	0	0	0	0	0	0	0	0	0
Florida Tribe of Eastern Creek TDSA (state)	0	0	0	0	0	0	0	0	0	0	0
Haliwa-Saponi TDSA (state)	9	33	28	10	0	0	9	139	16	0	0
Jena Band of Choctaw TDSA (state)	0	14	14	0	13	0	8	3	0	0	0
Klamath TDSA	22	50	39	8	0	0	10	22	24	11	0
Lumbee TDSA (state)	185	534	449	155	51	13	191	1,013	467	132	49
Meherrin TDSA (state)	2	30	1	0	0	0	0	0	20	3	0
Mohegan TDSA (state)	0	0	0	0	0	0	0	11	0	0	0
Ramapough TDSA (state)	0	14	0	22	0	0	0	0	0	5	0
United Houma Nation TDSA (state)	44	181	125	157	18	8	184	286	113	33	0
Waccamaw Siouan TDSA (state)	7	21	39	16	10	0	16	24	9	0	0
Wampanoag-Gay Head TDSA	0	2	9	10	6	4	0	8	7	10	3

Source: Census of Population and Housing, 1990: Summary Tape File 3C on CD-ROM [machine-readable datafiles]. Prepared by the Bureau of the Census. Washington, DC: The Bureau, 1992. *Notes:* 1. Tribal designated statistical areas (TDSAs) are areas, delineated outside Oklahoma by federally- and state-recognized tribes without a land base or associated trust lands, to provide statistical areas for which the Census Bureau tabulates data. TDSAs represent areas generally containing the American Indian population over which federally-recognized tribes have jurisdiction and areas in which state tribes provide benefits and services to their members. The names of TDSAs delineated by state-recognized tribes are followed by "(state)." The Census Bureau did not recognize TDSAs before the 1990 census.

★ 672 ★

Mortgages

Mortgage Status and Monthly Owner Costs of American Indians/Alaska Natives in Selected Tribal Jurisdiction Statistical Areas

| Tribal Jurisdiction Statistical Area[1] | Specified owner-occupied housing units - | | | | | | | | | | |
| | With a mortgage | | | | | | Not mortgaged | | | | |
	Less than $300	$400 $499	$500 $699	$700 $999	$1,000 $1,499	$1,500 or more	Less than $100	$100 $199	$200 $299	$300 $399	$400 or more
Absentee Shawnee-Citizens Band of Potawatomi TJSA	100	129	144	82	25	0	56	163	92	9	0
Caddo-Wichita-Delaware TJSA	27	7	6	0	0	0	9	30	2	0	0
Cherokee TJSA	1,407	1,750	1,024	468	94	13	956	2,287	624	113	21
Cheyenne-Arapaho TJSA	104	139	136	124	29	0	44	150	85	12	0
Chickasaw TJSA	684	524	425	181	38	0	206	695	182	40	17
Choctaw TJSA	1,223	837	321	88	42	0	562	967	176	60	27
Creek TJSA	928	1,368	1,184	819	254	46	405	1,332	482	109	64
Iowa TJSA	4	2	2	0	0	0	8	16	0	0	0
Kaw TJSA	36	14	18	15	6	0	7	11	19	0	0
Kiowa-Comanche-Apache-Fort Sill Apache TJSA	464	248	124	159	11	0	127	387	136	40	22
Otoe-Missouria TJSA	13	7	2	0	0	0	2	17	0	0	0
Pawnee TJSA	40	52	14	2	0	0	16	51	17	4	7
Sac and Fox TJSA	230	159	75	81	0	0	56	122	44	0	0
Seminole TJSA	75	36	34	25	0	0	65	150	46	0	0

[Continued]

★ 672 ★

Mortgage Status and Monthly Owner Costs of American Indians/Alaska Natives in Selected Tribal Jurisdiction Statistical Areas

[Continued]

Tribal Jurisdiction Statistical Area[1]	Specified owner-occupied housing units -										
	With a mortgage						Not mortgaged				
	Less than $300	$400 $499	$500 $699	$700 $999	$1,000 $1,499	$1,500 or more	Less than $100	$100 $199	$200 $299	$300 $399	$400 or more
Tonkawa TJSA	37	32	21	4	0	0	8	12	7	2	0
Creek-Seminole Joint Area TJSA	34	6	0	8	0	0	9	11	0	0	0
Iowa-Sac and Fox Joint Area TJSA	0	0	2	0	0	0	0	0	0	0	0

Source: Census of Population and Housing, 1990: Summary Tape File 3C on CD-ROM [machine-readable datafiles]. Prepared by the Bureau of the Census. Washington, DC: The Bureau, 1992. *Notes:* 1. Tribal jurisdiction statistical areas (TJSAs) are areas, delineated by federally recognized tribes in Oklahoma without a reservation, for which the Census Bureau tabulates data. TJSAs represent areas generally containing the American Indian population over which one or more tribal governments have jurisdiction. If tribal officials delineated adjacent TJSAs so that they include some duplicate territory, the overlap area is called a "joint use area," which is treated as a separate TJSA for census purposes.

★ 673 ★

Mortgages

Mortgage Status and Monthly Owner Costs of American Indians/Alaska Natives on Selected Reservations and Trust Lands

Data are shown for the 50 areas with the largest populations, in number of housing units.

American Indian Reservation and Trust Lands[1,2]	Specified owner-occupied housing units -										
	With a mortgage						Not mortgaged				
	Less than $300	$400 $499	$500 $699	$700 $999	$1,000 $1,499	$1,500 or more	Less than $100	$100 $199	$200 $299	$300 $399	$400 or more
Agua Caliente Reservation	0	0	0	0	4	3	0	0	0	0	0
Allegany Reservation	7	43	6	0	0	0	9	85	10	2	0
Blackfeet Reservation	135	57	29	11	0	0	53	162	47	7	0
Cheyenne River Reservation	31	25	1	0	0	0	44	40	50	2	2
Coeur d'Alene Reservation and Trust Lands, ID	52	6	0	2	0	0	20	20	0	0	0
Colorado River Reservation	84	35	32	4	4	0	47	95	33	0	4
Colville Reservation	135	71	30	4	0	0	55	62	5	2	3
Crow Reservation and Trust Lands, MT	89	54	5	0	0	0	24	113	5	16	14
Eastern Cherokee Reservation	456	85	19	0	0	0	208	200	24	0	0
Flathead Reservation	186	100	59	23	12	0	84	108	0	6	9
Fort Apache Reservation	282	25	0	21	0	0	606	391	34	43	0
Fort Berthold Reservation	77	40	21	3	0	0	27	40	11	2	0
Fort Hall Reservation and Trust Lands, ID	108	61	7	6	0	0	45	98	5	0	0
Fort Peck Reservation	102	95	49	25	6	0	34	191	41	27	10
Gila River Reservation	213	54	19	0	0	0	568	304	44	0	11
Hopi Reservation and Trust Lands, AZ	71	36	11	13	9	0	519	286	50	5	0
Isabella Reservation and Trust Lands, MI	0	28	14	0	0	0	0	12	5	0	0
Laguna Pueblo and Trust Lands, NM	225	43	7	10	0	0	166	138	33	8	3
Lake Traverse (Sisseton) Reservation	57	16	8	0	0	0	8	34	9	0	0
Leech Lake Reservation	82	130	19	0	0	0	62	101	48	0	0
Mississippi Choctaw Reservation and Trust Lands, MS	154	99	7	0	0	0	143	103	24	0	7
Muckleshoot Reservation and Trust Lands, WA	4	2	0	7	2	0	8	32	15	0	0
Navajo Reservation and Trust Lands, AZ-NM-UT	695	338	181	65	19	0	11,549	2,536	526	211	152
Nez Perce Reservation	116	52	10	6	0	0	50	53	10	1	0
Northern Cheyenne Reservation and Trust Lands, MT-SD	124	45	7	0	0	0	31	172	30	0	0
Omaha Reservation	36	27	6	4	0	0	7	17	8	0	0
Oneida (West) Reservation	43	75	33	19	2	0	17	63	18	10	14
Osage Reservation	228	206	83	75	9	0	59	214	110	7	0
Papago Reservation	187	29	4	0	0	0	953	181	34	5	0
Pine Ridge Reservation and Trust Lands, NE-SD	56	9	18	0	0	0	107	107	55	17	0
Port Madison Reservation	17	12	6	7	0	0	4	3	0	0	0
Puyallup Reservation and Trust Lands, WA	3	9	10	14	12	0	6	40	25	0	2
Red Lake Reservation	204	101	37	2	0	0	83	73	14	0	0
Rosebud Reservation and Trust Lands, SD	82	40	23	0	0	0	98	169	56	3	3
Salt River Reservation	210	52	0	6	6	0	156	44	19	12	0

[Continued]

★ 673 ★

Mortgage Status and Monthly Owner Costs of American Indians/Alaska Natives on Selected Reservations and Trust Lands

[Continued]

American Indian Reservation and Trust Lands[1,2]	Specified owner-occupied housing units -										
	With a mortgage						Not mortgaged				
	Less than $300	$400 $499	$500 $699	$700 $999	$1,000 $1,499	$1,500 or more	Less than $100	$100 $199	$200 $299	$300 $399	$400 or more
San Carlos Reservation	21	17	6	0	0	0	475	345	37	16	5
Sandia Pueblo	13	7	0	0	0	0	19	23	0	0	1
San Juan Pueblo	26	21	17	0	0	0	57	118	17	3	3
Santa Clara Pueblo	36	18	5	4	0	1	63	139	13	0	0
Southern Ute Reservation	40	9	2	7	0	0	10	17	5	3	0
Standing Rock Reservation	24	3	0	0	0	0	38	66	17	0	0
Taos Pueblo and Trust Lands, NM	86	6	5	0	0	0	86	95	24	2	0
Tulalip Reservation	26	20	18	9	0	0	15	34	6	2	0
Turtle Mountain Reservation and Trust Lands, ND–SD	273	90	0	7	0	0	38	163	117	2	11
Uintah and Ouray Reservation	32	16	17	2	0	0	35	93	41	4	6
White Earth Reservation	64	93	24	2	0	0	25	79	18	0	0
Wind River Reservation	154	43	30	3	0	0	122	72	12	7	0
Yakima Reservation and Trust Lands, WA	162	108	25	31	0	0	54	85	33	0	0
Yankton Reservation	64	20	2	0	0	0	9	26	7	0	0
Zuni Pueblo	83	21	0	0	0	0	198	437	117	39	0

Source: Census of Population and Housing, 1990: Summary Tape File 3C on CD-ROM [machine-readable datafiles]. Prepared by the Bureau of the Census. Washington, DC: The Bureau, 1992. *Notes:* 1. Federal American Indian reservations are areas with boundaries established by treaty, statute, and/or executive or court order, and recognized by the federal government as territory in which American Indian tribes have jurisdiction. State reservations are lands held in trust by state governments for the use and benefit of a given tribe. The reservations and their boundaries were identified for the 1990 census by the Bureau of Indian Affairs (BIA), Department of Interior (for federal reservations), and state governments (for state reservations). The names of American Indian reservations recognized by state governments, but not by the federal government, are followed by "state." Areas composed of reservation lands that are administered jointly and/or are claimed by two reservations, as identified by the BIA, are called "joint areas," and are treated as separate American Indian reservations for census purposes. Federal reservations may cross state boundaries, and federal and state reservations may cross county, county subdivision, and place boundaries. For reservations that cross state boundaries, only the portion of the reservations in a given state is shown in the data products for that state; the entire reservations are shown in data products for the United States. 2. Trust lands are property associated with a particular American Indian reservation or tribe, held in trust by the federal government. Trust lands may be held in trust either for a tribe (tribal trust lands) or for an individual member of a tribe (individual trust land). Trust lands recognized for the 1990 census comprised all tribal trust lands and inhabited individual trust lands located outside of a reservation boundary. As with other American Indian areas, trust lands may be located in more than one state. Only the trust lands in a given state are shown in the data products for that state; all trust lands associated with a reservation or tribe are shown in the data products for the United States. The Census Bureau first reported data for tribal trust lands for the 1980 census.

Public Assistance

★ 674 ★

CIAP Housing Funds, 1981-92

Data show fiscal year appropriations under the Comprehensive Improvement Assistance Program (CIAP), which is available to low-income rental projects through the Department of Housing and Urban Development.

Fiscal year	Appropriation
1981	14,218,093
1982	19,771,977
1983	22,870,830
1984	10,812,919
1985	11,228,545
1986	14,136,391

[Continued]

★ 674 ★

CIAP Housing Funds, 1981-92
[Continued]

Fiscal year	Appropriation
1987	28,770,482
1988	54,895,154
1989	44,687,046
1990	53,277,677
1991	67,365,000

Source: National Commission on American Indian, Alaska Native, and Native Hawaiian Housing. *Building the Future: A Blueprint for Change: "By Our Homes You Will Know Us."* Washington, DC: 1992, p. 34.

★ 675 ★

Public Assistance

Child Recipients of Welfare Benefits

These data show percent distribution by race/ethnicity of the more than 8.5 million children who received welfare benefits in the year ended September 1991.

Race/ethnicity	Percent
Black	40.1
White	33.5
Hispanic	18.5
Asian	3.7
Native American	1.3
Unknown	2.9

Source: Chavez, Linda. "Why make it easier to receive welfare?" *USA TODAY* (8 June 1994), p. 11A. Department of Health and Human Services.

★ 676 ★

Public Assistance

Food Stamp Administrative Costs in Reservation States - 1991

Costs per state are shown in dollars for fiscal year 1991.

State	Certification ($)	Issuance ($)	Combined ($)
Arizona	7,852,254	419,590	8,271,844
California	97,770,658	5,357,168	103,127,826
Colorado	3,863,062	2,169,025	6,032,087
Connecticut	5,935,780	410,529	6,346,309
Florida	29,618,972	4,047,310	33,666,282

[Continued]

★ 676 ★

Food Stamp Administrative Costs in Reservation
States - 1991
[Continued]

State	Certification ($)	Issuance ($)	Combined ($)
Idaho	2,546,709	241,684	2,788,393
Iowa	5,701,104	627,665	6,328,769
Kansas	2,822,777	234,636	3,057,413
Louisiana	20,221,346	3,273,564	23,494,910
Massachusetts	8,798,472	1,385,442	10,183,914
Maine	3,371,495	289,044	3,660,539
Michigan	14,705,326	2,492,927	17,198,253
Minnesota	11,078,956	1,421,881	12,500,837
Mississippi	9,320,344	1,549,428	10,869,772
Montana	2,586,125	261,435	2,847,560
Nebraska	2,595,203	720,452	3,315,655
Nevada	2,931,075	112,563	3,043,638
New Mexico	6,718,672	606,133	7,324,805
New York	70,809,264	10,849,483	81,658,747
North Carolina	19,869,908	1,822,476	21,692,384
North Dakota	1,579,676	293,749	1,873,425
Oregon	3,807,273	1,019,462	4,826,735
South Dakota	1,678,256	404,937	2,083,193
Texas	75,545,803	9,390,965	84,936,768
Utah	5,638,466	458,270	6,096,736
Washington	18,901,844	1,826,723	20,728,567
Wisconsin	6,904,023	2,086,452	8,990,475
Wyoming	838,383	22,663	861,046
Total	468,641,408	56,833,175	525,474,583

Source: U.S. General Accounting Office. *Food Stamp Program Provisions* (GAO/RCED-93-70R). Washington, DC: U.S. GAO, 1993, p. 19.

★ 677 ★

Public Assistance

Welfare-to-Work Programs by Type

The nation's 163 job-training programs cost the federal government $20 billion each year. Data show number of programs in operation, by type.

	Number
Total	4,604,000
Not required to participate	2,561,000
Not participating, though required	1,520,000
Participating, as required	523,000
Job-training programs	
Youths	19
Veterans	16

[Continued]

★ 677 ★

Welfare-to-Work Programs by Type
[Continued]

	Number
Native Americans	10
Displaced workers	10
The poor	9
Women/minorities	6
Migrants	5
Homeless	5
Refugees	4
Older workers	4

Source: Phillips, Leslie. "New welfare push, same old obstacles." *USA TODAY* (12 January 1995), p. 4A. Primary source: U.S. General Accounting Office.

Chapter 8
BUSINESS AND INDUSTRY

Businesses

★ 678 ★

Average Small Business Revenues in the U.S., by Sex and Race/Ethnicity, 1987

Ownership	Men	Women
White	189,000	70,000
Asian/Pacific Islander	107,000	64,000
Hispanic	66,000	88,000
African-American	50,000	41,000
American Indian/Alaska Native	47,000	32,000

Source: *Alaska Business Monthly* (June 1992), p. 50. Primary source: U.S. Bureau of the Census.

★ 679 ★

Businesses

Women in Corporate Management

The percent of women managers is shown, by race/ethnicity.

Ethnic group	Percent
Native American	0.5
White	96.7
Asian	1.9
African-American	0.9

Source: Baskerville, Dawn M. "Breaking through the glass ceiling," *Black Enterprise* 22 (August 1991), p. 37. Primary source: Heldrick and Struggles, *The Corporate Woman Officer*, Chicago, 1986.

★ 680 ★

Businesses

Minority-Owned Firms, 1987

Figures are shown for 1987, by race/ethnicity.

Ethnic group	Number of firms	% of all U.S. firms	1987 revenues (billions)	% of all U.S. revenues
Black	424,165	3.1	19.8	1.0
Hispanic	422,373	3.1	24.7	1.2
Asian/Pacific	355,331	2.6	33.1	1.7
American Indian and Alaskan	21,380	0.2	0.9	0.1

Source: Richards, Rhonda. "SBA squeezes minority merchants: commission wants change." *USA TODAY* (17 June 1992), p. 4B. Primary source: Economic Census (latest available data).

★ 681 ★

Businesses

Minority-Owned Firms, by Type, 1987

Data are shown for 1987.

Industry division, legal form of organization, and minority	All firms		Firms with paid employees				Relative standard error of estimate (%) for column -			
	Firms (number) A	Sales and receipts ($1,000) B	Firms (number) C	Sales and receipts ($1,000) D	Employees (number) E	Annual payroll ($1,000) F	A	B	C	D
All industries	1,213,750	77,839,943	248,149	56,463,624	836,483	9,508,592	-	-	-	-
Subchapter S corporations	42,212	23,300,949	30,783	22,137,767	291,319	4,056,980	-	-	-	-
Minority men	25,528	15,658,873	18,740	14,905,851	188,706	2,692,533	-	-	-	-
Minority women	16,684	7,642,076	12,043	7,231,916	102,613	1,364,447	-	-	-	-
American Indian and Alaska Native	360	138,126	242	128,463	2,088	27,654	3	1	3	1
Black	12,565	7,741,387	8,669	7,389,781	102,504	1,498,206	-	-	-	-
Hispanic	13,374	7,265,356	9,628	6,871,684	85,102	1,239,896	-	-	1	-
Asian and Pacific Islander	16,475	8,402,698	12,656	7,977,348	105,402	1,347,721	-	-	-	-
Individual proprietorships	1,129,705	46,164,026	196,600	27,818,283	426,636	4,406,130	-	-	-	-
Minority men	773,846	38,282,773	157,353	23,971,930	353,914	3,756,446	-	-	-	-
Minority women	355,859	7,881,253	39,247	3,846,353	72,722	649,684	-	-	1	1
American Indian and Alaska Native	20,454	674,173	3,247	396,429	5,864	71,237	1	1	3	2
Black	400,339	10,056,751	57,398	5,210,241	91,671	986,628	-	-	-	-
Hispanic	396,769	15,169,291	67,552	9,112,214	147,544	1,705,000	-	-	1	-
Asian and Pacific Islander	320,161	20,570,018	69,663	13,276,736	185,065	1,677,348	-	-	1	-
Partnerships	41,833	8,374,968	20,766	6,507,574	118,528	1,045,482	-	-	-	-
Minority men	26,067	5,905,347	13,428	4,610,225	80,807	731,690	-	-	1	-
Minority women	15,766	2,469,621	7,338	1,897,319	37,721	313,792	-	-	1	1
American Indian and Alaska Native	566	98,980	250	77,897	1,004	10,380	2	2	3	2

[Continued]

★ 681 ★

Minority-Owned Firms, by Type, 1987
[Continued]

Industry division, legal form of organization, and minority	All firms		Firms with paid employees				Relative standard error of estimate (%) for column -			
	Firms (number) A	Sales and receipts ($1,000) B	Firms (number) C	Sales and receipts ($1,000) D	Employees (number) E	Annual payroll ($1,000) F	A	B	C	D
Black	11,261	1,964,738	4,748	1,530,398	26,292	276,271	-	-	-	-
Hispanic	12,230	2,296,953	5,728	1,745,534	32,200	298,446	1	-	1	-
Asian and Pacific Islander	18,695	4,151,610	10,399	3,247,254	60,878	476,848	-	-	1	-

Source: 1987 Economic Censuses, Survey of Minority-Owned Business Enterprises: Summary, U.S. Department of Commerce, Bureau of the Census, 1991, p. 80. Primary source: 1987 Survey of Minority-Owned Businesses. *Minority-Owned Businesses.* Washington, D.C.: U.S. Government Printing Office, 1990. Detail may not add to total because of rounding and because a firm may be included in more than one minority group. This table is based on the 1972 SIC system.

★ 682 ★

Businesses

Minority-Owned Firms: Business Ownership, by Sex

Data are shown for 1987.

Minority	Firms (number)	Sales and receipts ($1,000,000)	% of all minority-owned firms by gender	
			Firms	Sales and receipts
All minority firms	1,213,750	77,840	100.0	100.0
Men	825,443	59,847	100.0	100.0
American Indian and Alaska Native	15,072	711	1.8	1.2
Black	265,889	13,377	32.0	22.1
Hispanic	307,348	20,442	36.9	33.8
Asian and Pacific Islander	243,442	25,988	29.3	42.9
Women	388,309	17,993	100.0	100.0
American Indian and Alaskan Native	6,308	200	1.6	1.1
Black	158,278	6,531	40.4	35.9
Hispanic	115,025	4,328	29.4	23.8
Asian and Pacific Islander	111,889	7,136	28.6	39.2

Source: "Minority-Owned Firms by Gender," *Minority-Owned Businesses,* p. 2. Primary source: 1987 Survey of Minority-Owned Businesses. *Minority-Owned Businesses,* Washington, D.C.: U.S. Government Printing Office, 1990. *Notes:* Detail in this table does not add to total because of duplication of some firms. Firms that were owned equally by two or more minorities are included in the data for each minority group but counted only once at total levels.

★ 683 ★
Businesses
Minority-Owned Firms: Employment Size

Employment size and minority	Firms (number) A	Sales and receipts ($1,000) B	Employees (number) C	Annual payroll ($1,000) D	Relative standard error of estimate (%) for column	
					A	B
All industries	1,213,750	77,839,943	836,483	9,508,592	-	-
With no paid employees	965,601	21,376,319	-	-	-	-
Minority men	635,920	16,358,957	-	-	-	-
Minority women	329,681	5,017,362	-	-	-	1
American Indian and Alaska Native	17,641	308,490	-	-	1	2
Black	353,350	5,632,	456	-	-	-
Hispanic	339,465	7,002,168	-	-	-	1
Asian and Pacific Islander	262,613	8,622,988	-	-	-	-
With paid employees	248,149	56,463,624	836,483	9,508,592	-	-
Minority men	189,521	43,488,036	623,427	7,180,669	-	-
Minority women	58,628	12,975,588	213,056	2,327,923	1	-
American Indian and Alaska Native	3,739	602,789	8,956	109,271	3	1
Black	70,815	14,130,420	220,467	2,761,105	-	-
Hispanic	82,908	17,729,432	264,846	3,243,342	1	-
Asian and Pacific Islander	92,718	24,501,338	351,345	3,501,917	-	-
No employees[1]	90,794	6,324,443	-	1,055,951	1	1
Minority men	71,210	5,275,213	-	893,258	1	1
Minority women	19,584	1,049,230	-	162,693	1	1
American Indian and Alaska Native	1,894	103,948	-	19,252	5	4
Black	31,414	1,495,861	-	295,167	-	-
Hispanic	33,717	2,300,522	-	457,870	1	1
Asian and Pacific Islander	24,372	2,461,292	-	290,507	1	1
1 to 4 employees	113,295	17,677,566	218,776	2,128,328	-	-
Minority men	85,291	13,901,557	165,046	1,648,380	-	-
Minority women	28,004	3,776,009	53,730	479,948	1	1
American Indian and Alaska Native	1,365	190,813	2,646	25,810	3	2
Black	29,238	3,565,200	54,936	541,404	-	-
Hispanic	35,239	5,208,198	68,367	696,933	1	-
Asian and Pacific Islander	48,466	8,867,263	94,757	883,105	-	-
5 to 9 employees	26,114	9,887,070	168,495	1,571,332	-	-
Minority men	19,626	7,652,265	126,728	1,192,794	-	-
Minority women	6,488	2,234,805	41,767	378,538	1	1
American Indian and Alaska Native	286	112,284	1,870	20,160	3	1
Black	6,060	1,984,302	38,851	385,923	-	-
Hispanic	8,221	3,075,801	53,181	526,090	1	-

[Continued]

★ 683 ★

Minority-Owned Firms: Employment Size

[Continued]

Employment size and minority	Firms (number) A	Sales and receipts ($1,000) B	Employees (number) C	Annual payroll ($1,000) D	Relative standard error of estimate (%) for column	
					A	B
Asian and Pacific Islander	11,788	4,801,877	76,139	654,046	1	-
10 to 19 employees	11,566	7,430,113	151,985	1,407,438	-	-
Minority men	8,697	5,748,744	114,252	1,063,083	-	-
Minority women	2,869	1,681,369	37,733	344,355	1	-
American Indian and Alaska Native	136	91,447	1,755	16,654	-	-
Black	2,443	1,650,580	31,978	338,183	-	-
Hispanic	3,671	2,433,738	48,330	491,931	1	-
Asian and Pacific Islander	5,419	3,316,649	71,301	573,764	1	-
20 to 49 employees	4,914	6,671,271	142,516	1,442,486	-	-
Minority men	3,636	4,902,599	105,178	1,054,968	-	-
Minority women	1,278	1,768,672	37,338	387,518	-	-
American Indian and Alaska Native	49	70,164	1,396	15,979	-	-
Black	1,143	1,933,049	33,630	415,857	-	-
Hispanic	1,582	2,126,435	46,142	477,564	1	-
Asian and Pacific Islander	2,187	2,601,780	62,820	552,254	-	-
50 to 99 employees	1,033	4,103,812	69,809	824,387	-	-
Minority men	745	2,968,384	50,200	572,507	1	-
Minority women	288	1,135,428	19,609	251,880	-	-
American Indian and Alaska Native	4	7,743	271	2,482	-	-
Black	328	1,493,038	22,363	306,820	-	-
Hispanic	349	1,370,194	23,335	269,919	-	-
Asian and Pacific Islander	368	1,296,402	24,885	262,097	1	-
100 employees or more	433	4,369,349	84,902	1,078,670	-	-
Minority men	316	3,039,274	62,023	755,679	-	-
Minority women	117	1,330,075	22,879	322,991	-	-
American Indian and Alaska Native	5	26,390	1,018	8,934	-	-
Black	189	2,008,390	38,709	477,751	-	-
Hispanic	129	1,214,544	25,491	323,035	-	-
Asian and Pacific Islander	118	1,156,075	21,443	286,144	-	-

Source: 1987 Economic Censuses, Survey of Minority-Owned Business Enterprises: Summary, U.S. Department of Commerce, Bureau of the Census, 1991, pp. 82-83. Primary source: 1987 Survey of Minority-Owned Businesses. *Minority-Owned Businesses*, Washington, D.C.: U.S. Government Printing Office, 1990. *Notes:* Detail may not add to total because of rounding and because a firm may be included in more than one minority group. 1. Firms reported annual payroll but did not report any employees on their payroll during specified period in 1987.

★ 684 ★

Businesses

Minority-Owned Firms: Sales and Receipts

Data are shown for 1987.

Receipts size and minority	All firms		Firms with paid employees				Relative standard error of estimate (%) for column -			
	Firms (number) A	Sales and receipts ($1,000) B	Firms (number) C	Sales and receipts ($1,000) D	Employees (number) E	Annual payroll ($1,000) F	A	B	C	D
All industries	1,213,750	77,839,943	248,149	56,463,624	836,483	9,508,592	-	-	-	-
Less than $5,000	357,180	767,373	6,191	18,018	1,356	13,264	-	-	2	2
Minority men	212,340	459,143	4,010	11,738	875	8,714	-	-	3	3
Minority women	144,840	308,230	2,181	6,280	481	4,550	-	1	4	4
American Indian and Alaska Native	7,621	16,163	94	287	14	150	2	3	24	29
Black	149,446	316,631	2,812	8,051	501	5,674	-	-	-	-
Hispanic	120,717	261,704	2,030	6,067	406	4,273	1	1	5	6
Asian and Pacific Islander	81,973	178,337	1,286	3,701	446	3,212	1	1	6	6
$5,000 to $9,999	202,669	1,365,675	11,094	77,435	2,208	27,831	-	-	2	2
Minority men	126,505	856,227	7,588	52,934	1,431	18,970	1	1	2	2
Minority women	76,164	509,448	3,506	24,501	777	8,861	1	1	3	3
American Indian and Alaska Native	3,971	26,520	318	2,178	28	757	3	4	13	13
Black	77,874	524,276	4,860	33,893	830	12,377	-	-	-	-
Hispanic	74,711	504,776	3,555	24,696	674	8,879	1	1	4	4
Asian and Pacific Islander	47,618	320,333	2,446	17,283	702	6,092	1	1	4	4
$10,000 to $24,999	251,749	3,920,362	30,368	510,301	12,744	136,941	-	-	1	1
Minority men	172,921	2,719,467	21,981	371,110	8,370	99,747	-	-	1	1
Minority women	78,828	1,200,895	8,387	139,191	4,374	37,194	1	1	2	2
American Indian and Alaska Native	4,153	63,104	651	10,834	173	2,754	3	3	8	8
Black	91,566	1,416,051	12,445	206,391	4,901	56,803	-	-	-	-
Hispanic	92,386	1,430,591	10,742	180,700	3,876	49,395	1	1	2	2
Asian and Pacific Islander	65,521	1,039,524	6,771	116,147	3,884	176,848	1	1	2	2
$25,000 to $49,999	147,247	5,162,808	39,875	1,452,814	33,125	338,811	-	-	1	1
Minority men	111,523	9,918,201	29,829	1,089,678	22,616	255,013	1	1	1	1
Minority women	35,724	1,244,607	10,046	363,136	10,509	83,798	1	1	1	1
American Indian and Alaska Native	2,085	72,868	635	22,976	507	5,307	4	4	7	7
Black	46,583	1,616,585	13,807	496,718	11,582	121,062	-	-	-	-
Hispanic	52,737	1,849,069	14,686	535,844	11,180	129,340	1	1	2	2
Asian and Pacific Islander	47,112	1,667,594	11,031	407,377	10,197	85,360	1	1	2	2
$50,000 to $99,999	109,235	7,672,302	50,833	3,672,971	78,494	746,614	-	-	1	1
Minority men	85,576	6,014,686	38,962	2,818,375	55,505	569,968	1	1	1	1
Minority women	23,659	1,657,616	11,871	854,596	22,989	176,646	1	1	1	1
American Indian and Alaska Native	1,848	127,880	791	54,899	1,060	13,011	5	5	5	5
Black	29,482	2,044,481	14,353	1,019,898	23,194	231,730	-	-	-	-
Hispanic	36,589	2,554,350	17,642	1,266,051	25,711	277,329	1	1	1	1
Asian and Pacific Islander	42,235	3,011,371	18,446	1,360,951	29,192	230,816	1	1	1	1

[Continued]

★ 684 ★

Minority-Owned Firms: Sales and Receipts
[Continued]

Receipts size and minority	All firms		Firms with paid employees				Relative standard error of estimate (%) for column -			
	Firms (number) A	Sales and receipts ($1,000) B	Firms (number) C	Sales and receipts ($1,000) D	Employees (number) E	Annual payroll ($1,000) F	A	B	C	D
$100,000 to $199,999	75,530	10,575,649	50,825	7,223,250	144,597	1,344,961	1	1	1	1
Minority men	60,282	8,437,235	40,166	5,708,013	107,865	1,050,795	1	1	1	1
Minority women	15,248	2,138,414	10,659	1,515,237	36,732	294,166	1	1	1	1
American Indian and Alaska Native	957	132,186	628	87,231	1,575	17,173	5	5	5	5
Black	15,942	2,201,517	11,086	1,552,069	33,591	330,816	-	-	-	-
Hispanic	23,711	3,308,844	15,927	2,251,181	43,490	467,072	1	1	1	1
Asian and Pacific Islander	35,671	5,039,149	23,670	3,401,617	67,305	543,159	1	1	1	1
$200,000 to $249,999	16,738	3,726,447	13,087	2,916,812	54,561	537,175	1	1	1	1
Minority men	13,576	3,023,041	10,507	2,342,444	41,677	424,906	1	1	1	1
Minority women	3,162	703,406	2,580	574,368	12,884	112,269	2	2	2	2
American Indian and Alaska Native	154	34,425	124	27,711	455	5,623	6	6	7	7
Black	3,116	693,241	2,491	554,446	10,752	115,103	-	-	-	-
Hispanic	5,105	1,137,501	4,052	902,989	16,715	190,127	2	2	2	2
Asian and Pacific Islander	8,484	1,888,270	6,511	1,452,094	26,986	229,835	2	2	2	2
$250,000 to $499,999	32,089	11,012,084	26,713	9,216,396	160,815	1,636,006	-	-	-	-
Minority men	25,873	8,870,936	21,398	7,375,467	122,942	1,280,040	-	-	-	-
Minority women	6,216	2,141,148	5,315	1,840,929	37,873	355,966	1	1	1	1
American Indian and Alaska Native	355	124,565	277	97,409	1,604	17,723	1	1	2	2
Black	5,843	2,009,503	4,994	1,727,663	30,931	342,475	-	-	-	-
Hispanic	9,581	3,290,917	8,078	2,789,838	50,969	566,462	1	1	1	1
Asian and Pacific Islander	16,584	5,683,919	13,595	4,683,806	78,949	725,621	-	-	-	-
$500,000 to $999,999	13,164	9,041,044	11,697	8,051,763	126,253	1,333,349	-	-	-	-
Minority men	10,570	7,257,529	9,358	6,442,079	98,296	1,038,699	-	-	-	-
Minority women	2,594	1,783,515	2,339	1,609,684	27,957	294,650	1	1	1	1
American Indian and Alaska Native	154	105,787	143	98,922	1,317	16,037	1	1	1	1
Black	2,366	1,636,463	2,134	1,474,381	25,295	290,403	-	-	-	-
Hispanic	4,292	2,933,649	3,843	2,635,973	41,930	474,069	-	-	-	-
Asian and Pacific Islander	6,476	4,448,267	5,687	3,916,417	58,886	565,818	-	-	-	1
$1,000,000 or more	8,149	24,596,199	7,466	23,323,864	222,330	3,393,640	-	-	-	-
Minority men	6,275	18,290,528	5,722	17,276,198	163,850	2,433,817	-	-	-	-
Minority women	1,874	6,305,671	1,744	6,047,666	58,480	959,823	-	-	-	-
American Indian and Alaska Native	82	207,781	78	200,342	2,223	30,736	-	-	-	-
Black	1,947	7,304,128	1,833	7,056,910	78,890	1,254,662	-	-	-	-
Hispanic	2,544	7,460,199	2,353	7,136,093	69,895	1,076,396	-	-	-	-
Asian and Pacific Islander	3,657	9,847,562	3,275	9,141,945	74,798	1,083,042	-	-	-	-

Source: 1987 Economic Censuses, Survey of Minority-Owned Business Enterprises: Summary, U.S. Department of Commerce, Bureau of the Census, 1991, p. 81. Primary source: 1987 Survey of Minority-Owned Businesses. *Minority-Owned Businesses*, Washington, D.C.: U.S. Government Printing Office, 1990. Detail may not add to total because of rounding and because a firm may be included in more than one minority group.

★ 685 ★

Businesses

Minority-Owned Firms: Trends in Firm Ownership, 1982-87

The number of firms owned and the percent change, from 1982 to 1987, are shown, by race/ethnicity.

Race/ethnicity	Number of firms		Percent change
	1982	1987	
Black	308,260	424,165	37.6
Hispanic	233,975	422,373	80.5
Asian and Pacific Islander	187,691	355,331	89.3
American Indian and Alaska Native	13,573	21,380	57.5
All minorities	741,640	1,213,750	63.7
All U.S. firms (including minorities)	12,000,000	13,700,000	14.2

Source: "Black entrepeneurship." *Wall Street Journal* (3 April 1992), p. R4. Primary source: Bureau of the Census.

★ 686 ★

Businesses

Minority-Owned Firms: Trends in Firm Sales, 1982-87

Firm sales and the percent change from 1982 to 1987, are shown, by race/ethnicity.

Race/ethnicity	Total sales (in millions of dollars)		Percent change
	1982	1987	
Black	9,619	19,763	105.5
Hispanic	11,759	24,732	110.3
Asian and Pacific Islander	12,654	33,124	161.8
American Indian and Alaska Native	495	911	84.0
All minorities	34,454	77,840	125.9
All U.S. firms	967,500	1,994,800	106.2

Source: "Black entrepeneurship." *Wall Street Journal* (3 April 1992), p. R4. Primary source: Bureau of the Census.

★ 687 ★

Businesses

Minority-Owned Firms: Firm Ownership per 1,000 Population, 1982-87

The number of firms owned, per 1,000 population, is shown, by race/ethnicity, for 1982-87.

Race/ethnicity	1982	1987	Percent change 1982-87
American Indian	8.8	11.8	34.1
Native American	7.4	10.3	39.2
Aleut	58.5	54.0	7.7
Eskimo	36.8	44.4	20.7
Blacks	11.3	14.6	29.2
Hispanics	14.3	20.9	46.2
Mexican	13.7	18.8	37.2
Puerto Rican	6.3	10.9	73.0
Cuban	41.4	62.9	51.9
Other Hispanic	14.2	22.9	61.3
Asian[1]	43.2	57.0	31.9
Asian Indian	51.3	75.7	47.6
Chinese	49.1	63.4	29.1
Japanese	59.3	66.1	11.5
Korean	68.0	102.4	50.6
Vietnamese	14.6	49.6	239.7
Filipino	25.5	32.8	28.6
Hawaiian	16.6	21.5	29.5
Non-Minority	61.9	67.1	8.4

Source: American Demographics (January 1992), p. 34. Primary source: Bureau of the Census, 1982 and 1987 Economic Census and population estimates. *Note:* 1. Data include Pacific Islanders.

★ 688 ★

Businesses

Minority-Owned Firms: Percent Distribution, by Industry

Percentages are shown for 1987.

Industry	American Indian and Alaskan Native	Black	Hispanic	Asian and Pacific Islander
Agricultural services, forestry fishing, and mining	10.0	20.0	45.0	26.0
Construction	3.0	34.0	52.0	12.0
Manufacturing	3.0	27.0	37.0	34.0
Transportation and public utilities	1.0	48.0	35.0	16.0
Wholesale trade	1.0	21.0	38.0	40.0
Retail trade	1.0	29.0	31.0	39.0
Finance, insurance, and real estate	1.0	35.0	29.0	36.0
Services	1.0	37.0	33.0	29.0
Industries not classified	2.0	38.0	36.0	25.0

Source: "Minority-Owned Firms by Industry Division: 1987," *Minority-Owned Businesses,* p. 8. Primary source: 1987 Survey of Minority-Owned Businesses. *Minority-Owned Businesses.* Washington, D.C.: U.S. Government Printing Office, 1990. Percent distributions may not add to 100, since duplication of firms exists among minority groups.

★ 689 ★

Businesses

Minority-Owned Firms: All Industries

The number of firms, employees, sales and receipts, and annual payroll is shown for all industries, by sex and race/ethnicity, for 1987. Dollars are shown in thousands.

Characteristic	All firms		Firms with paid employees				Relative standard error of estimate % for column			
	Firms (number) A	Sales and receipts ($1,000) B	Firms (number) C	Sales and receipts ($1,000) D	Employees (number) E	Annual payroll ($1,000) F	A	B	C	D
All industries	1,213,750	77,839,943	248,149	56,463,624	836,483	9,506,592	-	-	-	-
Minority men	825,441	59,846,993	189,521	43,488,036	623,427	7,180,669	-	-	-	-
Minority women	388,309	17,992,950	58,628	12,975,588	213,056	2,327,923	-	-	1	-
American Indian and Alaska Native	21,380	911,279	3,739	602,789	8,956	109,271	1	1	3	1
Men	15,072	711,166	2,881	468,016	6,660	85,144	1	1	3	1
Women	6,306	200,113	858	134,773	2,296	24,127	3	20	5	2
Black	424,165	19,762,876	70,815	14,130,420	220,467	2,761,105	-	-	-	-
Men	265,887	13,232,364	51,518	9,289,084	147,520	1,820,396	-	-	-	-
Women	158,278	6,530,512	19,297	4,841,336	72,947	940,709	-	-	-	-
Hispanic	422,373	24,731,600	82,908	17,729,432	264,846	3,243,342	-	-	1	-
Men	307,348	20,403,191	66,907	14,715,111	210,749	2,653,099	-	-	1	-
Women	115,025	4,328,409	16,001	3,014,321	54,097	590,243	1	1	1	1

[Continued]

★ 689 ★

Minority-Owned Firms: All Industries

[Continued]

Characteristic	All firms		Firms with paid employees				Relative standard error of estimate % for column			
	Firms (number) A	Sales and receipts ($1,000) B	Firms (number) C	Sales and receipts ($1,000) D	Employees (number) E	Annual payroll ($1,000) F	A	B	C	D
Asian and Pacific Islander	355,331	33,124,326	92,718	24,501,338	351,345	3,501,917	-	-	-	-
Men	243,442	25,988,493	69,675	19,370,068	264,873	2,698,681	-	-	-	-
Women	111,889	7,135,833	23,043	5,131,270	86,472	803,326	1	-	1	-

Source: 1987 Economic Censuses, Survey of Minority-Owned Business Enterprises: Summary, U.S. Department of Commerce, Bureau of the Census, 1991. *Notes:* A dash (-) represents or rounds to zero. Details may not add to total because of rounding and because a firm may be included in more than one minority group.

★ 690 ★

Businesses

Minority-Owned Firms: Agricultural Services

Data are shown for 1987. Trade groups are based on the 1972 Standard Industrial Classification (SIC) system.

Receipts size and minority	All firms		Firms with paid employees				Relative standard error of estimate % for column			
	Firms (number) A	Sales and receipts ($1,000) B	Firms (number) C	Sales and receipts ($1,000) D	Employees (number) E	Annual payroll ($1,000) F	A	B	C	D
Agricultural services, forestry, and fishing	36,864	1,372,297	7,087	858,401	21,706	260,062	-	1	2	1
Minority men	33,861	1,238,555	6,497	770,464	19,701	235,241	1	1	2	1
Minority women	3,003	133,742	590	87,937	2,005	24,821	4	4	6	4
American Indian and Alaska Native	3,661	104,446	371	30,109	486	8,950	2	5	12	8
Men	3,204	93,986	329	28,357	460	8,480	3	5	13	8
Women	457	10,460	42	1,752	26	470	12	23	39	19
Black	7,316	216,742	1,662	144,276	3,078	38,046	-	-	-	-
Men	6,645	176,988	1,482	112,995	2,564	31,652	-	-	-	-
Women	671	39,754	180	31,281	514	6,394	-	-	-	-
Hispanic	16,365	694,937	3,331	479,658	14,449	163,569	1	1	3	2
Men	15,211	645,694	3,096	446,248	13,309	150,316	1	1	3	2
Women	1,154	49,243	235	33,410	1,140	13,253	6	7	11	9
Asian and Pacific Islander	9,726	365,309	1,760	211,467	3,976	52,155	1	2	4	3
Men	8,975	330,533	1,622	189,712	3,635	47,386	1	2	4	3
Women	751	34,776	138	21,755	341	4,769	8	8	15	8
Agricultural services (SIC 07)	27,366	1,098,190	5,818	766,864	21,083	241,874	1	1	2	1
Minority men	25,241	994,220	5,363	689,959	19,131	218,459	1	1	2	1
Minority women	2,125	103,970	455	76,905	1,952	23,415	4	3	6	4
American Indian and Alaska Native	444	19,081	75	12,534	339	4,120	9	2	14	2
Black	6,155	189,980	1,474	134,886	2,984	36,210	-	-	-	-
Hispanic	14,752	648,290	3,210	464,607	14,197	160,618	1	2	3	2
Asian and Pacific Islander	6,184	248,865	1,093	161,548	3,836	43,482	2	2	4	3
Forestry (SIC 08)	728	21,520	186	13,316	317	3,486	-	-	-	-
Minority men	665	20,100	172	12,724	309	3,378	-	-	-	-
Minority women	63	1,420	14	592	8	108	-	-	-	-

[Continued]

★ 690 ★

Minority-Owned Firms: Agricultural Services
[Continued]

Receipts size and minority	All firms		Firms with paid employees				Relative standard error of estimate % for column			
	Firms (number) A	Sales and receipts ($1,000) B	Firms (number) C	Sales and receipts ($1,000) D	Employees (number) E	Annual payroll ($1,000) F	A	B	C	D
American Indian and Alaska Native	89	1,368	12	803	30	266	-	-	-	-
Black	417	11,416	119	6,129	85	1,274	-	-	-	-
Hispanic	184	8,263	45	6,065	195	1,882	-	-	-	-
Asian and Pacific Islander	43	861	11	664	17	160	-	-	-	-
Fishing, hunting, and trapping (SIC 09)	8,770	252,587	1,083	78,221	306	14,702	1	3	7	6
Minority men	7,955	224,235	962	67,781	261	13,404	1	3	7	7
Minority women	815	28,352	121	10,440	45	1,298	8	12	23	16
American Indian and Alaska Native	3,128	83,997	284	16,772	117	4,564	3	6	16	14
Black	744	15,346	69	3,261	9	562	-	-	-	-
Hispanic	1,429	38,384	76	8,986	57	1,069	3	3	13	4
Asian and Pacific Islander	3,499	115,583	656	49,255	123	8,513	2	5	8	9

Source: 1987 Economic Censuses, Survey of Minority-Owned Business Enterprises: Summary, U.S. Department of Commerce, Bureau of the Census, 1991, p. 9. Primary source: 1987 Survey of Minority-Owned Businesses. Minority-Owned Businesses, Washington, D.C., U.S. Government Printing Office, 1990. Arranged by the editors. Details may not add to total because of rounding and because a firm may be included in more than one minority group. Note: A dash (-) represents zero.

★ 691 ★

Businesses

Minority-Owned Firms: Construction

Data are shown for 1987. Trade groups are based on the 1972 Standard Industrial Classification (SIC) system.

Major industry group and minority	SIC code	All firms		Firms with paid employees				Relative standard error of estimate % for column			
		Firms (number) A	Sales and receipts ($1,000) B	Firms (number) C	Sales and receipts ($1,000) D	Employees (number) E	Annual payroll ($1,000) F	A	B	C	D
Construction		107,650	6,903,022	29,721	5,196,718	69,878	1,222,932	-	-	1	-
Minority men		101,791	5,933,726	27,594	4,384,423	59,918	1,037,318	-	-	1	-
Minority women		5,859	969,296	2,127	812,295	9,960	185,614	2	1	2	-
American Indian and Alaska Native		2,832	155,784	835	(D)	(D)	(D)	3	2	5	(D)
Men		2,606	132,389	769	102,303	1,445	25,038	3	3	5	3
Women		226	23,395	66	(D)	(D)	(D)	10	5	11	(D)
Black		36,763	2,174,399	11,081	1,668,952	27,427	424,665	-	-	-	-
Men		34,455	1,697,563	10,078	1,266,771	21,966	325,833	-	-	-	-
Women		2,308	476,836	1,003	402,181	5,461	98,832	-	-	-	-
Hispanic		55,516	3,438,706	14,717	2,646,244	34,684	631,477	-	1	2	1
Men		53,092	3,117,491	13,901	2,365,673	31,241	565,954	1	1	2	1
Women		2,424	321,217	816	280,571	3,443	65,523	5	2	6	1
Asian and Pacific Islander		13,391	1,224,190	3,330	(D)	(D)	(D)	1	1	2	(D)
Men		12,419	1,067,003	3,067	720,819	5,995	137,159	1	1	2	1
Women		972	157,187	263	(D)	(D)	(D)	5	1	7	(D)

[Continued]

★ 691 ★

Minority-Owned Firms: Construction
[Continued]

Major industry group and minority	SIC code	All firms		Firms with paid employees				Relative standard error of estimate % for column			
		Firms (number) A	Sales and receipts ($1,000) B	Firms (number) C	Sales and receipts ($1,000) D	Employees (number) E	Annual payroll ($1,000) F	A	B	C	D
General building contractors	15	17,236	1,981,974	5,846	1,575,624	14,984	280,998	1	1	2	1
Minority men		16,074	1,618,344	5,311	1,367,321	12,821	235,519	1	1	2	1
Minority women		1,162	363,630	535	308,303	2,163	45,479	4	1	4	1
American Indian and Alaska Native		461	34,219	175	28,153	251	5,269	6	5	11	5
Black		6,285	635,702	2,291	516,768	5,227	92,940	-	-	-	-
Hispanic		7,990	860,943	2,522	689,809	7,271	138,470	1	1	3	1
Asian and Pacific Islander		2,632	486,113	909	374,588	2,491	51,694	2	1	3	1
Heavy construction contractors	16	1,683	389,244	668	361,861	4,582	79,241	1	-	2	-
Minority men		1,546	357,742	588	331,703	4,216	70,387	2	-	2	-
Minority women		137	31,502	80	30,158	366	8,854	8	1	8	1
American Indian and Alaska Native		93	(D)	38	15,549	178	3,902	3	(D)	-	-
Black		638	155,949	275	144,259	2,118	32,911	-	-	-	-
Hispanic		859	205,100	318	192,606	2,137	39,942	2	1	5	1
Asian and Pacific Islander		107	(D)	40	15,996	208	3,746	10	(D)	4	2
Special trade contractors	17	87,920	4,209,682	23,008	3,102,746	49,530	844,885	-	-	1	1
Minority men		83,514	3,700,436	21,538	2,658,510	42,296	718,565	-	1	1	1
Minority women		4,406	509,246	1,470	444,236	7,234	126,320	3	1	3	1
American Indian and Alaska Native		2,268	97,410	619	72,247	1,166	19,299	3	3	6	4
Black		29,631	1,313,819	8,462	972,180	19,817	292,741	-	-	-	-
Hispanic		46,383	2,266,204	11,803	1,691,285	25,032	446,520	1	1	2	1
Asian and Pacific Islander		10,331	579,278	2,308	404,939	4,035	95,933	1	1	33	1
Subdividers and developers, n.e.c.	6552	811	322,122	199	156,487	782	17,808	2	-	2	-
Minority men		657	257,204	157	126,889	585	12,847	1	1	2	-
Minority women		154	64,918	42	29,598	197	4,961	6	-	3	1
American Indian and Alaska Native		10	(D)	3	(D)	(D)	(D)	-	(D)	-	(D)
Black		209	68,929	53	35,745	265	6,073	-	-	-	-
Hispanic		284	106,461	74	72,544	244	6,545	2	1	4	1
Asian and Pacific Islander		321	(D)	73	(D)	(D)	(D)	3	(D)	4	(D)

Source: 1987 Economic Censuses, Survey of Minority-Owned Business Enterprises: Summary, U.S. Department of Commerce, Bureau of the Census, 1991, p. 10. Primary source: 1987 Survey of Minority-Owned Businesses. *Minority-Owned Businesses*, Washington, D.C., U.S. Government Printing Office, 1990. Arranged by the editors. *Notes:* (D) stands for data withheld to avoid disclosure of competitive information. Details may not add to total because of rounding and because a firm may be included in more than one minority group. n.e.c. stands for not elsewhere classified. A dash (-) represents zero.

★ 692 ★

Businesses

Minority-Owned Firms: Farm Operators

Figures are shown in thousands.

Race/ethnicity	All farms		Farms with sales of of $10,000 and over	
	1982	1987	1982	1987
Total operators	2,241	2,088	1,143	1,060
White	2,187	2,043	1,127	1,046
Black	33	23	7	4
Asian or Pacific Islander	8	8	5	5
American Indian, Eskimos, and Aleuts	7	7	2	2
Other	6	7	2	2
Operators of Hispanic origin[1]	16	17	6	6

Source: U.S. Department of Commerce. Bureau of the Census. *1992 Statistical Abstract of the United States (112th ed.).* Washington, DC: U.S. Government Printing Office, p. 647. Primary source: U.S. Bureau of the Census, *1987 Census of Agriculture*, Vol. 1. *Notes:* 1. Operators of Hispanic origin may be of any race. 2. Excludes not reported.

★ 693 ★

Businesses

Minority-Owned Firms: Finance, Insurance, and Real Estate

Data are shown for 1987. Trade groups are based on the 1972 Standard Industrial Classification (SIC) system.

Major industry group and minority	SIC code	All firms		Firms with paid employees				Relative standard error of estimate % for column			
		Firms (number)	Sales and receipts ($1,000)	Firms (number)	Sales and receipts ($1,000)	Employees (number)	Annual payroll ($1,000)	A	B	C	D
		A	B	C	D	E	F				
Finance, insurance, and real estate		76,442	2,759,980	7,340	1,364,515	17,066	252,776	-	-	1	-
Minority men		47,936	1,942,427	5,388	997,955	12,337	179,468	1	1	1	1
Minority women		28,506	817,553	1,952	366,560	4,729	73,308	1	1	3	1
American Indian and Alaska Native		614	20,192	71	(D)	(D)	(D)	7	7	19	(D)
Men		389	11,508	44	4,420	167	2,021	9	11	21	6
Women		225	8,684	27	(D)	(D)	(D)	13	7	37	(D)
Black		26,989	804,252	2,514	464,389	5,938	94,718	-	-	-	-
Men		15,971	478,540	1,783	267,282	3,607	51,137	-	-	-	-
Women		11,018	325,712	731	197,107	2,331	43,581	-	-	-	-
Hispanic		22,106	864,282	2,236	433,851	4,960	80,882	1	1	2	1
Men		14,565	673,894	1,702	361,560	3,977	67,008	1	1	3	1
Women		7,541	190,388	534	72,291	983	13,874	2	2	5	3
Asian and Pacific Islander		27,297	1,086,855	2,558	(D)	(D)	(D)	1	1	3	(D)
Men		17,340	787,749	1,887	369,408	4,639	60,104	1	1	3	1
Women		9,957	299,106	671	(D)	(D)	(D)	2	2	6	(D)
Banking	60	86	(D)	82	88,897	881	14,146	-	(D)	-	-
Minority men		56	71,995	54	(D)	(D)	(D)	-	-	-	(D)
Minority women		30	(D)	28	(D)	(D)	(D)	-	(D)	-	(D)

[Continued]

★ 693 ★

Minority-Owned Firms: Finance, Insurance, and Real Estate
[Continued]

Major industry group and minority	SIC code	All firms		Firms with paid employees				Relative standard error of estimate % for column			
		Firms (number) A	Sales and receipts ($1,000) B	Firms (number) C	Sales and receipts ($1,000) D	Employees (number) E	Annual payroll ($1,000) F	A	B	C	D
American Indian and Alaska Native		1	(D)	1	(D)	(D)	(D)	-	(D)	-	(D)
Black		35	17,402	34	(D)	(D)	(D)	-	-	-	(D)
Hispanic		34	13,858	31	(D)	(D)	(D)	-	-	-	(D)
Asian and Pacific Islander		18	(D)	18	(D)	(D)	(D)	-	(D)	-	(D)
Credit agencies other than banks	61	175	(D)	141	30,116	624	9,775	-	(D)	-	-
Minority men		114	21,509	91	20,568	438	5,945	-	-	-	-
Minority women		61	(D)	50	9,548	186	3,830	-	(D)	-	-
American Indian and Alaska Native		1	(D)	1	(D)	(D)	(D)	-	(D)	-	(D)
Black		45	13,429	35	12,926	283	5,015	-	-	-	-
Hispanic		91	10,925	78	10,507	175	2,595	-	-	-	-
Asian and Pacific Islander		40	6,852	27	(D)	(D)	(D)	-	-	-	(D)
Security, commodity brokers and services	62	1,981	165,577	192	112,452	394	22,174	2	1	6	-
Minority men		1,521	147,545	153	101,256	334	19,776	2	1	8	-
Minority women		460	18,032	39	11,196	60	2,398	6	7	6	1
American Indian and Alaska Native		30	(D)	12	369	3	54	34	(D)	58	35
Black		711	22,723	62	11,031	77	2,856	-	-	-	-
Hispanic		525	89,792	67	69,857	173	12,707	4	1	12	1
Asian and Pacific Islander		733	(D)	52	31,234	142	6,559	4	(D)	13	-
Insurance carriers	63	78	13,132	38	(D)	(D)	(D)	-	-	-	(D)
Minority men		49	6,472	21	5,516	99	1,523	-	-	-	-
Minority women		29	6,660	17	(D)	(D)	(D)	-	-	-	(D)
American Indian and Alaska Native		-	-	-	-	-	-				
Black		36	6,220	16	4,532	52	611	-	-	-	-
Hispanic		33	5,086	15	4,567	71	1,115	-	-	-	-
Asian and Pacific Islander		9	1,826	7	(D)	(D)	(D)	-	-	-	(D)
Insurance agents, brokers, and services		64	20,793	576,848	305,429	3,979	62,749	1	1	2	1
Minority men		16,220	461,412	2,119	235,115	3,075	45,780	1	1	2	1
Minority women		4,573	115,436	457	70,314	904	16,969	2	2	6	2
American Indian and Alaska Native		152	5,051	20	2,321	40	500	15	21	27	1
Black		7,956	188,690	992	112,760	1,454	24,998	-	-	-	-
Hispanic		6,013	209,229	926	122,195	1,668	24,434	2	2	4	2
Asian and Pacific Islander		6,829	175,748	646	68,808	830	13,009	2	3	6	4
Real estate	65 pt.	46,253	1,671,457	3,864	772,820	10,604	133,755	-	1	2	1
Minority men		24,561	1,072,191	2,596	529,643	7,440	90,765	1	1	2	1
Minority women		20,692	599,266	1,268	243,177	3,164	42,990	1	1	3	1
American Indian and Alaska Native		370	12,746	33	7,710	150	1,668	10	7	31	7
Black		15,552	505,936	1,182	292,454	3,662	54,274	-	-	-	-
Hispanic		12,872	472,278	971	203,480	2,611	35,073	1	1	3	1
Asian and Pacific Islander		16,794	692,242	1,704	273,705	4,224	43,195	1	1	3	2
Combined real estate, insurance, etc.	66	7,959	189,043	430	35,734	333	6,138	1	2	5	3
Minority men		5,335	144,625	344	28,356	256	4,541	2	2	5	4
Minority women		2,624	44,418	86	7,378	77	1,597	3	5	10	9
American Indian and Alaska Native		59	1,212	4	411	9	96	21	34	-	-
Black		2,624	47,360	190	12,893	128	2,533	-	-	-	-

[Continued]

★ 693 ★

Minority-Owned Firms: Finance, Insurance, and Real Estate

[Continued]

Major industry group and minority	SIC code	All firms		Firms with paid employees				Relative standard error of estimate % for column			
		Firms (number) A	Sales and receipts ($1,000) B	Firms (number) C	Sales and receipts ($1,000) D	Employees (number) E	Annual payroll ($1,000) F	A	B	C	D
Hispanic		2,509	59,371	142	9,570	99	1,695	2	3	11	9
Asian and Pacific Islander		2,815	81,980	96	13,195	104	1,894	2	4	14	6
Holding and other investment officers	67 pt.	117	21,487	17	(D)	(D)	(D)	2	3	-	(D)
Minority men		80	16,678	10	(D)	(D)	(D)	4	3	-	(D)
Minority women		37	4,809	7	936	10	231	5	1	-	-
American Indian and Alaska Native		1	(D)	-	-	-	-	-	(D)	-	-
Black		30	2,492	3	(D)	(D)	(D)	-	-	-	(D)
Hispanic		29	3,743	6	(D)	(D)	(D)	-	-	-	(D)
Asian and Pacific Islander		59	(D)	8	(D)	(D)	(D)	4	(D)	-	(D)

Source: 1987 Economic Censuses, Survey of Minority-Owned Business Enterprises: Summary, U.S. Department of Commerce, Bureau of the Census, 1991, pp. 15-16. Primary source: 1987 Survey of Minority-Owned Businesses. *Minority-Owned Businesses*, Washington, D.C., U.S. Government Printing Office, 1990. Arranged by the editors. *Notes:* (D) stands for data withheld to avoid disclosures of competitive information. Details may not add to total because of rounding and because a firm may be included in more than one minority group.

★ 694 ★

Businesses

Minority-Owned Firms: Manufacturing

Data are shown for 1987. Trade groups are based on the 1972 Standard Industrial Classification (SIC) system.

Major industry group and minority	SIC code	All firms		Firms with paid employees				Relative standard error of estimate % for column			
		Firms (number) A	Sales and receipts ($1,000) B	Firms (number) C	Sales and receipts ($1,000) D	Employees (number) E	Annual payroll ($1,000) F	A	B	C	D
Manufacturing		29,879	3,961,128	10,126	3,584,420	76,741	946,089	-	-	1	-
Minority men		21,464	2,885,678	7,677	2,590,911	53,640	661,987	1	-	1	-
Minority women		8,415	1,075,450	2,449	993,509	23,101	284,102	1	-	2	-
American Indian and Alaska Native		911	63,563	148	(D)	(D)	(D)	4	1	5	(D)
Men		666	44,690	125	37,721	922	10,231	4	1	6	1
Women		245	18,873	23	(D)	(D)	(D)	10	3	6	(D)
Black		8,004	1,023,104	2,612	927,105	13,684	244,038	-	-	-	-
Men		6,349	639,407	2,111	563,806	8,719	146,829	-	-	-	-
Women		1,655	383,697	501	363,299	4,965	97,209	-	-	-	-
Hispanic		11,090	1,449,913	3,760	1,308,124	26,261	333,969	1	-	2	-
Men		8,358	1,085,513	2,890	967,467	18,468	242,123	1	1	2	1
Women		2,732	361,400	870	340,657	7,793	91,846	3	1	4	1
Asian and Pacific Islander		10,121	1,461,396	3,701	(D)	(D)	(D)	1	-	1	(D)
Men		6,253	1,135,387	2,616	1,041,615	26,077	269,851	1	-	2	-
Women		3,868	326,009	1,085	(D)	(D)	(D)	2	1	3	(D)
Food and kindred products	20	1,326	318,238	479	293,678	4,124	47,078	1	-	2	-
Minority men		871	252,347	360	233,092	3,200	35,092	2	1	2	-
Minority women		457	65,891	119	60,586	924	11,986	4	-	4	-
American Indian and Alaska Native		9	314	2	(D)	(D)	(D)	-	-	-	(D)
Black		286	60,595	70	57,181	699	11,019	-	-	-	-
Hispanic		589	151,632	240	140,141	2,100	23,442	3	1	3	1

[Continued]

★ 694 ★

Minority-Owned Firms: Manufacturing
[Continued]

Major industry group and minority	SIC code	All firms		Firms with paid employees				Relative standard error of estimate % for column			
		Firms (number)	Sales and receipts ($1,000)	Firms (number)	Sales and receipts ($1,000)	Employees (number)	Annual payroll ($1,000)	A	B	C	D
		A	B	C	D	E	F				
Asian and Pacific Islander		459	110,276	170	(D)	(D)	(D)	2	-	-	(D)
Tobacco manufactures	21	7	860	7	860	32	180	-	-	-	-
Minority men		7	860	7	860	32	180	-	-	-	-
Minority women		-	-	-	-	-	-	-	-	-	-
American Indian and Alaska Native		-	-	-	-	-	-	-	-	-	-
Black		-	-	-	-	-	-	-	-	-	-
Hispanic		7	860	7	860	32	180	-	-	-	-
Asian and Pacific Islander		-	-	-	-	-	-	-	-	-	-
Textile mill products	22	477	53,088	126	47,306	1,000	12,328	1	-	-	-
Minority men		225	35,093	72	31,285	581	6,852	-	-	-	-
Minority women		252	17,995	54	16,021	419	5,476	2	-	-	-
American Indian and Alaska Native		13	262	2	(D)	(D)	(D)	-	-	-	(D)
Black		74	9,954	25	9,384	115	3,070	-	-	-	-
Hispanic		188	21,361	56	18,894	437	5,229	1	-	-	-
Asian and Pacific Islander		208	22,337	47	(D)	(D)	(D)	3	-	-	(D)
Apparel and other textile products	23	6,536	847,492	2,720	794,509	36,611	278,739	1	1	2	1
Minority men		2,913	496,559	1,540	469,085	22,578	170,394	2	1	2	1
Minority women		3,623	350,933	1,180	325,424	14,033	108,345	2	1	3	1
American Indian and Alaska Native		76	(D)	6	(D)	(D)	(D)	14	(D)	24	(D)
Black		552	64,671	146	60,859	1,360	16,392	-	-	-	-
Hispanic		1,713	278,810	833	267,198	10,294	84,350	2	1	4	1
Asian and Pacific Islander		4,265	(D)	1,781	(D)	(D)	(D)	1	(D)	2	(D)
Lumber and wood products	24	5,046	344,167	1,838	278,091	5,056	68,168	1	-	1	1
Minority men		4,697	294,054	1,703	234,657	4,234	55,632	1	1	1	1
Minority women		349	50,113	135	43,434	822	12,536	4	1	6	1
American Indian and Alaska Native		274	22,230	78	18,796	407	5,155	7	2	10	1
Black		3,720	211,281	1,438	163,852	2,932	41,362	-	-	-	-
Hispanic		840	86,082	250	74,287	1,410	17,883	3	2	5	2
Asian and Pacific Islander		228	25,214	77	21,654	314	3,848	8	3	17	3
Furniture and fixtures	25	1,090	146,586	386	132,487	2,490	32,053	2	1	3	1
Minority men		931	127,483	340	114,921	2,151	26,779	2	1	4	1
Minority women		159	19,103	46	17,566	339	5,274	10	1	7	-
American Indian and Alaska Native		21	702	2	(D)	(D)	(D)	19	17	-	(D)
Black		226	29,812	65	27,429	545	7,960	-	-	-	-
Hispanic		657	88,946	249	80,165	1,617	19,810	3	1	5	1
Asian and Pacific Islander		202	28,309	73	(D)	(D)	(D)	3	-	-	(D)
Paper and allied products	26	195	(D)	51	(D)	(D)	(D)	-	(D)	-	(D)
Minority men		140	65,742	42	64,389	657	12,621	-	-	-	-
Minority women		55	(D)	9	(D)	(D)	(D)	-	(D)	-	(D)
American Indian and Alaska Native		2	(D)	-	-	-	-	-	(D)	-	-
Black		55	26,230	17	25,666	287	5,154	-	-	-	-
Hispanic		87	11,499	19	10,553	111	1,742	-	-	-	-
Asian and Pacific Islander		55	(D)	15	(D)	(D)	(D)	-	(D)	-	(D)

[Continued]

★ 694 ★

Minority-Owned Firms: Manufacturing
[Continued]

Major industry group and minority	SIC code	All firms		Firms with paid employees				Relative standard error of estimate % for column			
		Firms (number) A	Sales and receipts ($1,000) B	Firms (number) C	Sales and receipts ($1,000) D	Employees (number) E	Annual payroll ($1,000) F	A	B	C	D
Printing and publishing	27	4,823	523,128	1,626	462,676	6,394	115,930	1	1	3	1
Minority men		3,652	359,175	1,246	314,458	4,551	76,998	2	1	3	1
Minority women		1,171	163,953	380	148,218	1,843	38,932	4	2	6	2
American Indian and Alaska Native		50	2,501	11	2,192	58	680	19	1	-	-
Black		1,394	126,488	360	109,971	1,629	35,538	-	-	-	-
Hispanic		1,886	179,062	575	158,977	2,409	41,942	3	2	5	2
Asian and Pacific Islander		1,532	226,151	690	202,036	2,474	41,491	3	2	5	2
Chemicals and allied products	28	241	96,977	89	91,600	890	17,021	1	-	-	-
Minority men		195	87,925	74	83,257	806	14,815	2	-	-	-
Minority women		46	9,052	15	8,343	84	2,206	-	-	-	-
American Indian and Alaska Native		4	146	2	(D)	(D)	(D)	-	-	-	(D)
Black		65	57,468	23	56,511	498	10,329	-	-	-	-
Hispanic		72	20,157	28	19,432	179	3,135	-	-	-	-
Asian and Pacific Islander		100	19,206	36	(D)	(D)	(D)	3	-	-	(D)
Petroleum and coal products	29	8	(D)	6	(D)	(D)	(D)	-	(D)	-	(D)
Minority men		6	(D)	4	(D)	(D)	(D)	-	(D)	-	(D)
Minority women		2	(D)	2	(D)	(D)	(D)	-	(D)	-	(D)
American Indian and Alaska Native		-	-	-	-	-	-	-	-	-	-
Black		1	(D)	-	-	-	-	-	(D)	-	-
Hispanic		3	(D)	2	(D)	(D)	(D)	-	(D)	-	(D)
Asian and Pacific Islander		4	(D)	4	(D)	(D)	(D)	-	(D)	-	(D)
Rubber and miscellaneous plastics products	30	350	91,535	129	88,197	1,190	21,539	-	-	-	-
Minority men		260	74,426	101	71,610	870	16,501	-	-	-	-
Minority women		90	17,109	28	16,587	320	5,038	-	-	-	-
American Indian and Alaska Native		5	251	1	(D)	(D)	(D)	-	-	-	(D)
Black		71	11,844	29	11,383	214	4,231	-	-	-	-
Hispanic		176	50,765	62	48,960	698	12,891	-	-	-	-
Asian and Pacific Islander		101	30,244	38	(D)	(D)	(D)	-	-	-	(D)
Leather and leather products	31	362	35,834	92	31,313	590	7,701	3	-	-	-
Minority men		248	28,972	73	25,335	460	5,665	3	1	-	-
Minority women		114	6,862	19	5,978	130	2,036	6	-	-	-
American Indian and Alaska Native		18	212	2	(D)	(D)	(D)	-	-	-	(D)
Black		42	5,187	10	4,860	117	1,503	-	-	-	-
Hispanic		194	22,108	53	20,053	362	5,038	-	-	-	-
Asian and Pacific Islander		112	8,497	29	(D)	(D)	(D)	9	2	-	(D)
Stone, clay, and glass products	32	909	93,326	208	83,612	922	17,061	2	1	2	-
Minority men		595	63,485	172	56,673	654	11,906	3	1	3	-
Minority women		314	29,841	36	26,939	268	5,155	3	1	4	-
American Indian and Alaska Native		60	2,040	7	1,493	16	225	12	2	-	-
Black		193	30,428	61	29,637	349	5,742	-	-	-	-
Hispanic		400	38,880	106	33,782	370	7,203	3	1	5	1
Asian and Pacific Islander		263	22,175	35	18,717	187	3,897	9	1	-	-
Primary metal industry	33	219	97,553	66	(D)	(D)	(D)	4	-	-	(D)
Minority men		187	(D)	48	37,065	799	8,784	5	(D)	-	-

[Continued]

★ 694 ★

Minority-Owned Firms: Manufacturing
[Continued]

Major industry group and minority	SIC code	All firms		Firms with paid employees				Relative standard error of estimate % for column			
		Firms (number) A	Sales and receipts ($1,000) B	Firms (number) C	Sales and receipts ($1,000) D	Employees (number) E	Annual payroll ($1,000) F	A	B	C	D
Minority women		32	(D)	18	(D)	(D)	(D)	-	(D)	-	(D)
American Indian and Alaska Native		10	(D)	2	(D)	(D)	(D)	-	(D)	-	(D)
Black		54	8,122	12	7,420	76	772	-	-	-	-
Hispanic		104	53,897	32	(D)	(D)	(D)	-	-	-	(D)
Asian and Pacific Islander		51	(D)	20	(D)	(D)	(D)	19	(D)	-	(D)
Fabricated metal products	34	1,835	285,963	591	259,079	3,714	75,695	2	1	5	1
Minority men		1,563	189,915	485	166,400	2,527	44,356	2	1	5	1
Minority women		272	96,048	106	92,679	1,187	31,339	9	1	14	1
American Indian and Alaska Native		91	2,153	6	1,356	16	239	10	3	-	-
Black		338	116,191	106	111,785	1,271	33,167	-	-	-	-
Hispanic		1,140	107,976	386	91,969	1,792	28,303	2	2	7	2
Asian and Pacific Islander		275	60,548	94	54,614	651	14,166	3	1	5	1
Machinery, except electrical	35	2,003	249,327	701	222,707	3,074	63,193	2	1	4	1
Minority men		1,774	218,975	612	194,888	2,534	52,772	2	1	5	1
Minority women		229	30,352	89	27,819	540	10,421	10	2	9	2
American Indian and Alaska Native		34	4,090	8	3,635	44	1,042	11	6	17	6
Black		271	45,711	95	42,566	672	15,800	-	-	-	-
Hispanic		1,148	120,136	420	104,482	1,521	27,146	3	2	7	2
Asian and Pacific Islander		562	82,936	188	75,561	899	20,320	4	2	6	2
Electric and electronic equipment	36	1,037	314,557	250	298,577	4,333	79,415	1	-	3	-
Minority men		700	224,892	204	211,605	3,455	59,544	2	1	4	-
Minority women		337	89,665	46	86,972	878	19,871	5	-	3	-
American Indian and Alaska Native		8	4,250	3	4,236	59	630	31	-	-	-
Black		136	113,567	34	112,422	1,594	26,054	-	-	-	-
Hispanic		295	39,990	67	37,233	670	13,168	1	-	-	-
Asian and Pacific Islander		601	156,903	147	144,768	2,011	39,582	3	1	5	1
Transportation equipment	37	236	161,229	113	156,009	2,063	39,334	-	-	-	-
Minority men		197	146,418	89	141,533	1,761	34,806	-	-	-	-
Minority women		39	14,811	24	14,476	302	4,528	-	-	-	-
American Indian and Alaska Native		7	694	4	(D)	(D)	(D)	-	-	-	(D)
Black		57	69,685	24	68,917	902	18,396	-	-	-	-
Hispanic		129	74,747	66	70,875	938	17,821	-	-	-	-
Asian and Pacific Islander		48	17,023	22	(D)	(D)	(D)	-	-	-	(D)
Instruments and related products	38	187	26,979	78	(D)	(D)	(D)	-	-	-	(D)
Minority men		156	21,765	65	(D)	(D)	(D)	-	-	-	(D)
Minority women		31	5,214	13	4,706	59	1,082	-	-	-	-
American Indian and Alaska Native		3	14	-	-	-	-	-	-	-	-
Black		31	11,291	12	10,829	122	3,391	-	-	-	-
Hispanic		68	5,581	21	(D)	(D)	(D)	-	-	-	(D)
Asian and Pacific Islander		86	10,096	45	9,258	135	2,077	-	-	-	-
Miscellaneous manufacturing industries	39	2,990	170,602	570	124,418	1,920	27,606	2	2	4	1
Minority men		2,147	129,528	440	93,440	1,460	20,545	3	2	5	1
Minority women		843	41,074	130	30,978	460	7,061	5	2	9	1

[Continued]

★ 694 ★

Minority-Owned Firms: Manufacturing

[Continued]

Major industry group and minority	SIC code	All firms		Firms with paid employees				Relative standard error of estimate % for column			
		Firms (number) A	Sales and receipts ($1,000) B	Firms (number) C	Sales and receipts ($1,000) D	Employees (number) E	Annual payroll ($1,000) F	A	B	C	D
American Indian and Alaska Native		226	4,266	12	2,320	57	530	9	14	-	-
Black		438	(D)	85	16,433	302	4,158	-	(D)	-	-
Hispanic		1,394	(D)	288	53,451	858	11,821	3	(D)	7	3
Asian and Pacific Islander		969	68,340	190	54,365	741	11,650	4	2	7	1

Source: 1987 Economic Censuses, Survey of Minority-Owned Business Enterprises: Summary, U.S. Department of Commerce, Bureau of the Census, 1991, pp. 10-12. Primary source: 1987 Survey of Minority-Owned Businesses. *Minority-Owned Businesses*, Washington, D.C., U.S. Government Printing Office, 1990. Arranged by the editors. *Notes:* (D) stands for data withheld to avoid disclosure of competitive information. Details may not add to total because of rounding and because a firm may be included in more than one minority group. A dash (-) represents zero.

★ 695 ★

Businesses

Minority-Owned Firms: Mining

Data are shown for 1987. Trade groups are based on the 1972 Standard Industrial Classification (SIC) system.

Major industry group and minority	All firms		Firms with paid employees				Relative standard error of estimate % for column			
	Firms (number) A	Sales and receipts ($1,000) B	Firms (number) C	Sales and receipts ($1,000) D	Employees (number) E	Annual payroll ($1,000) F	A	B	C	D
Mining	1,613	103,075	147	76,961	859	14,532	3	1	3	1
Minority men	1,289	80,189	111	58,331	621	10,451	3	2	3	1
Minority women	324	22,886	36	18,630	238	4,081	7	1	7	-
American Indian and Alaska Native	106	4,062	8	1,882	28	522	11	5	-	-
Men	82	3,491	7	(D)	(D)	(D)	11	1	-	(D)
Women	24	571	1	(D)	(D)	(D)	31	37	-	(D)
Black	322	54,071	48	46,013	401	7,003	-	-	-	-
Men	221	38,462	29	31,906	222	3,750	-	-	-	-
Women	101	15,609	19	14,107	179	3,253	-	-	-	-
Hispanic	829	29,836	72	18,498	332	5,272	4	4	6	3
Men	684	25,109	62	15,763	291	4,678	4	5	6	3
Women	145	4,727	10	2,735	41	594	13	5	24	1
Asian and Pacific Islander	360	15,114	19	10,568	98	1,735	7	3	-	-
Men	303	13,128	13	(D)	(D)	(D)	8	4	-	(D)
Women	57	1,986	6	(D)	(D)	(D)	16	4	-	(D)
Metal mining	41	(D)	8	359	15	75	-	(D)	-	-
Minority men	38	(D)	7	(D)	(D)	(D)	-	(D)	-	(D)
Minority women	3	14	1	(D)	(D)	(D)	-	-	-	(D)
American Indian and Alaska Native	11	(D)	2	(D)	(D)	(D)	-	(D)	-	(D)
Black	6	75	3	52	2	13	-	-	-	-
Hispanic	16	244	1	(D)	(D)	(D)	-	-	-	(D)
Asian and Pacific Islander	9	274	2	(D)	(D)	(D)	-	-	-	(D)

[Continued]

★ 695 ★

Minority-Owned Firms: Mining

[Continued]

Major industry group and minority	All firms		Firms with paid employees				Relative standard error of estimate % for column			
	Firms (number) A	Sales and receipts ($1,000) B	Firms (number) C	Sales and receipts ($1,000) D	Employees (number) E	Annual payroll ($1,000) F	A	B	C	D
Anthracite mining	3	23	-	-	-	-	-	-	-	-
Minority men	1	(D)	-	-	-	-	-	(D)	-	-
Minority women	2	(D)	-	-	-	-	-	(D)		
American Indian and Alaska Native	-	-	-	-	-	-	-	-	-	-
Black	3	23	-	-	-	-	-	-	-	-
Hispanic	-	-	-	-	-	-	-	-	-	-
Asian and Pacific Islander	-	-	-	-	-	-	-	-	-	-
Bituminous coal and lignite mining	19	(D)	9	5,074	87	1,447	-	(D)	-	-
Minority men	16	4,311	6	(D)	(D)	(D)	-	-	-	(D)
Minority women	3	(D)	3	(D)	(D)	(D)	-	(D)	-	(D)
American Indian and Alaska Native	3	(D)	-	-	-	-	-	(D)	-	-
Black	9	3,968	6	(D)	(D)	(D)	-	-	-	(D)
Hispanic	4	58	1	(D)	(D)	(D)	-	-	-	(D)
Asian and Pacific Islander	3	(D)	2	(D)	(D)	(D)	-	(D)	-	(D)
Oil and gas extraction	1,448	73,870	100	54,299	543	9,737	3	2	4	1
Minority men	1,149	54,774	75	39,274	361	6,326	3	2	5	1
Minority women	299	19,096	25	15,025	182	3,411	7	2	10	-
American Indian and Alaska Native	80	2,441	5	(D)	(D)	(D)	14	9	-	(D)
Black	270	39,946	26	36,922	241	5,089	-	-	-	-
Hispanic	763	22,917	57	12,283	257	4,098	5	5	8	4
Asian and Pacific Islander	338	8,573	12	(D)	(D)	(D)	7	6	-	(D)
Nonmetallic minerals, except fuels	102	22,382	30	17,229	214	3,273	-	-	-	-
Minority men	85	(D)	23	(D)	(D)	(D)	-	(D)	-	(D)
Minority women	17	(D)	7	(D)	(D)	(D)	-	(D)	-	(D)
American Indian and Alaska Native	12	(D)	1	(D)	(D)	(D)	-	(D)	-	(D)
Black	34	10,039	13	(D)	(D)	(D)	-	-	-	(D)
Hispanic	46	6,617	13	(D)	(D)	(D)	-	-	-	(D)
Asian and Pacific Islander	10	(D)	3	(D)	(D)	(D)	-	(D)	-	(D)

Source: 1987 Economic Censuses, Survey of Minority-Owned Business Enterprises: Summary, U.S. Department of Commerce, Bureau of the Census, 1991, pp. 9-10. Primary source: 1987 Survey of Minority-Owned Businesses. *Minority-Owned Businesses*, Washington, D.C., U.S. Government Printing Office, 1990. Arranged by the editors. Details may not add to total because of rounding and because a firm may be included in more than one minority group. (D) stands for data withheld to avoid disclosure of competitive information. *Note:* A dash (-) represents zero.

★ 696 ★
Businesses

Minority-Owned Firms: Retail Trade

Major industry group and minority	SIC code	All firms		Firms with paid employees				Relative standard error of estimate % for column			
		Firms (number) A	Sales and receipts ($1,000) B	Firms (number) C	Sales and receipts ($1,000) D	Employees (number) E	Annual payroll ($1,000) F	A	B	C	D
Retail trade		226,140	26,903,914	72,310	21,614,740	319,048	2,522,579	-	-	-	-
Minority men		144,463	20,599,037	51,973	16,584,089	233,254	1,849,591	-	.	-	-
Minority women		81,677	6,304,877	20,337	5,030,651	85,794	672,988	1	-	1	-
Black		66,229	5,889,654	14,293	4,861,485	62,530	571,450	-	-	-	-
Men		36,389	3,812,061	9,274	3,124,476	39,383	350,570	-	-	-	-
Women		29,840	2,077,593	5,019	1,737,009	23,147	220,880	-	-	-	-
Hispanic		69,911	7,643,850	20,348	6,095,890	90,584	745,662	-	-	1	-
Men		46,179	6,216,518	15,114	5,011,191	70,394	590,518	1	-	1	-
Women		23,732	1,427,332	5,234	1,084,699	20,190	155,144	1	1	2	1
American Indian and Alaska Native		3,090	268,086	837	210,191	2,427	20,170	3	2	4	1
Men		1,683	202,941	534	163,835	1,730	14,722	4	2	5	2
Women		1,407	65,145	303	46,356	697	5,448	6	4	8	3
Asian and Pacific Islander		88,761	13,315,753	37,399	10,613,682	165,865	1,204,132	-	-	1	-
Men		61,356	10,514,603	27,390	8,398,758	123,261	905,725	1	-	1	-
Women		27,405	2,801,150	10,009	2,214,924	42,604	298,407	1	-	1	-
Building materials and garden supplies	52	2,690	467,932	971	407,114	3,737	49,022	1	1	2	1
Minority men		2,235	319,659	774	269,565	2,358	29,695	2	1	3	1
Minority women		455	148,273	197	137,549	1,379	19,327	5	1	3	1
Black		650	190,291	249	180,137	1,592	23,695	-	-	-	-
Hispanic		1,331	160,841	468	132,177	1,341	16,137	2	2	4	2
American Indian and Alaska Native		61	5,578	17	4,509	35	733	13	4	8	5
Asian and Pacific Islander		687	120,497	255	99,097	837	9,432	3	2	5	2
General merchandise stores	53	4,792	313,788	840	175,190	1,820	16,640	1	1	3	1
Minority men		3,359	219,268	607	113,058	1,129	9,512	2	2	4	1
Minority women		1,433	94,520	233	62,132	691	7,128	4	2	6	2
Black		1,064	44,343	194	26,097	306	2,569	-	-	-	-
Hispanic		1,152	54,795	146	30,974	406	3,237	3	2	10	2
American Indian and Alaska Native		72	8,394	29	6,658	47	385	15	7	15	9
Asian and Pacific Islander		2,564	210,192	481	113,638	1,080	10,612	2	2	5	2
Food stores	54	35,747	6,617,891	13,650	4,915,955	47,917	388,722	-	-	1	-
Minority men		27,146	5,288,873	10,467	3,923,594	37,116	301,489	1	-	1	-
Minority women		8,601	1,329,018	3,183	992,361	10,801	87,233	1	1	2	1
Black		8,952	1,001,462	2,664	719,575	7,946	65,389	-	-	-	-
Hispanic		9,599	1,835,802	3,569	1,383,998	14,010	1418,064	1	1	2	1
American Indian and Alaska Native		301	54,320	108	42,230	356	2,526	9	4	5	2
Asian and Pacific Islander		17,263	3,785,579	7,430	2,810,796	26,075	206,260	1	1	1	1
Automotive dealers and service stations	55	12,275	6,156,369	6,027	5,646,224	26,348	379,555	1	-	1	-
Minority men		10,982	5,122,074	5,329	4,654,304	21,890	304,893	1	-	1	-
Minority women		1,293	1,034,295	698	991,920	4,458	74,662	3	-	3	-
Black		3,690	2,155,680	1,689	2,041,434	9,370	160,026	-	-	-	-
Hispanic		5,627	2,100,213	2,475	1,853,478	9,378	128,153	1	-	2	-
American Indian and Alaska Native		222	65,257	88	55,793	330	3,754	8	1	5	1
Asian and Pacific Islander		2,831	1,880,502	1,825	1,735,791	7,540	90,595	1	-	1	-
Apparel and accessory stores	56	12,687	1,043,144	4,026	754,812	11,225	85,000	1	1	2	1
Minority men		7,416	702,997	2,420	508,514	7,176	54,025	1	1	2	1
Minority women		5,271	340,147	1,606	246,298	4,049	30,975	2	2	3	2

[Continued]

833

★ 696 ★

Minority-Owned Firms: Retail Trade
[Continued]

Major industry group and minority	SIC code	All firms		Firms with paid employees				Relative standard error of estimate % for column			
		Firms (number) A	Sales and receipts ($1,000) B	Firms (number) C	Sales and receipts ($1,000) D	Employees (number) E	Annual payroll ($1,000) F	A	B	C	D
Black		3,061	140,187	771	103,529	1,743	14,959	-	-	-	-
Hispanic		3,472	230,806	1,021	165,431 2	,651	21,258	2	2	3	2
American Indian and Alaska Native		85	5,994	36	4,992 8	8	516	11	4	14	4
Asian and Pacific Islander		6,208	677,045	2,242	489,078 6	,847	49,087	1	1	2	1
Furniture and home furnishings stores	57	7,536	961,045	2,399	756,200	6,338	79,599	1	1	1	1
Minority men		5,629	719,876	1,792	551,983	4,677	57,735	1	1	2	1
Minority women		1,907	241,169	607	204,217	1,661	21,864	3	1	3	1
Black		2,106	187,063	620	152,601	1,452	20,005	-	-	-	-
Hispanic		2,992	349,024	979	279,512	2,771	34,466	1	1	3	1
American Indian and Alaska Native		86	7,915	32	6,373	63	792	10	11	13	13
Asian and Pacific Islander		2,421	428,044	790	327,452	2,111	24,914	2	1	3	1
Eating and drinking places	58	52,202	6,324,180	30,586	5,620,474	186,687	1,198,209	-	-	1	-
Minority men		36,015	4,622,949	21,451	4,106,449	134,485	865,079	1	-	1	-
Minority women		16,187	1,701,231	9,135	1,514,025	52,202	333,130	1	1	1	1
Black		11,834	1,084,468	4,747	918,321	32,343	204,696	-	-	-	-
Hispanic		14,003	1,645,412	7,872	1,449,268	50,662	330,987	1	1	1	1
American Indian and Alaska Native		464	35,251	286	29,492	1,083	6,224	8	7	9	6
Asian and Pacific Islander		26,280	3,599,887	17,887	3,258,630	103,743	663,861	-	-	1	1
Miscellaneous retail	59	98,211	5,019,565	13,811	3,338,771	34,976	325,832	-	1	1	1
Minority men		51,681	3,603,341	9,133	2,456,622	24,423	227,163	1	1	1	1
Minority women		46,530	1,416,224	4,678	882,149	10,553	98,669	1	1	2	1
Black		34,870	1,086,160	3,359	719,791	7,778	80,111	-	-	-	-
Hispanic		31,735	1,266,957	3,818	801,052	9,365	93,360	1	1	3	1
American Indian and Alaska Native		1,799	85,377	241	60,144	425	5,240	5	4	10	3
Asian and Pacific Islander		30,507	2,614,007	6,489	1,779,200	17,632	149,371	1	1	2	1

Source: 1987 Economic Censuses, Survey of Minority-Owned Business Enterprises: Summary, U.S. Department of Commerce, Bureau of the Census, 1991, pp. 14-15. Primary source: 1987 Survey of Minority-Owned Businesses. *Minority-Owned Businesses,* Washington, D.C.: U.S. Government Printing Office, 1990. Arranged by the editors. Details may not add to total because of rounding and because a firm may be included in more than one minority group. *Notes:* This table is based on the 1972 SIC system. A Dash (-) indicates data were unavailable.

★ 697 ★

Businesses

Minority-Owned Firms: Services

Detail may not add to total because of rounding and because a firm may be included in more than one minority group. Data are shown for 1987. Industry groups are based on the 1972 Standard Industrial Classification (SIC) system.

Major industry group and minority	All firms		Firms with paid employees				Relative standard error of estimate (percent) for column --			
	Firms (Number) A	Sales and receipts ($1,000) B	Firms (numbers) C	Sales and receipts ($1,000) D	Employees (Number) E	Annual Payroll ($1,000) F	A	B	C	D
Services	562,559	21,990,719	98,110	14,577,051	280,181	3,384,329	-	-	-	-
Minority men	337,630	16,279,824	71,314	11,152,064	205,861	2,520,901	-	-	-	-
Minority women	224,929	5,710,895	26,796	3,424,987	74,320	863,428	-	-	1	-
American Indian and Alaska Native	7,604	178,165	1,073	108,396	2,297	24,390	2	2	5	2

[Continued]

★ 697 ★

Minority-Owned Firms: Services
[Continued]

Major industry group and minority	All firms		Firms with paid employees				Relative standard error of estimate (percent) for column --			
	Firms (Number) A	Sales and receipts ($1,000) B	Firms (numbers) C	Sales and receipts ($1,000) D	Employees (Number) E	Annual Payroll ($1,000) F	A	B	C	D
Men	4,422	121,878	744	76,074	1,409	16,262	3	3	6	3
Women	3,182	56,287	329	32,322	888	8,128	4	4	9	4
Black	209,547	6,120,084	29,963	3,888,212	89,700	1,077,437	-	-	-	-
Men	111,576	3,862,054	19,783	2,521,990	58,855	702,653	-	-	-	-
Women	97,971	2,258,030	10,180	1,366,222	30,845	374,784	-	-	-	-
Hispanic	184,372	6,031,406	29,750	3,774,117	74,427	941,588	-	-	1	1
Men	118,156	4,793,242	22,738	3,109,238	57,664	754,106	1	1	1	1
Women	66,216	1,238,164	7,012	664,879	16,763	187,482	1	1	2	1
Asian and Pacific Islander	165,342	9,880,868	38,176	6,962,276	117,946	1,387,293	-	-	1	-
Men	106,053	7,653,846	28,671	5,551,402	90,947	1,080,001	1	-	1	-
Women	59,289	2,227,022	9,505	1,410,874	26,999	307,292	1	1	2	1
Hotels and other lodging places	10,499	1,588,435	5,345	1,346,880	32,345	234,823	1	-	1	1
Minority men	7,498	1,245,764	4,134	1,060,050	25,073	180,130	1	1	1	1
Minority women	3,001	342,671	1,211	286,830	7,272	54,693	2	1	2	1
American Indian and Alaska Native	102	5,734	34	5,090	98	788	15	3	10	3
Black	1,734	128,256	553	94,028	2,698	22,334	-	-	-	-
Hispanic	973	112,551	315	92,996	2,284	23,342	4	1	6	1
Asian and Pacific Islander	7,809	1,366,121	4,507	1,177,169	27,682	192,406	1	1	1	1
Personal services	138,765	3,162,616	20,732	1,669,271	46,675	427,226	-	1	1	1
Minority men	68,771	1,927,822	12,067	1,097,981	29,342	270,185	1	1	1	1
Minority women	69,994	1,234,794	8,665	571,290	17,333	157,041	1	1	2	1
American Indian and Alaska Native	1,719	26,547	223	14,128	519	4,388	5	6	11	9
Black	56,772	959,696	6,246	427,283	12,108	109,773	-	-	-	-
Hispanic	44,872	893,064	6,111	430,645	13,688	129,379	1	1	2	2
Asian and Pacific Islander	36,392	1,318,400	8,304	819,467	21,249	190,277	1	1	2	1
Business services	166,666	4,510,917	19,755	2,592,828	63,552	799,677	-	-	1	1
Minority men	107,207	3,232,646	14,513	1,832,968	46,225	574,717	-	1	1	1
Minority women	59,459	1,278,271	5,242	759,860	17,327	224,960	1	1	2	1
American Indian and Alaska Native	2,532	48,601	319	23,585	545	6,238	5	5	12	5
Black	59,177	1,570,161	8,021	1,047,390	32,636	373,456	-	-	-	-
Hispanic	59,948	1,419,790	6,716	747,056	18,979	235,949	1	1	2	1
Asian and Pacific Islander	46,066	1,523,290	4,847	814,432	12,913	202,894	1	1	3	1
Auto repair, services, and garages	32,861	1,765,545	9,328	1,302,474	19,942	270,583	-	1	1	1
Minority men	30,814	1,580,288	8,503	1,142,551	17,218	230,066	1	1	1	1
Minority women	2,047	185,257	825	159,923	2,724	40,517	3	2	4	2
American Indian and Alaska Native	538	20,704	134	14,111	226	2,710	8	7	11	8
Black	11,801	426,584	2,767	271,836	4,543	57,223	-	-	-	-
Hispanic	15,824	836,738	4,522	622,052	9,749	139,178	1	1	2	1
Asian and Pacific Islander	5,072	499,491	2,022	405,607	5,592	74,176	2	1	2	1
Miscellaneous repair services	17,321	623,735	3,431	394,622	6,736	89,471	1	1	2	1
Minority men	15,834	557,412	3,050	344,546	5,839	76,923	1	1	3	1
Minority women	1,487	66,323	381	50,076	897	12,548	4	3	6	3
American Indian and Alaska Native	300	11,105	53	8,023	103	1,144	9	5	12	6
Black	5,197	154,027	895	101,433	1,827	25,996	-	-	-	-
Hispanic	8,337	302,456	1,837	193,150	3,130	43,812	1	2	4	2
Asian and Pacific Islander	3,601	163,272	685	97,614	1,786	19,569	2	2	5	2
Motion pictures	1,939	109,396	263	76,501	882	14,296	2	1	4	1
Minority men	1,371	78,202	188	52,916	712	9,050	2	1	5	1
Minority women	568	31,194	75	23,585	170	5,246	5	2	7	1
American Indian and Alaska Native	34	1,691	5	(D)	(D)	(D)	20	9	-	(D)
Black	733	61,911	72	48,867	358	9,006	-	-	-	-
Hispanic	694	24,880	107	14,278	344	2,877	3	3	7	2
Asian and Pacific Islander	505	22,730	82	(D)	(D)	(D)	5	4	10	(D)
Amusement and recreation services	28,430	858,082	2,256	484,502	5,451	99,085	1	1	3	1
Minority men	21,653	619,237	1,729	316,275	4,079	72,178	1	1	3	1
Minority women	6,777	238,845	527	168,227	1,372	26,907	2	1	6	-
American Indian and Alaska Native	556	15,698	57	11,602	212	1,663	8	3	23	2

[Continued]

★ 697 ★

Minority-Owned Firms: Services
[Continued]

Major industry group and minority	All firms		Firms with paid employees				Relative standard error of estimate (percent) for column --			
	Firms (Number) A	Sales and receipts ($1,000) B	Firms (numbers) C	Sales and receipts ($1,000) D	Employees (Number) E	Annual Payroll ($1,000) F	A	B	C	D
Black	13,250	502,847	965	316,336	2,021	62,094	-	-	-	-
Hispanic	9,528	203,812	800	89,891	1,518	19,948	2	3	8	4
Asian and Pacific Islander	5,307	142,451	467	70,229	1,736	16,188	2	3	7	3
Health services	80,753	6,399,878	23,508	4,727,372	66,568	889,621	-	-	1	1
Minority men	42,337	5,006,101	18,591	3,912,273	53,320	719,672	1	1	1	1
Minority women	38,416	1,393,777	4,917	815,099	13,248	169,949	1	1	2	1
American Indian and Alaska Native	488	20,840	91	13,417	205	2,293	10	11	18	11
Black	30,026	1,350,606	5,251	924,048	18,078	216,304	-	-	-	-
Hispanic	16,322	1,326,215	5,089	999,789	13,982	197,965	1	1	2	1
Asian and Pacific Islander	34,590	3,754,983	13,292	2,830,922	34,917	481,271	1	1	1	1
Legal services	10,887	809,756	3,572	608,052	7,121	120,514	1	1	1	1
Minority men	7,787	653,896	2,890	501,305	5,664	99,312	1	1	1	1
Minority women	3,100	155,860	682	106,747	1,457	21,202	2	1	3	2
American Indian and Alaska Native	169	11,153	52	8,400	105	1,916	8	4	10	2
Black	4,920	336,218	1,541	253,249	3,040	51,576	-	-	-	-
Hispanic	3,690	286,713	1,356	216,577	2,545	41,187	1	1	2	2
Asian and Pacific Islander	2,186	179,585	635	131,954	1,406	26,223	2	1	3	2
Educational services	10,124	173,474	574	104,556	2,764	34,429	1	1	3	-
Minority men	4,436	70,581	280	32,864	875	9,822	2	2	5	1
Minority women	5,688	102,893	294	71,692	1,889	24,607	2	1	5	-
American Indian and Alaska Native	210	1,051	3	214	4	38	12	7	-	-
Black	3,561	64,545	216	43,466	1,120	16,839	-	-	-	-
Hispanic	2,797	54,119	157	36,409	975	10,684	2	1	6	1
Asian and Pacific Islander	3,662	54,389	199	24,526	669	6,892	2	2	8	1
Social services	26,356	410,281	3,480	244,196	10,095	77,449	1	1	1	1
Minority men	4,121	128,058	844	95,455	3,916	31,745	3	1	3	1
Minority women	22,235	282,223	2,636	148,741	6,179	45,704	1	1	2	1
American Indian and Alaska Native	451	3,842	28	1,413	85	545	10	8	-	-
Black	13,210	224,137	2,229	139,407	6,005	47,262	-	-	-	-
Hispanic	8,840	100,321	697	45,344	1,886	13,215	2	2	7	4
Asian and Pacific Islander	4,038	84,553	549	59,699	2,225	17,039	3	2	4	1
Museums, botanical, zoological gardens	-	-	-	-	-	-	-	-	-	-
Minority men	-	-	-	-	-	-	-	-	-	-
Minority women	-	-	-	-	-	-	-	-	-	-
American Indian and Alaska Native	-	-	-	-	-	-	-	-	-	-
Black	-	-	-	-	-	-	-	-	-	-
Hispanic	-	-	-	-	-	-	-	-	-	-
Asian and Pacific Islander	-	-	-	-	-	-	-	-	-	-
Miscellaneous services	37,958	1,576,604	5,866	1,025,797	18,050	327,155	1	1	2	1
Minority men	25,801	1,179,817	4,525	762,880	13,598	247,101	1	1	2	1
Minority women	12,157	398,787	1,341	262,917	4,452	80,054	2	1	4	1
American Indian and Alaska Native	505	11,199	74	(D)	(D)	(D)	9	8	21	(D)
Black	9,166	341,096	1,207	220,869	5,266	85,574	-	-	-	-
Hispanic	12,547	470,747	2,043	285,930	5,347	84,052	1	1	3	1
Asian and Pacific Islander	16,114	771,603	2,587	(D)	(D)	(D)	1	1	3	(D)

Source: 1987 Economic Censuses, Survey of Minority-Owned Business Enterprises: Summary, U.S. Department of Commerce, Bureau of the Census, 1991, pp. 16-17. Primary source: 1987 Survey of Minority-Owned Businesses. *Minority-Owned Businesses,* Washington, D.C., U.S. Government Printing Office, 1990. Arranged by the editors. *Note:* A dash (-) represents zero.

★ 698 ★
Businesses

Minority-Owned Firms: Transportation and Utilities

Data are shown for 1987. Trade groups are based on the 1972 Standard Industrial Classification (SIC) system.

Major industry group and minority	All firms		Firms with paid employees				Relative standard error of estimate % for column			
	Firms (number) A	Sales and receipts ($1,000) B	Firms (number) C	Sales and receipts ($1,000) D	Employees (number) E	Annual payroll ($1,000) F	A	B	C	D
Transportation and public utilities	76,229	3,665,10,233	10,223	1,955,168	20,795	335,242	-	-	1	-
Minority men	68,052	3,052,314	8,710	1,482,705	15,900	262,551	-	-	1	1
Minority women	8,177	613,368	1,513	472,463	4,895	72,691	2	1	3	1
American Indian and Alaska Native	917	44,286	161	22,979	280	3,990	5	4	9	4
Men	764	38,602	136	19,981	241	3,490	5	4	10	4
Women	153	5,684	25	2,998	39	500	12	8	15	2
Black	36,958	1,573,342	4,987	786,091	9,910	153,959	-	-	-	-
Men	33,165	1,279,210	4,295	554,535	7,305	115,165	-	-	-	-
Women	3,793	294,132	692	231,556	2,605	38,794	-	-	-	-
Hispanic	26,955	1,380,981	3,989	725,484	8,006	135,592	1	1	3	1
Men	24,230	1,207,449	3,459	597,628	6,437	111,669	1	1	3	1
Women	2,725	173,532	530	127,856	1,569	23,923	4	2	7	2
Asian and Pacific Islander	11,940	691,480	1,154	432,638	2,750	45,784	1	1	3	1
Men	10,359	545,809	878	318,035	2,032	35,732	1	1	4	1
Women	1,581	145,671	276	114,603	718	10,052	4	2	6	1
Local and interurban passenger transit	22,037	454,980	1,106	86,151	2,722	23,571	1	1	3	1
Minority men	20,072	411,789	863	68,298	2,109	18,678	1	1	3	1
Minority women	1,965	43,191	243	17,853	613	4,893	3	3	6	3
American Indian and Alaska Native	95	2,941	13	1,357	40	265	13	12	26	-
Black	11,566	218,209	700	53,266	1,746	14,621	-	-	-	-
Hispanic	4,522	105,763	260	20,340	744	6,188	2	2	10	3
Asian and Pacific Islander	6,049	132,832	159	12,092	235	2,770	2	2	15	5
Trucking and warehousing	39,556	2,060,753	7,044	966,322	10,952	196,536	-	1	2	1
Minority men	37,005	1,842,679	6,372	811,677	8,818	161,792	-	1	2	1
Minority women	2,551	218,074	672	154,645	2,134	36,744	3	2	5	1
American Indian and Alaska Native	590	32,189	125	15,359	185	2,900	6	5	11	6
Black	19,663	1,010,229	3,632	465,617	5,504	98,309	-	-	-	-
Hispanic	17,304	906,583	2,936	426,794	4,499	85,692	1	1	4	2
Asian and Pacific Islander	2,214	121,853	377	61,832	786	12,228	3	2	6	3
Water transportation	339	37,000	89	31,814	572	7,820	1	-	-	-
Minority men	286	30,222	69	26,035	512	7,020	1	-	-	-
Minority women	53	6,778	20	5,779	60	800	7	1	-	-
American Indian and Alaska Native	12	695	3	452	10	127	-	-	-	-
Black	83	9,042	26	7,687	160	2,307	-	-	-	-
Hispanic	156	19,598	40	17,539	327	4,223	3	-	-	-
Asian and Pacific Islander	91	7,836	22	6,282	77	1,198	-	-	-	-
Transportation by air	462	29,332	51	15,919	239	4,279	3	-	-	-
Minority men	395	16,523	39	7,404	100	1,697	3	-	-	-
Minority women	67	12,809	12	8,515	139	2,582	5	-	-	-

[Continued]

★ 698 ★

Minority-Owned Firms: Transportation and Utilities
[Continued]

Major industry group and minority	All firms		Firms with paid employees				Relative standard error of estimate % for column			
	Firms (number) A	Sales and receipts ($1,000) B	Firms (number) C	Sales and receipts ($1,000) D	Employees (number) E	Annual payroll ($1,000) F	A	B	C	D
American Indian and Alaska Native	30	865	6	414	4	63	31	6	-	-
Black	117	11,485	12	7,860	121	2,447	-	-	-	-
Hispanic	222	10,895	23	4,022	67	1,116	2	-	-	-
Asian and Pacific Islander	101	6,154	10	3,623	47	653	8	-	-	-
Pipe lines, except natural gas	1	(D)	-	-	-	-	-	(D)	-	-
Minority men	1	(D)	-	-	-	-	-	(D)	-	-
Minority women	-	-	-	-	-	-	-	-	-	-
American Indian and Alaska Native	-	-	-	-	-	-	-	-	-	-
Black	-	-	-	-	-	-	-	-	-	-
Hispanic	-	-	-	-	-	-	-	-	-	-
Asian and Pacific Islander	1	(D)	-	-	-	-	-	(D)	-	-
Transportation services	10,665	895,539	1,479	706,588	4,018	62,172	1	-	2	-
Minority men	7,757	587,323	990	439,876	2,513	41,317	1	1	3	1
Minority women	2,908	308,216	489	266,712	1,505	20,855	2	1	3	1
American Indian and Alaska Native	134	6,296	8	4,711	34	494	13	3	-	-
Black	4,053	222,757	405	166,710	920	14,303	-	-	-	-
Hispanic	3,617	284,684	542	219,512	1,683	25,970	2	1	4	1
Asian and Pacific Islander	2,959	387,708	536	320,159	1,419	22,289	2	1	4	1
Communication	2,062	150,568	274	125,340	1,992	35,207	2	1	7	-
Minority men	1,537	130,548	219	109,567	1,583	28,928	2	1	8	-
Minority women	525	20,020	55	15,773	409	6,279	5	2	13	-
American Indian and Alaska Native	36	682	2	(D)	(D)	(D)	9	13	-	(D)
Black	896	81,785	118	71,953	1,334	20,779	-	-	-	-
Hispanic	756	38,852	115	28,851	533	10,451	4	2	16	1
Asian and Pacific Islander	385	32,355	40	(D)	(D)	(D)	5	1	5	(D)
Electric, gas, and sanitary services	1,107	(D)	180	23,034	300	3,657	2	(D)	5	1
Minority men	999	(D)	158	19,848	265	3,119	2	(D)	5	2
Minority women	108	4,280	22	3,186	35	538	6	4	16	5
American Indian and Alaska Native	20	618	4	(D)	(D)	(D)	-	-	-	(D)
Black	580	19,835	94	12,998	125	1,466	-	-	-	-
Hispanic	378	14,606	73	8,426	153	1,952	4	3	11	4
Asian and Pacific Islander	140	(D)	10	(D)	(D)	(D)	10	(D)	-	(D)

Source: 1987 Economic Censuses, Survey of Minority-Owned Business Enterprises: Summary, U.S. Department of Commerce, Bureau of the Census, 1991, p. 13. Primary source: 1987 Survey of Minority-Owned Businesses. *Minority-Owned Businesses*, Washington, D.C., U.S. Government Printing Office, 1990. Arranged by the editors. Details may not add to total because of rounding and because a firm may be included in more than one minority group. (D) stands for data withheld to avoid disclosure of competitive information. *Note:* A dash (-) represents zero.

★ 699 ★

Businesses

Minority-Owned Firms: Wholesale Trade

Data are shown for 1987. Trade groups are based on the 1972 Standard Industrial Classification (SIC) system.

Major industry group and minority	All firms		Firms with paid employees				Relative standard error of estimate % for column--			
	Firms (number) A	Sales and receipts ($1,000) B	Firms (number) C	Sales and receipts ($1,000) D	Employees (number) E	Annual payroll ($1,000) F	A	B	C	D
Wholesale trade	26,432	7,950,013	6,216	6,216	6,489,777	24,455	1	-	1	-
Minority men	20,685	6,087,858	4,812	4,844,929	17,588	323,063	1	-	1	-
Minority women	5,747	1,862,155	1,404	1,644,845	6,867	127,794	2	-	2	-
American Indian and Alaska Native	360	36,058	93	26,490	192	2,755	8	3	16	2
Men	292	29,709	75	20,846	159	2,283	10	3	20	3
Women	68	6,349	18	5,644	33	472	16	2	19	1
Black	5,519	1,327,479	1,256	1,169,608	6,156	115,944	-	-	-	-
Men	4,016	821,228	850	702,267	3,589	64,940	-	-	-	-
Women	1,503	506,251	406	467,341	2,567	51,004	-	-	-	-
Hispanic	10,154	2,445,416	2,309	1,991,736	9,119	157,537	1	-	2	-
Men	8,292	2,011,404	1,888	1,616,146	7,204	123,920	1	-	2	-
Women	1,862	434,012	421	375,590	1,915	33,617	4	1	4	1
Asian and Pacific Islander	10,654	4,188,852	2,622	3,337,014	9,192	177,221	1	-	2	-
Men	8,259	3,251,019	2,031	2,524,919	6,727	133,214	1	-	2	-
Women	2,395	937,833	591	812,095	2,465	44,007	4	1	3	1
Wholesale trade – durable goods	13,219	3,463,935	3,281	2,784,804	11,909	231,471	1	-	2	-
Minority men	10,513	2,673,962	2,519	2,100,024	8,764	169,669	1	-	2	-
Minority women	2,706	789,973	762	684,780	3,145	61,802	3	1	3	1
American Indian and Alaska Native	247	24,294	60	18,867	158	2,251	11	3	20	2
Black	2,792	628,729	731	559,469	3,309	63,196	-	-	-	-
Hispanic	5,080	1,056,969	1,218	851,385	4,744	84,530	1	1	2	1
Asian and Pacific Islander	5,238	1,775,057	1,305	1,367,633	3,789	82,773	2	1	3	1
Wholesale trade – nondurable goods	13,213	4,486,078	2,935	3,704,973	12,546	219,386	1	-	1	-
Minority men	10,172	3,413,896	2,293	2,744,905	8,824	153,394	1	-	2	-
Minority women	3,041	1,072,182	642	960,068	3,722	65,992	2	1	2	1
American Indian and Alaska Native	113	11,764	33	7,623	34	504	12	5	27	6
Black	2,727	698,750	525	610,139	2,847	52,748	-	-	-	-
Hispanic	5,074	1,388,447	1,091	1,140,351	4,375	73,007	1	1	3	-
Asian and Pacific Islander	5,416	2,413,795	1,317	1,969,381	5,403	94,448	1	-	2	-

Source: 1987 Economic Censuses, Survey of Minority-Owned Business Enterprises: Summary, U.S. Department of Commerce, Bureau of the Census, 1991, pp. 13-14. Primary source: 1987 Survey of Minority-Owned Businesses. *Minority-Owned Businesses*, Washington, D.C., U.S. Government Printing Office, 1990. Arranged by the editors. *Note:* A dash (-) represents zero.

★ 700 ★

Businesses

Minority-Owned Firms: Unclassified Firms

Data are shown for 1987.

Race/ethnicity	All firms		Firms with paid employees				Relative standard error of estimate % for column			
	Firms (number) A	Sales and receipts ($1,000) B	Firms (number) C	Sales and receipts ($1,000) D	Employees (number) E	Annual payroll ($1,000) F	A	B	C	D
Industries not classified	69,942	2,230,113	6,869	745,873	5,754	119,194	-	1	2	2
Minority men	48,270	1,747,385	5,445	622,165	4,607	100,098	1	1	2	2
Minority women	21,672	482,728	1,424	123,708	1,147	19,096	1	2	4	4
American Indian and Alaska Native	1,285	36,637	142	14,001	119	2,353	5	9	18	12
Men	964	31,972	118	(D)	(D)	(D)	7	10	19	(D)
Women	321	4,665	24	(D)	(D)	(D)	12	11	46	(D)
Black	26,518	579,749	2,399	174,289	1,643	33,845	-	-	-	-
Men	17,100	426,851	1,833	143,056	1,310	27,867	-	-	-	-
Women	9,418	152,898	566	31,233	333	5,978	-	-	-	-
Hispanic	25,075	752,271	2,396	255,830	2,024	47,794	1	2	4	3
Men	18,581	623,877	2,057	224,197	1,764	42,807	1	2	5	4
Women	6,494	128,394	339	31,633	260	4,987	3	4	12	12
Asian and Pacific Islander	17,739	894,509	1,999	306,801	2,028	36,011	1	1	4	3
Men	12,125	689,416	1,500	(D)	(D)	(D)	2	2	5	(D)
Women	5,614	205,093	499	(D)	(D)	(D)	3	3	9	(D)

Source: 1987 Economic Censuses, Survey of Minority-Owned Business Enterprises: Summary, U.S. Department of Commerce, Bureau of the Census, 1991, p. 17. Primary source: 1987 Survey of Minority-Owned Businesses. *Minority-Owned Businesses*, Washington, D.C.: U.S. Government Printing Office, 1990. Arranged by the editors. Details may not add to total because of rounding and because a firm may be included in more than one minority group. (D) stands for data withheld to avoid disclosure of competitive information. *Note:* A dash (-) indicates data were not available.

★ 701 ★

Businesses

Minority-Owned Firms: Midwestern States

Data are shown for 1987.

Geographic area and minority	All firms		Firms with paid employees				Relative standard error of estimate % for column			
	Firms (number) A	Sales and receipts ($1,000) B	Firms (number) C	Sales and receipts ($1,000) D	Employees (number) E	Annual payroll ($1,000) F	A	B	C	D
Illinois	43,247	3,106,646	8,631	2,271,936	30,662	356,981	-	-	1	-
Minority men	28,696	2,204,476	6,417	1,585,935	21,731	242,495	1	1	1	-
Minority women	14,551	902,170	2,214	686,001	8,931	114,486	1	1	2	1
American Indian and Alaska Native	193	7,213	48	(D)	(D)	(D)	14	10	26	(D)
Men	122	6,033	33	3,564	31	527	18	12	30	15
Women	71	1,180	15	(D)	(D)	(D)	24	17	53	(D)
Black	19,011	1,100,204	3,014	816,022	10,655	138,699	-	-	-	-
Men	11,608	693,830	2,146	495,536	6,799	81,077	-	-	-	-
Women	7,403	406,374	868	320,486	3,856	57,622	-	-	-	-

[Continued]

★ 701 ★

Minority-Owned Firms: Midwestern States
[Continued]

Geographic area and minority	All firms		Firms with paid employees				Relative standard error of estimate % for column			
	Firms (number) A	Sales and receipts ($1,000) B	Firms (number) C	Sales and receipts ($1,000) D	Employees (number) E	Annual payroll ($1,000) F	A	B	C	D
Hispanic	9,636	588,646	1,712	416,569	5,890	68,893	1	1	3	1
Men	6,778	422,253	1,338	288,645	4,463	47,511	2	1	3	1
Women	2,858	166,393	374	127,924	1,427	21,382	3	2	7	2
Asian and Pacific Islander	14,679	1,437,700	3,904	(D)	(D)	(D)	1	1	2	(D)
Men	10,352	1,099,540	2,931	812,551	10,574	114,746	1	1	2	1
Women	4,327	338,160	973	(D)	(D)	(D)	3	2	4	(D)
Indiana	9,063	660,646	2,111	534,487	9,871	102,775	1	-	1	-
Minority men	5,744	493,768	1,526	402,946	6,991	74,615	1	-	1	-
Minority women	3,319	166,878	585	131,541	2,880	28,160	1	1	2	1
American Indian and Alaska Native	90	3,221	15	2,361	33	331	12	5	16	-
Men	57	2,788	10	2,100	23	246	14	5	24	-
Women	33	433	5	261	10	85	21	10	-	-
Black	5,867	349,643	1,110	281,611	4,715	53,703	-	-	-	-
Men	3,563	241,909	761	195,440	2,882	33,585	-	-	-	-
Women	2,304	107,734	349	86,171	1,833	20,118	-	-	-	-
Hispanic	1,427	106,111	300	85,099	1,455	16,541	3	1	3	-
Men	1,016	93,216	250	77,746	1,310	15,111	3	1	4	-
Women	411	12,895	50	7,353	145	1,430	6	2	10	-
Asian and Pacific Islander	1,718	205,485	699	168,918	3,744	33,100	2	1	2	1
Men	1,132	157,786	512	129,413	2,814	26,189	2	1	2	1
Women	586	47,699	187	39,505	930	6,911	4	3	5	2
Iowa	1,785	119,792	490	101,511	2,344	18,255	1	1	2	1
Minority men	1,129	84,799	345	72,466	1,448	11,874	2	1	3	1
Minority women	656	34,993	145	29,045	896	6,381	3	1	4	1
American Indian and Alaska Native	43	1,302	8	764	11	110	17	19	18	18
Men	25	687	4	485	2	53	20	3	-	-
Women	18	615	4	279	9	57	30	40	37	50
Black	703	44,795	142	38,013	722	7,158	-	-	-	-
Men	449	31,835	104	27,027	327	4,039	-	-	-	-
Women	254	12,960	38	10,986	395	3,119	-	-	-	-
Hispanic	475	20,210	111	16,662	489	3,534	3	1	3	1
Men	308	12,403	77	9,715	328	2,216	3	1	4	1
Women	167	7,807	34	6,947	161	1,318	6	1	-	-
Asian and Pacific Islander	574	53,931	232	46,453	1,136	7,544	4	2	4	2
Men	350	40,062	161	35,412	796	5,622	5	2	5	3
Women	224	13,869	71	11,041	338	1,922	7	3	7	2
Kansas	5,164	300,722	1,166	237,248	4,627	48,993	1	-	2	-
Minority men	3,351	232,133	889	186,913	3,471	38,034	2	1	3	-
Minority women	1,813	68,589	277	50,335	1,156	10,959	3	1	4	1
American Indian and Alaska Native	231	(D)	33	5,426	79	631	14	(D)	23	2
Men	135	6,474	27	4,955	53	570	16	5	28	2
Women	96	(D)	6	471	26	61	21	(D)	-	-
Black	2,323	154,448	403	127,424	2,132	28,094	-	-	-	-

[Continued]

★ 701 ★

Minority-Owned Firms: Midwestern States
[Continued]

Geographic area and minority	All firms		Firms with paid employees				Relative standard error of estimate % for column			
	Firms (number) A	Sales and receipts ($1,000) B	Firms (number) C	Sales and receipts ($1,000) D	Employees (number) E	Annual payroll ($1,000) F	A	B	C	D
Men	1,451	122,595	307	104,092	1,893	24,081	-	-	-	-
Women	872	31,853	96	23,332	239	4,013	-	-	-	-
Hispanic	1,541	62,275	335	43,035	1,027	9,405	3	1	4	1
Men	1,088	44,752	265	29,071	575	5,457	4	2	6	1
Women	453	17,523	70	13,964	452	3,948	7	2	3	-
Asian and Pacific Islander	1,135	(D)	406	62,750	1,437	11,146	4	(D)	5	1
Men	721	59,768	299	49,940	979	8,172	6	2	5	1
Women	414	(D)	107	12,810	458	2,974	8	(D)	11	3
Michigan	21,032	1,230,777	4,131	922,413	15,975	170,356	-	-	-	-
Minority men	12,992	904,046	2,982	691,324	11,120	125,797	1	1	1	1
Minority women	8,040	326,731	1,149	231,089	4,855	44,559	1	1	2	1
American Indian and Alaska Native	305	(D)	42	(D)	(D)	(D)	10	(D)	13	(D)
Men	214	6,909	29	4,915	62	844	12	5	15	4
Women	91	(D)	13	(D)	(D)	(D)	21	(D)	27	(D)
Black	13,708	701,335	2,241	524,583	8,485	91,991	-	-	-	-
Men	8,112	489,595	1,553	372,031	5,561	63,416	-	-	-	-
Women	5,596	211,740	688	152,552	2,924	28,575	-	-	-	-
Hispanic	2,654	126,046	464	87,743	1,560	20,945	1	1	3	1
Men	1,788	104,064	354	75,333	1,260	18,420	2	1	3	1
Women	866	21,982	110	12,410	300	2,525	3	3	8	4
Asian and Pacific Islander	4,424	(D)	1,402	(D)	(D)	(D)	2	(D)	3	(D)
Men	2,916	313,276	1,058	248,593	4,347	44,348	3	2	3	2
Women	1,508	(D)	344	(D)	(D)	(D)	5	(D)	6	(D)
Minnesota	4,188	324,316	906	260,880	5,098	53,716	1	-	1	-
Minority men	2,690	226,943	625	179,651	3,068	34,980	1	-	2	-
Minority women	1,498	97,373	281	81,229	2,030	18,736	2	1	4	1
American Indian and Alaska Native	340	18,054	56	13,088	248	2,773	6	2	8	1
Men	227	14,003	39	9,981	186	2,295	7	2	9	1
Women	113	4,051	17	3,107	62	478	11	3	16	2
Black	1,448	124,915	224	101,434	1,727	21,557	-	-	-	-
Men	926	77,179	163	61,213	859	10,576	-	-	-	-
Women	522	47,736	61	40,221	868	10,981	-	-	-	-
Hispanic	751	29,061	122	20,341	299	3,598	3	1	5	-
Men	528	17,745	87	10,694	178	2,148	4	2	4	1
Women	223	11,316	35	9,647	121	1,450	7	1	12	1
Asian and Pacific Islander	1,684	153,953	509	126,937	2,842	25,965	2	1	2	1
Men	1,026	118,957	338	96,232	1,852	20,059	3	1	3	1
Women	658	34,996	171	28,705	990	5,906	4	2	5	2
Missouri	11,215	549,921	2,388	400,435	8,348	79,486	-	-	1	-
Minority men	7,111	404,289	1,729	301,724	6,018	61,214	1	1	1	1
Minority women	4,104	145,632	659	98,711	2,330	18,272	1	1	2	1
American Indian and Alaska Native	137	2,145	16	994	34	282	11	11	28	15
Men	94	1,485	11	563	18	179	13	14	39	23

[Continued]

★ 701 ★

Minority-Owned Firms: Midwestern States
[Continued]

Geographic area and minority	All firms		Firms with paid employees				Relative standard error of estimate % for column			
	Firms (number)	Sales and receipts ($1,000)	Firms (number)	Sales and receipts ($1,000)	Employees (number)	Annual payroll ($1,000)	A	B	C	D
	A	B	C	D	E	F				
Women	43	660	5	431	16	103	19	15	29	15
Black	7,832	336,094	1,306	239,602	4,831	50,354	-	-	-	-
Men	4,848	240,162	929	179,274	3,430	39,526	-	-	-	-
Women	2,984	95,932	377	60,328	1,401	10,828	-	-	-	-
Hispanic	1,247	49,677	258	32,830	765	8,022	3	2	5	2
Men	852	37,905	194	24,350	545	5,714	4	2	5	2
Women	395	11,772	64	8,480	220	2,308	7	2	9	1
Asian and Pacific Islander	2,056	164,617	824	129,157	2,757	21,347	2	1	2	1
Men	1,354	125,975	605	98,370	2,037	15,884	2	2	3	2
Women	702	38,642	219	30,787	720	5,463	4	2	5	2
Nebraska	1,921	81,448	423	63,608	1,555	12,345	1	-	2	-
Minority men	1,204	60,507	307	47,160	1,094	9,246	2	1	2	1
Minority women	717	20,941	116	16,448	461	3,099	3	1	1	-
American Indian and Alaska Native	66	1,611	18	947	18	204	11	9	21	16
Men	44	1,288	13	720	15	167	13	11	29	20
Women	22	323	5	227	3	37	20	3	-	-
Black	863	30,826	160	24,289	612	4,832	-	-	-	-
Men	483	21,338	104	16,984	451	3,738	-	-	-	-
Women	380	9,488	56	7,305	161	1,094	-	-	-	-
Hispanic	619	19,391	122	14,557	413	3,414	3	1	3	1
Men	421	16,759	104	12,907	343	3,054	3	1	4	1
Women	198	2,632	18	1,650	70	360	7	3	-	-
Asian and Pacific Islander	385	29,776	125	23,893	513	3,905	5	1	3	-
Men	261	21,220	87	16,588	286	2,288	6	1	5	1
Women	124	8,556	38	7,305	227	1,617	11	1	4	1
North Dakota	472	31,545	123	26,048	395	3,752	2	-	2	-
Minority men	344	19,866	95	15,327	299	2,413	2	-	-	-
Minority women	128	11,679	28	10,721	96	1,339	4	-	9	-
American Indian and Alaska Native	210	(D)	57	(D)	(D)	(D)	3	(D)	4	(D)
Men	151	8,686	40	(D)	(D)	(D)	3	1	-	(D)
Women	59	(D)	17	9,159	35	960	8	(D)	15	-
Black	57	1,207	9	670	8	96	-	-	-	-
Men	37	(D)	7	(D)	(D)	(D)	-	(D)	-	(D)
Women	20	(D)	2	(D)	(D)	(D)	-	(D)	-	(D)
Hispanic	88	2,167	14	1,279	35	315	2	-	-	-
Men	66	(D)	12	(D)	(D)	(D)	2	(D)	-	(D)
Women	22	(D)	2	(D)	(D)	(D)	-	(D)	-	(D)
Asian and Pacific Islander	119	(D)	43	(D)	(D)	(D)	5	(D)	-	(D)
Men	91	8,250	36	6,670	181	1,265	5	-	-	-
Women	28	(D)	7	(D)	(D)	(D)	11	(D)	-	(D)
Ohio	21,902	1,207,885	4,360	907,907	16,847	180,419	1	1	1	1
Minority men	13,762	909,518	3,214	698,066	11,518	130,162	1	1	1	1
Minority women	8,140	298,367	1,146	209,841	5,329	50,257	1	1	2	1

[Continued]

★ 701 ★

Minority-Owned Firms: Midwestern States
[Continued]

Geographic area and minority	All firms		Firms with paid employees				Relative standard error of estimate % for column			
	Firms (number)	Sales and receipts ($1,000)	Firms (number)	Sales and receipts ($1,000)	Employees (number)	Annual payroll ($1,000)	A	B	C	D
	A	B	C	D	E	F				
American Indian and Alaska Native	152	(D)	22	(D)	(D)	(D)	15	(D)	9	(D)
Men	87	4,370	11	3,341	35	360	18	4	-	-
Women	65	(D)	11	(D)	(D)	(D)	24	(D)	18	(D)
Black	15,983	625,665	2,548	439,841	8,888	96,243	-	-	-	-
Men	9,715	430,099	1,842	300,745	5,142	58,637	-	-	-	-
Women	6,268	195,566	706	139,096	3,746	37,606	-	-	-	-
Hispanic	1,989	191,797	420	164,503	2,263	31,382	4	1	6	1
Men	1,379	178,534	363	157,745	2,092	30,171	4	1	7	1
Women	592	13,263	57	6,758	171	1,211	8	7	17	8
Asian and Pacific Islander	3,859	(D)	1,392	(D)	(D)	(D)	2	(D)	2	(D)
Men	2,618	299,921	1,017	238,830	4,297	41,463	3	2	3	2
Women	1,241	(D)	375	(D)	(D)	(D)	5	(D)	6	(D)
South Dakota	539	25,488	153	19,858	328	2,798	2	-	2	-
Minority men	380	18,356	108	13,593	254	2,141	2	-	2	-
Minority women	159	7,132	45	6,265	74	657	4	1	5	1
American Indian and Alaska Native	267	11,166	75	8,240	153	1,366	3	1	3	-
Men	199	9,106	57	6,528	126	1,181	4	1	3	-
Women	68	2,060	18	1,712	27	185	8	2	8	1
Black	63	4,832	14	4,391	35	418	-	-	-	-
Men	41	(D)	10	(D)	(D)	(D)	-	(D)	-	(D)
Women	22	(D)	4	(D)	(D)	(D)	-	(D)	-	(D)
Hispanic	109	4,262	27	3,071	43	506	1	-	-	-
Men	86	(D)	19	(D)	(D)	(D)	2	(D)	-	(D)
Women	23	(D)	8	(D)	(D)	(D)	-	(D)	-	(D)
Asian and Pacific Islander	108	5,714	39	4,607	110	707	6	1	5	1
Men	62	4,443	24	3,638	88	534	6	1	-	-
Women	46	1,271	15	969	22	173	10	3	13	3
Wisconsin	4,689	417,655	1,154	343,643	5,921	58,166	1	1	2	1
Minority men	3,043	313,228	833	255,633	3,825	36,610	2	1	2	1
Minority women	1,646	104,427	321	88,010	2,096	21,556	3	1	5	1
American Indian and Alaska Native	307	(D)	89	18,280	520	3,808	10	(D)	14	5
Men	219	17,325	64	14,925	488	3,561	10	5	14	6
Women	88	(D)	25	3,355	32	247	24	(D)	37	2
Black	2,381	190,696	477	159,597	2,552	28,726	-	-	-	-
Men	1,474	124,027	334	101,710	1,066	11,860	-	-	-	-
Women	907	66,669	143	57,887	1,486	16,866	-	-	-	-
Hispanic	894	73,541	184	61,897	683	6,919	3	1	4	1
Men	612	61,712	136	52,099	548	5,624	3	1	5	1
Women	282	11,829	48	9,798	135	1,295	7	3	10	2
Asian and Pacific Islander	1,144	(D)	417	105,222	2,198	18,928	4	(D)	5	2

[Continued]

★ 701 ★

Minority-Owned Firms: Midwestern States

[Continued]

Geographic area and minority	All firms		Firms with paid employees				Relative standard error of estimate % for column			
	Firms (number)	Sales and receipts ($1,000)	Firms (number)	Sales and receipts ($1,000)	Employees (number)	Annual payroll ($1,000)				
	A	B	C	D	E	F	A	B	C	D
Men	766	111,350	309	87,632	1,745	15,743	5	2	5	2
Women	378	(D)	108	17,590	453	3,185	10	(D)	13	5

Source: 1987 Economic Censuses, Survey of Minority-Owned Business Enterprises: Summary, U.S. Department of Commerce, Bureau of the Census, 1991, pp. 18-28. Primary source: 1987 Survey of Minority-Owned Businesses. *Minority-Owned Businesses*, Washington, D.C., U.S. Government Printing Office, 1990. Arranged by the editors. Details may not add to total because of rounding and because a firm may be included in more than one minority group. (D) stands for data withheld to avoid disclosure of competitive information. *Note:* A dash (-) represents zero.

★ 702 ★

Businesses

Minority-Owned Firms: Northeastern States

Geographic area and industry division	All firms		Firms with paid employees				Relative standard error of estimate % for column			
	Firms (number)	Sales and receipts ($1,000)	Firms (number)	Sales and receipts ($1,000)	Employees (number)	Annual payroll ($1,000)				
Connecticut	8,236	620,841	1,765	449,393	5,626	76,850	1	1	1	-
Minority men	5,421	465,269	1,307	333,261	4,131	54,660	1	1	2	-
Minority women	2,815	155,572	458	116,132	1,495	22,190	2	1	3	1
American Indian and Alaska Native	88	(D)	9	785	13	155	14	(D)	23	19
Men	68	1,522	7	(D)	(D)	(D)	15	16	29	(D)
Women	20	(D)	2	(D)	(D)	(D)	30	(D)	-	(D)
Black	4,061	225,718	724	162,610	1,936	28,798	-	-	-	-
Men	2,493	157,903	503	113,908	1,275	18,826	-	-	-	-
Women	1,568	67,815	221	48,702	661	9,972	-	-	-	-
Hispanic	2,235	175,520	397	118,141	1,610	19,580	3	2	5	1
Men	1,603	148,314	319	100,913	1,307	14,379	3	2	5	1
Women	632	27,206	78	17,228	303	5,201	6	5	11	7
Asian and Pacific Islander	1,963	(D)	650	171,402	2,123	29,085	2	(D)	3	1
Men	1,314	160,687	489	(D)	(D)	(D)	3	1	3	(D)
Women	649	(D)	161	(D)	(D)	(D)	5	(D)	6	(D)
Maine	496	43,772	143	33,339	811	7,736	2	-	1	-
Minority men	330	38,286	104	29,650	714	6,894	2	-	1	-
Minority women	168	5,486	39	3,689	97	842	3	1	-	-
American Indian and Alaska Native	68	3,956	16	3,012	46	541	7	1	-	2
Men	43	2,724	10	2,194	23	350	6	-	-	-
Women	25	1,232	6	818	23	191	15	4	-	-
Black	131	5,151	31	3,706	80	675	-	-	-	-
Men	77	2,831	20	2,130	47	415	-	-	-	-
Women	54	2,320	11	1,576	33	260	-	-	-	-
Hispanic	139	12,061	42	9,504	173	1,768	2	-	3	-
Men	98	11,409	31	9,145	165	1,631	3	-	5	-
Women	41	652	11	359	8	137	-	-	-	-

[Continued]

★ 702 ★

Minority-Owned Firms: Northeastern States
[Continued]

Geographic area and industry division	All firms		Firms with paid employees				Relative standard error of estimate % for column			
	Firms (number)	Sales and receipts ($1,000)	Firms (number)	Sales and receipts ($1,000)	Employees (number)	Annual payroll ($1,000)				
Asian and Pacific Islander	165	22,786	56	17,260	514	4,772	3	-	-	-
Men	116	21,403	44	16,223	480	4,515	4	-	-	-
Women	49	1,383	12	1,037	34	257	7	2	-	-
Massachusetts	11,180	714,391	1,856	502,212	7,186	99,228	1	1	2	1
Minority men	7,041	505,79	1,359	346,994	4,662	69,567	1	1	2	1
Minority women	4,139	208,602	497	155,218	2,524	29,661	2	1	3	1
American Indian and Alaska Native	132	4,557	24	(D)	(D)	(D)	13	7	23	(D)
Men	102	3,907	20	2,433	42	742	15	7	27	6
Women	30	650	4	(D)	(D)	(D)	27	21	34	(D)
Black	4,761	251,946	628	182,043	2,683	41,186	-	-	-	-
Men	2,886	154,712	465	104,940	1,512	26,367	-	-	-	-
Women	1,875	97,234	163	77,103	1,171	14,819	-	-	-	-
Hispanic	2,636	173,969	411	118,907	1,346	19,736	2	1	3	1
Men	1,756	154,291	329	109,913	1,201	18,425	2	1	4	1
Women	880	19,678	82	8,994	145	1,311	3	6	8	4
Asian and Pacific Islander	3,784	292,291	803	(D)	(D)	(D)	2	1	3	(D)
Men	2,371	199,744	552	133,140	1,950	26,141	3	2	4	2
Women	1,413	92,547	251	(D)	(D)	(D)	4	2	6	(D)
New Hampshire	801	84,946	174	68,166	688	10,050	2	-	2	-
Minority men	523	51,037	126	38,082	431	5,862	3	1	3	-
Minority women	278	33,909	48	30,086	257	4,188	4	1		-
American Indian and Alaska Native	29	(D)	3	625	2	54	11	(D)	-	-
Men	24	1,254	3	625	2	54	13	1	-	-
Women	5	(D)	-	-	-	-	-	(D)	-	-
Black	229	31,198	49	27,295	246	4,179	-	-	-	-
Men	141	6,918	26	4,385	77	935	-	-	-	-
Women	88	24,280	23	22,910	169	3,244	-	-	-	-
Hispanic	244	12,818	49	8,248	120	1,333	4	2	5	2
Men	167	9,001	41	5,199	80	1,100	5	2	6	3
Women	77	3,817	8	3,049	40	233	8	4	-	-
Asian and Pacific Islander	304	(D)	74	32,034	320	4,485	5	(D)	4	-
Men	196	34,452	57	27,909	272	3,774	6	1	5	-
Women	108	(D)	17	4,125	48	711	10	(D)	-	-
New Jersey	38,914	3,075,652	7,181	2,119,310	22,765	326,973	-	-	1	-
Minority men	26,511	2,158,010	5,233	1,424,051	14,948	206,961	1	1	1	1
Minority women	12,403	917,642	1,948	695,259	7,817	120,012	1	1	2	1
American Indian and Alaska Native	135	(D)	17	5,467	42	328	15	(D)	19	8
Men	68	7,455	9	5,154	32	260	18	7	16	9
Women	67	(D)	8	313	10	68	23	(D)	35	24
Black	14,556	995,614	2,169	731,490	8,969	138,762	-	-	-	-
Men	9,123	514,016	1,500	330,719	4,882	64,672	-	-	-	-
Women	5,433	481,598	669	400,771	4,087	74,090	-	-	-	-
Hispanic	12,094	902,004	2,226	598,775	6,167	87,642	1	1	2	1
Men	8,991	733,236	1,714	481,002	4,618	67,051	1	1	2	1

[Continued]

★ 702 ★

Minority-Owned Firms: Northeastern States
[Continued]

Geographic area and industry division	All firms		Firms with paid employees				Relative standard error of estimate % for column			
	Firms (number)	Sales and receipts ($1,000)	Firms (number)	Sales and receipts ($1,000)	Employees (number)	Annual payroll ($1,000)				
Women	3,103	168,768	512	117,773	1,549	20,591	2	2	4	2
Asian and Pacific Islander	12,530	(D)	2,846	804,173	7,828	103,840	1	(D)	2	1
Men	8,593	921,973	2,061	617,690	5,536	76,368	1	1	2	1
Women	3,937	(D)	785	186,483	2,292	27,472	3	(D)	4	2
New York	99,148	6,553,732	15,658	4,377,469	49,823	720,487	-	-	1	-
Minority men	64,353	4,721,673	11,233	3,105,769	34,884	503,172	1	1	1	1
Minority women	34,795	1,832,059	4,425	1,271,700	14,939	217,315	1	1	2	1
American Indian and Alaska Native	445	25,008	95	15,048	251	3,663	11	10	20	11
Men	273	20,352	69	11,903	206	2,880	13	11	23	11
Women	172	4,656	26	3,145	45	783	20	23	39	31
Black	36,289	1,886,038	4,438	1,315,458	16,799	258,234	-	-	-	-
Men	20,834	1,184,246	3,025	796,586	10,321	151,197	-	-	-	-
Women	15,455	701,792	1,413	518,872	6,478	107,037	-	-	-	-
Hispanic	28,254	1,555,801	4,334	944,513	12,745	186,100	1	1	2	1
Men	20,222	1,245,276	3,279	755,775	9,507	145,512	1	1	3	1
Women	8,032	310,525	1,055	188,738	3,238	40,588	2	2	4	3
Asian and Pacific Islander	35,812	3,192,830	7,061	2,167,260	21,367	287,376	1	1	2	1
Men	24,118	2,337,569	5,035	1,576,506	15,583	211,006	1	1	2	1
Women	11,694	855,261	2,026	590,754	5,784	76,370	2	2	4	2
Pennsylvania	21,464	1,920,686	4,711	1,461,277	17,475	210,076	1	-	1	-
Minority men	14,191	1,372,696	3,561	1,026,754	12,252	148,701	1	1	2	1
Minority women	7,273	547,990	1,150	434,523	5,223	61,375	1	1	3	-
American Indian and Alaska Native	140	(D)	34	(D)	(D)	(D)	24	(D)	31	(D)
Men	70	3,089	25	992	31	176	25	39	41	19
Women	70	(D)	9	(D)	(D)	(D)	31	(D)	16	(D)
Black	11,728	747,417	1,970	568,904	7,325	93,781	-	-	-	-
Men	7,352	493,809	1,399	364,807	4,782	58,317	-	-	-	-
Women	4,376	253,608	571	204,097	2,543	35,464	-	-	-	-
Hispanic	2,650	247,081	531	182,890	1,880	27,091	2	1	3	1
Men	1,897	214,586	423	160,928	1,561	24,047	3	2	4	1
Women	753	32,495	108	21,962	319	3,044	4	3	6	2
Asian and Pacific Islander	7,049	(D)	2,193	(D)	(D)	(D)	2	(D)	3	(D)
Men	4,932	665,353	1,728	502,726	5,934	66,701	2	1	3	1
Women	2,117	(D)	465	(D)	(D)	(D)	5	(D)	6	(D)
Rhode Island	1,353	98,188	292	69,396	1,350	11,434	2	-	1	-
Minority men	937	75,194	212	52,487	997	7,633	2	-	2	-
Minority women	416	22,994	80	16,909	353	3,801	3	1	-	-
American Indian and Alaska Native	36	(D)	3	278	4	40	15	(D)	-	-
Men	22	964	2	(D)	(D)	(D)	19	12	-	(D)
Women	14	(D)	1	(D)	(D)	(D)	24	(D)	-	(D)
Black	489	18,209	70	11,988	356	2,957	-	-	-	-
Men	322	13,306	49	(D)	(D)	(D)	-	-	-	(D)
Women	167	4,903	21	(D)	(D)	(D)	-	-	-	(D)
Hispanic	426	40,471	97	27,116	292	3,503	2	1	4	1

[Continued]

★ 702 ★

Minority-Owned Firms: Northeastern States

[Continued]

Geographic area and industry division	All firms		Firms with paid employees				Relative standard error of estimate % for column			
	Firms (number)	Sales and receipts ($1,000)	Firms (number)	Sales and receipts ($1,000)	Employees (number)	Annual payroll ($1,000)				
Men	322	32,427	78	21,218	182	1,786	3	1	5	1
Women	104	8,044	19	5,898	110	1,717	6	2	-	-
Asian and Pacific Islander	436	(D)	129	30,581	706	5,032	4	(D)	-	-
Men	298	29,999	90	23,121	550	3,925	5	1	-	-
Women	138	(D)	39	7,460	156	1,107	9	(D)	-	-
Vermont	326	24,679	93	19,572	324	3,903	-	-	-	-
Minority men	209	18,806	65	14,655	227	3,026	-	-	-	-
Minority women	117	5,873	28	4,917	97	877	-	-	-	-
American Indian and Alaska Native	9	(D)	-	-	-	-	-	(D)	-	-
Men	6	120	-	-	-	-	-	-	-	-
Women	3	(D)	-	-	-	-	-	(D)	-	-
Black	98	6,682	27	5,626	84	1,076	-	-	-	-
Men	64	6,358	16	(D)	(D)	(D)	-	-	-	(D)
Women	34	3,324	11	(D)	(D)	(D)	-	-	-	(D)
Hispanic	118	5,383	24	3,367	48	569	-	-	-	-
Men	83	4,917	21	(D)	(D)	(D)	-	-	-	(D)
Women	35	466	3	(D)	(D)	(D)	-	-	-	(D)
Asian and Pacific Islander	102	(D)	42	10,579	192	2,258	-	(D)	-	-
Men	57	10,421	28	8,868	144	1,979	-	-	-	-
Women	45	(D)	14	1,711	48	279	-	(D)	-	-

Source: 1987 Economic Censuses, Survey of Minority-Owned Business Enterprises: Summary, U.S. Department of Commerce, Bureau of the Census, 1991, pp. 18-28. Primary source: 1987 Survey of Minority-Owned Businesses. *Minority-Owned Businesses,* Washington, D.C.: U.S. Government Printing Office, 1990. Arranged by the editors. Details may not add to total because of rounding and because a firm may be included in more than one minority group. (D) stands for data withheld to avoid disclosure of competitive information. *Note:* A dash (-) indicates data were unavailable.

★ 703 ★

Businesses

Minority-Owned Firms: Southern States

Data are shown for 1987.

Geographic area and minority	All firms		Firms with paid employees				Relative standard error of estimate % for column			
	Firms (number)	Sales and receipts ($1,000)	Firms (number)	Sales and receipts ($1,000)	Employees (number)	Annual payroll ($1,000)	A	B	C	D
	A	B	C	D	E	F				
Alabama	11,458	599,258	2,870	454,103	7,913	79,622	-	-	1	-
Minority men	7,654	454,182	2,187	351,113	5,677	56,020	-	-	-	-
Minority women	3,804	145,076	683	102,990	2,236	23,602	1	1	2	-
American Indian and Alaska Native	90	5,053	26	3,830	36	882	15	11	18	3
Men	70	4,898	22	3,730	32	859	19	11	20	3
Women	20	155	4	100	4	23	15	8	35	10
Black	10,085	439,966	2,337	320,594	5,562	59,450	-	-	-	-
Men	6,709	326,577	1,784	241,576	3,892	41,089	-	-	-	-

[Continued]

★ 703 ★

Minority-Owned Firms: Southern States
[Continued]

Geographic area and minority	All firms		Firms with paid employees				Relative standard error of estimate % for column			
	Firms (number)	Sales and receipts ($1,000)	Firms (number)	Sales and receipts ($1,000)	Employees (number)	Annual payroll ($1,000)	A	B	C	D
	A	B	C	D	E	F				
Women	3,376	113,389	553	79,018	1,670	18,361	-	-	-	-
Hispanic	397	30,006	97	23,366	647	4,855	3	1	3	-
Men	259	24,650	81	21,079	586	4,454	3	1	3	-
Women	138	5,356	16	2,287	61	401	6	3	-	-
Asian and Pacific Islander	917	125,771	417	107,553	1,691	14,642	5	1	4	1
Men	637	98,549	303	84,975	1,174	9,685	5	1	5	1
Women	280	27,222	114	22,578	517	4,957	10	3	9	2
Arkansas	5,371	284,537	1,181	215,133	3,648	36,982	-	-	1	-
Minority men	3,686	202,968	917	149,044	2,774	28,371	1	-	1	-
Minority women	1,685	81,569	264	66,089	874	8,611	1	-	2	-
American Indian and Alaska Native	91	3,141	11	1,694	32	219	12	4	14	6
Men	75	2,085	9	(D)	(D)	(D)	18	2	-	(D)
Women	16	1,056	2	(D)	(D)	(D)	18	2	-	(D)
Black	4,392	214,596	844	161,034	2,304	26,772	-	-	-	-
Men	2,953	146,669	658	105,938	1,685	19,912	-	-	-	-
Women	1,439	67,927	186	55,096	619	6,860	-	-	-	-
Hispanic	324	13,808	73	10,271	289	2,961	3	1	4	1
Men	230	11,007	59	(D)	(D)	(D)	4	1	5	(D)
Women	94	2,801	14	(D)	(D)	(D)	7	2	10	(D)
Asian and Pacific Islander	567	53,064	253	42,134	1,023	7,030	3	1	3	1
Men	430	43,256	191	34,145	862	5,818	4	1	4	1
Women	137	9,808	62	7,989	161	1,212	9	3	8	1
Delaware	2,039	127,249	478	93,477	1,950	19,585	1	-	-	-
Minority men	1,286	79,062	328	54,504	1,077	10,792	1	-	-	-
Minority women	753	48,187	150	38,973	873	8,793	1	-	1	-
American Indian and Alaska Native	43	(D)	7	664	13	178	11	(D)	-	-
Men	29	770	6	(D)	(D)	(D)	10	2	-	(D)
Women	14	(D)	1	(D)	(D)	(D)	25	(D)	-	(D)
Black	1,399	77,701	290	58,971	1,189	13,547	-	-	-	-
Men	869	43,060	198	29,012	559	6,598	-	-	-	-
Women	530	34,641	92	29,959	630	6,949	-	-	-	-
Hispanic	184	6,230	30	3,135	67	740	2	1	-	-
Men	130	4,728	24	2,218	33	482	-	-	-	-
Women	54	1,502	6	917	34	258	5	2	-	-
Asian and Pacific Islander	436	(D)	155	31,477	699	5,383	2	(D)	1	-
Men	273	31,177	102	(D)	(D)	(D)	3	-	-	(D)
Women	163	(D)	53	(D)	(D)	(D)	5	(D)	3	(D)
District of Columbia	9,722	602,789	1,412	478,635	6,046	89,017	-	-	-	-
Minority men	5,922	410,338	983	330,141	4,375	65,216	-	-	-	-
Minority women	3,850	192,451	429	148,494	1,671	23,801	-	-	1	-
American Indian and Alaska Native	28	865	2	(D)	(D)	(D)	21	5	-	(D)
Men	16	803	2	(D)	(D)	(D)	27	5	-	(D)
Women	12	62	-	-	-	-	35	34	-	-

[Continued]

★ 703 ★

Minority-Owned Firms: Southern States

[Continued]

Geographic area and minority	All firms		Firms with paid employees				Relative standard error of estimate % for column			
	Firms (number) A	Sales and receipts ($1,000) B	Firms (number) C	Sales and receipts ($1,000) D	Employees (number) E	Annual payroll ($1,000) F	A	B	C	D
Black	8,275	411,941	956	309,028	4,085	61,239	-	-	-	-
Men	5,021	272,015	666	205,493	2,952	44,429	-	-	-	-
Women	3,254	139,926	290	103,535	1,133	16,810	-	-	-	-
Hispanic	762	63,948	128	53,255	725	12,584	2	-	3	-
Men	446	50,703	91	43,328	611	10,857	3	-	3	-
Women	316	13,245	37	9,927	114	1,727	5	1	7	-
Asian and Pacific Islander	779	132,546	337	(D)	(D)	(D)	2	-	1	(D)
Men	484	91,897	229	(D)	(D)	(D)	3	-	-	(D)
Women	295	40,649	108	36,138	447	5,472	4	-	2	-
Florida	97,961	7,085,085	17,335	5,306,895	66,757	826,522	-	-	1	-
Minority men	69,121	5,541,004	12,741	4,127,260	48,311	627,190	-	-	1	-
Minority women	28,840	1,544,081	4,594	1,179,635	18,446	199,332	1	1	1	1
American Indian and Alaska Native	349	(D)	72	(D)	(D)	(D)	11	(D)	20	(D)
Men	184	11,893	38	9,857	103	1,148	15	6	28	6
Women	165	(D)	34	(D)	(D)	(D)	16	(D)	29	(D)
Black	25,527	1,211,648	4,919	829,865	13,583	161,949	-	-	-	-
Men	15,976	766,466	3,502	502,475	8,538	106,221	-	-	-	-
Women	9,551	445,182	1,417	327,390	5,045	55,728	-	-	-	-
Hispanic	64,413	4,949,151	9,924	3,743,959	42,375	563,088	-	-	1	-
Men	47,832	4,035,364	7,462	3,033,185	31,806	442,897	1	-	2	-
Women	16,581	913,787	2,462	710,774	10,569	120,191	2	1	2	1
Asian and Pacific Islander	8,553	(D)	2,670	(D)	(D)	(D)	2	(D)	2	(D)
Men	5,722	771,264	1,909	612,066	8,593	86,309	2	1	3	1
Women	2,831	(D)	761	(D)	(D)	(D)	3	(D)	4	(D)
Georgia	27,350	1,789,953	6,103	1,396,438	19,888	235,494	-	-	1	-
Minority men	17,974	1,322,369	4,639	1,035,932	15,254	179,657	-	-	1	-
Minority women	9,376	467,584	1,464	360,506	4,634	55,837	1	-	1	-
American Indian and Alaska Native	129	5,715	39	(D)	(D)	(D)	13	7	21	(D)
Men	97	4,229	30	2,126	42	638	16	10	26	14
Women	32	1,486	9	(D)	(D)	(D)	21	7	27	(D)
Black	21,283	1,179,730	4,079	916,426	12,306	163,527	-	-	-	-
Men	13,682	828,199	3,062	642,456	9,162	119,503	-	-	-	-
Women	7,601	351,531	1,017	273,970	3,144	44,024	-	-	-	-
Hispanic	1,931	145,252	480	115,841	2,375	27,796	3	1	5	1
Men	1,343	124,175	377	100,623	2,028	24,533	3	1	5	1
Women	588	21,077	103	15,218	347	3,263	6	3	12	3
Asian and Pacific Islander	4,092	463,354	1,533	(D)	(D)	(D)	2	1	2	(D)
Men	2,916	368,263	1,190	292,615	4,063	35,346	2	1	2	1
Women	1,176	95,091	343	(D)	(D)	(D)	4	2	5	(D)
Kentucky	4,979	233,007	1,010	174,534	3,518	33,088	1	1	1	-
Minority men	3,145	166,903	712	123,435	2,485	24,286	1	1	1	-
Minority women	1,834	66,104	298	51,099	1,033	8,802	2	1	3	1
American Indian and Alaska Native	24	1,705	7	1,575	17	203	10	1	-	-

[Continued]

★ 703 ★

Minority-Owned Firms: Southern States
[Continued]

Geographic area and minority	All firms		Firms with paid employees				Relative standard error of estimate % for column			
	Firms (number) A	Sales and receipts ($1,000) B	Firms (number) C	Sales and receipts ($1,000) D	Employees (number) E	Annual payroll ($1,000) F	A	B	C	D
Men	19	1,629	6	(D)	(D)	(D)	11	-	-	(D)
Women	5	76	1	(D)	(D)	(D)	28	17	-	(D)
Black	3,738	120,201	617	85,628	1,706	17,882	-	-	-	-
Men	2,330	73,993	418	48,960	1,084	11,888	-	-	-	-
Women	1,408	46,208	199	36,668	622	5,994	-	-	-	-
Hispanic	359	16,562	68	9,319	153	1,354	3	1	5	1
Men	249	12,326	54	(D)	(D)	(D)	4	1	6	(D)
Women	110	4,236	14	(D)	(D)	(D)	6	2	10	(D)
Asian and Pacific Islander	875	95,656	324	78,987	1,660	13,882	4	1	3	1
Men	557	79,485	237	66,076	1,276	11,.297	5	2	2	1
Women	318	16,171	87	12,911	384	2,858	10	3	11	3
Louisiana	20,766	841,624	3,868	554,426	8,662	96,918	-	-	1	1
Minority men	14,672	598,995	2,983	376,639	6,008	65,637	-	1	1	1
Minority women	6,094	242,629	885	177,787	2,654	31,281	1	-	1	-
American Indian and Alaska Native	225	(D)	50	(D)	(D)	(D)	12	(D)	25	(D)
Men	182	6,658	38	3,802	37	909	13	20	29	30
Women	43	(D)	12	(D)	(D)	(D)	24	(D)	47	(D)
Black	15,331	531,548	2,611	346,946	5,259	62,283	-	-	-	-
Men	10,585	348,017	1,948	210,202	3,431	39,018	-	-	-	-
Women	4,766	183,531	663	136,744	1,828	23,265	-	-	-	-
Hispanic	2,697	136,083	505	91,532	1,434	17,406	2	1	3	1
Men	1,983	108,285	414	71,688	1,004	12,519	2	1	3	1
Women	714	27,798	91	19,844	430	4,887	3	1	6	1
Asian and Pacific Islander	2,583	(D)	717	(D)	(D)	(D)	3	(D)	5	(D)
Men	1,988	139,325	594	93,607	1,569	13,27	3	3	5	3
Women	595	(D)	123	(D)	(D)	(D)	7	(D)	9	(D)
Maryland	32,445	1,605,358	5,352	1,086,549	15,505	197,205	-	1	1	1
Minority men	19,751	1,122,431	3,894	758,975	10,876	133,767	1	1	1	1
Minority women	12,694	482,927	1,458	327,574	4,629	63,438	1	1	3	1
American Indian and Alaska Native	123	9,411	25	8,035	96	1,451	18	5	11	4
Men	73	7,589	19	6,605	86	1,348	22	5	15	5
Women	50	1,822	6	1,430	10	103	32	11	-	-
Black	21,678	719,715	2,689	451,643	7,248	92,740	-	-	-	-
Men	12,383	508,379	1,920	334,432	5,152	69,185	-	-	-	-
Women	9,295	211,336	769	117,211	2,096	23,555	-	-	-	-
Hispanic	2,931	185,308	509	137,111	1,431	25,929	1	1	3	-
Men	1,882	117,413	389	84,162	991	15,451	2	1	3	1
Women	1,049	67,895	120	52,949	440	10,478	3	1	11	1
Asian and Pacific Islander	7,831	701,690	2,172	498,724	6,817	78,945	2	1	3	1
Men	5,492	495,143	1,600	338,639	4,691	48,410	2	2	3	2
Women	2,339	206,547	572	160,085	2,126	30,535	4	3	7	2
Mississippi	11,122	683,679	2,871	528,060	8,291	76,249	-	-	1	1
Minority men	7,849	506,013	2,203	388,563	6,056	54,992	-	1	1	1
Minority women	3,273	177,666	668	139,497	2,235	21,257	1	1	2	1

[Continued]

★ 703 ★

Minority-Owned Firms: Southern States
[Continued]

Geographic area and minority	All firms		Firms with paid employees				Relative standard error of estimate % for column			
	Firms (number)	Sales and receipts ($1,000)	Firms (number)	Sales and receipts ($1,000)	Employees (number)	Annual payroll ($1,000)				
	A	B	C	D	E	F	A	B	C	D
American Indian and Alaska Native	50	(D)	10	1,666	13	152	24	(D)	37	12
Men	42	1,207	7	(D)	(D)	(D)	28	13	50	(D)
Women	8	(D)	3	(D)	(D)	(D)	24	(D)	45	(D)
Black	9,667	531,929	2,249	410,481	5,760	60,171	-	-	-	-
Men	6,743	385,089	1,712	295,171	4,080	42,141	-	-	-	-
Women	2,924	146,840	537	115,310	1,680	18,030	-	-	-	-
Hispanic	308	12,490	70	6,509	147	1,073	3	2	5	3
Men	228	10,442	58	(D)	(D)	(D)	3	2	6	(D)
Women	80	2,048	12	(D)	(D)	(D)	7	3	12	(D)
Asian and Pacific Islander	1,128	(D)	551	110,700	2,404	15,069	3	(D)	5	3
Men	858	110,221	431	87,470	1,873	11,945	4	3	6	3
Women	270	(D)	120	23,230	531	3,124	11	(D)	13	6
North Carolina	24,149	1,136,114	5,394	839,087	16,531	165,884	-	-	1	-
Minority men	16,399	815,151	4,146	600,512	12,011	120,145	-	1	1	1
Minority women	7,750	320,963	1,248	238,575	4,520	45,739	1	1	2	-
American Indian and Alaska Native	1,758	(D)	547	63,434	1,151	14,140	4	(D)	6	3
Men	1,373	79,362	467	58,486	1,016	13,075	4	3	6	3
Women	385	(D)	80	4,948	135	1,065	10	(D)	17	10
Black	19,487	746,112	3,843	529,118	10,930	114,331	-	-	-	-
Men	13,079	505,561	2,930	349,987	7,866	78,968	-	-	-	-
Women	6,408	240,551	913	179,131	3,064	35,363	-	-	-	-
Hispanic	918	92,903	179	80,052	695	10,751	3	1	5	1
Men	614	65,503	128	56,796	466	8,574	4	1	6	1
Women	304	27,400	51	23,256	229	2,177	6	1	7	-
Asian and Pacific Islander	2,069	(D)	855	168,937	3,807	27,024	3	(D)	3	2
Men	1,385	166,700	638	136,563	2,692	19,728	4	2	4	2
Women	684	(D)	217	32,374	1,115	7,296	7	(D)	7	3
Oklahoma	8,659	299,270	1,431	195,387	4,248	39,143	1	1	2	1
Minority men	5,804	227,772	1,072	147,600	3,052	27,873	1	1	2	1
Minority women	2,855	71,498	359	47,787	1,196	11,270	2	2	4	2
American Indian and Alaska Native	2,051	57,294	268	33,812	456	5,489	3	2	6	3
Men	1,501	47,875	225	27,963	353	4,549	3	3	7	4
Women	550	9,419	43	5,849	103	940	7	4	11	2
Black	3,461	93,903	489	58,677	1,423	14,730	-	-	-	-
Men	2,187	63,532	361	37,334	882	8,805	-	-	-	-
Women	1,274	30,371	128	21,343	541	5,925	-	-	-	-
Hispanic	1,516	50,409	243	33,883	725	6,958	3	1	5	-
Men	1,087	40,004	190	27,186	493	5,002	3	1	5	1
Women	429	10,405	53	6,697	232	1,956	7	4	12	1
Asian and Pacific Islander	1,700	98,174	440	69,191	1,645	12,007	3	2	4	2
Men	1,087	76,804	300	55,239	1,325	9,537	4	2	5	2
Women	613	21,370	140	13,952	320	2,470	6	6	9	7
South Carolina	14,155	546,465	3,039	372,719	8,765	78,842	-	-	-	-
Minority men	9,612	412,355	2,373	283,381	6,885	61,198	-	-	-	-

[Continued]

★ 703 ★

Minority-Owned Firms: Southern States
[Continued]

Geographic area and minority	All firms		Firms with paid employees				Relative standard error of estimate % for column			
	Firms (number) A	Sales and receipts ($1,000) B	Firms (number) C	Sales and receipts ($1,000) D	Employees (number) E	Annual payroll ($1,000) F	A	B	C	D
Minority women	4,543	134,110	666	89,338	1,880	17,644	1	1	2	1
American Indian and Alaska Native	47	3,832	15	3,049	79	568	11	2	9	2
Men	41	3,108	11	(D)	(D)	(D)	13	2	12	(D)
Women	6	724	4	(D)	(D)	(D)	-	-	-	(D)
Black	12,815	444,201	2,567	290,463	6,888	65,975	-	-	-	-
Men	8,720	335,572	2,025	221,207	5,478	51,753	-	-	-	-
Women	4,095	108,629	542	69,256	1,410	14,222	-	-	-	-
Hispanic	393	15,997	79	9,294	216	1,932	4	2	6	1
Men	252	12,408	57	(D)	(D)	(D)	4	1	7	(D)
Women	141	3,589	22	(D)	(D)	(D)	9	6	9	(D)
Asian and Pacific Islander	918	83,892	386	71,316	1,621	10,653	4	2	3	2
Men	607	62,411	285	53,976	1,227	7,665	5	1	3	1
Women	311	21,481	101	17,340	394	2,988	8	5	10	5
Tennessee	12,606	600,234	2,785	427,083	8,381	74,766	-	-	1	-
Minority men	8,322	442,295	2,099	313,495	6,451	56,827	-	1	1	1
Minority women	4,284	157,939	686	113,588	1,930	17,939	1	1	1	1
American Indian and Alaska Native	90	(D)	18	2,314	30	240	12	(D)	21	9
Men	64	3,119	15	2,239	27	228	13	7	19	8
Women	26	(D)	3	75	3	12	24	(D)	81	81
Black	10,423	386,078	1,929	260,582	4,902	50,139	-	-	-	-
Men	6,712	263,319	1,425	173,859	3,676	36,463	-	-	-	-
Women	3,711	122,759	504	86,723	1,226	13,676	-	-	-	-
Hispanic	554	35,187	134	21,055	345	3,954	3	1	3	1
Men	415	30,985	110	18,866	304	3,528	3	1	3	1
Women	139	4,202	24	2,189	41	426	6	3	8	5
Asian and Pacific Islander	1,574	(D)	713	144,233	3,125	20,648	2	(D)	2	1
Men	1,161	146,014	556	119,174	2,456	16,760	2	2	3	2
Women	413	(D)	157	25,059	669	3,888	5	(D)	6	3
Texas	152,409	6,961,063	32,113	4,835,241	77,983	851,079	-	-	1	-
Minority men	109,456	5,702,720	25,603	4,008,148	62,070	703,712	-	-	1	-
Minority women	42,953	1,258,343	6,510	827,093	15,913	147,367	1	1	2	1
American Indian and Alaska Native	929	28,116	167	(D)	(D)	(D)	8	5	14	(D)
Men	618	21,619	130	14,679	337	3,199	9	6	16	6
Women	311	6,497	37	(D)	(D)	(D)	13	11	27	(D)
Black	35,725	1,084,014	5,570	679,204	12,374	137,101	-	-	-	-
Men	22,946	798,775	4,099	504,496	9,059	103,415	-	-	-	-
Women	12,779	285,239	1,471	174,708	3,315	33,686	-	-	-	-
Hispanic	94,754	4,108,076	20,845	2,886,579	49,942	555,868	-	1	1	1
Men	71,996	3,495,544	17,278	2,478,732	41,125	479,386	1	1	1	1
Women	22,758	612,532	3,567	407,847	8,817	76,482	1	2	3	2
Asian and Pacific Islander	21,753	1,787,067	5,704	(D)	(D)	(D)	1	1	2	(D)
Men	14,408	1,420,025	4,234	1,038,064	12,591	126,550	1	1	2	1
Women	7,345	367,042	1,470	(D)	(D)	(D)	2	2	4	(D)

[Continued]

★ 703 ★

Minority-Owned Firms: Southern States
[Continued]

Geographic area and minority	All firms		Firms with paid employees				Relative standard error of estimate % for column			
	Firms (number) A	Sales and receipts ($1,000) B	Firms (number) C	Sales and receipts ($1,000) D	Employees (number) E	Annual payroll ($1,000) F	A	B	C	D
Virginia	29,555	1,549,881	6,237	1,161,164	19,866	251,178	-	1	1	1
Minority men	19,503	1,137,589	4,688	839,131	12,900	167,215	1	1	1	1
Minority women	10,052	412,292	1,549	322,033	6,966	83,963	1	1	3	1
American Indian and Alaska Native	190	(D)	42	(D)	(D)	(D)	16	(D)	25	(D)
Men	68	4,886	22	3,885	44	1,154	15	16	19	20
Women	122	(D)	20	(D)	(D)	(D)	24	(D)	48	(D)
Black	18,781	810,569	3,530	610,435	11,094	143,513	-	-	-	-
Men	12,188	587,934	2,725	439,327	7,178	92,927	-	-	-	-
Women	6,593	222,635	805	171,108	3,916	50,586	-	-	-	-
Hispanic	2,716	140,917	483	103,186	1,605	28,485	2	1	3	1
Men	1,735	104,832	375	76,429	1,175	22,418	2	1	3	1
Women	981	36,085	108	26,757	430	6,067	3	1	10	1
Asian and Pacific Islander	7,973	(D)	2,209	(D)	(D)	(D)	2	(D)	3	(D)
Men	5,580	451,185	1,584	330,230	4,604	53,310	2	2	3	2
Women	2,393	(D)	625	(D)	(D)	(D)	4	(D)	6	(D)
West Virginia	1,446	127,700	428	109,604	1,391	14,994	1	1	1	1
Minority men	941	108,673	331	95,580	1,100	12,686	1	1	2	1
Minority women	505	19,027	97	14,024	291	2,308	2	2	3	2
American Indian and Alaska Native	28	1,438	8	1,015	15	144	15	1	-	-
Men	16	1,139	5	(D)	(D)	(D)	-	-	-	(D)
Women	12	299	3	(D)	(D)	(D)	36	3	-	(D)
Black	727	38,930	107	32,959	264	4,130	-	-	-	-
Men	430	33,090	82	29,124	196	3,521	-	-	-	-
Women	297	5,840	25	3,835	68	609	-	-	-	-
Hispanic	177	13,847	46	10,323	126	1,417	1	-	-	-
Men	130	12,960	40	(D)	(D)	(D)	1	-	-	(D)
Women	47	887	6	(D)	(D)	(D)	-	-	-	(D)
Asian and Pacific Islander	523	74,821	271	66,568	995	9,470	3	2	2	2
Men	369	62,653	207	56,939	783	7,850	4	2	3	2
Women	154	12,168	64	9,629	212	1,620	7	3	5	3

Source: 1987 Economic Censuses, Survey of Minority-Owned Business Enterprises: Summary, U.S. Department of Commerce, Bureau of the Census, 1991, pp. 18-28. Primary source: 1987 Survey of Minority-Owned Businesses. *Minority-Owned Businesses*, Washington, D.C., U.S. Government Printing Office, 1990. Arranged by the editors. Details may not add to total because of rounding and because a firm may be included in more than one minority group. (D) stands for data withheld to avoid disclosure of competitive information. *Note:* A dash (-) represents zero.

★ 704 ★
Businesses

Minority-Owned Firms: Western States

Data are shown for 1987.

Geographic area and minority	All firms		Firms with paid employees				Relative standard error of estimate % for column			
	Firms (number) A	Sales and receipts ($1,000) B	Firms (number) C	Sales and receipts ($1,000) D	Employees (number) E	Annual payroll ($1,000) F	A	B	C	D
Alaska	6,011	236,742	818	118,135	1,756	23,894	2	2	6	2
Minority men	4,553	193,273	636	99,240	1,451	20,670	2	2	8	2
Minority women	1,458	43,469	182	18,895	305	3,224	5	7	12	3
American Indian and Alaska Native	4,006	117,726	405	37,182	320	6,229	3	4	11	5
Men	3,256	98,566	325	30,933	257	5,465	3	4	13	6
Women	750	19,160	80	6,249	63	764	9	13	23	5
Black	507	14,444	81	9,050	200	2,181	-	-	-	-
Men	285	10,461	57	6,925	158	1,747	-	-	-	-
Women	222	3,983	24	2,125	42	434	-	-	-	-
Hispanic	502	27,412	86	18,099	282	3,926	5	3	11	2
Men	316	19,498	48	13,976	216	3,176	6	1	3	-
Women	186	7,914	38	4,123	66	750	9	9	25	8
Asian and Pacific Islander	1,028	78,378	250	54,286	957	11,591	7	3	10	1
Men	711	65,501	208	47,747	822	10,298	8	3	12	2
Women	317	12,877	42	6,539	135	1,293	14	12	-	-
Arizona	14,960	904,314	3,384	679,621	15,025	126,476	1	1	2	1
Minority men	10,191	714,866	2,721	535,350	12,055	101,134	1	1	3	1
Minority women	4,769	189,448	663	144,271	2,970	25,342	3	2	5	1
American Indian and Alaska Native	872	50,276	165	41,613	491	4,364	5	3	11	3
Men	648	38,471	132	31,381	417	3,521	6	3	13	2
Women	224	11,805	33	10,232	74	843	11	8	19	8
Black	1,811	91,439	319	68,032	1,601	14,161	-	-	-	-
Men	1,154	56,333	241	38,594	1,196	9,901	-	-	-	-
Women	657	35,106	78	29,438	405	4,260	-	-	-	-
Hispanic	9,845	513,125	2,206	384,281	8,969	78,329	1	1	3	1
Men	6,802	423,294	1,834	320,696	7,304	63,870	2	1	4	1
Women	3,043	89,831	372	63,585	1,665	14,459	4	3	7	2
Asian and Pacific Islander	2,526	253,109	736	187,903	3,988	867	2	1	2	1
Men	1,658	200,048	554	146,733	3,161	24,081	3	1	3	1
Women	868	53,061	182	41,170	827	5,786	5	3	5	2
California	324,584	25,022,349	72,765	18,244,209	264,410	2,953,274	-	-	1	-
Minority men	226,601	20,201,916	57,261	14,890,888	207,144	2,355,317	-	-	1	-
Minority women	97,983	4,820,433	15,504	3,353,321	57,266	597,957	1	1	1	1
American Indian and Alaska Native	3,280	162,179	631	109,621	1,572	21,332	5	4	8	4
Men	2,173	126,118	501	87,086	1,213	17,417	5	5	10	5
Women	1,107	36,061	130	22,535	359	3,915	8	6	16	6
Black	47,728	2,364,024	7,614	1,618,988	22,631	340,281	-	-	-	-
Men	29,627	1,621,645	5,466	1,103,238	16,174	238,186	-	-	-	-
Women	18,101	742,379	2,148	515,750	6,457	102,095	-	-	-	-
Hispanic	132,212	8,119,853	26,886	5,786,143	89,722	1,136,230	-	-	1	-
Men	95,254	6,772,518	22,127	4,886,061	72,588	939,893	1	-	1	1
Women	36,958	1,347,335	4,759	900,082	17,134	196,337	1	1	3	1
Asian and Pacific Islander	144,353	14,620,377	38,273	10,907,652	153,519	1,490,434	-	-	1	-

[Continued]

★ 704 ★

Minority-Owned Firms: Western States
[Continued]

Geographic area and minority	All firms		Firms with paid employees				Relative standard error of estimate % for column			
	Firms (number) A	Sales and receipts ($1,000) B	Firms (number) C	Sales and receipts ($1,000) D	Employees (number) E	Annual payroll ($1,000) F	A	B	C	D
Men	101,562	11,871,690	29,653	8,957,609	119,360	1,187,089	1	-	1	-
Women	42,791	2,748,687	8,620	1,950,043	34,159	303,345	1	1	2	1
Colorado	15,762	725,030	3,196	530,568	9,704	103,027	1	1	2	1
Minority men	10,314	546,308	2,372	397,272	7,080	77,051	1	1	3	1
Minority women	5,448	178,722	824	133,296	2,624	25,976	2	2	4	2
American Indian and Alaska Native	351	14,084	38	(D)	(D)	(D)	12	4	17	(D)
Men	226	12,332	31	9,770	104	1,087	14	5	21	1
Women	125	1,752	7	(D)	(D)	(D)	19	17	-	(D)
Black	2,871	105,849	414	69,259	1,051	15,794	-	-	-	-
Men	1,751	70,180	291	44,068	715	11,906	-	-	-	-
Women	1,120	35,669	123	25,191	336	3,888	-	-	-	-
Hispanic	9,516	394,410	1,813	290,756	4,601	56,903	2	2	4	2
Men	6,381	305,643	1,402	226,079	3,480	42,751	2	2	4	2
Women	3,135	88,767	411	64,677	1,121	14,152	4	4	8	4
Asian and Pacific Islander	3,192	215,875	952	(D)	(D)	(D)	2	2	3	(D)
Men	2,066	162,137	665	119,259	2,859	21,769	3	2	4	2
Women	1,126	53,738	287	(D)	(D)	(D)	4	3	6	(D)
Hawaii	32,705	1,721,407	4,618	1,157,349	15,671	184,967	-	1	2	1
Minority men	21,137	1,284,297	3,309	876,968	10,875	139,234	1	1	2	1
Minority women	11,568	437,110	1,309	280,381	4,796	45,753	2	2	3	2
American Indian and Alaska Native	106	6,239	16	5,512	48	675	21	3	15	2
Men	81	5,897	15	(D)	(D)	(D)	23	3	16	(D)
Women	25	342	1	(D)	(D)	(D)	54	10	-	(D)
Black	399	12,310	52	7,429	147	1,286	-	-	-	-
Men	254	8,125	41	(D)	(D)	(D)	-	-	-	(D)
Women	145	4,185	11	(D)	(D)	(D)	-	-	-	(D)
Hispanic	1,226	58,098	177	41,838	542	5,923	4	2	6	2
Men	822	50,190	135	37,597	459	5,200	5	2	8	2
Women	404	7,908	42	4,241	83	723	8	6	9	7
Asian and Pacific Islander	31,300	1,656,030	4,427	1,109,366	15,046	178,004	-	1	2	1
Men	20,186	1,228,047	3,158	833,809	10,367	133,163	1	1	2	1
Women	11,114	427,983	1,269	275,557	4,479	44,841	2	2	4	2
Idaho	1,541	70,760	362	53,922	1,173	10,286	2	1	4	1
Minority men	1,121	60,989	297	47,283	1,032	9,114	3	1	4	1
Minority women	420	9,771	65	6,639	141	1,172	5	3	8	3
American Indian and Alaska Native	80	6,965	17	(D)	(D)	(D)	11	-	-	(D)
Men	61	5,801	13	5,011	42	843	12	-	-	-
Women	19	1,164	4	(D)	(D)	(D)	25	2	-	(D)
Black	94	4,776	26	3,583	98	630	-	-	-	-
Men	67	3,026	16	1,981	69	352	-	-	-	-
Women	27	1,750	10	1,602	29	278	-	-	-	-
Hispanic	974	30,594	187	20,880	270	4,008	3	1	7	1
Men	731	26,000	153	17,965	220	3,564	3	1	8	1

[Continued]

★ 704 ★

Minority-Owned Firms: Western States
[Continued]

Geographic area and minority	All firms		Firms with paid employees				Relative standard error of estimate % for column			
	Firms (number) A	Sales and receipts ($1,000) B	Firms (number) C	Sales and receipts ($1,000) D	Employees (number) E	Annual payroll ($1,000) F	A	B	C	D
Women	243	4,594	34	2,915	50	444	7	4	11	2
Asian and Pacific Islander	433	30,671	143	(D)	(D)	(D)	5	1	4	(D)
Men	286	27,365	118	23,096	714	4,503	5	1	3	1
Women	147	3,306	25	(D)	(D)	(D)	10	6	20	(D)
Montana	989	46,819	236	36,276	763	6,238	2	1	2	-
Minority men	674	37,159	183	28,988	569	4,746	3	1	2	-
Minority women	315	9,660	53	7,288	194	1,492	5	1	7	-
American Indian and Alaska Native	405	16,510	83	12,619	157	1,609	5	2	7	-
Men	281	13,163	62	10,147	119	1,220	5	2	7	1
Women	124	3,347	21	2,472	38	389	10	4	18	1
Black	77	6,944	21	6,255	123	1,027	-	-	-	-
Men	45	4,054	15	3,798	61	403	-	-	-	-
Women	32	2,890	6	2,457	62	624	-	-	-	-
Hispanic	304	10,107	61	6,416	114	995	2	1	-	-
Men	215	9,026	53	5,951	95	890	2	1	-	-
Women	89	1,081	8	465	19	105	4	2	-	-
Asian and Pacific Islander	207	13,317	72	11,020	371	2,613	6	1	-	-
Men	135	10,953	54	9,126	296	2,239	6	1	-	-
Women	72	2,364	18	1,894	75	374	14	1	-	-
Nevada	4,116	271,038	915	201,131	4,072	42,892	1	-	2	-
Minority men	2,741	216,537	686	162,556	6,300	35,970	2	1	3	-
Minority women	1,375	54,501	229	38,575	772	6,922	3	1	4	1
American Indian and Alaska Native	150	8,712	33	6,967	75	897	11	2	11	2
Men	101	6,289	20	4,952	31	492	14	3	18	2
Women	49	2,423	13	2,015	44	405	19	3	-	-
Black	1,002	38,608	182	27,916	592	4,925	-	-	-	-
Men	591	24,798	120	18,124	427	3,274	-	-	-	-
Women	411	13,810	62	9,792	165	1,651	-	-	-	-
Hispanic	1,767	141,608	385	109,257	2,250	26,056	3	1	5	-
Men	1,274	124,395	322	97,961	2,017	23,858	3	1	6	-
Women	493	17,213	63	11,296	233	2,198	7	3	5	1
Asian and Pacific Islander	1,245	83,915	320	58,251	1,197	11,264	3	1	4	1
Men	818	62,405	228	42,418	855	8,536	4	1	4	1
Women	427	21,510	92	15,833	342	2,728	7	2	10	1
New Mexico	16,963	828,247	4,279	625,462	12,868	114,331	1	1	2	1
Minority men	12,174	688,118	3,523	529,463	10,273	94,535	1	1	2	1
Minority women	4,789	140,129	756	95,999	2,595	19,796	2	2	5	2
American Indian and Alaska Native	1,258	37,474	151	(D)	(D)	(D)	5	3	11	(D)
Men	782	25,051	98	17,916	276	3,378	7	3	9	3
Women	476	12,423	53	(D)	(D)	(D)	9	5	26	(D)
Black	587	27,133	110	20,762	481	4,284	-	-	-	-
Men	374	14,437	76	10,733	246	2,161	-	-	-	-
Women	213	12,696	34	10,029	235	2,123	-	-	-	-

[Continued]

★ 704 ★

Minority-Owned Firms: Western States
[Continued]

Geographic area and minority	All firms		Firms with paid employees				Relative standard error of estimate % for column			
	Firms (number) A	Sales and receipts ($1,000) B	Firms (number) C	Sales and receipts ($1,000) D	Employees (number) E	Annual payroll ($1,000) F	A	B	C	D
Hispanic	14,299	702,098	3,716	529,176	10,680	97,036	1	1	2	1
Men	10,450	600,900	3,126	463,471	8,776	82,502	1	1	2	1
Women	3,849	101,198	590	65,705	1,904	14,534	3	3	6	2
Asian and Pacific Islander	897	66,611	330	(D)	(D)	(D)	5	2	4	(D)
Men	619	50,911	242	40,108	1,025	6,898	6	3	5	4
Women	278	15,700	88	(D)	(D)	(D)	11	3	8	(D)
Oregon	5,725	476,830	1,575	379,657	6,651	57,417	1	1	2	1
Minority men	3,735	372,305	1,178	299,810	4,897	43,763	2	1	2	1
Minority women	1,990	104,525	397	79,847	1,754	13,654	3	2	3	1
American Indian and Alaska Native	333	19,200	47	14,242	217	2,790	8	4	13	1
Men	187	15,781	32	12,751	189	2,608	10	2	16	1
Women	146	3,419	15	1,491	28	182	13	19	25	7
Black	848	34,136	134	24,189	448	4,456	-	-	-	-
Men	510	20,417	85	13,982	279	2,805	-	-	-	-
Women	338	13,719	49	10,207	169	1,651	-	-	-	-
Hispanic	1,598	109,642	403	89,053	1,445	15,363	3	1	5	1
Men	1,118	84,628	325	68,964	1,194	12,859	4	1	5	1
Women	480	25,014	78	20,089	251	2,504	7	2	9	-
Asian and Pacific Islander	3,007	331,950	1,002	269,264	4,644	37,664	2	1	2	1
Men	1,962	269,254	744	221,050	3,328	28,302	2	1	3	1
Women	1,045	62,696	258	48,214	1,316	9,362	4	2	4	2
Utah	2,722	125,866	543	89,343	1,987	16,101	2	1	4	1
Minority men	1,718	104,670	448	77,636	1,578	13,930	3	1	4	1
Minority women	1,004	21,196	95	11,707	409	2,171	6	3	9	2
American Indian and Alaska Native	110	(D)	16	2,648	40	615	15	(D)	25	2
Men	66	3,066	12	2,544	40	596	17	2	31	2
Women	44	(D)	4	104	-	19	29	(D)	35	38
Black	202	8,615	35	5,619	110	1,212	-	-	-	-
Men	125	5,109	23	3,829	79	987	-	-	-	-
Women	77	3,506	12	1,790	31	225	-	-	-	-
Hispanic	1,300	47,255	228	31,506	657	6,056	3	2	7	1
Men	842	40,578	204	28,612	497	5,471	4	1	8	1
Women	458	6,677	24	2,894	160	585	8	7	-	-
Asian and Pacific Islander	1,129	(D)	270	50,313	1,196	8,338	4	(D)	5	1
Men	697	56,765	215	43,394	978	6,996	5	1	5	1
Women	432	(D)	55	6,919	218	1,342	10	(D)	16	4
Washington	13,408	1,103,835	3,413	899,335	14,242	141,891	1	1	2	-
Minority men	8,838	869,808	2,571	716,871	11,219	109,176	1	1	2	1
Minority women	4,570	234,027	842	182,464	3,023	32,715	2	1	4	1
American Indian and Alaska Native	682	47,803	126	36,180	314	6,057	9	4	19	3
Men	442	34,572	93	24,825	211	3,380	10	5	23	3
Women	240	13,231	33	11,355	103	2,677	17	5	31	4
Black	2,583	175,671	436	148,082	2,212	29,085	-	-	-	-

[Continued]

★ 704 ★

Minority-Owned Firms: Western States

[Continued]

Geographic area and minority	All firms		Firms with paid employees				Relative standard error of estimate % for column			
	Firms (number) A	Sales and receipts ($1,000) B	Firms (number) C	Sales and receipts ($1,000) D	Employees (number) E	Annual payroll ($1,000) F	A	B	C	D
Men	1,561	99,348	301	81,986	1,518	17,708	-	-	-	-
Women	1,022	76,323	135	66,096	694	11,377	-	-	-	-
Hispanic	2,686	141,196	553	108,472	2,333	21,424	2	1	2	-
Men	1,859	122,980	463	96,785	1,988	19,009	2	1	2	1
Women	827	18,216	90	11,687	345	2,415	4	2	4	1
Asian and Pacific Islander	7,559	744,585	2,322	611,190	9,455	86,223	2	1	2	1
Men	5,042	617,577	1,731	517,630	7,569	69,939	2	1	3	1
Women	2,517	127,008	591	93,560	1,886	16,284	4	3	6	2
Wyoming	885	39,712	229	29,973	799	6,431	1	-	2	-
Minority men	585	27,238	167	19,817	509	4,388	2	-	2	-
Minority women	300	12,474	62	10,156	290	2,043	3	-	3	-
American Indian and Alaska Native	79	(D)	17	2,273	61	666	3	(D)	-	-
Men	50	2,649	12	1,816	48	564	4	-	-	-
Women	29	(D)	5	457	13	102	-	(D)	-	-
Black	81	3,512	11	2,605	56	785	-	-	-	-
Men	51	1,776	8	1,006	15	224	-	-	-	-
Women	30	1,736	3	1,599	41	561	-	-	-	-
Hispanic	584	21,736	134	15,838	381	3,146	2	1	3	-
Men	394	13,909	94	9,307	207	2,034	2	1	3	1
Women	190	7,827	40	6,531	174	1,112	5	1	5	-
Asian and Pacific Islander	154	(D)	68	9,361	307	1,850	1	(D)	-	-
Men	102	9,319	54	7,792	245	1,582	-	-	-	-
Women	52	(D)	14	1,569	62	268	4	(D)	-	-

Source: 1987 Economic Censuses, Survey of Minority-Owned Business Enterprises: Summary, U.S. Department of Commerce, Bureau of the Census, 1991, pp. 18-28. Primary source: 1987 Survey of Minority-Owned Businesses. *Minority-Owned Businesses*, Washington, D.C., U.S. Government Printing Office, 1990. Arranged by the editors. Details may not add to total because of rounding and because a firm may be included in more than one minority group. (D) stands for data withheld to avoid disclosure of competitive information. *Note:* A dash (-) represents zero.

★ 705 ★

Businesses

Native American Owned Firms: Comparison to Minority and U.S. Firms - 1987

Data include American Indian, Aleut, and Eskimo business owners.

Industry	Native-owned firms (number)	Native sales and receipts ($ thous.)	Percent of -			
			Minority-owned		All U.S.	
			Firms	Sales and receipts ($ thous.)	Firms	Sales and receipts ($ thous.)
All industries	21,380	911,279	1.76	1.17	0.16	0.05
Agriculture, forestry, and fishing	3,661	104,446	9.93	7.61	1.03	0.51
Mining	106	4,062	6.57	3.94	0.09	0.03

[Continued]

★ 705 ★

Native American Owned Firms: Comparison to Minority and U.S. Firms - 1987
[Continued]

Industry	Native-owned firms (number)	Native sales and receipts ($ thous.)	Percent of -			
			Minority-owned		All U.S.	
			Firms	Sales and receipts ($ thous.)	Firms	Sales and receipts ($ thous.)
Construction	2,832	155,784	2.63	2.26	0.17	0.07
Manufacturing	911	63,563	3.05	1.60	0.21	0.03
Transportation and public utilities	917	44,286	1.20	1.21	0.15	0.06
Wholesale trade	360	36,058	1.36	0.45	0.08	0.01
Retail trade	3,090	268,086	1.37	1.00	0.14	0.05
Finance, insurance, and real estate	614	20,192	0.80	0.73	0.05	0.02
Services	7,604	178,165	1.35	0.81	0.13	0.04
Industries not classified	1,285	36,637	1.84	1.64	0.18	0.09

Source: Derived from *1987 Economic Censuses, Survey of Minority-Owned Business Enterprises: Summary*, U.S. Department of Commerce, Bureau of the Census, MB87-4, 1991. *Note:* Percentages may not add to 100 due to rounding.

★ 706 ★
Businesses

Native American Owned Firms, by Group and Legal Form of Organization

The number of firms owned and sales receipts, in thousands of dollars, are shown, by Native American group and legal form of organization.

Industry division, legal form of organization, and Native American group	All firms		Firms with paid employees				Relative standard error of estimate (percent) for column--			
	Firms (number) A	Sales and receipts ($1,000) B	Firms (number) C	Sales and receipts ($1,000) D	Employees (number) E	Annual payroll ($1,000) F	A	B	C	D
All industries	376,711	34,035,605	96,457	25,104,127	360,301	3,611,188	-	-	-	-
Subchapter S corporations	16,835	8,540,824	12,898	8,105,811	107,490	1,375,375	-	-	-	-
Aleut	13	5,611	6	(D)	(D)	(D)	-	-	-	(D)
Eskimo	14	9,398	13	(D)	(D)	(D)	14	1	16	(D)
American Indian	333	123,117	223	114,378	1,991	25,363	3	1	3	1
Individual proprietorships	340,615	21,244,191	72,910	13,673,165	190,929	1,748,585	-	-	1	-
Aleut	1,109	44,151	106	14,617	148	3,377	8	9	21	15
Eskimo	2,317	41,148	261	11,077	87	1,730	5	7	16	9
American Indian	17,028	588,874	2,880	370,735	5,629	66,130	2	1	3	1
Partnerships	19,261	4,250,590	10,649	3,325,151	61,882	487,228	-	-	1	-
Aleut	21	3,539	4	(D)	(D)	(D)	7	7	-	(D)
Eskimo	22	4,008	6	(D)	(D)	(D)	-	-	-	(D)
American Indian	523	91,433	240	74,371	951	9,652	3	2	3	2

Source: 1987 Economic Censuses, Survey of Minority-Owned Business Enterprises: Asian Americans, American Indians, and Other Minorities, U.S. Department of Commerce, Bureau of the Census, p. 104. *Notes:* A dash (-) represents zero. (D) stands for data withheld to avoid disclosure for individual companies.

★ 707 ★

Businesses

Native American Owned Firms, by Major Industry Group, 1987

The number of firms owned and sales receipts, in thousands of dollars, are shown, by Native American group and major industry, for 1987. This table is based on the 1972 Standard Industrial Classification (SIC) system.

| Major industry group and minority | All firms | | Firms with paid employees | | | | Relative standard error of estimated (percent)[1] for column- | | | |
	Firms (number) A	Sales and receipts ($1,000) B	Firms (number) C	Sales and receipts ($1,000) D	Employees (number) E	Annual payroll ($1,000) F	A	B	C	D
All Industries										
American Indian	17,884	803,424	3,343	559,484	8,571	101,145	1	1	3	1
Aleut	1,143	53,301	116	20,094	212	4,519	8	7	19	11
Eskimo	2,353	54,554	280	23,211	173	3,607	5	5	15	4
Agricultural services, forestry, and fishing										
American Indian	1,377	46,965	162	20,132	438	5,997	6	7	14	8
Aleut	671	34,207	52	7,743	48	2,196	10	10	32	20
Eskimo	1,613	23,274	157	2,234	-	757	5	10	23	37
Agricultural services	444	19,081	75	12,534	339	4,120	9	2	14	2
Forestry	89	1,368	12	803	30	266	-	-	-	-
Fishing, hunting and trapping	3,128	83,997	284	16,772	117	4,564	3	6	16	14
Mining										
American Indian	100	4,003	8	1,882	28	522	11	5	-	-
Aleut	-	-	-	-	-	-	-	-	-	-
Eskimo	6	59	-	-	-	-	-	-	-	-
Metal mining	11	(D)	2	(D)	(D)	(D)	-	(D)	-	(D)
Anthracite mining	-	-	-	-	-	-	-	-	-	-
Bituminous coal and lignite mining	3	(D)	-	-	-	-	-	(D)	-	(D)
Oil and gas extraction	80	2,441	5	(D)	(D)	(D)	14	9	-	(D)
Nonmetallic minerals, except fuels	12	(D)	1	(D)	(D)	(D)	-	(D)	-	(D)
Construction										
American Indian	2,749	148,012	823	116,258	1,594	28,524	3	3	5	3
Aleut	40	590	6	268	8	32	30	22	57	23
Eskimo	43	7,182	6	(D)	(D)	(D)	18	2	-	(D)
General building contractors	461	34,219	175	28,153	251	5,269	6	5	11	5
Heavy construction contractors	93	(D)	38	15,549	178	3,902	3	(D)	-	-
Special trade contractors	2,268	97,410	619	72,247	1,166	19,299	3	3	6	4
Subdividers and developers, n.e.c.	10	(D)	3	(D)	(D)	(D)	-	(D)	-	(D)
Manufacturing										
American Indian	875	60,221	144	51,452	1,275	13,472	4	1	6	1
Aleut	8	(D)	2	(D)	(D)	(D)	31	(D)	-	(D)
Eskimo	28	(D)	2	(D)	(D)	(D)	27	(D)	-	(D)
Food and kindred products	9	314	2	(D)	(D)	(D)	-	-	-	(D)
Tobacco manufacturers	-	-	-	-	-	-	-	-	-	-
Textile mill products	13	262	2	(D)	(D)	(D)	-	-	-	(D)
Apparel and other textile products	76	(D)	6	(D)	(D)	(D)	14	(D)	24	(D)
Lumber and wood products	274	22,230	78	18,796	407	5,155	7	2	10	1
Furniture and fixtures	21	702	2	(D)	(D)	(D)	19	17	-	(D)
Paper and allied products	2	(D)	-	-	-	-	-	(D)	-	-
Printing and publishing	50	2,501	11	2,192	58	680	19	1	-	-
Chemicals and allied products	4	146	2	(D)	(D)	(D)	-	-	-	(D)
Petroleum and coal products	-	-	-	-	-	-	-	-	-	-
Rubber and miscellaneous plastic products	5	251	1	(D)	(D)	(D)	-	-	-	(D)
Leather and leather products	18	212	2	(D)	(D)	(D)	-	-	-	(D)
Stone, clay and glass products	60	2,040	7	1,493	16	225	12	2	-	-
Primary metal industries	10	(D)	2	(D)	(D)	(D)	-	(D)	-	(D)
Fabricated metal products	91	2,153	6	1,356	16	239	10	3	-	-
Machinery, except electrical	34	4,090	8	3,635	44	1,042	11	6	17	6
Electric and electronic equipment	8	4,250	3	4,236	59	630	31	-	-	-
Transportation equipment	7	694	4	(D)	(D)	(D)	-	-	-	(D)

[Continued]

★ 707 ★

Native American Owned Firms, by Major Industry Group, 1987

[Continued]

Major industry group and minority	All firms		Firms with paid employees				Relative standard error of estimated (percent)[1] for column-			
	Firms (number) A	Sales and receipts ($1,000) B	Firms (number) C	Sales and receipts ($1,000) D	Employees (number) E	Annual payroll ($1,000) F	A	B	C	D
Instruments and related products	3	14	-	-	-	-	-	-	-	-
Miscellaneous manufacturing industries	226	4,266	12	2,320	57	530	9	14	-	-
Transportation and public utilities										
American Indian	819	41,675	152	22,483	270	3,881	5	4	9	4
Aleut	48	1,680	2	(D)	(D)	(D)	30	18	-	(D)
Eskimo	50	931	7	(D)	(D)	(D)	23	17	48	(D)
Local and interurban passenger transit	95	2,941	13	1,357	40	265	13	12	26	-
Trucking and warehousing	590	32,189	125	15,359	185	2,900	6	5	11	6
Water transportation	12	695	3	452	10	127	-	-	-	-
Transportation by air	30	865	6	414	4	63	31	6	-	-
Pipe lines, except natural gas	-	-	-	-	-	-	-	-	-	-
Transportation services	134	6,296	8	4,711	34	494	13	3	-	-
Communication	36	682	2	(D)	(D)	(D)	9	13	-	(D)
Electric, gas and sanitary services	20	618	4	(D)	(D)	(D)	-	-	-	-
Wholesale trade										
American Indian	340	34,585	91	(D)	(D)	(D)	9	3	17	(D)
Aleut	10	(D)	1	(D)	(D)	(D)	42	(D)	-	(D)
Eskimo	10	(D)	1	(D)	(D)	(D)	-	(d)	-	(D)
Wholesale trade-durable goods	247	24,294	60	18,867	158	2,251	11	3	20	2
Wholesale trade-nondurable goods	113	11,764	33	7,623	34	504	12	5	27	6
Retail trade										
American Indian	2,842	250,240	768	197,629	2,287	19,098	4	2	4	2
Aleut	91	5,564	27	3,688	28	339	24	20	37	27
Eskimo	157	12,282	42	8,874	112	733	17	3	20	1
Building materials and garden supplies	61	5,578	17	4,509	35	733	13	4	8	5
General merchandise stores	72	8,394	29	6,658	47	385	15	7	15	9
Food stores	301	54,320	108	42,230	356	2,526	9	4	5	2
Automotive dealers and service stations	222	65,257	88	55,793	330	3,754	8	1	5	1
Apparel and accessory stores	85	5,994	36	4,992	88	516	11	4	14	4
Furniture and home furnishings stores	86	7,915	32	6,373	63	792	10	11	13	13
Eating and drinking places	464	35,251	286	29,492	1,083	6,224	8	7	9	6
Miscellaneous retail	1,799	85,377	241	60,144	425	5,240	5	4	10	3
Finance, insurance and real estate										
American Indian	562	17,999	69	10,903	198	2,370	8	6	20	5
Aleut	29	1,238	2	(D)	(D)	(D)	40	55	-	(D)
Eskimo	23	955	-	-	-	-	46	82	-	-
Banking	1	(D)	1	(D)	(D)	(D)	-	(D)	-	(D)
Credit agencies other than banks	1	(D)	1	(D)	(D)	(D)	-	(D)	-	(D)
Security, commodity brokers and services	30	(D)	12	369	3	54	34	(D)	58	35
Insurance carriers	-	-	-	-	-	-	-	-	-	-
Insurance agents, brokers, and service	152	5,051	20	2,321	40	500	15	21	27	1
Real estate	370	12,746	33	7,710	150	1,668	10	7	31	7
Combined real estate, insurance, etc.	59	1,212	4	411	9	96	21	34	-	-
Holding and other investment offices	1	(D)	-	-	-	-	-	(D)	-	-
Services										
American Indian	7,132	168,784	1,007	102,075	2,218	22,837	2	3	5	3
Aleut	210	3,547	13	2,007	38	496	17	10	11	3
Eskimo	262	5,834	53	4,314	41	1,057	16	11	26	13
Hotels and other lodging places	102	5,734	34	5,090	98	788	15	3	10	3
Personal services	1,719	26,547	223	14,128	519	4,388	5	6	11	9
Business services	2,532	48,601	319	23,585	545	6,238	5	5	12	5

[Continued]

★ 707 ★

Native American Owned Firms, by Major Industry Group, 1987

[Continued]

Major industry group and minority	All firms		Firms with paid employees				Relative standard error of estimated (percent)[1] for column-			
	Firms (number) A	Sales and receipts ($1,000) B	Firms (number) C	Sales and receipts ($1,000) D	Employees (number) E	Annual payroll ($1,000) F	A	B	C	D
Auto repair, services and garages	538	20,704	134	14,111	226	2,710	8	7	11	8
Miscellaneous repair services	300	11,105	53	8,023	103	1,144	9	5	12	6
Motion pictures	34	1,691	5	(D)	(D)	(D)	20	9	-	(D)
Amusement and recreation services	556	15,698	57	11,602	212	1,663	8	3	23	2
Health services	488	20,840	91	13,417	205	2,293	10	11	18	11
Legal services	169	11,153	52	8,400	105	1,916	8	4	10	2
Educational services	210	1,051	3	214	4	38	12	7	-	-
Social services	451	3,842	28	1,413	85	545	10	8	-	-
Museums, botanical, zoological gardens	-	-	-	-	-	-	-	-	-	-
Miscellaneous services	505	11,109	74	(D)	(D)	(D)	9	8	21	(D)
Industries not classified										
American Indian	1,088	30,940	119	11,496	72	1,712	6	9	18	10
Aleut	36	2,296	11	1,732	40	505	45	57	86	74
Eskimo	161	3,401	12	773	7	136	15	26	80	19

Source: 1987 Economic Censuses, Survey of Minority-Owned Business Enterprises: Asian Americans, American Indians, and Other Minorities, U.S. Department of Commerce, Bureau of the Census, pp. 12-17. *Notes:* A dash (-) stands for zero. A (D) indicates data were withheld to avoid disclosure of individual companies.

★ 708 ★

Businesses

Native American Owned Firms: Percent Distribution by Industry

Data include American Indian, Aleut, and Eskimo business owners.

Industry	Number of firms	Share of firms (percent)	Sales and receipts ($000)	Share of sales (percent)
All industries	21,380	100.0	911,279	100.0
Agriculture, forestry, and fishing	3,661	17.1	104,446	11.5
Mining	106	0.5	4,062	0.4
Construction	2,832	13.2	155,784	17.1
Manufacturing	911	4.3	63,563	7.0
Transportation and public utilities	917	4.3	44,286	4.9
Wholesale trade	360	1.7	36,058	4.0
Retail trade	3,090	14.5	268,086	29.4
Finance, insurance, and real estate	614	2.9	20,192	2.2
Services	7,604	35.6	178,165	19.6
Industries not classified	1,285	6.0	36,637	4.0

Source: Derived from *1987 Economic Censuses, Survey of Minority-Owned Business Enterprises: Summary,* U.S. Department of Commerce, Bureau of the Census, MB87-4. *Note:* Percentages rounded to nearest tenth. Detail may not add to 100%.

★ 709 ★

Businesses

Native American Owned Firms, by State, 1987 - I

The number of firms owned and sales receipts, in thousands of dollars, are shown, by Native American group and state, for 1987.

Geographic area and Native American Group	All firms		Firms with paid employees				Relative standard error of estimated (percent)[1] for column-			
	Firms (number) A	Sales and receipts ($1,000) B	Firms (number) C	Sales and receipts ($1,000) D	Employees (number) E	Annual payroll ($1,000) F	A	B	C	D
United States										
American Indian	17,884	803,424	3,343	559,484	8,571	101,145	1	1	3	1
Aleut	1,143	53,301	116	20,094	212	4,519	8	7	19	11
Eskimo	2,353	54,554	280	23,211	173	3,607	5	5	15	4
Alabama										
American Indian	89	(D)	25	(D)	(D)	(D)	15	(D)	19	(D)
Aleut	1	(D)	1	(D)	(D)	(D)	-	(D)	-	(D)
Eskimo	-	-	-	-	-	-	-	-	-	-
Alaska										
American Indian	1,039	39,329	102	15,123	129	1,747	8	9	19	6
Aleut	821	37,253	63	9,072	83	2,234	9	9	26	17
Eskimo	2,146	41,144	240	12,987	108	2,248	5	6	16	7
Arizona										
American Indian	843	49,801	160	41,206	488	4,291	5	3	11	3
Aleut	11	(D)	1	(D)	(D)	(D)	86	(D)	-	(D)
Eskimo	18	(D)	4	(D)	(D)	(D)	39	(D)	87	(D)
Arkansas										
American Indian	91	3,141	11	1,694	32	219	12	4	14	6
Aleut	-	-	-	-	-	-	-	-	-	-
Eskimo	-	-	-	-	-	-	-	-	-	-
California										
American Indian	3,087	148,305	599	99,692	1,511	19,873	5	4	9	4
Aleut	112	5,103	28	(D)	(D)	(D)	25	35	49	(D)
Eskimo	81	8,771	4	(D)	(D)	(D)	30	9	35	(D)
Colorado										
American Indian	343	13,807	37	10,275	108	1,051	12	5	18	1
Aleut	2	(D)	1	(D)	(D)	(D)	-	(D)	-	(D)
Eskimo	6	(D)	-	-	-	-	59	(D)	-	-
Connecticut										
American Indian	87	2,087	9	785	13	155	14	13	23	19
Aleut	1	(D)	-	-	-	-	-	(D)	-	-
Eskimo	-	-	-	-	-	-	-	-	-	-
Delaware										
American Indian	42	1,177	7	664	13	178	11	1	-	-
Aleut	-	-	-	-	-	-	-	-	-	-
Eskimo	1	(D)	-	-	-	-	-	(D)	-	-
District of Columbia										
American Indian	28	865	2	(D)	(D)	(D)	21	5	-	(D)
Aleut	-	-	-	-	-	-	-	-	-	-
Eskimo	-	-	-	-	-	-	-	-	-	-
Florida										
American Indian	348	18,250	71	14,639	219	2,677	11	8	20	9
Aleut	1	(D)	1	(D)	(D)	(D)	-	(D)	-	(D)
Eskimo	-	-	-	-	-	-	-	-	-	-

[Continued]

★ 709 ★

Native American Owned Firms, by State, 1987 - I
[Continued]

Geographic area and Native American Group	All firms		Firms with paid employees				Relative standard error of estimated (percent)[1] for column-			
	Firms (number) A	Sales and receipts ($1,000) B	Firms (number) C	Sales and receipts ($1,000) D	Employees (number) E	Annual payroll ($1,000) F	A	B	C	D
Georgia										
American Indian	122	5,282	33	2,925	42	637	13	8	21	11
Aleut	-	-	-	-	-	-	-	-	-	-
Eskimo	7	433	6	(D)	(D)	(D)	64	9	75	(D)
Hawaii										
American Indian	89	6,201	16	5,512	48	675	22	3	15	2
Aleut	6	6	-	-	-	-	92	92	-	-
Eskimo	11	32	-	-	-	-	86	59	-	-
Idaho										
American Indian	76	6,786	16	5,836	53	948	11	-	-	-
Aleut	-	-	-	-	-	-	-	-	-	-
Eskimo	4	179	1	(D)	(D)	(D)	-	-	-	(D)
Illinois										
American Indian	182	6,876	39	3,720	40	558	15	11	29	14
Aleut	2	(D)	1	(D)	(D)	(D)	-	(D)	-	(D)
Eskimo	9	(D)	8	78	6	38	63	(D)	71	59
Indiana										
American Indian	84	3,203	15	2,361	33	331	12	5	16	-
Aleut	3	15	-	-	-	-	83	83	-	-
Eskimo	3	3	-	-	-	-	81	81	-	-
Iowa										
American Indian	43	1,302	8	764	11	110	17	19	18	18
Aleut	-	-	-	-	-	-	-	-	-	-
Eskimo	-	-	-	-	-	-	-	-	-	-
Kansas										
American Indian	225	7,643	33	5,426	79	631	14	5	23	2
Aleut	6	(D)	-	-	-	-	90	(D)	-	-
Eskimo	-	-	-	-	-	-	-	-	-	-
Kentucky										
American Indian	24	1,705	7	1,575	17	203	10	1	-	-
Aleut	-	-	-	-	-	-	-	-	-	-
Eskimo	-	-	-	-	-	-	-	-	-	-
Louisiana										
American Indian	221	7,585	49	4,456	48	1,072	12	17	25	26
Aleut	2	(D)	1	(D)	(D)	(D)	-	(D)	-	(D)
Eskimo	2	(D0	-	-	-	-	71	(D)	-	-
Maine										
American Indian	68	3,956	15	3,012	46	541	7	1	-	-
Aleut	-	-	-	-	-	-	-	-	-	-
Eskimo	-	-	-	-	-	-	-	-	-	-
Maryland										
American Indian	123	9,411	25	8,035	96	1,451	18	5	11	4
Aleut	-	-	-	-	-	-	-	-	-	-
Eskimo	-	-	-	-	-	-	-	-	-	-

[Continued]

★ 709 ★

Native American Owned Firms, by State, 1987 - I

[Continued]

Geographic area and Native American Group	All firms		Firms with paid employees				Relative standard error of estimated (percent)[1] for column-			
	Firms (number) A	Sales and receipts ($1,000) B	Firms (number) C	Sales and receipts ($1,000) D	Employees (number) E	Annual payroll ($1,000) F	A	B	C	D
Massachusetts										
American Indian	132	4,557	24	(D)	(D)	(D)	13	7	23	(D)
Aleut	-	-	-	-	-	-	-	-	-	-
Eskimo	-	-	-	-	-	-	-	-	-	-
Michigan										
American Indian	304	8,512	41	5,626	85	999	10	7	14	7
Aleut	-	-	-	-	-	-	-	-	-	-
Eskimo	1	(D)	1	(D)	(D)	(D)	-	(D)	-	(D)
Minnesota										
American Indian	333	17,984	56	13,088	248	2,773	6	2	8	1
Aleut	7	70	-	-	-	-	49	55	-	-
Eskimo	-	-	-	-	-	-	-	-	-	-

Source: 1987 Economic Censuses, Survey of Minority-Owned Business Enterprises: Asian Americans, American Indians, and Other Minorities, U.S. Department of Commerce, Bureau of the Census, pp. 27-35. *Notes:* A dash (-) stands for zero. A (D) indicates data were withheld to avoid disclosure of individual companies.

★ 710 ★

Businesses

Native American Owned Firms, by State, 1987 - II

The number of firms owned and sales receipts, in thousands of dollars, are shown, by Native American group and state, for 1987.

Geographic area and Native American Group	All firms		Firms with paid employees				Relative standard error of estimated (percent)[1] for column-			
	Firms (number) A	Sales and receipts ($1,000) B	Firms (number) C	Sales and receipts ($1,000) D	Employees (number) E	Annual payroll ($1,000) F	A	B	C	D
Mississippi										
American Indian	49	2,260	10	1,666	13	152	25	9	37	12
Aleut	-	-	-	-	-	-	-	-	-	-
Eskimo	1	(D)	-	-	-	-	-	-	-	-
Missouri										
American Indian	133	(D)	15	(D)	(D)	(D)	11	(D)	30	(D)
Aleut	1	(D)	1	(D)	(D)	(D)	-	(D)	-	(D)
Eskimo	3	3	-	-	-	-	82	82	-	-
Montana										
American Indian	405	16,510	83	12,619	157	1,609	5	2	7	-
Aleut	-	-	-	-	-	-	-	-	-	-
Eskimo	-	-	-	-	-	-	-	-	-	-
Nebraska										
American Indian	66	1,611	18	947	18	204	11	9	21	16
Aleut	-	-	-	-	-	-	-	-	-	-
Eskimo	-	-	-	-	-	-	-	-	-	-
Nevada										
American Indian	146	8,552	33	6,967	75	897	11	2	11	2
Aleut	-	-	-	-	-	-	-	-	-	-

[Continued]

★ 710 ★

Native American Owned Firms, by State, 1987 - II

[Continued]

Geographic area and Native American Group	All firms		Firms with paid employees				Relative standard error of estimated (percent)[1] for column-			
	Firms (number) A	Sales and receipts ($1,000) B	Firms (number) C	Sales and receipts ($1,000) D	Employees (number) E	Annual payroll ($1,000) F	A	B	C	D
Eskimo	4	160	-	-	-	-	92	92	-	-
New Hampshire										
American Indian	27	1,263	3	625	2	54	11	1	-	-
Aleut	2	(D)	-	-	-	-	-	(D)	-	-
Eskimo	-	-	-	-	-	-	-	-	-	-
New Jersey										
American Indian	131	6,104	15	(D)	(D)	(D)	15	8	21	(D)
Aleut	3	(D)	1	(D)	(D)	(D)	-	(D)	-	(D)
Eskimo	1	(D)	1	(D)	(D)	(D)	-	(D)	-	(D)
New Mexico										
American Indian	1,247	37,002	150	26,486	502	5,269	5	3	11	3
Aleut	3	(D)	1	(D)	(D)	(D)	44	(D)	-	(D)
Eskimo	8	(D)	-	-	-	-	94	(D)	-	-
New York										
American Indian	425	24,468	85	14,518	251	3,553	11	10	19	10
Aleut	10	10	-	-	-	-	95	95	-	-
Eskimo	10	530	10	530	-	110	95	95	95	95
North Carolina										
American Indian	1,757	89,708	547	63,434	1,515	14,140	4	3	6	3
Aleut	-	-	-	-	-	-	-	-	-	-
Eskimo	1	(D)	-	-	-	-	-	(D)	-	-
North Dakota										
American Indian	208	18,273	56	15,868	117	1,708	3	-	4	-
Aleut	-	-	-	-	-	-	-	-	-	-
Eskimo	2	(D)	1	(D)	(D)	(D)	-	(D)	-	(D)
Ohio										
American Indian	149	6,352	20	(D)	(D)	(D)	15	4	10	(D)
Aleut	2	(D)	1	(D)	(D)	(D)	-	(D)	-	(D)
Eskimo	1	(D)	1	(D)	(D)	(D)	-	(D)	-	(D)
Oklahoma										
American Indian	2,044	57,062	268	33,812	456	5,489	3	2	6	3
Aleut	3	228	-	-	-	-	84	84	-	-
Eskimo	4	4	-	-	-	-	88	88	-	-
Oregon										
American Indian	306	19,078	47	14,242	217	2,790	9	4	13	1
Aleut	20	101	-	-	-	-	34	45	-	-
Eskimo	7	21	-	-	-	-	53	51	-	-
Pennsylvania										
American Indian	139	(D)	33	14,115	354	3,698	24	(D)	31	1
Aleut	-	-	-	-	-	-	-	-	-	-
Eskimo	1	(D)	1	(D)	(D)	(D)	-	(D)	-	(D)
Rhode Island										
American Indian	36	(D)	3	278	4	40	15	(D)	-	-
Aleut	-	-	-	-	-	-	-	-	-	-
Eskimo	-	-	-	-	-	-	-	-	-	-

[Continued]

★ 710 ★

Native American Owned Firms, by State, 1987 - II
[Continued]

Geographic area and Native American Group	All firms		Firms with paid employees				Relative standard error of estimated (percent)[1] for column-			
	Firms (number) A	Sales and receipts ($1,000) B	Firms (number) C	Sales and receipts ($1,000) D	Employees (number) E	Annual payroll ($1,000) F	A	B	C	D
South Carolina										
American Indian	47	3,832	15	3,049	79	568	11	2	9	2
Aleut	-	-	-	-	-	-	-	-	-	-
Eskimo	-	-	-	-	-	-	-	-	-	-
South Dakota										
American Indian	267	11,166	75	8,240	153	1,366	3	1	3	-
Aleut	-	-	-	-	-	-	-	-	-	-
Eskimo	-	-	-	-	-	-	-	-	-	-
Tennessee										
American Indian	89	3,338	18	2,314	30	240	12	6	21	9
Aleut	-	-	-	-	-	-	-	-	-	-
Eskimo	1	(D)	-	-	-	-	-	(D)	-	-
Texas										
American Indian	872	27,049	165	17,916	387	3,847	8	5	14	6
Aleut	57	1,067	2	(D)	(D)	(D)	38	35	-	(D)
Eskimo	-	-	-	-	-	-	-	-	-	-
Utah										
American Indian	109	3,347	16	2,648	40	615	15	3	25	2
Aleut	1	(D)	-	-	-	-	-	(D)	-	-
Eskimo	-	-	-	-	-	-	-	-	-	-
Vermont										
American Indian	9	(D)	-	-	-	-	-	(D)	-	-
Aleut	-	-	-	-	-	-	-	-	-	-
Eskimo	-	-	-	-	-	-	-	-	-	-
Virginia										
American Indian	188	7,080	41	5,375	91	1,454	16	12	26	15
Aleut	1	(D)	1	(D)	(D)	(D)	-	(D)	-	(D)
Eskimo	1	(D)	-	-	-	-	-	(D)	-	-
Washington										
American Indian	602	42,976	112	33,256	295	5,500	10	4	21	3
Aleut	64	3,609	12	(D)	(D)	(D)	27	11	31	(D)
Eskimo	16	1,218	2	(D)	(D)	(D)	59	1	-	(D)
West Virginia										
American Indian	28	1,438	8	1,015	15	144	15	1	-	-
Aleut	-	-	-	-	-	-	-	-	-	-
Eskimo	-	-	-	-	-	-	-	-	-	-
Wisconsin										
American Indian	306	21,087	89	18,280	520	3,808	10	4	14	5
Aleut	-	-	-	-	-	-	-	-	-	-
Eskimo	1	(D)	-	-	-	-	-	(D)	-	-
Wyoming										
American Indian	76	3,299	17	2,273	61	666	3	-	-	-

[Continued]

★ 710 ★

Native American Owned Firms, by State, 1987 - II

[Continued]

Geographic area and Native American Group	All firms		Firms with paid employees				Relative standard error of estimated (percent)[1] for column-			
	Firms (number) A	Sales and receipts ($1,000) B	Firms (number) C	Sales and receipts ($1,000) D	Employees (number) E	Annual payroll ($1,000) F	A	B	C	D
Aleut	1	(D)	-	-	-	-	-	(D)	-	-
Eskimo	2	(D)	-	-	-	-	-	(D)	-	-

Source: 1987 Economic Censuses, Survey of Minority-Owned Business Enterprises: Asian Americans, American Indians, and Other Minorities, U.S. Department of Commerce, Bureau of the Census, pp. 27-35. *Notes:* A dash (-) stands for zero. A (D) indicates data were withheld to avoid disclosure of individual companies.

★ 711 ★

Businesses

Native American Owned Firms: Ownership for Selected Metropolitan Areas, 1987 - I

The number of firms owned and sales and receipts, in thousands, are shown, by Native American group and statistical area[1].

Geographic area	All firms		Firms with paid employees				Relative standard of estimate (percent)[1] for column -			
	Firms (number) A	Sales and receipts ($1,000) B	Firms (number) C	Sales and receipts ($1,000) D	Employees (number) E	Annual payroll ($1,000) F	A	B	C	D
Albuquerque, NM MSA										
Aleut	2	(D)	0	0	0	0	66	(D)	0	0
Eskimo	0	0	0	0	0	0	0	0	0	0
American Indian	180	10,065	25	7,913	182	1,559	14	7	8	4
Anaheim-Santa Ana, CA PMSA										
Aleut	0	0	0	0	0	0	0	0	0	0
Eskimo	4	1,032	3	(D)	(D)	(D)	35	9	47	(D)
American Indian	293	15,644	53	7,828	178	1,814	15	17	29	13
Anchorage, AK MSA										
Aleut	75	2,244	6	736	6	222	31	39	0	0
Eskimo	132	4,438	8	2,797	26	656	21	7	0	0
American Indian	116	7,571	10	5,439	23	197	21	11	0	0
Atlanta, GA MSA										
Aleut	0	0	0	0	0	0	0	0	0	0
Eskimo	0	0	0	0	0	0	0	0	0	0
American Indian	68	(D)	14	(D)	(D)	(D)	19	(D)	37	(D)
Austin, TX MSA										
Aleut	0	0	0	0	0	0	0	0	0	0
Eskimo	0	0	0	0	0	0	0	0	0	0
American Indian	34	1,086	8	940	14	236	35	20	47	23
Bakersfield, CA MSA										
Aleut	10	1,030	10	1,030	0	50	95	95	95	95
Eskimo	0	0	0	0	0	0	0	0	0	0
American Indian	86	4,656	5	3,605	181	1,614	26	13	28	13
Baltimore, MD MSA										
Aleut	0	0	0	0	0	0	0	0	0	0
Eskimo	0	0	0	0	0	0	0	0	0	0
American Indian	63	4,879	13	4,335	71	1,074	28	6	19	5

[Continued]

★ 711 ★

Native American Owned Firms: Ownership for Selected Metropolitan Areas, 1987 - I

[Continued]

Geographic area	All firms		Firms with paid employees				Relative standard of estimate (percent)[1] for column -			
	Firms (number)	Sales and receipts ($1,000)	Firms (number)	Sales and receipts ($1,000)	Employees (number)	Annual payroll ($1,000)	A	B	C	D
	A	B	C	D	E	F				
Bellingham, WA MSA										
Aleut	20	390	0	0	0	0	67	67	0	0
Eskimo	1	(D)	1	(D)	(D)	(D)	0	(D)	0	(D)
American Indian	36	1,450	21	1,347	11	193	56	43	92	47
Boston, MA PSMA										
Aleut	0	0	0	0	0	0	0	0	0	0
Eskimo	0	0	0	0	0	0	0	0	0	0
American Indian	61	1,925	10	(D)	(D)	(D)	22	6	45	(D)
Boulder-Longmont, CO PMSA										
Aleut	0	0	0	0	0	0	0	0	0	0
Eskimo	0	0	0	0	0	0	0	0	0	0
American Indian	38	2,108	5	(D)	(D)	(D)	34	12	0	(D)
Charlotte-Gastonia-Rock Hill, NC-SC MSA										
Aleut	0	0	0	0	0	0	0	0	0	0
Eskimo	0	0	0	0	0	0	0	0	0	0
American Indian	113,3,936	29	2,550	45	489	18	9	27	10	
Chicago, IL PMSA										
Aleut	1	(D)	1	(D)	(D)	(D)	0	(D)	0	(D)
Eskimo	3	(D)	2	(D)	(D)	(D)	48	(D)	72	(D)
American Indian	120	4,443	25	2,219	20	288	19	15	38	19
Columbus, OH MSA										
Aleut	0	0	0	0	0	0	0	0	0	0
Eskimo	0	0	0	0	0	0	0	0	0	0
American Indian	36	705	2	(D)	(D)	(D)	29	6	0	(D)
Dallas, TX PMSA										
Aleut	6	54	0	0	0	0	92	92	0	0
Eskimo	0	0	0	0	0	0	0	0	0	0
American Indian	185	7,463	44	5,973	111	1,504	16	7	29	7
Denver, CO PMSA										
Aleut	1	(D)	1	(D)	(D)	(D)	0	(D)	0	(D)
Eskimo	6	(D)	0	0	0	0	59	(D)	0	0
American Indian	161	2,557	16	902	31	186	19	20	31	9
Detroit, MI PMSA										
Aleut	0	0	0	0	0	0	0	0	0	0
Eskimo	1	(D)	1	(D)	(D)	(D)	0	(D)	0	(D)
American Indian	109	4,222	16	3,068	45	293	18	7	23	6
El Paso, TX MSA										
Aleut	4	8	0	0	0	0	87	87	0	0
Eskimo	0	0	0	0	0	0	0	0	0	0
American Indian	50	1,833	22	1,368	18	352	34	32	46	38
Fayetteville, NC MSA										
Aleut	0	0	0	0	0	0	0	0	0	0
Eskimo	0	0	0	0	0	0	0	0	0	0
American Indian	84	7,735	30	6,519	91	1,007	20	5	24	6

[Continued]

★ 711 ★

Native American Owned Firms: Ownership for Selected Metropolitan Areas, 1987 - I
[Continued]

Geographic area	All firms		Firms with paid employees				Relative standard of estimate (percent)[1] for column -			
	Firms (number) A	Sales and receipts ($1,000) B	Firms (number) C	Sales and receipts ($1,000) D	Employees (number) E	Annual payroll ($1,000) F	A	B	C	D
Fort Smith, AR-OK MSA										
Aleut	0	0	0	0	0	0	0	0	0	0
Eskimo	0	0	0	0	0	0	0	0	0	0
American Indian	63	1,278	7	(D)	(D)	(D)	19	7	49	(D)
Fort Worth-Arlington, TX PMSA										
Aleut	0	0	0	0	0	0	0	0	0	0
Eskimo	0	0	0	0	0	0	0	0	0	0
American Indian	73	(D)	13	(D)	(D)	(D)	25	(D)	48	(D)
Fresno, CA MSA										
Aleut	0	0	0	0	0	0	0	0	0	0
Eskimo	1	(D)	0	0	0	0	0	(D)	0	0
American Indian	42	(D)	18	1,523	34	438	39	(D)	54	13
Greensboro-Winston-Salem-High Point, NC MSA										
Aleut	0	0	0	0	0	0	0	0	0	0
Eskimo	0	0	0	0	0	0	0	0	0	0
American Indian	55	5,047	16	4,099	74	971	23	9	31	9

Source: *1987 Economic Censuses, Survey of Minority-Owned Business Enterprises: Asian Americans, American Indians, and Other Minorities,* U.S. Department of Commerce, Bureau of the Census, MB87-3, 1991. *Notes:* A (D) indicates data were withheld to avoid disclosing data from individual companies. 1. The metropolitan statistical areas (MSA's) for which data are shown are among those defined by the Office of Management and Budget as of June 30, 1987. An MSA is an integrated economic and social unit with a population nucleus of at least 50,000 inhabitants. Each MSA consists of one or more counties meeting standards of metropolitan character; in New England, cities and towns, rather than counties, are the component geographic units. An MSA with a population of 1 million or more may be subdivided into primary metropolitan statistical areas (PMSAs). A PSMA consists of a large urbanized county or a cluster of counties (cities and towns in New England) that demonstrates very strong internal economic and social links separate from the ties to other portions of its MSA. Where PMSAs are defined, the MSA of which they are component parts is redesignated a consolidated metropolitan statistical area (CMSA).

★ 712 ★

Businesses

Native American Owned Firms: Ownership for Selected Metropolitan Areas, 1987 - II

The number of firms owned and sales and receipts, in thousands, are shown, by Native American group and statistical area[1].

Geographic area	All firms		Firms with paid employees				Relative standard of estimate (percent)[1] for column -			
	Firms (number) A	Sales and receipts ($1,000) B	Firms (number) C	Sales and receipts ($1,000) D	Employees (number) E	Annual payroll ($1,000) F	A	B	C	D
Honolulu, HI MSA										
Aleut	6	6	0	0	0	0	92	92	0	0
Eskimo	11	32	0	0	0	0	86	59	0	0
American Indian	55	5,125	13	(D)	(D)	(D)	28	3	19	(D)
Houma-Thibodaux, LA MSA										
Aleut	0	0	0	0	0	0	0	0	0	0
Eskimo	0	0	0	0	0	0	0	0	0	0
American Indian	120	3,429	23	1,836	11	614	17	36	41	62
Houston, TX PMSA										
Aleut	11	308	0	0	0	0	86	92	0	0
Eskimo	0	0	0	0	0	0	0	0	0	0

[Continued]

★ 712 ★

Native American Owned Firms: Ownership for Selected Metropolitan Areas, 1987 - II
[Continued]

Geographic area	All firms		Firms with paid employees				Relative standard of estimate (percent)[1] for column -			
	Firms (number) A	Sales and receipts ($1,000) B	Firms (number) C	Sales and receipts ($1,000) D	Employees (number) E	Annual payroll ($1,000) F	A	B	C	D
American Indian	103	1,940	8	(D)	(D)	(D)	23	17	25	(D)
Kansas City, MO-KS MSA										
Aleut	0	0	0	0	0	0	0	0	0	0
Eskimo	0	0	0	0	0	0	0	0	0	0
American Indian	63	1,310	13	595	17	199	19	18	35	25
Las Cruces, NM MSA										
Aleut	1	(D)	1	(D)	(D)	(D)	0	(D)	0	(D)
Eskimo	0	0	0	0	0	0	0	0	0	0
American Indian	43	490	2	(D)	(D)	(D)	35	26	70	(D)
Las Vegas, NV MSA										
Aleut	0	0	0	0	0	0	0	0	0	0
Eskimo	4	160	0	0	0	0	92	92	0	0
American Indian	46	880	6	(D)	(D)	(D)	28	8	0	(D)
Lawton, OK MSA										
Aleut	0	0	0	0	0	0	0	0	0	0
Eskimo	0	0	0	0	0	0	0	0	0	0
American Indian	41	787	13	523	24	103	24	24	39	36
Los Angeles-Long Beach, CA PMSA										
Aleut	44	1,116	0	0	0	0	41	65	0	0
Eskimo	30	900	0	0	0	0	55	87	0	0
American Indian	722	37,045	148	24,328	238	3,626	10	7	19	8
Miami-Hialeah, FL PMSA										
Aleut	1	(D)	1	(D)	(D)	(D)	0	(D)	0	(D)
Eskimo	0	0	0	0	0	0	0	0	0	0
American Indian	49	1,027	5	280	13	98	32	53	40	30
Milwaukee, WI PSMA										
Aleut	0	0	0	0	0	0	0	0	0	0
Eskimo	0	0	0	0	0	0	0	0	0	0
American Indian	70	2,034	19	1,727	19	217	26	6	50	6
Minneapolis-St. Paul, MN-WI MSA										
Aleut	7	70	0	0	0	0	49	55	0	0
Eskimo	0	0	0	0	0	0	0	0	0	
American Indian	136	11,162	25	9,338	200	2,261	9	1	14	1
Modesto, CA MSA										
Aleut	2	(D)	2	(D)	(D)	(D)	71	(D)	71	(D)
Eskimo	0	0	0	0	0	0	0	0	0	0
American Indian	48	1,555	18	1,052	14	230	35	27	54	39
Nassau-Suffolk, NY PMSA										
Aleut	0	0	0	0	0	0	0	0	0	0
Eskimo	10	530	10	530	0	110	95	95	95	95
American Indian	24	4,776	14	3,963	46	794	25	23	25	26
New Orleans, LA MSA										
Aleut	2	(D)	1	(D)	(D)	(D)	0	(D)	0	(D)
Eskimo	0	0	0	0	0	0	0	0	0	0
American Indian	52	2,224	7	1,092	25	283	25	18	20	1

[Continued]

★ 712 ★

Native American Owned Firms: Ownership for Selected Metropolitan Areas, 1987 - II

[Continued]

Geographic area	All firms		Firms with paid employees				Relative standard of estimate (percent)[1] for column -			
	Firms (number) A	Sales and receipts ($1,000) B	Firms (number) C	Sales and receipts ($1,000) D	Employees (number) E	Annual payroll ($1,000) F	A	B	C	D
New York, NY PMSA										
Aleut	0	0	0	0	0	0	0	0	0	0
Eskimo	0	0	0	0	0	0	0	0	0	0
American Indian	180	6,444	23	(D)	(D)	(D)	18	23	43	(D)
Norfolk-Virginia Beach-Newport News, VA MSA										
Aleut	0	0	0	0	0	0	0	0	0	0
Eskimo	1	(D)	0	0	0	0	0	(D)	0	0
American Indian	34	1,405	9	1,290	13	634	35	54	42	59
Oakland, CA PMSA										
Aleut	3	15	0	0	0	0	82	82	0	0
Eskimo	0	0	0	0	0	0	0	0	0	0
American Indian	205	8,892	17	7,719	82	1,853	20	9	21	10
Oklahoma City, OK MSA										
Aleut	0	0	0	0	0	0	0	0	0	0
Eskimo	0	0	0	0	0	0	0	0	0	0
American Indian	320	8,406	32	4,339	75	870	9	8	12	13
Orlando, FL MSA										
Aleut	0	0	0	0	0	0	0	0	0	0
Eskimo	0	0	0	0	0	0	0	0	0	0
American Indian	48	2,509	17	2,208	21	431	30	41	47	46
Oxnard-Ventura, CA PMSA										
Aleut	12	1,702	10	(D)	(D)	(D)	80	77	95	(D)
Eskimo	0	0	0	0	0	0	0	0	0	0
American Indian	53	3,049	7	2,229	32	408	35	19	35	22
Philadelphia, PA-NJ PMSA										
Aleut	0	0	0	0	0	0	0	0	0	0
Eskimo	0	0	0	0	0	0	0	0	0	0
American Indian	60	14,797	16	(D)	(D)	(D)	28	6	18	(D)
Phoenix, AZ MSA										
Aleut	1	(D)	1	(D)	(D)	(D)	0	(D)	0	(D)
Eskimo	4	28	0	0	0	0	87	87	0	0
American Indian	198	13,728	30	11,628	132	866	11	2	27	2

Source: 1987 Economic Censuses, Survey of Minority-Owned Business Enterprises: Asian Americans, American Indians, and Other Minorities, U.S. Department of Commerce, Bureau of the Census, MB87-3, 1991. *Notes:* A (D) indicates data were withheld to avoid disclosing data from individual companies. 1. The metropolitan statistical areas (MSA's) for which data are shown are among those defined by the Office of Management and Budget as of June 30, 1987. An MSA is an integrated economic and social unit with a population nucleus of at least 50,000 inhabitants. Each MSA consists of one or more counties meeting standards of metropolitan character; in New England, cities and towns, rather than counties, are the component geographic units. An MSA with a population of 1 million or more may be subdivided into primary metropolitan statistical areas (PMSAs). A PSMA consists of a large urbanized county or a cluster of counties (cities and towns in New England) that demonstrates very strong internal economic and social links separate from the ties to other portions of its MSA. Where PMSAs are defined, the MSA of which they are component parts is redesignated a consolidated metropolitan statistical area (CMSA).

★ 713 ★
Businesses

Native American Owned Firms: Ownership for Selected Metropolitan Areas, 1987 - III

The number of firms owned and sales and receipts, in thousands, are shown, by Native American group and statistical area[1].

Geographic area	All firms		Firms with paid employees				Relative standard of estimate (percent)[1] for column -			
	Firms (number) A	Sales and receipts ($1,000) B	Firms (number) C	Sales and receipts ($1,000) D	Employees (number) E	Annual payroll ($1,000) F	A	B	C	D
Portland, OR PMSA										
Aleut	17	95	0	0	0	0	38	47	0	0
Eskimo	6	(D)	0	0	0	0	15	2	38	(D)
American Indian	103	6,512	10	(D)	(D)	(D)	15	2	38	(D)
Raleigh-Durham, NC MSA										
Aleut	0	0	0	0	0	0	0	0	0	0
Eskimo	0	0	0	0	0	0	0	0	0	0
American Indian	53	1,564	13	1,036	12	324	26	31	38	44
Reno, NV MSA										
Aleut	0	0	0	0	0	0	0	0	0	0
Eskimo	0	0	0	0	0	0	0	0	0	0
American Indian	31	1,322	7	808	16	145	16	0	0	0
Richmond-Petersburg, VA MSA										
Aleut	0	0	0	0	0	0	0	0	0	0
Eskimo	0	0	0	0	0	0	0	0	0	0
American Indian	35	2,490	15	2,393	48	485	31	1	16	1
Riverside-San Bernardino, CA PMSA										
Aleut	4	68	0	0	0	0	87	87	0	0
Eskimo	4	36	0	0	0	0	87	87	0	0
American Indian	211	9,124	58	6,857	83	1,352	19	16	32	19
Rochester, NY MSA										
Aleut	10	10	0	0	0	0	95	95	0	0
Eskimo	0	0	0	0	0	0	0	0	0	0
American Indian	27	593	1	(D)	(D)	(D)	49	67	0	(D)
Sacramento, CA MSA										
Aleut	0	0	0	0	0	0	0	0	0	0
Eskimo	0	0	0	0	0	0	0	0	0	0
American Indian	197	9,366	41	5,258	98	1,126	18	25	31	31
St. Louis, MO-IL MSA										
Aleut	1	(D)	1	(D)	(D)	(D)	0	(D)	0	(D)
Eskimo	0	0	0	0	0	0	0	0	0	0
American Indian	36	(D)	4	116	2	18	22	(D)	35	44
Salinas-Seaside-Monterey, CA MSA										
Aleut	0	0	0	0	0	0	0	0	0	0
Eskimo	10	90	0	0	0	0	95	95	0	0
American Indian	46	3,846	4	3,530	22	323	37	13	35	14
Salt Lake City-Ogden, UT MSA										
Aleut	1	(D)	0	0	0	0	0	(D)	0	0
Eskimo	0	0	0	0	0	0	0	0	0	0
American Indian	46	694	7	481	15	86	24	10	20	2
San Antonio, TX MSA										
Aleut	11	148	1	(D)	(D)	(D)	86	13	0	(D)
Eskimo	0	0	0	0	0	0	0	0	0	0
American Indian	61	530	3	260	13	72	35	12	47	20

[Continued]

★ 713 ★

Native American Owned Firms: Ownership for Selected Metropolitan Areas, 1987 - III

[Continued]

Geographic area	All firms		Firms with paid employees				Relative standard of estimate (percent)[1] for column -			
	Firms (number)	Sales and receipts ($1,000)	Firms (number)	Sales and receipts ($1,000)	Employees (number)	Annual payroll ($1,000)	A	B	C	D
	A	B	C	D	E	F				
San Diego, CA MSA										
Aleut	13	404	3	364	9	69	74	35	47	37
Eskimo	18	222	0	0	0	0	67	71	0	0
American Indian	374	13,718	66	7,960	78	1,104	14	17	29	19
San Francisco, CA PMSA										
Aleut	11	(D)	1	(D)	(D)	(D)	86	(D)	0	(D)
Eskimo	0	0	0	0	0	0	0	0	0	0
American Indian	131	4,149	13	1,977	27	350	22	27	46	42
San Jose, CA PMSA										
Aleut	0	0	0	0	0	0	0	0	0	0
Eskimo	0	0	0	0	0	0	0	0	0	0
American Indian	173	6,393	35	4,331	138	1,621	22	19	30	12
Santa Barbara-Santa Maria-Lompoc, CA MSA										
Aleut	2	(D)	2	(D)	(D)	(D)	71	(D)	71	(D)
Eskimo	0	0	0	0	0	0	0	0	0	0
American Indian	29	4,355	12	4,284	31	303	43	4	56	4
Santa Cruz, CA PMSA										
Aleut	0	0	0	0	0	0	0	0	0	0
Eskimo	0	0	0	0	0	0	0	0	0	0
American Indian	40	753	5	442	4	109	55	33	49	23
Santa Fe, NM MSA										
Aleut	0	0	0	0	0	0	0	0	0	0
Eskimo	0	0	0	0	0	0	0	0	0	0
American Indian	58	4,354	12	3,553	21	653	25	3	0	0
Santa Rosa-Petaluma, CA PMSA										
Aleut	1	(D)	0	0	0	0	0	(D)	0	0
Eskimo	11	(D)	1	(D)	(D)	(D)	86	(D)	0	(D)
American Indian	48	1,807	15	1,631	15	305	40	27	64	29
Seattle, WA PMSA										
Aleut	18	2,031	7	921	4	303	27	4	49	7
Eskimo	2	(D)	0	0	0	0	0	(D)	0	0
American Indian	243	15,006	29	10,905	78	2,548	16	10	33	2
Spokane, WA MSA										
Aleut	10	80	0	0	0	0	95	95	0	0
Eskimo	0	0	0	0	0	0	0	0	0	0
American Indian	44	1,034	4	(D)	(D)	(D)	38	11	33	(D)
Stockton, CA MSA										
Aleut	0	0	0	0	0	0	0	0	0	0
Eskimo	0	0	0	0	0	0	0	0	0	0
American Indian	53	2,090	2	(D)	(D)	(D)	36	16	0	(D)
Syracuse, NY MSA										
Aleut	0	0	0	0	0	0	0	0	0	0

[Continued]

★ 713 ★

Native American Owned Firms: Ownership for Selected Metropolitan Areas, 1987 - III

[Continued]

Geographic area	All firms		Firms with paid employees				Relative standard of estimate (percent)[1] for column -			
	Firms (number) A	Sales and receipts ($1,000) B	Firms (number) C	Sales and receipts ($1,000) D	Employees (number) E	Annual payroll ($1,000) F	A	B	C	D
Eskimo	0	0	0	0	0	0	0	0	0	0
American Indian	32	472	1	(D)	(D)	(D)	47	55	0	(D)

Source: 1987 Economic Censuses, Survey of Minority-Owned Business Enterprises: Asian Americans, American Indians, and Other Minorities, U.S. Department of Commerce, Bureau of the Census, MB87-3, 1991. *Notes:* A (D) indicates data were withheld to avoid disclosing data from individual companies. 1. The metropolitan statistical areas (MSA's) for which data are shown are among those defined by the Office of Management and Budget as of June 30, 1987. An MSA is an integrated economic and social unit with a population nucleus of at least 50,000 inhabitants. Each MSA consists of one or more counties meeting standards of metropolitan character; in New England, cities and towns, rather than counties, are the component geographic units. An MSA with a population of 1 million or more may be subdivided into primary metropolitan statistical areas (PMSAs). A PSMA consists of a large urbanized county or a cluster of counties (cities and towns in New England) that demonstrates very strong internal economic and social links separate from the ties to other portions of its MSA. Where PMSAs are defined, the MSA of which they are component parts is redesignated a consolidated metropolitan statistical area (CMSA).

★ 714 ★

Businesses

Native American Owned Firms: Ownership for Selected Metropolitan Areas, 1987 - IV

The number of firms owned and sales and receipts, in thousands, are shown, by Native American group and statistical area[1].

Geographic area	All firms		Firms with paid employees				Relative standard of estimate (percent)[1] for column -			
	Firms (number) A	Sales and receipts ($1,000) B	Firms (number) C	Sales and receipts ($1,000) D	Employees (number) E	Annual payroll ($1,000) F	A	B	C	D
Tacoma, WA PMSA										
Aleut	5	(D)	3	279	2	4	40	(D)	47	66
Eskimo	11	(D)	1	(D)	(D)	(D)	85	(D)	0	(D)
American Indian	17	5,252	8	5,149	53	541	18	2	30	2
Tampa-St. Petersburg-Clearwater, FL MSA										
Aleut	0	0	0	0	0	0	0	0	0	0
Eskimo	0	0	0	0	0	0	0	0	0	0
American Indian	54	901	14	(D)	(D)	(D)	29	44	72	(D)
Tucson, AZ MSA										
Aleut	10	10	0	0	0	0	95	95	0	0
Eskimo	0	0	0	0	0	0	0	0	0	0
American Indian	61	6,392	15	5,688	33	365	19	13	34	14
Tulsa, OK MSA										
Aleut	0	0	0	0	0	0	0	0	0	0
Eskimo	4	4	0	0	0	0	88	88	0	0
American Indian	540	11,113	64	5,559	77	1,055	7	5	13	4
Washington, DC-MD VA MSA										
Aleut	1	(D)	1	(D)	(D)	(D)	0	(D)	0	(D)
Eskimo	0	0	0	0	0	0	0	0	0	0
American Indian	176	5,546	23	3,226	37	403	16	7	41	6
Wichita, KS MSA										
Aleut	6	(D)	0	0	0	0	90	(D)	0	0
Eskimo	0	0	0	0	0	0	0	0	0	0
American Indian	42	3,363	8	2,638	16	197	23	1	0	0

[Continued]

★ 714 ★

Native American Owned Firms: Ownership for Selected Metropolitan Areas, 1987 - IV
[Continued]

Geographic area	All firms		Firms with paid employees				Relative standard of estimate (percent)[1] for column -			
	Firms (number) A	Sales and receipts ($1,000) B	Firms (number) C	Sales and receipts ($1,000) D	Employees (number) E	Annual payroll ($1,000) F	A	B	C	D
Yakima, WA MSA										
Aleut	0	0	0	0	0	0	0	0	0	0
Eskimo	0	0	0	0	0	0	0	0	0	0
American Indian	48	4,359	16	2,039	28	301	34	12	49	24

Source: 1987 Economic Censuses, Survey of Minority-Owned Business Enterprises: Asian Americans, American Indians, and Other Minorities, U.S. Department of Commerce, Bureau of the Census, MB87-3, 1991. *Notes:* A (D) indicates data were withheld to avoid disclosing data from individual companies. 1. The metropolitan statistical areas (MSA's) for which data are shown are among those defined by the Office of Management and Budget as of June 30, 1987. An MSA is an integrated economic and social unit with a population nucleus of at least 50,000 inhabitants. Each MSA consists of one or more counties meeting standards of metropolitan character; in New England, cities and towns, rather than counties, are the component geographic units. An MSA with a population of 1 million or more may be subdivided into primary metropolitan statistical areas (PMSAs). A PSMA consists of a large urbanized county or a cluster of counties (cities and towns in New England) that demonstrates very strong internal economic and social links separate from the ties to other portions of its MSA. Where PMSAs are defined, the MSA of which they are component parts is redesignated a consolidated metropolitan statistical area (CMSA).

★ 715 ★

Businesses

Employment by the Sault Ste. Marie Tribe of Chippewa, 1995

Number of persons employed by each business is shown as of January 1995.

Business	Location	No. of employees	Year opened
Vegas Kewadin Casino (Reservation)	Sault Ste. Marie, MI	1,120	1985
Mid-Jim Store (Reservation) (Gas station, 24-hour C-store)	Sault Ste. Marie, MI	16	1984
Kewadin Shores Casino	St. Ignace, MI	618	1987
Kewadin Inn (46-unit motel)	Sault Ste. Marie, MI	15	1988
Chippewa Service & Supply (Janitorial service & retail store)	Sault Ste. Marie, MI (downtown)	42	1989
Mid-Jim Store (Gas station, 24-hour C-store)	St. Ignace, MI	7	1991
Chi-Chuk Construction	Sault Ste. Marie, MI (downtown)	86	1992
Clarion Carriage House Hotel (Casino hotel)	Sault Ste. Marie, MI	260	1992
Dream Catcher Gift Shop	Sault Ste. Marie, MI	41	1992

[Continued]

★ 715 ★

Employment by the Sault Ste. Marie Tribe of Chippewa, 1995
[Continued]

Business	Location	No. of employees	Year opened
Dream Catcher Restaurant (Casino restaurant/lounge)	Sault Ste. Marie, MI	115	1992
Phoenix Accudrive (Remanufactures axles)	Kinross, MI	51	1992
Intermediary Relending Program (Private nonprofit finance company)	Traverse City, MI	3	1993
Northern Aviation (Air charter service)	Sault Ste. Marie, MI	3	1993
Northern Hospitality (Furniture, carpet, wallpaper, cabinets)	Sault Ste. Marie, MI	8	1993
Northstar Neon	Sault Ste. Marie, MI	32	1993
Demawating Sales & Rentals (Sales & rental of housing)	Kinross, MI	6	1994
Eagle Ridge Apartments	Marquette, MI	2	1994
Kewadin Inn (70-unit motel)	St. Ignace, MI	18	1994
Kewadin Slots/Mini-casino	Christmas, MI	80	1994
Kewadin Slots/Mini-casino	Hessel, MI	33	1994
Kewadin Slots/Mini-casino	Manistique, MI	62	1994
Special Plastic Products (Mfg. of plastic parts for autos)	Fair Haven, MI	100	1995
	Pontiac, MI	150[1]	1995

Source: Lam, Tina. "Chippewa Inc." *Detroit Free Press* (27 March 1995), p. 6A. Primary source: Sault Ste. Marie Chippewa Tribe annual reports. *Note:* 1. By end of 1995.

Industry Employment

★ 716 ★

Private Industry Employment by Occupation: United States

Data are shown for all industries, by race/ethnicity and sex, in 1993. Data do not include Hawaii.

Group	Total employ- ment	Officials and managers	Profes- sionals	Techni- cians	Sales workers	Office & clerical workers	Craft workers	Opera- tives	Laborers	Service workers
					Number of persons					
All employers	36,321,236	3,976,608	5,251,884	2,224,637	3,849,873	5,578,787	3,360,333	5,534,879	2,652,578	3,891,657
Male	19,425,287	2,789,118	2,613,254	1,182,134	1,675,551	959,091	2,975,681	3,750,207	1,740,266	1,739,985
Female	16,895,949	1,187,490	2,638,630	1,042,503	2,174,322	4,619,696	384,652	1,784,672	912,312	2,151,672
White	27,775,606	3,548,244	4,499,412	1,781,941	3,078,474	4,255,981	2,758,689	3,892,354	1,632,347	2,328,164
Male	15,053,016	2,520,475	2,274,476	969,838	1,363,715	683,719	2,470,132	2,720,268	1,075,082	975,311
Female	12,722,590	1,027,769	2,224,936	812,103	1,714,759	3,572,262	288,557	1,172,086	557,265	1,352,853
Minority	8,545,630	428,634	752,472	442,696	771,399	1,322,806	601,644	642,525	1,020,231	1,563,493
Male	4,372,271	268,643	338,778	212,296	311,836	275,372	505,549	1,029,939	665,184	764,674
Female	4,173,359	159,721	413,694	230,400	459,563	1,047,434	96,095	612,586	355,047	798,819
Black	4,603,282	209,045	291,045	233,294	409,174	779,365	310,167	949,143	496,476	925,573
Male	2,161,798	118,906	101,796	90,516	150,986	140,853	254,822	577,459	317,592	408,968
Female	2,441,484	90,139	189,249	142,778	258,188	638,612	55,345	371,684	178,884	516,605
Hispanic	2,630,746	121,908	141,708	105,293	262,685	357,871	218,759	507,227	432,335	482,960
Male	1,530,555	82,700	71,806	62,132	117,312	83,881	192,033	346,315	294,129	280,247
Female	1,100,191	39,208	69,902	43,161	145,373	273,990	26,726	160,912	138,206	202,713
Asian/Pacific Islander	1,134,536	84,561	303,279	94,572	80,155	162,276	53,609	152,509	71,411	131,153
Male	579,873	57,992	155,971	54,314	35,381	45,219	41,614	84,161	40,906	64,315
Female	554,663	26,569	147,308	40,258	44,774	117,057	11,995	68,348	31,516	66,838
American Indian/Alaskan Native	177,066	12,850	16,440	9,537	19,385	23,294	19,109	33,646	18,998	23,807
Male	100,045	9,045	9,205	5,334	8,157	5,519	17,080	22,004	12,557	11,144
Female	77,021	3,805	7,235	4,203	11,228	17,775	2,029	11,642	6,441	12,663
					Participation rate					
All employers	100.0	100.0	100.0	100.0	100.0	100.0	100.0	100.0	100.0	100.0
Male	53.5	70.1	49.8	53.1	43.5	17.2	88.6	67.8	65.6	44.7
Female	46.5	39.9	50.2	46.9	56.5	82.8	11.4	32.2	34.4	55.3
White	76.5	89.2	85.7	80.1	80.0	76.3	82.1	70.3	61.5	59.8
Male	41.4	63.4	43.3	43.6	35.4	12.3	73.5	49.1	40.5	25.1
Female	35.0	25.8	42.4	36.5	44.5	64.0	8.6	21.2	21.0	34.8
Minority	23.5	10.8	14.3	19.9	20.0	23.7	17.9	29.7	38.5	40.2
Male	12.0	6.8	6.5	9.5	8.1	4.9	15.0	18.6	25.1	19.6
Female	11.5	4.0	7.9	10.4	11.9	18.8	2.9	11.1	13.4	20.5
Black	12.7	5.3	5.5	10.5	10.6	14.0	9.2	17.1	18.7	23.8
Male	6.0	3.0	1.9	4.1	3.9	2.5	7.6	10.4	12.0	10.5
Female	6.7	2.3	3.6	6.4	6.7	11.4	1.6	6.7	6.7	13.3
Hispanic	7.2	3.1	2.7	4.7	6.8	6.4	6.5	9.2	16.3	12.4
Male	4.2	2.1	1.4	2.8	3.0	1.5	5.7	6.3	11.1	7.2
Female	3.0	1.0	1.3	1.9	3.8	4.9	0.8	2.9	5.2	5.2
Asian/Pacific Islander	3.1	2.1	5.8	4.3	2.1	2.9	1.6	2.8	2.7	3.4
Male	1.6	1.5	3.0	2.4	0.9	0.8	1.2	1.5	1.5	1.7
Female	1.5	0.7	2.8	1.8	1.2	2.1	0.4	1.2	1.2	1.7
American Indian/Alaskan Native	0.5	0.3	0.3	0.4	0.5	0.4	0.6	0.6	0.7	0.6
Male	0.3	0.2	0.2	0.2	0.2	0.1	0.5	0.4	0.5	0.3
Female	0.2	0.1	0.1	0.2	0.3	0.3	0.1	0.2	0.2	0.3

Source: U.S. Equal Employment Opportunity Commission. *Job Patterns for Minorities and Women in Private Industry, 1993.* Washington, DC: U.S. Government Printing Office, 1994, p. 1.

★ 717 ★

Industry Employment

Private Industry Employment: Air Transport Industry

Number of persons employed in each occupation is shown, by race/ethnicity, in 1993. Data are shown for selected industry sectors and do not include Hawaii.

Group	Total employ- ment	Officials and managers	Profes- sionals	Techni- cians	Sales workers	Office & clerical workers	Craft workers	Opera- tives	Laborers	Service workers
Scheduled air transportation										
All employers	370,707	23,814	54,981	6,117	39,366	53,482	65,335	27,522	14,124	85,966
White	298,260	20,690	51,835	5,382	29,650	41,962	54,041	19,864	7,301	67,535
Minority	72,447	3,124	3,146	735	9,716	11,520	11,294	7,658	6,823	18,431
Black	35,359	1,576	1,037	374	5,188	6,227	4,748	3,909	3,335	8,965
Hispanic	21,069	767	1,024	150	2,467	3,111	3,753	2,419	1,918	5,460
Asian/Pacific Islander	14,500	697	865	177	1,861	1,968	2,572	1,122	1,530	3,708
American Indian/Alaskan Native	1,519	84	220	34	200	214	221	208	40	298
Nonscheduled air transportation										
All employers	5,562	697	1,351	419	205	847	834	526	323	360
White	4,635	630	1,295	389	165	679	710	312	200	255
Minority	927	67	56	30	40	168	124	214	123	105
Black	368	18	15	11	14	82	29	102	58	39
Hispanic	416	41	25	11	17	66	80	77	40	59
Asian/Pacific Islander	125	6	10	7	9	19	9	35	23	7
American Indian/Alaskan Native	18	2	6	1	0	1	6	0	2	0

Source: U.S. Equal Employment Opportunity Commission. *Job Patterns for Minorities and Women in Private Industry, 1993.* Washington, DC: U.S. Government Printing Office, 1994, p. 26-27.

★ 718 ★

Industry Employment

Private Industry Employment: Apparel Industry

Number of persons employed in each occupation is shown, by race/ethnicity, in 1993. Data are shown for selected industry sectors and do not include Hawaii.

Group	Total employ- ment	Officials and managers	Profes- sionals	Techni- cians	Sales workers	Office & clerical workers	Craft workers	Opera- tives	Laborers	Service workers
Men's and boys' furnishings										
All employers	194,924	10,176	3,457	2,016	2,537	12,046	16,125	133,926	12,200	2,441
White	120,100	8,389	2,679	1,444	2,320	8,740	11,272	76,258	7,334	1,664
Minority	74,824	1,787	778	572	217	3,306	4,853	57,668	4,866	777
Black	40,979	731	206	173	127	1,326	3,010	31,942	2,928	536
Hispanic	28,570	818	276	338	61	1,560	1,442	22,123	1,733	219
Asian/Pacific Islander	3,967	199	285	57	24	385	354	2,527	124	12
American Indian/Alaskan Native	1,308	39	11	4	5	35	47	1,076	81	10
Women's and misses' outerwear										
All employers	56,090	3,810	1,776	868	3,831	6,392	6,356	26,655	5,548	854
White	38,721	3,332	1,516	674	3,411	4,622	4,554	16,804	3,212	596
Minority	17,369	478	260	194	420	1,770	1,802	9,851	2,336	258
Black	6,628	136	69	58	204	511	693	4,235	593	129
Hispanic	7,477	257	76	79	148	929	632	3,920	1,327	109

[Continued]

★ 718 ★

Private Industry Employment: Apparel Industry
[Continued]

	Total employ-ment	Officials and managers	Profes-sionals	Techni-cians	Sales workers	Office & clerical workers	Craft workers	Opera-tives	Laborers	Service workers
Asian/Pacific Islander	3,078	81	110	56	63	319	464	1,565	405	15
American Indian/Alaskan Native	186	4	5	1	5	11	13	131	11	5

Source: U.S. Equal Employment Opportunity Commission. *Job Patterns for Minorities and Women in Private Industry, 1993.* Washington, DC: U.S. Government Printing Office, 1994, p. 9.

★ 719 ★

Industry Employment

Private Industry Employment: Auto Sales

Number of persons employed in each occupation is shown, by race/ethnicity, in 1993. Data do not include Hawaii.

Group	Total employ-ment	Officials and managers	Profes-sionals	Techni-cians	Sales workers	Office & clerical workers	Craft workers	Opera-tives	Laborers	Service workers
All employers	78,460	9,114	2,574	4,820	18,384	11,135	10,504	12,421	6,661	2,847
White	63,058	8,318	2,035	3,838	14,796	9,569	8,571	10,127	4,040	1,764
Minority	15,402	796	539	982	3,588	1,566	1,933	2,294	2,621	1,083
Black	6,290	219	92	255	1,687	439	545	1,196	1,356	501
Hispanic	7,138	401	46	559	1,521	875	1,124	938	1,134	540
Asian/Pacific Islander	1,670	145	397	126	331	178	217	140	103	33
American Indian/Alaskan Native	304	31	4	42	49	74	47	20	28	9

Source: U.S. Equal Employment Opportunity Commission. *Job Patterns for Minorities and Women in Private Industry, 1993.* Washington, DC: U.S. Government Printing Office, 1994, p. 32.

★ 720 ★

Industry Employment

Private Industry Employment: Business Services

Number of persons employed in each occupation is shown, by race/ethnicity, in 1993. Data are shown for selected industry sectors and do not include Hawaii.

Group	Total employ-ment	Officials and managers	Profes-sionals	Techni-cians	Sales workers	Office & clerical workers	Craft workers	Opera-tives	Laborers	Service workers
Services to buildings										
All employers	228,765	11,601	2,763	2,528	4,683	8,347	11,635	9,607	11,375	166,226
White	92,592	8,275	2,236	2,046	3,713	6,485	8,399	5,938	4,089	51,411
Minority	136,173	3,326	527	482	970	1,862	3,236	3,669	7,286	114,815
Black	62,730	1,687	248	206	461	970	1,541	1,628	3,669	52,320
Hispanic	66,483	1,391	158	199	365	652	1,451	1,634	3,274	57,359
Asian/Pacific Islander	6,067	204	104	54	129	192	170	367	293	4,554

[Continued]

★ 720 ★

Private Industry Employment: Business Services
[Continued]

Group	Total employ-ment	Officials and managers	Profes-sionals	Techni-cians	Sales workers	Office & clerical workers	Craft workers	Opera-tives	Laborers	Service workers
American Indian/Alaskan Native	893	44	17	23	15	48	74	40	50	582
Miscellaneous business services										
All employers	928,206	101,785	140,366	51,325	46,823	158,432	46,496	86,780	35,941	260,258
White	679,516	91,096	121,366	42,046	36,032	120,792	37,846	57,447	19,915	152,976
Minority	248,690	10,689	19,000	9,279	10,791	37,640	8,650	29,333	16,026	107,282
Black	148,827	5,048	6,758	4,293	6,492	21,636	4,012	14,855	8,018	77,715
Hispanic	60,986	2,721	3,597	2,344	3,379	9,606	3,258	8,891	5,959	21,231
Asian/Pacific Islander	35,084	2,618	8,187	2,411	763	5,826	1,060	5,134	1,851	7,234
American Indian/Alaskan Native	3,793	302	458	231	157	572	320	453	198	1,102

Source: U.S. Equal Employment Opportunity Commission. *Job Patterns for Minorities and Women in Private Industry, 1993.* Washington, DC: U.S. Government Printing Office, 1994, p. 35.

★ 721 ★

Industry Employment

Private Industry Employment: Chemicals & Allied Products

Number of persons employed in each occupation is shown, by race/ethnicity, in 1993. Data are shown for selected industry sectors and do not include Hawaii.

Group	Total employ-ment	Officials and managers	Profes-sionals	Techni-cians	Sales workers	Office & clerical workers	Craft workers	Opera-tives	Laborers	Service workers
Industrial organic chemicals										
All employers	155,221	27,258	31,545	12,356	4,804	17,590	25,404	28,829	3,746	3,689
White	128,597	24,810	27,795	10,276	4,431	14,575	20,899	20,624	2,568	2,619
Minority	26,624	2,448	3,750	2,080	373	3,015	4,505	8,205	1,178	1,070
Black	16,421	1,278	1,503	1,289	204	2,130	2,845	5,528	827	817
Hispanic	6,615	615	642	433	113	636	1,416	2,302	266	192
Asian/Pacific Islander	3,025	471	1,528	323	44	204	125	240	42	48
American Indian/Alaskan Native	563	84	77	35	12	45	119	135	43	13
Plastics materials and synthetics										
All employers	190,815	22,003	28,619	16,158	3,056	14,789	45,241	48,266	10,557	2,126
White	158,062	20,072	25,196	13,790	2,832	12,768	38,613	36,232	6,898	1,661
Minority	32,753	1,931	3,423	2,368	224	2,021	6,628	12,034	3,659	465
Black	21,546	1,165	1,332	1,586	119	1,311	4,918	8,928	1,861	326
Hispanic	7,431	363	529	476	50	521	1,411	2,453	1,525	103
Asian/Pacific Islander	3,227	342	1,509	256	47	140	170	489	246	28
American Indian/Alaskan Native	549	61	53	50	8	49	129	164	27	8
Drugs										
All employers	259,664	44,873	60,146	17,745	39,624	33,317	18,267	34,833	5,831	5,028
White	206,929	39,955	49,185	13,590	34,351	26,985	14,631	21,821	3,310	3,101
Minority	52,735	4,918	10,961	4,155	5,273	6,332	3,636	13,012	2,521	1,927
Black	25,212	1,867	2,981	2,192	2,645	4,025	2,069	7,281	862	1,290
Hispanic	12,025	1,003	1,503	777	1,426	1,418	1,121	3,390	967	420
Asian/Pacific Islander	14,593	1,918	6,361	1,120	1,018	809	391	2,096	676	204
American Indian/Alaskan Native	905	130	116	66	184	80	55	245	16	13
Soaps, cleaners, and toilet goods										
All employers	125,628	20,970	13,713	5,657	13,997	18,961	10,256	23,796	16,616	1,662

[Continued]

★ 721 ★

Private Industry Employment: Chemicals & Allied Products

[Continued]

Group	Total employ-ment	Officials and managers	Profes-sionals	Techni-cians	Sales workers	Office & clerical workers	Craft workers	Opera-tives	Laborers	Service workers
White	96,222	18,616	11,612	4,591	12,868	15,622	8,159	15,635	8,048	1,071
Minority	29,406	2,354	2,101	1,066	1,129	3,339	2,097	8,161	8,568	591
Black	16,047	1,277	798	637	479	2,035	1,154	4,778	4,533	356
Hispanic	9,482	501	392	207	426	958	711	2,680	3,403	204
Asian/Pacific Islander	3,511	542	887	208	190	302	178	612	565	27
American Indian/Alaskan Native	366	34	24	14	34	44	54	91	67	4

Source: U.S. Equal Employment Opportunity Commission. *Job Patterns for Minorities and Women in Private Industry, 1993.* Washington, DC: U.S. Government Printing Office, 1994, pp. 13-14.

★ 722 ★

Industry Employment

Private Industry Employment: Commercial Banking

Number of persons employed in each occupation is shown, by race/ethnicity, in 1993. Data do not include Hawaii.

Group	Total employ-ment	Officials and managers	Profes-sionals	Techni-cians	Sales workers	Office & clerical workers	Craft workers	Opera-tives	Laborers	Service workers
All employers	1,002,942	211,534	165,360	24,625	23,017	554,566	3,062	7,817	982	11,979
White	761,242	185,651	136,539	18,482	18,973	385,249	2,516	4,953	661	8,218
Minority	241,700	25,883	28,821	6,143	4,044	169,317	546	2,864	321	3,761
Black	130,250	11,913	13,321	3,044	2,712	95,197	279	1,486	204	2,634
Hispanic	61,279	7,374	6,667	1,482	1,138	42,717	199	705	92	905
Asian/Pacific Islander	46,759	6,123	8,421	1,541	657	29,156	55	614	20	172
American Indian/Alaskan Native	3,412	473	412	76	77	2,247	13	59	5	50

Source: U.S. Equal Employment Opportunity Commission. *Job Patterns for Minorities and Women in Private Industry, 1993.* Washington, DC: U.S. Government Printing Office, 1994, p. 33.

★ 723 ★

Industry Employment

Private Industry Employment: Department & Variety Stores

Number of persons employed in each occupation is shown, by race/ethnicity, in 1993. Data do not include Hawaii.

Group	Total employ-ment	Officials and managers	Profes-sionals	Techni-cians	Sales workers	Office & clerical workers	Craft workers	Opera-tives	Laborers	Service workers
Department stores										
All employers	1,814,586	141,520	22,358	13,707	1,041,609	206,719	61,487	54,614	185,530	87,042
White	1,400,963	123,873	19,832	11,062	801,625	161,762	49,847	40,537	130,542	61,883
Minority	413,623	17,647	2,526	2,645	239,984	44,957	11,640	14,077	54,988	25,159
Black	230,446	9,850	1,080	1,565	132,434	26,438	5,495	6,871	31,852	14,861

[Continued]

★ 723 ★

Private Industry Employment: Department & Variety Stores
[Continued]

Group	Total employ-ment	Officials and managers	Profes-sionals	Techni-cians	Sales workers	Office & clerical workers	Craft workers	Opera-tives	Laborers	Service workers
Hispanic	136,245	5,549	646	716	78,312	13,900	4,652	5,256	19,003	8,211
Asian/Pacific Islander	38,335	1,877	710	328	23,853	3,836	1,267	1,655	3,101	1,708
American Indian/Alaskan Native	8,597	371	90	36	5,385	783	226	295	1,032	379
Variety stores										
All employers	120,566	12,384	1,025	957	64,858	11,268	7,452	2,365	15,706	4,551
White	98,989	11,174	953	857	52,236	9,982	6,732	2,031	12,501	2,523
Minority	21,577	1,210	72	100	12,622	1,286	720	334	3,205	2,028
Black	14,162	646	31	60	8,481	771	532	176	2,383	1,082
Hispanic	4,967	394	15	20	2,549	333	110	140	557	849
Asian/Pacific Islander	1,592	136	23	19	1,041	139	21	10	116	87
American Indian/Alaskan Native	856	34	3	1	551	43	57	8	149	10

Source: U.S. Equal Employment Opportunity Commission. *Job Patterns for Minorities and Women in Private Industry, 1993.* Washington, DC: U.S. Government Printing Office, 1994, p. 31.

★ 724 ★

Industry Employment

Private Industry Employment: Drugstores & Proprietary Stores

Number of persons employed in each occupation is shown, by race/ethnicity, in 1993. Data do not include Hawaii.

Group	Total employ-ment	Officials and managers	Profes-sionals	Techni-cians	Sales workers	Office & clerical workers	Craft workers	Opera-tives	Laborers	Service workers
All employers	57,663	6,796	4,675	2,456	22,172	7,422	1,095	6,671	5,285	1,091
White	43,394	5,926	3,820	1,944	15,494	6,107	892	4,670	3,757	784
Minority	14,269	870	855	512	6,678	1,315	203	2,001	1,528	307
Black	6,277	351	225	201	2,473	668	110	1,266	851	132
Hispanic	5,002	299	113	145	2,900	362	60	577	413	133
Asian/Pacific Islander	2,692	199	506	155	1,136	260	32	130	242	32
American Indian/Alaskan Native	298	21	11	11	169	25	1	28	22	10

Source: U.S. Equal Employment Opportunity Commission. *Job Patterns for Minorities and Women in Private Industry, 1993.* Washington, DC: U.S. Government Printing Office, 1994, p. 33.

★ 725 ★

Industry Employment

Private Industry Employment: Electronic/Electrical Equipment Industry

Number of persons employed in each occupation is shown, by race/ethnicity, in 1993. Data are shown for selected industry sectors and do not include Hawaii.

Group	Total employ- ment	Officials and managers	Profes- sionals	Techni- cians	Sales workers	Office & clerical workers	Craft workers	Opera- tives	Laborers	Service workers
Electric distributing equipment										
All employers	88,806	8,568	10,831	6,201	1,851	6,751	13,511	34,362	6,279	452
White	73,351	7,999	9,806	5,377	1,762	5,723	11,252	26,598	4,509	325
Minority	15,455	569	1,025	824	89	1,028	2,259	7,764	1,770	127
Black	8,292	227	286	292	36	570	1,383	4,889	541	68
Hispanic	4,254	155	177	196	29	260	572	1,784	1,042	39
Asian/Pacific Islander	2,576	162	530	315	19	164	262	958	147	19
American Indian/Alaskan Native	333	25	32	21	5	34	42	133	40	1
Electrical industrial apparatus										
All employers	134,342	12,862	17,270	8,601	3,256	9,184	20,706	49,478	12,064	921
White	113,133	12,069	15,925	7,675	3,102	8,075	17,684	38,436	9,422	745
Minority	21,209	793	1,345	926	154	1,109	3,022	11,042	2,642	176
Black	11,141	292	389	352	53	533	1,684	6,493	1,230	115
Hispanic	6,168	225	328	252	62	383	873	2,982	1,016	47
Asian/Pacific Islander	3,019	210	586	280	31	147	350	1,191	218	6
American Indian/Alaskan Native	881	66	42	42	8	46	115	376	178	8
Household appliances										
All employers	102,699	8,090	6,656	2,789	1,469	6,763	10,467	45,624	20,017	824
White	85,022	7,632	6,231	2,554	1,403	6,007	9,206	35,119	16,177	693
Minority	17,677	458	425	235	66	756	1,261	10,505	3,840	131
Black	12,869	236	204	150	27	498	864	8,346	2,457	87
Hispanic	3,491	120	78	61	31	200	283	1,722	953	43
Asian/Pacific Islander	1,016	76	125	21	7	48	73	301	365	0
American Indian/Alaskan Native	301	26	18	3	1	10	41	136	65	1
Electric lighting and wiring equipment										
All employers	86,820	7,936	5,410	2,887	2,326	6,412	13,943	33,279	13,934	693
White	63,667	7,261	4,880	2,401	2,184	5,248	11,537	22,047	7,660	449
Minority	23,153	675	530	486	142	1,164	2,406	11,232	6,274	244
Black	11,999	272	162	189	82	491	1,095	6,265	3,308	135
Hispanic	8,032	233	121	106	44	435	1,014	3,826	2,166	87
Asian/Pacific Islander	2,759	143	232	182	13	182	265	1,049	673	20
American Indian/Alaskan Native	363	27	15	9	3	56	32	92	127	2
Communications equipment										
All employers	318,707	46,327	108,398	35,338	6,183	40,422	20,263	53,848	5,253	2,675
White	256,303	41,910	93,400	28,218	5,455	30,908	16,696	34,754	3,110	1,852
Minority	62,404	4,417	14,998	7,120	728	9,514	3,567	19,094	2,143	823
Black	28,395	1,743	4,647	3,115	318	5,971	1,780	9,414	966	441
Hispanic	14,730	1,044	2,666	1,684	163	2,183	887	5,253	558	292
Asian/Pacific Islander	17,706	1,476	7,396	2,138	218	1,160	794	4,027	420	77
American Indian/Alaskan Native	1,573	154	289	183	29	200	106	400	199	13
Electronic components and accessories										
All employers	548,716	72,230	134,942	60,448	9,104	52,288	46,440	147,005	20,265	5,994
White	394,780	62,289	106,405	43,480	8,404	39,155	33,763	85,645	11,920	3,719
Minority	153,936	9,941	28,537	16,968	700	13,133	12,677	61,360	8,345	2,275
Black	38,230	1,993	4,383	3,981	180	4,334	3,618	15,617	3,021	1,103
Hispanic	49,733	2,659	5,492	5,006	239	5,105	5,037	21,920	3,333	942
Asian/Pacific Islander	63,047	5,012	18,231	7,683	251	3,405	3,735	22,643	1,900	187
American Indian/Alaskan Native	2,926	277	431	298	30	289	287	1,180	91	43
Misc. electrical equipment and supplies										
All employers	81,105	8,630	10,887	7,455	2,667	6,329	8,888	28,675	6,675	899
White	65,241	7,951	9,652	6,318	2,491	5,455	7,443	21,163	4,117	651
Minority	15,864	679	1,235	1,137	176	874	1,445	7,512	2,558	248
Black	7,620	236	314	402	77	408	839	3,987	1,187	170
Hispanic	4,287	177	246	308	50	278	381	1,876	925	46

[Continued]

★ 725 ★

Private Industry Employment: Electronic/Electrical Equipment Industry
[Continued]

Group	Total employ-ment	Officials and managers	Profes-sionals	Techni-cians	Sales workers	Office & clerical workers	Craft workers	Opera-tives	Laborers	Service workers
Asian/Pacific Islander	3,317	227	646	380	42	155	167	1,433	254	13
American Indian/Alaskan Native	640	39	29	47	7	33	58	216	192	19

Source: U.S. Equal Employment Opportunity Commission. *Job Patterns for Minorities and Women in Private Industry, 1993.* Washington, DC: U.S. Government Printing Office, 1994, pp. 21-23.

★ 726 ★

Industry Employment

Private Industry Employment: Fabricated Metals Industry

Number of persons employed in each occupation is shown, by race/ethnicity, in 1993. Data are shown for selected industry sectors and do not include Hawaii.

Group	Total employ-ment	Officials and managers	Profes-sionals	Techni-cians	Sales workers	Office & clerical workers	Craft workers	Opera-tives	Laborers	Service workers
Metal cans and shipping containers										
All employers	40,849	4,896	1,477	630	896	2,491	10,741	14,541	4,923	254
White	31,408	4,502	1,360	566	766	2,181	8,907	9,836	3,086	204
Minority	9,441	394	117	64	130	310	1,834	4,705	1,837	50
Black	4,599	202	41	26	61	166	868	2,639	838	28
Hispanic	4,028	124	32	27	56	100	784	1,980	909	16
Asian/Pacific Islander	605	47	42	10	10	29	143	253	65	6
American Indian/Alaskan Native	209	21	2	1	3	15	39	103	25	0
Cutlery, hand tools, and hardware										
All employers	65,268	6,298	3,501	2,236	2,457	4,950	10,372	27,301	7,495	658
White	50,054	5,879	3,203	1,961	2,315	4,244	8,494	18,797	4,688	473
Minority	15,214	419	298	275	142	706	1,878	8,504	2,807	185
Black	6,970	177	101	91	63	318	903	4,161	1,068	88
Hispanic	6,257	138	85	114	61	288	706	3,276	1,507	82
Asian/Pacific Islander	1,627	87	108	62	13	85	228	846	191	7
American Indian/Alaskan Native	360	17	4	8	5	15	41	221	41	8
Fabricated structural metal products										
All employers	190,091	18,947	15,656	10,285	4,652	13,769	41,316	57,625	25,585	2,256
White	150,805	17,685	13,843	9,228	4,481	12,003	33,488	41,496	17,019	1,562
Minority	39,286	1,262	1,813	1,057	171	1,766	7,828	16,129	8,566	694
Black	18,091	477	345	430	45	854	3,782	8,034	3,676	448
Hispanic	16,079	434	414	362	96	632	3,178	6,627	4,124	212
Asian/Pacific Islander	4,025	273	1,024	224	18	220	602	1,113	526	25
American Indian/Alaskan Native	1,091	78	30	41	12	60	266	355	240	9
Metal forgings and stampings										
All employers	108,440	9,349	5,030	3,900	1,366	5,891	23,126	44,086	14,559	1,133
White	89,168	8,667	4,633	3,588	1,326	5,276	20,407	33,597	10,869	805
Minority	19,272	682	397	312	40	615	2,719	10,489	3,690	328
Black	11,593	336	143	106	12	328	1,438	6,710	2,256	264
Hispanic	5,658	159	61	92	16	181	962	2,896	1,235	56
Asian/Pacific Islander	1,677	161	181	101	10	77	257	727	155	8
American Indian/Alaskan Native	344	26	12	13	2	29	62	156	44	0
Misc. fabricated metal products										
All employers	150,605	15,724	9,320	7,180	4,885	11,874	30,146	55,561	14,664	1,251
White	123,794	14,844	8,603	6,356	4,565	10,586	25,573	42,383	9,908	976
Minority	26,811	880	717	824	320	1,288	4,573	13,178	4,756	275
Black	12,302	330	178	282	163	592	1,924	6,862	1,796	175
Hispanic	10,343	299	158	303	104	502	1,848	4,555	2,497	77

[Continued]

★ 726 ★

Private Industry Employment: Fabricated Metals Industry
[Continued]

Group	Total employ-ment	Officials and managers	Profes-sionals	Techni-cians	Sales workers	Office & clerical workers	Craft workers	Opera-tives	Laborers	Service workers
Asian/Pacific Islander	3,655	190	361	219	47	151	705	1,560	404	18
American Indian/Alaskan Native	511	61	20	20	6	43	96	201	59	5

Source: U.S. Equal Employment Opportunity Commission. *Job Patterns for Minorities and Women in Private Industry, 1993.* Washington, DC: U.S. Government Printing Office, 1994, pp. 17-18.

★ 727 ★

Industry Employment

Private Industry Employment: Food & Kindred Products

Number of persons employed in each occupation is shown, by race/ethnicity, in 1993. Data are shown for selected industry sectors and do not include Hawaii.

Group	Total employ-ment	Officials and managers	Profes-sionals	Techni-cians	Sales workers	Office & clerical workers	Craft workers	Opera-tives	Laborers	Service workers
Meat products										
All employers	349,827	24,987	5,653	6,487	5,288	12,730	27,896	90,204	170,094	6,488
White	186,156	21,527	5,035	5,211	4,785	10,825	19,742	41,153	74,329	3,549
Minority	163,671	3,460	618	1,276	503	1,905	8,154	49,051	95,765	2,939
Black	79,293	2,089	340	695	354	1,209	4,781	25,397	42,650	1,778
Hispanic	67,536	1,066	148	417	105	548	2,750	18,591	42,961	950
Asian/Pacific Islander	13,253	186	105	112	32	83	422	4,345	7,852	116
American Indian/Alaskan Native	3,589	119	25	52	12	65	201	718	2,302	95
Dairy products										
All employers	109,338	11,921	3,918	3,414	8,329	11,086	13,248	32,555	22,194	2,673
White	91,177	11,029	3,632	2,962	7,274	9,623	11,281	26,410	16,769	2,197
Minority	18,161	892	286	452	1,055	1,463	1,967	6,145	5,425	476
Black	8,463	407	112	204	568	718	932	2,978	2,308	236
Hispanic	7,482	311	58	124	388	438	816	2,598	2,617	132
Asian/Pacific Islander	1,777	139	107	106	70	253	172	425	414	91
American Indian/Alaskan Native	439	35	9	18	29	54	47	144	86	17
Preserved fruits & vegetables										
All employers	163,573	14,533	6,448	4,084	2,935	10,548	20,982	41,029	59,990	3,024
White	102,369	13,080	5,719	3,170	2,689	8,992	16,421	25,827	24,727	1,744
Minority	61,204	1,453	729	914	246	1,556	4,561	15,202	35,263	1,280
Black	12,687	452	304	270	104	515	1,032	4,346	5,351	313
Hispanic	43,065	674	183	531	106	791	3,141	9,887	26,875	877
Asian/Pacific Islander	4,166	244	222	92	21	202	204	630	2,502	49
American Indian/Alaskan Native	1,286	83	20	21	15	48	184	339	535	41
Grain mill products										
All employers	77,874	12,230	6,314	3,365	4,392	8,602	9,024	22,263	10,620	1,064
White	64,274	11,385	5,663	2,952	4,241	7,394	7,799	17,130	6,880	830
Minority	13,600	845	651	413	151	1,208	1,225	5,133	3,740	234
Black	8,235	455	331	251	68	759	671	3,394	2,140	166
Hispanic	4,041	205	121	85	59	313	443	1,387	1,375	53
Asian/Pacific Islander	985	147	191	63	16	105	61	247	142	13
American Indian/Alaskan Native	339	38	8	14	8	31	50	105	83	2

[Continued]

★ 727 ★

Private Industry Employment: Food & Kindred Products
[Continued]

Group	Total employ-ment	Officials and managers	Profes-sionals	Techni-cians	Sales workers	Office & clerical workers	Craft workers	Opera-tives	Laborers	Service workers
Bakery products										
All employers	137,286	14,836	1,707	1,334	18,891	7,431	17,955	38,320	30,482	6,330
White	94,607	12,995	1,506	1,036	16,345	5,985	12,600	24,505	16,338	3,297
Minority	42,679	1,841	201	298	2,546	1,446	5,355	13,815	14,144	3,033
Black	24,501	1,047	103	175	1,251	833	2,953	8,374	8,091	1,674
Hispanic	14,803	551	44	76	1,102	429	1,972	4,572	4,923	1,134
Asian/Pacific Islander	2,790	188	53	43	134	161	347	710	964	190
American Indian/Alaskan Native	585	55	1	4	59	23	83	159	166	35
Beverages										
All employers	181,381	24,974	12,427	4,400	31,135	20,099	17,004	46,612	18,646	6,084
White	137,362	22,109	10,637	3,309	25,147	15,852	13,994	32,525	10,172	3,617
Minority	44,019	2,865	1,790	1,091	5,988	4,247	3,010	14,087	8,474	2,467
Black	24,012	1,567	939	549	3,410	2,466	1,346	8,305	3,684	1,746
Hispanic	16,494	906	481	393	2,131	1,329	1,387	5,119	4,301	447
Asian/Pacific Islander	2,543	324	347	134	288	345	200	465	360	80
American Indian/Alaskan Native	970	68	23	15	159	107	77	198	129	194

Source: U.S. Equal Employment Opportunity Commission. *Job Patterns for Minorities and Women in Private Industry, 1993.* Washington, DC: U.S. Government Printing Office, 1994, p. 6-7.

★ 728 ★

Industry Employment

Private Industry Employment: Freight Transport Industry

Number of persons employed in each occupation is shown, by race/ethnicity, in 1993. Data are shown for selected industry sectors and do not include Hawaii.

Group	Total employ-ment	Officials and managers	Profes-sionals	Techni-cians	Sales workers	Office & clerical workers	Craft workers	Opera-tives	Laborers	Service workers
Trucking and courier services										
All employers	691,347	73,783	27,378	7,575	25,761	78,037	37,872	271,469	136,424	33,048
White	540,586	63,014	25,330	6,633	19,769	61,010	32,120	213,796	92,354	26,560
Minority	150,761	10,769	2,048	942	5,992	17,027	5,752	57,673	44,070	6,488
Black	94,619	6,351	939	405	2,954	10,673	3,024	37,753	28,550	3,970
Hispanic	43,024	3,057	582	243	2,340	4,606	1,952	15,825	12,519	1,900
Asian/Pacific Islander	10,191	1,080	459	263	620	1,460	577	2,699	2,502	531
American Indian/Alaskan Native	2,927	281	68	31	78	288	199	1,396	499	87
Trucking terminal facilities										
All employers	5,195	375	195	248	81	468	220	3,137	392	79
White	4,574	360	177	225	81	434	186	2,762	278	71
Minority	621	15	18	23	0	34	34	375	114	8
Black	425	8	3	18	0	16	7	294	76	3
Hispanic	141	3	1	2	0	12	18	70	31	4
Asian/Pacific Islander	33	4	13	3	0	1	6	1	4	1
American Indian/Alaskan Native	22	0	1	0	0	5	3	10	3	0

Source: U.S. Equal Employment Opportunity Commission. *Job Patterns for Minorities and Women in Private Industry, 1993.* Washington, DC: U.S. Government Printing Office, 1994, p. 26.

★ 729 ★

Industry Employment

Private Industry Employment: Furniture and Home Furnishings Stores

Number of persons employed in each occupation is shown, by race/ethnicity, in 1993. Data do not include Hawaii.

Group	Total employment	Officials and managers	Professionals	Technicians	Sales workers	Office & clerical workers	Craft workers	Operatives	Laborers	Service workers
All employers	41,847	5,259	1,368	546	8,826	9,944	2,237	6,791	5,834	1,042
White	30,750	4,697	1,233	422	6,707	7,436	1,497	4,234	3,875	649
Minority	11,097	562	135	124	2,119	2,508	740	2,557	1,959	393
Black	5,414	256	43	51	1,003	1,205	290	1,252	1,175	139
Hispanic	4,236	223	50	52	783	998	365	887	645	233
Asian/Pacific Islander	1,263	77	40	20	310	283	60	344	113	16
American Indian/Alaskan Native	184	6	2	1	23	22	25	74	26	5

Source: U.S. Equal Employment Opportunity Commission. *Job Patterns for Minorities and Women in Private Industry, 1993.* Washington, DC: U.S. Government Printing Office, 1994, p. 32.

★ 730 ★

Industry Employment

Private Industry Employment: Grocery Stores

Number of persons employed in each occupation is shown, by race/ethnicity, in 1993. Data do not include Hawaii.

Group	Total employment	Officials and managers	Professionals	Technicians	Sales workers	Office & clerical workers	Craft workers	Operatives	Laborers	Service workers
All employers	1,601,271	140,778	16,018	7,706	1,052,123	60,504	54,060	96,288	96,082	77,712
White	1,249,802	124,389	13,614	6,251	813,468	50,867	44,417	71,148	68,385	57,263
Minority	351,469	16,389	2,404	1,455	238,655	9,637	9,643	25,140	27,697	20,449
Black	174,268	7,554	651	421	124,937	4,419	3,926	10,713	12,448	9,199
Hispanic	139,253	6,629	850	819	88,801	3,988	4,542	12,162	12,584	8,878
Asian/Pacific Islander	27,159	1,736	804	155	17,948	924	905	1,237	1,523	1,927
American Indian/Alaskan Native	10,789	470	99	60	6,969	306	270	1,028	1,142	445

Source: U.S. Equal Employment Opportunity Commission. *Job Patterns for Minorities and Women in Private Industry, 1993.* Washington, DC: U.S. Government Printing Office, 1994, p. 31.

★ 731 ★

Industry Employment

Private Industry Employment: Health Care Industry

Number of persons employed in each occupation is shown, by race/ethnicity, in 1993. Data are shown for selected industry sectors and do not include Hawaii.

Group	Total employ-ment	Officials and managers	Profes-sionals	Techni-cians	Sales workers	Office & clerical workers	Craft workers	Opera-tives	Laborers	Service workers
Nursing and personal care facilities										
All employers	845,204	50,273	133,040	100,220	2,087	67,484	11,270	17,916	13,510	449,404
White	561,013	43,955	108,040	73,045	1,863	53,386	7,789	11,797	7,530	253,608
Minority	284,191	6,318	25,000	27,175	224	14,098	3,481	6,119	5,980	195,796
Black	198,943	3,817	11,604	18,902	157	8,777	2,262	4,104	3,844	145,476
Hispanic	48,287	1,224	2,639	3,602	43	3,421	808	1,343	1,596	33,611
Asian/Pacific Islander	33,174	1,140	10,357	4,216	20	1,679	357	547	488	14,370
American Indian/Alaskan Native	3,787	137	400	455	4	221	54	125	52	2,339
Hospitals										
All employers	3,436,239	234,537	1,298,175	555,455	6,031	610,988	47,066	37,243	21,944	627,800
White	2,655,559	207,103	1,105,821	425,508	4,659	468,816	37,910	25,828	13,458	366,456
Minority	780,680	27,434	192,354	126,947	1,372	142,172	9,156	11,415	8,486	261,344
Black	467,090	15,159	77,566	76,607	802	92,767	5,201	7,528	5,790	185,670
Hispanic	158,257	6,000	29,617	25,876	284	35,560	2,753	2,769	2,068	53,330
Asian/Pacific Islander	142,881	5,767	80,077	22,438	266	12,133	1,032	967	519	19,682
American Indian/Alaskan Native	12,452	508	5,094	2,026	20	1,712	170	151	109	2,662

Source: U.S. Equal Employment Opportunity Commission. *Job Patterns for Minorities and Women in Private Industry, 1993.* Washington, DC: U.S. Government Printing Office, 1994, p. 36.

★ 732 ★

Industry Employment

Private Industry Employment: Household Furniture Production

Number of persons employed in each occupation is shown, by race/ethnicity, in 1993. Data are shown for selected industry sectors and do not include Hawaii.

Group	Total employ-ment	Officials and managers	Profes-sionals	Techni-cians	Sales workers	Office & clerical workers	Craft workers	Opera-tives	Laborers	Service workers
All employers	177,047	12,146	3,152	2,210	6,243	11,369	38,390	71,868	29,521	2,148
White	138,109	11,255	2,953	2,044	5,555	10,177	31,656	53,280	19,729	1,460
Minority	38,938	891	199	166	688	1,192	6,734	18,588	9,792	688
Black	25,571	411	64	77	374	517	4,713	12,820	6,055	540
Hispanic	10,958	315	32	56	220	468	1,595	4,774	3,376	122
Asian/Pacific Islander	1,639	64	42	24	79	96	313	752	253	16
American Indian/Alaskan Native	770	101	61	9	15	111	113	242	108	10

Source: U.S. Equal Employment Opportunity Commission. *Job Patterns for Minorities and Women in Private Industry, 1993.* Washington, DC: U.S. Government Printing Office, 1994, p. 10.

★ 733 ★

Industry Employment

Private Industry Employment: Instrumentation Industry

Number of persons employed in each occupation is shown, by race/ethnicity, in 1993. Data are shown for selected industry sectors and do not include Hawaii.

Group	Total employ-ment	Officials and managers	Profes-sionals	Techni-cians	Sales workers	Office & clerical workers	Craft workers	Opera-tives	Laborers	Service workers
Measuring and controlling devices										
All employers	191,391	25,978	42,184	21,446	5,732	22,248	21,086	42,733	7,049	2,935
White	159,120	24,092	37,487	17,855	5,383	18,861	17,564	30,351	5,171	2,356
Minority	32,271	1,886	4,697	3,591	349	3,387	3,522	12,382	1,878	579
Black	10,718	491	851	1,005	119	1,368	1,306	4,606	706	266
Hispanic	10,805	557	1,006	1,015	122	1,296	1,345	4,188	995	281
Asian/Pacific Islander	9,929	739	2,691	1,481	93	604	795	3,355	148	23
American Indian/Alaskan Native	819	99	149	90	15	119	76	233	29	9
Medical instruments and supplies										
All employers	225,297	29,627	33,690	19,824	15,050	28,606	17,278	63,077	15,704	2,441
White	168,912	26,940	28,580	14,994	14,101	23,214	13,258	38,176	7,951	1,698
Minority	56,385	2,687	5,110	4,830	949	5,392	4,020	24,901	7,753	743
Black	17,304	862	1,074	1,232	439	1,992	1,270	7,569	2,553	313
Hispanic	22,731	967	1,476	1,697	343	2,459	1,866	10,256	3,291	376
Asian/Pacific Islander	15,423	780	2,465	1,819	135	833	827	6,716	1,808	40
American Indian/Alaskan Native	927	78	95	82	32	108	57	360	101	14

Source: U.S. Equal Employment Opportunity Commission. *Job Patterns for Minorities and Women in Private Industry, 1993.* Washington, DC: U.S. Government Printing Office, 1994, p. 25.

★ 734 ★

Industry Employment

Private Industry Employment: Insurance Industry

Number of persons employed in each occupation is shown, by race/ethnicity, in 1993. Data are shown for selected industry sectors and do not include Hawaii.

Group	Total employ-ment	Officials and managers	Profes-sionals	Techni-cians	Sales workers	Office & clerical workers	Craft workers	Opera-tives	Laborers	Service workers
Life insurance										
All employers	327,518	50,277	71,190	40,774	33,559	125,698	1,566	1,260	338	2,856
White	267,361	45,701	60,721	32,692	29,125	95,135	1,259	859	256	1,613
Minority	60,157	4,576	10,469	8,082	4,434	30,563	307	401	82	1,243
Black	36,993	2,576	5,877	5,014	1,946	20,280	189	251	59	801
Hispanic	13,113	939	2,040	1,650	1,035	6,907	100	96	18	328
Asian/Pacific Islander	9,143	971	2,396	1,323	1,261	3,018	15	50	3	106
American Indian/Alaskan Native	908	90	156	95	192	358	3	4	2	8
Health insurance and medical service plans										
All employers	262,904	34,370	65,717	35,708	10,236	111,456	1,197	1,038	228	2,954
White	203,938	30,441	55,300	27,168	9,057	78,478	925	626	141	1,802
Minority	58,966	3,929	10,417	8,540	1,179	32,978	272	412	87	1,152
Black	40,386	2,528	6,158	6,610	693	23,090	185	268	61	793
Hispanic	9,481	718	1,700	810	348	5,439	51	112	22	281
Asian/Pacific Islander	8,111	580	2,401	993	107	3,908	26	28	2	66
American Indian/Alaskan Native	988	103	158	127	31	541	10	4	2	12

[Continued]

★ 734 ★

Private Industry Employment: Insurance Industry

[Continued]

Group	Total employment	Officials and managers	Profes- sionals	Techni- cians	Sales workers	Office & clerical workers	Craft workers	Opera- tives	Laborers	Service workers
Fire, marine, and casualty insurance										
All employers	392,918	59,584	117,762	35,062	11,991	161,186	1,985	2,279	524	2,545
White	324,628	54,076	101,901	29,455	9,987	124,424	1,694	1,665	366	1,870
Minority	68,290	5,508	16,671	5,607	2,004	36,762	291	614	158	675
Black	38,894	3,246	9,593	2,990	805	21,280	108	322	73	477
Hispanic	17,499	1,242	3,770	1,297	1,022	9,571	160	225	75	137
Asian/Pacific Islander	10,715	857	3,014	1,243	150	5,315	21	51	8	56
American Indian/Alaskan Native	1,182	163	294	77	27	596	2	16	2	5

Source: U.S. Equal Employment Opportunity Commission. *Job Patterns for Minorities and Women in Private Industry, 1993.* Washington, DC: U.S. Government Printing Office, 1994, pp. 33-34.

★ 735 ★

Industry Employment

Private Industry Employment: Laundry, Cleaning & Garment Services

Number of persons employed in each occupation is shown, by race/ethnicity, in 1993. Data do not include Hawaii.

Group	Total employment	Officials and managers	Profes- sionals	Techni- cians	Sales workers	Office & clerical workers	Craft workers	Opera- tives	Laborers	Service workers
All employers	82,069	7,629	539	610	9,580	5,229	4,052	28,872	22,636	2,992
White	45,637	6,762	490	515	8,282	4,131	2,704	12,820	8,368	1,565
Minority	36,432	867	49	95	1,298	1,098	1,348	16,052	14,268	1,357
Black	17,658	419	25	50	589	604	597	8,128	6,543	703
Hispanic	16,580	401	16	27	651	405	670	6,860	7,003	547
Asian/Pacific Islander	1,898	41	7	16	48	78	68	942	606	92
American Indian/Alaskan Native	296	6	1	2	10	11	13	122	116	15

Source: U.S. Equal Employment Opportunity Commission. *Job Patterns for Minorities and Women in Private Industry, 1993.* Washington, DC: U.S. Government Printing Office, 1994, p. 35.

★ 736 ★

Industry Employment

Private Industry Employment: Leather Footwear Industry

Number of persons employed in each occupation is shown, by race/ethnicity, in 1993. Data do not include Hawaii.

Group	Total employment	Officials and managers	Profes- sionals	Techni- cians	Sales workers	Office & clerical workers	Craft workers	Opera- tives	Laborers	Service workers
All employers	59,638	5,729	2,408	801	4,080	4,777	7,448	23,937	9,725	733
White	47,316	5,197	2,172	713	3,477	4,102	5,997	18,978	6,081	599
Minority	12,322	532	236	88	603	675	1,451	4,959	3,644	134
Black	3,906	133	67	21	239	268	341	1,975	809	53

[Continued]

★ 736 ★

Private Industry Employment: Leather Footwear Industry
[Continued]

Group	Total employ-ment	Officials and managers	Profes-sionals	Techni-cians	Sales workers	Office & clerical workers	Craft workers	Opera-tives	Laborers	Service workers
Hispanic	6,876	303	70	46	267	319	979	2,397	2,427	68
Asian/Pacific Islander	728	59	88	15	78	61	78	277	60	12
American Indian/Alaskan Native	812	37	11	6	19	27	53	310	348	1

Source: U.S. Equal Employment Opportunity Commission. *Job Patterns for Minorities and Women in Private Industry, 1993.* Washington, DC: U.S. Government Printing Office, 1994, p. 15.

★ 737 ★
Industry Employment

Private Industry Employment: Lodging Industry

Number of persons employed in each occupation is shown, by race/ethnicity, in 1993. Data are shown for the hotel and motel sectors and do not include Hawaii.

Group	Total employ-ment	Officials and managers	Profes-sionals	Techni-cians	Sales workers	Office & clerical workers	Craft workers	Opera-tives	Laborers	Service workers
All employers	653,316	60,152	12,268	4,989	21,550	80,957	33,248	23,583	23,993	395,576
White	364,413	49,335	9,711	3,950	16,945	55,472	22,425	10,642	9,921	186,012
Minority	288,903	10,817	2,557	1,039	4,605	25,485	10,823	9,941	14,072	209,564
Black	116,857	4,629	1,027	389	2,242	12,736	3,710	4,018	5,365	82,731
Hispanic	127,280	3,826	708	442	1,379	7,994	4,457	4,400	7,547	96,527
Asian/Pacific Islander	41,552	2,161	756	192	883	4,358	2,503	1,381	1,014	28,304
American Indian/Alaskan Native	3,214	191	66	16	101	397	153	142	146	2,002

Source: U.S. Equal Employment Opportunity Commission. *Job Patterns for Minorities and Women in Private Industry, 1993.* Washington, DC: U.S. Government Printing Office, 1994, p. 34.

★ 738 ★
Industry Employment

Private Industry Employment: Lumber & Wood Products

Number of persons employed in each occupation is shown, by race/ethnicity, in 1993. Data are shown for selected industry sectors and do not include Hawaii.

Group	Total employ-ment	Officials and managers	Profes-sionals	Techni-cians	Sales workers	Office & clerical workers	Craft workers	Opera-tives	Laborers	Service workers
Sawmills and planing mills										
All employers	71,981	6,532	3,381	1,498	991	4,044	15,363	22,550	16,941	681
White	56,419	6,200	3,172	1,317	934	3,495	13,272	16,223	11,277	529
Minority	15,562	332	209	181	57	549	2,091	6,327	5,664	152
Black	11,459	179	115	113	39	437	1,431	5,005	4,011	129
Hispanic	2,570	60	25	20	12	59	342	823	1,218	11

[Continued]

★ 738 ★

Private Industry Employment: Lumber & Wood Products
[Continued]

Group	Total employ- ment	Officials and managers	Profes- sionals	Techni- cians	Sales workers	Office & clerical workers	Craft workers	Opera- tives	Laborers	Service workers
Asian/Pacific Islander	429	37	58	32	3	27	51	108	113	0
American Indian/Alaskan Native	1,104	56	11	16	3	26	267	391	322	12
Millwork, plywood & structural members										
All employers	99,618	7,173	2,021	1,786	2,335	5,475	20,304	32,951	26,819	754
White	80,885	6,738	1,919	1,668	2,270	5,024	17,415	25,283	19,920	648
Minority	18,733	435	102	118	65	451	2,889	7,668	6,899	106
Black	12,304	245	35	44	19	262	1,910	5,246	4,491	52
Hispanic	4,942	114	23	49	35	138	741	1,923	1,883	36
Asian/Pacific Islander	938	39	42	19	7	40	121	325	333	12
American Indian/Alaskan Native	549	37	2	6	4	11	117	174	192	6

Source: U.S. Equal Employment Opportunity Commission. *Job Patterns for Minorities and Women in Private Industry, 1993.* Washington, DC: U.S. Government Printing Office, 1994, pp. 9-10.

★ 739 ★

Industry Employment

Private Industry Employment: Machinery and Computer Equipment Industry

Number of persons employed in each occupation is shown, by race/ethnicity, in 1993. Data are shown for selected industry sectors and do not include Hawaii.

Group	Total employ- ment	Officials and managers	Profes- sionals	Techni- cians	Sales workers	Office & clerical workers	Craft workers	Opera- tives	Laborers	Service workers
Farm and garden machinery										
All employers	54,398	5,169	3,648	3,140	1,422	4,802	9,232	17,714	7,999	1,272
White	45,302	4,913	3,484	2,943	1,392	4,359	8,159	13,924	5,015	1,113
Minority	9,096	256	164	197	30	443	1,073	3,790	2,984	159
Black	6,111	137	73	133	9	287	707	2,739	1,908	118
Hispanic	2,489	80	38	38	18	124	287	892	975	37
Asian/Pacific Islander	325	25	47	21	2	20	41	102	66	1
American Indian/Alaskan Native	171	14	6	5	1	12	38	57	35	3
Construction and related machinery										
All employers	143,649	16,660	16,707	10,217	3,702	12,999	31,661	41,716	8,480	1,507
White	126,989	15,857	15,677	9,459	3,538	11,620	27,797	35,494	6,233	1,314
Minority	16,660	803	1,030	758	164	1,379	3,864	6,222	2,247	193
Black	8,610	324	340	340	44	807	1,737	3,742	1,157	119
Hispanic	5,414	190	201	221	83	379	1,499	1,841	942	58
Asian/Pacific Islander	1,785	219	439	154	20	135	370	371	65	12
American Indian/Alaskan Native	851	70	50	43	17	58	258	268	83	4
Metalworking machinery										
All employers	101,385	10,840	7,964	6,340	4,039	7,875	27,772	30,656	5,127	772
White	86,645	10,272	7,444	5,825	3,910	7,121	24,397	23,202	3,918	556
Minority	14,740	568	520	515	129	754	3,375	7,454	1,209	216
Black	6,543	191	136	185	41	372	1,486	3,344	644	144
Hispanic	5,714	176	96	174	60	264	1,280	3,170	429	65
Asian/Pacific Islander	2,164	168	261	139	20	86	527	835	124	4
American Indian/Alaskan Native	319	33	27	17	8	32	82	105	12	3
Special industry machinery										
All employers	118,436	13,875	14,057	8,979	4,173	11,567	26,271	30,145	8,448	921
White	102,301	13,204	13,101	8,006	3,992	10,396	23,537	23,623	5,761	681
Minority	16,135	671	956	973	181	1,171	2,734	6,522	2,687	240
Black	7,706	257	245	291	38	597	1,263	3,603	1,268	144
Hispanic	5,297	192	218	378	98	386	1,019	1,868	1,068	70

[Continued]

★ 739 ★

Private Industry Employment: Machinery and Computer Equipment Industry

[Continued]

Group	Total employ-ment	Officials and managers	Profes-sionals	Techni-cians	Sales workers	Office & clerical workers	Craft workers	Opera-tives	Laborers	Service workers
Asian/Pacific Islander	2,533	179	463	259	34	125	349	808	292	24
American Indian/Alaskan Native	599	43	30	45	11	63	103	243	59	2
General industry machinery										
All employers	195,179	23,313	23,177	12,513	5,804	17,318	40,469	58,240	12,930	1,415
White	168,706	22,089	21,196	11,537	5,598	15,598	35,245	46,541	9,819	1,083
Minority	26,473	1,224	1,981	976	206	1,720	5,224	11,699	3,111	332
Black	14,625	455	498	388	59	968	2,617	7,581	1,827	232
Hispanic	7,402	344	471	331	90	492	1,677	2,888	1,026	83
Asian/Pacific Islander	3,579	326	944	220	44	183	675	973	200	14
American Indian/Alaskan Native	867	99	68	37	13	77	255	257	58	3
Computer and office equipment										
All employers	356,139	47,336	131,952	43,079	21,889	36,046	18,885	50,352	5,213	1,387
White	282,638	41,804	110,766	34,414	18,654	28,286	14,985	30,273	2,439	1,017
Minority	73,501	5,532	21,186	8,665	3,235	7,760	3,900	20,079	2,774	370
Black	25,391	2,023	5,776	3,027	1,626	3,942	1,683	6,292	884	138
Hispanic	18,155	1,147	3,483	2,392	651	2,409	1,298	5,444	1,146	185
Asian/Pacific Islander	28,715	2,235	11,618	3,048	875	1,245	851	8,094	716	33
American Indian/Alaskan Native	1,240	127	309	198	83	164	68	249	28	14
Refrigeration and service machinery										
All employers	110,099	10,913	8,524	5,559	2,078	8,356	18,851	45,868	8,969	981
White	88,345	10,159	7,880	5,052	1,995	7,429	15,758	33,328	5,952	792
Minority	21,754	754	644	507	83	927	3,093	12,540	3,017	189
Black	12,678	318	211	227	17	464	1,785	8,184	1,348	124
Hispanic	6,555	234	142	137	49	334	1,000	3,218	1,392	49
Asian/Pacific Islander	2,055	165	266	122	11	109	219	916	236	11
American Indian/Alaskan Native	466	37	25	21	6	20	89	222	41	5
Misc. industrial and commercial machinery										
All employers	30,134	3,038	1,987	1,661	993	2,366	6,551	11,063	2,118	357
White	24,714	2,858	1,822	1,500	958	2,087	5,624	8,165	1,457	243
Minority	5,420	180	165	161	35	279	927	2,898	661	114
Black	2,311	55	31	62	8	142	346	1,295	324	48
Hispanic	2,176	63	28	51	20	95	388	1,192	275	64
Asian/Pacific Islander	820	54	101	42	3	26	168	367	57	2
American Indian/Alaskan Native	113	8	5	6	4	16	25	44	5	0

Source: U.S. Equal Employment Opportunity Commission. *Job Patterns for Minorities and Women in Private Industry, 1993.* Washington, DC: U.S. Government Printing Office, 1994, pp. 19-21.

★ 740 ★

Industry Employment

Private Industry Employment: Manufacturing-Durable Goods

Number of persons employed in each occupation is shown, by race/ethnicity, in 1993. Data do not include Hawaii.

Group	Total employ-ment	Officials and managers	Profes-sionals	Techni-cians	Sales workers	Office & clerical workers	Craft workers	Opera-tives	Laborers	Service workers
All employers	7,006,445	761,229	1,032,890	438,816	174,769	562,111	1,168,232	2,196,122	591,274	81,002
White	5,611,529	695,966	896,732	367,045	160,194	470,380	973,132	1,585,636	403,744	58,700
Minority	1,394,916	65,263	136,158	71,771	14,575	91,731	195,100	610,486	187,530	22,302
Black	693,710	26,595	37,062	25,494	6,583	45,377	102,889	339,690	95,531	14,489
Hispanic	423,304	17,521	27,074	20,714	4,828	30,353	65,229	179,006	72,295	6,284

[Continued]

★ 740 ★

Private Industry Employment: Manufacturing-Durable Goods

[Continued]

Group	Total employ-ment	Officials and managers	Profes-sionals	Techni-cians	Sales workers	Office & clerical workers	Craft workers	Opera-tives	Laborers	Service workers
Asian/Pacific Islander	246,219	18,330	68,997	23,627	2,654	13,441	21,544	80,290	16,160	1,176
American Indian/Alaskan Native	31,683	2,817	3,025	1,936	510	2,560	5,438	11,500	3,544	353

Source: U.S. Equal Employment Opportunity Commission. *Job Patterns for Minorities and Women in Private Industry, 1993.* Washington, DC: U.S. Government Printing Office, 1994, p. 3.

★ 741 ★

Industry Employment

Private Industry Employment: Mining

Number of persons employed in each occupation is shown, by race/ethnicity, in 1993. Data do not include Hawaii.

Group	Total employ-ment	Officials and managers	Profes-sionals	Techni-cians	Sales workers	Office & clerical workers	Craft workers	Opera-tives	Laborers	Service workers
All employers	337,741	47,557	53,243	19,798	7,090	32,878	71,411	74,434	26,426	4,904
White	281,928	44,247	47,263	16,361	5,977	25,803	59,447	59,259	20,523	3,048
Minority	55,813	3,310	5,980	3,437	1,113	7,075	11,964	15,175	5,903	1,856
Black	22,191	1,104	2,007	1,412	521	3,867	4,002	5,911	2,347	1,020
Hispanic	24,624	1,384	1,623	1,254	448	2,389	6,079	7,682	3,073	692
Asian/Pacific Islander	4,516	439	2,068	526	92	492	325	370	123	81
American Indian/Alaskan Native	4,482	383	282	245	52	327	1,558	1,212	360	63

Source: U.S. Equal Employment Opportunity Commission. *Job Patterns for Minorities and Women in Private Industry, 1993.* Washington, DC: U.S. Government Printing Office, 1994, p. 2.

★ 742 ★

Industry Employment

Private Industry Employment: Paper and Allied Products

Number of persons employed in each occupation is shown, by race/ethnicity, in 1993. Data are shown for selected industry sectors and do not include Hawaii.

Group	Total employ-ment	Officials and managers	Profes-sionals	Techni-cians	Sales workers	Office & clerical workers	Craft workers	Opera-tives	Laborers	Service workers
Pulp mills										
All employers	25,911	3,076	1,698	915	273	1,395	6,853	8,645	2,760	296
White	22,441	2,932	1,609	815	264	1,249	6,155	6,942	2,232	243
Minority	3,470	144	89	100	9	146	698	1,703	528	53
Black	2,694	83	45	66	5	119	559	1,398	381	38
Hispanic	296	28	13	13	1	14	38	126	57	6
Asian/Pacific Islander	162	16	28	14	1	5	21	54	22	1
American Indian/Alaskan Native	318	17	3	7	2	8	80	125	68	8
Paper mills, except building paper										
All employers	158,856	17,236	13,760	4,925	2,869	10,723	39,561	51,318	16,908	1,556

[Continued]

★ 742 ★

Private Industry Employment: Paper and Allied Products
[Continued]

Group	Total employment	Officials and managers	Professionals	Technicians	Sales workers	Office & clerical workers	Craft workers	Operatives	Laborers	Service workers
White	137,619	16,265	12,807	4,483	2,654	9,511	35,578	41,625	13,423	1,273
Minority	21,237	971	953	442	215	1,212	3,983	9,693	3,485	283
Black	15,757	585	513	335	132	879	2,920	7,726	2,440	227
Hispanic	3,471	184	121	58	62	222	712	1,291	787	34
Asian/Pacific Islander	1,021	142	274	28	16	53	114	252	128	14
American Indian/Alaskan Native	988	60	45	21	5	58	237	424	130	8
Paperboard mills										
All employers	29,433	3,547	1,367	777	387	1,775	9,254	8,376	3,738	212
White	24,306	3,376	1,297	673	375	1,561	7,748	6,396	2,735	145
Minority	5,127	171	70	104	12	214	1,506	1,980	1,003	67
Black	3,886	108	38	90	3	167	1,157	1,587	678	58
Hispanic	908	37	14	8	6	29	262	292	254	6
Asian/Pacific Islander	158	14	14	4	1	11	36	40	37	1
American Indian/Alaskan Native	175	12	4	2	2	7	51	61	34	2
Paperboard containers and boxes										
All employers	112,176	11,893	3,130	1,694	4,107	7,864	23,442	37,865	21,495	686
White	85,962	10,963	2,849	1,519	3,961	6,913	18,558	26,586	14,086	527
Minority	26,214	930	281	175	146	951	4,884	11,279	7,409	159
Black	14,332	464	120	76	61	508	2,682	6,433	3,888	100
Hispanic	9,784	340	68	60	51	306	1,849	4,163	2,896	51
Asian/Pacific Islander	1,444	74	83	29	9	89	226	460	472	2
American Indian/Alaskan Native	654	52	10	10	25	48	127	223	153	6
Converted paper and paperboard products										
All employers	180,308	19,604	14,540	5,176	8,068	15,430	32,400	55,508	27,765	1,817
White	143,564	18,285	13,371	4,514	7,571	13,821	26,879	40,178	17,597	1,348
Minority	36,744	1,319	1,169	662	497	1,609	5,521	15,330	10,168	469
Black	20,827	641	402	311	253	934	3,014	9,174	5,806	292
Hispanic	11,986	387	206	234	169	455	1,915	4,916	3,553	151
Asian/Pacific Islander	3,248	238	517	100	51	165	470	1,022	665	20
American Indian/Alaskan Native	683	53	44	17	24	55	122	218	144	6

Source: U.S. Equal Employment Opportunity Commission. *Job Patterns for Minorities and Women in Private Industry, 1993.* Washington, DC: U.S. Government Printing Office, 1994, pp. 11-12.

★ 743 ★

Industry Employment

Private Industry Employment: Petroleum Refining

Number of persons employed in each occupation is shown, by race/ethnicity, in 1993. Data do not include Hawaii.

Group	Total employment	Officials and managers	Professionals	Technicians	Sales workers	Office & clerical workers	Craft workers	Operatives	Laborers	Service workers
All employers	111,375	18,095	21,800	6,188	5,543	12,435	33,430	11,316	1,894	674
White	89,415	16,111	18,615	4,923	4,341	9,184	25,895	8,544	1,339	463
Minority	21,960	1,984	3,185	1,265	1,202	3,251	7,535	2,772	555	211
Black	11,816	1,047	1,200	644	869	1,711	4,379	1,556	277	133
Hispanic	6,531	581	781	315	210	883	2,504	960	241	56
Asian/Pacific Islander	2,714	266	1,074	239	54	507	409	143	9	13
American Indian/Alaskan Native	899	90	130	67	69	150	243	113	28	9

Source: U.S. Equal Employment Opportunity Commission. *Job Patterns for Minorities and Women in Private Industry, 1993.* Washington, DC: U.S. Government Printing Office, 1994, p. 14.

★ 744 ★

Industry Employment

Private Industry Employment: Primary Metals Industry

Number of persons employed in each occupation is shown, by race/ethnicity, in 1993. Data are shown for selected industry sectors and do not include Hawaii.

Group	Total employ-ment	Officials and managers	Profes-sionals	Techni-cians	Sales workers	Office & clerical workers	Craft workers	Opera-tives	Laborers	Service workers
Iron and steel foundries										
All employers	189,101	20,359	10,834	5,634	3,145	11,691	57,346	60,793	17,454	1,826
White	153,907	18,870	10,063	5,023	2,900	10,230	48,053	45,608	11,755	1,405
Minority	35,194	1,489	771	630	245	1,461	9,293	15,185	5,699	421
Black	23,352	828	322	334	148	945	6,372	10,489	3,625	289
Hispanic	9,832	397	165	235	65	435	2,708	3,800	1,903	124
Asian/Pacific Islander	1,563	221	236	49	20	58	133	749	91	6
American Indian/Alaskan Native	447	43	48	12	12	23	80	147	80	2
Rolling and drawing										
All employers	94,370	9,839	3,880	3,172	1,300	5,312	18,693	39,813	11,192	1,169
White	70,889	9,003	3,597	2,649	1,231	4,613	15,302	26,070	7,538	886
Minority	23,481	836	283	523	69	699	3,391	13,743	3,654	283
Black	15,526	502	143	275	32	447	2,061	9,398	2,446	222
Hispanic	6,950	239	48	181	26	185	1,156	3,965	1,101	49
Asian/Pacific Islander	721	71	80	52	10	46	107	282	67	6
American Indian/Alaskan Native	284	24	12	15	1	21	67	98	40	6
All employers	85,986	9,631	5,099	2,963	1,455	4,990	17,954	36,130	6,961	803
White	70,487	8,920	4,694	2,604	1,402	4,416	15,449	27,767	4,596	639
Minority	15,499	711	405	359	53	574	2,505	8,363	2,365	164
Black	9,046	361	132	185	21	298	1,475	5,247	1,208	119
Hispanic	4,685	196	86	105	22	212	837	2,326	867	34
Asian/Pacific Islander	1,444	124	175	48	6	52	129	636	268	6
American Indian/Alaskan Native	324	30	12	21	4	12	64	154	22	5

Source: U.S. Equal Employment Opportunity Commission. *Job Patterns for Minorities and Women in Private Industry, 1993.* Washington, DC: U.S. Government Printing Office, 1994, pp. 16-17.

★ 745 ★

Industry Employment

Private Industry Employment: Printing & Publishing

Number of persons employed in each occupation is shown, by race/ethnicity, in 1993. Data are shown for selected industry sectors and do not include Hawaii.

Group	Total employ-ment	Officials and managers	Profes-sionals	Techni-cians	Sales workers	Office & clerical workers	Craft workers	Opera-tives	Laborers	Service workers
Newspapers										
All employers	292,850	36,117	47,417	8,795	36,332	48,174	38,156	41,591	29,090	7,178
White	236,687	32,603	42,200	7,463	30,421	37,665	33,084	30,251	18,608	4,392
Minority	56,163	3,514	5,217	1,332	5,911	10,509	5,072	11,340	10,482	2,786
Black	33,423	1,833	2,669	649	3,600	6,560	2,585	6,783	6,800	1,944
Hispanic	15,838	1,175	1,470	389	1,673	2,797	1,856	3,251	2,620	607

[Continued]

★ 745 ★

Private Industry Employment: Printing & Publishing

[Continued]

Group	Total employ- ment	Officials and managers	Profes- sionals	Techni- cians	Sales workers	Office & clerical workers	Craft workers	Opera- tives	Laborers	Service workers
Asian/Pacific Islander	5,767	373	954	251	512	991	466	1,108	906	206
American Indian/Alaskan Native	1,135	133	124	43	126	161	165	198	156	29
Commercial printing										
All employers	176,521	15,292	8,297	5,808	7,982	20,264	46,162	38,315	32,574	1,827
White	149,943	14,492	7,729	5,294	7,554	17,901	40,492	30,289	24,918	1,274
Minority	26,578	800	568	514	428	2,363	5,670	8,026	7,656	553
Black	12,966	344	247	216	266	1,149	2,574	4,001	3,847	322
Hispanic	10,129	291	145	156	101	811	2,336	3,156	2,946	187
Asian/Pacific Islander	2,988	137	158	124	48	338	640	741	763	39
American Indian/Alaskan Native	495	28	18	18	13	65	120	128	100	5

Source: U.S. Equal Employment Opportunity Commission. *Job Patterns for Minorities and Women in Private Industry, 1993.* Washington, DC: U.S. Government Printing Office, 1994, p. 12.

★ 746 ★

Industry Employment

Private Industry Employment: Retail Trade

Number of persons employed in each occupation is shown, by race/ethnicity, in 1993. Data do not include Hawaii.

Group	Total employ- ment	Officials and managers	Profes- sionals	Techni- cians	Sales workers	Office & clerical workers	Craft workers	Opera- tives	Laborers	Service workers
All employers	5,677,285	509,620	85,264	52,753	2,586,528	475,842	171,095	269,811	430,656	1,095,716
White	4,298,787	445,756	73,900	42,615	2,002,117	375,935	136,498	197,093	293,069	731,804
Minority	1,378,498	63,864	11,364	10,138	584,411	99,907	34,597	72,718	137,587	363,912
Black	717,411	32,387	4,206	4,515	311,461	55,011	14,122	35,208	71,630	188,871
Hispanic	496,266	22,072	2,996	3,624	202,212	32,301	15,934	29,609	53,891	133,627
Asian/Pacific Islander	129,065	7,826	3,836	1,765	55,692	10,555	3,752	5,872	8,873	30,894
American Indian/Alaskan Native	35,756	1,579	326	234	15,046	2,040	789	2,029	3,193	10,520

Source: U.S. Equal Employment Opportunity Commission. *Job Patterns for Minorities and Women in Private Industry, 1993.* Washington, DC: U.S. Government Printing Office, 1994, p. 4.

★ 747 ★

Industry Employment

Private Industry Employment: Rubber & Plastics Products

Number of persons employed in each occupation is shown, by race/ethnicity, in 1993. Data are shown for selected industry sectors and do not include Hawaii.

Group	Total employ-ment	Officials and managers	Profes-sionals	Techni-cians	Sales workers	Office & clerical workers	Craft workers	Opera-tives	Laborers	Service workers
Tires and inner tubes										
All employers	73,238	7,872	5,964	2,969	920	2,915	8,600	40,493	2,561	944
White	61,253	7,252	5,441	2,607	865	2,590	7,813	32,052	1,896	737
Minority	11,985	620	523	362	55	325	787	8,441	665	207
Black	9,968	432	264	302	31	274	602	7,431	447	185
Hispanic	989	76	52	35	19	39	78	480	199	11
Asian/Pacific Islander	505	72	194	10	4	6	39	164	13	3
American Indian/Alaskan Native	523	40	13	15	1	6	68	366	6	8
Miscellaneous plastics products										
All employers	315,102	29,005	14,230	11,295	6,172	19,851	47,991	126,866	57,259	2,433
White	241,716	26,619	13,063	9,969	5,918	17,573	40,035	90,353	36,469	1,717
Minority	73,386	2,386	1,167	1,326	254	2,278	7,956	36,513	20,790	716
Black	33,648	946	368	568	98	1,059	3,377	18,120	8,765	347
Hispanic	30,490	901	300	486	116	936	3,536	14,277	9,627	311
Asian/Pacific Islander	8,145	454	475	234	35	239	874	3,665	2,115	54
American Indian/Alaskan Native	1,103	85	24	38	5	44	169	451	283	4

Source: U.S. Equal Employment Opportunity Commission. *Job Patterns for Minorities and Women in Private Industry, 1993.* Washington, DC: U.S. Government Printing Office, 1994, pp. 14-15.

★ 748 ★

Industry Employment

Private Industry Employment: Services

Number of persons employed in each occupation is shown, by race/ethnicity, in 1993. Data do not include Hawaii.

Group	Total employ-ment	Officials and managers	Profes-sionals	Techni-cians	Sales workers	Office & clerical workers	Craft workers	Opera-tives	Laborers	Service workers
All employers	9,613,652	861,552	2,557,136	1,081,360	205,482	1,679,543	288,963	354,675	258,750	2,326,191
White	7,036,286	759,028	2,166,066	836,946	163,962	1,260,490	221,318	223,616	137,136	1,267,724
Minority	2,577,366	102,524	391,070	244,414	41,520	419,053	67,645	131,059	121,614	1,058,467
Black	1,433,980	50,386	155,901	141,203	22,120	252,409	31,059	68,848	61,170	650,884
Hispanic	695,237	26,723	65,062	51,026	13,159	110,150	26,865	44,144	50,601	307,507
Asian/Pacific Islander	410,304	23,063	161,527	47,859	5,583	50,199	8,255	16,273	8,450	89,095
American Indian/Alaskan Native	37,845	2,352	8,580	4,326	658	6,295	1,466	1,794	1,393	10,981

Source: U.S. Equal Employment Opportunity Commission. *Job Patterns for Minorities and Women in Private Industry, 1993.* Washington, DC: U.S. Government Printing Office, 1994, p. 5.

★ 749 ★

Industry Employment

Private Industry Employment: Stone, Clay, and Glass Industry

Number of persons employed in each occupation is shown, by race/ethnicity, in 1993. Data are shown for selected industry sectors and do not include Hawaii.

Group	Total employ-ment	Officials and managers	Profes-sionals	Techni-cians	Sales workers	Office & clerical workers	Craft workers	Opera-tives	Laborers	Service workers
Glass and glassware, pressed or blown										
All employers	70,025	6,540	3,565	1,942	459	3,602	15,454	23,307	14,539	617
White	57,536	6,058	3,225	1,765	424	3,300	13,660	17,894	10,715	495
Minority	12,489	482	340	177	35	302	1,794	5,413	3,824	122
Black	7,627	276	193	87	13	174	1,039	3,568	2,205	72
Hispanic	3,572	88	40	63	11	92	565	1,439	1,235	39
Asian/Pacific Islander	982	91	98	21	5	27	102	284	345	9
American Indian/Alaskan Native	308	27	9	6	6	9	88	122	39	2
Misc. nonmetallic mineral products										
All employers	70,430	7,316	5,150	2,730	3,754	5,053	10,421	26,171	9,331	504
White	57,179	6,829	4,731	2,431	3,317	4,216	8,726	19,947	6,590	392
Minority	13,251	487	419	299	437	837	1,695	6,224	2,741	112
Black	7,682	224	148	156	207	431	919	3,981	1,545	71
Hispanic	4,160	151	75	89	128	330	590	1,750	1,015	32
Asian/Pacific Islander	1,220	100	189	49	94	69	144	408	160	7
American Indian/Alaskan Native	189	12	7	5	8	7	42	85	21	2

Source: U.S. Equal Employment Opportunity Commission. *Job Patterns for Minorities and Women in Private Industry, 1993.* Washington, DC: U.S. Government Printing Office, 1994, pp. 15-16.

★ 750 ★

Industry Employment

Private Industry Employment: Telephone Communications

Number of persons employed in each occupation is shown, by race/ethnicity, in 1993. Data do not include Hawaii.

Group	Total employ-ment	Officials and managers	Profes-sionals	Techni-cians	Sales workers	Office & clerical workers	Craft workers	Opera-tives	Laborers	Service workers
All employers	771,874	153,416	63,937	40,966	57,425	277,663	157,867	15,620	1,695	3,285
White	586,713	127,107	51,657	33,935	40,560	188,577	131,358	10,176	1,332	2,011
Minority	185,161	26,309	12,280	7,031	16,865	89,086	26,509	5,444	363	1,274
Black	119,424	15,595	5,106	4,180	10,160	64,196	15,625	3,334	232	996
Hispanic	44,786	6,416	2,045	1,623	5,153	18,899	8,656	1,653	106	235
Asian/Pacific Islander	17,577	3,710	4,918	1,086	1,252	4,630	1,543	395	11	32
American Indian/Alaskan Native	3,374	588	211	142	300	1,361	685	62	14	11

Source: U.S. Equal Employment Opportunity Commission. *Job Patterns for Minorities and Women in Private Industry, 1993.* Washington, DC: U.S. Government Printing Office, 1994, p. 27.

★ 751 ★

Industry Employment

Private Industry Employment: Textile Mill Products

Number of persons employed in each occupation is shown, by race/ethnicity, in 1993. Data are shown for selected industry sectors and do not include Hawaii.

Group	Total employ-ment	Officials and managers	Profes-sionals	Techni-cians	Sales workers	Office & clerical workers	Craft workers	Opera-tives	Laborers	Service workers
Weaving mills, cotton										
All employers	98,048	6,758	1,738	2,083	528	5,236	14,706	54,308	10,770	1,921
White	66,151	6,171	1,630	1,755	489	4,433	11,590	32,624	6,291	1,168
Minority	31,897	587	108	328	39	803	3,116	21,684	4,479	753
Black	29,854	541	85	307	25	748	2,925	20,259	4,236	728
Hispanic	1,172	24	8	12	11	38	113	767	186	13
Asian/Pacific Islander	793	19	13	5	3	10	66	616	49	12
American Indian/Alaskan Native	78	3	2	4	0	7	12	42	8	0
Knitting mills										
All employers	87,346	5,538	1,254	1,965	1,086	4,858	10,313	52,597	8,730	1,005
White	59,905	4,944	1,096	1,686	1,008	4,214	7,847	33,314	5,102	694
Minority	27,441	594	158	279	78	644	2,466	19,283	3,628	311
Black	20,158	414	59	201	37	473	1,542	14,824	2,332	276
Hispanic	4,722	97	63	38	21	104	673	2,626	1,078	22
Asian/Pacific Islander	1,453	60	31	32	19	41	155	1,003	105	7
American Indian/Alaskan Native	1,108	23	5	8	1	26	96	830	113	6
Yarn and thread mills										
All employers	93,437	7,007	1,776	2,361	617	5,010	15,493	51,988	7,349	1,836
White	66,074	6,434	1,665	1,884	602	4,306	12,375	33,418	4,075	1,315
Minority	27,363	573	111	477	15	704	3,118	18,570	3,274	521
Black	24,012	465	58	377	6	631	2,785	16,413	2,803	474
Hispanic	1,544	38	7	61	5	35	132	997	254	15
Asian/Pacific Islander	1,292	42	42	33	4	19	123	828	180	21
American Indian/Alaskan Native	515	28	4	6	0	19	78	332	37	11

Source: U.S. Equal Employment Opportunity Commission. *Job Patterns for Minorities and Women in Private Industry, 1993.* Washington, DC: U.S. Government Printing Office, 1994, p. 8.

★ 752 ★

Industry Employment

Private Industry Employment: Toys & Sporting Goods Industry

Number of persons employed in each occupation is shown, by race/ethnicity, in 1993. Data do not include Hawaii.

	Total employ-ment	Officials and managers	Profes-sionals	Techni-cians	Sales workers	Office & clerical workers	Craft workers	Opera-tives	Laborers	Service workers
All employers	58,259	5,890	3,587	2,078	2,175	5,603	5,862	23,943	8,431	690
White	44,404	5,376	3,223	1,789	1,998	4,824	4,767	16,399	5,598	430
Minority	13,855	514	364	289	177	779	1,095	7,544	2,833	260
Black	4,632	122	83	106	73	276	349	2,465	1,096	62
Hispanic	6,152	250	97	117	81	331	566	3,351	1,179	180

[Continued]

★ 752 ★

Private Industry Employment: Toys & Sporting Goods Industry
[Continued]

	Total employment	Officials and managers	Profes-sionals	Techni-cians	Sales workers	Office & clerical workers	Craft workers	Opera-tives	Laborers	Service workers
Asian/Pacific Islander	2,749	128	172	61	18	160	156	1,528	516	10
American Indian/Alaskan Native	322	14	12	5	5	12	24	200	42	8

Source: U.S. Equal Employment Opportunity Commission. *Job Patterns for Minorities and Women in Private Industry, 1993.* Washington, DC: U.S. Government Printing Office, 1994, p. 25.

★ 753 ★

Industry Employment

Private Industry Employment: Transportation Equipment Industry

Number of persons employed in each occupation is shown, by race/ethnicity, in 1993. Data are shown for selected industry sectors and do not include Hawaii.

	Total employment	Officials and managers	Profes-sionals	Techni-cians	Sales workers	Office & clerical workers	Craft workers	Opera-tives	Laborers	Service workers
Motor vehicles and equipment										
All employers	864,525	70,927	81,811	27,273	8,842	34,123	143,999	420,636	61,476	15,438
White	693,921	63,231	71,995	24,257	7,865	28,996	127,642	312,847	45,908	11,180
Minority	170,604	7,696	9,816	3,016	977	5,127	16,357	107,789	15,568	4,258
Black	128,665	5,103	4,937	1,721	433	3,449	11,582	87,541	10,269	3,630
Hispanic	27,464	1,107	1,229	674	414	1,201	3,487	15,265	3,562	525
Asian/Pacific Islander	11,713	1,233	3,437	493	101	357	751	3,783	1,501	57
American Indian/Alaskan Native	2,762	253	213	128	29	120	537	1,200	236	46
Aircraft and parts										
All employers	439,549	54,742	126,328	36,093	1,169	40,080	105,957	62,887	7,061	5,232
White	365,726	50,589	110,966	30,960	1,055	32,949	86,215	44,532	4,844	3,616
Minority	73,823	4,153	15,362	5,133	114	7,131	19,742	18,355	2,217	1,616
Black	30,890	1,562	4,384	1,909	30	3,629	8,999	8,441	987	949
Hispanic	23,694	1,293	3,592	1,473	58	2,223	7,462	6,321	757	515
Asian/Pacific Islander	16,945	1,002	6,961	1,516	18	1,019	2,711	3,154	430	134
American Indian/Alaskan Native	2,294	296	425	235	8	260	570	439	43	18
Ship and boat building and repairing										
All employers	79,556	8,323	6,900	3,350	282	3,357	37,909	13,165	5,426	844
White	62,138	7,662	6,345	3,123	273	2,895	28,228	9,585	3,391	636
Minority	17,418	661	555	227	9	462	9,681	3,580	2,035	208
Black	11,412	425	371	109	3	324	6,543	2,005	1,471	161
Hispanic	4,198	164	75	61	5	85	2,100	1,201	473	34
Asian/Pacific Islander	1,528	48	96	50	1	45	884	326	70	8
American Indian/Alaskan Native	280	24	13	7	0	8	154	48	21	5

Source: U.S. Equal Employment Opportunity Commission. *Job Patterns for Minorities and Women in Private Industry, 1993.* Washington, DC: U.S. Government Printing Office, 1994, p. 24.

★ 754 ★

Industry Employment

Private Industry Employment: Transportation & Public Utilities

Number of persons employed in each occupation is shown, by race/ethnicity, in 1993. Data do not include Hawaii.

Group	Total employ-ment	Officials and managers	Profes-sionals	Techni-cians	Sales workers	Office & clerical workers	Craft workers	Opera-tives	Laborers	Service workers
All employers	3,501,987	461,370	356,493	178,271	176,257	704,444	609,308	590,848	258,933	166,063
White	2,731,421	399,508	309,931	143,884	131,969	507,749	511,162	438,601	163,191	120,426
Minority	770,566	61,862	46,562	29,387	44,288	196,695	98,146	152,247	95,742	45,637
Black	461,643	34,680	20,011	15,603	25,584	129,366	54,678	97,923	57,090	26,708
Hispanic	217,880	16,820	11,077	8,478	13,243	48,837	32,800	43,435	30,417	12,773
Asian/Pacific Islander	72,381	8,542	14,199	4,266	4,601	14,969	7,145	7,064	6,144	5,451
American Indian/Alaskan Native	18,662	1,820	1,275	1,040	860	3,523	3,523	3,825	2,091	705

Source: U.S. Equal Employment Opportunity Commission. *Job Patterns for Minorities and Women in Private Industry, 1993.* Washington, DC: U.S. Government Printing Office, 1994, p. 3.

★ 755 ★

Industry Employment

Private Industry Employment: Utilities

Number of persons employed in each occupation is shown, by race/ethnicity, in 1993. Data are shown for selected industry sectors and do not include Hawaii.

	Total employ-ment	Officials and managers	Profes-sionals	Techni-cians	Sales workers	Office & clerical workers	Craft workers	Opera-tives	Laborers	Service workers
Electric services										
All employers	344,011	52,206	67,180	30,270	1,915	58,873	91,697	29,658	7,915	4,297
White	295,120	48,467	59,843	26,505	1,586	45,653	80,522	23,524	6,057	2,963
Minority	48,891	3,739	7,337	3,765	329	13,220	11,175	6,134	1,858	1,334
Black	30,934	2,142	3,318	2,160	276	9,036	7,527	4,344	1,166	965
Hispanic	12,320	1,040	1,830	1,092	31	3,290	2,795	1,434	527	281
Asian/Pacific Islander	3,835	372	2,017	346	7	529	279	169	80	36
American Indian/Alaskan Native	1,802	185	172	167	15	365	574	187	85	52
Gas production and distribution										
All employers	110,263	17,259	16,372	7,995	2,443	25,598	25,416	11,241	2,437	1,502
White	86,289	15,465	13,827	6,532	2,211	17,499	19,852	8,077	1,722	1,104
Minority	23,974	1,794	2,545	1,463	232	8,099	5,564	3,164	715	398
Black	13,447	1,010	1,116	512	101	4,832	3,146	1,993	479	258
Hispanic	8,201	537	767	651	102	2,677	2,088	1,064	198	117
Asian/Pacific Islander	1,619	173	595	203	14	425	147	43	13	6
American Indian/Alaskan Native	707	74	67	97	15	165	183	64	25	17
Combination utility services										
All employers	183,491	26,394	32,867	16,955	591	35,465	51,421	13,818	4,307	1,673
White	150,355	23,931	28,330	14,341	524	25,779	43,305	9,884	3,070	1,191
Minority	33,136	2,463	4,537	2,614	67	9,686	8,116	3,934	1,237	482
Black	18,055	1,153	1,716	1,291	37	6,095	4,448	2,274	696	345
Hispanic	9,152	711	979	799	26	2,313	2,755	1,147	329	93

[Continued]

★ 755 ★

Private Industry Employment: Utilities
[Continued]

	Total employ- ment	Officials and managers	Profes- sionals	Techni- cians	Sales workers	Office & clerical workers	Craft workers	Opera- tives	Laborers	Service workers
Asian/Pacific Islander	4,242	480	1,700	419	2	1,001	399	139	86	16
American Indian/Alaskan Native	1,687	119	142	105	2	277	514	374	126	28

Source: U.S. Equal Employment Opportunity Commission. *Job Patterns for Minorities and Women in Private Industry, 1993.* Washington, DC: U.S. Government Printing Office, 1994, pp. 27-28.

★ 756 ★

Industry Employment

Private Industry Employment: Wholesale - Durable Goods

Number of persons employed in each occupation is shown, by race/ethnicity, in 1993. Data are shown for selected industry sectors and do not include Hawaii.

Group	Total employ- ment	Officials and managers	Profes- sionals	Techni- cians	Sales workers	Office & clerical workers	Craft workers	Opera- tives	Laborers	Service workers
Motor vehicles & automotive equipment										
All employers	115,578	15,209	11,658	3,031	7,748	17,017	9,293	33,586	15,235	2,801
White	93,663	13,884	9,919	2,714	7,187	13,985	8,040	25,507	10,672	1,755
Minority	21,915	1,325	1,739	317	561	3,032	1,253	8,079	4,563	1,046
Black	12,423	500	615	137	245	1,652	623	5,626	2,319	706
Hispanic	6,208	301	300	79	237	828	500	1,966	1,731	266
Asian/Pacific Islander	2,913	482	790	98	57	494	119	347	466	60
American Indian/Alaskan Native	371	42	34	3	22	58	11	140	47	14
Electrical goods										
All employers	105,431	18,667	18,158	8,046	9,208	18,827	5,987	19,693	5,775	1,070
White	80,441	16,162	15,159	6,187	8,331	14,302	4,828	11,527	3,267	678
Minority	24,990	2,505	2,999	1,859	877	4,525	1,159	8,166	2,508	392
Black	9,822	595	735	478	331	1,945	639	3,816	1,062	221
Hispanic	7,864	593	665	538	276	1,565	324	2,545	1,241	117
Asian/Pacific Islander	6,913	1,258	1,555	809	250	935	180	1,696	180	50
American Indian/Alaskan Native	391	59	44	34	20	80	16	109	25	4
Machinery, equipment, and vehicles										
All employers	218,563	30,913	34,004	27,310	24,194	36,687	25,125	26,501	11,500	2,329
White	180,175	27,992	29,285	22,116	21,707	29,683	21,306	18,881	7,699	1,506
Minority	38,388	2,921	4,719	5,194	2,487	7,004	3,819	7,620	3,801	823
Black	18,367	1,311	1,744	2,294	1,223	4,001	1,501	3,700	2,010	583
Hispanic	12,443	721	1,009	1,568	841	2,081	1,692	2,765	1,593	173
Asian/Pacific Islander	6,575	744	1,864	1,174	352	782	473	975	151	60
American Indian/Alaskan Native	1,003	145	102	158	71	140	153	180	47	7
Miscellaneous durable goods										
All employers	39,638	5,481	3,071	1,243	4,235	7,336	3,495	6,696	6,726	1,355
White	29,981	4,810	2,594	981	3,547	5,744	2,933	4,716	3,735	921
Minority	9,657	671	477	262	688	1,592	562	1,980	2,991	434
Black	4,625	203	140	113	383	733	241	1,206	1,478	128
Hispanic	3,038	148	100	82	185	528	225	528	1,049	193
Asian/Pacific Islander	1,843	300	233	63	106	308	81	216	437	99
American Indian/Alaskan Native	151	20	4	4	14	23	15	30	27	14

Source: U.S. Equal Employment Opportunity Commission. *Job Patterns for Minorities and Women in Private Industry, 1993.* Washington, DC: U.S. Government Printing Office, 1994, pp. 28-29.

★ 757 ★

Industry Employment

Private Industry Employment: Wholesale - Nondurable Goods

Number of persons employed in each occupation is shown, by race/ethnicity, in 1993. Data are shown for selected industry sectors and do not include Hawaii.

	Total employ-ment	Officials and managers	Profes-sionals	Techni-cians	Sales workers	Office & clerical workers	Craft workers	Opera-tives	Laborers	Service workers
Drugs, proprietaries, and sundries										
All employers	88,328	13,167	11,003	4,448	24,277	12,765	2,806	12,012	6,406	1,444
White	72,373	11,880	9,390	3,493	20,945	10,549	2,133	8,155	4,846	982
Minority	15,955	1,287	1,613	955	3,332	2,216	673	3,857	1,560	462
Black	8,111	564	479	390	1,996	1,298	240	2,036	885	223
Hispanic	4,816	403	235	219	858	614	352	1,458	488	189
Asian/Pacific Islander	2,744	287	883	336	359	268	76	322	164	49
American Indian/Alaskan Native	284	33	16	10	119	36	5	41	23	1
Groceries and related products										
All employers	293,475	35,124	8,890	4,750	49,772	33,473	13,850	79,497	61,473	6,646
White	233,684	32,192	8,013	4,072	44,539	28,507	10,957	59,052	41,490	4,862
Minority	59,791	2,932	877	678	5,233	4,966	2,893	20,445	19,983	1,784
Black	30,524	1,332	321	268	2,180	2,255	1,298	11,011	10,865	994
Hispanic	23,558	1,125	259	273	2,334	1,986	1,399	8,174	7,351	657
Asian/Pacific Islander	4,641	378	263	117	601	625	135	924	1,486	112
American Indian/Alaskan Native	1,068	97	34	20	118	100	61	336	281	21
Chemicals and allied products										
All employers	23,632	4,015	2,758	1,221	2,768	3,553	2,038	4,795	2,320	164
White	19,280	3,714	2,424	1,026	2,607	3,030	1,633	3,650	1,095	101
Minority	4,352	301	334	195	161	523	405	1,145	1,225	63
Black	2,471	144	111	77	76	305	252	786	683	37
Hispanic	1,331	77	67	83	48	153	131	281	470	21
Asian/Pacific Islander	468	68	147	32	27	51	17	54	67	5
American Indian/Alaskan Native	82	12	9	3	10	14	5	24	5	0

Source: U.S. Equal Employment Opportunity Commission. *Job Patterns for Minorities and Women in Private Industry, 1993.* Washington, DC: U.S. Government Printing Office, 1994, p. 30.

★ 758 ★

Industry Employment

Private Industry Employment: Women's Apparel Stores

Number of persons employed in each occupation is shown, by race/ethnicity, in 1993. Data do not include Hawaii.

	Total employ-ment	Officials and managers	Profes-sionals	Techni-cians	Sales workers	Office & clerical workers	Craft workers	Opera-tives	Laborers	Service workers
All employers	21,144	3,560	895	387	5,463	3,746	918	2,365	2,572	1,238
White	15,497	3,212	807	315	4,388	2,592	649	1,566	1,123	845
Minority	5,647	348	88	75	1,075	1,154	269	799	1,449	393
Black	3,034	156	44	38	704	591	75	654	596	176
Hispanic	1,858	120	18	17	238	427	132	105	637	164

[Continued]

★ 758 ★

Private Industry Employment: Women's Apparel Stores
[Continued]

	Total employ-ment	Officials and managers	Profes-sionals	Techni-cians	Sales workers	Office & clerical workers	Craft workers	Opera-tives	Laborers	Service workers
Asian/Pacific Islander	702	67	25	17	123	127	62	38	198	45
American Indian/Alaskan Native	53	5	1	0	10	9	0	2	18	8

Source: U.S. Equal Employment Opportunity Commission. *Job Patterns for Minorities and Women in Private Industry, 1993.* Washington, DC: U.S. Government Printing Office, 1994, p. 32.

Casinos and Gaming

★ 759 ★

Gaming Revenues in the U.S., by Sector, 1993

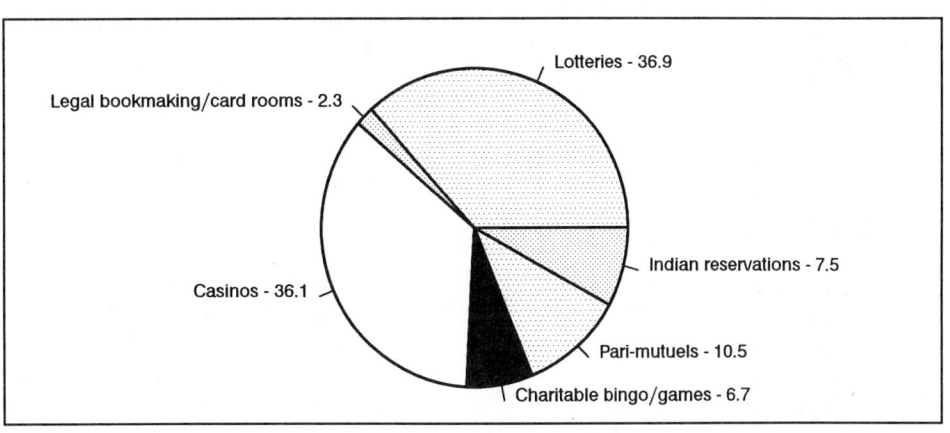

Figures show percent distribution of gross revenues of gambling enterprises. Total revenues were more than $30 billion in 1993.

	Percent of revenues
Lotteries	36.9
Casinos	36.1
Pari-mutuels	10.5
Indian reservations	7.5
Charitable bingo/games	6.7
Legal bookmaking/card rooms	2.3

Source: "The next throw." *The Economist* (18 March 1995), p. 28. Christiansen; National Conference of State Legislatures.

★ 760 ★
Casinos and Gaming

Gaming Revenues by State, 1992

```
All others - 24
California - 14
Minnesota - 11
Wisconsin - 9
Washington - 6
Arizona - 6
        Michigan - 3
        South Dakota - 3
      Nebraska - 2
      Colorado - 2
   Connecticut - 1
          Chart shows data from column 1.
```

Data show estimated gaming revenue and net income in millions of dollars for states with tribal gaming operations.

State	No. of tribes with gaming operations	Gross revenues ($ mil.)	Net profit to tribes ($ mil.)
Michigan	3	48.7	12.2
Wisconsin	9	77.0	19.3
Minnesota	11	63.0	15.8
California	14	95.6	23.9
Colorado[1]	2	11.0	2.7
South Dakota	3	23.1	5.8
Connecticut	1	180.0	45.0
Nebraska	2	6.3	1.6
Washington	6	14.0	3.5
Arizona	6	7.0	1.8
All others	24	42.0	10.5

Source: Johnson, Dirk. "Economies come to life on Indian reservations." *The New York Times (National)* (3 July, 1994), p. 11. Primary source: Census Bureau; National Indian Policy Center. *Note:* 1. Estimate based on partial year operations.

★ 761 ★

Casinos and Gaming

Annual Revenues from Bingo, by Area, 1987

Area	Annual gross revenue
Aberdeen	5,076,083
Albuquerque	1,200,000
Anadarko	2,887,428
Billings	339,381
Eastern	65,000,000
Juneau	0
Minneapolis	40,450,000
Muskogee	18,776,029
Navajo	0
Phoenix	unknown
Portland	15,000,000
Sacramento	106,900,000

Source: U.S. Senate Select Committee on Indian Affairs. *Gaming Activities on Indian Reservations and Lands*, S. Hrg. 100-341. Washington, DC: U.S. Government Printing Office, 1988, p. 238.

★ 762 ★

Casinos and Gaming

Tribal Casinos, by Year Started

1992 - 28
1990 - 14
1991 - 9
Pending - 3

Three casinos are currently pending.

Year	Number started
1990	14
1991	9
1992	28
Pending	3

Source: Vancura, Cliff. "USA Snapshots: reservations up the ante." *USA TODAY* (4 December 1992), p. 1A. Primary source: National Indian Gaming Association.

★ 763 ★

Casinos and Gaming

Michigan: Indian Casino Payout to Government

In the first year of a 20-year profit-sharing compact with the state of Michigan, tribes made payments of $17.6 million to the state and to local communities. Shown are the amounts paid by each tribe.

Casinos	Tribe	Members	Paid to state (dollars)	Paid to localities (dollars)
Ojibwa Casino Ojibwa II	Keweenaw Bay Community	3,500	719,416	179,854
Lac Vieux Casino	Lac Vieux Desert Band of Lake Superior Chippewa	250	279,936	94,984
Chip-In Casino/Motel	Hannahville Potawatomi Indian Community	400	880,138	220,034
Vegas Kewadin Casino Kewadin Shores Casino Slot parlors: Hessel, Manistique, and Christmas	Sault St. Marie Tribe of Chippewas	22,000	3,811,158	952,789
King's Club Tribal Casino	Bay Mills Band of Chippewa	1,082	120,942	30,235
Leelanau Sands Casino	Grand Traverse Band of Chippewa and Ottawa	2,500	1,357,480	370,729
Soaring Eagle	Saginaw Chippewa Indian Tribe	1,700	6,784,480	1,696,000

Source: Weeks, George and Don Weeks. "Indian-run casinos produce jackpot for state, municipalities: they shared $17.6 million in first-year payouts under Indian Gaming Compact." *The Detroit News* (25 December 1994), p. 4C. Primary source: Detroit News research.

★ 764 ★

Casinos and Gaming

Minnesota: Expenditures of Gaming Facilities, 1991

Figures are shown in millions of dollars.

Expenditure type	Amount
Salaries and wages	27.6
Payroll taxes and benefits	4.2
Payroll-related total	31.8
Advertising and promotion	7.1
Utilities	.9
Other operating	49.2

[Continued]

★ 764 ★

Minnesota: Expenditures of Gaming Facilities, 1991
[Continued]

Expenditure type	Amount
Operations-related total	57.2
Total	89.0

Source: U.S. Senate Select Committee on Indian Affairs. *Implementation of the Indian Gaming Regulatory Act*, S. HRG. 102-660, Pt. 2. Washington, DC: U.S. Government Printing Office, 1992, p. 283. *Notes:* Participating members include the following tribes: Bois Forte, Leech Lake, Lower Sioux, Mille Lacs Chippewa, Prairie Island Sioux, and Shakopee Sioux.

★ 765 ★

Casinos and Gaming

Minnesota: How Gambling Facilities Compare With Minnesota's Largest Corporate Employers

Tribal gaming includes all gaming groups together[1].

Company name	Rank	Minnesota employment
3M	1	23,000
Dayton Hudson Corporation	2	21,650
Northwest Airlines Inc.	3	17,600
Mayo Foundation	4	16,500
Health One Corp.	5	11,000
Honeywell Inc.	6	11,000
IBM Corporation	7	9,300
Lifespan Inc.	8	8,800
Norwest Corporation	9	8,151
Unisys Corporation	10	8,000
U.S. West	11	7,316
Fairview Hospital & Health Services	12	7,000
Northern States Power Company	13	7,000
First Bank System Inc.	14	6,426
Fingerhut Corporation	15	5,800
Kmart Corporation	16	5,700
Health East Corp.	17	5,050
Control Data Corporation	18	4,864
J.C. Penney Company Inc.	19	4,800
Tribal gaming	*	4,730
Burlington Northern Railroad Inc.	20	4,500
United Parcel Service	21	4,200
The Prudential	22	4,100
Sears, Roebuck and Company	23	4,033

[Continued]

★ 765 ★

Minnesota: How Gambling Facilities Compare With Minnesota's Largest Corporate Employers

[Continued]

Company name	Rank	Minnesota employment
Gateway/Rainbow Foods Inc.	24	4,000
Anderson Corporation	25	3,960

Source: U.S. Senate Select Committee on Indian Affairs. *Implementation of the Indian Gaming Regulatory Act*, S. HRG. 102-660, Pt. 2. Washington, DC: U.S. Government Printing Office, 1992, p. 16. Primary source: Minnesota Department of Trade and Economic Development, *Report of Minnesota's Largest Corporate Employers*, September 10, 1991. *Notes:* 1. Participating members include the following tribes: Bois Forte, Leech Lake, Lower Sioux, Mille Lacs Chippewa, Prairie Island Sioux, and Shakopee Sioux.

★ 766 ★

Casinos and Gaming

Minnesota: Out-of-State Visitor Expenditures at Gaming Facilities, 1991

Data include bus visitors only.

Expenditure type	In-state expenditure
Lodging	9,350,000
Meals	1,813,000
Miscellaneous	1,364,000
Total expenditures	12,527,000

Source: U.S. Senate Select Committee on Indian Affairs. *Implementation of the Indian Gaming Regulatory Act*. S. HRG. 102-660, Pt. 2. Washington, DC: U.S. Government Printing Office, 1992, p. 23. *Notes:* Participating members include the following tribes: Bois Forte, Leech Lake, Lower Sioux, Mille Lacs Chippewa, Prairie Island Sioux, and Shakopee Sioux.

★ 767 ★

Casinos and Gaming

Minnesota: Reported Revenues from Gaming, 1991

Figures are shown in millions of dollars.

Revenue sources	Amount
Video	99.3
Blackjack	28.5
Bingo and pull-tabs	11.0
Concessions & other	4.2
Total	143.0

Source: U.S. Senate Select Committee on Indian Affairs. *Implementation of the Indian Gaming Regulatory Act*, S. HRG. 102-660, Pt. 2. Washington, DC: U.S. Government Printing Office, 1992, p. 282. *Notes:* Participating members include the following tribes: Bois Forte, Leech Lake, Lower Sioux, Mille Lacs Chippewa, Prairie Island Sioux, and Shakopee Sioux.

★ 768 ★

Casinos and Gaming

New Mexico: Indian Gaming Fiscal Impact

Figures show fiscal impacts attributed to Indian gaming.

Fiscal impacts attributed to -	Amount (dollars)
Tax revenue from gaming employee expenditures	211,872
Tax revenue from gaming tourist expenditures	1,208,183
Total tax revenue from Indian gaming	1,204,183

Source: Stanton, Mark J. "Economic benefits: study shows job and tourism growth." *New Mexico Business Journal* vol. 17, no. 12 (December 1994), p. S4. Primary source: New Mexico Indian Gaming Association; The Center for Applied Research, 1993.

★ 769 ★

Casinos and Gaming

Oneida Tribe of Wisconsin: Reported Growth from Gaming Enterprises, 1976 to 1992

	1976	1992
Employment	150	1000+
Tribal members (%)		80.0
Non-tribal members (%)		20.0
Rate of unemployment (%)	40.1	17.9
Land holding (acres)	2,500	6,000
Nongaming enterprises		Radisson Hotel
		4 convenience stores
		Environmental lab
		Farm

Source: U.S. Senate Select Committee on Indian Affairs. *Implementation of the Indian Gaming Regulatory Act*, S. HRG. 102-660, Pt. 2. Washington, DC: U.S. Government Printing Office, 1992, pp. 302-303.

Minerals

★ 770 ★

U.S. Coal Mining Acreage from Indian Leases

```
┌─────────────────────────────────────────────────┐
│  ┌──────────────────────────────────────────┐    │
│  │ U.S. Total - 115,630                     │    │
│  ├──────────────────────────────┐           │    │
│  │ Arizona - 64,858             │           │    │
│  ├──────────────────┐           New Mexico - 36,026 │
│  │                  │                            │
│  ├────────┐ Montana - 14,746                     │
│  │        │                                      │
│  └────────┘   Chart shows data from column 1.    │
└─────────────────────────────────────────────────┘
```

Figures are shown for 1990, by state. Chart shows royalties in thousands of dollars.

State	Acres leased	Production (thousand short tons)	Royalties[1] ($ thou.)
New Mexico	36,026	12,174	30,055
Arizona	64,858	12,621	29,237
Montana	14,746	2,731	1,500
U.S. Total	115,630	27,526	60,791

Source: U.S. Department of Energy. Energy Information Administration. Office of Coal, Nuclear, Electric, and Alternate Fuels. *Coal Data: A Reference.* Washington, DC: U.S. DOE, November 1991, p. 49. Primary source: U.S. Department of the Interior, Minerals Management Service, Royalty Management Program, *Mineral Revenues: The 1990 Report on Receipts from Federal and Indian Leases. Notes:* Totals may not equal sum of components because of independent rounding. 1. Current dollars.

★ 771 ★

Minerals

Coal Leases on Indian Lands, 1984-93

Data show number of leases and total acres leased for producing Indian onshore coal leases as of December 31 of each year.

Year	Number of leases	Acres
1984	6	155,918
1985	7	195,918
1986	6	155,630
1987	7	195,918
1988	7	155,918
1989	8	156,141
1990	6	115,630
1991	6	113,194

[Continued]

★ 771 ★

Coal Leases on Indian Lands, 1984-93

[Continued]

Year	Number of leases	Acres
1992	6	123,998
1993	6	123,998

Source: U.S. Department of the Interior. Minerals Management Service. Royalty Management Program. *Mineral Revenues 1993: Report on Receipts from Federal and Indian Leases.* Washington, DC: Minerals Management Service, p. 99.

★ 772 ★

Minerals

Coal Leases on Indian Lands, by State

Shown are total leases and total acres leased for producing Indian onshore coal leases as of December 31, 1993.

State	Number	Acres
Arizona	3	64,858
Montana	1	14,746
New Mexico	2	44,394
Total	6	123,998

Source: U.S. Department of the Interior. Minerals Management Service. Royalty Management Program. *Mineral Revenues 1993: Report on Receipts from Federal and Indian Leases.* Washington, DC: Minerals Management Service, p. 98.

★ 773 ★

Minerals

Mineral Leases on Federal and Indian Lands

Summary data are shown for volume sales of selected minerals in calendar year 1993. OCS stands for Outer Continental Shelf.

Leases	U.S. total	OCS	Federal onshore	Indian	Federal and Indian total
Oil in barrels (mil. bls.)					
Sales volume	2,496	363	127	15	505
% U.S. total production		14.5	5.1	0.6	20.2
Gas in Mcf (mil.)					
Sales volume	19,353	4,533	1,709	189	6,431
% U.S. total production		23.4	8.8	1.0	33.2
Coal in tons (mil. s.t.)					
Sales volume	947	NA	258	28	286
% U.S. total production		NA	27.2	3.0	30.2

[Continued]

★ 773 ★

Mineral Leases on Federal and Indian Lands
[Continued]

Leases	U.S. total	OCS	Federal onshore	Indian	Federal and Indian total
Lead in tons (000 s.t.)					
Sales volume	390	NA	199	NA	199
% U.S. total production		NA	51.0	NA	51.0
Phosphate in tons (000 s.t.)					
Sales volume	38,733	NA	5,874	990	6,864
% U.S. total production		NA	15.2	2.6	17.7
Potash in tons (000 s.t.)					
Sales volume	3,381	NA	1,723	NA	1,723
% U.S. total production		NA	51.0	NA	51.0
Sodium in tons (000 s.t.)					
Sales volume	10,246	NA	4,627	NA	4,627
% U.S. total production		NA	45.2	NA	45.2

Source: U.S. Department of the Interior. Minerals Management Service. Royalty Management Program. *Mineral Revenues 1993: Report on Receipts from Federal and Indian Leases.* Washington, DC: Minerals Management Service, p. 24. Primary source: U.S. production totals are from "Mineral Commodity Summaries," Bureau of Mines, DOI, and "Monthly Energy Review," U.S. Department of Energy. Federal and Indian totals are from Minerals Management Service records. *Notes:* 1993 U.S. production data are estimated. Data by calendar year are rounded: oil, including crude oil and condensate, in millions of barrels; natural gas in millions of Mcf; coal, including anthracite, bituminous, and lignite, in millions of short tons; and lead, phosphate, potash, and sodium in thousands of short tons.

★ 774 ★

Minerals

Mineral Leases on Indian Lands

Revenues from mineral leases on Indian lands are shown for calendar years 1984-1993.

Year	Royalties ($)	Minimum Royalties ($)	Rents ($)	Bonuses ($)	Total ($)
1984	128,386,900	-	3,576,549	-	131,963,449
1985	139,424,708	-	3,372,750	-	142,797,458
1986	105,028,658	-	3,018,833	-	108,047,491
1987	104,787,583	-	1,206,406	-	105,993,989
1988	112,282,668	-	1,255,603	-	113,538,271
1989	122,429,802	-	1,454,523	-	123,884,325
1990	151,992,888	-	438,483	-	152,431,371
1991	145,185,355	-	1,819,916	-	147,005,271
1992	156,397,215	-	1,366,413	-	157,763,628
1993	166,371,356	-	1,860,669	-	168,232,025
1984-93	1,332,287,133	-	19,370,145	-	1,351,657,278

Source: U.S. Department of the Interior. Minerals Management Service. Royalty Management Program. *Mineral Revenues 1993: Report on Receipts from Federal and Indian Leases.* Washington, DC: Minerals Management Service, pp. 8-9. Primary source: Bureau of Indian Affairs. *Notes:* A dash indicates data not given in original source. Most Indian leases retain rental provisions after the lease is producing. Indian rent revenues represent fiscal year data from Bureau of Indian Affairs (BIA) records for the period 1984-87. Indian rent revenues represent calendar year data from Minerals Management Service (MMS) records for producing leases during the period 1988-93. Indian bonus revenues are collected by BIA.

★ 775 ★

Minerals

Mineral Leases on Indian Lands, Summary

Data show royalty revenues collected from federal and Indian mineral leases in the U.S. from 1920-93. Data do not include rents and bonuses.

	Oil production (mil. bbl.)	Gas production (mil. Mcf)	Coal production (Mil. short tons)	Other production
1920-93				
Volume	1,343	4,609	544	NA
Value ($ mil.)	9,455	4,480	6,918	2,402
Royalties ($ mil.)	1,362	597	519	259
1990				
Volume	15	127	28	NA
Value ($ mil.)	330	220	532	74
Royalties ($ mil.)	52	30	61	9
1991				
Volume	14	132	32	NA
Value ($ mil.)	283	210	544	71
Royalties ($ mil.)	44	29	63	9
1992				
Volume	15	150	28	NA
Value ($ mil.)	280	249	548	76
Royalties ($)	46	35	66	9
1993				
Volume	15	189	28	NA
Value ($)	244	342	542	171
Royalties ($)	40	48	65	13

Source: U.S. Department of the Interior. Minerals Management Service. Royalty Management Program. *Mineral Revenues 1993: Report on Receipts from Federal and Indian Leases.* Washington, DC: Minerals Management Service, pp. 14-15. Primary source: U.S. Geological Survey and the Minerals Management Service, Department of the Interior. *Note:* Data are rounded. NA stands for not available.

★ 776 ★
Minerals

Mineral Revenues on Indian Lands, by Commodity

Volume, sales value, and royalties, by commodity and state, from Indian mineral leases. Data are shown for calendar year 1993.

Leases	Sales volume	Sales value ($)	Royalties received ($)
Chat			
Oklahoma	197,034	197,034	59,110
Coal			
Arizona	12,257,727	264,025,579	32,999,499
Montana	3,517,511	28,040,475	1,785,621
New Mexico	12,316,224	249,852,677	29,964,701
Subtotal	28,091,462	541,918,731	64,749,821
Copper			
Arizona	190,565	122,712,533	6,580,246
Gas			
Arizona	49,150	38,927	4,866
Colorado	88,743,753	143,541,639	18,666,573
Michigan	23	66	8
Montana	1,701,053	3,189,847	481,561
New Mexico	51,673,798	99,842,377	12,922,892
North Dakota	107,177	116,433	17,391
Oklahoma	25,093,022	51,584,467	9,034,465
Texas	2,118,952	4,677,144	878,613
Utah	8,292,811	20,930,432	3,202,965
Wyoming	11,226,343	17,648,161	2,821,107
Subtotal	189,006,082	341,569,493	48,030,441
Gas lost			
New Mexico	-128,749	-188,751	-23,594
Utah	300	732	91
Subtotal	-128,449	-188,019	-23,503
Gas plant products			
Colorado	-1,287,232	-432,948	-27,302
Montana	335,548	93,868	8,962
New Mexico	18,413,998	4,314,967	307,095
North Dakota	361,669	106,119	9,876
Oklahoma	6,457,786	1,769,880	210,328
Utah	10,316,085	3,217,631	361,641
Wyoming	559,438	237,606	10,082
Subtotal	35,157,292	9,307,123	880,682
Gypsum			
New Mexico	404,445	1,617,780	336,248
Limestone			
Oklahoma	223,478	938,608	24,583

[Continued]

★ 776 ★

Mineral Revenues on Indian Lands, by Commodity
[Continued]

Leases	Sales volume	Sales value ($)	Royalties received ($)
Oil			
Arizona	85,711	1,407,826	231,635
Colorado	128,491	2,061,257	398,970
Michigan	630	11,028	1,540
Montana	1,016,902	15,771,788	2,424,425
New Mexico	1,167,505	19,629,051	2,859,905
North Dakota	148,941	2,465,491	371,120
Oklahoma	2,046,793	35,283,885	5,101,160
South Dakota	4,805	60,964	12,193
Texas	165,853	2,883,637	564,507
Utah	7,837,548	137,830,240	23,007,348
Wyoming	1,998,419	26,496,232	5,385,643
Subtotal	14,601,598	243,901,399	40,358,446
Oil lost			
Colorado	26	363	47
Utah	690	21,697	3,616
Wyoming	140	2,228	402
Subtotal	856	24,288	4,065
Phosphate			
Idaho	990,014	14,655,816	1,823,056
Sand and gravel			
Arizona	2,121,546	8,271,765	1,352,763
California	827,143	4,373,269	584,924
Nevada	422,312	1,554,294	145,813
New Mexico	1,670,244	4,737,845	1,142,297
Oklahoma	161,970	471,266	23,451
Washington	559,517	1,190,872	229,904
Subtotal	5,762,732	20,599,311	3,479,152
Silica sand			
Arizona	33,115	745,088	14,570
Sulfur			
North Dakota	35	572	71
Uranium			
Washington	16,058	355,044	54,368
Total		1,298,354,801	166,371,356

Source: U.S. Department of the Interior. Minerals Management Service. Royalty Management Program. *Mineral Revenues 1993: Report on Receipts from Federal and Indian Leases.* Washington, DC: Minerals Management Service, pp. 82-83.

★ 777 ★
Minerals

Mineral Revenues on Indian Lands, 1937-93

Data show summary of sales volume, sales value, and royalties by State and commodity from Indian mineral leases in calendar years 1937-93.

State/commodity	1937-88	1989	1990	1991	1992	1993	1937-93
Alaska							
Gas in Mcf							
Volume	277,556	0	0	0	0	0	277,556
Sales volume ($)	39,269	0	0	0	0	0	39,269
Royalties ($)	6,541	0	0	0	0	0	6,541
Arizona							
Oil in barrels							
Volume	19,048,598	164,464	135,709	108,734	126,408	117,987	19,701,900
Sales volume ($)	107,434,182	2,589,452	2,330,655	1,654,596	2,185,278	2,429,422	118,623,585
Royalties ($)	17,445,680	423,267	381,290	272,042	360,929	402,942	19,286,150
Gas in Mcf							
Volume	12,842,337	17,294	15,254	7,517	7,640	12,441	12,902,483
Sales value ($)	2,704,000	11,760	14,963	8,042	10,418	14,700	2,763,883
Royalties($)	339,720	1,446	1,870	1,005	1,302	1,844	347,187
Coal in tons							
Volume	129,124,096	11,550,000	11,602,674	12,318,335	11,118,215	12,621,393	188,334,713
Sales value ($)	1,400,031,309	184,684,500	124,925,051	238,341,308	226,502,328	243,469,458	2,417,953,954
Royalties ($)	50,553,214	9,078,969	5,887,427	21,7369,989	19,374,672	29,236,716	135,870,987
Other products							
Sales value ($)	307,035,583	12,161,076	17,927,276	18,141,340	34,554,658	30,679,027	420,498,960
Royalties ($)	30,118,571	1,212,695	2,176,490	2,944,098	4,495,482	4,155,102	45,102,438
Total royalties							
All minerals ($)	98,457,185	10,716,377	8,447,077	24,957,134	24,232,385	33,796,604	200,605,762
California							
Other products							
Sales value ($)	22,701,952	2,771,676	3,724,398	3,780,110	792,547	10,398,711	44,169,394
Royalties ($)	2,293,287	346,460	446,928	452,022	46,546	1,291,546	4,876,789
Royalties							
All minerals ($)	2,293,287	346,460	446,928	452,022	46,546	1,291,546	4,876,789
Colorado							
Oil in barrels							
Volume	3,654,759	588,257	318,938	298,018	136,452	124,430	5,120,854
Sales value ($)	31,737,548	10,310,421	5,198,591	4,785,313	2,293,182	2,543,710	56,868,765
Royalties ($)	4,704,789	1,749,512	954,293	766,856	329,878	332,234	8,837,562
Gas in Mcf							
Volume	513,764,410	17,829,157	18,989,709	20,743,420	24,288,051	36,584,090	632,198,837
Sales value ($)	280,076,318	34,846,076	37,125,686	37,274,001	36,961,936	56,451,514	482,735,531

[Continued]

★ 777 ★

Mineral Revenues on Indian Lands, 1937-93
[Continued]

State/commodity	1937-88	1989	1990	1991	1992	1993	1937-93
Royalties ($)	35,387,180	4,511,366	4,787,410	4,663,647	4,643,232	6,599,683	60,592,518
Coal in tons							
Volume	1,659	0	0	0	0	0	1,659
Sales value ($)	7,723	0	0	0	0	0	7,723
Royalties ($)	198	0	0	0	0	0	198
Other products							
Sales value ($)	2,300,305	589,285	355,423	99,965	679,729	2,363,452	6,388,159
Royalties ($)	277,259	102,132	54,367	12,344	82,662	279,369	808,133
Total royalties							
All minerals	40,369,426	6,363,010	5,796,070	5,442,847	5,055,772	7,211,286	70,238,411
Florida							
Oil in barrels							
Volume	4,688	0	0	0	0	0	4,688
Sales value ($)	51,367	0	0	0	0	0	51,367
Royalties ($)	6,422	0	0	0	0	0	6,422
Other products							
Sales value ($)	451,024	0	0	0	0	0	451,024
Royalties ($)	45,103	0	0	0	0	0	45,103
Total royalties							
All minerals	51,525	0	0	0	0	0	51,525
Idaho							
Other products							
Sales value ($)	180,087,533	20,026,962	18,231,839	20,562,230	22,681,048	16,439,381	278,028,993
Royalties	15,620,361	2,461,808	2,278,980	2,365,726	2,430,332	1,764,968	26,922,175
Total royalties							
All minerals ($)	15,620,361	2,461,808	2,278,980	2,365,726	2,430,332	1,746,968	26,922,175
Michigan							
Oil in barrels							
Volume	37,822	2,127	1,307	1,502	1,911	1,588	46,257
Sales value ($)	334,636	37,483	22,638	24,240	33,718	35,474	488,189
Royalties ($)	43,127	6,432	2,982	3,550	5,072	5,163	66,326
Gas in Mcf							
Volume	0	1,030	108	22,072	416	98	23,724
Sales value ($)	0	670	63	21,189	1,016	273	23,211
Royalties ($)	0	28	8	2,649	126	34	2,845

[Continued]

★ 777 ★

Mineral Revenues on Indian Lands, 1937-93
[Continued]

State/commodity	1937-88	1989	1990	1991	1992	1993	1937-93
Total royalties							
All minerals ($)	43,127	6,460	2,990	6,199	5,248	5,197	69,171
Minnesota							
Other products							
Sales value ($)	178,461	0	0	0	0	0	178,461
Royalties ($)	6,455	0	0	0	0	0	6,455
Total royalties							
All minerals	6,455	0	0	0	0	0	6,455
Montana							
Oil in barrels							
Volume	88,199,829	1,591,378	1,259,170	1,053,218	994,782	1,038,722	94,137,099
Sales value ($)	505,566,025	24,436,384	20,179,391	14,936,681	16,531,892	21,939,267	603,589,640
Royalties ($)	68,490,633	3,324,434	2,846,750	2,232,566	2,567,636	3,402,852	82,864,871
Gas in Mcf							
Volume	24,134,005	1,412,892	1,177,288	1,407,422	1,171,877	1,372,922	30,676,406
Sales value ($)	21,640,203	3,236,678	2,178,272	2,313,424	2,015,268	2,639,673	34,023,518
Royalties ($)	3,281,820	461,908	313,201	330,412	284,935	367,577	5,039,853
Coal in tons							
Volume	41,814,690	1,168,836	1,231,669	1,926,826	2,614,973	2,730,964	51,487,958
Sales value ($)	339,530,820	13,378,181	10,987,034	14,990,558	18,855,032	18,422,448	416,164,073
Royalties ($)	20,982,894	812,464	708,859	1,126,593	1,489,332	1,499,932	26,620,074
Other products							
Sales value ($)	17,235,190	101,786	4,872	14,601	25,988	29,315	17,411,752
Royalties ($)	1,015,355	15,890	700	910	1,037	1,924	1,035,716
Total royalties							
All minerals ($)	93,770,702	4,614,696	3,869,510	3,690,481	4,342,940	5,272,185	115,560,514
Nevada							
Other products							
Sales value ($)	3,330,226	1,748,149	1,292,587	1,956,496	1,802,314	1,276,614	11,406,886
Royalties ($)	325,924	157,822	102,684	156,701	150,129	103,042	1,006,302
Total royalties							
All minerals ($)	325,924	167,822	102,684	156,701	150,129	103,042	1,006,302
New Mexico							
Oil in barrels							
Volume	101,537,542	1,803,995	2,363,197	1,932,611	1,490,661	1,358,619	110,486,625
Sales value ($)	669,222,293	20,201,618	38,333,688	26,333,852	26,409,382	30,130,817	810,331,650
Royalties ($)	93,150,355	2,743,651	5,115,260	3,587,417	3,499,813	4,175,026	112,271,522

[Continued]

★ 777 ★

Mineral Revenues on Indian Lands, 1937-93
[Continued]

State/commodity	1937-88	1989	1990	1991	1992	1993	1937-93
Gas in Mcf							
Volume	1,613,422,067	16,225,790	16,571,091	19,053,982	24,707,624	38,505,580	1,728,486,134
Sales value ($)	1,155,855,959	47,300,933	35,469,326	36,611,000	42,749,789	67,979,864	1,385,966,871
Royalties ($)	150,956,195	6,176,038	4,695,317	4,809,241	5,458,029	8,406,848	180,501,668
Coal in tons							
Volume	147,188,950	10,210,329	11,157,838	11,984,923	13,249,499	12,173,961	205,965,500
Sales value ($)	1,136,426,894	209,236,271	306,648,588	237,139,427	253,595,409	269,740,481	2,412,787,070
Royalties ($)	37,801,422	19,585,540	23,885,088	23,825,185	26,813,923	30,054,848	161,966,006
Other products							
Sales value ($)	699,428,292	3,223,336	2,749,069	4,732,756	13,064,068	6,087,903	729,285,424
Royalties ($)	100,781,031	399,487	343,865	585,752	1,602,034	948,599	104,660,768
Total royalties							
All minerals ($)	382,689,003	28,904,716	34,039,530	32,807,595	37,373,799	43,585,321	559,399,964
North Dakota							
Oil in barrels							
Volume	8,934,463	94,303	114,391	127,483	93,598	122,459	9,486,697
Sales value ($)	46,025,910	1,420,936	1,944,077	1,896,403	1,587,414	2,635,200	55,509,940
Royalties ($)	6,096,236	191,603	272,804	275,635	230,633	395,625	7,462,536
Gas in Mcf							
Volume	10,474,796	30,002	190,826	140,620	136,706	185,369	11,158,319
Sales value ($)	1,642,755	24,256	124,586	125,150	77,684	174,895	2,169,326
Royalties ($)	211,370	3,324	15,824	16,334	10,165	23,732	280,749
Coal in tons							
Volume	2,921	0	0	0	0	0	2,921
Sales value ($)	8,834	0	0	0	0	0	8,834
Royalties ($)	540	0	0	0	0	0	540
Other products							
Sales value ($)	5,006,608	1,335	23,955	137,263	82,662	95,961	5,347,784
Royalties ($)	380,308	167	2,994	13,412	8,828	12,191	417,900
Total royalties							
All minerals ($)	6,688,454	195,094	291,622	305,381	249,626	431,548	8,161,725
Oklahoma							
Oil in barrels							
Volume	358,704,177	4,086,478	3,764,771	3,221,375	2,926,504	2,447,881	375,151,186
Sale value ($)	1,647,616,913	51,392,515	65,121,512	49,782,893	51,139,525	52,876,286	1,927,929,644
Royalties ($)	208,370,481	8,046,769	8,433,077	6,523,640	7,063,189	7,957,300	246,394,456

[Continued]

★ 777 ★

Mineral Revenues on Indian Lands, 1937-93

[Continued]

State/commodity	1937-88	1989	1990	1991	1992	1993	1937-93
Gas in Mcf							
Volume	832,554,807	45,096,525	57,375,400	45,578,928	40,978,372	37,303,356	1,058,887,388
Sales value ($)	195,755,788	102,710,719	81,475,935	71,473,941	65,413,470	60,351,360	1,177,181,213
Royalties ($)	105,346,113	10,172,241	8,636,325	8,464,378	8,105,099	9,300,449	150,024,605
Coal in tons							
Volume	9,375,686	0	0	0	0	0	9,375,686
Sales value ($)	37,232,091	0	0	0	0	0	37,232,091
Royalties ($)	1,050,777	0	0	0	0	0	1,050,777
Other products							
Sales value ($)	313,427,795	1,321,352	2,602,963	2,742,994	3,315,661	3,632,751	327,043,516
Royalties ($)	24,070,366	139,978	303,188	202,080	255,916	338,679	25,310,207
Total royalties							
All minerals ($)	338,837,737	18,358,988	17,372,590	15,190,098	15,424,204	17,596,428	422,780,045
South Dakota							
Oil in barrels							
Volume	75,669	841	6,375	6,389	5,781	6,888	101,943
Sales value ($)	1,155,700	17,038	88,770	72,719	81,431	121,475	1,537,133
Royalties ($)	198,061	3,408	17,754	14,544	16,243	24,295	274,305
Coal in tons							
Volume	15,876	0	0	0	0	0	15,876
Sales value ($)	72,302	0	0	0	0	0	72,302
Royalties ($)	3,175	0	0	0	0	0	3,175
Other products							
Sales value ($)	5,950,624	0	0	0	0	0	5,950,624
Royalties ($)	474,609	0	0	0	0	0	474,609
Total royalties							
All minerals ($)	675,845	3,408	17,754	14,544	16,243	24,295	752,089
Texas							
Oil in barrels							
Volume	0	0	0	0	29,655	129,948	159,603
Sales value ($)	0	0	0	0	548,322	2,964,277	3,512,599
Royalties ($)	0	0	0	0	68,540	555,390	623,930
Gas in Mcf							
Volume	0	0	0	0	256,610	1,329,895	1,586,505
Sales value ($)	0	0	0	0	397,745	2,433,707	2,831,452
Royalties ($)	0	0	0	0	50,116	443,073	493,189

[Continued]

★ 777 ★

Mineral Revenues on Indian Lands, 1937-93
[Continued]

State/commodity	1937-88	1989	1990	1991	1992	1993	1937-93
Total royalties							
All minerals ($)	0	0	0	0	118,656	998,463	1,117,119
Utah							
Oil in barrels							
Volume	391,226,853	8,182,235	7,800,045	7,161,520	6,762,666	7,193,799	428,327,118
Sales value ($)	2,923,143,699	128,820,858	138,514,859	109,382,351	125,647,412	161,668,148	3,587,177,327
Royalties ($)	439,742,797	18,824,315	19,858,199	18,919,988	24,880,001	538,442,670	
Gas in Mcf							
Volume	273,532,962	6,896,952	6,953,376	4,828,629	6,419,454	4,820,609	303,451,982
Sales value ($)	214,590,288	16,523,387	13,800,057	9,691,972	13,196,980	12,849,810	280,652,494
Royalties ($)	32,654,170	2,322,417	2,015,060	1,586,466	2,005,646	2,187,760	42,771,519
Other products							
Sales value ($)	163,306,625	6,771,898	3,480,708	2,774,385	1,753,902	2,658,367	180,745,885
Royalties ($)	10,082,362	985,901	499,509	311,171	206,018	297,327	12,382,288
Total royalties							
All minerals ($)	482,479,329	22,132,633	22,372,768	18,115,007	21,131,652	27,365,088	593,596,477
Washington							
Gas in Mcf							
Volume	2,939	0	0	0	0	0	2,939
Sales value ($)	1,170	0	0	0	0	0	1,170
Royalties ($)	146	0	0	0	0	0	146
Other products							
Sales value ($)	48,660,404	63,732	33,456	33,261	27,620	520,108	49,338,581
Royalties ($)	5,021,901	7,967	4,182	4,264	3,615	49,958	5,091,887
Total royalties							
All minerals ($)	5,002,047	7,967	4,182	4,264	3,615	49,958	5,092,033
Wisconsin							
Other products							
Sales value ($)	40,711	0	0	0	0	0	40,711
Royalties ($)	3,271	0	0	0	0	0	3,271
Total royalties							
All minerals ($)	3,271	0	0	0	0	0	3,271
Wyoming							
Oil in barrels							
Volume	241,326,302	3,463,830	3,225,966	2,965,278	2,903,945	2,775,325	256,660,646
Sale value ($)	1,251,394,952	45,987,552	50,040,829	38,141,657	43,644,439	53,113,393	1,482,322,822
Royalties ($)	176,985,399	7,106,979	7,931,388	6,153,059	7,773,964	10,076,457	216,027,246

[Continued]

★ 777 ★

Mineral Revenues on Indian Lands, 1937-93
[Continued]

State/commodity	1937-88	1989	1990	1991	1992	1993	1937-93
Gas in Mcf							
Volume	306,965,458	10,215,245	6,272,923	11,330,346	16,485,447	6,825,391	358,094,810
Sales value ($)	210,688,160	22,678,369	12,418,389	17,838,303	29,708,116	16,831,502	310,162,839
Royalties ($)	31,257,771	3,615,217	1,775,283	2,617,909	4,071,330	2,419,975	45,760,485
Other products							
Sales value ($)	6,161,853	213,547	263,178	54,103	9,689	3,811	6,706,181
Royalties ($)	580,334	27,023	38,227	3,701	411	527	650,223
Total royalties							
All minerals ($)	208,823,504	10,749,219	9,744,898	8,774,669	11,848,705	12,496,959	262,437,954
Indian Totals							
Oil in barrels							
Volume	1,212,750,702	19,977,908	18,989,869	16,876,128	15,472,363	15,317,646	1,299,384,616
Sales value ($)	7,183,683,225	295,214,257	321,775,010	247,010,705	269,801,995	330,457,469	8,647,942,661
Royalties ($)	1,015,233,980	42,420,370	45,813,797	36,046,679	40,835,885	52,207,285	1,232,557,996
Gas in Mcf							
Volume	3,587,971,337	97,724,887	107,545,975	103,112,936	114,452,197	126,939,751	4,137,747,083
Sales value ($)	2,682,993,910	227,332,848	182,607,277	175,357,022	190,532,422	219,727,298	3,678,550,777
Royalties ($)	359,441,026	27,263,985	22,240,298	22,492,041	24,632,980	29,750,975	485,821,305
Coal in tons							
Volume	327,523,878	22,929,165	23,992,181	26,230,084	26,982,687	27,526,318	455,184,313
Sales value ($)	2,913,309,973	407,298,952	442,560,673	490,471,293	498,952,769	531,632,387	5,284,226,047
Royalties ($)	110,392,220	29,476,973	30,481,374	46,691,767	47,677,927	60,791,496	325,511,757
Other products							
Sales value ($)	1,775,303,186	48,994,134	50,689,724	55,029,504	78,790,386	74,185,401	2,082,992,335
Royalties ($)	191,096,497	5,867,330	6,252,114	7,052,181	9,283,010	9,243,132	228,794,264
Total royalties							
All minerals ($)	1,676,163,723	105,028,658	104,787,583	112,282,668	122,429,802	151,992,888	2,272,685,322

Source: U.S. Department of the Interior. Minerals Management Service. Royalty Management Program. *Mineral Revenues 1993: Report on Receipts from Federal and Indian Leases*. Washington, DC: Minerals Management Service, pp. 75-81.

★ 778 ★

Minerals

Mineral Revenues on Indian Lands, 1937-93: All Indian Lands

Data show summary of sales volume, sales value, and royalties commodity from Indian mineral leases in calendar years 1937-93.

State/commodity	1937-88	1989	1990	1991	1992	1993	1937-93
Indian land totals							
Oil in barrels							
Volume	1,268,594,607	15,472,363	15,317,646	14,176,197	15,332,033	14,601,598	1,343,494,444
Sales value ($)	8,047,683,197	269,801,995	330,457,469	283,383,813	279,711,971	243,901,399	9,454,939,844
Royalties ($)	1,139,514,826	40,835,885	52,207,285	44,431,636	46,386,064	40,358,446	1,363,734,142
Gas in Mcf							
Volume	3,896,355,135	114,452,197	126,939,751	131,985,320	149,685,398	189,006,082	4,608,423,883
Sales value ($)	3,268,291,057	190,532,422	219,727,298	210,187,959	248,754,839	341,569,493	4,479,063,068
Royalties ($)	431,437,350	24,632,980	29,750,975	29,223,094	34,630,655	48,030,441	597,705,495
Coal in tons							
Volume	400,675,308	26,982,687	27,526,318	32,090,432	28,144,767	28,091,462	543,510,974
Sales value ($)	4,253,640,891	498,952,769	531,632,387	543,959,584	547,885,670	541,918,731	6,917,990,032
Royalties ($)	217,042,334	47,677,927	60,791,496	62,883,284	65,918,888	64,749,821	519,063,750
Other products							
Sales value ($)	1,930,016,548	78,790,386	74,185,401	70,640,984	75,611,044	170,965,178	2,400,209,541
Royalties ($)	210,268,122	9,283,010	9,243,132	8,647,341	9,461,608	13,232,648	260,135,861
Total royalties							
All minerals	1,998,262,632	122,429,802	151,992,888	145,185,355	156,397,215	166,371,356	2,740,639,248

Source: U.S. Department of the Interior. Minerals Management Service. Royalty Management Program. *Mineral Revenues 1993: Report on Receipts from Federal and Indian Leases.* Washington, DC: Minerals Management Service, p. 78.

★ 779 ★

Minerals

Mineral Revenues on Indian Lands, 1937-93: Alaska

Data show summary of sales volume, sales value, and royalties by commodity from Indian mineral leases in calendar years 1937-93.

State/commodity	1937-88	1989	1990	1991	1992	1993	1937-93
Alaska							
Gas in Mcf							
Volume	277,556	0	0	0	0	0	277,556
Sales volume ($)	39,269	0	0	0	0	0	39,269
Royalties ($)	6,541	0	0	0	0	0	6,541

[Continued]

★ 779 ★

Mineral Revenues on Indian Lands, 1937-93: Alaska
[Continued]

State/commodity	1937-88	1989	1990	1991	1992	1993	1937-93
Total royalties, all minerals	6,541	0	0	0	0	0	6,541

Source: U.S. Department of the Interior. Minerals Management Service. Royalty Management Program. *Mineral Revenues 1993: Report on Receipts from Federal and Indian Leases.* Washington, DC: Minerals Management Service, pp. 75-81.

★ 780 ★
Minerals

Mineral Revenues on Indian Lands, 1937-93: Arizona

Data show summary of sales volume, sales value, and royalties by commodity from Indian mineral leases in calendar years 1937-93.

State/commodity	1937-88	1989	1990	1991	1992	1993	1937-93
Arizona							
Oil in barrels							
Volume	19,457,505	126,408	117,987	116,939	87,672	85,711	19,992,222
Sales volume ($)	114,008,885	2,185,278	2,429,422	2,322,258	1,585,035	1,407,826	123,938,704
Royalties ($)	18,522,279	360,929	402,942	384,726	259,247	231,635	20,161,758
Gas in Mcf							
Volume	12,882,402	7,640	12,441	358,699	394,732	49,150	13,705,064
Sales value ($)	2,738,765	10,418	14,700	277,677	380,899	38,927	3,461,386
Royalties($)	344,041	1,302	1,844	45,683	63,199	4,866	460,935
Coal in tons							
Volume	164,595,105	11,118,215	12,621,393	17,877,672	12,951,372	12,257,727	231,421,484
Sales value ($)	1,947,982,168	226,502,328	243,469,458	284,020,527	264,235,116	264,025,579	3,230,235,176
Royalties ($)	87,259,599	19,374,672	29,236,716	33,174,586	33,054,106	32,999,499	235,099,178
Other products							
Sales value ($)	355,265,275	34,554,658	30,679,027	28,194,247	36,798,858	131,729,386	617,221,451
Royalties ($)	36,451,854	4,495,482	4,155,102	3,261,684	4,244,011	7,947,579	60,555,712
Total royalties							
All minerals ($)	142,577,773	24,232,385	33,796,604	36,866,679	37,620,563	41,183,579	316,277,583

Source: U.S. Department of the Interior. Minerals Management Service. Royalty Management Program. *Mineral Revenues 1993: Report on Receipts from Federal and Indian Leases.* Washington, DC: Minerals Management Service, p. 75.

★ 781 ★
Minerals

Mineral Revenues on Indian Lands, 1937-93: California

Data show summary of sales volume, sales value, and royalties by commodity from Indian mineral leases in calendar years 1937-93.

State/commodity	1937-88		1989		1990		1991		1992		1993		1937-93
California													
Other products													
Sales volume ($)	32,978,136	0	792,547	0	10,398,711	0	6,226,845	0	4,569,201	0	4,373,269	0	59,338,709
Royalties ($)	3,538,697		46,546		1,291,546		682,736		474,087		584,924		6,618,536
Total royalties, all minerals	3,538,697		46,546		1,291,546		682,736		474,087		584,924		6,618,536

Source: U.S. Department of the Interior. Minerals Management Service. Royalty Management Program. *Mineral Revenues 1993: Report on Receipts from Federal and Indian Leases.* Washington, DC: Minerals Management Service, pp. 75-81.

★ 782 ★
Minerals

Mineral Revenues on Indian Lands, 1937-93: Colorado

Data show summary of sales volume, sales value, and royalties by commodity from Indian mineral leases in calendar years 1937-93.

State/commodity	1937-88	1989	1990	1991	1992	1993	1937-93
Colorado							
Oil in barrels							
Volume	4,859,972	136,452	124,430	89,151	165,532	128,491	5,504,028
Sales volume ($)	52,031,873	2,293,182	2,543,710	1,741,764	3,159,855	2,061,257	63,831,641
Royalties ($)	8,175,450	329,878	332,234	231,983	524,866	398,970	9,993,381
Gas in Mcf							
Volume	571,326,696	24,288,051	36,584,090	41,618,059	59,788,870	88,743,753	522,349,519
Sales value ($)	389,322,081	36,961,936	56,451,514	57,045,444	84,731,177	143,541,639	768,053,791
Royalties($)	49,349,603	4,643,232	6,599,683	7,047,036	10,990,326	18,666,573	97,296,453
Coal in tons							
Volume	1,659	0	0	0	0	0	1,659
Sales value ($)	7,723	0	0	0	0	0	7,723
Royalties ($)	198	0	0	0	0	0	198
Other products							
Sales value ($)	3,344,978	679,729	2,363,452	140,653	-129,325	-432,585	5,966,902
Royalties ($)	446,102	82,662	279,369	11,833	-12,289	-27,255	780,422
Total royalties							
All minerals ($)	57,971,353	5,055,772	7,211,286	7,290,852	11,502,903	19,038,288	108,070,454

Source: U.S. Department of the Interior. Minerals Management Service. Royalty Management Program. *Mineral Revenues 1993: Report on Receipts from Federal and Indian Leases.* Washington, DC: Minerals Management Service, p. 76.

★ 783 ★

Minerals

Mineral Revenues on Indian Lands, 1937-93: Florida

Data show summary of sales volume, sales value, and royalties by commodity from Indian mineral leases in calendar years 1937-93.

State/commodity	1937-88	1989	1990	1991	1992	1993	1937-93
Florida							
Oil in barrels							
Volume	4,688	0	0	0	0	0	4,688
Sales volume ($)	51,367	0	0	0	0	0	51,367
Royalties ($)	6,422	0	0	0	0	0	6,422
Other products							
Sales value ($)	451,024	0	0	0	0	0	451,024
Royalties ($)	45,103	0	0	0	0	0	45,103
Total royalties							
All minerals ($)	51,525	0	0	0	0	0	51,525

Source: U.S. Department of the Interior. Minerals Management Service. Royalty Management Program. *Mineral Revenues 1993: Report on Receipts from Federal and Indian Leases.* Washington, DC: Minerals Management Service, p. 76.

★ 784 ★

Minerals

Mineral Revenues on Indian Lands, 1937-93: Idaho

Data show summary of sales volume, sales value, and royalties by commodity from Indian mineral leases in calendar years 1937-93.

State/commodity	1937-88	1989	1990	1991	1992	1993	1937-93
Idaho							
Other products							
Sales value ($)	238,908,564	22,681,048	16,439,381	14,892,748	13,683,175	14,655,816	321,260,732
Royalties ($)	22,726,875	2,430,332	1,764,968	2,098,051	1,750,810	1,823,056	32,594,092
Total royalties							
All minerals ($)	22,726,875	2,430,332	1,764,968	2,098,051	1,750,810	1,823,056	32,594,092

Source: U.S. Department of the Interior. Minerals Management Service. Royalty Management Program. *Mineral Revenues 1993: Report on Receipts from Federal and Indian Leases.* Washington, DC: Minerals Management Service, p. 76.

★ 785 ★

Minerals

Mineral Revenues on Indian Lands, 1937-93: Michigan

Data show summary of sales volume, sales value, and royalties commodity from Indian mineral leases in calendar years 1937-93.

State/commodity	1937-88	1989	1990	1991	1992	1993	1937-93
Michigan							
Oil in barrels							
Volume	42,758	1,911	1,588	788	797	630	48,472
Sales volume ($)	418,997	33,718	35,474	16,598	15,665	11,028	531,480
Royalties ($)	56,091	5,072	5,163	2,291	2,112	1,540	72,269
Gas in Mcf							
Volume	23,210	416	98	5	54	23	23,806
Sales volume ($)	21,922	1,016	273	13	151	66	23,441
Royalties ($)	2,685	126	34	2	19	8	2,874
Total royalties							
All minerals	58,776	5,198	5,197	2,293	2,131	1,548	75,143

Source: U.S. Department of the Interior. Minerals Management Service. Royalty Management Program. *Mineral Revenues 1993: Report on Receipts from Federal and Indian Leases.* Washington, DC: Minerals Management Service, pp. 75-81.

★ 786 ★

Minerals

Mineral Revenues on Indian Lands, 1937-93: Minnesota

Data show summary of sales volume, sales value, and royalties commodity from Indian mineral leases in calendar years 1937-93.

State/commodity	1937-88	1989	1990	1991	1992	1993	1937-93
Minnesota							
Other products							
Sales value ($)	178,461	0	0	0	0	0	178,461
Royalties ($)	6,455	0	0	0	0	0	6,455
Total royalties							
All minerals	6,455	0	0	0	0	0	6,455

Source: U.S. Department of the Interior. Minerals Management Service. Royalty Management Program. *Mineral Revenues 1993: Report on Receipts from Federal and Indian Leases.* Washington, DC: Minerals Management Service, pp. 75-81.

★ 787 ★
Minerals

Mineral Revenues on Indian Lands, 1937-93: Montana

Data show summary of sales volume, sales value, and royalties commodity from Indian mineral leases in calendar years 1937-93.

State/commodity	1937-88	1989	1990	1991	1992	1993	1937-93
Montana							
Oil in barrels							
Volume	92,103,595	994,782	1,038,722	873,540	940,203	1,016,902	96,967,744
Sales volume ($)	565,118,481	16,531,892	21,939,267	16,561,864	16,228,556	15,771,788	652,151,848
Royalties ($)	76,894,383	2,567,636	3,402,852	2,601,748	2,411,597	2,424,425	90,302,641
Gas in Mcf							
Volume	28,131,607	1,171,877	1,372,922	1,091,463	1,376,812	1,701,053	34,845,734
Sales value ($)	29,368,577	2,015,268	2,639,673	1,908,925	2,265,278	3,189,847	41,387,568
Royalties($)	4,387,341	284,935	367,577	272,733	339,656	481,561	6,133,803
Coal in tons							
Volume	46,142,021	2,614,973	2,730,964	2,979,447	2,299,856	3,517,511	60,284,772
Sales value ($)	378,886,593	18,855,032	18,422,448	18,395,721	11,591,274	28,040,475	474,191,543
Royalties ($)	23,630,810	1,489,332	1,499,932	1,367,295	1,175,285	1,785,621	30,948,275
Other products							
Sales value ($)	17,356,449	25,988	29,315	30,381	32,868	93,868	17,568,869
Royalties ($)	1,032,855	1,037	1,824	1,702	3,385	8,962	1,049,765
Total royalties							
All minerals ($)	105,945,389	4,342,940	5,272,185	4,243,478	3,929,923	4,700,569	128,434,484

Source: U.S. Department of the Interior. Minerals Management Service. Royalty Management Program. *Mineral Revenues 1993: Report on Receipts from Federal and Indian Leases.* Washington, DC: Minerals Management Service, pp. 75-81.

★ 788 ★
Minerals

Mineral Revenues on Indian Lands, 1937-93: Nevada

Data show summary of sales volume, sales value, and royalties commodity from Indian mineral leases in calendar years 1937-93.

State/commodity	1937-88	1989	1990	1991	1992	1993	1937-93
Nevada							
Other products							
Sales value ($)	8,327,458	1,802,814	1,276,614	988,381	1,148,408	1,554,294	15,097,969
Royalties ($)	753,131	150,129	103,042	82,116	96,307	145,813	1,330,538

[Continued]

★ 788 ★

Mineral Revenues on Indian Lands, 1937-93: Nevada
[Continued]

State/commodity	1937-88	1989	1990	1991	1992	1993	1937-93
Total royalties All minerals	753,131	150,129	103,042	82,116	96,307	145,813	1,330,538

Source: U.S. Department of the Interior. Minerals Management Service. Royalty Management Program. *Mineral Revenues 1993: Report on Receipts from Federal and Indian Leases.* Washington, DC: Minerals Management Service, p. 78.

★ 789 ★

Minerals

Mineral Revenues on Indian Lands, 1937-93: New Mexico

Data show summary of sales volume, sales value, and royalties commodity from Indian mineral leases in calendar years 1937-93.

State/commodity	1937-88	1989	1990	1991	1992	1993	1937-93
New Mexico							
Oil in barrels							
Volume	107,637,345	1,490,661	1,358,619	1,133,772	1,284,980	1,167,505	114,072,882
Sales value ($)	754,091,451	26,109,382	30,130,817	23,585,103	23,490,282	19,629,051	877,036,086
Royalties ($)	104,596,683	3,499,813	4,175,026	3,343,961	3,441,379	2,859,905	121,916,767
Gas in Mcf							
Volume	1,665,272,930	24,707,624	38,505,580	39,267,452	45,142,344	51,673,798	1,864,569,728
Sales value ($)	1,275,237,218	42,749,789	67,979,864	61,866,890	76,521,999	99,842,377	1,624,198,137
Royalties ($)	166,636,791	5,458,029	8,406,848	7,494,313	9,505,570	12,922,892	210,424,443
Coal in tons							
Volume	180,542,040	13,249,499	12,173,961	11,233,313	12,893,539	12,316,224	242,408,576
Sales value ($)	1,889,451,180	253,595,409	269,740,481	241,543,336	272,059,280	249,852,677	3,176,242,363
Royalties ($)	105,097,235	26,813,923	30,054,848	28,341,403	31,689,497	29,964,701	251,961,607
Other products							
Sales value ($)	710,133,453	13,064,068	6,087,903	12,135,489	11,268,429	10,481,841	763,171,183
Royalties ($)	102,110,135	1,602,034	948,599	1,718,742	1,812,566	1,762,046	109,954,122
Total royalties							
All minerals	478,440,844	37,373,799	40,585,321	40,898,419	46,449,102	47,509,544	694,256,939

Source: U.S. Department of the Interior. Minerals Management Service. Royalty Management Program. *Mineral Revenues 1993: Report on Receipts from Federal and Indian Leases.* Washington, DC: Minerals Management Service, p. 78.

★ 790 ★
Minerals

Mineral Revenues on Indian Lands, 1937-93: North Dakota

Data show summary of sales volume, sales value, and royalties commodity from Indian mineral leases in calendar years 1937-93.

State/commodity	1937-88	1989	1990	1991	1992	1993	1937-93
North Dakota							
Oil in barrels							
Volume	9,270,640	93,598	122,459	227,303	202,633	148,941	10,065,574
Sales value ($)	51,287,326	1,587,414	2,635,200	4,355,127	3,646,932	2,465,491	65,977,490
Royalties ($)	6,836,278	230,633	395,625	683,755	560,405	371,120	9,077,816
Gas in Mcf							
Volume	10,836,244	136,706	185,369	134,269	232,426	107,177	11,632,191
Sales value ($)	1,916,747	77,684	174,895	156,410	111,027	116,433	2,553,196
Royalties ($)	246,852	10,165	23,732	24,438	16,786	17,391	339,364
Coal in tons							
Volume	2,921	0	0	0	0	0	2,921
Sales value ($)	8,834	0	0	0	0	0	8,834
Royalties ($)	540	0	0	0	0	0	540
Other products							
Sales value ($)	5,169,161	82,662	95,961	60,235	155,682	106,691	5,670,392
Royalties ($)	396,881	8,828	12,191	7,198	18,764	9,947	453,809
Total royalties							
All minerals	7,480,551	249,626	431,548	715,391	595,955	398,458	9,871,529

Source: U.S. Department of the Interior. Minerals Management Service. Royalty Management Program. *Mineral Revenues 1993: Report on Receipts from Federal and Indian Leases.* Washington, DC: Minerals Management Service, p. 78.

★ 791 ★
Minerals

Mineral Revenues on Indian Lands, 1937-93: Oklahoma

Data show summary of sales volume, sales value, and royalties commodity from Indian mineral leases in calendar years 1937-93.

State/commodity	1937-88	1989	1990	1991	1992	1993	1937-93
Oklahoma							
Oil in barrels							
Volume	369,776,801	2,926,504	2,447,881	2,501,264	2,424,784	2,046,793	382,124,027
Sales value ($)	1,823,913,833	51,139,525	52,876,286	50,377,582	44,426,228	35,283,885	2,058,017,339
Royalties ($)	231,373,967	7,063,189	7,957,300	7,445,752	6,775,600	5,101,160	265,716,968
Gas in Mcf							
Volume	980,605,660	40,978,372	37,303,356	34,631,405	26,087,004	25,093,022	1,144,698,819

[Continued]

★ 791 ★

Mineral Revenues on Indian Lands, 1937-93: Oklahoma

[Continued]

State/commodity	1937-88	1989	1990	1991	1992	1993	1937-93
Sales value ($)	1,051,416,383	65,413,470	60,351,360	51,642,176	46,500,233	51,584,467	1,326,908,089
Royalties ($)	132,619,057	8,105,099	9,300,449	8,135,186	7,559,284	9,034,465	174,753,540
Coal in tons							
Volume	9,375,686	0	0	0	0	0	9,375,686
Sales value ($)	37,232,091	0	0	0	0	0	37,232,091
Royalties ($)	1,050,777	0	0	0	0	0	1,050,777
Other products							
Sales value ($)	320,095,104	3,315,661	3,632,751	4,382,983	3,186,489	3,376,788	337,989,776
Royalties ($)	24,715,612	255,916	338,679	377,181	446,559	317,472	26,451,419
Total royalties							
All minerals	389,759,413	15,424,204	17,596,428	15,958,119	14,781,443	14,453,097	467,972,704

Source: U.S. Department of the Interior. Minerals Management Service. Royalty Management Program. *Mineral Revenues 1993: Report on Receipts from Federal and Indian Leases.* Washington, DC: Minerals Management Service, p. 78.

★ 792 ★

Minerals

Mineral Revenues on Indian Lands, 1937-93: South Dakota

Data show summary of sales volume, sales value, and royalties commodity from Indian mineral leases in calendar years 1937-93.

State/commodity	1937-88	1989	1990	1991	1992	1993	1937-93
South Dakota							
Oil in barrels							
Volume	89,274	5,781	6,888	5,512	5,706	4,805	117,966
Sales value ($)	1,334,227	81,431	121,475	96,134	90,314	60,964	1,784,545
Royalties ($)	233,767	16,243	24,295	19,227	17,862	12,193	323,587
Coal in tons							
Volume	15,876	0	0	0	0	0	15,876
Sales value ($)	72,302	0	0	0	0	0	72,302
Royalties ($)	3,175	0	0	0	0	0	3,175
Other products							
Sales value ($)	5,950,624	0	0	0	0	0	5,950,624
Royalties ($)	474,609	0	0	0	0	0	474,609
Total royalties							
All minerals	711,551	16,243	24,295	19,227	17,862	12,193	801,371

Source: U.S. Department of the Interior. Minerals Management Service. Royalty Management Program. *Mineral Revenues 1993: Report on Receipts from Federal and Indian Leases.* Washington, DC: Minerals Management Service, p. 78.

★ 793 ★

Minerals

Mineral Revenues on Indian Lands, 1937-93: Texas

Data show summary of sales volume, sales value, and royalties commodity from Indian mineral leases in calendar years 1937-93.

State/commodity	1937-88	1989	1990	1991	1992	1993	1937-93
Texas							
Oil in barrels							
Volume	0	29,655	129,948	143,160	160,376	165,853	628,992
Sales value ($)	0	548,322	2,964,277	2,949,989	3,109,556	2,883,637	12,455,781
Royalties ($)	0	68,540	555,390	575,472	580,685	564,507	2,344,594
Gas in Mcf							
Volume	0	256,610	1,329,895	2,131,788	2,492,135	2,118,952	8,329,380
Sales value ($)	0	397,745	2,433,707	3,133,728	4,147,486	4,677,144	14,789,810
Royalties ($)	0	50,116	443,073	576,606	752,980	878,613	2,701,388
Total royalties							
All minerals	0	118,656	998,463	1,152,078	1,333,665	1,443,120	5,045,982

Source: U.S. Department of the Interior. Minerals Management Service. Royalty Management Program. *Mineral Revenues 1993: Report on Receipts from Federal and Indian Leases.* Washington, DC: Minerals Management Service, p. 78.

★ 794 ★

Minerals

Mineral Revenues on Indian Lands, 1937-93: Utah

Data show summary of sales volume, sales value, and royalties commodity from Indian mineral leases in calendar years 1937-93.

State/commodity	1937-88	1989	1990	1991	1992	1993	1937-93
Utah							
Oil in barrels							
Volume	414,370,653	6,762,666	7,193,799	6,638,655	7,681,932	7,837,548	450,485,253
Sales value ($)	3,299,861,767	125,647,412	161,668,148	141,378,735	150,196,064	137,830,240	4,016,582,366
Royalties ($)	494,642,681	18,919,988	24,880,001	21,602,056	25,067,256	23,007,348	608,119,330
Gas in Mcf							
Volume	292,211,919	6,419,454	4,820,609	6,401,441	8,863,289	8,292,811	327,009,523
Sales value ($)	254,605,704	13,196,980	12,849,810	18,440,102	21,355,488	20,930,432	341,378,516
Royalties ($)	38,578,113	2,005,646	2,187,760	3,187,615	3,299,076	3,202,965	52,461,175
Other products							
Sales value ($)	176,333,616	1,753,902	2,658,367	1,871,708	3,818,719	3,240,060	189,676,372
Royalties ($)	11,878,943	206,018	297,327	227,317	519,516	365,348	13,494,469

[Continued]

★ 794 ★

Mineral Revenues on Indian Lands, 1937-93: Utah

[Continued]

State/commodity	1937-88	1989	1990	1991	1992	1993	1937-93
Total royalties All minerals	545,099,737	21,131,652	27,365,088	25,016,988	28,885,848	26,575,661	674,074,974

Source: U.S. Department of the Interior. Minerals Management Service. Royalty Management Program. *Mineral Revenues 1993: Report on Receipts from Federal and Indian Leases.* Washington, DC: Minerals Management Service, p. 78.

★ 795 ★

Minerals

Mineral Revenues on Indian Lands, 1937-93: Washington

Data show summary of sales volume, sales value, and royalties commodity from Indian mineral leases in calendar years 1937-93.

State/commodity	1937-88	1989	1990	1991	1992	1993	1937-93
Washington							
Gas in Mcf							
Volume	2,939	0	0	0	0	0	2,939
Sales value ($)	1,170	0	0	0	0	0	1,170
Royalties ($)	146	0	0	0	0	0	146
Other products							
Sales value ($)	48,790,853	27,620	520,108	527,810	763,737	1,545,916	52,176,044
Royalties ($)	5,038,314	3,615	49,958	41,032	70,259	284,272	5,487,450
Total royalties							
All minerals	5,038,460	3,615	49,958	41,032	70,259	284,272	5,487,596

Source: U.S. Department of the Interior. Minerals Management Service. Royalty Management Program. *Mineral Revenues 1993: Report on Receipts from Federal and Indian Leases.* Washington, DC: Minerals Management Service, p. 78.

★ 796 ★

Minerals

Mineral Revenues on Indian Lands, 1937-93: Wisconsin

Data show summary of sales volume, sales value, and royalties commodity from Indian mineral leases in calendar years 1937-93.

State/commodity	1937-88	1989	1990	1991	1992	1993	1937-93
Wisconsin							
Other products							
Sales value ($)	40,711	0	0	0	0	0	40,711
Royalties ($)	3,271	0	0	0	0	0	3,271

[Continued]

★ 796 ★

Mineral Revenues on Indian Lands, 1937-93: Wisconsin

[Continued]

State/commodity	1937-88	1989	1990	1991	1992	1993	1937-93
Total royalties All minerals	3,271	0	0	0	0	0	3,271

Source: U.S. Department of the Interior. Minerals Management Service. Royalty Management Program. *Mineral Revenues 1993: Report on Receipts from Federal and Indian Leases.* Washington, DC: Minerals Management Service, p. 78.

★ 797 ★

Minerals

Mineral Revenues on Indian Lands, 1937-93: Wyoming

Data show summary of sales volume, sales value, and royalties commodity from Indian mineral leases in calendar years 1937-93.

State/commodity	1937-88	1989	1990	1991	1992	1993	1937-93
Wyoming							
Oil in barrels							
Volume	250,981,376	2,903,945	2,775,325	2,446,113	2,377,418	1,998,419	263,482,596
Sales value ($)	1,385,564,990	43,644,439	39,998,439	53,113,393	39,998,659	26,496,232	1,582,581,197
Royalties ($)	198,176,825	7,773,964	10,076,457	7,540,665	6,745,055	5,385,643	235,698,609
Gas in Mcf							
Volume	334,783,972	16,485,447	6,825,391	6,350,739	5,307,732	11,226,343	380,979,624
Sales value ($)	263,623,221	29,718,116	16,831,502	15,716,594	12,741,101	17,648,161	356,268,695
Royalties ($)	39,266,180	4,074,330	2,419,975	2,439,482	2,103,759	2,821,107	53,124,833
Other products							
Sales value ($)	6,692,681	9,689	3,811	1,189,504	314,803	239,834	8,450,322
Royalties ($)	649,285	411	527	137,749	37,633	10,484	836,089
Total royalties							
All minerals	238,092,290	11,848,705	12,496,959	10,117,896	8,886,447	8,217,234	289,659,531

Source: U.S. Department of the Interior. Minerals Management Service. Royalty Management Program. *Mineral Revenues 1993: Report on Receipts from Federal and Indian Leases.* Washington, DC: Minerals Management Service, p. 78.

★ 798 ★

Minerals

Royalties from Mineral Leases on Indian Lands

Royalties are shown, by type, from 1984-93.

Lease	1984	1985	1986	1987	1988	1989	1990	1991	1992	1993	1984-93
Oil royalties	75,973,022	75,025,974	42,420,370	45,813,797	36,046,679	40,835,885	52,207,285	44,431,636	46,386,064	40,358,446	499,499,158
Gas royalties	37,295,148	35,853,169	27,263,985	22,240,298	22,492,041	24,632,980	29,750,975	29,223,094	34,630,655	48,030,441	311,412,786
Coal royalties	7,613,759	23,403,3366	29,476,973	30,481,374	46,691,767	47,677,927	60,791,496	62,883,284	65,918,888	64,749,821	439,688,625
Other royalties	7,504,971	5,142,229	5,867,330	6,252,114	7,052,181	9,283,010	9,243,132	8,647,341	9,461,608	13,232,648	81,686,564
Minimum royalties	-	-	-	-	-	-	-	-	-	-	-
Rents	3,576,549	3,372,750	3,018,833	1,206,406	1,255,603	1,454,523	438,483	1,819,916	1,366,413	1,860,669	19,370,145
Bonuses	-	-	-	-	-	-	-	-	-	-	-
Totals	131,963,449	142,797,458	108,047,491	105,993,989	113,538,271	123,884,325	152,431,371	147,005,271	157,763,628	168,232,025	1,351,657,278

Source: U.S. Department of the Interior. Minerals Management Service. Royalty Management Program. *Mineral Revenues 1993: Report on Receipts from Federal and Indian Leases.* Washington, DC: Minerals Management Service, pp. 10-13. A dash (-) indicates no data given in original source. Most Indian leases do not contain minimum royalty provisions. Most Indian leases retain rental provisions after the lease is producing. Indian rent revenues represent fiscal year data from Bureau of Indian Affairs (BIA) record for the period 1984-87. Indian rent revenues represent calendar year data from Minerals Management Service (MMS) records for the period 1988-93. Indian bonus revenues are collected by the BIA.

★ 799 ★

Minerals

Oil and Gas Leases, 1984-93

Data show number of leases and total acreage of producing and producible Indian onshore oil and gas leases, as of December 31 of each year.

Year	Number	Acres
1984	4,392	1,594,148
1985	4,601	1,842,803
1986	4,701	1,647,920
1987	4,819	1,625,772
1988	4,349	1,600,469
1989	4,223	1,565,123
1990	4,137	1,607,407
1991	4,158	1,605,970
1992	4,166	1,710,998
1993	4,1209	1,708,028

Source: U.S. Department of the Interior. Minerals Management Service. Royalty Management Program. *Mineral Revenues 1993: Report on Receipts from Federal and Indian Leases.* Washington, DC: Minerals Management Service, p. 97.

★ 800 ★

Minerals

Oil and Gas Leases on Indian Lands, by State

Data show number of leases and total acreage of producing and producible Indian onshore oil and gas leases, by state, as of December 31, 1993.

State	Number	Acres
Arizona	15	69,096
Colorado	170	457,362
Michigan	3	60
Montana	444	106,743
New Mexico	465	555,296
North Dakota	36	7,511
Oklahoma	2,087	201,649
South Dakota	1	160
Texas	8	3,267
Utah	789	255,437
Wyoming	91	51,447
Total	4,109	1,708,028

Source: U.S. Department of the Interior. Minerals Management Service. Royalty Management Program. *Mineral Revenues 1993: Report on Receipts from Federal and Indian Leases.* Washington, DC: Minerals Management Service, p. 96.

★ 801 ★

Minerals

Other Minerals Leased on Indian Lands, by State

Data show number of leases and total acreage for producing Indian onshore leases of various minerals, as of December 31, 1993.

State/mineral	Leases	Acres
Arizona		
Copper	3	6,734
Sand-gravel	4	796
Silica sand	1	640
California		
Sand-gravel	4	1,545
Idaho		
Phosphate	20	4,022
Nevada		
Sand-gravel	1	100
New Mexico		
Gypsum	1	800
Sand-gravel	9	1,870
Oklahoma		
Chat	3	265
Limestone	1	18
Sand-gravel	5	4,556

[Continued]

★ 801 ★

Other Minerals Leased on Indian Lands, by State
[Continued]

State/mineral	Leases	Acres
Washington Sand-gravel	7	224
Total	59	21,570

Source: U.S. Department of the Interior. Minerals Management Service. Royalty Management Program. *Mineral Revenues 1993: Report on Receipts from Federal and Indian Leases.* Washington, DC: Minerals Management Service, pp. 100-101.

Tobacco

★ 802 ★

Tax Exempt Cigarette Sales on Indian Reservations

Number of packs sold and state tax revenue losses are shown, by state, FY 1983[1].

State	Sales (thousands of packs)	Percent of total sales	Revenue loss (in thousands of dollars)[2]
United States, total	189,822	0.6	43,130
Alabama	0	0	0
Alaska	0	0	0
Arizona	27,397	8.6	4,657
Arkansas	0	0	0
California	115[3]	[4]	17
Colorado	Minimal	-	-
Connecticut	0	0	0
Delaware	0	0	0
Washington D.C.	0	0	0
Florida	59,777	4.5	15,542
Georgia	0	0	0
Hawaii	0	0	0
Idaho	5,399	5.0	707
Illinois	0	0	0
Indiana	0	0	0
Iowa	0	0	0
Kansas	180	[4]	34
Kentucky	0	0	0
Louisiana	0	0	0
Maine	0	0	0
Maryland	0	0	0
Massachusetts	0	0	0

[Continued]

★ 802 ★

Tax Exempt Cigarette Sales on Indian Reservations
[Continued]

State	Sales (thousands of packs)	Percent of total sales	Revenue loss (in thousands of dollars)[2]
Michigan	169	[4]	42
Minnesota	2,026	0.4	486
Mississippi	0	0	0
Missouri	0	0	0
Montana	15,902	17.4	2,544
Nebraska	4,002	2.3	880
Nevada	3,324	2.4	690
New Hampshire	0	0	0
New Jersey	0	0	0
New Mexico	13,476	10.3	2,021
New York	6,356	0.3	1,525
North Carolina	0	0	0
North Dakota	1,050	1.3	231
Ohio	0	0	0
Oklahoma	9,295	2.1	1,673
Oregon	500	0.2	94
Pennsylvania	0	0	0
Rhode Island	0	0	0
South Carolina	0	0	0
South Dakota	139[5]	0.2	21
Tennessee	0	0	0
Texas	0	0	0
Utah	NA[6]	-	-
Vermont	0	0	0
Virginia	0	0	0
Washington	21,427	4.9	6,214
West Virginia	0	0	0
Wisconsin	19,132	3.8	5,740
Wyoming	156[1,7]	0.2	122

Source: Advisory Commission on Intergovernment Relations. *Cigarette Tax Evasion: A Second Look.* Washington, DC: ACIR, March 1985, Table 3-9. Primary source: Compiled by ACIR staff from data provided by state revenue departments. *Notes:* The data for Indian reservations were provided by state tax administrators. In the case of South Dakota, the information was obtained from the Minnesota revenue department as the Indians in South Dakota are supplied by a Minnesota wholesaler. 1. Montana and Nebraska figures are for CY 1983. Wyoming number is for FY 1984. 2. Losses are based on state cigarette and sales tax rates as of November 1, 1983. 3. Minimum estimate. 4. Less than 0.1 percent. 5. Total sales on Indian reservations are 1,384,400 packs. Only this small amount is not taxed. 6. NA is not explained in the original text. 7. Total sales are 260,000 packs; 40 percent are taxed.

Chapter 9
LAND AND WATER MANAGEMENT

░░

Land Ownership

░░

★ 803 ★

Largest 10 Reservations

Navajo
Windriver
Pine Ridge
San Carlos
Fort Apache
Hopi
Crow
Cheyenne River
Tohono O'Odham
Yakima

Acreage is shown for the ten largest Indian reservations.

Reservation (state)	Acreage (millions)
Navajo (Arizona, New Mexico, Utah)	16.0
Windriver (Wyoming)	1.9
Pine Ridge (South Dakota)	1.8
San Carlos (Arizona)	1.8
Fort Apache (Arizona)	1.7
Hopi (Arizona)	1.6
Crow (Montana)	1.5
Cheyenne River (South Dakota)	1.4
Tohono O'Odham (Arizona)[1]	1.2
Yakima (Washington)	1.1

Source: "Indians will ask Clinton to live up to expectations." *Detroit News* (24 April 1994), p. 5A. Primary source: Bureau of Indian Affairs. *Note:* 1. Formerly Papago.

★ 804 ★

Land Ownership

Federally Recognized Reservations, by Acreage, State, and Population, 1990 - I

Reservation	State	Acreage	Tribal land	Population	Indians
Poarch Creek	AL	213	213	212	149
Camp Verde	AZ	653	653	618	569
Cocopah	AZ	6,009	6,009	515	436
Fort Apache	AZ	1,664,972	1,664,972	10,394	9,825
Fort McDowell	AZ	24,680	24,680	640	560
Fort Yuma	AZ-CA	43,561	35,435	2,084	1,160
Gila Bend	AZ	10,404	10,404	0	0
Gila River	AZ	371,933	274,278	9,540	9,116
Havasupai	AZ	188,077	188,077	423	400
Hopi	AZ	1,561,213	1,560,993	7,360	7,061
Hualapai	AZ	992,463	992,463	822	802
Kaibab	AZ	120,413	120,413	165	102
Maricopa (AK-Chin)	AZ	21,840	21,840	446	405
Tohono O'Odham (Papago)	AZ	2,774,450	2,773,850	8,730	8,480
Pascua Yaqui	AZ	895	895	2,412	2,284
Payson Community	AZ	85	85	102	97
Salt River	AZ	50,506	26,072	4,852	3,533
San Carlos	AZ	1,826,541	1,826,541	7,294	7,110
San Juan Southern Paiute	AZ	0	0	204	204
San Xavier	AZ	71,095	30,412	1,172	1,073
Yavapai	AZ	1,398	1,398	176	134
Colorado River	AZ-CA	225,995	220,116	7,865	2,345
Fort Mojave	AZ-CA-NV	32,697	32,697	758	592
Navajo	AZ-NM-UT	15,662,413	14,715,093	148,451	143,405
Aqua Caliente Reservation	CA	23,173	2,139	20,206	117
Alturas Rancheria	CA	20	20	5	5
Augustine Reservation	CA	502	342	0	0
Barona Rancheria	CA	5,181	5,181	537	373
Benton Paiute Reservation	CA	160	160	63	52
Berry Creek Rancheria	CA	33	33	2	2
Big Bend Rancheria	CA	40	40	3	3
Big Lagoon Rancheria	CA	20	9	22	19
Big Pine Reservation	CA	279	279	452	331
Big Sandy Reservation	CA	76	...	51	38
Big Valley Reservation	CA	38	38	108	90
Bishop Reservation	CA	875	875	1,408	935
Blue Lake Rancheria	CA	4	0	58	30
Bridgeport Indian Colony	CA	40	40	49	37
Buena Vista	CA	0	...	1	1
Cabazon Reservation	CA	1,382	954	819	20
Cahuilla Reservation	CA	18,884	18,272	104	82
Campo Reservation	CA	15,480	15,010	281	143
Capitain Grande Reservation	CA	15,753	15,753	0	0
Cedarville Rancheria	CA	20	17	8	6
Chemehuevi Reservation	CA	30,654		358	95

[Continued]

★ 804 ★

Federally Recognized Reservations, by Acreage, State, and Population, 1990 - I
[Continued]

Reservation	State	Acreage	Tribal land	Population	Indians
Chicken Ranch Rancheria	CA	3	3	73	10
Cloverdale Rancheria	CA	0	0	1	1
Cold Springs Rancheria	CA	155	155	192	159
Colusa Rancheria	CA	273	278	22	19
Cortina Rancheria	CA	640	640	30	22
Coyote Valley Rancheria	CA	58	58	135	122
Cuyapaipe Reservation	CA	4,103	4,100	0	0
Dry Creek Rancheria	CA	75	75	75	38
Elk Valley Rancheria	CA	0	0	77	32
Enterprise Rancheria	CA	40	40	5	5
Fort Bidwell Reservation	CA	3,335	3,335	118	107
Fort Independence Reservation	CA	234	234	69	38
Greenville Rancheria	CA	0		24	7
Grindstone Rancheria	CA	80	80	103	102
Hoopa Valley	CA	85,445	85,432	2,143	1,733
Hopland Rancheria	CA	48	22	189	142
Inaja-Cosmit Reservation	CA	852	852	0	0
Jackson Rancheria	CA	331	331	21	13
Jamul Indian Village	CA	6	6	0	0
Karuk Tribe	CA	243	11	421	33
La Jolla Reservation	CA	8,541	7,588	152	121
La Posta Reservation	CA	3,556	3,672	10	3
Laytonville Rancheria	CA	200	200	142	129
Likely Rancheria	CA	1	1	0	0
Lone Pine Reservation	CA	237	237	244	168
Lookout Rancheria	CA	40	40	17	12
Los Coyotes Rancheria	CA	25,049	25,049	58	42
Manchester Point Rancheria	CA	363	363	200	178
Manzanita Reservation	CA	3,579	3,579	84	47
Mesa Grande Reservation	CA	20	120	96	72
Middletown Rancheria	CA	109	109	79	18
Montgomery Creek Rancheria	CA	72	72	11	9
Mooretown	CA	0	0	225	79
Morongo Reservation	CA	32,362	30,968	1,072	1,070
North Fork Rancheria	CA	80	0	4	0
Pala Reservation	CA	11,893	10,319	1,071	563
Pauma & Yulma Reservation	CA	5,877	5,877	148	137
Pechanga reservation	CA	4,394	2,626	398	289
Picayune Rancheria	CA	29	0	32	15
Pinoleville Rancheria	CA	3	0	130	77
Potter Valley Rancheria	CA	3		1	1
Quartz Valley Rancheria	CA	24	0	124	19
Ramona Reservation	CA	560	560	0	0
Redding Rancheria	CA	31	0	101	79
Redwood Valley Rancheria	CA	170	170	142	14

[Continued]

★ 804 ★

Federally Recognized Reservations, by Acreage, State, and Population, 1990 - I

[Continued]

Reservation	State	Acreage	Tribal land	Population	Indians
Resighini Rancheria	CA	228	228	28	26
Rincon Reservation	CA	4,276	3,612	1,352	379
Roaring Creek Rancheria	CA	80	80	18	18
Robinson Rancheria	CA	103	68	139	113
Rohnerville Rancheria	CA	0	0	8	8
Round Valley Reservation	CA	30,538	13,601	1,183	577
Rumsey Rancheria	CA	185	185	8	4
San Manuel Reservation	CA	658	658	80	56
San Pasqual Reservation	CA	1,380	1,380	512	212
Santa Rosa Rancheria	CA	170	179	323	284
Santa Rosa Reservation	CA	11,093	11,093	50	37
Santa Ynez Reservation	CA	127	127	279	213
Santa Ysabel Reservation	CA	15,527	15,527	169	150
Sheep Ranch Rancheria	CA	1	1	0	0
Sherwood Valley Rancheria	CA	350	292	15	9
Shingle Springs Rancheria	CA	160	160	18	7
Smith River Rancheria	CA	30	0	104	72
Soboba Reservation	CA	5,916	5,036	369	308
Stewart's Point Rancheria	CA	40	40	91	86
Sulphur Bank Rancheria	CA	50	50	93	90
Susanville Rancheria	CA	150	150	454	154
Sycuan Reservation	CA	640	371	4	0
Table Bluff Rancheria	CA	...	0	48	43
Table Mountain Rancheria	CA	61	37	51	48
Timbi-Sha W. Shoshone	CA	40	40	55	55
Torres-Martinez Reservation	CA	24,024	18,223	4,462	143
Trinidad Rancheria	CA	47	44	78	59
Tule River Reservation	CA	55,356	55,356	798	745
Tuolumne Rancheria	CA	336	336	135	107
Twenty-Nine Palms Reservation	CA	402	402	0	0
Upper Lake Rancheria	CA	19	0	76	28
Viejas Reservation	CA	1,609	1,609	411	227
XL Ranch	CA	9,255	9,255	35	27
Yurok Tribe	CA	3,669	3,669	1,357	463
Southern Ute	CO	310,002	307,561	7,804	1,044
Ute Mountain	CO-NM-UT	477,850	477,850	1,320	1,264
Mashantucket Pequot	CT	1,201	1,201	83	55
Big Cypress	FL	42,728	42,728	484	447
Brighton	FL	35,805	35,805	524	402
Hollywood	FL	481	481	1,394	481
Miccosukee	FL	75,146	74,812	94	94
Sac & Fox	IA	3,540	3,535	577	564
Omaha	IA-NE	26,792	9,596	5,227	1,908
Coeur d'Alene	ID	67,981	21,268	5,802	749
Duck Valley	ID	289,819	289,819	1,101	1,022

[Continued]

★ 804 ★

Federally Recognized Reservations, by Acreage, State, and Population, 1990 - I

[Continued]

Reservation	State	Acreage	Tribal land	Population	Indians
Fort Hall	ID	522,510	260,837	5,114	3,035
Kootenai	ID	2,072	18	65	61
Nez Perce	ID	85,661	36,409	16,160	1,863
Iowa	KS	1,072	866	172	83
Kickapoo	KS	6,660	3,505	478	370
Pottawatomi	KS	21,479	2,939	279	502
Sac & Fox	KS-NE	354	309	210	49
Chitimacha	LA	283	283	286	212
Coushatta	LA	154	154	36	33
Tunica-Biloxi	LA	134	134	29	16
Indian Township	ME	23,000	23,000	617	541
Penobscot	ME	127,838	60,143	517	430
Pleasant Point	ME	200	200	572	523
Bay Mills	MI	2,209	2,209	461	403
Grand Traverse	MI	...	...	228	208

Source: Russell, George. *The American Indian in Question.* Phoenix, AZ: Thunderbird Enterprises, Copyright 1992, pp. 13-18. Published with permission. *Notes:* Three dots (...) indicates that data were not available at the time of the original source's publication.

★ 805 ★

Land Ownership

Federally Recognized Reservations, by Acreage, State, and Population, 1990 - II

Reservation	State	Acreage	Tribal land	Population	Indians
Hannahville Community	MI	3,411	3,411	181	173
Isabella	MI	138,240	676	22,944	795
Lac Vieux Desert	MI	104	104	124	119
L'Anse	MI	13,765	5,764	3,293	724
Sault Ste. Marie	MI	293	293	768	554
Nett Lake	MN	41,864	30,354	358	346
Deer Creek	MN	...	...	186	6
Fond du Lac	MN	21,932	4,898	3,229	1,106
Grand Portage	MN	44,844	37,679	306	207
Leech Lake	MN	27,853	15,530	8,669	3,390
Lower Sioux Community	MN	1,745	1,745	259	225
Mille Lacs	MN	3,863	3,795	470	428
Prairie Island Community	MN	571	571	60	56
Red Lake	MN	564,452	564,452	3,699	3,602
Sandy Lake	MN	...	...	37	36
Shakopee	MN	293	293	203	153

[Continued]

★ 805 ★

Federally Recognized Reservations, by Acreage, State, and Population, 1990 - II

[Continued]

Reservation	State	Acreage	Tribal land	Population	Indians
Upper Sioux Community	MN	745	745	49	43
Vermillion Lake	MN	...	...	91	87
White Earth	MN	56,078	54,125	8,727	2,759
Mississippi Choctaw	MS	17,926	17,715	4,073	3,932
Blackfeet	MT	937,838	302,072	8,849	7,025
Crow	MT	1,517,406	408,444	6,370	4,724
Flathead	MT	627,070	581,907	21,259	5,130
Fort Belknap	MT	588,756	188,017	2,508	2,338
Fort Peck	MT	904,683	391,769	10,595	5,782
Rocky Boy's	MT	108,334	108,334	1,954	1,882
Northern Cheyenne	MT	436,948	318,072	3,923	3,542
Santee Sioux	NE	9,358	6,943	758	425
Winnebago	NE	27,538	4,241	2,341	1,156
Eastern Cherokee	NC	56,573	56,461	6,527	5,388
Devils Lake Sioux	ND	53,239	16,229	3,588	2,676
Fort Behold	ND	419,362	69,509	5,395	2,999
Turtle Mountain	ND	33,319	8,618	7,106	6,772
Acoma Pueblo	NM	263,611	263,291	2,590	2,551
Alamo (Navajo)	NM	63,108	43,335	1,271	1,228
Canoncito	NM	76,813	68,144	1,189	1,177
Cochiti Pueblo	NM	50,669	50,669	1,342	666
Isleta Pueblo	NM	211,034	211,026	2,915	2,699
Jemez Pueblo	NM	89,619	89,617	1,750	1,738
Jicarilla Apache	NM	823,580	823,580	2,617	2,375
Laguna Pueblo	NM	461,099	458,933	3,731	3,634
Mescalero Apache	NM	460,678	460,678	2,695	2,516
Nambe Pueblo	NM	19,076	19,076	1,402	329
Picuris Pueblo	NM	14,947	14,947	1,882	147
Pojoaque Pueblo	NM	11,602	11,602	2,556	177
Ramah Community	NM	146,953	99,353	194	191
Sandia Pueblo	NM	22,871	22,871	3,971	358
San Felipe Pueblo	NM	48,930	48,859	2,434	1,859
San Ildefonso Pueblo	NM	26,196	26,196	1,499	347
SAn Juan Pueblo	NM	12,237	12,235	5,209	1,276
Santa Ana Pueblo	NM	61,414	61,414	593	481
Santa Clara Pueblo	NM	45,748	45,744	10,193	1,246
Santo Domingo Pueblo	NM	69,260	69,260	2,992	2,947
Taos Pueblo	NM	95,341	95,334	4,745	1,212
Tesuque Pueblo	NM	16,813	16,811	697	232
Zia Pueblo	NM	117,680	117,680	637	637
Zuni Pueblo	NM-AZ	409,182	406,969	7,412	7,073
Carson Colony	NV	160	160	248	235
Dresslerville Colony	NV	40	40	152	144
Duckwater	NV	3,815	3,815	135	115
Ely Colony	NV	100	100	59	52

[Continued]

★ 805 ★

Federally Recognized Reservations, by Acreage, State, and Population, 1990 - II
[Continued]

Reservation	State	Acreage	Tribal land	Population	Indians
Fallon Colony & Res	NV	8,180	3,540	546	506
Fort McDermitt	NV-OR	16,497	16,352	396	387
Las Vegas Colony	NV	3,723	3,723	80	72
Lovelock Colony	NV	20	20	94	80
Moapa River	NV	71,955	71,955	375	190
Pyramid Lake	NV	476,689	476,689	1,388	959
Reno-Sparks Colony	NV	29	29	264	262
Summit Lake	NV	10,863	10,098	7	6
Te-Moak	NV	13,050	13,050	949	831
Walker River	NV	323,406	313,690	802	620
Washoe	NV	3,672	3,672	157	65
Winnemucca Colony	NV	340	340	67	61
Yerington	NV	1,632	1,632	428	324
Yomba	NV	4,718	4,718	95	88
Goshute	NV-UT	7,489	7,489	99	98
Allegany	NY	30,984	...	7,315	1,062
Cattaraugus	NY	22,013	...	2,178	2,051
Oil Springs	NY	640	...	5	0
Oneida	NY	32	...	37	37
Onondaga	NY	7,300	...	771	2
St. Regis Mohawk	NY	14,640	...	1,978	1,923
Tonawanda	NY	495	...	501	453
Tuscarora	NY	5,778	...	772	310
Osage	OK	168,794	675	41,645	6,161
Burns Paiute	OR	11,466	932	163	151
Coos, Lower Umpqua & Siuslaw	OR	6	6	4	1
Cow Creek	OR	28	28	58	11
Grand Ronde	OR	9,811	9,811	57	1
Siletz	OR	3,673	3,673	5	0
Umatilla	OR	85,256	16,643	2,502	1,029
Warm Springs	OR	643,507	592,143	3,076	2,820
Narragansett	RI	...	...	31	17
Cheyenne River	SD	1,395,905	954,398	7,743	5,100
Crow Creek	SD	125,483	65,018	1,756	1,531
Flandreau Santee Sioux	SD	2,183	3,183	279	249
Lower Brule	SD	130,239	104,244	1,123	994
Pine Ridge	SD-NE	1,780,444	709,112	12,215	11,182
Standing Rock	SD-ND	847,254	356,039	7,956	4,870
Lake Traverse (Sisseton)	SD-ND	105,543	17,104	10,733	2,821
Rosebud	SD	954,572	529,954	9,696	8,043
Yankton	SD	36,559	16,706	6,269	1,994
Alabama-Coushatta	TX	4,600	4,600	478	477
Ysleta Del Sur Pueblo	TX	...	...	292	211
Northwestern Shoshoni	UT	...	...	0	0
Paiute	UT	425	425	645	323

[Continued]

★ 805 ★

Federally Recognized Reservations, by Acreage, State, and Population, 1990 - II
[Continued]

Reservation	State	Acreage	Tribal land	Population	Indians
Skull Valley	UT	17,445	17,284	32	32
Uintah & Ouray	UT	1,021,558	1,007,238	17,224	2,650
Chehalis	WA	2,076	76	491	308
Colville	WA	1,063,043	1,023,640	6,957	3,788
Hoh	WA	443	443	96	74
Jamestown Klallam	WA	11	8	22	4
Kalispel	WA	4,557	1,970	100	91
Lower Elwah	WA	427	427	137	130
Lummi	WA	7,678	635	3,147	1,594
Makah	WA	27,244	24,967	1,214	940
Muckleshoot	WA	1,275	106	3,841	864
Nisqually	WA	930	195	578	365
Nooksack	WA	1	1	556	412
Ozette	WA	719	719	12	0
Port Gamble	WA	1,303	1,303	552	377
Port Madison	WA	2,872	86	4,834	388
Puyallup	WA	103	73	32,406	937
Quileute	WA	814	804	381	303
Quinault	WA	129,221	7,466	1,216	943
Sauk-Suiettle	WA	23	23	124	69
Shoalwater	WA	335	335	131	66
Skokomish	WA	2,987	162	614	431
Spokane	WA	133,302	105,383	1,502	1,229
Squaxin Island	WA	971	145	157	127
Stillaquamish	WA	...	...	113	96
Swinomish	WA	3,602	565	2,282	585
Tulalip	WA	10,667	7,511	7,103	1,204
Upper Skagit	WA	74	74	180	162
Yakima	WA	1,130,286	904,411	27,668	6,307
Bad River	WI	56,558	23,451	1,070	868
Lac Courte Oreilles	WI	48,139	22,062	2,408	1,771
Lac du Flambeau	WI	44,726	30,344	2,434	1,432
Menominee	WI	222,552	222,552	3,397	3,182
Oneida	WI	2,751	2,366	18,033	2,447
Potawatomi	WI	11,692	11,292	1,082	266
Red Cliff	WI	7,495	5,458	857	727
St. Croix	WI	1,940	1,940	505	462
Sokaogon Chippewa Community	WI	1,694	1,694	357	311
Stockbridge	WI	15,603	15,447	581	447
Wisconsin Winnebago	WI	4,245	632	700	570
Wind River	WY	1,888,558	1,793,420	21,851	5,676

Source: Russell, George. *The American Indian in Question.* Phoenix, AZ: Thunderbird Enterprises, Copyright 1992, pp. 13-18. Published with permission. *Notes:* Three dots (...) indicates that data were not available at the time of the original sources publication.

★ 806 ★

Land Ownership

How Some Sovereign Nations Compare in Size to Selected Indian Areas

Indian areas are shown in boldface type.

Nation/Tribe	Square miles
Navajo	21,838
Costa Rica	19,575
Dominican Republic	18,816
Bhutan	18,147
Denmark	16,619
Switzerland	15,941
Netherlands	14,125
Taiwan	13,886
Belgium	11,781
Lesotho	11,716
Albania	11,100
Equatorial Guinea	10,852
Burundi	10,747
Haiti	10,714
Rwanda	10,166
El Salvador	8,260
Israel	7,993
Fiji	7,055
Swaziland	6,704
Kuwait	6,178
Qatar	6,000
Papago	4,460
Jamaica	4,411
Lebanon	4,015
Gambia	4,005
Hopi	3,862
Cyprus	3,572
White Mountain Apache	2,947
Wind River tribes	2,947
San Carlos Apache	2,855
Pine Ridge Sioux	2,600
Crow tribe	2,434
Cheyenne River Sioux	2,210
Yakima tribe	1,711
Uintah and Ouray	1,581
Colville tribe	1,569
Hualapai tribe	1,551
Fort Peck Sioux	1,534
Rosebud Sioux	1,526
Blackfeet tribe	1,420
Standing Rock Sioux	1,320
Jicarilla Apache tribe	1,159
Trinidad and Tobago	1,979
Western Samoa	1,130

[Continued]

★ 806 ★

How Some Sovereign Nations Compare in Size to Selected Indian Areas

[Continued]

Nation/Tribe	Square miles
Fort Belknap	1,027
Luxembourg	999
Flathead tribe	960
Ute Mountain Ute	917
Red Lake Chippewa	882
Warm Springs tribe	881
Fort Hall Shoshone	817
Pyramid Lake Paiute	742
Mauritius	720
Mescalero Apache	719
Northern Cheyenne	678
Laguna Pueblo	652
Fort Berthold	651
Zuni Pueblo	636
Sisseston	629
Pima	582
Walker River	500
Tonga	269
Bahrain	231
Singapore	226
Quinault	200
Kaibab Piute	188
Andorra	179
Barbados	166
Rocky Boy's Chippewa-Cree	162
Nez Perce	137
Hoopa Valley	134
Malta	122
Maldives	112
Coeur d'Alene	108
Liechtenstein	62
San Marino	23.50
Nauru	8
Monaco	.60
Vatican City	.17

Source: Deloria, Jr., Vine. *Behind the Trail of Broken Treaties: An Indian Declaration of Independence*. Austin, TX: University of Texas Press, pp. 166-168. Published with permission.

★ 807 ★

Land Ownership

Land Ownership of Lands Under BIA Jurisdiction, by Selected Reservation and Indian Ownership, 1991

The number of tracts owned is shown, by selected reservation and type of ownership, 1991.

Reservation	Number of tracts owned solely by -			Number tracts with multiple owners		Total tracts
	One Indian	Tribe	Others	At least one Indian owner	No Indian owners	
Blackfeet	1,640	1,800	18	3,571	7	7,036
Cheyenne River	2,103	5,549	11	2,809	2	10,474
Colville	771	2,744	17	1,884	66	5,482
Crow	2,244	823	44	3,696	3	6,810
Fort Berthold	1,831	4,243	16	2,610	8	8,708
Fort Peck	1,928	1,232	7	3,702	27	6,896
Pine Ridge	2,409	3,435	85	4,726	6	10,661
Rosebud	629	2,766	7	2,961	47	6,410
Standing Rock	1,483	2,363	6	5,402	13	9,267
Turtle Mountain	401	101	5	409	1	917
Wind River	845	1,186	22	2,128	47	4,228
Yakima	916	2,892	15	2,236	30	6,089
Total	17,200	29,134	253	36,134	257	82,978

Source: U.S. General Accounting Office. *Indian Programs: Profile of the Land Ownership at 12 Reservations* (GAO/RCED-92-96BR). Washington, DC: U.S. GAO, February 1992, p. 12.

★ 808 ★

Land Ownership

Land Tract Owners on Selected Reservations, 1991

The number of Indian owners is shown, by selected reservation and tribal membership status, for 1991.

Reservation	Indian Owners		
	Members	Non-Members	Total[1]
Blackfeet	4,715	508	5,223
Cheyenne River	4,586	514	5,100
Colville	3,665	499	4,164
Crow	3,143	144	3,287
Fort Berthold	3,232	137	3,369
Fort Peck	5,743	728	6,471
Pine Ridge	12,910	2,490	15,400
Rosebud	9,811	2,226	12,037
Standing Rock	10,333	1,254	11,587
Turtle Mountain	4,524	126	4,650
Wind River	3,904	888	4,792

[Continued]

★ 808 ★

Land Tract Owners on Selected Reservations, 1991
[Continued]

Reservation	Indian Owners		
	Members	Non-Members	Total[1]
Yakima	3,508	273	3,781
Total	70,074	9,787	79,861

Source: U.S. General Accounting Office. *Indian Programs: Profile of Land Ownership at 12 Reservations* (GAO/RCED-92-96BR). Washington, DC: U.S. GAO, February 1992, p. 24. *Notes:* 1. Coding errors in the BIA database led to some double counting of the Indian owners; therefore, the total number of Indian owners is slightly overstated.

★ 809 ★

Land Ownership

Land Tract Ownership Records, by Selected Reservation and Size of Ownership Interest, 1991

The number of ownership records the BIA maintains is shown, by selected reservation and size of ownership interest, for 1991. As shown in the table, over 620,000 (about 67 percent) of the Indian individual ownership records are for interests of 2 percent or less.

Reservation	Number of records with percentage ownership interest of -						Total Indian records[1]
	100	51-99	26-50	11-25	3-10	2 or less	
Blackfeet	1,541	203	1,957	6,673	24,325	69,224	113,923
Cheyenne River	2,028	70	2,198	5,748	12,011	14,487	36,542
Colville	776	151	1,173	2,443	6,859	14,323	25,725
Crow	2,078	465	2,449	7,239	22,931	74,498	109,660
Fort Berthold	1,891	170	1,510	4,909	14,356	38,793	61,629
Fort Peck	1,932	195	2,444	6,710	19,000	47,040	77,321
Pine Ridge	2,198	209	2,855	8,212	24,559	81,881	119,914
Rosebud	566	72	1,203	4,024	14,968	73,758	94,591
Standing Rock	1,326	134	2,854	10,153	36,743	95,570	146,780
Turtle Mountain	423	43	251	795	2,250	9,760	13,522
Wind River	804	187	923	3,012	13,087	65,950	83,963
Yakima	914	226	1,302	3,622	12,174	25,228	43,465
Total	16,477	2,125	21,119	63,540	203,263	620,511	927,035

Source: U.S. General Accounting Office. *Indian Programs: Profile of the Land Ownership at 12 Reservations* (GAO/RCED-92-96BR). Washington, DC: U.S. GAO, February 1992, p. 23. *Notes:* 1. This distribution excludes historical records for original allottees no longer having any ownership interests in the land and for 24 other Indians with less than one ten-millionth of one percent ownership interests.

★ 810 ★

Land Ownership

Land Tract Ownership Records, by Selected Reservation and Type of Ownership Interest, 1991

The number of ownership records the BIA maintains is shown, by selected reservation and type of ownership, for 1991.

Reservation	Number of ownership records				Total ownership records
	Tribal interests	Individual Indians	Non-Indians	Other[1]	
Blackfeet	5,235	115,514	2,784	789	124,322
Cheyenne River	9,005	37,182	377	32	46,596
Colville	4,949	28,471	1,381	107	34,908
Crow	3,120	111,825	783	724	116,452
Fort Berthold	7,684	64,096	582	62	72,424
Fort Peck	2,572	79,110	2,021	50	83,753
Pine Ridge	16,660	121,126	800	156	138,742
Rosebud	24,309	95,684	1,169	108	121,270
Standing Rock	9,526	147,517	2,065	243	159,351
Turtle Mountain	494	13,699	504	20	14,717
Wind River	4,548	86,128	1,245	895	92,816
Yakima	6,226	47,808	212	85	54,331
Total	94,328	948,160	13,923	3,271	1,059,682

Source: U.S. General Accounting Office. *Indian Programs: Profile of the Land Ownership at 12 Reservations* (GAO/RCED-92-96BR) Washington, DC: U.S. GAO, February 1992, p. 22. *Note:* 1. Other includes corporations and government.

★ 811 ★

Land Ownership

Land Tract Ownership Records, by Selected Reservation and Type of Surface, 1991

The number of ownership records the BIA maintains is shown, by selected reservation and type of surface, for 1991[1].

Reservation	Number of records maintained for tract ownership of -			Total ownership records[2]
	Surface only	Subsurface only	Both surface & subsurface	
Blackfeet	64,924	36,662	22,708	124,294
Cheyenne River	7,842	23,180	15,574	46,596
Colville	5,459	19,970	9,577	34,906
Crow	38,487	33,544	44,406	116,437
Fort Berthold	25,614	41,011	5,799	72,424
Fort Peck	12,239	38,090	33,424	83,753
Pine Ridge	11,521	24,206	103,015	138,742
Rosebud	19,645	37,620	64,005	121,270
Standing Rock	18,658	80,027	60,666	159,351

[Continued]

★ 811 ★

Land Tract Ownership Records, by Selected Reservation and Type of Surface, 1991
[Continued]

Reservation	Number of records maintained for tract ownership of -			Total ownership records[2]
	Surface only	Subsurface only	Both surface & subsurface	
Turtle Mountain	3,297	3,722	7,698	14,717
Wind River	25,496	52,753	14,564	92,813
Yakima	952	6,739	46,598	54,289
Total	234,134	397,524	427,934	1,059,592

Source: U.S. General Accounting Office. *Indian Programs: Profile of the Land Ownership at 12 Reservations* (GAO/RCED-92-96BR), Washington, DC: U.S. GAO, February 1992, p. 21. *Notes:* 1. Land held for individual Indians and tribes includes both surface and subsurface (oil, gas, and mineral) components. These are accounted for as separate tracts when their ownership differs; they are otherwise treated as one tract. The BIA does not maintain records for land tracts that have been sold or transferred to non-Indian ownership and are, therefore, no longer the responsibility of the Interior Department. 2. Excludes 90 records where the tract resource code was not specified.

★ 812 ★

Land Ownership

Land Tracts Under BIA Jurisdiction, by Selected Reservation and Degree of Individual Indian Ownership Interests, 1991

Figures are shown, by selected reservation, for 1991. To illustrate extreme cases of an Indian individual having ownership interest in many tracts, this table shows both the number of tracts and the number of separate ownership interests held by an Indian individual at each of the 12 reservations. It also shows the number of tracts where the Indian individual's interest is 2 percent or less.

Reservation	Number of tracts	Ownership interests	Number of tracts with ownership of 2 percent or less
Blackfeet	113	301	68
Cheyenne River	41	93	23
Colville	19	75	3
Crow	241	616	151
Fort Berthold	82	203	30
Fort Peck	73	191	2
Pine Ridge	44	199	19
Rosebud	50	150	36
Standing Rock	112	195	70
Turtle Mountain	2	58	0

[Continued]

★ 812 ★

Land Tracts Under BIA Jurisdiction, by Selected Reservation and Degree of Individual Indian Ownership Interests, 1991
[Continued]

Reservation	Number of tracts	Ownership interests	Number of tracts with ownership of 2 percent or less
Wind River	194	413	98
Yakima	95	121	34

Source: U.S. General Accounting Office. *Indian Programs: Profile of the Land Ownership at 12 Reservations* (GAO/RCED-92-96BR). Washington, DC: U.S. GAO, February 1992, p. 18.

★ 813 ★

Land Ownership

Land Tracts Under BIA Jurisdiction, by Selected Reservation and Individual Indian Ownership With Multiple Tract Ownership, 1991

The number of consolidated interests is shown, by selected reservation, for 1991.

Reservation	Number of Indians with ownership in -								Total Indian owners
	1 tract	2 tracts	3-5 tracts	6-10 tracts	11-25 tracts	26-50 tracts	51-100 tracts	Over 100 tracts	
Blackfeet	794	464	730	939	1,260	787	217	30	5,221
Cheyenne River	1,282	635	1,391	973	717	90	5	0	5,093
Colville	1,408	623	878	562	568	40	1	0	4,080
Crow	618	303	405	295	568	569	441	85	3,284
Fort Berthold	494	309	456	555	965	471	112	0	3,362
Fort Peck	1,585	1,001	1,080	860	1,392	463	50	2	6,433
Pine Ridge	4,346	2,056	3,229	2,791	2,597	368	13	0	15,400
Rosebud	3,025	2,196	2,582	2,038	1,808	373	12	0	12,034
Standing Rock	2,741	1,296	2,523	1,428	2,180	1,241	165	6	11,580
Turtle Mountain	2,120	1,314	1,052	163	1	0	0	0	4,650
Wind River	726	668	842	728	1,066	644	158	8	4,840
Yakima	962	439	599	626	798	294	15	0	3,733
Total	20,101	11,304	15,767	11,958	13,920	5,340	1,189	131	79,710

Source: U.S. General Accounting Office. *Indian Programs: Profile of the Land Ownership at 12 Reservations* (GAO/RCED-92-96BR). Washington, DC: U.S. GAO, February 1992, p. 17.

★ 814 ★

Land Ownership

Land Tracts Under BIA Jurisdiction, by Selected Reservation and Largest Number of Owners on a Single Tract, 1991

Figures are shown for selected reservations in 1991.

Reservation	Indian owners	Other owners	Total owners	Indian interests of 2 percent or or less	Tribal affiliations represented
Blackfeet	242	43	285	240	3
Cheyenne River	223	10	233	214	9
Colville	120	18	138	112	6
Crow	345	2	347	338	4
Fort Berthold	243	23	266	229	7
Fort Peck	335	10	345	326	12
Pine Ridge	407	12	419	406	9
Rosebud	367	7	374	364	6
Standing Rock	531	11	542	523	16
Turtle Mountain	335	27	362	331	6
Wind River	317	5	322	310	5
Yakima	160	2	162	148	3

Source: U.S. General Accounting Office. *Indian Programs: Profile of the Land Ownership at 12 Reservations* (GAO/RCED-92-96BR). Washington, DC: U.S. GAO, February 1992, p. 16.

★ 815 ★

Land Ownership

Land Tracts Under BIA Jurisdiction, by Selected Reservation and Number of Indian Owners, 1991

The number of tracts owned is shown, by selected reservation and number of Indian owners, for 1991.

Reservation	Number of tracts with -							Total tracts
	Two Indian owners	3-10 Indian owners	11-25 Indian owners	26-50 Indian owners	51-100 Indian owners	101-300 Indian owners	Over 300 Indian owners	
Blackfeet	381	1,141	960	667	351	71	0	3,571
Cheyenne River	535	1,416	645	177	30	6	0	2,809
Colville	476	753	435	163	52	5	0	1,884
Crow	490	1,403	933	481	261	122	6	3,696
Fort Berthold	352	999	675	377	174	33	0	2,610
Fort Peck	635	1,447	987	422	179	31	1	3,702
Pine Ridge	634	1,840	1,234	588	283	145	2	4,726
Rosebud	296	1,021	770	468	266	135	5	2,961
Standing Rock	411	1,958	1,640	858	414	111	10	5,402
Turtle Mountain	81	139	102	40	25	21	1	409

[Continued]

★ 815 ★

Land Tracts Under BIA Jurisdiction, by Selected Reservation and Number of Indian Owners, 1991

[Continued]

Reservation	Number of tracts with -							Total tracts
	Two Indian owners	3-10 Indian owners	11-25 Indian owners	26-50 Indian owners	51-100 Indian owners	101-300 Indian owners	Over 300 Indian owners	
Wind River	169	561	611	371	270	145	1	2,128
Yakima	297	875	636	332	86	10	0	2,236
Total	4,757	13,553	9,628	4,944	2,391	835	26	36,134

Source: U.S. General Accounting Office. *Indian Programs: Profile of the Land Ownership at 12 Reservations* (GAO/RCED-92-96BR). Washington, DC: U.S. GAO, February 1992, p. 14.

★ 816 ★

Land Ownership

Land Tracts Under BIA Jurisdiction, by Selected Reservation and Shared Ownership, 1991

The number of tracts owned is shown, by selected reservation and shared ownership, for 1991.

Reservation	Number of tracts owned by -				Total tracts
	Indians only	Indians and the tribe	Indians and non-Indians	Indians, tribe, and non-Indians	
Blackfeet	1,830	646	534	561	3,571
Cheyenne River	2,097	430	241	41	2,809
Colville	741	533	404	206	1,884
Crow	2,564	631	265	236	3,969
Fort Berthold	1,543	646	206	215	2,610
Fort Peck	2,265	294	826	317	3,702
Pine Ridge	2,546	1,672	176	332	4,726
Rosebud	1,120	1,168	177	496	2,961
Standing Rock	3,000	1,072	683	647	5,402
Turtle Mountain	258	23	70	58	409
Wind River	979	565	178	406	2,128
Yakima	1,141	972	42	81	2,236
Total	20,084	8,652	3,802	3,596	36,134

Source: U.S. General Accounting Office. *Indian Programs: Profile of the Land Ownership at 12 Reservations* (GAO/RCED-92-96BR). Washington, DC: U.S. GAO, February 1992, p. 13.

★ 817 ★

Land Ownership

Land Tracts Under BIA Jurisdiction, by Selected Reservation and Size of Consolidated Indian Ownership, 1991

The number of consolidated interests is shown, by selected reservation and size of interest, for 1991. As the table shows, 431,074, or over 60 percent, of the consolidated Indian ownership is represented by interests of 2 percent or less.

Reservation	Number of consolidated ownership interests totaling -						Total
	100 percent	51-99 percent	26-50 percent	11-25 percent	3-10 percent	2 percent or less	
Blackfeet	1,709	416	1,935	6,306	20,983	48,899	80,248
Cheyenne River	2,119	194	2,188	5,386	9,402	10,257	29,546
Colville	854	249	1,066	2,093	5,787	10,180	20,229
Crow	2,189	755	2,225	6,941	18,503	48,094	78,707
Fort Berthold	1,981	340	1,384	4,813	11,890	26,494	46,902
Fort Peck	2,062	513	2,394	6,076	15,606	29,789	56,440
Pine Ridge	2,324	451	2,884	7,339	20,845	60,986	94,829
Rosebud	612	190	1,238	3,819	12,993	55,552	74,404
Standing Rock	1,444	371	3,008	9,852	32,140	70,372	117,187
Turtle Mountain	432	103	242	734	1,685	6,437	9,633
Wind River	892	255	891	3,078	11,325	46,437	62,878
Yakima	1,057	271	1,259	3,550	9,845	17,577	33,559
Total	17,675	4,108	20,714	59,987	171,004	431,074	704,562

Source: U.S. General Accounting Office. *Indian Programs: Profile of the Land Ownership at 12 Reservations* (GAO/RCED-92-96BR). Washington, DC: U.S. GAO, February 1992, p. 19.

★ 818 ★

Land Ownership

Land Tracts Under BIA Jurisdiction, by Selected Reservation and Smallest Individual Indian Ownership Interests, 1991

This table shows extreme examples of fractioned ownership at each reservation in terms of the size of the ownership interest. For each reservation, it shows the smallest interest held by an Indian individual and identifies the land equivalent of that ownership interest. In some cases, the land size equivalent is smaller than the dimensions of this page.

Reservation	Tract acreage	Percentage ownership of tract	Land equivalent of ownership interest	
			Square feet	Inches
Blackfeet	80.00	0.0002900	10.11	38.1 x 38.1
Cheyenne River	647.21	0.0004962	139.89	142.0 x 142.0
Colville	160.00	0.0006955	48.47	83.5 x 83.5
Crow	160.00	0.0000100	.70	10.0 x 10.0
Fort Berthold	80.00	0.0002624	9.15	36.3 x 36.3
Fort Peck	40.00	0.0001200	2.09	17.4 x 17.4
Pine Ridge	474.14	0.0000047	0.97	11.8 x 11.8

[Continued]

★ 818 ★

Land Tracts Under BIA Jurisdiction, by Selected Reservation and Smallest Individual Indian Ownership Interests, 1991

[Continued]

Reservation	Tract acreage	Percentage ownership of tract	Land equivalent of ownership interest	
			Square feet	Inches
Rosebud	320.00	0.0000047	0.66	9.7 x 9.7
Standing Rock	320.00	0.0000025	0.35	7.1 x 7.1
Turtle Mountain	7.50	0.0000192	0.06	2.9 x 2.9
Wind River	80.00	0.0000100	.35	7.1 x 7.1
Yakima	80.00	0.0001929	6.72	31.1 x 31.1

Source: U.S. General Accounting Office. *Indian Programs: Profile of the Land Ownership at 12 Reservations* (GAO/RCED-92-96BR). Washington, DC: U.S. GAO, February 1992, p. 20. *Notes:* Smallest ownership share represents the smallest share that is at least one ten-millionth of one percent. Attempts to identify ownership interest smaller than one ten-millionth of one percent were not made.

★ 819 ★

Land Ownership

Land Tracts Under BIA Jurisdiction, by Selected Reservation and Two Percent or Less Consolidated Indian Ownership, 1991

The number of tracts owned is shown, by selected reservation and consolidated Indian ownership interests of two percent or less per tract, for 1991. The Indian Land Consolidation Act generally provides that ownership interests of 2 percent or less will transfer, or escheat, to the tribe upon the death of an Indian.

Reservation tracts	Number of tracts with Indian interests of 2 percent or less								
	None	One	2-10	11-25	26-50	51-100	101-300	Over 300	Total
Blackfeet	1,722	42	602	468	453	247	37	0	3,571
Cheyenne River	2,055	26	381	258	68	20	1	0	2,809
Colville	1,237	18	306	226	69	27	1	0	1,884
Crow	2,013	41	690	389	280	189	91	3	3,696
Fort Berthold	1,501	28	394	335	236	91	25	0	2,610
Fort Peck	2,159	53	669	481	214	103	22	1	3,702
Pine Ridge	2,570	46	847	559	374	214	115	1	4,726
Rosebud	1,256	40	534	506	292	216	113	4	2,961
Standing Rock	2,594	41	1,126	787	523	240	85	6	5,402
Turtle Mountain	235	4	67	38	25	22	17	1	409
Wind River	731	64	416	360	253	212	91	1	2,128
Yakima	1,211	45	446	320	169	37	8	0	2,236
Total	19,284	448	6,478	4,727	2,956	1,618	606	17	36,134

Source: U.S. General Accounting Office. *Indian Programs: Profile of the Land Ownership at 12 Reservations* (GAO/RCED-92-96BR). Washington, DC: U.S. GAO, February 1992, p. 15.

★ 820 ★

Land Ownership

Land Tracts Under BIA Jurisdiction, by Selected Reservation, 1991

The number and acreage of tracts are shown, by selected reservation and selected characteristics, for 1991[1].

Reservation	Number of acres	Number of tracts	Number of tracts			Acreage of tracts		Average tract acreage
			Less than 40 acres	40-159 acres	160 acres or more	Smallest tract	Largest tract	
Blackfeet	1,238,021	7,036	792	3,434	2,810	0.001	5,365.7	176
Cheyenne River	2,004,773	10,474	449	2,830	7,195	0.001	2,800.0	191
Colville	1,233,098	5,482	1,195	2,027	2,260	0.050	6,133.0	225
Crow	1,680,246	6,810	957	2,899	2,954	0.030	23,025.0	247
Fort Berthold	1,190,544	8,708	728	4,192	3,788	0.010	827.5	137
Fort Peck	1,390,345	6,896	1,204	2,355	3,337	0.001	2,994.4	202
Pine Ridge	2,050,492	10,661	694	2,744	7,223	0.001	1,000.6	192
Rosebud	1,134,906	6,410	197	1,242	4,971	0.001	1,735.7	177
Standing Rock	1,244,016	9,267	3,018	1,854	4,395	0.010	2,290.0	134
Turtle Mountain	42,453	917	528	335	54	0.145	471.5	46
Wind River	2,158,925	4,228	1,256	2,437	535	0.310	662,515.2	511
Yakima	1,149,734	6,089	1,212	2,658	2,219	0.060	3,200.0	189
Total	16,517,553	82,978	12,230	29,007	41,741	-	-	199

Source: U.S. General Accounting Office. *Indian Programs: Profile of the Land Ownership at 12 Reservations* (GAO/RCED-92-96BR). Washington, DC: U.S. GAO, February 1992, p. 9. *Notes:* A dash (-) stands for not applicable. 1. Because BIA maintains separate tract records for surface and subsurface resources when ownership is different, the number of acres shown in the table does not always represent surface acres.

★ 821 ★

Land Ownership

Land Tracts Under BIA Jurisdiction, by Surface and Subsurface Use and Selected Reservation, 1991

The number of tracts is shown, by surface and subsurface use and selected reservation, for 1991.

Reservation	Tracts			Total tracts managed[1]
	Surface only	Subsurface only	Both surface and subsurface	
Blackfeet	3,204	1,417	2,412	7,033
Cheyenne River	2,457	3,501	4,516	10,474
Colville	880	1,369	3,231	5,480
Crow	3,195	1,406	2,205	6,806
Fort Berthold	2,169	5,436	1,130	8,708
Fort Peck	1,717	2,405	2,774	6,896
Pine Ridge	1,282	1,713	7,666	10,661
Rosebud	870	1,375	4,165	6,410
Standing Rock	1,473	3,911	3,883	9,267
Turtle Mountain	193	168	556	917
Wind River	1,414	1,394	1,417	4,225

[Continued]

★ 821 ★

Land Tracts Under BIA Jurisdiction, by Surface and Subsurface Use and Selected Reservation, 1991

[Continued]

Reservation	Tracts			Total tracts managed[1]
	Surface only	Subsurface only	Both surface and subsurface	
Yakima	252	299	5,531	6,082
Total	19,106	24,394	39,456	82,959

Source: U.S. General Accounting Office. *Indian Programs: Profile of the Land Ownership at 12 Reservations* (GAO/RCED-92-96BR). Washington, DC: U.S. GAO, February 1992, p. 10. *Notes:* 1. Excludes 19 tracts for which the BIA database did not specify the resource type (i.e., surface, subsurface, or both).

Land Use

★ 822 ★

Acreage of Indian Lands, by State

Acreages are shown, by ownership and state, for 1990.

State	Ownership			Total
	Tribal	Individual	Government	
Alabama	213.00	0.00	0.00	213.00
Alaska	86,773.00	884,099.50	0.09	970,872.59
Arizona	19,775,958.14	311,579.05	90,697.55	20,178,234.74
Arkansas	0.00	2.78	0.00	2.78
California	520,048.66	66,769.39	808.04	587,626.09
Colorado	795,210.99	2,804.68	32.14	798,047.81
Connecticut	1,637.79	0.00	0.00	1,637.79
Florida	153,874.24	0.00	333.33	154,207.57
Idaho	609,621.91	327,300.63	32,531.88	969,454.42
Iowa	3,550.00	0.00	0.00	3,550.00
Kansas	7,218.54	23,762.60	1.00	30,982.14
Louisiana	414.59	0.00	0.00	414.59
Maine	163,570.15	0.00	0.00	163,570.15
Massachusetts	157.00	0.00	0.00	157.00
Michigan	14,410	9,276.28	0.00	23,687.18
Minnesota	779,137.52	50,337.60	103.10	829,578.22
Mississippi	20,486.16	0.00	192.41	20,678.57
Missouri	0.00	374.37	0.00	374.37
Montana	2,671,416.07	2,868,123.84	11,802.80	5,551,342.71
Nebraska	2,141,995.79	43,208.37	6.79	2,185,210.95
Nevada	1,147,087.55	78,528.56	4,945.91	1,230,562.02
New Mexico	7,252,325.70	630,293.42	270,276.14	8,152,895.26
New York	118,199.40	0.00	0.00	118,199.40

[Continued]

★ 822 ★

Acreage of Indian Lands, by State
[Continued]

State	Ownership			Total
	Tribal	Individual	Government	
North Carolina	56,508.87	0.00	112.16	56,621.03
North Dakota	214,005.96	627,288.84	623.57	841,918.37
Oklahoma	96,838.56	1,000,164.91	2,297.96	1,099,301.45
Oregon	660,366.77	135,052.36	378.08	795,797.21
Rhode Island	1,800.00	0.00	0.00	1,800.00
South Dakota	2,399,530.95	2,121,188.19	1,605.27	4,522,324.41
Texas	4,628.98	0.00	0.00	4,628.98
Utah	2,286,447.57	32,838.09	87.45	2,319,373.11
Washington	2,097,842.03	467,785.11	3,163.64	2,568,790.78
Wisconsin	338,097.10	80,345.36	1.00	418,443.46
Wyoming	1,908,095.44	101,537.25	1,296.15	2,010,928.84
State totals	46,327,469.33	9,862,661.18	421,296.48	56,611,426.99

Source: Bureau of Indian Affairs. Office of Public Affairs.

★ 823 ★

Land Use

Acreage of Indian Lands, by State and Area Office, 1990

Acreages are shown, by ownership, state, and area office, for 1990.

Area/state	Ownership			Total
	Tribal	Individual	Government	
Aberdeen Area				
South Dakota	2,399,530.95	2,121,188.19	1,605.27	4,522,324.41
North Dakota	214,005.96	627,288.84	623.57	841,918.37
Nebraska	2,141,671.00	42,976.14	6.79	2,184,653.93
Aberdeen total	4,755,207.91	2,791,453.17	2,235.63	7,548,896.71
Albuquerque area				
Arizona	10,085.70	54,699.17	126.82	64,911.69
New Mexico	3,673,320.44	8,578.05	-	3,681,898.49
Utah	5,921.08	8,578.05	-	14,499.13
Colorado	795,210.99	2,408.88	32.14	797,652.01
Texas	-	-	-	-
Albuquerque total	4,484,538.21	74,264.15	158.96	4,558,961.32
Anadarko area				
Oklahoma	28,513.57	411,159.74	1,472.34	441,145.65
Texas	4,628.98	-	-	4,628.98
Kansas	7,218.54	23,762.60	1.00	30,982.14
Nebraska	324.79	232.23	-	557.02
Colorado	-	395.80	-	395.80
Anadarko total	40,685.88	435,550.37	1,473.34	477,709.59

[Continued]

★ 823 ★

Acreage of Indian Lands, by State and Area Office, 1990
[Continued]

Area/state	Ownership			Total
	Tribal	Individual	Government	
Billings area				
Montana	2,089,509.37	2,867,723.84	11,079.68	4,968,312.89
Wyoming	1,908,095.44	101,537.25	1,296.15	2,010,928.84
Billings total	3,997,604.81	2,969,261.09	12,375.83	6,979,241.73
Muskogee Area				
Oklahoma	68,324.99	589,005.17	825.64	658,155.80
Arizona	-	0.35	-	0.35
Arkansas	-	2.78	-	2.78
Missouri	-	374.37	-	374.37
Montana	-	400.00	-	400.00
New Mexico	-	0.16	-	0.16
Muskogee total	68,324.99	589,782.83	825.64	658,933.46
Navajo area				
Arizona	9,989,462.71	85,620.37	753.90	10,075,836.98
New Mexico	3,579,005.26	621,715.21	229,482.64	4,430,203.11
Utah	1,184,783.66	9,741.80	5.99	1,194,531.45
Navajo total	14,753,251.63	717,077.38	230,242.53	15,700,571.54
Eastern area				
North Carolina	56,508.87	-	112.16	56,621.03
New York	118,199.40	-	-	118,199.40
Florida	153,874.24	-	333.33	154,207.57
Mississippi	20,486.16	-	192.41	20,678.57
Louisiana	414.59	-	-	414.59
Alabama	213.00	-	-	213.00
Maine	163,570.15	-	-	163,570.15
Connecticut	1,637.79	-	-	1,637.79
Rhode Island	1,800.00	-	-	1,800.00
Massachusetts	157.00	-	-	157.00
Eastern total	516,861.20	0.00	637.90	517,499.10
Minneapolis area				
Wisconsin	338,097.10	80,345.36	1.00	418,443.46
Minnesota	779,137.52	50,337.60	103.10	829,578.22
Michigan	14,410.90	9,276.28	-	23,687.18
Iowa	3,550.00	-	-	3,550.00
Minneapolis total	1,135,195.52	139,959.24	104.10	1,275,258.86
Phoenix area				
Arizona	9,776,409.73	171,259.16	89,816.83	10,037,485.72
Nevada	1,147,087.55	78,528.56	4,945.91	1,230,562.02
Utah	1,095,742.83	14,518.24	81.46	1,110,342.53
California	114,876.55	8,704.00	84.92	123,665.47
Oregon	16,936.00	-	-	16,936.00

[Continued]

★ 823 ★

Acreage of Indian Lands, by State and Area Office, 1990
[Continued]

Area/state	Ownership			Total
	Tribal	Individual	Government	
Idaho	145,545.00	-	-	145,545.00
New Mexico	-	-	40,793.50	40,793.50
Phoenix total	12,296,597.66	273,009.96	135,722.62	12,705,330.24
Portland area				
Washington	2,097,842.03	467,785.11	3,163.64	2,568,790.78
Oregon	643,430.77	135,052.36	378.08	778,861.21
Idaho	464,076.91	327,300.63	32,531.88	823,909.42
Montana	581,906.70	-	723.12	582,629.82
Portland total	3,787,256.41	930,138.10	36,796.72	4,754,191.23
Sacramento area				
California	405,172.11	58,065.39	723.12	463,960.62
Sacramento total	405,172.11	58,065.39	723.12	463,960.62
Juneau area				
Alaska	86,773.00	884,099.50	0.09	970,872.59
Juneau total	86,773.00	884,099.50	0.09	970,872.59
Total	46,327,469.33	9,862,661.18	421,296.48	56,611,426.99

Source: Bureau of Indian Affairs. Office of Public Affairs. *Note:* A dash (-) represents zero.

★ 824 ★

Land Use

Ownership and Land Use Class of Lands Under BIA Jurisdiction - Aberdeen Area
[Acres]

	Open grazing	Forest grazing	Commercial forest lands	Non-commercial forest lands	Dry farming	Irrigation projects	Private irrigation	Wild Lands (Non-recr.)[1]	Wild lands (recr.)[2]	Other uses (non-agric.)
Tribally Owned										
Indian Use	1,881,834	47,970	47,678	190,139	52,514	14,916	-	-	124,210	55,029
Non-Indian Use	395,993	489	-	676	75,007	3,043	2,922	-	9,926	4,824
Idle	51,801	303	200	303	10,150	623	-	-	525	28,371
Individually Owned										
Indian Use	1,566,185	7,169	27,621	81,776	70,456	803	1,104	-	46,310	30,657
Non-Indian Use	862,215	2,246	4,172	3,185	253,563	483	-	-	9,342	6,293
Idle	83,350	850	-	4,850	7,502	-	-	-	-	1,983
Government Owned										
Indian Use	35,305	401	400	192	-	30	-	-	-	1,373

[Continued]

★ 824 ★

Ownership and Land Use Class of Lands Under BIA Jurisdiction - Aberdeen Area
[Continued]

	Open grazing	Forest grazing	Commercial forest lands	Non-commercial forest lands	Dry farming	Irrigation projects	Private irrigation	Wild Lands (Non-recr.)[1]	Wild lands (recr.)[2]	Other uses (non-agric.)
Non-Indian Use	964	-	-	60	-	-	-	-	-	302
Idle	2,299	-	-	-	57	-	-	-	-	760

Source: U.S. Department of the Interior. Bureau of Indian Affairs. *Natural Resource Information System.* Data are for 1993 and were processed on March 30, 1995. *Notes:* A dash (-) stands for data not provided in original source. 1. Lands with a primary use other than recreation or wildlife but with significant secondary use for recreation or wildlife. 2. Lands such as dense forest, marshes, or other inaccessible areas, suitable only for recreation or wildlife.

★ 825 ★

Land Use

Ownership and Land Use Class of Lands Under BIA Jurisdiction - Albuquerque Area

[Acres]

	Open grazing	Forest grazing	Commercial forest lands	Non-commercial forest lands	Dry farming	Irrigation projects	Private irrigation	Wild Lands (Non-recr.)[1]	Wild lands (recr.)[2]	Other uses (non-agric.)
Tribally Owned										
Indian Use	1,990,670	1,455,307	480,665	1,176,306	1,760	14,352	8,696	-	197,116	556,227
Non-Indian Use	31,456	26,592	-	532	752	2,355	1,756	-	3,183	16,805
Idle	75,746	-	-	-	34	9,692	7,264	-	-	-
Individually Owned										
Indian Use	37,143	24,916	1,538	24,533	300	783	-	-	-	94
Non-Indian Use	214	-	-	-	-	1,001	-	-	-	73
Idle	-	-	-	-	-	-	71	-	-	-
Government Owned										
Indian Use	40	-	-	-	-	-	-	-	-	27
Non-Indian Use	-	-	-	-	-	-	-	-	-	12
Idle	-	-	-	-	-	-	-	-	-	-

Source: U.S. Department of the Interior. Bureau of Indian Affairs. *Natural Resource Information System.* Data are for 1993 and were processed on March 30, 1995. *Notes:* A dash (-) stands for data not provided in original source. 1. Lands with a primary use other than recreation or wildlife but with significant secondary use for recreation or wildlife. 2. Lands such as dense forest, marshes, or other inaccessible areas, suitable only for recreation or wildlife.

★ 826 ★
Land Use

Ownership and Land Use Class of Lands Under BIA Jurisdiction - Anadarko Area

[Acres]

	Open grazing	Forest grazing	Commer-cial forest lands	Non-com-mercial forest lands	Dry farming	Irriga-tion projects	Private irriga-tion	Wild Lands (Non-recr.)[1]	Wild lands (recr.)[2]	Other uses (non-agric.)
Tribally Owned										
Indian Use	57	19	77	84	121	-	-	-	-	1,417
Non-Indian Use	11,002	1,285	-	1,241	4,373	-	-	-	-	53
Idle	165	8	-	8	-	-	-	-	-	612
Individually Owned										
Indian Use	5,485	1,797	110	6,759	18,027	-	-	-	-	452
Non-Indian Use	128,495	25,969	57	27,266	115,329	-	-	-	50	2,984
Idle	17,241	2,048	120	1,486	3,539	5	-	-	1,422	7,048
Government Owned										
Indian Use	-	-	-	-	-	-	-	-	-	1
Non-Indian Use	-	-	-	-	10	-	-	-	-	-
Idle	-	-	-	-	-	-	-	-	-	198

Source: U.S. Department of the Interior. Bureau of Indian Affairs. *Natural Resource Information System.* Data are for 1993 and were processed on March 30, 1995. *Notes:* A dash (-) stands for data not provided in original source. 1. Lands with a primary use other than recreation or wildlife but with significant secondary use for recreation or wildlife. 2. Lands such as dense forest, marshes, or other inaccessible areas, suitable only for recreation or wildlife.

★ 827 ★
Land Use

Ownership and Land Use Class of Lands Under BIA Jurisdiction - Billings Area

[Acres]

	Open grazing	Forest grazing	Commer-cial forest lands	Non-com-mercial forest lands	Dry farming	Irriga-tion projects	Private irriga-tion	Wild Lands (Non-recr.)[1]	Wild lands (recr.)[2]	Other uses (non-agric.)
Tribally Owned										
Indian Use	2,299,462	574,275	255,753	354,465	167,422	20,147	9,409	-	16,937	10,004
Non-Indian Use	308,243	28,180	-	-	53,161	4,724	15	-	204	1,853
Idle	2,689	-	-	-	1,775	3,067	2,084	-	-	-
Individually Owned										
Indian Use	1,108,378	41,414	53,665	64,073	186,857	28,428	7,030	-	14,849	14,253
Non-Indian Use	981,333	-	-	-	243,349	48,966	1,506	-	25	240
Idle	6,337	-	-	-	10,485	4,524	726	-	-	5,500
Government Owned										
Indian Use	577	148	11	137	53	113	-	-	-	7,664

[Continued]

★ 827 ★

Ownership and Land Use Class of Lands Under BIA Jurisdiction - Billings Area

[Continued]

	Open grazing	Forest grazing	Commercial forest lands	Non-commercial forest lands	Dry farming	Irrigation projects	Private irrigation	Wild Lands (Non-recr.)[1]	Wild lands (recr.)[2]	Other uses (non-agric.)
Non-Indian Use	-	-	-	-	-	41	-	-	-	569
Idle	-	-	-	-	-	-	-	-	-	-

Source: U.S. Department of the Interior. Bureau of Indian Affairs. *Natural Resource Information System*. Data are for 1993 and were processed on March 30, 1995. Notes: A dash (-) stands for data not provided in original source. 1. Lands with a primary use other than recreation or wildlife but with significant secondary use for recreation or wildlife. 2. Lands such as dense forest, marshes, or other inaccessible areas, suitable only for recreation or wildlife.

★ 828 ★

Land Use

Ownership and Land Use Class of Lands Under BIA Jurisdiction - Eastern Area

[Acres]

	Open grazing	Forest grazing	Commercial forest lands	Non-commercial forest lands	Dry farming	Irrigation projects	Private irrigation	Wild Lands (Non-recr.)[1]	Wild lands (recr.)[2]	Other uses (non-agric.)
Tribally Owned										
Indian Use	30,507	850	260,607	139,857	3,288	10	27,671	-	63,659	5,617
Non-Indian Use	-	-	-	-	-	-	-	-	-	12
Idle	210	-	881	1,408	175	-	-	-	-	-
Individually Owned										
Indian Use	-	-	22,427	-	-	-	-	-	-	-
Non-Indian Use	-	-	-	-	-	-	-	-	-	-
Idle	-	-	-	83,078	-	-	-	-	-	-
Government Owned										
Indian Use	-	-	-	-	-	-	-	-	-	-
Non-Indian Use	-	-	-	-	-	-	-	-	-	-
Idle	-	-	-	-	-	-	-	-	-	-

Source: U.S. Department of the Interior. Bureau of Indian Affairs. *Natural Resource Information System*. Data are for 1993 and were processed on March 30, 1995. Notes: A dash (-) stands for data not provided in original source. 1. Lands with a primary use other than recreation or wildlife but with significant secondary use for recreation or wildlife. 2. Lands such as dense forest, marshes, or other inaccessible areas, suitable only for recreation or wildlife.

★ 829 ★

Land Use

Ownership and Land Use Class of Lands Under BIA Jurisdiction - Juneau Area

[Acres]

	Open grazing	Forest grazing	Commer-cial forest lands	Non-com-mercial forest lands	Dry farming	Irriga-tion projects	Private irriga-tion	Wild Lands (Non-recr.)[1]	Wild lands (recr.)[2]	Other uses (non-agric.)
Tribally Owned										
Indian Use	-	-	-	-	-	-	-	-	-	-
Non-Indian Use	-	-	-	-	-	-	-	-	-	-
Idle	-	-	-	-	-	-	-	-	-	-
Individually Owned										
Indian Use	141,460	-	204,419	53,141	5	-	-	-	776,093	278
Non-Indian Use	-	-	-	95,953	-	-	-	-	-	-
Idle	-	-	-	-	35	-	-	-	-	-
Government Owned										
Indian Use	-	-	-	-	-	-	-	-	-	-
Non-Indian Use	-	-	-	-	-	-	-	-	-	-
Idle	-	-	-	-	-	-	-	-	-	-

Source: U.S. Department of the Interior. Bureau of Indian Affairs. *Natural Resource Information System.* Data are for 1993 and were processed on March 30, 1995. *Notes:* A dash (-) stands for data not provided in original source. 1. Lands with a primary use other than recreation or wildlife but with significant secondary use for recreation or wildlife. 2. Lands such as dense forest, marshes, or other inaccessible areas, suitable only for recreation or wildlife.

★ 830 ★

Land Use

Ownership and Land Use Class of Lands Under BIA Jurisdiction - Minneapolis Area

[Acres]

	Open grazing	Forest grazing	Commer-cial forest lands	Non-com-mercial forest lands	Dry farming	Irriga-tion projects	Private irriga-tion	Wild Lands (Non-recr.)[1]	Wild lands (recr.)[2]	Other uses (non-agric.)
Tribally Owned										
Indian Use	3,377	10,600	801,080	115,474	12,189	700	10	-	162,189	26,327
Non-Indian Use	-	-	-	-	1,569	698	-	-	-	4,013
Idle	864	-	-	-	-	-	-	-	-	1,096
Individually Owned										
Indian Use	-	-	128,393	7,915	123	-	-	-	6,714	26,287
Non-Indian Use	-	-	22,221	-	282	-	-	-	-	-
Idle	-	-	2,697	-	40	-	-	-	-	-
Government Owned										
Indian Use	-	-	72	-	-	-	-	-	-	-

[Continued]

★ 830 ★

Ownership and Land Use Class of Lands Under BIA Jurisdiction - Minneapolis Area

[Continued]

	Open grazing	Forest grazing	Commer-cial forest lands	Non-com-mercial forest lands	Dry farming	Irriga-tion projects	Private irriga-tion	Wild Lands (Non-recr.)[1]	Wild lands (recr.)[2]	Other uses (non-agric.)
Non-Indian Use	-	-	-	-	-	-	-	-	-	-
Idle	-	-	-	-	-	-	-	-	-	-

Source: U.S. Department of the Interior. Bureau of Indian Affairs. *Natural Resource Information System.* Data are for 1993 and were processed on March 30, 1995. *Notes:* A dash (-) stands for data not provided in original source. 1. Lands with a primary use other than recreation or wildlife but with significant secondary use for recreation or wildlife. 2. Lands such as dense forest, marshes, or other inaccessible areas, suitable only for recreation or wildlife.

★ 831 ★

Land Use

Ownership and Land Use Class of Lands Under BIA Jurisdiction - Muskogee Area

[Acres]

	Open grazing	Forest grazing	Commer-cial forest lands	Non-com-mercial forest lands	Dry farming	Irriga-tion projects	Private irriga-tion	Wild Lands (Non-recr.)[1]	Wild lands (recr.)[2]	Other uses (non-agric.)
Tribally Owned										
Indian Use	14,177	30,379	30,675	3,894	9,209	-	-	-	-	4,462
Non-Indian Use	10,772	876	9	765	3,308	-	-	-	-	1,904
Idle	9,035	2,225	-	80	8,099	-	-	-	-	950
Individually Owned										
Indian Use	155,336	18,303	22,203	66,704	10,105	-	-	-	-	6,405
Non-Indian Use	277,574	30,391	-	11,152	10,071	-	-	-	-	1,607
Idle	1,269	-	205	-	-	-	-	-	-	1,049
Government Owned										
Indian Use	9	10	10	-	-	-	-	-	-	643
Non-Indian Use	-	179	-	-	-	-	-	-	-	3
Idle	-	-	-	-	-	-	-	-	-	10

Source: U.S. Department of the Interior. Bureau of Indian Affairs. *Natural Resource Information System.* Data are for 1993 and were processed on March 30, 1995. *Notes:* A dash (-) stands for data not provided in original source. 1. Lands with a primary use other than recreation or wildlife but with significant secondary use for recreation or wildlife. 2. Lands such as dense forest, marshes, or other inaccessible areas, suitable only for recreation or wildlife.

★ 832 ★

Land Use

Ownership and Land Use Class of Lands Under BIA Jurisdiction - Navajo Area

[Acres]

	Open grazing	Forest grazing	Commer-cial forest lands	Non-com-mercial forest lands	Dry farming	Irriga-tion projects	Private irriga-tion	Wild Lands (Non-recr.)[1]	Wild lands (recr.)[2]	Other uses (non-agric.)
Tribally Owned										
Indian Use	8,575,189	3,246,289	663,783	2,582,506	9,570	12,980	12,846	-	1,014,554	105,892
Non-Indian Use	-	-	-	-	4,398	400	-	-	-	-
Idle	-	-	-	-	80,611	8,434	11,691	-	-	295
Individually Owned										
Indian Use	590,212	107,094	3,600	105,779	925	84	-	-	291	3,000
Non-Indian Use	-	-	-	-	-	-	-	-	-	-
Idle	-	-	-	-	150	-	-	-	-	-
Government Owned										
Indian Use	217,840	4,000	-	4,000	-	-	-	-	-	8,490
Non-Indian Use	-	-	-	-	-	-	-	-	-	1,500
Idle	-	-	-	-	-	-	-	-	-	-

Source: U.S. Department of the Interior. Bureau of Indian Affairs. *Natural Resource Information System.* Data are for 1993 and were processed on March 30, 1995. *Notes:* A dash (-) stands for data not provided in original source. 1. Lands with a primary use other than recreation or wildlife but with significant secondary use for recreation or wildlife. 2. Lands such as dense forest, marshes, or other inaccessible areas, suitable only for recreation or wildlife.

★ 833 ★

Land Use

Ownership and Land Use Class of Lands Under BIA Jurisdiction - Phoenix Area

[Acres]

	Open grazing	Forest grazing	Commer-cial forest lands	Non-com-mercial forest lands	Dry farming	Irriga-tion projects	Private irriga-tion	Wild Lands (Non-recr.)[1]	Wild lands (recr.)[2]	Other uses (non-agric.)
Tribally Owned										
Indian Use	7,681,487	1,871,723	796,179	1,191,888	9,474	82,236	6,486	-	475,843	1,091,914
Non-Indian Use	91,375	-	-	-	-	75,420	11,776	-	37,910	54,444
Idle	218,848	82,166	-	-	539	31,864	7,150	-	-	113,177
Individually Owned										
Indian Use	43,868	-	-	-	-	14,045	13,281	-	45,983	2,996
Non-Indian Use	2,029	-	-	-	-	20,936	6,561	-	543	3,282
Idle	14,783	-	-	-	-	24,051	2,213	-	-	1,758
Government Owned										
Indian Use	79,136	-	-	-	-	-	-	-	-	1,304

[Continued]

★ 833 ★

Ownership and Land Use Class of Lands Under BIA Jurisdiction - Phoenix Area

[Continued]

	Open grazing	Forest grazing	Commer-cial forest lands	Non-com-mercial forest lands	Dry farming	Irriga-tion projects	Private irriga-tion	Wild Lands (Non-recr.)[1]	Wild lands (recr.)[2]	Other uses (non-agric.)
Non-Indian Use	-	-	-	-	-	-	-	-	-	2
Idle	-	-	-	-	-	120	-	-	-	85

Source: U.S. Department of the Interior. Bureau of Indian Affairs. *Natural Resource Information System.* Data are for 1993 and were processed on March 30, 1995. *Notes:* A dash (-) stands for data not provided in original source. 1. Lands with a primary use other than recreation or wildlife but with significant secondary use for recreation or wildlife. 2. Lands such as dense forest, marshes, or other inaccessible areas, suitable only for recreation or wildlife.

★ 834 ★

Land Use

Ownership and Land Use Class of Lands Under BIA Jurisdiction - Portland Area

[Acres]

	Open grazing	Forest grazing	Commer-cial forest lands	Non-com-mercial forest lands	Dry farming	Irriga-tion projects	Private irriga-tion	Wild Lands (Non-recr.)[1]	Wild lands (recr.)[2]	Other uses (non-agric.)
Tribally Owned										
Indian Use	783,534	1,674,389	1,973,756	391,260	15,860	8,094	4,054	-	182,130	16,505
Non-Indian Use	186,086	281,422	35	-	10,080	29,397	9,286	-	1,350	5,158
Idle	4,877	45,617	-	-	12,975	4,118	2,462	-	-	365
Individually Owned										
Indian Use	215,434	151,795	277,763	12,249	9,336	23,486	4,368	-	10,925	7,601
Non-Indian Use	149,110	18,164	-	80	114,339	64,219	15,536	-	-	6,552
Idle	18,701	4,382	-	-	17,870	23,270	1,596	-	-	1,311
Government Owned										
Indian Use	2,023	217	2,082	16	34	40	-	-	29,900	24
Non-Indian Use	10,970	-	-	-	2,329	110	-	-	42,123	58
Idle	-	-	-	-	-	-	-	-	-	3

Source: U.S. Department of the Interior. Bureau of Indian Affairs. *Natural Resource Information System.* Data are for 1993 and were processed on March 30, 1995. *Notes:* A dash (-) stands for data not provided in original source. 1. Lands with a primary use other than recreation or wildlife but with significant secondary use for recreation or wildlife. 2. Lands such as dense forest, marshes, or other inaccessible areas, suitable only for recreation or wildlife.

Environmental Issues

★ 835 ★

BIA Dam Safety

67 BIA dams are shown, by combined hazard/safety classifications, task force rank among all of the Department of Interior's high- and significant-hazard dams, and relative rank among the BIA's priority dams.

Dam/rating	Interior rank	Relative BIA rank	Area office
High hazard dams/unsatisfactory safety rating			
Ganado	12	4	Navajo
Round Rock	14	6	Navajo
Black Lake	34	16	Portland
Pablo	42	22	Portland/ Flathead
Ponca	96	41	Aberdeen
High Hazard dams/poor safety rating			
Black Rock	4	1	Albuquerque
Dulce	6	2	Albuquerque
Bonneau	9	3	Billings
Washakie	21	7	Billings
McDonald	22	8	Portland/ Flathead
Santa Ana	23	9	Albuquerque
Lower Dry Fork	26	11	Portland/ Flathead
Tula Stone	29	13	Phoenix
Weber	31	14	Phoenix
Jocko	33	15	Portland/ Flathead
Many Farms	35	17	Navajo
Standing Rock	36	18	Aberdeen
Acomita	38	19	Albuquerque
Rosebud	47	24	Aberdeen
White Clay	56	29	Aberdeen
He Dog	61	31	Aberdeen
Upper Dry Fork	66	33	Portland/ Flathead
Oglala	72	37	Aberdeen
Barmelee	95	40	Aberdeen
Crow	117	45	Portland/ Flathead
Tabor	129	47	Portland/ Flathead
Assayi	186	53	Navajo
Elgo	242	57	Phoenix
Lower Two Medicine	274	62	Billings

[Continued]

★ 835 ★

BIA Dam Safety
[Continued]

Dam/rating	Interior rank	Relative BIA rank	Area office
Significant-hazard dams/unsatisfactory safety rating[1]			
Significant-hazard dams/poor safety rating			
Equalizer	25	10	Portland
Crow Creek	27	12	Aberdeen
Tsaile	206	54	Navajo
High-hazard dams/conditionally poor safety rating			
Captain Tom	39	20	Navajo
Lower Mundo	40	21	Albuquerque
Wheatfields	53	28	Navajo
Kicking Horse	69	34	Portland
Lake Mescalero	71	36	Albuquerque
Cutter	113	44	Navajo
Wild Horse	243	58	Phoenix
Hubbart	248	59	Portland/ Flathead
Bottle Hollow	254	60	Phoenix
Willow Creek	322	64	Billings
Significant-hazard dams/conditionally poor safety rating			
Indian Lake	45	23	Portland
High-hazard dam/fair or satisfactory safety rating			
Ninepipe (Fair)	137	49	Portland/ Flathead
Little Bitteroot (Satisfactory)	157	50	Portland
Red Lake (Fair)	237	56	Navajo
Mission (Fair)	267	61	Portland/ Flathead
Significant-hazard dams/fair or satisfactory safety rating			
Headgate Rock (fair)	335	65	Phoenix
Tat Momolikot (Satisfactory)	354	67	Phoenix
High-hazard dams/no safety rating			
Canyon Diablo	13	5	Navajo
Indian Scout Lake	50	26	Aberdeen
Agency	60	30	Billings
East Fork	49	25	Billings
Kyle	89	39	Aberdeen
Ghost Hawk	169	51	Aberdeen
Ring Thunder	173	52	Aberdeen

[Continued]

★ 835 ★

BIA Dam Safety
[Continued]

Dam/rating	Interior rank	Relative BIA rank	Area office
Allen	227	55	Aberdeen
Blackfoot	275	63	Portland
Blue Canyon	348	66	Navajo
Significant-hazard dams/no safety rating			
Ray Lake	63	32	Billings
La Jara	70	35	Albuquerque
Wanblee	74	38	Aberdeen
Hell Roaring	110	46	Portland
Twin (Turtle) Lake	130	48	Portland
Low-or unclassified hazard dams			
Pasture Canyon	51	27	Phoenix
Tuve	98	42	Phoenix
Wauneka	104	43	Navajo

Source: U.S. General Accounting Office. *Indian Programs: BIA and Indian Tribes Are Taking Action to Address Dam Safety Concerns* (GAO/RCED-92-50). Washington, DC: U.S. GAO, February, 1992, pp. 16-18. *Note:* 1. None in this category.

★ 836 ★

Environmental Issues

Coal Mining Effluent Limitations

Performance standards apply to each coal mining operation on Indian lands on or after December 16, 1977. Figures are given in milligrams per liter, except for pH.

Effluent characteristics	Maximum allowable[1]	Average of daily values for 30 consecutive discharge days[1]
Iron, total	7.0	3.5
Manganese, total	4.0	2.0
Total suspended solids[2]	70.0	35.0
pH[3]	Within the range 6.0 to 9.0	-

Source: Office of the Federal Register. National Archives and Records Administration. *Code of Federal Regulations* Vol. 25 (April 1991), p. 558. *Notes:* Discharges from areas disturbed by surface coal mining and reclamation operations must meet all applicable Federal and Tribal laws and regulations and, at a minimum, the above numerical of effluent limitations. 1. Based on representative sampling. 2. In Arizona, Colorado, Montana, New Mexico, North Dakota, South Dakota, Utah, and Wyoming, total suspended solids limitations will be determined on a case-by-case basis, but they must not be greater than 45 mg/l (maximum allowable) and 30 mg/l (average of daily value for 30 consecutive discharge days) based on a representative sampling. 3. Where the application of neutralization and sedimentation treatment technology results in inability to comply with the manganese limitations set forth, the regulatory authority may allow the pH level in the discharge to exceed to a small extent the upper limit of 9.0 in order that the manganese limitations will be achieved.

★ 837 ★

Environmental Issues

Concerns About Transporting Nuclear Waste Materials Near or Across Indian Lands - I

"The Nuclear Regulatory Commission identified fifteen Indian tribal jurisdictions that are transited by or adjacent to designated spent-fuel shipping routes. These tribes have an obvious and immediate interest in the possibility of a transportation incident involving radioactive materials. With the assistance of the National Congress of American Indians, fifteen of these tribal jurisdictions were chosen for inclusion in the survey. All were contacted by project staff, and twelve agreed to participate." This table presents highlights from this survey, showing some of the more poignant questions asked and responses by the participating tribes.

Tribe	Question 1: Lead agency for radiological assessment at the scene	Question 2: Document identifying lead agency	Question 3: Document identifying support agency	Question 4: Local jurisdictions exercising own emergency response authority	Question 5: Written emergency response plan
Acoma Pueblo state and county public safety authorities	Rely entirely on New Mexico	New Mexico disaster protocol	County call list	None	No
Navajo Nation Response Commission and Navajo Environmental Protection Administration	Navajo Nation Emergency	In process of development	No documentation; cooperative agreements being sought with state and local jurisdictions in Arizona, New Mexico, and Utah	Highway rights-of-way in affected state	In process

[Continued]

★ 837 ★

Concerns About Transporting Nuclear Waste Materials Near or Across Indian Lands - I
[Continued]

Tribe	Question 1: Lead agency for radiological assessment at the scene	Question 2: Document identifying lead agency	Question 3: Document identifying support agency	Question 4: Local jurisdictions exercising own emergency response authority	Question 5: Written emergency response plan
Nez Perce Tribe	None	None	None	None	No
Onondaga Nation	None	None	None	None	No
Pyramid Lake Paiute Tribe	Bureau of Indian Affairs police	Nevada DOT calls appropriate state agency	None	None	No
San Filipe Pueblo	Bureau of Indian Affairs police, county fire dept.	Informal agreement, tribal authorities call state and local police	None	None	No, one in discussion
Sandia Pueblo	Bureau of Indian Affairs, Indian Health Service, and volunteer fire department	None	None	Some pockets of private land	No
Seneca Nation	None assigned, most likely Health Department of the Seneca	No documentation	Received SARA Title III grant for training; will include several tribal agencies	None	No plan
Shoshone-Bannock Tribes	Tribal police	Plan in process; participating with 8 local jurisdictions under SARA Title III to create regional umbrella plan	SARA hazmat plan will be appendix to Tribal Basic Emergency Plan also in process	No autonomous jurisdictions within reservation, but private industrial operation has its own personnel; concurrent jurisdiction with state on highway rights-of-way	Draft plan in process
Te-Moak Tribe	Bureau of Indian Affairs police	None	None	None	No
Umatilla Indian Reservation	No designed agency, but have public health and safety agencies that would be involved	None	None	No autonomous jurisdictions within reservation, but Possessory and Usage Rights Area extends into 4 states; situation unclear	No, use Indian Health Service Plan
Yakima Indian Nation	Tribal police	No official document	No	Indian Health Service (1 staff member)	No

Source: Vilardo, Frank J. and others. U.S. Nuclear Regulatory Commission. Division of Safeguards and Transportation. Office of Nuclear Material Safety and Safeguards. *Survey of State and Tribal Emergency Response Capabilities for Radiological Transportation Incidents* (NRC FIN D1054). Washington, DC: U.S. NRC, pp. 4-4 to 4-5.

★ 838 ★
Environmental Issues

Concerns About Transporting Nuclear Waste Materials Near or Across Indian Lands - II

"The Nuclear Regulatory Commission identified fifteen Indian tribal jurisdictions that are transited by or adjacent to designated spent-fuel shipping routes. These tribes have an obvious and immediate interest in the possibility of a transportation incident involving radioactive materials. With the assistance of the National Congress of American Indians, fifteen of these tribal jurisdictions were chosen for inclusion in the survey. All were contacted by project staff, and twelve agreed to participate." This table presents highlights from this survey, showing some of the more poignant questions asked and responses by the participating tribes.

Tribe	Question 22: Professional specialists available to contribute their expertise for emergency response	Question 23: and 24 Portable radiation-detection equipment (type and location)	Question 25: Dedicated emergency response vehicles	Question 26: Emergency field kits	Question 27: Communications network
Acoma Pueblo	No trained personnel	2 or 3 devices received 2 years ago; no one knows how to use them	None	None	Telephone/radio with State
Navajo Nation	2 health-physics technicians and 1 radiation monitor	All equipment at one location: 1 each Low-, medium-, and high-range beta-gamma instrument 3 low-energy gamma detectors 6 alpha-particle detectors, 3 instruments that determine concentration of radon decay products Also, certified sources and equipment for calibration	None	None	Tribal public safety
Nez Perce Tribe	No trained personnel	No detection instruments	None	None	None
Onondaga Nation	No trained personnel	No detection instruments	None	None	None
Pyramid Lake Paiute Tribe	No trained personnel	No detection instruments	None	None	Radio from Bureau of Indian Affairs police to county dispatch
San Felipe Pueblo	1 communications specialist and 1 site coordinator	No detection instruments	None	None	Radio contact with state authorities
Sandia Pueblo	No trained personnel	No detection instruments	None	None	Fire and police radio link to Bureau of Indian Affairs
Seneca Nation	No trained personnel	No detection instruments	None	First aid only	Tribal police and fire radio
Shoshone-Bannock Tribes	2 radiation monitors and 2 communication specialists	Bureau of Indian Affairs has 2 portable instruments, but these have never been taken out of their boxes	None	First aid only	Tribal police base station and portable units; access to state net
Te-Moak Tribe	No trained personnel	No detection instruments	None	None	None
Umatilla Indian Reservation	Sanitarian on temporary assignment to Indian Health Service is trained as radiation monitor	Beta-gamma detectors and alpha-particle detectors are available at one location	None	Not tribe's	None
Yakima Indian Nation	No trained personnel	No detection instruments	None	None	Tribal police radio

Source: Vilardo, Frank J. and others. U.S. Nuclear Regulatory Commission. Division of Safeguards and Transportation. Office of Nuclear Material Safety and Safeguards. *Survey of State and Tribal Emergency Response Capabilities for Radiological Transportation Incidents* (NRC FIN D1054). Washington, DC: U.S. NRC, p. 4-27.

★ 839 ★
Environmental Issues

Concerns About Transporting Nuclear Waste Materials Near or Across Indian Lands - III

"The Nuclear Regulatory Commission identified fifteen Indian tribal jurisdictions that are transited by or adjacent to designated spent-fuel shipping routes. These tribes have an obvious and immediate interest in the possibility of a transportation incident involving radioactive materials. With the assistance of the National Congress of American Indians, fifteen of these tribal jurisdictions were chosen for inclusion in the survey. All were contacted by project staff, and twelve agreed to participate." This table presents highlights from this survey, showing some of the more poignant questions asked and responses by the participating tribes.

Tribe	Question 28: Number of trained radiological emergency response teams	Question 29: Number of team members trained in radiological emergency response procedures (RERO or equivalent)	Question 30: Location of trained radiological emergency response team
Acoma Pueblo	0	0	Not applicable
Navajo Nation	0	0	Not applicable
Nez Perce Tribe	0	0	Not applicable
Onondaga Nation	0	0	Not applicable
Pyramid Lake Paiute Tribe	0	0	Not applicable
San Felipe Pueblo	0	0	Not applicable
Sandia Pueblo	0	0	Not applicable
Seneca Nation	0	0	Not applicable
Shoshone-Bannock Tribes	0	0	Not applicable
Te-Moak Tribe	0	0	Not applicable
Umatilla Indian Reservation	0	1[1]	Only 1 trained person
Yakima Indian Nation	0	0	Not applicable

Source: Vilardo, Frank J. and others. U.S. Nuclear Regulatory Commission. Division of Safeguards and Transportation. Office of Nuclear Material Safety and Safeguards. *Survey of State and Tribal Emergency Response Capabilities for Radiological Transportation Incidents* (NRC FIN D1054). Washington, DC: U.S. NRC, p. 4-20. *Note:* 1. An employee of the Indian Health Service on temporary assignment.

Public Lands

★ 840 ★

Land Legislation in the 102nd Congress

The American Mining Congress (AMC) monitors congressional legislation in order to track public land laws that may affect the mining industry. This table shows pending legislation as of the 102nd Congress, as counted by the AMC tracking system.

Characteristic	Number of bills
Wilderness-related bills	108
Bills that refer to wild and scenic rivers	55
National Parks-related bills	37
Bills refer to Endangered Species	148
Native Americans-related bills	97
Bills refer to "Indians"	545

Source: Hale, Alma. "Public lands legislation: drowning in a sea of bills." *AMC Journal* (August 1992), p. 6.

★ 841 ★

Public Lands

Public Lands in Selected States

The American Mining Congress (AMC) monitors congressional legislation in order to track public land laws that may affect the mining industry. Data show acreage of public lands in each state and the percentage of total lands they encompass. There are approximately 622 million acres of land administered by the U.S. government.

State	Total acreage	Public lands	Percentage
Alaska	365,481,000	247,802,244	67.8
Arizona	72,688,000	31,491,364	43.3
California	100,206,720	61,042,577	60.9
Colorado	66,485,760	22,647,838	34.0
Idaho	52,933,120	33,121,958	62.5
Montana	93,271,040	25,862,496	27.7
Nevada	70,264,320	57,803,208	82.2
New Mexico	77,766,400	25,747,308	33.1
Oregon	61,598,720	29,668,752	48.1
Utah	52,696,960	33,611,395	63.8

[Continued]

★ 841 ★

Public Lands in Selected States
[Continued]

State	Total acreage	Public lands	Percentage
Washington	42,693,760	12,373,150	28.9
Wyoming	62,343,040	30,407,258	48.7

Source: Hale, Alma. "Public lands legislation: drowning in a sea of bills." *AMC Journal* (August 1992), p. 5.

Chapter 10
GOVERNMENT RELATIONS

Employment

★ 842 ★

Federal and Civilian Employment, 1992

This table shows percent distribution of workers in each sector by race/ethnicity.

Group	All federal workers	U.S. civilian workers
White	71.8	77.0
Male	43.8	42.1
Female	28.0	34.9
Black	17.2	10.6
Male	6.7	5.2
Female	10.5	5.4
Hispanic	5.6	8.9
Male	3.3	5.4
Female	2.3	3.5
Asian/Pacific	3.5	2.6
Male	2.1	1.4
Female	1.4	1.2
Native American	1.9	0.9
Male	0.9	0.5
Female	1.0	0.4
Total	100.0	100.0

Source: "Minorities in government." *Manpower Comments* (April/May 1994), p. 20. Primary source: U.S. Merit Systems Protection Board and *Career Opportunity News* (March/April 1994).

★ 843 ★

Employment

Employment in Key Federal Jobs, by Race/Ethnicity

Data show numbers of white and minority men and women employed in key jobs at 25 federal agencies, by race/ethnicity and general schedule (GS) pay level. Figures are for fiscal years 1984 and 1990.

Year and grade	White		Black		Hispanic		Asian		Native American	
	Men	Women	Men	Women	Men	Women	Men	Women	Men	Women
1984										
<11	76,469	51,791	8,384	13,857	4,967	2,867	1,882	2,029	1,558	2,254
11	46,159	19,208	3,085	4,556	1,705	644	1,430	983	456	282
12	49,518	8,728	2,788	2,260	1,423	243	1,792	281	375	115
13	35,414	4,060	1,697	805	721	118	873	134	228	32
14	21,001	1,861	991	275	369	47	464	84	127	12
15	14,170	1,231	463	92	336	42	671	202	51	4
Total	242,731	86,879	17,408	21,845	9,521	3,961	7,112	3,713	2,795	2,699
1990										
<11	68,174	52,800	8,290	15,665	5,670	3,952	2,407	2,490	1,589	1,932
11	47,132	27,033	3,991	6,810	2,641	1,495	2,173	2,315	590	459
12	53,598	15,954	3,581	4,134	2,391	639	2,668	783	503	204
13	40,404	8,399	2,304	1,716	1,261	266	1,394	337	281	78
14	26,359	3,950	1,265	570	618	119	638	135	203	37
15	16,057	2,044	615	196	454	68	997	366	67	12
Total	251,724	110,180	20,046	29,091	13,035	6,539	10,277	6,426	3,233	2,722

Source: U.S. General Accounting Office. *Affirmative Employment: Assessing Progress of EEO Groups in Key Federal Jobs Can Be Improved* GAO/GGD-93-65. Washington, DC: U.S. GAO (March 1993), p. 59. Primary source: Office of Personnel Management.

★ 844 ★

Employment

White Collar Federal Employment, by Race/Ethnicity

Data show percent distribution of employees by race/ethnicity for each general schedule (GS) pay level. SES stands for Senior Executive Service.

Race/ethnicity	GS 1-10	GS 11-13	GS 14-15	SES
White	65.0	81.0	88.0	92.0
Black	24.0	11.0	6.0	5.0
Hispanic	6.0	4.0	2.0	2.0
Native American	2.0	1.0	1.0	1.0
Asian/Pacific Islander	3.0	4.0	3.0	1.0

Source: "Federal diversity." *Manpower Comments* (January/February 1994), p. 28. Primary source: Merit Systems Protection Board and *The Washington Post*.

★ 845 ★

Employment

Native American Men in Key Federal Jobs

These data show the number of Native American men per 1,000 white men at each general schedule (GS) pay level in fiscal years 1984 and 1990. Figures refer to employment in 25 federal agencies.

GS	Native American men per 1,000 white men		Ratio
	1984	1990	
<11	20	23	1.15
11	10	13	1.3
12	8	9	1.13
13	6	7	1.17
14	6	8	1.33
15	4	4	1

Source: U.S. General Accounting Office. *Affirmative Employment: Assessing Progress of EEO Groups in Key Federal Jobs Can Be Improved* GAO/GGD-93-65. Washington, DC: U.S. GAO (March 1993), p. 35. Primary source: Office of Personnel Management.

★ 846 ★

Employment

Native American Women in Key Federal Jobs

These data show the number of Native American women per 1,000 white men at each general schedule (GS) pay level in fiscal years 1984 and 1990. Figures refer to employment in 25 federal agencies.

GS	Native American women per 1,000 white men		Ratio
	1984	1990	
<11	29	28	0.97
11	6	10	1.67
12	2.3	4	1.74
13	0.9	1.9	2.11
14	0.6	1.4	2.33
15	0.3	0.7	2.33

Source: U.S. General Accounting Office. *Affirmative Employment: Assessing Progress of EEO Groups in Key Federal Jobs Can Be Improved* GAO/GGD-93-65. Washington, DC: U.S. GAO (March 1993), p. 36. Primary source: Office of Personnel Management.

★ 847 ★

Employment

Native Americans Employed, Hired, and Separated From Key Federal Jobs

These data show numbers of Native American men and women per 1,000 white men employed in, hired for, and separated from key federal jobs in fiscal years 1984 and 1990.

GS	Native American men per 1,000 white men		Native American women per 1,000 white men	
	1984	1990	1984	1990
Hired	8	12	9	12
Employed	12	13	11	11
Separated	12	13	8	12

Source: U.S. General Accounting Office. *Affirmative Employment: Assessing Progress of EEO Groups in Key Federal Jobs Can Be Improved* GAO/GGD-93-65. Washington, DC: U.S. GAO (March 1993), p. 42. Primary source: Office of Personnel Management.

★ 848 ★

Employment

Number of Full-Time State and Local Government Employees, by Sex and Race/Ethnicity, 1990: U.S. Summary

Annual salary	Total		American Indian Alaska Native		White		Black		Hispanic		Asian	
	Number	Percent	Number	Percent	Number	Percent	Number	Percent	Number	Percent	Number	Percent
Male												
100-7,900	18,886	49.8	149	0.4	14,733	38.8	2,970	7.8	920	2.4	114	0.3
8,000-11,900	69,181	37.9	498	0.3	39,724	21.8	22,740	12.5	5,945	3.3	274	0.2
12,000-15,900	229,659	39.5	1,934	0.3	146,625	25.2	61,961	10.7	17,884	3.1	1,255	0.2
16,000-19,900	406,326	46.5	3,184	0.4	284,873	32.6	86,471	9.9	28,324	3.2	3,474	0.4
20,000-24,900	583,235	51.9	3,422	0.3	435,728	38.8	99,904	8.9	36,948	3.3	7,233	0.6
25,000-32,900	786,335	62.6	3,962	0.3	609,236	48.5	112,876	9.0	46,865	3.7	13,396	1.1
33,000-42,900	603,595	71.6	2,707	0.3	483,250	57.3	65,685	7.8	36,957	4.4	14,996	1.8
43,000-Plus	374,137	78.6	1,236	0.3	311,370	65.4	29,563	6.2	17,885	3.8	14,083	3.0
Total	3,071,354	57.2	17,092	0.3	2,335,539	43.3	482,170	9.0	191,728	3.6	54,825	1.0
Female												
100-7,900	19,069	50.2	100	0.3	14,586	38.4	3,520	9.3	762	2.0	101	0.3
8,000-11,900	113,129	62.1	620	0.3	75,196	41.2	30,540	16.8	6,249	3.4	524	0.3
12,000-15,900	351,550	60.5	2,201	0.4	241,407	41.5	85,723	14.7	20,084	3.5	2,135	0.4
16,000-19,900	467,700	53.5	2,662	0.3	318,643	36.5	111,412	12.7	29,602	3.4	5,381	0.6
20,000-24,900	540,928	48.1	2,594	0.2	365,502	32.5	127,721	11.4	34,273	3.0	10,838	1.0
25,000-32,900	468,883	37.4	2,204	0.2	333,124	26.5	93,613	7.5	26,371	2.1	13,571	1.1
33,000-42,900	239,252	28.4	870	0.1	170,135	20.2	43,104	5.1	13,122	1.6	12,021	1.4
43,000-Plus	101,901	21.4	385	0.1	74,165	15.6	15,954	3.4	4,567	1.0	6,830	1.4
Total	2,302,412	42.8	11,636	0.2	1,592,758	29.6	511,587	9.5	135,030	2.5	51,401	1.0
Total												
100-7,900	37,955	100.0	249	0.7	29,319	77.2	6,490	17.1	1,682	4.4	215	0.6

[Continued]

★ 848 ★

Number of Full-Time State and Local Government Employees, by Sex and Race/Ethnicity, 1990: U.S. Summary

[Continued]

Annual salary	Total		American Indian Alaska Native		White		Black		Hispanic		Asian	
	Number	Percent	Number	Percent	Number	Percent	Number	Percent	Number	Percent	Number	Percent
8,000-11,900	182,310	100.0	1,118	0.6	114,920	63.0	53,280	29.2	12,194	6.7	798	0.4
12,000-15,900	581,209	100.0	4,135	0.7	388,032	66.8	147,684	25.4	37,968	6.5	3,390	0.6
16,000-19,900	874,026	100.0	5,846	0.7	603,516	69.1	197,883	22.6	57,926	6.6	8,855	1.0
20,000-24,900	1,124,163	100.0	6,016	0.5	801,230	71.3	227,625	20.2	71,221	6.3	18,071	1.6
25,000-32,900	1,255,218	100.0	6,166	0.5	942,360	75.1	206,489	16.5	73,236	5.8	26,967	2.1
33,000-42,900	842,847	100.0	3,577	0.4	653,385	77.5	108,789	12.9	50,079	5.9	27,017	3.2
43,000-Plus	476,038	100.0	1,621	0.3	385,535	81.0	45,517	9.6	22,452	4.7	20,913	4.4
Total	5,373,766	100.0	28,728	0.5	3,918,297	72.9	993,757	18.5	326,758	6.1	106,226	2.0

Source: U.S. Equal Employment Opportunity Commission. *Job Patterns for Minorities and Women in State and Local Government, 1990.* Washington, DC: U.S. Government Printing Office, 1991, p. 1.

★ 849 ★

Employment

Number of Full-Time State and Local Government Employees, by Sex and Race/Ethnicity, 1990: Officials and Administrators

Annual salary	Total		Indian		White		Black		Hispanic		Asian	
	Number	Percent	Number	Percent	Number	Percent	Number	Percent	Number	Percent	Number	Percent
Male												
100-7,900	2,401	77.6	1	0.0	2,239	72.4	125	4.0	30	1.0	6	0.2
8,000-11,900	1,366	56.1	4	0.2	1,182	48.6	140	5.8	36	1.5	4	0.2
12,000-15,900	2,114	42.5	8	0.2	1,821	36.6	186	3.7	88	1.8	11	0.2
16,000-19,900	4,921	49.6	19	0.2	4,280	43.1	401	4.0	210	2.1	11	0.1
20,000-24,900	11,637	56.5	43	0.2	10,287	49.9	882	4.3	388	1.9	37	0.2
25,000-32,900	31,735	57.9	127	0.2	27,559	50.3	2,773	5.1	1,090	2.0	186	0.3
33,000-42,900	51,491	66.7	232	0.3	45,336	58.7	3,883	5.0	1,557	2.0	483	0.6
43,000-Plus	100,076	79.1	304	0.2	88,209	69.8	6,900	5.5	2,941	2.3	1,722	1.4
Total	205,741	68.7	738	0.2	180,913	60.4	15,290	5.1	6,340	2.1	2,460	0.8
Female												
100-7,900	693	22.4	2	0.1	641	20.7	42	1.4	5	0.2	3	0.1
8,000-11,900	1,067	43.9	22	0.9	941	38.7	71	2.9	31	1.3	2	0.1
12,000-15,900	2,856	57.5	12	0.2	2,542	51.1	209	4.2	86	1.7	7	0.1
16,000-19,900	5,000	50.4	31	0.3	4,339	43.7	464	4.7	151	1.5	15	0.2
20,000-24,900	8,960	43.5	47	0.2	7,578	36.8	923	4.5	384	1.9	28	0.1
25,000-32,900	23,046	42.1	95	0.2	16,491	30.1	5,016	9.2	1,252	2.3	192	0.4
33,000-42,900	25,718	33.3	106	0.1	20,015	25.9	4,281	5.5	982	1.3	334	0.4
43,000-Plus	26,360	20.9	63	0.0	20,550	16.3	4,187	3.3	846	0.7	734	0.6
Total	93,720	31.3	378	0.1	73,097	24.4	15,193	5.1	3,737	1.2	1,315	0.4
Total												
100-7,900	3,094	100.0	3	0.1	2,880	93.1	167	5.4	35	1.1	9	0.3
8,000-11,900	2,433	100.0	26	1.1	2,123	87.3	211	8.7	67	2.8	6	0.2
12,000-15,900	4,970	100.0	20	0.4	4,363	87.8	395	7.9	174	3.5	18	0.4
16,000-19,900	9,921	100.0	50	0.5	8,619	86.9	865	8.7	361	3.6	26	0.3

[Continued]

★ 849 ★

Number of Full-Time State and Local Government Employees, by Sex and Race/Ethnicity, 1990: Officials and Administrators

[Continued]

Annual salary	Total		Indian		White		Black		Hispanic		Asian	
	Number	Percent	Number	Percent	Number	Percent	Number	Percent	Number	Percent	Number	Percent
20,000-24,900	20,597	100.0	90	0.4	17,865	86.7	1,805	8.8	772	3.7	65	0.3
25,000-32,900	54,781	100.0	222	0.4	44,050	80.4	7,789	14.2	2,342	4.3	378	0.7
33,000-42,900	77,209	100.0	388	0.4	65,351	84.6	8,164	10.6	2,539	3.3	817	1.1
43,000-Plus	126,456	100.0	367	0.3	108,759	86.0	11,087	8.8	3,787	3.0	2,456	1.9
Total	299,461	100.0	1,116	0.4	254,010	84.8	30,483	10.2	10,077	3.4	3,775	1.3

Source: U.S. Equal Employment Opportunity Commission. *Job Patterns for Minorities and Women in State and Local Government, 1990.* Washington, DC: U.S. Government Printing Office, 1990, p. 4.

★ 850 ★

Employment

Number of Full-Time State and Local Government Employees, by Sex and Race/Ethnicity, 1990: Professionals

Annual salary	Total		Indian		White		Black		Hispanic		Asian	
	Number	Percent	Number	Percent	Number	Percent	Number	Percent	Number	Percent	Number	Percent
Male												
100-7,900	1,866	54.0	11	0.3	1,656	47.9	110	3.2	57	1.6	32	0.9
8,000-11,900	1,265	39.2	5	0.2	1,095	33.9	128	4.0	21	0.7	16	0.5
12,000-15,900	5,035	32.4	32	0.2	3,900	25.1	827	5.3	251	1.6	25	0.2
16,000-19,900	24,557	35.8	173	0.3	19,063	27.8	3,943	5.8	1,162	1.7	216	0.3
20,000-24,900	72,267	38.6	612	0.3	56,607	30.2	10,663	5.7	3,346	1.8	1,039	0.6
25,000-32,900	163,673	43.8	932	0.2	134,457	36.0	17,067	4.6	7,025	1.9	4,192	1.1
33,000-42,900	181,345	54.3	747	0.2	150,791	45.2	14,839	4.4	7,519	2.3	7,449	2.2
43,000-Plus	147,867	71.7	397	0.2	124,245	60.2	8,008	3.9	5,745	2.8	9,472	4.6
Total	597,875	50.2	2,909	0.2	491,814	41.3	55,585	4.7	25,126	2.1	22,441	1.9
Female												
100-7,900	1,589	46.0	0	0.0	1,271	36.8	245	7.1	47	1.4	26	0.8
8,000-11,900	1,961	60.8	7	0.2	1,521	47.1	373	11.6	44	1.4	16	0.5
12,000-15,900	10,499	67.6	73	0.5	7,848	50.5	2,002	12.9	509	3.3	67	0.4
16,000-19,900	43,966	64.2	323	0.5	32,443	47.3	8,853	12.9	2,067	3.0	280	0.4
20,000-24,900	114,876	61.4	639	0.3	85,927	45.9	22,299	11.9	4,868	2.6	1,143	0.6
25,000-32,900	210,247	56.2	915	0.2	160,725	43.0	34,996	9.4	8,246	2.2	5,365	1.4
33,000-42,900	152,582	45.7	490	0.1	111,248	33.3	24,756	7.4	6,739	2.0	9,349	2.8
43,000-Plus	58,372	28.3	212	0.1	41,736	20.2	8,150	4.0	2,656	1.3	5,618	2.7
Total	594,092	49.8	2,659	0.2	442,719	37.1	101,674	8.5	25,176	2.1	21,864	1.8
Total												
100-7,900	3,455	100.0	11	0.3	2,927	84.7	355	10.3	104	3.0	58	1.7
8,000-11,900	3,226	100.0	12	0.4	2,616	81.1	501	15.5	65	2.0	32	1.0
12,000-15,900	15,534	100.0	105	0.7	11,748	75.6	2,829	18.2	760	4.9	92	0.6
16,000-19,900	68,523	100.0	496	0.7	51,506	75.2	12,796	18.7	3,229	4.7	496	0.7
20,000-24,900	187,143	100.0	1,251	0.7	142,534	76.2	32,962	17.6	8,214	4.4	2,182	1.2
25,000-32,900	373,920	100.0	1,847	0.5	295,182	78.9	52,063	13.9	15,271	4.1	9,557	2.6
33,000-42,900	333,927	100.0	1,237	0.4	262,039	78.5	39,595	11.9	14,258	4.3	16,798	5.0

[Continued]

★ 850 ★

Number of Full-Time State and Local Government Employees, by Sex and Race/Ethnicity, 1990:
Professionals
[Continued]

Annual salary	Total		Indian		White		Black		Hispanic		Asian	
	Number	Percent	Number	Percent	Number	Percent	Number	Percent	Number	Percent	Number	Percent
43,000-Plus	206,239	100.0	609	0.3	165,981	80.5	16,158	7.8	8,401	4.1	15,090	7.3
Total	1,191,967	100.0	5,568	0.5	934,533	78.4	157,259	13.2	50,302	4.2	44,305	3.7

Source: U.S. Equal Employment Opportunity Commission. *Job Patterns for Minorities and Women in State and Local Government, 1990.* Washington, DC: U.S. Government Printing Office, 1990, p. 5.

★ 851 ★
Employment

Number of Full-Time State and Local Government Employees, by Sex and Race/Ethnicity, 1990:
Protective Service

Annual salary	Total		Indian		White		Black		Hispanic		Asian	
	Number	Percent	Number	Percent	Number	Percent	Number	Percent	Number	Percent	Number	Percent
Male												
100-7,900	3,541	63.1	61	1.1	2,842	50.6	478	8.5	145	2.6	15	0.3
8,000-11,900	6,512	68.2	56	0.6	4,921	51.5	1,148	12.0	364	3.8	23	0.2
12,000-15,900	35,914	75.8	253	0.5	26,288	55.5	7,741	16.3	1,523	3.2	109	0.2
16,000-19,900	98,924	82.7	960	0.8	76,332	63.8	16,400	13.7	4,963	4.1	269	0.2
20,000-24,900	146,292	84.8	740	0.4	115,610	67.0	22,569	13.1	6,881	4.0	492	0.3
25,000-32,900	226,986	89.9	962	0.4	183,608	71.9	29,483	11.6	11,719	4.6	1,214	0.5
33,000-42,900	196,812	90.7	658	0.3	155,404	71.6	23,060	10.6	15,285	7.0	2,405	1.1
43,000-Plus	52,641	92.3	166	0.3	42,809	75.1	4,305	7.6	4,539	8.0	822	1.4
Total	767,622	86.8	3,856	0.4	607,814	68.8	105,184	11.9	45,419	5.1	5,349	0.6
Female												
100-7,900	2,073	36.9	12	0.2	1,348	24.0	602	10.7	107	1.9	4	0.1
8,000-11,900	3,039	31.8	15	0.2	2,243	23.5	628	6.6	149	1.6	4	0.0
12,000-15,900	11,449	24.2	78	0.2	7,524	15.9	3,442	7.3	381	0.8	24	0.1
16,000-19,900	20,667	17.3	185	0.2	13,872	11.6	5,634	4.7	918	0.8	58	0.0
20,000-24,900	26,222	15.2	164	0.1	16,756	9.7	8,110	4.7	1,132	0.7	60	0.0
25,000-32,900	28,268	11.1	140	0.1	16,888	6.6	9,287	3.6	1,758	0.7	195	0.1
33,000-42,900	20,274	9.3	65	0.0	11,393	5.2	6,475	3.0	2,047	0.9	294	0.1
43,000-Plus	4,363	7.7	13	0.0	2,813	4.9	971	1.7	484	0.8	82	0.1
Total	116,355	13.2	672	0.1	72,837	8.2	35,149	4.0	6,976	0.8	721	0.1
Total												
100-7,900	5,614	100.0	73	1.3	4,190	74.6	1,080	19.2	252	4.5	19	0.3
8,000-11,900	9,551	100.0	71	0.7	7,164	75.0	1,776	18.6	513	5.4	27	0.3
12,000-15,900	47,363	100.0	331	0.7	33,812	71.4	11,183	23.6	1,904	4.0	133	0.3
16,000-19,900	119,591	100.0	1,145	1.0	90,204	75.4	22,034	18.4	5,881	4.9	327	0.3
20,000-24,900	172,514	100.0	904	0.5	132,366	76.7	30,679	17.8	8,013	4.6	552	0.3
25,000-32,900	255,254	100.0	1,102	0.4	200,496	78.5	38,770	15.2	13,477	5.3	1,409	0.6
33,000-42,900	217,086	100.0	723	0.3	166,797	76.8	29,535	13.6	17,332	8.0	2,699	1.2

[Continued]

★ 851 ★

Number of Full-Time State and Local Government Employees, by Sex and Race/Ethnicity, 1990: Protective Service
[Continued]

Annual salary	Total		Indian		White		Black		Hispanic		Asian	
	Number	Percent	Number	Percent	Number	Percent	Number	Percent	Number	Percent	Number	Percent
43,000-Plus	57,004	100.0	179	0.3	45,622	80.0	5,276	9.3	5,023	8.8	904	1.6
Total	883,977	100.0	4,528	0.5	680,651	77.0	140,333	15.9	52,395	5.9	6,070	0.7

Source: U.S. Equal Employment Opportunity Commission. *Job Patterns for Minorities and Women in State and Local Government, 1990.* Washington, DC: U.S. Government Printing Office, 1990, p. 7.

★ 852 ★

Employment

Number of Full-Time State and Local Government Employees, by Sex and Race/Ethnicity, 1990: Technicians

Annual salary	Total		Indian		White		Black		Hispanic		Asian	
	Number	Percent	Number	Percent	Number	Percent	Number	Percent	Number	Percent	Number	Percent
Male												
100-7,900	701	43.7	1	0.1	597	37.2	70	4.4	25	1.6	8	0.5
8,000-11,900	2,760	36.0	12	0.2	2,096	27.3	402	5.2	240	3.1	10	0.1
12,000-15,900	14,966	38.0	127	0.3	11,114	28.2	2,638	6.7	998	2.5	89	0.2
16,000-19,900	35,024	43.5	318	0.4	27,465	34.1	4,828	6.0	2,028	2.5	385	0.5
20,000-24,900	61,716	50.3	418	0.3	49,090	40.0	7,505	6.1	3,525	2.9	1,178	1.0
25,000-32,900	89,203	63.9	403	0.3	73,108	52.3	8,617	6.2	4,728	3.4	2,347	1.7
33,000-42,900	61,736	82.1	249	0.3	52,071	69.2	4,726	6.3	2,984	4.0	1,706	2.3
43,000-Plus	31,438	90.1	110	0.3	26,462	75.8	2,202	6.3	1,829	5.2	835	2.4
Total	297,544	59.3	1,638	0.3	242,003	48.2	30,988	6.2	16,357	3.3	6,558	1.3
Female												
100-7,900	902	56.3	6	0.4	738	46.0	122	7.6	24	1.5	12	0.7
8,000-11,900	4,917	64.0	29	0.4	3,491	45.5	930	12.1	440	5.7	27	0.4
12,000-15,900	24,413	62.0	115	0.3	17,134	43.5	5,795	14.7	1,223	3.1	146	0.4
16,000-19,900	45,568	56.5	266	0.3	32,376	40.2	10,098	12.5	2,325	2.9	503	0.6
20,000-24,900	61,063	49.7	275	0.2	40,956	33.4	14,389	11.7	3,708	3.0	1,735	1.4
25,000-32,900	50,471	36.1	208	0.1	34,734	24.9	9,414	6.7	3,649	2.6	2,466	1.8
33,000-42,900	13,495	17.9	60	0.1	9,535	12.7	2,099	2.8	1,012	1.3	789	1.0
43,000-Plus	3,453	9.9	12	0.0	2,521	7.2	499	1.4	202	0.6	219	0.6
Total	204,282	40.7	971	0.2	141,485	28.2	43,346	8.6	12,583	2.5	5,897	1.2
Total												
100-7,900	1,603	100.0	7	0.4	1,335	83.3	192	12.0	49	3.1	20	1.2
8,000-11,900	7,677	100.0	41	0.5	5,587	72.8	1,332	17.4	680	8.9	37	0.5
12,000-15,900	39,379	100.0	242	0.6	28,248	71.7	8,433	21.4	2,221	5.6	235	0.6
16,000-19,900	80,592	100.0	584	0.7	59,841	74.3	14,926	18.5	4,353	5.4	888	1.1
20,000-24,900	122,779	100.0	693	0.6	90,046	73.3	21,894	17.8	7,233	5.9	2,913	2.4
25,000-32,900	139,674	100.0	611	0.4	107,842	77.2	18,031	12.9	8,377	6.0	4,813	3.4
33,000-42,900	75,231	100.0	309	0.4	61,606	81.9	6,825	9.1	3,996	5.3	2,495	3.3

[Continued]

★ 852 ★

Number of Full-Time State and Local Government Employees, by Sex and Race/Ethnicity, 1990: Technicians
[Continued]

Annual salary	Total		Indian		White		Black		Hispanic		Asian	
	Number	Percent	Number	Percent	Number	Percent	Number	Percent	Number	Percent	Number	Percent
43,000-Plus	34,891	100.0	122	0.3	28,983	83.1	2,701	7.7	2,031	5.8	1,054	3.0
Total	501,826	100.0	2,609	0.5	383,488	76.4	74,334	14.8	28,940	5.8	12,455	2.5

Source: U.S. Equal Employment Opportunity Commission. *Job Patterns for Minorities and Women in State and Local Government, 1990*. Washington, DC: U.S. Government Printing Office, 1990, p. 6.

★ 853 ★

Employment

Number of Full-Time Local Government Employees, by Sex and Income Level, 1990: Counties

Annual salary	Total		Indian		White		Black		Hispanic		Asian	
	Number	Percent	Number	Percent	Number	Percent	Number	Percent	Number	Percent	Number	Percent
Male												
100-7,900	9,303	46.0	51	0.3	7,597	37.6	1,213	6.0	397	2.0	45	0.2
8,000-11,900	22,698	32.3	206	0.3	15,844	22.6	5,116	7.3	1,451	2.1	81	0.1
12,000-15,900	65,587	33.9	622	0.3	49,090	25.4	11,579	6.0	3,969	2.1	327	0.2
16,000-19,900	100,803	41.8	523	0.3	79,383	32.9	13,658	5.7	6,144	2.5	995	0.4
20,000-24,900	121,749	47.3	682	0.3	96,663	37.6	15,006	5.8	7,538	2.9	1,860	0.7
25,000-32,900	123,477	53.1	677	0.3	98,827	42.5	13,811	5.9	7,813	3.4	2,349	1.0
33,000-42,900	86,811	58.7	416	0.3	70,430	47.6	7,710	5.2	5,766	3.9	2,489	1.7
43,000-Plus	71,248	71.2	288	0.3	60,346	60.3	4,337	4.3	3,977	4.0	2,300	2.3
Total	601,676	47.6	3,565	0.3	478,180	37.9	72,430	5.7	37,055	2.9	10,446	0.8
Female												
100-7,900	10,916	54.0	68	0.3	8,929	44.2	1,366	6.8	494	2.4	59	0.3
8,000-11,900	47,468	67.7	212	0.3	36,419	51.9	8,283	11.8	2,364	3.4	190	0.3
12,000-15,900	127,950	66.1	747	0.4	100,510	51.9	19,003	9.8	6,964	3.6	726	0.4
16,000-19,900	140,565	58.2	685	0.3	104,572	43.3	23,469	9.7	9,929	4.1	1,910	0.8
20,000-24,900	135,381	52.7	596	0.2	95,344	37.1	24,535	9.5	11,432	4.4	3,474	1.4
25,000-32,900	109,069	46.9	453	0.2	80,673	34.7	17,319	7.4	7,503	3.2	3,121	1.3
33,000-42,900	61,198	41.3	244	0.2	43,233	29.2	9,105	6.2	4,446	3.0	4,170	2.8
43,000-Plus	28,846	28.8	99	0.1	21,556	21.5	3,551	3.5	1,637	1.6	2,003	2.0
Total	661,393	52.4	3,104	0.2	491,236	38.9	106,681	8.4	44,769	3.5	15,653	1.2
Total												
100-7,900	20,219	100.0	119	0.6	16,526	81.7	2,579	12.8	891	4.4	104	0.5
8,000-11,900	70,166	100.0	418	0.6	52,263	74.5	13,399	19.1	3,815	5.4	271	0.4
12,000-15,900	193,537	100.0	1,369	0.7	149,600	77.3	30,582	15.8	10,933	5.6	1,053	0.5
16,000-19,900	241,368	100.0	1,308	0.5	183,955	76.2	37,127	15.4	16,073	6.7	2,905	1.2
20,000-24,900	257,130	100.0	1,278	0.5	192,007	74.7	39,541	15.4	18,970	7.4	5,334	2.1
25,000-32,900	232,546	100.0	1,130	0.5	179,500	77.2	31,130	13.4	15,316	6.6	5,470	2.4
33,000-42,900	148,009	100.0	660	0.4	113,663	76.8	16,815	11.4	10,212	6.9	6,659	4.5
43,000-Plus	100,094	100.0	387	0.4	81,902	81.8	7,888	7.9	5,614	5.6	4,303	4.3
Total	1,263,069	100.0	6,669	0.5	969,416	76.8	179,061	14.2	81,824	6.5	26,099	2.1

Source: U.S. Equal Employment Opportunity Commission. *Job Patterns for Minorities and Women in State and Local Government, 1990*. Washington, DC: U.S. Government Printing Office, 1990, p. 15.

★ 854 ★

Employment

Number of Full-Time Local Government Employees, by Sex and Income Level, 1990: Special Districts

Annual salary	Total		Indian		White		Black		Hispanic		Asian	
	Number	Percent	Number	Percent	Number	Percent	Number	Percent	Number	Percent	Number	Percent
Male												
100-7,900	975	42.7	8	0.4	533	23.4	202	8.9	205	9.0	27	1.2
8,000-11,900	5,390	25.7	12	0.1	1,969	9.4	2,343	11.2	1,004	4.8	52	0.3
12,000-15,900	9,800	25.6	26	0.1	4,517	11.8	3,885	10.1	1,228	3.2	144	0.4
16,000-19,900	13,550	33.1	64	0.2	7,133	17.4	4,870	11.9	1,268	3.1	215	0.5
20,000-24,900	25,352	47.6	174	0.3	15,382	28.9	6,964	13.1	2,366	4.4	466	0.9
25,000-32,900	66,905	62.7	351	0.3	41,296	38.7	18,912	17.7	5,053	4.7	1,293	1.2
33,000-42,900	44,961	68.1	497	0.8	32,404	49.1	7,329	11.1	3,415	5.2	1,315	2.0
43,000-Plus	33,190	79.0	170	0.4	24,112	57.4	6,147	14.6	1,310	3.1	1,451	3.5
Total	200,123	54.0	1,302	0.4	127,346	34.4	50,652	13.7	15,850	4.3	4,973	1.3
Female												
100-7,900	307	57.3	7	0.3	875	38.3	353	15.5	62	2.7	10	0.4
8,000-11,900	15,565	74.3	31	0.1	8,678	41.4	5,395	25.7	1,384	6.6	77	0.4
12,000-15,900	28,540	74.4	63	0.2	16,077	41.9	10,089	26.3	1,997	5.2	314	0.8
16,000-19,900	27,445	66.9	76	0.2	16,809	41.1	8,529	20.8	1,647	4.0	324	0.8
20,000-24,900	27,906	52.4	149	0.3	19,002	35.8	6,611	12.4	1,524	2.9	570	1.1
25,000-32,900	39,812	37.3	150	0.1	27,783	26.0	8,700	8.2	1,910	1.8	1,269	1.2
33,000-42,900	21,047	31.9	94	0.1	15,672	23.7	3,398	5.1	778	1.2	1,105	1.7
43,000-Plus	8,844	21.0	40	0.1	6,294	15.0	1,800	4.3	247	0.6	463	1.1
Total	170,466	46.0	610	0.2	111,300	30.0	44,875	12.1	9,549	2.6	4,132	1.1
Total												
100-7,900	2,282	100.0	15	0.7	1,408	61.7	555	24.3	267	11.7	37	1.6
8,000-11,900	20,955	100.0	43	0.2	10,647	50.8	7,738	36.9	2,388	11.4	139	0.7
12,000-15,900	38,340	100.0	89	0.2	20,594	53.7	13,974	36.4	3,225	8.4	458	1.2
16,000-19,900	40,995	100.0	140	0.3	24,002	58.5	13,399	32.7	2,915	7.1	539	1.3
20,000-24,900	53,258	100.0	322	0.6	34,434	64.7	13,575	25.5	3,890	7.3	1,036	1.9
25,000-32,900	106,717	100.0	501	0.5	69,079	64.7	27,612	25.9	6,963	6.5	2,562	2.4
33,000-42,900	66,008	100.0	501	0.9	48,076	72.8	10,727	16.3	4,194	6.4	2,420	3.7
43,000-Plus	42,034	100.0	210	0.5	30,403	72.3	7,947	18.9	1,557	2.7	1,914	4.6
Total	370,589	100.0	1,912	0.5	238,646	64.4	95,527	25.8	25,399	6.9	9,105	2.5

Source: U.S. Equal Employment Opportunity Commission. *Job Patterns for Minorities and Women in State and Local Government, 1990.* Washington, DC: U.S. Government Printing Office, 1990, p. 24.

★ 855 ★

Employment

Number of Full-Time Local Government Employees, by Sex and Income Level, 1990: Cities

Annual salary	Total		Indian		White		Black		Hispanic		Asian	
	Number	Percent	Number	Percent	Number	Percent	Number	Percent	Number	Percent	Number	Percent
Male												
100-7,900	5,732	56.0	73	0.7	4,261	41.6	1,081	10.6	292	2.9	25	0.2
8,000-11,900	22,655	59.7	161	0.4	10,596	27.9	9,228	24.3	2,617	6.9	53	0.1
12,000-15,900	74,004	60.3	492	0.4	41,058	33.4	23,853	19.4	8,292	6.8	309	0.3
16,000-19,900	145,888	61.8	853	0.4	90,394	38.3	39,933	16.9	13,633	5.8	1,075	0.5
20,000-24,900	210,384	64.7	1,015	0.3	143,760	44.2	45,441	14.0	17,580	5.4	2,588	0.8
25,000-32,900	300,364	76.4	1,337	0.3	222,911	56.7	48,139	12.2	22,403	5.7	5,574	1.4
33,000-42,900	249,284	82.7	978	0.3	194,102	64.4	30,294	10.0	17,646	5.9	6,264	2.1
43,000-Plus	137,875	85.5	494	0.3	112,563	69.8	11,846	7.3	8,320	5.2	4,652	2.9
Total	1,146,186	72.2	5,403	0.3	819,645	51.6	209,815	13.2	90,783	5.7	20,540	1.3
Female												
100-7,900	4,501	44.0	21	0.2	3,044	29.7	1,231	12.0	190	1.9	15	0.1
8,000-11,900	15,273	40.3	86	0.2	9,164	24.2	4,886	12.9	1,083	2.9	54	0.1
12,000-15,900	48,776	39.7	295	0.2	32,403	26.4	12,249	10.0	3,609	2.9	220	0.2
16,000-19,900	90,017	38.2	446	0.2	51,675	21.9	29,141	12.4	7,775	3.3	980	0.4
20,000-24,900	114,987	35.3	506	0.2	60,366	18.6	41,698	12.8	9,754	3.0	2,663	0.8
25,000-32,900	92,670	23.6	455	0.1	55,592	14.1	25,112	6.4	7,222	1.8	4,289	1.1
33,000-42,900	52,255	17.3	208	0.1	30,728	10.2	14,308	4.7	3,687	1.2	3,324	1.1
43,000-Plus	23,337	14.5	96	0.1	14,965	9.3	4,918	3.1	1,389	0.9	1,969	1.2
Total	441,816	27.8	2,113	0.1	257,937	16.2	133,543	8.4	34,709	2.2	13,514	0.9
Total												
100-7,900	10,233	100.0	94	0.9	7,305	71.4	2,312	22.6	482	4.7	40	0.4
8,000-11,900	37,928	100.0	247	0.7	19,760	52.1	14,114	37.2	3,700	9.8	107	0.3
12,000-15,900	122,780	100.0	787	0.6	73,461	59.8	36,102	29.4	11,901	9.7	529	0.4
16,000-19,900	235,905	100.0	1,299	0.6	142,069	60.2	69,074	29.3	21,408	9.1	2,055	0.9
20,000-24,900	325,371	100.0	1,521	0.5	204,126	62.7	87,139	26.8	27,334	8.4	5,251	1.6
25,000-32,900	393,034	100.0	1,792	0.5	278,503	70.9	73,251	18.6	29,625	7.5	9,863	2.5
33,000-42,900	301,539	100.0	1,186	0.4	224,830	74.6	44,602	14.8	21,333	7.1	9,588	3.2
43,000-Plus	161,212	100.0	590	0.4	127,528	79.1	16,764	10.4	9,709	6.0	6,621	4.1
Total	1,588,002	100.0	7,516	0.5	1,077,582	67.9	343,358	21.6	125,492	7.9	34,054	2.1

Source: U.S. Equal Employment Opportunity Commission. *Job Patterns for Minorities and Women in State and Local Government, 1990.* Washington, DC: U.S. Government Printing Office, 1990, p. 18.

★ 856 ★

Employment

Number of Full-Time Local Government Employees, by Sex and Income Level, 1990: Towns

Annual salary	Total		Indian		White		Black		Hispanic		Asian	
	Number	Percent	Number	Percent	Number	Percent	Number	Percent	Number	Percent	Number	Percent
Male												
100-7,900	619	60.7	0	0.0	608	59.6	10	1.0	1	0.1	0	0.0
8,000-11,900	367	39.6	3	0.3	350	37.8	10	1.1	3	0.3	1	0.1
12,000-15,900	1,477	34.2	3	0.1	1,355	31.4	92	2.1	27	0.6	0	0.0

[Continued]

★ 856 ★

Number of Full-Time Local Government Employees, by Sex and Income Level, 1990: Towns
[Continued]

Annual salary	Total		Indian		White		Black		Hispanic		Asian	
	Number	Percent	Number	Percent	Number	Percent	Number	Percent	Number	Percent	Number	Percent
16,000-19,900	4,904	43.8	13	0.1	4,593	41.1	229	2.0	62	0.6	7	0.1
20,000-24,900	13,968	66.1	22	0.1	13,269	62.8	541	2.6	124	0.6	12	0.1
25,000-32,900	25,120	83.4	39	0.1	24,221	80.5	627	2.1	200	0.7	33	0.1
33,000-42,900	16,599	89.4	23	0.1	16,145	87.0	313	1.7	102	0.5	16	0.1
43,000-Plus	6,726	92.4	10	0.1	6,607	90.8	75	1.0	23	0.3	11	0.2
Total	69,780	73.8	113	0.1	67,148	71.0	1,897	2.0	542	0.6	80	0.1
Female												
100-7,900	401	39.3	1	0.1	397	38.9	2	0.2	1	0.1	0	0.0
8,000-11,900	559	60.4	0	0.0	532	57.5	12	1.3	12	1.3	3	0.3
12,000-15,900	2,839	65.8	4	0.1	2,712	62.8	94	2.2	25	0.6	4	0.1
16,000-19,900	6,284	56.2	4	0.0	6,067	54.2	146	1.3	46	0.4	21	0.2
20,000-24,900	7,167	33.9	7	0.0	6,842	32.4	249	1.2	52	0.2	17	0.1
25,000-32,900	4,985	16.6	9	0.0	4,776	15.9	149	0.5	33	0.1	18	0.1
33,000-42,900	1,961	10.6	1	0.0	1,902	10.2	48	0.3	7	0.0	3	0.0
43,000-Plus	553	7.6	0	0.0	523	7.2	18	0.2	6	0.1	6	0.1
Total	24,749	26.2	26	0.0	23,751	25.1	718	0.8	182	0.2	72	0.1
Total												
100-7,900	1,020	100.0	1	0.1	1,005	98.5	12	1.2	2	0.2	0	0.0
8,000-11,900	926	100.0	3	0.3	882	95.2	22	2.4	15	1.6	4	0.4
12,000-15,900	4,316	100.0	7	0.2	4,067	94.2	186	4.3	52	1.2	4	0.1
16,000-19,900	11,188	100.0	17	0.2	10,660	95.3	375	3.4	108	1.0	28	0.3
20,000-24,900	21,135	100.0	29	0.1	20,111	95.2	790	3.7	176	0.8	29	0.1
25,000-32,900	30,105	100.0	48	0.2	28,997	96.3	776	2.6	233	0.8	51	0.2
33,000-42,900	18,560	100.0	24	0.1	18,047	97.2	361	1.9	109	0.6	19	0.1
43,000-Plus	7,279	100.0	10	0.1	7,130	98.0	93	1.3	29	0.4	17	0.2
Total	94,529	100.0	139	0.1	90,899	96.2	2,615	2.8	724	0.8	152	0.2

Source: U.S. Equal Employment Opportunity Commission. *Job Patterns for Minorities and Women in State and Local Government, 1990.* Washington, DC: U.S. Government Printing Office, 1990, p. 21.

★ 857 ★

Employment

Number of Part-Time State and Local Government Employees, by Job Category, 1990

Job category	Total		Indian		White		Black		Hispanic		Asian	
	Number	Percent	Number	Percent	Number	Percent	Number	Percent	Number	Percent	Number	Percent
Male												
Officials/administrators	14,052	60.7	52	0.2	12,159	52.5	999	4.3	558	2.4	284	1.2
Professionals	50,679	31.9	245	0.2	41,006	25.8	4,780	3.0	2,020	1.3	2,628	1.7
Technicians	29,642	40.3	233	0.3	23,849	32.5	2,762	3.8	1,689	2.3	1,109	1.5
Protective service workers	71,537	70.0	348	0.3	62,879	61.6	5,067	5.0	2,737	2.7	506	0.5
Paraprofessionals	73,755	36.4	381	0.2	53,124	26.2	12,698	6.3	5,750	2.8	1,802	0.9
Administrative support	48,840	22.4	943	0.4	35,654	16.3	7,119	3.3	3,171	1.5	1,953	0.9
Skilled craft workers	26,333	68.4	257	0.7	20,098	52.2	3,934	10.2	1,698	4.4	346	0.9
Service-maintenance	180,025	61.0	1,321	0.4	133,741	45.3	30,469	10.3	12,073	4.1	2,421	0.8
Total	494,863	44.5	3,780	0.3	382,510	34.4	67,828	6.1	29,696	2.7	11,049	1.0
Female												
Officials/administrators	9,108	39.3	34	0.1	7,062	30.5	1,089	4.7	688	3.0	235	1.0

[Continued]

★ 857 ★

Number of Part-Time State and Local Government Employees, by Job Category, 1990
[Continued]

Job category	Total		Indian		White		Black		Hispanic		Asian	
	Number	Percent	Number	Percent	Number	Percent	Number	Percent	Number	Percent	Number	Percent
Professionals	108,057	68.1	380	0.2	92,059	58.0	8,575	5.4	3,174	2.0	3,869	2.4
Technicians	43,828	59.7	209	0.3	34,719	47.3	5,284	7.2	2,338	3.2	1,278	1.7
Protective service workers	30,605	30.0	145	0.1	24,516	24.0	4,733	4.6	1,070	1.0	141	0.1
Paraprofessionals	128,628	63.6	653	0.3	97,163	48.0	21,553	10.6	7,264	3.6	1,995	1.0
Administrative support	169,596	77.6	911	0.4	131,857	60.4	22,502	10.3	10,265	4.7	4,061	1.9
Skilled craft workers	12,151	31.6	69	0.2	9,649	25.1	1,781	4.6	537	1.4	115	0.3
Service-maintenance	115,018	39.0	768	0.3	86,117	29.2	20,292	6.9	6,253	2.1	1,588	0.5
Total	616,991	55.5	3,169	0.3	483,142	43.5	85,809	7.7	31,589	2.8	13,282	1.2
Total												
Officials/administrators	23,160	100.0	86	0.4	19,221	83.0	2,088	9.0	1,246	5.4	519	2.2
Professionals	158,736	100.0	625	0.4	133,065	83.8	13,355	8.4	5,194	3.3	6,497	4.1
Technicians	73,470	100.0	442	0.6	58,568	79.7	8,046	11.0	4,027	5.5	2,387	3.2
Protective service workers	102,142	100.0	493	0.5	87,395	85.6	9,800	9.6	3,807	3.7	647	0.6
Paraprofessionals	202,383	100.0	1,034	0.5	150,287	74.3	34,251	16.9	13,014	6.4	3,797	1.9
Administrative support	218,436	100.0	1,854	0.8	167,511	76.7	29,621	13.6	13,436	6.2	6,014	2.8
Skilled craft workers	38,484	100.0	326	0.8	29,747	77.3	5,715	14.9	2,235	5.8	461	1.2
Service-maintenance	295,043	100.0	2,089	0.7	219,858	74.5	50,761	17.2	18,326	6.2	4,009	1.4
Total	1,111,854	100.0	6,949	0.6	865,652	77.9	153,637	13.8	61,285	5.5	24,331	2.2

Source: U.S. Equal Employment Opportunity Commission. *Job Patterns for Minorities and Women in State and Local Government, 1990.* Washington, DC: U.S. Government Printing Office, 1991, p. 2.

Federal Expenditures

★ 858 ★

BIA FTE Summary, 1975-95 - Part I

Since 1982 the Bureau of Indian Affairs (BIA) has used the Full-Time Equivalent (FTE) process to track and control employment levels throughout the organization. FTE hours are shown by fiscal year.

Operation of Indian programs	FY 75	FY 76	FY 77	FY 78	FY 79	FY 80	FY 81	FY 82	FY 83	FY 84
Education										
School operations	7,691	6,676	5,686	5,678	5,187	4,466	6,052	5,124	5,778	5,047
Johnson O'Malley	2	1				7				
Continuing education	294	68	89	86	88	267	306	357	262	248
Tribe/Agency operations									38	
Subtotal	7,987	6,745	5,775	5,764	5,275	4,740	6,358	5,481	6,078	5,295
Tribal services										
Tribal government services	150	179	191	207	195	177	228	204	112	126
Social services	439	375	392	380	392	372	439	294	37	42
Law enforcement	352	348	483	460	472	556	633	567	48	54
Self-determination service		48	37	36	48	149	128	94	20	20
Employment development	262	393	354	367	390	364	213	204	27	100
Housing	124	107	121	118	101	103	130	92		69
Tribe/agency operations									1,175	977
Subtotal	1,327	1,450	1,578	1,568	1,598	1,721	1,771	1,455	1,419	1,388

[Continued]

★ 858 ★

BIA FTE Summary, 1975-95 - Part I

[Continued]

Operation of Indian programs	FY 75	FY 76	FY 77	FY 78	FY 79	FY 80	FY 81	FY 82	FY 83	FY 84
Navajo/Hopi Settlement			6	16	9	31	79	45	54	66
Economic development										
Business enterprise development	202	188	225	233	233	204	312	165	60	55
Road maintenance	277	254	226	244	268	374	491	392	6	8
Tribe/agency operations									532	494
Subtotal	479	442	451	477	501	678	803	557	598	557
Natural resources dev.										
Forestry and agriculture	95	819	1,091	1,051	1,118	1,201	1,478	1,303	324	373
Minerals & mining	11	9	23	17	27	31	29	33	9	16
Tribe/agency operations									964	895
Subtotal	964	828	1,114	1,068	1,145	1,232	1,507	1,336	1,297	1,284
Trust responsibilities										
Indian Rights Protection	27	32	73	74	93	92	116	121	156	151
Real estate/Fin. trust	704	645	723	718	680	737	842	809	356	231
Tribe/agency operations									661	630
Subtotal	731	677	796	792	778	829	958	930	1,173	1,012
Facilities management	1,551	1,497	1,586	1,575	1,828	1,585	1,760	1,522	1,304	1,413
General administration										
Management & Admin.	293	1,379	1,578	1,566	1,616	1,708	1,623	1,544	932	969
ADP services									68	
Program management								170	157	157
Tribe/agency operations									536	502
Subtotal	293	1,379	1,578	1,566	1,616	1,708	1,623	1,714	1,693	1,628
Total OIP	13,332	13,018	12,884	12,826	12,550	12,424	14,859	13,040	13,616	12,643
Construction	728	549	510	517	493	505	869	603	158	80
Reimbursable programs	516	548	403	435	443	483	1,140	1,411	1,080	1,849
Total FTE	14,576	14,115	13,797	13,778	13,486	13,412	16,868	15,054	14,854	14,572

Source: U.S. Senate Committee on Indian Affairs. *Fiscal Year 1995 Budget.* 103rd Cong., 2nd sess., March 3, 9, 1994 and April 13, 1994. Washington, DC: U.S. Government Printing Office, 1994, p. 213. Primary source: Bureau of Indian Affairs.

★ 859 ★

Federal Expenditures

BIA FTE Summary, 1975-95 - Part II

Since 1982 the Bureau of Indian Affairs (BIA) has used the Full-Time Equivalent (FTE) process to track and control employment levels throughout the organization. FTE hours are shown by fiscal year.

Operation of Indian programs	FY 85	FY 86	FY 87	FY 88	FY 89	FY 90	FY 91	FY 92	FY 93	FY 94	FY 95
Education											
School operations	4,618	4,274	3,775	3,764	3,749	3,486	3,361	3,902	4,015	3,906	3,806
Continuing education	249	252	277	286	273	265	253	166	240	234	232
Tribe/Agency operations	27	26	214	19	23	20	20	21	17	17	17
Subtotal	4,894	4,552	4,266	4,069	4,045	3,771	3,634	4,089	4,272	4,157	4,055
Tribal services											
Tribal government services	90	82	72	72	83	72	76	77	85	84	75
Social services	32	34	34	36	37	29	33	26	44	44	41

[Continued]

★ 859 ★

BIA FTE Summary, 1975-95 - Part II
[Continued]

Operation of Indian programs	FY 85	FY 86	FY 87	FY 88	FY 89	FY 90	FY 91	FY 92	FY 93	FY 94	FY 95
Law enforcement	41	35	40	47	46	52	48	47	54	54	46
Self-determination service	30	35	19	17	18	16	9	7	7	7	7
Employment development	22	81		6	6	6	5	4	2	2	1
Housing									73	71	69
Tribe/agency operations	905	853	883	934	943	956	906	1,060	1,019	1,014	993
Subtotal	1,120	1,120	1,048	1,112	1,133	1,131	1,077	1,221	1,284	1,276	1,232
Navajo/Hopi Settlement	64	56	52	71	47	31	35	21	23	23	23
Economic development											
Business enterprise development	57	52	61	50	46	44	44	26	49	52	52
Road maintenance	2	3	1	5	411				378	363	363
Tribe/agency operations	466	450	558	459	59	57	50	52	53	53	55
Subtotal	525	505	620	514	516	101	94	78	480	468	470
Natural resources dev.											
Forestry and agriculture	487	280	427	689	693	208	212	241	219	218	238
Minerals & mining	14	30	14	44	39	27	23	20	19	19	19
Tribe/agency operations	857	1,086	1,126	915	893	830	844	811	370	867	872
Subtotal	1,358	1,396	1,567	1,648	1,625	1,065	1,079	1,072	1,108	1,104	1,129
Trust responsibilities											
Indian Rights Protection	60	58	126	122	103	72	70	77	88	91	73
Real estate/Fin. trust	285	543	305	310	366	364	425	454	510	514	515
Tribe/agency operations	580	377	560	515	505	485	478	506	537	534	537
Subtotal	925	978	991	947	974	921	973	1,037	1,156	1,139	1,125
Facilities management	1,415	1,220	1,231	1,036	1,073	1,032	1,003	363	332	318	317
General administration											
Management & Admin.	740	726	684	664	774	714	706	743	809	824	665
ADP services	94	94	121	132	124	116	127	154	156	153	152
Program management	109	128	122	100	100	105	112	252	122	122	121
Consolidated training							1	1	2	0	0
Indian Gaming									9	9	9
Tribe/agency operations	428	543	485	481	500	490	517	726	576	566	511
Subtotal	1,371	1,491	1,412	1,377	1,498	1,425	1,463	1,876	1,674	1,674	1,458
Total OIP	11,672	11,318	11,197	10,774	10,911	9,477	9,358	9,757	10,308	10,159	9,809
Construction	146	144	130	148	99	50	646	710	154	193	181
Miscellaneous payments				6	19	20	31	27	25	25	25
Reimbursable programs	2,097	2,118	1,924	1,996	2,117	3,105	2,570	2,519	2,587	2,499	2,473
Total FTE	13,915	13,580	13,251	12,924	13,146	12,652	12,605	13,013	13,074	12,876	12,488

Source: U.S. Senate Committee on Indian Affairs. *Fiscal Year 1995 Budget.* 103rd Cong., 2nd sess., March 3, 9, 1994 and April 13, 1994. Washington, DC: U.S. Government Printing Office, 1994, p. 213. Primary source: Bureau of Indian Affairs.

★ 860 ★
Federal Expenditures

Federal Programs of Assistance to Native Americans, 1988-90 - I

Obligations represent actual dollars spent; appropriations are total amounts allotted at the beginning of the year.

Government agency and program	Appropriations ($)			Obligations ($)		
	1988	1989	1990	1988	1989	1990
Food and Nutrition Service						
Food Distribution Program on Indian Reservations	56,099	57,854	60,140	55,680	57,079	60,140
Nutrition Program for the Elderly (Title VI)	138,009	141,293	143,482	137,558	140,863	143,482
Food Stamp Program	12,678,507,000	12,915,329,000	15,969,589,000	12,338,327,000	12,859,527,000	15,522,412,000
National School Lunch Program	3,068,167	3,025,352	3,115,124	2,934,996	3,082,247	3,213,869
School Breakfast Program	479,819	514,498	563,926	473,190	513,032	564,367
Special Milk Program for Children	21,500	19,925	20,309	22,119	19,905	20,943
Summer Food Service Program	137,649	147,824	170,872	136,312	146,672	163,344
Child and Adult Care Food Program	599,836	655,932	757,288	613,076	677,431	716,866
Supplemental Food Program for Women, Infants and Children (WIC)	1,802,363	1,929,362	2,126,000	1,802,430	1,928,926	2,126,398
Agricultural Stabilization and Conservation Service (ASCS)						
Forestry Incentives Program	N/A	N/A	N/A	N/A	N/A	N/A
Agricultural Conservation Program	N/A	N/A	N/A	N/A	N/A	N/A
Emergency Conservation Program	N/A	N/A	N/A	N/A	N/A	N/A
Water Bank Program	N/A	N/A	N/A	N/A	N/A	N/A
Wool and Mohair Payment Program	N/A	N/A	N/A	N/A	N/A	N/A
Indian Acute Distress Donation Program	N/A	N/A	N/A	N/A	N/A	N/A
Livestock Feed Program	N/A	N/A	N/A	N/A	N/A	N/A
Conservation Reserve Program	N/A	N/A	N/A	N/A	N/A	N/A
Natural Resources and Environment						
Soil Conservation Service	N/A	N/A	N/A	N/A	N/A	N/A
Soil Survey Program	N/A	N/A	N/A	N/A	N/A	N/A
Technical Assistance Program	N/A	N/A	N/A	N/A	N/A	N/A
Great Plains Conservation Programs	N/A	N/A	N/A	N/A	N/A	N/A
Resource Conservation and Development Program	N/A	N/A	N/A	N/A	N/A	N/A
Soil and Water Conservation Program	N/A	N/A	N/A	N/A	N/A	N/A
Watershed Projects	N/A	N/A	N/A	N/A	N/A	N/A
Forest Service						
Range Management Program	N/A	N/A	N/A	N/A	N/A	N/A
Special Land Use Program	N/A	N/A	N/A	N/A	N/A	N/A
Senior Community Service Employment Program	N/A	N/A	N/A	N/A	N/A	N/A
Cooperative Forest Management Program	N/A	N/A	N/A	N/A	N/A	N/A
Forest Products Utilization Program	N/A	N/A	N/A	N/A	N/A	N/A
Forest Pest Management Program	N/A	N/A	N/A	N/A	N/A	N/A
Forestry Incentives Program	N/A	N/A	N/A	N/A	N/A	N/A
Free Use Timber Program	N/A	N/A	N/A	N/A	N/A	N/A
Job Corps Civilian Conservation Program	N/A	N/A	N/A	N/A	N/A	N/A
Rural Community Fire Protection Program	N/A	N/A	N/A	N/A	N/A	N/A
Small Community and Rural Development						
Farmers Home Administration (FMHA)						
Indian Out Reach Program	N/A	N/A	N/A	N/A	N/A	N/A
Indian Land Acquisition Loans	2,000,000	2,000,000	N/A	461,330	120,000	N/A
Farm Ownership Loan Program	755,000,000	819,000,000	N/A	477,000,000	400,100,000	N/A
Farm Ownership Loans for Socially Disadvantaged Persons	N/A	N/A	10,913,300	N/A	N/A	11,149,680
Farm Operating Loan Program	3,050,000,000	3,531,000,000	N/A	1,793,000,000	1,735,000,000	N/A
Water and Waste Disposal Systems for Rural Communities						
Grants	109,395,000	116,895,000	N/A	119,359,170	122,698,510	N/A
Loans	330,380,000	332,880,000	N/A	330,380,000	332,879,900	N/A
Watershed Protection and Flood Prevention Loans	8,000,000	8,000,000	N/A	148,200	0	N/A
Resource Conservation and Development Loans	1,207,000	600,000	N/A	0	0	N/A
Industrial Development Grants	6,500,000	6,500,000	N/A	6,500,000	6,500,000	N/A
Community Facility Loans	95,700,000	95,700,000		95,700,000	95,700,000	N/A
Direct	N/A	N/A	94,381,000	N/A	N/A	N/A
Guarantee	N/A	N/A	23,229,000	N/A	N/A	N/A
Rural Housing Loan Program	N/A	N/A	1,310,804,000	N/A	N/A	N/A
Rural Housing Site Development Loans	600,000	600,000	N/A	N/A	400,000	N/A
Rental and Cooperative Housing Loan Program	515,100,000	554,900,000	571,900,000	N/A	544,900,000	N/A
Housing Preservation Grant Program	19,140,000	19,140,000	19,140,000	N/A	N/A	N/A
Business and Industrial Loans Program	95,700,000	295,700,000	165,000,000	95,400,000	99,100,000	N/A
Rural Electrification Administration (REA)						
Rural Electrification Loan Program	N/A	N/A	N/A	N/A	N/A	N/A
Rural Telephone Loan Bank	N/A	N/A	N/A	N/A	N/A	N/A

[Continued]

★ 860 ★

Federal Programs of Assistance to Native Americans, 1988-90 - I

[Continued]

Government agency and program	Appropriations ($)			Obligations ($)		
	1988	1989	1990	1988	1989	1990
Rural Telephone Bank Loan Program	N/A	N/A	N/A	N/A	N/A	N/A
Rural Economic Development Loan and Grant Program	N/A	N/A	N/A	N/A	N/A	N/A
Department of Commerce						
Office of Intergovernmental Affairs	N/A	N/A	N/A	N/A	N/A	N/A
Economic Development Administration (EDA)						
Planning Assistance	22,995,000	22,995,000	N/A	22,751,000	22,956,000	N/A
Public Works Impact Program	N/A	N/A	N/A	N/A	N/A	N/A
Public Works and Development Facilities Assistance	126,000,000	126,400,000	N/A	123,613,000	123,843,000	N/A
Loan Guarantees for Business Development	150,000,000	150,000,000	N/A	0	2,508,000	N/A
Technical Assistance	1,916,000	1,916,000	N/A	1,962,000	1,849,000	N/A
Special Economic Development and Adjustment Assistance	24,657,000	24,657,000	N/A	24,673,000	27,156,000	N/A
EDA Regional Offices	N/A	N/A	N/A	N/A	N/A	N/A
Minority Business Development Agency						
Indian Business Development Center (IBDC) Program	1,495,000	1,495,000	1,495,000	1,495,000	1,495,000	1,495,000
MBDA Regional Offices	N/A	N/A	N/A	N/A	N/A	N/A
National Oceanic and Atmospheric Administration						
Anadromous Fish Grants	N/A	N/A	N/A	N/A	N/A	N/A
Alaska Eskimo Whaling Commission Grants	427,950	350,000	350,000	427,950	330,000	330,000
National Telecommunications and Information Administration						
Public Telecommunications Facilities Program	18,000,000	18,000,000	N/A	19,000,000	22,000,000	N/A
Department of Defense						
National Guard Programs for Benefit to American Indians						
American Indian Program	N/A	N/A	N/A	N/A	N/A	N/A
Procurement Technical Assistant Program	500,000	500,000	600,000	500,000	500,000	N/A
Department of the Army	N/A	N/A	N/A	N/A	N/A	N/A
Corps of Engineers						
Missouri River Division						
Development of Shoreline Recreation Potential at Lake Oahe	8,000	6,000	4,000	N/A	N/A	N/A
Development of Shoreline Recreation Potential at Lake Sakakawea	10,000	10,000	5,000	N/A	N/A	N/A
Natural Resource Work at Lake Oahe	N/A	N/A	24,000	N/A	N/A	N/A
Native American Loop Trail	N/A	N/A	N/A	N/A	N/A	N/A
Crow Creek Sioux Wildlife Mitigation Contract	N/A	45,000	90,000	N/A	N/A	N/A
Lower Brule Sioux Wildlife Mitigation Contract	N/A	45,000	90,000	N/A	N/A	N/A

Source: Walke, Roger. *Federal Programs of Assistance to Native Americans: A Report Prepared for the Senate Select Committee on Indian Affairs of the United States Senate,* S. Prt. 102-62, Washington, DC: U.S. Government Printing Office, December 1991, pp. 1-83. *Notes:* (N/A) indicates that information was not available. 1. The allotments awarded to tribes/tribal organizations is taken from a percentage of state's allotment. 2. Referred to as draw downs in the original source.

★ 861 ★

Federal Expenditures

Federal Programs of Assistance to Native Americans, 1988-90 - II

Obligations represent actual dollars spent; appropriations are total amounts allotted at the beginning of the year.

Government agency and program	Appropriations ($)			Obligations ($)		
	1988	1989	1990	1988	1989	1990
Department of Defense (cont.)						
North Pacific Division						
Grays Harbor Navigation Improvement	N/A	N/A	990,000	N/A	N/A	N/A
Puyallup River, WA	N/A	31,000	38,000	N/A	N/A	N/A
Howard A. Hanson Dam Flood Control and Low Flow Enhancement	N/A	N/A	N/A	N/A	N/A	N/A
Elwha Flood Damage Reduction Project	162,000	950,000	N/A	N/A	N/A	N/A
Neah Bay Shore Projection Project	N/A	15,000	290,000	N/A	N/A	N/A
Cultural Resources Curation Centers	26,000	42,000	114,000	N/A	N/A	N/A
Wildlife Mitigation at the Chief Joseph Dam	200,000	200,000	200,000	N/A	N/A	N/A
North Central Division						
Upper Mississippi Headwaters						
(St. Paul Monitoring Equipment)	120,000	120,000	120,000	N/A	N/A	N/A
Upper Mississippi Headwaters						
(St. Paul District Low Flow Plan)	230,000	230,000	230,000	N/A	N/A	N/A

[Continued]

★ 861 ★

Federal Programs of Assistance to Native Americans, 1988-90 - II
[Continued]

Government agency and program	Appropriations ($)			Obligations ($)		
	1988	1989	1990	1988	1989	1990
Upper Mississippi Nine Foot Channel	2,000	2,000	2,000	N/A	N/A	N/A
Mission Project Cemetery Stabilization	48,000	48,000	48,000	N/A	N/A	N/A
Indian Business Initiative	N/A	N/A	N/A	N/A	N/A	N/A
Department of the Air Force						
Special Emphasis Program	N/A	N/A	N/A	N/A	N/A	N/A
Air Force Distinguished EEO Awards	N/A	N/A	N/A	N/A	N/A	N/A
Department of Education						
Indian education - Formula Grants to Local Education Agencies						
and Tribal Schools	45,670,000	49,248,000	50,828,000	N/A	N/A	N/A
Indian Education - Special Programs and Projects	7,907,000	8,307,000	8,200,000	N/A	N/A	N/A
Indian Education - Adult Indian Education	3,000,000	4,000,000	4,078,000	N/A	N/A	N/A
Indian Education - Grants to Indian - Controlled Schools	3,500,000	3,500,000	3,451,000	N/A	N/A	N/A
Indian Education - Fellowships for Indian Students	1,600,000	1,600,000	1,587,000	N/A	N/A	N/A
Indian Education - Technical Assistance Centers	2,200,000	2,268,000	2,268,000	2,200,000	2,268,000	2,268,000
Additional Education Department Programs						
Office of Vocational and Adult Education						
Vocational Education - Indians and Hawaiian Natives						
Indians	N/A	10,808,990	11,010,277	N/A	N/A	N/A
Hawaiians	N/A	2,161,798	2,202,055	N/A	N/A	N/A
Office of Elementary and Secondary Education						
Native Hawaiian Model Curriculum Development - Kamehameha						
Elementary Education Program (KEEP)	N/A	N/A	N/A	N/A	395,200	494,000
Native Hawaiian Family - Based Education Centers	N/A	N/A	N/A	N/A	1,778,400	2,765,000
Native Hawaiian Gifted and Talented	N/A	N/A	N/A	N/A	790,000	741,000
Office of Special Education and Rehabilitative Services						
Native Hawaiian Special Education	N/A	N/A	N/A	N/A	494,000	741,000
Office of Educational Research and Improvement						
Library Services for Indian Tribes and Hawaiian Natives	N/A	N/A	N/A	N/A	2,448,700	2,419,120
Jacob K. Javits Gifted and Talented Students	N/A	N/A	N/A	N/A	7,900,000	8,880,000
Department to Energy						
Weatherization Assistance Programs	161,000,000	161,000,000	N/A	N/A	N/A	N/A
Office of Minority Economic Impact						
Minority Financial Institution Deposit Program	N/A	N/A	N/A	N/A	N/A	N/A
Minority Undergraduate Training for Energy Related Careers						
Training Program (MUTEC)	N/A	N/A	1,000,000	N/A	N/A	N/A
Minority Honors Training Program	402,000	402,000	417,000	N/A	N/A	N/A
Bid or Proposal Loan Program	N/A	N/A	N/A	N/A	N/A	N/A
State Energy Conservation Program (SECP)	N/A	N/A	N/A	9,519,000	9,519,000	9,555,000
Energy Extension Service (EES)	N/A	N/A	N/A	3,968,000	3,844,050	3,983,000
Institutional Conservation Program (ICP)	25,100,000	25,100,000	25,200,000	N/A	N/A	N/A
Department of Energy Regional and Local Contacts	N/A	N/A	N/A	N/A	N/A	N/A
Department of Health and Human Services						
Office of Human Development Services						
Administration for Children, Youth and Families						
Head Start	1,202,324,000	1,235,000,000	1,386,315,000	38,570,020	41,520,689	46,983,000
Child Welfare Services	239,350,000	246,679,000	252,647,751	239,350,000	246,679,000	252,647,751
Administration for Native Americans	29,679,000	29,975,000	31,710,574	29,679,000	29,974,988	31,710,574
Office of Policy, Planning and Legislation						
Family Violence Prevention and Services	8,138,000	8,219,000	8,273,000	8,138,000	8,227,000	8,273,000
Administration on Aging						
American Indian Native Programs	7,500,000	9,345,000	11,107,970	7,500,000	9,345,000	11,170,970
Native Hawaiian Program	N/A	1,365,000	1,433,000	N/A	N/A	N/A
Title VI - Grants for Native Americans						
Public Health Service						
Indian Health Service						
Health Management Development Program	N/A	N/A	N/A	13,064,189	15,688,238	16,500,000
Health Professions Recruitment Program for Indians	575,000	625,000	640,000	N/A	625,000	640,000
Health Professions Preparatory and Pregraduate						
Scholarship Program for Indians	2,058,000	2,119,000	2,160,000	N/A	1,327,596	2,160,000
Health Professions Scholarship Program for Indians	3,926,000	4,058,000	4,883,000	N/A	4,644,781	4,883,000
Indian Health service - Direct Services	928,824,500	1,002,623,500	1,185,910,000	N/A	N/A	N/A
National Institutes of Health						
Minority Biomedical Research Support Program (MBRS)	28,500,000	28,100,000	29,700,000	N/A	N/A	N/A

[Continued]

★ 861 ★

Federal Programs of Assistance to Native Americans, 1988-90 - II

[Continued]

Government agency and program	Appropriations ($)			Obligations ($)		
	1988	1989	1990	1988	1989	1990
Family Support Administration						
Office of Community Services						
Low Income Home Energy Assistance Program (LIHEAP)	1,532,000,000	1,383,000,000	1,393,000,000	N/A	N/A	N/A
Community Services Block Grant Programs (CSBG)[1,2]	1,793,022	1,687,048	1,689,827	729,325	1,683,328	2,453,739
Department of Housing and Urban Development						
Indian Housing Program	130,400,000	96,000,000	N/A	N/A	N/A	N/A
Comprehensive Improvement Assistance Program (CIAP)						
Modernization for Public Housing Agencies and Indians Authorities	54,000,000	43,000,000	N/A	N/A	N/A	N/A
Operating Subsidies for Public Housing Agencies and Indian housing Authorities	50,000,000	50,500,000	54,400,000	N/A	N/A	N/A
Community Development Block Grants for Indian Tribes and Alaskan Native Villages	25,500,000	27,000,000	26,200,000	27,000,000	N/A	N/A
Federal Housing Administration (FHA)						
Section 248 Mortgage Insurance on Indian Reservations	N/A	N/A	N/A	N/A	N/A	N/A
Section 247 Mortgage Insurance for Hawaiian Homelands	N/A	N/A	N/A	N/A	N/A	N/A
Indian Program Field Offices of the Department of Housing and Urban Development	N/A	N/A	N/A	N/A	N/A	N/A
Department of the Interior						
Bureau of Indian Affairs						
Office of Administration						
Indian Property Acquisition - Transfer of Federally Owned Buildings, Improvements and or Facilities (Public Law 991 Transfer)	N/A	N/A	N/A	N/A	N/A	N/A
Indian Property Acquisition - Transfer of Indian School Properties (Public Law 47 Transfer)	N/A	N/A	N/A	N/A	N/A	N/A
Office of Indian Education Programs						
Indian Education - Contracts/Grants with Indian Tribal Organizations	N/A	N/A	N/A	55,268,100	57,285,500	68,563,300
Indian Education - Federal Schools (Indian Schools)	N/A	N/A	N/A	177,890,000	175,286,000	187,596,000
Indian Education - Higher Education Grant Program	N/A	N/A	N/A	30,680,000	30,436,000	29,766,000
Adult Education	N/A	N/A	N/A	3,141,000	3,138,000	3,181,000
Johnson O'Malley Educational Assistance	N/A	N/A	N/A	20,400,000	23,000,000	23,252,000

Source: Walke, Roger. *Federal Programs of Assistance to Native Americans: A Report Prepared for the Senate Select Committee on Indian Affairs of the United States Senate,* S. Prt. 102-62, Washington, DC: U.S. Government Printing Office, December 1991, pp. 83-162. *Notes:* (N/A) indicates that information was not available. 1. The allotments awarded to tribes/tribal organizations is taken from a percentage of state's allotment. 2. Referred to as draw downs in the original source. 1. The allotments awarded to tribes/tribal organizations is taken from a percentage of state's allotment. 2. Referred to as draw downs in the original source.

★ 862 ★

Federal Expenditures

Federal Programs of Assistance to Native Americans, 1988-90 - III

Obligations represent actual dollars spent; appropriations are total amounts allotted at the beginning of the year.

Government agency and program	Appropriations ($)			Obligations ($)		
	1988	1989	1990	1988	1989	1990
Department of the Interior (cont.)						
Tribally Controlled Community Colleges (TCCC)	N/A	N/A	N/A	12,836,000	13,800,000	17,124,000
Office of Tribal Services						
Indian Housing Assistance - Housing Improvement Program (HIP)	22,827,000	22,823,000	22,463,000	N/A	N/A	N/A
Indian Judicial Services - Contracts with Indian Tribal Organizations	N/A	N/A	N/A	9,061,000	9,399,000	10,527,000
Indian Law Enforcement Services	51,223,000	52,713,000	55,126,000	N/A	N/A	N/A
Self-Determination Grants - Indian Tribal Governments	N/A	N/A	13,500,000	N/A	N/A	N/A
Social Services - General Assistance	N/A	N/A	N/A	50,443,000	51,025,000	52,630,000
Social Services - Child and Family Services	N/A	N/A	N/A	17,602,000	18,899,000	24,488,000
Social Services - Indian Child Welfare Act Title II Grants	N/A	N/A	N/A	N/A	N/A	N/A
Social Services - Child Welfare Assistance	N/A	N/A	N/A	15,943,000	16,792,000	16,402,000

[Continued]

★ 862 ★

Federal Programs of Assistance to Native Americans, 1988-90 - III
[Continued]

Government agency and program	Appropriations ($)			Obligations ($)		
	1988	1989	1990	1988	1989	1990
Office of Trust and Economic Development						
Financial Assistance - Guaranteed Loan Program	N/A	3,400,000	4,800,000	N/A	N/A	43,600,000
Financial Assistance - Direct Loan Program	N/A	N/A	N/A	N/A	N/A	8,900,000
Financial Assistance - Expect Assistance Fund	N/A	N/A	N/A	N/A	N/A	716,485
Financial Assistance - Indian Business Development Grant Program	7,000,000	7,000,000	7,000,000	N/A	6,907,159	N/A
Division of Energy and Minerals - Minerals Resource Inventory Program	7,885,000	5,724,000	4,997,000	7,742,478	5,643,638	4,997,000
Environmental Services Staff - Indian Lands - Environmental Quality Services	1,259,000	1,321,000	1,727,000	1,259,000	1,321,000	1,727,000
Division of Forestry - Indian Forests - Management, Protection and Development	N/A	32,617,000	35,965,000	N/A	32,617,000	35,965,000
Division of Forestry - Indian Forests - Fire Suppression and Emergency Pre-Suppression	N/A	N/A	29,645,000	N/A	43,645,000	43,744,000
Division of Real Estate Services	26,967,000	27,482,000	26,311,000	22,153,331	26,845,330	25,546,764
Division of Real Estate Services - Appraisals	3,645,000	3,311,000	3,435,000	3,361,595	3,165,272	3,163,208
Division of Water and Land Resources - Indian Lands - Range Management	24,982,000	26,701,000	24,542,000	24,595,000	26,102,000	23,457,000
Division of Water and Land Resources - Indian Lands - Soil and Moisture Conservation	24,982,000	21,701,000	24,542,000	24,595,000	26,102,000	23,457,000
Area Offices - Bureau of Indian Affairs						
Indian Arts and Crafts Board						
Indian Arts and Crafts Development	N/A	N/A	N/A	912,000	900,000	912,000
Minerals Management Services (MMS)						
Royalty Management Program	N/A	N/A	N/A	N/A	N/A	N/A
Bureau of Land Management	N/A	N/A	N/A	N/A	N/A	N/A
Land Conveyances and Exchanges Benefiting American Indians	N/A	N/A	N/A	N/A	N/A	N/A
Surveys of Indian Lands	N/A	N/A	N/A	N/A	N/A	N/A
Employment of Wildlife Control Work	N/A	N/A	N/A	N/A	N/A	N/A
Management of Indian Mineral Leases	N/A	N/A	N/A	N/A	N/A	N/A
Bureau of Reclamation	N/A	N/A	N/A	N/A	N/A	N/A
Office of Native Americans Affairs	N/A	N/A	N/A	N/A	N/A	N/A
Department of Justice						
Civil Rights Division	N/A	N/A	N/A	N/A	N/A	N/A
Community Relations Service	N/A	N/A	N/A	N/A	N/A	N/A
Office of Justice Programs						
Office of Juvenile Justice and Delinquency Prevention (OJJDP)	N/A	N/A	N/A	N/A	N/A	N/A
Office for Victims of Crime (OVC)						
Children's Justice Act Discretionary Grant Program for Native Americans	0	0	531,000	N/A	N/A	531,000
Discretionary Grant Assistance to Victims of Federal Crime in Indian Country	0	1,000,000	700,000	N/A	1,700,000	1,700,00
Department of Labor						
Employment and Training Administration	59,713,000	58,996,000	58,193,000	59,713,000	58,996,000	58,193,000
Office of Special Targeted Programs	59,713,000	58,996,000	58,193,000	59,713,000	58,996,000	58,193,000
Indian and Native American Employment and Training Programs	59,713,000	58,996,000	58,193,000	59,713,000	58,996,000	58,193,000
Department of Transportation						
Federal Highway Administration						
Indian Employment and Contracting Preference	N/A	N/A	N/A	N/A	N/A	N/A
Supportive Services	N/A	N/A	N/A	N/A	N/A	N/A
Indian Reservation Road Program	80,000,000	80,000,000	80,000,000	80,000,000	78,500,000	77,640,000
National Highway Traffic Safety Administration						
American Indian Highway Safety Program	528,295	541,630	548,850	N/A	N/A	N/A
Urban Mass Transportation Administration						
Section 6 Program - Research, Development and Demonstration Projects	9,000,000	7,000,000	8,000,000	N/A	N/A	393,417
Section 18 Program - Formula Grants	65,000,000	65,000,000	66,000,000	N/A	N/A	11,000,000

[Continued]

★ 862 ★

Federal Programs of Assistance to Native Americans, 1988-90 - III
[Continued]

Government agency and program	Appropriations ($)			Obligations ($)		
	1988	1989	1990	1988	1989	1990
Section 20 Program - Human Resource Programs	1,500,000	1,000,000	1,000,000	N/A	N/A	139,433
United States Coast Guard						
Cooperative Education Program (CO-OP)	N/A	N/A	N/A	N/A	N/A	N/A
Minority Officer Recruiting Effort (M.O.R.E)	N/A	N/A	N/A	N/A	N/A	N/A
Federal Aviation Administration						
Disadvantaged Business Enterprise Program (DBE)	N/A	N/A	N/A	N/A	N/A	N/A
Action						
Vista (Volunteers in Service to America)	19,828,000	21,647,000	23,615,000	19,769,000	21,589,000	N/A
Student Community Service Program (SCS)	1,310 000	1,352,000	893,000	N/A	N/A	N/A
Program Demonstration and Development Division						
Minigrant Program	158,000	150,000	0	N/A	N/A	N/A
Volunteer Demonstration Program	621,000	754,000	0	N/A	N/A	N/A
Technical Assistance Program	124,000	46,000	0	N/A	N/A	N/A
Drug Alliance Program	1,541,000	1,600,000	1,314,000	N/A	N/A	N/A
Retired Senior Volunteer Program (RSVP)	30,608,000	30,862,000	31,487,000	N/A	N/A	N/A
Foster Grandparent Program (FGP)	57,413,000	58,928,000	59,623,000	N/A	N/A	N/A
Senior Companion Program (SCP)	23,104,000	25,135,000	26,692,000	N/A	N/A	N/A
Environmental Protection Agency						
Office of Air and Radiation						
Air Pollution Control Program Support	N/A	N/A	N/A	N/A	N/A	N/A
Air Pollution Control Manpower Training	N/A	N/A	N/A	240,000	400,000	200,000
Air Pollution Control - Technical Training	N/A	N/A	N/A	241,000	241,000	245,000
Air Pollution Control - National Ambient Air and Source Emission Data	N/A	N/A	N/A	1,170,000	1,085,000	1,485,000
Air Information Center	N/A	N/A	N/A	43,000	32,000	32,000
Office of Pesticides and Toxic Substances						
Pesticides use Regulation Program	N/A	N/A	N/A	N/A	N/A	N/A
Office of Solid Waste and Emergency Response						
Solid Waste Management - Assistance Grants	N/A	N/A	N/A	0	2,800,000	3,950,000
Office of Water						
Municipal Wastewater Treatment Construction Grants Program	N/A	11,000,000	4,705,000	1,596,854	1,596,854	1,596,854
Wetlands Protection Program on Indian Lands	N/A	25,000	30,000	N/A	N/A	N/A
Indian Water Quality Management Programs	N/A	N/A	N/A	489,898	489,898	489,898
Indian Public Water Supply Program	N/A	669,000	786,000	N/A	40,000	N/A
National Pollutant Discharge Elimination System Permits and State Sludge Management Program on Indian Lands	N/A	N/A	N/A	N/A	N/A	N/A
Indian Underground Injection Control Program	N/A	525,000	558,900	N/A	N/A	N/A

Source: Walke, Roger. *Federal Programs of Assistance to Native Americans: A Report Prepared for the Senate Select Committee on Indian Affairs of the United States Senate*, S. Prt. 102-62, Washington, DC: U.S. Government Printing Office, December 1991, pp. 165-256. *Notes:* (N/A) indicates that information was not available. 1. The allotments awarded to tribes/tribal organizations is taken from a percentage of state's allotment. 2. Referred to as draw downs in the original source.

★ 863 ★

Federal Expenditures

Federal Programs of Assistance to Native Americans, 1988-90 - IV

Obligations represent actual dollars spent; appropriations are total amounts allotted at the beginning of the year.

Government agency and program	Appropriations ($)			Obligations ($)		
	1988	1989	1990	1988	1989	1990
Environmental Protection Agency (cont.)						
Indian Ground Water Protection Program	N/A	N/A	N/A	N/A	N/A	N/A
Equal Employment Opportunity Commission	N/A	N/A	N/A	N/A	N/A	N/A
Tribal Employment Rights Office Program (TERO)	N/A	N/A	N/A	N/A	N/A	N/A

[Continued]

★ 863 ★

Federal Programs of Assistance to Native Americans, 1988-90 - IV
[Continued]

Government agency and program	Appropriations ($)			Obligations ($)		
	1988	1989	1990	1988	1989	1990
Federal Emergency Management Agency	N/A	N/A	N/A	N/A	N/A	N/A
Emergency Management Assistance Program	54,123,000	58,123,000	61,123,000	54,160,038	58,116,000	N/A
Disaster Assistance Program	120,000,000	1,208,000,000	1,185,159,000	189,608,000	138,563,000	N/A
Sara Title III 305(A) Training Grants	142,000	0	150,000	142,000	N/A	150,000
U.S. Fire Administration						
National Fire Information Reporting System (NFIRS) Pilot Initiative with Amerind Risk Management Corp	N/A	N/A	N/A	N/A	N/A	N/A
National Community Volunteer Fire Prevention Program - Projects with an Indian Focus on Inclusion	N/A	N/A	N/A	N/A	N/A	N/A
Fema Regional Office	N/A	N/A	N/A	N/A	N/A	N/A
State Officials Responsible for Disaster Operations	N/A	N/A	N/A	N/A	N/A	N/A
Legal Services Corporation	7,022,000	7,022,000	7,304,000	N/A	N/A	N/A
National Endowment for the Arts	167,731,000	165,081,000	158,567,000	N/A	N/A	N/A
National Endowment for the Humanities	140,435,000	153,000,000	156,910,000	N/A	N/A	N/A
National Science Foundation						
Comprehensive Programs						
Career Access Opportunities in Science and Technology (ACCESS)	N/A	N/A	N/A	N/A	7,000,000	N/A
Alliances for Minority Participation (AMP)	N/A	N/A	N/A	N/A	N/A	N/A
Programs for Students						
Research Assistantships for Minority High School Students (RAMHSS)	N/A	N/A	N/A	N/A	27,035	N/A
Research Careers for Minority Scholars (RCMS)	N/A	N/A	N/A	N/A	2,000,000	N/A
Creativity Awards for Graduate Study in Engineering for Women, Minorities, and Disabled Persons	N/A	N/A	N/A	N/A	N/A	N/A
Minority Graduate Fellowship Program (MGF)	N/A	N/A	N/A	N/A	2,400,000	N/A
Postdoctoral and Faculty Research Opportunities						
Minority Postdoctoral Research Fellowships - Biological, Behavioral and Social Sciences Directorate	N/A	N/A	N/A	N/A	N/A	N/A
Minority Research Initiative Program (MRI)	N/A	N/A	N/A	N/A	3,400,000	N/A
Research Improvement in Minority Institutions Program (RIMI)	N/A	N/A	N/A	N/A	4,850,000	N/A
Minority Research Centers of Excellence (MRCE)	N/A	N/A	N/A	N/A	5,800,000	N/A
Computer and Information Science and Engineering (CISE) - Institutional Infrastructure in Minority Institutions	N/A	N/A	N/A	N/A	1,100,000	N/A
Nuclear Regulatory Commission	N/A	N/A	N/A	N/A	N/A	N/A
Office of Personnel Management						
Training Assistance to American Indian Tribal Organizations	N/A	N/A	N/A	N/A	N/A	N/A
Inter-Governmental Mobility of Federal, State, and Local Employees	N/A	N/A	N/A	N/A	N/A	N/A
Small Business Administration						
Minority Small Business and Capital Ownership Development	N/A	N/A	N/A	N/A	N/A	N/A
Minority Business Development - Procurement Assistance	N/A	N/A	N/A	N/A	N/A	N/A
Management and Technical Assistance for Disadvantaged Businesses	N/A	N/A	N/A	N/A	N/A	N/A
8(A) Participant Loans	0	5,000,000	5,000,000	N/A	N/A	N/A
Office of Business Development	46,133,000	51,338,000	5,122,000	45,912,000	51,338,000	5,122,000
Economic Injury Disaster Loans	N/A	N/A	N/A	5,708,600	78,762,500	N/A
Physical Disaster Loans	N/A	N/A	N/A	245,000,000	146,000,000	N/A
Economic Opportunity Loans						
Direct	N/A	N/A	N/A	17,100,000	17,100,000	17,000
Guarantee	N/A	N/A	N/A	32,800,000	33,900,000	0
Small Business Loans						
Direct	N/A	N/A	N/A	0	0	0
Guarantee	N/A	N/A	N/A	2,421,300,000	2,606,600,000	3,200,000,000
Veterans Loans Program	N/A	N/A	N/A	16,900,000	16,800,000	17,000,000
Handicapped Assistance Loans						
Direct	N/A	N/A	N/A	11,700,000	11,900,000	12,000,000
Guarantee	N/A	N/A	N/A	200,000	1,600,668	0
State and Local Development Company Loans	N/A	N/A	50,000,000	39,096,312	44,120,000	N/A
Certified Development Company Loans	450,000,000	365,000,000	422,228,000	291,986,000	329,247,000	N/A
Office of Women's Business Ownership	N/A	N/A	N/A	N/A	2,000,000	2,000,000
Small Business Pollution Control Loan Program	N/A	N/A	N/A	N/A	N/A	N/A
Procurement Assistance	15,635,000	15,444,000	16,223,000	15,635,000	15,444,000	16,223,000
Procurement Automated Source System	1,145,000	1,200,000	1,138,000	1,145,000	1,200,000	1,138,000
Small Business Development Centers	N/A	N/A	N/A	N/A	44,908,000	49,338,000
Surety Bond Guarantees	N/A	N/A	N/A	N/A	1,151,562,493	1,250,000,000
Small Business Investment Companies (SBIC)						
Direct	N/A	N/A	N/A	35,900,000	36,000,000	N/A

[Continued]

★ 863 ★

Federal Programs of Assistance to Native Americans, 1988-90 - IV
[Continued]

Government agency and program	Appropriations ($)			Obligations ($)		
	1988	1989	1990	1988	1989	1990
Guarantee	N/A	N/A	N/A	117,500,000	50,200,000	N/A
Service Corps of Retired Executives (SCORE)	2,120,000	2,500,000	2,500,000	2,120,000	2,500,000	2,500,000
Smithsonian Institution						
National American Resources at the Smithsonian Institution						
National Museum of National History/National Museum of Man	N/A	N/A	N/A	N/A	N/A	N/A
National Anthropological Archives	N/A	N/A	N/A	N/A	N/A	N/A
National Museum of American History	N/A	N/A	N/A	N/A	N/A	N/A
Office of Folklife Programs						
Office of Elementary and Secondary Education	N/A	N/A	N/A	N/A	N/A	N/A
Office of Fellowships and Grants	N/A	N/A	N/A	N/A	N/A	N/A
Quincentenary Programs	N/A	N/A	N/A	N/A	N/A	N/A

Source: Walke, Roger. *Federal Programs of Assistance to Native Americans: A Report Prepared for the Senate Select Committee on Indian Affairs of the United States Senate*, S. Prt. 102-62, Washington, DC: U.S. Government Printing Office, December 1991, pp. 256-326. *Notes:* (N/A) indicates that information was not available. 1. The allotments awarded to tribes/tribal organizations is taken from a percentage of state's allotment. 2. Referred to as draw downs in the original source.

★ 864 ★

Federal Expenditures

HUD Subsidies to IHAs, 1981-90

Data show operating subsidies provided by the Department of Housing and Urban Development (HUD) to Indian Housing Authorities (IHAs), by year.

Fiscal year	Appropriation
1981	11,463,408
1982	16,723,969
1983	22,730,642
1984	19,623,329
1985	27,131,857
1986	33,512,149
1987	46,124,433
1988	49,813,998
1989	55,200,515
1990	58,150,423

Source: National Commission on American Indian, Alaska Native, and Native Hawaiian Housing. *Building the Future: A Blueprint for Change: "By Our Homes You Will Know Us."* Washington, DC: 1992, p. 36.

★ 865 ★

Federal Expenditures

HUD Subsidies to IHAs, FY90

This table shows operating subsidies provided by the Department of Housing and Urban Development (HUD) to Indian Housing Authorities (IHAs) in fiscal year 1990, by program type.

Subsidy	Amount ($)
PFS funding	45,432,016
Insurance premiums	307,804
Mutual help subsidies	9,298,138
Turnkey III subsidies	716,268
Subsidy for Alaska	2,396,197

Source: National Commission on American Indian, Alaska Native, and Native Hawaiian Housing. *Building the Future: A Blueprint for Change: "By Our Homes You Will Know Us."* Washington, DC: 1992, p. 36.

Government Representation

★ 866 ★

Federal Judgeships by Race/Ethnicity and Sex - 1994

Number of federal judges, including Supreme Court judges, is shown for each race/ethnicity, as of 20 June 1994. As of that date, there were 837 seats, of which 88 were vacant.

Race/ethnicity and sex	Number of judges
White males	549
White females	98
Black males	48
Hispanic males[1]	29
Black females	13
Asian-American males	5
Native American males	1

Source: Mauro, Tony. "Last gasp scramble to clear up backlogs." *USA TODAY* (27 June 1994), p. 2A. Primary source: Alliance for Justice. *Note:* 1. Hispanics may be of any race.

★ 867 ★

Government Representation

Native Americans, Women, and Other Minorities in Congress, 1991 and 1993

Women - 31	
Blacks - 25	
Hispanics - 14	
Asians - 6	
Native American - 1	

Chart shows data from column 1.

Data include non-voting delegates.

Group	1991	1993
Women	31	54
Blacks	25	39
Hispanics	14	19
Asians	6	9
Native American	1	1

Source: Wolf, Richard. "Speaker Foley's back and in top form." *USA TODAY* (7 December 1992), p. 10A. Primary source: *USA TODAY* research.

Military Personnel

★ 868 ★

Military Service by Civilian Veterans Age 16 and Older in Selected Alaska Native Villages - Part I

Data are shown for the 50 areas with the largest populations, in number of persons.

Alaska Native Village Statistical Area[1]	May 1975 or later only				Vietnam era no Korean conflict nor WW II	Korean conflict, no WW II
	Sept. 1980 or later only		May 1975 to Aug. 1980 only	May 1975 to Aug 1980 & Sept. 1980 or later		
	Less than 2 yrs. of service	2 or more yrs. of service				
Akiachak	0	0	8	0	8	0
Akutan	0	32	16	0	20	0
Alakanuk	4	0	3	0	2	0
Andreafsky	4	5	6	0	24	0
Angoon	0	4	1	0	22	0
Aniak	0	0	3	7	22	0
Barrow	5	5	24	2	102	0
Bethel	9	71	36	7	177	8

[Continued]

★ 868 ★

Military Service by Civilian Veterans Age 16 and Older in Selected Alaska Native Villages - Part I

[Continued]

Alaska Native Village Statistical Area[1]	May 1975 or later only				Vietnam era no Korean conflict nor WW II	Korean conflict, no WW II
	Sept. 1980 or later only		May 1975 to Aug. 1980 only	May 1975 to Aug 1980 & Sept. 1980 or later		
	Less than 2 yrs. of service	2 or more yrs. of service				
Chevak	2	6	2	0	16	4
Copper Center	0	4	5	0	26	0
Craig	0	12	0	6	70	0
Dillingham	7	7	5	5	87	0
Emmonak	2	2	2	2	5	0
Fort Yukon	0	4	4	0	14	0
Galena	0	1	4	0	34	0
Gambell	0	4	2	0	13	0
Grouse Creek Group	0	0	0	5	50	2
Hoonah	0	22	0	0	40	0
Hooper Bay	0	6	2	0	8	2
Kake	0	0	2	0	28	0
Kasigluk	0	3	0	3	2	0
King Cove	0	0	8	2	7	0
King Salmon	0	13	5	5	52	0
Kipnuk	0	4	0	0	6	0
Klawock	0	6	8	0	37	0
Kotlik	0	0	0	0	5	0
Kotzebue	8	32	10	4	94	0
Kwethluk	0	5	0	0	2	0
McGrath	0	2	4	0	36	3
Mountain Village	0	2	2	3	20	0
Naknek	0	5	2	2	42	0
Ninilchik	2	48	76	6	444	7
Noorvik	0	12	6	0	8	0
Pilot Station	0	0	0	2	11	0
Point Hope	3	2	4	0	24	0
Quinhagak	0	0	0	0	5	0
St. Paul	3	10	19	0	20	0
Salamatof	3	2	12	0	72	0
Sand Point	0	3	6	0	27	0
Savoonga	1	2	3	0	4	0
Selawik	0	0	3	0	8	0
Shishmaref	0	0	1	0	3	0
Stebbins	0	5	2	0	8	0
Togiak	0	0	0	0	10	0
Tok	0	2	7	0	62	1
Toksook Bay	0	3	0	2	0	0
Unalakleet	0	0	7	0	50	0
Unalaska	0	149	35	0	206	0

[Continued]

★ 868 ★

Military Service by Civilian Veterans Age 16 and Older in Selected Alaska Native Villages - Part I

[Continued]

Alaska Native Village Statistical Area[1]	May 1975 or later only		May 1975 to Aug. 1980 only	May 1975 to Aug 1980 & Sept. 1980 or later	Vietnam era no Korean conflict nor WW II	Korean conflict, no WW II
	Sept. 1980 or later only					
	Less than 2 yrs. of service	2 or more yrs. of service				
Wainwright	0	2	4	0	5	0
Yakutat	0	2	12	2	27	0

Source: Census of Population and Housing, 1990: Summary Tape File 3C on CD-ROM [machine-readable datafiles]. Prepared by the Bureau of the Census. Washington, DC: The Bureau, 1992. Notes: 1. Alaska Native villages (ANVs) constitute tribes, bands, clans, groups, villages, communities, or associations in Alaska that are recognized pursuant to the Alaska Native Claims Settlement Act of 1972, Public Law 92-203. Because ANVs do not have legally designated boundaries, the Census Bureau has established Alaska Native village statistical areas (ANVSAs) for statistical purposes. For the 1990 census, the Census Bureau cooperated with officials of the nonprofit corporation within each participating Alaska Native Regional Corporation (ANRC), as well as other knowledgeable officials, to delineate boundaries that encompass the settled area associated with each ANV.

★ 869 ★

Military Personnel

Military Service by Civilian Veterans Age 16 and Older in Selected Alaska Native Villages - Part II

Data are shown for the 50 areas with the largest populations, in number of persons.

Alaska Native Village Statistical Area[1]	Vietnam era, Korean conflict, and WWII	Feb. 1955 to to July 1964 only	Korean conflict, no Vietnam era nor WWII	Korean conflict and WW II, no Vietnam era	WW II, no Korean conflict, nor Vietnam era	WW I	Other service
Akiachak	0	4	10	0	6	0	2
Akutan	0	0	0	0	2	0	0
Alakanuk	0	5	7	0	4	0	4
Andreafsky	0	4	2	0	2	0	0
Angoon	0	9	9	0	6	0	0
Aniak	0	3	10	0	4	0	0
Barrow	0	31	19	2	14	0	0
Bethel	0	48	37	0	32	0	0
Chevak	3	5	10	0	2	0	3
Copper Center	0	12	8	2	5	0	0
Craig	0	18	16	9	12	0	0
Dillingham	0	35	26	0	21	0	3
Emmonak	0	6	0	0	2	0	2
Fort Yukon	0	5	3	0	3	0	0
Galena	0	11	5	0	4	0	0
Gambell	0	2	0	0	0	0	0
Grouse Creek Group	0	1	15	0	13	0	0
Hoonah	0	7	13	0	11	0	0
Hooper Bay	0	2	2	0	2	0	4
Kake	0	11	8	2	5	0	0
Kasigluk	0	3	0	0	1	0	0
King Cove	0	10	1	0	6	0	0
King Salmon	0	14	15	0	2	0	0
Kipnuk	0	1	1	0	2	0	0
Klawock	0	15	8	0	12	0	0

[Continued]

★ 869 ★

Military Service by Civilian Veterans Age 16 and Older in Selected Alaska Native Villages - Part II
[Continued]

Alaska Native Village Statistical Area[1]	Vietnam era, Korean conflict, and WWII	Feb. 1955 to to July 1964 only	Korean conflict, no Vietnam era nor WWII	Korean conflict and WW II, no Vietnam era	WW II, no Korean conflict, nor Vietnam era	WW I	Other service
Kotlik	0	5	0	0	0	0	0
Kotzebue	0	33	19	0	33	0	2
Kwethluk	0	0	0	0	2	0	0
McGrath	0	14	4	0	5	0	0
Mountain Village	0	9	3	0	0	0	0
Naknek	0	12	4	0	4	0	0
Ninilchik	9	146	150	29	327	0	4
Noorvik	0	4	7	0	6	0	0
Pilot Station	0	2	1	0	0	0	0
Point Hope	0	0	6	0	0	0	0
Quinhagak	0	0	0	0	0	0	0
St. Paul	0	7	3	0	9	0	0
Salamatof	0	14	11	2	16	0	0
Sand Point	0	14	12	0	5	0	0
Savoonga	0	0	7	0	0	0	0
Selawik	0	0	2	0	2	0	0
Shishmaref	0	5	2	0	8	0	0
Stebbins	0	0	5	0	0	0	0
Togiak	0	0	9	0	3	0	0
Tok	0	29	13	3	32	0	0
Toksook Bay	0	0	0	0	0	0	0
Unalakleet	0	0	4	0	17	0	0
Unalaska	0	49	27	3	3	2	0
Wainwright	0	4	0	0	5	0	3
Yakutat	0	5	12	0	10	0	0

Source: Census of Population and Housing, 1990: Summary Tape File 3C on CD-ROM [machine-readable datafiles]. Prepared by the Bureau of the Census. Washington, DC: The Bureau, 1992. *Notes:* 1. Alaska Native villages (ANVs) constitute tribes, bands, clans, groups, villages, communities, or associations in Alaska that are recognized pursuant to the Alaska Native Claims Settlement Act of 1972, Public Law 92-203. Because ANVs do not have legally designated boundaries, the Census Bureau has established Alaska Native village statistical areas (ANVSAs) for statistical purposes. For the 1990 census, the Census Bureau cooperated with officials of the nonprofit corporation within each participating Alaska Native Regional Corporation (ANRC), as well as other knowledgeable officials, to delineate boundaries that encompass the settled area associated with each ANV.

★ 870 ★

Military Personnel

Military Service by Civilian Veterans Age 16 and Older in Selected Tribal Designated Statistical Areas - Part I

Data show number of persons.

Tribal Designated Statistical Area[1]	May 1975 or later only				Vietnam era no Korean conflict nor WW II	Korean conflict, no WW II
	Sept. 1980 or later only		May 1975 to Aug. 1980 only	May 1975 to Aug 1980 & Sept. 1980 or later		
	Less than 2 yrs. of service	2 or more yrs. of service				
Apache Choctaw TDSA (state)	13	95	79	15	412	38
Chickahominy TDSA (state)	9	15	6	9	122	7
Clifton Choctaw TDSA (state)	0	0	10	0	19	0
Coharie TDSA (state)	205	1,338	658	214	3,342	364
Coquille Indian TDSA	668	2,918	2,227	588	15,819	687
Delaware-Muncie TDSA (state)	0	0	0	0	13	0
Florida Tribe of Eastern Creek TDSA (state)	0	0	0	0	0	10
Haliwa-Saponi TDSA (state)	0	17	35	0	83	0
Jena Band of Choctaw TDSA (state)	81	403	185	69	2,165	225
Klamath TDSA	57	375	261	67	1,691	122
Lumbee TDSA (state)	46	359	221	43	932	36
Meherrin TDSA (state)	30	400	199	29	1,234	49
Mohegan TDSA (state)	20	280	213	65	868	21
Ramapough TDSA (state)	0	0	0	0	25	0
United Houma Nation TDSA (state)	953	3,347	2,782	777	22,410	635
Waccamaw Siouan TDSA (state)	8	32	16	0	83	0
Wampanoag-Gay Head TDSA	12	54	17	15	320	6

Source: Census of Population and Housing, 1990: Summary Tape File 3C on CD-ROM [machine-readable datafiles]. Prepared by the Bureau of the Census. Washington, DC: The Bureau, 1992. *Notes:* 1. Tribal designated statistical areas (TDSAs) are areas, delineated outside Oklahoma by federally- and state-recognized tribes without a land base or associated trust lands, to provide statistical areas for which the Census Bureau tabulates data. TDSAs represent areas generally containing the American Indian population over which federally-recognized tribes have jurisdiction and areas in which state tribes provide benefits and services to their members. The names of TDSAs delineated by state-recognized tribes are followed by "(state)." The Census Bureau did not recognize TDSAs before the 1990 census.

★ 871 ★

Military Personnel

Military Service by Civilian Veterans Age 16 and Older in Selected Tribal Designated Statistical Areas - Part II

Data shown number of persons.

Tribal Designated Statistical Area[1]	Vietnam era, Korean conflict, and WWII	Feb. 1955 to to July 1964 only	Korean conflict, no Vietnam era nor WWII	Korean conflict and WW II, no Vietnam era	WW II, no Korean conflict, nor Vietnam era	WW I	Other service
Apache Choctaw TDSA (state)	43	249	394	90	941	0	16
Chickahominy TDSA (state)	0	40	59	0	60	0	13
Clifton Choctaw TDSA (state)	0	0	10	0	7	0	0
Coharie TDSA (state)	195	963	1,553	182	3,178	5	107
Coquille Indian TDSA	451	5,619	6,841	1,620	18,645	256	592
Delaware-Muncie TDSA (state)	0	0	0	0	5	0	6
Florida Tribe of Eastern Creek TDSA (state)	10	0	0	0	44	0	0

[Continued]

★ 871 ★

Military Service by Civilian Veterans Age 16 and Older in Selected Tribal Designated Statistical Areas - Part II

[Continued]

Tribal Designated Statistical Area[1]	Vietnam era, Korean conflict, and WWII	Feb. 1955 to to July 1964 only	Korean conflict, no Vietnam era nor WWII	Korean conflict and WW II, no Vietnam era	WW II, no Korean conflict, nor Vietnam era	WW I	Other service
Haliwa-Saponi TDSA (state)	0	8	67	12	77	0	11
Jena Band of Choctaw TDSA (state)	116	724	767	187	1,992	0	62
Klamath TDSA	72	623	819	130	1,812	25	60
Lumbee TDSA (state)	7	276	323	58	742	0	15
Meherrin TDSA (state)	40	413	499	95	1,573	3	50
Mohegan TDSA (state)	52	335	463	102	838	13	24
Ramapough TDSA (state)	0	0	10	0	22	0	0
United Houma Nation TDSA (state)	395	9,236	11,059	1,671	24,489	70	638
Waccamaw Siouan TDSA (state)	0	0	50	0	18	0	0
Wampanoag-Gay Head TDSA	0	156	314	34	567	0	6

Source: Census of Population and Housing, 1990: Summary Tape File 3C on CD-ROM [machine-readable datafiles]. Prepared by the Bureau of the Census. Washington, DC: The Bureau, 1992. *Notes:* 1. Tribal designated statistical areas (TDSAs) are areas, delineated outside Oklahoma by federally- and state-recognized tribes without a land base or associated trust lands, to provide statistical areas for which the Census Bureau tabulates data. TDSAs represent areas generally containing the American Indian population over which federally-recognized tribes have jurisdiction and areas in which state tribes provide benefits and services to their members. The names of TDSAs delineated by state-recognized tribes are followed by "(state)." The Census Bureau did not recognize TDSAs before the 1990 census.

★ 872 ★

Military Personnel

Military Service by Civilian Veterans Age 16 and Older in Selected Tribal Jurisdiction Statistical Areas - Part I

Data show number of persons.

Tribal Jurisdiction Statistical Area[1]	May 1975 or later only				Vietnam era no Korean conflict nor WW II	Korean conflict, no WW II
	Sept. 1980 or later only		May 1975 to Aug. 1980 only	May 1975 to Aug 1980 & Sept. 1980 or later		
	Less than 2 yrs. of service	2 or more yrs. of service				
Absentee Shawnee-Citizens Band of Potawatomi TJSA	153	398	517	195	4,722	320
Caddo-Wichita-Delaware TJSA	14	11	25	2	186	22
Cherokee TJSA	460	1,721	1,892	365	14,307	671
Cheyenne-Arapaho TJSA	129	446	589	200	5,254	178
Chickasaw TJSA	372	717	958	225	8,662	481
Choctaw TJSA	241	767	922	68	6,910	374
Creek TJSA	798	3,230	3,148	866	22,687	695
Iowa TJSA	7	14	17	1	158	7
Kaw TJSA	0	21	45	0	521	18
Kiowa-Comanche-Apache-Fort Sill Apache TJSA	399	2,516	1,305	728	7,808	1,333
Otoe-Missouria TJSA	2	9	4	0	96	0
Pawnee TJSA	4	57	66	9	513	33
Sac and Fox TJSA	39	215	213	33	1,459	105
Seminole TJSA	14	79	103	19	626	17
Tonkawa TJSA	10	41	37	10	370	11

[Continued]

★ 872 ★

Military Service by Civilian Veterans Age 16 and Older in Selected Tribal Jurisdiction Statistical Areas - Part I

[Continued]

Tribal Jurisdiction Statistical Area[1]	May 1975 or later only		May 1975 to Aug. 1980 only	May 1975 to Aug 1980 & Sept. 1980 or later	Vietnam era no Korean conflict nor WW II	Korean conflict, no WW II
	Sept. 1980 or later only					
	Less than 2 yrs. of service	2 or more yrs. of service				
Creek-Seminole Joint Area TJSA	4	0	3	0	52	0
Iowa-Sac and Fox Joint Area TJSA	0	6	3	0	37	0

Source: Census of Population and Housing, 1990: Summary Tape File 3C on CD-ROM [machine-readable datafiles]. Prepared by the Bureau of the Census. Washington, DC: The Bureau, 1992. Notes: 1. Tribal jurisdiction statistical areas (TJSAs) are areas, delineated by federally recognized tribes in Oklahoma without a reservation, for which the Census Bureau tabulates data. TJSAs represent areas generally containing the American Indian population over which one or more tribal governments have jurisdiction. If tribal officials delineated adjacent TJSAs so that they include some duplicate territory, the overlap area is called a "joint use area," which is treated as a separate TJSA for census purposes.

★ 873 ★

Military Personnel

Military Service by Civilian Veterans Age 16 and Older in Selected Tribal Jurisdiction Statistical Areas - Part II

Data shown number of persons.

Tribal Jurisdiction Statistical Area[1]	Vietnam era, Korean conflict, and WWII	Feb. 1955 to to July 1964 only	Korean conflict, no Vietnam era nor WWII	Korean conflict and WW II, no Vietnam era	WW II, no Korean conflict, nor Vietnam era	WW I	Other service
Absentee Shawnee-Citizens Band of Potawatomi TJSA	214	1,464	1,553	424	2,983	6	90
Caddo-Wichita-Delaware TJSA	10	80	115	8	279	0	0
Cherokee TJSA	311	5,112	6,984	1,409	15,535	158	408
Cheyenne-Arapaho TJSA	138	1,663	2,423	304	4,617	74	88
Chickasaw TJSA	317	3,124	4,093	822	10,314	120	310
Choctaw TJSA	321	2,572	3,264	797	8,483	88	265
Creek TJSA	475	8,447	10,204	2,078	21,968	180	576
Iowa TJSA	8	65	63	7	144	2	2
Kaw TJSA	6	246	205	85	623	10	21
Kiowa-Comanche-Apache-Fort Sill Apache TJSA	899	1,593	2,285	993	5,516	43	179
Otoe-Missouria TJSA	4	36	56	6	88	0	3
Pawnee TJSA	11	298	284	27	666	8	12
Sac and Fox TJSA	48	685	866	176	2,036	34	62
Seminole TJSA	41	250	392	88	1,121	0	11
Tonkawa TJSA	12	117	165	45	568	3	7
Creek-Seminole Joint Area TJSA	0	11	54	7	97	6	4
Iowa-Sac and Fox Joint Area TJSA	5	11	14	6	28	0	0

Source: Census of Population and Housing, 1990: Summary Tape File 3C on CD-ROM [machine-readable datafiles]. Prepared by the Bureau of the Census. Washington, DC: The Bureau, 1992. Notes: 1. Tribal jurisdiction statistical areas (TJSAs) are areas, delineated by federally recognized tribes in Oklahoma without a reservation, for which the Census Bureau tabulates data. TJSAs represent areas generally containing the American Indian population over which one or more tribal governments have jurisdiction. If tribal officials delineated adjacent TJSAs so that they include some duplicate territory, the overlap area is called a "joint use area," which is treated as a separate TJSA for census purposes.

★ 874 ★

Military Personnel

Military Service by Civilian Veterans Age 16 and Older on Selected Reservations and Trust Lands - Part I

Data are shown for the 50 areas with the largest populations, in number of persons.

American Indian Reservation and Trust Lands[1,2]	May 1975 or later only		May 1975 to Aug. 1980 only	May 1975 to Aug 1980 & Sept. 1980 or later	Vietnam era no Korean conflict nor WW II	Korean conflict, no WW II
	Sept. 1980 or later only					
	Less than 2 yrs. of service	2 or more yrs. of service				
Agua Caliente Reservation	0	104	44	17	387	21
Allegany Reservation	3	67	42	8	211	4
Blackfeet Reservation	6	82	43	3	277	0
Cheyenne River Reservation	2	41	52	5	172	3
Coeur d'Alene Reservation and Trust Lands, ID	6	33	26	3	214	24
Colorado River Reservation	15	41	46	0	214	0
Colville Reservation	10	30	45	4	278	8
Crow Reservation and Trust Lands, MT	39	83	35	7	152	0
Eastern Cherokee Reservation	22	54	11	7	254	20
Flathead Reservation	30	81	104	6	835	8
Fort Apache Reservation	0	42	63	0	87	0
Fort Berthold Reservation	11	31	18	9	189	0
Fort Hall Reservation and Trust Lands, ID	15	5	33	0	118	0
Fort Peck Reservation	23	49	64	2	350	0
Gila River Reservation	4	43	53	0	128	0
Hopi Reservation and Trust Lands, AZ	0	44	94	0	101	0
Isabella Reservation and Trust Lands, MI	23	172	117	23	591	8
Laguna Pueblo and Trust Lands, NM	2	28	21	0	150	0
Lake Traverse (Sisseton) Reservation	5	34	50	7	204	9
Leech Lake Reservation	7	62	37	20	299	22
Mississippi Choctaw Reservation and Trust Lands, MS	0	0	38	5	67	0
Muckleshoot Reservation and Trust Lands, WA	2	35	19	10	119	9
Navajo Reservation and Trust Lands, AZ–NM–UT	98	350	643	27	2,113	0
Nez Perce Reservation	27	91	60	22	589	23
Northern Cheyenne Reservation and Trust Lands, MT–SD	6	30	16	0	157	0
Omaha Reservation	7	21	29	3	81	2
Oneida (West) Reservation	21	77	79	6	644	17
Osage Reservation	88	156	119	11	1,550	85
Papago Reservation	44	52	15	0	120	30
Pine Ridge Reservation and Trust Lands, NE–SD	25	116	44	0	275	0

[Continued]

★ 874 ★

Military Service by Civilian Veterans Age 16 and Older on Selected Reservations and Trust Lands - Part I

[Continued]

American Indian Reservation and Trust Lands[1,2]	May 1975 or later only				Vietnam era no Korean conflict nor WW II	Korean conflict, no WW II
	Sept. 1980 or later only		May 1975 to Aug. 1980 only	May 1975 to Aug 1980 & Sept. 1980 or later		
	Less than 2 yrs. of service	2 or more yrs. of service				
Port Madison Reservation	7	57	50	25	247	16
Puyallup Reservation and Trust Lands, WA	42	340	238	105	1,440	92
Red Lake Reservation	0	27	16	0	57	0
Rosebud Reservation and Trust Lands, SD	33	113	75	0	280	5
Salt River Reservation	0	26	27	0	49	0
San Carlos Reservation	0	40	31	5	73	0
Sandia Pueblo	5	30	22	9	133	6
San Juan Pueblo	6	57	37	3	175	0
Santa Clara Pueblo	16	71	48	4	323	20
Southern Ute Reservation	6	40	33	4	271	6
Standing Rock Reservation	21	66	68	6	263	0
Taos Pueblo and Trust Lands, NM	9	37	32	0	150	5
Tulalip Reservation	0	52	45	0	330	8
Turtle Mountain Reservation and Trust Lands, ND – SD	10	7	61	0	168	0
Uintah and Ouray Reservation	10	39	37	5	440	8
White Earth Reservation	4	16	34	4	293	13
Wind River Reservation	42	141	77	45	698	0
Yakima Reservation and Trust Lands, WA	18	58	95	10	475	15
Yankton Reservation	4	27	26	4	154	2
Zuni Pueblo	0	51	19	0	137	0

Source: Census of Population and Housing, 1990: Summary Tape File 3C on CD-ROM [machine-readable datafiles]. Prepared by the Bureau of the Census. Washington, DC: The Bureau, 1992. *Notes:* 1. Federal American Indian reservations are areas with boundaries established by treaty, statute, and/or executive or court order, and recognized by the federal government as territory in which American Indian tribes have jurisdiction. State reservations are lands held in trust by state governments for the use and benefit of a given tribe. The reservations and their boundaries were identified for the 1990 census by the Bureau of Indian Affairs (BIA), Department of Interior (for federal reservations), and state governments (for state reservations). The names of American Indian reservations recognized by state governments, but not by the federal government, are followed by "state." Areas composed of reservation lands that are administered jointly and/or are claimed by two reservations, as identified by the BIA, are called "joint areas," and are treated as separate American Indian reservations for census purposes. Federal reservations may cross state boundaries, and federal and state reservations may cross county, county subdivision, and place boundaries. For reservations that cross state boundaries, only the portion of the reservations in a given state is shown in the data products for that state; the entire reservations are shown in data products for the United States. 2. Trust lands are property associated with a particular American Indian reservation or tribe, held in trust by the federal government. Trust lands may be held in trust either for a tribe (tribal trust lands) or for an individual member of a tribe (individual trust land). Trust lands recognized for the 1990 census comprised all tribal trust lands and inhabited individual trust lands located outside of a reservation boundary. As with other American Indian areas, trust lands may be located in more than one state. Only the trust lands in a given state are shown in the data products for that state; all trust lands associated with a reservation or tribe are shown in data products for the United States. The Census Bureau first reported data for tribal trust lands for the 1980 census.

★ 875 ★

Military Personnel

Military Service by Civilian Veterans Age 16 and Older on Selected Reservations and Trust Lands - Part II

Data are shown for the 50 areas with the largest populations, in number of persons.

American Indian Reservation and Trust Lands[1,2]	Vietnam era, Korean conflict, and WWII	Feb. 1955 to to July 1964 only	Korean conflict, no Vietnam era nor WWII	Korean conflict and WW II, no Vietnam era	WW II, no Korean conflict, nor Vietnam era	WW I	Other service
Agua Caliente Reservation	43	188	480	159	1,983	22	59
Allegany Reservation	4	109	131	10	392	0	8
Blackfeet Reservation	0	41	89	8	164	0	0
Cheyenne River Reservation	2	119	144	15	151	5	1
Coeur d'Alene Reservation and Trust Lands, ID	8	133	88	34	273	6	4
Colorado River Reservation	24	91	99	31	345	0	12
Colville Reservation	3	96	131	18	248	0	9
Crow Reservation and Trust Lands, MT	0	38	83	9	144	0	10
Eastern Cherokee Reservation	0	54	75	0	135	0	0
Flathead Reservation	30	288	375	71	854	20	23
Fort Apache Reservation	0	36	80	0	114	0	16
Fort Berthold Reservation	0	48	82	3	136	0	4
Fort Hall Reservation and Trust Lands, ID	0	51	61	0	82	6	5
Fort Peck Reservation	0	154	188	6	274	8	0
Gila River Reservation	0	17	68	9	104	0	9
Hopi Reservation and Trust Lands, AZ	0	46	44	0	90	0	0
Isabella Reservation and Trust Lands, MI	0	227	299	19	624	0	19
Laguna Pueblo and Trust Lands, NM	0	10	75	11	78	0	0
Lake Traverse (Sisseton) Reservation	0	177	206	15	384	0	0
Leech Lake Reservation	2	116	254	29	400	0	5
Mississippi Choctaw Reservation and Trust Lands, MS	9	9	6	0	39	0	0
Muckleshoot Reservation and Trust Lands, WA	13	47	79	13	114	0	14
Navajo Reservation and Trust Lands, AZ–NM–UT	0	421	697	43	1,319	0	38
Nez Perce Reservation	8	323	347	46	855	6	19
Northern Cheyenne Reservation and Trust Lands, MT–SD	0	19	47	9	57	0	0
Omaha Reservation	2	63	107	2	170	0	5
Oneida (West) Reservation	7	289	259	19	342	0	17
Osage Reservation	42	546	845	165	1,518	31	75
Papago Reservation	0	31	57	0	112	0	10
Pine Ridge Reservation and Trust Lands, NE–SD	0	52	204	33	212	0	11
Port Madison Reservation	19	69	62	13	172	3	3
Puyallup Reservation and Trust Lands, WA	55	494	456	109	900	8	29
Red Lake Reservation	0	59	37	11	61	0	0
Rosebud Reservation and Trust Lands, SD	6	68	110	9	157	0	2

[Continued]

★ 875 ★

Military Service by Civilian Veterans Age 16 and Older on Selected Reservations and Trust Lands - Part II

[Continued]

American Indian Reservation and Trust Lands[1,2]	Vietnam era, Korean conflict, and WWII	Feb. 1955 to to July 1964 only	Korean conflict, no Vietnam era nor WWII	Korean conflict and WW II, no Vietnam era	WW II, no Korean conflict, nor Vietnam era	WW I	Other service
Salt River Reservation	0	33	41	30	202	0	10
San Carlos Reservation	0	35	24	8	81	0	0
Sandia Pueblo	0	48	55	3	88	5	5
San Juan Pueblo	0	57	63	0	106	2	0
Santa Clara Pueblo	1	108	139	28	311	0	0
Southern Ute Reservation	0	123	149	24	265	2	2
Standing Rock Reservation	1	38	89	16	194	0	4
Taos Pueblo and Trust Lands, NM	0	62	65	7	155	4	0
Tulalip Reservation	28	147	129	38	282	5	6
Turtle Mountain Reservation and Trust Lands, ND – SD	0	56	42	0	113	0	0
Uintah and Ouray Reservation	7	128	192	34	392	0	0
White Earth Reservation	2	145	194	22	322	8	6
Wind River Reservation	0	327	313	41	758	14	32
Yakima Reservation and Trust Lands, WA	8	168	278	44	595	0	14
Yankton Reservation	0	77	168	7	224	3	0
Zuni Pueblo	0	59	75	4	89	0	0

Source: Census of Population and Housing, 1990: Summary Tape File 3C on CD-ROM [machine-readable datafiles]. Prepared by the Bureau of the Census. Washington, DC: The Bureau, 1992. *Notes:* 1. Federal American Indian reservations are areas with boundaries established by treaty, statute, and/or executive or court order, and recognized by the federal government as territory in which American Indian tribes have jurisdiction. State reservations are lands held in trust by state governments for the use and benefit of a given tribe. The reservations and their boundaries were identified for the 1990 census by the Bureau of Indian Affairs (BIA), Department of Interior (for federal reservations), and state governments (for state reservations). The names of American Indian reservations recognized by state governments, but not by the federal government, are followed by "state." Areas composed of reservation lands that are administered jointly and/or are claimed by two reservations, as identified by the BIA, are called "joint areas," and are treated as separate American Indian reservations for census purposes. Federal reservations may cross state boundaries, and federal and state reservations may cross county, county subdivision, and place boundaries. For reservations that cross state boundaries, only the portion of the reservations in a given state is shown in the data products for that state; the entire reservations are shown in data products for the United States. 2. Trust lands are property associated with a particular American Indian reservation or tribe, held in trust by the federal government. Trust lands may be held in trust either for a tribe (tribal trust lands) or for an individual member of a tribe (individual trust land). Trust lands recognized for the 1990 census comprised all tribal trust lands and inhabited individual trust lands located outside of a reservation boundary. As with other American Indian areas, trust lands may be located in more than one state. Only the trust lands in a given state are shown in the data products for that state; all trust lands associated with a reservation or tribe are shown in data products for the United States. The Census Bureau first reported data for tribal trust lands for the 1980 census.

★ 876 ★

Military Personnel

VA Home Loan Benefit Utilization, 1988

Data show number of veterans participating in the VA (Veterans Affairs) Loan Guaranty Program and participation rate of all veterans compared to Native American veterans.

Group	Population	Number participating	Veteran population participating in loan guaranty program (%)
Veterans	27,424,000[6]	186,000[2]	0.67[5]
Native Americans	159,900[3]	1,536[2]	0.96[1]
Native American veterans on Trust land	21,204[4]	15[8]	0.07[7]

Source: National Commission on American Indian, Alaska Native, and Native Hawaiian Housing. *Building the Future: A Blueprint for Change: "By Our Homes You Will Know Us."* Washington, DC: 1992, p. 45. Primary source: U.S. Department of Veterans Affairs, *Final Report: Assessment of the Utilization of the VA Home Loan Benefit by Native American Veterans Living on Trust Land* (28 November 1990). *Notes:* 1. Estimated participation rate. 2. American Indian, Alaska Native, and Asian/Pacific Islander. For calendar year ending December 31, 1988: *Loan Guaranty Division, Property Management Operations, Minority Participation*, Report Number RCS20-0201. 3. "Statistical Brief, Native American Veterans," Department of Veterans Affairs, October 1985, Publication Number SB70-85-3. 4. *Characteristics of American Indians by Tribes and Selected Areas: 1980*, Section 2, U.S. Department of Commerce, Bureau of the Census, Publication Number PC80-2-1C. 5. *1987 Survey of Veterans*, Department of Veterans Affairs, July 1989. 6. "1986 Total, Veteran Population Projects by Age and Period of Service, 1980-2040," Department of Veterans Affairs, May 1989. 7. Hard data are not available to determine the number of participating Native American veterans on trust status land for CY89. A participation rate of .001 would result from 21 loans made to Native American veterans on trust status land for CY88. Our best judgment is that this figure (21) is significantly higher than the actual number of loans made to Native American veterans on trust status land in CY88. 8. These 15 loans represented loans denoted "VA" by BIA area office title plants. These loans were made from 1961 to 1992. We believe that all 15 of these loans were direct loans made to handicapped veterans living on trust lands for specially adapted housing. The BIA title plants record all land transactions on the reservations. No other source of data exists to determine the number of Native American veterans participating in the loan guaranty program and living on trust land.

Tribal Enrollment

★ 877 ★

Tribal Enrollment - Aberdeen Area

Data are shown in number of persons. Census population figures are based on self-reported responses and may be lower than the tribally enrolled population. The number of persons in ICWA (Indian Child Welfare Act) may exceed the number of tribally enrolled persons, since a child needn't be enrolled and may be only a descendant to receive benefits.

Tribe	Tribal enrollment	Res. pop.	Census 1980 pop.	Census 1990 pop.	No. on ICWA
Cheynenne River Sioux	9,841	5,137	1,557	5,100	12,828
Crow Creek Sioux	3,000	2,699	1,484	1,531	2,957
Flandreau Santee Sioux	544	448	126	249	529
Fort Berthold	9,200	2,663	2,651	2,999	3,965
Fort Totten/Devils Lake Sioux	3,700	3,780	2,258	2,676	4,452
Lower Brule Sioux	1,685	994	854	994	1,087
Omaha Tribe of Nebraska	4,000	1,860	1,329	1,908	3,088
Pine Ridge Oglala Sioux	17,775	20,206	11,941	11,182	21,846
Rosebud Sioux Tribe	15,438	17,128	5,688	8,043	13,422
Santee Sioux	2,200	498	430	425	529
Sisseton-Wahpeton Sioux	9,277	3,323	2,723	0	3,141
Standing Rock Sioux	10,109	10,308	4,800	4,870	6,153
Turtle Mountain Chippewa	25,000	9,889	3,955	6,772	11,370
Winnebago Tribe of Nebraska	3,100	1,189	1,122	1,156	1,732
Yankton Sioux	5,700	3,075	1,704	1,994	3,604
Total	120,569	83,197	42,622	49,899	90,703

Source: U.S. Department of the Interior. Bureau of Indian Affairs. Unpublished data, 12 April 1994.

★ 878 ★

Tribal Enrollment

Tribal Enrollment - Albuquerque Area

Data are shown in number of persons. Census population figures are based on self-reported responses and may be lower than the tribally enrolled population. The number of persons in ICWA (Indian Child Welfare Act) may exceed the number of tribally enrolled persons, since a child needn't be enrolled and may be only a descendant to receive benefits.

Tribe	Tribal enrollment	Res. pop.	Census 1980 pop.	Census 1990 pop.	No. on ICWA
Acoma Pueblo	3,886	4,350	2,354	2,551	6,291
Cochiti Pueblo	917	921	796	666	1,298
Isleta Pueblo	3,133	2,979	2,249	2,699	4,027
Jemez Pueblo	2,465	2,378	1,488	1,738	2,774

[Continued]

★ 878 ★

Tribal Enrollment - Albuquerque Area
[Continued]

Tribe	Tribal enrollment	Res. pop.	Census 1980 pop.	Census 1990 pop.	No. on ICWA
Jicarilla Apache Tribe	2,702	2,920	1,696	2,375	3,255
Mescalero Apache Tribe	2,938	3,252	1,945	2,516	3,686
Nambe Pueblo	398	435	175	329	634
Picuris Pueblo	222	221	124	147	304
Pojoaque Pueblo	76	102	37	177	250
Pueblo of Laguna	6,492	7,542	3,526	3,634	7,355
Pueblo of San Felipe	2,465	2,398	1,787	1,859	2,749
Pueblo of Sandia	394	321	220	358	300
Pueblo of Santa Ana	582	549	347	481	660
Pueblo of Santo Domingo	3,234	3,446	2,140	2,947	4,136
San Ildefonso Pueblo	556	632	478	347	665
San Juan Pueblo	1,927	1,935	1,146	1,276	2,238
Santa Clara Pueblo	1,237	1,582	318	1,246	1,829
Southern Ute Indian Tribe	1,119	732	812	1,044	2,257
Taos Pueblo	1,931	1,631	1,042	1,212	1,681
Tesuque Pueblo	324	328	229	232	400
Ute Mountain Ute	1,626	1,436	997	1,264	0
Ysleta del Sur Pueblo	1,112	801	0	211	1,025
Zia Pueblo	668	694	602	637	892
Zuni Indian Tribe	7,663	8,299	5,929	7,073	8,973
Total	48,067	49,884	30,437	37,019	57,679

Source: U.S. Department of the Interior. Bureau of Indian Affairs. Unpublished data, 12 April 1994.

★ 879 ★

Tribal Enrollment

Tribal Enrollment - Anadarko Area

Data are shown in number of persons. Census population figures are based on self-reported responses and may be lower than the tribally enrolled population. The number of persons in ICWA (Indian Child Welfare Act) may exceed the number of tribally enrolled persons, since a child needn't be enrolled and may be only a descendant to receive benefits.

Tribe	Tribal enrollment	Res. pop.	Census 1980 pop.	Census 1990 pop.	No. on ICWA
Absentee Shawnee	2,346	1,034	0	0	1,233
Alabama & Coushatta of Texas	0	0	490	477	475
Apache Tribe of Oklahoma	1,118	832	0	0	1,013
Caddo Tribe of Oklahoma	2,948	894	0	0	905
Cheyenne-Arapaho Tribes of Oklahoma	9,152	4,339	0	0	7,606
Citizen Band Potawatomi	11,018	4,233	0	0	6,200
Comanche Tribe of Oklahoma	3,372	4,718	0	0	5,028
Delaware Tribe of Western Oklahoma	1,012	326	0	0	326
Fort Sill Apache Tribe of Oklahoma	327	95	0	0	114
Iowa Tribe of Kansas and Nebraska	2,035	478	31	83	275
Iowa of Oklahoma	367	204	0	0	300

[Continued]

★ 879 ★

Tribal Enrollment - Anadarko Area
[Continued]

Tribe	Tribal enrollment	Res. pop.	Census 1980 pop.	Census 1990 pop.	No. on ICWA
Kaw Tribe of Oklahoma	338	559	0	0	610
Kickapoo Tribe of Kansas	1,319	610	372	370	0
Kickapoo Tribe of Oklahoma	1,914	921	0	0	1,402
Kiowa Tribe of Oklahoma	9,106	4,823	0	0	5,288
Otoe Missouria Tribe of Oklahoma	1,561	1,306	0	0	1,425
Pawnee Tribe of Oklahoma	2,439	2,229	0	0	1,050
Ponca Tribe of Oklahoma	2,014	2,387	0	0	2,606
Prairie Band of Potawatomi of Kansas	3,739	1,328	333	502	610
Sac & Fox of Missouri in Kansas/Nebraska	295	48	0	49	20
Sac & Fox of Oklahoma	2,201	1,554	0	0	1,665
Tonkawa Tribe of Oklahoma	211	763	0	0	186
Wichita Tribe of Oklahoma	1,449	869	0	0	868
Total	60,281	34,550	1,226	1,481	39,200

Source: U.S. Department of the Interior. Bureau of Indian Affairs. Unpublished data, 12 April 1994.

★ 880 ★

Tribal Enrollment

Tribal Enrollment - Billings Area

Data are shown in number of persons. Census population figures are based on self-reported responses and may be lower than the tribally enrolled population. The number of persons in ICWA (Indian Child Welfare Act) may exceed the number of tribally enrolled persons, since a child needn't be enrolled and may be only a descendant to receive benefits.

Tribe	Tribal enrollment	Res. pop.	Census 1980 pop.	Census 1990 pop.	No. on ICWA
Assiniboine & Sioux/Fort Peck	8,794	5,495	4,422	5,782	7,034
Blackfeet Tribe of Montana	13,503	7,179	5,084	7,025	7,919
Crow Tribe of Montana	8,070	6,226	4,083	4,724	6,968
Gros Ventre & Assiniboine	4,782	2,310	1,711	0	3,652
Northern Cheyenne Tribe of Montana	5,621	3,197	3,010	3,542	4,681
Rocky Boy's Chippewa Cree	3,968	2,682	1,445	1,882	2,992
Shoshone & Arapahoe/Wind River	6,305	4,935	4,170	5,676	7,972
Total	51,043	32,024	23,925	28,631	41,218

Source: U.S. Department of the Interior. Bureau of Indian Affairs. Unpublished data, 12 April 1994.

★ 881 ★

Tribal Enrollment

Tribal Enrollment - Eastern Area

Data are shown in number of persons. Census population figures are based on self-reported responses and may be lower than the tribally enrolled population. The number of persons in ICWA (Indian Child Welfare Act) may exceed the number of tribally enrolled persons, since a child needn't be enrolled and may be only a descendant to receive benefits.

Tribe	Tribal enrollment	Res. pop.	Census 1980 pop.	Census 1990 pop.	No. on ICWA
Cayuga Nation of New York	421	421	0	0	449
Chitimacha Tribe of Louisiana	520	246	159	212	415
Eastern Cherokee Reservation	8,822	6,110	4,830	5,388	10,619
Gay Head Wampanoag	0	0	0	0	609
Houlton Band of Maliseets	485	289	0	0	557
Louisiana Coushatta	300	537	0	33	695
Mashantucket Pequot Tribe	69	80	20	55	577
Miccosukee Tribe of Florida	275	525	0	94	577
Mississippi Choctaw Tribe	5,067	4,832	2,648	3,932	5,824
Narragansett Tribe	1,170	2,058	0	17	2,310
Oneida Nation of New York	800	520	0	37	1,164
Onodaga Nation of New York	1,543	1,034	604	2	1,034
Passamaquoddy (Pleasant Point)	2,478	602	506	523	1,655
Passamaquoddy Tribe (Ind. Twnp.)	895	895	333	541	1,126
Penobscot Tribe of Maine	1,852	1,073	406	417	2,111
Poarch Band of Creeks	1,822	1,480	0	149	2,087
Seminole Tribe of Florida	1,700	1,537	740	0	2,429
Seneca Nation of New York	5,744	5,744	2,758	0	6,538
St. Regis Band of Mohawks	2,500	3,242	1,729	1,923	5,644
Tonawanda Band of Senecas of New York	0	699	442	453	689
Tunica-Biloxi Tribe of Louisiana	208	153	0	16	441
Tuscararora Nation of New York	975	664	881	310	664
Total	37,646	32,731	16,056	14,102	48,214

Source: U.S. Department of the Interior. Bureau of Indian Affairs. Unpublished data, 12 April 1994.

Tribal Enrollment - Gallup and Phoenix Areas

Data are shown in number of persons. Census population figures are based on self-reported responses and may be lower than the tribally enrolled population. The number of persons in ICWA (Indian Child Welfare Act) may exceed the number of tribally enrolled persons, since a child needn't be enrolled and may be only a descendant to receive benefits.

Tribe	Tribal enrollment	Res. pop.	Census 1980 pop.	Census 1990 pop.	No. on ICWA
Gallup Area					
Navajo Nation	280,000	185,661	108,356	143,405	195,470
Phoenix Area					
Ak Chin Commun. of Papago Indians	488	525	403	0	650
Battle Mountain (Te-Moak)	442	231	0	0	521
Chemehuevi Tribe of California	106	107	9	95	132
Cocopah Tribe of Arizona	967	677	407	436	701
Colorado River Tribes	2,300	2,459	1,989	2,345	2,361
Duckwater Shoshone of Nevada	319	123	147	115	120
Elko Colony (Te-Moak)	147	684	0	0	1,280
Ely Indian Colony of Nevada	319	225	76	52	279
Fallon (Paiute Shoshone)	737	758	307	356	904
Fort McDermitt Paiute & Shoshone	671	671	416	387	744
Fort McDowell Mohave/Apache	430	633	415	560	887
Fort Mojave Tribe of Arizona	536	703	189	592	739
Gila River	11,670	11,700	6,904	9,116	11,700
Goshute	371	135	45	98	416
Havasupai Tribe of Arizona	430	460	255	400	606
Hopi Tribe of Arizona	8,500	9,617	6,606	7,061	10,258
Hualapai Tribe of Arizona	1,100	1,300	833	802	1,800
Kaibab Band of Paiute of Arizona	200	89	47	102	212
Las Vegas Tribe of Paiute	56	43	89	72	114
Lovelock Tribe of Paiute of Nevada	192	230	113	80	329
Moapa Band of Paiute Indians	249	171	153	190	330
Paiutes of Utah	577	420	0	323	650
Pascua Yaqui Tribe of Arizona	1,822	2,759	471	2,284	8,229
Pyramid Lake Paiute	1,370	1,589	699	959	1,603
Quechan Indian Tribe/Ft. Yuma	3,150	2,108	1,113	1,160	3,019
Reno Sparks Colony	730	742	444	262	724
Salt River Pima/Maricopa	4,198	5,117	2,490	3,533	4,328
San Carlos Apache of Arizona	7,157	7,826	6,013	7,110	10,501
Shoshone-Paiute/Duck Valley	1,151	1,640	962	1,022	1,584
Skull Valley Goshutes	83	89	13	32	113
South Fort (Te-Moak)	90	148	0	0	257
Summit Lake Paiute Tribe	4	16	0	6	112
Te Moak	216	1,165	79	0	0
Tohono O'Odham	16,675	16,531	7,052	0	18,900
Tonto Apache Tribe of Arizona	112	123	0	0	165
Ute Indian Tribe	3,079	3,130	1,990	0	3,205
Walker River Paiute Tribe	803	830	452	620	941
Washoe Tribe of Nevada	2,104	784	443	65	1,597
Wells Colony (Te-Moak)	242	102	0	0	180
White Mountain Apache Tribe	8,840	8,726	7,010	0	13,575

[Continued]

★ 882 ★

Tribal Enrollment - Gallup and Phoenix Areas
[Continued]

Tribe	Tribal enrollment	Res. pop.	Census 1980 pop.	Census 1990 pop.	No. on ICWA
Winnemucca Colony	83	83	35	61	161
Yavapai Apache	520	635	136	0	800
Yavapai-Prescott	47	114	160	134	136
Yerington Paiute	384	419	116	324	445
Yomba Shoshone	187	144	0	88	144
Total	83,954	86,781	49,031	40,842	106,452

Source: U.S. Department of the Interior. Bureau of Indian Affairs. Unpublished data, 12 April 1994.

★ 883 ★

Tribal Enrollment

Tribal Enrollment - Juneau Area

Data are shown in number of persons. Census population figures are based on self-reported responses and may be lower than the tribally enrolled population. The number of persons in ICWA (Indian Child Welfare Act) may exceed the number of tribally enrolled persons, since a child needn't be enrolled and may be only a descendant to receive benefits.

Tribe	Tribal enrollment	Res. pop.	Census 1980 pop.	Census 1990 pop.	No. on ICWA
Alaska Tribes	44,936	0	0	0	0
Atka	0	0	93	0	70
Chenega	0	0	0	0	68
Copper Center	0	0	117	0	0
Eagle	0	0	56	0	46
Fort Yukon	0	0	381	0	529
Gambell	0	0	407	0	530
Kanatak	0	0	0	0	90
Kenaitze	0	0	0	0	535
Nome-Eskimo Community	0	0	0	0	1,717
Perryville	0	0	103	0	107
Pitka's Point	0	0	73	0	135
Platinum	0	0	46	0	59
Pt. Graham	0	0	138	0	157
Scammon Bay	0	0	212	0	347
Selawik	0	0	515	0	597
St. Paul	0	0	563	0	529
Stebbins	0	0	354	0	397
Tanana	0	0	292	0	289
Tatitlek	0	0	50	0	109
Tlingit-Haida Tribes	0	0	0	0	0
Total	44,936	0	3,400	0	6,310

Source: U.S. Department of the Interior. Bureau of Indian Affairs. Unpublished data, 12 April 1994.

★ 884 ★

Tribal Enrollment

Tribal Enrollment - Minneapolis Area

Data are shown in number of persons. Census population figures are based on self-reported responses and may be lower than the tribally enrolled population. The number of persons in ICWA (Indian Child Welfare Act) may exceed the number of tribally enrolled persons, since a child needn't be enrolled and may be only a descendant to receive benefits.

Tribe	Tribal enrollment	Res. pop.	Census 1980 pop.	Census 1990 pop.	No. on ICWA
Bad River Chippewa	4,664	1,538	694	868	1,578
Bay Mills Chippewa	915	605	279	403	630
Fond du Lac Chippewa	2,820	3,038	471	1,106	3,045
Forest County Potawatomi	783	460	0	266	510
Grand Portage Chippewa	770	308	201	207	337
Grand Traverse Chippewa	1,702	1,351	0	208	844
Hannahville Chippewa	408	328	202	173	347
Keweenaw Bay Chippewa	2,408	785	640	0	910
Lac Courte Oreilles Chippewa	5,217	2,279	1,133	1,771	3,201
Lac Vieux Desert Chippewa	201	0	0	119	346
Lac du Flambeau Chippewa	2,706	1,420	1,091	1,432	1,484
Leech Lake Chippewa	5,478	4,930	2,612	3,390	6,060
Lower Sioux Community	620	237	69	225	279
Menominee Tribe of Wisconsin	6,380	3,684	2,467	3,182	4,725
Mille Lacs Chippewa	2,189	942	281	428	1,209
Nett Lake Chippewa (Bois Forte)	2,101	1,491	531	346	2,016
Oneida of Wisconsin	10,309	4,875	1,762	2,447	5,129
Prairie Island Sioux	304	191	82	56	185
Red Cliff Chippewa	2,830	1,471	586	727	1,502
Red Lake Band of Chippewa	7,198	4,092	2,832	3,602	5,341
Sac & Fox of Iowa	1,026	737	454	564	853
Saginaw Chippewa	1,702	954	447	0	2,216
Sault Ste. Marie Chippewa	14,870	8,700	0	554	9,281
Shakopee Mdewakanton Sioux	60	218	76	0	242
Sokaogon Chippewa	1,399	413	107	311	545
St. Croix Chippewa	759	1,288	360	462	1,409
Stockbridge-Munsee	1,653	846	566	447	936
Upper Sioux Indian Community	148	148	53	43	177
White Earth Chippewa	9,660	4,268	2,585	2,759	4,615
Wisconsin Winnebago Tribe	3,970	2,763	377	370	2,738
Total	96,250	54,360	20,958	26,466	62,790

Source: U.S. Department of the Interior. Bureau of Indian Affairs. Unpublished data, 12 April 1994.

★ 885 ★

Tribal Enrollment

Tribal Enrollment - Muskogee Area

Data are shown in number of persons. Census population figures are based on self-reported responses and may be lower than the tribally enrolled population. The number of persons in ICWA (Indian Child Welfare Act) may exceed the number of tribally enrolled persons, since a child needn't be enrolled and may be only a descendant to receive benefits.

Tribe	Tribal enrollment	Res. pop.	Census 1980 pop.	Census 1990 pop.	No. on ICWA
Cherokee Nation of Oklahoma	85,986	87,059	0	0	100,206
Chickasaw Nation of Oklahoma	36,000	12,369	0	0	26,265
Choctaw Nation of Oklahoma	50,000	26,884	0	0	28,411
Creek Nation of Oklahoma	38,000	56,244	0	0	68,000
Eastern Shawnee Tribe of Oklahoma	1,392	351	0	0	300
Miami Tribe of Oklahoma	1,270	239	0	0	204
Modoc Tribe of Oklahoma	135	102	0	0	49
Osage Tribe of Oklahoma	26,000	8,147	0	6,161	10,594
Ottawa Tribe of Oklahoma	1,579	246	0	0	420
Peoria Tribe of Oklahoma	2,132	424	0	0	258
Quapaw Tribe of Oklahoma	2,000	559	0	0	678
Seminole Nation of Oklahoma	15,000	1,106	0	0	8,407
Seneca-Cayuga Tribe of Oklahoma	2,200	693	0	0	874
Wyandotte Tribe of Oklahoma	2,872	366	0	0	658
Total	264,566	197,789	0	6,161	245,324

Source: U.S. Department of the Interior. Bureau of Indian Affairs. Unpublished data, 12 April 1994.

★ 886 ★

Tribal Enrollment

Tribal Enrollment - Portland Area

Data are shown in number of persons. Census population figures are based on self-reported responses and may be lower than the tribally enrolled population. The number of persons in ICWA (Indian Child Welfare Act) may exceed the number of tribally enrolled persons, since a child needn't be enrolled and may be only a descendant to receive benefits.

Tribe	Tribal enrollment	Res. pop.	Census 1980 pop.	Census 1990 pop.	No. on ICWA
Burns Paiute Tribe	320	207	161	151	217
Chehalis	491	775	151	308	815
Coeur d'Alene	1,216	1,100	457	749	2,187
Colville Confederated Tribes	7,308	3,880	3,248	3,788	5,296
Confed. Tribes of Warm Springs	2,517	3,179	2,067	2,820	3,337
Confed. Salish & Kootenai	6,481	6,669	3,504	5,130	7,002
Confed. Tribes of the Umatilla	1,249	1,652	946	1,029	2,932
Coos, Lower Umpqua & Siuslaw	351	266	0	1	340
Cow Creek - Umpqua Indians	763	382	0	11	396
Grand Ronde Community	2,457	923	0	1	3,072

[Continued]

★ 886 ★

Tribal Enrollment - Portland Area
[Continued]

Tribe	Tribal enrollment	Res. pop.	Census 1980 pop.	Census 1990 pop.	No. on ICWA
Hoh Tribe of Washington	137	94	29	74	89
Jamestown Klallam	237	389	0	4	408
Kalispel	211	232	94	91	150
Klamath Tribe	2,477	2,313	0	0	2,488
Kootenai Tribe of Idaho	82	108	55	61	150
Lower Elwah Tribal Community	537	1,099	38	130	1,142
Lummi Tribe	2,676	2,846	1,258	1,594	3,415
Makah Tribe	1,569	960	799	940	1,963
Metlakatla Indian Community	1,394	1,424	875	0	1,685
Muckleshoot Tribe	797	2,963	428	864	3,301
Nez Perce Tribe	3,250	2,455	1,060	1,863	2,577
Nisqually Indian Community	332	1,455	21	365	1,527
Nooksack Indian Tribe	1,015	454	0	412	635
Port Gamble Community	645	645	317	377	1,685
Puyallup Tribe	1,329	7,987	900	937	9,072
Quileute	723	597	273	303	824
Quinault Indian Nation	2,367	2,260	974	943	2,398
Sauk-Suiattle Indian Tribe	183	210	0	69	220
Shoalwater Bay Tribe	134	134	31	66	544
Shoshone-Bannock & NW Band	3,818	6,617	2,500	3,035	7,220
Siletz Indians	1,976	1,309	0	0	1,579
Skokomish Tribe of Washington	643	829	342	431	1,103
Spokane Tribe	2,025	1,248	1,045	1,229	1,229
Squaxin Island Tribe	431	1,311	59	127	1,541
Stillaguamish Tribe	155	461	0	96	537
Suquamish Tribe	665	652	0	388	1,680
Swinomish Indian Tribal Commun.	412	646	381	585	802
Tulalip Tribes of Washington	2,043	1,710	749	1,204	2,231
Upper Skagit Tribe	504	350	0	162	367
Yakima	7,607	6,706	4,957	6,307	13,997
Total	63,527	69,497	27,719	36,645	92,153

Source: U.S. Department of the Interior. Bureau of Indian Affairs. Unpublished data, 12 April 1994.

★ 887 ★

Tribal Enrollment

Tribal Enrollment - Sacramento Area

Data are shown in number of persons. Census population figures are based on self-reported responses and may be lower than the tribally enrolled population. The number of persons in ICWA (Indian Child Welfare Act) may exceed the number of tribally enrolled persons, since a child needn't be enrolled and may be only a descendant to receive benefits.

Tribe	Tribal enrollment	Res. pop.	Census 1980 pop.	Census 1990 pop.	No. on ICWA
Agua Caliente	232	232	91	117	286
Alturas	20	10	0	5	8
Augustine	0	0	0	0	8
Barona	140	420	183	373	472
Benton	125	84	9	52	48
Berry Creek	202	225	0	2	304
Big Lagoon	23	27	0	19	22
Big Pine	403	413	265	331	385
Big Sandy	175	110	0	38	188
Big Valley	206	211	0	90	211
Bishop	1,016	1,350	867	935	1,350
Blue Lake Rancheria	17	23	0	30	33
Bridgeport	53	80	20	37	58
Buena Vista	1	1	0	0	1
Cabazon	25	25	0	20	29
Cahuilla	260	148	30	82	227
Campo	214	115	96	143	234
Capitan Grande	0	36	0	0	36
Cedarville	20	13	6	6	25
Chicken Ranch	6	10	0	10	10
Cloverdale	7	7	0	0	273
Cold Springs	265	265	0	159	265
Colusa	20	69	0	19	71
Cortina	105	106	0	22	150
Coyote Valley	238	201	0	122	274
Cuyapaipe	5	17	0	0	0
Dry Creek	140	163	18	38	163
Elk Valley Rancheria	150	260	0	32	190
Enterprise	347	360	0	5	360
Fort Bidwell Reservation	132	135	116	107	177
Ft. Independence	96	123	42	38	129
Greenville	64	317	0	7	317
Grindstone	143	155	62	102	171
Hoopa Valley	1,700	2,049	1,481	1,733	2,393
Hopland	234	290	0	142	304
Inaja-Cosmit Reservation	16	17	0	0	17
Jackson	27	28	0	13	29
Jamul	54	60	0	0	63
Karuk Tribe of California	1,682	2,133	0	33	5,040
La Jolla	493	385	158	121	534
La Posta	16	14	0	3	9
Laytonville	140	504	204	129	529

[Continued]

★ 887 ★

Tribal Enrollment - Sacramento Area
[Continued]

Tribe	Tribal enrollment	Res. pop.	Census 1980 pop.	Census 1990 pop.	No. on ICWA
Lone Pine	140	296	171	168	296
Los Coyotes	201	212	58	42	212
Manchester	499	253	68	178	253
Manzanita	64	52	0	47	71
Mesa Grande	334	70	0	72	70
Middletown	64	66	29	18	99
Mooretown	134	425	0	0	808
Morongo	779	996	343	527	1,067
Northfork	262	280	0	0	280
Pala	598	585	441	563	750
Pauma & Yuima	137	132	63	137	138
Pechanga	694	725	44	289	725
Picayune	30	20	0	15	769
Pinoleville	0	161	0	77	169
Pit River Tribe	724	731	66	1	2,329
Potter Valley	0	2	0	0	107
Quartz Valley	250	102	0	19	264
Ramona	1	3	0	0	0
Redding Rancheria	1,657	2,610	0	79	2,740
Redwood Valley	120	124	0	14	112
Resighini	72	879	15	26	89
Rincon	496	457	236	379	683
Robinson	177	211	0	113	211
Rohnerville	110	129	0	1	298
Round Valley	2,399	656	314	577	1,080
Rumsey	29	51	11	4	51
San Manuel	70	80	26	56	80
San Pasqual	268	435	144	212	435
Santa Rosa	129	135	0	37	356
Santa Rosa Rancheria	320	362	173	284	135
Santa Ynez	168	223	0	213	312
Santa Ysabel	300	953	178	150	953
Sheep Ranch	0	0	0	0	0
Sherwood Valley	233	155	0	9	274
Shingle Springs	263	263	0	7	185
Smith River Rancheria	500	402	0	72	188
Soboba	517	725	242	308	725
Stewarts Point	194	248	62	86	248
Sulphur Bank	152	140	101	90	221
Susanville	109	406	92	154	565
Sycuan	20	120	28	0	126
Table Bluff	70	218	0	43	239
Table Mountain	95	115	0	48	115
Timbi-Sha	213	188	0	0	188
Torres-Martinez	343	290	51	143	261
Trinidad Rancheria	250	123	46	59	128

[Continued]

★ 887 ★

Tribal Enrollment - Sacramento Area
[Continued]

Tribe	Tribal enrollment	Res. pop.	Census 1980 pop.	Census 1990 pop.	No. on ICWA
Tule River	601	850	436	745	957
Tuolume	102	614	67	107	288
Twenty-Nine Palms	10	16	0	310	14
Upper Lake	154	150	0	28	188
Viejas	70	222	150	227	213
Yurok Tribe	0	0	396	463	3,622
Total	24,334	28,857	7,699	12,312	40,080

Source: U.S. Department of the Interior. Bureau of Indian Affairs. Unpublished data, 12 April 1994.

Politics and Voting

★ 888 ★

Admired Qualities in Political Leaders - Upper Skagit Tribe

Data shown are part of the results of a study of the Upper Skagit Tribe conducted from 1985-87 and reflects responses by a randomly selected group of voters.

Quality	Percentage of those reporting quality
Objectivity/impartiality	95.0
Knowledge of dealing with bureaucracies (e.g. BIA, social services, IHS, and state government)	82.0
Ability to communicate with tribal members	71.0
Education	61.0
Knowledge of tribal traditions	33.0
Knowledge of the reservation	26.0

Source: Miller, Bruce G. "Women and tribal politics: is there a gender gap in Indian elections?" *American Indian Quarterly* (Winter 1994), p. 35.

★ 889 ★

Politics and Voting

Upper Skagit Tribal Voting Participation, 1985-87

Distribution of persons participating in tribal elections is shown by sex and age group of voters.

Age group	Women	Percent	Men	Percent	Total	Percent
18-27 years	134	15.2	107	12.1	241	27.4
28-37 years	90	10.2	101	11.5	191	21.7
38-47 years	101	11.5	73	8.3	174	19.8
48-57 years	51	5.8	66	7.5	117	13.3
57 years and older	93	10.6	65	7.4	158	17.9
Totals	469	53.2	412	46.8	881	100.0

Source: Miller, Bruce G. "Women and tribal politics: is there a gender gap in Indian elections?" *American Indian Quarterly* (Winter 1994), p. 32.

Chapter 11
LAW AND LAW ENFORCEMENT

Arrests

★ 890 ★

Arrest Rate by Race, 1992

Total arrests are shown with percent distribution of arrestees by race.

[10,950 agencies; 1992 estimated population 213,130,000]

Offense charged	Total arrests					Percent[1]				
	Total	White	Black	American Indian or Alaskan Native	Asian or Pacific Islander	Total	White	Black	American Indian or Alaskan Native	Asian or Pacific Islander
Total	11,876,204	8,030,171	3,598,259	130,770	117,004	100.0	67.6	30.3	1.1	1.0
Murder and nonnegligent manslaughter	19,463	8,466	10,728	107	162	100.0	43.5	55.1	0.5	0.8
Forcible rape	33,332	18,490	14,258	291	293	100.0	55.5	42.8	0.9	0.9
Robbery	153,246	57,837	93,392	608	1,409	10.0	37.7	60.9	0.4	0.9
Aggravated assault	434,471	258,545	168,744	3,629	3,553	100.0	59.5	38.8	0.8	0.8
Burglary	359,306	243,637	109,165	2,840	3,664	100.0	67.8	30.4	0.8	1.0
Larceny-theft	1,290,278	853,558	404,707	14,293	17,720	100.0	66.2	31.4	1.1	1.4
Motor vehicle theft	171,136	99,874	67,481	1,355	2,426	100.0	58.4	39.4	0.8	1.4
Arson	16,275	12,430	3,572	135	138	100.0	76.4	21.9	0.8	0.8
Violent crime[2]	640,512	343,338	287,122	4,635	5,417	100.0	53.6	44.8	0.7	0.8
Property crime[3]	1,836,995	1,209,499	584,925	18,623	23,948	100.0	65.8	31.8	1.0	1.3
Total Crime Index[4]	2,477,507	1,552,837	872,047	23,258	29,365	100.0	62.7	35.2	0.9	1.2
Other assaults	911,374	584,668	308,170	10,567	7,969	100.0	64.2	33.8	1.2	0.9
Forgery and counterfeiting	88,573	57,377	29,804	492	900	100.0	64.8	33.6	0.6	1.0
Fraud	345,768	223,483	118,931	1,531	1,823	100.0	64.6	34.4	0.4	0.5
Embezzlement	11,699	8,022	3,476	52	149	100.0	68.6	29.7	0.4	1.3
Stolen property; buying, receiving, possessing	136,411	77,622	56,817	755	1,217	100.0	56.9	41.7	0.6	0.9
Vandalism	262,084	199,657	57,295	2,707	2,425	100.0	76.2	21.9	1.0	0.9
Weapons; carrying, possessing, etc.	203,739	115,377	85,072	1,055	2,235	100.0	56.6	41.8	0.5	1.1
Prostitution and commercialized vice	86,932	53,922	31,541	485	984	100.0	62.0	36.3	0.6	1.1

[Continued]

★ 890 ★

Arrest Rate by Race, 1992
[Continued]

Offense charged	Total arrests					Percent[1]				
	Total	White	Black	American Indian or Alaskan Native	Asian or Pacific Islander	Total	White	Black	American Indian or Alaskan Native	Asian or Pacific Islander
Sex offenses (except forcible rape and prostitution)	91,454	72,366	17,280	861	947	100.0	79.1	18.9	0.9	1.0
Drug abuse violations	919,561	546,430	364,546	3,500	5,085	100.0	59.4	39.6	0.4	0.6
Gambling	15,021	7,194	6,756	59	1,012	100.0	47.9	45.0	0.4	6.7
Offenses against family and children	83,770	56,124	24,437	1,044	2,165	100.0	67.0	29.2	1.2	2.6
Driving under the influence	1,317,968	1,155,884	132,894	17,797	11,393	100.0	87.7	10.1	1.4	0.9
Liquor laws	441,781	378,288	47,388	12,147	3,958	100.0	85.6	10.7	2.7	0.9
Drunkenness	663,573	534,629	113,496	13,627	1,821	100.0	80.6	17.1	2.1	0.3
Disorderly conduct	604,612	394,210	199,055	7,788	3,559	100.0	65.2	32.9	1.3	0.6
Vagrancy	28,611	14,563	13,588	359	101	100.0	50.9	47.5	1.3	0.4
All other offenses (except traffic)	2,950,424	1,818,980	1,067,226	30,326	33,892	100.0	61.7	36.2	1.0	1.1
Suspicion	15,336	7,572	7,634	24	106	100.0	49.4	49.8	0.2	0.7
Curfew and loitering law violations	74,428	56,752	15,607	703	1,366	100.0	76.3	21.0	0.9	1.8
Runaways	145,578	114,214	25,199	1,633	4,532	100.0	78.5	17.3	1.1	3.1

Source: Maguire, Kathleen and Ann L. Pastore, eds., *Sourcebook of Criminal Justice Statistics 1993*. U.S. Department of Justice, Bureau of Justice Statistics. Washington, DC: U.S. Government Printing Office, 1994, p. 432. Primary source: U.S. Department of Justice, Federal Bureau of Investigation, *Crime in the United States, 1992*, (Washington, DC: USGPO, 1993), pp. 235-237. *Notes:* Estimates by the U.S. Bureau of the Census indicate that on July 1, 1992, whites comprised 83.5 percent, blacks 12.4 percent, and other racial categories 4.1 percent of the total U.S. resident population (U.S. Department of Commerce, Bureau of the Census, "U.S. Population Estimates, by Age, Sex, Race, and Hispanic Origin: 1990 to 1992," Washington, DC: U.S. Department of Commerce, September 1993. (Mimeographed.) Table 1) 1. Because of rounding, percents may not add to total. 2. Violent crimes are offenses of murder, forcible rape, robbery, and aggravated assault. 3. Property crimes are offenses of burglary, larceny-theft, motor vehicle theft, and arson. 4. Includes arson.

★ 891 ★
Arrests

Arrest Rate by Race and Age Group - 1992

Total number of arrests and percent distribution are shown[1].

Offense charged	Arrests under 18						Arrests 18 and older					
	Total	Total	White	Black	American Indian or Alaskan Native	Asian or Pacific Islander	Total	Total	White	Black	American Indian or Alaskan Native	Asian or Pacific Islander
Total	1,939,456	100.0	70.0	27.3	1.0	1.7	9,936,748	100.0	67.1	30.9	1.1	0.8
Murder and nonnegligent manslaughter	2,829	100.0	41.0	57.4	0.4	1.1	16,634	100.0	43.9	54.7	0.6	0.8
Forcible rape	5,364	100.0	52.2	45.9	1.0	0.9	27,968	100.0	56.1	42.2	0.9	0.9
Robbery	40,354	100.0	37.8	60.2	0.4	1.5	112,892	100.0	37.7	61.2	0.4	0.7
Aggravated assault	63,683	100.0	56.3	41.9	0.7	1.0	370,788	100.0	60.1	38.3	0.9	0.8
Burglary	122,439	100.0	75.2	22.2	1.0	1.6	236,867	100.0	64.0	34.6	0.7	0.7
Larceny-theft	401,375	100.0	72.6	24.2	1.2	2.0	888,903	100.0	63.3	34.6	1.1	1.1
Motor vehicle theft	75,706	100.0	58.3	38.9	1.0	1.8	95,430	100.0	58.4	39.8	0.6	1.1
Arson	7,946	100.0	83.0	15.2	0.7	1.1	8,329	100.0	70.1	28.4	0.9	0.6
Violent crime[2]	112,230	100.0	49.1	49.1	0.6	1.2	528,282	100.0	54.6	43.9	0.7	0.8

[Continued]

★ 891 ★

Arrest Rate by Race and Age Group - 1992
[Continued]

Offense charged	Arrests under 18						Arrests 18 and older					
	Total	Total	White	Black	American Indian or Alaskan Native	Asian or Pacific Islander	Total	Total	White	Black	American Indian or Alaskan Native	Asian or Pacific Islander
Property crime[3]	607,466	100.0	71.5	25.6	1.1	1.8	1,229,529	100.0	63.1	34.9	1.0	1.0
Total Crime Index[4]	719,696	100.0	68.0	29.2	1.1	1.7	1,757,811	100.0	60.5	37.6	0.9	1.0
Other assaults	143,368	100.0	62.5	35.0	1.0	1.5	768,006	100.0	64.5	33.6	1.2	0.8
Forgery and counterfeiting	7,018	100.0	78.3	19.3	1.0	1.3	81,555	100.0	63.6	34.9	0.5	1.0
Fraud	15,019	100.0	53.4	44.3	0.5	1.8	330,749	100.0	65.1	33.9	0.4	0.5
Embezzlement	669	100.0	69.4	29.0	0.6	1.0	11,030	100.0	68.5	29.8	0.4	1.3
Stolen property; buying, receiving, possessing	36,265	100.0	58.9	39.1	0.7	1.3	100,146	100.0	56.2	42.6	0.5	0.7
Vandalism	117,855	100.0	82.0	16.1	0.9	1.1	144,229	100.0	71.5	26.6	1.2	0.8
Weapons; carrying, possessing, etc.	46,221	100.0	61.6	36.5	0.6	1.4	157,518	100.0	55.2	43.3	0.5	1.0
Prostitution and commercialized vice	1,095	100.0	69.0	29.2	0.7	1.0	85,837	100.0	61.9	36.4	0.6	1.1
Sex offenses (except forcible rape and prostitution)	16,599	100.0	72.9	25.0	0.7	1.3	74,855	100.0	80.5	17.5	1.0	1.0
Drug abuse violations	73,886	100.0	52.2	46.6	0.4	0.8	845,675	100.0	60.1	39.0	0.4	0.5
Gambling	1,088	100.0	24.4	74.4	0.6	0.6	13,933	100.0	49.7	42.7	0.4	7.2
Offenses against family and children	3,917	100.0	75.7	20.8	0.6	2.8	79,853	100.0	66.6	29.6	1.3	2.6
Driving under the influence	11,942	100.0	91.9	5.4	2.1	0.6	1,306,026	100.0	87.7	10.1	1.3	0.9
Liquor laws	97,203	100.0	91.7	5.3	2.4	0.6	344,578	100.0	83.9	12.3	2.8	1.0
Drunkenness	15,093	100.0	87.9	9.9	1.7	0.5	648,480	100.0	80.4	17.3	2.1	0.3
Disorderly conduct	109,610	100.0	66.5	32.1	0.7	0.7	495,002	100.0	64.9	33.1	1.4	0.6
Vagrancy	3,435	100.0	66.6	32.5	0.3	0.6	25,176	100.0	48.8	49.5	1.4	0.3
All other offenses (except traffic)	294,508	100.0	68.3	278.6	0.8	2.3	2,655,916	100.0	60.9	37.0	1.1	1.0
Suspicion	4,963	100.0	62.8	35.6	X	1.6	10,373	100.0	42.9	56.5	0.2	0.3
Curfew and loitering law violations	74,428	100.0	76.3	21.0	0.9	1.8	X	X	X	X	X	X
Runaways	145,578	100.0	78.5	17.3	1.1	3.1	X	X	X	X	X	X

Source: Maguire, Kathleen and Ann L. Pastore, eds., *Sourcebook of Criminal Justice Statistics 1993*. U.S. Department of Justice, Bureau of Justice Statistics. Washington, DC: U.S. Government Printing Office, 1994, p. 433. Primary source: U.S. Department of Justice, Federal Bureau of Investigation, *Crime in the United States, 1992*, (Washington, DC: USGPO, 1993), pp. 235-237. *Notes:* Estimates by the U.S. Bureau of the Census indicate that on July 1, 1992, whites comprised 83.5 percent, blacks 12.4 percent, and other racial categories 4.1 percent of the total U.S. resident population (U.S. Department of Commerce, Bureau of the Census, "U.S. Population Estimates, by Age, Sex, Race, and Hispanic Origin: 1990 to 1992," Washington, DC: U.S. Department of Commerce, September 1993. (Mimeographed.) Table 1) 1. Because of rounding, percents may not add to total. 2. Violent crimes are offenses of murder, forcible rape, robbery, and aggravated assault. 3. Property crimes are offenses of burglary, larceny-theft, motor vehicle theft, and arson. 4. Includes arson.

★ 892 ★

Arrests

Arrest Rate in Cities by Race - 1992

Data are shown by offense charged and race, for 1992.

[7,615 agencies; 1992 estimated population 145,842,000]

Offense charged	Total arrests					Percent[1]				
	Total	White	Black	American Indian or Alaskan Native	Asian or Pacific Islander	Total	White	Black	American Indian or Alaskan Native	Asian or Pacific Islander
Total	9,105,947	5,886,380	3,023,380	98,592	97,600	100.0	64.6	33.2	1.1	1.1
Murder and nonnegligent manslaughter	14,999	5,475	9,331	54	139	100.0	36.5	62.2	0.4	0.9
Forcible rape	24,950	12,283	12,257	155	255	100.0	49.2	49.1	0.6	1.0
Robbery	135,319	49,301	84,239	506	1,273	100.0	36.4	62.3	0.4	0.9
Aggravated assault	335,834	186,847	143,574	2,382	3,031	100.0	55.6	42.8	0.7	0.9
Burglary	265,964	169,365	91,905	1,705	2,989	100.0	63.7	34.6	0.6	1.1
Larceny-theft	1,091,343	708,972	353,919	12,954	15,498	100.0	65.0	32.4	1.2	1.4
Motor vehicle theft	136,503	75,550	57,842	957	2,154	100.0	55.3	42.4	0.7	1.6
Arson	11,858	8,667	2,994	86	111	100.0	73.1	25.2	0.7	0.9
Violent crime[2]	511,102	253,906	249,401	3,097	4,698	100.0	49.7	48.8	0.6	0.9
Property crime[3]	1,505,668	962,554	506,660	15,702	20,752	100.0	63.9	33.7	1.0	1.4
Total crime index[4]	2,016,770	1,216,460	456,061	18,799	25,450	100.0	60.3	37.5	0.9	1.3
Other assaults	716,614	437,119	265,036	8,034	6,425	100.0	61.0	37.0	1.1	0.9
Forgery and counterfeiting	64,989	40,218	23,629	353	789	100.0	61.9	36.4	0.5	1.2
Fraud	204,748	122,891	79,458	854	1,545	100.0	60.0	38.8	0.4	0.8
Embezzlement	8,339	5,429	2,783	37	90	100.0	65.1	33.4	0.4	1.1
Stolen property; buying, receiving, possessing	109,786	58,622	49,568	539	1,057	100.0	53.4	45.1	0.5	1.0
Vandalism	209,75	154,366	51,164	2,159	2,066	100.0	73.6	24.4	1.0	1.0
Weapons; carrying, possessing, etc.	165,612	88,821	74,152	765	1,874	100.0	53.6	44.8	0.5	1.1
Prostitution and commercialized vice	83,269	51,155	30,691	470	953	100.0	61.4	36.9	0.6	1.1
Sex offenses (except forcible rape and prostitution)	65,722	49,613	14,701	585	823	100.0	75.5	22.4	0.9	1.3
Drug abuse violations	718,055	398,720	312,857	2,286	4,192	100.0	55.5	43.6	0.3	0.6
Gambling	13,124	5,919	6,250	36	919	100.0	45.1	47.6	0.3	7.0
Offenses against family and children	46,915	31,517	12,706	654	2,038	100.0	67.2	27.1	1.4	4.3
Driving under the influence	803,938	702,724	84,113	10,747	6,354	100.0	87.4	10.5	1.3	0.8
Liquor laws	349,728	294,020	42,033	10,269	3,406	100.0	84.1	12.0	2.9	1.0
Drunkenness	554,266	437,645	103,722	11,396	1,503	100.0	79.0	18.7	2.1	0.3
Disorderly conduct	531,322	335,324	187,021	5,781	3,196	100.0	63.1	35.2	1.1	0.6
Vagrancy	26,956	13,285	13,231	342	98	100.0	49.3	49.1	1.3	0.4
All other offenses (except traffic)	2,215,657	1,294,457	868,967	22,593	29,640	100.0	58.4	39.2	1.0	1.3
Suspicion	13,861	6,260	7,489	11	101	100.0	45.2	54.0	0.1	0.7

[Continued]

★ 892 ★

Arrest Rate in Cities by Race - 1992

[Continued]

Offense charged	Total arrests					Percent[1]				
	Total	White	Black	American Indian or Alaskan Native	Asian or Pacific Islander	Total	White	Black	American Indian or Alaskan Native	Asian or Pacific Islander
Curfew and loitering law violations	70,504	53,605	15,242	643	1,014	100.0	76.0	21.6	0.9	1.4
Runaways	116,017	88,210	22,501	1,239	4,067	100.0	76.0	19.4	1.1	3.5

Source: Maguire, Kathleen and Ann L. Pastore, eds., *Sourcebook of Criminal Justice Statistics 1993.* U.S. Department of Justice, Bureau of Justice Statistics. Washington, DC: U.S. Government Printing Office, 1994, p. 436. Primary source: U.S. Department of Justice, Federal Bureau of Investigation, *Crime in the United States, 1992,* (Washington, DC: USGPO, 1993), pp. 244-246. *Notes:* 1. Because of rounding, percents may not add to total. 2. Violent crimes are offenses of murder, forcible rape, robbery, and aggravated assault. 3. Property crimes are offenses of burglary, larceny-theft, motor vehicle theft, and arson. 4. Includes arson.

★ 893 ★

Arrests

Arrest Rate in Cities by Race and Age Group - 1992

Number of arrests and percent distribution are shown by offense charged, age group, and race, for 1992[1].

Offense charged	Total	Arrests under 18					Total	Arrests 18 and older				
		Total	White	Black	American Indian or Alaskan Native	Asian or Pacific Islander		Total	White	Black	American Indian or Alaskan Native	Asian or Pacific Islander
Total	1,617,737	100.0	68.1	29.2	1.0	1.7	7,488,210	100.0	63.9	34.1	1.1	0.9
Murder and nonnegligent manslaughter	2,350	100.0	37.4	61.2	0.3	1.1	12,649	100.0	36.3	62.4	0.4	0.9
Forcible rape	4,167	100.0	45.8	52.4	0.7	1.0	20,783	100.0	49.9	48.5	0.6	1.0
Robbery	36,667	100.0	37.2	60.8	.04	1.6	98,652	100.0	36.1	62.8	0.4	0.7
Aggravated assault	51,730	100.0	53.9	44.5	0.6	1.0	284,104	100.0	56.0	42.4	0.7	0.9
Burglary	90,055	100.0	72.1	25.4	0.8	1.8	175,909	100.0	59.4	39.3	0.6	0.8
Larceny-theft	346,684	100.0	71.8	24.9	1.3	2.0	744,659	100.0	61.8	35.9	1.1	1.2
Motor vehicle theft	61,701	100.0	55.5	41.7	0.9	1.9	74,802	100.0	55.2	42.9	0.6	1.3
Arson	6,265	100.0	81.5	16.8	0.7	1.1	5,593	100.0	63.7	34.7	0.8	0.8
Violent crime[2]	94,914	100.0	46.7	51.5	0.5	1.2	416,188	100.0	50.4	48.2	0.6	0.8
Property crime[3]	504,705	100.0	70.0	26.9	1.1	1.9	1,000,963	100.0	60.9	37.0	1.0	1.1
Total crime index[4]	599,619	100.0	66.3	30.8	1.1	1.8	1,417,151	100.0	57.8	40.3	0.9	1.0
Other assaults	119,397	100.0	60.7	36.8	0.9	1.6	597,217	100.0	61.1	37.0	1.2	0.8
Forgery and counterfeiting	5,723	100.0	76.6	20.9	1.1	1.4	59,266	100.0	60.5	37.8	0.5	1.2
Fraud	13,383	100.0	50.2	47.5	0.4	1.8	191,365	100.0	60.7	38.2	0.4	0.7
Embezzlement	541	100.0	68.4	29.8	0.6	1.3	7,798	100.0	64.9	33.6	0.4	1.1
Stolen property; buying, receiving, possessing	30,893	100.0	56.4	41.6	0.7	1.3	78,893	100.0	52.2	46.5	0.4	0.8
Vandalism	95,153	100.0	80.1	17.9	0.8	1.1	114,602	100.0	68.2	29.8	1.2	0.9
Weapons; carrying, possessing, etc.	39,641	100.0	60.2	37.8	0.6	1.4	125,971	100.0	51.6	47.0	0.4	1.1
Prostitution and commercialized vice	999	100.0	68.4	29.8	0.7	1.1	82,270	100.0	61.3	36.9	0.6	1.1
Sex offenses (except forcible rape and prostitution)	12,173	100.0	68.5	29.3	0.5	1.7	53,549	100.0	77.1	20.8	1.0	1.2
Drug abuse violations	63,211	100.0	49.5	49.4	0.4	0.7	654,844	100.0	56.1	43.0	0.3	0.6

[Continued]

★ 893 ★

Arrest Rate in Cities by Race and Age Group - 1992

[Continued]

Offense charged	Total	Arrests under 18					Total	Arrests 18 and older				
		Total	White	Black	American Indian or Alaskan Native	Asian or Pacific Islander		Total	White	Black	American Indian or Alaskan Native	Asian or Pacific Islander
Gambling	1,032	100.0	24.2	75.0	0.2	0.6	12,092	100.0	46.9	45.3	0.3	7.6
Offenses against family and children	3,158	100.0	73.2	22.9	0.5	3.4	43,757	100.0	66.7	27.4	1.5	4.4
Driving under the influence	7,599	100.0	91.3	6.0	2.1	0.6	796,339	100.0	87.4	10.5	1.3	0.8
Liquor laws	73,772	100.0	90.7	6.1	2.6	0.7	275,956	100.0	82.3	13.6	3.0	1.1
Drunkenness	13,019	100.0	87.2	10.7	1.6	0.5	541,247	100.0	78.8	18.9	2.1	0.3
Disorderly conduct	99,209	100.0	65.2	33.4	0.7	0.7	432,113	100.0	62.6	35.6	1.2	0.6
Vagrancy	3,051	100.0	64.2	34.8	0.3	0.73	23,905	100.0	47.4	50.9	1.4	0.3
All other offenses (except traffic)	244,909	100.0	66.5	30.3	0.8	2.4	1,970,748	100.0	57.4	40.3	1.1	1.2
Suspicion	4,734	100.0	61.8	36.6	X	1.6	9,127	100.0	36.6	63.0	0.1	0.3
Curfew and loitering law violations	70,504	100.0	76.0	21.6	0.9	1.4	X	X	X	X	X	X
Runaways	116,017	100.0	76.0	19.4	1.1	3.5	X	X	X	X	X	x

Source: Maguire, Kathleen and Ann L. Pastore, eds., *Sourcebook of Criminal Justice Statistics 1993*. U.S. Department of Justice, Bureau of Justice Statistics. Washington, DC: U.S. Government Printing Office, 1994, pp. 437-438. Primary source: U.S. Department of Justice, Federal Bureau of Investigation, *Crime in the United States, 1992*, (Washington, DC: USGPO, 1993), pp. 244-246. *Notes:* An X stands for not applicable. 1. Because of rounding, percents may not add to total. 2. Violent crimes are offenses of murder, forcible rape, robbery, and aggravated assault. 3. Property crimes are offenses of burglary, larceny-theft, motor vehicle theft, and arson. 4. Includes arson.

★ 894 ★

Arrests

Arrest Rate in Rural Counties by Race - 1992

Arrest rates are shown in percent, by offense charged, age group, and race, for 1992.

Offense charged	Total arrests	Percent[1]				
		Total	White	Black	American Indian or Alaskan Native	Asian or Pacific Islander
Total	937,627	100.0	81.2	14.9	2.7	1.2
Murder and nonnegligent manslaughter	1,507	100.0	71.1	25.6	2.8	0.5
Forcible rape	2,974	100.0	78.3	17.6	3.3	0.8
Robbery	2,700	100.0	56.3	39.9	1.9	2.0
Aggravated assault	30,802	100.0	75.4	20.9	3.0	0.6
Burglary	31,657	100.0	82.5	13.3	2.9	1.2
Larceny-theft	48,411	100.0	80.4	16.1	1.7	1.8
Motor vehicle theft	8,187	100.0	82.4	12.6	3.6	1.4
Arson	1,490	100.0	87.7	9.4	2.0	0.9
Violent crime[2]	37,983	100.0	74.1	22.2	2.9	0.7
Property crime[3]	89,745	100.0	81.4	14.7	2.3	1.6

[Continued]

★ 894 ★

Arrest Rate in Rural Counties by Race - 1992
[Continued]

Offense charged	Total arrests	Percent[1]				
		Total	White	Black	American Indian or Alaskan Native	Asian or Pacific Islander
Total crime index[4]	127,728	100.0	79.3	16.9	2.5	1.3
Other assaults	64,433	100.0	77.2	18.3	3.1	1.5
Forgery and counterfeiting	8,031	100.0	77.7	20.3	1.4	0.6
Fraud	57,801	100.0	76.2	22.8	0.8	0.2
Embezzlement	1,124	100.0	85.4	9.3	0.9	4.4
Stolen property; buying, receiving, possessing	7,017	100.0	80.7	16.7	2.1	0.5
Vandalism	18,661	100.0	87.3	9.5	2.3	1.0
Weapons; carrying, possessing, etc.	10,234	100.0	74.8	21.5	2.0	1.7
Prostitution and commercialized vice	189	100.0	86.8	11.1	2.1	X
Sex offenses (except forcible rape and prostitution)	9,464	100.0	90.7	6.3	2.3	0.7
Drug abuse violations	60,195	100.0	78.6	18.9	1.5	0.9
Gambling	496	100.0	55.4	28.0	4.6	11.9
Offenses against family and children	10,141	100.0	74.9	20.9	3.3	0.8
Driving under the influence	214,426	100.0	84.9	10.9	2.7	1.5
Liquor laws	42,944	100.0	91.5	4.2	3.5	0.7
Drunkenness	50,413	100.0	89.5	6.8	3.5	0.2
Disorderly conduct	31,243	100.0	81.6	12.1	5.6	0.7
Vagrancy	350	100.0	82.9	15.1	2.0	X
All other offenses (except traffic)	212,246	100.0	77.6	18.4	2.8	1.2
Suspicion	226	100.0	85.0	14.2	0.4	0.4
Curfew and loitering law violations	1,455	100.0	69.4	3.4	4.0	23.2
Runaways	8,810	100.0	88.2	4.7	2.7	4.4

Source: Maguire, Kathleen and Ann L. Pastore, eds., *Sourcebook of Criminal Justice Statistics 1993.* U.S. Department of Justice, Bureau of Justice Statistics. Washington, DC: U.S. Government Printing Office, 1994, p. 444. Primary source: U.S. Department of Justice, Federal Bureau of Investigation, *Crime in the United States, 1992,* (Washington, DC: USGPO, 1993), pp. 262-264. *Notes:* An X stands for not applicable. 1. Because of rounding, percents may not add to total. 2. Violent crimes are offenses of murder, forcible rape, robbery, and aggravated assault. 3. Property crimes are offenses of burglary, larceny-theft, motor vehicle theft, and arson. 4. Includes arson.

★ 895 ★

Arrests

Arrest Rate in Rural Counties by Race and Age Group - 1992

Arrest rates are shown in percent, by offense charged, age group, and race, for 1992[1].

Offense charged	Total arrests	Arrests under 18					Total arrests	Arrests 18 and older				
		Total	White	Black	American Indian or Alaskan Native	Asian or Pacific Islander		Total	White	Black	American Indian or Alaskan Native	Asian or Pacific Islander
Total	88,270	100.0	85.3	8.7	3.1	2.8	849,357	100.0	80.8	15.5	2.6	1.0
Murder and nonnegligent manslaughter	106	100.0	71.7	24.5	2.8	0.9	1,401	100.0	71.1	25.7	2.8	0.4
Forcible rape	347	100.0	81.0	13.3	4.3	1.4	2,627	100.0	78.0	18.1	3.2	0.7
Robbery	360	100.0	53.6	39.4	3.3	3.6	2,340	100.0	56.7	39.9	1.7	1.8
Aggravated assault	2,500	100.0	72.8	22.7	3.4	1.1	28,302	100.0	75.6	20.8	3.0	0.6
Burglary	10,290	100.0	86.9	7.2	3.6	2.2	21,367	100.0	80.4	16.3	2.6	0.8
Larceny-theft	11,321	100.0	85.9	8.1	2.5	3.5	37,090	100.0	78.7	18.6	1.4	1.3
Motor vehicle theft	3,205	100.0	83.6	9.3	5.0	2.2	4,982	100.0	81.6	14.8	2.8	0.8
Arson	399	100.0	89.2	4.8	3.3	2.8	1,091	100.0	87.2	11.1	1.6	0.2
Violent crime[2]	3,313	100.0	71.6	23.6	3.5	1.4	34,670	100.0	74.4	22.1	2.9	0.7
Property crime[3]	25,215	100.0	86.1	7.8	3.3	2.8	64,530	100.0	79.6	17.4	1.9	1.1
Total crime index[4]	28,528	100.0	84.4	9.7	3.3	2.7	99,200	100.0	77.8	19.0	2.3	0.9
Other assaults	5,314	100.0	75.1	17.2	4.1	3.6	59,119	100.0	77.4	18.4	3.0	1.3
Forgery and counterfeiting	437	100.0	90.6	6.6	2.1	0.7	7,594	100.0	76.9	21.0	1.4	0.6
Fraud	585	100.0	83.2	13.5	2.6	0.7	57,216	100.0	76.1	22.9	0.8	0.2
Embezzlement	41	100.0	92.7	7.3	X	X	1,083	100.0	85.1	9.3	0.9	4.6
Stolen property; buying, receiving, possessing	1,133	100.	86.8	9.6	2.6	1.0	5,884	100.0	79.5	18.1	2.0	0.5
Vandalism	6,903	100.0	91.9	4.6	2.2	1.3	11,758	100.0	84.6	12.3	2.3	0.9
Weapons; carrying, possessing, etc.	1,063	100.0	75.0	19.2	2.9	2.9	9,171	100.0	74.8	21.8	1.9	1.5
Prostitution and commercialized vice	14	100.0	57.1	42.9	X	X	175	100.0	89.1	8.6	2.3	X
Sex offenses (except forcible rape and prostitution)	1,410	100.0	89.4	7.0	2.9	0.7	8,054	100.0	90.9	6.2	2.1	0.7
Drug abuse violations	2,443	100.0	73.2	20.1	2.2	4.5	57,752	100.0	78.8	18.9	1.5	0.8
Gambling	17	100.0	41.2	29.4	29.4	X	479	100.0	55.9	28.0	3.8	12.3
Offenses against family and children	260	100.0	89.2	6.9	2.7	1.2	9,881	100.0	74.6	21.3	3.4	0.8
Driving under the influence	2,269	100.0	90.8	4.9	3.3	1.0	212,157	100.0	84.9	10.9	2.7	1.5
Liquor laws	10,634	100.0	94.5	1.3	3.6	0.6	32,310	100.0	90.5	5.2	3.5	0.8
Drunkenness	871	100.0	92.7	2.6	3.7	1.0	49,542	100.0	89.4	6.9	3.5	0.2
Disorderly conduct	2,956	100.0	84.2	11.0	3.4	1.4	28,287	100.0	81.3	12.2	5.8	0.7
Vagrancy	92	100.0	91.3	8.7	X	X	258	100.0	79.8	17.4	2.7	X
All other offenses (except traffic)	12,972	100.0	81.6	12.1	2.9	3.4	199,274	100.0	77.3	18.8	2.8	1.1
Suspicion	63	100.0	93.7	6.3	X	X	163	100.0	81.6	17.2	0.6	0.6
Curfew and loitering law violations	1,455	100.0	69.4	3.4	4.0	23.2	X	X	X	X	X	X
Runaways	8,810	100.0	88.2	4.7	2.7	4.4	X	X	X	X	X	X

Source: Maguire, Kathleen and Ann L. Pastore, eds., *Sourcebook of Criminal Justice Statistics 1993.* U.S. Department of Justice, Bureau of Justice Statistics. Washington, DC: U.S. Government Printing Office, 1994, pp. 445-446. Primary source: U.S. Department of Justice, Federal Bureau of Investigation, *Crime in the United States, 1992,* (Washington, DC: USGPO, 1993), pp. 262-264. *Notes:* An X stands for not applicable. 1. Because of rounding, percents may not add to total. 2. Violent crimes are offenses of murder, forcible rape, robbery, and aggravated assault. 3. Property crimes are offenses of burglary, larceny-theft, motor vehicle theft, and arson. 4. Includes arson.

★ 896 ★

Arrests

Arrest Rate in Suburban Areas by Race - 1992

Arrest rates in suburban areas are shown in percent by offense charged, and race, for 1992[1].

(5,476 agencies; 1992 estimated population 90,592,000).

Offense charged	Total arrests					Percent[2]				
	Total	White	Black	American Indian or Alaskan Native	Asian or Pacific Islander	Total	White	Black	American Indian or Alaskan Native	Asian or Pacific Islander
Total	4,280,290	3,240,742	999,493	18,485	21,570	100.0	75.7	23.4	0.4	0.5
Murder and nonnegligent manslaughter	4,607	2,774	1,792	14	27	100.0	60.2	38.9	0.3	0.6
Forcible rape	10,663	7,328	3,218	62	55	100.0	68.7	30.2	0.6	0.5
Robbery	34,109	15,561	18,240	131	177	100.0	45.6	53.5	0.4	0.5
Aggravated assault	140,007	97,915	40,645	611	836	100.0	69.9	29.0	0.4	0.6
Burglary	127,218	97,530	28,484	464	740	100.0	6.7	22.4	0.4	0.6
Larceny-theft	458,298	326,481	125,423	2,015	4,379	100.0	71.2	27.4	0.4	1.0
Motor vehicle theft	51,019	34,592	15,784	246	397	100.0	67.8	30.9	0.5	0.8
Arson	6,604	5,600	928	35	41	100.0	84.8	14.1	0.5	0.6
Violent crime[3]	189,386	123,578	63,895	818	1,095	100.0	65.3	33.7	0.4	0.6
Property crime[4]	643,139	464,203	170,619	2,760	5,557	100.0	72.2	26.5	0.4	0.9
Total crime index[5]	832,525	587,781	234,514	3,578	6,652	100.0	70.6	28.2	0.4	0.8
Other assaults	312,391	231,042	78,123	1,519	1,707	100.0	74.0	25.0	0.5	0.5
Forgery and counterfeiting	33,335	23,608	9,453	94	180	10.0	70.8	28.4	0.3	0.5
Fraud	149,511	101,760	46,757	392	602	100.0	68.1	31.3	0.3	0.4
Embezzlement	3,980	2,948	995	9	28	100.0	74.1	25.0	0.2	0.7
Stolen property; buying, receiving, possessing	49,341	32,957	15,847	165	372	10.0	66.8	32.1	0.3	0.8
Vandalism	101,867	85,930	15,055	362	520	100.0	84.4	14.8	0.4	0.5
Weapons; carrying, possessing, etc.	65,463	44,842	19,948	203	470	100.0	68.5	30.5	0.3	0.7
Prostitution and commercialized vice	9,657	6,928	2,637	22	70	100.0	71.7	27.3	0.2	0.7
Sex offenses (except forcible rape and prostitution)	31,773	27,128	4,358	127	160	100.0	85.4	13.7	0.4	0.5
Drug abuse violations	278,694	197,852	79,479	630	733	100.0	71.0	28.5	0.2	0.3
Gambling	2,711	1,574	1,068	8	61	100.0	58.1	39.4	0.3	2.3
Offenses against family and children	42,594	29,738	12,645	110	101	100.0	69.8	29.7	0.3	0.2
Driving under the influence	593,583	541,408	46,498	2,556	3,121	100.0	91.2	7.8	0.4	0.5
Liquor laws	167,716	153,055	12,960	1,016	685	100.0	91.3	7.7	0.6	0.4
Drunkenness	205,153	178,569	24,253	1,751	580	100.0	87.0	11.8	0.9	0.3
Disorderly conduct	204,505	157,051	45,960	839	655	100.0	76.8	22.5	0.4	0.3
Vagrancy	4,470	3,238	1,190	20	22	100.0	72.4	26.6	0.4	0.5
All other offenses (except traffic)	1,110,673	764,303	337,351	4,592	4,427	100.0	68.8	30.4	0.4	0.4
Suspicion	3,518	2,873	620	14	11	100.0	81.7	17.6	0.4	0.3

[Continued]

★ 896 ★

Arrest Rate in Suburban Areas by Race - 1992
[Continued]

Offense charged	Total arrests					Percent[2]				
	Total	White	Black	American Indian or Alaskan Native	Asian or Pacific Islander	Total	White	Black	American Indian or Alaskan Native	Asian or Pacific Islander
Curfew and loitering law violations	24,264	20,587	3,441	102	134	100.0	84.8	14.2	0.4	0.6
Runaways	52,566	45,570	6,341	376	279	100.0	86.7	12.1	0.7	0.5

Source: Maguire, Kathleen and Ann L. Pastore, eds., *Sourcebook of Criminal Justice Statistics 1993.* U.S. Department of Justice, Bureau of Justice Statistics. Washington, DC: U.S. Government Printing Office, 1994, p. 440. Primary source: U.S. Department of Justice, Federal Bureau of Investigation, *Crime in the United States, 1992,* (Washington, DC: USGPO, 1993), pp. 271-273. *Notes:* 1. Includes suburban city and county law enforcement agencies within metropolitan areas. Excludes central cities. Suburban cities and counties are also included in other groups. 2. Because of rounding, percents may not add to total. 3. Violent crimes are offenses of murder, forcible rape, robbery, and aggravated assault. 4. Property crimes are offenses of burglary, larceny-theft, motor vehicle theft, and arson. 5. Includes arson.

★ 897 ★

Arrests

Arrest Rate in Suburban Areas by Race and Age Group - 1992

Arrest rates are shown in percent by offense charged, age group, and race, for 1992[1].

Offense charged	Total arrests	Arrests under 18 (Percent[2])					Total arrests	Arrests 18 and older (Percent[2])				
		Total	White	Black	American Indian or Alaskan Native	Asian or Pacific Islander		Total	White	Black	American Indian or Alaskan Native	Asian or Pacific Islander
Total	723,000	100.0	77.8	21.0	0.5	0.8	3,557,290	100.0	75.3	23.8	0.4	0.4
Murder and nonnegligent manslaughter	621	100.0	52.8	45.9	0.2	1.1	3,986	100.0	61.4	37.8	0.3	0.5
Forcible rape	1,809	100.0	65.7	33.4	0.6	0.3	8,854	100.0	69.3	29.5	0.6	0.6
Robbery	8,775	100.0	44.7	53.9	0.5	0.9	25,334	100.0	46.0	53.3	0.3	0.4
Aggravated assault	22,184	100.0	65.7	33.1	0.4	0.8	117,823	100.0	70.7	28.3	0.4	0.6
Burglary	48,681	100.0	81.1	17.7	0.4	0.8	78,537	100.0	73.9	25.3	0.3	0.4
Larceny-theft	149,673	100.0	77.0	21.3	0.5	1.2	308,625	100.0	68.4	30.3	0.4	0.8
Motor vehicle theft	22,924	100.0	68.2	30.0	0.6	1.2	28,095	100.0	67.4	31.7	0.4	0.5
Arson	3,587	100.0	88.7	10.2	0.3	0.8	3,017	100.0	80.1	18.6	0.8	0.5
Violent crime[3]	33,389	100.0	59.9	38.8	0.4	0.8	155,997	100.0	66.4	32.6	0.4	0.5
Property crime[4]	224,865	100.0	77.2	21.2	0.5	1.1	418,274	100.0	69.5	29.4	0.4	0.7
Total crime index[5]	258,254	100.0	74.9	23.5	0.5	1.1	574,271	100.0	68.6	30.3	0.4	0.7
Other assaults	53,254	100.0	71.0	27.9	0.4	0.7	259,137	100.0	74.6	24.4	0.5	0.5
Forgery and counterfeiting	2,458	100.0	84.5	13.3	0.7	1.6	30,877	100.0	69.7	29.6	0.2	0.5
Fraud	5,169	100.0	55.1	43.0	0.3	1.6	144,342	100.0	68.5	30.9	0.3	0.4
Embezzlement	209	100.0	64.6	33.0	1.0	1.4	3,771	100.0	74.6	24.6	0.2	0.7
Stolen property; buying, receiving, possessing	13,871	100.0	68.6	29.8	0.4	1.2	35,470	100.0	66.1	33.0	0.3	0.6
Vandalism	51,589	100.0	87.3	11.8	0.3	0.5	50,278	100.0	81.3	17.9	0.4	0.5
Weapons; carrying, possessing, etc.	16,165	100.0	72.3	26.3	0.3	1.1	49,298	100.0	67.3	31.8	0.3	0.6
Prostitution and commercialized vice	223	100.0	71.7	27.8	0.4	X	9,434	100.0	71.7	27.3	0.2	0.7
Sex offenses (except forcible rape and prostitution)	6,397	100.0	80.7	18.4	0.4	0.4	25,376	100.0	86.6	12.5	0.4	0.5

[Continued]

★ 897 ★

Arrest Rate in Suburban Areas by Race and Age Group - 1992
[Continued]

Offense charged	Total arrests	Arrests under 18 (Percent[2])					Total arrests	Arrests 18 and older (Percent[2])				
		Total	White	Black	American Indian or Alaskan Native	Asian or Pacific Islander		Total	White	Black	American Indian or Alaskan Native	Asian or Pacific Islander
Drug abuse violations	21,401	100.0	68.1	31.0	0.3	0.6	257,293	100.0	71.2	28.3	0.2	0.2
Gambling	222	100.0	27.0	72.1	0.5	0.5	2,489	100.0	60.6	36.5	0.3	2.4
Offenses against family and children	1,510	100.0	84.8	14.9	0.1	0.2	41,084	100.0	69.3	30.2	0.3	0.2
Driving under the influence	4,917	100.0	95.0	4.2	0.6	0.2	588,666	100.0	91.2	7.9	0.4	0.5
Liquor laws	43,341	100.0	94.6	4.4	0.6	0.3	124,375	100.0	90.1	8.9	0.6	0.4
Drunkenness	5,436	100.0	92.0	6.6	0.8	0.5	199,717	100.0	86.9	12.0	0.9	0.3
Disorderly conduct	43,445	100.0	75.7	23.5	0.3	0.4	161,060	100.0	77.1	22.2	0.4	0.3
Vagrancy	1,092	100.0	83.7	15.6	0.4	0.4	3,378	100.0	68.8	30.2	0.5	0.5
All other offenses (except traffic)	116,302	100.0	74.8	24.0	0.5	0.7	994,371	100.0	68.1	31.1	0.4	0.4
Suspicion	915	100.0	80.2	19.1	X	0.7	2,603	100.0	82.2	17.1	0.5	0.2
Curfew and loitering law violations	24,264	100.0	84.8	14.2	0.4	0.6	X	X	X	X	X	X
Runaways	52,566	100.0	86.7	12.1	0.7	0.5	X	X	X	X	X	X

Source: Maguire, Kathleen and Ann L. Pastore, eds., *Sourcebook of Criminal Justice Statistics 1993.* U.S. Department of Justice, Bureau of Justice Statistics. Washington, DC: U.S. Government Printing Office, 1994, 441-442. Primary source: U.S. Department of Justice, Federal Bureau of Investigation, *Crime in the United States, 1992,* (Washington, DC: USGPO, 1993), pp. 271-273. *Notes:* An X stands for not applicable. 1. Includes suburban city and county law enforcement agencies within metropolitan areas. Excludes central cities. Suburban cities and counties are also included in other groups. 2. Because of rounding, percents may not add to total. 3. Violent crimes are offenses of murder, forcible rape, robbery, and aggravated assault. 4. Property crimes are offenses of burglary, larceny-theft, motor vehicle theft, and arson. 5. Includes arson.

Crimes

★ 898 ★

Crime Rate in United States and Indian Country, 1992

Data show offenses reported per 100,000 population, by crime and area.

Offense	U.S. total	Suburban counties[1]	Rural counties[2]	Suburban areas[3]	Indian Country[4]
Murder/non-negligent manslaughter	9.3	6.0	5.3	5.0	10.6
Forcible rape	42.8	37.3	27.3	33.7	32.5
Robbery	263.6	114.2	17.0	116.0	162.6
Aggravated assault	441.8	318.6	176.7	310.0	273.3
Burglary	1,168.2	991.6	701.4	957.1	250.5
Motor vehicle theft	631.5	395.5	116.6	400.9	67.1

Source: Peak, Ken. "Policing and crime in Indian Country: history, issues, challenges." *Journal of Contemporary Criminal Justice* vol. 10, no. 2 (May 1994), p. 90. Primary source: FBI, *Crime in the United States 1992: Uniform Crime Reports. Notes:* Data unavailable for larceny-theft. 1. 1,239 agencies in suburban counties. 2. 2,416 agencies in rural counties. 3. 5,949 agencies in suburban counties. 4. Indian Country data provided by the Bureau of Indian Affairs, Division of Law Enforcement, Central Office, as reported in the annual report and based on data provided by approximately 200 BIA and tribal police agencies. Figures are based on a population of 739,000 in Indian Country.

★ 899 ★

Crimes

Homicide Rates for American Indians, by Reservation County

Homicide rates are shown for 114 counties that include reservation land. Data for 1980-87 are shown per 100,000 persons.

County, state	Homicide rate
Bingham, ID	6.41
Franklin, NY	6.74
Prince of Wales, AK	8.21
Montezuma, CO	8.32
Cattaraugus, NY	8.43
Dewey, SD	8.70
Carson City, NV	9.36
Elko, NV	9.46
NezPerce, ID	9.82
Del Norte, CA	10.43
Tulare, CA	10.92
Taos, NM	11.13
Brown, WI	11.18
Yavopai, AZ	11.27
Sonoma, CA	11.75
Grays Harbor, WA	11.89
McKinley, NM	12.72
Ashland, WI	12.81
Lake, MT	12.87
Washington, ME	13.14
Snohomish, WA	13.17
Menominee, WI	13.58
Mahnomen, MN	13.59
Ferry, WA	14.09
San Juan, NM	15.68
Washoe, NV	15.77
Charles Mix, SD	15.97
Coconino, AZ	16.07
Whatcom, WA	16.81
San Juan, UT	17.01
Mendocino, CA	17.16
Outagamie, WI	17.26
Rolette, ND	17.27
Benson, ND	17.34
Osage, OK	17.54
Clark, NV	18.33
Stevens, WA	18.39
Mohave, AZ	18.59
Apache, AZ	19.04
St. Louis, MN	19.40
Graham, AZ	2023
Riverside, CA	21.06
Big Horn, MT	21.14
Okanogan, WA	21.21

[Continued]

★ 899 ★

Homicide Rates for American Indians, by Reservation County
[Continued]

County, state	Homicide rate
Humboldt, NV	21.32
Navajo, AZ	21.42
Brown, KS	21.84
Bannock, ID	22.37
Pierce, WA	22.84
Bernalillo, NM	22.92
Jackson, NC	22.93
Tuolumne, CA	23.38
Hill, MT	23.43
Becker, MN	23.59
Pima, AZ	23.83
Skagit, WA	24.44
La Plata, CO	24.72
Rio Ariba, NM	25.72
Beltrami, MN	27.53
Jackson, KS	27.97
Thurston, NB	28.23
Thurston, NB	28.23
Neshoba, MS	28.47
Klickitat, WA	28.98
Humboldt, CA	29.14
Mountrail, ND	29.39
Day, SD	29.52
Lyman, SD	29.67
Brouward, FL	30.01
Yakima, WA	30.61
Benewah, ID	30.72
King, WA	31.14
Valencia, NM	32.89
Wood, WI	32.92
Hendry, FL	33.61
Jefferson, OR	33.90
Burnett, WI	34.09
Inyo, CA	34.26
Sioux, ND	34.80
Unitah, UT	34.95
Leake, MS	35.54
Yellowstone, MT	35.82
Umatilla, OR	36.89
Koochiching, MN	38.71
Nye, NV	38.82
Maricopa, AZ	39.59
Fremont, WY	39.63
Missoula, MT	39.82
Glacier, MT	40.17

[Continued]

★ 899 ★

Homicide Rates for American Indians, by Reservation County
[Continued]

County, state	Homicide rate
Modoc, CA	40.36
Sawyer, WI	40.38
Mason, WA	40.47
Fresno, CA	41.04
Shannon, SD	41.28
Yuma, AZ	42.20
Pondera, MT	42.39
Glades, FL	42.64
Gila, AZ	42.74
Blaine, MT	42.77
Buffalo, SD	42.87
Wasco, OR	44.71
Roberts, SD	44.84
Pinal, AZ	45.28
Roosevelt, MT	48.98
McLean, ND	49.52
Otero, NM	50.39
Imperial, CA	50.41
Swain, NC	54.80
Newton, MS	54.95
Kootnai, ID	59.15
Knox, NB	60.28
Todd, SD	61.98
Polk, WI	63.21
Lewis, ID	64.94
Rosebud, MT	71.93
Corson, SD	72.18
Sauk, WI	73.26
Marshall, SD	97.51
Douglas, NV	103.52
Harney, OR	127.55
Idaho, ID	140.06

Source: Bachman, Ronet. "An analysis of American Indian homicide: a test of social disorganization and economic deprivation at the reservation county level." *Journal of Research in Crime and Delinquency* 28, no. 4 (November 1991), pp. 461-465. Primary source: Department of Health and Human Services, Indian Health Services.

Death Penalty

★ 900 ★

Death Row Prisoners, by Race/Ethnicity and State, 1994

Data show the number of prisoners under sentence of death in each state, as of April 20, 1994.

Jurisdiction	Total	Race, ethnicity					
		White	Black	Hispanic	Native American	Asian	Unknown
United States[1]	2,848	1,423	1,138	208	50	20	9
Federal statutes	5	1	3	1	0	0	0
U.S. military	8	1	6	0	0	1	0
Alabama	122	68[2,3]	52[2,4]	1	0	1	0
Arizona	119	80[4,5,6]	14[7]	20[4,6]	4	0	1
Arkansas	41	24	15[6]	1	1[6]	0	0
California	383	166[2,8]	143[5]	54[5]	13	6	1
Colorado	3	2	0	1	0	0	0
Connecticut	5	3	2	0	0	0	0
Delaware	15	7	8	0	0	0	0
Florida	330	184[7,9,10]	112[5]	32[5]	1	1	0
Georgia	109	60	49[11]	0	0	0	0
Idaho	23	21	0	2[6]	0	0	0
Illinois	161	52[5]	98[2,6]	8[5]	0	0	3
Indiana	51	31[6]	19[6,12]	1	0	0	0
Kansas	0	NA	NA	NA	NA	NA	NA
Kentucky	25	19[5]	6[4]	0	0	0	0
Louisiana	42	11	29	2	0	0	0
Maryland	14	3	11	0	0	0	0
Mississippi	52	21[4,5,6]	31[11]	0	0	0	0
Missouri	84	47[13]	33[6]	1[5]	1	1	1
Montana	8	6	0	0	2	0	0
Nebraska	10	6	3	0	1	0	0
Nevada	66	36	23[5,6]	7	0	0	0
New Hampshire	0	NA	NA	NA	NA	NA	NA
New Jersey	9	3[6]	5	1	0	0	0
New Mexico	2	2	0	0	0	0	0
North Carolina	132	71[9]	52[5]	1	4	1	3
Ohio	127	60	62	3	2	0	0
Oklahoma	118	72[4,6,13]	29[5]	2	13[6]	2	0
Oregon	14	12	0	1	1	0	0
Pennsylvania	170	60[5]	101[2,6,11]	7	0	2	0
South Carolina	55	27[4]	27[4]	0	1	0	0
South Dakota	1	1	0	0	0	0	0
Tennessee	100	65[5]	31[6]	1	2	1	0
Texas	386	167[4,13]	150[2,14]	60[10]	5	4	0
Utah	11	8	2	1	0	0	0
Virginia	46	24[4]	22[4]	0	0	0	0

[Continued]

★ 900 ★

Death Row Prisoners, by Race/Ethnicity and State, 1994
[Continued]

Jurisdiction	Total	Race, ethnicity					
		White	Black	Hispanic	Native American	Asian	Unknown
Washington	13	9	3	0	0	1	0
Wyoming	0	NA	NA	NA	NA	NA	NA

Source: Maguire, Kathleen and Ann L. Pastore (eds.). U.S. Department of Justice. U.S. Bureau of Justice Statistics. *Sourcebook of Criminal Justice Statistics 1993.* Washington, DC: U.S. Government Printing Office, 1994, p. 666. Primary source: Table constructed by *Sourcebook* staff from data provided by the NAACP Legal Defense and Educational Fund, Inc. *Notes:* NA stands for not applicable. The NAACP Legal Defense and Educational Fund, Inc. periodically collects data on persons on death row. As of Apr. 20, 1994, 37 jurisdictions, the Federal Government, and the United States military had capital punishment laws; and 34 jurisdictions, the Federal Government, and the United States military had at least 1 prisoner under sentence of death. Between Jan. 1, 1973 and Apr. 20, 1994, an estimated 1,379 convictions or sentences, have been reversed or vacated on grounds other than constitutional. Between Jan. 1, 1973 and May 30, 1990, an estimated 558 death sentences have been vacated as unconstitutional. 1. Detail will not add to total because inmates sentenced to death in more than one state are listed in the respective state totals, but each is counted only once at the national level. 2. Includes two females. 3. Includes three males who were juveniles at the time of their offenses. 4. Includes one male who was a juvenile at the time of his offense. 5. Includes one female. 6. Includes one male sentenced to death in the state but serving another sentence in another state. 7. Includes two males sentenced to death in the state but serving another sentence in another state. 8. Includes three males sentenced to death in the state but serving another sentence in another state. 9. Includes four females. 10. Includes four males who were juveniles at the time of their offenses. 11. Includes two males who were juveniles at the time of their offenses. 12. Includes one female sentenced to death in the state but serving another sentence in another state. 13. Includes three females. 14. Includes six males who were juveniles at the time of their offenses.

★ 901 ★
Death Penalty

Defendants and Victims in Capital Crimes by Race/Ethnicity, 1976-93

Data show distribution of persons since the reinstitution of the death penalty in 1976.

Race/ethnicity	Number
White defendant	
White victim	147
Black victim	1
Asian victim	1
Black defendant	
White victim	69
Black victim	33
Asian victim	2
Hispanic victim	1
Hispanic defendant	
White victim	7
Hispanic victim	5
Asian victim	1
Native American defendant	
White victim	2

Source: Mauro, Tony. "After 199 executions, nation still divided." *USA TODAY* (28 April 1993), p. 4A. Primary source: NAACP Legal Defense and Educational Fund; FBI.

★ 902 ★

Death Penalty

Executions by Race/Ethnicity, 1976-93

| White - 108 |
| Black - 77 |
| Hispanic - 12 |
| Native American - 2 |

Data show distribution of persons executed under the death penalty since its reinstitution in 1976.

Race/ethnicity	Number
White	108
Black	77
Hispanic[1]	12
Native American	2

Source: Mauro, Tony. "After 199 executions, nation still divided." USA TODAY (28 April 1993), p. 4A. Primary source: NAACP Legal Defense and Educational Fund; FBI. Note: 1. Hispanics can be of any race.

Hate Crimes

★ 903 ★

Bias Motivations in Reported Hate Crimes, 1991 and 1992

Number and percent distribution of crimes are shown, by race/ethnicity, religion, and sexual orientation.

	1991		1992	
	Number	Percent[1]	Number	Percent[1]
Total	4,755	100.0	8,075	100.0
Race	2,963	62.3	5,050	62.5
Anti-white	888	18.7	1,664	20.6
Anti-black	1,689	35.5	2,884	35.7
Anti-American Indian/Alaskan Native	11	0.2	31	0.4
Anti-Asian/Pacific Islander	287	6.0	275	3.4
Anti-multiracial group	88	1.9	198	2.5
Ethnicity	450	9.5	841	10.4
Ant-Hispanic	242	5.1	498	6.2
Anti-other ethnicity/national origin	208	4.4	343	4.2
Religion	917	19.3	1,240	15.4
Anti-Jewish	792	16.7	1,084	13.4

[Continued]

★ 903 ★

Bias Motivations in Reported Hate Crimes, 1991 and 1992
[Continued]

	1991 Number	1991 Percent[1]	1992 Number	1992 Percent[1]
Anti-Catholic	23	0.5	18	0.2
Anti-Protestant	26	0.5	29	0.4
Anti-Islamic (Moslem)	10	0.2	17	0.2
Anti-other religion	51	11.1	77	1.0
Anti-multireligious group	11	0.2	14	0.2
Anti-atheism/agnosticism/etc.	4	0.1	1	[2]
Sexual orientation	425	8.9	944	11.7
Anti-homosexual	421	8.9	928	11.5
Anti-heterosexual	3	0.1	13	0.2
Anti-bisexual	1	0.0	3	[2]

Source: Maguire, Kathleen and Ann L. Pastore (eds.). U.S. Department of Justice. U.S. Bureau of Justice Statistics. *Sourcebook of Criminal Justice Statistics 1993.* Washington, DC: U.S. Government Printing Office, 1994, p. 375. Primary source: Table provided to *Sourcebook* staff by the U.S. Department of Justice, Federal Bureau of Investigation. *Notes:* The data were obtained from the Federal Bureau of Investigation's statistical program on hate crimes. Data for 1991 were supplied by 2,771 law enforcement agencies in 32 states. Data for 1992 were supplied by 6,180 law enforcement agencies in 41 states and the District of Columbia. 1. Because of rounding, percents may not add to totals. 2. Less than 0.05 percent.

★ 904 ★

Hate Crimes

Hate Crime Offenses, 1993

Data show number of incidents, offenses, victims, and offenders, by bias motivation, for 1993.

Bias motivation	No. of incidents	No. of offenses	No. of victims	No. of known offenders
Total[1]	6,746	7,969	8,293	7,421
Racial:	4,168	5,085	5,288	5,419
Anti-White	1,299	1,600	1,637	2,544
Anti-Black	2,467	2,985	3,117	2,421
Anti-American Indian/Alaska Native	24	36	40	45
Anti-Asian/Pacific Islander	236	274	293	254
Anti-multiracial group	133	190	201	155
Ethnicity/National Origin:	583	701	735	645
Anti-Hispanic	329	414	446	451
Anti-other ethnicity/national origin	254	287	289	194
Religion:	1,189	1,245	1,287	363
Anti-Jewish	1,054	1,104	1,146	290
Anti-Catholic	30	31	31	15
Anti-Protestant	25	25	25	11
Anti-Islamic	11	13	13	6

[Continued]

★ 904 ★

Hate Crime Offenses, 1993
[Continued]

Bias motivation	No. of incidents	No. of offenses	No. of victims	No. of known offenders
Anti-other religion	55	58	58	15
Anti-multireligious group	11	11	11	23
Anti-Atheism/Agnosticism/etc.	3	3	3	3
Sexual Orientation:	806	938	983	994
Anti-male homosexual	582	665	682	776
Anti-female homosexual	111	133	140	94
Anti-homosexual	84	111	132	99
Anti-heterosexual	28	28	28	25
Anti-bisexual	1	1	1	0

Source: U.S. Department of Justice. Federal Bureau of Investigation. Criminal Justice Information Services Division. *Criminal Justice Information Services Uniform Crime Reports: Hate Crime - 1993*. Washington, DC: FBI, June 1994, p. 4. *Notes:* 1. Data are not available for 161 incidents recorded in Florida, 377 in Minnesota, and 400 in Pennsylvania.

★ 905 ★

Hate Crimes

Hate Crime Suspects by Race/Ethnicity, 1993

Data show distribution of suspects in 7,684 crimes related to hate or prejudice in 1993.

Race/ethnicity	No. of suspects
White	3,797
Black	2,599
Native American	81
Asian/Pacific Islander	42
Mixed race	398
Race unknown	504

Source: Shanker, Thom and Linnet Myers. "Frequency of hate crimes in U.S. alarms FBI director." *Chicago Tribune* (29 June 1994), p. 7. Primary source: FBI.

Juvenile Delinquents

★ 906 ★

Native American Youths in the Minnesota Correctional System

Data from the Minnesota Criminal Justice Analysis Center show that a disproportionate percentage of juveniles in the correctional system are Native Americans.

"- In 1990 minority youth accounted for 8% of Minnesota juvenile population ages 10 to 17.
- Native American youth account for 1.6% (7,914) of the approximate 484,115 juveniles between ages 10 to 17 in Minnesota for 1990.
- In the seven (7) county metro area Native American youth account for 1.5% (3,491) of approximately 232,764 juveniles between ages 10 to 17."

Source: U.S. Senate Committee on Indian Affairs. *Proposed Amendments to the American Indian Religious Freedom Act: Hearing Before the Committee on Indian Affairs.* 103rd Cong., 1st sess., 8 March 1993, Minneapolis, MN, pt. 3. Washington, DC: U.S. Government Printing Office, 1993, pp. 248-249. Primary source: Heart of the Earth Corrections Program, *Re-Entry Services Project*, pp. 15-16.

★ 907 ★
Juvenile Delinquents

Delinquents: Runaway and Homeless Centers

Use of runaway and homeless centers by youths is shown for fiscal year 1989. Data are shown, by race/ethnicity and by sex, for the U.S.

Race, ethnicity	Total (N=34,819)	Female (N=19,670)	Male (N=15,149)
Hispanic	9.4	9.3	9.4
American Indian or Alaskan Native	2.6	2.8	2.4
Asian or Pacific Islander	3.7	4.0	3.4
Black, non-Hispanic	19.5	18.8	20.5
White, non-Hispanic	64.8	65.1	64.4

Source: U.S. Department of Justice. Office of Justice Programs. Bureau of Justice Statistics. *Sourcebook of Criminal Justice Statistics, 1990.* Washington, DC: U.S. Government Printing Office, 1991, p. 577. Primary source: U.S. Department of Health and Human Services, Office of Human Development Services, "Annual Report to the Congress on the Runaway and Homeless Youth Program, Fiscal Year 1989," pp. 56, 57, 59. Washington, DC: U.S. Department of Health and Human Services. (Mimeographed). Table adapted by *Sourcebook* staff.

Law Officers

★ 908 ★

Assaults on Federal Officers, 1981-92

Data are shown by department and agency.

Department and agency	Number of officers assaulted											
	1981	1982	1983	1984	1985	1986	1987	1988	1989	1990	1991	1992
Total	728	712	580	672	808	628	690	880	751[1]	1,1254[1]	63[1]	661[1]
U.S. Department of the Interior	29	22	11	47	30	9	33	35	33	38	96	167
Bureau of Indian Affairs	22	19	7	20	6	6	9	9	8	5	[2]	110
National Park Service	7	3	4	27	24	3	24	26	25	33	96	57
U.S. Department of Justice	316	252	1743	143	211	192	310	312	570	968	404	376
Bureau of Prisons	111	115	59	60	51	61	33	146	161	185	[3]	[3]
Drug Enforcement Administration	95	63	18	32	92	53	80	70	77	65	47	66
Federal Bureau of Investigation	42	40	22	32	32	37	14	18	17	24	31	50
Immigration and Naturalization Service[4]	46	22	18	14	21	31	118	37	288	409	296	228[5]
U.S. and Assistant U.S. attorney	8	4	5	4	8	7	45	6	6	269[6]	[4]	[4]
U.S. Marshals Service	14	8	21	4	7	4	20	35	21	16	30	32
U.S. Department of the Treasury	333	395	396	438	524	369	270	647	99	73	127	89
Bureau of Alcohol, Tobacco, and Firearms	31	9	15	5	17	16	5	7	18	7	31	36
Internal Revenue Service	251	347	334	409	465	323	220	391	18[7]	3	1	9
U.S. Customs Service	25	15	19	3	15	4	21	51	21	35	66	7
U.S. Secret Service	26	24	28	21	27	26	24	18	42	28	29	37
Judicial branch	24	22	21	19	23	23	41	26	23	36	[4]	[4]
U.S. Capitol Police	NA	NA	NA	10	10	10	7	8	8	16	17	5
U.S. Postal Service	26	21	9	12	10	26	29	32	18	23	39	24
Postal Inspectors	4	6	2	1	5	5	10	13	7	6	[8]	[8]
Postal Security Police	22	15	7	11	5	21	19	19	11	17	[8]	[8]

Source: Maguire, Kathleen and Ann L. Pastore (eds.). U.S. Department of Justice. U.S. Bureau of Justice Statistics. *Sourcebook of Criminal Justice Statistics 1993.* Washington, DC: U.S. Government Printing Office, 1994, p. 398. Primary source: U.S. Department of Justice, Federal Bureau of Investigation, *Assaults on Federal Officers, 1979*, p. 7; *1981*, p. 4, Table 1, FBI Uniform Crime reports (Washington, DC: USGPO); *Law Enforcement Officers Killed and Assaulted, 1983*, FBI Uniform Crime reports (Washington, DC: USGPO, 1984), p. 49, Table 1; *Law Enforcement Officers Killed and Assaulted, 1985*, FBI Uniform Crime Reports (Washington, DC: U.S. Department of Justice, 1986), p. 52; and *Law Enforcement Officers Killed and Assaulted, 1987*, p. 51; *1989*, p. 61; *1990*, p.51; *1992*, p. 73, FBI Uniform Crime Reports (Washington, DC: USGPO). Table adapted by *Sourcebook* staff. *Notes:* NA stands for data not separately enumerated, tabulated or otherwise available. These data were compiled from reports of investigations conducted by the Federal Bureau of Investigation, the U.S. Department of Treasury, the U.S. Postal Service, and the U.S. Capitol Police. The Federal Bureau of Investigation is responsible for the investigation of assaults on personnel of the U.S. Department of the Interior, the U.S. Department of Justice, and the Federal judiciary. Customarily, the U.S. Department of the Treasury, the U.S. Postal Service, and the U.S. Capitol Police investigate assaults against officers assigned to their agencies. All assaults and threats of assault are included in the analysis even though no injury to an officer may have resulted, as are assaults that resulted in the death of an officer (Source, *1990*, p. 2). 1. Beginning in 1989, totals and subtotals may not be directly comparable due to modifications in reporting procedures, failures to report, or changes in Federal agencies included. 2. No report concerning assaults on Bureau of Indian Affairs officers was received for 1991. 3. Beginning in 1991, assault statistics from the Bureau of Prisons, U.S. and Assistant U.S. attorneys, and the judicial branch were no longer collected. 4. Beginning in 1989, the variation in Immigration and Naturalization Service figures is due to changes in reporting procedures. 5. Covers only Border Patrol Division. 6. Increase in U.S. and Assistant U.S. attorney figures due to change in reporting procedures. 7. Decrease in Internal Revenue Service figures due to change in reporting procedures. 8. Beginning in 1991, the U.S. Postal Service no longer differentiates between Inspectors and Security Police in its report.

★ 909 ★

Law Officers

Native American Representation in Federal Law Enforcement Occupations, 1991

The estimated number of persons needed to reach full representation per capita population is shown, for selected groups.

Agency	Occupation series[1]	American Indian Men	American Indian Women	Hispanic Men	Hispanic Women	White Men	White Women	Black Men	Black Women	Asian Men	Asian Women
Drug Enforcement Administration	1811		3		10		101	23	56		
Federal Bureau of Investigation	1811	34	6	45	36			476	206		4
U.S. Immigration and Naturalization Service	1801	.82	2			19	37	13	.34	4	2
	1802		2			200	155		.62	30	15
	1811	5	2			120	22	66	29		
	1869	17	3			482	242	282	96	18	4
	2181	.23	.01	.37	.05		3	.96	.18		.03
U.S. Marshals Service	0082	3	.84	11	3			39	16	3	2
	1811		.89	3	6		19	14	37	11	3
Bureau of Alcohol, Tobacco and Firearms	1811	7	3		3		2	29	25	4	
U.S. Customs Service	1801	2	.65		6		42	15	15	.63	2
	1811	5	4		6		20	171	65		3
	2181	2	.06	.75	.26		8	3	.87	4	.14
Internal Revenue Service	1811	5	3	72		69		128	7		
U.S. Secret Service	0083	7	2	33	9		50			8	2
	1811	5	2	20	14		66	61	38		2
U.S. Postal Service	1811	6	2	39	11			27	12		

Source: U.S. General Accounting Office. *Federal Affirmative Employment: Status of Women and Minority Representation in Federal Law Enforcement Occupations* (GAO/T-GGD-93-2). Washington, DC: U.S. GAO, (1 October 1992), p. 10. *Notes:* Except when the estimated number was less than 1 person, each fraction of a person was rounded to the next whole person; for example, 21.6 was rounded to 22 people. 1. Occupation series represent the following groups: 0082, U.S. Marshal; 0083, Police; 1801, General inspection, investigation, and compliance; 1802, Compliance inspection and support; 1811, Criminal investigation; 1896, Border Patrol Agent; 2181, Aircraft operation.

★ 910 ★

Law Officers

New York City: Police Officers, by Race/Ethnicity, 1992

Distribution of police officers is shown by race/ethnicity.

Race/ethnicity	Number of officers
White	20,098
Hispanic	3,688[1]
Black	3,121
Native American	28
Asian-Pacific Islander	219

Source: Frankel, Bruce. "Change looms large for troubled NYC police force." *USA TODAY* (7 October 1992), p. 8A. Primary source: *USA TODAY* research. *Note:* 1. Hispanics can be of any race.

Legal Aid

★ 911 ★

Federally Funded Legal Aid

The Legal Services Corporation (LSC) receives an annual appropriation. A specific amount of the appropriation is allocated to Native American programs and components.

	Fiscal year		
	1988	1989	1990[1]
LSC total	305,500,000	308,555,000	321,000,000
Native American	7,022,000	7,022,000	7,304,000

Source: Walke, Roger. *Federal Programs of Assistance to Native Americans: A Report Prepared for the Senate Select Committee on Indian Affairs of the United States Senate.* Washington, DC: U.S. Government Printing Office, (December 1991), p. 272. *Notes:* 1. The 1990 funding levels are based on Public Law 101-162. They do not reflect sequestration required by applicable Executive orders issued pursuant to Public Law 100-119, and the Balanced Budget and Emergency Deficit Control Reaffirmation Act of 1987 (the so-called "Gramm-Rudman- Hollings") sequestration reductions. The final sequestration reduction was approximately 1.4 percent.

Prisons

★ 912 ★

Adults on Probation, by Race, 1989

Regions and jurisdictions	Probation population 12/31/89	Number of adults on probation				
		American Indian/ Alaska Native	White	Black	Asian/ Pacific Islander	Other, unknown, or not reported
U.S. total	2,520,479	13,387	1,173,870	512,395	4,281	816,546
Federal	59,146	746	43,436	13,753	1,106	105
State	2,461,333	12,641	1,130,434	498,642	3,175	816,441
Northeast	443,794	351	171,155	82,625	644	189,019
Connecticut	42,842	-	29,990	12,852	-	-
Maine	6,851	70	6,721	50	10	-
Massachusetts	88,529	-	-	-	-	88,529
New Hampshire	2,991	-	2,841	-	-	150
New Jersey	66,753	-	-	-	-	66,753
New York	128,707	281	63,554	44,187	371	20,314
Pennsylvania	89,491	0	62,677	25,509	263	1,042
Rhode Island	12,231	-	-	-	-	12,231

[Continued]

★ 912 ★

Adults on Probation, by Race, 1989
[Continued]

Regions and jurisdictions	Probation population 12/31/89	Number of adults on probation				
		American Indian/ Alaska Native	White	Black	Asian/ Pacific Islander	Other, unknown, or not reported
Vermont	5,399	-	5,372	27	-	0
Midwest	542,765	4,827	224,397	67,709	647	245,185
Illinois	93,944	-	-	-	-	93,944
Indiana	61,861	-	-	-	-	61,861
Iowa	13,722	-	-	-	-	13,722
Kansas	22,525	276	17,713	4,369	94	73
Michigan	121,436	998	56,506	9,023	188	54,721
Minnesota	58,648	2,139	48,265	4,748	-	3,496
Missouri	45,251	40	33,375	11,505	30	301
Nebraska	12,627	495	10,228	1,389	185	330
North Dakota	1,652	166	1,468	12	6	0
Ohio	78,223	26	34,774	29,842	58	13,523
South Dakota	2,716	-	-	-	-	2,716
Wisconsin	30,160	687	22,068	6,821	86	498
South	986,508	3,482	611,892	336,438	775	33,921
Alabama	26,475	-	11,188	15,239	48	0
Arkansas	17,572	4	11,133	6,287	3	145
Delaware	9,701	16	5,616	4,064	5	0
District of Colombia	10,351	-	517	9,834	-	-
Florida	192,495	130	135,715	49,649	271	6,730
Georgia	125,441	73	66,280	59,040	5	43
Kentucky	8,062	-	-	-	-	8,062
Louisiana	32,295	-	15,710	16,377	-	208
Maryland	84,456	84	42,607	40,583	337	845
Mississippi	7,333	4	3,193	4,127	9	0
North Carolina	72,325	1,612	37,470	32,720	66	457
Oklahoma	24,240	1,558	17,174	5,472	30	6
South Carolina	29,652	-	15,657	13,880	-	115
Tennessee	30,906	-	6,563	7,257	-	17,086
Texas	291,156	-	227,100	64,056	-	-
Virginia	19,085	-	11,451	7,413	-	221
West Virginia	4,963	1	4,518	440	1	3
West	488,266	3,981	122,990	11,870	1,109	348,316
Alaska	3,335	828	2,170	302	35	0
Arizona	27,650	-	-	-	-	27,650
California	285,018	-	-	-	-	285,018
Colorado	26,378	37	18,248	2,220	14	5,859
Hawaii	11,377	-	-	-	-	11,377
Idaho	4,025	137	3,823	54	11	0
Montana	3,459	416	3,001	31	5	6
Nevada	7,324	92	5,340	1,290	39	563

[Continued]

★ 912 ★

Adults on Probation, by Race, 1989
[Continued]

Regions and jurisdictions	Probation population 12/31/89	Number of adults on probation				
		American Indian/ Alaska Native	White	Black	Asian/ Pacific Islander	Other, unknown, or not reported
New Mexico	5,660	231	3,828	244	0	1,357
Oregon	31,878	606	29,548	1,660	64	-
Utah	5,524	140	4,961	196	57	170
Washington	74,254	1,494	52,071	5,873	884	13,932
Wyoming	2,384	-	-	-	-	2,384

Source: U.S. Department of Justice. Bureau of Justice Statistics. Office of Justice Programs. *Correctional Populations in the United States, 1989* (NCJ- 130445). Washington, DC: U.S. Government Printing Office, (October 1991), p. 31. *Notes:* 1. The state estimated all numbers in the detailed categories. 2. The state estimated all data.

★ 913 ★
Prisons

Characteristics of Native Americans Incarcerated in Minnesota Facilities

Data from the Heart of the Earth Survival School (HOTESS) Corrections program are shown, as amended in 1992 from a funding proposal submitted for the 1989-90 school year.

"- According to data derived from the Minnesota Criminal Justice Statistical Centre (MCJSAC) as of 1991 Native Americans account for 1.1% (49,909) of the total population of 4,375,099 in the state of Minnesota.

- As of January 1, 1992, 270 Native American adult men and 15 adult women account for 8.3% of the total population of 3,453 in Minnesota adult correctional facilities.

- 35% of correctional facilities' populations are functionally illiterate.

- Average grade level of students entering HOTESS Corrections Education Program is less than 6th grade.

- 50.9% of Native American offenders have not completed high school or GED equivalence.

- 91.2% of Native American offenders are listed as unskilled.

- Imprisonment rate for the employed offender is 4.9%, for the unemployed offender 24.4%.

- Unemployment on the reservations for Native Americans runs as high as 95%; in the metropolitan centers as high as 70%.

- Approximately 98.7% of all offenses committed by Native American offenders were committed while under the influence of alcohol and/or drugs.

- Approximately 75% who fail to complete voluntary or mandated chemical dependency programs are returned to correctional facilities for the remainder of their sentences.

[Continued]

★ 913 ★

Characteristics of Native Americans Incarcerated in Minnesota Facilities
[Continued]

- A study by the Minnesota Department of Corrections (DOC) on recidivism indicates that 47% of Native American offenders gaining supervised release return for violations within the first thirty (30) months, with 25% of this figure returning with new compounded charges; 32% return in the first eleven (11) months of their release with one-third (1/3) of this figure returning with new compounded charges.

- Black population recidivism at 43% with 24% returning with new compounded charges within 30 months of release.

- White population recidivism at 32% with 24% returning with new compounded charges within 30 months of release."

Source: U.S. Senate Committee on Indian Affairs. *Proposed Amendments to the American Indian Religious Freedom Act: Hearing Before the Committee on Indian Affairs.* 103rd Cong., 1st sess., 8 March 1993, Minneapolis, MN, pt. 3. Washington, DC: U.S. Government Printing Office, 1993, pp. 246-247. Primary source: Heart of the Earth Corrections Program. *Re-Entry Services Project,* 1992, pp. 10-11.

★ 914 ★

Prisons

Native American Prisoners in Federal and State Correctional Institutions, by State, 1991

A 1991 survey of federal and twenty-three state correctional system shows the following population data on Native American prisoners.

	Number
Federal Bureau of Prisons	974
Alaska	769
Arizona	412
California	678
Colorado	80
Hawaii	831
Idaho	92
Kansas	74
Minnesota	285
Montana	231
Nebraska	90
Nevada	90
New Mexico	100
New York	208
North Carolina	421
North Dakota	122
Oklahoma	744
Oregon	156
South Dakota	341
Utah	59
Washington	336

[Continued]

★ 914 ★

Native American Prisoners in Federal and State Correctional Institutions, by State, 1991

[Continued]

	Number
Wisconsin	164
Wyoming	60

Source: U.S. Senate Committee on Indian Affairs. *Proposed Amendments to the American Indian Religious Freedom Act: Hearing Before the Committee on Indian Affairs.* 103rd Cong., 1st sess., 8 March 1993, Minneapolis, MN, pt. 3. Washington, DC: U.S. Government Printing Office, 1993, p. 235. Primary source: Testimony by Vernon Bellecourt and Ted Means of the Heart of the Earth Survival School Corrections Program.

★ 915 ★

Prisons

Prisoners, by Race and State, 1991

Number of prisoners is shown, as of December 31, 1991.

| Region and jurisdiction | Number of prisoners | | | | | |
	Prisoner population 12/31/91	White	Black	American Indian/ Alaska Native	Asian/ Pacific Islander	Not known
U.S. total	824,133	385,347	395,245	7,407	3,423	32,711
Federal	71,608	46,868	22,727	1,222	791	0
State	752,525	338,479	372,518	6,185	2,632	32,711
Northeast	131,866	56,815	66,442	214	338	8,057
Connecticut[2,3]	10,977	3,053	5,144	7	26	2,747
Maine	1,579	1,522	37	16	4	0
Massachusetts[3]	9,155	4,410	3,036	14	51	1,644
New Hampshire	1,533	1,443	80	5	5	0
New Jersey[3]	23,483	6,762	15,005	4	41	1,671
New York[4]	57,862	28,181	29,151	135	155	240
Pennsylvania[3]	23,388	8,470	13,090	28	45	1,755
Rhode Island[2]	2,771	1,856	899	5	11	0
Vermont[2,5]	1,118	1,118	[1]	[1]	[1]	0
Midwest	155,917	71,227	79,217	1,394	130	3,949
Illinois[3]	29,115	8,055	18,306	49	28	2,677
Indiana	13,008	8,000	4,971	30	7	0
Iowa	4,145	3,089	940	69	15	32
Kansas[3]	5,903	3,329	2,145	81	33	315
Michigan[3]	36,423	14,586	20,985	137	25	690
Minnesota[3]	3,472	1,960	1,051	287	1	173
Missouri	15,897	8,547	7,317	30	3	0
Nebraska	2,495	1,564	830	95	0	6
North Dakota	492	397	4	88	3	0
Ohio[5]	35,744	16,433	19,311	0	0	0
South Dakota	1,374	992	32	350	[1]	0

[Continued]

★ 915 ★

Prisoners, by Race and State, 1991
[Continued]

Region and jurisdiction	Number of prisoners					
	Prisoner population 12/31/91	White	Black	American Indian/ Alaska Native	Asian/ Pacific Islander	Not known
Wisconsin	7,849	4,275	3,325	178	15	56
South	301,866	104,969	181,341	1,249	374	13,933
Alabama[3]	16,760	5,958	10,793	6	2	1
Arkansas[3]	7,766	3,302	4,437	3	1	23
Delaware[2,3]	3,717	1,175	2,449	2	3	88
District of Columbia[2,5]	10,455	218	10,237	0	0	0
Florida[3]	46,533	18,383	27,185	0	105	860
Georgia	23,644	7,613	15,931	20	6	74
Kentucky	9,799	6,672	3,123	2	0	2
Louisiana[6]	20,003	5,168	14,834	[1]	[1]	1
Maryland	19,291	4,581	14,638	6	0	66
Mississippi[3]	8,904	2,437	6,410	7	9	41
North Carolina	18,903	6,747	11,522	421	11	202
Oklahoma[3]	13,340	7,522	4,652	760	0	406
South Carolina	18,269	6,099	12,120	13	2	35
Tennessee[6]	11,474	5,857	5,503	[1]	[1]	114
Texas[3]	51,677	15,013	24,520	6	193	11,945
Virginia[3]	19,829	6,942	12,769	2	41	75
West Virginia	1,502	1,282	218	1	1	0
West	162,876	105,468	45,518	3,328	1,790	6,772
Alaska[2,5]	2,706	1,488	339	847	32	0
Arizona	15,415	12,271	2,633	498	12	1
California	101,808	61,594	35,205	662	[1]	4,347
Colorado[5]	8,392	5,990	1,937	108	27	330
Hawaii[2,3,5]	2,700	642	155	34	1,470	399
Idaho[5]	2,143	1,997	32	94	15	5
Montana	1,478	1,189	20	269	0	0
Nevada[3]	5,503	3,141	1,719	77	50	516
New Mexico	3,119	2,680	316	97	4	22
Oregon	6,732	4,994	923	147	51	617
Utah	2,625	2,264	222	67	36	36
Washington	9,156	6,345	1,966	372	91	382
Wyoming[3]	1,099	873	51	56	2	117

Source: U.S. Department of Justice. Bureau of Justice Statistics. *Correctional Populations in the United States, 1991* (NCJ-142729). Washington, DC: Bureau of Justice Statistics, August 1993, p. 57. *Notes:* All data for Arizona, California, Florida, Georgia, Illinois, Indiana, Iowa, Massachusetts, Michigan, Texas, and Wyoming are custody rather than jurisdiction counts. 1. Not reported. 2. Figures include both jail and prison inmates; jails and prisons are combined in one system. 3. Hispanic prisoners reported under "unknown race." 4. New York includes all Hispanic inmates under "White." 5. Race was estimated. 6. Louisiana and Tennessee reported persons whose race was neither black nor white under "other race." These persons are here reported under "unknown race."

Victim Assistance

★916★

Children's Justice Act Funding for Native Americans, 1990

From the source: "In 1988, while Congress was considering the reauthorization of the Victims of Crime Act, the Department of Justice successfully proposed an amendment to reduce the amount of CJA [Children's Justice Act] funds available to the States through HHS [Health and Human Services]. This was proposed to allow Indian tribes to participate in the grant program. As a result of the amendment, $675,000 is now available to Native Americans to 1)promote systemic improvements in the way child abuse cases are investigated and prosecuted in Indian Country and 2)ensure that child victims are treated in a manner that prevents or limits the onset of additional trauma."

Recipient	Amount (dollars)
Assiniboine and Sioux Tribes (Fort Peck Indian Reservation, MT)	50,000
Cherokee Nation of Oklahoma	52,000
Crow-Creek Sioux Tribe (Crow-Creek Reservation, SD)	41,000
Gila River Indian Community (Gila River Indian Reservation, AZ)	43,000
Hopi Tribe (Hopi Reservation, AZ)	45,000
Mississippi Band of Choctaw (Choctaw Reservation, MS)	40,000
Nez Perce Tribe (Nez Perce Reservation, ID)	50,000
Ogalala Sioux Tribe (Pine Ridge Reservation, SD)	60,000
Pueblo of Santa Clara, New Mexico	30,000
South Puget Sound Intertribal Agency/ Intertribal Family Services[1]	55,000
Total	466,000

Source: U.S. Department of Justice. Office of Justice Programs. Office for Victims of Crime. *OVC Bulletin: Victim Programs to Serve Native Americans* (February 1992), p. 4. *Notes:* 1. On behalf of the Chehalis, Skokomish, Squaxin Island, Quileuta, Jamestown Klallam, Makah, Lower Elwha, and Shoalwater Bay Tribes of Washington.

★ 917 ★

Victim Assistance

Victim Assistance Grants for Native Americans, 1988-89

Funding for grants to Native American victims of federal crimes, totaling $1.8 million as of February 1992, is shown by state. Funding, designated by the Office for Victims of Crime (U.S. Dept. of Justice), has been made available to states containing areas of Indian Country where the Federal Government has authority to investigate and prosecute crimes.

State	Amount (dollars)
First Year (1988) Indian Grants	
Arizona	250,500
Michigan	90,500
North Dakota	100,500
Oregon	35,500
South Dakota	195,500
Utah	50,000
Washington	170,600
Wisconsin	35,500
Wyoming	75,500
Second Year (1989) Indian Grants	
Idaho	115,500
Kansas	40,500
Minnesota	40,500
Montana	200,500
Nevada	105,500
New Mexico	200,500

Source: U.S. Department of Justice. Office of Justice Programs. Office for Victims of Crime. *OVC Bulletin: Victim Programs to Serve Native Americans* (February 1992), p. 4.

Chapter 12
CANADA

Population

★ 918 ★

Aboriginal Population by Sex and Age, 1991

Data show number of persons in each category. Figures are based on 20-percent sample data from the Canadian 1991 Census.

Characteristics	Population with Aboriginal origins and/or Indian Registration			Population with Aboriginal origins[4]	Population with North American Indian origins[1]		Population with Metis origins		Population with Inuit origins		Total Canadian population
	Total[2]	On Indian Reserve[3]	Off Indian Reserve[3]		Single responses	Multiple responses[5]	Single responses	Multiple responses[5]	Single responses	Multiple responses[5]	
Total population[6]	1,016,335	189,365	826,970	1,002,670	365,375	418,605	75,150	137,500	30,090	19,170	26,994,040
Males, total	493,880	97,575	396,305	489,085	178,675	203,340	37,005	67,040	15,190	9,685	13,337,675
0-4 years	69,545	13,615	55,925	68,865	23,270	30,055	4,435	10,550	2,371	1,505	976,090
5-9 years	61,475	12,170	49,305	60,940	21,075	26,310	4,205	9,025	1,985	1,180	974,540
10-14 years	55,035	11,110	43,920	54,530	19,725	22,680	3,875	7,795	1,740	1,065	964,895
15-19 years	49,210	10,255	38,955	48,690	18,080	19,460	3,830	6,955	1,500	970	963,325
20-24 years	43,755	8,655	35,100	43,175	16,400	17,045	3,435	5,500	1,655	845	985,875
25-34 years	88,455	15,520	72,935	87,560	31,300	37,930	6,295	11,475	2,505	1,740	2,402,050
35-44 years	61,420	10,615	50,805	60,960	21,410	27,345	4,410	8,195	1,470	1,185	2,159,900
45-54 years	32,880	6,825	26,050	32,595	12,935	12,625	3,140	3,980	885	620	1,483,685
55-64 years	18,475	4,610	13,865	18,260	7,810	6,125	1,925	2,105	670	395	1,169,455
65-74 years	9,250	2,700	6,550	9,180	4,285	2,760	960	1,030	295	120	835,405
75 years and older	4,385	1,500	2,880	4,325	2,380	995	495	430	115	60	424,445
Females, total	522,455	91,790	430,670	513,595	186,700	215,265	38,150	70,460	14,900	9,480	13,656,370
0-4 years	66,620	12,770	53,850	66,020	22,930	28,290	4,480	9,810	2,245	1,450	927,920
5-9 years	60,020	11,915	48,105	59,395	20,515	26,075	3,820	8,525	1,860	1,100	931,120
10-14 years	52,355	10,485	41,870	51,915	18,525	21,955	3,700	7,520	1,575	940	914,730
15-19 years	49,305	9,585	39,720	48,760	18,250	19,400	3,975	6,850	1,485	885	910,905
20-24 years	48,790	8,185	40,605	48,095	17,910	19,445	3,590	6,535	1,590	1,040	974,720
25-34 years	103,325	14,770	88,560	101,060	34,520	44,685	6,955	14,425	2,605	1,905	2,438,280
35-44 years	71,145	9,385	61,765	69,305	23,755	31,430	5,155	9,175	1,560	1,105	2,193,680
45-54 years	35,485	6,110	29,380	34,460	13,865	13,510	2,840	4,060	950	515	1,476,755
55-64 years	19,290	4,250	15,040	18,815	8,635	5,975	1,830	2,065	630	300	1,215,780

[Continued]

1063

★ 918 ★

Aboriginal Population by Sex and Age, 1991

[Continued]

Characteristics	Population with Aboriginal origins and/or Indian Registration			Population with Aboriginal origins[4]	Population with North American Indian origins[1]		Population with Metis origins		Population with Inuit origins		Total Canadian population
	Total[2]	On Indian Reserve[3]	Off Indian Reserve[3]		Single responses	Multiple responses[5]	Single responses	Multiple responses[5]	Single responses	Multiple responses[5]	
65-74 years	10,680	2,630	8,050	10,395	4,985	3,095	1,225	1,015	225	165	1,017,525
75 years and older	5,440	1,705	3,735	5,365	2,810	1,400	570	485	160	70	654,945

Source: Statistics Canada. *Profile of Canada's Aboriginal Population.* Ottawa: Industry, Science and Technology Canada, 1995. 1991 Census of Canada. Catalogue number 94-325, p. 8. Copyright, 1995. Used with permission. *Notes:* 1. Some respondents reported a combination of different Aboriginal/non-Aboriginal origins. These combinations of Aboriginal responses are counted under each relevant Aboriginal group. Therefore, the sum of the responses is greater than the total population reporting an Aboriginal ancestry. 2. This category includes 1,002,675 people who provided Aboriginal ancestry and 13,660 people who reported that they are registered but did not indicate any Aboriginal origins. 3. Some Indian reserves and settlements were incompletely enumerated during the 1991 Census due to the fact that on some Indian reserves or settlements, enumeration was not permitted or was interrupted before it could be completed. Some Indian reserves and settlements were enumerated late or the quality of the collected data was considered inadequate. These geographic areas (a total of 78) are called incompletely enumerated Indian reserves and Indian settlements. Data for 1991 are therefore not available for the incompletely enumerated reserves and settlements and are not included in the tabulations. Because of missing data, users are cautioned that for the affected geographic areas, comparisons between 1986 and 1991 are not exact. While for higher level geographic areas (Canada, provinces, census metropolitan areas and census agglomerations) the impact of missing data is very small, the impact can be significant for smaller areas, where the affected reserves and settlements account for a higher proportion of the population. 4. Total is derived by adding the single and multiple response columns of the population with Aboriginal origins. There is no double counting of the population in this total. 5. Refers to respondents who reported more than one ancestry. The sum of multiple response columns for each Aboriginal group is greater than the total population with Aboriginal origins who reported multiple ancestry. 6. All characteristics exclude institutional residents and are based on weighted sample data (20%).

★ 919 ★

Population

Aboriginal Population, by Age Group, 1991

Data show percent distribution of Canada's Aboriginal population. Figures are based on self-reported responses to the 1991 Aboriginal Peoples Survey. This survey provided data for approximately 626,000 persons who identified with an Aboriginal group and/or who were registered Indians as defined by the Indian Act of Canada. Nearly 25% of persons identifying themselves as North American Indian were between the ages of 5 and 14 years.

Age group	Canada's total population	Population identifying as North American Indian
Total	100.0	100.0
0-14 years	7.1	14.0
5-14 years	14.0	23.4
15-24 years	14.2	19.4
25-34 years	17.9	17.6
35-54 years	27.1	18.4
55 years and older	19.7	7.2

Source: Statistics Canada. *The Daily* (30 March 1993), p. 10. Primary source: Statistics Canada. *1991 Aboriginal Peoples Survey.* Ottawa: Statistics Canada, 1993. Catalogue number 94-327. *Notes:* 181 Indian reserves and settlements (representing approximately 2,000 people) who participated in the 1991 Census did not participate in the Aboriginal Peoples Survey.

★ 920 ★

Population

Aboriginal Population, by Metropolitan Area, 1991

Data show number of persons in each census metropolitan area. Figures are based on 20-percent sample data from the Canadian 1991 Census.

Characteristics	Population with Aboriginal origins[3]	Population with Aboriginal origins				Population with North American Indian origins[1]			
		Single responses	Multiple responses[4]	Registered under the Indian Act[5]	Member of an Indian Band/First Nation[5]	Single responses	Multiple responses[4]	Registered under the Indian Act[5]	Member of an Indian Band/First Nation[5]
St. John's	1,160	205	955	55	35	105	660	35	35
Halifax	6,710	830	5,875	705	650	720	5,080	650	620
St. John	2,180	100	2,080	110	65	80	1,960	105	55
Chicoutimi-Jonquiere	2,005	1,020	990	365	335	740	890	310	280
Quebec[2]	6,715	2,590	4,125	1,150	990	2,135	3,710	1,045	890
Sherbrooke	2,035	545	1,490	50	35	495	1,425	50	30
Trois-Rivieres	2,105	865	1,235	260	245	645	1,175	215	200
Montreal[2]	44,650	12,735	31,915	3,255	2,660	10,290	28,815	2,895	2,440
Ottawa-Hull	30,890	6,920	23,975	3,480	2,355	5,385	20,565	3,190	2,185
Oshawa	5,345	785	4,560	570	525	675	4,260	570	525
Toronto	40,045	6,440	33,600	4,920	4,235	5,645	30,520	4,750	4,105
Hamilton	11,020	2,295	8,725	1,910	1,660	2,115	8,220	1,845	1,620
St. Catherines-Niagara	9,000	1,470	7,525	1,320	980	1,360	7,005	1,285	970
Kitchener	5,835	710	5,120	480	420	600	4,635	470	405
London	7,820	2,015	5,805	1,905	1,575	1,940	5,490	1,865	1,560
Windsor	7,545	595	6,950	485	410	575	6,485	480	405
Sudbury	7,040	2,175	4,865	2,095	1,810	2,015	4,105	2,020	1,740
Thunder Bay	6,980	3,345	3,635	3,695	3,290	3,185	2,805	3,585	3,200
Winnepeg	44,970	21,410	23,560	14,935	13,070	12,145	11,330	12,670	11,290
Regina	12,965	7,680	5,085	6,345	5,555	5,795	2,805	6,175	5,415
Saskatoon	14,225	7,945	6,280	6,050	5,310	5,685	3,405	5,665	4,960
Cagary	24,375	6,810	17,565	5,390	4,885	4,720	12,495	5,060	4,635
Edmonton	42,695	16,580	26,115	11,055	9,505	9,650	15,930	9,830	8,665
Vancouver	42,795	12,570	30,225	11,605	10,030	10,850	25,850	11,290	9,810
Victoria[2]	10,210	3,510	6,695	3,445	3,015	3,175	5,750	3,355	2,945

Source: Statistics Canada. *Canada's Aboriginal Population by Census Subdivisions and Census Metropolitan Areas: Aboriginal Data.* Ottawa: Industry, Science and Technology Canada, 1994. 1991 Census of Canada. Catalogue number 94-326, p. 100. Copyright, 1995. Used with permission. *Notes:* 1. Some respondents reported a combination of different Aboriginal/non-Aboriginal origins. These combinations of Aboriginal responses are counted under each relevant Aboriginal group. Therefore, the sum of the responses is greater than the total population reporting an Aboriginal ancestry. 2. Excludes Census data for one or more incompletely enumerated Indian reserves or settlements (see footnote 3). 3. Some Indian reserves and settlements were incompletely enumerated during the 1991 Census due to the fact that on some Indian reserves or settlements, enumeration was not permitted or was interrupted before it could be completed. Some Indian reserves and settlements were enumerated late or the quality of the collected data was considered inadequate. These geographic areas (a total of 78) are called incompletely enumerated Indian reserves and Indian settlements. Data for 1991 are therefore not available for the incompletely enumerated reserves and settlements and are not included in the tabulations. Because of missing data, users are cautioned that for the affected geographic areas, comparisons between 1986 and 1991 are not exact. While for higher level geographic areas (Canada, provinces, census metropolitan areas and census agglomerations) the impact of missing data is very small, the impact can be significant for smaller areas, where the affected reserves and settlements account for a higher proportion of the population. 4. Total is derived by adding the single and multiple response columns of the population with Aboriginal origins. There is no double counting of the population in this total. 5. Refers to respondents who reported more than one ancestry. The sum of multiple response columns for each Aboriginal group is greater than the total population with Aboriginal origins who reported multiple ancestry.

★ 921 ★

Population

Aboriginal Population, by Province and Territory, 1991

Data show percent distribution of Canada's Aboriginal population. Figures are based on self-reported responses to the 1991 Aboriginal Peoples Survey. This survey provided data for approximately 626,000 persons who identified with an Aboriginal group and/or who were registered Indians as defined by the Indian Act of Canada.

	Canada's total population	Population identifying as North American Indian
Canada	100.0	100.0
Number	26,994,045	460,680
Newfoundland	2.1	0.8
Prince Edward Island	0.5	0.2
Nova Scotia	3.3	1.9
New Brunswick	2.7	1.1
Quebec	25.2	9.0
Ontario	37.0	22.3
Manitoba	4.0	14.4
Saskatchewan	3.6	13.0
Alberta	9.3	14.1
British Columbia	12.0	20.2
Yukon	0.1	0.9
Northwest Territories	0.2	2.1

Source: Statistics Canada. *The Daily* (30 March 1993), p. 10. Primary source: Statistics Canada. *1991 Aboriginal Peoples Survey*. Ottawa: Statistics Canada, 1993. Catalogue number 94-327. *Notes:* 181 Indian reserves and settlements (representing approximately 2,000 people) who participated in the 1991 Census did not participate in the Aboriginal Peoples Survey.

★ 922 ★

Population

Aboriginal Identity in Quebec

"According to 1991 Census figures, Quebecers claiming aboriginal heritage leaped 70 percent between 1986 and 1991, the highest increase of any province in Canada....

"In metropolitan Montreal—the area most directly affected by the Oka confrontation—the number of people claiming aboriginal heritage doubled to 44,645 from 22,700 between 1986 and 1991....

[Continued]

★ 922 ★

Aboriginal Identity in Quebec
[Continued]

"From coast to coast, a little over a million Canadians claimed aboriginal roots at census time in 1991. They accounted for 3.7 percent of Canada's population....

"Across the province, 41 percent of Quebecers citing aboriginal ancestry said they identified with their group. That compared with 62 percent across Canada."

Source: Peritz, Ingrid. "More Quebecers claiming aboriginal roots; Statistics Canada cites greater pride in Indian heritage for trend." *The Gazette (Montreal)* (31 March 1993), p. B1.

★ 923 ★

Population

Geographic Mobility of the Aboriginal Population, 1991

Data show number of persons in each category. Figures are based on 20-percent sample data from the Canadian 1991 Census.

Characteristics	Population with Aboriginal origins and/or Indian Registration			Population with Aboriginal origins[4]	Population with North American Indian origins[1]		Population with Metis origins		Population with Inuit origins		Total Canadian population
	Total[2]	On Indian Reserve[3]	Off Indian Reserve[3]		Single responses	Multiple responses[5]	Single responses	Multiple responses[5]	Single responses	Multiple responses[5]	
Total population[6]	1,016,335	189,365	826,970	1,002,670	365,375	418,605	75,150	137,500	30,090	19,170	26,994,040
Total population 1 year and older[7]											
by place of residence 1 year ago	980,445	183,430	797,020	967,155	353,140	403,130	72,650	132,245	29,155	18,425	26,430,895
Non-movers	727,910	155,330	572,580	718,655	264,745	300,445	50,755	96,585	22,540	14,070	22,108,675
Movers	252,535	28,100	224,435	248,505	88,395	102,685	21,895	35,655	6,610	4,355	4,322,225
Intraprovincial movers	230,505	36,795	203,710	226,825	82,340	92,950	19,515	31,915	6,325	3,875	3,767,625
Interprovincial movers	20,085	1,110	18,780	5,560	8,515	2,320	3,555	285	440	319,200	
External migrants	1,945	190	1,755	1,900	500	1,215	65	185	-	35	235,395

Source: Statistics Canada. *Profile of Canada's Aboriginal Population.* Ottawa: Industry, Science and Technology Canada, 1995. 1991 Census of Canada. Catalogue number 94-325, p. 8. Copyright, 1995. Used with permission. *Notes:* 1. Some respondents reported a combination of different Aboriginal/non-Aboriginal origins. These combinations of Aboriginal responses are counted under each relevant Aboriginal group. Therefore, the sum of the responses is greater than the total population reporting an Aboriginal ancestry. 2. This category includes 1,002,675 people who provided Aboriginal ancestry and 13,660 people who reported that they are registered but did not indicate any Aboriginal origins. 3. Some Indian reserves and settlements were incompletely enumerated during the 1991 Census due to the fact that on some Indian reserves or settlements, enumeration was not permitted or was interrupted before it could be completed. Some Indian reserves and settlements were enumerated late or the quality of the collected data was considered inadequate. These geographic areas (a total of 78) are called incompletely enumerated Indian reserves and Indian settlements. Data for 1991 are therefore not available for the incompletely enumerated reserves and settlements and are not included in the tabulations. Because of missing data, users are cautioned that for the affected geographic areas, comparisons between 1986 and 1991 are not exact. While for higher level geographic areas (Canada, provinces, census metropolitan areas and census agglomerations) the impact of missing data is very small, the impact can be significant for smaller areas, where the affected reserves and settlements account for a higher proportion of the population. 4. Total is derived by adding the single and multiple response columns of the population with Aboriginal origins. There is no double counting of the population in this total. 5. Refers to respondents who reported more than one ancestry. The sum of multiple response columns for each Aboriginal group is greater than the total population with Aboriginal origins who reported multiple ancestry. 6. All characteristics exclude institutional residents and are based on weighted sample data (20%). 7. Population residing in Canada, excluding all persons in collective households and Canadians (military and government personnel) in households outside Canada.

★ 924 ★

Population

Inuit Population, by Age Group, 1991

Data show percent distribution of Canada's Inuit population. Figures are based on self-reported responses to the 1991 Aboriginal Peoples Survey. This survey provided data for approximately 626,000 persons who identified with an Aboriginal group and/or who were registered Indians as defined by the Indian Act of Canada. The Inuit population showed the largest proportion of young persons of any of the Aboriginal groups surveyed. More than 40 percent of persons who identified themselves as Inuit were younger than age 15.

Age group	Canada's total population	Population identifying as Inuit Indian
Total	100.0	100.0
0-14 years	7.1	17.0
5-14 years	14.0	25.5
15-24 years	14.2	20.3
25-34 years	17.9	16.6
35-54 years	27.1	14.2
55 years and older	19.7	6.3

Source: Statistics Canada. *The Daily* (30 March 1993), p. 11. Primary source: Statistics Canada. *1991 Aboriginal Peoples Survey.* Ottawa: Statistics Canada, 1993. Catalogue number 94-327. *Notes:* 181 Indian reserves and settlements (representing approximately 2,000 people) who participated in the 1991 Census did not participate in the Aboriginal Peoples Survey.

★ 925 ★

Population

Inuit Population, by Province and Territory, 1991

Data show percent distribution of Canada's Inuit population. Figures are based on self-reported responses to the 1991 Aboriginal Peoples Survey. This survey provided data for approximately 626,000 persons who identified with an Aboriginal group and/or who were registered Indians as defined by the Indian Act of Canada.

	Canada's total population	Population identifying as Inuit
Canada	100.0	100.0
Number	26,994,045	36,215
Newfoundland	2.1	13.0
Prince Edward Island	0.5	-
Nova Scotia	3.3	0.2
New Brunswick	2.7	0.2
Quebec	25.2	19.4
Ontario	37.0	2.2

[Continued]

★ 925 ★

Inuit Population, by Province and Territory, 1991
[Continued]

	Canada's total population	Population identifying as Inuit
Manitoba	4.0	1.3
Saskatchewan	3.6	0.4
Alberta	9.3	3.7
British Columbia	12.0	1.4
Yukon	0.1	0.2
Northwest Territories	0.2	58.1

Source: Statistics Canada. *The Daily* (30 March 1993), p. 11. Primary source: Statistics Canada. *1991 Aboriginal Peoples Survey*. Ottawa: Statistics Canada, 1993. Catalogue number 94-327. *Notes:* 181 Indian reserves and settlements (representing approximately 2,000 people) who participated in the 1991 Census did not participate in the Aboriginal Peoples Survey.

★ 926 ★

Population

Metis Population, by Age Group, 1991

Data show percent distribution of Canada's Metis population. Figures are based on self-reported responses to the 1991 Aboriginal Peoples Survey. This survey provided data for approximately 626,000 persons who identified with an Aboriginal group and/or who were registered Indians as defined by the Indian Act of Canada. As was the case with the North American Indian population, a large proportion of persons identifying themselves as Metis were age 15 years and younger.

Age group	Canada's total population	Population identifying as Metis
Total	100.0	100.0
0-14 years	7.1	14.1
5-14 years	14.0	23.7
15-24 years	14.2	18.6
25-34 years	17.9	18.4
35-54 years	27.1	18.3
55 years and older	19.7	6.9

Source: Statistics Canada. *The Daily* (30 March 1993), p. 11. Primary source: Statistics Canada. *1991 Aboriginal Peoples Survey*. Ottawa: Statistics Canada, 1993. Catalogue number 94-327. *Notes:* 181 Indian reserves and settlements (representing approximately 2,000 people) who participated in the 1991 Census did not participate in the Aboriginal Peoples Survey.

★ 927 ★

Population

Metis Population, by Province and Territory, 1991

Data show percent distribution of Canada's Metis population. Figures are based on self-reported responses to the 1991 Aboriginal Peoples Survey. This survey provided data for approximately 626,000 persons who identified with an Aboriginal group and/or who were registered Indians as defined by the Indian Act of Canada.

	Canada's total population	Population identifying as Metis
Canada	100.0	100.0
Number	26,994,045	135,285
Newfoundland	2.1	1.5
Prince Edward Island	0.5	-
Nova Scotia	3.3	0.2
New Brunswick	2.7	0.1
Quebec	25.2	6.4
Ontario	37.0	8.9
Manitoba	4.0	24.6
Saskatchewan	3.6	20.0
Alberta	9.3	28.6
British Columbia	12.0	6.7
Yukon	0.1	0.1
Northwest Territories	0.2	2.9

Source: Statistics Canada. *The Daily* (30 March 1993), p. 11. Primary source: Statistics Canada. *1991 Aboriginal Peoples Survey*. Ottawa: Statistics Canada, 1993. Catalogue number 94-327. *Notes:* 181 Indian reserves and settlements (representing approximately 2,000 people) who participated in the 1991 Census did not participate in the Aboriginal Peoples Survey.

★ 928 ★

Population

Metis Population in Saskatchewan

"According to preliminary data released from the census earlier this year, there are only 32,800 Metis in Saskatchewan. Metis Society of Saskatchewan estimates have the number of Metis in the province at around 80,000....

"[Metis local president Robert] Doucette estimated there were 10,000 to 15,000 Metis living in the Saskatoon region alone based on the results of the 1986 census.

"The official statistics from that census said there were 21,560 Metis in Saskatchewan.

[Continued]

★ 928 ★

Metis Population in Saskatchewan
[Continued]

"The census results showed only about 135,000 Canadians reported their origins as Metis."

Source: Campbell, Jeff. "Census takers way out of line say Metis." *New Breed Magazine* (April 1993), p. 5.

The Family

★ 929 ★

Marital Status of the Aboriginal Population, 1991

Data show number of persons in each category. Figures are based on 20-percent sample data from the Canadian 1991 Census.

Characteristics	Population with Aboriginal origins and/or Indian Registration			Population with Aboriginal origins[4]	Population with North American Indian origins[1]		Population with Metis origins		Population with Inuit origins		Total Canadian pop.
	Total[2]	On Indian[3] Reserve	Off Indian[3] Reserve		Single responses	Mult. responses[5]	Single responses	Mult. responses[5]	Single responses	Mult. responses[5]	
Total population[6]	1,016,335	189,365	826,970	1,002,670	365,375	418,605	75,150	137,500	30,090	19,170	26,994,040
Single (never married), total	664,970	129,140	535,830	657,720	244,805	267,240	49,700	90,900	21,340	12,535	12,234,655
Single (never married), 15 yrs. of age and older	299,925	57,065	242,855	296,050	118,755	111,865	25,185	37,675	9,565	5,290	6,545,355
Legally married (and not separated)	252,010	45,575	206,435	247,800	83,535	111,855	16,370	34,315	7,045	5,310	11,639,965
Legally married and separated	29,420	4,260	25,165	28,780	11,510	11,195	2,685	3,895	400	330	602,335
Widowed	23,170	6,340	16,830	22,705	11,595	6,210	2,470	1,965	855	295	1,244,365
Divorced	46,765	4,050	42,715	45,665	13,935	22,105	3,930	6,425	450	705	1,272,715

Source: Statistics Canada. *Profile of Canada's Aboriginal Population*. Ottawa: Industry, Science and Technology Canada, 1995. 1991 Census of Canada. Catalogue number 94-325, pp. 8-9. Copyright, 1995. Used with permission. *Notes:* 1. Some respondents reported a combination of different Aboriginal/non-Aboriginal origins. These combinations of Aboriginal responses are counted under each relevant Aboriginal group. Therefore, the sum of the responses is greater than the total population reporting an Aboriginal ancestry. 2. This category includes 1,002,675 people who provided Aboriginal ancestry and 13,660 people who reported that they are registered but did not indicate any Aboriginal origins. 3. Some Indian reserves and settlements were incompletely enumerated during the 1991 Census due to the fact that on some Indian reserves or settlements, enumeration was not permitted or was interrupted before it could be completed. Some Indian reserves and settlements were enumerated late or the quality of the collected data was considered inadequate. These geographic areas (a total of 78) are called incompletely enumerated Indian reserves and Indian settlements. Data for 1991 are therefore not available for the incompletely enumerated reserves and settlements and are not included in the tabulations. Because of missing data, users are cautioned that for the affected geographic areas, comparisons between 1986 and 1991 are not exact. While for higher level geographic areas (Canada, provinces, census metropolitan areas and census agglomerations) the impact of missing data is very small, the impact can be significant for smaller areas, where the affected reserves and settlements account for a higher proportion of the population. 4. Total is derived by adding the single and multiple response columns of the population with Aboriginal origins. There is no double counting of the population in this total. 5. Refers to respondents who reported more than one ancestry. The sum of multiple response columns for each Aboriginal group is greater than the total population with Aboriginal origins who reported multiple ancestry. 6. All characteristics exclude institutional residents and are based on weighted sample data (20%).

★ 930 ★

The Family

Domestic Violence Among Aboriginals

"Statistics show that 1 of every 10 women in Canada has experienced violence, but a recent study done specifically on Aboriginal Family Violence released evidence that 8 of every 10 Native women experience violence and 4 of every 10 Native children are abused in some way."

Source: Fiddler-Berteig, Ona. "Aboriginal women: uniting against family violence." *New Breed* (April 1990), p. 8.

Education

★ 931 ★

Postsecondary Education of the Aboriginal Population

"...old stereotypes about untrainability and poor education of native people are slowly giving way to new developments that may dramatically change the aboriginal workforce of the future. Statistics from Indian and Northern Affairs Canada reveal that the number of Indian and Inuit people participating in postsecondary programs has increased from a 1975-76 figure of 2,500 to a 1990-91 high of 18,000."

Source: Helin, Calvin. "First Nations business." *New Breed* (January 1992), p. 11.

★ 932 ★

Education

School Enrollment and Attainment of the Aboriginal Population, 1991

Data show number of persons in each category. School attendance is shown for persons between the ages of 15 and 24 years; educational attainment is shown for persons age 15 years and older. Figures are based on 20-percent sample data from the Canadian 1991 Census.

Characteristics	Population with Aboriginal origins and/or Indian Registration			Pop. with Abor-iginal	Population with North Amer. Indian origins[1]		Population with Metis origins		Population with Inuit origins		Total Canadian responses[5]
	Total[2]	On Indian Reserve[3]	Off Indian Reserve[3]		Single	Mult.	Single	Mult.	Single origins[4]	Mult. responses	
Total population[6]	1,016,335	189,365	826,970	1,002,670	365,375	418,605	75,150	137,500	30,090	19,170	26,994,040
Total population 15-24 yrs. by school attendance	191,060	36,680	154,375	188,720	70,645	75,355	14,830	25,845	6,230	3,740	3,832,820
Not attending school	93,700	21,455	72,245	92,545	38,895	32,235	7,620	11,815	3,905	1,730	1,468,300

[Continued]

★ 932 ★

School Enrollment and Attainment of the Aboriginal Population, 1991

[Continued]

Characteristics	Population with Aboriginal origins and/or Indian Registration			Pop. with Abor-iginal	Population with North Amer. Indian origins[1]		Population with Metis origins		Population with Inuit origins		Total Canadian responses[5]
	Total[2]	On Indian Reserve[3]	Off Indian Reserve[3]		Single	Mult.	Single	Mult.	Single origins[4]	Mult. responses	
Attending school full-time	87,605	14,415	73,195	86,595	29,170	38,260	6,530	12,570	2,090	1,800	2,124,995
Attending school part-time	9,750	810	8,940	9,580	2,580	4,855	685	1,435	230	210	239,530
Total population 15 years + by highest level of schooling	651,290	117,290	355,995	641,005	239,330	263,230	50,630	84,270	18,315	11,920	21,304,735
Less than grade 9[7]	119,845	42,785	77,055	118,220	69,135	20,325	12,780	9,385	8,610	1,440	2,959,910
Grades 9-13											
without secondary certificate	209,595	37,645	171,945	205,965	79,625	79,735	19,195	27,835	3,995	3,260	5,170,345
with secondary certificate	69,400	6,150	63,250	68,210	17,990	36,245	4,475	10,405	740	1,350	3,146,345
Trades certificate or diploma	22,245	3,640	18,605	21,965	7,905	9,315	1,600	2,985	615	480	846,885
Other non-university educ. only[8]											
without certificate	54,345	8,510	45,835	53,570	19,210	22,785	3,820	7,370	1,680	1,000	1,393,720
with certificate	96,070	12,270	83,800	94,600	27,360	47,780	5,710	13,805	2,230	2,230	3,362,480
University											
without degree											
without certificate	24,755	2,515	22,245	24,355	7,040	12,735	1,020	4,100	185	595	936,910
with certificate[9]	24,265	2,410	21,855	23,820	6,550	13,320	1,130	3,410	165	545	1,068,400
with degree	30,775	1,365	29,410	30,280	4,510	20,975	900	4,975	80	1,015	2,419,745

Source: Statistics Canada. *Profile of Canada's Aboriginal Population.* Ottawa: Industry, Science and Technology Canada, 1995. 1991 Census of Canada. Catalogue number 94-325, p. 8. Copyright, 1995. Used with permission. *Notes:* 1. Some respondents reported a combination of different Aboriginal/non-Aboriginal origins. These combinations of Aboriginal responses are counted under each relevant Aboriginal group. Therefore, the sum of the responses is greater than the total population reporting an Aboriginal ancestry. 2. This category includes 1,002,675 people who provided Aboriginal ancestry and 13,660 people who reported that they are registered but did not indicate any Aboriginal origins. 3. Some Indian reserves and settlements were incompletely enumerated during the 1991 Census due to the fact that on some Indian reserves or settlements, enumeration was not permitted or was interrupted before it could be completed. Some Indian reserves and settlements were enumerated late or the quality of the collected data was considered inadequate. These geographic areas (a total of 78) are called incompletely enumerated Indian reserves and Indian settlements. Data for 1991 are therefore not available for the incompletely enumerated reserves and settlements and are not included in the tabulations. Because of missing data, users are cautioned that for the affected geographic areas, comparisons between 1986 and 1991 are not exact. While for higher level geographic areas (Canada, provinces, census metropolitan areas and census agglomerations) the impact of missing data is very small, the impact can be significant for smaller areas, where the affected reserves and settlements account for a higher proportion of the population. 4. Total is derived by adding the single and multiple response columns of the population with Aboriginal origins. There is no double counting of the population in this total. 5. Refers to respondents who reported more than one ancestry. The sum of multiple response columns for each Aboriginal group is greater than the total population with Aboriginal origins who reported multiple ancestry. 6. All characteristics exclude institutional residents and are based on weighted sample data (20%). 7. Includes "Never attended school or never attended kindergarten only". 8. Refers to courses completed at postsecondary non-university institutions which normally require a secondary school graduation certificate or equivalent for entrance, *as well as* to other courses in related or like institutions (such as private trade schools or adult vocational centres) which may *not* require secondary school graduation for entrance. 9. Includes "Other non-university certificate or diploma" and "Trades certificate or diploma".

Culture

★ 933 ★

First Language of Aboriginal Population, 1991

Data show number of persons in each category. Figures are based on 20-percent sample data from the Canadian 1991 Census.

Characteristics	Population with Aboriginal origins and/or Indian Registration			Pop. with Abori-ginal origins[4]	Population with North Amer. Indian origins[1]		Population with Metis origins		Population with Inuit origins		Total Canadian pop.
	Total[2]	On Indian Reserve[3]	Off Indian Reserve[3]		Single responses	Mult. responses[5]	Single responses	Mult. responses[5]	Single responses	Mult. responses[5]	
Total population[6]	1,016,335	189,365	826,970	1,002,670	365,375	418,605	75,150	137,500	30,090	19,170	26,994,040
Single responses	994,775	181,395	813,375	981,460	352,515	414,335	73,405	135,235	29,465	18,815	26,663,790
English	699,075	85,090	613,980	688,685	195,140	338,950	53,685	111,750	6,915	15,670	16,169,880

[Continued]

★ 933 ★

First Language of Aboriginal Population, 1991
[Continued]

Characteristics	Population with Aboriginal origins and/or Indian Registration			Pop. with Aboriginal origins⁴	Population with North Amer. Indian origins¹		Population with Metis origins		Population with Inuit origins		Total Canadian pop.
	Total²	On Indian Reserve³	Off Indian Reserve³		Single responses	Mult. responses⁵	Single responses	Mult. responses⁵	Single responses	Mult. responses⁵	
French	123,355	2,070	121,285	121,420	28,110	66,685	11,080	17,715	475	1,020	6,502,865
Non-official languages⁷	172,345	94,240	78,115	171,360	129,260	8,705	8,635	5,775	22,070	2,125	3,991,050
Aboriginal languages⁷	171,805	94,160	77,645	171,340	129,245	8,700	8,635	5,775	22,065	2,125	172,610
Cree	73,375	45,690	27,695	73,140	66,815	5,675	6,735	4,315	25	95	73,780
Inktitut	24,005	20	23,985	24,005	20	130	15	45	21,965	2,000	24,100
Ojibway	21,870	14,625	7,245	21,800	19,895	880	950	390	10	10	21,985
Montagnais-Naskapi	7,315	5,770	1,545	7,320	7,150	135	15	30	15	-	7,340
Micmac	6,010	5,340	665	6,000	5,910	85	-	20	-	-	6,020
Dakota	3,500	2,995	505	3,485	3,430	30	25	10	-	-	3,510
Blackfoot	3,440	2,470	965	3,440	3,395	35	10	10	-	-	3,435
South Slave	3,295	995	2,295	3,290	3,110	95	60	80	10	10	3,330
Wakashan languages	2,895	1,945	950	2,880	2,805	55	15	10	10	10	2,905
Salish languages	2,470	1,900	565	2,460	2,330	125	10	10	-	-	2,470
Chipewayan	2,220	910	1,315	2,215	1,835	150	205	100	10	-	2,230
Dogrib	2,140	10	2,135	2,140	2,080	20	40	10	-	-	2,140
Carrier	1,720	1,230	485	1,700	1,650	40	10	10	-	-	1,720
Chilcotin	855	858	270	845	840	10	10	-	-	-	850
Kutchin-Gwich'in (Loucheux)	445	-	440	445	405	25	10	10	10	10	445
Tsimshian	340	165	175	340	320	15	-	-	-	-	340
Mohawk	300	35	265	295	285	10	-	-	-	-	300
Malecite	235	170	65	235	225	10	10	-	-	-	235
Kutenai	155	110	45	155	145	10	-	-	-	-	155
Haida	100	65	30	95	90	-	-	-	-	10	100
Tlingit	90	35	50	85	80	10	-	-	-	-	90
North Slave (Hare)	40	-	40	40	30	10	-	-	-	-	40
Other Aboriginal languages	15,005	9,105	5,900	14,915	13,150	1,170	530	745	30	-	15,095
Multiple responses	21,565	7,965	13,600	21,215	12,860	4,270	1,745	2,260	625	350	330,250
English and Aboriginal langauges	8,035	3,945	4,090	7,905	6,310	515	230	160	580	230	8,140
French and Aboriginal languages	340	170	170	335	210	45	30	15	30	15	350
Other multiple responses	13,190	3,850	9,335	12,975	6,330	3,715	1,480	2,090	20	105	321,760

Source: Statistics Canada. *Profile of Canada's Aboriginal Population.* Ottawa: Industry, Science and Technology Canada, 1995. 1991 Census of Canada. Catalogue number 94-325, p. 8. Copyright, 1995. Used with permission. *Notes:* 1. Some respondents reported a combination of different Aboriginal/non- Aboriginal origins. These combinations of Aboriginal responses are counted under each relevant Aboriginal group. Therefore, the sum of the responses is greater than the total population reporting an Aboriginal ancestry. 2. This category includes 1,002,675 people who provided Aboriginal ancestry and 13,660 people who reported that they are registered but did not indicate any Aboriginal origins. 3. Some Indian reserves and settlements were incompletely enumerated during the 1991 Census due to the fact that on some Indian reserves or settlements, enumeration was not permitted or was interrupted before it could be completed. Some Indian reserves and settlements were enumerated late or the quality of the collected data was considered inadequate. These geographic areas (a total of 78) are called incompletely enumerated Indian reserves and Indian settlements. Data for 1991 are therefore not available for the incompletely enumerated reserves and settlements and are not included in the tabulations. Because of missing data, users are cautioned that for the affected geographic areas, comparisons between 1986 and 1991 are not exact. While for higher level geographic areas (Canada, provinces, census metropolitan areas and census agglomerations) the impact of missing data is very small, the impact can be significant for smaller areas, where the affected reserves and settlements account for a higher proportion of the population. 4. Total is derived by adding the single and multiple response columns of the population with Aboriginal origins. There is no double counting of the population in this total. 5. Refers to respondents who reported more than one ancestry. The sum of multiple response columns for each Aboriginal group is greater than the total population with Aboriginal origins who reported multiple ancestry. 6. All characteristics exclude institutional residents and are based on weighted sample data (20%). 7. Some Aboriginal languages may be under-reported due to one or more incompletely enumerated Indian reserves or settlements.

★ 934 ★

Culture

Knowledge of Official Languages by the Aboriginal Population, 1991

Data show number of persons in each category. Figures are based on 20-percent sample data from the Canadian 1991 Census.

Characteristics	Population with Aboriginal origins and/or Indian Registration			Population with Aboriginal origins⁴	Population with North American Indian origins¹		Population with Metis origins		Population with Inuit origins		Total Canadian population
	Total²	On Indian Reserve³	Off Indian Reserve³		Single responses	Multiple responses⁵	Single responses	Multiple responses⁵	Single responses	Multiple responses⁵	
Total population⁶	1,016,335	189,365	826,970	1,002,670	365,375	418,605	75,150	137,500	30,090	19,170	26,994,040
English only	810,775	164,135	646,635	799,695	306,680	319,260	61,510	110,210	22,150	16,250	18,106,765
French only	67,740	9,655	58,085	66,615	26,090	29,220	5,780	5,550	885	440	4,110,300

[Continued]

★ 934 ★

Knowledge of Official Languages by the Aboriginal Population, 1991
[Continued]

Characteristics	Population with Aboriginal origins and/or Indian Registration			Population with Aboriginal origins[4]	Population with North American Indian origins[1]		Population with Metis origins		Population with Inuit origins		Total Canadian population
	Total[2]	On Indian Reserve[3]	Off Indian Reserve[3]		Single responses	Multiple responses[5]	Single responses	Multiple responses[5]	Single responses	Multiple responses[5]	
Both English and French	115,925	3,905	112,020	114,510	18,615	69,610	7,480	21,355	585	1,940	4,398,655
Neither English nor French	21,895	11,665	10,230	21,850	13,990	510	375	385	6,470	530	378,320

Source: Statistics Canada. *Profile of Canada's Aboriginal Population.* Ottawa: Industry, Science and Technology Canada, 1995. 1991 Census of Canada. Catalogue number 94-325, p. 8. Copyright, 1995. Used with permission. *Notes:* 1. Some respondents reported a combination of different Aboriginal/non-Aboriginal origins. These combinations of Aboriginal responses are counted under each relevant Aboriginal group. Therefore, the sum of the responses is greater than the total population reporting an Aboriginal ancestry. 2. This category includes 1,002,675 people who provided Aboriginal ancestry and 13,660 people who reported that they are registered but did not indicate any Aboriginal origins. 3. Some Indian reserves and settlements were incompletely enumerated during the 1991 Census due to the fact that on some Indian reserves or settlements, enumeration was not permitted or was interrupted before it could be completed. Some Indian reserves and settlements were enumerated late or the quality of the collected data was considered inadequate. These geographic areas (a total of 78) are called incompletely enumerated Indian reserves and Indian settlements. Data for 1991 are therefore not available for the incompletely enumerated reserves and settlements and are not included in the tabulations. Because of missing data, users are cautioned that for the affected geographic areas, comparisons between 1986 and 1991 are not exact. While for higher level geographic areas (Canada, provinces, census metropolitan areas and census agglomerations) the impact of missing data is very small, the impact can be significant for smaller areas, where the affected reserves and settlements account for a higher proportion of the population. 4. Total is derived by adding the single and multiple response columns of the population with Aboriginal origins. There is no double counting of the population in this total. 5. Refers to respondents who reported more than one ancestry. The sum of multiple response columns for each Aboriginal group is greater than the total population with Aboriginal origins who reported multiple ancestry. 6. All characteristics exclude institutional residents and are based on weighted sample data (20%).

★ 935 ★
Culture

Language Spoken at Home by the Aboriginal Population, 1991

Data show number of persons in each category. Figures are based on 20-percent sample data from the Canadian 1991 Census.

Characteristics	Population with Aboriginal origins and/or Indian Registration			Population with Aboriginal origins[4]	Population with North American Indian origins[1]		Population with Metis origins		Population with Inuit origins		Total Canadian population
	Total[2]	On Indian Reserve[3]	Off Indian Reserve[3]		Single responses	Multiple responses[5]	Single responses	Multiple responses[5]	Single responses	Multiple responses[5]	
Total population[6]	1,016,335	189,365	826,970	1,002,670	365,375	418,605	75,150	137,500	30,090	19,170	26,994,040
Single responses	989,815	177,250	812,570	976,420	348,200	414,020	73,465	135,440	28,540	18,800	26,506,310
English	767,500	102,040	665,460	756,005	232,315	353,500	60,305	120,125	9,545	16,320	18,220,175
French	105,945	2,375	103,565	104,250	28,245	56,140	9,265	12,170	435	815	6,211,240
Non-official languages	116,375	72,830	43,545	116,160	87,645	4,380	3,895	3,150	18,560	1,670	2,074,900
Aboriginal languages[7]	116,000	72,790	43,210	115,885	87,585	4,260	3,855	3,120	18,550	1,635	116,310
Cree	50,650	37,855	12,795	50,615	44,485	2,865	3,105	2,290	20	65	50,765
Inktitut	20,035	15	20,020	20,030	10	85	10	30	18,445	1,560	20,075
Ojibway	12,055	10,095	1,960	12,030	11,505	250	260	135	10	-	12,100
Montagnais-Naskapi	6,990	5,625	1,370	6,995	6,850	125	10	35	10	-	7,000
Micmac	4,350	4,210	145	4,350	4,330	15	-	-	-	-	4,355
Dakota	2,480	2,420	60	2,480	2,475	-	10	-	-	-	2,480
Blackfoot	1,705	1,540	165	1,695	1,690	10	-	-	-	-	1,705
South Slave	2,045	760	1,285	2,045	1,975	35	35	25	-	-	2,045
Wakashan languages	600	470	130	600	590	10	-	-	10	-	600
Salish languages	500	460	45	495	495	-	-	-	-	-	500
Chipewayan	930	515	415	935	795	45	85	40	-	10	940
Dogrib	1,625	10	1,625	1,625	1,580	15	30	-	-	-	1,630
Carrier	750	635	110	730	725	10	-	-	-	-	750
Chilcotin	540	470	65	535	535	-	-	-	-	-	540
Kutchin-Gwich'in (Loucheux)	50	-	50	50	45	-	-	-	-	-	50
Tsimshian	45	35	10	45	45	-	-	-	-	-	45
Other Aboriginal languages	10,600	7,655	2,945	10,580	9,410	790	310	565	65	10	10,680
Multiple responses	26,525	12,115	14,405	26,255	17,175	4,585	1,685	2,060	1,550	365	487,730
English and Aboriginal langauges	10,880	6,065	4,815	10,795	8,390	430	215	210	1,495	255	11,650

[Continued]

★ 935 ★

Language Spoken at Home by the Aboriginal Population, 1991
[Continued]

Characteristics	Population with Aboriginal origins and/or Indian Registration			Population with Aboriginal origins[4]	Population with North American Indian origins[1]		Population with Metis origins		Population with Inuit origins		Total Canadian population
	Total[2]	On Indian Reserve[3]	Off Indian Reserve[3]		Single responses	Multiple responses[5]	Single responses	Multiple responses[5]	Single responses	Multiple responses[5]	
French and Aboriginal languages	425	225	195	425	370	15	10	10	25	10	6,965
Other multiple responses	15,220	5,825	9,395	15,035	8,415	4,140	1,460	1,840	35	100	469,120

Source: Statistics Canada. *Profile of Canada's Aboriginal Population.* Ottawa: Industry, Science and Technology Canada, 1995. 1991 Census of Canada. Catalogue number 94-325, p. 8. Copyright, 1995. Used with permission. *Notes:* 1. Some respondents reported a combination of different Aboriginal/non-Aboriginal origins. These combinations of Aboriginal responses are counted under each relevant Aboriginal group. Therefore, the sum of the responses is greater than the total population reporting an Aboriginal ancestry. 2. This category includes 1,002,675 people who provided Aboriginal ancestry and 13,660 people who reported that they are registered but did not indicate any Aboriginal origins. 3. Some Indian reserves and settlements were incompletely enumerated during the 1991 Census due to the fact that on some Indian reserves or settlements, enumeration was not permitted or was interrupted before it could be completed. Some Indian reserves and settlements were enumerated late or the quality of the collected data was considered inadequate. These geographic areas (a total of 78) are called incompletely enumerated Indian reserves and Indian settlements. Data for 1991 are therefore not available for the incompletely enumerated reserves and settlements and are not included in the tabulations. Because of missing data, users are cautioned that for the affected geographic areas, comparisons between 1986 and 1991 are not exact. While for higher level geographic areas (Canada, provinces, census metropolitan areas and census agglomerations) the impact of missing data is very small, the impact can be significant for smaller areas, where the affected reserves and settlements account for a higher proportion of the population. 4. Total is derived by adding the single and multiple response columns of the population with Aboriginal origins. There is no double counting of the population in this total. 5. Refers to respondents who reported more than one ancestry. The sum of multiple response columns for each Aboriginal group is greater than the total population with Aboriginal origins who reported multiple ancestry. 6. All characteristics exclude institutional residents and are based on weighted sample data (20%). 7. Some Aboriginal languages may be under-reported due to one or more incompletely enumerated Indian reserves or settlements.

★ 936 ★

Culture

Native Language Speakers in Canada

"A report prepared by staff at the Woodland Cultural Centre...entitled *Language Development and Delivery Framework Consultants Program*...contains a wealth of information about what is being done and what can be done to revitalize ancestral languages.

"As of September 1994 the language council study showed that in 16 First Nations with a combined population of 43,635 there were only 1,415 fluent speakers. That number represents slightly over 3%."

Source: Barnsley, Paul. "Chiefs Assembly wants language policies." *Tekawennake* (1 March 1995), p. 6. Woodland Cultural Centre and the Sweetgrass First Nations Language Council.

★ 937 ★

Culture

Religious Affiliations of the Aboriginal Population, 1991

Data show number of persons in each category. Figures are based on 20-percent sample data from the Canadian 1991 Census.

Characteristics	Population with Aboriginal origins and/or Indian Registration			Population with Aboriginal origins[4]	Population with North American Indian origins[1]		Population with Metis origins		Population with Inuit origins		Total Canadian population
	Total[2]	On Indian Reserve[3]	Off Indian Reserve[3]		Single responses	Multiple responses[5]	Single responses	Multiple responses[5]	Single responses	Multiple responses[5]	
Total population[6]	1,016,335	189,365	826,970	1,002,670	365,375	418,605	75,150	137,500	30,090	19,170	26,994,040
Catholic	463,500	96,595	366,905	457,225	185,265	165,915	48,985	66,730	5,420	4,750	12,335,255
Protestant	361,090	71,975	289,115	356,725	122,775	156,330	15,015	42,025	23,495	11,005	9,780,715
Aboriginal religions	10,130	4,650	5,485	9,905	8,275	1,245	290	360	25	-	10,840
Other religions[7]	6,715	765	5,950	6,570	1,665	3,680	220	1,275	80	265	1,480,870
No religious affiliation	174,895	15,375	159,520	172,250	47,395	91,430	10,640	27,105	1,070	3,150	3,386,365

Source: Statistics Canada. *Profile of Canada's Aboriginal Population.* Ottawa: Industry, Science and Technology Canada, 1995. 1991 Census of Canada. Catalogue number 94-325, p. 8. Copyright, 1995. Used with permission. *Notes:* A dash (-) stands for nil or zero. 1. Some respondents reported a combination of different Aboriginal/non-Aboriginal origins. These combinations of Aboriginal responses are counted under each relevant Aboriginal group. Therefore, the sum of the responses is greater than the total population reporting an Aboriginal ancestry. 2. This category includes 1,002,675 people who provided Aboriginal ancestry and 13,660 people who reported that they are registered but did not indicate any Aboriginal origins. 3. Some Indian reserves and settlements were incompletely enumerated during the 1991 Census due to the fact that on some Indian reserves or settlements, enumeration was not permitted or was interrupted before it could be completed. Some Indian reserves and settlements were enumerated late or the quality of the collected data was considered inadequate. These geographic areas (a total of 78) are called incompletely enumerated Indian reserves and Indian settlements. Data for 1991 are therefore not available for the incompletely enumerated reserves and settlements and are not included in the tabulations. Because of missing data, users are cautioned that for the affected geographic areas, comparisons between 1986 and 1991 are not exact. While for higher level geographic areas (Canada, provinces, census metropolitan areas and census agglomerations) the impact of missing data is very small, the impact can be significant for smaller areas, where the affected reserves and settlements account for a higher proportion of the population. 4. Total is derived by adding the single and multiple response columns of the population with Aboriginal origins. There is no double counting of the population in this total. 5. Refers to respondents who reported more than one ancestry. The sum of multiple response columns for each Aboriginal group is greater than the total population with Aboriginal origins who reported multiple ancestry. 6. All characteristics exclude institutional residents and are based on weighted sample data (20%). 7. "Other religions" includes Eastern Orthodox, Jewish, Eastern non-Christian, para-religious groups, and other not elsewhere classified.

Health and Health Care

★ 938 ★

AIDS in Northern Ontario

Aboriginal vulnerability to the AIDS (acquired immunodeficiency syndrome) virus, as reported in the *Calgary Herald*.

"An Ontario study released earlier this year found that AIDS could be easily spread through the populations of remote, northern aboriginal communities because of low awareness and the lack of preventative measures during sex.

"Ted Myers, the main author of the $400,000 study, estimated there could be a one infection per 212 Indians in 11 northern Ontario communities, about five times the rate in the rest of the country."

Source: Aubry, Jack. "AIDS hits aboriginals hard." *Calgary Herald* (10 May 1993).

Business and Industry

★ 939 ★

Aboriginal Land and Resource Control

"...Aboriginal people control an impressive chunk of Canadian resources and over 20 percent of Canada's land mass. They have already settled claims valued at $2 billion, and by the end of this century, they will own or control 30 percent of the land in Canada and have settled claims totalling over $7 billion. This total does not include the worth of the natural resources on this land. We may be heading into the so-called "information age," but land and other natural resources remain very important for Canada. Resource development provides over 20 percent of Canada's Gross Domestic Product and 12 percent of all jobs...."

Source: Jamieson, Ron. "Mutual opportunities through partnership." *Canadian Business Review* vol. 21, no. 2 (Summer 1994), p. 16. *Notes:* Article discusses at length the advantages of business partnering between aboriginal people and non-aboriginal businesses.

★ 940 ★
Business and Industry

Aboriginal Music Industry in Canada

"...Few aboriginal artists sell more than 5,000-10,000 units in a market that is driven primarily by direct-mail sales....

"...According to Kashtin's manager, Claude Ranger, the duo has sold 225,000 units of its self-titled 1990 debut album on the Group Concept Musique label and 125,000 units of the 1992 album "Innu.""

"...Another example of aboriginal success in the music business is a 20-year-old, Winnipeg, Manitoba-based label/distributor, the Sunshine Group of Companies. The firm had $1.5 million in sales in 1993, according to president Nes Michaels....

"...Aside from Kashtin, sales of contemporary Canadian aboriginal product have been unimpressive overall. The vast majority of releases are from small independent labels or from regional cultural organizations selling fewer than 5,000 copies. Exceptions include [Lawrence] Martin's 1993 album "Wapistan," which has sold 10,000 units, according to First Nations Music label head Vic Wilson....

"...[Susan] Aglukark's album "Artic [sic] Rose," first issued on the Aglukark Entertainment label in 1992 and re-released by EMI last April, has chalked up total sales of 30,000 units, according to Tim Trombley, VP of talent acquisition and artist development at EMI Music Canada...."

Source: LeBlanc, Larry. "Canada's aboriginal musicians seek mainstream recognition." *Billboard* vol. 106, no. 36 (3 September 1994), p. 1. *Notes:* Article presents extensive discussion of the Canadian aboriginal music industry, including types of music, target audiences, and outlets.

Social and Economic Conditions

★ 941 ★

Selected Socioeconomic Characteristics of Canadian Aboriginals

"—Estimated total population of aboriginal and Metis people in Canada: 1.1 million.

—Average annual income for aboriginal men (1986 census): $26,400

—Average annual income for aboriginal women: $18,540

—Unemployment average on remote reserves: 90%

—Unemployment in urban centres: more than 20%

—Percentage of reserve children who don't finish high school: more than 75%

—Percentage of federal penitentiary inmates who are aboriginal: more than 10%

—Percentage of women's prison inmates in Manitoba, Saskatchewan and the Northwest Territories who are aboriginal: more than 70%

—Suicide rate for aboriginal people: 142 per 100,000 or more than three times the national average."

Source: Seeseequasis, Paul. "Home and Native lands: aboriginal workers & unions." *Our Times* (August/ September 1994), pp. 22-27. 1986 census; StatsCanada; PSAC aboriginal survey.

★ 942 ★

Social and Economic Conditions

Housing Tenure of the Aboriginal Population, 1991

Data show number of persons residing in each type of dwelling. Figures are based on 20-percent sample data from the Canadian 1991 Census. For historical and statutory reasons, shelter occupancy on Indian reserves does not lend itself to the usual classification by standard tenure categories (i.e. owned or rented). Therefore, in 1991, a special category "Band Housing" was created. In 1986, dwellings on Indian reserves were all classified in the "On Reserve" category. Previous to 1986, dwellings on Indian reserves were classified as being owned or rented.

| Characteristics | Population with Aboriginal origins and/or Indian Registration | | | Population with Aboriginal origins[4] | Population with North American Indian origins[1] | | Population with Metis origins | | Population with Inuit origins | | Total Canadian population |
	Total[2]	On Indian Reserve[3]	Off Indian Reserve[3]		Single responses	Multiple responses[5]	Single responses	Multiple responses[5]	Single responses	Multiple responses[5]	
Total population[6]	1,016,335	189,365	826,970	1,002,670	365,375	418,605	75,150	137,500	30,090	19,170	26,994,040
Persons residing in owned dwellings	441,560	48,685	392,885	435,965	111,015	228,125	30,615	72,930	5,050	10,230	18,635,345

[Continued]

★ 942 ★

Housing Tenure of the Aboriginal Population, 1991
[Continued]

Characteristics	Population with Aboriginal origins and/or Indian Registration			Population with Aboriginal origins[4]	Population with North American Indian origins[1]		Population with Metis origins		Population with Inuit origins		Total Canadian population
	Total[2]	On Indian Reserve[3]	Off Indian Reserve[3]		Single responses	Multiple responses[5]	Single responses	Multiple responses[5]	Single responses	Multiple responses[5]	
in rented dwellings	447,895	24,090	423,805	440,365	140,960	180,960	42,550	61,020	24,865	8,700	7,978,535
in Band housing	116,835	116,310	520	116,440	110,280	5,225	845	2,165	10	30	117,825

Source: Statistics Canada. *Profile of Canada's Aboriginal Population.* Ottawa: Industry, Science and Technology Canada, 1995. 1991 Census of Canada. Catalogue number 94-325, pp. 24-25. Copyright, 1995. Used with permission. *Notes:* 1. Some respondents reported a combination of different Aboriginal/non-Aboriginal origins. These combinations of Aboriginal responses are counted under each relevant Aboriginal group. Therefore, the sum of the responses is greater than the total population reporting an Aboriginal ancestry. 2. This category includes 1,002,675 people who provided Aboriginal ancestry and 13,660 people who reported that they are registered but did not indicate any Aboriginal origins. 3. Some Indian reserves and settlements were incompletely enumerated during the 1991 Census due to the fact that on some Indian reserves or settlements, enumeration was not permitted or was interrupted before it could be completed. Some Indian reserves and settlements were enumerated late or the quality of the collected data was considered inadequate. These geographic areas (a total of 78) are called incompletely enumerated Indian reserves and Indian settlements. Data for 1991 are therefore not available for the incompletely enumerated reserves and settlements and are not included in the tabulations. Because of missing data, users are cautioned that for the affected geographic areas, comparisons between 1986 and 1991 are not exact. While for higher level geographic areas (Canada, provinces, census metropolitan areas and census agglomerations) the impact of missing data is very small, the impact can be significant for smaller areas, where the affected reserves and settlements account for a higher proportion of the population. 4. Total is derived by adding the single and multiple response columns of the population with Aboriginal origins. There is no double counting of the population in this total. 5. Refers to respondents who reported more than one ancestry. The sum of multiple response columns for each Aboriginal group is greater than the total population with Aboriginal origins who reported multiple ancestry. 6. All characteristics exclude institutional residents and are based on weighted sample data (20%).

★ 943 ★

Social and Economic Conditions

Income of the Aboriginal Population, 1991

Data show number of persons in each income category, for persons age 15 years and older of both sexes. Figures are based on 20-percent sample data from the Canadian 1991 Census. All data refer to persons with income.

Characteristics	Population with Aboriginal origins and/or Indian Registration			Population with Aboriginal origins[4]	Population with North American Indian origins[1]		Population with Metis origins		Population with Inuit origins		Total Canadian population
	Total[2]	On Indian Reserve[3]	Off Indian Reserve[3]		Single responses	Multiple responses[5]	Single responses	Multiple responses[5]	Single responses	Multiple responses[5]	
Total population[6]	1,016,335	189,365	826,970	1,002,670	365,375	418,605	75,150	137,500	30,090	19,170	26,994,040
Both sexes 15 years and older with income	575,190	104,910	470,285	566,385	209,475	236,495	42,955	75,535	15,300	10,620	19,424,885
Under $1,000[7]	40,940	14,535	26,405	40,495	21,130	12,205	2,590	4,490	1,185	515	681,410
$1,000-$2,999	50,905	12,795	38,110	50,050	22,280	16,930	4,325	5,920	1,775	710	995,260
$3,000-$4,999	43,705	12,045	31,655	43,175	20,120	13,985	3,425	5,155	1,475	780	908,890
$5,000-$6,999	43,770	8,720	35,050	43,025	17,860	15,720	3,815	5,225	1,275	830	1,081,730
$7,000-$9,999	61,810	14,420	47,390	60,650	26,900	20,585	5,440	7,170	1,780	895	1,712,340
$10,000-$14,999	86,225	16,255	69,970	84,825	33,490	32,270	7,525	11,450	2,155	1,310	2,741,385
$15,000-$19,999	57,960	9,375	48,585	56,960	20,240	24,720	4,340	7,455	1,350	980	2,002,490
$20,000-$24,999	48,325	6,290	42,030	47,545	14,730	22,665	3,195	7,120	1,045	925	1,910,110
$25,000-$29,999	37,720	4,000	33,720	37,115	10,330	18,715	2,555	5,555	875	770	1,618,455
$30,000-$39,999	53,040	4,175	48,865	52,315	12,820	28,415	3,235	7,880	1,200	1,280	2,488,295
$40,000-$49,999	27,415	1,450	25,970	27,055	5,490	15,985	1,365	4,255	690	810	1,479,755
$50,000 and over	23,375	840	22,535	23,165	4,075	14,300	1,135	3,850	490	815	1,804,755
Average income ($)	16,967	10,621	18,383	16,983	13,194	20,334	14,890	18,651	15,090	21,378	24,001
Median income ($)	12,333	7,970	13,798	12,338	9,631	16,129	10,796	14,161	10,252	16,019	18,832

[Continued]

★ 943 ★

Income of the Aboriginal Population, 1991
[Continued]

Characteristics	Population with Aboriginal origins and/or Indian Registration			Population with Aboriginal origins[4]	Population with North American Indian origins[1]		Population with Metis origins		Population with Inuit origins		Total Canadian population
	Total[2]	On Indian Reserve[3]	Off Indian Reserve[3]		Single responses	Multiple responses[5]	Single responses	Multiple responses[5]	Single responses	Multiple responses[5]	
Standard error of average income ($)	45	69	52	46	60	81	137	157	157	374	13

Source: Statistics Canada. *Profile of Canada's Aboriginal Population.* Ottawa: Industry, Science and Technology Canada, 1995. 1991 Census of Canada. Catalogue number 94-325, p. 8. Copyright, 1995. Used with permission. *Notes:* 1. Some respondents reported a combination of different Aboriginal/non-Aboriginal origins. These combinations of Aboriginal responses are counted under each relevant Aboriginal group. Therefore, the sum of the responses is greater than the total population reporting an Aboriginal ancestry. 2. This category includes 1,002,675 people who provided Aboriginal ancestry and 13,660 people who reported that they are registered but did not indicate any Aboriginal origins. 3. Some Indian reserves and settlements were incompletely enumerated during the 1991 Census due to the fact that on some Indian reserves or settlements, enumeration was not permitted or was interrupted before it could be completed. Some Indian reserves and settlements were enumerated late or the quality of the collected data was considered inadequate. These geographic areas (a total of 78) are called incompletely enumerated Indian reserves and Indian settlements. Data for 1991 are therefore not available for the incompletely enumerated reserves and settlements and are not included in the tabulations. Because of missing data, users are cautioned that for the affected geographic areas, comparisons between 1986 and 1991 are not exact. While for higher level geographic areas (Canada, provinces, census metropolitan areas and census agglomerations) the impact of missing data is very small, the impact can be significant for smaller areas, where the affected reserves and settlements account for a higher proportion of the population. 4. Total is derived by adding the single and multiple response columns of the population with Aboriginal origins. There is no double counting of the population in this total. 5. Refers to respondents who reported more than one ancestry. The sum of multiple response columns for each Aboriginal group is greater than the total population with Aboriginal origins who reported multiple ancestry. 6. All characteristics exclude institutional residents and are based on weighted sample data (20%). 7. Includes loss.

★ 944 ★

Social and Economic Conditions

Employment Equity in Saskatchewan

"Saskatchewan Metis are being left by the wayside by current employment equity programs says MSS President Gerald Morin....

"Morin presented the case for hiring more Metis during Saskatchewan Human Rights Commission Hearings on September 28 [1993].

"'Under employment equity programs, the proportion of Aboriginal people in the work force has increased from about 2.6 percent to 2.9 percent. At that rate of change, it would take 150 years to achieve the employment equity targets,' he told the commission.

"Saskatchewan Natives make up about 15 percent of the total provincial population."

Source: Campbell, Jeff. "Metis underrepresented in hiring says Morin." *New Breed Magazine* (October 1993), p. 12.

★ 945 ★

Social and Economic Conditions

Native Unemployment in Canada

"...figures released [by Statistics Canada] on September 20 [1993], show Native unemployment was 25 percent in 1991 compared with 10 percent across Canada. The survey showed unemployment among Metis was 22 percent, the lowest rate among Native groups, with Indians on reserves suffering 31 percent unemployment."

Source: "Native unemployment more than double national rate." *New Breed Magazine* (October 1993), p. 6.

★ 946 ★

Social and Economic Conditions

Industry Employment of the Aboriginal Population, 1991

Data show number of persons in each category for persons age 15 years and older, for both sexes. Figures are based on 20-percent sample data from the Canadian 1991 Census. Industry divisions are based on 1980 [Canadian] industrial classification.

Characteristics	Population with Aboriginal origins and/or Indian Registration			Population with Aboriginal origins[4]	Population with North American Indian origins[1]		Population with Metis origins		Population with Inuit origins		Total Canadian population
	Total[2]	On Indian Reserve[3]	Off Indian Reserve[3]		Single responses	Multiple responses[5]	Single responses	Multiple responses[5]	Single responses	Multiple responses[5]	
Total population[6]	1,016,335	189,365	826,970	1,002,670	365,375	418,605	75,150	137,500	30,090	19,170	26,994,040
Persons of both sexes, age 15 and older[7]	462,475	63,205	399,270	455,535	143,085	211,225	32,700	66,780	12,810	9,730	15,509,255
Agricultural and related services	10,605	1,760	8,845	10,465	3,370	5,005	775	1,665	20	125	570,275
Fishing and trapping	5,425	2,090	3,330	5,340	3,150	965	395	410	335	240	56,625
Logging and forestry	10,100	2,850	7,250	9,950	4,695	3,295	1,100	1,230	40	110	117,835
Mining (incl. milling), quarrying, and oil well industries	8,490	530	7,960	8,435	2,030	3,670	1,080	1,715	220	210	202,300
Manufacturing	47,700	3,365	44,330	46,925	12,515	25,940	2,820	6,120	410	860	2,235,630
Construction	35,630	4,945	30,685	35,125	11,460	14,835	3,500	5,355	945	550	1,005,280
Transportation and storage	18,720	1,660	17,060	18,465	4,695	8,990	1,650	3,045	530	482	620,645
Communication and other utilities	13,210	920	12,290	13,095	2,750	7,090	860	1,905	650	415	507,150
Wholesale trade	14,060	415	13,645	13,945	2,585	8,125	760	2,660	185	380	653,340
Retail trade	53,275	3,995	49,280	52,555	12,415	27,410	3,335	8,605	1,740	1,385	2,039,380
Finance and insurance	9,455	235	9,225	9,340	1,760	5,695	460	1,505	60	270	609,265
Real estate operator and insurance agent industries	4,695	140	4,555	4,630	825	2,595	345	850	135	155	252,930
Business services	18,050	540	17,510	17,840	3,305	11,090	980	2,985	190	425	869,300
Government services	70,160	24,905	45,260	69,195	35,625	20,460	4,090	7,075	3,460	1,245	1,200,295
Educational services	27,515	5,390	22,125	27,040	9,570	11,845	1,525	3,860	1,215	640	1,051,435
Health and social services	38,615	3,810	34,805	37,845	11,655	17,825	2,650	5,855	910	805	1,371,325

[Continued]

★ 946 ★

Industry Employment of the Aboriginal Population, 1991

[Continued]

Characteristics	Population with Aboriginal origins and/or Indian Registration			Population with Aboriginal origins[4]	Population with North American Indian origins[1]		Population with Metis origins		Population with Inuit origins		Total Canadian population
	Total[2]	On Indian Reserve[3]	Off Indian Reserve[3]		Single responses	Multiple responses[5]	Single responses	Multiple responses[5]	Single responses	Multiple responses[5]	
Accommodation, and food & beverages	43,440	3,260	40,180	42,595	12,080	19,580	3,940	7,115	835	760	1,070,405
Other service industries	33,310	2,385	30,925	32,755	8,585	16,795	2,415	4,800	930	680	1,075,825

Source: Statistics Canada. *Profile of Canada's Aboriginal Population.* Ottawa: Industry, Science and Technology Canada, 1995. 1991 Census of Canada. Catalogue number 94-325, pp. 20-21. Copyright, 1995. Used with permission. *Notes:* 1. Some respondents reported a combination of different Aboriginal/non-Aboriginal origins. These combinations of Aboriginal responses are counted under each relevant Aboriginal group. Therefore, the sum of the responses is greater than the total population reporting an Aboriginal ancestry. 2. This category includes 1,002,675 people who provided Aboriginal ancestry and 13,660 people who reported that they are registered but did not indicate any Aboriginal origins. 3. Some Indian reserves and settlements were incompletely enumerated during the 1991 Census due to the fact that on some Indian reserves or settlements, enumeration was not permitted or was interrupted before it could be completed. Some Indian reserves and settlements were enumerated late or the quality of the collected data was considered inadequate. These geographic areas (a total of 78) are called incompletely enumerated Indian reserves and Indian settlements. Data for 1991 are therefore not available for the incompletely enumerated reserves and settlements and are not included in the tabulations. Because of missing data, users are cautioned that for the affected geographic areas, comparisons between 1986 and 1991 are not exact. While for higher level geographic areas (Canada, provinces, census metropolitan areas and census agglomerations) the impact of missing data is very small, the impact can be significant for smaller areas, where the affected reserves and settlements account for a higher proportion of the population. 4. Total is derived by adding the single and multiple response columns of the population with Aboriginal origins. There is no double counting of the population in this total. 5. Refers to respondents who reported more than one ancestry. The sum of multiple response columns for each Aboriginal group is greater than the total population with Aboriginal origins who reported multiple ancestry. 6. All characteristics exclude institutional residents and are based on weighted sample data (20%). 7. Population age 15 and older who worked in 1990 or 1991.

★ 947 ★

Social and Economic Conditions

Labor Status of the Aboriginal Population, 1991

Data show number of persons in each category for persons age 15 years and older, for both sexes. Figures are based on 20-percent sample data from the Canadian 1991 Census.

Characteristics	Population with Aboriginal origins and/or Indian Registration			Population with Aboriginal origins[4]	Population with North American Indian origins[1]		Population with Metis origins		Population with Inuit origins		Total Canadian population
	Total[2]	On Indian Reserve[3]	Off Indian Reserve[3]		Single responses	Multiple responses[5]	Single responses	Multiple responses[5]	Single responses	Multiple responses[5]	
Total population[6]	1,016,335	189,365	826,970	1,002,670	365,375	418,605	75,150	137,500	30,090	19,170	26,994,040
Persons of both sexes, age 15 and older	651,290	117,295	533,995	641,005	239,330	263,225	50,630	84,275	18,315	11,925	21,304,735
In the labor force	418,565	54,710	363,855	412,335	126,325	195,535	29,265	60,895	10,302	8,875	14,474,940
Employed	337,500	37,900	299,600	332,575	92,065	167,660	21,795	51,605	7,865	7,470	13,005,500
Unemployed	81,065	16,810	64,255	79,765	34,255	27,875	7,470	9,285	2,455	1,410	1,469,440
Not in the labor force	232,725	62,585	170,140	228,670	113,005	67,690	21,365	23,380	7,995	3,050	6,829,795
Unemployment rate (percent)	19.4	30.7	17.7	19.3	27.1	14.3	25.5	15.2	23.8	15.9	10.2
Participation rate (percent)	64.3	46.6	68.1	64.3	52.8	74.3	57.8	72.3	56.3	74.4	67.9
Experienced labor force	400,050	49,345	350,705	394,175	116,500	190,750	27,575	59,255	9,790	8,630	14,220,230
Worked in 1990 or 1991	462,475	63,205	399,270	455,530	143,085	211,225	32,695	66,785	12,810	9,730	15,509,250
Did not work in 1990 or 1991	188,815	54,090	134,725	185,470	96,245	52,000	17,935	17,490	5,505	2,195	5,795,485

[Continued]

★947★

Labor Status of the Aboriginal Population, 1991
[Continued]

Characteristics	Population with Aboriginal origins and/or Indian Registration			Population with Aboriginal origins[4]	Population with North American Indian origins[1]		Population with Metis origins		Population with Inuit origins		Total Canadian population
	Total[2]	On Indian Reserve[3]	Off Indian Reserve[3]		Single responses	Multiple responses[5]	Single responses	Multiple responses[5]	Single responses	Multiple responses[5]	
Percent who worked in 1990 or 1991[7]	71.0	53.9	74.8	71.1	59.8	80.2	64.6	79.2	69.9	81.6	72.8

Source: Statistics Canada. *Profile of Canada's Aboriginal Population.* Ottawa: Industry, Science and Technology Canada, 1995. 1991 Census of Canada. Catalogue number 94-325, pp. 20-21. Copyright, 1995. Used with permission. *Notes:* 1. Some respondents reported a combination of different Aboriginal/non-Aboriginal origins. These combinations of Aboriginal responses are counted under each relevant Aboriginal group. Therefore, the sum of the responses is greater than the total population reporting an Aboriginal ancestry. 2. This category includes 1,002,675 people who provided Aboriginal ancestry and 13,660 people who reported that they are registered but did not indicate any Aboriginal origins. 3. Some Indian reserves and settlements were incompletely enumerated during the 1991 Census due to the fact that on some Indian reserves or settlements, enumeration was not permitted or was interrupted before it could be completed. Some Indian reserves and settlements were enumerated late or the quality of the collected data was considered inadequate. These geographic areas (a total of 78) are called incompletely enumerated Indian reserves and Indian settlements. Data for 1991 are therefore not available for the incompletely enumerated reserves and settlements and are not included in the tabulations. Because of missing data, users are cautioned that for the affected geographic areas, comparisons between 1986 and 1991 are not exact. While for higher level geographic areas (Canada, provinces, census metropolitan areas and census agglomerations) the impact of missing data is very small, the impact can be significant for smaller areas, where the affected reserves and settlements account for a higher proportion of the population. 4. Total is derived by adding the single and multiple response columns of the population with Aboriginal origins. There is no double counting of the population in this total. 5. Refers to respondents who reported more than one ancestry. The sum of multiple response columns for each Aboriginal group is greater than the total population with Aboriginal origins who reported multiple ancestry. 6. All characteristics exclude institutional residents and are based on weighted sample data (20%). 7. Percentage who worked in 1990 or 1991 is derived by dividing those who worked in 1990 or 1991 by the population age 15 and older (excluding institutional residents).

★948★
Social and Economic Conditions

Work Status of the Aboriginal Population, 1991

Data show number of persons in each category for persons age 15 years and older, for both sexes. Figures are based on 20-percent sample data from the Canadian 1991 Census. Persons who worked full-year, full-time worked 49-52 weeks in 1990, mostly full-time. Persons who worked part year or part-time worked 49-52 weeks in 1990, mostly part-time, or worked less than 49 weeks total.

Characteristics	Population with Aboriginal origins and/or Indian Registration			Population with Aboriginal origins[4]	Population with North American Indian origins[1]		Population with Metis origins		Population with Inuit origins		Total Canadian population
	Total[2]	On Indian Reserve[3]	Off Indian Reserve[3]		Single responses	Multiple responses[5]	Single responses	Multiple responses[5]	Single responses	Multiple responses[5]	
Total population[6]	1,016,335	189,365	826,970	1,002,670	365,375	418,605	75,150	137,500	30,090	19,170	26,994,040
Worked full year, full-time	170,230	16,155	154,075	167,900	42,350	89,760	10,265	25,805	3,850	4,140	7,718,780
Avg. employment income ($)	28,755	21,787	29,485	28,796	25,291	30,806	25,767	29,256	27,880	32,756	33,714
Standard error	88	213	94	89	151	125	328	270	329	651	21
Worked part year or part-time	246,110	37,160	208,955	242,305	80,305	106,150	18,000	35,635	8,025	5,045	6,752,260
Avg. employment income ($)	10,769	8,084	11,247	10,765	9,603	11,751	10,377	11,122	8,275	11,161	14,430
Standard error	52	100	58	52	88	82	171	141	146	344	15
Composition of total income[7]											
Total (%)	100.0	100.0	100.0	100.0	100.0	100.0	100.0	100.0	100.0	100.0	100.0
Employment (%)	78.30	59.82	80.68	78.36	67.99	84.22	71.83	82.53	76.28	85.88	77.78
Govt. transfer payments (%)	17.92	37.78	15.36	17.88	28.87	11.61	24.83	13.73	21.64	10.67	11.42
Other income (%)	3.78	2.40	3.95	3.76	3.14	4.17	3.34	3.75	2.08	3.45	10.80

Source: Statistics Canada. *Profile of Canada's Aboriginal Population.* Ottawa: Industry, Science and Technology Canada, 1995. 1991 Census of Canada. Catalogue number 94-325, pp. 20-21. Copyright, 1995. Used with permission. *Notes:* 1. Some respondents reported a combination of different Aboriginal/non-Aboriginal origins. These combinations of Aboriginal responses are counted under each relevant Aboriginal group. Therefore, the sum of the responses is greater than the total population reporting an Aboriginal ancestry. 2. This category includes 1,002,675 people who provided Aboriginal ancestry and 13,660 people who reported that they are registered but did not indicate any Aboriginal origins. 3. Some Indian reserves and settlements were incompletely enumerated during the 1991 Census due to the fact that on some Indian reserves or settlements, enumeration was not permitted or was interrupted before it could be completed. Some Indian reserves and settlements were enumerated late or the quality of the collected data was considered inadequate. These geographic areas (a total of 78) are called incompletely enumerated Indian reserves and Indian settlements. Data for 1991 are therefore not available for the incompletely enumerated reserves and settlements and are not included in the tabulations. Because of missing data, users are cautioned that for the affected geographic areas, comparisons between 1986 and 1991 are not exact. While for higher level geographic areas (Canada, provinces, census metropolitan areas and census agglomerations) the impact of missing data is very small, the impact can be significant for smaller areas, where the affected reserves and settlements account for a higher proportion of the population. 4. Total is derived by adding the single and multiple response columns of the population with Aboriginal origins. There is no double counting of the population in this total. 5. Refers to respondents who reported more than one ancestry. The sum of multiple response columns for each Aboriginal group is greater than the total population with Aboriginal origins who reported multiple ancestry. 6. All characteristics exclude institutional residents and are based on weighted sample data (20%). 7. Totals may not add to 100% due to rounding.

★ 949 ★

Social and Economic Conditions

Aboriginal Opinions on Community Problems

Results show number of persons age 15 and older endorsing each method as a solution to problems in aboriginal communities. Data are based on a survey of 625,710 aboriginals in 1991.

Solution	Persons endorsing
More policing	31,015
Family counseling	30,780
Improved community services	27,610
More employment	21,228
Self-government	4,240
Return to traditional lifestyle	3,385

Source: Johnson, William. "Out of touch; Indian leaders are building on sand." *The (Montreal) Gazette* (30 June 1993), p. B3. Primary source: Statistics Canada.

Government Relations

★ 950 ★

First Nations Membership of the Aboriginal Population, 1991

Membership is shown for the 49 major groups of First Nations. These include a total of 601 subdivisions, known as Indian Bands/ Frist Nations. Data show number of persons in each category. Figures are based on 20-percent sample data from the Canadian 1991 Census.

Characteristics	Population with Aboriginal origins and/or Indian Registration			Population with Aboriginal origins[4]	Population with North American Indian origins[1]		Population with Metis origins		Population with Inuit origins		Total Canadian population
	Total[2]	On Indian Reserve[3]	Off Indian Reserve[3]		Single responses	Multiple responses[5]	Single responses	Multiple responses[5]	Single responses	Multiple responses[5]	
Total population[6]	1,016,335	189,365	826,970	1,002,670	365,375	418,605	75,150	137,500	30,090	19,170	26,994,040
First Nations membership[7]											
Cree	119,810	68,050	51,760	117,195	99,565	13,130	3,610	5,670	55	120	119,810
Ojibway (Chippewa)	76,335	35,105	41,230	73,350	59,460	10,695	2,160	2,685	100	85	76,335
Micmac	14,625	9,545	5,080	13,650	11,775	1,690	115	80	15	15	14,625
Montagnais-Naskapi	12,025	7,650	4,385	11,500	10,020	890	475	210	15	10	12,030
Blackfoot	11,670	7,285	4,390	11,470	10,615	780	55	80	-	10	11,670
Dakota	10,040	6,425	3,615	9,755	8,960	650	105	135	10	-	10,035
Halkomelem (Cowichan)	9,360	6,240	3,120	8,885	7,650	1,210	30	80	10	-	9,360
Chipewyan	9,350	4,685	4,665	9,210	7,185	1,425	470	870	50	20	9,350
Mohawk	9,305	235	9,070	8,130	5,610	2,390	75	95	-	45	9,305
Carrier	6,910	3,670	3,240	6,520	5,665	760	20	85	20	-	6,915
Algonquin	5,780	2,420	3,360	5,270	3,720	1,160	230	270	-	-	5,785
Slave	5,120	1,700	3,415	5,070	4,420	445	130	205	25	10	5,120
Shuswap	4,920	2,960	1,965	4,745	3,925	805	10	45	-	-	4,925
Gitskan	4,560	2,495	2,060	4,395	3,715	670	-	45	-	10	4,560
Coast Tsimshian	4,550	1,945	2,600	4,285	3,640	600	20	50	10	10	4,545
Nootka	4,325	2,000	2,325	4,100	3,560	485	45	25	-	-	4,325
Kwakiutl	4,120	1,875	2,245	3,890	3,150	710	20	45	-	-	4,120
Ntlakapamux (Thompson)	3,925	1,990	1,945	3,750	2,925	780	25	30	-	-	3,925
Nishga	3,635	1,510	2,120	3,470	3,035	420	-	55	-	-	3,635
Attikamek (Tete-de Boule)	3,420	3,045	370	3,400	3,290	80	25	25	-	-	3,420
Dogrib	2,845	10	2,840	2,830	2,515	205	80	110	-	10	2,845
Lillooet	2,570	1,200	1,370	2,500	2,100	375	20	10	-	-	2,570

[Continued]

★ 950 ★

First Nations Membership of the Aboriginal Population, 1991
[Continued]

Characteristics	Population with Aboriginal origins and/or Indian Registration			Population with Aboriginal origins[4]	Population with North American Indian origins[1]		Population with Metis origins		Population with Inuit origins		Total Canadian population
	Total[2]	On Indian Reserve[3]	Off Indian Reserve[3]		Single responses	Multiple responses[5]	Single responses	Multiple responses[5]	Single responses	Multiple responses[5]	
Okanagan	2,275	1,510	760	2,185	1,720	460	-	30	-	-	2,275
Haida	2,270	1,015	1,250	2,165	1,680	470	10	25	-	20	2,270
Squamish	2,030	1,130	900	1,970	1,665	305	-	10	-	-	2,030
Kutchin (Loucheux)	1,995	10	1,985	1,970	1,550	320	65	80	15	90	1,990
Straits Salish	1,900	1,445	455	1,810	1,695	110	-	-	-	-	1,900
Malecite	1,705	905	795	1,510	1,055	445	10	10	-	-	1,705
Chilcotin	1,705	1,020	685	1,650	1,550	95	10	-	-	-	1,705
Tutchone	1,160	125	1,485	1,575	1,150	405	15	35	10	10	1,610
Heiltsuk (Bella Bella)	1,580	1,040	540	1,520	1,375	145	10	-	-	-	1,575
Huron	1,450	-	1,450	1,200	715	330	125	55	-	10	1,455
Beaver	1,405	740	665	1,365	1,055	190	95	90	10	10	1,400
Tahltan	1,330	285	1,050	1,275	1,000	245	15	15	10	-	1,335
Hare	1,180	10	1,170	1,175	995	130	30	85	10	10	1,180
Tlingit	1,170	260	905	1,105	740	325	15	30	15	20	1,170
Bella Coola	980	655	325	960	830	130	-	-	-	-	980
Haisla	955	520	430	915	790	125	10	-	-	-	955
Abenaki	945	230	715	810	485	225	85	35	-	-	945
Sarcee (Sarsi)	810	685	125	785	720	65	-	10	-	-	810
Comox	800	170	635	765	485	265	15	20	-	10	800
Kaska	705	130	575	670	510	145	10	-	10	10	700
Sekani	630	290	335	615	525	85	15	-	-	-	630
Delaware	590	335	250	560	485	70	-	-	-	-	590
Kutenai (Kootenay)	565	340	225	525	430	95	-	-	-	-	570
Sechelt	565	365	205	515	425	90	-	10	-	-	565
Han	495	10	485	480	270	205	10	10	-	10	500
Potawatomi	85	-	80	80	10	70	-	-	-	-	80

Source: Statistics Canada. *Profile of Canada's Aboriginal Population.* Ottawa: Industry, Science and Technology Canada, 1995. 1991 Census of Canada. Catalogue number 94-325, pp. 12-15. Copyright, 1995. Used with permission. *Notes:* 1. Some respondents reported a combination of different Aboriginal/non-Aboriginal origins. These combinations of Aboriginal responses are counted under each relevant Aboriginal group. Therefore, the sum of the responses is greater than the total population reporting an Aboriginal ancestry. 2. This category includes 1,002,675 people who provided Aboriginal ancestry and 13,660 people who reported that they are registered but did not indicate any Aboriginal origins. 3. Some Indian reserves and settlements were incompletely enumerated during the 1991 Census due to the fact that on some Indian reserves or settlements, enumeration was not permitted or was interrupted before it could be completed. Some Indian reserves and settlements were enumerated late or the quality of the collected data was considered inadequate. These geographic areas (a total of 78) are called incompletely enumerated Indian reserves and Indian settlements. Data for 1991 are therefore not available for the incompletely enumerated reserves and settlements and are not included in the tabulations. Because of missing data, users are cautioned that for the affected geographic areas, comparisons between 1986 and 1991 are not exact. While for higher level geographic areas (Canada, provinces, census metropolitan areas and census agglomerations) the impact of missing data is very small, the impact can be significant for smaller areas, where the affected reserves and settlements account for a higher proportion of the population. 4. Total is derived by adding the single and multiple response columns of the population with Aboriginal origins. There is no double counting of the population in this total. 5. Refers to respondents who reported more than one ancestry. The sum of multiple response columns for each Aboriginal group is greater than the total population with Aboriginal origins who reported multiple ancestry. 6. All characteristics exclude institutional residents and are based on weighted sample data (20%). 7. Some First Nations may be under-reported due to one or more incompletely enumerated Indian reserves or settlements.

Listing of Sources

The following listing shows all sources used in *SRNNA-2* in the format in which the sources appear referenced under each table. In addition to these sources, the originators of the data frequently cited additional sources on which they based their work. Those sources are shown with each table but, because of the diversity of the citations, have not been extracted and included here.

1987 Economic Censuses, Survey of Minority-Owned Business Enterprises: Asian Americans, American Indians, and Other Minorities, U.S. Department of Commerce, Bureau of the Census, MB87-3, 1991. Tables: 706-707, 709-714

1987 Economic Censuses, Survey of Minority-Owned Business Enterprises: Summary, U.S. Department of Commerce, Bureau of the Census, 1991. Tables: 681, 683-684, 689-691, 693-704

1994 Statistical Abstract of the United States on CD-ROM [machine-readable datafiles]. CD-8A-94. Washington, DC: U.S. Department of Commerce, Economics and Statistics Administration, Bureau of the Census, Data User Services Division, January 1995. Tables: 109, 226, 277, 380, 433

Advisory Commission on Intergovernment Relations. *Cigarette Tax Evasion: A Second Look*. Washington, DC: ACIR, March 1985, Table 3-9. Table: 802

Alaska Business Monthly (June 1992). Table: 678

American Demographics (January 1992). Table: 687

Anderson, D. Michael and Gregory M. Christenson, "Ethnic breakdown of AIDS related knowledge and attitudes from the National Adolescent Student Health Survey," *Journal of Health Education*, Vol. 22, No. 1, January/February 1991. Tables: 459-462

Anderson, Mary. "Census figures misleading: Navajo claim to be largest tribe." *Indian Country Today* (3 December 1992). Table: 111

Annual Report to Congress: Indian Civil Service Retirement Act, P.L. 96-135, FY 89. Tables: 516-518

Anquoe, Bunty. "1990 Census shows Indians still high in unemployment." *Lakota Times* (12 August 1992). Table: 574

Atkins, Elizabeth. "Racial bias still widespread in the media, study finds." *Detroit News* (24 July 1994). Tables: 534-536

Aubry, Jack. "AIDS hits aboriginals hard." *Calgary Herald* (10 May 1993). Table: 938

Bachman, Ronet. "An analysis of American Indian homicide: a test of social disorganization and economic deprivation at the reservation county level." *Journal of Research in Crime and Delinquency* 28, no. 4 (November 1991). Table: 899

Barnsley, Paul. "Chiefs Assembly wants language policies." *Tekawennake* (1 March 1995). Table: 936

Baskerville, Dawn M. "Breaking through the glass ceiling," *Black Enterprise* 22 (August 1991). Table: 679

"Black entrepeneurship." *Wall Street Journal* (3 April 1992). Tables: 685-686

Bureau of Indian Affairs. Office of Public Affairs. Tables: 822-823

Cage, Mary Crystal. "Fewer Students Get Bachelor's Degrees in 4 Years, Study Finds". *Chronicle of Higher Education* (15 July 1992). Table: 341

Campbell, Jeff. "Census takers way out of line say Metis." *New Breed Magazine* (April 1993). Table: 928

Campbell, Jeff. "Metis underrepresented in hiring says Morin." *New Breed Magazine* (October 1993). Table: 944

Carter, James and Dominique de Menil. "USA can't point finger at others on human rights." *USA TODAY* (10 December 1992). Table: 223

Census of Population and Housing, 1990: Summary Tape File 1 on CD-ROM, U.S. Bureau of the Census, Washington, D.C. 1991. Tables: 114-115, 506

Census of Population and Housing, 1990: Summary Tape File 3C on CD-ROM [machine-readable datafiles]. Prepared by the Bureau of the Census. Washington, DC: The Bureau, 1992. Tables: 153-220, 227-230, 232-271, 297-308, 311-318, 323-334, 408-423, 538-545, 558-573, 585-604, 606-609, 619-634, 638-653, 656-663, 666-673, 868-875

Chavez, Linda. "Why make it easier to receive welfare?" *USA TODAY* (8 June 1994). Table: 675

Chronicle of Higher Education Almanac (1 September 1994). Table: 346

Chronicle of Higher Education Almanac (7 September 1994). Table: 335

Deloria, Jr., Vine. *Behind the Trail of Broken Treaties: An Indian Declaration of Independence.* Austin, TX: University of Texas Press, pp. 166-168. Published with permission. Table: 806

"The demographics of school board service." *American School Board Journal* (January 1993). Table: 366

"Federal diversity." *Manpower Comments* (January/February 1994). Table: 844

Fiddler-Berteig, Ona. "Aboriginal women: uniting against family violence." *New Breed* (April 1990). Table: 930

Frankel, Bruce. "Change looms large for troubled NYC police force." *USA TODAY* (7 October 1992). Table: 910

"Gender gap continues to close on S.A.T.'s." *New York Times (National Edition)* (25 August 1994). Table: 347

Grobsmith, Elizabeth S. and Beth R. Ritter, "The Ponca Tribe of Nebraska: the process of restoration of a federally terminated tribe," *Human Organization* vol. 51, No. 1, 1992. Table: 100

Hale, Alma. "Public lands legislation: drowning in a sea of bills." *AMC Journal* (August 1992). Tables: 840-841

Halmo, David B., Richard W. Stoffle, and Michael J. Evans. "Paitu Nanasuagaindu Pahonupi (Three Sacred Valleys): cultural significance of Gosiute, Paiute, and Ute plants." *Human Organization* vol. 52, No. 2, 1993. Table: 430

Helin, Calvin. "First Nations business." *New Breed* (January 1992). Table: 931

"Heterosexually acquired AIDS - United States, 1993." *JAMA*, vol. 271, no. 13 (6 April 1994). Table: 463

Indian Health Service, Maternal and Child Health Bureau, and the Robert Wood Johnson Foundation. *The State of Native American Youth Health, February, 1992*. Tables: 279-286, 289-296, 491-493

''Indians will ask Clinton to live up to expectations.'' *Detroit News* (24 April 1994). Table: 803

Jamieson, Ron. "Mutual opportunities through partnership." *Canadian Business Review* vol. 21, no. 2 (Summer 1994). Table: 939

Johnson, Dirk. "Economies come to life on Indian reservations." *The New York Times (National)* (3 July, 1994). Table: 760

Johnson, William. "Out of touch; Indian leaders are building on sand." *The (Montreal) Gazette* (30 June 1993). Table: 949

Jones, Lee R., and others, *The 1990 Science Report Card: NAEP's Assessment of Fourth, Eighth, and Twelfth Graders*, Prepared by Educational Testing Service under contract with the National Center for Education Statistics, Office of Educational Research and Improvement, U.S. Department of Education, March, 1992. Tables: 349-356

Jones, Richard. Congressional Research Service. *American Indian Policy: Background, Nature, History, Current Issues, Future Trends, Congressional Research Service Report No. 87227*. Washington, DC: CRS, 1980. Table: 101

Kennedy, Richard D. M.S. and Roger E. Deapen, Ph.D., "Differences between Oklahoma Indian infant mortality and other races," *Public Health Reports* Vol. 106, No. 1 (January-February 1991). Tables: 478-482

Lam, Tina. "Chippewa Inc." *Detroit Free Press* (27 March 1995). Table: 715

LeBlanc, Larry. "Canada's aboriginal musicians seek mainstream recognition." *Billboard* vol. 106, no. 36 (3 September 1994). Table: 940

Lewin, David I. "Washington window: across the gender divide." *Mechanical Engineering* (October 1993). Table: 533

Lewin, Tamar. "Study points to increase in tolerance of ethnicity." *The New York Times* (8 January 1992). Table: 431

Maguire, Kathleen and Ann L. Pastore (eds.). U.S. Department of Justice. U.S. Bureau of Justice Statistics. *Sourcebook of Criminal Justice Statistics 1993*. Washington, DC: U.S. Government Printing Office, 1994. Tables: 890-897, 900, 903, 908

Manpower Comments (December 1993). Tables: 396-398

Mauro, Tony. "After 199 executions, nation still divided." *USA TODAY* (28 April 1993). Tables: 901-902

Mauro, Tony. "Last gasp scramble to clear up backlogs." *USA TODAY* (27 June 1994). Table: 866

McCauley, Elfrieda. "Native American school libraries: a survey." *School Library Journal* (April 1991). Table: 361

Mental Health, United States, 1994. Manderscheid, R.W. and Sonnenschein, M.A., eds. DHHS Pub. No. (SMA)94-3000. Washington, DC: U.S. Government Printing Office, 1994. Table: 488

Miller, Bruce G. "Women and tribal politics: is there a gender gap in Indian elections?" *American Indian Quarterly* (Winter 1994). Table: 888-889

"Minorities in government." *Manpower Comments* (April/May 1994). Table: 842

"Minority-Owned Firms by Gender." *Minority-Owned Businesses*. Table: 682

"Minority-Owned Firms by Industry Division: 1987." *Minority-Owned Businesses*. Table: 688

National Advisory Council on Indian Education. *Toward the Year 2000: Listening to the Voice of Native America*, 17th Annual Report to the United States Congress, Fiscal Year 1990. Tables: 368-369, 371-373, 385, 388, 391

National Center for Health Statistics. *Health, United States, 1993*. Hyattsville, MD: Public Health Service, May 1994. Tables: 436-437, 439, 443-445, 458, 476, 525

National Commission on American Indian, Alaska Native, and Native Hawaiian Housing. *Building the Future: A Blueprint for Change: "By Our Homes You Will Know Us."* Washington, DC: 1992. Tables: 674, 864-865, 876

National Science Board. *Science & Engineering Indicators—1993* (NSB 93-1). Washington, DC: U.S. Government Printing Office, 1993. Tables: 365, 382, 393-395, 537

"Native unemployment more than double national rate." *New Breed Magazine* (October 1993). Table: 945

"The next throw." *The Economist* (18 March 1995). Table: 759

Office of the Federal Register. National Archives and Records Administration. *Code of Federal Regulations: Indians*, Title 25, Revised as of April 1, 1994. Tables: 84-85

Office of the Federal Register. National Archives and Records Administration. *Code of Federal Regulations: Indians*, Title 25, Revised as of April 1, 1991. Table: 836

Peak, Ken. "Policing and crime in Indian Country: history, issues, challenges." *Journal of Contemporary Criminal Justice* vol. 10, no. 2 (May 1994). Table: 898

Peritz, Ingrid. "More Quebecers claiming aboriginal roots; Statistics Canada cites greater pride in Indian heritage for trend." *The Gazette (Montreal)* (31 March 1993). Table: 922

Peterson, Dan E., MD, MPH and others. "Behavioral risk factors of Chippewa Indians living on Wisconsin reservations." *Public Health Reports* vol. 109, no. 6 (November/December 1994). Table: 526

Phillips, Leslie. "New welfare push, same old obstacles." *USA TODAY* (12 January 1995). Table: 677

"Ranking of total combined non-white population of states, 1990," *Black Issues in Higher Education* vol. 8 (29 August 1991). Table: 108

Report on the Americas Volume XXV, No. 3, (December 1991). Table: 110

Richards, Rhonda. "SBA squeezes minority merchants: commission wants change." *USA TODAY* (17 June 1992). Table: 680

Rith-Najarian, Stephen J. MD and others. "Reducing amputations caused by diabetes in American Indians: a simple strategy." *The (IHS) Provider* (February 1993). Table: 469

Russell, George. *The American Indian in Question.* Phoenix, AZ: Thunderbird Enterprises, Copyright 1992, pp. 13-18. Published with permission. Tables: 804-805

Schwartz, John. "Preserving endangered speeches: researchers begin an aggressive effort to keep Native American languages alive." *The Washington Post National Weekly Edition* (21-27 March 1995). Table: 407

Seeseequasis, Paul. "Home and Native lands: aboriginal workers & unions." *Our Times* (August/September 1994). Table: 941

Shanker, Thom and Linnet Myers. "Frequency of hate crimes in U.S. alarms FBI director." *Chicago Tribune* (29 June 1994). Table: 905

Snipp, C. Matthew. *American Indians: The First of This Land.* New York, NY: Russell Sage Foundation, p. 22. Published by permission. Table: 83

Staimer, Marcia. "USA snapshots: states with the most Native Americans." *USA TODAY* (27 November 1992). Table: 112

Stanton, Mark J. "Economic benefits: study shows job and tourism growth." *New Mexico Business Journal* vol. 17, no. 12 (December 1994). Table: 768

Statistics Canada. *Canada's Aboriginal Population by Census Subdivisions and Census Metropolitan Areas: Aboriginal Data.* Ottawa: Industry, Science and Technology Canada, 1994. 1991 Census of Canada. Catalogue number 94-326, p. 100. Copyright, 1995.Used with permission. Table: 920

Statistics Canada. *Profile of Canada's Aboriginal Population.* Ottawa: Industry, Science and Technology Canada, 1995. 1991 Census of Canada. Catalogue number 94-325, p. 8. Copyright, 1995. Used with permission. Tables: 918, 923, 929, 932-935, 937, 942-943, 946-948, 950

Statistics Canada. *The Daily* (30 March 1993). Tables: 919, 921, 924-927

"Students of color earn more Ph.Ds." *Higher Education & National Affairs, ACE* (10 January 1994). Table: 389

Thornton, Russell. *American Indian Holocaust and Survival: A Population History Since 1492*. Norman, OK University of Oklahoma Press, 1987, p. 26. Published by permission. Table: 1-8, 24-25, 38-51, 80-82, 221-222, 224

Thornton, Russell. *We Shall Live Again: The 1870 and 1890 Ghost Dance Movements as Demographic Revitalization*. New York, NY: Cambridge University Press, 1986, p. 22. Published by permission. Table: 11, 16, 23

Toomey, Kathleen E., Alisa G. Oberschelp, and Joel R. Greenspan, "Sexually transmitted diseases and Native Americans: trends in reported gonorrhea and syphilis morbidity, 1984-88," *Public Health Reports* Vol. 104, No. 6, (November/December 1989). Tables: 501-504

Truesdell, Dr. Leon E. U.S. Department of Commerce. Bureau of the Census. Fifteenth Census of the United States: 1930, *The Indian Population of the United States and Alaska*. Washington, DC: U.S. Government Printing Office, 1937. Tables: 12-15, 17-18, 21-22, 29-30, 31-37, 64-65, 72-73, 78-79, 90-94

U.S. Bureau of the Census, Subject Reports, PC80-2-1D, Part II, *American Indians, Eskimos, and Aleuts on Identified Reservations and in the Historic Areas of Oklahoma (Excluding Urbanized Areas)*, U.S. Government Printing Office, Washington, DC, 1986. Tables: 424-429

U.S. Bureau of the Census. *1990 Census of Population: Characteristics of American Indians by Tribe and Language*. CP3-7. Washington, DC: The Bureau, 1994. Tables: 117-152, 309-310, 321-322, 404-406, 546-557

U.S. Bureau of the Census. *Indian Population in the United States and Alaska, 1910*. Washington, DC: U.S. Government Printing Office, 1915. Tables: 10, 19-20, 26-28, 52-63, 66-71, 74-77, 86-89, 95-98

U.S. Bureau of the Census. *Statistical Abstract of the United States: 1992* (112th edition). Washington, DC: U.S. Government Printing Office, 1992. Table: 113, 692

U.S. Bureau of the Census. *Statistical Abstract of the United States, 1993*. (113th edition) Washington, DC: U.S. Government Printing Office, 1993. Table: 107

U.S. Department of Education. *A Profile of the American Eighth Grader*. Washington, DC: U.S. Department of Education, 1990. Tables: 272-273, 319

U.S. Department of Education. National Center for Education Statistics. *The Condition of Education 1994*. Washington, DC: U.S. Government Printing Office, 1994. Tables: 340, 342-343, 348, 360, 362, 381, 532

U.S. Department of Education. National Center for Education Statistics. Office of Educational Research and Improvement. *Digest of Education Statistics, 1994*. Lanham, MD: Bernan, November 1994. Tables: 320, 336-339, 344-345, 357-359, 363-364, 367, 374, 376, 379, 384, 386-387, 390, 392, 399-403

U.S. Department of Education. Office of Educational Research and Improvement. Postsecondary Education Statistics Division. *Trends in Racial/Ethnic Enrollment in Higher Education: Fall 1980 Through Fall 1990*. Washington, DC: U.S. Government Printing Office. Tables: 375, 377-378

U.S. Department of Energy. Energy Information Administration. Office of Coal, Nuclear, Electric, and Alternate Fuels. *Coal Data: A Reference*. Washington, DC: U.S. DOE, November 1991. Table: 770

U.S. Department of Health. Public Health Service. Indian Health Service. *Inpatient Summary Data for Indian Health Service Hospitals by Area and Facility October Through March, Fiscal Year 1994*. Rockville, MD: IHS, April 1994. Table: 514

U.S. Department of Health. Public Health Service. Indian Health Service. *Inpatient Summary Data for Tribally Operated Hospitals by Area and Facility October Through March, Fiscal Year 1994*. Rockville, MD: IHS, 6 June 1994. Table: 513

U.S. Department of Health and Human Services. National Center for Health Statistics. *Health, United States, 1993*. Hyattsville, MD: Public Health Service, May 1994. Table: 434

U.S. Department of Health and Human Services. Public Health Service. Alcohol, Drug Abuse, and Mental Health Administration. Office for Substance Abuse Prevention. *Breaking New Ground For American Indian and Alaska Native Youth: Program Summaries* (OSAP Technical Report-3). Rockville, MD: U.S. DHHS. Tables: 287-288, 495-497, 500

U.S. Department of Health and Human Services. Public Health Service. *Healthy People 2000*. Washington, DC: U.S. Government Printing Office, 1993,. Table: 466

U.S. Department of Health and Human Services. Public Health Service. Indian Health Service. Office of Planning, Evaluation, and Legislation. Division of Program Statistics. *Regional Differences in Indian Health - 1994*, Rockville, MD: U.S. Department of Health and Human Services, Public Health Service. Tables: 457, 475

U.S. Department of Health and Human Services. Public Health Service. Indian Health Service. Office of Planning, Evaluation, and Legislation. Division of Program Statistics. *Trends in Indian Health - 1993*, Rockville, MD: U.S. Department of Health and Human Services, Public Health Service. Tables: 432, 435, 438, 441-442, 446-455, 464-465, 467, 470-471, 473-474, 477, 483-487, 489-490, 494, 505, 507-512, 515, 519-524

U.S. Department of Health and Human Services. Public Health Service. Substance Abuse and Mental Health Services Administration. Office of Applied Studies. *National Drug and Alcoholism Treatment Unit Survey (NDATUS)*, 1991 Main Findings Report. DHHS Publication No. (SMA) 92-2007, 1993. Table: 528

U.S. Department of Health and Human Services. Public Health Service. Substance Abuse and Mental Health Services Administration. Office of Applied Studies. *State Resources and Services Related to Alcohol and Other Drug Problems, Fiscal Year 1992: An Analysis of State Alcohol and Drug Abuse Profile Data*. Prepared by the National Association of State Alcohol and Drug Abuse Directors, Incorporated. DHHS Publication No. (SMA) 94-2092. Rockville, MD: Department of Health and Human Services, 1994. Tables: 527, 529

U.S. Department of the Interior. Bureau of Indian Affairs. Unpublished data, 12 April 1994. Tables: 877-887

U.S. Department of the Interior. Bureau of Indian Affairs. *U.S. Indian Population (1962) and Land (1963)*. Washington, DC: U.S. Government Printing Office, November 1963. Table: 102-104

U.S. Department of the Interior. Bureau of Indian Affairs. Albuquerque Area Office. Division of Administration. *Fact Book*. U.S. Department of the Interior, February 1989. Table: 9, 99

U.S. Department of the Interior. Bureau of Indian Affairs. *Natural Resource Information System*. Tables: 824-834

U.S. Department of the Interior. Minerals Management Service. Royalty Management Program. *Mineral Revenues 1993: Report on Receipts from Federal and Indian Leases*. Washington, DC: Minerals Management Service. Tables: 771-801

U.S. Department of Justice. Bureau of Justice Statistics. *Correctional Populations in the United States, 1991* (NCJ-142729). Washington, DC: Bureau of Justice Statistics, August 1993. Table: 915

U.S. Department of Justice. Bureau of Justice Statistics. Office of Justice Programs. *Correctional Populations in the United States, 1989* (NCJ-130445). Washington, DC: U.S. Government Printing Office, October 1991. Table: 912

U.S. Department of Justice. Federal Bureau of Investigation. Criminal Justice Information Services Division. *Criminal Justice Information Services Uniform Crime Reports: Hate Crime - 1993*. Washington, DC: FBI, June 1994. Table: 904

U.S. Department of Justice. Office of Justice Programs. Bureau of Justice Statistics. *Sourcebook of Criminal Justice Statistics, 1990*. Washington, DC: U.S. Government Printing Office, 1991. Table: 907

U.S. Department of Justice. Office of Justice Programs. Office for Victims of Crime. *OVC Bulletin: Victim Programs to Serve Native Americans* (February 1992). Tables: 916-917

U.S. Equal Employment Opportunity Commission. *Job Patterns for Minorities and Women in Private Industry, 1993*. Washington, DC: U.S. Government Printing Office, 1994. Tables: 716-758

U.S. Equal Employment Opportunity Commission. *Job Patterns for Minorities and Women in State and Local Government, 1990*. Washington, DC: U.S. Government Printing Office, 1990. Tables: 848-857

U.S. General Accounting Office. *Affirmative Employment: Assessing Progress of EEO Groups in Key Federal Jobs Can Be Improved* GAO/GGD-93-65. Washington, DC: U.S. GAO (March 1993). Tables: 843, 845-847

U.S. General Accounting Office. *Diabetes: Status of the Disease Among American Indians, Blacks and Hispanics*. Washington, DC: U.S. GAO, 1992. Table: 468, 472

U.S. General Accounting Office. *Federal Affirmative Employment: Status of Women and Minority Representation in Federal Law Enforcement Occupations* (GAO/T-GGD-93-2). Washington, DC: U.S. GAO, (1 October 1992). Table: 909

U.S. General Accounting Office. *Food Stamp Program Provisions* (GAO/RCED-93-70R). Washington, DC: U.S. GAO, 1993. Table: 676

U.S. General Accounting Office. *Indian Health Service: Basic Service Mostly Available - Substance Abuse Problems Need Attention* (GAO/HRD-93-48). Washington, DC: U.S. GAO, 1993. Tables: 498-499

U.S. General Accounting Office. *Indian Programs: BIA and Indian Tribes Are Taking Action to Address Dam Safety Concerns* (GAO/RCED-92-50). Washington, DC: U.S. GAO, February, 1992. Table: 835

U.S. General Accounting Office. *Indian Programs: Profile of the Land Ownership at 12 Reservations* (GAO/RCED-92-96BR). Washington, DC: U.S. GAO, February 1992. Tables: 116, 807-821

U.S. Senate Committee on Indian Affairs and Committee on Agriculture. *Barriers to Participation in Food Stamp and Other Nutrition Programs of the Department of Agriculture by People Residing on Indian Lands*. 103rd Cong., 1st sess., 25 May 1993. Table: 655

U.S. Senate Committee on Indian Affairs. *Fiscal Year 1995 Budget*. 103rd Cong., 2nd sess., March 3, 9, 1994 and April 13, 1994. Washington, DC: U.S. Government Printing Office, 1994. Tables: 370, 858-859

U.S. Senate Committee on Indian Affairs. *Health Care Reform in Indian Country, and the American Health Care Security Act: Hearing Before the Committee on Indian Affairs*. 103rd Cong., 2nd sess. on S. 1757, 31 January 1994. Washington, DC: U.S. Government Printing Office, 1994. Table: 456

U.S. Senate Committee on Indian Affairs. *Indian Child Protection and Family Violence Prevention Act: Hearing Before the Committee on Indian Affairs*. 103rd Cong., 1st sess., (28 October 1993). Tables: 276, 278

U.S. Senate Committee on Indian Affairs. *Indian Housing and Related Facilities*. 103rd Cong., 1st. sess., 12 January 1993. Table: 665

U.S. Senate Committee on Indian Affairs. *Proposed Amendments to the American Indian Religious Freedom Act: Hearing Before the Committee on Indian Affairs*. 103rd Cong., 1st sess., 8 March 1993, Minneapolis, MN, pt. 3. Washington, DC: U.S. Government Printing Office, 1993. Tables: 906, 913-914

U.S. Senate Committee on Small Business. *Small Business Development in Indian Country*. 103rd Cong., 1st sess. on Small Business Development in Indian Country. Washington, DC: U.S. Government Printing Office (3 September 1993). Table: 575, 637

U.S. Senate Select Committee on Indian Affairs. *Gaming Activities on Indian Reservations and Lands*, S. Hrg. 100-341. Washington, DC: U.S. Government Printing Office, 1988. Table: 761

U.S. Senate Select Committee on Indian Affairs. *Implementation of the Indian Gaming Regulatory Act*, S. Hrg. 102-660, Pt. 2. Washington, DC: U.S. Government Printing Office, 1992. Tables: 764-767, 769

Usdansky, Margaret L. "A new U.S. workforce evolves: job shifts reflect progress of Hispanics and women." *USA TODAY* (29 January 1993). Table: 530-531

Usdansky, Margaret L. "California's mix offers a look at the future." *USA TODAY* (4 December 1992). Table: 225

Usdansky, Margaret L. "USA's decade of change: 'diverse' fits nation better than 'normal'." *USA TODAY* (29 May 1992). Table: 105

Vancura, Cliff. "USA Snapshots: reservations up the ante." *USA TODAY* (4 December 1992). Table: 762

Vilardo, Frank J. and others. U.S. Nuclear Regulatory Commission. Division of Safeguards and Transportation. Office of Nuclear Material Safety and Safeguards. *Survey of State and Tribal Emergency Response Capabilities for Radiological Transportation Incidents* (NRC FIN D1054). Washington, DC: U.S. NRC. Tables: 837-839

Vobejda, Barbara. "Birth rate among teenage girls declines slightly." *The Washington Post* (26 October 1994). Table: 440

Walke, Roger. *Federal Programs of Assistance to Native Americans: A Report Prepared for the Senate Select Committee on Indian Affairs of the United States Senate,* S. Prt. 102-62, Washington, DC: U.S. Government Printing Office, December 1991. Tables: 383, 860-863, 911

Weeks, George and Don Weeks. "Indian-run casinos produce jackpot for state, municipalities: they shared $17.6 million in first-year payouts under Indian Gaming Compact." *The Detroit News* (25 December 1994). Table: 763

Welch, William M. "Census ruling may remap politics." *USA TODAY* (10 August 1994). Table: 106

Wolf, Richard. "Speaker Foley's back and in top form." *USA TODAY* (7 December 1992). Table: 867

Woodward, Jeanne M. *America's Racial and Ethnic Groups: Their Housing in the Early Nineties*. Bureau of the Census. Current Housing Reports, Series H121/94-3. Washington, DC: U.S. Government Printing Office. Tables: 231, 274-275, 576-584, 605, 610-618, 635-636, 654, 664

Keyword Index

The Keyword Index lists every topic, company or business, agency, organization, brand, or personal name mentioned in *Statistical Record of Native North Americans, 2nd Edition* tables. Citations are arranged alphabetically, word by word, then letter by letter. Each index citation is followed by page and table reference numbers. Page numbers are preceded by "p." or "pp." Page references do not necessarily identify the page on which a table begins. In cases where tables span two or more pages, references point to to the page on which the index term actually appears, which may be the second or subsequent page of a table. Table reference numbers appear in brackets ([ ]). This index, too, is extensively cross-referenced to direct users to related subjects or terms. Geographic acronyms used in this index are: ANVSA (Alaska Native Village Statistical Area); CMSA (Consolidated Statistical Metropolitan Statistical Area); MSA (Metropolitan Statistical Area); PMSA (Primary Metropolitan Statistical Area); TDSA (Tribal Designated Statistical Area); and TJSA (Tribal Jurisdiction Statistical Area).

Numbers following p. or pp. are page references. Numbers in [ ] are table references.

Numbers following p. or pp. are page references. Numbers in [ ] are table references.

Keyword Index

Akiachak continued:
— rooms per housing unit, p. 733 [601]
— school enrollment, p. 459 [331]
— school enrollment by race/ethnicity in, pp. 451-452 [323-324]
— sewage disposal methods, p. 753 [623]
— telephone availability, p. 763 [631]
— urban vs. rural population, p. 326 [205]
— water sources for housing, p. 758 [627]

Akiak
— population by age, pp. 256, 258, 260 [153-155]
— population by sex and race, p. 273 [162]

Akokisa
— population in Texas, 1690-1890, p. 21 [24]

Akutan
— children and type of family in, p. 350 [227]
— children in households, pp. 356, 361 [232, 236]
— class of workers in, p. 656 [538]
— educational attainment, pp. 422, 427 [301, 305]
— educational attainment and employment status in, pp. 435, 437 [311-312]
— elderly persons in, p. 417 [297]
— employment in, pp. 661, 690-691 [542, 558-559]
— employment of family members, p. 379 [252]
— geographic mobility in, p. 335 [213]
— home heating in, p. 749 [619]
— household income, p. 783 [650]
— household type and relationship in, pp. 366-367 [240-241]
— housing by year built, p. 729 [597]
— housing costs and income, p. 800 [666]
— housing tenure, pp. 714, 724 [585, 593]
— housing tenure by race, p. 719 [589]
— income and poverty, pp. 790, 792 [656-657]
— income by race, p. 769 [638]
— income by source, pp. 774-775 [642-643]
— language spoken at home, pp. 534, 539-541 [408, 412-414]
— linguistic isolation in, p. 534 [408]
— marital status of females in, pp. 388, 392 [260, 264]
— marital status of males in, p. 397 [268]
— median income of families in, p. 383 [256]
— military service, pp. 1008, 1010 [868-869]
— monthly housing costs, p. 804 [670]
— occupations in, pp. 699, 701 [566-567]
— persons in housing units, pp. 375, 738 [248, 606]
— place of birth, p. 340 [217]
— population by age, pp. 256, 258, 260 [153-155]
— population by race/ethnicity, p. 331 [209]
— population by sex and race, p. 273 [162]
— rooms per housing unit, p. 733 [601]
— school enrollment, p. 459 [331]
— school enrollment by race/ethnicity in, pp. 451-452 [323-324]
— sewage disposal methods, p. 753 [623]
— telephone availability, p. 763 [631]
— urban vs. rural population, p. 326 [205]
— water sources for housing, p. 758 [627]

Alabama
— ability to speak English, 1910, p. 133 [86]
— adults on probation, p. 1056 [912]
— alcohol treatment programs, p. 646 [527]
— American Indian languages spoken at home, p. 533 [406]

Alabama continued:
— blood status, 1910, pp. 68, 78 [55, 59]
— cigarettes and tax exemptions, p. 942 [802]
— drug treatment programs, p. 650 [529]
— Indian and white mixed-bloods, 1910, p. 86 [62]
— Indian lands, pp. 964, 966 [822-823]
— Native American owned firms, p. 864 [709]
— population, p. 181 [113]
— population, 1890-1930, p. 17 [21]
— population, 1900-1980, p. 344 [222]
— population, 1910-1930, pp. 37, 40, 51 [31-32, 36]
— population by race/ethnicity, p. 173 [107]
— population by tribe, pp. 206, 215, 224, 234, 244, 252 [126, 131, 136, 141, 146, 151]
— poverty in, p. 789 [655]
— prison population, p. 1060 [915]
— prisoners on death row, p. 1047 [900]
— school attendance, 1910, pp. 95, 106 [67, 71]
— urban and rural population, 1930, p. 19 [22]

Alabama and Coushatta Reservation
— acreage, tribal lands, and population, p. 950 [805]
— land trusteeship termination, pp. 165, 167 [102]
— population by age, pp. 279, 281, 283 [165-167]
— population by sex and race, p. 310 [189]
— traditional occupations, pp. 552, 554 [424-425]

Alabama Coushatta
— population by region, p. 192 [118]
— population by state, pp. 210, 212, 214-215, 217 [128-132]
— restoration of federal recognition, p. 164 [100]
— tribal enrollment, p. 1021 [879]

Alabama Quassarte
— population by region, p. 192 [118]
— population by state, pp. 210, 212, 214-215, 217 [128-132]

Alabama [language]
— spoken at home, p. 529 [404]

Alakanuk
— children and type of family in, p. 350 [227]
— children in households, pp. 356, 361 [232, 236]
— class of workers in, p. 656 [538]
— educational attainment, pp. 422, 427 [301, 305]
— educational attainment and employment status in, pp. 435, 437 [311-312]
— elderly persons in, p. 417 [297]
— employment in, pp. 661, 690-691 [542, 558-559]
— employment of family members, p. 379 [252]
— geographic mobility in, p. 335 [213]
— home heating in, p. 749 [619]
— household income, p. 783 [650]
— household type and relationship in, pp. 366-367 [240-241]
— housing by year built, p. 729 [597]
— housing costs and income, p. 800 [666]
— housing tenure, pp. 714, 724 [585, 593]
— housing tenure by race, p. 719 [589]
— income and poverty, pp. 790, 792 [656-657]
— income by race, p. 769 [638]
— income by source, pp. 774-775 [642-643]
— language spoken at home, pp. 534, 539-541 [408, 412-414]
— linguistic isolation in, p. 534 [408]
— marital status of females in, pp. 388, 392 [260, 264]

Numbers following p. or pp. are page references. Numbers in [ ] are table references.

Numbers following p. or pp. are page references. Numbers in [ ] are table references.

Keyword Index

Alaskan Athabaskans continued:
— school enrollment, p. 447 [321]
Alatna
— population by age, pp. 256, 258, 260 [153-155]
— population by sex and race, p. 273 [162]
Albania
— land area, p. 952 [806]
Albany, GA MSA
— population, p. 181 [114]
Albany-Schenectady-Troy, NY MSA
— population, pp. 176, 181 [109, 114]
Alberta
— Aboriginal population, p. 1066 [921]
— Inuit population, p. 1069 [925]
— Metis population, p. 1070 [927]
Albuquerque Area
— bingo revenues, p. 909 [761]
— child abuse investigations, p. 403 [276]
— hospitals, p. 635 [514]
— Indian lands, p. 965 [823]
— land ownership, p. 968 [825]
— YPLL rates, p. 590 [457]
Albuquerque, NM MSA
— firm ownership, p. 869 [711]
— population, pp. 177, 181 [109, 114]
Alcohol
— crime and, pp. 1057-1058 [913]
— death rate reductions and, p. 576 [442]
— motor vehicle risk behaviors and, p. 405 [280]
— nutritional counseling and, p. 644 [524]
— risk factors of Wisconsin Chippewa, p. 646 [526]
— use by students, p. 413 [290]
Alcohol treatment
— for adolescents, p. 624 [498]
— for adults, p. 625 [499]
— programs by state, p. 646 [527]
— programs by type, p. 648 [528]
Aleknagik
— population by age, pp. 256, 258, 260 [153-155]
— population by sex and race, p. 273 [162]
Aleut
— ability to speak English, 1910, p. 141 [89]
— Alaskan population, 1910, p. 24 [26]
— blood status, 1910, p. 73 [56]
— illiteracy, 1910, p. 118 [76]
— language, 1910 and 1930, p. 149 [91]
— Native American owned firms, pp. 861-877 [707, 709-714]
— population, p. 180 [113]
— school attendance, 1910, p. 104 [70]
— substance abuse prevention programs, p. 623 [497]
Alexander
— population by age, pp. 256, 258, 260 [153-155]
— population by sex and race, p. 273 [162]
Alexander Valley, CA
— land trusteeship termination, p. 166 [102]
Alexandria, LA MSA
— population, p. 181 [114]
Algebra
— course enrollment, p. 470 [343]

Algonquian
— Alaskan population, 1910, p. 22 [26]
— blood status, 1910, p. 64 [54]
— educational attainment, p. 431 [309]
— illiteracy, 1910, p. 111 [74]
— Indian and white mixed-bloods, 1910, p. 84 [62]
— labor force status, pp. 666, 668 [546-547]
— language, 1910 and 1930, pp. 142-143, 148 [90-91]
— population, 1910-1930, pp. 30, 33 [29-30]
— population by state, pp. 201-202, 204, 206, 208 [123-127]
— population by U.S. region, p. 190 [117]
— school enrollment, p. 447 [321]
Algonquian [language]
— spoken at home, p. 527 [404]
Alibamu
— ability to speak English, 1910, p. 136 [88]
— blood status, 1910, pp. 68, 78 [55, 59]
— illiteracy, 1910, p. 114 [75]
— language, 1910 and 1930, p. 144 [90]
— marital status, 1910, pp. 154, 159 [95, 97]
— school attendance, 1910, p. 95 [67]
Alienation from social values
— and substance abuse, pp. 410-411 [287]
Alimony
— households receiving, p. 788 [654]
Allakaket
— population by age, pp. 256, 258, 260 [153-155]
— population by sex and race, p. 273 [162]
Allegany Reservation, NY
— acreage, tribal lands, and population, p. 950 [805]
— children and type of family on, p. 353 [230]
— children in households, pp. 359, 364 [235, 239]
— class of workers in, p. 659 [541]
— educational attainment, pp. 425, 429 [304, 308]
— educational attainment and employment status on, pp. 441, 443 [317-318]
— elderly persons on, p. 420 [300]
— employment on, pp. 664, 695, 697 [545, 564-565]
— geographic mobility on, p. 338 [216]
— home heating on, p. 752 [622]
— household income, p. 786 [653]
— household type and relationship, pp. 372-373 [246-247]
— housing by year built, p. 731 [600]
— housing costs and income, p. 802 [669]
— housing tenure, pp. 717, 727 [588, 596]
— housing tenure by race, p. 722 [592]
— income and poverty, pp. 796-797 [662-663]
— income by race, p. 772 [641]
— income by source, pp. 780, 782 [648-649]
— language spoken at home, pp. 537, 547-548, 550 [411, 421-423]
— linguistic isolation, p. 537 [411]
— marital status of females on, pp. 391, 395 [263, 267]
— marital status of males on, p. 399 [271]
— median family income on, p. 386 [259]
— military service, pp. 1015, 1017 [874-875]
— monthly housing costs, p. 807 [673]
— occupations on, pp. 705, 707 [572-573]
— persons in housing units, pp. 377, 741 [251, 609]
— place of birth, p. 342 [220]

Numbers following p. or pp. are page references. Numbers in [ ] are table references.

1102

Numbers following p. or pp. are page references. Numbers in [ ] are table references.

1104

Numbers following p. or pp. are page references. Numbers in [ ] are table references.

Numbers following p. or pp. are page references. Numbers in [ ] are table references.

Numbers following p. or pp. are page references. Numbers in [ ] are table references.

Keyword Index

Atsina
— language, 1910 and 1930, p. 142 [90]
— population, 1910-1930, p. 32 [29]
— population by state, pp. 218, 220, 222, 224, 226 [133-137]
— population by U.S. region, p. 193 [119]
— school enrollment, 1930, pp. 107, 109 [72-73]

Atsina [language]
— spoken at home, p. 527 [404]

Atsugewi
— spoken at home, p. 528 [404]

Attendance patterns
— secondary school, p. 486 [364]

Attention deficit disorder
— and substance abuse, p. 411 [287]

Attrition of tribes
— 1600-1907, p. 9 [11]

Auburn
— land trusteeship termination, p. 166 [102]

Audiologists
— employed by Indian Health Service, pp. 637, 639 [516, 518]

Augusta, GA – SC MSA
— population, p. 182 [114]

Augustine Reservation, CA
— acreage, tribal lands, and population, p. 945 [804]
— extensions of trust and land restrictions, p. 126 [84]
— population by age, pp. 279, 281, 283 [165-167]
— population by sex and race, p. 310 [189]
— traditional occupations, pp. 552, 554 [424-425]
— tribal enrollment, p. 1029 [887]

Auk
— ability to speak English, 1910, p. 141 [89]
— Alaskan population, 1910, p. 28 [28]
— blood status, 1910, p. 73 [56]
— illiteracy, 1910, p. 119 [76]
— language, 1910 and 1930, p. 149 [91]
— school attendance, 1910, p. 104 [70]

Austin-San Marcos, TX MSA
— firm ownership, p. 869 [711]
— population, pp. 176, 182 [109, 114]

Austrians
— perceptions of, p. 564 [431]

Auto parts manufacturing
— employment by, p. 878 [715]

Auto production
— employment, p. 903 [753]

Auto repair
— minority-owned firms, p. 834 [697]
— Native American owned firms, p. 863 [707]

Auto sales
— employment, pp. 881, 905 [719, 756]
— minority-owned firms, p. 833 [696]
— Native American owned firms, p. 862 [707]

Axle remanufacturing
— employment by, p. 878 [715]

Aymara
— spoken at home, p. 528 [404]

Aztecan
— spoken at home, p. 530 [405]

Bachelor's degrees
— completion rates, p. 468 [341]
— engineering, p. 521 [396]

Bad River Chippewa
— acreage, tribal lands, and population, p. 951 [805]
— population by region, p. 191 [118]
— population by state, pp. 210-211, 213, 215-216 [128-132]
— tribal enrollment, p. 1026 [884]

Bad River Reservation, WI
— population by age, pp. 279, 281, 283 [165-167]
— population by sex and race, p. 310 [189]
— traditional occupations, pp. 552, 554 [424-425]

Bahrain
— land area, p. 953 [806]

Bakersfield, CA MSA
— firm ownership, p. 869 [711]
— population, pp. 177, 182 [109, 114]

Bakery products industry
— employment, p. 887 [727]

Baltimore, MD MSA
— firm ownership, p. 869 [711]
— population, p. 182 [114]

Bangor, ME MSA
— population, p. 182 [114]

Banking
— employment, p. 883 [722]
— employment by tribe, pp. 675, 679 [551, 553]
— Native American owned firms, p. 862 [707]

Bannock
— ability to speak English, 1910, p. 138 [88]
— blood status, 1910, pp. 69, 80 [55, 59]
— educational attainment, p. 431 [309]
— illiteracy, 1910, p. 115 [75]
— labor force status, pp. 666, 668 [546-547]
— language, 1910 and 1930, p. 146 [91]
— marital status, in 1910, pp. 156, 161 [96, 98]
— population, 1910-1930, p. 43 [33]
— population by state, pp. 201, 203, 205-206, 208 [123-127]
— population by U.S. region, p. 190 [117]
— school attendance, 1910, p. 98 [68]
— school enrollment, p. 447 [321]

Barbados
— land area, p. 953 [806]

Barbareno, Santa Ynez
— language, 1910 and 1930, p. 144 [90]

Barmelee
— dam safety, p. 975 [835]

Barona Rancheria, CA
— acreage, tribal lands, and population, p. 945 [804]
— population by age, pp. 279, 281, 283 [165-167]
— population by sex and race, p. 310 [189]
— traditional occupations, pp. 552, 554 [424-425]
— tribal enrollment, p. 1029 [887]

Barrio Libre
— population by state, pp. 248, 250-251, 253-254 [148-152]
— population by U.S. region, p. 200 [122]

Barrow, AK
— children and type of family in, p. 350 [227]
— children in households, pp. 356, 361 [232, 236]

Numbers following p. or pp. are page references. Numbers in [ ] are table references.

Numbers following p. or pp. are page references. Numbers in [ ] are table references.

Keyword Index

Numbers following p. or pp. are page references. Numbers in [ ] are table references.

Numbers following p. or pp. are page references. Numbers in [ ] are table references.

Numbers following p. or pp. are page references. Numbers in [ ] are table references.

Budgets continued:
— Office of Indian Education, p. 489 [368]

Budsage
— cultural significance of, p. 563 [430]

Buena Vista
— acreage, tribal lands, and population, p. 945 [804]
— land trusteeship termination, p. 165 [102]
— tribal enrollment, p. 1029 [887]

Buffalo – Niagara Falls, NY CMSA
— population, pp. 176, 182 [109, 114]

Building materials
— minority-owned firms, p. 833 [696]
— Native American owned firms, p. 862 [707]

Building services
— employment, p. 881 [720]

Bureau of Alcohol, Tobacco and Firearms
— Native American representation in law enforcement, p. 1054 [909]

Bureau of Indian Affairs
See also: BIA
— child abuse investigation, p. 403 [276]
— dam safety, p. 975 [835]
— employment, p. 163 [99]
— expenditures for education, p. 490 [369]
— FTE summary by year, pp. 996-997 [858-859]
— land jurisdiction, pp. 967-974 [824-834]
— use of in 1872, p. 8 [9]

Bureau of Alcohol, Tobacco, and Firearms (BATF)
— Native American representation in law enforcement, p. 1054 [909]

Burglary
— arrests for, pp. 1033-1034 [890-891]
— arrests in cities, pp. 1036-1037 [892-893]
— arrests in rural counties, pp. 1038, 1040 [894-895]
— arrests in suburbs, pp. 1041-1042 [896-897]
— crime rate in U.S. and Indian Country, p. 1043 [898]

Burlington, NC MSA
— population, p. 182 [114]

Burlington, VT MSA
— population, p. 182 [114]

Burners (cooking)
— in housing, p. 747 [615]

Burns Paiute
— population by state, pp. 228, 230, 233, 235, 237 [138-142]
— population by U.S. region, p. 196 [120]
— tribal enrollment, p. 1027 [886]

Burns Paiute Reservation and Trust Lands, OR
— acreage, tribal lands, and population, p. 950 [805]
— population by age, pp. 280, 282-283 [165-167]
— population by sex and race, p. 310 [189]
— traditional occupations, pp. 553-554 [424-425]

Burt Lake Band
— population by state, pp. 248, 250, 252-253, 255 [148-152]
— population by U.S. region, p. 200 [122]

Burt Lake Ottawa
— population by state, pp. 228, 230, 232, 234, 236 [138-142]
— population by U.S. region, p. 195 [120]

Burundi
— land area, p. 952 [806]

Business
— agricultural services, forestry, and fishing, p. 822 [690]
— bingo, p. 909 [761]
— employment by tribe, pp. 675, 679 [551, 553]
— employment size, p. 815 [683]
— finance, insurance, and real estate, p. 825 [693]
— gaming, pp. 907, 913 [759, 767]
— in midwestern states, p. 840 [701]
— in neighborhoods, p. 746 [613]
— in southern states, p. 848 [703]
— in western states, p. 855 [704]
— minority-owned firms, p. 819 [685]
— Native American owned firms, pp. 859, 861, 863-864, 866, 869, 871, 874, 876 [705, 707-714]
— occupational goals of high school seniors, p. 471 [345]
— ownership, pp. 814, 821 [682, 688]
— resource development in Canada, p. 1078 [939]
— retail trade, p. 833 [696]
— sales and receipts, p. 817 [684]
— Sault Ste. Marie Chippewa Tribe, p. 877 [715]
— tribal gaming by state, p. 908 [760]
— women in corporate management, p. 812 [679]

Business administration
— faculty, full-time, p. 524 [401]
— fellowships given for, p. 492 [371]

Business & repair services
— employment in ANVSAs, p. 691 [559]
— employment in TDSAs, p. 693 [561]
— employment in TJSAs, p. 694 [563]
— employment on reservations and trust lands, p. 697 [565]

Business services
— employment, p. 881 [720]
— employment in Canada, p. 1082 [946]
— minority-owned firms, p. 834 [697]
— Native American owned firms, p. 862 [707]

Bustle makers
— on reservations, pp. 554, 558, 561 [425, 427, 429]

Cabazon Reservation, CA
— acreage, tribal lands, and population, p. 945 [804]
— extensions of trust and land restrictions, p. 126 [84]
— population by age, pp. 280, 282-283 [165-167]
— population by sex and race, p. 310 [189]
— traditional occupations, pp. 553-554 [424-425]
— tribal enrollment, p. 1029 [887]

Cache Creek
— land trusteeship termination, p. 165 [102]

Cachil Dehe Rancheria, CA
— traditional occupations, pp. 553-554 [424-425]

Cactus, fishhook
— cultural significance of, p. 563 [430]

Cactus, hedgehog
— cultural significance of, p. 563 [430]

Caddo
— ability to speak English, 1910, p. 135 [87]
— blood status, 1910, pp. 66, 76 [54, 58]
— educational attainment, p. 431 [309]
— epidemics, 1528-1892, pp. 122-123 [80]
— illiteracy, 1910, p. 112 [74]
— Indian and white mixed-bloods, 1910, p. 85 [62]

Numbers following p. or pp. are page references. Numbers in [ ] are table references.

1113

Numbers following p. or pp. are page references. Numbers in [ ] are table references.

California Area
— YPLL rates, p. 590 [457]

California Athapaskans
— population, 1910-1930, p. 35 [30]
— school enrollment, 1930, pp. 108, 110 [72-73]

California Rancherias
— restoration of federal recognition, p. 164 [100]

California tribes
— educational attainment, p. 431 [309]
— labor force status, pp. 666, 668 [546-547]
— population by state, pp. 201, 203, 205, 207-208 [123-127]
— population by U.S. region, p. 190 [117]
— population, pre-European to 1980, p. 54 [39]
— population, prehistory to 1900, p. 20 [23]
— school enrollment, p. 447 [321]

Camp Verde Reservation, AZ
— acreage, tribal lands, and population, p. 945 [804]
— population by age, pp. 280, 282-283 [165-167]
— population by sex and race, p. 310 [189]
— traditional occupations, pp. 553-554 [424-425]

Campo
— extensions of trust and land restrictions, p. 126 [84]
— population by region, p. 192 [118]
— population by state, pp. 211-212, 214, 216, 218 [128-132]
— tribal enrollment, p. 1029 [887]

Campo Reservation, CA
— acreage, tribal lands, and population, p. 945 [804]
— population by age, pp. 280, 282-283 [165-167]
— population by sex and race, p. 310 [189]
— traditional occupations, pp. 553-554 [424-425]

Can production
— employment, p. 886 [726]

Canada
— Aboriginal identity in, pp. 1066-1067 [922]
— Aboriginal musicians, p. 1078 [940]
— Aboriginal population, pp. 177, 1063-1064, 1066-1067, 1071, 1073-1075, 1077, 1079-1080, 1082-1085 [110, 918-919, 921, 923, 929, 933-935, 937, 942-943, 946-948, 950]
— Aboriginal population by census area, p. 1065 [920]
— AIDS in, p. 1077 [938]
— ancestral language use in, p. 1076 [936]
— domestic violence in, p. 1072 [930]
— education in, p. 1072 [931]
— employment equity in, p. 1081 [944]
— European contact and population, p. 5 [7]
— Inuit population, p. 1068 [925]
— Inuit population by age, p. 1068 [924]
— Metis population, pp. 1070-1071 [927-928]
— Metis population by age, p. 1069 [926]
— opinions on aboriginal community problems, p. 1085 [949]
— population, p. 4 [6]
— resource development in, p. 1078 [939]
— smallpox epidemics, 1520-1797, p. 125 [83]
— socioeconomic characteristics, p. 1079 [941]
— unemployment in, p. 1082 [945]

Canada, Central
— European contact and population, p. 5 [7]
— population, p. 4 [6]

Canadian Indians [in the U.S.]
— educational attainment, p. 431 [309]
— labor force status, pp. 666, 668 [546-547]
— population, 1910-1930, p. 52 [37]
— population by state, pp. 201, 203, 205, 207, 209 [123-127]
— population by U.S. region, p. 190 [117]
— school enrollment, p. 447 [321]

Cancer
— death rates for urban Indians, p. 589 [456]

Canoncito Reservation, NM
— acreage, tribal lands, and population, p. 949 [805]
— population by age, pp. 280, 282-283 [165-167]
— population by sex and race, p. 310 [189]
— traditional occupations, pp. 553-554 [424-425]

Canton, OH MSA
— population, p. 182 [114]

Cantwell
— population by age, pp. 256, 258, 261 [153-155]
— population by sex and race, p. 274 [162]

Canyon Diablo
— dam safety, p. 976 [835]

Canyon Village
— population by age, pp. 256, 259, 261 [153-155]
— population by sex and race, p. 274 [162]

Capital punishment
— by race/ethnicity, pp. 1048-1049 [901-902]

Capitan Grande Reservation, CA
— acreage, tribal lands, and population, p. 945 [804]
— extensions of trust and land restrictions, p. 126 [84]
— population by age, pp. 280, 282-283 [165-167]
— population by region, p. 193 [118]
— population by sex and race, p. 310 [189]
— population by state, pp. 211-212, 214, 216, 218 [128-132]
— traditional occupations, pp. 553, 555 [424-425]
— tribal enrollment, p. 1029 [887]

Captain Tom
— dam safety, p. 976 [835]

Car sales
— employment, p. 881 [719]

Cardiovascular disease
— and death, p. 582 [447]

Carex sp. (sedge)
— cultural significance of, p. 563 [430]

Caribbean Islands
— population estimates for 1492, pp. 2-3 [3-4]

Carl Albert (ADA), OK
— hospitals, p. 636 [514]

Carnegie units, p. 466 [339]
— foreign language, p. 469 [342]

Carrier
— as mother tongue, p. 1074 [933]
— spoken at home, p. 1075 [935]

Carrot, wild
— cultural significance of, p. 563 [430]

Carson Colony, NV
— acreage, tribal lands, and population, p. 949 [805]
— population by age, pp. 280, 282-283 [165-167]
— population by sex and race, p. 310 [189]
— traditional occupations, pp. 553, 555 [424-425]

Numbers following p. or pp. are page references. Numbers in [ ] are table references.

1115

Numbers following p. or pp. are page references. Numbers in [ ] are table references.

Numbers following p. or pp. are page references. Numbers in [ ] are table references.

Numbers following p. or pp. are page references. Numbers in [ ] are table references.

Numbers following p. or pp. are page references. Numbers in [ ] are table references.

1119

Numbers following p. or pp. are page references. Numbers in [ ] are table references.

Numbers following p. or pp. are page references. Numbers in [ ] are table references.

Numbers following p. or pp. are page references. Numbers in [ ] are table references.

Numbers following p. or pp. are page references. Numbers in [ ] are table references.

Keyword Index

1123

Numbers following p. or pp. are page references. Numbers in [ ] are table references.

Numbers following p. or pp. are page references. Numbers in [ ] are table references.

Numbers following p. or pp. are page references. Numbers in [ ] are table references.

Keyword Index

Numbers following p. or pp. are page references. Numbers in [ ] are table references.

Numbers following p. or pp. are page references. Numbers in [ ] are table references.

Numbers following p. or pp. are page references. Numbers in [ ] are table references.

1131

Numbers following p. or pp. are page references. Numbers in [ ] are table references.

Numbers following p. or pp. are page references. Numbers in [ ] are table references.

Numbers following p. or pp. are page references. Numbers in [ ] are table references.

Numbers following p. or pp. are page references. Numbers in [ ] are table references.

Numbers following p. or pp. are page references. Numbers in [ ] are table references.

Dresslerville Colony, NV
— acreage, tribal lands, and population, p. 949 [805]
— population by age, pp. 284, 286-287 [168-170]
— population by sex and race, p. 312 [190]
— traditional occupations, pp. 553, 555 [424-425]

Drill teams
— high school senior participation, p. 483 [359]

Drinking
— risk factors of Wisconsin Chippewa, p. 646 [526]
— suicide risk and, p. 408 [283]

Driver
— population estimates before 1492, p. 2 [2]
— population estimates for North America before 1492, p. 1 [1]

Driving
— by high school seniors, p. 482 [358]

Driving under the influence
— arrests for, pp. 1034-1035 [890-891]
— arrests in cities, pp. 1036, 1038 [892-893]
— arrests in rural counties, pp. 1039-1040 [894-895]
— arrests in suburbs, pp. 1041, 1043 [896-897]
— risk factors of Wisconsin Chippewa, p. 646 [526]

Drug abuse violations
— arrests for, pp. 1034-1035 [890-891]
— arrests in cities, pp. 1036-1037 [892-893]
— arrests in rural counties, pp. 1039-1040 [894-895]
— arrests in suburbs, pp. 1041, 1043 [896-897]

Drug Enforcement Administration
— Native American representation in law enforcement, p. 1054 [909]

Drug-Free Schools and Communities (Set-Aside)
— expenditures, p. 490 [369]

Drug production
— employment, p. 882 [721]

Drugs
— exposure in school, p. 484 [360]
— motor vehicle risk behaviors and, p. 405 [280]
— treatment programs, pp. 648, 650 [528-529]
— use by adolescents, p. 410 [286]
— use by students, p. 413 [290]

Drugstores
— employment, pp. 884, 906 [724, 757]

Drunkenness
— arrests for, pp. 1034-1035 [890-891]
— arrests in cities, pp. 1036, 1038 [892-893]
— arrests in rural counties, pp. 1039-1040 [894-895]
— arrests in suburbs, pp. 1041, 1043 [896-897]

Dry Creek Rancheria, CA
— acreage, tribal lands, and population, p. 946 [804]
— population by age, pp. 284, 286-287 [168-170]
— population by sex and race, p. 312 [190]
— traditional occupations, pp. 553, 555 [424-425]
— tribal enrollment, p. 1029 [887]

Dryers, clothes
— in housing, p. 747 [615]

Dubuque, IA MSA
— population, p. 183 [114]

Duck Valley
— population by state, pp. 239, 241, 243, 245, 247 [143-147]
— population by U.S. region, p. 198 [121]

Duck Valley continued:
— tribal enrollment, p. 1024 [882]

Duck Valley Reservation, ID-NV
— acreage, tribal lands, and population, p. 947 [804]
— population by age, pp. 284, 286-287 [168-170]
— population by sex and race, p. 312 [190]
— traditional occupations, pp. 553, 555 [424-425]

Duckwater Reservation, NV
— acreage, tribal lands, and population, p. 949 [805]
— population by age, pp. 284, 286-287 [168-170]
— population by sex and race, p. 312 [190]
— traditional occupations, pp. 553, 555 [424-425]

Duckwater Shoshone of Nevada
— tribal enrollment, p. 1024 [882]

DUI
— arrests for, pp. 1034-1035 [890-891]
— arrests in cities, pp. 1036, 1038 [892-893]
— arrests in rural counties, pp. 1039-1040 [894-895]
— arrests in suburbs, pp. 1041, 1043 [896-897]
— risk factors of Wisconsin Chippewa, p. 646 [526]

Dulce
— dam safety, p. 975 [835]

Dull Knife Memorial College
— adult education, p. 494 [373]

Duluth, MN-WI MSA
— population, p. 183 [114]

Durable goods, wholesale
— employment, p. 905 [756]

Dutch
— perceptions of, p. 564 [431]

Duwamish
— language, 1910 and 1930, p. 145 [90]
— population by state, pp. 238, 240, 242, 244, 246 [143-147]
— population by U.S. region, p. 197 [121]

Eagle
— population by age, pp. 257, 259, 261 [153-155]
— population by sex and race, p. 274 [162]
— tribal enrollment, p. 1025 [883]

Eagle Butte, SD
— hospitals, p. 635 [514]

Eagle Ridge Apartments
— employment by, p. 878 [715]

East Fork
— dam safety, p. 976 [835]

East North Central Region
— ability to speak English, 1910, p. 131 [86]
— American Indian languages spoken at home, p. 532 [406]
— population, p. 180 [113]
— population, 1890-1930, pp. 16-17 [21]
— population by race/ethnicity, p. 172 [107]
— population by tribe, pp. 189, 191, 193, 195, 197, 199, 202, 211, 220, 230, 240, 249 [117-122, 124, 129, 134, 139, 144, 149]
— school attendance, 1910, p. 105 [71]
— urban and rural population, 1910-1930, p. 13 [17]
— urban and rural population, 1930, pp. 18-19 [22]

East South Central Region
— ability to speak English, 1910, p. 132 [86]
— American Indian languages spoken at home, pp. 532-533 [406]
— population, p. 180 [113]

Numbers following p. or pp. are page references. Numbers in [ ] are table references.

Numbers following p. or pp. are page references. Numbers in [ ] are table references.

Numbers following p. or pp. are page references. Numbers in [ ] are table references.

Numbers following p. or pp. are page references. Numbers in [ ] are table references.

Numbers following p. or pp. are page references. Numbers in [ ] are table references.

Numbers following p. or pp. are page references. Numbers in [ ] are table references.

Numbers following p. or pp. are page references. Numbers in [ ] are table references.

Numbers following p. or pp. are page references. Numbers in [ ] are table references.

Numbers following p. or pp. are page references. Numbers in [ ] are table references.

Numbers following p. or pp. are page references. Numbers in [ ] are table references.

Keyword Index

Numbers following p. or pp. are page references. Numbers in [ ] are table references.

Numbers following p. or pp. are page references. Numbers in [ ] are table references.

1149

Keyword Index

Numbers following p. or pp. are page references. Numbers in [ ] are table references.

Numbers following p. or pp. are page references. Numbers in [ ] are table references.

Numbers following p. or pp. are page references. Numbers in [ ] are table references.

Numbers following p. or pp. are page references. Numbers in [ ] are table references.

Hat Creek continued:
— school attendance, 1910, p. 98 [68]
Hate crimes, p. 1049 [903]
— incidents, offenses, and victims, p. 1050 [904]
— race/ethnicity of suspect, p. 1051 [905]
Havasupai
— ability to speak English, 1910, p. 140 [89]
— acreage, tribal lands, and population, p. 945 [804]
— illiteracy, 1910, p. 117 [76]
— language, 1910 and 1930, p. 148 [91]
— population by state, pp. 248, 250-251, 253, 255 [148-152]
— population by U.S. region, p. 200 [122]
— school attendance in 1910, p. 103 [70]
— tribal enrollment, p. 1024 [882]
Havasupai Reservation, AZ
— population by age, pp. 288, 290-291 [171-173]
— population by sex and race, p. 313 [191]
— traditional occupations, pp. 553, 555 [424-425]
Havasupai [language]
— spoken at home, p. 529 [404]
Hawaii
— adults on probation, p. 1056 [912]
— alcohol treatment programs, p. 647 [527]
— American Indian languages spoken at home, p. 533 [406]
— cigarettes and tax exemptions, p. 942 [802]
— drug treatment programs, p. 650 [529]
— minority-owned firms, p. 855 [704]
— Native American owned firms, p. 865 [709]
— Native American prison population, p. 1058 [914]
— population, p. 181 [113]
— population, 1900-1980, p. 345 [222]
— population by race/ethnicity, p. 174 [107]
— population by tribe, pp. 208, 216, 226, 236, 246, 254 [127, 132, 137, 142, 147, 152]
— poverty in, p. 789 [655]
— prison population, p. 1060 [915]
Hay fever
— in adolescents, p. 619 [492]
— outpatient services, p. 642 [522]
Hazardous waste
— transportation of, pp. 978, 980 [837-838]
He Dog
— dam safety, p. 975 [835]
Head Start (Health and Human Services)
— expenditures, p. 491 [369]
Headaches
— in adolescents, p. 619 [492]
Headgate Rock
— dam safety, p. 976 [835]
Health
— AIDS, p. 591 [458]
— AIDS-related deaths, p. 580 [445]
— birth weight, pp. 572-573 [438-439]
— births, pp. 566-567 [432-434]
— deaths, pp. 582-583 [446, 448]
— deaths of Omahas, 19th century, p. 124 [82]
— diabetes and death, pp. 598-599 [466-467]
— diabetes prevalence, p. 599 [468]
— diabetes-related amputations, p. 600 [469]

Health continued:
— diabetes research, p. 602 [472]
— epidemics in Texas, 1528-1892, p. 122 [80]
— infant mortality rates, pp. 612-613 [483-484]
— leading causes of death, pp. 584-589, 608, 615-616 [449-455, 477, 486-487]
— malignant neoplasms and death, p. 601 [471]
— maternal deaths, p. 614 [485]
— risk factors of Wisconsin Chippewa, p. 646 [526]
— smallpox epidemics, 1520-1797, p. 125 [83]
— suicide attempts by adolescents, p. 415 [293]
— teenage mothers, p. 574 [440]
— tuberculosis and death, p. 603 [473]
— tumors and death, p. 601 [470]
— venereal disease, pp. 626-628 [502-504]
Health aides/technicians
— employed by Indian Health Service, pp. 637-638 [516, 518]
Health and Human Services
— expenditures, p. 491 [369]
Health and Social Services
— employment in Canada, p. 1082 [946]
Health care
— accreditation of IHS labs, p. 633 [510]
— AIDS education, pp. 592-593, 595 [459-462]
— community-based substance abuse prevention, p. 621 [495]
— community health services, p. 639 [519]
— dental services, pp. 604-605 [474-475]
— employment, p. 890 [731]
— employment in ANVSAs, p. 691 [559]
— employment in TDSAs, p. 693 [561]
— employment in TJSAs, p. 694 [563]
— employment on reservations and trust lands, p. 697 [565]
— hospitals, pp. 634-635 [513-514]
— IHS employment, pp. 637-638 [516, 518]
— IHS public health nursing, p. 640 [520]
— IHS service population, p. 636 [515]
— leading causes of hospitalization, pp. 630-631 [507-508]
— minority-owned firms, p. 834 [697]
— Native American owned firms, p. 863 [707]
— outpatient services, pp. 641-643 [521-523]
— psychiatric services, p. 617 [488]
— substance abuse prevention, pp. 412, 623, 625 [288, 497, 500]
— substance abuse treatment, pp. 624-625, 650 [498-499, 529]
Health education
— and community health services, p. 639 [519]
Health educators
— employed by Indian Health Service, pp. 637, 639 [516, 518]
Health insurance industry
— employment, p. 891 [734]
Health promotion
— public health services and, p. 640 [520]
Health sciences
— doctorates conferred, p. 513 [390]
— faculty, full-time, p. 524 [401]
— master's degrees conferred, p. 510 [387]
Healy Lake
— population by age, pp. 257, 260, 262 [153-155]
— population by sex and race, p. 275 [162]

Numbers following p. or pp. are page references. Numbers in [ ] are table references.

1155

Numbers following p. or pp. are page references. Numbers in [ ] are table references.

Hoh continued:
— population by state, pp. 202-203, 205, 207, 209 [123-127]
— population by U.S. region, p. 190 [117]
— tribal enrollment, p. 1028 [886]

Hoh Reservation, WA
— acreage, tribal lands, and population, p. 951 [805]
— population by age, pp. 288, 290-291 [171-173]
— population by sex and race, p. 313 [191]
— traditional occupations, pp. 553, 555 [424-425]

Hokan languages
— spoken at home, p. 528 [404]

Holding and other investment offices
— Native American owned firms, p. 862 [707]

Holding offices
— minority-owned firms, p. 825 [693]

Hollywood Reservation, FL
— acreage, tribal lands, and population, p. 947 [804]
— population by age, pp. 288, 290, 292 [171-173]
— population by sex and race, p. 313 [191]
— traditional occupations, pp. 553, 555 [424-425]

Holy Cross
— population by age, pp. 257, 260, 262 [153-155]
— population by sex and race, p. 275 [162]

Home economics
— doctorates conferred, p. 513 [390]
— full-time faculty, p. 524 [401]
— master's degrees conferred, p. 510 [387]

Home furnishings stores
— employment, p. 889 [729]
— minority-owned firms, p. 833 [696]

Home loans
— veterans' utilization, p. 1019 [876]

Home placements, multiple
— substance abuse and, p. 411 [287]

Homeless centers
— youths in, p. 1052 [907]

Homeless Children and Youth Program
— budget appropriations and requests, p. 491 [370]

Homemaker services
— community health services, p. 639 [519]

Homework assignments
— completion of, p. 467 [340]

Homicide, pp. 584-585 [449-450]
— and death, pp. 576, 583, 586-587, 589, 616 [442, 447, 451-452, 456, 487]
— in reservation counties, p. 1044 [899]

Honduras
— Native population, p. 177 [110]
— population estimates, 1500, p. 3 [5]

Honolulu, HI MSA
— Native-owned firms, p. 871 [712]
— population, pp. 176, 184 [109, 114]

Honor societies
— high school, p. 481 [357]

Hoonah
— children and type of family in, p. 350 [227]
— children in households, pp. 356, 361 [232, 236]
— class of workers in, p. 657 [538]
— educational attainment, pp. 422, 427 [301, 305]

Hoonah continued:
— educational attainment and employment status in, pp. 435, 437 [311-312]
— elderly persons in, p. 418 [297]
— employment in, pp. 661, 690-691 [542, 558-559]
— employment of family members, p. 379 [252]
— geographic mobility in, p. 336 [213]
— home heating in, p. 749 [619]
— household income, p. 784 [650]
— household type and relationship in, pp. 366-367 [240-241]
— housing by year built, p. 729 [597]
— housing costs and income, p. 800 [666]
— housing tenure, pp. 715, 724 [585, 593]
— housing tenure by race, p. 720 [589]
— income and poverty, pp. 790, 792 [656-657]
— income by race, p. 769 [638]
— income by source, pp. 774-775 [642-643]
— language spoken at home, pp. 535, 539-540, 542 [408, 412-414]
— linguistic isolation in, p. 535 [408]
— marital status of females in, pp. 389, 393 [260, 264]
— marital status of males in, p. 397 [268]
— median income of families in, p. 384 [256]
— military service, pp. 1009-1010 [868-869]
— monthly housing costs, p. 804 [670]
— occupations in, pp. 699, 701 [566-567]
— persons in housing units, pp. 375, 739 [248, 606]
— place of birth, p. 340 [217]
— population by age, pp. 257, 260, 262 [153-155]
— population by race/ethnicity, p. 331 [209]
— population by sex and race, p. 275 [162]
— rooms per housing unit, p. 734 [601]
— school enrollment, p. 459 [331]
— school enrollment by race/ethnicity in, pp. 451, 453 [323-324]
— sewage disposal methods, p. 754 [623]
— telephone availability, p. 763 [631]
— urban vs. rural population, p. 326 [205]
— water sources for housing, p. 758 [627]

Hoopa
— educational attainment, p. 432 [309]
— labor force status, pp. 667, 669 [546-547]
— population by state, pp. 219-222, 224, 226 [133-137]
— population by U.S. region, p. 193 [119]
— school enrollment, p. 448 [321]
— tribal enrollment, p. 1029 [887]

Hoopa Valley Reservation, CA
— acreage, tribal lands, and population, p. 946 [804]
— extensions of trust and land restrictions, p. 126 [84]
— land area, p. 953 [806]
— population by age, pp. 289-290, 292 [171-173]
— population by sex and race, p. 313 [191]
— traditional occupations, pp. 553, 555 [424-425]

Hooper Bay
— children and type of family in, p. 350 [227]
— children in households, pp. 356, 361 [232, 236]
— class of workers in, p. 657 [538]
— educational attainment, pp. 422, 427 [301, 305]
— educational attainment and employment status in, pp. 436-437 [311-312]
— elderly persons in, p. 418 [297]

Numbers following p. or pp. are page references. Numbers in [ ] are table references.

Numbers following p. or pp. are page references. Numbers in [ ] are table references.

Keyword Index

Numbers following p. or pp. are page references. Numbers in [ ] are table references.

Numbers following p. or pp. are page references. Numbers in [ ] are table references.

Keyword Index

Numbers following p. or pp. are page references. Numbers in [ ] are table references.

Keyword Index

Numbers following p. or pp. are page references. Numbers in [ ] are table references.

Numbers following p. or pp. are page references. Numbers in [ ] are table references.

Numbers following p. or pp. are page references. Numbers in [ ] are table references.

Numbers following p. or pp. are page references. Numbers in [ ] are table references.

Keyword Index

Numbers following p. or pp. are page references. Numbers in [ ] are table references.

Numbers following p. or pp. are page references. Numbers in [ ] are table references.

Numbers following p. or pp. are page references. Numbers in [ ] are table references.

Numbers following p. or pp. are page references. Numbers in [ ] are table references.

Keyword Index

1171

Numbers following p. or pp. are page references. Numbers in [ ] are table references.

Klawock continued:
— educational attainment and employment status in, pp. 436-437 [311-312]
— elderly persons in, p. 418 [297]
— employment in, pp. 662, 690-691 [542, 558-559]
— employment of family members, p. 379 [252]
— geographic mobility in, p. 336 [213]
— home heating in, p. 749 [619]
— household income, p. 784 [650]
— household type and relationship in, pp. 366, 368 [240-241]
— housing by year built, p. 729 [597]
— housing costs and income, p. 800 [666]
— housing tenure, pp. 715, 725 [585, 593]
— housing tenure by race, p. 720 [589]
— income and poverty, pp. 791-792 [656-657]
— income by race, p. 770 [638]
— income by source, pp. 774, 776 [642-643]
— language spoken at home, pp. 535, 539-540, 542 [408, 412-414]
— linguistic isolation in, p. 535 [408]
— marital status of females in, pp. 389, 393 [260, 264]
— marital status of males in, p. 397 [268]
— median income of families in, p. 384 [256]
— military service, pp. 1009-1010 [868-869]
— monthly housing costs, p. 805 [670]
— occupations in, pp. 700-701 [566-567]
— persons in housing units, pp. 375, 739 [248, 606]
— place of birth, p. 340 [217]
— population by age, pp. 263, 265, 268 [156-158]
— population by race/ethnicity, p. 332 [209]
— population by sex and race, p. 276 [163]
— rooms per housing unit, p. 734 [601]
— school enrollment, p. 459 [331]
— school enrollment by race/ethnicity in, pp. 451, 453 [323-324]
— sewage disposal methods, p. 754 [623]
— telephone availability, p. 763 [631]
— urban vs. rural population, p. 327 [205]
— water sources for housing, p. 759 [627]

Klikitat
— ability to speak English, 1910, p. 137 [88]
— blood status, 1910, pp. 69, 79 [55, 59]
— illiteracy, 1910, p. 115 [75]
— language, 1910 and 1930, p. 146 [91]
— marital status, 1910, pp. 155, 161 [96, 98]
— school attendance, 1910, p. 97 [68]

Knaiakhotana
— ability to speak English, 1910, p. 140 [89]
— Alaskan population, 1910, p. 23 [26]
— blood status, 1910, p. 72 [56]
— illiteracy, 1910, p. 118 [76]
— school attendance, 1910, p. 104 [70]

Knik
— population by age, pp. 263, 265, 268 [156-158]
— population by sex and race, p. 276 [163]

Knitting mills
— employment, p. 902 [751]

Knoxville, TN MSA
— population, pp. 177, 185 [109, 114]

Koasati
— language, 1910 and 1930, p. 144 [90]

Koasati continued:
— spoken at home, p. 529 [404]

Kobuk
— population by age, pp. 263, 265, 268 [156-158]
— population by sex and race, p. 276 [163]

Kokhanok
— population by age, pp. 263, 265, 268 [156-158]
— population by sex and race, p. 276 [163]

Kokomo, IN MSA
— population, p. 185 [114]

Koliganek
— population by age, pp. 263, 265, 268 [156-158]
— population by sex and race, p. 276 [163]

Kongiganak
— population by age, pp. 263, 265, 268 [156-158]
— population by sex and race, p. 276 [163]

Konkow
— educational attainment, p. 432 [309]
— labor force status, pp. 667, 669 [546-547]
— population by state, pp. 219, 221, 223, 225, 227 [133-137]
— population by U.S. region, p. 194 [119]
— school enrollment, p. 448 [321]

Koosharem
— land trusteeship termination, p. 167 [102]

Kootenai
See also: Kutenai
— educational attainment, pp. 432, 434 [309-310]
— employment by occupation, p. 688 [557]
— labor force status, pp. 667, 669-670, 672 [546-549]
— population by state, pp. 219, 221, 223, 225, 227, 239, 241, 243-244, 246 [133-137, 143-147]
— population by U.S. region, pp. 194, 198 [119, 121]
— school enrollment, pp. 448, 450 [321-322]
— substance abuse prevention, p. 623 [497]
— tribal enrollment, p. 1028 [886]

Kootenai Reservation, ID
— acreage, tribal lands, and population, p. 948 [804]
— population by age, pp. 289, 291-292 [171-173]
— population by sex and race, p. 313 [191]
— traditional occupations, pp. 556, 558 [426-427]

Kopagmiut
— Alaskan population, 1910, p. 25 [26]

Korean War
— veterans in ANVSAs, pp. 1008, 1010 [868-869]
— veterans in TDSAs, p. 1012 [870-871]
— veterans in TJSAs, pp. 1013-1014 [872-873]
— veterans on reservations and trust lands, pp. 1015, 1017 [874-875]

Kotlik
— children and type of family in, p. 351 [227]
— children in households, pp. 356, 361 [232, 236]
— class of workers in, p. 657 [538]
— educational attainment, pp. 422, 427 [301, 305]
— educational attainment and employment status in, pp. 436-437 [311-312]
— elderly persons in, p. 418 [297]
— employment in, pp. 662, 690-691 [542, 558-559]
— employment of family members, p. 379 [252]
— geographic mobility in, p. 336 [213]
— home heating in, p. 749 [619]

Numbers following p. or pp. are page references. Numbers in [ ] are table references.

1173

Numbers following p. or pp. are page references. Numbers in [ ] are table references.

Numbers following p. or pp. are page references. Numbers in [ ] are table references.

Numbers following p. or pp. are page references. Numbers in [ ] are table references.

Numbers following p. or pp. are page references. Numbers in [ ] are table references.

Laundry facilities
— in housing, p. 747 [615]
Laundry services
— employment, p. 892 [735]
Law and legal studies
— doctorates conferred, p. 513 [390]
— fellowships given for, p. 492 [371]
— master's degrees conferred, p. 510 [387]
Law enforcement
See also: Crime; Prisons
— arrest rates by race, pp. 1034-1042 [890-897]
— death penalty by race/ethnicity, pp. 1048-1049 [901-902]
Law officers
See also: Police officers
— assaults on, p. 1053 [908]
— Native American representation, p. 1054 [909]
Lawrence, KS MSA
— population, p. 185 [115]
Lawton, OK MSA
— hospitals, p. 636 [514]
— Native American owned firms, p. 872 [712]
— population, p. 185 [115]
Laytonville Rancheria, CA
— acreage tribal land, and population, p. 946 [804]
— population by age, pp. 289, 291-292 [171-173]
— population by sex and race, p. 313 [191]
— traditional occupations, pp. 556, 558 [426-427]
— tribal enrollment, p. 1029 [887]
Lead
— mineral leases, p. 916 [773]
Leadership
— admired qualities, p. 1031 [888]
Learning disabilities
— in adolescents, p. 619 [492]
Leather and leather products
— employment, p. 892 [736]
— minority-owned firms, p. 827 [694]
— Native American owned firms, p. 861 [707]
Lebanon
— land area, p. 952 [806]
Leech Lake Chippewa
— extensions of trust and land restrictions, p. 126 [84]
— population by region, p. 191 [118]
— population by state, pp. 210-211, 213, 215-216 [128-132]
— tribal enrollment, p. 1026 [884]
Leech Lake Reservation, MN
— acreage, tribal lands, and population, p. 948 [805]
— children and type of family on, p. 354 [230]
— children in households, pp. 360, 364 [235, 239]
— class of workers in, p. 660 [541]
— educational attainment, pp. 425, 430 [304, 308]
— educational attainment and employment status on, pp. 442, 444 [317-318]
— elderly persons on, p. 420 [300]
— employment on, pp. 664, 696, 698 [545, 564-565]
— geographic mobility on, p. 338 [216]
— home heating on, p. 752 [622]
— household income, p. 786 [653]
— household type and relationship, pp. 372-373 [246-247]

Leech Lake Reservation, MN continued:
— housing by year built, p. 732 [600]
— housing costs and income, p. 803 [669]
— housing tenure, pp. 718, 727 [588, 596]
— housing tenure by race, p. 723 [592]
— income and poverty, pp. 796-797 [662-663]
— income by race, p. 772 [641]
— income by source, pp. 780, 782 [648-649]
— language spoken at home, pp. 538, 547, 549, 551 [411, 421-423]
— linguistic isolation, p. 538 [411]
— marital status of females on, pp. 391, 396 [263, 267]
— marital status of males on, p. 400 [271]
— median family income on, p. 387 [259]
— military service, pp. 1015, 1017 [874-875]
— monthly housing costs, p. 807 [673]
— occupations on, pp. 705, 707 [572-573]
— persons in housing units, pp. 378, 742 [251, 609]
— place of birth, p. 343 [220]
— population by age, pp. 289, 291-292 [171-173]
— population by race/ethnicity, p. 334 [212]
— population by sex and race, p. 313 [191]
— rooms per housing unit, p. 737 [604]
— school enrollment, pp. 458, 462 [330, 334]
— school enrollment by race/ethnicity on, p. 456 [329]
— sewage disposal methods, p. 757 [626]
— telephone availability, p. 766 [634]
— traditional occupations, pp. 556, 558 [426-427]
— urban vs. rural population, p. 330 [208]
— water sources for housing, p. 762 [630]
Leelanau
— population by region, p. 191 [118]
— population by state, pp. 210-211, 213, 215-216 [128-132]
Leelanau Sands Casino
— profit-sharing compact in Michigan, p. 910 [763]
Legal agencies
— substance abuse prevention programs, p. 622 [496]
Legal aid
— federal assistance, p. 1055 [911]
Legal services, p. 1055 [911]
— minority-owned firms, p. 834 [697]
— Native American owned firms, p. 863 [707]
Legal Services Corporation
— federal assistance, p. 1055 [911]
Legislation
— public lands, p. 982 [840]
Legislators
— on reservations, pp. 552, 556, 560 [424, 426, 428]
Leisure activities
— participation by high school seniors, p. 482 [358]
Lenni-Lenape
— population by region, p. 192 [118]
— population by state, pp. 211-212, 214, 216, 218 [128-132]
Lesotho
— land area, p. 952 [806]
Levelock
— population by age, pp. 263, 265, 268 [156-158]
— population by sex and race, p. 276 [163]
Lewiston-Auburn, ME MSA
— population, p. 185 [115]

Numbers following p. or pp. are page references. Numbers in [ ] are table references.

Numbers following p. or pp. are page references. Numbers in [ ] are table references.

Numbers following p. or pp. are page references. Numbers in [ ] are table references.

Numbers following p. or pp. are page references. Numbers in [ ] are table references.

Numbers following p. or pp. are page references. Numbers in [ ] are table references.

Numbers following p. or pp. are page references. Numbers in [ ] are table references.

Numbers following p. or pp. are page references. Numbers in [ ] are table references.

Numbers following p. or pp. are page references. Numbers in [ ] are table references.

Numbers following p. or pp. are page references. Numbers in [ ] are table references.

1187

Numbers following p. or pp. are page references. Numbers in [ ] are table references.

Numbers following p. or pp. are page references. Numbers in [ ] are table references.

Numbers following p. or pp. are page references. Numbers in [ ] are table references.

Numbers following p. or pp. are page references. Numbers in [ ] are table references.

Numbers following p. or pp. are page references. Numbers in [ ] are table references.

Numbers following p. or pp. are page references. Numbers in [ ] are table references.

Keyword Index

Numbers following p. or pp. are page references. Numbers in [ ] are table references.

Numbers following p. or pp. are page references. Numbers in [ ] are table references.

Numbers following p. or pp. are page references. Numbers in [ ] are table references.

Numbers following p. or pp. are page references. Numbers in [ ] are table references.

Keyword Index

Numbers following p. or pp. are page references. Numbers in [ ] are table references.

Numbers following p. or pp. are page references. Numbers in [ ] are table references.

Keyword Index

Numbers following p. or pp. are page references. Numbers in [ ] are table references.

Numbers following p. or pp. are page references. Numbers in [ ] are table references.

Numbers following p. or pp. are page references. Numbers in [ ] are table references.

Numbers following p. or pp. are page references. Numbers in [ ] are table references.

Numbers following p. or pp. are page references. Numbers in [ ] are table references.

Keyword Index

Numbers following p. or pp. are page references. Numbers in [ ] are table references.

Numbers following p. or pp. are page references. Numbers in [ ] are table references.

Numbers following p. or pp. are page references. Numbers in [ ] are table references.

Numbers following p. or pp. are page references. Numbers in [ ] are table references.

Numbers following p. or pp. are page references. Numbers in [ ] are table references.

Numbers following p. or pp. are page references. Numbers in [ ] are table references.

Numbers following p. or pp. are page references. Numbers in [ ] are table references.

Numbers following p. or pp. are page references. Numbers in [ ] are table references.

Keyword Index

1215

Numbers following p. or pp. are page references. Numbers in [ ] are table references.

Numbers following p. or pp. are page references. Numbers in [ ] are table references.

Numbers following p. or pp. are page references. Numbers in [ ] are table references.

Numbers following p. or pp. are page references. Numbers in [ ] are table references.

1219

Numbers following p. or pp. are page references. Numbers in [ ] are table references.

Numbers following p. or pp. are page references. Numbers in [ ] are table references.

Numbers following p. or pp. are page references. Numbers in [ ] are table references.

Numbers following p. or pp. are page references. Numbers in [ ] are table references.

1223

Keyword Index

Numbers following p. or pp. are page references. Numbers in [ ] are table references.

Numbers following p. or pp. are page references. Numbers in [ ] are table references.

Keyword Index

Numbers following p. or pp. are page references. Numbers in [ ] are table references.

Numbers following p. or pp. are page references. Numbers in [ ] are table references.

Keyword Index

Numbers following p. or pp. are page references. Numbers in [ ] are table references.

Numbers following p. or pp. are page references. Numbers in [ ] are table references.

Numbers following p. or pp. are page references. Numbers in [ ] are table references.

Numbers following p. or pp. are page references. Numbers in [ ] are table references.

Numbers following p. or pp. are page references. Numbers in [ ] are table references.

Numbers following p. or pp. are page references. Numbers in [ ] are table references.

Keyword Index

1233

Savoonga continued:
—water sources for housing, p. 759 [627]
Sawmills
—employment, p. 893 [738]
Saxman
—population by age, pp. 264, 267, 269 [156-158]
—population by sex and race, p. 277 [163]
Scammon Bay
—population by age, pp. 264, 267, 269 [156-158]
—population by sex and race, p. 277 [163]
—tribal enrollment, p. 1025 [883]
Scenic rivers
—and public lands legislation, p. 982 [840]
Schaghticoke
—educational attainment, p. 434 [310]
—employment by occupation, p. 689 [557]
—labor force status, pp. 670, 672 [548-549]
—population by state, pp. 239, 241, 243-244, 246 [143-147]
—population by U.S. region, p. 198 [121]
—school enrollment, p. 450 [322]
Schaghticoke Reservation, CT
—population by age, pp. 300-301, 303 [180-182]
—population by sex and race, p. 318 [194]
—traditional occupations, pp. 560-561 [428-429]
Scholarships
—expenditures, p. 491 [369]
Scholastic Aptitude Test (SAT)
—average scores, pp. 472-473 [346-347]
School-limiting conditions
—in adolescents, p. 620 [492]
School-to-Work
—budget appropriations and requests, p. 491 [370]
Schools
See also: Education
—adolescent concerns, pp. 415-416 [294-295]
—attendance, 1910, pp. 90, 93, 96, 99, 102 [66-70]
—dropouts and substance abuse, p. 410 [287]
—drug exposure, p. 484 [360]
—emotional stress and, p. 407 [282]
—enrollment, 1900-1930, pp. 89-90 [64-65]
—enrollment, 1930, pp. 107, 109 [72-73]
—enrollment by race/ethnicity in ANVSAs, pp. 451-452 [323-324]
—enrollment by race/ethnicity in TDSAs, pp. 453-454 [325-326]
—enrollment by race/ethnicity in TJSAs, p. 455 [327-328]
—enrollment by race/ethnicity on reservations and trust lands, pp. 456-457 [329-330]
—enrollment by tribal group, pp. 447, 449 [321-322]
—enrollment in ANVSAs, p. 459 [331]
—enrollment in TDSAs, p. 460 [332]
—enrollment in TJSAs, p. 461 [333]
—enrollment on reservations and trust lands, p. 462 [334]
—environment of, p. 486 [364]
—expenditures, p. 490 [369]
—libraries in, p. 484 [361]
—performance factors, p. 406 [281]
—preparedness for class, p. 467 [340]
—public health services, p. 640 [520]
—risk behavior and, p. 413 [290]

Schools continued:
—school board service, p. 488 [366]
—students' reasons for attendance, p. 485 [363]
—substance abuse prevention programs, pp. 412, 622 [288, 496]
—teacher qualifications, p. 487 [365]
—type attended, p. 445 [319]
Science
—bachelor's degrees earned, p. 515 [393]
—course enrollment, pp. 470, 473 [343, 348]
—doctorates conferred, p. 519 [395]
—experiments by students, pp. 474-475 [349-350]
—graduate enrollment, p. 505 [382]
—master's degrees conferred, p. 517 [394]
—proficiency levels, pp. 476-480 [351-356]
—students' attitudes, p. 477 [352]
—workforce, p. 656 [537]
Sclerocactus pubispinus (fishhook cactus)
—cultural significance of, p. 563 [430]
Scotch
—perceptions of, p. 564 [431]
Scotts Valley
—land trusteeship termination, p. 166 [102]
Scranton-Wilkes-Barre-Hazleton, PA MSA
—population, pp. 176, 187 [109, 115]
Sealaska
—population by state, pp. 201-202, 204, 206, 208 [123-127]
—population by U.S. region, p. 189 [117]
Seatbelt use
—by adolescents, p. 405 [280]
Seattle Indian Center
—adult education, p. 495 [373]
Seattle-Tacoma-Bremerton, WA CMSA
—population, pp. 176, 187 [109, 115]
Seattle, WA PMSA
—Native American owned firms, p. 875 [713]
Secondary schools
—attendance patterns, p. 486 [364]
—course enrollment, pp. 469-470, 473 [342-343, 348]
—curriculum, p. 466 [339]
—enrollment by race/ethnicity in ANVSAs, pp. 451-452 [323-324]
—enrollment by race/ethnicity in TDSAs, pp. 453-454 [325-326]
—enrollment by race/ethnicity in TJSAs, p. 455 [327-328]
—enrollment by race/ethnicity on reservations and trust lands, pp. 456-457 [329-330]
—enrollment in 1900-1930, pp. 89-90 [64-65]
—enrollment in ANVSAs, p. 459 [331]
—enrollment in TDSAs, p. 460 [332]
—enrollment in TJSAs, p. 461 [333]
—enrollment on reservations and trust lands, p. 462 [334]
—federal expenditures, p. 490 [369]
—preparedness for class, p. 467 [340]
—public school enrollment, p. 446 [320]
—teachers, p. 488 [367]
Security brokers
—minority-owned firms, p. 825 [693]
—Native American owned firms, p. 862 [707]
Security officers
—occupational goals of high school seniors, p. 471 [345]

Numbers following p. or pp. are page references. Numbers in [ ] are table references.

Numbers following p. or pp. are page references. Numbers in [ ] are table references.

Keyword Index

1235

Numbers following p. or pp. are page references. Numbers in [ ] are table references.

Numbers following p. or pp. are page references. Numbers in [ ] are table references.

Shishmaref continued:
— class of workers in, p. 657 [538]
— educational attainment, pp. 423, 427 [301, 305]
— educational attainment and employment status in, pp. 436-437 [311-312]
— elderly persons in, p. 418 [297]
— employment in, pp. 662, 690, 692 [542, 558-559]
— employment of family members, p. 380 [252]
— geographic mobility in, p. 336 [213]
— home heating in, p. 750 [619]
— household income, p. 784 [650]
— household type and relationship in, pp. 366, 368 [240-241]
— housing by year built, p. 729 [597]
— housing costs and income, p. 800 [666]
— housing tenure, pp. 715, 725 [585, 593]
— housing tenure by race, p. 720 [589]
— income and poverty, pp. 791-792 [656-657]
— income by race, p. 770 [638]
— income by source, pp. 774, 776 [642-643]
— language spoken at home, pp. 535, 539, 541-542 [408, 412-414]
— linguistic isolation in, p. 535 [408]
— marital status of females in, pp. 389, 393 [260, 264]
— marital status of males in, p. 397 [268]
— median income of families in, p. 384 [256]
— military service, pp. 1009, 1011 [868-869]
— monthly housing costs, p. 805 [670]
— occupations in, pp. 700, 702 [566-567]
— persons in housing units, pp. 375, 739 [248, 606]
— place of birth, p. 340 [217]
— population by age, pp. 264, 267, 269 [156-158]
— population by race/ethnicity, p. 332 [209]
— population by sex and race, p. 278 [163]
— rooms per housing unit, p. 734 [601]
— school enrollment, p. 459 [331]
— school enrollment by race/ethnicity in, pp. 452-453 [323-324]
— sewage disposal methods, p. 754 [623]
— telephone availability, p. 763 [631]
— urban vs. rural population, p. 327 [205]
— water sources for housing, p. 759 [627]

Shivwitz
— land trusteeship termination, p. 167 [102]

Shoalwater Bay Tribe
— Children's Justice Act funding, p. 1061 [916]
— population by state, pp. 249-250, 252-253, 255 [148-152]
— population by U.S. region, p. 200 [122]
— tribal enrollment, p. 1028 [886]

Shoalwater Reservation, WA
— acreage, tribal lands, and population, p. 951 [805]
— population by age, pp. 300-301, 303 [180-182]
— population by sex and race, p. 318 [194]
— traditional occupations, pp. 560-561 [428-429]

Shoshone
— ability to speak English, 1910, p. 138 [88]
— blood status, 1910, pp. 69, 80 [55, 59]
— educational attainment, p. 434 [310]
— employment by occupation, p. 689 [557]
— illiteracy, 1910, p. 115 [75]
— Indian and white mixed-bloods, 1910, p. 87 [63]
— labor force status, pp. 670, 672 [548-549]

Shoshone continued:
— language, 1910 and 1930, p. 146 [91]
— marital status, 1910, pp. 156, 161 [96, 98]
— marital status, 1910 and 1930, p. 152 [94]
— population, pp. 178, 189 [111, 116]
— population, 1910-1930, pp. 43-44 [33]
— population by state, pp. 239, 241, 243, 245-247 [143-147]
— population by U.S. region, p. 198 [121]
— school attendance, 1910, p. 99 [68]
— school enrollment, p. 450 [322]
— school enrollment, 1930, pp. 108, 110 [72-73]
— tribal enrollment, p. 1022 [880]

Shoshone-Bannock
— substance abuse prevention, p. 623 [497]
— tribal enrollment, p. 1028 [886]

Shoshone-Paiute
— educational attainment, p. 434 [310]
— employment by occupation, p. 689 [557]
— labor force status, pp. 670, 672 [548-549]
— population by state, pp. 239, 241, 243, 245, 247 [143-147]
— population by U.S. region, p. 198 [121]
— school enrollment, p. 450 [322]
— tribal enrollment, p. 1024 [882]

Shoshone [language]
— spoken at home, p. 531 [405]

Showers
— in housing, p. 747 [615]

Shreveport, LA MSA
— population, p. 187 [115]

Shungnak
— population by age, pp. 265, 267, 270 [156-158]
— population by sex and race, p. 278 [163]

Shuswap, Songish
— language, 1910 and 1930, p. 149 [91]

Sia
— ability to speak English, 1910, p. 135 [87]
— illiteracy, 1910, p. 113 [74]
— language, 1910 and 1930, p. 144 [90]
— school attendance, 1910, p. 94 [67]

Sidarumiut
— Alaskan population, 1910, p. 27 [27]

Sierra Madre
— smallpox epidemics, 1520-1797, p. 125 [83]

Sierra Miwok
— spoken at home, p. 530 [405]

Sihasapa
— ability to speak English, 1910, p. 139 [88]
— blood status, 1910, pp. 71, 81 [56, 60]
— illiteracy, 1910, p. 116 [75]
— Indian and white mixed-bloods, 1910, p. 88 [63]
— marital status, 1910, pp. 156, 162 [96, 98]
— school attendance, 1910, p. 101 [69]

Siletz
— acreage, tribal lands, and population, p. 950 [805]
— educational attainment, p. 434 [310]
— employment by occupation, p. 689 [557]
— extensions of trust and land restrictions, p. 129 [85]
— labor force status, pp. 670, 672 [548-549]
— land trusteeship termination, p. 166 [102]

Numbers following p. or pp. are page references. Numbers in [ ] are table references.

1238

Numbers following p. or pp. are page references. Numbers in [ ] are table references.

Keyword Index

Numbers following p. or pp. are page references. Numbers in [ ] are table references.

Numbers following p. or pp. are page references. Numbers in [ ] are table references.

Numbers following p. or pp. are page references. Numbers in [ ] are table references.

Numbers following p. or pp. are page references. Numbers in [ ] are table references.

Numbers following p. or pp. are page references. Numbers in [ ] are table references.

Numbers following p. or pp. are page references. Numbers in [ ] are table references.

Numbers following p. or pp. are page references. Numbers in [ ] are table references.

Tatitlek
— population by age, pp. 270-272 [159-161]
— population by sex and race, p. 278 [164]
— tribal enrollment, p. 1025 [883]

Tawakoni
— language, 1910 and 1930, p. 143 [90]

Tax exemptions
— and cigarettes, p. 942 [802]

Tax revenue
— from Indian gaming in New Mexico, p. 913 [768]

Tazlina
— population by age, pp. 270-272 [159-161]
— population by sex and race, p. 278 [164]

TDSAs
— children and type of family in, p. 352 [228]
— children in households, pp. 358, 362 [234, 237]
— class of workers in, p. 658 [539]
— educational attainment, pp. 424, 428 [302, 306]
— educational attainment and employment status in, pp. 438-439 [313-314]
— elderly persons in, p. 418 [298]
— employment in, pp. 663, 692-693 [543, 560-561]
— employment of families, p. 380 [253]
— geographic mobility in, p. 337 [214]
— home heating methods, p. 750 [620]
— household income, p. 785 [651]
— household type and relationship in, p. 369 [242-243]
— housing by year built, p. 730 [598]
— housing costs and income, p. 801 [667]
— housing occupancy in, p. 716 [586]
— housing tenure, p. 726 [594]
— housing tenure by race, p. 721 [590]
— income and poverty, pp. 793-794 [658-659]
— income by race, p. 771 [639]
— income by source, p. 777 [644-645]
— language spoken at home, pp. 543-544 [415-417]
— linguistic isolation in, p. 536 [409]
— marital status of females in, pp. 390, 394 [261, 265]
— marital status of males in, p. 398 [269]
— median income of families in, p. 385 [257]
— military service, p. 1012 [870-871]
— monthly housing costs, p. 806 [671]
— occupations in, pp. 702-703 [568-569]
— persons in housing units, p. 740 [607]
— persons per household, p. 376 [249]
— place of birth, p. 341 [218]
— population by age, pp. 321-322 [197-199]
— population by race/ethnicity, p. 333 [210]
— population by sex and race, p. 323 [200]
— rooms per housing unit, p. 735 [602]
— school enrollment, p. 460 [332]
— school enrollment by race/ethnicity in, pp. 453-454 [325-326]
— sewage disposal methods, p. 755 [624]
— telephone availability, p. 764 [632]
— urban vs. rural population, p. 328 [206]
— water sources for housing, p. 760 [628]

Te-Moak
— tribal enrollment, p. 1024 [882]

Te-Moak Reservation and Trust Lands, NV
— acreage, tribal lands, and population, p. 950 [805]
— population by age, pp. 304-306 [183-185]
— population by sex and race, p. 319 [195]
— traditional occupations, pp. 560, 562 [428-429]
— tribal enrollment, p. 1024 [882]

Te-Moak Western Shoshone
— population by state, pp. 239, 241, 243, 245, 247 [143-147]
— population by U.S. region, p. 198 [121]

Tea, Indian
— cultural significance of, p. 563 [430]

Teachers
— as abuse confidants, p. 417 [296]
— colleges and universities, pp. 523-524 [399-401]
— high school, p. 488 [367]
— mathematics, p. 487 [365]
— occupational goals of high school seniors, p. 471 [345]
— public schools, p. 488 [367]
— vocational schools, p. 488 [367]

Technical assistance
— FHA loans, p. 799 [665]
— public health services, p. 640 [520]

Technical Support (Agency & MIS)
— expenditures, p. 490 [369]

Technicians
— employment by tribe, pp. 681, 686 [554, 556]
— employment in ANVSAs, p. 699 [566]
— employment in TDSAs, p. 702 [568]
— employment in TJSAs, p. 704 [570]
— employment of, pp. 879-906 [716-758]
— employment on reservations and trust lands, p. 705 [572]
— government employees, p. 991 [852]
— occupational goals of high school seniors, p. 471 [345]
— part-time workers, pp. 995-996 [857]

Technicians, health
— employed by Indian Health Service, pp. 637-638 [516, 518]

Teenagers
— teenage mothers, p. 574 [440]

Tehachapi
— language, 1910 and 1930, p. 146 [91]

Telephone communications
— employment, p. 901 [750]

Telephones
— availability in ANVSAs, p. 763 [631]
— availability in TDSAs, p. 764 [632]
— availability in TJSAs, p. 765 [633]
— availability on reservations and trust lands, p. 765 [634]

Television news
— employment, p. 655 [536]

Television viewing
— high school seniors, p. 482 [358]

Telida
— population by age, pp. 270-272 [159-161]
— population by sex and race, p. 278 [164]

Teller
— population by age, pp. 270-272 [159-161]
— population by sex and race, p. 278 [164]

Temecula
— extensions of trust and land restrictions, p. 126 [84]

Numbers following p. or pp. are page references. Numbers in [ ] are table references.

1247

Numbers following p. or pp. are page references. Numbers in [ ] are table references.

Numbers following p. or pp. are page references. Numbers in [ ] are table references.

Numbers following p. or pp. are page references. Numbers in [ ] are table references.

Numbers following p. or pp. are page references. Numbers in [ ] are table references.

Keyword Index

Numbers following p. or pp. are page references. Numbers in [ ] are table references.

Keyword Index

Numbers following p. or pp. are page references. Numbers in [ ] are table references.

Keyword Index

Numbers following p. or pp. are page references. Numbers in [ ] are table references.

Unalakleet continued:
— geographic mobility in, p. 336 [213]
— home heating in, p. 750 [619]
— household income, p. 784 [650]
— household type and relationship in, pp. 367-368 [240-241]
— housing by year built, p. 730 [597]
— housing costs and income, p. 800 [666]
— housing tenure, pp. 715, 725 [585, 593]
— housing tenure by race, p. 720 [589]
— income and poverty, pp. 791, 793 [656-657]
— income by race, p. 770 [638]
— income by source, pp. 775-776 [642-643]
— language spoken at home, pp. 535, 539, 541-542 [408, 412-414]
— linguistic isolation in, p. 535 [408]
— marital status of females in, pp. 389, 393 [260, 264]
— marital status of males in, p. 398 [268]
— median income of families in, p. 384 [256]
— military service, pp. 1009, 1011 [868-869]
— monthly housing costs, p. 805 [670]
— occupations in, pp. 700, 702 [566-567]
— persons in housing units, pp. 376, 739 [248, 606]
— place of birth, p. 340 [217]
— population by age, pp. 270-272 [159-161]
— population by race/ethnicity, p. 332 [209]
— population by sex and race, p. 279 [164]
— rooms per housing unit, p. 734 [601]
— school enrollment, p. 460 [331]
— school enrollment by race/ethnicity in, pp. 452-453 [323-324]
— sewage disposal methods, p. 754 [623]
— telephone availability, p. 764 [631]
— urban vs. rural population, p. 327 [205]
— water sources for housing, p. 759 [627]

Unalaska
— children and type of family in, p. 351 [227]
— children in households, pp. 357, 362 [232, 236]
— class of workers in, p. 657 [538]
— educational attainment, pp. 423, 428 [301, 305]
— educational attainment and employment status in, pp. 436, 438 [311-312]
— elderly persons in, p. 418 [297]
— employment in, pp. 662, 690, 692 [542, 558-559]
— employment of family members, p. 380 [252]
— geographic mobility in, p. 336 [213]
— home heating in, p. 750 [619]
— household income, p. 784 [650]
— household type and relationship in, pp. 367-368 [240-241]
— housing by year built, p. 730 [597]
— housing costs and income, p. 800 [666]
— housing tenure, pp. 715, 725 [585, 593]
— housing tenure by race, p. 720 [589]
— income and poverty, pp. 791, 793 [656-657]
— income by race, p. 770 [638]
— income by source, pp. 775-776 [642-643]
— language spoken at home, pp. 535, 539, 541-542 [408, 412-414]
— linguistic isolation in, p. 535 [408]
— marital status of females in, pp. 389, 393 [260, 264]
— marital status of males in, p. 398 [268]
— median income of families in, p. 384 [256]
— military service, pp. 1009, 1011 [868-869]

Unalaska continued:
— monthly housing costs, p. 805 [670]
— occupations in, pp. 700, 702 [566-567]
— persons in housing units, pp. 376, 739 [248, 606]
— place of birth, p. 340 [217]
— population by age, pp. 270-272 [159-161]
— population by race/ethnicity, p. 332 [209]
— population by sex and race, p. 279 [164]
— rooms per housing unit, p. 734 [601]
— school enrollment, p. 460 [331]
— school enrollment by race/ethnicity in, pp. 452-453 [323-324]
— sewage disposal methods, p. 754 [623]
— telephone availability, p. 764 [631]
— urban vs. rural population, p. 327 [205]
— water sources for housing, p. 759 [627]

Unaligmiut
— ability to speak English, 1910, p. 141 [89]
— Alaskan population, 1910, p. 27 [27]
— blood status, 1910, p. 73 [56]
— illiteracy, 1910, p. 118 [76]
— school attendance, 1910, p. 104 [70]

Uncompahgra Band of Utes
— extensions of trust and land restrictions, p. 129 [85]

Undernutrition
— nutritional counseling, p. 644 [524]

Unemployment
— by tribal group, pp. 666, 668, 670-671 [546-549]
— in Canada, p. 1082 [945]
— in South Dakota and reservations, p. 709 [575]
— on reservations, p. 708 [574]
— on reserves [Canada], p. 1079 [941]
— substance abuse and, p. 411 [287]
— urban, p. 1079 [941]

United Houma Nation TDSA (state)
— children and type of family in, p. 352 [228]
— children in households, pp. 359, 363 [234, 237]
— class of workers in, p. 658 [539]
— educational attainment, pp. 424, 428 [302, 306]
— educational attainment and employment status in, pp. 438-439 [313-314]
— elderly persons in, p. 419 [298]
— employment in, pp. 663, 693 [543, 560-561]
— employment of families, p. 381 [253]
— geographic mobility in, p. 337 [214]
— home heating in, p. 751 [620]
— household income, p. 785 [651]
— household type and relationship in, pp. 369-370 [242-243]
— housing by year built, p. 730 [598]
— housing costs and income, p. 801 [667]
— housing tenure, pp. 716, 726 [586, 594]
— housing tenure by race, p. 721 [590]
— income and poverty, pp. 793-794 [658-659]
— income by race, p. 771 [639]
— income by source, pp. 777-778 [644-645]
— language spoken at home, pp. 536, 543-544 [409, 415-417]
— linguistic isolation in, p. 536 [409]
— marital status of females in, pp. 390, 394 [261, 265]
— marital status of males in, p. 398 [269]
— median family income in, p. 385 [257]

Numbers following p. or pp. are page references. Numbers in [ ] are table references.

Numbers following p. or pp. are page references. Numbers in [ ] are table references.

Numbers following p. or pp. are page references. Numbers in [ ] are table references.

1259

Keyword Index

Numbers following p. or pp. are page references. Numbers in [ ] are table references.

Numbers following p. or pp. are page references. Numbers in [ ] are table references.

Numbers following p. or pp. are page references. Numbers in [ ] are table references.

Numbers following p. or pp. are page references. Numbers in [ ] are table references.

1263

Numbers following p. or pp. are page references. Numbers in [ ] are table references.

Numbers following p. or pp. are page references. Numbers in [ ] are table references.

Numbers following p. or pp. are page references. Numbers in [ ] are table references.

Numbers following p. or pp. are page references. Numbers in [ ] are table references.

Numbers following p. or pp. are page references. Numbers in [ ] are table references.

Numbers following p. or pp. are page references. Numbers in [ ] are table references.

Numbers following p. or pp. are page references. Numbers in [ ] are table references.

Numbers following p. or pp. are page references. Numbers in [ ] are table references.